THE ROUGH GUIDE TO

Italy

*Maranello
Stelabar S.A. -
ROSSO*

*Stelabar S.A. - Strada dei Censiti, 21
47891 Falciano - Repubblica di San Marino
Tel: 0549 970614*

There are more than two hundred Rough Guide titles
covering destinations from Alaska to Zimbabwe
and subjects from Acoustic Guitar to Travel Health

Forthcoming travel guides include
Devon & Cornwall • Malta
Tenerife • Vancouver

Forthcoming reference guides include
Cuban Music • Personal Computers
Pregnancy & Birth • Trumpet & Trombone

Rough Guides Online
www.roughguides.c

D0290155

ROUGH GUIDE CREDITS

Text editor: Lucy Ratcliffe and Sam Thorne
Series editor: Mark Ellingham

Production: Helen Ostick, Julia Bovis, Ed Wright
Picture research: Louise Boulton, Sharon Martins

ACKNOWLEDGEMENTS

Rob Andrews would like to thank Alvaro Arnaiz, Leila Calvarano, Ciccio Cario, Alberto Cozza, Evelina Pallone, Agata Scamporrino and Elena Valente. **Martin Dunford** thanks Lucy Ratcliffe for her patience – and not taking no for an answer! **Jeffrey Kennedy** special thanks to: Dr Stefano Contoli, Saku, Clark Lawrence, Brunetta Barbieri, Suzanne Hartley, Elizabeth Geoghegan, Maria McCourt, Elaine O'Reilly, Aloma Valentini and Lila Yawn. **James McConnachie** wants to say thank you to Kate, Fede and Cristina in Venice, Daniella and Monica in Verona, Alessio and his family in Padua, Ishai in Bolzano, and Jonathan and Lucy in London. **Lucy Ratcliffe** ringrazia Mario e Lucia, e Alessandro e Barabara, per la loro generosa ospitalità; special thanks to Luca for all his support and inside information. **Helena Smith** thanks Massimina Caneva at Liaisons Abroad for a wonderful itinerary. Also, on Ischia: Alessandro at *Il Moresco* for his kind help; Signor Matera at the Castello Aragonese; and Lady Walton at La Mortella – thanks too to Eduardo and his friends for the low-down on Naples. Not forgetting Markie for sharing the highs and lows in Napoli; Chiara for putting up with the Amalfi Coast; and Dan and Matthew – a big *cin-cin*! **Matthew Teller** would like to thank tourist-office staff throughout Tuscany and Liguria. Of particular help were, in no particular order: Micaela and Alessandra of ENIT, London; Roberta Glorio of APT Genoa, and our guide

Natascia Clemente; Mrs Moro of APT Riviera dei Fiori, San Remo; Dr Franco Orio of Consorzio Portofino Coast, Rapallo; Gian Guido D'Amico of APT Tigullio, S. Margherita Ligure; Marinella Mariotti, La Spezia; Erika in Giglio Porto; Rossana Bartolini of APT Arezzo; Ambra Nepi of Ambra Nepi Comunicazione, Florence; Dr Paolo Bresci of APT Pistoia; Dr Umberto Gentini of APT Arcipelago Toscano, Portoferraio; Roberta Berni and Elisa of APT Florence; Francesca Bellandi and staff of "Pisa è"; Luca Frediani in Carrara; *La Vedetta* in Livorno; Luigina Benci of APT Siena; staff of Consorzio Turistico di Volterra and our guide Giulia Munday; and Luigi Cerroni in Pitigliano. Also thanks to Sam Thorne for kicking things off; and especially to Lucy Ratcliffe for her flexibility and understanding. **Celia Woolfrey** thanks Tom Bateman; Luciano di Battista; *Masseria Salinola*, Ostuni; Riccardo de Melis; *Hotel Le Gole*, Celano; Enrico Pizzuti; Elisabetta Bernadini; *Villa Vignola*, Vasto; Anna Maria d'Orazio; Carmelo Silla; Renato and Silvana Pinto; Edoardo Betti and Alessandra at ENIT London; Lucy Ratcliffe, Jonathan Buckley and Sam Thorne.

Thanks also to Narrell Leffman and Amy Brown for extra Basics research; Elaine Pollard and Russell Walton for proofreading; James McConnachie for indexing; Ed Wright for cartography; Julie Sanderson for help with the letters; and Helen Ostick for typesetting.

PUBLISHING INFORMATION

This fifth edition published April 2001 by
Rough Guides Ltd, 62–70 Shorts Gardens,
London WC2H 9AH.
Distributed by the Penguin Group:
Penguin Books Ltd, 27 Wrights Lane, London W8 5TZ
Penguin Putnam, Inc. 375 Hudson Street, NY 10014,
USA
Penguin Books Australia Ltd, 487 Maroondah Highway,
PO Box 257, Ringwood, Victoria 3134, Australia
Penguin Books Canada Ltd, 10 Alcorn Avenue, Toronto,
Ontario, Canada M4V 1E4
Penguin Books (NZ) Ltd, 182–190 Wairau Road,
Auckland 10, New Zealand
Typeset in Linotron Univers and Century Old Style to an
original design by Andrew Oliver.
Printed in the United Kingdom by Clays Ltd, St Ives Plc.
Illustrations in Part One and Part Three by Edward Briant.

Illustrations on p.1 & p.1059 by Link Hall
Euro banknotes draft design on p.1 © EWI.
© Ros Belford, Martin Dunford & Celia Woolfrey.
No part of this book may be reproduced in any form
without permission from the publisher except for the
quotation of brief passages in reviews.
1184pp – Includes index
A catalogue record for this book is available from the
British Library.
ISBN 1-85828-692-1

The publishers and authors have done their best to
ensure the accuracy and currency of all the information
in *The Rough Guide to Italy*, however, they can accept
no responsibility for any loss, injury, or inconvenience
sustained by any traveller as a result of information or
advice contained in the guide.

THE ROUGH GUIDE TO

Italy

written and researched by

Ros Belford, Martin Dunford & Celia Woolfrey

with additional contributions by

Rob Andrews, Sheila Brownlee, Jeffrey Kennedy, Ellen
Leopold, Catherine McBeth, James McConnachie, Gordon
McLachlan, Lucy Ratcliffe, Helena Smith & Matthew Teller

ROUGH
GUIDES

We set out to do something different when the first Rough Guide was published in 1982. Mark Ellingham, just out of university, was travelling in Greece. He brought along the popular guides of the day, but found they were all lacking in some way. They were either strong on ruins and museums but went on for pages without mentioning a beach or taverna. Or they were so conscious of the need to save money that they lost sight of Greece's cultural and historical significance. Also, none of the books told him anything about Greece's contemporary life – its politics, its culture, its people and how they lived.

So with no job in prospect, Mark decided to write his own guidebook, one which aimed to provide practical information that was second to none, detailing the best beaches and the hottest clubs and restaurants, while also giving hard-hitting accounts of every sight, both famous and obscure, and providing up-to-the-minute information on contemporary culture. It was a guide that encouraged independent travellers to find the best of Greece, and was a great success, getting shortlisted for the Thomas Cook travel guide award,

and encouraging Mark, along with three friends, to expand the series.

The Rough Guide list grew rapidly and the letters flooded in, indicating a much broader readership than had been anticipated, but one which uniformly appreciated the Rough Guide mix of practical detail and humour, irreverence and enthusiasm. Things haven't changed. The same four friends who began the series are still the caretakers of the Rough Guide mission today: to provide the most reliable, up-to-date and entertaining information to independent-minded travellers of all ages, on all budgets.

We now publish more than 150 titles and have offices in London and New York. The travel guides are written and researched by a dedicated team of more than 100 authors, based in Britain, Europe, the USA and Australia. We have also created a unique series of phrasebooks to accompany the travel series, along with an acclaimed series of music guides, and a best-selling pocket guide to the Internet and World Wide Web. We also publish comprehensive travel information on our Web site:

www.roughguides.com

HELP US UPDATE

We've gone to a lot of effort to ensure that the fifth edition of *The Rough Guide to Italy* is accurate and up-to-date. However, things change – places get "discovered", opening hours are notoriously fickle, restaurants and rooms raise prices or lower standards. If you feel we've got it wrong or left something out, we'd like to know, and if you can remember the address, the price, the time, the phone number, so the better.

We'll credit all contributions, and send a copy of the next edition (or any other *Rough Guide* if you prefer) for the best letters. Please mark letters: "Rough Guide Italy Update" and send to:
Rough Guides, 62–70 Shorts Gardens, London WC2H 9AH, or Rough Guides, 4th Floor, 345 Hudson St, New York, NY 10014.
Or send email to: mail@roughguides.co.uk
Online updates about this book can be found on Rough Guides' Web site at **www.roughguides.com**

THE AUTHORS

Ros Belford first travelled to Italy when she was eighteen, and has written and edited several books and numerous articles about the country. She now writes about travelling with her daughter, Ismene, for *Condé Nast Traveller*, and as this fifth edition of *The Rough Guide to Italy* goes to press, is expecting her second child.

Martin Dunford was born and raised in southeast London. After years of travelling and various dead-end jobs, he took up travel writing, authoring several books and co-founding the Rough Guide series. He is now editorial director of Rough Guides and spends weekends plotting the resurgence of Charlton Athletic FC.

Celia Woolfrey grew up in England and Australia and first visited Italy on a round-Europe interrailing trip. She has been back many times and has a weak spot for staying in mountain refuges and recovering in great hotels. She is author of a book of London walks (published by Duncan Petersen), and has contributed to the Rough Guides to New York and Scandinavia and *Condé Nast Traveller* magazine. She writes a weekly column in the *Guardian* "Weekend" magazine and is currently compiling a guide to special places to stay in central and southern Italy.

READERS' LETTERS

Thanks to all the readers who took the trouble to write in with their comments on the previous edition (apologies for any omissions or misspellings): David Arthur, Beverly Averill, Adrian Banfield, Peter & Paula Barrett, Colette Barron, Dr Giles W. Becker & Jon R. Naylor, Anders Berglund, Adrian Bessop, Paul Biesta, Mari Borghesi, Claudia Brackenbury, Ruth Brandwood-Dixon, Rachel Brasier, Richard Brooks, Mrs J. Brown, Joan Brown, Lucy Brown, Chris Burin, Revd. J. Noel Burke, Peter Butler, John Cameron & Ann Beaton, Holly Cartlidge, Ute Christiansen, Mike Clements, Patricia Compter, Rosamund Connell, Jim Cook & Ulrike Sieglohr, Audrey Coyle, Peter Croft, Brenda J. Cronini, Martin Cross, James Donalson, Xuela Edwards, Kirsten Empson, Anna Evans, Eve Fernandez, Adrian & Lisa Foldies, Jessica Forbess, Christopher Gallagher, Joanne Garner, Romina Gentini, Karan Granat, Malcolm Grieve, Anthea Grimason, Jonathan Gunz, Karta Guy & Octavia Hartlan, Eddie Halliday, Joan Hammond, Rebecca Harding, Sarah Harding, Melissa Hayes, Anne Healion, Sally Holdstock, Kevin Hubbard, Graham Hughes, Stephen Hyrnczak, David Johnson, "Jollerton", Bridgett Jones, Peter Jones, Chris Kershaw & Karen Pearce, Justin Kerswell, Kinda, Andrew & Sarah Knightly-Brown, Johanna Kollar, Alastair Lack, Nick & Gill Lakin, Irene Lamont, Jeroen Lauen, Adrian Legge, Brian Lowery, Mausumi Majumdar, Martin Mann, Laura Mason, Byron Mathioudakis, Duncan McCosham, Amanda McCullough, Linda McGhee, Perry Merkel, Luciano Michel, Isabel Montiero, Helen Moore, Madeleine Moore, Harry Mount, Trilokesh Mukherjee, Shahid Nawaz, V.L. Nicholson, David Nugent, Ivan Nutbrown & Jennie Kitteringham, Jenny Ogilvie, Sarah O'Hagan, Anne O'Mahony, Jezz Osborn, Linda Payne, Karen Pearce, Piergiorgio Pescali, Anne Peter, John Pitt, Natalija Porodnik, Vicky Porter, Celia Price, Max & Julia Prola, Matthew Rankin, Tammy Ratoff & Keith Fradgley, Wendy A. Reid, Mr J. Richardson, M. Richmond, Yvonne Riddell, A.N. ap Robert, Mrs C. Anne Robertson, Simon Rowe, Eric & Sally Rowland, Ralph M. Ruge, Raleigh St Lawrence, Craig J. Sallinger, Michael Salmon, Jackie Sanders, Yvette Saunders & John Delaunay, Carl Scarpa, "SeaOtter6", Julian Seeley, Ella Sharp, Anne Sheedy, Cathy Shrank, Angela Smith, Matthew Smith & Emily Nance, Tim Smith, Annie Stephenson, Barbara & David Struggles, Genevieve Symonds, Elina Talvitie, Joyce Templeton, John Tetney, Peter Tomaney, Ruth Tovim, B.W.B. Turner, Simon Vicary, Paul Viera, Silvia Viviani, David Wakeling, Kirstie Warner, Marie Watton, Keith Weaver, John Whatley, Roger Wikeley, Diederick J. Wolters, Bernice Wyle.

CONTENTS

Introduction xii

• CHAPTER 4: TRENTINO-ALTO ADIGE · 233–269

• CHAPTER 5: VENICE & THE VENETO · 270–367

• CHAPTER 6: FRUILI-VENEZIA GIULIA · 368–393

• CHAPTER 7: EMILIA ROMAGNA · 394–449

• CHAPTER 8: TUSCANY · 450–579

• CHAPTER 9: UMBRIA

• CHAPTER 10: MARCHE

• CHAPTER 11: ROME & LAZIO

• CHAPTER 12: ABRUZZO & MOLISE

• CHAPTER 13: CAMPANIA   812–874

• CHAPTER 14: PUGLIA   875–916

• CHAPTER 15: CALABRIA & BASILICATA   917–955

• CHAPTER 16: SICILY   956–1020

● CHAPTER 17: SARDINIA 1021–1058

PART THREE CONTEXTS 1060

MAP LIST

MAP SYMBOLS

Major road	Castle
Minor road	Cave
Footpath	Church (regional maps)
Railway	Gates
National boundary	Hospital
Regional boundary	Parking
Chapter division boundary	Bus/taxi stop
Ferry route	Post office
Hydrofoil route	Information office
River	Telephone office
Wall	Airport
Cable car	Built up area
Mountain range	Building
Mountain peak	Cathedral/church (town maps)
Pass	Cemetery
Ancient site/place of interest	National park
Campsite	Park

INTRODUCTION

O f all European countries, **Italy** is perhaps the hardest to classify. It is a modern, industrialized nation. It is the harbinger of style, its designers leading the way with each season's fashions. But it is also, to an equal degree, a Mediterranean country, with all that that implies. Agricultural land covers much of the country, a lot of it, especially in the south, still owned under almost feudal conditions. In towns and villages all over the country, life grinds to a halt in the middle of the day for a siesta, and is strongly family-oriented, with an emphasis on the traditions and rituals of the Catholic Church which, notwithstanding a growing scepticism among the country's youth, still dominates people's lives here to an immediately obvious degree.

Above all Italy provokes reaction. Its people are volatile, rarely indifferent to anything, and on one and the same day you might encounter the kind of disdain dished out to tourist masses worldwide, and an hour later be treated to embarrassingly generous hospitality. If there is a single national characteristic, it's to embrace life to the full: in the hundreds of local festivals taking place across the country on any given day, to celebrate a saint or the local harvest; in the importance placed on good food; in the obsession with clothes and image; and above all in the daily domestic ritual of the collective evening stroll or passeggiata – a sociable affair celebrated by young and old alike in every town and village across the country.

Italy only became a unified state in 1861 and, as a result, Italians often feel more loyalty to their region than the nation as a whole – something manifest in different cuisines, dialects, landscape and often varying standards of living. There is also, of course, the country's enormous cultural legacy: Tuscany alone has more classified historical monuments than any country in the world; there are considerable remnants of the Roman Empire all over the country, notably of course in Rome itself; and every region retains its own relics of an artistic tradition generally acknowledged to be among the world's richest.

Yet there's no reason to be intimidated by the art and architecture. If you want to lie on a beach, there are any number of places to do it: development has been kept relatively under control, and many resorts are still largely the preserve of Italian tourists. Other parts of the coast, especially in the south of the country, are almost entirely undiscovered. Beaches are for the most part sandy, and doubts about the cleanliness of the water have been confined to the northern part of the Adriatic coast and the Riviera. Mountains, too, run the country's length – from the Alps and Dolomites in the north right along the Apennines, which form the spine of the peninsula – and are an important reference-point for most Italians. Skiing and other winter sports are practised avidly, and in the five national parks, protected from the national passion for hunting, wildlife of all sorts thrives.

Where to go

The **north** is "discovered" Italy. The regions of **Piemonte** and **Lombardy**, in the northwest, make up the richest and most cosmopolitan part of the country, and the two main centres, Turin and Milan, are its wealthiest large cities. In their southern reaches, these regions are flat and scenically dull, especially Lombardy, but in the north the presence of the Alps shapes the character of each: skiing and hiking are prime activities, and the lakes and mountains of Lombardy are time-honoured tourist territory. **Liguria**, the small coastal province to the south, has long been known as the "Italian Riviera" and is accordingly crowded with sun-seeking holiday-makers for much of the summer season.

Nonetheless it's a beautiful stretch of coast, and its capital, Genoa, is a bustling port with a long seafaring tradition.

Much of the most dramatic mountain scenery lies within the smaller northern regions. In the far northwest, the tiny bilingual region of **Valle d'Aosta** is home to some of the country's most frequented ski resorts, and is bordered by the tallest of the Alps – the Matterhorn and Mont Blanc. Moving east, **Trentino-Alto Adige**, another bilingual region, and one in which the national boundary is especially blurred, marks the beginning of the Dolomites mountain range, where Italy's largest national park, the Stelvio, lies amid some of the country's most memorable landscapes.

The Dolomites stretch into the northeastern regions of the **Veneto** and **Friuli-Venezia Giulia**. However here the main focus of interest is, of course, Venice; a

THE NORTH–SOUTH DIVIDE

Italy breaks down into twenty regions, which in turn divide into different provinces. Some of these regional boundaries reflect long-standing historic borders, like Tuscany, Lombardy or the Veneto; others, like Friuli-Venezia Giulia or Molise, are more recent administrative divisions, often established in recognition of quite modern distinctions. But the sharpest division is between north and south. The **north** is one of the most advanced industrial societies in the world, its people speak Italian with the cadences of France or Germany and its "capital", Milan, is a thoroughly European city. The **south**, derogatively known as *il mezzogiorno*, begins somewhere between Rome and Naples, and is by contrast one of the most economically depressed areas in Europe; and its history of absolutist regimes often seems to linger in the form of the spectre of organized crime and the remote hand of central government in Rome.

The economic backwardness of the south is partly the result of the historical neglect to which it was subjected by various foreign occupiers. But it is also the result of the deliberate policy of politicians and corporate heads to industrialize the north while preserving the underdeveloped south as a convenient reservoir of labour. Italy's industrial power and dynamism, based in the north, was built on the back of exploited southerners who emigrated to the northern industrial cities of Turin, Milan and Genoa in their millions during the Fifties and Sixties. Even now, Milan and Turin have very sizeable populations of *meridionali* – southerners – working in every sector of the economy.

This north–south divide is something you'll come up against time and again, wherever you're travelling. To a northerner the mere mention of Naples – a kind of totem for the south – can provoke a hostile response; and you may notice graffiti in northern cities against *terroni* (literally "those of the land"), the derogatory northern nickname for southerners. In recent years this hostility has been articulated through the rise of the Lega Nord, who have promoted the future independence of northern Italy and campaigned vigorously against immigration from outside Italy.

Oddly enough, the Lega Nord's campaign against the entrenchment and vested interests of the Italian political establishment, not to mention organized crime and the Mafia (whose power has spread to the north of the country), backfired to some extent when it became clear that the centre of the *tangentopoli* ("bribesville") corruption scandals was, after all, Milan itself. Most northern Italians were forced to revise their simplistic view of the south as a drain on the country's resources, and look to sort out the problems in their own political backyard. These massive political upheavals seemed to dissipate the north–south divide for a while and give most Italians a greater sense of unity than ever before, if only by virtue of their opposition to the old political establishment.

unique city, and every bit as beautiful as its reputation would suggest (although this means you won't be alone in appreciating it). If the crowds are too much, there's also the arc of historic towns outside the city – Verona, Padua and Vicenza, all centres of interest in their own right, although rather overshadowed by their illustrious neighbour. To the south, the region of **Emilia-Romagna** has been at the heart of Italy's postwar industrial boom and has a standard of living on a par with Piemonte and Lombardy, although it's also a traditional stronghold of the Italian Left. Its coast is popular among Italians, and Rimini is about Italy's brashest, tackiest (and trendiest) seaside resort, with a high reputation on the clubbing scene. You may do better to ignore the beaches altogether, however, and concentrate on the ancient centres of Ravenna, Ferrara, Parma and the regional capital of Bologna, one of Italy's liveliest, most historic but least appreciated cities.

Central Italy represents perhaps the most commonly perceived image of the country, and **Tuscany**, with its classic rolling countryside and the art-packed towns of Florence, Pisa and Siena, to name only the three best-known centres, is one of its most visited regions. Neighbouring **Umbria** is similar in all but its tourist numbers, though it gets busier every year, as visitors flock into towns such as Perugia, Spoleto and Assisi. Further east still, **Marche** may in time go the same way, but for the moment is comparatively untouched, its highlights being the ancient towns of Urbino and Áscoli Piceno. South of Marche, the hills begin to pucker into mountains in the twin regions of **Abruzzo** and **Molise**, Italy's first really remote area if you're travelling north to south, centring on the country's highest peak – the Gran Sasso d'Italia. Molise, particularly, is a taster of the south, as is **Lazio** to the west, in part a poor and sometimes desolate region whose often rugged landscapes contrast with the more manicured beauty of the other central regions. Lazio's real focal point, though, is **Rome**, Italy's capital and the one city in the country which owes allegiance neither to the north *or* south, its people proudly aloof from the rest of the country's squabbles. Rome is a tremendous city quite unlike any other, and in terms of historical sights outstrips everywhere else in the country by a long way.

The **south** proper begins south of Rome, with the region of **Campania**, which is as far as many tourists get. Naples is a petulant, unforgettable city, the spiritual heart of the Italian south, and on hand nearby are some of Italy's finest ancient sites in Pompeii and Herculaneum, not to mention the country's most spectacular stretch of coast around Amalfi. **Basilicata** and **Calabria**, which make up the instep and toe of Italy's boot, are harder territory but still rewarding, the emphasis less on art, more on the landscape and quiet, unspoilt coastlines. **Puglia**, also in the "heel" of Italy, has underrated pleasures, notably the landscape of its Gargano peninsula, the souk-like quality of its capital Bari, and the Baroque glories of Lecce in the far south. As regards **Sicily**, the island is really a law unto itself, a wide mixture of attractions ranging from some of the finest preserved Hellenistic treasures in Europe, to a couple of Italy's fanciest beach resorts in Taormina and Cefalù, not to mention some gorgeous upland scenery. Come this far south and you're closer to Africa than Milan, and it shows, in the climate, the architecture and the cooking – with couscous featuring on many menus in the west of the island. **Sardinia**, too, feels far removed from the Italian mainland, especially in its relatively undiscovered interior, although you may be content to explore its fine beaches, which are among Italy's best.

AVERAGE TEMPERATURES

	Jan	Feb	March	April	May	June	July	Aug	Sept	Oct	Nov	Dec
Ancona	5.7	5.8	9.4	13.6	17.6	22.3	24.9	24.3	21.1	16.6	12.6	7.4
Bari	8.4	8.5	10.8	13.9	17.5	21.9	24.5	24.3	21.7	18.2	14.8	10.2
Bologna	2.5	3.4	8.6	13.8	18.1	23.3	26.0	25.4	21.3	15.2	9.7	3.9
Cagliari	10.5	11.0	13.0	15.0	18.5	22.5	25.5	25.5	23.0	19.0	15.0	12.5
Florence	5.6	5.8	9.9	13.3	17.4	22.1	25.0	24.5	21.2	15.8	11.2	6.0
Genoa	8.4	8.7	11.5	14.5	17.8	21.9	24.6	25.0	21.8	18.1	18.1	13.3
Milan	1.9	3.8	8.6	13.2	17.3	22.2	24.8	23.9	20.3	13.7	8.5	3.0
Naples	8.7	8.7	11.4	14.3	18.1	22.3	24.8	24.8	22.3	18.1	14.5	10.3
Palermo	10.3	10.4	13.0	16.2	18.7	23.0	25.3	25.1	23.2	19.9	16.8	12.6
Rome	7.4	8.0	11.5	14.4	18.4	22.9	25.7	25.5	22.4	17.7	13.4	8.9
Trieste	5.3	4.8	8.6	12.9	17.1	21.2	24.0	23.3	20.4	15.1	11.0	6.3
Venice	3.8	4.1	8.2	12.6	17.1	21.2	23.6	23.3	20.4	15.1	10.5	5.0

°C = (°F - 32) multiplied by 5/9

Climate: when to go

Italy's **climate** is one of the most hospitable in the world, with a general pattern of warm, dry summers and mild winters. There are, however, marked regional variations, ranging from the more temperate northern part of the country to the firmly Mediterranean south. **Summers** are hot and dry along the coastal areas, especially as you move south, cool in the major mountain areas – the Alps and Apennines. **Winters** are mild in the south of the country, Rome and below, but in the north they can be at least as cold as anywhere in the northern hemisphere, sometimes worse, especially across the plains of Lombardy and Emilia-Romagna, which can be very inhospitable indeed in January.

As for **when to go**, if you're planning to visit fairly touristed areas, especially beach resorts, avoid July and August, when the weather can be too hot and the crowds at their most congested. August is when the Italians go on holiday so expect the crush to be especially bad in the resorts and the scene in the major historic cities – Rome, Florence, Venice – to be slightly artificial as the only people around are fellow tourists. The nicest time to visit, in terms of the weather and lack of crowds, is April to late June, or September and October. If you're planning to swim, however, bear in mind that only the south of the country may be warm enough outside the May to September period.

PART ONE

THE

BASICS

GETTING THERE FROM BRITAIN

The easiest way to get to Italy from Britain is to fly; and the prices of the cheapest tickets can even be cheaper than those for the long train journey. Deals change all the time, and prices depend on where you want to fly to and often on how far in advance you can book. The majority of flights go to Milan and Rome, with Bologna, Pisa, Naples, Turin and Venice in the second tier; frequent onward connections are possible from these gateway cities to smaller regional airports.

Costs broadly reflect the distance and popularity of the place you're travelling to – flights to Milan, for instance, can be a great deal cheaper than those to Palermo.

BY PLANE

A **scheduled flight** is the most obvious if not always the cheapest option. Of scheduled airlines flying the Italian routes, British Airways (BA) and Alitalia operate daily direct flights to most of the major Italian cities from London Heathrow or Gatwick. From Manchester flights go direct to Milan and Rome, from Birmingham and Glasgow they are only direct to Milan. Low-cost airlines – Go, Ryanair and Buzz – fly from Stansted to a number of destinations across the country – a distinct advantage if you want to avoid the major gateway cities.

You will see some very cheap flights advertised with **low-cost airlines**, and while there are certainly some bargains to be had (in 2000 Ryanair had one-way flights to Turin for £9) they do not always work out the least expensive. The major **scheduled carriers** now operate the same system of first-come, first-served on the cheaper seats, and prices depend more on how

TRAVEL AGENTS

Alpha Flights, 37 King's Exchange, Tileyard Rd, London N7 9AH (☎020/7609 8188).

CTS Travel, 44 Goodge St, London W1P 2AD (☎020/7290 0620).

Flight File, 46 Victoria Rd, Surbiton, Surrey KT6 4JL (☎020/8296 0309).

Italflights, 125 High Holborn, London WC1V 6QA (☎020/7405 6771).

Italia nel Mondo, 6 Palace St, London SW16 5HY (☎020/7828 9171).

Italy Sky Shuttle, 227 Shepherd's Bush Rd, London W6 7AS (☎020/8748 1333).

Itavia Travel Ltd, 152 Bury Old Rd, Manchester M7 4QY (☎0161/740 5095, *www.itavia.co.uk*).

North South Travel, Moulsham Mill Centre, Parkway, Chelmsford, Essex CM2 7PX (☎01245/608291).

STA Travel, Telesales Europe (☎020/7361 6161, *www.statravel.co.uk*). Branches in London, Aberdeen, Brighton, Bristol, Cambridge, Cardiff, Edinburgh, Exeter, Glasgow, Leeds, Liverpool, Manchester, Newcastle, Oxford, and Southampton, as well as on university campuses throughout Britain.

Trailfinders, European Flights (☎020/7937 5400, *www.trailfinders.co.uk*). Branches in Birmingham, Bristol, Cambridge, Glasgow, London, Manchester and Newcastle.

Travel Bug, 597 Cheetham Hill Rd, Manchester M8 5EJ (☎0161/721 4000).

Usit CAMPUS, Call Centre (☎0870/2401010, *www.usitcampus.co.uk*). Branches in London, Aberdeen, Birmingham, Brighton, Bristol, Cambridge, Coventry, Edinburgh, Glasgow, Manchester, Oxford, Sheffield and in YHA shops and on university campuses all over Britain.

far in advance you book and how popular the flight is than the season or even the distance.

Most flights cost around £90–£150 return, though it's quite possible to pay significantly less if you're able to be flexible – and more if you're not. Be prepared to pay £200-£250 in high season, when the cheaper seats get booked up months in advance. In general fares to cities further south

AIRLINES IN BRITAIN

Alitalia ☎0870/5448259, www.alitalia.co.uk
British Airways ☎0345/222111, www.britishairways.com
British Midland ☎0870/6070555, www.britishmidland.co.uk
Buzz ☎0870/2407070, www.buzzaway.com
Go ☎0845/6054321, www.go-fly.com
Meridiana ☎020/7839 2222, www.meridiana.it
Ryanair ☎0541/569569, www.ryanair.com

cost around £40 more. Restrictions on the cheapest scheduled tickets, including low-cost airlines, are normally that you must stay a Saturday night abroad and you cannot change the details of your ticket without paying an additional fee; they're also rarely valid for longer than a month.

Most airlines now offer direct phone or Internet booking, with many of the low-cost carriers operating a **ticketless system** – you are given a reference number to check in with at the airport.

Travel agents will often be able to do you a deal on a direct **charter flight**, although you'd be advised to make enquiries weeks in advance during peak season; you can also track down deals on charters direct through a number of specialist tour operators (see box opposite). To find agents offering discounted flights, scour the classified sections in the weekend **newspapers** – the *Guardian*, *Sunday Times* and *Observer* especially – and if you live in London, *Time Out* magazine and the *Evening Standard* newspaper. Teletext, Ceefax and the **Internet** are also good sources of information, and there are useful sites specializing in bargain deals – try *www.lastminute.com*, *www.travelocity.com*, *www.cheapflights.co.uk* or *www.bargainholidays.com*.

There are a number of **flight specialists to Italy** (see box on previous page for addresses)

offering a wide array of flights to a broad selection of Italian cities; or you could approach a **student/youth travel specialist** like Usit CAMPUS or STA Travel (again, see box on previous page for details), who offer all kinds of discounted fares, though these won't necessarily beat the deals you could find yourself. Using one of these outfits – and setting aside cut-price airlines – you can expect to pay £100–120 to one of the major gateways in low season and even during the height of summer you should be able to find something for significantly under £200.

Most agents, and some airlines, offer "**open-jaw**" deals, whereby you can fly into one Italian city and back from another – a good idea if you want to make your way across the country, and sometimes no more expensive than a standard charter or scheduled return. Consider also a **package deal** (see below), which takes care of flights and accommodation for an all-in price.

PACKAGES AND ORGANIZED TOURS

Italy stands somewhat apart from other European package destinations: it's not especially cheap and has avoided the big hotel build-ups that have blighted parts of Spain and Greece. And it's as much a venue for specialist interest and touring holidays as the standard sun-sand-sea packages. The Italian State Tourist Office (see p.24) provides a comprehensive list of tour operators.

Having said that, there's no shortage of **travel-plus-accommodation** deals on the market, and if you're keen to stay in one (or two) places, they can work out to be very good value. Many companies offer travel at rates as competitive as you could find on your own, and any travel agent can fill you in on all the latest offers. Obviously, it's cheapest to travel out of season, something we'd recommend anyway as resorts and sights are much less crowded, and the weather, in the south at least, is often still warm enough for swimming. **Prices** for package deals start at about £400 per person per week for half-board in a hotel during May in Amalfi or Sorrento, and they can be as high as £1000, although you may be able to do it a little cheaper in less popular resorts or somewhere more geared to mass tourism like Rimini. In high season (Easter, July & Aug), prices are higher, and you can expect to pay as much as £1200 for a week's half-board in Amalfi, Sorrento or Taormina, although your travel agent might come up with some good, last-minute deals. Restored

BRITISH SPECIALIST TOUR OPERATORS

Alternative Travel Group (☎01865/513333, *www.atg-oxford.co.uk*). All-inclusive walking holidays in Tuscany, Umbria and Sicily, including truffle- and flower-themed tours. Costly but well organized.

Citalia (☎020/8686 5533, *www.citalia.co.uk*). Hotel and villa packages all over Italy, plus tailor-made itineraries, self-catering holidays and car rental.

Crystal (☎020/8939 5405, *www.crystalholidays.co.uk*). Hotel packages, two-centre holidays, city breaks and fly-drives.

CV Travel (☎020/7591 2811). Luxurious restored farmhouses, villas and palazzi.

Explore Worldwide (☎01252/319448, *www.exploreworldwide.co.uk*). Walking in Tuscany, Alpine trails and volcano hikes in Sicily.

Interhome (☎020/8891 1294, *www.interhome.co.uk*). Holiday homes all over Italy; you arrange your own transport. Budget choices for 4–10 people at £50 or less per person per week, even in high season.

Italia nel Mondo (☎020/7828 9171). Beach holidays, self-catering apartments and villas and room reservations throughout Italy. Web site (*www.thesicilianexperience.com*) lists holidays in Sicily.

Italiatour (☎01883/623363, *www.alitalia.it/italiatour*). Package deals, city breaks (including ones to coincide with football matches), winter-sun holidays and specialist Italian cuisine tours.

Landmark Trust (☎01628/825925, *www.landmarktrust.co.uk*). Four properties: a Palladian villa near Vicenza, the home of Keats in Rome, the Brownings' home in Florence, and the old monastery of Sant'Antonio at Tivoli.

Liaisons Abroad (☎020/7376 4020, *www.liasonsabroad.com*). Specialists in booking for festivals, opera, concerts, theatre and football, as well as hotel accommodation.

Long Travel (☎01694/722193). Small company specializing in southern Italy. Flights and accommodation, including self-catering on organic farms, from a buffalo farm in Campania to *trulli* in Puglia, and weekends in Naples with the services of an English guide. Good value.

Magic of Italy (☎020/8939 5453). City breaks and hotel and villa packages throughout Italy.

Sunvil (☎020/8568 4499, *www.sunvil.co.uk*). Hotel and villa packages, city breaks and fly-drives.

Time Off (☎020/7235 8070). Short-break specialists for Milan, Florence, Venice and Rome.

Vacanze in Italia (☎01798/869461, *www.indiv-travellers.com*). Country farmhouses, villas and apartments throughout Italy, concentrating on the Lakes, Tuscany and Umbria.

Voyages Ilena (☎020/7924 4440, *www.voyagesilena.co.uk*). Self-catering and hotel accommodation in Sardinia, backed up by detailed local information and a full travel-booking service.

villas and farmhouses are a popular option but are no bargain: you should reckon on about £700 a week to rent the average four-bedded Tuscan farmhouse in August, rather less out of season and in less discovered areas. A cheaper alternative is agriturismo (see p.35).

Some operators organize **specialist holidays** to Italy – walking tours, art and archeology holidays, Italian food and wine jaunts, short breaks to coincide with opera festivals or even football matches. However, they don't come cheaply: accommodation, food, local transport and the services of a guide are nearly always included, and a week's half-board holiday can cost anything from £500–700 per person, rising to well over £1000 for full board. There's also a plethora of operators selling **short-break deals** to Italian cities: for

these, reckon on spending upwards of £300 per person for three nights in Florence in a three-star hotel during low season and upwards of £350 between April and October; though special offers can sometimes cut prices drastically, especially for late bookings.

If you want to rent a car in Italy, it's well worth checking with tour operators (and flight agents) before you leave, as some **fly-drive** deals work out very cheaply. Crystal (see box above) have good prices, starting at around £280 a week per person in summer, but check out also Citalia – and see p.30 for more on car rental.

BY TRAIN

Travelling **by train** to Italy won't save much money, and can even end up costing more than

INFORMATION AND TICKET OFFICES

TRAINS

Eurostar, EPS House, Waterloo Station, London SE1 8SE (☎0870/5186186, www.eurostar.com).

Italian State Railways (☎020/7724 0011 – but you'll have a hard time getting through; www.fs-on-line.com).

Rail Choice, Delta House, 175 Borough High St, London SE1 1XP (☎020/7939 9915, www.railchoice.com). Internet and telephone rail ticket agency.

Rail Europe, 179 Piccadilly, London W1V 0BA and International Rail Centre, Victoria Station, London SW1V 1JY (☎0870/584 8848, www.raileurope.co.uk). Sells rail journeys for Italy, sleepers and couchettes as well as InterRail and Euro-Domino passes.

Ultima Travel, 424 Chester Rd, Little Sutton, South Wirral L66 3RB (☎0151/339 6171).

BUSES

Eurolines, National Express (☎08705/808 080 or 01582/404 511, www.eurolines.co.uk).

the plane, but it can be a leisurely way of getting to the country and you can stop off in other parts of Europe on the way. As you'd expect, the choice of routes and fares is hugely complex, but most trains pass through Paris and head down through France towards Milan. A return ticket to Milan, using Eurostar under the Channel and the superfast TGV through France, costs around £180, and takes around twelve hours, but advance-booked fares, discounts (including for under-26s) and special offers are legion. Using slower trains won't cut the cost very significantly and neither will using the train and ferry route, which is now barely used and accordingly, badly timetabled.

From London the main cost is getting across the channel to Brussels or Paris: a return ticket to Paris on **Eurostar**, through the Channel Tunnel, costs anything from £90 to £160, depending on how far in advance you book and whether or not you are under 26; prices to Brussels are similar, but the journey to Italy takes at least three hours longer. Bear in mind that if you travel via Paris you'll have to change both trains and stations which means lugging your bags on the metro from the Gare du Nord to the Gare de Lyon. From either Brussels or Paris the trains south are fast and frequent, although once again the cost and journey time depends on whether you take the TGV through France or make a slower journey on ordinary trains – one option is to travel through Switzerland.

If you're doing a lot of train travel it can often make sense to get an **InterRail pass**, valid for one month's unlimited rail travel in specified zones. You'll need the two-zone version (£235, £169 for under-26s) to get from Britain to Italy –

which is grouped with Turkey, Greece and Slovenia; if you want to explore further afield than this, get the all-zone version (£309/£209). The pass also gives discounts on cross-Channel services, including Eurostar, and is valid on the Bríndisi–Corfu–Patras route to Greece. InterRail is available from major train stations and youth/student travel agencies, but you need to have been resident in Europe for at least six months to qualify.

Finally, senior citizens holding a Senior Citizen Railcard can purchase a **Rail Europe Senior Card** for £5, which allows thirty-percent discounts on rail fares throughout Europe, including Italy, as long as the journey crosses an international border, plus thirty percent off most ferry crossings.

Details on all international rail tickets and passes are best obtained by calling personally at major train stations or by contacting the agents listed in the box above. Don't expect much help from travel agents on planning routes, however, or the Italian State Railways office to answer the phone.

For details of passes for use solely within Italy, see p.28.

BY BUS

It's difficult to see why anyone would want to travel to Italy by **bus,** unless they have a phobia of flying – and of trains. National Express Eurolines (see box above), do, however, have occasional bargain offers – at the time of writing a return ticket to Milan costs £69, if booked two weeks in advance; the normal price for under-26s is £112. The Milan service departs three times a week (daily in summer) and takes twenty two hours; the journey on to Rome will add a gruelling nine hours – and a light £15 – to the trip.

There are direct services from London to Turin, Milan, Bologna, Florence and Rome, with less frequent services to Parma, Siena, Venice, Verona, Genoa and Naples. If you are really keen on buses the Eurolines pass gives you unlimited travel between forty-eight European cities for either thirty or sixty days; high-season prices for under-26s or over-60s are £195 for thirty days, or £227 for sixty days; for adults £245 and £283 respectively.

BY ROAD: FERRIES AND EUROTUNNEL

There's no one fixed route to Italy if you're travelling with **your own vehicle**. The best cross-Channel options for most drivers will be the standard ferry/hovercraft links between Dover and Calais (with Hoverspeed or P&O Stena), Folkestone and Boulogne (Hoverspeed), or Newhaven and Dieppe (P&O Stena). Crossing using Eurotunnel (24hr service, departs every 15min at peak periods) will speed up the initial part of the journey, although overall there are no great savings on time to be made since there's still a long way to go once you reach France. Any travel agent can provide up-to-date cross-Channel schedules and make advance bookings – which are essential in season.

As regards **routes**, from northern France, the Alpine route, via Germany and Switzerland, is probably the shortest as the crow flies, but can be pretty arduous; most drivers hotfoot it to the south of France and then switch east into northern Italy. The Automobile Association (AA; ☎0800/435980, *www.theaa.co.uk*) and Royal Automobile Club (RAC, ☎0800/550550, *www.rac.co.uk*) both provide comprehensive route-planning services, as well as offering insurance, general advice on all aspects of driving to Italy and details of useful contact organizations. The AA has special deals for Channel crossings, with an overnight stay and breakdown assistance policy included.

FERRY ROUTES TO ITALY

CROSS-CHANNEL TICKETS

Note: for Eurostar passenger services, see box opposite.

Eurotunnel (☎0870/5353535, *www.eurotunnel.com*). To Calais.

Hoverspeed (☎0870/524 0241, *www.hoverspeed.co.uk*). To Boulogne and Calais.

P&O Stena Line (☎0870/6000600, *www.posl.com*). To Calais and Dieppe.

Sea France (☎0870/5711711, *www.seafrance.com*). Dover to Calais.

AGENTS FOR FERRIES TO ITALY

Serena Holidays, 40–42 Kenway Rd, London SW5 0RA (☎020/7373 6548 or 020/7373 6549). Agents for Adriatica (Albania, Greece and Croatia); Moby Lines (Corsica); Siremar (Sicily); and Tirrenia (Malta, Tunisia, Sardinia and Sicily).

Southern Ferries, 179 Piccadilly, London W1V 9DB (☎020/7491 4968). Represent Corsica Marittima (Corsica); SNCM (France).

Viamare Travel, Graphic House, 2 Sumatra Rd, London NW6 1PU (☎020/7431 4560, *ferries@viamare.com*). Agents for Fraglines (Greece); Jadrolinja (Croatia); Linee Lauro (Albania and Tunisia); Marlines (Greece); Strintzis (Greece); Transeuropea (Yugoslavia);Ventouris (Greece).

GETTING THERE FROM IRELAND

Both Aer Lingus and Alitalia have direct flights from Dublin to Milan daily, from where connections to regional airports are frequent; flights to Rome are less often, usually around three times a week. It's possible to find deals for around IR£250/€288.00 if you book a long time in advance, but prices are usually significantly higher (IR£300–450 /€346.00–518.00), and unless you're in a hurry it's likely to make more sense to pick up an inexpensive flight to London, Brussels or Paris especially if you are heading for the south of Italy.

There are many daily flights from Dublin to London, operated by Ryanair, Aer Lingus and British Midland: the cheapest is Ryanair – which also flies from Kerry, Cork and Knock – starting at around IR£60/€76.18 for a return to Stansted (sometimes as low as £IR30/€38.09), though the cost of the journey across London, added to Britain's high airport taxes, may in fact make the total as much as Aer Lingus or British Midland fares straight to Italy. Avoiding these costs, Virgin Express now flies from Shannon to Brussels twice a day and budget deals can be found on Ryanair from Dublin to Brussels or Paris, from where connections to the major Italian airports are frequent.

From **Belfast**, British Airways and British Midland fly to Heathrow, but the cheapest options are the British European flights to Gatwick and Stansted, starting at around £60 return, though prices depend very much on availability. For the best **youth/student deals** from either city, contact Usit (see box below).

AIRLINES AND AGENTS IN IRELAND

AIRLINES

Aer Lingus Belfast ☎0845/9737747; Dublin ☎01/886 8888; Cork ☎021/4327155; Limerick ☎061/474 239; www.aerlingus.com

Alitalia ☎01/677 5171; www.alitalia.co.uk

British Airways Belfast ☎08457/222111; Dublin ☎1800/626747; www.britishairways.com

British Midland Belfast ☎0870/6070555; Dublin ☎01/283 8833; www.britishmidland.co.uk

British European, Belfast ☎0870/567 6676.

Ryanair Belfast ☎0870/1569 569; Dublin ☎01/609 7881; www.ryanair.com

Virgin Express ☎061/704470; www.virgin-express.com

TRAVEL AGENTS

Budget Travel, 134 Lower Baggot St, Dublin 2 (☎01/661 1866). Flight-only charters and scheduled.

Thomas Cook, 11 Donegall Place, Belfast BT1 5AJ (☎028/9088 3900); 118 Grafton St, Dublin 2 (☎01/677 1721). www.thomascook.co.uk; Mainstream package holiday and flight agent, with occasional discount offers.

United Travel, Stillorgan Bowl, Stillorgan, County Dublin (☎01/283 2555). Scheduled flights, charters and packages to Italy.

Usit, Dublin reservations: ☎01602/1600, Belfast reservations ☎028/9032 7111. Branches at: 19 Aston Quay, O'Connell Bridge, Dublin (☎01/602 1777); Fountain Centre, College St, Belfast BT1 6ET (☎028/9032 4073). www.usit.ie; Student and youth specialist.

GETTING THERE FROM THE USA AND CANADA

You can fly to Italy direct from a number of US and Canadian cities: the main points of entry are Rome and Milan, although there are plenty of connecting flights on to other Italian cities from those two gateways. Prices are quite competitive, making Italy a feasible entry-point for Europe as a whole. Many airlines and agents also offer "open-jaw" tickets, enabling you to fly into one Italian city and out from another, travelling overland in between. Another good option is to travel via elsewhere in Europe (particularly Britain or Germany), since there's a broad range of well-priced flights from all over North America. A Eurail pass (see box on p.12) may be a useful option if Italy is part of a longer European trip, since you can use it to get from any part of Europe to Italy.

SHOPPING FOR TICKETS

Barring special offers, the cheapest fare is usually an **Apex ticket**, although this will carry certain restrictions: you have to book – and pay – at least 21 days before departure, spend at least seven days abroad (maximum stay three months), and you tend to get penalized if you change your schedule. There are also winter **Super Apex** tickets, sometimes known as "Eurosavers" – slightly cheaper than an ordinary Apex, but limiting your stay to between seven and 21 days. Some airlines also issue **Special Apex** tickets to people younger than 24, often extending the maximum stay to a year. Many airlines offer **youth or student fares** to under 26s; a passport or driving licence is sufficient proof of age, though these tickets are subject to availability and can have eccentric booking conditions. It's worth remembering that most cheap return fares involve spending at least one Saturday night away and that many will only give a percentage refund if you need to cancel or alter your journey, so make sure you check the restrictions carefully before buying a ticket.

You can normally cut costs further by going through a **specialist flight agent** – either a consolidator, which buys up blocks of tickets from the airlines and sells them at a discount, or a discount agent, which deals in blocks of tickets offloaded by the airlines, and often offers special student and youth fares and a range of other travel-related services such as travel insurance, rail passes, car rentals, tours and the like. Bear in mind, though, that penalties for changing your plans can be stiff. Some agents specialize in **charter flights**, which may be cheaper than anything available on a scheduled flight, but again departure dates are fixed and withdrawal penalties are high (check the refund policy). If you travel a lot, **discount travel clubs** are another option – the annual membership fee may be worthwhile for cut-price air tickets and car rental. Finally, **students** should be able to take advantage of discounted air fares from various travel agents; while a couple of agents (see box overleaf) also offer very cheap **courier flights** – though these carry severe restrictions on trip duration and the amount of luggage allowed.

Don't automatically assume that tickets purchased through a travel specialist will be the cheapest – once you get a quote, check with the airlines and you may turn up an even better deal. Be advised also that the pool of travel companies is swimming with sharks – exercise caution and never deal with a company that demands cash up front or refuses to accept payment by credit card.

Regardless of where you buy your ticket, fares will depend on the **season** and are highest between June and August; they drop during the "shoulder" seasons, September–October and April–May, and you'll get the best prices during the low season, November–March (excluding Christmas and New Year, when prices are hiked up and seats are at a premium.

AIRLINES, AGENTS AND OPERATORS IN NORTH AMERICA

AIRLINES

Air Canada US ☎1-800/776-3000l; Canada ☎1-800/247-2262; *www.aircanada.ca*

Air France US ☎1-800/237-2747; Canada ☎1-800/667-2747; *www.airfrance.com*

Alitalia US ☎1-800/223-5730; Canada ☎1-800/361-8336; *www.alitalia.com*

American Airlines ☎1-800/433-7300; *www.americanairlines.com*

British Airways US ☎1-800/247-9297; Canada ☎1-800/243-6822; *www.britishairways.com*

Canadian Airlines US ☎1-800/426-7000; Canada ☎1-800/665-1177; *www.aircanada.ca*

Continental Airlines; ☎1-800/231-0856; *www.continental.com*

Delta Airlines US ☎1-800/241-4141; Canada ☎1-800/221-1212; *www.delta.com*

Iberia ☎1-800/772-4642; *www.iberia.com*

Icelandair ☎1-800/223-5500; *www.icelandair.com*

KLM US ☎1-800/447-4747; Canada ☎1-800/361-5073; *www.klm.com*

Lufthansa US ☎1-800/645-3880 or 1-800/399-LUFT; Canada ☎1-800/563-5954; *www.lufthansa.com*

Northwest US ☎1-800/447-4747; Canada ☎1-800/581-6400; *www.nwa.com*

Sabena ☎1-800/955-2000; *www.sabena.com*

SAS ☎1-800/221-2350; *www.flysas.com*

Swissair US ☎1-800/221-4750; Canada ☎1-800/267-9477; *www.swissair.com*

TWA ☎1-800/892-4141; *www.twa.com*

DISCOUNT TRAVEL COMPANIES

Air Brokers International, 150 Post St, Suite 620, San Francisco, CA 94108 (☎1-800/883-3273, *www.airbrokers.com*). Consolidator.

Air Courier Association, 15000 W 6th Ave, Suite 203, Golden, CO 80401 (☎1-800/282-1202 or 303/278-8810, *www.aircourier.org*). Courier flight broker, often with flights from New York to Milan or Rome.

Airhitch, 2641 Broadway, 3rd Floor, Suite 100, New York, NY 10025 (☎212/326-2009, *www.airhitch.org*). Standby-seat broker: For a price, they will get you on a flight close to your preferred destination, within a week.

Cheap Tickets, 115 E 57th St, Suite 1510, New York, NY 10022 (☎1-800/377-1000, *www.cheaptickets.com*). Discounted tickets for international destinations.

Council Travel, Head Office: 205 E 42nd St, New York, NY 10017 (☎1-800/2COUNCIL or ☎212/822-2700 in New York, *www.counciltravel.com*). Student and youth travel organization offering discounted air fares, rail passes and travel gear. For those over 26, it acts like a regular travel agency.

Educational Travel Center, 438 N Frances St, Madison, WI 53703 (☎1-800/747-5551, *www.edtrav.com*). Student/youth discount agent with good prices on flights to Rome and Milan.

Encore Travel Club, 4501 Forbes Blvd, Lanham, MD 20706 (☎1-800/444-9800, *www.preferredtraveller.com*). Discount travel club.

Interworld Travel, 800 Douglass Rd, Suite 140, Coral Gables, FL 33134 (☎1-800/468-3796, *www.interworldtravel.com*). Consolidator.

Last Minute Travel Club, 100 Sylvan Rd, Suite 600, Woburn, MA 01801 (☎1-800/LAST-MIN).Travel club specializing in standby deals.

New Frontiers/Nouvelles Frontières, Head Offices: 12 E 33rd St, New York, NY 10016 (☎1-800/366-6387 or 212/779-0600, *www.newfrontiers.com*); 1001 Sherbrook East, Suite 720, Montréal, PQ H2L 1L3 (☎514/526-8444). French discount travel firm with summer charters to Rome. Other branches in LA, San Francisco and Québec City.

Now Voyager, 74 Varick St, Suite 307, New York, NY 10013 (☎212/431-1616, *www.nowvoyagertravel.com*). Courier flight broker.

STA Travel, Head Office: 10 Downing St, New York, NY 10018 (nationwide ☎1-800/777-0112, *www.statravel.com*). Worldwide specialist in independent travel for students and under-26s only, with branches in the Los Angeles, San Francisco and Boston areas.

TFI Tours International, Head Office: 34 W 32nd St, 12th Floor, New York, NY 10001 (☎1-800/745-8000, *www.tfitoursinternational.com*). Consolidator; other offices in Las Vegas, San Francisco, Los Angeles.

Travac, Head Office: 989 6th Ave, 16th Floor, New York, NY 10018 (☎1-877/872-8221 or 212/630-3316); 2601 East Jefferson St, Orlando, FL 32803 (☎407/896-0014); *www.travac.com*. Consolidator and charter broker. Current fares available from their fax line, 1-888/872-8327.

Travel Avenue, 10 S Riverside Plaza, Suite 1404, Chicago, IL 60606 (☎1-800/333-3335, *www.travelavenue.com*). Discount travel agent.

Travel Cuts, Head Office: 187 College St, Toronto, ON M5T 1P7 (☎1-800/667-2887 or 416/979-2406, *www.travelcuts.com*). Canadian student travel organization with branches all over the country.

Travelers Advantage, 3033 S Parker Rd, Suite 900, Aurora, CO 80014 (☎1-800/548-1116, *www.travelersadvantage.com*). Discount travel club.

UniTravel, 11737 Administration Drive, Suite 120, St Louis, MO 63146 (☎1-800/325-2222, *www.unitravel.com*). Consolidator.

Worldtek Travel, 111 Water St, New Haven, CT 06511 (☎1-800/243-1723, *www.worldtek.com*). Discount travel agency.

Worldwide Discount Travel Club, 11601 Biscayne Blvd, Suite 310, North Miami, FL 33181 (☎305/534-2082). Discount travel club.

NORTH AMERICAN TOUR OPERATORS

Note: Although phone numbers are given here, you're better off making tour reservations through your local travel agent. An agent will make all the phone calls, sort out any booking complications and arrange flights, insurance and the like – all at no extra cost to you.

Adventure Center (☎1-800/228-8747, *www.adventurecenter.com*). Hiking specialist with tours in Tuscany, Sicily and the Alps, for $795 upwards (Volcano Hike in Sicily starts at $830), not including flights.

American Express Vacations (☎1-800/241-1700, *www.americanexpress.com*). Individual and escorted programmes to Italy; can also plan city stays, offering competitive hotel rates.

Archaeological Tours (☎212/986-3054). Fully escorted 14- to 17-day tours of Sicily, southern Italy and ancient Rome, starting at around $4000, land only or $5650 including airfare.

BCT Scenic Walking (☎1-800/473-1210, *www.bctwalk.com*). Four diverse walking tours led by locals, from $2195, land only.

Central Holidays (☎1-800/935-5000, *www.centralh.com*). General-interest tours, starting at $2369 all-inclusive; also fly-drives and city breaks.

Ciclismo Classico (☎1-800/866-7314, *www.ciclismoclassico.com*). Luxury walking and cycling vacations; $2395–3595, land only.

CIT Tours (☎1-800/CIT-TOUR; in Canada call Toronto on 1-800/387-0711 or Montréal on 1-800/361-7799; *www.cit-tours.com*). Specializing exclusively in tours to Italy.

Dailey-Thorp (☎212/307-1555, *www.daileythorp.com*). Specializes in opera and classical music tours, lasting 7–21 days.

Donna Franca Tours (☎1-800/225-6290, *www.donnafranca.com*). Huge variety of tours, from cooking courses to golf. Cooking courses start at $829–889 and scenic tours range from $1795–3000, including air travel.

EIS (European Incoming Services) (☎1-800/443-1644). Italy specialist offering escorted and independent tours of varying lengths, with prices averaging $2000.

Globus-Cosmos (☎1-800/221-0090, *www.globusandcosmos.com*). Escorted and independent tours; prices start around $1500, land only.

Italiatour (US ☎1-800/ 845-3365; Canada 1-888/515-5245; *www.italiatour.com*). Offers fly-drive tours, escorted and individual programmes, in conjunction with Alitalia.

Mountain Travel-Sobek (☎1-800/227-2384, *www.mtsobek.com*). Wilderness specialist – adventure itineraries, including hiking, from around $2200 land-only. Their Tuscany walking tour runs in the Spring and Fall and starts at $3190.

New Frontiers (☎1-800/366-6387, *www.newfrontiers.com*). Affordable tours, using charter flights to keep costs down.

FROM THE USA

Alitalia, the national airline of Italy, fly the widest choice of routes between the USA and Italy. They fly direct every day from New York, Boston, Miami, Chicago and Los Angeles to Milan and Rome. As for American-based airlines, Delta Airlines fly daily from New York non-stop, or from Chicago and Los Angeles to Rome and Milan with stopovers in either New York or a European city; TWA fly daily from LA and Chicago via New York to Milan and Rome; and American Airlines only fly direct to Milan from Chicago and Miami. If you're looking for alternatives, or specifically want a

European stopover, other airlines with services to Italy include: British Airways (via London); Air France (via Paris); Lufthansa (via Frankfurt or Münich); Iberia (via Madrid); Sabena (via Brussels); Swissair (via Zürich); Icelandair (via Luxembourg); KLM (via Amsterdam); and SAS (via Copenhagen) – all of which have services to, at least, Rome and Milan.

The **direct scheduled fares** charged by each airline don't vary as much as you might think, and you'll more often than not be basing your choice around things like flight timings, routes and gateway cities, ticket restrictions, and even the airline's reputation for comfort and service. It's a

---

EUROPEAN RAIL PASSES FROM NORTH AMERICA AND AUSTRALASIA

There are a number of European rail passes that can only be purchased before leaving home, though consider carefully how much travelling you are going to be doing: these all-encompassing passes only really begin to pay for themselves if you intend to see a fair bit of Italy and the rest of Europe.

The best-known and most flexible is the **Eurail Youthpass** (for under-26s) which costs US$388/A$733 for fifteen days, and there are also one-month and two-month versions; if you're 26 or over you'll have to buy a first-class **Eurail** pass, which costs US$522/A$854 for the fifteen-day option. You stand a better chance of getting your money's worth out of a **Eurail Flexipass**, which is good for a certain number of travel days in a two-month period. This too comes in under-26/first-class versions: ten days in two months cost US$458/A$872 for under 26s, US$654/A$1245 for over 26s. A scaled-down version of the Flexipass, the **Europass** allows travel in France, Germany, Italy, Switzerland and Spain for five days in two months US$348/A$662, fifteen days in two months US$728/A$1385; the under-26 version, the **Europass Youth**, costs about US$233/A$443 and up. These passes can be bought from the agents listed below and also from many regular travel agents, especially youth and student specialists (see listings on pp.10–11).

North Americans and Australasians are also eligible to purchase **more specific passes** valid for travel in Italy only – see p.28 for details.

RAIL CONTACTS IN NORTH AMERICA

DER Travel, 9501 W Devon St, Suite 301, Rosemont, IL 60018 (☎1-800/421-2929, *www.dertravel.com*). Eurail and Italian passes.

Forsyth Travel Library, 226 Westchester Ave, White Plains, NY 10604 (☎1-800/367-7984, *www.forsyth.com*). Eurail passes.

Italian State Railways, c/o CIT Tours, 342 Madison Ave, Suite 207, New York, NY 10173 (☎1-800/223-7987, ☎310/338-8616 in LA, *www.cit-tours.com*). Eurail and Italian passes.

Rail Europe, 226 Westchester Ave, White Plains, NY 10604 (☎1-800/4EURAIL, 1-800/361-RAIL in Canada, *www.raileurope.com*). Official Eurail agent in North America; also sells a wide range of European regional and individual country passes.

ScanTours, 3439 Wade St, Los Angeles, CA 90066 (☎1-800/223-7226, *www.scantours.com*). Eurail and European country passes.

RAIL CONTACTS IN AUSTRALIA AND NZ

Rail Plus, Australia Level 3, 459 Little Collins St, Melbourne vic 3000 (☎1300/555 003 or 03/9642 8644, *info@railplus.com.au*); New Zealand Level 2, 6 Parnell Rd, Auckland 1 (☎09/303 2484).

CIT, 2/263 Clarence St, Sydney (☎02/9267 1255, *www.cittravel.com.au*), plus offices in Melbourne, Brisbane, Adelaide and Perth.

long flight, something like 9 hours from New York, Boston and the eastern Canadian cities, 12 hours from Chicago, and 15 hours from Los Angeles, so it's as well to be fairly comfortable and to arrive at a reasonably sociable hour.

The cheapest **round-trip fares** to Rome or Milan, travelling midweek in low season, start at around $650 from New York or Boston to Rome, rising to around $750 during the shoulder season, and to about $950 during the summer. Flights from LA work out about $200 on top of these round-trip fares; from Miami or Chicago, add on about $100. Note that flying on weekends ordinarily adds $60 to the round-trip fare, while taxes added to each fare usually run to another $70.

FROM CANADA

The only airline to fly **direct** to Italy from Canada is Alitalia, which flies from Toronto and Montréal to Rome or Milan for a low-season fare of Can$1060 midweek, increasing to around Can$1320 in high season. Remember to add on Can$55–65 in taxes and another Can$100 or so for any connecting flights. Flights to Italy take around 9 hours from the eastern Canadian cities, 15 hours from the west. Other airlines to consider are British Airways (from Toronto, Montréal and Vancouver via London to Rome); Lufthansa (from Calgary, Montréal, Toronto and Vancouver via Frankfurt to Milan, Rome or Venice); and KLM (via Amsterdam).

PACKAGES AND ORGANIZED TOURS

There are dozens of companies operating **group travel and tours** in Italy, ranging from full-blown luxury escorted tours to small groups sticking to specialized itineraries. Prices vary wildly, so check what you are getting for your money (many don't include the cost of the airfare). Reckon on paying at least US$1500/C$2250 for a 10-day touring vacation, and as much as US$5000/C$7500 for a fourteen-day escorted specialist package.

GETTING THERE FROM AUSTRALIA & NEW ZEALAND

There are no direct flights to Italy from Australia or New Zealand. All flights require either a transfer or stopover en route – often a welcome break as flying time is upwards of 21 hours. Several airlines fly to both Milan and Rome via an Asian or European city. Fares are highest between mid-May and August and at Christmas; low season is October to mid-November and mid-January to February; while the rest of the year is classed as shoulder season. Tickets purchased direct from the airlines tend to be expensive; travel agents generally offer much better deals, and have the latest information on special offers and stopovers. They can often also help with accommodation packages, tours and car rental, as well as organizing your visa and travel insurance. It's also worth checking out Web sites like *www.travel.com.au* and *www.sydneytravel.com* for discounted fares.

If you're planning to visit Italy as part of a wider world trip, then **Round-the-World** tickets offer greater flexibility and are better value than a standard return flight. There are numerous airline combinations to choose from; for example, a straightforward ticket (no backtracking) from Sydney or Auckland to Honolulu, then Vancouver, London, Rome/Milan, Bangkok, Singapore and back home, starts at A$2099/NZ$2399. However, more comprehensive and flexible routes are

AIRLINES

Alitalia (Australia ☎02/9244 2400 or 07/3407 7278; New Zealand ☎09/ 302 1452; *www .alitalia.it*). Three times weekly to Milan from Sydney and Auckland via Bangkok (refuelling) with connections to other destinations in Italy: code share with Qantas.

British Airways (Australia ☎02/8904 8800; New Zealand ☎09/356 8690; *www.british-airways.com*). Three flights a week to Rome from Auckland with a transfer in LA and London; and from major Australian gateways via Bangkok or Singapore and London with onward connections to other destinations in Italy.

Cathay Pacific (Australia ☎13 1747 or ☎02/9931 5500; New Zealand ☎09/379 0861; *www.cathaypacific.com*). Daily to Rome from Sydney, Melbourne, Brisbane, Cairns, Perth and Auckland, with a transfer in Hong Kong.

Garuda (Australia ☎1300/365 330; New Zealand ☎09/366 1855 or 1800/128 510). Several flights weekly from major cities in Australia and New Zealand to Rome, with either a transfer or an overnight stop in Denpasar or Jakarta and a transfer in either Frankfurt or Amsterdam.

Japan Airlines (JAL) (Australia ☎02/9272 1111; New Zealand ☎09/379 9906; *www.japanair.com*). Daily flights to Rome from Brisbane and Sydney, and several flights a week from Cairns and Auckland, with either a transfer or overnight stop in Tokyo or Osaka.

Malaysian Airlines (Australia ☎13 2627; New Zealand ☎09/373 2741 or 008/657 472; *www.malaysiaair.com*). Three flights a week to Rome with a transfer in Kuala Lumpur.

Qantas (Australia ☎13/1313; New Zealand ☎09/357 8900 or 0800/808 767; *www.qantas.com*). Daily flights to Rome from major cities in Australia and New Zealand with a transfer in either Singapore or Bangkok: code share with Alitalia.

Singapore Airlines (Australia ☎02/9350 0262 or 13 1011; New Zealand ☎09/303 2129 or 0800/808 909; *www.singaporeair.com*). Daily flights to Rome and Milan from Brisbane, Sydney, Melbourne, Perth and Auckland with either a transfer or overnight stop in Singapore.

Sri Lankan Airlines (Australia ☎02/9244 2234; New Zealand ☎09/308 3353). Three flights a week to Rome from Sydney with a transfer or overnight stop in Colombo.

Thai Airways (Australia ☎1300/651 960; New Zealand ☎09/377 3886; *www.thaiair.com*). Daily flights to Rome from Sydney, Melbourne, Brisbane and Auckland with a transfer in Zurich and either a transfer or overnight stop in Bangkok.

DISCOUNT TRAVEL AGENTS

Anywhere Travel, 345 Anzac Parade, Kingsford, Sydney (☎02/9663 0411, *anywhere@ozemail.com.au*).

Budget Travel, 16 Fort St, Auckland, plus branches around the city (☎09/366 0061 or 0800/808 040).

Destinations Unlimited, 220 Queen St, Auckland (☎09/373 4033).

Flight Centre Australia: 82 Elizabeth St, Sydney, plus branches nationwide (☎02/9235 3522, nearest branch ☎13 1600). New Zealand: 350 Queen St, Auckland (☎09/358 4310), plus branches nationwide; *www.flightcentre.com.au*.

Northern Gateway, 22 Cavenagh St, Darwin (☎08/8941 1394, *oztravel@norgate.com.au*).

STA Travel Australia: 855 George St, Sydney; 256 Flinders St, Melbourne; other offices in state capitals and major universities (nearest branch ☎13 1776, fastfare telesales ☎1300/360 960); New Zealand: 10 High St, Auckland (☎09/309 0458, fastfare telesales ☎09/366 6673), plus branches in Wellington, Christchurch, Dunedin, Palmerston North, Hamilton and at major universities. *www.statravel.com.au*

offered by "One World" and "Star Alliance" allowing you to take in other destinations in the USA, Canada, Europe, Asia as well as South America and Africa; prices are mileage-based from A$/NZ$2700, for a max of 29,000 miles up to A$/NZ$3700 for 39,000 miles

If you are planning to see some of Europe by **train** on your way to or from Italy, see box on p.12 for information on the European rail passes that must be bought before you leave home; and see pp.5–6 for details of routes from Britain.

Student Uni Travel, 92 Pitt St, Sydney (☎02/9232 8444, *sydney@backpackers.net*) branches in Brisbane, Cairns, Darwin, Melbourne and Perth.

Thomas Cook *www.thomascook.com.au*; Australia: 175 Pitt St, Sydney (☎02/9231 2877); 257 Collins St, Melbourne (☎03/ 9282 0222); plus branches in other state capitals (local branch ☎13 1771, Thomas Cook Direct telesales ☎1800/801 002); New Zealand: 191 Queen St, Auckland (☎09/379 3920).

Trailfinders, 8 Spring St, Sydney (☎02/9247 7666); 91 Elizabeth St, Brisbane (☎07/3229 0887); Hides Corner, Shield St, Cairns (☎07/4041 1199).

Travel.com.au, 76–80 Clarence St, Sydney (☎02/9249 5444 or 1800 000 447, *www.travel.com.au*).

USIT Beyond, cnr Shortland St and Jean Batten Place, Auckland (☎09/379 4224 or 0800/788 336, plus branches in Christchurch, Dunedin, Palmerston North, Hamilton and Wellington; *www.usitbeyond.co.nz*

SPECIALIST OPERATORS

Adventure Specialists, 1/69 Liverpool St, Sydney (☎02/9261 2927). Overland and adventure tour agent for a wide range of companies offering tours in Italy.

The Adventure Travel Company, 164 Parnell Rd, Parnell, Auckland (☎09/379 9755, *advakl@hot.co.nz*). NZ agent for Peregrine and Exodus' cycling and walking tours.

Adventure World, Australia: 73 Walker St, North Sydney (☎02/9956 7766 or 1300/363 055), plus branches in Adelaide, Brisbane, Melbourne and Perth; New Zealand: 101 Great South Rd, Remuera, Auckland (☎09/524 5118). Agents for an array of international adventure travel companies that operate trips to Italy. *www .adventureworld.com.au*

Allways Travel, 4/372 Eastern Valley Way, Chatswood, Sydney (☎1800/259 297, *www .allwaysdive.com.au*). All inclusive dive package holidays to prime dive sites in the Mediterranean.

CIT, 263 Clarence St, Sydney (☎02/9267 1255, *www.cittravel.com.au*); also offices in Melbourne, Adelaide, Brisbane and Perth. Specializes in city tours and accommodation packages, plus bus and rail passes and car rental.

Intrepid Adventure Travel, 12 Spring St, Fitzroy, Melbourne (☎1300 360 667 or 03/9473 2626, *www.intrepidtravel.com.au*). Agents for

Imaginative Traveller's trekking holidays through regional Italy.

Italia Mia, 101 Bridport St, Albert Park, Melbourne (☎03/9682 8098). Specializes in Italian travel arrangements.

Peregrine Adventures, 258 Lonsdale St, Melbourne (☎03/9662 2700 or 1300 655 433, *www.peregrine.net.au*), plus offices in Brisbane, Sydney, Adelaide and Perth. Specialize in walking and cycling adventures throughout Italy.

Silke's Travel, 263 Oxford St, Darlinghurst, Sydney (☎1800 807 860 or 02/9380 5835, *www.silkes.com.au*) Tailored holidays for gay and lesbian travellers.

Travel Plan, 118 Edinburgh Rd, Castlecrag, Sydney (☎02/9958 1888 or 1300/130 754). Skiing and snowboarding in the Italian Alps.

Walkabout Gourmet Adventures, PO Box 52, Dinner Plain, Victoria (☎03/5159 6556, *walkaboutAus@compuserve.com*). Food, wine and walking tours in Lazio, including cooking seminars.

Yalla Tours, 661 Glen Huntley Rd, Caulfield, Melbourne (☎1300/362 844, *www.yallatours.com.au*). Wide range of accommodation plus walking, cycling through Tuscany and Umbria, and food and wine tours, They also organize train journeys, car rental and cruises.

FROM AUSTRALIA

Round-trip fares to Rome or Milan with the major airlines from the main eastern cities in Australia cost around A$1600 in low season, to A$2600 high season; fares from Perth are approx-imately A$100 less. You are likely to get most **flexibility** by travelling with Alitalia, Thai, Cathay Pacific, British Airways or Qantas, which offer a range of discounted Italian tour packages and air passes, although the cheapest fares at around A$1499–2400 are generally with Garuda to Milan or Rome and Sri Lankan Airlines to Rome.

FROM NEW ZEALAND

Round-trip fares to Rome from Auckland are around NZ$2000 low season, NZ$2600 shoulder season and NZ$3200 high season, though fares from Christchurch are between NZ$150 and NZ$350 higher depending on the airline. Alitalia flies in conjunction with other carriers (from Auckland via Sydney and Bangkok/Singapore to Rome or Milan); British Airways to Rome from Auckland via Singapore/Bangkok or LA; Qantas to Rome from Auckland, Chistchurch or Wellington; JAL to Rome from Auckland (with inclusive overnight stop in Tokyo/Osaka); Malaysia and Thai to Rome from Auckland via Kuala Lumpur and Bangkok respectively.

RED TAPE AND VISAS

British, Irish and other EU citizens can enter Italy and stay as long as they like on pro-

duction of a valid passport. **Citizens of the United States, Canada, Australia and New Zealand need only a valid passport, too, but are limited to stays of three months. All other nationals should consult the relevant embassy about visa requirements.**

Legally, you're required to register with the police within three days of entering Italy, though if you're staying at a hotel this will be done for you. Although the police in some towns have become more punctilious about this, most would still be amazed at any attempt to register yourself down at the local police station while on holiday. However, if you're going to be living here for a while, you'd be advised to do it; see p.55 for more details.

ITALIAN EMBASSIES AND CONSULATES ABROAD

Australia: Getaway, Level 45, 1 Macquarie Place, Sydney, NSW 2000 (☎02/9392 7900); 509 St Kilda Rd, Melbourne, VIC 3004 (☎03/9867 5744); 12 Grey St, Deakin, ACT 2600 (☎02/6273 3333).

Britain: 38 Eaton Place, London SW1X 8AN (☎020/7235 9371); 32 Melville St, Edinburgh EH3 7HA (☎0131/226 3631); 111 Piccadilly, Manchester M1 2HY (☎0161/236 9024).

Canada: 275 Slater St, Ottawa, Ontario K1P 5H9 (☎613/232-2401); 3489 Drummond St, Montréal, Quebec H3G 1X6 (☎514/849-8351); 136 Beverley St, Toronto (☎416/977-1566).

Ireland: 63–65 Northumberland Rd, Dublin 4 (☎01/660 1744); 7 Richmond Park, Belfast (☎028/9066 8854).

New Zealand: 34 Grant Rd, Thorndon, Wellington (☎04/499 4186).

USA: 690 Park Ave, New York (☎212/737- 9100 or 439-8600); 12400 Wilshire Blvd, Suite 300, Los Angeles (☎310/820-0622); 1601 Fuller St NW, Washington DC (☎202/328-5500).

INSURANCE AND HEALTH COVER

As an EU country, Italy has free reciprocal health agreements with other member states. To take advantage, EU citizens will need form E111, available over the counter from main post offices. There are no inoculations required nor any particular health hazards to beware of beyond those of taking care when travelling in an unknown place. Still, you're as likely to fall ill or have an accident here as anywhere else, so it's as well to make sure you're covered by adequate travel insurance.

A typical **travel insurance** policy usually provides cover for the loss of baggage, tickets and – up to a certain limit – cash or cheques, as well as cancellation or curtailment of your journey. Most of them exclude so-called dangerous sports

unless an extra premium is paid: in Italy this can include skiing, windsurfing, trekking and mountaineering. Read the small print and benefits tables of prospective policies carefully; coverage can vary wildly for roughly similar premiums. Many policies can be chopped and changed to exclude coverage you don't need – for example, sickness and accident benefits can often be excluded or included at will. If you do take medical coverage, ascertain whether benefits will be paid as treatment proceeds or only after return home, and whether there is a 24-hour medical emergency number. When securing baggage cover, make sure that the per-article limit – typically under £500 equivalent – will cover your most valuable possession. If you need to make a claim, you should keep receipts for medicines and medical treatment, and in the event you have anything stolen, you must obtain an official statement from the police. Bank and credit cards often have certain levels of medical or other insurance included and you may automatically get travel insurance if you use a major credit card to pay for your trip.

Even with an E111, **UK citizens** would do well to take out an insurance policy before travelling to cover against theft, loss and illness or injury. Travel agents and tour operators are likely to require some sort of insurance when you book a package holiday, though according to UK law they can't make you buy their own (other than a £1 premium for "schedule airline failure"). If you have a good all-risks home insurance policy it *may* cover your

ROUGH GUIDES TRAVEL INSURANCE

Rough Guides now offer their own travel insurance, customized for our readers by a leading UK broker and backed by a Lloyds underwriter. It's available for anyone, of any nationality, travelling anywhere in the world, and we are convinced that this is the best-value scheme you'll find.

There are two main **Rough Guide insurance** plans: Essential, for effective, no-frills cover, starting at £11.75 for two weeks; and Premier – more expensive but with more generous and extensive benefits. Each offer European or Worldwide cover, and can be supplemented with a "Hazardous Activities Premium" if you plan to indulge in

sports considered dangerous, such as skiing, scuba-diving or trekking. Unlike many policies, the Rough Guides schemes are calculated by the day, so if you're travelling for 27 days rather than a month, that's all you pay for. You can alternatively take out annual multi-trip insurance, which covers you for all your travel throughout the year (with a maximum of sixty days for any one trip).

For a policy quote, call the Rough Guides Insurance Line on UK freefone ☎0800 015 0906, or, if you're calling from outside Britain on (☎+44) 1243 621 046. Alternatively, you can get a quote or buy online at *www.roughguides.com/insurance*.

possessions against loss or theft even when overseas. Many private medical schemes such as BUPA or PPP also offer coverage plans for abroad, including baggage loss, cancellation or curtailment and cash replacement as well as sickness or accident.

Americans and **Canadians** should also check that they're not already covered. Canadian provincial health plans usually provide partial cover for medical mishaps overseas. Holders of official student/teacher/youth cards are entitled to meagre accident coverage and hospital in-patient benefits. Students will often find that their student health coverage extends during the vacations and for one term beyond the date of last enrolment. Homeowners' or renters' insurance often covers theft or loss of documents, money and valuables while overseas, though conditions and maximum amounts vary from company to company.

COSTS, MONEY AND BANKS

Until the euro currency is introduced in 2002 (see box below), the Italian unit of money is the lira (plural lire), abbreviated as L or £. The exchange rate hovers around L3000 to the pound sterling, about L1800 to the US dollar. Banknotes come in denominations of L1000, L2000, L5000, L10,000, L50,000 and L100,000, and coins as L50, L100, L200, L500 and L1000; there is more than one version of almost any coin, so check your change.

In recent years the economic boom and the glut of visitors in the more touristy cities have conspired to increase prices in Italy. However, the weak lira – and now, the weak euro (see box below) – often results in highly favourable exchange rates for sterling and US dollars, which helps keep real costs down. Generally you'll find the south much less expensive than the north: as a broad guide, expect to pay most in Venice, Milan, Florence and Bologna, less in Rome, while in Naples and Sicily prices come down to fairly reasonable levels.

AVERAGE COSTS

A number of **basic things** are reasonably inexpensive: a pizza or plate of pasta with a beer (the

---

THE EURO

Italy is one of twelve European Union countries who have changed over to a single currency, the **euro** (€). The transition period, which began on January 1, 1999, is however lengthy: euro notes and coins are not scheduled to be issued until January 1, 2002, with lira remaining in place for cash transactions, at a fixed rate of 1936.27 lire to 1 euro, until they are scrapped entirely at the end of February, 2002.

Even before euro cash appears in 2002, you can opt to pay in euros by credit card and you can get travellers' cheques in euros – you should not be charged commission for changing them in any of the twelve countries in the euro zone (also known as "Euroland"), nor for changing from any of the old Euroland currencies to any other (French francs to lira, for example).

All prices in this book are given in lira and the exact equivalent in euros. When the new currency takes over completely, prices are likely to be rounded off – and if decimalization in the UK is anything to go by, rounded up.

Euro notes will be issued in **denominations** of 5, 10, 20, 50, 100, 200 and 500 euros, and coins in denominations of 1, 2, 5, 10, 20 and 50 cents and 1 and 2 euros.

staple cheap meal in a restaurant) will set you back between £5/$8 and £10/$16 on average, though in some of the larger, more visited cities – Florence and Venice, for example – it can be difficult to find appealing venues in this price range; Rome and Naples, on the other hand, are no problem. Buses and trains are cheap too: the rail journey from Rome to Milan on an Intercity train, for instance, costing just £46/$74 for a second-class return – a five-and-a-half-hour, six-hundred-kilometre trip. **Drinking**, by contrast, is pricey – unless you stick to wine. Soft drinks and coffee cost around the same as in Britain and more than in North America; a large glass of beer can cost up to £3/$5 if you decide to sit down. **Room rates** start at a bottom line of £15/$24 for the most basic double room in a one-star hotel, although again in Milan, Florence or Venice it's hard to find anything under £25/$40. Overall, in central Italy, if you're watching your budget – camping, buying food from shops and markets – you could get by on around £25/$40 a day; a more realistic **average daily budget** – staying in one-star hotels, taking trains and eating one cheap meal out a day – would be approaching £40/$64, perhaps a little less in the south; while to live reasonably well you probably need to spend at least £50/$80 a day.

Bear in mind, too, that the **time of year** can make a big difference. During the height of summer, in July and August when the Italians take their holidays, hotel prices can escalate; outside the season, however, you can often negotiate much lower rates. Apart from state museums and sites, which are free to under-18s and over 65s, and half price to people under 26, there are few **reductions** or discounts: only a handful of museums accept ISIC cards, and buses and trains never do.

CREDIT AND DEBIT CARDS, AND TRAVELLERS' CHEQUES

The most painless way of dealing with your money is probably by using **credit** or **debit cards,** which, in conjunction with your personal identification number (PIN), give you access to cash dispensers (Bancomat). Found even in small towns, these accept all major cards, with a minimum withdrawal of L50,000/€25.82 and a maximum of L500,000/€258.23 per day. Cards can also be used for cash advances over the counter in banks and for payment in most hotels, restaurants, petrol stations and some shops; for all these transactions you will pay a fee of 1.5 percent, but the rate of exchange will be in your favour. If you have an Australian or New Zealand key or debit card, arrange for cirrus, plus or maestro withdrawl facilities to be added before you leave home. You will be charged for withdrawing cash but the rates compare favourably.

A safer option is to carry your money in the form of **travellers' cheques,** available from any British high-street bank, whether or not you have an account, as well as post offices and some building societies. Most American and Canadian banks sell American Express cheques, and they're widely accepted; your local bank will probably also sell one or more of the other brands. To find the nearest bank that sells a particular brand, or to buy cheques by phone or over the Internet, contact the following companies: American Express (☎1-800/673-3782, *www.americanexpress.com*), Citicorp (☎1-800/645-6556, *www.citicorp.com*), MasterCard International/Thomas Cook (☎1-800/223-7373, *www.thomascook.com*), Visa (☎1-800/227-6811, *www.visa.com*). The usual fee for travellers' cheque sales is 1 or 2 percent, and it pays to get them in either sterling or dollars. Make sure to keep the purchase agreement and a record of cheque serial numbers safe and separate from the cheques themselves. In the event that cheques are lost or stolen, the issuing company will expect you to report the loss forthwith to their nearest office; most companies claim to replace lost or stolen cheques within 24 hours.

You'll usually – though not always – pay a small commission when you **exchange money** using travellers' cheques – again around 1 percent of the amount changed, although some banks will make a standard charge per cheque regardless of its denomination – usually around L6000/€3.10. It's worth knowing that Thomas Cook offices don't charge for cashing their own cheques, and American Express offices don't charge for cashing anyone's cheques.

It's an idea to have at least some Italian/euro **cash** for when you first arrive. You can buy lire over the counter in British banks; most American banks will need a couple of days' notice.

BANKS AND EXCHANGE

In Italy, you'll get the best rate of exchange (*cambio*) at a **bank**. There are a few nationwide banking chains – the Banca Nazionale del Lavoro, Crédito Italiano and Cassa di Risparmio, among others – as well as regional chains like the Banca di Roma, Banco di Napoli or Banco di Sicilia. **Banking hours** are normally Monday to Friday mornings from 8.30am until 1pm, and for an hour in the afternoon (usually 3–4pm). There are local variations on this and banks are usually open only in the morning on the day before a public holiday. Be warned that changing travellers' cheques in a bank can entail a long wait – up to half an hour – so make sure you're in the right queue. Outside banking hours, the larger **hotels** will change money or travellers' cheques, although if you're staying in a reasonably large city the rate is invariably better at the train station **exchange bureaux** – normally open evenings and weekends. Check the "Listings" sections of the main city accounts in the Guide for locations and specific opening hours.

EMERGENCY CASH

If you run out of money, or there is some kind of emergency, you can have **money sent out** by contacting your bank at home and have them wire the cash to the nearest bank (see box), but bear in mind that this is an expensive way to send and receive money abroad and can, in some cases take weeks not hours; it should be considered only as a last resort. Many banks have reciprocal arrangements with banks in Italy through which

transfers are likely to prove less expensive – check with your bank before travelling.

Alternatively you can use a specialist money wiring agency (see box below). The cash should be available for collection, usually in local currency, from the company's local agent (who will make a small charge of roughly £1/$1.50 for tax) within a few minutes of being sent. Western Union or Moneygram charge on a sliding scale (in the UK, roughly £12 for sending £100, £35 for £500, £80 for £2000), so sending larger amounts of cash is better value. Thomas Cook have a much cheaper flat rate (£25 in the UK) but it takes one or two days for the money to arrive.

WIRE SERVICES

American Express MoneyGram: Australia (☎1800/230 100); Britain (☎0800/8971.8971); Ireland (☎01850/205800); New Zealand (☎09/379 8243 or 0800/262 263); USA and Canada (☎1-800/543-4080); *www .moneygram.com*

Western Union: Australia (toll-free ☎1800/649 565 except Brisbane ☎3229 8610); Britain (☎0800/833 833); Ireland (☎1800/395395); New Zealand (☎09/270 0050; USA and Canada (☎1-800/325-6000); *www.westernunion.com*

TRAVELLERS WITH DISABILITIES

Facilities in Italy aren't particularly geared towards disabled travellers, though people are helpful enough and progress is gradually being made in the areas of accessible accommodation, transport and public buildings. The historical and, in some cases, crumbling fabric of many of Italy's cities and villages presents particular problems.

The Italian State Tourist Office (see p.24 for addresses) can supply you with detailed information about facilities and accommodation in Rome and Florence and a booklet in English, *Servicing for Disabled People*, published by the Italian State Railways, listing their services. *Cooperativa Sociale* has a useful Web site – *www .coincociale.it* – with some pages in English and a

wealth of information, tips and links in Italian. If you do not use a wheelchair all the time but your walking capabilities are limited, remember that you are likely to need to cover greater distances while travelling (often over rougher terrain and in hotter temperatures) than you are used to. And if you use a wheelchair, have it serviced before you go and carry a repair kit.

Read your travel **insurance** small print carefully to check that pre-existing medical conditions are not excluded. And use your travel agent to make your journey simpler: airline or bus companies can cope better if they are expecting you, with a wheelchair provided at airports and staff primed to help. A medical certificate of your fitness to travel, provided by your doctor, is also

CONTACTS FOR TRAVELLERS WITH DISABILITIES

BRITAIN AND IRELAND

Disability Action Group, 2 Annadale Ave, Belfast BT7 3JH (☎028/9079 1900). Information on access for disabled travellers abroad.

Holiday Care Service, 2nd Floor, Imperial Buildings, Victoria Rd, Horley, Surrey RH6 7PZ (☎01293/774535). Provides information on all aspects of travel.

Irish Wheelchair Association, Blackheath Drive, Clontarf, Dublin 3 (☎01/833 8241). A national voluntary organization working with

disabled people and offering related services for holidaymakers.

RADAR, 12 City Forum, 250 City Rd, London EC1V 8AS (☎020/7250 3222; Minicom ☎020/7250 4119). A good source of advice on holidays and travel abroad.

Tripscope, The Courtyard, Evelyn Rd, London W4 5JL (☎ & Minicom 020/8580 7021). National telephone information service offering transport and travel advice, free of charge.

USA AND CANADA

AccessAbility Travel, 186 Alewife Brook Parkway, Cambridge, MA 02138-1102 (☎1-800/610-5640; TTY ☎1-800/228-5379). A division of FPT Travel Management Travel group, with tours to Italy and travel information for disabled travelers.

Access First, 45-A Pleasant St, Malden, MA 02148 (☎1-800/557-2047; TTY ☎617/397-8610). Specializes in trips to Italy.

Jewish Rehabilitation Hospital, 3205 Place Alton Goldbloom, Laval, PQ H7V 1R2 (☎514/688-9550 ext 226). Guidebooks and travel information.

Mobility International USA, PO Box 10767, Eugene, OR 97440 (Voice and TDD: ☎541/343-1284, *www.miusa.org*). Information and referral services, access guides, tours and exchange programmes. Annual membership $35 (includes quarterly newsletter).

Society for the Advancement of Travel for the Handicapped (SATH), 347 5th Ave, Suite

610, New York, NY 10016 (☎212/447-7284, *www.sath.org*). Non-profit travel-industry referral service that passes queries on to its members as appropriate; allow plenty of time for a response.

Travel Information Service, Moss Rehabilitation Hospital, 1200 West Tabor Rd, Philadelphia, PA 19141 (☎215/456-9600). Telephone information and referral service.

Twin Peaks Press, Box 129, Vancouver, WA 98666 (☎360/694-2462 or 1-800/637-2256, *www.disabilitybookshop.virtualave.net*). Publisher of the *Directory of Travel Agencies for the Disabled* ($19.95), listing more than 370 agencies worldwide; *Travel for the Disabled* ($19.95); the *Directory of Accessible Van Rentals* ($12.95); and *Wheelchair Vagabond* ($19.95), loaded with personal tips.

Wheels Up!, P.O. Box 509, Fanwood, NJ 07023 (☎1-888/389-4335, *www.wheelsup.com*). Provides discounted air fare, tour and cruise prices for disabled travelers, and also publishes a free monthly newsletter.

AUSTRALIA AND NEW ZEALAND

ACROD (Australian Council for Rehabilitation of the Disabled) PO Box 60, Curtin ACT 2605 (☎02/6282 4333); 24 Cabarita Rd, Cabarita NSW 2137 (☎02/ 9743 2699). Lists of travel agencies and tour operators for people with disabilities.

Disabled Persons Assembly, 4/173–175 Victoria St, Wellington (☎04/801 9100). Resource centre with lists of travel agencies and tour operators for people with disabilities.

extremely useful; some airlines or insurance companies may insist on it. Finally, don't forget any medication you may require – carried with you if

you fly – and a prescription, including the generic name, in case of emergency.

HEALTH

EU citizens can take advantage of Italy's health services under the same terms as the residents of the country, but you'll need form E111, available from any main post office. The Australian Medicare system also has a reciprocal health-care arrangement with Italy.

Vaccinations are not required, and Italy doesn't present any more **health worries** than anywhere else in Europe; the worst that's likely to happen to you is suffering from the extreme heat in summer or from an upset stomach (shellfish is the usual culprit). The **water** is perfectly safe to drink and you'll find public fountains (usually button- or tap-operated) in squares and city streets everywhere, though look out for *acqua non potabile* signs, indicating that the water is unsafe to drink. It's worth taking insect repellent, as even inland towns, most notoriously Milan, suffer from a persistent **mosquito** problem, especially in summer. For information on the possible health implications of travelling with children, see p.60.

PHARMACIES

An Italian **pharmacist** (*farmacia*) is well qualified to give you advice on minor ailments and to dispense prescriptions (most speak good English too), and there's generally one open all night in the bigger towns and cities. A rota system operates, and you should find the address of the one currently open on any *farmacia* door or listed in the local paper. Condoms (*profilático*) are available over the counter from all pharmacists and most supermarkets; some pharmacists have late-night dispensers too. The pill (*la píllola*) is available by prescription only.

DOCTORS AND HOSPITALS

If you need **treatment**, go to a doctor (*médico*); every town and village has one. Ask at a pharmacy, or consult the local Yellow Pages (under *Azienda Unità Sanitaria Locale* or *Unità Sanitaria Locale*). The Italian Yellow Pages also list some specialist practitioners in such fields as acupuncture and homeopathy, the latter much more common in Italy than in some countries. If you're eligible, take your E111 with you to the doctor's: this should enable you to get free treatment and prescriptions for medicines at the local rate – about ten percent of the price of the medicine. For repeat medication, take any empty bottles or capsules with you to the doctor's – the brand names often differ.

If you are **seriously ill** or involved in an **accident**, go straight to the nearest hospital and go straight to *Pronto Soccorso* (casualty), or phone ☎113 and ask for *ospedale* or *ambulanza*. Throughout the Guide, you'll find listings for pharmacists, hospitals and emergency services in all the major cities. Major train stations and airports also often have first-aid stations with qualified doctors on hand.

Incidentally, try to avoid going to the **dentist** (*dentista*) while you're in Italy. These aren't covered by the *mutua* or health service, and for the smallest problem you'll pay through the teeth. Take local advice, or consult the local Yellow Pages.

If you don't have a spare pair of glasses, take a copy of your prescription so that an **optician** (*óttico*) can make you up a new pair should you lose or damage them.

INFORMATION AND MAPS

Before you leave, it may be worth calling the Italian State Tourist Office (ENIT, *www.enit.it*) for a selection of maps and brochures, though you'll have to be persistent to get through on the phone and bear in mind that nearly all of the same bumph can easily be picked up in Italy.

TOURIST OFFICES

Most Italian towns and main city train stations and airports have a **tourist office**, usually known as an **APT** (*Azienda per Il Turismo*) or just *ufficio turistico*, and signposted by the standard "i" symbol. Note that not all places with the symbol are impartial information offices, however, and that not all information offices are called APTs; there are any number of acronyms, including EPT (*Ente Provinciale per il Turismo*); IAT (*Ufficio di Informazione e Accoglienza Turistica*); and AAST (*Azienda Autónoma di Soggiorno e Turismo*, a smaller local outfit). When there isn't one of any of these, there will sometimes be a Pro Loco office, usually run by businesses in smaller villages, which will have much the same kind of information but generally keep much shorter hours. All of these vary in degrees of usefulness, and apart from the main cities and tourist areas the staff aren't likely to speak English. But you should always be able at least to get a free town plan, a list of accommodation and a local listings booklet in Italian, and some will reserve you a room and sell places on guided tours.

USEFUL INTERNET ADDRESSES

Italian Web sites have proliferated in recent years and provide a wealth of information; we've listed a few of the more useful ones here. For the Internet addresses of the major travel and accommodation organizations, see the relevant sections.

Football *www.football.it*
League tables, news and links.

In Italy *www.initaly.com*
Travel tips, campsites, services and etiquette.

Italian Ministry for Arts and the Environment *www.beniculturali.it*
Museums, temporary exhibitions, performances and so on – in Italian language only.

Italian State Railways (FS)
www.fs-on-line.com
Timetable information in Italian and English.

Italian Yellow Pages *www.paginegialle.it*
Online phone book.

Italian National Parks *www.parks.it*
Contacts and wildlife information.

Italytour 68 *www.italytour.com*
Shopping, fashion, trains and hotels.

Museums *www.museionline.it*
Links to museums and exhibition sites, dates, events.

Opera *www.operabase.com*
Listings and contact details for the country's major venues.

Venere *www.venere.it*
Probably the best site for accessing the Web pages of those hotels that have them – and booking rooms online.

Weather *www.meteo.it*
Forecasts – in Italian , but with self-explanatory symbols.

ITALIAN STATE TOURIST OFFICES ABROAD

Note: ENIT is on the Web at www.enit.it

Australia: contact the consulate, Level 45, 1 Macquarie Place, Sydney 2000, NSW (☎02/9392 7900).

Canada: 1 Place Ville Marie, Suite 1914, Montréal, Québec H3B 2C3 (☎514/866-7667); 175 Bloor St East, Suite 907, South Tower, Toronto, ON M4W 3R8 (☎416/925-4882); *www.italiantourism.com.*

Ireland: 47 Merrion Square, Dublin 2 (☎01/766 397).

New Zealand: apply to the embassy, 34 Grant Rd, Thorndon, Wellington (☎04/473 5339).

UK: 1 Princes St, London W1R 8AY (☎020/7408 1254).

USA: 630 5th Ave, Suite 1565, New York, NY 10111 (☎212/245-5618; brochure requests ☎212/245-4822); 500 North Michigan Ave, Suite 2240, Chicago, IL 60611 (☎312/644-0996; brochure requests ☎312/644-0990); 12400 Wilshire Blvd, Suite 550, Los Angeles, CA 90025 (☎310/820-1898; brochure requests ☎310/820-0098); *www.italiantourism.com*

Opening hours vary, but larger city and resort offices are likely to be open Monday to Saturday 9am to 1pm and 4 to 7pm, and sometimes for a short period on Sunday mornings; smaller offices may open weekdays only, while Pro Loco times are notoriously erratic – some open for only a couple of hours a day, even in summer. If the tourist office isn't open and all else fails, the local telephone office, most hotels, and bars with phones should all have a copy of the local *Tuttocittà* (a supplement to the main telephone directories), which carries listings and phone numbers of essential services, adverts for restaurants and shops, together with indexed maps of the appropriate city.

MAPS

The **town plans** we've printed should be fine for most purposes, and practically all tourist offices give out maps of their local area for free. However, if you want an indexed town plan, Studio FMB cover most towns and cities, and Falk and Touring Club Italiano (TCI) also do decent plans of the major cities. The clearest and best-value large-scale commercial **road map** of Italy is the Michelin 1:1,000,000 one; Michelin also produce 1:400,000 maps covering the whole of Italy,

including Sicily and Sardinia, which are equally good value. There are also the 1:800,000 and 1:400,000 maps produced by the Touring Club Italiano, covering north, south and central Italy, although these are a little more expensive; TCI also produce excellent 1:200,000 maps of the individual regions, which are indispensable if you are touring a specific area in depth. Alternatively, the Automobile Club d'Italia (see p.30 for address) issues a good, free 1:275,000 road map, available from State Tourist Offices. Local tourist offices also often have road maps of varying quality to give away.

For **hiking** you'll need at least a scale of 1:50,000. Studio FMB and the TCI cover the major mountain areas of northern Italy to this scale, but for more detailed, down-to-scale 1:25,000 maps, the Istituto Geografico Centrale series covers central and northwest Italy and the Alps; Kompass also publish these areas to the same scale. The Apennines and Tuscany are covered by Multigraphic (Firenze), easiest bought in Italy, while Tabacco produce a good series detailing the Dolomites and the northeast of the country. In Italy, the Club Alpino Italiano is a good source of hiking maps; we've supplied details of branches throughout the Guide.

BOOK AND MAP OUTLETS

BRITAIN AND IRELAND

Blackwell's Map and Travel Shop, 53 Broad St, Oxford OX1 3BQ (☎01865/792 792).

Daunt Books, 83 Marylebone High St, London W1M 3DE (☎020/7224 2295); 193 Haverstock Hill, London NW3 4QL (☎020/7794 4006).

Easons Bookshop, 40 O'Connell St, Dublin 1 (☎01/873 3811).

Fred Hanna's Bookshop, 1 Dawson St, Dublin 2 (☎01/677 1255).

Heffers, 20 Trinity St, Cambridge CB2 1TY (☎01223/568 522).

Hodges Figgis Bookshop, 56–58 Dawson St, Dublin 2 (☎01/677 4754).

Italian Bookshop, 7 Cecil Court, London WC2N 4EZ (☎020/7240 1634).

James Thin Melven's Bookshop, 29 Union St, Inverness IV1 1QA (☎01463/233500).

John Smith and Sons, at Tiso Outdoor, 50 Cooper St, Glasgow G4 0DL (☎0141/552 4394).

National Map Centre, 22–24 Caxton St, London SW1H 0QU (☎020/7222 2466, www.mapsworld.com).

Newcastle Map Centre, 55 Grey St, Newcastle upon Tyne NE1 6EF (☎0191/261 5622, www.newtraveller.com).

Stanfords, 12–14 Long Acre, London WC2E 9LP (☎020/7836 1321); at Usit CAMPUS, 52 Grosvenor Gardens, London SW1W 0AG; 156 Regent St, London W1R 5TA; 29 Corn St, Bristol BS1 1HT (☎0117/929 9966). *

The Map Shop, 30a Belvoir St, Leicester LE1 6QH (☎0116/247 1400).

The Travel Bookshop, 13–15 Blenheim Crescent, London W11 2EE (☎020/7229 5260, www.thetravelbookshop.co.uk).

Waterstone's, UK-wide chain: 91 Deansgate, Manchester M3 2BW (☎0161/832 1992, www.waterstones.co.uk); Queens Building, 8 Royal Ave, Belfast BT1 1DA (☎028/9024 7355); 7 Dawson St, Dublin 2 (☎01/679 1260); 69 Patrick St, Cork (☎021/276522).

*Note: maps by mail or phone order are available from Stanfords, ☎020/7836 1321, sales @stanfords.co.uk.

USA AND CANADA

Book Passage, 51 Tamal Vista Blvd, Corte Madera, CA 94925 (☎1-800/999-7999 or 415/927-0960, www.bookpassage.com).

California Map & Travel Center, 3312 Pico Blvd, Santa Monica, CA 90405 (☎310/396-6277, www.mapper.com).

The Complete Traveler Bookstore, 199 Madison Ave, New York, NY 10016 (☎212/685-9007); 3207 Fillmore St, San Francisco, CA 94123 (☎415/923-1511).

Curious Traveller Travel Bookstore, 101 Yorkville Ave, Toronto, ON M5R 1C1 (☎1-800/268-4395).

International Travel Maps, 530 W Broadway, Vancouver, BC V5Z 1E9 (☎604/879-3621, www.itmb.com).

Open Air Books and Maps, 25 Toronto St, Toronto, ON M5C 2R1 (☎416/363-0719).

Phileas Fogg's Books, Maps and More, #87 Stanford Shopping Center, Palo Alto, CA 94304 (☎1-800/233-FOGG in California; ☎1-800/533-FOGG elsewhere in US).

Rand McNally, 24 stores across the US; call ☎1-800/333-0136 ext 2111 for the location of your nearest store); online at www.randmcnally.com.

Sierra Club Bookstore, 6014 College Ave, Oakland, CA 94618 (☎510/658-7470, www .sierraclubbookstore.com).

Travel Books & Language Center, 4437 Wisconsin Ave NW, Washington, DC 20016 (☎1-800/220-2665).

AUSTRALIA AND NEW ZEALAND

The Map Shop, 6 Peel St, Adelaide (☎08/8231 2033).

Specialty Maps, 46 Albert St, Auckland (☎09/307 2217).

Worldwide Maps and Guides, 187 George St, Brisbane (☎07/3221 4330).

Walkers Bookshop, 96 Lake St, Cairns

(☎07/4051 2410).

Mapworld, 173 Gloucester St, Christchurch (☎03/374 5399, www.mapworld.co.nz)

Mapland, 372 Little Bourke St, Melbourne (☎03/9670 4383)

Perth Map Centre, 1/884 Hay St, Perth (☎08/9322 5733)

GETTING AROUND

The easiest way of travelling around Italy is by train. The Italian train system is one of the least expensive in Europe, reasonably comprehensive, and, in the north of the country at least, very efficient – and is far preferable over long distances to the fragmented, localized and sometimes grindingly slow bus service. Local buses, though, can be very efficient, and where it is actually a better idea to take a bus we've said as much in the text. Planes are expensive and are best reserved for longer journeys where time is tight. Ferries ply to all the Italian islands, and also serve international routes to Greece, Albania, Croatia, Malta, Yugoslavia, Corsica and Tunisia (see boxes on pp.522, 653, 894, 907 & 1020). We've detailed train, bus and ferry frequencies in the "Travel Details" section at the end of each chapter of the Guide: note that these refer to regular working-day schedules, (ie Monday to Saturday); services may be much reduced or even non-existent on Sundays.

TRAINS

Operated by Italian State Railways (Ferrovie dello Stato, or FS), there are seven types of train in Italy. At the top of the range are the **"Pendolino"** (CiS) and "Eurostar Italia" (ES), an Intercity service; in first class your ticket includes newspapers and a meal; reservations are included in the ticket price. **Eurocity** trains connect the major Italian cities with centres such as Paris, Vienna, Hamburg and Barcelona, while Intercity trains link

the major Italian centres; reservations are advised on both of these services (and are sometimes compulsory anyway) and a supplement in the region of thirty percent of the ordinary fare is payable. (Make sure you pay your supplement before getting on board; otherwise you'll have to cough up a far bigger surcharge to the conductor.) **Diretto, Espresso** and **Interregionale** trains are the common-or-garden long-distance expresses, calling only at larger stations; and lastly there are the **Regionale** services, which stop at every place with a population higher than zero (and on which smoking is not allowed). For information on trains call ☎1478.88.088, or visit the useful Web site at *www.fs-on-line.com*.

In addition to the routes operated by FS, there are a number of **privately run** lines, using separate stations though charging similar fares. Where they're worth using, these are detailed in the text.

TIMETABLES

Timings and route information for the FS network are posted up at train stations, and we give a rough idea of frequencies and journey times in the "Travel Details" sections at the end of each chapter. If you're travelling extensively it would be worth investing in a copy of either the twice-yearly *Tutt'Italia* timetable (L7500/€15.49), which covers the main routes, or the three regional timetables (free) covering every line in northern, central and southern Italy; they're normally on sale at train-station newspaper stands. Pay attention to the **timetable notes**, which may specify the dates between which some services run (*Si effetua dal . . . al . . .*), or whether a service is seasonal (*periódico*, denoted by a vertical squiggle); *laborativo* or *feriale* is the word for the Monday to Saturday service, represented by two crossed hammers; and *festivo* means that a train runs only on Sundays and holidays, symbolized by a cross.

FARES

Fares are inexpensive, calculated by the kilometre and easy to work out for each journey. The timetables give the prices per kilometre but as a rough guide, a single second-class one-way fare from Rome to Milan currently costs about L70,000/€ 36.15 by Intercity. **Sleepers** are available on many long-distance services, and prices vary according to the length of journey and whether or not you're sharing. A *cuccetta*, or couchette, costs a flat fee of an extra L21,000/€10.85, while a place in a sleeping compartment costs a lot more (from about L70,000/€36.15). In summer it's often worth making a **seat reservation** on the main routes, which can get very busy; this is something you're obliged to do anyway on the faster trains. Reservations can be made either at any staffed station booking

office in Italy, or via Italian State Railways agents in the UK, US or Australia (see pp.6 and 12).

All stations have machines in which passengers must stamp their ticket before embarking on their journey. Look out for them as you come on to the platform: if you fail to **validate your ticket** you may be given a spot-fine of L30,000/€15.49, though foreigners are often indulged. Return tickets are valid within two months of the outward journey, but as two one-way tickets cost the same it's hardly worth bothering.

RAIL PASSES AND DISCOUNTS

The Europe-wide **InterRail** and **Eurail** passes (see p.6 & p.12) give unlimited travel on the FS network, although you'll be liable for supplements on the faster trains.

If you're travelling exclusively in Italy by train you might want one of the many rail passes available on the FS system, though you'd have to cover a lot of ground to make the price worth it. **Euro-Domino/Freedom** passes are valid on the Italian network; coming from the UK these give three days' unlimited rail travel within a month for £87/under-26s £65, five days' for £106/£80, or eight days' for £133/£102; discounts of 25 percent are included for the journey to Italy. Passes are available from rail agents in the UK (see p.6) and must be bought at least a week before you make your first journey. For North Americans, the passes are slightly different and give eight days' unlimited travel for US$266/Can$399, fifteen days for US$332/ Can$498, twenty one days for US$386/Can$579, and thirty days for US$465/Can$697.

A variant of this – the **Italy Flexi Railcard** – is available to North American and Australasian travellers, but not to Europeans. Prices start at US$209/Can$313/A$170 for four days' travel in nine; US$293/Can$439/A$238 for eight days' travel in twenty one; and US$375/Can$562/A$306 for twelve days' travel in thirty. Note that these passes must be bought outside Italy, and US citizens are charged an additional $15 for all Italian rail passes (see p.12 for details of US and Australian rail contacts).

In addition, there are three other specific Italian passes, available to all travellers from the same agencies and also at major city train stations within Italy. The **Italy Railcard** gives unlimited travel on all FS trains except Eurostar Italia expresses, but unless you're moving on practically every day it isn't likely to be worth the money. Approximate costs (depending on exchange rate) work out at £128/US$195/A$320 for eight days, £158/US$263/A$395 for fifteen days; passes are also available for twenty one and thirty days and occasional offers give you a couple of extra days free. The **Italy Flexicard** is essentially the same as the Eurodomino pass (see above), but there are no discounts for under-26s; four days' travel within the month costs £96, eight days' £132 and twelve days' £172. The other option is the **Kilometric/Chilométrico** ticket, giving 3000km worth of travel on a maxi-

mum of twenty separate journeys. It costs L214,000/€110.42 but you have to pay supplements on faster trains and unless you're travelling in a group (the ticket is valid for five people), you're unlikely to cover this sort of distance on an Italian holiday anyway.

Two discount cards – the **Cartaverde** for under-26s, and the **Carta d'argento** for over-65s – come into their own if you're going to be spending a long time in the country. Valid for one year, they give a 20 percent discount on any fare, cost L40,000/€20.66, and are available from main train stations in Italy. Bear in mind, too, that children aged 4–12 qualify for a 50 percent discount on all journeys, and **children** under 4 (not occupying a seat) travel free.

BUSES

Trains don't go everywhere and sooner or later you'll have to use **regional buses** (*autobus*). Almost everywhere is connected by some kind of bus service, but in out-of-the-way places schedules can be sketchy and are drastically reduced – sometimes non-existent – at weekends, especially on Sundays, something you need to watch out for on the timetable. Bear in mind also that in rural areas schedules are often designed with the working and/or school day in mind – meaning a frighteningly early start if you want to catch that day's one bus out of town, and occasionally a complete absence of services during school holidays.

There isn't a national **bus company,** although a few companies do operate services beyond their own immediate area. **Bus terminals** can be anywhere in larger towns, though often they're sensibly placed next door to the train station; wherever possible we've detailed their whereabouts in the text, but if you're not sure ask for directions to the *autostazione*. In smaller towns and villages, most buses pull in at the central piazza. **Timetables** are worth picking up if you can find one, from the local company's office, bus stations or on the bus. Buy **tickets** immediately before you travel from the bus station ticket office, or on the bus itself; on longer hauls you can try to buy them in advance direct from the bus company, but seat reservations are not normally possible. If you want to get off, ask *posso scéndere?;* "the next stop" is *la próssima fermata.*

City buses are always cheap, usually costing a flat fare of between L1000/€0.52 and L2000/€1.03; it's normally a bit cheaper down south. Invariably you need a ticket before you get on the bus and once you've bought your ticket it is only valid for about an hour; within that time, however, you can use it on as many journeys as you like. **Tickets** are available from a variety of sources, commonly newsagents and tobacconists, but also from any shop displaying the *biglietti* symbol, including many campsite shops and hotel front desks. Once on board, you must cancel your ticket in the machine at the back of the bus. The whole system is based on trust, though in most cities checks for fare-dodging are regularly made, and hefty spot-fines are levied against offenders.

PLANES

ATI, the domestic arm of Alitalia, operate **flights** all over Italy. However, it's only worth taking a plane within Italy if you want to cover a large distance quickly: ordinary prices are quite high, pricier than even the most expensive express train.

As an example of ordinary one-way fares, Venice–Rome will cost from around L250,000/ €129.11, Milan–Naples about L300,000/ €154.94, though a limited number of cheaper seats are available on each flight, these tend to sell out fairly quickly on popular routes. If you book a flight from London to Italy with Alitalia you qualify for their **Visit Italy Pass**, which gives you three internal flights for £80 – a bargain if you're making long hops from north to south.

FERRIES AND HYDROFOILS

Italy has a well-developed network of **ferries** and **hydrofoils** operated by a number of different private companies. Large car ferries connect the major islands of Sardinia and Sicily with the mainland ports of Genoa, Livorno, La Spezia, Civitavecchia, Fiumicino and Naples, while the smaller island groupings – the Tremiti islands, the Bay of Naples islands, the Pontine islands – are usually linked to a number of nearby mainland towns. Fares are reasonable, although on some of the more popular services – to Sardinia, certainly – you should book well in advance in summer, especially if you're taking a vehicle across. Remember, too, that frequencies are drastically reduced outside the summer months, and some services stop altogether. You'll find a broad guide to journey times and frequencies in the "Travel Details" section at the end of relevant chapters; for full up-to-date schedules, and prices, contact the local tourist office – and see p.7 for a list of ferry agents in the UK.

DRIVING

Travelling **by car** in Italy is relatively painless, though cities can be hard work. The roads are good, the motorway, or *autostrada* network very comprehensive, and the notorious Italian drivers rather less erratic than their reputation suggests – though their regard for the rules of the road is sometimes lax to say the least. The best plan is to avoid driving in cities as much as possible; the congestion, proliferation of complex one-way systems and occasional incidents of naked aggression can make it a nightmare.

Parking is very often a headache too. If you get fed up of driving around and settle for a space in a *zona di rimozione* (tow-away zone), don't expect your car to be there. A handy gadget to have is a small clock-like dial which you set and stick in the windscreen, to indicate when you parked and that you're still within the allowed limit: rental cars generally come equipped with these, and some tourist offices have them too. Parking at night is easier than during the day, but make sure you are not parked in a street that turns into a market in the morning. Increasing numbers of cities operate a colour-coded parking scheme: **blue zone** parking spaces (delineated by a blue line) usually have a maximum stay of one or two hours; they cost around L1000–1500/ €0.52–0.78 per hour (pay at meters or to attendants) but are sometimes free between 1 and 3pm and on Sundays. **White-zone** spaces (white lines) are free and unlimited in some cities, but reserved for residents in other cities; **yellow-zone** spaces are almost always reserved for residents. Note that walled towns which exclude cars often allow tourists to drive into the city to drop off baggage at a hotel. Car parks, often small enclosed garages, are universally expensive, costing L25,000–35,000/€12.91–18.08 a day in big cities; be aware that it's not unknown for hotels to state that they have parking and then direct you to the nearest paying garage.

Most **motorways** are **toll-roads**. Take a ticket as you come on and pay on exit; in automatic booths the amount due is flashed up on a screen in front of you. Major credit cards are accepted; follow the "Viacard" sign. Rates aren't especially high but they can mount up on a long journey: as a general rule, you'll pay around L35,000/€8.08 driving a small car from Rome to Florence. Since other roads can be frustratingly slow, tolls are well worth it over long distances. **Petrol** per litre costs around L2200/€1.12 for four-star and L2100/€1.08 for unleaded; for unleaded petrol, look for the sign "Senza Piombo".

As regards **documentation**, if you're bringing your own car you need a valid driving licence plus an international green card of insurance, and an **international driving permit** if you're a non-EU licence holder. In Australia these are available from state motoring organization offices in major towns and cities; in New Zealand contact your local Automobile Association office. In North America get in touch with the American Automobile Association (*www.aaa.com*), the Canadian Automobile Association (*www.caa.ca*), or your local branch for details of the procedure. It's compulsory to carry your car documents and passport while you're driving, and you may be required to present them if stopped by the police – not an uncommon occurrence.

Rules of the road are straightforward: drive on the right; at junctions, where there's any ambiguity, give precedence to vehicles coming from the right; observe the speed limits – 50kph in built-up areas, 110kph on country roads, 130kph on motorways (for camper vans, these limits are reduced to 50kph, 80kph and 100kph respectively); and don't drink and drive. Roundabouts can be tricky until you get the hang of them as cars entering the larger ones have right of way, unlike smaller ones, on which you give way to the right.

If you **break down**, dial ☎116 at the nearest phone and tell the operator where you are, the type of car and your registration number: the nearest office of the Automobile Club d'Italia (ACI), Via Marsala 8, 00185 Rome (☎803.116 for 24hr assistance), the Italian national motoring organization, will be informed and they'll send someone out to fix your car – although it's not a free service and can work out very expensive if you need a tow. For peace of mind, you might prefer to join the ACI outright, and so qualify for their discounted repairs scheme (alternatively it might be easier to arrange cover with a motoring organization in your home country before you leave). Any ACI office in Italy can tell you where to get **spare parts** for your particular car: see the "Listings" sections in the Guide for details of local addresses.

CAR RENTAL

Car rental in Italy is pricey, especially in high season, at around £200/US$320 per week for a small hatchback, with unlimited mileage. The major chains have offices in all the larger cities and at airports, train stations, etc: addresses are detailed in the "Listings" sections at the end of city accounts throughout the Guide. Local firms can be less expensive and often have an office at the airport, but generally the best deals are to be had by arranging things in advance, through one of the agents listed in the box below or with Italian specialist tour operators like Crystal or Citalia when you book your flight or holiday. You will need a credit card to act as a deposit when picking up your car.

SAFETY

Never leave anything visible in the car when you're not using it, including the radio. Certain

---

CAR RENTAL

AUSTRALIA		NORTH AMERICA	
Avis	☎1-800/225 533	Auto Europe	☎1-800/223-5555
Hertz	☎1-800/550 067	Avis	☎1-800/331-1084
Renault Eurodrive	☎02/9299 3344	Europe by Car	☎1-800/223-1516
		in New York	☎212/581-3040
IRELAND		in Canada	☎1-800/252-9401
Avis	☎01/874 5844	Hertz	☎1-800/654-3001
Hertz	☎01/676 7476	in Canada except Toronto	☎1-800/263-0600
Holiday Autos	☎01/872 9366	in Toronto	☎416/620-9620
NEW ZEALAND		**UK**	
Avis	☎09/526 5231	Autos Abroad	☎020/7287 6000
Fly and Drive Holidays	☎09/366 0759	Avis	☎0990/900500
Hertz	☎09/309 0989	Hertz	☎0990/996699
		Holiday Autos	☎0990/300400
		National Car Rental	☎01895/233300

economically depressed cities have appalling reputations for theft – in Naples, some rental agencies won't insure a car left anywhere except in a locked garage. If you're taking your own vehicle, consider installing a detachable car-radio, and depress your aerial and tuck in your wing mirrors when you park. Most cities and ports have **garages** where you can leave your car; these are a safe enough option.

However you get around on the roads, bear in mind that the **traffic** can be heavy on main roads and appalling in city centres – and although Italians are by no means the world's worst drivers they don't win any safety prizes either. The secret is to make it very clear what you're going to do – and then do it. A particular danger for foreign drivers is the large number of scooters that can appear suddenly from the blind spot or dash across junctions and red lights with alarming recklessness. Contrary to popular belief, Italians don't go round sounding their horns all the time – in fact, it's taken as a sign of letting things get to you if you resort to such crude tactics. There are exceptions to this rule, though – notably in Naples, which has anarchic tendencies all of its own.

Finally, don't assume that as a **pedestrian** you're safe; even on crossings with traffic lights you can be subject to some close calls.

HITCHHIKING

Hitchhiking (*autostop*) is moderately possible in Italy, especially in the north, but as elsewhere in Europe, is generally inadvisable. If you're determined, remember that hitching on motorways is illegal, eliciting an on-the-spot fine; stand on a slip-road or at one of the service areas. Bear in mind also that you should **never hitch alone** –

this applies particularly to women in the south. Always ask where the car is headed (*Dov'è diretto?*) before you commit yourself, and if you want to get out say *Mi fa scéndere*.

CYCLING AND MOTORBIKING

Cycling is seen as more of a sport than a way of getting around in much of Italy, but as well as racing clubs on the move you'll see mountain bikes, touring cycles laden with panniers, and people of all ages on shopping bikes, often with a toddler balanced on the cross-bar. Italians in small towns and villages are welcoming to cyclists, and hotels and hostels will take your bike in overnight for safekeeping. Although there's usually a good cycle shop in most small towns, tyres and wheels for touring bikes (700mm x 28 or 30mm) are hard to come by. On the islands, in the mountains, in major resorts and larger cities it's usually possible to **rent** a bike, but generally facilities for this are few and far between. In the UK, the Cyclists' Touring Club (Cotterell House, 69 Meadrow, Godalming, Surrey GU7 3HS; ☎01483/417 217) can provide members with advice and help on planning a tour.

An alternative is to tour by **motorbike**, though again there are relatively few places to rent one. **Mopeds** and **scooters**, on the other hand, are relatively easy to find: everyone in Italy, from kids to grannies, rides one of these, and, although they're not really built for any kind of long-distance travel, for shooting around towns and islands they're ideal. We've detailed outlets in the text; roughly speaking you should expect to pay up to L50,000/€25.82 a day for a machine. Crash helmets are compulsory, though in the south at least it's a law that seems to be largely ignored.

ACCOMMODATION

Accommodation in Italy is strictly regulated and, while never especially cheap, is at least fairly reliable: hotels are star-rated and are required to post their prices clearly in each room. Most tourist offices have details of hotel rates in their town or region, and you can usually expect them to be broadly accurate. Whatever happens, establish the *full* price of your room *before* you accept it. In popular resorts and the major cities booking ahead is advisable, particularly during July or August, while for Venice, Rome and Florence it's pretty well essential to book ahead from Easter until late September. You can do this relatively painlessly through room-booking agencies (see

below) or travel agents, but we've given phone numbers – and fax numbers where available – throughout the Guide if you want to book direct. Make sure you get confirmation of the booking by fax, email or letter, it is far from uncommon to arrive and find all knowledge of your booking is denied. The phrases on pp.1134–1137 should help you get over the language barrier, but in many places you should be able to find someone who speaks at least some English.

HOTELS

Hotels in Italy come tagged with a sometimes confusing variety of names, and, although the differences have become minimal of late, you will still find the various names used for what are always basically private hotel facilities. A **locanda** is his-

---

DAY HOTELS

One peculiar Italian institution is the *albergo diurno* or **day hotel** – not as sleazy as it sounds in fact, but an establishment providing bathrooms, showers, cleaning services, hairdressers and the like for a fixed rate, usually around L10,000/€5.17. You'll often find them at train stations, and they're usually open daily from 6am to midnight. Useful for a fast cleanup if you're on the move.

ROOM-BOOKING AGENCIES IN THE UK

There are several UK-based **accommodation agencies** that will book affordable hotels in major tourist cities, plus the Lakes, the Amalfi coast and Tuscany – a useful option if you don't speak Italian and can't face complicated long-distance phone calls.

Accommodation Line Ltd, 1st Floor, 46 Maddox St, London W1R 9PB (☎020/7409 1343).

HPS, Archgate, 823–825 High Rd, Finchley, London N12 8UB (☎020/8446 0126).

Room Service, 42 Riding House St, London W1P 7PL (☎020/7636 6888).

---

torically perhaps the most basic option, although the word is, oddly enough, sometimes appropriated to denote somewhere quite fancy. You will also find **pensione**, although there is nowadays very little difference between these and a regular **albergo** or **hotel**. **Prices** vary greatly between the poor south and the wealthy north, as well as between well-touristed honeyspots and more rural areas. The official star system is based on facilities (TV in rooms, swimming pool, etc) rather than character or comfort – or even price.

In very busy places it's not unusual (as well as finding everywhere full) to have to stay for a minimum of three nights, and many proprietors will add the price of **breakfast** to your bill whether you want it or not; try to ask for accommodation only – you can always eat more cheaply in a bar.

ACCOMMODATION PRICES

Hotels in this guide have been categorized according to the price codes outlined below. They represent the minimum you can expect to pay for a double room in high season, excluding the cost of breakfast, which you may not be able to avoid. Outside the main tourist areas high season can mean just July and August; in places like Florence or Venice the prices stay high from March through to November. For hostels, prices per person per night in lire are quoted in the Guide and assume Hostelling International (HI) membership.

① Up to L60,000/€30.99 The cheapest kind of one-star hotels; most rooms will have shared facilities and may be quite bleak. You may find places in this category heavily booked due to the fact that they're often used as cheap permanent accommodation. Credit cards are only rarely accepted at these places.

② L60,000–90,000/€30.99–46.48. The standard one-star hotel, normally with a mixture of rooms with shared and private facilities, and in most cases comfortable enough for a shortish stay. This is probably the most commonly recommended category in this book, although in Venice, Florence and some other northern cities and resorts, you'll be extremely lucky to find one-star places at this price.

③ L90,000–120,000/€46.48–61.98. Mainly two-star hotels, which may have some rooms with shared facilities. You will sometimes have a TV and telephone at this price, too.

④ L120,000–150,000/€61.98–77.47. In Venice and Florence there are one-stars in this category. Elsewhere, this price will get you a room in an attractive two-star, or even a three-star hotel, generally with private bath, telephone and TV.

⑤ L150,000–200,000/€77.47–103.29. This should get you a room with private bath, TV and telephone pretty much everywhere in Italy, and in the south of the country and more remote places, you could be looking at something fairly swanky.

⑥ L200,000–250,000/€103.29–129.11. Usually a good three-star or moderate four-star; expect high standards and a range of facilities including a pool and formal restaurant.

⑦ L250,000–300,000/€129.11–154.94. These should be special hotels, either by virtue of their location or facilities. Again, in Venice and Florence, you'll be paying this sort of price for rooms that would fall into one of the lower categories elsewhere.

⑧ L300,000–400,000/€154.94–206.58. We have only recommended somewhere in this category if it is really special, if it enjoys a wonderful location, a superb site or building – perhaps an old convent or manor house – or if the service and food are just too good to miss.

⑨ Over L400,000/€206.58. The sky's-the-limit category, populated by a select few of the most celebrated hotels in Italy.

Be warned, too, that in major seaside resorts you will often be forced to take **half- or full-pension** in high season. You can cut costs slightly by cramming three into a double room, but most hotels will charge an extra thirty-five percent for this. Note also that people travelling alone may sometimes be clobbered for the price of a double room even when taking a single, though it can also work the other way round – if all their **single rooms** are taken, a hotelier may well put you in a double room but only charge the single rate.

YOUTH HOSTELS

There are around fifty official **HI youth hostels** in Italy, charging between L13,000/€6.71 and L30,000/€15.49 a night for a dormitory bed; breakfast, when not included, comes to about L2000/€1.03, and showers may be charged as an extra at approximately L1000/€0.51. You can easily base a tour of the country around them, although for two people travelling together they don't always represent a massive saving on the cheapest double hotel room – especially if you take into account the bus fare you might have to fork out to reach some of them. If you're travelling on your own, on the other hand, hostels are usually more sociable and can work out a lot cheaper; many have facilities such as inexpensive restaurants and self-catering kitchens that enable you to cut costs further. In a few cases, too – notably Castroreale in Sicily and Verona and Montagnana in the Veneto – the hostels are beautifully located and in many ways preferable to any hotel.

YOUTH HOSTEL ASSOCIATIONS

England and Wales Youth Hostel Association (YHA), Trevelyan House, 8 St Stephen's Hill, St Albans, Herts AL1 2DY (☎01727/845047, www.yha.org.uk). London shop (☎020/7836 8541) and information office (☎0870/870 8808), 14 Southampton St, London WC2 7HY.

Scotland Scottish Youth Hostel Association (SYHA), 7 Glebe Crescent, Stirling FK8 2JA (☎01786/451 181).

Ireland An Oige, 61 Mountjoy St, Dublin 7 (☎01/830 4555, www.irelandyha.org); Youth Hostel Association of Northern Ireland, 22 Donegall Rd, Belfast BT12 5JN (☎028/9032 4733).

USA Hostelling International-American Youth Hostels (HI-AYH), 733 15th St NW, Suite 840, Washington, DC 20005 (☎1-800/444-6111, www.hiayh.org).

Canada Hostelling International/Canadian Hostelling Association, Suite 400, 205 Catherine St, Ottawa, ON K2P 1C3 (☎613/237-7884 or 1-800/663 5777, www.hostellingintl.ca).

Australia Youth Hostel Association (YHA), 422 Kent St, Sydney (☎02/9261 1111, www.yha.com.au).

New Zealand Youth Hostel Association (YHA), 173 Gloucester St, Christchurch (☎03/379.9970, www.yha.co.nz).

Italy Associazione Italiana Alberghi per la Gioventù (AIG), Via Cavour 44, 00184 Rome (☎06.487.1152, fax 06.488.0492, www.hostels-aig.org).

Virtually all of the Italian hostels are members of the official International Youth Hostel Federation, and strictly speaking you need to be a member of that organization in order to use them – you can join through your home country's youth hostelling organization (see box above). Many hostels, however, allow you to join on the spot, or will simply charge you a supplement. If you choose to pay the supplement you will receive a stamp in the card they give you; once you have collected six stamps, you are deemed to have paid the membership fee.

Member or not, you will need to reserve well ahead in the summer months, most efficiently by using Hostelling International's **International Booking Network** which, for a small fee, enables you to book (including online) at hostels in selected Italian cities from your home country up to six months in advance (see box above for details of head offices). For more out-of-the-way hostels, you need to contact the hostel direct at least fifteen days in advance, sending approximately a thirty-percent deposit with your booking. We've listed most of the hostels in the Guide, and there's a full list of hostels, with fax and phone numbers, available from branches of the Italian State Tourist Office (see box on p.24 for addresses).

In some cities, including Rome, it's also possible to stay in **student accommodation** vacated by Italian students for the summer. This is usually confined to July and August, but accommodation is generally in individual rooms and can work out a lot cheaper than a straight hotel room. Again you'll need to book in advance: we've listed possible places in the text, and you should contact them as far ahead as possible to be sure of a room.

You will also come across accommodation operated by **religious organizations** – convents (normally for women only), welcome houses and the like, again with a mixture of dormitory and individual rooms, which can sometimes be a way of cutting costs as well as meeting like-minded people. Most operate a curfew of some sort, and you should bear in mind that they don't always work out a great deal cheaper than a bottom-line one-star hotel. Information can be found in the local tourist offices or through the Associazione Cattólica Internazionale al Servizio della Giovane, Via Urbana 158, 00184 Rome (☎06.488.1489), which has offices in major towns.

CAMPING

Camping is not as popular in Italy as it is in some European countries, but there are plenty of sites, mostly on the coast and mostly open April to September (though winter "camping" – in caravans and camper vans – is popular in ski areas). The majority are well equipped and often have bungalows, mainly with four to six beds. However, if you're camping, it doesn't always work out a great deal cheaper than staying in a hotel or hostel once you've added the cost of a tent and vehicle. Local tourist offices have details of nearby sites, and prices range from L6000–10,000/€3.10–5.17 per person daily, plus L7000–17,000/€3.62–8.78 for each caravan or tent, and around L6000/€3.10 for each vehicle. If you're camping extensively, the Touring Club Italiano (*www.touringclub.it*) publishes a comprehensive guide to campsites countrywide, *Campeggi e Villaggi Turistici*, available from bookshops before you leave or once you're there (L32,000/€16.53). If you don't need something this detailed, you can obtain a simple list of addresses and telephone numbers, along with a location map, free of charge from the Italian State Tourist Office; visit *www.camping.it* to book campsites in advance.

VILLAS, AGRITURISMO AND RIFUGI

If you're not intending to travel around a lot it might be worth considering renting a villa or **farmhouse** for a week or two. Most tend to be located in the affluent northern areas of Italy – especially Tuscany and Umbria. They don't come cheap, but are of a very high standard, and often enjoy marvellous locations; British-based tour operators who rent villas, either on their own or in conjunction with a flight or fly-drive package, are detailed on p.5.

Bed and breakfast schemes are a relatively new arrival, the best ones offering a good way to get a flavour of Italian home life; they're not necessarily cheaper than an inexpensive hotel, however. Caffeletto (*www.caffeletto.it*) is one of the best (and most expensive), allowing you to specify your needs by email, while *www.bbitalia.it* has a less showy list.

The **agriturismo** scheme, which has grown considerably in recent years, enables farmers to rent out converted barns and farm buildings to tourists through a centralized booking agency, and

has found favour with city-bound Italians intent on rediscovering "country ways" and keen to feast on rustic delicacies. Some tourist apartments or other converted farm buildings cost about the same as a one-star hotel and are available for a minimum of a week, with rates starting from L500,000/€258.23 for places with two beds. Other set-ups let you have rooms on a nightly basis, with meals (comprising at least four courses) for around L15,000/€7.75 extra. There are often a wide range of activites on offer, such as horse riding, hunting and mountain biking, plus escorted walks and excursions. For a full list of properties, contact Agriturist, Corso V. Emanuele 101, 00168 Rome (☎06.852.1342, *www .agriturist.com*); another useful resource is the guide *Agriturismo e vacanze in campagna*, published by Touring Club Italiano, costing L34,000/€37.58 and available from bookshops in Italy as well as from specialist outlets overseas. Agriturist has also produced a book, *Vacanza in Fattoria* (Farm Holidays), available in English, in the UK for £19.95, from travel bookshops (see p.25).

Finally, if you're planning on hiking and climbing, there is the **rifugi** network, consisting of about five hundred mountain huts, owned by the Club Alpino Italiano (CAI), that non-members can stay in for L15,000–20,000/€7.75–10.35 a night; there are also private *rifugi* that charge around double this. Most are fairly spartan, with bunks in unheated dorms, but their sitings can be magnificent and usually leave you well placed to continue your hike the next day. They are obliged to take you if you turn up on the off-chance, but it's better to book in advance; CAI, Via S. Pellico 6, Milan 201221 (☎02.614.1378, *www.cai.it*) provides a full list of huts. Bear in mind that the word *rifugio* can be used for anything from a smart chalet-hotel to a snack bar at the top of a cable-car line. We've indicated in the text where this is the case.

FOOD AND DRINK

Although it has long been popular primarily for its cheapness and convenience, Italian food occupies a revered place as one of the world's great cuisines. The southern Italian diet especially, with its emphasis on olive oil, fresh and plentiful fruit, vegetables and fish, is one of the healthiest in Europe, and there are few national cuisines that can boast so much variety in both ingredients and cooking methods. Italy's wines, too, are among the finest and most diverse in Europe and the international image of cheap fizz and rough reds is long out of date.

THE BASICS OF ITALIAN CUISINE

Although the twentieth century has done much to blur the **regional differences** of Italian food, they are still there – and often highly evident, with the French influence strong in Piemonte, Austrian flavours in Alto Adige, and even Greek in Calabria (regional cuisine and specialities to seek out are highlighted in "Regional Food and Wine" boxes at the beginning of Guide chapters). Italy has remained largely untouched by the latter-day boom in non-indigenous eating, partly due to its lack of any substantial colonial legacy but also because of the innate chauvinism of Italian eating habits. The exceptions are the Chinese restaurants that crop up in every town, the ubiquitous burger bars, and recently Spanish, Japanese and North African cuisine has started to pop up in more cosmopolitan towns especially, of course, Rome and Milan. More usually, the exotic option is sampling cooking from other parts of the coun-

try. Milan tends to be the favourite melting-pot, with restaurants specializing in food from all regions.

True to the stereotype that every Italian believes that Italian food is the best in the world and that mamma's is always the perfect example, many restaurants are simply an extension of the home dining table. Adventure is not usually on the menu. There has been some limited experimentation with new, "trendier" ingredients like wholewheat pasta and brown rice, but probably the best you'd get if you asked a waiter for any such thing would be a raised eyebrow; request a wholewheat pizza and you'd certainly be laughed out of sight. **Vegetarian restaurants**, too, have been slow to catch on, and you're only likely to find them in major cities, but there are always plenty of non-meat choices on every menu.

Perhaps the most striking thing about eating in Italy is how deeply embedded in the culture it really is. Food is celebrated with gusto: **traditional meals** tend to consist of many courses and can seem to last forever, starting with an antipasto, followed by a risotto or a pasta dish, leading on to a fish or meat course, cheese, and finished with fresh fruit and coffee. Even everyday meals are a scaled-down version of the full-blown affair. **Shopping for food** is a serious matter. Supermarkets have yet to make any real impact on the dominance of the traditional store in town centres, and foodstores of every description abound. Street markets, too, can be exhilarating, selling bountiful, fresh and flavoursome produce. Happily, the Italians as yet haven't adopted the heavy cropping methods which result in completely tasteless produce – even a simple raw tomato can be a revelation.

Foods like bread and cheese are still made with an eye on quality. **Bread** is almost entirely made by small bakeries and tends to get heavier, crustier and more salty the further south you go (for eating with salty hams, salami and cheeses there is *pane senza sale*). **Cheese** is often factory produced, with large firms like the Milan-based Galbani marketing common varieties like Bel Paese, Gorgonzola and Taleggio. But cheesemaking also remains in the hands of local farmers working to traditional recipes: local tastes are much in evidence.

BREAKFAST, SNACKS AND ICE CREAM

Most Italians start their day in a bar, their **breakfast** consisting of a coffee with hot milk (*cappuccino*) and a *brioche* or *cornetto* – a jam-, custard- or chocolate-filled croissant, which you usually help yourself to from the counter and eat standing at the bar. Breakfast in a hotel (*prima colazione*) is often a limp affair of bread and processed meats, often not worth the price.

At other times of the day, **sandwiches** (*panini*) can be pretty substantial, a bread stick or roll packed with any number of fillings. A sandwich bar (*paninoteca*) in larger towns and cities, and in smaller places a grocer's shop (*alimentari*) will normally make you up whatever you want; you'll pay L3000–5000/€1.55–2.58 each. Bars may also offer *tramezzini*, ready-made sliced white bread with mixed fillings – less appetizing than the average *panino* but still tasty and slightly cheaper at around L3000/€1.55 a time. Toasted sandwiches (*toast*) are common, too: in a *paninoteca* you can get whatever you want toasted; in ordinary bars it's more likely to be a variation on cheese or ham with tomato.

If you want hot **takeaway food** there are a number of options. It's possible to find slices of pizza (*pizza rustica* or *pizza al taglio*) pretty much everywhere, and you can get most of the things already mentioned, plus pasta, chips, even full hot meals, in a **távola calda**, a sort of stand-up snack bar that's at its best in the morning when everything is fresh. Some are self-service and have limited seating, too. The bigger towns have these, and there's often one inside larger train stations. Another alternative is a **rosticceria**, where the speciality is spit-roast chicken but other fast foods such as slices of pizza, chips and hamburgers, or stuffed roasted vegetables, are also often served.

Other sources of quick snacks are **markets**, some of which sell takeaway food from stalls, including *focacce* – oven-baked pastries topped with cheese or tomato or filled with spinach, fried offal or meat – and *arancini* or *supplì* – deep-fried balls of rice with meat (*rosso*) or butter and cheese (*bianco*) filling. **Supermarkets**, also, are an obvious stop for a picnic lunch: the major department store chains, Upim and Standa, often have food halls.

Italian **ice cream** (*gelato*) is justifiably famous: a cone (*un cono*) is an indispensable accessory to the evening *passeggiata*. Most bars have a fairly good selection, but for real choice go to a **gelateria**, where the range is a tribute to the Italian imagination and flair for display. You'll sometimes have to go by appearance rather than attempting to decipher their exotic names, many of which don't even mean much to Italians: often the basics – chocolate and strawberry – are best. There's no problem locating the finest gelateria in town – it's the one that draws the crowds – and we've noted the really special places throughout the Guide. If in doubt, go for the places that make their own ice cream, denoted by the sign "Produzione Propria" outside.

PIZZA

Pizza is now a worldwide phenomenon, but Italy remains the best place to eat it. The creations served up here – especially in the city where pizza started, Naples – are wholly different from the soggy concoctions that have taken over the international fast-food market. Everywhere in Italy pizza comes thin and flat, not deep-pan, and the choice of toppings is fairly limited, with none of the dubious pineapple and sweetcorn variations. It's easy to find pizzas cooked in the traditional way, in wood-fired ovens (*forno a legna*) rather than the squeaky-clean electric ones, so that the pizzas arrive blasted and bubbling on the surface and with a distinctive charcoal taste.

Pizzerias range from a stand-up counter selling slices to a fully fledged sit-down restaurant, and on the whole they don't sell much else besides pizza, soft drinks and beer. Some straight restaurants often have pizza on the menu, too. A basic cheese and tomato pizza (*margherita*) costs around L6000–8000/€3.10–4.13 (sometimes less in the south, often more in the north), a fancier variety L8000–15,000/€4.13–7.75, and it's quite acceptable to cut it into slices and eat it with your fingers. Consult our food glossary (overleaf) for the different kinds of pizza.

MEALS: LUNCH AND DINNER

Full **meals** are often elaborate affairs, generally served in either a **trattoria** or a **ristorante**. Traditionally, a trattoria is a cheaper and more basic purveyor of homestyle cooking (*cucina casalinga*), while a ristorante is more upmarket, with aproned waiters and tablecloths, though these days the two are often interchangeable. The main differences you'll notice now are to do

A LIST OF FOOD AND DISHES

Basics and snacks

Aceto	Vinegar	Olive	Olives
Aglio	Garlic	Pane	Bread
Biscotti	Biscuits	Pane integrale	Wholemeal bread
Burro	Butter	Panino	Bread roll/sandwich
Caramelle	Sweets	Patatine	Crisps (potato chips)
Cioccolato	Chocolate	Patate fritte	Chips (French fries)
Focaccia	Oven-baked snack	Pepe	Pepper
Formaggio	Cheese	Pizzetta	Small cheese-and-tomato pizza
Frittata	Omelette	Riso	Rice
Gelato	Ice cream	Sale	Salt
Grissini	Bread sticks	Uova	Eggs
Maionese	Mayonnaise	Yogurt	Yoghurt
Marmellata	Jam	Zúcchero	Sugar
Olio	Oil	Zuppa	Soup

Pizzas

Calzone	Folded pizza, often with cheese, ham and tomato	Margherita	Cheese and tomato
		Marinara	Tomato and garlic
Capricciosa	Literally "capricious"; topped with whatever they've got in the kitchen, usually including baby artichoke, ham and capers	Napoli/ Napoletana	Tomato, cheese, anchovy, olive oil and oregano
		Quattro formaggi	"Four cheeses", usually including mozzarella, fontina, gruyère and gorgonzola
Cardinale	Ham and olives		
Funghi	Mushroom; tinned, sliced button mushrooms unless it specifies fresh, funghi freschi	Quattro stagioni	"Four seasons"; the toppings split into four sections, usually including ham, pepper, onion, mushrooms, artichokes, olives, etc
Frutti di mare	Seafood; usually mussels, prawns, squid and clams		

Antipasti and starters

Antipasto misto	Starter of seafood, vegetables, and cold meats	Insalata russa	Salad of diced vegetables in mayonnaise
Caponata	Mixed aubergine, olives, tomatoes and anchovies	Melanzane alla parmigiana	Aubergine with tomato and parmesan cheese
Caprese	Tomato and mozzarella salad with basil	Peperonata	Green and red peppers stewed in olive oil
Crespolina	Pancake, usually stuffed	Pomodori ripieni	Stuffed tomatoes
Insalata di mare	Seafood salad	Prosciutto	Ham
Insalata di riso	Rice salad	Salame	Salami

The first course (*il primo*): soups, pasta . . .

Brodo	Clear broth	Maccheroni	Macaroni (tubular pasta)
Cannelloni	Large tubes of pasta, stuffed	Minestrina	Clear broth with small pasta shapes
Farfalle	Butterfly-shaped pasta		
Fettuccine	Narrow pasta ribbons	Minestrone	Thick vegetable soup
Gnocchi	Small potato and dough dumplings	Pasta al forno	Pasta baked with minced meat, eggs, tomato and cheese
Lasagne	Lasagne		

Pasta e fagioli	Pasta with beans	Spaghettini	Thin spaghetti
Pastina in brodo	Pasta pieces in clear broth	Stracciatella	Broth with egg
Penne	Smaller version of rigatoni	Tagliatelle	Pasta ribbons, another word
Ravioli	Ravioli		for fettucine
Rigatoni	Large, grooved tubular pasta	Tortellini	Small rings of pasta, stuffed
Risotto	Cooked rice dish, with sauce		with meat or cheese
Spaghetti	Spaghetti	Vermicelli	Thin spaghetti ("little worms")

... and pasta sauce (*salsa*)

Amatriciana	Cubed bacon and tomato sauce	Peperoncino	Olive oil, garlic and fresh
Arrabbiata	Spicy tomato sauce, with		chillies
	chillies ("Angry")	Pesto	Sauce with ground basil,
Bolognese	Meat sauce		garlic and pine nuts
Burro	Butter	Pomodoro	Tomato sauce
Carbonara	Cream, ham and beaten egg	Puttanesca	Tomato, anchovy, olive oil
Funghi	Mushroom		and oregano ("Whorish")
Panna	Cream	Ragù	Meat sauce
Parmigiano	Parmesan cheese	Salvia	Sage
		Vóngole	Sauce with clams

The second course (*il secondo*): meat (*carne*) ...

Agnello	Lamb	Fégato	Liver	Pancetta/	Bacon
Bistecca	Steak	Involtini	Meat slices,	Speck	
Carpaccio	Thin slices of		rolled and	Pollo	Chicken
	raw beef		stuffed	Polpette	Meatballs
Cervella	Brain, usually	Lepre	Hare	Rognoni	Kidneys
	calves'	Lingua	Tongue	Salsiccia	Sausage
Cinghiale	Wild boar	Maiale	Pork	Saltimbocca	Veal with ham
Coniglio	Rabbit	Manzo	Beef	Spezzatino	Stew
Costolette	Cutlet, chop	Mortadella	Salami-type	Tacchino	Turkey
or cotoletta			cured meat	Trippa	Tripe
Fégatini	Chicken livers	Ossobuco	Shin of veal	Vitello	Veal

... fish (*pesce*) and shellfish (*crostacei*)

Acciughe	Anchovies	Gámberi	Prawns	Sampiero	John Dory
Anguilla	Eel	Granchio	Crab	Sarde	Sardines
Aragosta	Lobster	Merluzzo	Cod	Sgombro	Mackerel
Baccalà	Dried salted cod	Ostriche	Oysters	Sógliola	Sole
Calamari	Squid	Pesce spada	Swordfish	Tonno	Tuna
Céfalo	Grey mullet	Polpo	Octopus	Triglie	Red mullet
Cozze	Mussels	Riccio di mare	Sea urchin	Trota	Trout
Déntice	Sea Bream	Rospo	Monkfish	Vóngole	Clams ·
Gamberetti	Shrimps				

Vegetables (*contorni*), herbs (*erbe aromatice*) and salad (*insalata*)

Asparagi	Asparagus	Carciofi	Artichokes	Cávolo	Cabbage
Basílico	Basil	Carciofini	Artichoke hearts	Cetriolo	Cucumber
Bróccoli	Broccoli	Carotte	Carrots	Cipolla	Onion
Cápperi	Capers	Cavolfiori	Cauliflower		Continues over

Fagioli	Beans	Lenticchie	Lentils	Pomodori	Tomatoes
Fagiolini	Green beans	Melanzane	Aubergine	Radicchio	Red salad
Finocchio	Fennel	Orígano	Oregano		leaves
Funghi	Mushrooms	Patate	Potatoes	Spinaci	Spinach
Insalata verde/	Green salad/	Peperoni	Peppers	Zucchini	Courgettes
mista	mixed salad	Piselli	Peas		

Some terms and useful words

Affumicato	Smoked	Al dente	Firm, not	Pizzaiola	Cooked with
Arrosto	Roast		overcooked		tomato sauce
Ben cotto	Well done	Ai ferri	Grilled without	Ripieno	Stuffed
Bollito/lesso	Boiled		oil	Al sangue	Rare
Alla brace	Barbecued	Al forno	Baked	Allo spiedo	On the spit
Brasato	Cooked in wine	Fritto	Fried	Stracotto	Braised, stewed
Congelato	Frozen	Grattugiato	Grated	Surgelato	Frozen
Cotto	Cooked	Alla griglia	Grilled	In umido	Stewed
	(not raw)	Alla milanese	Fried in egg and		
Crudo	Raw		breadcrumbs		

Sweets (dolci), fruit (frutta), cheeses (formaggi) and nuts (noci)

Amaretti	Macaroons	Gorgonzola	Soft, strong,	Pignoli	Pine nuts
Ananas	Pineapple		blue-veined	Pistacchio	Pistachio nut
Anguria/	Watermelon		cheese	Provola/	Smooth, round
Coccómero		Limone	Lemon	Provolone	mild cheese,
Arance	Oranges	Macedonia	Fruit salad		made from
Banane	Bananas	Mándorle	Almonds		buffalo or
Cacchi	Persimmons	Mele	Apples		sheep milk.
Ciliegie	Cherries	Melone	Melon		Sometimes
Dolcelatte	Creamy blue	Mozzarella	Soft white		smoked
	cheese		cheese, made	Ricotta	Soft, white
Fichi	Figs		from buffalo's		sheep cheese
Fichi d'India	Prickly pears		milk	Torta	Cake, tart
Fontina	Northern Italian	Parmigiano	Parmesan	Uva	Grapes
	cheese, used	Pecorino	Strong, hard	Zabaglione	Dessert with
	in cooking		sheep cheese		eggs, sugar.
Frágole	Strawberries	Pere	Pears		marsala wine
Gelato	Ice cream	Pesche	Peaches	Zuppa	Trifle
				Inglese	

Drinks

Acqua	Mineral water	Latte	Milk	Bianco	White
minerale		Limonata	Lemonade	Rosato	Rosé
Aranciata	Orangeade	Selz	Soda water	Secco	Dry
Bicchiere	Glass	Spremuta	Fresh fruit juice	Dolce	Sweet
Birra	Beer	Spumante	Sparkling wine	Litro	Litre
Bottiglia	Bottle	Succo	Concentrated	Mezzo	Half
Caffè	Coffee		fruit juice with	Quarto	Quarter
Cioccolata	Hot chocolate		sugar	Caraffa	Carafe
calda		Tè	Tea	Salute!	Cheers!
Ghiaccio	Ice	Tónica	Tonic water		
Granita	Iced drink, with	Vino	Wine		
	coffee or fruit	Rosso	Red		

with opening times: often trattorias, at least in rural areas, will be open at lunchtime – there won't be a menu and the waiter will simply reel off a list of what's on that day. In large towns both will be open in the evening, but there'll be more choice in a ristorante, which will always have a menu and sometimes a help-yourself antipasto buffet. In either, pasta dishes go for around L8000–10,000/€4.13–5.17, and there's usually no problem just having this; the main fish or meat courses will normally be anything between L10,000/€5.17 and L15,000/€7.75.

At the end of the meal ask for the bill (*il conto*); bear in mind that almost everywhere you'll pay a cover charge (*coperto*) on top of your food of around L3000/€1.55 a head. In many trattorias this doesn't amount to much more than an illegible scrap of paper; if you want to check it, ask to have a **receipt** (*ricevuta*), something all bars and restaurants are legally bound to provide anyway (indeed they – and you – can be fined if you don't take the receipt with you and the same applies to shops and bars). In more expensive places service (*servizio*) will often be added on top of the cover charge, generally about ten percent. If service isn't included you can choose to **tip** about the same amount, but unless you're particularly pleased with the service it's common just to leave a few coins.

Other types of eating places include those that bill themselves as everything – trattoria ristorante-pizzeria – and perform no function very well, serving mediocre food that you could get at better prices elsewhere. Look out also for spaghetterias, restaurant-bars which serve basic pasta dishes and are often the hangout of the local youth. Osterie are common too, basically an old-fashioned restaurant or pub-like place specializing in home cooking, though some extremely upmarket places with pretensions to established antiquity borrow the name. In our listings, we've indicated the regular weekly **closing day**.

Traditionally, a meal (lunch is *pranzo*, dinner is *cena*) starts with **antipasto** (literally "before the meal"), a course generally served only in *ristoranti* and consisting of various cold cuts of meat, seafood and various cold vegetable dishes. *Prosciutto* is a common antipasto dish, ham either cooked (*cotto*) or just cured and hung (*crudo*) and served alone or with mozzarella cheese. A plateful of various antipasti from a self-service buffet will set you back L8000–10,000 /€4.13–5.17 a head, an item chosen from the menu a few thousand less. The next course, **il primo**, consists of a soup, risotto or pasta dish, and is followed by **il secondo** – the meat or fish course, usually served alone, except for perhaps a wedge of lemon or tomato. Watch out when ordering fish, which will either be served whole or by weight: 250g is usually plenty for one person, or ask to have a look at the fish before it's cooked. You may need quite an appetite to tackle all three courses; those on a budget will fill up best with just pasta, though portions can be quite small – in most places to it's fine to eat just a pasta course and nothing else.

Vegetables or salads – **contorni** – are ordered and served separately, and sometimes there won't be much choice: potatoes will usually come as chips (*patate fritte*), but you can also find boiled (*lesse*) or roast (*arrostite*), while salads are either green (*verde*) or mixed (*mista*). If there's no menu, the verbal list of what's available can be bewildering; if you don't understand, just ask for what you want. Everywhere will have pasta with tomato sauce (*pomodoro*) or meat sauce (*al ragù*). Afterwards you nearly always get a choice of fresh fruit (*frutta*) and a selection of **desserts** (*dolci*) – sometimes just ice cream or *macedonia* (fresh fruit salad), but often more elaborate items, like *cassata* (ice cream made with ricotta) or *zuppa inglese* (spongecake or trifle). Sadly, the indulgent dessert of *zabaglione* is rarely available at any but the most upmarket places.

Italy isn't a bad country to travel in if you're a **vegetarian**, but unless you're determined you can end up eating endless plates of pizza and pasta with tomato sauce. There are, however, other pasta sauces without meat, some superb vegetable *antipasti* and if you eat fish and seafood you should have no problem at all. Salads, too, are fresh and good. The only real difficulty is one of comprehension: Italians don't understand someone not eating meat, and stating the obvious doesn't always get the point across. Saying you're a vegetarian (*Sono vegetariano/a*) and asking if a dish has meat in it (*c'è carne dentro?*) might still turn up a poultry or prosciutto dish. Better is to ask what a dish is made with before you order (*com'è fatto?*) so that you can spot the non-meaty meat. **Vegans** will have a much harder time, though pizzas without cheese (*marinara* – nothing to do with fish – is a common option) are a good standby, vegetable soup is usually just that and the fruit is excellent.

DRINKING

Although many Italian children are brought up on wine and a *mezzo* (half-litre carafe) is a standard accompaniment to any meal, there's not a great emphasis on dedicated **drinking** in Italy. You'll rarely see drunks in public, young people don't devote their nights to getting wasted, and women especially are frowned upon if they're seen to be overindulging. Nonetheless there's a wide choice of alcoholic drinks available, often at low prices; soft drinks come in multifarious hues, thanks to the abundance of fresh fruit; and there are also mineral water and crushed-ice drinks: you'll certainly never be stuck if you want to slake your thirst.

WHERE TO DRINK

Traditional **bars** are less social centres than functional places and are all very similar to each other – brightly lit places, with a chrome counter, a Gaggia coffee machine and a picture of the local football team on the wall. You'll come here for ordinary drinking: a coffee in the morning, a quick beer, a cup of tea, but people don't generally idle away the day or evening in bars. Indeed in some more rural areas it's difficult to find a bar open much after 9pm. Where these places do fit into the general Mediterranean pattern is with their lack of set licensing hours and the fact that children are always allowed in; there's often a telephone and you can buy snacks and ice creams as well as drinks.

An **osteria** can be a more congenial setting, often a traditional place where you can usually try local specialities with a glass of wine; real wine enthusiasts, however, should head for an **enoteca**, though many of these are more oriented towards selling wine by the case than by the glass. Cities offer a much greater variety of places to sit and drink in the evening, sometimes with live music or DJs. The more energetic or late-opening of these are have taken to calling themselves **pubs**, a spill-over from the outrageous success of Irish pubs, at least one of which you'll find in almost every city, packed to the rafters with the local talent. Beer, particularly in its draught form, *alla spina*, has become fashionable in recent years.

In **traditional bars**, the routine rarely varies. It's cheapest to drink standing at the counter (there's often nowhere to sit anyway), in which case you pay first at the cash desk (*la cassa*), pre-sent your receipt (*scontrino*) to the barperson and give your order. There's always a list of prices (*listino prezzi*) behind the bar. It's customary to leave a small coin on the counter for the barperson, although no one will object if you don't. If there's waiter service, just sit where you like, though bear in mind that to do this will cost perhaps twice as much, especially if you sit outside (*fuori*) – the difference is shown on the price list as *távola* (table) or *terrazzo* (any outside seating area). Late-night bars and pubs rarely operate on the *scontrino* system; you may be asked to pay up front, in the English manner, or be presented with a bill. If not, head for the counter when you leave – the barperson will have kept a rough but surprisingly accurate tally.

COFFEE, TEA, SOFT DRINKS

One of the most distinctive smells in an Italian street is that of fresh **coffee**, usually wafting out of a bar (most trattorias and pizzerias don't serve hot drinks). It's always excellent: the basic choice is either small and black (*espresso*, or just *caffé*), which costs around L1000–L1500/€0.52–0.77 a cup, or white and frothy (*cappuccino*, for about L2000/€1.03), but there are scores of variations. If you want your espresso watered down, more like an American black coffee, ask for a *caffé lungo* or *Americano*; with a drop of milk is *caffé macchiato*; very milky coffee is *caffé latte*. Coffee with a shot of alcohol – and you can ask for just about anything in your coffee – is *caffé corretto*. Many places also now sell decaffeinated coffee (ask for Hag, even when it isn't); while in summer you might want to have your coffee cold (*caffé freddo*). For a real treat ask for *caffé granita* – cold coffee with crushed ice, usually topped with cream.

If you don't like coffee, there's always **tea**. In summer you can drink this cold too (*tè freddo*) – excellent for taking the heat off. Hot tea (*tè caldo*) comes with lemon (*con limone*) unless you ask for milk (*con latte*). Milk itself is drunk hot as often as cold, or you can get it with a dash of coffee (*latte macchiato*) and sometimes as milk shakes – *frappe* or *frullati*.

Alternatively, there are various **soft drinks** (*analcóliche*) to choose from. A **spremuta** is a fresh fruit juice, squeezed at the bar, usually orange, lemon or grapefruit. You might need to add sugar to the lemon juice (*di limone*), but the orange (*d'arancia*) is invariably sweet enough on its own, especially the crimson-red variety, made from blood oranges. There are also crushed-ice **granitas**, big in Sicily and offered in several flavours other than coffee, and available with or without whipped cream (*panna*) on top. Otherwise there's the usual range of fizzy drinks and concentrated juices: Coke is as prevalent as it is everywhere, though the diet or light versions less so; the homegrown Italian version, Chinotto, is less sweet – good with a slice of lemon. **Tap water** (*acqua normale)* is quite drinkable, and you won't pay for it in a bar. Italians drink more **mineral water** (*acqua minerale*) than any other country in Europe, certainly at least a bottle with every meal. Either still (*senza gas* or *naturale*) or sparkling (*con gas* or *frizzante*), it costs about L2500/€1.29 a bottle.

BEER AND SPIRITS

Beer (*birra*) is always a lager-type brew which usually comes in one-third or two-third litre bottles, or on draught (*alla spina)*, measure for measure more expensive than the bottled variety. A small beer is a *píccola*, (20cl or 25cl), a larger one (usually 40cl) a *media*. The chaepest and most common brands are the Italian Moretti, Peroni and Dreher, all of which are very drinkable; if this is what you want, either state the brand name or ask for *birra nazionale* or *birra chiara* – otherwise you may be given the more expensive imported beer. You may also come across darker beers (*birra nera* or *birra rossa*), which have a sweeter, maltier taste and in appearance resemble stout or bitter.

All the usual **spirits** are on sale and known mostly by their generic names. There are also Italian brands of the main varieties: the best Italian brandies are Stock and Vecchia Romagna. A generous shot of these costs about L2500/€1.29, imported stuff much more.

The homegrown Italian firewater is **grappa**, originally from Bassano di Grappa in the Veneto but now available just about everywhere. It's made from the leftovers from the winemaking process (skins, stalks and the like) and is something of an acquired taste; should you acquire it, it's probably the cheapest way of getting plastered. The more expensive *distillato*, extravagantly made from the grape itself, will suit more refined tastes.

You'll also find **fortified wines** like Martini, Cinzano and Campari; ask for a Campari-soda and you'll get a ready-mixed version from a little bottle; a slice of lemon is a *spicchio di limone*, ice is *ghiaccio*. You might also try Cynar – believe it or not, an artichoke-based sherry often drunk as an aperitif. There's also a daunting selection of **liqueurs**. Amaro is a bitter after-dinner drink, Amaretto much sweeter with a strong taste of almond, Sambuca a sticky-sweet aniseed concoction, traditionally served with a coffee bean in it and set on fire (though, increasingly, this is something put on to impress tourists). Another sweet alternative, originally from Sorrento, is *Limoncello* or *limoncino*, a lemon-based liqueur best drunk in a frozen vase-shaped glass. Strega is another drink you'll see behind every bar, yellow, herb-and-saffron based stuff in tall, elongated bottles: about as sweet as it looks but not unpleasant.

WINE

Just as Italy's food has suffered from stereotyped images, so too has its **wine**. Lambrusco was one of the first Italian wines to sell well overseas, despite (or because of) its reputation as cheap party plonk, while cheap Soave, Valpolicella and Chianti continue to shift units. But the finer wines are now well established abroad, though often the very best wines are kept for the home market. A few pointers in the right direction are given in the "Regional Food and Wine" box at the beginning of each chapter. Nudged along by the DOC laws (see box overleaf), standards have been steadily increasing in recent years. Many producers have been turning their hands to making higher **quality wines**, and besides the finer tuning of established names such as Barolo and Orvieto, there's a good deal of experimentation going on everywhere. Southern winemakers are no longer content to see nearly all of their produce sold north to beef up table-wine blends, while in Tuscany, Trentino-Alto Adige and Friuli, French grape varieties such as Chardonnay, Sauvignon Blanc and the Pinots are joining old Italian favourites with startling success.

They don't waste drinking time in Italy with dialogue or veneration, however; neither is there much time for the snobbery often associated with "serious" wine drinking. Light **reds** such as those made from the dolcetto grape are hauled out of the fridge in hot weather, while some full-bodied **whites** are drunk at near room temperature. Wine is still very cheap, though unless your aim is to get legless as cheaply as possible, it's wise to avoid the very cheapest plonk. In restaurants you'll invariably be offered red (*rosso*) or white (*bianco*) – rarely rosé (*rosato*). If you're

THE DENOMINAZIONE D'ORIGINE SYSTEM

The **Denominazione d'Origine** system is the key to understanding what to look for in Italian wine, but it shouldn't be seen as any sort of guarantee. The denomination is a certification of origin, not of quality, and while it may mean a wine will be drinkable, stick to it too rigidly and you could be missing out on an awful lot.

Denomination zones are set by governmental decree. They specify where a certain named wine may be made, what grape varieties may be used, the maximum yield of grapes per hectare and how long the wine should be aged. **Denominazione d'Origine Controllata** (DOC) guarantees the origin of the wine and that it has been made to the specification of the rules for the zone in which it's produced. Vino da távola is simply wine that does not conform to the DOC laws, though it's not necessarily wine you'd sooner pour down the sink than drink. **Denominazione d'Origine Controllata e Garantita** (DOCG) is the only designation at the moment that actually has any real meaning. Wines sold under this label not only have to conform to the ordinary DOC laws, but are also tested by government-appointed inspectors. There are only currently eighteen such wines, but more are planned.

Though it's undoubtedly true that the DOC system has helped lift standards, the laws have come under fire from both growers and critics for their rigidity, constraints and anomalies. Chianti, for instance, can be a quaffable lunchtime drink, a wine of pedigree to be treated with reverence, or – depending on the vintage – it can be appalling. All will have a DOC. Some claim too that the restrictions of the DOCG are losing their credibility. With big reds such as Barolo the ageing term can destroy all the fruitiness of the wine, while the entry of Albana di Romagna, a somewhat ordinary white, to DOCG status, with others to follow, has caused consternation. Increasingly, producers eager to experiment have begun to disregard the regulations and make new wines that are sometimes expensive and among Italy's best wines, though they're still offically labelled da távola (the nickname super vini da távola has emerged). The Sicilian Corvo, red and white, is perhaps the best-known non-DOC label, a modern wine that goes for a little over twice the price of ordinary table plonk. Tuscany also produces some excellent table wines.

unsure about what to order, don't be afraid to try the local stuff (ask for *vino sfuso*, or simply *un mezzo* – a half litre – or *un quarto* – a quarter), sometimes served straight from the barrel, particularly down south. It's often very good, and cheap at an average of around L6000/€3.10 a litre. Bottled wine is pricier but still very good value; expect to pay around L12,000/€6.20 a bottle in a restaurant, less than half that from a shop or supermarket. In bars you can buy a glass of wine for about L1000–3000/€0.51–1.55, depending on quality.

COMMUNICATIONS: POST, PHONES AND THE MEDIA

Opening hours of main post offices are usually Monday–Saturday 8.30am–7.30pm; others are likely to be open Monday–Friday 8.30am–5pm and Saturday 8.30am–noon, and offices in smaller towns may close altogether on Saturday. Note too that offices may close an hour earlier on the last working day of the month. Stamps (*francobolli*), are sold in *tabacchi* too, as well as in some gift shops in the tourist resorts; they will often also weigh your letter. The Italian postal system is one of the worst in Europe, but if you're determined to write, airmail letter rates are L800/€0.41 anywhere within the European Union, and L1500/€0.77 to North America, Australia and New Zealand. Letters can be sent poste restante to any Italian post office, by addressing them "Fermo Posta" followed by the name of the town. When picking something up take your passport, and make sure they check under middle names and initials – and every other letter when all else fails – as filing is often diabolical.

TELEPHONES

Public **telephones**, run by **Telecom Italia**, come in various forms, usually with clear instructions in English. At the time of writing, **coin-operated** phones take L100, L200 and L500 coins; you need at least L200 to start a call, even to toll-free numbers (the money is refunded at the end of the call). Most phones will only accept **telephone cards** (*carte* or *schede telefoniche*), available from tabacchi and newsstands for L5000, L10,000 or L15,000, but there's sometimes one nearby that takes coins. Note that the perforated corner of these cards must be torn off before they can be used. If you can't find a phone box, bars will often have a phone you can use – look for the red phone symbol.

Telephone numbers change with amazing frequency in Italy, a practice which has resulted in numbers having anything between four and eight digits, not including the code which is usually somewhere between two and four digits long. The codes are now an integral part of the number and always need to dialled, regardless of whether or not you are in the zone you are telephoning. If in doubt, consult the local directory – there's a copy in most Italian bars, hotels and, of course, telephone offices. Numbers beginning ☎800, ☎147 and ☎167 are free; ☎170 will get you through to an English speaking operator, ☎176 to international directory enquiries.

CODES FOR MAJOR ITALIAN CITIES

Calling Italy **from abroad**, dial the access code (☎00 from Britain and New Zealand, ☎011 from the US and Canada, ☎0011 from Australia), followed by 39, then the area code including the first zero (the major towns are listed below), then the subscriber number. If calling **within Italy** the area code must always be used, even when dialling locally; all telephone numbers listed in the Guide include the relevant code.

Bari ☎080	Bologna ☎051	Florence ☎055
Genoa ☎010	Milan ☎02	Naples ☎081
Palermo ☎091	Rome ☎06	Turin ☎011
	Venice ☎041	

PHONING ABROAD FROM ITALY

For direct **international calls from Italy**, dial ☎00 followed by the country code (given below), the area code (minus its first zero), and finally the subscriber number. **Country Direct** services enable you to speak to an operator in your home country, and to make collect (reverse-charge) calls.

UK: 44 **Ireland**: 353 **USA & Canada**: 1 **Australia**: 61 **New Zealand**: 64

COUNTRY DIRECT SERVICES

Australia: Telstra ☎172 1061; Optus ☎172 1161
Canada: ☎172 1001
Ireland: ☎172 0353
New Zealand: ☎172 1064
UK: BT ☎172 0044
USA: AT&T ☎172 1011; MCI ☎172 1022; Sprint ☎172 1877

You can make **international calls** from any booth that accepts cards or any other booth labelled *interurbano*; put in at least L2000 to be sure of getting through. Alternatively, use a special **international phone card** (*carta telefonica internazionale*) available from post offices for L12,500, L25,000, L50,000 and L100,000; all cardphones accept them, but before each call you need to dial ☎1740 and the PIN number on the back of the card. One of the cheapest ways to make international calls, however, is to get hold of a phone card before you leave: in the UK, from **British Telecom** (☎0800/345144) or **Cable & Wireless** (☎0500/100505); in the US, from **AT&T** (☎1-800/543-3117) or **MCI** (☎1-800/444-3333, *www.mci.com*); in Australia, from **Telstra** (☎1800/038 000) or **Optus** (☎1300/300 937); and in New Zealand, from **Telecom NZ** (☎04/801 9000). Simple user instructions are supplied with the cards and the cost of the connected call is added to your domestic bill or a credit card account. You can also make **international reversed charge** or **collect calls** (*cárico al destinatario*) by dialling ☎172 followed by the country code (see box above), which will connect you to an operator in your home country.

Phone **tariffs** are among the most expensive in Europe, though prices drop to a reduced rate off peak. For domestic calls a reduced rate is charged on weekday nights (6.30pm–8am) and at weekends (from 1pm on Saturday through to 8am Monday morning); it's cheaper to dial internationally between 10pm and 8am Monday to Saturday, and all day on Sunday. Unusually, it's often less expensive to make calls from your hotel than to use the pricey public telephones, whether for domestic or international calls.

Mobile phones work on the GSM European standard. You will hardly see an Italian without his or her *telefonino*, but if you are going to join them make sure you have made the necessary "roaming" arrangements before you leave home – which may involve paying a hefty (refundable) deposit.

FAX AND EMAIL

Nearly every Italian town has a **fax office**, but the cost of faxing from these places is usually fairly high: for faxes within Italy, expect to pay at least L5000/€2.58 for the first page and L2500/€1.29 for each subsequent page, plus the cost of the call; for international faxes it's about L10,000/€5.16 for the first and L5000/€2.58 for subsequent pages, plus the cost of the call. A cheaper, fiddlier alternative is to use one of Telecom Italia's Pubblifax machines, found in the larger phone offices where you'll find groups of public telephones; these only charge the cost of the call plus L2000/€1.03 per page.

Internet cafés, often a simple Internet point without café facilities, are now common in cities and even in smaller towns, allowing you to log on for between L10,000/€5.16 and L15,000/€7.75 an hour. We've detailed options in all the major cities under "Listings", and most tourist offices will print out a sheet of likely places; otherwise check out *www.cyberiacafe.net/cyberia/guide /ccafe. htm* for a list of cybercafés. Organizing a free Internet mail address at sites like *www.hotmail.com* and *www.yahoo.com* is a handy, reliable way of keeping in contact with home. Travelling with a laptop and a modem enables you to log in to your own service provider – and many provide local-access numbers – but many travellers find this isn't as glitch-free as it should be. Note that lower-grade hotels tend to have the non-standard chunky Italian four-pin phone-plug whereas more expensive places almost always use the standard US-style RJ11 phone-plug.

NEWSPAPERS

The **Italian press** is fairly regionally based, but there are some newspapers that are available all over the country. The centre-left *La Repubblica* and authoritative right-slanted *Corriere della Sera* are the two most widely read and available, published nationwide with local supplements. The traditionally radical *Il Manifesto* has in recent years lost ground to *L'Unità*, the party organ of the Democratic Left (formerly the Communist Party), which has won recognition as the best-designed and most readable newspaper. *Paese Sera* is another broadly left-wing daily read widely in the south. Of other provincial newspapers, *La Stampa* is the daily of Turin, *Il Messaggero* of Rome – both rather stuffy, establishment sheets. *Il Mattino* is the more readable organ of Naples and the Campania area, while other southern editions include the *Giornale di Sicilia and La Gazzetta del Sud*. Perhaps the most avidly read newspapers of all, however, are the specialist sports papers, most notably the *Corriere dello Sport* and the pink *Gazzetta dello Sport* – both essential reading if you want to get a handle on the Italian football scene.

English-language newspapers can be found for around three times their home cover price in all the larger cities and most of the more established resorts, usually a day late, though in Milan and Rome you can sometimes find the papers on the day of publication, especially those such as *The Times*, the *Financial Times*, the *Guardian*, the *European*, the *New York Times*, the *Wall Street Journal* and the *International Herald Tribune*, which publish a European edition. Conversely, in the remoter parts of the country it's not unusual for papers to be delayed by several days.

TV AND RADIO

If you get the chance, try to watch some Italian **TV**, if only to size up the pros and cons of dereg-ulation. Although the much-vaunted programmes with stripping housewives and the like do exist, the output is otherwise pretty bland, with the accent on ghastly quiz shows, shopping channels, cathartic chat shows in which the famous and not-so-famous air their dirty linen, and soaps, plus a heavy smattering of American imports. Nevertheless, the three national channels, RAI 1, 2 and 3, have the odd worthy programme; RAI 3 remains broadly left-wing, with its output leaning more towards the cultural and intellectual, and is the outlet for local news and features. Satellite television is fairly widely distributed, and three-star hotels and above almost always offer the usual mix of BBC World, CNN and French-, German- and Spanish-language news channels, as well as MTV and Eurosport.

The situation in **radio** is if anything even more anarchic, with the FM waves crowded to the extent that you continually pick up new stations whether you want to or not. This means there are generally some good stations if you search hard enough, but on the whole the RAI stations are again the more professional – though even with them daytime listening is virtually undiluted Euro-pop.

OPENING HOURS AND PUBLIC HOLIDAYS

Increasingly, there is a trend towards more flexible opening hours. Most shops and businesses in Italy open from Monday to Saturday from around 8am until 1pm, and from about 4pm until 7pm, though many shops close on Saturday afternoons and Monday mornings, and in the south the day can begin and end an hour later. In the north some businesses work to a 9am–5pm day to facilitate international dealings. Traditionally, everything except bars and restaurants closes on Sunday, though most towns have a *pasticceria* open in the mornings, while in large cities and tourist areas, Sunday opening is becoming more common.

The other factors that can disrupt your plans are **national holidays** and local **saints' days** and festivals. In **August**, particularly during the weeks either side of *Ferragosto*, when most of the country flees to the coast, many towns are left half-deserted, with shops, bars and restaurants closed and a reduced public transport service. Local religious holidays don't generally close down shops and businesses for the whole day, but they do mean that accommodation space may be tight. The country's official **national holidays**, on the other hand, close everything down, except bars and restaurants. These are:

January 1 (New Year's Day)

January 6 (Epiphany)

Pasquetta (Easter Monday)

April 25 (Liberation Day)

May 1 (Labour Day)

August 15 (*Ferragosto*; Assumption of the Blessed Virgin Mary)

November 1 (*Ognissanti*; All Souls Day)

December 8 (*Immaccolata*; Immaculate Conception of the Blessed Virgin Mary)

December 25 (*Natale*; Christmas)

December 26 (*Santo Stefano*; St Stephen's Day)

CHURCHES, MUSEUMS AND ARCHEOLOGICAL SITES

The rules for visiting **churches** are much as they are all over the Mediterranean. **Dress modestly**, which usually means no shorts for men or women and covered shoulders for women, and try to avoid wandering around during a service. Most churches open in the early morning, around 7 or 8am for Mass, and close around noon, opening up again at 4pm and closing at 7 or 8pm. In more remote places, some churches will only open for early morning and evening services, while others are closed at all times except Sundays and on religious holidays; if you're determined to take a look, you may have to ask around for the key.

Another problem you'll face – and this applies to the whole country – is that lots of churches, monasteries, convents and oratories are **closed for restoration** (*chiuso per restauro*). We've indicated in the text the more long-term closures, though you might be able to persuade a workman or priest/curator to show you around even if there's scaffolding everywhere.

Most museums and sites are closed on Mondays. **Opening hours** for state-run **museums** are generally from 9am until 7pm, Tuesday to Saturday, and from 9am until 1pm on Sunday. Most other museums roughly follow this pattern too, although they are more likely to close for a couple of hours in the afternoon, and have shorter opening hours in winter. Many large museums also run late-night openings in summer (till 10pm or later Tues–Sat, or 8pm Sun). The opening times of **archeological sites** are more flexible: most sites open every day, often Sunday included, from 9am until late evening – frequently specified as one hour before sunset, and thus changing according to the time of year. In winter, times are drastically cut, if only because of the darker evenings; 4pm is a common closing time. They, too, are sometimes closed on Monday.

Admission prices for state-run museums vary between L4000/€2.07 and L8000/€4.13, although for major sites such as the Forum in Rome and the Uffizi in Florence you'll be paying around L12,000/€6.20, and even higher for the Vatican. Under-18s and over-65s get in free on production of documentary proof of age, such as a passport; under-26s get half-price entry; students can often, but not always, get entry at discounted prices – an ISIC card is the safest bet. Some sites, churches and monasteries are nominally free to get in, but you are expected to tip the custodian to open things up and show you around: L1000/€0.52 per person in your party should do it. Otherwise, expect to make a donation. For the latest information on museums, the Web site *www.beniculturali.it/home.htm* is useful.

FESTIVALS

Italy has few national festivals, but there is no shortage of celebrations, saints' days being the usual excuse for some kind of binge. All cities, small towns and villages have their local saint, who is normally paraded through the streets amid much noise and spectacle. There is no end of other occasions for a *festa* – either to commemorate a local miracle or historic event, or to show off the local products or artistic talent. Many happen at Easter, or in May, September or around Ferragosto (August 15); the local tourist office will have details and exact dates.

Recently there's also been a revival of the **carnival** (*Carnevale*), the last fling before Lent, although the anarchic fun that was enjoyed in the past has generally been replaced by elegant, self-conscious affairs, with ingenious costumes and handmade masks. Venice has the most famous carnival – a well-organized event that is so popular it sometimes takes over the entire city centre – and there are other, equally large and perhaps more fun events such as at Viareggio in Tuscany and Acireale in Sicily, while smaller towns will often put on a parade. A carnival usually lasts for the five days before Ash Wednesday; because it's connected with Easter the dates can change from year to year – count on some time between the end of February and end of March.

RELIGIOUS AND TRADITIONAL FESTIVALS

Perhaps the most widespread local event in Italy is the **religious procession**, some of which can be very dramatic affairs. Many – perhaps all – have strong pagan roots, marking important dates on the calendar and only relatively recently sanctified by the Church. One of the best known takes place in the small village of **Cocullo** in the Abruzzi mountains, on May 6 (St Dominic Abate's Day), when a statue of the saint, swathed in snakes, is carried through the town – a ritual that certainly dates back to pre-Christian times. **Good Friday**, for obvious reasons, is also a popular time for processions. In many towns and villages models of Christ taken from the Cross are paraded through towns accompanied by white-robed, hooded figures singing penitential hymns. The west coast of Sicily sees many of these, as do other places across the south – **Táranto, Reggio, Bari, Bríndisi**. On the following Saturday a procession of flagellants makes its way through **Nocera Tirinese** in Calabria. Later on in the year, elaborate *presepi* (nativity scenes)

FESTIVALS DIARY

AGRIGENTO Almond blossom festival (March).

ALBA Giostra delle Cento Torri, Palio and costume parade (1st Sun in Oct).

AMALFI Sant'Andrea's day (June 27).

AOSTA Fiera di Sant'Orso – thousand-year-old fair (End of Jan).

AREZZO Giostra del Saracino – jousting by knights in armour (1st Sun in Sept).

ASCOLI PICENO Torneo della Quintana – jousting (1st weekend in Aug).

ASSISI Holy Week celebrations (Easter); Calendimaggio spring *festa* (1st week in May).

ASTI Bareback riders from villages around take part in Palio (3rd Sun in Sept).

BARI Sagra di San Nicola – pilgrims follow a boat carrying the saint's image for a ceremony out at sea, in honour of the 47 sailors who saved his bones from raiders (1st weekend in May).

BRISIGHELLA Medieval festival (End of June).

CAGLIARI Sagra di Sant Efisio – thousands of pilgrims accompany the saint's statue in carts, on horseback or on foot (May 1).

CAMOGLI Sagra del Pesce – procession of boats, with a fish fry-up (2nd Sun in May).

CAMPOBASSO Sagra dei Misteri (Beginning of June).

COCULLO Festa di San Domenico Abate – procession through the village with a statue of the saint swathed in snakes (1st week in May).

DIANO MARINA Festival del Mare – fireworks (Aug 15).

DOLCEACQUA Festa di San Sebastiano – saint's day celebrated with a tree covered with Communion hosts carried through town (Jan 20).

ENNA Celebrations for Holy Week (Easter).

FAVIGNANA La Mattanza – ritual slaughter of tuna (May/June).

FELTRE Medieval Palio (1st weekend in Aug).

FLORENCE Scoppio del Carro – firework display in the Piazza del Duomo (Easter Sun); Festa di San Giovanni – fireworks and the Gioco di Calcio Storico, a rough-and-tumble football game played between the four quarters of the city in medieval costume (June 24 & 28).

FOLIGNO Torneo della Quintana – six hundred medieval knights in jousting contest (2nd weekend in Sept).

GENOA Festa di San Giovanni (June 24).

GUBBIO Festa dei Ceri (May 5); Crossbow matches against San Sepolcro (Last Sun in May).

LA SPEZIA Rowing contests in Palio del Golfo (Aug).

---

are displayed during the days leading up to **Christmas** in **Naples** and **Verona** (in Naples especially *presepi* are a popular local craft), and the nativity figures are prominent in the large-scale Mercato di Sant'Ambrogio in **Milan**. At **Epiphany** (January 6) a toy-and-sweet fair, dedicated to the good witch Befana, lasts until dawn around the fountains of Piazza Navona in **Rome**. On the same day a procession of the *Rei Magi* (Three Kings) passes through Milan, and there are live tableaux at **Rivisondoli** in Abruzzo. There are plenty of other festive events, for instance the famous Festa di San Gennaro in **Naples**, where much superstition surrounds the miraculous liquefaction of the saint's blood three times a year.

Other ritual celebrations bear less of the Church's imprint, and a Communist mayor and local bishop will jointly attend a town's saint's day celebration, where the separate motivations to make some money, have a good time and pay some spiritual dues all merge. Superstition and a desire for good luck are part of it, too. In **Gubbio** there's a mad race to the Church of San Ubaldo (May 5) with the *Ceri* – three phallic wooden pillars each eight metres high. Similar obelisks are carried around in other places. On September 3 a ninety-foot-tall *Macchina di Santa Rosa*, illuminated with tiny oil lamps, is paraded through **Viterbo**, and at **Nola**, near Naples, around June 22, eight *gigli* (lilies) are carried through the streets. Phallic though these may seem, the giant towers are more likely to be associated with an ancient, goddess-worshipping culture.

The number of practising Catholics in Italy is dwindling, and until recently many *feste* were dying out. But interest in many festivals has been revived over the last decade or so, especially in **pilgrimages**. These are as much social occasions as spiritual journeys, some of them more important to people than Christmas, and they still attract massive crowds. As many as a million pilgrims travel through the night, mostly on foot, to

LUCCA Torchlight processions as part of Luminaria di Santa Croce (Aug 14).

LUNGRO Albanian celebrations (Easter).

MAROSTICA Human chess game (Every even year 2nd weekend in September)

MASSA MARITTIMA Crossbow competition (May 24).

MILAN Mercato di Sant'Ambrogio, also known as O Bei! O Bei! (December).

MONTEPULCIANO Bravio delle Botte, barrel-rolling race preceded by procession, drums and flag-throwing (Last Sun in Aug).

NAPLES Festa di San Gennaro Gathering in the cathedral to witness the liquefaction of the saint's blood (1st Sun in May, Sept 19, Dec 16).

NOCERA TIRINESE Flagellants' procession through the village (Easter Sat).

NORCIA Crossbow matches and processions (March 20–21).

NOVOLI Bonfires in honour of Sant'Antonio Abate (Jan 17).

ORVIETO Corpus Christi procession (Mid-June).

PIANA DEGLI ALBANESI Byzantine celebrations (Easter and Epiphany).

PISA Luminaria – festival of lights (June 16–17); Gioco del Ponte, tug-of-war game over main bridge, preceded by historical procession (June 26); Historical regatta in costume (July 26 & 27).

PISTOIA Giostra dell Orso – Joust of the Bear (July 25).

PORTO CESAREO Luminaria – festival of lights (Aug 22).

ROME Befana, toy-and-sweet fair in Piazza Navona (Jan 6 – Epiphany); Festa de'Noantri – dancing, songs and floats in Trastevere's piazzas (July 16–24).

SAN MARCO IN LAMIS Fracchie – ritual of pagan origin in which bundles of burning wood are hauled through the streets (Good Friday).

SAN SEPOLCRO Crossbow matches against Gubbio (2nd weekend in Sept).

SIENA Palio in medieval Campo (July 2 & Aug 16).

TAGGIA Festa della Maddalena with Dance of Death in main piazza (Sun nearest to July 22).

VENICE Carnevale (Feb/March); Il Redentore – gondola procession, fireworks, to commemorate the end of a sixteenth-century plague (3rd week in July); Regatta (1st Sun in Sept).

VENTIMIGLIA Regatta and processions (Aug 9–10).

VIAREGGIO Carnevale (Feb/March).

VITERBO Procession of the Macchina di Santa Rosa (Sept 3).

---

the **Shrine of the Madonna di Polsi** in the inhospitable Aspromonte mountains in Calabria, while Sardinia's biggest festival, the **Festa di Sant'Efisio**, sees a four-day march from Cágliari to Pula and back, to commemorate the saint's martyrdom. And there are other shrines and sanctuaries all over Italy, mostly in inaccessible hilltop locations, some of them visited regularly by families from the surrounding area keen for a day out, others just the subject of a once-a-year trek.

Other traditions survive: on the **Day of the Dead** (All Saints' Day) on November 1, children receive presents, given on behalf of dead relatives, to make them feel that the people they were close to still think of them. There are festivals that evoke local pride in tradition, too, medieval contests like the **Palio** horse race in Siena perpetuating allegiances to certain competing clans; Palio races take place in a few other centres, Alba and Asti in Piemonte for example, though most have been revived more to support the tourist industry than anything else and can't compete with the seriousness and vigour of Siena's contest. Other towns put on crossbow, jousting and flag-twirling contests, marching bands in full medieval costume accompanying the event with enthusiastic drumming; these are far from staged affairs, with fierce rivalry between participants.

FOOD FESTIVALS

Food-inspired *feste* are more low-key affairs than the religious events, but no less enjoyable for it, usually celebrating the local speciality of the region to the accompaniment of dancing, music from a local brass band and noisy fireworks at the end of the evening. There are literally hundreds of food festivals, sometimes advertised as *sagre*, and every region has them – look in the local papers or ask at the tourist office during summer and autumn and you're bound to find something going on. Most are modest affairs, meant for the locals and little publicized – but there are a few exceptions. In **Tivoli**, near Rome, the town's fountains run with wine on the second Sunday in October; the same happens in **Città della Pieve** in Umbria, in April, during the Festa delle Fontane, and at nearby **Panicale**. Other notable events are **Orvieto**'s wine festival each June, **Bolzano**'s in the second half of March or the beginning of April, and the truffle fair and Palio in **Alba** on the first Sunday in October. Generally though, the smaller events are better, giving you a chance to join in the dancing and sample the cooking.

ARTS FESTIVALS

The home-town pride that sparks off many of the food festivals also expresses itself in some of the **arts festivals** spread across Italy, particularly in the central part of the country – based in ancient amphitheatres or other ruins or marking the work of a native composer, and sometimes going on for as long as a month. Perhaps the most prestigious is the **Venice** film festival in August and September. **Spoleto**'s summer Festival dei Due Mondi (Festival of the Two Worlds) is also well known, a two-month-long event of classical concerts, films, ballet, street theatre and perfor-

mance art, with its venue the open spaces of the ancient walled town, that is the biggest arts festival in the country nowadays. The Sferisterio in **Macerata** in Marche and the Roman arena in Verona are two equally dramatic places to hear music in the summer months. Similarly there's the Panatenee Pompeiane music festival, held in the ruins of **Pompeii** during the last week of August. **Bologna**'s summer festival often tries something different, with live bands playing in its medieval palace courtyards and screenings of soap opera or art movies in unexpected places. Other festivals remember a particular composer: Puccini's music is celebrated from the end of July to mid-August in Torre del Lago, near **Viareggio**, Rossini's in **Pésaro** from mid-August to September. And it's worth noting the dates of the Italian **opera season**, which begins in December and runs through until May or June. The principal opera houses are La Scala in Milan, the Teatro dell'Opera in Rome, La Fenice in Venice (currently closed after fire, but there is a temporary replacement), the Teatro Comunale in Florence and the Teatro San Carlo in Naples. But there are also other, more modest venues that have regular performances of opera throughout these months.

ARTS FESTIVALS

CITTA DI CASTELLO Chamber Music Festival (Aug & Sept).

CLUSONE Jazz Festival (September).

FIESOLE Estate Fiesolana – music, cinema, ballet, theatre (Mid-June to Aug).

FLORENCE Maggio Musicale Fiorentino (May & June).

LUCCA Opera and theatre festival at Barga (Last half of July).

MARTINA FRANCA Festivale della Valle d'Itria – opera, classical and jazz recitals (End of July & 1st week of Aug).

NAPLES International Music Festival (Last half of May); Neapolitan song contest at Piedigrotta (First half of Sept).

PERUGIA Umbria Jazz Festival (July & Aug).

RAVELLO Opera and Music Festival (June–Sept).

RAVENNA Basilica di San Vitale organ music recitals (July & Aug); Music Festival (June & July).

ROME Opera at Baths of Caracalla and concerts at Campidoglio (July); at the Basilica of

Maxentius (All summer); and at the Accademia Nazionale di Santa Cecilia and Accademia Filarmonica Romana (Winter).

SIENA Settimane Musicali – musical weeks (Aug).

SORRENTO International Cinema Convention (Oct–Dec).

SPOLETO Festival dei Due Mondi (End of June–Aug).

STRESA Settimane Musicali (End of Aug–Sept).

SIRACUSA Greek drama in ancient theatre (May & June).

TAORMINA International film festival concerts and plays in the Greek theatre (July & Aug).

TURIN Settembre Musica (Sept).

UMBÉRTIDE Rock festival (Summer).

VENICE International Film Festival (Aug & Sept).

VERONA International Opera Festival (June–Aug); International Film Festival (June).

VITERBO Baroque Music Festival (Mid-June to July).

SPORTS AND OUTDOOR PURSUITS

Spectator sports are popular in Italy, especially the hallowed *calcio* (football), and there is undying national passion for frenetic motor and cycle races. When it comes to participation, though, you get the impression that there isn't the same compulsion to hit the hell out of a squash ball or sweat your way through an aerobics class after work as there is, say, in Britain or the States. All the same, the notion of staying fit has lately been absorbed into the general obsession with *bella figura* (looking good), especially when it offers the opportunity to wear the flashiest designer gear. Members-only sports clubs, gyms and public sports facilities have mushroomed over the last decade and it's usually possible to find places where you can work out or join in a competitive game. Otherwise, the country's natural advantages provide plenty of scope for keeping in trim in the most enjoyable ways possible.

For visitors to Italy, the most accessible activities are centred around the mountains, which you can climb, ski, paraglide, raft or simply explore on foot. And, with so much coastline, as well as the lakes region, there are plenty of opportunities for swimming, sailing and windsurfing; Campania, Calabria and Sicily are particularly popular for scuba diving and snorkelling.

You can get a guide and map suggesting **sailing itineraries** round the coast of southern Italy from the Italian State Tourist Office (see p.24).

SPORT

If you are at all interested in the game, it would be a shame to leave Italy without attending a *partita* or **football** match; *calcio* is the national sport and is followed fanatically by millions of Italians. The **season** starts around the end of August, takes a break during the latter part of December and early part of January, and finishes up, with the Italian Cup final, in June. The **Italian League** is split into four principal divisions, Serie A, Serie B, and Serie C1 and C2; matches are normally played on Sunday afternoons, occasionally Sunday evenings, and there is a good chance that on any weekend there will be a team from one of the above divisions playing not too far away. Serie A, is of course, the most prestigious division, comprising eighteen teams; the bottom-placed four are relegated each season, to be replaced by the top four from Serie B, although there are some clubs whom it would be unimaginable to see in Serie B – teams like Juventus, Inter Milan and AC Milan.

Inevitably, **tickets** for Serie A matches are not cheap, starting at about L30,000/€15.49 for "Curva" seats at each end of the ground, where the *tifosi* or hard-core fans go, rising to L50,000/€25.82 for the *Distinti* or corner seats, and up to L70,000–150,000/€36.15–77.47 for seats in the "Tribuna", along the side of the pitch. We've given details of where to buy tickets for the major clubs and how to get to their grounds in the "Listings" sections at the end of major city accounts. Once at the football match, get into the atmosphere of the occasion by knocking back *borghetti* – little vials of cold coffee with a drop of spirit added.

Italy's chosen sport after football is **basketball**, introduced from the United States after World War II. Most cities have a team, and Italy is now ranked among the foremost in the world. Other stateside imports are **baseball** and **American football**. In a country that has produced Ferrari, Maserati, Alfa Romeo and Fiat, it should come as no surprise that **motor racing** gives Italians such a buzz. There are grand prix tracks at Monza near Milan (home of the Italian Grand Prix) and at Imola, where the San Marino Grand Prix is held.

The other sport popular with participants and crowds of spectators alike is **cycling.** At weekends especially, you'll often see a club pack out, dressed in bright team kit, whirring along on their slender machines. The annual Giro d'Italia (tour of Italy) in the second half of May is a prestige event that attracts scores of international participants each year, closing down roads and creating great excitement.

OUTDOOR PURSUITS

With the Alps right on the doorstep, it's easy to spend a weekend on the pistes from Milan, Turin, Bologna or Venice, and the Abruzzi mountains offer some **skiing** reachable from Rome or Naples in resorts such as Campo Felice and Roccardo; tourist offices should have details of resorts in their areas. *Settimane Bianche* (White Weeks), a package of accommodation in a ski resort, can be excellent value and are relatively easy to arrange. Contact the regional tourist offices in Val d'Aosta, Trentino-Alto Adige or your chosen resort in autumn for brochures: these specify prices, participating hotels and contact details; then you book your accommodation direct and arrange your own transport. Extras such as equipment rental and lift passes are equally inexpensive, with a three-day pass costing between L84,000–140,000/€43.34–72.24. Snow can be unreliable on this southerly, sunnier side of the Alps, but snow cannon keep a guaranteed core of pistes open.

In summer, the **hiking** and **climbing** are second to none, and are detailed in the Trentino-Alto Adige chapter, starting on p.233. **Mountain-biking** has also taken off in a big way in the last five years with plenty of rental outlets (charging about L30,000/€15.49 a day), and the added advantage that some cable-car companies offer special deals whereby they take the slog out of getting the bike up and you get to freewheel down.

Waterskiing, sailing and **windsurfing** are also popular at seaside resorts as well as on Lake Garda (see p.223 for more on the latter), with equipment and lessons easy to arrange. Swimming in anything but the sea is harder than you might imagine – there are few municipal pools (note that swimming caps are often obligatory), but you can always make the occasional hotel with a pool a priority. Ùstica, off Sicily's northern coast, hosts an annual **marine festival** from mid-June through to August: activities, exhibitions and events take place on both land and sea. **Canoeing** and **kayaking** have boomed in recent years, particularly in the mountain areas of the North. The Amici del Fiume has a Web site (*www.services.csi.it/~fiume*) with useful links, though not all the pages are translated into English.

The use of gym facilities or tennis courts usually entails acquiring club membership. In country areas it's becoming increasingly easy to find stables offering **riding** lessons or holidays – agriturismo agencies (see p.35) and local tourist offices can help with arrangements.

TROUBLE AND THE POLICE

Despite what you hear about the Mafia, most of the crime you're likely to come across in Italy is of the small-time variety, prevalent in the major cities and the south of the country, where gangs of *scippatori* or "snatchers" operate. Crowded streets or markets and packed tourist sights are the places to be wary of; *scippatori* work on foot or on scooters, disappearing before you've had time to react. As well as handbags, they whip wallets, tear off visible jewellery and, if they're really adroit, unstrap watches.

You can **minimize the risk** of this happening by being discreet: don't flash anything of value, keep a firm hand on your camera, and carry shoulderbags, as Italian women do, slung across your body. It's a good idea, too, to entrust money and credit cards to hotel managers. Never leave anything valuable in your car, and try to park in car parks on well-lit, well-used streets. On the whole it's common sense to avoid badly lit areas completely at night and deserted inner-city areas by

EMERGENCIES

For help in an **emergency**, call one of the following national emergency telephone numbers.

☎112 for the police (Carabinieri).

☎113 for any emergency service, including ambulance (Soccorso Pubblico di Emergenza).

☎115 for the fire brigade (Vigili del Fuoco).

☎116 for road assistance (Soccorso Stradale).

☎118 for an ambulance (Ambulanza).

day. Confronted with a robber, your best bet is to submit meekly: it's an excitable situation where panic can lead to violence – though very few tourists see anything of this.

THE POLICE

If the worst happens, you'll be forced to have some dealings with the **police.** In Italy these come in many forms, their power split ostensibly to prevent any seizure of power. You're not likely to have much contact with the **Guardia di Finanza**, responsible for investigating smuggling, tax evasion and other finance-related felonies; and the **Vigili Urbani**, or town police, are mainly concerned with directing the traffic and punishing parking offences; while the **Polizia Stradale** patrol motorways. You may, however, have dealings with the **Carabinieri**, with their military-style uniforms and white shoulder belts, who deal with general crime, public order and drug control. These are the ones Italians are most rude about, but a lot of jokes concerning their supposed stupidity stem from the usual north–south prejudice. The Carabinieri tend to come from southern Italy – joining the police is one way to escape the poverty trap – and they are posted away from home so as to be well out of the sphere of influence of their families. The **Polizia Statale**, the other general crime-fighting force, enjoy a fierce rivalry with the **Carabinieri** and are the ones you'll perhaps have most chance of coming into contact with, since **thefts** should be reported to them. You'll find the address of the **Questura** or police station in the local telephone directory (in smaller places it may be just a local *commissariato*), and we've included details in the major city listings. The *Questura* is also where you're supposed to go to obtain a *permesso di soggiorno* **if you're staying** for any length of time, or a **visa extension** if you require one (see "Red Tape and Visas", p.16).

In any brush with the authorities, your experience will depend on the individuals you're dealing with. Apart from **topless bathing** (permitted, but don't try anything more daring) and **camping rough**, don't expect a soft touch if you're picked up for any offence, especially if it's drugs related. **Drugs** are generally frowned upon by everyone above a certain age, and universal hysteria about *la* *droga*, fuelled by the serious problem of heroin addiction all over Italy, means that any distinction between the "hard" and "soft" variety has become blurred. Theoretically everything is illegal above the possession of a few grams of cannabis or marijuana "for personal use", though there's no agreed definition of what this means and you can expect at least a fine for this. In general the south of Italy is more intolerant than the north, and in any case, if found with suspicious substances you can be kept in jail for as long as it takes for them to analyse the stuff, draw up reports and wait for the bureaucratic wheels to grind – which could be several weeks and sometimes months. For the nearest **embassy or consulate** see "Listings" in the Rome, Milan and Naples accounts – though bear in mind that they're unlikely to be very sympathetic or do anything more than put you in touch with a lawyer.

WOMEN. . . AND SEXUAL HARASSMENT

The degree of freedom Italian women enjoy is comparable to that in Britain or the USA, despite the somewhat outdated reputation of Italian men as predatory lotharios.* In previous editions of this guide we have mentioned whistling, hissing and catcalling being part of the Roman experience for some women. Actually this kind of behaviour is quite rare: you are just as likely to find an intrinsic courtesy in day-to-day communications where men will take a great deal of care to show respect. It's all too easy to overreact to unwelcome overtures; don't take a little light-hearted flirting or an appreciative *ciao bella!* too seriously.

One thing that is dangerous is being drawn into making generalizations – the two female authors of this guide for example have had very different experiences researching the book – but Italy is an easy country to travel around for a woman, whether alone or with female friends. Certainly there is none of the alcohol-fuelled agressive abuse from men that you might find in English cities; occasionally you might find yourself walking into a café and finding that you have invaded an all-male preserve, or be on the receiving end of a stupid comment from a group of adolescent boys. However, if you're on holiday without a male partner at any of the resorts popular with northern

European tourists the assumption will be made that you are looking for a quick fling – fine if you are, but irritating if you're not.

Basically, as long as you recognize that you are in a different culture, and as long as you only do what you feel comfortable doing, you don't need to be unduly concerned. It is advisable to try and modify your dress and behaviour to conform more closely with that of local women. Not only should this reduce the level of hassle you get, but it will also mean you're less likely to offend people's sensibilities. Incidentally, greater respect seems to be accorded to older women – so, for once, age can work in your favour.

CONTACTS FOR WOMEN TRAVELLERS

In most places in Italy, women are basically as liberated as they are in the UK or US – even if few will admit to being feminist, a label that carries largely negative connotations in Italy. This social stigma has resulted in a low level of structured activity such as women's groups and helpline organizations; despite this, women have secured great advances in the fields of equality at work and good maternity rights. Another statistic that may confound your preconceptions is that Italy's birth rate is one of the lowest in Europe.

Periodicals such as **Noi Donne** are good sources of information on culture, news and politics relating to women. Rome, Bologna and Milan are the places with most action, although this is fairly limited: **il riflusso**, the general term to describe the fall-off in political activity since the Seventies, has affected the women's movement as it has others. The Centro Documentazione

---

*The problems with Italian men stemmed from problems caused by the traditional adoration of the male-child that lingers on into adult life. After all, it is said that Jesus Christ himself had some of the attributes of the typical Italian male: he thought he was the son of God, lived at home till he was thirty, and thought his mother was a virgin.

Donne (Via Galliera 8, Bologna; ☎051.233.863), the Unione delle Donne Italiane (Via della Lungara 19, Trastevere, Rome; ☎06.687.2130), and the Centro Studi Storiche sul Movimento di Liberazione delle Donne (Corso di Porta Nuova 32, Milan; ☎02.2900.5987), are organizations with an academic or institutional slant on women's issues. For contacts and Internet discussion groups try the **Spazio Donna** (womens' space) in La Città Invisibile at *www.citinv.it*. Italy's first woman-focussed Internet portal is *www.supereva.it* – it is laid out very much like a women's magazine, though has a "politica e societa" section with some interesting contacts.

SEXUAL HARASSMENT

If you do experience persistent **pestering** it isn't usually accompanied by any kind of violent intent, but it can be annoying and frustrating nevertheless. **Silent indifference** is often the most effective policy, as is looking as confident as possible – if you feel threatened it's always a good idea to look as though you know where you are going,

even if you don't. Any attempt to hurl Italian insults in the direction of the transgressor is, at best, likely to cause ridicule – and at worst, could well inflame the situation further.

One thing that's worth mentioning is that the Italian **sex industry** is a thriving business, and a woman on her own wandering around a town may in some places be taken to be a prostitute looking for business. Even such an innocent occupation as waiting alone at a bus stop can bring unwelcome attention – this obviously doesn't mean every street or bus stop but there are certain places (one particular road in Rimini, for example) where car doors will mysteriously spring open as you pass by; you can pretty quickly work out what's going on and the obvious thing to do is walk somewhere else.

Flashers in parks are another common occurrence, and, as parks are often a pick-up place, your motives for sitting quietly in the sun may be misconstrued. This doesn't mean it's impossible to go there, just that it's more relaxing if you pick a spot where there are other people around.

WORK AND STUDY

All EU citizens are eligible to work in Italy. The two main bureaucratic requirements are a *libretto di lavoro* and *permesso di soggiorno*, respectively a work and residence permit, both available from the *Questura* (police station). For the first you must have a

letter from your employers saying they are prepared to take you on; for the second (which is also necessary if you want to buy a car or have a bank acount in Italy), you'll need a passport, passport photos, and a lot of patience. Work permits are pretty impossible for non-EU citizens to obtain: you must have the firm promise of a job that no Italian could do before you can even apply to the Italian embassy in your home country. A useful publication to have is *Live and Work in Italy* by Victoria Pybus, published by Vacation Work in the UK, costing £10.99, a comprehensive guide and full of practical information.

WORK

The obvious choice is to **teach English**, for which the demand has expanded enormously in recent years. You can do this in two ways: freelance private lessons, or through a language

WORK, STUDY AND VOLUNTEER PROGRAMMES

ITALY

Ministero Lavoro E Previdenza Sociale, Divisone 11, Via Flavia 6, 1-00187 Rome. Job placement information.

BRITAIN

Central Bureau for Educational Visits and Exchanges, 10 Spring Gardens, London SW1A 2BN (☎020/7389 4004). The Central Bureau administers a number of exchanges, including LEONARDO DA VINCI (vocational training) and LINGUA (language training opportunities).

Commission of the European Communities, 8 Storey's Gate, London SW1P 3AT (☎020/7463 8177). The publications office produces a series of fact sheets on issues relating to work and study in Europe.

European Programme, The Prince's Trust, 18 Park Square East, London NW1 4LH (☎0800/842842). Offers a number of "Go and See" grants to young people between 18 and 25 with ideas for European partnerships.

Italian Cultural Institute, 39 Belgrave Square, London SW1X 8NX (☎020/7235 1461). Produces a list of institutions running all sorts of courses; will also give basic advice on job hunting.

USA

American Institute for Foreign Study, River Plaza, 9 West Broad St, Stamford, CT 06902 (☎1-800/727-AIFS, *www.aifs.org*). Language study and cultural immersion for the summer or school year.

Council on International Educational Exchange (CIEE), 205 E 42nd St, New York, NY 10017 (☎1-888/COUNCIL, *www.counciltravel.com*). The non-profit parent organization of Council Travel and Council Charter, CIEE runs a volunteer programme in Italy. It also publishes two excellent resource books, *Work, Study, Travel Abroad* and *Volunteer! The Comprehensive Guide to Voluntary Service in the US and Abroad.*

Institute of International Education, 809 UN Plaza, New York, NY 10017 (recorded information ☎212/984-5413, *www.iie.org*). Contact IIE's Publications Service to order its annual study-abroad directory.

InterExchange Program, 161 6th Ave, New York, NY 10013 (☎212/924-0446, *www.interex-*

change.org). Information on work programmes and au pair positions.

Italian Cultural Institute, 686 Park Ave, New York, NY 10021 (☎212/879-4242, *www.italcult-ny.org*); Suite 104, 1717 Massachusetts Ave NW, Washington, DC 20036 (☎202/387-5161). Publishes a directory of study courses for English-speaking students and helps with job openings.

Office of Overseas Schools, US Department of State, Room 245, SA-29, Washington, DC 20522-2902 (☎703/875-7800, *www.state.gov*). Produces a list of schools for potential EFL teachers to contact.

Volunteers for Peace, 43 Tiffany Rd, Belmont, VT 05730 (☎802/259-2759, *www.vfp.org*). Non-profit organization with links to a huge international network of "workcamps", two- to four-week programmes that bring volunteers together from many countries to carry out needed community projects. Most workcamps are in summer, with registration in April–May. Annual directory costs $15.

AUSTRALIA AND NEW ZEALAND

Australians Studying Abroad (ASA), 1st Floor, High St, Armadale, Victoria, (☎03/9509 1955 or toll-free 1800 645 755, *www.asatravinfo.com.au*). All-inclusive lecture tours taking in art and culture of Rome, Florence, Sienna, Urbino, Verona, Ravenna and Venice.

CIT, 263 Clarence St, Sydney (☎02/9267 1255); offices in Melbourne, Adelaide, Brisbane and Perth. No NZ office – enquire to Australian offices.

Nacel Australia, 35 Kavenagh St, Leederville, WA (☎08/9388 3371).

Southern Cross Cultural Exchange, PO Box 142, Somerville, VIC (☎03/5978 6788).

school. **Private lessons** generally pay best, and you can charge around L30,000–42,000 /€15.49–21.70 an hour, though there's scope for bargaining. Advertise in bars, shop windows and local newspapers, and, most importantly, get the news around by word-of-mouth that you're looking for work, emphasizing your excellent background, qualifications and experience. An advantage of private teaching is that you can start at any time of the year (summer especially is a good time for schoolchildren and students who have to retake exams in September); the main disadvantage is that it can take weeks to get off the ground, and you need enough money to support yourself until then. You'll find the best opportunities for this kind of work in the tourist resorts and the bigger towns and cities.

Teaching in schools, you start earning immediately. It usually involves more hours per week, often in the evening, at a lower rate per hour, though the amount you get depends on the school. Don't accept anything less than L15,000/€7.75 an hour (approximately £5/US$8), while the bigger schools should pay much more than this. For the less reputable places, you can get away without any qualifications and a bit of bluff, but you'll need to show a TEFL (Teaching of English as a Foreign Language) certificate for the more professional establishments. For the main language schools, it's best to apply in writing before you leave (look for the ads in the *Guardian* and *Times Education Supplement,* and contact the Italian Cultural Institute; see box opposite for details), preferably before the summer, though

you can also find openings in September. If you're looking on the spot, sift through the phone books and do the rounds on foot, asking to speak to the *direttore* or his/her secretary; don't bother to try in August when everything is closed. The best teaching jobs of all are with a university as a *lettore*, a job requiring fewer hours than the language schools and generally providing a fuller pay-packet. Universities require English-language teachers in most faculties, and you can write to the individual faculties (addressed to Ufficio di Personale). Strictly speaking you could get by without any knowledge of Italian while teaching, though it obviously helps a lot.

If teaching's not up your street, there's the possibility of **courier work** in the summer, especially around the seaside resorts. These are good places for finding **bar/restaurant work**, too – not the most lucrative of jobs, though you should make enough to keep you over the summer. You'll have to ask around for both types of work, and some knowledge of Italian is essential. **Au pairing** is another option: sift through the ads in *The Lady* to find openings.

STUDYING

One way of spending time in Italy is to combine a holiday with learning the language, or taking one of many summer courses on myriad aspects of Italian art and culture. There are a great many places where you can do this, usually offering language courses of varying levels of intensity for between one and three months – see box opposite for useful contacts.

DIRECTORY

ADDRESSES These are usually written as the street name followed by the number – eg Via Roma 69. *Interno* refers to the flat number – eg *interno* 5 (often abbreviated as int.). Confusingly, some towns (notably Florence and Genoa) have two parallel systems for numbering properties, one for shops and restaurants and another for businesses and private residences; sometimes a shop or restaurant is suffixed by the letter "r", meaning that Via Garibaldi 15r might be in an entirely different place from Via Garibaldi 15. Watch out for addresses with "s/n" rather than a street number, which refers to the fact that they have no number, or are *senza numero*.

AIRPORT TAX Nearly always included in the price of your ticket.

BARGAINING Not really on in shops and restaurants, though you'll find you can get a "special price" for some rooms and cheap hotels if you're staying a few days or off season, and that things like boat or bike rental and guided tours (especially out of season) are negotiable. In markets, you can in theory haggle for everything except food.

BEACHES Most beaches are clearly signposted *spiaggia* but you'll have to pay for access to the best parts of the better ones (referred to as lidos), plus a few thousand lire to rent a sun bed and shade and use the showers all day. Although technically the few metres immediately by the water cannot be sectioned off, it's debatable whether it's worth the hassle of trying to enforce your rights. During winter most beaches look like

rubbish dumps: it's not worth anyone's while to clean them until the season starts at Easter. Some beaches, particularly along the north coast of Sicily are prone to invasions of jellyfish (*meduse*) from time to time. These are not dangerous, but can cause quite a sting, so take local advice and believe, if you will, the Italian train of thought that they are a sign of unpolluted water.

CAMPING GAZ Easy enough to buy for the small, portable, camping stoves, either from a hardware store (*ferramenta*) or camping/sports shops; remember you can't carry canisters on aeroplanes.

CHILDREN Children are adored in Italy and will be made a fuss of in the street, and welcomed and catered for in bars and restaurants (though be warned that there's no such thing as a smoke-free environment, with chain-smoking the norm). Hotels normally charge around thirty percent extra to put a bed or cot in your room, though kids pay less on trains (see "Getting Around", p.26). The only hazards when travelling with children in summer are the heat and sun. Very high factor suncreams are quite difficult to find although chemists usually sell sunblock. Bonnets or straw hats are plentiful in local markets. Take advantage of the less intense periods – mornings and evenings – for travelling, and use the quiet of siesta-time to recover flagging energy. The rhythms of the southern climate soon modify established patterns, and you'll find it more natural carrying on later into the night, past normal bedtimes. In summer, it's not unusual to see Italian children out at midnight, and not looking any the worse for it.

CIGARETTES The state monopoly brand – MS, jokingly referred to as *Morte Sicura* ("certain death") or *Merda Secca* ("dried shit") – are the most widely smoked cigarettes, strong and aromatic and selling for around L4200/€2.17 for a pack of twenty. Younger people tend to smoke imported brands these days – all of which are slightly more expensive, at around L4500–5500/€2.32–2.84 per pack. You buy cigarettes from *tabacchi*, recognizable by a sign displaying a white "T" on a black or blue background, but not from bars. After hours you'll have to use automatic, hole-in-the-wall vending machines; these are hardly more expensive than *tabacchi*, accept notes and are found on practically every street corner in major cities.

CONTRACEPTION Condoms (*preservativi, pro-filàttici*) are available over the counter from all pharmacies (some also have vending machines after hours) and some supermarkets; the pill (*la píllola*) is available from pharmacies by prescription only.

DEPARTMENT STORES There are two main nationwide chains, Upim and Standa. Neither is particularly posh, and they're good places to stock up on toiletries and other basic supplies; branches of both stores sometimes have a food hall attached.

ELECTRICITY The supply is 220V, though anything requiring 240V will work. Most plugs are three round pins though you'll find the older 2-pin plug in some places: a travel plug adapter is useful.

GAY AND LESBIAN LIFE Homosexuality is legal in Italy, and the age of consent is 14. The Gay "World Pride" march took place in Rome in July 2000, and although condemned, predictably enough, by the pope, the size of the turn-out (over a quarter of a million) and the largely sympathetic press coverage have been read as signs that homosexuality is becoming more widely accepted in Italy. Attitudes are most tolerant in the northern cities: Bologna is generally regarded as the gay capital, and Milan, Turin and to a lesser extent Rome all have well-developed gay scenes; there are also a few *spiagge gay* (gay beaches) dotted along the coast, and the more popular gay resorts include Taormina and Rimini. Away from the big cities and resorts, though, activity is more covert. You'll notice, in the South especially, that overt displays of affection between (all) men – linking arms during the passeggiata, kissing in greeting, etc – are common. The line determining what's acceptable, however, is finely drawn. The national gay organization, ARCI-Gay, Piazza di Porta Saragozza 2, PO Box 691, 40100 Bologna (☎051.644.7054, *arcigl@iperbole.it*), and at Via dei Mille 23, Rome (☎06.446.5839), affiliated to the youth section of the ex-Communist Party, has branches in most big towns; *Babilonia* (*www.babilonia.net*) is the national gay magazine, published monthly.The Italian lesbian organization, Collegamento tra Lesbiche Italiane, is based at Via San Francesco di Sales 1a, Rome (☎06.686.4201), but is mainly a campaigning force; ARCI-Lesbica, Via dei Monti di Petralata 16, (☎06.418.0369, *www.women.it/~arciles/roma*) is a more general organization and the Web site has lots of useful links.

LAUNDRIES Coin-operated laundromats, sometimes known as *tintorie*, are rare outside large cities, and even there numbers are sparse; see the "Listings" sections of the main city accounts for addresses. More common is a *lavanderia*, a service-wash laundry, but this will be more expensive. Although you can usually get away with it, washing clothes in your hotel room can cause an international incident – simply because the room's plumbing often can't cope with all the water. It's better to ask if there's somewhere you can wash your clothes.

PUBLIC TOILETS Almost unheard of outside train and bus stations, and usually the only alternative is to dive discreetly into a bar or restaurant. In stations and some smarter establishments, there might be an attendant who guards the facilities, dispenses paper (*carta*) – and expects a tip of a few hundred lire. Standards have improved over the last few years and you'll find most places to be very clean, though it's advisable not to be without your own toilet roll.

TAKE HOME Top of the list of many Italian goodies worth taking home is a *caffeteria* – the many-sided coffee-makers that are surprisingly cheap in Italy; Upim and Standa usually have a good selection, as do markets. Obviously clothes and shoes make tempting souvenirs, too, but don't expect any bargains; in Milan, especially, prices are sky-high, though if you're in the market for designer threads, this is as cheap a place as any.

TIME Italy is always one hour ahead of Britain, seven hours ahead of US Eastern Standard Time and ten hours ahead of Pacific Time.

VACCINATIONS None required.

WAR CEMETERIES Anzio and Cassino are just the best known of a number of fiercely contested battles on Italian soil during World War II. Information and a list of Allied cemeteries are available from the Commonwealth War Graves Commission, 2 Marlow Rd, Maidenhead, Berkshire SL6 7DX (☎01628/634 221).

WATER Safe everywhere, including drinking fountains, although people often prefer the taste of bottled water.

PART TWO

THE

GUIDE

CHAPTER ONE

PIEMONTE AND VALLE D'AOSTA

F ringed by the French and Swiss Alps and grooved with mountain valleys, there are no less "Italian" regions than **Piemonte** and **Valle d'Aosta**, in the extreme northwest of the country. French was spoken in Piemonte until the end of the nineteenth century and still influences Piemontese dialects; Valle d'Aosta remains bilingual. Piemonte (literally "at the foot of the mountains", and indeed more than forty percent of its surface is mountainous) is one of Italy's wealthiest regions, known for its fine wines and food and for being home to key Italian corporations such as Fiat and Olivetti. The mighty River Po, Italy's longest, begins here, and the towns of its vast plain – which stretches right across northern Italy – have grown rich on both manufacturing and rice, cultivated in sweeping paddy fields.

Turin, on the main rail and road route from France to Milan, is the obvious first stop: despite being Italy's second industrial city, it retains a Baroque core and is well placed for days out. South of Turin, **Alba** and **Saluzzo** are perhaps the most enticing centres, the former a good base for visiting the wine cantinas, the latter convenient if you want to explore the western valleys; **Asti**, to the southeast, really comes to life during its famous medieval Palio. For the rest, winter sports and walking are the main activities, with **Sestriere** the main skiing centre and the ascent of **Monviso** in the far west appealing to the climbing fraternity. Greater challenges – and more spectacular views – are to be found in the adjoining region of **Valle d'Aosta**. Cut off from Switzerland and France by the highest of the Alps – **Monte Rosa**, the **Matterhorn** and **Mont Blanc** – and with a **national park** around the **Gran Paradiso** mountain, this is serious skiing and hiking country. The main town of **Aosta** itself repays a visit, and the surrounding countryside is sprinkled with **castles**.

Although the western shore of **Lago Maggiore** is actually in Piemonte, we've treated all the lakes as a region and covered them in the "Lombardy and the Lakes" chapter; the Maggiore account starts on p.195.

ACCOMMODATION PRICE CODES

Throughout this guide, prices per person are given for **youth hostels** and assume Hostelling International (HI) membership. **Hotel** accommodation is coded on a scale from ① to ⑨, reflecting the cost of the cheapest double room in each establishment in high season. The price bands to which these codes refer are as follows:

① Up to L60,000/€30.99
② L60,000–90,000/€30.99–46.48
③ L90,000–120,000/€46.48–61.98
④ L120,000–150,000/€61.98–77.47
⑤ L150,000–200,000/€77.47–103.29

⑥ L200,000–250,000/€103.29–129.11
⑦ L250,000–300,000/€129.11–154.94
⑧ L300,000–400,000/€154.94–206.58
⑨ over L400,000/€206.58

(See p.32 for a full explanation.)

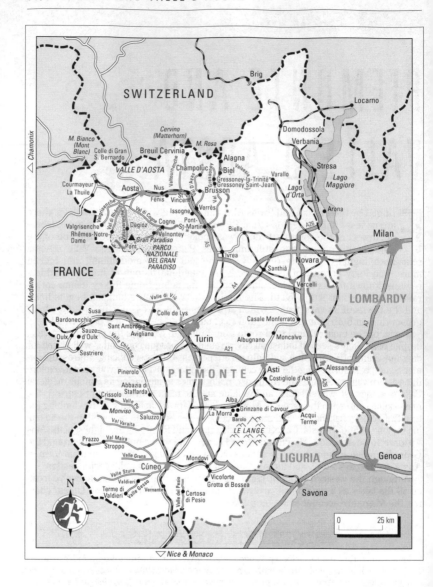

PIEMONTE

Many of the dishes in **Piemonte**'s swankiest restaurants derive from the tables of the Piemontese aristocracy, in particular the Savoy dukes and kings who ruled the region from the eleventh century, making Turin their capital in 1574. Their presence is clearly visible today in the grandiose architecture of central Turin and in their ostentatious hunting palace at Stupinigi just outside the city.

Piemonte and the Savoys were at the heart of the Italian Unification movement in the nineteenth century, which, under King Vittorio Emanuele II and the Piemontese states-man Camillo Cavour, succeeded in dragging the various regions of Italy together under Savoy rule. Rome became the new capital, much to the disquiet of the Piemontese aris-tocracy and bourgeoisie, who acted quickly to save the region's not inconsiderable influence, setting up industries such as Fiat and Olivetti that were destined to change the face of Italian as well as Piemontese society. These days Piemonte is second only to Lombardy in national wealth and power.

Getting around Piemonte is fairly easy. The network of trains and buses is compre-hensive, and your own transport is only necessary for the more out-of-the-way places. You can get to most places from Turin; Alba makes a good base for exploring Le Langhe, Saluzzo for the western valleys.

REGIONAL FOOD AND WINE

Piemonte and Valle d'Aosta is a paradise for gastronomes and connoisseurs of vintage wines. Rich Piemontese cuisine betrays close links with France through dishes like *fon-duta* (fondue) and its preference for using **butter** and **cream** in cooking. As in most of the north, olive oil and tomatoes are relatively uncommon, although immigrants from the south to towns like Turin have brought their cooking with them. Piemonte is perhaps most famous for its white **truffles**, the most exquisite of which come from around the town of Alba and are ferociously expensive. Their most usual use is a few shavings to subtly perfume a dish of pasta or a risotto. Watch out too for *porcini* mushrooms, chest-nuts, and, more specifically, the **bagna caoda** – a sociable local variation on the fondue in which everyone dips vegetables into a sauce of oil, anchovies, garlic, butter and cream. In Valle d'Aosta they prepare good rich **soups** like *soupe à la Valpellineuntze*, with cab-bage, or *soupe à la cogneintze*, with rice.

The rolling vine-clad hills of Le Langhe and Monferrato produce classy, traditional **wines** like Barolo, Bardolino, Barbera and Nebbiolo. These fine reds need ageing, and Barolo in particular can be very expensive. More suitable for everyday drinking are wines made from the dolcetto grape, notably Dolcetto d'Alba, drunk young and lightly chilled. Probably the most famous is the sparkling Asti (wine makers dropped the "spumante" from the name in 1994 in a bid for a new image) – a sweet wine, though there has been a trend in recent years to make dry spumante. Martini and Cinzano vermouths are also produced in and around Turin, a fusion of the region's wines with at least thir-teen of the wild herbs that grow on its mountains. The traditional version to drink, now a brand name, is Punt e Mes ("point and a half") – one part bitter to half-a-part sweet.

Turin (Torino)

"Do you know Turin?" asked Nietzsche. "It is a city after my own heart . . . a princely residence of the seventeenth century, which has only one taste giving commands to everything, the court and its nobility. Aristocratic calm is preserved in everything; there are no nasty suburbs." Although **TURIN**'s traffic-choked streets are no longer calm, and its suburbs are as dreary as any in Italy, the city centre's gracious Baroque thoroughfares, opulent palaces, sumptuous churches and splendid collections of Egyptian antiquities and northern European paintings are still there – a pleasant sur-prise to those who might have been expecting satanic factories and little else.

Turin's suburbs were built by a new dynasty, **Fiat** (Fabbrica Italiana di Automobili Torino), whose owner, Gianni Agnelli, is reckoned to be the most powerful man in Italy. Although the only sign of Agnelli's power appears to be the number of Fiats that cram Turin's streets (as they do those of every other Italian city), it's worth remembering that Fiat owns Alfa Romeo, Lancia, Autobianchi and Ferrari too, accounting for more than sixty percent of the Italian car market. But there are other, more hidden branches of the Agnelli empire. Stop for a Cinzano in one of the city's many *fin de siècle* cafés and you're drinking an Agnelli vermouth; buy the *La Stampa* or *Corriere della Sera* newspapers and you're reading newsprint produced by the Agnelli family. Support the Juventus football team and you're supporting the Agnellis who own it; or go for a Club Med skiing holiday at the nearby resort of Sestriere and you'll sleep in hotels built by Agnelli's grandfather. Wielding such power, Agnelli and friends are seen as a political force in a country where governments are relatively transient. Foreign governments often take more notice of Agnelli than they do of Italy's elected leaders: as Henry Kissinger once said, Gianni Agnelli "is the permanent establishment". Terrorists too recognized where the roots of Italian power lay: the Red Brigade was founded on the factory floors of Fiat, and Fiat executives were as much targets as were politicians.

Some history

The Torinese are accustomed to absolutism. From 1574 Turin was the seat of the Savoy dukes, who persecuted Piemonte's Protestants and Jews, censored the press and placed education of the nobles in the extreme hands of the Jesuits. The Savoys gained a royal title in 1713, and a few years later acquired Sardinia, which whetted their appetite for more territory. After more than a century of military and diplomatic wrangling with foreign powers, the second monarch, Carlo Emanuele III (who promised to "eat Italy like an artichoke"), teamed up with the liberal politician of the Risorgimento, Cavour, who used the royal family to lend credibility to the Unification movement. In 1860 Garibaldi handed over Sicily and southern Italy to Vittorio Emanuele, and though it was to take a further ten years for him to seize the heart of the artichoke – Rome – he was declared king of Italy.

The capital was moved to Rome in 1870, leaving Turin in the hands of the Piemontese nobility. It became a provincial backwater where a tenth of the 200,000 population worked as domestic servants, with a centre decked out in elaborate finery, its cafés – decorated with chandeliers, carved wood, frescoes and gilt – only slightly less ostentatious than the rooms of the Savoy palaces. World War I brought plenty of work, but also brought food shortages and, in 1917, street riots which spread throughout the north, establishing Turin as a centre of labour activism. Gramsci led occupations of the Fiat factory here, going on to found the Communist Party.

By the Fifties Turin's population had soared to 700,000, the increase mainly made up of migrant workers from the poor south, who were housed in shanty towns outside the city and shunned as peasants by the Torinese. Blocks of flats were eventually built for the workers – the bleak Mirafiori housing estates – and by the Sixties Fiat was employing 130,000 workers, with a further half million dependent on the company in some way. Not surprisingly, Turin became known as Fiatville. Today there are fewer people involved in the industry, and Fiat's famous Lingotto factory has been turned into a conference centre and performance space, yet the gap left behind has been filled by some of the biggest names from other industries, especially those belonging to the worlds of textiles and fashion (Armani, Valentino, Cerruti and Ungaro), publishing (Einandi and UTET), and banking; the Banca Popolare di Novara is the most important co-operative bank in Europe.

Arrival, information and city transport

Turin's main **train station**, Porta Nuova (☎011.668.9290), is on Corso Vittorio Emanuele II, at the foot of Via Roma – convenient for the city centre and hotels. Some trains also stop at Porta Susa (☎011.538.513) on Corso Inghilterra, west of the centre. Close by, on the corner of Corso Inghilterra and Corso Vittorio Emanuele II, is the main **bus station** (☎011.433.2525), the arrival and departure point for most intercity and all international coaches; buses to Saluzzo and Cúneo arrive and leave from the top of Corso Marconi, near the junction with Via Nizza. The bus station is linked to Via Nizza (near Porta Nuova) and Porta Susa by bus #60. Turin's **airport**, Caselle (information ☎011.567.6361 or 011.567.6362), is 15km north of the city, connected by buses every 30 to 45 minutes with the Corso Inghilterra bus station (35-minute journey; tickets cost L6000/€3.10).

There are three **tourist offices**: a main one on the corner of Piazza Castello and Via Garibaldi (daily 9am–7.30pm; ☎011.535.181, *www.turismotorino.org*), and smaller ones at the train station (daily 8.30am–7.30pm; ☎011.531.327) and the airport (daily 9am–7.30pm; ☎011.567.8124). They are very well organized with detailed information and suggested itineraries as well as a free hotel reservation service. **What's on** listings and **ticket outlets** are detailed on pp.79–80.

City transport

Most of Turin's sights are within walking distance of Porta Nuova station, although if you're pushed for time the **tram and bus** network provides a fast and efficient way of getting around. Tickets must be bought before you board – L1400/€0.72 from *tabacchi*, although it's worth asking at the tourist offices for details of current discount tickets. Of **routes** you might use a lot, tram #4 goes north through the city from Porta Nuova, along Via XX Settembre to Piazza della Repubblica. Other useful routes are tram #1 between Porta Susa and Porta Nuova, tram #15 from Porta Nuova to Via Pietro Micca, bus #61 from Porta Nuova across the river and bus #34 from Porta Nuova to the Museo dell'Automobile. The main **taxi** ranks are at the bus and train stations and the airport, or dial ☎011.5730, 011.5737 or 011.3399.

Accommodation

The majority of the city's **hotels** – in all price ranges – are close by Porta Nuova station; while not the most salubrious part of town, it has been cleaned up in recent years. The streets opposite Porta Nuova, close to Piazza Carlo Felice, although slightly more expensive, are less eventful, and there are also other attractive options dotted around the city. Wherever you choose to stay, bear in mind that demand is usually high, especially during the skiing season and trade fairs (when prices also rise), and it's a good idea to phone in advance. As the majority of Turin's hotels cater to the business trade however, at weekends and during August it's often possible to negotiate a discount.

Hotels

Artua, Via Brofferio 1 (☎011.517.5301, fax 011.517.5141). Comfortable hotel with air-conditioning, plus safe parking. Has a sister hotel, *Solferino* (☎011.561.3444, fax 011.562.2241), next door, with similar facilities. Both ④.

Astoria, Via XX Settembre 4 (☎011.562.0653, fax 011.562.5866). Good-value hotel just off Piazza Carlo Felice, with very pleasant rooms, all with satellite TV, and extremely friendly management. ⑤.

Canelli, Via San Dalmazzo 7 (☎011.537.166). A neat, simple but gloomy hotel close to the pedestrian area of Via Garibaldi. As the cheapest hotel in town, this place is often full – book well in advance. ①.

Conte Biancamano, Corso Vittorio Emanuele II 73 (☎011.562.3281, fax 011.562.3789). If you feel like splashing out a bit, go for this hotel set in an old palace with panelled ceilings and large rooms. ⑤.

Hotel Liberty, Via Pietro Micca 15 (☎011.562.8801, fax 011.562.8163). Comfortable *belle époque*-style rooms on the edge of the medieval quarter. ⑤.

Montevecchio, Via Montevecchio 13 (☎011.562.0023, fax 011.562.3047). That rare thing – a quiet hotel near the train station. This one also has good facilities, with TV and telephone in all rooms. ④.

Roma & Rocca Cavour, Piazza Carlo Felice 60 (☎011.561.2772, fax 011.562.8137). Old-style hotel close to the station, overlooking a noisy square with a small park and fountain. Generally good value, though avoid the poor breakfast at L12,000/€6.20 extra. ⑤.

San Carlo, Piazza San Carlo 197 (☎011.562.7846). Well located in one of Turin's most representative central squares. Try to get a room with a view. ③.

Sila, Piazza Carlo Felice 80 (☎011.544.086). Convenient location almost opposite the main train station. Good lodgings with decent facilities. ③.

Urbani, Via Saluzzo 7 (☎011.669.9047, fax 011.669.3226). First choice for comfort and value in the station area. Very pleasant rooms, individually furnished, many with balconies overlooking the inner courtyard. Located on a quiet street a minute's walk from Porta Nuova. ④.

Victoria, Via Nino Costa 4 (☎011.561.1806). Very comfortable place in a quiet central position. Eclectic furnishings and its own garden. ⑧.

Villa Sassi, Strada Traforo del Pino 47 (☎011.898.0556, fax 011.890.095). A luxurious eighteenth-century villa set in its own parkland in the hills above the city. Rooms are elegant, many with original features. Closed Aug. ⑨.

Hostel and campsite

Ostello Torino, Via Alby 1 (☎011.660.2939). Bus #52 from Porta Nuova. The official HI hostel, with beds in clean modern dormitories, and dinners for L12,000/€6.20. Mid-Feb to Christmas. L18,000/€9.30, including breakfast.

Villa Rey, Strada Val San Martino Superiore 27 (☎011.819.0117). The most convenient of the city's campsites, not far from the youth hostel. Take bus #61 from Porta Nuova, and then bus #54. End of March to end of Nov.

The City

The grid street-plan of Turin's Baroque centre makes it easy to find your way about. **Via Roma** is the central spine of the city, a grand affair lined with designer shops and ritzy cafés, although nowadays on the grubby side. It is punctuated by the city's most elegant piazzas, most notably **Piazza San Carlo**, close to which are some of the most prestigious museums. **Piazza Castello** forms a fittingly grandiose, if hectic, conclusion to Via Roma, with its royal palaces awash in a sea of traffic. From here you can walk in a number of directions. To the west, **Via Pietro Micca** leads to a cluster of pedestrianized shopping streets, more relaxed than Via Roma and a good area to head to during the evening passeggiata in summer. North lies **Piazza della Repubblica**, a vast and rather shabby square given over to a daily market. To the southeast, the porticoes of **Via Po** forge down to the river, a short walk along which is the extensive **Parco del Valentino**, home to some of the city's best nightlife. Beyond lies the engaging **Museo dell'Automobile**, while the hills **across the river**, which are peppered with the Art Deco villas of the richest Torinese, shelter the **Basilica di Superga** and the **Stupingi Palace**.

Porta Nuova and around

As you step out of **Porta Nuova** station, you'll notice immediately Turin's measured symmetry, although the area around the station is seedy, with prostitutes and street-hasslers cruising the once-elegant arcades of Via Nizza and Corso Vittorio Emanuele II.

To the west of here, the **Galleria Civica d'Arte Moderna e Contemporanea** at Via Magenta 31 (Tues–Sun 9am–7pm; *www.gam.intes.it*; L10,000/€5.17) features a good selection of twentieth-century work by artists as varied as De Chirico, Chillida, Warhol, Fontana and Basilico. The overall quality of the permanent collection is tempered by an unexceptional floor-and-a-half of work from the last two hundred years of the Torinese school, but as the gallery is on the international circuit for touring exhibitions and loans there is often more than enough to compensate.

Back at Porta Nuova, crossing the road brings you to the neat gardens of **Piazza Carlo Felice**, beyond which lies **Via Roma**, the stamping ground of the well heeled. Halfway down Via Roma, **Piazza San Carlo** is known with some justification as the parlour of Turin, a grand oval space fronted by Baroque facades, the porticoes of which house elegant cafés. Holding court is an equestrian statue of the Savoy duke Emanuele Filiberto raising his sword in triumph after securing Turin's independence from the French and Spanish at the battle of San Quintino in 1574, while the entrance to the square is guarded by the twin Baroque churches of **San Carlo** and **Santa Cristina**. Behind the churches two nudes represent Turin's two rivers – the Po and the Dora.

Around the corner from Piazza San Carlo, the **Museo Egizio**, Via Accademia delle Scienze 6 (Tues–Sat 9am–7pm, Sun 9am–2pm; *www.multix.it/museoegizio_to*; L12,000/€6.20), holds a superb collection of Egyptian antiquities, gathered together in the late eighteenth century under the aegis of Carlo Emanuele III. There are decorated mummy cases and an intriguing assortment of everyday objects, including castanets, sandals, a linen tunic dating from 2300 BC, and even food – eggs, pomegranates and grain, recognizable despite their shrivelled, darkened state. Also interesting is the small Nubian temple dedicated by Tutmosis III to Ellesija, although the undoubted highlights are a **statue of Ramses II**, very much praised by Champollion, and the **Tomb of Kha and Mirit**. The tomb, discovered in 1906 at Deir-el-Medina, home of the architects, masons and painters of the nearby royal necropoli, is that of a 1400 BC architect, Kha, and his wife Mirit. The burial chamber contains the tools of Kha's trade – cubits, a case for balances, pens and a writing tablet – and more ordinary daily items: a bed with a headrest, clothes, generous rations of food, even a board game to while away the posthumous hours. And to ensure that Mirit kept up appearances, she was provided with a cosmetic case, wig, comb, and tweezers.

Above the museum, the **Galleria Sabauda** (Tues, Wed & Fri–Sun 9am–2pm, Thurs 10am–7pm; L8000/€4.13) was built around the Savoys' private collection and is still firmly stamped with their taste: a middling miscellany of Italian paintings – work from Piemontese, Florentine, Venetian and Bolognese schools – supplemented by a fine collection of Dutch and Flemish works. Of the Italian paintings, the most interesting is the fifteenth-century *Archangel Raphael and Tobias* by Antonio and Piero Pollaiuolo, an ultra-realistic work that amply demonstrates the Pollaiuolo brothers' studies in anatomy. Among the first artists to do this, the brothers were once considered ahead of their time, as a look at the rarefied, almost ethereal painting of the same subject by their contemporary, Filippino Lippi, shows. The northern European collection is more engaging. Alongside a number of French paintings, there are debauched peasant scenes by Flemish artists, notably works by Pieter Brueghel, David Teniers Jnr, and a bucolic *Amarilli and Mirtillo* by Van Dyck. Take a look too at the intriguing *Vanity of Human Life* by Jan Brueghel. On a more elevated level, Hans Memling's *Passion of Christ* tells the story of Christ's final days in a Renaissance city setting.

Piazza Castello and around

Via Roma continues north through the heart of Turin, passing near some of the key monuments of the Savoys and the Italian Unification. The **Museo Nazionale del Risorgimento**, Via Accademia della Scienze 5 (Tues–Sat 9am–7pm, Sun 9am–1pm; L8000/€4.13), housed in the double-fronted **Palazzo Carignano**, birthplace of Vittorio

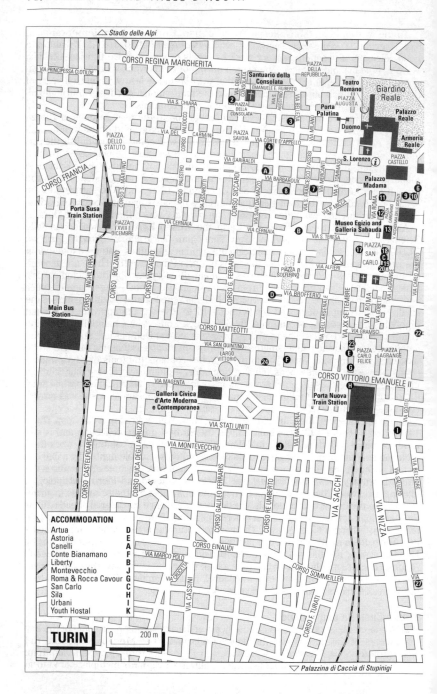

△ Stadio delle Alpi

CORSO REGINA MARGHERITA

VIA PRINCIPESSA CLOTILDE

Santuario della Consolata

EMANUELE E. FILIBERTO

PIAZZA DELLA REPUBBLICA

Teatro Romano

Giardino Reale

Palazzo Reale

PIAZZA AUGUSTA

Porta Palatina

Duomo

Armeria Reale

VIA S. CHIARA

PIAZZA DELLA CONSOLATA

VIA DEL CARMINE

VIA DEL VALDOCCO

PIAZZA SAVOIA

VIA CORTE D'APPELLO

PIAZZA DELLO STATUTO

CORSO FRANCIA

VIA GARIBALDI

S. Lorenzo

PIAZZA CASTELLO

Palazzo Madama

VIA BARBAROUX

Porta Susa Train Station

PIAZZA XVIII DICEMBRE

VIA CERNAIA

VIA CERNAIA

VIA S. TERESA

Museo Egizio and Galleria Sabauda

Main Bus Station

PIAZZA SOLFERINO

VIA ALFIERI

PIAZZA SAN CARLO

VIA BROFFERIO

CORSO MATTEOTTI

VIA SAN QUINTINO

LARGO VITTORIO

EMANUELE II

VIA MAGENTA

Galleria Civica d'Arte Moderna e Contemporanea

CORSO VITTORIO EMANUELE II

Porta Nuova Train Station

VIA STATI UNITI

VIA MONTEVECCHIO

PIAZZA CARLO FELICE

PIAZZA LAGRANGE

VIA MARCO POLO

VIA CROCETTA

CORSO EINAUDI

CORSO SOMMEILLER

ACCOMMODATION

Artua	D
Astoria	E
Canelli	A
Conte Bianamano	F
Liberty	B
Montevecchio	J
Roma & Rocca Cavour	G
San Carlo	C
Sila	H
Urbani	I
Youth Hostel	K

TURIN   0   200 m

▽ Palazzina di Caccia di Stupinigi

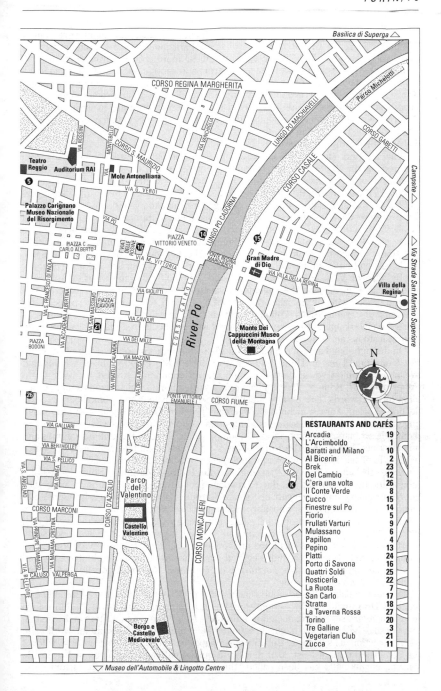

Basilica di Superga △

CORSO REGINA MARGHERITA

Parco Michelotti

Campsite △

△ Via Strada San Martino Superiore

VIA ROSSINI
MONTEBELLO
CORSO S. MAURIZIO
VIA VANCHIGLIA
LUNGO PO MACHIAVELLI
CORSO GABETTI
CORSO CASALE

Teatro Reggio
Auditorium RAI
Mole Antonelliana
⑤

VIA G. VERDI

Palazzo Carignano
Museo Nazionale
del Risorgimento

VIA PO

LUNGO PO CADORNA

PIAZZA C. CARLO ALBERTO

PIAZZA VITTORIO VENETO
VIA DELLE ROSINE
⑯
VIA M. VITTORIA

⑭

⑮

PONTE REGINA MARGHERITA

Gran Madre di Dio

VIA VILLA DELLA REGINA

Villa della Regina

VIA FRANCESCO DI PAOLA
VIA ACCADEMIA ALBERTINA
VIA SAN MASSIMO
PIAZZA CAVOUR
VIA GIOLITTI

VIA CAVOUR

㉑

VIA DEI MILLE

PIAZZA BODONI

River Po

CORSO CAIROLI

Monte Dei Cappuccini Museo della Montagna

VIA FRATELLI CALANDRA
VIA MAZZINI
VIA DELLA ROCCA

N

PONTE VITTORIO EMANUELE I

CORSO FIUME

㉖

VIA GALLIARI

VIA BERTHOLLET

VIA S. PELLICO

VIA S. ANSELMO
VIA ORMEA
VIA SALUZZO

Parco del Valentino

CORSO D'AZEGLIO

CORSO MONCALIERI

K

CORSO MARCONI

VIA PRINCIPE TOMMASO
VIA MADAMA CRISTINA

Castello Valentino

VIA BELFIORE
CALUSO VALPERGA

Borgo e Castello Medioevale

RESTAURANTS AND CAFÉS	
Arcadia	19
L'Arcimboldo	1
Baratti and Milano	10
Al Bicerin	2
Brek	23
Del Cambio	12
C'era una volta	26
Il Conte Verde	8
Cucco	15
Finestre sul Po	14
Fiorio	5
Frullati Varturi	9
Mulassano	6
Papillon	4
Pepino	13
Platti	24
Porto di Savona	16
Quattri Soldi	25
Rosticeria	22
La Ruota	7
San Carlo	17
Stratta	18
La Taverna Rossa	27
Torino	20
Tre Galline	3
Vegetarian Club	21
Zucca	11

▽ Museo dell'Automobile & Lingotto Centre

Emanuele II, is worth a visit. The first meetings of the Italian parliament were held in the palace's circular Chamber of the Subalpine Parliament, and the building was the powerbase of leaders like Cavour, who ousted the more radical Garibaldi to an early retirement on the island of Caprera near Sardinia. It's ironic, then, that the most interesting sections of the museum are those dedicated to Garibaldi: portraits showing him as a scruffy, long-haired revolutionary, some of his clothes – an embroidered fez, a long stripey scarf and one of the famous red shirts – adopted during his exile in South America, where he trained himself by fighting in various wars of independence. These shirts became the uniform of his army of a thousand volunteers who seized southern Italy and Sicily from the Bourbons.

What Vittorio Emanuele II made of the eccentrically dressed revolutionary who secured half the kingdom for him is undocumented, but you feel sure that his residence – and that of the princes of Savoy for more than two hundred years – the sixteenth-century **Palazzo Reale** (guided tours every 40min Tues–Sun 9am–7pm; L8000/€4.13), at the head of the sprawling, traffic-choked Piazza Castello, wouldn't have impressed Garibaldi. Designed by Castellamonte, to the specifications of Madama Reale Cristina of France, this nouveau-riche palace with an unexceptional facade hides glitzy rooms gilded virtually top-to-bottom and decorated with bombastic allegorical paintings. Around the rooms you'll find comical collections of chinoiserie, with lions, cockerels and fat laughing Chinamen, a thousand-piece dinner set and a particularly flashy vase of Meissen porcelain encrusted with golf balls and birds. If this isn't enough, look in also on the seventeenth-century church of **San Lorenzo**, tucked behind the left wing of the palace. Designed by Guarini, who was also responsible for the Palazzo Carignano, it's scalloped with chapels, crowned by a complex dome supported on overlapping semicircles, and lined with multicoloured marble, frescoes and stucco festoons and statuettes.

On the right-hand side of the Palazzo Reale is the **Armeria Reale** (Mon, Wed, Fri & Sat 9am–2pm, Tues & Thurs 1.30–7pm; L8000/€4.13), a collection of armour and weapons spanning seven centuries and several continents started by King Carlo Alberto in 1837. Pride of place is given to his stuffed horse, which stands among cases of guns and swords. There's also a gallery of suits of armour and a blood-curdling collection of oriental arms, including gorgeously jewelled Turkish sheaths and intimidating Japanese masks. The same building houses the **Biblioteca Reale** (open only to bona fide scholars, or for special exhibitions), which, along with countless volumes and manuscripts, has a collection of drawings by artists including Leonardo da Vinci, Bellini, Raphael, Tiepolo and Rembrandt, part of it sometimes on display.

Across the square from the Palazzo Reale, the **Palazzo Madama** (closed for restoration at the time of writing but due to reopen around the end of 2001) is an altogether more appealing building, with an ornate Baroque facade by the early eighteenth-century architect Juvarra, who also redesigned the piazza and many of the streets leading off it. Inside, the originally fifteenth-century palace incorporates parts of a thirteenth-century castle and a Roman gate. If open, it's worth looking in also for some of the building's original furniture and frescoes and the **Museo Civico dell'Arte Antica** – a collection that includes everything from early Christian gold jewellery and oriental ceramics to a famous *Portrait of an Unknown Man* by Antonello da Messina and an inlaid Gothic commode.

Behind the Palazzo Reale – and reached through a small passage – is the fifteenth-century **Duomo**, on Via XX Settembre. The only example of Renaissance architecture in Turin, it was severely damaged in a fire in 1997 but is open to visitors and worshippers despite being decked in purple satin to hide scaffolding and restoration work – the reconstruction of its fantastic Holy Shroud Chapel, designed by Guarini in 1668, will not be completed until at least 2010. Luckily a quick-thinking fireman rescued from the blazing chapel what has been called "the most remarkable forgery in history", the

Turin Shroud – a piece of cloth imprinted with the image of a man's body that has been claimed as the shroud in which Christ was wrapped after his crucifixion. One of the most famous medieval relics, it made world headlines in 1989 after carbon-dating tests carried out by three universities all concluded it was a fake, made between 1260 and 1390 – although no one is any the wiser about how the medieval forgers actually managed to create the image. Most of the time you can't see the shroud itself; it is locked away and officially only on display once every twenty-five years, although in reality the possibility of a glimpse is more frequent, as it is sometimes brought out for special occasions (it's worth checking at the tourist office for details). If you don't get to see the real thing, head to the left of the nave, where there's a photographic reproduction, on which the face of a bearded man, crowned with thorns, is clearly visible, together with marks supposed to have been left by a double-thonged whip, spear wounds and bruises that could have been caused carrying a cross. For those whose interest is still not satiated, there is a museum that covers the history and science of the shroud, **Museo della Sindone** (daily 9am–noon & 3–7pm; *www.sindone.org/it/museo.htm*; L9000/€4.65), on Via S. Domenico 28.

The only relics of Turin's days as a small Roman colony are visible from outside the duomo: the scant remains of a **theatre** and the impressive **Porta Palatina** – two sixteen-sided towers flanking an arched passageway. Beyond, the massive **Piazza della Repubblica** is another Juvarra design, though his grand plan for it is marred nowadays by the seedy buildings of the Porta Palazzo **market**, selling fruit, veg, clothes and bric-a-brac daily. Of more interest, behind the Porta Palazzo, is the Saturday-morning Balôn, or **flea market**, home to fortune-tellers (Turin is reputed to be the centre of the Italian occult) and black marketeers. On the second Sunday of each month there's a Gran Balôn with opportunities to buy collectable items including lace, toys, secondhand furniture and books.

Behind Piazza della Repubblica stands Turin's most elaborate church, the **Santuario della Consolata**, built to house an ancient statue of the Madonna, Maria Consolatrice, the protector of the city. Designed by Guarini, the church has an impressive decorative altar by Juvarra, and outside its pink-and-white Neoclassical facade there are shops crammed with votive objects, which the more devout Torinese buy to offer to the statue, housed in an ancient crypt below the church. Not to be missed is the series of paintings in the church, featuring people being "saved" from such disasters as being gored by a bull, cutting overhead electricity cables with garden shears, exploding chip pans, and numerous accidents involving prams and trams. After all this, you may well want to head across the road to the beautiful old café *Al Bicerin* (see p.78) for a pick-me-up.

Down to the river: Parco del Valentino and the Museo dell'Automobile

The scruffy porticoes of Via Po lead down to the river from Via Roma, ending just before the bridge in the vast arcaded Piazza Vittorio Veneto. Turn off halfway down, along Via Montebello, to the **Mole Antonelliana**, whose bishop's-hat dome, topped by a pagoda-like spire balancing on a mini-Greek temple, is a distinctive landmark and has been adopted as the city's emblem. Designed as a synagogue in the nineteenth century by the eccentric architect Antonelli, the building was ceded to the local council by Turin's Jewish community while still under construction because of escalating costs. Always a rather preposterous white elephant, the decision to house the new **Museo del Cinema** there (Tues–Sun 9am–7pm; L13,000/€6.71) seems a suitable way to celebrate the sheer spectacle of the building. Turin's involvement with cinema goes back to the early years of the twentieth century, when it was one of the first Italian cities to import and experiment with the new medium invented by the Lumière brothers. The interesting museum covers the early days of the magic lantern and experimental moving pictures, the development of the cinema as a global phenomenon, and twenty-first-century special effects.

Across the bridge from the **Piazza Vittorio Veneto** there is the Pantheon-like **Gran Madre di Dio** church. Behind the church, a path takes you up the hill to the **Museo Nazionale della Montagna Duca degli Abruzzi** at Via Giardino 39 (daily 9am–7pm; *www.museomontagna.org*; L4000/€2.07), a fascinating museum dedicated to the mountain environment and its people.

South along the river from Piazza Vittorio Veneto is the riverside **Parco del Valentino**, which you're most likely to visit at night, as it holds some of the best of Turin's clubs. But in the daytime it makes a pleasant place to wind down after the hum of the city centre, its curving lanes, formal flower beds and fake hills covering half a million square metres – making it one of Italy's largest parks. Within the grounds are two castles, one real, the other a fake. The ornate **Castello Valentino** was another Savoy residence, used mainly for wedding feasts and other extravagant parties, and nowadays seat of the university's faculty of architecture. The **Borgo e Castello Medioevale** (daily 9am–8pm; free) and, inside, the **Rocca Medioevale** (Tues–Sun 9am–7pm; L5000/€2.58, free first Fri of the month 2–7pm) date from an industrial exhibition held in 1884 and are a synthesis of the best houses and castles of medieval Piemonte and Valle d'Aosta, built with the same materials as the originals and using the same construction techniques. You may balk at the bogusness of the thing, and it does feel a little like Disneyland, but it actually conjures up a picture of life in a fifteenth-century castle far better than many of the originals, kitted out as it is with painstaking replicas of intricately carved Gothic furniture. The castle is based on those at Fénis and Verrès (see pp.98 and 96), and the frescoes are reproductions of those at Manta (see p.83).

A longish walk from here, along the river, takes you to the **Museo dell'Automobile** at Corso Unità d'Italia 40 (Tues–Sun 10am–6.30pm; L10,000/€5.17; bus #34 from Via Nizza), Italy's only motor museum. Even if you know nothing about cars, this has some appeal – you'll spot models you haven't seen since your childhood and others familiar from films, as the museum traces the development from the early cars, handcrafted for a privileged minority, to the mass-produced family version. There's one of the first Fiats, a bulky 1899 model, close to a far sleeker version, built only two years later and, just three decades later, the first small Fiat family-targeted vehicle, a design which was still on the streets in the Sixties. Look also at the gleaming Isotta Fraschini driven by Gloria Swanson in *Sunset Boulevard*, still with the initials of Norma Desmond, the character she played, on the side. The pride of the collection is the 1907 Itala which won the Peking-to-Paris race in the same year; you can read of its adventures in Luigi Barzini's book *Peking to Paris*.

Out from the centre: the Basilica di Superga and Stupinigi Palace

South of the river, Turin fades into decrepit suburbs, beyond which lie the wooded hills that conceal the fancy villas of the city's industrialists, including that of Gianni Agnelli. For a taste of the views enjoyed by Turin's mega-rich, take bus #70 up to the **Parco della Rimembranza**, with 10,000 trees planted in honour of the Torinese victims of World War I and crowned with an enormous light-flashing statue of Victory. Alternatively, head out to the grandiose Baroque **Basilica di Superga**, from which there are fine panoramas across the city to the Alps (tram #15 followed by a shuttle bus).

The basilica, yet another design from Filippo Juvarra, stands high on a hill above the rest of the city, a position that is the key to its existence. In 1706 King Vittorio Amadeo climbed the hill in order to study the positions of the French and Spanish armies who had been besieging the city for four months, and vowed that he would erect a temple to the Madonna on this site if she were to aid him in the coming battle. Turin was spared, and the king immediately set Juvarra to work, flattening the top of the hill and producing over the next 25 years the circular basilica you see today. An elegant dome, pierced by windows and supported on pairs of white columns, is flanked by delicately scalloped onion-domed towers and rises above a Greek temple entrance, though the most striking thing about the building these days is the graffiti – names dating back to the beginning of the century scratched into the interior pillars. Many Torinese come here not to pay homage to the Virgin, nor even to the splendid tombs of the Savoys, but to visit the tomb of the 1949 Torino football team, all of whom were killed when their plane crashed into the side of the hill. If you happen to go to a match between Torino and Juventus, you may well hear the sinister chant from the Juventus supporters, "Superga, Superga".

The other nearby attraction worth making a trip out of town for is the Savoy dynasty's luxurious hunting lodge, the **Palazzina di Caccia di Stupinigi** (Tues–Sun 10am–7pm; L8000/€4.13). Another Juvarra creation, built in the 1730s and perhaps his finest work, this symmetrical fantasy with a generous dash of Rococo was awarded UNESCO World Heritage status in 1997. The exterior of the palace has been restored, and the interior is as luxurious as it ever was: the most extravagant room, the oval Salone Centrale, is a dizzying triumph of optical illusion that merges fake features with real in a superb trompe l'oeil. Other rooms are decorated with hunting motifs: Diana, goddess of hunting, bathes on bedroom ceilings, hunting scenes process across walls, and even the chapel is dedicated to St Uberto, patron saint of the hunt. And everywhere there are opulent wall-coverings – gilded brocades, hand-painted silk, carefully inked rice paper – and delicate eighteenth-century furniture, including gilded four-posters, inlaid desks and cabinets, even a marvellous marble bath, decorated with a relief of an imperial eagle, installed by Pauline Bonaparte. To get there, take bus #41sb from Corso Vittorio Emanuele II; on the way you'll pass through the bleak Mirafiori suburbs on the west side of the city, built for workers at the nearby Fiat plant.

Eating and drinking

Torinese **cuisine** shows strong French influences, especially evident in the winter dish of *bagna caoda*. Fungi and game in autumn, and truffles used as flavouring, are also classics. *Agnolotti* and *cappelletti* are the best-known dishes, followed by meat *buji* (boiled) or braised in wine. Cheeses to look out for are *tomini, robiole* and *tume*. The humble *grissini* (bread sticks) found wrapped in greaseproof paper on every restaurant table across the land reach new heights in Turin (they were allegedly invented to tempt the appetite of the sickly boy-king Vittorio Amedeo II in the seventeenth century). The sweets, too, are marvellous, many of them invented in the Savoy kitchens to tempt the royal palates: among the decadent delights are *spumone piemontese*, a mousse of mascarpone cheese with rum; *panna cotta*, smooth, rich cooked cream; and light pastries like *lingue di gatto* (cat's tongues) and *baci di dama* (lady's kisses). Turin is also credited as the home of *zabaglione*, used to fill *bignole*, or iced choux pastries; Spanish friar San Pasquale Bayon, a gifted cook and parish priest of the city's church of San Tommaso in the sixteenth century, is said to have invented the egg yolk, sugar and Marsala mixture.

There are plenty of **restaurants** in which to indulge in these dishes all over the city, as well as any number of cheaper eating places serving the kind of food you can find anywhere in the country. For food on the run, there are **snack bars** and **takeaways** on Via Nizza, some tempting **delicatessens** on Via Lagrange and a superb rosticceria on Corso Vittorio Emanuele II for DIY lunches. For a drink, a snack, a pastry or an ice cream, you should also look in on one of the city's *fin de siècle* **cafés**, which are a Turin institution. The prices are steep, but the atmosphere more than compensates.

Restaurants

Arcadia, Galleria Subalpina 16. Try this place for an eclectic mix of Italian food and sushi. It's affordable at lunchtime, but pricier in the evening. Closed Sun & Aug.

L'Arcimboldo, Via Santa Chiara 54. Specializes in *pasta fresca*, with a choice of a hundred sauces, all at low prices. Closed Sun.

Del Cambio, Piazza Carignano 2 (☎011.546.690). Historic, formal shrine to Piemontese food much frequented by expense-account types. A great opportunity to feast on traditional dishes, such as beef in Barolo or Cavour's favourite of *fianziera* (veal, sweetbreads and *porcini*, cooked with butter and wine); prices are suitably extravagant and booking is advisable. Closed Mon, Sun & Aug.

C'era una volta, Corso Vittorio Emanuele II 41. Simple, delicious Piemontese cuisine at moderate prices. Closed Sun.

Il Conte Verde, Via Bellezia 15. Piemontese specialities – try the *tartrà*, a soufflé of cheese, herbs and cream. Closed Sun.

Cucco, Corso Casale 89. A big Art Nouveau place near the river at Ponte Margherita serving typical Piemontese cooking with a choice of around 30 antipasti. There's a set menu for L45,000/€23.20 or you can eat à la carte. Closed Mon.

Finestre sul Po, Lungo Po Cadorna 1. A new place that's on the waterfront near Piazza Vittorio Veneto. You eat well for a relatively modest price from a menu of Italian and Piemontese dishes. No closing day.

Porto di Savona, Piazza Vittorio Veneto 2. Cheap and cheerful restaurant very popular with students and businesspeople alike, attracted primarily by the bargain formula of *piatto unico* and dessert. Closed Tues lunchtime and all day Mon.

Quattro Soldi, Corso Castelfidardo 7. Reliable, good-value neighbourhood pizzeria-ristorante in the southwest corner of town. Closed Wed.

La Taverna Rossa, Via Valperga Caluso. Excellent pizza and simple dishes at low prices down by the Parco del Valentino. No closing day.

Tre Galline, Via Bellezia 37 (☎011.436.6553.). The oldest restaurant in Turin, with a lovely panelled interior and a fixed menu for L50,000/€25.82 (a bit more for à la carte). Don't miss the sweet-and-sour (*agrodolce*) rabbit. Booking advisable. Closed Mon lunchtime, all day Sun & Aug.

Vegetarian Club, Via San Massimo 17. Reasonably priced vegetarian restaurant with a good selection of dishes and a quiet outside terrace. Closed Mon.

Cafés

Baratti and Milano, Piazza Castello 29. Established in 1873 and preserving its nineteenth-century interior of mirrors, chandeliers and carved wood, in which genteel Torinese ladies sip leisurely teas. Great hot chocolate.

Al Bicerin, Piazza della Consolata 5. Walk into this tiny, beautiful place and you feel a bit like you're stepping into a museum. Try a *bicerin* – a Piemontese speciality of coffee fortified with brandy, cream and chocolate.

Fiorio, Via Po 8. Once the haunt of Cavour, this is the best place in the city to eat ice cream. Their *gianduia* (hazlenut chocolate) flavour is legendary, as are the real-fruit sorbets.

Mulassano, Piazza Castello 15. A cosy café first opened in 1900, with marble fittings and a beautiful ceiling. Traditionally the favourite of actors and singers from the nearby Teatro Regio.

Pepino, Piazza Carignano 8. Ritzy café with summer garden, famed for its ice creams. Try the violet-flavoured *pinguino* or the outrageously rich cream-and-chocolate concoction of *pezzo duro*.

Platti, Corso Vittorio Emanuele II 72. Art Nouveau-furnished café dating from 1870 that hosts art exhibitions and occasional live music.

San Carlo, Piazza San Carlo 156. Where the heroes of the Risorgimento met in the nineteenth century, this rather glitzily restored café with gilt pilasters and an immense chandelier combines a restaurant and ice cream parlour.

Stratta, Piazza San Carlo 156. The oldest *confetteria* in Turin, dating back to 1836. *Marron glacé* is a speciality.

Torino, Piazza San Carlo 204. A good place for a leisurely aperitif or cocktail, of which the most popular is the *Torino*'s very own "Elvira", made with Martini, vodka and various secret ingredients. Famous regulars were writer Cesare Pavese and Luigi Einaudi (a Torinese economist who became the second President of the Italian Republic).

Zucca, Via Roma 294. Pastries and *tramezzini*, plus a famous *aperitivo della casa*.

Snacks, takeaways and self-service places

Brek, Piazza Carlo Felice (closed Sun) and Piazza Solferino (closed Mon). Slick, high-quality self-service, with tables outside in summer.

Frullati Varturi, Piazza Castello 15. Very central lunchtime option, with sandwiches and an array of fresh local and tropical fruits, ready for the liquidizer.

Papillon, Via Corte d'Appello 3. Sandwiches, snacks and full meals.

Rosticceria, Via Gramsci 12. Inexpensive place, very crowded at lunchtime, serving everything from *arancini* (fried rice balls) to whole roast chickens.

La Ruota, Via Barbaroux 11. Good place for a quick lunch, eat in or takeaway.

Nightlife and entertainment

Turin's **nightlife** is more sedate than that of, say, Milan, but there is a reasonably varied mix of clubs and bars here, with the most lively spots down on the embankment bordered by the Parco del Valentino, known locally as the **Murazzi** – the best advice is just to wander down there and see what takes your fancy. Problems with drugs and theft have given the place a bit of a reputation and there's often quite a heavy police/carabinieri presence – so watch your wallet and take it easy. The area is especially popular on summer weekends when a big crowd spills out of the bars and onto the riverfront jetties. For a more tranquil alternative try the medieval area around Piazza Emanuele Filiberto and Via Santa Chiara.

Getting down to the business of **drinking**, you'll find that birrerias, extremely popular in the 1980s, have been supplemented by new vinerias – wine bars – where you can also order up a substantial snack (known locally as a *marenda sinoira*). Note that some **clubs** require membership cards, which cost between L12,000/€6.20 and L15,000/€7.75, but your first drink is usually included in this. After that, although drink prices can be inflated, the measures are relatively generous – bar staff usually keep pouring until they think it looks big enough (often until it's about the equivalent of a triple).

The city has an impressive agenda of **live music** in July and September, with many well-publicized open-air performances, some of them free. The season kicks off with **jazz** in the second week of July courtesy of the JVC Jazz Festival (☎011.561.3926) at the Piazzetta and Giardini Reale, which attracts international names such as Tito Puente and João Gilberto. For **rock** fans, the Pellerossa Festival (☎011.434.3333) in the third and fourth weeks of July offers an eclectic mix of Italian and foreign bands – previous headliners have included Bob Dylan and Sonic Youth – with affordable tickets. However, the festival takes place outside town at the Certosa Reale and the Parco dalla Chiesa, and you'll need a car to get there. For most of September a major festival called, appropriately enough, Settembre Musica mixes **jazz**, **world music**, **classical music** and **performance art** (☎011.442.4777) at various venues around town. Check the Web site *www.comune.torino.it* and links for listings.

Turin is also the home of the prestigious **RAI National Symphony Orchestra**, which performs in, among other places, the Lingotto centre, the former Fiat factory converted to a conference centre and performance space by architect Renzo Piano in 1995. Turin's **opera** house, the Teatro Regio (☎011.881.5241), is one of the best in the country and is recognizable from its pod-like Seventies architecture.

The city's Il Teatro Stabile (☎011.517.6246), one of Italy's principal publicly funded **theatre** companies, is acclaimed for its productions of major works by nineteenth- and twentieth-century European writers; they normally perform at the Casignano Theatre on Piazza Carignano. For new writers and experimental work, look out for shows by the Gruppo della Rocca, the Teatro dell'Angolo, the Teatro Juvarra and the Laboratorio Teatro Settimo. There are also four international **film** festivals held in Turin each year, among them a women's film festival in March and a "cinema of homosexual themes" in April; contact the tourist office for details.

For **what's on listings**, opening hours and so on, check the pages of the Turin daily, *La Stampa*, particularly its Tuesday and Friday supplements, or the weekly *News Spettacolo*. There's also a free monthly bilingual publication available in hotels and bars, *Un Ospite a/A guest in Torino*, which has a list of events and exhibitions as well as suggestions for itineraries; the Web site address is *www.ospite.it*. Failing that you can get information on events, exhibitions, festivals and the like from either the Informacittà office, on Piazza Palazzo di Città (Mon–Fri 8.30am–4pm; ☎011.442.3602), or the Vetrina per Torino office, Piazza San Carlo 159 (Mon 3–7pm, Tues–Sat 9am–1pm; ☎011.442.4740); the latter also sells tickets for most events.

Bars, birrerias, clubs and vinerias

AEIOU, Via Spanzotti 3 (☎011.385.8580). Off Corso Francia, this is a large, modern club in a former warehouse, with a wide selection of cocktails – and music. A good place to go if you just want to dance.

Centralino, Via delle Rosine 16 (☎011.837.500). Jazz concerts and avant-garde productions; membership card required.

La Contea, Corso Quintino Sella 132. Birreria situated across the river that features live jazz and other styles under a trompe l'oeil fresco of a square. Food, too, is served on the terrace under a pergola in summer. Closed Sun.

Doctor Sax, Murazzi di Lungo Po Cadorna 4. African rhythms and exhibitions of contemporary art. Closed Mon.

Hiroshima Mon Amour, Via Bossoli 83 (☎011.317.6636). Live music, avant-garde performances, alternative theatre and cabaret in a converted school.

Jumping Jester, Via Mazzini 2. Old-style wooden interior with huge TV screen on which football matches are shown live. Serves a top pint of cold Caffreys or Tennants.

Lucky Nugget Saloon, Corso Vittorio Emanuele II 40. Open late and popular with an eclectic bunch of customers – you can have just a drink or choose from a full range of Mexican food. There are three floors: chill out upstairs or downstairs, or if you're pining to dance on a few tables, head straight for the central section. Closed Mon.

Magazzino di Gilgamesh, Piazza Moncenisio 13b. Birreria and coffee shop with music, plus an international restaurant on the third floor, and cabaret and country music. Closed Sun.

Nuev Caval Brons, Piazza San Carlo 157. Bar (and restaurant) with a help-yourself canapé selection that Henry VIII would have been proud of. Closed Sat lunch & all day Sun.

Roar Roads, Via Carlo Alberta 3. Despite the dubious name, a very passable pub just off Via Po that pulls in locals and foreigners. Closed Sun.

The Shamrock Inn, Corso Vittorio Emanuele II 34. The place for an authentic pint of Irish stout, frequented from about 10.30pm onwards by Torinese and a smattering of Brits, Australians and Scandinavians. Good-value sandwiches for around L5000/€2.58. Closed Sun.

Tre Galli, Via Sant'Agostino 25. Busy vineria with a long wine list of local and Italian wines by the bottle or glass (for the latter, ask for a *mescita a calice*) and plates of cheeses, ham, *salumi* and homemade *grissini*. Laid-back atmosphere and tables outside on the piazza in summer. Open until 2am. Closed Sun.

Listings

Books and newspapers Libreria Luxembourg, Via C. Battisti 7, has an excellent range of British and American paperbacks. English-language newspapers and magazines can be bought from the newsagents in Porta Nuova station and Libreria Internazionale de La Stampa, Via Roma 80.

Car parks The Porta Nuova car park (daily 7am–10pm; L1500/€0.78 per 30min) is the most central place to leave your vehicle.

Car rental Avis, Corso Turati 15 (☎011.501.107); Europcar, Via Madama Cristina 272 (☎011.650.3603); Hertz, Via Magellano 12 (☎011.502.080). All these companies also have desks at Porta Nuova station and the airport.

Chocolate Turin is a major centre for chocolate production, its most famous product being the hazelnut chocolate *Gianduiotto*, which dates back to the nineteenth century. Some even claim that it was the Torinese who introduced chocolate to France when chocolate making for export began in 1678. Peyrano at Corso Moncalieri 47 and Croci Bruno at Via Principessa Clotilde 61a both have an excellent selection; the latter is slightly less expensive.

Closing days Some shops are closed on Monday morning. Be prepared for the summer shutdown (First Mon–last Sat of Aug), when there's only a limited public transport service, and many restaurants, food shops and other businesses are closed.

Exchange Outside normal banking hours you can exchange money at Porta Nuova station (daily 7.10am–1.40pm & 2.10–8.30pm).

Football Turin's two teams, Juventus (*www.juventus.it*) and Torino (*www.toroclub.it*), play on Saturday and Sunday afternoons at the Stadio dell' Alpi, Strada Altessano 131, Continassa, Venaria Reale (☎011.738.0081), although it's rumoured that Torino may soon be moving to a new stadium. Stadio dell' Alpi is reachable by tram #9 only when there's a game on; at other times (to see the hightech architecture of the stadium, for example) take bus #72. Although Juventus is the most popular team in Italy (a recent poll found that one-third of all Italians support them), most of the locals support the underdogs, Torino.

Hospital Ospedale Molinette, Corso Bramante 88–90 (☎011.633.1633); for 24hr emergency medical attention call ☎5747.

Internet access *@h!*, Via Montebello 13 (Mon–Fri 10am–1pm & 2–7pm; ☎011.815.4058, *www.ahto2000.com*; L10,000/€5.17 per hour).

Laundries Alba, Via San Secondo 1; Lava Aschiuga, Via Berthollet 18, with other branches at Via de Nanni 84 and Piazza della Repubblica 5.

Markets In addition to the Porta Palazzo on Piazza della Repubblica, and the weekly Balòn and monthly Gran Balòn markets behind Porta Palazzo (see p.75), there's often some heavily discounted designer fashion (the genuine thing, from end-of-line clearances) at the Crocetta market around Via Cassini and Via Marco Polo (Tues–Fri morning & all day Sat) – not exactly street market prices, but still much cheaper than in the shops.

Pharmacist Boniscontro, Corso Vittorio Emanuele II 66 (☎011.538.271) is an all-night chemist.

Police ☎113. City police station at Corso XI Febbraio 22 (☎011.460.6060). Dial ☎112 for Carabinieri.

Post office The central post office is at Via Alfieri 10 (Mon–Fri 8.30am–2.30pm, Sat 8.30am–1pm).

Shopping Via Roma is good for designer labels, and there is trendier, less expensive fare in the pedestrianized streets bordered by Via Pietro Micca, Via Monte Pietá, Via dei Mercanti and Via San Francesco d'Assisi. Sellers of secondhand clothes and costume jewellery, book binders, tailors and dress makers cluster in the narrow streets around Via Barbaroux, Via San Tommaso and Via Monte di Pieta, off Via Garibaldi.

Telephones There are Telecom Italia offices at Via Roma 18 and at the Porta Nuova and Porta Susa stations (daily 7am–10pm).

West of Turin: the Susa and Chisone valleys

The main route to France from Turin runs through the **Susa Valley**, passing the region's main ski resorts. The one real sight, the **Sacra di San Michele**, a forbidding fortified abbey anchored atop a rocky hill, is an easy day-trip from Turin. **Susa** itself, reached by a minor branch of the rail line, was once a modest Roman town and is now a modest provincial town – a pleasant stopover but with little else to lure you.

Sacra di San Michele

The closest town to the **Sacra di San Michele** is **AVIGLIANA**, half an hour by train from Turin and connected with the abbey by infrequent buses. It's a grotty sort of place, though, and if you don't mind walking it's much nicer to push on to the next stop on the train route, **SANT'AMBROGIO**, a small village at the foot of San Michele's hill, from where it's a steep 60- to 90-minute hike to the abbey.

The walk is worth it, both for the views and for the opportunity it affords to soak up the spooky atmosphere that surrounds the glowering abbey, reached by a long flight of stairs hewn into the rock – the *Scalone dei Morti* ("Stairs of the Dead"). Corpses used to be laid out here for local peasants to come and pay their respects, setting a morbid tone that's continued with the abbey buildings proper, from the Romanesque entrance arch carved with signs of the zodiac to the Gothic-Romanesque abbey church.

Susa

A further 25km down the valley from Sant'Ambrogio, **SUSA** is a possible stopover if it's late, a likeable, rather scruffy old town with a few one-star **hotels**, such as the *du Park*, Via Mazzini 15 (☎0122.622.273; ④), and the three-star *Napoleon*, Via Mazzini 44 (☎0122.622.855; ⑤).

While most of Italy was ruled by the Romans, Susa and western Piemonte remained in the hands of the Gauls. The best-known of its Gaulish leaders, Cottius, was much admired by the Romans, with whom he reached a peaceful arrangement, and there are a handful of Gaulish/Roman remains scattered around the town centre, notably in **Piazza San Giusto**, where there's a redoubtable defensive gate. The adjacent Romanesque **Cattedrale** has a fine campanile, but its most interesting features are the external frescoes – a *Crucifixion* and an *Entry into Jerusalem*. Just above the piazza, Cottius erected the **Arco di Augusto** in honour of the Roman emperor; its top is decorated with a processional frieze and gives views down into a small park laid out around the remains of some **Roman Baths**.

From Susa you can make an excursion to the **Abbey of Novalesa**, 10km away at the foot of Rocciamelone in the Cenischia Valley, close by the French border. The church here is a relatively recent, eighteenth-century structure, but part of the cloister and walls date back to the eighth century, while the four chapels, one of which is decorated with frescoes, were built in the tenth century.

In the opposite direction, southeast, at the end of the Chisone Valley, **PINEROLO** is worth a short stop. It's a small town with a medieval centre that was for centuries the seat of the Acaia princedom, precursors of the House of Savoy. You can walk around the frescoed courtyard of their **palace**, halfway up the hill, where you'll also find the church of **San Maurizio**, burial place of the Acaia princes, decorated with fifteenth-century frescoes. In the town centre, there's a Gothic **Duomo** and the huge covered **Cavallerizza Caprilli** or parade ground for horses. The **Museo della Cavalleria** (Tues–Thurs 9–11.15am & 3–5.15pm, Fri–Sun 9–11.30am; free) gives a good sense of the town's glory days, with displays relating to the prestigious former cavalry school of Pinerolo. There are lots of objects – uniforms, arms and spurs, trophies and documents, even a stuffed horse – pertaining to the brilliance of the horsemen and their steeds, as well as displays of bridles, horseshoes, tools and the like, and a rather sad section devoted to the tanks and jeeps that have come to replace horses in the military.

The Piemontese ski resorts

Close to the French border are Piemonte's principal purpose-built ski resorts – well used by British tour operators and really far cheaper if you take a package. The snow is in any case notoriously unreliable, and resorts have been known to close down midseason, though Sestriere has lately protected itself against the weather by installing Europe's largest artificial snow-machine.

Of the main three resorts, **BARDONECCHIA** is a weekenders' haunt, a modern resort with small chalet-style hotels. **SAUZE D'OULX**, a little way south, is known as the Benidorm of the Alps and attracts hordes of youngsters who treat skiing as a hangover cure. Apart from a few winding streets of old houses, it's an ugly, sprawling place, and its lift-passes are expensive. Linked by lift to Sauze d'Oulx, **SESTRIERE** was the dream resort of Mussolini and the Fiat baron, Giovanni Agnelli, though it's now very overdeveloped. Agnelli conceived an aristocratic mountain retreat, favoured by the young and beautiful, though he was not unaware of the fast-growing tourist industry. The story goes that he insisted the height of the sinks be raised to prevent "common tourists" from pissing in them. Nowadays, the reality is a bland resort that dribbles over a bleak mountain, dominated by two cylindrical towers, both now owned by Club Med.

Saluzzo and the western valleys

A flourishing medieval town, and later the seat of one of Piemonte's few Renaissance courts, **SALUZZO**, 57km south of Turin, retains much of its period appeal. Flaking ochre-washed terraces and Renaissance houses with painted trompe l'oeil landscapes line stepped cobbled streets climbing up to a castle, now a prison. A pleasant place to stay and wander, the town has the added attraction of regular bus services into the Po, Varaita and Maira valleys, which cut through the foothills of the Monviso mountain towards France.

There are a few things around town worth seeing. Just below the castle, the Gothic church of **San Giovanni** has a number of thirteenth- and fourteenth-century frescoes and the tomb of the leading light of Renaissance Saluzzo, Marchese Ludovico II, anachronistically depicted like a medieval knight beneath a fancily carved canopy. Close by, the Gothic **Casa Cavassa** is a fifteenth-century palace with an arcaded courtyard that doubled as home for one of Ludovico's ministers and now houses the town's **Museo Civico** (Wed–Sun: April–Sept 9am–12.15pm & 3–6.15pm; Oct–March 9am–12.15pm & 2–5.15pm; L6000/€3.10). Inside are period furniture and paintings, including the gorgeously gilded *Madonna della Misericordia*, with the Madonna sheltering Ludovico, his wife and the population of Saluzzo in the folds of her cloak.

That's about all there is to the town centre, but just to the south of Saluzzo, a five-minute bus ride from outside the train station, there's the **Castello di Manta** – a medieval fortress that was transformed into a refined residence by the Saluzzo marquises in the fifteenth century (Tues–Sun 10am–1pm & 2–5pm; L6000/€3.10). Though from the outside it's as plain and austere as Saluzzo's castle, it's worth visiting for the late-Gothic frescoes in the Baronial Hall. One of these illustrates the myth of the fountain of youth, elderly people processing towards the magical waters while others impatiently rip off their clothes to plunge in. The other, *Nine Heroes and Nine Heroines*, depicts idealized chivalrous courtiers and exquisite damsels, with china-pale faces and elaborate costumes, standing beneath stylized trees with coats of arms hanging from the branches.

Saluzzo's **tourist office** is at Via Griselda 6, in front of the town hall (Tues–Fri 8am–12.30pm & 2–5pm, Sat 8am–noon; ☎0175.46.710, *www.comune.saluzzo.cn.it*), and can provide information on the whole of the western valleys region. Among the **hotels**, the cheapest is the *Persico* in Vicolo Mercati (☎0175.41.213; ②), which also has a very good **restaurant** serving traditional cuisine (closed Fri); or there are a couple of three-stars, the *Astor* at Piazza Garibaldi 39 (0175.45.506; ④) and the *Griselda* at Corso XXVII Aprile 13 (0175.47.484; ④).

Valle Po

West of Saluzzo, close to the French border, lies the source of the River Po, which flows right across industrial northern Italy, gathering the waste from its thousands of factories before finally discharging into the Adriatic. The Alpine-style resort of **CRISSOLO** lies towards the end of the valley, and you can hike (or take a minibus in summer) to the **Pian del Re**, a grassy plain around the source of the Po, walking on to the entrance of the **Pertuis de la Traversette**, a 75-metre-long tunnel (currently closed) built by Saluzzo's Marquis Ludovico, to ease the trading route into France for his mule trains. According to one theory, the pre-tunnel pass was used by Hannibal and his elephants.

Crissolo is also a good base for climbing **Monviso**, Piemonte's highest mountain, reachable by way of a long rocky scramble in about six hours from the *Quintino Sella rifugio* (see below), two to three hours beyond the Pian del Re. Even if you don't want to scale the summit, the walk to the *rifugio* is lovely, passing a series of **mountain lakes**; or, if you prefer, it's possible to do a **circuit of the lakes**, turning off the main trail just before Lago Chiaretto, from where a path leads past Lago Superiore and back to Pian del Re. There are also **caves** near Crissolo, the **Grotta del Rio Martino** above the town, with stalactites and a subterranean lake and waterfall. The quick route here takes half an hour from Crissolo but is steep; the slower, easier route takes an hour. Unless you're an experienced caver, it's advisable to go with a guide, arranged through Crissolo's tourist office.

Crissolo's **hotels** are all on the main street, the Via Provinciale. The *Albergo Serenella* at no. 18 (☎0175.94.944; ②) is cheap and open year-round, as is the *Club Alpino* at no. 32 (☎0175.94.925; ③). Another small hotel at Pian del Re, the *Pian del Re* (☎0175.94.967; ②), is open mid-June to mid-September, while the *Quintino Sella rifugio*, near the Lago Grande del Viso, is open at Easter and from June 20 to October 4, and sometimes in winter; at all times it's advisable to phone in advance (☎0175.94.943). The majority of **restaurants** are in the hotels, so you may find taking half-board a better deal.

Val Varaita

To the south of the Valle Po, **Val Varaita**'s only draw is the rustic-style furniture that has been produced here since the eighteenth century, when the locals decided to capitalize on the vogue among Torinese and Genovese aristocrats for building country villas in the area. The industry continues to flourish, these days patronized by wealthy Torinese weekenders, and has brought much-needed prosperity to the area, though sadly its distinctly un-rustic factories and a preponderance of fake Alpine apartment blocks have ruined the look of the place irreparably.

Cúneo and around

There's not much to bring you to **CÚNEO**, the main town of southern Piemonte. Its severely geometric modern centre has less appeal than its extensive bus and rail connections, and the old town – what there is left of it – is dark and gloomy. Even its one "sight", the museum (weekdays only) in the restored Gothic church of **San Francesco** behind the bus station, is only of limited interest: the collection ranges from medieval frescoes to a folk section with traditional costumes, kitchen utensils and an ancient bike.

The **tourist office** is at Corso Nizza 17 (Mon–Sat 9.30am–12.30pm & 3–6.30pm, Sun 9.30am–12.30pm; ☎0171.66.615 or 0171.693.258). If you want to stay, there are a couple of reasonable **hotels**: the *Cavallo Nero* at Piazza Seminario 8 (☎0171.692.168; ③) and the similarly priced *Ligure* at Via Savigliano 11 (☎0171.681.942; ③).

The valleys

What does bring people to Cúneo are the valleys to the south of the town, which are popular for their sulphurous spas and summer and winter resorts. Of the main valleys, the **Valle Stura** is much visited by botanists for its many rare species of flowers; the

Valle Gesso, whose name means gypsum or chalk, is characterized by its vast walls of limestone, unusual in Piemonte, and some of it has been set aside as the huge **Parco Naturale dell'Argentera-Valle Gesso**, in which you can stay in various refuges, take the waters at **TERME DI VALDIERI**, or visit the botanical gardens at **VALDIERI**. The **Valle del Pesio** shouldn't be missed in spring at least, when a waterfall, known for obvious reasons as the *Piss del Pesio*, is in full pelt; there's also a twelfth-century monastery, the **Certosa di Pesio**, which boasts a missionary museum. Trains to France run through the verdant **Valle Vermenagna**, part of which is given over to the **Parco Naturale di Palanfre**, visitable from **VERNANTE**. Again, the appeal is mainly botanical, with over 800 species of trees and flowers growing at some 3000m above sea level, along with lots of birds and mammals.

Val Maira, actually to the north of Cúneo but still considered one of its valleys, is a quiet and narrow valley, known as the "Emerald Valley" for its greenery; its drama is heightened if you take the bus from Cúneo, recklessly hurtling around craggy cliffs, the driver seemingly oblivious to the sheer drops below. There's not much beyond this, though the villages, with their traditional rubble and wood houses perched high above the river, are very picturesque, particularly **ELVA**, in the hills above **STROPPO** (ask in the cafés for the unofficial taxi driver). If you're walking, get a **map** from Saluzzo before heading out. The best base is the *Gentil Locando* (☎0171.99.139; ①), located at the Marmara Bridge, between Stroppo and the small village of Prazzo, with clean rooms and a good-value restaurant. There are no hotels at Stroppo, just a **campsite** near the turn-off for Elva.

Mondoví and around

Half an hour by train from Cúneo, **MONDOVÍ** is a town split into two: the lower half – Breo – is modern and sleepily suburban, while the upper half, Piazza, is an uneasy combination of crumbling medieval and exuberant Baroque. Neither is especially exciting, but the town gives access to some interesting fifteenth-century frescoes, a sanctuary and some caves nearby.

Time in Mondoví is best spent in Piazza, built around a large square on which stand a turretted medieval palace and an exotic Baroque church, the seventeenth-century **Chiesa della Missione**, whose interior is decorated with an incredible trompe l'oeil by Andrea Pozzo, a cloudy heaven with angels seemingly suspended in mid-air. If you've time, you can laze around in the **Belvedere**, to the north of Piazza, a garden occupying the site of a thirteenth-century church destroyed except for its campanile in the last century. The campanile was used by a physicist in the eighteenth century to establish topographical measurements; though you can't climb up, the views from garden-level stretch north to the hills of Le Langhe and south to the foothills of the Alps.

Bastia

One of the attractions of Mondoví is its proximity to the hamlet of **BASTIA**, 10km northeast, where the church of **San Fiorenzo** – from the outside a modest rustic structure – holds some brilliantly coloured late-Gothic frescoes. Completed around 1472, the panels were worked on by at least four artists; they're absorbing pieces, with lively if predictable scenes from the lives of Christ and various saints, including a stunning hell, infested with vicious monsters. **Buses** run to Bastia from the train station at Mondoví but are badly timed for returning.

The Santuario di Vicoforte

A twenty-minute bus ride (from the train station) east of Mondoví, the **Santuario di Vicoforte** is another popular trip from the town, an imposing Baroque church crowned by what is claimed as the world's largest elliptical dome. It's liveliest on Sundays – like most Italian sanctuaries as much a place for a good day out as for devotions, purpose-built arcaded crescents housing restaurants, pastry, souvenir and clothes shops.

According to legend the sanctuary owes its existence to a hunter who, while out in the woods, discovered a pillar painted with a picture of the Madonna and Child – said by a second legend to have been erected as a votive offering by a poor baker whose bread wouldn't rise. In fact, the sanctuary was begun in 1598 on the orders of King Carlo Emanuele I, and eventually finished in 1890. The frescoed pillar is nowhere to be seen, and the 36-metre dome is rather a disappointment. But the kitsch **museum** provides some compensation: a haphazard collection of ecclesiastical bric-a-brac laid out in a labyrinth of rooms around the dome and towers. The exhibits range from gaudy treasures to ceremonial costumes and photos of those cured of their ailments by a visit here.

Grotta di Bossea

Twenty-four kilometres south of Vicoforte, the **Grotta di Bossea** (daily 9am–noon & 2–6pm; guided visits L10,000/€5.17) is the third of Mondoví's surrounding sights, a long-established subterranean tourist attraction filled with contorted stalactites and stalagmites, waterfalls and lakes and a subterranean scientific laboratory, set up to monitor the caves' wildlife – which includes seven unique species. On display is the skeleton of the *Ursius spelaeus*, an underground monster over three metres long and two metres high that lived here between 25,000 and 40,000 years ago. Sadly, reaching the caves without your own transport is virtually impossible.

Alba and Le Langhe

Northeast of Cúneo, the town of **Alba** and the surrounding **Le Langhe** hills mean two things to the Italians: white truffles and red wine. The region supplies some of the finest of both – the **truffles** are more delicate and aromatic than the black variety found further south, and the **wines** range from the "King of Italian reds", Barolo, to the light and fragrant Nebbiolo. There are a number of wine museums and cantinas in the hill-villages around Alba, the best being those at Barolo, Annunziata and Grinzane di Cavour – all accessible direct by bus from Alba.

Although these big cantinas all sell wine, you'll get a better deal at one of the smaller family-owned establishments scattered around the region. Most of the area's very different wines all come from the same grape, Nebbiolo, and the final taste is dependent on the soil: sandy soil produces the grapes for the light red, **Nebbiolo**, calcium and mineral-rich soil those for the more robust **Barolo**.

Alba

Whether or not you want to taste wine, **ALBA** repays a visit, for its central core of red-brick medieval towers, Baroque and Renaissance palaces and cobbled streets lined with gastronomic shops is one of Piemonte's most alluring. And if you come in October, there's a chance to see the town's hilarious annual donkey race – a skit on nearby Asti's prestigious Palio.

Of things to see, the late-Gothic **Duomo** on the central Piazza Risorgimento has been gaudily restored and holds some fine Renaissance stalls, inlaid with cityscapes, musical instruments, and fake cupboards whose contents seem to be on the verge of falling out. But Alba is primarily a place to stroll and eat. **Via Vittorio Emanuele**, the main drag, leads up to the centre from Piazza Savona, and is a fine, bustling street, with the most tempting of Alba's local produce on display – wines, truffles, cheeses, weird and wonderful varieties of mushroom, and the wickedly sticky *nocciola*, a nutty, choco-latey cake. **Via Cavour** is another pleasant medieval street with plenty of wine shops, behind which the **donkey race** and displays of medieval pageantry attract the crowds during the festival at the beginning of October. There's also an annual **truffle festival** later in the month, when you could blow your whole budget on a knobbly truffle or a meal in one of the many swanky restaurants. At the end of April/beginning of May, the Vinum festival gives the chance to taste five hundred Barolo, Nebbiolo, Barbaresco and Roero wines.

Practicalities

The **tourist office** (Mon–Fri 9am–1pm & 2–6pm, Sat 9am–noon; ☎0173.36.2562, *www.comune.alba.cn.it*) is on Via Emanuele 19 and has maps of Alba and information on the surrounding area. If you want to **stay**, you could try the very basic *Leon d'Oro*, Piazza Marconi 2 (☎0173.441.901; ②); the more comfortable *Piemonte*, Piazza Rossetti 6 (☎0173.441.354; ③); or the *Hotel Savona*, a good three-star handy for the train station, located at Piazza Savona 2 (☎0173.440.440; ③), with especially good deals for triples. You'll need to plan ahead to be sure of a room, especially during the October festival. The best place to sample **Albese cooking** is the excellent *Osteria dell'Arco*, at Piazza Savona 5 (closed Mon lunchtime & all day Sun), which has a particularly fine selection of local cheeses.

If you have your own transport, the village of **NEIVE**, about 13km north of Alba, makes a good alternative overnight stop. Here *Il Contea*, Piazza Cocito 8 (☎0173.671.126; ③), a **restaurant** with **rooms**, offers excellent food and some of the best Barbaresco, Dolcetto and Barolo wines from the vineyards around. Rooms are comfortable, with antique beds and whitewashed walls.

Around Alba: the hills of Le Langhe

Eight kilometres south of Alba, the castle of **Grinzane di Cavour** was rented by the Cavour family in the nineteenth century and served as a weekend retreat for Camillo Cavour. Nowadays it's the seat of Piemonte's regional *enoteca*, or winery, and has a pricey restaurant serving local specialities. The upstairs **folk museum** (daily except Tues: June–Sept 9am–noon & 2.30–6.30pm; Oct–Dec & Feb–May 9am–noon & 2–6pm; L5000/€2.58) holds various bits of Cavour trivia and a surprisingly engaging display of agricultural equipment, ranging from a ferret trap and grappa distillery to winter boots made of hay and a contraption for cleaning the cocoons of silkworms. In the afternoons there are wine-tasting sessions, and although there are inevitably some extremely expensive wines, many are affordable.

A few kilometres southwest of Grinzane, in the heart of Le Langhe, **BAROLO** is the best-known name among Italian wines, its peach- and ochre-washed houses set among extensive vineyards. It's a small village but is very geared up to the steady stream of wealthy gastronomes and wine connoisseurs who come here. You can visit the *Enoteca Regionale del Barolo*, housed in a flaking turreted castle on Piazza Falletti (daily except Thurs 10am–12.30pm & 3–6.30pm; free; tastings at weekends L4000/€2.07 a glass or L10,000/€5.17 for three), or indulge yourself with a **night** and a **meal** at the *Hotel Barolo*, Via Lo Mondo 2 (☎0173.563.54; ④), whose restaurant – an imperious place with a stiff dress code – is renowned hereabouts.

Just north of Barolo, **LA MORRA** is an earthy old village, with good views over the undulating vineyards from outside the *Belvedere* **restaurant** (☎0173.50.190; closed Mon) on Piazza Castello, which offers classic Albese cooking including wonderful *agnolotti* (a meal comes to around L60,000/€30.99). The village is home to the Cantina Comunale di La Morra (Wed–Fri 11am–12.30pm & 2.30–5.30pm, Sat & Sun

10am–12.30pm & 2.30–6pm; free), in which you can taste and buy wine. There are also some good food shops, with a wide range of local cheeses, and if you're there on a Monday, you can pick up bargains at the market. As for staying over, there's the *Italia* **hotel** at Via Roma 30 (☎0173.50.609; ③).

The Cantina Comunale has maps of **walks** through the vineyards, best of which is the one to **ANNUNZIATA**, about half an hour down the hill, where there's a private wine museum, the **Museo "Ratti" dei Vini d'Alba** at Frazione Annunziata 2 (Mon–Fri 8.30am–noon & 2.30–6pm, Sat & Sun phone in advance, ☎0173.50.185; free), housed in a Renaissance abbey next to the firm's cantina. Laid out in a musty cellar, the museum has a number of intriguing exhibits – a massive barrel for treading grapes, a primitive wine tanker, consisting of an elongated barrel on a rickety cart, and a collection of Roman wine jugs found in the area. Best of all, there's a letter from an Arctic explorer, congratulating the Ratti on the fact that their Barolo had stood up to the rigours of travel and climate on an expedition to the North Pole. Wine at the Ratti cantina is expensive, and you can only buy it in lots of six. It's far cheaper and is sold in single bottles at the small family cantina, Oberto Severino, a kilometre or so up the road back towards La Morra.

Asti and around

The wine connection continues in **Asti**, 30km north of Alba, and the capital of Italy's sparkling wine industry, being the most famous producer of *spumante*. For most of the year Asti itself is fairly sedate, a small town, not unattractive, but it becomes the focus of attention in September every year, as it gears up for its Palio. Though it's taken nothing like as seriously as Siena's more famous event (see p.541), and has to some extent been revived for tourists, you'd be mad to miss it if you're near here at the right time. The surrounding area hides a fine Romanesque abbey near **Albugnano**, the more profane attraction of steamy spa waters at **Acqui Terme**, and a rare glimpse of Italy's Jewish history in the grand synagogue of **Casale Monferrato**.

Asti

In the run-up to its annual Palio, **ASTI** throws off its sedate air and hosts street banquets and a medieval market. On the day of the race itself, the third Sunday in September, there's a thousand-strong procession of citizens dressed as their fourteenth-century ancestors, before the frenetic bare-backed horse race around the arena of the Campo del Palio – followed by the awarding of the *palio* (banner) to the winner and all-night feasting and boozing.

The rest of the year the Campo del Palio is a vast, bleak car park, and there's frankly not a lot to see. The arcaded **Piazza Alfieri** is officially the centre of town, behind which the **Collegiata di San Secondo** (Mon–Sat 10.45am–noon & 3.30–5.30pm, Sun 3.30–5.30pm) is dedicated to the city's patron saint, built on the site of the saint's martyrdom in the second century. There's nothing left of the second-century church but there is a fine sixth-century crypt, its columns so slender that they seem on the verge of toppling over. As for the rest of the church, it's a slick, early-Gothic construction, with neat red-brick columns topped with tidily carved capitals and in the left aisle a polyptych by one of Asti's Renaissance artists, Gandolfino d'Asti. The Palio banners are also kept here, housed in a heavily ornate Baroque chapel, along with the Carroccio – a sacred war chariot used in medieval times.

The main street, **Corso Alfieri**, slices through the town from the Piazza Alfieri, to the east of which the church of **San Pietro** at Corso Alfieri 2 (Tues–Fri 9am–1pm & 3–5pm, Sat 10am–1pm & 3–6pm, Sun 10am–1pm) has a circular twelfth-century

Baptistry, now used as an exhibition space, and a **museum**, housed in what was a pilgrim's hospice, displaying an odd – and badly labelled – assortment of Roman and Egyptian artefacts. At the other end of the Corso, the **Torre Rossa** is a medieval tower with a chequered top, built on the foundations of the Roman tower in which San Secondo, a Roman soldier, was imprisoned before being killed.

Practicalities

Asti's **tourist office** is on Piazza Alfieri (Mon–Sat 9.30am–1pm & 2.30–6.30pm, plus occasional summer Sundays 10am–1pm; ☎0141.530.357, fax 0141.538.200), and has information on the Palio and maps of the town. If you're intending to go to Asti on the Palio weekend, book a **room** well in advance; at other times there should be little problem. The best of the affordable options are the conveniently sited *Cavour* at Piazza Marconi 18 (☎0141.530.222; ③) and the slightly cheaper *Genova*, Corso Alessandria 26 (☎0141.593.197; ②). As somewhere renowned for its food perhaps should, Asti has a wide choice of **restaurants**, ranging from basic and cheap pizzerias like *Monna Laura*, Via Cavour 30 (closed Mon), to places serving local cuisine like *Trattoria Aurora*, Viale Partigiana 58 (closed Mon), and the excellent *Gener Neuv*, Lungotanaro dei Pescatori 4 (closed Sun evening and Mon). If you're into *spumante* or want to sample the other wines of the region, there is a **wine festival** from the second Friday to the third Sunday in September, the Festa della Douya d'Or, with wine tastings in the piazzas of the *centro storico* from early evening until midnight.

Around Asti

Although Alba is a better base for visiting vineyards and wine museums, **COSTIGLIOLE D'ASTI**, a short bus ride south of Asti, is the centre of Asti Spumante production; it has the Cantina dei Vini di Costigliole d'Asti at Via Roma 9 (open weekends only), and a predictably pricey gastronomic **restaurant** in its castle.

Immediately east of Asti, the area around the industrial provincial capital of **ALESSANDRIA**, is scattered with castles, though all are privately owned and only occasionally opened to the public. Alessandria itself is famous for being the home of the Borsalino hat (the kind with the dented crown, favoured by American gangsters), but there is little reason to step foot outside the station unless you're interested in modern Italian architecture, in which case you might like to check out the exterior of two of Ignazio Gardella's seminal works: the tuberculosis clinic at Via Gasparolo 2–4 and the Borsalino Company's residential building at Corso Borsalino 15–17.

ACQUI TERME, to the south, is a spa town, with a steaming sulphurous spring, La Bollente, gurgling up from a pavilion in its slightly shabby main piazza. The efficacy of Acqui's spas earned the attention of Romans from Pliny to Seneca, but there's only one substantial relic from its Roman heyday – an aqueduct below the main bridge. The seventeenth-century Castello dei Paleologi, next to the cathedral, contains an **archeological museum** (Tues–Sat 10am–noon & 3–6pm; L4000/€2.07), displaying the remains of mosaics and statues from the Roman spa.

North of Asti, **CASALE MONFERRATO** has the dubious distinction of being cement capital of Italy, but it's also home to the country's most sumptuous **synagogue**, tucked down an alley off Via Saloman Olmer, the first left off the main Via Roma (Sat & Sun 10am–12.30pm & 3–6.30pm, on weekdays ring next door for entrance). A rich, gold-encrusted affair with a voluptuously curving pulpit and a "museum of treasures" laid out in the closed-off women's gallery, the synagogue is a leftover from the days when there was a sizeable Jewish population in Piemonte, most of whom had fled from Spain in the sixteenth century to escape persecution. Casale was home to nearly 200 Jewish families, who lived here in peace until Mussolini's racial laws (brought in mainly to appease Hitler) forced many to leave.

Between Asti and Casale Monferrato is the small town of **MONCALVO**, tucked into a fold in the hills and surrounded by fields of sunflowers, vineyards and acres of corn. If you have the cash and want to spoil yourself in restful surroundings, head for the *Locanda di Sant'Uffizio* (☎0141.916.292; ⑦), 4km south of Moncalvo at Cioccaro di Penango, a luxury hotel in a seventeenth-century ecclesiastical palace, with antique-filled rooms, a gourmet restaurant and a swimming pool. If the *menu degustazione* seems a little excessive, there are plenty of agriturismo places to eat at nearby, or try the *Ametista* at Piazza Antico Castello 14 (closed Wed) in Moncalvo itself, which offers country dishes such as pepperoni flan with *bagna caoda*.

Most easily reached with your own transport, the **Abbazia di Vezzolano** (daily 9am–1pm & 2–5pm, open until 6pm on Sun), in the village of **ALBUGNANO**, deep in a valley to the northwest of Asti, displays some of the area's best late-Romanesque architecture. According to legend the abbey was founded by Charlemagne, who had a religious vision on the site in the eighth century. Outside it has a fancily arcaded and sculpted facade and a secluded Romanesque cloister. Inside, there's a stone rood screen carved with expressive scenes from the life of Mary, and a row of naive, rustic-looking saints.

Eastern Piemonte: Vercelli and Novara

A less typically Mediterranean landscape than the area **east of Turin** would be difficult to imagine. The vast paddy fields here produce more rice than anywhere in Europe, on a deadly flat plain across which road and rail cut on their way to Milan. For about half the year the fields are flooded (with warm water in winter), and are at their most evocative in autumn when the weak sun filters through the mists, making the stalk-spiked waters gleam. Most people are ready to move on, though, just as soon as the novelty wears off.

Vercelli

The centre of Piemonte's – indeed Europe's – rice-growing region is **VERCELLI**, where business people come to wheel and deal over prices in the Borsa del Riso, or rice stock exchange. If you've time to spare between trains, the **Basilica of Sant'Andrea**, just across from the station, is worth a peek. Built in the thirteenth century by a cardinal, its construction was funded with revenues from a Cambridgeshire monastery granted him by King Henry III as a reward for helping to establish him on the English throne. As the revenues were vast, it took only nine years to complete – an incredible feat at a time when churches frequently took over a century to build – and today it's an important church architecturally, one of the first in Italy to incorporate Gothic elements: pointed arches, slender columns shooting up to the vaults, and tall, slim conical-roofed belltowers flanking the facade.

The **Cattedrale di Sant'Eusebio**, at the end of Via Bicchieri, also deserves a visit, built on the site of a much more ancient basilica and with some fine old treasures and manuscripts in its library. Otherwise Vercelli's most atmospheric spot is **Piazza Cavour**, just off the main Corso Libertà, surrounded by pleasantly scruffy arcades and the scene of the Tuesday market. Close by, on Via Borgogna, the large **Museo Pinacoteca Borgogna** (summer Tues & Fri 2.30–5pm, Sat & Sun 9.30am–noon; winter Tues & Fri 3–5.30pm, Sat & Sun 9.30am–noon; free) holds the work of relatively unknown local artists together with the odd Brueghel and Jan Steen and some frescoes taken from local churches.

Vercelli's **tourist office** is at Viale Garibaldi 90 (Mon–Fri 8am–noon & 2.30–6.30pm; ☎0161.257.888). Finding a **room** in Vercelli can be a problem, with the hotels often full with rice-trade reps and the overspill from Turin's industrial fairs; it's advisable to phone in advance. The cheapest options are the *Rondinella*, Corso Gastaldi 15 (☎0161.250.835; ①), outside the bus station and a couple of minutes' walk to the right of the train station, and the *Valsesia*, at Via G. Ferraris 104 (☎0161.250.842; ②); both hotels have **restaurants** with very reasonably priced food.

Novara

NOVARA, twenty minutes further down the train line towards Milan, makes for a more elegant, unhurried stopover than Vercelli, its main street, **Corso Cavour**, neatly paved with half-moon cobbles and lined with *pasticcerie* and old-fashioned tearooms. That said, there's not much left of historic Novara: the medieval **Broletto** houses an open-air cinema in summer, and the **Duomo** is an overblown Neoclassical creation which dwarfs all around to Lilliputian proportions; inside are bits and pieces from earlier churches – a fifth-century **Baptistry** with tenth-century frescoes of the Apocalypse, and a frescoed twelfth-century chapel – both open only in the morning. A couple of blocks north, the weird three-tiered dome of the church of **San Gaudenzio** with its syringe-like spire dominates the whole town. It was built by Antonelli, a nineteenth-century architect responsible for a similar monstrosity, the Mole in Turin.

Novara's **tourist office** is centrally placed at Piazza Matteotti 1 (Mon–Thurs 8am–2.15pm & 3.30–6pm, Fri 8am–2.15pm). The cheapest **hotel** is the *Cristallo* on Largo Cantelli 7 (☎0321.452.681; ②), though you might prefer to splash out on a little more comfort at the *Garden*, at Corso Garibaldi 25 (☎0321.625.094; ③). There's a reasonable **pizzeria**, *Le Tre Lanterne*, at Via dei Tornielli 1, just off Piazza Gramsci at the end of Corso Cavour.

Northern Piemonte: Biella, Varallo and Valsesia

The main attraction of northern Piemonte is really the mountains, especially the dramatic Alpine **Valsesia**, which winds up to the foot of Monte Rosa on the Swiss border. On the way, stop off at two of the region's most visited sanctuaries, the **Santuario d'Oropa** near **Biella** and the **Sacro Monte** at **Varallo**. From here you're well poised either for Piemonte's mountains or those of Valle d'Aosta, a few kilometres west. Worth a slight detour is the magical train ride that starts at **Domodossola**, conveniently en route if you're heading for Switzerland or down to Milan.

Biella and Ivrea

A short train ride northwest from Novara, the provincial capital of **BIELLA** is known for its wool industry, its periphery choked with mills and the hilltop upper town with the mansions and villas of wool barons. It's not an especially rewarding place, apart perhaps from its small medieval quarter, reachable by funicular or by strolling up its many arcaded lanes. But it does give access to the **Santuario d'Oropa** (daily 7.30am–noon & 2–6pm; free), a forty-minute bus ride northwest of Biella at the foot of Monte Mucrone. Founded in the fourth century by St Eusebio to house a black statue of the Madonna and Child, this is an odd sort of attraction, and can't really compete with the sanctuary at Varallo (see overleaf) for sheer sensationalism. But it's the most venerated of Piemonte's shrines, the main church an immense neo-Baroque concoction, and it's a good starting-point also for **walks** into the surrounding mountains. If you wish, you can **stay at the sanctuary** itself, which has around 700 rooms (book through the

Biella tourist office; see below). A cable car runs regularly up Monte Mucrone as far as the (closed) *Albergo Savoia*, where a network of marked trails begins. One of the nicest and easiest is to the **Lago Mucrone**, a small mountain lake; more energetic is the hike up to the summit of Monte Mucrone itself – a two-hour trek.

Biella's **tourist office** is at Piazza Vittorio Veneto 3 (Mon–Sat 9am–12.30pm & 3–6.30pm, Sun 9am–12.30pm; ☎015.351.128, *www.atl.biella.it*). Though you should definitely move on if you can, you may need to stay overnight in Biella. The choice of **hotels** is limited, but you could try the three-star *Principe* at Via Gramsci 4 (☎015.252.2003; ④). If you do stay, swing by *La Baracca* at Via Costa di Riva 11b, a **nightclub** and art gallery in a converted nineteenth-century factory building that makes great use of light and glass.

IVREA, to the southwest of Biella, is well worth a visit in the week leading up to Shrove Tuesday, when there's a week-long **carnival**, featuring piping, drumming, masked balls, historic processions and fireworks, culminating in a bizarre three-day "Battle of the Oranges" when the whole town and hundreds of spectators turn out to pelt each other with oranges; it's important to know that you have to wear a red hat if you don't want to be a target. At the end of each day, the town is covered in a thick carpet of orange pulp, and the following morning there's a traditional handing out of polenta and cod. For a **place to stay**, try the small *Luca* at Corso Garibaldi 58 (☎0125.48.697; ②), or head 3km northeast out of town to the *Castello San Giuseppe* at Chiaverano d'Ivrea (☎0125.424.370; ⑤), a four-star hotel in a converted Carmelite monastery.

Varallo and Sacro Monte

Some 50km by train north of Novara, **VARALLO** marks the beginning of northern Piemonte's more picturesque reaches, surrounded by steep wooded hills and filled with Art Deco villas and Baroque *palazzi*. It's a pretty place in itself, very pleasant for a short visit, but most people come to see the sanctuary of **Sacro Monte**, just outside the town and connected by bus five times daily from the train station.

If you've only come for Sacro Monte you could make straight there from the station; if you want to see the town first – and it is worth a wander – the centre is a five-minute walk to the right along Corso Roma. On the way you pass the church of **San Gaudenzio**, anchored to a creeper-covered cliff and surrounded by arcades. It's less impressive inside, though there's a polyptych by the sixteenth-century Varallo-born artist Gaudenzio Ferrari, responsible for much of the work at Sacro Monte. The main street, **Corso Umberto I**, lined with shuttered and balconied palaces, winds through the town from here towards the River Serio. There's more work by Gaudenzio Ferrari in the church of **Madonna delle Grazie**, off to the north of Corso Umberto I at the end of Via Don Maio, where an entire wall is covered with colourful and detailed scenes from the life of Christ.

The **tourist office** is at Corso Roma 38 (Tues–Sun except some winter Sundays 9am–1pm & 3–7pm; ☎0163.51.280 or 0163.53.091). If you want to **stay over** in Varallo, try the *Monte Rosa* at Via Regaldi 4 (☎0163.51.100; ③), a wonderful, friendly, rambling old hotel a brisk five-minute walk away from the town centre. For **food**, the restaurant *Fra Dolcino*, opposite the station in Piazza Marconi 3, does falafel, couscous and kebabs, as well as good pizzas (closed Thurs).

Sacro Monte

Crowning the hill above Varallo, **Sacro Monte** (daily 7.30am–12.15pm & 2.15–6.30pm; free) is a complex of 45 chapels, each housing a 3-D tableau of painted statues against frescoed scenery representing a scene from the life of Christ. Founded in the fifteenth century by a friar anxious to popularize Catholicism in a region in which heresy was rife, Sacro Monte emphasizes sensationalism and spectacle, calculated to work upon the emotions of the uneducated. The sanctuary is at its best when busy: to get a measure of its continuing popularity, you need to visit on a Sunday, when it's full of families, pensioners and nuns, all of whom picnic in the shady grounds after finishing their pilgrimage.

Inevitably a bizarre spectacle, depicting the whole range of key biblical episodes from the Fall to Christ's birth, life and death, the tableaux don't pull any punches. The *Massacre of the Innocents* (#11) has a floor littered with dead babies, while Herod's army prepares to spear, hack and slash more. And the chapels (#30–41) that retell the events of Christ's passion are flagrant emotional manipulation, with crazed flagellators, spitting soldiers and a series of liberally blood-splattered Christs. By the time you reach the *Road to Calvary* (#36) you almost flinch at the sight of a flaked-out Christ being viciously kicked. Dominating the central piazza of the sanctuary, the Baroque **Basilica** offers some relief, the highlight being the cupola – a nice piece of optical trickery, encrusted with figures perched on bubblegum clouds.

Valsesia

From Varallo the main road follows the River Sesia to the foot of multipeaked Monte Rosa, whose massive bulk heads four Italian valleys and spreads north into Switzerland. **Valsesia**, the most easterly valley, is also the most dramatic – worth going for the ride even if you don't want to launch a hiking or skiing assault on the mountains.

Flanked by dark pine-wooded slopes crowned with a toothed ridge of rock, the road winds up the valley, the perspective changing at every turn. It's a well-touristed area (mainly by Italians and Germans), and traditional houses with slate roofs and wood-slatted balconies mingle with Alpine-style villas and apartments. The villages are crowded for much of the summer, and with weekend skiers in the winter. September is the quietest month, when many of the hotels close, but the weather up the mountains is unpredictable then, and hiking can be hazardous.

The Valsesia villages were founded in the thirteenth century by religious sects from the Swiss Valais, known as Walser, in search of land and the freedom to worship. There are reckoned to be around 3000 true Walsers in the valleys of Monte Rosa, and in most bars and shops you'll still hear people speaking a dialect based on ancient German. If you want to see how these isolated communities lived and worked, there's a **Walser Museum** (July daily 2–6pm; Aug 1–21 daily 10am–noon & 2–6pm; Aug 22–June Sat & Sun 2–6pm or by appointment, ☎0163.922.935; free), a traditionally furnished seventeenth-century house in the hamlet of **PEDEMONTE**, ten minutes' walk out of Alagna.

ALAGNA, at the head of the valley, right below Monte Rosa, is the most convenient place to stay, whether you want to ski or hike. Popular and predominantly modern, it has a cluster of wood-slatted Walser houses to the south, with a tiny network of overgrown tracks winding in between them. Some houses still function as farms, with hay hanging to dry on the slats and wood stacked behind, while others are holiday homes, with geraniums tumbling from window boxes. Alagna's cheapest **hotel** is the *Mirella*, in the suburb of Bonda (☎0163.922.965; ③); there are also the more central but more expensive *Genzianella*, Via Centro 33 (☎0163.922.915; ⑤), the *Monte Rosa* on the same street (☎0163.922.994; ④), and the *Cristallo* (☎0163.91.285; ⑤), next to the **tourist office** (Tues–Sun 9am–1pm & 3–6pm; ☎0163.922.988) on the appropriately named Piazza degli Alberghi.

There are lots of **walks** among the foothills, all of which are well marked from Alagna. If you're interested in seeing more than mountain scenery, follow a path 5km back down the valley to **RIVA VALDOBBIA**, whose church facade is covered with a colourful late sixteenth-century fresco of *The Last Judgement*. However, the toughest and most spectacular hikes are those on **Monte Rosa** itself. It's possible to save time and energy by taking the cable car up to Punta Indren (3260m), from where you can walk to one of the many *rifugi;* most of these are open from June to September, but check at the tourist office in Alagna before setting out. Failing that, you could walk down into the next valley, Val Gressoney in Valle d'Aosta (see opposite).

All these walks involve a good deal of scree-crossing and some sobering drops, and none are to be taken lightly – you'll need a good **map** (the FMB map of the four Monte Rosa valleys shows all paths, *rifugi* and pistes as does the Kompass *Monte Rosa* map), and you should monitor the weather carefully. There's also an ambitious long-distance circuit of Monte Rosa, starting at Alagna, taking in Val Gressoney, Val d'Ayas and Zermatt across the Swiss border: you'll need five days if you make use of ski-lifts and cable cars, and a good deal longer than that if you don't.

Skiing in the area is organized by Monterosa Ski, who have an office in Alagna, and equipment is available for rent in the village. However, the runs are narrow, and though experienced skiers can cross into Val Gressoney, it involves walking as well as off-piste skiing. The valleys are also popular for **canoeing and rafting**, and several centres organize classes and excursions: contact the Canoa Club Valsesia on Via Vetti in Varallo (☎0163.542.45) for more information.

Domodossola and over the border to Locarno

At the foot of the Simplon Pass, but handily situated on the main train line between Milan and Bern, in Switzerland, and with frequent trains (15 daily) from Novara, is the little town of **DOMODOSSOLA**. With its arcaded medieval centre and market square, it warrants a visit in its own right, but is more famous as the starting point of a scenic train ride. "La Vigezzina", a small, pale-blue train, connects Domodossola with Locarno, across the border in Switzerland, taking in the vineyards and chestnut forests of the Val Vigezzo and Centovalli along the way. The scenery is gorgeous, and, although the ride is pricier than the regular train, it is well worth it; InterRail passes are valid in any case, if you have one. The journey to Locarno takes an hour and a half, but you can get off and explore at any of the pretty flower-strewn stations en route; when you want the next train to stop, just remember to raise the red and white signal on the platform. An alternative way back is to take the hydrofoil from Locarno across Lago Maggiore to Arona (covered in the "Lombardy and the Lakes" chapter, see p.196).

VALLE D'AOSTA

Fringed by Europe's highest mountains, Mont Blanc, the Matterhorn and Monte Rosa, veined with valleys and studded with castles, **Valle d'Aosta** is undeniably picturesque. The central Aosta valley cuts right across the region, following the River Dora to the foot of Mont Blanc on the French border. Along the river are most of the feudal castles for which Valle d'Aosta is famed – the majority built by the Challant family, who ruled the region for seven centuries. Although the castles are pretty from the outside, and easily accessible by bus or train, few are absorbing enough to warrant a special trip into the region. But as skiing and walking country, Valle d'Aosta is unsurpassed.

Valle d'Aosta is the least Italian of all the regions. Its landscape and architecture are Swiss, the official language French, and in some valleys the locals, whose ancestors emigrated from Switzerland, still speak a dialect based on German. In fact, although Italian is more widely spoken than French, bilingualism is an essential part of Valle d'Aosta's identity, which is quite distinct from other parts of the north – a distinctiveness reflected in its greater administrative and financial autonomy.

Aosta, the regional capital, is the only town of any size and, with its attractive cobbled streets and good shopping, it makes an excellent staging post on the way to the smaller mountain resorts. As for the countryside, the main valley is for the most part rather bland, and it's in the more scenic tributary valleys that you'll want to spend most of your time. The eastern valleys are the most touristed, with ski resorts and narrow, winding roads that can get choked with holiday traffic. If you're walking, you're best off heading for the valleys in the west, inside the protected zone of Italy's largest national park, the **Gran Paradiso**. The valleys here can also be busy – the mountain *rifugi* as well as the hotels get packed in summer – but development is restrained.

Getting around on public transport demands patience. Buses run from Piemonte along the main valley past most of the castles, but buses into many of the tributary valleys are rare. The road branches off at Aosta into Switzerland via the Grand-St-Bernard Pass (where you can stop to take clichéd photos of the famous dogs) and forks again some 30km further west at Pré-St-Didier: both branches run into France – the southern via the Petit-St-Bernard Pass to Chambéry, the northern to Chamonix through the Mont Blanc tunnel. Because of the border posts, the road is much used by long-distance lorries, which are something of an earache and eyesore. Trains are less regular and run only as far as Pré-St-Didier, but by using a combination of the two, you can get just about everywhere, though for serious exploration of the quieter valleys, your own vehicle is a definite advantage.

The road to Aosta and the eastern valleys

The tributary valleys in **eastern Valle d'Aosta** have suffered most from the skiing industry, although experienced mountain hikers may be allured by the challenge of climbing Monte Rosa and the Matterhorn from **Valtournenche**. Less ambitious walkers will find most to do in the **Val Gressoney**, which still has a number of traditional villages settled by the Swiss Walsers, while in the main Aosta valley there are two of the region's more interesting castles, **Issogne** and **Fénis**.

Val Gressoney

The **Val Gressoney** is the first of the Valle d'Aosta valleys, but you could be forgiven for thinking you'd stepped into an ad-maker's Switzerland. The grass is velvety green, the River Lys crystal clear, the traditional houses wood-slatted and the modern ones gleaming Alpine chalets, while the craggy head of the valley is overlooked by one of Monte Rosa's shimmering glaciers. As you might expect from such natural advantages, the valley gets busy, especially at weekends and holidays: the walking is good, and the skiing isn't bad either, with pistes laid out on rocky south-facing slopes that are great for catching the sun but which get a little slushy by the afternoon in late season.

At the mouth of the valley, **PONT-ST-MARTIN** was named for the single-spanned Roman bridge that dominates the village. According to legend it was donated by the devil in exchange for the first soul that crossed it. However, St Martin tricked him by sending a dog over, thus securing a bridge for the villagers and his own immortalization in the village's name. Pont-St-Martin's usefulness as a bus and train terminus outweighs its attractiveness, and there's little reason to hang around – especially as buses run fairly regularly up the valley.

The valley comes into its own at **GRESSONEY-ST-JEAN** and **GRESSONEY-LA-TRINITÉ**. These are popular but attractive resorts, especially La Trinité, which is close to the head of the valley and is cheaper than St-Jean, with some good, homely hotels. It also makes a convenient starting-point for walks, though be warned that the true beginning of the summer walking season doesn't start until late June: between Easter and then, most hotels are closed. If you want to do more than wander along the river, a track leads up to the lovely mountain lake, **Gabiet** – a two- to three-hour walk (you can go part way by ski-lift or cable car) – from where you can continue over the mountain into the Valsesia, doing the last part of the descent by cable car if you're tired. Val Gressoney's Walser settlements can be reached by footpaths from La Trinité; one of the nicest is **BIEL**, with some eighteenth-century houses (maps available from La Trinité's tourist office, see below). The Walsers still speak their German dialect, and French and Italian too, and the trilingual signs you'll see are not only for the benefit of tourists.

La Trinité's **tourist office** (Mon–Wed, Fri & Sat: March–Sept 9am–7pm; Oct–Feb 10am–5pm) is on the main piazza, across the river from the bus stop. Most **hotels** in the area are quite expensive, but the *Gressoney*, for example, at Via Lys 3 in St-Jean (☎0125.355.986; ⑨), has huge king-sized beds and is worth splashing out on if you feel like some four-star comfort (avoid eating there though and have a pizza in the village instead). At Gabiet is the one-star *Del Ponte* (☎0125.366.180; ③), and there are a couple of less expensive places around St-Jean too: *La Stella* at Località Steina (☎0125.355.068; ③) and *Grünes Wasser* on the Strada Regionale 41 at no. 14 (☎0125.355.403; ③).There are also a couple of **campsites** just beyond St-Jean: *Località La Pineta* (☎0125.355.370) and *Camping Gressoney* (☎0125.355.264).

Verrès and Issogne

Buses and trains continue up the main valley to **VERRÈS**, an undistinguished village overlooked by the gloomy cube of its virtually impregnable fourteenth-century **fortress** (Sun 10am–6pm; L6000/€3.10). This is a stark, primitive place, built by the lord of the town, Ibelto di Challant, primarily as a military stronghold. The spartan soldiers' quarters give some idea of the conditions under which they lived; the Challants' quarters are barely more comfortable, although their fortress does go down in the history books as one of the first to install a toilet. If you need a **room** in Verrès for the night, there are some very basic ones in the *Hotel Ghibli* (☎0125.929.316; ①), at Viale Stazione 9, three minutes' walk from the train station.

The castle at **ISSOGNE** (daily: March–Sept 9am–6pm; Oct–Feb 10am–5pm; L10,000/€5.17) is of greater interest than its counterpart at Verrès – though another residence of the Challants, it's a far more comfortable and civilized dwelling. Few buses go there, but it's only a short walk from the bus stop outside Verrès. Set unceremoniously in the centre of Issogne village, from the outside the castle resembles a municipal building, and you'll probably wonder why you bothered to come. But the well-preserved interior is one of Valle d'Aosta's best examples of a late-Gothic ducal residence – with an arcaded courtyard, some vivid frescoes and coffered-ceilinged rooms filled with Gothic furniture.

In the centre of the courtyard is an unusual fountain – a wrought-iron pomegranate tree with water spurting from the lower branches. The courtyard's walls are patched with painted coats of arms, and in the shelter of one of the arcades is a colourful and bustling fresco of a medieval high street. From here, you pass through to the kitchens, a beautifully furnished dining room, a couple of chapels with ornate polyptychs, and into the Countess of Challant's bedroom, whose bedside chair conceals a commode. After seeing the castle, it's worth a look-in at the **exhibition of costume** (same hours and ticket as castle), which features well-researched reconstructions of those worn in the courtyard frescoes.

Val d'Ayas

Branching off the main valley, and headed by the huge mass of Monte Rosa, **Val d'Ayas** is one of the region's most beautiful valleys – large, open and flanked by thickly wooded slopes. As a result, it tends to be overwhelmed by visitors, and the tourist-geared villages are chock-full of trippers and skiers at the weekend and during high season – and correspondingly dead at other times of the year.

The main ski resort, **CHAMPOLUC**, at the head of the valley, is connected by a series of chair lifts to Staffal in the Val Gressoney. It's also the base for the tough ascent (4hr minimum; route #62) of the **Testa Grigia** (3315m) – although you can cheat on this by taking the funicular and ski-lift part of the way. From the top there's a superb view across the peaks of the Matterhorn to Mont Blanc; however, unless you can afford a **guide** (contact the Alpine Guide Association of Champoluc on ☎0125.308.960, or the Champoluc tourist office, at Via Varasc 16, ☎0125.307.113, fax 0125.307.785) the climb is strictly for the experienced.

BRUSSON, further down the valley, is a better base for less demanding walks. There's a trail (3hr 30min; route #6) up to seven mountain lakes, starting with a long climb through a dense wood up to a waterfall – the water drops 30m, and is most impressive in spring when the snow is melting.

The **hotel** *Beau Site* at Rue Trois Villages 2 (☎0125.300.144; ③), on the edge of Brusson, is clean, simple and has a good **restaurant**. In Champoluc hotels are expensive, but the *Cré-Forné* hotel (☎0125.307.197; ③) at **CREST** (connected with Champoluc by funicular) is a good alternative. There are also **campsites** between Brusson and Champoluc: try the *Camping Deans* (☎0125.300.297) in località Extrapieraz.

Valtournenche and the Matterhorn (Cervino)

VALTOURNENCHE, headed by the Matterhorn, or Cervino as the Italians call it, should be one of the most spectacular of Italy's mountain valleys, but unfortunately the main towns are overdeveloped and hydroelectric works ruin the views on the plains. The international ski resort Breuil-Cervinia is a purely functional modern resort, and even the Matterhorn is a let-down, with tribes of skiers ensuring that its glacier is grubby for much of the year. That said these are the Alps, and if you can't manage to carry on to the other valleys further west, you will at least get a taste of chocolate-box chalets and flower-covered meadows straight out of Heidi.

Breuil-Cervinia
BREUIL-CERVINIA was one of Italy's first ski resorts, built in the prewar years as part of Mussolini's drive for a healthy nation. In its day the ski lifts, soaring to 3500m, broke all records, and its grand hotels ensured the patronage of Europe's wealthy. Today the wealthy are cossetted in modern buildings outside the resort, leaving the tacky streets of the town for packaged hordes attracted by a large skiing area with lots of easy runs.

If you want to climb the **Matterhorn** (4476m), you should seriously consider approaching from Zermatt in Switzerland; the Italian route is strictly for experts. If undeterred, you'll need the FMB map, which covers Valtournenche and the Monte Rosa valleys, and to be very well equipped. There are two *rifugi* on the way, *Duca degli Abruzzi* (☎0166.949.145; mid-July to mid-Sept), two hours fifteen minutes from Breuil in Orionde (2800m), and the *Rifugio Jean A Carrel* (☎0166.948.169; open all year) – where most people stay the night – four hours beyond (3850m). From the *Carrel rifugio* it's a tough climb to the summit, even with the ropes that have been fitted along the more dangerous stretches of the route.

The less agile members of the smart set now head to **ST VINCENT**, an unattractive spa resort near the industrial town of Chatillon at the mouth of the valley. There's a famous **casino** here, but a distinct lack of Monte Carlo glitz on the streets. If you end up with time to spare between buses, the parish **church** (Parrocchiale) is quite interesting, with the excavations of the baths of a Roman villa around the outside and lively frescoes inside.

Nus and the Castello di Fénis

NUS, further up the main valley from Chatillon, is a small, pretty village, overlooked by a ruined castle, that makes a good base for the **Castello di Fénis** 2km away (daily: March–Sept 9am–7pm; Oct–Feb 10am–5pm; L6000/€3.10). Backed by wooded hills and encircled by two rows of turreted walls, the castle is a fairy-tale cluster of towers decorated with scalloped arcades. These defences were primarily aesthetic, with the real job of protecting the valley being left to the less prettified fortresses of nearby Nus and Quart, while the Fénis branch of the Challant counts concentrated on refining their living quarters with fine Gothic frescoes. The best of these is in the courtyard, above the elaborate twin staircase that leads to the upper storeys. A courtly St George rescues a damsel in distress from the clutches of a tremendous dragon, overlooked by a tribe of protective saints brandishing moral statements on curling scrolls.

There's a **hotel** in Fénis – *La Chatelaine* (☎0165.764.264; ①), in località Chez Sapin, open year-round. However, as Nus has a train station and is close to the main road for buses, you may find it more convenient to sleep there: the *Florian* at Via Risorgimento 3 (☎0165.767.968; ②), has clean and comfortable doubles and is also open all year.

Aosta and around

The attractive mountain town of **AOSTA** was founded by the Romans in 25 BC after they disposed of the local tribe by auctioning them off in a slave market. It was primarily a military camp, but little survives from the era. More remains of medieval Aosta, its narrow cobbled streets and overhanging upper storeys giving the place a very alpine air. The town's key attraction though is its position: encircled by the **Alps**, and with access to the lovely valleys of the **Parco Nazionale del Gran Paradiso**, the ski resorts of **Mont Blanc**, and a sprinkling of castles in between, it's an ideal base for exploring the northwest of the region, before heading on to Switzerland or France.

The Town

The centre of town is marked by **Piazza E. Chanoux** and its pavement cafés, from where Via Porta Pretoria and Via Sant'Anselmo lead east, forming the main axis of the town centre and the principal street for window-shopping and people-watching. At the far end, the **Porta Pretoria** is one of the town's most impressive sights: two parallel triple-arched gateways which formed the main entrance into the Roman town. The space in between was for soldiers to keep a check on visitors to the town, and a family of medieval nobles later made their home above it, building a tower which now houses temporary exhibitions.

North of the gate there are further relics of the Roman occupation in the **Teatro Romano** (daily: April–Sept 9am–8pm; rest of year 9am–6.30pm; free), of which a section of the four-storeyed facade remains, 22m high and pierced with arched windows. Unfortunately for some years it has been hidden behind scaffolding, and no one will risk estimating a date for completion of the restoration. Close by, the medieval **Torre Fromage** at Via du Baillage is now a contemporary art exhibition-space (daily 9.30am–12.30pm & 2.30–6.30pm).

A short walk east of here, outside the main town walls off Via Sant'Anselmo, the church of **Sant'Orso** houses a number of tenth-century frescoes behind its dull facade, hidden up in the roof where you can examine them at close quarters from specially constructed walkways – though you'll need to find the sacristan to get up there. If you can't find him, content yourself with the fifteenth-century choir stalls, carved with a menagerie of holy men and animals, ranging from bats and monkeys to a tonsured

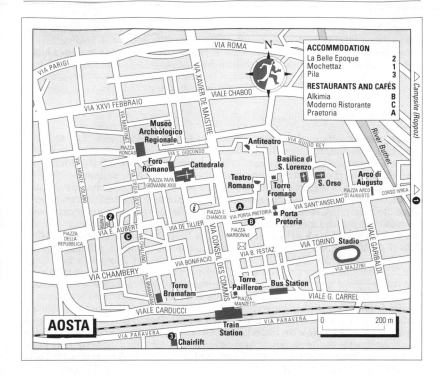

monk. There are even better carvings on the eye-level capitals of the intimate Romanesque **cloisters** (daily 9am–6.30pm) – mostly scenes from the story of Christ, with an undue emphasis on donkeys and sheep. The **priorate**, closed at the time of writing but forecast to reopen at the end of 2001, has terracotta decorations on its outside walls and an octagonal tower which rises above the complex. Nearby are the recently discovered fifth-century remains of the **Basilica of San Lorenzo** (daily 9am–7pm; free), which are well-explained (in Italian) and worth a peek on your way past.

At the far end of Via Sant'Anselmo, the **Arco di Augusto** was erected in 25 BC to celebrate the seizure of the territory from the local Salassi tribe and to honour Emperor Augustus, after whom the town was named Augusta Praetoria (Aosta is a corruption of Augusta). Though the arch loses something islanded in a sea of traffic and topped by an ugly eighteenth-century roof, it's a sturdy-looking monument, the mountains behind only adding to its measure of dignity. Beyond is a well-preserved **Roman bridge**, its single arch spanning the dried-up bed of the River Buthier.

On the other side of the centre of town, the **Foro Romano** on Piazza Giovanni XXIII is the misleading name for another Roman relic, a vaulted passage under the actual forum area, the purpose of which is unclear. Nearby, is the **Museo Archaeologico Regionale** (daily 9am–7pm; free), with interesting exhibits on the settlements based around Aosta since Celtic times. The **Cattedrale** next door looks unpromising from the outside, but masks a Gothic interior with even more fantastically carved choir stalls than Sant'Orso's, with a mermaid, lion and snail among the saints. Remains of a fourth-century baptistry are visible through the floor; better are the mosaics on the presbytery pavement showing the two rivers of earthly paradise and Christ, holding the sun and moon, surrounded by the symbols of the months. There are more treasures in the cathedral **museum** (April–Sept Mon–Sat 9.30–11.30am & 3–5.30pm; Sun 3–5.30pm; rest of the year by appointment, ☎0165.40.413; L4000/€2.07) – gold-, silver- and gemencrusted reliquaries and equally ornate chalices, crucifixes and caskets for relics.

Practicalities

Aosta's **tourist office** (June–Sept daily 9am–1pm & 3–8pm; Oct–May Mon–Sat 9am–1pm & 3–8pm, Sun 9am–1pm; ☎0165.236.627, *www.regione.vda.it/turismo*) is at Piazza E. Chanoux 8 and has maps and other information on the town and around. You can get to most places within the region by bus from the **bus station** on Viale G. Carrel, but some of the more remote valleys are served by only one bus a week out of season. Trains run from the **train station** at Piazza Manzetti, south of the centre, west along the main valley only as far as Pré-St-Didier. The best bet is to arm yourself with the combined bus and train timetable from the tourist office and use both.

The first choice for a **hotel room** would be *La Belle Epoque* at Via d'Avise 8, off Via Aubert (☎0165.262.276; ②), which is modern, clean and compact. Alternatively, the *Mochettaz*, Corso Ivrea 107 (☎0165.43.706; ②), charges slightly less, while the *Albergo Pila*, Via Paravera 12b (☎0165.43.398; ②), is good value, though it's a ten-minute walk from the centre of town on the far side of the train line. All these hotels are open year-round. There are a number of **campsites** nearby: *Milleluci*, about a kilometre away in località Roppoz (☎0165.235.278; year-round), is just on the outskirts of town. Finding **somewhere to eat** is no problem: you could try the *Praetoria*, Via Sant'Anselmo 9 (closed Thurs), a family-style trattoria; the *Alkimia* at Via Porta Pretoria 43 (closed Mon), for snacks; or the *Moderno Ristorante*, Via E Aubert 21, a friendly, lively place with a wide choice of dishes (closed Thurs). Otherwise Via E. Aubert and Via Porta Pretoria are the best streets to trawl.

West from Aosta: three castles

Both road and rail run west from Aosta through the main valley, passing a number of **castles**. All of these are easy to reach on public transport, and after visiting you can catch a bus into the valleys of the Gran Paradiso National Park.

The first of the castles is the thirteenth-century **Castello di Sarre**, accessible by bus or train from Aosta (July & Aug daily 9am–8pm; L10,000/€5.17). It's a ten-minute walk up a hill covered with apple orchards from the St Maurice train station; coming by bus, walk from the bus stop up the main road and take the unmarked turning just before the toll-booth. Sarre is the former hunting lodge of Vittorio Emanuele II, who actually bought the castle by mistake. He had set his sights on the castle of Aymaville opposite, but the agent sent to buy the castle was confused about the direction in which the river flowed, and ended up buying Sarre instead.

Vittorio Emanuele made the best of a bad job, permanently stamping the halls of the castle with his astounding taste in interior decor, pushing the hunting-lodge motif to its limits, with horns of wild ibex lining the main gallery, thousands of white chamois skulls studding the stuccoed festoons and horn-sprouting medallions that surround the stuffed heads of ibex. Pride of place is given to the first ibex slain by the king. The custodian claims that many died a natural death, but this was hardly the impression that Vittorio Emanuele, in his guise as macho huntsman, intended to convey. The rest of the castle is well patronized by diehard Italian monarchists who come to pay their respects to Savoy family trees, portraits and photographs and walls plastered with magazine features on the now-exiled Italian royals.

Five minutes further along the rail line, the **Castello di Saint-Pierre** (March 15–31 daily 9am–noon & 2–6pm; April to mid-Oct daily 9am–7pm; L5000/€2.58) perches on a rocky cliff, a crenellated and turreted castle that dates from the twelfth century but is mostly the result of a restyling in the eighteenth century. There's a small **natural history museum** inside with an array of stuffed birds, but unless this appeals you'd do well to press on.

A short walk along the main road beyond St-Pierre, set on a low hill above the river and invisible from the road, **Sarriod de La Tour** is less a castle than a medieval tower with farm buildings built around it, but it's a refreshingly rustic place with some appealing frescoes.

North from Aosta: the Col di San Bernardo

Immediately north of Aosta, the **Col di San Bernardo** (2473m) leads the way into Switzerland; it was named after the legendary **monastery** that for centuries provided shelter to travellers on the main pilgrim route from Northern Europe to Rome, and was the home of the eponymous big brown-and-white dogs who rescued Alpine travellers in distress. The history of the mountain pass is well documented in the **museum** (June–Sept daily 9am–6pm; 6 Swiss francs) housed in the monastery, although you'll need your passport to visit as it's situated just over the border in Switzerland. The spectacular pass is open only during summer, but the border is open year-round by way of a tunnel.

The Gran Paradiso National Park

For some of Valle d'Aosta's most beautiful mountains and valleys you need to make for the south of the region, down to the **Parco Nazionale di Gran Paradiso** – Italy's first national park, spread around the valleys at the foot of 4061-metre-high Gran Paradiso mountain.

Oddly enough the park owes its foundation to King Vittorio Emanuele II, who donated his extensive hunting park to the state in 1922, ensuring that the population of ibex that he and his hunters had managed to reduce to near-extinction survived. There are now around 3500 ibex here and about 6000 chamois, living most of the year above the tree line but descending to the valleys in winter and spring. The most dramatic sightings are during the mating season in November and December, when if you're lucky you'll see pairs of males fighting it out for the possession of a female. You might also see golden eagles nesting, and there are a number of rare types of alpine flower – most of which can be seen in the botanical garden in the Cogne Valley.

The park's three valleys – **Cogne**, **Valsavarenche** and **Val de Rhêmes** – are popular, but tourist development has been cautious and well organized. The hotels are good (you get far more for your money than you would in one of the nearby towns) and the campsites not too vast – though once you are inside the park boundaries you can pitch a tent between the hours of 9pm and 6am only. There are a few mountain *rifugi* and *bivacci* (unoccupied shelters) between which run well-marked footpaths. Though it's primarily a summer resort for walkers, the cross-country skiing is also good, and every winter a 45-kilometre Gran Paradiso Trek is organized at Cogne (contact the tourist office in Cogne for details – see below). The starting-point for the ascent of Gran Paradiso itself is **Pont** in the Valsavarenche, while **Cogne** gives access to the Alta Via 2, a long, high-level mountain trail.

There are regular buses throughout the year from Aosta to Cogne, but Valsavarenche and Val de Rhêmes are served by buses only in summer. At other times driving into either of these valleys is easiest from the village of **INTROD**, about 2km from **VILLENEUVE**, which is on the main bus route and a walkable distance from the castles of Saint-Pierre and Sarriod de la Tour.

Val di Cogne

The **Val di Cogne** is the principal, most popular and most dramatic section of the park. Its lower reaches are narrow, the road running above the fast-flowing Grand Eyvia River overlooked by sheer wavy-ridged mountains. Further on, the valley broadens out around the main village, **COGNE**, which is surrounded by gentle green meadows with glacier-covered mountains rising beyond.

The **tourist office** here, in the centre of the village (Mon–Sat 9am–12.30pm & 3–6pm, Sun 9am–12.30pm; ☎0165.74.040, *www.cogne.org*), has maps with descriptions in English of walks, one of which is an easy, scenic stroll that follows the river, with the glaciers in view for most of the way. **VALNONTEY** is a small village and starting-point for the steep, three-hour walk up to the *Rifugio V. Sella* (☎0165.74.310; Easter–Sept), a demanding hike that is incredibly popular on summer Sundays and in early August. The path passes a **botanical garden** (mid-June to mid-Sept daily 9.30am–12.30pm & 2.30–6.30pm; L3000/€1.55), with rare Alpine flora, then zigzags up through a forest and onto exposed mountainside before reaching the *rifugio*, set on a grassy plateau. At the mountain tarn of Lago Loson, a fifteen-minute walk from the *rifugio*, you may well spot **ibex** or more timid **chamois**, especially at sunset and sunrise, when there are fewer people around. Hardened hikers who can cope with a stretch of climbing can press on over the **Colle de Lauson** to the Val de Rhêmes.

There's a **campsite**, *Vallee de Cogne*, close to Cogne village in località Fabrique (☎0165.74.079; year-round), and two at Valnontey: *Lo Stambecco* (☎0165.74.152; mid-May to mid-Sept) and *Gran Paradiso* (☎0165.749.204; mid-May to mid-Sept). As for **hotels**, Cogne's most reasonable are the *Stambecco*, at Rue des Clementines 21 (☎0165.74.068; ④), and the *Bouton d'Or* at Viale Cavagnet 15 (☎0165.74.268; ④), which also has very reasonable singles. Both are open all year, although they can get booked up quickly in high season, and it's advisable to call ahead. Groups of two to six people may want to consider staying in one of the *Bellevue* hotel's self-contained **chalets** on Rue des Clementines (☎0165.74.825), which work out at about L200,000/€103 per person per night for half board – not the budget option, but the food is excellent.

Staying in Valnontey may be a better bet if you want to do some walking. There are a handful of affordable **alberghi** in the cluster of stone and wood chalets that make up the village centre: try *Herbetet* (☎0165.74.180; ③; mid-May to mid-Sept), the *Petit Dahu* (☎0165.74.146; ④), or the *Paradisia* (☎0165.74.158; ③; April–Oct). Stock up on picnic food and provisions before you leave Cogne because all Valnontey has to offer in the way of shops are lots of souvenir stalls and some "panoramic" restaurants.

Cogne's choice of **restaurants** is more limited, since most people stay on a half-pension basis, but you could try the rustic *Brasserie Bon Bec* on Rue Bourgeo, or the couple of **takeaways** and plenty of *salumerie* that will make up sandwiches for you.

Valsavarenche

Although not as spectacular as the Val di Cogne, **Valsavarenche**, the next valley west, has its own kind of beauty, attracting seasoned walkers rather than gentle amblers. The most popular route is the **ascent of Gran Paradiso**, from **PONT** at the end of the valley. Though reckoned to be the easiest of the higher Alps to climb, it is nevertheless a climb rather than a hike, with no path marked beyond the *Rifugio Vittorio Emanuele II* (☎0165.95.920; March 23–Sept 19), two and a half hours from Pont.

If you feel safer walking along footpaths, the best of the hikes are from the main village of **DEGIOZ**, otherwise known as Valsavarenche, up to the *Rifugio Orvielles* (2hr

30min) and then on to a series of high mountain lakes. This takes seven hours, but you can shorten it a bit by taking path #3a down to Pont. Less taxing is the two-hour walk from Pont towards the glacier **Grand Etret** at the head of the valley, although the first stretch is boring.

The only **hotel** in Degioz is the *Parco Nazionale* (☎0165.905.706; ③; New Year & mid-May to Sept), but in Pont there is the *Genzianella* (☎0165.95.393; ③; June–Sept). The area is well supplied with **campsites**, of which perhaps the nicest is *Pont Breuil* (☎0165.95.458; June–Sept), actually in Pont, with a well-stocked site shop (there's no other for miles); ibex come down to graze on the grassy meadow around the tents – so have your camera at the ready in the evening and early morning. There's also a site at località Pia de la Presse, *Gran Paradiso* (☎0165.95.451; June–Sept). There are **places to eat** in Degioz, but at Pont you'll have to cook for yourself, or ask at one of the hotels.

Val di Rhêmes

The least touristed but most open of the valleys, **Val di Rhêmes**, is also headed by glaciers. The best place to stay is **BREUIL**, a small hamlet outside Rhêmes-Notre-Dame at the end of the valley, from which most of the walks start. There's a fairly easy path along the river to a waterfall, the Cascata di Goletta, at its most spectacular after the spring snow-melt, and from here you can continue to the mountain lake of Goletta and the *Rifugio Albergo Benevolo* (☎0165.936.143; March 6–Sept 20). In Breuil, the *Hotel Breuil* (☎0166.949.537; ⑦) is conveniently central and is open all year, as is the *Edelweiss*, Via Guido Rey 18 (☎0166.949.078; ⑤), which has its own sauna and fitness facilities should hiking up and down mountains not prove exhausting enough. Further out, in Avouil, the *Leonardo Carrel* (☎0166.949.077; ②) is a fine **pensione** with good food and appealingly wood-panelled, Alpine-style rooms.

Arvier and Valgrisenche

Valgrisenche, a few kilometres west from Val di Rhêmes, is the wildest and least accessible of Valle d'Aosta's valleys. It's stunningly beautiful, narrow with rocky snow-dusted ridges rising above dark pine woods, although the upper reaches are defaced by the concrete dam of a reservoir. The only buses from Aosta into the valley are at 7am and 6pm in summer, and at 5.30am in winter, although buses and trains stop year-round at **ARVIER** at the mouth of the valley – one of the region's most appealing villages, with a small medieval core of twisting streets and stone houses alongside a gorge spanned by a Roman bridge. Arvier produces *L'Enfer d'Arvier*, reckoned to be the region's best wine. You really need your own transport to explore this area, but the effort is worth it.

In the village of **VALGRISENCHE** itself, the *Frassy* hotel (☎0165.97.100; ②) makes a good base, although it's only open July to mid-September. Nearby the hamlet of **BONNE** above the reservoir is a good starting point for **walks**. These include the four-to five-hour ascent of the glaciated Testa del Rutor (3486m). There are many other walks, but none of them is easy – make sure you carry the Kompass *Gran Paradiso* map. The only **hotel** in Bonne is the *Perret* (☎0165.97.107; ②), open all year and with a restaurant and bar.

The northwest: around Mont Blanc

Dominated by the snowy peaks of **Mont Blanc** (Monte Bianco to the Italians), the northern reaches of Valle d'Aosta are scenically stunning but also very popular. The most sensational views are from the cable cars that glide and swoop (at times alarmingly so) across the mountain to Chamonix in France. However, the trip is expensive, even if you take a bus back to Italy through the eleven-kilometre-long Mont Blanc tunnel, and the service is often suspended because of bad weather.

La Thuile and Testa d'Arpy

If the cable car seems too pricey, you can walk up to the **Testa d'Arpy** from the sprawling resort of **LA THUILE**, on the road to the Petit-St-Bernard Pass into France, for sweeping views of the peaks and glaciers of Mont Blanc. Buses run from Pré-St-Didier at the end of the Valle d'Aosta railway line to La Thuile, from where it's just over two hours' walk by path or road to the old *La Genzianella* hotel at the top of the Colle San Carlo. From here a path leads through woods to Testa d'Arpy in around ten minutes, a natural balcony with a bird's-eye view up the valley to Mont Blanc. It's well worth having a good map (FSB *Monte Bianco*), not so much to find your way as to identify the peaks and glaciers spread out before you.

As for La Thuile, it's rather an overdeveloped resort, and it makes sense to pass through quickly, after calling in at the **tourist office**, at Via Collomb 4 (daily 9am–12.30pm & 3–6pm; ☎0165.884.179, *www.lathuile.it*), for maps – and to sleep instead up the mountain at *Du Glacier* (☎0165.884.137; ⑨), in the little hamlet of Golette; it's open all year but phone in advance to check that there's room. Of the other walks starting from the hotel the most interesting is the 45-minute hike to **Lago d'Arpy**, from where a path leads down into La Thuile.

Courmayeur and Mont Blanc

COURMAYEUR is the smartest and most popular of Valle d'Aosta's ski resorts, much used by package-tour operators. The skiing is good, though there's little to challenge experts, and the scenery is magnificent, but, predictably, what remains of the old village is enmeshed in a web of ersatz Alpine chalets and après-ski hangouts.

If you simply want a week of skiing, you'll probably do better to take a package; if you've come to hike or take the big-dipping cable cars across to Chamonix, the most convenient place to stay is **LA PALUD**, 5km outside Courmayeur (three buses a day).

The **cable car** runs from La Palud to Punta Helbronner all year round, but continues to Chamonix only between April and September. There are between ten and twelve departures a day, depending on the time of year, roughly hourly starting at 8.30am – although ultimately the regularity depends on the weather. To be sure of good views, you'll need to set out early since it's usually cloudy by midday; be sure also to get there in plenty of time, especially on summer weekends, as it's much used by summer skiers. Even if it's blazing hot in the valley, the temperature plunges to freezing-point at the top, so take some warm clothes.

There are good walks along the two valleys at the foot of the Mont Blanc glaciers, both of which have seasonal **campsites** accessible by bus from Courmayeur. Val Ferret to the west is the more interesting option – you can walk back from Frebouze over Monte de la Saxe, with some stunning views of Mont Blanc en route.

If you do end up having to spend a night in Courmayeur, the cheapest **hotel** is the *Venezia* at Via delle Villette 2 (☎0165.842.461; ③); or there's the *Crampon*, on the same street at no. 8 (☎0165.842.385; ⑤; Christmas–April & July to mid-Sept), which also has a **restaurant**. Hotels in La Palud include the *Chalet Joli* (☎0165.869.722; ④) and the extremely comfortable *Vallee Blanche* (☎0165.89.7002; ④).

travel details

TRAINS

Alba to: Asti (8 daily; 1hr).

Aosta to: Pré-St-Didier (14 daily; 50min).

Asti to: Casale Monferrato (6 daily; 50min).

Cúneo to: Limone Piemonte (14 daily; 30min).

Novara to: Biella (20 daily; 1hr 10min); Varallo (9 daily; 1hr 30min).

Turin to: Aosta (17 daily; 2hr); Asti (33 daily; 30min–1hr); Cúneo (9 daily; 1hr 30min); Milan Centrale (24 daily; 1hr 45min); Modane (8 daily; 1hr 25min–2hr 25min); Novara (27 daily; 1hr 15min); Vercelli (23 daily; 1hr).

Verrès to: Aosta (14 daily; 30min–1hr 10min); Turin (13 daily; 1hr 10min–1hr 45min).

BUSES

Alba to: Barolo (6 daily; 30min); Grinzane (6 daily; 1hr).

Aosta to: Aymavilles (22 daily; 25min); Cogne (6 daily; 50min); Courmayeur (20 daily; 1hr); Pont Valsavarenche (3 daily; 1hr 10min); Rhêmes St Georges (3 on weekdays Sept–June; 45min; July & Aug 2 daily, going on to Rhêmes Notre Dame; 1hr); Valgrisenche (mid-June to mid-Sept 2 daily; mid-Sept to mid-June Mon, Tues & Sat only; 1hr 30min).

Biella to: Ivrea (6 daily; 2hr 25min); Santuario di Oropa (9 daily; 40min).

Chatillon to: Breuil Cervinia (6 daily; 1hr–1hr 30min).

Cogne to: Valnontey (July & early Sept 9 daily; Aug 22 daily; 15 min).

Cúneo to: Dronero (Val Maira; 22 daily; 35min); Valle Stura (7 daily; 1hr–1hr 20min).

Pont-St-Martin to: Gressoney La Trinité (7 daily; 1hr 20min).

Pré-St-Didier to: Courmayeur (15 daily; 10–25min); La Thuile (7 daily; 25min).

Saluzzo to: Crissolo (3 daily; 2hr); Cúneo (17 daily; 1hr); Val Varaita (3 daily; 1hr 15min).

Turin (Corso Inghilterra) to: Alagna (1 daily; 3hr); Aosta (12 daily; 2–3hr); Cervinia (1 daily; 2hr 15min); Chamonix/Geneva (1 daily; 3hr 15min–4hr 30min); Champoluc (2 daily; 3hr 30min); Courmayeur (7 daily; 3–4hr); Gressoney La Trinité (4 daily; 2hr 10min–3hr 10min); Ivrea (12 daily; 1hr 15min); Locarno (1 daily; 4hr); Lugano via Novara (1 daily; 3hr).

Turin (Corso Marconi) to: Cúneo (8 daily; 2hr 45min); Saluzzo (10 daily; 1hr 20min).

Verrès to: Champoluc (6 daily; 1hr 10min).

CHAPTER TWO

LIGURIA

S
heltering on the seaward side of the mountains that divide Piemonte from the coast, **Liguria** is the classic introduction to Italy for travellers journeying overland through France. There's an unexpected change as you cross the border from Nice and Monaco: the **Italian Riviera** (as Liguria's commercially developed strip of coast is known) has more variety of landscape and architecture than its French counterpart, and is generally less frenetic. The mountains which, in places, drop sheer to the sea are treated as an irrelevance by most visitors eager to press on to their chosen resort, but Liguria's lofty hinterland can offer respite from the standard format of beach, beach and more beach. Teetering on slopes carpeted with olives and vines are isolated mountain villages that retain their own rural culture and cuisine.

The chief city of the region is **Genoa**, an ancient, sprawling port often acclaimed as the most atmospheric of all Italian cities. It has a dense and fascinating old quarter that is complemented by a vibrant social and ethnic mix and a newly energized dockside district. The city stands midway between two distinct stretches of coastline. To the west is the **Riviera di Ponente**, one long ribbon of hotels packed out in summer with Italian families who book a year ahead to stay in their favourite spot. Picking your route carefully means you can avoid the worst of it. **San Remo**, the *grande-dame* of Riviera resorts, is flanked by hillsides covered with glasshouses, and is a major centre for the worldwide export of flowers; **Albenga** and **Noli** are attractive medieval centres that have also retained a good deal of character; and **Finale Ligure** is a thoroughly pleasant Mediterranean seaside town.

On Genoa's eastern side is the more rugged **Riviera di Levante**. Umbrella pines grow horizontally on the cliff-faces overlooking the water, and in the evening a glassy calm falls over the little bays and inlets. Walks on **Monte di Portofino** and in the coastal scenery of the famed **Cinque Terre** take you through scrubland and vineyards for memorable vistas over broad gulfs and jutting headlands. This mix of mountains and fishing villages accessible only by boat appealed to the early nineteenth-century Romantics, who "discovered" the Riviera in the eighteenth century, preparing the way for other artists and poets and the first package tourists. Now the whole area explodes

---

ACCOMMODATION PRICE CODES

Throughout this guide, prices per person are given for **youth hostels** and assume Hostelling International (HI) membership. **Hotel** accommodation is coded on a scale from ① to ⑨, reflecting the cost of the cheapest double room in each establishment in high season. The price bands to which these codes refer are as follows:

① Up to L60,000/€30.99
② L60,000–90,000/€30.99–46.48
③ L90,000–120,000/€46.48–61.98
④ L120,000–150,000/€61.98–77.47
⑤ L150,000–200,000/€77.47–103.29

⑥ L200,000–250,000/€103.29–129.11
⑦ L250,000–300,000/€129.11–154.94
⑧ L300,000–400,000/€154.94–206.58
⑨ over L400,000/€206.58

(See p.32 for a full explanation.)

REGIONAL FOOD AND WINE

Liguria belongs geographically to the north, but its benign Mediterranean climate, and to some extent its cooking, belong further south. Traditionally, the recipes from this region make something out of nothing; this is a legacy of the hardships of life here in the past, and is mirrored by a reserve in the Ligurian character that has given the people an undeserved reputation among other Italians for meanness. The best-known of all Ligurian specialities is **pesto**. Invented by the Genoese to help their long-term sailors fight off scurvy, it's made with chopped basil, garlic, pine-nuts and grated sharp cheese (pecorino or parmesan) ground up together in olive oil – traditionally with a pestle and mortar, from where the name arises. It's used as a sauce for pasta (often flat *trenette* noodles, or knobbly little potato-flour shapes known as **trofie**), or stirred into soup to make *minestrone alla genovese*. Otherwise, **fish** dominates – not surprising in a region where more than two-thirds of the population live on the coast. Local **anchovies** are a common antipasto, while pasta with a variety of fish and seafood sauces appear everywhere (mussels, scampi, octopus and clams are all excellent); there's also a host of specific dishes such as *ciuppin* or fish soup, *burrida di seppie* (cuttlefish stew), or fish *in carpione* (marinated in vinegar and herbs). Salt **cod** (*bacalà*) and wind-dried cod (*stoccofisso*) are big local favourites, often served fried. Other dishes to look out for are *cima alla genovese* (cold stuffed veal) and the widely available *torta pasqualina*, a spinach-and-cheese pie with eggs. The latter is served as fast food, as are other kinds of *torta* and golden **focaccia** bread, often flavoured with olives, sage or rosemary. Chickpeas grow abundantly along the coast and crop up in **farinata**, a kind of chickpea pancake displayed in broad round baking trays that you'll see everywhere, and in *zuppa di ceci*, another dish rarely found outside Liguria. Pastries, too, are excellent: Genoa is famous for its **pandolce**, a sweet cake laced with dried fruit, nuts and candied peel.

Liguria's soil and aspect aren't suited to vine-growing, although plenty of local **wine** – mainly white – is quite drinkable. The steep, terraced slopes of the Cinque Terre are home to an eponymous white wine and the sweet, expensive dessert wine called Sciacchetrà, made from partially dried grapes. From the Riviera di Ponente, look out for the crisp whites of Pigato (from Albenga) and Vermentino (from Imperia), as well as the acclaimed Rossese di Dolceacqua, Liguria's best red.

into quite a ruck every July and August, with resorts like **Portofino** qualifying as amongst the most expensive in the country – although nearby **Santa Margherita Ligure** has its unpretentious moments, and **Lévanto** is a great place to make for if you just want to soak up the sun on a budget. Visiting out of season, of course, is a peaceful way to enjoy the beauty without the hubbub.

In the summer months, though, the only real way to avoid the crowds is to travel inland. Minor roads and mule tracks link villages built spiral-fashion around hilltops, originally as protection against Saracen invasion. A testing long-distance footpath, the **Alta Via dei Monti Liguri** runs from pass to mountain pass along the length of Liguria, but aside from the odd section accessible on public transport from the coast it's mainly for hardened pros. Nonetheless, high-altitude resorts such as **Santo Stefano d'Aveto** and **Torriglia** offer plenty of summer walking (and, in places, winter skiing) that can lift you a world away from the resorts down below on the sea.

In a **car**, the shore road is for the most part a disappointment: the coast is extremely built up, and in fact you get a much better sense of the beauty of the region by taking the east–west *autostrada* which cuts through the mountains a few kilometres inland by means of a mixture of tunnels and viaducts. Fleeting bursts of daylight between tunnels give glimpses of the string of resorts along the coast, silvery olive groves and a brilliant sea. However, the easiest way to take in the region is by **train**: there are regular services stopping just about everywhere and, because the track is forced to squeeze

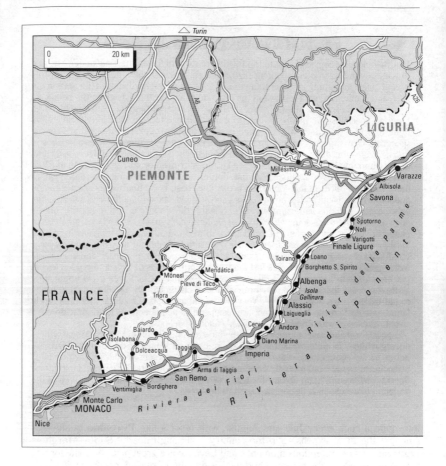

along the narrow coastal strip, stations are invariably centrally located in towns and villages.

Liguria's regional **tourist office** is based at Piazza Matteotti 9, Genoa (☎010.530.8201, *www.turismo.liguriainrete.it*) – check out their encyclopedic website, which has information in English on every town and village in the region, plus the option to reserve at any hotel, campsite or agriturismo farmhouse. The excellent spiral-bound **Liguria Tourist Atlas**, published by the regional government in collaboration with cartographers DeAgostini, is invaluable if you're spending any time in the region and has useful detailed plans of town centres.

GENOA

GENOA (**Genova** in Italian) is "the most winding, incoherent of cities, the most entangled topographical ravel in the world." So said Henry James, and the city is still marvellously eclectic, full of pace and rough-edged style. Sprawled behind the huge

port – Italy's largest and an increasingly popular stopoff for international cruise liners – is a dense and fascinating warren of medieval alleyways, a district which has more zest than all the coastal resorts put together.

Genoa made its money at sea, through trade, colonial exploitation and piracy. By the thirteenth century, on the heels of a major role in the **Crusades**, the Genoese were roaming the Mediterranean, bringing back ideas as well as goods: the city's architects were using Arab pointed arches a century before the rest of Italy. The San Giorgio banking syndicate effectively controlled the city for much of the fifteenth century, and cold-shouldered **Columbus** (who had grown up in Genoa) when he sought funding for his voyages of exploration. With Spanish backing, he opened up new Atlantic trade routes which ironically reduced *Genova La Superba* ("the proud") to a backwater. Following foreign invasion, in 1768 the Banco di San Giorgio was forced to sell the Genoese colony of Corsica to the French, and a century later, the city became a hotbed of radicalism: **Mazzini**, one of the main protagonists of the Risorgimento, was born here, and in 1860 **Garibaldi** set sail for Sicily with his "Thousand" from the city's harbour. Around the same time, Italy's industrial revolution began in Genoa, with steelworks and shipyards spreading along the coast. These suffered heavy **bombing** in World War II, and the subsequent economic decline hobbled Genoa for decades.

Things started to look up in the 1990s. State funding to celebrate the 500th anniversary of Columbus's 1492 voyage paid to renovate some of the city's late-Renaissance palaces and the old port area, with Genoa's most famous son of modern times, **Renzo Piano** (best known as the co-designer of Paris's Pompidou Centre), taking a leading role. The city is to be the focus of world attention for the G8 summit in July 2001 (*www.genoa-g8.it*), an event which marks a L90 billion programme to prepare for a well-earned role as **European Capital of Culture** in 2004.

The tidying-up hasn't sanitized the **old town**, however; the core of the city, between the two stations and the waterfront, is still dark and slightly threatening. But despite the sleaze, the overriding impression is of a buzzing hive of activity – food shops nestled in the portals of former palaces, carpenters' workshops sandwiched between designer furniture outlets, everything surrounded by a crush of people and the squashed vowels of the impenetrable Genoese dialect that has, over the centuries, absorbed elements of Neapolitan, Calabrese and Portuguese. Aside from the cosmopolitan street-life, you should seek out the **Cattedrale di San Lorenzo** with its fabulous treasury, small medieval churches such as **San Donato** and **Santa Maria di Castello**, and the Renaissance *palazzi* that contain Genoa's **art** collections and furniture and decor from the grandest days of the city's illustrious past.

Arrival, city transport and information

There are two big **train stations** in Genoa. **Stazione Principe**, on Piazza Acquaverde just above the port on the west side of the centre, is the main one, although a number of mainline trains also pass through **Stazione Brignole** on Piazza Verdi, to the east of the centre. Buses #33 and #37, among others, ply between the two. There's a staffed left-luggage office at Principe (daily 6am–10pm; L5000/€2.58 per piece for 12hr), and lockers at Brignole (daily 24hr; L4000/€2.06 for 6hr; 30hr maximum). If you're arriving at Principe after dark, cling on to your valuables while moving through the station and avoid the notorious Via di Prè alley nearby, which is the core territory of Genoa's lowlife. **Buses** arrive on Piazza della Vittoria, a few minutes' walk south of Brignole.

The **Aeroporto Cristoforo Colombo** (*www.airport.genova.it*) is 6km west of the city centre. "Volabus" #100 runs to Stazione Principe, Piazza de Ferrari on the edge of the Old Town, and Piazza Verdi outside Stazione Brignole (every 30min; takes 25min; information ☎010.558.2414). Buy your L5000/€2.58 ticket on the bus.

Getting around the centre is best done **on foot**, resorting to Genoa's AMT **buses** (information ☎010.558.2414), only for trips to outlying sights. Public transport tickets, available from *tabacchi* and newspaper stands, cost L1500/€0.77 for 90 minutes, or L5000/€2.58 all day, and are valid on buses, all the city's various **funiculars** and **lifts**, the expanding metro system which serves the suburban commuter belt, and local trains between Voltri and Nervi (although not on the narrow-gauge mountain line to Casella; see p.126). AMT also runs **Giro Giro Tour** buses daily around the major city sights with multilingual guides aboard, starting from Piazza Caricamento (Mon–Fri 3.30pm, Sat & Sun 10am; L25,000/€12.91; lasts 1hr 40min; ☎010.254.3431) – although, of course, you won't see any of the old quarter this way. Another good way to get a flavour of the city is from **a boat**; see "Listings" on p.124 for details.

The main **tourist office** (toll-free ☎1674.69.838, *www.apt.genova.it*) is at the Porto Antico, in the modern Palazzina Santa Maria on the western side of the flyover (daily 9am–6.30pm; ☎010.248.711). Additional branches are at Stazione Principe (daily 7am–9pm; ☎010.246.2633); the airport (Mon–Sat 8am–8pm; ☎010.601.5247); and at Stazione Marittima near the cruise terminal (May–Sept daily 9am–6.30pm;

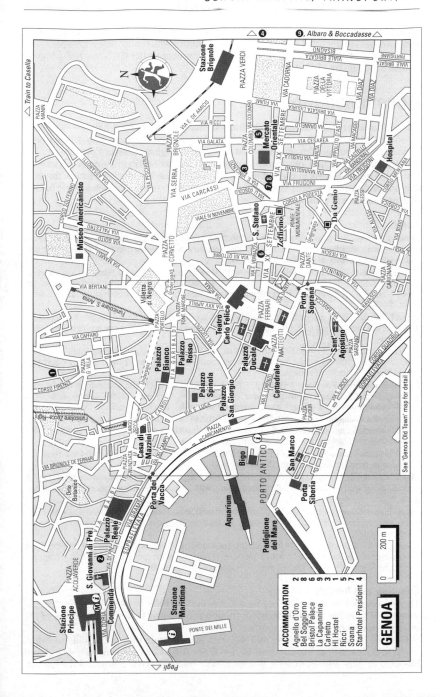

ACCOMMODATION
Agnello d'Oro   2
Bel Soggiorno   8
Bristol Palace   6
La Capannina   9
Carletto   3
HI Hostel   1
Ricci   5
Soana   7
Starhotel President 4

GENOA

☎010.246.3686). Beware, though, that Genoa's tourist industry is undergoing a complete overhaul in the build-up to the 2004 celebrations, which may well encompass new locations and changes in opening times; for details, contact the city's tourism administration, at Via Roma 11/3 (☎010.576.791).

Accommodation

There's no shortage of **accommodation**, but many of the budget hotels – especially those around the train stations – are grimy and depressing, and you need to look hard to find the exceptions. The area just west of Stazione Brignole (Piazza Colombo and Via XX Settembre) is much preferable to anything around Stazione Principe. There's a handful of quality hotels in the old quarter – though you should steer clear of the one-star places down by the port (on and around Via di Prè), some of which are the haunts of drug-dealers and prostitutes.

Hotels

Agnello d'Oro, Vico Monachette 6 (☎010.246.2084, fax 010.246.2327). Comfortable, modernized rooms – some with balconies – in a seventeenth-century palace alongside the Palazzo Reale and within spitting distance of Stazione Principe. ④.

Bel Soggiorno, Via XX Settembre 19/2 (☎010.542.880, fax 010.581.418). Run by a gregarious German woman (who speaks English), this is a welcoming place although the standard of the rooms – both en suite and not – doesn't quite measure up to the cosiness of the lobby and breakfast room. ②–③.

Bristol Palace, Via XX Settembre 35 (☎010.592.541, fax 010.561.756). Grand old pile full of antique furniture, old masters and an Edwardian sense of order and discretion. Rooms are large, attractive and air-conditioned. ⑧.

Cairoli, Via Cairoli 14/4 (☎010.246.1454, fax 010.246.7512, *cairoli@rdn.it*). A very friendly two-star hotel, whose brightly furnished, modern, soundproofed rooms all have private bath, TV and telephone. One of the city's best deals. ③.

La Capannina, Via Tito Speri 7 (☎010.317.131, fax 010.362.2692). Down a sidestreet off the river walkway near the charming fishing cove of Boccadasse, well east of the centre (bus #17). Characterful rooms and a tranquil location make it something of a bargain. ③.

Carletto, Via Colombo 16/4 (☎010.588.412, fax 010.589.615). Less than ten minutes' walk from Stazione Brignole, just off busy Via San Vincenzo, this has clean, ordinary rooms – some en suite, some with shared bathroom – and friendly management. ②.

City, Via San Sebastiano 6 (☎010.5545, fax 010.586.301). Four-star Best Western hotel in a great central location, round the corner from the theatre. ⑥.

Major, Vico Spada 4 (☎010.247.4174, fax 010.246.9898). A great location in the old town, just off Via Luccoli, along with clean and well-furnished rooms with TV and telephone, make this a great bargain. ①.

Ricci, Piazza Colombo 4/8 (☎010.592.746, fax 010.590.380). A slightly institutional one-star in a rather grim apartment building. But it's handy for Stazione Brignole, and the shared-bath rooms are clean enough. ①.

Soana, Via XX Settembre 23/8 (☎010.562.814, fax 010.561.486). A good location right by the Porta Monumentale, and very friendly, with a mixture of rooms – some are plain and basic, others are lovely and fully modernized. One of the best choices in the area. ①–②.

Camping and hostels

The few **campsites** within the city boundaries include *Villa Doria* at Via al Campeggio Villa Doria 15 in Pegli (☎010.696.9600) though you'd do far better to stay at one of the coastal resorts and commute into town.

Genoa's HI **hostel** is a clean and well-run place situated up in the hills of Righi, north of the centre, at Via Costanzi 120 (☎ & fax 010.242.2457, *hostelge@iol.it*; closed late Dec & Jan). From Stazione Brignole, take bus #40; from Stazione Principe you need bus #35, then switch at the fifth stop onto bus #40. Bed and breakfast costs L23,000/€11.88, and there are cheap meals as well as maps and information on offer. Check-in is 3.30–6pm.

GENOA ADDRESSSES

Note that Genoa is one of the handful of Italian cities that, for some reason, has an unnecessarily complicated double system of street-numbering: commercial establishments (such as bars and restaurants) have **red** numbers (*rosso*), while all other buildings have **black** numbers (*nero*) – and the two systems don't run in tandem. This means, for example, that Via Banchi 35r might be next-door to Via Banchi 89n, but several hundred metres from Via Banchi 33n. There's no logic or purpose to it at all.

The City

Genoa's atmospheric **Old Town** spreads outwards from the port in a confusion of tiny alleyways (*caruggi*), bordered by **Via Gramsci** along the waterfront and by **Via Balbi** and **Via Garibaldi** to the north. The caruggi are lined with high buildings, usually six or seven storeys, set very close together. Tiny grocers, textile workshops and bakeries jostle for position with boutiques, design outlets and goldsmiths amidst a flurry of shouts, smells and scrawny cats. Not for nothing is Genoa the only European city to be mentioned in the *Arabian Nights*.

The cramped layout of the area reflects its medieval politics. Around the thirteenth and fourteenth centuries, the city's principal families – Doria, Spinola, Grimaldi and Fieschi – marked out certain streets and squares as their territory, even extending their domains to include churches: to pray in someone else's chapel was to risk being stabbed in the back. New buildings on each family's patch had to be slotted in wherever they could, resulting in a maze of crooked alleyways that was the battleground of dynastic feuds which lasted well into the eighteenth century. Genoa has, however, remained relatively free of fire, not least because each building's kitchens were invariably placed on the topmost storey.

The Palazzo Ducale and around

From 1384 to 1515, except for brief periods of foreign domination, Genoa was ruled by a doge, resident at the **Palazzo Ducale** in Piazza Matteotti, right in the heart of the old town. The present building, with its huge vaulted atrium, was built in the sixteenth century – its wide steps up from the courtyard were designed with the doge's grand processions in mind. The building now makes a splendid exhibition hall (times and prices vary; *www.palazzoducale.genova.it*) and houses archives and libraries, as well as hosting shows and concerts; it's scheduled to be the location of the G8 conference in July 2001. The dour **Gesù** church across the square, where locals come to siesta on hot summer afternoons, was designed by Pellegrino Tibaldi at the end of the sixteenth century and contains a mass of marble and gilt stucco and some fine Baroque paintings, including Guido Reni's *Assumption* in the right aisle and two works by Rubens: the *Miracles of St Ignatius* on the left and the *Circumcision* on the high altar.

An alley between the two leads through to **Piazza de Ferrari**, overlooked by a statue of Garibaldi in front of the grand facade of the Carlo Felice opera house; from here, Via XX Settembre heads east towards Brignole, while Via Roma cuts north to skirt the old town.

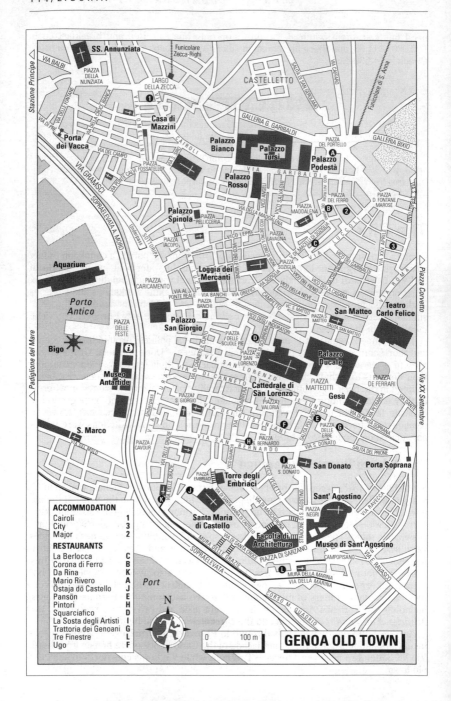

GENOA OLD TOWN

ACCOMMODATION

Cairoli	1
City	3
Major	2

RESTAURANTS

La Berlocca	C
Corona di Ferro	B
Da Rina	K
Mario Rivero	A
Ostaja dö Castello	J
Pansön	E
Pintori	H
Squarciafico	D
La Sosta degli Artisti	I
Trattoria dei Genoani	G
Tre Finestre	L
Ugo	F

0   100 m

Cattedrale di San Lorenzo

West of Piazza Matteotti, bulking out the north side of Via San Lorenzo which cuts down to the port, is the **Cattedrale di San Lorenzo**. There's an entrance from the street, but you should first go round to take in the main western **facade**, an elaborate confection of twisting, fluted columns and black-and-white striped stone – high-quality Carrara marble alternating with local slate – that was added by Gothic craftsmen from France in the early thirteenth century, a hundred years or so after the main building had been constructed. The **stripes** here, like other examples throughout the city, were a sign of prestige: families could use them only if they had a permit, awarded for "some illustrious deed to the advantage of their native city". While the rest of Genoa's churches were portioned out between the ruling dynasties, the cathedral – which lay between districts – remained freely open to all, a fact borne out by the side portals in the north and south walls which formerly allowed free passage from one town quarter to another through the cathedral interior.

The **interior** houses the Renaissance chapel of St John the Baptist, whose ashes – legend has it – once rested in the thirteenth-century sarcophagus. After a particularly bad storm in medieval times, priests carried his casket through the city down to the port to placate the sea, and a commemorative procession still takes place each June 24 in honour of the saint. The Baptist's reliquary is in the **Museo del Tesoro** (Mon–Sat 9–11.30am & 3–5.30pm; L10,000/€5.16; *www.comune.genova.it/ musei*), housed in an atmospheric crypt, along with a polished quartz plate on which, legend says, Salome received his severed head. Also on display are a glass vessel said to have been given to Solomon by the Queen of Sheba and used at the Last Supper, a lock of hair that's supposedly from the Virgin Mary, and a piece of the True Cross. Artefacts from Byzantine and later times include delicate jewelled crosses and reliquaries – along with a British artillery shell fired from the sea during World War II that fell through the roof but miraculously failed to explode.

North of San Lorenzo

The district around the cathedral has changed dramatically in the last few years, with an influx of art shops and trendy fashion outlets along the main Via San Lorenzo. One block north, just off Piazza San Lorenzo, a narrow winding alley, **Vico del Filo**, doglegs its way crazily westwards down to Piazza Caricamento on the portside; a local insult for one who is particularly dim is to describe them as being "as stupid as the Vico del Filo".

An unnamed lane leads north from San Lorenzo through tiny **Piazza Invrea** – shamed by having had a 1960s concrete eyesore cemented onto the side of a medieval residence – to the rather swanky little shopping square of **Campetto** and adjacent **Via degli Orefici**, "Street of the Goldsmiths". Unlike the generic, machine-produced gold jewellery found in Florence, much of what is on offer in Genoa is still made by hand at upper-floor workshops in the area of Campetto, sold in shops such as *L'Oro degli Sforza* on the square at relatively affordable prices. Linked to Campetto is genteel **Piazza Soziglia**, with a good mixture of bars and places to eat, among them *Klainguti*, one of Genoa's oldest coffee-houses (see p.123). From here **Via Luccoli** heads north, continuing the web with glitzy boutiques and design outlets galore, while a few steps to the west is **Piazza Lavagna**, home to Genoa's thriving Mercato dei Pulci, the daily flea market. Via Garibaldi, and the sixteenth-century *palazzi* of Genoa's mercantile dynasties, is a short stroll north (see p.117).

A little east of Campetto and Piazza Soziglia is the city's prettiest small square, **Piazza San Matteo**. This lay in the territory of the Doria family, who went one step further than merely striping the twelfth-century church of **San Matteo** in black and white: they ordered elaborate testimonials to the family's worthiness to be carved on the facade of the church and their adjoining palaces. Andrea Doria, the most illustrious of the clan, lived in the palace on the left corner of the square (the other palaces on the square were home to the rest of the family) before he built his lavish palace down on the waterfront (see p.116). He is now buried in the crypt, which the sacristan will open for you. Peek in too at the pretty little cloister adjoining the church.

Piazza Banchi and Piazza Caricamento

Heading west from Campetto on Via degli Orefici brings you out into a thriving commercial zone centred on **Piazza Banchi**, a tiny, enclosed market square of secondhand books, records, fruit and flowers which was once the heart of the medieval city. The little church of **San Pietro in Banchi** overlooking the square was built in the sixteenth century after a plague: with little money to spare, the city authorities sold plots of commercial space in arcades around the church terrace in order to fund construction of the main building, an economic model that is familiar today but was virtually unknown at the time.

It's a short stroll west from Piazza Banchi out into the open spaces of Genoa's port. The sea once came up to the vaulted arcades of Via Sottoripa, which runs alongside the main **Piazza Caricamento**; these days the waterfront is blocked off by containers and fences, but there's been a market here since the twelfth century, when small boats used to come ashore from galleys at anchor. Fruit and vegetable stalls still line the arcade, now interspersed with fly pitches selling sunglasses and pirated CDs.

On the southern edge of the square is the **Palazzo di San Giorgio**, a brightly painted fortified palace built in 1260 from the stones of a captured Venetian fortress. After the great sea-battle of Curzola in 1298, the Genoese used the building to keep their Venetian prisoners under lock and key; among them was one **Marco Polo**, who met a Pisan writer named Rustichello inside and spun tales of adventure to him of worlds beyond the seas. After their release, Rustichello published the stories in a single volume that became one of the most famous books of all time, translated into English as *The Travels of Marco Polo*. In 1408, the building was taken over by the Banco di San Giorgio, a syndicate established to finance the war against Venice, which in the sixteenth century steered the city from trading to banking, thus turning Genoa into the

---

THE CROSS OF ST GEORGE

If you're a football fan wandering around Genoa, you may legitimately be wondering why the locals seem so taken with the England team as to hang English flags of **St George** from every window. The truth is, however, that the flag – a red cross on a white background – was first acquired by the Genoese, and only came to be the English national emblem courtesy of some crafty deal-making.

The legend of St George originated in the early Christian era in the Middle East with tales of the bravery of an Arab or Turkish warrior: the hero is still venerated today in ordinary churches across Syria, Turkey, Palestine and as far afield as Armenia. The familiar story of dragon-baiting and princess-saving was brought to Europe during the Crusades. Genoese sailors, the master navigators of the day, safely escorted the waves of European armies to and from the Holy Land, and in gratitude, the newly – and temporarily – victorious Crusader kings of Middle Eastern territories granted the Genoese the honour of flying the flag of their local saint protector, St George.

For centuries afterwards, Genoese ships flying the St George's cross remained immune from attack by pirates – although whether it was respect for the saint, fear of violent retribution, or the attraction of Genoese payoffs which kept the bandits away is open to question. However, some time in the sixteenth or seventeenth centuries, English sea-captains, who had long suffered at the hands of pirates, formally requested the right to fly the favoured emblem. And never slow to spot a nice little earner, the Genoese agreed a price.

leading financial centre of the day. These days, the palazzo is home to the harbour authorities, but you can ask the guardian on the door to let you in to see the medieval Sala dei Protettori and beautiful Sala Manica Lunga, with decor restored to its thirteenth-century grandeur following bomb damage in World War II.

The Galleria Nazionale di Palazzo Spinola

From Piazza Banchi, the animated medieval lane **Via San Luca** heads north, lined with shops selling counterfeit designer clothes and accessories. This street was in Spinola family territory, and when the last of the family died, in 1958, their grand residence became the excellent **Galleria Nazionale di Palazzo Spinola**, located beside Piazza Pelliceria (Tues–Sat 9am–8pm, Sun 1–8pm; L8000/€4.13; under-25s half-price; joint ticket with Palazzo Reale L12,000/€6.20). Room 2 holds portraits by Van Dyck of Matthew, Mark, Luke and John as men of books, while on the third upper floor are an intensely mournful *Ecce Homo* by the Sicilian master Antonello da Messina and the splendid *Adoration of the Magi* by Joos van Cleve, sawn into planks when stolen from the church of San Donato in the 1970s. Don't miss the little **terrace**, way up on the spine of the roof and shaded with orange and lemon trees.

The way north passes through a hectic and rather seedy neighbourhood centred on the vibrant **Via della Maddalena** alley, crowded with shops and stalls that ring with shouts in French and Arabic from the predominantly West and North African streettraders, doing business alongside Genoa's burgeoning red-light trade (mostly serviced by women from developing countries, kidnapped and kept in virtual enslavement by local pimps). Steep lanes rise north of Via della Maddalena, lifting you out of the mêlée and into the ordered calm of Via Garibaldi.

Along Via Garibaldi

When newly made fortunes encouraged Genoa's merchant bankers to move out of the cramped old town in the mid-sixteenth century, artisans' houses were pulled down to make way for the Strada Nuova, later named **Via Garibaldi**, on the northern fringe of the quarter. To walk along the surprisingly narrow street is to stroll through a Renaissance architect's drawing pad – sculpted facades, stucco work and medallions decorate the exterior of the three-storey *palazzi*, while the big courtyards are almost like private squares. Take a look, for instance, at no. 7, the heavily stuccoed **Palazzo Podestà**, with its grotto and fountain on the far side of its small courtyard, or the splendid **Palazzo Tursi**, a few doors along, the largest of Genoa's palaces and now the town hall, with a glassed-in main courtyard that is the street's most impressive.

The first building at the western end of Via Garibaldi is the **Galleria di Palazzo Bianco**, Genoa's finest art gallery (Tues, Thurs & Fri 9am–1pm, Wed & Sat 9am–7pm, Sun 10am–6pm; L6000/€3.10; joint ticket with Palazzo Rosso L10,000/€5.16; free on Sun; *www.comune.genova.it/musei*). In room 1 a small but potent image of San Fabiano hangs alongside a strikingly similar portrait of San Antonio; the former is by Francesco Brea, the latter by his father Antonio Brea, both Genoese. At the top of the stairs is a radiant *SS Sebastian, Francis and John the Baptist* by Fra' Filippo Lippi, but most rooms on the upper floor are filled with Flemish works. Room 4 holds a *Madonna and Child* by Joos van Cleve and a dark, brooding Christ by Hans Memling, while room 6 has a gloriously detailed celebration of a Netherlandish winter by Jan Wildens, showing a woman tumbling immodestly on the ice and some poor character about to be pelted with snowballs while in the privy. The piercing gaze of Van Dyck's Christ dominates room 7, despite Rubens's ageing *Venus and Mars* cavorting bawdily nearby, while room 8 has some festive tavern scenes by Jan Steen. Room 9 holds Veronese's giant *Crucifixion*, while next door is a dramatic *Ecce Homo* by Caravaggio. A surfeit of work by the Genoese painter Bernardo Strozzi completes the collection.

Across the road is the less prestigious **Galleria di Palazzo Rosso** (same times and prices). Room 2 has an effeminate *St John the Baptist* by Leonardo da Vinci and a striking *Portrait of a Young Man* by Dürer, but it's the topmost floor that is the main attraction, with every room restored to its original Baroque grandeur and bedecked with chandeliers, mirrors and an excess of gilding. Frescoes cover the ceilings, while rooms 13 and 14 display a series of splendid portraits by Van Dyck of the Brignole-Sale family, who built the palace in 1671.

Along Via Balbi

A few minutes' walk west of Via Garibaldi is the house at Via Lomellini 11 where Giuseppe Mazzini, one of the most influential activists of Italian Unification, was born in 1805; it now displays documents and relics from his life as the **Museo di Risorgimento** (Tues & Thurs–Sat 9am–1pm; L6000/€3.10). Past traffic-heavy Piazza della Nunziata, overlooked by the giant sixteenth-century church of **Santissima Annunziata del Vastato**, which boasts one of the most exuberantly decorated interiors in the city, you'll come to the main road of **Via Balbi**, laid out a few decades after Via Garibaldi.

The Palazzo Reale

At Via Balbi 10 sits the vast and absorbing **Palazzo Reale** (Sun, Mon & Tues 9am–1.45pm, Wed–Sat 9am–7pm; L8000/€4.13; under-25s half-price; joint ticket with Palazzo Spinola L12,000/€6.20), built by the Balbi family in the early seventeenth century and later occupied by the Durazzo dynasty and the Savoyard royals. You enter through the huge atrium, which looks onto the elegant courtyard garden behind, and climb grand staircases. The first big room is the **ballroom**, with gilt stucco ceilings and Chinese vases. To the left are four drawing-rooms, featuring a huge watercolour of the crossing of the Red Sea painted on silk by Romanelli, grand marble fireplaces and bronze candelabra. These rooms lead through to the stunning hall of mirrors, where Joseph II, Emperor of Austria, is said to have remarked in 1784 – with a flourish of disingenuous flattery – that the palace appeared more of a royal residence than his own simple pad back in Vienna. The room was designed in the 1730s by Gerolamo Durazzo and the best of its statues are four exquisite works in marble and gold by Filippo Parodi: the first pair, facing each other nearest the door, are Hyacinth and Venus, while at the far end of the room are Adonis and Clizia. Doors lead through to the private quarters of the Duke of Genoa, with the **duke's bedchamber** featuring a sumptuous Baroque ceiling fresco and the duke's bathchamber holding elegant furniture carved in England in the 1820s.

On the way back through to the east wing of the building, you pass along a **chapel gallery** behind the ballroom, covered in trompe l'oeil frescoes by Lorenzo de Ferrari (1733). The adjacent **throne room**, its walls covered in deep red velvets and an excess of gold, is dotted with dozens of "C.A." monograms in honour of Carlo Alberto, King of Savoy. Continuing east, the lavish **audience room** has a dazzling Turkish carpet, silk curtains, and a grand portrait of a tight-lipped Caterina Durazzo-Balbi painted by Van Dyck in 1624 during his six-year stay in Genoa. Alongside, the **king's bedchamber** has parquet wooden flooring made by English carpenters in 1843, an exquisite Murano glass chandelier, and Van Dyck's first canvas of the Crucifixion, also dating from 1624, while the King's Bathchamber features the Savoyard motto *Je atans mon astre* ("I await my destiny" in archaic French) set into the floor. You then move into the **queen's quarters**, a series of rooms featuring a ghostly pale *Crucifixion* by the Neapolitan master Luca Giordano and a *St Lawrence* (1616) by Bernardo Strozzi. Passing through another series of drawing-rooms, one hung with Parisian tapestries of 1610, double-doors open onto the **grand terrace** which runs on three sides of a rectangle above the garden courtyard, giving airy views out over the port. Adjacent on the east side is the crumbling Teatro Falcone, where once the virtuoso Genoese violinist Paganini played.

Around Stazione Principe

Via Balbi continues west to the grandiose **Stazione Principe**, fronted by Piazza Acquaverde with a central statue of Columbus. Immediately below the train station, the drab run of portfront buildings is broken by the elegant loggia of the twelfth-century **Commendà**, a former convent, hospital and lodging-house for crusading knights, now gutted and converted to a temporary exhibition space. The oddly double-apsed church of **San Giovanni di Prè**, whose landmark campanile was added in the late twelfth century, was originally reserved solely for the use of the Knights of Malta, or Knights Hospitallers, who ran the Commendà next door and who have left behind them the legacy of a host of Maltese crosses used as decoration on buildings all over town. From here, the busy and notoriously seedy **Via di Prè** runs parallel with the waterfront Via Gramsci and is the first real street of the old town; partway along is the Bagnaschi hardware shop, occupying a perfectly preserved former hospital dating from 1353. Via di Prè skirts the port as far as the twelfth-century **Porta dei Vacca**, from where alleys run you into the heart of the old quarter.

From Piazza Acquaverde, Via Doria runs west down to the ferry terminal, past the lavish gardens of the huge **Palazzo del Principe Doria Pamphilj**, built in the early 1530s by Andrea Doria, who made his reputation and fortune attacking Turkish fleets and Barbary pirates and liberating the Genoese republic from the French and Spanish. The gardens back onto the *fin-de-siècle* **Stazione Marìttima**, which was once the departure point for steamers to New York and Buenos Aires but nowadays handles ferries to Corsica, Sardinia and Sicily (see p.125). It was from the **Ponte dei Mille** (Jetty of the Thousand) in front of the ferry terminal that **Giuseppe Garibaldi**, ex-mercenary and spaghetti salesman, persuaded his thousand Red Shirts to set off for Sicily in two clapped-out paddle steamers, armed with just a few rifles and no ammunition. Their mission, to support a Sicilian uprising and unite the island with the mainland states, greatly annoyed some northern politicians, who didn't want anything to do with the undeveloped south – an attitude which echoes in Italian politics to this day. About 1km further round the port is Genoa's restored sixteenth-century lighthouse, the **Lanterna** (*www.lanterna.provincia.genova.it*), as well as the **Matitone**, a postmodern polygonal tower housing municipal offices which comes to a sharp point above the industrial area of the port – giving rise to its sardonic nickname of "The Big Pencil".

The Porto Antico

The *sopraelevata*, or elevated highway, shoots along the waterfront above Piazza Caricamento, dividing the city from the ancient port, or **Porto Antico** (*www.portoantico .it*), long-since finished as a commercial concern but revitalized during the 1990s with the aim of bringing people down to the harbour again. Old warehouses have been converted into exhibition spaces, open stages host waterside performances, and there's an ice-skating rink, a cinema, a children's play area and a swimming pool. It's now a pleasant place to stroll, with cafés and pricey waterside bistros fronting the marina.

The visual centrepiece of the development is the **Bigo** – a curious multi-armed contraption, brainchild of Renzo Piano, intended to recall the harbourside cranes of old. One of the arms hauls a circular elevator up more than sixty metres to give visitors a superb all-round view over the city (daily 11am–1pm & 2–6pm; L6000/€3.10). South of the Bigo is the old Porta Siberia, with the **Molo Vecchio** (Old Wharf) just beyond; this was formerly where condemned prisoners would be led, to take the Last Sacrament at the little church of **San Marco** halfway along, before arriving at the gallows overlooking Piazza Cavour. The main feature of the area is a gigantic former cotton warehouse,

WHALE-WATCHING

The waters off the Ligurian coast as far south as Corsica comprise a World Wildlife Fund-monitored **International Whale Sanctuary**, home to 12 species of whale as well as dolphins and plenty of other marine life. It's easy to join summer boat excursions from towns along the Riviera for whale-watching, or *avvistamento cetacei*, in open sea (June–Sept at least twice weekly). All must be **booked in advance** and comprise a full day on board, including a light lunch and commentary from local WWF experts.

Main operators are Alimar (☎010.256.775, *www.alimar.ge.it*) and Cooperativa Battellieri (☎010.265.712, *www.battellierigenova.it*) – their boats start from **Genoa** (L60,000/€30.99) and pick up from **Savona** (L55,000/€28.41); Alimar's also pick up from **Alassio** (L50,000/€25.82 with lunch, or L40,000/€20.66 without). Different boats depart Porto Maurizio harbour in **Imperia** (☎0183.280.110; L50,000/€25.82), while from **San Remo** the operator is Riviera Line (☎0184.505.055, *www.rivieraline.it*; L70,000/€36.15).

now a commercial shopping centre with bars, cinemas, music stores and the **Padiglione del Mare e della Navigazione**, a small museum tracing the history of Genoa's relationship with the sea (March–Sept Mon–Fri 10.30am–6pm, Sat & Sun 10.30am–7pm; Oct–Feb Sat & Sun 10.30am–6pm; L9000/€4.65; joint ticket with Aquarium L25,000/€12.91).

Just north of the Bigo is the pride and joy of the city, the **Acquario di Genova** (July & Aug daily 9.30am–11pm; rest of year Mon–Fri 9.30am–7pm, Sat & Sun 9.30am–8pm, Oct–Feb closed Mon; last entry 1hr 30min before closing; L19,000/€9.81; joint ticket with Padiglione L25,000/€12.91; *www.acquario.ge.it*). This is Europe's largest aquarium, and houses sea creatures from all the world's major habitats. They have the world's largest reconstruction of a Caribbean coral reef, complete with moray eels, turtles and angelfish, and a growing number of species from the coral reefs and forests of Madagascar. Although the whole affair boasts a fashionably ecology-conscious slant and excellent background information (delivered in Italian and English), the larger beasts – including grey sharks, dolphins, seals and an enclosure containing a group of Humboldt penguins – can't help but seem pathetically imprisoned. It's best to avoid visiting on the weekend, when it can be a struggle just to glimpse the creatures between the human bodies.

South of San Lorenzo

The section of the old town south of the Cattedrale di San Lorenzo is less visited than the attraction-packed districts to the north, and more residential. Many of Genoa's students and young professionals live in the upper floors of the old buildings lining Via dei Giustiniani and Via San Bernardo, generating a lively bar-culture in the surrounding alleys.

From the cathedral and Piazza Matteotti, narrow **Salita Pollaiuoli** plunges you into the gloom between high buildings down to a crossroads with **Via San Bernardo**, a long, straight thoroughfare built by the Romans and now one of Genoa's most characterful old-town streets, with grocers and bakers trading behind the portals of palaces decorated in the fifteenth and sixteenth centuries. On the south side of the crossroads is tiny **Piazza San Donato**, a quiet square overlooked by the church of San Donato, whose decorous octagonal Byzantine-style campanile peeks over the roofs of this run-down quarter of town, not unlike the polygonal Matitone office-block rising above the industrial port further west. A crumbly, bare Romanesque church with a Roman architrave surviving over its door, San Donato's stark simplicity is refreshing after the self-importance of the nearby Gesù on Piazza Matteotti.

Piazza Sarzano and around

A shrine stuck on the side wall of San Donato faces up Stradone San Agostino, laid out in the eighteenth century and now home to a quirky array of bars and workshops. Partway up, stairs lead you into Ignazio Gardella's **architecture faculty** of the university, with a tranquil internal garden courtyard giving expansive views over the city. At the top of the street is the long, narrow bulge of **Piazza Sarzano**, originally home to Genoa's many ropemaking workshops and, due to its enormous length, still the scene for medieval-style jousting tournaments. The piazza is marked by the mosaic spire of the newly rebuilt church of **Sant'Agostino**; alongside it is the unique triangular cloister of the thirteenth-century monastery, which now houses the **Museo di Sant'Agostino** (Tues–Sat 9am–7pm, Sun 9am–12.30pm; L6000/€3.10), displaying Roman and Romanesque masonry fragments, led by the graceful tomb of Margherita of Brabant, sculpted in 1312 by Giovanni Pisano and now with only a part surviving.

Sneak down behind a remnant of the city wall at the southeastern corner of Piazza Sarzano alongside the church of San Antonio, and an alley lined with pretty houses will lead you down into the tranquil little enclosed piazza of **Campopisano**. It was here, during the wars between Genoa and Pisa, that Pisan prisoners were brought in chains, executed and buried; today, the pavement sports pretty mosaics in local *rissëu* style, using smooth white stones collected from the beach and black stones – or *serpentinita* – quarried from dark veins of slate that snake their way across nearby hillsides.

North from Piazza Sarzano streets connect to the **Porta Soprana**, a twin-towered stone gateway featuring impressive Gothic arches (surprisingly dating from as early as 1155) that now stands as the focus for a rather upmarket collection of bars and terrace cafés.

Modern Genoa

In the nineteenth century, Genoa began to expand beyond its old-town constraints. The newer districts begin with the large central **Piazza de Ferrari**, from where **Via XX Settembre** runs a straight course east through the commercial centre of the city towards Stazione Brignole. This grand boulevard features big department stores, shops selling designer clothes, and pavement cafés beneath its neon-lit arcades. There are prized delicatessens in the side-streets around Stazione Brignole and Piazza Colombo, and a bustling covered **Mercato Orientale** partway along, in the cloisters of an old Augustinian monastery. At the eastern end of Via XX Settembre, the small park outside the Brignole train station (hub for city buses) extends south into **Piazza della Vittoria**, a huge and dazzling white square built during the Fascist period that now serves as the long-distance bus station.

Walking north from Piazza de Ferrari takes you up to **Piazza Corvetto** – built by the Austrians in the nineteenth century and now a major confluence of traffic and people. Across the other side of the square, a thoughtful-looking statue of Giuseppe Mazzini marks the entrance to the **Villetta di Negro**, a lushly landscaped park whose artificial waterfalls and grottoes scale the hill. At the top, the **Museo d'Arte Orientale Edoardo Chiossone** (Tues & Thurs–Sun 9am–1pm; L6000/€3.10), holds a collection of oriental art that includes eighteenth-century sculpture and paintings and samurai armour. Chiossone was a printer and engraver for the Italian mint, and on the strength of his banknote engraving skills, he was invited by the Meiji dynasty to establish the Japanese Imperial Mint. He lived in Japan from 1875 until his death in Tokyo in 1898, building up an fascinating and extensive collection.

If you're not satisfied with the view from the Villetta di Negro, you can take the Art Nouveau-style public lift from **Piazza del Portello** up to the **Castelletto**, which offers a great panorama over the port and the roofs of the old town; a **funicular** also leaves from the same place up to the residential **Sant'Anna** district, although the views from here aren't as good (ordinary bus tickets are valid for both). When Genoa ran out of building space, plots for houses were hewn out of the hillside behind, like the steps of an amphitheatre, and the funicular enables you to see this at close quarters, as the carriages edge past people's front windows. Another funicular runs from Largo Zecca, further west, to the suburb of **Righi**, where you can admire vistas of the city below and wander off on any of a number of paths all around, although most locals' motives for coming up here are more prosaic – to sit in the various panoramic restaurants for extended sessions of family dining.

The outskirts: Albaro, Boccadasse and Staglieno

For a spot of relaxation, head out of town to the eastern waterfront suburb of **Albaro**, at the end of Corso Italia, a broad boulevard that runs along the seafront beyond the giant Fiera exhibition area (bus #31 from Stazione Brignole). This is the place to jog, stroll, pose at one of the private lidos, or to watch the sun set from a café table. From Albaro, you can walk or take bus #42 to **Boccadasse**. Once an outlying fishing port, this village is now part of the city, with boats pulled up on the pebble beach, nets hanging out to dry, some arty shops, and costly restaurants in which to sample the catch of the day.

Another good outing is to the **Staglieno cemetery** (daily 8am–5pm; free), on a hill northeast of the centre above the Bisagno valley. Bus #34 runs from Stazione Principe through Piazza Nunziata and Piazza Corvetto to the cemetery. This is still Genoa's major burial ground, laid out between 1844 and 1851, and is a veritable city of the dead, crammed with Neoclassical porticoes, Gothic chapels and statuary galore. The entrance gates lead you into a vast quadrangle dominated by a Neoclassical **Pantheon** holding monuments to a clutch of famous nineteenth-century Genoese, including **Nino Bixio**, second-in-command on Garibaldi's expedition to Sicily. Behind and to the right of the Pantheon is the mausoleum of **Giuseppe Mazzini**, fronted by two squat Doric columns. One of the most sentimental monuments is the statue of **Teresa Campodonico**, a seller of nuts, whose life savings went to reproduce her slight, bent figure; carved below is a poem recounting how she sold her nuts in sunshine and in rain so as to gain her daily bread and propel her image into future ages. In the Protestant section of the cemetery you'll find the grave of **Constance Lloyd**, Oscar Wilde's wife, who died in 1898 at the age of forty, less than a year after Wilde had been released from prison, having long since changed her name and the names of their two sons in shame to Holland.

Eating, drinking and nightlife

You could spend several days checking out the scores of places to **eat** in Genoa, from basic trattorias to elegant nineteenth-century *caffès*. The cheapest, around the port, are often open only at lunchtime.

On first impressions, life **after dark** looks sparse but a bit of time rooting around in the old town will turn up a good choice of convivial bars and small clubs, some of them with live music.

Drinks, snacks and light meals

Piazza Caricamento is one of the best places to head for a quick lunch on the hoof, the arcades (*sottoripe*) along the edge of the piazza lined with cafés serving **focaccia**, *panini* and deep-fried seafood. There are also lots of places in the old town selling **farinata** (Genoa's home-grown snack, made from chickpea flour and olive oil) – two that stand out are *Antica Sciamadda* at Via Ravecca 19r (closed Mon), and *Tugnin* on Piazza Tommaseo. *Forno Patrone*, Via Ravecca 72r (closed Wed afternoon) is one of the city's top bakeries. Centuries of Turkish influence has produced Genoese variations on Middle Eastern confectionery, including candied fruit (best sampled at *Romanengo* in Via Soziglia) and slabs of *pandolce* as served up at *Profumo* in Via del Portello.

Bar Berto, Piazza delle Erbe 6r. Relaxed café-bar founded in 1904 by Mr Berto who walked some 15km west to the ceramics centre of Albisola in order to collect colourful bits of broken tile to decorate the walls of his new bar. Whether inside or out beneath the terrace awning, this is a trendy spot for coffee, beer or a reasonably priced light meal. Open daily.

Doge Bar, Piazza Matteotti 84r. Small, civilized little nook alongside the Palazzo Ducale for daytime sandwiches and coffee. Closed Sun.

Klainguti, Piazza Soziglia 98r. An Austrian-built *salon* dating from 1828, selling cakes and ice cream under chandeliers. They still produce the hazelnut croissant known as a *Falstaff*, which was much esteemed by Giuseppe Verdi, who spent forty winters in Genoa – "Thanks for the Falstaff, much better than mine," he wrote to the bakers. No closing day.

Café La Madeleine, Via della Maddalena 103r. A wonderful little café-theatre, haunt of writers, poets, musicians and story-tellers, with plenty of readings and small concerts. Closed Mon.

Caffè Mangini, Via Roma at Piazza Corvetto. One of Genoa's most venerable *pasticcerie*, in business since the early 1800s and still top-notch today. No closing day.

Caffetteria Orefici, Via degli Orefici 25r. Fragrant temple to the art of coffee-making, with a range of specialist coffees and perfect results every time. Closed Sun.

Café Roger, Via Sant'Agostino. A quirky spot designed in riotous style after the Frank Zappa song "The Dangerous Kitchen" – every shelf is wonky, fake meat-cleavers dangle overhead, plastic sharks rise out of the sink, phoney electric cables snake around the basins, and so on. The staff, music, and clientele make this a fun stop for a daytime coffee or evening beer. No closing day.

Caffè degli Specchi, Salita Pollaiuoli 43r. Hidden in an alley opposite the Palazzo Ducale, this has been a prime spot since 1917 for Genovese artists, writers and intellectuals to take coffee while admiring themselves in the mirrors (*specchi*) which cover the magnificent tiled interior. The place still offers much the same ambience and old-time service, along with some tapas in the evening. Closed Sun.

Restaurants

La Berlocca, Via del Macelli di Soziglia 45r (☎010.247.4162). Young bistro-style establishment in the old town, offering something more adventurous than traditional Ligurian dishes. Closed Mon.

Da Genio, Salita San Leonardo 61r (☎010.588.443). This long-established restaurant, off Via Fieschi at the top of a steep hill above Piazza Dante, is highly regarded for great Ligurian food, served in a reasonably informal atmosphere, at moderate prices. Closed Sun & Aug.

Kilt, Via Bisagno 8. Self-service canteen dishing out three-course meals for L16,000/€8.26. No closing day. *Kilt 2* (closed Sun) is on Piazza San Matteo.

Mario Rivaro, Via del Portello 16r. Decent local dishes and seafood soups, from L20,000/€10.33 a dish. Closed Sun.

Östaja dö Castello, Salita Santa Maria di Castello 32r. Great old-town family-run trattoria serving Genoese specialities – mainly, but not exclusively, fish. Moderate to low prices. Closed Sun.

Pansön, Piazza delle Erbe 5r (☎010.246.8903). Venerable Genoese institution, in the same family since 1790; diners select from a fishy menu priced high to keep the riff-raff away. Closed Sun eve.

Pintori, Via di San Bernardo 68r. Family-run trattoria serving Sardinian specialities along with, on occasion, vegetarian dishes such as *torte di verdura* (check in advance for availability). Closed Sun & Mon.

Da Rina, Mura delle Grazie 3r. High-quality, simple Genoese cooking in fairly unpretentious surroundings down near the waterfront. Lots of fish and classic Ligurian dishes such as *cima alla genovese*. Moderately priced. Closed Mon.

Squarciafico, Piazza Invrea 3r (☎010.247.0823, *www.squarciafico.it*). Atmospheric cantina in the wine-cellar of a fifteenth-century mansion just off Piazza San Lorenzo. Calm, modern decor and innovative, carefully prepared food complement each other perfectly; be prepared for L45,000/€23.24 per person. Closed Aug.

Trattoria dei Genoani, Piazza delle Erbe 8r. Sociable little trattoria in a lively area founded and patronized by supporters of the Genoa football club – don't go shouting for Sampdoria here – which offers down-the-line takes on Genoese and Ligurian dishes, for affordable prices. No closing day.

Tre Finestre, Scalinata di San Antonio 2a. A tiny old-time trattoria off Piazza Sarzano. There's no menu (the waitress will just rattle off the dishes of the day), and the food is cheap, plain and hearty. Join in the good old-fashioned accordion singalong on Friday nights. Closed Mon–Thurs eve, and all day Sun.

Ugo, Via Giustiniani 86r. Convivial trattoria in the heart of the student quarter near San Donato, with a boisterous, friendly group of regulars who pack in at shared tables to wolf the Genovese and Ligurian nosh – heavy on pesto and seafood. A hearty meal for two can come in at under L30,000/€15.49. Well worth checking out. Closed Sun & Mon.

Zeffirino, Via XX Settembre 20r (☎010.591.990). Expensive – expect to pay around L80,000/€42.32 (excluding wine) for a three- to four-course meal of between-two-stools trad/mod cuisine – but this is where Frank Sinatra and Pavarotti have also dined and so has ineffable star quality. Closed Wed.

Nightlife

The best source of information on **nightlife** is the local daily paper *Il Secolo XIX*; in summer you can supplement this with *Genova by Night,* the tourist office's free what's-on guide. The student magazine *La Rosa Purpurea del Cairo* also has information on music, theatre and cinema; it's published monthly and is available from bars and some Via Balbi bookshops in term-time.

There are plenty of **bars** along the seamy waterfront Via Gramsci, in between the strip joints and brothels, but more attractive places to drink can be found on the side roads off Via XX Settembre and around Piazza delle Erbe. *Moretti* on Via San Bernardo is a beery student dive; *Le Corbusier*, Via San Donato 36r, is consistently popular; *Eprie Rosse*, Via Ravecca 54r, is a characterful wine-bar. The *Britannia* pub at Vico Casana 76r, off Piazza di Ferrari, has pints of Guinness and burgers and chips. The *Louisiana* **club** on Via San Sebastiano has live trad jazz most nights from around 10pm, but you'll find more happening joints tucked away in the southern part of the old town: the *Quaalude*, beneath the "Massari" signboard at Piazza Sarzano 14, is an underground club that features live bands and/or dance parties on Fridays and Saturdays – ask around in local bars for the latest news.

Theatre and opera

The two main **theatres** in Genoa are the Teatro della Corte, Via E.F. Duca d'Aosta, and the Teatro Duse, Via Bacigalupo, who advertise their performances on the same hoardings around town and sell tickets to both venues (☎010.534.2200, *www.teatro-di-genova.it.net*). The Teatro Carlo Felice in Piazza de Ferrari (☎010.589.329, *www.carlofelice.it*), is Genoa's main **opera house**; its performances are often oversubscribed, but it's still worth an enquiry. Chamber music concerts take place in some of Genoa's palaces over summertime.

Listings

Airlines Alitalia, via XXII Ottobre 12 (☎1478.65.642); British Airways (☎1478.12.266); Delta (☎1678.64.114); Meridiana (☎0789.69.300).

Banks Plenty are clustered next to Stazione Principe in Piazza Acquaverde, along Via Balbi, and on Via XX Settembre.

Boats Alimar (☎010.256.775, *www.alimar.ge.it*) and Cooperativa Battellieri (☎010.265.712, *www.battellierigenova.it*) offer 45min tours by boat around the port, departing from alongside the aquarium (every 30min, daily 10am–5pm; L10,000/€5.16). Alimar also do romantic tours by night (July

& Aug daily 9pm). Both companies run plenty of summer excursions west and east along the Riviera (generally L15–25,000/€7.74–12.90 one-way), departing either from the Aquarium or from Calata Zingari next to the Stazione Maríttima. Routings along the eastern coast are also operated by Golfo Paradiso, based in Camogli (☎0185.772.091, *www.golfoparadiso.it*), whose boats depart from Calata Mandraccio, just south of the Bigo. For whale-watching see p.120.

Bookshops Feltrinelli, Via XX Settembre 233, has some English-language paperbacks, but Di Stefano (*www.distefano.it*) at Porto Antico and Via Ceccardi 40r, has a better selection.

Car rental Europcar (airport ☎010.650.4881); Hertz, Via Casaregis 76 (☎010.570.265; airport ☎010.651.2422); Maggiore, Corso Sardegna 275 (☎010.839.2153); airport ☎010.651.2467); Sixt, Via Montevideo 111r (☎010.313.024); Swiss Rent, Via Canevari 191 (☎010.882.248).

Consulates UK, Piazza Vittoria 15 (☎010.564.833); USA, Via Dante 2 (☎010.584.492).

Doctor Call ☎010.354.022 for a doctor on call; First Aid emergency is on ☎113.

Ferries Any of the shipping agencies under the arcades along Piazza Caricamento can give current details of the long-distance ferries departing regularly to Bastia (Corsica), Olbia or Porto Torres (both Sardinia), Palermo (Sicily) and further afield to Barcelona, Tunis and around the Med. Main operators are: Corsica Tours, Piazza Dante 5a (☎010.593.301, *www.corsicaferries.com*); Grimaldi, Via Fieschi 17 (☎010.589.362; *www.grimaldi.it*); Moby, Ponte Asseretto (☎010.252.755, *www.mobylines.it*); and Tirrenia, Ponte Colombo (☎010.275.8041).

Flight information ☎010.601.5410.

Football Genoa's premier side, the sporadically successful Sampdoria, play at the Luigi Ferraris stadium, up behind Stazione Brignole. They share the stadium with the city's other major team, Genoa – founded in 1893 as the Genoa Cricket and Athletic Club, originally for British expatriates only. Bus #12 from Piazza Caricamento and bus #37 from Stazione Principe, Piazza Corvetto and Stazione Brignole, both pass near the stadium; or you can walk it in 15–20min from Brignole.

Hospitals Ospedale Galliera, Mura delle Cappuccine 14 (☎010.56.321), is the city's most central hospital, situated just south of Piazza Vittoria, while Ospedale Evangelico, Corso Solferino 1a (☎010.55.221) is English-speaking. For an emergency ambulance, call ☎010.5551.

Internet access Amazingly, Genoa had no public access points at the time of writing, but word had it that a cybercafé was due to open on Via Ravecca in the old town.

Parking There are a dozen or so central car parks, all of which cost L30–35,000/€15–18 per day; the largest is beneath Piazza della Vittoria (open 24hr). The old quarter is barred to traffic.

Pharmacies Ponte Monumentale, Via XX Settembre 115r (☎010.564.430) and Farmacia Pescetto, Via Balbi 185r (☎010.246.2697) are both English-speaking and open 24hr.

Police Carabinieri ☎112; Polizia ☎113; coastguard police ☎010.267.451. Genoa's police HQ is on ☎010.53.631.

Post office Via Dante 4 (Mon–Sat 8.10am–7.40pm; staff at window 15 speak English). Sub-post offices are at both train stations, open same hours.

Taxis Radio Taxi Genova ☎010.5966.

Train information ☎1478.88.088.

Travel agents CTS, Via San Vincenzo 119 (☎010.564.366 or 010.532.748); Giver Viaggi, Via XX Settembre 14 (☎010.570.1241 or 010.585.010); Nouvelles Frontieres, Via Brigata Bisagno 19r (☎010.553.6474).

Around Genoa

Genoa has spilled over its old city limits to sprawl some 30km along the coast, with good bus and train connections to most of its outlying parts, including the popular parks and promenades at **Nervi** to the east and **Pegli** to the west. If you can, though, head north inland: the terraced hills are at their most verdant in spring, when the blossom is out and the vines are flourishing. Several small villages make good bases for scenic walking, or you can sit back and let the train take the strain with an hour-long ride on a clanky old narrow-gauge line from Genoa up to the rustic hill-village of **Casella**. See the box on p.127 for details of how to access hikes on the alta via long-distance mountain trail.

Nervi

Genoa's mainly residential suburbs extend east to **NERVI** (accessible by local train or bus #15 from Piazza Cavour), a neat resort spread around a small harbour with a handful of bars along the seafront. Much of the centre of Nervi is given over to exotic flowers and plants: walking left out of the train station brings you into the **Parco di Villa Gropallo**, with, alongside, the **Parco di Villa Serra**, which hosts an open-air cinema during August (information from the Genoa tourist office). The park slopes down to a romantic seafront promenade with a few bars and fish restaurants, while joining it to the east are the lavish rose-gardens of the **Parco di Villa Grimaldi**. Following the lovely **promenade** east around the cliffs of the Sant'Ilario headland brings you to the **Museo Civile G. Luxoro**, holding a small collection of furniture, textiles and clocks (Tues–Sat 9am–1pm; L6000/€3.10). Semi-suburban though Nervi is, it still feels a long way from city life among the orange trees and the dreamy villa gardens.

Pegli

Near the airport west of Genoa is the industrial suburb of **Sestri Ponente**, a grim collection of blast furnaces, smelting works and housing projects. Local trains and the slow buses #1, #2 or #3 from Piazza Caricamento pass through here to **PEGLI**, and the romantic **Villa Durazzo-Pallavicini**, which is set in lavish grounds landscaped in nineteenth-century fantasy style (gardens Tues–Sun: April–Sept 9am–7pm; Oct–March 9am–5pm; L7000/€3.61). The villa now houses the **Museo Civico di Archeologia Ligure** (Tues–Thurs 9am–7pm, Fri–Sun 9am–1pm; L6000/€3.10), where items unearthed from cave burials in the hills along the west coast include the skeleton of a "Young Prince" with seashell crown and ceremonial dagger.

Genoa's northern hinterland

Many Genoese escape the city in summer by heading for the hills. The Genoa **tourist office** has the useful *Antola and its Valleys* booklet in English, complete with itinerary suggestions, a map and details of walks. AMT **buses** from Genoa's Piazza della Vittoria serve all the larger villages. Look out wherever you are for breads and pastas made with local chestnut flour, as well as *scarpignon*, ravioli stuffed with a meat and walnut paste.

Narrow-gauge **trains** – worth taking just for the sake of it – leave roughly hourly from a station in Genoa's Piazza Manin, connected to Brignole by bus #33 and Principe by bus #34/. The FGC trains (☎010.837.321) aren't covered by Genoa's normal bus tickets: one-way fares to Casella are L3100/€1.60 (L4300/€2.22 on Sun). They start off climbing through the Val Bisagno – from an early stop, **Trensasco**, there's a scenic three-hour walk that heads back down into Genoa past three medieval hill-fortresses – and coil northwards up to **CASELLA**, in a wooded dell at the foot of Monte Maggio (55min from Genoa). This little town is the trailhead for a number of hiking routes in the picturesque **Valle Scrivia** (*www.altavallescrivia.it*). If you show a train ticket at the little office in front of Casella station, you can **rent a mountain-bike** for L7000/€3.61 per hour, or L20,000/€10.33 per day (bookings on ☎010.967.7520). Casella has a couple of **hotels**, of which the *Magenta* is the better bet, Piazza XXV Aprile 20 (☎010.967.7113; ②); there are half-a-dozen **restaurants**, including *Camugin* (closed Mon) in front of the church, known for its fresh fish, and *Chiara* (closed Mon) with a wood-fired pizza oven.

Northeast of Genoa, buses follow the SS225 road over the Passo di Scoffera to little **TORRIGLIA**, which offers the photogenic ruins of a medieval castle and plenty of hiking trails into the mountains of the **Parco Naturale dell'Antola** (*www.parks.it*). The **tourist office** is at Via N.S. della Provvidenza 3 (☎010.944.931, *www.telecentroantola.it*)

WALKING THE ALTA VIA

The **Alta Via dei Monti Liguri** is a long-distance high-level trail covering the length of Liguria, from Ventimiglia in the west all across the ridge-tops to Ceparana on the Tuscan border above La Spezia in the east, a total distance of some 440km. The mountains, which form the connection between the Alps and the Apennines, aren't high – rarely more than 1500m – and the scenic route, which makes full use of the many passes between peaks, is correspondingly easygoing. The whole thing, which would take weeks to complete in full, has been divided up into 43 stages of between about two and four hours each, making it easy to dip in and out. Trail support and maintenance is generally good, with *rifugi* dotted along the path and distinctive waymarks (red-white-red "AV" signs).

A sample walk starts from point 26 – **Crocetta d'Orero**, on the Genoa–Casella train line: heading east from Crocetta, an easy route covers 7.8km to point 27, **Colle di Creto** (2hr 30min, and served by Genoa buses), with a diversion along the way to a lovely botanical path in and around the deserted hamlet of **Ciaé**. Another sample walk, the very first stage of all, from **Ventimiglia** to La Colla, sidelining to **Dolceacqua**, is outlined on p.129, and we've given details of access to hikes between points 32 and 34 above **Chiávari** on p.144. Unfortunately, access from the main coastal towns to most other parts of the alta via can be tricky, and requires juggling with route itineraries and bus timetables.

For information on the alta via, your best bet is the **Associazione Alta Via dei Monti Liguri**, based at the Centro Studi Unioncamere Liguri, Via San Lorenzo 15/1 in Genoa (☎010.247.1876, fax 010.247.1522, *www.lig.camcom.it*), which produces a full-colour wall-map of the route along with detailed English descriptions and timings of all 43 stages (plus hotels and restaurants along the way). Books and an eight-pamphlet guide to the trail are on sale in bookshops. The same information is at *www.parks.it* – click on "Grand Itineraries". **Club Alpino Italiano** offices in the major towns have information on *rifugi*, and the **Federazione Italiano Escursionismo** (FIE) publishes detailed guides to all the inland paths of Liguria.

---

and the basic *Della Posta* **hotel** is at Via Matteotti 39 (☎010.944.050; ②). From Torriglia, the SS45 heads northeast along the Val Trebbia through **Montebruno**, famed for its richly decorated fifteenth-century Santuario dell'Assunta (containing a Byzantine carving of the Madonna) and its mushroom-shaped chocolates called *funghetti*. Minor roads from Montebruno serve the mountain community of **FONTANIGORDA**, set further east amongst beech and chestnut woods and famous for its thirteen fountains. A scenic walking trail from here heads up and over the Passo di Esola to **Rezzoáglio** (see p.144), which lies within striking distance of Santo Stefano d'Aveto. Fontanigorda's **hotels** include the good-value *Fontanella*, Piazza Roma 7 (☎010.952.000, fax 010.542.825; ②), with en suite and shared-bath rooms, and the adequate *Augustus*, Via Fontana Vecchia 1 (☎010.952.014; ③), both with **restaurants**. The main SS45 continues over the mountains to Piacenza (see p.427).

Off to the west of Bolzaneto a few kilometres north of Genoa, a minor road off the SS35 heads to the hilltop sanctuary of **Madonna della Guardia**, for centuries the prime pilgrimage spot for the Genoese. The SS35 continues north up the valley, with buses passing through tiny **Ronco Scrivia**, which has an attractive medieval bridge over the river with three pointed arches, and **Isole del Cantone**, where a minor road climbs right up a wild side-valley towards Vobbia; a few kilometres into the valley, high up on the left (north) side, you'll spot the towers of the **Castello della Pietra**, a thirteenth-century castle, recently restored, which sits in a dramatic spot wedged between rock pinnacles above the thick forest; if you have the puff, climb the steep path up to it for spectacular valley views.

THE RIVIERA DI PONENTE

The *autostrada* gives the most positive impression of the **Riviera di Ponente** ("Western Riviera"), the umbrella title for the stretch of Ligurian coast between the French border and Genoa. From its elevated viaducts, the marinas and resorts way below are mere specks in a stunning panorama of glittering sea and acres of glasshouses. If you exit the *autostrada* and venture down to the coastal road to see things close-up, you'll find that the Riviera towns are generally fairly functional places, occasionally sporting an attractive medieval quarter but always overflowing with hotels and apartment blocks. Yet these resorts have their good points – chiefly the sandy beaches, comparatively low prices and lack of pretentiousness. However, with a very mild and sunny climate, they have their winter devotees too – but are much less crowded out of high season.

Just about every settlement along this stretch of coast is a resort of some kind, either well-developed family-targeted places like **Finale Ligure**, small, better-preserved villages like **Noli**, or grand old resorts like **San Remo**; the attractive medieval town of **Albenga** manages happily to fall somewhere in between. Some of these places – San Remo, for example, or the border town of **Ventimiglia** – also make good bases for travelling into the mountain areas behind the coast, where stone villages and agricultural communes reveal the more private side of the region. Walkers can explore sections of the Alta Via dei Monti Liguri (see box on previous page) or loop through attractive and little-visited hill-towns like **Baiardo**, **Taggia** or **Dolceacqua**. In the large resort of **Alassio**, an organization of local hoteliers – the Consorzio Riviera Palmhotels – at Via Leonardo da Vinci 139 (☎0182.648.270, fax 0182.600.961, *www.palmhotels.it*) offer a booking service along the whole coast.

Ventimiglia and around

Barely 6km east of the border, **VENTIMIGLIA** is the first stop inside Italy, a scruffy frontier town that had several centuries of minor prosperity courtesy of the constant border traffic, but is now experiencing hard times. In 1995 the **Schengen** agreement, permitting unhindered passage between France and Italy, rendered Ventimiglia's time-honoured role as customs post and refreshment point redundant. Even the excuse of stopping to spend your last lire will evaporate after 2002, when the currency is unified on both sides of the border. The main advantage of breaking your journey here is that hotels offer considerably better value than those in other nearby resorts, and it makes a good base for country walks.

The huge **train station** is in the centre of the modern quarter on the eastern bank of the River Roia. A block in front of the forecourt runs the main Via Cavour, with the **tourist office** at no. 61 (Mon–Sat 8am–7pm; ☎ 0184.351.183, *www.apt.rivieradeifiori.it*) and the covered flower market nearby. Across the river is the crumbling medieval quarter up on its hill, the most prominent sight being the Romanesque **Cattedrale dell'Assunta** with its twelfth-century campanile and, behind it, an eleventh-century polygonal **Baptistry**. About 1km east of the station, alongside the main road and rail tracks, lie a small late-second-century AD **amphitheatre**, town gate and remains of Roman Albintimilium with the nearby Forte dell'Annunziata, Via Verdi 41, displaying a small collection of finds in the **Museo Archeologico G. Rossi** (Tues–Sat 9am–12.30pm & 3–5pm, Sun 10am–12.30pm; L4000/€2.06). The best day to visit is Friday, when a colourful clothes, food and junk **market** takes over the centre of town, and French bargain-hunters stream across the border.

The priciest **hotel** is *La Riserva*, 5km northwest in Castel d'Appio, at Via Peidago 79 (☎0184.229.533, fax 0184.229.712, *www.lariserva.it*; ⑥; Easter–Sept) – grand views from the terrace and a pool raise it well out of the ordinary. The pleasant *Sea Gull*, Passeggiata Marconi 24 (☎0184.351.726, fax 0184.231.217, *www.seagullhotel.it*; ③) has its own patch of beach below the medieval quarter. Of the occasionally grotty low-end choices, *XX Settembre*, Via Roma 16 (☎0184.351.222; ②) and *Villa Franca*, Corso Repubblica 12 (☎0184.351.871, fax 0184.33.434; ①) stand out, the latter close to the station. For **food**, try the excellent *Usteria d'a Porta Marina* (closed Tues eve & Wed), overlooking the river at Via Trossarelli 22: the celebrated *branzino* (sea-bass) in local Rossese wine is expensive, but they have three-course menus for L30,000/€15.49. Other less pricey places line the promenades on the east side of the river; one option is the *Terrazzino*, which has a rock-bottom *menu fisso* for L18,000/€9.30.

Around Ventimiglia

From Via Cavour in front of Ventimiglia's train station, bus #1a heads west for 5km to the village of **MÓRTOLA INFERIORE**, famed for the spectacular hillside **Giardini Botanici "Hanbury"** (daily: mid-June to Sept 9am–7pm; April to mid-June & Oct 10am–6pm; rest of year 10am–5pm, closed Wed; L12,000/€6.20). These gardens were laid out in 1867 by Sir Thomas Hanbury, a London spice merchant, and are powerfully atmospheric, with hidden corners and pergola-covered walks tumbling down to the sea. A half-hour walk further west along the coast road – or a few minutes on bus #1a – is the frontier post. A scramble down the hillside brings you to the caves of **Balzi Rossi** (Tues–Sun 9am–7pm; free), where were discovered remains of prehistoric civilizations dating back to the Paleolithic age; a small **Museo Preistorico** (same hours; L4000/€2.06) houses a collection of artefacts, crude fertility sculptures and bones from hippos, rhinos and elephants.

A walk to Dolceacqua
The area's best walk comprises Stage One of the **Alta Via dei Monti Liguri** hiking trail (see box p.127). The 10km route (which takes an easy 3hr) begins from Ventimiglia tourist office; walk east for a few minutes along Via Cavour, which becomes Corso Genova, and then duck north beneath the train tracks via an underpass which is marked with the first of the red-and-white "AV" waymarkers. From here, you climb out of the town through vineyards onto a ridge running between the valleys of the Roia and the Nervia, past the votive chapel of **San Giacomo**, through the ancient hamlet of **Ciaixe** and up to **La Colla**.

From La Colla, the trail continues along a side-path that takes you east down to the medieval riverside village of **DOLCEACQUA**, best-known for its excellent Rossese red wine and its olive oil. Piles of black olives crowd the village at harvest time, spread out on cloths on the ground prior to processing. The Nervia, crossed by an elegant 33m single-span medieval bridge, runs from the new part of town, or **borgo**, alongside the valley road, to the steep, stone alleyways of the older quarter, the **terra**, which are arranged in concentric circles around slopes topped by the blank-eyed ruins of a castle that once belonged to the Doria family. A theatre festival and concerts are staged here every summer (contact the tourist office for details, see below), and Dolceacqua is also the scene of a more ancient festival, rooted in fertility rites: on the Sunday nearest to January 20, a laurel tree hung with coloured Communion wafers is carried through the village as part of the procession of St Sebastian. For ideas on **walks** in the beautiful Upper Nervia Valley, ask at the **tourist office**, Via Patrioti Martiri 58 (daily

10am–1pm & 4–7pm; ☎0184.206.666). **Buses** run between Dolceacqua and Ventimiglia.

San Remo and around

Set on a broad sweeping bay between twin headlands, **SAN REMO** had its heyday as a classy resort in the sixty years or so up to the outbreak of World War II, when the Empress Maria Alexandrovna headed a substantial Russian community in the town (Tchaikovsky completed *Eugene Onegin* and wrote his Fourth Symphony in San Remo in 1878) and wealthy Europeans paraded on the Corso Imperatrice. Some of the grand hotels overlooking the sea, especially those near the train station, are now grimy and crumbling, but others in the ritzier western parts of town are still in pristine condition, opening their doors to Europe's blue-rinse nobility season after season. San Remo is blessed with the Riviera's most famous **casino** after the one in Monte Carlo, and it remains a showy, old-fashioned town, with a good deal of life.

San Remo's premier annual event is the **Festival della Canzone**, held every February, where Italy's finest pop performers compete for the giddy honour of representing the motherland in the Eurovision Song Contest. No less melodramatic is the **Campionato Mondiale di Fuochi d'Artificio**, or World Fireworks Championship (*www.sanremo.it/fuochi*), an annual fixture in late June and early July which sees lavish pyrotechnic displays bursting nightly over the port.

Arrival, information and accommodation

The **train station** is centrally located beside the sea with the **tourist office** just across the road at Largo Nuvoloni 1 (Mon–Sat 8am–7pm, Sun 9am–1pm; ☎0184.571.571, *www.sanremonet.com* and *www.apt.rivieradeifiori.it*). The main **bus station** is five minutes' walk east along Corso Matteotti on Piazza Colombo. Local Riviera Trasporti buses from here or the train station shuttle around town and up to Taggia (see p.132); one-hour tickets cost L1650/€0.85. Trips along the coast by **boat** are run by Riviera Line, Molo di Levante 35 (March–Oct daily 10am & 3pm; lasts 1hr 30min; L21,000/€10.84; ☎0184.505.055, *www.rivieraline.it*); they also do whale-watching excursions (see p.120). For **Internet** access, head to Mailboxes Etc at Corso Cavalotti 86, beside *Hotel Méditerranée* (Mon–Sat 8.30am–6.30pm, Sat 9am–1pm; L5000/€2.58 for 15min). For advice on **hiking**, visit the Club Alpino Italiano office, Piazza Cassini 13 (Tues & Fri 9.30–10.30pm, Wed & Sat 6–7pm).

Finding **accommodation** is usually no problem; note, though, the usual insistence on half- or full-board in high season. The *Royal Hotel*, Corso Imperatrice 80 (☎0184.5391, fax 0184.661.445, *www.royalhotelsanremo.com*; ⑨), is probably the finest in Liguria, complete with a vast heated saltwater swimming pool set into its tropical garden and a resident orchestra to accompany afternoon tea and formal dinner. Cream of the four-star crop is the *Astoria West End*, Corso Matuzia 8 (☎0184.667.701, fax 0184.663.318, *astoria@tourism.it*; ⑧), dripping with *fin-de-siècle* elegance. The *Paradiso*, Via Roccasterone 12 (☎0184.571.211, fax 0184.578.176, *www.italiaabc.it*; ⑤), is in a quiet location above the town's bustle, with its own secluded garden and sunny, modern rooms. The *Maristella*, right by the sea at Corso dell'Imperatrice 77 (☎0184.667.881, fax 0184.667.655, *hmcps@tin.it*; ③), is a friendly place with attractive Liberty-style decor. To the east of the station, on and between Corso Matteotti and Via Roma, you'll find a number of budget hotels, including the cosy *Albergo Al Dom* at Corso Mombello 13 (☎0184.501.460; ②) and the welcoming *Matuzia* at Corso Matteotti

121, top floor (☎ & fax 0184.577.070; ②). There's a **campsite** west of town, *Villaggio dei Fiori*, Via Tiro a Volo 3 (☎0184.660.635, fax 0184.662.377, *www.seasun.net*).

The Town

The tourist office is housed in the **Palazzo di Riviera**, a prime example of the kind of floral Liberty-style architecture that is arrayed all along the palm-lined **Corso Imperatrice** boulevard which lines the seafront west of the centre. (Partway towards the grandest and most luxurious palace hotels further west on Corso Matuzia, you'll pass the **Giardini Marsaglia**, a public park centred on an auditorium that stages regular summer concerts.) Directly opposite the tourist office is an onion-domed **Russian Orthodox church** (daily 9.30am–12.30pm & 3–6.30pm), built in the 1920s and more impressive on the outside than within. About 100m further east you'll come to San Remo's landmark **Casino**, a white Liberty-style palace with grand staircases and distinctive turrets that still stands as the epitome of the town's old-fashioned sense of monied leisure, playing an active part in its nightlife to this day (see overleaf). **Corso degli Inglesi** winds around and above the casino, home to dozens of villas in varying states of repair, including one close to the junction of Via Fratelli Asquascati complete with stained-glass irises and majolica tiles.

From the casino, the main **Corso Matteotti**, lined with cocktail bars, *gelaterie*, cinemas and clothes stores, heads east into the commercial centre of town. Lurid neon signs on sidestreets point to private clubs and by-the-hour hotels, all rubbing shoulders with a handful of expensive restaurants. The cross-street **Corso Mombello** connects south to the Giardini Veneto on the seafront alongside the harbour, and north to the main central square **Piazza Eroi Sanremesi**. This huge, rambling space is partly taken up by market-stalls and terrace cafés, and partly backs onto the Gothic **Cattedrale di San Siro** (daily 7–11.15am & 3–6pm), which features unusual twelfth-century bas reliefs above its side doors and a processional black crucifix within. A short way east of the cathedral, at Corso Matteotti 143, is the impressive Renaissance Palazzo Borea d'Olmo, still owned by the family of the same name and now housing the **Museo Civico** (Tues–Sat 9am–12.30pm & 3–6.30pm, Sun 9am–noon; L4000/€2.06), but its array of local finds and paintings is less memorable than the sumptuous frescoed interior. **Piazza Colombo** is just east of the museum, with Via Asquasciati heading down to the sea. If you follow the harbourside promenade east for 1km, you'll come to the marina and – on the north side of the tracks – the **Giardino Ormond**, which is filled with date-palms, yuccas, olive-trees, jacaranda, bougainvillea and even a grand cedar of Lebanon.

San Remo's most fascinating quarter – which stands in stark contrast to the glamour and bustle of the seafront districts – is its **old town**, accessible up steep lanes north of Piazza Eroi Sanremesi and Piazza Cassini. Known as **La Pigna** or the "Pine-Cone", its kasbah-like arched passageways and alleys leading nowhere come as quite a surprise after the busy modern streets below. It's worth clambering up to the highest point, not only for the ethereal experience of wandering through the quarter itself, but also for the views from the gardens at the peak across the whole of the town and surrounding countryside.

If you can drag yourself out of bed early enough, San Remo offers one of the liveliest and most engaging spectacles on the Riviera: the **wholesale flower market** in Armea, 4km east of town (Mon–Fri 4am–8am). You'll know when you're approaching by the sight of waiters running around with trays of espresso, and the woven boxes for flowers attached to the vans and Vespas outside. Some eighty tonnes of flowers a day are shipped out of here, around Italy and the world. The market itself is strictly for trade, but no one minds bystanders as long as they don't get in the way.

Eating, drinking and nightlife

San Remo is well served for **restaurants**, most of which offer the local speciality of *sardenàira*, a kind of cheese-less pizza topped with tomatoes, olives, capers, garlic and fresh oregano. *Cantine Sanremesi*, Via Palazzo 7, is a convivial small tavern on a central shopping street that serves snacks and simple fare. Piazza Eroi Sanremesi is ringed by pizzeria-restaurants, most with decent tourist menus; best is *Graziella* (closed Mon). Up in the old town, just off Piazza dei Dolori, *Osteria della Costa* (closed Sun) does an excellent rabbit stew but its few tables are snapped up early. Moving up the price scale, *Nuovo Piccolo Mondo*, Via Piave 7 (☎0184.509.012; closed Sun & Mon) is a cosy little trattoria serving choice Ligurian dishes on an alley off Corso Matteotti, while *Vittorio*, round the corner at Piazza Bresca 16 (☎0184.501.924; closed Wed) is an excellent place for mid-price fish and seafood. *Bagatto*, Corso Matteotti 145 (☎0184.531.925; closed Sun & July) is the easiest-going of San Remo's many formal restaurants, serving top-quality local cuisine for around L60,000/€30.99 without wine.

For **nightlife**, San Remo's famous **Casino** comes out tops every time (daily 2pm–3am). Admission is free to the slot machines, but not to the evocative Belle Epoque gaming rooms (Mon–Thurs L5000/€2.58, Fri–Sun L15,000/€7.75). The dress-code is jacket and tie for both American and French gaming rooms, but you can get away with jeans and sneakers in the slot machine area. It's worth the effort to get in, even if you then eschew the James Bondery downstairs in favour of a quiet evening on the roof garden (where drinks aren't too expensive). Elsewhere around town, there's no shortage of **clubs** and **bars**, and in summer there are open-air jazz, blues and folk **concerts** around the harbour and in the various parks.

Inland from San Remo

Corso degli Inglesi coils up from San Remo's seafront Casino around the peak of **Monte Bignone** through a landscape of vines and silvery olive trees which is green and lush even in the height of summer. **BAIARDO** – reachable by bus – makes the best centre if you plan to stay in this region, a hill-town comprising little more than a few houses around a church with wide views over several valleys, and mule tracks and footpaths meandering through the fields and vineyards. The only place to stay is the two-star *La Greppia* (☎0184.673.310; ②), although the village of **APRICALE**, clinging to a pinnacle of rock some 8km southwest of Baiardo, has *La Favorita* (☎0184.208.186, fax 0184.208.247; ②) along with part of its ancient walls and gates, a ruined twelfth-century castle and views of **Perinaldo** perched even higher in the distance. About 2km west of Apricale and 4km north of Dolceacqua (see p.129) is the village of **Isolabona**, where you can pick up buses for Ventimiglia.

The Valle Argentina

The Valle Argentina ("Silver Valley") heads inland from the bustling seaside resort of **Arma di Taggia**, 6km east of San Remo. Sleepy, crumbling **TAGGIA**, 3km north, is known for its sixteen-arched **Romanesque bridge**, the *taggiasca* black olive that is famed for giving top-quality oil (*www.taggiasca.com*), and a collection of work by Ligurian artists in the black-and-white stone convent church of **San Domenico** just outside the old walls (daily 9am–noon & 3–5pm; donations). If you can, time a visit for the third Sunday in July, when the ancient *festa* of the Magdalene culminates in a "Dance of Death" performed by two men, traditionally from the same two families, accompanied by the local brass and woodwind band.

Some 25km further up the valley is the tiny village of **TRIORA**. The trip here from San Remo is worth doing in its own right, the bus wending its way past small settlements with ancient bridges and farms linked to the main road across the valley by a rope and pulley system. Triora is within sight of Monte Pietradura, which stays snowcapped until April. In 1588, after an unexpected famine, two hundred women in this isolated community were denounced by the Inquisition as **witches**: thirty were tortured, fourteen were burned at the stake, and one woman committed suicide before she could be executed. Documents from the trial are preserved in the **Museo Etnografico** in the village (May–Dec Mon–Sat 3–6.30pm, Sun 10.30am–noon & 3–6pm; Jan–April Sun only; L2000/€1.03), and a commemorative plaque adorns the overgrown Cabotina just outside the village, supposed scene of the witches' gatherings. Also worth seeking out is the celebrated Sienese painter Taddeo di Bartolo's *Baptism of Christ* (1397), hung in the baptistry of the Romanesque-Gothic **Collegiata** church. Triora is known for its flat bread, *Pane di Triora*, and the village has a single **hotel**, the peaceful *Colombo d'Oro*, Corso Italia 66 (☎0184.94.051, fax 0184.94.089; ②), converted from an old monastery.

From San Remo to Genoa

There's not a great deal to divert you on the first stretch of coast east of San Remo as far as Albenga. This stretch is shoulder-to-shoulder beach resorts, which offer little diversity and stay unrelentingly busy all summer long (when it can be hard to find accommodation, despite the hundreds of hotels), although the crush does ease a bit out of season.

Some 30km east of San Remo is the provincial capital of **IMPERIA**, formed in 1923 when Mussolini linked twin townships on either side of the River Impero. Imposing **Porto Maurizio**, on the western bank, is the more attractive of the two, ascending the hillside in a series of zigzags from a marina and small beach. Its stepped old quarter is dominated by a massive late-eighteenth-century cathedral and a series of Baroque churches and elegant villas. Quieter **Oneglia**, 2km east, is still very much wedded to the sea, with an active population of fisherfolk; just behind its station at Via Garessio 13 is the **Museo dell'Olivo**, paid for by the town's leading olive-oil dynasty, the Fratelli Carli (Mon & Wed–Sun: Aug 4–8pm; rest of year 9am–noon & 3–6.30pm; free; *www.oliocarli.it*), housing modern displays devoted to the history of Liguria's green nectar. The **tourist office** is at Viale Matteotti 37 in Porto Maurizio (Mon–Sat 8am–7pm; ☎0183.660.140), where you'll also find the comfortable **hotels** *Croce di Malta*, overlooking the old harbour at Via Scarincio 148 (☎0183.667.020, fax 0183.63.687, *www.hotelcrocedimalta.com*; ④) and *Ambra*, on Via Rambaldo 9 (☎0183.63.715; ②).

East of Imperia, olive plantations take over from flowers along what has been dubbed the **Riviera dei Olivi**. Two big beach resorts – Diano Marina and **ALASSIO**, the latter with a spectacular 4km fine-sand beach and motorboat trips out to the Isola Gallinara island nature reserve – bookend a couple of slightly less frenetic spots: **Cervo** is a picturesque spiral of cottages that primps and preens itself for the tourist trade, while **LAIGUEGLIA**, a quiet ex-fishing port with a couple of porticoed streets to wander, offers a more palatable slice of beach life than its big-time neighbours.

A walk up the steps from the junction of Via Mimosa and the main Via Roma in Laigueglia takes you away from the coast through a cluster of holiday homes to the old **Roman road** near the top of the hill. From here, follow the *strada privata* into the woods and take the signposted path for the ruins of the **Castello di Andora** and what is held to be the best Romanesque church on the Riviera (a 45min walk). Even if you never get to the church and castle, the walk along mule tracks between olive groves and woods is one of the most appealing parts of this bit of coast, with plenty of shaded places to dream away the afternoon. From the castle you can either backtrack or walk on through the outskirts of the village of **Andora** to its train station.

Albenga

Beyond Alassio the terrain grows more mountainous, and the rail line and road stick close to the sea for the 8km journey to the small market town of **ALBENGA**. With silting up of the river estuary, Albenga long ago lost its port and merits a visit these days to explore its pleasingly business-like old quarter, still within medieval walls. The **train station** is 800m east of the old town via the twin parallel boulevards of Viale dei Mille and Viale Martiri della Libertà; the latter leads to the **tourist office** at no. 1 (Mon–Sat 9am–12.30pm & 3–7pm, Sun 9am–12.30pm; ☎0182.558.444, *www.italianriviera.com*), and on to **Piazza San Michele** at the heart of the old town. This small square is dominated by the elegant **cathedral**, the main part of which was built in the eleventh century and enlarged in the early fourteenth. Diagonally opposite in the Torre Comunale is the **Museo Civico Ingauno** (Tues–Sun 10am–noon & 3–6pm; L3000/€1.55), displaying interesting ancient artefacts and providing access to Albenga's big draw, the **Baptistry**. This ingenious building went up alongside the cathedral in the fifth century, and combines an unusual ten-sided exterior with a more orthodox octagonal interior. Inside are fragmentary mosaics showing the Apostles represented by twelve doves.

Behind the baptistry to the north, the archbishop's palace houses the diverting **Museo Diocesano** (Tues–Sun 10am–noon & 3–6pm; donations). Taking pride of place are the remains of the fifteenth-century frescoes that adorned what used to be a chapel and the bishop's own bedchamber (the latter decorated by Provençal artists with a mixture of sombre and bright flower patterns to represent night and day). A few metres west, where Via Medaglie d'Oro crosses Via Ricci, is the thirteenth-century **Loggia dei Quattro Canti**, marking the town centre of Roman Albingaunum. Some 500m north of here, beyond Piazza Garibaldi and along Viale Pontelungo, you'll find the odd sight of an elegant, arched 150m bridge spanning nothing much: the **Pontelungo** was built here in the twelfth century to cross the river, which shifted course soon afterwards.

The pleasant *Italia*, Viale Martiri della Libertà 8 (☎0182.50.405, fax 0182.570.273; ②), is an old 1930s-style **hotel** with only shared-bath rooms. Alternatively, down on the seafront *Sole Mare*, Lungomare Colombo 15 (☎0182.51.817, fax 0182.52.752; ④) has a range of rooms including some bargains. The *Lungomare* **campsite** is at the mouth of the river off Strada Vicinale Avarenna (☎0182.51.449, fax 0182.52.525). Albenga's least expensive **restaurants** are off Via Medaglie d'Oro on the alley Via Torlaro. *Da Puppo*, a characterful little place with a wood-burning pizza oven and good *farinata* is at no. 20, while at no. 13 is *Il Vecchio Mulino* (closed Thurs) serving basic trattoria food from L9000/€4.65. Pricey *Osteria dei Leoni*, behind the baptistry at Via Lengueglia 49 (closed Mon), has a good range of local dishes, while the popular *Babette*, Viale Pontelungo 26 (closed Mon & Tues), hosts Greek-, French- and Italian-themed dinners.

The caves of Toirano

Nurseries of artichokes and petunias, interspersed with garden centres and caravan sites, line the coast between Albenga and the town of **Borghetto Santo Spirito**, transfer point for buses a few kilometres inland to the spectacular caves of **TOIRANO**, set halfway up a rocky hillside outside the well-preserved medieval village centre. There are three main cave complexes (daily: July & Aug 9.30am–6pm; rest of year 9am–noon & 2–5pm; L15,000/€7.75; *www.toirano.it*). The stalactite-adorned **Grotta della Bàsura** – dialect for "The Witch's Cave" – was the home of Stone Age inhabitants some eighty thousand years ago. These early troglodytes apparently shared their cave-dwellings with local bears: there's a mass of bear bones in the underground Bear Cemetery, and dozens of prehistoric foot- and pawprints left in what was once mud. A path leads on to the **Grotta di Santa Lucia**, containing remarkable stalagmite and stalactite formations, with a natural spring which was dedicated in the Middle Ages to St Lucy, patron saint of eyesight, after several miraculous cures were effected here. Further on, there are guided tours around **Grotta del Colombo** which lead you through the beautiful caverns formed in the limestone over millions of years by the action of water.

Finale Ligure

Busy **FINALE LIGURE** is overtly committed to tourism, yet it manages to remain attractive. The majority of tourists are Italian families; only around 10pm on summer nights does the place come alive, as people pack the outdoor restaurants, seafront fairground and open-air cinema, while an extended passeggiata fills the promenade and the old alleys. There are three parts to the town. **Finalmarina** is the main bit, with the **train station** at its western end, a good pebbly beach, a promenade lined with palms, and narrow shopping streets set back from the seafront that hold the **tourist office** at Via San Pietro 14 (Mon–Sat 9am–12.30pm & 3.30–7pm, Sun 9am–noon; ☎019.681.019, *www.italianriviera.com*). The bars in the vicinity of Piazza Vittorio Emanuele II and the adjoining Piazza di Spagna, the main public space in the centre of this spread-out resort, are the points to which everyone eventually gravitates. **Finalpia** is a small district five minutes' walk to the east on the other side of the River Sciusa focused around the twelfth-century church of Santa Maria di Pia (rebuilt in florid early-eighteenth-century style) and its adjacent sixteenth-century cloistered abbey. **Finalborgo** is a medieval walled quarter set on a slight hill 2km inland from Finalmarina and overlooked by bare rock-faces that are a favourite with free climbers, who gather at *Bar Gelateria Centrale* in Finalborgo's Piazza Garibaldi at weekends. The area's wider fame comes from the **Grotte delle Arene Candide**, among Europe's most important caves for prehistoric remains; they're closed for excavation, but some finds are on display at the **Museo Civico** in Finalborgo's church of Santa Caterina (June–Sept Tues–Sat 10am–noon & 3–6pm, Sun 9am–noon; rest of year slightly shorter hours; L5000/€2.58). The same church hosts an interesting bric-à-brac and antiques **market** on the first weekend of each month during summer.

In high season virtually all the hotels insist on full pension, and you'd do better staying up the coast at Noli (see below), unless you opt for the *Castello Wuillermin* HI **hostel** which occupies an old castle high above the train station at Via Caviglia 46 (☎019.690.515, *hostelfinaleligure@libero.it*; L20,000/€10.33; mid-March to mid-Oct). *Eurocamping* is a well-run riverside **campsite** at Via Calvisio 37 in Finalpia (☎019.601.240; April–Sept). The best places **to eat** need some hunting out. *Da Tonino*, Via Bolla 5, has outside seating and good pizzas. *Gnabbri*, next to the church of San Giovanni Battisti at Via Pollupice 1 (closed Thurs) is a friendly trattoria whose atmosphere and reasonably priced menu feels a million miles away from the brash seafront pizza parlours. Up in Finalborgo is *Ai Torchi*, Via dell'Annunziata 12 (☎019.690.531; June, July & Sept closed Tues; Aug open daily; Oct–May closed Mon & Tues; also closed Jan), occupying an ancient olive-oil factory and serving expensive pasta and fish dishes with care and some style.

The tourist office has information on picturesque inland **walks**, the **Sentieri Parlanti**, which zigzag across the hills past the excellent mid-priced *La Briga* restaurant (☎019.698.579; closed Tues & Wed and in winter), where you can fill up on *ortica* (nettle) and *tartufo nero* (black truffle) lasagne. You can rent **mountain-bikes** on Via Brunenghi in Finalborgo – from Raceware at no. 124, and R.C. Bike at no. 65.

Noli

The Via Aurelia heads northeast from Finale Ligure past the small Capo di Noli, where the sea is inviting and the inlets are accessible from the road. **NOLI**'s beaches aren't great but otherwise this is the nicest resort along this part of the Riviera, topped by a castle whose battlements march down the hill to meet the walls of the small but pretty old town. Aside from half-a-dozen medieval towers, Noli's grid of old streets hides the majestic Romanesque church of **San Paragorio** near the train station, notable for its crypt, its frescoes, a thirteenth-century bishop's throne of inlaid wood kept behind glass in an interior chapel, and a twelfth-century *Volto Santo* (True Likeness of Christ) similar to the one at Lucca in Tuscany (see p.517). The **tourist office** faces the sea at Corso Italia 8 (Mon–Sat 9am–noon & 3.30–6.30pm, Sun 9am–noon; ☎019.749.9003), and a number of the town's thirteenth-century palaces have been converted into **hotels**, most of which have popular **restaurants** attached. *Miramare*, Corso Italia 2 (☎019.748.926; ④) is top choice, an old fortress updated with all mod cons. *Albergo Triestina*, down a medieval street off the seafront at Via da Noli 16 (☎019.748.024; ④), offers a personal, welcoming ambience, while *Da Ines* at Via Vignolo 1 (☎019.748.5428, fax 019.748.086; ③), has pleasant, well-equipped rooms, and is an especially convivial place to eat. The **beaches** are broad and sandy some 3km further up the coast at **SPO-TORNO**, but this once-tranquil little place has lost just about all of the character it could claim in 1926, when D.H. Lawrence holed up there to write *Lady Chatterley's Lover*.

Savona

First impressions of **SAVONA**, 17km northeast of Noli, aren't up to much: it's a functional city much rebuilt after a hammering in World War II. However, its port infrastructure and ugly outskirts hide a picturesque **medieval centre** worth exploring – especially when it's taken over on summer Saturdays by a huge antiques and bric-à-brac market. The town's main claim to fame is as the *Città dei Papi*, City of Popes: local boy Francesco Della Rovere became **Pope Sixtus IV** in 1471, and had a large private chapel built within the Vatican (named the Sistine Chapel after himself) and his nephew Giuliano, who became **Pope Julius II** in 1503, commissioned Michelangelo to decorate the chapel's ceiling.

Savona lies at the southern end of a time-honoured route over the mountains, and the town's links with Turin are maintained to this day via the *autostrada* and main train line. The **train station** is in the west of town, across the River Letimbro from the old quarter which nestles in the curve of the old port and bristles with medieval towers. Via Don Minzoni, to the left of the station as you walk out, heads east across the river to the parks of Piazza del Popolo, from where the main **Via Paleocapa**, lined by Art Nouveau arcades, continues east to the port. Savona's **tourist office** is nearby at Via Guidobono 125r (Mon–Sat 9am–12.30pm & 3.30–7pm; ☎019.840.2321). The Dominican church of San Giovanni marks the point where Via Pia heads south into the atmospheric old quarter, which is dominated by the **Duomo** and its attached **Cappella Sistina**, a Baroque extravaganza commissioned by Sixtus IV in memory of his parents.

Above the old town is the huge **Priamàr** fortress, built in 1528 by the Genoese as a sign of their superiority over the defeated Savonese. These days it houses four major museums, led by the **Pinacoteca Civica** (July & Aug Mon–Sat 8.30am–1pm & 6.30–11.30pm; rest of year Mon–Sat 8.30am–1pm, Tues & Thurs until 6.30pm; L4000/€2.06), with a collection of mostly mediocre Baroque paintings overshadowed by a striking Renaissance *Crucifixion* by Donato de' Bardi. The interesting **Museo d'Arte Sandro Pertini** (Mon–Sat 8.30am–1pm), displaying modern Italian art collected by Pertini, one-time President of Italy, and the **Museo Renata Cuneo** (closed for renovation at the time of writing) housing contemporary sculpture by Cuneo, a Savona local, share a joint L4000/€2.06 admission ticket. Completing the array is the **Museo Civico** (Tues–Sat 10am–noon & 3–5pm, Sun 3–5pm; L4000/€2.06), which has Greek and Etruscan bits and bobs along with some Islamic and Byzantine ceramics.

There are no **hotels** in the old town, but the decent *Riviera Suisse*, Via Paleocapa 24 (☎019.850.853, fax 019.853.435; ③) is very close by. The more convenient and enticing of Savona's two HI **hostels** is *Fortezza del Priamar* in the old fortress (☎ & fax 019.812.653, *priamarhostel@iol.it*; L22,000/€11.36; bus #2). The best **campsite** is *Buggi*, at Via N.S. del Monte 15 (☎019.804.573).

THE RIVIERA DI LEVANTE

The glorious stretch of coast **east from Genoa**, dubbed the **Riviera di Levante**, is not the place to come for a relaxing beach holiday. As ever, visiting out of season eases the claustrophobia, but in summer, catching some rays in the most popular resort towns involves fighting for a small piece of pebble beach or concrete jetty (the beaches aren't as good as those on the other side of Genoa), while sitting in the waterfront restaurants and cafés means running the gauntlet of some highly competitive posing. Ports that once eked a living from fishing and coral diving have been transformed by a solid thirty years of tourism; the coastline is still wild and extremely beautiful in parts, but predictably the sense of remoteness has gone. It's pointless protesting against the stranglehold that tourism has: once you accept that wandering around ex-fishing villages with hordes of others is inevitable, you can appreciate the attractions this area still holds.

Away from the resorts, the cliffs and bays are covered with pine and olive trees, best seen from the vantage points along the footpaths criss-crossing the headland of the **Monte di Portofino**. The harbour towns of **Camogli** on the Golfo Paradiso and **Santa Margherita Ligure** on the Golfo Tigullio are favourite subjects for arty picture postcards, while super-chic **Portofino** on the southern tip of the headland effortlessly pulls in the international jetset. More digestible nightlife is better served at big, feisty resorts such as **Rapallo**. Further east, the main road heads inland, bypassing the spectacular **Cinque Terre** and joining the train line at the port of **La Spezia**, which stands at the head of the idyllic Golfo dei Poeti and gives access to romantic waterside villages such as **Portovénere**. From La Spezia, there's easy access by road or rail to Pisa or Parma, and by sea to Corsica.

The Golfo Paradiso

East of Genoa, roads and train lines follow a folded coastline that forms an elegant curve modestly dubbed the **Golfo Paradiso**. The characterful resort of **Camogli** avoids the worst of the blandness that undermines resorts further east and has a good deal going for it. The hamlet of **San Fruttuoso** – best known for its picturesque abbey – occupies a narrow cove at the southern tip of the **Monte di Portofino** headland and is only accessible by boat or on foot.

Recco

Allied bombing in 1944 to cut the coastal rail line virtually destroyed **RECCO** – at the head of the gulf 18km east of Genoa – and the town that has sprung up in its place is unremarkable but for its gastronomy. People come here specifically to eat at some of the best **restaurants** in Liguria. If your wallet is fat, book a table at either *Da-ö Vittorió*, Via Roma 160 (☎0185.74.029, fax 0185.723.605; ⑨; restaurant closed Thurs), a characterfully renovated century-old building 500m north of the town centre, or the modern villa-style *Manuelina*, Via Roma 300 (☎0185.74.128, fax 0185.721.095, *manuelina @manuelina.it*; ⑤; restaurant closed Wed) some 300m further north set in its own garden; both establishments are also hotels. They are acclaimed for their *focaccia al formaggio* (Recco's speciality), *minestrone alla genovese* and local *troffiette recchelline* (pasta with green beans, potatoes and pesto). Eating well in Recco needn't cost a lot, however: *La Baracchetta*, a hut on the Via Marinai d'Italia waterfront with outside tables, also does outstanding *focaccia al formaggio*.

Camogli

CAMOGLI – 2km southeast of Recco – was the "saltiest, roughest, most piratical little place", according to Dickens when he visited in 1884. It's had its rough edges knocked off since then, but remains one of the most attractive small resorts along this stretch of the coast, well connected by road, rail and boat. The town's name, a contraction of *Casa Moglie* (House of Wives), comes from the days when voyages lasted for years and the women ran the port while the men were away. In its day, Camogli supported a huge fleet of 700 vessels, which once saw off Napoleon. The town declined in the age of steam, but the crumbling arcades by the harbour and the dark flight of steps into the town centre still have the "smell of fish, and seaweed, and old rope" that Dickens relished.

The **train station** is just south of the beach; turn right towards the centre for the small **tourist office**, 50m north at Via XX Settembre 33 (Mon–Sat 8.30am–noon & 3–7pm, Sun 9am–1pm; ☎0185.771.066). Summer **boats** shuttle over from Genoa's Porto Antico in an hour (L10,000/€5.16), using the old harbour on the north side of town, separated from the unimpressive pebble beach to the south by a promontory occupied by the medieval **Castello della Dragonara**. You can wander up through the alleyways to the castle, which nowadays is home to the rather humdrum **Acquario Tirrenico** (Tues–Sun 10am–noon, also Fri–Sun afternoons: summer 3–7pm; winter 2–6pm; L4000/€2.06), housing tanks full of marine life.

The best **hotel** is the lavish *Cenobio dei Dogi*, in its own waterfront park at Via Cuneo 34 (☎0185.7241, fax 0185.772.796; ⑧); once the summer palace of Genoa's doges, it boasts its own beach, pool, tennis courts, restaurants and tasteful guest rooms. *La Camogliese*, Via Garibaldi 55 (☎0185.771.402, fax 0185.774.024; ③), is a friendly spot excellently situated by the water (take the steps down opposite the station); it has pleasant rooms and they don't insist on full pension. Otherwise, try the spartan *Selene*, Via Cuneo 15 (☎0185.770.149, fax 0185.770.195; ②). The *Camogliese* hotel has a quality mid-priced **restaurant** (closed Wed in winter). The much pricier *Vento Ariel* on the harbourfront (☎0185.771.080; closed Wed) serves only fish brought that day directly from the nets into the kitchen. Away from the sea, *Don Riccardo* on Salita Priaro (the flight of steps up from the fishing harbour), does affordable Mexican food, and Revello is a fine bakery at Via Garibaldi 183.

Fish aside, Camogli makes its living from **ferries** operated by Golfo Paradiso, Via Scalo 3 (☎0185.772.091, *www.golfoparadiso.it*). Departures to tranquil **Punta**

OPEN OR WRAPPED?

If you're visiting Camogli on the second Sunday in May, you won't be able to miss the **Sagra del Pesce**, preceded on the Saturday night by fireworks and a huge bonfire. This generous – and smelly – event has its origins in celebrating the munificence of the sea and retains its ancient resonance for Camogli's fisherfolk even today. Thousands of fish are plucked fresh from the waves, flipped into a giant frying-pan set up on the harbourfront and distributed free of charge to all and sundry as a demonstration of the sea's abundance (and in the hope for its continuation). In recent years the event has been beset by quibbles: bureaucrats have suggested that the frying-pan – some five metres across – is a health hazard, and there have even been allegations that frozen fish is defrosted out at sea and then passed off as fresh, but local enthusiasm for the festival hasn't waned one bit.

Chiappa, ideal for a spot of swimming and basking in the sun, and **San Fruttuoso** (see below), are most frequent (May–Sept at least hourly; Oct–April 3 weekdays, hourly at weekends; around L8000/€4.13), with a special **night excursion** offering the most romantic views of the gulf plus 3hr in San Fruttuoso for dinner or a stroll (July & Aug 3–5 weekly; L16,000/€8.26). There are also boats east to the **Cinque Terre** (June–Sept 3–4 weekly; L20,000/€10.32), which stop beforehand at **Portofino** and continue to **Portovénere**, as well as plenty more west to **Recco** and **Genoa** (L10,000/€5.16).

San Fruttuoso

The enchanting thousand-year-old abbey of **SAN FRUTTUOSO** is one of the principal draws along this stretch of the Riviera, occupying a picturesque little bay at the southern foot of Monte di Portofino. The only way to get there is **on foot** (see overleaf) or **by boat**, dozens of which shuttle backwards and forwards from practically every harbour along the coast. On summer weekends, boats crammed with tourists ply to and fro, and the tiny harbour and church may be uncomfortably crowded. Out of season, however (or at twilight, courtesy of the occasional night cruises), San Fruttuoso is peaceful and an excellent place for doing very little; while wandering through the abbey, the only sound is the waves on the beach outside.

The **Abbazia di San Fruttuoso** (May–Sept Tues–Sun 10am–6pm; March, April & Oct Tues–Sun 10am–4pm; Nov–Feb Sat & Sun 10am–4pm; L6000/€3.10) was originally built to house the relics of the third-century martyr St Fructuosus, which were brought here from Spain after the Moorish invasion in 711. It was rebuilt in 984 with an unusual Byzantine-style cupola and distinctive waterside arches. In later centuries it became a Benedictine abbey which exerted a sizeable degree of control over the surrounding countryside. The Doria family took over in the sixteenth century and added the defensive **Torre dei Doria** nearby. Find a quiet moment, if you can, to explore the small, elegant church, with its compact little cloister and half-dozen Doria tombs. Off the headland, a 1954 bronze statue known as the **Cristo degli Abissi** (Christ of the Depths) rests eight fathoms down on the seabed, to honour the memory of divers who have lost their lives at sea and to protect those still working beneath the waves.

There's a handful of simple **restaurants** on San Fruttuoso's beach serving fish and steamed mussels, and one place **to stay** – the tiny *Da Giovanni* (☎0185.770.047; ④).

Portofino and the Golfo del Tigullio

Matching the Golfo Paradiso on the western side of the Monte di Portofino headland is the **Golfo del Tigullio** on the eastern side, a broad arc of a bay named after the local Tigullian tribe of pre-Roman antiquity. The gulf stretches 28km from the rocks and inlets around the millionaire's playground of **Portofino** and its friendlier neighbour **Santa Margherita Ligure** to head east along a dramatically beautiful – and densely touristed – coastline. There are virtually no quiet parts in summer with the main focus being the large resort of **Rapallo**. The way to avoid the high-season crowds, as usual in Liguria, is to head inland; buses from the quiet town of **Chiávari** wind their way north into the wooded hills, accessing plenty of hiking trails between tranquil stone-built villages and eventually terminating way up above 1000m at the winter skiing retreat of **Santo Stefano d'Aveto**.

The Consorzio Portofino Coast runs an information and hotel-booking service for the area, based at Via Lamarmora 17/6, Rapallo (☎0185.270.222, fax 0185.230.054, *www.portofinocoast.it*).

WALKS AROUND PORTOFINO

The Portofino headland – protected as the Parco Naturale Regionale di Portofino (*www.parks.it*) and encircled by cliffs and small coves – is one of the most rewarding areas for **walking** on the Riviera coast. At 612m, **Monte di Portofino** is high enough to be interesting but not so high as to demand any specialist hiking prowess. The trails cross slopes of wild thyme, pine and holm oak, enveloped in summer in the constant whirring of cicadas. From the summit, the view over successive headlands is breathtaking. Not many people walk these marked paths, maybe because their early stages are fairly steep – but they aren't particularly strenuous, levelling off later and with plenty of places to stop.

One of the best trails skirts the whole headland, beginning in Camogli, on the western side of the promontory. The path rises gently for 1km south to **San Rocco** (221m), then follows the coast south to a viewpoint above Punta Chiappa, before swinging east to the scenic **Passo del Bacio** (200m), rising to a ridge-top and then descending gently through the olive-trees and palms to **San Fruttuoso** (3hr from Camogli). It continues east over a little headland and onto the wild and beautiful cliff-tops above **Punta Carega**, before passing through the hamlets of Prato, Olmi (279m) and Cappelletta and down steps to **Portofino** (4hr 30min from Camogli).

There are plenty of alternative routes. About 1km south of San Rocco, an easier path forks inland up to **Portofino Vetta** and **Pietre Strette** (452m), before leading down again through the foliage to San Fruttuoso (2hr 30min from Camogli). **Ruta** is a small village 250m up on the north side of Monte di Portofino, served by buses from Camogli, Santa Margherita and Rapallo; a peaceful, little-trod trail from Ruta heads up to the summit of the mountain (2hr), or diverts partway along to take you across country to Olmi and on to Portofino (2hr 30min from Ruta).

Portofino

There's no escaping the beauty of **PORTOFINO**, tucked into a protected inlet surrounded by lush cypress- and olive-clad slopes, yet it manages to be both attractive and off-putting at the same time. This picture-pretty village has been effortlessly drawing in Europe's jetset royals, filmstars and other glitterati since the *dolce vita* days of Bogart and Bacall, Sophia Loren, Burton and Taylor, and Princess Grace, all of whom holidayed here – its snob rating remains impeccable. The village lies at the end of a narrow and treacherously winding road 5km south from Santa Margherita, but thanks to continuous traffic the bus journey can take longer than the boats that shuttle regularly to and from all nearby ports. Once you've arrived and surveyed the expensive restaurants and lace shops by the water, there's not much to do other than watch everyone else do the same; bear in mind, though, that a couple of peaceful harbourside beers will leave you little change from L40,000/€20.66.

To get a sense of Portofino's idyllic setting follow the footpath which heads south from the harbour up onto the headland. Five minutes from the village is the church of **San Giorgio**, said to contain relics of St George. A further ten minutes up is the **Castello Brown** (Tues–Sun 10am–6pm; L4000/€2.06); there's not much to see, but you can look down on pint-sized Portofino from the terrace. The scenic path continues south for a quarter-hour down to the **Faro** (lighthouse) on the very tip of the promontory. The only way back is up the same path. Northwest from the village, steeply stepped paths head through vineyards and orchards to Olmi and on to San Fruttuoso (see box above for more). The best sandy **beach** is the sparkling cove at **Paraggi**, 3km north of Portofino on the corniche road (buses will stop on request) – not exactly remote, but less formal than Portofino, with a couple of bars set back from the water.

The **tourist office** is at Via Roma 35 (daily 9.30am–1.30pm & 2–6.30pm; ☎0185.269.024, *www.apttigullio.liguria.it*). **Accommodation** is absurdly expensive year-round. The *Eden* stands within its own delightful gardens in the centre (☎0185.269.091, fax 0185.269.047; ⑦), but if money is no object, you'll want to shell out with style at the *Splendido*, Viale Baratta 16 (☎0185.267.801, fax 0185.267.806, *www. orient-expresshotels.com*; ⑨) – prices are astronomical but this is held to be one of Italy's best hotels. **Eating out**, whether at the hotels or, for example, at the super-chic seafood restaurant *Il Pitosforo* on the harbour (☎0185.269.020, closed Mon & Tues), which in summer opens only in the evening, is best left to those who don't read their credit card statements.

Santa Margherita Ligure

SANTA MARGHERITA LIGURE is a thoroughly attractive, palm-laden small resort tucked into an inlet, replete with grand hotels, garden villas and views of the glittering bay. In the daytime, trendy young Italians cruise the streets or whizz around the harbour on jetskis, while the rest of the family sunbathes or crams the *gelaterie*. Santa Margherita is cheaper to stay in than Portofino and less crowded than Rapallo, and makes a good base both for taking boats and trains up and down the coast and for exploring the countryside on foot. The **train station** overlooks the harbour from the north; behind the waterfront Piazza Veneto 250m south is the **tourist office**, Via XXV Aprile 2 (Mon–Sat 9am–12.30pm & 3.30–6.30pm, Sun 9.30am–12.30pm; ☎0185.287.485, *www.apttigullio.liguria.it*).

The town is also famous for its **watersports** – the European Dive-In Center, Via Canevaro 2 (☎0185.293.017, *www.europeandc.com*) is one outfit offering waterskiing, sailing and diving; the tourist office has a list of others and there's a handful of places on the harbourfront offering **boats for rent**. **Walking** trails cross the Monte di Portofino headland: marked paths from Santa Margherita to Pietre Strette (1hr 30min) and Olmi (1hr 40min) link in with the trails outlined in the box opposite. The best **beaches** are out of town, accessible by bus: south towards Portofino is Paraggi (see opposite), while to the north the road drops down to a patch of beach in the bay of **San Michele di Pagana**. Dedicated art fiends should come to see the *Crucifixion* by Van Dyck in the church of San Michele, but the beach bars and crystal-clear water are likely to prove stronger incentives to visit.

As ever, check in case the **hotels** insist on half- or full-pension. Best mid-price option is *Fasce*, Via Bozzo 3 (☎0185.286.435, fax 0185.283.580, *www.hotelfasce.it*; ④) which has pleasantly furnished modern rooms, a roof terrace, free bikes, parking, and an excellent, inexpensive restaurant. *Annabella*, Via Costasecca 10 (☎0185.286.531; ③), has attractive bathless rooms; and welcoming *Nuova Riviera*, Via Belvedere 10 off Piazza Mazzini (☎0185.287.403, fax 0185.290.083; ③) is on a quiet residential street. Although there are several stuffy grand hotels vying for top-dog status, you may prefer the pleasant, modern suite-style rooms at the seafront *Lido Palace*, Via Doria 3 (☎0185.285.821, fax 0185.284.708; ⑥), which also has private parking.

Trattoria Baicin, just back from the waterfront park at Via Algeria 5 (closed Mon), is a fine **restaurant**, with a three-course set menu for L30,000/€15.49 and excellent seafood. *Da Pezzi*, Via Cavour 21 (closes 9pm & closed Sat), is a long-established locals' hangout serving basic pasta and grills. On the same street at no. 29 is a good *focacceria*, with opposite it a bar-gelateria that can make up a big salad for L8000/€4.13. Of the many seafront restaurants, one to aim for is *Da Alfredo*, Piazza Martiri 37 (closed Tues), which does good pizzas. Head south behind the squat harbourfront *castello* to reach the old port, where you'll find a clutch of old-style fish restaurants, including *L'Ancora*, Via Maragliano 7 (closed Tues), an excellent-value, mid-priced place; and the swankier *Dei Pescatori*, Via Bottaro 43 (☎0185.286.747; closed Wed & Thurs).

BOATS ON THE TIGULLIO COAST

Dozens of **boats** serve all points on the Tigullio coast, run by companies based in Genoa (see p.142), Camogli (see p.138) and La Spezia (see p.151), along with the main local operator – Servizio Marittimo del Tigullio, Via Palestro 8/1b, Santa Margherita (☎0185.284.670). You should **book ahead** to guarantee a place in high summer.

The most popular line shuttles to and fro between **Rapallo**, **Santa Margherita**, **Portofino** and **San Fruttuoso**, taking 15min between each (summer: hourly every day; winter: 2 on Sun). There are also lovely **night excursions** on the same route (July & Aug 2–8 weekly). The most you'll pay for a one-way fare is L13,000/€6.71. Boats also connect to **Chiávari** (June–Sept 1–7 weekly; L14,000/€7.23), and then on to the **Cinque Terre** (L25,000/€12.91). Some continue to **Portovénere** (L30,000/€15.49). The best-value round-trip cruise ticket is the **"Super Cinque Terre"**, which gives stops of 1hr in Riomaggiore, 3hr for lunch in Monterosso and 1hr in Vernazza (June–Sept 2 weekly; L38,000/€19.63).

Rapallo

RAPALLO is a highly developed resort town – three times bigger than Santa Margherita – with an expanse of glass-fronted restaurants and plush hotels crowding around a south-facing bay. Earlier this century it was a backwater, and writers in particular came for the bay's extraordinary beauty, of which you now get an inkling only early in the morning or at dusk. Max Beerbohm lived in Rapallo for the second half of his life, and attracted a literary circle to the town; Ezra Pound wrote the first thirty of his *Cantos* here between 1925 and 1930, D.H. Lawrence stayed for a while and Hemingway also dropped by (but came away muttering that the sea was flat and boring). The resort's striking landmarks are the large **marina** and the **castle**, now converted into an exhibition space, stuck out at the end of a small causeway. Unlike most of the Tigullio resorts, Rapallo does have an existence separate from its tourist trade, particularly around the **old town**, a grid of cobbled streets behind the stone Saline Gate: this is the commercial centre and venue for the Tuesday fish and vegetable market, while the busy Thursday market at Piazza Cile to the northwest of the centre beneath the train tracks is a good place to buy cheap clothing.

The **tourist office** is at Via Armanda Diaz 9 (Mon–Sat 9am–12.30pm & 3.30–6.30pm, Sun 9.30am–12.30pm; ☎0185.230.346, *www.apttigullio.liguria.it*), and can provide details of diving outfits in the town and places to rent boats. The **hotels** are headed by the lavish *Excelsior Palace*, Via San Michele di Pagana 8 (☎0185.230.666, fax 0185.230.214, *www.thi.it*; ⑨). Welcoming *Stella*, Via Aurelia Ponente 6 (☎0185.50.367, fax 0185.272.837, *www.hotelstella-riviera.com*; ④) and *Riviera*, nearby at Piazza IV Novembre 2 (☎0185.50.248, fax 0185.65.668, *www.tigullio.net/hotelriviera*; ⑤), are both converted villas a block in from the sea, the former with parking and some discount shared-bath rooms. Best bargain is the *Bandoni*, in a fine old palazzo within sight and smell of the sea at Via Marsala 24 (☎0185.50.423, fax 0185.57.206; ③): its modest rooms are tastefully furnished and the management are flexible about full pension. The *Rapallo* **campsite** is at Via San Lazzaro 4 (☎0185.262.018; June–Sept).

Many **restaurants** in Rapallo and along the Tigullio coast serve the local speciality *bagnun*, a dish based on anchovies, tomato, garlic, onion and white wine. You'll find good trattorias in the alleys behind the mediocre seafront restaurants: *Da Mario*, Piazza Garibaldi 23 (closed Wed), is moderately priced, with tables outside under medieval porticoes. *U Bansin*, Via Venezia 49 (closes 8.30pm & closed Sun), is an affordable old town restaurant. *Zi Teresa*, opposite the train station at Corso Italia 33 (closed Wed), has a good mixed menu of pizzas, pasta and more expensive fish dishes. *Nin Hao*, a pleasant Chinese with its own garden at Piazza Molfino 4 (no closing day) has good-value set menus, from as little as L15,000/€7.75 for lunch. For just a drink or a snack, try the pubby *Taverna Paradiso* down a side alley off Via Mazzini 73 (open evenings only), or the *Gallo Nero*, Via Magenta 10.

Santuario di Montallegro

The best excursion from Rapallo is on the **cable car** (*funivia*; L13,000/€6.71 return), which rises every thirty minutes from Via Castegneto, ten minutes' walk inland from Rapallo's castle, up to the **Santuario di Montallegro** (612m). The church was founded in 1557 when a Byzantine icon of the Madonna appeared miraculously in the hands of one Giovanni Chichizola, and it's in a superb setting overlooking a steep, green valley, with views across the whole of the sparkling bay. A *festa* commemorating the miracle is held during the first three days of July, when the coffer of the Madonna is carried through Rapallo, and a fireworks contest culminates in the mock burning of the castle.

Alternative ways up to Montallegro include following a relatively easy footpath from Rapallo station (1hr). This continues to the summit of Monte Rosa above the church (another 30min), or diverts east across the hilltops and down to Chiávari (4hr 30min from Rapallo). Bus #92 runs from Rapallo station to Montallegro.

Chiávari

Most of the 9km train journey from Rapallo east to **CHIÁVARI** is through tunnels, so for an idea of the scenery you need to dawdle on bus #9, which follows the mad coast road around several headlands. Some of the villas and gardens are spectacular, surrounded by wisteria, fig trees and mini olive groves. The overriding attraction, however, is the sea, brilliant turquoise coves appearing as the bus takes another bend; you can stop off at any of the signs that point *al mare* – though you probably won't be alone when you get there.

Chiávari, itself, however, by contrast, sits on a flat, featureless bit of coastline. Called Clavarium ("Keys") by the Romans for the access it gave them to the inland valleys, it's still a good starting-point for trips into the mountains and has a characterful, untouristed old quarter. **Boats** shuttle all summer long west to Rapallo and east to the Cinque Terre (see box opposite), and the **bus** and **train** stations are beside each other in the town centre, forming a barrier between the seafront to the south and the large public gardens of **Piazza Nostra Signora dell'Orto** to the north. The **tourist office** is opposite the station at Corso Assarotti 1 (Mon–Sat 9.30am–12.30pm & 3.30–6.30pm, Sun 9.30am–12.30pm; ☎0185.325.198, *www.apttigullio.liguria.it*). Wander through the piazza, with its ochre **cathedral**, into the peaceful old quarter of medieval arcades lined with food shops and outlets for macramé, a craft brought back from the Middle East by local sailors. The pretty main square, **Piazza Mazzini**, hosts a thriving market each morning. East along Via Martiri is Piazza Matteotti and the crumbling seventeenth-century Palazzo Rocca, now home to the **Civica Galleria** (Sat & Sun 10am–noon & 4–7pm; free), displaying paintings by Genoese artists. Next door in the same palazzo is the more engaging **Museo Archeologico** (Tues–Sat 9am–1.30pm, also second & fourth Sun of month 9am–1.30pm; free), with finds from a nearby seventh- to eighth-century necropolis.

The *Dell'Orto* is a comfortable three-star **hotel** beside the cathedral at Piazza N.S. dell'Orto 3 (☎0185.322.356, fax 0185.322.215; ③), although you may prefer the peace and quiet to be found at the plusher *Monterosa*, at the north edge of the old town arcades, Via Marinetti 6 (☎0185.300.321, fax 0185.312.868, *www.gattei.it/monterosa*; ④). The cheapest option is *Villa Le Rose*, west of the centre at Salita Bacezza 13 (☎0185.303.493; ①). The *Al Mare* **campsite** is at Via Preli 30 (☎ & fax 0185.304.633). There are lots of pleasant **eateries** on the old town squares. *Da Vittorio,* just north of

Piazza Mazzini (closed Thurs), is a workers' café serving tasty local dishes, while *Cantine Reggiana*, under the old town arcades at Via Martiri di Liberazione 27 (closed Mon) does a delicious *minestrone alla genovese*. *Ideal Bar*, Piazza N.S. dell'Orto 31 (closed Sun), has **Internet** access.

Inland from Chiávari

Bus #11 from Chiávari station follows the main route **inland** from the coast, passing through isolated villages and hillsides terraced up to the snowline. It's good country-side for hiking, and gives the chance to hook up with the **Alta Via dei Monti Liguri** long-distance trail (see box p.127). The town at the end of the road, Santo Stefano d'Aveto (2hr by bus from Chiávari), is worth a visit for its own merits – fresh, cool air, dramatic mountain scenery and a complete change of culture and environment from the seaside bustle.

The road from Chiávari heads up through a succession of villages to **BOR-ZONASCA**, where you'll find the comfortable *Ü Rustegü* **hotel** (☎0185.341.005, fax 0185.341.060, *www.valdivara.com*; ③) and the very basic *Da Beppe* (☎0185.341.008; ①), along with the information centre for the **Parco Naturale Regionale Aveto**, which covers the countryside of the high valleys, Via Marré 75a (☎0185.340.311, *www.parks.it*).

Increasingly narrow, winding roads climb to the hamlet of **LA SQUAZZA** (721m), from where a 45min walk heads up to the **Passo del Bozale** (963m), an ancient pass midway between points 32 and 33 of the alta via. The trail northwest down the other side of the pass to the peaceful rural village of **Cabanne** (2hr) has sections of original Roman paving; if this doesn't appeal, you can head along the ridge southwest to point 32, the **Passo della Forcella** (875m; 1hr 30min), or northeast to point 33, the **Passo delle Lame** (1300m; 2hr 30min) and on to the **Riserva dell'Agoraie**, a botanic reserve encompassing three small lakes on the northern slopes of Monte degli Abeti. Just past the reserve, a path heads down to **MAGNASCO** (823m; 3hr 30min from Passo delle Lame), passing on the way the lovely little **Lago delle Lame** and the rural three-star *Lago delle Lame* hotel (☎0185.870.036; ③). Passo della Forcella, Cabanne and Magnasco are all stops on the Chiávari–Santo Stefano bus route.

Some 8km up the road from Cabanne, **REZZOÁGLIO** (715m), is the trailhead for a relatively easy walk northwest over the Passo di Esola (1304m) to the resort of **Fontanigorda** (819m; see p.127). Rezzoáglio's *Americano* **hotel**, Via Roma 14 (☎0185.870.336; ②), has a choice of en suite or bathless rooms, and the nearby *Villa Cella* restaurant (☎0185.86.646) provides **horses** and guides.

The bus winds on to **SANTO STEFANO D'AVETO** (1017m), largest of the mountain resorts. A host of trails lead onto the slopes of the three mountains which loom over the town to 1800m and provide reasonably reliable downhill and cross-country skiing in winter. One of the most pleasant walks is to the tiny, chilly **Lago Nero** (1540m), a five-hour round-trip. The **tourist office** is at Piazza del Popolo 6 (☎0185.88.046), and **hotels** include the three-star *Grand Hotel Siva*, Via Marconi 5 (☎ & fax 0185.88.091; ③), and bargain *Montesanto*, Via Statale 67 (☎0185.899.030; ①).

The Cinque Terre

The stupendous folded coastline of the **Cinque Terre** ("Five Lands") stretches between the pleasant beach resort of Lévanto and the major port of La Spezia. The area is named for five tiny villages wedged into a series of coves between sheer cliffs; their comparative remoteness, and the dramatic nature of their position on a stunning coast-line, make them the principal scenic highlight of the whole Riviera.

The only fly in the ointment – and a big, ugly fly it is too – is the quantity of visitors the Cinque Terre attract. Although local skills such as viticulture and fishing are happily thriving, the centres of all the villages have lost a good deal of their character to a tide of kitschy souvenir shops and overpriced, under-quality restaurants that service the day-trippers who crowd in all summer long. Things are undoubtedly quieter out of season, but even in August you really shouldn't bypass the area – the scenery is breathtaking, there is some lovely walking between villages, and nearby **Lévanto** is a comfortable base away from the worst of the crowds. However, you should also be under no illusions that you might find some tranquil, private little paradise: you won't, but you'll be able to buy any number of "Pasta of Italy" tea-towels in recompense.

Transport around the Cinque Terre

The three principal ways to get to and around the villages of the Cinque Terre are trains, boats and Shanks's pony. If you're on a fast **train**, you'll zip through without seeing much more than a few tantalizing glimpses of turquoise water as the train speeds from one tunnel to the next. Regular slow trains stop at every village, and local stations sell a Cinque Terre day ticket (*biglietto giornaliero*) for L5500/€2.83, covering travel between all five villages and Lévanto until midnight.

Boats from every company on the Riviera shuttle along this bit of coast all summer long. Make sure to confirm which of the four waterside villages you'll be stopping at (Corniglia has no harbour), and specify if you want a one-way ticket, rather than the more usual round-trip cruise tickets. Hopping between Cinque Terre villages by boat is easy, with between five and eight a day (April–Oct) going in both directions – although watch out for a lull between about noon and 2.30pm.

The most satisfactory way to get around is **on foot**: there's a network of trails (see box p.149) linking the villages along the coast or up on the ridge-tops that offer spectacular views. However, the coastal path in particular can get uncomfortably crowded throughout the summer months.

Trying to tour the area by **car or motorbike** truly isn't worth the effort. All five villages do now have road access, although the roads are narrow, exceptionally steep, not very scenic and punctuated by corkscrew bends. There's also virtually no public parking anywhere (one small toll area at Riomaggiore and another at Monterosso, both of which fill up by mid-morning). To get to Vernazza, for instance, you must park way back at a barrier placed across the access road and then walk a steep kilometre down into the village. You'd do better to leave your vehicle in Lévanto or La Spezia.

Lévanto

Heading east out of the big resort of Sestri Levante, the train line and coastal road disappear into a series of tunnels that last almost until La Spezia. The slow bus route loops through coastal resorts and past red marble quarries inland before arriving at the unpretentious small town of **Lévanto**, last settlement before the Cinque Terre. Its sandy **beach** – the best for miles around – inexpensive hotels and good transport links make it a perfect base for exploring, more congenial than staying in one of the five villages themselves. The only real sights in the town are architectural remnants from Lévanto's thirteenth-century heyday, including the **Loggia Comunale** on the central Piazza del Popolo, the black-and-white striped church of **Sant'Andrea** above the piazza, and the odd surviving stretch of medieval wall here and there. The huge Wednesday market draws crowds of shoppers.

The **tourist office** is on the central arcaded Piazza Cavour (Mon–Sat 9.30am–12.30pm & 3–6pm, Sun 10am–12.30pm; ☎0187.808.125), while the **train station** is ten minutes' walk inland from the seafront. The finest **hotel** is *Stella Maris*, Via

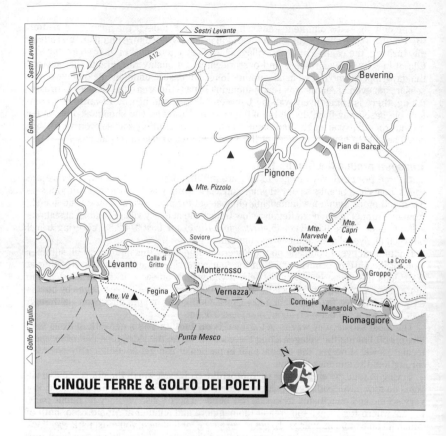

CINQUE TERRE & GOLFO DEI POETI

Marconi 4 (☎0187.808.258, fax 0187.807.351, *www.hotelstellamaris.it*; ⑤), with a handful of characterful rooms in the nineteenth-century Palazzo Vannoni, plus some others (④) in a more modern annexe on Piazza Staglieno. The venerable old *Nazionale*, Via Jacopo da Levanto 20 (☎0187.808.102, fax 0187.800.901, *www.nazionale.it*; ④), has comfortable, attractive rooms, plus parking. The *Europa*, Via Dante Aligheri 41 (☎0187.808.126, fax 0187.808.594; ③) is another charmingly old-fashioned place with parking. *Pensione Garden* occupies the first floor of a modern apartment building 20m from the beach, at Corso Italia 6 (☎0187.808.173; ②; April–Sept): its functional rooms are pleasant, but none has a bathroom. The *Gentile*, a block back from the sea at Via Jacopo 27 (☎0187.808.551; ②), is a good alternative. The best of a handful of **campsites** is *Acqua Dolce*, Via Semenza 5 (☎0187.807.365, fax 0187.808.465).

The town's best **restaurant** is the expensive *Araldo*, Via Jacopo 24 (closed Tues except in July & Aug), featuring fresh local ingredients served with care and attention beneath a vaulted, painted ceiling. Don't miss the local specialities *gattafin*, deep-fried vegetable ravioli, and *cotolette di acciughe*, fried stuffed anchovies. For more casual fare, *Caffè Roma*, Piazza Staglieno 10 (closed Tues), as well as being a popular hangout, has a small restaurant at the back that serves moderately priced pasta, pizzas and fish. *Pizzeria Miky*, Corso Italia 52 (closed Wed), is another cheap pizzeria.

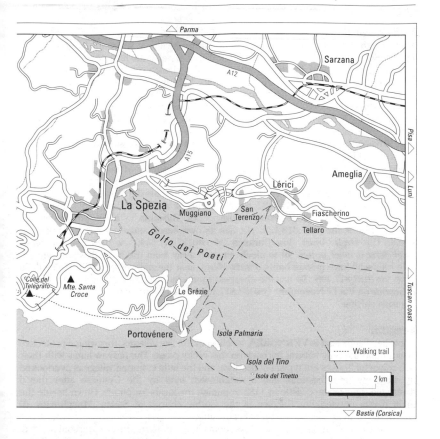

The Cinque Terre villages

The five Cinque Terre villages are **Monterosso**, **Vernazza**, **Corniglia**, **Manarola** and **Riomaggiore**. All of them can get crowded, but they're all nonetheless winningly charming, shoehorned into rocky coves or clinging to precipitous cliffs surrounded by painstakingly terraced vineyards. Principally fishing ports for centuries, in recent decades the five have diversified into **wine**. The Cinque Terre label is one of Liguria's better whites, but is less famous than the dessert wine Sciacchetrà, made from grapes which are left to dry on open-air racks until late autumn; they end up much sweeter than normal, like raisins, and in turn produce a full-bodied, heavily alcoholic and (because of the quantity of grapes that goes into it) expensive wine that you savour sip by sip, or dunk dry *biscotti* into after a meal. Despite the impact of tourism, exacerbated in the 1990s by the construction of roads to each village, wine-making, olive-growing and fishing for the delectable local anchovies remain the major occupations.

Local businesses have set up the Consorzio Turistico Cinque Terre as a central **information and booking service**, based at Piazza Garibaldi 29, Monterosso al Mare (☎0187.817.838 or 0187.778.336, *www.cinqueterre.it*) – their Web site is especially useful.

Monterosso al Mare

Tucked into a bay on the east side of the jutting headland of Punta Mesco, **MONTEROSSO** is the chief village of the Cinque Terre. It's also the largest of the five – population 1800 – and most developed, with the modern beach resort of **Fegina** occupying the shore just west of the old village. Beaches, both free and toll, are broad and picturesque; they're separated from the narrow lanes of the old quarter by a hill, atop which is the seventeenth-century **Convento dei Cappuccini**. In the centre of the old village is the striped thirteenth-century church of **San Giovanni Battista**. Monterosso's most recent claim to fame is as the hometown of the Nobel Prize-winning poet Eugenio Montale; his *Ossi di Seppia* (Cuttlefish Bones) is a collection of early poems about his youth in Monterosso.

Monterosso has the Cinque Terre's sole official **tourist office**, on Via del Molo (☎0187.817.204, *www.aptcinqueterre.sp.it*; June–Sept), as well as a Pro Loco tourist association office at Via Fegina 38 (☎0187.817.506). Top **hotel** is the *Porto Roca*, Via Corone 1 (☎0187.817.502, fax 0187.817.692, *www.portoroca.it*; ⑧; March–Oct) in a blissful location with sea-views from every room. *Villa Adriana*, Via IV Novembre 23 (☎0187.818.109, fax 0187.818.128; ⑤), has its own beach and even some car-parking space. The *Degli Amici*, Via Buranco 36 (☎0187.817.544, fax 0187.817.424, *www.cinqueterre.it/hotel_amici*; ④) is nicely situated away from the hubbub; its unremarkable rooms all have private baths. *Punta Mesco*, near the rail bridge at Via Molinelli 35 (☎ & fax 0187.817.495; ③) has the cheapest rooms in town. Pick of the **restaurants** is *Il Gigante* on Via IV Novembre (☎0187.817.401; closed Mon), with pricey but excellent Ligurian cuisine.

Vernazza

A few headlands east is **VERNAZZA**, loveliest of the five villages, throwing a protective arm around the only natural harbour on this rocky coast. The narrow lanes with their tall, colourful houses are typical of the area, and the little cramped village is overlooked by stout medieval bastions and a watchtower, built by the Genoese after they'd destroyed the previous castle in 1182 to punish the locals for piracy. Down beside the main piazza overlooking the sea is the Gothic church of **Santa Margherita di Antiochia**, with an elegant octagonal campanile.

There are two **hotels**: plain, bathless rooms in the *Barbara*, Piazza Marconi 30 (☎ & fax 0187.812.398; ②) occupy the top floor of one of the oldest buildings in the village, overlooking the main square beside the harbour, while the friendly *Sorriso*, further up into the village at Via Gavino 4 (☎0187.812.224; ③) has both en suite and bathless options. A handful of places offer **rooms** – in summer, ask at the Monterosso tourist office in advance for details, since you're likely to find them all full if you turn up without a booking. Poor-value **restaurants** ring the main Piazza Marconi; the *Sorriso* hotel is better value, and *Osteria Il Baretto*, Via Roma 31 (☎0187.812.381; no closing day) may lack a sea view but has excellent *antipasti di mare* in recompense. *Bar Marlin*, Via Roma 43, has **Internet** access. Also on Via Roma you'll spot a sales outlet of the **Cooperativa Agricola Cinque Terre**, where you can sample the local wines.

Corniglia

CORNIGLIA is the smallest of the five, and also the most remote: the village clings to a high cliff 90m above the sea, and its only access to the water (and the train station) is via a long flight of steps. Floral-decorated squares fill the village, and the little Gothic church of **San Pietro** boasts an exquisite marble rose window. There are no hotels, but plenty of places offering **rooms**, and a handful of unremarkable eateries. Oddly for a hilltop village, Corniglia stands out for its **beaches**. On the southern side of the village's rocky promontory is the **Spiaggone di Corniglia**, a narrow stretch of pebbles

WALKS IN THE CINQUE TERRE

There's plenty of **walking** to be done in and around the Cinque Terre, but you should note a couple of precautions. Most of the paths are unshaded, and in summer temperatures can soar: you should wear a hat and carry a water-bottle for even a short stroll. Walking shoes are also advisable – paths are rocky and uneven at the best of times. Take note of weather forecasts in spring and autumn, as rainstorms can brew up rapidly and make paths treacherously slippery. Tourist offices in Monterosso, Lévanto and La Spezia have plenty of maps and information, and can advise on good itineraries.

The most popular and accessible route is the 11km Blue Trail (*Sentiero Azzurro*), signed either with blue waymarkers or as route no. 2; this hugs the shoreline between all five villages, offering spectacular scenery the whole way along. Due to the gradients, covering it from east to west (5hr) is considerably easier than from west to east; if you start early, walking west also means you'll have the sun behind you most of the way. Follow the red and white stripes painted on walls, trees and gates from **Riomaggiore** station to the start of the Blue Trail, a stretch called the **Via dell'Amore** (Lovers' Path), which winds above the waves past lemon trees in every backyard. In spring, before the sun has turned everything except the vines to dust, you'll walk beneath cliffs covered with wildflowers. An easy twenty minutes covers the kilometre west to **Manarola**, from where a less crowded and more spectacular path climbs slightly and then heads on for 3km to the station at **Corniglia**, passing rock-cut steps leading down to the pebbly beach. Steep steps lead up into the centre of Corniglia itself (1hr from Manarola). It's a fairly leisurely ninety-minute walk for the 4km on to **Vernazza**, with just a couple of difficult spots and the attraction of access to the lovely beach at Guvano. Note that if you're attempting things in the other direction, the Vernazza–Corniglia walk is a tough-going 2hr-plus hike. The walk from Vernazza to **Monterosso** is the hardest westbound stretch, two hours to cover 3km, with first a steep climb up to 180m and then a sharp descent into Monterosso.

Other routes run perpendicular to the coastline, heading steeply up the slopes to give breathtaking coastal views, often passing old churches in the hills above each township. These routes link up with the long trail no. 1, or *Sentiero Rosso*, that runs from Portovénere (east of Riomaggiore) along the ridge-tops to Lévanto, a full-day (9–10hr) hike covering some 23km. Nonetheless, it's easy to split things up manageably. As an example, trail no. 3 climbs from Riomaggiore past the Santuario di Montenero church up to the **Colle del Telegrafo** viewpoint (516m; 1hr 30min), from where trail no. 1 heads west, giving expansive views along the coast as far as Monterosso; through the chestnut woods, some 3km west of Colle del Telegrafo, is **La Croce** (637m; 1hr), where trail no. 01 returns you steeply down to Riomaggiore (1hr). Another, yet more scenic, option would be to follow trail no. 7 up from Vernazza 3km through vineyards and past dry stone walls to the church at San Bernardino, then Casa Fornacchi and the ridge-top at **Cigoletta** (612m; 1hr 30min). Cigoletta is another junction point on the *Sentiero Rosso*, from where a trail heads further up to the peak of **Monte Marvede** (667m; 45min) high above Corniglia, with panoramic vistas over the whole coast; the lovely trail no. 6 heads down from Marvede through more vineyards and patches of forest to Manarola (3.5km; 1hr 45min).

Another highly rewarding walk is trail no. 10, which leads from Monterosso station up through pine woods and onto a flight of steps that emerge at the San Antonio church on the high point of the **Punta Mesco** headland (1hr), giving a spectacular panorama along the length of the Cinque Terre coastline. The walk north along the tops from there to **Monte Vè o Focone**, and the descent on trail no. 14 into Lévanto, are both easy (total 3hr from Monterosso).

that has relatively easy access from the footpath towards Manarola. Here you'll find the *Villaggio Marino Europa* (☎0187.812.279; April–Sept) – a **campsite** and set of spartan bungalows sleeping up to six (③).

The Cinque Terre's best beach is the wild and tranquil **Spiaggia di Guvano**, on the northern side of Corniglia's promontory. Follow the signs from the north side of the train station, which will lead you to a disused rail tunnel with an entryphone: ask for the *spiaggia*, and you'll be buzzed through the gate for a long walk through the tunnel (a kilometre or more) to the beach itself, where you must pay L5000/€2.58 admission. Once there, the attractions of warm, clear water, lovely scenery and relative peace and quiet might persuade you to throw off your social bonds – this is one of the few beaches in Liguria to permit **nudity** (although bear in mind that you are overlooked by walkers on the footpath to Vernazza).

Manarola
MANAROLA is almost as enchanting as Vernazza, its pastel-shaded houses crowded impossibly up the sides of a prominent headland of dark rock. The fourteenth-century church of San Lorenzo in the village has another beautiful rose window. On the road from Manarola to Corniglia above the village is the hamlet of **Groppo**, home to the **Cooperativa Agricola Cinque Terre**, which offers tastings and direct sale of the local wines (Mon–Sat 10am–noon & 2–6pm; ☎0187.920.435).

Manarola's two **hotels** are outstanding. Family-run *Ca' d'Andrean*, Via Discovolo 101 (☎0187.920.040, fax 0187.920.452; ③) takes a real pride in its service and its few, airy rooms (some with balcony); *Marina di Piccolo*, Via Discovolo 192 (☎0187.920.103, fax 0187.920.966; ④) has six pleasant rooms in the main building and four in a less inviting annexe. The small non-HI **hostel** *Ostello 5 Terre* is a clean, friendly place 300m up the hill from the station at Via Riccobaldi 21 (☎0187.920.215, fax 0187.920.218, *www. cinqueterre.net/ostello*; L30,000/€15.49); you may need to book several weeks ahead in summer for dorm beds or en suite rooms.

Riomaggiore
Lively **RIOMAGGIORE** is the easternmost of the Cinque Terre, with a relatively easy road link to the outside world that makes it also the most crowded of the five. Nonetheless, its vividly multicoloured houses piling up the steep slopes above the romantic little harbour, with no two on the same level, give the place a bizarre charm that remains untempered by the café crowds. Aside from the requisite rose window, the church of **San Giovanni Battista** houses a striking wooden *Crucifixion* by Maragliano. Riomaggiore is also the starting-point for the twenty-minute walk on the **Via dell'Amore** (Lovers' Path) to Manarola (see box on previous page).

The town's Web site *www.tamnet.it/riomaggiore/homepage2* gives plenty of background. The only **hotel** is the pleasantly modern *Villa Argentina*, in a lovely spot at Via De Gasperi 37 (☎ & fax 0187.920.213; ④). Otherwise, your best bet is **private rooms**; English-speaking Roberto and Luciano Fazioli (Scalinata della Tagliata 6h; ☎0187.920.587) manage various properties in Riomaggiore and Manarola from clean, simple rooms to self-catering apartments with terraced balconies overlooking the harbour (②). For **food**, *La Lanterna* (closed Tues) has a good, moderately priced pasta and seafood menu, and a great location in the pinched harbour (to get there, walk under the train line from the bottom of the main street); while *Contravelaccio* on Via Colombo also has various inexpensive menus. *Ripa del Sole*, Via De Gasperi 4 (☎0187.920.143) serves acclaimed gourmet menus for L80,000/€42.32.

The Golfo dei Poeti

After the beauty of the Golfo Paradiso and Golfo del Tigullio, and the drama of the Cinque Terre, Liguria still has a final flourish. Hard up against the Tuscan border is the majestic Golfo di La Spezia, an impressive sweeping panorama of islands and rough headlands renamed the **Golfo dei Poeti** in 1919 by Italian playwright Sam Benelli for the succession of romantic souls who fell in love with the place. Petrarch was the first; Shelley lived and died on these shores; Byron was another regular; and D.H. Lawrence passed the pre-World War I years here. The town at the head of the gulf is workaday **La Spezia**, a major naval and shipbuilding centre with a fine art gallery. Small resorts line the fringes of the bay, linked by buses which swing around on twisting roads or boats which shuttle across the glittering blue water – **Portovénere**, sitting astride a spit of land to the southwest, and **Lérici** on the southeastern shore, both of them pleasant and highly picturesque stopovers.

Dozens of **boats** embark on rapid, half-day and all-day excursions throughout the summer – and on certain days in winter too – between just about every port along this coast. Local tourist offices have precise details of sailings. The principal operator is Navigazione Golfo dei Poeti, Via Mazzini 21 in La Spezia (☎0187.732.987, *www. navigazionegolfodeipoeti.it*); others include In-Tur, Viale Italia (☎0187.24.324), and Battellieri del Golfo, Banchina Revel (☎0187.21.010). Fares are low: from La Spezia to Isola Palmaria is L6000/€3.10; from Lérici across the bay to Portovénere L8000/€4.13; and from Portovénere around the three islands of Palmaria, Tino and Tinetto L13,000/€6.71.

La Spezia

Up until a few years ago, most travel guides dismissed **LA SPEZIA** with a few curt comments. This ordinary working town was known mainly for its huge mercantile port and the largest naval base in the country – until the **Museo Amedeo Lia** – probably the finest collection of medieval and Renaissance art in Liguria – put it on the tourist map. Art aside, realistically priced hotels and restaurants make it a good base from which to explore both the Golfo dei Poeti and the Cinque Terre.

La Spezia's position, sandwiched between the hills and the sea, proved an early attraction to conquerors, with its strategic importance reflected in the number of Genoese castles that stud the hills. These were the town's first fortifications, yet it took **Napoleon** to capitalize on what is one of Europe's finest natural harbours and construct a naval and military complex at La Spezia early in the nineteenth century. The naval presence made the town a prime target in World War II and most of the centre had to be rebuilt following Allied **bombing**; it's now characterized by rather drab buildings lining a regular grid of streets behind the palm-fringed harbourfront promenade of **Viale Mazzini**. At the eastern end, opposite the Porto Mercantile, sits the 1970s **Cattedrale Cristo Re**, overlooking Piazza Europa and distinguished by a boldly minimalist white tower curving against a hilly backdrop. At the western end are some lovely **public gardens**, a short distance from **Piazza Chiodo** and La Spezia's *raison d'être* – the vast naval **Arsenale**, which was rebuilt after destruction in World War II. There's no public admittance to the complex itself, but just to the left of the entrance is the engaging **Museo Tecnico Navale** (Mon & Fri 2–6pm, Tues–Thurs & Sat 9am–noon & 2–6pm, Sun 8.30am–1.15pm; L3000/€1.55), which contains battle relics and models.

From the public gardens it's a short stroll inland on Via Prione to Piazza Beverini and the striped Duomo of **Santa Maria Assunta** housing a polychrome terracotta by Andrea della Robbia. Behind the church is the lively marketplace of **Piazza Cavour**, from where the **Museo Amedeo Lia** is 100m east at Via Prione 234 (Tues–Sun: mid-June to Aug 10am–1pm & 5–8pm; rest of year 10am–6pm; L12,000/€6.20; *www.castagna.it/mal)*. This impressive place occupies a seventeenth-century former Franciscan convent that has undergone careful and intelligent renovation. It was opened in December 1996 following the donation of more than a thousand artworks to the city by Lia, a private collector. Pricey it may be, but you can go in and out as many times as you like during the day with the same ticket.. Highlights include a lovely

Madonna with Child by Giampietrino that launches the small but exceptionally high-quality sixteenth-century collection in Rooms VI and VII, which also takes in Pontormo's sharp-eyed *Self-Portrait*, a supremely self-assured *Portrait of a Gentleman* by Titian, and Bellini's *Portrait of an Attorney*. Upstairs in room XI are bronzes by Giambologna and Ammannati. Room XII houses the museum's most celebrated item, the famous *Addolorata*, a half-statue of a sorrowful Madonna made by Benedetto da Maiano in polychrome terracotta in the fifteenth century.

Practicalities

The **train station** is a steep ten-minute walk above the town centre – head left out of the station and then follow the curving Via XX Settembre all the way down until it hits the first of three long, parallel boulevards which run along the front of the port: these three are Via Chiodo, then palm-lined Viale Mazzini, and then the principal traffic street of Viale Italia. The ferries to Corsica, Sardinia, the Cinque Terre and around the Golfo dei Poeti leave from the Porto Mercantile, on the central waterfront.

There are two **tourist offices** – on platform 1 of the train station (June–Sept daily 9am–1pm & 3–6pm; Oct–May Mon–Sat 9am–12.30pm & 2–5pm, Sun 9am–12.30pm; ☎0187.718.997) and just back from the port at Viale Mazzini 47 (daily 9am–1pm & 3–6pm; ☎0187.770.900, *www.laspezianet.it* and *www.aptcinqueterre.sp.it*). The main **bus station** is on Piazza Chiodo, at the western end of Via Chiodo in front of the naval arsenal, from where ATC buses depart towards Tuscany and into the countryside valleys. Buses to Portovénere and Lérici depart either from the train station forecourt, or from Piazza Cavour.

There are several **hotels** near the train station: the *Terminus* is right outside at Via Paleocapa 21 (☎0187.703.436, fax 0187.714.935; ①); the slightly more comfortable *Parma* is down the steps in front of the station at Via Fiume 143 (☎0187.743.010, fax 0187.743.240; ②); while the *Venezia*, Via Paleocapa 10 (☎0187.733.465; ③) is better in terms of decor and service. Near Piazza Cavour is the *Flavia*, Vicolo della Stagno 7 (☎0187.736.060; ①), with bargain doubles. Closer to the water, on one of the old centre's few pretty streets, the *Nuovo Spezia*, Via F. Cavalotti 31 (☎0187.735.164; ②), has basic rooms furnished with a haphazard selection of ancient furniture. The *Jolly* overlooks the bay at Via XX Settembre 2 (☎0187.739.555, fax 0187.22.129; ⑤), part of a chain and replete with all comforts.

For **food**, the daily covered market in Piazza Cavour is a good place to buy picnic supplies; it takes over the whole square on Saturday mornings. You can get *farinata* at *La Pia* on Via Magenta, and good pizzas at *Da Giulio*, Via San Agostino 29 (closed Wed). There's a cluster of restaurants between Via del Prione and the Arsenale, where prices

---

FERRIES TO CORSICA

Happy Lines is the main **ferry** operator between La Spezia and **Bastia** on the island of Corsica (France), running boats most days between mid-April and late September. The crossing takes five hours and costs L33,000/€17.04 per person (much more on summer weekends), plus L82,000/€42.35 for a car. Departures are all in the daytime, but you can book a bargain cabin onboard either for the night before you depart or for the night after you dock (checkout is at 6.30am, however); two-person cabins cost from L42,000/€21.69, four-person ones from L55,000/€28.40. You can get tickets from any travel agent in La Spezia, Happy Lines at Via Maralunga 45 (☎0187.564.530, *www.happylines.it*) or on the dockside.

There are also 12-hour crossings to **Olbia** on Sardinia, but you'll find much lower prices, shorter crossing-times and more regular service from Piombino or Livorno in Tuscany.

are kept in check by the naval clientele (many are closed in August); *Da Luciano*, Via Colombo 27, is another low-priced possibility in this part of town. Down near the seafront lurks *Da Dino*, Via Da Passano 19 (closed Sun evening & Mon), a down-to-earth eatery offering good-value menus of fish and other local fare, and *La Posta*, Via Don Minzoni 24 (closed Sat & Sun), in much the same mould. *La Muraglia*, Via Prione 44 (no closing day), is an excellent, inexpensive Chinese with plenty of authentic dishes.

Portovénere

The ancient, narrow-laned village of **PORTOVÉNERE** sits astride a spit of land on the very tip of the southwestern arm of the bay, blessed with breathtaking views, a memorably tranquil atmosphere and a string of three islets just offshore, each smaller and rockier than the last. The **bus** ride from La Spezia is a frenetic affair, with some hair-raising bends, but it gives fine views of the bay and the islands; however, the views are just as good from the **boats** which depart as regularly as buses – and the chances of holding onto your breakfast are much higher.

You enter through a twelfth-century towered **gate** built by the Genoese, who fortified this spot in opposition to Pisan forces that had taken Lérici across the bay. In the upper part of the village is the twelfth-century church of **San Lorenzo**, renowned for the remarkable treasures in its vestry, including four ivory caskets (three Syrian and one Byzantine) from about the year 1000. Higher up still is the sixteenth-century fortified **castello**, with panoramic views out over this most beautiful spot from its terraced gardens. Portovénere's characteristic rose- and yellow-painted tower-houses were aligned to form a defensive wall, now transformed into a trendy waterside strip known as the Palazzata, which spreads out at the end of the promontory to the church of **San Pietro** on the very tip of dry land, built with a banded facade and an elegant campanile in the thirteenth century over the ruins of a Roman **temple to Venus**; the village got its name from the Latin *Portus Veneris*, or Port of Venus. The views from the terrace in front of the church out to the three islands and across to the Cinque Terre coast are magnificent. One of the rocky coves around the base of the church is the **Grotto Arpaia**, a favoured spot of Lord Byron's where he came to seek inspiration and from where he swam across the bay to visit Shelley at San Terenzo (see below). To this day, the gulf has the nickname of the "Baia di Byron", but swimming is discouraged in favour of the **boats** which shuttle regularly to and from Lérici.

Boats from Portovénere also tour the three **islands** that lie south of the peninsula, all but the nearest of which lie in a military zone and so can only be viewed from the water. (Note, though, that island excursions paid for in Portovénere cost quite a bit more than the same things booked and begun in La Spezia – see opposite.) **Isola Palmária** is the largest, 500m south of Portovénere, with the Grotta Azzurra cave as its star attraction. Next is the **Isola del Tino**, a rocky islet marked with a lighthouse and the remains of a Romanesque abbey. Finally comes the yet tinier **Isola del Tinetto**, also home to a monastic community in centuries gone by.

Practicalities

Portovénere's **tourist office** is at Piazza Bastreri 7 (Mon–Sat 9am–noon & 3–6pm, Sun 9am–noon; ☎0187.790.691, *www.aptcinqueterre.sp.it*), alongside the least expensive **hotel**, two-star *Genio* (☎0187.790.611; ④). Of the four upscale choices, the pick is the *Royal Sporting*, a short walk outside the village on the beach, Via dell'Olivo 345 (☎0187.790.326, fax 0187.777.707; ⑥), with pleasant, cool interior courtyards, spectacular views and a huge salt-water swimming pool. In a different vein, *Locanda Lorena* offers half-a-dozen simple bathless rooms: nothing special but for its remote location on the Isola Palmaria, at Via Cavour 4 (☎0187.792.370; ④; April–Sept).

There's a wealth of places to **eat**. The century-old *Antica Osteria del Carrugio* (closed Thurs) is at Via Capellini 66, in the shadow of the castle; its affordable specialities are anchovies, sheep's cheese and stuffed mussels (which are cultivated on poles in Portovénere's harbour). Down on the photogenic harbourfront Calata Doria are a handful of pricier places, including *La Taverna del Corsaro* (✶0187.900.622), famous for its version of Portovénere's *zuppa di datteri* (razor-clam soup), and the acclaimed *Iseo* (✶0187.790.610; closed Wed), the village's best restaurant.

Lérici and around

East of La Spezia, you'll pass several kilometres of dockyards, foundries and thriving heavy industry; the sprawl is eventually brought up short at the boundary of a protected nature reserve which covers the southern half of the gulf shore.

First of the string of small resorts here is **SAN TERENZO**, marked by its prominent castle. There's a good sandy beach and a choice of accommodation but, predictably, most of the **hotels** will insist on full- or half-pension in high season. The best deals are, strangely enough, right on the seafront, at the *Nettuno*, Via Mantegazza 1 (✶0187.971.093; ②) and the *Trieste*, a few doors down at no. 13 (✶0187.970.610; ②), alongside which is the **Villa Magni**, where Shelley spent some productive months in 1822, before setting off to meet Leigh Hunt at Livorno, "full of spirits and joy", according to Mary Shelley's account. On the way back, his boat, the *Ariel*, went down near Viareggio, and Shelley drowned, aged thirty. Plans to turn the house into a multimedia **Museo P.B. Shelley** are well under way.

About 2km, or a thirty-minute walk, south of San Terenzo lies **LÉRICI**, an upwardly mobile resort of garden villas, seafront bars, trattorias and gift shops. Piazza Garibaldi, behind the marina, acts as the bus station. The **tourist office** is on the seafront north of Piazza Garibaldi, at Via Biaggini 6 (Tues–Sat 9.30am–12.30pm & 3.30–6pm, Sun 9.30am–12.30pm; ✶0187.967.346, *www.aptcinqueterre.sp.it*), and has details of the regular **boats** across to Portovénere. The circuitous route up to the Pisan-built castle from Piazza Garibaldi passes through **Via del Ghetto**, the old Jewish quarter once populated by Livornese merchants, and up the steep **Salita Arpara**, derived from a medieval word meaning "the place where hawks nest". At the top, the **castle** (Mon & Wed–Sun 9am–1pm & 3–7pm; L2000/€1.03) has fabulous views from the highest terrace right across to Portovénere and the three islands and back towards La Spezia. Inside, apart from a Gothic chapel, much of the interior is given over to a museum of geopaleontology, documenting prehistoric dinosaur life in the area.

Lérici's two most pleasant **hotels** are near the tourist office: the *Shelley & Delle Palme* is at Via Biaggini 5 (✶0187.968.204, fax 0187.964.271; ⑤) and the *Byron* is at no. 19 (✶0187.967.104, fax 0187.967.409, *www.cdh.it/hb*; ④); both have dreamy sea views from balconied rooms. The sole inexpensive option is the modern *Del Golfo*, inland at Via Gerini 37 (✶0187.967.400, fax 0187.965.733; ②). For **eating**, the outdoor pizzerias that line Lérici's harbour provide an attractive setting as the sun goes down. Amongst many are the popular *Il Giogo*, Via Petriccioli 44 (closed Mon), where you can indulge in pizzas, interesting seafood and home-made desserts; and the elegant *La Piccola Oasi*, Via Cavour 60 (closed Tues), which offers a simple set menu.

Fiascherino and Tellaro

The quiet 5km stretch of coast, accessible by bus or on foot, south to Tellaro seems to belong to another world, far from both La Spezia's bustle and Lérici's monied exclusivity: the water is improbably clear here and the many coves and inlets are irresistible places to bask. Partway along the road, signs direct you to a path down to a *spiaggia libera*, or public beach, an expanse of shingle and sand surrounded by wooded slopes. The next inlet south is sparklingly clear **FIASCHERINO**, accessible along Via D.H.

Lawrence. One of the most pleasant **campsites** on the Riviera is here – take the steps inland from the car park, and turn right for *Campeggio Gianna* (☎ & fax 0187.966.411; April–Sept), set on a terraced and shaded hillside.

Ten minutes' walk south of Fiascherino is the quiet fishing village of **TELLARO**, comparatively untouched by tourism, with stone houses packed tightly on the spur of rock over the slipway, and alleyways stalked by cats. The road ends in a cluster of bars and a couple of places **to stay**. If money is tight head for *Delle Ondine* (☎0187.965.131; ②), in a lovely location, but otherwise make sure you've booked ahead to stay at *Miranda* (☎0187.968.130, fax 0187.964.032; ⑤), a delightful little family-run inn with just seven en suite rooms; half-pension here is no hardship, since the pricey **restaurant** has won a reputation that extends well beyond Liguria's borders for its innovative and stylish presentation of fish and seafood. The mixing of flavours and ideas that goes on in this small kitchen makes Tellaro well worth a gastronomic detour.

travel details

TRAINS

Genoa to: Alassio (every 30min; 1hr–1hr 25min); Albenga (every 30min; 1hr 10min); Bologna (every 2–3hr; 3hr); Camogli (every 20min; 30–50min); Finale Ligure (every 30min; 1hr); Imperia (every 30min; 1hr 45min); La Spezia (hourly; 1hr 10min–2hr 10min); Milan (hourly; 2hr); Naples (every 2–3hr; 8hr); Pisa (every 2hr; 2hr 30min); Rapallo (every 20min; 30min); Rome (every 1–2hr; 6hr); San Remo (every 30min; 2hr–2hr 40min); Santa Margherita (every 20min; 20min–1hr); Ventimiglia (every 30min; 2hr 55min).

BUSES

Camogli to: Ruta (every 30min–1hr; 25min).

Chiávari to: Rezzoaglio (6 daily; 1hr 25min); Santo Stefano d'Aveto (6 daily; 1hr 55min).

Finale Ligure to: Borghetto Santo Spirito (every 15min; 25min).

Genoa to: Rovegno (5 daily; 1hr 50min); Torriglia (hourly; 1hr 10min).

La Spezia to: Lérici (every 10min; 20min); Portovénere (every 30min; 20min).

Lérici to: Tellaro (every 30min; 10min).

Rapallo to: Chiávari (hourly; 30min); Montallegro (every 2hr; 40min); Santa Margherita (every 20min; 10min).

San Remo to: Apricale (3 daily; 40min – change at Ventimiglia); Baiardo (4 daily; 1hr 15min).

Santa Margherita to: Portofino (every 15–20min; 15min).

Ventimiglia to: Dolceacqua (14 daily; 18min); La Mortola (9 daily; 15min).

FERRIES

Genoa to: Arbatax (2 weekly; 19hr); Bastia (1 weekly; 9hr); Cágliari (2 weekly in summer; 20hr); Olbia (at least 7 weekly in summer; 13hr); Palermo (4 weekly; 23hr); Porto Torres (7 weekly; 12hr).

La Spezia to: Bastia (5 weekly; 5hr); Olbia (7 weekly; 11hr 30min).

CHAPTER THREE

LOMBARDY AND THE LAKES

Lombardy, Italy's richest and most developed region, often seems to have more in common with its northern European neighbours than with the rest of Italy. Given its history, this is hardly surprising: it was ruled for almost two centuries by the French and Austrians and takes its name from the northern Lombards, who invaded the region and ousted the Romans. As a border region, accessible through numerous mountain passes, Lombardy has always been vulnerable to invasion, just as it has always profited by being a commercial crossroads. It was long viewed by northerners as the capital of Italy – emperors from Charlemagne to Napoleon came to Lombardy to be crowned king – and northern European business magnates continue to take Lombardy's capital, Milan, more seriously than Rome, the region's big businesses and banks wielding political as well as economic power across the nation.

The region's landscape has paid the price for economic success: industry chokes the peripheries of towns, sprawls across the Po plain in the south, and even spreads its polluting tentacles into the northern lakes and mountain valleys. Nonetheless Lombardy has its attractions: the upper reaches of its valleys are largely unspoilt; its towns and cities all retain wanderable medieval cores; and the stunning scenery and lush vegetation of the lakes make it easy to forget that the water is not sparkling clean.

As for Lombardy's people, from the cossetted residents of the provincial towns to Milan's workaholics, they hardly fit the popular image of Italians. In fact, they don't have much time for a substantial proportion of their compatriots: urban northerners are rather dismissive of the south, derisive of Rome and historically all too ready to exploit the so-called *terroni* (literally earth-people) – a highly insulting term for southern Italians who leave their poverty-stricken villages to find work in the north.

ACCOMMODATION PRICE CODES

Throughout this guide, prices per person are given for **youth hostels** and assume Hostelling International (HI) membership. **Hotel** accommodation is coded on a scale from ① to ⑨, reflecting the cost of the cheapest double room in each establishment in high season. The price bands to which these codes refer are as follows:

① Up to L60,000/€30.99
② L60,000–90,000/€30.99–46.48
③ L90,000–120,000/€46.48–61.98
④ L120,000–150,000/€61.98–77.47
⑤ L150,000–200,000/€77.47–103.29

⑥ L200,000–250,000/€103.29–129.11
⑦ L250,000–300,000/€129.11–154.94
⑧ L300,000–400,000/€154.94–206.58
⑨ over L400,000/€206.58

(See p.32 for a full explanation.)

REGIONAL FOOD AND WINE

Lombardy is distinctive in its **variations** in culinary habits – rice, for example, might form the bulk of the diet in some areas but would rarely be eaten in others, and food varies even from town to town. The short-grain rice used for **risottos** is grown in the paddy fields of the Ticino Valley, and other staples include green pasta and **polenta**. The latter is found all over northern Italy: made from maize meal boiled and patiently stirred for around forty minutes, watched with an eagle eye so it doesn't go lumpy. Polenta can be eaten straightaway, or else left to cool and then sliced and grilled and served as an accompaniment to meat.

The sophisticated recipes of Milanese urbanites contrast sharply with the more rustic dishes of the Alpine foothills and lakes. The latter are sometimes known as **piatti poveri** (poor food): devised over centuries, these employ imagination and often time-consuming techniques to make up for the lack of expensive ingredients. *Pizzoccheri*, buckwheat noodles found in the Valtellina Valley, are an example of this. *Risotto alla Milanese*, on the other hand, golden yellow from saffron, is Milan's most renowned culinary export, and, it is said, only truly **Milanese** if it has been cooked with the juices of roast veal flavoured with sage and rosemary. *Ossobucco* (shin of veal) is another Milanese favourite, as are *biscotti* – handmade biscuits flavoured with nuts, vanilla and lemon and sold by weight at specialist shops all over the city. *Panettone*, the soft, eggy cake with sultanas, also originated here.

From Cremona comes **mostarda di frutta** (pickled fruit with mustard), the traditional condiment to serve with boiled meats (*bollito misto*). Another meaty dish is *La Casoêula*, a pork stew said to be of Spanish origin. Stuffed pastas and veal are also popular, as are wild fungi.

Lombardy is also one of the largest cheese-making regions in the country. As well as Gorgonzola and Bel Paese there are numerous local **cheeses**, the parmesan-like Grana Padano and the smooth, rich Mascarpone (used in sweet dishes) being only the best known.

Although Lombardy is not well known internationally for its wines, Milan supermarket shelves bulge with basic **wines** from the Oltrepò Pavese, and the northern areas of Valtellina and around Brescia make good reds such as Franciacorta, as well as Ca' Del Bosco, a white sparkler.

Milan, a natural gateway to the region, and where you may well arrive, dominates the plain that forms the southern part of Lombardy. The towns across here – **Pavia**, **Cremona**, **Mantua** – flourished during the Middle Ages and Renaissance, and retain their historical character today, albeit encircled by burgeoning suburbs. To the north, Lombardy is quite different, the lakes and low mountains of the edge of the Alps sheltering fewer historic towns, though **Bergamo** and **Brescia** are notable exceptions. This has long been popular tourist territory, particularly around the lakes of **Maggiore**, **Como** and **Garda**, and wealthy Italian holiday-makers and day-trippers are much in evidence. Although the western shore of Lago Maggiore and the eastern and northern shores of Lago di Garda are, strictly speaking, in Piemonte, Veneto and Trentino respectively, the **lakes region** and all its resorts are all covered in this chapter.

MILAN AND SOUTHERN LOMBARDY

Much of Lombardy's wealth is concentrated in the cities and towns of the broad Po plain, which forms the southern belt of the region. It's a wealth that is obvious throughout the area in the well-preserved medieval towns and the ugly industrial estates that surround them, not to mention the pollution – the Po is Italy's most polluted river, and

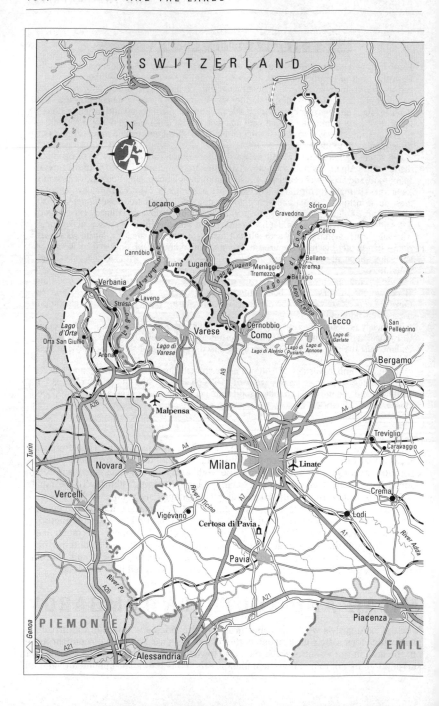

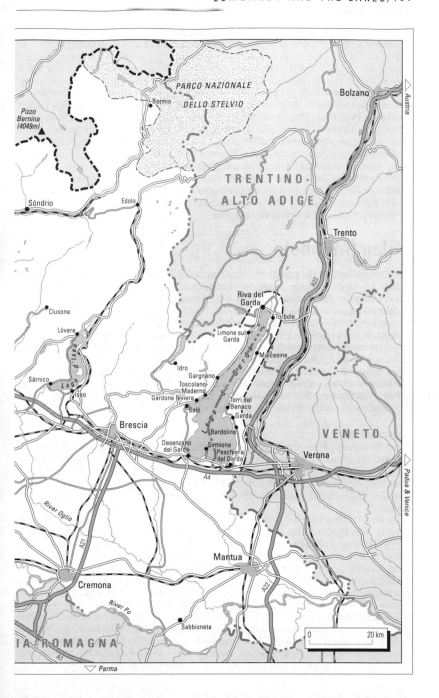

air pollution in Milan is sometimes so dangerous that the traffic police don gas masks.
Despite all this, the area is well worth exploring. **Milan** may be polluted, but it's an
upbeat city, with some great classical and contemporary art galleries and a splendid
cathedral, as well as world-famous designer stores and a lively night scene. As a first
taste of Italy it can be daunting; given time, though, and taken on its own, contemporary terms, it is a stimulating place to be. **Pavia**, to the south, is a pretty medieval town
that makes a cheaper – and rather more peaceful – alternative base for this part of
Lombardy, its cobbled streets and ancient churches taking a firm back seat in terms of
sights to its **Certosa**, just outside. Heading east, **Cremona** was the birthplace of the
violin and home of Stradivari, and has a neat, well-preserved centre, though it's not the
kind of place you'd want to stay long. **Mantua**, in the far eastern corner of the region,
is by contrast Lombardy's most visually appealing city, at least from a distance,
although what you really come for are the remains of the powerful Gonzaga family, who
ruled here for 300 years from their extravagant ducal palace and their later Palazzo Te,
on the outskirts of the city, which contains some of the finest (and most steamily erotic) fresco-painting of the entire Renaissance.

Milan (Milano)

The dynamo behind the country's "economic miracle", **MILAN** is a city like no other
in Italy. It's foggy in winter, muggy in summer, and is closer in outlook, as well as distance, to London than to Palermo. This is no city of peeling palazzi, cobbled piazzas and
la dolce vita, but one in which time is money, the pace fast, and where consumerism and
the work-ethic rule the lives of its power-dressed citizens.

Because of this most people pass straight through, and if it's summer and you're keen
for sun and sea this might well be the best thing you can do; the weather, in August especially, can be off-puttingly humid. But at any other time of year it's well worth giving
Milan more of a chance. It's a historic city, with enough churches and museums to keep
you busy for a week – the Accademia Brera, duomo and the church of Santa Maria delle
Grazie – but there are also parks and cafés to relax in, and the contemporary aspects of
the place represent the leading edge of Italy's fashion and design industry.

Some history

Milan first stepped into the historical limelight in the fourth century when Emperor
Constantine issued the **Edict of Milan** here, granting Christians throughout the
Roman Empire the freedom to worship for the first time. The city, under its charismatic bishop, Ambrogio (St Ambrose), swiftly became a major centre of Christianity –
many of today's churches stand on the sites, or even retain parts, of fourth-century predecessors.

Medieval Milan rose to prominence under the ruthless regime of the Visconti
dynasty, who founded what is still the city's most spectacular building, the florid late-
Gothic **Duomo**, and built the first, heavily fortified nucleus of the **Castello** – which,
under their successors, the Sforza, was extended to house what became one of the
most luxurious courts of the Renaissance. This was a period of much building and
rebuilding, notably under the last Sforza, Lodovico, who employed the architect
Bramante to improve the city's churches and **Leonardo da Vinci** to paint *The Last
Supper* and design war-machines to aid him in his struggles with foreign powers and
other Italian states. Leonardo's inventions didn't prevent Milan falling to the French in
1499, marking the beginning of almost four centuries of foreign rule. Later, the Austrian
Habsburgs took control, during their time commissioning the **Teatro della Scala** and
founding the **Brera** art gallery, which, during Milan's short spell under Napoleon, was
filled with paintings looted from churches and private collections.

Mussolini made his mark on the city too. Arrive by train and you emerge into the massive white megalith of the central **station** built on his orders; the main tourist office is housed in one half of the pompous twin **Arengario**, from which he would address crowds gathered in Piazza Duomo. And with stark irony it was on the now major road junction of **Piazzale Loreto** that the dead dictator was strung up for display to the baying mob.

Arrival

Most international and domestic **trains** pull in at the main **Stazione Centrale**, northeast of the city centre on Piazza Duca d'Aosta, at the hub of the metro network on lines MM2 and MM3. Quite a few trains, especially those from stations in the Milan region – Bergamo, Pavia, Como and the other western lakes – terminate at **Garibaldi**, **Lambrate**, **Porta Genova** and **Nord**, all on MM2 (the metro stop for Milan Nord is "Cadorna"), although these often also stop at Centrale. International and long-distance **buses** arrive at and depart from Piazza Castello, in front of the Castello Sforzesco. Information and tickets are available from the Autostradale bus office (☎02.801.161) on the piazza, or Zani Viaggi (☎02.867.131), on the corner of Piazza Castello and Foro Buonaparte. As for arrival **by car**, the city is encircled by a multi-laned toll road, the Tangenzianale, from which there are links onto the *autostradas* for Venice and Turin (A4), Genoa (A7), and the "Autostrada del Sole" (A1) for Bologna, Florence, Rome and the south.

Milan has two **airports**, both used by domestic and international traffic. **Malpensa** (☎02.7485.2200), 50km northeast of the city, is the main one, connected by direct bus with the Stazione Centrale (every 20 mins 5.20am–10.30pm; 1hr; L13,000/€6.71) and by the new FNME train, the Malpensa Express (every 30min 6.30am–1.30am; 40min; information ☎02.27.723, *www.malpensaexpress.com*), with Milano Nord (the early morning and late evening services are replaced by a bus from Via Leopardi, just to the left of the station). It costs L15,000/€7.75, although Air Italia and Lufthansa passangers are entitled to discounts. Check when you buy your ticket that your airline hasn't arranged a similar deal. Milan's other airport, **Linate** (☎02.7485.2200), is just 7km from the city centre: special airport buses connect it with the air terminal on Piazza Luigi di Savoia, on the east side of Stazione Centrale (every 20min 5.40am–7pm, every 30min 7–9pm; 20min; L4500/€2.32). Ordinary ATM urban transport **buses** (#73) also run every ten minutes from 5.30am until around midnight between Linate and Piazza San Babila in the city centre, and they don't take much longer; tickets cost L1500/€0.78 and should be bought before you get on the bus from the airport newsagent, or, if you have change, from the ticket machine at the bus stop. Bear in mind, too, that there's a twice-daily connecting bus service between Linate and Malpensa, a 75-minute journey.

Information

Milan has two main **tourist offices**, one tucked away between two jewellery shops down a corridor off the main upper level of the Stazione Centrale (Mon–Sat 9am–6pm; ☎02.7252.4360), and another, larger office in the city centre at Via Marconi 1, on the corner of Piazza Duomo (Mon–Fri 8.30am–8pm, Sat 9am–1pm & 2–7pm, Sun 9am–1pm & 2–5pm; ☎02.7252.4301, fax 02.7252.4350); there are also information desks at the airports (daily 9am–4pm). The tourist office publish *Milano Mese* (*www.vivimilano.it*), a monthly booklet which can be worth picking up for its **listings** and general information. *Hello Milan* also gives good monthly rundowns of cultural events and the like, and *Milan Where, When, How*, has comprehensive listings concentrating on shopping, sport, bars, clubs and discos; both are available free in hotel lobbies, bars or the tourist office in Piazza Duomo. The pullouts in either *Corriere della Sera* on Wednesdays, or *La Repubblica* on Thursdays, are another valuable source of listings.

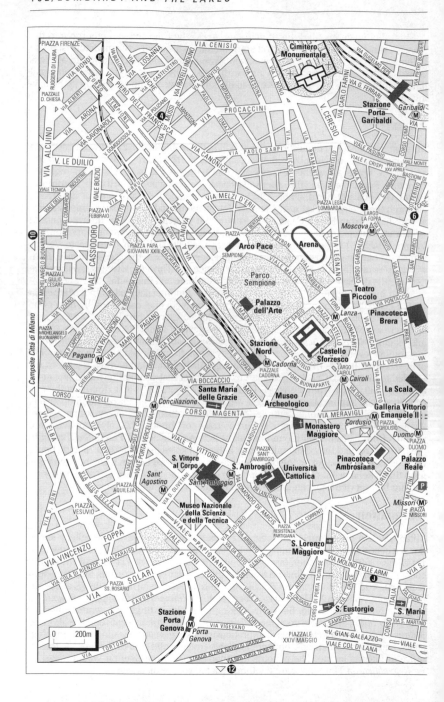

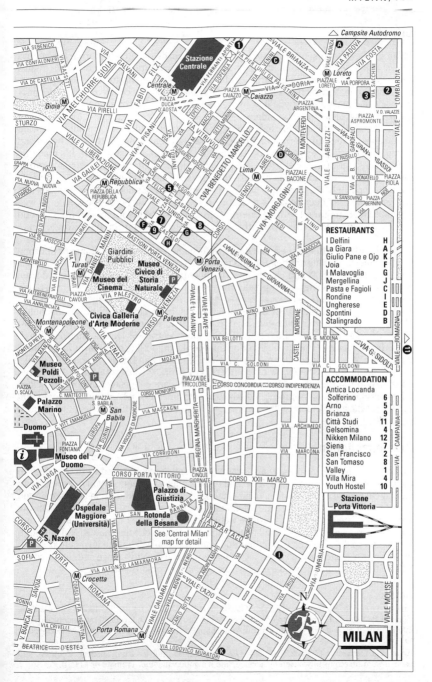

△ *Campsite Autodromo*

Stazione
Centrale

RESTAURANTS

I Delfini	H
La Giara	A
Giulio Pane e Ojo	K
Joia	F
I Malavoglia	G
Mergellina	J
Pasta e Fagioli	C
Rondine	I
Ungherese	E
Spontini	D
Stalingrado	B

ACCOMMODATION

Antica Locanda Solferino	6
Arno	5
Brianza	9
Città Studi	11
Gelsomina	4
Nikken Milano	12
Siena	7
San Francisco	2
San Tomaso	8
Valley	1
Villa Mira	4
Youth Hostel	10

Stazione
Porta Vittoria

See 'Central Milan'
map for detail

MILAN

N

City transport

Milan's street-plan resembles a spider's web, with roads radiating out from the central Piazza Duomo. The bulk of the city is encircled by three concentric ring roads, although the suburbs and industrial estates are now spilling out towards a fourth ring, the Tangenzianale, which links the main *autostradas*. The city centre is, however, fairly compact, and most of what you'll want to see is within the first or second rings, each of them marking ancient city boundaries.

In spite of this, the streets can be smoggy and packed, and at some point you'll want to make use of the **public transport** system – an efficient network of trams, buses and metro. The **metro** is easiest to master (and the fastest and most useful). It's made up of four lines, the red MM1, green MM2, yellow MM3, and blue *passante ferroviario*, meeting at the four main hubs of Stazione Centrale, Duomo, Cadorna and Loreto (see our map opposite). The system is not comprehensive, but it's adequate for sightseeing. However, you may need to use a **tram** or **bus** to get to your hotel: the system is well organized and integrated with the metro. Buses, trams and the metro run from around 6am to midnight, after which **nightbuses** take over, following the metro routes until 1am.

For all **public transport enquiries** the information office at the Duomo or Stazione Centrale metro stations are helpful, and have free route maps. **Tickets**, valid for 75 minutes, cost L1500/€0.78 and can be used for one metro trip and as many bus and tram rides as you want. They are on sale at tobacconists, bars and at the metro station newsagents; most outlets close at 8pm so it's best to buy a few tickets in advance, or a carnet of ten for L14,000/€7.23. Some stations have automatic ticket machines, although only the newer ones give change. You can also buy a one-day (L5000/€2.58) or two-day ticket (L9000/€4.65) from the Stazione Centrale or Duomo metro stations.

Taxis don't cruise the streets, so don't bother trying to flag one down. Either head for a taxi rank – on Piazza Duomo, Largo Cairoli, Piazza San Babile, Stazione Centrale, etc – or phone one of the following numbers: ☎02.6767, 02.5353 or 02.8585. Apart from taxis, **driving** in the city is best avoided: the streets are congested and parking close on impossible. Parking in prohibited zones is not worth it; you'll be fined if caught and have your car impounded by the police (see "Listings", p.179 for details of city-centre car parks).

Accommodation

Milan is still more a business than a tourist city, and its **accommodation** is geared to the expense-account traveller: prices tend to be high, and whenever you're here there's a good chance that many hotels, of all categories, will be booked up in advance. If you want to be sure of a room, phone ahead and get them to fax you back to confirm the reservation. The area around Stazione Centrale, and across to Corso Buenos Aires and Piazzale Loreto, is home to a good proportion of the city's cheaper hotels, and although many cater to the area's considerable red-light trade, you will be fine if you choose with care. We've also included a sprinkling of places around the city centre and the so-called "Città Studi", or university quarter, further east from Corso Buenos Aires.

Hotels

Antica Locanda Solferino, Via Castelfidardo 2 (☎02.657.0129, fax 02.657.1361). Between the Giardini Pubblici and Parco Sempione, this is *the* hotel to be seen in; favoured by models and lefty intellectuals alike, and only a stone's throw from shopper's heaven. Book in advance. MM Moscova. ⑥.

Arno, Via Lazzaretto 17 (☎02.670.5509). Off Viale Tunisia, not far from Stazione Centrale, and packed from March to July. Friendly service, and it's good value too. Tram #4 or #11. ③.

Brianza, Via P. Castaldi 16 (☎02.2940.4819, fax 02.2953.1145). Respectable, basic one-star in the vicinity of the Stazione Centrale. Entrance on Via Lazzaretto. MM Repubblica or Pta Venezia. ②.

Cinque Giornate, Piazza Cinque Giornate 6 (☎02.546.3433). Two-star hotel a ten-minute walk from Piazza Duomo; it often has rooms when other places are full. MM Duomo or S. Babila. ④.

Città Studi, Via Saldini 24 (☎02.744.666, fax 02.713.122). University-quarter hotel that is a good deal if you get one of the rooms without bathroom. Bus #61, #90 or #91. ④.

Gelsomina, V. Pier della Francesca 4/7 (☎02.3419.1742). Comfortable, friendly *pensione*; all rooms are en suite. Tram #33 or #29 from MM Garibaldi, or buses #57 or #94. ③.

Nikken Milano, V. Fumagalli 4 (☎02.5810.7065, fax 02.5811.5066). A relaxed four-star hotel in the heart of the Navigli district. MM Cordusio. ⑦.

Rovello, Via Rovello 18a (☎02.8646.4654, fax 02.7202.3656). City-centre hotel, close to Castello Sforzesco, with nice rooms at two-star prices. MM Cairoli. ⑥.

San Francisco, Viale Lombardia 55 (☎02.236.1009, fax 02.2668.0377). Family-run hotel with simple rooms and a small garden several blocks east of Piazzale Loreto, in the student area. Bus #56. ⑤.

San Tomaso, Viale Tunisia 6 (☎ & fax 02.2951.4747). Very popular and friendly *pensione* in a building full of such places. Separate, clean bathrooms and a notice board crammed with testimonials from travellers. MM Centrale or Repubblica. ③.

Siena, Via P. Castaldi 17 (☎02.2951.6180, fax 02.2951.4615). Stazione Centrale area hotel, with small, spotless rooms with tiled floors and shower; entrance actually on Via Lazzaretto. MM Repubblica or Pta Venezia. ④.

Valley, Via Soperga 19 (☎02.6698.7252). Very pleasant rooms, very close to Stazione Centrale, just two blocks to the east. MM Centrale. ④.

Vecchia Milano, Via Borromei 4 (☎02.875.042). City-centre two-star hotel situated on the north side of Piazza Cordusio, in a very nice part of town. MM Cordusio or Cairoli. ⑤.

Villa Mira, Via Sacchini 19 (☎02.2952.5618). Two blocks from Piazzale Loreto, this is a quiet, family-run place with nicely furnished, clean rooms. MM Loreto. ②.

Hostel

Ostello Piero Rotta, Viale Salmoiraghi 1, on the corner of Via Martino Bassi (☎02.3926.7095). A HI hostel housed in a large modern building with a garden, out in the northwest suburbs near the San Siro stadium. Open 7–9am and 3.30–11pm; 12.30am curfew. You can't book ahead, so it's best to arrive early, especially in summer. MM1 to QT8, signposted from there. L26,000/€13.43, including breakfast.

Camping

Autodromo, Parco di Monza, Monza (☎039.387.771). In a park near the renowned Formula One circuit, north of Milan. Trains run from Stazione Centrale to Monza station, from where it's a short bus ride. Open from early May to the end of September only.

Città di Milano, Via G. Airaghi 61(☎02.4820.0134). The nearest campsite to the centre, but still a metro trip and a bus ride away. MM1 to De Angeli, then bus #72. Open all year.

The City

Historic Milan lies at the centre of a web of streets, within the inner **Cerchia dei Navigli**, which follows the route of the medieval city walls. **Piazza del Duomo** is the city centre's main orientation point: most of the city's major sights lie within this area, as well as the swankiest designer shops and most elegant cafés. Visits to **art galleries and museums**, the **Duomo** and other churches can be punctuated with designer window-shopping in the so-called Quadrilatero d'Oro, or sipping overpriced drinks among the designer-dressed clientele of the pavement cafés of the **Galleria Vittorio Emanuele** or around the **Pinacoteca di Brera** art gallery. The second *cerchia*, the **Viali**, skirts behind the centre's two large parks – the **Parco Sempione** and **Giardini Pubblici** – to the canal sides of the **Navigli** in the south, following the tracks of defensive walls built during the Spanish occupation. Within lie the **Castello Sforzesco** and the church of **Santa Maria delle Grazie**, which houses Milan's most famous painting, Leonardo's *The Last Supper*. What follows is a wedge-by-wedge account of the city: Milan is not an easily wanderable city, so make a judicious selection, walking a little but where necessary hopping between places by way of the metro or other public transport.

Piazza del Duomo

The unquestioned hub of the city is **Piazza del Duomo**, a large, mostly pedestrianized square that's rarely quiet at any time of day. Harassed Milanese hurry out of the metro station deftly avoiding the pigeon-feed sellers and ice cream vendors; designer-dressed kids hang out on the steps of the cathedral; harassed tour-guides gather together their flocks; and well-preserved women stiletto-click across the square to glitzy cafés.

The **Duomo** is the world's largest Gothic cathedral, begun in 1386 under the Viscontis and completed nearly five centuries later. The finishing touches to the facade were finally added in 1813, and from the outside at least it's an incredible building, notable as much for its decoration as its size and with a front that's a strange mixture of Baroque and Gothic. The marble, chosen specially by the Viscontis, comes from the quarries of Candoglia near Lago Maggiore and continues to be used in renovation today – the fabric not surprisingly under severe attack from Milan's polluted atmosphere.

Inside the duomo, a green, almost subterranean half-light filters through the stained glass windows, lending the marble columns a bone-like hue that led the French writer Suarés to compare the interior to "the hollow of a colossal beast". By the entrance, the brass strip embedded in the pavement with the signs of the zodiac alongside is Europe's largest sundial, laid out in 1786. A beam of light still falls on it through a hole in the ceiling, though changes in the Earth's axis mean that it's no longer accurate. To the right, the sixteenth-century statue of St Bartholomew, with his flayed skin thrown like a toga over his shoulder, is one of the church's more gruesome statues, with veins, muscles and bones sculpted with anatomical accuracy, the draped skin retaining the form of knee, foot, toes and toenails.

At the far end of the church, suspended high above the chancel, a large crucifix contains the most important of the duomo's holy relics – a nail from Christ's cross, which was crafted to become the bit for the bridle of Emperor Constantine's horse. The cross is lowered once a year, on September 14, the Feast of the Cross, by a device invented by Leonardo da Vinci. Close by, beneath the presbytery, the **Scurolo di San Carlo** (daily 9am–noon & 2.30–6pm; L2000/€1.03) is an octagonal crypt designed to house the remains of St Charles Borromeo, the zealous sixteenth-century cardinal who was canonized for his unflinching work among the poor of the city and whose reforms antagonized the higher echelons of the corrupt Church. He lies here in a glass coffin, clothed, bejewelled, masked and gloved, wearing a gold crown attributed to Cellini. Borromeo was also responsible for the large altar in the north transept, erected in order to close off a door which allowed the locals to use the cathedral as a short cut to the market. Adjacent to Borromeo's resting-place, the **treasury** features extravagant evangelical covers, Byzantine ivory-work and heavily embroidered vestments.

Back towards the entrance you'll find the cathedral's fourth-century **Battistero Paleocristiano** (daily 9.30am–5.15pm; L3000/€1.55), where St Ambrose baptized St Augustine in 387 AD. Augustine had arrived in Milan three years earlier with his illegitimate son, and after sampling various religions, pagan and Christian, was eventually converted to Christianity by Ambrose, then the city's bishop. Outside again, from the northwest end of the cathedral you can get to the cathedral **roof** (second weekend in Feb to first week in Nov daily 9am–5.45pm; rest of year daily 9am–4.15pm; L6000/€3.10 to walk, L9000/€4.65 for the elevator), where you can stroll around the forest of tracery, pinnacles and statues while enjoying fine views of the city and on clear days even the Alps. The highlight is the central spire, its lacy marble crowned by a gilded statue of the Madonna looking out over the bodies of the roof sunbathers.

Across the way from the cathedral, the **Museo del Duomo** (daily 9.30am–12.30pm & 3–6pm; L10,000/€5.17), housed in a wing of the Palazzo Reale on the southern side of the piazza, holds casts of a good many of the 3000 or so statues and gargoyles that spike the duomo. You can also see how it might have ended up, in a display of entries for a late nineteenth-century competition of new designs for the facade. The scheme came to nothing – partly because the winner died, but mostly because the Milanese had grown attached to the duomo's distinctive hybrid frontage.

South of Piazza del Duomo

The area south of Piazza del Duomo is relatively thin on tourist attractions, with few real targets and unalluring streets. However, the charming church of **San Satiro** (daily 8–11am & 3.30–6.30pm), off the busy shopping street of Via Torino, is a study in ingenuity, commissioned from Milan's foremost Renaissance architect, Bramante, in 1476. Originally the oratory of the adjacent ninth-century church of San Satiro, it was transformed by Bramante into a long-naved basilica by converting the long oblong oratory into the transept and adding a wonderful trompe l'oeil apse onto the back wall.

Five minutes away, just off Via Torino at Piazza Pio 2, the **Pinacoteca Ambrosiana** (Tues–Sun 10am–5.30pm; L12,000/€6.20) was founded by another member of the Borromeo family, Cardinal Federico Borromeo, in the early seventeenth century. The cardinal collected ancient manuscripts, assembling one of the largest libraries in Europe, though what you come here for now is his art collection, stamped with his taste for Jan Brueghel, sixteenth-century Venetians and some of the more kitsch followers of Leonardo. Among many mediocre works, there is a rare painting by Leonardo da Vinci, *Portrait of a Musician*, a cartoon by Raphael for the School of Athens, and a Caravaggio considered to be Italy's first ever still life. The museum's quirkiest exhibit, however, is a lock of Lucrezia Borgia's hair – put for safe-keeping in a glass phial ever since Byron (having decided that her hair was the most beautiful he had ever seen) extracted one as a keepsake from the library downstairs where it used to be kept unprotected.

Cutting across Via Torino and Via Mazzini to Corso di Porta Romano, one of the city's busiest radial roads, takes you to the church of **San Nazaro**. It's something of a minor sight, but the severe octagonal chapel which serves as its vestibule was the

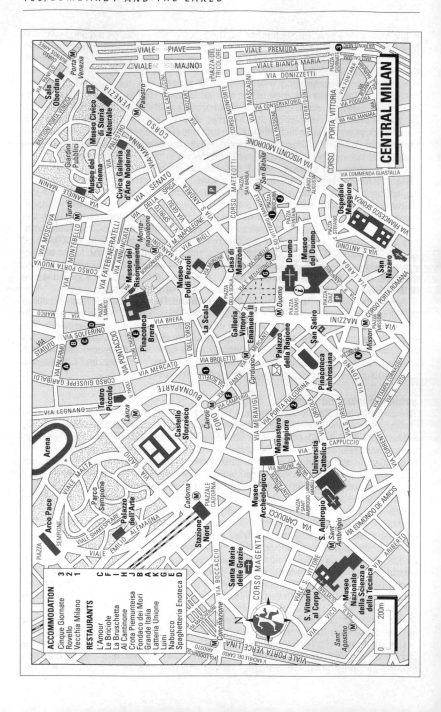

CENTRAL MILAN

family church of one of the city's better-known traitors – the *condottiere* Giangiacomo Trivulzio, who led the French attack on Milan to spite his rival Lodovico Sforza and was rewarded by being made the city's French governor. His tomb and those of his family are contained in niches around the walls, the inscription above Giangiacomo's reading, "He who never rested now rests: silence."

Behind San Nazaro, the **Ospedale Maggiore** – once known locally as the "Ca' Granda" (Big House) – was an ambitious project undertaken by the Florentine architect Filarete to unite the city's numerous hospitals and charitable institutions on one site. His hopes of introducing Renaissance architecture to Milan were dampened by local architects who, as soon as Filarete returned to Florence, introduced the late-Gothic elements clearly visible on the facade. To get a clearer idea of Filarete's intentions, step inside to look at the courtyards – eight small ones formed by two crucifixes, separated by a ninth rectangular one. Today the building houses the city's university.

North of Piazza del Duomo

Almost as famous a Milanese sight as the duomo is the gaudily opulent **Galleria Vittorio Emanuele II**, a cruciform glass-domed gallery designed in 1865 by Giuseppe Mengoni, who was killed when he fell from the roof a few days before the inaugural ceremony. Though the prices in its cafés are extortionate, it's worth splashing out once to indulge in some people-watching – eke your drink out for long enough and you'll see what seems like the city's whole population shove or stroll through depending on the time of day. In one of the lulls take a look at the circular mosaic beneath the glass cupola, composed of the symbols that made up the cities of the newly united Italy: Romulus and Remus for Rome, a fleur-de-lys for Florence and a bull for Turin – the indentation in the last is because it's considered good luck to stand on the bull's testicles.

The left arm of the gallery leads towards **Piazza dei Mercanti**, surrounded by medieval palaces which were once the seats of guilds and other city organizations. The square was the commercial centre of medieval Milan and the city's financial hub until the turn of the twentieth century, when the Borsa or Stock Exchange – then housed in the sixteenth-century **Palazzo dei Giureconsulti** on Via Mercanti – was moved north to Piazza degli Affari. Now the square is one of the city's more peaceful spots, dominated by the **Palazzo della Ragione**, built in the early thirteenth century to celebrate Milan winning autonomy from the emperor. The upper storey was added four centuries later, by another imperial figure, Empress Maria Theresa.

The main branch of Galleria Vittorio Emanuele leads through to Piazza della Scala and the world-famous **La Scala** opera house, designed by Piermarini and opened in 1778 with an opera by Antonio Salieri – a well-known name in his own right then, though more famous now (thanks to Peter Schaffer's play *Amadeus*) for his rivalry with Mozart than for his music. La Scala is still to a great extent the social and cultural centre of Milan's elite, and although Sixties protests have since led to a more open official policy on the arts in Milan, it remains as exclusive a venue as it ever was, with ticket prices sky-high. The small **museum** (May–Oct daily 9am–noon & 2–5pm; Nov–April Mon–Sat same hours; L6000/€3.10), featuring composers' death masks, plaster casts of conductors' hands, and a rugged statue of Puccini in a capacious overcoat, may be the only chance you get to see the interior.

Another big-name nineteenth-century figure lived only a block away from La Scala at Via Morone 1, just off the busy street that now bears his name. The **house of Alessandro Manzoni** (Tues–Fri 9.30am–noon & 2–4pm; free), who wrote the great Italian novel of the last century, *The Betrothed*, now contains a small museum of memorabilia, though it won't mean much if you haven't read the book.

The star attraction of this area, however, is the **Museo Poldi Pezzoli** at Via Manzoni 12 (Tues–Sun 10am–6pm; L10,000/€5.17), comprising pieces assembled by the nineteenth-century collector Gian Giacomo Poldi Pezzoli. Much of this is made up of rather dull rooms of clocks, watches, cutlery and jewellery, but the Salone Dorato upstairs contains a number of intriguing paintings, including a portrait of a portly *San Nicola da Tolentino* by Piero della Francesca, part of an altarpiece on which he worked spasmodically for fifteen years. St Nicholas looks across at two works by Botticelli, one a gentle *Madonna del Libro*, among the many variations of the Madonna and Child theme which he produced at the end of the fifteenth century, the other a mesmerizing *Deposition*, painted towards the end of his life in response to the monk Savonarola's crusade against his earlier, more humanistic canvases. Also in the room is one of Italy's most famous portraits, *Portrait of a Young Woman* by Pollaiuolo, whose anatomical studies are evidenced in the subtle suggestion of bone structure beneath the skin of this ideal Renaissance woman.

The Brera district and Pinacoteca di Brera

North of La Scala, **Via Brera** sets the tone for the city's arty quarter with its small galleries and art shops. There's nothing resembling an artist's garret, however: Via Brera and the streets around it are the terrain of the rich, reflected in the café prices and designer styles of those who can afford to sit outside them.

The Brera district gives its name to Milan's most prestigious art gallery, the **Pinacoteca di Brera** at Via Brera 28 (Tues–Fri & Sun 8.30am–7.30pm, Sat 8.30am–11pm; L12,000/€6.20), originally set up by Napoleon, who filled the building with works looted from the churches and aristocratic collections of French-occupied Italy, opening the museum to the public in 1809. It's a fine gallery, Milan's best by far, but it's also very large, and unless you're keen on making several exhaustive visits you need to be very selective, dipping into the collection guided by your own personal tastes.

Not surprisingly, most of the museum's paintings are Italian and predate the twentieth century. The Brera does display modern work, including paintings by Modigliani, De Chirico and Carrà, but it's the Renaissance which provides the museum's core. There's a good representation of Venetian painters – works by Bonifacio and, a century later, Paolo Veronese, the latter weighing in with a depiction of *Supper in the House of Simon* which got him into trouble with the Inquisition, who considered the introduction of frolicking animals and unruly kids unsuitable subject matter for a religious painting. Tintoretto's *Deposition* was more starkly in tune with requirements of the time, a scene of intense concentration and grief over Christ's body, painted in the 1560s. Gentile Bellini's *St Mark Preaching in St Euphemia Square* introduces an exotic note, the square bustling with turbaned men, veiled women, camels and even a giraffe. There are also paintings by Gentile's follower, Carpaccio, namely *The Presentation of the Virgin* and *The Disputation of St Stephen*, while the *Pietà* by Gentile's more talented brother, Giovanni, has been deemed "one of the most moving paintings in the history of art".

Look out also for *The Dead Christ*, a painting by Giovanni Bellini's brother-in-law, Mantegna: it's an exercise in virtuosity really, but an ingenious one – Christ, lying on a wooden slab, viewed from the wrinkled and pierced soles of his feet upwards. Although he was a contemporary of Mantegna, Crivelli's work, nearby, is quite different, his paintings creating a fairyland for his pale, perfect Madonnas, hermetically sealed from the realities of time and decay.

The rooms that follow hold yet more quality work, of which Piero della Francesca's chill *Madonna with Angels, SS and Federigo da Montefeltro* is the most famous painting. But take a look too at Raphael's *Marriage of the Virgin*, whose lucid, languid Renaissance mood is in sharp contrast to the grim realism of Caravaggio's *Supper at Emmaus* – set in a dark tavern and painted a century later. Less well known but equally realistic are the paintings of Lombardy's brilliant eighteenth-century realist, Ceruti –

known as Il Pitochetto (The Little Beggar) for his unfashionable sympathy with the poor, who stare out with reproachful dignity from his canvases. As his main champion, Roberto Longhi, said, his figures are "dangerously larger than life", not easily transformed into "gay drawing room ornaments".

The Quadrilatero d'Oro and the Giardini Pubblici

The shopping quarter to the northeast of Piazza del Duomo – the few hundred square yards bordered by Via Monte Napoleone, Via Sant'Andrea, Via Spiga and Via Borgospesso, the so-called **Quadrilatero d'Oro** – is home to the shops of all the big designer names, along with design studios and contemporary art galleries. The area is well worth a stroll, if only to observe the better-heeled Milanese searching out the perfect objet d'art for their elegant pads. Indeed, to leave Milan without looking in the windows of its fashionable boutiques would be to miss out on a crucial aspect of the city.

Just to the north of the shopping quarter, the **Museo del Risorgimento** at Via Borgonuovo 23 (Tues–Sun 9am–1pm & 2–6pm; free) charts the course of Italian Unification through a well-presented combination of paintings, proclamations, cuttings and photographs – though it helps to have some knowledge of the Italian Unification to appreciate it.

Along Via Fatebenefratelli from here, the heavily trafficked Piazza Cavour marks the corner of the city's oldest public park, the **Giardini Pubblici**, designed by Piermarini shortly after completing La Scala. Relandscaped in the nineteenth century to give it a more rustic look, its shady avenues and small lake are ideal for recuperating from Milan's twin doses of culture and carbon monoxide fumes. On the left side of the park, the basement of the Palazzo Dugnani houses Milan's **Museo del Cinema** (Tues–Fri 3–6.30pm; L5000/€2.58), comprising an unlabelled collection of cameras, film-cutting apparatus and other equipment from the early days of cinema. The curator will do his best to persuade you to buy a catalogue, but the free leaflets are perfectly adequate.

Across the road from the park in the Villa Reale, the **Civica Galleria d'Arte Moderna**, Via Palestro 16 (daily 9.30am–5.30pm; free), is one of Milan's most palatable galleries, housed in Napoleon's former in-town residence, which now doubles as the civic registry office. The main building holds nineteenth-century Italian art and sculpture – including striking political works by the painter Giuseppe Pellizza da Volpedo, canvases by the self-styled romantic *scapigliati* (wild-haired) movement of the late nineteenth century, impressive sculptures by Marino Marini, and a less arcane selection of paintings by Corot, Millet and various French Impressionists. Also worth a look are the works of the Futurists – Boccioni, Balla and Morandi. In the grounds, the **Padiglione d'Arte Contemporanea** (Tues–Sun 9.30am–5.30pm; *www.pac-milano.org*; L10,000/ €5.17) is a venue for temporary and often prestigious exhibitions of national and international contemporary art. Overlooking the gardens, in a light airy annexe, the small **Collezione Vismara** has Picasso's *Battle of the Centaurs* – a spontaneously simple charcoal complete with finger smudges – and minor but appealing works by Matisse, Dufy and their Italian contemporaries.

Just to the northeast of the park is **Spazio Oberdan**, Viale Vittorio Veneto 2 (Tues & Thurs 10am–10pm, Wed & Fri–Sun 10am–7.30pm; ☎02.7740.6300, *www.provincia. milano.it*), one of the city's most important venues for cultural events and very good temporary exhibitions on art, photography and sculpture.

On the east side of the Giardini Pubblici, the **Civico Museo di Storia Naturale**, Corso Venezia 55 (Mon–Fri 9am–6pm, Sat & Sun 9.30am–6.30pm; free), completes the round of museums, with a fairly predictable natural history collection. It's reckoned to be Italy's best, but really the stuffed animals and dinosaur-bits are best reserved for one of Milan's rainy afternoons: even then, parts of it are closed, as it's currently undergoing what may prove to be a lengthy restoration.

The Castello Sforzesco

At the far end of Via Dante from Piazza del Duomo, **Castello Sforzesco** rises imperiously from the mayhem of Foro Buonaparte, a congested and distinctly un-forum-like road and bus terminus laid out by Napoleon in self-tribute. He had a vision of a grand new centre for the Italian capital, laid out along Roman lines, but he only got as far as constructing an arena, a triumphal arch and these two semicircular roads before he lost Milan to the Austrians a few years later. The arena and triumphal arch still stand behind the castle in the **Parco Sempione**, a notorious hangout for junkies and prostitutes.

The red-brick castle, the result of numerous rebuildings, is, with its crenellated towers and fortified walls, one of Milan's most striking landmarks. Begun by the Viscontis, it was destroyed by mobs rebelling against their regime in 1447, and rebuilt by their successors, the Sforzas. Under Lodovico Sforza the court became one of the most powerful, luxurious and cultured of the Renaissance, renowned for its ostentatious wealth and court artists like Leonardo and Bramante. Lodovico's days of glory came to an end when Milan was invaded by the French in 1499, and from then until the end of the nineteenth century the castle was used as a barracks by successive occupying armies. Just over a century ago it was converted into a series of museums.

The castello's buildings are grouped around three courtyards, one of which, the Corte Ducale, formed the centre of the residential quarters, which now contain the **Museo d'Arte Antica** and the **Pinacoteca del Castello** (daily 9am–5.40pm; free). The Museo d'Arte Antica holds fragments of sculpture from Milan's demolished churches and palaces, a run-of-the-mill collection saved by the inclusion of Michelangelo's *Rondanini Pietà*, which the artist worked on for the last nine years of his life. It's an unfinished but oddly powerful work, with much of the marble unpolished and a third arm (indicating a change of position for Christ's body) hanging limply from a block of stone to his right.

The first room of the **Pinacoteca**, upstairs, contains a cycle of monochrome frescoes illustrating the Griselda story from Boccaccio's *Decameron* – a catalogue of indignities inflicted by a marquis on his wife in order to test her fidelity. It was intended as a celebration of the patience and devotion of one Bianca Pellegrini, and if you decide to push on into the first room of the main picture gallery, you'll see what she looked like: Bianca was used as a model for the Madonna in a polyptych by Benedetto Bembo. In the same room are works by Bellini, Crivelli and Lippi, and one of Mantegna's last works, a dreamy evocation of the *Madonna in Glory among Angels and SS*. There are also lots of paintings by Vincenzo Foppa, the leading artist on the Milanese scene before Leonardo da Vinci, in the next room; look out too for the polyptych by De' Tatti, in which the castle makes an appearance as a fanciful setting for the Crucifixion, and for Arcimboldi's bizarre *Primavera* – a portrait of a woman composed entirely of flowers, heralded as a sixteenth-century precursor of Surrealism.

The castle's other museums are housed in the Sforza fortress, the **Rocchetta**, to the left of the Corte Ducale (same times). Of these, the **museum of applied arts** is of limited interest, containing wrought-iron work, ceramics, ivory and musical instruments. The small, well-displayed **Egyptian collection** in the dungeons is rather better, with impressive displays of mummies and sarcophagi and papyrus fragments from *The Book of the Dead*. There's also a small and deftly lit **prehistoric collection**, which has as its centrepiece an assortment of finds from the Iron Age burial grounds of the Golasecca civilization, south of Lago Maggiore.

Santa Maria delle Grazie and around

Apart from Parco Sempione, good for a wander or lakeside picnic, the area around the Castello Sforzesco has little to detain you, and there are more interesting pickings to the south, beyond the busy streets of the financial district, skirted by Corso Magenta. The **Museo Archeologico**, in the ex-Monastero Maggiore at Corso Magenta 15

(Tues–Sun 9.30am–5.30pm; free), is well worth a visit. The displays of glass phials, kitchen utensils and jewellery from Roman Milan are compelling, and though there's a scarcity of larger objects, there is a colossal head of Jove, found near the castle, a torso of Hercules and a smattering of mosaic pavements unearthed around the city.

But what really brings visitors into this part of town is the church of **Santa Maria delle Grazie** – famous for its mural of the *Last Supper* by Leonardo da Vinci. First built as a Gothic church by the fifteenth-century architect Solari, Santa Maria delle Grazie was partially rebuilt under a dissatisfied Lodovico Sforza by the more up-to-date Bramante, who tore down Solari's chancel and replaced it with a massive dome supported by an airy Renaissance cube. Lodovico also intended to replace the nave and facade, but was unable to do so before Milan fell to the French, leaving an odd combination of styles – Solari's Gothic vaults, decorated in powdery blues, reds and ochre, illuminated by the light that floods through the windows of Bramante's dome. A side door leads into Bramante's cool and tranquil cloisters, outside of which there's a good view of the sixteen-sided drum the architect placed around his dome.

Leonardo's *Last Supper* – signposted **Cenacolo Vinciano** – is one of the world's great paintings and most resonant images. However, art of this magnitude doesn't come easy: visits must be booked by telephone preferably 3 or 4 days in advance (reservations Mon–Fri 9am–7pm ☎02.8942.1146; viewing Tues–Sat 9am–6.30pm, Sun 9am–7.30pm; L12,000/€6.20, plus L2000/€1.03 obligatory booking fee). Henry James likened the painting to an "illustrious invalid" that people visited with "leave-taking sighs and almost death-bed or tip-toe precautions"; certainly it's hard, when you visit the painting, decayed and faded on the refectory wall, not to feel that it's the last time you'll see it. Restoration is virtually perpetual due to its fragile nature, but the main part of the fresco is free from scaffolding. That the work survived at all is something of a miracle. Leonardo's decision to use oil paint rather than the more usual faster-drying – and longer-lasting – fresco technique with watercolours led to the painting disintegrating within five years of its completion. A couple of centuries later Napoleonic troops billetted here used the wall for target practice. And in 1943 a bomb destroyed the building, amazingly leaving only the *Last Supper*'s wall standing. Well-meaning restoration over the centuries has also meant that little of Leonardo's original colouring has survived, but despite this the painting still retains its power. Leonardo spent two years on it, searching the streets of Milan for models. When the monks complained that the face of Judas was still unfinished, Leonardo replied that he had been searching for over a year among the city's criminals for a sufficiently evil face, and that if he didn't find one he would use the face of the prior. Whether or not Judas's face is modelled on the prior's is unrecorded, but Leonardo's Judas does seem, as Vasari wrote, "the very embodiment of treachery and inhumanity".

A couple of blocks south, at Via S. Vittore 21, the **Museo Nazionale della Scienza e della Tecnica** (Tues–Fri 9.30am–4.50pm, Sat & Sun 9.30am–6.20pm; L12,000/€6.20) is dedicated to Leonardo and is inspired by his inventions, with reconstructions of some of his wackier contraptions, including the famous flying machine. Less compelling are the general sections on physics, astronomy, telecommunications and musical instruments. There are also collections of steam trains, aeroplanes and even an ocean liner.

The nearby church of **Sant'Ambrogio** (Mon–Sat 7am–noon & 3–7pm, Sun 7am–1pm & 3.30–8pm) was founded in the fourth century by Milan's patron saint. St Ambrose, as he's known in English, is even today an important name in the city: the Milanese refer to themselves as Ambrosiani, have named a chain of banks after him, and celebrate his feast day, December 7, with the opening of the Scala season and a big street market around the church. Ambrose's remains still lie in the church's crypt, but there's nothing left of the original church in which his most famous convert, St Augustine, first heard him preach.

The present church, the blueprint for many of Lombardy's Romanesque basilicas, is, however, one of the city's loveliest, reached through a colonnaded quadrangle with column capitals carved with rearing horses, contorted dragons and an assortment of bizarre predators. Inside, to the left of the nave, a freestanding Byzantine pillar is topped with a "magic" bronze serpent, flicked into a loop and symbolizing Aaron's rod – an ancient tradition held that on the Day of Judgement it would crawl back to the Valley of Jesophat. Look, too, at the pulpit, a superb piece of Romanesque carving decorated with reliefs of wild animals and the occasional human, most of whom are intent upon devouring one another. There are older relics further down the nave, notably the ciborium, reliefed with the figures of saints Gervasius and Protasius – martyred Roman soldiers whose clothed bodies flank that of St Ambrose in the crypt. A nineteenth-century autopsy revealed that they had been killed by having their throats cut. Similar investigations into St Ambrose's remains restored the reputation of the anonymous fifth-century artist responsible for the mosaic portrait of the saint in the Cappella di San Vittorio in Ciel d'Oro (to the right of the sacristry). Until then it was assumed that Ambrose owed his crooked face to a slip of the artist's hand, but the examination of his skull revealed an abnormally deep-set tooth, suggesting that his face would indeed have been slightly deformed.

Outside (entrance to the left of the choir) is Bramante's unfinished **Cortile della Canonica**. The side that Bramante did complete, a novel concoction incorporating knobbly "tree trunk" columns and a triumphal arch, was shattered by a bomb in the last war and reconstructed from the fragments. The second side was added only in 1955 and leads to a modest museum (Mon & Wed–Fri 10am–noon & 3–5pm, Sat & Sun 3–5pm; L3000/€1.55), whose only memorable exhibit is St Ambrose's bed.

South of the centre: Navigli and Ticinese

Flanking the city's two canals, just south of the Cerchia Viali, the streets of the **Navigli** quarter feel a long way from the city centre, their peeling houses and waterside views much sought after by the city's would-be bohemians. A thriving inland port from the fifteenth century until the 1950s, the Naviglio Pavese – which links Milan with Pavia – and the Naviglio Grande – which runs to the west – are part of a network of rivers and canals covering the whole of Italy's northern plain, making ports or even naval bases of landlocked cities. They were also much used by travellers: the ruling families of the North used them to visit one another, Prospero and Miranda escaped along the Navigli in *The Tempest*, and they were still being used by Grand Tourists in the eighteenth century; Goethe, for example, describes the discomfort and hazards of journeying by canal. These days there's not much to do other than browse in its artists' studios and antique shops, but it's a peaceful area, good for idle strolling, and at night its bars and clubs are among the city's best.

Back towards the centre, the **Ticinese** is another arty district, though as yet less a prey to regeneration than Navigli. On the southern edge of the quarter, at the bottom of Corso di Porta Ticinese, the nineteenth-century **Arco di Porta Ticinese** is an Ionic gateway on a noisy traffic island built to celebrate Napoleon's victory at Marengo – and, after his demise, dedicated to peace. As you walk north up the Corso, the only obvious signs of trendification are secondhand clothes shops, a few bars and the occasional club, and the musty decadence makes it one of Milan's more intriguing areas.

Ticinese also boasts two important churches. The first, **Sant'Eustorgio**, at the bottom end of the Corso, was built in the fourth century to house the bones of the Magi, said to have been brought here by St Ambrose. It was rebuilt in the eleventh century, but in the twelfth century was virtually destroyed by Barbarossa, who seized the Magi's bones and deposited them in Cologne Cathedral. Some of the bones were returned in 1903 and are kept in a Roman sarcophagus in the right transept. The main reason for visiting the church, however, is to see the **Portinari Chapel** commissioned from the

Florentine architect Michelozzi in the 1460s by one Portinari, an agent of the Medici bank, to house the remains of St Peter the Martyr. Peter, one of Catholicism's less attractive saints, was banned from the Church for allegedly entertaining women in his cell, then cleared of the charge and given a job as an Inquisitor. His death was particularly nasty – he was axed in the head by a member of the sect he was persecuting – but the martyrdom led to almost immediate canonization and the dubious honour of being deemed Patron of Inquisitors. The chapel, with its simple geometric design, has been credited with being Milan's first real Renaissance building, although it was Bramante who really developed the style. Inside, you are treated to scenes from the life of St Peter in frescoes by Foppa and reliefs carved on the sides of his elaborate tomb.

Further up the Corso, the fourteenth-century **Porta Ticinese** and sixteen Corinthian columns – **the Colonne di San Lorenzo**, scavenged from a Roman ruin – stand outside the church of **San Lorenzo**. It's an evocative spot – an odd contrast to the backdrop of grubby bars and rattling trams – and *the* place to hang out at night before hitting the Navigli and Ticinese clubs and bars. San Lorenzo, apparently considered by Leonardo da Vinci to be the most beautiful church in Milan, was founded in the fourth century, when it was the largest centrally planned church in the western Roman Empire. The current structure is a sixteenth-century renovation of an eleventh-century rebuilding, a shaky edifice under threat from the vibrating tramlines outside. Inside, the most interesting feature is the **Cappella di San Aquilino** (daily 9am–6pm; L2000/€1.03), much of which has survived from the fourth century. There are fragments of fourth-century mosaics on the walls, including one in the left apse where the tiles have crumbled away, revealing the artist's original sketches. Behind the altar, steps lead down to what is left of the original foundations, a jigsaw of fragments of Roman architecture looted from an arena.

Eating

Food in workaholic Milan, at lunchtime at least, is more of a necessity than a pleasure, with the city centre dominated by *paninoteche* and fast-food outlets. Don't despair, however: there are plenty of good-value – and some extremely good – restaurants here, and you can eat as well and as reasonably as in any other part of Italy.

Restaurants

Though many restaurants in the **centre** of Milan are pricey, expense-account places, there are a few survivors from a time when the city wasn't dominated by the fashion crowd and business execs. Just outside the immediate centre, the **Ticinese** and **Navigli** areas are full of restaurants and cafés; we've also included a number of options around **Stazione Centrale and Piazzale Loreto**, since this is the part of town you're most likely to be staying in, as well as a handful of places that are simply worth going a little bit out of your way for.

CITY CENTRE

L'Amour, V. Solferino 25. Trendy hangout, with a lively atmosphere and serving good food. Not cheap but very Milanese. MM Moscova. Closed Mon.

Le Briciole, Via Camperio 17. Busy, convivial place off Piazza Castello that offers reasonable pizzas, straight meals, and a great antipasto table. MM Cairoli. Closed Mon and Sat lunch.

La Bruschetta, Piazza Beccaria 12. Two minutes from Piazza Duomo and always packed, so expect a long wait. Good location and decent pizzas at moderate prices, and a free bruschetta when you eventually get a table. MM San Babila or Duomo. Closed Sun.

Al Cantinone, Via Agnello 19. Famous old trattoria and bar, with home-made pasta, grilled meat dishes and choice wine. Not exactly leisurely dining, but good, moderately priced food – and you couldn't get more central. MM San Babila or Duomo. Closed Sun.

Fondaco dei Mori, Via Solferino 33. North-African cuisine with a self-service buffet; eat as much as you can for a set price. Set in the courtyard of a palazzo, the restaurant is part of an Islamic cultural institute, so you'll need to fill in a membership form (free). MM Moscova.

Grand' Italia, Via Palermo 5. Centrally placed, bustling restaurant serving good pizza and *focaccie* cooked in a wood-burning oven, and delicious daily specials. MM Moscova. Closed Mon.

Latteria Unione, Via Unione 6, near the church of San Satiro off Via Torino. Set in the front part of an *alimentari* shop, serving excellent Italian vegetarian food. MM Missori. Open lunchtimes only.

Nabucco, Via Fiori Chiari 10. Chic little restaurant, simply furnished, whose menu encompasses a wide range of salads, imaginative fish dishes, and home-made pastries and puddings. Moderately priced. MM Lanza. Closed Tues.

Spaghetteria Enoteca, Via Solferino 3. Located under a clothes shop, and perhaps the cheapest place to sit down and fill up in the Brera area. MM Moscova. Closed Mon and Tues.

Ungherese, Largo La Foppa 5. Home-style Hungarian food in small, unpretentious surroundings, though not cheap. MM Moscova. Closed Wed.

STAZIONE CENTRALE, PIAZZALE LORETO AND AROUND

I Delfini, Via Lecco 7. Not worth going out of your way for, but a good choice in the Stazione Centrale area, with reasonable pizzas and a good antipasto bar. MM Pta. Venezia. Closed Sun.

La Giara, Viale Monza 10. Supremely affordable Pugliese restaurant with a very limited menu – good *antipasti*, grilled meats, home-made Pugliese bread and hearty wine. You eat at wooden tables and benches, which you'll have to share when things get busy. MM Loreto. Closed Wed.

Joia, Via P. Castaldi 18 (☎02.2952.2124). Upmarket vegetarian food worth tracking down. MM Pta. Venezia. Closed Sun.

I Malavoglia, Via Lecco 4 (☎02.2953.1387). Warm, southern hospitality and excellent Sicilian food at moderate prices. Open evenings only and Sunday lunch. MM Pta. Venezia. Closed Mon & Aug.

Pasta e Fagioli, Via Venini 54. The speciality here, as the name suggests, is pasta and beans, but it's also worth trying their *scamorza* – mozzarella grilled on the fire. MM Caiazzo. Closed Tues.

TICINESE, NAVIGLI AND AROUND

Da Giulio, Corso San Gottardo 38. Lively local haunt, just off the Naviglio Grande, that's both a takeaway joint and an ordinary sit-down restaurant. Has a huge array of different fish and seafood dishes, pizzas, roast chicken, polenta, etc. Good for lunch. MM Genova. Closed Mon.

Mergellina, Via Molino delle Armi 48. Busy place around the corner from Porta Ticinese that serves decent pizza at low prices. MM Missori. Closed Tues.

Osteria Briosca, Via Ascanio Sforza 13. Reasonably priced restaurant with a pleasant, woody atmosphere and occasional live music. MM Genova. Closed Sun.

Ponte Rosso, Ripa di Porta Ticinese 23. Charming restaurant – with hospitable owners – set right on the Naviglio Grande. The food is great, and prices are very reasonable. MM Genova. Closed Sun.

Premiata, Alzaia Naviglio Grande 2. Extremely loud and busy pizzeria that has a queue running out of the door, despite cramming in as many tables as possible. There's a second branch a little further north at Via de Amicis 24, which is just as popular. Both MM Genova.

FURTHER AFIELD...

Giulio pane e ojo, V. Muratori 10 (☎02.545.6189; booking essential). Simple trattoria with excellent food at reasonable prices. MM Porta Romana. Closed Sat lunch and Sun.

Rino Vecchia Napoli, Via Chevez 4. Off the beaten track, but worth the effort of getting there: *Rino* won the European Pizza Championship a few years ago. Good prices and a massive choice. Tram #33 or bus #56. Closed Sun & Mon lunch.

Rondine, Via Spartaco 13. Just out of the city centre, but worth a trip for its traditional dishes, along with some more creative ones, in simple, homely surroundings. Try to get there early. Bus #84. MM Porta Romana. Closed Wed.

Stalingrado, Via Biondi 4. Long-standing politically oriented eatery that caters to a young clientele and is also open as a pub. Reasonable prices and a small outside eating area for the summer. Bus #61 or #78. Closed Sun.

Snacks and fast food

Amico, Piazza Duomo 5; Piazza Cinque Giornate; Corso Beunos Aires at Piazza Lima. Chain of self-service restaurants that has several branches around the city centre.

Brek, Piazza Cavour; Piazzetta Giordano 1; Via Lepetit 20. Chain of good-value self-service restaurants with an excellent choice of salads and freshly cooked main courses.

Burghy, Piazza Duomo 17; Via Cordusio; Piazza Argentina. Chain of self-service burger joints that's more popular with the Milanese than *McDonald's*.

Ciao, Duomo Centre, Piazza Duomo; Via Dante, on the corner with Via Meravigli; Corso Europa 12; Corso Buenos Aires 7; Via Fabio Filzi 8. Citywide chain with good, reasonably priced food.

Crota Piemunteisa, Piazza Beccaria 10. Centrally placed bar and *paninoteca* with a vast array of chunky sandwiches, and wooden tables to eat and drink at. MM Duomo.

Luini, Via S. Radegonda 16, just east of the duomo. You almost have to fight your way through the crowds at lunchtime to get hold of one of their delicious *panzerotti* (deep fried mini calzone). MM Duomo. Closed Aug.

Panino Giusto, Corso Garibaldi 125, Piazza Beccaria. Popular places that serve a huge selection of sandwiches. A good lunch stop between sights. MM Duomo or MM Porta Romana.

Spontini, Via Spontini 2. One kind of pizza only: tomato, cheese and anchovies on a thick, soft base served in various sized portions; at lunchtime there is lasagna too. Great value. MM Lima or Loreto.

Food markets and supermarkets

For real low-budget eating, there are **street markets** every day except Sunday scattered through the city, selling all the cheese, salami and fruit you need for a picnic lunch. A complete list is given daily in the *Corriere della Sera* under the heading "Mercati". The most central **supermarkets** are Standa at Via Torino 37 and in Piazza Castello, Esselunga at Viale Piave 38, near Porta Venezia, and the tightly packed Centro Commerciale in the Stazione Centrale (daily 5.30am–midnight).

Nightlife: bars, clubs, live music

Milan has perhaps Italy's best **nightlife**. This centres on two main areas: the streets around the Brera gallery, and the canal-side Navigli and the adjacent Ticinese quarter, south of the city, where there are any number of lively bars, restaurants and nightclubs, some hosting regular live bands.

The city's **clubs** are at their hippest midweek, particularly on Thursdays – at weekends out-of-towners flood in and any self-respecting Milanese trendy either stays at home or hits a bar. Many places have obscure door policies, often dependent on the whim of the bouncer; assuming you get in, you can expect to pay L20,000–30,000/ €10.33–15.49 entry, which usually includes your first drink. As for **live music**, Milan scores high on jazz, and the rock scene is relatively good by Italian standards: there are regular gigs by local bands, and the city is a stop on the circuit for big-name touring bands.

If you need an antedote to the expensive designer side of Milan's nightlife, check out the very healthy alternative scene, which revolves around the city's many **Centri Sociali**. Born out of the student protests of the late Sixties, these centres are essentially squatted buildings, where committees organize cheap, sometimes free, entertainment, such as concerts and film showings. They also contain bars and – often good – vegetarian restaurants, and are an established part of the social scene, accepted by neighbours and even sometimes receiving local funding. Worth checking out are *Gargliano*, in Via Gargliano, ten minutes' walk north of Garibaldi Station, and *Conchetta*, on Via Conchetta, five minutes' walk south of Porta Ticinese and the flagship, *Leoncavallo*, which you can contact on ☎02.670.5185 or *csleo@tiscalinet.it*.

For details of **what's on listings** see p.161.

Cafés, bars and pubs

Arco della Pace, Piazzi Sempione 2a. Located in the arch itself, this café is a relaxed place for a drink in the summer when you can spill out onto the pavement and listen to the concerts in the nearby park. Open Wed–Fri.

Bar Magenta, Via Carducci 13. Twenties decor, enduringly popular to the point of bursting at weekends. Good for sandwich lunches as well as late-night drinks. Closed Mon.

Camparino, Piazza Duomo 21. Probably Milan's oldest bar, and the inventor of Campari. Prices are high even by Milanese standards. Closed Wed.

Alla Fontanella, Alzaia Naviglio Pavese 4, just around the corner from the Naviglio Grande. Bar renowned for its unusual-shaped beer-glasses; there are bibs available for those concerned about spillages. Usually packed with an unpretentious crowd. Open until 3am.

Luca's Bar, Colonne di San Lorenzo. Unassuming by day, this Ticinese bar kicks into action in the evening, when the Milanese youth congregate on the pavement outside. Closed Sun.

Morigi, Via Morigi. Authentic old wine bar in a lively part of town. Closed Sun.

Osteria del Pallone, Via Gorizia 30, corner Alzaio Naviglio Grande. Old-fashioned and sometimes raucous osteria right on the canal. Closed Mon.

Racana Pub, Via Sannio 18. Irish-style pub with real ale and Guinness on draught – and occasional Celtic music. Out of the centre, though – bus #90 or #91. Closed Mon.

Venues and clubs

Capolinea, Via Lodovico Il Moro 119 (☎02.8912.2024). Founded in 1969, this place is a jazz milestone where all the best performers, Italian and foreign, have played. Named for the terminus (*capolinea*) of tram #19.

De Sade, corner of Via Valtellina and Via Piazza (☎02.688.8898). Posey club, popular hangout for models.

Hollywood, Corso Como 15 (☎02.659.8996). Long-established as the place to go if you want to be surrounded by beautiful people.

Magazzini Generali, Via Pietrasanta 14 (☎02.5521.1313). Hip venue set in an ex-warehouse, with a mixture of club nights and live music.

Plastic, Viale Umbria 120 (☎02.743.674). Club with live and recorded music that hosts a Gothic and punky crowd.

Prego, Via Besenzanica 3 (☎02.4407.5653). A disco that sometimes has gigs. Each night of the week tends to host a different type of music.

Propaganda, Via Castelbarco 11–13 (☎02.5831.0682). Medium-sized venue south of the city centre, close to the Navigli canals. Rock bands in the winter, themed disco nights in the summer.

Rolling Stone, Corso XXII Marzo 32 (☎02.733.172). Enormous hall that doubles as a club and concert venue, sometimes used for big-name rock bands; the music is very loud.

Sabor, Via Molino delle Armi 18–24 (☎02.5831.3584). Popular, sweaty Latin-American venue in the Ticinese district.

Scimmie, Via Ascanio Sforza 49 (☎02.8940.2874). Ticinese club that is one of Milan's most popular venues, with a different band every night and jazz-fusion predominating. Small, noisy and smoky, but with a restaurant – and a barge on the canal in summer.

Zelig, Viale Monza 140 (☎02.255.1774). A slightly pretentious and overpriced venue for arty happenings, cabaret, theatre, and the like.

Opera, theatre and cinema

Many of Milan's tourists are in the city for just one reason – **La Scala**, Via dei Filodrammatici 2 (box office open daily noon–6pm, plus 15min after the start of each performance for ticket collection only; ☎02.7200.3744, fax 02.887.9297, *www.lascala .milano.com*), one of the world's most prestigious opera houses. The opera season runs from December through to July, and there's usually also a season of classical concerts between September and November. Not surprisingly, seats for the opera sell out months in advance, but you can book tickets via their Web site if you get in early enough. The average price of a ticket is about L75,000/€38.74. There is also often a reasonable chance of picking up a cheaper seat in the gods on the day, or one of around 200 standing places; get there an hour or so before the performance starts.

Of Milan's **theatres**, the Teatro Piccolo, Via Rovello 2 (☎02.7233.3222, *www. piccoloteatro.org*), is a classical theatre, with a traditional repertoire, and is reckoned to be one of Italy's best. Teatro dell'Elfo, Via Ciro Menotti 11 (☎02.716.791), reachable on bus #60, puts on more original plays. Count on paying around L30,000/€15.49 for a seat at either of these places.

As for **cinema**, Sound and Motion Pictures (*www.anteospaziocinema.com*; L9000/ €4.65) show a selection of original language films at the following cinemas: the Arcobaleno, Viale Tunisia 11 (☎02.2940.6054; MM Porta Venezia), the Anteo, Via Milazzo 9 (☎02.659.7732), and the Mexico, Via Savona 57 (☎02.4895.1802). The Fondazione Cineteca Italiana is based at the Spazio Oberdan (see p.171), and has an excellent programme of international arthouse films. In the summer months outdoor cinema is organized at several venues, including the Parco di Villa Ghirlanda, Cinisello Balsamo Via Frova 10 (☎02.617.3005; *www.comune.cinisello-balsamo.mi.it*); see newspaper for listings.

Listings

Airlines Aer Lingus, Galleria Passarella 2 (☎02.7600.0080); Alitalia, Via Albricci 5 (☎02.2499.2700); Air Canada, Viale Regina Giovanna 8 (☎02.2940.9189); American Airlines, Via Vittor Pisani 19 (☎02.6791.4400); British Airways, Corso Italia 8 (☎147.812.266); Qantas, Piazza Velasca 4 (☎02.864.287).

Airport enquiries ☎02.7485.2200 (daily 7am–11pm) for both Linate and Malpensa airports.

American Express Via Brera 3 (Mon–Fri 9am–5pm; ☎02.876.674).

Books The American Bookstore, on Largo Cairoli, is the best source of English-language books in the city centre.

British Council Via Manzoni 38 (library open Tues–Fri 10am–6pm, Sat 2–5pm; general enquiries ☎02.772.221).

Bus enquiries ☎02.4803.2403 (Mon–Sat 8am–8pm).

Car rental Avis, Europcar, Hertz and Maggiore all have desks at Stazione Centrale, and at both airports.

Car parks Central car parks include Autosilo Diaz, Piazza Diaz 6, just south of Piazza Duomo; Garage Traversi, on Via Bagutta, close to Piazza San Babila; and Garage Venezia, Corso Venezia 11, near Piazza Oberdan.

Consulates Australia, Via Borgogna 2 (☎02.777.041); Canada, Via V. Pisani 19 (☎02.67.581); UK, Via San Paolo 7 (☎02.723.001); USA, Via Bigli 11 (☎02.771.9031).

Doctors English-speaking doctors: Dr A. Waygood, Via Visconti Venosta 5 (☎02.5501.1538); Dr J. Weston, Via San Paolo 15 (☎02.7200.4080); Dr G. Gottardi, Via Boscovich 31 (☎02.6707.5732).

Exchange Out of normal banking hours you can change money and travellers' cheques at the Stazione Centrale office (daily 7am–11pm), where there's also a 24-hour automatic currency-exchange machine, or at the Money Shop on Piazza Duomo 17 (daily 9am–8pm). Both airports have exchange facilities.

Football Milan's two teams are Inter Milan and AC Milan. They play on alternate Sundays at the G. Meazza stadium (San Siro), Via Piccolomini 5 (☎02.4870.0457); MM Lotto, then a longish walk. There are hourly guided tours around the stadium (Mon–Sat 11am–8pm from Gate 4, Piazalle dello Sport; Sun 9am–noon from Gate 21/22, Piazzale Axum; L12,000/€6.20). You can buy match tickets here for AC Milan games, from branches of Cariplo banks (☎02.88.661) and from Milan Point, on Via Verri 8 (☎02.796.481); and for Inter games from Inter F.C. Admin office, Piazza Duse 1 (☎02.77.151) and branches of Banca Popolare Milano (☎02.77.011).

Gay Milan Milan is something of a focus for gays, with northern Italy's only gay bookshop, the Babel Bookshop, Via San Nicolas 10 (☎02.669.2986), making for a good meeting-place for gay men. Run by a Milan-based gay publishing house, Babilonia, it issues a monthly magazine of the same name that is available at most newsagents. *After Line Disco Pub*, Via Sammartini 25, is a popular bar not far from the Stazione Centrale; *Querelle*, Via de Castillia 20, is a gay bar with snacks and music; *Nuova Idea*, Via de Castiesa 30, is the biggest gay disco in Italy; and *Transfer Club*, at Via Breda 158, is also a very popular nightclub.

Hospital There is a 24-hour casualty service at the Ospedale Maggiore Policlinico, Via Francesco Sforza 35 (☎02.551.0809), a short walk from Piazza Duomo.

Internet access *Terzomillennio*, Via Lazzaretto (Mon–Fri 9am–9pm, Sat 9am–6pm; ☎02.205.2121); *Internet Enjoy*, Via Medici 6 (Mon–Sat 10am–8pm; ☎02.7209.4544). Both L10,000/ €5.17 per hour.

Laundries There's a coin-operated laundry in the Brera district, Via Anfiteatro 9, and another, the Lavanderia Automatica, on Via Lombardini 4. Near the Stazione Centrale, try the Lavanderia at Via Tadino 6.

Pharmacy The Stazione Centrale (☎02.669.0935), which has English-speaking assistants, and Carlo Erba, on Piazza Duomo (☎02.8646.4832); both have 24-hour services. Bracco, Via Boccaccio 26 (☎02.469.5281), is sometimes open all night. Rotas are published in *Corriere della Sera*, and are usually posted on *farmacia* doors.

Police Phone ☎113. Head office at Via Fatebenefratelli 11 (☎02.62.261), near the Brera.

Post office Via Cordusio 4, off Piazza Cordusio – not the building marked "Poste", but around the corner (Mon–Fri 8.30am–1.50pm, Sat 8.30am–noon).

Shopping The "Quadrilatero d'Oro" – Via Monte Napoleone and around – is the place for the big fashion designers (and their sky-high prices), while on the peripheries are youth-oriented shops like Fiorucci on Piazza San Babila; Corso Buenos Aires is home to most of the more middle-range clothes stores and chains. You can get designer cast-offs at the (early) Saturday morning market on Viale Papiniano, near the Porta Genova train station. If you're on a budget, and can't make the Papiniano market, check out the *blochisti*, or warehouses selling last season's lines at half-price: try Gastone, Via Vanzetti 20, Emporio, Via Prina 11, or Il Salvagente, on Via Bronzetti.

Swimming pools Cozzi, Viale Tunisia 35 (☎02.659.9703), is perhaps the most convenient place if you're dying for a swim, close to Stazione Centrale. There's also the Lido di Milano, Piazzale Lotto 15 (☎02.366.100), which has both indoor and open-air pools.

Telephones International calls can be made either from Telecom Italia offices in Galleria V. Emanuele II (8am–9.30pm) or at the Stazione Centrale (8am–8pm).

Train enquiries Ferrovie dello Stato (daily 7am–9pm; ☎147.888.088); Ferrovie Nord (daily 9am–6pm; ☎02.20.222).

Travel agents CTS, Via Sant'Antonio 2 (☎02.5830.4751), and CIT in the Galleria Vittorio Emanuele II (☎02.863.701), are the best source of train tickets, discounted flights, etc.

Women By Italian standards, Milan is not a difficult city for women. The Libreria delle Donne at Via Dogana 2, close to the duomo, sells feminist literature and has information on women's groups, events and publications. *Cicip e Ciciap*, Via Gorani 9, is a women-only café/bar/restaurant with occasional exhibitions and readings. There's also a women-only disco at *Sottomarino Giallo*, Via Donatello 2.

South of Milan: Pavia and Vigévano

Furthest west of the string of historic towns that spread across the Lombardy plain, **Pavia** and **Vigévano** are close enough to Milan to be seen on a day-trip, but still retain clear identities of their own. Pavia should not be missed if you're in Milan for any length of time, and indeed could serve as a feasible and perhaps more palatable base for seeing the larger city. Vigévano is more of a backwater, and as such hardly a place to stay, but its central Renaissance square and ramshackle castle could make a pleasant half-day out from either Pavia or Milan.

Pavia and around

Medieval **PAVIA** was known as the city of a hundred towers. And although only a handful remain – one of the best collapsed in 1989 – the medieval aspect is still strong, with numerous Romanesque and Gothic churches tucked away in a wanderable web of narrow streets and cobbled squares. The town is not, however, stranded in the past – its ancient university continues to thrive, ensuring an animated street life and reasonably lively night-time scene.

Pavia reached its zenith in the Dark Ages when it was capital of the Kingdom of the Lombards. After their downfall it remained a centre of power, and the succession of emperors who ruled northern Italy continued to come to the town to receive the Lombards' traditional iron crown. This all came to an end in the fourteenth century when Pavia was handed over to the Viscontis and became a satellite of Milan. The Viscontis, and later the Sforzas, did, however, found the university and provide the town with its prime tourist attraction – the nearby Certosa di Pavia.

Arrival, information and accommodation

Regular **trains** make the thirty-minute journey between Pavia and Milan, but connections from Pavia to the other cities of the Lombardy plain are infrequent and slow. **Bus** services for the area are slightly better and will drop you at the bus station round the corner from the train station, on the western edge of the town centre. Buses #3 and #6 connect the train station with the centre, or it's about a ten minute walk down Corso Cavour to Piazza della Vittoria. The **tourist office** is near Stazione Centrale – turn left as you leave the train station, then right after the bus station – at Via F. Filzi 2 (Mon–Sat 8.30am–12.30pm & 2–6pm; ☎0382.22.156).

Pavia's few **hotels** tend to get filled with the overspill from Milan's commercial fairs, and finding somewhere to stay can be more difficult than you might imagine, especially as there are very few cheap options. The most reasonable choices are the *Aurora*, Via Vittorio Emanuele 25 (☎0382.23.664; ③), or *Stazione*, Via Bernardino De Rossi 8 (☎0382.35477; ③), both near the station. There is also a **campsite**, the *Ticino*, Via Mascherpa 10 (☎0382.527.094; April–Nov) – take bus #4 from the train station.

The Town

It's Pavia as a whole that appeals, rather than any specific sight. Just wandering around town is the nicest way to spend time here: pick any side street and you're almost bound to stumble on something of interest – a lofty medieval tower, a pretty Romanesque or Gothic church, or just a silent, sleepy piazza. Getting lost is difficult, as long as you bear in mind that the centre is quartered by the two main streets: Corso Cavour, which becomes Corso Mazzini, and Corso Strada Nuova.

One piazza that is neither sleepy nor silent is the central **Piazza della Vittoria**, a large cobbled rectangle surrounded by tatty buildings, housing bars, *gelaterie* and restaurants. At the eastern end steps lead down to an **underground market**, while at the square's southern end the **Broletto**, medieval Pavia's town hall, abuts the rear of the rambling and unwieldy **Duomo** – an early Renaissance sprawl of protruding curves and jutting angles that was only finally completed in the 1930s. The west front of the duomo, facing **Piazza del Duomo**, has been tidied up since the collapse of the adjacent Torre Civica in March 1989, which killed four people.

The best of the town's churches is the Romanesque **San Michele**, a five-minute walk away on Via Cavallotti. The friezes and capitals on its broad sandstone facade are carved into a menagerie of snake-tailed fish, griffins, dragons and other beasts, some locked in a struggle with humans, representing the fight between good and evil. It's also worth looking in on the church of **San Pietro in Ciel d'Oro**, on the other side of the centre at the top of Strada Nuova, dating from 1132 and containing a superb fourteenth-century altarpiece. Nearby, the **Castello Visconteo** (Tues–Sat 9am–1.30pm, Sun 9am–12.30pm; L5000/€2.58) was initiated by Galeazzo II Visconti in 1360, and added to by the Sforzas. The austere exterior originally housed luxurious apartments, the majority of which were in the wing of the quadrangle destroyed by the French in 1527. But the castle was used as a barracks until 1921, and although it's been restored the rooms that remain are hardly stunning. The **Museo Civico** inside includes an art gallery with a handful of Venetian paintings, an archeology collection with Roman jewellery, pottery and glassware, and a museum of sculpture displaying architectural fragments, mosaics and sculptures rescued from the town's demolished churches – most impressive of which are the reconstructed eleventh- and twelfth-century portals.

Eating and drinking

For a quick **lunch**, the *Punto Bar*, Strada Nuova 9, is a good *paninoteca*, with at least thirty varieties of sandwich and plenty of space to sit down. For a more substantial feed in more subdued surroundings, try the *Bar del Senatore*, on Via del Senatore, off Corso Cavour. Of regular **restaurants**, the *Piedigrotta*, near the church at the far end of Via Teodolinda (closed Wed), does good, reasonably priced pizza and pasta, as does the *Marechiaro*, right on Piazza della Vittoria (closed Mon). If you're feeling flush, try the *Vecchia Pavia*, by the duomo at Via Cardinale Riboldi 2 (closed Wed), an elegant place with adventurous local cooking – though at a price.

The Certosa di Pavia

Ten kilometres from Pavia, the **Certosa di Pavia** (summer Tues–Sun 9–11.30am & 2.30–6pm; winter closes as early as 4.30pm; free) is one of the most extravagant monasteries in Europe, commissioned by Gian Galeazzo Visconti in 1396 as the family mausoleum. Visconti intended the church here to resemble Milan's late-Gothic cathedral. It took a century to build, and by the time it was finished tastes had changed – and the Viscontis had been replaced by the Sforzas. But the architect appointed to finish the building, Amadeo, did so in style, festooning the facade with a fantasia of inlaid marble, twisted columns and friezes that say more about the wealth of the families that financed the complex than the contemplative Carthusian order it was built for. The Certosa is actually reachable from both Milan and Pavia, either by bus or by train. Buses are most frequent, hourly from Piazza Castello in Milan or from Pavia's bus station, dropping you a fifteen-minute walk from the Certosa. If you arrive by train, turn left out of the station and walk around the Certosa walls until you reach the entrance – also a fifteen-minute walk.

The monastery lies at the end of a tree-lined avenue, part of a former Visconti hunting range that stretched all the way from Pavia's castello. You can see the **church** unaccompanied, a Gothic building on the inside though no less splendid than the facade, its paintings, statues and vaults combining to create an almost ballroom glamour; look out for the tombs of Lodovico Il Moro and Gian Galeazzo Visconti, which are masterpieces of the early Renaissance. But to visit the rest of the monastery you need to join a **guided tour** of just under an hour, led by one of the monks released from the Carthusian strict vow of silence. It is in Italian, but well worth doing even if you don't understand a word. The tour begins in the church and then moves on to the **small cloister**, with fine terracotta decoration and a geometric garden around a fountain. Further on, the **great cloister** is stunning for its size and tranquillity, and also offers an insight into life in the complex. It is surrounded on three sides by the **monks' houses**, each consisting of two rooms, a chapel, a garden and a loggia, with a bedroom above. The hatches to the side of the entrances were to enable food to be passed through without any communication. There is also a **refectory** with a frescoed ceiling, which was used for occasional communal eating; the Bible was read throughout the silent meal from the pulpit (with a hidden entrance). The dining room is divided by a blind wall which allowed the monastery to feed pilgrims staying in their guesthouse without compromising the rules of their closed order. The tour is free but voluntary contributions to upkeep are collected on your way out. The final call is the Certosa **shop**, stocked with honey, chocolate, souvenirs and the famous Chartreuse liqueur; give yourself time before leaving to sample the different varieties of the liqueur at the kiosk outside the entrance – yellow is strong, green stronger.

Vigévano

An hour by bus to the west of Pavia, **VIGÉVANO** is Lombardy at its most comfortably wealthy, a smug little town of boutiques, antiques dealers and – most significantly – shoe shops. The shoe industry is Vigévano's mainstay, and there are signs of the bedrock of the town's prosperity all over the centre. If you go on a Sunday, Italy's only **shoe museum** is open on Corso Cavour (10.30am–12.30pm & 3–6pm; closed Aug & Dec), with a collection of some of the weirdest and wackiest excesses of shoe design in the country.

As for the town itself, most of it is pretty unremarkable, and there'd be little reason to visit were it not for the **Piazza Ducale**, which is something special, surrounded on three sides by well-preserved and delicately frescoed arcades, the embodiment of Renaissance harmony. Designed by Bramante and heavily influenced by Leonardo, even the Baroque front of the **Duomo** doesn't spoil the proportions, deftly curved to conceal the fact that the church is set at a slight angle to the square.

Otherwise the **Castello** (Tues–Sun 8.30am–1.30pm; L4000/€2.07) is about all Vigévano has to offer. A Visconti and later Sforza stronghold now in the final throes of a lengthy restoration, the castle's still semi-dilapidated state is part of its attraction: it's largely unsupervised, especially in the mornings, which means you can go just about wherever you want, scrambling up rickety flights of steps to the upper floors, or down dank passages to the dungeons. The oldest part of the castle is the Rocca Vecchia, a fort built by the Visconti to defend the road to Milan, to which it is connected by a covered walkway. The Sforzas retained the castle's military function, but added the elegant Palazzo Ducale, still mostly unrestored, the Loggia delle Dame, an open walkway for the noblewomen's evening passeggiata, and the Falconiera, another open gallery used for the training of falcons. On the right of the courtyard, the **stables** (summer Mon–Fri 2–8pm, Sat & Sun 2–10pm; winter daily 2–6pm; free), designed by Leonardo, offer some insight into how the Sforza troops lived and worked – cathedral-like quarters for the horses, and a loft above for soldiers and hay.

For a good overhead view of both the Castello and the Piazza Ducale, climb the **Torre del Bramante** (Tues–Fri 10am–noon & 3.30–5.30pm, Sat & Sun 10am–12.30pm & 2.30–6.30pm; L2500/€1.29), a tower that was begun in 1198, before the Castello, and completed by Bramante at the end of the fifteenth century. The entrance is next to that of the Castello.

Cremona

A cosy provincial town situated bang in the middle of the Po plain, **CREMONA** is known for its violins. Ever since Andrea Amati established the first violin workshop here in 1566, and his son Nicolo and pupils Stradivari and Guarneri continued and expanded the industry, Cremona has been a focus for the instrument, attracting both tourists and musicians worldwide. Today around a hundred violin makers maintain the tradition started by the Amati family: there's an internationally famous school of violin making here, and there are frequent classical concerts, as well as a string festival held every third October.

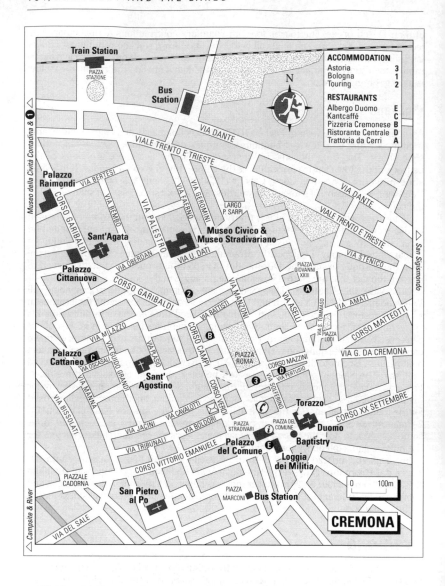

All this said, Cremona is a quiet, relatively unexciting town, and not an obvious place to spend a night, and most people treat it as a day-trip from Milan or as a stopover en route to the richer pickings of Mantua or Bergamo. However, its lack of overnight visitors can be appealing in itself – certainly there are places to stay and a small crop of pleasant restaurants – and it can be a nice idea to give yourself time to wind down here, but not long enough to get bored.

Arrival, information and accommodation

Cremona's **train station** is on Via Dante, on the northern edge of the city centre, ten minutes' walk from the focal Piazza del Comune; bus #1 runs regularly to the Piazza Cavour, also in the centre. Most intercity buses stop at the train station or at the **bus station** next door.

The **tourist office** is on the Piazza del Comune, opposite the duomo (Mon–Sat 9.30am–noon & 3–6pm, Sun 9.45am–noon; ☎0372.23.233, *www.cremonaturismo.com*), and has maps, leaflets and details of classical concerts. They also have lists of violin makers' workshops (Botteghe Liutarie) and will be able to tell you if the school of violin making in Palazzo Raimondi is open for visits.

If you want to stay over in Cremona, the cheapest **hotel** is the *Bologna*, Piazzale Risorgimento 7 (☎0372.24.258; ①) – turn right off Piazza Stazione – whose main advantage is its proximity to the stations. For a centrally placed alternative, you could try the *Touring*, Via Palestro 3, close to the junction of Via Palestro and Corso Garibaldi (☎0372.36.976; ②), although it's slightly bleak. A better bet, and not much more expensive is the *Astoria*, close to Piazza del Comune at Via Bordigallo 19, off Via Solferino (☎0372.461.616, fax 0372.461.810; ③); it's best to book in advance here. There's a **campsite**, the *Parco al Po*, on Via Lungo Po Europa (☎0372.21.268, fax 0372.27.137; May–Sept); take bus #1 (direction Viale Po) from the train station.

The City

The centre of Cremona is **Piazza del Comune**, a slightly disjointed medieval square, with a west side formed by the red-brick **Loggia dei Militia** – formerly headquarters of the town's militia – and the arched **Palazzo del Comune**, and the northeast corner marked by the gawky Romanesque **Torazzo**, built in the mid-thirteenth century and bearing a fine Renaissance clock dating from 1583. At 112m, the Torazzo claims to be Italy's highest medieval tower, and if you've the energy you can ascend for some excellent views over the rest of Cremona and around (March–Nov daily 10.30am–noon & 3–6pm; rest of year same hours weather permitting or by appointment; ☎0372.27.633; L8000/€4.13). Next door, the **Duomo**, connected to the Torazzo by way of a Renaissance loggia, is a mixed-looking church, with a fine west facade made up of Classical, Romanesque and fancy Gothic features, focusing on a rose window from 1274. Originally conceived as a basilica, its transepts were added when the Gothic style became more fashionable – presumably explaining its slightly squat appearance inside. Its most significant interior features are its sixteenth-century nave frescoes, including a superb trompe l'oeil by Pordenone on the west wall, showing the *Crucifixion* and *Deposition*, and the fifteenth-century pulpits, decorated with finely tortured reliefs.

Next to the duomo, the octagonal **Baptistry** dates from the late twelfth century, and is currently under restoration. Immediately opposite the duomo, the **Palazzo del Comune** has a very select exhibition of some of Cremona's most historic violins in its upstairs **Sala dei Violini** (Tues–Sat 8.30am–6.30pm, Sun 10am–6pm; L6000/€3.10), including a very early example made by Andrea Amati in 1566 for the court of Charles IX of France, as well as later instruments by Amati's son, Guarneri, and Stradivari. You can hear recordings of the different instruments being played and you'll also catch a glimpse of the opulent state rooms of the Palazzo del Comune itself.

If you've come to Cremona primarily for the violins, the pilastered **Palazzo Affaitati**, north of the square at Via Palestro 17, will also be of interest. It holds the **Museo Stradivariano** (Tues–Sat 8.30am–6pm, Sun 10am–6pm; L5000/€2.58), which contains models, paper patterns, tools and acoustic diagrams from Stradivari's workshop, along with more violins, violas, viols, cellos and guitars, many of which have elaborately carved scrolls, hanging impotently in glass cases; an enlightening video is also shown (alternately in English and Italian), which helps to unravel the mysteries of the violin maker's art. The instruments have to be played regularly to keep them in trim, and you could try asking the custodian when the next work-out is due. In the same building (entrance around the corner in Via U. Dati), the **Museo Civico** (same hours; L10,000/€5.17) is a decidedly provincial and rather pedestrian collection of mainly Cremonese art, redeemed only by being superbly displayed in striking galleries. Alongside the art are changing exhibitions drawn from the bizarre artefacts and natural history specimens accumulated by Ponzone, the museum's nineteenth-century founder.

Turning left off Via Palestro onto Via Bertesi, you approach the **Palazzo Raimondi**, a dignified building made distinctive by its frescoed cornice. Conceived by the humanist Raimondi, it now houses the prestigious International School of Violin Making and its associated **Museo Organologico**, which is used mainly by the school, although visits can be arranged in advance (☎0372.386.89).

Southwest of Piazza del Comune, on Via Tibaldi, the church of **San Pietro al Po** has better (and more visible) frescoes than the duomo; indeed its walls are coated with paintings and intricate stuccos, also dating from the sixteenth century. It's all pretty excessive, but there's sophisticated optical trickery in the trompe l'oeil work of Antonio Campi in the transept vaults. Look in also on the refectory next door for Bernadino Gatti's hearty fresco of the *Feeding of the Two Thousand*.

If you like the church of San Pietro al Po, you'll love that of **San Sigismondo** on the eastern edge of town (bus #3 from the train station, bus #2 from Piazza Cavour). Built by Francesco and Bianca Sforza in 1441 to commemorate their wedding – Cremona was Bianca's dowry – its Mannerist decor is among Italy's best, ranging from Camillo Boccaccino's soaring apse fresco to the *Pentecost* by Giulio Campi in the third bay of the nave, plagiarized from Mantegna's ceiling in the Camera degli Sposi at Mantua. Other highlights include Giulio's *Annunciation* on the entrance wall, in which Gabriel is seemingly suspended in midair, and the gory John the Baptist in the second left chapel, by Giulio's younger brother Antonio.

There's a rather different attraction on the opposite edge of town (bus #3 from the train station): the **Museo della Civiltà Contadina**, stuck on the edge of an industrial estate at Via Castelleone 51 (Tues–Sat 8.30am–6pm, Sun 9.15am–12.15pm & 3–6pm; L5000/€2.58), a possible contender for Italy's muddiest museum. A display of agricultural history laid out in an old farm, it's a scruffy place, and sporadic labelling (in Italian only) makes working out the uses of the various pieces of agricultural apparatus virtually impossible. But the farm itself, with its row of tiny workers' cottages, the larger houses of the foreman and *padrone*, the immense stable, and the small chapel, built so that time wasn't wasted in travelling to church, is sufficient to give you a good picture of the strict hierarchy and slave-like existence that governed the lives of Italian agricultural labourers over several centuries.

Eating and drinking

For **food**, the excellent *gastronomie* that cluster along Corso Garibaldi and the Corso Campi make good places to put together a picnic, while *Pizzeria Cremonese*, Piazza Roma 39 (closed Mon), is a cheap and popular place to sit down and eat. There are also lots of places to try local specialities: the *Trattoria da Cerri*, Piazza Giovanni XXIII 3 (closed Tues & Wed), off Via Aselli, and the *Ristorante Centrale*, off Via Solferino at Via Pertusio 4 (closed Thurs), are both very good, if not especially cheap. *Albergo Duomo*, on Via Gonfalonieri 13, down the side of the Palazzo Comunale is a popular place, worth booking if you want a table outside in the evening (☎0372.352.96). If it's on the menu, try a *bollito misto* – a mixture of boiled meats, served with Cremonese *mostarda di* *frutta*, consisting of fruit suspended in a sweet mustard syrup. Around Piazza del Comune and Piazza della Pace there are several very pleasant pavement cafes and *gelaterie* in which to while away the time. Three minutes' walk out of the centre of town, the charming Palazzo Cattaneo on Via Oscasali houses a new cultural association cum bar-café, *Kantcaffé* (daily 3pm–midnight), which organizes a programme of temporary exhibitions and concerts using the palace building, the wine vaults and the garden. The bar itself, with tables and chairs dotted around the leafy garden, is a wonderfully tranquil spot, and it also has a computer for Internet access.

Mantua (Mantova) and around

Aldous Huxley called it the most romantic city in the world; and with an Arabian nights skyline rising above its three encircling lakes, **MANTUA (MANTOVA)** is undeniably evocative. It was the scene of Verdi's *Rigoletto*, and its history is one of equally operatic plots, most of them perpetuated by the Gonzagas, one of Renaissance Italy's richest and most powerful families, who ruled the town for three centuries. Its centre of interlinking cobbled squares retains its medieval aspect, and there are two splendid palaces: the **Palazzo Ducale**, containing Mantegna's stunning fresco of the Gonzaga family and court, and **Palazzo Te**, whose frescoes by the flashy Mannerist Giulio Romano have entertained and outraged generations of visitors with their combination of steamy erotica and illusionistic fantasy.

But hazy sunsets reflected in tranquil lakes, and the town's melodramatic history, are only half the story. Outside the few traffic-free streets of the historic centre the roads are lined with grimy Fascist-era buildings and jammed with cars, while the outskirts have been desecrated by chemical, plastics and paper works that are reputedly responsible for lining the bed of the largest lake, Superiore, with mercury. Nevertheless, the core of the city is still appealing, especially on Thursdays when Piazza Mantegna, Piazza dell'Erbe and the streets around are filled with a large market.

The state of these same streets aroused the ire of a visiting pope in 1459, who complained that Mantua was muddy, marshy, riddled with fever and intensely hot. His host, Lodovico II Gonzaga, was spurred into action: he could do little about the heat (Mantua can still be unbearably hot and mosquito-ridden in summer) but he did give the city an elaborate facelift, ranging from paving the squares and repainting the shops, to engaging Mantegna as court artist and calling in the prestigious architectural theorist Alberti to design the monumental church of Sant'Andrea – one of the most influential buildings of the early Renaissance. Lodovico's successors continued the tradition of artistic patronage, and although most of the thousands of works of art once owned by the Gonzagas are now scattered around Europe, the town still has plenty of relics from the era.

Arrival, information and accommodation

Mantua's old centre is a ten-minute walk from the **train station** on Piazza Don E. Leoni and the **bus station**, just beyond on Piazza Mondadori, off Corso Vittorio Emanuele II. Bus #1 runs from the train station to the centre of town. The **tourist office**, in the centre of town at Piazza Mantegna 6 – the entrance is actually on Piazza dell'Erbe (Mon–Sat 8.30am–12.30pm & 3–6pm, Sun 9.30am–12.30pm; ☎0376.328.253) – has the usual maps and hotel lists as well as information on boat and bike trips in the Po Valley and agriturismo in the region. **Bicycles** can be rented by the hour or the day from La Rigola (☎0376.366.677) at the end of Via Accademia on the lake.

As in most parts of northern Italy, **hotels** get booked up quickly, and it's advisable to phone ahead. Mantua has only one cheap hotel: the *Peter Pan*, Cittadella Piazza Giulia 3 (☎0376.392.638; ②), ten minutes' walk across the lake from the centre. In the town

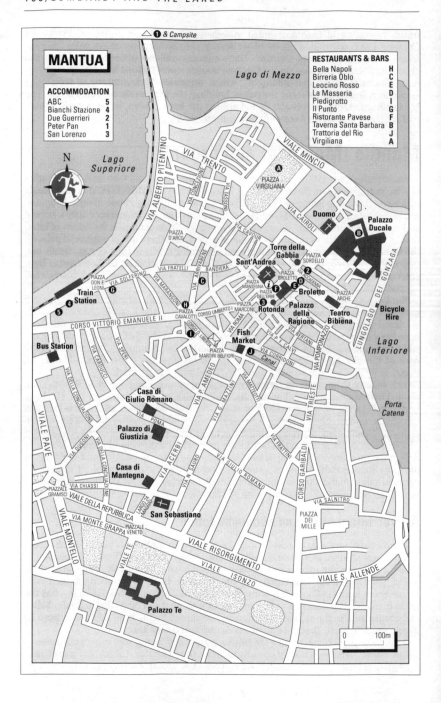

itself, and right opposite the station, the *ABC*, Piazza Don Leoni 25 (☎0376.322.329; ③), is good value with breakfast included and free use of bicycles, while the pleasant *Bianchi Stazione*, next door at Piazza Don Leoni 24 (☎0376.326.465, fax 0376.321.504; ⑤), offers more comfort at correspondingly higher prices. Another possibility, right on the square overlooking the Palazzo Ducale, is the run-down *Due Guerrieri*, Piazza Sordella 52 (☎0376.325.596, fax 0376.329.645; ⑤), and at the top end of the scale is the *San Lorenzo*, Piazza Concordia 14 (☎0376.220.500, fax 0376.327.194; ⑨). Unfortunately, there's no youth hostel here, the only other option being the small (ten plots only) and expensive **campsite**, *Corte Chiara* (☎0376.390.804; May–Sept), north of Mantua, outside of Porto Mantovano on the road to Marmirolo.

The City

The centre of Mantua is made up of four interlinking squares, the first of which, **Piazza Mantegna**, is a small, wedge-shaped open space at the end of the arcaded shopping thoroughfare of **Corso Umberto**. It's dominated by the facade of Alberti's church of **Sant'Andrea**, an unfinished basilica that says a lot about the ego of Lodovico II Gonzaga, who commissioned it. He felt that the existing medieval church was neither impressive enough to represent the splendour of his state nor large enough to hold the droves of people who flocked to Sant'Andrea every Ascension Day to see the holy relic of Christ's blood which had been found on the site. The relic is still there, and after years of dispute about its authenticity (it was supposed to have been brought to Mantua by the soldier who pierced Christ's side), Pope Pius II settled the matter in the fifteenth century by declaring it had miraculously cured him of gout.

Work started on the church in 1472, with the court architect, Luca Fancelli, somewhat resentfully overseeing Alberti's plans. There was a bitchy rivalry between the two, and when, on one of his many visits, Alberti fell and hurt a testicle, Fancelli gleefully told him that "God lets men punish themselves in the place where they sin". Inside, the church is roofed with one immense barrel vault, echoing the triumphal arch of the facade, which gives it a rather cool and calculated feel. The octagonal balustrade at the crossing stands above the crypt where the holy relic is kept in two vases, copies of originals designed by Cellini and stolen by the Austrians in 1846; to see them, ask the sacristan. The painter Mantegna is buried in the first chapel on the left, his tomb topped with a bust of the artist that's said to be a self-portrait; the wall-paintings in the chapel were designed by the artist and executed by students, one of whom was Correggio.

Opposite Sant'Andrea, sunk below the present level of the adjoining **Piazza dell'Erbe**, is Mantua's oldest church, the eleventh-century **Rotonda** (daily 10am–noon & 2.30–4.30pm), which narrowly escaped destruction under Lodovico's city-improvement plans, only to be partially demolished in the sixteenth century and used as a courtyard by the surrounding houses. Rebuilt at the beginning of this century and beautifully restored in the last few years, it still contains traces of twelfth- and thirteenth-century frescoes. Piazza dell'Erbe itself is one of the town's most characterful squares, with a small daily market and cafés and restaurants sheltering in the arcades below the thirteenth-century **Palazzo della Ragione**, whose impressive wooden-vaulted main hall is viewable during occasional temporary exhibitions. At the north end of the square, a passage leads under the red-brick **Broletto**, or medieval town hall, into the smaller **Piazza Broletto**, where you can view two reminders of how "criminals" were treated under the Gonzagas. The bridge to the right has metal rings embedded in its vault, to which victims were chained by the wrists, before being hauled up by a pulley and suspended in mid-air; while on your far left – actually on the corner of Piazza Sordello – the tall medieval **Torre della Gabbia** has a cage attached in which prisoners were displayed. The Broletto itself is more generous to deserving Mantuans, and is dedicated to the city's two most famous sons: Virgil, a statue of whom overlooks the square, and Tazio Nuvolari, Italy's most celebrated racing driver, whose career is mapped in a small **museum** (April–Oct Tues, Wed & Fri–Sun 10am–1pm & 3.30–6.30pm; rest of year by appointment ☎0376.325.691; L5000/€2.58).

If you have the time, it's well worth making a short diversion off Via Broletto up Via Accademia to the eighteenth-century **Teatro Scientifico** or **Bibiena** (daily 9.30am–12.30pm & 3–6pm; L4000/€2.07), designed by Antonio Bibiena, whose brother designed the Bayreuth Opera House. This is a much smaller theatre, at once intimate and splendid, its curving walls lined with boxes calculated to make their inhabitants more conspicuous than the performers. A thirteen-year-old Mozart gave the inaugural concert here: his impression is unrecorded, but his father was fulsome in his praise for the building, writing that he had never in his life seen anything more beautiful. Concerts are still given – details from the theatre or tourist office.

Beyond Piazza Broletto, **Piazza Sordello** is a large, sombre square, headed by the Baroque facade of the **Duomo** and flanked by grim crenellated palaces built by the Gonzagas' predecessors, the Bonalcosi. The duomo conceals a rich interior, designed by Giulio Romano after the church had been gutted by fire. As for the palaces, the two on the left are now owned by the successors of Baldassare Castiglione, a relative of the Gonzagas, who made himself unpopular at the Mantuan court by setting his seminal handbook of Renaissance behaviour, *The Book of the Courtier*, in the rival court of Urbino. Opposite, the **Palazzo del Capitano** and **Magna Domus** were taken by Luigi Gonzaga when he seized Mantua from the Bonalcosi in 1328, the beginning of three hundred years of Gonzaga rule.

The Palazzo Ducale

The Palazzo del Capitano and Magna Domus form the core of the **Palazzo Ducale**, an enormous complex that was once the largest palace in Europe (Tues–Sun 8.45am–7.15pm; June–Sept Sat until 11pm; L12,000/€6.20). At its height it covered 34,000 square metres, had a population of over a thousand, and when it was sacked by the Habsburgs in 1630 eighty carriages were needed to carry the two thousand works of art contained in its five hundred rooms. Only a proportion of these rooms are open to visitors, and to see them you have to take a guided tour that takes you through to the Sala dei Specchi and then allows you to wander freely through the grounds and the Castello di San Giorgio. The tours are conducted in Italian only and are fairly indiscriminate; save your energy for the rooms that deserve it.

At the time of Luigi's coup of 1328, the Gonzagas were a family of wealthy local peasants, living outside the city on vast estates with an army of retainers. On seizing power Luigi immediately nominated himself Captain of the People – an event pictured in one of the first paintings you'll see on your tour – and the role quickly became a hereditary one, eventually growing in grandeur to that of marquis. During this time the Gonzagas did their best to make Mantua into a city which was a suitable reflection of their increasing influence, commissioning sought-after Renaissance artists like Mantegna to depict them in their finery. Lodovico II's grandson, Francesco II, further swelled the Gonzagan coffers by hiring himself out as a mercenary for various other Italian city-states – money his wife, Isabella d'Este, spent amassing a prestigious collection of paintings, sculpture and objets d'art. Under Isabella's son, Federico II, Gonzaga fortunes reached their height; his marriage to the heiress of the duchy of Monferrato procured a ducal title for the family, while he continued the policy of self-glorification by commissioning an out-of-town villa for himself and his mistress. Federico's descendants were for the most part less colourful characters, one notable exception being Vincenzo I, whose debauchery and corruption provided the inspiration for Verdi's licentious duke in *Rigoletto*. After Vincenzo's death, the now bankrupt court was forced to sell many of the family treasures to England's King Charles I (many of the works are still in London's Victoria and Albert Museum) just three years before it was sacked by the Habsburgs.

The first rooms of the palace are the least impressive. There is a thirteenth-century sculpture of a seated Virgil, a painting from 1494 by Domenico Morone showing the *Expulsion of the Bonatosi* from the square outside, and, perhaps most interestingly, the fragments of a half-finished fresco by Pisanello, discovered in 1969 behind two layers of plaster and thought to depict either an episode from an Arthurian romance or the (idealized) military exploits of the first marquis, Gianfrancesco Gonzaga. Whatever its subject, it's a powerful piece of work, charged with energy, in which faces, costumes and landscape are minutely observed.

Further on, through the Sala dello Zodiaco, whose late sixteenth-century ceiling is spangled with stars and constellations, is the **Salone dei Fiume** ("Room of the Rivers"), in which Baroque trompe l'oeil goes over the top to create a mock garden complete with painted creepers and two ghastly fountains surrounded by stalactites and stalagmites. The **Sala dei Specchi** ("Hall of the Mirrors") has a notice outside signed by Monteverdi, who worked as court musician to Vincenzo I and gave frequent concerts of new works – notably the world's first modern opera, *L'Orfeo*, written in 1607. Vincenzo also employed Rubens, whose *Adoration of the Magi* in the **Salone degli Arcieri**, next door, shows the Gonzaga family of 1604, including Vincenzo with his handlebar moustache. The picture was originally part of a triptych, but Napoleonic troops carried off two-thirds of it after briefly occupying the town in 1797 and chopped the remaining third into saleable chunks of portraiture. Although most have been traced, and some returned to the palazzo, there are still a few gaps. Around the room is a curious frieze of horses, glimpsed behind curtains.

The Castello di San Giorgio contains the palace's principal treasure, however: Mantegna's frescoes of the Gonzaga family – among the painter's most famous works, splendidly restored in the so-called **Camera degli Sposi** and depicting the Marquis Lodovico and his wife Barbara with their family. They're naturalistic pieces of work, giving a vivid impression of real people, of the relationships between them and of the tensions surrounding something that is happening, or about to happen. In the main one Lodovico discusses a letter with a courtier while his wife looks on; their youngest daughter leans on her mother's lap, about to bite into an apple, while an older son and daughter (possibly Barbarina) look towards the door, where an ambassador from another court is being welcomed – lending some credence to the theory that negotiations are about to take place for Barbarina's marriage. The other fresco, *The Meeting*, takes place out of doors against a landscape of weird rock formations and an imaginary city with the Gonzagan arms above the gate. Divided into three sections by fake pilasters, it shows Gonzagan retainers with dogs and a horse in attendance on Lodovico, who is welcoming his son Francesco back from Rome, where he had just become the first Gonzaga to be made a cardinal. In the background are the Holy Roman Emperor Frederick III and the King of Denmark – a selection which apparently annoyed the Duke of Milan, who was incensed that the "two most wretched men in the world" had been included while he had been omitted. Lodovico's excuse was that he would have included the duke had he not objected so strongly to Mantegna's uncompromising portrait style. If you have time before the guide sweeps you out, have a look at the ceiling, another nice piece of trompe l'oeil, in which two women, peering down from a balustrade, have balanced a tub of plants on a pole and appear to be on the verge of letting it tumble into the room – an illusionism that was to be crucial in the development of the Gonzaga's next resident artist of any note, Giulio Romano, whose Palazzo Te – see overleaf – should not be missed.

Finally, the private **apartments of Isabella d'Este**, on the ground floor, are sometimes on view. Though they once housed works by Michelangelo, Mantegna and Perugino, only the unmoveable decorations remain – inlaid cupboards and intricately carved ceilings and doors. A ruthless employer, Isabella would threaten her artists and craftsmen with the dungeon if she thought they were working too slowly, and had no compunction about bullying Mantegna on his death-bed to give her a piece of sculpture she particularly coveted. She was more deferential to Leonardo da Vinci, however, who did two drawings of her but ignored her suggestion that one be converted into a portrait of Christ. Isabella also collected dwarfs, whose job it was to cheer her up while her husband was away fighting. For centuries it was assumed that the suite of miniature rooms beyond Isabella's apartments was built for the dwarfs; in fact it's a scaled-down version of the St John Lateran basilica in Rome, built for Vincenzo.

South of the centre: to the Palazzo Te

A twenty-minute walk from the centre of Mantua, at the end of the long spine of Via Principe Amedeo and Via Acerbi, the Palazzo Te is the later of the city's two Gonzaga palaces, and equally compelling in its way; and you can take in a few of Mantua's more minor attractions on the way there.

The first thing to look at on the way is Giulio Romano's **Fish Market**, to the left off Piazza Martiri Belfiori, a short covered bridge over the river, which is still used as a market building. Following Via Principe Amedeo south, the **Casa di Giulio Romano**, off to the right at Via Poma 18, overshadowed by the monster-studded Palazzo di Giustizia, was also designed by Romano – like much of his Mantuan work, it was meant to impress the sophisticated, who would have found the licence taken with the Classical rules of architecture witty and amusing. A five-minute walk away on busy Via Giovanni Acerbi, the more austere brick **Casa del Mantegna** was also designed by the artist, both as a home and private museum, and is now used as a contemporary art-space and conference centre (during exhibitions daily 10am–12.30pm & 3–6pm). Across the road, the church of **San Sebastiano** (Tues–Sun 10am–12.30pm & 4–6pm; L3000/€1.55) was the work of Alberti, and is famous as the first Renaissance church to be built on a central Greek cross plan, described as "curiously pagan" by Nicholas Pevsner. Lodovico II's son was less polite: "I could not understand whether it was meant to turn out as a church, a mosque or a synagogue." Its days as a consecrated building are over and it now contains commemorative plaques forming a monument to the fallen Mantuan soldiers of World War II.

At the end of Via Giovanni Acerbi, across Viale Te, the **Palazzo Te** (Mon 1–6pm, Tues–Sun 9am–6pm; L12,000/€6.20) was designed for playboy Federico Gonzaga and his mistress, Isabella Boschetta, by Giulio Romano; it's the artist/architect's greatest work and a renowned Renaissance pleasure dome. When the palace was built, Te – or Tejeto, as it used to be known – was an island connected to the mainland by bridge, an ideal location for an amorous retreat away from Federico's wife and the restrictions of life in the Palazzo Ducale. Built around a square courtyard originally occupied by a labyrinth, these days it houses modest but appealing collections of Egyptian artefacts and modern art, although the main reason for visiting is to see Giulio's amazing decorative scheme.

A tour of the palace is like a voyage around Giulio's imagination, a sumptuous world where very little is what it seems. In the **Camera del Sole e delle Luna**, the sun and the moon are represented by a pair of horse-drawn chariots viewed from below, giving a fine array of bottoms on the ceiling; in the **Sala dei Cavalli**, dedicated to the prime specimens from the Gonzaga stud-farm (which was also on the island), portraits of horses stand before an illusionistic background in which simulated marble, fake pilasters and mock reliefs surround views of painted landscapes through nonexistent windows. The function of the **Sala di Psiche**, further on, is undocumented, but the sultry frescoes, and the proximity to Federico's private quarters, might give a few clues, the ceiling paintings telling the story of Cupid and Psyche with some more dizzying "sotto in su" (from the bottom up) works by Giulio, among others clumsily executed by his pupils. On the walls, too, are racy pieces, covered with orgiastic wedding-feast scenes, at which drunk and languishing gods in various states of undress are attended by a menagerie of real and mythical beasts. Don't miss the severely incontinent river-god in the background, included either as a punning reference to Giulio's second name, Pippi (The Pisser), or as encouragement to Federico who, according to his doctors, suffered from the "obstinate retention of urine". Other scenes show Mars and Venus having a bath, Olympia about to be raped by a half-serpentine Jupiter and Pasiphae disguising herself as a cow in order to seduce a bull – all watched over by the giant Polyphemus, perched above the fireplace, clutching the pan-pipes with which he sang of his love for Galatea before murdering her lover.

Polyphemus and his fellow giants are revenged in the extraordinary **Sala dei Giganti** beyond – "the most fantastic and frightening creation of the whole Renaissance", according to the critic Frederick Hartt – showing the destruction of the giants by the gods. As if at some kind of advanced disaster movie, the destruction appears to be all around: cracking pillars, toppling brickwork, and screaming giants, mangled and crushed by great chunks of architecture, appearing to crash down into the room. Stamp your feet and you'll discover another parallel to twentieth-century cinema – the sound-effects that Giulio created by making the room into an echo chamber.

Eating and drinking

Mantua is an easy place to **eat** well and cheaply, with plenty of reasonably priced restaurants throughout its centre, many serving Mantuan specialities like *spezzatino di Mantua* (normally donkey stew), *agnoli in brodo* (pasta stuffed with cheese and sausage in broth) or the delicious *tortelli di zucca* (pasta stuffed with pumpkin).

On a **budget**, there are a couple of decent self-service places – *Il Punto*, almost opposite the train station on Via Solferino 36 (daily except Sun noon–2.30pm & 7.30–9.15pm), and the *Virgiliana*, Piazza Virgiliana 57, although this is only open weekday lunchtimes (noon–2pm). If all you want is a pizza, try *Piedigrotto*, Corso Libertá 15 (closed Wed), and *Bella Napoli*, Piazza Cavalotti 14 (closed Tues), both decent, standard **pizzerias** on the edge of the old town. *La Masseria*, Piazza Broletto 7 (closed Thurs), is a popular, lively place with a wide selection of other dishes as well as good pizzas.

Among **restaurants** with a more local flavour, the *Leoncino Rosso*, just through the arch off Piazza Broletto (closed Sun), is friendly and informal – and a good place just to drink – and the *Taverna Santa Barbara*, Piazza Santa Barbara 19 (closed Mon), inside the Palazzo Ducale complex itself, is an atmospheric setting for local specialities. Try also *Ristorante Pavesi* (closed Thurs), one of several very pleasant but more expensive options in Piazza Erbe, or *Trattoria del Rio* at Via Pescheria 23 (closed Fri), right by the fish market, which serves inexpensive traditional Mantovan dishes. For just a **drink**, either before or after dinner, try *Birreria Oblo*, Via Arrivabene 50, a pubby place with a great selection of beers, almost matched by a good range of sandwiches.

Grazie and Sabbioneta

There's not much to see within easy reach of Mantua, and the countryside – the Mantuan plain – is for the most part flat and dull. The closest real attraction is at **GRAZIE**, a ten-minute bus ride west, where the church of **Santa Maria delle Grazie** has an interior chock-full of weird votive offerings, wax and wooden mannequins in clothes petrified with age standing in niches, surrounded by wooden hearts, breasts, hands and feet nailed up by the recipients of miracle cures. There's even a stuffed crocodile hanging from the ceiling. Alongside the church, a path leads down to the marshes, rich in rare birds and wildlife. For **boat trips** along the Po contact Montonavi Andes at Piazza Sordello 8, Mantua (☎0376.322.875) or Motonave Sebastiano N. at Via Ostigliese est 272, Governolo (☎0376.668.134).

Further out, fifty minutes by bus from Mantua bus station (3–9 daily), **SABBIONETA** is a more interesting target, an odd little place with the air of an abandoned film set, where imperious Renaissance palaces gaze blankly over deserted and dusty piazzas. The town is the result of the obsessive dream of Vespasiano Gonzaga, member of a minor branch of the Mantuan family, to create the ideal city, but it has now been abandoned by all but the oldest inhabitants, a handful of agricultural workers and the tourist board.

Sabbioneta was an anachronism even as it was being built. In the sixteenth century it was no more than an agricultural village, nominal capital of an insignificant state on the Mantuan border struggling to maintain its independence from the foreign powers who had colonized most of Lombardy. Unperturbed, its ruler, Duke Vespasiano, was keen to create an ideal state on the model of ancient Athens and Rome, and he uprooted his subjects from their farm cottages, forcing them to build and then inhabit the new city, which held a Greek and Latin Academy and a Palladian theatre as well as a couple of ducal residences. After Vespasiano's death, Sabbioneta returned to – and has remained in – its former state: a small agricultural village like hundreds of others throughout Italy.

To get inside any of the town's buildings you have to take a **guided tour**. These are arranged by the **tourist office** at Via Gonzaga 31 (April–Sept Tues–Sat 9.30am–12.30pm & 2.30–6pm, Sun 9.30am–12.30pm & 2.30–7pm; Oct–March closes one hour earlier; ☎0375.52.039, *www.unh.net/sabbioneta*), by the main piazza and bus stop. The tours start with the **Palazzo del Giardino**, Vespasiano's private residence, decorated with frescoed models of civilized behaviour, ranging from Roman emperors to the Three Graces. Next stop is the **Teatro Olimpico**, copied from Palladio's theatre of the same name in Vicenza, in which the only spectators are pallid marble gods, fake-bronze emperors and ghostly painted courtiers. The **Palazzo Ducale**, around the corner, holds painted wooden statues of four of the Gonzagas, including Vespasiano (with the ruffle and beard), sitting imperiously on horseback. What remains of the palace's decor is likewise concerned with the show of strength – frescoed elephants and friezes of eagles and lions. Close by, the **Chiesa dell'Incoronata** is remarkable mainly for its trompe l'oeil roof, which appears to be three times higher in than out – perhaps an apt comment on Vespasiano, a bronze statue of whom sits beneath, dressed as a Roman emperor and looking reluctant to leave his dream city.

NORTHERN LOMBARDY: LAKES AND MOUNTAINS

"One can't describe the beauty of the **Italian lakes**, nor would one try if one could." Henry James's sentiment hasn't stopped generations of writers trying to describe the region in pages of purple prose. In fact, the lakes just about deserve it: their beauty is extravagant, and it's not surprising that the most melodramatic and romantic of Italy's opera composers – Verdi, Rossini and Bellini – rented lakeside villas in which to work. British and German Romantic poets also enthused about the area, and in doing so implanted them firmly in northern European imaginations. The result is a massive influx every summer of package tourists from cooler climes, come to savour the Italian dream and to take large gulps at what Keats called "the beaker of the warm south".

It would, however, be unwise literally to drink the lakes' waters, even though considerable efforts have been made in recent years to clean them up. Most *comunes* have installed purification plants, and although there is still some way to go before the lakes are totally clean, swimming is safe in most areas. Where it is not, the local *comune* is obliged to erect a warning notice. **Garda** is the cleanest lake, and one of the best centres in Europe for windsurfing and sailing, although you'll have to share the water with huge numbers of like-minded enthusiasts. If watersports don't appeal,

Como is the most scenically stunning of the lakes: surrounded by tall peaks that rise more or less directly from the water's edge, the luxuriance of its vegetation is equalled by the opulence of the local villas and *palazzi*; and when such things begin to cloy, there are good hikes in its mountainous hinterland. The shores of **Maggiore** are much flatter, and many of its *fin-de-siècle* resorts are rather sedate. There are, however, some good walks, and you shouldn't miss the gardens on Isola Bella. Though the picture-postcard charms of Orta San Giulio, the main village on **Lago d'Orta**, ensure that it is thronged with people at Easter and in summer, it's a romantic base in spring or autumn, and while the other minor lakes – **Lago d'Iseo** and **Lago Ledro** – are tame by comparison, you might want to stay on Iseo's islet, where there are some pleasant hikes.

The hilly terrain between the lakes is sliced up by **mountain valleys**: their lower reaches are largely residential and harbour light industry, with their rivers frequently reduced to a trickle by hydroelectric works, but the upper reaches are in parts unspoilt, with plenty of possibilities for hikes. There are also a handful of small ski resorts, but none worth going out of your way for. Of the two main cities, **Brescia** is really best avoided; **Bergamo** makes a much nicer place to stay, with an old walled hilltop centre that ranks as one of the loveliest in Italy. If you're lucky enough to find a room there, it's also a good base for trips to lakes Como and Iseo and the mountainous country in between.

Getting around the lakes

The three biggest lakes are all well served by **ferries**, which zigzag from shore to shore, docking at jetties that are usually conveniently positioned on the main lakeside piazzas or in the centre of the larger towns' promenades. The regular boats are pretty slow, and if you're in a hurry, you might want to pay extra for a **hydrofoil**; timings are listed in red in the timetables, which are available at all tourist offices and the ticket offices on the jetties themselves, and include a table of tariffs. Prices vary from lake to lake (Maggiore is the cheapest, with a one-stop hop costing L2000/€1.03; on Garda, the distances between villages are longer and an average journey costs around L10,000/€5.16) and day passes are available on all of them. However, unless you're doing two or three long journeys, they're no bargain; the Garda pass, for example, will cost you L40,000/€20.66.

In addition, there are fairly regular **buses** up and down the shores, a cheaper but far less interesting way of travelling. Timetables are often posted on bus stops, and again some of the better-organized tourist offices have copies. Be warned, though, that in Garda and Maggiore, which have one shoreline in Lombardy and another in, respectively, Veneto and Piemonte, it can be impossible to get hold of timetables for the "rival" region's buses.

Lago Maggiore and Lago d'Orta

For generations of overland travellers, **Lago Maggiore** has been the first taste of Italy. Road and railway from Switzerland run along its shores and, for travellers weary of the journey and the cool grandeur of the Alps, the first glimpse of Maggiore's limpid waters, gentle green hills and the hint of exotic vegetation can seem a promising taster of the country. Unmistakably Mediterranean in atmosphere, with citrus trees, palms and oleanders lining the lakeside proms and a peaceful, serene air, this is not somewhere for thrill-seekers, but is a beautiful place to chill out for a while.

Orange blossom, vines, clear air and the verbena that flourishes on its shores continue to draw the tourists, and to stay in the most popular resorts of Pallanza, Stresa and Baveno, you'll need to book in advance in peak season. The lake has always been a favourite with the British: Queen Victoria stayed at the Villa Clara at Baveno, and nineteenth-century travellers on their Grand Tour raved about it, although Robert Southey reckoned the Villa Borromeo on Isola Bella, now Maggiore's biggest tourist attraction, to be "one of the most costly efforts of bad taste in all Italy".

The western shore

The majority of the tourists who flock to Lago Maggiore head for the western shore, from where the jewel of the lake, the sumptuous gardens and villas of the **Isole Borromee**, is easily accessible. Miraculously however, the area has not completely lost it's charm and the established resorts of **Stresa** and **Baveno** are punctuated with smaller, less-saturated places where your money goes further and you might even hear some Italian in addition to English and German. Three such villages are **Arona**, the first stop from the south, **Verbania**, with ferry links to the eastern shore, and **Cannobio**, a convenient pad for exploring Maggiore's hilly hinterland. The southern reaches of the shore are rather drab, but you'll have more chance of finding a room there in high season.

Arona

ARONA, uninteresting in itself, is on the main railway line, and its cheap hotels make it a useful base for visiting the rest of the lake. The one sight here is a thirty-metre-high **copper statue** of St Charles Borromeo, who was born in the now ruined Castle of Arona. It's hollow and, if you don't suffer from claustrophobia or vertigo, climb up into its empty head and look out across the lake (April–Oct daily 8.30am–12.30pm & 2–6.30pm; Oct closes at 5pm; Nov–March Sat & Sun 9am–12.30pm & 2–5pm; L4000/€2.07).

If you decide to **stay** in Arona, the *Lido* campsite (☎0322.243.383) is right on the lake shore, a short walk from the train station. The cheapest hotels are the *Ponte*, Via Torini 19 (☎0322.45.317; ①), and the *Antico Gallo*, Via Botelli 13 (☎0322.243.137; ①); both have a bar and restaurant, but neither has en-suite rooms.

Stresa

The Maggiore of the tourist brochures begins at **STRESA**, whose popularity as a resort began in 1906 with the construction of the Simplon Tunnel. Its elegant lakeside promenade is now trodden by elderly visitors for whose benefit the main square in its mellow old centre is filled with ranks of café tables dedicated to the mass consumption of outsize ice-cream sundaes; at night the cobbled streets sway to the sound of Muzak and accordion players.

The town's hotels are quite expensive, and there's not a lot to do in Stresa other than catch a boat to the Isole Borromee (something that can be just as easily done from any number of other villages), making it difficult to recommend Stresa as a base – although fans of classical music might want to catch a concert or two at its prestigious **international music festival**, held annually in late August and early September. If you are here for any length of time, after strolling up and down the promenade, where the *Grand Hotel des Iles Borromees* (☎0323.938.938, fax 0323.32.405; ⑨) was used as a location by Hemingway in *A Farewell to Arms*, you might want to laze around at Stresa's **Lido** (open summer only) to the north, close to the Mottarone cable car station. From here, you can also catch a cable car up **Monte Mottarone** (daily every 20min 9.20am–noon & 1.40–5pm; L11,000/€5.68 one way, L18,000/€9.30 return). It's hardly the most sensational of hills, but undeserving of Ruskin's derision – he referred to it as "the stupidest of mountains" and thought the views of the Alps dull. Ruskin's mood or the weather must have been bad, for the views stretch from Monte Rosa on the Valle d'Aosta/Swiss border across to the Adamello. Its wooded western slopes are now a favourite destination for family outings, and on summer Sundays the roadside is lined with everything-but-the-kitchen-sink picnickers. If you want to range a bit further, you can rent mountain bikes near the summit (L30,000/€15.49 per day). Lago d'Orta lies on the other side of the mountain, and though it is possible to walk down to the lake, it's a tedious three-hour tramp.

Stresa's Pro Loco **tourist office** at Via Canonica 8 (summer daily 10am–12.30pm & 3–6.30pm; winter Mon–Fri 10am–12.30pm & 3–6.30pm, Sat 10am–12.30pm; ☎0323.31.308, fax 0323.3133.2561, *www.lagomaggiore.it*), as well as dispensing the usual local information, has programmes for the festival of classical music; tickets for this are on sale at the *cambio*/excursion booking booth on the lakefront, opposite the *Regina Palace Hotel* – expect to pay around L30,000/€15.49. If you want to **stay** in Stresa, the cheapest and most congenial option is the *Orsola*, Via Duchessa di Genova 45 (☎0323.31.087; ②), a comfortable place with good-value single and double rooms, and just three minutes' walk from the train station – turn right out of the station, and the hotel is just to the left down Via Duchessa di Genova. Otherwise the well-maintained villa of *Mon Toc*, Via Duchessa di Genova 69 (☎0323.30.282; ③) – turn right from the train station up Via Duchessa di Genova – is not greatly more expensive, and there are rooms above the *Chez Osvaldo* restaurant, at Via Anna Maria Bolongaro 57 (☎0323.31.948; ②); turn right out of the station and keep on straight ahead along the upper edge of the town for about ten minutes, and the street is off to the left. If you don't mind being a ferry ride from the mainland, you could also consider the *Elvezia* on Isola Bella (see below).

The best places for **meals** are the *Ristorante Venezia*, Via Duchessa di Genova (closed Wed), which does interesting salads and risottos as well as wood-fired pizzas, the *Orsola*, next door, and the *Osteria degli Amici* at Via Anna Maria Bolongaro 27 (closed Wed); all are reasonably priced. For snacks and booze, the *Red Baron*, five minutes' walk along from the train station at Via Roma 63, is an amiable place run by a friendly English woman who serves up great sandwiches, hearty *bruschette* and beer on tap. Finally, don't miss the *Casa del Caffè*, Via Anna Maria Bolongaro 26, one of the town's few authentic (and cheap) bars.

The Isole Borromee

The three visitable **Isole Borromee** are all served by regular ferries from Stresa, either from Piazza Marconi or Piazzale Lido, further up the lakeside promenade. Of the islands, **Isola Bella** (mid-March to late Sept daily 9am–noon & 1.30–5.30pm; Oct closes 5pm; L13,000/€6.71) is the best known and most gloriously excessive of all the lakes' gardens, though three centuries ago it was little more than a barren rock. In the seventeenth century Count Carlo III Borromeo decided to create an island paradise for his wife Isabella, and commissioned the architect, Angelo Crivelli, to transform it into a sumptuous Baroque oasis. Tons of soil were brought across from the mainland, a villa, fountains and statues were built, white peacocks imported, and ten terraces of orange and lemon trees, camellias, magnolias, box trees, laurels and cypresses carved out. The centrepiece, however, is a four-tiered confection of shell-, mirror- and marble-encrusted grottoes, topped with a suitably melodramatic unicorn, mini-obelisks, and various Greek gods and cute cherubs in attendance. Inside, ritzy rooms are opulently furnished, and there are more artificial grottoes and a collection of eighteenth-century marionettes in the cellar. Isola Bella really is worth seeing, though as Maggiore's main tourist attraction, every inch of the island not occupied by the palace and garden is taken up by restaurants with multilingual menus and stalls selling lace, pottery, the ubiquitous Pinnochio puppet and assorted gimcrackery. Unfortunately, the only hotel on the island, the delightfully old-fashioned *Elvezia*, at Lungo Lago V. Emanuele 18 (☎0323.30.043), is currently only open as a restaurant.

Hemingway's favourite island, **Isola dei Pescatori**, once an island of fishermen, retains a certain charm, despite the regular invasions of sightseers. Along with the obligatory trinket stands and restaurants there are a few ordinary bars and shops, and it's not a bad place to hang around for an hour or so. Ferries move on to **Isola Madre** (same hours as Isola Bella; L13,000/€6.71), larger and less visited than Isola Bella, with a small, tasteful palazzo stacked with portraits of the Borromeos in a luxuriant but less formal garden. Tiny **San Giovanni**, the fourth Borromean island, has a villa once owned by Toscanini, but is closed to the public.

Further north

If you're on a tight budget you might consider staying at **BAVENO**, up the coast from Stresa, which has ten campsites and a couple of reasonably priced hotels, and a beach backed by craggy mountains. Queen Victoria stayed at the Villa Clara (now Castello Branca) in 1879, establishing Baveno as a fashionable resort among the pre-jet set, although predictably it's now been colonized by British package operators. From here you can reach the tiny Lago Mergozzo, an arm of Maggiore, cut off from the rest of the lake by silt, or take the lovely road up to Monte Camoscio.

Again, there's not a great deal to do, though if you stay at the *Parisi* **campsite**, Via Piave 50 (☎0323.923.156; April–Sept), it's safe to swim from its narrow pebbly beach. There's a good-value **hotel** directly opposite the *imbarcadero*: the *Posta*, Piazza Dante 16 (☎0323.924.509; ②). Alternatively there's the slightly more expensive *La Ripa*, Via Sempione 11 (☎0323.924.589; ③), right on the lakeside but backed by the busy main road; turn left out of the *imbarcadero* and follow the coast road for around five minutes. The **tourist office**, on Piazzale Dante Alighieri 14 (May–Sept Mon–Sat 9am–12.30pm & 3–6pm, Sun 9am–noon; Oct–April Mon–Fri same hours, closed Sat afternoon; ☎0323.924.632), has lists of all hotels and campsites.

Further up the lake is **PALLANZA**, which along with the industrial quarters of Suna and Intra makes up the town of **VERBANIA**, whose name recalls *Verbanum* – the name used by the Romans for the whole, verbena-shored lake. Verbania's winter climate is the mildest on the lake, which enabled a retired Scottish soldier, Captain Neil McEachern, to create in the Thirties the most botanically prestigious garden of all the lakes, at the **Villa Táranto**. The grounds (April–Oct daily 8.30am–sunset; last admission 6.30pm; L11,000/€5.68) contain 20,000 species of plant – including giant Amazonian lilies, lotus blossoms, Japanese maple, and *Melia azederach*, a sacred Indian tree – laid out with cool geometric accuracy around fountains and pools.

A short walk south of Villa Táranto, Pallanza's lakefront is lined with manicured flower beds and dapper *gelaterie*, bars and hotels, but on the hill behind there's a more down-to-earth quarter in which the souvenir shops are almost outnumbered by *alimentari*, fruit shops and *pasticcerie*. If you want to escape the tourist-oriented lakeside bars, head up the hill to the *Bottinelli*, Via Ruga 16, a pasticceria with an unprettified wood-panelled bar with a pool table and outsize TV.

Cannobio

CANNOBIO is perhaps the most appealing place to stay on the western shore of the lake, its lakefront road of pastel-washed houses giving onto a series of stepped alleyways leading into a tightly tangled old village of stone houses. The only sight as such is the **Santuario della Pietà**, a Bramante-inspired church with a curious openwork cupola. It was built on the site of a 1522 miracle, when a picture of the *Pietà* suddenly began to bleed; shortly afterwards Cannobio remained unscathed while the plague ravished other villages nearby, and superstitious religious minds could do nothing but link the two events. Carlo Borromeo, anxious as ever to boost the morale of Catholics in the face of the snowballing power of the Protestant church, ordered a chapel to be built to house the painting. It's still there, though curiously there's no sign of blood stains.

Cannobio is well served by both ferries and buses, and you could catch one of the latter from the jetty up the Val Cannobina, a rarely visited valley punctuated by a few ancient stone-built hamlets. From Falmonta at the end of the bus route you could walk or drive up to the winter resort of Malesco from where you can pick up the privately run FART train to Locarno in Switzerland (see p.94).

To the far left of the lakefront (as you face the village) a ramp-like street leads up to the main drag, **Via Marconi**. At the head of Via Marconi is the SS34 coast road, on which you'll find the **tourist office** (Mon–Sat 9am–noon & 4.30–7pm, Sun 9am–noon; ☎0323.71.212) and a couple of supermarkets. Sadly, Cannobio's **hotels** are expensive: perhaps the best value is offered by the newly refurbished *Antica Stallera*, Via P. Zacchero (☎0323.715.95; ④), the attractive *Hotel Pironi*, Via G. Marconi 35 (☎0323.706.24; ⑥), and the swish *Elvezia*, Viale Rimembranza 1 (☎0323.70.142; ④). Otherwise, try the cheaper (and scruffier) *Giardino*, on Via Veneto – the SS34 – at no. 24 (☎0323.71.482; ②), or the much more appealingly positioned but grotty *Cannobio* on the lakefront (☎0323.71.390; ③). If the prices are getting too much for you, head out of town on the SS34: just past the River Cannobino is the very popular *La Residence* **campsite** (☎0323.71.190; March–Oct) where, in addition to tent pitches, there are **rooms** in a clean, modern villa (③). There are also simple rooms to be had above a nearby pizzeria: cross the road and follow the signposts for *Locanda del Fiume*, Via Darbedo 26 (☎0323.70.192; ③).

As for **eating**, *Verbano*, by the lake (closed Wed), is one of Cannobio's more reasonable café-restaurants, serving hot dishes and sandwiches, and as good a place as any to waste an hour or so. The *Osteria La Streccia*, up a narrow cobbled alley off the lakefront (closed Tues), has the best food on offer in Cannobio in a rustic, low-ceilinged dining room. Up in the village, the *Ristorante Antica Stallera*, Via P. Zacchero 7 (closed Tues), is a pleasant and reasonably priced place for lunch or dinner, where you can eat homemade pasta in the garden under a vine-covered trellis. The only place to go at night, for draught beer and snacks, is *Birreria Scurrone* on Vicolo Scurrone, reached through a tunnelling alleyway at the southern end of the lakefront.

The eastern shore

In general there is little of great interest on the eastern side of Lago Maggiore, although any of the smaller centres make feasible bases for the rest of the lake, or for hiking into the hills behind. From **MACCAGNO**, an improbably steep track leads straight out from the village into the hills, from where there are paths to the Lago Delio and Valle Veddasca. Most interestingly, you can walk to the village of Curiglia, beyond which, from Ponte di Piero, an acute mule track climbs to the isolated village of **MONTEVIASCO**, 500m above. There's no road to Monteviasco, and until recently the mule track was its only link with the world. Nowadays, however, there's a cable car.

Monteviasco was allegedly founded by four deserters from the occupying Spanish army who abducted four girls from a neighbouring village. In fact, there are scarcely any of their descendants left in the village now – most of the covetably picturesque drystone houses have been snapped up as holiday homes.

Back in Maccagno, the *Albergo della Torre Imperiale* on Piazza Roma (☎0332.560.142; ②), at the foot of the village near the lake, has basic doubles above a simple restaurant and bar, and there's a **campsite** on the waterfront – *Camping Lido* (☎0332.560.250).

Just to the south of Maccagno, **LUINO**, a sizeable town and tourist centre, is really only worth visiting on Wednesdays when it hosts Maggiore's biggest market. The *centro storico* (follow sign off the main road to the left of the *imbarcadero*) is no great shakes but is reasonably well stocked with food and especially wine shops. If you've spent any time in Lombardy's art galleries you may already be familiar with the work of Bernardino Luino, one of Leonardo's followers. It's assumed that he hailed from Luino, and if you like his work, you should take a look at the campanile he frescoed at the oratory of **SS Pietro e Paolo**.

Luino's **tourist office** (Mon–Sat 9am–noon & 3–6.45pm; ☎0332.530.019) is across the road from the jetty. For **food**, you could try the *pizza al trancio* outlet at Via Pellegrini 42 or the *Pizzeria Marinella*, Via Alessandro Manzoni 46 (closed Mon), just off Piazza Giovanni XXIII at the top of the *centro storico*; the latter offers a good selection of classic pizzas and veggie variations, for around the L9000/€4.65 mark, until 1am in summer. Luino's best ice cream is sold at *Pasticceria Chiara*, at Via Manzoni 22, also in the old town.

South of Luino, **LAVENO** (also accessible by L16,000/€8.26 car ferry from Intra in around 20min) specializes in bizarre attractions. At Christmas there's a floodlit underwater crypt, and, even if you're not into ceramics – its main industry – a visit to the entertainingly kitsch **museum** (July & Aug Tues–Sun 10am–noon & 3.30–6.30pm; Sept–June Tues–Thurs 2.30–5.30pm, Fri–Sun 10am–noon & 2.30–5.30pm; L2500/€1.29), 3km down the road at **CERRO**, is a must. The collection reaches the height of tastelessness in the gilded green aspidistra containers, a lavatory bowl decorated inside with pastoral scenes and an Art Nouveau bidet perched on a stand of leaves.

From Laveno a cable car climbs up to the **Sasso del Ferro** for great views of the Alps. On its southern slopes, but visible only from the lake, is the **Santuario di Santa Caterina del Sasso** (daily 8.30am–noon & 2–6pm). In the early twelfth century a wealthy moneylender, Alberto Besozzi, was sailing on the lake when his boat sank. He prayed to St Catherine of Alexandria and was safely washed up on shore, afterwards giving up usury and becoming a hermit in a cave on the hillside. When his prayers averted a plague the locals built a church which became popular with pilgrims, especially after a boulder fell on the roof but was miraculously wedged just above the altar instead of falling on the priest saying Mass. The boulder finally crashed through in 1910, and the church was closed until recently for fear of further rockfalls.

Towards the foot of the lake, **ANGERA** is a sizeable village with a small, quiet beach dominated by an imposing twelfth-century castle, the **Rocca** (March–Oct daily 10.30am–12.30pm & 4–6pm; L8000/€4.13), more appealing for the character it gives the shore than for the self-congratulatory Visconti frescoes inside – battle scenes celebrating their seizure of the Rocca from the Torriani family. Little did the Viscontis know that just over 100 years later they would lose the castle to the pious and powerful Borromeo family, who ended up owning much of the lake and producing Milan's saint, Charles Borromeo.

Lago d'Orta

The locals call **Lago d'Orta** "Cinderella", capturing perfectly the reticent beauty of this small lake with its deep blue waters and intriguing island. Orta is on the books of several package-holiday companies, as well as being a popular target for the weekend-long passeggiata that occurs from Easter onwards, but nevertheless is perhaps the only place on the lakes which really has retained a faded nineteenth-century charm. Try, if you can, to go mid-week or out of season.

Orta San Giulio and the hinterland

Occupying the tip of a peninsula on the lake's eastern shore, **ORTA SAN GIULIO** is a romantic little town where narrow cobbled streets run between pastel-washed houses and palaces with elaborate wrought-iron balconies. It is, not surprisingly, Lago d'Orta's main attraction, and on summer Sundays the approach roads hum with traffic and the alleyways with day-trippers. Life centres on two piazzas: **Piazzetta Ernesto Ragazzoni**, and **Piazza Motta** – open to the lake and looking directly on to Isola San Giulio – where visitors congregate in three *gelaterie* (of which *Venus* is the best). Somewhat out of place among the pavement cafés is the **Palazzo della Comunità**, Orta's diminutive town hall, decorated with faded frescoes and supported on an arcaded loggia. From the piazza you can walk out of the village along Via Giovanetti to a lakeside promenade popular with smooching couples, or catch a boat to the island (see below). Above the town is the **Sacro Monte**, 21 chapels dedicated to St Francis of Assisi and containing some awful tableaux of painted terracotta statues acting out scenes from the saint's life against frescoed B-movie backgrounds. They make up a devotional route still followed by pilgrims, though as many visitors come simply to picnic, admire the views of the lake and inhale the pine-scented air.

Orta San Giulio's **tourist office** is just out of town, up the hill on Via Panoramica (Tues–Sat 9am–noon & 3–6pm, Sun 10am–noon & 3–5pm; ☎0322.905.614); it's well organized, with bus timetables as well as information on hotels. **Accommodation** in Orta San Giulio is pricey, but one of the better (and cheaper) places to stay is the *Olina* (☎0322.905.656, fax ☎0322.905.645; ④), at Via Olina 40 in the village centre, offering reliably comfortable rooms and with one of the Orta's best restaurants downstairs; it also has apartments in the village for longer stays, with weekly rates starting at L490,000/€253.06. If you can't get into the *Olina*, a double at the three-star *Santa Caterina*, a large, cream-coloured villa at Via Marconi 10 (☎0322.915.875, fax 0322.915.865; ④), will cost you the same; turn left out of the train station and head downhill – it's about a five-minute walk.

Finding **snack** food is a challenge, but the *Pizzeria Campana*, just off the main piazza at Via Giovanetti 41, isn't bad for simple dishes as well as pizza and has a neighbourly bar frequented by locals. *Bar Edera*, signposted off Via Olina, does reasonably priced crepes, *piadine* and *pizzette*. With more to spend, you'll eat very well at the **restaurant** below the hotel *Olina* (closed Wed), which serves excellent local specialities and thoughtful extras like aperitifs on the house; just beyond Piazzetta Ragazzoni in the *centro storico*, the *Antico Agnello*, Via Olina 18 (booking advised at weekends, ☎0322.90.259; closed Tues), is equally good, with Lombard dishes, great puddings and congenial service.

Isola San Giulio

Orta's highlight is the **Isola San Giulio**, a tiny island-village dominated by a severe white seminary and the tower of its twelfth-century basilica. Boats leave every fifteen minutes, and the return journey costs L4000/€2.07; the last boat back is at 7.30pm. The San Giulio of the town and island was a priest who in 390 AD decided to found a sanctuary on the island. The locals refused to row him over, as the island was supposedly seething with monsters and snakes, and Giulio is said to have crossed on foot using his staff as a rudder and his cloak as a sail. Once there, he banished the snakes, founded his sanctuary and earned himself a sainthood. The **Basilica** (May–Sept Mon–Sat 9.30–10.45am & 2–6.45pm, Sun 9.30am–12.15pm & 2–6.45pm; Oct–March closes 5.30pm) has a redoubtable black marble pulpit, carved with venomous-looking griffins and serpents, recalling the myth. The massive vertebrae in the sacristy is said to have belonged to one of the island's dragons; scientists reckon it's a whalebone.

The Varesotto

The **Varesotto** is the least attractive but richest of the lake provinces, a major industrial region that produces everything from shoes and silk to helicopters. Its three small lakes are badly polluted, and, lying blandly on the plain, cannot compete with nearby

Maggiore and Como for scenic splendour. The provincial capital, **Varese**, is worthy of a place on your itinerary only if you have to make train or bus connections, or want to visit the province's more interesting pickings at **Castiglione Olona** or **Castelseprio**.

Varese

VARESE is a gracious purpose-built town of gardens, marble Fifties villas and rectangular Fascist-era buildings, fringed with shoe factories. Its inhabitants are every bit as obsessed with style as the Milanese and look almost as perfect as the window-display mannequins in the designer shops that line the main street, Corso Matteotti.

The centre of town is **Piazza Monte Grappa**, not far from the city's main attraction, the formal gardens around the long, pink **Palazzo Estense**, built in the eighteenth century for the Este Dukes of Modena (daily 8am–sunset, until 11pm July & Aug; free). The *raison d'être* of modern Varese is to provide alternative accommodation for the thousands who visit Milan's trade fairs, especially the fashion shows in April and October. Consequently, the majority of the **hotels** are aimed at an expense-account clientele, though there are a half-dozen two-stars in the price category ③ range, and a cheaper option in the shape of the *Stadio*, Via Bolchini 24 (☎0332.224.069; ②), which also has rooms for up to four people – there's also a reasonably priced restaurant next door. For inexpensive meals and snacks such as roast beef and fresh salads, there's *Bistrot* on the corner of Via Manzoni and Via Mazzini. The **tourist office** at Via Carobbio 2 (June–Sept Mon–Fri 9am–12.30pm & 3.15–7pm, Sat 9am–12.30pm & 3–6pm; Oct–May Mon–Fri 9am–12.30pm & 3–6.30pm, Sat 9am–12.30pm) can give the full picture.

Castiglione Olona and Castelseprio

One of the best excursions you can make from Varese is to **CASTIGLIONE OLONA**, a Renaissance-style village just twenty minutes by bus from Varese's Piazza Kennedy (#B45), built by Cardinal Branda Castiglione in the fifteenth century and inspired by the architecture he had seen in Florence. Masolino, a pupil of Masaccio, created the limpid frescoes you can see in the hilltop **Collegiata** and its **baptistry**. And there are more frescoes in the **Casa dei Castiglioni** on the sleepy main square, including one of Vezprem, Hungary, as described to Masolino by the cardinal, who was bishop there for a while. Castiglione Olona livens up on the first Sunday in the month, when an antiques market is held.

Further along the #B45 bus route, **CASTELSEPRIO** is less attractive but worth visiting for its intriguing seventh-century church, **Santa Maria Foris Portas**, which has exotic Byzantine-style frescoes of *Christ's Infancy*, discovered during the last war by a partisan hiding in the church.

North of Varese: hiking routes

More attractive than the three lakes near Varese is **Lago di Ghirla**, a tarn deep in a valley, the Valganna, near the Swiss border. There's a **campsite** on the side away from the B37 road and plenty of opportunities for stiff hikes – it's best to avoid going on the weekends in summer though, when the area is very crowded.

There are a number of other country and forest **treks** to the north of Varese, the most interesting of which is the haul across to Maccagno on Lago Maggiore (see p.199). The walk starts at Porto Ceresio at the foot of Lago Lugano near the Swiss border and takes ten days; you could, though, pick it up at any point along the route. The booklet *Via Verde Varesina*, available only in Italian from local bookshops, is useful for information on how to get to starting-points on public transport and for places to eat and stay over; its maps, however, are poor, and unless you can read its route descriptions you'll need to buy a decent map as well.

Lago di Como

Of all the Italian lakes, it's the forked **Lago di Como** that comes most heavily praised. Wordsworth thought it "a treasure which the earth keeps to itself", though what he would think of the place now is anyone's guess: the lake is still surrounded by abundant vegetation but it can get very busy and the principal towns of **Como** and **Lecco** are not these days particularly attractive destinations. At times, though, as you're zigzagging up the lake on a steamer, it can seem almost ridiculously romantic, and if you want to do more than indulge in *belle époque* dreams, you could try one of several great walks through the lake's mountainous hinterland – and in most places the water is clean enough for swimming. Of the lake's other towns and villages, three are outstanding: **Varenna** and **Bellagio** for unrepentant romantics and **Menaggio** if you want a pleasant, affordable base for walking, swimming or cycling.

Como Town

COMO can be a dispiriting place to arrive, with none of the picture-postcard prettiness you may be expecting from a lakeside town. As the nearest resort to Milan and a popular stopoff on the main road into Switzerland, it's both heavily touristed – though the atmosphere doesn't feel as forced as in some of the other lake towns as many of the tourists are Italian – and, on the outskirts at least, fairly industrialized. Apart from tourism, the main industry is a rarefied one – Como is the main silk-supplier for Milan's fashion designers – but it doesn't make its factories any more endearing. If you have time to spare, the old town is not a bad place to wander or eat in, and the funicular ride has great views across the lake, but really you'd do best using the town as a transport hub and moving on to one of the lake's more attractive resorts.

Lakeside **Piazza Cavour** is a bleak space bounded by ugly metal-and-glass hotels and banks with a couple of pricey pavement cafés. To the left is a little lakeside park set around a curious temple, now the **Museo Alessandro Volta** (April–Sept Tues–Sun 10am–noon & 3–6pm; Oct–March 10am–noon & 2–4pm; L4000/€2.07), dedicated to Como's most useful son, a pioneer in electricity who gave his name to the volt – some of the instruments he used to conduct his experiments are displayed inside.

Beyond, compellingly illuminated at night, is the **Villa Olmo**, an eighteenth-century Neoclassical pile in magnificent grounds. The villa itself is a popular venue for congresses, but when the villa is delegate-free the **gardens** are open to the public (Mon–Sat 9am–noon & 3–6pm). From Piazza Cavour Via Plinio leads up to the **Broletto**, prettily striped in pink, white and grey, and with a fifteenth-century balcony designed for municipal orators. Next door, the splendid **Duomo** (daily: summer 7.30am–noon & 3–7pm; winter 7am–noon & 3–7pm) was begun at the end of the fourteenth century but wasn't completed until the eighteenth, when the Baroque genius Juvarra added the cupola. The church is reckoned to be Italy's best example of Gothic-Renaissance fusion: the Gothic spirit clear in the fairy-tale pinnacles, rose windows and buffoonish gargoyles; that of the Renaissance in its portals (with rounded rather than ogival arches) and in the presence of the two pagans flanking the main west door – the Elder and Younger Plinys, both of whom were born in Como. There was nothing unusual in the sequestration of classical figures by Christians in the Renaissance, but the presence, especially of Pliny Junior, does seem somewhat inappropriate, since his only connection with Christianity was to order the assassination of two deaconesses. Inside, the Gothic aisles are hung with rich Renaissance tapestries (some woven with perspective scenes) and if you've a few spare coins you could illuminate a heavy-lidded Leonardesque *Madonna* and an *Adoration of the Magi* by Luini, and a languid *Flight to Egypt* by Gaudenzio Ferrari.

The second of Como's churches, the Romanesque **Sant'Abbondio**, left along Via Regina from the main train station, struggles to hold its own in a dreary suburb. Built in the eleventh century, it was stripped of later encrustations in the nineteenth century and returned to its original simplicity. Once inside you can forget the brutal surroundings as you wander down the serene aisles to the apse with its colourful fourteenth-century frescoes, the most appealing of which depicts the Magi dreaming of Christ under striped and patterned blankets.

If you have time, head down to the lake shore to the right of Piazza Cavour, by Como Lago station, and take a **funicular** (roughly every thirty minutes 6am–10.30pm; L7000/€3.62) up to **Brunate**, a small hilltop resort that's a good starting-point for hikes and has great views up the lake.

Practicalities

Como has three **train stations**: Como San Giovanni, on the main line from Chiasso to Milan, and Como Borghi and Como Lago, from where trains run to Milan Nord, Saronno, Varese Nord and Novara Nord. Como Lago is, as its name suggests, on the lake shore, opposite the **ferry jetty** and across the road from the **bus station**. Como San Giovanni, ten minutes' walk from the lake and old centre, is connected with the jetty (and the bus station across the road) by buses #4 and #7. Como Borghi is on the southern side of the town centre, a short walk down Via Sirtori from Viale Battisti. Como San Giovanni has a small **tourist office**, but the main office is situated on Piazza Cavour (Oct–May Mon–Sat 9am–1pm & 2.30–6pm, Sun 9.30am–12.30pm; June–Sept Mon–Sat same hours, Sun 2.30–6pm; ☎031.269.712, *www.lakecomo.com*).

Como's **youth hostel** is at the *Villa Olmo*, Via Bellinzona 2 (☎031.573.800; L16,000/€8.26; March–Nov); it also serves dinner (L15,000/€7.75), has laundry facilities, rents out bikes, and can get you a discount on the funicular. To get there take bus #1 or #6 from Como San Giovanni or walk for twenty minutes along Via Borgo Vico (on the left as you walk down the steps from the main train station). An alternative for women is the *Ostello per la Protezione della Giovane* at Via Borgo Vico 182 (☎031.573.540; L21,000/€10.85). Grotty as Via Borgo Vico is, it also holds some of the town's cheaper **hotels** and is close enough to Como San Giovanni. The *Sole*, at Via Borgo Vico 91, is about as rough and ready as they come in Como (☎031.573.382; ②); for around the same price, you could stay more centrally at the nicely positioned but very basic *Teatro Sociale*, in a fine arcade right by the duomo at Via Maestri Comacini 8 (☎031.264.042; ②). Prices rise abruptly in the two-star bracket, but the *Fontana*, behind Piazza Cavour at Via D. Fontana 19 (☎ & fax 031.271.110; ④), is at least a fairly central choice.

The liveliest of the cheaper **places to eat** is *La Scuderia*, Piazza Matteotti 4 (closed Tues), right next to the bus station; the pizzas here are pretty standard, so go for something simple. Alternatively, try the *Osteria del Gallo* at Via Vitani 16, centrally located and good value. Opposite the duomo in the restaurant of *Teatro Sociale* (see above), at Via Maestri Comacini, you can get a good set meal for L30,000/€15.49. If you crave something sweet, try the pastries at *Belli* on Via Vittorio Emanuele, or the ice creams at *Bolla* on Via Pietro Boldoni.

The western shore

The first port-of-call by steamer on the **western shore** of Lake Como is **CERNOBBIO** (also accessible by frequent bus from Como's Piazza Matteotti), whose main claim to fame is the nearby **Villa d'Este** hotel (☎031.34.81, fax 031.348.844, *www.villadeste.it*; ⑨), a palatial sixteenth-century confection in an opulent garden which has for some time ranked among Europe's most luxurious hotels. Greta Garbo once stayed, and it still manages to fill itself with guests willing to pay for the chance to wander like Garbo among the statues, fountains and grottoes of its extravagant gardens. If your pockets aren't up to this, you'll have to content yourself with glimpses of its gardens from the steamer.

Although pleasant enough, Cernobbio is otherwise pretty undistinguished, though it has a good waterfront market on Wednesdays and Sundays, and a **Lido** (summer Tues–Sat 8.30am–6pm), should you fancy spending a day at the poolside. It is also the starting-point for the 130-kilometre trail through the mountains on Como's west shore, known as the *Via dei Monti Lariani*. The **tourist office**, Via Regina 33b (Mon–Sat 10am–1pm & 4–8pm; ☎031.510.198), has maps and booklets detailing the route and the various *rifugi* along the way.

At **TORNO** on the opposite shore, where the steamer also stops, you'll find the **Villa Pliniana**, which was built in the sixteenth century on the site of one of Pliny the Younger's many villas. A spring behind it feeds a pool, and still gushes out at six-hour intervals as Pliny Jnr described it. Rossini composed here, and Shelley tried to rent the place, describing it as magnificent but in ruins with "ill-furnished apartments".

Further up the western shore, **ARGEGNO**'s lakeside cafés screen a hilly village of ancient houses with wooden eaves protruding over steep stepped alleyways. Served by regular ferries, it's a convenient base, as well as a peaceful place to potter around. The cheapest of Argegno's three **hotels** is *La Griglia*, at Via Milano 14 (☎031.821.147; ②); otherwise there's the *Argegno*, on the lakefront (☎031.821.455; ③), or the most expensive option of the *Lago Belvedere*, at Via Milano 8 (☎031.821.116; ④).

Ferries move on from Argegno to the **Isola Comacina**, Como's only island. Anything further removed from the greenery of Maggiore's islands would be hard to imagine. Comacina, uninhabited save for a handful of artists, is a wild place where you can wander through the ruins of nine abandoned churches. One of the earliest settlements on the lake, it was conquered by the Romans, and, later, when the barbarians invaded, it became a refuge for the wealthy citizens of Como. It developed into a centre of resistance, and in the turmoil of the Middle Ages, attracted an eclectic mix of dethroned monarchs, future saints and the pirate Federico Barbarossa. Eventually it allied with Milan against Como, an unfortunate move which led to the island being sacked by Como and razed to the ground. Abandoned for centuries, it was eventually bought by a local, Auguste Caprini, who outraged Italy by selling it to the King of Belgium after World War I. Diplomatically, the king decided to return it, and the island is now administered by a joint Belgian/Italian commission, who built three houses there for artists.

Incongruously, the island has been home since 1947 to an extremely exclusive restaurant, the *Locanda dell'Isola*, whose former clients range from Arnold Schwarzenegger and Sylvester Stallone to Ursula Andress and the Duchess of Kent. If you don't wish to spend all your budget on one meal, bring a picnic, as the snack bar by the jetty overcharges even for simple sandwiches.

The Tremezzina

Sheltered by a headland, the shore above Isola Comacina, known as the **Tremezzina**, is where Como's climate is at its gentlest, the lake at its most tranquil and the vegetation at its most lush. Lined with cypresses and palms, it's lovely at any time of year, but unbeatable in spring, when it's awash with colour and heady with the scent of flowering bushes.

LENNO, in the south of the Tremezzina, is the site of another of Pliny the Younger's villas, from which, he reported, he could fish from his bedroom window. Just inland at **MEZZEGRA**, in 1944, two families of evacuees staying at the Villa Belmonte witnessed a rather different scene from their windows. A car drew up and a burly man in a black beret, nervously clutching the lapels of his coat, got out, followed by a woman and a tall pale man with a machine gun. The burly man was Mussolini, the woman his mistress,

Claretta Petacci, and the tall man the partisan leader, Walter Audisio. Audisio pulled the trigger and Claretta flew at him, grasping the barrel of the gun; Audisio shot twice more, but the trigger jammed. He took his driver's machine gun and pointed it at Mussolini, who said "Shoot me in the chest"; Audisio shot first at Claretta, killing her outright, and then complied with Mussolini's last request.

TREMEZZO, like Como's other resorts, has its fair share of *belle époque* palaces, villas and hotels, but overall it's a sedate, rather middle-aged resort. Although you might want to move on to somewhere livelier, it's a pleasant place to pause before or after visiting the Villa Carlotta (see below). The best lunch-spot is *Jookjoint*, on the lakefront, which does brilliant sandwiches. If you do want to sleep here, choose between the *Darsena* (☎0344.40.423; ②) at the waterfront on the southern edge of the village or the slightly more expensive *Azalea* (☎0344.40.424; ②), though both suffer traffic noise from the main road around the lake.

A couple of minutes' walk north along the lakeside road is the **Villa Carlotta** (daily: April–Sept 9am–6pm; March & Oct 9–11.30am & 2–4.30pm; L12,000/€6.20), which has its own *imbarcadero* between Tremezzo and Cadenabbia (see below). Pink, white and Neoclassical, it was built by a Prussian princess for her daughter, Carlotta, and now houses a collection of pompous eighteenth-century statues, including Canova's meltingly romantic *Cupid & Psyche* and a frieze of Alexander entering Babylon commissioned by Napoleon – though he was exiled before he could pay for it. The bill was picked up by a count, who in return got himself included as a member of Alexander's army (he's at the end, along with the artist). The villa's greatest attraction, however, is the fourteen-acre **garden**, a beautifully ordered collection of camellias, rhododendrons and azaleas.

CADENABBIA, five minutes' walk north of the villa, has little to hold you – it's a rather downmarket resort that lacks Tremezzo's architectural panache. Head instead to **MENAGGIO** a few kilometres further on, a bustling village and lively resort that is a good base for hiking and cycling in the mountains as well as sunbathing and swimming. The **ferry jetty** is about five minutes' walk from the main square, Piazza Garibaldi, in and around which you'll find most of Menaggio's lakeside cafés and restaurants. The **tourist office** here (Mon–Sat 9am–noon & 3–6pm; ☎0344.32.924) is unusually well organized, with practical information on the town and maps on walks in the area. Swimming in the lake is safe here, and there's a beach and vast pool at the **Lido** (late-June to mid-Sept daily 9am–7pm), as well as **water-skiing** and other waterborne activities at the Centro Lago Service on Via Lago Castelli (☎0344.32.003).

If you decide to stay, Menaggio's **youth hostel**, the *Ostello La Primula*, Via IV Novembre 86 (☎0344.32.356, fax 0344.31.677; L17,000/€8.78; mid-March to mid-Nov), is just outside the village, overlooking the main road; bookings are encouraged. A happening place, it rents out **bikes** by the day, organizes hikes and language courses, and can arrange discounts on horse-riding and boat rental, and at the Lido, as well as serving excellent three-course meals for about L15,000/€7.75. The more convenient of the two **campsites** is the *Lido* (☎0344.31.150; May–Sept); the other, the *Europa* (☎0344.31.187; April–Sept), is slightly further out on the road heading north. If you need a **hotel**, try the *Garni Corona* on Largo Cavour (☎0344.32.006; ②), next to Piazza Garibaldi with views over the lake, or the rooms above the *Vapore* restaurant (☎0344.32.229; ②) just off the same piazza – the **restaurant** itself (closed Wed) has reasonably priced meals (including a standard tourist menu). Another good choice for simple meals is *Trattoria da Gino* (no closing day), Via Camozzi 16, while *La Paolino* (no closing day), on the lakefront near Piazza Garibaldi, is good but more expensive and has no set menu. The gelateria at Via Camozzi 22 makes its own ice cream, and the *Garni Corona* (see above) serves a good *frullati* and apple pie. Menaggio is a treasure trove for self-caterers, with a couple of big supermarkets and some excellent delicatessens, plus a *tavola calda* on the main road through town.

There's a good selection of **hikes** to be done around Menaggio, ranging from a two-and-a-half hour walk to the pretty village of **CARDANO**, to the fifty-kilometre *Sentiero delle 4 Valli*, which leads through four valleys to Lago Lugano. The tourist office has descriptions of routes in English, including details of how to get to the various starting-points on public transport, but take a map as well.

The north

The next major steamer stop is **GRAVEDONA**, not a particularly pretty place but one of the few towns on the lake as old as Como. Wordsworth set off on a moonlight hike from here, got lost, and, stuck on a rock in the middle of nowhere, was unable to sleep because he was "tormented by the stings of insects". Medieval Gravedona, along with nearby Dongo and Sorico, formed part of an independent republic, victimized in the fifteenth century by the inquisitor Peter of Verona for daring to doubt that the pope was God's earthly representative. The people got rid of Peter by hacking him to death, but the pope rewarded him for his devotion to duty by swiftly canonizing him and deeming him Patron of Inquisitors. There's a prophetic twelfth-century carving in the lakeside church of **Santa Maria del Tiglio** (open July–Sept, at other times get the key from the green house on the road) – a centaur pursuing a deer, an early Christian symbol for the persecution of the Church.

If you want to stay over, the *Locanda Serenella* (☎0344.89.452; ②) and the *Serenella* **campsite**, beyond the church and down towards the lake, are both open from April to September or October. Beyond Gravedona the lake sides flatten out and the building gets more haphazard, although as the winds are good for **sailing** and **windsurfing** there are a number of **campsites** and cheap, modern **hotels** to the north of **DOMASO** – a not unattractive small town.

The northeastern shore, Bellagio and Lecco and the central zone

The **eastern shore** of the lake, stretching from the flat marshes of the north to Como's left branch, **Lago Lecco**, overshadowed by the saw-like ridge of Monte Resegone, is often sunless and consequently less visited than the western shore. The triangle of land between the two branches – the **central zone** – is lusher and sunnier, busy on the coast but with plenty of quiet villages and three small lakes inland. There are fewer places to stay, however, and these are not easily accessible, except Colico, Bellano and Varenna on the main shore and Bellagio on the central triangle, which are all served by steamer and hydrofoil.

The northeastern shore

At the top end of the lake's eastern shore – opposite Gravedona – **COLICO** is the final stop for Como steamers, a small industrial centre whose only attraction is a restored eleventh-century abbey, the **Abbazia di Piona**, on the tip of the promontory just above the steamer landing. From here, steamers and hydrofoils head back down the eastern shore, stopping off at **BELLANO**, a tiny town of silk and cotton mills, near to which is a steep gorge with walkways (Easter–Sept daily 9.30am–1pm & 2.30–7.30pm; Oct–Nov Thurs, Sat & Sun 10am–1pm & 3–6.30pm), suspended above a roaring river.

Further south, **VARENNA** is a relaxed, immediately likeable place, shaded by pines and planes, and almost completely free of souvenir shops. If you are feeling energetic, you could haul up the hill to the **Castello de Vezio**, allegedly founded by the Lombard Queen Theodolinda, for some great views. If you're not, it's a short walk south, past the **tourist office** on Piazza San Giorgio (May–Sept Mon–Sat 9.30am–12.30pm & 3.30–6.30pm; ☎0341.830.367), along the main road to the **Villa Cipressi**, a nineteenth-century villa now occupied by a hotel. For L3000/€1.55 (or L5000/€2.58 including

Monastero, see below) you get access to its gardens (March–Oct daily 9am–6.30pm), which are voluptuously terraced and swooningly scented enough to make even die-hard cynics gush. After this, the gardens of the **Villa Monastero** next door (April 15–Oct daily 10am–noon & 2–6.30pm; L3000/€1.55, or L5000/€2.58 for this and Cipressi) seem tame, so it's no great hardship, if, as often happens, they are closed for conferences. Continue along the road for about a kilometre and you'll come to the small village of **FIUMELATTE**, which is named after the waterfall which froths its way through the centre in winter and spring – though it's a rather disappointing dribble in summer.

If you've got the cash, it's easy to be seduced into **staying** in Varenna at the *Villa Cipressi* (☎0341.830.113; ⑤) and, although the bedrooms are more ascetic than you might imagine, the public rooms are superb. Other attractive options include the *Milano*, overlooking the water, just off the main square (☎0341.830.298; ⑤), and *Olivedo*, directly opposite the *imbarcadero* (☎0341.830.115; ③); the latter is Victorian in style, stuffed with old prints and knick-knacks. There are no budget options in Varenna but the cheapest and perfectly comfortable – if a little garish – rooms are in the friend-ly *Albergo Beretta* on Via per Esino 1 (☎ & fax 0341.830.132; ③) just up the road from the Lido. The best place to **eat** is *Vecchia Varenna*, hidden in the arcades along the lake-side promenade (closed Mon) – though it's not cheap, you may be tempted by such classic dishes as *gnocchi* with game sauce and trout with pine nuts. For snacks, *Il Mole*, a little further round the bay, is very pleasant, and has a good selection of salads.

Bellagio
Cradled by cypress-spiked hills on the tip of the triangle separating Como's two "legs", **BELLAGIO** has been called the most beautiful town in Italy. With a promenade plant-ed with oleanders and limes, *fin-de-siècle* hotels painted shades of butterscotch, peach and cream, and a hilly old centre of steep cobbled streets and alleyways – to say noth-ing of its tremendous location – it's certainly a contender.

The lake is clean enough to swim in here, which you can do from the **Lido** (Easter–Oct daily 8am–midnight) at the end of the promenade, or if you can't stand the piped music, do as the local kids do and have a dip at the tiny harbour less than 1km out of town in the other direction; follow the signs to the *Ristorante La Punta*. The gar-dens of the **Villa Melzi** behind (April–Oct daily 9am–6.30pm; L5000/€2.58) are no great shakes, but it's well worth making the effort to book onto a guided tour around the gorgeous gardens of the **Villa Serbelloni**, splendidly sited on a hill above the town. Built on the site of one of Pliny the Younger's villas, it is now owned by the Rockefeller Foundation, and is perhaps the best place to appreciate Bellagio's genteel English air. It was once a favourite haunt of European monarchs, and it's not hard to imagine them strolling among the grottoes and statues of the extravagant garden and gushing over the views of the two branches of the lake. The sumptuously frescoed interior is closed to visitors, but there are guided tours around the **gardens** (April–Oct Tues–Sun 11am & 4pm; book at the tourist office; L6000/€3.10). At the foot of the hill is a classy hotel, also called *Villa Serbelloni* (☎031.950.216, fax 031.951.529, *www.villaserbelloni.it*; ⑨), whose guests numbered Churchill, recovering from the war in late 1945, and John F. Kennedy.

Bellagio's **tourist office**, on Piazza della Chiesa (Easter–Oct daily 9am–noon & 3–6pm; Nov–Easter Mon & Wed–Sat same hours; ☎031.950.204, *www.fromitaly.net /bellagio*), is a helpful source of information. If you're **staying**, the least expensive rooms are at the *Suisse*, Piazza Mazzini 8 (☎031.950.335; ②), a slightly down-at-heel hotel on the lakefront, boasting a fine restaurant. Alternatively try the *Giardinetto*, Via Roncati 12 (☎031.950.168; ②; March–Oct), with a garden where you can picnic, or *Il Perlo Panoramico* (☎031.950.229; ③; March–Oct), with views of the lake. If you have your own transport, you could opt for *La Pergola* (☎031.950.263, fax 031.950.253; ⑤), set in a stunning location in Pescallo, just over the hill to the Lecco arm of the lake – and with a good restaurant.

Bellagio's **restaurants** range from cheap snack bars to pricey establishments that cater to the beautiful people. For snacks and light meals, try *La Lanterna* at Salita Serbelloni 15 (closed Thurs), an animated hangout that serves pasta, omelettes and sandwiches. For an excellent pizza, head for *La Grotta*, Salita Cernaia 14 (closed Mon), clearly signposted from the lakefront. A cheap, full meal can be had at the *Bistro del Ritorno*, Via E. Vitali 8, which does a good-value menu, but if money's no object, splash out at *Bilacus*, on Salita Serbelloni, which is reckoned to be the town's best restaurant. Another good bet is *La Punta* (☎031.951.888; you'll need to book at weekends and in high season), which serves excellent food at good prices and offers lovely views over the lake. The best places for ice cream are *Il Sorbetto* at the top of Salita Serbelloni, and the *Gelateria del Borgo* at Via Garibaldi 46. **Nightlife** in Bellagio centres on a couple of trendy bars: *Divina Commedia*, an American-style bar and creperie, clearly signposted off Via Garibaldi (closed Wed), frescoed with *putti*, poppies and dippy blond angels, where they also do good food; and the similarly styled *Spiritual Café*, a music and video bar at Salita Plinio 12 (closed Wed).

Lecco and around

Flanked by mountains of scored granite, Como's eastern fork is austere and fjord-like, at its most atmospheric in the morning mists. The villages wedged along the shoreline are far more workaday than those of the rest of the lake, and **LECCO**, at its foot, is a frantic commercial centre. You almost certainly won't want to stay in Lecco, but its public transport connections are good, and there are some challenging hikes in the nearby mountains. Trains run to Como, Milan and Bergamo, and back up the eastern shore by way of Varenna to Sondrio, and there are buses into the mountain villages. **Buses** leave from outside the **train station**, from where it's a brisk five-minute walk to the **ferry station** (go straight down the central street, Via Cavour, and across Piazza Garibaldi, to the shore and turn right). Lecco's business-like **tourist office** is on Via N. Sauro, off Piazza Garibaldi (Mon–Sat 9am–12.30pm & 2.30–6.30pm; June same hours plus Sun 9am–12.30pm; ☎0341.362.360, *www.cot.it*). If you need to **stay**, the only central hotel is the *Moderno* on Piazza Diaz, outside the train station (☎0341.286.519; ③). There are a number of **snack bars** and pizzerias around the station, though none of them is particularly special.

If you've time to kill you could pop into Lecco's **Basilica**, which boasts a set of fourteenth-century Giottesque frescoes, and the birthplace of Alessandro Manzoni, author of the great nineteenth-century novel *I Promessi Sposi* ("The Betrothed"). The **Villa Manzoni**, on Via Amendola (head left out of the station along Via Sassi then Via Marconi), is open as a museum (Tues–Sun 9.30am–2pm; L5000/€2.58).

Above Lecco at the end of the road to **MALNAGA** a **cable car** – and paths #1, #7 and #18 – climb up to the **Piani d'Erna**, from where trails lead further into the mountains. Alternatively, buses from outside the train station run up to **PIANI RESINELLI**, another starting-point for hikes. These are not Sunday afternoon strolls, however, and unless you are experienced, you really should get hold of a reliable walking book as well as a good map before you go. Many of the walks involve scaling a *via ferrata* (see box on p.238). Some stretches are vertical, and once you've started it's often impossible to turn back – the *vie ferrate* are popular and there will probably be a queue behind you.

The Valchiavenna and Valtellina

Trains run north of Colico into the **Valchiavenna**, a flat-bottomed valley into which Lake Como extended right up until Roman times. It left behind the **Lago di Mezzola**

– not worth getting off the train for, but a pleasant enough distraction before you hit the rusty corrugated-iron buildings of Novate. Further on, you could stop at **CHIAVENNA**, at the end of the train line, to visit one of the many *crotti*, natural cellars in the rocks (across the rail line), which for centuries have been used for maturing wine, salami, cured meats and cheeses. Most are now inns and restaurants, the most authentic of which is the *Crotto Torricelli*, where you sit at granite tables. The town otherwise is nothing special, and the old centre definitely looks best when lit up at night, but there are interesting walks up to the **Marmitte dei Giganti**, potholes formed by glaciation. The cheapest **hotel** is the *Elvezia*, at Via Garibaldi 3 (☎0343.32.165; ②), but this is such a depressing place you might prefer to pay a little more and stay next door in the more civilized *Flora* at Via Don Guanella 10 (☎0343.32.254; ②). You'll see both hotels as soon as you step out of the train station. For a bit more, you can loll by the swimming pool and get the three-star treatment at the *Crimea*, Via Pratogiano 16 (☎0343.34.343; ③). From Chiavenna you can catch a bus to St Moritz in Switzerland, from where the *trenino rosso* (see below) takes a scenic mountain route back across the border to Tirano.

Unless you're a keen skier, or are heading for eastern Switzerland or Trentino, there's little to draw you to the **Valtellina**, east of Lake Como, one of Italy's less appealing Alpine valleys. Cut through by road and rail, it's mined for minerals and iron ore and is prone to landslides. The train continues up from Lake Como to the region's main centre, **SONDRIO**, a modern and undistinguished town, but well known for its wine, which is on sale in many of its shops. The **tourist office** is at Via C. Battisti 12 (☎0342.512.500), though distractions are few – apart from the **Museo Valtellinese** at Via del Gesù 8 (Mon 2.30–4.30pm, Tues–Fri 9am–noon & 2.30–4.30pm, Sat 9am–noon; free), a museum of local traditions with small art and archeological sections. You'd do better to catch a train on to **TIRANO**, a similarly bland town, but one which gives access to the private **RhB trenino rosso**, which follows a stunning route through the mountains to St Moritz in Switzerland. InterRail and Eurail passes are valid; otherwise the return journey costs around L50,000/€25.82 (depending on the exchange rate). If you wanted, you could pick up a bus in St Moritz and return to Italy via Chiavenna.

A prettier valley, the **Val Malenco**, runs off to one side of the Valtellina, and is easily accessible by bus from Sondrio. Head up as high as possible to the tiny village of **CHIAREGGIO**, where you can stay at *Locanda Pian del Lupo* (☎0342.451.601; ②) before heading off on a network of footpaths past brilliantly clear tarns, well served by mountain *rifugi*. The tourist office in Sondrio (see above) has details, including maps, or you could buy the local Kompass map.

Further up Valtellina from Tirano, to which it's connected by bus, **BORMIO** is a very prestigious but snooty and unfriendly ski resort that was once an important stopover on the trade routes between Venice and Switzerland. It still retains a core of cobbled streets and frescoed palaces from the fifteenth and sixteenth centuries within a sprawl of hotels for its many skiers: it hosted the 1985 World Alpine Ski Championships and is now one of Europe's largest areas for summer skiing. Close by, the huge **Parco Nazionale dello Stelvio** (see p.261) is a good place for walks and challenging climbs, as well as skiing. Details can be gleaned from the **tourist office** in Bormio at Via Roma 131b (Mon–Sat 9am–12.30pm & 2.30–6pm, Sun 9.30am–12.30pm; ☎0342.903.300) – where you can also pick up maps, details of *rifugi*, and information on the town – or from the national park **visitors' centre**, Via Monte Braulio 56 (Mon–Fri 9am–1pm & 2.30–6.30pm, only until 5pm on Fri; plus Sat & Sun in summer 9am–12.30pm & 2–7pm; ☎0342.910.100). If you're sleeping over in Bormio, the *Villa Rina*, at Via Milano 77 (☎0342.901.674; ②), has reasonable doubles, but prices vary greatly with the time of year.

Bergamo

Just 50km northeast of Milan, yet much closer to the mountains in look and feel, **BERGAMO** is a city with a split identity, made up of two distinct parts – **Bergamo Bassa**, the lower, more modern centre, and **Bergamo Alta**, clinging to the hill 1200 feet above the Lombardian plain. Bergamo Bassa is no great shakes, a mixture of suburbs and pompous Neoclassical town planning; but Bergamo Alta is one of northern Italy's loveliest city centres, a favourite retreat for the work-weary Milanese, who flock here at weekends seeking solace in its fresh mountain air, wanderable streets and the lively, but easy-going pace of its life.

Bergamo owes much of its magic to the Venetians, who ruled the town for over 350 years, building houses and palaces with fancy Gothic windows and adorning many a facade and open space with the Venetian lion – symbol of the republic. The most striking feature, however, is the ring of gated walls. Now worn, mellow and overgrown with creepers, these kept alien armies out until 1796, when French Revolutionary troops successfully stormed the city, throwing off centuries of Venetian rule.

Arrival, information and accommodation

The **train station** is right at the end of Bergamo Bassa's central avenue, Viale Giovanni XXIII, which becomes Via Vittorio Emanuele II. To the right are the two **bus stations**: the SAB, serving the northern mountains and valleys, and the Stazione Autolinee, serving all other destinations. Bus #1 runs from the train station to the **funicular station** at the foot of the hill, from where you can make the ascent by cable car to Piazza Mercato delle Scarpe for no extra charge as long as you show your bus ticket – otherwise it costs L1500/€0.78. Alternatively you can get bus #1A from Viale Papa Giovanni XXIII, along the central avenue and up to Bergamo Alta.

The **tourist office**, at Viale Vittorio Emanuele II 20 (Mon–Fri 9am–12.30pm & 2–5.30pm; ☎035.210.204, *www.bergamo.it*), is a ten-minute walk up from the train station and has maps and information on the town and province; there's also a second office up in Bergamo Alta at Vicolo Aquila Nera 2, off Piazza Vecchia (April–Oct daily 9am–12.30pm & 2–5.30pm; ☎035.232.730).

Bergamo is not somewhere to arrive on spec, even out of season: itinerant workers based in the new town's factories take up all the cheaper **accommodation**, and it's not unusual to discover that the only vacancies are in four-star hotels. Help is at hand in the form of the **youth hostel** (☎ & fax 035.361.724; L25,000/€12.91 per person for a family room or a dorm, L35,000/€18.08 per person for a double, triple or single room), which features breakfast included in the price, meals for L14,000/€7.23, bathrooms in every room, balconies, bicycles for hire (L15,000/€7.75 per day), a garden to flop in, and disabled-accessible facilities – there's also a great view of the *città alta*. To get to the hostel, take bus #14 from Porta Nuova, direction S. Colombana, and get off just after the modern church at the stop signposted for the *ostello* – it's at the top of the rather steep steps on the right.

Bergamo's cheaper **hotels** are in **Bergamo Bassa**, though with doubles at uninspiring one-star establishments clocking in around the ③ mark, it's all relative. West of the station, ten minutes' walk along Via Bonomelli, are the *Quarenghi*, Via Quarenghi 33 (☎035.319.914; ③), a dreary but friendly, family-run hotel that is pricey considering none of the rooms has a private bathroom; and the very shabby two-star *San Giorgio*, on Via San Giorgio 10, the continuation of Via Paleocapa (☎035.212.043; ③).

A better option is to dig deeper into your pockets and stay in one of the pleasanter hotels in **Bergamo Alta**: the *Agnello d'Oro*, Via Gombito 22 (☎035.249.883, fax

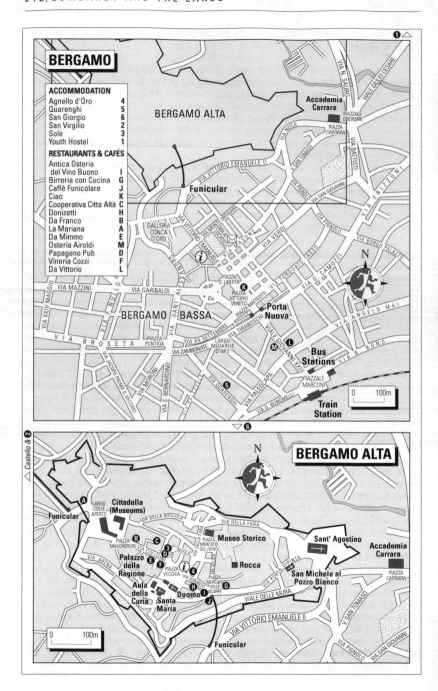

BERGAMO

ACCOMMODATION
Agnello d'Oro	4
Quarenghi	5
San Giorgio	6
San Virgilio	2
Sole	3
Youth Hostel	1

RESTAURANTS & CAFÉS
Antica Osteria del Vino Buono	I
Birreria con Cucina	G
Caffè Funicolare	J
Ciao	K
Cooperativa Citta Altà	C
Donizetti	H
Da Franco	B
La Mariana	A
Da Mimmo	E
Osteria Airoldi	M
Papageno Pub	D
Vineria Cozzi	F
Da Vittorio	L

035.235.612; ④), and the *Sole*, Via Rivola 2 (☎035.218.238; ④), are old traditional spots, and both have well-regarded restaurants to boot. There is also the option of the small, wonderfully positioned *San Vigilio*, Via San Vigilio 15 (☎035.253.179, fax 035.402.081; ⑤), near the castle at the top of the second funicular or on bus route #21 from Colle Aperto.

The City

However you get to Bergamo, you'll arrive in **BERGAMO BASSA**, which spreads north from the railway station in an uneasy blend of Neoclassical ostentation, Fascist severity and tree-lined elegance. At the heart of things, the mock-Doric temples of the **Porta Nuova** mark the entrance to **Sentierone**, a spacious piazza with gardens, surrounded by nineteenth-century arcades and frowned down upon by the **Palazzo di Giustizia**, built in the bombastic rectangular style of the Mussolini era. This is the liveliest part of the lower city, busy most of the day and especially during the evening passeggiata, but it has no great appeal, and you'd be wise to save your energy for **BERGAMO ALTA**, easily walkable using the **funicular** at the top end of Viale Vittorio Emanuele II, or by taking bus #1A from the train station, which drops you just inside the northwestern gate of Porta Alessandro at Largo Colle Aperto.

Bergamo Alta

From Piazza Mercato delle Scarpe, Via Gombito leads up to **Piazza Vecchia**, enclosed by a harmonious miscellany of buildings, ranging from wrought-iron-balconied houses containing cafés and restaurants to the opulent Palladian-style civic library. Stendhal rather enthusiastically dubbed the square "the most beautiful place on earth", and certainly it's a striking open space, the most imposing building the medieval **Palazzo della Ragione**, a Venetian-Gothic-style structure that stretches right across the piazza, lending a stagey feel to things, especially at night when the wrought-iron lamps are switched on. Court cases used to be heard under the open arcades that form the ground floor, and, following a guilty verdict, condemned criminals were exhibited there. The piazza itself was the scene of more joyous celebrations in 1797, when the French formed the Republic of Bergamo. A "tree of liberty" was erected, and the square, carpeted with tapestries, was transformed into an open-air ballroom in which – as a symbol of the new democracy – dances were led by an aristocrat partnered by a butcher.

To the right of the Palazzo della Ragione is the entrance to the massive **Torre Civica**, or Torre del Campanone, which you can ascend by lift (May to mid-Sept daily 10am–8pm, Fri & Sat until 10pm; mid-Sept to Oct Mon–Fri 9.30am–12.30pm & 2–7pm, Sat & Sun 10am–7pm; Nov–Feb Sat & Sun 10.30am–12.30pm & 2–6pm; March & April Wed–Sun 10.30am–12.30pm & 2–8pm; L2000/€1.03). Its fifteenth-century bell, which narrowly escaped being melted down by the Germans to make arms during World War II, still tolls every half-hour. Afterwards, walk through the palazzo's arcades to the **Piazza del Duomo** and the **Duomo** on the left – though this is of less interest than the church of **Santa Maria Maggiore** in front, a rambling Romanesque church garnished with a scalloped Gothic porch crowned by two loggias sheltering statues of saints. Inside, Santa Maria is an extraordinarily elaborate church, its ceiling marzipanned with ornament in the worst tradition of Baroque excess, encrusted with gilded stucco, painted vignettes and languishing statues. There's a piece of nineteenth-century kitsch too – a monument to Donizetti, the Bergamo-based composer of highly popular romantic comedies with memorable melodies and predictable plots who died from syphilis here in 1848. As the town's most famous son, his death was much grieved, and bas-relief *putti* stamp their feet and smash their lyres in misery over the event. More subtly, the intarsia biblical scenes on the choir stalls – designed by Lotto, and executed by a local craftsman – are remarkable not only for their intricacy but for the incredible colour-range of the natural wood.

Even the glitziness of Santa Maria is overshadowed by the Renaissance decoration of the **Cappella Colleoni** next door (April–Oct daily 9am–12.30pm & 2–6.30pm; Nov–March Tues–Sun 9am–12.30pm & 2–4.30pm). Built onto the church in the 1470s, the chapel is a gorgeously extravagant confection of pastel-coloured marble carved into an abundance of miniature arcades, balustrades and twisted columns, and capped with a mosque-like dome. Commissioned by Bartolomeo Colleoni, a Bergamo mercenary in the pay of Venice, it was designed by the Pavian sculptor Amadeo – responsible for the equally excessive Certosa di Pavia. The interior is almost as opulent, with a ceiling fres-coed in the eighteenth century by Tiepolo sheltering Colleoni's sarcophagus, encrust-ed with reliefs and statuettes, and topped with a gleaming gilded equestrian statue. There's also the more modest tomb of his daughter, Medea, who died aged 15. Note Colleoni's coat-of-arms on the gate as you enter, the smoothness of the third "testicle" (supposedly biologically true) bears witness to the local tradition that rubbing it will bring you luck.

Take a look, too, at the nearby **Baptistry** (visits by appointment, ☎035.210.223), removed from the interior of Santa Maria Maggiore in the seventeenth century when christenings were transferred to the duomo. After some time in storage it was eventu-ally reconstructed outside the **Aula della Curia** ("Bishop's Court"; Mon–Fri 9am–12.30pm; free), alongside the Cappella Colleoni, which contains thirteenth- and fourteenth-century frescoes of the life of Christ, including an odd scene in which Christ judges the damned, holding a dagger, Damocles-like, in his teeth. Behind, at the back of Santa Maria Maggiore, is the bulging and recently restored, although still closed to the public, **Tempietto di Santa Croce**, dating from the tenth century.

Leading out of Piazza Vecchia, **Via Colleoni** also memorializes Bartolomeo Colleoni; it's a narrow street but one of the upper city's main pedestrian thoroughfares, leading to the brink of Bergamo Alta and lined with pastry shops selling chocolate and marzi-pan cakes topped with birds (*uccelli*). **Luogo Pio Colleoni**, Via Colleoni 9–11 (May–July Sun 10am–1pm & 2–7pm; L1500/€0.78), was Colleoni's Bergamo resi-dence; it was also the headquarters of a charitable institution that he set up to provide dowries for poor women – the Venetians ruled that no woman could marry without one. Only two rooms of the original house still exist. The first displays the original Amadeo statues from the front of the Cappella Colleoni and some average frescoes depicting Colleoni; the second was once the meeting room for the charity's council members, who these days continue a modernized version of their good work from upstairs, giv-ing financial aid and lodgings to widows. Also upstairs, there's a small **museum** (visits by appointment only, ☎035.218.568) containing copies of Colleoni's arms; the originals were found when his tomb was opened. At the end of Via Colleoni, Piazza Mascheroni lies at the entrance to the **Cittadella**, a military stronghold built by Barnabo Visconti that originally occupied the entire western headland. The remaining buildings now house a small theatre and two **museums**: one of **archeology** (Tues–Sun 9am–12.30pm & 2.30–6pm; free) and the other of **natural history** (Tues–Fri 9am–12.30pm & 2.30–6pm, Sat & Sun 9am–7.30pm; free).

There are good views from here across the **Colle Aperto** (Open Hill) to Bergamo Bassa, though for really outstanding views you need to walk up to the **Castello**, perched on the summit of San Vigilio, which rises up from Porta Sant'Alessandro. A funicular operates in summer but the walk is pleasant, up a steep narrow road over-looking the gardens of Bergamo's most desirable properties, and past very attractive but rather pricey bars and restaurants. In the grounds of the castle there's a maze of underground passages to explore that used to run right down to Bergamo Alta. If you're interested in the subterranean world, there are **guided tours** of the tunnels under the Venetian wall (the wall that encloses Bergamo Alta) organized by the Gruppo

Speleologico Le Nottole (☎035.251.233; hours and price vary according to season and size of group).

Returning to the Colle Aperto, you can either walk back through the city or follow the old **walls** around its circumference – the whole circuit takes a couple of hours. The most picturesque stretch is between the Colle Aperto and Porta San Giacomo, from where a long flight of steps leads down into the lower city. Alternatively, returning through the upper city to Piazza Mercato delle Scarpe, you can turn down Via San Pancrazio and then into Piazza Mercato del Fieno, to see the **Museo Storico** (Tues–Sun 9.30am–4pm; free). Housed in the ex-convent of San Francesco, it currently spans the history of the city during the Unification and is relatively small, but there are plans to display the rest of the collection, which covers the last hundred years, as and when funds allow. Heading east from here you'll climb to Via Rocca, which leads up to the grounds of the **Rocca**, where there is little to attract your attention, apart from a view over eastern Bergamo, before you delve into the twisting streets of the **medieval quarter** below.

The Accademia Carrara

Just below the upper town, close to the city walls, the **Accademia Carrara** (Tues–Sun 9.30am–1pm & 2.30–7pm; L5000/€2.58) is one of Bergamo's most important sights and among Lombardy's best collections of art. You can walk down here from the old city, along the steep Via Porta Dipinta and through the Porta Sant'Agostino, to see portraits by Pisanello and Botticelli, works by Giovanni Bellini and Crivelli, Carpaccio and Lotto – all carefully and imaginatively displayed with the layperson in mind. There are also paintings by the Lombard realists Foppa and Bergognone, Spanish-style portraits by Moroni, an elegant idealized *St Sebastian* by Raphael and canvases by Titian and Palma il Vecchio. Don't miss the room dedicated to works by the twentieth-century Bergamo-born sculptor Giacomo Manzù, best known for his stylized bronzes of cardinals. While you're in this area, take a stroll across the road to the **Galleria d'Arte Moderna e Contemporanea** (prices and times vary according to each exhibition), which hosts top-quality touring exhibitions of work by twentieth-century artists and designers.

Eating and drinking

One of the pleasures of Bergamo is its food, easily enjoyable whether you're on a tight budget and restricted to assembling picnics from the many *salumerie* and bakeries in the old town, or can afford to graze around the city's terrific **osterie**. For some, one of the town's attractions are the local game-bird specialities (hunting and devouring the wildlife around Bergamo is a major occupation).

If you're on a tight budget the cheapest places for a sit-down meal are the university *mensa* on Via San Lorenzo, and the self-service restaurant *Ciao* at Piazza Vittorio Veneto 15 in Bergamo Bassa (10 percent discount with a card obtained from the youth hostel; closed Mon). Browsing around cafés and *osterie* is more fun, though. For **picnic food**, stock up on rustic-style pies at the Salumeria Mangili at Via Gombito 8, or on *pane greco* (bread topped with aubergine and tomato) from Forno tre Soldi, Via Colleoni 13a, and decadent pastries at Nessi, Via Gombito 34. You'll find the best **ice cream** in town under the luxuriant Bergamasc balconies of *La Mariana*, in the corner of Colle Aperto in the *città altà*.

Antica Osteria del Vino Buono, Piazza Mercato delle Scarpe, at the top of the funicular (☎035.247.993). Convivial osteria, offering a reasonably priced menu. Closed Mon.

Birreria con Cucina, Via Porta Dipinta 30b. Long, dark pub-like place in Bergamo Altà, serving snacks, pizzas and more substantial meals. Closed Mon.

Caffè Funicolare, in the funicular station on Piazza Mercato delle Scarpe. Serves good-value snacks, has a terrace with a great view. Stays open until 2am. Closed Tues.

Cooperativa Citta Altà, Vicolo Sant'Agata, clearly signposted off Via Colleoni. A cheery amalgam of café, canteen and bar open until 2am.This co-operative venture in Bergamo Altà boasts low prices, a happy hour on Thursdays, and a pergola where you can idle away the afternoon admiring the distant hills. Closed Wed.

Da Franco, Via Colleoni 8. Serves hearty polenta dishes and other local specialities with a good value set menu. Closed Mon.

Da Mimmo, Via Colleoni 17. Dishes up reasonably priced pizzas in rather plush surroundings with good views over the surrounding hillsides. Closed Tues.

Da Vittorio, Via Papa Giovanni XXIII 21 (☎ 035.218.222). This place has rightly been known as Bergamo's top restaurant for years and continues to serve first-rate cuisine at relatively reasonable prices. Closed Wed.

Donizetti, Via Gombito 17a. Excellent both for a slap-up meal and a *degustazione* platter of local meats and cheeses; its tables are laid out in a covered market space.

Osteria Airoldi, Viale Giovanni XXIII 18. Handily placed near the bus and train stations, this place features wonderful creations in aspic upstairs and a good-value restaurant downstairs. Closed Sun lunch.

Papageno Pub, Via Colleoni. Serves hot meals, sandwiches and salads. Closed Thurs.

Vineria Cozzi, Via Colleoni 22a. Classy wine bar in Bergamo Altà with around 300 wines to choose from and an excellent cold buffet. Closed Wed.

Around Bergamo

Industrial development has done a pretty thorough job of ruining much of the countryside around Bergamo, particularly in the **Valle Seriana** northeast of the town, where factories and apartment blocks compete for space with forests and mountains, and rivers have been reduced to streams by hydroelectric power. Persevere, however: the upper reaches of the valley are still fairly unspoilt and easily accessible by bus from Bergamo.

Clusone

CLUSONE is the first stop worth making in the Valle Seriana, a picturesque hilltop town whose **Chiesa dei Disciplini** (above the centre, a ten-minute walk from the bus station) draws people from all over. There's little of interest inside the church, but the two fifteenth-century frescoes on its outside wall more than compensate. The upper fresco, *The Triumph of Death*, concentrates on the attitude of the wealthy towards death, with three noblemen returning from the hunt, discovering an open tomb containing the worm-infested corpses of the pope and emperor. A huge skeleton, representing Death, balances on the edge of the tomb, while other skeletons take aim at people gathered around the tomb – incorruptible figures, uninterested in the bribes being offered them. The *Dance of Death* below continues the moral tale, contrasting the corrupt upper classes with a procession of contented commoners, each dancing his way towards death quite happily, above an inscription inviting those who have genuinely served God to approach without fear and join the dance.

Clusone itself is worth a wander, especially on Mondays when the steep curving streets are taken over by a market selling local sausage and cheeses. The **tourist office** (Mon, Tues, Thurs & Fri 10am–noon & 3–5pm, Sat 9am–noon & 3–6pm, Sun 9am–noon; ☎0346.21.113) is on Piazza dell'Orologio, named for the fiendishly complicated sixteenth-century clock on the tower of the Palazzo Comunale. If you have the time and patience, you can work out the date, the sign of the zodiac, the duration of the night and the phase of the moon. The tourist office has information on local walks and hotels, and they will also be able to provide details of the internationally renowned **jazz festival** which is held in July. Of several one-star hotels, the cheapest is the *San Marco* on Via G. Marconi (☎0346.21.269; ①).

Val Cavallina

From Clusone you can take a bus to Lago d'Iseo (see below) or further up the Valle Seriana, though this is of little interest unless you're a committed skier. The same is true of the **Val Cavallina**, which has also suffered from industrial development, with much of it ruined by small factories and tacky housing. The holiday area around Lago d'Endine isn't too bad, but you're more likely to pass through the valley only on your way up to Lago d'Iseo.

Beyond Lago d'Endine, to the northwest, **CANTONIERA DELLA PRESOLANA** is a large ski resort with some swanky hotels, dating back to the turn of the century. It has fifteen slopes, an ice rink, ski and sled hire, and, surprisingly, a number of reasonable one-star hotels. **Val di Scalve**, beyond Presolana, is famous for the **Gorge of the Dezzo**, a narrow chasm forged by the torrents of the River Scalve, whose overhanging rocks are spectacular even if the river has been reduced to a miserable trickle by hydroelectric works.

Val Brembana

Northwest of Bergamo the **Val Brembana** follows a mountain-fringed route that was well-trodden in the Middle Ages by caravans of mules transporting minerals from the Valtellina to the cities of the plain. The road is now frequented mostly by weekend skiers heading up to Foppolo and by less energetic Italians en route to **SAN PELLE-GRINO TERME** to take the waters. San Pellegrino has been Lombardy's most fashionable spa since the turn of the century, and it's from this period that its extravagant main buildings – the grand hotels and casino – date.

Lago d'Iseo and the Val Camonica

Lago d'Iseo raises your expectations: descending from Clusone, the road passes through steep gorges, thick forests and stark angular mountains, at the foot of which lies the lake. As it's the fifth largest of the northern lakes, and the least known outside Italy, you'd imagine it to be more undiscovered than the others but the apartment blocks, harbourside boutiques, ice cream parlours and heavy industry of **LOVERE** put paid to any notions that Iseo might have escaped either tourist exploitation or industrialization. This doesn't deter the Italians, who flock to Lago d'Iseo's resorts for its fish restaurants, watersports and low-key hikes, but unless any of these appeal, or you want to use it as a base for the ascent of Monte Gugliemo or for exploring the prehistoric rock carvings in the Val Camonica, there's little point in hanging around.

There is one retreat, however: the traffic-free **Monte Isola**, accessible by **ferry** (hourly) from Iseo town at the south of the lake. It's Italy's largest lake-island, over 3km long and rising to 600m. As there's a large campsite, and space in its hotels for 200 people, you're unlikely to get much solitude in high season; but out of season it's well worth a visit, either to be utterly lazy or to take a walk right around the edge of the island, for great views across the lake. There are a couple of cheap **hotels**: the *Bellavista* (☎030.988.6106; ②) in the village of **SIVIANO** on the northwest corner of the island, and the *Sensole* (☎030.988.6203; ②) in **SENSOLE**. The **campsite** (☎030.982.5221; April–Oct) is at **CARZANO** on the northeast tip of the island.

The attractions of **ISEO** town are purely practical: **trains** from Brescia stop here, as do buses. If you need to **stay** here, try the *Milano*, Lungolago Marconi 4 (☎030.980.449; ②), a reasonably priced hotel in the centre, or the pricier but very pleasant option, the *Ambra*, Porta Gabriele Rosa 2 (☎030.980.130; ④). Iseo's **tourist office** at Lungolago Marconi 23 (Mon–Sat 9am–12.30pm & 3–6pm, Sun 9am–noon; closed Sat pm and Sun in winter; ☎030.980.209) has maps and details of walks, the most worthwhile of which is the hike from Marone, halfway along the eastern side of the lake, up a steep and winding road to the village of **ZONE**. The reward is the extraordinary rock formations – soaring pinnacles formed by the erosion of the debris brought down by the glacier that gouged out the lake basin. If they look strangely familiar, it could be because Leonardo is said to have visited them, reproducing their peaks in his *Virgin of the Rocks* in the Louvre.

From Zone a track leads up to **Monte Gugliemo** (1949m), the ascent taking about three and a half hours. There's a *rifugio* near the summit: ask around in Zone before you leave to check it's open; if the warden's not there you'll be given the key.

Val Camonica

Like Lago d'Iseo, the **Val Camonica** would be outstandingly beautiful were it not for the indiscriminate scattering of light industry that mars its lower reaches. Road and railway run up from the lake, following the River Oglio through the spa town of Boario to **CAPO DI PONTE**, whose **national park** (Tues–Sun 9am–sunset; L8000/€4.13), a fifteen-minute walk from the town, contains prehistoric rock carvings spanning an incredible 8000 years – remnants from the culture of the Camuni tribe who holed up here to escape northern invaders from 5000 BC until the Romans colonized the area several thousand years later, together with the even older works that inspired the Camuni's art. There are carvings throughout the valley, but the most concentrated group is in the park, beginning with the **Great Rock** in front of the site's shop, where a set of stick-and-blob figures gives a taste of Camuni life over a thousand-year period. There are hunters, agricultural workers, a religious ceremony presided over by priests, and a Bronze Age burial in which the corpse is surrounded by his weapons and tools. To see how the civilization developed into the Iron Age, head for Rock 35, carved with a blacksmith, and Rock 23, with a four-wheeled wagon transporting an urn. Carvings in other parts of the valley include some in the hamlet of **BEDOLINO** outside **CEMMO**, about 2km above Capo di Ponte on the other side of the Oglio, where there's a rock with a carving of a **Bronze Age map** showing huts, fields, walls, streams and canals.

Brescia and around

Famed for its arms industry and chill Fascist-era piazza, **BRESCIA** is a rather ugly industrial town and one that is, unsurprisingly, not on most travellers' itineraries – although you may pass through on the way to Venice or up to the lakes. If you do, the architectural contrasts of its disjointed centre may provide some temporary light relief, but your overall impression will most likely be a negative one.

Arrival, information and accommodation

Brescia's main advantage is its convenience: it is on the main Milan–Verona railway line, giving you access to the cities of the Veneto as well as those of Lombardy; local trains run up to Lecco, Lago d'Iseo, and the Camonica Valley, while the rest of the province, including the main resorts of Garda and several more distant destinations, is covered by direct buses, which leave from the two **bus terminals** outside the **train station**. This is south of the centre, a short bus ride or fifteen-minute walk from the city centre. Brescia has two **tourist offices**, one at Piazza Loggia 6 (Mon–Sat: April–Sept 9.30am–6.30pm; Oct–March 9.30am–12.30pm & 2–5pm; ☎030.240.0357, *www. bresciaholiday.com*, *www.asm.brescia.it/musei*), the other at Corso Zanardelli 34 (Mon–Fri 9am–12.30pm & 3–6pm, Sat 9am–12.30pm; ☎030.43.418 or 030.45.052).

Of Brescia's **hotels**, *Ai Giardini*, Via Rubuffone 13, just beyond Porta Venezia (☎030.292.250; ①), is very cheap, if some way out of the centre; take bus #Q from the

△ Lago d'Idro

RESTAURANTS & BARS
Altamira	A
BarBar	B
Bersiglieria	E
Osteria dell'Elfo	C
Osteria Vecchio Botticino	D

ACCOMMODATION
Al Giardini	2
Albergo San Marco	5
Albergo Stazione	4
Duomo	1
Solferino	3

BRESCIA

train station or any that runs through Porta Venezia. Other hotels include the *San Marco* at Via Spalto 15 (☎030.45.541; ②), and the plain but handily placed *Albergo Stazione* on Vicolo Stazione 15/17, off Viale Stazione (☎030.377.4614; ②), or *Solferino*, Via Solferino 1 (☎030.46.300; ②), opposite the bus station. With a little more money, you could try *Duomo*, very conveniently placed at Via Cesare Beccaria 17 (☎030.375.8751; ③).

The City

Brescia's centre is grouped around the four piazzas beyond the main Corso Palestro. **Piazza del Mercato** is a sprawling cobbled square of more interest to the stomach than the eye – there's a weekday market, a supermarket, and small shops selling local salamis and cheeses nestling under its dark porticoes. **Piazza della Vittoria** is quite different, a disquieting reminder of the Fascist regime embodied in the clinical auster-ity of Piacentrini's gleaming marble rectangles. The arcades, boutiques, *gelaterie* and *pasticcerie* ensure that the square is well frequented in the passeggiata hour.

Alongside the post office, Via 24 Maggio leads to Brescia's prettiest square, **Piazza della Loggia**, dating back to the fifteenth century, when the city invited Venice in to rule and protect it from Milan's power-hungry Viscontis. The Venetian influence is clearest in the fancily festooned **Loggia**, in which both Palladio and Titian had a hand, and in the **Torre dell'Orologio**, modelled on the campanile in Venice's Piazza San Marco. In the northeast corner is the **Porta Bruciata**, a defensive medieval tower-gate, which in 1974, as part of the Strategy of Tension, was the scene of a Fascist bomb attack during a left-wing march, in which eight people were killed and over a hundred injured.

To the south of Porta Bruciata, a small side street leads to **Piazza Paolo VI**, one of the few squares in Italy to have two cathedrals – though, frankly, it would have been better off without the second, a heavy Mannerist monument that took over two hundred years to complete. The old twelfth-century cathedral, or **Rotonda** (April–Oct daily except Tues 9am–noon & 3–7pm; Nov–March Sat & Sun 10am–noon & 3–6pm), is quite a different matter, a simple circular building of local stone, whose fine proportions are sadly difficult to appreciate from the outside as it is sunk below the current level of the piazza. Inside, glass set into the transept pavement reveals the remains of Roman baths (a wall and geometrical mosaics) and the apse of an eighth-century basilica which burned down in 1097. Most interesting is the fine red marble tomb of Berardo Maggi, a thirteenth-century Bishop of Brescia, opposite the entrance, decorated on one side with a full-length relief of the cleric, on the other by reliefs showing other ecclesiasts and dignitaries processing through a lively crowd of citizens to celebrate the peace Maggi had brought to the town's rival Guelph and Ghibelline factions.

Behind Piazza del Duomo, Via Mazzini leads to Via dei Musei, along which lie the remains of the Roman town of Brixia, though there's not a lot to see. There's a **theatre**, currently in the process of excavation and visible only through a wire fence, but the most substantial monument is the **Capitolino,** a Roman temple built in 73 AD, now reconstructed with red brick. Unfortunately it is presently closed for restoration work (call ☎030.377.4999 for latest details). Behind the temple are three reconstructed *celle*, probably temples to the Capitoline trinity of Jupiter, Juno and Minerva, which now house fragments of carved funerary monuments and mosaic pavements.

Further along Via dei Musei, the abbey of **San Salvatore e Santa Giulia** (Tues–Sun: June–Sept 10am–5pm; Oct–May 9.30am–1pm & 2.30–5pm; L5000/€2.58) thrived from the eighth century until it was suppressed in 1798. It's currently undergoing restoration and a consequent reshuffle of its museum exhibits, so only certain sections will be open, although the most important pieces should be on display somewhere. Inside are three churches, the oldest being **San Salvatore**, whose present structure dates back to the twelfth century but includes the remains of an original crypt built in 762 to house the relics of St Julia. **Santa Maria in Solario**, built in the twelfth century as a private chapel for the Benedictine nuns who lived at the abbey, is covered in frescoes painted mainly by Floriano Ferramola during the early 16th century (various dates are visible). Those in the central apse show the marriage of St Catherine to the baby Jesus – a clear reference to the nuns' spiritual marriage to God – while St Scolastica, St Benedict's sister, makes several appearances in her capacity as patron saint to the Benedictine nuns. St Julia's particularly gruesome tale – strung from a tree by her own hair, her breasts were then cut off, from which sprang two angels – is depicted on the left wall. The late-sixteenth-century church of **Santa Giulia** is not as interesting but does contain further frescoes by Ferramola.

Churches aside, the complex also houses the **civic museum**, which, although still in the process of coming together, is the culmination of the work done by two of Brescia's major museums. The **Roman museum** has jewellery, glassware, sculptures and bronzes, fragments of mosaic pavements and a life-sized winged *Victory*. The prize exhibits at the **museum of Christian art** include a fourth-century ivory reliquary chest carved with lively biblical scenes and an eighth-century crucifix presented to the convent by Desiderius, King of the Lombards – made of wood overlaid with silver and encrusted with over two hundred gems and cameos. Look also at the remains of the

Byzantine Basilica of San Salvatore and the remnants of the **Roman villa**, which have been found under a large part of the abbey; those mosaics that are visible are in a beautiful state of preservation.

Behind the museum, Via Piamarta climbs up the **Cydnean Hill**, the core of early Roman Brixia, mentioned by Catullus, though again the remains are scanty. There are a few fragments of a gate just before you reach the sixteenth-century church of **San Pietro in Oliveto**, so called because of the olive grove surrounding it, and the hill itself is crowned by the **Castello** – a monument to Brescia's various overlords, begun in the fifteenth century by Luchino Visconti and added to by the Venetians, French and Austrians over the years. The resultant confusion of towers, ramparts, halls and courtyards makes a good place for an atmospheric picnic, and holds a complex of museums including Italy's largest **museum of arms,** the **Museo del Risorgimento** and a **model railway museum** (Tues–Sun: June–Sept 10am–5pm; Oct–May 9.30am–1pm & 2.30–5pm: L5000/€2.58).

More appealing perhaps is Brescia's main art gallery, the **Pinacoteca Tosio-Martinengo** (Tues–Sun: June–Sept 10am–5pm; Oct–May 9.30am–1pm & 2.30–5pm; L5000/€2.58), which consists of a well laid-out collection mainly made up of the works of minor local artists, including a beautiful black *Sant'Apollonia* by Vincenzo Foppa. The rooms devoted to the "Nativity" and "Town and Province" are worth a look, as are those of the seventeenth-century realist Ceruti, who, unusually for his time, specialized in painting the poor (see p.170).

Eating and drinking

Brescia is nowhere near as well endowed with **restaurants** as Bergamo, and none are especially cheap. However, if you're flat broke, *BarBar*, opposite the Rotonda (closed Wed), is a good place to fill up on bar snacks for free. *Bersaglieria*, at Corso Magenta 38 (closed Mon), is a decent pizzeria, cheap and with the option of vegetarian pizza on a wholemeal ("integrale") base; while for a more unusual evening meal there's organic food at *Altamira*, just off the northern end of Piazza Paolo VI on Vicolo Agostino (closed Mon), though this can be quite expensive. Other good bets include *Osteria Vecchio Botticino*, at Piazzale Arnaldo 6 (closed Sun), on the eastern edge of town, and *Osteria dell Elfo*, near the cathedral at Piazza del Vescovado 1b (booking advisable, ☎030.377.4858; closed Mon) – a fine, inexpensive restaurant serving a seasonally varied menu that includes great pasta, intriguing trout-filled ravioli, and carrot cake.

Around Brescia

With Lago di Garda and the mountains of Val Trompia so easily accessible from Brescia, there seems little point in making do with the distinctly run-of-the-mill attractions of the countryside closest to the city. But if you're keen on wine you might want to make for the area between Brescia and Lago d'Iseo, known as the **Franciacorta** – a hilly wine-producing district, rising from the bland built-up lowlands around the city, which got its name from the religious communities that lived there from the eleventh century onwards. These communities and their land were exempt from tax and known as the Corti Franche, or free courts. The wine-producers soon moved in, attracted by the possibility of owning vineyards in a duty-free haven, and though the Franciacorta is no longer tax free, the extremely drinkable wine continues to flow – and is available from shops all over the region.

With a further half-day to spare in Brescia, you could also head out to the **Abbazia di Rodengo** (group visits by appointment only, ☎030.610.182 and ask for Padre Landra, but brush up your Italian first; if you're alone they might show you around 9–11am, 3–3.30pm or 4.30–5.30pm, if there's someone free), just outside the village of the same name, which has a sumptuously frescoed church, with some gorgeous stucco-work and a generous dash of trompe l'oeil, and another room decorated with scantily clad figures surging into a cloudy heaven. The most interesting thing about a visit here is the insight you get into the lives of the five monks who live here – their primitive kitchen, tatty library and silently austere corridors. Entrance is free, although if Don Antonio shows you round he'll probably ask you to send him stamps for his collection; if you wish, the monks will put you up and feed you for no charge, although you should bear in mind that they're pretty poor themselves.

Getting to the abbey, bear in mind that express buses take the *autostrada* – keep a sharp lookout for the yellow signs as the drivers are apt not to stop; the abbey is a ten-minute signposted walk from the bus stop. If your bus is a local one, get off in Rodengo village centre and walk back along the main road towards the motorway.

Val Trompia, Lago d'Idro and Lago di Ledro

You may be able to ignore the arms industry in Brescia, but its impact is unavoidable when you pass through the **Val Trompia**, directly north of the city. The industry dates back over four hundred years, started by the Venetians, keen to utilize the rich iron ore deposits of the area and to whom it became so indispensable that during the sixteenth century restrictions were actually placed on people's movements out of the region. The centre of today's (much diminished) arms industry is **GARDONE VAL TROMPIA**, where the Beretta company has its headquarters.

The valley beyond Gardone is crammed with industry as far as Lavone, and hiking becomes possible only at **BOVEGNO**. From this small village paths lead up to Monte Muffetto (4hr) and, even better, to Monte Crestoso and its tiny tarns (5hr 30min), though you'll need a tent, as there are no *rifugi*. If you're without a tent, there are two *rifugi* further on – *Croce Domini* (1992m) at the head of the valley, and *Bonardi* (1743m) above the lovely Passo del Maniva. From either base you can walk down to Lago d'Idro or climb Monte Colombino, again with a couple of tarns. The map to get is the Kompass Carta Turistica, *Le Tre Valli Bresciane*. There are also a few cheap hotels at the ski resorts of **COLLIO** and **SAN COLUMBANO**; try the tiny *Belvedere* (☎030.927.259; ①) in the latter.

From close to the *rifugio Croce Domini* a steep track climbs over into the broad Valle della Berga and up to **BAGOLINO** on the road to Lago d'Idro. Bagolino is quiet, preserving many of its medieval houses and a church, **San Rocco**, that has a startlingly realistic cycle of fifteenth-century frescoes. If you want to avoid Idro's unremarkable resorts, this is the place to stay: the *Cavallino* hotel at Via San Giorgio 164 (☎0365.99.108; ②) is quite reasonable, and buses run fairly frequently to and from the lake.

Lago d'Idro is a reasonably pretty lake, except for its marshy upper reaches where the effect is spoiled by a sand-dredger. Tourism is family oriented, but as there's no road running along the upper reaches of the east shore, you should be able to find a quiet beach there. Although bathing in the lake is said to induce a skin rash, few people are able to resist its cool, clear waters; there are also walks in the area if you want to do more than swim and laze around. Marked paths climb up into the hills from the east shore, and from **ANFO** on the west shore a track leads past the *rifugio Rosa di Baramone* to Bagolino. Again, you'll need the Kompass map mentioned above.

Idro's resorts are uniformly bland, but if you want to stay over, *Al Lago*, Via Lago 10 (☎0365.809.026; ①), at Anfo, has cheap doubles, as does the *Geny*, Via Capovalle 7 (☎0365.83.291; ②), at **CRONE**, on the bus route from Idray, 2km away. Of the **campsites**, the most convenient are the two at Anfo and a couple at Vantone on the east shore – both on the bus route from Brescia.

Northeast from Idro, via Ponte Caffaro, you reach the point which the Austrian border ran through until 1918. From here a road leads to **Lago di Ledro** in the Val Sabbia, only 2km long and slightly less across, and a good bolt-hole if you want to get away from the frantic northwest of Lake Garda. Quieter than Idro, and far preferable, it has a couple of **campsites** and a **hotel**, the *Mezzolago* (☎0464.508.181; ①), which is open all year.

Lago di Garda

Lago di Garda is the largest and cleanest of the Italian lakes, and also the most popular. Tourism is relatively recent – beginning only this century when the road around its shores was completed – and it has none of the Victorian-era resorts that line the shores of Como and Maggiore. Indeed, the only celebrity English visitor to spend much time around the lake was D. H. Lawrence, whose *Twilight in Italy* details many of the lake's attractions.

For all that, Lake Garda is now firmly on the tour operators' schedules, and much of the development has been feverish; its resorts are each year invaded by a fair number of package-holiday clients, as well as huge numbers of Germans, French and Italians attracted by some of Europe's best windsurfing and the gentle climate. Winters are mild, summers tempered by breezes – the northern *sover*, which blows down the lake from midnight and through the morning, and the *ova*, blowing from the south in the afternoon and evening. Along the so-called Riviera Bresciana, on the most sheltered stretch of the western shore, are lush groves of olives, vines and citrus trees – fruits used for Garda's main products: olive oil, citrus syrups and Bardolino, Soave and Valpolicella wines. Scenically the shores of the lake are varied: the rich vegetation of its middle reaches gives way to the rugged north, where the lake narrows and is tightly enclosed by craggy mountains; the southern shores, 16km at their widest, are backed by a gentle plain.

Desenzano, Sirmione and the southern shore

Within easy striking distance of the Milan–Venice *autostrada* and railway, the **southern shore** of Lake Garda is predictably well touristed. **DESENZANO DEL GARDA**, the lake's largest town, is a major rail junction and the best starting-point for visiting Garda. Buses tend to connect with trains, and there are several ferries daily up to Riva and other resorts. The town itself holds little to detain you. The lakefront, lined with bars and restaurants, is quite attractive, though it's hard to ignore the busy main road running alongside. If you do end up with time to fill, head for the **castle**, from where there are spectacular views, or the **Roman villa** on Via Crocifisso: the villa is definitely worth visiting, a formerly large and luxurious home that preserves some good mosaics (March to mid-Oct Tues–Sat 8.30am–7pm, Sun 9am–6pm; mid-Oct to Feb Tues–Sat 8.30am–4.30pm, Sun 9am–4.30pm; L4000/€2.07).

A short but infrequent train ride from Desenzano, **SAN MARTINO DELLA BATTAGLIA** was the site of a famous battle, where Napoleon III and Vittorio Emanuele II defeated the Austrians in 1859. The **Torre di San Martino** (daily: April–Sept 9am–12.30pm & 2–7pm; Oct–March closes 5pm; L6000/€3.10) was built in 1893 to commemorate the victory, and has paintings and sculptures of the leading figures plus a good view of the battlefield and Lake Garda from the top. Behind it is a battle museum.

Horrified by the extent of the slaughter, a Swiss man, Henry Dunant, was inspired to found the Red Cross, writing a short book, *A Memory of Solferino*, suggesting the formation of "relief societies for the purpose of having care given to the wounded in wartime, by zealous, devoted and thoroughly qualified volunteers". Dunant bankrupted himself over founding the Red Cross and was discovered in the last years of his life in a home for impoverished men. He was awarded the first ever Nobel prize, but never moved from the home. There's a monument to Dunant and the Red Cross 11km southeast of San Martino, at **SOLFERINO** – a paved path along the crest of the hill lined with tablets set into a wall, bearing the names of countries who ratified the Geneva Convention. There are also good views from the nearby fortress and a small **museum** (same hours as Torre di San Martino; L3000/€1.55) of battle memorabilia on the fringes of the village.

Sirmione and around

The original inhabitants of Desenzano's villa may well have come to **SIRMIONE**, spread along a narrow promontory protruding 4km into the lake, to seek cures in its sulphurous springs – it still retains the remains of a Roman spa. It is a popular spot, in a beautiful setting, though these days it's suffocated with luxury hotels, souvenir stands and tourists. You're unlikely to want to stay, and in any case most of the hotels are pricey and usually full, but it's worth a brief visit to take in the town's handful of sights and laze around on the surrounding lidos.

Most people head for the **Rocca Scaligera** (daily except Mon: April–Sept 9am–6pm; Oct–March 9am–1pm; L8000/€4.13), a fairy-tale castle with boxy turreted towers almost entirely surrounded by water, built by the Veronese Scaligeri family in the thirteenth century when they ruled Garda. There's not much to see inside, and, although the views from its battlements are lovely, they don't really warrant the high entrance fee.

You can escape the crowds by walking out beyond the town to the peninsula's triangular and traffic-free hilly head, covered in cypresses and olive groves. The church of **San Pietro** here has thirteenth-century frescoes inside, and its shady grounds make for a good picnic stop. A path leads along the edge of the peninsula, passing bubbling hot sulphur springs, to the **Lido** (May–Oct daily 8am–midnight) where you can eat, drink, swim in the lake or sunbathe on the pontoon or nearby rocks. If you continue, you'll reach a fenced-off area at the tip of the peninsula. The signs warn of landslides, but most people ignore these since the flat rocks are good for sun-soaking. Swimming or paddling is tricky, however, as underwater the rocks are slippery. There's a gate here up to the **Grotte di Catullo** (March to mid-Oct Tues–Sat 8.30am–7pm, Sun 9am–6pm; mid-Oct to Feb Tues–Sat 8.30am–4.30pm, Sun 9am–4.30pm; L8000/€4.13), touted as Catullus's villa, although the white ruins are actually of a Roman spa: there's a hot sulphur spring 300m under the lake, and people still come to Sirmione to take the waters. Catullus did, however, retire to the town, coming all the way from the Black Sea by boat, hauling it overland when necessary so that he could keep it on the lake. The ruins, scattered on the hillside among ancient olive trees, are lovely, and there are superb views across the lake to the mountains. There's a small antiquarium with fragments of mosaics and frescoes, and below the site, though not accessible from it, a beach.

If you want to stay in Sirmione, booking ahead is essential in July and August. If you haven't booked, the **tourist office** (April–Oct daily 9am–8pm; Nov–March Mon–Fri 9am–12.30pm & 3–6pm, Sat 9am–12.30pm; ☎030.916.114) by the bus station has a list of **rooms**, but don't count on these being free either. Of the **hotels**, the *Grifone*, Via Bocchio 4 (☎030.916.014; ②), on the waterfront overlooking the castle, and *La Magnolia*, Via Vittorio Emanuele 43 (☎030.916.135; ②), on the main thoroughfare beyond the castle, are both reasonably priced and pleasant. The nearest **campsite** is the *Sirmione*, Via Sirmioncino 9 (☎030.990.4665; March–Oct), at Colombare, 3km south of Sirmione, on the lakefront; head along Via Colombare out of town towards the mainland – though this too gets extremely crowded.

The western shore

Less built-up, and with reputedly cleaner water than the northern reaches of the lake, the lower reaches of the **western shore** are studded with campsites which make for cheap and reasonably convenient bases. If you're not heading for the campsites, **SALÓ** is worth a stop, splendidly sited on a bay at the foot of the luxuriant Riviera Bresciana and a good place to stock up on local produce. Saló gave its name to Mussolini's short-lived last republic, instituted here after his rescue from the Abruzzi by the Nazis. Though it retains a handful of buildings from the fifteenth century – notably the duomo and town hall – when it was the Venetian Empire's main garrison town, these are unlikely to detain you for long. Better to detour 6km inland to **PUEGNAGO DEL GARDA**, where you can sample the rosé wines – Grapello and Chiaretto – that the Comincioli vineyard has been producing since the sixteenth century.

Gardone Riviera and Il Vittoriale

A few miles further up the shore **GARDONE RIVIERA** was once the most fashionable of Garda's resorts and still retains its symbols of sophistication, though the elegant promenade, lush gardens, opulent villas and ritzy hotels now have to compete with more recent – and less tasteful – tourist tack. It is famous for the consistency of its climate, and has Garda's most exotic botanical garden, the **Giardino Botanico Hruska** (mid-March to mid-Oct daily 9am–6.30pm; L8000/€4.13), laid out among artificial cliffs and streams.

The highlight of Gardone, and indeed of the whole lake, is **Il Vittoriale** (Tues–Sun: April–Sept 8.30am–8pm; Oct–March 9am–12.30pm & 2–5.30pm; *www.vittoriale.gs. net.it*; L30,000/€15.49), the home of Italy's most notorious and extravagant twentieth-century writer, Gabriele D'Annunzio. Weight of numbers means that tickets for the house itself are restricted at peak times (Sundays, national holidays, some days in July & Aug), when you must arrive well before the opening times to be sure of a ticket for the house – even then, be prepared for a scrum. Once tickets for the house are sold out, you can only visit the grounds, the mausoleum, a small musuem and the ship *Puglia*, beached somewhat incongruously among cypress trees in the park, for a reduced fee of L12,000/€6.20.

Born in 1863, D'Annunzio was no ordinary writer. He did pen some exquisite poetry and a number of novels, but he became better known as a soldier and socialite, leading his own private army and indulging in much-publicized affairs with numerous women, including the actress Eleonora Duse. When berated by his friends for treating her cruelly, he simply replied, "I gave her everything, even suffering". He was a fervent supporter of Mussolini, providing the Fascist Party with their (meaningless) war cry, *eia! eia! alalá*, though Mussolini eventually found his excessive exhibitionism an embarrassment (his boasts of eating dead babies, certainly, were bad publicity), and in 1925 presented him with this villa – ostensibly as a reward for his patriotism, in reality to shut him up.

Once D'Annunzio had had the house "de-Germanized", as he put it (the house had been confiscated from the German art critic Henry Thode), it didn't take him long to transform Mussolini's Liberty-style gift into the Hollywood studio look-alike you see now. Outside, rammed into the cypress-covered hillside, is the prow of the battleship *Puglia* used in D'Annunzio's so-called "Fiume adventure". Fiume (now Rijeka), on the North Adriatic, had been promised to Italy before they entered World War I, but was eventually handed over to Yugoslavia instead. Incensed, D'Annunzio gathered together his army, occupied Fiume, and returned home a national hero. D'Annunzio's personality makes itself felt from the start in the two reception rooms – one a chilly and formal room for guests he didn't like, the other warm and inviting for those he did. Il Duce was apparently shown to the former, where the mirror has an inscription reputedly aimed at him – "Remember that you are made of glass and I of steel."

Nor was dining with D'Annunzio a reassuring experience: roast baby may not have featured on the menu, but in the glitzy dining room, as a warning to greedy guests, pride of place was given to a gilded and embalmed tortoise who had died of overeating. In fact D'Annunzio rarely ate with his guests, retreating instead to the Sala di Lebbroso, where he would lie on a bier surrounded by leopard skins and contemplate death. The rest of the house is no less bizarre: the bathroom has a bathtub hemmed in by hundreds of objects, ranging from Persian ceramic tiles, through Buddhas, to toy animals; and the Sala del Mappamondo, as well as the huge globe for which it is named, contains an Austrian machine-gun and books, including an immense version of *The Divine Comedy*. Suspended from the ceiling of the auditorium adjoining the house is the biplane that D'Annunzio used in a famous flight over Vienna in World War I.

Gardone's **tourist office** is at Via Repubblica 39, the cobbled street that runs parallel with the lakefront through the village (April–June Mon–Sat 9am–12.30pm & 4–7pm, closed Thurs afternoon; July–Sept same hours plus Thurs 4–7pm & Sun 9am–12.30pm; Oct–March Mon–Sat 9am–12.30pm & 3–6pm, closed Thurs afternoon; ☎ & fax 0365.20.347). If you want to **stay** over in Gardone, there are functional doubles at the very basic *Nord*, Via Zanardelli 18 (☎0365.20.707; ②), on the main coast road by the most central bus stop. Head down towards the lake and for a bit more you can have a room with bath on the lakeside at the *Diana*, Lungolago D'Annunzio 30 (☎0365.21.815; ③). Alternatively, walk up the hill on the other side of the main road towards Il Vittoriale until Via Roma meets Via dei Colli and you'll come to the pleasantly located *Hohl*, Via dei Colli 4 (☎0365.20.160; ③; March–Oct), which has a garden.

There are a couple of **places to eat** up in the old village around Il Vittoriale, but you're better off going back down the hill to *La Terrazza* at Via Roma 53 (closed Tues except July & Aug), where you can get good pizzas and snacks, and great views, or, if you want to splash out, to *Agli Angeli*, 2 Piazzetta Giuseppe Garibaldi (no closing day), which has interesting pasta and fish courses. Down by the lakeside, *Ciar de Luna* at Via Repubblica 34 (closed Tues) is a congenial place open until 3am, with snacks such as bruschetta or gnocchi, full meals in the restaurant section – and Beck's on tap.

San Michele

Up in the mountains behind Gardone is the little Alpine village of **SAN MICHELE**. There are six buses daily from Gardone and Saló, but as the views along the road are splendid, it's worth walking the hour or so uphill. The *Colomber Hotel* (☎0365.21.108; ②), 500m inland – follow the signs to the *Refugio G. Pirlo M. Spino* – is a good base if you want to do some walking to the springs and waterfalls in the surrounding hills. The owners will give suggestions for **walks**, but for more ambitious hikes, there are maps marked with footpaths available from CAI, Via San Carlo 17, in Saló. The hotel also has a good restaurant with lots of local specialities and well-chosen wine.

Toscalano-Maderno to Limone sul Garda

A ten-minute bus ride up the coast brings you to **TOSCALANO-MADERNO**, two villages long since united by tourist sprawl. There are only two reasons for visiting. One is the regular **ferry** that plies across the lake to Garda's loveliest village, Torri del Benaco (see p.229), the other a long though narrow shingle **beach**. Beyond is **GARGNANO**, now a good place for sailing but once the headquarters of Mussolini's puppet Republic of Saló. The puppeteers were the Nazis, who placed him here in Villa Feltrinelli largely to keep him out of harm's way. The dictator had by this time lost all credibility and he sank into depression; although he installed his mistress, Claretta Petacci, in nearby Il Vittoriale, the cold, damp rooms and heavy Nazi presence in the woods outside put paid to any passion.

Gargnano is still more a working village than a resort, which is exactly the attraction. It's worth a stop to wander around the abandoned olive factory or the lakefront villas with their boathouses, or just to relax with an ice cream or a drink in one of the cafés. The main sight in the village is the thirteenth-century church of **San Francesco** – the columns in its cloisters are carved with citrus fruits, a reference to the fact that the Franciscans were credited with introducing the cultivation of citrus fruit to Europe. A 3km stroll along the road which leads north from the port takes you through olive and lemon groves, past Villa Feltrinelli (now a conference centre for Milan University) to the eleventh-century chapel of **San Giacoma Calina**. On the side facing the lake, under the portico where the fishermen keep their equipment, are some thirteenth-century frescoes, incredible for the fact that they are still visible despite the obvious lack of attention.

Gargnano's **tourist office** (Mon–Sat 10am–noon & 3.30–7pm; ☎0365.71.222) is housed in the ex-Palazzo Communale, which has two cannonballs wedged in the lake side of the building as a reminder of the naval bombings suffered in July 1866 during the war of independence from the Austrians. If you fancy **staying** the night, you could try the *Tiziana-Garnì* on Via Dosso 51 (☎0365.71.342; ②), just off the main road, which has lake views and friendly owners, or the more upmarket *Villa Giulia* on Viale Rimembranze 20 (☎0365.71.022, fax 0365.72.774; ⑥), a very comfortable lake-side option. There is also a campsite, *Rucc*, at Via Rimembranze 23 (☎0365.71.805).

Further north among citrus groves is **LIMONE SUL GARDA**, a pretty, stone-built village jammed on the slopes between the mountains and the lake. Unfortunately it's been ruined by tourism. The steep cobbled streets are lined with stalls selling souvenirs, leather jackets and sequined T-shirts; the old stone facades are studded with plastic signs advertising restaurants and hotels; and as you elbow your way through the crowds you'll dig into more German and British than Italian ribs. Unless you're aching to eat chicken and chips, frankfurters and sauerkraut, you're better off staying away.

Riva del Garda

At the northwest tip of the lake, **RIVA DEL GARDA** is the best known of the lake's resorts. It's been a resort since the late nineteenth century and retains some stylish pastel-painted hotels, which in high season and on sunny Sundays form an elegant backdrop for a portside crammed with gaudy excursion coaches. There's an old town behind this, which is pleasant enough, but the main reason for basing yourself here is the fact that Riva currently boasts Garda's only youth hostel.

There's not a great deal to do or see, except for the severe moated **castle** (daily 9.30am–12.30pm & 2.30–5.30pm; L4000/€2.07) alongside the port, still undergoing lengthy renovation, but open at least for visiting the modest collection of **art** pertaining to the region.

The lakefront is lined with **gelaterie and pizzerias**, and there's a good *pizza al taglio* place on Via Gazzoletti, just off the port area, and an English-style pub, *All'Oca*, at Via Santa Maria 9, which is cosy on a chilly day. For a more substantial meal try the *Vaticano* at Via Santa Maria 8 (no closing day), a reasonably priced restaurant where you can eat in the garden. If you're staying at Riva you'll need a map, available from the **tourist office** (May–June Mon–Sat 9am–noon & 3–6.30pm; July–Sept same hours plus Sun 10am–noon & 4–6.30pm; Oct–April Mon–Fri 8.30am–12.15pm & 2.30–5.15pm; ☎0464.554.444, *www.gardatrentino.com*) in the Giardini di Porta Orientale, on the far side of the castle. If you decide to **stay**, you'll find the youth hostel at Piazza Cavour 10 (☎0464.554.911; L19,000/€9.81; April–Oct), but little to choose from when it comes to cheap hotels. Your best bet is either *La Montanara* at Via Montanara 18–20 (☎0464.554.857; ①) at the top of Via Concordia, which runs up from the castle, or the *Vittoria* at Via Dante 39 (☎0464.554.398; ②), just before the entrance to the historic centre if you're coming from the bus station.

The eastern shore

Overlooked by the mountains of the Monte Baldo chain, the main resorts of Garda's **eastern shore** are heavily touristed and have none of the charming flaking palaces of the western side. Head for **Torbole** in the north if you're a keen windsurfer or attracted by any of the myriad of other activities on offer. Along the shore to the south, **Malcesine** has a lovely old centre that is nowadays hidden under postcard stands and trilingual pizza menus. It is however still a good base for escapes by bike or on foot into the mountains. Further south still, **Torri del Benaco** is a gorgeous old village, popular but not yet ruined by tourism, while **Garda** and **Bardolino** are bustling resorts, the former a favourite haunt of Italian holiday-makers.

Between June and September you will need to book **accommodation** ahead in nearly all the resorts. There are several types of **bus passes** which give you unlimited journeys between Riva and any of the towns down to Verona, and from June to September there is also a service to transport you and your bike. However, the deals change frequently so check with the APT (*www.apt.vr.it*) or tourist offices.

Torbole

TORBOLE, at the top of the lake, played an important role in the fifteenth-century war between the Viscontis and the Venetians, when a fleet of warships was dragged overland here and launched into the lake. Nowadays it's still the water that dominates, since Torbole's main diversions are sailing and windsurfing, and the place has a fresh feeling, something added to by the suntanned faces you'll encounter in the many bars and fast-food joints. If you're a sports freak, this is a great place to stay, with plenty of brisk young things in dazzling lycra whizzing around on rollerblades or mountain bikes, and a more buzzing café life than in other resorts around the lake. Windsurfing enthusiasts come here from all over Europe, and it's obvious why once you see the speed at which they skim across the water when the afternoon wind gets up. It's also a good place for beginners, and in the mornings, when the wind is gentler, the water is full of wobbling novices attempting to circle their instructors.

The **tourist office** (April & May Mon–Sat 9am–noon & 3–6.15pm; June–Oct Mon–Sat 9am–noon & 3–6.30pm, Sun 10am–noon & 4–6.30pm; Nov–March 9am–noon & 2.30–5.15pm; ☎0464.505.177, *www.torbole.com*) is conveniently located on the lakefront between the jetty and the centre; it has a huge range of information on different courses, places to rent bikes and boards and routes for every imaginable sport. If it's closed, there is a freephone service outside to a substantial number of the **hotels** (phone numbers are listed on a board). The *Casa Nataly*, on Piazza Alpini (☎0464.505.341; ②), is just off the main road on the edge of town and also rents apartments by the week; the *Casa Romani* (☎0464.505.113; ②) charges about the same and is in a handy location just off the main road directly opposite the ferry jetty; it has two swimming pools and some rooms with use of a kitchen. A slightly more upmarket alternative is *Casa Morandi*, on Via Matteoti (☎0464.505.239; ②), a spick-and-span place with old-fashioned furnishings and a café-restaurant next door, usefully positioned on a main road above town right next to a bus stop. *Monte Baldo*, at the heart of things on Lungolago Verona (☎0464.505.121; ③), overlooking the port, is another good bet.

Malcesine

Backed by the slopes of Monte Baldo and blessed with the same windsurfer-friendly winds as Torbole, **MALCESINE**, 14km further south, has been inundated with British and German package tourists in the last few years and the crowds temper much of the appeal of what is left of the old town. The main sight is a thirteenth-century turreted **Castello** (daily: summer 9.30am–6.30pm; winter 10am–12.30pm & 2–6pm; L6000/ €3.10), built, like Sirmione's, by the Scaligeri family. Goethe was imprisoned here briefly in 1786, having been arrested on suspicion of being a spy – he'd been caught making sketches of the lake castle's towers. In 1439, the warships of the Venetian fleet were transported over the 320-metre-high San Giovannia pass to Malcesina by means of filling in the small River Cameras with earth and hauling the ships uphill over tree-trunk rollers, *Fitzcarraldo*-style. They went on to rule the nearby towns of Lazise and Peschiera, and eventually Brescia (see p.218), but by May 1509 they lost their hard-won territory after battles with the army commanded by Louis XII of France.

For more active pursuits you need to head up Monte Baldo. Although there are well-marked trails up the mountain, you can save energy by taking a **funicular** (daily: April–Oct every thirty minutes 8am–6pm; L20,000/€10.33 return-trip, L24,000/€12.39 with bike), but be prepared for long queues in summer. If you want to mountain bike, there are wheels for hire at G. Furioli in Piazza Matteotti, who even transport the bikes to the top, from where you can make a panoramic descent; you can also take your own bike up on one of the four trips especially for bikes, three in the morning and one at lunchtime.

The **tourist office** at Via Capitanato 6–8 (June–Oct Mon–Sat 9am–1pm & 3–7pm, Sun 9am–1pm; Nov–May closed Sun; ☎045.740.0044, fax 045.740.1633), north along the lake from the port, has maps of signposted walks in the hills behind. Most **hotels** in Malcesine get swallowed up by package companies, so the choice is limited. The *Catullo*, in Via Priori 11 (☎045.740.0352; ③), has a pool and is very reasonable, as is the *Primavera* on Via Gardesana (☎045.740.0091; ①). Another good deal is *Gardesana* on the main road through town and within walking distance of the bus station (☎045.740.0121; ②), though you'll need to book months in advance for July and August. Many of Malcesine's **restaurants** are aimed at the town's German visitors: the *Speck Stube*, Via Molina 1, is one of the better of the Teutonic-style eateries; or else try the more Italian *Gondoliere* on Piazza Matteotti – the seafood is particularly recommended.

Torri del Benaco and the Punta San Vigilio

To the south of Malcesine, **TORRI DEL BENACO** is the prettiest and least spoilt of all the lake towns. Its old centre consists simply of one long cobbled street, Corso Dante, crisscrossed with tunnelling alleyways and lined with mellow stone *palazzi*. At one end of the street is the **castle**, illuminated at night and with a long glasshouse built along one side to protect the lemon trees inside during cold weather. Inside the castle there is a small **anthropological museum** (April, May & Oct daily 9.30am–12.30pm & 2.30–6pm; June–Sept daily 9.30am–1pm & 4.30–7.30pm; Nov–March Sun 2.30–5.30pm; L5000/€2.58). Beyond the castle, the port area is a piazza planted with limes and chestnuts, at night swinging to the strains of the live musicians at swanky pavement cafés.

Torri is a fine place to stay, and there are a number of reasonable **hotels**, among which the *Onda*, located on Via per Albisano two minutes' walk from the village centre (☎045.722.5895; ②), is certainly the best option. Each spotlessly clean room has its own balcony or terrace and the friendly owner provides a first-rate breakfast. If there's no room, the *Belvedere* (☎045.722.5088; ②) opposite is a good bet. On the main road to the south of the village is the *Lido* (☎045.722.5084; ①), on the lakeside, or for a more central, pricey choice there is the *Gardisena* on Piazza Calderini (☎0457.225.411, fax 0457.225.771; ⑤), just round the corner from the **tourist office** (April–June & Sept Mon–Sat 9am–1pm & 3–6pm; July & Aug daily 9am–1pm & 3–7pm; ☎045.722.5120). For **food**, *La Regata* on the lakefront does hearty sandwiches; *La Grotta*, also on the lakefront, is good value with excellent pasta dishes; and, for more refined fare, *El Trincero*, Vicolo Chiesa 5, off Piazza Chiesa (closed Mon), a bulge in Corso Dante, serves *schiacciata* – flat bread bases topped with olive paté, or *porcini* and truffles – and sophisticated pasta dishes which have a wide following. For **drinks**, try *Don Diego* on Via Faese, an alleyway off Corso Dante, easily recognizable by the graffitied doors, where you can drink local Bardolino wine or its notorious and moderately priced *sangria*.

If you fancy a **swim,** there's a lido in Torri (with a disco in season), but you'd probably be better off heading south for the white shingle beaches at **Punta San Vigilio,** a hilly headland a short bus ride away. There's an excellent pay beach, with sun loungers and picnic tables scattered on grassy slopes planted with pines and planes, or, if you want to save your money, you can take a footpath about 100m from the first gate to several smaller coves – one of which is unofficially nudist. There's also an extremely exclusive hotel here, which numbers Churchill and Prince Charles among its famous ex-guests. Should you happen to be on the Punta on May 25, which is the only day they're open, you could visit the immaculate formal gardens of the **Villa Guarienti,** a tidy Renaissance creation by Sanmicheli.

Garda

GARDA is a lively, flourishing resort, popular with Italians as well as foreigners, and the evening passeggiata along its tree-lined prom is good fun if you're into people-watching. Not long ago it was a fishing village, although now the narrow windy alleys and cottages of its old centre are studded with souvenir shops and snack bars. Even the fifteenth-century **Loggia della Losa,** originally a dock for the palace behind, is now a gelateria.

Like Torri, Garda is well placed for beach-bumming days on the Punta San Vigilio, but if you want to do something more energetic, you could follow the pleasant route from the church of Santa Maria Maggiore up to a seventeenth-century hermitage, the **Eremo dei Camoldolesi** – open for prayer only, but you can visit the shop, which sells produce from their gardens and orchards (daily 10.30am–noon & 3.30–5pm). The monks here were ousted by Napoleon in 1810 but bought the place back later in the century – though they only began to live there again in 1972. Each monk enjoys the luxury of a four-roomed house and garden.

If you want to stay in Garda, the most fairly priced **hotels** are the *Speranza* on the central square, Piazzale Roma 2 (☎045.725.5046; ③), and the more comfortable *Giardinetto* on Via V. Bellini 1 (☎045.725.5051, fax 045.627.8302; ④) where the rooms all have lake views and there is a good restaurant downstairs (closed Tues). The **tourist office** is in the centre of town on the inland side of the main road, at Via Don Gnocchi 23 (April–Sept Mon–Sat 9am–7pm, Sun 9am–1pm; Oct–March Mon–Sat 9am–1pm & 3–6pm; ☎045.627.0384), and it has daily information on which hotels have rooms available. Alternatively there are houses with **rooms to rent;** if you want to fix up somewhere like this directly, try Mauro Consolino, Via Monte Baldo 13 and Via Antiche Mura 4 (☎045.725.6113 and 045.725.5561), or Giorgio Ferri, Via delle Viole (☎045.725.5409). There are two **campsites:** the three-star *Serenella* (☎045.721.1333), halfway between Garda and Bardolino on the main road; and two-star *La Rocca* (☎045.721.1111), slightly nearer and on the same road a five-minute walk from town (in the Verona direction), next to the main road – though there are plenty of lakeside spots.

The best places to **eat** in Garda are outside the centre: *Al Ponte Sel*, Via Monte Baldo 75 (closed Mon), does a good set menu which includes wine; and *Rasole*, Via San Bernardo 95 (closed Tues), does decently priced home-made pasta, though it's a good thirty-minute walk from town. Slightly more expensive, *La Val*, on Via Val Molini (no closing day), the first left-turn along the road to Costermano, is known for its grilled trout. In town, *Taverna Fregosa*, at Corso Vittorio Emanuele 37 (no closing day), does a delicious half roast chicken. Garda is fairly animated at **night:** head either for the *Taverna* on the lakefront just off Piazza Catullo, *Bar Taitu* on Vicolo Cieco Forni off Corso Vittorio Emanuele (the old town's main street), or to an ersatz Greek cocktail bar, perplexingly titled *Taverna Goethe*, Via delle Viole, off Via San Bernardo.

Bardolino, Lazise and Gardaland

BARDOLINO is a spruce little resort, popular with British and German visitors, which is, as you might have guessed, the home of the light, red Bardolino wine – the town is at its most animated between mid-September and mid-October, when the *Festa di Uva* (Festival of the Grape) is held. At other times of year, apart from strolling along its lush palm- and pine-planted promenade, there's not a lot to do, although the church of **San Zeno**, tucked in the corner of a dusty yard just off the main coast road, is worth a brief look. It was built in the eighth century, and its Latin-cross form and high domed ceiling became a prototype for later Romanesque churches. Otherwise, concentrate on sampling Bardolino wine at the unlikely-looking bar on Via Cesare Battisti, which has no name outside but is commonly known as *Da Romaldi*, or try the ice cream at *Cristallo* on the lakefront near the ferry jetty, which sells the biggest and best ice creams on the lake, in a repertoire of flavours ranging from *mascarpone* to *panna cotta* with fresh forest fruits.

The walled village of **LAZISE**, further down the shore, was once a major Venetian port and retains a (privately owned) **castle** and, on the harbour, an arcaded medieval **customs house**. Originally used for building and repairing boats for the Venetian fleet, it was later used to house sheep, whose urine was used to make nitrogen, a vital ingredient in gunpowder. Nowadays Lazise is crammed with cafés, pizzerias and *gelaterie* and plenty of summer visitors, but it's not a bad place to escape to out of season, when it reverts to being a sleepy lakeside village. If you want to **stay**, go for the *Tecla* at Via Cansignorio 12 (☎045.758.0032; ②), above a wine shop just off Corso Cangrande. The **tourist office** (Mon–Sat: April–Oct 9am–1pm & 3–7pm; Nov–March closes one hour earlier; ☎045.758.0114) is on Via F. Fontana near the harbour, and has maps and leaflets about the village.

Finally, if you have kids to amuse, or just want a daft day out, you can catch a bus from any of the east shore villages to **Gardaland**, Italy's most popular amusement park, at Castelnuovo del Garda (April–June & Sept daily 9.30am–6.30pm; July & Aug daily 9am–midnight; Oct Sat & Sun 9.30am–6.30pm; ☎045.644.9777, *www.gardaland.it*; L38,000/€19.63, children under ten L32,000/€16.53). It's pricey, and you pay extra for some of the attractions, but its various rides and themed entertainments attract around two million visitors a year; with restless children in tow, you might just want to join them.

travel details

TRAINS

Bergamo to: Brescia (20 daily; 45min–1hr); Lecco (18 daily; 35min).

Brescia to: Capo di Ponte (7 daily; 2hr); Cremona (12 daily; 45min); Iseo (12 daily; 40min); Parma (9 daily; 1hr 30min–1hr 50min); Verona (42 daily; 35min–1hr).

Cremona to: Mantua (18 daily; 1hr).

Lecco to: Bergamo (16 daily; 35min); Sondrio (19 daily; 1hr 25min).

Milan Centrale to: Arona (10 daily; 50min); Bergamo (15 daily; 50min); Brescia (40 daily; 1hr 30min); Certosa di Pavia (3 daily; 25min); Como (20 daily; 40min); Desenzano (18 daily; 1hr 15min); Lecco (12 daily; 1hr 20min); Pavia (37 daily; 25min); Peschiera (20 daily; 1hr 25min); Stresa (10 daily; 1hr 5min); Varese (4 daily; 1hr 10min).

Milan Lambrate to: Certosa di Pavia (13 daily; 30min); Cremona (12 daily; 1hr 35min); Pavia (18 daily; 25min).

Milan Porta Garibaldi to: Arona (11 daily; 1hr 10min); Bergamo (27 daily; 55min); Varese (17 daily; 1hr).

Milan Porta Genova to: Vigévano (28 daily; 35min).

Pavia to: Certosa di Pavia (14 daily; 10min); Cremona (11 daily; 2hr 20min); Mantua (6 daily; 3hr).

Sondrio to: Tirano (14 daily; 30min).

BUSES

Bergamo to: Clusone (23 daily; 1hr).

Brescia to: Gardone Riviera (33 daily; 1hr 5min); Iseo (2 daily; 30–55min).

Chiesa to: Chiareggio (2 daily; 30min).

Como to: Argegno (15 daily; 45min); Bellagio (12 daily; 1hr 10min); Cernobbio (every 30min; 20min); Colico (5 daily; 2hr 20min); Menaggio (16 daily; 1hr 10min); Tremezzo (14 daily; 1hr); Varese (38 daily; 1hr 10min).

Cremona to: Bergamo (4 daily; 2hr 20min); Brescia (12 daily; 1hr 25min); Iseo (2 daily; 2hr).

Gardone Riviera to: Limone (3 daily; 1hr); Riva del Garda (3 daily; 1hr 15min).

Mantua to: Peschiera (9 daily; 1hr 10min); Sabbioneta (4 daily; 50min); Verona (6 daily; 1hr 20min).

Menaggio to: Lugano (9 daily; 1hr).

Milan to: Cremona (8 daily; 2hr).

Pavia to: Vigévano (8 daily; 1hr).

Peschiera to: Garda (12 daily; 30min).

Sondrio to: Chiesa (6 daily; 30min).

Tirano to: Bormio (15 daily; 1hr).

FERRIES

Como to: Bellagio (4 daily; 2hr); Cernobbio (19 daily; 15min); Lenno (4 daily; 1hr 40min); Varenna (3 daily; 2hr 20min).

Desenzano to: Garda (3 daily; 1hr); Gardone Riviera (4 daily; 1hr 45min); Gargnano (2 daily; 2hr 30min); Malcesine (2 daily; 3hr 15min); Riva del Garda (2 daily; 4hr 10min); Saló (5 daily; 1hr 30min); Sirmione (10 daily; 20min).

Lenno to: Bellagio (4 daily; 20min); Menaggio (4 daily; 35min); Varenna (3 daily; 50min).

Stresa to: Intra (15 daily; 1hr); Isola Bella (21 daily; 5min); Isola dei Pescatori (20 daily; 10min); Isola Madre (19 daily; 30min); Pallanza (20 daily; 35min); Villa Taranto (11 daily; 45min).

HYDROFOILS

Arona to: Locarno (2 daily; 2hr), stopping at Stresa, Baveno, Pallanza, Intra, Luino, Cannobio.

Como to: Colico (5 daily; 1hr 30min), stopping at Argegno, Tremezzo, Bellagio, Menaggio, Varenna, Gravedona.

Desenzano to: Riva del Garda (3 daily; 2hr 20min), stopping at Sirmione, Peschiera (1 daily), Bardolino, Garda, Salò, Torri del Benaco (1 daily), Maderno, Malcesine, Limone.

CHAPTER FOUR

TRENTINO-ALTO ADIGE

Trentino-Alto Adige is something of an anomaly: a mixed **German-Italian** region, much of which has only been part of Italy since 1919. Before then Alto Adige was known as the South Tyrol and was part of Austria. At the end of World War I, Austria ceded South Tyrol to the Italians, and, in a bid to make the new territory instantly Italian, Mussolini turned the name on its head, naming it after the upper reaches of the Adige River, which bisects the region. Many Tyroleans opted for resettlement in Germany, but others stayed and have clung tenaciously to their language, culture and traditions.

Even now, one of the first things you'll notice about **Alto Adige** is its German character. Gothic onion-domed churches dot the landscape of vineyards and forests, street signs are in German, and there's sauerkraut and strudel on the menu. By contrast **Trentino**, just to the south, is 98 percent Italian-speaking, and the food and architecture belong more to the Mediterranean world than to the Alps. Both parts of the region enjoy semi-autonomy from central government, along with one of the highest standards of living in Italy, a consequence of special grants and aid they receive from Rome – intended to defuse the ethnic tension that has existed ever since enforced union took place.

If some German speakers are unwilling to remain part of Italy, there are right-wing Italian speakers who would be equally pleased to see them go. Friction between the two camps flared up in the Sixties, when Germanic activists staged disturbances. Talks between the Austrian and Italian governments brought about a package of concessions and promises from central government, known as the *pachetto*, all the provisions of which have now been implemented. These days, the **political climate** has shifted slightly: in the 1993 general elections, the fascist MSI (Movimento Sociale Italiano), once the most popular party among Italian-speakers, lost votes; and German-speakers moved away from the extreme nationalist Union Für Südtirol towards the Northern League and the Greens.

Tourism, farming and wine production are the mainstays of the economy, and there are plenty of good, reasonably cheap guesthouses and agriturism places in the mountains

---

ACCOMMODATION PRICE CODES

Throughout this guide, prices per person are given for **youth hostels** and assume Hostelling International (HI) membership. **Hotel** accommodation is coded on a scale from ① to ⑨, reflecting the cost of the cheapest double room in each establishment in high season. The price bands to which these codes refer are as follows:

① Up to L60,000/€30.99
② L60,000–90,000/€30.99–46.48
③ L90,000–120,000/€46.48–61.98
④ L120,000–150,000/€61.98–77.47
⑤ L150,000–200,000/€77.47–103.29

⑥ L200,000–250,000/€103.29–129.11
⑦ L250,000–300,000/€129.11–154.94
⑧ L300,000–400,000/€154.94–206.58
⑨ over L400,000/€206.58

(See p.32 for a full explanation.)

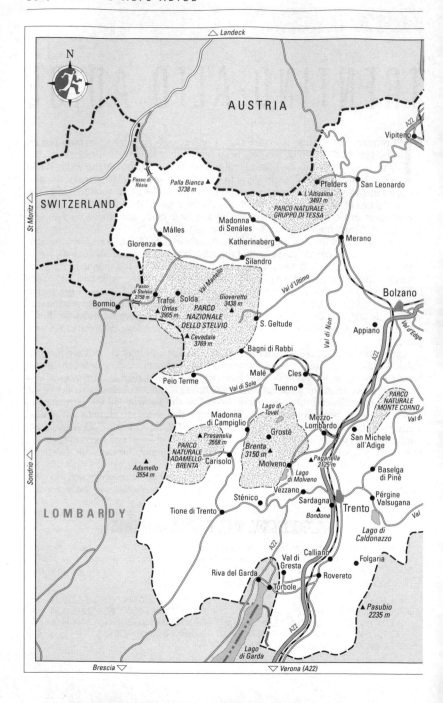

and vineyards. Although the region's resorts can be lethargic, the landscape, dominated by the stark and jagged **Dolomites**, is among the most beautiful in the country. Circling the spiked towers of rock that characterize the range, a network of trails follows the ridges, varying in length from a day's walk to a two-week trek; the long-distance trails, called *alte vie*, can be picked up from the small resorts.

The chief towns of **Trento** and **Bolzano** are the transport hubs for the region. Trento gives access to most of the western Dolomites: the **Pale di San Martino**, a cluster of enormous peaks encircling the high, rocky plain above San Martino di Castrozza; the **Catinaccio** (or Rosengarten) range between the Val di Fassa and Bolzano; the **Gruppo di Sella**, with its *vie ferrate* (see box on p.238); and the glacier-topped **Marmolada**. Still in the western Dolomites, but with easier access from Bolzano, are the **Alpe di Siusi**, a magical plateau of grass and wetland, high above the valley. The *alpe* are enclosed by the peaks of **Sasso Lungo** (or Langkofel) and **Sciliar** (or Schlern); to the north is the quieter Odle (or Geisler Gruppe). Even further to the west, on the other side of Trento, are the **Dolomiti di Brenta**, a collection of wild peaks above the meadows of Valle Rendena.

The eastern Dolomites start on the opposite side of the Adige Valley, past Passo di Campolongo and Corvara, with activity focusing on **Cortina d'Ampezzo**, self-styled "Queen of the Dolomite resorts" – though actually just across the regional border in the Veneto. In summer, avoid the overpopulated peaks like the **Tre Cime di Lavaredo**

REGIONAL FOOD AND WINE

Trentino-Alto Adige, as its name suggests, is really two regions: Alto Adige with its unreservedly Germanic traditions, and Trentino, which mixes mountain influences with more Italian flavours from the south. Another influence is the weather: in this mountainous region, with only a couple of snow-free months a year, the diet tends to be dominated by carbohydrates. There's no such thing as a light supper in Trentino.

A **typical meal** starts with some kind of salami *(lucanicche* in local dialect), often paper-thin slices of salt beef, followed by Tyrolean *canederli* – bread dumplings flavoured with *speck* (smoked ham) and accompanied by a melted butter dressing – or *strangolapreti*, bread and spinach gnocchi. Game and rabbit with polenta are popular as *secondi*. Desserts are often based on apples, pears or plums, readily available from the local orchards. Other sweet treats include *Soffiato alla Trentina*, a meringue trifle, and *Zelten Trentino*, a rich fruitcake flavoured with grappa and usually eaten at Christmas.

As you travel north into Alto Adige the menu becomes more Germanic, with *knödel* (dumplings) and goulash, sausages with horseradish sauce *(salsa al cren)*, sauerkraut, *apfel strudel*, *sachertorte* and all manner of sweet tarts and pastries. If you're really keen to sample some of Alto Adige's cuisine, try to co-ordinate your visit with the Törggelen season (see box on p.259).

Vines have been cultivated here since Roman times, and Trentino-Alto Adige produces more **DOC wines** than any other region in Italy. Most famous are the Pinot Grigios and Chardonnays, which are bright and aromatic from being grown at high altitudes and in cool conditions. These also provide wine makers with the raw material for some outstanding traditional-method sparkling wines, often marketed under the spumante Trentino Classico label. Despite the excellence of the whites, local wine makers actually make more reds, achieving considerable success with local varieties like Teróldego and Schiava (known as Vernatsch in German-speaking areas). Red wines made from Schiava are good when young: look out for the pale-red Kalterersee (Caldaro) and the fuller, more fruity St Magdalene (Santa Maddalena); those made from the Lagrein grape variety are more robust, such as the strong, dark Lagrein Dunkel, or the Kretzer rosé from Bolzano's vineyards at Gries. Also worth seeking out is the rare **vin santo** from Trentino's Valle dei Laghi – a luscious dessert wine made from local Nosiola grapes.

and head for **Sorapiss** or **Monte Pelmo** to the south, or **Le Tofane** and the mountains of the **Fánes-Sénnes-Bráies** group to the west. In winter, Cortina comes into its own as an upmarket ski resort with excellent, if expensive, facilities.

Hiking and skiing

The official **hiking** season lasts from June 20 to September 20; this is when most refuges and cable cars are open, though you'll find some also have a winter season. Cable cars sometimes close in mid-September. These dates may seem rigid, but they're based on long experience of climate in the area: snow can linger in the high country until late June, and winter closes in early. Some refuges open or close early or late according to local conditions. Nearby *rifugi* are the best place to phone for information on cable cars and weather conditions.

Routes are well-established, with a large number of well-marked day walks and a series of longer trails, known as **alte vie**. Four of these run north–south between the Val Pusteria (Pustertal) and the Veneto, and four from the Val d'Isarco (Eisacktal) south, each stage requiring five to eight hours' walking from one mountain refuge to the next. Some of the initial ascents are strenuous, but once you are up on the ridges the paths level out and give superb views across the valleys and glaciers. (As a rule of thumb, an averagely fit person takes around three hours to ascend 1000m.) Parts of the trails are exposed, or have snowfields across them, but alternative routes are always available. Alta Via 1, between the Lago di Bráies (Pragser Wildsee) and Belluno, is the most popular, so much so that you should think twice about going between mid-July and August because of the crowds, not to mention the summer heat.

There aren't many guides in English to the trails. Tourist offices usually have details of the day walks in the locality, often quite detailed and with good maps. The larger branches sometimes have guides to Alte Vie 1 and 2; Martin Collins's *Alta Via: High Level Walks in the Dolomites* (Cicerone) details walks along Alte Vie 1 and 2; and if you read Italian or German Alpina Verlag's *Dolomite Alte Vie/Dolomiten Hohenwegel 1–10*, is an extremely thorough option – available free from larger tourist offices. As for maps, the *alte vie* are marked on the Kompass 1:50,000 and Tabacco 1:25,000 maps, along with the multitude of other shorter trails which can be followed without guides. These maps are on sale everywhere in the Dolomites.

As for **skiing and winter sports**, Trento's excellent *Snow Info* brochure and Bolzano's skiing booklet (published by the provincial tourist offices) give details of chair lifts, altitude and length of runs in each resort, plus maps; try also *www. dolomitisuperski.com*. From December, you can get the latest on snow conditions in Trentino on ☎0461.916.666 and in Bolzano on ☎0471.271.177; Bolzano's weather Web site, *www.provinz.bz.it/meteo* is very useful. *Settimane Bianche* ("White Weeks") are bargain package deals offering full- or half-board and a ski-pass: information is available from Italian tourist offices before you leave, and also from regional offices in Italy. For specific details of places to stay, and prices, ask for the information leaflets published each October by local tourist offices. If you take a car and want to ski at more than one resort, the one-week Dolomiti Superski gives you access to 1200km of runs, 460 cable cars and chair lifts, and costs L60,000/€30.99 per day, though the more days you buy the cheaper it gets – a week costs L300,000/€154.93. Note that ski buses are free in some places.

Rifugi

The most convenient places to stay once you're high up are the **rifugi** (refuges). Solidly constructed, usually two- or three-storey buildings, they provide dormitory accommodation, meals and a bar. Some have hot showers, but just as many have only freezing

VIE FERRATE

Vie ferrate (literally "iron ways") are a peculiarly Italian phenomenon. The easiest way to describe them is as aided rock-climbs. Consisting of permanently fixed metal ladders, pegs and cables, onto which climbers' karabiners can be clipped, they provide access to routes which would otherwise be too difficult. Many *vie ferrate* were begun as far back as the late nineteenth century as mountaineering really took off in Europe; others were put in place by the Alpini troops during World War I to assist the climbs that were a matter of survival for the soldiers fighting in the mountains. Many more have been created since, by volunteers from local Club Alpino Italiano groups.

All are clearly marked on both Kompass and Tabacco maps as a line of little black dots or crosses, but *vie ferrate* are definitely not for beginners or vertigo-sufferers. You need to be confident belaying, have the proper equipment (including helmet, ropes, two self-locking karabiners and a chest- or seat-harness) – and you must know what you're doing. Incidentally, it's not advisable to climb a *via ferrata* in a thunderstorm either; it might just become one long lightning conductor.

Of course, once you've done a few straightforward paths up in the mountains you may be inspired to tackle some *ferrate*, and there are plenty of people around who will teach you. Individual guides charge by the hour, and so become more affordable if you can assemble a small group. Otherwise, enrol on a mountain skills course: both Trentino and Alto Adige provincial tourist offices keep lists of guides and mountaineering schools, but you'll need to book well in advance.

GUIDES AND MOUNTAINEERING SCHOOLS

Alpinschule Südtirol, Jungmannstrasse 8, Campo Tures (☎0474.690.012). Courses throughout the Dolomites, from ice-climbing to *vie ferrate*. The school is run by the famous mountaineer Hans Kammerlander.

Collegio Guide Alpine (☎0461.981.207, *b.f.v@pronet.it*). Central number for Alpine guides in the province of Trentino. For Alto Adige, call ☎0471.976.357.
Scuola Alpinismo Orizzonti Trentini, Via Petrarca 8 (☎0461.230.141). Trento-based guides.

cold water. Blankets are provided, and sheets can be rented for a nominal charge. All are open from June until around September or October, and some also operate in the skiing season; we've given opening periods as a guide, but these are still subject to prevailing weather conditions. If you're planning a long trek that relies on refuges for accommmodation, you should definitely call ahead; at the same time, you can check that the place isn't likely to be packed out by a large party – nobody is ever turned away, but overflow accommodation is either on a mattress in the bar or even in the hen house. **Emergency calls** can be made from the refuges; to call Soccorso Alpino (Alpine Rescue), dial ☎118. A full list of refuges, with phone numbers, is available from the provincial tourist offices in Bolzano and Trento. For more on *rifugi*, see "Accommodation" in Basics, p.35

TRENTINO

Unlike Alto Adige to the north, where you sometimes wonder if you've crossed the border into Austria, **Trentino** is unmistakably Italian. The main centre is **Trento**, which like its smaller cousin to the south, Rovereto, was established in the Middle Ages as a market town in a predominantly wine-growing area. Trento makes an excellent base for travelling into the mountains, where countless trails cross the awesome terrain (over fifty percent of the area is covered with forest). Close to Rovereto, one of the more unusual trails is the **Sentiero della Pace** ("Path of Peace"), which snakes across the province along the World War I front. A long campaign of attrition took place in these peaks, claiming 460,000 dead – many from the cold – and 947,000 wounded on the Italian side alone. The trail occasionally enters galleries carved through rock, or old fortifications pitted with bullet holes.

Up in the mountains, a traditional way of life still thrives. In the summer months, farmers base themselves in a *malga* (hut) on the upper pastures and cut timber and hay, bringing their animals and wood down to the village as soon as winter starts. The first snowfall is the starting signal for Trentino's other major earner, tourism: the area is crisscrossed with ski-lifts and runs, and also offers facilities for other winter sports, such as ice-skating on the lakes and ice-waterfall climbing.

Trento

Straddling the Adige Valley, **TRENTO**, just three hours from Venice by train, is a quiet provincial centre that makes one of the best bases for exploring the region, not least because of its bus services to the mountains. Overshadowed by Monte Bondone, it's beautifully sited too, encircled by mountains and exuding a relaxed pace of life. It wasn't always so, however. From the tenth to the eighteenth centuries, Trento was a powerful bishopric ruled by a dynasty of princes; it was the venue of the Council of Trent in the sixteenth century, when the Catholic Church, threatened by the Reformation in northern Europe, met to plan its countermeasures – meetings that spanned a total of eighteen years. Later, throughout the nineteenth century, ownership of the city, which remained in Austrian hands, was hotly contested, and it only became properly part of Italy in 1918, after the conclusion of World War I.

Arrival, information and accommodation

Trento's main **bus and train stations** are almost next door to each other at Piazza Dante and Via Pozzo. A secondary, combined station – **Trento-Malé**, run by a private company – is on Via Dogana, just beyond the train station, with trains up to Cles in the Val di Non, Malé in the Vale di Sole (the line is being extended further north to Fucine, due for completion around 2002) and buses to Madonna di Campiglio and Molveno. Tickets and information on Trento-Malé connections can be had from the office at the station (☎0461.238.350, *www.fertm.it*).

The **tourist office** at Via Alfieri 4, across the park from the main train station (Mon–Sat 9am–6pm, Sun 9am–1pm; ☎0461.983.880), has information specifically on Trento, including copies of *Trentino Mese*, the monthly guide to life in the town. The **regional information centre** is at Via Romagnosi 11 (Mon–Fri 9am–12.30pm & 2.30–5pm; ☎0461.839.000) and has details on mountain refuges, transport, hiking and skiing possibilities, and agriturismo in the province. Ask too for their free *Guida ai Trasporti nel Trentino*, which details all the bus and train schedules in the province.

For **accommodation** close to the central Piazza Duomo, there are three inexpensive places: *Al Cavallino Bianco*, Via Cavour 29 (☎0461.231.542; ②) is mildly shabby, but the cheapest are: the *Venezia*, Piazza Duomo 45 (☎0461.234.559, fax 0461.234.114; ②), which is plain but comfortable, with a few rooms overlooking the piazza and others in a thirteenth-century tower, and the rather more luxurious *Aquila d'Oro*, next door, at Via Belenzani 76 (☎ & fax 0461.986.282; ④). Close to the main station, the smart *Hotel America*, at Via Torre Verde 50 (☎0461.983.010, fax 0461.230.603; ③), is the only other affordable hotel anywhere near the centre. In Cagnola, in the hills overlooking Trento to the east, the *Villa Madruzzo*, Via Ponto Alto 26 (☎0461.986.220, fax 0461.986.361; ③), is good value and also serves regional cuisine; take bus #9 (L1500/€0.77), a twenty-

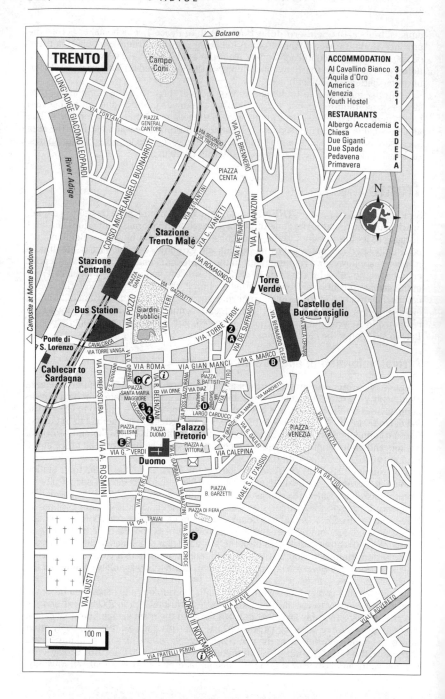

minute journey. For those on a budget there's the friendly **youth hostel**, *Giovane Europa*, at Via Manzoni 17 (☎ & fax 0461.234.567; L22,000/€11.36 including breakfast), which has a midnight curfew. The nearest **campsite** is a stiff hike away at the end of a cable-car ride, on Monte Bondone, which overlooks town from across the river (see "Around Trento" on p.243).

The Town

Trento was known as Tridentum to the Romans, a name celebrated by the eighteenth-century Neptune fountain in the central **Piazza Duomo**, a pleasant square ringed by arcades, shops and cafés and giving onto streets lined with frescoed palaces, notably via Belanziani, many of them built in the sixteenth century when Trento was an important market town. Architecture buffs might like to pick up an excellent guide to the palaces, *Renaissance Trento*, from the tourist information office. The three most significant meetings of the Council of Trent – convened to confront the growth of Protestantism and to establish the so-called Counter-Reformation – took place in the **Duomo** between 1545 and 1563. The building itself was begun in the thirteenth century, but wasn't completed until the sixteenth. Inside, the arched, colonnaded steps flanking the nave are a dramatic touch to an otherwise plain building. There are fresco fragments in the nave and an enormous carved marble baldachin over the altar – a replica of the one in St Peter's, Rome – although the most interesting part lies under the church, where a medieval crypt and foundations of an early Christian basilica (built over the tomb of St Vigilio, the third bishop of Trento) were discovered in 1977.

In the late 1970s, excavations uncovered the remains of an early Christian Basilica. The neighbouring **Museo Diocesano Tridentino e Basilica Paleocristiana** (Mon–Sat 9.30am–12.30pm & 2.30–6pm; L5000/€2.58), housed in the Palazzo Pretorio, includes large annotated paintings of the sessions of the Council of Trent and some carved altarpieces from the church of San Zeno in the Val di Non. Hidden away in cell-like side rooms are some ornate reliquaries and an impressive cycle of fifteenth-century Flemish tapestries. The building is appealing in itself, too, with its fishtail battlements and heavy studded doors and a view from the upper floor of the frescoed palaces around the square.

The most powerful of the Trento princes was Bernardo Clesio, who in the late fifteenth and early sixteenth centuries built up much of the town's art collection, a good proportion of which is held in the **Castello del Buonconsiglio** (Tues–Sat 9am–noon & 2–5.30pm; L9000/€4.65), another venue of the Council of Trent, a short walk from Piazza Duomo on the eastern side of the town centre. It's two castles really: the thirteenth-century **Castelvecchio** and the extension built in 1530 called the **Magno Palazzo**, in which several rooms frescoed with classical subjects by the Dossi Family and Romanino lead off a quiet inner courtyard. Upstairs is the **Museo Provinciale d'Arte**, whose highlight is the *Ciclo dei Mesi* ("Cycle of the Months"), hidden at the end of a narrow passageway in the Torre d'Aquila (ask at the ticket desk to be taken there). These fifteenth-century frescoes show details from farming and courtly life and – reflecting the castle's role in the nineteenth century – soldiers confined to barracks; in a case of life imitating art, soldiers also added their own touches by scribbling on the borders and drawing in beards.

The ditch around the castle was the place of execution for two celebrated Trentese, Cesare Battisti and his comrade Fabio Filzi. Born in 1875, Battisti was a man of his times, a combination of romantic idealist and guerrilla fighter. He set up the socialist-irredentist newspaper *Il Popolo* as a forum for protest against Austrian rule, and used Italy's entry into World War I as an opportunity to step up his campaign to eject Austrian forces from the Tyrol. The stratagem was unsuccessful: in 1916 he led an attempt to take Monte Pasubio to the south of Trento, but he was arrested by the

Austrians and shot as a traitor. You can visit his and Filzi's cells in the castle, as well as a small museum to the Risorgimento and Liberation of Trentino.

Eating, drinking and nightlife

You can **eat** well in Trento and the surrounding area, feasting on unfussy local specialities. Gourmands will appreciate the special L85,000/€43.90 six-course and L55,000/€28.41 four-course menus at *Osteria a le due Spade* on Via Dom Archangelo Rizzi 11 (west of the duomo off Via G. Verdi; closed Mon lunch & all day Sun), with sophisticated dishes to savour in a low-ceilinged, wood-panelled room. For about the same price, try the restaurant attached to the *Albergo Accademia* at Vicolo Collico 6, off Piazza Sta. Maria Maggiore (☎0461.981.580; no closing day), which serves marvellous local specialities. Otherwise try the slightly less pricey *Chiesa*, on Via San Marco (closed Sun), with fish a speciality. If you're feeling more budget-concious, *Due Giganti*, at Via Simonino 14 (closed Sun), is a good-value self-service place, offering simple fixed-price menus or pasta dishes from L6000/€3.10. There are also a couple of good *rosticcerie* on Via Santa Croce, near the market, plus the lively *Pedavena* at Via Santa Croce 15 (closed Tues), which stays open until midnight and serves excellent, cheap Trentese dishes such as *canederli* and *strangolapreti* (spinach gnocchi). *Primavera*, at

---

TRAVELLING THE WINE ROAD

Wine enthusiasts are well catered for in Trentino, with a wine road (Strada di Vino or Südtiroler Weinstrasse) that enables you to indulge in a happy combination of sightseeing and **sampling local food and wine**. Head out of Trento on the trunk road to Bolzano, and take the right turning, signposted for Lavis, from where the wine road is clearly marked.

The vines are often strung on wide pergolas, the traditional method of viticulture here since Roman times, which allows the breezes blowing up the Adige Valley from Lake Garda to circulate around the grapes, giving a beneficial cooling effect. Farmers and wine makers who are part of the agriturismo network advertise their establishments with a **yellow sign**: anything with a farm name and a knife and fork symbol is usually worth investigating. Often the owners will have converted a room in their farmhouse into a small informal restaurant, and will serve a set meal, accompanied by their own (or local) wine for around L15,000/€7.75. Most of the goodies will be home-made: *nostra produzione* is the phrase to look out for, applied across the menu to anything from salami to sausages to goat's cheese. It helps to have a few words of Italian or German at your disposal so you can chat – you will probably be shown around the farm or cantina (winery) if you express an interest.

---

via Suffragio 92, is popular for inexpensive Italian standards and has outside seating under the arches.

One of the best ways to sample **regional cooking** is to follow your nose along the wine road (see box above), but there are also more formal places to try local delicacies. South of town, try *Marlene*, in località Margone di Ravina (☎0461.349.148; closed Thurs & all June).

Trento doesn't resound with **nightlife**, but there are a couple of good bars that stay open late. *Pub Stube*, at Via del Suffragio 51 (closed Sun), is the centre of the German-speaking scene, while inevitably, students head for one of the two Irish pubs, *Murphy's*, on Piazza Duomo, or the *Irish Pub* on Via G. Verdi.

Around Trento

Cable cars run from Ponte San Lorenzo, near Trento's bus station (every 15–30min; L1500/€0.77), to **SARDAGNA**, on the lower slopes of the towering Monte Bondone. There's some skiing in winter, and a scattering of holiday homes belonging mostly to Trentese; for committed **campers** there's *Camping Mezavia* (☎0461.948.178; June–Sept & Dec–April), two hours' trek from the top of the cable car. Also popular with locals are the resorts of **Lavarone** and **Folgaria** to the south, or **Pergine** to the west near **Lago di Caldonazzo**, where there is a free beach and lido (buses from Trento).

An enlightening half-day trip from the city (and reachable by local bus) is a visit to the **ethnographic museum** (Museo degli Usi e Costumi della Gente Trentina; Tues–Sat: summer 10am–12.30pm & 2.30–7pm; winter 9am–12.30pm & 2.30–6pm; L5000/€2.58) at **SAN MICHELE ALL'ADIGE**. One of the largest of its kind in Europe, with exhibits ranging from re-creations of village houses (complete with muddy boots drying by the stove) to displays on hunting, grazing and wine making, the museum gives a real flavour of what life in Trentino was like until the twentieth century.

The rail line south from Trento runs between the scree-covered slopes of the Adige Valley, where the only sight for miles might be a station platform in the middle of nowhere or the blank fortifications of a castle or World War I stronghold. Hanging on an outcrop above the village of **CALLIANO**, 9km north of Rovereto, **Castel Beseno** is one of the few castles that have been restored and is open to the public (April–Sept Tues–Sun 9am–noon & 2–5.30pm; Oct–March Tues–Sat 9am–noon & 2–5pm; L6000/€3.10, combined ticket with Castello del Buonconsiglio L13,000/€6.71). It's more of a fortified town than a castle in fact, spreading across the hilltop at the valley entrance and once providing a bulwark between the Venetians and the Tyrolese. A bloody but decisive battle was fought here in 1487, after which the Venetians gave up all hope of seizing Trentino at all. The castle is a twenty-minute walk from the village of **Besenello**, which is connected with Trento (and Rovereto – see below) by bus. At weekends buses run all the way to the castle from Besenello's main piazza.

Rovereto

About 45 minutes south of Trento by bus, **ROVERETO** is the largest town in the area between Trento and Verona. The gilded lion of St Mark over the gateway into the old town dates from the fifteenth century, when Rovereto was an outpost of the Venetian Empire, as do the extensions to the castle, now the **Museo della Guerra** (mid-March to June, Oct & Nov Tues–Sun 8am–12.30pm & 2–6pm; July–Sept Tues–Sun 8.30am–6.30pm; L10,000/€5.16). Along the dark stone streets of the old town on Via della Terra, the **Museo Depero** (Tues–Sun: April–Sept 10am–12.30pm & 2.30–7pm; Oct–March 9–11.30am & 2.30–6pm; L4000/€2.07) has a collection of Futurist art ranging from Fortunato Depero's advertising designs (Campari posters among others) to semi-abstract work. Cassettes and word-pictures – including an evocative one of the New York subway – complement the more conventional stuff. If you're obliged to stay in Rovereto, there's a **youth hostel**, *Ancona*, at Via della Scuola 16 (☎0464.433.707; L25,000/€12.91) 400m from the train station.

Monte Pasubio

Some of the most bloody engagements of World War I took place around **Monte Pasubio**, to the southeast of Rovereto. The recently created **Sentiero della Pace** ("Path of Peace") follows the front, from the Órtles mountains east across the ranges to Marmolada, the trail littered with old bullets and barbed wire. Tourist offices can provide free maps (Kompass, 1:50,000) of the entire route. The opposing armies dug fortresses in the rock and cut tunnels into the glaciers, but protection from enemy fire did not ensure safety – in the winter of 1916, one of the hardest in living memory, around 10,000 soldiers died in avalanches. The historian G.M. Trevelyan, commander of a British Red Cross ambulance unit in the campaign, described one fortress as "four storeys of galleries, one above the other, each grinning with cannon and machine guns. There were also medieval-looking wooden machines for pouring volleys of rock down the gullies by which the enemy might attempt to ascend... Our work lay, of course, at the foot of the *teleferiche*, or aerial railways which fed the war on those astonishing rock citadels: the sick and wounded came down the wires in cages, hundreds of feet in the air." The Campana dei Caduti, made out of melted-down cannon, tolls every evening in memory of the dead of both sides, from the Colle di Miravalle, a hill just outside Rovereto.

The Dolomiti di Brenta

The sawtoothed peaks and glaciers of the **Dolomiti di Brenta**, northwest of Trento, give these ranges a rougher character than the rest of the Dolomites, yet throughout you can choose your own level of walking. While steep, few peaks rise above 3000m, and the paths are easy to follow but strenuous, while less demanding trails circle the side valleys. The range is circled by a good slow road, the southern half of which passes through the quiet lake resort of **Malveno** before it is joined by the road from Trento. The circuit then turns north passing the frescoed churches and wooded valleys of the **Valle Rendena** before arriving at the main resort of **Madonna di Campiglio**, the best base for climbing, walking or skiing in the area. The northern half of the Brenta is bounded by **Val di Non** and **Val di Sole**, both served by the private Trento-Malè railway line and home to a smattering of castles and other sights.

Climbers come here for the towers of Cima Tosa and Cima Brenta, the original reason for *vie delle bochette* – iron ladders knocked into the rock to give access to these ascents; their position, clinging tenaciously to the rock walls, is sensational (see box on p.238 for more on these *vie ferrate*). There are enough regular, marked footpaths for two or three days' high-altitude walking; Kompass produce the best map for the area. Trento's tourist office has a free guide to the Dolomiti di Brenta in English.

Up the Valle Rendena

Buses from Trento to Madonna di Campiglio skirt Monte Bondone and wind their way past a series of patchy hills and villages, passing **Lago di Toblino**, just outside **VEZZANO**, where **Castel Toblino** – now a restaurant – sits on a spit of land jutting into the lake. The castle is steeped in the legend of a medieval love affair between one Claudia Particella and Carlo Emanuele Madruzzo, Prince-Bishop of Trento. The bishop apparently asked the pope, in vain, to allow him to leave the Church; undeterred, the two lovers returned to the castle, but one night, during a trip on the lake, they mysteriously drowned. Whether it was murder, accident or suicide is unknown. In the restaurant, a four-course meal will set you back by L60,000/€30.99, but there's also a lakeside bar selling beer, coffee and sandwiches for a fraction of the price.

From Lago di Toblino, the road continues west, turning into the **Valle Rendena** at Tione di Trento, where a more remote landscape of pasture and forest begins. This quiet valley is a good place to rest up, with an wonderfully eccentric roadside **hotel**, *Pub-Museum da Giorgio* (☎0465.321.541; ④) at Iavré, 6km north of Tione and a couple of small **campsites** reasonably close to villages; one of these is *Faè della Val Rendena* (☎0465.57.178; June–Sept & Dec–April) north of Pinzolo, near **Sant'Antonio di Mavignola**.

Small churches like the lone Sant'Antonio, just before Borzago, are decorated with fresco cycles by Baschenis, one of the many Bergamasque artists who worked in the area. At **CARISOLO**, the church of **Santo Stefano** has frescoes of a *danse macabre* on an outside wall, and others inside depicting the legend of Charlemagne's passage through the Val di Campiglio on the way to his coronation in Rome. Before Madonna, several turnings off the main road lead high up west into the Adamello range, the most beautiful being the **Val di Genova**, which begins 2km from Carisolo. The road follows the cascading river up through a pine forest, along a deteriorating road past several waterfalls, spectacular in spring when the snow begins to melt. Most impressive is the **Cascata di Nárdis**, 4km from the turn-off, where several channels spill down the granite rock walls of the mountainside. Facing the waterfall is the *Albergo Cascate Nardis* (☎0465.501.454; ⑤), with a restaurant; it's a good place to stop, though busy with day-trippers in summer. From here, it's another 13km to **BÉDOLE** (1614m), and a further two to three hours' hike from there along trail 212 to the *Rifugio Città di Trento* (☎0465.501.193; March–Sept) at 2480m, within reach of the Adamello glaciers.

A short way before Carisolo, at **CADERZONE**, a turning off the Valle Rendena follows a much less trodden trail (221) which heads steeply up to the small lakes of **San Giuliano** and **Garzone** (two and a half hours' walk). There's a small, very basic refuge between the two, and a second path (230) heads north then descends to Pinzolo (two hours' descent). A further 3km up the valley is the ski village of **PINZOLO**. It's much smaller than its neighbour Madonna di Campiglio (ski-lift passes cover both resorts), but well worth a look for its church of San Vigilio, decorated with another sixteenth-century fresco of the danse macabre by Simone Baschenis.

Madonna di Campiglio

The major village in the Valle Rendena is **MADONNA DI CAMPIGLIO**, an upmarket ski resort with plenty of chair lifts and runs for all levels of skiing. About eight **buses** a day run from Trento to the main square, not far from the **tourist office** on Via Pradalago 4 (Mon–Sat 9am–noon & 3–6.30pm, Sun 9am–noon; ☎0465.442.000). Another service runs at about the same frequency to Malé, 23km north, from where you can pick up trains back to Trento. In summer, the climbing and walking in the Dolomiti di Brenta are superb, and you may want to stay at Madonna, if only to reach the trailheads. Luckily, out of the skiing season, the village tends to be deserted except for a sprinkling of walkers, and there are often good off-season deals to be had in three-star **hotels**. A good, central place is *La Montanara* (☎0465.441.105; ④), though the least expensive places in town are a few minutes' walk down via Vallesina – follow the yellow signs for the *Rifugio Vallesinella*; try the *Garni Bucaneve* (☎0465.441.271; ④), the *Garni dei Fiori* (☎0465.442.310; ④) and the *Norma* (☎0465.441.110; ④).

The best way to approach the trailheads is by cable car from **Carlo Magno**, 3km north of the village centre, to Grostè (mid-June to mid-Sept daily 8.30am–12.30pm & 2–5pm; L19,000/€9.81 one way, L26,000/€13.43 return) – see below. Another possibility is to head west, taking Funivia Cinque Laghi (July to mid-Sept, same times and prices as above) from the centre of town to *Rifugio Pancugolo* (☎0465.443.270) at 2064m, in the Presanella group. From the refuge, paths include a five-hour route via **Lago Ritorto** and **Lago Gelato** back down to the valley.

Trails from Grostè

Once you're at **GROSTÈ** (2437m) you can plan your own routes as long as you have a decent hiking map, such as the one produced by Kompass. The *Rifugio Graffer*, by the cable car terminus, at 2262m, was closed at the time of writing, but is due to re-open soon (☎0465.986.462; June 20 to Sept 20 & Dec 1 to April 30). It is close to the trails and will have overnight accommodation and a restaurant. From the cable-car station, trail

316 sets out across boulder-strewn slopes towards refuges *Sella* and *Tuckett* (both ☎0465.507.287; June–Sept), about 5km (1hr 30min) away, where you can eat a large meal and bask on the veranda, thousands of feet above the valley.

Trail 328, which later becomes 318 (called the Sentiero Bogani), starts just past the refuges; there are difficult boulders to negotiate at first, but then there's an easy path which has been blasted out of the side of the rock walls. A shrine in a small overhang commemorates the lives lost in these peaks, but by this time, about four hours from Grostè, the *Rifugio Brentei* (☎0465.441.244; June–Sept), set at 2176m, is in sight, mid-way between Cima Brenta and Cima Tosa. There are some difficult ascents a short distance from the refuge, but it's more than likely that by this stage you won't be capable of anything other than staring across the vast ravine at the Adamello glaciers in the distance. Next day, if you can cope with snowfields, you could either trek up to the **Bocca di Brenta** and cross over the ridge to meet trail 319 down to Molveno (see below; 3hr 30min), or simply return to Madonna via trails 318 and 316 (3hr 30min).

Molveno

The lakeside village of **MOLVENO**, surrounded by the peaks of the Brenta Alta, is a marginally cheaper place to stay than Madonna. Although the cheapest places go quickly, particularly in high season, the **tourist office** here, above the lake in the small town centre, at Piazza Marconi 5 (Mon–Sat 9am–12.30pm & 3–6.30pm, Sun 9.30am–12.30pm; ☎0461.586.086, *www.molvenohappyholiday.it*) should be able to help you find a **room** for the night. *Albergo Italia* (☎0461.586.915; ⑤) and the plainer *Garni Alpenrose*, just back from the campsite (☎0461.586.169; ③) are both on Via Lungolago, with views of the lake. Failing these, there's a swish **campsite**, *Campeggio Spiaggia Lago di Molveno* (☎0461.586.978, *www.campingspiaggio.com*), on the water's edge.

There are few **easy trails** from Molveno into the Brenta massif – paths often disappear into nothing but *vie ferrate* across the rocks; fortunately these are all marked on maps, so you just need to plan your route carefully. If you decide to approach the Brenta group from this side, a cable car runs from the village to **Pradel** (1500m), where there's an albergo, *Rifugio Pradel* (☎0461.586.903), and from where trails lead through the beeches and pines of the **Val delle Seghe** in the shadow of Croz dell'Altissimo (2339m). An easy circular route winds back to Molveno (2hr 30min), or technically more demanding paths take you higher up, past *Rifugio Tosa* at 2439m, and *Rifugio Tommaso Pedrotti* at 2491m (both ☎0461.948.115).

The most prodigious of nineteenth-century climbers, Francis Fox Tuckett, opened up a difficult new route to Cima Brenta from Molveno, now known as the **Bochetta di Tuckett**. As ice axes hadn't been invented, he negotiated snowfields with a ladder and alpenstock, and carried joints of meat and bottles of wine for mountaintop breakfasts. The landscape where he "roamed amongst toppling rocks, and spires of white and brown and bronze coloured stone" is almost unchanged but for the *bochetta*, descending from the pass down to the *Tuckett* and *Sella* refuges (see above). More paths skirt Cima Tosa and lead to Pinzolo via *Rifugio Dodici Apostoli* (☎0465.501.309), a stone-built refuge for the hardy set at 2498m, with only cold water to wash in.

From Molveno, the road follows the lake south then descends down to **Ponte Arche**, where you can pick up buses on the Madonna–Trento route. It's a beautiful trip through a valley which hasn't benefited from, or been blighted by, ski tourism, but there are only two buses daily.

Val di Non and Val di Sole

The steep **Val di Non**, where apple orchards cover every available terraced slope, skirts the northern edges of the Brenta group. You see the best of the valley by car, taking the turning for Tuenno off the N43 from Trento to **CLES**, at the head of the Val di Non. Cles is also served by buses, and trains on the private Trento-Malé line. Lying close to the shore of the artificial **Lago di Santa Giustina**, Cles presents a strange mixture, with a hydroelectric dam on the lake to the northeast and several (privately owned) castles around, including the turreted **Castel Cles**, which has good frescoes by Fogolino.

Across the lake from Cles, the **Santuario di San Romedio** (always open), reachable by car or a 45-minute walk uphill from **SANZENO** (follow the signs past *Ristorante Mulino*), is a popular pilgrimage shrine, the legendary home of Romedius, a hermit who lived with his bear on the side of the cliff. The sanctuary is a complex of several churches built between the eleventh and eighteenth centuries; with its gateway and isolated position surrounded by forest, it feels like a private citadel. Votive offerings and hordes of crutches line the walls of the narrow stone stairwell up to the atmospheric highest chapel, said to be the saint's retreat. A brown mother-bear, her mate and their offspring pad around their family den on one side of the grounds.

From Cles, the **Parco Nazionale dello Stelvio** is just an hour or so's drive via Malé and Bagni di Rabbi or Pejo Terme; the last two villages are both off the N42, although if you're relying on buses, access to the park is much easier from Merano (see p.259). **MALÉ** itself, in the **Val di Sole** (*www.valdisole.net*), has the **Museo Della Civiltà Solandra** in Via Trento (June 22–Sept 12 Mon–Sat 10am–noon & 4–7pm; free but donations gratefully received), which takes an evocative look at how life once was in the valley, and tells of seasonal migration as far afield as Russia. A good selection of walking literature and maps is available from the **tourist office** on Piazza Regina Elena (Mon–Sat 9am–noon & 4–7pm, Sun 10am–noon; ☎0463.901.280).

East of Trento

To the **east of Trento**, the **Valsugana** and the **Val di Fiemme** are joined by road, making a wide loop. Halfway around, a group of stunning pinnacles and bare peaks called the **Pale di San Martino** appears: formed as a coral reef sixty million years ago, their rock is so pale it glares even at dawn. It is now incorporated in the **Parco Naturale Panevéggio**, a gentler, wooded area with many walks, trails and campsites. The nearest resort to the Pale is **San Martino di Castrozzo**, the terminus for buses travelling the loop in both directions.

Valsugana

Most people take the bus along the **Valsugana** to get to a market in one of its modern and busy towns, such as Caldonazzo. There's nothing to see between the towns except rows of fruit trees and vineyards, and later, as the Brenta Valley closes in to become a narrow gorge, a succession of hydroelectric plants. What makes the trip interesting is the terrain to the north, in particular the **Cima d'Asta**, a mountain dotted with bright blue, icy tarns and crossed by the Sentiero della Pace ("Path of Peace", see p.239). You reach the westerly part of this from **Panarotta**, in the mountains above Lago di Caldonazzo, from where the trail – at this point an ancient ridgeway path and wartime patrol route – follows a course across the peaks towards Passo di Rolle (see "Parco Naturale Panevéggio", p.249).

If you're travelling by public transport from Trento to San Martino di Castrozza you have no choice but to travel the long way round, via Fonzaso in the Veneto; most services head east by **train** from Trento to Primolano, where you have to change for the **bus** on to San Martino. By **car**, though, there's a short cut if you turn off at Borgo Valsugana and cut through the foothills, climbing through an increasingly Alpine landscape to rejoin the main road at Imer.

Imer, Mezzano and Fiera di Primiero

IMER and, a couple of kilometres east, **MEZZANO** are archetypal tourist villages, decked out with geraniums and credit card stickers, attracting people by the busload, but away from the main roads you can easily escape the crowds. The valley itself is wide, with hay meadows spreading either side, and, outside from the main tourist centres, makes a good place to rest up, with easy paths running into the foothills. One possibility is the path east from Imer along the lush **Val Noana** to the reservoir under the slopes of Monte Pavione (a 3hr 30min round trip). As far as **accommodation** goes, self-sufficiency is an advantage, as you'll be competing with bus tours for the cheap hotels. An alternative to Alpine-style hotels in the villages is *Camping Calavise*, a (well-signposted) couple of kilometres off the main valley road (☎0439.67.468) or, further up the valley, *Rifugio Fonteghi* (☎0439.67.043), a forty-five-minute walk along the path on the south side of the reservoir.

About 4km further on from Imer, **FIERA DI PRIMIERO** is a larger resort and market town with a tourist office (Mon–Sat 9am–noon & 3–7pm, Sun 9.30am–12.30pm; ☎0439.62.407). It's a major crossroads in the area, from where buses run up to the beginning of the Val Canali and to Passo Cereda (1369m). The mountains around Fiera were worked for silver from the thirteenth century, and local miners paid for the town's fifteenth-century church. Now the ranges are crossed by hiking trails.

Trails to the north of Passo Cereda take you up into the high plateau of the **Pale di San Martino**. One path follows a long ridge of rock before passing down into **Val Canali**, described by Amelia Edwards in the nineteenth century as the most "lonely, desolate and tremendous scene . . . to be found this side of the Andes". Things have changed since the arrival of Alta Via 2 – followed by a bar, visitor centre, refuge and campsite – but the valley retains a feeling of isolation. The official site, *Castelpietra* (☎0439.62.426), is opposite the National Park centre, and there are further places to camp at the head of the glen. *Rifugio Treviso* (☎0439.62.311; end of June–Sept) is a possible overnight stop, while the more luxurious *Cant del Gal* (☎0439.62.997; ③), further down the valley, also has a good restaurant specializing in game and wild mushrooms, though it's fairly expensive.

A stiff ascent from *Rifugio Treviso* brings you onto the **Altopiano delle Pale** at Passo di Pradidali, where eagles can be seen circling above the barren plateau and the silence is broken every so often by a trickle of falling stones. Once you are at this altitude, there are many possibilities for linking up with other trails across the stark upland; local tourist offices publish a useful 1:35,000 map which shows the various paths, though you shouldn't rely on it for navigation. *Rifugio Pedrotti alla Rosetta* (☎0439.682.578; June–Sept), at 2581m, is the nearest place with accommodation (a 2hr 30min hike north); facilities include coldwater washbasins, a restaurant and bar. The *rifugio* is also the base of the Orizzonti Trentini alpine guides (see "Vie ferrate" box on p.238).

San Martino di Castrozza and around

The road into **SAN MARTINO DI CASTROZZA** twists and turns, and you feel like you're in the middle of nowhere until the resort's new hotels appear around the corner; the sensation is even more marked if you're heading up over the Passo di Rolle (see opposite). After Cortina d'Ampezzo, San Martino is one of the smarter Dolomite resorts, but it has a more relaxed atmosphere in its cafés and a less pretentious way of going about things. The **tourist office**, next to the bus stop, at Via Passo Rolle 165 (Mon–Sat 9am–noon & 3–7pm, Sun 9.30am–12.30pm; ☎0439.768.867, *www.san martino.com*) may be able to help with finding a cheapish **room**. Otherwise, try the *Biancaneve* (☎0439.68.135; ③) or the slightly more expensive *Suisse* (☎0439.68.087; ③); both are on Via Dolomiti, which runs off the main square just up from the tourist office.

The alternative is to pitch a tent at the village **campsite**, *Sass Maor* (☎0439.68.347), about a kilometre from the centre. Heading out of San Martino, **buses** south to Fiera di Primiero and Imer run at least hourly. The service north over the Passo di Rolle runs less often, but you can count on at least six daily for much of the summer.

A number of **trails**, chair lifts and cable cars head off into the mountains, making San Martino one of the best bases in the area. The strongest attraction is again the **Pale di San Martino**; a cable-car ride from San Martino (daily 8am–5pm; journey up L18,000/€9.30, down L16,500/€8.52, return-trip L28,000/€14.46) takes you up to *Rifugio Pedrotti alla Rosetta*, perched on the edge of the Altopiano – see opposite for details. The Colverde cable car from the village runs to the foot of the Pale, from where the Rosetta cable car takes you up to the highland.

Up on the summits, even in the summer, you should be prepared for snow, wind and rain – as well as scorching sun and the most stupendous views. From the chair-lift terminus, you can make for *Rifugio Pradidali* at 2278m (☎0439.64.180), a walk and descent of three hours. A more ambitious walk would be to continue on from the refuge over the **Passo di Ball**, returning from there to San Martino or descending over into **Val Canali** at *Rifugio Cant del Gal* (see opposite). If you prefer the relative security of a guided trek, ask at the desk of the Gruppo Guide Alpine (☎0439.768.795), in the same building as the tourist office, they run graded excursions most days in July and August.

Parco Naturale Panevéggio

Out of San Martino, traffic files up to **Passo di Rolle**, a beautiful stretch of high moorland dotted with avalanche breaks and a few sheep. There are only two buses a day, so a car really helps here. At the pass, a chair lift takes you up to Baita Segantini, a log-cabin bar from where you can see **Cimon della Pala**'s summit. It takes thirty minutes or so to walk back down to the pass, where there are several more bars and restaurants.

The Passo di Rolle falls within the **Parco Naturale Panevéggio** (*www.parcopan.org*), an area of firs, rowan and larch that once provided timber for the Venetian fleet and wood for Stradivarius violins. Skirted by nature trails, it has a **visitors' centre** (summer daily 9am–12.30pm & 2–6pm; winter Sat & Sun 9am–12.30pm & 2–6pm; L2000/€1.03) 7km on from the pass, outside **PANEVÉGGIO** village, with excellent displays on the wildlife of the area and offering guided walks into the forest (L4000/€2.07). In the remoter parts of the park you might catch a glimpse of white alpine hare or marmot – a creature resembling a large guinea pig, which stands up on its hind legs to act as sentinel for the burrow and emits a distinctive screech. After a few days trekking in the Pale, you may want to take it easy, and Panevéggio's fields are good for sunbathing and sleep. There's an unusually pleasant **camping area** next to Lago Panevéggio, though the atmosphere is spoiled when the lake is dry. The entrance is at the end of the track marked "Area della Sosta", just past the village; facilities are minimal and stays are limited to 24 hours. There's a proper campsite, *Bellamonte* (☎0462.576.119), 4km down the road to Predazzo (see below).

Val di Fiemme

Once out of the confines of the park, **PREDAZZO** is the first town you come to in the **Val di Fiemme**, at the turn-off for the Val di Fassa. The town itself has become something of a pilgrimage site for geologists, owing to the extensive collection of local rocks and fossils in the newly enlarged **Museo Civico** on Piazza Santi Filippo e Giacomo (closed for restoration but reopening imminently). Surprisingly accessible to non-experts, the displays include samples of the Dolomitic calcite rock first identified by, and named after, the French mineralogist Dieudonné Sylvain Guy Tancrède de Gratet de Dolomieu.

Predazzo is a useful point to overnight, and **bus** connections to Trento and Bolzano are reasonable. A good **hotel** is the *Maria* (☎0462.502.394; ③), five minutes' walk from the centre on the main Corso Dolomiti. *Camping Villa Verde* (☎0462.502.394) is a thirty-minute walk east, from the central bus station, but has spectacular views.

Throughout the valley, hotel hoardings are ubiquitous, and even the tiniest villages hereabouts have a plan of the mountain ranges with chair lifts marked, but behind the modern Dolomites tourist industry, this is an ancient region that from the twelfth to the seventeenth centuries was virtually autonomous. A local parliament met at the *Banco de la reson*, a circle of stone benches surrounded by trees in **CAVALESE**, the next town along, and the Magnifica Communità of Cavalese is still relatively powerful, administering extensive communal land. A short way beyond the town centre, on the road to Tésero, is a small **tourist office** (Mon–Sat 9am–noon & 3.30–7pm; July & Aug also Sun 9am–noon) which can arrange visits to the medieval **Palazzo della Communità**. This was the Bishop of Trento's summer palace, and now houses a small **museum and gallery** (guided tours only; July & Aug daily 4.30, 5.30 and 6.30pm; rest of year for hours contact the tourist office; free). Wood-panelled rooms redolent of sawdust and polish, with fine wooden ceilings and painted friezes, contain the original valley statutes, together with some unremarkable paintings by local seventeenth-century artists. The building's lack of fortifications indicates that Trento's bishop felt safe from the armed rebellions that had plagued him in the city, and its exterior is covered in frescoes depicting St Virgilio (Trento's patron saint) enthroned in the centre of a trompe l'oeil pediment.

Many people pause at Cavalese simply to stroll the cobbled streets, grazing at some of the cake and ice cream shops, or to take the cable car up to the **Catena dei Lagorai**. This mountain chain, concealing a string of lakes, is accessible on foot from any of the small villages along the main road. There was a tragic accident here in February 1998, in which a number of skiers were killed when a low-flying US airforce aeroplane sliced through the wires of their cable-car; the lift has since re-opened (July, Aug & Dec–Easter; L22,000/€11.36 return). Leisurely day-trips are feasible, but if you feel inspired once you're up on the ridges, either follow the paths towards Passo di Rolle, or go west. A day or two of walking west (via refuges) brings you to the Val dei Mócheni, which was colonized in medieval times by German farmers travelling south, and has kept its own language and Gothic script. The first farmers were joined later by speculators searching for the rich seams of copper and silver which lay in the mountains. For somewhere to **stay**, in Cavalese, the *Laurino* (☎0462.340.151; ④) has recently been refitted and is a good choice.

TÉSERO, 4km from Cavalese on the higher road, is, for most people, simply a staging post on their way to the mountains. The town's only attraction is the parish church, frescoed with *Cristo della Domenica* (Christ of the Sabbath) and symbols of everything banned on a Sunday.

The Catinaccio and Gruppo di Sella

Heading north from Predazzo, the Val di Fassa penetrates deep into the western Dolomites, passing through one of the heartlands of **Ladino** culture (see box on p.252). Access to the famously roseate peaks of the **Catinaccio** (Rosengarten) range is simple enough from **Vigo di Fassa**, the valley's main resort. The area is popular with German walkers, drawn to the dramatic serrated peaks, but once above the whine of the cable cars there's plenty of wilderness to lose yourself in.

At the head of the Val di Fass, **Canazei** makes a good springboard for the high plateaus of the **Gruppo di Sella**, and the gentler trail of the **Viel del Pan**, which leads down to the tiny resort of **Arabba**. Just across the border on the northern side of the Sella group, Alto Adige (Sdtirol), **Corvara** is a much larger resort with a sizeable Ladino population.

Catinaccio

The long belt of sheer rock walls and towers which makes up the **Catinaccio** (**Rosengarten**) range is an awesome sight, described by local judge and nineteenth-century writer Theodor Christomannos as a "gigantic fortification. . . the gate into the kingdom of immortal ghosts, of high-flying giants". Rosengarten gets its German name from the roses that legend says used to grow here. King Laurino, saddened when his daughter married and left him alone, put a spell on the roses so that no one would see them again by day or night, but forgot to include dawn and dusk in his curse, which is when the low sun gives the rock a roseate glow.

The trails across the range cater for all levels of hiking ability, but the going gets tough on the ridges, from where you can see as far as the Stubaier Alps, on the border with Austria. The most popular approach to Catinaccio is from **VIGO DI FASSA**, a bus stop on the Trento–Canazei route with a few three-star **hotels**; try the simple *Renato*, via Solar, 15 (☎0462.764.006; ③), the smarter *Gambrinus* (☎0462.764.159; ④), or the slightly more luxurious *Vael* (☎0462.764.110; ④). Alternatively, there's the *Rifugio Roda de Vael* (☎0462.764.450; June–Sept), a ninety-minute walk away from the village along trails 547 and 545.

The trek to **Torri del Vájiolet** from Vigo di Fassa is the preferred route up onto the range; the cable car from the village to *Rifugio Ciampedie* (☎0462.764.432; mid-June to mid-Oct) covers most of the ascent; a well-beaten trail leads from the terminus through the woods to the basic *Rifugio Gardeccia* (☎0462.763.152; mid-June to mid-Oct). From here it's a steep walk up to a refuge under the Torri, although the severity of the ascent doesn't discourage hordes of summer Sunday walkers. A stiff zigzagging climb from here brings you to *Rifugio Re Alberto* (☎0462.763.428; June–Sept), three hours from *Rifugio Ciampedie*; there's also alternative accommodation nearby at the *Rifugio Passo Santner* (☎0471.642.230; June–Sept) or the *Rifugio Vájiolet* (☎0462.763.292; mid-June to Sept).

Paths lead **south** across the range and eventually down to Passo di Costalunga and the Lago di Carezza, a beautiful little lake reflecting the peaks of the Latemar range, from where you can catch a bus to Bolzano. There are more choices to the **north**, where there are a number of trails onto Monte Sciliar (Schlern), with variations in height of no more than around 500m. *Rifugio Bolzano-Schlern* (☎0471.612.024; June–Sept), near the summit of Monte Sciliar, is a good two days' trek from *Rifugio Re Alberto*; you can stop overnight at *Rifugio Alpe di Tires* (*Tierser Alplhütte*; ☎0471.727.958), in between the two. From Sciliar, paths descend onto the wetland plateau of the Alpe di Siusi (see p.262).

For a change of pace, head to the **Museo Instituto Culturale Ladino** (closed for restoration until 2001) for an excellent introduction to Ladino culture (see box overleaf). Located in a renovated hayloft next to the parsonage of the Parish church of San Giovanni, the tiny village next to Vigo di Fassa (in walking distance), the museum has intriguing exhibits on myths and rites of the Ladini.

Canazei

CANAZEI is a relatively modern town at the head of the Val di Fassa and, for the area, a buzzing summer and winter resort. It's from there that you head for the high passes – the **Gruppo di Sella** for hard trails, or the easier **Viel del Pan**, opposite Marmolada. The Sella Ronda Card gives use of a selection of lifts and public transport (buses run by the SAD company) around the Gruppo di Sella. It's available at ski lifts for L30,000/€15.49 per day. Canazei itself makes a good base to **stay**: *La Zondra* (☎0462.601.233; ④) and the *Ciamorc* (☎0462.602.426; ③), are both on Via Pareda, while the *Giardino delle Rose* (☎0462.602.221; ③) and *Albergo Centrale* (☎0462.602.340; ③)

LADINO COUNTRY

The meeting-point of Trentino, Alto Adige and the Veneto is home to a distinct cultural group, the **Ladini**. Their language, Ladin, was once spoken over a wide area, from Austria down to the River Po (in what's now Emilia-Romagna), but now survives only in a few valleys in the Dolomites, and in Swiss Engadine, preserved by the relative remoteness of the mountainous territory. There are around 40,000 speakers, but Ladin is especially prevalent in the area around the Sella group – the Val di Fassa, the Val Badia, the Val Gardena and Livinallongo.

The history of the Ladini is recorded in their epics, which recount tales of battles, treachery and reversals of fortune. Around 4000 AD, the Ladini were constantly threatened with invasion by Germanic tribes from the north and others from the Po Valley. Christianity later emerged as a major threat, but the Ladini absorbed and transformed the new religion, investing the new saints with the powers of more ancient female divinities. The rudimentary Castello di Thurn at San Martino di Badia, a bleak outpost of the bishop-princes of Bressanone, is testimony to the Church's attempt to keep the Val di Badia under its control. In 1452, Bishop Nicolo Cusano railed against a woman from the Val di Fassa who said she had met the goddess Diana in the woods, and there was a strong pagan undercurrent to the cult of Santa Giuliana, whose sword-wielding image is painted on the plaster of houses in the Fassa and Badia valleys.

The Cësa di Ladins, in **Ortisei** (see p.263) and the Museo Instituto Culturale Ladino, near **Vigo di Fassa** (see previous page), are excellent places to find out more, but the latter is closed until an uncertain date in 2001. Meanwhile, villages in the area around Vigo contain sections of the museum devoted to working life in Ladino country (mid-June to mid-Sept Mon–Sat 10am–noon & 3–7pm; outside season call tourist information in Vigo di Fassa ☎0462.764.093, *www.fassa.com*). **Moena** is home to a restored nineteenth-century cooperage (*Botega da Pinter*) at Via Dolomiti 3; **Pera di Fassa** houses a restored watermill (*Molin de Pezol*) at Via Jumela 6; and a working, antique sawmill (*La Sia*) can be seen at Via Pian Trevisan at Penia, just outside **Canazei**. Tourist offices, notably the one in **Corvara** (see opposite), have details of occasional festivals, exhibitions and events.

are pleasantly located on via Dolomiti, in the middle of the village; *Villa Ester* (☎0462.601.254; ③) is also centrally located, next to the swimming pool. From Canazei a switchback road (of 27 bends) climbs relentlessly for 12km and is often busy with busloads of tourists heading for the scenic Great Dolomites Road (see p.268), and determined cyclists making the thousand-metre ascent.

Halfway up the switchback road out of Canazei, the cable car at Pradel leads to **Passo Sella** (2240m), one of the most impressive of the Dolomite passes. Paths climb from here onto the jagged peaks of the **Sasso Lungo** (Langkofel) and follow the ridges down onto the Alpe di Siusi. Even up on the summits, saxifrage grows between cracks in the rock, and the silence is broken only by the occasional buzzing of a beetle. It takes two days to walk from the Sella pass, via *Rifugio Vicenza* (☎0471.797.315; June–Sept) into the Val Gardena (Grödnertal), where there are buses to Bolzano.

Just past Pradel the road forks. The right-hand turning takes you up to **Passo Pordoi** (2242m), an astonishing vantage point between the Gruppo di Sella and Marmolada – at 3246m the highest Dolomite, its rounded peak permanently shrouded by a glacier. From here, peaks radiate in every direction, giving you a chance to identify the distinctive shapes of each of the main Dolomite ranges. In the foreground, the Sasso Lungo mountains look like a jagged, gloved hand, flanked by two prominent peaks; the Gruppo di Sella is squat and chunky; and Sciliar (Schlern), just visible in the distance, comprises a flat rocky tabletop, culminating in two peaks. A small road winds downwards to Passo Folzarego, and ultimately Cortina d'Ampezzo, but Passo Pordoi itself is where many of the trails start. It's also another occasion for joining Alta Via 2, which dips down to the main road here. Most of the tourist buses stop at this point, and a collection of cafés and stalls have taken advantage of their location around the trail-heads to charge rather inflated prices; the cheapest of the three **hotels** here is the *Pordoi* (☎0462.601.115; ③).

The Gruppo di Sella

The **Gruppo di Sella** lies to the north of Passo Pordoi and resembles a lunar landscape, with an arid plateau surrounded by pink, dolomitic peaks and crisscrossed by many fairly difficult trails. For less confident walkers, there's a choice of two less demanding paths: either stick to the Alta Via 2, which crosses from one edge of the massif to the other, or break away at Sass de Mesdi, from where a trail circles down to the Sella pass. Both routes take a couple of days, with overnight stops at *Rifugio Cavazza* (*Pisciaduhutte*; ☎0471.836.292; July–Sept) or *Rifugio Boè* (*Boè Hutte*; ☎0471.847.303; June–Sept). The Gruppo di Sella is an excellent place to walk, with views across the ranges down to Passo Gardena (Sellajoch, 2137m), from where Corvara and the Val Badia are within striking distance, as are the Odle (Geisler) group across the valley. There are bus services to Sella Ronda, and you can also pick up buses to Bolzano from **Selva**, 11km away in the Val Gardena.

Viel del Pan

Some much less ambitious walking can be undertaken from Passo Pordoi, starting just past the *Albergo Savoia*, again following the route of Alta Via 2 but in the opposite direction. A narrow path cut into the turf traverses the mountainside opposite Marmolada, where Austrian battalions hid under the glacier in 8km of gallery during World War I. Even if you're not a great walker, a twenty-minute stroll along this easy trail is worthwhile for the views of the Dolomites, which are far better than those from the road.

From the seventeenth century this path was on the grain-smuggling route called the **Viel del Pan** ("trail of bread" in Venetian dialect), and it remained busy enough in the nineteenth century for the Guardia di Finanza to set up armed patrols along it. The contrast between the glacier on Marmolada and the peaks of the Sella group – 360 degrees of mountain – is superb. The path descends to **Lago Fedaia**, from where there are irregular buses in summer back to Canazei. The *Rifugio Marmolada Castiglioni* (☎0462.601.117) is on the edge of the reservoir. On the northern side of the ridge lies **ARABBA**, a small resort with family-run hotels in the centre and scattered in the peaceful pastures around, from where a cable-car system runs up to the Dolomites. For somewhere to **stay**, the *Albergo Posta* (☎0436.79.105; ②) is basic but central and ageing gracefully, while the *Garni Emma* (☎0436.79.116; ②) has a family atmosphere and sits beside a small stream. The larger, more professional *Pensione Marilena* (☎0436.79.128; ③) is right at the foot of the cable car. The only bus service from here is the one that goes from Belluno to Corvara.

Corvara

The central town of the Ladini (see box opposite), **CORVARA**, is primarily a ski resort, and the most visible sign of the language is a page or two in Ladino in local newspapers. Corvara also makes a good base for the excellent trails of the nearby Fánes Park, a bus ride away, where most of the Ladini legends are based. The **tourist office** at Strada Col Alp 36 (Mon–Sat 9am–noon & 3–6pm, Sun 10am–2pm & 4–6pm; ☎0471.836.176) has details of **hotels and rooms** in private houses. The *Monti Pallidi* (☎0471.836.081; ②), Strada Col Alp 75, is good value, as is the *Laura* (☎0471.836.340; ③), at no. 44, round the corner, opposite the church. There's also a **campsite**, *Camping Colfosco* (*Colfuschg*; ☎0471.836.515; May–Sept & Dec–Easter). A few buses leave for Brunico and Belluno from outside the tourist office.

ALTO ADIGE (SÜDTIROL)

Austria officially begins at the Brenner Pass, but it can feel as though the border is some way south, around Bolzano, where the villages are Tyrolean in looks and German is spoken everywhere. **Alto Adige** (Südtirol) was Italy's prize for co-operation with the Allies in World War I. When the Fascists came to power in 1923, despite the fact that German speakers outnumbered Italian speakers by about ten to one, a process of Italianization was imposed on the area. Cartographers remade maps, substituting Italian place-names for German, people were stripped of their own names and forced to adopt Italian ones, the teaching of German in schools was banned and stonemasons were even brought in to chip away German inscriptions from tombstones. Most telling was the change of the region's name and orientation – what had been the *South* Tyrol became the *Upper* Adige. But colonization wasn't just linguistic, as Italian workers from other regions were encouraged to settle, particularly in the towns. A large number of German speakers took the hint and emigrated, but after World War II many remained – along with the rival claims of Austria and Italy for control over the area. Both parties came to an agreement ratified under the Paris Peace Treaty of 1946 that Austria would give up its claim to the region on condition that Italy took steps to redress some of the cultural damage perpetrated under Fascism.

In 1948 some fancy footwork by the Italian government led to the union of Italian-speaking Trentino with German-speaking Alto Adige. In the new Trentino-Alto Adige region, German speakers were a minority and, as such, were entitled to very few of the compensatory measures agreed under the Paris Peace Treaty. After violent protests in the Sixties, a package of concessions was hastily agreed, including a statute drawn up in 1971 which deemed that two-thirds of all public jobs and houses should be reserved for German speakers (a fair reflection of the ethnic mix at the time) and that all public servants should be bilingual in German and Italian. This has since been upheld, partly due to pressure from the SVP (Südtiroler Volkspartei). Funds have been channelled into the area by successive governments, with the result that unemployment is low compared with the national average, and per capita, income high. However, the right-wing MSI (Movimento Sociale Italiano), who argue for repeal of the 1971 act, gained strength during the Eighties, commanding something like fifty percent of the local Italian vote in some places, and in 1987 secured the election of their first-ever local deputy, a lawyer who declared Mussolini "a great man", and actively encouraged neo-fascist sympathizers to move into the province to swell their numbers.

A petty apartheid still exists in the education system, for example: there are separate entrances to the German and Italian sections of the same school and many young German speakers commute across the Austrian border to Innsbruck University. A spate of violence in the late Eighties increased the profile of the dispute in Italy, although those responsible were later arrested in Austria (said to be sympathetic to the secessionist cause). But as Italy moves closer into the European Union, the central and regional governments have become more tolerant of ethnic diversity, with German gaining ground as the official language of preference. But while political pressures may have declined, on social occasions the two groups remain surprisingly separate – some bars and restaurants, particularly in Bolzano, make their allegiances clear.

Travelling around Alto Adige is not as eventful as it might sound from this background, although a few German phrases will certainly ease your way, particularly in more rural areas, and in some places English may be more favourably received than Italian. There are few hints of tension to outsiders – quite the reverse, in fact, as even the big towns have a leisurely pace of life, and the high valleys are utterly peaceful. Although you can get close to some mountainous land around **Bolzano**, the provincial capital, the Dolomites region proper only begins to pay dividends once you head east, high up into the ranges between here and **Cortina d'Ampezzo**, just across the border in the Veneto. Alternatively, make for the glacial ranges to the west, in the **Ortles** group, in sight of the Swiss and Austrian Alps.

It's worth noting that provincial **bus** companies stick fairly rigidly to towns within their territory, so that some places which look like they should be easy to get to from Bolzano say, often are not. For example, there are more frequent buses to Canazei from Trento, and this is the case for other towns in the northern part of Trentino. If you're **driving** outside the summer months, be aware that many passes can remain closed until well after Easter. Approach roads all have signs indicating whether the pass is open, or you can call Bolzano's information line on ☎0471.200.198. The Südtirol's official **Web site**, *www.hallo.com*, (in German, English and Italian) has some useful links and reams of information about the province, with pages devoted to individual towns and resorts.

Bolzano (Bozen)

Situated on the junction of the rivers Talvera (Talfer) and Isarco (Eisack) near the southern limit of the province, **BOLZANO** (BOZEN) is Alto Adige's chief town. For centuries a valley market town and way station, Bolzano's fortunes in the Middle Ages vacillated as the Counts of Tyrol and the Bishops of Trento competed for power. The town passed to the Habsburgs in the fourteenth century, then at the turn of the nineteenth century Bavaria took control, opposed by Tyrolese patriot and military leader Andreas Hofer. His battle in 1809 to keep the Tyrol under Austrian rule was only temporarily successful, as in the same year the Austrian Emperor ceded the Tyrol to the Napoleonic kingdom of Italy. More changes followed, as Bolzano was handed back to Austria until after World War I, whereupon it passed, like the rest of the province, to Italy. Nowadays, in both winter and summer, the town is a busy tourist resort, and its pavement cafés and generally relaxed pace of life make it a good, if uneventful, place to rest up or use as a base for trips into the mountains. An unmissable pleasure is the local wine: Bolzano is at the head of the wine road (Strada di Vino/Südtiroler Weinstrasse; see box on p.242), which runs south to the border with Trentino, and it's especially well known for its Chardonnay.

Arrival, information and accommodation

Bolzano's **bus station**, centrally placed at Via Perathoner 4, serves most of the small villages and resorts in the province; the **train station** is a few minutes' walk south of here through the park down via Stazione. There is a city **tourist office** at Piazza Walther 8 (Mon–Fri 9am–6.30pm, Sat 9am–12.30pm; ☎0471.307.000), and a **regional office** just off the square at Piazza Parrochia 11/12 (Mon–Thurs 8.30am–1pm & 3–6.30pm, Fri 8.30am–2.30pm; ☎0471.307.040). Their "Alpine Desk" (Mon–Fri 9am–noon & 2–5pm; ☎0471.473.809) has information on weather conditions and advisability of routes. The Club Alpino Italiano at Piazza Erbe 46 (daily except Sat 11am–noon & 5–7pm; ☎0471.978.172), on the top end of the square, is also a good source of local hiking information. For Internet access, the bus station café has an arcade-style Internet machine which accepts ordinary phonecards. It's inexpensive but slow so a better option is *Vecchia Bolzano*, via Isarco 19, a pub popular with teenagers right opposite the Duomo.

Accommodation options are somewhat limited, particularly in summer. The best budget places are off Piazza Walther: *Kolpinghaus*, Via Ospedale 3 (☎0471.308.400, fax 0471.973.917, *www.kolping.it/bz*; ③) is a religious-run hostel with single and double rooms, while the *Croce Bianca* on Piazza del Grano (*Weisses Kreuz*; ☎0471.977.552; ②)

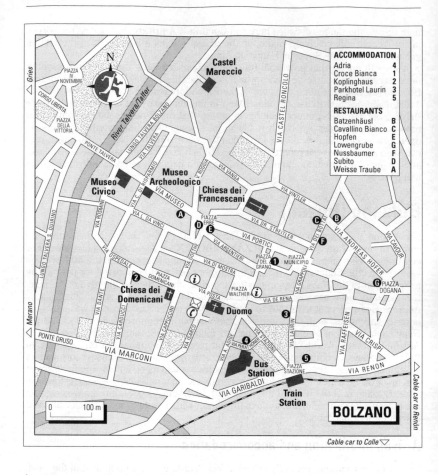

is a more conventional cheap albergo. Convenient for transport, but characterless, are the inexpensive *Hotel Adria*, Via Perathoner 17 (☎0471.975.735, *adriahot@tin.it*; ④), immediately opposite the bus station, and *Hotel Regina*, opposite the train station on Via Renon (☎0471.972.195, fax 0471.978.944; ④). For luxury, the *Parkhotel Laurin*, Via Laurin 4 (☎0471.975.735, *www.laurin.it*; ⑦) has a restaurant, garden and swimming pool. One way of escaping the summer humidity is to stay in the hills above town at Colle (Kohlern), reached by a ten-minute cable car (L6000/€3.10) from Via Campiglio, itself a twenty-minute walk from the train station. The *Klaushof*, Colle 14 (☎0471.329.999; ③) is one of several hotels on the same road. The tourist office has details of rooms to let in farmhouses and in a few private houses in town. For **campers**, the *Moosbauer* site (☎0471.918.492) is on the main Bolzano–Merano road.

The Town

Central Bolzano definitely looks like a part of the German-speaking world. Restaurants serve *speck*, *gulasch* and *knödel*, and bakers sell black bread and *sachertorte*. The centre of town is **Piazza Walther**, whose pavement cafés, around its statue of the *minnesinger* (troubadour) Walther von der Vogelweide, are the town's favoured meeting places; with just a L10,000/€5.16 deposit you can borrow bicycles for use around town from here. Converted into a cathedral as recently as 1964, the **Duomo** (Dom), on the edge of the square, resembles a parish church: built in the fourteenth and fifteenth centuries, and restored after being bombed in World War II, it has a striking green-and-yellow mosaic roof and elaborately carved spire. The fourteenth-century **Franciscan church** on Via dei Francescani is also worth seeking out, embellished with a carved wooden altarpiece by Hans Klocher and with elegant, frescoed cloisters from the same period.

A couple of streets west of Piazza Walther, on Via Cappuccini, the **Chiesa dei Domenicani** (Dominican monastery) has frescoes of fifteenth-century courtly life painted on the walls of the decaying cloisters, framed by a growth of stone tracery. The Cappella di San Giovanni, built at the beginning of the fourteenth century, retains frescoes by painters of the Giotto school, including a *Triumph of Death* underneath a starry vault. Follow the street north to **Piazza Erbe**, site of a daily fruit and vegetable market, from where the oriel windows and eleventh-century arcades of **Via Portici** lead off to the right.

On the west side of the old town stands one of Alto Adige's more important museums, the recently opened **Museo Archeologico** (Tues–Sun 10am–5pm, Thurs until 7pm, *www.iceman.it*; L10,000/€5.16), a ten-minute walk west of the centre at Via Museo (Museumstrasse) 43. Once the seat of the Austro-Hungarian National Bank, and then the Banco d'Italia, the building's four floors trace the region's history and developing culture from the end of the last Ice Age to the early Middle Ages, through exhibits, reconstructions, models and multimedia presentations. At the heart of the museum is the Iceman, nicknamed "Ötzi", the superbly preserved mummy of an early Copper Age male discovered in the ice of the Ötzaler Alps in 1991. Visitors can only view the mummy through a small window in a high-tech refrigeration unit, its preservation depends on remaining in an identical climate to the one in which he was discovered. At around 5300 years old, "Ötzi", his clothing, and his attendant possessions provide an unprecedented insight into the everyday culture of his time.

Continuing westwards down Via Museo takes you to a pleasant park alongside the River Talvera (Talfer). Bolzano's German and Gothic quarter ends on the other side of the Ponte Talvera, where **Piazza della Vittoria** signals the edge of the Italian town, much of it laid out by Mussolini's favourite architect, Marcello Piacentini. The epic triumphal arch on the square was commissioned by Mussolini in 1928 and is something of a controversial monument. Until a recent clean-up it was covered with graffiti and surrounded by low railings, and it was even bombed by German-speaking separatists in the late-1980s. The piazza is now the site of relatively sedate activity, hosting a big general market on Saturdays.

If you've time, follow Corso Libertà from the square to the leafy suburb of Gries, on the left bank, where the Gothic **Parrocchiale** in the main square, overshadowed by a Baroque church nearby, contains a richly carved and painted fifteenth-century altarpiece by Michael Pacher (see p.265 for more on this Tyrolean artist).

Eating and drinking

If you're just after a lunchtime snack, try *wurstel* and *apfel strudel,* the commonest **street foods**, available from stalls on Piazza del Grano and via Stazione, and the cafés of Via dei Portici. Via Museo is a good source of decent local **restaurants**; the *Weisse Traube* (*Uva Bianca*) at no. 17a (closed Sun), for example, offers a set lunch for L23,000/€11.88. Along Via dei Bottai there's the *Cavallino Bianco* (*Weisses Rössel*) at no. 6 (closed July), a *bierkeller* with a menu heavy on Tyrolean specialities. *Batzenhäusl*, Via A. Hofer 30 (closed Tues), is good too, an old wine bar with a lively atmosphere, as is *Lowengrube*, Piazza Dogana 3, a *bierlokal* with good food and *weissbier* on tap. *Hopfen*, a restaurant on the corner of the fruit market at Piazza Erbe, is highly recommended for its beer brewed on the premises and huge plates of meaty Tyrolean specialities. It's worth noting that despite being a tourist destination Bolzano practically closes down on Sunday, supermarkets included, though on Sunday evenings, and late every night, it's possible to get **pizza** and ice cream from *Subito*, on Piazza Erbe.

If you're after **nightlife** Bolzano is surprisingly dull for a town of its size, but it's easy to meet young people as there are only three venues. *Nadamas*, on Piazza Erbe 44, is a Latin-themed bar, while just off Via Museo, on Vicolo Erbe, are *Casanova* and the inevitable Irish pub next door. The one central disco, *Mirò*, is on Piazza Domenicani and only gets going on Fridays and Saturdays.

Around Bolzano

Bolzano is hemmed in by mountains terraced high with vineyards, across which a couple of footpaths up from the valley basin give a brief taste of the countryside. The **Passeggiata del Guncinà** starts at the end of Via Knoller near Gries' Parrocchiale, while the other, the **Passeggiata Sant'Osvaldo**, begins at Via Rencio, behind the train station, traverses some hillside terraces, and brings you down to the path next to the River Talvera.

Just north of the town centre, the thirteenth-century **Castello Róncolo** (Schloss Runkelstein; mid-June to Sept daily 10am–8pm; Oct to mid-June Tues–Sun 10am–6pm; L10,000/€5.16), reachable by bus #12 from the station, is easy enough to get to, with frescoes of courtly life showing people hunting, dancing and generally having a good time, as well as a group of knights on horseback and the legendary lovers Tristan and Isolde.

There's a whole clutch of castles just southwest of Bolzano at **APPIANO** (EPPAN AN DER WEINSTRASSE). One of the few that hasn't fallen to rack and ruin or been turned into a hotel or restaurant is **Schloss Moos Schulthaus** (Easter–Oct Tues–Sun, tours at 10am, 11am, 4pm & 5pm; L5000/€2.58), which was saved from crumbling away just in time and turned into a museum. Its original Tyrolean kitchen, complete with huge great hearth, has been kept intact, and there are some newly uncovered frescoes depicting "the war of cats and mice".

From the ruined battlements of nearby **Schloss Hocheppan** (April–June & Sept–Nov daily except Tues 9am–5pm; July daily 9am–5pm) you can see thirty or so other fortresses and castles, testifying to the cut and thrust of medieval politics in these parts. Hocheppan was the stronghold of the Counts of Eppan, rulers of the area until the powerful Counts of Tyrol took over after a series of bloody battles. The Hocheppan chapel by the side of the ruins is worth a look for its very secular frescoes: women flirting at the altar, and one of the earliest representations of the ubiquitous *knödel*, or dumpling, which still features heavily on most South Tyrolean menus.

Monte Renòn (Rittner) gives a taste of the high peaks around Bolzano. A cable car (open all year dawn to dusk; every 20min) ascends from Via Renòn (Rittnerstrasse) to Soprabolzano (Oberbozen), from where a tram service or footpaths lead to some of the other small villages, past a forest of eroded earth pillars, thirty minutes' walk north of Collalbo. A good time to come up here is in summer, around St Bartholomew's Day (August 24), when hundreds of farmers from outlying villages congregate on Renòn for the annual horse fair.

You might also visit the area south of Bolzano to eat; some of the farmhouses serve typical South Tyrolean dishes in their wood-panelled dining rooms (see "Törggelen", opposite).

TÖRGGELEN

To get a flavour of Alto Adige's edible specialities, it's well worth timing your visit for the Törggelen season. This roughly coincides with the grape harvest, from about the end of September to the beginning of December, and traditionally marked the passage of the year – celebrating a golden time of clear autumnal weather before winter really set in. Farmers and innkeepers lay on a spread of *speck* (smoked ham), local cheese and roast chestnuts, accompanied by wines from the surrounding hills, to which you apply yourself after a walk (or just a cable-car ride) up the mountain. Good areas to embark on your Törggelen expedition are found just south of Bolzano, around the wine road (see p.242), and the villages of Termano (Tramin), Caldaro (Kaltern) and Appiano (Eppan), or the Valle d'Isarco around Bressanone (Brixen). Just a few suggestions to whet your appetite: *Törglkeller* at Località Bichl 2 at Caldaro (closed Sun); *Loosmannhof* (☎0471.365.237), Località Signato/Signat; and *Wieser* (☎0471.662.376; closed Wed) at Appiano (Eppan).

Merano and the Giogáia di Tessa

MERANO (MERAN) an hour north by train from Bolzano, lies close to two great mountain ranges. The closest, the **Giogáia di Tessa** (Texelgruppe), less than 10km away, is characterized by steep traverses across pastureland, with old snow still on the slopes in summer; watercourses irrigate the south-facing slopes, planted below with vines, peach and apple trees. Further west, the **Ortles** mountains – an unbelievable expanse of glaciers and rocky spurs – straddle the border with Valtellina and are included within the Parco Nazionale dello Stelvio, one of Italy's major national parks (see p.261). Both ranges offer isolated trails, away from tourist routes, with bus services to most villages.

Merano itself sits on a bend in the River Passirio, a sedate spa town surrounded by a ring of mountains, and, incongruously, by semitropical plants. Mild spring and autumn weather attracted Central Europeans at the turn of the century, and a resort of *fin de siècle* hotels, neat gardens and promenades evolved. The town's old nucleus is **Via dei Portici**, running west from the Gothic **Duomo** and fifteenth-century castle; around it are plenty of shopping streets and the Thermal Centre, which still provides radioactive water cures. It's mainly a retirement resort, but you may decide to stay in Merano for bus connections to the Parco Naturale di Tessa to the north, or the Ortles mountains in the Parco Nazionale dello Stelvio to the southwest. If you're here on Easter Monday, head for the hippodrome to the south of the centre, where Tyrolean musicians astride huge Haflinger horses parade around the stadium, with much horn-blowing and flag-waving before the actual races start. In summer, twice-weekly classical concerts are held – some in atmospheric castles. Perhaps more tempting, though, is the **grape fest** in the third week of October, marked by a procession, concerts and stands groaning under the weight of gastronomic delights.

Buses arrive and leave directly outside the **train station** on Piazza Stazione, 10 minutes' walk from the centre of town. The **tourist office** is at Corso Libertà 35 (March–Nov Mon–Fri 9am–6.30pm, Sat 9.30am–6pm, Sun 10am–12.30pm; Dec–Feb Mon–Fri 9am–12.30pm & 2.30–6.30pm; ☎0473.235.223, *www.meraninfo.it*). Three of the least expensive central **hotels** are: the *Santer Klause* on Passeirerg, just off Pfarrplatz (☎0473.234.086; ③); *Tyrol*, closer to the train station at Via XXX Aprile 8 (☎0473.449.719; ③); and *Villa Betty*, just across the river from the station, on Via Petrarca (☎0473.233.949; ②). The best places to **eat** in town are the *Weinstube Haisrainer*, Via dei Portici 100, serving Italian and Tyrolean dishes, and the *Weinstube Batzenhäusl* a few doors along at no. 84. **Campers** should use *Camping Meran*, Via

Piave 44 (☎0473.231.249; Easter–Nov): turn right out of the station, cross the river by way of Via Rezia and Via Petrarca, and Via Piave is the third turning on the right.

For **hiking** advice and information, consult the Club Alpino Italiano office, Via Carlo Wolff, or Merano's Alpine association, the Alpenverien Südtirol, at Via Galilei 45 (☎0473.237.134), an alley off Corso Libertà.

Parco Naturale di Tessa (Naturpark Texelgruppe)

The mountain chains around Merano belong to a separate geological period from the Dolomites, and are actually part of the Zillertaler and Ötztaler ranges of the eastern Alps. Their foothills, called the **Giogáia di Tessa** (Texelgruppe), begin immediately north of the town. Two high-level paths, the north and south sections of the **Meraner Höhenweg**, encircle this massif. The gentler **southern route** (marked as route 24 on signs) overlooks Merano, the built-up Val Venosta (Vinschgau), and the neighbouring peaks, and is crowded even out of season. The total walking time is 24 hours, and every few kilometres there's a dairy farm offering bed and breakfast or a rifugio for overnight stops. **Buses** go from Merano to the beginning of the route at Hof Unterpferl in Katherinaberg (#105), and to Ulfas, just west of Sankt Leonhard, where it ends – plus several points along the way, including **Castel Tirolo** (mid-March to mid-Nov Tues–Sun 10am–5pm; L7000/€3.62), where a cable car ascends to a couple of *rifugi* and souvenir shops at **Hochmuter**. The castle's tenth-century frescoed chapel is worth the visit, if you can fight your way through the crowds of other tourists who pack the lanes around. Below Tirolo Castle is **Brunnenburg**, a neo-Gothic pile that's all fishtail battlements and conical towers, where American poet Ezra Pound spent the last years of his life. His grandson now runs a rather surreal **art gallery** in the same building (April–Nov daily except Tues 9.30am–5pm; L3000/€1.55), all its works being linked by the theme of "bread".

The **northern** stretch of the Meraner Höhenweg is an entirely different trail, running at a higher altitude but still below the snowline, through isolated pastures and rocky terrain. The comparative scarcity of *rifugi* makes it necessary to plan overnight stops in advance. The first section of the trail, Katherinaberg–Montfert–Eishof, is a walk of four hours; you then pick up the path from Eishof to *Rifugio Stettiner* (no accommodation; 3hr 30min); Stettiner to Pfelders (3hr 30min) is the last part. For places to stay in **KATHERINABERG**, try the *Katherinabergerhof* (☎0473.670.171; ③), the *Schnalsburg* (☎0473.89.145; ③), or the *Hotel Am Fels* (☎0473.679.139; ④); in **PFELDERS**, there's *Edelweiss* (☎0473.646.713; ③) and *Panorama* (☎0473.646.727; ③) – all much of a muchness.

From *Rifugio Stettiner* there's another option, the **Pfelderer Höhenweg**, which runs east to the Zwickauer Shelter, crosses the path here, and traverses the pastures of Obere Schneid. There are some sheer drops down to the valley, and you need crampons above the snowline, but this is an excellent walk, which gives a hint of how isolated these small valleys were until recently. If you don't feel equipped for this, but want to extend the route, continue past Pfelders to Ulfas (4hr), and from there on to Vipiteno (2–3 days), where you either link up with the main Bolzano-to-Innsbruck railway or carry on eastwards along the **Pfunderer Höhenweg** (see p.266).

A bus travels north from Merano along the Val Passiria to **SANKT LEONHARD**, skirting the edge of the Texelgruppe, and, on the other side, Merano's ski resorts on the slopes of Punta Cervina (Hirzer Spitze). A network of paths cross the summer pastures around Sankt Leonhard: one of these leaves **Sankt Martino**, 4km south of Sankt Leonhard, and makes the steep ascent (2hr 30min) to **Pfandleralm**, the home village of Andreas Hofer. Originally an innkeeper, wine merchant and cattle dealer, he fought for the Tyrol's return to Austria after it had been ceded to Bavaria in 1805. After successful uprisings against occupying Bavarian and Napoleonic troops, he became self-styled commander-in-chief of the South Tyrol, attracting strong popular support. However, larger political forces overtook him. When the Tyrol was ceded to the French by Austria's Emperor Francis I, Hofer was arrested in 1810 and executed under Napoleon's orders in Mantua. At Pfandleralm a memorial to him stands on the edge of the meadow, and in the Sandwirt guesthouse at Sankt Leonhard, there's a small **museum** in his memory (Mon–Sat 8am–noon & 2–6pm; L2000/€1.03).

The other road out of Sankt Leonhard follows the Val Passiria west to **MOSO** (MOOS), at the head of the Val di Plan (Pfelderer Tal). From Moso the old military road leads to **SANKT MARTIN AM SCHNEEBERG** (2hr). An eerie trail leads through a peat gulley to *Rifugio Schneeberghütte* (40 mattress beds & 10 bunks; ☎0473.647.045; May 15 to Oct 15), surrounded by spoil heaps and ruined buildings – the remains of Europe's highest mining settlement (2355m), opened in 1660 within sight of the glaciers on Austria's Pan di Zucchero (Zuckerhütl) mountain.

Parco Naturale dello Stelvio

The Parco Nazionale dello Stelvio (or the Stilfser National park) is one of Italy's major national parks; it covers the whole **Ortles** range, and is topped by one of Europe's largest glaciers (the Ghicciaio dei Forni) and crossed by the Passo dello Stelvio, which misses being the highest pass in the Alps by just twelve metres. Tourism has made its mark, and the park is as crisscrossed by ski lifts as anywhere in the Alps. But it's still a remarkable place. People come here for the high trails and glacier skiing in summer, or for the chance of seeing species such as the red and roe deer, elk, chamois, golden eagles and ibex. One of the best valleys for spotting wildlife is the sheer-sided Val Zebrù, off the Valfurva, the smallest of the valleys, accessible from Bormio (see p.210).

There are buses to the park's various points of access but perhaps the place to head first is **SILANDRO** (SCHLANDERS), in the long, relatively wide Val Venosta (Vinschgau), with its **visitors' centre** (Mon–Fri 8.30am–noon & 3–7pm, Sat 9am–noon; ☎0473.730.155) and information on *rifugi* and trails. If you're all hiked out, there's a good castle, **Coira**, but more frequently known by its German name of **Churburg**, 20km away on the road to Malles (Mals; buses from Merano). It was owned by the Lords of Matsch at the turn of the thirteenth century, when it was just one castle in a whole chain stretching from Bavaria to just north of Milan and was battled over by various knights in armour – whose suits, some weighing nearly 25kg, can be seen in the **armoury** (March 20 to Oct 31 Tues–Sat 10am–noon & 2–4.30pm; L10,000/€5.16).

The valleys

Three main valley roads thread their way from the Val Venosta (Vinschgau) into the foothills of the Ortles range: Val d'Ultimo, Val Martello (Martelltal) and Val di Solda (Suldental). A traditional place of hiding in an area renowned for mountain warfare, the isolated **Val d'Ultimo** was opened up this century, and buses now run from Merano to the village of **SANKT GERTRAUD**. Around the lower slopes are startling green pastures and some ancient larches, but the main attraction of coming here lies higher up, where trails lead over rock-strewn moorland to *Rifugio Canziani* (*Höchster Hütte*; 3hr; no accommodation), dramatically surrounded by the glaciers and peaks of **Zufrittspitze**. If you're feeling less energetic, the valley is still a good place for some shorter walks, using the village as base. *Utnerhof*, Hauptstrasse 114 (☎0473.798.117; ②) is one of a handful of **hotels** in the village, while for **food** you should splash out at *Genziana*, Via Fontana Bianca 116 – amazing meals for around L50,000/€25.82 a head; there are rooms available too (☎0473.798.085; ①).

Further west, **Val Martello** (Martelltal) is equally beautiful, its lower slopes covered with silver birches. A bus travels from Merano to Silandro, and another from Silandro into Val Martello, passing the ruins of Cartel Montani and an aviary for falcons at Morter. At the head of the valley, **PARADISO DEL CEVEDALE** (2088m) is one of the busiest bases for climbers and cross-country skiers, lying close to Monte Cevedale (Zufall Spitze; 3757m); other trails lead through high passes to Val d'Ultimo and Val di Solda.

One of the main roads through the park is the awe-inspiring route over the **Passo dello Stelvio** (2758m), one of the highest and last to open – it is known to stay closed until July. A single bus from Merano makes the journey to the pass (late June to mid-Sept), passing the turn-off to the Val di Solda on the way; an alternative route is to take the frequent service from Merano to **Spondigna** and wait for one of the two afternoon buses from Malles there. **TRAFOI**, up at 1543m, is a lonely hamlet perched by the side of the road towards the beginning of the main climb, but there are a few good pensions just short of the village and bus stop: try the *Tuckett* (☎0473.611.722; ③) or the *Trafoi* (☎0473.611.728; ③). A cable car leads up to *Rifugio Forcola* (no accommodation), at 2250m, from where a fine path continues up and round to the Passo dello Stelvio (4hr). The pass marked the frontier between Italy, Switzerland and Austria until 1918, and **Pizzo Garibaldi** (Dreisprachenspitze), a spur of rock fifteen minutes' walk from the pass, is the symbolic meeting place for the three main languages of the area. The road continues down through switchbacks and startling gradients to Bormio.

A better choice in this area is to turn off just short of Trafoi towards **SOLDA**, 8km west. Set in an isolated tributary valley hanging over the main road, it's been a major climbing and skiing centre since the nineteenth century – there's even a tiny, eccentric **museum** (Tues–Sat 4–6pm; free) celebrating Solda's existence as a mountain resort. There's now a helpful **tourist office** (Mon–Sat 9am–noon & 2–6pm, Aug also open Sun 9am–noon & 2–6pm; ☎0473.613.015, *www.sulden.suedtirol.com*) and a large range of **accommodation**. In the lower town, best for restaurants and services, are *Paulmichl* (☎0473.613.064; ③), right next to the tourist office, and *Ortlerhof*, the first hotel on the way into town (summer only; ☎0473.613.052; ②). Ten minutes' walk away, in the upper part of town, the *Garni des Alpes* (☎0473.613.062; ②) is excellent value, and has a resident climbing/skiing guide. Although Solda attracts fairly serious climbers and skiers, you don't have to be experienced to attempt some of the trails. There are easy paths (2hr) up to *Rifugio-Albergo Città di Milano* (*Schaubach Hütte*; ☎0473.613.002; June–Sept) at 2581m, or more difficult trails to *Rifugio Payer* (☎0473.613.010; July–Sept) at 3020m, a fantastic viewpoint and base for the ascent of **Ortles** (3905m).

Alpe di Siusi (Seiser Alm)

The grasslands of the **Alpe di Siusi** (Seiser Alm), to the north of Bolzano, are Europe's largest Alpine plateau, extending over sixty square kilometres high above the rest of the valley under the peaks of **Sciliar** (Schlern) national park. The valley roads give you little idea of what lies above.

The bus from Bolzano goes to Siusi, from where another service ascends to the Alpe. On the way, the road climbs through a series of loops past the Hauenstein forest, the ruins of a castle which was once the home of Osvald of Wolkenstein (1377–1445) – the last *minnesinger* (troubador) of the South Tyrol – and the onion-domed church of **San Valentino** (St Valentiskirchlein). Buses terminate at **SALTRIA** (SALTNER), at the heart of the wetlands in a relatively unspoilt area, where the only evidence of human activity is dairy farming and some logging in the woods. Horses graze on the tough grass which grows up here, picking their way between the bogs and streams; small huts and clumps of pine are dotted across the plateau. Paths lead off the Alpe di Siusi to *rifugi* in the peaks, or there are four **hotels** that are more or less the only buildings at Saltria: *Ritsch* is one of the simpler (☎0471.727.910; ②).

Sciliar (Schlern) and Sasso Lungo (Langkofel)

The **Parco Nazionale dello Sciliar**, which spreads over this area, is named after **Sciliar** (Schlern), a flat-topped, sheer mountain which splits off at one end into two peaks, Cima Euringer and Santner. Trails lead onto Sciliar from Tires (Tiers), Fié Am Sciliar (Völs Am Schlern) or Siusi (Seis), all involving long, steep climbs up to the summit (2563m). In the heyday of the spa resort, **FIÉ AM SCILIAR** was famous for its curative hay baths – presumably only beneficial if you didn't suffer from hayfever. Schloss Prösels, the fairly simple **castle** (guided tours daily: April–Oct 11am, 2pm & 3pm; July & Aug extra tours at 10am, 4pm & 5pm; L5000/€2.58) here was once the seat of the Lords of Völs, patrons of the arts and staunch campaigners against witchcraft and superstition.

Just before the peak of Sciliar is *Rifugio Bolzano al Monte Pez* (*Schlernhaus*; ☎0471.612.024; Jun–Oct,) one of the original Alpine huts from the 1880s. The cable car from Hoferalp, above Umes di Fiè (Ums), cuts out 1000m of ascent. In summer, paths can be crowded, but the day-trippers tend to disappear back down into the valley by evening, when the teeth of **Sasso Lungo** (Langkofel) become blunted by cloud.

Trails onto Sasso Lungo spring from the path between Saltria and **Monte Pana**, above Santa Cristina in the Val Gardena (see below). Half a day's walking brings you to *Rifugio Vicenza* (*Langkofelhütte*; ☎0471.797.315; June 20–Sept 30); from here paths lead across the mountain down to Passo di Sella (Sellajoch).

Val Gardena (Grödnertal)

Trails and chair lifts connect the Alpe with the **Val Gardena** (Grödnertal), a valley of squeaky-clean guesthouses and a continuous stream of tourist buses. The main village in the valley, **ORTISEI** (SANKT ULRICH), has for centuries been a big producer of religious sculpture and, more recently, hand-carved wooden toys, several families each perpetuating a particular design. Three thousand woodcarvers in the valley still make furniture and religious statues, but Ortisei, like the neighbouring villages of **Santa Cristina** and **Selva** (Wolkenstein), is now mainly a ski resort, within easy reach of the **Sella Ronda**, a route of ski-runs and lifts encircling the Gruppo di Sella that make up the heart of the Dolomite skiing area. The massive circuit takes at least a day to complete. The **Cësa di Ladins** at Reziastrasse 83 (summer daily 10am–noon & 3–7pm; free; for winter hours call ☎0471.797.554) celebrates local Ladino culture (see box on p.252), the natural history of the area and local-boy-made-good Luis Trenker, a documentary filmmaker in the 1930s. **Buses** make the journey back to Bolzano, or you can drive in the other direction towards the Passo di Sella or Passo di Gardena.

Valle d'Isarco and Val Pusteria

The attraction of the four-hour bus trip from Bolzano to Cortina d'Ampezzo isn't so much what you see of the **Valle d'Isarco** (Eisacktal) and **Val Pusteria** (Pusertal), but the access it gives to the beginning of the *alte vie* and quieter routes into the **Val di Funes** (Villnöss), the Odle group, and the isolated ridges to the north of Val Pusteria. Largely untouched by tourism, these are great places to walk. In the side valleys dippers dart in and out of the streams and the sawing of timber cuts through the air. Higher up, you're likely to see marmots, and chamoix betray their presence with a tumbling of stones.

The Valle d'Isarco (Eisacktal) and around

The main village of the southern Valle d'Isarco (Eisack), **CHIUSA** (KLAUSEN), is served by trains from Bolzano and Bressanone (Brixen), and buses that continue into the **Val di Funes**, a little to the north. **SANTA MADDALENA** (SANKT MAGDALE-NA), surrounded by tracts of pasture, lies 10km into the valley, at the base of Le Odle. This quiet village is a good place for an overnight stop with a few reasonable **hotels**, such as the two-star *Gasthof Hofmann* on Hofman Johann (☎0474.948.014; ③). Another bus climbs halfway up the mountain to Zanseralm, from where it's one hour's walk to *Rifugio Genova* (☎0472.840.132; July–Sept) at 2301m. The level paths take you above the larch forests that fill the valley, and give fantastic views of the peaks. A four-hour circular trail called the Sentiero delle Odle (Adolf Munkel Weg) traverses the grass slopes beneath the teeth of the range, from Zanseralm via Saint Renon or to Brogles-Alm, and back down to the valley. Alta Via 2 is a short walk from Saint Renon.

Bressanone (Brixen)

Alta Via 2 can also be picked up in the foothills above **BRESSANONE** (BRIXEN), whose bishops – in constant rivalry with the neighbouring Counts of Tyrol – ruled the area as an independent state for a thousand years. The complex of buildings which made up their base is still the focus of the town, centred on Piazza del Duomo (Dom Platz), and preserves a medieval character, though rather diluted by bourgeois tidiness.

The **Duomo**, modernized in the eighteenth century, is the most imposing building in the complex: the interesting part lies to the side, in the cloisters, which were frescoed in the fourteenth century. The cathedral **treasury** is now kept in the Museo Diocesano (see below), where vestments belonging to Bressanone's bishop-princes are hung. Their strong influence in the region is evident from the present given by Emperor Henry II to Bishop Albuino: a tenth-century Byzantine silk cloak, spread with the stylized eagle that was the bishop's personal emblem. The bishop's palace, next to the duomo, houses the **Museo Diocesano** (mid-March to Nov Tues–Sun 10am–5pm; L6000/€3.10), furnished in predictably grand style, with an overwhelming collection of crib scenes in the **crypt** (Jan, Feb & Dec 10 daily 2–5pm; L4000/€2.07). For more secular pleasures, head for the **Novacella Monastery** (Kloster Neustift), 3km away and reachable by bus (at least hourly), which produces well-regarded wine and sells direct to the public via its own cellar in the old smithy. If you can get a group together, take a guided tour around the beautifully frescoed medieval **cloisters** (Easter–Oct Mon–Sat 10am, 11am, 2pm, 3pm & 4pm; Nov to Easter Mon-Fri 11am & 3pm, Sat 11am; L6500/€3.36; ☎0472.836.189).

Bressanone's **tourist office** (Mon–Sat 8.30am–12.30pm & 2.30–6pm; ☎0472.836.401, *www.brixen.org*), opposite the bus station, has information on trails around the town and further afield. There are some excellent, inexpensive **places to stay** in the old town, including *Golden Traube*, Via Portici Minori 9 (☎0472.836.552; ①), *Tallero*, Via Mercato Vecchio 35 (☎0472.830.577; ②) and the small, family-run *Mayrhofer*, Via Tratten 17 (☎0472.836.327; ②). If you're feeling flush, the *Elephant*, Via Rio Bianco 4 (☎0472.832.750; *elephant.brixen@acs.it*; ④), is one of the longest-established grand hotels in the Dolomites, furnished in elegant Tyrolean style and with excellent food and service. There are two **campsites** 5km north in Varna (Vahrn): the *Löwenhof* (*Al Leone*) is at Via Lago di Varna 60 (☎0472.836.216; closed Nov), while the other, *Zum See* (*Al Lago*), is near Lake Varna, at Via Lago di Varna 129 (☎0472.832.169; April–Oct); several buses travel here on weekdays, fewer at weekends. The narrow streets around the edge of Piazza Duomo have some old-established Tyrolean **restaurants** – like *Fink*, Via Portici Minori 4 (closed Tues evening & all Wed), and *Oste Scuro* in front of the cathedral (closed Sun evening & all Mon), and there's a *mensa* on Via Fallmerayer. For picnics, try the shops in the old arcades or the Monday market on Brennerstrasse.

Val Pusteria (Pusertal)

The road through the **Val Pusteria** (Pusertal), a wide valley of maize fields and hay meadows, sweeps around the northern edge of the Dolomites. Most of the *alte vie* start from points along the main road through the valley, which is served by bus from Brunico. The train route branches off the main Bolzano–Innsbruck line at Fortezza, heading on to Bressanone, Brunico and Dobbiaco on its way to Innichen. For walkers, many of the *alte vie* start in the Val Pusteria: Alta Via 1 starts from Lago di Bráies (Pragser Wildsee), Alta Via 3 from Villabassa (Niederdorf), Alta Via 4 from San Candido (Innichen) and Alta Via 5 from Sesto (Sexten). There are also lesser-known trails to the north, for example the Alta Via di Fundres (Pfunderer Höhenweg) – see p.266 for details.

Brunico (Bruneck)

An influx of people from the surrounding villages arrives daily in the otherwise sleepy market town of **BRUNICO** (BRUNECK), which is also the transport centre of the region, with buses along the valley and to most of the small places higher up in the hills. Brunico was home of painter and sculptor Michael Pacher (c1435–98): if you have some time to kill, go and look at his *Vine Madonna* in the parish church of the village of San Lorenzo, 4km southwest of town. Pacher is probably the most famous Tyrolean painter and woodcarver, straddling German Gothic and the more spare, Italian styles; there's something vaguely unsavoury about this particular Madonna and her pudgy child, gripping a bunch of black grapes, but it's refreshing to see work in its original setting rather than in a museum.

The Brunico **tourist office**, opposite the bus station in Via Europa (Mon–Fri 9am–12.30pm & 3–6pm, Sat 9am–noon; ☎0474.555.722), has details of **places to stay**. The central *Blitzburg*, Via Europa 10 (☎0474.555.837; ③), and *Corona* (*Krone*) at Via Ragen di Sopra 8 (☎0474.411.108; ③) are reasonable options. For **campers** there's the *Camping Scheisstand*, Via Dobbiaco 4 (☎0474.401.326; May–Sept). A stopping **train** makes the journey along the Val Pusteria from here to the end of the line at Dobbiaco; **buses** from Brunico to Cortina d'Ampezzo also go through Dobbiaco (see p.267).

Vipiteno (Sterzing)

Situated on the busy route north from Bolzano to Innsbruck, **VIPITENO** (STERZING) is easy enough to get to. This close to the Austrian border it's hardly surprising that much of Vipiteno is typically Tyrolean, with geranium-filled balconies and wood-panelled old inns. The porticoed main street, however, **Via Città Nuova** (Neustadtstrasse), is more reminiscent of places further south, lined with elegant, battlemented *palazzi* erected in Renaissance times by a locally based Florentine bank. At one end, the **Torre di Città** was rebuilt in 1867 after fire destroyed the fifteenth-century original. The late-Gothic **Palazzo Comunale** on the square behind, is worth a visit for its attractive galleried courtyard and a collection of fifteenth- and sixteenth-century paintings and sculptures (Mon–Sat 8.30am–noon & 2.30–6pm L2500/€1.29). Also worth tracking down is the **Museo Civico**, on Via della Commenda (May–Oct Tues–Sat 10am–noon & 2–5pm; L3000/€1.55), five minutes' walk from the centre, near the hospital. The museum is essentially an exhibition of local carving, the highlight being an altarpiece by Hans Multscher, a fifteenth-century sculptor and painter from Ulm. His work shows a keen sense of realism, as exemplified in an altarpiece of 1459. Several of his carved wooden figures can be seen in the nearby parish church of **Santa Maria in Vibitin**.

If you decide to **stay** in Vipiteno, the elegant, friendly *Wipptalerhof*, Via Città Nuova 4 (☎0472.765.428; ③) is undoubtedly the first choice. If it's fully booked, the tranquil *Pension Schneider*, Eduard Ploner Strasse 1 (☎0472.765.288; ③) is well-situated on a quiet side-street just above Via Città Vecchia, the extension of Via Città Nuova.

Parco Naturale Fánes-Sénnes-Bráies

If you have a limited amount of time to spend in the **Parco Naturale Fánes-Sénnes-Bráies**, east of Brunico, you should aim for the upper slopes of **Alpe di Fánes**, where you pick up some of the best ridgeway paths. You can get here by taking a bus from either Corvara (see p.253) or Brunico to **Longega** (Zwischenwasser), and then walking 4km to **San Vigilio Di Marebbe**, in a side valley, where the tourist office can advise on routes up into the mountains. A regular jeep taxi service runs from San Vigilio to *Rifugio Fánes* (☎0474.501.097; Dec 20 to April 30 & June 10 to Oct 15) and *Rifugio La Varella* (☎0474.501.079; March 19 to April 25 & June 19 to Oct 19), both around 2000m up on the Alpe di Fánes Piccola. Footpaths cross the grassy plateaus, passing small tarns and the rocks of **Castel de Fánes**, home of Dolasilla, the mythical princess of the Ladini. The lakes are fed by underground streams, which you can sometimes hear, burbling deep beneath your feet.

Perhaps the best way to see the park, however, is to walk the section of Alta Via 1 that runs through it, a hike which takes three to four days, with overnight stops at refuges. The trail starts at **Lago di Bráies** (Pragser Wildsee), a deep-green lake surrounded by pines, 8km off the main road through the Val Pusteria – an extraordinary place (according to legend, the lake is a gateway to underground caverns), although you should avoid it in July and August, when crowds descend on the trails. To get here, take a bus from **Corvara** to **Brunico** and then another bus towards **Dobbiaco** (see opposite), asking the driver to drop you at the turn-off, which is between **Monguelfo** (Welsberg) and **Villabassa** (Niederdorf), around thirty minutes out of Brunico; buses also go all the way to the lake from Dobbiaco.

Also accessible from Brunico by cable car (L22,000/€11.36 return) is the **Plan de Corones**, surrounded by jagged peaks. Here, legend has it, Dolasilla was crowned at the top of the mountain with the *raiëta* – a crystal that harnessed powerful forces.

Alta Via Val di Fundres (Pfunderer Höhenweg)

The high-level **Alta Via Val di Fundres** (Pfunderer Höhenweg) follows the ridges north of Brunico. Although it's in the lower part of the Zillertal Alps, the path gives a feeling of the high mountains, with views across to the glaciers of Gran Pilastro (Hochfeiler) on the Austrian border. It's an exhilarating area, often subject to snow, ice and scorching sun in the same day. Access to the path is at Kleines Tor (2374m) on Monte Sommo (Sambock), a steep climb along path 29 from **Selva Dei Molini** (Mühlwald), 24km from Brunico. The walk takes four to five days, with overnight stops in *rifugi* or *bivacci*. The nearest big village is **CAMPO TURES** (SAND IN TAUFERS), where the wonderfully evocative medieval castle, **Schloss Taufers** (visits by guided tour only: Dec to mid-June Tues, Fri & Sun at 3pm & 4pm; mid-June to mid-July & Sept–Oct daily at 10am, 11am, 2pm, 3.15pm & 4.30pm; mid-July to end of Aug daily every 30min 10–11.30am & 1–5pm; L6000/€3.10) has dozens of wood-panelled rooms, including one haunted by a woman whose husband was murdered on their wedding day. The dungeons boast a particularly gruesome array of torture instruments, but perhaps the most appealing aspect of the castle is its setting: stark grey walls, bristling with towers, stand in contrast to the glistening backdrop of the Zillertal glaciers.

From Kleines Tor the path drops down to the Winnebach Valley, then climbs to *Fritz Walde Hütte*. A steep path crosses the Hochsagescharte Col (2650m), drops to Passenjoch (2410m) and then, after a westerly descent to *Gampes Hütte* (2223m), makes a spectacular traverse across steep pasture that eventually descends to the Eisbrugger Valley. The end of the route at **Vipiteno** (see previous page) is reached via **Boden** and the Weitenber Valley. Early on the last day you can be descending across pasture just emerging from snow, and in the evening be eating pizza in town, listening to kids roar around on motorbikes. It's possible to do half of the walk by joining the path above **Fundres**, or the top of the Val di Valles (Valser Tal), where there's accommodation at *Brixner Hütte* (☎0472.547.131; mid-June to mid-Sept).

Dobbiaco (Toblach) and around
In the eastern part of the Val Pusteria, civilization and streams of car-borne German tourists resume at **DOBBIACO**, a stultifying resort and spa town where Gustav Mahler spent his summers between 1908 and 1910, at the junction of roads into the Val di Sesto (Sextental) and the Val di Landro (Höhlenstein Tal). The latter takes you south past Lago di Dobbiaco onto the Alemagna, the pilgrims' route from Germany to Rome. From the lake there's a superb view of the intimidating peaks of the Tre Cime di Lavaredo, rising to 2999m. The Val di Landro bus rounds the outer peaks of the Cristallo mountain group, where the road is flanked by forest on either side, before emerging at Cortina d'Ampezzo.

Cortina d'Ampezzo and around

The 1956 Winter Olympics were staged at **CORTINA D'AMPEZZO** (it still has the Pista Olimpica di Bob), an event which began the transformation of the town from a small resort to a city in the mountains. Its main reason for existing now is the skiing season – roughly Christmas to Easter – when the population rises from 7000 to around 40,000, packing out the designer-clothes and antiques shops, as well as the slopes around the city. Cortina is the Italian equivalent of Saint Moritz, attracting actors, artists – and the rich. The place encourages a kind of Hollywood existence: taking sleighs down the mountain after a meal at a glamorous restaurant, or renting helicopters to seek out off-piste skiing. Out of season the place is dead; although it has a summer hiking season of sorts, between July and September when the cable cars operate. The ranges are less crowded on the side that faces away from the city, and are better approached from the smaller resorts of Corvara, Alleghe and San Vigilio di Marebbe. The setting is stunning, however, surrounded by a great circle of mountains which includes Monte Pelmo and Antelao, the Gruppo delle Marmarole, and Monte Sorapiss, Cristallo and Tofane.

Cortina's **tourist office** is at Piazzetta San Francesco 8 (daily 9am–12.30pm & 3.30–6.30pm; ☎0436.3231, *www.sunrise.it/dolomiti*). Their hiking map is good, with refuge phone numbers and an indication of how long trails take to walk. The bad news is that **staying** here is expensive: prices climb exponentially in August and during the peak ski season. One of the cheaper places worth trying to book ahead is the central *Albergo Cavallino*, Corso Italia 142 (☎0436.2614; ③), which was being refitted at the time of writing but is due to re-open soon. Otherwise try the large *Hotel Impero*, Via Cesare Battisti 66 (☎0436.4246; ⑥), which sometimes has good deals, or the modern *Villa Nevada*, on Ronce 64 (☎0436.4778; ④), across the other side of town. Women who write far enough in advance may be able to get a bed in one of the convent hostels: names and addresses to try are Rev. Suore Canossiane, *Regina Mundi*, Via Grignes 9, or Rev. Suore Francescane, *Casa dello Studente San Francesco*, Via Cianderies 33. The tourist office has further details and lists of rooms available in private houses. In summer, there's the option of **camping** at one of a number of sites: *Cortina* (☎0436.867.575), *Dolomiti* (☎0436.2485) and *Rochetta* (☎0436.5063) are all 2km to the south at **Campo**, while *Olympia* (☎0436.5057) is at **Fiames**, 5km north.

Away from the hotel dining rooms, cafés and ice cream parlours are about the only sources of sustenance, though the central *Croda Café*, Corso Italia 163, has good-value pizza and a wide, if more expensive, à la carte menu. Campers and self-caterers will appreciate the **food** section of the large Cooperativa department store in the centre of town.

Apart from the tortuous **bus** routes via Bolzano and Belluno, there are long-distance services to Cortina from Milan, Padua and Bologna; the **bus station** is on Via Marconi, above town. The nearest **train station** is Calalzo, 32km east; a connecting bus runs every hour.

Around Cortina

Cortina is better known for trips by road and cable car than for mountain trails, with many drivers heading for the **Great Dolomites Road** (a scenic route between Cortina and Bolzano) and its passes. In summer there are buses to the small lake at **Misurina** (3 or 4 daily) and to the **Tre Cime di Lavaredo**, three mountain peaks to the northeast of the city – both extremely busy areas in high season.

One of the alternatives is to head south by bus towards Belluno in the Veneto (see p.366), passing through Titian's home town of **PIEVE DI CADORE**, with many paintings attributed to him and his family in the Parrocchiale. The one most likely to be authentic is in the third chapel on the left, and the altarpiece of the *Last Supper*, by his cousin Cesare is rather fine. **Titian's birthplace** is represented by a stone and wood house on Via Arsenale (late June to mid-Sept Tues–Sun 9.30am–12.30pm & 4–7pm; L2500/€1.29). Although it has been equipped with furniture and a fireplace from the fifteenth century, the present structure dates from the 1800s.

Sporting, Piazza Municipio 21 (☎0435.31.262; ②) is the most comfortable of Pieve di Cadore's inexpensive **hotels**; the **tourist office** (Mon–Sat 9am–noon & 3–6pm, Sun 10am–12.30pm; ☎0435.31.644), just down the road in a village called **TAI DI CADORE**, has the full list of accommodation. Among the handful of cafés and **bars**, *Caffè Tiziano* (closed Mon), in the vaults of the old Palazzo della Magnifica Comunità Cadorina, offers snacks, great cocktails and pool on full-size tables.

Alleghe and Monte Civetta

Without your own vehicle, it can be difficult to reach the most interesting mountains in these parts. One place you can get to by bus is the small village of **ALLEGHE**. The lake here was created after a huge rock avalanche in the eighteenth century – a common occurrence in the area. Now a peaceful summer and winter resort, Alleghe borders the northeastern edge of the lake, its aquamarine waters reflecting the pine forests around. Towering above is Monte Civetta, essentially Alleghe's main attraction, and the village makes a good base in between walks or climbs. The best of several two-star **hotels** in Alleghe is the *Alpenrose*, a five-minute walk up from the village centre at Via Coldai 85 (☎0437.723.929; ④); otherwise the *Garni La Nava*, Corso Italia 43 (☎0437.523.340; ③) is in a good position right beside the lake, near the town centre. *Camping Alleghe*, 2km away at Masarè (☎0437.723.737), is open for the summer and skiing seasons. **Places to eat** in town include the *enoteca* in Piazza Kennedy (closed Tues); don't miss the cakes in the pasticceria on the same square. Also on Piazza Kennedy is the **tourist office** (Mon–Sat 8.30am–noon & 3.30–6.30pm, Sun 9am–noon; ☎0437.523.333), geared up to provide information on cable cars and difficulty of footpaths; it also sometimes has English-language guides to the *alta via* routes.

For trips around the lake, the *Hotel Alleghe*, at the bottom of town, rents mountain **bikes** at L40,000/€20.66 per day. But the classic trip from Alleghe is the walk up to **Monte Civetta**: from Fontanive just above the village take footpath 564 all the way up through steep meadows and summer pastures until you join Alta Via 1 at the Pian dei Sech. From there it's a last haul (about an hour) to *Rifugio Sonino* at Coldai (also signposted as *Rifugio Coldai*; 2132m; ☎0437.789.160; late June to Sept). If avoiding the three- or four-hour slog up the mountain appeals, then take the **cable car** from the village to Piani di Pezze and the **chair lift** from there to Col dei Baldi (July–Aug daily 8.30am–5.30pm; L9000/€4.65 return). If you're lucky enough to be at the Col on a clear evening, head for Lago Coldai just beyond the refuge for views of the great rock wall of Civetta, rippling with rock chimneys and pipes, glowing red in the sunset.

Hardened hikers can continue on Alta Via 1, the next day of which takes you across small snowfields and past windows in the rock which offer dizzying glimpses of the valley and the Dolomite groups. A couple of hours from Coldai, *Rifugio Tissi* is perched improbably on an incline, on a vast slab of rock, and is cheerfully shambolic, with accommodation available (☎0437.721.644; late June to mid-Sept). From here you can continue on Alta Via 1, past *Rifugio Vazzoler* down to Listolade in the valley (5hr; hourly buses to Alleghe), or head straight down the steep trail 563 for three hours to Masare (20min walk from Alleghe), dipping your feet in a waterfall on the way.

travel details

TRAINS

Bolzano to: Bressanone (25 daily; 30min); Merano (hourly; 40min); Trento (30 daily; 35–50min); Vipiteno (14 daily; 1hr).

Brunico to: Dobbiaco (15 daily; 30min).

Fortezza to: Brunico (15 daily; 40min); Dobbiaco (15 daily; 1hr).

Trento to: Bologna (10 daily; 3hrs); Bolzano (30 daily; 35–50min); Cles (Trento-Malé line; hourly; 1hr); Malé (Trento-Malé line; hourly; 1hr 35min); Rovereto (28 daily; 15min); Venice (3 daily; 2hr 45min); Verona (28 daily; 1hr 10min).

BUSES

Note that buses are significantly less frequent on Saturdays, and rare on Sundays and public holidays.

Bolzano to: Canazei (3 daily; 1hr 45min); Corvara (7 daily; 1hr); Fiè (16 daily; 30min); Lago di Carezzo (5 daily; 55min); Merano (hourly; 1hr); Predazzo (7 daily; 2hr); Selva (8 daily; 1hr 20min); Siusi (every 30min; 45min); Vigo di Fassa (4 daily; 1hr 20min).

Bressanone to: Brunico (hourly; 1hr); San Pietro (3 daily; 45min); Santa Maddalena (2 daily; 55min); Siusi (6 daily; 40min).

Brunico to: Bressanone (hourly; 1hr); Campo Tures (every 30min; 20min); Corvara (hourly; 1hr 10min); Dobbiaco (10 daily; 45min); Plan de Corones cable-car terminal (8 daily; 15min); San Vigilio di Marebbe (6 daily; 35min); Siusi (3 daily; 1hr 30min; change at Prato Isarco).

Cortina d'Ampezzo to: Belluno (6 daily; 2hr); Calalzo (10 daily; 1hr); Dobbiaco (6 daily; 45min); Pieve di Cadore (10 daily; 50min).

Corvara to: Belluno (2 daily; 2hr 45min); Longega (8 daily; 45min).

Dobbiaco to: Brunico (10 daily; 45min); Cortina d'Ampezzo (6 daily; 45min); Lago Bráies (5 daily; 25min); Villabassa (10 daily; 10 min).

Fiera di Primiero to: Passo di Cereda (1–2 daily; 25min).

Merano to: Moso (at least hourly; 1hr 10min); Passo dello Stelvio (1 daily; 3hr); San Leonardo (every 30min; 50min); Katherinaberg (6 daily; 50min); Santa Geltrude (9 daily; 1hr 25min); Silandro (every 30min; 1hr); Solda (2 daily; 2hr 30min).

San Martino di Castrozza to: Feltre, Veneto (9 daily; 1hr 20min); Fiera di Primiero (9 daily; 30min); Imer (9 daily; 40min); Predazzo (2 daily; 1hr).

Siusi to: Ortisei (5 daily; 40min); Santa Cristina (4 daily; 1hr); Selva (4 daily; 1hr); Tires (4 daily; 45min).

Trento to: Belluno (1 daily; 2hr 40min); Canazei (6 daily; 2hr 40min); Fiera di Primiero (3 daily, bus and train connection; 2hr 30min); Madonna di Campiglio (9 daily; 2hr); Molveno (3 daily; 2hr); Predazzo (6 daily; 1hr 45min); Rovereto (hourly; 40min); San Martino di Castrozza (3 daily, bus and train connection; 3hr); Tione (11 daily; 1hr); Vigo di Fassa (6 daily; 2hr 15min).

CHAPTER FIVE

VENICE AND THE VENETO

The first-time visitor to **Venice** arrives with a heavy freight of expectations, most of which turn out to be well founded. All the photographs you've seen of the Palazzo Ducale, of the Basilica di San Marco, of the palaces along the Canal Grande – they've simply been recording the extraordinary truth. All the bad things you've heard about the city turn out to be right as well. Economically and socially ossified, it is losing people by the year and plays virtually no part in the life of modern Italy. It is deluged with tourists – the annual influx exceeding Venice's population two-hundredfold. Occasionally things get so bad that entry into the city is barred to those who haven't already booked a room. And it is expensive – the price of a good meal almost anywhere else in Italy will get you a lousy one in Venice, and its hoteliers make the most of a situation where demand will always far outstrip supply.

As soon as you begin to explore Venice, though, every day will bring its surprises, for this is an urban landscape so rich that you can't walk for a minute without coming across something that's worth a stop. And although it's true that Venice can be unbearably crowded, things aren't so bad beyond the magnetic field of San Marco and the kitsch-sellers of the vicinity, and in the off-season (October to Christmas and January to Easter) it's even possible to have parts of the centre virtually to yourself. As for keeping your costs down, Venice has plenty of markets in addition to the celebrated Rialto, there are some good-value eating places, and you can, with planning, find a bed without spending a fortune.

Tourism is far from being the only strand to the economy of the **Veneto**, however. The rich, flat land around the Po supports some of Italy's most productive farms and vineyards, and industrial development around the main towns rivals even the better-known areas around Milan, making the region one of the richest in Europe. At

---

ACCOMMODATION PRICE CODES

Throughout this guide, prices per person are given for **youth hostels** and assume Hostelling International (HI) membership. **Hotel** accommodation is coded on a scale from ① to ⑨, reflecting the cost of the cheapest double room in each establishment in high season. The price bands to which these codes refer are as follows:

① Up to L60,000/€30.99
② L60,000–90,000/€30.99–46.48
③ L90,000–120,000/€46.48–61.98
④ L120,000–150,000/€61.98–77.47
⑤ L150,000–200,000/€77.47–103.29

⑥ L200,000–250,000/€103.29–129.11
⑦ L250,000–300,000/€129.11–154.94
⑧ L300,000–400,000/€154.94–206.58
⑨ over L400,000/€206.58

(See p.32 for a full explanation.)

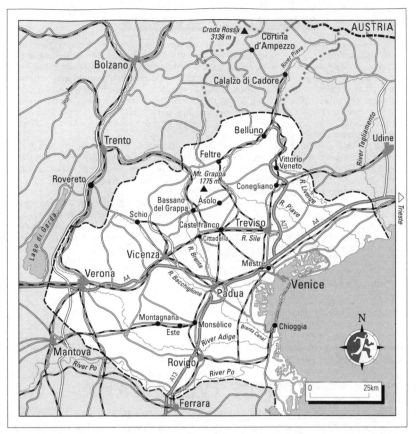

Marghera, just over the lagoon from Venice, the Veneto has the largest industrial complex in the country, albeit one that is now in decline. But tourism is important, and the region has more tourist accommodation than any other in Italy. After Venice, it's **Padua** and **Verona** that are the main attractions, with their masterpieces by Giotto, Donatello and Mantegna and a profusion of great buildings from Roman times to the Renaissance. None of the other towns of the Veneto can match the cultural wealth of these two former rivals to Venice, but there are nonetheless plenty of places between the plains of Polésine in the south and the mountains in the north that justify a detour – the Palladian city of **Vicenza**, for instance, the fortified settlements of **Montagnana**, **Cittadella** and **Castelfranco**, or the idyllic upland town of **Ásolo**.

For outdoor types, much of the Veneto is dull, consisting of flatlands interrupted by gentle outcrops around Padua and Vicenza. The interesting terrain lies in its northern part, especially in the area above **Belluno** and **Vittorio Veneto**, where the wooded slopes of the foothills – excellent for walking – soon give way to the savage precipices of the eastern Dolomites. Because most of the high peaks of the Dolomites lie within Trentino-Alto Adige, and the mountains of the eastern Dolomites are most easily explored as part of a tour of the range as a whole, the area of the Veneto to the north of Belluno is covered in the "Trentino-Alto Adige" chapter, starting on p.233. Similarly,

---

REGIONAL FOOD AND WINE

The Veneto vies with Lombardy for the risotto-making crown, while Venice specializes in fish and **seafood**, together with exotic ingredients like pomegranates, pine nuts and raisins, harking back to its days as a port and merchant city. The **risottos** tend to be more liquid than those to the west, usually with a seafood base although peas (*bisi* in dialect) are also common, as are other seasonal vegetables – spinach, asparagus, pumpkin. The red salad leaf raddichio also has its home in the Veneto, as does the renowned Italian dessert, tiramisu. Polenta is eaten too, while **pork** in all forms features strongly, together with heavy **soups** of beans, rice and root vegetables. Gnocchi tend to be served in an unusual sweet-sour sauce.

Pastries and **sweets** are also an area of Venetian expertise. Look out for the thin oval biscuits called *baicoli*, the ring-shaped cinnamon-flavoured *bussolai* (a speciality of the Venetian island of Burano), and *mandolato* – a cross between nougat and toffee, made with almonds. The Austrian occupation has left its mark in the form of the ubiquitous strudel and the cream- or jam-filled *krapfen* (doughnuts).

The Veneto has been very successful at developing **wines** with French and German grape varieties, notably Merlot, Cabernet, Pinot Bianco, Pinot Grigio, Müller-Thurgau, Riesling, Chardonnay and Gewürztraminer. The quintessentially Italian Bardolino, Valpolicella and Soave are all from the Verona region and, like so many Italian wines, taste better near their region of origin. This is also true of the more rarely exported Prosecco, a light champagne-like wine from the area around Conegliano: don't miss the chance to sample Prosecco Rosé and the delicious Cartizze, the finest type of Prosecco. **Grappa**, the local firewater, is associated particularly with the upland town of Bassano di Grappa, where every *alimentari* is stocked with a dozen varieties. Made from grape husks, juniper berries or plums, *grappa* is very much an acquired taste, but beware – the acquisition can be a damaging process.

---

the eastern shore of Lago di Garda is covered as part of the lakes region in the "Lombardy and the Lakes" chapter, starting on p.156.

VENICE (VENEZIA)

The monuments that draw the largest crowds are the **Basilica di San Marco** – the mausoleum of the city's patron saint – and the **Palazzo Ducale** – the home of the doge and all the governing councils. Certainly these are the most dramatic structures in the city: the first a mosaic-clad emblem of Venice's Byzantine origins, the second perhaps the finest of all secular Gothic buildings. Every parish rewards exploration, though – a roll-call of the **churches** worth visiting would feature over fifty names, and a list of the important paintings and sculptures they contain would be twice as long. Two of the distinctively Venetian institutions known as the **scuole** retain some of the outstanding examples of Italian Renaissance art – the **Scuola di San Rocco**, with its sequence of pictures by Tintoretto, and the **Scuola di San Giorgio degli Schiavoni**, decorated with a gorgeous sequence by Carpaccio.

Although many of the city's treasures remain in the buildings for which they were created, a sizeable number have been removed to one or other of Venice's **museums**. The one that should not be missed is the **Accademia**, an assembly of Venetian painting that consists of virtually nothing but masterpieces; other prominent collections include the museum of eighteenth-century art in the **Ca'Rezzonico**, and the **Museo Correr**, the civic museum of Venice – but again, a comprehensive list would fill a page.

The cultural heritage preserved in the museums and churches is a source of endless fascination, but you should discard your worthy itineraries for a day and just wander – the anonymous parts of Venice reveal as much of the city's essence as the highlighted attractions. And equally indispensable for a full understanding of Venice's way of life and development are expeditions to the **northern and southern islands** of the lagoon, where the incursions of the tourist industry are on the whole less obtrusive.

A brief history

Small groups of fishermen and hunters were living on the mudbanks of the Venetian lagoon at the start of the Christian era, but it was with the barbarian invasions of the fifth century that sizeable communities began to settle on the mudbanks. The first mass migration was provoked by the arrival in the Veneto of **Attila the Hun**'s hordes in 453, and the rate of settlement accelerated a century later, when, in 568, the **Lombards** swept into northern Italy.

The loose confederation of island communes that began to develop in the sixth century owed political allegiance to Byzantium, and until the end of the seventh century its senior officials were effectively controlled by the Byzantine hierarchy of Ravenna. But with the steep increase in the population of the islands which resulted from the strengthening of the Lombard grip on the Veneto in the later seventh century, the ties with the empire grew weaker, and in 726 the settlers chose their own leader of the provincial government – their first **doge**.

The control of Byzantium soon became no more than nominal, and the inhabitants of the lagoon signalled their independence through one great symbolic act – the theft of the body of **St Mark** from Alexandria in 828. St Mark displaced Byzantium's St Theodore as the city's patron, and a basilica was built alongside the doge's castle to accommodate the relics. These two buildings – the **Basilica di San Marco** and the **Palazzo Ducale** – were to remain the emblems of the Venetian state and the repository of power within the city for almost one thousand years.

Before the close of the tenth century the Venetian **trading networks** were well established through concessions granted by Byzantium in the markets of the East and the exploitation of the waterways of northern Italy to distribute the goods from the Levant. By the early twelfth century Venetian merchants had won exemption from all tolls within the eastern empire and were profiting from the chaos that followed the **First Crusade**, which had been launched in 1095. Prosperity found expression in the fabric of the city: the present-day basilica and many of its mosaics are from this period; and at the end of the century the Piazza was brought to something close to its modern shape. The **Fourth Crusade**, diverted to Constantinople by the Venetians, set the seal on their maritime empire. They brought back shiploads of treasure (including the horses of San Marco) from the **Sack of Constantinople** in 1204, but more significant was the division of the territorial spoils, which left "one quarter and half a quarter" of the Roman Empire under Venice's sway and gave the Republic a chain of ports that stretched almost without a break from the lagoon to the Black Sea.

For almost all the fourteenth century, the defeat of Genoa – Venice's main rival in the eastern markets – preoccupied Venice's rulers, who finally secured the Republic's economic and political supremacy after the defeat of the Genoese in the **War of Chioggia** (1379–80). It was during the Genoese campaigns that the **constitution** of Venice arrived at a state that was to endure until the fall of the Republic, the largest step in this evolution being the **Serrata del Maggior Consiglio** of 1297, a measure which restricted participation in the government of the city to those families already involved in it. A revolt of disgruntled aristocrats in 1310 led to the creation of the **Council of Ten** to supervise internal security – intended to be an emergency measure, it was made permanent in 1334 and became the most secretive and most feared state institution.

Venetian foreign policy was predominantly eastward-looking from the start, but a degree of intervention on the mainland was necessary to maintain its continental trade routes. By the middle of the fifteenth century, Venice was in possession of a mainland empire that was to survive virtually intact until the coming of Napoleon.

But while Venice was advancing at home, the **Ottoman Turks** were emerging as a threat to the colonial empire. Constantinople fell to the Sultan's army in 1453, and with their capture of the main fortresses of the Morea (Peloponnese) in 1499, the Turks gained control of the access to the Adriatic.

Distrust of Venice's ambitions on the mainland and fear of Turkish expansion provoked the formation of the **League of Cambrai** in 1508. Headed by Pope Julius II, Louis XII, Emperor Maximilian and the King of Spain, it pitted almost every power in Europe against the Venetians, in a pact that set out to destroy Venice's empire as a prelude to conquering the Turks. When the fighting finished in 1516, Venice's subtle diplomacy had ensured that it still possessed nearly all the land it had held a decade before, but many of the cities of the Veneto had been sacked, great swaths of the countryside ruined, and the Venetian treasury bled almost dry. Worse was to come. After Vasco da Gama's voyage to India via the Cape of Good Hope, the slow and expensive land routes across Asia to the markets of Venice could now be bypassed by the merchants of northern Europe. The economic balance of Europe now began to tilt in favour of the Portuguese, the English and the Dutch.

After the **Sack of Rome** in 1527 the whole Italian peninsula, with the sole exception of Venice, came under the domination of Emperor Charles V. Hemmed in at home, Venice saw its overseas territory further whittled away by the Turks as the century progressed: by 1529 the Ottoman Empire extended right along the southern Mediterranean to Morocco, and even the great naval success at **Lepanto** in **1571** was quickly followed by the surrender of Cyprus.

At the start of the seventeenth century a row with Rome, concerning the extent of papal jurisdiction within the Republic, culminated in 1606 with the excommunication of the entire city. After a year of arguments the **Papal Interdict** was lifted, damaging the prestige of the papacy throughout Europe. Relations with the **Habsburgs** were no easier. The Austrian branch caused trouble by encouraging pirate raids on Venetian shipping, and in 1618 the more devious Spanish wing attempted to subvert the Venetian state by a wildly ambitious plot that has always been known as **The Spanish Conspiracy**. But the **Turks** caused the most lasting damage, taking the one remaining stronghold in the eastern Mediterranean, Crete, in 1669.

Venice in the eighteenth century became a political nonentity, reduced to pursuing a policy of unarmed neutrality. At home, the economy remained healthy, but the division between the upper stratum of the aristocracy and the ever-increasing poorer section was widening, and all attempts to dampen discontent within the city by democratizing its government were stifled by the conservative elite.

Politically moribund and constitutionally ossified, Venice was renowned not as one of the great powers of Europe, but rather as its playground, a city of casinos and perpetual festivals. **Napoleon** brought the show to an end. On May 12, 1797, the Maggior Consiglio met for the last time, voting to accede to Napoleon's demand that it dismantle the machinery of government. In October, Napoleon relinquished Venice to the Austrians, but returned in 1805 to join the city to his Kingdom of Italy, and it stayed under French rule until after Waterloo. It then passed back to the Austrians and remained a Habsburg province until united with the Kingdom of Italy in 1866.

During the French occupation a large number of buildings were demolished to facilitate urban improvement schemes, and modernization projects were continued under the Austrians. They created most of the *rii terrà* (infilled canals), constructed two new bridges across the Canal Grande, and built a rail link with the mainland.

Yet Venice in the nineteenth century was almost destitute. Eclipsed as an Adriatic port by Trieste (the Austrians' preference), Venice achieved large-scale expansion in the area of **tourism**, with the development of the **Lido** as Europe's most fashionable resort. It was the need for a more substantial economic base that led, in the wake of World War I, to the construction of the industrial complex on the marshland across the lagoon from

Venice, at **Marghera**, a processing and refining centre to which raw materials would be brought by sea. In 1933 a road link was built to carry the workforce between Venice and the steadily expanding complex, but it was not until after World War II that Marghera's growth accelerated. The factories of Marghera are essential to the economy of the province, but they have caused terrible problems too: apart from polluting the environment of the lagoon, they have siphoned many people out of Venice and into the cheaper housing of Mestre, making Mestre-Marghera today more than three times larger than the historic centre of Venice, where the population has dropped since the last war from around 170,000 to about 80,000. No city has suffered more from the tourist industry than Venice – about 10 million people visit the city each year, and around half of those don't even stay a night – though without them Venice would barely survive at all.

Arrival

If you are arriving **by air**, you'll touch down in one of two airports: **Treviso**, 30km inland from Venice, or at Venice's Marco Polo airport. The former is used chiefly by charter companies, many of whom provide a bus link from the airport into Venice. If such a service isn't provided, take the #6 bus from right outside the arrivals building into Treviso (30min), from where there are regular bus and train connections to Venice. Nearly all scheduled flights and some charters arrive at **Marco Polo**, around 7km north of Venice, on the edge of the lagoon. If you're on a package holiday, the cost of transport to the city centre, either by land or by water, might already be covered. If it's not, don't succumb to the touts for the **water-taxis** – this will cost you in the region of L130,000/€67.08, though the cost becomes less extortionate when shared out between a group. Ordinary **car-taxis** are ranked outside the arrivals hall, and cost about L50,000/€25.82 to Piazzale Roma, site of the Venice bus terminal. The alternatives are to take one of the hourly Alilaguna **water buses** to the landing stage near San Marco (L17,000/€8.78; journey time 1hr), or one of the ATVO (Azienda Trasporti Veneto Orientale) **buses** that are scheduled to meet incoming and outgoing flights (L5000/€2.58; 20min). The cheapest option is to wait for the next ACTV (Azienda del Consorzio Trasporti Veneziano) **bus** #5, which runs every twenty minutes (L1500/€0.77, plus a small supplement for large pieces of luggage; 30min). The ticket offices for the water buses and the land buses are in the arrivals hall; the latter will sell you a ticket for the ATVO rather than the ACTV bus unless you make clear your preference for *il cinque*. You can also get ACTV bus tickets (but not passes) from the *tabacchi* in the departures area, which you reach by turning right outside the arrivals hall.

People arriving **by car** must leave their vehicle either on the mainland or at the car parks of Venice itself – at **Piazzale Roma** or the ever-expanding **Tronchetto**, Europe's largest car park. Prices at these two vary according to the time of year, the length of stay and the size of car, but it's never a cheap option (from about L40,000/€20.66 per day), and in summer the tailbacks can be horrendous. Better to use the open-air **San Giuliano** car park at Mestre, which operates only in summer, at Easter and during the *Carnevale*. ACTV buses connect with central Venice. The newly expanded terminal at Fusina, however, is now open year-round and ACTV water buses connect directly to Piazza San Marco, making this route one of the most pleasant ways to arrive in Venice.

Arriving **by train or bus**, you simply get off at the end of the line. The **Piazzale Roma** bus station and **Santa Lucia** train station are just five minutes' walk from each other, at the top of the Canal Grande, and both are well served by *vaporetto* (water bus) services to the core of the city. The **left luggage** office at the train station charges L5000/€2.58 per item per twelve hours; it's found at the end of platform 14. The lockers alongside platform 1 are slightly more expensive at L3000/€1.55 per six hours.

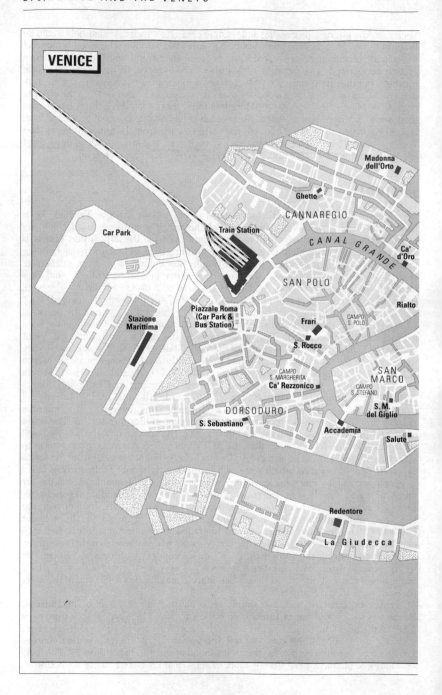

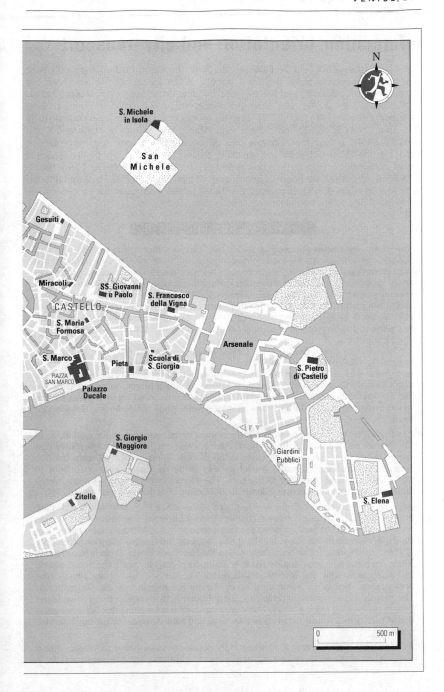

S. Michele
in Isola

San
Michele

Gesuiti

Miracoli

SS. Giovanni
e Paolo

S. Francesco
della Vigna

CASTELLO

S. Maria
Formosa

Arsenale

S. Marco

Pieta

Scuola di
S. Giorgio

S. Pietro
di Castello

PIAZZA
SAN MARCO

Palazzo
Ducale

S. Giorgio
Maggiore

Giardini
Pubblici

Zitelle

S. Elena

0   500 m

Information, orientation and city transport

The main **tourist office** is in the Palazzina del Santi, the waterfront building on the west side of the Giardinetti Reale, within a minute of the Piazza San Marco (Mon–Sat 10am–6pm; ☎041.522.6356) and has a central info line (*www.provincia.venezia.it/aptve*). It also hosts a good Web site (*www.govenice.com*), or you could try the excellent *www.governice.com*. (☎041.522.8711). Smaller offices operate at the train station (daily 8am–7pm; ☎041.529.8727), on Piazza San Marco 71f (Mon–Sat 9.30am–5.30pm; ☎041.520.8964), in the airport arrivals area (Mon–Sat 9.30am–8pm) and on the Lido at Gran Viale 6 (May–Oct daily 9.30am–3.30pm; ☎041.526.5721). There are seasonal tourist information offices (green cabins) dotted around the city (Feb–Oct 10am–1pm & 1.30–5pm), on Campo San Felice (Cannaregio), Campo dei Frari (San Polo) and Riva dei Sette Martiri (Castello). The free map distributed by these offices is fine for general ori-

---

WATER-BUS ROUTES

The **water-bus routes** operated by ACTV can seem bewilderingly complicated, and in the past the company has seemed bent on maximizing the confusion by altering routes and numbers for no readily apparent reason. Recent changes have rationalized the situation, but this is no guarantee for the future; in particular note that the water buses which currently make a circuit of the far eastern side of the city may return to their previous route through the Arsenale. As a rule, the routes displayed at each *vaporetto* stop are reliable, although in the outlying parishes they sometimes take a few months to get round to posting up the current map. The map handed out by the tourist offices never gives the complete picture.

What follows is a run-through of the most useful services. Times given are approximate, as it will depend on exactly where along the route you pick up the bus, so if you need to catch an early or late *vaporetto*, check at a ticket office; most of the vendors speak some English. Be warned that so many services call at San Marco, San Zaccaria, Rialto and the train station, that the bus stops at these points are spread out over a long stretch of waterfront, so you might have to walk past several stops before finding the one you need.

#1: The perversely named *accelerato* is the slowest of the water buses, the workhorse of the system, and the one you'll use most often; it's also one of the very few routes that seem exempt from alterations. It starts at the Piazzale Roma, calls at all stops bar San Samuele on the Canal Grande, works its way along the San Marco waterfront to Sant'Elena, and then goes over to the Lido. The #1 runs every 20min 5–6.30am, every 10min 6.30am–9.45pm, and every 20min 9.45–11.45pm. For the night service, see #N.

#82: This all-year service circles the southern island of San Polo/Dorsoduro, travelling in both directions along the route. What you'll most likely need to know is that it runs from the train and bus stations down the Canal Grande to San Marco, and it's faster than the #1, as there are fewer stops. It calls at San Zaccaria, San Giorgio Maggiore, Giudecca (Zitelle, Redentore and Palanca), Zàttere, San Basilio, Sacca Fisola, Tronchetto, Piazzale Roma, train station, Canal Grande (usually Rialto, Sant' Angelo, San Tomà, San Samuele and Accademia) and San Marco at Vallaresso. The service runs every 10min from 6am–8.30pm, then every 20min until 11pm, though the section from San Tomà to San Marco runs only every 20min through the day. Earlier in the morning (from 5–8am) and later in the evening (after 8.30pm) there is a restricted service along this latter section – the #82 acting as a shuttle between San Zaccaria and Sant' Angelo. For the night service see #N.

#41/42: The circular service, running right round the main island of Venice, with a short detour at the northern end to San Michele and Murano. The #41 travels anticlock-

entation, but not much else. Far more useful is the English-Italian magazine *Un Ospite di Venezia*, produced weekly in summer and monthly in winter, which gives up-to-date information on exhibitions, special events and *vaporetto* timetables – it's free from the main tourist office, and from the receptions of the posher hotels. There are a number of dedicated **Internet** sites. One of the best, though not really designed for tourists (most pages are in Italian) can be found at *www.provincia.venezia.it*, with links to museums

If you're aged between 14 and 29, you are elligible for a **Rolling Venice** card, which entitles you to discounts at some shops, restaurants, cinemas, museums and exhibitions, plus reductions on some transport services, all of which are detailed in a leaflet that comes with the card. The card costs L5000/€2.58, is valid for a year, and is worth buying if you're in town for a week or longer and aim to make the most of every minute. Only the following places issue it: Agenzia Transalpino, at the train station; Assessorato alla Gioventù, Corte Contarina 1529 (just west of San Marco); Agenzia Arte e Storia, Santa Croce 659 (near Campo della Lana); Associazione Italiana Alberghi per la

---

wise, the #42 clockwise and both run every 20min from 7am to 8pm. Earlier and later in the day, a commuter service shuttles between Murano and Venice every 10–20min, following the #51/52 route on from the Fondamente Nove in the appropriate direction.

#51/52: Similar to the #41/42, this much-altered route also circles Venice, but heads out to the Lido (rather than Murano) at the easternmost end of the circle. The #51 runs anticlockwise, the #52 clockwise, and both run fast through the Guidecca canal, stopping only at Zattere and Santa Marta between San Marco and Piazzale Roma. Both run every 20min from 7am–9.30pm. Early in the morning and late in the evening a reduced service begins from and terminates at Murano instead of the Lido, cutting out the northeasternmost flank of Venice between Fondamente Nove and the Lido. This applies to the #51 in the mornings (4.30–7am) and evenings (8–11pm) and to the #52 after 8pm only. After 11pm the #52 becomes a shuttle between the Lido and the train station via the Guidecca canal; this route runs until 12.30pm and connects through to Rialto.

#N: The night service (11.30pm–4.30am) is a selective fusion of the #1 and #82 routes, running from Piazzale Roma to the Lido, down the Canal Grande. Stops are as follows: Lido, Giardini, San Zaccaria, Vallaresso, Accademia, San Samuele, San Tomà, Rialto, Ca' d'Oro, San Stae, San Marcuola, train station, Piazzale Roma, Tronchetto, Sacca Fisola, San Basilio, Zattere, Palanca, Redentore, Zitelle, San Giorgio and San Zaccaria – then retracing its route. It runs along the whole of the route in both directions every 30–40min, and from Rialto to Tronchetto every 20min. Another night service connects Venice with the Murano stops, running to and from Fondamente Nove every 30min between midnight and 4am.

Fast links: You're less likely to need the #61/62, a fast weekday link between Piazzale Roma and the Lido down the Giudecca canal, or the #71/72, which connects Murano directly to the transport termini and San Marco. The #4/G2: is a super-fast tourist service which leaves every 20min from the train station (via the bus station, car park and Giudecca canal) for San Marco. It was designed as a special millennial-year service, but may continue to run into 2001/2002.

Lagoon routes: Heading out into the lagoon, the #6, #12, #13 and #14 connect Venice with the northern islands (including Murano, Burano, Torcello and the Lido) while the #20 runs from San Marco to the southern islands. Details are given in the appropriate sections (see pp.315–320).

NB: In addition to the longer routes, some *vaporetti* and *motoscafi* operate as *traghetti* across the Canal Grande and over to the nearer islands: for example, if you want to go from San Zaccaria over to San Giorgio Maggiore, you need only pay the lower *traghetto* fare of L3000/€1.55. If your journey is a short single-stop trip across a body of water, a *traghetto* fare almost certainly applies – it'll be shown on the tariff list on the ticket booth.

Gioventù, Calle del Castelforte 3101 (near the Scuola di San Rocco); and Agenzia Transalpino (in the train station).

The transport system

Venice has two interlocking street-systems – the canals and the pavements – and contrary to what you might expect, you'll be using the latter for most of the time. Apart from services #1 and #82, which cut through the city along the Canal Grande, the water buses skirt the city centre, connecting points on the periphery and the outer islands. In most cases the speediest way of **getting around** is on foot. Distances between major sights are extremely short (you can cross the whole city in an hour), and once you've got your general bearings you'll find that navigation is less daunting than it seems on arrival.

The water buses

There are two basic types of boat: the **vaporetti**, which are the lumbering workhorses used on the Canal Grande stopping service and other heavily used routes, and the **motoscafi**, smaller vessels employed on routes where the volume of traffic isn't as great. On both types there's a **flat-rate fare** of L6000/€3.10 for any one continuous journey, or L10,000/€5.16 return unless it's a traghetto journey (see below), in which case the fare is L2000/€1.03. On return journeys (and some one-way routes – look at the top of your ticket to see if there is a date printed) you'll have to stamp your ticket in the yellow machine, usually placed right by the landing stage.

Tickets are available from most landing stages, from *tabacchi*, from shops displaying the ACTV sign, and from the two ACTV public offices – at Piazzale Roma (daily 6am–midnight), and in Calle dei Fuseri, close to the northwest corner of the Piazza (Mon–Fri 7.30am–6pm, Sat 7.30am–1pm). The latter is your best source of free up-to-date colour maps of the main routes – the tourist offices seem to run out of them very quickly. In the remoter parts of the city, you may not be able to find anywhere to buy a ticket, particularly after working hours, when the booths at the landing stages tend to close down. If necessary you can pay on board for the normal price, but make sure you ask the attendant immediately as there's a L26,000/€30.99 spot-fine for not having a valid ticket and inspections are frequent.

ACTV produces three travel cards: a 24-hour ticket (L18,000/€9.30); a three-day ticket (L35,000/€18.08), and a seven-day ticket (L60,000/€60.000), all of which are valid on all water- and land-buses within Venice. There are also three itinerary tickets covering particular routes: these cost L15,000/€7.75 each and are valid for twelve hours unlimited use on either the Canal Grande, the islands of the Northen Lagoon (including Torcello, Burano and Murano) or to and from Chioggia via Pellestrina. The **Carta Venezia**, which gives huge reductions on all ACTV buses, is not available to non-residents.

Traghetti

There are only three bridges along the Canal Grande – at the train station, Rialto and Accademia – so the **traghetti** (gondola ferries) that cross it can be useful time-savers. Costing just L700/€0.36, they are also the only cheap way of getting a ride on a gondola – though it's *de rigueur* to stand in a traghetto rather than sit. In summer most of the Canal Grande *traghetti* run from early morning to around 7–9pm daily; in the winter months some *traghetti* operate until about 5pm, while others are suspended altogether. The gondola *traghetti* across the Canal Grande are as follows: San Marco–Salute; Santa Maria del Giglio–Salute; San Barnaba–San Samuele; San Tomà–Santo Stefano; Riva del Carbon–Riva del Vin (near Rialto); Santa Sofia–Pescheria; San Marcuola–Fondaco dei Turchi; train station–San Simeone.

Gondolas

The **gondola** is no longer a form of transport but rather an adjunct of the tourist industry. That said, it can be a delightful way of lifting your eyes from the map or dinnerplate
and relishing the sheer sense of being in Venice, and the cost isn't all that offputting
when split among a small group. To hire one costs L120,000/€61.97 per up to 50min for up
to six passengers, rising to L150,000/€77.47 between 8pm and 8am; you pay an extra
L60,000/€30.99 for every additional 25 minutes. Further hefty surcharges will be
levied should you require the services of an on-board accordionist or tenor – and a surprising number of people do, despite the strangulated voices and hackneyed repertoire
of most of the aquatic Carusos. Even though the tariff is set by the local authorities, it's
been known for some gondoliers to try to extort even higher rates than these – if you
do decide to go for a ride, establish the charge before setting off.

To minimize the chances of being ripped off by a private individual making a few million lire on the side, only take a boat from one of the following **official gondola stands**:
west of the Piazza at Calle Vallaresso, Campo San Moisè or Campo Santa Maria del
Giglio; immediately north of the Piazza at Bacino Orseolo; on the Molo, in front of the
Palazzo Ducale; outside the *Danieli* hotel on Riva degli Schiavoni; at the train station;
at Piazzale Roma; at Campo Santa Sofia, near the Ca' d'Oro; at San Tomà; or by the
Rialto Bridge on Riva Carbon.

Accommodation

The virtually limitless demand for **accommodation** in Venice has pushed prices to such
a level that it's possible to pay in excess of L200,000/€103.29 for a double room in a one-
star hotel in high season. What's more, the **high season** here is longer than anywhere
else in the country – it is officially classified as running from March 15 to November 15
and then from December 21 to January 6, but many places don't recognize the existence
of a low season any more. At any time during the official high season it's wisest to book
your place at least two months in advance, whether it's a hostel bed or a five-star suite,
and for June, July and August it's virtually obligatory. Should you bowl into town unan-
nounced in high summer, the booking offices (see below) may be able to dig out something in the hotels of mainland Mestre or way out in the lagoon at the unlovely neighbouring resorts of Jesolo and Cavallino (a thirty-minute boat ride), but rooms here
would be nobody's free choice, which is why we have not included them in our listings.
During the winter it's possible to bargain for a reduced-rate room, but many hotels –
especially the cheaper ones – close down from November to February or even March,
so you might have to put in a bit of legwork before finding somewhere.

If there is no space in any of the places listed below, try one of the following **booking offices**: at the train station (summer 8am–9pm; winter 8am–7pm); on the
Tronchetto (9am–7pm) in the multistorey car park at Piazzale Roma (summer
9am–10pm; winter 9am–7pm); at Marco Polo airport (9am–10pm); at the *autostrada's*
Venice exit (11am–7pm). They only deal with hotels (not hostels) and take a deposit
that's deductible from your first night's bill.

Hotels

Venice has around two hundred hotels, ranging from spartan one-star joints to five-star
establishments charging a million lire a night, and what follows is a rundown on the
best choices in all categories. Though there are some typical anomalies, the star system is a broadly reliable indicator of quality, but always bear in mind that you pay
through the nose for your proximity to the **Piazza San Marco**. So if you want maximum comfort for your money, decide how much you can afford and then look for a

place outside the San Marco sestiere – after all, it's not far to walk, wherever you're staying.

Be warned that although **breakfast** should be optional, most hotels include it in their price and simply refuse to take guests who don't want to pay a ludicrous extra charge for a jug of coffee and a puny croissant – breakfast at the humblest one-star can add L20,000/€10.32 per person onto your bill. By law, the price of a room must be displayed on the back of its door; if it's not, or if the price doesn't correspond to what you're being charged, complain first to the management and then to the *Questura* (see p.330).

San Marco

Ai Do Mori, Calle Larga S. Marco, S. Marco 658 (☎041.520.4817, fax 041.520.5328). Very friendly, and situated a few paces off the Piazza, this recently refitted hotel is a top recommendation for budget travellers. The top-floor room, with its private terrace looking over the roofs of the Basilica and the Torre dell'Orologio, is one of the most attractive one-star rooms in the city. ③.

Ala, Campo S. Maria del Giglio, S. Marco 2494 (☎041.520.8333, fax 041.520.6390, *www.hotelala.it*). If you want to stay in the city's aristocratic accommodation zone but can't stretch to the prices of the Bauer Grünwald and its coevals, the three-star Ala is a logical choice. There are more welcoming places in Venice, but the rooms are spacious and the Ala has a perfect location, on a square whose mouth opens onto the Canal Grande. ⑦.

Casa Petrarca, Calle delle Colonne, S. Marco 4394 (☎041.520.0430). The cheapest hotel within a stone's throw of the Piazza. Phone first, as it only has seven rooms, though they may be able to accommodate you nearby. Extremely hospitable, with English-speaking staff. ③.

La Fenice et des Artistes, Campiello Fenice, S. Marco 1936 (☎041.523.2333, fax 041.520.3721, *fenice@fenicehotels.it*). This large three-star was a favoured hangout of the opera crowd, performers and audience alike. With La Fenice turned into a building site for the next few years, it might have more vacancies than it used to. ⑦.

Fiorita, Campiello Nuovo, S. Marco 3457 (☎041.523.4754, fax 041.522.8043, *www.locandafiorita.com*). Just nine rooms, but they have recently been refurbished in a beguiling Venetian style. Welcoming management, and there's a nearby traghetto across the Canal Grande. ⑤.

Flora, Calle Larga XXII Marzo, S. Marco 2283a (☎041.520.5844, fax 041.522.8217). Some of the rooms are too cramped, but this large three-star is very close to the Piazza and has a peaceful little garden, too. ⑦.

Al Gambero, Calle dei Fabbri, S. Marco 4687 (☎041.522.4384, fax 041.520.0431, *hotelgamb@tin.it*). Large and recently refurbished hotel in an excellent position a short distance off the north side of the Piazza; the rooms are well maintained, and many of them overlook a canal that's on the standard gondola route from the Bacino Orseolo. Has more single rooms than many Venice hotels. There's a boisterous Franco-Italian bistro on the ground floor. ③.

Kette, Piscina S. Moisè, S. Marco 2053 (☎041.520.7766, fax 041.522.8964). A favourite with the upper-bracket tour companies, mainly on account of its quiet location in an alleyway parallel to Calle Larga XXII Marzo. In season there's nothing under L450,000/€232.40, but out of season prices halve. ⑧.

Noemi, Calle dei Fabbri, San Marco 909 (☎041.523.8144). The rooms are basic (only two of the fifteen have bathrooms) and the decor is dowdy, but the one-star Noemi is right in the thick of the action, just a minute's walk north of the Piazza, and its prices are lower than rival one-stars (though they don't include breakfast). ③.

San Samuele, Salizzada S. Samuele, S. Marco 3358 (☎ & fax 041.522.8045). A friendly one-star place close to the Palazzo Grassi, with rooms distinctly less shabby than some at this end of the market, if not exactly plush. ④.

Dorsoduro

Accademia Villa Maravege, Fondamenta Bollani, Dorsoduro 1058 (☎041.521.0188, fax 041.523.9152, *pension.accademia@flashnet.it*). Once the Russian embassy, this seventeenth-century villa has a devoted following, not least on account of its courtyard, which occupies a promontory at the convergence of two canals, with a view of a small section of the Canal Grande, and its small garden. To be sure of a room, get your booking in at least three months ahead. ⑥.

Agli Alboretti, Rio Terrà Foscarini, Dorsoduro 884 (☎041.523.0058, fax 041.521.0158, *www.cash.it/ alboretti*). Good two-star very close to the Accademia. Avoid murky room 19 and you can't go wrong. ⑥.

Antico Capon, Campo S. Margherita, Dorsoduro 3004b (☎ & fax 041.528.5292). Antique rooms above a pizzeria-restaurant on an atmospheric square in the heart of the student district. An annexe is due to open on the other side of the square in late 2001. ⑤.

La Calcina, Záttere ai Gesuati, Dorsoduro 780 (☎041.520.6466, fax 041.522.7045, *lacalcina@iol,it*). Unpretentious and charismatic three-star hotel in the house where Ruskin wrote much of *The Stones of Venice*. From some of the rooms you can gaze across to the Redentore, a church that gave the old man apoplexy. ⑦.

Domus Cavanis, Rio Terrà Foscarini, Dorsoduro 898 (☎041.520.7374). Technically a Catholic-run hostel, a complete refit has made it more like a hotel. If it wasn't for the rules (11.30pm curfew; separate male and female rooms unless married), this would be the best bargain in the city, given the location on the street going down the left of the Accademia. ④.

Messner, Rio Terrà dei Catacumeni, Dorsoduro 216/237 (☎041.522.7443, fax 041.522.7266, *a.nardi@flashnet.it*). Excellent location on one of Dorsoduro's quiet, yet central, canals, just behind the Accademia. Modern, smart rooms throughout – those in the annexe are less expensive. ⑤.

Montin, Fondamenta di Borgo, Dorsoduro 1147 (☎041.522.7151, fax 041.520.0255). The *Montin* is known principally for its upmarket and once-fashionable restaurant; few people realise that it offers some of Venice's most charismatic accommodation, though there are only five rooms. Excellent location too. ⑤.

Pausania, Fondamenta Gherardini, Dorsoduro 3942 (☎041.522.2083, fax 041.522.2989). A fourteenth-century Gothic palazzo, with many original features, houses this quiet, comfortable and rather romantic three-star. Expensive, but good value for money in the off-season, when you can pick up a double for under L120,000/€61.97. Very close to San Barnaba church, just five minutes from the Accademia. ⑦.

Seguso, Záttere ai Gesuati, Dorsoduro 779 (☎041.528.6858, fax 041.522.2340). There are no bad rooms in this two-star – those that don't face Giudecca overlook an attractive side-canal. Essential to book months ahead, as it's another one with a great word-of-mouth reputation. ⑥.

San Polo

Alex, Rio Terrà Frari, S. Polo 2606 (☎ & fax 041.523.1341). A longstanding budget-travellers' favourite, this one-star hotel is decorated in 1960s style, but bearably so. The supermarket in front is useful for picnics and breakfast. ③.

Ca' Fóscari, Calle della Frescada, Dorsoduro 3887b (☎041.710.401, fax 041.710.817, *valtersc@tin.it*). Quiet, well decorated and relaxed one-star, tucked away in a micro-alley near S. Tomà. Just eleven rooms, so it's quickly booked out. ③.

San Cassiano-Ca' Favretto, Calle della Rosa, S. Croce 2232 (☎041.524.1768, fax 041.721.033). Beautiful three-star, with some rooms looking across the Canal Grande towards the Ca' d'Oro. ⑧.

Sturion, Calle del Sturion, S. Polo 679 (☎041.523.6243, fax 041.522.8378). Immaculate three-star on a wonderful site a few yards from the Canal Grande, close to the Rialto. Run by an exceptionally welcoming management that offers free trips to Murano, concert tickets and other goodies. ⑧.

Al Sole, Fondamenta Minotto, S. Croce 136 (☎041.710.844, fax 041.714.398, *www.corihotels.it*). Huge three-star hotel in gorgeous Gothic palazzo on a tiny canal. A wonderful place to stay. ⑧.

Tivoli, Crosera S. Pantalon, Dorsoduro 3638 (☎041.524.2460, fax 041.522.2656). This two-star is the biggest moderately priced hotel in the immediate vicinity of the Frari and S. Rocco, so often has space when the rest are full. ⑤.

Cannaregio

Adua, Lista di Spagna, Cannaregio 233a (☎041.716.184). Clean one-star on the third floor. The refit has left the décor rather spartan, but the management and prices are benign. The rooms in their annexe round the corner are around L20,000/€10.32 less expensive. ③.

Bernardi Semenzato, Calle dell'Oca, Cannaregio 4363/6 (☎041.522.7257, fax 041.522.2424, *mtfepoli@tin.it*). The big advantages of this two-star are its location (in a tiny alleyway close to Campo S. Apostoli) and its owners, who speak good English and are immensely helpful. ⑤.

Al Gobbo, Campo S. Geremia, Cannaregio 312 (☎041.715.001). Rather more genteel than most of its fellow one-stars on the adjacent Lista di Spagna; the better – and more expensive – rooms overlook an attractive small garden and include a bathroom. ④.

Hesperia, Calle Riello, Cannaregio 459 (☎041.715.251, fax 041.715.112, *hesperia@shineline.it*). Sixteen-room two-star in a secluded alleyway just beyond the Palazzo Savorgnan, close to the Cannaregio canal. Rooms are small but very homely, and come complete with Murano glass fittings (not the garish variety). ⑤.

Rossi, Lista di Spagna, Cannaregio 262 (☎041.715.164, fax 041.717.784). Modern and characterless rooms, but among the best value in the ugly cluster near the station. It helps if you book early and speak French, as years of inclusion in the *Guide Routard* have drawn a loyal and almost exclusively young, French clientele. ④.

Villa Rosa, Calle della Misericordia, Cannaregio 389 (☎041.718.976, fax 041.716.569, *villarosa@ve.nettuno.it*). Clean, fairly large one-star secreted in a narrow alley off the Lista di Spagna, well away from the hubbub but still near the station. The best rooms have a small terrace. ⑤.

Castello

Bucintoro, Riva S. Biagio, Castello 2135 (☎041.522.3240, fax 041.523.5224). Almost completely characterless, despite its great age, the two-star *Bucintoro* nonetheless has one trump card – virtually all 28 of its rooms look out over the water towards San Giorgio Maggiore and the Lido. ⑦.

Casa Linger, Salizzada Sant'Antonin, Castello 3541 (☎041.528.5920, fax 041.528.4851). Set back in a quiet part of Castello near Vivaldi's church of La Pieta, this is just far enough from the piazza to escape the crowds. The simple rooms are just a step above mildly shabby, but the more expensive en suite rooms have great views. ④.

Casa Verardo, Calle della Chiesa, Castello 4765 (☎041.528.6127, fax 041.523.2765, *casaverardo@tin.it*). Just off Campo Santi Filippo e Giacomo, a couple of minutes from San Marco and similarly close to Campo Santa Maria Formosa. Friendly new management, though it's the same wonderful hotel, with its sumptuous grand salon and fine terrace. Most of the nine rooms have a bath or shower. ⑥.

Corona, Calle Corona, Castello 4464 (☎041.522.9174). Friendly budget place not far from the *Casa Verardo*, next door to a glassmaker's. The cheapest you'll find anywhere, but with just six rooms, all without bathrooms. ③.

Danieli, Riva degli Schiavoni, Castello 4196 (☎041.522.6480, fax 041.520.0208, *www.sheraton.com*). No longer the most expensive hotel in Venice (the *Bauer* and *Cipriani* share the title), but no other place can compete with the glamour of the *Danieli*. Balzac stayed here, as did Wagner and Dickens. This magnificent Gothic palazzo affords just about the most sybaritic hotel experience on the Continent – provided you book a room in the old part of the building, not the modern extension. Most double rooms cost around L800,000/€413.20, though some come in at a couple of hundred thousand more. ⑨.

Gabrielli Sandwirth, Riva degli Schiavoni, Castello 4110 (☎041.523.1580, fax 041.520.9455). Another converted Gothic palace, with a lovely courtyard. *Danieli*-style views across the Bacino di San Marco, for a fraction of the price. Four-star doubles start at L270,000/€13.94. ⑦.

Paganelli, Riva degli Schiavoni, Castello 4182 (☎041.522.4324, fax 041.523.9267, *hotelpag@tin.it*). This two-star is a great place to stay, as long as you get one of the rooms on the lagoon side – the ones in the annexe look onto San Zaccaria, which is a nice enough view, but not really in the same league. ⑤.

La Residenza, Campo Bandiera e Moro, Castello 3608 (☎041.528.5315, fax 041.523.8859). Even though the rooms are a touch bare, this fourteenth-century palazzo is a mid-budget gem (in Venetian terms), occupying much of one side of a tranquil square just off the main waterfront. A tad pricier than the average two-star, but worth the money. ⑥.

Sant'Anna, Corte del Bianco, Castello 269 (☎ & fax 041.528.6466, *santanna@libero.it*). Although it's in one of the remotest parts of the city, beyond the far end of Via Garibaldi, this one-star has been discovered in recent years – so book well in advance. ③.

Silva, Fondamenta del Rimedio, Castello 4423 (☎041.523.7892, fax 041.528.6817). One-star overlooking a quiet canal to the north of San Marco. ④.

Hostels and institutions

Venice's hostels, most of which are run by religious foundations, are generally comfortable, well run and inexpensive by Venetian standards – moreover, even in the high season they might well have a place or two to spare. The tourist office regularly produces a simple typed list of all hostel accommodation in the city; if the places listed below are full up, ask for a copy of it at the San Marco branch.

Domus Civica, Calle Campazzo, S. Polo 3082 (☎041.721.103). A student house in winter, but open to travellers July to October. A little awkward to find: it's off Calle della Lacca, to the west of San Giovanni Evangelista. Most rooms are double; showers free; no breakfast; 11.30pm curfew; single L42,000/€21.67, double L70,000/€36.15 with 20 percent discount for ISIC card holders.

Foresteria Santa Fosca, S. Maria dei Servi, Cannaregio 2372 (☎041.715.775). Student-run hostel in an atmospheric former Servite convent in a quiet part of Cannaregio, with dorm beds and double rooms. Check-in 4–7pm; 11.30pm curfew. L30,000/€15.49 dorm bed, with some double rooms available.

Foresteria Valdese, S. Maria Formosa, Castello 5170 (☎041.528.6797). Installed in a palazzo at the end of Calle Lunga S. Maria Formosa, with flaking frescoes and a large salon. Run by Waldensians, it's principally a hostel for grown-ups, with occasional school groups. Two large dorms, and a couple of rooms for two to four people. It also has a couple of self-catering flats for three to six people. Registration 9am–1pm & 6–8pm. Prices range from L28,000/€14.46 for a dorm bed to L40,000/€20.66 for a room.

Ostello Venezia, Fondamenta delle Zitelle, Giudecca 86 (☎041.523.8211, fax 041.523.5689). The city's HI hostel occupies a superb location looking over to San Marco, but it's run with a certain briskness – notices demand "perfect sobriety and cleanliness". The waiting room opens at 1.30pm in summer and 4pm in winter for the 6pm registration. Curfew at 11pm, chucking-out time 9.30am. Gets so busy in July and August that written reservations must be made by April. If it's full, they use a local school with camp-beds as an annexe. Breakfast and sheets included in price, but bear in mind that you'll have to pay for a boat over to the main island. No kitchen, but full (and excellent) meals at L14,000/€7.23. Luggage can't be left here after you've checked out. L27,000/€13.94 per bed, HI card necessary, but you can join on the spot for L30,000/€15.49.

Suore Canossiane, Fondamenta del Ponte Piccolo, Giudecca 428 (☎041.522.2157). Women-only hostel near the Palanca vaporetto stop. Open 8am–noon & 2–10pm – you must arrive in person, as there's no booking. L20,000/€10.32 per bed.

Suore Mantellate, Calle Buccari, Castello 10 (☎041.522.0829). Another convent-run hostel in a quiet part of the lagoon, near Sant'Elena vaporetto stop. Rooms of two to six beds available; essential to book ahead as gets booked up by groups. Closed Aug. L55,000/€28.41 per bed including breakfast.

Camping

If you're coming from the airport and want to pitch your tent promptly, you could settle for one of the two large sites nearby, which at least have the benefit of frequent bus connections to Piazzale Roma: the *Marco Polo*, Via Triestina 167 (☎041.541.6033; Feb 15–Nov 15), which is within walking distance of the airport; and the friendlier *Alba d'Oro*, Via Triestina 214b (☎041.541.5102; April–Sept), which also has bungalows, just beyond the airport – take bus #5 from Piazzale Roma to the airport, then walk or take bus #15 (every 20min) to Cánoghera, the fourth stop.

More attractive sites are to be found on the outer edge of the lagoon on the **Litorale del Cavallino**, which stretches from the Punta Sabbioni to Jésolo and has a total of around 60,000 pitches, many of them quite luxuriously appointed. The #14 vaporetto stops close to the relatively cheap *Miramare*, Lungomare Dante Alighieri 29 (☎041.966.150; April–Sept) and a bit further away the more luxurious and expensive *Marina di Venezia*, Via Montello 6 (☎041.966.146; April–Sept). However, there's a minimum stay of three days here, and the price can be a problem; when you've added on the fare for the forty-minute boat trip into the city you're not left with a particularly economical proposition.

Alternatively, back on the mainland, the municipal site at **Fusina**, Via Moranzani 79 (☎041.547.0064; Jan–Sept), has 650 places. *Vaporetti* now connect Fusina to central Venice all year, or you can take the bus to Mestre and change there for bus #1.

There are also several sites at **Sottomarina**, the resort attached to Chioggia, at the southern end of the lagoon (see p.321), but getting between there and the centre of Venice involves, at best, a fifty-minute bus journey each way.

The City

The 118 islands of central Venice are divided into six districts known as *sestieri*, and the houses within each *sestiere* are numbered in a sequence that makes sense solely to the functionaries of the post office – this explains how buildings facing each other across an alleyway can have numbers that are separated by hundreds.

The sestiere of **San Marco** is the zone where the majority of the essential sights are clustered, and is accordingly the most expensive and most crowded district of the city. On the east it's bordered by **Castello**, and on the north by **Cannaregio** – both of which become more residential, and poorer and quieter, the further you go from the centre. On the other side of the Canal Grande, the largest of the *sestieri* is **Dorsoduro**, stretching from the fashionable quarter at the southern tip of the canal to the docks in the west. **Santa Croce**, named after a now demolished church, roughly follows the curve of the Canal Grande from Piazzale Roma to a point just short of the Rialto, where it joins the smartest and commercially most active of the districts on this bank – **San Polo**.

To the uninitiated, the boundaries of the *sestieri* seem arbitrary. So, although in some instances we've used *sestieri* as broad indicators of location, the boundaries of our sections have been chosen for their practicality and do not, except in the case of San Marco, exactly follow the city's official divisions.

THE BIGLIETTO CUMULATIVO AND CHORUS PASS

In an attempt to make sure that tourists go to see more than just the big central sights, the entry charges for several museums have been combined in one **Biglietto Cumulativo**. Costing L18,000/€9.30, the ticket allows one visit to each of the following attractions before the end of the year in which you buy the ticket: Palazzo Ducale, Museo Correr (along with the Museo Archeologico and Biblioteca Nazionale Marciana), Palazzo Mocenigo, Museo del Merletto (Burano) and Museo Vetrario (Murano). It's available at the Correr and Palazzo Ducale, each of which can be visited only with the Biglietto Cumulativo – at the other places you have the option of paying an entry charge just for that attraction.

In addition, thirteen churches that charge for entry (either to the whole structure or just part) are now part of the **Chorus Pass** scheme (*www.chorus-ve.org*). For L15,000/€7.75 you can buy a pass that allows one visit to each of the churches over a one-year period, or for L10,000/€5.16 you can buy one that allows entry to any six on the same day. Individual entrance fees at each of the participating churches are L3000/€1.55, and nearly all the churches observe the same opening hours: Monday to Saturday 10am to 5pm, and Sunday 3pm to 5pm. The churches involved are: Santa Maria del Giglio, Santo Stefano, Santa Maria Formosa, Santa Maria dei Miracoli, the Frari, San Polo, San Giacomo dell'Orio, San Stae, Sant'Alvise, Madonna dell'Orto, San Pietro di Castello, Redentore and San Sebastiano.

San Marco

The section of Venice enclosed by the lower loop of the Canal Grande – a rectangle smaller than 1000 metres by 500 – is, in essence, the Venice of the travel brochures. The plush hotels are concentrated here, in the sestiere of **SAN MARCO**, as are the swankier shops and the best-known cultural attractions of the city. But small though this area is, you can still lose the hordes within it.

"The finest drawing-room in Europe" was how Napoleon described its focal point, the **Piazza San Marco** – the only *piazza* in Venice, all other squares being *campi* or *campielli*. Less genteel phrases might seem appropriate on a suffocating summer afternoon, but you can take some slight consolation from the knowledge that the Piazza has always been congested. Neither is the influx of foreigners a modern phenomenon – its parades, festivities and markets have always drawn visitors from all over the Continent and beyond, the biggest attraction being a huge international trade fair known as the **Fiera della Sensa**, which kept the Piazza buzzing for the fortnight following the Ascension Day ceremony of the marriage of Venice to the sea. The coffee shops of the Piazza were a vital component of eighteenth-century high society, and the two survivors from that period – *Florian* and *Quadri* – are still the smartest and most expensive in town: an espresso in *Florian* will set you back at least L10,000/€5.16, plus a supplement for the thrill of hearing the band's rendition of *My Way* or the best of Lloyd-Webber.

The Basilica di San Marco

The **Basilica di San Marco** is the most exotic of Europe's cathedrals, and no visitor can remain dispassionate when confronted by it. Herbert Spencer found it loathsome – "a fine sample of barbaric architecture", but to John Ruskin it was a "treasure-heap . . . a confusion of delight". Delightful or not, it's certainly confusing, increasingly so as you come nearer and the details emerge; some knowledge of the history of the building helps bring a little order out of chaos.

Although San Marco is open from 6.30am on most days for prayer, tourists are asked not to enter before 9am and the main body of the church is often roped off before this time; the basilica usually closes at 5.30pm. Admission fees totalling L8000/€4.13 are charged for certain parts of the church. Sections of the basilica will almost certainly be under restoration or closed off for some other reason; though restoration of the Cappella Zen and Baptistry has at last been completed, there's no sign of either being reopened in the near future.

THE STORY OF THE BASILICA

According to the **legend of St Mark's annunciation**, the Evangelist was moored in the lagoon, on his way to Rome, when an angel appeared and told him that his body would rest there. (The angel's salute – *Pax tibi, Marce evangelista meus* – is the text cut into the book that the Lion of St Mark is always shown holding.) The founders of Venice, having persuaded themselves of the sacred ordination of their city, duly went about fulfilling the angelic prophecy, and in 828 the body of St Mark was stolen from Alexandria and brought here.

Modelled on Constantinople's Church of the Twelve Apostles, the shrine of St Mark was consecrated in 832, but in 976 both the church and the Palazzo Ducale were ruined by fire during an uprising against the doge. The present basilica was originally finished in 1094 and embellished over the succeeding centuries. The combination of ancient structure and later decorations is, to a great extent, what makes San Marco so bewildering, but the picture is made yet more complicated by the addition of ornaments looted from abroad that are sometimes older than the building itself and in some cases

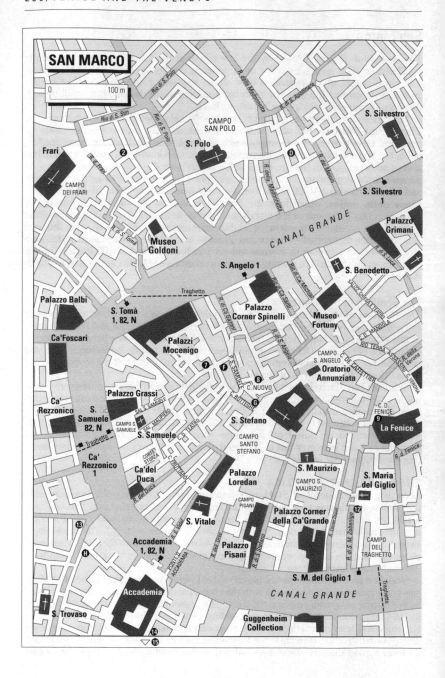

SAN MARCO

0   100 m

S. Silvestro

CAMPO SAN POLO

Rio di S. Polo

R. della Madonnetta

R. di S. Agostin

Rio di S. Stin

Frari

S. Polo

CAMPO DEI FRARI

R. dei Frari

S. Silvestro 1

Rio di S. Tomà

Museo Goldoni

R. della Madonnetta

R. dei Maroni

CANAL GRANDE

Palazzo Grimani

R. di S. Luca

S. Angelo 1

Traghetto

Ponte Ca' Michiel

Rio di Ca' Michiel

S. Benedetto

SAL. Chiesa O Teatro

Palazzo Balbi

Palazzo Corner Spinelli

Museo Fortuny

C. D. MANDOLA

RIO TERRA ASSASSINI

R. della Verona

C. VERONA

S. Tomà 1, 82, N

R. di Ca' Garzoni

R. di S. Angelo

Ca'Foscari

Palazzi Mocenigo

7

CAMPO S. ANGELO

C. DE FABBRI

Oratorio Annunziata

F

P. S. SAMUELE

8

C. NUOVO

C. D. FENICE

Palazzo Grassi

G

BOTTEGHE

9

La Fenice

Ca' Rezzonico

S. Samuele 82, N

SAL. S. SAMUELE

SAL. MALIPIERO

S. Stefano

R. d. Fenice

CAMPO S. SAMUELE

S. Samuele

R. DEL TEATRO

CAMPO SANTO STEFANO

Tragetto

CORTE' STORZA

Ca' Rezzonico 1

Ca' del Duca

CRUTOTON

S. Maurizio

S. Maria del Giglio

R. del Duca

Palazzo Loredan

CAMPO S. MAURIZIO

12

13

CAMPO PISANI

Palazzo Corner della Ca'Grande

R. di S. M. Zobenigo

CAMPO DEL TRAGHETTO

H

S. Vitale

R. di S. Vidal

Accademia 1, 82, N

R. dei Folco

Palazzo Pisani

PONTE D' ACCADEMIA

R. di S. Stefano

R. Corner Zaguri

Traghetto

S. M. del Giglio 1

Accademia

CANAL GRANDE

S. Trovaso

14

15

Guggenheim Collection

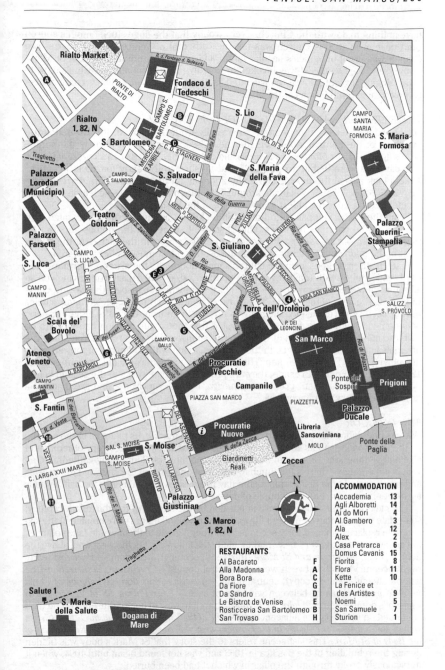

Rialto Market

Fondaco d. Tedeschi

S. Lio

CAMPO SANTA MARIA FORMOSA

S. Maria Formosa

Rialto 1, 82, N

PONTE DI RIALTO

S. Bartolomeo

Palazzo Loredan (Municipio)

Traghetto

S. Salvador

S. Maria della Fava

Teatro Goldoni

Palazzo Querini-Stampalia

Palazzo Farsetti

S. Luca

CAMPO S. LUCA

S. Giuliano

CAMPO MANIN

Scala del Bovolo

Torre dell'Orologio

P. DEI LEONCINI

San Marco

Ateneo Veneto

CAMPO S. FANTIN

Procuratie Vecchie

Campanile

PIAZZA SAN MARCO

PIAZZETTA

Ponte dei Sospiri

Prigioni

S. Fantin

Procuratie Nuove

Libreria Sansoviniana

Palazzo Ducale

S. Moise

CAMPO S. MOISE

MOLO

Ponte della Paglia

Giardinetti Reali

Zecca

C. LARGA XXII MARZO

Palazzo Giustinian

S. Marco 1, 82, N

N

Salute 1

S. Maria della Salute

Dogana di Mare

Traghetto

RESTAURANTS

Al Bacareto	F
Alla Madonna	A
Bora Bora	C
Da Fiore	G
Da Sandro	D
Le Bistrot de Venise	E
Rosticceria San Bartolomeo	B
San Trovaso	H

ACCOMMODATION

Accademia	13
Agli Alboretti	14
Ai do Mori	4
Al Gambero	3
Ala	12
Alex	2
Casa Petrarca	6
Domus Cavanis	15
Fiorita	8
Flora	11
Kette	10
La Fenice et des Artistes	9
Noemi	5
San Samuele	7
Sturion	1

have nothing to do with the Church. Every trophy that the doge stuck onto his church (and bear in mind this church was not the cathedral of Venice but the doge's own chapel) was proof of Venice's secular might and so of the spiritual power of St Mark. Conversely, the Evangelist was invoked to sanctify political actions and rituals of state – the doge's investiture was consecrated in the church, and military commanders received their commissions at the altar.

THE EXTERIOR, NARTHEX AND LOGGIA DEI CAVALLI

Of the exterior features that can be seen easily from the ground, the **Romanesque carvings** of the **central door** demand the closest attention – especially the middle arch's figures of *The Months and Seasons* and outer arch's series of *The Trades of Venice*. The carvings were begun around 1225 and finished in the early fourteenth century. Take a look also at the mosaic above the doorway on the far left – *The Arrival of the Body of St Mark* – which was made around 1260 (the only early mosaic left on the main facade) and includes the oldest known image of the basilica.

From the Piazza you pass into the vestibule known as the **narthex**, decorated with the first of the church's **mosaics**: Old Testament scenes on the domes and arches, together with *The Madonna with Apostles and Evangelists* in the niches of the bay in front of the main door – dating from the 1060s, the oldest mosaics in San Marco.

A steep staircase goes from the church's main door up to the **Museo Marciano** and the **Loggia dei Cavalli** (daily 9.45am–4.30pm; L3000/€1.55). Apart from giving you an all-round view, the loggia is also the best place from which to inspect the **Gothic carvings** along the apex of the facade. The **horses** outside are replicas, the genuine articles having been removed inside, allegedly to protect them from the risks of atmospheric pollution, although some cynics have insisted that the rescue mission had more to do with the marketing strategies of Olivetti, who sponsored the operation. You'll find the originals just behind the loggia, in the **Galleria**, along with oddments of mosaic and a fine polyptych by Paolo Veneziano. Thieved from the Hippodrome of Constantinople in 1204 during the Fourth Crusade, they are probably Roman works of the second century – the only such ancient group, or *quadriga*, to have survived – and are made of a bronze that is very rich in copper.

THE INTERIOR

With its undulating floor of twelfth-century patterned marble, its plates of eastern stone on the lower walls, and its 4000 square metres of **mosaics** covering every other inch of wall and vaulting, the interior of San Marco is the most opulent of any cathedral. One visit is not enough – there's too much to take in at one go, and the shifting light reveals and hides parts of the decoration as the day progresses; try calling in for half an hour at the beginning and end of a couple of days.

The majority of the mosaics were in position by the middle of the thirteenth century; some date from the fourteenth and fifteenth centuries, and others were created in the sixteenth to replace damaged early sections. A thorough guide to them would take volumes, but an inventory of the very best might include the following. On the west wall, above the door – *Christ, the Virgin and St Mark* (thirteenth century); west dome – *Pentecost* (early twelfth century); arch between west and central domes – *Crucifixion, Resurrection* (the latter a fifteenth-century copy); central dome – *Ascension*; east dome – *Religion of Christ Foretold by the Prophets*; between windows of apse – *Four Patron SS of Venice*; north transept's dome – *Acts of St John the Evangelist*; arch to west of north transept's dome (and continued on upper part of adjacent wall) – *Life of the Virgin and Life of the Infant Christ*; wall of south aisle – *The Agony in the Garden*; west wall of south transept – *Rediscovery of the Body of St Mark*. This last scene refers to the story that St Mark's body was hidden during the rebuilding of the basilica in 1063 and was not found again until 1094, when it miraculously broke through the pillar in which it had been buried.

From the south transept you can enter the **Sanctuary** (Mon–Sat 9.45am–4.30pm, Sun 1.30–4.30pm; L3000/€1.55), where, behind the altar, you'll find the most precious of San Marco's treasures – the **Pala d'Oro** (Golden Altar Panel). Commissioned in 976 in Constantinople, the Pala was enlarged, enriched and rearranged by Byzantine gold-smiths in 1105, then by Venetians in 1209 (to incorporate some less cumbersome loot from the Fourth Crusade) and again (finally) in 1345. The completed screen holds 83 enamel plaques, 74 enamelled roundels, 38 chiselled figures, 300 sapphires, 300 emer-alds, 400 garnets, 15 rubies, 1300 pearls and a couple of hundred other stones.

In a corner of the south transept is the door of the **Treasury** (Mon–Sat 9.45am–4.30pm, Sun 1.30–4.30pm; L2000/€1.03), a small but dazzling line-up of chal-ices, reliquaries, candelabra and so on – a fair proportion of which owes its presence here to the great Constantinople robbery of 1204.

The **Baptistry** – off the south aisle – was altered to its present form by the four-teenth-century Doge Andrea Dandolo, whose tomb (facing the door) was thought by Ruskin to have the best monumental sculpture in the city. Dandolo also ordered the cre-ation of the **mosaics** depicting *Scenes from the Lives of Christ and John the Baptist*, works in which the hieratic formality of Byzantine art is blended with the rich detail of the Gothic.

The adjoining **Cappella Zen** was created between 1504 and 1521 by enclosing the piazzetta entrance to the narthex, in order to house the tomb of Cardinal Giambattista Zen, whose estate was left to the city on condition that he was buried within San Marco. The late thirteenth-century **mosaics** on the vault show *Scenes from the Life of St Mark*. The chapel is sometimes known as the Chapel of the Madonna of the Shoe, taking its name from the *Virgin and Child* by Antonio Lombardo (1506) on the high altar.

Back in the main body of the church, there's still more to see on the lower levels of the building. Don't overlook the **rood screen**'s marble figures of *The Virgin, St Mark and the Apostles*, carved in 1394 by the dominant sculptors in Venice at that time, Jacobello and Pietro Paolo Dalle Masegne. The **pulpits** on each side of the screen were assembled in the early fourteenth century from miscellaneous panels (some from Constantinople); the new doge was presented to the people from the right-hand one. The tenth-century **Icon of the Madonna of Nicopeia** (in the chapel on east side of north transept) is the most revered religious image in Venice; it used to be one of the most revered in Constantinople. A beautiful mid-fifteenth-century mosaic cycle of *Scenes from the Life of the Virgin*, one of the earliest Renaissance works in Venice, is to be seen in the adjacent **Cappella della Madonna dei Mascoli**. And on the north side of the nave stands a marble kiosk fabricated to house a painting of the *Crucifix* on the altar; this arrived in Venice in 1205, and in 1290 achieved its current exalted status by spouting blood after an assault on it.

The Palazzo Ducale

The Palazzo Ducale (daily: April–Oct 9am–7pm; Nov–March 9am–4pm; entrance with Biglietto Cumulativo, see box on p.286) was far more than the residence of the doge – it was the home of all of Venice's governing councils, many of its courts, a sizeable number of its civil servants and even its prisons. The government of Venice was admin-istered through an intricate system of elected committees and councils – a system designed to limit the power of any individual – but for the last 500 years of the repub-lic's existence only those families listed in the register of noble births and marriages known as the *Libro d'Oro* (Golden Book) were entitled to play a part in the system.

At the head of the network sat the **doge**, the one politician to sit on all the major coun-cils of state and the only one elected for life; he could be immensely influential in steer-ing policy and in making appointments, and restrictions were accordingly imposed on his actions to reduce the possibility of his abusing that power – his letters were read by censors, for example, and he wasn't permitted to receive foreign delegations alone. The privileges of the job far outweighed the inconveniences, though, and men campaigned for years to increase their chances of election.

Like San Marco, the Palazzo Ducale has been rebuilt many times since its foundation in the first years of the ninth century. It was with the construction of a new hall for the Maggior Consiglio (Great Council) in 1340 that the palazzo began to take on its present shape. The hall was constructed parallel to the waterfront and was inaugurated in 1419; three years later, it was decided to extend the building along the piazzetta, copying the style of the fourteenth-century work – the slightly fatter column on the piazzetta side, under a tondo of *Justice*, is where the two wings meet.

The principal entrance to the palazzo – the **Porta della Carta** – is one of the most ornate Gothic works in the city. It was commissioned in 1438 by Doge Francesco Fóscari from Bartolomeo and Giovanni Bon, but the figures of Fóscari and his lion are replicas – the originals were pulverized in 1797 by the head of the stonemason's guild, as a favour to Napoleon. Fóscari's head survived the hammering, however, and is on display inside.

Tourists no longer enter the building by the Porta della Carta, but instead are herded through a doorway on the lagoon side. Once through the ticket hall you emerge in the courtyard, opposite the other end of the passageway into the palazzo – the **Arco Fóscari**. This also was commissioned from the Bons by Doge Fóscari but finished a few years after his death by Antonio Rizzo and Antonio Bregno. In 1483 a fire demolished most of the wing to your right, and led to more work for Rizzo – he designed the enormous staircase (Scala dei Giganti) and much of the new wing. Reconstruction continued under Pietro Lombardo, Spavento and Scarpagnino, and finally Bartolomeo Monopola, who completed the courtyard in about 1600 by extending the arcades along the other two sides.

Parts of the Palazzo Ducale can be marched through fairly briskly. Acres of canvas cover the walls, but many of the paintings are just wearisome exercises in self-aggrandizement. But other sections you will not want to rush, and, if you're there in the high season, it's a good idea to buy your ticket within half an hour of the opening time. A word of warning – restoration work is continually in progress in the Palazzo Ducale, and there's never any indication before you go in as to which bits are under wraps; it's a distinct possibility that some of the highlights will be hidden from view.

The itinerary begins on the left side of the courtyard, where the finest of the capitals from the palazzo's exterior arcade are displayed in the **Museo dell'Opera**. Upstairs, the route takes you through the doge's private apartments then on to the **Anticollegio**, the room in which embassies had to wait before being admitted to the presence of the doge and his cabinet. As regards the quality of its paintings, this is one of the richest rooms in the Palazzo Ducale: four pictures by **Tintoretto** hang on the door walls, and facing the windows is **Veronese's** *Rape of Europa*.

The cycle of paintings on the ceiling of the adjoining **Sala del Collegio** is also by Veronese, and he features strongly again in the most stupendous room in the building – the **Sala del Maggior Consiglio**. Veronese's ceiling panel of *The Apotheosis of Venice* is suspended over the dais from which the doge oversaw the sessions of the city's general assembly; the backdrop is **Tintoretto's** immense *Paradiso*, painted towards the end of his life, with the aid of his son, Domenico. At the opposite end there's a curiosity: the frieze of portraits of the first 76 doges (the series continues in the Sala dello Scrutinio – through the door at the far end) is interrupted by a painted black veil, marking the place where **Doge Marin Falier** would have been honoured had he not conspired against the state in 1355 and been beheaded for his crime.

From here you descend quickly to the underbelly of the Venetian state, crossing the **Ponte dei Sospiri** (Bridge of Sighs) to the **prisons**. Before the construction of these cells in the early seventeenth century all prisoners were kept in the Piombi (the Leads), under the roof of the Palazzo Ducale, or in the Pozzi (the Wells) in the bottom two storeys; the new block was occupied mainly by petty criminals. The route finishes with a detour through the Pozzi, but if you want to see the Piombi, and the rooms in which the day-to-day administration of Venice took place, you have to go on the **Itinerari Segreti del Palazzo Ducale**, a guided tour through the warren of offices and passageways that interlocks with the public rooms of the building. It's not cheap (L24,000/€12.39), but well worth the price. Tickets must be booked in advance by asking at the Palazzo or phoning ☎041.522.4951; the tour is held every day except Wednesday at 10am and noon in Italian and at 10.30am in English.

The Campanile and Torre dell'Orologio

Most of the landscape of the Piazza dates from the great period of urban renewal that began at the end of the fifteenth century and went on for much of the following century. The one exception – excluding San Marco itself – is the **Campanile** (daily 9.45am–4pm; L8000/€4.13), which began life as a lighthouse in the ninth century and was modified frequently up to the early sixteenth. The present structure is in fact a reconstruction: the original tower collapsed on July 14, 1902 – a catastrophe that injured nobody and is commemorated by faked postcard photos ostensibly taken at the very instant of the disaster. The collapse reduced to rubble the **Loggetta** at the base of the campanile, but somehow it was pieced together again; built between 1537 and 1549 by Sansovino, it has served as a meeting-room for the nobility, a guardhouse and the place at which the state lottery was drawn. At 99 metres, the campanile is the tallest structure in the city, and from the top you can make out virtually every building, but not a single canal.

The other tower in the Piazza, the **Torre dell'Orologio**, was built between 1496 and 1506. A restoration lasting several years has prevented people from taking the staircase up past the innards of the clock and onto the terrace on which the so-called Moors stand.

The Procuratie and Museo Correr

Away to the left of the Torre dell'Orologio stretches the **Procuratie Vecchie**; begun around 1500 by Codussi, this block housed the offices of the **Procurators of St Mark**, a committee of nine men whose responsibilities included the upkeep of the basilica and other public buildings. A century or so after taking possession, the procurators were moved to the opposite side of the Piazza, into the **Procuratie Nuove**. Napoleon converted these apartments and offices into a royal palace and then, having realized that the building lacked a ballroom, remedied the deficiency by smashing down the church of San Geminiano in order to connect the two Procuratie with a new wing for dancing.

Generally known as the **Ala Napoleonica**, this short side of the Piazza is partly occupied by the **Museo Correr** (daily: April–Oct 9am–7pm; Nov–March 9am–5pm; entrance with Biglietto Cumulativo, see box on p.286), an immense triple-decker museum with a vast **historical collection** of coins, weapons, regalia, prints, paintings and miscellanea. Much of this is heavy going unless you have an intense interest in Venetian history, though there's an appealing exhibition of Venetian applied arts, and one show-stopping item in the form of the original blocks and a print of Jacopo de'Barbari's astonishing aerial view of Venice, engraved in 1500. The **Quadreria** on the second floor is no rival for the Accademia's collection (see p.296), but it does set out clearly the evolution of painting in Venice from the thirteenth century to around 1500 (though not all of its pictures are by Venetians), and it contains some gems. The *Pietà* by Cosmé Tura and the *Transfiguration* and *Dead Christ Supported by Angels* by Giovanni Bellini stand out, along with a **Carpaccio** picture usually known as *The Courtesans*, although its subjects are really a couple of terminally bored, bourgeois ladies dressed in the eccentric manner prevalent in the late fifteenth century.

Accessed from within the Correr is the **Museo Archeologico** (times and ticket as above). In many cities a collection of Greek and Roman sculpture as comprehensive as this one would merit a strong recommendation; in Venice you needn't feel guilty about leaving it for a rainy day. A further section is devoted to the **Museo del Risorgimento**, (included in the Museo Correr ticket) which acts as a shrine to Daniele Manin, five of the fifteen rooms being devoted to his rebellion against the Austrians. The final part of the Correr, part of the Biblioteca Nazionale Marciana, is the **Libreria Sansoviniana** (times and ticket as above), which looks down onto the Piazzetta (see below). These historic rooms of the library were only recently opened to the public and it's worth perservering as far as this end of the museum if only to see the Staircase, stuccoed by Vittoria, and adjacent Antechamber. The latter, designed by Palladio's follower Scamaozzi, has a remarkable Titian *Wisdom* in the centre of the ceiling, surrounded by mesmerizing trompe l'oeil perspective. In the main hall are reproductions of some of the more precious of the library's million volumes, while staring down pensively from the walls are frescoes of philosophers and Virtues by Veronese, Tintoretto and others.

The Piazzetta

The **Piazzetta** – the open space between San Marco and the waterfront pavement known as the Molo – was the area where the politicians used to gather before meetings; known as the *broglio*, its wheeling and dealing probably gave rise to the English word "imbroglio". Facing the Palazzo Ducale is Sansovino's masterpiece and the most consistently admired Renaissance building in the city – the **Libreria Sansoviniana** (see above). Work was well advanced on the building when, in December 1545, a severe frost resulted in a major collapse, a setback that landed the architect in prison for a while. Completion came in 1591, two decades after Sansovino's death.

Attached to the library, with its main facade to the lagoon, Sansovino's first major building in Venice, the **Zecca** (Mint), was built between 1537 and 1545 on the site of the thirteenth-century mint. By the beginning of the fifteenth century the city's prosperity was such that the Venetian coinage was in use in every European exchange, and the doge could with some justification call Venice "the mistress of all the gold in Christendom".

The piazzetta's two **columns** were brought here from the Levant at the end of the twelfth century, in company with a third, which fell off the barge and still lies somewhere just off the Molo. The figures perched on top are St Theodore (it's a copy – the original is in the Palazzo Ducale), patron saint of Venice when it was dependent on Byzantium, and a Chimera, customized to look like the Lion of St Mark. Public executions were carried out between the columns, the techniques employed ranging from straightforward hanging to burial alive, head downwards. Superstitious Venetians avoid passing between them.

Sometimes the heads of freshly dispatched villains were mounted on the **Pietra del Bando**, the stump of porphyry at the other end of the piazzetta, against the corner of San Marco. Its routine use, however, was as one of the two stones from which the laws of the republic were proclaimed (the other is at the Rialto). The Pietra del Bando was brought back to Venice from Acre after the Venetian defeat of the Genoese there in 1256; the two square pillars near to it, with their fine fifth-century Syrian carving, were probably hauled away from Constantinople in 1204.

North of the Piazza

The **Mercerie**, a chain of glitzy streets that starts under the clock tower and finishes at the Campo San Bartolomeo, is the most direct route between the Rialto and San Marco and has therefore always been the main land thoroughfare of the city and a prime site for its shopkeepers. For those immune to the charms of window-shopping there's little reason to linger until you reach the church of **San Salvador**, (Mon-Sat 10am-noon &

5-7pm, Sun 9am-12.30pm & 5-7.30pm; free) an early sixteenth-century church cleverly planned in the form of three Greek crosses placed end to end. It has a couple of Titian paintings – an altarpiece of the *Transfiguration* (1560) and an *Annunciation* (1566), whose awkwardly embarking angel is often blamed on the great man's assistants. The end of the south transept is filled by the tomb of Caterina Cornaro, who for a while was Queen of Cyprus before being manoeuvred into surrendering the island to Venice (see p.361).

The **Campo San Bartolomeo**, close to the foot of the Rialto bridge, is at its best in the evening, when it's as packed as any bar in town. For a crash-course in the Venetian character, hang around the statue of Goldoni for a while at about 7pm. If the crush gets a bit too much, you can retire to the nearby **Campo San Luca**, another focus of after-work gatherings but not as much of a pressure-cooker as San Bartolomeo, though – like San Bartolomeo – the presence of a *McDonald's* has increased the traffic.

Beyond Campo San Luca is **Campo Manin**, on the south side of which is a sign for the spiral staircase known as the **Scala del Bovolo** (*bovolo* means "snail shell" in Venetian dialect), a piece of flamboyant engineering dating from around 1500 (March–Oct daily 11am–4pm; L3000/€1.55). The **Museo Fortuny** (closed for repair, but sections sometimes open Tues–Sun 10am–6pm) is also close at hand, similarly tucked away in a spot you'd never accidentally pass, but signposted with small eye-level posters. In addition to making his famous silk dresses, which were said to be fine enough to be threaded through a wedding ring, **Mariano Fortuny** (1871–1949) was a painter, architect, engraver, photographer, theatre designer and sculptor; the museum reflects his versatility, but you'll probably come out wishing there were more of his frocks on display.

West of the Piazza

Although it too has its share of fashionable shops – much of the broad Calle Larga XXII Marzo, for example, is dedicated to the beautification of the well-heeled and their dwellings – the area to the **west of the Piazza** is less frenetic than the streets to the north. None of the first-division tourist sights are here, but the walk from the Piazza to the Accademia bridge, through a succession of campi each quite unlike its predecessor, isn't lacking in worthwhile diversions.

Heading west from the Piazza, you soon reach the hypnotically dreadful **San Moisè** (Mon–Sat 3.30–7pm, Sun 9am–12pm & 3.30–7pm; free), runaway winner of any poll for the ugliest church in Venice. The facade sculpture, featuring a species of camel unknown to zoology, was created in 1668 by Heinrich Meyring; and if you think this is in dubious taste, wait till you see his altarpiece of *Mount Sinai with Moses Receiving the Tablets*.

Halfway along the Calle Larga XXII Marzo, on the right, is the Calle del Sartor da Veste, which takes you over a canal and into the Campo San Fantin, where the Renaissance church of **San Fantin** has a graceful domed apse by Sansovino. Across the campo is the wreckage of Venice's largest and oldest theatre, **La Fenice**, opened in December 1792, rebuilt in 1836 after the place had been wrecked by fire, and now a burned-out husk once again, in the wake of the fire that ripped though the building on the night of January 29, 1996, just as a phase of restoration was coming to a close. Criminal investigations are proceeding (it seems almost certain that the fire was started deliberately), and La Fenice is officially supposed to be opening in 2001, but given that the building is still a burnt-out shell four years on, that seems very unlikely. In the interim, opera and ballet performances are being held over on Tronchetto, in a vast tent called the Palafenice (see p.326) and, from March 2001, in the newly restored Teatro Malibran (ask at tourist office for details).

Back on the main road to the Accademia, another very odd church awaits – **Santa Maria del Giglio**, otherwise known as Santa Maria del Zobenigo (Mon–Sat

10am–5pm, Sun 3–5pm; entrance with Chorus Pass, see box on p.286, or L3000/€1.55). You can stare at this all day and still not find a single Christian image. The statues are of the five Barbaro brothers who financed the rebuilding of the church in 1678; Virtue, Honour, Fame and Wisdom hover respectfully around them; and the maps in relief depict the towns the brothers graced in the course of their exemplary military and diplomatic careers.

The tilting campanile that soon looms into view over the vapid church of San Maurizio belongs to Santo Stefano, which stands at the end of the next campo – the **Campo Santo Stefano**. Large enough to hold several clusters of tourists and natives plus a kids' football match or two, the Campo Santo Stefano is always lively but never feels crowded, and has, in *Paolin*, one of the best ice cream places in Venice (see review on p.326). To those few non-Venetians to whom his name means anything, Francesco Morosini is known as the man who lobbed a missile through the roof of the Parthenon towards the end of the seventeenth century. He lived at the Canal Grande end of the campo (no. 2802) and is buried in **Santo Stefano** (Mon–Sat 10am–5pm, Sun 1–5pm; entrance with Chorus Pass, see box on p.286, or L3000/€1.55), a thirteenth-century church that was rebuilt in the fourteenth and altered again in the first half of the fifteenth; the Gothic doorway and the ship's keel roof both belong to this last phase. The best paintings are in the sacristy – *The Agony in the Garden*, *The Last Supper* and *The Washing of the Disciples' Feet*, all late works by Tintoretto.

Dorsoduro

Some of the finest architecture in Venice, both domestic and public, is to be found in the sestiere of **DORSODURO**, a situation partly attributable to the stability of its sand-banks – *Dorsoduro* means "hard back". Yet for all its attractions, not many visitors wander off the strip that runs between the main sights of the area – the Ca' Rezzonico, the Accademia and the Salute. The sestiere has a bafflingly complex border, so for clarity's sake we have taken the curve of the Canal Grande–Rio di Ca' Fóscari–Rio Nuovo as the boundary between Dorsoduro and the rest of central Venice.

The Galleria dell'Accademia

The **Galleria dell'Accademia** (summer Mon 9am–2pm, Tues–Sat 9am–10pm, Sun 9am–8pm; winter Tues–Sat 9am–7pm, Mon & Sun 9am–2pm; L12,000/€6.20) is one of the finest specialist collections of European art, following the history of Venetian painting from the fourteenth to the eighteenth centuries. When it was established in 1807, its exhibits came largely from churches and convents that were then being suppressed; indeed, the buildings that the Accademia has occupied since then include two former religious buildings – the church of Santa Maria della Carità, rebuilt by Bartolomeo Bon in the 1440s, and the incomplete Convento dei Canonici Lateranensi, partly built by Palladio in 1561.

The Accademia is the third component – with San Marco and the Palazzo Ducale – of the triad of obligatory tourist sights in Venice, but admissions are restricted to batches of 300 people at a time. So, if you're visiting in high summer and don't want to wait, get here about 1pm when most people are having lunch.

TO THE EARLY RENAISSANCE

The gallery is laid out in a roughly chronological succession of rooms going anticlockwise. The first room at the top of the stairs is the fifteenth-century assembly room of the Scuola and houses works by the earliest known individual Venetian painters. **Paolo Veneziano** (from the first half of the fourteenth century) and his follower **Lorenzo Veneziano** are the most absorbing.

Room 2 moves on to works from the late fifteenth and early sixteenth centuries, with large altarpieces that are contemplative even when the scenes are far from calm.

Carpaccio's strange and gruesome *Crucifixion and Glorification of the Ten Thousand Martyrs of Mount Ararat* (painted around 1512) and his *Presentation of Jesus in the Temple* accompany works by **Giovanni Bellini** and **Cima da Conegliano**.

In the west room you can observe the emergence of the characteristically Venetian treatment of colour in works from the early Renaissance, but there's nothing here as exciting as the small paintings in rooms 4 and 5, a high point of the collection. Apart from an exquisite *St George* by **Mantegna** and a series of **Giovanni Bellini** Madonnas, this section contains **Giorgione**'s enigmatic *Tempest* – nobody has ever satisfactorily explained what, if anything, is going on here, and the picture may well have been equally opaque to the person for whom it was created in 1500.

HIGH RENAISSANCE
Room 6 introduces one of the heavyweights of Venetian painting, Jacopo Robusti, known as **Tintoretto**. The *Creation of the Animals* features a few species that must have followed the unicorn into extinction. Another big name represented here is **Titian** (Tiziano Vecellio), with a not particularly interesting *John the Baptist* (early 1540s). One of the most compelling paintings in the gallery is in room 7, the *Young Man in his Study* by **Lorenzo Lotto** (1528).

Room 10 is dominated by epic productions, and an entire wall is filled by **Paolo Veronese**'s *Christ in the House of Levi*. Originally called *The Last Supper*, this picture provoked a stern reaction from the Court of the Holy Office: it was too irreverent for such a holy subject, they insisted – why were there "Germans and buffoons and suchlike things in this picture? Does it appear to you fitting that at our Lord's last supper you should paint buffoons, drunkards, Germans, dwarfs, and similar indecencies?" Veronese fielded all their questions and responded simply by changing the title, which made the work acceptable. The pieces by **Tintoretto** in here include three legends of St Mark: *St Mark Rescues a Slave* (1548), which was the painting that made his reputation, *The Theft of the Body of St Mark* and *St Mark Saves a Saracen* (both 1560s). All of these show Tintoretto's love of energy and drama – from the physical or psychological drama of the subject matter, emphasized by the twisting poses of the people depicted, to the technical energy of his brush strokes, perception of colour and use of light. Opposite is an emotional late **Titian**, a pietà (1570s) intended for his own tomb in the Frari (see p.301).

THE EIGHTEENTH CENTURY
Room 11 contains a number of works by **Giambattista Tiepolo**, the most prominent painter of eighteenth-century Venice, including two shaped fragments rescued from the wreckage of the Scalzi (1743–45) and *The Translation of the Holy House of Loreto* (1743), a sketch for the same ceiling. There's also more from **Tintoretto**; the *Madonna dei Tesorieri* (1566), with its sumptuously painted velvets, shows facial types still found in Venice today.

The following stretch of seventeenth- and eighteenth-century paintings isn't too enthralling – the highlights are portraits by **Rosalba Carriera** and interiors by **Pietro Longhi** in room 17. Carriera's work popularized the use of pastel as a medium; look for her moving *Self-Portrait in Old Age* (1740s), executed just before she went blind. Longhi is not the most brilliant of painters in the Accademia, but his illustrative work is fascinating for the insights it gives into eighteenth-century Venice. (For more, including the famous *Rhinoceros*, go to the Ca' Rezzonico; see p.299.)

THE VIVARINIS, THE BELLINIS AND CARPACCIO
Around the corner and to the right are more works from the fifteenth and early sixteenth centuries. Pieces by the Vivarini family feature strongly; **Alvise Vivarini**'s *Santa Chiara* is outstanding. **Giovanni Bellini** is represented by four triptychs painted, with

workshop assistance, for this church in the 1460s. The extraordinary *Blessed Lorenzo Giustinian* is by his brother, **Gentile**; one of the oldest surviving Venetian canvases, and Gentile's earliest signed work, it was possibly used as a standard in processions, which would account for its state.

The magnificent cycle of pictures painted around 1500 for the Scuola di San Giovanni Evangelista, mainly illustrating the miracles of the Relic of the Cross, is displayed in room 20, off a corridor to the left. All of the paintings are replete with fascinating local details, but particularly rich are **Carpaccio's** *Cure of a Lunatic* and **Gentile Bellini's** *Recovery of the Relic from the Canale di San Lorenzo* and *Procession of the Relic in the Piazza*. The next room contains a complete cycle of pictures by **Carpaccio** illustrating the *Story of St Ursula*, painted for the Scuola di Sant'Orsola at San Zanipolo (1490–94). Restored in the mid-1980s, the paintings form one of Italy's most unforgettable groups. The legend is that Hereus, a British prince, proposed marriage to Ursula, a Breton princess. She accepted on two conditions: that Hereus convert to Christianity, and that he should wait for three years, while she went on a pilgrimage. The pilgrimage, undertaken with a company of 11,000 virgins, ended with a massacre near Cologne by the Huns – as Ursula had been forewarned in a dream.

Finally, in room 24 (the former hostel of the Scuola), there's **Titian's** *Presentation of the Virgin* (dating from 1539). It was painted for the place where it hangs, as was the triptych by **Antonio Vivarini** and **Giovanni d'Alemagna** (1446), another of the oldest Venetian canvases.

The Guggenheim and the Salute

Within five minutes' walk of the Accademia, beyond the Campo San Vio, is the unfinished Palazzo Venier dei Leoni, home of Peggy Guggenheim for thirty years until her death in 1979, now the base for the **Guggenheim Collection** (daily except Tues 10am–6pm; L12,000/€6.20, *www.guggenheim.org*). Her private collection is an eclectic, quirky choice of mainly excellent pieces from her favourite modernist movements and artists. Prime pieces include Brancusi's *Bird in Space* and *Maestra*, De Chirico's *Red Tower* and *Nostalgia of the Poet*, Max Ernst's *Robing of the Bride*, sculpture by Laurens and Lipchitz, paintings by Malevich and collages by Schwitters.

Continuing along the line of the Canal Grande, you come to Santa Maria della Salute, better known simply as the **Salute** (daily 9am–noon & 3–5pm), built to fulfil a Senate decree of October 22, 1630, that a new church would be dedicated to Mary if the city were delivered from the plague that was ravaging it – an outbreak that was to kill about a third of the population. Work began in 1631 on **Baldessare Longhena's** design and was completed in 1681, though the church was not consecrated until November 9, 1687, five years before Longhena's death. Thereafter, every November 21, the Signoria headed a procession from San Marco to the Salute, over a specially constructed pontoon bridge, to give thanks for the city's good health (*salute* meaning "health" and "salvation") – and even today the festival of the Salute is a major event on the Venetian calendar.

In 1656, a hoard of **Titian** paintings from the suppressed church of Santo Spirito were moved here and are now housed in the **sacristy** (L2000/€1.03). The most prominent of these is the altarpiece of *St Mark Enthroned with SS Cosmas, Damian, Sebastian and Rocco* (the plague saints). The *Marriage at Cana*, with its dramatic lighting and perspective, is by **Tintoretto** (1561), and features likenesses of a number of the artist's friends.

The **Dogana di Mare** (Customs House), with its Doric facade (1676–82), occupies the spur formed by the meeting of the Canal Grande with the Giudecca canal; known as the Punta Dogana, the very tip of the promontory is a great spot to have a picnic, particularly at sunset. The gold ball, noticeable from anywhere on this busy stretch of water, is a weathervane, topped by a figure representing either Justice or Fortune.

Along the Záttere to San Sebastiano

Stretching from the Punta della Dogana to the Stazione Marittima, the **Záttere** (Rafts) was originally the place where most of the bulky goods coming into Venice were unloaded, and is now a popular place for a picnic lunch or a Sunday stroll. Its principal sight is the church of Santa Maria del Rosario, invariably known as the **Gesuati** (Mon–Sat 8.30am–noon & 5–6pm, Sun 5–6pm; L2000/€1.03) – worth a call for its paintings by **Giambattista Tiepolo**: three ceiling frescoes of *Scenes from the Life of St Dominic* and an altarpiece of *Madonna with three Dominican Saints*.

A diversion to the right straight after the Gesuati takes you past the **squero di San Trovaso**, the busiest gondola workshop left in Venice, and on to the church of **San Trovaso**. Venetian folklore has it that this church was the only neutral ground between the rival working-class factions of the Nicolotti and the Castellani, who would celebrate intermarriages and other services here, but came and went through separate doors. It is a large dark church, whose paintings are properly visible only in the morning; they include a pair of fine paintings by **Tintoretto** (*The Temptation of St Anthony* and *The Last Supper*), and the two large pictures begun by Tintoretto at the very end of his life, *The Adoration of the Magi* and *The Expulsion from the Temple*.

The church of **San Sebastiano** (daily 10am–5pm; entrance with Chorus Pass, see box on p.286, or L3000/€1.55), right up by the Stazione Marittima (erratic opening hours) was built between 1505 and 1545 and was the parish church of **Paolo Veronese**, who provided most of its paintings and is buried here. He was first brought in to paint the ceiling of the sacristy with a *Coronation of the Virgin* and the *Four Evangelists*, followed by the *Scenes from the Life of St Esther* on the ceiling of the church. He then painted the dome of the chancel (since destroyed), and with the help of his brother, Benedetto, moved on to the walls of the church and the nuns' choir. The paintings around the high altar and the organ came last, painted in the 1560s.

Ca' Rezzonico and around

From San Sebastiano it's a straightforward walk back towards the Canal Grande along Calle Avogaria and Calle Lunga San Barnaba, a route that deposits you in Campo San Barnaba, just yards from the **Ca' Rezzonico**, now the **Museo del Settecento Veneziano** – the Museum of Eighteenth-Century Venice (closed for repairs until 2002). Having acquired the Ca' Rezzonico in 1934, the *comune* of Venice set about furnishing and decorating it with eighteenth-century items and materials (or their closest modern equivalent), so giving the place the feel of a well-appointed house rather than of a formal museum. On the applied arts side of the collection, the plentiful and outlandish carvings by **Andrea Brustolon** are as likely to elicit revulsion as admiration. As for the paintings, the highlights are **Pietro Longhi**'s affectionate illustrations of Venice social life and the frescoes painted towards the end of his life by **Giandomenico Tiepolo**. Although painted at a time when this type of work was going out of fashion, these frescoes of clowns and carnival scenes (created originally for his own house) are among Giandomenico's best-known images. Fans of his father's slightly more flamboyant style won't come away disappointed either.

The nearby **Campo Santa Margherita** is a wide but friendly space, with a daily **market** and a clutch of shops that contribute to the quarter's distinctive atmosphere. The **Scuola Grande dei Carmini** (summer Mon–Sat 9am–noon & 3–6pm, Sun 9am–1pm; winter Mon–Sat 9am–4pm, Sun 9am–1pm; L8000/€4.13), on the west of the campo, is a showcase for Giambattista Tiepolo, whose ceiling paintings in the main upstairs hall, painted in the early 1740s, centre on a panel of *The Virgin in Glory*.

San Polo

For practical reasons, the district we have labelled **SAN POLO** covers an area over twice the size of the sestiere of the same name, including a huge chunk of the sestiere of Santa Croce and a bit of Dorsoduro, and is bounded by the Canal Grande and the Rio Nuovo–Rio di Ca' Fóscari. You cannot stray unwittingly over either of these canals, which is more than can be said for the boundaries of the *sestieri*.

From the Rialto to the museum of modern art

Relatively stable building land and a good defensive position drew some of the earliest lagoon settlers to the high bank (*rivo alto*) above the Canal Grande that was to develop into the **Rialto** district. While the political centre of the new city grew up around San Marco, the Rialto became the commercial zone. In the twelfth century, Europe's first state bank was opened here, and the financiers of the district were the weightiest figures on the international exchanges for the next three centuries and more. The state offices that oversaw all maritime business were here as well, and in the early sixteenth century the offices of the exchequer were installed in the new **Palazzo dei Camerlenghi**, at the foot of the Rialto bridge.

The connection between wealth and moral turpitude was exemplified by the Rialto, where the fleshpots were as busy as the cash desks. A late sixteenth-century survey showed that there were about 3000 patrician women in the city, but well over 11,000 prostitutes, the majority of them based in the banking quarter. One Rialto brothel, the *Casteletto*, was especially esteemed for the literary, musical and sexual talents of its staff, and a perennial Venetian bestseller was a catalogue giving the addresses and prices of the city's most alluring courtesans.

It was through the markets of the Rialto that Venice earned its reputation as the bazaar of Europe. Virtually anything could be bought or sold here: Italian fabrics, precious stones, silver plate and gold jewellery, spices and dyes from the Orient. Trading had been going on here for over 400 years when, in 1514, a fire destroyed everything in the area except the church. The possibility of relocating the business centre was discussed but found little favour, so reconstruction began almost straight away, the **Fabbriche Vecchie** (the arcaded buildings along the Ruga degli Orefici and around the Campo San Giacomo) being finished five years after the fire, and Sansovino's **Fabbriche Nuove** (running along the Canal Grande from Campo Cesare Battisti) following about thirty years later.

Today's Rialto market is tamer than that of Venice at its peak, but it's still one of the liveliest spots in the city, and one of the few places where it's possible to stand in a crowd and hear nothing but Italian spoken. There's a shoal of memento-sellers by the church and along the Ruga degli Orefici; the market proper lies between them and the Canal Grande – mainly fruit stalls around the **Campo San Giacomo**, vegetable stalls and butchers' shops as you go through to the **Campo Battisti**, after which you come to the fish market. (The fish market and many of the other stalls close for the day at 1pm, but some re-open in the late afternoon.) There are excellent cheese shops around the junction of **Ruga degli Orefici** and **Ruga Vecchia San Giovanni**; the Ruga Vecchia has a number of good *alimentari* among the kitsch-merchants.

A popular Venetian legend asserts that the city was founded on Friday, March 25, 421 AD at exactly midday; from the same legend derives the claim that the church of **San Giacomo di Rialto** (daily 10am–noon; free) was founded in that year, and is thus the oldest church in Venice. It might actually be the oldest; what is not disputed is that the church was rebuilt in 1071 and that parts of the present structure date from then – for instance, the interior's six columns of ancient Greek marble have eleventh-century Veneto-Byzantine capitals. As you walk away from the Rialto, following roughly the curve of the Canal Grande, you enter a district which becomes labyrinthine even by

Venetian standards. A directionless stroll between the Rio delle Beccerie and the Rio di San Zan Degolà will satisfy any addict of the picturesque: you cannot walk for more than a couple of minutes without coming across a workshop crammed into a ground-floor room or a garden spilling over a canalside wall.

The church of **San Cassiano** (Mon–Sat 9.45–11.30am & 4.30–7pm; free) is a building you're bound to pass as you wander out of the Rialto. Don't be put off by its barn-like appearance: it contains three paintings by **Tintoretto**, *The Resurrection, The Descent into Limbo* and *The Crucifixion*. The first two have been mauled by restorers, but the third is one of the greatest pictures in Venice, a startling composition dominated not by the cross but by the ladder on which the executioners stand.

Nearby, and signposted from San Cassiano, is the **Ca' Pésaro**, in which you'll find both the **Galleria d'Arte Moderna** and **Museo Orientale** (both closed at time of writing, check with the tourist office for updates on progress). Pieces bought from the Biennale make up much of the modern collection, and its backbone consists of work by a range of Italian artists, many of whom will be unfamiliar. As for the oriental galleries, the jumble of lacquer work, armour, screens, weaponry and so forth will appeal chiefly to the initiated.

Campo San Polo

The largest square in Venice after the Piazza, the **Campo San Polo** used to be the city's favourite bullfighting arena as well as the site of weekly markets and occasional fairs. Nowadays it's a combination of outdoor social centre and children's sports stadium.

The bleak interior of **San Polo** church (Mon–Sat 10am–5pm, Sun 3–5.30pm; entrance with Chorus Pass, see box on p.286, or L3000/€1.55) should be visited for a *Last Supper* by **Tintoretto** and **Giandomenico Tiepolo's** paintings of the *Stations of the Cross*, a series painted when the artist was only twenty. The sober piety of these pictures will come as a surprise if you've been to the Ca' Rezzonico, though it often seems that his interest was less in the central drama than in the society portraits that occupy the edges of the stage.

Calle Madonetta, going off the campo in the direction of Rialto, is the beginning of a sequence of busy **shopping streets**, in which you'll find a couple of good *pasticcerie* and a host of shoe and clothes shops. Salizzada San Polo and Calle dei Saonéri, on the opposite side of the *campo*, are effectively a continuation of these streets, which together comprise this side of the Canal Grande's answer to the Mercerie.

The Frari

The Franciscans were granted a large plot of land near San Polo in about 1250, not long after the death of St Francis; replacement of their first church by the present Santa Maria Gloriosa dei Frari – more generally known simply as the **Frari** (Mon–Sat 9am–6pm, Sun 1–6pm; entrance with Chorus Pass, see box on p.286, or L3000/€1.55) – began in the mid-fourteenth century and took over a hundred years. This mountain of brick is not an immediately attractive building but, whatever your predilections, its collection of paintings, sculptures and monuments will gain the church a place on your list of Venetian highlights.

As every guide to the city points out, Venice is relatively impoverished as far as major paintings by **Titian** are concerned: apart from the Salute and the Accademia, the Frari is the only building in Venice with more than a single significant work by him. One of these – the *Assumption*, painted in 1518 – you will see almost immediately as you look towards the altar through the fifteenth-century monks' choir, a swirling, dazzling piece of compositional and colouristic bravura for which there was no precedent in Venetian art. The other Titian masterpiece here, the *Madonna di Ca' Pésaro*, is more static but was equally innovative in its displacement of the figure of the Virgin from the centre of the picture.

Wherever you stand in the Frari, you'll be facing something that deserves your attention, but three or four pieces apart from the Titians stand out from the rest. Two funerary monuments embodying the emergence in Venice of Renaissance sculptural technique flank the Titian *Assumption*: on the left the **tomb of Doge Niccolò Tron**, by **Antonio Rizzo** and assistants, dating from 1476; on the right, the more chaotic **tomb of Doge Francesco Fóscari**, carved by **Antonio and Paolo Bregno** shortly after Fóscari's death in 1457. The wooden statue of *St John the Baptist*, in the first chapel to the right, was commissioned from **Donatello** in 1438 by Florentine merchants in Padua; recent work has restored its luridly naturalistic appearance. Still moving to the right, the third chapel houses a typically vivid *Christ on the Sarcophagus* by **Bartolomeo Vivarini**. Head through the door on the right for the sacristy, where on the altar (the site for which it was created) is a picture that alone would justify a visit to the Frari – the *Madonna and Child with SS Nicholas of Bari, Peter, Mark and Benedict*, painted in 1488 by **Giovanni Bellini**. In the words of Henry James, "it is as solemn as it is gorgeous and as simple as it is deep".

Two massive tombs take up much of the nave. One is the bombastic **monument to Titian**, built in the mid-nineteenth century on the supposed site of his grave. He died in the 1576 plague epidemic, in around his ninetieth year, and was the only casualty of that outbreak to be given a church burial. Opposite is a tomb of similarly pompous dimensions but of redeeming peculiarity: the **Mausoleum of Canova**, erected in 1827 by pupils of the sculptor, following a design he had made for the tomb of Titian.

The Scuola Grande di San Rocco and San Rocco church

At the rear of the Frari is a place you should on no account miss: the **Scuola Grande di San Rocco** (daily: summer 9am–5.30pm; winter 10am–4pm; L9000/€4.65). St Rocco (St Roch) was attributed with the power to cure the plague and other serious illnesses, so when the saint's body was brought to Venice in 1485, this *scuola* began to profit from donations from people wishing to invoke his aid. In 1515 it commissioned this prestigious new building, and soon after its completion in 1560, work began on the decorative scheme that was to put the Scuola's rivals in the shade – a cycle of more than fifty major paintings by **Tintoretto**.

THE TINTORETTO PAINTINGS

To appreciate the evolution of Tintoretto's art you have to begin in the smaller room on the upper storey – the **Sala dell'Albergo**. In 1564 the Scuola held a competition for the contract to paint its first picture. The subject was to be *The Glorification of St Roch*, and Tintoretto won the contest by rigging up a finished painting in the very place for which the winning picture was destined – the centre of the ceiling. The protests of his rivals, who had simply submitted sketches, were to no avail. Virtually an entire wall of the Sala is occupied by the stupendous *Crucifixion*, a painting that reduced Ruskin to a state of dumbfounded wonder. His loquacious guide to the cycle concludes: "I must leave this picture to work its will on the spectator; for it is beyond all analysis, and above all praise." The pictures on the entrance wall – *Christ before Pilate, Christ Crowned with Thorns* and *The Way to Calvary* – inevitably suffer from such company, but they deserve close scrutiny.

Tintoretto finished the Sala in 1567 and eight years later he started on the main upper hall, a project he completed in 1581. The Old Testament subjects depicted in the three large panels of the **ceiling**, with their references to the alleviation of physical suffering, are coded declarations of the Scuola's charitable activities: *Moses Striking Water from the Rock, The Miracle of the Brazen Serpent* and *The Miraculous Fall of Manna*. The paintings around the walls, all based on the New Testament, are an amazing feat of sustained inventiveness, in which every convention of perspective, lighting, colour and even anatomy is defied. A caricature of the irascible Tintoretto (with a jarful of paint-

THE SCUOLE

The institutions known as the **scuole** seem to have originated in the thirteenth century with the formation of the flagellant orders, whose public scourgings were intended to purge the sins of the world. The interaction between these societies of flagellants and the lay brotherhoods established by the city's branches of the mendicant orders (the Franciscans and the Dominicans) gave rise in 1260 to the formation of the confraternity called **Scuola di Santa Maria della Carità**, the first of the so-called **scuole grande**. By the middle of the sixteenth century there were five more of these major confraternities – **San Giovanni Evangelista, San Marco, Santa Maria della Misericordia, San Rocco** and **San Teodoro** – plus scores of smaller bodies known as the **scuole minore**, of which there were once as many as four hundred.

The *scuole grande*, drawing much of their membership from the wealthiest professional and mercantile groups, and with rosters of up to six hundred men, received subscriptions that allowed them to fund lavish architectural and artistic projects, of which the Scuola Grande di San Rocco is the most spectacular example. The *scuole minore*, united by membership of certain guilds (eg goldsmiths at the Scuola dei Battioro e Tiraori, shoemakers at the Scuola dei Calerghi), or by common nationality (as with San Giorgio degli Schiavoni, the Slavs' *scuola*), generally operated from far more modest bases. Yet all *scuole* had the same basic functions – to provide assistance for their members (eg dowries and medical aid), to offer a place of communal worship, and to distribute alms and services in emergencies (anything from plague relief to the provision of troops). To an extent, the *scuole* also acted as a kind of political safety valve. The councils of state were the unique preserve of the city's self-designated patrician class, but the *scuole* were open only to traders, doctors, lawyers, artisans and civil servants. They had no real power, but a wealthy private club like the Scuola Grande di San Rocco could, if it chose, act as an effective pressure group. Like all other Venetian institutions, the *scuole* came to an end with the coming of Napoleon, who disbanded them in 1806. Most of their possessions were scattered, and their headquarters were in time put to new uses – thus the Scuola Grande di San Marco became the city hospital, the Scuola Grande di Santa Maria della Carità became the galleries of the Accademia, the Scuola Grande di Maria della Misericordia has become a sports hall. Two of the *scuole*, however, were revived in the middle of the nineteenth century and continue to function as charitable bodies in the magnificently decorated buildings they commissioned centuries ago – they are the Scuola di San Giorgio degli Schiavoni and Scuola Grande di San Rocco.

brushes) is incorporated into the trompe l'oeil carvings by the seventeenth-century sculptor **Francesco Pianta**.

Displayed on easels, either in the *sala* or main hall – they are often moved – are a handful of paintings that are understandably missed by many visitors, given the competition. *Christ Carrying the Cross* is now generally thought to be an early **Titian**, though some still maintain Giorgione's authorship; Titian's *Annunciation* is similarly influenced by the earlier master. Two early **Tiepolo** paintings, also on easels, relieve the eyes with a wash of airy colour.

The paintings on the ground floor were created between 1583 and 1587, when Tintoretto was in his late sixties. The turbulent *Annunciation* is one of the most arresting images of the event ever painted, and there are few Renaissance landscapes to match those of *The Flight into Egypt* and the small paintings of *St Mary Magdalen* and *St Mary of Egypt*.

THE CHURCH

Yet more paintings by Tintoretto adorn the neighbouring church of **San Rocco** (8am–12.30pm & 3–5pm; free). On the south wall of the nave you'll find *St Roch Taken to Prison*, and below it *The Pool of Bethesda* – though only the latter is definitely by

Tintoretto. In the chancel are four large works, all of them difficult to see properly: the best are *St Roch Curing the Plague Victims* (lower right) and *St Roch in Prison* (lower left); the two higher pictures are *St Roch in Solitude* and *St Roch Healing the Animals*, though the second is again a doubtful attribution.

San Pantaleone

To the south of San Rocco runs the teeming Crosera San Pantalon, the atmosphere in whose shops, cafés and bars has a lot to do with the proximity of the university. Between this street and the Rio di Ca' Fóscari stands the church of **San Pantaleone** (daily 8–11am & 4.30–7pm; free), which possesses a *Coronation of the Virgin* by Antonio Vivarini and Giovanni d'Alemagna (in the chapel to the left of the chancel) and Veronese's last painting, *San Pantaleone Healing a Boy* (second chapel on right). The church can also boast of having the most melodramatic **ceiling** in the city: *The Martyrdom and Apotheosis of San Pantaleone*. It kept **Gian Antonio Fumiani** busy from 1680 to 1704 but he never got the chance to bask in the glory of his labours – he died in a fall from the scaffolding on which he'd been working.

Cannaregio

In the northernmost section of Venice, **CANNAREGIO**, you can go from one extreme to another in a matter of minutes: it is a short distance from the bustle of the train station and the execrable Lista di Spagna to areas which, although no longer rural – Cannaregio comes from *canna*, meaning "reed" – are still among the quietest and prettiest parts of the whole city. The district also has the dubious distinction of containing the world's original ghetto.

The station area

The first building worth a look in the vicinity of the station is to the left as you come out of it – the **Scalzi** church also called Santa Maria di Nazareth (daily 6.30am–noon & 3.30–7pm; free. Built in the 1670s for the barefoot (*scalzi*) order of Carmelites, the interior, by Baldessare Longhena, is a joy for aficionados of the Baroque. There are frescoes by Giambattista Tiepolo in the first chapel on the left and the second on the right, but his major work in the church, the ceiling, was destroyed in 1915 by an Austrian bomb. A couple of fragments, now in the Accademia, were all that was salvaged.

Foreign embassies used to be concentrated in this area, so that the Venetian authorities could keep an eye on them all together, and the **Lista di Spagna** takes its name from the Spanish embassy, which used to be at no. 168. The street is now completely given over to the tourist trade, with shops and stalls, bars, restaurants and hotels all competing for the same desperate trade. If you are hunting for trinkets, food or a bed, you'll find things better and cheaper elsewhere.

The church of **San Geremia** (Mon–Sat 8am–noon & 3–7pm, Sun 9.15am–12.15pm & 3–7pm; free) is chiefly notable for being the present home of **St Lucy**, martyred in Syracuse in 304, stolen from Constantinople by Venetian crusaders in 1204, and ousted from her own Palladian church in 1863 when it was demolished to build the station. Lucy tore her own eyes out after an unwanted suitor kept complimenting her on their beauty, and hence became the patron saint of eyesight: the glass case on the high altar contains her desiccated body. Architecturally, the church's main point of interest is the twelfth-century campanile, one of the oldest in the city.

The ballroom of the **Palazzo Labia**, next door to the church, contains frescoes by Giambattista Tiepolo and his assistants (1745–50), illustrating the story of Anthony and Cleopatra. The present owners, RAI (the state radio service), allow the public in to see them on Wednesdays, Thursdays and Fridays from 3pm to 4pm (for an appointment call ☎041.781.277).

The **Canale di Cannaregio** was the main entrance to Venice before the road and rail bridges were built; walk along it to get to the church of **San Giobbe**. The physical afflictions with which God permitted Satan to test the faith of Job – he was smitten with "sore boils from the sole of his foot unto his crown" – made Job particularly popular with the Venetians, who suffered regularly from malaria, plague and a plethora of damp-related diseases. The church was built on the site of an oratory by the Venetian Gothic architect Antonio Gambello, later assisted by Pietro Lombardo, who introduced Tuscan Renaissance elements. Lombardo's contribution, his first work in Venice, consists of the doorway and, inside, the statues of *SS Anthony, Bernardino and Louis* and the chancel. Its choicest paintings – Giovanni Bellini's *Madonna Enthroned with Saints* and Carpaccio's *Presentation in the Temple* – have been removed to the drier atmosphere of the Accademia.

The Ghetto

The Venetian **Ghetto** was, in a sense, the first in the world: the word comes from the Venetian dialect *getar* (to found), or *geto* (foundry), which is what this area was until 1390. It was in 1516 that all the city's Jews were ordered to move to the island of the Ghetto Nuovo, an enclave that was sealed at night by Christian curfew guards – whose wages were paid for by the Jews. Distinctive badges or caps had to be worn by all Jews, and there were various economic and social restraints on the community, although oppression was lighter in Venice than in most other parts of Europe (it was one of the few states to tolerate the Jewish religion). When Jews were expelled en masse from Spain in 1492 and Portugal in 1497, many of them came here.

Each wave of Jewish immigrants established its own synagogues with their distinctive rites. The **Scola Levantina**, founded in 1538, and the **Scola Spagnola**, possibly founded about twenty years later, reflect the wealth of these particular groups, who were important traders within the Venetian state; the latter was redesigned around 1584 by Longhena (the profession of architect was barred to Jews), a project that influenced the alteration of the other synagogues. These two are still used today for services, and can be viewed, with the Scola al Canton and the Scola Italiana, in a fascinating and multilingual hourly tour of the area, organized by the **Jewish Museum** in Campo Ghetto Nuovo (daily except Sat: June–Sept 10am–7pm; Oct–May 10am–4.30pm; L5000/€2.58, or L12,000/€6.20 with tour); the collection in the museum itself is mainly of silverware, embroidery and other liturgical objects. Try the excellent Web site, *www.jewishvenice.org*, for links and more information.

The Ghetto looks quite different from the rest of Venice. The Jewish population grew to about 4000 and, even though they were allowed to spread into the **Ghetto Vecchio** and the **Ghetto Nuovissima**, there was gross overcrowding. As the Ghetto buildings were not allowed to be more than one-third higher than the surrounding houses, the result was a stack of low-ceilinged storeys – seven is the usual number. Napoleon removed the gates of the Ghetto in 1797 but the Austrians replaced them in 1798, and Venice's Jews didn't achieve equal rights with other Venetians until Unification with Italy in 1866. After the depredations of the Holocaust, the Jewish population is now growing again, with many Hasidic Jews, often younger people from the US and Israel, once more living and working in and around the Ghetto.

Sant'Alvise, Madonna dell'Orto and around

The area northeast of the Ghetto is one of the most restful parts of Venice. The long *fondamente*, dotted with food shops, bars and trattorias; the red walls and green shutters of the houses; the blue and yellow hulls of the boats – together they create a scene reminiscent of Henry James's vision of the essence of Venice: "I simply see a narrow canal in the heart of the city – a patch of green water and a surface of pink wall."

A few minutes north of the Ghetto stands the church of **Sant'Alvise** (Mon–Sat 10am–5pm, Sun 3–5pm; entrance with Chorus Pass, see box on p.286, or L3000/€1.55). Commissioned by Antonia Venier, daughter of Doge Antonio Venier, after the saint appeared to her in a vision in 1388, the church has one outstanding picture, the recently restored *The Road to Calvary* by Giambattista Tiepolo, painted in 1743. His *Crown of Thorns* and *Flagellation*, slightly earlier works, are on the right-hand wall of the nave. Normally under the nuns' choir, to the right as you enter the church, but on view in the sacristy whilst restoration work is ongoing, are eight small tempera paintings, generally known as *The Baby Carpaccios* thanks to Ruskin's speculative attribution; they do date from Carpaccio's infancy (around 1470), but they're not actually by him.

A circuitous stroll eastwards brings you to the Gothic church of **Madonna dell'Orto** (Mon–Sat 10am–5pm, Sun 3–5pm; entrance with Chorus Pass, see box on p.286, or L3000/€1.55). Dedicated to St Christopher in about 1350, the church was renamed after a large stone *Madonna* by Giovanni de'Santi, found discarded in a local vegetable garden (*orto*), began to work miracles; brought inside the church in 1377, the figure can still be seen (now heavily restored) in the Cappella di San Mauro. The main sculpture on the **facade** is a fifteenth-century *St Christopher* by the Florentine Nicolò di Giovanni; Bartolomeo Bon designed the portal in 1460, shortly before his death. The **interior** was messed around in the 1860s, and although some of the overpainting was removed during restoration work of the 1930s, its appearance still owes much to nineteenth-century interference. Scraps of fresco on the arches and the painted beams give an idea of how it must have looked in the sixteenth century. This was the first church in Venice to be given a thorough restoration job after the floods of 1966; the floor was relaid, the lower walls rebuilt, chapels restored to their pre-1864 layout and all the paintings were cleaned. The *St Christopher* over the door was the first Istrian stonework to be restored in Venice.

This is Tintoretto's parish church: he is buried here, in the chapel to the right of the high altar. So too are his son and daughter, Domenico and Marietta. And there are a number of paintings by the artist here, notably the colossal *Making of the Golden Calf* and *The Last Judgment*, which flank the main altar. Others include Tintoretto's *The Presentation of the Virgin in the Temple*, at the end of the right aisle; *The Vision of the Cross to St Peter* and *The Beheading of St Paul*, on each side of the chancel's *Annunciation* by Palma il Giovane; and *St John the Baptist and Other SS* by Cima da Conegliano on the first altar on the right. In the first chapel on the left there should also be a *Madonna and Child* by Giovanni Bellini, but it was stolen a couple of years back.

From the Ca' d'Oro to the Gesuiti

Back towards the Canal Grande, the main thoroughfare of eastern Cannaregio, the **Strada Nova**, was carved through the houses in 1871–72, and is now a bustling and eclectic shopping street where you can buy anything from spaghetti to surgical trusses. Nearly halfway along is the inconspicuous *calle* named after, and leading to, the **Ca' d'Oro** – a Gothic palace much altered by restoration, and whose finest feature, the facade, is best seen from the water anyway. Inside the **Galleria Giorgio Franchetti** (daily 9am–6pm; L6000/€3.10) is a museum put together from the bequest of the man who owned and repaired the house at the start of this century, and from a few state collections. One of the prize exhibits is in the courtyard – Bartolomeo Bon's sculpted wellhead; others include a *St Sebastian* by Mantegna and a beautifully carved *Young Couple* by Tullio Lombardo. Big names such as Tintoretto and Titian are here, but not at their best; you'll get more out of pieces from less exalted artists – for instance, the views of *The Piazzetta facing San Giorgio* and *Quayside with the Salute* by Francesco Guardi.

At the eastern end of the Strada Nova you come to the Campo dei Santi Apostoli, a general meeting-point and crossroads, and the church of **Santi Apostoli** (daily 7.30–11.30am & 3–7pm; free). The exterior is unexceptional, other than the curious 24-

hour clock on the campanile, but give the interior a look for the Cappella Corner: the design of the chapel is attributed to Mauro Codussi, the altar painting of the *Communion of St Lucy* is by Giambattista Tiepolo, and the tomb of Marco Corner (father of Caterina Cornaro) is attributed to Tullio Lombardo.

Just inland from the Fondamente Nuove, the northern edge of this zone, is the **Gesuiti** church, as Santa Maria Assunta is familiarly known (daily 10am–noon & 5–7pm; free). The Jesuits began work on their church in 1714, and it took fifteen years to inlay the marble walls of the interior and carve its marble "curtains" – with a result that is jaw-droppingly impressive even if you hate Baroque architecture. The *Martyrdom of St Lawrence* by Titian, on the first altar on the left, is a night scene made doubly obscure by the lighting arrangements.

Castello

Our designation of **CASTELLO** includes all the eastern section of the city, and is bounded in the northwest by the Rio dei Santi Apostoli and Rio dei Gesuiti, and in the southwest by the canal that winds from the side of the post office at the Rialto to the back of San Marco. In terms of its tourist appeal, centre stage is occupied by the huge **Santi Giovanni e Paolo**, a place saturated with the history and mythology of Venice. Within a few minutes' walk of here you will find a trio of fascinating churches, **Santa Maria dei Miracoli**, **Santa Maria Formosa** and **San Zaccaria**, as well as the beguiling Carpaccio paintings in the Scuola di San Giorgio degli Schiavoni, to name just the highlights of the western part of this district.

Once the industrial hub of the city and the largest manufacturing site in Europe, the **Arsenale** area (the eastern section of the Castello sestiere) is now predominantly a residential quarter and has little to offer of cultural significance. It would be a mistake, however, to leave it entirely unexplored. In the summer of odd-numbered years the Biennale art show sets up shop in its custom-built pavilions here, and at other times its open spaces – the **Giardini Garibaldi**, **Giardini Pubblici** and **Parco della Rimembranze** – are a good antidote to the claustrophobia that overtakes most visitors to Venice at some point.

The Miracoli and around

If you head into Castello by walking north from the Rialto bridge, you'll pass the cosy church of **San Giovanni Crisostomo**, (Mon–Sat 8.15am–12.15pm & 3–7pm Sun 3–7pm; free) built around 1500 to designs by Mauro Codussi. It has a magnificent late painting by Giovanni Bellini, *SS Jerome, Christopher and Augustine*, and a fine altarpiece by Sebastiano del Piombo – *St John Chrysostom with SS John the Baptist, Liberale, Mary Magdalen, Agnes, and Catherine*. Round the back of the church is the Corte Seconda del Milion, a tiny courtyard hemmed in by ancient buildings, one of which – though nobody is sure which – was Marco Polo's family home.

Sitting on the lip of a canal just a minute to the north of Corte Seconda del Milion, the church of Santa Maria dei Miracoli – known simply as the **Miracoli** (Mon–Sat 10am–5pm, Sun 3–5pm; entrance with Chorus Pass, see box on p.286, or L3000/€1.55) – is one of the most attractive buildings in Europe. It was built in the 1480s to house a painting of the Madonna (still the altarpiece) which was believed to have performed a number of miracles, such as reviving a man who'd spent half an hour lying at the bottom of the Giudecca canal. The church is thought to have been designed by Pietro Lombardo; certainly he and his two sons Tullio and Antonio oversaw the building and executed much of the carving. Typically for Renaissance architecture in Venice, richness of effect takes precedence over classical correctness – the Corinthian pilasters are set below the Ionic, so that the viewer can better appreciate the carving on the Corinthian.

The marble-lined interior contains some of the most intricate decorative sculpture to be seen in Venice. The half-length figures of two saints and the *Annunciation* on the balustrade of the raised galleries at the east end are attributed to Tullio Lombardo; the rest of the attributions for the carvings at this end are arguable between the two brothers and their father. Ruskin was greatly distressed by the children's heads carved to the side of the top of the altar steps: "The man who could carve a child's head so perfectly must have been wanting in all human feeling, to cut it off, and tie it by the hair to a vine leaf."

Campo Santi Giovanni e Paolo

After the Piazza, the **Campo Santi Giovanni e Paolo** – or, in its Venetian dialect form, **San Zanipolo** – is the most impressive open space in Venice. Dominated by the huge brick church from which it gets its name, it also has the most beautiful facade of any of the *scuole grande* and one of the finest Renaissance equestrian monuments.

THE COLLEONI STATUE AND THE SCUOLA GRANDE DI SAN MARCO

The *condottiere* **Bartolomeo Colleoni** began his wayward career in Venice's army in 1429. In the succeeding years he defected to Milan, re-enlisted for Venice, fled again, and finally signed up for good in 1455 – whereupon Venice suffered an outbreak of peace, which meant that in the twenty years leading up to his death in 1475 (see p.214) Colleoni was called upon to fight only once. When he died, Colleoni left a handsome legacy to the republic on condition that a monument should be erected to him in the square before San Marco, an impossible proposition to Venice's rulers, with their cult of anonymity. They got around this dilemma with a splendid piece of disingenuousness, interpreting the will in a way that allowed them to raise the monument before the Scuola Grande di San Marco, rather than the basilica, and still claim the money.

The commission for the monument was won by **Andrea Verrocchio** in 1481, and difficulties dogged this stage of the proceedings too. Having virtually completed the horse, Verrocchio heard that another artist was being approached to sculpt the rider, and he retaliated by mutilating the work he'd done and galloping off to Florence. The matter was eventually smoothed over, and Verrocchio was working again on the piece when he died at the end of June 1488. **Alessandro Leopardi** was then called in to finish the work and produce the plinth for it, which he gladly did – even adding his signature on the horse's girth and appending *del Cavallo* to his name.

An unimprovable backdrop to Colleoni, the **Scuola Grande di San Marco** has provided a sumptuous facade and foyer for the Ospedale Civile since its suppression in the early nineteenth century. The facade was started by Pietro Lombardo and Giovanni Buora in 1487, and finished in 1495 by Mauro Codussi after a row between Pietro and Buora and the Scuola. It works better in sections rather than as a unity: the perspectival panels by Tullio and Antonio Lombardo don't quite bring off the intended illusion, but only the hardhearted will not be charmed by them individually.

THE CHURCH OF SANTI GIOVANNI E PAOLO

The **church of Santi Giovanni e Paolo** (Mon–Sat 7.30am–12.30pm & 3.30–6pm, Sun 4–6pm; free), the Dominican equivalent to the Frari, was founded in 1246, rebuilt and enlarged from 1333, and finally consecrated in 1430. The sarcophagus of Doge Giacomo Tiepolo, who originally gave the site to the Dominicans, is on the left of the door outside.

The **interior** is stunning for its sheer size: approximately 90 metres long, 38 metres wide at the transepts and 33 metres high in the centre. It seems more spacious now than it would have up to 1682, when the wooden choir, placed similarly to that of the Frari, was demolished. The simplicity of the design, a nave with two aisles and gracefully soaring arches, is offset by the huge number of tombs and monuments around the walls. Contrary to the impression created, not all of the doges are buried here, just 25 of them.

The **west wall** is devoted to the Mocenigo family: above the door is the tomb of Doge Alvise Mocenigo and his wife by Pietro Lombardo; to the right is the monument to Doge Giovanni Mocenigo by Tullio Lombardo; and on the left the superb monument to Doge Pietro Mocenigo by Pietro Lombardo, assisted by his sons.

In the **south aisle**, after the first altar, is the monument to the Venetian military commander Marcantonio Bragadin, to which is attached one of Venice's grisliest stories. In 1571 Bragadin was double-crossed by the Turks to whom he had been obliged to surrender Famagusta: tortured and humiliated for days by his captors, he was eventually skinned alive. Some years later the skin was brought back to Venice, and today it sits in that urn high up on the wall.

The next altar has a superb **Giovanni Bellini** polyptych, showing *St Vincent Ferrer, with SS Christopher and Sebastian*, and an *Annunciation* and pietà above, still in the original frame. At the far end of this aisle, before you turn into the transept, you'll see a small shrine with the **foot of St Catherine of Siena**: most of her body is in Rome, her head is in her house in Siena, one foot's here, and other little relics are scattered about Italy.

The **south transept** has a painting by **Alvise Vivarini**, *Christ Carrying the Cross* (1474), and **Lorenzo Lotto**'s *St Antonine* (1542), painted in return for nothing more than his expenses and permission to be buried in the church. Sadly, Lotto was eventually driven from his home town by the jealousies and plots of other artists (including Titian), and died and was buried in the monastery at Loreto.

On the right of the chancel is the tomb of Doge Michele Morosini, selected by Ruskin as "the richest monument of the Gothic period in Venice". The tomb of Doge Andrea Vendramin, opposite, was singled out as its antithesis – only the half of the effigy's head that would be visible from below was completed by the artist, a short cut denounced by Ruskin as indicative of "an extreme of intellectual and moral degradation". Tullio Lombardo is thought to have been the culprit, with help from others – maybe his father and brother.

The **Cappella del Rosario**, at the end of the north transept, was virtually destroyed by fire in 1867; its paintings by Tintoretto, Palma il Giovane and others were lost. Of their replacements, the best are **Veronese**'s ceiling panels and *Adoration*.

Funerary sculpture is the main attraction of the **north aisle**. To the left of the sacristy door is the monument to Doge Pasquale Malipiero by Pietro Lombardo, one of the earliest in Renaissance style in Venice.

Santa Maria Formosa and around

South of San Zanipolo lies Campo di Santa Maria Formosa, an atmospheric square with a modest but mouthwatering morning market. The church of **Santa Maria Formosa** (Mon–Sat 10am–5.30pm, Sun 3–5.30pm; entrance with Chorus Pass, see box on p.286, or L3000/€1.55) was built by San Magno, Bishop of Oderzo in the seventh century, who was inspired by a dream in which he saw a buxom (*formosa*) figure of the Madonna. The present building is another Codussi effort, dating from 1492. Palma il Vecchio's altarpiece of *St Barbara*, the church's outstanding picture, was admired by George Eliot as "an almost unique presentation of a hero-woman". Bartolomeo Vivarini's *Madonna della Misericordia*, in a side chapel, is a fine example of one of the warmest Catholic symbols – here she's shown sheltering a group of parishioners under her cloak.

The Renaissance Palazzo Querini-Stampalia, just round the corner from Santa Maria Formosa, houses the **Pinacoteca Querini-Stampalia** (Tues–Thurs & Sun 10am–1pm & 3–6pm, Fri & Sat 10am–1pm & 3–10pm; L12,000/€6.20). Unless you have a voracious appetite for seventeenth- and eighteenth-century Venetian painting, you'll get most pleasure from earlier pieces such as Palma il Vecchio's portraits of *Francesco Querini* and *Paola Priuli Querini* and Giovanni Bellini's *The Presentation in the Temple*. Apart from that, the main interest is in the eighteenth-century decor of the rooms, and it's worth taking advantage of the unusual late opening times at the weekend, when you can often savour the atmosphere of the palace in peace or take in a classical concert (included in the price; ☎041.271.1411). The basement, and some of the entranceways were remodelled in 1963 by the Venetian architect **Carlo Scarpa**. Most impressive is his garden, a characteristically curious mixture of brutalism and whimsy.

San Zaccaria and the Riva

The Campo San Zaccaria, a few yards off the waterfront, has a more torrid past than most – the convent here was notorious for its libidinous goings-on (officials were once sent to close down the nuns' parlour, only to be met with a barrage of bricks), and in 864 Doge Pietro Tradonico was murdered here as he returned from vespers. The towering church of **San Zaccaria** (daily 10am–noon & 4–6pm; free), a pleasing mixture of Gothic and Renaissance, was started by Antonio Gambello and finished after his death in 1481 by Mauro Codussi, who was responsible for the facade from the first storey upwards. Inside is one of the city's most stunning altarpieces, a *Madonna and Four SS* by Giovanni Bellini. A small fee gets you into the rebuilt remnants of the old church, the Cappella di Sant'Atanasio and Cappella di San Tarasio; here you'll find an early Tintoretto, the *Birth of John the Baptist*, and three wonderful altarpieces by Antonio Vivarini and Giovanni d'Alemagna. Floor mosaics from the ninth and twelfth centuries can be seen through panels in the present floor level, and downstairs is a spooky, waterlogged, ninth-century crypt.

The principal waterfront of the area, the **Riva degli Schiavoni**, stretches right back to the Molo. It's a favourite walk, particularly as the sun goes down, and many notables have lived or stayed in houses and hotels here: Petrarch and his daughter lived at no. 4145 for a while, Henry James stayed nearby at no. 4161 when he was finishing *The Portrait of a Lady*, and the *Hotel Danieli*, at the far end, has accommodated George Sand, Charles Dickens, Proust, Wagner and the ever-present Ruskin.

Halfway along the Riva stands the **Pietà** church (or Santa Maria della Visitazione), famous as the place where Vivaldi was choirmaster – he was also violin teacher to the attached orphanage. Giorgio Massari won a competition to redesign the church in 1736, and it's possible that he consulted with Vivaldi on its acoustics; building didn't actually begin until 1745, and the facade was even more delayed – it was only finished in 1906. The church is still used for concerts, and when the box office is open you can sometimes peer over the ropes at the interior, which, in its newly restored form, looks like a wedding-cake turned inside out – and it has one of Venice's most ostentatious ceiling paintings, Giambattista Tiepolo's *The Glory of Paradise*.

The Greek quarter and the Scuola di San Giorgio degli Schiavoni

Stroll north along the flank of the pietà and you'll enter the quarter of Venice's Greek community, identifiable from a distance by the alarmingly tilted campanile of **San Giorgio dei Greci**. The Greek presence was strong in Venice from the eleventh century, and grew stronger after Constantinople's capture by the Turks in 1453; by the close of the fifteenth century they had founded their own church, college and school here. The present *scuola*, designed (like the college) by Longhena in the seventeenth century, now houses the **Museo Dipinti Sacri Bizantini** (Mon–Sat 9am–12.30pm & 1.30–4.30pm, Sun 10am–5pm; L7000/€3.62). Although many of the most beautiful of the exhibited works (mainly fifteenth to eighteenth century) maintain the traditions of icon painting in terms of composition and use of symbolic figures rather than attempts at realism, it's fascinating to see how some of the artists absorbed Western influences. The **church** contains icons dating back to the twelfth century and a lot of work by

Michael Danaskinàs, a sixteenth-century Cretan artist.

From here it's a hundred metres or so to the **Scuola di San Giorgio degli Schiavoni**, whose ground-floor hall (Tues–Sat 10am–12.30pm & 3.30–6pm, Sun 9.30am–12.30pm; L5000/€2.58) would get onto anyone's list of the ten most beautiful rooms in Europe. Venice's resident Slavs (*Schiavoni*), most of whom were traders, set up a *scuola* to look after their interests in 1451; the present building dates from the early sixteenth century, and the whole interior looks more or less as it would have then. Entering it, you step straight from the street into the superb lower hall, the walls of which are decorated with a cycle created by Vittore Carpaccio between 1502 and 1509. Originally painted for the upstairs room, but moved here when the building was rearranged in 1551, the sequence of pictures consists chiefly of scenes from the lives of SS George, Tryphone and Jerome (the Dalmatian patron saints). Outstanding among them is *The Vision of St Augustine*, depicting the moment that Augustine was told in a vision of Jerome's death.

San Francesco della Vigna

Somewhat stranded on the northern edge of Castello, the church of **San Francesco della Vigna** (daily 8am–noon & 3.30–7pm; free) takes its name from the vineyard that was here when the Franciscans were given the site in 1253. The present church building was begun in 1534, designed and supervised by Sansovino, but the design was modified during construction, and Palladio was later brought in to provide the facade. Although smaller than the two great mendicant churches of San Zanipolo and the Frari, it feels less welcoming – probably attributable to the cold colouring added to the more calculated Renaissance architecture. However, there are some fine works of art that make the trek worthwhile – but be sure to have a pocketful of coins for the (necessary) light boxes. The ones you shouldn't miss are: *SS Jerome, Bernard and Ludovic*, attributed to Antonio Vivarini (left of main door); the sculptures of *Prophets* and *Evangelists* by the Lombardo family (in the chapel left of the chancel); and a *Sacra Conversazione* by **Veronese** (fifth chapel on the north side).

The Arsenale and Museo Storico Navale

A corruption of the Arabic *darsin'a* (house of industry), the very name of the **Arsenale** is indicative of the strength of Venice's trading links with the eastern Mediterranean, and the workers of these dockyards and factories were the foundations upon which the city's mercantile and military supremacy rested. Construction of the Arsenale commenced in the early years of the twelfth century, and by the third decade of the fifteenth century it had become the base for some 300 shipping companies, operating around 3000 vessels in excess of 200 tons. The productivity of the Arsenale was legendary: for the visit of Henry III of France in 1574 the Arsenalotti built a complete ship while the state reception for the king was in progress.

Expansion of the Arsenale continued into the sixteenth century – Sanmicheli's covered dock for the state barge (the *Bucintoro*) was built in the 1540s, for example, and da Ponte's gigantic rope-factory (the Tana) in 1579. By then, though, the maritime strength of Venice was past its peak; militarily too, despite the conspicuous success at Lepanto in 1571, Venice was on the wane, and the recapture of the Morea at the end of the seventeenth century was little more than a glorious interlude in a longer story of decline. When Napoleon took over the city in 1797 he burned down the wharves, sank the last *Bucintoro* and confiscated the remnant of the Venetian navy.

Under Austrian occupation the docks were reconstructed, and they stayed in continuous service until the end of 1917, when, having built a number of ships for the Italian navy in World War I, they were dismantled to prevent them being of use to the enemy. Since then it has been used by the navy for storage and repairs, and as a venue for part of the Biennale, but plans exist to extend the Museo Storico Navale into the

Arsenale buildings and to convert other parts into sports halls, accommodation for the University of Architecture and premises for ACTV.

There is no public access to the Arsenale complex. You can get a look at part of it, however, from the bridge connecting the Campo Arsenale and the Fondamenta dell'Arsenale. The main **gateway** to the Arsenale, built by Antonio Gambello in 1460, was the first structure in Venice to employ the classical vocabulary of Renaissance architecture. The four **lions** to the side of the gateway must be the most-photographed in the city: the two on the right were probably taken from Delos (at an unknown date), the left-hand one of the pair being positioned here to mark the recapture of Corfu in 1716; the larger pair were brought back from Piraeus in 1687 by Francesco Morosini after the reconquest of the Morea.

Nearby, on the other side of the Rio dell'Arsenale and facing the lagoon, is the **Museo Storico Navale** (Mon–Fri 8.45am–1.30pm, Sat 8.45am–1pm; L3000/€1.55). Chiefly of interest for its models of Venetian craft from the gondola to the *Bucintoro* (these models were the equivalents of blueprints), the museum gives a comprehensive picture of the working life of the Arsenale and the smaller boatyards of Venice; but if you want to get a flavour of the city's history from a single museum visit, then you should give priority to the Correr (see p.293).

San Pietro di Castello

In 1808 the greater part of the canal connecting the Bacino di San Marco to the broad inlet of the Canale di San Pietro was filled in to form what is now **Via Garibaldi**, the widest street in the city and the busiest commercial area in the eastern district. If you follow your nose along the right-hand side of the street you'll soon be crossing the Ponte di Quintavalle onto the island of **San Pietro**, once the ecclesiastical centre of Venice, but nowadays a slightly down-at-heel place where the chief activity is the repairing of boats.

By 775 the settlement here had grown sufficiently to be granted the foundation of a bishopric under the authority of the Patriarch of Grado. From the beginning, the political and economic nucleus of the city was in the Rialto and San Marco areas, and the relationship between the Church and the geographically remote rulers of the city was never to be close. In 1451 the first **Patriarch of Venice** was invested, but still his seat remained at Castello, and things stayed that way until 1807 (ten years after the republic had ceased to exist), when the patriarch was at last permitted to install himself in San Marco.

As with the Arsenale, the hidden history of San Pietro is perhaps more interesting than what you can actually see. The church – which takes its name from the castle that used to stand here – is basically a grandiose derivative of a plan by Palladio and has little to recommend it. The most intriguing object inside is the so-called Throne of St Peter (in the south aisle), a marble seat made from an Arabic funeral stone inscribed with texts from the Koran. The lurching campanile, rebuilt by Codussi in the 1480s, was the first tower in Venice to be clad in stone.

Sant'Elena

Located at the eastern limit of the city, beyond the area in which the Biennale is held, the island of **Sant'Elena** was enlarged tenfold during the Austrian administration, partly to form exercise grounds for the troops. Much of the island used to be covered by the meadow of Sant'Elena, a favourite recreation area in the last century, but which has since been usurped by houses, leaving only a strip of park along the waterfront. Still, the walk out here is the nearest you'll get to country pleasures in Venice, and the **church of Sant'Elena** – next to the city's football stadium – is worth a visit. The city's football team recently enjoyed a run in Italy's top flight *Serie A*, although they were inevitably demoted at the end of an unhappy 2000 season.

A church was first erected here in the thirteenth century, following the acquisition of the body of St Helena (the mother of Constantine), and substantially rebuilt in 1435. The spartan Gothic interior has recently been restored, as have the cloister and campanile (the latter so zealously that it now looks like a power-station chimney), but the main attraction is the doorway to the church, an ensemble created in the 1470s by Antonio Rizzo. The sculptural group in the lunette – a monument to Comandante Vittore Cappello, showing him kneeling before St Helena – is the district's one major work of art.

The Canal Grande

The **CANAL GRANDE** is Venice's main thoroughfare. Almost four kilometres long and between thirty and seventy metres wide (but at no point much deeper than five metres), it divides the city in half – three *sestieri* to the west and three to the east. The majority of the most important palaces in Venice stand on the Canal Grande, and the main facades of all of them are on the canalside, many properly visible only from the water. The account that follows is mainly a brief guide to these palaces – the major churches and other public buildings are covered in the appropriate geographical sections.

Left Bank

The first of the major palaces to come into view is the **Palazzo Labia** (completed around 1750). The main facade of the building stretches along the Cannaregio canal, but from the Canal Grande you can see how the side wing wraps itself round the campanile of the neighbouring church – such interlocking is common in Venice, where maximum use has to be made of available space. (See p.304 for details of the interior.)

Not far beyond stands the **Palazzo Vendramin-Calergi**, built by Mauro Codussi at the start of the sixteenth century. This was the first Venetian palace constructed in accordance with the classical rules of Renaissance architecture as formulated by Alberti, and is frequently singled out as the Canal Grande's masterpiece. The round-arched windows enclosing two similar arches are identifying characteristics of Codussi's designs. Richard Wagner died here in 1883; the size of the palace can be gauged from the fact that his rented suite of fifteen rooms occupied just a part of the mezzanine level.

Just after the Rio di San Felice comes the most beguiling palace on the canal – the **Ca' d'Oro**. Incorporating fragments of a thirteenth-century palace that once stood on the site, the Ca' d'Oro was begun in the 1420s and acquired its nickname – "Golden House" – from the gilding that used to accentuate much of its carving. It now houses a large art collection, details of which are given on p.306.

Close to the far side of the Rio dei Santi Apostoli stands the **Ca' da Mosto**. The arches of the first floor and the carved panels above them are remnants of a thirteenth-century Veneto-Byzantine building, among the oldest structures to be seen on the Canal Grande. From the fifteenth to the nineteenth centuries this was one of Venice's most famous hotels, the *Albergo del Lion Bianco*.

As the canal turns, the **Ponte di Rialto** (Rialto Bridge) comes into view. The huge building before it, with five arches at water level, is the **Fondaco dei Tedeschi**, once the headquarters of the city's German merchants. Reconstructed in 1505 after a fire and renovated several times since (most recently to accommodate the main post office), it once had frescoes by Giorgione and Titian on its exterior walls, the remains of which are now in the Ca' d'Oro. The bridge itself was built in 1588–91, superseding a succession of wooden and sometimes unreliable structures; until 1854, when an iron bridge was built at the Accademia, this was the only point at which the Canal Grande could be crossed on foot.

Immediately before the next canal is Sansovino's first palace in Venice, the **Palazzo Dolfin-Manin**. It dates from the late 1530s, a period when other projects by him – the library, the mint and the Loggetta – were transforming the city centre. The **Palazzo Loredan** and the **Palazzo Farsetti**, standing side by side at the end of the Fondamenta del Carbon, are heavily restored thirteenth-century palaces; the former was the home of Elena Corner Piscopia, who in 1678 graduated from Padua University, thereby becoming the first woman to obtain a degree.

Work began on the **Palazzo Grimani** (near-side of the Rio di San Luca) in 1556, to designs by Sanmicheli, but was not completed until 1575, sixteen years after his death. Ruskin, normally no fan of Renaissance architecture, made an exception for this colossal palace, declaring it "simple, delicate, and sublime".

On the approach to the sharp bend in the canal there stands a line of five buildings, the first four of which belonged to the Mocenigo family. This group consists of: the **Palazzo Mocenigo-Nero**, a late sixteenth-century building; the double **Palazzo Mocenigo**, built in the eighteenth century as an extension to the Nero house, and home to Byron for a couple of years; and the **Palazzo Mocenigo Vecchio**, a Gothic palace remodelled in the seventeenth century, reputedly haunted by the ghost of the philosopher-alchemist Giordano Bruno, whose betrayal by Giovanni Mocenigo in 1592 led ultimately to his torture and execution. The fifth palace is the **Palazzo Contarini delle Figure**, named after the almost invisible figures at the water entrance.

The vast pristine building round the bend is the **Palazzo Grassi**, built in 1748–72; owned by Fiat – hence the lavish renovation – it's now a conference centre and venue for Venice's glossiest exhibitions.

The Santa Maria del Giglio landing stage is virtually in the shadow of one of the Canal Grande's most imposing buildings – Sansovino's **Palazzo Corner della Ca' Grande**. The house that used to stand here was destroyed when a fire lit to dry out a stock of sugar in one of its rooms ran out of control; Sansovino's replacement was built from 1545 onwards.

Opposite the church of the Salute, squeezed into a line of fifteenth- and seventeenth-century buildings, is the narrow **Palazzo Contarini-Fasan**, a Gothic palace with unique wheel tracery on the balconies. It's popularly known as the House of Desdemona, for no good reason.

Right bank

The first attraction on the right bank is the **Fondaco dei Turchi**. Originally a private house, then from the 1620s until 1838 the base for Turkish traders in the city, the Fondaco was savagely restored in the last century. Whatever the shortcomings of the work, however, the building's towers and water-level arcade give a reasonably precise picture of a typical Veneto-Byzantine palace. It now houses the Museo di Storia Naturale (Natural History Museum).

A short distance beyond stands Longhena's thickly ornamented **Ca' Pésaro**, finished in 1703, long after the architect's death. Unusually, this has a stone-clad side facade: most houses in Venice have plain brick sides, either because of the cost of stone or to allow for a later building to be attached. Ca' Pésaro now contains the Galleria d'Arte Moderna and the Museo Orientale (see p.301).

There's nothing especially engrossing now until you reach the Rialto markets, which begin with the neo-Gothic **Pescheria** (fish market), built in 1907. The older buildings that follow it, the **Fabbriche Nuove di Rialto** and (set back from the water) the **Fabbriche Vecchie di Rialto**, are by Sansovino and Scarpagnino respectively, and replaced buildings destroyed by fire in 1514. The large building at the base of the Rialto bridge is the **Palazzo dei Camerlenghi** (1525), once home to the Venetian exchequer.

The cluster of Gothic palaces at the Volta constitutes one of the city's architectural glories. Built in 1435, the **Ca' Fóscari** (currently being restored and under wraps until late 2001, though the painted fabric cover gives you an idea), which Ruskin thought "the noblest example in Venice" of late Gothic, was the home of Doge Francesco Fóscari, whose extraordinarily long term of office came to an end with his forced resignation, an event partly attributable to the unrelenting feud conducted against him by the Loredan family and its allies. He died in 1457, only weeks after leaving the Palazzo Ducale. Adjoining the Ca' Fóscari are a pair of joined buildings of the same period – the **Palazzi Giustinian**. Wagner wrote the second act of *Tristan* while living here.

A little further on comes Longhena's **Ca' Rezzonico**, as gargantuan as his Ca' Pésaro but less aggressive. It was begun in 1667 as a commission from the Bon family, but their ambition exceeded their financial resources and they were obliged in 1750 to sell out to the Rezzonico, who completed the palace and even tacked a ballroom and staircase onto the back. Much of the interior of the Ca' Rezzonico is open to the public, as it houses the Museo del Settecento Veneziano (see p.299). The unfinished **Palazzo dei Leoni** (soon after the Campo San Vio) would have been the largest palace on the canal, but its construction, begun in 1759, never progressed further than the first storey – probably owing to the ruinous cost. The stump of the building and the platform on which it is raised are occupied by the Guggenheim collection of modern art (see p.298).

The one domestic building of note between here and the **Dogana di Mare** (Customs House) at the end of the canal is the miniature **Palazzo Dario**, two along from the Palazzo dei Leoni. Compared by Henry James to "a house of cards that hold together by a tenure it would be fatal to touch", the palace was built in the late 1480s not for a patrician family but for Giovanni Dario, a civil servant. The multicoloured marbles of the facade are characteristic of the work of the Lombardo family, and the design may actually be by the founder of the dynasty, Pietro Lombardo.

The northern islands

The islands lying to the north of Venice – **San Michele, Murano, Burano** and **Torcello** – are the places to visit when the throng of tourists in the main part of the city becomes too oppressive, and are the source of much of the glass and lace work you will have seen in many shops in Venice.

To get to them, the main **vaporetto** stop is the Fondamente Nuove, though you can also get the #72 (every 20min) direct from the train station. From the Fondamente Nuove, the #41 (every 20min) will take you to San Michele and Murano. The #12 (every 30min) runs directly from the Fondamente Nuove to Murano's Faro stop, and straight on to Burano and Torcello; it takes 45 minutes to get to Burano, from where it's a short hop to Torcello.

San Michele

The high brick wall around the cemetery island of **San Michele** gives way by the landing stage for the elegant white facade of **San Michele in Isola**, designed by Mauro Codussi in 1469. With this building, Codussi not only helped introduce Renaissance architecture to Venice, but also promoted the use of Istrian stone. Easy to carve yet resistant to water, it had been used as damp-proofing at ground level, but never before for a complete facade; it was to be used on the facades of most major buildings in Venice from the Renaissance onwards.

The main part of the island, through the cloisters, is the city **cemetery** (daily: summer 7.30am–6pm; winter 7.30am–4pm), established by Napoleonic decree and nowadays maintained by the Franciscans, as is the church. The majority of Venetians lie here for just ten years or so, when their bones are dug up and removed to an ossuary and the land recycled. Only those who can afford it stay longer. The cemetery is laid out in sections – ask at the entrance for the little give-away map – the most dilapidated of which is for the Protestants (no. XV), where any admirers can find **Ezra Pound's** grave. In section XIV are the Greek and Russian Orthodox graves, including the restrained memorial stones of **Igor and Vera Stravinsky** and the more elaborate tomb of **Serge Diaghilev** – always strewn with flowers.

Even with the grave-rotation system, the island is reaching full capacity, so in 1998 a competition was held for the **redevelopment** of San Michele. The winning entry, from English architect David Chipperfield, places a sequence of formal courtyards alongside a new funerary chapel and crematorium (the Church's line on space-saving cremation having become more flexible of late). On the eastern side of San Michele two foot-bridges will connect with a rectangular expanse of reclaimed land, site of a trio of tomb buildings overlooking two tiers of waterside gardens, which in turn will overlook central Venice. Making much use of Istrian stone and earthenware plasterwork, Chipperfield's creation promises to be an austerely beautiful addition to the cityscape – and there's a certain appropriateness to the fact that Venice's first great architectural project of the twenty-first century will be a cross between a necropolis and a philosopher's retreat.

Murano

Chiefly famed now as the home of Venice's **glass-blowing** industry, **Murano**'s main *fondamente* are crowded with shops selling the mostly revolting products of the furnaces. However, don't despair: Murano does have other things to offer.

The glass furnaces were moved to Murano from Venice as a safety measure in 1291, and so jealously did the Muranese guard their industrial secrets that for a long while they had the European monopoly on glass mirror-making. The glass-blowers of Murano were accorded various privileges not allowed to other artisans, such as being able to wear swords. From 1376 the offspring of a marriage between a Venetian noble-man and the daughter of a glass-worker were allowed to be entered into the Libro d'Oro, unlike the children of other cross-class matches.

Far more interesting than most of the finished products is the performance of their manufacture. There are numerous **furnaces** to visit, all free of charge on the assumption that you will then want to buy something, though you won't be pressed too hard to do so. Many of the workshops are to be found along Fondamenta dei Vertrai, traditionally a glassworking centre, as the name suggests.

When the Venetian Republic fell to Napoleon in 1797, there were seventeen churches on Murano; today only two are open. The first is **San Pietro Martire** (daily 8am–12.30pm & 1.30–6.30pm; free), a Dominican Gothic church begun in 1363 and largely rebuilt after a fire in 1474. Its main attraction is a large and predictably elegant Giovanni Bellini: the *Madonna and Child with SS Mark and Augustine, and Doge Barbarigo* (1488); a second Bellini (an *Assumption*) is at present being restored.

THE GLASS MUSEUM

Close by, along Fondamenta Cavour, you'll find the **Museo Vetrario** in the Palazzo Giustinian (daily except Wed: summer 10am–5pm; winter 10am–4pm; L8000/€4.13). Perhaps the finest single item is the dark blue Barovier marriage cup, dating from around 1470; it's on show in room 1 on the first floor, along with some splendid Renaissance enamelled and painted glass. But every room contains some amazing creations: glass beakers that look as if they are made from veined stone; sixteenth-century platters that look like discs of crackled ice; stupendously ugly nineteenth-century decorative pieces, with fat little birds enmeshed in trellises of glass. A separate room contains a fascinating exhibition on the history of Murano glass techniques, this time fully explained in English. Look out for the extraordinary *murine in canna* – the technique of placing different coloured rods together to form an image in cross-section. Not all of the modern and contemporary section is on display as it is in the process of being moved into this building, but the collection contains a few pieces of functional glassware that try to look like modernist sculptures, and one or two modernist sculptures that end up looking like giant pieces of functional ware. However, there are some interesting works – like the baby by Alfredo Borbini which looks as though it's carved from lava, and the mirror with gold leaf by Piero Fornasetti.

SANTI MARIA E DONATO

Murano's main draw is the Veneto-Byzantine church of **Santi Maria e Donato**, which was founded in the seventh century and rebuilt in the twelfth (daily 8am–noon & 4–7pm; free). Its beautiful **mosaic floor**, dated 1141 in the nave, mingles abstract patterns with images of beasts and birds – an eagle carries off a deer; two roosters carry off a fox, slung from a pole. The church was originally dedicated to Mary, but in 1125 was rededicated when the relics of St Donato were brought here from Kefallonia. Four splendid bones from an unfortunate dragon that was slain by the holy spit of Donato are now hanging behind the altar. Above these, in the apse, is a twelfth-century **mosaic of the Madonna** and fifteenth-century frescoes of the Evangelists. A guidebook to the church is available, proceeds of which go towards restoration work.

Burano

The main route into **Burano** is a narrow street full of lace shops which soon opens out to reveal the brightly painted houses of the village itself; the colours used to be symbolic, but the meanings have become muddled over time and people now paint their houses whatever colour takes their fancy.

This is still largely a fishing community, the lagoon's main yield being shellfish of various kinds, such as *vongole* (tiny clams) and small crabs. (The catch can be bought either here, on the Fondamenta Pescheria, or back in Venice, at the Rialto.) It's a solitary business; one or two people have even built themselves vulnerable-looking houses out on the slightly higher mud-flats, constructed largely from material scavenged from the lagoon tips.

As the men of Burano live mainly from the water, so the women are to a large extent dependent on **lace making**. Making Burano-point and Venetian-point lace is extremely exacting work – highly skilled, mind-bendingly repetitive, and taking an enormous toll on the eyesight. Each woman specializes in one particular stitch, and so each piece is passed along a sort of "production line" during its construction. The skills are taught at the **Scuola dei Merletti** (daily except Tues: April–Oct 10am–5pm; Nov–March 10am–4pm; L8000/€4.13). It's in the spacious Piazza Baldessare Galuppi and combines a lace school with a museum, and is well worth a visit before you buy anything. (Much of the work in the shops is machine produced and imported.) The school was opened in 1872 after the indigenous crafting of lace nearly died out; the museum shows work dating back to the sixteenth century, but most was produced in the past hundred years.

Torcello

Torcello has come full circle: settled as early as the fifth century, the seat of the Bishop of Altinum from 638, and the home of about 20,000 people by the fourteenth century, it was then eclipsed by Venice, and by 1600 was largely deserted. Today the total population of Torcello is about 100, and there is little visible evidence of the island's prime – two churches and a couple of buildings round a dusty square, and pottery shards half-buried in the fields.

The main reason people come here today is to visit Venice's first cathedral, **Santa Maria dell'Assunta** (daily 10.30am–5.30pm, closes 5pm in winter; L5000/€2.58, including audio-guide). An early church on the site became a cathedral after the Bishop of Altinum arrived with other emigrants from the mainland. The present Veneto-Byzantine building is on pretty much the same plan as the seventh-century one, but it was largely rebuilt in the 860s and altered again in 1008. Inside, the waterlogged crypt is the only survival of the body of the original church; the baptistry also dates from the seventh century, but circular foundations in front of the main doors are all that remain of it.

The dominant tone of the interior is created by its watery green-grey marble columns and panelling; the mosaic floor is eleventh-century, but two wooden panels lift to reveal the original floor underneath. A stunning twelfth-century **mosaic** of the Madonna and Child, on a pure gold background, covers the semi-dome of the apse, resting on an eleventh-century mosaic frieze of the Apostles. In the centre of the frieze, below the window, is an image of St Heliodorus, the first Bishop of Altinum, whose remains were brought here by the first settlers. It's interesting to compare this image with the gold-plated face mask given to his remains in a Roman sarcophagus in front of the original seventh-century altar. Ruskin described the view from the **campanile** (April–Oct daily 11am–5pm; L3000/€1.55), completed in the twelfth century, as "one of the most notable scenes in this wide world"; after thirty years of being unsafe to visit, the pigeons have been evicted and it has been restructured and cleaned, so now you can see for yourself. It's a 50-metre, easy-going climb to the top; a group leaves every thirty minutes, and tickets are available from the postcard stall at Santa Maria dell'Assunta.

The church of **Santa Fosca** (same hours and ticket as Santa Maria) was built in the eleventh and twelfth centuries to house the body of the eponymous saint, brought to Torcello from Libya some time before 1011 and now resting under the altar. Much restored, the church retains the Greek cross form and a fine exterior apse, and inside, the elegant brick arches and cornerings leading up to its wooden dome. Despite the tourists, both these churches manage to maintain a meditative calm.

In the square outside sits the curious **chair of Attila**. Local legend has it that if you sit in it you will be wed within a year. Behind it is the **Museo dell'Estuario** (Tues–Sun: April–Sept 10am–12.30pm & 2–5.30pm; Oct–March 10am–12.30pm & 2–4pm; L3000/€1.55), which includes thirteenth-century beaten gold figures, sections of mosaic heads, and jewellery. It's all nicely laid out, and worth a visit.

The southern islands

The section of the lagoon to the south of the city, enclosed by the long islands of the **Lido** and **Pellestrina**, has far fewer outcrops of solid land than the northern half: once you get past **Giudecca** and **San Giorgio Maggiore** – which are in effect detached pieces of central Venice – and clear of the smaller islands that dot the water off the middle section of the Lido, you could, on certain days, look in the direction of the mainland and think you were out in the open sea. The nearer islands are the more interesting: the farther-flung settlements of the southern lagoon have played as significant a role in the history of Venice as the better-known northern islands but nowadays they have little going for them other than the pleasure of the trip.

San Giorgio Maggiore

The prominence of Palladio's church of **San Giorgio Maggiore** (daily 9.30am–noon & 2.30–5pm; free) almost forces you to have an opinion as to its architectural merits. Ruskin didn't much care for it: "It is impossible to conceive a design more gross, more barbarous, more childish in conception, more servile in plagiarism, more insipid in result, more contemptible under every point of rational regard." Palladio's successors were more impressed, though, and it was to prove one of the most influential Renaissance church designs. For more on Palladio, see box on p.343.

The finely calculated proportions and Counter-Reformation austerity of the interior reminded Ruskin merely of an assembly room; in his opinion, its paintings were what justified opening the door. Two pictures by Tintoretto hang in the chancel: *The Fall of Manna* and *The Last Supper*, perhaps the most famous of all his images. They were painted as a pair in 1592–94, the last years of the artist's life; another Tintoretto of the same date – a *Deposition* – hangs in the Cappella dei Morti, approached through the door on the right of the choir.

On the left of the choir a corridor leads to the **campanile** (L3000/€1.55); rebuilt in 1791 after the collapse of its predecessor, it's one of the two best vantage points in the city – the other being the campanile of San Marco.

The ex-Benedictine monastery next door to the church, now the base of the combined arts research institute, craft school and naval college known as the **Fondazione Giorgio Cini**, is one of the architectural gems of Venice, and a regular venue for exhibitions (the only time when the Fondazione is open to the public; phone ☎041.528.9900 for details). It incorporates a 128-metre-long dormitory, designed by Giovanni Buora around 1494, a double staircase and a library by Longhena, a magnificent refectory by Palladio and two adjoining cloisters, one planned by Giovanni Buora and built by his son, the other designed by Palladio.

Giudecca

In the earliest records of Venice, the island of **Giudecca** was known as Spina Longa, a name clearly derived from its shape; the modern name might refer to the Jews (*Giudei*) who were based here from the late thirteenth century, or to the disruptive noble families who, from the ninth century, were shoved onto this chain of islets to keep them quiet (*giudicati* meaning "judged"). Before the banks of the Brenta became the prestigious site for one's summer abode, Giudecca was where the wealthiest aristocrats of early Renaissance Venice built their villas, and in places you can still see traces of their gardens. The present-day suburb is a strange mixture of decrepitude and vitality. The boatyards and fishing quays on the south side are interspersed with half-abandoned factories and roofless sheds, and even the side facing the city presents a remarkable economic contrast: at the western edge is the derelict neo-Gothic fortress of the Mulino Stucky, a flour mill built in 1895, and at the other stands the *Cipriani*, the most expensive hotel in Venice.

The Franciscan church of the **Redentore** (Mon–Sat 10am–5pm, Sun 3–5pm; L3000/€1.55), designed by Palladio (see p.343) in 1577, is Giudecca's main monument. In 1575–76 Venice suffered an outbreak of bubonic plague that annihilated nearly 50,000 people – virtually a third of the city's population. The Redentore was built in thanks for Venice's deliverance, and every year until the downfall of the republic the doge and his senators attended a Mass in the church on the Feast of the Redentore to express their continuing gratitude. The procession walked to the church over a pontoon bridge from the Záttere, a ceremony perpetuated by the people of Venice on the third Sunday in July.

The long-overdue restoration of the interior has cleared the clutter, revealing the genius of Palladio's original conception. The bright, clean plasterwork, in particular, reflects the masterful use of different intensities of light in the various parts of the church to draw the eye – and the mind – inward and upward. As the architect wrote, "Among all colours, none can be more suitable for temples than white because the purity of the colour is more acceptable to God". The best paintings in the church, including a *Madonna with Child and Angels* by Alvise Vivarini, are in the sacristy, where you'll be greatly edified by a gallery of eighteenth-century wax heads of illustrious Franciscans, arranged in glass cases all round the room.

San Lazzaro degli Armeni

No foreign community has a longer pedigree in Venice than the Armenians: they were established by the end of the thirteenth century, and for around five hundred years have had a church within a few yards of the Piazza (in Calle degli Armeni). They are far less numerous now, and the most conspicuous sign of their presence is the Armenian island by the Lido, **San Lazzaro degli Armeni** (daily 3–5pm; L10,000/€5.16; take vaporetto #20 just before 3pm), identifiable from the city by the onion-shaped top of its campanile. The Roman Catholic Armenian monastery here was founded in 1717 by Manug di Pietro (known as Mechitar "The Consoler"), and derived its name from the island's past function as a leper colony – Lazarus being the patron saint of lepers.

The Armenian monks have always had a reputation as scholars and linguists, and the monastery's collection of precious manuscripts and books – the former going back to the fifth century – is a highlight, along with a Tiepolo ceiling panel and the room in which Byron stayed while lending a hand with the preparation of an Armenian–English dictionary.

The Lido and the southern lagoon

For about eight centuries, the **Lido** was the focus of the annual hullaballoo of Venice's "Marriage to the Sea", when the doge went out to the Porto di Lido to drop a gold ring into the brine and then disembarked for Mass at San Nicolò al Lido. It was then an unspoilt strip of land, and remained so into the last century. Within thirty years it had become the smartest bathing resort in Italy, and although it's no longer as chic as it was when Thomas Mann set *Death in Venice* here, there's less room on its beaches now than ever before. But unless you're staying at one of the flashy hotels that stand shoulder to shoulder along the seafront, or are prepared to pay a ludicrous fee to rent one of their beach hutches for the day, you won't be allowed to get the choicest Lido sand between your toes. The ungroomed public beaches are at the northern and southern ends of the island – though why people would want to jeopardize their health in these filthy waters is a mystery.

The Film Festival occupies the Lido's Palazzo del Cinema in late August and early September, but the place has little else to recommend it – although inveterate gamblers in possession of a snappy wardrobe might want to investigate the summer casino.

FROM THE LIDO TO CHIOGGIA

The trip across the lagoon to **Chioggia** is a more protracted business than simply taking the land bus from Piazzale Roma, but it will give you a curative dose of salt air and a good knowledge of the lagoon. From Gran Viale Santa Maria Elisabetta – the main street from the Lido landing stage to the seafront – the more or less hourly bus #11 goes down to **Alberoni**, where it drives onto a ferry for the five-minute hop to Pellestrina; the 10km to the southern tip of Pellestrina are covered by road, and then you switch from the bus to a steamer for the 25-minute crossing to Chioggia. The entire journey takes about eighty minutes, and costs L8000/€4.13 for a through-ticket, including the cost of the hop from San Zaccaria to the Lido – but be sure to check the timetable carefully at Gran Viale Santa Maria Elisabetta – not every #11 goes all the way to Chioggia. The quickest way **back to Venice** is by bus from the duomo or Sottomarina to Piazzale Roma, but it's a dispiriting drive, only about ten minutes quicker than the island-hop route and just a thousand lire cheaper (and ACTV passes are not valid, as this is an extra-urban bus service). All in all, your best plan is to get an ACTV pass, and do the entire trip to Chioggia by island-hopping.

The fishing village of **Malamocco**, about 5km into the expedition, is the successor of the ancient settlement which in the eighth century was the capital of the lagoon confederation. In 810 the town was taken by Pepin, son of Charlemagne, and there followed one of the crucial battles in Venice's history, when Pepin's fleet, endeavouring to reach the islands that were to become Venice, became jammed in the mudbanks and was swiftly massacred. After the battle, the capital was promptly transferred to the safer islands of Rivoalto. In 1107 the old town of Malamocco was wiped out by a tidal wave. As the boat crosses from Pellestrina Cimitero to Chioggia, you get the best possible view of what could be described as the last great monument of the republic – the

NEIL SETCHFIELD

The porticoes of Piazza San Carlo, Turin

MICHAEL JENNER

La Mortola gardens, Liguria

PETER WILSON

JAMES MORRIS, AXIOM

The Canal Grande, Venice

Palazzo Ducale, Venice

NEIL SETCHFIELD

Moschino shop display, Milan

PETER W.LSON

The Sala dei Specchi in Mantua's Palazzo Ducale

LEE KAREN STOW

GREG EVANS

Madonna di Campiglio

Crivelli's gardens on Isola Bella

GREG EVANS

SARAH QUILL, VENICE PICTURE LIBRARY

Mosaics, San Marco, Venice

Rialto fish market, Venice

SARAH QUILL, VENICE PICTURE LIBRARY

First day of the Carnevale, Venice

Murazzi. This colossal wall of Istrian boulders, 4km long and 14m thick at the base, was constructed at the sides of the Porto di Chioggia to protect Venice from the battering of the sea, and did its job perfectly from the year of its completion (1782) until the flood of November 1966.

CHIOGGIA

In 1379 **Chioggia** was the scene of the most serious threat to Venice since Pepin's invasion, when the Genoese, after copious shedding of blood on both sides, took possession of the town. Protracted siege warfare resulted in the nearly complete destruction of medieval Chioggia before the surrender of the enemy in June 1380. From then until the arrival of Napoleon's ships nobody broke into the Venetian lagoon.

Modern Chioggia is the second largest settlement in the lagoon after Venice and one of Italy's busiest fishing ports. It's not the most charming of places, and you can see virtually everything worth seeing in a hour's walk along the Corso del Popolo, the principal street in Chioggia's grid layout. The main attractions are the **fish market** (Tues–Sat mornings) and the **Duomo**, which was Longhena's first major commission and possesses some good, if grisly, eighteenth-century paintings.

Buses run from the duomo to **Sottomarina**, Chioggia's downmarket answer to Venice's Lido. On the beaches of Sottomarina you're a fraction closer to nature than you would be on the Lido, and the resort does have one big plus – after your dip you can go back to the Corso and have a fresh seafood meal that's cheaper than any you'd find in Venice's restaurants and better than most.

Eating and drinking

In the early 1990s, the reliably objective judges of the Accademia della Cucina ventured that it was "a rare privilege" to eat well in Venice, and there's more than an element of truth to Venice's reputation as a place where mass tourism has produced homogenized menus and slapdash standards. Venice has fewer good moderately priced **restaurants** than any other major Italian city, it has more really bad restaurants than any other, and in some of the very expensive establishments you're paying not for a fine culinary experience but for the event of dining in a posh Venetian restaurant. However, things have been getting better recently, an improvement due in part to the efforts of the Ristorante della Buona Accoglienza, an association of restaurateurs determined to present the best of genuine Venetian cuisine at sensible prices. In the Venetian context, "sensible" means in the region of L50,000/€25.82 per person, but even in the lower price ranges there are plenty of acceptable little places hidden away in the city's quieter quarters – and some are rather more than merely acceptable.

More than anywhere else in Italy, the division between **bars** and restaurants is often difficult to draw – many of the places listed below under "Restaurants" have a bar area on the street side of the dining room, while some of the "Bars" have basic sit-down areas for eating. We've classified our bars and restaurants according to which aspect of the business draws most of the customers, but if you're looking for a simple meal in a particular area of the city, be sure to check both sets of listings.

Restaurants

Virtually every budget restaurant in Venice advertises a set-price **menù turistico** for as little as L25,000/€12.91, which at its best will offer a choice of three or four dishes for each course. This can be a cheap way of sampling Venetian specialities (though you'd be better off with *cicchetti*, tapas-like portions served in bars), but the quality and certainly the quantity won't be up to the mark of an **à la carte** meal. As a general rule, value for money tends to increase with the distance from San Marco; plenty of restaurants within a short radius of the Piazza offer menus that seem to be reasonable, but you'll probably find the food unappetizing, the portions tiny and the service abrupt. And quality of food aside, an evening expedition into the maze of **Dorsoduro** and **San Polo** or lively **Cannaregio**, the best *sestieri* for dining, is an excellent way to get yourself off the beaten track.

We've supplied the phone numbers for those places where **booking** is advisable; Sunday lunch is particularly busy. Wherever possible, we've also supplied the day of the week on which each restaurant is closed, but bear in mind that many restaurateurs take their annual holiday in August, and that quite a few places close down in the dead weeks of January and early February.

San Marco

Al Bacareto, Calle Crosera 3447. Inexpensive to moderately priced dishes such as the excellent *risotto alla pescatore* (fisherman's risotto) can be eaten either in the dining room or standing at the bar area (the cheaper option). Handy for the Palazzo Grassi. Closed Sun.

Bora Bora, Calle Stagneri. Buzzing, young, good-value pizzeria-restaurant, down an alley off Campo S. Bartolomeo. Ten percent discount for *Rough Guide* readers. Closed Wed.

Da Fiore, Calle delle Botteghe 3461. Established in the mid-1990s, this popular (and expensive) restaurant offers genuine Venetian cuisine in a classy trattoria-style setting. The anteroom is a nice small bar that's open to all, though most of the customers are waiting to go through. Open until midnight. Closed Tues.

Le Bistrot de Venise, Calle dei Fabbri 4685 (*www.bistrotdevenise.com*). This place is done up as a facsimile of a wood-panelled French bistro, but the menu is based on old-style Venetian recipes. The reasonably priced food is fine, though the atmosphere has suffered by proximity to the tourist honeypot of the Piazza. But *Le Bistrot* has preserved something of its role as a community arts centre, with poetry readings, live music and exhibitions. The bar opens at 9am, the kitchen at noon, and food is served until 15min before closing. Open until 1am. No closing day.

Rosticceria San Bartolomeo, Calle della Bissa 5423. Hidden under the arches leading east of Campo San Bartolomeo, downstairs it's a sort of glorified snack-bar, serving pizzas and set meals starting at around L18,000/€9.30 – the trick is to first grab a place at the long tables along the windows, then order from the counter. Good if you need to refuel quickly and cheaply, but can't face another pizza. The rudimentary restaurant upstairs isn't really worth the extra. Closed Mon.

Dorsoduro

Ai Carmini, Calle delle Pazienze, Rio Terrà Scozzera 2893b. If you're looking for a good, inexpensive tourist menu of Venetian specialties, you won't find better, and at L20,000/€10.32 you certainly won't find a better price. Open until 2am. Closed Sun.

Ai Cugnai, Piscina del Forner 857. A few yards to the east of the Accademia, but remarkably unspoilt considering how close it is to one of the city's biggest tourist draws, this is a moderately priced and very welcoming little trattoria, run by a family of gregarious Venetian senior citizens. Closed Mon.

Da Gianni, Fondamenta Záttere 918a. Nicely sited and reasonably priced restaurant-pizzeria, right by the Záttere vaporetto stop. Slightly better than nearby *Alle Záttere*, though the terrace isn't as appealing. Closed Wed.

Montin, Fondamenta di Borgo 1147 (☎041.522.7151). Very highly rated, but the quality is more erratic than you'd expect for the money; you'll pay in the region of L60,000/€30.99 here for what would cost L40,000/€20.66 in some places. It's always been a place for the literary/artistic set – Pound, Hemingway, Peggy Guggenheim and Visconti, for example – and the restaurant doubles as a commercial art gallery. Closed Tues & Wed.

Ai Quattro Ferri, Calle Lunga S. Barnaba. Simple, easy-going and cheap osteria with delicious *cicchetti* and a menu that changes daily. Just off Campo S. Barnaba. Closed Sun.

San Trovaso, Fondamenta Priuli 1016. An efficient two-storey restaurant-pizzeria which is packed most nights with a mix of tourists and locals. Straightforward food in robust portions. Closed Mon.

Al Sole di Napoli, Campo Santa Margherita 3023. Cheap and very cheerful pizzeria – especially pleasant in summer, when its tables colonize the campo. Closed Dec.

San Polo

Crepizza, Calle S. Pantalon 3757. One of the favourites with the university crowd; excellent cheap pizzas and crepes, just south of the Frari. Closed Tues.

Do Spade, Sottoportego delle Do Spade 860. Larger than the nearby *Do Mori* (see p.325), and more touristy – though friendly enough – the tables and menus make it just about qualify as a restaurant. Almost impossible to locate from a map – walk past the *Do Mori* and keep going as straight as possible. Closed Wed, and Sun outside Aug.

Jazz Club 900, Campiello del Sansoni, 900. Follow your nose towards one of the best pizza ovens you'll find in the city, or just follow the signpost off the Ruga Vecchia San Giovanni, by the Rialto bridge. The atmosphere is eccentric, with a dark, heavily pannelled interior and non-stop jazz – live on Thurdsays only. Open until midnight. Closed Mon.

Alla Madonna, Calle della Madonna 594 (☎041.522.3824). Roomy, bustling seafood restaurant that's been going strong for four decades. Little finesse, but the moderate prices here represent good value for money, and many locals rate its kitchen as one of the city's best. Be wary of the wine list, which is expensive for anything beyond the ordinary house carafe. Closed Wed.

Al Nono Risorto, Sottoportego de Siora Bettina 2338. Busy pizzeria-restaurant just off Campo S. Cassiano; has a pleasant garden and a predominantly twenty-something following. Inexpensive to moderate prices. Open until midnight. Closed Wed.

Da Sandro, Campiello dei Meloni. Split-site pizzeria-trattoria, with rooms on both sides of the campiello and tables on the pavement. Often frenetic, though not aggressively so. The pizzas are the best thing they do. Inexpensive to moderate prices. Closed Fri.

La Zucca, Ponte del Megio 1762 (☎041.524.1570). Long a well-respected restaurant, *La Zucca* was once a vegetarian establishment (its name means "pumpkin") but now goes against the Venetian grain by featuring a lot of meat – chicken, lamb, goose, turkey. The quality remains high, the prices reasonable, and the canalside setting is a delight. Closed Sun.

Cannaregio

Alla Pallazina, Rio Terá San Leonardo 1509. Cosy, romantic setting by one of the lovelier bridges, the Ponte delle Guglie, which spans the Cannaregio Canal. The location draws the tourists, and you could pay less elsewhere, but the Venetian cuisine is as good as you'll find anywhere near the station. Open Mon–Thurs from 7pm only; Fri–Sun also open for lunch.

Anice Stellato, Fondamenta Madonna dell'Orto (☎041.720.744). Hugely popular with Venetians for the superb, reasonably priced meals and unfussy atmsophere. Rather too far out for most tourists, though, situated as it is on the northernmost Cannaregio canal. If you can't get a table – it's frequently booked solid – drop by for the excellent *cicchetti* at the bar. Closed Mon.

Casa Mia, Calle dell'Oca 4430. Always heaving with locals, who usually order from the pizza list rather than the menu, though the standard dishes are reliable enough. Closed Tues.

Gam Gam, Fondamenta di Cannaregio 122. A Refreshing change from everything *a la Venexiana*, with an intriguing menu of Israeli, Eastern European and Venetian cuisine, and a mixed clientele of discerning New Yorkers and curious locals. The *cholent*, a chick pea stew, and *latkas*, potato balls, are particularly good. Excellent for vegetarians and, of course, it's all kosher. Ten percent discount for *Rough Guide* readers. Party night Fridays.

Alla Vedova Ca' d'Oro, Calle del Pistor 3912. Just off the Strada Nova, opposite the alley leading to the Ca' d'Oro, this trattoria is vaguely reminiscent of a Victorian parlour, albeit one that's heaving with Venetians, especially later on in the evening. A small blackboard acts as a menu, with a short list of Venetian standards.

Castello

Aciugheta, Campo S. Filippo e Giacomo 4357. A bar with a pizzeria-trattoria next door. The closest spot to San Marco to eat without paying through the nose. Closed Wed.

Corte Sconta, Calle del Pestrin 3886 (☎041.522.7024). Secreted in a tiny lane to the east of San Giovanni in Brágora, this restaurant offers wonderful seafood dishes and far better than average house wine. The *menù degustazione*, costing L70,000/€36.15 (without wine), is probably the best meal that sum will get you in the entire city. Booking absolutely essential. Closed Sun & Mon.

Al Mascaron, Calle Lunga S. Maria Formosa 5225 (☎041.522.5995). Has an arty feel and interesting bar food, but definitely two types of clientele – Italians and non-Italians – with service to match each. Has a good reputation among the locals though and gets very busy, so book if you can. Closed Sun.

Da Remigio, Salizzada dei Greci 3416 (☎041.523.0089). Brilliant, good-value neighbourhood trattoria, serving gorgeous home-made gnocchi. Be sure to book – the locals pack this place every night. Closed Mon evening and Tues.

Dai Tosi, Calle Secco Marina 738. Terrific and moderately priced pizzeria-trattoria, with excellent home-made pasta as well as delicious pizzas. A really buzzing place when the Biennale is on, and devoid of tourists outside the festival. Open until 11.30pm. Closed Wed.

Giudecca

Altanella, Calle dell' Erbe 268 (☎041.522.7780). Highly recommended for its beautiful and reasonably priced fish dishes and the terrace overlooking the island's central canal. Closed Mon.

Harry's Dolci, Fondamenta S. Biagio 773 (☎041.522.4844). Despite the name, sweets aren't the only things on offer here – the kitchen of this offshoot of *Harry's Bar* (see below) is rated by many as the equal of its ancestor. It's actually less expensive, but you're nonetheless talking about a place where the set menu costs L85,000/€43.86 a head, drink excluded. Still, if you want to experience Venetian culinary refinement at its most exquisite, this is it. Closed Tues.

Bars and snacks

Stand at a traditional Venetian **bar**, known as a *bácaro*, any time of the day and you won't have to wait long before someone drops by for a reviving *ombra*, a tiny glass of wine customarily downed in one. The origins of the word are obscure, but may come from the tradition of wine-sellers in the Piazza keeping their bottles cool by standing in the *ombra*, or shade. Most bars also serve some kind of food, ranging from fat little sandwiches in soft white bread, Venice's famous **tramezzini**, through the traditional **cicchetti**, tapas by another name, to proper cooked meals.

San Marco

Bácaro Jazz, Salizzada Fondaco dei Tedeschi. Formerly a branch of *Wendy Burger* (who presumably found the going a bit tough when *McDonald's* moved into town), this place has been reborn as a jazz-themed bar with a menu of old-style *cicchetti*, and is proving a big hit with cool Venetian kids. Open 4pm–2am. Closed Wed.

Da Carla, Sottoportego Corte Contarina. Hidden down a sottoportego off Frezzeria, a couple of paces from the Piazza, *Da Carla* somehow preserves an almost exclusively local clientele, with workers dropping in for simple pasta dishes and salads at L10,000/€5.16 a plate.

Devil's Forest, Calle Stagneri. The liveliest bar in the vicinity of Campo San Bartolomeo, and a convincing facsimile of a British pub, with a good range of beers and a dartboard – though the food is a lot better than you'd find in most real pubs. Open 8am–midnight.

Harry's Bar, Calle Vallaresso 1323. Most glamorous bar in town since time immemorial; famed in equal measure for its cocktails, its sandwiches and its celebrity league prices. Open 3pm–1am. Closed Mon.

Leon Bianco, Salizzada S. Luca 4153. Wood-panelled bar between Campo San Luca and Campo Manin. Good range of sandwiches, and a decent selection of more substantial fare, including excellent value plates of ready-cooked pasta. Open 8am–8pm. Closed Sun.

Vino Vino, Ponte delle Veste 2007. Very close to the Fenice opera house, this is a slightly posey wine bar, but it does stock more than 100 wines. It also serves relatively inexpensive meals as well. Open 10am–midnight. Closed Tues.

Al Volto, Calle Cavalli 4081. This dark little bar is an *enoteca* in the true sense of the word – 1300 wines from Italy and elsewhere, some cheap, many not; good snacks, too. Closed Sun.

Dorsoduro

Il Caffé, Campo S. Margherita. Tiny, buzzing bar known as Caffé Rosso with an elegant interior and outside tables. Opposite Antico Capon, on the largest and most studeny *campo*.

Cantina del Vino già Schiavi, Fondamenta Nani 992. Great bar and wine shop opposite San Trovaso – do some sampling before you buy. Closed Sun.

Corner Pub, Calle della Chiesa 684. Very near the Guggenheim, this place usually has a few arty foreigners in attendance, but they are always outnumbered by locals. Open until 2am. Closed Tues.

San Polo

Antica Ostaria Ruga Rialto, Ruga Vecchia S. Giovanni. Lively bar with a young crowd, though lacking in atmosphere on quiet nights. Good for *cicchetti* and an *ombra*.

Do Mori, Calle Do Mori 429. Hidden just off Ruga Vecchia S. Giovanni, this is the best bar in the market area. Delicious snacks and terrific atmosphere. Open 9am–1pm & 5–8pm. Closed Wed afternoon and all day Sun.

Café Noir, Crosera San Pantalon. Along with the adjacent, and un-marked *Caffè Blu*, this is the absolute favourite student bar. Warm, cosmopolitan atmosphere, with a trendy crowd dropping in for a *spritz* or dabbling on the Internet in the small room at the back.

Cannaregio

Fiddler's Elbow, Corte dei Pali. Self-styled "Irish pub"; usually has a few Venetian lads trying to act rowdily and a smattering of Brits showing them how it's really done, but most of the kids are content with sipping a small glass of Guinness for an hour. Open 5pm–midnight. Closed Wed.

Iguana, Fondamenta della Misericordia 2517. Sits on the borderline between *bácaro* and Mexican cantina, serving reasonably-priced Tex-Mex fare to a young crowd. Live Latin and jazz Tues. Open until 1am; happy hour 6–7.30pm. Closed Mon.

Paradiso Perduto, Fondamenta della Misericordia 2540. Lashings of simple (but not inexpensive) Venetian food are served at the refectory-like tables of *Paradiso Perduto*, but essentially this place is Venice's leading boho bar, attracting students, arty types and the gay community. The bar opens around 7.30pm, the kitchen gets going at 8pm, and the doors close at midnight or later, depending on how things are going. Bar prices higher when live music is playing – usually Sun. Closed Wed.

Cantina Vecia Carbonera, Rio Terrà della Maddalena 2329. Old-style *bácaro* atmosphere, with a young, stylish clientele and playlist. Good wine and plenty of space to sit down. Live jazz on Thursday and Sunday, except in August when the gourmet snacks take over. Open until 2am at weekends. Closed Tues and Wed lunchtime and all day Mon.

Castello

Alla Rampa, Salizzada S. Antonin 3607. Utterly traditional *bácaro* with a nautical flavour. Great for a cheap *ombra* (L1000/€0.52), if you don't mind being the only customer who isn't Venetian, male and over forty.

Cafés, pasticcerie and ice cream

As in every Italian city, the **cafés** are central to social life, and you'll never be more than a couple of minutes from a decent one. In addition to their marvellous local confections, many **pasticcerie** also serve coffee, but will have at most a few bar stools. Strict budgeting is further jeopardized by Venice's **gelaterie**, where ice cream comes in forms you're unlikely to have experienced before.

General areas in which to find good cafés and *pasticcerie* include **Campo Santa Margherita**, **Crosera San Pantalon**, running just south of San Rocco, and **Campiello Meloni** (between S. Polo and S. Aponal), which has a couple of excellent *pasticcerie* whose doors remain open on Sundays.

Florian, Piazza S. Marco 56–59. Opened in 1720 by Florian Francesconi, and frescoed and mirrored in a passable pastiche of that period, this is the café to be seen in. A simple cappuccino will set you back around L10,000 if the band's performing, and you'll have to take out a mortgage for a cocktail. Closed Wed.

Nico, Záttere ai Gesuati; Dorsoduro. A high point of a wander in the area, celebrated for an artery-clogging creation called a *gianduiotto* – a paper cup containing a block of praline ice cream drowned in whipped cream. Closed Thurs.

Paolin, Campo S. Stefano; San Marco. Thought by many to be the makers of the best ice cream in Venice; certainly their pistachio is amazing, and the outside tables have one of the finest settings in the city. Closed Fri.

Rosa Salva, Campo S. Luca, Calle Fiubera and Merceria S. Salvador; all San Marco. Venice's premier catering chain: excellent coffee, very good pastries, but slightly surgical ambience.

Tonolo, Crosera S. Pantalon; San Polo. The busiest café on one of the busiest streets of the student district; especially hectic on Sunday mornings, when the fancy *Tonolo* cakes are in high demand for the day's main meal. Closed Mon.

Takeaways, markets and shops

The campi, parks and canalside steps make **picnicking** a pleasant alternative in Venice, and if you're venturing off to the outer islands it's often the only way of refuelling. Don't try to picnic in the piazzas, though – the bylaws against it are strictly enforced.

Takeaway **pizza** is all over the place, but most of it is pretty miserable fare in Venice. The widest range of take-away pizza slices (*pizza al taglio*) and pies is offered by *Cip Ciap*, across the canal from the west side of Santa Maria Formosa, at Calle Mondo Nuovo 5799 (closed Tues) – their spinach and ricotta pie is especially tasty and filling.

Open-air **markets** for fruit and vegetables are held in various squares every day except Sunday; check out Santa Maria Formosa, Santa Margherita, Campiello dell'Anconetta, Rio Terrà San Leonardo and the barge moored by Campo San Barnaba. The market of markets, however, is the one at the Rialto, where you can buy everything you need for an impromptu feast – it's open Monday to Saturday 8am to 1pm, with a few stalls opening again in the late afternoon.

Virtually every parish has its **alimentari** and most of them are good; one worth singling out is Aliani Gastronomia in Ruga Vecchia S. Giovanni (San Polo) – scores of cheeses, meats and salads that'll have you drooling. Alternatively, you could get everything from one of Venice's well-hidden **supermarkets**. Most central is Su.Ve., on the corner of Salizzada S. Lio and Calle Mondo Nuovo (Castello); others are on Campo S. Margherita (Dorsoduro), Rio Terrà Frari (San Polo), Záttere Ponte Lungo (Dorsoduro) and close to the youth hostel on the main Giudecca waterfront.

Nightlife, shows and festivals

Except when the *Carnevale* is in full swing, Venice after dark is pretty moribund. Locals head to Mestre and the mainland for nightlife, as high rents and zealous noise policing close down as many late bars as manage to open. That said, the city's calendar of special events is often impressive, though the bias is definitely towards high culture. To find out what's on in the way of concerts and films, check *Un Ospite di Venezia*, or go to *www.boxoffice.it* and search under Venezia; for news of events outside the mainstream, check the posters.

Concerts and cinema

Prior to the calamitous fire of 1996, **La Fenice** was the third-ranking Italian opera house after Milan's La Scala and Naples' San Carlo. While the building is being reconstructed, a process that is expected to last into 2002, performances are now held in a vast marquee called the **Palafenice**, over on Tronchetto; a special water bus transports ticket-holders from San Marco to the tent. Tickets for Palafenice can be bought from the temporary box office in the Cassa di Risparmio building on Campo S. Luca (Mon–Fri 8.30am–1.30pm; ☎041.521.0161), or at Palafenice itself (☎041.786.511, fax 041.786.505, *www.tin.it/fenice*), where the box office is open from two hours before the start of the night's show. Prices usually range from L30,000/€15.49 to L60,000/€36.15; the opera season runs from late November to the end of June, punctuated by ballet performances. From March 2001 opera performances (as well as concerts) will also be held at the newly restored **Teatro Malibran**; ask at the tourist office for booking details.

Music performances at the **Goldoni** (box office 9.30am–12.30pm & 4–6pm; ☎041.520.5422, *teatrogo@tin.it*) are somewhat less frequent than at La Fenice; the repertoire here isn't as straitlaced, with a **jazz** series cropping up every now and then. For most of the year the Goldoni specializes in the works of the eponymous writer. **Classical** concerts, with a strong bias towards the eighteenth century, are also performed at three Scuole Grande (San Giovanni Evangelista, San Rocco and San Teodoro), at the Palazzo Mocenigo (San Stae) and Palazzo Querini-Stampalia (☎041.271.1411), and at the churches of Santo Stefano, the Frari, San Samuele, Zitelle, San Barnaba, the Ospedaletto and the Pietà (the most regularly used – it specializes in Vivaldi in particular). The average ticket price for these concerts is L30,000/€15.49 (often with a L10,000/€5.16 reduction for students and children), which is expensive for performances more often distinguished by enthusiasm than professionalism – for the same price you can get to hear real stars at La Fenice.

Venice's **cinemas** show a typically depressing selection of the worst Hollywood offering badly dubbed into Italian. But between June and August, however, an open-air cinema in Campo S. Polo shows dubbed or Italian-language films to a high-spirited local audience. Films start each night at around 9pm, and it's worth the trip if only for the atmosphere.

Late bars

Upbeat and downmarket from the theatre and classical concerts, some **bars** play music late and approach a **pub** (current jargon for the ubiquitous "disco-bar") atmosphere. We've listed likely venues under bars (pp.324–5), but trends and nights change so fast that it can be best to head for one or two areas and just follow the noise. The best nightlife is found along the Fondamenta della Misericordia, in Cannaregio, where *La Bagatela, Iguana* and *Paradiso Perduto* (see "Bars") stay open late and have occasional DJs or live music. Dorsoduro, on and around the studenty Campo S. Margherita, is another good bet, though many bars close earlier; try *DuChamp*, which stays open until 1am. To really get down, however, there's only one option, *Casanova* (☎041.534.7479, *www.casanova.it*), on the Lista di Spagna. As a huge, old-fashioned **disco-club** it would be half empty anywhere else. In Venice it's packed from Wednesday to Saturday, and has a good-time atmosphere as a result. The current regime is salsa (Wed), student/indie-pop (Thurs), classic dance (Fri), house (Sat); don't even think about arriving before 2am.

Exhibitions – and the Biennale

In addition to those permanent museums that hold one-off exhibitions from time to time, Venice has numerous venues for temporary shows, of which the Fiat-owned **Palazzo Grassi** (☎199.139.139, *www.palazzograssi.it*) maintains the highest standards. There's also the **Venice Biennale** (☎041.521.8842, *www.labiennale.org*), set up in 1895 as a showpiece for international contemporary art and held from June to September of every odd-numbered year. Its permanent site in the Giardini Pubblici has pavilions for about forty countries (the largest for Italy's representatives), plus space for a thematic international exhibition. Supplementing this central part of the Biennale is the **Aperto** ("Open"), a mixed exhibition showing the work of younger, or less established artists – often more exciting than the main event. The Aperto takes over spaces all over the city: the salt warehouses on the Záttere, for instance, or the Corderie in the Arsenale. Over and above this, various sites throughout the city host fringe exhibitions, installations and performances, particularly in the opening weeks. Exhibits from earlier years, plus a fabulous collection of magazines and catalogues from all over the world, are kept in the **archive** in the Palazzo Corner della Regina, close to Ca' Pésaro; entrance is free.

Festivals

The *Carnevale* and the Film Festival might be the best publicized of the city's festivals, but the calendar is strewn with other special events, most of them with religious or commemorative origins.

Carnevale

The Venice **Carnevale** occupies the ten days leading up to Lent, finishing on Shrove Tuesday with a masked ball for the glitterati and dancing in the Piazza for the plebs. Revived spontaneously in the 1970s, it is now supported by the city authorities, who organize various pageants and performances. (Details from the San Marco tourist office – see p.278) Apart from these events, *Carnevale* is an endless parade. During the day people don costumes and go to the Piazza to be photographed, while business types can be seen doing their shopping in the classic white mask, black cloak and tricorne hat. In the evening some congregate in the remoter squares, while those who have spent hundreds of pounds on their costumes install themselves in the windows of Florian's and pose for a while. Many private palaces open their doors to themed feasts, some of which you'll be able to visit; ask at the tourist office for more details. **Masks** are on sale throughout the year in Venice, but special mask and costume shops magically appear during *Carnevale*, and Campo San Maurizio sprouts a marquee with mask-making demonstrations and a variety of designs for sale.

La Sensa

The feast of **La Sensa** happens in May on the Sunday after Ascension Day – the latter the day on which the doge performed the wedding of Venice to the sea. The ritual has recently been revived – a distinctly feeble procession that ends with the mayor and a gang of other dignitaries getting into a present-day approximation of the *Bucintoro* (the state barge) and sailing off to the Lido. Of more interest is the **Vogalonga** (long row), held on the same day. Open to any crew in any class of rowing boat, it covers a 32-kilometre course from the Bacino di San Marco out to Burano and back; the competitors arrive at the mouth of the Canal Grande anywhere between about 11am and 3pm.

Santa Maria della Salute

Named after the church of the Salute, this centuries-old feast day is a reminder of the devastating plague of 1630–31. The church was built in thanks for deliverance from the outbreak, and every November 21 since then the Venetians have processed over a pontoon bridge across the Canal Grande to give thanks for their good health, or to pray for sick friends and relatives. It offers the only chance to see the church as it was designed to be seen – with its main doors open, and with hundreds of people milling up the steps and round the building.

La Festa del Redentore

Another plague-related festival, this time to mark the end of the 1576 epidemic. Celebrated on the third Sunday in July, the day is centred on Palladio's church of the Redentore, which was built by way of thanksgiving for the city's escape. A bridge of boats is strung across the Giudecca canal to allow the faithful to walk over to the church, and on the Saturday night hundreds of people row out for a picnic on the water. The night ends with a grand fireworks display, after which it's traditional to make for the Lido to watch the sun rise.

The Regata Storica

Held on the first Sunday in September, the **Regata Storica** is the annual trial of strength and skill for the city's gondoliers and other expert rowers. It starts with a procession of richly decorated historic craft along the Canal Grande course, their crews all decked out in period dress. Bystanders are expected to support contestants in the main event, and may even be issued with appropriate colours.

The Film Festival

The **Venice Film Festival** – the world's oldest – takes place on the Lido every year in late August and early September. The tourist office will have the festival programme a few weeks in advance, as will the two cinemas where the films are shown – the main **Palazzo del Cinema** (Lungomare G. Marconi) and the **Astra** (Via Corfu). Tickets are available for the general public, but you have to go along and queue for them on the day of performance. Outside the festival season, the Palazzo and Astra are run as ordinary commercial cinemas.

Listings

ACTV enquiries Piazzale Roma, daily 7.30am–8pm (☎041.528.7886, *www.activ.it*).

Airlines Alitalia, Salizzada S. Moisè, San Marco 1463 (☎041.520.0355); British Airways, Riva degli Schiavoni, Castello 4191 (☎041.528.5026); TWA, Salizzada S. Moisè, San Marco 1475 (☎041.520.3219).

Airport enquiries ☎041.260.6111, *www.veniceairport.it*.

American Express The American Express office is in Salizzada S. Moisè, a couple of minutes' walk west of the Piazza; Mon–Fri 9am–5.30pm, Sat 9am–12.30pm; emergency number ☎041.1678.72.000 (toll-free).

Banks Banca Commerciale Italiana, Calle Larga XXII Marzo, San Marco 2188; Banca d'Italia, Campo S. Bartolomeo, San Marco 4799; Banca Credito Italiano, Campo S. Salvador, San Marco; Banco Ambrosiano Veneto, Calle Goldoni, San Marco 4481; Banco di Roma, Mercerie dell'Orologio, San Marco 191; Banco San Marco, Calle Larga XXII Marzo, San Marco 383.

Car rental At Marco Polo airport: Eurodollar (☎041.541.5570); Hertz (☎041.541.6075); Italy by Car (☎041.541.6049). At Piazzale Roma: Autorent (☎041.520.9907); Avis (☎041.522.5825); Eurodollar (☎041.528.9551); Europcar (☎041.523.8616); Hertz (☎041.528.3524); Mattiazzo (☎041.528.9494); Sixt (☎167.018.668).

Consulates and embassies The British consulate is opposite the Accademia in the Palazzo Querini, Dorsoduro 1051 (☎041.522.7207); this office is staffed by an honorary consul – the closest full consulate is in Milan. The nearest US consulate is also in Milan. Travellers from Ireland, Australia, New Zealand and Canada should contact their Rome embassies.

Exchange There are clusters of exchange bureaux (*cambios*) where most tourists gather – near San Marco, the Rialto and the train station. Open late every day of the week, they can be useful in emergencies, but their rates of commission and exchange tend to be steep. The best rates are at American Express and the main banks (see above).

Hospital Ospedale Civile, Campo SS. Giovanni e Paolo (☎041.523.0000).

Internet access A number of dedicated Internet points have opened in the last couple of years, most charging around L10,000/€5.16 per 30min, though rates tend to drop the longer you stay online. *Venetian Navigator* has two of the most convenient places, both near Piazza San Marco, on Spadaria and Casselleria. The large *Internet Café* on Campo S. Stefano is also well-potistioned, near the Ponte dell'Accademia. *Play the Game* can be found just northeast of the Piazza, on Calle Lunga S. Maria Formosa, in Castello. *Omniservice* is a short walk from near Piazzale Roma, behind the Giardini ex-Papadópoli on Fondamenta dei Tolentini. Dorsoduro and San Polo are well-served, with

Internet Points on Campo S. Margherita and Calle Lunga S. Pantalon; nearby, on Crosera S.Pantalon is the congenial *Café Noir* (see p.325).

Laundries In Salizzada del Pistor, Cannaregio 4553, near SS. Apostoli; or Lavaget, on Fondamenta Pescaria, Cannaregio 1269, off Rio Terrà S. Leonardo.

Left luggage The desk at the end of platform 14 in the train station charges L5,000/€2.58 per item per 12 hours. The lockers alongside platform 1 are slightly more expensive at L3000/€1.55 per 6 hours. Both open 24hr.

Lost property If you lose anything on the train or at the station, call ☎041.785.238; at Piazzale Roma or on the bus, call ☎041.522.4576; at the airport call ☎041.260.6436; on the *vaporetti* call ☎041.272.2179; and anywhere in the city itself call the town hall on ☎041.520.8844.

Passports In the event of a lost passport, notify the *Questura* in Mestre, at Via Nicoldi 24 (☎041.271.5511) and then your consulate or embassy (see previous page).

Police To notify police of a theft, report to the carabinieri's Pronto Intervento Stranieri office on Fondamenta S. Lorenzo (☎041.520.4777); in emergencies, ring ☎113.

Post offices Venice's main post office is in the Fondaco dei Tedeschi, near the Rialto bridge. Any poste restante should be addressed to Fermo Posta, Fondaco dei Tedeschi, 80100 Venezia; it can be collected Mon–Sat 8.15am–6.45pm – take your passport with you. Stamps are on sale Mon–Sat 8.15am–7pm; the telegram service operates round the clock. The principal branch post offices are in Calle dell'Ascensione, immediately west of the Piazza (Mon–Fri 8.10am–1.25pm, Sat 8.10am–noon) and at Záttere 1406 (same hours). Stamps can also be bought in *tabacchi*, as well as in some gift shops.

Public toilets On most *campi* you'll now see a small, often yellow, sign directing you to the nearest toilet; the charge is L1000/€0.52. Toilets are to be found in most of the city's bars as well – it's diplomatic to buy a drink before availing yourself of the facility, but it's not a legal requirement. In practice it's best to ask in places off the main thoroughfares, if only for the sake of the long-suffering restaurateurs. *McDonald's* on Campo San Bartolomeo is a supremely well-sited venue, right by the Rialto.

Telephones All Venice's public call-boxes accept phonecards (the vast majority accept nothing but cards), but for lengthy long-distance calls it might be best to go to one of the two main Telecom Italia offices, where you can dial direct and be charged afterwards. The offices are at Piazzale Roma (daily 8am–9.30pm) and adjoining the main post office (Mon–Fri 8.30am–12.30pm & 4–7pm).

Train enquiries Central enquiries ☎147.888.088; Venice enquiries ☎041.785.111, *www. fs-on-line.com*.

THE VENETO

Virtually every acre of the Veneto bears the imprint of Venetian rule. In **Belluno**, right under the crags of the Dolomites, the style of the buildings declares the town's former allegiance. A few kilometres away, the Lion of St Mark looks over the central square of the hill-town of **Feltre**, as it does over the market square of **Verona**, on the Veneto's western edge. On the flatlands of the Po basin (the southern border of the region) and on farming estates all over the Veneto, the elegant **villas** of the Venetian nobility are still standing.

> Note that the area of the Veneto to the **north of Belluno** is covered as part of the Dolomites (see the *Trentino-Alto Adige* chapter, p.233), while the eastern shore of **Lago di Garda** is covered with the rest of the lakes region in the *Lombardy and the Lakes* chapter (see p.156).

Yet the Veneto is as diverse culturally as it is geographically. The aspects of Verona that make the city so attractive were created long before the expansion of Venice's *terra firma* empire, and in **Padua** – a university seat since the thirteenth century – the civilization of the Renaissance displays a character quite distinct from that which evolved in Venice. Even in **Vicenza**, which reached its present form mainly during its long period of subservience, the very appearance of the streets is proof of a fundamental independence.

Nowadays this is one of Italy's wealthiest regions. Verona, Padua, Vicenza and **Treviso**, 30km north of Venice, are all major industrial and commercial centres, while intensive dairies, fruit farms and vineyards (around Conegliano, for example) have made the Veneto a leading agricultural producer too.

The Veneto's densest concentration of industry is at **Mestre** and **Marghera**, the grim conurbation through which all road and rail lines from Venice pass before spreading out over the mainland. It's less a city than an economic life-support system for Venice, and the negative impression you get on your way through is entirely valid. Some people trim their holiday expenses by staying in Mestre's cheaper hotels (Venice's tourist offices will supply addresses), but venturing further inland is a more pleasurable cost-cutting exercise.

The Brenta

The southernmost of the three main rivers that empty into the Venetian lagoon, the **Brenta** caused no end of trouble to the earliest settlers on both the mainland and the islands, with its frequent flooding and its deposits of silt. By the sixteenth century, though, the canalization of the river had brought it under control, and it became a favoured building site for the Venetian aristocracy. Some of these Venetian villas were built as a combination of summer residence and farmhouse – many, however, were intended solely for the former function. The period from mid-June to mid-November was the season of the *villeggiatura*, when the patrician families of Venice would load their best furniture onto barges and set off for the relative coolness of the Brenta.

Around one hundred **villas** are left standing on the river between Padua and Venice: some are derelict, a large number are still inhabited and a handful are open to the public. Of this last category, two are outstanding – the **Villa Fóscari** and the **Villa Pisani** – both of which are easily accessible by bus from Venice: four ACTV buses go to the former (L1400/€0.72), and the hourly Padua buses go past the latter (L4000/€2.07). Don't be tempted by the widely advertised boat trips along the Brenta – they cost upwards of L100,000/€51.65 and stop longer for lunch than at any of the villas.

The Villa Fóscari

The **Villa Fóscari** at **MALCONTENTA** (May–Oct Tues & Sat 9am–noon; L10,000/€5.16) was designed in 1559 by Palladio (see box on p.343) and is the nearest of his villas to Venice. Most of Palladio's villas fall into two broad groups: those built on cohesive farming estates, with a central low block for living quarters and wings for storage and associated uses (the Villa Barbaro at Maser and the Villa Emo near Castelfranco); and the large, single-block villas, built for landowners whose fields were dispersed or in some way unsuitable for the construction of a major building. The Villa Fóscari is the masterpiece of this second group, powerfully evoking the architecture of ancient Rome by its heavily rusticated exterior, its massive Ionic portico and its two-storey main hall – a space inspired by the baths of Rome.

The frescoes in the living rooms include what is said to be a portrait of a woman of the Fóscari family who was exiled here as punishment for an amorous escapade, and whose subsequent misery, according to legend, was the source of the name Malcontenta. The reality is more prosaic – the area was known by that name long before the Fóscari arrived, either because of some local discontent over the development of the land or because of the political *malcontenti* who used to hide out in the nearby salt marshes.

The Villa Pisani

The **Villa Pisani** (or Nazionale) at **STRA** (Tues–Sun: April–Sept 9am–6pm; Oct–March 9am–4pm; L8000/€4.13), virtually on the outskirts of Padua, looks more like a product of the *ancien régime* than a house for the Venetian gentry. Commissioned by way of celebration when Alvise Pisani was elected Doge of Venice in 1735, it was the biggest such residence to be built in Venetian territory during that century. It has appealed to megalomaniacs ever since: Napoleon bought it off the Pisani in 1807 and handed it over to Eugène Beauharnais, his stepson and Viceroy of Italy; and in 1934 it was the place chosen for the first meeting of Mussolini and Hitler.

Most of what you see is unexciting and sparsely furnished. But stick with it for the ballroom, its ceiling covered with a fresco of *The Apotheosis of the Pisani Family*, painted by Giambattista Tiepolo at the age of 66; a dazzling performance, it's as full of blue space as it could be without falling apart. And if you're trying to puzzle out what's going on – the Pisani family, accompanied by Venice, are being courted by the Arts, Sciences and Spirits of Peace, while Fame plays a fanfare in praise of the Pisani and the Madonna looks on with appropriate pride.

Padua

Extensively reconstructed after the damage caused by bombing in World War II, and hemmed in by the sprawl that has accompanied its development as the most important economic centre of the Veneto, **PADUA** (PADOVA) is not immediately the most alluring city in northern Italy. It is, however, one of the most ancient, and plentiful evidence remains of its impressive lineage. A large student population creates a young, vibrant atmosphere and the city has undoubtedly the best nightlife within reach of Venice. As a result, more and more people use Padua as a base from which to make day-trips to its overcrowded neighbour.

A Roman municipium from 45 BC, the city thrived until the barbarian onslaughts and the subsequent Lombard invasion at the start of the seventh century. Recovery was slow, but by the middle of the twelfth century, when it became a free commune, Padua was prosperous once again. The university was founded in 1221, and a decade later the city became a place of pilgrimage following the death here of St Anthony.

In 1337 the **Da Carrara** family established control. Under their domination, Padua's cultural eminence was secured – Giotto, Dante and Petrarch were among those attracted here – but Carraresi territorial ambitions led to conflict with Venice, and in 1405 the city's independence ended with its conquest by the neighbouring republic. Though politically nullified, Padua remained an artistic and intellectual centre: Donatello and Mantegna both worked here, and in the seventeenth century Galileo researched at the university, where the medical faculty was one of the most ambitious in Europe. With the fall of the Venetian Republic the city passed to Napoleon, who handed it over to the Austrians, after whose regime Padua was annexed to Italy in 1866.

Arrival, information and accommodation

Trains arrive in the north of the town, just a few minutes' walk up Corso del Popolo from the old city walls. The main **bus station** is at Piazzale Boschetti, immediately north of the walls to the east of the Corso; however, you'll find **local buses** for the city and for

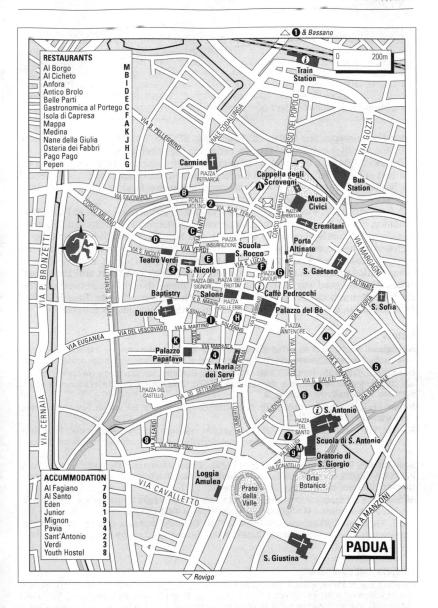

all the nearby towns described in this chapter also stop at the train station. The main **tourist office**, at the train station (summer Mon–Sat 9am–7pm, Sun 9am– 12.30pm; winter Mon–Sat 9.20am–5.45pm, Sun 9am–noon; ☎049.875.2077, *www.padova.it/apt*), stocks free maps and lists of accommodation, and there is a booth at Piazza del Santo

The comprehensive ticket called **Padova Arte** costs L15,000/€7.75 and allows one visit to the Musei Civici (including the Cappella Scrovegni), the Palazzo della Ragione, Baptistry, Scuola del Santo, Museo Antoniano and the Orto Botanico within one year of purchase. It is available at the tourist office and the above museums and monuments. If you're heading south of Padua it might also be worth getting the **Padova Itinerante** card, which costs L15,000/€7.75 and gives access to various sites around Padua, including the castle at Monsélice (see p.340) and the Petrarch's housr (see p.340).

(Mon–Sat 9am–6pm, Sun 9.30am–12.30pm; ☎049.875.3087) which is only open in summer. Another all-year office in Piazzetta Pedrocchi is planned to open soon.

Internet points can be found at the unmistakeably decorated *American Dream Pub*, just east of Piazza dell' Erbe, and at the large *Ludoteca* on Piazza Petrarca, just behind the Basilica del Carmine, in the north of town. Both keep café hours (don't expect them to be open in the late afternoon) and close late.

A few years ago it was infinitely simpler to find an inexpensive room in Padua than in Venice; it's still the case that the average cost is lower, but availability can be a problem given the growing popularity of the city as a base for Venice. If you're visiting in high season, be prepared for a slightly protracted search, but don't despair – Padua has plenty of reasonably priced hotels, and the tourist office has a full list. If you don't mind being a little further from the centre you could try Padua's new **"Bed and Breakfast"** places. This is a good way to see an Italian family home, though bear in mind that this can have its drawbacks in terms of noise, getting home late and so on. Ring Koko Nor (☎049.864.3394, *kokornor@intercity.it*), the group which co-ordinates the scheme.

Hotels

Al Fagiano, Via Locatelli 45 (☎049.875.3396). Fairly large two-star near the basilica. The rooms have a rather spartan Eighties' style but are clean and of a decent size, with huge double beds. ④.

Eden, Via C.Battisti 255 (☎049.650.484). A mixed bag of rooms, but most are a cut above the average one-star and all doubles have showers and TV. Excellent value given the location near Piazza del Santo, in the university quarter. ②.

Junior, Via L. Faggin 2 (☎049.611.756). Acceptable one-star, close to the station. Just seven rooms, some with shared bathrooms. ①.

Mignon, Via Belludi 22 (☎049.661.722). Comfortable, relatively plush two-star between Prato delle Valle and the basilica. They also have rooms that sleep three and four, which can work out cheaper. ③.

Sant'Antonio, Via San Fermo 118 (☎049.875.1393). Pleasant two-star in the northern part of central Padua. Slightly faded modern interiors, but decent enough; the best rooms, at the back, have a view over the canal and the lovely Ponte Molino. ②.

Al Santo, Via del Santo 147 (☎049.875.2131). Ordinary one-star right by the basilica. Needs a refit, but the rooms are clean and bright and all doubles have a bathroom. ②.

Verdi, Via Dondi dell'Orologio 7 (☎049.875.5774). Centrally located and inexpensive one-star. Simple rooms with wooden floors and ill-matched furnishings; just three bathrooms between fifteen rooms. ①.

Hostels and campsites

Ostello Città di Padova, Via A. Aleardi 30 (☎049.875.2219, fax 049.654.210). Padua's HI hostel is a short walk west of the Prato della Valle – or take bus #3 or #18 from the train station. Very quiet and friendly, with washing machines, Internet access and bike hire, but has an 11pm curfew. Check-in 7–9.30am and 5–11pm. L23,000/€11.88, including breakfast.

Montegrotto Terme, Strada Romana Aponense 104 (☎049.793.400). This is the nearest campsite to Padua – 15km from the city centre, but frequent trains take around 15min; a very upmarket site, it boasts not merely a swimming pool but thermal baths too. March to mid-Nov.

The City

From the train station, the Corso del Popolo, later the Corso Garibaldi lead south through a gap in the Renaissance city walls towards the centre of the city, passing after a short distance the **Cappella degli Scrovegni** and **Musei Civici** (Tues–Sun: Feb–Oct 9am–7pm; Nov–Jan 9am–6pm; entrance included in Padova Arte ticket, see box opposite; €5.16 for joint ticket; Cappella is also open on its own on Mon; L7000/€3.62). For many people the **Giotto frescoes** (L2000/€1.03 surcharge; ☎049.820.4550) in the Scrovegni, considered to be one of the key works in the development of European art, are *the* reason for coming to Padua, but even if you're no expert the chapel exerts an extraordinary presence. If anything the sense of drama has been increased by the new airlock entrance system, recently installed in an attempt to reverse the damage caused to the frescoes by high levels of humidity borne by the breath and clothing of visitors. At the time printed on your ticket, the glass door to the waiting room slides open to allow the next set of visitors in – and immediately shuts again, anyone left outside being forced to pay up and book another slot. Once inside, a high-tech system adjusts the air humidity of the waiting room down to that of the chapel itself and filters away the worst of the spores and pollution. Fourteen minutes later another door leading to the chapel itself opens and you have exactly a quarter of an hour to take in the frescoes before being ejected through a third glass door back into the grounds of the museum. Visits are restricted to a maximum of twenty-five people at a time and given the popularity of the Scrovegni it's worth booking around three days in advance. If you're travelling in a group, however, or at weekends during high season it's worth booking as much as a month ahead; out of season, you can usually just turn up and wait.

The chapel was commissioned in 1303 by Enrico Scrovegni in atonement for his father's usury, which was so vicious that he was denied a Christian burial. As soon as the walls were built, Giotto was commissioned to cover them with illustrations of the life of Mary, the life of Jesus and the story of the Passion; the finished cycle, arranged in three tightly-knit tiers and painted against a backdrop of saturated blue, is one of the high points in the development of European art. The Scrovegni series is a marvellous demonstration of Giotto's innovative attention to the inner nature of his subjects. In terms of sheer physical presence and the relationships between the figures and their environment, Giotto's work takes the first important strides towards realism and humanism. The Joachim series on the top row of the north wall (on your right as you walk in) is particularly powerful – note the exchange of looks between the two shepherds in the *Arrival of Joachim*. Beneath the main pictures are shown the vices and virtues in human (usually female) form, while on the wall above the door is a *Last Judgement* – in rather poor condition and now thought to be only partly by Giotto – with rivers of fire leading from God to hell. Directly above the door is a portrait of Scrovegni presenting the chapel; his tomb is at the far end, behind the altar with its statues by **Giovanni Pisano**.

The neighbouring **Musei Civici degli Eremitani** (same hours and ticket as above), formerly the monastery of the Eremitani, is a superbly presented three-part museum complex. The archeological collection, on the ground floor, has a vast array of pre-Roman, Roman and paleo-Christian objects. Upstairs, the vast **Museo d'Arte** houses an extensive assembly of fourteenth- to nineteenth-century art from the Veneto and further afield. The collection is arranged in chronological order, and it's a fairly long walk through tracts of workaday stuff, but names such as Titian, Tintoretto and Tiepolo leaven the mix. Spectacular highpoints are provided by the Giotto *Crucifixion* that was once in the Scrovegni chapel, and a fine *Portrait of a Young Senator* by Bellini. The Capodilista collection, an offshoot of the main gallery, has a pair of mysterious Titian and Giorgione landscapes, and some good Luca Giordano grotesques. The **Museo Bottacin**, for more specialist tastes, was founded in 1865 and contains over 50,000 coins, medals and seals, making it one of the most important museums of its type in the world.

The Eremitani

The nearby church of the **Eremitani**, built at the turn of the fourteenth century, was almost completely wrecked by an Allied bombing raid in 1944 and has been fastidiously rebuilt (summer Mon–Sat 8.15am–12.15pm & 4–6pm, Sun 9.30am–12.15pm & 4–6pm; winter Mon–Sat closes 5.30pm, Sun closes 5pm). Photographs to the left of the apse show the extent of the damage, the worst aspect of which was the near-total destruction of **Mantegna**'s frescoes of the lives of St James and St Christopher – the war's severest blow to Italy's artistic heritage.

Produced between 1454 and 1457, when Mantegna was in his mid-twenties, the frescoes were unprecedented in the thoroughness with which they exploited fixed-point perspective – a concept central to Renaissance humanism, with its emphasis on the primacy of individual perception. The extent of his achievement can now be assessed only from the fuzzy photographs and the sad fragments preserved in the chapel to the right of the high altar. On the left wall is the *Martyrdom of St James*, put together from fragments found in the rubble; and on the right is the *Martyrdom of St Christopher*, which had been removed from the wall before the war.

Piazza del Santo and the basilica

Apart from the encampment of stalls selling decorated candles and outsize souvenir rosaries, the main sight of the Piazza del Santo, a 10min walk south, is Donatello's **Monument to Gattamelata** (which translates literally as "The Honeyed Cat"), as the *condottiere* Erasmo da Narni was known. He died in 1443 and this monument was raised ten years later, the earliest large bronze sculpture of the Renaissance. A direct precursor to Verrocchio's monument to Colleoni in Venice, it could hardly be more different: Gattamelata was known for his honesty and dignity, and Donatello has given us an image of comparative sensitivity and restraint, quite unlike Verrocchio's image of power through force. The modelling of the horse makes a double allusion: to the equestrian statue of Marcus Aurelius in Rome, and to the horses of San Marco.

Within eighteen months of his death, St Anthony had been canonized and his tomb was attracting enough pilgrims to warrant the building of the Basilica di San Antonio, or **Il Santo** (daily: summer 6.30am–7.45pm; winter 6.30am–7pm). It was not until the start of the fourteenth century that the church reached a state that enabled the saint's body to be placed in the Cappella del Santo (in the left transept). Plastered with such votive offerings as photographs of limbs healed by the saint's intervention, the shrine is irresistible to the voyeur. The chapel's more formal decoration, quite ignored by the religiose and voyeuristic alike, includes the most important series of relief sculpture created in sixteenth-century Italy, a sequence of nine marble panels showing scenes from the life of St Anthony. Carved between 1505 and 1577, most have the names of their sculptors incised into the base, Antonio Lombardo, Tullio Lombardo and Jacopo Sansovino being among the most famous.

Adjoining the chapel is the Cappella della Madonna Mora (named after its fourteenth-century French altar statue), which in turn gives onto the Cappella del Beato Luca, whose fourteenth-century frescoes include a lovely image of St James lifting a prison tower to free a prisoner. Back in the aisle, just outside the Cappella del Santo, is Padua's finest work by Pietro Lombardo, the monument to Antonio Roselli (1467). More impressive still are the high altar's bronze sculptures and reliefs by Donatello (1444–45), the works that introduced Renaissance classicism to Padua. Built onto the farthest point of the ambulatory, the **Cappella del Tesoro** (daily 7am–1pm & 2.30–7pm) houses the tongue and vocal chords of St Anthony, as well as a host of lesser relics. For more on St Anthony and the basilica, enter the cloisters (on the south side of the basilica) and follow the signs for the **Museo Antoniano** (summer daily 9am–1pm & 2.30–6.30pm; winter Tues–Fri 10am–1pm & 2–5pm, Sat & Sun 9am–1pm & 2–5pm; L5000/€2.58), which includes the **Mostra Antoniana** (closes 30min earlier; free). The former, on the first floor, is a collection of paintings (including the fresco of *St Anthony and St Bernardino* by **Mantegna**), ornate incense holders, ceremonial robes and other paraphernalia linked to the basilica; the latter, on the ground floor, is a history of votive gifts.

The south side of the piazza

To the left as you leave the basilica are the **Oratorio di San Giorgio** and **Scoletta del Santo**. The oratory (daily: April–Sept 9am–12.30pm & 2.30–7pm; Oct–March 9am–12.30pm & 2.30–5pm; L3000/€1.55) was founded in 1377 as a mortuary chapel, and its frescoes by **Altichiero di Zevio** and **Jacopo Avanzi** were completed soon after. One wall is adorned by the wonderfully titled *St Lucy Remains Immoveable at an Attempt to Drag Her with the Help of Oxen to a House of Ill Repute.*

The Scoletta (same hours as above; L3000/€1.55) was founded soon after Anthony's canonization, though this building only goes back as far as the early fifteenth century. The ground floor is still used for religious purposes, while upstairs is maintained to look pretty much as it would have in the sixteenth century, with its fine ceiling and paintings dating mainly from 1509–15. Four of the pictures are said to be by Titian.

Next door to the Scuola, the **Museo al Santo** is used for one-off exhibitions, often drawing on the resources of the Musei Civici.

One way to relax from all this art is to stroll round the corner to the **Orto Botanico**, the oldest botanic gardens in Europe (summer daily 9am–1pm & 3–6pm; winter Mon–Sat 9am–1pm; L5000/€2.58). Planted in 1545 by the university's medical faculty as a collection of medicinal herbs, the gardens are laid out much as they were originally, and the specimens on show haven't changed too much either. Goethe came here in 1786 to see a palm tree that had been planted in 1585; the selfsame tree still stands.

The Prato della Valle and Santa Giustina

A little to the south sprawls the **Prato della Valle**, claimed to be the largest town square in Italy; it's a generally cheerless area, ringed by over-wide roads, but the vast Saturday market and the summer funfair do a lot to make it jollier.

One side is fronted by the sixteenth-century **Basilica di Santa Giustina** (summer daily 8.30am–noon & 3–7pm; winter Mon–Fri closes 5.30pm, Sat closes 6.45pm, Sun closes 7.30pm). A pair of fifteenth-century griffins, one holding a knight and the other a lion, are the only notable adornments to the unclad brick facade; the freezing interior has little of interest except a huge *Martyrdom of St Justina* by Paolo Veronese (in the apse), some highly proficient carving on the choir stalls, and the sarcophagus which once contained the relics of Luke the Evangelist (apse of left transept).

More appealing are the vestiges of the church's earlier incarnations. In the right transept a stone arch opens onto the **Martyrs' Corridor**, a composite of fifth- to twelfth-century architectural fragments that leads to the **Sacellum di Santa Maria e San Prosdocimo**, burial place of St Prosdocimus. He was the first bishop of Padua back in the fourth century, when the church was founded, and is depicted here on a fifth-century panel. The fifteenth-century **old choir**, reached by a chain of corridors from the left-hand chapel of the right transept, has choir stalls inset with splendid marquetry panels.

To the university

Via Umberto I leads up towards the **university**, the main block of which is the **Palazzo del Bò** (The Ox – named after an inn that used to stand here). Established in September 1221, the University of Padua is older than any other in Italy except that of Bologna, and the coats of arms which encrust the courtyard and Great Hall attest to the social and intellectual rank of its alumni. The first permanent **anatomy theatre** was built here in 1594, a facility that doubtless greatly helped William Harvey, who went on to develop the theory of blood circulation after taking his degree here in 1602. Galileo taught physics here from 1592 to 1610, declaiming from a lectern that is still on show. And in 1678 Elena Lucrezia Corner Piscopia became the first woman to collect a university degree when she was awarded her doctorate in philosophy here – there's a statue of her in the courtyard. The Bò is only open for guided visits, which should be booked in advance (March–Oct Mon, Wed & Fri 3pm & 4pm, Tues, Thurs & Sat 10am & 11am; L5000/€2.58; ☎049.820.9773).

The central squares

The area north and west of the university forms the hub of the city. A little way up from the university, on the left, is the **Caffè Pedrocchi**, which used to be the city's main intellectual salon; it's no longer that, but it does have a multiplicity of functions – chic café, concert hall and conference centre.

The **Piazza della Frutta** and **Piazza dell' Erbe**, the sites of Padua's daily markets, are lined by bars, restaurants and shops. Separating them is the extraordinary **Palazzo della Ragione** or **Salone** (Tues–Sun: Feb–Oct 9am–7pm; Nov–Jan 9am–6pm; L7000/€3.62); at the time of its construction in the 1210s, this vast hall was the largest room to have been built on top of another storey. Its decoration would once have been as astounding as its size, but the original frescoes by Giotto and his assistants were destroyed by fire in 1420, though some by Giustio de'Menabuoi have survived; most of the extant frescoes are by Nicola Miretto (1425–40) depicting an astrological calendar distinctively Medieval in its complexity. Mainly used as the city council's assembly hall, it was also a place where Padua's citizens could plead for justice – hence the appellation *della Ragione*, meaning "of reason". The unmissable wooden horse with disproportionately gigantic gonads is modelled on Donatello's *Gattamelata*, and was made for a joust in 1466 (closed off for restoration work at the time of writing).

The duomo and baptistry

Close by is Padua's **Duomo** (Mon–Sat 7.30am–noon & 3.45–7.30pm, Sun 7.45am–1pm & 3.45–8.30pm), an unlovely church whose architect cribbed his design from drawings by Michelangelo. The adjacent Romanesque **baptistry**, though, is one of the unproclaimed delights of Padua (daily: June–Sept 9.30am–1.30pm & 3–7pm; Oct–May 9.30am–1pm & 3–6pm; L3500/€1.81). Built by the Da Carraras in the thirteenth century, and still in use today, it's lined with fourteenth-century frescoes by Giusto de'Menabuoi, a cycle which makes a fascinating comparison with Giotto's in the Cappella degli Scrovegni. The influence of Giotto is plain, but in striving for greater realism Giusto has lost Giotto's monumentality and made some of his figures awkward and unconvincing. Yet many of the scenes are delightful, and the vibrancy of their colours, coupled with the size and relative quiet of the building, make for a memorable visit.

Eating, drinking and nightlife

Catering for the midday stampede of ravenous students, Padua's **bars** generally produce weightier **snacks** than the routine *tramezzini* – slabs of pizza and sandwiches vast enough to satisfy a glutton are standard – and there's a surprisingly good choice of self-service restaurants offering good-value full menus. Although open for lunch and dinner, they do close earlier than other restaurants in the evening; the hot-plates are often turned off by 9pm. For a passeggiata and a place to sit and watch the world go by, the main areas to head for are Piazza dell' Erbe, Piazza Duomo and Piazza Cavour, but for the real action the bars in the narrow streets around these piazzas and the University are the liveliest, with a student-based clientele.

Restaurants

Anfora, Via Soncin 13 (☎049.656.629). Lively bohemian restaurant that doubles up as a bar between restaurant hours (12.30–3.15pm & 8–11.30pm). Get there early or book in advance. Closed Sun.

Antico Brolo, Corso Milano 22 (☎049.664.555). Located on a busy road but the garden is quite secluded. Expect to pay around L60,000/€30.99 for a full meal à la carte, or go for the pizza menu. Closed Mon.

Belle Parti, Via Belle Parti 11 (☎049.875.1822). Set in a tiny street running between Via Verdi and Via S. Lucia. This is somewhere to go on a special occasion, with an excellent menu and a relaxed atmosphere. Closed Sun.

Al Borgo, Via Belludi 56. Wood-fired oven pizzeria with tables outside looking onto the Piazza del Santo; popular with locals and tourists alike. Closed Sun.

Al Cicheto, via Savonarola, 59 (☎049.871.9794). On the posh side of what an osteria can be, but the atmosphere is young and friendly, and you can get inexpensive lunches and pizza, though there is a more luxurious evening menu. Try to book the conservatory section, which overlooks the canal. Closed Sun.

Gastronomica al Portego, Via Dante 9. Self-service restaurant with local dishes. Closed Sun evening and all day Mon.

L'Isola di Capresa, via Marsilio di Padova 11–15 (☎049.876.0244). One of central Padova's best restaurants, situated just north of Piazza della Fruta and renowned for its fish and seafood dishes. A meal will cost you at least L40,000/€20.66 per head, though there is a tourist menu for L35,000/€18.08.

Mappa, Via Matteotti 17. Not far from the train station, another self-service restaurant, open until 9pm. Closed Sat.

Medina, via S.G. Barbarigo, 18. Small, bustling pizzeria, often packed with students enjoying excellent pizza and salads. Closed Tues.

Nane della Giulia, via Santa Sofia 1. An unusual mix of trendy and unpretentious. Go for the reasonably priced Veneto and vegetarian specialities earlier in the evening and the bar atmosphere later. Live piano, tango or jazz Wed and Thurs. Closed Mon.

Osteria dei Fabbri, Via dei Fabbri 13 (☎049.650.336). Excellent mid-range trattoria; you'll be lucky to get a seat without booking. Closed Sun.

Pago Pago, Via Galilei 59. Simple, traditional pizzeria/trattoria with prices to match. Closed Sat.

Pepen, Piazza Cavour. With a wonderful range of pizzas and seats on the square in the summer, this is one of Padua's best-sited pizzerias. Closed Sun.

Bars and nightlife

Your best bet, as usual, is to head for the centre and follow the throng. A good place to start is the unmarked *Bar Nazionale*, at Piazza dell' Erbe 40, on the northeast corner (closed Sun); there's the benefit of a gelateria next door, too. After around eleven the crowds disperse, mostly to out-of-town clubs, though the places listed below tend to stay pretty lively until at least 2am, though things are quieter outside university terms.

Padua's main theatre is the **Teatro Verdi** on Corso Milano hosting opera and big-name dramatists; details of the season's events can be obtained from the tourist office or in the bilingual information booklet *Padova Today*, distributed in some bars and most hotels. Of the local newspapers, the most comprehensive for listings is *Il Mattino*, but for more offbeat events check out the posters up around the city, particularly in the university area.

Extra Extra, via Ciamician, 145. Padova's flashiest disco. Buzzing after 2am from Thursday to Saturday, dead the rest of the time. If you can't get a taxi, it's an inadvisable thirty-minute walk back to the centre by way of via Sório.

Joyce's Irish Pub, Riviera S. Benedetto 154. Irish pubs are all the rage in Italy and this one is particularly popular; head west of Piazza Duomo down via Vescovado and the pub is just across an attractive part of the canal. Open until 2am. Closed Sun.

Limbo, via San Fermo, just south of Piazza Petrarca. Another popular disco-pub. Open until 3am. Closed Sun.

Victoria Pub, via Savonarola, off Piazza Petrarca. Ghastly underground fake English pub (to complete the UK selection), but it really pulls in the punters, and at least it doesn't shut at 11pm. Open until 2am. Closed Sun.

South of Padua

Of the small towns to the **south of Padua** the most enticing are **Monsélice**, which has a superbly restored castle, and **Montagnana**, whose medieval town walls have survived in almost pristine form. And if you need a rest from urban pursuits, the green **Colli Euganei** (Euganean Hills) offer a pleasant excursion, while the **Po Delta**'s nature reserves and beaches are the quietest stretches of coastline in the area. The Padova Itinerante card (see box on p.334), available from tourist offices, gives access to many of the sights in the area.

The Colli Euganei

A few kilometres to the southwest of Padua the **Colli Euganei** (Euganean Hills) rise abruptly out of the plains, their slopes patched with vineyards between the scattered villages, villas and churches. Between Padua and the hills lie the spa towns of **ÁBANO TERME** and **MONTEGROTTO TERME**, which for much of the year are crowded with people looking for cures or beauty treatment from the radioactive waters and mud baths. Largely composed of big and expensive modern hotels, these really are places to avoid unless you're hell-bent on trying to poach yourself in the hot springs.

A car is a great advantage for exploring the Colli Euganei proper, as buses are few and far between. The **villas** of the region are its major architectural attractions, but many of them remain in private hands and can only be viewed from a distance. An exception is the **Villa Barbarigo** (March–Oct daily 9am–noon & 1.30–sunset; L9500/€4.90) at **VALSANZIBIO**, which is famous for its extraordinary gardens; laid out in 1699, they feature a maze and fantastical Baroque gateways.

The gem of the Colli Euganei is the medieval village of **ARQUÀ PETRARCA**, most easily reached by bus from Este (3 daily), though it is walkable in about an hour by the back road. The poet **Francesco Petrarca** (Petrarch) spent the last summers of his life here, and this is where he died. His **house** (Tues–Sun: Feb–Sept 9am–12.30pm & 3–6.30pm; Oct–Jan 9am–12.30pm & 2.30–5pm; L6000/€3.10) still stands, and his desk and chair are still intact, as are various parts of the original fabric of the interior – though the frescoes, illustrating his works, were retouched in the seventeenth century. (Petrarch's sarcophagus is in the centre of the village, with one epitaph penned by him and another by his son-in-law, who placed it here.

Monsélice

Served by nine daily trains from Padua, the attractive town of **MONSÉLICE** is far more accessible than the villages nearer to the city. In earlier times it perched on the pimple of volcanic rock round the base of which it now winds, and you pass through the remnants of its defensive walls on your way from the train station to the central Piazza

Mazzini. A little way beyond the square stands Monsélice's main sight – the **Castello di Ezzelino**, or **Ca' Marcello** (guided tours only: April–Nov Tues–Sun 9am, 10am, 11am, 3pm & 4pm; L10,000/€5.16). Dating back to the eleventh century, the house was expanded in the thirteenth century by Ezzelino da Romano, who added the square tower across the courtyard. The interior was altered by the Da Carraras in the fourteenth century, and linking the two main sections is a fifteenth-century bit added by the Marcello family. The castle's immaculate appearance is down to Count Vittorio Cini, who inherited the derelict building after it had been in the tender care of the army during World War I and sank a fortune into restoring it and furnishing each section in the appropriate style.

The **Duomo Vecchio**, higher up the hill, retains fourteenth-century fresco fragments and has a Romano-Gothic polyptych on the high altar. Just beyond it, a gateway guarded by two Venetian lions gives onto the Via Sette Chiese, a private road leading up to the **Villa Duodo**. The seven churches of the road's name are a small-scale version of the seven pilgrimage churches of Rome, arranged as a line of chapels leading up to the church of **San Giorgio** at the top. Sinners could earn forgiveness by praying their way up to San Giorgio, where rows of martyred saints are arranged in wood and glass cabinets. However, it's not possible to go up the steps to the **Rocca** – Ezzelino's citadel – as it's currently undergoing restoration, although it may be open to the public when the work is finished.

The **tourist office** is on Piazza Mazzini (Mon–Sat 10am–12.30pm & 3–6pm, Sun 10am–1pm & 3–6pm; ☎0429.783.026). If you want to **stay**, there's a superb new youth hostel in a sixteenth-century palace at the far end of via San Stefano (☎0429.783.125, *ostellomonselice@libero.it*; L35,000/€18.07) or try the two-star *Cavallino*, Via Petrarca 2 (☎0429.72.242; ③), or the three-star *Ceffri*, Via Orti 7 (☎0429.783.111; ④). The best option for **eating** is the trattoria-pizzeria *Al Campiello*, at Riviera G.B. Belzoni 2 (closed Wed).

Este

If you're dependent on public transport, about the best base from which to roam around the Colli Euganei is the ceramics-producing town of **ESTE**, on the southern edge of the range and just an eight-minute train ride from Monsélice. Sporadic buses run up into the hills from here, and the chief **tourist office** of the Colli Euganei, the Pro Loco Sud-Est, is at Piazza Maggiore 9 (Mon–Fri 10am–noon & 4–6pm; ☎0429.3635).

Right out of the piazza, you come face to face with the ruined **Castello dei Carraresi**, parts of which went to build the nearby sixteenth-century palace that now houses the **Museo Nazionale Atestino** (daily 9am–7pm; L4000/€2.07). The Veneto's outstanding collection of pre-Roman artefacts is installed on the first floor, while much of the ground floor is given over to Roman remains. The room devoted to medieval pieces includes a *Madonna and Child* by Cima that was once stolen from the local church of Santa Maria della Consolazione and is now here for safekeeping.

The Baroque **Duomo**, the plan of which anticipates the pietà in Venice, contains a huge altarpiece of *St Thecla* by G. B. Tiepolo – unusually, it is set in a scene of pestilence and death rather than in one of his light-filled heavens.

There's a pair of good two-star **hotels** in Este: the *Leon d'Oro*, Viale Fiume 20 (☎0429.602.949; ②); and the *Beatrice d'Este*, Via Rimembranze 1 (☎0429.600.533; ③). For **food**, try *Al Gambero*, Via d'Azeglio 6 (closed Sat), or *Da Piero Ceschi*, Piazza Trento 16 (closed Thurs).

Montagnana

The pride of **MONTAGNANA**, fifteen minutes down the train line from Este, is its **medieval city walls**, raised by the tyrant Ezzelino da Romano after he had virtually flattened the town in 1242. With a circumference of nearly two kilometres and twenty-four polygonal towers spaced at regular intervals, these are among the finest medieval fortifications in the country.

Gates pierce the walls at the cardinal points of the compass, the entrances to the east and west being further reinforced by fortresses. The eastern gate (Porta Padova) is protected by the **Castello di San Zeno**, built by Ezzelino in 1242, and now houses the **Museo Civico e Archeologico** (guided tours Wed–Fri 11am, Sat & Sun 11am & 4pm; L3000/€1.55), which displays objects uncovered around the town. On the western side, the **Rocca degli Alberi** was built by the Da Carrara clan in 1362 to keep the roads from Mantua and Verona covered.

The centre of Montagnana is the Piazza Vittorio Emanuele, dominated by the late-Gothic **Duomo**; Veronese's altarpiece, a *Transfiguration*, is less engaging than the huge anonymous painting of the *Battle of Lepanto* on the left as you enter – it's said to represent accurately the ships and their positions at one point in the battle.

The **tourist office** is in Castel San Zeno (Mon 9.30am–12.30pm, Wed–Sat 9.30am–12.30pm & 3.30–6.30pm, Sun 10am–1pm & 4–7pm; ☎0429.81.320). For **accommodation** the two-star hotels *Concordia*, Via San Zeno 148 (☎0429.81.673; ③), and *Ezzelino*, Via Praterie 1 (☎0429.82.035; ②), are both reasonable (the latter is above the *Pizzeria Ezzelino*). The **youth hostel** is stunning, installed as it is in Rocca degli Alberi (reception open 7.30–9.30am & 3.30–11pm; ☎0429.81.076; L16,000/€8.26; April to mid-Oct). The least expensive decent **meal** in Montagnana is served at *Pizzeria al Palio* on Piazza Trieste (closed Tues), but for just a little more you can eat wonderful home-made dishes at *Da Stona*, Via Carrarese 51 (closed Mon). The hotels listed above also have **restaurants**. If you're stopping for a picnic in Montagnana, be sure to sample the delicious local *prosciutto*, which is exported all over the world.

Come to Montagnana on the first Sunday in September and you'll see its **Palio** – a poor relative of the costumed horse races in Siena, but enthusiastically performed, and rounded off by a firework display.

Vicenza

Europe's largest producer of textiles and the focus of Italy's "Silicon Valley", **VICENZA** is a very sleek city, where it can seem that every second car is a BMW. Modern prosperity hasn't ruined the look of Vicenza, though. The centre of the city, still partly enclosed by medieval walls, is an amalgam of Gothic and Classical buildings that today looks much as it did when the last major phase of construction came to an end at the close of the eighteenth century. This historic core is compact enough to be explored in a day, but the city and its environs really require a short stay to do them justice.

In 1404 Vicenza was absorbed by Venice, and the city's numerous Gothic palaces reflect its status as a Venetian satellite. But in the latter half of the sixteenth century the city was transformed by the work of an architect who owed nothing to Venice and whose rigorous but flexible style was to influence every succeeding generation – Andrea di Pietro della Gondola, alias Palladio.

The City

The main street of Vicenza, the **Corso Andrea Palladio**, cuts right through the old centre from the Piazza del Castello down to the Piazza Matteotti, and is lined with palaces, all of them now occupied by shops, offices and banks. Palladio's last palace, the fragmentary **Palazzo Porto-Breganze**, stands on the southern side of Piazza Castello; no. 163 on the Corso, the **Casa Cogollo**, is known as the Casa del Palladio, though he never lived there and few people think he designed it.

PALLADIO

Born in Padua in 1508, Andrea di Pietro (or della Gondola) began his career as an apprentice stonemason in Vicenza. At thirty he became the protégé of a local nobleman, Count Giangiorgio Trissino, the leading light of the humanist Accademia Olimpico – a learned society which still meets in Vicenza. Trissino gave the architect his classicized name, **Palladio**, directed his architectural training, brought him into contact with the dominant class of Vicenza and, perhaps most crucially, took him to Rome – the first of many trips he made through Italy, sketching Imperial Roman remains.

Between 1540 and his death in 1580, Palladio created around a dozen palaces and public buildings in Vicenza, nearly twenty villas in the countryside of the Veneto and two important religious buildings in Venice. But unlike the pioneers of Renaissance Classicism – architects such as Alberti, Brunelleschi and Bramante – Palladio's reputation does not rest on a particular transformation of architectural style. Instead, his fame – and he is arguably the most influential architect in the world – rests on the way he is considered to have perfected existing values of harmony and proportion.

In particular, his lasting influence stems from *I Quattro Libri dell'Architettura* or "The Four Books of Architecture", a treatise he published in 1570, towards the end of his career. Other architects had written important works of theory, but Palladio's is unique in its practical applicability, serving almost as a text book for Classical architecture. As the style spread into the rest of Europe and beyond, it was to Palladio's book that architects like Inigo Jones (and later, Thomas Jefferson) turned, finding both inspiration and guidance in his examples.

Today, Palladio has perhaps become the victim of his own success. The ubiquity of neo-Classicism in second-rate churches and third-rate bank buildings can make it hard to sense the freshness and brilliance of his designs, though it still shines through in masterpieces like the Basilica in Vicenza, the Villa Barbaro near Ásolo and the churches of the Redentore and San Giorgio Maggiore in Venice. Even if you're inclined to agree with Herbert Read's opinion that "in the back of every dying civilization there sticks a bloody Doric column", you might leave the region converted.

The Museo Civico and Teatro Olimpico

The Corso ends with one of the architect's most imperious buildings, the **Palazzo Chiericati** (begun in 1550), now home of the **Museo Civico**, also known as the Pinacoteca (mid-June to Aug Tues–Sun 9am–7pm; Sept to mid-June 9am–5pm; L5000/€2.58). The core of the picture collection is made up of Vicentine artists, none of whose work will knock you flat on your back; it's left to a few more celebrated names – Memling, Tintoretto, Veronese, Tiepolo – and some fine fifteenth-century painting to make the visit memorable.

Across the Piazza Matteotti is the one building in Vicenza you shouldn't fail to go into – the **Teatro Olimpico**, the oldest indoor theatre in Europe (same hours & ticket as Museo Civico). Approached in 1579 by the members of the Olympic Academy (a society dedicated to the study of the humanities) to produce a design for a permanent theatre, Palladio devised a covered amphitheatre derived from his reading of Vitruvius and his studies of Roman structures in Italy and France. He died soon after work commenced, and the scheme was then overseen by Scamozzi, who added to Palladio's design the backstage perspective of a classical city, creating the illusion of long urban vistas by tilting the "streets" at an alarming angle. The theatre opened on March 3, 1585, with an extravagant production of *Oedipus Rex*, and is still used for plays and concerts.

The Piazza dei Signori

At the hub of the city, the **Piazza dei Signori**, stands the most awesome of Palladio's creations – the **Basilica**. Designed in the late 1540s (but not finished until the second

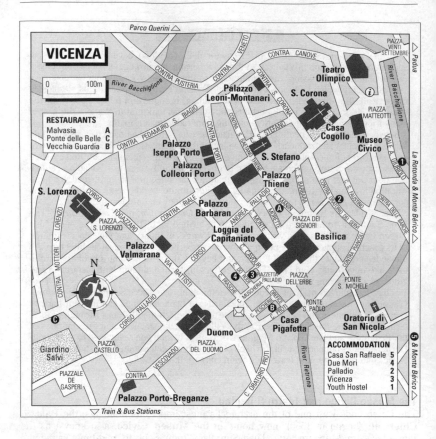

decade of the next century), this was Palladio's first public project and the one that secured his reputation. The monumental regularity of the basilica disguises the fact that the Palladian building is effectively a stupendous piece of buttressing – the Doric and Ionic colonnades enclose the fifteenth-century hall of the city council, an unstable structure that had defied a number of attempts to prop it up before Palladio's solution was put into effect. The vast Gothic hall is often used for good contemporary architecture exhibitions (Tues–Sun: summer 10am–7pm; winter 9am–5pm; price varies).

As in the sixteenth century, a daily fruit, vegetable and flower market is pitched at the back of the basilica, in the **Piazza dell' Erbe**; if you're shopping for picnic food, you'll save money by going down the slope and over the river, where the shops are a good bit cheaper. On Tuesdays a general market spreads along the roads between the basilica and the duomo.

A late Palladio building, the unfinished **Loggia del Capitaniato**, faces the basilica across the Piazza dei Signori. Built as accommodation for the Venetian military commander of the city, it's decorated with reliefs in celebration of the Venetian victory over the Turks at Lepanto in 1571.

VICENZA'S MUSEUMS

Two different **biglietti cumulativi** are on offer in Vicenza: the L12,000/€6.20 ticket allows you one visit to the Teatro Olimpico, the Museo Civico and the less than enthralling Museo Naturalistico-Archeologico; the L14,000/€7.23 ticket gives admission to these three plus the Museo del Risorgimento, a rather specialized museum that's a long way out of the city centre. Individually, each site charges L6000/€3.10 for admission. You can also buy two more expensive cards, but these are poor value unless you plan to make a very comprehensive visit. The "Vicenza Card – Musei e Palazzi" costs L20,000/€10.35 and gets you into all the places above plus the Gallerie di Palazzo Leoni-Montanari, and gives free entrance to exhibitions at the Basilica Palladiana and Palazzo Barbaran. You'd do better paying the individual entrance fees at La Rotonda and the Villa Valmarana than buying the Vicenze e le Ville card at L40,000/€20.66.

The churches

The **Duomo** was bombed flat in 1944 and carefully reconstructed after the war; it's a rather gloomy place, chiefly distinguished as one of the few Italian cathedrals to be overwhelmed by its secular surroundings. Far more interesting is **Santa Corona** (daily: summer 8.30am–noon & 2.30–6pm; winter 9.30am–noon & 3–6pm), on the other side of the Corso Palladio (at the Piazza Matteotti end), a Dominican church dating from the mid-thirteenth century. Here you'll find two of the three great church paintings in Vicenza – *The Baptism of Christ*, a late work by Giovanni Bellini, and *The Adoration of the Magi*, painted in 1573 by Paolo Veronese. The cloisters now house a run-of-the-mill **Museo Naturalistico-Archeologico** (Tues–Sun: mid-June to Aug 9am–7pm; Sept to mid-June 9am–5pm; see box above for admission prices).

The nearby **Santo Stefano** (Mon–Sat 8.30–10am & 5.30–7pm) contains the third of the city's fine church paintings: Palma Vecchio's typically stolid and voluptuous *Madonna and Child with SS George and Lucy*.

The palazzi and the parks

Santo Stefano faces a corner of the huge **Palazzo Thiene**, another of Palladio's palaces. It was planned to occupy the entire block down to Corso Palladio, but in the end work progressed no further than the addition of this wing to the existing fifteenth-century house. The facade of the old building is in Contrà Porti, a street that amply demonstrates the way in which the builders of Vicenza grafted new houses onto old without disrupting the symmetry of the street; the palaces here span two centuries, yet the overall impression is one of cohesion. Facing Palazzo Thiene is the Palazzo Barbaran, which houses a research institute for Palladian architecture (*www.cisapalladio.org*) and often has excellent exhibitions, usually, but not always, on classical architects.

Outstanding buildings on Contrà Porti are the fourteenth-century **Palazzo Colleoni Porto** (no. 19) and Palladio's neighbouring **Palazzo Iseppo Porto**, designed a few years after the Thiene palace. The parallel Corso A. Fogazzaro completes the itinerary of major Palladian buildings, with the **Palazzo Valmarana** (no. 16), perhaps the most eccentric of Palladio's projects – notice the gigantic stucco figures at the sides of the facade, where you'd expect columns to be.

At the end of Contrà Santa Corona, two blocks east of Contrà Porti, the **Palazzo Leoni-Montanari** (Fri–Sun 10am–6pm; see box above for admission prices; *www.palazzomontanari.com*) houses a rather specialized gallery with a collection of art from the Veneto that is respectable enough, if not up to the standards of Venice, or even Padua. Eighteenth-century painting is best represented, including landscape works by Canaletto and Guardi, and there's a rather surprising collection of Russian icons.

Contrà Porti takes you towards the Pusterla bridge and the **Parco Querini**, the biggest expanse of green in the city, enlivened by a decorative hillock populated by ducks, rabbits and peacocks. Vicenza's other refuge for the brick-wearied, the **Giardino Salvi** (at the end of the road running straight up from the train station), is a more modest, artificial affair of winding gravel paths and fountains.

The outskirts – Monte Bérico and the villas

In 1426 Vicenza was struck by bubonic plague, during the course of which outbreak the Virgin appeared twice at the summit of **Monte Bérico** – the hill on the southern edge of the city – to announce the city's deliverance. The chapel raised on the site of her appearance became a place of pilgrimage, and at the end of the seventeenth century it was replaced by the present **Basilica di Monte Bérico**. Bus #18 climbs the hill from the bus station every thirty minutes or so; on foot it takes around 25 minutes from the centre of town.

Pilgrims regularly arrive here by the busload, and the glossy interior of the church is immaculately maintained to receive them; a well-stocked shop in the cloister sells devotional trinkets to the faithful. Those in search of artistic fulfilment should venture into the church for Montagna's pietà (in the chapel to the right of the apse) and *The Supper of St Gregory the Great* by Veronese (in the refectory). The latter, the prototype of *The Feast in the House of Levi* in Venice's Accademia, was used for bayonet practice by Austrian troops in 1848 – the small reproduction nearby shows what a thorough job the vandals and subsequent restorers did.

Carry on towards the summit of the hill and you'll come to the **Museo del Risorgimento e della Resistenza**, some ten minutes' walk beyond the basilica. The museum houses an impressively thorough display, paying particular attention to Vicenza's resistance to the Austrians in the mid-nineteenth century and to the efforts of the anti-fascist Alpine fighters a century later, but for many visitors the main attraction will be the extensive wooded parkland laid out on the slopes below the Villa Guiccioli, the main building (mid-June to Aug 9am–7pm; Sept to mid-June 9am–5pm; museum L6000/€3.10; park free).

The Villa Valmarana

Ten minutes' walk away from Monte Bérico is the **Villa Valmarana "ai Nani"**, an undistinguished house made extraordinary by the decorations of Giambattista and Giandomenico Tiepolo (mid-March to April Tues & Fri 2.30–5.30pm, Wed, Thurs, Sat & Sun 10am–noon & 2.30–5.30pm; May–Sept Tues–Sat 10am–noon & 3–6pm; Oct–Nov 5 Tues–Sat 10am–noon & 2–5pm; L10,000/€5.16). *Nani*, by the way, means "Dwarves", the significance of which becomes clear when you see the garden wall. To get there, go back down the hill, head along Via M. D'Azeglio for 100m, then turn right into the cobbled Via S. Bastiano, which ends at the villa.

There are two parts to the house: the Palazzina, containing six rooms frescoed with brilliant virtuosity by Giambattista (scenes based on Virgil, Tasso and Ariosto – you're handed a brief guide to the paintings at the entrance); and the Foresteria, one room of which is frescoed by Giambattista and six by Giandomenico, whose predilections are a little less heroic than his father's.

La Rotonda

From the Villa Valmarana the narrow Strada Valmarana descends the slope to one of Europe's most imitated buildings – Palladio's Villa Capra, known to most people as **La Rotonda** (March 15–Nov 4: villa Wed 10am–noon & 3–6pm; L10,000/€5.16, including gardens; grounds only Tues–Thurs same hours; L5000/€2.58) because of its centrally-planned structure: the square outer walls symbolize the physical world while the circle within represents the idea of divine perfection. More obviously, the villa's shape and hill-top position emphasizes its domination of the surrounding countryside. La Rotonda is unique among Palladio's villas (see box on p.343) in that it was designed not as the main building of a farm but as a pavilion in which entertainments could be held and the landscape enjoyed. Only a tour of the lavishly decorated interior will fully reveal the subtleties of the Rotonda; the grounds are little more than an attractive belt of grass from which to view the villa and surrounding countryside.

Practicalities

The **train station** is a ten-minute walk southwest of the historic centre; head straight ahead through the park to reach Piazza del Castello. The **tourist office** is at the far end of Corso Palladio, alongside the entrance to the Teatro Olimpico, at Piazza Matteotti 12 (Mon–Sat 9am–1pm & 2.30–6pm, Sun 9am–1pm; ☎0444.320.854, *www.ascom.vi.it/ aptvicenza*). For **listings**, pick up a copy of the local papers *Il Gazzettino* or *Il Giornale di Vicenza*. **Internet** access can be found in the main library, on Contra Riale, one block west of Palazzo Barbaran.

Vicenza's one-star **hotels** are all on very noisy roads, or above bars or restaurants, or some way out of the centre – or a combination of these drawbacks. Of the two-stars within a few yards of the Piazza dei Signori, the following are worth trying – graceful *Due Mori*, Contrà Do Rode 26 (☎0444.321.886; ③), which has some beautifully furnished and spacious rooms; the capacious *Vicenza*, Stradella dei Nodari 5/7 (☎0444. 321.512; ③); and, friendliest of the bunch, *Palladio*, Via Oratorio dei Servi 25 (☎0444. 321.072; ③). The brand-new **youth hostel**, viale Giuriolo, 7 (☎0444.540.222) is in a superb position just off Piazza Matteoti, opposite the Museo Civico. If centrality isn't an issue, enquire after the two-star *Casa San Raffaele*, Viale X Giugno 10 (☎0444.545.767; ③), which is due to re-open by summer 2001 and enjoys a beautiful position on the slope of Monte Bérico. Wherever you decide to stay, phone ahead to book a room if you're going in summer or early autumn – some places close down in August, and Vicenza's popularity as a conference centre can make it tricky to find rooms, especially in September.

The best budget **restaurant** is the *Antica Casa della Malvasia*, Contrà delle Morette 5 (closed Mon), a bustling, roomy inn just off the Piazza dei Signori: the food is variable but it has live music on Tuesday and Thursday, is open till at least 1am on Friday and Saturday, and the bar's superb too. Equally popular, but somewhat less basic, is the *Vecchia Guardia*, close to the basilica at Contrà Pescheria Vecchia 11 (closed Thurs). For a posher, more intimate atmosphere, head just beyond the Piazza del Castello to the *Trattoria Ponte delle Belle*, Contrà Ponte delle Belle, 5 (☎0444.320.647; closed Sun), which specializes in Tyrolean cuisine, but also does Vicentine specialities. Note that there are few restaurants in central Vicenza and many close in August.

As for **bars** in the centre of the city, the *Malvasia* (see above) is excellent, but the most atmospheric is *Il Grottino*, under the basilica at Piazza dell' Erbe 2 (closed Sun). It has a good range of wines, stays open till 2am and has live music on Wednesdays and Fridays in summer. Among the **cafés** and *pasticcerie* along the Corso and around the basilica, *Sorarù*, in the Piazzetta Andrea Palladio, next to the basilica, is highly recommended, as is the neighbouring *Gran Caffè Garibaldi*. The best **ice creams** in town are at *Tutto Gelato*, Contrà Frasche 26 (between the basilica and the duomo), though the *Gran Caffè Garibaldi* runs it close. If you want to buy your own food, the *alimentari* on the Corso are excellent, especially Il Ceppo at no. 196; Porro, just south of the basilica on Contrà Orefice, is also good.

Verona

With its wealth of Roman sites and streets of pink-hued medieval buildings, the easy-going city of **VERONA** has more in the way of sights than any other place in the Veneto except Venice itself. Unlike Venice, though, it's not a city overwhelmed by the tourist industry, important though that is to the local economy. Verona is the largest city of the mainland Veneto, its economic success largely due to its position at the crossing of the major routes from Germany and Austria to central Italy and from the west to Venice and Trieste.

Verona's initial development as a **Roman** settlement was similarly due to its straddling the main east–west and north–south lines of communication. A period of decline in the wake of the disintegration of the Roman Empire was followed by revival under the Ostrogoths, who in turn were succeeded by the Franks: Charlemagne's son, Pepin, ruled his kingdom from here. By the twelfth century Verona had become a city-state, and in the following century approached the zenith of its independent existence with the rise of the **Scaligers**. Ruthless in the exercise of power, the Scaligers were at the same time energetic patrons of the arts, and many of Verona's finest buildings date from their rule.

With the fall of their dynasty a time of upheaval ensued, Gian Galeazzo Visconti of Milan emerging in control of the city. Absorption into the Venetian Empire came in 1405, and Verona was governed from Venice until the arrival of Napoleon. Verona's history then shadowed that of Venice: a prolonged interlude of Austrian rule, brought to an end by the Unification of Italy in 1866.

Arrival, information and accommodation

If you're flying to Verona's Valerio Catullo **airport** at Villafranca, 10km away, you can get into the city by a regular APT bus (every 20min 7am–midnight; L7000/€3.62) from the airport to the train station and Piazza Cittadella, near the city centre. Otherwise, unless you're staying in the youth hostel, you're only likely to need a **bus** if you don't fancy the fifteen-minute walk from the **train** and **bus stations** to the centre. To walk to the centre from here, turn right outside the train station (keeping to the right-hand side of the road – there are some busy junctions) then left at the main junction with the broad Corso Porta Nuova, which leads straight to Piazza Bra, site of the Arena and the hub of Verona. Bus tickets must be bought before boarding the bus, either from the machines alongside bay A or from the *tabacchi* inside the train station ticket hall. They cost L1500/€0.77 and are valid for any number of journeys within an hour.

The main **tourist office** is on the central Piazza Bra, within the old town walls beside the Palazzo Municipale (Mon–Sat 9am–6pm; ☎045.806.8680, *www.verona-apt.net*). There is an additional office at the train station (daily 9am–6pm; ☎045.800.0861) and a **room-finding service**, Cooperativa Albergatori Veronesi (CAV), at Via Patuzzi 5 (Mon–Fri 9am–6.30pm; ☎045.800.9844); Via Patuzzi runs parallel to Via Leoncino off Piazza Gallieno in the southeast corner of Piazza Bra. You can **rent bikes** in summer from stalls in Piazza Bra. For **Internet** access, head for the small shop on platform 1 at the train station (Mon–Sat 7.30am–7.30pm) or to *Diesis*, on via Sottoriva 15 (Mon–Thurs 11am–11pm, Fri & Sat 11am–midnight, Sun 3pm–8pm; L15.000/€7.75 per hour).

Hotels

Aurora, Piazzetta XIV Novembre 2 (☎045.594.717, fax 045.801.0860). Upmarket two-star hotel with a warm atmosphere and many rooms overlooking the Piazza dell' Erbe. The staff are friendly and knowledgeable, and speak good English. ⑤.

Al Castello, Corso Cavour 43 (☎045.800.4403). Tiny one-star just off the central Corso Cavour, with simple but dark rooms. ④.

Catullo, Via Valerio Catullo 1 (☎045.800.2786). The most economical hotel near the centre, just off the main shopping artery of Via Mazzini. Large rooms with shabby gentility and plenty of light. ③.

Cavour, Vicolo Chiodo 4b (☎045.590.166). A one-star, recently renovated, in a small street that runs south off Corso Cavour. Choose between cutesy rooms in blue and white, or the posher and slightly pricier annexe, which has been done up as a rural villa, all terracotta floors and beams. ⑤.

Ciopeta, Vicolo Teatro Filarmonica 2 (☎045.800.6843, fax 045.803.3722). The excellent location behind the Arena and the family atmosphere make this hotel a bargain, especially if you manage to book room 8, which has a balcony. ④.

Mazzanti, Via Mazzanti 6 (☎045.800.6813, fax 045.801.1262). A sizeable two-star with restaurant just west of Piazza dei Signori. The rooms are less characterful than you'd think, given the rambling old building and location in the heart of the historic centre. ④.

Il Torcolo, Vicolo Listone 3 (☎045.800.7512, fax 045.800.4058). Nicely turned-out two-star hotel within 100m of the Arena. Extremely welcoming owners – and a favourite with the opera crowds, so book ahead. ⑥.

Hostels and campsites

Campeggio Castel San Pietro, Via Castel S. Pietro 2 (☎045.592.037). Along with the hostel site, this is the most pleasant and convenient place to camp near Verona – take a bus to Via Marsala.

Casa della Giovane, Via Pigna 7 (☎045.596.880). Spartan, convent-run hostel for women, with an 11pm curfew, although there is some flexibility for guests with opera tickets. L22,000/€11.36, plus some double rooms at L25,000/€12.91.

Ostello della Gioventù, Salita Fontana del Ferro 15 (☎045.590.360). The official HI hostel is in a beautiful old building behind the Teatro Romano; as it's quite a walk from the centre, it's best to take a bus (#73, or 90 on Sundays) to Piazza Isolo then walk up the hill. There's an 11.30pm curfew, but there's some flexibility extended to guests with concert tickets. It does reasonably priced evening meals. Also has a campsite. L20,000/€10.32.

The City

Coming from the train station, you pass Verona's south gate, the **Porta Nuova**, and come onto the long Corso Porta Nuova, which ends at the battlemented arches that precede the **Piazza Bra**. Here stands the mightiest of Verona's Roman monuments, the **Arena**. Dating from the first century AD, the Arena has survived in remarkable condition, despite the twelfth-century earthquake that destroyed all but four of the arches of the outer wall. The interior (Tues–Sun 9am–6pm, closes 3.30pm during the opera season, usually July–Aug; L6000/€3.10) was scarcely damaged by the tremor, and nowadays audiences come to watch gargantuan opera productions where once crowds of around 20,000 packed the benches for gladiatorial contests and the like. Originally measuring 152m by 123m overall, and thus the third largest of all Roman amphitheatres, the Arena is still an awesome sight – and as an added treat offers a tremendous urban panorama from the topmost of the 44 pink marble tiers.

The Casa di Giulietta and San Fermo

Heading north from the Arena, **Via Mazzini** is a narrow traffic-free street lined with generally expensive clothes, shoe and jewellery shops. A left turn at the end leads to the Piazza dell' Erbe (see p.352), while a right takes you into **Via Cappello**, a street named after the family that Shakespeare turned into the Capulets – and on the left, at no. 23, is the **Casa di Giulietta** (Juliet's House) (Tues–Sun 9am–6.30pm; L6000/€3.10 or see box on p.352 for details of combined tickets). In fact, although the "Capulets" and the "Montagues" (Montecchi) did exist, Romeo and Juliet were entirely fictional creations. The house itself, constructed at the start of the fourteenth century, is in a fine state of preservation, but is largely empty.

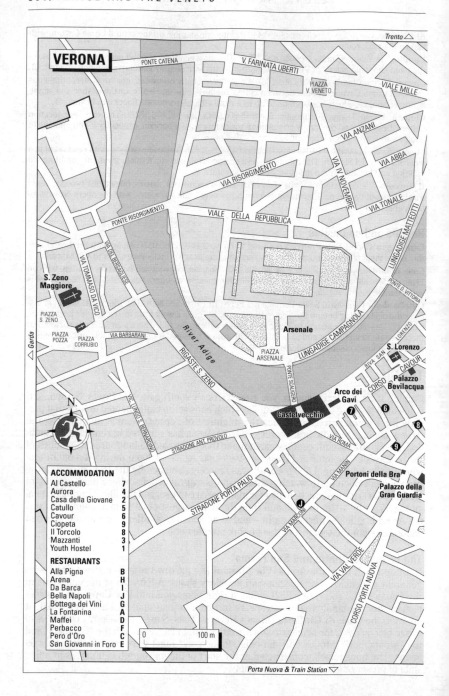

VERONA

Trento △

PONTE CATENA

V. FARINATA UBERTI

PIAZZA
V. VENETO

VIALE MILLE

VIA ANZANI

VIA ABBA

VIA RISORGIMENTO

VIA IV NOVEMBRE

VIALE DELLA REPUBBLICA

VIA TONALE

LUNGADIGE MATTEOTTI

PONTE RISORGIMENTO

PONTE D. VITTORIA

VIA TOMMASO DA VICO

VIA DEL BERSAGLIERE

S. Zeno
Maggiore

PIAZZA
S. ZENO

△ Garda

PIAZZA
POZZA

PIAZZA
CORRUBIO

VIA BARBARANI

River Adige

Arsenale

PIAZZA
ARSENALE

LUNGADIGE CAMPAGNOLA

RIGASTE S. ZENO

PONTE SCALIGERO

RIVA SAN LORENZO

S. Lorenzo

CORSO CAVOUR

Palazzo
Bevilacqua

Arco dei
Gavi

7

6

8

Castelvecchio

VIA ROMA

9

VIC. LUNGO S. BERNARDINO

N.

STRADONE ANT. PROVOLO

VIA MANIN

Portoni della Bra

Palazzo della
Gran Guardia

STRADONE PORTA PALIO

J

VIA MARCONI

VIA VAL VERDE

CORSO PORTA NUOVA

ACCOMMODATION
Al Castello   7
Aurora   4
Casa della Giovane 2
Catullo   5
Cavour   6
Ciopeta   9
Il Torcolo   8
Mazzanti   3
Youth Hostel   1

RESTAURANTS
Alla Pigna   B
Arena   H
Da Barca   I
Bella Napoli   J
Bottega dei Vini   G
La Fontanina   A
Maffei   D
Perbacco   F
Pero d'Oro   C
San Giovanni in Foro E

0   100 m

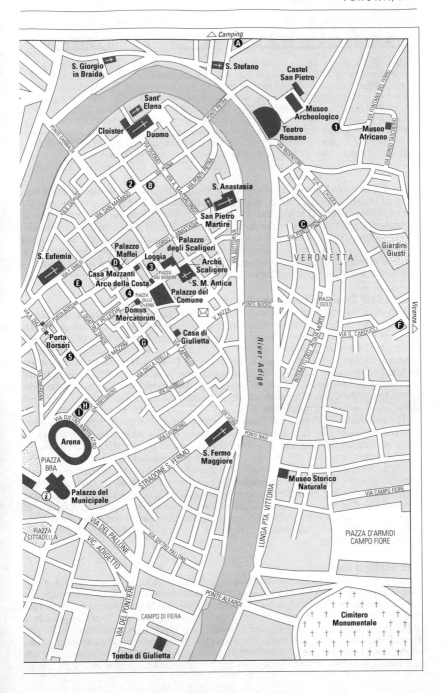

△ Camping
A
S. Giorgio in Braida
S. Stefano
Castel San Pietro
Sant' Elena
Museo Archeologico
Cloister
Duomo
Teatro Romano
Museo Africano
❶
② **B**
S. Anastasia
San Pietro Martire
C
VERONETTA
Giardini Giusti
Palazzo Maffei
Palazzo degli Scaligeri
S. Eufemia
Loggia
③
Arche Scaligere
Casa Mazzanti
D
Arco della Costa
S. M. Antica
E
④
Palazzo del Comune
Domus Mercatorum
PIAZZA ISOLO
PONTE NUOVO
Casa di Giulietta
F
Porta Borsari
⑤
G
VIA G. CARDUCCI
Vicenza △
Arena
H
PIAZZA BRA
S. Fermo Maggiore
PONTE NAVI
Museo Storico Naturale
ⓘ
Palazzo del Municipale
PIAZZA CITTADELLA
PIAZZA D'ARMIDI CAMPO FIORE
River Adige
LUNGA PTA. VITTORIA
PONTE ALEARDI
CAMPO DI FIERA
Cimitero Monumentale
Tomba di Giulietta

VERONA'S CHURCHES, MUSEUMS AND MONUMENTS

There is a **biglietto unico** for Verona's principal churches, which costs L8,000/€4.13 and allows entry to San Zeno, San Lorenzo, the Duomo (including the baptistry and archeological findings), Sant'Anastasia and San Fermo; it can be bought at any of the churches. Alternatively you can buy individual tickets at L3000/€1.55. If you're planning to be very busy, it might be worth getting the **Verona Card**, which costs L22,000/€11.36 and gives free access to all the museums, buses and churches in the city for three days. Be careful which day you buy it, however, as almost everything shuts on a Monday and the card doesn't carry over after the weekend. A third card, costing L52,000/€26.85, throws in entrance to Gardaland, the lake's answer to Disneyworld (see p.232).

Via Cappello leads into Via Leoni with its Roman gate, the **Porta Leoni**, and a segment of excavated Roman street, exposed three metres below today's street level. At the end of Via Leoni and across the road rises the red-brick **San Fermo** church, whose inconsistent exterior betrays the fact that it consists of two churches combined. Flooding forced the Benedictines to superimpose a second church on the one founded in the eighth century. The Gothic upper church has no outstanding works of art but is graceful enough; the Romanesque lower church, entered from the left of the choir, has impressive low vaulting, sometimes obscured by exhibitions.

Piazza dell' Erbe and Piazza dei Signori

Originally a major Roman crossroads and the site of the forum, **Piazza dell' Erbe** is still the heart of the city. As the name suggests, the market used to sell mainly vegetables, but nowadays it has been largely taken over by ugly, semi-permanent booths selling clothes, souvenirs, antiques and fast food. The rich variety of buildings framing the square is far more attractive. Most striking are the **Domus Mercatorum** (on the left as you look from the Via Cappello end), which was founded in 1301 as a merchants' warehouse and exchange, the fourteenth-century **Torre del Gardello** and, to the right of the tower, the **Casa Mazzanti**, whose sixteenth-century murals are best seen after dark, under enhancing spotlights.

The neighbouring **Piazza dei Signori** used to be the chief public square of Verona. Much of the right side is taken up by the **Palazzo del Capitano**, which is separated from the Palazzo del Comune by a stretch of excavated Roman street. Facing you as you come into the square is the medieval **Palazzo degli Scaligeri**, residence of the Scaligers; a monument to more democratic times extends from it at a right angle – the fifteenth-century **Loggia del Consiglio**, former assembly hall of the city council and Verona's outstanding early-Renaissance building. The rank of Roman notables along the roof includes Verona's most illustrious native poet, Catullus. For a dizzying view of the city, take a sharp right as soon as you come into the square, and go up the twelfth-century **Torre dei Lamberti** (Tues–Sun 9.30am–6pm; L4000/€2.07 by lift, L3000/€1.55 on foot).

The Scaliger tombs

Passing under the arch linking the Palazzo degli Scaligeri to the Palazzo del Capitano, you come to the little Romanesque church of Santa Maria Antica, in front of which are ranged the **Arche Scaligeri**, some of the most elaborate Gothic funerary monuments in Italy. Over the side entrance to the church, an equestrian statue of **Cangrande I** ("Big Dog"; d.1329) gawps down from his tomb's pyramidal roof; the statue is a copy, the original being displayed in the Castelvecchio (see opposite). The canopied tombs of the rest of the clan are enclosed within a wrought-iron palisade decorated with ladder motifs, the emblem of the Scaligers – the family name was della Scala, "scala" meaning ladder. **Mastino I** ("Mastiff"; d.1277), founder of the dynasty, is buried in the simple tomb against the wall of the church; **Mastino II** (d.1351) is to the left of the entrance, opposite the most florid of the tombs, that of **Cansignorio** ("Top Dog"; d.1375).

Sant'Anastasia, San Pietro Martire and the duomo

Going on past the Arche Scaligeri, and turning left along Via San Pietro, you come to **Sant'Anastasia** (Mon–Sat 9am–6pm, Sun 1–6pm; L3000/€1.55), Verona's largest church. Started in 1290 and completed in 1481, it's mainly Gothic in style, with undertones of the Romanesque. The fourteenth-century carvings of New Testament scenes around the doors are the most arresting feature of its bare exterior; the interior's highlight is Pisanello's delicately coloured fresco of *St George and the Princess* (in the sacristy), a work in which the normally martial saint appears as something of a dandy.

To the left of Sant'Anastasia's facade is an eye-catching tomb, the free-standing monument to Guglielmo di Castelbarco (1320) by Enrico di Rigino. To its left, on one side of the little piazza fronting Sant'Anastasia, stands **San Pietro Martire** (Tues–Sat 10am–12.30pm & 4–7.30pm), deconsecrated since its ransacking by Napoleon. Numerous patches of fresco dot the walls, making for an atmospheric interior, though the highlight is the vast lunette fresco on the east wall. Easily the strangest picture in Verona, it is thought to be an allegorical account of the Virgin's Assumption, though the bizarre collection of animals appears to have little connection with a bemused-looking Madonna.

Verona's red-and-white-striped **Duomo** (Mon–Sat 9am–6pm, Sun 1.30–6pm; L3000/€1.55) lies just round the river's bend, past the Roman **Ponte Pietra**. Consecrated in 1187, it's Romanesque in its lower parts, developing into Gothic as it goes up; the two doorways are twelfth century – look for the story of Jonah and the whale on the south porch, and the statues of Roland and Oliver, two of Charlemagne's paladins, on the west. The interior has fascinating architectural details around each chapel and on the columns – particularly fine is the Cappella Mazzanti (last on the right). In the first chapel on the left, an *Assumption* by Titian occupies an architectural frame by Sansovino, who also designed the choir.

To the Castelvecchio

After the Arena and the Teatro Romano, Verona's most impressive Roman remnant is the **Porta dei Borsari** (on the junction of Via Diaz and Corso Porta Borsari), a structure which was as great an influence on the city's Renaissance architects as the amphitheatre. Now reduced to a monumental screen straddling the road, it used to be Verona's largest Roman gate; the inscription dates it at 265, but it's almost certainly older than that.

Some way down Corso Cavour, which starts at the Porta dei Borsari, stands the **Arco dei Gavi**, a first-century Roman triumphal arch which was re-built in 1930 after Napoleon's troops tore down the original. This is your best vantage point from which to admire the **Ponte Scaligero**; built by Cangrande II between 1355 and 1375. It was the turn of the German army to indulge in wanton destruction this time: they blew up the bridge in 1945, but the salvaged material was used for reconstruction. The stretch of shingle on the opposite bank is a popular spot for picnics, sunbathing and just watching the water flow by, rich in colour from the glacial deposits upstream.

The fortress from which the bridge springs, the **Castelvecchio** (Tues–Sun 9am–6.30pm; L6000/€3.10), was commissioned by Cangrande II at around the same time and became the stronghold for Verona's subsequent rulers. Opened as the city museum in 1925, it was damaged by bombing during World War II, but opened again after scrupulous restoration in 1964. The Castelvecchio's collection of paintings, jewellery, weapons and other artefacts flows through a labyrinth of chambers, courtyards and passages that is fascinating to explore in itself. The equestrian figure **Cangrande I**, removed from his tomb, is strikingly displayed on an outdoor pedestal; his expression is disconcerting at close range, the simpleton's grin being difficult to reconcile with the image of the ruthless warlord. Outstanding among the paintings are two works by Jacopo Bellini, two *Madonna*s by Giovanni Bellini, another *Madonna* by Pisanello, Veronese's *Descent from the Cross*, a Tintoretto *Nativity*, a Lotto portrait and works by Giambattista and Giandomenico Tiepolo. The real joy of the museum, however, is in wandering round the medieval pieces; beautiful sculpture and frescoes by the often nameless artists of the late Middle Ages.

San Zeno Maggiore

A little over a kilometre northwest of the Castelvecchio is the **Basilica di San Zeno Maggiore** (Mon–Sat 9am–6pm, Sun 1–6pm; L3000/€1.55), one of the most significant Romanesque churches in northern Italy. A church was founded here, above the tomb of the city's patron saint, as early as the fifth century, but the present building and its campanile were put up in the first half of the twelfth century, with additions continuing up to the end of the fourteenth. Its large rose window, representing the Wheel of Fortune, dates from the early twelfth century, as does the magnificent portal, whose lintels bear relief sculptures representing the months – look also for St Zeno trampling the devil. The reliefs to the side of the portal are also from the twelfth century and show scenes from the Old Testament on the right, and scenes from the New Testament on the left (except for the bottom two on both sides, which depict scenes from the life of Theodoric the Great). Extraordinary bronze panels on the doors depict scenes from the Bible and the Miracles of San Zeno, their style influenced by Byzantine and Ottoman art; most of those on the left are from around 1100, and most of the right-hand panels date from a century or so later. Areas of the lofty and simple interior are covered with frescoes, some superimposed upon others, some defaced by ancient graffiti. Diverting though these are, the one compulsive image in the church is the high altar's luminous *Madonna and Saints* by Mantegna.

North of the Adige

On the other side of Ponte Garibaldi, and right along the embankments or through the public gardens, is **San Giorgio in Braida**, in terms of its works of art the richest of Verona's churches. A *Baptism* by Tintoretto hangs over the door, while the main altar, designed by **Sanmicheli**, incorporates a marvellous piece by **Paolo Veronese** – the *Martyrdom of St George*.

It's a short walk along the embankments, past the twelfth-century church of **Santo Stefano** and the Ponte Pietra, to the first-century-BC **Teatro Romano** (Tues–Sun: July–Aug 9am–3pm; Sept–June 9am–6.30pm; L5000/€2.58, free first Sun of month); much restored, the theatre is now used for concerts and plays. High above it, and reached by a rickety-looking lift, the **Museo Archeologico** (same hours & ticket) occupies the buildings of an old convent; its well-arranged collection features a number of Greek, Roman and Etruscan finds.

If you continue up via Santa Chiara from the Teatro Romano you'll come to the finest formal gardens in Verona, the **Giardini Giusti** at Via Giardini Giusti 2 (daily: summer 9am–8pm; winter 9am–sunset; L7000/€3.62). Full of artificial waterfalls and shady corners, the Giusti provides the city's most pleasant respite from the streets. One last spot on this side of the river might profitably fill an hour or so – the **Museo Storico Naturale** (Mon–Sat 9am–7pm, Sun 2–7pm; L4000/€2.07), opposite the church of San Fermo at Lungadige Porta Vittoria 9. As well as fossilized mammoths and tigers from local cave sites, the museum has an offbeat section on faked natural wonders – unicorn horns, monstrous animals and the like. If you've got any energy left to walk up the hill, the **Museo Africano** (Tues–Sat 9am–noon & 3–6pm, Sun 3–6pm; L5000/€2.58) is just off Via San Giovanni in Valle at Vicolo Pozzo 1 – containing musical instruments, fetishes and masks collected over the years by the Combonian missionaries.

Eating, drinking and nightlife

Your money goes a lot further in Verona than it does in Venice: numerous **trattorias** offer full meals for around L25,000/€12.91 (especially in the Veronetta district, on the east side of the river), while on almost every street corner there's a bar where a glass of house wine will set you back a mere L1000/€0.52. As the Veneto produces more DOC wine than any other region in Italy, it's not surprising that Italy's main wine fair, Vinitaly, is held in Verona; it takes place in April and offers abundant sampling opportunities. For non-alcoholic pleasure, sit outside one of the *gelaterie* in Piazza dell' Erbe and indulge in an incredible concoction of fruit, cream and ice cream; another place to make for is *Gelateria Pampanin*, by Ponte Garibaldi. **Nightlife** is varied, and genuinely goes on into the night, in contrast to Venice's late-evening shutdown.

Restaurants

Arena, Vicolo Tre Marchetti 1. Good pizzeria for a late-night bite, as it's open till 1am. Situated in a tiny alley between Via Mazzini and Via Anfiteatro off the northeast side of the Arena. Closed Mon.

Bella Napoli, via Marconi 14. The best pizzas in Verona, in a distinctly Neapolitan atmosphere. Closed Mon.

Trattoria da Barca, Vicolo Tre Marchette 19b (☎045.803.0463). A couple of steps north of the Arena, with a deeply classy ambience, this is the perfect spot for a pre- or post-opera meal of Veronese specialities. Closed Sun.

Bottega dei Vini, Vicolo Scudo di Francia 3a. Just off the north end of Via Mazzini, this is simply the best restaurant in Verona and has one of the largest selections of wines you'll find anywhere in Italy, though it's slightly touristy as a result. Open until midnight. Closed Tues.

Maffei, Piazza dell' Erbe 38 (☎045.801.015). Superb restaurant in a lovely Baroque palazzo, complete with courtyard. You can eat superbly for around L60,000/€30.99, not including wine. Closed July & Aug, plus Sun (and Mon in winter).

Osteria La Fontanina, Piazzetta Fontanina. One of the best old-world *osterie* on the left (west) bank of the Adige, with restaurant-style atmosphere and prices.

Osteria Perbacco, Via Carducci 48. Moderately priced Veronetta restaurant with a very attractive garden. Especially good fish and vegetarian dishes. Closed Wed.

Osteria alla Pigna, Via Pigna 4. Elegant traditional restaurant in between the duomo and Piazza dell' Erbe. Easily among the top five of the thirty or so *osterie tipiche* dotted around the historic centre. A main course will set you back around L25,000/€12.91. Closed Sun & Mon lunch.

Pero d'Oro, Via Ponte Pignolo 25. Another good Veronetta trattoria, with a family atmosphere. Serves inexpensive but genuine Veronese dishes. Closed Mon.

San Giovanni in Foro, Corte San Giovanni in Foro 4. Pizzas to rival *Bella Napoli* with outside seating in a courtyard just off Corso Porta Borsari. Closed Tues.

Bars

Al Carro Armato, Vicolo Gatto 2a. One of the most atmospheric bars in the city, with live music on Sunday evenings in winter. Open until 2am. Closed Wed.

Caffe dell' Erbe, Piazza dell' Erbe 32. Known universally as Mazzanti, this is the loudest, youngest and coolest of the late-opening bars on the square.

Al Mascaron, Piazza San Zeno 16. A five-minute walk west from Castelvecchio takes you beyond the bustle to a quiet square where you'll find a crowd of young Veronese. Fine wines and an urbane atmosphere earlier on, popular disco-bar later. Closed Mon.

Osteria al Duomo, Via Duomo 7a. Best of the city's bars, little changed by twentieth-century fashion, and enlivened on Wednesday afternoons (5–8pm) and Friday nights in winter by a traditional singalong. Open 4pm–midnight. Closed Thurs.

Osteria al Vino, Via Sottoriva 9. Rumbustious and full of locals: Verona's traditional *osterie* don't come much more authentic than this.

Al Ponte, Via Ponte Pietra. Sip a glass in the garden here and enjoy a marvellous view of Ponte Pietra and the Teatro Romano. Open till 3am. Closed Wed.

Ai Preti, Via Acqua Morta 27. Popular osteria over in the Veronetta district; the pasta and wine are cheap, and musicians often drop by to play. Closes 8pm.

Nightlife

Music and **theatre** are the dominant art forms in the cultural life of Verona. In July and August an opera festival takes place in the **Arena**, always featuring a no-expense-spared production of *Aida*. To get the best (or last-minute) seats, call in at the office on via Dietro Anfiteatro 6b, which opens late on performance nights; if you can't make it in person you can now book by phone or online (☎045.800.5151, *www.arena.it*). **Big rock events** crop up on the Arena's calendar too. A season of ballet and of Shakespeare and other dramatists in Italian is the principal summer fare at the **Teatro Romano**. Some of the Teatro events are free; for the rest, cheapskates who don't mind inferior acoustics can park themselves on the steps going up the hill alongside the theatre. The box office at the Teatro Romano also sells tickets for the Arena and vice versa.

From October to May **English-language films** are shown every Tuesday at the Cinema Stimate in Piazza Cittadella. The **disco** scene is much more lively than in Venice, with venues coming and going; look in the local paper, *L'Arena* (there's a copy in every bar), to find out where they are and what days they're open. The *Spettacoli* section of *L'Arena* is the best source of up-to-date information on entertainment in Verona.

Treviso

The local tourist board are pitching it a bit high when they suggest that the waterways of **TREVISO** may remind you of Venice, but the old centre of this brisk provincial capital is certainly more alluring than you might imagine from a quick glance on your way to or from the airport. Treviso was an important town long before its assimilation by Venice in 1389, and plenty of evidence of its early status survives in the form of Gothic churches, public buildings and, most dramatically of all, the paintings of **Tomaso da Modena** (1325–79), the major artist in north Italy in the years immediately after Giotto's death. The general townscape within Treviso's sixteenth-century walls is often appealing too – long porticoes and frescoed house facades give many of the streets an appearance quite distinct from those of other towns in the region.

The City

These features are well preserved in the main street of the centre, **Calmaggiore**, where modern commerce (epitomized by the omnipresent Benetton, a Trevisan firm) has reached the sort of compromise with the past that the Italians seem to arrange better than anyone else. Modern building techniques have played a larger part than you might think in shaping that compromise – Treviso was pounded during both world wars and on Good Friday 1944 was half destroyed in a single bombing raid.

The early thirteenth-century **Palazzo dei Trecento**, at the side of the **Piazza dei Signori**, was one casualty of 1944 – a line round the exterior shows where the restoration began. The adjoining **Palazzo del Podestà** is a nineteenth-century structure, concocted in an appropriate style.

Of more interest are the two churches at the back of the block: **San Vito** and **Santa Lucia**. The tiny, dark chapel of Santa Lucia has extensive frescoes by Tomaso da

Modena and his followers; San Vito has even older paintings in the alcove through which you enter from Santa Lucia, though they're not in a good state. The cathedral of Treviso, **San Pietro**, stands at the end of Calmaggiore (Mon–Sat 7.30am–noon & 3.30–7pm, Sun 7.30am–1pm & 3.30–8pm). Founded in the twelfth century, San Pietro was much altered in succeeding centuries, and then rebuilt to rectify the damage of 1944. The interior is chiefly notable for the crypt – a thicket of twelfth-century columns with scraps of medieval mosaics – and the Cappella Malchiostro, with fragmentary frescoes by Pordenone and an *Annunciation* by Titian.

Just over the River Sile from the railway station is the severe Dominican church of **San Nicolò** (Mon–Fri 8am–12.30pm & 3.30–7pm), which has frescoes dating from the thirteenth to the sixteenth centuries. Some of the columns are decorated with paintings by Tomaso da Modena and his school, of which the best are the *SS Jerome* and *Agnes* (by Tomaso) on the first column on your right as you enter; there's also a towering *St Christopher*, on the wall of the right aisle, painted around 1410 and attributed to Antonio da Treviso. Equally striking, but far more graceful, is the composite *Tomb of Agostino d'Onigo* on the north wall of the chancel, created in 1500 by Antonio Rizzo (who did the sculpture) and Lorenzo Lotto (who painted the attendant pages). The figures of Agnes and Jerome are an excellent introduction to Tomaso da Modena, but for a comprehensive demonstration of his talents you have to visit the neighbouring **Seminario**, where the chapter house is decorated with a series of forty *Portraits of Members of the Dominican Order*, executed in 1352 (Mon–Fri: summer 8am–6pm; winter 8am–12.30pm & 3–5.30pm; free).

The Santa Caterina district

Treviso has a second great fresco cycle by Tomaso da Modena – *The Story of the Life of St Ursula*, now housed in the deconsecrated church of **Santa Caterina**, on the other side of the centre from San Nicolò – unfortunately it's closed and the restoration of this building seems to be eternal. The area around the church is a pleasant one, with its antiques sellers and furniture restorers, and the hubbub of the stalls around the fish market. There are a couple of other churches worth a look, too. To the north of Santa Caterina is the rebuilt thirteenth-century church of **San Francesco**, an airy building with a ship's-keel roof and patches of fresco, including a *Madonna and Saints* by Tomaso da Modena (chapel to north of chancel). To the south, at the end of Via Carlo Alberto – one of the most attractive streets in the town – stands the **Basilica di Santa Maria Maggiore**, which houses the most venerated image in Treviso, a fresco of the Madonna originally painted by Tomaso but subsequently retouched.

The Museo Civico

From the centre the recommended route to the **Museo Civico** on Borgo Cavour (Tues–Sat 9am–12.30pm & 2.30–5pm, Sun 9am–noon; L3000/€1.55) is along Via Riccati, which has a number of fine old houses. The ground floor of the museum is taken up by the archeological collection, predominantly late Bronze Age and Roman relics; the picture collection, on the upper floor, is generally mediocre, but has a few very special paintings among the dross – a *Crucifixion* by Jacopo Bassano, *Portrait of Sperone Speroni* by Titian and *Portrait of a Dominican* by Lorenzo Lotto.

Practicalities

The **tourist office** is right in the centre, at Piazza Monte di Pietà 8 (Mon–Sat 9am–12.30pm & 2–6pm; ☎0422.547.632, *www.sevenonline.it/tvapt*); it dispenses useful leaflets not just on Treviso but on attractions throughout Treviso province. From the train station, head straight across the bridge, bending slightly left at the first roundabout to reach the centre.

There are only three hotels in the centre, and you'd only choose to stay at one of them, the reasonably priced and pleasant *Campeol*, close to the tourist office, at Piazza Ancilotto 8 (☎0422.56.601; ④); reception is at the *Beccherie* restaurant, on the opposite side of the tiny piazza. Second choice would be the four-star *Continental*, a short walk from the train station at Via Roma 16 (☎0422.411.216; ⑦); aimed at Eurobusiness types, it's not the most charismatic hotel in the Veneto, but it is conveniently located, well maintained and, with 142 beds, is almost certain to have space.

Treviso's **restaurants** have a far higher reputation than its hotels, the leader of the pack being *El Toulà da Alfredo*, at Via Collalto 26 (☎0422.540.275; closed Sun evening & Mon), where you shouldn't expect to see change from L100,000/€51.65 per person. If that's too steep, try the homely *Toni del Spin*, a few steps from the church of San Vito at Via Inferiore 7 (☎0422.543.829; closed all day Sun & Mon lunchtime), or the *Beccherie* (see above; closed Sun evening and Mon), both of which provide superb Trevisan cuisine at around L45,000/€23.24 per head. The most popular **bars and cafés** in Treviso are those clustered underneath the Palazzo dei Trecento and spread along Calmaggiore and Via XX Settembre. One of these, *Nascimben*, Via XX Settembre 3, serves perhaps the best **ice cream** in town.

Castelfranco Veneto and Cittadella

CASTELFRANCO VENETO once stood on the western edge of Treviso's territory, and battlemented brick walls that the Trevisans threw round the town in 1199 to protect it against the Paduans still encircle most of the old centre (or *castello*). Of all the walled towns of the Veneto, only two – Cittadella (see opposite) and Montagnana (see p.341) – bear comparison with Castelfranco, and the place would merit an expedition on the strength of this alone. But Castelfranco was also the birthplace of **Giorgione** and possesses a painting that single-handedly vindicates Vasari's judgement that Giorgione's place in Venetian art is equivalent to Leonardo da Vinci's in that of Florence.

The painting in question – *The Madonna and Child with SS Francis and Liberale*, usually known simply as the *Castelfranco Madonna* – hangs in the **Duomo** (daily: summer 8am–noon & 3.30–7pm; winter 9am–noon & 3–6pm), in a chapel to the right of the chancel. Giorgione is the most elusive of all the great figures of the Renaissance: including the *Castelfranco Madonna*, only six surviving paintings can indisputably be attributed to him, and so little is known about his life that legends have proliferated to fill the gaps – for instance, the one that attributes his death in 1510, aged not more than 34, to his catching bubonic plague from a mistress. The paintings themselves have compounded the enigma, and none is more mysterious than this one, in which formal abstraction is combined with an extraordinary fidelity to physical texture, while the demeanour of the figures suggests a melancholic preoccupation. It was commissioned to commemorate Matteo Costanza, towards whose tombstone the gazes of the three figures are directed. You'll notice piles of coins in a space beneath a grill underfoot: there's no legend here, it's just an air-conditioning vent – not that the superstitious seem to mind. The minor works by Palma Vecchio and others in the **sacristy** are worth a look, though the experience is somewhat anticlimactic after the *Madonna*; ask the sacristan to let you in.

In a first-floor room of the adjacent **Casa Giorgione** there's a rather dull chiaroscuro frieze that's wishfully attributed to the artist (Tues–Sun 9am–12pm & 3–6pm; often closed weekday mornings in winter; L2500/€1.29), and an exhibition of reproductions (the originals are scattered around the world, mostly in Washington and the UK), just to show you what you're missing.

To get from the **train station** to the centre, turn left as you leave the station, then follow the curve of the road to the right, heading straight up Borgo Pieve to the southeast corner of the town walls. The walled city is tiny, and even a gentle stroll will quickly get you from one end to the other, but a good way to soak in the atmosphere is to eat at the **restaurant** *Al Castello*, at via Preti 11, just 200m down from the Duomo, which has outside tables and serves excellent, reasonably priced lunches.

Cittadella

When Treviso turned Castelfranco into a garrison, the Paduans promptly retaliated by reinforcing the defences of **CITTADELLA**, 15km to the west, on the train line to Vicenza. The fortified walls of Cittadella were built in the first quarter of the thirteenth century, and are even more impressive than those of its neighbour. You enter the town through one of four rugged brick gateways; if you're coming from the train station it'll be the Porta Padova, the most daunting of the four, flanked by the **Torre di Malta**. The tower was built as a prison and torture chamber by the monstrous Ezzelino da Romano, known to those he terrorized in this region in the mid-thirteenth century as "The Son of Satan". His atrocities earned him a place in the seventh circle of Dante's *Inferno*, where he's condemned to boil eternally in a river of blood. There's not much else to Cittadella, but it's definitely worth hopping off the train for a quick circuit of the walls.

Bassano del Grappa and Maróstica

Situated on the River Brenta where it widens on its emergence from the hills, **BAS-SANO** has expanded rapidly this century, though its historic centre remains largely unspoiled by twentieth-century mistakes. It's better known for its manufacturers and produce, and for the events of the two world wars (see below), than for any outstanding architecture or monuments, but the airy situation on the edge of the mountains, and the quiet charm of the old streets make it well worth the trip. For centuries a major producer of ceramics and wrought iron, Bassano is also renowned for its **grappa** distilleries and culinary delicacies such as porcini (dried mushrooms), white asparagus and honey.

Almost all of Bassano's sights lie between the Brenta and the train station; go much further in either direction and you'll quickly come to recently developed suburbs. Walking away from the station, you cross the orbital Viale delle Fosse to get to **Piazza Garibaldi**, one of the two main squares. Here, the cloister of the fourteenth-century church of San Francesco now houses the **Museo Civico** (Tues–Sat 9am–6.30pm, Sun 3.30–6.30pm; L8000/€4.13, ticket includes the Palazzo Sturm – see overleaf, *www. x-land.it/museobassano*). Downstairs the rooms are devoted to Roman and other archeological finds. Upstairs is a collection including paintings by the da Ponte family (better known as the Bassano family). Jacopo Bassano is the most famous, though his works can be sentimental and derivative; his son Francesco is better represented by some brooding portraits. Don't miss the tucked-away medieval rooms, which conceal a couple of typically luminous Bartolomeo Vivarini works, and a compelling *Crucifixion* by the fourteenth-century Padovan artist Guariento. Other rooms are devoted to a number of plaster works by Canova, two thousand of whose drawings are owned by the museum, and to the great baritone Tito Gobbi, who was born ion Bassano.

Overlooking the other side of the piazza is the **Torre Civica**, once a lookout tower for the twelfth-century inner walls, now a clock tower with spurious nineteenth-century battlements and windows. Beyond Piazza Libertà with its fifteenth-century Loggia (once home of the Venetian military commander), Piazzetta Montevecchio leads to a little jumble of streets and stairways running down to the river and the **Ponte degli Alpini**. The river was first bridged at this point in the late twelfth century, and replacements or repairs have been needed at regular intervals ever since, mostly because of flooding; the present structure was designed by Palladio in 1568, and built of wood in order to make the bridge as flexible as possible. Nardini, a grappa distillery founded in 1779 (Tues–Sun 8am–8pm), stands at this end of the bridge; these days the distilling process takes place elsewhere, but there's still the original shop and bar where you can sample before you select your bottle.

From here, if you follow Via Ferracina downstream for a couple of minutes you'll come to the eighteenth-century **Palazzo Sturm** (June–Sept Tues–Sat 9am–12.30pm, Sun 10am–12.30pm & 3.30–6.30pm; April, May & Oct Tues–Sat 9am–12.30pm, Sun 3.30–6.30pm; Nov–March Fri 9am–12.30pm, Sat & Sun 3.30–6.30pm; same ticket as Museo Civico – see previous page), a showcase for the town's famed majolica ware.

Various streets and squares in Bassano commemorate the dead of the two world wars. The major **war memorial**, however, is out of town on **Monte Grappa**. A vast, circular, tiered edifice with a "Via Eroica" leading to a war museum, it holds 12,000 Italian and Austro-Hungarian dead; less a symbol of mourning and repentance than a declaration of future collaboration, it was built by the Fascists in 1935. Buses go up there from Bassano during the summer months.

Practicalities

The **tourist office** is just within the easternmost ambit of the town walls, at Largo Corona d'Italia 35 (Mon–Sat 9am–12.30pm & 2–5pm, Sat 9am–12.30pm; ☎0424.524.351), their free magazine called *Bassano News* gives up-to-date information about the city's facilities and events. The train station is just beyond, across the busy main road.

For **accommodation**, there's only one hotel actually in the old centre, *Al Castello*, Piazza Terraglio, 19 (☎0424.228665; ④), right by the castle. The other hotels are a short distance out, though the *Belvedere*, on the main Viale delle Fosse, just east of the walls (☎0424.529.845, *www.bonotto.it*; ⑤), and the *Victoria*, at Viale Diaz 33, just across the Ponte Nuovo, on the west bank of the Brenta (☎0424.503.620, *victoriahotel@pn.itnet.it*; ④), are within easily walkable distance of the centre and are just as good. Otherwise, there's a hostel, *Istituto Cremona*, Via Chini 6 (☎0424.522.032; L15,000/€7.75), and the inexpensive *Alla Favorita*, Via S. Giorgio 11 (☎0424.502.030; ③), which is a good fifteen minutes from the centre, west across the river, beyond Piazza Santa Trinita.

As for **food**, the *Antica Osteria*, Via Matteotti 7 (closed Mon), has good bar snacks, while the old-fashioned *Trattoria del Borgo*, Via Margnan 7, which has a garden, and *El Piron*, Via Z. Bricito 12 (closed Sat), are recommended for a full meal, at around L30,000/€15.49.

Maróstica

Seven kilometres to the west of Bassano (and a fifteen-minute hop on the regular bus), the walled town of **MARÓSTICA** was yet another stronghold of Ezzelino da Romano, whose fortress glowers down on the old centre from the crest of the hill of Pausolino. The Ezzelini controlled Maróstica for quite a while – Ezzelino III was preceded by Ezzelino the Stutterer and Ezzelino the Monk – but it was another despotic dynasty, the Scaligers of Verona, who constructed the **town walls** and the Castello Inferiore (lower castle).

In front of the castle is Piazza Castello, the central square of the town, onto which is painted the board for the **Partita a Scacchi**, the town's principal claim to fame. The game's origin was an everyday chivalric story of rival suitors, the only unusual aspect being that the matter was decided with chess pieces rather than swords. The game was played with live pieces here in the square, and is re-enacted with great pomp on the second weekend of September of even-numbered years. Fourteenth-century costumes worn for the game are displayed in the **Castello Inferiore** (guided tours only Mon–Sat 10am, 10.45am, 11.30am, 3.30pm, 4.15pm, 5pm and 5.45pm & Sun 10am, 10.45am, 11.30am, 3.30pm & 6pm; L1000/€0.52, *www.telemar.it/marostica.htm*).

Ásolo and the Villa Barbaro

Known as "la Città dai cento orizzonti" (the city with a hundred horizons), the medieval walled town of **ÁSOLO** presides over a tightly grouped range of nearly thirty gentle peaks in the foothills of the Dolomites. In 1234 Ezzelino da Romano wrested the town from the Bishop of Treviso; on his death in 1259 the townspeople ensured that the dynasty died with him by massacring the rest of his family, who were at that time in nearby San Zenone.

The end of the fifteenth century was marked by the arrival of Caterina Cornaro (see below) – her celebrated court was attended by the likes of Cardinal Bembo, one of the most eminent literary figures of his day, who coined the verb *Asolare* to describe the experience of spending one's time in pleasurable aimlessness. Later writers and artists found the atmosphere equally convivial: Gabriele d'Annunzio wrote about the town, and Robert Browning's last published work – *Asolando* – was written here.

There are regular **buses** to Ásolo from Bassano; if you want to get there from Venice, it's quickest to take a train to Treviso, from where there are buses at least hourly (some change at Montebelluna) – in addition to the direct Ásolo services, all the buses to Bassano go through Ásolo and Masèr (see p.362).

The Town

The bus drops you at the foot of the hill, from where a connecting minibus (L1500/€0.77 return) shuttles up into the town. Memorabilia of Ásolo's celebrated residents are gathered in the **Museo Civico** in Piazza Maggiore, which has long been in the throes of restoration. Especially diverting are the portraits, photos and personal effects of **Elenora Duse**. An actress in the Sarah Bernhardt mould, Duse was almost as well known for her tempestuous love life as for her roles in Shakespeare, Hugo and Ibsen, and she came to Ásolo to seek refuge from public gossip. Although she died in Pittsburgh while on tour in 1924, her wish was to be buried in Ásolo, and so her body was transported back here, to the church of Sant'Anna. The main interest of the art collection is provided by a pair of dubiously attributed Bellinis, a portrait of Ezzelino painted a good couple of centuries after his death and a brace of large sculptures by Canova.

The Teatro Duse occupies a major part of the **Castello**, which has been largely restored, though there's still little to see other than the view from the ramparts. From 1489 to 1509 this was the home of **Caterina Cornaro**, one of the very few women to have played a major part in Venetian history. Born into one of Venice's most powerful families, Caterina was married to Jacques II, King of Cyprus. Within a year of the wedding Jacques was dead, and there followed nearly a decade of political pressure from Venice's rulers, who wanted to get their hands on the strategically vital island. In 1489 she was finally forced to abdicate in order to gain much-needed weapons and ships against a Turkish attack. Brought back to Venice to sign a deed "freely giving" Cyprus to the Republic, she was given the region of Ásolo as a sign of Venice's indebtedness. Eventually Ásolo too was taken away from her by the Emperor Maximilian, and she sought asylum in Venice, where she died soon after, in 1510.

If you're driving, you may want to head out to **Possagno**, 8km from Ásolo (also served by buses from Bassano, an hour's ride away), birthplace of the sculptor Antonio Canova. The **Gipsoteca**, (May–Sept Tues–Sat 9am–noon & 3–6pm, Sun 9am–noon & 3–7pm; Oct–April Tues–Sat 9am–noon & 2–5pm, Sun 9am–noon & 2–6pm;

L5000/€2.58) in the centre of the village, next to the sculptor's house, contains a huge collection of Canova's inimicable preparatory casts, as well as works by Luca Giordano and Palma il Giovane. For modern architecture enthusiasts, the brilliant gallery design is by Carlo Scarpa, who left his subtle mark on museums throughout the Veneto.

Practicalities

The **tourist office** is at Piazza G. D'Annunzio 2 (Mon–Sat 9am–12.30pm & 3–6pm; ☎0423.529.046). Accommodation is all but impossible to find. The cheapest of the **hotels** is the *Duse*, a reasonable-quality three-star at Via Browning 190 (☎0423.55.241; ⑤); the place is booked solid on the second weekend of every month, when a large antiques fair takes over the centre of town. Of the two four-star hotels the *Villa Cipriani*, Via Canova 298 (☎0423.523.411, *www.sheraton.com/villacipriani*; ⑨), is a long-standing favourite with Europe's crowned heads and mega-rich showbiz types; doubles start at L475,000/€245.34. Above the main square, the new *Albergo al Sole*, Via Collegio 33 (☎0423.528.399, *albergoalsole@sevenonline.it*; ⑥), is rapidly making a name for itself, with impeccable facilities and a breathtaking view from the breakfast terrace.

For around L45,000/€23.24 you can get a fine meal at the best **restaurant** in town, *Ca' Derton*, Piazza G. D'Annunzio (☎0423.529.648; closed Sun evening & Mon); the more basic *Cornaro* just off Piazza Garibaldi, in Via Regina Cornaro (closed Mon), has a good range of pizzas plus the standard *primi* and *secondi*.

The Villa Barbaro at Masèr

Touring the villas of the Veneto, you become used to mismatches between the quality of the architecture and the quality of the decoration, but at the **Villa Barbaro** at **MASÈR** (Tues, Sat & Sun: summer 3–6pm, winter 2.30–5pm; L9500/€4.90, *www.tvol.it/villadimaser*), a few kilometres northeast of Ásolo, you'll see the best of two of the central figures of Italian civilization in the sixteenth century – **Palladio** (see p.343) and **Paolo Veronese**, whose careers crossed here and nowhere else. If you're reliant on public transport, a visit is best made by bus from Bassano via Ásolo (at least 9 daily), or from Treviso – the services from Treviso to Ásolo all pass through Masèr.

The **villa** was built in the 1550s for Daniele and Marcantonio Barbaro, men whose humanist training and diverse cultural interests made the process of designing the house far more of a collaborative venture than were most of Palladio's other projects. The entire ground floor was given over to farm functions – dovecotes in the end pavilions, stables and storage space under the arcades, administrative offices on the lower floor of the central block. The avenue of trees, the sculptures and the very structure of the villa draw you in from the fields, down the projecting central axis of the building and through to the extravagant nymphaeum watered by a spring – the source of the fertility of the land.

This theme of fertility is echoed again and again in the living quarters of the *piano nobile*, in a series of **frescoes** by Veronese that has no equal in northern Italy. The more abstruse scenes are decoded in an excellent guidebook on sale in the villa, but most of the paintings require no footnotes. The walls of the Villa Barbaro are the most resourceful display of trompe l'oeil you'll ever see: servants peer round painted doors, a dog sniffs along the base of a flat balustrade in front of a landscape of ruins, a huntsman (probably Veronese himself) steps into the house through an entrance that's a solid wall. (Inevitably, it's speculated that the woman facing the hunter at the other end of the house was Veronese's mistress.)

In the grounds in front of the villa stands Palladio's **Tempietto**, the only church by him outside Venice and one of his last projects; commissioned by Marcantonio a decade after his brother's death, it was built in 1580, the year Palladio himself died. It is currently closed for restoration and no-one seems to know when, if ever, the work will be complete.

Just by the bus stop and crossroads, 300m from the villa, the *Locanda di Masèr* (closed Wed) is a gem, serving superb local cuisine at bargain prices – perfect for a late lunch before the villa opens.

Feltre

The historic centre of **FELTRE**, spread along a narrow ridge overlooking the modern town, owes its beguiling appearance to the calamity of 1509, when, in the course of the War of the League of Cambrai, the troops of the Imperial Army decided to punish the place for its allegiance to Venice by wiping much of it from the face of the planet. The Venetians took care of the reconstruction, and within a few decades the streets looked pretty much as they do nowadays. You're not going to find architecture students on every street corner, but you'd have to travel a long way to get a better idea of how an ordinary town looked in sixteenth-century Italy.

There are no direct **trains** to Feltre from Venice, but Feltre is a stop for the twelve-daily Padua-to-Belluno trains, which you can intercept at Castelfranco. The journey from Padua to Feltre takes ninety minutes, and it's a further thirty to Belluno.

From the station the shortest route to the old town is to cross straight over into Viale del Piave, over Via Garibaldi (where there's a decent range of bars, restaurants and hotels) and along Via Castaldi, which brings you to the **Duomo** and **Baptistry**, at the foot of the ridge. The main objects of interest in the duomo are a sixth-century Byzantine cross and a tomb by Tullio Lombardo. At the top of the steps that go past the side of the baptistry, on the other side of the road, is the town's south gate, under which begins a long covered flight of steps that takes you up into the heart of the old town. You come out by the sixteenth-century **Municipio**, the portico of which was designed by Palladio. The keep of the medieval *castello* rises behind the platform of the **Piazza Maggiore**.

To the left, the main street of Feltre, **Via Mezzaterra**, slopes down to the fifteenth-century Porta Imperiale. Nearly all the houses here are sixteenth century, and several have external frescoes by the town's most important painter, Lorenzo Luzzo – better known as Il Morto da Feltre (The Dead Man), a nickname prompted by the pallor of his skin. Via L. Luzzo, the equally decorous continuation of Via Mezzaterra on the other side of the piazza, leads to the **Museo Civico** (Tues–Sun 10am–1pm & 3–6pm; L8000/€4.13), which contains Il Morto's *Madonna with SS Vitus and Modestus* and other pieces by him, plus paintings by Cima and Gentile Bellini and a display of Roman and Etruscan finds. Il Morto's finest work is generally held to be the fresco of the *Transfiguration* in the **Ognissanti** church; this building is unlikely to be open in the foreseeable future, but if you want to try your luck, go out of the Porta Oria, right by the Museo Civico, down the dip and along Borgo Ruga for a couple of hundred metres.

Feltre has another, more unusual museum – the **Museo Rizzarda** at Via del Paradiso 8, parallel to Via Mezzaterra (June–Sept Tues–Sun 10am–1pm & 4–7pm; L3000/€1.55). This doubles as the town's collection of modern art and an exhibition of wrought-iron work, most of it by **Carlo Rizzarda** (1883–1931), ex-owner of the house. This is more appealing than it sounds, rescued by the remarkable finesse of Rizzarda's pieces.

Conegliano

North of Treviso, around the amiable town of **CONEGLIANO**, the landscape ceases to be boring. The surrounding hills are patched with vineyards, and the production of wine (*Prosecco* in particular) is central to the economy of the district. Italy's first wine-growers' college was set up in Conegliano in 1876, and there's a large grape festival in the last weekend of September, with parades and a banquet. It's a rewarding place for tourists too, as two well-established **wine routes** meet here: the Strada dei Vini del Piave, which runs for 68km southeast to Oderzo, and the more rewarding Strada del Prosecco, the first to be established in Italy, a 42-kilometre journey west to Valdobbiádene. Access to Conegliano itself is straightforward, as nearly all the regular Venice-to-Udine trains stop here.

The old centre of Conegliano, adhering to the slope of the Colle di Giano, is right in front of you as you come out of the station; just follow the road ahead and climb the steps to Via XX Settembre. This is the original main street, whose most decorative feature is the unusual facade of the **Duomo**: a fourteenth-century portico, frescoed in the sixteenth century, which joins seamlessly the buildings on each side. The interior of the church has been much rebuilt, but retains fragments of fifteenth-century frescoes; the major adornment of the church, though, is the magnificent altarpiece of *The Madonna and Child with Saints and Angels*, painted in 1493 by Giambattista Cima, the most famous native of Conegliano.

Cima's birthplace, no. 24 Via G.B. Cima (at rear of duomo), has now been converted into the **Casa Museo di G. B. Cima** (summer Fri 9am–noon & 3.30–7pm, Sat 3.30–7pm, Sun 10am–noon & 3.30–7pm; winter Sat & Sun 3–6pm; L1000/€0.52), which consists mainly of reproductions of his paintings and archeological finds made during the restoration of the house. The painting tradition is kept alive in the **Galleria d'Arte Moderna**, Palazzo Sarcinelli, on Via XX Settembre, which hosts occasional exhibitions that are more important than you'd expect in a town of this size. More variable in quality, but certainly picturesque, is the **art festival** held in September, when local painters set up stalls right along the Contrada Granda.

The **Museo Civico** (Tues–Sun: April–Sept 10am–12.30pm & 3.30–7pm; Oct–March 10am–12.30pm & 3–6.30pm; L3000/€1.55) is housed in the tallest surviving tower of the reconstructed castello on top of the hill. It's reached most quickly by the steep and cobbled Calle Madonna della Neve, which begins at the end of Via Accademia, the street beside the palatial Accademia cinema, and follows the town's most impressive stretch of ancient wall. The museum has some damaged frescoes by Pordenone and a small bronze horse by Giambologna, but most of the paintings are "Workshop of . . ." or "School of . . . ", and the displays of coins, maps, war memorabilia, armour and so forth are no more fascinating than you'd expect. But it's a lovingly maintained place, and the climb through the floors culminates on the tower's roof, from where you get a fine view across the gentle vine-clad landscape.

Practicalities

Conegliano's **tourist office** is on Via XX Settembre (Tues–Sat 9am–12.30pm & 3–6pm, Sun 9.30am–12.30pm & 4–6.30pm; ☎0438.21.230). Via XX Settembre has all you'll need in the way of **cafés**, **bars** and **food shops**; the three-star *Canon d'Oro* **hotel** at no. 129 (☎0438.34.246, *www.sevenonline.it/canondoro*; ④) is the best base for a tour of the Conegliano vineyards. If money's tight, you could stay at one of the very basic one-stars a couple of kilometres from the centre of town: the *Parè*, Via Vecchia Trevigiana 3/5 (☎0438.64.140; ②), or the nearby *Dei Mille*, above a trattoria at Via Dei Mille 22 (☎0438.61.618; ①). Bus #1 from the train station and buses to Treviso go past the former; ask to be let off at Parè. Top recommendation for low-cost **eating** is the superb *Alla Corona* trattoria, Via Beato Ongaro 29 (closed Mon), where a meal of genuine local dishes should cost around L40,000/€20.66; you get to it by continuing along Via XX Settembre past the *Canon d'Oro*.

Vittorio Veneto

The name **VITTORIO VENETO** first appeared on the map in 1866 when, to mark the Unification of Italy and honour the first king of the new country (Vittorio Emanuele II), the neighbouring towns of Cèneda and Serravalle (not previously the best of friends) were knotted together and rechristened. A new town hall was built midway along the avenue connecting the two towns, and the train station was constructed opposite, thus ensuring that the visitor steps straight from the train into a sort of no-man's-land. It's here, too, that you'll find the tourist office and bus station.

Cèneda

CÈNEDA, the commercial centre of Vittorio Veneto, is primarily worth a visit for the **Museo della Battaglia** (Tues–Sun: May–Sept 10am–noon & 4.30–6.30pm; Oct–April 10am–noon & 3–5pm; L5000/€2.58), whose loggia was built by Sansovino. The dull cathedral is right next door; turn right out of the station and keep going until you see the sign for the centre. The museum is dedicated to the climactic Battle of Vittorio: fought in October 1918, this was the final engagement of World War I for the Italian Army and marked the end of the Austro-Hungarian empire, which is why most towns in Italy have a Via Vittorio Veneto.

Overlooking town is the imposing Castello di San Martino, once a Lombard stronghold and now the bishop's palace, which is why you won't be allowed in. The only other building that merits a look in Cèneda is the church of **Santa Maria del Meschio**, where you'll find a splendid *Annunciation* by Andrea Previtali, a pupil of Giovanni Bellini. If you turn left off the Cèneda–Serravalle road instead of going right for the cathedral square, you'll soon come across it.

Serravalle

SERRAVALLE, wedged up against the mouth of the gorge between the Col Visentin and the Cansiglio, is an entirely different proposition from its reluctant twin. Once through its southern gate you are into a town that has scarcely seen a demolition since the sixteenth century, though the effect is spoiled by the main road which tears right through the centre. Most of the buildings along Via Martiri della Libertà, Via Roma and Via Mazzini, and around the stage-like Piazza Marcantonio Flaminio, date from the fifteenth and sixteenth centuries – the handsomest being the shield-encrusted Loggia Serravallese. This is now the home of the **Museo del Cenedese** (May–Sept 10am–noon & 4–6.30pm; Oct–April 10am–noon & 3–5pm; closed Tues; same ticket as Museo della Battaglia – see above), a jumble of sculptural and archeological bits and pieces, detached frescoes and minor paintings. The **Palazzo Minucci de Carlo** (daily 9am–noon; ☎0438.571.93) has a ragbag collection of minor paintings, tapestries and old furniture, but you'll need to make an appointment to get inside.

Your time will be more profitably spent in **San Lorenzo dei Battuti** (daily except Tues: May–Sept 3–4pm; Oct–April 2–3pm; same ticket as Museo della Battaglia – see above; ☎0438.571.03), immediately inside the south gate, which is decorated with frescoes painted around 1450. Uncovered in 1953 and restored to rectify the damage done when Napoleon's lads used the chapel as a kitchen, this is one of the best-preserved fresco cycles in the Veneto. If it's closed, ask at the museum for the (rather grumpy) custodian; at present he won't open the church while he's looking after the Museo del Cenedese, but you can be more certain of gaining access on a Sunday, or if you ring ahead.

Practicalities

The **tourist office**, at Piazza del Popolo 18 (daily 9am–12.30pm & 3–6pm, Sat & Sun closes 5.30pm; ☎0438.57.243), is good for information on the ski resorts and walking terrain around the town. Most homely of the local **hotels** is the *Locanda Leon d'Oro*, a small three-star at Via Cavour 8 (☎0438.940.740; ③), opposite the gate into Serravalle; it has a fine and moderately priced restaurant. Immediately beside the bus stop, opposite the town hall, is the more formal *Hotel Flora* (☎0438.536.25; ④), which has a good fish restaurant. If you're determined to save money, they can direct you to the basic but friendly *Cairoli*, on Piazza Meschio (☎0438.536.43; ①) – it's a good fifteen-minute walk down the main Via Dante Aligheri, in the opposite direction from Serravalle, but bus #1 runs between the two every fifteen minutes.

Belluno

The most northerly of the major towns of the Veneto, **BELLUNO** was once a strategically important ally of Venice, and today is the capital of a province that extends mainly over the eastern Dolomites. Although the urban centres to the south are not far away, Belluno's focus of attention lies clearly to the north – the network of the Dolomiti-Bus company radiates out from here, trains run regularly up the Piave Valley to Calalzo, and the tourist handouts are geared mostly to hikers and skiers. Just one train a day runs from Venice to Belluno directly, but it's just as quick anyway to go from Venice to Conegliano and change there; from Padua there are twelve trains daily.

Its position is Belluno's main attraction, but the old centre calls for an hour or two's exploration if you're passing through. The hub of the modern town, and where you'll find its most popular bars and cafés, is the wide **Piazza dei Martiri**, off the south side of which a road leads to the Piazza del Duomo, the kernel of the old town. The sixteenth-century **Duomo**, an amalgam of the Gothic and classical, and built in the pale yellow stone that is a feature of the buildings in Belluno, was designed by Tullio Lombardo; it has had to be reconstructed twice after earthquake damage, in 1873 and 1936. There are a couple of good paintings inside: one by Andrea Schiavone (first altar on right) and one by Jacopo Bassano (third altar on right). The stately **campanile**, designed in 1743 by Filippo Juvarra, offers one of the great views of the Veneto.

Occupying one complete side of the Piazza del Duomo is the residence of the Venetian administrators of the town, the **Palazzo dei Rettori**, a frilly late-fifteenth-century building dolled up with Baroque trimmings. A relic of more independent times stands on the right – the twelfth-century **Torre Civica**, all that's left of the medieval castle. Continuing round the piazza, in Via Duomo, along the side of the town hall, you'll find the **Museo Civico** (Mon & Sat 10am–noon, Tues–Fri 10am–noon & 3–6pm; L4000/€2.07): the collection is strong on the work of Belluno's three best-known artists – the painters Sebastiano and Marco Ricci and the sculptor-woodcarver **Andrea Brustolon** – all of whom were born here between 1659 and 1673.

Via Duomo ends at the **Piazza del Mercato**, a tiny square hemmed in by porticoed Renaissance buildings. The principal street of the old town, **Via Mezzaterra**, goes down to the medieval **Porta Ruga** (veer left along the cobbled road about 50m from the end), from where the view up into the mountains will provide some compensation if you haven't managed to find the campanile open.

Practicalities

The **tourist office**, at Piazza dei Martiri 7 (Mon–Sat 9am–12.30pm & 3–6pm, Sun 10am–12.30pm), is a good source of leaflets on Belluno and its province, but if you want specialized information on mountain pursuits you should also call at ASVI Viaggi, Piazza dei Martiri 27e (Mon–Fri 9am–12.30pm & 3–7pm, Sat 9am–12.30pm).

The cheapest **hotels** in town are the *Taverna*, Via Cipro 7 (☎0437.25.192; ③), and *Centrale*, Via Loreto 2 (☎0437.943.349; ②); both are basic (only the *Centrale* has private bathrooms) but also very close to Piazza dei Martiri. Pick of the central three-stars are *Alle Dolomiti*, just off the piazza at Via Carrera 46 (☎0437.941.660; ④), and *Astor*, Piazza dei Martiri 26e (☎0437.942.094; ④), but both places are functional rather than atmospheric. The best **restaurant** in town is *Terracotta*, near the train station, at Borgo Garibaldi 61 (☎0437.942.644; closed Sat); a three-course meal should cost around L45,000/€23.24.

travel details

TRAINS

Belluno to: Calalzo (10 daily; 1hr); Conegliano (15 daily; 1hr–1hr 30min); Vittorio Veneto (15 daily; 30min).

Conegliano to: Belluno (15 daily; 1hr–1hr 30min); Udine (30 daily; 1hr 15min); Venice (34 daily; 1hr); Vittorio Veneto (15 daily; 25min).

Monsélice to: Este (9 daily; 10min); Montagnana (9 daily; 25min); Padua (9 daily; 20min); Venice (6 daily; 50min).

Padua to: Bassano (10 daily; 1hr 5min); Belluno (12 daily; 2hr); Feltre (12 daily; 50min); Milan (25 daily; 2hr 30min); Monsélice (9 daily; 25min); Venice (every 30min; 35min); Verona (25 daily; 55min); Vicenza (25 daily; 20min).

Treviso to: Castelfranco Veneto (hourly; 25min); Cittadella (hourly; 35min); Udine (hourly; 1hr 10min–1hr 30min); Venice (30 daily; 30min); Vicenza (hourly; 1hr).

Venice to: Bassano (14 daily; 1hr); Belluno (1 daily; 2hr); Castelfranco Veneto (at least every 2hr; 50min); Conegliano (34 daily; 1hr); Milan (25 daily; 2hr 50min–3hr 50min); Monsélice (6 daily; 50min); Padua (every 30min; 35min); Treviso (30 daily; 30min); Trieste (14 daily; 2hr 10min); Udine (hourly; 2hr); Verona (at least 25 daily; 1hr 30min); Vicenza (25 daily; 55min); Vittorio Veneto (4 daily; 1–2hr).

Verona to: Milan (30 daily; 1hr 40min); Padua (25 daily; 50min); Venice (25 daily; 1hr 30min); Vicenza (30 daily; 30min).

Vicenza to: Castelfranco (hourly; 40min); Cittadella (hourly; 30min); Milan (30 daily; 1hr 40min); Padua (25 daily; 20min); Treviso (hourly; 1hr); Venice (25 daily; 55min); Verona (30 daily; 30min).

BUSES

Bassano to: Ásolo (15 daily; 30min); Maróstica (hourly; 15min); Masèr (8 daily; 40min); Possagno (every 1–2hr; 40min).

Treviso to: Ásolo (hourly; 50min); Bassano (hourly; 1hr 20min); Padua (every 30min; 1hr 10min); Venice (every 20min; 55min).

Venice to: Malcontenta (hourly; 20min); Strà (every 30min; 45min).

Vicenza to: Bassano (hourly; 1hr 10min); Maróstica (hourly; 40min).

CHAPTER SIX

FRIULI-VENEZIA GIULIA

The geographical complexity of **Friuli-Venezia Giulia** – around eight thousand square kilometres of alps, limestone plateau, alluvial plain and shelving coastlands – is mirrored in its social diversity. The mountainous north is ethnically and linguistically Alpine; the old peasant culture of Friuli, though now waning, still gives a degree of coherence to the area south of the mountains; **Udine** seems Venetian, and **Grado**, slumbering in its Adriatic lagoons, Byzantine-Venetian; while **Aquileia**, a few kilometres north of Grado, is still redolent of its Roman and early Christian past. And **Trieste** itself, the regional capital, is a Habsburg city, developed with Austrian capital to be the empire's great southern port. In spirit and appearance it is central European, more like Ljubljana in Slovenia than anywhere else in the region with the possible exception of **Gorizia**.

If one thing unites the different parts of the region, it's how far removed they are from the conventional image of Italy, a remoteness that intensifies the further east you travel. This area has always been a bridge between the Mediterranean world and central Europe – that hazy multinational entity which begins, according to Eric Newby at least, at Monfalcone, north of Trieste. It has been invaded – sometimes enriched, often laid waste – from east and west and north, by the Romans, Huns, Goths, Lombards, Nazis and even the Cossacks. Venice in its heyday controlled the coast and plain as far as Udine; Napoleonic France succeeded the Venetian Republic, to be supplanted in turn by the Habsburgs. Earlier this century the region saw some of the fiercest fighting of World War I on the **Carso** (the plateau inland from Trieste), where artillery shells splintered the limestone into deadly shrapnel and the hills are still scarred with trenches. Vast war memorials and ossuaries punctuate the landscape: the bones of 60,000 soldiers lie at Oslavia, near Gorizia; 100,000 at Redipuglia; 25,000 in the Udine ossuary.

ACCOMMODATION PRICE CODES

Throughout this guide, prices per person are given for **youth hostels** and assume Hostelling International (HI) membership. **Hotel** accommodation is coded on a scale from ① to ⑨, reflecting the cost of the cheapest double room in each establishment in high season. The price bands to which these codes refer are as follows:

① Up to L60,000/€30.99
② L60,000–90,000/€30.99–46.48
③ L90,000–120,000/€46.48–61.98
④ L120,000–150,000/€61.98–77.47
⑤ L150,000–200,000/€77.47–103.29

⑥ L200,000–250,000/€103.29–129.11
⑦ L250,000–300,000/€129.11–154.94
⑧ L300,000–400,000/€154.94–206.58
⑨ over L400,000/€206.58

(See p.32 for a full explanation.)

There was less loss of life in World War II, but just as much terror. Fuelled by widespread and long-standing anti-Slavism, Italian Fascism in Trieste was especially virulent, and the city held Italy's only death camp. One of the strangest sideshows of the war was staged north of Udine: Cossack troops, led by White Russian officers, made an alliance with the Nazis and invaded Carnia, on the promise of a Cossack homeland among the Carnian mountains once the Reich was secure. No more invading armies have taken this road, but the last border dispute between Italy and Yugoslavia was not settled until the 1970s, and when neighbouring Slovenia became independent in June 1991 the border posts with Italy were the scene of brief but fierce confrontations between Slovene and Yugoslav troops. Despite Italian fears, however, the fighting did not spill across the border.

While the Friulani want Italian nationality, they don't care for the baggage of Italian identity. Respect for Rome and the government is in short supply, and enthusiasm for the separatist north Italian "League" movement has spread from Lombardy in recent years. It is unlikely that this marks the birth of Friulian separatism, but there's no doubt that the people here have their own ways and traditions, fostering a strong sense of identity. The local dialect, *friulano*, is undergoing something of an official revival – many road signs are bilingual in Italian and *friulano*, while studies of the dialect's history and many local variants are published by the Società Filologica Friulana in Udine.

REGIONAL FOOD AND WINE

Friuli-Venezia Giulia was once the poorest of the northern regions, with a dialect that's almost a language of its own and culinary influences from both Austria and the former Yugoslavia. *Jota*, a **soup** of sauerkraut and barley, is a traditionally cheap and filling dish, a reminder of harder times; the basic broth is given some pizzazz by the addition of *brovada*, a local mix of turnips steeped in a wooden cask full of grape pressings for about ninety days.

Perhaps a more appealing gourmet product is the succulent **ham** from San Daniele, delicious in both its cooked and cured forms. Friuli-Venezia Giulia's Slavic origins are evident in recipes that include yoghurt, rye bread, cumin and fennel seeds, and some unusual sweet-sour dishes – one combines sultanas and chocolate with spinach and potatoes; another has spices and dried fruit with polenta or pasta. Trieste's **gnocchi** tops the lot: gnocchi the size of eggs are stuffed with a pitted prune, rolled in breadcrumbs, browned in butter and sprinkled with cinnamon and sugar. Other dishes you might come across are *Cialzons* (ravioli from Carnia) stuffed with spinach and ricotta; pork pot-roasted in milk; rich, spicy *muset* sausage boiled and served with lentils or polenta; and a whole range of fish broths made from squid, octopus, mackerel, sardines and clams.

Friuli-Venezia Giulia makes some of the most stylish Italian white **wines** from local varieties like Tocai and Ribolla Gialla, as well as international varieties. The best and best-known wines come from Collio, the eastern hills, either Collio Goriziano near Gorizia, or the Colli Orientali Friulani, near Udine; look out for this, or the abbreviated form of COF, on the label. Tocai is the one to go for – dry, with the flavour of pears, citrus and herbs; wines from Picolit and Verduzzo are also good, along with the more familiar Pinot Bianco, Chardonnay and Sauvignon Blanc varieties. Reds, including Pinot Nero, Cabernet Franc and Merlot, taste better for ageing. The region's other wines are easy-drinking whites and aromatic reds from Isonzo, rather tart, fruity reds from Carso, and quaffable, inexpensive Merlot, Cabernet Sauvignon and Cabernet Franc from Grave del Friuli and Aquileia.

(Pier Paolo Pasolini, who grew up in Casarsa, near Pordenone, wrote his early poetry in *friulano*.) Economically the region is in fairly good shape: Udine and Pordenone are thriving, while Trieste is a focus for container traffic and is becoming a centre of computer technology and electronics.

Tourism is growing too. Increasing numbers of visitors, mostly Italian and German, are discovering places which almost rival the claims of the neighbouring Veneto, with none of the crowds or the cynical attitudes to tourists. Notwithstanding it's post-industrial atmosphere, Trieste makes a good base for walking trips into the extraordinary, cave-riven landscape of the Carso, with the option of a day at one of the purpose-built beach resorts along the **Triestine Riviera** – which isn't as glamorous as it sounds. **Udine**, with its beautiful Venetian centre and excellent art collections, is within easy reach to the north, as is tiny **Cividale del Friuli**, which preserves a picturesque historic centre perched on the gorge of the Natisone, as well as some fascinating Lombard remains. The archeologically minded will head straight for **Aquileia**, however, which has some of the most important Roman and early Christian remains in Italy, and is fifteen minutes from the lagoon resort of **Grado**, which conceals a tiny early Christian centre amid the beach hotels. Further north, towards the Austrian border, the **Carnia** is struggling to develop itself as a rival to the Dolomites for skiing and hiking, though in truth it has little over its neighbour other than peace and quiet.

Trieste

Backed by the green and white cliffs of a limestone plateau and facing the blue Adriatic, **TRIESTE** has a potentially idyllic setting; close up, however, the place reveals uninviting water and an atmosphere of run-down haughtiness. The city itself is rather strange: a capitalist creation built to play a role that no longer exists, though like so many ports in Europe, the seediness that long prevailed is now giving way to a nascent optimism. Trieste was Tergeste to the Romans, who captured it in 178 BC, but although signs of their occupancy are scattered throughout the city (the theatre off Corso Italia, for instance, and the arch by Piazza Barbacan), what strikes you straightaway is its modernity. With the exception of the castle and cathedral of San Giusto, and the tiny medieval quarter below, the city's whole pre-nineteenth-century history seems dim and vague beside the massive Neoclassical architecture of the **Borgo Teresiano** – the name given to the modern city centre, after Empress Maria Theresa (1740–80), who initiated the development.

Trieste was constructed largely with Austrian capital to serve as the Habsburg Empire's southern port. It briefly eclipsed Venice as the Adriatic's northern port, but its brief heyday drew to a close after 1918, when it finally became Italian and discovered that, for all its good intentions, Italy had no economic use for it. The city languished for sixty years, and is only now making a new role for itself. Computer-based firms are cropping up while seaborne trade goes through the container port on the south side of Trieste, leaving the old quays as windblown car parks.

Lying on the political and ethnic fault-line between the Latin and Slavic worlds, Trieste has long been a city of political extremes. In the last century it was a hotbed of *irredentismo* – an Italian nationalist movement to "redeem" the Austrian lands of Trieste, Istria (see D'Annunzio on p.225) and the Trentino. After 1918 the tensions increased, leading to a strong Fascist presence in Friuli-Venezia Giulia. Yugoslavia and the Allies fought over Trieste until 1954, when the city and a connecting strip of coast were secured for Italy, though a definitive border settlement was not reached until 1975. Tito kept the Istrian peninsula, whose fearful Italian population emigrated in huge numbers: Fiume (Rijeka), for example, lost 58,000 of its 60,000 Italians. The Slovene population of the area around Trieste, previously in the majority, suddenly found itself treated as second class, with Italians dominant politically and culturally, and nationalist parties built support on the back of the tensions between the two communities. The neo-Fascist MSI party does well here, and Trieste shocked the rest of Italy in February 2000 by inviting Jorg Haider, founder of Austria's right-wing Freedom Party to the city. Yet nationalism has long provoked the development of its antithesis and there is an intense socialist and intellectual tradition which is intimately connected with the city's café culture. Numerous foreign writers based themselves around Trieste, most famously James Joyce (see below), and Rainer Maria Rilke, and native literati include Umberto Saba and Italo Svevo.

Arrival, information and accommodation

Trieste's Piazza Libertà **bus station** is right by the central **train station,** ten minutes' walk from the town centre. The main **tourist office** is rather hidden away on the third

---

JOYCE IN TRIESTE

From 1905 to 1915, and again in 1919–20, **James Joyce** and his wife Nora lived in Trieste. After staying at Piazza Ponterosso 3 for a month, they moved to the third-floor flat at Via San Nicolò 30. (In 1919 the poet Umberto Saba bought a bookshop on the ground floor at the same address. The two writers seem never to have met, though they had a common friend in the novelist Italo Svevo.) There is no plaque in Via San Nicolò, but there is one on via Bramante 4, quoting the postcard that Joyce despatched in 1915 to his brother Stanislaus, whose Irredentist sympathies had landed him in an Austrian internment camp. The postcard announced that the first chapter of James's new work, *Ulysses*, was finished.

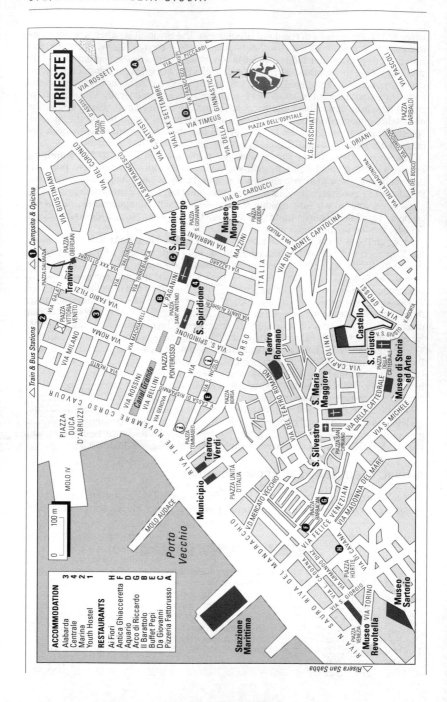

floor at Via San Nicolò 20 (Mon–Fri 9am–7pm, Sat 9am–1pm; ☎040.369.881), but there's an equally helpful office at Riva 3 Novembre 9 (daily 9am–7pm; ☎040.347.8312) and a good Web site at *www.triestetourism.it*. For information on the Friuli-Venezia Giulia region, go to the tourist office at Via G. Rossini 6 (Mon–Thurs 8.30am–12.30pm & 2–4.30pm, Fri 8.30am–12.30pm; ☎040.365.152, *www.fvgpromo.it*).

Accommodation in Trieste is uninspiring. The cheapest decent **hotels** are all between the train station and the town centre and are fairly uniformly dull but acceptable. The large *Marina*, Via Galatti 14 (☎040.369.298; ②) is probably the best bet, but otherwise try the *Centrale*, Via Ponchielli, 1 (☎040.639.482; ③; mid-March to Oct) or the *Alabarda*, Via Valdirivo 22 (☎040.630.269; ②). There's also a **youth hostel**, 7km out of the city at Viale Miramare 331 (☎040.224.102; L20,000/€10.32) – take a #36 bus from the station to Grignano and ask the driver to drop you at Bivio al Miramare, from where it's a five-minute walk straight down along Viale Miramare. The nearest **campsite** is the *Obelisco* (☎040.211.655), on an airy site 7km away in the hills below Opicina, take bus #4 or the *tranvia* (cable tramway) from Piazza Oberdan, stop at the obelisk, cross over the tracks where you'll see a sign to the campsite which is a minute's walk away.

The City

Trieste's modern life takes place in the grid-like streets of the Borgo Teresiano, but the focal point of the city's pre-modern history, and its prime tourist site, is the hill of **San Giusto**, named after the patron saint of the city. At the very summit of the hill, overlooking the remnants of the Roman forum, is the **Castello** (daily: April–Sept 9am–7pm; Oct–March 9am–5pm; L2000/€1.03, L3000/€1.55 including museum), a fifteenth-century Venetian fortress. There's nothing much to see inside, but a walk round the ramparts is *de rigueur* and there are fine views of the new town and the busy port below, while beyond the city confines the high escarpment of the Carso looms over the Adriatic. Its **museum** (Tues–Sun 9am–1pm; L3000/€1.55, including castle) houses a small collection of antique weaponry.

More interesting is the **Cattedrale di San Giusto** (Mon–Sat 8am–noon & 2.30–6.30pm, Sun 8am–1pm & 3.30–8pm), built on the ruins of a first century AD Roman structure. Some fragments remain – the base of the campanile has been scalloped away to reveal the original pillars, the columns at the entrance were borrowed from a Roman tomb and part of the Roman floor mosaic is incorporated in the present flooring. In around 1050 an earlier Christian chapel was replaced by two churches, the Basilica di Santa Maria Assunta and the Capella di San Giusto. The site was further expanded in the early thirteenth century in an extraordinary stroke of pragmatic architectural genius: the two adjacent buildings were bridged by a high beamed vault, forming the current cathedral nave and leaving a double aisle on each side. The complex history of the building becomes clearer if you study the arches in the interior, or look down on the apse from the castle wall behind. As it stands today, the cathedral is a typically Triestine synthesis of styles, with a serene, largely Romanesque interior only marred by an ugly modern choir. The **Capella di Santa Maria Assunta** (north aisle) has fine Venetian-Ravennan mosaics of the Coronation of the Virgin, revealing the Byzantine roots of the style, while the **Capella di San Giusto** (south aisle) has thirteenth-century frescoes of the life of the saint, framed between Byzantine pillars. The facade is predominantly Romanesque, but includes a Gothic rose window.

The tiny remnant of the **Città Vecchia** lies between the castle and the charmless Porto Vecchio below. On the cobbled Via della Cattedrale, the **Museo Civico di Storia ed Arte** (Tues–Sun 9am–1pm; L3000/€1.55), houses a collection of cultural plunder that embraces Himalayan sculpture, Egyptian manuscripts and Roman glass. Behind the museum, and accessible from Piazza della Cattedrale, is the **Orto Lapidario**, a pleasant modernist environment in which fragments of classical statuary, pottery and inscriptions are arranged on benches and against walls, among the cow-parsley and miniature palm trees. The little Corinthian temple on the upper level contains the remains of J.J.Winckelmann (1717–68), the German archeologist and theorist of Neoclassicism, who was murdered in Trieste by a man to whom he had shown off his collection of antique coins.

Further down Via della Cattedrale are a couple of ill-matched churches. The imposing **Santa Maria Maggiore** is little more than another brutish Baroque creation, but its tiny early Romanesque neighbour, **San Silvestro**, is worth a look for its unusual state of preservation; it's now used by adherents of the rare Helvetic-Waldensian sect. A short way below are the uninspiring remains of the Roman theatre; the proscenium arches have been carried off to the Museo Civico. There's little else of note in the old city, though some of the buildings of the old town are at last being restored and there's an antiques fair on the third Sunday of every month. Mosaic enthusiasts may want to stop off at the remains of the **Basilica Paleocristiana** (Wed 10am–noon; free) under the building at via Madonna del Mare 11. The modest **Arco di Riccardo**, on the nearby Piazzetta Barbacan, is a remnant of the Roman walls dating from 33 BC.

To the north, Trieste's new town, the **Borgo Teresiano**, is dominated by heavy Neoclassical architecture imported from nineteenth-century Vienna, with wide boulevards and a waterfront spoilt by a busy main road. The focus of the main grid of streets is **Piazza S. Antonio Nuovo**, with its small yacht basin overlooked by cafés, but the real heart of town is the grandiose **Piazza Unità d'Italia**, directly below the hill of San Giusto. Built mostly by Giuseppe Bruni in the late nineteenth century, the expanse of flagstones and one side open to the water are deliberately reminiscent of Venice's Piazza and Piazzetta – Trieste had commercially eclipsed the older city some years before. Projecting into the harbour nearby, the **Molo Audace**, named after the first boat of Italian soldiers to land here in 1918, is the venue for the evening passeggiata.

Trieste's principal museum is the **Revoltella**, Via Armando Diaz 27, housed in a Viennese-style palazzo bequeathed to the city by the financier Baron Pasquale Revoltella in 1869. Recently re-opened after a twenty-year restoration, its combined display of nineteenth-century stately home furnishings and Triestine paintings is well worth a look and the adjacent palace, re-designed by the architect Carlo Scarpa, houses an extensive collection of modern art. (Mon & Wed–Sat 10am–1pm & 3–7.30pm, Sun 10am–6pm; July–Aug open until midnight; L5000/€2.58). The nearby **Museo Sartorio**, in Largo Papa Giovanni XXIII (Tues–Sun 9am–1pm; L5000/€2.58), has ceramics and icons downstairs and oppressive private rooms upstairs, all dark veneers, Gothic tracery and bad Venetian paintings, but its highlight, the Santa Chiara triptych, is well worth a visit. Dating back to the early fourteenth century, the backs of its side panels have been attributed to Paolo Veneziano, and the central panel contains thirty-six beautifully restored miniature scenes from the life of Christ. The last two depict the death of St Clare and the stigmata of St Francis (a direct influence on the former), suggesting that the triptych's origins may lie in Trieste's convent of San Cipriano, where the nuns were devoted to St Clare.

A vastly more pleasant domestic interior is the **Museo Morpurgo**, north of San Giusto at Via Imbriani 5 (Tues–Sun 9am–1pm; L3000/€1.55). The palazzo was left to the city by the merchant and banker Mario Morpurgo di Nilma, and its apartments have not really been touched since their first decoration in the 1880s. With its sepia photographs and other memorabilia, it feels less like a museum than like a home whose owners went on holiday and never came back.

One of the ugliest episodes of recent European history is embodied by the **Risiera di San Sabba**, overlooking the southern flank of Trieste's port at Ratto della Pileria 43 (mid-April to May & Nov 1–5 Tues–Sat 9am–6pm, Sun 9am–1pm; rest of the year Tues–Sun 9am–1pm; free), on the #10 bus route. Once a rice-hulling plant, this was one of only two concentration camps in Italy (the other was near Carpi in Emilia-Romagna;

see p.414) and now houses a permanent exhibition that serves as a reminder of Fascist crimes in the region. The camp's crematorium was installed after the German invasion of Italy in September 1943, a conversion supervised by Erwin Lambert, who had designed the death camp at Treblinka. Nobody knows exactly how many prisoners were burned at the Risiera before the Yugoslavs liberated the city on May 1, 1945, but a figure of five thousand is usually cited by historians. Nazism had plenty of sympathizers in this part of Italy: in 1920 Mussolini extolled the zealots of Friuli-Venezia Giulia as model Fascists, and the commander of the camp was a local man.

Eating and drinking

Triestine **cuisine** is as mixed as its population, with goulash, potato noodles and cheese dumplings on many menus, as well as some superb fish dishes. The local *terrano*, a very sharp red wine grown only on the limestone highlands, was reputedly the favourite of the Roman empress Livia and is supposed to be good for the blood. It's delicious in any event and should be tried, ideally as an accompaniment to the heavy Triestine food. For less stolid meals, investigate the **osmizze** (see box on p.378), impromptu eating places, often in the hinterland of the Carso, which offer the simplest of local produce at rock-bottom prices. Trieste is most famous in Italy for its **coffee**, imported and even roasted here – you'll be pushed to find a better or a stronger cup anywhere. Via C. Battisti is a good street for **food shops** – cheeses, cooked meats, olives and pasta in its many guises are piled high in the windows.

Restaurants

Two restaurants in the new town are perfect for snack meals and lunches: *Buffet Pepi*, on Via Cassa di Risparmio 3 (closed Sun), a favourite student place, emphasizes Trieste's Austrian connections with excellent sausages, gammon and bowls of steaming sauerkraut. *Da Giovanni*, Via S. Lazzaro 14 (closed Sun), serves simple meals at bench tables, the hams hanging from the ceiling and the barrels of wine behind the bar lending a distinctly rustic air. For an inexpensive meal, head for the ramshackle streets behind the castle, where the *Arco di Riccardo*, adjoining the Roman arch of the same name, at Via del Trionfo 3, serves excellent meals in a welcoming atmosphere (closed Mon).

More expensive places tend to specialize in fish; *branzino* and *sogliola* – sea bass and sole – are local favourites. *Aquario*, on Via Crispi, serves superb fish and seafood at reasonable prices, while the very popular *Trattoria dell'Antica Ghiacceretta* in Via dei Fornelli (closed Sun) concentrates on the food rather than the decor. Plusher, but still excellent, is *Ai Fiori*, on Piazza Hortis 7 (closed Sun & Mon; ☎040.300.633) a classy trattoria on a leafy square between the Riva and the castle hill. For meat, and steak in particular, the prestigious restaurant of *Antica Trattoria Suban*, way out to the east of the city at Via Comici 2 (closed Mon, Tues, & part of Aug), deserves its reputation, but is pricey.

Viale XX Settembre has a number of lively **pizza** places among the bars and cinemas, *Pizzeria Fattorusso*, just off Viale XX Settembre at Via Rosetti 3 is good, and less canteen-like in atmosphere than its rivals. Otherwise *Il Barattolo*, on Piazza Sant'Antonio (closed Mon in winter) is very popular for pizza and decent Italianate food, and is centrally located.

Cafés and gelaterie

Trieste's association with **coffee** dates back to the mid-eighteenth century, when trading began and when the first coffee shops opened in emulation of Vienna. Even now it's the leading coffee port in the Mediterranean – eighty percent of Italy's coffee arrives here, and the city's mayor is currently one Riccardo Illy, from the famous Illy coffee clan. Triestines treat coffee with great seriousness. One of the pleasures of walking around the city centre is the unexpected scent of roasting beans that wafts through the streets and there's a plethora of places in which to sample the various imports and a vast range of ways in which the coffee can be served.

Trieste's favourite **café** is the *Caffè San Marco* (closed Wed), which has occupied its premises on Via C. Battisti for some eighty years. It's a huge, relaxed place with a clientele of all ages chatting and playing chess in the mahogany and mirrored Art Nouveau-style interior. Much of the historic style of the *Caffè Tommaseo* on Piazza Tommaseo (closed Mon) – a rendezvous for Italian nationalists in the last century – was lost in a recent refurbishment, but the almost equally famous *Caffè degli Specchi*, in Piazza Unita (closed Thurs), is still a classy spot from which to watch the world go by. For a quick pastry, try the *Caffè Pasticceria Pirona* on Largo Barriera Vecchia, one of whose regulars was James Joyce during his Triestine sojourn. The best place to sample the product however, is at a *torrefazione* – a café that roasts and sells beans, as well as grinding them; try the *Caffè Colombiana* in Via Carducci near the Via Coroneo junction, *La Triestina* on Piazza Cavana or the *Crèmcaffè* in Piazza Goldoni.

For **ice cream**, the best spot is the leafy Viale XX Settembre, known as the "Acquedotto", where citizens stroll in the evening and most of the city's numerous cinemas are to be found. *Zampolli* is superb, but there are many to choose from. The Viale is sometimes less congenial at its Piazza San Giovanni end, a gathering place for young *fascisti*. The original *Zampolli* is at Via Ghega 10 and is still considered the best.

Bars and nightlife

Many of the city's **bars** are as glossy as the top-notch cafés, though there is one survival of old Trieste, the *Osteria de Libero*, on the castle hill at Via Risorta 7 (closed Sun), which can hardly have changed in a hundred years. The bar in the Galleria Protti – which runs north from the Piazza Borsa, inside the Assicurazioni Generali building – has a Thirties' nightclub feel. For late drinking, Via Madonna del Mare, on the castle hill, has a number of bars whose names, managements and popularity come and go each year – it's best to follow your ears to where the crowds are. In the new town, *Public House*, Via San Lazzaro 9 (closed Sun), is a trendy, upmarket wine bar, while the *Caffè della Musica*, at Via Rosetti 6 (closed Sun), off Viale XX Settembre is younger and more studenty than most, and has occasional live music. After midnight, the most popular **nightspots** are east down the Riva: *Benningans Pub* and *Tender* are fairly tacky, but full to bursting on weekend nights; the most central disco, *Mandracchio*, is on the Passo di Piazza, off Piazza Unita, and comes with similar warnings.

Listings

Airport information ☎0481.773.224.

Bus information ☎040.77.951 or freephone ☎1670.16.675 (Mon–Thurs 8am–noon & 2–3.30pm, Fri 8am–noon). For AECT buses down the coast, call freephone ☎800.016.675. Timetables and tickets can be bought from newsagents and tobacconists. Town buses cost a standard L1400/€0.72 for any journey made within an hour of purchase, buses within the province cost L1700/€0.88, except private AECT and SAITA services.

Car rental Avis, Piazza della Libertà (☎040.421.521); Europcar, Via Mazzini 1 (☎040.367.944); Maggiore, at the train station (☎040.421.323).

Club Alpino Italiano Via Donota 2 (☎040.630.464).

Consulates UK, Vicolo delle Ville 16 (Tues & Fri 9am–12.30pm; ☎040.302.884); US Consular Agent, Via Roma 15 (Mon–Fri 10am–noon; ☎040.660.177).

Festivals and events During the summer there are programmes of musical events at the castle of San Giusto, and the Verdi opera house (☎040.672.2500) has a summer season, performing mostly operetta. The Festa dell'Unità runs from end of July to mid-August – check the timetable in *Il Piccolo*, Trieste's daily paper, which should also have details of the festivals in the Carso villages (see below).

Hospital Ospedale Maggiore, Piazza dell'Ospedale (☎040.399.1111); in an emergency, dial ☎118.

Internet access *Sportnet*, Piazza Squero Vecchio, just west of Piazza Unita (Mon–Sat 9am–1pm & 3.30–7.30pm); *Caffè Internet*, Viale XX Settembre (Mon–Sat).

Police The *Questura* is on Via Teatro Romano (☎040.379.0111).

Post office The main post office is in Piazza Vittorio Veneto (Mon–Sat 8am–7.30pm).

Taxis at train station ☎040.418.822; Radio Taxi ☎040.307.730.

Telephones Telecom Italia, Piazza Tommaseo 4b (8am–10pm) or at the train station (8am–10pm).

Train information ☎147.888.088.

Travel agent Agemar, Piazza Duca degli Abruzzi 1a (☎040.363.222) – for ferry tickets to Grado and Ligano, Pirano (Slovenia), Brioni and Rovigno (Croatia).

Around Trieste: the Carso

The **Carso** is the Italian name for the limestone uplands that rise from the plain of the Veneto south of Monfalcone and eventually merge into the Istrian plateau. Although within thirty minutes' bus ride of Trieste, it feels like an entirely different country, and is geologically, botanically and socially distinct from anywhere else in Italy. Most of the Carso now lies within Slovenia (its Slovene name is Kras), and even the narrow strip inside Italy, though supporting a population of just 20,000, remains distinctively Slovene in culture, boasting villages with names like Zagradec and Koludrovica. The dour villages of thick-walled houses seem to hunker down against the *bora*, the northeasterly wind which can blast this area at any time of year – when it's especially fierce, ropes are strung along the steeper streets in Trieste.

Like all limestone country, the environment is harsh: arid in summer and sometimes snowbound in winter. The surface of the plateau is studded with sink-holes left by streams which have slowly carved their way underground, sometimes reappearing miles away on the coast, as at San Giovanni del Timavo (see p.381). The abundance of caves has even led to the German name for the area, *karst*, becoming the standard geographical term for this type of landscape. In other places – near Aurisina, for instance – the land is scarred with World War I trenches.

The distinctive landscape and natural environment have led to proposals for creating a National Park. There is fine **walking** to be had, and several bus services run to the Carso from Trieste, including the #42, #43, #44 and #46. The tourist office publishes a useful map of the network of numbered footpaths in the Carso; it shouldn't be used for serious navigation, but is a useful guide to what's possible – and it would be difficult to get yourself seriously lost. If the scenery isn't as grand as the Dolomites, the pace is gentler, especially if you can break your expedition at an *osmizza* (see box overleaf).

Grotta Gigante and Rupingrande

The most picturesque way up into the Carso is to take the *tranvia* (cable tramway; 7.30am–8pm; every 20min; L1400/€0.72 from Trieste's Piazza Oberdan to the village of Opicina, at the edge of the plateau. From here it's a pleasant thirty-minute walk to the **Grotta Gigante** (guided visits; daily: April–Sept every 30min 10am–6pm; March & Oct hourly 10am–4pm; Nov–Feb hourly 10am–noon & 2–4pm; L13,000/€6.71), the world's largest accessible cave, and the second largest natural chamber anywhere in the world. At 107m deep by 208m broad, the dome of St Peter's would fit comfortably inside. It's a steady 11°C inside, so come prepared.

To get there on foot, walk straight down the road from the tram station, then take the first left along Via di Prosecco. After the railway bridge, take a sharp right down a slip road signposted *Officine Laborante*, then turn left, crossing over the small railway line. A path to the left leads through sparse woods and farmland for twenty minutes, passing through a tunnel under the main road before bringing you out at the approach road to the cave. The route is much easier to follow in reverse, and you can save yourself the outgoing walk by taking bus #42 from the far side of the small square opposite the tram stop.

The cave itself, while impressive in scale, is utterly devoid of life, killed off by the electric lights and the spores and germs brought in by visitors. Like most of the caves in the Carso, it was created by the erosive action of a river, in this case the Timavo, which sank deeper and deeper underground before changing course. The cave is now dry. The stalactites and stalagmites grew later, formed by deposits of calcium carbonate and colourful metal oxides. The two long "pillars" in the centre of the cave are in fact wires sheathed in plastic. At the bottom end two super-accurate pendulums are suspended, used to measure seismic shifts in isolation from surface noise and air currents.

Close to the cave are *Milic*, a pleasant trattoria (closed Mon), and the *Centro Sportivo Mario Ervatti* (☎040.225.047), the only bike-rental place in the area – useful should you not have a car but want to explore more of the Carso.

The sights to head for are in and around the village of **RUPINGRANDE**, just 3km northeast of the cave, which acts as something of a cultural capital. A short walk east of the village is a fortress built in the fourteenth century to defend the area from Turkish incursions while in Rupingrande itself, the **Casa Carsica** (Easter–Sept Sun & public holidays only; free) exhibits old furniture and costumes, as well as works by local artisans. Every two years the village hosts an important Slovene folk festival, the **Nozze carsiche** (Carso weddings), on the four days leading up to the last Sunday in August.

Strada Vicentina and Val Rosandra

Two walking areas near the city can be particularly recommended. The **Strada Vicentina** (or Napoleonica) is some 2kms long, curving along the hillside above the city, between the *Obelisco* campsite and the hamlet of **BORGO NAZARIO** (near Prosecco). It's a scenic but unstrenuous walk, partly shadowed by trees and partly cut through almost sheer limestone cliffs. Roughly half way along is the truncated pyramid of the **Tempio Mariano** at Monte Grisa, built in 1967 on the site of a local place of pil-

---

OSMIZZE

Perhaps the best way to experience the Slovene culture of the Carso is to find an **osmizza**, an informal restaurant where farmers sell their own produce, such as home-cured meats, cheese, olives, bread and wine. A frequent bonus is a stunning view over the bay of Trieste or the limestone hills behind the city. The problem with *osmizze* is that they are temporary, don't advertise, and usually lie off the beaten track – which makes them all the more worth tracking down. Your best bet is to buy a copy of the Slovene newspaper, *Primorski Dnevnik*, preferably the Sunday edition, which usually prints up-to-date lists; it's easily available but not always on display, so you'll probably have to ask for it. If you can't make sense of the Slovene listings, enlist the help of someone in a tourist office or a hotel. Otherwise as long as you don't mind taking a few detours, just take a #44 bus from outside the station in Trieste, get off at the villages Contovello or Prosecco, and start asking if there is an *osmizza* nearby. You'll know you are getting warm when you see arrows on clumps of leaves suspended from archways and lamp-posts: they point the way to the nearest *osmizza*.

grimage. The structure isn't exactly easy on the eye, but the interior is impressive and on a clear day the views are superb. Access to the Strada Vicentina couldn't be simpler: *Obelisco* is a stop on the *tranvia*, and the Borgo Nazario end is near Via San Nazario, where the #42 bus stops on its way back to Trieste station.

The other area, the **Val Rosandra**, is very different. This miniature wilderness of limestone cliffs and sumac trees is the local rock-climbing headquarters and is criss-crossed with paths. Take bus #40 or #41 from Trieste's bus station to **BAGNOLI DELLA ROSANDRA** and follow the road at the back of the square toward the hills. After about 500m or so the tarmac gives way to a path bordered on the right by a minia-ture Roman aqueduct – now resembling little more than a stone-lined ditch – and on the left by a stream with pools for bathing. After thirty minutes the little sanctuary church of Santa Maria in Siaris appears, perched on a spur of rock high on the right. You can climb up to it easily enough and a steep path continues up to the top of the plateau beyond. Beyond this is a waterfall, accessible by a steep path, then the tiny hamlet of Bottazzo – the last habitation before Slovenia. At the border a sign advertises a friend-ship path linking communities on either side of the frontier. Don't be tempted to inves-tigate; only locals are allowed to cross unpatrolled borders, and the military are fairly active in the area as it's a busy crossing point for illegal immigrants.

Other paths lead across the valley and up to the villages of **Mocco**, where there's a ruined castle, the most rewarding expedition, although strenuous, is across the slopes of **Monte Carso**. It's simplest to begin at **SAN DORLIGO DELLA VALLE**, where bus #40 terminates. Walk uphill through town past the general store to a fountain where there's a signpost to the beginning of the walk. After 100m, the unsurfaced track divides into two paths at a small spring. Take the left fork here and follow the path marked #46 as it rises gently across the contours of Monte Carso. After about an hour the trail steepens to bring you out onto the plateau. Be wary of taking the smaller paths that branch uphill off the main trail; these are local shortcuts, but often peter out among faded signs warning of old mines – the explosive type. At the top of the mountain is a beautiful undulating plateau of mixed woodland and grasses, the path running within metres of the Slovene border. A number of roughly marked steep paths turn down into to Val Rosandra, but you'll need good grip and a head for heights; the last, #17, proba-bly has the gentlest gradient.

The Triestine Riviera

The thirty-odd kilometres of coastline either side of Trieste, from Múggia to the south and as far as Duino in the north, are optimistically known as the **Triestine Riviera**. While beaches aren't as fine as you'll find further down the Adriatic, or even at nearby Grado or Lignano, some fine walks, historic sites and castles are worth a day-trip. Frequent buses trace the coast road, and in summer ferries (see p.393) call at all the coastal towns.

Múggia

Directly south across the bay from Trieste, 11km away by road, MÚGGIA, the last rem-nant of Venice's Istrian possessions, is now reduced to little more than a popular spot for lunch expeditions from Trieste, though the town comes into its own during carnival time. The ferry-trip across the bay from Trieste (summer only) can be a good enough reason in itself to visit, but there are also appealing signs of the past, particularly in the brightly painted buildings on the main square. On the east side of the piazza, the fif-teenth-century **Duomo** reveals its origins in its Venetian-Gothic arches and a bas-relief of Christ Pantocrator in the lunette above the main door; the handsome **Palazzo dei**

Rettori, on the north side of the square, displays the tell-tale *leone marciano*, the lion of St Mark. The piazza is backed by a handful of narrow streets and tumbledown houses, many of which date back to Venetian times, though the only house of any architectural note is the so-called **Casa Veneta**, on Via Dante Aligheri, with more Venetian-Gothic arches. There are plans to turn the house opposite into a museum for local archeological finds.

On the seaward side of the piazza, the tiny *mandracchio* is now used as a basin for pleasure boats, while the working harbour just beyond is spoilt only by the unrivalled view of Trieste's industrial backside. Múggia's handful of **fish restaurants** are all within spitting distance of the water. Top recommendation, and not just for the name, is the *Trattoria Lilibontempo* (closed Tues), at Riva Nazario Sauro 10, known as the *ex-Hitler* after the former proprietor, who bore an unnerving resemblance to the Nazi dictator. The most formal – and expensive – of the *trattorie* is the *Lido* (closed Mon), 200m along the waterfront, but a decent meal can be had at the inexpensive *Alle Rose*, at Via Roma 5 (closed Mon), the main road running behind town.

Bus #20 runs back to Trieste every 30min, but it's worth visiting **Múggia Vecchia**, on the hilltop hard against the Slovene border and less than 20km from Croatia. It's a steep twenty-minute walk past Múggia's fourteenth-century castle and town walls, but bus #27 from outside the **train station**, 100m inland from the main road, runs every 40min for those who don't fancy the climb. The old village has a few oddments of ancient foundations, but the main reason to visit is the lovely **Santuario di Santa Maria Assunta**, a largely tenth-century structure, though much rebuilt in the twelfth and fifteenth centuries. Inside, there is just enough light coming through the narrow Romanesque windows to illuminate some peeling Veneto-Byzantine frescoes, mostly of the thirteenth century, and an unusual pulpit supported on four slender, carved columns. From the hill behind the sanctuary on a clear day you can see as far as Fiume and Grado.

Barcola and Miramare

BARCOLA, 2km west of Trieste and connected to the city by buses #6 and #36 from the bus station, is the nearest beach resort. Developed during Trieste's great days at the end of the nineteenth century, it is now really a suburb that comes to life in summer, when all Trieste seems to come here to chat, play cards, sunbathe and swim. Despite the cargo ships and tankers moored in the harbour, the water is moderately clean. Just short of the resort, perched on the slope of the limestone escarpment, is the **Faro della Vittoria**, the second tallest lighthouse in the world after New York's Statue of Liberty.

Standing at the tip of a rocky promontory 7km from Trieste, the salt-white castle of **MIRAMARE** is the area's prime tourist attraction. The Archduke Ferdinand Maximilian, Emperor Franz Josef's younger brother, was once forced ashore here by a squall, and resolved to buy the site. He built his dream castle and laid out its grounds between 1856 and 1870, but never lived to see it completed – having accepted Napoleon III's offer to make him the Emperor of Mexico, Maximilian was executed by his Mexican opponents in 1867, in the line of imperial duty. His wife Carlotta later went mad, and the legend was born that anyone who spends a night in Miramare will come to a bad end.

The park makes an excellent spot for a picnic, but the real draw is the kitsch **interior** (daily: summer 9am–7pm, plus July–Aug Fri & Sat 8.30am–11.30pm; winter 9am–4pm; L8000/€4.13), a remarkable example of regal decadence. The "Monarchs' Salon", for instance, is embellished with portraits of a King of Norway, the Emperor of Brazil, a Czar of Russia – anyone, no matter how fraudulent or despotic, as long as they're nominal monarchs. This softens you up for the bedroom and its images of the most important events in the history of this area, pride of place going to the construction of the castle, of course. Other rooms are panelled and furnished like a ship's quarters, reflecting Maximilian's devotion to the Austrian Navy.

There are a number of ways **to get to Miramare**, of which the simplest is to take the #36 bus from Piazza Oberdan, though the private SAITA service from the bus station is quicker. Trains heading west from Trieste also stop, and in summer there's a boat service from the harbour. In July and August a *son et lumière* called "the Romance of Maximilian of Mexico and Charlotte of Habsburg" is performed beside the sea, with a regular performance in English; check with the tourist office or the castle (☎040.224.143) for information on dates and times.

Duino and Sistiana

The village of **DUINO**, 14km northwest along the coast from Trieste, is dominated by its two castles, the **Castello Vecchio** and the fifteenth-century **Castello Nuovo**, seat of the princes of Thurn and Taxis down to the present day. It was in the latter that Rainer Maria Rilke began the great *Duino Elegies*, a work dedicated to his host, the incumbent princess. Access to the Castello Nuovo is prearranged and granted only to large guided groups (ask at the tourist office in Trieste), while the Castello Vecchio is now just a ruined eyrie above the sea.

A pleasant footpath, the Sentiero Rilke, runs 3km back along the coast to the **campsite** (May–Sept; ☎040.299.264) at **SISTIANA**, where there's a large harbour backed by woods, and a **beach**. Bus #44 and the much faster SAITA bus to Monfalcone run from Trieste's bus station to Sistiana and Duino.

San Giovanni del Timavo

Buses from Trieste to Monfalcone go on to **SAN GIOVANNI DEL TIMAVO**, stopping just above the Gothic church of San Giovanni in Tuba, built on the site of a fifth-century basilica. A few metres away, the River Timavo swells and bubbles up from the limestone just below road level, at the end of a subterranean course of some 40kms. A stroll around the woods reveals numerous smaller springs, the water a strange deep green and icy cold. The mouth of the Timavo has long been seen as a powerful place; in the *Aeneid*, Virgil describes the water "resounding against the cliffs with a great sound", though these days most of the noise comes from the nearby road. The Greek historian Strabo says there was a sacred wood here, where white horses were sacrificed to Diomedes, god-hero of the Trojan Wars. Above the road, beside an ugly modern church, is the so-called **Grotte del Mitreo**, a deep cave with its own clutch of local legends. The site is dangerous, however, and you should only go with a guide (ask at the tourist office in Trieste).

Aquileia, Grado and around

Bordered by the Tagliamento in the west and the Isonzo in the east, and drained by other rivers flowing into the sandy, shallow waters at the head of the Adriatic, the triangle of flatlands west of Trieste and south of Udine seems unpromising territory for a visitor – mile upon mile of maize fields, punctuated by telegraph poles, streams, level roads and newish villages. Yet at **Aquileia,** the dull fields of this secretive region have yielded up a wealth of Roman remains, while the glorious **Basilica** ranks among the most important monuments of early Christendom. Tucked away in the lagoons, just to the south, the popular resort of **Grado** with its beaches and crowds of holiday-makers has a completely different atmosphere, though it too preserves some beautiful early Christian remains. If you don't have your own transport, **buses** are the way to explore the region: they leave Udine for Grado at least every hour, calling at Palmanova and Aquileia on the way; from Trieste, change at **Monfalcone**, from where buses leave hourly for Aquileia and Grado.

Aquileia

Forty-five kilometres west of Trieste, **AQUILEIA** was established as a **Roman colony** in 181 BC, its location at the eastern edge of the Venetian plain – on the bank of a navigable river a few kilometres from the sea – being ideal for defensive and trading purposes. It became the nexus for all Rome's dealings with points east and north, and by 10 BC, when the Emperor Augustus received Herod the Great here, Aquileia was the capital of the Regio Venetia et Histria and the fourth most important city in Italy, after Rome, Milan and Capua. In 314 the famous Patriarchate of Aquileia was founded, and under the first patriarch, Theodore, a great basilica was built. Sacked by Attila in 452 and again by the Lombards in 568, Aquileia lost the patriarchate to Grado, which was protected from invasion by its lagoons. It regained its primacy in the early eleventh century under **Patriarch Poppo**, who rebuilt the basilica and erected the campanile, a landmark for miles around. But regional power inevitably passed to Venice, and in 1751 Aquileia lost its patriarchate for the last time, to Udine. The sea has long since retreated, and the River Natissa is a reed-clogged stream. Aquileia is now a dusty little town of 3500 people, bisected by Via Giulia Augusta, the main road to Grado, but the remnants of its ancient heyday make it one of northeast Italy's most important archeological sites.

Aquileia's rich history is made visible in the layers of the vast **Basilica** (daily: May–Oct 8.30am–7pm; Nov–April 8.30am–12.30pm & 2.30–5.30pm; some summer evenings also open 9pm–midnight; free), just east of the main road. The earliest part, Theodore's extraordinary **mosaic pavement**, was discovered below the nave floor at the beginning of the twentieth century and is thought to be the earliest surviving remnant of any Christian church. The mosaic undulates the full length of the nave in a riotous sequence of colours, patterns and images, many of which draw on Roman iconography. As far as the red line extending across the nave aisle there is no explicitly Christian imagery, though pagan symbolism was frequently adopted and adapted by the early Church. Look for the blond angel bearing the laurel wreath and palm frond – whether it represents the Pax Romana or Christian Victory, no one can be sure. Beyond the line the Biblical story of Jonah begins, complete with waves, whale and fish everywhere – a motif not unconnected to the nearby Adriatic. Other mosaics from Theodore's original basilica, depicting a whole bestiary, have been discovered around the base of the campanile (access from inside the basilica).

In 1348 an earthquake destroyed much of Poppo's work but the building is still superb, the Gothic elements of the reconstruction – all points above the capitals – harmonizing perfectly with the Romanesque below. The fine nave ceiling, like the steeple of the campanile, dates from the early sixteenth century. The ninth-century **crypt** under the chancel (L2000/€1.03) has very beautiful twelfth-century frescoes telling the story of St Hermagora, the legendary first bishop of Aquileia, including a gory beheading scene and a moving descent from the cross.

A couple of minutes' walk from the basilica, on the other side of the main road, on Via Roma, is the **Museo Archeologico** (daily 9am–2pm; L8000/€4.13). Worked stone and everyday items litter the fields around Aquileia, but the finer pieces have been collected here, ranging from precise surgical needles and delicate coloured glass to great piles of jumbled masonry. The two courtyards, in particular, resemble a junkyard of Roman stone, with hundreds of funerary monuments; concerts are occasionally held here in summer. Its worth persevering up to the top floor of the museum where two extraordinary bronze heads are displayed side by side. One is a fantastical relief in the

Hellenistic style, the other a naturalistic bust which may portray a dictator of the third century AD; the cruel expression certainly supports the speculation. On the ground floor rows of marble sculptures and busts mostly derive from the Roman tombs which once lined the roads into Aquileia.

The **Museo Paleocristiano** (daily 9am–2pm; free), housed in the shell of a Benedictine monastery in the northern part of the town, opposite the campsite on Via Germina, is recommended solely to those insatiable for more mosaic pavements. Most of the patterns are geometric, but the mosaic on the mezzanine level is attractive, with Christ represented as a peacock and the apostles by their various animals. There are various pieces of early Christian carving and sculpture, but the fifteen-minute riverside walk to the museum from the basilica is perhaps the best reason to go, taking you past the sad remnants of the quays of Aquileia. From the museum you can loop back along the main road, past the forum, to the basilica.

The **tourist office** is in Piazza Capitolo (summer daily except Thurs 8.20am–6pm; winter Sat & Sun 10am–noon), beside the basilica. In the newer part of town, west of the main road past the Museo Archeologico, you'll find the least expensive of Aquileia's two **hotels**, the *Aquila Nera*, Piazza Garibaldi 5 (☎0431.91.045; ②), with an excellent **restaurant** attached. If they're full, try the upmarket *Hotel Patriarchi*, on the main road by the bus stop (☎0431.919.595, *www.hotelpatriarch.it*; ⑤), or head along Via Gemina past the Museo Paleochristiana, where rooms are available in **private houses** (①). Also on Via Gemina is *Camping Aquileia* (☎0431.919.583; mid-May to mid-Sept).

Grado and around

Some 11km south of Aquileia, isolated among lagoons at the end of a causeway, is the ancient island-town of **GRADO**, through which Aquileia once traded with Syria, Cyprus, Arabia and Asia Minor. But Grado is no miniature Venice, despite its parallel history and situation, the tiny historic centre being all but lost among the concrete buildings of the large, modern resort.

For relaxing on the **beach**, however, this is one of the best places in the northern Adriatic, the resort extending eastwards along the length of the sandy island. The water is warm and safe as a bath, and almost as shallow – indeed, the name of the town comes from the gentle angle of its shore. The free beaches are at the western end; if you want a locker, deckchair and shower facilities, you will have to pay a few thousand lire to one of the businesses on the Lungomare Adriatico.

It's worth finding the **historic centre**, however, for its three early-Christian buildings, grouped close together in the heart of a miniature network of old streets. The exteriors are of fairly rustic brick construction, though enlivened by fragments of carved Roman marble. The sixth-century **Basilica** was heavily restored between the 1930s and 1950s, but preserves a bizarre parade of ill-matched nave pillars topped by an assortment of Corinthian capitals; it's thought that these were borrowed from various Roman buildings in Aquileia. The pulpit is of similarly hybrid origins, perched on six slender Roman columns under a Venetian canopy that resembles an oriental tent. Venice's presence is also felt in the fourteenth-century silver *pala* on the high altar. The mosaic pavement, while not as impressive as Aquileia's, is beautiful, the pattern being formed by an endless knot.

The adjacent octagonal **Baptistry** also dates back to the fifth century and the arrival of the first Christians in the lagoon. The church of **Santa Maria delle Grazie**, on its far side, is from the same period as the basilica, and has another mongrel collection of columns and capitals. From the outside it's possible to see how the ground level has sunk over the centuries.

Ten buses per day make the one-hour run to Udine, and there's also a half-hourly bus connection from Cervignano train station, on the Venice–Trieste line. The best way to visit Grado, though, is by boat from Trieste; on Wednesdays, Fridays and Sundays the little steamer *Dionea* calls morning and evening at the Molo Torpediniere on its way from and to the city (see "Travel Details" on p.393).

Grado's **tourist office**, at Viale Dante Alighieri 72 (daily: June–Aug 8am–7pm; Sept–May 9am–6pm; ☎0431.899.220; *aptgrado@tin.it*), has details of **boats**, which run to Venice and Trieste in summer, and the town's **hotels**, the majority of which are fairly expensive and sometimes insist on your taking full pension. Three cheaper hotels are the *Villa Marin*, Via dei Provveditori 20 (☎0431.80.789, fax 0431.85.534; ②), overlooking the seafront wall between the two beaches; the *Sirenetta*, Via Milano 1 (☎0431.80.404; ②), on the western beach; and *Al Sole Meuble*, Viale del Sole 31 (☎& fax 0431.80.370; ②), which is near the beach, but at its eastern end, a good ten minutes' walk from the centre. The best local **campsites** are at Grado Pineta, around 3km east of the town and served by regular buses: *Camping al Bosco* (☎0431.80.485), *Camping Punta Spin* (☎0431.80.732) and *Camping Europa* (☎0431.80.877).

A cluster of good **restaurants** is found in the old streets around the basilica. The tiny *Santa Lucia* (closed Mon), secreted in an alleyway at Calle Corbato 2, serves good pizza, while the *Tavernetta all'Androna* (closed Mon) is more expensive but has a lovely courtyard under the basilica's east wall. The *Enoteca La Sentina*, opposite, is good for wine and snacks. For Grado's fish specialities, head just west to *Trattoria de Toni*, in Piazza Duca d'Aosta, or the *Trattoria Alla Borsa*, Via Conte di Grado, behind the marina.

A few kilometres westwards across the lagoons lies the purpose-built resort complex of **LIGNANO SABBIADORO**. Hemingway used to shoot duck on this sandy, pine-wooded peninsula at the mouth of the Tagliamento, but nowadays it appeals to beach-niks only and, like Grado, is especially popular with German tourists. Its 100,000-plus beds get booked pretty solid in summer – the **tourist office** at Via Latisana 42 (daily 8.30am–12.30pm & 3–7pm; ☎0431.71.821) will winkle out whatever hotel and campsite vacancies there are. If you do get washed up here, the wine and cakes at *Enoteca-bar Scarpa*, Vicolo Marano 9, will cheer you up. **LIGNANO PINETA**, 4km away east, is less high-rise but equally dedicated to the beach; there's a pleasant **campsite** here, the *Pino Mare* (☎0431.428.454), a few steps from the shore on Viale Adriatico.

Gorizia

As with other towns in this region, the tranquillity of present-day **GORIZIA** – virtually midway along the Trieste–Udine rail line – belies the turbulence of its past. The castle that dominates the old centre was the power-base of the dukes of Gorizia, who ruled the area for four centuries. After their eclipse, Venice briefly ruled the town at the start of the sixteenth century, before the Habsburgs took over. It was controlled from Vienna uninterruptedly until August 8, 1916, when the Italian army occupied it – but only until the rout at Caporetto, some 50km north. The border settlement after World War II literally split houses in Gorizia down the middle. Italy kept the town proper but lost its eastern perimeter to what was then Yugoslavia, where the new regime resolved to build its own Gorizia: **Nova Gorica** – "New Gorizia"– is the result.

The town's appearance, like that of Trieste, is distinctly central European, stamped with the authority of Empress Maria Theresa. Numerous parks and gardens – thriving in the area's mild climate – further enhance the *fin de siècle* atmosphere. Again like Trieste, it's a major shopping town for Slovenes, which explains the large number of electrical goods, clothes and food shops, and the good cafés and restaurants.

The main sight in town is the **Borgo Castello**, the quarter built round the castle by the Venetians, mostly in the sixteenth century. It's a pleasant place to wander, and the collection of local folkloric items and handicrafts passes a half-hour or so, but the view from the castle walls is more inspiring. The graceful rooms of the **Castle** itself (Tues–Sun: April–Sept 9.30am–1pm & 3–7.30pm; Oct–March 9.30am–6pm; L6000/€3.10) host occasional exhibitions, though these are of mostly local interest. The **Museo Provinciali** (Tues–Sun: summer 10am–7pm; winter 10am–1pm & 3–6.30pm; L6000/€3.10), in the Borgo just down from the castle entrance, is again fairly dry, with collections on textiles, fashion and World War I – the latter interesting enough for Italian speakers.

One of the finest of its Neoclassical buildings is the **Palazzo Attems** in Piazza De Amicis, built by Nicolo Pacassi, Maria Theresa's favourite architect. After restoration work is complete – at some uncertain date – it is due to house the town archives and picture gallery, the latter including some nice pieces, among them an altarpiece by Antonio Guardi. In what was once the Jewish quarter, the **Synagogue**, at Via Ascoli 19 (Mon, Fri & Sat 6–8pm; summer Tues & Thurs 6–8pm, winter 4–7pm; free), is also of Neoclassical design; the serene interior resembles those in Venice's Ghetto.

Probably the strangest sight in Gorizia is the crypt in the Franciscan monastery at **Castagnavizza** – Kostanjevica, rather, for the monastery lies across the border in Nova Gorica. This is the burial place of the last of the French Bourbons. After Louis Philippe was ousted by the bloodless revolution of July 1830, the Bourbons were exiled from France; the family eventually arrived in Gorizia in 1836, and the Habsburgs allowed them to stay. To judge by the impassioned entries in the visitors' book, the silence of the crypt is regularly disturbed by French royalists, whose withered bouquets line the walls. The French state must reckon that the republic is now strong enough to withstand any monarchist pressure, for there has been a recent agreement to return these royal relics, although the dates have yet to be decided. The monastery was also home to Brother Stanislav Skrabec (1844–1918), an important Slovene linguist, and the library of 10,000 books includes a rare copy of the first Slovene grammar, inscribed by its author, Adam Bohoric (1584). The easiest approach is to take a taxi up the hill once you're across the border; walking is the best way back. Once there, ring the bell; there's no charge, but you should offer a donation.

For information on the current status of the Palazzo Attems, ask at the **tourist office** at Via Roma 5, on the first floor (May–Sept Mon–Fri 9am–1pm & 3–6pm; Oct–April 9am–1pm & 3–5pm; ☎0481.386.225), which also supplies information on the province of Gorizia as a whole. For accommodation, the only one-star **hotel** is the excellent *Sandro* at Via S. Chiara 18 (☎0481.533.223; ②), not far from the central Piazza della Vittoria. If that's full, try the comfortable but bland *Alla Transalpina* at Via Caprin 30 (☎0481.530.291; ③); the restaurant is overpriced, and it's a good 2km northeast of the centre, right on the Slovene border, but bus #1 runs every 15min from the train station through town, terminating opposite the hotel.

Gorizia is better served by **places to eat**. The *Osteria Panesale* (closed Sun), Corso Verdi 11, on the way into the old ghetto, serves beautiful local food in simple, classy surroundings. At the other end of the scale, *Al Sabatino* (closed Sun), at Via Mameli 4, is a traditional workers' trattoria serving local dishes in distinctly ordinary surroundings. More urbane is *Alle Lune*, Via Oberdan (closed Sun eve & Mon), but the prices are still moderate.

Udine and around

It is fitting that the best artworks in **UDINE**, seventy one kilometres northwest of Trieste, are by Giambattista Tiepolo: his airy brilliance suits this town. Running beside and beneath the streets are little canals called *rogge*, diverted from the Torre and Cormor rivers, and these bright streams reflect light onto the walls and through the roadside greenery. Comfortable and bourgeois, Udine is the second city of

Friuli-Venezia Giulia, and some say that although it has less than half the population of Trieste, it will gain the ascendancy sooner or later. Certainly it's already far more attractive to visitors, with its galleries, fine churches and well-preserved historic buildings around Piazza Libertà. Udine seems everything that Trieste is not – delicate, untroubled, successful.

Along with Cividale, Tricesimo and Zuglio, Udine was one of the frontier bastions of Imperial Rome, and by the sixth century AD it was far more than a garrison colony. Legend has it that the castle-topped hill at the heart of Udine was built by Attila's hordes, using their helmets as buckets, so that their leader could relish the spectacle of Aquileia in flames, 36km away. But it was not until the thirteenth century that it started to become a regional centre. Patriarch Bertoldo di Andechs (1218–51) can be seen as the father of Udine – he established two markets (the "old market" in Via Mercatovecchio, and the new one in Piazza Matteotti, still a marketplace), moved the patriarchate from Cividale to the castle of Udine, and set up a city council. In 1362 the dukes of Austria acquired the place by treaty, but not for long: Venice, now hungry for territory, captured Udine in 1420, after several assaults and sieges. The city was ruled by Venetian governors for almost 400 years – until 1797, when the Venetian Republic surrendered to Napoleon. Even now, the old aristocracy of Udine speak a version of Venetian dialect, while the humbler Udinese, many of whom have migrated from the countryside, speak *friulano*.

The City

The place to start any exploration of Udine is at the foot of the hill, in the **Piazza Libertà**, a square whose architectural ensemble is matched by few cities in Italy. The fifteenth-century **Palazzo del Comune** is a clear homage to the Palazzo Ducale in Venice, and the clock tower facing the palazzo, built in 1527, similarly has a Venetian model – the lion on the facade and the bronze "Moors" who strike the hours on top of the tower are explicit references to the Torre dell'Orologio in Piazza San Marco. The statue at the north end of the square is a bad allegory of *Peace*, donated to the town by Emperor Franz I to commemorate the Habsburg acquisition of Udine.

To walk up to the **Castello**, go through the **Arco Bollani**, designed by Palladio, and onward up the graceful Venetian Gothic gallery, the **Loggia del Lippomano** on the right. The sixteenth-century *castello*, built and decorated by local artists, houses an excellent **Galleria d'Arte Antica** (Tues–Sat 9.30am–12.30pm & 3–6pm, Sun 9.30am–12.30pm; L4000/€2.07, free Sun), containing works by Carpaccio, Bronzino and Tiepolo, as well as an indifferent Carvaggio and an interesting historical painting by Palma Il Giovanni showing St Mark putting the city under the patronage of St Hermagora, first bishop of Aquileia; Piazza Libertà is clearly visible on the right. There are fine views across the city from the grassy terrace outside the castle, a good spot for a picnic.

North from the Piazza Libertà is **Via Mercatovecchio**, once the mercantile heart of the city and now the busiest shopping street. The little chapel of **Santa Maria**, incorporated into the Palazzo del Monte di Pietà in Via Mercatovecchio, is a beauty: viewed through the glass booth from the street, the interior, with its cloudy Baroque frescoes by Giulio Quaglio (1694), has a pristine, subaqueous appearance.

Due west lies the **Piazza Matteotti**, with galleries on three sides and the fine Baroque facade of San Giacomo on the fourth. The square's importance as the centre of public life in Udine is proved by the outside altar on the first-floor balcony of **San Giacomo**; mass was celebrated here on Saturdays so that selling and buying could go on uninterrupted in the market below. As well as being the town's main market, this was the setting for tournaments, plays and carnivals. The fountain in the middle of the square was designed in 1543 by Giovanni da Udine, a pupil of Raphael, who also had a hand in building the castle.

Off the south side of Piazza Libertà is the **Duomo** (7am–noon & 4–8pm), a Romanesque construction that was given a Baroque refit in the eighteenth century. Altarpieces and frescoes by Giambattista Tiepolo are the main attraction – they decorate the first two chapels on the right and the chapel of the Sacrament, a little way beyond. A series of frescoes painted by Tiepolo in collaboration with his son, Giandomenico, can be seen in the tiny **Oratorio della Purità** opposite – ask the sacristan in the duomo to show you.

But Udine's outstanding works of art are the Giambattista Tiepolo frescoes in the nearby **Gallerie del Tiepolo** in the beautifully furnished **Palazzo Arcivescovile** (Wed–Sun 10am–noon & 3.30–6.30pm; L7000/€3.62, including Museo Diocesano – see below). Painted in the late 1720s, these luminous and consummately theatrical scenes add up to a sort of Rococo epic of the Old Testament. *Fall of the Rebel Angels* is the first work you see as you climb the staircase, while the finest room, the Gallery, is at the top, immediately on your right. Every surface is painted with either trompe l'oeil architectural details or scenes from the story of Abraham, Isaac and Jacob. To the left is a sequence of rooms decorated in rich colours: watch for Tiepolo's *Judgement of Solomon* in the Red Room, and Bambini's wonderful *Triumph of Wisdom* in the serene Delfino library. Also inside the Palazzo Arcivescovile and arranged around the Tiepolo galleries is the **Museo Diocesano**, with an assortment of sculpture and funerary monuments, as well as an exhibition of naive art – popular sculptures from Friuli's churches spanning the Gothic, Renaissance and Baroque periods.

On the edge of the old town in Piazza Diacono, the **Galleria d'Arte Moderna** (Tues–Sat 9.30am–12.30pm & 3–6pm, Sun 9.30am–12.30pm; L4000/€2.07, free Sun) gives a reasonable overview of Italian art in the twentieth century, plus a glimpse of a few foreign greats.

Practicalities

Udine's **train** and **bus stations** are close together in the south of the town, on Viale Europa Unità; Via Roma leads from the train station into the centre. The **tourist office** is at Piazza 1° Maggio 7 (May–Sept Mon–Fri 9am–1pm & 3–6pm; Oct–April 9am–1pm & 3–5pm; ☎0432.295.972). **Internet** access can be found to the north of town, at Tempo Reale, Via Gemona 86. **Hotel** options are surprisingly limited: cheap, central but rather grim is *Al Vecchio Tram*, Via Brennari 32 (☎0432.502.516; ①). It's worth paying the extra to stay at *Quo Vadis*, Piazzale Cella 28 (☎0432.21.091; ③), a ten-minute walk east along Viale Europa Unitá from the train station, or the new *Al Bue*, at Via Pracchiuso 75 (☎0432.299.070; ③), just north of Piazza 1° Maggio. The student **hostel** *Residenza Grande* (☎0432.26.058; ①) in Via Zoletto, off Via Aquileia may also be able to put you up.

Udine has scores of **restaurants**, including the unpretentious *Trattoria all'Allegria*, Via Grazzano 18 (closed Mon), which does simple local dishes in the dining room beside the bar. Just north of Piazza Marconi, the *Osteria Sbarco dei Pirati*, at Via Bartolini 12 (closed Sun), is lively and has a room built out over the *rogga*, while the excellent *Ai Frati*, on Piazzetta Antonini (closed Sun), serves local dishes on a shaded terrace. Try the Carnian speciality of *cialzons* or little ravioli (available Sundays only) at *Al Vecchio Stallo*, an osteria in a converted stables at Via Viola 7 (closed Wed), just inside the ring road, near Piazzale XXVI Luglio; prices are reasonable, and in summer you can eat in the small inner courtyard, surrounded by greenery and Udine's ancient buildings. South of the old town, the *Spaghetteria Da Ciccio*, on Via Grazzano (closed Sun), serves famously vast portions at budget prices to an appreciative student crowd. For **ice-cream**, *Il Buon Gelato*, in the old town at Via Manin 14b lives up to its name.

Later in the evening, students and young Udinese head for Piazza Matteotti and Via Sarpi. On the latter, *Teresina* is a livelier **enoteca** than most, with a good garden, while the apparently unnamned *Tapas*, at Via Sarpi 1, and *Al Capello*, two doors down (both closed Sun), pull in a young crowd. The inevitable Irish **pub**, Caffè Caucigh, at Via Gemona 28, is unsurprisingly popular and has live music on Fridays. Students hangout in the *St James* and *Al Marinaio* bars in Via Grazzano, and the *Locanda Medievale* on Viale Sottomonte is popular for its enterprising mix of cured ham and house music, but **nightlife** is otherwise limited, especially outside term. In summer, however, there's a busy programme of cultural events – theatre, music, dance – in and around the town, and throughout the Ferroviario arts cinema at Via Cernaia 2 is always worth checking out.

Cividale del Friuli

Lying only 17km east of Udine and connected to it by train and bus, **CIVIDALE DEL FRIULI** is a gem of a town, much prized by the Friulani but pretty well unknown to outsiders. It was founded in 50 BC by Julius Caesar where the Natisone Valley opens into the plain, and in the sixth century became the capital of the first Lombard duchy. In the eighth century the Patriarch of Aquileia moved here, inaugurating Cividale's most prosperous period.

The Town

The old town lies on the same side as the rail and coach stations, and the visitor need never cross the river; though a walk over the Devil's Bridge is *de rigueur*. Just walking around the town, within the oval ring bisected by Via Carlo Alberto and Corso Mazzini, is a pleasure; the pace of life is provincially serene, and many of the buildings have interesting histories and respectable architecture. Cividale has been the main market town in the Natisone Valley for 200 years, and today you hear Italian, *friulano*, and Slovene dialects spoken in the street. There are some remarkable tourist sights, too.

The tiny **Tempietto Longobardo** (daily: April–Oct 9am–1pm & 3–6.30pm; Nov–March 10am–1pm & 3.30–5.30pm; L4000/€2.07), poised above the Natisone off Piazza San Biagio, is a uniquely fine example of Lombard art. Constructed in the eighth century, largely from older fragments, much of the elaborate stucco work inside the chapel was reduced to rubble in the terrible earthquake of 1222. The delicate interior preserves faded frescoes and carved stalls from its use as a convent chapel in the late fourteenth century, but the eye is drawn to the east wall where an exquisite stucco arch is flanked by six female figures. Whether they represent saints, queens or nuns is uncertain, but the luminous, smiling statues are among the most splendid surviving works of art from the eighth century.

Two other beautiful Lombard pieces are to be found in the **Museo Cristiano** (Mon–Sat 9.30am–noon & 3–6.30pm, Sun 10am–1pm & 3–6.30pm; free), housed in the precincts of the fifteenth-century Duomo. The Altar of Ratchis was carved for Ratchis, Duke of Cividale and King of the Lombards at Pavia, who died as a Benedictine monk at Montecassino in 759; the reliefs of *Christ in Triumph* and the *Adoration of the Magi* are delicate and haunting. The other highlight is the Baptistry of Callisto, named after Callisto de Treviso, the first Patriarch of Aquileia to move to Cividale. He lived here from 730 to 756 and initiated the building of the patriarchal palace, the cathedral and this octagonal baptistry, which used to stand beside the cathedral. It's constructed from older Lombard fragments, the columns and capitals dating from the fifth century.

The **Duomo** itself (same hours as Museo Cristiano) houses a twelfth-century masterpiece of silversmithery: the *pala* (altarpiece) named after Pellegrino II, the patriarch who commissioned it and donated it to the town; it depicts the Virgin seated between the archangels Michael and Gabriel, who are flanked by 25 saints and framed by saints, prophets and the patron himself.

Also in Piazza del Duomo is the **Museo Archeologico** (daily 8.30am–2pm; L4000/€2.07), which houses an excellent exhibition on the Lombards on the first floor, incorporating local finds including some beautiful gold *fibulae*. On the ground floor is a hotchpotch of late Roman and early Christian pieces, the highlight being a second-century mosaic of a wild-eyed head identified as Neptune, which reveals a subtle sense of perspective.

Just a stone's throw from the fifteenth-century Ponte del Diavolo, in Via Monastero Maggiore, is a cellar-like cavern called the **Ipogeo Celtico** (daily 8am–6pm; key from the bar *All' Ipogeo* on Via P. d'Aquileia if closed). The hypogeum was probably used as a tomb for Celtic leaders between the fifth and second centuries BC, but there is still some dispute whether it's artificial or was merely adapted by its users. Either way, the spectral faces carved on the walls make it a most unsettling place.

Practicalities

The **tourist office** is just off Piazza Duomo at Via P. d'Aquileia 10 (Mon–Fri 9am–1pm & 3–6pm, closes 5pm in winter; ☎0432.731.398). Most visitors are day-trippers from Udine, but you could stay at Cividale's least expensive **hotel**, *Pomo d'Oro*, Piazza S. Giovanni 20 (☎0432.731.489; ③), a little way out of town beyond the train station. More comfortable and with exceptional views, is the pricier *Castello*, Via del Castello 20 (☎0432.733.242; ⑤) – it's a couple of kilometres north of the town, on a hill above the road to Tarcento and Faedis. The restaurant is good, and on a sunny day the terrace at the *Castello* is the best place for a leisurely lunch, well worth the taxi trip from the town centre if you don't feel like walking.

The town's smartest **café** is the *San Marco*, opposite the Duomo in the loggia of the sixteenth-century town hall – well placed for watching passers-by. There are good **restaurants**, but they tend to be expensive and largely aimed at tourists. *Zorutti*, Borgo di Ponte 9 (closed Mon), situated just across the Natisone by the Ponte del Diavolo, and the expensive *Alla Frasca*, Via de Rubeis 10 (closed Mon), one block north from Piazza Duomo, are good, the latter boasting a vast array of truffle and mushroom dishes. For Friulian specialities, *Al Fortino*, Via C. Alberto 46 (closed Mon), heading out of town from Piazza P. Diacono, and *Da Nardini*, Piazzetta de Portis 6 (closed Thurs), off C. Alberto, are good but touristy. A favourite with discerning locals is the excellent *Trattorie Dominissini*, at Stretta Stellini 18 (closed Mon) – take a right just short of the Ponte del Diavolo.

Palmanova

Once ranked as the strongest fortress in all Europe, **PALMANOVA** is a massive Venetian garrison town built in 1593 in the form of a nine-pointed star, its symmetrical streets converging on a large hexagonal piazza. Guided tours are conducted through the tunnels in the fortifications, and the **Civico Museo Storico,** at Borgo Udine 4 (daily except Wed 10am–noon & 4–7pm; L5000/€2.58), fills out the story further. Apart from this military curiosity, there is no reason to visit the town.

Pordenone and around

Heading west to **Pordenone**, a workaday provincial capital best known for its favourite son, the architect of the same name, there seems little reason to get off the train, particularly with the attractions of the Veneto waiting just a few minutes away. But the frequency of trains – they run hourly from Udine to Venice – means that it is possible to hop on and off, and in the pleasantly low-key towns you'll have most of the sites all to yourself.

Codroipo

CODROIPO is a peaceful little town on the main railway line, midway between Udine and Pordenone, that would have nothing to recommend it were the huge **Villa Manin** not just 3km to the southeast, where it completely dominates the little village of Passariano. As the only public transport to the villa from Codroipo consists of three daily buses, the best way to get there is to walk: straight ahead from the station, and bear left in the main square – you could easily pick up a lift.

Friuli's best-known country house, the Villa Manin was built in 1738 and later enlarged for Lodovico Manin, the pitiful last doge of Venice. In 1797 Napoleon stayed here when he signed the Treaty of Campoformio, which gave Venice to Austria. The greater part of the interior, much of it coated in run-of-the-mill frescoes, is impressive solely for its size, and is used as an exhibition centre in the summer; the arena created by its great frontal galleries is used for open-air concerts. The villa contains a mediocre **museum** (Tues–Sun 9am–12.30pm & 3–6pm; free); more alluring is the ramshackle **park** (Tues–Sun 9am–6pm; free), where reedy ponds, birdsong and lichen-green statues create a congenial atmosphere for an afternoon doze.

Pordenone

The westernmost of Friuli-Venezia Giulia's three large towns, **PORDENONE** was once a thriving river port, but is now the region's main manufacturing centre, specializing in light industries especially white goods, textiles and ceramics. As such, the town was hardly set up for tourism, with few specific sights, but the historic centre is carefully preserved and worth a visit. From the train station go straight ahead along Via Mazzini, then take the third right down **Corso Vittorio Emanuele** to the Gothic-Renaissance **Palazzo Communale**.

Over the road from the palazzo is the **Museo Civico Ricchieri** (Tues–Fri 9.30am–12.30pm & 3–6pm; L4000/€2.07); it's predominantly a second-string collection of Venetian art, but it does have a clutch of works by the finest local artist, Giovanni Antonio de' Sacchis, better known simply as Il Pordenone. Many of the paintings in the museum were removed from the Duomo after the 1976 earthquake. The **Duomo** itself, mainly a late-Gothic structure, is notable only for its Romanesque campanile, and some works by Pordenone – the first altarpiece on the right, and the two (not three, whatever the sign may say) least damaged frescoes belonging to the right-hand pillar at the end of the nave.

If you want to see more of Pordenone's work in his home town, search out the parish churches of Roraigrande, Torre, Villanova and Vallenoncello – for information about access, ask at the helpful **tourist office**, Corso Vittorio Emanuele 38 (Mon–Fri: May–Sept 9am–1pm & 3–6pm; Oct–April 9am–1pm & 3–5pm; ☎0434.21.912). There's an **Internet** café on Piazzetta dei Domenicani, just beyond the swish *Hotel Moderno*. **Accommodation** in Pordenone is poor, with just a handful of ugly business hotels. The *Minerva*, Piazzale XX Settembre (☎0434.26.066, *www.hotelminerva.it*; ④), however, is smart enough, if hardly home from home. Otherwise try the more expensive *Park Hotel*, via Mazzini 43 (☎0434.27.901; ④), which is near the train station but has little else in its favour.

The choices for **eating** are much better. La *Vecia Osteria del Moro* (☎0434.28.658; closed Sun) is a beautiful old restaurant a step away from the Palazzo Communale where you eat superbly for around L40,000/€20.66 a head. For budget meals, *Da Zelina* is just behind the Palazzo and serves good pizza.

San Vito and Sesto Al Reghena

You really need a car to get around, but it is possible to make a short trip across country from Pordenone to Portogruaro on the main railway line between Trieste and Venice, taking in a couple of sleepy local attractions on the way. At least six **buses** run from Pordenone's Piazza Risorgimento to **SAN VITO AL TAGLIAMENTO**, which has lapsed into slumber since its medieval heyday, retaining a handsome piazza overlooked by a few minor *palazzi*, the thirteenth-century **Torre Raimonda** and a rather plain cathedral. The Torre Raimonda houses a dull **Museo Civico** (Mon–Fri 10am–noon & 3–6.30pm; free), but the main reason to visit is the **Museo Provinciale della Vita Contadina** (Mon–Sat 9am–1pm; free), which gives a sense of the everyday realities of tradional peasant life in Friuli.

Four **buses** from San Vito (more on weekdays) serve **SESTO AL REGHENA**, 10km south which is the chief draw of the area. In the centre of the village, the fortified **Santa Maria in Sylvis** (daily 8am–7pm; June–Aug 8am–noon & 2.30–7pm; free) is one of the oldest inhabited abbeys in the world, having been founded by the Lombards in the eighth century. The interior of the tenth-century chapel is heavily frescoed, though much is barely visible now; one exception is the unusual image of Christ crucified on the tree of Jesse – the tree of life – in the south transept. But the abbey's treasures are found in the crypt, which houses three important pieces of stonework, including a carved Lombard chest known as St Anastia's Urn, a fourteenth-century altar panel in bas-relief and an extraordinary German pietà from the fifteenth century.

Transport on to **PORTOGRUARO**, a large industrial town just over the border in the Veneto, is similarly sparse, with around four buses daily. There's little reason to linger here other than to stroll down the main street, which locals claim looks like the Canal Grande without the water. It is indeed lined with arcades and Venetian-Gothic *palazzi*, but that needn't stop you getting straight on the train.

Gemona and the Carnia

The peak district in the north of Friuli is known as the **Carnia**, a name given to it by the Celtic tribes who settled here in the fourth century BC. If you're approaching the area by road or rail from Udine, you could make a stop at **GEMONA**, a little town that was largely destroyed in the 1976 earthquake, when almost 1000 people were killed and around 15,000 houses destroyed. The historic centre, on the steep-sided hilltop, has been devotedly reconstructed and feels disconcertingly like a film set. The cathedral, once a marvellous Romanesque-Gothic specimen, is notable for the enormous four-teenth-century statue of St Christopher on the facade.

Gemona is a good staging post on the way into the Carnia, with a couple of fine and inexpensive **hotels**. The better one is the *Agli Amici*, a couple of kilometres out of the centre at Via G. Odo 44 (☎0432.981.013; ②) – turn right outside the station then head along Via Piovega, following the yellow signs; the alternative is the *Si-Si*, Via Piovega 15 (☎0432.981.158; ③). There's an excellent **trattoria** at the *Agli Amici*, while *Al Falomo*, Via Bini 11 (closed Wed), on the main street just down from the Duomo has pizzas and an inexpensive tourist menu.

The Carnia proper begins north of Gemona, around the headwaters of the River Tagliamento, and comprises two distinct areas. To the west, hay meadows and orchards give way to the Alpine uplands and pastures of the **Alpi Carniche**, which share the culture of the eastern Dolomites. To the east, the high, sheer and often bar-ren limestone peaks of the **Alpi Giulie** are divided by deep, forested valleys that radi-ate towards the borders with Austria in the north and Slovenia in the east. Both of these ranges are hardly known even within Italy, yet the area has a lot to offer the hiker and climber. Linguists should get a kick out of it too, as the villagers speak strange variants of *friulano*, German and Slovene.

If you want to plan a Carnia walking trip in advance, call in at the Udine office of the *Società Alpina Friulana*, Via Odorico da Pordenone 3 (daily 5–7.30pm plus Mon, Thurs, Fri 9–11pm; ☎0432.504.290, *safcai@tin.it*).

Western Carnia

The lush valleys and flower-filled meadows of the **western Carnia** attract hundreds of walkers from June to September, when the numerous *rifugi* are open for business. One of the best bases for the northern part of this region is the village of **ARTA TERME**, about 35km north of Gemona – there are buses direct from Udine and services from Gemona, changing at Tolmezzo. There's cheap **accommodation** at the central *Miramonti* at Via Umberto I 22 (☎0433.920.76; ②) and *Comune Rustico* at Via Fontana 14 (☎0433.922.18; ②), with slightly dearer rooms at the *Gortani* at Via Umberto I 47 (☎0433.928.754; ③). At **PIANO D'ARTA**, 1km away, you'll find another couple of options – *Pensione Cozzi* at Via Marconi 13–15 (☎0433.920.39; ②) and *Belvedere* at Via Marconi 39 (☎0433.92.006; ③). The **tourist office**, Via Umberto I 15 (May–Sept Mon–Sat 9am–noon & 4–7pm, Sun 9am–12.30pm; Oct–April Mon–Sat 9am–noon & 3–6pm, Sun 9am–12.30pm; ☎0433.929.290), has masses of information on the beautifully secluded local refuges and on the fourteen waymarked *Club Alpino* **walks** in the surrounding highlands. If these treks sound too energetic, you could always just spend L9000/€4.65 on a visit to the **thermal pool** of the pagoda-style spa complex close to the tourist office.

Between **Tolmezzo**, where you're likely to have to change buses, and **FORNI DI SOPRA** is a thickly wooded area. After the rural peasantry moved out to the cities and the trees moved in, the area was designated the **Parco Naturale Dolomite Friulane**. The Forni **tourist office**, at Via Cadore 1 (Mon–Sat 9am–12.30pm & 3–6pm; July & Aug also Sun 10am–12.30pm; ☎0433.886.767), has lots of information on activities such as mountain biking, horse-riding and **hikes**. They can also help with *rifugi*, as well as provide lists of **accommodation** in town. The cluster of villages that comprise Forni lies about 70km northwest of Gemona, at the foot of the Passo di Mauria, the mountain pass between the Carnia and the eastern Dolomites. It really feels like the end of the road; seven buses arrive here direct from Udine every day but the services onwards are sporadic. In Forni itself, the *Albergo Centrale* (☎0433.88.062; ③) is a good choice, but most of the places to stay are in **VICO**, a hamlet set back a little from Forni; try the *Roma*, on Via Nazionale 97 (☎0433.88.027; ②). The only **campsite** hereabouts is the *Tornerai* (☎0433.88.035), 2km away in **STINSANS**.

The Forni region is celebrated for its **food**, with many of its dishes incorporating some of the wild plants found in the vicinity. The mountain refuges are excellent places to sample these local specialities. Especially good is the nearby and spectacularly sited *Varmost* (June–Sept), on the slopes of Monte Crusicalas – there's a cable car in operation (June–Aug & Dec–March; L12,000/€6.20 return ticket, L28,500/€14.72, including a meal at the refuge). In Forni itself, the places to eat are *Varmost* (closed Wed), with polenta and *frico* (a cheese and potato dish) or hearty sausages and goulash to eat in or take away, plus a L21,000/€10.85 tourist menu, or the *Pizzeria Coopera* (no regular closing day); both are on the main road through town, Via Nazionale. Forni also has a branch of the *Club Alpino Italiano* on Via Vittorio Veneto, on the square behind the bus stop (July & Aug daily 5–7pm; Sept–June Fri, Sat & Sun 5–7pm), which organizes walks of varying degrees of difficulty.

Eastern Carnia

The place to head for in the **eastern Carnia** is **TARVISIO**, a small mountain resort 65km northeast of Gemona and just 7km from the Austrian border. Four buses a day come here from Udine, and eight trains – if you're coming by train, make sure you get out at Tarvisio Città station, perversely more central than Tarvisio Centrale.

The town receives a steady flow of Austrian visitors, who pour into town for the cheap Italian booze, the strange mix of *bierkeller* and café nightlife, and the first-rate ski slopes. More robust types set off from here on the Carnia's one high-level **long-distance trail**: the *Traversata Carnica*, which runs all the way to Sesto, just below the border. Information on this and all other healthy Tarvisio pursuits is available from the **tourist office**, right by the bus stop on Via Roma (summer Mon–Fri 9am–12.30pm & 3.30–6pm, Sat & Sun 9am–1pm; rest of year closed Sun; ☎0428.2135, *www.tarvisiano.org*). The nicest place **to stay** in Tarvisio is the *Albergo Valle Verde*, just outside the village on Via Priesnig (☎0428.2342; ③) – it has a wonderful **restaurant** too, serving such specialities as gnocchi with smoked ricotta. There are a couple of cheaper places in Tarvisio itself: the *Al Cacciatore*, on the noisy Via Dante (☎0428.2082; ②), and *Al Mangart* at Via Vittorio Veneto 39 (☎0428.2246; ②). The nearest **campsite** is the *Da Cesco* at Camporosso, 4km from Tarvisio (☎0428.2918).

For a taste of the splendours of the **Parco Regionale delle Alpi Giulie**, you could hop onto one of the summer buses to the **Laghi di Fusine** – two peaceful, wooded, blue-green lakes within 9km of Tarvisio. The smaller of the pair, and the nearer to Tarvisio, is **Lago Inferiore**, where there's **accommodation** at the *Capanna Edelweiss* (☎0428.61.050; ②). However, the best walks are from **Lago Superiore**, a short distance up the road, from where there's a marked five-hour circular trail via the *Rifugio Zacchi* (☎0428.61.195; June–Sept).

travel details

TRAINS

Trieste to: Gorizia (25 daily; 30min); Udine (25 daily; 1hr 20min); Venice (15 daily; 1hr 40min).

Udine to: Cividale (hourly; 20min); Conigliano (31 daily; 1hr 15min); Gemona (12 daily; 30min); Gorizia (13 daily; 30min); Palmanova (12 daily; 30min); Pordenone (28 daily; 30min); Tarvisio (11 daily, many including transfer to bus; 2hr); Trieste (13 daily; 1hr 10min); Venice (28 daily; 1hr 45min–2hr 15min).

BUSES

Gemona to: Tolmezzo (2 daily; 30min).

Tolmezzo to: Arta Terme (10 daily; 20min); Forni di Sopra (7 daily; 1hr 20min).

Trieste to: Duino (hourly; 30min); Grado (14 daily; 1hr–1hr 30min); Lignano (1 daily in summer; 2hr); Monfalcone (for Aquileia and Grado; hourly; 45 min); Tolmezzo (1 daily; 3hr); Udine (27 daily; 1hr 15min).

Udine to: Aquileia (16 daily; 40min); Arta Terme (10 daily; 1hr); Cividale (20 daily; 20min); Codroipo (hourly; 20min); Pordenone (hourly; 40min); Forni di Sopra (8 daily; 1hr 20min); Gemona (9 daily; 50min); Grado (12 daily; 1hr); Lignano (12 daily; 1hr); Palmanova (16 daily; 20min); Porenone (hourly; 40 min); Tarvisio (4 daily; 2hr 20min); Tolmezzo (14 daily; 50min); Trieste (9 daily; 1hr).

FERRIES

Trieste to: Barcola (July to mid-Sept hourly; 30min); Duino (July–Sept 3 daily via Grignano and Sistiana; 1hr 45min); Grado (June–Sept Wed, Fri & Sun; 1 daily; 1hr); Lignano (Tues, Thurs & Sat 1 daily; 1hr 10min); Múggia (mid-June to Oct every 90min; 30min). CROATIA: Brioni (June–Sept Tues–Sun; 4hr); Rovigno (June–Sept Tues–Sun; 3hr 10min); SLOVENIA: Pirano (Wed, Fri & Sun; 1 daily; 1hr 50min).

CHAPTER SEVEN

EMILIA-ROMAGNA

S et between Lombardy and Tuscany, and stretching from the Adriatic coast almost to the shores of the Mediterranean, **Emilia-Romagna** is the heartland of northern Italy. It is two provinces really: Emilia to the east and the Romagna to the west – the former Papal States, joined together after Unification. Before the papacy took charge in the area, it was a patchwork of ducal territories, ruled over by a handful of families – the Este in Ferrara and Modena, the Farnese in Piacenza and Parma, and lesser dynasties in Ravenna and Rimini – who created sparkling Renaissance courts, combining autocracy with patronage of the arts alongside a continual jockeying for power with the Church. Their castles and fortresses remain, preserved in towns with restored medieval centres which, apart from a few notable exceptions, are relatively off the tourist track, since many visitors are put off by the extreme weather (searingly hot in summer, close to freezing in winter), or are sidetracked by the more immediate pleasures of Tuscany and Umbria.

The region's landscape is a varied one, ranging from the foothills of the Apennine mountains in the south to the flat fields of the northern plain, the Pianura Padana, interrupted only by windbreaks of poplars, shimmering in the breeze. The area has grown wheat since Roman times, and nowadays its industry and agribusinesses are among Italy's most advanced – there are currently more pigs than people in the Po Valley. Emilia-Romagna remains one of the richest regions in Italy, holding some of the country's most successful small-scale, specialist industrial enterprises.

Carving a dead-straight route through the heart of Emilia-Romagna, from Piacenza to Rimini on the coast, the **Via Emilia** is a central and obvious reference point, a Roman military road constructed in 187 BC that was part of the medieval pilgrim's route to Rome, and the way east to Ravenna and Venice. The towns that grew up along here are among Emilia's most compelling. **Bologna**, the region's capital, is one of Italy's largest cities. Despite having one of the most beautifully preserved city centres in the country, some of its finest food, and inhabitants whose openness and seemingly unflappable temperaments contrast markedly with the stressed-out Milanese, it has been relatively neglected by tourists, and most people pass straight through – definitely a mistake.

ACCOMMODATION PRICE CODES

Throughout this guide, prices per person are given for **youth hostels** and assume Hostelling International (HI) membership. **Hotel** accommodation is coded on a scale from ① to ⑨, reflecting the cost of the cheapest double room in each establishment in high season. The price bands to which these codes refer are as follows:

① Up to L60,000/€30.99
② L60,000–90,000/€30.99–46.48
③ L90,000–120,000/€46.48–61.98
④ L120,000–150,000/€61.98–77.47
⑤ L150,000–200,000/€77.47–103.29

⑥ L200,000–250,000/€103.29–129.11
⑦ L250,000–300,000/€129.11–154.94
⑧ L300,000–400,000/€154.94–206.58
⑨ over L400,000/€206.58

(See p.32 for a full explanation.)

REGIONAL FOOD AND WINE

Emilia-Romagna has a just reputation for harbouring the richest, most lavish food in Italy, with its most famous specialities of **parmesan** cheese (*parmigiano-reggiano*), egg pasta, **Parma ham** (generically known as *prosciutto di Parma*) and balsamic vinegar. Despite its current foodie connotations, **balsamic vinegar** started off as a cottage industry, with many Emilian families distilling and then re-distilling local wine to form a dark liquor that is then matured in wooden barrels for at least twelve years. Bologna is regarded as the gastronomic capital of Italy, and Emilia is the only true home of **pasta** in the North: often lovingly hand-made, the dough is formed into lasagne, tortellini stuffed with ricotta cheese and spinach, pumpkin or pork, and other fresh pastas served with *ragù* (meat sauce), cream sauces or simply with butter and parmesan – *alla parmigiana* usually denotes something cooked with parmesan. Modena and Parma specialize in *bollito misto* – boiled **meats**, such as flank of beef, trotters, tongue and spicy sausage; another Modenese dish is *zampone* – stuffed pig's trotter. Romagna's cuisine is more Southern in orientation. While ingredients such as butter, cheese, mushrooms, chestnuts and meat feature in Emilia, Romagna tends more toward onions, garlic and olive oil; the region is second only to Sicily for the amount of **fish** caught in its waters.

Emilia and Romagna only became one in 1947 – their **wines**, like their respective landscapes and people, are quite different. Emilia is synonymous with **Lambrusco**, but don't despair: buy only DOC Lambrusco and be amazed by the dark, often blackberry-coloured wine that foams into the glass and cuts through the fattiness of the typically meaty Emilian meal. There are four DOC zones for Lambrusco and you get a glimpse of three of them, all around Modena, from the Via Emilia, each supporting neat rows of high-trellised vines. The fourth zone extends across the plains and foothills of the Apennines, in the province of Reggio Emilia. Other wines to try, both whites, are Trebbianino Val Trebbia and Monterosso Val D'Arda, while the lively Malvasia (also white) from the Colli di Parma goes well with the celebrated local ham.

Heading east towards the Adriatic coast, you come to the Romagna, a flatter, drier province where the wines have less exuberance but more body and are dominated by Albana and Sangiovese. The sweeter versions of **Albana** are often more successful at bringing out the peachy, toasted-almond flavours of this white. The robust red of **Sangiovese**, from the hills around Ímola and Rimini, comes in various "weights" – all around the heavy mark. Much lighter is Cagnina di Romagna, which is best drunk young (within six months of harvest) and is particularly good with roast chestnuts.

Bologna also gives easy access to places like **Modena** and **Parma** (each just an hour or so away by train): wealthy provincial towns that form the smug core of Emilia and hold some of its finest and most atmospheric architecture, as well as giving access to routes south into the **Apennines**. With a car you can dip into the foothills at will from any of these points, sampling local cuisine and joining in the festivals; and even by bus it's possible to get a taste of the area, which at its best can be very beautiful, not at all like the functional plain to the north. If you're a keen hiker, there's the Grand Escursione Apenninica, a 25-day-long trek following the backbone of the range from refuge to refuge, and which can be accessed from the foothills south of **Reggio Emilia**.

The north of Emilia-Romagna is less interesting than the Via Emilia stretch, the Po disgorging into the Adriatic from its bleak **delta** (which it shares with the Veneto), a desolate region of marshland and lagoons that is mainly of appeal to birdwatchers. However, **Ferrara**, just half an hour north of Bologna, is one of the most important Renaissance centres in Italy, formerly under the tutelage of the Este family; and **Ravenna**, a short way east from here, preserves probably the finest set of Byzantine mosaics in the world in its churches and mausoleums. The coast south is an overdeveloped ribbon of settlement, although **Rimini**, at its southern end, provides a spark of interest, with its wild seaside strip concealing a surprisingly historic town centre.

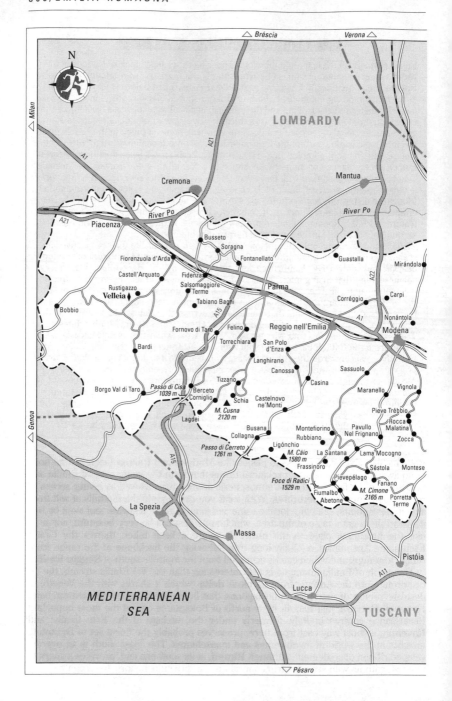

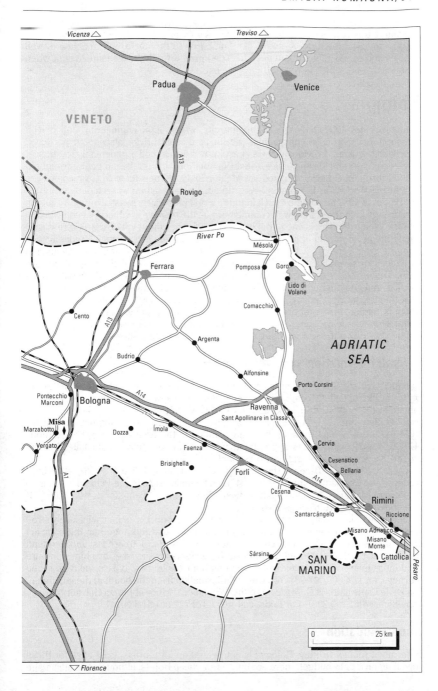

None of this comes cheap, though: Emilia is a wealthy area that makes few concessions to tourists; the tone is, rather like Lombardy to the north, well mannered, well dressed and comfortable. If you need to economize, it would be a shame to stint when it comes to food, which is where the region excels.

Bologna

Emilia's capital, **BOLOGNA**, is a thriving city, whose light engineering and hi-tech industries have brought conspicuous wealth to the old brick palaces and porticoed streets and squares. Previously, it was best known for its food – undeniably the richest in the country – and for its politics. "Red Bologna" became the Italian Left's stronghold and spiritual home, having evolved out of the resistance movement to German occupation during World War II. Consequently, Bologna's train station was singled out by fascist groups in 1980 for a bomb attack in Italy's worst postwar terrorist atrocity. A glassed-in jagged gash in the station wall commemorates the tragedy in which 84 people died.

After Venice, the city is one of the best looking in the country. The city centre is startlingly medieval in plan, a jumble of red brick, tiled roofs and balconies radiating out from the great central square of Piazza Maggiore. There are enough monuments and curiosities for several days' leisured exploration, but Bologna is really enjoyable just for itself. Thanks to its university, which makes up one-fifth of the city's population of 500,000, and an enlightened local government, there's always something happening – be it theatre, music, the city's strong summer festival, or just the café and bar scene, which is among northern Italy's most convivial. The only problem is expense; nightlife, particularly, can leave your wallet steamrolled, and finding a low-priced place to stay can be very difficult, especially during one of the major trade shows.

Arrival, information and city transport

Bologna's **train station** (enquiries ☎147.888.088, 7am–9pm) lies on the edge of the city centre at Piazza delle Medaglie d'Oro, near Porta Galliera; all long-distance buses terminate at the **bus station**, next door on Piazza XX Settembre. Bus #25 connects the train station and Piazza del Nettuno, the city centre. The **airport** (enquiries ☎051.647.9615) is northwest of the centre, linked to the train station by the Aerobus (L7000/€3.62), which runs approximately every twenty minutes and takes around twenty-five minutes if the traffic is reasonably light.

There are **tourist offices** at the airport (daily 8am–8pm; ☎051.647.2036), at the train station (Mon–Sat 9am–7pm; ☎051.251.947), and a main office in the Palazzo d'Accursio at Piazza Maggiore 6 (Mon–Sat 8.30am–7pm, Sun 8.30am–2pm; ☎051.246.541, *www.comune.bologna.it/bolognaturismo*).

Once you're in the city centre, the best way to **get around** is on foot: a leisurely stroll downtown beneath some of the 25 miles of porticoes that link together the compact *centro storico* is most appealing. **Buses** (enquiries ☎051.245.400) are fast and frequent; tickets cost L1800/€0.93 each from *tabacchi*, newsstands or ticket machines and are valid on as many buses as you like within one hour (or buy a Citypass, valid for seven journeys, for L14,000/€7.23). You can get information from the booth at the junction of Via Delle Lame and Via G. Marconi or the "Via Libera" office at Piazza Galvani 4c (daily 7am–8pm; ☎051.290.290). For **taxis**, call ☎051.372.727 or 051.534.141.

Accommodation

In terms of **places to stay**, Bologna is not geared up for tourists, least of all for those travelling on a tight budget: there are only a few cheap **hotels**, although one advantage

Is that some are reasonably central, and there is no feasibly placed campsite. The tourist offices have hotel lists and the CST (the Centre for Tourist Services, toll-free ☎800.856.065 or 051.648.7583) can book rooms for you.

Hotels

Accademia, Via Belle Arti 6 (☎051.232.318, fax 051.263.590, *www.hotelaccademia.it*). In the heart of the university quarter, this large hotel has modest-sized doubles. ③.

Al Cappellorosso, Via Dé Fusari 9 (☎051.261.891, fax 051.227.179, *cappellorosso@tin.it*). Understated chic right in the heart of the centre, a fourteenth-century building completely remodeled with business travellers in mind. ⑨.

Arcoveggio, Via L. Spada 27 (☎ & fax 051.355.436). The best-value option close to the train station – from where it is a 15-minute walk northwards, or take bus #25 to Piazza dell'Unità. ⑤.

Centrale Via della Zecca 2 (☎051.225.114, fax 051.235.162). Good-value hotel, in the heart of the city, with great views from the top-floor rooms. ④.

Commercianti Via De' Pignattari 11 (☎051.233.052, fax 051.224.733, *hotcom@tin.it*). Luxury in one of the centre's historic buildings, A twelfth-century palazzo, which has been luxuriously refurbished, right in the centre of town. ⑨.

Corona D'Oro Via Oberdan 12 (☎051.236.456 fax 051.262.279, *hhotcoro@tin.it*). Four-star opulence in a former palazzo close to the twin towers. ⑨.

Garisenda, Via Rizzoli 9, Galleria del Leone 1 (☎051.224.369, fax 051.221.007). Excellent views from this centrally located, clean hotel, but the staff are less than friendly and rather inefficient. All baths are down the hall. ③.

Minerva, Via De' Monari 3 (☎ & fax 051.239.652). Very basic rooms located conveniently halfway between the station and Piazza Maggiore. ③.

Orologio, Via IV Novembre 10 (☎051.231.253, fax 051.260.552, *hotoro@tin.it*). One of Bologna's better three-star hotels overlooking a corner of Piazza Maggiore. Book well in advance. ⑧.

Panorama, Via Livraghi 1 (☎051.221.802, fax 051.266.360). Just off Ugo Bassi, this place has a range of accommodation, varying from three- and four-bedded rooms to ordinary doubles – all sharing clean and pleasant bathrooms down the corridor. Helpful owners. ③.

Roma, Via D'Azeglio 9 (☎051.226.322, fax 051.239.909, *hotelroma@mailbox.dsnet.it*). On one of the centre's major pedestrian arteries, quiet and refined, comfortably and unpretentiously furnished. ⑦.

Rossini, Via Bibbiena 11 (☎051.237.716, fax 051.268.035). In the student quarter, just off Piazza Verdi, a friendly place with clean and comfortable, if rather basic, rooms. ③.

San Donato, Via Zamboni 16 (☎051.235.395, fax 051.230.547, *www.bestwestern.it/sandonato_bo*). In an elegant old building, which has been restored and updated, located in a delighful little piazza, a stone's throw from the two towers. ⑦.

Hostels

The **San Sisto**, Via Viadagola 14, and the **Due Torri**, Via Viadagola 5 (☎051.501.810), are the city's two official youth hostels, 6km outside the centre of town. The first is the old hostel, closed for refurbishing at the time of writing; the second is a newer, purpose-built place that costs L20,000/€10.33. To get to the hostel take bus #93 from Porta San Donato (last service 10.45pm). There's a curfew of midnight and the hostel is closed from December 19 to January 20.

Outside Bologna

Thirty minutes by car northeast of Bologna, just outside the town of Budrio, nestled amidst a magnificent stand of poplars, is the *Villa Montefano*, Via Volpino 13 (☎051.692.9587, *www.montefano.com*; ①). It's a seventeenth-century country villa that's now best described as a residential cultural centre – the brainchild of a young American, Clark Lawrence. Grand, frescoed rooms offer cosy accommodation for up to 8 guests, family-style; everyone pitches in with cleaning and cooking duties. There's an ongoing cultural programme, known throughout the area, of art exhibitions, classical and jazz concerts and readings, plus impromptu parties and other events that keep the

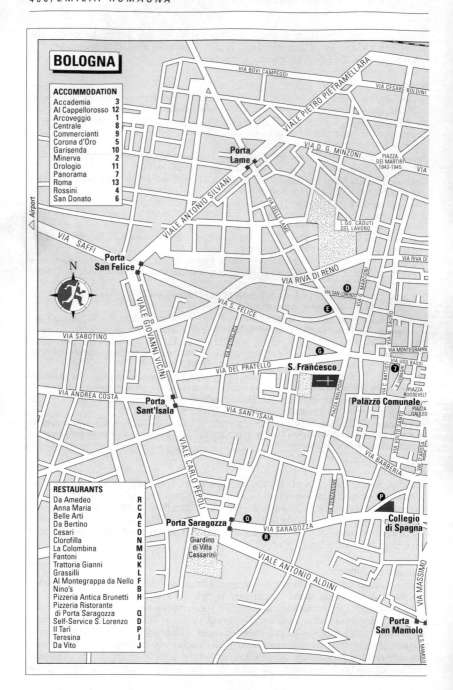

BOLOGNA

ACCOMMODATION
Accademia	3
Al Cappellorosso	12
Arcoveggio	1
Centrale	8
Commercianti	9
Corona d'Oro	5
Garisenda	10
Minerva	2
Orologio	11
Panorama	7
Roma	13
Rossini	4
San Donato	6

RESTAURANTS
Da Amedeo	R
Anna Maria	C
Belle Arti	A
Da Bertino	E
Cesari	O
Clorofilla	N
La Colombina	M
Fantoni	G
Trattoria Gianni	K
Grassilli	L
Al Montegrappa da Nello	F
Nino's	B
Pizzeria Antica Brunetti	H
Pizzeria Ristorante di Porta Saragozza	Q
Self-Service S. Lorenzo	D
Il Tarì	P
Teresina	I
Da Vito	J

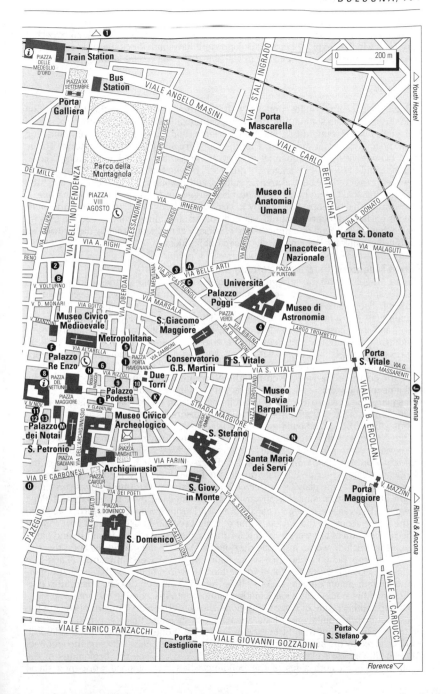

atmosphere lively. A stimulating mix of Italians and foreigners, it makes an excellent base from which to explore Ferrara, Bologna and Ravenna. Check the Web site for seasonal programmes – and do be sure to call ahead to reserve and for directions.

The City

Bologna's city centre is quite compact, with most things of interest within the main ring road. From the train station, **Via dell'Indipendenza** leads into the centre; it is one of Bologna's main thoroughfares, lined with cinemas and bars and always busy, finishing up at the linked central squares of **Piazza Maggiore** and **Piazza del Nettuno**. To the right of here lies the commercial district, bordered by office blocks along Via G. Marconi, and to the left the university quarter. The one thing you will notice quickly is how well preserved the central area actually is, and although this can be frustrating, too – it's not unusual to find notices on churches suggesting you return in a year's time – the reward is a city centre that is a joy to stroll around. Above all you'll notice the city's famous porticoes – ochre-coloured, vaulted colonnades lining every street into the city centre that make a vivid first impression, especially at night, and that by day provide an unofficial catwalk for Bologna's well-turned-out residents.

Piazza Maggiore, Piazza del Nettuno and around

Piazza Maggiore and the adjacent **Piazza del Nettuno** make up the notional pulse of the city and are the obvious area to make for first, with an activity that seems almost constant. Their cafés are packed out through the morning for the market, afterwards thinning out just a little before passeggiata. The squares are a quintessentially social place, and they host, as you might expect, the city's principal secular and religious buildings: the church of San Petronio, Palazzo Re Enzo and Palazzo Comunale – all impressive for their bulk alone, with heavy studded doors and walls pitted with holes from the original scaffolding.

At the centre of Piazza del Nettuno, the **Neptune Fountain** is a symbol of the city and a haunt of pigeons, styled in extravagant fashion by Giambologna in 1566. Across the square, the **Palazzo Re Enzo** takes its name from its time as the prison-home of Enzo, king of Sicily, confined here by papal supporters for two decades after the Battle of Fossalta in 1249. If the building looks rather dour, it's partly thanks to controversial architect Alfonso Rubbiani, who restored (purists would say rebuilt) many of Bologna's medieval structures in the early part of this century. Next door to the Palazzo Re Enzo, **Palazzo Podestà** fills the northern side of Piazza Maggiore, built at the behest of the Bentivoglio clan, who ruled the city during the fifteenth century, before papal rule was re-established. On the piazza's western edge, the **Palazzo Comunale** gives some indication of the political shifts in power, its facade adorned by a huge statue of Pope Gregory XIII as an affirmation of papal authority. Through a small courtyard, stairs lead to the upper rooms of the palace, some of which remain in use as local government offices while others are worth visiting for their galleries of ornate furniture and paintings, which include works by Vitale da Bologna, Simone dei Crocefessi and others of the Bolognese School. On the same floor is the **Museo Morandi** (Tues–Sun 10am–6pm; L8000/€4.13), devoted to the life and works of one of Italy's most important twentieth-century painters. As well as the 200 works on display, a faithful reconstruction of his studio offers a fascinating glimpse into his working methods.

On the southern side of Piazza Maggiore, the church of **San Petronio** is one of the finest Gothic brick buildings in Italy, an enormous structure that was originally intended to have been larger than St Peter's in Rome, but money and land for the side aisle were diverted by the pope's man in Bologna towards a new university, and the architect Antonio di Vicenzo's plans had to be modified. You can see the beginnings of the planned aisles on both sides of the building: when they stopped work they sliced through the window arches and left only the bottom third of the facade decorated with the marble geometric patterns intended to cover the whole. There are models of what the church was supposed to look like in the museum (daily except Tues 10am–12.30pm; free). Notwithstanding its curtailment, San Petronio is a fine example of late fourteenth-century architecture. Above the central portal is a beautiful carving of *Madonna and Child* by visiting artist Jacopo della Quercia. Within, the side chapels contain a host of treasures; the fourth chapel on the north aisle, the Cappella Bolognini, features remarkable frescoes by Giovanni da Modena and a gilded altarpiece by Jacopo di Paolo. The most unusual feature is the astronomical clock – a long brass meridian line set at an angle across the floor, with a hole left in the roof for the sun to shine through onto the right spot.

The ornately decorated building next door to San Petronio is the Palazzo dei Notai ("Notaries"), a fourteenth-century reminder that it was Bologna's legal scholars who, in the Middle Ages, laid the first foundations of contemporary European law. In the opposite direction, across Via dell'Archiginnasio from San Petronio, the **Palazzo dei Banchi** is more of a set-piece than a palazzo, basically a facade designed by the Renaissance architect Vignola to unify a set of medieval houses that didn't really fit with the rest of the square. Adjacent, the **Museo Civico Archeologico** (Tues–Fri 9am–2pm, Sat & Sun 9am–1pm & 3.30–7pm; L8000/€4.13) is rather stuffy, but has good displays of Egyptian and Roman antiquities, and an Etruscan section that is one of the best outside Lazio, with finds drawn from the Etruscan settlement of Felsina, which predated Bologna; there are reliefs from tombs, vases and a bronze *situla*, richly decorated, from the fifth century BC.

Just north of the museum, **Via Clavature** – together with nearby Via Pescerie Vecchie and Via Draperie – is home to a grouping of market stalls and shops that makes for one of the city's most enticing sights and provides proof positive of Bologna's gourmet proclivities. In autumn especially the market is a visual and aural feast, with fat porcini mushrooms, truffles in baskets of rice, thick rolls of *mortadella*, hanging pheasants, ducks and hares, and skinned frogs by the kilo. The church of **Santa Maria della Vita**, in Via Clavature, is worth a look for its outstanding pietà by Nicola dell'Arca – seven life-sized terracotta figures that are among the most dramatic examples of Renaissance sculpture you'll see.

Down the street in the other direction, Bologna's old university – the **Archiginnasio** – was founded at more or less the same time as Piazza Maggiore was laid out, predating the rest of Europe's universities, although it didn't get a special building until 1565, when Antonio Morandi was commissioned to construct the present building on the site until then reserved for San Petronio. Centralizing the university on one site was a way of maintaining control over students at a time when the Church felt particularly threatened by the Reformation. You can wander freely into the main courtyard, covered with the coats of arms of its more famous graduates, and perhaps even attend a lecture – Umberto Eco lectures here on semiotics. In the mornings it's also possible to visit the main upstairs **library**, and, most interestingly, the **Teatro Anatomico** (Mon–Sat 9am–1pm, free), the original medical faculty dissection theatre. Tiers of seats surround an extraordinary professor's chair, covered with a canopy supported by figures known as *gli spellati* – "the skinned ones". Not many dissections went on, due to prohibitions of the Church, but when they did (usually around carnival time), artists and the general public used to turn up as much for the social occasion as for studying the body.

Outside the old university, **Piazza Galvani** remembers the physicist Luigi Galvani with a statue. One of Bologna's more successful scientists, Galvani discovered electrical currents in animals, thereby lending his name to the English language in the word "galvanize". A few minutes south, down Via Garibaldi, is **Piazza San Domenico**, with its strange canopied tombs holding the bones of medieval law scholars. Bologna was instrumental in sorting out wrangles between the pope and the Holy Roman emperor in the tenth and eleventh centuries, earning itself the title of "La Dotta" (The Learned) and forming the basis for the university's prominent law faculties. The church of **San Domenico** was built in 1251 to house the relics of St Dominic, which were placed in the so-called *Arca di San Domenico*: a fifteenth-century work that was ostensibly the creation of Nicola Pisano – though in reality many artists contributed to it. Pisano and his pupils were responsible for the reliefs illustrating the saint's life; the statues on top were the work of Pisano himself; Nicola dell'Arca was responsible for the canopy (this was the work that earned him his name); and the short-haired angel and figures of saints Proculus, with a cloak over his shoulder, and Petronius, holding the model of the city, were the work of a very young Michelangelo. While you're in the church, try also to see the **Museo di San Domenico** (Tues–Sat 10am–noon & 3–5pm, Sun 3–5pm; free) displaying a very fine polychrome terracotta bust of St Dominic by Nicolò dell'Arca along with paintings, reliquaries and vestments, and, beyond, the intricately inlaid mid-sixteenth-century choir stalls.

Just to the east of San Domenico, on a little hill, stands **San Giovanni in Monte**, worth a visit for its stunning collection of paintings from the Bolognese school. Built on an ancient temple, the present structure dates from the thirteenth to fifteenth centuries. The facade's great portal is by Domenico Berardi, and the harmonious interior features unusual partly frescoed columns, a fifteenth-century stained glass tondo, inlaid choir stalls, and a chapel decorated by Guercino.

The university quarter

Bordered by Via Oberdan to the west and Strada Maggiore to the south, the eastern section of Bologna's *centro storico* preserves many of the older **university** departments, housed for the most part in large seventeenth- and eighteenth-century palaces. This is perhaps the most pleasant part of the city to while away the day – or night – amid a concentration of low-budget bars, restaurants and shops aimed at the student population. It is also the place to scour for information on events around town: posters plaster the walls along Via Zamboni and the lanes off it – Via delle Moline, Via Belle Arti, Via Mentana – and the bars and cafés are often promoting some happening or other.

Via Rizzoli leads into the district from Piazza Maggiore, ending up at Piazza di Porta Ravegnana, where the **Torre degli Asinelli** (daily 9am–6pm; closes 5pm in winter; L3000/€1.55), next to the perilously leaning **Torre Garisenda**, are together known as the **Due Torri**, the only two remaining of literally hundreds of towers that were scattered across the city during the Middle Ages. The former makes a good place from which to get an overview of the city centre and beyond, out over the red-tiled roofs across the hazy, flat plains and southern hills beyond.

Walking southeast from the Due Torri, Via Santo Stefano leads down to its medieval gateway, past a complex of four – but originally seven – churches, collectively known as **Santo Stefano**. It's an attractive complex set in a wide piazza at the conjunction of several narrow porticoed streets. Three of the churches face on to the piazza, of which the striking polygonal church of **San Sepolcro** (closed noon–3.30pm), reached through the church of **Crocifisso**, is about the most interesting. The basin in its courtyard, called "Pilate's Bowl", dates from the eighteenth century, while on the inside the bones of St Petronius, held in a tomb modelled on the church of the holy sepulchre in Jerusalem, provide a macabre focus typical of the relic-obsessed Middle Ages. A doorway leads from here through to **Santi Vitale e Agricola**, Bologna's oldest church, built from discarded Roman fragments in the fifth century, while the fourth church, the **Trinità**, lies across the courtyard and is home to a small museum (daily 9am–noon & 3.30–6pm; free) containing a reliquary of St Petronius, a thirteenth-century fresco of the Massacre of the Innocents, and a handful of later paintings.

From here, follow Via Gerusalemme up to Strada Maggiore, where, a little way down on the right, the Gothic church of **Santa Maria dei Servi** dates from 1386. It's arguably Bologna's most elegant church, with a beautiful portico and fourteenth-century ceiling frescoes by Vitale da Bologna – a rare chance to see the work of the so-called "father" of Bolognese painting *in situ*. A chapel also holds a *Madonna Enthroned* by Cimabue. Across Strada Maggiore, Piazza Aldrovandi has a good daily street market, and is lined on one side by the **Museo Civico d'Arte Industriale** and the **Museo Davia Bargellini** (both Tues–Sat 9am–2pm, Sun 9am–1pm; free), an eclectic mixture made up of the art collection of the Davia family and displays of textiles, glassware and furniture; the entrance is on Strada Maggiore. Further north from here, Via Petroni leads through to **Piazza Verdi**, at the heart of the university district and at lunchtimes packed with students grabbing some of the city's cheapest food. **Via Zamboni** bisects Piazza Verdi, around and along which are many of the old palaces housing various parts of the university. A large number of these buildings were decorated by members of the Bolognese academies, which were prominent in Italian art after 1600. Tibaldi, better known as an architect, turned his hand to fresco in the main building, the **Palazzo Poggi** at no. 33 (Mon–Fri 9am–12.30pm; check with the tourist office as times are subject to frequent change; free). His fresco of Ulysses here was influenced by Michelangelo's Sistine Chapel and has played a part in the well-publicized row over the latter's restoration, with art historians using Tibaldi's fresco as proof that they have got Michelangelo's colours right. On the fourth floor of the building, the fascinating 300-year-old **Specola** or observatory draws most people here, its small **Museo di Astronomia** (closed at the time of writing; Mon–Fri 8.30am–5.30pm; ☎051.209.9369; free) home to a number of eighteenth-century instruments and a frescoed map of the constellations – painted just seventy years after Galileo was imprisoned for his heretical statements about the cosmos.

A little way down Via Zamboni, in Piazza Rossini, is the church of **San Giacomo Maggiore** (☎051.225.970), a Romanesque structure begun in 1267 and enlarged over the centuries. The target here is the Bentivoglio Chapel, decorated with funds provided by one Annibale Bentivoglio to celebrate the family's victory in a local feud in 1488. Lorenzo Costa painted frescoes of the *Apocalypse*, the *Triumph of Death* and a *Madonna Enthroned* as well as of the Bentivoglio family – a deceptively pious-looking lot, captured in what was a fairly innovative picture in its time for the careful characterizations of its patrons. Further frescoes by Costa, along with Francesco Francia, decorate the **Oratorio di Santa Cecilia**; they show gory episodes from the lives of saints Cecilia and Valerian. And there's a tomb of Anton Galeazzo Bentivoglio by Quercia opposite the chapel – one of the artist's last works.

Piazza Rossini is named after the nineteenth-century composer, who studied at the **Conservatorio G.B. Martini** on the square. The library here is among the most important music libraries in Europe; some of the original manuscripts are on display to the public along with a few paintings. Further north up Via Zamboni, around Porta San Donato, are many of the university's faculty buildings, including that of the **Museo di Anatomia Umana**, recently re-opened in it's original rooms at Via Zamboni 33 (Mon–Fri 9am–5pm ☎051.244.467; free). An odd place to visit, perhaps, but it would be a shame to leave Bologna without seeing its highly idiosyncratic (and beautiful) **waxworks**. These were used until the nineteenth century for medical demonstration, and they are as startling as any art or sculpture in the city. There were two Italian schools of waxworks: the Florentine method, where they used limbs, organs and bones to make moulds to cast the wax; and the Bolognese, where everything was sculpted, even tiny veins and capillaries, which were rolled like Plasticine. The boundaries between "art" and "science" were not rigidly drawn, and in Bologna in the early eighteenth century the workshops of Anna Morandi Mazzolini and Ercole Lelli turned out figures that were much more than just clinical aids. Mazzolini, for example, created a self-portrait in the midst of a brain dissection, pulling back a scalp with wispy hairs attached; other figures, unnervingly displayed in glass cases, are modelled like classical statues, one carrying a sickle, the other a scythe.

Close by, the collection of paintings in the **Pinacoteca Nazionale** at Via Belle Arti 56 (Tues–Sat 9am–2pm, Sun 9am–1pm; L8000/€4.13) may provide some light relief, concentrating mainly (though not exclusively) on the work of Bolognese artists. There are canvases by the fourteenth-century painter Vitale da Bologna, later works by Francia and Tibaldi, and paintings from the city's most productive artistic period, the early seventeenth century, when Annibale and Agostino Carracci, Guido Reni and Guercino ("The Cross-eyed") were active here.

The Metropolitana, Museo Civico and the church of San Francesco

There's much less of interest to the north and west of Bologna's central piazzas. The city's cathedral, the **Metropolitana di San Pietro**, is on the right out of Piazza del Nettuno, two blocks down Via dell'Indipendenza from Piazza del Nettuno. Originally a tenth-century building, it's been rebuilt many times and is these days more enjoyable for its stately atmosphere than any particular features. The **Museo Civico Medioevale e dal Rinascimento** (Mon & Wed–Fri 9am–2pm, Sat & Sun 9am–1pm & 3.30–7pm; L8000/€4.13), opposite, is of more interest, housed in the Renaissance Palazzo Fava at Via Manzoni 4 and decorated with frescoes by Carracci and members of the Bolognese School depicting the *History of Europa, Jason's Feats* and scenes from the *Aeneid*. The museum collection itself includes bits of armour, ceramics, numerous tombs and busts of various popes and other dignitaries, and a *Madonna and SS* by Jacopo della Quercia.

West of Piazza del Nettuno, at the end of Via Ugo Bassi, the basilica of **San Francesco** (daily 6.30am–noon & 3–7pm) is a huge Gothic brick pile supported by flying buttresses that was heavily restored in the 1920s and partly rebuilt after World War II. Inside there are a beautiful and very ornate altarpiece from 1392 and a pleasant cloister.

Eating, drinking and nightlife

Eating and **drinking** are the mainstays of Bolognese social life. Eating especially is important to the Bolognese: the city is known as "La Grassa" ("The Fat"), the result of a rich culinary tradition, and the emphasis on food here can be taken to extremes. People travel a long way to eat at the top restaurants, which are said to be the best in Italy, and even the simplest restaurants and the many *osterie* often serve dishes of a very high standard. Certainly the lack of a fancy menu or elaborate decor shouldn't rule out further investigation, and you should endeavour to try some local specialities while you're here. Handmade lasagne, tagliatelle and tortellini (small, shaped pasta with a stuffing of ham, sausage, chopped chicken, pork and veal, eggs, nutmeg and parmesan) are excellent and regarded with great affection by residents of Bologna, to the extent that elaborate stories explain their origin: the first tortellini are said to have been made by a Bolognese innkeeper trying to re-create the beauty of Venus's navel.

Bologna has any number of chic **bars** if all you want to do is drink, most notably on and around Via Zamboni, in the student quarter. It also has a good selection of **osterie**, which have been the mainstay of Bolognese **nightlife** for several hundred years – pub-like places, open late, where you go more to drink than eat, though you can get excellent snacky (if sometimes pricey) food. The Bolognese like to go out late, around 10.30 or 11pm, and most *osterie* stay open until around 2am. The city also has a good variety of **clubs**, with music to suit most tastes: the more established places are mentioned on p.409, but check for details of what's happening, and look out for posters advertising events around the university quarter and Piazza Verdi in particular. Bologna's enlightened city council encourages open-air **raves** by giving subsidies and making entrance either free or very inexpensive – the most well-known being "Made in Bo". They happen on weekends in summer, off Via Stalingrado in the area around the Fiera and the Parco di Nord.

As for **the arts and cultural attractions**, the city has also tried to curb the general August exodus by mounting a summer arts festival, called Bo Est, with concerts and videos at night in the courtyards of the civic buildings. Ferragosto is an especially good time to be here, when everyone takes to the hills for all-night revelry in one of the parks outside town.

For **information** the main tourist office in Piazza Maggiore has lists of nightclubs, *osterie* and forthcoming events. Bologna currently lacks a regular "what's on" guide of its own, but for rock concerts and venues, you could try asking at the Rock Shop, Via Mazzini 146, or looking in the weekly supplement of the national newspaper *La Repubblica*. Or, if you want to stop by the British Council, Corte Isolani 8 (☎051.225.142) you can pick up a copy of *Talk About*, which lists some of the main goings-on around town.

Restaurants

Anna Maria, Via Belle Arti 17a (☎051.266.894). A favourite with the orchestra from the Teatro Comunale nearby; the *sfogline* (pasta-makers) work out front at lunchtime. Especially worth trying are the *tortellini al gorgonzola*. Closed Mon.

Da Amedeo, Via Saragozza 88. A good place to try *tortellini in brodo* (in clear broth) and other Emilian specialities, including game. The vegetable dishes and desserts are reliable. Closed Sat.

Belle Arti, Via Belle Arti 14. A noisy, studenty place with friendly service and extra-large pizzas. Closed Wed.

Da Bertino, Via Delle Lame 55. The place to come for no-nonsense Bolognese peasant-style cooking. *Bollito* and *arrosto* (boiled and roast meats) are brought to your table on a metal trolley, accompanied by a range of traditional relishes. Closed Sun.

Cesari, Via dé Carbonesi 8 (☎051.226.769). One of Bologna's perennial top choices for quality Emilian cuisine and friendly service. Closed Sun.

Clorofilla, Strada Maggiore 64c. A non-smoking vegetarian restaurant – just the place if the "fat of Bologna" has been weighing you down. Closed Sun.

La Colombina, Vicolo Colombina 5 (☎051.231.706). Very attractive, very authentic, and fairly expensive, but excellent value if you're looking for authentic Bolognese specialities. Closed Tues.

Fantoni, Via del Pratello 11. Family-style Bolognese food on one of the oldest streets in the city. Amazing value for money, but open lunchtimes only. Closed Sun.

Trattoria Gianni, Via Clavature 18 (☎051.229.434). Definitely one of the top options in Bologna. Try the ultra-traditional *bolliti*, a variety of meats boiled in the Emilian way. Moderate prices. Closed Sunday evenings and Mon.

Grassilli, Via del Luzzo 3 (☎051.222.961). Way up in the expensive category, serving Emilian dishes that have been adapted with flair to suit modern tastes, accompanied by exceptionally good service. An experience to remember, though you'll definitely need to book ahead. Closed Wed.

Al Montegrappa da Nello, at the Piazza del Nettuno end of Via Montegrappa. Try the very Emilian antipasti, in which each prosciutto is described according to the town it comes from. There are around half a dozen non-meat dishes on the menu too. Closed Mon, throughout Aug, plus Sat & Sun in summer.

Nino's, Via Volturno 9c (off Via dell'Indipendenza). Pizzeria that serves a good selection of pizzas as well as home-made pasta – try the lasagne. Closed Mon.

Pizzeria Antica Brunetti, Via Caduti di Cefalonia 5 (☎051.234.441). An elegant old wood-panelled restaurant on two floors, handily located close to Piazza Maggiore, that specializes in fish and seafood dishes and pizza. Moderately priced. Closed Wed.

Pizzeria Ristorante di Porta Saragozza, Via Saragozza 7. Friendly and lively, serving enormous pizzas at moderate prices. Many gay clientele. Closed Wed.

Self-Service S. Lorenzo, Via S. Lorenzo 4. Convenient cafeteria/restaurant off Via Marconi, serving traditional Bolognese dishes. Closed Sat evenings.

Il Tari, Via Collegio di Spagna 13. A trattoria and pizzeria featuring fish dishes, such as delicious *spaghetti allo scoglio* – with mussels and galletti mushrooms. Enormous salads, too. Closed Thurs.

Teresina, Via Oberdan 4. A great family run restaurant serving regional dishes as well as very good southern Italian food, including fish (L50,000–60,000/€25.83–30.99 for a full meal), with tables outside in summer. Closed Sun.

Da Vito, Via Mario Musolesi 9. (☎051.349.809). Though difficult to find, this trattoria is famous throughout Bologna for its *carpaccio* (air-dried beef), served with brioche and cheese. Closed Wed.

Osterie

Birreria del Pratello, Via del Pratello 24a. Bustling, pub-like osteria serving a good range of German beers. Food available. Closed Sun.

Il Cantinone, Via del Pratello 56a. A lively *enoteca* offering a dozen or more wines by the glass and beer on tap. Food available too. Closed Wed.

Enoteca des Arts, Via San Felice 9. Tiny, dark and atmospheric bar serving cheap, local wine. Open all day Mon–Sat.

Marione, Via San Felice 137. Close to the city gate, an old, smoky and dark osteria, with good wine and snacks. Closed Wed.

Da Matusel, Via Bertolini 2. Close by the university, a popular and noisy place with reasonably priced food. Closed Sun.

Del Montesino, Via del Pratello 74b. A chatty, convivial place serving a handful of snacks including substantial, southern-inspired salads and good *crostini* (various toppings spread on toasted bread). The house wine is very drinkable, though there are other, more expensive options. Closed Mon.

Del Moretto, Via San Mamolo 5. One of Bologna's best *osterie*, situated just outside Porto San Mamolo. Large and lively, with a mixture of young and old, especially favoured by musicians and artists. Closed Sun.

Dell'Orsa, Via Mentana 1f. Has live jazz during the winter. Stick with the bruschetta; the other dishes are fairly pricey. Closed Mon.

Poeti, Via Poeti 1. An old palazzo that has been an osteria since the fifteenth century. Trades on its reputation, which means its prices are slightly inflated; occasional live music. Closed Mon.

Senzanome, Via Senzanome 42a. Off Via Saragozza, this was a favourite drinking place for cart drivers in the seventeenth century when the osteria was famed for its sausage – made, it is claimed, from bull's testicles. The place now serves good home-made pasta and has a wide choice of beers and wines. Arrive after 10pm if you just want to drink. Closed Mon.

Del Sole, Vicolo Ranocchi 1d. One of the oldest *osterie* right in the heart of the historic centre. At lunch you can assemble a picnic from the nearby market and eat it here, so long as you buy a glass of wine to wash it all down. Evening opening is limited to the hour between 8 and 9pm. Closed Sun.

Snacks, bars, cafés and ice cream

Altero, Via dell'Indipendenza 33; Via Ugo Bassi 10. Part of a mensa-style chain, and the best place for pizza by the slice.

Caffè Commercianti, Strada Maggiore 23c. Atmospheric and very central snack and cocktail bar. Open every day.

C'entro, Via dell'Indipendenza 45. Smart cafeteria, with tables outside in summer. Closed Sun.

Frulé, Via Clavature. On the corner of Piazza del Francia, this is the place for *frullati* and ice cream.

Gianni, Via Montegrappa 11. Fine spot to eat ice cream, with tables outside in the summer.

Impero, Via dell'Indipendenza 39. Excellent croissants and pastries for breakfast – and later. Closed Mon.

All'Inzu, Via del Pratello 5a. Small, trendy bar with board games and enormous video screen; Closed Sun.

Mocambo,Via d'Azeglio 1. A tiny bar where the slickest Bolognese sip their aperitifs. Closed Sun.

Il Piccolo Bar, Piazza Verdi. Famous student hangout open later than most other bars.

Pino, Via Castiglione 65. The main branch of Bologna's best-known ice cream chain.

Bar Rosa Rose, Via Clavature 18b. A small, chic bar with meals and tables outside, popular with Bologna's new left at *aperitivo* hour. Closed Tues.

La Torinese, Piazza Re Enzo 1. Hot chocolate to die for – no seats so you just stand at the counter. Closed Thurs.

Ugo, Via San Felice 24. Considered by locals to offer the best home-made ice cream in town. Closed Mon & Tues & Oct–March.

Zanarini, Piazza Galvani 1. Where the chic Bolognese gather for their *aperitivi*; suitably smart and expensive. Closed Mon.

Clubs and live music venues

Blade Runner, Via S. Isaia 57d. Designer disco-bar with dance floor in basement – a favourite with hip young Bolognese. Closed Tues.

Café Caracol, Piazza Galileo. Centrally placed Mexican bar by the police station that's open until 2am, serves great food, and has a small dance floor. Cheap cocktails too during the club's happy hour (7.30–8.30pm). Closed Sun.

Candilejas, Via Bentini 20. Salsa and merengue music, alternating with indie stuff. To get there take bus #27 from Piazza del Nettuno to the suburb of Corticella (a 25min journey); nightbus #62 runs, on the hour, back into town. Closed Sun.

Cantina Bentivoglio, Via Mascarella 4b. On the edge of the university quarter, and as much an osteria as a club. Live bands, often including jazz, play at around 9.30pm in the cellars of this six-teenth-century palazzo, where the food and wine are excellent. Closed Mon.

Cassero, Piazza di Porta Saragozza 2. Actually inside the city gate itself, this is a mostly male, gay club with café and bookshop open sporadically during the day but hotting up around 10pm or 11pm with a bar and dancing at night, and a beautiful roof garden with some good views over the city.

Down Town, Via delle Moline 16b. Off the left-hand side of Via dell'Independenza, about halfway down, as you head away from the train station. Live bands playing a mix of jazz, bluegrass and coun-try – simple eats, a well-stocked bar and plenty of atmosphere. Things start to kick off around 11pm. Closed Mon.

Link, Via Fioravanti 14 (☎051.370.971). Just behind the train station, this *centro sociale* has a cyber-style bar upstairs and enormous dance floor downstairs. Avant-garde performance art and live bands early on, with ambient or techno sounds later. No entrance fee, except for gigs. Daily 10pm–5am.

Palazzo dei Congressi, Piazza Costituzione 4 (☎051.637.5165). The venue for bands commanding bigger audiences; get there on bus #18 from Via Rizzoli, just off Piazza Maggiore. Tickets from Fonte dell'Oro, Galleria Accuisio 14, off Via Rizzoli (☎051.235.324).

Porto di Mare, Via Sampieri. Right behind the Due Torri, with good live bands at the weekend and a Greek taverna downstairs. Open 10.30pm–2.30am; closed Mon.

Vicolo Bolognetti, Vicolo Bolognetti 2. More of an open-air bar than a club, set in the middle of an impressive cloister. Open summer only, but a great place to while away balmy evenings.

Listings

Books English books from Feltrinelli International, Via Zamboni 7.

Car rental Avis, Viale Pietramellara 35 (☎051.255.024); Europcar, Via Amendola 12 (☎051.247.101); Hertz, Via Amendola 16a (☎051.254.830); Maggiore (Budget) Via Cairoli 4 (☎051.252.525). All the major companies also have desks at the airport.

Cinema Adriano, Via San Felice 52, shows films in their original language on Mondays; Arena Puccini, Via Serlio 25, is a summer-only outdoor cinema; Lumiere, Via Pietralata 55a, is an excellent film club that occasionally offers non-dubbed classics; Tiffany, Piazza di Porta Saragozza 5, on Wednesdays.

Hospital In an emergency, dial ☎118; or go to the Pronto Soccorso (24hr casualty) at the Ospedale San Orsola Generale, Via Massarenti 9 (☎051.636.3345); bus #14 from Via Rizzoli.

Internet access Central tourist office, Piazza Maggiore 6 (see p.398; free). Otherwise, there's *La Linea* in Piazza Re Enzo (8pm–2am; ☎051.296.013; free) or *Internet Point* on Via Ranzani 5/12 (10am–10pm; ☎051.247.474; L12,000/€6.20 per hr).

Laundry Laundromat, Via Petroni 38, is the most central coin-op/drop-service laundry; Onda Blu, Via S. Donato 4b–c, just beyond the city wall, and Via Sargoza 34a–b, daily 8am–10pm.

Markets There are a couple of great indoor food markets in the city centre: the large and lively Mercato delle Erbe, Via Ugo Bassi 2 (Mon–Sat 7.15am–1pm & 5–7pm, closed Thurs & Sat afternoon); and another on Via Clavature (same opening hours); there's also a smaller open-air market at Piazza Aldrovandi, along Strada Maggiore, closed Thursday afternoons. Finally, there's the open-air La Montagnola market, held in Piazza VIII Agosto on Fridays and Saturdays, dawn until dusk, which sells just about everything, but is especially good for new and secondhand clothes.

Pharmacy Night services rotate; look outside the Farmacia Comunale in Piazza Maggiore or dial ☎192.

Police In an emergency dial ☎113. Otherwise their main office is Piazza Galileo 7 (☎051.640.1111).

Post office City's main post office is on Piazza Minghetti (Mon–Fri 8.15am–6.30pm, Sat 8.15am–1pm).

Shops Some of Bologna's most colourful sights are inside its many food stores, particularly those between Piazza Maggiore and the Due Torri, epitomized by Tamburini at Via Caprarie 1, which has a sizeable array of the different ways of eating the "fat of Bologna". The most convenient supermarket is the Co-op, at Via Montebello 2, behind the train station.

Swimming pool Viale Costa 174 (☎051.615.2520; Mon & Wed–Sat 10.30am–10.30pm, Tues 2.30-10.30pm; call to confirm, as the hours change from season to season).

Telephones Telecom Italia, Piazza VIII Agosto (24hr); Via Fossalta 4e (daily 8am–10pm).

Travel agents CTS, Largo Respighi 2g (☎051.261.802); University Viaggi, Via Zamboni 16e (☎051.236.255).

Women's bookshop Libreria delle Donne, Via Avesella 2.

On from Bologna: south to Tuscany

In the heat of the summer the need to get out of Bologna becomes pressing, and the hills that start almost as soon as you leave the city gates take you high enough to catch some cooling breezes. The most obvious destination for a short trip is the eighteenth-century shrine of **Santuario di Madonna di San Luca**, close on 4km outside the city but connected by way of the world's longest portico, which meanders across the hillside in a series of 666 arches – a shelter for pilgrims on the trek to the top. Bus #20 from the station drops you at the start of the route, by Porta Saragozza southwest of the centre. Further south, the N325 passes through **PONTECCHIO MARCONI**, where the physicist Guglielmo Marconi lived in the late nineteenth century, and from where, in 1895, he sent the first radio message ever – to his brother on the other side of the hill. Marconi lies in a specially designed mausoleum in the village, close to the remains of the boat, *Elettra*, from which Marconi lit up the warship *Sydney* while anchored in Genoa in 1930. A stop here is also a convenient time to try the local speciality of *crescente ripiena* (a kind of bread stuffed with cheese and herbs), at Sasso Marconi, a few kilometres down the road.

The route on from here towards Pistoia is a beautiful one, taking you above the Setta Valley, past chestnut groves and small villages. It's a well-trafficked road, though, and the backroads are the greatest attraction. **MARZABOTTO**, a few kilometres on from Sasso Marconi and accessible by direct bus from Bologna, is known as the site of the massacre by the Nazis of 1800 people during World War II. It also sports the remains of an Etruscan town, **Misa** (daily 8am–7pm; free), just outside. The site marks out the residential areas, the city gates, streets and drains; fragments of foundations from temples and some tombs remain – evidence of a town of highly skilled craft workers that was much more than just a staging-post between Etruria and the Po Valley. The **museum** (daily 9am–noon & 3–6.30pm; L4000/€2.07) contains a variety of finds, from the remains of the piped water system to household objects inscribed *mi Venelus* ("I belong to Venel") or *mi Sualus* ("I belong to Sualu").

Modena and around

Though only thirty minutes northwest by train, **MODENA** has a quite distinct identity from Bologna. It proclaims itself the "spiritual capital" of Emilia, highlighting the two cities' long and sometimes intense rivalry. Indeed, Modena does have a number of

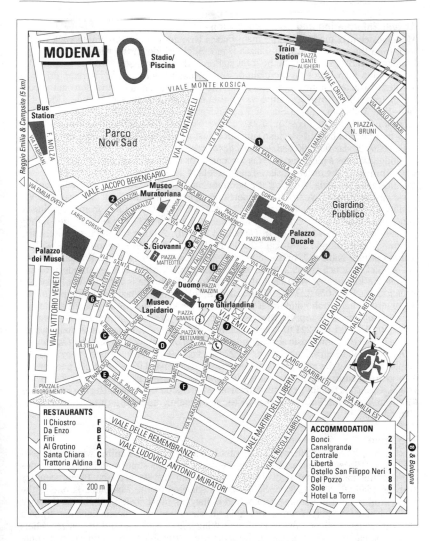

MODENA

Stadio/Piscina

Train Station

PIAZZA DANTE ALIGHIERI

VIALE MONTE KOSICA

VIALE CRISPI

VIA PAOLO FERRARI

Bus Station

Reggio Emilia & Campsite (5 km)

F. MOLZA

F. FABRIANI

Parco Novi Sad

VIA A. FONTANELLI

VIA GANACETO

VIA SANT'ORSOLA

CORSO VITTORIO EMANUELE II

PIAZZA N. BRUNI

VIA EMILIA OVEST

VIALE JACOPO BERENGARIO

VIA CERCA BELLE ARTI

VIA FERRARIS

CORSO CAVOUR

Giardino Pubblico

Museo Muratoriana

VIA R. RAMAZZINI

VIA P. SAURO

VIA L. POMPOSA

VIA TAGLI

PIAZZA SANDOMENICO

LARGO CORSICA

VIA CASTELMARALDO

S. Giovanni

PIAZZA MATTEOTTI

VIA C. SIGONIO

VIA C. TASSONI

VIA S. GEMINIANO

PIAZZA ROMA

Palazzo Ducale

Palazzo dei Musei

VIA VITTORIO VENETO

VIA S. AGOSTINO

RUA MURA

VIA CARTERIA

VIA MALATESTA

VIA SANTA EUFEMIA

VIA C. FALLOPPA

VIA CESARE BATTISTI

VIA BLASIA

VIA FARINI

VIA FONTERASO

VIA VINCENZO

VIA GORZI

CORSO CANAL GRANDE

VIALE DEI CADUTI IN GUERRA

VIALE V. REITER

Duomo

PIAZZA MAZZINI

Museo Lapidario

Torre Ghirlandina

VIA EMILIA

PIAZZA GRANDE

CORSO CANALCHIARO

VIA S. CARLO

VIA S. VINCENZO

N

CORSO DUOMO

RUA PIOPPA

VIA DELLE ORDINE

PIAZZA XX SETTEMBRE

VIA D. UNIVERSITÀ

VIA MONDATORA

CORSO CANAL GRANDE

LARGO GARIBALDI

VIA DEI SERVI

VIA CAMATTA

VIA CANALINO

VIA MARTIRI DELLA LIBERTÀ

VIALE MARTIRI DELLA LIBERTÀ

VIA STELLA

LARGO S. FRANCESCO

RUA FRATI MINORI

VIA FRANCESCO SELMI

VIA S. PAOLO

VIA SARAGOZZA

VIA EMILIA EST

PIAZZALE RISORGIMENTO

VIALE DELLE REMEMBRANZE

VIALE NICOLA FABRIZI

8 & Bologna

RESTAURANTS	
Il Chiostro	F
Da Enzo	B
Fini	E
Al Grotino	A
Santa Chiara	C
Trattoria Aldina	D

VIALE LUDOVICO ANTONIO MURATORI

ACCOMMODATION	
Bonci	2
Canalgrande	4
Centrale	3
Libertà	5
Ostello San Filippo Neri	1
Del Pozzo	8
Sole	6
Hotel La Torre	7

0   200 m

claims to fame: its outskirts are fringed with prosperous industry – knitwear and ceramics factories on the surrounding plain make a healthy profit, and Ferrari build their prestige motor cars close by, testing the Formula 1 monsters on the racetrack at nearby Fiorano; Pavarotti is a native of the town and gives regular summer concerts in the Parco Novi Sad near the train station; while the cathedral is considered perhaps the finest Romanesque building in Italy. Of things to see, top of most people's list are the rich collections of paintings and manuscripts built up by the Este family, who decamped here from Ferrara in 1598, after it was annexed by the Papal States, and ruled the town until the nineteenth century. But really the appeal of Modena is in wandering its labyrinthine old centre, finishing up the day with some good food and nightlife.

Arrival, information and accommodation

Modena's centre, marked by the main Piazza Grande, is a fifteen-minute walk southwest from the **train station** on Piazza Dante Alighieri, down the wide Corso Vittorio Emanuele II. Bus #7 connects the train station with the main street of Via Emilia. The **bus station** for villages on the plain or in the Apennines is on Via Fabriani, off Viale Monte Kosica, ten minutes' walk east from the train station and northeast from the centre of town. The **tourist office** is in the main square Piazza Grande (Mon–Sat 9am–1pm & 3–7pm, closed Sun & Wed afternoon; ☎059.206.660; you can go **online** there for two hours at a cost of L7500/€3.87). You can also take your questions to the very friendly and helpful ModenaTur office, just around the block at Via Scudari 8/10 (☎059.220.022, fax 059.206.688, *www.modenatur.net*).

Modena makes a nice place to stay for a night or two, and there are a few reasonably priced **hotels** in the narrow palace-lined streets of the city centre. However, places are at a premium, especially during the summer months, and you should really book in advance at any time of year. The cheapest option, just east off the Via Emilia, is *Del Pozzo*, Via del Pozzo 72a (☎059.360.350; ②); take bus #7 from the train station. Otherwise, try the *Bonci*, Via Ramazzini 59 (☎059.223.634; ③) – or the slightly pleasanter *Sole*, Via Malatesta 45 (☎059.214.245; ②). Among the smarter hotels, the *Centrale*, Via Rismondo 55 (☎059.218.808, fax 059.238.201; ⑤) is a good choice, with or without private bath, and, on the other side of the main artery of Via Emilia, *Hotel La Torre*, Via Cervetta 5 (☎059.222.615, fax 059.216.316; ④) offers spotless modern rooms in a period building. A very central and comfortable choice is *Libertà*, Via Blasia, 10 (☎059.222.365, fax 059.222.502, *hliberta@tin.it*; ⑤), off quiet Piazza Mazzini, just a couple of streets behind the duomo. If you're in the mood for full Modenese elegance in a garden setting, the top of the list is the *Canalgrande*, Corso Canalgrande 6 (☎059.217.160, fax 059.221.674, *www.canalgrandehotel.it*; ⑦), close to the main piazza. There is also the more basic accommodation option of the city's **hostel**, the *Ostello San Filippo Neri*, Via Sant'Orsola 52 (☎059.222.556, fax 059.243.548), situated very near the station and one of the city's well tended parks, which costs L23,000/€11.88 per person. The nearest **campsite** is *International Camping Modena* at Via Cave di Ramo 111 (☎059.332.252), Località Bruciata, 5km from Modena on the way to Reggio Emilia; bus #19 from Viale Monte Kosica, close by the train station, takes you right there in about 10 minutes.

The Town

Modena's tight, concentric medieval centre is bisected by **Via Emilia**, which runs past the edge of **Piazza Grande**, the nominal centre of town, its stone buildings and arcades forming the focus of much of its life. Dominating the square, the twelfth-century **Duomo** (daily 6.30am–12.30 & 3.30–7pm), dedicated to the Madonna, is one of the finest products of the Romanesque period in Italy. Its most striking feature is the west facade, just off the piazza, whose portal is supported by two majestic lions and fringed with marvellous reliefs – the work of one Wiligelmus, who also did the larger reliefs that run along the wall. Look also at the sculpture on the south side of the church, some of which is by Wiligelmus, some of which – in the final arch – is much later, from the fourteenth century. Inside, the duomo is a lovely Romanesque church, rising to a high choir, supported again by lions and crouched figures and friezed with polychrome reliefs depicting New Testament stories – the *Last Supper* stands out particularly. Under the choir is the plain stone coffin of St Geminianus, the patron saint of Modena. Have a look too at Begarelli's terracotta tableaux of the *Shepherds* in the south aisle.

Beside the main entrance to the duomo, the **Museo Lapidario** (Wed–Sun 10am–12.30pm & 4–7pm; L6000/€3.10) has stone bits and pieces from the duomo and around the town, while on the other side of the church, the lurching **Torre Ghirlandina** was begun at the same time as the duomo but completed 200 years later.

Until recently it contained the *Secchia Rapita* (now in the Palazzo Comunale), a wooden bucket stolen during a raid by the Modenese on Bologna in 1325, and often cited as evidence of the long-standing rivalry between the two towns. The Modenese, who supported Re Enzo (the son of the emperor), swore enmity when the Bolognese took him prisoner after a thirteenth-century battle, liberating the bucket from Bologna until well into the next century in an attempt to even the score. The seventeenth-century poet Tassoni wrote a mock heroic verse on the subject, which apparently retains its significance in people's minds and is still the object of occasional student stunts.

The other main focus for your wanderings around Modena is at the far, northwestern end of Via Emilia, a five-minute walk from Piazza Grande, where the **Palazzo dei Musei** houses the city museums and art galleries. Through an archway lined with Roman tombstones – Piazza Matteotti was on the site of a necropolis – a staircase leads off to the right up to the **Biblioteca Estense**, on the first floor (Mon–Sat 9am–1pm; L5000/€2.58). This is only partly open to non-students, but what is on display is worth a look: letters between monarchs, popes and despots, with great wax seals, filed away for hundreds of years, old maps, and the prize treasure, Borso d'Este's bible – the *Bibbia di Borso d'Este* – arguably the most decorated book in the world. The **Museo d'Arte Medievale e Moderna e Etnologia** (Tues–Sat 9am–noon, plus Tues & Sat 4–7pm, Sun 10am–1pm & 4–7pm; L4000/€2.07), on the second floor, is the newest part of the museum, with a large collection of artefacts of archeological and artistic significance, while on the top floor, the **Galleria Estense** (Tues–Sun 8.30am–7.30pm; L8000/€4.13) is perhaps the highlight of all the collections. Made up of the picture collection of the Este family, it contains paintings of the local schools, from the early Renaissance through to the works of the Caraccis, Guercino and Guido Reni, a sculpture of St Monica in terracotta attributed to Nicolo Dell'Arca, as well as portable altars, Madonnas and triptychs by lesser-known Emilian artists like Cosmé Tura, who painted the Palazzo Schifanoia in Ferrara (see p.433). There's also a bust of Francesco I d'Este by Bernini, a portrait of the same man by Velazquez, and Venetian works by Tintoretto and Veronese.

Five minutes' walk away in an undisturbed corner of town, off Via N. Sauro at Via Pomposa 1, is another museum, the **Museo Muratoriana** (daily 9am–noon; free). This contains possessions and works of Ludovico Antonio Muratori, the Jesuit priest, historiographer and intellectual whose ideas helped break the monopoly of the Church over education in the eighteenth century.

Eating, drinking and nightlife

Like Bologna, Modena is a terrific place to **eat**, with a large array of restaurants in all price ranges. Try if you can to sample some of the local pork-based specialities, like *ciccioli* – flaky pork scratchings laid out in bars in the evening – or, in a restaurant, *zampone* (pig's trotters, boned and filled with minced meat) or *cotechino* – the same thing, but stuffed inside an animal bladder.

At the bottom end of the price scale, Giusti, Via Farini 75 (closed 12.30–5.30pm), a delicatessen since the seventeenth century, is a good source of picnic food; Giusti also run a bar, a few doors up, which is a good place for ready-made sandwiches. There is a self-service restaurant, *Il Chiostro*, at Via San Geminiano 3 (closed Sun), and a reasonable *mensa* at Via Leodino 9. Up a notch, the ristorante-pizzeria *Al Grotino*, Via del Taglio 26 (closed Wed), and the *Trattoria Aldina*, Via Albinelli 40 (closed Mon), are both decent, affordable standbys. If you want to try Modenese specialities, *Da Enzo*, Via Coltellini 17 (☎059.225.177; closed Mon), is a nice, slightly old-fashioned place to do so – though not especially cheap; there's also *Santa Chiara*, on Via Ruggera (☎059.225.302; closed Sun), a swish restaurant with adventurous contemporary local cooking. Nearby *Fini*, off Largo San Francesco (☎059.223.314; closed Mon & Tues), is a pricey and rather upscale establishment, but the food is delectable in the extreme.

Around Modena

At first glance the countryside **around Modena** looks bland and uninviting – discount furniture and lighting stores, crumbling farmhouses the size of mansions, and factories. Further north onto the plain, wide vistas of maize fields, rows of pollarded fruit trees and vines strung up from pergolas are broken only occasionally by a line of poplar trees shimmering in the heat.

You might, however, want to venture out to visit the **Galleria Ferrari**, at Via Dino Ferrari 43 in **MARANELLO**, south of Modena (Tues–Sun 9.30am–12.30pm & 2.30–6pm; L15,000/€7.75), an exhibition centre dedicated to the racing dynasty; it's reachable on the regular ATCM Blu-bus to Maranello from Modena bus station on Via Molza. On display are the cups and trophies won by the Ferrari team over the years, an assortment of Ferrari engines, along with vintage and contemporary examples of the cars themselves and a reconstruction of Enzo Ferrari's study.

CARPI, the region's main centre, around 15km north, is also worth a few hours of your time. The town's central **Piazza dei Martiri** is an enormous and impressive open space, almost worth the trip alone, and the sixteenth-century **Castello del Pio**, a mass of ornamental turrets and towers, holds another interesting museum inside – the **Museo al Deportato** (Thurs, Sat, Sun & public hols 9.30am–12.30pm & 3.30–6.30pm; free). German occupying forces in World War II held prisoners awaiting deportation to concentration camps at a site in Fossoli, 6km to the north – the camp sheds still stand, dilapidated, in a field – and the museum has displays on the camps and the conditions for the prisoners, neatly putting them into context with information on political and racial exile. The most sobering aspect of the museum is its layout; you progress through the almost bare rooms accompanied by a long ribbon of quotes painted on the walls, taken from prisoners' letters. Some were proud to have stood by their ideals, others expressed a fear of death or simply their frustration at dying so young.

The activity outside in the square provides some welcome relief with slick clothing stores running the length of its sixteenth-century red-brick **Portico Lungo**. At one end of the square are a couple of cafés and the bright ochre **Teatro Comunale**, at the other the Renaissance **Cattedrale** with Baroque facade. *Bar Tazza d'Oro* opposite the theatre does a brisk trade (try the iced tea in summer), but for more substantial **snacks** head for the *Bottega della Pizza* at Via Berengario 13. The rest of Carpi is unexciting, so it's unlikely that you'll want to hang around town. There are trains and buses every hour to Modena, but if you do want to stay try the **rooms** at *Albergo da Giorgio* at Via G. Rocca 1–5 (☎059.685.365; ③).

About 10km northeast of Modena, and reachable by bus, **NONANTOLA** is best known for its **abbey**, founded in 752 by Anselmo – then an abbot, later made a saint. The abbey seems at first unprepossessing, rebuilt as it was in red-brick in the thirteenth century, but the portal more than makes up for it, flanked by stone lions and topped by carvings executed by the workshop of Wiligelmus, who worked also on Modena's and (probably) Cremona's cathedrals. The carvings tell some familiar stories, in an earthy, vernacular style, perhaps best exemplified by the figures of the asses in the nativity scene. Also featured in the series of carvings are St Adrian and St Sylvester, both of whom are buried in the monastic interior – the church is in fact dedicated to St Sylvester.

South of Modena

To the **south of Modena** lie the foothills of the Apennines, covered by turkey oak, hornbeam and hazel woods. Narrow roads corkscrew into the mountains, from which you can climb by foot onto the *crinale* – the backbone of the Apennine range. Trails lead along the succession of peaks above the treeline, steep slopes on either side, to some glacial lakes, although the routes are most impressive for the views they give across the breadth of Italy on either side.

For many, the main attraction of the **small villages** in the foothills is **food**. The tourist office can advise you on "gourmet itineraries" to find the real Modenese cuisine, but they're not really necessary: restaurant signs by the side of the road invite you in to try cuisine *"alla tua nonna"* – "like grandma used to make" – often involving mortadella, salami or *crescente* (a kind of pitta bread eaten with a mixture of oil, garlic, rosemary and parmesan). Variations on the same theme include *gnocco ritto* – fried dough diamonds eaten with salami or ham. Higher in the mountains you can still find *ciacci* – chestnut-flour pancakes, filled with ricotta and sugar – and walnuts (which should be picked on or around the night of St John the Baptist, June 24) that go to make *nocino* liqueur.

Vignola, Zocca and the Riserva dei Sassi Rocca Malatina

VIGNOLA produces some of the best cherries in Italy and is an impressive sight in April, when it is surrounded by blossom and people come from all around for the spring festival. At other times Vignola is worth a visit for its castle, the **Rocca di Vignola** (Tues–Fri 9am–noon & 3.30–7pm, Sat & Sun 10am–noon & 3.30–7pm; free), which is particularly well preserved; one of many castles built in the fifteenth and sixteenth centuries to defend the crossings along the River Panaro into the neighbouring state of Bologna. It is a mammoth specimen, with enormous watchtowers on each corner, and fancy brickwork – a castle style you see in other parts of Emilia.

The *Antica Osteria da Bacco*, on the main road that skirts the castle, serves classic local pasta dishes and a good *nocino* (walnut) liqueur. It also has an *enoteca* around the back on Via Selmi, where you can try a glass of locally produced wine, albeit in a rather serious atmosphere. If you need to **stay**, the *Eden* hotel, at Via Cesare Battisti 49 (☎059.772.847, fax 059.771.477; ③), is uninviting but the only one in town.

En route to Zocca, the **Riserva dei Sassi Rocca Malatina** is named after the giant outcrop of rock, partly eroded into strange pinnacles and popular with climbers, located near the village of **Rocca Malatina** itself. If you have your own transport, take the turning off the main road for a look at **PIEVE TRÉBBIO**, an eleventh-century Romanesque church with separate polygonal baptistry and belltower, the oldest church in the Modenese Apennines. Much of it was reconstructed at the beginning of this century, including the facade, but plenty of intricate medieval carving remains, as well as some fine Romanesque capitals inside – though it's only open on Sunday.

ZOCCA, 9km further on, is a quiet market town with buses from Modena, and a couple of affordable hotels. *Jolì*, Via Pineta 20–22 (☎059.987.052; ③), in front of the church, is comfortable and inviting; as is *Lenzi*, Via Cavour 14 (☎059.987.039, fax 059.986.680; ③), to the left off Via della Pace; and there's a **campsite** 2km southwest of town, the *Montequestiolo*, at Via Montequestiolo 184 (☎059.985.137; open mid-June to mid-September) – take Via Roma, then Via Rosola and follow the signs. One exceptionally relaxing – although very basic – place to stay is *Tizzano* (☎059.989.581; ②), 6km from Zocca, a former fortress farmhouse that's now an informal osteria with rooms. Still a working farm, it's in an unsually peaceful spot, looking across the orchards straight through to Monte Cimone, with only the hilltop town of Monte Corone between you and the mountains. The food is excellent and very reasonably priced too. It's about 10 minutes from Zocca through the village of Monte Ombraro; follow the signs to *Tizzano*.

Fourteen kilometres south of Zocca, the road between Castel d'Aiano and Abetaia is beautiful, a lush landscape with the only sign of life an occasional farm with geese and hens scratching in a steeply raked orchard. **MONTESE** set back 4km from the main road, is worth a quick detour, especially around the third weekend in July when the wild black cherry festival is in full swing, and from then until mid-August when there's medieval singing, dancing and classical concerts in the castle above town. The Montese **tourist office** (daily 9am–noon & 3–7pm; ☎059.981.4911, *www.provincia.modena.it/ turismoappennino/montese/index.htm*) – in reality a wooden hut in the town centre – also rents out tandems by the hour or by the half or full day.

Pievepélago and Lago Santo

A little further west, the SS12 from Modena becomes really beautiful after Pavullo nel Frignano, especially in spring when the colours are startling – white blossom against bright green meadows. There is not much reason to stop until **Lama Mocogno,** except perhaps to sample the award-winning traditional fare at the *Parco Corsini* in Pavullo (Viale Martiri 11 (☎0536.20.129). *Camping Valverde* (☎0536.44.045; June–Aug), is a peaceful place to camp. At **La Santona,** *prodotti del sottobosco* (specialities of the woods – berries, fungi etc) are on sale in summer and autumn, when people from Bologna and the other main towns around visit the area, mainly to eat.

PIEVEPÉLAGO is a modern-looking market town with a couple of inexpensive **places to stay**, of which the *Albergo Bucaneve* is the more appealing, 1km up the road from the village at Via Giardini 31 (☎0536.71.383; ③). Three ATCM buses a day make the trip here from Bologna via Vignola, six daily from Modena, and it's well worth a stop if you're passing through. *La Capanna Celtica*, Via Roma 24, serves an exceptional blend of Emilian and Tuscan cooking, though not especially cheaply. In the evenings *Birreria-Paninoteca Il Cantuccio* is lively and is open on Tuesdays, when practically all else is closed. An easy path leads up from the town to **Lago Santo** a small lake in a large glacial basin. The hike takes about 3 hours (follow the red and white flashes painted on rocks along the way). Or, in summer, there's a bus that takes you up. If you want to **stay**, try the very friendly *Rifugio Vittoria* (☎0536.71.509, *www.rifugiovittoria.it*; ②) right next to the lake, in whose restaurant you can sample porcini mushrooms, game and fruits of the forest. Check the rifugio's Web site for detailed information on hiking trails and seasonal activities in the area.

Séstola, Fanano and around

Buses make the trip east along the Scoltenna gorge from Pievepélago to SÉSTOLA, whose trattorias and hotels make it seem like a teeming metropolis compared with the tiny hamlets around. In reality, the town nucleus is quite tiny, but there are some good **places to eat**, including the *Ristorante Pizzeria Il Campanaccio* on Corso Libertà (closed Wed), which serves such mountain food as *tagliatelle ai porcini* or *porcini trifolati* and a good selection of wines at very reasonable prices. The *Sport* at Via delle Ville 116 (☎0536.62.502; ②) is a basic but welcoming lodge-like **hotel**; the *Regina*, Via Cimone 23 (☎0536.62.336; ③), is an attrative chalet-style establishment.

Perched at 1020m, Séstola gives good views of the countryside around; a cable car takes you even higher so you can look back down over Séstola and its ninth-century castle (August 8.30am–12.30pm & 2–6pm; L3500/€1.81; during the ski season 8am–5.20pm; included in ski pass). In winter, Séstola is one of the best ski resorts in the area. A four-kilometre hike will take you up to the **Pian del Falco** (1530m), where there's accommodation at the *Rifugio Pian del Falco* (☎0536.61.113 fax 0536.61.232, *www.sestolaonline.it/baitadelsole*; ③). A high path winds around the head of the Rio Vésale to **Passo del Lupo** (1550m), 4.5km later, and, soon after, the **Lago della Ninfa**, surrounded by beech and larch trees.

In late spring, when the snow has melted, the wide, cultivated valley below is ideal for some easy cycling, or you could tackle the climb up to Pian Cavallaro high on Monte

Cimone's slopes – allow around six hours for the round-trip. A mule track south to **Madonna del Trogolino**, a seventeenth-century oratory, begins the ascent, after which you skirt Monte Cervarola and veer southwest to climb towards **Passo del Lupo** at 1550m. For a while you stay relatively level as you follow the **Cresta del Gallo** watershed, after which a turning to the west brings you into a natural rocky amphitheatre, followed by a steep ascent to **Pian Cavallaro** (1861m) itself. Your efforts are rewarded by awesome views spanning ridge after ridge, before eventually dropping off to Lombardy and the Veneto. Either retrace your steps to Pian del Falco, or press on down to Séstola, where you can pick up a bus to Modena. Pick up trail maps either at the hotels in Séstola or the rifugio in Pian del Falco.

FANANO, just under 6km from Séstola (reachable by bus every 2–3 hours from Modena via Séstola), is a more attractive village of ancient slate-roofed houses. It's a stop on the old pilgrim's route between Modena and Pistoia, and its origins are probably connected with the Benedictine monastery founded here in 752 by St Anselmo. Every three years – and next due in 2004 – on Good Friday, a torchlight procession threads its way through the medieval streets decorated with greenery. A clutch of tiny oratories includes the **Chiesa di San Giuseppe** and **L'Oratorio del Santi Sacramento**, both with magnificent Baroque gilded wooden altars. If you decide to stay, there are half a dozen inexpensive **hotels**, including the recently renovated *La Pace* at Via Roma 2–6 (☎0536.68.865, fax 0536.69.478; ③) and the central *Sole* at Via C. Foli 4 (☎0536.68.070; ③) a medieval building in the centre of the village.

Montefiorino and around

A series of steep, switchback roads marks the approach to **MONTEFIORINO**, a small village often swathed in fog in spring and autumn and topped by a correspondingly grim thirteenth-century **fortress**. The seat of the partisan republic in the summer of 1944, the area was the focus of some intense wartime resistance activity, its mountain farms and haylofts making ideal hide-outs. Sabotage of transport and communication links, or harbouring prisoners of war, was punishable by death, and the many people shot in reprisals are remembered in the **Museo della Repubblica**, in the ground-floor rooms of the fortress (Tues–Sat 9am–12.30pm & 3–6pm; L2000/€1.03).

From the village, you can hike down the mule track (20min) to **RUBBIANO** and look at some weird stone carvings in the eleventh-century parish church of **Santa Maria** (closed at the time of writing because of earthquake damage; telephone the church office in Montefiorino ☎536.965.916 for the latest information). As all over this area, these are the work of the stonemasons of Como, renowned for their skill in the Middle Ages. Circles, spirals, wheels, all reminiscent of the sun, symbolize light and strength and ward off darkness and evil. The highly stylized and enigmatic faces superseded the ancient custom of human sacrifices, in which the bodies of the victims were buried in the building's foundations to appease the gods.

A side road covers the 11km from Montefiorino to **FRASSINORO**, worth the trip for a meal of local rabbit or chicken, and home-made pasta at the moderately priced *Piacentini*, in the alleyway of the same name (☎0536.969.817; closed Thurs, booking advisable).

Reggio Emilia

About twenty-five kilometres northwest up the Via Emilia from Modena, **REGGIO EMILIA** is a very different place from Modena, a quiet, ancient town that makes a good place to rest up for a while. It's admittedly sparse on sights, and has an air of neglect about it, but it's a pleasant enough town to wander through and is a feasible jumping-off point for travelling into the Reggiano Apennines.

The Town

Reggio is built around two central squares, **Piazza Prampolini** and **Piazza San Prospero**, and the **Palazzo del Municipio** with its fishtail battlements. Like other towns in the area, the centre is closed to traffic, and bicycles clank across the cobbles from all directions. Piazza San Prospero comes alive on market days (Tues & Fri), its stalls and the shops selling a staggering array of fruit, vegetables, salami and cheese, including the local *parmigiano-reggiano*. Around the square, the buildings squeeze up so close to the church of **San Prospero** that they seem to have pushed it off balance so that it now lurches to one side. Built in the sixteenth century, its facade is decorated with columns and statues in niches, guarded by six lions in rose-coloured Verona marble – a marked contrast to the unclad octagonal campanile next to it. Via Broletto leads through into **Piazza Prampolini**, skirting the side of the **Duomo**, which displays an awkward amalgamation of styles. Underneath the marble tacked on in the sixteenth century, it's possible to see the church's Romanesque facade, with incongruously Mannerist statues of Adam and Eve lounging over the medieval portal, although all else that remains of the original building are the apse and enormous crypt. The niche of the disproportionate central octagonal tower sports – in gleaming copper – an outsized group of the Madonna and donors that looms weirdly over the rest of the facade and the entire piazza. The dusty interior houses a painting of the *Assumption* by Guercino and many tombs, including one for a noted sixteenth-century clockmaker/inventor, Cherubino Sforzani, whose tomb bears a symbolic hourglass carved in marble.

At right angles to the duomo is the sugar-pink **Palazzo del Capitano del Popolo**. The Italian tricolour of red, white and green was proclaimed here as the official national flag of Italy, when Napoleon's Cispadane Republic was formed in 1797. Walking north from here, the four **Musei Civici** along Via Spallanzani (Tues–Sun 9am–noon, Sat & Sun also 3–6pm; free), on the edge of Piazza della Vittoria, are made up of an eighteenth-century private collection of archeological finds, fossils and paintings. In the corner of the square, the **Galleria Parmeggiani** (same hours) houses an important collection of Spanish, Flemish and Italian art, including sculptures and bronzes, as well as costumes and textiles. Nearby stands the church of **Madonna della Ghiara**, built in the seventeenth century and decorated with Bolognese School frescoes of scenes from the Old Testament and a *Crucifixion* scene by Guercino.

Practicalities

Reggio is on the main rail line between Bologna and Milan. The **train station** is on Piazza Marconi I, just east of the old centre; the **bus station** is on the west side of the public gardens on Via Raimondo Franchetti. The **tourist office** is in the main Piazza Prampolini (Mon–Sat 8.30am–1pm & 2.30–5.30pm, Sun 9am–noon; ☎0522.451.152, *www.municipio.re.it/turismo*), and there's a very helpful Club Alpino Italiano office at Viale Mille 32 (☎0522.436.685). As in may places in Emilia-Romagna, the central tourist office offers free **internet** access, as does *Qui Qua Navigator*, Piazza Fontanesi 4 (9am–7.30pm Mon–Sat; ☎0522.406.172, www.*quiqua.it*).

If you're planning **to stay** over, be aware that hotel space is somewhat limited: from Easter to June because of tourists, and then in the autumn due to endless trade fairs. There's a **youth hostel**, *Ostello Tricolore*, 500m from the train station at Via dell'Abbadessa 8, open all year (☎0522.454.795; L18,000/€9.30). For a little more money the *Ariosto* on Via San Rocco 12 (☎0522.437.320, fax 0522.452.514; ③) is a central and reasonably priced choice. Or, if you want a taste of fabulous luxury in historic Palazzo del Capitano del Popolo, located just outside the main piazza, stay at the *Posta*, Piazza del Monte 2 (☎0522.432.944, fax 0522.452.602, *hotelposta@citynet.re.it*; ⑦). For **food**, *La Zucca*, on the southern edge of the historic centre in Piazza

Fontanesi (closed Thurs), is a good place to sample local dishes; as is *Canossa*, at Via Roma 37 (closed Wed), which specializes in various ham antipasti. *La Casseruola*, not far from the central piazza on Via S. Carlo 5a (closed Tues), is a bustling pizzeria, with tables outside.

South of Reggio

Very much in a different vein, the foothills **south of Reggio** are cheese country: you'll see many signs along the roadside advertising the local *parmigiano-reggiano*, and the village of **CASINA**, 27km outside Reggio on the N63 to La Spezia, holds a popular Festa del Parmigiana in August, when the vats of cheese mixture are stirred with enormous wooden paddles. The countryside itself is a mixture of lush pastures and scraggy uplands, with some footpaths around, though there's better walking higher up in the mountains.

With your own transport, you can take the side road leading from Casina to **CANOS-SA**. This was the seat of the powerful Da Canossa family, whose most famous member, the Countess Mathilda of Tuscany (La Gran Contessa), was a big name here in the eleventh century – unusually so in a society largely controlled by warlords and the clergy. She was known for donning armour and leading her troops into battle herself, and at the age of 43 scandalized the nobility by marrying a youth of seventeen. During the battles between Pope Gregory VII and the Holy Roman Emperor Henry IV, she supported the pope and helped draw the excommunicated emperor here as a penitent to apologize to the pontiff. Henry was apparently left waiting outside in the snow for three days before the castle doors were opened. The remains of the **Castle** (summer Tues–Sun 9am–3pm; free) are largely thirteenth-century, but it's really the location – on a rocky outcrop looking towards the mountains in one direction and over the neighbouring castle at Rossena and the towns strung out over the plain in the other – which is impressive.

People from the surrounding towns are fond of coming out here at weekends to eat in the local **restaurants**, and it's a popular area for **hiking** or cross-country skiing. You may also see people armed with plastic bags for collecting **mushrooms**, or filling bottles with mineral water from the springs off the mountains. There are few specific centres to aim for, though, and you're most likely to travel along these valleys if you're driving over the mountains to the coast. It's tortuous going and the view changes constantly as you switchback your way across the mountain ridges or through small villages with austere, high-walled houses backing directly onto the roadside. The best times to come are late spring and early summer; in autumn, the fog often descends, clearing only momentarily for a brief glimpse of a chestnut grove or scree-filled riverbed hundreds of metres below.

High in the hills paths lead onto the mountain *crinale*. **Castelnovo Ne'Monti** in the foothills is a possible base for these walks. Further on, at **Busana**, the road forks to the left, descending through a series of hairpin bends bordered by plenty of falling rock signs, in the Secchia Valley, climbing back up the other side through Cinquecerri to **Ligonchio** – another good starting-point for walks away from cable cars and ski lifts onto nearby **Monte Cusna** (2120m). Close by here are the Prati di Sara, a windswept expanse of grassland with small tarns and the occasional tree. As you ascend, you have more of a view across the layers of ridges, often half-obscured in the mist. It's possible to stay overnight in some of the refuges that group along the GEA (Grand Escursione Apenninica) route, a 25-day trek that weaves its way back and forth across the border between Emilia and Tuscany. The Club Alpino Italiano office in Reggio (see opposite) should have information on this route; if it all seems too daunting, they also sometimes organize weekend treks.

Parma

Generally reckoned to have one of the highest standards of living in Italy, **PARMA**, about thirty kilometres along the Via Emilia northwest of Reggio, is about as comfortable a town as you could wish for. The measured pace of its streets, the abundance of its restaurants and the general air of provincial affluence are almost cloying, especially if you've arrived from the south. Not surprisingly, if you're travelling on a tight budget, Parma presents a few difficulties – the cheap hotels are usually full, and, although the restaurants are excellent, food too can cost a bomb. That said, it's a friendly enough place, with plenty to see. A visit to the opera can be an experience: the audience are considered one of the toughest outside La Scala and don't pull any punches if they consider a singer to be performing badly. And the city's works of art include the legacy of two great artists – Correggio and Parmigianino.

Arrival, information and accommodation

Parma's **train station** is fifteen minutes' walk from the central Piazza Garibaldi, or a short ride on buses #1–#6, #8 & #9, and #12–#15. The local **bus station** is next to the river, at the junction of Viale IV Novembre and Viale P. Toschi. Despite the sign in the Piazza Duomo, the **tourist office** is in fact at Via Melloni 1b (Mon–Sat 9am–7pm, Sun 9am–1pm; ☎0521.218.889, ☎ & fax 052.234.735, *www.turismo.comune.parma.it/turismo*). You can check email or go **online** for free but you need to reserve a time in advance (Mon–Sat 9am–1pm & 3–7pm, Thurs 9am–7pm; ☎0521.218.749).

Accommodation

Finding a **place to stay** can be tricky and you'd be well advised to book in advance. There's an official **youth hostel**, *Cittadella*, just south of the town centre, in the Parco Cittadella (☎0521.961.434; L17,000/€8.78; April–Oct) – take bus #9 from the station (8pm–midnight nightbus #E).

Amorini, Via Gramsci 37 (☎ & fax 0521.983.239). A basic but spotless choice on the university side of the river. Used by relatives visiting patients in the nearby hospital. ③.

Button, Borgo Salina 7 (☎0521.208.039). Small but very well-appointed rooms just south of Piazza Garibaldi. ③.

Lazzaro, Via XX Marzo 14 (☎0521.208.944). A tiny, homey establishment with its own restaurant, on the east side of Piazza Garibaldi. ③.

Leon d'Oro, Viale A. Fratti 4 (☎0521.773.182; ②). Just to the left of the station, attractive, though basic, rooms and its own restaurant. ②.

Starhotel du Parc, Viale Piacenza 12c (☎0521.292.929, fax 0521.292.828, *www.starhotels.it*). Luxurious old palace on the north side of the Parco Ducale. ⑨.

Torino, Via A. Mazza 7 (☎0521.281.046, fax 0521.230.725). Very comfortable rooms right in the heart of things. ③.

The Town

Parma's main street, **Via Mazzini**, and its continuation, **Strada della Repubblica**, run east from the river, past **Piazza Garibaldi** – which, together with the narrow streets and alleyways that wind to the south and west, forms the fulcrum of Parma. The mustard-coloured **Palazzo del Governatore** forms the backdrop of the square, behind which the Renaissance church of the **Santa Maria della Steccata** (daily 9am–noon & 3–6pm) was apparently built using Bramante's original plan for St Peter's as a model. Inside there are frescoes by a number of sixteenth-century painters, notably Parmigianino, who spent the last ten years of his life on this work, eventually being

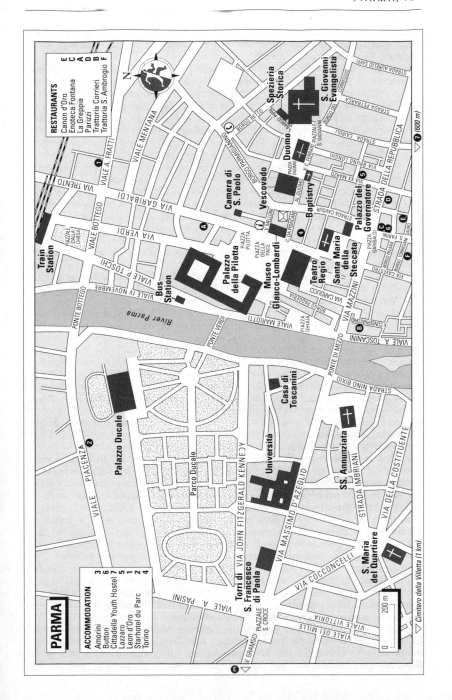

PARMA

ACCOMMODATION

Amorini 3
Button 6
Cittadella Youth Hostel 7
Lazzaro 5
Leon d'Oro 1
Starhotel du Parc 2
Torino 4

RESTAURANTS

Canon d'Oro E
Enoteca Fontana C
La Greppia A
Parizzi D
Trattoria Corrieri B
Trattoria S. Ambrogio F

sacked for breach of contract by the disgruntled church authorities. A year later he was dead, aged 37, "an almost savage or wild man" who had become obsessed with alchemy, according to Vasari.

Five minutes' walk away – turn right off Strada Cavour – the slightly gloomy **Piazza Duomo** forms part of the old *centro episcopale*, away from the shopping streets of the commercial centre. The beautiful Lombard-Romanesque **Duomo** (daily 9am–12.30pm & 3–7pm), dating from the eleventh century, holds earlier work by Parmigianino in its south transept, painted when the artist was a pupil of Correggio – who painted the fresco of the *Assumption* in the central cupola. Finished in 1534, this is among the most famous of Correggio's works, the Virgin Mary floating up through a sea of limbs, faces and swirling drapery, which attracted some bemused comments at the time. One contemporary compared it to a "hash of frogs' legs", while Dickens, visiting much later, thought it a sight that "no operative surgeon gone mad, could imagine in his wildest delirium". Correggio was paid for the painting with a sackful of small change to annoy him, since he was known to be a great miser. The story goes that he carried the sack of coins home in the heat, caught a fever and died at the age of 40. Before you leave, take a look at the relief of the *Deposition* on the west wall of the south transept, an impressive piece of work by the architect Benedetto Antelami that dates from 1178. Look too at the frieze that runs the length of the nave above the arches – also by Correggio.

There's a more significant work by Antelami outside the duomo, in the form of the beautiful octagonal **Baptistry** (daily 9am–12.30pm & 3–6pm; L3000/€1.55), its sugary pink Verona marble facing, four storeys high, encircled by a band of sculpture and topped off by some slim turrets. The three elaborately carved portals serve as a meeting place in the evening. Bridging the gap between the Romanesque and Gothic styles, this is considered Antelami's finest work; started in 1196, the architect sculpted the frieze that surrounds the building and was also responsible for the reliefs inside, including the polychrome figures above the door and a series of fourteen statues, representing the months and seasons, that have been painstakingly scrubbed down and restored. Take the spiral staircase to the top for a closer view of the thirteenth-century frescoes on the rib-vaulted ceiling. There's more work by Correggio in the cupola of the church of **San Giovanni Evangelista** behind the duomo (daily 6.30am–noon & 3.30–8pm) – a fresco of the *Vision of St John* at Patmos. Next door, the **Spezieria Storica di San Giovanni Evangelista**, at Borgo Pipa 1 (daily 9am–1.45pm; L4000/€2.07), is a thirteenth-century pharmacy that preserves its medieval interior.

A short walk northwest from here, the **Camera di San Paolo** in the former Benedictine Convent on Via Melloni (daily 9am–1.45pm; L4,000/€2.07), houses more frescoes by Correggio done in 1519; above the fireplace, the abbess who commissioned the work is portrayed by Correggio as the Goddess Diana. Around the corner on Piazza della Pace, the **Museo Glauco-Lombardi** at Via Garibaldi 15 (☎0521.233727; Tues–Sat 10am–3pm, Sun 9am–1pm; L8000/€4.13), recalls later times, with a display of memorabilia relating to Marie-Louise of Austria, who reigned here after the defeat of her husband Napoleon at Waterloo. She set herself up with another suitor (much to the chagrin of her exiled spouse) and expanding the Parma violet perfume industry.

Just across from here, it's hard to miss Parma's biggest monument, the **Palazzo della Pilotta**, surrounded by vast expanses of wonderfully green lawn set off by modern fountains. Begun for Alessandro Farnese – the wiley Pope Paul III – in the sixteenth century, this building was reduced to a shell by World War II bombing, though it's been rebuilt and now houses a number of Parma's museums.

Inside is Parma's main art gallery, the **Galleria Nazionale** (daily 9am–1.45pm; L12,000/€6.20, including the Teatro Farnese), a modern, hi-tech display that includes more work by Correggio and Parmigianino, and the remarkable *Apostles at the Sepulchre* and *Funeral of the Virgin* by Carracci – massive overwhelming canvases, suspended either side of a gantry at the top of the building. The **Teatro Farnese** (Mon 8.30am–2pm, Tues–Sun 8.30am–7.30pm; L4000/€2.07, or L12,000/€6.20 including the Galleria Nazionale), which you pass through to get to the gallery, in the former arms room of the palace, was almost entirely destroyed by the bombing in 1944. The restored theatre, still used occasionally, with an extended semicircle of seats three-tiers high, made completely of wood, in a facsimile of Palladio's Teatro Olympico at Vicenza, houses Italy's first revolving stage. On the lower floor, the **Museo Archeologico Nazionale** (Tues–Sun 9am–6.30pm; L4000/€2.07) is a less essential stop but is still worth a glance, with finds from the Etrusco-Roman city of Velleia (see p.427) and the prehistoric lake villages around Parma, as well as the table top on which the Emperor Trajan notched up a record of his gifts to the poor.

Across the river from the Palazzo della Pilotta, the **Parco Ducale** is a set of formal gardens laid out in the eighteenth century around the sixteenth-century **Palazzo Ducale** (Mon–Sat 8am–noon; free) built for Ottaviano Farnese. Just south, the **Casa di Toscanini** on Via R. Tanzi (Tues–Sat 10am–1pm & 3–6pm, Sun 10am–1pm; L3000/€1.55) is the birthplace of the composer who debuted in the Teatro Regio here (see below), and just one of the sights that recall Parma's strong musical heritage. Further south still, on the same side of the river, the embalmed body of the violinist Niccolo Paganini rests under a canopy in the **Cimitero della Villetta** (daily: summer 8am–12.30pm & 4–7pm; winter 8am–12.30pm & 2.30–5pm).

Eating, drinking and nightlife

Parma is not well known for its nightlife, and the locals tend to prefer long sessions in the various (excellent) restaurants, or else dress up and head for the theatre or opera. For **picnic food**, the market by the river on Piazza Ghiaia is the best source both of ingredients and sandwiches and ready-made dishes at a number of *tavole calde*; there's also a small *tavola calda* at Borgo Sant'Ambrogio 2, off the Piazza Garibaldi end of Strada della Repubblica. For more substantial **meals**, also close by Piazza Garibaldi, the *Enoteca Fontana*, Strada Farini 24, is a great authentic old bar, with long wooden tables, a huge choice of different wines and a menu that includes sandwiches, steaming bowls of pasta and hot and cold daily specials – a good bet for lunch. *Trattoria Corrieri* is a popular place, tucked away off the main street at Via Conservatorio 1 (closed Sun), with excellent fare that is not too expensive. *Trattoria San Ambrogio* (closed Mon), at Borgo Piero Torrigiani 4a, is similar with fresh pasta and a meat-dominated menu that leans towards game. The *Lazzaro* hotel, centrally placed (see p.420 for address), has a decent restaurant serving a good array of local dishes (closed Sun). Up a bracket in price, opera *apassionati* eat at *Canon d'Oro*, Via N. Sauro 3a (closed Wed) – expensive but entertaining. Top choices for local gourmets are *La Greppia*, Via Garibaldi 39a (☎0521.233.686, closed Mon & Tues) and *Parizzi*, Via Repubblica 71 (☎0521.285.952, closed Mon throughout the year, Sun eves in summer), both with a wide range of specialities, including five types of ham. For **later on** in the evening, *Bottiglia Azzurra*, Borgo Felino 63 (closed Sun), serves a good choice of wines and hot snacks and stays open until 2am.

Opera is big in Parma: the Teatro Regio, at Via Garibaldi 16a (☎0521.218.678, *www.teatrostabileparma.com*), is renowned for its discerning audiences. It's not unknown for supporters of one singer to gather in cliques during the opera and discuss his or her virtues with supporters of a rival. Viale Basetti, next to the river, is also the home of one of the top **theatre** companies in Europe, the Colletivo di Parma, who perform between October and April at the Teatro Due, Viale Basetti 12a (☎0521.230.242), and whose shows draw on a tradition of comedy and political theatre – Dario Fo was a founder member and has often returned.

South of Parma

The countryside **around Parma** is a strange mixture: some of the major roads follow bleak gorges, skirting the edge of blank rock walls for miles; others, looking for all the world as if they lead nowhere, emerge into open meadows and orchards, rich farmland stretching far into the distance.

Prime targets are any of the **medieval castles** strung out across the foothills. **TORRECHIARA**, about 20km south and connected with Parma by hourly buses, has a fifteenth-century **castle** that provides a superb vantage point over the surrounding area. There are also frescoes by Bembo in the **Camera d'Oro** (Tues–Fri 9am–1.45pm, Sat & Sun 9am–6.15pm; L4000/€2.07).

One of the most famous Parma hams (*Prosciutto di Langhirano*) comes from the foothills around **LANGHIRANO**, which is a few kilometres further on and also linked by regular bus with Parma. The experts say the ham cures so successfully here because of the unique mixture of clear mountain air and sea breezes blowing over the Apennines from Liguria; it is served simply with butter, so as not to mask the fine flavour. The town itself has grown into a mass of stainless steel warehouses – there's nothing of interest unless you want to carry a haunch of meat round with you for the rest of your holiday. But the countryside around, particularly near Calestano, is beautiful. Apart from the rail route, the fast way over the mountains is by **autostrada**, the A15, which snakes its way in and out of a succession of tunnels, giving quick glimpses of lush, hidden valleys, vines and orchards. Women risk life and limb by climbing over the barriers to sell **mushrooms** on the hard shoulder: They tie plastic bags, which fill with air and act like crazy dirigible balloons, to the trees, so you can see them from a distance. Despite this, lots of drivers don't and instead sail across the three lanes at the last minute, screeching to a halt to inspect the latest harvest. You have been warned.

The slower N62 gives access to the *crinale* of the mountains: the trails are a popular attraction for walkers these days but served a quite different purpose in the last war, when adults and children made the long journey by foot, carrying sacks of salt from the coast to trade for food. The writer Eric Newby was hidden by villagers in these mountains as an escaped prisoner of war in 1943, and the book chronicling his experiences, *Love and War in the Apennines*, captures the beauty of the region and its stupendous views across the full width of Italy.

CORNIGLIO, reached by bus from Parma, is a centre for hiking or skiing, and there are places to stay in most villages nearby – in Bosco di Corniglio, 10km away, try the picturesque and comfortable *Ghirardini* (☎0521.889.123 or 0521.889.001, *info100laghi. bosco@libero.it*; generally closed Thurs; ②). More buses squeeze themselves round the tight bends to the small villages of Monchio (16km), Trefiumi (20km) and Prato Spilla (23km from Corniglio), leaving you on the lower slopes of **Monte Malpasso** (1716m) – glistening with small lakes and tarns.

Take a bus from Corniglio to **LAGDEI**, 14km away, from where a 45-minute walk up a mule path leads to Lago Santo; an easier option is to take the sporadically working ski lift (August daily 8.30am–12.30pm & 1.30–5.30pm; other summer months Sat & Sun 8.30am–12.30pm & 1.30–5.30pm; winter, in good weather only, Sun 8.30am–12.30pm & 1.30–5.30pm). There are **mountain refuges** for overnight stops at Lagdei (☎0521.889.136 or 0521.889.118), and, better still, near the summit of Monte Orsaro (1831m), *Rifugio Mariotti* (☎0521.889.334). For more demanding trekking, join the GEA route at **RIGOSO** (5km from the trail), connected with Parma by five or six buses a day. For information on maps, trekking trails etc, call the **Parco dei Cento Laghi** office on ☎0521.354.112.

West to Piacenza

The Via Emilia continues west from Parma, with small towns mushrooming out from the edges of the road, but mostly it's just a ribbon of shops and roadside cafés. **FIDEN-ZA**, the first place of any size, has a Lombard-Romanesque **cathedral** with a richly decorated facade worked on by followers of the Parma master, Antelami. As Fidenza was a major staging-post on the pilgrimage route to Rome, the carvings depict pilgrims and more domestic subjects – appropriately enough for such an intensive salami-producing region – strings of sausages festoon one figure, others show hunting scenes. The building itself is an important – and relatively rare – example of architecture from during the Romanesque-Gothic transition period. If you're in the area on a Wednesday or a Saturday don't miss the extensive **market** that takes over the town. **Places to eat** are good here too: if you fancy a treat, the *Antica Trattoria al Duomo* in Piazza Duomo (closed Mon) has a fine reputation for its fish, with a fixed-price menu for L65,000/€33.57. For snacks, head for the *Birreria-Paninoteca* at the station end of Via Benedetto Bacchini.

The countryside **to the north** of here is the *bassa*, flat, low country (where Bertolucci filmed *1900*) cut by drainage ditches and open fields growing wheat and corn, sugar beet and vines. In summer it's scorching hot and almost silent, with an odd, still beauty all its own, but generally it's seen as a place to pass through on your way to somewhere else. The small towns and villages of the region are quiet and mainly undistinguished. **SORAGNA** is a good place to be on the first weekend in May for its grand agricultural *festa*, with local wine, cheese and salami tasting. At any time of year, the aroma wafting out of the *salumerie* in the main square may tempt you to sample its array of local produce, also available at *Birreria-Paninoteca Stella d'Oro*, on the side alley Via Mazzini. The small market town is dominated by the tenth-century palace of **Rocca di Soragna** (Tues–Sun: April–Oct 9–11am & 3–6pm; Nov & March 9–11am & 2–4.30pm; L9000/€4.65), still owned by the local Meli Lupi family, who ran the town between the fourteenth and eighteenth centuries. The dozen or so rooms are furnished with the original sixteenth-century pieces and decorated with frescoes, some by Parmigianino, one of the most elegant of the early Mannerist artists; more of his work appears in Parma's churches and at the Rocca San Vitale in Fontanellato.

The village of **FONTANELLATO**, a few kilometres northeast of Fidenza, was the site of the camp where Eric Newby was imprisoned, but is perhaps better known as a centre for the production of parmesan cheese. Its central square is dominated by the **Rocca San Vitale** (summer daily 9.30–11.30am & 3–6pm; winter Tues–Sun closes 5pm; L7000/€3.62), a fifteenth-century moated castle that the Sanvitale family called home until the onset of World War II. Inside there are some ancient pieces of furniture and a fresco of the legend of *Diana and Actaeon* by Parmigianino. Further north, **BUS-SETO**, the childhood home of Giuseppe Verdi, is an appealing little battlemented town that holds a few mementoes of the nineteenth-century composer in its **Museo Civico** (April–Nov Tues–Sun 9.30am–noon & 2.30–5pm; L5000/€2.58). There's more Verdi memorabilia in the nearby village of **LE RONCOLE**, in the **house** where he was born (Tues–Sun: April–Sept 9.30am–12.30pm & 3–7pm; Oct & Nov 9.30am–noon & 2.30–5pm; L4000/€2.07; ☎0524.92.487) – a veritable industry has grown up around the composer's birthplace, with regular opera performances during summer. And Verdi's **villa**, a couple of kilometres outside Busseto at **SANT'AGATA DI VILLANOVA**, is open for guided tours (Jan to mid–Nov Tues–Sun 9–11.40am & 2.30–5.45pm; L10,000/€5.17; ☎0523.830.000), which includes a mock-up of the Milan hotel room where he died.

South of the Via Emilia, there's the same emphasis on epicurean matters in the villages as in other parts of the province: festivals are common, celebrating local cheese, bilberries, or chestnuts and mushrooms, and the whole village will turn out for a big party. With your own transport, the area is well worth dawdling through, though you can easily reach the town of **SALSOMAGGIORE TERME**, 9km from Fidenza, by train or bus; the **tourist office** is at Viale Romagnosi 7, off Piazza del Popolo (Mon–Sat 9am–12.30pm & 3.30–6.30pm, Sun 10am–12.30pm; ☎0524.580.211, *www.turismo. comune.salsomaggiore-terme.pr.it/iatsalso*). It's a major local town, popular with Italians anxious to detoxify their systems with its springs. The domed Piscina Termale on Via d'Azeglio (☎0524.574.577) is a relaxed way to join in; or you can go for the full treatment either at the fabulous Art Nouveau Terme Berzieri (open to the general public in summer) in the town centre 100m from Piazza Libertà, or the more businesslike Terme Zoja in Parco Mazzini, ten minutes' walk from the tourist office. Some of the grander hotels offer treatments, too. Out of season, the place is suitably sedate, but in summer it springs into life, mostly revolving around an almost constant passeggiata.

There is no shortage of places to stay; the **tourist office** (see above), has a full list, but the majority of Salsomaggiore's **hotels** are only open between April and November. *Valentini*, Viale Porro 10 (☎0524.578.251, fax 0524.578.266; ⑤) is an elegant old hotel with its own pool, spa and parklands. *Albergo Villino Cervia*, Vicolo Cervia 6, off Via Romagnosi (☎0524.572.234, fax 0524.572.983; ③) and *Albergo Venezia*, Vicolo Venezia 5 (☎0524.573.100; ③), are both bang in the centre of town. *Camping Arizona* (☎0524.565.648), between Salsomaggiore and Tabiano Bagni, boasts swimming pools, sports facilities and wooden bungalows as well as pitches. **Café life** is important in the town; there's a full complement of *gelaterie* and *pasticcerie*, but not many inexpensive places to eat. One of the few is *La Porchetta* (closed Tues) next to the Palazzo dei Congressi, a very popular place serving massive pieces of pizza wrapped in several layers of prosciutto, or more substantial dishes that include rather incongruous Tyrolean specialities. For something more refined, *Alle Querce di Giorgio*, Via Parma 85 (closed Mon), offers lake views and a menu specializing in porcini mushrooms, truffles and homemade pasta. Even more up-market is *Al Tartufo*, Viale Marconi 30 (☎0524. 573.696; July, August and Nov–April closed Wed) which features sumptuous local fare; try the *tagliolini al tartufo*.

Walks around Salsomaggiore cover some beautiful countryside: the tourist office booklet, *Carnet dell'Ospite*, details around eight routes. A five-kilometre walk south (or a bus from the station, Salsomaggiore to Pellegrino Parmense) takes you past the vineyard at **Contignaco**, which sells direct to the public. On the opposite side of the road, the simple Romanesque church of **San Giovanni** contains a sixteenth-century fresco of St Lucia on one of its columns and other, fourteenth-century frescoes.

To the east, buses run from Salsomaggiore to the modern spa town of **Tabiano Bagni**, from where you can get a taxi, or sometimes a bus, or walk the 2.5km to **TABIANO CASTELLO** for a meal at *Locanda del Colle da Oscar*, a fifteenth-century castle inn and staging post serving marvellous food in a warm and lively atmosphere (☎0524.565.676; closed Mon). The castle itself is privately owned, but everyone seems to ignore the "keep out" signs and wanders into the grounds all the same.

Heading west from Salsomaggiore, you can strike out on foot across the dead flat Parco Fluviale dell Stirone to Castell'Arquato, passing on the way *Ristorante Agrituristica Montà dell'Orto* (☎0523.947.146), which offers snacks, draught wine and typical regional dishes at the weekend and on holidays. To get there by car from Salsomaggiore, follow the road to Piacenza for 5km until you get to Castelnuovo Fogliani, which borders the park. If you want to stay, there's a good place to **camp** under the trees behind the farmhouse, with cooking and shower facilities. **CASTELL'ARQUATO** itself lies further on, a small town with a beautiful medieval piazza, set on a hillside overlooking the Arda Valley. Among a collection of ageing buildings there is the thirteenth-century **Palazzo del Podestà**, a Romanesque basilica and the **Rocca Viscontea** from the fourteenth century, though you can only admire them from the outside. At weekends plenty of people do just that, and then repair to one of the many **restaurants and cafés** in town. *Café Trattoria Garibaldi*, just inside the old town walls, serves game and inexpensive simple dishes. The **tourist office** (Mon–Fri 9am–1pm; ☎0523.803.091) is on the edge of the main piazza just outside the town walls. There are a couple of cheap **places to stay**, notably *Locanda Le Rose* in the suburb of Case Ilariotti (☎0523.895.548; ①), and in the town itself, the hotel *San Carlo*, Via Dante Alighieri 41 (☎0523.805.138; ②).

The road continues south from here, through Lugagnano, following the line of the River Arda through gentle hills to **BARDI**, overshadowed by its eleventh-century **castle** on an outcrop of rock, reachable by way of one daily bus from Parma. A side turning from Lugagnano into steeper, narrower lanes takes you to **VELLEIA**, 5km west of **RUSTIGAZZO** (six buses a day from Piacenza), where there are the remains of a provincial Roman town, excavated in the eighteenth century (daily 9am–1hr before sunset; free). Velleia was the capital of a vast mountainous area inhabited in the first five centuries AD and named after the Ligurian tribe attracted here by the salt springs in the area. The road continues south through woods of beech to the belt of mountains – the Apennino Piacentino – stretching from Bobbio down to Borgo Val di Taro.

Piacenza

PIACENZA marks the end of the Via Emilia and the border with Lombardy. It's a small, unassuming city, its attractions often passed over in favour of Parma or Modena (or Cremona in Lombardy, see p.183), and, despite a small industrial district across the Po, there's a definite feeling of grass growing between the tracks. Travellers are scarce enough to attract a few stares as they cross the main square, and although it's interesting enough to merit perhaps half a day of your time, you'd probably be better off staying in one of the Via Emilia's more animated centres, if not pressing on to Milan.

The Town

Piazza dei Cavalli marks the centre of town, so called because of its two famous bronze equestrian statues, one on each side of the square, often quoted as being among the finest examples of Baroque sculpture. Cast in the early part of the seventeenth century by Francesco Mochi, a pupil of Giambologna, they're impressive works certainly, convincingly poised for action. One of the riders is Alessandro Farnese, a mercenary for Philip II of Spain; the other his son Ranuccio I. Behind, the **Palazzo de Comune**, "Il Gotico", is a fine red-brick palace, built in 1280 – an elegant example of Lombard-Gothic architecture, topped by fishtail battlements.

The church of **San Francesco**, just off the square, dates from the same period and sports an imposing Gothic interior. West of here, back towards the train station, the main shopping street of **Via XX Settembre** leads down to the **Duomo**, a grand Lombard-Romanesque church that has been altered many times since it was built between 1122 and 1233. The interior is lovely, with a high, plain nave supported by stout columns and cupola decorated with frescoes by Guercino – though these may be more difficult to see than the fine frescoes in the transepts and apses. From the duomo, follow Via Chiapponi up to the church of **San Antonino** – known as "Il Paradiso" for the twelfth-century bas-reliefs on its portal. Beyond, a couple of minutes' walk away from here on Via San Siro, the **Galleria Ricci-Oddi** with its collection of nineteenth-century Italian art, is closed for restoration.

The other place to visit in Piacenza is the **Museo Civico** (Tues–Sat 9.30–11am, Sun 10.30am–noon, plus Sat & Sun also 2.30–4pm; L4500/€2.32). It holds displays of Romanesque and later sculpture, roomfuls of armour and weapons, lots of paintings, including a depiction of the *Madonna and Child with John the Baptist* by Botticelli, and, in the same room, the so-called *"fegato di Piacenza"*. Very much the star exhibit of the museum, this is a bronze Etruscan representation of a sliced sheep's liver, marked with the names of Etruscan deities, that was (like real sheep livers) used to divine the future. As for the building, it's a huge affair, begun by Paciotto in 1558 and only half completed by Vignola some years later for the Farnese family: one room is still decorated with heroic frescoes of Alessandro Farnese, though most were carted off to Naples by the Bourbons, where they remain.

Practicalities

The **train station** is fifteen minutes' walk east of Piazza dei Cavalli, on Piazzale Marconi. The **tourist office** is at Piazzetta dei Mercanti 7, next to Piazza dei Cavalli (Tues–Sat 9.30am–12.30pm & 3.30–6.30pm; ☎0523.329.324, *www.provincia. piacenza.it/turismo*), and has maps of the town and other information. Cheap **hotels** are virtually non-existent, but the *Milano* is very central on Viale Risorgimento 47–49 (☎0523.336.843, fax 0523.385.101; ③). Piacenza is considered the gateway to Emilian cooking for people coming from Piemonte and Lombardy, but despite this, **places to eat** in the centre of town are rather thin on the ground. One of the best – and most central – restaurants is *Trattoria Agnello*, right behind the Palazzo del Comune at Via Calzolai 2 (closed Mon), an unpretentious place with great food and moderate prices that is justifiably popular. *La Pireina*, ten minutes' walk north of Piazza dei Cavalli at Via Borghetto 137 (closed Sun and Mon), is more expensive, but its menu of Piacentine specialities is well worth the splurge.

East along the Via Emilia from Bologna

East of Bologna, the Via Emilia takes in much less of interest than it does on its way west, passing through a clutch of small towns – some of them, like **Forlì**, industrialized and mostly postwar, others, like **Faenza**, with medieval piazzas surrounded by towers and battlements. Both started life as Roman way-stations and were under the rule of the Papal States for much of their subsequent history. The **lowlands** to the north are farmed intensively and were the heart of the cooperative movement that spawned the now left-wing local administration. On the southern side lie hilly vineyards and pastures, narrow gorges that lead up into the mountains and a couple of ski resorts around Monte Fumaiolo (1407m).

Ímola and Dozza

About 30km out of Bologna, **ÍMOLA** might be worth a short stop if you're heading east; it's well known as a centre for machinery and ceramic ware, and for the San Marino Grand Prix, which gained a certain notoriety following the death of Ayrton Senna here in 1994. It's a pleasant town, with a thirteenth-century castle and some grey-walled Renaissance palaces, but there is nothing extraordinary about it.

The city's various art and historical collections are divided among the four main museums, all of which have limited opening hours, but can be visited during the week by telephoning ☎0542.602.609. The **Pinacoteca** at Via Sacchi 4 (summer Sat 10am–1pm & 3.30–6.30pm, Sun 3.30–6.30pm; winter closes 6pm; L5000/€2.58) holds work by local fifteenth- to eighteenth-century artists; the **Museo Archeologico e Naturalistico** in Via Verdi 7 (Sun: summer 3.45–6.45pm; winter 3.15–6.15pm; L5000/€2.58) has an extensive display of rare plants and beetles; and the **Palazzo Tozzoni** at Via Garibaldi 18 (mid-Sept to April Sat 9am–noon & 2.45–6.45pm, Sun

2.45–6.45pm; L5000/€2.58) has a vast armoury dating from the thirteenth to the nineteenth centuries. You can buy a combined ticket for all the museums (L10,000/€5.17).

For places to **eat** there's *Osteria del Merlo* at Via Callegherie 13, off Viale A. Costa near the train station, or if money is no object, head for the hallowed *Ristorante San Domenico* at Via G. Sacchi 1 (☎0542.29.000; closed Mon all day & Sun evening; booking essential), which is consistently rated one of the country's top restaurants. If you want to stay the night, the *Moderno*, Via XX Settembre 22 (☎0542.231.22; ③), is well situated and has its own restaurant serving local specialities.

Back towards Bologna but easier to reach by bus from Ímola, the village of **DOZZA**, set on a hill surrounded by vineyards, is a popular place for a Sunday afternoon outing, with hordes of people descending to view the kitsch murals on the outside of the houses, created during the Biennale del muro dipinto, held every other year during the first two weeks of September (the next is planned for 2002.) The village also has an annual Sagra dell'Albana, in honour of the fragrant white wine produced locally, which you can taste at any time of year along with 500 of the region's other wines, in Emilia-Romagna's official *enoteca* housed in the castle, which also has a wine museum.

Faenza and Brisighella

East of Ímola, cypress trees and umbrella pines, gentler hills and vineyards signal the fact that you're leaving Emilia and entering the Romagna – although strictly speaking there's no distinct boundary between the two regions. **FAENZA**, 12km from Ímola, gives its name to the faïence-ware it has been producing for the last 600 years. This style of decorated ceramic ware reached its zenith in the fifteenth and sixteenth centuries, and the town is worth a visit for the vast **Museo delle Ceramiche** alone (May–Oct Tues–Sat 9am–7pm, Sun 9.30am–1pm & 3–7pm; Nov–April Tues–Fri 9am–1.30pm, Sat & Sun 9.30am–1pm & 3–6pm; L10,000/€5.17); it's at Viale Baccarini 19 – take Corso D. Baccarini from the station, and it's on the left. The massive collection includes early work painted in the characteristic blue and ochre, and later more colourful work, often incorporating portraits and landscapes. There's a section devoted to ceramics from other parts of the world, too, including ceramic art by Picasso, Matisse and Chagall.

Faenza is still home to one of Italy's leading ceramics schools, teaching techniques of tin-glazing first introduced in the fourteenth century – the ceramics are decorated after glazing and are given a final lead-based, lustrous wash. The town is also a major production centre, with small workshops down most of its sidestreets; the **tourist office** in Piazza del Popolo 1 (June–Oct Mon–Sat 9.30am–12.30pm & 3.30–6.30pm, Sun 9.30am–12.30pm; Nov–May Tues–Sat 9.30am–12.30pm & 4–6pm; ☎0546.25.231) has details of where to buy.

The rest of Faenza is fairly ordinary, although the town's medieval centre is appealing enough. The long, crenellated **Palazzo del Podesta** and the **Piazza del Popolo** together make up Faenza's medieval heart, linked to **Piazza Martiri della Libertà**, the main marketplace, through an archway. There's a market here on Tuesday, Thursday and Saturday mornings, when the trattorias that surround it are packed out. Another good time to be in Faenza is for the Palio del Niballo (jousting and flag twirling), which takes place on the last Sunday in June. If you want to **stay** in Faenza, bed-and-breakfast options are around half the price of the hotels – ask the tourist office for the list of *affittacamere*. The best hotel in town is the *Vittoria*, Corso Garibaldi 23 (☎0546.21.508, fax 0546.29.136; ⑤), a few blocks away from the Duomo, featuring nineteenth-century decor and a dining room with a frescoed ceiling. **Eating** prospects are favourable – try the *Osteria del Mercato* in Piazza Martiri della Libertà (closed Sun), a good, lively place frequented by locals.

South of Faenza, and accessible by train, the village of **BRISIGHELLA**, halfway up a hillside, is famed for its restaurants (visited by people from as far afield as Milan) and its **Via degli Asini** – a raised, covered lane once part of the town fortifications, used to protect mule trains carrying olive oil and clay for making ceramics. The medieval fortress topping the cliffs over the town was held first by the local Manfredi family, then successively by Cesare Borgia, the Venetians and the pope. It now houses a **Museo del Lavoro Contadino** (summer daily 10am–noon & 3.30–7pm; winter Sat 2.30–4.30pm only; L3500/€1.81) with a collection of tools and other objects evoking the region's traditional rural life. The thirteenth-century **Torre dell'Orologio** sits on a spur of rock opposite, while below the town, down by the River Lamone, is the **Pieve del Tho** – an eleventh-century church, built on top of the remains of an earlier temple to Jupiter. It's worth coming here at carnival time and in July for the Feste Medievali as well as the Sagra della Polenta, del Tartufo (truffle) and dell'Ulivo in October, November and December respectively.

Of Brisighella's **restaurants**, *La Grotta Osteria con Uso di Cucina* serves excellent Romagnolo dishes, albeit at very high prices – although it does offer an affordable fixed-price menu (☎0546.81.829; closed Tues); or there's the more modest *Tre Colli*, Via Gramsci 9 (closed Mon), the other side of the level crossing below town. Brisighella's **hotels** are disappointing – all are expensive for their standard of accommodation. Stay in an agriturismo place instead; the **tourist office** at Porta Gabolo 5 (Mon–Fri 10am–noon & 4–6pm; ☎0546.81.166) has details of these.

Forlì

FORLÌ, administrative capital of the Romagna, is a mainly modern place with office blocks and dual carriageways around the centre, but the heart of the town is closed to traffic and is an interesting if low-key place to visit. It's unlikely that you will want to stay here unless Fascist architecture is your sort of thing, although you might want to stop off for its couple of museums. Benito Mussolini, who was born a few miles away at Predappio, was editor of the Forlì newspaper and spokesman of the radical wing of the Socialist Party (PSI) before he left the town in 1912 to edit the *Avanti* paper in Milan. The city is an important Romagnolo agricultural centre; its **Museo Etnografico**, Corso della Republica 72 (Tues–Fri 9am–2pm, Sat 9am–1.30pm, Sun 9am–1pm; L4000/ €2.07), gives a good rundown on peasant life early last century and today. The same building also houses the **Museo Romagnolo del Teatro** (same hours; separate admission charge L4000/€2.07), where antique musical instruments, documents and mementos of the city's cultural life are displayed; there are scores of posters from the old Teatro Comunale, as well as exhibits associated with the most celebrated local opera singers.

Ferrara

Thirty minutes' train ride north of Bologna, **FERRARA** was the residence of the Este dukes, an eccentric dynasty that ranked as a major political force throughout Renaissance times. The Este kept the main artists of the day in commissions and built a town which, despite a relatively small population, was – and still is – one of the most elegant urban creations of the period.

When there was no heir, the Este were forced to hand over Ferrara to the papacy and leave for good. Life in Ferrara effectively collapsed: eighteenth-century travellers found a ghost town of empty streets and clogged-up canals infested with mosquitoes. Since then Ferrara has picked itself up, dusted itself down, and is now the centre of a key fruit-producing area, to which the expanse of neat, pollarded trees outside town testifies. It's a popular stop for tourists travelling up from Bologna to Venice, but they rarely stay, leaving the city centre enjoyably tourist-free by the evening.

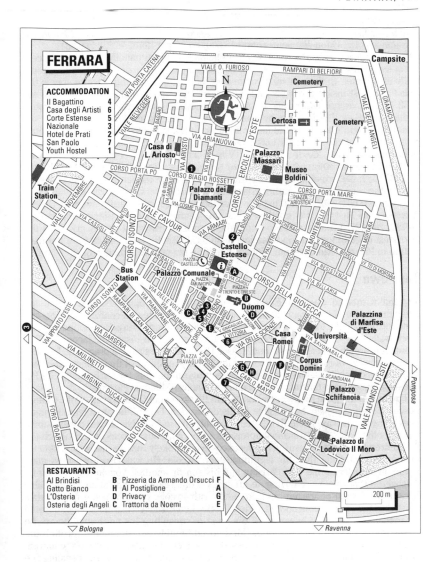

FERRARA

ACCOMMODATION
Il Bagattino	4
Casa degli Artisti	6
Corte Estense	5
Nazionale	3
Hotel de Prati	2
San Paolo	7
Youth Hostel	1

RESTAURANTS
Al Brindisi		Pizzeria da Armando Orsucci	F
Gatto Bianco	H	Al Postiglione	A
L'Osteria	D	Privacy	G
Osteria degli Angeli	C	Trattoria da Noemi	E

Arrival, information and accommodation

Ferrara's **train station** is just west of the city walls, a fifteen-minute walk along Viale Cavour from the centre of town around the *castello*; buses #1, #2, #6, #9 and #11 run from the train station to the centre of town, of which #2 and #11 are the most direct. The **bus station** is just southwest of the main square, on Corso Isonzo. The main **tourist office** is in the *castello* courtyard (daily 9am–1pm & 2–6pm; ☎0532.209.370, *www.provincia.fe.it*) and has plenty of maps and bumph on the town. You can check your **email** at the *Centro Servizio Link*, Via Ariosto 57a (daily 9am–1pm & 3–6.30pm;

July & Aug 9am–1pm only; ☎0532.241.579; L12,000/€6.20/hr), or at *Internet Point*, Via San Romano 123 (Mon–Sat 9am–8pm; L15,000/€7.75 per hour; ☎0532.769.831).

Ferrara has a number of affordable **hotels**, most of them handily placed in the centre of town, although again you need to book ahead to be sure of finding a place, especially in summer. In the centre, a convenient, but not too exciting place to stay is the *San Paolo*, just inside the walls and off Piazza Travaglio at Via Baluardi 9 (☎ & fax 0532.762.040, *www.hotelsanpaolo.it*; ③). Or opt for the much more central and refurbished *Hotel de Prati,* close by the *castello* at Via Padiglioni 5 (☎0532.241.905, *www.hoteldeprati.com*; ③) or the funky, friendly *Casa degli Artisti*, in the medieval quarter at Via Vittoria 66 (☎0532.761.038; ②). Closer to the main piazza, you'll find a much finer choice, the *Corte Estense*, Via Correggiari 4a (☎0532.242.176, fax 0532.246.4050532; ⑥), and *Il Bagattino*, Corso Porta Reno 24 (☎0532.241.887, fax 0532.206.387; ③), which has its own trattoria around the corner. If everything else is full, try the very central but rather characterless *Nazionale*, Corso Porta Reno 32 (☎ & fax 0532.209.604; ③), which usually has rooms. Ferrara's **youth hostel**, Ostello Estense, lies just to the northwest of the centre at Corso Biagio Rossetti 24 (☎0532.204.227; L23,000/€11.88) while the **campsite**, *Estense* (May–Sept), is on the northeast edge of town at Via Gramicia 5 (☎0532.752.396); take bus #1 from the train station to Piazzale San Giovanni, from where it's a ten-minute walk north.

The Town

The bulky, moated **Castello Estense** (Tues–Sun 9.30am–5pm; L8000/€4.13) dominates the centre of Ferrara, built in response to a late fourteenth-century uprising and generally held at the time to be a major feat of military engineering. But behind its grim brick walls, the Este court thrived, supporting artists like Pisanello, Jacopo Bellini, Mantegna, and the poets Ariosto and Tasso. The Este dukes were a pragmatic lot, with a range of ways of raising cash: keeping tax levels just ahead of their court expenses, boosting cashflow by selling official titles, putting up the tolls for traffic along the Po, and supplying troops for the various rulers of Naples, Milan or Florence.

The first of the **Este** to live here was Nicolò II, who commissioned the castle, though descendants were really responsible for its decoration. One of the most famous members of the family was Nicolò III d'Este, who took over in 1393. Nicolò was a well-known patron of the arts, but he was most notorious for his amorous liaisons and, although the 27 children he admitted to siring seems excessive, it's likely that he was responsible for many more offspring than his legitimate heir, Ercole. He was also a ruthless man, reputedly murdering his wife Parisina and his son by another woman, Ugo, when he discovered that they were having an affair. Two other sons, Leonello and Borso, also became renowned characters and, together with Ercole, oversaw some of Ferrara's most civilized years. Leonello was a friend of the Renaissance man Alberti and became a caricature of the time by virtue of his habit of consulting his horoscope before he chose what to wear in the morning. Borso loved hunting and thundered through the woods at Mesola on horseback, dressed in velvet and jewels. Ercole's children, Beatrice and Isabella, married into the Sforza and Gonzaga families, thus sealing the Este's status as one of the most glittering of Renaissance dynasties. Ercole's grandson, Alfonso I, married Lucrezia Borgia, who continued to support the retinue of artists and poets, patronizing Titian and Ariosto – as did the last Este duke, Alfonso II, who invited Tasso and Guarini to his court.

It's hard to credit all this as you walk through the castle now, most of which is used as offices and inaccessible to the public. The few rooms that you can see go some way to bringing back the days of Este magnificence, especially the *saletta* and Salone dei Giochi or games rooms, decorated by Sebastiano Filippi with vigorous scenes of wrestling, discus-throwing, ball-tossing and chariot-racing – beautifully restored and full of interest. Otherwise it's rather a cold, draughty place on the whole, perhaps at its most evocative in the dungeons, where the sound of water lapping in the moat conjures an image of Este enemies: Ugo and Parisina were incarcerated down here before their execution, and Ferrante and Giulio Este were detained in the dungeon for most of their lives after attempting to depose Alfonso I.

Just south of here, the crenellated **Palazzo Comunale**, built in 1243 but since much altered and restored, holds statues of Nicolò III and another son, Borso, on its facade – though they're actually twentieth-century reproductions. Walk through the arch into the pretty enclosed square of **Piazza Municipio** for a view of the rest of the building. Opposite the Palazzo Comunale, the **Duomo** is a mixture of Romanesque and Gothic styles and has an undeniably impressive facade, centring on a carved central portal that was begun in the mid-twelfth century by Wiligelmus (of Modena cathedral fame) and finished a century or so later. Much of the carving depicts the *Last Judgement*, with the damned souls grimacing on the central frieze and hell itself depicted on the central lunette, while below the frieze bodies climb out of their coffins. Inside, the main part of the church has the grandeur of a ballroom, with sparkling chandeliers, but is much less intriguing than the exterior carving, and it's upstairs, in the **museum** (Mon–Sat 10am–noon & 3–5pm, Sun 10am–noon & 4–6pm; free), that the real treasures are kept. The highlight of the collection is a set of bas-reliefs illustrating the labours of the months, which formerly adorned the outside of the cathedral. There are also illuminated manuscripts, two organ shutters decorated by Cosimo Tura, one of the Annunciation, another showing St George killing the dragon, and a beautiful *Madonna* by della Quercia.

The long arcaded south side of the duomo flanks **Piazza Trento e Trieste**, whose rickety-looking rows of shops herald the arcades of the appealing **Via San Romano** that runs off the far corner of the square, and – beyond – the labyrinth of alleyways that make up Ferrara's medieval quarter; the arched **Via delle Volte**, a long street running east parallel to Via Carlo Mayr, is one of the most characteristic. On the wider streets above the tangled medieval district are a number of the Renaissance palaces once inhabited by Ferrara's better-heeled families. Most give nothing away with their anonymous facades – all you get is the occasional glimpse of a roof garden or courtyard inside a closing doorway – but a handful are open to the public and give an idea of what life must have been like for the privileged few during Ferrara's heyday. The **Casa Romei**, at Via Savonarola 30 (Tues–Sat 8.30am–7.30pm & Sun 8.30am–2pm; L4000/€2.07), is a typical building of the time, with frescoes and graceful courtyards alongside artefacts rescued from various local churches. Just beyond is the house, at no. 19, where the monk Savaranola was born and lived for twenty years, while behind the palace, the monastery church of **Corpus Domini** at Via Pergolata 4 (Mon–Fri 9.30–11.30am & 3.30–5.30pm; free), holds the tombs of Alfonso I and II d'Este and Lucrezia Borgia.

Palaces and museums

Two minutes southeast of Corpus Domini, the **Palazzo Schifanoia** – the "Palace of Joy" – at Via Scandiana 23 (Tues–Sun 9am–7pm; L8000/€4.13) is one of the grandest of Ferrara's palaces. It belonged to the Este family, and Cosimo Tura's frescoes inside transplanted their court to Arcadia. In the marvellous Salone dei Mesi (the "rooms of the months"), the blinds are kept closed to protect the colours, and the room seems silent and empty compared with what's happening on the walls, which are split into three bands. Borso features in many of the court scenes, on the lowest band, surrounded by friends and hunting dogs, along with groups of musicians, weavers and embroiderers with white rabbits nibbling the grass at their feet. Above, each section is topped with a sign of the zodiac and, above that, various mythological scenes.

On nearby Corso della Giovecca, at no. 170, the **Palazzina di Marfisa d'Este** (Tues–Sun 9.30am–1pm & 3–6pm; L4000/€2.07), has more frescoes, this time by

Filippi, and although its gloomy interior is less impressive than the Schifanoia complex, in summer the loggia and orange grove are a welcome refuge from the heat. In the other direction, to the south, the **Palazzo di Lodovico Il Moro**, Via XX Settembre 124, (Tues–Sun 9am–7.30pm; summer Saturdays 9am–10.30pm; L8000/€4.13) holds the city's well-organized archeological museum, with finds from Spina, the Graeco-Etruscan seaport and trading colony near Commachio, displayed together with a dugout canoe from one of the prehistoric lake villages in the Po Delta.

There are some more impressive palaces north of the *castello*, along and around **Corso Ercole I d'Este** – named after Ercole I, who succeeded to the throne in 1441 after his father died, probably poisoned, and who promptly disposed of anyone likely to pose a threat. His reputation for coldness earned him the names "North Wind" and "Diamond", but he certainly got things done, consolidating his power by marrying Eleanor of Aragon, daughter of the Spanish King of Naples, and laying out the northern quarter of the city, the so-called "Herculean Addition", on such a grand scale that Ferrara was tagged the first modern city in Europe. He wasn't a puritanical ruler either; writers of the time describe grand events consisting of many hours of feasting, with sugar castles full of meat set up for the crowd to storm. The **Palazzo dei Diamanti**, a little way down the Corso on the left, named after the diamond-shaped bricks that stud its facade, was at the heart of Ercole's town-plan and is nowadays used for temporary modern art exhibitions as well as being home to the **Pinacoteca Nazionale** (Tues, Wed, Fri & Sat 9am–2pm, Sun 9am–1pm, Thurs 9am–7pm; L8000/€4.13), the **Museo Michelangelo Antonioni** (daily 9am–1pm & 3–6pm; L4000/€2.07), and the **Museo del Risorgimento e della Resistenza** (Mon–Sat 9am–2pm & 3–7pm, Sun 9am–noon & 3.30–6.30pm; L3000/€1.55). You can safely give the last a miss, and, at the moment, the Museo Antonioni holds only a rather unexciting collection of the film director's paintings but will eventually be a museum dealing with his pivotal role in Italian cinema. The Pinacoteca, however, holds works from the Ferrara and Bologna schools in rooms with ornately decorated wooden ceilings, notably paintings by Dossi, Garofalo and Guercino, and a spirited St Christopher by "Il Bastianino" (Sebastiano Filippi). Around the corner, at Corso Porta Mare 9, the **Palazzo Massari** (daily 9am–1pm & 3–6pm; L4000/€2.07) has a small **photographic gallery** and the **Documentario della Metafisica** – a collection of transparencies of work by the Scuola Metafisica, the proto-surrealist group founded here by Giorgio de' Chirico in 1917. However, most of the impressive palace is given over to the **Museo Boldini** (daily 9am–1pm & 3–6pm; L8000/€4.13) and the **Museo d'Arte Moderna e Contemporanea** (daily 9am–1pm & 3–6pm; L4000/€2.07), both housing fairly brain-numbing collections of work by local nineteenth-century artists.

Eating and drinking

Ferrara has a good range of **restaurants** and trattorias with prices to suit most pockets. At the bottom end of the scale, but one of the most charming is *Pizzeria da Armando Orsucci*, Via Saraceno 116 (closed Thurs), featuring not just pizza but also a relatively new Ferraran treat, of Genovese origins – a kind of chickpea-flour pie, *torta di ceci*, eaten by the slice right out of the oven, with a dash of black pepper – locals line up for it. *Al Postiglione*, off Corso Martiri di Libertà at Vicolo del Teatro 4 (closed Sun), on the east side of the *castello*, is a *paninoteca* with any number of sandwich combinations, hot and cold, as well as home-made pasta and lots of different beers and wines (open until midnight). Among the regular restaurants, the attractive and atmospheric *Privacy*, Via Carlo Mayr 45 (closed Thurs), does good pizzas and more elaborate regional fare at moderate prices and is open till 2am. *Trattoria Da Noemi*, Via Ragno 31 (closed Tues), is an affable, family-run restaurant with a short and very simple pasta-and meat-based menu at moderate prices, while *Il Bagattino* (see p.432; closed Mon) is an attractive, affordable trattoria a few steps from the duomo. *Osteria degli Angeli*, Via delle Volte 4 (closed Mon), is a convivial, rather pricey place, open late, with lots of different wines and good food, and at upscale *L'Osteria*, Via Romei 51 (closed Mon), the *tortelli di zucca* (pumpkin ravioli) is definitely something special. Probably the best all-round choice for charm, fun, good food and drink is *Al Brindisi*, Via degli Adelardi 11 (closed Mon), just to the left of the duomo. It's Ferrara's oldest osteria, once frequented by the likes of Cellini, Titian and Copernicus, with a magnificent wine selection, which the proud sommelier will be delighted to tell you about. Food prices are very reasonable, but some of the wines are Italy's finest and are priced accordingly.

The Po Delta

"So ugly it's beautiful" is a somewhat contrary summing up of the **Po Delta**, east of Ferrara: an expanse of marshland and lagoons culminating in small fingers of land poking out into the Adriatic. Most of the traffic is just passing through, and it's not surprising that the tourist authorities have decided on some heavy promotion.

The River Po splits into several channels, trickling to the sea through these wetlands. Etruscan traders set up the port of Spina here between the fourth and third centuries BC, when the sea covered much of the land from Comacchio to Ravenna. Partly due to drainage schemes, the briny waters have since retreated by 12km, and the area becomes a bit less marshy each year – an advantage for local farmers but a threat to the many varieties of sea and shore **birds** that inhabit the area. The two main lagoons of **Valli di Comacchio** and **Valle Bertuzzi** have been designated as nature reserves to protect at least some of the wetlands and now constitute one of Europe's most highly regarded birdwatching areas, providing a habitat for nesting and migrating birds, including herons, egrets, curlews, avocets and terns.

Another threat to the area's wild (and human) life is **pollution**: 136,000 tonnes of nitrates; 250 tonnes of arsenic and 60 tonnes of mercury are pumped into the River Po every day, and spillages from oil refineries are further cause for anxiety. Not surprisingly, swimming in the river is banned, as is use of the water for irrigation or drinking purposes. Though you might not fancy it having read this, the best way to see the delta is by **boat**. There are a number of people in the surrounding area who run guided tours. Sig. Schiavi Vincensino, Via Vicolo del Farol (☎0533.999.815), or Sig. Dante Passarella, c/o *Ristorante USPA* (☎0533.999.817), both in Gorino, take out boats in summer if enough people are interested. Boats also leave from Valle Fole, south of Comacchio; ask at the tourist office in Comacchio at Piazza Folegatti 28 (Mon–Fri 9am–noon; ☎0533.310.147) for details.

Comacchio

The main town of the region, **COMACCHIO** is a small fishing town intersected by a network of canals, with a famous local attraction in its triple-bridge or **Trepponti**, built in 1634, which crosses three of the canals. Comacchio is an eel-port, and the time to visit is autumn, when wriggling masses of the creatures are fished out of the canals on their way to the Sargasso Sea. Not surprisingly, eel (*anguille*) is a central ingredient in the local cuisine and there are several places around town to try the different ways they're prepared or other regional dishes like fish risotto, or *fritto misto*.

The **beach developments** directly east of Comacchio are not particularly inviting, especially bearing in mind the proximity of the nasty waters of the Po, but it's interesting to see the cantilever nets set up either side of the channels running out to the sea. Incidentally, Comacchio's harbour is named Porto Garibaldi, after the Risorgimento hero who was left on the shore with his wife, Anita, and their companion Leggero, as the last Garibaldini were captured off the coast by the Austrian navy.

North of Comacchio: Pomposa Abbey and around

About 20km north of Comacchio, and connected by buses from the port, the **Abbey of Pomposa** is about all the area has to offer in the way of orthodox sights, a lonely collection of buildings, saved from complete oblivion by the main road to Chioggia and numerous bus tours in summer. At the centre of a complex that includes a Lombard-Romanesque campanile, a chapter house and refectory is an eighth-century **Basilica** containing frescoes by Vitale di Bologna and the Bolognese School, though the abbey is better known for one of its monks, Guido d'Arezzo, who in the early eleventh century invented the musical scale here. Only a few hundred years after Pomposa was built, it went into decline, the delta becoming marshier and malarial, and those who weren't killed off by the disease were left to scratch a living from hunting and fishing. The monks finally abandoned their abbey in the seventeenth century.

From Pomposa a minor road leads to Volano, following the **Valle Bertuzzi**, an expanse of water and small islets given over to the Riserva Natura Pineta di Volano. On the other side of the estuary is the **Bosco della Mésola** (Sat & Sun 8am–dusk; free), an ancient wood planted by the Etruscans, now surrounded by fields of peppers and artichokes. It has been much reduced in size by commercial logging, but it's the only woodland in the vicinity and deer lurk among its oak and juniper trees. You can rent bicycles at the gate – reachable by taking a bus from Ferrara towards Goro, getting off at stop no. 15 and walking the 2km back down the road to the left-hand turning.

GORO itself, the next port up the coast, is used by deep-sea drifters as well as smaller local boats, and is one of the most thriving, if bleakest, harbours along this stretch. Catches are either packed in ice and loaded directly into the container lorries, or else sold at the co-operative nearby. In theory it's all strictly for trade but some informal private bargaining does go on at the quayside. The road from Goro inland keeps company with drainage ditches that have a water level higher than the surrounding fields. The main village here is **MÉSOLA**, where a noisy Saturday market invades the courtyard and the porticoes by the castle. From Mésola the road west follows the course of one of the Po's main channels – the Po di Goro – which also marks the border with the Veneto.

South of Comacchio: Alfonsine and the Museo del Senio

The countryside around the lagoons of the Valli di Comacchio is a combination of farm and marshland. Buildings are rare and the only sign of life is the odd heron or scavenging bird. **ALFONSINE**, the main centre of the area, is on the Ferrara–Ravenna rail line, although there's little to tempt you off the train. Not much of the pre-1944 town survived heavy bombing during World War II, and only the **Museo del Senio** (Mon–Sat 8am–1pm, Tues & Thurs also 2.30–5.30pm; free) on Piazza della Resistenza is worth seeing. This documents the war, including the "Gothic Line" held by the Germans across the Apennines, and the role of Italian partisans in their defeat. The many objects and photographs include an esoteric collection of pictures of gates made from leftover anti-slip tank tracking (you still see lots of them around), as well as the Bailey bridges used to cross the ditches and canals.

Ravenna and around

When **RAVENNA** became capital of the Western Roman Empire fifteen hundred years ago, it was more by quirk of fate than design. The Emperor Honorius, alarmed by armies invading from the north, moved his court from Milan to this obscure town on the Romagna coast around 402; it was easy to defend, surrounded by marshland, and was situated close to the port of Classis – at the time the biggest Roman naval base on the Adriatic. Honorius's anxiety proved well founded: Rome was sacked by the Goths in 410 and sank into a decline matched only by Ravenna's ensuing prosperity, and the town became the Roman capital almost by default. After enjoying a period of great monumental adornment as chief city of the empire, Ravenna, too, was conquered by the Goths in 476. However, the new conquerors – and new emperors – were also Christians and continued to embellish the city lavishly, particularly the Ostrogoth Theodoric, making it one of the most sought-after towns in the Mediterranean. It wasn't long before Byzantine forces annexed the city to the Eastern Empire and made it into an exarchate, under the rule of Constantinople.

The Byzantine rulers were responsible for Ravenna's most glorious era, keen to outdo rival cities with magnificent palaces, churches and art, and the city became one of the most compelling cultural centres in the world. The growing importance of Venice brought some further prosperity, but the sixteenth century saw the sack of the city and

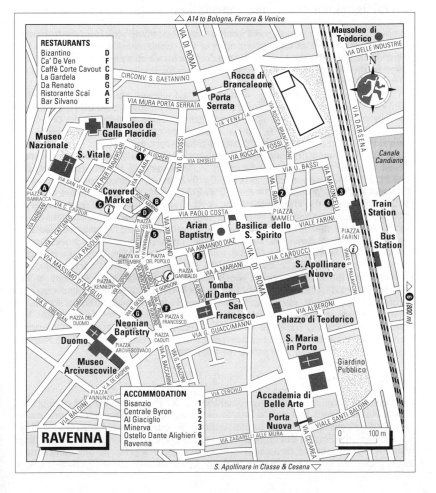

its absorption into the Papal States, since when the Adriatic shoreline has receded, and an eleven-kilometre-long canal through a vast industrial complex now links Ravenna's port to the sea. But remnants of the dazzling Byzantine era are still thick on the ground – not least a set of mosaics at San Vitale that is generally acknowledged to be the crowning achievement of Byzantine art extant anywhere in the world.

Unlike Florence or Venice, say, tourism seems almost incidental to the life of the town, although the nearby **Mirabilandia**, a Disneyesque theme-park, helps bring in the crowds during summer. Bombs levelled much of Ravenna in the last world war, but enough has survived to warrant a couple of days' unhurried exploration. Churches and mosaics could easily monopolize your time, but foot traffic past the cafés in the main square, and noisy restaurants, make the city an appealing destination just for itself. Nightlife is sparse, but the family-oriented lido towns a couple of kilometres away provide some excitement in summer.

Arrival, information and accommodation

Ravenna has a compact centre, and it's only a short, ten-minute walk from the **train station** on Piazza Farini, on the eastern edge of the centre, along Viale Farini and Via Armando Diaz to the central square, Piazza del Popolo, which with the adjoining streets makes up the old centre. The **bus station** is across the tracks behind the train station, in Piazzale Aldo Moro.

There's an information office, with maps, just outside the station on the left (Mon–Sat 6.15am–8pm), next to a place that rents bikes, and a main **tourist office** at Via Salara 8 (Mon–Sat 8.30am–7pm, closes 6pm in winter, Sun 9am–noon & 3–6pm; ☎0544.35.404, www.*racine.ra.it*). To go **online**, you can use the computers at the Central Post Office, Piazza Garibaldi (Mon–Fri 8am–2pm; free).

The district around the train station is a good place to find **somewhere to stay**. Almost opposite the station, the *Ravenna*, Viale Maroncelli 12 (☎0544.212.204, fax 0544.212.077; ③), is very inviting, as is the slightly more expensive *Minerva*, just across the street at Viale Maroncelli 1 (☎ & fax 0544.213.711; ③). Not much further from the station, and one of the cheapest options, is *Al Giaciglio*, Via Rocca Brancaleone 42 (☎0544.39.403; ②), with its own restaurant and a good lunch menu that changes every day. If you prefer to stay right in the historic centre, there are two very comfortable choices: the *Centrale Byron*, two blocks from the central piazza, at Via IV Novembre 14 (☎0544.212.225, fax 0544.34.114; ③) and, a little farther toward San Vitale, the *Bisanzio*, Via Salara 30 (☎0544.217.111, fax 0544.32.539; ⑥), part of the Best Western chain. Not far away from the station there's a **youth hostel**, the *Ostello Dante Alighieri*, at Via Nicolodi 12 (☎0544.421.164; L25,000/€12.91; April–Oct), with some family rooms and evening meals available. You can get there on bus #1 from outside the train station, or it's a ten-minute walk – south out of the station, east under the tracks, follow Via Candiano and then bear southeast down Via T. Gulli; Via Nicolodi goes off to the right. The closest **campsite** to Ravenna is down in the nearby coastal resort of Punta Marina, to which there are regular buses from the train station.

The City Centre

The centre of Ravenna is without question **Piazza del Popolo**, an elegant open space, arcaded in one corner, that was laid out by the Venetians in the fifteenth century and is now filled with café tables. A few blocks south of the square, across Piazza Garibaldi on Via Alighieri, the **Tomba di Dante** is a site of local pride, a small Neoclassical building which was put up in the eighteenth century to enclose a previous fifteenth-century tomb. Dante had been chased out of Florence by the time he arrived in Ravenna, and he was sheltered here by the Da Polenta family – then in control of the city – while he finished his *Divine Comedy*. He died in 1381 and was laid to rest in the adjoining church of **San Francesco**, a much-restored building, elements of which date from the fourth century. File down the stairs in front of the choir for a look at the waterlogged crypt, dating from the tenth century, complete with goldfish and remnants of a mosaic floor. You might want to look in, too, on the **Museo Dantesco**, situated in San Francesco's cloister on Via Alighieri (daily 9.30am–noon & 3.30–6pm; L3000/€1.55 or Visit Card, see box below) – though its collection of paintings, bronzes and various artefacts relating to Dante is pretty deadly unless you're absolutely fanatical about the man.

From June to October a "Visit Card" is available which allows you into six of the main sights for L9000/€4.65 – certainly worthwhile if you intend to visit more than two monuments. The **combined ticket** includes everything except the National Museum (at San Vitale) and Theodoric's Mausoleum; they can be purchased from any participating site.

A couple of minutes' walk west of here, a grouping of buildings around **Piazza del Duomo** shelters the **Duomo** itself, with its cylindrical – and slightly tipsy – tower. Originally a fifth-century building, the duomo was completely destroyed by an earthquake in 1733 and rebuilt in unexceptional style soon after. It's not particularly worth a second glance, but the **Museo Arcivescovile** (daily 9.30am–6.30pm; L5000/€2.58 joint ticket with the Neonian Baptistry, or Visit Card, see box above), inside the Bishop's Palace behind it next door, is fascinating, with fragments of mosaics from around the city and the palace's sixth-century Oratorio Sant'Andrea, which is adorned with mosaics of birds in a meadow above a Christ dressed in the armour, cloak and gilded leather skirt of a Roman centurion. There are also fragments from the original cathedral, an ornate ivory throne from Alexandria, which belonged to Bishop Maximian in the sixth century, and a circular marble calendar from the same time, used for calculating the date of Easter and related holy days according to the nineteen-year cycle of the Julian calendar.

The **Neonian Baptistry**, on the same side of the duomo, by the belltower (daily 9.30am–6.30pm; L5000/€2.58 joint ticket with the Museo Arcivescovile, or Visit Card, see box above), is a conversion from a Roman bathhouse. The original floor level has sunk into the marshy ground, and the remains of the previous building are now three metres below. The choice of building was a logical one: baptisms involved total immersion in those days, and the mixture of styles works well – the marble inlaid designs from the bathhouse blend in with the mosaics of prophets on the arches round the sides. Mosaics of the baptism of Christ and portraits of the twelve Apostles decorate the dome, which is made of hollow terracotta tubes.

East of here, **Via di Roma**, lined with bland, official-looking palaces, cuts right through the modern centre of Ravenna and sees much of its traffic. Halfway up on the right, the basilica of **Sant'Apollinare Nuovo** (daily 9.30am–6.30pm; L5000/€2.58, joint ticket with the Arian Baptistry, or Visit Card, see box above) – called Nuovo to distinguish it from the church of the same name at Classe (see p.442) – dates from the sixth century, built by Theodoric and with mosaics that rank among Ravenna's most impressive. There are just two of these, running the length of either side of the nave. Each shows ceremonial processions of martyrs – one side male, the other female – bearing gifts for Christ and the Virgin enthroned through an avenue of date palms. Some of the scenery is more specific to Ravenna: you can make out what used to be the harbour at Classe with the city in the background, from which rises Theodoric's palace. As a Goth, Theodoric belonged to the Arian branch of Christianity which didn't accept the absolute divinity of Christ, a heresy stamped out by Constantinople as much for political as theological reasons. When the Byzantine rule began, they removed many of the figures that had been placed here under Theodoric's reign. In the mosaics that you can see just above the entrance door, it is clear that whoever was under the arches pictured in the mosaics has been substituted with mosaics of drapery. In fact, if you look very closely at the columns to the left of the building labelled "PALA TIUM", you can still discern outstretched hands, possibly Theodoric's, though no one actually knows for sure. When Theodoric built the church in the early 500s, he dedicated it to Jesus, but when the Byzantines took over it was rededicated to St Martin, who was known for his anti-heretic campaigns and is shown at the head of the line of male devotees. Still later, in the ninth century, it was rededicated yet again to the present eponymous saint.

Five minutes' walk away, north up Via di Roma, the **Arian Baptistry**, also built by Theodoric, beside the **Basilica dello Santo Spirito** (daily 8.30am–7pm; L5000/€2.58 joint ticket with the Sant'Apollinare Nuovo, or Visit Card) recalls this struggle, in name at least, with a fine mosaic ceiling showing the twelve Apostles and the baptism of Christ.

San Vitale and around

In terms of monuments, Ravenna's biggest draw is the area ten minutes' walk northwest of the city centre, around the basilica of San Vitale, which holds the finest of the mosaics and is now gathered together into one big complex, including the mausoleum of Galla Placida and the National Museum.

San Vitale (daily 9am–7pm; L6000/€3.10, or Visit Card; includes Mausoleo di Galla Placidia), which was begun in 525 under the Roman emperor Theodoric and finished in 548 under the Byzantine ruler Justinian, is a fairly typical Byzantine church, and its Eastern-inspired arrangement of void and solid, dark and light, was unique for an Italian building of the time. The Byzantines had a mathematical approach to architecture, calling it the "application of geometry to solid matter", and it shows in the building, based on two concentric octagons, its central dome supported by eight columns, and with eight recesses extending from each side – one of which is a semicircular apse that glitters with mosaic. The design was the basis for the great church of Aghia Sofia in Istanbul, built fifteen years later.

There were definite rules about who appeared where in **mosaics** – the higher up and further to the east, the more important or holy the subject. The series in the basilica starts with Old Testament scenes spread across the semicircular lunettes of the choir; the triumphal arch shows Christ, the Apostles and sons of St Vitalis. Further in, on the semi-dome of the apse, a beardless Christ stands between two angels, presenting a model of the church to St Vitalis and Bishop Ecclesius. But what could have been simply a rigid hierachy preserved in stone is enlivened by fields and rivers teeming with frogs, herons and dolphins. Of the mosaics on the side walls of the apse, the two processional panels are the best surviving portraits of the Emperor Justinian and his wife Theodora – he's on the left and she's on the right – and a rich example of Byzantine mosaic technique. The small glass *tesserae* are laid in sections, alternate rows set at slightly different angles to vary the reflection of light and give an impression of depth. Colour is used emblematically too, with gold backgrounds to denote either holiness or high status. As an extra sign of superiority, Justinian's foot rests on that of his general, Belisarius, who defeated the Goths then holding Ravenna and reclaimed the city, while next to Theodora, on the right, is the wife of Belisarius, Antonina, and their daughter.

Theodora looks a harsh figure under her finery, and she certainly had a reputation for calculated cruelty, arranging "disappearances" of anyone who went against her. According to the sixth-century chronicler Procopius, in his "Secret History" of the court, her rise to power was meteoric. When young she made a living as a child prostitute and circus performer with her two sisters, and later became a courtesan and an actor in bizarre sex shows. She travelled the Middle East, and when she returned brought herself to the attention of the emperor, Justinian. To the horror of the court, he rejected the well brought-up daughters of his Roman peers and lived with Theodora, giving her the rank of patrician. He was unable to marry her until his mother, the empress, was dead and the law changed; the two then embarked on a reign of staggering corruption and legalized looting.

Across the grass from the basilica is the tiny **Mausoleo di Galla Placidia** (daily 9am–7pm; L6000/€3.10, or Visit Card; includes San Vitale), named after the half-sister of Honorius, who was responsible for much of the grandeur of Ravenna's early days, though despite the name and the three sarcophagi inside, it's unlikely that the building ever held her bones. Galla Placidia was taken hostage when the Goths sacked Rome, and created a scandal for the Roman world by marrying one of her kidnappers, Ataulf, going into battle with him as his army forged south. Later they reigned jointly over the Gothic kingdom; when Ataulf was assassinated the Romans took her back for a ransom of corn, after which she was obliged to marry a Roman general, Constantius. Their son formally became the Emperor Valentinian III at the age of six; as his regent, Galla Placidia assumed control of the Western Empire.

Inside the building, filtered through thin alabaster windows, the light falls on mosaics that glow with a deep blue lustre, most in an earlier style than those of San Vitale, full of Roman and naturalistic motifs. Stars around a golden cross spread across the vaulted ceiling; the Gospels are four volumes on the shelves of a small cupboard, and there are symbolic representations of the Apostles – the lion of St Mark and the ox of St Luke are set in the sky at the points where you would expect to see the constellations of Leo and Taurus. At each end are representations of St Lawrence, with the gridiron on which he was martyred, and the Good Shepherd, with one of his flock, at the entrance end.

Adjacent to San Vitale on the southern side, housed in the former cloisters of the church, the **Museo Nazionale** (Tues–Sun 8.30am–6.30pm; L8000/€4.13) contains various items from this and later periods – fifteenth-century icons, early Byzantine glass, embroidery from Florence. Among the most eye-catching exhibits is a sixth-century statue of Hercules capturing a stag, possibly a copy of a Greek original and a very late example of classically inspired subject matter; and the so-called "Veil of Classis", decorated with portraits of Veronese bishops of the eighth and ninth centuries.

Still within Ravenna but a bit of a hike north of the train station, lies one more early sixth-century monument that's worth the effort: the **Mausoleo di Teodorico**, Theodoric's Mausoleum (8.30am–7pm; L6000/€3.10). This ten-sided, all-but entirely monolithic curiosity is unique in Western architecure. In fact, its design owes much to Syrian models of its day, and the whole is constructed of Istrian limestone – the 300-ton cupola being a single, although cracked, chunk. No one knows exactly why it was thought necessary to bring this material here all the way from the Middle East – or, for that matter, how it was manoeuvered into place. Inside the decagonal second storey sits an ancient porphyry bathtub, pressed into use as the royal sarcophagus.

Eating and drinking

Central Ravenna is not exactly filled with **places to eat,** and you need to know in advance where to go to avoid fruitless wandering. For lunch, the self-service *Bizantino*, just inside the covered market on Piazza A. Costa, is excellent value; the market itself stays open until 2pm and is a good source of picnic supplies. The very friendly *Bar Silvano*, Piazza Einaudi 7 (closed Sun), just up from Piazza del Popolo, offers delicious appetizers with drinks, and makes good sandwiches and even full meals, with outside seating. On the way to or from San Vitale, on Via S. Vitale 22, you can pop into the *Caffè Corte Cavour*, where the inner courtyard is particularly inviting. For a full meal, don't forget the varied and tempting lunch menu at *Al Giaciglio* hotel (see p.438). *Da Renato*, close by the cathedral square at Via R. Gessi 9, serves traditional local food, specializing in wild mushrooms in autumn; nearby, towards Piazza San Francesco, *Ca' De Ven*, at Via C. Ricci 24 (closed Mon), is a wood-panelled *enoteca* with a large selection of Emilia-Romagnan wine, and some food. Behind the covered market, *La Gardela*, Via Ponte Marino 3 (closed Thurs), is a pleasant and very central place with a varied menu and moderate prices – ask for the daily specials; *Ristorante Scai*, Piazza Barracca 20 (closed Mon), at the end of Via Cavour, is a roast-meat and game speciality restaurant, though a moderately priced one, that also serves pizzas.

Around Ravenna: Sant'Apollinare in Classe

South of Ravenna about 6km, by train or buses #4 and #44 from the station, the remains of the old port of **Classe** (Tues–Sun 9am–7pm; L4000/€2.07) are very thin indeed – the buildings have been looted for stone and the ancient harbour has now completely disappeared under the silt of the River Uniti. One building however, does survive – the church of **Sant'Apollinare in Classe**, which was spared because it was the burial place of Ravenna's patron saint. It's a typical basilical church, quite large in extent, with a beautifully proportioned brick facade concealing an interior holding more fine mosaics. There's a marvellous allegorical depiction of the *Transfiguration* in the apse, with Christ represented by a large cross in a star-spangled universe, flanked by Constantine IV granting privileges to the church of Ravenna, with St Apollinaris pictured in prayer in a naturalistic landscape below. Altogether, it's an odd site, with an otherworldly feel quite at odds with its position close to the *autostrada*.

Nearby, the **Pineta di Classe** is a long belt of umbrella pines that runs the length of the coast; the **Pineta San Vitale** runs north. This is closed to visitors during summer due to the fire risk; at other times it's a popular cycling route – though the thick belt of smog that sometimes rests over the tops of the trees can rather destroy any bucolic appeal it might have. There's easy access to Ravenna's lido towns of **Marina Romea**, **Marina di Ravenna** or **Punta Marina** by bus from here, both resorts with some upmarket villas that make for quiet, peaceful places to stay once you've driven through Ravenna's heavy industry to get there. **PORTA CORSINI**, between Marina Romea and Marina di Ravenna, is interesting for its working port, large and modern enough to take tankers but still with old-fashioned cantilevered nets used for fishing the side channels. Just before the port, you pass the **Capanno Garibaldi**, a reconstruction of the hut in which Garibaldi hid on his epic 800-kilometre march from Rome after the fall of the short-lived Roman republic in 1849. Garibaldi's life-long partner Anita, who often fought alongside him, died on the way and he was unable to stop for long enough to bury her. After Marina Romea, take a left through the pinewoods towards the Strada Romea (SS309), where you'll find places to picnic under the umbrella pines well away from the sight of the industrial area – as well as some places for viewing the tolerant bird life that still frequents the lagoon, which is part of the Po Delta nature reserve (see p.435).

The coast to Rimini

From Ravenna, a slow train runs down to Rimini, past a number of resorts that blur into one after a while. It's not an enticing part of Italy, and if the sea is what you're after you may just as well push on to Rimini, which is at least compelling through its sheer excess. But if you're tempted to linger, **CERVIA** might be the place to do it, a fishing and salt-producing village that has grown into something of a resort only in the last thirty or so years. On the first Sunday after Ascension, the town's bishop sails out into the Adriatic, accompanied by a flotilla of small boats in a ceremonial "marriage to the sea", throwing a wedding ring into the water.

Cervia's **old town** consists of a ring of porticoed houses around Piazza Garibaldi, built in the eighteenth century for the workers who worked on the salt beds a little way inland, southwest of town. At the height of production, this huge salt pan produced 500 thousand quintals (one quintal equals 100kg) of salt a year. The seventeenth-century **Torre**, just off Piazza Garibaldi, stored a mere 170 thousand quintals and is now the **Museo della Civiltà Salinara** (daily: summer 4–7pm & 8.30–11pm, closed Thurs evening; winter 9.30am–noon; free). Close by, in the porticoes of Viale Roma 86, is Cervia's **tourist office** (☎0544.974.400; May–Sept daily 9am–noon & 3–6pm). For **snacks**, try the self-service *Pizzeria-Rosticceria La Terrazza* on Piazza Carlo Pisacane, which adjoins Piazza Garibaldi.

A fifteen-minute walk from Piazza Garibaldi is Cervia's main reason for a visit – a stretch of clean, sandy **beach**, serviced by scores of small, family-run hotels lining the grid of streets along the seafront. Of these, *Ascot* at Viale Titano 14 (☎0544.72.318; ③) is excellent value for a three-star hotel and is situated only a few blocks from the beach. Cervia's **campsites** are well-equipped places away from the town centre in Pinarella and Milano Maríttima. The closest is *Camping Adriatico* at Via Pinarella 90 (☎0544.71.537). There's a beach tourist office at Viale Roma 86 (mid-May to mid-Sept daily 9am–12.40pm & 3–6pm; ☎0544.974.400), and plenty of bike-rental places (the closest one a couple of blocks along Viale Volturno from the tourist office), not to mention any number of places with tennis, windsurfing, water-skiing and sailing facilities on the side roads near the beach.

CESENATICO, 8km to the south, also grew on the strength of its fishing industry, but has since developed into a large resort, with restaurants lining its central port-canal, designed by Leonardo da Vinci for Cesare Borgia in 1502. Many of the boats here are still primarily fishing vessels, but the port area is a popular venue for a night out. The open-air, floating Museo della Marineria (free), on the canal, is a collection of old fishing and trading vessels, best seen in the summer, when the unfurled sails are most impressive. Otherwise, there's nothing much to keep you if you don't go in for the grill-pan variety of sunbathing apart from a couple of good, budget places to eat: *La Crêpe* on Via Mazzini – two minutes walk over the canal in the Ravenna direction – offers a choice of twenty different piadini (the Romagnolo version of filled pitta bread), as well as crepes. A couple of doors down, at no. 34, there's a good rosticceria serving fish kebabs, *fritto misto* and pasta dishes.

Rimini

RIMINI is one of the least pretentious towns in Italy, the archetypal seaside resort, with a reputation for good if slightly sleazy fun that puts it on a par with Blackpool or Torremolinos. It's certainly brash enough to bear the comparison, and there's plenty of money in evidence; but Rimini is never downright tacky. Rather, it's a traditional family resort, to which some Italians return year after year, to stay in their customary *pensione* and be looked after by a hardworking *padrona di casa* as if they were relatives. Indeed the warmth of hoteliers in this part of Italy has undoubtedly added to the tourist industry's success. The resort is best avoided in August, unless you feel you can cope with teeming crowds. Out of season, it's a pleasant-enough town, but many hotels, restaurants, shops, etc, are closed and the atmosphere is almost eerily quiet.

There's another, less savoury side to the town: Rimini is known across Italy for its fast-living and chancy nightlife, and there's a thriving hetero- and transsexual prostitution scene alongside the town's more wholesome attractions. The road between the train station and the beach can be particularly full of kerb-crawlers, and, although it's rarely dangerous, women on their own – after dark at any rate – should be wary in this part of town.

Rimini was 95 percent destroyed in the last war; however, the town does have a much-ignored old centre that is worth at least a morning of your time. The extensive beach operation you see now had been built over the last forty years until the "Adriatic slime slick" (a mass of gloopy algae) hit business badly at the beginning of the 1980s. The clean-up operation seems to have been almost completely successful – and, despite occasional recurrences, a daunting number of holidaymakers troop once more through the city's airport. The beach, the crowds and the wild cruising are what you really come for: Rimini is still the country's best place to party.

Arrival, information and getting around

The train station is situated in the centre of Rimini, on Piazzale Cesare Battisti, ten min-utes' walk from both the sea and the old centre; the town's main bus station is just south of here on Via Clementini; and bus #9 runs from the airport (information ☎0541.715.711), to the train station (7km) every thirty minutes. Tickets cost L1700/€0.88, and can be bought at the airport bar. There's a **tourist office** right out-side the train station on Via Dante Alighieri (April–Sept Mon–Sat 8am–7pm, Sun 9.30am–12.30pm; Oct–March Mon–Sat 9.30am–12.30pm & 3.30–6.30pm; ☎0541.51.331). They have a list of hotels and will help find a room, or pass you onto the Promozione Alberghiera – see below – except in the peak of the season (first two weeks in August), when normally you don't stand a chance if you haven't booked ahead. The main tourist office, at Piazza Federico Fellini 3 on the seafront (April–Sept Mon–Sat 8.30am–7pm, Sun 9.30am–12.30pm; Oct–March Mon–Sat 9.30am–12.30pm & 3.30–6.30pm; ☎0541.56.902, *www.riminiturismo.it*), offers the same service and a board outside showing vacancies when everything else is closed. For accommodation, you can bypass the tourist office altogether and go straight to the Promozione Alberghiera for somewhere to stay (June–Sept daily 8am–8pm; ☎0541.52.269); they have offices in the station and opposite the beachfront tourist office. The Centro di Informazione Comunale, in the Municipio on Piazza Cavour (Mon–Fri 8.30am–1pm & 2–7pm, Sat 9am–1pm; ☎0541.704.112), gives information on cultural events, often in English.

Getting around is best done on foot, at least within the town centre. But if you need to use the buses, buy an orange ticket from a tobacconist or newsstand; it gives 24 hours' unlimited travel in Rimini and the surrounding area (including Santarcángelo, Riccione and Bellaria) for L5000/€2.58; an eight-day ticket costs L20,000/€10.33. There are also a couple of nightbus services – details in "Nightlife" section on p.447.

Accommodation

Despite its 1600 hotels, accommodation can be a problem in Rimini, and in high season especially you may have to take full pension, which can make it very expensive. At the beginning of the season (before Easter) and towards the end (late September), some hoteliers will negotiate a price for room only, but in the depths of low season you should bear in mind that the town is pretty much dead, and the few hotels that remain open are largely geared to people here on business. All the hotels listed here are within a five-minute walk of the beach. To get to the beach area from the station, go out to the right – northwest – all the way to the end of the plane trees, and then turn right again – northeast – through the underpass. The name of the beach area's main artery changes every ten blocks or so, but the section nearest the station underpass is called Viale Amerigo Vespucci.

One of the first nice **hotels** you'll come to along the tree-lined streets is the bright and friendly *Villa Lalla*, Viale Vittorio Veneto 22 (☎0541.55.155, fax 0541.23.570, *www.villalalla.com*; ③). A little closer to the beach is the delightful *Villa Adriatica*, Viale Vespucci 3 (☎0541.54.599, fax 0541.26.962, *villaadriatica@iper.net*; ③), with a pool and all amenities. Further down the main thoroughfare towards the south, there's the chic luxurious four-star *La Gradisca*, Viale Fiume 1 (☎0541.25.200, fax 0541.56.299, *gradisca@metha.com*; ⑤), where the décor inside and out is like the over-the-top set of a Fellini film. Next, a few blocks further south, comes one of the best of Rimini's more affordable hotels, the *Verudella*, Viale Tripoli 238 (☎0541.391.124; ③), quite smart, and run by a friendly brother-and-sister management. The *Carducci*, Viale Carducci 15 (☎0541.391.780; ②) is appealing, and spotless too, down a quiet side street two blocks south of Piazzale Tripoli. Down another leafy side street between Piazzale Tripoli and Piazzale B. Croce, the welcoming, if rather basic, *Donau*, Viale Alfieri 12 (☎0541.381.302; ③), does a wonderful buffet breakfast, as does the *Nancy*, Viale Leopardi 11 (☎0541.381.731; ④), an attractive villa in a lush garden, in a street parallel one block further south. A much more basic choice is the *Bel Ami* at Via Metastasio 4 (☎0541.381.643; ②), located in a peaceful, shady side street, three blocks south of Piazzale B. Croce.

Among the **campsites** reachable by bus from Rimini station are *Camping Italia International,* 2km along the coast at Via Toscanelli 112, Viserba (☎0541.722.882; bus #2, #4 or #8 from outside the station; late May to Sept 20); *Camping Belvedere*, 5km up the coast at Via Grazia Verenin 9, Viserbella, (☎0541.720.960; bus #4 from the station; June–Sept); and *Camping Maximum International,* close to the airport at Viale Principe di Piemonte 57, Miramare (☎0541.372.602; bus #10 or #11 from the station; May–Sept). Further from the city, there are also smaller, more attractive sites, worth considering if you have your own transport – *Comunità Agro-Turistica La Ruspante* (☎0541.758.057; summer months only), at Via Balduccia 862, San Ermete – 9km from Rimini – with a swimming pool; and *Camping Green* (☎0541.346.929; April–Nov) at Via Vespucci 8, San Mauro Mare, 15km north of Rimini. The latter is also just 1km north from Gatteo a Mare or 1km south from Bellária station.

The Town

There are two parts to Rimini. The belt of land east of the rail line is taken up mostly by holiday accommodation, leading down to the main drag of souvenir shops, restaurants and video arcades that stretches 9km north to the suburbs of Viserba and Torre Pedrera and 7km south to Miramare. Out of season, hotel windows are boarded up and neon signs are wrapped in black plastic to protect against the gales, and Rimini's activity contracts around the Parco dell'Indipendenza and the old town, inland. This is the second, often unseen part of Rimini, a ten-minute walk west from the train station – stone buildings clustered around the twin squares of Piazza Tre Martiri and Piazza Cavour, bordered by the port-canal and town ramparts.

On the southern and northern edges of the old centre respectively, the **Arco d'Augusto** and **Ponte Tiberio** sit just inside the ramparts, built at the beginning of the first century AD and BC respectively and testifying to Rimini's importance as a Roman colony. The patched-up Arco was built at the point where Via Emilia joined Via Flaminia. Rimini's other Roman remains consist of the **Anfiteatro**, of which there are sparse foundations off Via Roma, just south of the train station.

The city passed into the hands of the papacy in the eighth century and was subject to a series of disputes that left it in the hands of the Guelph family of Malatesta. Just south of the Ponte Tiberio, **Piazza Tre Martiri** and **Piazza Cavour** are the two main squares. Piazza Cavour has a statue of Pope Paul V and the Gothic **Palazzo del Podestà**; the square was rebuilt in the 1920s, and purists argue that it was ruined, although its fishtail battlements are still impressive enough. Buskers play here, and bikes and Vespas converge from all directions. Opposite, beyond the sixteenth-century fountain incorporating Roman reliefs, the **Porticus Piscarias** shades bookstalls worth a browse. **Castel Sigismondo**, in the adjoining **Piazza Malatesta**, designed and built in 1446 by Sigismondo Malatesta, holds a museum of ethnography, **Museo delle Culture Extraeuropee "Dinz Rialto"** (Mon–Fri 8.30am–1.30pm, Sat & Sun 3.30–6.30pm; L4000/€2.07), with a fine collection of Oceanic and pre-Columbian art. The **Museo della Città** at Via L. Tonini 1 (daily 9am–1.30pm & 3.30–6.30pm, closed Mon afternoon; L6000/€3.10) has a collection of works of art dating from the fourteenth to the nineteenth centuries, the highlight of which is Giovanni Bellini's pietà.

The Malatesta family provided the town's best-known monument, the **Tempio Malatestiano** just east of here on Via 4 Novembre (daily 7.30am–12.30pm & 3.30–7pm; free), a strange-looking building because it was left unfinished, but nevertheless one of the masterworks of the Italian Renaissance. Originally a Franciscan Gothic church, in 1450 Leon Battista Alberti transformed the building for Sigismondo Malatesta, a *condittiero* with an unparalleled reputation for evil, and it's an odd mixture of private chapel and personal monument. His long list of alleged crimes include rape, incest, plunder and looting, not to mention the extreme oppression of his subjects. The temple kept, rather disingenuously, its dedication to St Francis, but this didn't faze the pope at the time, Pius II, who condemned its graceful blend of pagan ornaments and classical hedonism, branding it "a temple of devil-worshippers".

Pius was angered enough to publicly consign Sigismondo to hell, burning an effigy of him in the streets of Rome. This had no effect on Sigismondo, who treated the church as a private memorial chapel to his great love, Isotta degli Atti. Their initials are linked in emblems all over the church, and the Malatesta armorial bearing – the elephant – appears almost as often. Trumpeting elephants, with their ears flying upwards, or elephants with their trunks entwined, decorate the screens between the side aisles and naves; chubby putti, nymphs and shepherds play, surrounded by bunches of black grapes, in a decidedly un-Christian celebration of humanism. There are a number of fine artworks, now restored and very spick and span: a *Crucifix* attributed to Giotto, friezes and reliefs by Agostino di Duccio and a fresco by Piero della Francesca of Sigismondo himself. All in all, it's an appropriate attraction for Rimini, its qualities of pleasurable extravagance almost an emblem for a town that thrives on excess.

Eating and drinking

As far as **eating** goes, the seafront is the best place to do it cheaply, with hundreds of pizza bars for on-your-feet refuelling. There are also some extremely ritzy places, where formal dress is obligatory, but most of the interesting restaurants are in the old town.

For **snacks**, Via Garibaldi, which leads inland from Piazza Tre Martiri, has several pizza-by-the-slice places or seek out a shop on Via Bonsi selling *piada* – pitta-type bread with hot fillings of mozzarella, tomato and prosciutto. The tiny rosticceria nearby at Via Garibaldi 65 has three or four tables, which are usually full by 7.30pm – though it closes at 9pm. You can grab a variety of snacks, from well-made burgers to seafood salad, at the *Paninoteca* at Corso d'Augosto 226; there are places to sit and a good jukebox.

For **sit-down food**, *Osteria de Börg*, at Via Forzieri 12 (closed Mon), is definitely the place to head for first, a relaxed and moderately priced place serving Romagnolo cooking with innovations, such as *cappelletti* (filled pasta) in carrot sauce, fish kebabs, meat roasted over an open fire and a dozen different vegetable dishes. *Pic-Nic*, Via Tempio Malatestiano 30 (closed Mon), does reasonably priced pizzas, as well as pasta, crepes – and game. *Rimini Key* (closed Tues) has a number of special menus from L20,000/€10.33 as well as pizzas, and is in a prime location for catching Rimini's evening cruising along the seafront on Piazzale Croce. *Buliroun*, Piazza Kennedy 2 (closed Mon), is fairly reliable, while *Acero Rosso,* on the other side of the Ponte Tiberio, at Viale Tiberio 11 (closed Mon), is a more expensive fish restaurant. Among the top restaurants along the seafront, *Lo Squero,* (closed Tues) Lungomare Tintori 7, offers great shellfish on a leafy terrace with beach views. For a change of cuisine, try the very affordable Chinese food at *Il Mandarino*, Via Dante 39 (closed Wed), between the station and the old town.

In the suburb of Covignano, en route to *Paradiso* (see "Nightlife" below), the *Dalla Maria* at Via Grazie 81, is a good-value restaurant serving dependable Romagnolo cooking for L40,000/€20.66. Another restaurant that merits the journey is *Bastian Contrario* (the name means "Awkward Customer"; closed Mon), 5km out of town at Via Marecchiese 312 in Spadarolo (bus #20), serving well-priced regional cooking. A bargain version of the same is available at *La Baracca* (closed Wed) on the same road at no. 373.

Nightlife

Rimini's **nightlife** happens along the seafront. Above all Rimini is a place to go **clubbing**: the town has become the Italian Ibiza and is a favourite destination for those who want to club the summer away. The evening's cruising starts at 10pm or 11pm, along the seafront, shortly after which people then move on to the first club, either in their cool convertibles and jeeps or by a nightbus called the Blue Line, which operates through the night (10.30pm–sunrise) and serves two routes: the first along the length of the coast, from Bellariva to Cattólica; the second from Rimini to Covignano for club *Paradiso*. Pick up either route at Piazzale Kennedy; nightly bus passes cost L4000/€2.07, tickets available on board. For up-to-date information on the Rimini club scene, check the **listings** in the weekly *Chiamami Città* or the widely available *Guida d'Estate*.

Paradiso, at Via Covignano 260 (☎0541.751.132), is perhaps the most consistently popular club, with great dance music as well as various happenings, such as fashion shows, performances and other, often art-based events, featuring guest spots by DJs, designers and artists from other European countries.

Other places with style and good dance music are scattered among the small resorts that fringe Rimini, again all served by the Blue Line bus. **Riccione** has a lively club scene centred around garage and techno with *Pascià* at Via Sardegna 30 (☎0541.604.207), *Prince* at Via Tre Baci 49 (☎0541.691.209) and, probably the most famous club in Italy, *Cocoricò*, at Via Chieti 44 (☎0541.605.183), where thousands congregate every weekend under an enormous glass pyramid to rave to the latest in Italian techno. To the south of Riccione are *Byblos* – revival/commercial sounds – at Piazza Castello 24 (☎0541.690.252), in **Misano Monte**; and *Echoes Trade Mark* – trance and techno – at Via Del Carro 40 (☎0541.610.350), in **Misano Adriatico**.

For **quieter evenings**, *Arena Astra*, at Viale Vespucci 131, Misano Adriatico, to the south, shows alternative and rerun movies in the open air in July and August. More sedately still, there's a classical music festival, the Sagra Musicale Malatestiana, throughout the summer in the Tempio Malatesta. It's also worth checking at the tourist office or in the listings (see above) to see if and when the independent film festivals in Bellaria (to the north) and the Rimini-Cinema in Rimini itself are running – both appropriate events for Fellini's home town.

Listings

Airport enquiries ☎0541.715.711.

Car rental Avis, Viale Trieste 160 (☎0541.51.256); Europcar, Via Giovanni XXIII 126 (☎0541.54.746); Mondaini, Viale Tripoli 160 (☎0541.782.646).

Emergency ☎112.

Doctor Rimini Soccorso on 24hr call on ☎118 , or Infermi hospital ☎0541.705.111.

Internet access Main tourist office (see p.444) L4000/€2.07 per hr.

Laundry Lavanderia Italia '90, 11e Viale Giusti, just off the seafront between Piazzale Tripolo and Piazzale B. Croce.

Pharmacy Via IV Novembre 39/41 (daily except Thurs 8.30am–12.30pm & 4–8pm; ☎0541.24.414); when closed, details of all-night services are posted outside.

Post office Main office on Largo Giulio Cesare (Mon–Fri 8.15am–5.30pm, Sat 8.15am–1pm); smaller branch at Piazzale Tripoli 4 (Mon–Fri 8.10am–1.30pm, Sat 8.10–11.50am).

Taxis Radiotaxi Cooperative (☎0541.50.020 or 0541.51.488); 24hr rank outside the train station.

Telephones Telecom Italia at Piazza Ferrari 34 (summer daily 8am–10pm).

Travel agent Miramare, Piazza Ferrari 22 (☎0541.28.820), does discount tickets.

Around Rimini: Santarcángelo and San Marino

The countryside around Rimini is attractive: small hilltop towns and lush gentle valleys covered with firs and chestnuts, much of it connected to the coast by bus. **SANTARCÁNGELO**, 11km inland and easily accessible by bus or train from Rimini, is worth the short trip for its steep medieval streets and thirteenth-century **fortress** (June–Sept Tues, Thurs & Sat 10am–noon & 4–7pm; L5000/€2.58). Carved into the hillside on the edge of the village are some artificial caves, a dank hide-out for early Christians in the seventh century. The best bet for local **accommodation** is the campsite at *La Ruspante* (see p.445), but if you need advice follow signs to the **tourist office** at Via C. Battisti 5 (closed Oct–April, ☎0541.624.270, *iat.santarcangelo@iper.net*). It's also worth visiting Santarcángelo for the village's **restaurants**, of which *Da Lazaroun* at Via del Platano 21 (closed Thurs) is recommended. *Osteria della Violina*, Vicolo d'Enzi 4 (booking advisable, ☎0541.620.416; closed Wed), occupies a seventeenth-century palazzo with internal courtyard, and has a cheaper section downstairs serving *piatti poveri* "poor dishes", which are chalked up on a board and washed down with *Sangiovese* wine.

Santarcángelo is very different from the region's second tourist attraction (after the beach), the **REPUBLIC OF SAN MARINO** – an unashamed, though not entirely unpleasant, tourist destination that trades on its nearly two millennia of precariously maintained autonomy. Said to have been founded around 300 AD by a monk fleeing the persecutions of Diocletian, it has its own mint, produces its own postage stamps, and has an army of around a thousand men. The ramparts and medieval-style buildings of the citadel above Borgomaggiore, also called "San Marino", restored this century, are mildly interesting; there is a trumped-up **waxworks museum** in Via Lapicidi Marini 17 (daily: April–Sept 8.30am–6.30pm; Oct–March 8.30am–12.30pm & 2–5.30pm; L6000/€3.10), a **stamp museum** in Piazza Belzotti in Borgomaggiore (Mon & Thurs 8.15am–6pm, Tues, Wed & Fri, 8.15am–2.15pm; free), and other places where you can view suits of armour, as well as tacky souvenir shops and restaurants. And you can also get your passport officially stamped, for only L2000/€1.03, by the border guards or at the **information** office at Contrada del Collegio (Mon–Fri 8.30am–6.30pm, Sat & Sun 9am–1pm & 2–6pm, ☎0549.882410 or 0549.882.914). But all the touristy tawdriness aside, it's a good place just to stroll around; the walk up through town to the **rocce**, battlemented castles along the highest three ridges, is worth the effort for the all-round views. Below, in Borgomaggiore, is Giovanni Michelucci's "fearless and controversial" modernist church, built in the 1960s, with a roof that seems to cascade down in waves.

travel details

TRAINS

Bologna to: Ancona (hourly; 2hr 15min); Cesena (20 daily; 1hr); Faenza (hourly; 45min); Ferrara (hourly; 30min); Fidenza (hourly; 1hr 10min); Florence (hourly; 1hr); Forlì (hourly; 50min); Ímola (hourly; 30min); Milan (hourly; 2hr 35min); Modena (every 30 min; 20min); Parma (every 30 min; 50min); Piacenza (hourly; 1hr 30min); Ravenna (13 daily; 1hr 20min); Reggio Emilia (every 30 min; 40min); Rimini (hourly; 1hr 20min).

Faenza to: Brisighella (15 daily; 10min).

Ferrara to: Ravenna (16 daily; 1hr 15min); Rimini (9 daily; 2hr 15min).

Fidenza to: Busseto (14 daily; 15min); Cremona (15 daily; 35min); Salsomaggiore (every 30 min; 7min).

Modena to: Carpi (hourly; 12min); Mantua (14 daily; 1hr 20min); Verona (9 daily; 2hr).

Parma to: Brescia (10 daily; 2hr); La Spezia (8 daily; 2hr 15min).

Piacenza to: Cremona (6 daily; 30min).

Rimini to: Santarcángelo (6 daily; 8min).

BUSES

Bologna to: Ímola (every 15min; 1hr); Marzabotto (hourly; 15min); Sasso Marconi (every 15min; 45min); Vergato (hourly; 1hr); Vignola (hourly; 1hr).

Ferrara to: Bosco della Mesola (3 daily; 2hr); Codigoro (1 daily; 2hr 45min); Comacchio (10 daily; 1hr 10min).

Fidenza to: Fontanellato (3 daily; 25min); Soragna (9 daily; 20min); Tabiano (8 daily; 10min).

Forlì to: Bertinoro (8 daily; 25min).

Ímola to: Dozza (5 daily; 15min).

Modena to: Carpi (20 daily; 40min); Fanano (8 daily; 2hr); Fossoli (6 daily; 17min); Montefiorino (5 daily; 1hr 50min); Pievepélago (7 daily; 3hr 10min); Sestola (7 daily; 2hr); Vignola (8 daily; 40min).

Parma to: Bardi (5 daily; 1hr 10min); Busseto/Le Roncole (5 daily; 1hr); Calestano (7 daily; 1hr); Corniglio (2 daily; 1hr 20min); Fontanellato (6 daily; 35min); Langhirano (hourly; 45min); Monchio (3 daily; 2hr); Noceto (9 daily; 35min); Rigoso (3 daily; 2hr 30min); Roncole Verdi (5 daily; 50min); Salsomaggiore Terme (10 daily; 1hr); Soragna (5 daily; 40min); Torrechiara (hourly; 30min).

Piacenza to: Bobbio (12 daily; 1hr 15min); Castell'Arquato (10 daily; 1hr); Lugagnano (10 daily; 1hr); Rustigazzo (6 daily; 1hr).

Ravenna to: Classe (every 30 min; 10min); Marina di Ravenna (every 30 min; 20min); Marina Romea (10 daily: 20min); Mésola (2 daily; 2hr); Punta Marina (every 30 min; 15min).

Reggio Emilia to: Busana (3 daily; 1hr 55min); Casina (15 daily; 50min); Castelnuovo ne'Monti (15 daily; 1hr 20min); Ligonchio (3 daily; 2hr 30min).

Rimini to: Rome (2 daily in summer, 2 weekly in winter; 5hr 30min); San Marino (hourly; 30min); Santarcángelo (hourly; 30min).

Salsomaggiore to: Tabiano Bagni (hourly; 20min).

CHAPTER EIGHT

TUSCANY

T uscany harbours the classic landscapes of Italy, familiar from Renaissance paintings and TV travel shows alike, with their backdrop of medieval hill-towns, rows of slender cypress trees, vineyards and olive groves, and artfully sited villas and farmhouses. It's a picture that has long held an irresistible attraction for northern Europeans.

The expat's perspective may be distorted, but Tuscany is indeed the essence of Italy in many ways. The national language evolved from Tuscan dialect, a supremacy ensured by Dante, who wrote the *Divine Comedy* in the vernacular of his birthplace, Florence, and Tuscan writers such as Petrarch and Boccaccio. But what makes this area pivotal to the culture of Italy and all of Europe is the **Renaissance**, which fostered painting, sculpture and architecture that comprise an intrinsic part of a Tuscan tour. The very name by which we refer to this extraordinarily creative era was coined by a Tuscan, Giorgio Vasari, who wrote in the sixteenth century of the "rebirth" of the arts. **Florence** was the most active centre of the Renaissance, flourishing principally through the all-powerful patronage of the Medici dynasty. Every eminent artistic figure from Giotto onwards – Masaccio, Brunelleschi, Alberti, Donatello, Botticelli, Leonardo da Vinci, Michelangelo – is represented here, in an unrivalled gathering of churches, galleries and museums.

Few people react entirely positively to Florence's crowds and its rather draining commercialism. **Siena** provokes less ambiguous responses. This is one of the great medieval cities of Europe, almost perfectly preserved, and with superb works of art in its religious and secular buildings. Its beautiful Campo – the central, scallop-shaped market square – is the scene, too, of Tuscany's one unmissable festival, the **Palio**, which sees bareback horse-riders careering around the cobbles amid the brightest display of pageantry this side of Rome. Other major cities, **Pisa** and **Lucca**, provide convenient entry points to the region, either by air (via Pisa's airport) or along the coastal rail route from Genoa. **Arezzo** serves as the classic introduction to Tuscany if you're approaching from the south (Rome) or east (Perugia). All three have their splendours – Pisa its Leaning Tower, Lucca a string of Romanesque churches, Arezzo an outstanding fresco cycle by Piero della Francesca.

ACCOMMODATION PRICE CODES

Throughout this guide, prices per person are given for **youth hostels** and assume Hostelling International (HI) membership. **Hotel** accommodation is coded on a scale from ① to ⑨, reflecting the cost of the cheapest double room in each establishment in high season. The price bands to which these codes refer are as follows:

① Up to L60,000/€30.99
② L60,000–90,000/€30.99–46.48
③ L90,000–120,000/€46.48–61.98
④ L120,000–150,000/€61.98–77.47
⑤ L150,000–200,000/€77.47–103.29

⑥ L200,000–250,000/€103.29–129.11
⑦ L250,000–300,000/€129.11–154.94
⑧ L300,000–400,000/€154.94–206.58
⑨ over L400,000/€206.58

(See p.32 for a full explanation.)

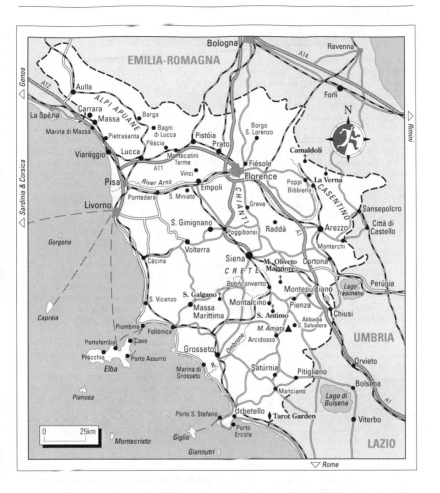

Tucked away to the west and south of Siena are dozens of small **hill-towns** that, for many, epitomize the region. **San Gimignano** is the best-known, and is worth visiting as much for its spectacular array of frescoes as for its much-photographed bristle of medieval tower-houses, though it's now a little too popular for its own good. **Montepulciano**, **Pienza** and **Cortona** are each superbly located and dripping with atmosphere, but the best candidates for a Tuscan hill-town escape are little-mentioned places such as **Volterra**, **Massa Maríttima** or **Pitigliano**, in each of which tourism has yet to undermine local character.

If the Tuscan **countryside** has a fault, it's the popularity that its seductiveness has brought, and you may find lesser-known sights proving most memorable – remote monasteries like **Monte Oliveto Maggiore**, the sulphur spa of **Bagno Vignoni**, or the striking open-air art gallery of the **Tarot Garden**. The one area where Tuscany fails to impress is its over-developed **coast**, with uninspired beach-umbrella compounds filling every last scrap of sand. The Tuscan **islands** have rather more going for them – **Elba**

REGIONAL FOOD AND WINE

Tuscan cooking has been a seminal influence in Italian cuisine generally. Its guiding principle is simplicity: classic Tuscan *antipasti* are peasant fare: *bruschetta* is stale bread, toasted and dressed with oil and garlic, *crostini* is toast and pâté. **Olive oil** is the essential flavouring, used as a dressing for salads, a medium for frying and to drizzle over bread or vegetables and into soups and stews just before serving.

Soups are very popular – Tuscan menus always include either *ribollita*, a hearty stew of vegetables, beans and chunks of bread and/or *zuppa di farro*, thick with spelt (a barley-like grain). Fish restaurants around the region try to copy *cacciucco*, a spiced fish and seafood soup, but the best place in Italy to try it is the town of its birth, Livorno. White cannellini **beans** (*fagioli*) are another favourite, turning up in salads, with pasta (*tuoni e lampo*) or just dressed with olive oil. Tuscany is not known for its **pasta**, but many towns in the south serve *pici*, a local variety of thick spaghetti. **Meat** is kept plain, often grilled, and Florentines will often profess to liking nothing better than a good *bistecca alla fiorentina* (rare char-grilled steak), or the simple rustic dishes of *arista* (roast pork loin stuffed with rosemary and garlic) or *pollo alla diavola* (chicken flattened, marinated and then grilled with herbs). Hunters' fare such as *cinghiale* (wild boar) and *coniglio* (rabbit) often turns up in hill-town *trattorie*. Spinach is often married with ricotta to make gnocchi, used as a pasta filling, and in *crespoline* (pancakes) or between two chunks of *focaccia* and eaten as a street or bar snack. Sheep's milk *pecorino* is the most widespread Tuscan **cheese** (best in Pienza), but the most famous is the oval *marzolino* from the Chianti region, which is eaten either fresh or ripened. **Dessert** menus will often include *cantuccini*, hard, almond-flavoured biscuits to be dipped in a glass of Vinsanto (sweet dessert wine) – best known as *biscottini* in Prato – but Siena is the main source of sweet treats, such as almond macaroons and *panforte*, a rich and sticky cake full of nuts and fruit.

Tuscany has some of Italy's finest **wines**. Three top names, which all bear the exclusive DOCG mark (and price-tags to match), are Chianti Classico, Brunello di Montalcino and Vino Nobile di Montepulciano – not the sort of thing you'd knock back at a trattoria. There are dozens of other Chianti varieties, most of them excellent, but it can be difficult to find a bargain: it's worth finding out which labels to aim for before buying. Both Montalcino and Montepulciano produce *rosso* varieties that are more pocket-friendly, and other names to look for include Carmignano and Rosso delle Colline Lucchesi. Two notable whites are dry Vernaccia di San Gimignano and the fresh Galestro. Tuscany is also renowned for Vinsanto, a sweet, strong dessert wine made from grapes left to dry in the sun.

may be a victim of its own allure, but the smaller islands such as **Giglio** and **Capraia** retain a tranquil isolation.

Tuscany's **tourist office** is based at Via di Novoli 26, I-50127 Firenze (☎055.438.2111, *www.turismo.toscana.it*) – their Web site gives access to a comprehensive accommodation database and links to all fifteen of Tuscany's area tourist offices. Finding **accommodation** can be a major problem in the summer: you should definitely reserve in advance, even at budget level. Be warned that the region is also expensive, even by northern Italian standards, with few hotel doubles costing less than L80,000/€42.32 in high season (L100,000/€51.65 in Florence). **Agritourism** is big business, with a plethora of family-run places dotted around the countryside offering anything from budget rooms in a farmhouse up to luxury apartments within restored castles or Renaissance villas set amidst wine estates. The regional government's Web site (*www.agriturismo.regione.toscana.it*) has plenty of information. Call the toll-free number ☎800.570.530 for timetable and fare information for all forms of **transport** – trains, buses and boats.

FLORENCE (FIRENZE)

Since early in the nineteenth century **FLORENCE** has been celebrated as the most beautiful city in Italy. Stendhal staggered around its streets in a perpetual stupor of delight; the Brownings sighed over its idyllic charms; and E.M. Forster's *Room with a View* portrayed it as the great southern antidote to the sterility of Anglo-Saxon life. For most people Florence comes close to living up to the myth only in its first, resounding impressions. The pinnacle of Brunelleschi's stupendous cathedral dome dominates the cityscape, and the close-up view is even more breathtaking, with the multicoloured **Duomo** rising behind the marble-clad **Baptistry**. Wander from there down towards the River Arno and the attraction still holds: beyond the broad Piazza della Signoria, site of the towering **Palazzo Vecchio**, the river is spanned by the medieval shop-lined **Ponte Vecchio**, with the gorgeous church of **San Miniato al Monte** glistening on the hill behind it.

Yet after registering these marvellous sights, it's hard to stave off a sense of disappointment, for much of Florence is a city of narrow streets and heavy-set, oppressively dour *palazzi* that show only iron-barred windows and massive, studded doors to the outside world. The alienating effects of this physical entrenchment are redoubled both by an unending tide of **mass tourism**. You'll find light relief to be in short supply.

The fact is, the best of Florence is to be seen indoors. Under the patronage of the **Medici** family, the city's artists and thinkers were instigators of the shift from the medieval to the modern world-view, and churches, galleries and museums are the places to get to grips with their achievement. The development of the Renaissance can be plotted in the vast picture collection of the **Uffizi** and in the sculpture of the **Bargello** and the **Museo dell'Opera del Duomo**. Equally revelatory are the fabulously decorated chapels of **Santa Croce** and **Santa Maria Novella**, forerunners of such astonishing creations as Masaccio's superb frescoes in the **Cappella Brancacci**, and Fra' Angelico's serene paintings in the monks' cells at **San Marco**. The Renaissance emphasis on harmony and rational design is expressed with unrivalled eloquence in Brunelleschi's architecture, specifically in the churches of **San Lorenzo**, **Santo Spirito** and the **Cappella dei Pazzi**. The full genius of Michelangelo, the dominant creative figure of sixteenth-century Italy, is on display in the fluid design of San Lorenzo's **Biblioteca Laurenziana** and the marble statuary of the **Cappelle Medicee** and the **Accademia** – home of the *David*. Every quarter of Florence can boast a church or collection worth an extended call, and the enormous **Palazzo Pitti** south of the river constitutes a museum district on its own.

Some history

The Roman colony of Florentia was established in 59 BC; expansion was rapid, based on trade along the Arno. In the sixth century AD the city fell to the barbarian hordes of

---

PLANNING A VISIT

Three days is the minimum to get a feel for Florence and its trappings. Since many museums close on Mondays, and many churches close to tourists on Sundays, you'd do best to schedule a midweek visit. Watch out, too, for **opening-times**: some museums only open in the mornings, the Baptistry only opens in the afternoons, and almost all churches close in the middle of the day. The famous sights, notably the Duomo and the Uffizi, can get absurdly overcrowded – on a whistle-stop visit, it makes sense to reject them in favour of the under-visited Bargello, Cappella Brancacci and Cappelle Medicee. Booking entry to museums in advance is strongly recommended (see p.455).

Totila, then the **Lombards** and then Charlemagne's **Franks**. In 1078 Countess Mathilda of Tuscia supervised the construction of new fortifications, and in the year of her death – 1115 – granted Florence the status of an **independent city**. Around 1200, the first *Arti* (Guilds) were formed to promote the interests of traders and bankers in the face of conflict between the pro-imperial **Ghibelline** faction and the pro-papal **Guelphs**. In 1260, the Guelph-backed regime of Florence's *Primo Popolo*, a government of the mercantile class, was ousted after Siena's Ghibelline army defeated Florence. By the 1280s the Guelphs were back in power through the *Secondo Popolo*; the exclusion of the nobility from government in 1293 was the most dramatic measure in a programme of political reform that invested power in the *Signoria*, a council drawn from the major guilds. The mighty Palazzo della Signoria – now known as the **Palazzo Vecchio** – was raised as a visible demonstration of authority over a huge city: at this time, Florence had a population around 100,000, a thriving mercantile sector and a highly developed banking system (the **florin** was common currency across Europe). Strife within the Guelph camp marked the start of the fourteenth century, and then in the 1340s the two largest banks collapsed and the **Black Death** struck, destroying up to half the city's population.

The political rise of **Cosimo de' Medici**, later dubbed Cosimo il Vecchio ("the Old"), was to some extent due to his family's sympathies with the smaller guilds. The **Medici** fortune had been made by the banking prowess of Cosimo's father, Giovanni Bicci de' Medici, and Cosimo used the power conferred by wealth to great effect. Through his patronage of such figures as Brunelleschi and Donatello, Florence became the centre of artistic activity in Italy.

The ascendancy continued under Cosimo's grandson **Lorenzo il Magnifico**, who ruled the city at the height of its artistic prowess. Papal resentment of Florentine independence found an echo in the jealousy of the Pazzi family, one of the city's main rivals to the Medici. The two camps colluded in the **Pazzi conspiracy** of 1478, in which Lorenzo was wounded and his brother Giuliano murdered. Before Lorenzo's death in 1492, the Medici bank failed, and in 1494 Lorenzo's son Piero was obliged to flee. Florentine hearts and minds were seized by the charismatic Dominican monk **Girolamo Savonarola**, who preached on the decadence and corruption of the city. Artists departed in droves. In a symbolic demonstration of the new order, Savonarola and his child spies set about collecting all the trappings of Florence's Medicean culture – books, paintings, tapestries, fancy furniture and clothes – and piled them high in Piazza della Signoria in a **Bonfire of the Vanities**. But such a graphic assault on the past signalled a turning-point: within a year, Savonarola had been found guilty of heresy and treason, and burned alive at the same spot.

After Savonarola, the city functioned peaceably under a republican constitution headed by Piero Soderini, whose chief adviser was his friend **Niccolò Machiavelli**. In 1512 the Medici returned, and in 1516, Giovanni de' Medici became **Pope Leo X**, granting Michelangelo and Leonardo da Vinci major commissions. After the assassination of the tyrannical transvestite Alessandro de' Medici in 1537, Florentine power was handed to a new Cosimo, who seized the Republic of Siena and, in 1569, took the title **Cosimo I**, Grand Duke of Tuscany. The great traditions of Florentine art descended into farce as sycophants such as **Giorgio Vasari** plastered the city with fawning images of Medici power and glory.

Florence's decline was slow and painful. The later Medicis were each more ridiculous than the last: **Francesco** spent most of his thirteen-year reign indoors, obsessed by alchemy; **Ferdinando II** sat back as harvests failed, plagues ran riot and banking and textiles slumped to nothing; the virulently anti-Semitic **Cosimo III** spent 53 years in power cracking down on dissidents; and **Gian Gastone** spent virtually all his time drunk in bed. When Gastone died, in 1737, the Medici line died with him.

Under the terms of a treaty signed by Gian Gastone's sister, **Anna Maria Ludovica**, Florence – and the whole Grand Duchy of Tuscany – passed to Francesco of Lorraine,

FLORENCE'S MUSEUMS

EU citizens under 25 and over 65 get a fifty-percent discount at state-run **museums**, and everyone under 20 gets a twenty-five percent discount at city-run museums. Note that most forbid entry one hour before stated closing times.

There are three museum passes. The L10,000/€5.16 **Musei Fiorentini carnet** gives fifty percent off all the city-run museums (the Cappella Brancacci, Palazzio Vecchio, Santa Maria Novella and half-a-dozen small collections; *www.comune.firenze.it/servizi_pubblici/arte/musei*) plus the private Museo Marini. The L20,000/€10.33 Palazzo Pitti **biglietto cumulativo** gives free entry to the Pitti and the Bóboli gardens for three days. Best of all is the three-day L25,000/€12.91 **Michelangelo itinerary ticket**, giving free entry to the unmissable trio of the Accademia, Cappelle Medicee and Bargello. All these grant only one admission to each museum.

All **state-run** museums (*www.sbas.firenze.it*) allow you to **book in advance**, thereby cutting down on the time you're otherwise likely to spend waiting in very long lines. Currently, it's possible to book at the Uffizi (with or without the Corridoio Vasariano), the Accademia, the Bargello, the Cappelle Medicee, the Museo di San Marco, the Museo Archeologico, and all the Pitti museums. You have to call **Firenze Musei** on ☎055.294.883 (Mon–Fri 8.30am–6.30pm, Sat 8.30am–12.30pm) and state which museums you want, the day and time you wish to enter, and your name; they then give you a **reservation number**. You can reserve from an hour to a year in advance for anything up to thirty people. On the day, you head straight to the dedicated reservations pickup desk, quote your name and number and pay the museum admission charge (in cash only) plus a L3000/€1.55 booking fee per person.

At the time of writing, the only way to pay by **credit card** was online at *www.weekendafirenze.com* or *english.firenze.net*, a minimum of three days in advance. There's a service fee totalling L10,700/€5.52 extra per ticket. Once you're in Florence, you can book **in person** at any of the above museums for entry to any other.

the future Francis I of Austria. Austrian rule lasted until the coming of the French in 1799; after a fifteen-year interval of French control, the Lorraine dynasty was brought back, remaining in residence until the Risorgimento upheavals of 1859. Absorbed into the united Italian state in the following year, Florence became the **capital** of the Kingdom of Italy in 1861, a position it held until 1875.

After 1890, large swathes of the medieval city were **demolished** by government officials and developers; buildings that had stood in the area of what is now Piazza della Repubblica since the early Middle Ages were pulled down to make way for undistinguished office blocks, and old quarters around Santa Croce and Santa Maria Novella were razed. In 1944, the retreating German army blew up all the city's bridges except the Ponte Vecchio and destroyed swathes of medieval architecture. A disastrous **flood** in November 1966 drowned several people and wrecked buildings and works of art. Restoration of damage caused by the flood, and by a 1993 **Mafia car-bomb** that killed five people outside the Uffizi, is still going on. Indeed, monuments and paintings are the basis of Florence's survival in the new century, a state of affairs that gives rise to considerable popular discontent. The development of new industrial parks on the northern outskirts is the latest and most ambitious attempt to break Florence's ever-increasing dependence on its seven million annual **tourists**.

Arrival, information and orientation

Florence's main **train station** is Santa Maria Novella, or "Firenze SMN". Many city and all inter-urban **buses** stop outside. Between 1.30am and 4am, trains stop instead at the

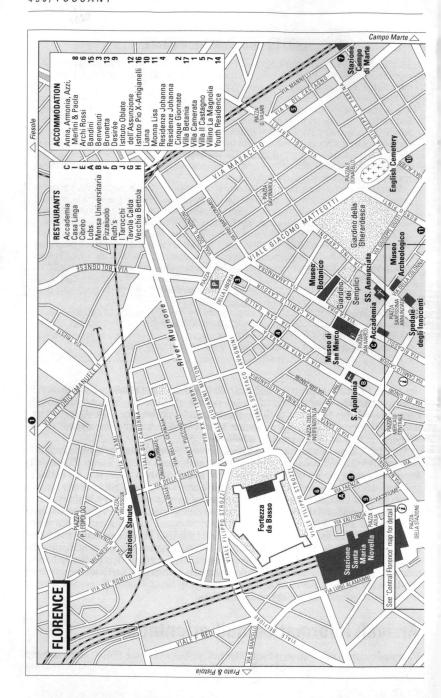

FLORENCE

ACCOMMODATION

Anna, Armonia, Azzi,	8
Merlini & Paola	6
Archi Rossi	15
Bandini	3
Benvenuti	13
Brunetta	9
Desirée	
Istituto Oblate	12
dell'Assunzione	16
Istituto Pio X-Artigianelli	10
Liana	11
Monna Lisa	4
Residenze Johanna	2
Residenze Johanna	17
Cinque Giornate	1
Villa Betania	5
Villa Camerata	7
Villa Il Castagno	14
Villino La Magnolia	
Youth Residence	

RESTAURANTS

Accademia	C
Casa Linga	I
Cibrèo	E
Lobs	A
Mensa Universitaria	B
Pizzaiuolo	F
Ruth's	D
I Tarocchi	G
Tavola Calda	J
Vecchia Bettola	H

Campo Marte △

△ Fiesole

Stazione Campo di Marte

Via Mannelli

Via del Castagno

Piazza G. Vasari

Via Masaccio

English Cemetery

Piazzale Donatello

Giardino della Gherardesca

Museo Archeologico

Museo Botanico

Giardino dei Semplici

SS. Annunziata

Piazza Santissima Annunziata

Accademia

Spedale degli Innocenti

Museo di San Marco

Piazza San Marco

Viale Giacomo Matteotti

Via Camillo Cavour

Via San Gallo

Via Santa Reparata

River Mugnone

Via Trieste

Viale Filippo Strozzi

Fortezza da Basso

Stazione Statuto

Piazza G. Leopoldo

Piazza G. Vusseux

S. Apollonia

Piazza della Libertà

Viale Spartaco Lavagnini

Viale Don Minzoni

Viale Giovanni Milton

Via XX Settembre

Via Faenza

Via Valfonda

Stazione Santa Maria Novella

Piazza della Stazione

Piazza Mercato Centrale

Via Luigi Alamanni

Viale F. Redi

Via del Romito

Viale Belfiore

△ Prato & Pistoia

See 'Central Florence' map for detail

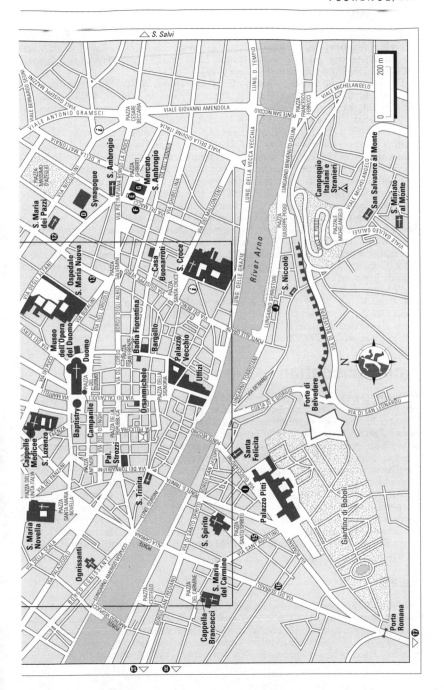

eastern Campo di Marte station, served by nightbus #70. Florence's **Aeroporto Amerigo Vespucci** (*www.safnet.it*), 5km northwest in Perètola, is linked to SMN station by ATAF city bus #62 (every 25min; L1500/€0.77) and SITA buses (hourly; L6000/€3.10). For details of parking, see p.494.

The main **tourist office** is just north of the duomo at Via Cavour 1r (Mon–Sat 8.15am–7.15pm, Sun 8.30am–6.30pm; shorter hours in winter; ☎055.290.832 or 055.290.833, *infoturismo@provincia.fi.it*). There's a smaller office at **Piazza Stazione 4** (Mon–Sat 8.30am–7pm, Sun 8.30am–1.30pm; shorter hours in winter; ☎055.212.245); another one at **Borgo Santa Croce 29r** (same hours; ☎055.234.0444); an information counter within the APT's headquarters at **Via Manzoni 16** (Mon–Sat 9am–6pm; ☎055.23.320); and a desk at **Vespucci airport** (daily 7.30am–11.30pm; ☎055.315.874). Aside from maps and brochures, the most useful item these offices can give you is a photocopied list of the up-to-date opening hours and entrance charges for all the city's museums, which change often. The fat little freebie magazine *Florence Concierge Information*, available from tourist offices, is crammed with ads, walking itineraries and practical information. Florence's excellent what's-on guide is *Firenze Spettacolo*, available monthly from newsagents (L3500/€1.81; *www.firenzespettacolo. it*). On the **Internet**, the APT (*www.firenze.turismo.toscana.it*), the province (*www.provincia.fi.it*) and the municipality (*www.comune.fi.it*) are outclassed by some very useful commercial sites (notably *www.mega.it*, *www.arca.net/florence.htm* and *english.firenze.net*).

ATAF city **buses** have a range of tickets (L1500/€0.77 for 1hr; L2500/€1.29 for 3hr; L6000/€3.10 for 24hr; or the *biglietto multiplo* giving four one-hour rides for L5800/€2.99). Most routes originate at or pass by the train station, where you can get more information from the ATAF kiosk (Mon–Sat 7.15am–1.15pm, Tues & Thurs also 2.45–5.45pm; ☎055.565.0222, *www.ataf.net*).

Accommodation

On the whole, Florence's **accommodation** is over-priced: it is true to say that the welcome and the service you receive is often not on a par with that of other places in Italy. You should always **book in advance**. If you leave it to the last minute, or to save you phoning round, you could get the Consorzio Informazioni Turistiche Alberghiere (ITA) to book for you – they charge from L3000/€1.55 to ten times that, according to the class of hotel, and only take bookings over the counter. There are ITA offices at the Agip service area on the A11 *autostrada* west of Florence (daily 8.30am–8.15pm); at the Chianti Est service area on the A1 *autostrada* to the south (March–Nov same times); and within Florence's train station (daily 8.30am–8.15pm) – in high season, be prepared to spend a couple of hours queueing here. Five upmarket hotels offer substantial **discounts to students** – see the APT's excellent brochure *Studying in Florence: A Guide* for details. The other option is to save money staying outside Florence, at Fiesole, Prato, Pistoia, Empoli or Greve in Chianti, all of which are within a thirty-minute radius by bus or train (see p.495).

Hotels

Prices at the down-market end of Florence's **hotels** have a high-season average in one-star places of around L140,000/€72.30 – and that's without breakfast, which is virtually compulsory in summer, slapping as much as an extra L15,000/€7.75 per person onto the bill. From October to April prices come down a little, and if you arrive in the low season – roughly January to Easter, plus November – you'll find many discounts.

FLORENCE ADDRESSES

Street-numbering runs in relation to the river. If the street or square is parallel to the river, numbers start from the east and proceed towards the west. If the street is perpendicular to the river, the numbering starts from the end nearest the river bank. Odd numbers are on the left side of the street, even on the right.

However, beware that Florence has a complicated double system of street-numbering: commercial establishments (such as bars and restaurants) have **red** numbers (*rosso*), while private buildings have black or blue numbers – and the two systems don't run in tandem. This means, for example, that Via Mosca 35r might be next-door to Via Mosca 89, but several hundred metres from Via Mosca 33. There's no logic or purpose to it at all.

The central area

Alessandra, Borgo Santi Apostoli 17 (☎055.283.438, fax 055.210.619, *www.hotelalessandra.com*). Occupying a sixteenth-century palazzo, steps from the Uffizi, this stylish two-star is justifiably popular. ⑥.

Bavaria, Borgo degli Albizi 26 (☎& fax 055.234.0313). Excellent one-star installed in a sixteenth-century frescoed palazzo, with disappointingly modern interiors and helpful staff. ⑤.

Dali, Via dell'Oriuolo 17 (☎& fax 055.234.0706, *www.hoteldali.com*). Discreet little one-star on a street just behind the Duomo, with cosily furnished rooms (three en suite), a peaceful courtyard and limited parking. ④.

Firenze, Piazza dei Donati 4 (☎055.214.203, fax 055.212.370). Modernized one-star bang in the heart of things, with 54 clean, generic doubles, the best on the upper floors. ④.

Hermitage, Vicolo Marcio 1 (☎055.287.216, fax 055.212.208, *www.hermitagehotel.com*). This welcoming little three-star is steps from the Ponte Vecchio; reception is alongside the roof garden, while above-average guest rooms fill the lower floors, some with river views. ⑧.

Orchidea, Borgo degli Albizi 11 (☎& fax 055.248.0346). Lovely little *locanda* in a twelfth-century palazzo run by a friendly Anglo-Italian couple. Four singles and three doubles, with shared bathrooms. ③.

Scoti, Via Tornabuoni 7 (☎& fax 055.292.128, *hotelscoti@hotmail.com*). Bags of character and a superb central location. The lounge features amazing floor-to-ceiling frescoes and the rooms are light and spacious (none with private bathrooms). ③.

The western city centre

Anna (☎055.239.8322), **Armonia** (☎055.211.146), **Azzi** (☎ & fax 055.213.806), **Marini** (☎055.284.824), **Merlini** (☎055.212.848, fax 055.283.939) and **Paola** (☎055.213.682), all Via Faenza 56. With most of its rooms overlooking the garden, the *Azzi* is the most pleasant of the six one-stars occupying the upper floors of this building, but it tends to get block-booked by a tour operator. The others are all at least tolerable. All ③.

Desirée, Via Fiume 20 (☎055.238.2382, fax 055.291.439, *www.italyhotel.com*). A comfortable two-star with stained-glass windows, simulated antique furniture, and a bath in every room. ⑤.

Elite, Via della Scala 12 (☎055.215.395, fax 055.213.832). Usefully located two-star with pleasant, friendly management and occasional bargain prices. ④.

Ferretti, Via delle Belle Donne 17 (☎055.238.1328, fax 055.219.288, *www.emmeti.it/hferretti*). Pleasant little place in a side-street, with clean bathrooms, better-than-average breakfasts, helpful and informative staff and free Internet access. ④.

Gigliola (☎055.287.981) and **La Romagnola** (☎055.211.597), both Via della Scala 40. Pick of the low-end bunch on this street – a midnight curfew is the only drawback. With a total of 42 rooms between them, they often have space when the others are full. Both ③.

The northern city centre

Casci, Via Cavour 13 (☎055.211.686, fax 055.239.6461, *www.hotelcasci.com*). Excellent family-run two-star. Only two of its 25 rooms face onto busy Via Cavour, both of which are triple-glazed; some of the others look onto the peaceful rear garden. ⑥.

Loggiato dei Serviti, Piazza Santissima Annunziata 3 (☎055.289.592, fax 055.289.595, *www.venere.it/firenze*). A monastery overlooking one of Florence's loveliest squares, with vaulted ceilings, original antiques and all mod cons. Twenty percent student discount (Dec–Feb). ⑧.

Residenze Johanna, Via Bonifacio Lupi 14 (☎055.481.896, fax 055.482.721). Comfortable old place on a residential street just north of San Marco offering peace and quiet in TV-free, phone-free rooms, some of them en suite. ③.

South of the river

Bandini, Piazza Santo Spirito 9 (☎055.215.308, fax 055.282.761). Vast rooms, gorgeous decor and great views from the top-deck loggia make this one of Florence's most attractive – if overpriced – one-stars. ⑤.

Lungarno, Borgo San Jacopo 14 (☎055.27.261, fax 055.268.437, *www.lungarnohotels.com*). Picture windows in all public rooms take full advantage of the romantic Arno view, as do the balconies attached to the best of the blue-and-cream liveried guest rooms. ⑨.

Villa Betania, Viale Poggio Imperiale 23 (☎& fax 055.222.243, *www.villabetania.it*). Fifteenth-century villa 1km south of Porta Romana that has its own, lush gardens and private parking. Fifteen percent student discount (July, Aug & Nov–Feb). Bus #11. ⑦.

Further north and east

Benvenuti, Via Cavour 112 (☎055.572.141, fax 055.586.727, *www.utenti.tripod.it/firenzebenvenuti*). A first-choice two-star in the university quarter, on the corner of Piazza Libertà and Via Matteotti. Bus #1 or #7 to Libertà. ④.

Brunetta, Borgo Pinti 5 (☎055.240.360, fax 055.247.8134). Inexpensive and well placed, a five-minute walk to the east of the duomo, with functional shared-bath rooms. Bus #14 to Salvemini. ③.

Liana, Via V. Alfieri 18 (☎055.246.6004, fax 055.234.4595, *www.venere.it/firenze/liana*). Little hotel that was once the British Embassy and maintains a similar tone, with refined interior decor and a cool, discreet atmosphere. Bus #6 to D'Azeglio. ⑥.

Monna Lisa, Borgo Pinti 27 (☎055.247.9751, fax 055.247.9755, *www.monnalisa.it*). A grim facade conceals a charming and elegant hotel, furnished with original antiques and decor. Go for one of the larger rooms overlooking the lovely internal garden. Bus #6 to Colonna. ⑨.

Residence Johanna Cinque Giornate, Via delle Cinque Giornate 12 (☎ & fax 055.473.377). Quiet villa on a residential street way north; you're given a set of keys and left alone. It has a nice little garden, six good-value en suite doubles, and private parking. Bus #4 or #28 to Statuto. ④.

Villa Il Castagno, Via A. del Castagno 31 (☎055.571.701, fax 055.572.027). Pleasant two-star in a residential area, with plenty of on-street parking. Rooms are generically comfortable. Bus #10, #11 or #17 to Ponte al Pino. ④.

Villino La Magnolia, Via Mannelli 135 (☎055.246.6015, fax 055.226.8900, *www.villinolamagnolia.it*). Tasteful conversion of a family home near Campo di Marte, with marble floors, spacious high-ceilinged guest rooms and modern bathrooms. Internet access and easy parking. Bus #12 to Campo Marte. ⑤.

Hostels and campsites

As well as **hostels**, Florence has student houses, most of them run by religious bodies, which are open to young tourists in summer (June–Oct). A new HI hostel, *Ostello del Carmine*, opens in 2001 at Via del Leone 35, just west of Santo Spirito; prices hadn't been set and the phone number hadn't been assigned at the time of writing; for information, contact *Villa Camerata* (see opposite), surf to *www.hostels-aig.org* or consult the tourist office.

Hostels

Archi Rossi, Via Faenza 94r (☎055.290.804, fax 055.230.2601). A bright and friendly hostel east of the station, with airy rooms and inexpensive meals. Bed in a dorm is L26,000/€13.42; in an en suite quad L35,000/€18.08. Curfew 12.30am.

Istituto Gould, Via dei Serragli 49 (☎055.212.576, fax 055.280.274). Excellent place near Santo Spirito: ask for a quieter back room. Singles are L55,000/€28.40, doubles L78,000/€40.28; also triples and quads. Check in Mon–Fri 9am–1pm & 3–7pm, Sat 9am–1pm. Bus #11, #36 or #37 to Serragli.

Istituto Oblate dell'Assunzione, Borgo Pinti 15 (☎055.248.0582, fax 055.234.6291). Just east of the duomo. Run by nuns but open to men and women. Singles L55,000/€28.40; doubles L110,000/€56.81. No breakfast; midnight curfew. Open late-June, July & Sept.

Istituto Pio X – Artigianelli, Via dei Serragli 106 (☎055.225.044 or 055.225.008). Quality hostel with friendly, relaxed staff. Aim to arrive by 9am, as its 64 beds soon get snapped up. Singles are L25,000/€12.91; doubles, triples and quads at L23,000/€11.87 per person. Minimum stay two days. Midnight curfew. Bus #11, #36 or #37 to Serragli.

Santa Monaca, Via Santa Monaca 6 (☎055.268.338, fax 055.280.185, *www.ostello.it*). Very popular 115-bed non-HI hostel near Santo Spirito. Separate male and female dorms, kitchen and laundry facilities, free hot showers and inexpensive meals. L25,000/€12.91 for a dorm bed. Curfew 1am. Bus #11, #36 or #37 to Serragli.

Suore Oblate dello Spirito Santo, Via Nazionale 8 (☎055.239.8202, fax 055.239.8129). Near the station. Run by nuns, and open to women and married couples only; very clean and pleasant. Doubles L80,000/€42.32; triples L90,000/€46.48. Midnight curfew (mid-June to Oct).

Villa Camerata, Viale Righi 2 (☎055.601.451, fax 055.610.300). HI hostel occupying a sixteenth-century frescoed villa in a beautiful park below Fiesole. Films in English; inexpensive meals; midnight curfew. Dorms L25,000/€12.91; also doubles. Bus #17a or #17b, plus a walk up the hill.

Youth Residence Firenze, Viale Sanzio 16 (☎055.233.5558, fax 055.230.6392, *european@dada.it*). Upmarket non-smoking hostel west of Santo Spirito; small all-en suite dorms (max five beds per room); indoor swimming pool; no curfew. Bus #12 to Sanzio.

Campsites

Italiani e Stranieri, Viale Michelangelo 80 (☎055.681.1977). Always crowded, owing to a superb hillside location and regular late-night disco. Kitchen facilities. Bus #13. April–Oct.

Panoramico, Via Peramonda 1, Fiesole. See p.496.

Villa Camerata, Viale Righi 2 (☎055.600.315). Small, basic, year-round site in the grounds of the HI hostel. Midnight curfew.

The City

Greater Florence now spreads several kilometres down the Arno Valley and onto the hills north and south of the city, but the major sights are contained in an area that can be crossed on foot in under thirty minutes.

A short walk southeast from the train station brings you to **Piazza del Duomo**, site of the **Duomo** itself and the neighbouring **Baptistry**. The compact district from here south to the river is the inner core, the area into which most of the tourists are packed, and which boasts the best-preserved medieval parts of Florence and the majority of its fashionable streets. Just south of the duomo is Florence's outstanding sculpture gallery, the **Bargello**. The large **Piazza della Signoria**, some 300m south of the duomo, is overlooked by the **Palazzo Vecchio** and the famous picture gallery of the **Uffizi**.

West of the duomo, and backing onto the train station, is the unmissable church of **Santa Maria Novella**. Immediately north of the duomo is the grand church of **San Lorenzo**, at the heart of a throng of market stalls around the covered **Mercato Centrale**. Clustered together just northeast of San Lorenzo are the monastery of **San Marco**, with its paintings by Fra' Angelico; the **Accademia**, home of Michelangelo's *David*; and **Piazza Santissima Annunziata**, Florence's most attractive square. The main attraction in the eastern quarters of the city centre is the vast Franciscan church of **Santa Croce**.

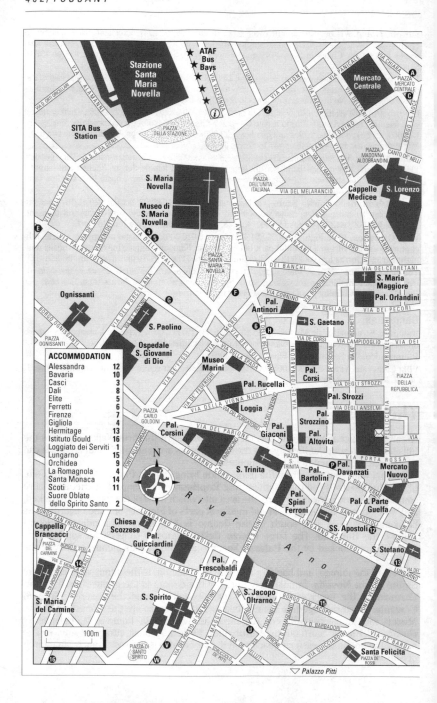

ACCOMMODATION

Alessandra	12
Bavaria	10
Casci	3
Dali	8
Elite	5
Ferretti	6
Firenze	7
Gigliola	4
Hermitage	13
Istituto Gould	16
Loggiato dei Serviti	1
Lungarno	15
Orchidea	9
La Romagnola	4
Santa Monaca	14
Scoti	11
Suore Oblate	
dello Spirito Santo	2

▽ *Palazzo Pitti*

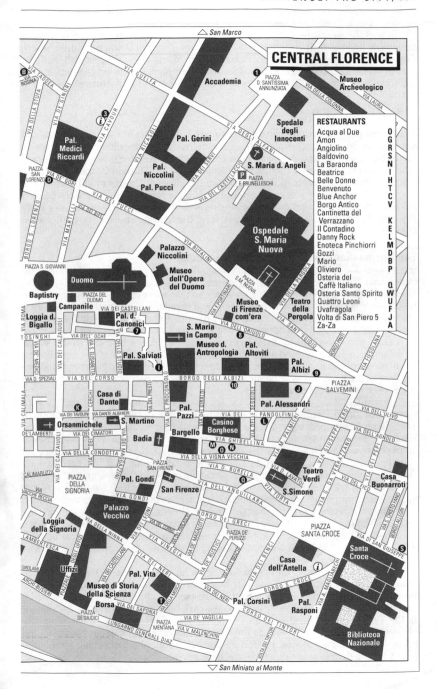

△ San Marco

CENTRAL FLORENCE

Accademia

PIAZZA D. SANTISSIMA ANNUNZIATA ❶

Museo Archeologico

Pal. Medici Riccardi

Pal. Gerini

Spedale degli Innocenti

Pal. Niccolini

Pal. Pucci

S. Maria d. Angeli

PIAZZA F. BRUNELLESCHI

PIAZZA SAN LORENZO D

RESTAURANTS

Acqua al Due	O
Amon	G
Angiolino	R
Baldovino	S
La Baraonda	N
Beatrice	I
Belle Donne	H
Benvenuto	T
Blue Anchor	C
Borgo Antico	V
Cantinetta del Verrazzano	K
Il Contadino	E
Danny Rock	L
Enoteca Pinchiorri	M
Gozzi	D
Mario	B
Oliviero	P
Osteria del Caffè Italiano	Q
Osteria Santo Spirito	W
Quattro Leoni	U
Uvafragola	F
Volta di San Piero 5	J
Za-Za	A

Palazzo Niccolini

Ospedale S. Maria Nuova

Duomo

Museo dell'Opera del Duomo

PIAZZA S. GIOVANNI

PIAZZA S.M. NUOVA

Baptistry

Campanile

PIAZZA DEL DUOMO

Museo di Firenze com'era

Teatro della Pergola

Loggia d. Bigallo

Pal. d. Canonici ❼

S. Maria in Campo ❽

TOSINGHI

Pal. Salviati ❶

Museo d. Antropologia

Pal. Altoviti

Pal. Albizi ❾

Casa di Dante K

Pal. Pazzi ❿

J

Pal. Alessandri

PIAZZA SALVEMINI

Orsanmichele

S. Martino

Casino Borghese

L

Badia

Bargello

S. Simone

Teatro Verdi

Casa Buonarroti

San Firenze

Pal. Gondi

PIAZZA DELLA SIGNORIA

Palazzo Vecchio

PIAZZA SANTA CROCE

Loggia della Signoria

Casa dell'Antella ⓘ

Santa Croce S

Uffizi

Pal. Vita

Museo di Storia della Scienza

Borsa

Pal. Corsini

Pal. Rasponi

Biblioteca Nazionale

▽ San Miniato al Monte

South of the river – preferably via the medieval **Ponte Vecchio**, which is still picturesquely lined with shops perched over the water – lies the **Oltrarno** district, where the array of museums within the **Palazzo Pitti** exerts the strongest pull, and the church of **Santo Spirito** stands at the focus of a lively student quarter. Overlooking the city from the south is the lavish hilltop church of **San Miniato al Monte**.

Piazza del Duomo

Traffic and people gravitate towards the square at the heart of Florence, **Piazza del Duomo**, beckoned by the pinnacle of Brunelleschi's extraordinary dome, which dominates the cityscape in a way unmatched by any architectural creation in any other Italian city. Yet even though the magnitude of the **Duomo** is apparent from a distance, the first full sight of the church and the adjacent **Baptistry** still comes as a jolt, the colours of their patterned exteriors making a startling contrast with the dun-coloured buildings around them. The square is at its romantic best in the very early morning, lit by low, pale sunlight and free from the heaving crowds that gather soon after 8am.

The Duomo (Santa Maria del Fiore) and around

It was some time in the seventh century when the seat of the Bishop of Florence was transferred from San Lorenzo to the ancient church that stood on the site of the **Duomo**. In the thirteenth century, it was decided that a new cathedral was required, to reflect more accurately the wealth of the city and to put the Pisans and Sienese in their place. **Arnolfo di Cambio**, entrusted with the project in 1294, designed a massive vaulted basilica focused on a domed tribune embraced by three polygonal tribunes. He died eight years later, but by 1418 everything was in place to bear the weight of the dome which he had envisaged as the church's crown. The conception was magnificent: the dome was to span a distance of nearly 42m and rise from a base some 54m above the floor of the nave. It was to be the largest dome ever constructed – but nobody had yet worked out how to build the thing.

A committee of the masons' guild was set up to ponder the problem, and it was to them that **Filippo Brunelleschi** presented himself. Some seventeen years before, in 1401, Brunelleschi had been defeated by Ghiberti in the competition to design the Baptistry doors (see p.466), and had spent the intervening time studying classical architecture and developing new theories of engineering. He won the commission on condition that he work jointly with Ghiberti – a partnership that did not last long (though Ghiberti's contribution to the project was probably more significant than his colleague ever admitted). The key to the dome's success was the construction of two shells: a light outer shell about one metre thick, and an inner shell four times thicker. Brunelleschi's genius was to lay the brickwork in a herringbone pattern in cantilevered rings, thus allowing the massively heavy dome to support itself as it grew, without the use of scaffolding. On March 25, 1436 – Annunciation Day, and the Florentine New Year – the completion of the dome was marked by the papal consecration of the cathedral.

The duomo's overblown and pernickety main **facade** is a nineteenth-century imitation of a Gothic front, its marble cladding quarried from the same sources as the first builders used – white stone from Carrara (see p.520), red from the Maremma, green from Prato. The south side is the oldest part, but the most attractive adornment is the **Porta della Mandorla**, on the north side. This takes its name from the almond-shaped frame that contains the relief of *The Assumption of the Virgin*, sculpted by Nanni di Banco around 1420. Note that limited numbers of people are permitted inside the duomo at any one time, and long **queues** often form outside. If you can, come early.

INSIDE THE DUOMO

The duomo's **interior** (Mon–Sat 10am–5pm, Sun 1.30–5pm; closes at 3.30pm on first Sat of month & every Thurs; free) is a vast enclosure of bare masonry in stark contrast to the fussy exterior. Today the fourth-largest church in Europe, it once held a congregation of ten thousand to hear Savonarola preach – the ambience is more that of a public assembly hall than of a devotional building. Initially, the most conspicuous pieces of decoration are two memorials to *condottieri* (mercenary commanders) in the north aisle – Uccello's monument to **Sir John Hawkwood**, painted in 1436, and Castagno's monument to **Niccolò da Tolentino**, created twenty years later. Just beyond, Domenico do Michelino's *Dante Explaining the Divine Comedy* makes the dome only marginally less prominent than the mountain of Purgatory. The enamelled terracotta reliefs over the doorways to the two **sacristies**, on each side of the altar, are by Luca della Robbia, who also cast the bronze doors of the north sacristy. These sheltered Lorenzo de' Medici after his brother Giuliano had been mortally stabbed on the altar steps by the Pazzi conspirators. Judged by mere size, the major work of art in the duomo is the fresco of *The Last Judgement* inside the dome, though a substantial number of Florentines are of the opinion that Vasari and Zuccari's effort does nothing but deface Brunelleschi's masterpiece and want it stripped away. Below the fresco are seven stained-glass roundels designed by Uccello, Ghiberti, Castagno and Donatello; they are best inspected from the gallery immediately below them, which forms part of the route up **inside the dome** (Mon–Fri 8.30am–6.20pm, Sat 8.30am–5pm; closes at 3.20pm on first Sat of month; L10,000/€5.16). The gallery is the queasiest part of the climb, most of which winds between the brick walls of the outer and inner shells of the dome, up to the very summit with its stunning views over the city.

In the 1960s remnants of the duomo's predecessor, the **Cripta di Santa Reparata**, were uncovered beneath the west end of the **nave** (Mon–Sat 10am–5pm; L5000/€2.58). A detailed model helps make sense of the jigsaw of Roman, early Christian and Romanesque remains, areas of mosaic and patches of fourteenth-century frescoes. Also down here is the **tomb of Brunelleschi**, one of the few Florentines ever honoured with burial inside the duomo.

THE CAMPANILE

Alongside Italy's most impressive cathedral dome is perhaps its most elegant bell-tower. The **Campanile** (daily: March–Oct 9am–6.50pm; Nov–Feb 9am–4.20pm; L10,000/€5.16) was begun in 1334 by **Giotto**, who was no engineer: after his death in 1337 Andrea Pisano and Francesco Talenti took over the teetering, half-built edifice, and immediately doubled the thickness of the walls to stop it collapsing. The first storey is studded with two rows of remarkable bas-reliefs; the lower, illustrating the *Creation of Man* and the *Arts and Industries*, was carved by Pisano himself, the upper by his pupils. The figures of *Prophets* and *Sibyls* in the second-storey niches were created by Donatello and others. The parapet at the top of the tower has the advantage of letting you view the dome as a foreground counterpoint to Florence's cityscape.

The Baptistry

The **Baptistry** is the oldest building in Florence, generally thought to date from the sixth or seventh century. Although its mysterious origins lie in the depths of the Dark Ages, no building better illustrates the special relationship between Florence and the Roman world. Throughout the Middle Ages the Florentines chose to believe that the baptistry was originally a Roman temple to Mars, a belief bolstered by the interior's inclusion of Roman granite columns. The pattern of its marble cladding, applied in the eleventh and twelfth centuries, is clearly classical in inspiration, and the baptistry's most famous embellishments – its gilded bronze doors – mark the emergence of a self-conscious interest in the art of the ancient world, the birth of the Renaissance.

After Andrea Pisano's success with the **south doors** in 1336, the merchants' guild held a competition in 1401 for the job of making a new set of doors. The two finalists were Brunelleschi and **Lorenzo Ghiberti** – and the latter won the day. Ghiberti's **north doors** show a new naturalism and classical sense of harmony, but their innovation is timid in comparison with his sublime **east doors**. These remarkable works of art are these days reverentially dubbed "The Gates of Paradise", supposedly after a remark made by Michelangelo – but, in fact, the area between a baptistry and a cathedral is formally known in Italy as the *paradiso*. Unprecedented in the subtlety of their modelling, these Old Testament scenes are a primer of early Renaissance art, using perspective, gesture and sophisticated grouping of their subjects to convey the human drama of each scene. Ghiberti has included a self-portrait in the frame of the left-hand door – his is the fourth head from the top of the right-hand band. All the panels now set in the door are replicas, with the originals on display in the Museo dell'Opera (see below); the original competition entries are in the Bargello (see p.468).

You **enter** through the south doors (Mon–Sat noon–6.30pm, Sun 8.30am–1.30pm; L5000/€2.58). Inside, both the semi-abstract mosaic floor and the magnificent mosaic ceiling – including a fearsome platoon of demons at the feet of Christ in judgement – were created in the thirteenth century. To the right of the altar is the **tomb of John XXIII**, the schismatic pope who died in Florence in 1419 while a guest of his financial adviser and close friend, Giovanni di Bicci de' Medici. The monument, draped by an illusionistic marble canopy, is the work of Donatello and his pupil Michelozzo.

The Museo dell'Opera del Duomo

At Piazza del Duomo 9, behind the east end of the duomo, is the **Museo dell'Opera del Duomo** (Mon–Sat 9.30am–6.30pm, Sun 8am–2pm; L10,000/€5.16), second only to the Bargello and far easier to take in on a single visit. It's also one of the few museums in the city to provide extensive English notes.

In the large ground-floor hall is a glassy-eyed *Madonna* by **Arnolfo di Cambio**, a ramrod-straight statue of *Boniface VII*, one of the most unpleasant of all medieval popes (in comedy hat), and four seated figures of the Evangelists (including **Donatello's** fine *St John*) wrenched from the duomo's demolished sixteenth-century facade. Giovanni di Bondo's *St Sebastian* is in the end room, eye-catching if only for the ludicrous number of arrows piercing the hapless saint. On the mezzanine is the highlight of the museum – **Michelangelo's** angular and anguished pietà. This was one of his last works, carved when he was almost eighty and intended for his own tomb: Vasari records that the face of the hooded Nicodemus is a self-portrait. Dissatisfied with the quality of the marble, Michelangelo mutilated the group by hammering off the left leg and arm of Christ; his pupil Tiberio Calcagni restored the arm, then finished off the figure of Mary Magdalene, turning her into a whey-faced supporting player.

Upstairs in room II are **Donatello's** figures for the campanile, the most powerful of which is the prophet *Habbakuk*, the intensity of whose gaze allegedly prompted the sculptor to seize it and yell "Speak, speak!" Donatello also created one of the ornate *cantorie* (choir-lofts) here, competing with **Luca della Robbia's** opposite, created at the same time and featuring crowds of laughing, dancing children. Room III is dominated by expression of a very different side of Donatello: his haggard wooden figure of *Mary Magdalene* stares into the middle distance, a wild presence amidst cases full of rich vestments, jewelled reliquaries, and a huge silver-gilt **altar** from the Baptistry, a dazzling meditation on the life of John the Baptist. Returning through room II leads you through a corridor lined with ropes and pulleys used in the construction of the dome (as well as Brunelleschi's **death-mask**) to a room full of wooden models submitted as part of a 1588 facade-designing competition and plans from the nineteenth-century reconstruction. The second upper floor was under restoration at the time of writing.

You return to ground level into the newly covered **courtyard** – where Michelangelo worked from 1501 to 1504 on his *David*. Today, it displays in sealed cases of nitrogen Ghiberti's original **bronze panels** for the baptistry's east doors.

Orsanmichele and the Badìa

The main route south from Piazza del Duomo is the arrow-straight **Via dei Calzaiuoli**, Florence's main street today as in Roman times – a catwalk for the Florentine passeggiata between the campanile and Piazza della Signoria. Halfway down the street is the opening into **Piazza della Repubblica**, created in the nineteenth century by razing the old Jewish quarter and markets which once stood here in an attempt to give Florence a grand public square. It's a characterless place, impressive solely for its size.

Partway along Via dei Calzaiuoli is the church of **Orsanmichele** (daily 9am–noon & 4–6pm; closed first & last Mon of month; free). Often unintentionally bypassed by visitors dazzled by the ice-cream parlours and shoe-shops, it stands three storeys high like a military tower. From the ninth century, the church of *San Michele ad Hortum* ("at the garden") stood here, replaced in 1240 by a grain market and after a fire in 1304 by a merchants' loggia. In 1380 the loggia was walled in and dedicated exclusively to religious functions, while two upper storeys were added for use as emergency grain stores. Restoration is in progress on the **exterior sculpture**: outstanding on the east side (Via dei Calzaiuoli) are *John the Baptist* by Ghiberti, the first life-size bronze statue of the Renaissance; on the north side Donatello's *St George*; and on the west side *St Matthew* and *St Stephen* by Ghiberti. You **enter** from the west (daily 9am–noon & 4–6pm; closed on first and last Mon of month: free). The rectangular interior is dominated by the vast tabernacle by Orcagna, carved with delicate reliefs and studded with coloured marble and glass. It frames a *Madonna* painted in 1347 by Bernardo Daddi as a replacement for a miraculous image of the Virgin destroyed by the 1304 fire, whose powers this picture is said to have inherited. You can get to the vaulted halls of the **upstairs granary** – one of the city's most imposing medieval interiors – via the building opposite the church door (same hours as church); climb all the stairs to the footbridge three storeys up. Aside from admiring the hall itself, you might also get the chance to see some of the church's statues – this doubles as the restorers' workshop.

Opposite Orsanmichele, the narrow Via Tavolini heads east a block or two to **Via del Proconsolo**, the other main route between Piazza del Duomo and Piazza della Signoria. On the corner, more or less across the road from the Museo del Bargello, is the huge **Badìa Fiorentina** (undergoing long-term restoration; at the time of writing open Mon 3–6pm only). This ancient Benedictine abbey was founded late in the tenth century. In the 1280s it was overhauled, probably under the direction of Arnolfo di Cambio; later work has smothered much of the old church, but the narrow campanile – Romanesque at its base, Gothic higher up – has come through intact. The **interior** is deliciously musty and gloomy. Immediately on the left as you enter is Filippino Lippi's *Madonna and St Bernard*. An unmarked door from the choir, immediately right of the high altar, leads to a staircase giving access to the upper storey of the tranquil, fifteenth-century **Chiostro degli Aranci** (Cloister of Oranges – named after the fruit trees that the monks cultivated here), the walls of which are brightened by a vivid fresco cycle of the life of St Benedict, thought to be the work of Giovanni di Consalvo, a Portuguese contemporary of Fra Angelico.

The Bargello

To get a comprehensive idea of the Renaissance achievement in Florence, two museum calls are essential: one to the Uffizi and one to the **Museo Nazionale del Bargello** (Tues–Sat 8.30am–1.50pm; also open on second & fourth Sun, and first, third & fifth

Mon of month same times; L8000/€4.13; see box on p.455 for details of combined tickets and advance reservations; *www.sbas.firenze.it*). This outstanding museum is installed in the dauntingly fortress-like Palazzo del Bargello on Via del Proconsolo, halfway between the duomo and the Palazzo Vecchio. Nowhere else in Italy is there so full a collection of sculpture from the period, and yet the Bargello is normally uncrowded. The palazzo was built in 1255, and soon became the seat of the *Podestà*, the chief magistrate. Numerous malefactors were tried, sentenced and executed here and the building acquired its present name in the sixteenth century, after the resident *Bargello*, or police chief.

The courtyard and ground floor

From the ticket desk, you enter the beautiful Gothic **courtyard**, which is plastered with the coats of arms of the *Podestà* and contains, among many other pieces, six allegorical figures by **Ammannati** from the fountain of the Palazzo Pitti courtyard. The left room holds **Tino di Camaino**'s accomplished *Madonna and Child*, and the others hold paraphernalia as well as some pieces removed from Orsanmichele. At the foot of the courtyard steps is the **Michelangelo Room** (room B), focusing on the artist within whose shadow every Florentine sculptor of the sixteenth century laboured. The tipsy, soft-bellied figure of *Bacchus* was his first major sculpture, carved at the age of 22 – a year before the great pietà in Rome. A decade later, Michelangelo's style had evolved into something less immediately seductive, as is shown by the *Pitti Tondo*, the stern grandeur of which prefigures the prophets of the Sistine Chapel ceiling, on which he was then about to start work. The square-jawed bust of *Brutus*, Michelangelo's sole work in the genre, is a coded celebration of anti-Medicean republicanism, having been made in 1540 soon after the murder of the tyrannical Duke Alessandro de' Medici. Works by Michelangelo's followers and contemporaries are ranged in the immediate vicinity; some would command prolonged attention in different company, including **Cellini**'s *Bust of Cosimo I*, and **Giambologna**'s voluptuous *Florence Defeating Pisa*, eclipsed by his more famous *Mercury*. Comic relief is provided by the reliably awful **Bandinelli**, whose coiffured *Adam and Eve* look like a grandee and his wife taking an *au naturel* stroll through their estate.

The upper floors

At the top of the courtyard staircase, the **loggia** has been turned into an aviary for Giambologna's bronze birds, brought here from the Medici villa at Castello (see p.497). The doorway to the right at the top of the stairs opens into the fourteenth-century Salone del Consiglio Generale (room H), where the presiding genius is **Donatello**. Vestiges of the sinuous Gothic manner are evident in the drapery of his marble *David*, placed against the left wall, but there's nothing antiquated in the *St George*, carved just eight years later for the tabernacle of the armourers' guild at Orsanmichele and installed in a replica of its original niche at the far end of the room. If any one sculpture could be said to embody the shift of sensibility that occurred in Renaissance Florence, this is it: whereas St George had previously been little more than a symbol of valour, this alert, tense figure represents not the act of heroism but the volition behind it. In front stands Donatello's sexually ambiguous bronze *David*, cast in the early 1430s as the first freestanding nude figure since classical times and memorably described by Mary McCarthy as "a transvestite's and fetishist's dream." Back opposite the entrance door is Donatello's strange, jubilant figure known as *Amor Atys*, dating from the end of the 1430s, while his breathtakingly vivid bust of *Niccolò da Uzzano* nearby shows that he was just as comfortable with portraiture. The less complex humanism of **Luca della Robbia** is embodied in the glazed terracotta Madonnas set round the walls, while Donatello's master, **Ghiberti**, is represented by his relief of *The Sacrifice of Isaac*, his successful entry in the competition for the baptistry doors. The treatment of the same theme submitted by **Brunelleschi** – and rejected – is displayed close by. Most of the rest of this floor is occupied by a collection of **European and Islamic applied art**, of so high a standard that it would constitute an engrossing museum in its own right. Elsewhere is dazzling carved **ivory** from Byzantium and medieval France.

The sculptural display resumes upstairs, with **Giovanni della Robbia**'s pietà and **Andrea della Robbia**'s exquisite busts of a young woman and a boy. The Sala dei Bronzetti (room P) is Italy's best assembly of small Renaissance bronzes, with plentiful evidence of Giambologna's virtuosity at table-top scale. Lastly, rooms Q and R are devoted mainly to Renaissance portrait busts, including a small bronze group of *Hercules and Antaeus* by **Antonio Pollaiuolo**, possessing a power out of all proportion to its size.

Piazza della Signoria

Even though it sets the stage for the **Palazzo Vecchio** and the **Uffizi**, Florence's main civic square – the frenetic **Piazza della Signoria** – doesn't quite live up to its role. Too many of its buildings are bland nineteenth-century efforts, and the surface of the square resembles the deck of an aircraft carrier. In the 1970s, it was decided to restore the piazza's ancient paving stones, but when the "restorers" returned the first batch, it was found that they had sandblasted chunks off them rather than rinsing them carefully. Some of the original stones then turned up in the yard of a builders' merchant and on the front drives of a number of Tuscan villas. The subsequent scandal brought corruption charges against contractors and politicians; meanwhile, new archeological evidence of twelfth-century Florence beneath the piazza was covered up in order to preserve the tourist trade.

What little charm the Piazza della Signoria does possess comes from its peculiar array of **statuary**, a miscellany collected at the foot of the Palazzo Vecchio. The line-up starts with Giambologna's equestrian statue of *Cosimo I* and continues with Ammannati's fatuous *Neptune Fountain* and copies of Donatello's *Marzocco* (the city's heraldic lion), his *Judith and Holofernes* and Michelangelo's *David*. Near Ammannati's fountain is a small plaque set into the pavement to mark the location of Savonarola's **Bonfire of the Vanities** (see p.454) and his execution pyre. The square's grace-note, the **Loggia della Signoria**, was built in the late fourteenth century as a dais for city officials during ceremonies; only in the late eighteenth century did it become a showcase for some of the city's more melodramatic sculpture. In the corner nearest the Palazzo Vecchio stands a figure that has become one of the iconic images of the Renaissance, Benvenuto Cellini's *Perseus* (removed for restoration at the time of writing, and likely to be under wraps for some time). Equally attention-seeking is Giambologna's last work, *The Rape of the Sabines*, epitome of the Mannerist obsession with spiralling forms.

The Palazzo Vecchio

Florence's fortress-like town hall, looming above the square as an icon of the city's power and authority, is the **Palazzo Vecchio** (mid-June to mid-Sept: Mon & Fri 9am–11pm, Tues, Wed & Sat 9am–7pm, Thurs & Sun 9am–2pm; rest of year Mon–Wed, Fri & Sat 9am–7pm, Thurs & Sun 9am–2pm; L11,000/€5.68; see box on p.455 for details of combined tickets and advance reservations; *www.comune.fi.it/nuovopalazzovecchio*). The building was begun in 1299 to serve as the home of the Signoria, the highest tier of the city's republican government. Local folklore has it that its misshapen plan was due to the fact that the Guelph government refused to encroach on land previously owned by the hated Ghibellines, and so squeezed the building instead. The most radical overhaul came in 1540, when **Cosimo I** – recently installed as Duke of Florence – moved his retinue here from the Palazzo Medici. The Medici were only in residence for nine years before moving to the Palazzo Pitti, largely at the insistence of Cosimo's wife, but the enlargement and refurbishment instigated by Cosimo continued throughout the period of his rule. Much of the decoration of the state rooms comprises a relentless eulogy of Cosimo and his clan, but in among the propaganda are some excellent works of art, including some seminal examples of Mannerism, Cosimo I's court style. The **entrance**, which is alongside the copy of Michelangelo's *David* mobbed night and day by snap-happy crowds, leads into a lovely internal **courtyard** designed by Michelozzo. The ticket office is on the same level at the rear; signs point you upstairs to begin the tour.

Giorgio Vasari, court architect from 1555 until his death in 1574, was responsible for much of the sycophantic decor in the state apartments. His limited talents were given full rein in the huge **Salone dei Cinquecento** at the top of the stairs, built at the end of the fifteenth century as a council assembly hall. This room might have become one of Italy's most extraordinary showcases of Renaissance art, when in 1503 Leonardo da Vinci and Michelangelo were commissioned to fresco opposite walls of the chamber. Unfortunately, Leonardo abandoned the project after his experimental fresco technique went wrong, and Michelangelo's ideas existed only on paper when he was summoned to Rome by Pope Julius II. (His preparatory sketch was so much admired, studied and copied by subsequent artists that it fell to pieces from over-handling, and is now lost.) A few decades later, the hack Vasari stepped in, and painted over Leonardo's failed attempts with drearily bombastic murals celebrating Cosimo's military prowess. Michelangelo's *Victory*, facing the entrance door, was sculpted for Julius's tomb but was donated to the Medici by the artist's nephew; Vasari installed it here to mark Cosimo's defeat of the Sienese.

Stairs rise from the corridor past an intriguing fireworks fresco of 1558 showing the Piazza della Signoria during celebrations for the feast of John the Baptist. Turn left at the top and you enter the **Quartiere degli Elementi** – the decor plays second fiddle to the romantic rooftop views from the terrace. Back at the top of the stairs, head straight on and you cross a gallery at the rear of the Salone dei Cinquecento into the private apartments of **Eleanor**, Cosimo I's wife. Star turn here is the tiny and exquisite **chapel**, superbly and vividly decorated by Bronzino in the 1540s.

Through a handful of rooms is the frescoed **Sala d'Udienza**, once an audience chamber, which boasts lovely views over the piazza below and a stunning gilt-coffered ceiling by Giuliano da Maiano, who was also responsible, with his brother Benedetto, for the intarsia work on the doors and the lovely doorway that leads into the **Sala dei Gigli**, a room that takes its name from the lilies (*gigli*) that adorn most of its surfaces. The room has another splendid ceiling by the Maiano brothers, and frescoes by Domenico Ghirlandaio. The highlight of the room is **Donatello's** original *Judith and Holofernes*, a copy of which sits down below in the piazza. Commissioned by Cosimo il Vecchio, the piece originally served as a fountain in the Palazzo Medici, but was

---

SECRET PASSAGEWAYS

Secret passageways between rooms within the Palazzo Vecchio are explorable on guided tours (Mon–Fri 9.30am & 11am, Sat 3.30pm, 4.30pm & 5.30pm, Sun 10am, 11am & noon; mid-June to mid-Sept also Mon & Fri 9.30pm; L13,000/€6.71; reserve on ☎055.276.8224). You're led up the **Staircase of the Duke of Athens**, built in 1342 within the thickness of the exterior walls, to the **private apartments** of Cosimo I and the strange **Studiolo of Francesco I**, a windowless cell created as a retreat for Cosimo's introverted son and decorated by several of Florence's prominent Mannerist artists. Another spiral staircase heads up to the **Tesoretto**, Cosimo's beautifully decorated private study, and up into the vast space above the Salone dei Cinquecento.

removed to the Piazza della Signoria after the expulsion of the Medici in 1494, to be displayed as a mark of vanquished tyranny. Donatello froze the action at the moment Judith's arm begins its scything stroke, a dramatic conception that no other sculptor of the period would have attempted.

The two small side-rooms are the Cancellaria, **Machiavelli**'s office for fifteen years and now containing a bust and portrait of the much-maligned political thinker; and the lovely **Sala delle Carte**, decorated with 57 maps painted in 1563 by the Medici court astronomer Fra' Ignazio Danti, depicting in some detail what was then the entire known world.

The Museo di Storia della Scienza

At the rear of the Palazzo Vecchio runs Via dei Leoni, named after lions that were moved here from the piazza after Cosimo I objected to the smell. Heading down to the river the street becomes Via dei Castellani, which then opens into **Piazza dei Giudici**, so called because of the tribunal that met in what's now the excellent **Museo di Storia della Scienza** (June–Sept Mon & Wed–Fri 9.30am–5pm, Tues & Sat 9.30am–1pm; Oct–May Mon & Wed–Sat 9.30am–5pm, Tues 9.30am–1pm; L12,000/€6.20; *galileo.imss.firenze.it*). Stop in if you fancy a glimpse of the Renaissance that includes neither heroic male nudes nor tortured saintly visages.

Long after Florence had declined from its artistic apogee, the intellectual reputation of the city was maintained by its scientists. Grand Duke Ferdinando II and his brother Leopoldo, both of whom studied with **Galileo**, founded the Academy of Experiment at the Pitti in 1657, and the instruments made and acquired by this academy are the core of the museum, which has extensive English notes. The **first upper floor** features timepieces and measuring instruments (such as beautiful Arab astrolabes), as well as a massive armillary sphere made for Ferdinando I to prove the fallacy of Copernicus's heliocentric universe. Galileo's original instruments are on show here, such as the lens with which he discovered the four moons of Jupiter. On the **top floor** is the huge lens made for Cosimo III, with which Faraday and Davy managed to ignite a diamond by focusing the rays of the sun. The medical section is full of alarming surgical instruments and wax anatomical models for teaching obstetrics.

The Uffizi

Ranged around a grand U-shaped courtyard between Piazza della Signoria and the river, the **Galleria degli Uffizi** (Tues–Sat 8.30am–6.50pm, Sun 8.30am–1.50pm; L12,000/€6.20; see box on p.455 for details of advance reservations; *www.uffizi. firenze.it* and *www.arca.net/uffizi*) holds Italy's greatest art collection, and is the city's key attraction. Perhaps that's why the gallery's directors feel no shame in making you queue for two hours or more for admission – there are often queues even to pick up reserved tickets – then climb dozens of internal stairs to reach the gallery level (or queue again for two ancient six-person lifts). Should you fancy a spot of refreshment, there's a rooftop café with excellent views – which charges an insulting L5000/€2.58 for a thimbleful of bitter espresso. The single set of public toilets is located at the far end of the uppermost storey. You'd be justified in wondering where all those admission fees end up.

The curators have, it's true, finally launched a programme of modernization and expansion – with the upshot being that the masterpiece you came specifically to see, or the room it hangs in, may be undergoing renovation when you visit. In the meantime they appear to hold no truck with newfangled ideas of how to run a museum: staff posted at each corner sternly discourage solo meanderings from room to room (there is a fixed, chronological route through the gallery, and you are not permitted to backtrack); there are few directional signs on the grimy plaster walls, no information boards at all, barely any public seating, and the display and lighting of some of the star works – most of which are shielded behind reflective, fingermarked glass – is appalling. The Uffizi remains unmissable, but you must be prepared to suffer for your art.

The main picture rooms open off a corridor that runs all the way round the uppermost level of the U-shaped building, is crammed higgledy-piggledy with **classical statuary**, and boasts a **ceiling** decorated in ornate Grotesque style that is an artwork in itself. The paintings are hung chronologically, with each block of rooms forming a neat, self-contained unit. So many masterpieces are collected here that you should put aside **three or four hours** as the minimum to be able to take in the gallery's key works; this gives time for only a few brief pauses, and means that you'll be skipping some rooms altogether. If time or energy is short, it makes sense to limit yourself to an hour or two exploring the first fifteen rooms, where the Florentine Renaissance works are concentrated, leaving the rest for another time.

The elongated U-shaped building originated in 1560, when Duke Cosimo I ordered **Giorgio Vasari** to design a block of government offices (*uffizi*) to fill a site between the Palazzo Vecchio and the river that was, at that time, occupied by houses and a church. After Vasari's death, work was continued by **Buontalenti**, who – under orders from Francesco I – glazed the upper storey so that it could house his art collection. Each of the succeeding Medici added to the family's trove of art treasures, and the accumulated collection was preserved for public inspection by the last member of the family, Anna Maria Lodovica, whose will specified that it should be left to the people of Florence and never be allowed to leave the city. During the nineteenth century, a large proportion of the sculpture was transferred to the Bargello, while many of the antiquities went to the Museo Archeologico, leaving the Uffizi itself as essentially a gallery of paintings.

ROOMS 1–9: FROM CIMABUE TO FRA' FILIPPO LIPPI

Room 1 (which is usually closed) houses an assembly of antique sculpture, used as a source-book by Renaissance artists. The gestation period of the Renaissance can be studied in **room 2**, where three altarpieces of the Maestà (*Madonna Enthroned*) by Cimabue, Duccio and Giotto dwarf everything around them, and demonstrate the softening of the Byzantine style into a more tactile form of representation. A high point in the comparatively conservative art of fourteenth-century Siena (room 3) is Martini's *Annunciation*, with its eloquently expansive background of plain gold. Florence's only first-rank Gothic painter, Lorenzo Monaco, features amid the collection of other *trecento* artists (**rooms 5 & 6**), with a majestic *Coronation of the Virgin* and an *Adoration of the Magi*; the spangled version of the latter subject by Gentile da Fabriano is the epitome of International Gothic, cramming every inch of the flattened picture plane with often highly naturalistic detail.

In **room 7**, Piero della Francesca is represented by paired portraits of *Federico da Montefeltro* and *Battista Sforza*; the panels are backed by images of the Duke surrounded by the cardinal virtues and his wife by the theological virtues. Paolo Uccello's curiously measured *Battle of San Romano* – demonstrating the artist's obsessional interest in perspectival effects more successfully than his grasp of the realities of war – once hung in Lorenzo il Magnifico's bedchamber, in company with depictions of the same skirmish that now reside in the Louvre and London's National Gallery. Among the plentiful works by Fra' Filippo Lippi in **room 8** is his celebrated *Madonna and Child with Two Angels*. Close by there's a fine *Madonna* by Botticelli.

ROOMS 10–16: FROM BOTTICELLI TO LEONARDO DA VINCI

The works upon which Botticelli's reputation rests are gathered in the merged **rooms 10–14**: *Primavera, The Birth of Venus, Adoration of the Magi* and *The Madonna of the Magnificat*. Even when their meaning remains opaque – and few pictures have occasioned as much scholarly argument as the *Primavera* – these paintings are irresistibly fresh in both their conception and execution. *The Birth of Venus* takes as its source the myth that the goddess emerged from the waves intact after the sea had been impregnated by the castration of Uranus – an allegory for the creation of beauty through the mingling of the spirit (Uranus) and physicality. The painting shows a radiantly beautiful Venus being blown to shore by Zephyrus, god of the west wind, and the nymph Cloris; she is about to step – with oddly filth-lined toenails – onto land, to be clothed by Hora, daughter of Aurora, goddess of the dawn. The *Primavera* on the nearby wall is generally held to show the triumph of Venus, who stands as the central focus of the painting. Zephyrus, on the right, chases Cloris and transmutes her into Flora, symbol of natural fertility (who is endowed with one of the most reproduced smiles in the history of art). The Three Graces, expressions of physical beauty, dance together while Mercury, tantalizingly clad only in a loose robe, chases away the clouds of winter.

Though the Uffizi doesn't own a finished painting entirely by Leonardo da Vinci, works in **room 15** comprise a full sketch of his career. From his formative years there's the celebrated and precisely handled *Annunciation* (mainly by Leonardo) along with the landscape and single angel in profile that he painted aged 18 in Verrocchio's *Baptism*. The incomplete sketch for *The Adoration of the Magi* in the same room encapsulates Leonardo's later radicalism, with its vortex of figures round Mary and the infant Christ. **Room 16**, the enigmatically titled Map Room, is usually kept closed.

ROOMS 17–24: FROM BRONZINO TO HOLBEIN

Room 18, the octagonal **Tribuna**, was the original Medici gallery and now houses the most important of the Medici sculptures, principal among which is the Medici Venus, a first-century BC copy of the Praxitelean Aphrodite of Cnidos. Also in this room are del Sarto's flirtatious *Portrait of a Girl* and some chillingly precise portraits by Bronzino – especially compelling are *Bartolomeo Panciatichi*, *Lucrezia Panciatichi* and *Eleanor of Toledo with Giovanni de' Medici*. Vasari's portrait of Lorenzo il Magnifico and Bronzino's of Cosimo il Vecchio are deceptively immediate – each was painted long after the death of its subject.

Room 20 is largely devoted to Cranach and Dürer, including the latter's *Portrait of the Artist's Father*, his earliest authenticated painting. Highlights in the following sequence of rooms (**21–23**) are a perplexing *Sacred Allegory* by Giovanni Bellini and Holbein's *Portrait of Sir Richard Southwell*.

ROOMS 25–45: FROM MICHELANGELO TO GOYA

The main attraction in **room 25** is Michelangelo's only completed easel painting, the virtuoso *Holy Family*, widely known as the "Doni Tondo" (a *tondo* – a circular artwork – commissioned by the Doni family). An unusually robust and powerful, bare-armed Mary reaches back to take the Christ child from Joseph, watched by a young John the Baptist in an animal skin. The contorted gestures and cold, almost metallic, colours were revolutionary for the time, as was the innovation of including nude figures in an ostensibly religious painting. The *maniera*, or style and execution, of this work was studied and imitated by Florentine painters of the sixteenth century in what became known as the Mannerist movement – as can be gauged from *Moses Defending the Daughters of Jethro* in **room 27** by Rosso Fiorentino, one of the pivotal figures of Mannerism, and works by Bronzino and the mercurial Pontormo. Separating the two Mannerist groups is **room 26** containing Andrea del Sarto's sultry *Madonna of the Harpies* and a number of compositions by Raphael, including the lovely *Madonna of the Goldfinch* and *Pope Leo X with Cardinals Giulio dei Medici and Luigi de' Rossi* – as shifty a group of ecclesiastics as ever was gathered in one frame. **Room 28** is almost entirely given over to another of the titanic figures of sixteenth-century art, Titian. His *Flora* and *A Knight of Malta* are stunning, but most eyes tend to swivel towards the famous *Venus of Urbino*, just about the most fleshy and provocative of all Renaissance nudes.

A brief diversion through the painters of the sixteenth-century Emilian school follows, centred on Parmigianino, whose *Madonna of the Long Neck* is one of the definitive Mannerist creations. **Rooms 31 to 35** feature artists from Venice and the Veneto, with outstanding paintings by Paolo Veronese (*Holy Family with St Barbara*), Tintoretto (*Leda*) and G.B. Moroni (*Count Pietro Secco Suardi*). Sebastiano del Piombo's *Death of Adonis* which formerly hung here was torn to shreds in 1993 by a Mafia bomb and is still being pieced together.

In **room 41**, dominated by Rubens and Van Dyck, it is one of the less demonstrative items that makes the biggest impact – Rubens' *Portrait of Isabella Brandt*. His equally theatrical contemporary, Caravaggio, has a cluster of pieces in **room 43**, including a sultry, come-hither *Bacchus*. Next is a showcase for the portraiture of Rembrandt – the *Self-Portrait as an Old Man*, painted five years or so before his death, is one of his most melancholic works, its poignancy enhanced by the proximity of another self-portrait from decades earlier. Portraits also seize the attention in the following room of eighteenth-century works (**room 45**), especially the two of Maria Theresa painted by Goya. **Room 42** between these is an impressively ceilinged hall packed with classical statuary, while in an alcove at the top of the exit stairs – misleadingly entitled **rooms 36 & 37** – squats one of Florence's talismans, the Wild Boar, a Roman copy of third-century-BC Hellenistic sculpture. This tusked beast was the model for the Porcellino which stands today in the Mercato Nuovo.

THE CORRIDOIO VASARIANO

A door on the west corridor between rooms 25 and 34 opens onto the **Corridoio Vasariano**, a passageway built by Vasari to link the Palazzo Vecchio to the Palazzo Pitti through the Uffizi. You must reserve at least one day ahead for a **guided tour** (Tues, Wed, Fri & Sat 9am, 10.30am, 1pm & 2.30pm, Sun 9am & 10.30am; L50,000/€25.82; ☎055.294.883). Winding its way down to the river, over the Ponte Vecchio on an upper level, through the church of Santa Felicita and into the Giardino di Bóboli, it gives a fascinating series of clandestine views of the city, and is completely lined with paintings, the larger portion of which comprises a **gallery of self-portraits**. Once past the portrait of Vasari, the series proceeds chronologically, its roll-call littered with illustrious names: Andrea del Sarto, Bronzino, Bernini, Rubens, Rembrandt, Van Dyck, Velazquez, Hogarth, Reynolds, Delacroix, Ingres, and others.

The western city centre

Several streets in central Florence retain their medieval character, especially in the district west of Piazza della Signoria. Forming a gateway to this quarter is the **Mercato Nuovo** (summer daily 9am–7pm; winter Tues–Sat 9am–5pm), whose souvenir stalls are probably the busiest in the city; there's been a market here since the eleventh century, though the present loggia dates from the sixteenth. Usually a small group is gathered round the bronze boar known as **Il Porcellino**, trying to gain some good luck by getting a coin to fall from the animal's mouth through the grill below his head. An aimless amble through the streets beyond will give you some idea of the feel of Florence in the Middle Ages, when every important house was an urban fortress. The fourteenth-century **Palazzo Davanzati**, Via Porta Rossa 13, looks much as it did when first inhabited, and nowadays houses the **Museo della Casa Fiorentina Antica** (closed indefinitely for long-term restoration; ask at the tourist office for latest details). Virtually every room of the reconstructed interior is furnished and decorated in medieval style, using genuine artefacts assembled from a variety of sources.

Santa Trìnita and around

Via Porta Rossa culminates at Piazza Santa Trìnita, not so much a square as a widening of the city's classiest street, **Via de' Tornabuoni**, which heads south across the Arno on the city's most stylish bridge, the **Ponte Santa Trìnita**. This was ostensibly designed by Ammannati, but the curve of its arches so closely resembles the arc of Michelangelo's Medici tombs that the credit probably should be his; it was rebuilt stone by stone after the retreating Nazis had blown up the original in 1944. **Santa Trìnita** (Mon–Sat 8am–noon & 4–6pm, Sun 4–6pm) was founded in the eleventh century, but piecemeal additions have lent it a pleasantly hybrid air: the largely Gothic interior contrasts with Buontalenti's Mannerist facade of 1594. The interior is notable for **Ghirlandaio**'s decoration of the **Cappella Sassetti** (second to the right of the altar). His frescoes of the *Life of St Francis* are concerned as much with a portrayal of fifteenth-century Florence as with their religious themes: the saint is shown healing a sick child in Piazza Santa Trìnita, and the lunette above the altar is set in Piazza della Signoria (the figure with a hand on his hip is a self-portrait). Elsewhere in the church is **Luca della Robbia**'s powerful composition for the tomb of Benozzo Federighi, Bishop of Fiesole, occupying a wall of the chapel second to the left of the altar and framed by a ceramic border of flowers and greenery.

Heading north from Santa Trìnita is **Via de' Tornabuoni**, home to Cartier, Versace, Armani and the famous local firms Ferragamo and Gucci. Conspicuous wealth is nothing new here, for looming above everything is the vast **Palazzo Strozzi**, the last, the largest and the least subtle of Florentine Renaissance palaces. Filippo Strozzi bought and demolished a dozen town houses to make space for Giuliano da Sangallo's strongbox in stone (1536). When Giovanni Rucellai – one of the richest businessmen in the city and an esteemed scholar into the bargain – decided in the 1450s to commission a new house, he turned to Leon Battista Alberti. The **Palazzo Rucellai**, just west of the Strozzi house in Via della Vigna Nuova, was the first building in Florence to follow the rules of Classical architecture. You can see an even more refined example of Alberti's work, the Cappella di San Sepolcro, in the **Cappella Rucellai** behind the house·at Via della Spada 18 (Sat 5.30pm for Mass only; closed July–Sept). The church of San Pancrazio on Via della Spada has been converted into the slick **Museo Marino Marini** (Mon & Wed–Sat 10am–5pm, Sun 10am–1pm; summer also Thurs until 11pm; closed Aug; L8000/€4.13; see box on p.455 for details of combined tickets and advance reservations; *www.fol.it/clients/marini*). Marini (1901–80) was one of Italy's foremost sculptors of the twentieth century, and this spacious conversion displays variations on his familiar horse-and-rider theme.

Ognissanti

In medieval times a major area of cloth production – the foundation of the Florentine economy – lay in the west of the city. **Ognissanti**, or All Saints, the main church of this quarter located on Borgo Ognissanti, five minutes' walk west of Via de' Tornabuoni, was founded in 1256 by a Benedictine order who wove woollen cloth. Three hundred years later the Franciscans took it over and renovated it in Baroque style; inside is the habit worn by St Francis of Assisi when he received the stigmata atop Monte Verna in September 1224 (see p.577). The young face squeezed between the Madonna and the dark-cloaked man in **Ghirlandaio**'s *Madonna della Misericordia* fresco, over the second altar on the right, is said to be that of Amerigo Vespucci – later to set sail on voyages that would give his name to America. Just beyond this, on opposite sides of the nave, are mounted **Botticelli**'s *St Augustine* and Ghirlandaio's more earthbound *St Jerome*, both painted in 1480. In the same year Ghirlandaio painted the bucolic *Last Supper* that covers one wall of the **refectory**, reached through the cloister entered to the left of the church (Mon, Tues & Sat 9am–noon).

Santa Maria Novella

The focus of the western city centre is the large, pleasant **Piazza Santa Maria Novella** in front of the church it was named after, which has a lethargic backwater atmosphere, favoured as a spot for picnic lunches and after-dark loitering.

From the beguiling green, white and pink patterns of its marble facade, you'd never guess that the church of **Santa Maria Novella** was the Florentine base of the Dominican order, fearsome vigilantes of thirteenth-century Catholicism. The architects of the Gothic **interior** (Mon–Fri 7am–noon & 3.30–6pm, Sat 7am–noon & 3.30–5pm, Sun 3.30–5pm) were capable of great ingenuity – the distance between the columns diminishes with proximity to the altar, a device to make the nave appear from the entrance to be longer than it is. **Masaccio's** extraordinary 1427 fresco of *The Trinity*, one of the earliest works in which perspective and classical proportion were rigorously employed, is painted onto the wall halfway down the left aisle. **Filippino Lippi's** frescoes for the **Cappella di Filippo Strozzi** (immediately to the right of the chancel) are a fantasy vision of classical ruins in which the narrative often seems to take second place, and one of the first examples of an archeological interest in Roman culture. As a chronicle of fifteenth-century life in Florence, no series of frescoes is more fascinating than **Domenico Ghirlandaio's** behind the high altar; the work was commissioned by Giovanni Tornabuoni – which explains why certain ladies of the Tornabuoni family are present at the birth of John the Baptist and of the Virgin. **Brunelleschi's** *Crucifix*, popularly supposed to have been carved as a response to Donatello's uncouth version at Santa Croce, hangs in the Cappella Gondi, left of the chancel. At the end of the left transept is the raised **Cappella Strozzi**, whose faded frescoes by Nardo di Cione (1350s) include an entire wall of visual commentary on Dante's *Inferno*. The magnificent altarpiece by Nardo's brother Andrea (better known as **Orcagna**), is a piece of propaganda for the Dominicans – Christ is shown bestowing favour simultaneously on both St Peter and St Thomas Aquinas, a figure second only to St Dominic in the order's hierarchy.

THE MUSEO DI SANTA MARIA NOVELLA

More remarkable paintings are on display in the spacious Romanesque conventual buildings to the left of the church, entered through a separate door into the **Museo di Santa Maria Novella** (Mon–Thurs, Sat & Sun 9am–2pm; L5000/€2.58; see box on p.455 for details of combined tickets and advance reservations). The cloisters, just beyond the ticket desk, are more richly decorated than any others in Florence. The first set, the Romanesque **Chiostro Verde**, features frescoes of *Stories from Genesis* by **Paolo Uccello** and his workshop. Look out for Uccello's windswept image of *The Flood*, on the right as you enter, rendered almost unintelligible by the telescoping perspective and the double appearance of the ark (before and after the flood), the flanks of which form a receding corridor in the centre of the image. On the left, the ark is rising on the deluge; on the right it has come to rest as the waters subside. In the foreground, two men fight each other in their desperation to stay alive (the chequered lifebelt that one of them is wearing is a favourite Uccello device for demonstrating a mastery of perspective). In the right foreground there's a preview of the universal devastation, with a crow gobbling an eyeball from one of the drowned.

Off the cloister opens what was once the chapter-house of the immensely rich convent, the **Cappellone degli Spagnuoli** (Spanish Chapel), which received its new name after Eleanor of Toledo reserved it for the use of her Spanish entourage. Its fresco cycle by Andrea di Firenze, an extended depiction of the triumph of the Catholic Church, was described by Ruskin as "the most noble piece of pictorial philosophy in Italy". The left wall depicts the *Triumph of Divine Wisdom*: Thomas Aquinas is enthroned below the Virgin and Apostles amidst winged Virtues and biblical notables. The more spectacular right wall depicts the *Triumph of the Church*, and includes at the bottom a building supposed to be Florence's cathedral, a pinky-purple creation imagined eighty years before its actual completion. Before it stand the pope and the Holy Roman Emperor, society's ultimate spiritual and temporal rulers. To the right is a group of pilgrims; the saved are shown being marshalled towards a friar who hears their confession (which removes the taint of mortal sin) before dispatch towards St Peter and the Gate of Paradise.

The northern city centre

The busy quarter north of the duomo and east of the train station is packed with shops and commerce. Focus of the area is Florence's main food market, the vast covered **Mercato Centrale** (Mon–Sat 7am–2pm; also Sat & the day before a public holiday 4–8pm; *www.firenzesanlorenzo.com*). Butchers, *alimentari*, tripe sellers, greengrocers, pasta stalls and bars are all gathered under one roof, charging prices lower than you'll readily find elsewhere. All around is a hectic **street market** (Mon–Sat 8.30am–7pm; *www.sanlorenzo-market.com*), thronged with stalls selling leather bags, belts, clothes and shoes – plus racks of football shirts from all the most famous teams in Europe.

San Lorenzo
Founded in the fourth century, **San Lorenzo**, on the piazza of the same name (Mon–Sat 7am–noon & 3.30–5.30pm, Sun 3.30–5.30pm), has a good claim to be the oldest church in Florence, and was the city's cathedral for almost three centuries. Although Michelangelo sweated to produce a scheme for San Lorenzo's facade, the bare brick of the exterior has never been clad; it's a stark, inappropriate prelude to the powerful simplicity of Brunelleschi's interior, one of the earliest Renaissance church designs. Inside are two striking **bronze pulpits** by **Donatello**. Covered in densely populated and disquieting reliefs, chiefly of scenes preceding and following the *Crucifixion*, these are the artist's last works and were completed by his pupils. Close by, at the foot of the altar steps, a large disc of multicoloured marble marks the grave of Cosimo il Vecchio, the artist's main patron. Further pieces by Donatello (who is buried here) adorn the **Sagrestia Vecchia** off the left transept (usually Mon, Wed, Fri & Sat 10am–noon, Tues & Thurs 4–6pm) – the two pairs of bronze doors, the large reliefs of *SS Cosmas and Damian* and *SS Lawrence and Stephen*, the cherub-filled frieze, and the eight terracotta tondi. The table of milky marble in the centre of the room is the tomb of Cosimo il Vecchio's parents, Giovanni Bicci de' Medici and Piccarda Bueri.

At the top of the left aisle of San Lorenzo a door leads out to the cloister, and the staircase immediately on the right goes up to the **Biblioteca Laurenziana** (Mon–Sat 9am–1pm). Wishing to create a suitably grandiose home for the precious manuscripts assembled by Cosimo il Vecchio and Lorenzo il Magnifico, Pope Clement VII (Lorenzo's nephew) asked **Michelangelo** to design a new Medici library in 1524. The vestibule of the building he came up with is a revolutionary showpiece of Mannerist architecture, delighting in paradoxical display – brackets that support nothing, columns that sink into the walls rather than stand out from them, and a flight of steps so large that it almost fills the room, spilling down like a solidified lava flow. You pass from this deliberately eccentric space into the tranquil, architecturally correct reading room. Almost everything here is the work of Michelangelo, even the inlaid desks.

THE CAPPELLE MEDICEE
Some of Michelangelo's most celebrated Florentine works are in San Lorenzo's Sagrestia Nuova, part of the **Cappelle Medicee** (Medici Chapels; Tues–Sat 8.30am–5pm; also open on first, third & fifth Sun and second & fourth Mon of month same times; L11,000/€5.68; see box on p.455 for details of combined tickets and advance reservations; *www.sbas.firenze.it*). Entrance to the chapels is round the back of

San Lorenzo, on Piazza Madonna degli Aldobrandini, and leads directly into the low-vaulted **crypt**, last resting-place of a clutch of minor Medici tossed down here in 1791 by Ferdinand III. After filing through the crypt, you climb steps into the **Cappella dei Principi** (Chapel of the Princes), a gloomy, marble-plated octagonal hall built as a mausoleum for Cosimo I and his ancestors. Morbid and dowdy, it was the most expensive building project ever financed by the family.

Follow the corridor leading on to the **Sagrestia Nuova**, one of the earliest Mannerist buildings, begun by Michelangelo in 1520 and intended as a tribute to, and subversion of, Brunelleschi's Sagrestia Vecchia. Architectural connoisseurs go into raptures over the complex cornices of the alcoves and other such sophistications, but you might be more drawn to the fabulous **Medici tombs**, carved by Michelangelo. To the left is the **tomb of Lorenzo**, Duke of Urbino, grandson of Lorenzo il Magnifico. Michelangelo depicted him as a man of thought, and his sarcophagus bears figures of *Dawn* and *Dusk*, the times of day whose ambiguities appeal to the contemplative mind. Opposite is the **tomb of Giuliano**, Duke of Nemours, youngest son of Lorenzo il Magnifico. As a man of action, his character is symbolized by *Day* and *Night*. Contrary to these idealized images, Giuliano was in fact an easygoing but feckless individual, while Lorenzo combined ineffectualness with arrogance; both died young and unlamented of tuberculosis, combined in Lorenzo's case with syphilis. Michelangelo was not unaware of the ironies – critics have suggested that Lorenzo's absurd hat may well be a gentle hint as to the subject's feeble-mindedness. Their effigies were intended to face the equally grand tombs of Lorenzo il Magnifico and his brother Giuliano, two Medici who had genuine claims to fame and honour, but the only part of the project realized by Michelangelo is the serene **Madonna and Child**, the last image of the Madonna he ever sculpted and one of the most affecting, now flanked by *Cosmas* and *Damian*, patron saints of doctors (*medici*) and thus of the dynasty.

The Palazzo Medici-Riccardi

On the northeastern edge of Piazza San Lorenzo stands the **Palazzo Medici-Riccardi** (Mon, Tues & Thurs–Sun 9am–7pm; L8000/€4.13), built by Michelozzo in the 1440s for Cosimo il Vecchio and for a century or more the principal seat of the Medici in the city. With its heavily rusticated exterior, this monolithic palace was the prototype for such houses as the Palazzo Pitti and Palazzo Strozzi, but was greatly altered in the seventeenth century by its new owners, the Riccardi family, who took over after Cosimo I moved out. Thanks to its restored Gozzoli **frescoes** – some of the most charming in all Florence – it now rates as a major sight. However, as only fifteen people are allowed to view these paintings at any one time, the queues can be overwhelming. You should visit the ticket office (through the palace courtyard to the rear) and **book in advance** for a timed visit the following day.

Of Michelozzo's original scheme, only the upstairs **chapel** remains intact, its interior covered by a brilliantly colourful narrative fresco of the *Procession of the Magi*, painted around 1460 by Benozzo Gozzoli. It shows the pageant of the Compagnia dei Magi, the most patrician of the city's religious confraternities, through a glowing, dream-like landscape dotted with castles; dogs and fabulous animals trot along beside. It's known that several of the Medici household are featured, but putting names to these prettified faces is a problem. The man leading the cavalcade on a white horse is certainly Piero il Gottoso, sponsor of the fresco. Lorenzo il Magnifico is probably the young king in the foreground, riding the grey horse seen in full profile, while his brother, Giuliano, is probably the one preceded by the black bowman. The artist himself is in the crowd on the far left, his red beret signed with his name in gold. A second staircase ascends from the courtyard to the **Sala di Luca Giordano**, a gilded and mirrored gallery notable for its *Madonna and Child* by Fra' Filippo Lippi, kept in a grotesque black metal box to the left of the door. Luca Giordano's overblown ceiling fresco of *The Apotheosis of the*

Medici, painted after the Riccardi family had bought the building in 1659, is either deftly tongue-in-cheek or utterly shameless.

The Accademia

Florence's first Academy of Drawing – indeed, Europe's first – was founded northeast of San Lorenzo on Via Ricasoli in the mid-sixteenth century by Bronzino, Ammannati and Vasari. In 1784, Grand Duke Pietro Leopoldo opened the onsite **Galleria dell'Accademia** (Tues–Sun 8.30am–6.50pm, Sat until 10pm; L15,000/€7.75; see box on p.455 for details of combined tickets and advance reservations; *www.sbas.firenze.it*). The gallery has an impressive collection of paintings, especially of Florentine altarpieces from the fourteenth to the early sixteenth centuries – but the pictures are not what pull the crowds. Everyone comes here to see the most famous sculpture in the world, **Michelangelo's** *David*.

Seeing the *David* for the first time can be something of a shock. The conception of the piece was revolutionary. Instead of, as was common, portraying a static warrior David in full armour, with the head of Goliath lying trophy-like at his feet, Michelangelo chose to emphasize human thought and motivation. This David, as well as breaking with tradition by being completely nude (thus recalling classical statuary), is frozen in mid-movement. He is gazing intently over his left shoulder with a stone in his other hand, sizing up Goliath while shifting his weight onto his right foot prior to loading his sling and firing off the stone. The poise of the figure comes in its balance between head and hands, between thought and action.

Michelangelo spent almost three years working beneath a temporary shelter set up in the courtyard of the Opera del Duomo, sculpting the *David* from a tall but very narrow block of flawed Carrara marble which had already been partly worked by others and abandoned. The completed statue is one of the few that Michelangelo created with a main frontal view, as opposed to being viewable in the round – largely because of the block's limitations. He finished it, the largest nude to have been sculpted since classical times, in early 1504 at the age of 29. It was then carted on a four-day procession through the city to its display site in front of the Palazzo Vecchio, suffering attacks as it went from pro-Medici supporters who saw it as symbolizing the recent overthrow of Medicean and Savonarolan rule. Since then, the *David* has become an emblem of the city's pride and of the illimitable ambition of the Renaissance artist. In 1873, it was moved to this specially designed tribune in the Accademia for conservation reasons, and was replaced outside the Palazzo Vecchio by a marble copy.

But herein lies the shock of a first viewing, which so upsets many in the scrum that gathers at *David*'s feet. Michelangelo seems blithely to have abandoned all normal human **proportion**. *David*'s head and hands are obviously far too big, his arms are too long, his legs are too short. Laser-wielding scientists even determined in 2000 that he is wall-eyed. For many people this undermines the whole work: the *David* is an incomparable show of technical bravura but how can it represent the ideal of male beauty? And yet this piece of monumental public sculpture was not designed to be examined up close. On the plinth in Piazza della Signoria *David*'s feet would have been way above head height. In the Accademia, you could reach out and touch his toes (but for a perspex shield installed after a tourist took a hammer to the sculpture's left foot in 1991). Without the benefit of being able to view the work from a position well back as Michelangelo envisaged – which would give the illusion of lengthening the legs and shortening the trunk and arms – the *David* appears hopelessly gangling. Equally, scrutinizing a close-up, full-face image of *David*'s frowning features is a modern preoccupation: from below, in profile and at a distance, the eyes that do in fact point in slightly different directions appear perfectly focused. In the words of Marc Levoy, the scientist from Stanford University who discovered the squint, "He optimized each eye for its appearance as seen from the side... It's a typical Michelangelo trick." Proportion, it seems, is in the eye of the beholder.

Michelangelo once described the process of sculpting as being the liberation of the form from within the stone, a notion that seems to be embodied by the stunning unfinished **Slaves** that line the approach to the *David*. His procedure, clearly demonstrated here, was to cut the block as if it were a deep relief, and then to free the three-dimensional figure. Carved in the 1520s and 1530s, these immensely powerful creations, writhing as if to pull themselves free of the stone, were intended for the tomb of Pope Julius II; in 1564 the artist's nephew gave them to the Medici, who installed them in the grotto of the Bóboli gardens. In their midst here is another unfinished work, *St Matthew*.

The Museo di San Marco

Just north of the Accademia is the lively **Piazza San Marco**, a meeting-place for Florence's many art students. One side of the square is taken up by the Dominican convent and church of San Marco, now deconsecrated to house the **Museo di San Marco** (Tues–Fri 8.30am–1.50pm, Sat 8.30am–6.50pm; also open on second & fourth Sun of month 8.30am–6.50pm, and on first, third & fifth Mon of month 8.30am–1.50pm; L8000/€4.13; see box on p.455 for details of advance reservations; *www.sbas.firenze.it*). In the 1430s, the convent was the recipient of Cosimo il Vecchio's most lavish patronage: he financed Michelozzo's enlargement of the buildings, and went on to establish a vast public library here. Ironically, the convent became the centre of resistance to the Medici later in the century – Savonarola was prior of San Marco from 1491. Meanwhile, as Michelozzo was altering and expanding the convent, its walls were being decorated by one of its friars, **Fra' Angelico**, a painter in whom a medieval simplicity of faith was uniquely allied to a Renaissance sophistication of manner.

The **Ospizio dei Pellegrini** (Pilgrims' Hospice) contains around twenty paintings by Fra' Angelico, most brought here from other churches in Florence. A *Deposition* and a small *Last Judgement* are outstanding – the former remarkable for its aura of tranquillity, as though the minds of its protagonists were already fixed on the Resurrection. Across the cloister, in the **Sala Capitolare**, is a powerful fresco of the *Crucifixion*, painted by Angelico and assistants in 1441. At the rear of this room, the **refectory** – with a lustrous *Last Supper* by Ghirlandaio – forms an ante-room to the *foresteria* (guest rooms). The key work, for the drama of its setting and the lucidity of its composition, is the famous **Annunciation** at the summit of the main staircase. All round this upper floor are ranged 44 tiny **dormitory cells**, each frescoed either by Angelico himself or by his assistants – don't miss the *Noli me tangere* (cell 1), the *Annunciation* (cell 3), the *Transfiguration* (cell 6) and the *Coronation of the Virgin* (cell 9). In all likelihood, the marvellous *Madonna Enthroned*, on the facing wall, is by Angelico too. The anachronistic monastic onlookers in several of the scenes are St Dominic (with the star above his head) and St Peter Martyr (with the split skull); the latter, responsible for a massacre of Florentine heretics in the thirteenth century, is the city's home-produced Dominican saint. Michelozzo's **library**, a room that seems to exude an atmosphere of calm study, is off the corridor to the right, at the end of which is the pair of rooms used by Cosimo il Vecchio when he came here on retreat.

The **church** of San Marco, greatly altered since Michelozzo's intervention, is worth a visit for two works on the second and third altars on the right: a *Madonna and Saints*, painted in 1509 by Fra' Bartolommeo (like Fra' Angelico, a friar at the convent), and an eighth-century mosaic of *The Madonna in Prayer*, brought here from Constantinople.

Piazza Santissima Annunziata

The Accademia stands between Piazza San Marco to the west and, to the east, **Piazza Santissima Annunziata**, the locals' favourite square on account of its lovely porticoes and church. Until the seventeenth century the Florentine year used to begin on March 25, the Feast of the Annunciation – hence the city's predilection for paintings of the

Annunciation, and the popularity of the Annunziata church, which is still the place for society weddings. The festival is marked by a huge fair in the square and the streets leading off it. Giambologna's final work, the equestrian statue of Grand Duke Ferdinando I, holds the centre of the square; it was cast by his pupil Pietro Tacca, creator of the two bizarre **fountains**, on each of which a pair of aquatic monkeys dribble water at two bewhiskered sea-slugs.

The tone of the square is set by Brunelleschi's **Spedale degli Innocenti** (Mon, Tues & Thurs–Sun 8.30am–2pm; L5000/€2.58), opened in 1445 as the first foundlings' hospital in Europe, and which still incorporates an orphanage – Luca della Robbia's ceramic tondi of swaddled babies advertise the building's function. The convent, centred on two beautiful cloisters, now contains a miscellany of Florentine Renaissance art including one of Luca della Robbia's most charming Madonnas and an incident-packed *Adoration of the Magi* by Ghirlandaio.

The church of **Santissima Annunziata** (daily 7.30am–12.30pm & 4–6.30pm) is the mother church of the Servite order, which was founded by seven Florentine aristocrats in 1234. Its dedication took place in the fourteenth century, in recognition of its miraculous image of the Virgin which, left unfinished by the monastic artist, was purportedly completed by an angel. It attracted so many pilgrims that the Medici commissioned **Michelozzo** to rebuild the church in the second half of the fifteenth century in order to accommodate them. In the Chiostro dei Voti, the atrium that Michelozzo built onto the church, are some beautiful frescoes mainly painted in the 1510s, including a *Visitation* by **Pontormo** and a series by **Andrea del Sarto**, whose *Birth of the Virgin* achieves a perfect balance of spontaneity and geometrical order. Much of the church interior's gilt and stucco fancy dress was perpetrated in the seventeenth and eighteenth centuries, but the ornate tabernacle of the miraculous image, cordoned by candles and lanterns to the left of the entrance, was produced by Michelozzo. His patron, Piero il Gottoso, made sure that nobody remained unaware of his largesse: an inscription in the floor reads "The marble alone cost 4000 florins". The painting encased in marble has been repainted into obscurity, and is rarely shown anyway; far more interesting are the frescoes of *The Vision of St Jerome* and *The Trinity* by **Andrea del Castagno** in the first two chapels on the left. Separated from the nave by a triumphal arch is the unusual tribune, begun by Michelozzo but completed to designs by Alberti. The adjoining Chiostro dei Morti, entered from the left transept, is worth visiting for Andrea del Sarto's calculatedly informal *Madonna del Sacco*, painted over the door.

THE MUSEO ARCHEOLOGICO

Just off the square is the **Museo Archeologico**, Via della Colonna 38 (Mon 4–7pm, Tues & Thurs 8.30am–7pm, Wed & Fri–Sun 8.30am–2pm; summer Sat also 9pm–midnight; L8000/€4.13; see box on p.455 for details of advance reservations). This is the pre-eminent collection of its kind in northern Italy, though modernization is perpetually in progress, and they are still rectifying damage caused by the flood of 1966. Its special strength is its **Etruscan** finds. On the ground floor, pride of place goes to the *François Vase*, an Attic bowl from the sixth century BC. It's been restored twice – once after its discovery in Chiusi in 1845, and again after a butter-fingered member of staff converted it into a 638-piece jigsaw in 1900. The two upper floors are arranged with variable clarity. Outstanding among the **Roman** pieces is the nude known as the *Idolino*, probably a copy of a fifth-century BC original. The **Greek** head of a horse, in the same room, once adorned the garden of the Palazzo Medici, where it was studied by Donatello and Verrocchio. In the long gallery stand the *Arringatore* (Orator), the only known Etruscan large bronze from the Hellenistic period; and a *Chimera*, a bizarre triple-headed bronze monster of the fifth century BC discovered at Arezzo and much admired by Cosimo I's retinue of Mannerist artists.

The eastern city centre

The 1966 flood permanently changed the character of the eastern city centre. Before the deluge it had been one of the more densely populated districts of the city, packed with tenements and small workshops. But **Piazza Santa Croce**, a short stroll east of Piazza della Signoria, and the streets around it lie lower than the surrounding area, and were devastated when the Arno burst its banks. Many of the residents moved out permanently in the following years. Leather shops and jewellers are still in evidence, but the souvenir stalls are now a more conspicuous presence.

The piazza has traditionally been one of the city's main arenas: the Medici used it for self-aggrandizing pageants, and under Savonarola it was the principal site for the ceremonial execution of heretics. It's still sometimes used for the **Gioco di Calcio Storico**, a football tournament between the city's four *quartieri*; the game is held three times in St John's week (the last week of June), and is characterized by incomprehensible rules and a degree of violence from which the heavy sixteenth-century costumes offer inadequate protection.

Santa Croce

Florence's two most lavish churches after the duomo were the headquarters of the two preaching orders; the Dominicans occupied Santa Maria Novella, while the Franciscans were based at the giant church of **Santa Croce** (summer Mon–Sat 8am–6.30pm, Sun 3–5.30pm; winter Mon–Sat 8am–12.30pm & 3–5.30pm, Sun 3–5.30pm), famed as the mausoleum of Florence's eminent citizens. Over 270 tombstones pave the floor of the church, while grander monuments commemorate the likes of Ghiberti, Michelangelo, Machiavelli and Galileo. **Dante** has a monument in the church as well as a supremely dramatic statue overlooking the piazza outside – although he is actually buried in Ravenna, where he died.

Inside the door is Vasari's monument to **Michelangelo**, whose body was brought back from Rome to Florence in July 1574; he requested this position so that when the graves of the dead fly open on Judgement Day, the first thing to catch his eye would be Brunelleschi's cathedral dome. On the opposite side of the church is the tomb of **Galileo**, made in 1737, when it was finally agreed to give the great scientist a Christian burial. Back in the right aisle, the Neoclassical cenotaph to **Dante** is immediately after the second altar, while against the third pillar there's a beautiful pulpit by Benedetto da Maiano, carved with scenes from the life of St Francis. The side door at the end of the aisle is flanked by Donatello's gilded stone relief of *The Annunciation* and Bernardo Rossellino's tomb of the humanist **Leonardo Bruni**, a design which has spawned innumerable imitations.

The dazzling chapels at the east end of Santa Croce are a compendium of Florentine fourteenth-century art, showing the extent of Giotto's influence and the full diversity of his followers. The two immediately to the right of the chancel are entirely covered with frescoes by **Giotto**: beside the chancel is the **Cappella Bardi**, featuring scenes from the life of St Francis, while next to it is the **Cappella Peruzzi** with a cycle on the lives of St John the Baptist and John the Evangelist. On the south side of the right transept is the **Cappella Baroncelli**, featuring the first night scene in Western painting, Taddeo Gaddi's *Annunciation to the Shepherds*. On the north side of the left transept, the second **Cappella Bardi** houses a wooden Crucifix by **Donatello** – supposedly criticized by Brunelleschi as resembling a "peasant on the Cross".

THE MUSEO DELL'OPERA DI SANTA CROCE

Santa Croce's most celebrated attractions have been hived off to form the separate, and little-explored, **Museo dell'Opera di Santa Croce**, entered to the right of the main steps of the church (March–Oct Mon, Tues & Thurs–Sun 10am–7pm; rest of year closes 6pm; L8000/€4.13). Standing at the far end of the **Primo Chiostro**, a peaceful expanse of grass hard up against the church wall, is one of Florence's architectural gems, Brunelleschi's **Cappella dei Pazzi**. If one building could be said to typify the spirit of the early Renaissance, this is it. Brunelleschi designed the chapel in the 1430s and worked on it between 1442 and 1446, though it was only completed after his death. The building is geometrically perfect without seeming pedantic, and is exemplary in the way its decorative detail harmonizes with the design. The polychrome lining of the portico's shallow cupola is by **Luca della Robbia**, as is the tondo of *St Andrew* over the door; inside, Luca also produced the blue-and-white tondi of the *Apostles*.

As you exit the chapel, to your left hides Santa Croce's spacious **Secondo Chiostro**, also by Brunelleschi, and perhaps the most peaceful spot in the centre of Florence (although restoration means access is often restricted). A building between the two houses a damaged *Crucifixion* by **Cimabue** on the right wall, which has become the emblem of the havoc caused by the 1966 flood – six metres of filthy water surged into the church, tearing the artwork from its mounting. Also in this room are Taddeo Gaddi's fresco of the *Last Supper* and *Crucifixion* and **Donatello**'s enormous gilded *St Louis of Toulouse*, made for Orsanmichele.

South of the river

Visitors to Florence might perceive the Arno as merely a brief interruption in the urban fabric, but Florentines talk as though a ravine divided their city. North of the river is *Arno di quà* ("over here"), while the south side is *Arno di là* ("over there"), also known as the **Oltrarno**, literally "Beyond the Arno". Though traditionally an artisans' quarter, the Oltrarno has always contained prosperous enclaves, and many of the ruling families chose to settle in this area. Nowadays some of the city's swankiest shops line Borgo San Jacopo, while the windows of Via Maggio are an amazing display of palatial furnishings.

The direct route from the city centre to the heart of Oltrarno crosses the river on the **Ponte Vecchio**, the only bridge not mined by the retreating Nazis in 1944. Built in 1345 to replace an ancient wooden bridge, the bustling thoroughfare has always been loaded with shops propped over the water. Up until the sixteenth century, butchers, fishmongers and tanners occupied the bridge, but in 1565 the Medici had the Corridoio Vasariano (see p.474) constructed over the arcades as a private passageway between the Palazzo Vecchio and the Palazzo Pitti. For a generation, the noble nostrils suffered the stench rising from the bridge, until in 1593 Ferdinando I ejected the butchers and installed goldsmiths instead. Today, still replete with jewellery firms, the bridge is crammed with sightseers and big-spending shoppers during the day, and also remains busy after the shutters come down, when street traders set out their stalls and the local lads hang around the bust of Cellini.

Santa Felìcita, at the southern end of the bridge, is worth a visit (Mon–Sat 9am–noon & 3–6pm, Sun 10–11am & noon–1pm) for the paintings by **Pontormo** in the Cappella Capponi, just inside the door on the right. His weirdly erotic *Deposition* is one of the masterworks of Florentine Mannerism, its jarring colours slicing through the chapel's gloom. There's no sign of any standard imagery, or even the Cross: instead, androgynous figures clad in billows of drapery – metallic blue, puce green and bubblegum pink – bear the lifeless body of Christ like a mournful trophy, backed only by a solitary, ghostly cloud.

The Palazzo Pitti

Although the Medici later took possession of the largest palace in Florence – the **Palazzo Pitti** – it still bears the name of the man for whom it was built. Luca Pitti was a prominent rival of Cosimo il Vecchio, and much of the impetus behind the building of his new house came from a desire to trump the Medici. No sooner was the palace completed, however, than the Pitti's fortunes began to decline. By 1549 they were forced, ironically, to sell out to the Medici. The palace then became the Medici's family pile, growing in bulk until the seventeenth century, when it achieved its present gargantuan proportions. Today, the palazzo and the pavilions of the grand **Giardino di Bóboli** hold eight museums.

Many of the paintings gathered by the Medici in the seventeenth century are now arranged in the **Galleria Palatina**, a labyrinthine suite of 26 rooms in the right-side upper-floor wing of the palace (Tues–Sun 8.30am–6.50pm, Sat until 10pm; L12,000/€6.20; see box on p.455 for details of combined tickets and advance reservations). The ticket office is on the ground floor, just off the main courtyard. You'll need at least a couple of hours to do the gallery justice. The pictures are hung three deep in places, as they would have been in the days of their acquisition, and conform to no ordering principle except that of making each room as varied as possible. There are half-a-dozen excellent works by **Raphael** here, including, in room 5, portraits of Angelo Doni and his wife Maddalena – her pose copied directly from the *Mona Lisa* – and the celebrated *Madonna della Seggiola*, or Madonna of the Chair, in which the figures are curved into the rounded shape of the picture with no sense of artificiality. An even larger contingent of supreme works by **Titian** includes a number of his most trenchant portraits – among them *Pietro Aretino*, the preening *Cardinal Ippolito de' Medici*, and the disconcerting *Portrait of an Englishman* in room 2, a picture that makes the viewer feel as closely scrutinized as was the subject. **Rubens'** *Consequences of War* packs more of a punch than most other Baroque allegories. The gallery's outstanding sculpture is **Canova's** *Venus Italica* in room 1, commissioned by Napoleon.

Much of the rest of this floor comprises the **Appartamenti Monumentali** (same hours and ticket as Galleria Palatina) – the Pitti's state rooms, renovated by the dukes of Lorraine in the eighteenth century, and then again by Vittorio Emanuele when Florence became Italy's capital. On the floor above is the **Galleria d'Arte Moderna** (Tues–Sat 8.30am–1.50pm; also open on first, third & fifth Sun and second & fourth Mon of month same times; joint ticket with Galleria del Costume L8000/€4.13, or see box on p.455 for details of combined tickets and advance reservations). This displays a chronological survey of primarily Tuscan art from the mid-eighteenth century to 1945. Most rewarding are the products of the Macchiaioli, the Italian division of the Impressionist movement; most startling, however, are the sublime specimens of sculptural kitsch, such as Antonio Ciseri's *Pregnant Nun*. The left-side wing of the palace is given over to the **Museo degli Argenti** (same hours as Galleria d'Arte Moderna; L4000/€2.06; see box on p.455 for details of combined tickets and advance reservations) – a collection of luxury artefacts, including Lorenzo il Magnifico's trove of antique vases, displayed in one of the four splendidly frescoed reception rooms on the ground floor. The **Galleria del Costume** (same hours and ticket as Galleria d'Arte Moderna) is housed in the Palazzina della Meridiana, the eighteenth-century southern wing of the Pitti, and across the palace gardens is the **Museo delle Porcellane** (Museum of Porcelain; Mon–Sat 9am–1.30pm; also open on first, third & fifth Sun and second & fourth Mon of month same times; L4000/€2.06).

The Bóboli Gardens and the Belvedere

The **Giardino di Bóboli** is the Pitti's enormous formal garden (daily: June–Aug 9am–7.30pm; April, May & Sept 9am–6.30pm; March & Oct 9am–5.30pm; Nov–Feb 9am–4.30pm; closed first and last Mon of month; L4000/€2.06; see box on p.455 for details of combined tickets and advance reservations). Created when the Medici took possession of the Palazzo Pitti, it continued to expand into the early seventeenth century. Today, it is the only extensive area of greenery in the centre of the city, and thus tends to get crowded in the areas close to the gates; it gets quieter in the heart of the garden, however, as the sharp gradients of its avenues take their toll. Of all the garden's Mannerist embellishments, the most celebrated is the **Grotta del Buontalenti**, close to the entrance to the left of the palace facade, beyond the turtle-back figure of Cosimo I's court dwarf (as seen on a thousand postcards). In amongst the fake stalactites are shepherds and sheep that look like calcified sponges, while embedded in the corners are replicas of Michelangelo's *Slaves*, replacing the originals that were here until 1908. In the deepest recesses of the cave stands Giambologna's *Venus Emerging from her Bath*, leered at by attendant imps. The vast **amphitheatre** facing the palace courtyard was designed in the early seventeenth century as an arena for Medici festivities. A set-piece of comparable scale is the fountain island **Isolotto**, best approached along the central cypress avenue known as the *Viottolone*, many of whose statues are Roman originals. Carry straight on from here and you'll come to the **Porta Romana** entrance, which takes its name from the fourteenth-century city gate in the street outside.

It's sometimes possible to leave the gardens by the gate that leads to the precincts of the **Forte di Belvedere** (daily 9am–8pm; free, except during temporary exhibitions). This star-shaped fortress was built on the orders of Ferdinando I in 1590, ostensibly for the city's protection but really to intimidate the Grand-Duke's fellow Florentines. Art exhibitions are sometimes held in the box-like palace in the centre of the fortress, but they rarely offer any inducement to turn away from the incredible **urban panorama**. East from the Belvedere, and also accessible on Costa San Giorgio which coils up from Piazza Santa Felicita, stretches the best-preserved section of Florence's fortified walls, an attractive if tiring route to San Miniato (see overleaf).

Santo Spirito

The charmingly lived-in **Piazza Santo Spirito**, on the south side of the Ponte Santa Trinita, with its lolling students, market stalls and cafés, and the neighbouring streets with their furniture workshops and antiques showrooms, together encapsulate the self-sufficient character of the quarter, a character not yet hopelessly compromised by the encroachments of tourism. Don't be deterred by the vacant facade of the church of **Santo Spirito** (daily 9am–noon & 4–6pm; closed Wed afternoon) – the interior, one of Brunelleschi's last projects, prompted Bernini to describe it as "the most beautiful church in the world". It's so perfectly proportioned it seems artless, yet the plan is extremely sophisticated – a Latin cross with a continuous chain of 38 chapels round the outside and a line of 35 columns running in parallel right round the building. Unfortunately a Baroque baldachin covers the high altar, but this is the sole disruption of Brunelleschi's arrangement.

The Cappella Brancacci

In 1771 fire wrecked the Carmelite convent and church of **Santa Maria del Carmine** some 300m west of Santo Spirito, but somehow the flames did not damage the frescoes of the church's **Cappella Brancacci**, a cycle of paintings that is one of the essential sights of Florence (Mon & Wed–Sat 10am–5pm, Sun 1–5pm; L6000/€3.10; see box on p.455 for details of combined tickets and advance reservations). The frescoes adorn one side-chapel of the Carmine, which is barricaded off from the chancel and nave and instead has to be entered on a back route through the cloister. The ticket office is to the right of the church entrance, and your money allows you to view the stunning frescoes, in a maximum group of thirty, for an utterly inadequate fifteen minutes.

The decoration of the chapel was begun in 1424 by **Masolino** and **Masaccio**, the former aged 41 and the latter 22. Within a short time the elder was taking lessons from the younger, whose grasp of the texture of the real world, of the principles of perspective, and of the dramatic potential of the biblical texts they were illustrating far exceeded that of his precursors. Three years later Masaccio was dead, but (in the words of

Vasari), "All the most celebrated sculptors and painters since Masaccio's day have become excellent and illustrious by studying their art in this chapel." Michelangelo used to come here to make drawings of Masaccio's scenes – and had his nose broken on the chapel steps by a young sculptor whom he enraged with his condescending attitude.

The Brancacci frescoes are as startling a spectacle as the restored Sistine Chapel in Rome, the brightness and delicacy of their colours and the solidity of the figures exemplifying what Bernard Berenson singled out as the tactile quality of Florentine art. The small scene on the left of the entrance arch is the quintessence of Masaccio's art. Depictions of **The Expulsion of Adam and Eve** had never before captured the desolation of the sinners so graphically – Adam presses his hands to his face in bottomless despair, Eve raises her head and screams. In contrast to the emotional charge of Masaccio's couple, Masolino's almost dainty *Adam and Eve* on the opposite arch pose as if to have their portraits painted – highly reminiscent of Bandinelli's unintentionally comic sculpture in the Bargello.

St Peter is chief protagonist of most of the remaining scenes, two of which are especially compelling. The *Tribute Money* on the upper left wall, is the most widely praised, a complex narrative by Masaccio showing Peter, under Christ's instruction, fetching money from the mouth of a fish to pay a sum demanded by the city authorities of Capernaum. Masaccio's *St Peter Healing the Sick*, to the left of the altar, depicts the shadow of the stern saint curing the infirm as it passes over them, a miracle invested with the aura of a solemn ceremonial.

The cycle was suspended in 1428 when Masaccio left for Rome, where he died, and work did not resume until 1480, when the frescoes were completed by **Filippino Lippi**. He finished the *Raising of Theophilus's Son and St Peter Enthroned* (lower left wall), which depicts St Peter bringing the son of the Prefect of Antioch to life and then preaching to the people of the city from a throne. The three figures to the right of the throne are thought to be portraits of Masaccio, Alberti and Brunelleschi. Masaccio originally painted himself touching Peter's robe, but Lippi considered such physical contact to be improper and painted out the arm; you can clearly see where the arm used to be. There's another portrait in the combined scene of *St Peter before Agrippa* and *St Peter's Crucifixion* (lower right wall): the central figure looking out from the painting in the trio right of the crucifixion is Botticelli, Lippi's teacher. Lippi's most distinctive contribution, though, is *The Release of St Peter* on the right-hand side of the entrance arch, where there's a touching intimacy in the relationship between saint and counselling angel.

San Miniato al Monte

The brilliant, multicoloured facade of **San Miniato al Monte** on a steep hillside in the Oltrarno lures troops of visitors up from the south bank of the Arno. Most routes pass through or alongside the broad **Piazzale Michelangelo** just below the church: buses #12 and #13 stop here, there's free parking or it's twenty minute's walk from the city centre. The spectacular views from here of Brunelleschi's dome floating above the city are worth a special journey in themselves.

The church itself more than fulfils the promise of its appearance from a distance: **San Miniato** is the finest Romanesque church in Tuscany. The church's dedicatee, St Minias, belonged to a Christian community that settled in Florence in the third century; according to legend, after his martyrdom his corpse was seen to carry his severed head over the river and up the hill to this spot, where a shrine was subsequently erected to him. Construction of the present building began in 1013 with the foundation of a Cluniac monastery. The gorgeous marble facade – alluding to the baptistry in its geometrical patterning – was added towards the end of that century, though the external mosaic of *Christ between the Virgin and St Minias* dates from the thirteenth. The **interior** (daily: summer 7.30am–7pm; winter 8am–noon & 2.30–6pm) is like no other in the city, with the choir raised on a platform above the large crypt; its general form has changed little since the mid-eleventh century. The main structural addition is the Cappella del Cardinale del Portogallo, a paragon of artistic collaboration: the basic design was by Antonio Manetti (a pupil of Brunelleschi's), the tomb was carved by Antonio Rossellino, and the terracotta decoration of the ceiling is by Luca della Robbia. The majority of the frescoes along the aisle walls were painted in the fifteenth century; the most extensive are the sacristy's *Scenes from the Life of St Benedict*, painted in the 1380s by Spinello Aretino.

Eating, drinking and entertainment

Florence's gastronomic reputation has suffered under the pressure of mass tourism, and many locals swear there's scarcely a single genuine Tuscan **restaurant** left in the city. But don't dispair – this is an exaggeration – a decent meal isn't hard to come by if you explore away from the touristy central streets.

Florentines have always seemed to prefer wine to coffee, and the city can't really claim to have a **café** tradition like that of Rome or Turin – **bars** are both more plentiful and generally more attractive places to rest your weary limbs. The university and the annual influx of language students and other young visitors keeps the **nightlife** lively, while **classical music** events such as the prestigious Maggio Musicale maintain Florence's standing as the cultural focus of Tuscany.

Restaurants, pizzerias and snack-bars

In gastronomic circles, Florentine cuisine is often accorded as much reverence as Florentine art but quality cooking doesn't come cheap in Florence – most of the **restaurants** that meet with local approval cost L60,000/€30.99-plus per person, including wine. Yet there are some more affordable and congenial places in districts that have a bit of local colour to them, such as Santa Croce and around Santo Spirito. One thing to be aware of is that many restaurants in Florence will only serve full meals – check the menu outside if you're thinking of just popping in for a quick lunchtime plate of pasta.

At the lower end of the market, one option for a rapid stomach-filler is the **friggitoria**, a frequently nameless place serving fried food such as polenta and croquettes, while a **rosticceria** is usually a bit less basic, serving first courses and roast meat dishes often for takeaway only, although some have seating. We've divided the listings below by price: **expensive** means an average full meal (excluding wine) costs more than about L60,000/€30.99 per person; **inexpensive** means you can eat for L25,000/€12.91 or less; **mid-priced** is between the two.

Inexpensive

Amon, Via Palazzuolo 26r. This hole-in-the-wall is open until 11pm, churning out Egyptian falafel sandwiches for a bargain L4000/€2.06, plus meat kebabs and super-sticky desserts. Closed Mon.

Belle Donne, Via delle Belle Donne 16r. Bustling trattoria with banks of fresh flowers. Share a table and choose from the blackboard menu; especially busy at lunchtime. Closed Sat & Sun.

Benvenuto, Via Mosca 15r. Don't be misled by the entrance, which looks more like the doorway to a delicatessen than a trattoria; the gnocchi and *arista* are delicious and straightforward. Closed Wed & Sun.

Blue Anchor, Piazza del Mercato Centrale 44r. It may fall short of pretensions to being a Scottish pub, but you can nonetheless get Scottish and English beers to wash down its all-day breakfasts (bacon, eggs and all), toasted sandwiches and main meals, which include full Sunday lunch (roast beef and yorkshire pudding). Students with ID get ten percent discount at lunchtime (not valid for the breakfast). Open until 2am. No closing day.

Cantinetta del Verrazzano, Via dei Tavolini 18–20. Great central place for pizza, sandwiches or pastries, owned by a prestigious Chianti vineyard. Take away, sit down briefly by the counter, or grab a table in the pleasant rooms at the back to sample the wine. Closed Mon.

Casalinga, Via Michelozzi 9r. Long-established, traditional family-run trattoria east of Santo Spirito that serves up some of the best low-cost authentic Tuscan dishes in town. Paper tablecloths and brisk service add to the allure. Closed Sun.

Danny Rock, Via Pandolfini 13. Looks fast-foody but does top crepes. Big screens show concerts and sporting events. Students holding ID and cinema ticket get ten percent off. Open daily until 1am.

I Tarocchi, Via de' Renai 12. Quality basic pizzeria. Students with ID can claim a 15 percent late-night discount on all food (10pm–midnight). Closed Mon.

Il Contadino, Via Palazzuolo 69r. Very basic meals at around L25,000/€12.91, with often a lot of backpackers in the queue. Closed Sat.

Mario, Via Rosina 2r. A San Lorenzo fixture for decades, serving generations of students and market workers with no-nonsense lunches in no-nonsense surroundings. Be prepared to queue and share a table. Closed Sun.

Mensa Universitaria, Via San Gallo 25a. Not far from the San Lorenzo market, this is the cheapest deal in town. Only open to students with ID (Mon–Sat noon–2.15pm & 6.45–8.45pm; closed mid-July to mid-Sept). There are smaller *mensas* at Via dei Servi 25a (same hours) and at Piazza Santissima Annunziata 2 (noon–2.15pm only).

Pizzaiuolo, Via de' Macci 113r (☎055.241.171). Many Florentines reckon the pizzas here are the best in the city, something not unconnected with the fact that the owners are Neapolitan. The ambience is friendly and high-spirited, but space is at a premium: you'd should book a table. Closed Sun.

Volta di San Pietro 5. Highly recommended *friggitoria* in a tiny alley off Borgo degli Albizi, between the duomo and Sant'Ambrogio. Serves hamburgers, sausages and salads, and you can wash your snack down with a glass of wine from *All'Antico Noè*, in front of the *friggitoria* – which also does excellent sandwiches.

Mid-priced

Accademia, Piazza San Marco 7r. Usefully located alongside the Accademia, this family-run place has had high praise from *Rough Guide* readers for its versatile menu – from pizzas and salads to a full Tuscan blowout – and its pleasant, English-speaking staff. No closing day.

Acqua al Due, Via della Vigna Vecchia 40r (☎055.284.170). Always packed, chiefly on account of its *assaggio di primi* – a succession of pasta dishes shared by everyone at the table. No closing day.

Angiolino, Via Santo Spirito 36r (☎055.239.8976). Ambience alone makes this place worth a visit – it's one of the city's prettiest old-fashioned trattorias. Dried flowers and chillis hang from the brick-vaulted ceiling, set off by wicker-clad Chianti bottles and red checked tablecloths. The menu is short, Tuscan and to the point. Closed Mon.

Baldovino, Via San Giuseppe 22r (☎055.241.773). First-rate and very stylish contemporary-looking restaurant run by a charming Scottish couple. It's especially known for its pizzas, but the menu is chock-full of other excellent Tuscan and Italian dishes. Also good snacks from the adjacent wine bar. Closed Mon.

Borgo Antico, Piazza Santo Spirito 6r. A popular and boisterous trattoria. A good choice if you're more interested in the atmosphere than gourmet food. No closing day.

Gozzi, Piazza San Lorenzo 8r. Over the road from the market, this is a traditional lunchtime trattoria with long, shared tables and low prices. Closed Sun.

Lobs, Via Faenza 75r (☎055.212.478). Quirky all-wood fish restaurant, where there are no *antipasti* or *primi* – only fishy main courses, which come in "light", "small" or "big" portions, plus vegetables. Around midnight, the champagne flows as the place mutates into what they call a "fish-pub". There's a good budget set-menu at lunchtime for under L20,000/€10.33. Closed Mon.

Osteria del Caffè Italiano, Via Isola delle Stinche 11r (☎055.289.368). This rambling wood-panelled place, with casual lunch parlour, wine bar and smarter restaurant sections serves first-rate Tuscan food throughout (steer clear of the lacklustre vegetarian offering). Closed Mon.

Osteria Santo Spirito, Piazza Santo Spirito 16r (☎055.238.2383). Trendy, modern-looking osteria, serving simple, hearty Tuscan dishes with contemporary flair. There's no problem ordering a snack or single course. Outside tables in summer. No closing day.

Quattro Leoni, Via Vellutini 1r. A young, relaxed place arranged around an impressive three-room medieval interior. They only serve full meals, and direct you across the road to the *Caffè degli Artigiani* if you just want a snack. The menu is very Florentine: as a starter try the *finocchiona*, a type of Tuscan salami. Closed Wed in winter.

Ruth's, Via Farini 2a (☎055.248.0888). Quality North African/Middle Eastern cuisine that happens also to be meat-free and kosher, a couple of doors down from the synagogue. Indulge in a Tunisian fish couscous, or alternatively plump for falafel, home-made hummus and/or the delectable Syrian nut-based dip *muhammara*. Closed Fri eve & Sat lunch.

Tavola Calda, Sant'Ambrogio market. A superb lunch-only place for mouthwatering Tuscan dishes such as *topini di patate*, a first course of potatoes topped with a variety of sauces. Closed Sun.

Uvafragola, Piazza Santa Maria Novella 9r. The best of the clutch of pizzeria places lining this square, handy for rapid, uncomplicated nosh. Closed Wed.

Vecchia Bettola, Viale Lodovico Ariosto 32r. Long trestle tables give this place something of the atmosphere of a drinking den, which is what it once was; the menu has a good repertoire of Tuscan meat dishes. Closed Sun & Mon.

Zà-zà, Piazza del Mercato 26r. The best of several archetypal San Lorenzo trattorias. The old stone-walled interior has just a few tables; there's a bigger canteen below ground. Set menus for around L20,000/€10.33 are a steal. Closed Sun.

Expensive

La Baraonda, Via Ghibellina 67r (☎055.234.1171). This cosy little place has an appealing domesticity about it, and the varied menu always takes in fish dishes and vegetarian options as well as the house speciality *polpettone di vitello in umido* (stewed veal meatloaf). Students with ID get a twenty percent discount at lunchtime. Closed Sun & Mon lunch.

Beatrice, Via del Proconsolo 31r (☎055.239.8123). It's hard to imagine a more beautiful dining room; perfect for a smoochy date. The medieval painted ceiling alone is worth the price of a meal. Enter via the lobby of *Hotel Cavour*. Closed Mon.

Cibrèo, Via de'Macci 118r (☎055.234.1100). Superb food with creative takes on Tuscan classics in a relaxed, tasteful dining room with friendly and professional service. Allow at least L80,000/€42.32 in the posh part of the restaurant, but round the corner in Via del Verrocchio there's a backroom section where prices are far lower. Closed Sun & Mon.

Enoteca Pinchiorri, Via Ghibellina 87 (☎055.242.777). Florence's best restaurant, with two Michelin stars. The food is sublime and sophisticated, and as for wine, you've a choice of 80,000 different bottles. The eight-course set menus are slightly less taxing on your wallet than the à la carte. Closed Mon & Wed lunch, and all day Sun.

BUYING PICNIC FOOD

One way to cut eating costs is to retire with a **picnic** to the Bóboli gardens or squares such as Santissima Annunziata, Santa Croce or Santa Maria Novella. The easiest option is to call in at San Lorenzo's **Mercato Centrale** (Mon–Sat 7am–2pm, plus Sat 4–8pm), where everything can be bought under one roof. Almost as comprehensive, and even cheaper, is the **Mercato Sant'Ambrogio** over by Santa Croce (Mon–Fri 7am–2pm). The American bakery Mr Jimmy's, Via San Niccòlo 47, has bagels, brownies, muffins, banana bread and cheesecake. If you're in the centre with closing time approaching Via dei Tavolini, off Via dei Calzaiuoli, is a good street in which to assemble a picnic: Grana Market at no. 11r has cheeses and Semelino at no. 18r bakes wonderful bread. Every district has its *alimentari*, selling the choicest Tuscan produce. The unnamed one close to Santa Trinita at Via Parione 19 prepares delicious sandwiches (eg smoked salmon and *stracchino* cheese), and has a few seats, so you can linger over a glass of wine. Vera, at the southern end of Ponte Santa Trinita at Piazza Frescobaldi 3r, takes the prize for the ultimate Florentine deli; other excellent central *alimentari* include Tassini at Borgo Santi Apostoli 24r and Alessi Paride at Via delle Oche 27–29r.

Oliviero, Via delle Terme 52r (☎055.240.618). Currently enjoying a reputation for some of the city's best food. The innovative cuisine is predominantly Tuscan, but includes influences from around Italy (especially the South), served with formality. Desserts, for once, are a cut above the usual, led by an acclaimed *soufflé*. Closed Sun.

Cafés, gelaterie, bars and pubs

Pavement **cafés** are not really part of the Florentine scene. Smaller, less ostentatious venues are more the city's style – one-room cafés, bars or *pasticcerie*, or places that combine the functions of all three. Many line the big tourist streets around Piazza della Signoria, but it takes only a little effort to find places where prices are lower and non-Florentine faces fewer: a short walk north from the duomo gets you into the university area around San Marco, and it's just as easy to cross the river into Oltrarno, the city centre's most down-to-earth quarter. Many of the café/pasticceria-style places are at their busiest first thing in the morning, as the locals stop off for a quick coffee and a pastry such as a *budino di riso* (small rice cake) or a simple *brioche* or *cornetto*. Devotees of Italian **ice cream** will find plenty of *gelaterie* in Florence to sample some wacky concoctions without straying far off the main drags. The city has a fair spread of **bars** and **pubs** to fuel an evening's entertainment, and classier, specialist **wine-bars** are coming back into fashion after a hiatus: one of the focal points of a Florentine parish is the *vinaio*, an institution that's part wine cellar, part snack bar and part social centre.

Cafés

Caffè Amerini, Via della Vigna Nuova 63r. Stylish and intimate, with a clientele like the medieval/Art Deco/modern decor: eclectic. Ideal for a snack lunch, aperitif, or lingering on a rainy afternoon. Closed Sun.

Caffè Cibrèo, Via A. del Verrocchio 5r. It's a long way to come just for a drink, but the glorious wood-panelled interior is the prettiest in the city, and the cakes and desserts are outstanding. Open until 1am. Closed Sun & Mon.

Caffè Italiano, Via della Condotta 56r. A veritable oasis just steps away from the madness of Via dei Calzaiuoli. Elegant downstairs bar with silver teapots and wonderful cakes, and a secret little room upstairs with red velvet banquettes. Lunch is excellent. Closed Sun.

Caffèllatte, Via degli Alfani 39r. This vaguely alternative place is good for breakfast and brunch, featuring a wide range of teas and healthy snacks as well as terrific organic bread baked onsite. The *caffè latte*, served piping hot in big bowls, is phenomenal. Open until midnight. Closed Sun.

Caffè Notte, Via delle Caldaie 28r. Appealingly down-to-earth talking-shop just south of Santo Spirito, open from breakfast until 2am during the week, 3am at weekends. Closed Sun & Mon.

Caffè Rivoire, Piazza Signoria 5r. Every city has its Rivoire – a historic café whose central position and traditional reputation has seen it swamped by mass tourism. But if you want to people-watch on Florence's main square, this is the place to do so. The café's main claim to fame is its thick hot chocolate, but in summer, go for the refreshing *aperitivo della casa* (Campari, Martini, tonic and Punt & Mes). Closed Mon.

Capocaccia, Lungarno Corsini 12r. Voted as the locals' favourite night-time rendezvous, this stylish, trendy haunt doubles as a daytime café and evening snackery. Closed Sun & Mon.

Giacosa, Via de' Tornabuoni 83r. Public living-room of Florence's gilded youth, this was the birthplace of the Negroni cocktail – equal parts Campari, gin and vermouth. Closed Sun.

Hemingway, Piazza Piattellina 9r. Chocolate is the owners' passion (they're big cheeses in the Chocolate Appreciation Society, and offer desserts to die for), but the swathes of speciality teas, gourmet coffees, cocktails, food and wines are all excellent. Open until 1am. Closed Mon.

Procacci, Via de'Tornabuoni 64r. Famous café-shop that doesn't serve coffee, just cold drinks. Its fame comes from the extraordinary truffle rolls (*tartufati*), which are delicious but not very filling.

Ruggini, Via de' Neri 76r. Dessert-packed pasticceria close to the Uffizi that is smart without being intimidating. Closed Mon.

Gelaterie

Festival del Gelato, Via del Corso 75r. Over 100 varieties, with some exotic combinations (including carrot and spinach) and good *semifreddi*, but third-rate compared to *Vivoli*. Closed Mon.

Frilli, Via San Niccolò 57. Excellent ice creams made from seasonal fruit. Closed Wed.

Perchè No!, Via de' Tavolini 19r. Very central and highly regarded gelateria with a vast range of flavours; go for the rum-laced *tiramisù* ice cream. Students with ID can get discounts on the thick milkshakes. Closed Tues in winter.

Vivoli, Via Isola delle Stinche 7r. Operating from unprepossessing premises in a side street close to Santa Croce, this is the best ice cream maker in Florence – some say in Italy. An institution, creating subtle and sublime flavours. Closed Mon.

Pubs, bars and wine bars

All'Antico Vinaio, Via de' Neri 65r. Good rough-and-ready joint, close to the Uffizi, featuring a range of half-cut local characters sliding off their chairs. Closed Sun.

Apollo, Via dell'Ariento 41r. Narrow DJ-bar near San Lorenzo that rapidly crams after 11pm. No closing day.

Cabiria, Piazza Santo Spirito 4r. Cultish alternative bar, though still cosy and laid-back. Plenty of punters (locals and foreigners) sit out on the piazza. Closed Tues.

Caffè La Torre, Lungarno Cellini 65r. Alongside a medieval tower on the waterfront and notable for two things. First is the free buffet of food to accompany drinks (7–9pm); second is the late opening, until 4am every day.

Caracao, Via Ginori 10r. Pseudo-Latin American dive, with a big wooden bar and ranks of tequila bottles. Half-price happy hour (5.30–7pm). Closed Mon.

Casa del Vino, Via dell'Ariento 16r. Wine bar located just west of the Mercato Centrale, and passed by thousands of tourists daily but visited by only a handful. Florentines pitch up for a drink, a natter and an assault on a fine range of panini and *crostini*. Closed Sun.

Dolce Vita, Piazza del Carmine 6r. Trendy, modern-looking bar that's often a venue for small-scale art exhibitions. Dress to preen. Closed Sun.

Enoteca Baldovino, Via San Giuseppe 18r. Bright, modern and painted in warm ochre tones, this is a stylish, friendly little place to buy a range of gastronomic goodies and sample wines by the bottle or glass. Very convenient for Santa Croce. Closed Mon.

Enoteca de' Giraldi, Via de' Giraldi 4r (☎055.216.518, *www.koinecenter.com*). Old-fashioned central wine-bar and bistro, with vaulted ceilings, stone columns and marble-topped tables. Concentrates on local wines, and, uniquely, offers English-language classes in tasting and recognizing the reds, rosés and whites of Tuscany and central Italy. Closed Sun & Aug.

Fiaschetteria La Mescita, Via degli Alfani 70r. Low-key student *vinaio* in the university area; serves veggie as well as traditional *crostini*. Closed Sun.

Fiddler's Elbow, Piazza Santa Maria Novella. Florence's most popular Irish pub is an invariably heaving affair (outside tables relieve the crush). No closing day.

Fuori Porta, Via del Monte alla Croci. If you decide to climb up to San Miniato and regret your decision halfway, console yourself at Florence's most famous wine-bar. There are over 400 wines by the bottle – the choice by the glass changes every few days – and a wide selection of grappas and malt whiskies. Closed Sun.

Genesi, Piazza del Duomo 20r. Cool central bar with sofas and jazzy sounds. Closed Mon.

Lochness, Via dei Benci 19r. Quality imitation of a British student bar, crowded, windowless and covered in graffiti. Admission L10,000/€5.16. Closed June–Sept.

Rex, Via Fiesolana 25r. Long-established night-time fixture near Santa Croce, friendly and with eye-catching decor. Cocktails are good, tapas are excellent and the DJ outstanding. No closing day. Quieter *Caffè Piansa*, just round the corner at Borgo Pinti 18r, makes a good alternative, and has a happy hour when students can get two glasses of wine for L6000/€3.10 (5–8pm).

Le Volpi e L'Uva, Piazza dei Rossi 1r. This discreet little daytime place just over the Ponte Vecchio typifies the atmosphere of the Oltrarno – relaxed, mellow and welcoming. The owners concentrate on the interesting wines of small producers, and provide high-quality snacks to help them down (the cheeses in particular are tremendous). Closed Sun & Mon.

Nightlife and entertainment

Florentine **nightlife** has a reputation for catering primarily to the middle-aged and affluent, but like every university town it has its pockets of activity, and by hanging around
the San Marco or Santo Spirito quarters you should pick up news of any impromptu
events. For gay and lesbian nightlife, see Listings, p.494. The city's sizeable population
of British and American students ensures a supply of English-language **films**, and the
highbrow cultural calendar is filled out with seasons of **classical music, opera and
dance** to rival the best in Europe.

You can find **information** in English about concerts and shows at the kiosks in
Piazza Repubblica and inside the Palazzo Vecchio; otherwise, consult the tourist
offices, check out advertising hoardings around town or get hold of the *Firenze
Spettacolo* monthly listings magazine (see p.458 for details). The **ticket agency** Box
Office, at Via Alamanni 39 (☎055.210.804, *www.boxoffice.it*) and Chiasso de' Solderini 8r
off Via Porta Rossa (☎055.219.402), has information and tickets for all events, concerts
and festivals – but permanently busy phones.

Clubs and live music venues

Andromeda, Via dei Cimatori 13. Central club that heaves at weekends, with music covering all
bases from Euro-dance to Caribbean. Admission around L25,000/€12.91. Closed Sun.

Be Bop, Via dei Servi 28r. Classy rock, jazz and blues cellar, often crammed solid with students.
Generally open nightly.

Central Park, Parco delle Cascine. Currently one of the city's best clubs, with adventurous, wide-
ranging music and a superb sound system. Admission L15,000/€7.75. Wandering in the park outside is unsafe, doubly so for women; take a taxi there and back. Closed Sun–Wed in winter.

Chiodo Fisso, Via Dante Alighieri 16r. Good central venue for folk and sometimes jazz. Open nightly.

Jazz Club, Via Nuova de' Caccini 3. Florence's foremost jazz venue has been a fixture for years in
this side-street off Borgo Pinti. The L10,000/€5.16 annual membership fee gets you down into the
medieval brick-vaulted cellar, where the atmosphere is informal and there's live music most nights.
Gigs often decamp to suburban parks in the summer – check before heading out. Closed Sun.

Pongo, Via Verdi 59r. An afternoon bar and cybercafé that mutates into the city's most refreshingly unpretentious club, with no dress code, live music most nights and some excellent DJing to boot.
Admission L10,000/€5.16 (includes first drink). Closed Sun & June–Sept.

Film

There are a couple of **cinemas** showing films undubbed. Cinema Astro, in Piazza San
Simone near Santa Croce (no phone), screens English-language films six nights weekly, while Cinema Goldoni, Via dei Serragli 109 (☎055.222.437) and Odeon Original
Sound, Via Sassetti 1 (☎055.214.068, *www.cinehall.it*) run VO (original-language) films
once or twice a week. Most cinemas close in the summer months, when **open-air
screens** take over – usually at the Forte Belvedere, above the Bóboli gardens, and at
the Palacongressi, near the train station on Viale Strozzi. Tickets are around
L12,000/€6.20, often less for students.

Classical music, opera and dance

The **Maggio Musicale Fiorentino** is one of Europe's leading festivals of **opera** and
classical music, lasting from late April to early July. Events are staged at the Teatro
Comunale, the tiny Teatro Goldoni, the Teatro della Pergola, the Palazzo dei Congressi,
and occasionally in the Bóboli gardens. Tickets from L20,000/€10.33 to
L160,000/€82.63 go on sale in early April from the Teatro Comunale box office, Corso
Italia 16 (☎055.211.158 or 055.213.535, *www.maggiofiorentino.com*) as well as from
Liaisons Abroad (see p.5). Day tickets are sold from the theatre box office an hour
before each performance for L20,000/€10.33.

The Teatro Comunale is the city's major concert venue, hosting the **symphony orchestra** under the direction of Zubin Mehta, which performs a new programme every week during the winter concert season (Jan–March), as well as a prestigious **opera and ballet** season in the autumn (Sept–Dec). The Teatro della Pergola, at Via della Pergola 12 (☎055.247.9651), built in 1656 and believed to be Italy's oldest theatre, hosts seasons of **chamber concerts** by the Amici della Musica that draw in world-class performers (Jan–April & Oct–Dec), while the Florence Chamber Orchestra (☎055.783.374, *www.videosoft.it/orchest*) performs every two weeks (April–June & Sept–Oct) in Orsanmichele church. The **Estate Fiesolana** summer festival concentrates on chamber and symphonic music, with most events held in Fiesole's open-air Roman amphitheatre (see p.497). July's three-week **Florence Dance Festival** showcases first-rate classical, traditional and contemporary dance; get tickets and information from the festival offices at Borgo della Stella 23r (☎055.289.276, *www. florencedance.org*) or the Box Office agency (see opposite).

Listings

Airlines Air France, Borgo SS Apostoli 9 (☎1478.84.466); Alitalia, Piazza dell'Oro 1 (☎1478.65.642); British Airways (☎1478.12.266); Garuda, Via Palagio degli Spini 1 (☎055.337.1201); Lufthansa, Via Lamberti 39r (☎055.340.838); Meridiana, Lungarno Vespucci 28r (☎055.230.2416); SAS, Lungarno Acciaioli 8 (☎055.238.2701); TWA, Via Vecchietti 4 (☎055.239.6856); United, Via Vecchietti 4 (☎055.289.460).

Bike, scooter and motorbike rental There are 17 Bike Points (*Punti Bici*) around the city (all Mon–Sat 8am–7.30pm) where the council provides bikes for a nominal L1000/€0.52 per day in exchange for a photocopy of your passport, although you must bring the bikes back in the evening. Central locations are: Piazza Stazione, the Mercato Centrale, Piazza Cestello, Porta Romana, Piazza Strozzi, Via della Ninna beside the Uffizi, and Piazza San Marco. One of the best commercial outlets is Florence by Bike, Via San Zanobi 120r (daily 9am–7.30pm; ☎055.488.992, *www.florencebybike.it*): push bikes are L4000/€2.06 per hour or L20,000/€10.33 per day; 21-gear mountain bikes start from L30,000/€15.49 per day; electric scooters are L60,000/€30.99 per day; and a two-person 125cc touring scooter is L120,000/€61.97 per day. They have discount weekend rates, and lower prices for students. Other similarly priced outlets include Alinari at Via Guelfa 85r (☎055.280.500) and Via dei Bardi 35 (☎055.234.6436); and Motorent, Via San Zanobi 9r (☎055.490.113).

Books Aside from the chain bookshops Feltrinelli, Via Cavour 12r, and Seeber, Via de' Tornabuoni 68r, good general outlets are Paperback Exchange, Via Fiesolana 31r (*www.dada.it/paperback*); BM Bookshop, Borgognissanti 4r; and After Dark, Via de' Ginori 47r. City Lights, Via San Niccolo 23, concentrates on Beat literature and organizes plenty of readings; Il Viaggio, Via Ghibellina 117r, specializes in travel books, guides and maps; The Cinema Bookshop is at Via Guelfa 14r; and Libreria delle Donne, Via Fiesolana 2b, is a women's bookshop.

Car rental Avis, Borgo Ognissanti 128r (☎055.213.629), and at the airport (☎055.315.588); Europcar, Borgo Ognissanti 53r (☎055.236.0073 or ☎167.013.942, airport ☎055.318.609); Hertz, Via Maso Finiguerra 33r (☎055.239.8205, airport ☎055.307.370); Holiday Autos, Via Palagio degli Spini 1 (☎055.337.1201); Italy by Car/Thrifty, Borgo Ognissanti 134r (☎055.287.161, airport ☎055.300.413); Maggiore/National, Via Maso Finiguerra 31r (☎055.210.238 or ☎1478.67.067, airport ☎055.311.256); Program (lowest daily rate), Borgo Ognissanti 135r (☎055.282.916); Sixt (airport ☎055.309.790).

City tours Enjoy Florence (toll-free ☎800.274.819) run walking tours from the Thomas Cook office at Lungarno Acciaiuoli 6r (Mon–Sat 10am; L30,000/€15.49; takes 3hr). Gentle small-group 3-hour bike tours are run by Florence by Bike, Via San Zanobi 120r (☎055.488.992, *www.florencebybike.it*; leaving daily 9.15am & 3pm; L45,000/€23.24).

Consulates Netherlands, Via Cavour 81 (☎055.475.249); South Africa, Piazza Saltarelli 1 (☎055.281.863); UK, Lungarno Corsini 2 (☎055.284.133); USA, Lungarno Vespucci 38 (☎055.239.8276). For the Rome embassies of Australia, Canada, Ireland and New Zealand, see p.747.

Exchange Banks are concentrated around Via de' Tornabuoni and Piazza della Repubblica, and some open for a few hours on Saturday. There are dozens of exchange kiosks, most with none-too-favourable rates or commissions. Try American Express, Via Dante Alighieri 22r (Mon–Fri

9am–5.30pm, Sat 9am–12.30pm; ☎055.50.981), or Thomas Cook, Lungarno Acciaiuoli 6r (Mon–Sat 9am–6pm, Sun 9am–2pm; ☎055.289.781 or ☎167.004.488).

Flight information For flights from Florence-Perètola (Aeroporto Amerigo Vespucci), call ☎055.306.1702 (international) or ☎055.306.1700 (domestic). For all flights from Pisa (Aeroporto Galileo Galilei), call ☎050.500.707, or go to the Air Terminal check-in desk on platform 5 of Florence's Santa Maria Novella train station (daily 7am–5pm; ☎055.216.073). You can buy train tickets here to Pisa airport (plus a service charge of L2000/€1.03) and check your bags in too. The cutoff time is 15min before the train leaves, and you must still allow a minimum of 35min at the airport end before your flight departs in order to get through passport control and security. Advance check-in is not available if you're flying with Ryanair.

Football Florence's soccer team, Fiorentina, is one of Italy's most glamorous sides. They won the Italian cup in 1996 and came close to a league championship in 1999. Games are played on alternate Sundays (except in June & July) at Stadio Artemio Franchi east of Campo di Marte, served by the special match-day bus #52 from the train station. Tickets start at L30,000/€15.49, but you should consult the tourist office in advance about availability.

Gay and lesbian life Florence's history is scattered with some of history's greatest gay and bisexual artists (Michelangelo, Leonardo and Botticelli, among others). The support group Azione Gay e Lesbica is at Via San Zanobi 54r (☎055.476.557). Of the handful of gay- and lesbian-friendly bar/cafés around town is the arty, relaxed *Piccolo Caffè*, Borgo Santa Croce 23r (daily 5pm–1.30am). The key men-only venues are *Crisco Bar*, Via S. Egidio 43r (Mon & Wed–Sun 10pm–late) and *Tabasco Disco-Bar*, Piazza S. Cecilia 3 (Tues–Sun 10pm–late). The women's bookshop Libreria delle Donne, Via Fiesolana 2b, has contacts and information for lesbian visitors. *Yag*, Via dei Macci, is a gay-friendly cybercafé and bar.

Internet access Florence has dozens of cybercafés, all of which charge around L6000/€3.10 per thirty minutes, and all of which knock L1000/€0.52 off if you can show student ID. Long hours, from mid-morning until late at night (slightly truncated on Sundays), are common. Check out *Internet Train*, Via Guelfa 24a, Via Oriuolo 40r, Borgo San Jacopo 30r, Via de' Benci 36r, or Via Giacomini 9 (*www.internettrain.it*); *The NetGate*, Via San Egidio 10r, Via Cavour 144r, Via dei Cimatori 17r, or Via Nazionale 156r (*www.thenetgate.it*); *MeridiaNet*, Borgo San Frediano 5r (☎055.264.5507); *Odus Intercomm*, Via del Porcellana 20r (*www.odusintercomm.com*); *Webpuccino*, Via de' Conti 22r (☎055.277.6469); or, if you prefer an iMac, *IntoTheWeb*, Via de' Conti 23r (☎055.264.5628).

Laundry Wash & Dry is in several central locations (Via Ghibellina 143r, Via Nazionale 129r, Via della Scala 52r, Via dei Serragli 87r, Via dei Servi 105r, and Via del Sole 29r), all open daily 8am–10pm.

Left luggage There's a staffed counter at the train station (daily 4.15am–1.30am; L5000/€2.58 per piece for 12hr).

Lost property The city office, Via Circondaria 19 (Mon–Wed, Fri & Sat 9am–noon; ☎055.328.3942) receives property handed in to police (☎055.4977) or the railway police (☎055.212.296). If you lost items on a train, call ☎055.235.2190; at Vespucci airport ☎055.308.023.

Medical facilities There's a first aid station on Piazza Duomo. The Guardia Medica Turistica, Via Santa Rosa 13 (Mon–Fri 8am–2pm, Sat 8am–1pm; ☎055.228.5789), it charges L25,000/€12.91 for a consultation. IAMAT, Via Lorenzo il Magnifico 59 (☎055.475.411), has English-speaking doctors on call, day or night (L150,000/€77.47). Otherwise, the Ospedale Santa Maria Nuova, Piazza Santa Maria Nuova 1 (☎055.27.581) has a 24hr emergency room. The Associazione Volontari Ospedalieri (☎055.425.0126) are volunteers on 24hr call who help foreigners in medical difficulties by providing advice and interpreting.

Parking The only legal street parking is in a blue space (max 2hr, 8am–8pm). Firenze Parcheggi (☎055.272.011, *www.firenzeparcheggi.it*) controls all city car parks, including the 24-hour guarded car park "Parterre" at Piazza della Libertà; with a chit from your hotel you pay L15,000/€7.75 for 24 hours here, and get free bike rental plus a voucher for L5000/€2.58 off a taxi ride. The most central parking is on Piazza Brunelleschi, northeast of the duomo (L2000/€1.03 per hour). There's free parking south of the river at Piazzale Michelangelo – watch out for a long-running scam whereby bogus parking attendants direct you into a free space, thus implying there's a charge (there isn't). If you've been towed, phone ☎055.308.249 and be prepared for a cash fine of L150,000/€77.47.

Pharmacies Comunale della Stazione inside the train station (☎055.289.435); Molteni, Via Calzaiuoli 7r (☎055.289.490); and All'Insegna del Moro, Piazza San Giovanni 20r (☎055.284.013) are all open 24hr daily.

INTER-URBAN BUSES

Florence has an alphabet soup of **bus companies** operating on different routes to destinations within Tuscany and in the neighbouring regions. All of them are headquartered at one or other of the bays around Santa Maria Novella train station.
ATAF, Piazza Stazione (☎055.565.0222); **CAP**, Largo Alinari 9 (☎055.214.637); **CLAP**, c/o Lazzi, Piazza Stazione 1 (☎0583.587.897); **COPIT**, Largo Alinari 9 (☎0571.74.194); **Eurolines**, c/o Lazzi Express (☎055.215.155); **Lazzi**, Piazza Stazione 1 (☎055.215.155); **LFI**, c/o Lazzi, Piazza Stazione 1 (☎0575.39.881); **RAMA**, c/o Lazzi, Piazza Stazione 1 (☎0564.454.169); **SITA**, Via Santa Caterina da Siena 15 (local and regional ☎800.373.760; long-haul ☎055.214.721); **SULGA**, Piazza Adua (☎075.500.9641).

Arezzo SITA, Lazzi
Assisi SULGA
Bettolle* LFI
Empoli Lazzi
Fiesole ATAF
Greve in Chianti SITA
Grosseto RAMA
Livorno Lazzi
Lucca CLAP, Lazzi
Perugia Lazzi, SITA, SULGA
Pisa Lazzi
Pistoia COPIT, Lazzi
Poggio a Caiano CLAP

Poggibonsi† SITA
Prato CAP, Lazzi
Sansepolcro SITA
Siena SITA
Viareggio Lazzi
Vinci COPIT
Volterra SITA
* change for Montepulciano
† change for San Gimignano

Florence city buses ATAF
International buses Eurolines

Police Emergency: Carabinieri ☎112; Police ☎113. The tourist police are at Via Pietrapiana 50r, off Piazza de' Ciompi (☎055.203.911). The city police (emergency ☎055.36.911) are at the train station, Palazzio Vecchio and Via delle Terme. The *Questura* police HQ, for passport problems, reporting thefts and so on, is at Via Zara 2 (☎055.49.771).

Post office Central post office is at Via Pellicceria 3 (Mon–Sat 8.15am–6pm; telegram office open 24hr; poste restante at counters 23 & 24). Other post offices are at Via Pietrapiana 53, Via Cavour 71r, and Via Barbadori 40r.

Taxis Radio taxis are on ☎055.4798, ☎055.4242 and ☎055.4390. Main stands are the train station and Piazza della Repubblica.

Train information ☎1478.88.088.

Around Florence

Within the area of Greater Florence, city buses run northeast to the hill-village of **Fiesole** and to the nearest of the various **Medici villas** – originally country retreats, now all but consumed by the suburbs. To the south towards Siena lie the hills and vineyards of **Chianti**, Italy's premier wine region. Around thirty minutes northwest of Florence on the train or bus route towards Lucca lie the neighbours **Prato** and **Pistoia**, both of them full of art and historic architecture, and both serving as fine day-trips or alternative bases in the area. Finally, on the train or bus journey west to Pisa, there are worthwhile diversions to **Vinci** – Leonardo's birthplace – and hilltop **San Miniato**.

Fiesole

A long-established Florentine retreat from the summer heat and crowds, **FIESOLE** spreads over a cluster of hilltops 8km northeast of the city. It predates Florence by several millennia: the Etruscans held out so long up here that the Romans were forced to set up permanent camp in the valley below – thus creating the beginnings of the settlement that was to become Florence. The **views** of Florence, which highlight just how extraordinary Brunelleschi's cathedral dome is, are unmissable, and the airiness of the place makes it great for kicking back.

The central square of Fiesole, **Piazza Mino**, is a long, gently sloping arena lined with shaded cafés and named after the fifteenth-century sculptor Mino da Fiesole, who has two fine pieces in the **Duomo** that dominates the north side of the square (daily 7am–noon & 3–6pm). Nineteenth-century restoration ruined the duomo's exterior, and the interior is something like a stripped-down version of Florence's San Miniato, although there's relief from the austerity in the Cappella Salutati, to the right of the choir: it contains Mino's panel of the *Madonna and Saints*. Behind the duomo lie the interesting **Museo Archeologico** (daily 9.30am–7pm; winter closes 5pm; L12,000/€6.20) and the adjacent **Museo Bandini** (same hours and ticket as above), housing a local canon's collection of medieval Florentine and Tuscan art. Gates give onto the Area Archeologica behind (same hours and ticket), featuring a 2000-seat **Roman theatre** built in the first century BC, a baths complex and an **Etruscan temple** dedicated to Minerva.

Fiesole's two other major churches are reached by Via San Francesco, which rises steeply from Piazza Mino, partway up broadening into a terrace giving a spectacular panorama of Florence. **Sant'Alessandro** (daily 10am–noon & 3–5pm) was founded in the sixth century on the site of Etruscan and Roman temples and has beautiful *marmorino cipollino* (onion marble) columns adorning its basilical interior. The Gothic church of **San Francesco** (same hours) occupies the site of the acropolis; across one of the convent's tiny cloisters there's a chaotic museum of pieces brought back from Egypt and China by missionaries. An alternative descent back to Piazza Mino is through the public park, entered by a gate facing San Francesco's facade. Another lovely walk heads southwest from Piazza Mino for 1.5km down the narrow, winding Via Vecchia Fiesolana (which branches off the main road) to the hamlet of **SAN DOMENICO**. Fra' Angelico was once prior of the Dominican **monastery** here, and the church retains a 1420 *Madonna and Angels* by him (first chapel on the left), and the chapter house also has a Fra' Angelico fresco of *The Crucifixion* (ring the bell at no. 4 for entry).

Practicalities

ATAF city **bus** #7 runs every fifteen minutes from Florence train station through Piazza San Marco to the Piazza Mino. The **tourist office** is just off the square, behind the cathedral on Via Portigiani 3 (Mon–Sat 8.30am–7.30pm, Sun 10am–7pm; ☎055.598.720, *www.comune.fiesole.fi.it/infoturismo*). There is **Internet** access here (10min free), and at the branch of Internet Train (*www.internettrain.it*) within Il Segnalibro, Piazza Mino 12.

Best of Fiesole's few **hotels** is the stunning *Villa San Michele*, a fourteenth-century former monastery at Via Doccia 4 (☎055.567.8200, fax 055.567.8250, *www.orient-expresshotels.com*; ⑨). On the slope below, is the light and stylish *Villa Fiesole*, Via Beato Angelico 35 (☎055.597.252, fax 055.599.133, *www.villafiesole.it*; ⑦); half-board here is no hardship, since the food is as impressive as the terrace views. Both have private parking. *Villa Sorriso*, Via Gramsci 21 (☎055.59.027, fax 055.597.8075; ③), is a pleasant, unfussy mid-price option. The **campsite** *Panoramico*, 3km east at Via Peramonda 1 (☎055.599.069, fax 055.59.186), is Florence's best. Ranged around Piazza Mino are a handful of **restaurants**, including *Mario* at no. 9r (☎055.59.143; closed Tues), with a shaded terrace and good salads; and the pizza/pasta *Etrusca* at no. 2r (closed Thurs). *India*, Via Gramsci 43a (☎055.599.900; closed Tues) has quality mid-priced North Indian cuisine – plenty of mughlai and tandoori dishes – as well as both veggie and meat-based *thalis*.

Fiesole's big party is the **Estate Fiesolana** (*www.comune.fiesole.fi.it/estatefiesolana*), a festival of music, dance and drama held in the Roman amphitheatre from June to September, which incorporates the prestigious international **Florence Dance Festival** during July, see p.493. July 6 is the day of **St Romolo**, patron saint of Fiesole, celebrated with a procession and festivities.

The Medici villas

The finest country houses of the Florentine hinterland are, predictably enough, those built for the **Medici**. The earliest of these grand villas were intended as fortified refuges to which the family could withdraw when the political temperature in the city became a little too hot, but as the Medici became established and the risk of challenge lessened, the villas became more ostentatious, signifying the might of the dynasty through their sheer luxuriousness. The **northern outskirts** of Florence hold a clutch of them, these days often to be reached through unattractive industrial sprawl. All, however, boast delightful gardens.

The **Villa della Petraia** (daily: June–Aug 9am–7.30pm; April, May & Sept 9am–6.30pm; March & Oct 9am–5.30pm; Nov–Feb 9am–4.30pm; closed first & fourth Mon of month; joint ticket including Villa di Castello gardens L4000/€2.06; bus #28) was adapted from a medieval castle in the 1570s and 1580s by Buontalenti. Vittorio Emanuele II glassed over the interior courtyard to convert it into a ballroom; its walls are covered by a seventeenth-century fresco cycle glorifying the Medici. Giambologna's bronze statue of *Venus*, now transplanted to a small room indoors, used to adorn the marble fountain on the upper terrace of the magnificent **garden**. A little under 1km northwest down the hill from La Petraia stands the Baroque **Villa di Castello** (bus #28; villa closed to public; gardens same hours and ticket as Villa della Petraia). This house was bought in 1477 by Lorenzo and Giovanni de' Medici, principal patrons of Botticelli – the *Birth of Venus* and *Primavera* both used to hang here. The fame of the villa rests on its spectacular **garden**: Montaigne was delighted by its labyrinths, fountains and myriad tricks, and judged it the best garden in Europe. The outstanding eccentricities are Ammannati's shivering figure of *January*, the triple-bowled fountain topped by the same artist's *Hercules and Antaeus*, and the Grotto degli Animali, an artificial cave against whose walls stands a menagerie of sculpted creatures. Also within walking distance of Petraia is **Villa di Careggi**, the meeting place for Lorenzo il Magnifico's academy of Platonic scholars and now a nursing home set amidst expansive woodland with variable opening hours.

Nothing remains of Francesco I's favourite villa, the **Villa Demidoff** at **PRATOLINO**, 12km north of Florence, except its expansive **park** (April–Sept Thurs–Sun 10am–8pm; March Sun 10am–6pm; Oct Sun 10am–7pm; L5000/€2.58; *www.provincia.fi.it*; bus #25), and even this is but a shadow of its earlier self. The mechanical toys, trick fountains and other practical jokes that Buontalenti installed here were the most ingenious of their day. Only Giambologna's immense *Appennino* sculpture – a grizzled man-mountain who gushes water – survives from the original garden, but the park is still one of the most pleasant green spaces near Florence.

In the small town of **POGGIO A CAIANO**, 18km west of Florence and 7km south of Prato, is the romantic **Villa Medicea "Ambra"** (open daily for guided tours on the half-hour: June–Aug 9.30am–5.30pm; April, May & Sept 9.30am–4.30pm; March & Oct 9.30am–3.30pm; Nov–Feb 9.30am–2.30pm; closed on second and third Mon of month; L4000/€2.06). The villa is served by CLAP buses from Florence, and CAP from Prato; pick up from the Prato tourist office (see p.501) the excellent "weekend guide" *Prato: In and Around*, giving information on the villa, places to eat and walks nearby. Lorenzo il Magnifico bought a farmhouse on this site in 1480 and had it rebuilt as a grand rural palace by Giuliano da Sangallo. An impressive double-staircase sweeps up to the imposing entrance loggia, commissioned by Lorenzo's son Giovanni, the future Pope Leo X. Inside, the focal point is the double-height *salone*, which the architect made out of the original courtyard; its sixteenth-century frescoes include works by Pontormo and del Sarto. The **gardens**, modified by the Lorraine princes into an English-style landscape, contain some magnificent old trees. To cap the afternoon in style, take a local bus 5km southwest to the village of **CARMIGNANO** where, in the church of San Michele, hangs Pontormo's *Visitazione* (c.1530), one of the outstanding works of the Mannerist period: its combination of superbly realized colour in the women's drapes, profound emotion and the mesmeric quality of all four faces is electrifying.

The Chianti region

Ask a sample of northern Europeans to describe their idea of paradise, and the odds are it will sound much like **Chianti**, the territory of vineyards and hill-towns that stretches between Florence and Siena. The climate is drenched in luminescent sunlight during the long summer and rarely grim even in the pit of winter. And to cap it all, there's the **wine** – the one Italian vintage everyone's heard of (*www.chianticlassico. com*). Visitors from Britain and other similarly ill-favoured climes were long ago alerted to Chianti's charms, and the rate of immigration has been so rapid since the 1960s that the region is now wryly dubbed "**Chiantishire**". Yet it would be an exaggeration to say that Chianti is losing its character in the way that many of Italy's coastal towns have lost theirs. The tone of certain parts has been altered, but concessions to tourism have been more or less successfully absorbed into the rhythm of local life.

If you're relying on **buses**, the best targets are the two main towns, **Greve in Chianti** and **Radda in Chianti**. Three SITA **buses** a day run from Florence through Greve and Castellina to Radda. Five TRA-IN buses a day run from Radda through Castellina (but not Greve) to Siena. But the only realistic way to get to know the region is with **your own transport**, following the "Chiantigiana", the SS222 that snakes its way between Florence and Siena through the most beautiful parts of Chianti. The Florence APT's excellent *Il Chianti cartoguida turistica* 1:70,000 contour map pinpoints every lane and farmhouse. Florence by Bike, see p.493, run full-day tours of Chianti **by bike** – an easy 32km route or a harder 70km (L97,000/€50.09 for either tour includes an English-speaking guide and all equipment).

Greve in Chianti

The "Chiantigiana" road meanders south through picture-pretty wine-villages for 28km to the amiable market town of **GREVE IN CHIANTI**. Cafés, restaurants and *enoteche* line the arcades of its attractive central **Piazza Matteotti**. This long, sloping triangle hosts the regular Saturday market and is overlooked by a statue of local boy **Giovanni da Verrazzano**, who became, in 1524, the first European to see Manhattan island.

Greve's **tourist office** is in a hut in the Parco di Sant'Anna, alongside the main Viale Verrazzano 1km north of Piazza Matteotti (Mon–Fri 10am–1pm & 3–6pm, Sat 11am–1pm & 4–6pm; ☎055.854.6287, *comunegreve@ftbcc.it*; check out also *www. greve-in-chianti.com*). Chianti'Pop has **Internet** access, Via Roma 36 (☎055.854.6280, *www.chiantipop.net*; L3000/€1.55 for 15min). For **picnic** supplies, head for Macelleria Falorni, Chianti's most famous butcher, a fixture on Piazza Matteotti since 1729 (*www.falorni.it*), and then choose a bottle from the Enoteca di Gallo Nero, Piazzetta Santa Croce 8 (*www.chianticlassico.it*). Greve's September **wine fair** is one of the largest such events in Tuscany. *Albergo del Chianti* is a straightforward three-star **hotel** at Piazza Matteotti 86 (☎& fax 055.853.762, *www.albergodelchianti.it*; ④), with air-con and a pool. Hilltop *Castello Vicchiomaggio*, Via Vicchiomaggio 4 (☎055.854.709, fax

SMILE, MY LADY

About 3km south of Greve is **Villa Vignamaggio**, set amidst formal Italian gardens at the centre of a beautiful old estate founded by the Gherardini family in the fourteenth century. In 1479, Antonio Maria Gherardini celebrated the birth of a new baby, Lisa, at Vignamaggio. It seems that, around the age of 24, Lisa sat for a portrait by one of Tuscany's most celebrated artists of the day, **Leonardo da Vinci**, shortly after her marriage to the wealthy Florentine silk merchant Francesco del Giocondo. The likeness famously captured the smile of La Gioconda, whose noble title was "Ma Donna Lisa" ("my lady") – shortened to *Mona Lisa*.

055.853.911, *www.vicchiomaggio.it*; ⑤) is a more luxurious option: a ninth-century castle resplendent amidst vineyards, boasting a top-flight restaurant, old-fashioned rooms and apartments, and regular half-day cookery classes. But the most charming choice is *Villa Vignamaggio*, 3km south of Greve, at Via Petriolo 5 (☎055.854.661, fax 055.854.4468, *www.vignamaggio.com*; ⑤) with a choice of en suite rooms and self-contained apartments within the main villa, and a handful of small cottages dotted around the grounds. It was here that Kenneth Branagh filmed *Much Ado About Nothing*. There's no restaurant in this **agriturismo**, but the owners prepare a classic Tuscan dinner for their guests twice a week. Best **restaurant** is the pricey, traditional-style *Giovanni da Verrazzano*, Piazza Matteotti 28 (☎055.853.189; closed Mon). Around the square you'll also find the easygoing *Mangiando Mangiando* at no. 80 (closed Mon), with an open kitchen serving light meals, and inexpensive *Nerbone di Greve* at no. 22 (closed Tues).

Radda in Chianti

A ridge 22km south of Greve is occupied by the well-heeled town of **Castellina in Chianti**: its walls, fortress and the covered perimeter walkway all bear testimony to an embattled past on the frontline between Florence and Siena, which lies a further 21km south. From Castellina, the SS429 branches east 22km to **RADDA IN CHIANTI**. The street plan of this minuscule but historic town is focused on **Piazza Ferrucci**, where the frescoed and shield-studded Palazzo Comunale faces a church raised on a high platform.

Within the palazzo's portico is the Pro Loco **tourist office** (Mon–Sat 10am–1pm & 3–7pm, Sun 10am–1pm; ☎& fax 0577.738.494, *proradda@chiantinet.it*), which will book rooms in the area for free. They also have maps outlining a series of scenic **walks** in the vicinity.

There's a handful of well-kept **rooms** above the central *Girarrosto* restaurant, Via Roma 41 (☎0577.738.010; ②), and simple comforts in the seven doubles above the 1950s-style *Bottega di Giovannino*, Via Roma 6 (☎ & fax 0577.738.056; ③). One of the region's quirkier **agriturismi** is *La Penisola*, 3km northwest of Radda (☎ & fax 0577.738.080, *www.chiantinet.it/penisola*; ③), home to a free-roaming herd of goats which provide milk (for soap) and cashmere (for hand-woven scarves and shawls). The unpretentious, family-run *Girarrosto* **restaurant**, Via Roma 41 (☎0577.738.010; closed Wed), is packed at weekends but far from expensive. The Michelin-starred *Ristorante Vignale* on the main road at Via XX Settembre 23 (☎0577.738.094; closed Thurs) is a more upmarket option. *Bar Dante*, at the entrance to Radda on Piazza Dante Aligheri, is a comfortable, convivial place to sample some wines or relax with a light lunch in the sunshine. Plenty of agencies in Radda act as **tour operators** for Chianti, reserving at *agriturismi* and conducting guided visits to country estates and wine-tastings; two of the biggest are A Bit Of Tuscany, Via Roma 39 (☎0577.738.637, *www.chiantinet.it/*

traveltuscany) and ChiantiMania, Via Trentro e Trieste 12 (☎0577.738.979, *www. chiantiservices.com*). The latter also has **Internet** access (L4000/€2.06 for 15min).

Prato

Taking its name from the meadow (*prato*) where a great market was held in antiquity, **PRATO** – capital of its own little province 15km northwest of Florence – has been Italy's chief textile city since the early Middle Ages. Even though recent recession has cut into export sales, it still produces three-quarters of all Italy's woollen cloth. Its proximity to Florence (just half-an-hour away) makes it feasible as a cut-price alternative base.

Prato's *centro storico* is enclosed within a rough hexagon of walls, making orientation straightforward. From the square in front of Stazione Centrale, cross the bridge to Piazza Europa and continue on Viale Vittorio Veneto to Piazza San Marco, which is framed by the city walls. Directly ahead, past the prominent **Henry Moore** sculpture *Square Form with Cut* (1974) in the centre of the piazza, rises the white-walled **Castello Imperatore** (under restoration at the time of writing), built in the thirteenth century for Emperor Frederick II. Concerts are held in the courtyard in summer, and the ramparts offer fine views. Just below the castle to the north is Prato's major Renaissance monument, Giuliano Sangallo's church of **Santa Maria delle Carceri** (daily 7am–noon & 4–7pm), which makes a decorative gesture towards the Romanesque with its bands of green and white marble. The interior is lightened by an Andrea della Robbia frieze. The route to the duomo passes through Piazza del Comune, home to the **Museo Civico e Galleria Comunale** (under restoration at the time of writing; most of the paintings have been removed to the Museo di Pittura Murale, see below), which contains a ramshackle collection of Florentine art, including work by Fra' Filippo Lippi and a predella by Bernardo Daddi narrating the story of Prato's holy relic, the Girdle of the Madonna (see box opposite).

Piazza Duomo, one block north of Piazza del Comune, forms an effective space for the Pisan-Romanesque facade of the **Duomo** (daily 7am–12.30pm & 3–6.30pm, Sun until 8pm), distinguished by an Andrea della Robbia terracotta over the portal and, on the corner, a strange and beautiful external pulpit designed by Donatello and Michelozzo. The sensuous frescoes behind the high altar were created between 1452 and 1466 by **Fra' Filippo Lippi**, and depict the martyrdoms of St John the Baptist and St Stephen. During the period of his work, Lippi – though nominally a monk – became infatuated with a young nun called Lucrezia; they later had a child together, Filippino. Lucrezia is said to be the model for the dancing figure of Salome, while Filippo has painted himself as one of those mourning St Stephen; he's third from the right. To see the heavily corroded original panels of Donatello's pulpit, look in at the adjacent **Museo dell'Opera del Duomo** (under restoration at the time of writing). The museum's other main treasure is Maso di Bartolomeo's tiny reliquary for the Sacred Girdle, while some equally important works are housed in the **Museo di Pittura Murale** (Mon & Wed–Sun 10am–1pm & 3.30–7pm; L5000/€2.58), a five-minute walk west of the duomo.

The **Museo d'Arte Contemporaneo Luigi Pecci** is one of Italy's leading museums of contemporary art, housed in striking premises designed by Italo Gamberini on the eastern edge of town at Viale della Repubblica 277 (Mon & Wed–Sun 10am–7pm; permanent collection free; special exhibitions around L12,000/€6.20; *www.comune. prato.it/pecci*; bus #7 or #8). Along with work by Italian artists such as Marco Bagnoli and Michelangelo Pistoletto, there is plenty to see by international big names, including Sol LeWitt, Anish Kapoor and the huge, glittering *Colonna cadente* sculpture in steel by Anne and Patrick Poirier.

THE HOLY GRAIL OF PRATO

The main treasure held by Prato's cathedral is the **Holy Girdle**, a green woollen belt decorated with gold brocade that was, according to legend, given by the Virgin Mary to St Thomas – "Doubting Thomas" – at the moment of her ascension to heaven. The girdle stayed somewhere in the Holy Land for a millennium, until the crusading knight Michele of Prato fell in love with a Jerusalemite girl named Maria, and received the Holy Girdle as part of her marriage dowry. The couple set off together for Italy, but Maria died during the long journey and Michele arrived back in Prato in 1141 alone; he hid the Girdle away and kept his own counsel until thirty years later when, on his deathbed, he granted the relic to the cathedral provost. Since then, the Girdle (*Cintola*, or *Cingolo*) has served as a rallying focus for Prato during its feuds with neighbouring Pistoia and Florence. For centuries, it has been solemnly brought out for public display from the external pulpit of the cathedral to the accompaniment of dignified ceremony and much veneration – currently at Christmas, Easter, on May 1, August 15 and, most importantly, on September 8 during the ancient Prato Fair.

Practicalities

All **trains** (including services direct from Bologna) stop at Stazione Centrale; slow Florence–Pistoia trains also stop at the more convenient Stazione Porta al Serraglio, 150m north of Piazza Duomo. CAP and Lazzi **buses** from Florence stop at Piazza Duomo, while Lazzi buses from Pistoia, Lucca and local villages pass through both train station forecourts. The **tourist office** (Mon–Sat: summer 9–6.30pm; winter 9am–1pm & 3–6pm; ☎0574.24.112, *www.prato.turismo.toscana.it*) is on Piazza Santa Maria delle Carceri, 500m west of Stazione Centrale in the centre of the old town – it has excellent English booklets on local walks and attractions.

Near the Luigi Pecci museum is the lavish five-star **hotel** *Art Hotel Museo*, Via della Repubblica 289 (☎0574.5787, fax 0574.578.880, *www.arthotel.it*; ⑦), but the most agreeable central hotel is the *Flora*, Via Cairoli 31 (☎0574.33.521, fax 0574.40.289, *www.texnet.it/utenti/comm/hotelflora*; ⑤). Prato has a single one-star, the *Roma*, Via Carradori 1 (☎0574.31.777, fax 0574.604.351; ②), and several two-stars, including the once-grand *Stella d'Italia* at Piazza Duomo 8 (☎& fax 0574.27.910; ③). The HI **hostel** *Villa Fiorelli* is in Parco di Galceti, 3km from the station by bus #13 (☎0574.697.611, fax 0574.697.6256; L25,000/€12.91).

Mattei, Via Ricasoli 20 (closed Mon) is a venerable old **café** in business since 1858, famed for its *biscotti*. The atmospheric **restaurant** *Osteria Cibbè*, Piazza Mercatale 49 (☎0574.607.509; closed Sun), serves up decent, fairly priced local food in an intimate, friendly setting on a huge piazza 200m east of the tourist office. For pricier Pratese cooking, head for *Osvaldo Baroncelli*, Via Fra Bartolomeo 13 south of Piazza Europa (☎0574.23.810; closed Sat lunch & Sun), a long-established, formal little place. The *Pirana*, Via Valentini 110 (☎0574.25.746; closed Sat lunch & Sun) is acclaimed as one of Tuscany's best fish restaurants. *Salomé*, in Hotel Flora (see above), is a vegetarian restaurant open evenings only (closed Sun). The rabbit in Prato's hat, however, is its numerically and culturally strong Chinese community; exploit the fact at the affordable *Hua Li Du*, Via Marini 4 (closed Tues lunch). The *Loch Ness*, Via Santo Stefano 24 (open nightly), tries to be a Scottish **pub**; what it lacks in authenticity, it makes up for in whisky.

Pistoia

PISTOIA, 18km northwest of Prato and also capital of its own province, is one of the least visited cities in Tuscany – an unjustified ranking for this quiet, well-preserved medieval city just 35 minutes by train from Florence (and about the same by bus). Pistoia was known throughout medieval times for its feuding and was condemned by Dante, Machiavelli and others; Michelangelo referred to the Pistoiese as "the enemies of heaven". An important metalworking centre, it left a legacy to the world in the *pistole*, originally the name of a dagger but later the title given to the first local firearms.

Piazza Duomo and around

The superb medieval complex of **Piazza Duomo** is the heart of the town, and scene of many events and celebrations throughout Pistoia's July festival (see below). If you've arrived from Pisa or Lucca, the style of the **Duomo** itself will be immediately familiar, with its tiered arcades and striped decoration of black and white marble. Set into this soberly refined front is a tunnel-vault portico of bright terracotta tiles by Andrea della Robbia, creator also of the *Madonna and Child* above the door. The **interior** (daily 8.30am–12.30pm & 3.30–7pm) has an outstanding array of sculptural pieces, one of which is part of the entrance wall – a font designed by Benedetto da Maiano, showing incidents from the life of John the Baptist. Off the right aisle is the Cappella di San Jacopo (Mon–Sat 10am–noon & 4–5.45pm, Sun 11.20am–noon & 4–5.30pm; L3000/€1.55), endowed with one of the richest pieces of silverwork to be seen in Italy, the **Altarpiece of St James**. Weighing almost a ton and populated with 628 figures, it was begun in 1287 and completed by Brunelleschi in 1456.

Adjoining the duomo, the Palazzo dei Vescovi (Bishop's Palace) was bought early in the twentieth century by a local bank, who supplied the cash needed for restoration; they now show the building off as the **Museo della Cattedrale**, entered through the tourist office (tours Tues, Thurs & Fri 10am–1pm & 3–5pm; Oct–April also second & fourth Sun of the month 4pm; L7000/€3.61; book ahead on ☎0573.369.272). Both the duomo and the palace – occupied by successive bishops until 1786 – were built on the site of a huge villa which stood at the centre of Roman Pistoia; guides lead you through a warren of underground rooms showing bits of the Roman wall, stairways and various levels of excavated street, and then head up into the interior of the palace amidst rooms displaying treasures from various parts of the building's past. The chief exhibit is the huge golden **reliquary of St James** by Lorenzo Ghiberti (1407), housed in the frescoed "Sacristy of Beautiful Treasure" mentioned by Dante; you'll also see the name-scratchings of Roman slaves on ceramic kitchenware, a decorated glass beaker from twelfth-century Egypt which found its way to Pistoia as the "Cup of St Hedwig", and pottery from the Syrian city of Raqqa.

Opposite the duomo is the dapper Gothic **Baptistry** (Tues–Sat 9.30am–12.30pm & 3–6pm, Sun 9.30am–12.30pm), possibly designed by Nicola Pisano; there's nothing under the vast conical brick ceiling but a font, made by Lanfranco da Como in 1226, and the interior's emptiness is sometimes filled by shows of contemporary art. On the opposite side of the piazza, the Palazzo Comunale contains the **Museo Civico** (Tues–Sat 10am–7pm, Sun 9am–12.30pm; L6000/€3.10; joint ticket with Museo Diocesano and Centro Marini L12,000/€6.20), where the customary Tuscan welter of medieval and Renaissance pieces is bolstered by an impressive showing of Baroque hyperactivity. To the side of the Palazzo Comunale, the Palazzo Rospigliosi on Via Ripa del Sale contains the **Nuovo Museo Diocesano** (Tues, Thurs & Fri 10am–1pm & 4–7pm, Wed & Sat 10am–1pm; L6000/€3.10; joint ticket with Museo Civico and Centro Marini L12,000/€6.20), a typical small-town collection of historical and ecclesiastical oddments.

The rest of the town

Behind the Palazzo Comunale, across Via Pacini, is **San Bartolomeo in Pantano**, or "St Bartholomew in the Swamp" (daily 8.30am–noon & 4–6pm), named for the marshy ground on which the church was raised in the eighth century, and with a rectangular pulpit sculpted in 1250 by Guido da Como. The **Ospedale del Ceppo**, 100m north along Via Pacini, was embellished in the fifteenth century with a portico emblazoned with Giovanni della Robbia's startlingly colourful terracotta frieze of the *Theological Virtues* and the *Seven Works of Mercy*, a panoply of Renaissance types and costume. A couple of minutes over to the west, the twelfth-century **Sant'Andrea** (daily 8.30am–12.30pm & 3.30–7pm) has a corridor-slim aisle with a spectacular pulpit carved by Giovanni Pisano in 1297, showing scenes from the life of Christ and the Last Judgement.

Barely 100m south of the baptistry, Via Cavour is now the main street of the city's inner core, but was once the settlement's outer limit – as the name of the majestic **San Giovanni Fuorcivitas** ("outside the walls") proclaims. The church was founded in the eighth century, but rebuilt between the twelfth and fourteenth centuries, when it received the dazzlingly striped green-and-white flank that serves as its facade. The interior (daily 8am–noon & 4–6.30pm), though lit only feebly by the slit windows, is just as remarkable for its pulpit, another of Pistoia's exquisite thirteenth-century trio, carved in 1270 by a pupil of Nicola Pisano.

Via Crispi leads due south to Piazza Garibaldi, where the **Cappella del Tau** (Mon–Sat 9am–2pm) preserves a chaos of fourteenth- and fifteenth-century frescoes. A couple of doors away, in the Palazzo del Tau, is the engaging **Centro Marino Marini** (Tues–Sat 9am–1pm & 3–7pm, Sun 9am–12.30pm; L6000/€3.10, free on Sat afternoon; joint ticket with Museo Civico and Museo Diocesano L12,000/€6.20), showing a selection of etchings, engravings, sculptures, drawings and watercolours by this important modern artist and Pistoia local.

A few kilometres east in the suburb of **SANTOMATO**, reachable by COPIT bus #19 (direction Tobbiana or Bagnolo), is the remarkable **Fattoria di Celle** art centre, featuring an array of contemporary sculpture and installations set amidst a large area of parkland around a seventeenth-century villa, including constructions in steel and wire by Dennis Oppenheim, in polished green and white marble by Robert Morris, and in stone by Richard Serra. The centre is open from April to September, by appointment only; contact them in advance (fax 0573.473.486) or on the day (☎0573.479.907, calls taken 8.45–10am).

Practicalities

Lazzi **buses** from Florence, Prato, Lucca or Pisa leave you at the **train station**, from where short Via XX Settembre points the way north to Piazza Treviso and the gate into the old town. COPIT buses from Poggio a Caiano, Empoli and Vinci use instead Piazza San Francesco, northwest of the centre. Note that **parking** is heavily restricted during the Wednesday and Saturday morning markets held in the central streets. The **tourist office** is at Piazza Duomo 4 (Mon–Sat 9am–1pm & 3–6pm, June–Sept also Sun same times; ☎0573.21.622) and also houses the Pistoia Bookshop, which offers **Internet** access (L5000/€2.58 per half-hour) and bike rental (L20,000/€10.33 per day).

The best **hotel** in town is the friendly, air-conditioned *Leon Bianco*, Via Panciatichi 2 (☎0573.26.675, fax 0573.26.704, *www.promonet.it/leonbianco*; ⑤). Two-star *Albergo Firenze*, Via Curtatone e Montanara 42 (☎0573.23.141, fax 0573.21.660; ③), and *Piccolo Ritz*, Via Vannucci 67 (☎0573.26.775, fax 0573.27.798; ④), are useful mid-range options. Downmarket choice is *Albergo Autisti*, off Piazza Lucchese at Viale Pacinotti 89 (☎0573.21.771; ②). The best **restaurant** accolade is claimed by the mid-priced *San Jacopo*, Via Crispi 15 (☎0573.27.786; closed Mon & Tues lunch), with friendly service and excellent food. *Il Pollo d'Oro*, Via Attilio Frosini 132 (closed Mon) has wood-fired pizzas and excellent *frutti di mare*, while *Da Mone*, Via Verdi 3 (closed Sun), offers straightforward mid-priced Tuscan fare. Cheaper options include the pleasant *Lo Storno*, a traditional osteria at Via del Lastrone 8 (closed Sun), a few doors from the atmospheric *La Bottegaia* wine-cellar at no. 4 (closed Sun lunch & Mon).

Key festival is the **Luglio Pistoiese**, a programme of concerts and events throughout July which includes openair performances in Piazza Duomo by world-class jazz and blues acts under the "Pistoia Blues" banner (*www.pistoia-blues.com*). The *Giostra dell'Orso* medieval pageant and joust is on July 25.

West to Pisa

Two main roads and rail lines head west from Florence. The A11 *autostrada* shadows the train track northwest through Prato and Pistoia to Lucca. An alternative is the SS67 road, which heads due west from Florence down the valley of the Arno to Pisa, a pleasant enough journey of an hour or so. Along the way you'll pass through the industrial town of **Empoli**, marking the turnoff into the hills north to **Vinci**. A little west of Empoli, past the turning south to Siena and across the border in the Provincia di Pisa, is the medieval village of **San Miniato**, perched high on its rock above the pretty Valdarno.

Empoli and Vinci

Most people don't bother with **EMPOLI**, a modern and heavily industrial town 32km west of Florence, but it does have a quality museum of Renaissance art. If you can spare time, head left out of the station on Viale Martino and then right on Via Leonardo da Vinci to reach the ancient arcaded Piazza Farinata degli Uberti, overlooked by the **Museo della Collegiata** (Tues–Sun 9am–noon & 4–7pm; joint ticket with Museo Leonardiano in Vinci L8000/€4.13), with Masolino's moving fresco of the pietà in the Baptistry, a cloister full of technicolour Della Robbia terracottas, and works by Monaco and Fra' Filippo Lippi upstairs. Opposite the station is the comfortable **hotel** *Il Sole*, Piazza Don Minzoni 18 (☎0571.73.779, fax 0571.79.871; ④), while the more spartan *Plaza* is a short walk east of the Collegiata at Piazza della Vittoria 11 (☎0571.74.751; ②).

Occupying the picturesque vine- and olive-planted southern slopes of Montalbano 11km north of Empoli, **VINCI** is inextricably associated with **Leonardo da Vinci**, who was born on April 15, 1452, in nearby Anchiano and baptized in Vinci's church of Santa Croce. Vinci itself is a torpid little village that suffers from a surfeit of tour-groups (especially at weekends). The main sight is the thirteenth-century castle, now home to the **Museo Leonardiano** (daily: March–Oct 9.30am–7pm; Nov–Feb 9.30am–6pm; L7000/€3.61; joint ticket with Museo Collegiata in Empoli L8000/€4.13), packed with models reconstructed from Leonardo's notebook drawings – his celebrated bicycle, helicopter and multi-barrelled machine-gun are all on display.

Buses from Empoli drop off just below the castle hill; at the top of the hill, next to the castle, the helpful **tourist office** (daily: March–Oct 10am–7pm; Nov–Feb 10am–3pm; ☎0571.568.012, *www.comune.vinci.fi.it*) has details of some lovely country walks, including a trip to the hamlet of Anchiano where Leonardo was born. At the foot of the village hill is the **Museo Ideale Leonardo da Vinci** (daily 10am–1pm & 3–7pm; L5000/€2.58; *www.museoleonardo.it*), an uninspiring enterprise housed in a dank wine-cellar that jumbles together models with old olive-presses and antique prints. Vinci's best **hotel** is the tranquil *Alexandra*, Via dei Martiri 82 (☎0571.56.224, fax 0571.567.972; ⑤), but **restaurants** tend to be overly touristy; for simple, cheap food make for the *Bar-Trattoria Centrale*, Via Fucini 16 (closed Tues).

San Miniato

The strategic village of **SAN MINIATO**, midway between Pisa and Florence (42km from both), was given its landmark fortress by the Holy Roman Emperor Frederick II in 1236. Today it's an attractive mid-journey stopoff, split between a modern valley-floor settlement with train and bus stations (see below) and the original medieval village on its hilltop with a warren of attractive cobbled alleys. Dominating the old quarter's central **Piazza del Popolo** is the fourteenth-century church of **San Domenico**; its windows, glazed with odd greenish-yellow glass, do nothing to aid appreciation of its frescoes and trompe l'oeil decoration. There's a market in its cloisters every Sunday. A narrow street climbs to **Piazza della Repubblica**, which is jazzed up by seventeenth-century *sgraffiti* on the long facade of the religious seminary; part of the ground floor is a row of rare, restored fourteenth-century shops. Opposite the seminary a flight of steps rises to the **Prato del Duomo**, overlooked by a tower of the imperial fortress. The red brick **Duomo**, dedicated to St Genesius, the patron saint of actors, is hacked-about Romanesque, with an interior of Baroque gilding and marbling. Next door, the tiny **Museo Diocesano** (Tues–Sun 9am–noon & 3.30–6pm; Jan–Easter Sat & Sun same times; L3000/€1.55) has a *Crucifixion* by Fra' Filippo Lippi and a terracotta bust of Christ by Verrocchio. From the Prato del Duomo it's a short walk up to the tower of the **Rocca**, which was restored after damage in the last war; the spectacular view from the top is worth the climb. Dante's *Inferno* perpetuates the memory of Pier della Vigna, treasurer to Frederick II, who was imprisoned and blinded here, a fate that drove him to suicide by jumping from the tower – as the inscription on a graffitied stone at the base of the tower records.

The **train station**, down in the Arno valley, is a ten-minute walk from the modern part of town, **San Miniato Basso**, from where it's a steep 4km climb to **San Miniato Alto**, the old quarter. (You'd do best to leave your **car** in one of the large car parks just below Alto's embankment walls and walk the last bit up; parking in the historic centre is difficult.) **Buses** shuttle from the train station, through Basso, up the hill past the Piazzale Dante Alighieri car park and on up Corso Garibaldi into Alto, dropping off at the central **Piazza del Popolo**, where you'll find the **tourist office** (June–Oct daily 9.30am–1pm & 3.30–7.30pm; Nov–May Mon–Sat 9am–1pm & 3–6.30pm, Sun 10am–1pm & 3–7.30pm; ☎0571.42.745, *ufficio.turismo@penteres.it*).

The most characterful place **to stay** is the Convento di San Francesco, on the opposite side of the Rocca from the seminary (☎0571.43.051, fax 0571.43.398; ②); this is still a monastic community, and the simple rooms are en suite and very quiet. Otherwise, head for the *Centro Turistico San Martino*, Via Battisti 70 (☎0571.401.469, fax 0571.403.712; *www.ponteverde.it*; ③), a fifteenth-century hillside convent now converted to a conference centre, with functional en suite rooms. The *Palazzo Buonaparte* on Piazza Buonaparte (☎0571.418.258; ②) is the most illustrious of a handful of places around town offering private self-catering rooms; Napoleon dropped in here to see a relative on June 29, 1797. Best of the few **restaurants** is the atmospheric *L'Antro di Bacco*, Via IV Novembre 5 (☎0571.43.319; closed Wed eve & Sun), hidden away behind a delicatessen and renowned for its white truffles, served with much ceremony during November. *Canapone*, Piazza Buonaparte (closed Mon), is another favourite local eatery.

PISA, LUCCA AND THE COAST

Thanks to its Leaning Tower, **Pisa** is known by name to just about every visitor to Italy, though it remains an underrated place, seen by most people on a whistle-stop day-trip that takes in little of its majestic architecture, less of its atmospheric medieval quarters, and none of its street life. Genteel **Lucca** nearby, its walled old town crammed with Romanesque churches, is even less explored.

Tuscany's **coast** is a mixed bag, too over-developed to be consistently attractive. North of Pisa, the succession of beach resorts feature the backdrop of the mighty Alpi Apuane, which harbour the marble quarries of Carrara. South from Pisa, past the untouristed port of **Livorno**, are a hundred scrubby strips of hotels and campsites. The Tuscan shoreline is at its best in the **Maremma** region, where you'll find the protected

Monti dell'Uccellina reserve and the wild, wooded peninsula of **Monte Argentario**. Tuscany's **islands** offer a breath of fresh air, from the scenic walks on **Elba** to the remoteness of **Giglio** or little **Capraia**.

Pisa

Since the beginning of tourism, **PISA** has been known for just one thing – the **Leaning Tower**, which serves around the world as a shorthand image for Italy. It is indeed a freakishly beautiful building, a sight whose impact no amount of prior knowledge can

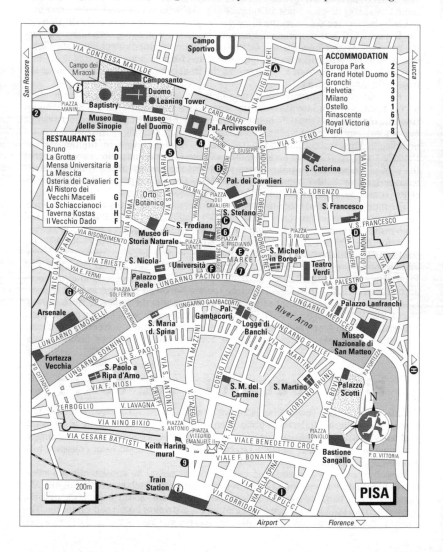

blunt. Yet it is just a single component of Pisa's breathtaking **Campo dei Miracoli**, or Field of Miracles, where the **Duomo**, **Baptistry** and **Camposanto** complete a dazzling architectural ensemble. These, and a dozen or so churches and palazzi scattered about the historic centre, belong to Pisa's "Golden Age", from the eleventh to the thirteenth centuries, when the city was one of the maritime powers of the Mediterranean. The so-called "Pisan Romanesque" **architecture** of this period, with its black and white marble facades inspired by the Moorish designs of Andalucia, is complemented by some of the finest medieval **sculpture** in Italy, much of it from the workshops of Nicola and Giovanni Pisano. The city's political zenith came late in the eleventh century with a series of victories over the **Saracens**: the Pisans brought back from Arab cultures long-forgotten ideas of science, architecture and philosophy. Decline set in with defeat by the Genoese in 1284, followed by the silting-up of Pisa's harbour. From 1406 the city was governed by Florence, whose Medici rulers re-established the University of Pisa, one of the intellectual forcing houses of the Renaissance; **Galileo** was one of the teachers there. Subsequent centuries saw Pisa fade into provinciality.

Arrival, information and orientation

Pisa Centrale **train** station (information ☎1478.88.088) is about 1km south of the Arno. Lazzi **buses** from Florence, Prato, Pistoia and Carrara arrive at the nearby Piazza Vittorio Emanuele II, while other buses from Volterra, Lucca and Livorno arrive at Piazza San Antonio alongside it. From here, the Leaning Tower is about 25 minutes' walk north, or a ride on CPT city bus #1 from outside the station. Alternatively, you could take a local train five minutes to the more convenient **Pisa San Rossore** station, 200m west of Piazza Manin (also served by local trains from Lucca and some from Viareggio).

Pisa's **Aeroporto Galileo Galilei** (information ☎050.500.707, *www.pisa-airport.com*) is 2km south of Centrale station. Hourly trains run from Pisa Aeroporto station to Pisa Centrale and on to Florence, 1hr 15mins away. CPT city bus #3 departs from the airport every fifteen minutes, and passes the train station, runs along the south bank of the Arno, over Ponte Solferino, to Piazza Manin and then out to the hostel. A taxi to the centre costs around L10,000/€5.16.

Pisa's APT **tourist office** is snug against the walls amidst the tangle of stalls just outside the gate of the Campo dei Miracoli, at Via Cammeo 2 off Piazza Manin (May–Sept daily 8am–8pm; Oct–April daily 8.30am–5pm; ☎050.560.464, *www.pisa.turismo. toscana.it*). In the same office, the adjacent desk is staffed by the **Consorzio Turistico "Pisa è"**, the city's official hotel-booking service (Mon–Fri 9.30am–6pm, Sat 9.30am–1pm; Oct–March Mon–Fri closes 5pm; ☎050.830.253, *www.pisae.com*). There's also a small APT office at the **train station** (May–Sept daily 8am–6pm; Oct–April daily 9am–5pm; ☎050.42.291), and another at the **airport** (May–Sept daily 10am–10pm; Oct–April daily 10am–5pm; ☎050.503.700). All of these also stock information for towns such as San Miniato (see p.504) and Volterra (see p.555) that lie within the Provincia di Pisa.

Accommodation

Most visitors hurry through Pisa on a day-trip – this is their loss, but it means that **accommodation** is usually not too hard to find. Staying in the centre of town brings you away from the touristy haunts and into local life a bit more, but beware that many low-end hotels are filled by students during the academic year.

Hotels

Europa Park, Via Andrea Pisano 23 (☎050.500.732, fax 050.554.930). Smallish, comfortable and well-run modern three-star hotel, with parking. It's on a characterless street, but is barely two minutes' stroll from the Campo dei Miracoli. ④.

Gronchi, Piazza Arcivescovado 1 (☎050.561.823). Most characterful of Pisa's low-end hotels, in a perfect position within spitting distance of the Tower. Twenty-three rooms share four bathrooms. Midnight curfew. ②.

Grand Hotel Duomo, Via Santa Maria 94 (☎050.561.894, fax 050.560.418). Good choice, a modern four-star with comforts (including parking), a couple of minutes' stroll from the Leaning Tower. ⑧.

Helvetia, Via G. Boschi 31 (☎050.553.084). One-star in an excellent location just off the Campo dei Miracoli with en suite and shared-bath rooms, kept spotless by the friendly staff. Midnight curfew. ③.

Milano, Via Mascagni 14 (☎050.23.162, fax 050.44.237). One of the better low-end choices around Piazza Stazione, in a side-street right opposite the station, with shared-bath and en suite rooms. ②.

Rinascente, Via del Castelletto 28 (☎ & fax 050.580.460). Very popular budget rooms – en suite and not – occupying an old palazzo just off Piazza dei Cavalieri. ②.

Royal Victoria, Lungarno Pacinotti 12 (☎050.940.111, fax 050.940.180). Tastefully furnished palazzo overlooking the Arno, with character, old-fashioned elegance and private parking. Also some bargain non-en suite rooms. ⑤.

Verdi, Piazza della Repubblica 5 (☎050.598.947, fax 050.598.944). A competent and welcoming three-star hotel occupying a restored palazzo well away from the tourist bustle in a quiet square near San Matteo. ⑤.

Campsite and hostel

Campeggio Torre Pendente, Viale delle Cascine 86 (☎050.561.704, fax 050.561.734). A large, well-maintained site signposted 1km west of the Campo dei Miracoli, with a laundry, bar, restaurant and shop. April to mid-Oct.

Ostello, Centro Turistico Madonna dell'Acqua, Via Pietrasantina 15 (☎ & fax 050.890.622). Despite the signs, this non-HI hostel is a 45min hike from Campo dei Miracoli; instead take bus #3 from the station or Piazza Manin, which stops outside. The staff are very welcoming and there's a supermarket nearby, but make sure you have mosquito repellent in summer: it's right by a marsh. L22,000/€11.36 per person.

The City

Since it was first laid out in the mid-eleventh century, Pisa's ecclesiastical centre has been known as the **Campo dei Miracoli** (Field of Miracles; also Piazza dei Miracoli or Piazza Duomo; *www.duomo.pisa.it*). The four major buildings – the **Duomo**, its Bell-tower (which almost immediately slipped to become the **Leaning Tower**), the **Baptistry** and the monumental cemetery of the **Camposanto** – were built on a broad swathe of grassy lawn just within the northern walls of the city. Nowhere else in Italy are the key buildings of a city arrayed with such precision, and nowhere is there so beautiful a contrast of stonework and open meadow. However, the turf rests on highly unstable sandy soil, which accounts for the tower's lean; take a look at the baptistry and you'll see that it leans the other way from the tower.

The rest of the city centre makes for some fine wandering, through alleys that have largely retained their medieval appearance. Southeast, on the river, is the **Museo Nazionale di San Matteo**, a fine collection of ecclesiastical art and sculpture, while

---

The five museums and monuments in and around Campo dei Miracoli – the Duomo, Baptistry, Museo dell'Opera, Camposanto and Museo delle Sinopie – share a complicated system of **ticketing**. Admission to the duomo costs L3000/€1.55. Admission to any two sights costs L10,000/€5.16. Admission to any three including the duomo costs L13,000/€6.71. Admission to the four excluding the duomo costs L15,000/€7.75. Admission to all five costs L18,000/€9.30. Students pay L2000/€1.03 admission to each sight.

You can get tickets only from the **ticket offices** at the Museo delle Sinopie, the Museo dell'Opera and the Camposanto.

west along the Arno is the lavish **Palazzo Reale** mansion and the city's huge **Arsenale**, the latter currently housing a display of items taken from ongoing excavations at the newly discovered site of Pisa's ancient harbour. One of Pisa's biggest surprises lurks in an unregarded piazza south of the river near the train station: covering one wall of an open bus station is the last-ever mural by US artist **Keith Haring**.

The Leaning Tower of Pisa

The view from the Porta Nuova gate over the serene architectural ensemble laid out on the Campo dei Miracoli would be memorable enough, even were it not for the desperately comic sight of the **Leaning Tower** (*torre.duomo.pisa.it*) sticking out jauntily from behind the duomo, wearing its rakishly angled bell-chamber like a pork-pie hat. It is a lunatic vision, slouched over far enough to topple any second – or so it seems.

Two of the most telling facts about the tower (*Torre Pendente* in Italian) are that it has always tilted, and that no one ever put their name to the project, as though the masons involved somehow knew it was doomed. Twelve years after work began on the tower in 1173, it started to subside, but in the opposite direction from the current lean. Masons inserted wedge-shaped stones to correct the problem, whereupon the whole tower tilted crazily the other way. Work was halted when it was only three storeys high. A century or so later, after much calculation, architects added three more uneven storeys, tilted to counterbalance the lean, and then in 1350 Tommaso Pisano completed the stack with a lopsided bell-chamber. A couple of centuries later, **Galileo** exploited the overhang in one of his celebrated experiments, dropping items of different mass off the top to demonstrate the constancy of gravity.

An ill-advised attempt to correct the southerly lean in the mid-nineteenth century involved digging a trench all the way round the base of the tower; this made things considerably worse and, along with lowering of the water table throughout the twentieth century, has brought the structure to the edge of crisis. By 1990, the top leant more than five metres from vertical and the tower was finally declared off-limits to visitors. Since then, scientists and engineers have joined forces to save the thing. The lean had previously worsened by about one millimetre a year, but attempts to stabilize the tower and stop it buckling under its own weight by wrapping **steel bands** around the lowest storey caused the tower to shift that amount in the first ten weeks of 1991 alone. The decision was taken to stabilize the tower by shoring up its northern side with 800 tonnes of **lead ingots** piled at its base – unsightly, but successful – as a prelude to fixing cables to the deep bedrock and wrapping them around the foundations. Engineers started to drill down beside the tower in 1995, whereupon it lurched another couple of millimetres in a single night. Further stabilization ensued, and in 1998 **steel cables** were stretched from counterweights on the north side of the square to hold the tower steady. Then the master plan went into operation: an array of **rotating drills** ranged around the north base of the tower removed silt and sand from beneath the foundations – a little on this side, a little on that – as the tower's reactions were minutely scrutinized. The tower slowly began to correct its lean and settle. By summer 2000, the overhang had been reduced by five degrees, or 15cm, and the tower was back to its 1870 position. The plan is continuing, with one ingot of lead a week removed and transferred underground to help anchor the cables strung around the foundations. When all is complete, the tower will still lean – the tourist board insisted on that – but by some 50cm less than in 1990, approximately as much as in Galileo's day.

At the time of writing, the authorities propose to re-open the tower to the public in a grand ceremony on June 17, 2001, the Day of San Ranieri, patron saint of Pisa – although this is dependent on continued success with the stabilizing operation. More than a million people climbed the tower in 1989, but it is still unclear what public access will now be granted; numbers of visitors, and possibly how far up the 293 internal stairs they can climb, may be limited.

The rest of the Campo dei Miracoli

Pisa's breathtaking **Duomo** (March–Oct Mon–Sat 10am–7.40pm, Sun 1–7.40pm; Nov–Feb Mon–Sat 10am–12.45pm, Sun 3–4.45pm; L3000/€1.55; see box on p.508 for details of combined tickets) was begun in 1064 and completed around a century later. With its four levels of variegated colonnades and its subtle interplay of dark grey marble and white stone, the duomo is the archetype of Pisan Romanesque, a model often imitated in buildings across Tuscany, but never surpassed. Squares and discs of coloured marble are set into the magnificent facade, but the soberly graceful effect of the primary grey and white is such that you notice these strong tones only when you look closely. Entry is through the huge bronze doors of the **Portale di San Ranieri**, close to the Leaning Tower. These were cast in 1180 by Bonnano Pisano, first architect of the tower, with powerfully diagrammatic biblical scenes. The vast interior is defined by the crisp black and white marble of the long arcades, which recalls the Moorish architecture of Cordoba. A notable survivor from the medieval building is the apse mosaic of *Christ in Majesty*, completed by Cimabue in 1302. The acknowledged highlight, however, is the **pulpit** sculpted by **Giovanni Pisano**. This was packed away after a 1595 fire and was only rediscovered in 1926. The last of the great series of three pulpits created in Tuscany by Giovanni and his father Nicola (the others are in Siena and Pistoia), it is a work of amazing virtuosity with, for instance, the story of the Passion condensed into a single panel.

You exit the duomo at the main western facade. Directly ahead is the circular **Baptistry** (daily: April–Sept 8am–7.40pm; March & Oct 9am–5.40pm; Nov–Feb 9am–4.40pm; see box on p.508 for details of combined tickets), a bizarre but pleasing building with its three storeys of Romanesque arcades peaking in a crest of Gothic pinnacles and a dome shaped like the stalk end of a lemon. This is the largest baptistry in Italy, begun in 1152 by a certain Deotisalvi ("Godsaveyou"), who left his name on a column to the left of the door; it was worked on in the thirteenth century by Nicola and Giovanni Pisano, and completed late in the fourteenth century. Inside you're immediately struck by the plainness of the vast interior, with its unadorned arcades and bare dome, and by its astonishing acoustics. Overlooking the massive raised font is Nicola Pisano's **pulpit**, sculpted in 1260, half a century before his son's work in the cathedral. There are **stairs** to the upper gallery, and more stairs from there up inside the dome.

The screen of sepulchral white marble running along the north edge of the Campo dei Miracoli is the perimeter wall of what has been called the most beautiful cemetery in the world – the **Camposanto** (same hours as baptistry). According to legend, the Archbishop Ubaldo Lanfranchi had Pisan knights on the Fourth Crusade of 1203 bring a cargo of soil back to Pisa from the hill of Golgotha, in order that eminent Pisans might be buried in holy earth. The building enclosing this sanctified site was completed almost a century later and takes the form of an enormous Gothic cloister. However, when Ruskin described the Camposanto as one of the most precious buildings in Italy, it was the **frescoes** that he was praising. Paintings once covered over two thousand metres of cloister wall, but now the brickwork is mostly bare: **incendiary bombs** dropped by Allied planes on July 27, 1944, set the roofing on fire and drenched the frescoes in molten lead. The most important survivor is the remarkable *Triumph of Death* cycle, a ruthless catalogue of morbid horrors painted within a few months of the Black Death of 1348.

Near the Leaning Tower is the absorbing **Museo dell'Opera del Duomo** (daily: April–Sept 8am–7.20pm; March & Oct 9am–5.20pm; Nov–Feb 9am–4.20pm; see box on p.508 for details of combined tickets). Room 7 contains Giovanni Pisano's affecting *Madonna del Colloquio*, so called because of the intensity of the gazes exchanged by the Madonna and Child. In room 11 is the *Pisan Cross*, which incited the Pisan contingent on the First Crusade to invade Jerusalem. Upstairs, room 15 has beautiful examples of intarsia, the art of inlaid wood, much practised in Pisa in the fifteenth and sixteenth centuries.

On the south side of the Campo, the only gap in the souvenir stalls is for the **Museo delle Sinopie** (same hours as baptistry). After the damage wreaked on the Camposanto, restorers removed its *sinopie* (a *sinopia* is a monochrome sketch over which a fresco is painted). These great plates of plaster now hang from the walls of this hi-tech museum, but getting sense from them is a rather scholastic enterprise. You may get more reward from **walking on the ramparts**; access is at the northwest corner of the lawns (daily: July & Aug 8am–8pm; March–June, Sept & Oct 9am–6pm; L4000/€2.06), and you can also climb up inside the medieval **Torre di Santa Maria** here to look down into the Camposanto.

Piazza dei Cavalieri and the eastern quarters

Away from the Campo dei Miracoli, Pisa takes on a very different character. Few tourists penetrate far into its squares and arcaded streets, with their Romanesque churches and – especially along the Arno's banks – ranks of fine palazzi. With the large student population it can be a lively place, particularly during the summer festivals and the monthly market, when the main streets on either side of the river become one continuous bazaar.

Piazza dei Cavalieri opens unexpectedly from the narrow backstreets, the central civic square of medieval Pisa. The curving **Palazzo dei Cavalieri**, covered in sgraffiti and topped with busts of the Medici, adjoins the church of **Santo Stefano**, which still houses banners captured from Turkish ships by the Knights of St Stephen – a grand title for a gang of state-sponsored pirates. On the other side of the square is the Renaissance-adapted **Palazzo dell'Orologio**, in whose tower the military leader Ugolino della Gherardesca was starved to death with his sons and grandsons in 1208, as punishment for his alleged duplicity with the Genoese enemy – as described in Dante's *Inferno* and Shelley's *Tower of Famine*. Via Dini heads east to the arcaded **Borgo Stretto**, Pisa's smart street, its windows glittering with consumer desirables that seem out of kilter with the city's unshowy style. More typically Pisan is the atmospheric **market** in and around Piazza Vettovaglie (Mon–Fri morning & all day Sat). The Borgo meets the river at the traffic-knotted **Piazza Garibaldi**, at the foot of the Ponte di Mezzo.

At the eastern end of the riverfront road Lungarno Mediceo is the **Museo Nazionale di San Matteo** (Tues–Sat 9am–7pm, Sun 9am–2pm; L8000/€4.13; joint ticket with Palazzo Reale L12,000/€6.20; *www.ambientepi.arti.beniculturali.it*). Most of the major works of art from Pisa's churches are now gathered here, including a *St Paul* by a young Masaccio, an oddly festive *Crucifixion* by Gozzoli, and another *Crucifixion* by Turino Vanni that clearly shows the Leaning Tower. The sculpture collection is led by two outstanding works – Donatello's gilded bronze bust of an introspective *San Lussorio*, and Andrea and Nino Pisano's *Madonna del Latte*, a touchingly crafted work showing Mary breastfeeding the baby Jesus.

The western quarters

A main route south from the Campo dei Miracoli is **Via Santa Maria**, which starts out clogged with touristy shops. Where Via dei Mille heads east for Piazza dei Cavalieri, the smaller Via Ghini cuts west to the gate of the **Orto Botanico**, the oldest university botanical gardens in the world, founded in 1543 (Mon–Fri 8am–5.30pm, Sat 8am–1pm; free). Via Santa Maria continues south in a much more subdued vein, crooking its way down to meet the river alongside the second of Pisa's leaning towers, the campanile of **San Nicola**, which starts off cylindrical, then becomes octagonal, then finally hexagonal on top.

Alongside San Nicola, fronting onto the Arno, is the **Museo Nazionale di Palazzo Reale**, Lungarno Pacinotti 46 (Mon–Sat 9am–2pm; L6000/€3.10; joint ticket with San Matteo L12,000/€6.20), displaying painting, sculpture and furniture belonging to the

Medici, Lorraine and Savoy dynasties which occupied the house. Lavish sixteenth-century Flemish tapestries share space with antique weaponry, ivory miniatures and porcelain. A largely undistinguished collection of painting is led by **Bronzino**'s famous portrait of Cosimo I's wife, Eleanor of Toledo. Just as memorable, however, is the lovely river **view** from the balcony.

West along the Arno is the vast **Arsenale**, built in the late sixteenth century to house the ships of the Order of St Stephen. In a twist of fate, it is again housing a naval fleet, though one from much earlier. In December 1998, during excavations to expand Pisa San Rossore train station, archeologists stumbled on the extensive, well-preserved remains of port facilities and ships dating from Etruscan and Roman times. Sixteen ships were uncovered, dating from between the first century BC and the sixth century AD, eight of them entire – one of which may turn out to be the only complete Roman warship yet discovered – along with a vast hoard of artefacts. Currently, the museum, known as **Le Navi Antiche di Pisa**, occupies one wing of the arsenal (Mon–Fri 10am–7pm, Sat & Sun 11am–1pm & 2–10pm; L5000/€2.58; *www.navipisa.it*), but the authorities are planning to expand the displays to fill the whole building in the near future.

Just west of the arsenal rises the **Torre Guelfa** of the Fortezza Vecchia or Cittadella Vecchia (Tues–Sun: June–Aug 10am–1pm & 5–8pm, Sat & Sun until 10pm; March–May, Sept & Oct 10am–1pm & 3–6pm; L3000/€1.55; joint ticket with Santa Maria della Spina L4000/€2.06). This ancient fortress, originally built in the thirteenth century, once stood guard over Pisa's harbour but now punctuates an otherwise little-explored district. Pisa is a low-rise city, and the **view** from the tower is spectacular.

South of the river

The middle of the **Ponte di Mezzo**, the city's central bridge, is a perfect spot from which to admire the sweep of Pisa's palazzo-lined waterfront and the **Logge di Banchi** on the south side of the bridge. Formerly the city's silk and wool market, this is now the scene for student gatherings and assignations after dark; it stands at the head of the main **Corso Italia**, a street that gets progressively shabbier as it nears the train station. On the church of San Antonio, just off Piazza Vittorio Emanuele II, is the last work of US artist **Keith Haring**. Haring completed the vibrant, imaginative mural in a week in June 1989 while seriously ill; he died eight months later. His bendy, cartoonish figures radiate colour above what is now the bus station, tragically unregarded, and indeed, quite often obscured by parked buses.

A five-minute walk west of the Ponte di Mezzo is the turreted oratory of **Santa Maria della Spina**. The little church dates from 1230, but was rebuilt in 1323 in the finest flourish of Pisan Gothic by a merchant who had acquired a thorn (*spina*) of Christ's crown. The tiny single-naved **interior** (same hours as Torre Guelfa, above; L2000/€1.03; joint ticket with Torre Guelfa L4000/€2.06) has mullioned windows on the river side, but has lost most of its furnishings.

Eating and drinking

Restaurants in the environs of the Leaning Tower are not good value (although the many **bars** and **cafés** benefit from the views). A few blocks south, around Piazza Cavalieri and Piazza Dante, you'll find predominantly local places, many with prices reflecting student finances. Although most kitchens serve up standard Tuscan fare, you'll also find Pisan dishes, including *baccalà alla Pisana* (dried cod) and plenty of seafood.

Bruno, Via Bianchi 12 (☎050.560.818). Outside the historic centre, northeast of the Leaning Tower, this traditional *antica trattoria* is known for its top-notch, and pricey, Pisan cuisine. Closed Mon eve & Tues.

La Grotta, Via San Francesco 103 (☎050.578.105). Comfortable, quiet old osteria in a cave-like setting, with the motto "wine, bread and company". Locals crowd in at the benches to sample unfussy Tuscan nosh. Closed for lunch and all day Sun.

Mensa Universitaria, Via Martiri. Student refectory off Piazza Cavalieri; the cheapest meals in town. Closed Sat & Sun eve, and mid-July to mid-Sept.

La Mescita, Via Cavalca 2. This small restaurant in the warren of the Piazza Vettovaglie market is an academic institution, patronized by students and professors alike. Set menus (including vegetarian) from L35,000/€18.08. Closed Mon, and Tues & Wed lunch.

Osteria dei Cavalieri, Via San Frediano 16 (☎050.580.858, *www.toscana.net/pisa/odc*). Outstanding quality, with English-speaking staff and a calm, fresh atmosphere. The fish is exquisite, Tuscan meat and game dishes are expertly prepared, and their vegetarian options are excellent. Eat à la carte or choose from a welter of set menus starting at L30,000/€15.49. Closed Sat lunch & Sun.

Al Ristoro dei Vecchi Macelli, Via Volturno 49 (☎050.20.424). Acclaimed as Pisa's best restaurant, with a wide range of sophisticated, innovative takes on Tuscany's gourmet traditions – choose from meat or fish set menus for upwards of L50,000/€25.82. Closed Sun lunch & Wed.

Lo Schiaccianoci, Via Vespucci 104 (☎050.21.024). Wonderful, if tiny, upper-midpriced fish and seafood restaurant in an hard-to-reach location east of the station. Closed Sun.

Taverna Kostas, Via del Borghetto 39. Longstanding local favourite, offering a mix of Greek and Mediterranean cooking, as well as Pisan seafood. Closed Sun lunch & Mon.

Il Vecchio Dado, Lungarno Pacinotti 21 (☎050.580.900). Quality pizzeria on the waterfront with a friendly welcome, classy food (the fish dishes are excellent) and lively atmosphere. Closed Wed & Thurs lunch.

Entertainment

Pisa's big traditional event is the **Gioco del Ponte**, held on the last Sunday in June every year, when twelve teams from the north and south banks of the city stage a series of battles, pushing a seven-tonne carriage over the Ponte di Mezzo. The event, first mentioned in 1568, is still held in medieval costume with much ceremony. June 17 sees the **Regata di San Ranieri**, where four rowing teams race in costume in honour of the patron saint of Pisa; it is preceded the night before by the **Luminaria di San Ranieri**, when all the waterfront buildings and the Leaning Tower are illuminated. Italy's four great maritime republics (Amalfi, Pisa, Genoa and Venice) take turns to host the **Regata delle Antiche Repubbliche Marinare**, which comes round to Pisa in late May or early June of 2002. Four eight-man crews from each of the cities race against each other on the Arno, in between festivities and parades.

Look out for **concerts** at the Teatro Comunale Verdi, Via Palestro 40, and for more offbeat and contemporary shows (even the odd rock concert) held in a former church at the end of Via San Zeno. The city also has an adventurous **arts cinema**, Cinema Nuove, in Piazza Stazione.

Listings

Airlines Air Dolomiti (☎167.013.366); Alitalia (☎1478.65.642); American (☎02.6791.4400); British Airways (☎1478.12.266); Continental (☎055.476.454); Delta (☎1678.64.114); KLM (☎06.652.9286); Lufthansa (☎02.8066.3025); Meridiana (☎055.230.2416); Ryanair (☎050.503.770); TWA (☎055.239.6856); United (☎1678.825.181).

Books Libreria Internazionale, Via Rigattieri 33, stocks English books.

Car rental Autoeuropa (☎050.506.883), Avis (☎050.42.028), Europcar (☎050.41.017), Hertz (☎050.43.220), Liberty Rent (☎050.48.088), National/Maggiore (☎050.42.574), Program (☎050.500.296), Sixt (☎050.46.209), Thrifty (☎050.45.490), Travelcar (☎050.44.424). All are based at the airport.

Hospital Santa Chiara, Via Roma 67 (☎050.992.111).

Internet access Internet Planet, Piazza Cavallotti 3 (☎050.830.702, *www.internetplanet.it*); Internet Point, Via dei Mille 3 (☎050.830.701, *www.koinepisa.it*). Both have long opening-hours and charge L3000/€1.55 for 15min (less for students). Internet Surf, open daily until 1am at Via Carducci 5 (☎050.830.800, *www.internetsurf.it*), lets you pay by credit card.

Laundry OndaBlu, Via San Francesco 8a.

Left luggage At the airport (daily 8am–8pm; L5000/€2.58 per piece per day).

Lost property At the airport (☎050.849.400).

Parking There are car parks outside the Porta Nuova, just west of the Campo dei Miracoli, and west of the train station on Via Battisti. Parking in the historic centre is severely restricted: yellow spaces are off-limits, blue spaces are charged by the hour, day and night, and white spaces are free only if you display a chit from your hotel, signed, stamped and dated. The airport long-term car park P2 is free.

Police The *Questura* is at Via Mario Lalli 1 (☎050.583.511).

Post office Piazza Vittorio Emanuele II (Mon–Fri 8.15am–7pm, Sat 8.15am–noon).

Taxi Radio Taxi Pisa ☎050.541.600.

Lucca

LUCCA, 17km northeast of Pisa, is the most graceful of Tuscany's provincial capitals, set inside a ring of Renaissance walls fronted by gardens and huge bastions. It's quiet without being dull and absorbs its few tourists with ease.

The city lies at the heart of one of Italy's richest agricultural regions, and it has prospered since Roman times. Its heyday was the eleventh to fourteenth centuries, when the silk trade brought wealth and, for a time, political power. Lucca first lost its independence to Pisa in 1314, then, under Castruccio Castracani, forged an empire in the west of Tuscany. Pisa and Pistoia both fell, and, but for Castracani's untimely death in 1325, Lucca might well have taken Florence. In subsequent centuries it remained largely independent until falling into the hands of Napoleon and the Bourbons. The composer **Giacomo Puccini** was born here in 1858. Today Lucca is reckoned among the wealthiest and most conservative cities in Tuscany, its prosperity gained largely through **silk** and high-quality **olive oil**.

Arrival and information

Lucca's **train station** (information ☎1478.88.088) is just outside the walls to the south. Frequent Lazzi and CLAP **buses** from Florence, and Lazzi ones from Pisa and Livorno, arrive at the western Piazzale Verdi. The focus of Lucca's compact historic centre is the vast Piazza Napoleone, but its social heart is **Piazza San Michele** just to the north. The "long thread", Via Fillungo, heads northeast to the extraordinary circular **Piazza Anfiteatro**. Further east, beyond the Fosso ("ditch"), lies San Francesco.

The main **tourist office** is in the north of town, at Piazza Santa Maria (daily: April–Sept 9am–7pm; Oct–March 9am–5pm; ☎0583.53.549, *www.lucca.turismo.toscana.it*). Other offices are in the Cortile degli Svizzeri, behind Piazza Napoleone (same times; ☎0583.4171) and on Piazzale Verdi (daily: April–Sept 9am–7pm; Oct–March 9am–2pm; ☎0583.419.689). They all have (English) **audioguides** for a self-guided town walk (L15,000/€7.75) which lasts one hour twenty minutes, or you can dot around between the sights. The **Lucchese Settembre** festival features plenty of activity throughout September, centred on a candlelit procession on the 13th. Consult the tourist office for details of affiliated events, such as jazz and classical **concerts** (including Puccini opera) and **art** shows.

Accommodation

Accommodation can be difficult at almost any time of year; if you turn up without a booking, be prepared to move on to Pisa or Pistoia. There are very few **hotels** within

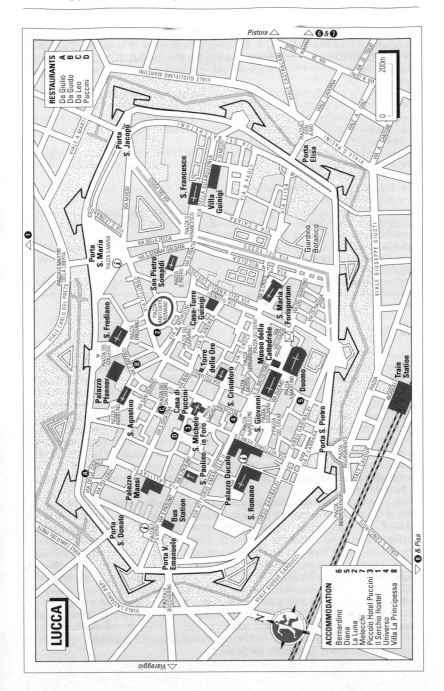

the walls, although some good-value **private rooms** ease the burden (consult the tourist office). The non-HI **hostel** *Il Serchio* is 3km north of town at Via del Brennero 673 (☎& fax 0583.341.811; L19,000/€9.82; bus #6; March–Oct). It's often full, and the summer peak is reserved for groups, but you can camp in the back garden (midnight curfew).

Bernardino, Via di Tiglio 108 (☎0583.953.356, fax 0583.491.765). A two-star 600m east of Porta Elisa that is a shade higher-quality than the nearby *Stipino*, with all-en suite rooms. ③.

Diana, Via del Molinetto 11 (☎0583.492.202, fax 0583.467.795, *aldiana@tin.it*). Located within the walls a block west of the duomo, this nine-room two-star would be a fine budget choice were it not for the frequency of complaints about surly staff. ③.

La Luna, Corte Compagni 12 (☎0583.493.634, fax 0583.490.021). A thirty-room three-star within the walls, with characterful rooms ranged around an internal courtyard and free parking – but well-beaten for price by the *Puccini*. ⑤.

Melecchi, Via Romana 37 (☎0583.950.234). Lucca's only one-star has nine rooms, none with bathroom, and is about 750m east of Porta Elisa. ②.

Piccolo Hotel Puccini, Via di Poggio 9 (☎0583.55.421, fax 0583.53.487, *hotelpuccini@onenet.it*). Friendly three-star with just fourteen rooms, steps from the Casa di Puccini and San Michele. First choice within the walls for character and welcome. ④.

Universo, Piazza del Giglio 1 (☎0583.493.678, fax 0583.954.854). Lucca's not-so-grand grand hotel, a venerable old three-star pile right in the centre with a varying set of rooms that match the staff for unpredictable charm. ⑥.

Villa La Principessa, SS del Brennero 1616, Massa Pisana (☎0583.370.037, fax 0583.379.136). A beautifully appointed nineteenth-century country villa set in lovely grounds (with pool) 3km south of town. ⑨.

The City

Lucca is a delightful place simply to wander at random, with much of the historic centre free from traffic. The historical heart of town is the site of the Roman forum, now the square surrounding **San Michele in Foro** (daily 7.30am–12.30pm & 3–6pm), a church with one of Tuscany's most exquisite **facades**. Most of the present structure dates from the century after 1070, but the church is unfinished, as the money ran out before the body of the building could be raised to the level of the facade. The effect is wonderful, the upper loggias and the windows fronting air. Its Pisan-inspired intricacy is a triumph of poetic eccentricity: each of its myriad columns is different – some twisted, others sculpted or candy-striped. The impressive **campanile** is Lucca's tallest. It would be hard to follow this act and the **interior** barely tries; the best work of art is a beautifully framed painting of *SS Jerome, Sebastian, Roch and Helena* by Filippino Lippi in the right-hand nave.

The composer **Giacomo Puccini** was born a few metres away, on December 22, 1858, at Corte San Lorenzo 9; his father and grandfather had both been organists at San Michele. The family home is now a study centre and small museum, the **Casa di Puccini** (Tues–Sun: June–Sept 10am–6pm; March–May & Oct–Dec 10am–1pm & 3–6pm; L5000/€2.58; *www.puccini.it*). Inside you'll find the Steinway on which Puccini wrote *Turandot* and some scores and ephemera. Just west of here is the **Museo Nazionale di Palazzo Mansi**, Via Galli Tassi 43 (Tues–Sat 9am–7pm, Sun 9am–2pm; L8000/€4.13; joint ticket with Museo Guinigi L12,000/€6.20). This seventeenth-century palazzo is worth seeing for its magnificent Rococo decor: from a vast, frescoed **Music Salon**, you pass through three drawing-rooms hung with seventeenth-century Flemish tapestries to a gilded **bridal suite**, complete with lavish canopied bed. Rooms 11–14 in the far wing hold an indifferent **Pinacoteca**, the highlight of which is Pontormo's portrait of Alessandro de' Medici.

The Duomo and around

It needs a double-take before you realize why the **Duomo** looks odd. The building is fronted by a severely assymetric facade – its right-hand arch and loggias are squeezed by the belltower, which was already in place from an earlier building. Nonetheless, little detracts from its overall grandeur, created by the repetition of tiny columns and loggias and by the stunning **atrium**, whose bas-reliefs are some of the finest sculptures in the city. The carvings over the left-hand door – a *Deposition, Annunciation, Nativity* and *Adoration of the Magi* – are by **Nicola Pisano**. Other panels display a symbolic labyrinth, a Tree of Life (with Adam and Eve at the bottom and Christ at the top), a bestiary of grotesques and the months of the year.

The **interior** (Mon–Sat 7am–6.30pm, Sun 9.30am–6.45pm) is best known for the contribution of **Matteo Civitali** (1435–1501), who is represented here most famously by the *Tempietto*, a gilt-and-marble octagon halfway down the church. Some fanatically intense acts of devotion are performed in front of it, directed at the **Volto Santo** (Holy Face), a cedarwood crucifix with bulging eyes popularly said to be a true effigy of Christ carved by Nicodemus, an eyewitness to the Crucifixion. Legend has it that the *Volto Santo* came to Lucca of its own volition, first journeying by boat from the Holy Land, and then brought by oxen guided by divine will. The effigy attracted pilgrims from all over Europe: King William Rufus of England used to swear by it (*"Per sanctum vultum de Lucca!"*). The **Tomb of Ilaria del Carretto** (1410), originally situated in the north transept, is now in the sacristy to the south following lengthy restoration (Mon–Fri 9.30am–5.45pm, Sat 9.30am–6.30pm, Sun 9–9.50am, 11.30–11.50am & 1–6pm; L3000/€1.55; joint ticket with Museo della Cattedrale and San Giovanni L8000/€4.13). Considered the masterpiece of Sienese sculptor **Jacopo della Quercia**, it consists of a raised dais and the sculpted body of Ilaria, second wife of Paolo Guinigi, one of Lucca's medieval big shots. In a touching, almost sentimental gesture, the artist has carved the family dog at her feet. Also within the sacristy is a superb *Madonna Enthroned* by **Ghirlandaio**.

Occupying a converted twelfth-century building opposite the duomo is the **Museo della Cattedrale** (daily 10am–6pm; Nov–April Mon–Fri closes 5pm; L6000/€3.10; joint ticket with Tomb of Ilaria and San Giovanni L8000/€4.13). This contains some unnerving Romanesque stone heads, human and equine and, in room II on the upper floor, a reliquary from Limoges decorated with stories from the life of St Thomas à Becket alongside the *Croce dei Pisani*, an ornate fifteenth-century gold crucifix. West of the duomo is the church of **San Giovanni** (same hours; L2000/€1.03; joint ticket with Tomb of Ilaria and Museo della Cattedrale L8000/€4.13). This was Lucca's cathedral until 715, and excavations here have unearthed a tangle of remains, from Roman mosaics to traces of a Carolingian church.

North to San Frediano

Via Cenami leads from the duomo north to the **Torre delle Ore**, the city's clock tower since 1471. From here, **Via Fillungo** cuts through Lucca's luxury shopping district.

San Frediano is again Pisan-Romanesque, featuring a magnificent thirteenth-century exterior mosaic of *Christ in Majesty*, with the Apostles gathered below. The **interior** (Mon–Sat 7.30am–12.30pm & 3–6pm, Sun 9am–1pm & 3–6pm except during services) lives up to the facade's promise – a delicately lit, hall-like basilica. Facing the door is the **Fonta Lustrale**, a huge twelfth-century font executed by three unknown craftsmen. Set behind the font is an *Annunciation* by Andrea della Robbia, festooned with trailing garlands of ceramic fruit. The left-hand of the two rear chapels houses the incorrupt body of **St Zita** (died 1278), a Lucchese maidservant who achieved sainthood from a white lie: she used to give bread from her household to the poor, and when challenged one day by her boss as to the contents of her apron, she replied "only roses and flowers" – into which the bread was transformed. She is commemorated on April 27 by a flower market outside the church. Lucca's best frescoes – **Amico Aspertini's** sixteenth-century scenes of the *Arrival of the Volto Santo*, the *Life of St Augustine* and *The Miracle of St Frediano* – occupy the second chapel of the left aisle. Frediano, an Irish monk, is said to have brought Christianity to Lucca in the sixth century and is depicted here saving the city from flood.

A short distance south, at Via degli Asili 33, is the **Palazzo Pfanner** (daily 10am–6pm; gardens L3000/€1.55, tour of house L3000/€1.55, both L5000/€2.58). The palazzo, housing a textiles collection, is less interesting than its rear loggia and exquisite statued gardens with fountain. They can be seen to good effect from the city walls just nearby, which also yield a good overview of another fine church, **Sant'Agostino**.

East of San Frediano is the remarkable **Piazza Anfiteatro**. This ramshackle circuit of medieval buildings, built on the foundations of the Roman amphitheatre that once stood here (arches and columns of which can still be discerned), is now ringed by cafés. South past a covered market looms the **Torre Guinigi**, the fifteenth-century home of Lucca's leading family and one of the strangest sights in town: its battlemented tower is surmounted, 44m up, by a **holm oak** whose roots have grown into the room below. You can climb the tower from Via Sant'Andrea (daily: March–Sept 9am–7.30pm; Oct 10am–6pm; Nov–Feb 10am–4.30pm; L5000/€2.58).

East to San Francesco

Running from north to south across town is a canal and Via del Fosso, across which is the church of **San Francesco**, fronted by a relatively simple facade and adjoining a crumbling brick convent. Behind the church is Lucca's key collection of painting, sculpture, furniture and applied arts, the **Museo Nazionale di Villa Guinigi**, housed in the family's much-restored mansion (Tues–Sat 9am–7pm, Sun 9am–2pm; L4000/€2.06). Its lower floor has mainly sculpture and archeological finds, with numerous Romanesque pieces and works by della Quercia and Matteo Civitali. Upstairs are lots of big sixteenth-century paintings and more impressive works by early Lucchese and Sienese masters, as well as fine Renaissance offerings from such as Fra' Bartolommeo.

Eating, drinking and entertainment

Lucca has some high-quality **restaurants**. Local specialities include *zuppa di farro*, a thick soup made with spelt (a type of grain) and *capretto*, mountain goat, often roasted. *Puccini*, opposite the composer's house at Corte San Lorenzo 1 (☎0583.316.116; closed Tues & Wed lunch in summer; all day Tues in winter), has a light touch and classy approach to its exquisite pasta and especially good fish dishes: this is top choice for a lunch to remember, or a romantic dinner date. *Da Giulio in Pelleria*, Via della Conce 45 (☎0583.55.948; closed Sun & Mon) is a lively trattoria always packed in the evenings – the food is not exceptional, but the atmosphere is. *Da Leo*, Via Tegrini 1 (closed Sun), is a locals' haunt with solid Tuscan cooking; and *Da Guido*, Via Cesare Battisti 28 (closed Sun) is a heartwarming place with much joviality and truly unbeatable prices. Lucca's most famous **café-bar** is *Caffè di Simo* at Via Fillungo 58, once Puccini's favourite haunt and still with an appealing turn-of-the-century ambience. Of the bars around Piazza San Michele, *Casali* at no. 40 is the most alluring.

The town's **food shops** are equally good. Caniparoli in Via San Paolina is a wonderful chocolate shop; La Cacioteca, Via Fillungo 242, sells a wide variety of cheeses; Forno Amedeo Giusti, Via Santa Lucia 18, is the town's top bakery, with delicious fresh *focaccia*; Pellegrini on Piazza San Michele has pizza by the slice; and Pasticceria Taddeucci on the same square has a stunning interior of wood-panelling and mosaic tiles to match its selection of cakey delights.

The **Lucchese Settembre** festival features plenty of activity throughout September, centred on a **candlelit procession** on the 13th, when the bejewelled *Volto Santo* is carried through the streets from San Frediano to the duomo. Consult the tourist office for details of affiliated September events, such as **classical concerts** (including performances of a Puccini opera) at the intimate, four-tiered Teatro Comunale in Piazza del Giglio, as well as **jazz** happenings and **art** exhibitions. Another key musical event is the summertime **Estate Musicale Lucchese**, often featuring big-name international stars performing in Piazza Anfiteatro.

Listings

Bike rental Cicli Barbetti, Via Anfiteatro 23; or Cicli Bizzari on Piazza Santa Maria (L4000/€2.06 per hour).
Hospital Campo di Marte, in Via dell'Ospedale (☎0583.9701).
Internet access There's a cybercafé near San Frediano at Via Battisti 58 (L3000/€1.55 for 15min), or a change office at Via Pescheria 7, just off San Michele (Mon–Sat 1–7pm; L8000/€4.13 for 30min, or 15min free if you change the equivalent of US$200).
Lost property c/o Comune di Lucca, Via Battisti 10 (☎0583.442.388).
Parking Outside the walls, parking is free for all; inside, only hotel customers can park for free.
Police The *Questura* is at Via Cavour 38 (☎0583.4551).
Post office Via Vallisneri 2 (Mon–Fri 8.15am–7pm, Sat 8.15am–12.30pm).

North of Pisa

The coast from near Pisa north to the Ligurian border is a solid strip of unattractive beach resorts. This **Riviera della Versilia** ought to be otherwise, given the backdrop of the **Alpi Apuane** mountains, but the beaches share the coastal plain with a railway, *autostrada* and clogged urban roads – and, on top of this, the sea is not the cleanest in Italy. The resort of **Viareggio** provides a lively diversion on a coastal journey north to the stunning Cinque Terre (see p.144). Otherwise, the only real appeal lies inland, hiking in the Alpi Apuane and exploring the famed marble quarrying centre of **Carrara**.

Viareggio

VIAREGGIO, 22km northwest of Pisa, is a large and once-elegant nineteenth-century resort, which continues to aim – with limited success – for a well-heeled clientele. It has its attractions, with a fair amount of nightlife (including big-name concerts and hot dance clubs) complemented by some neat Art Deco buildings along Passeggiata Margherita. But the beaches are private and charge upwards of L25,000/€12.91 for admission, and in season the hotels are either full or demand *pensione completa*. Aim instead for Viareggio's famously boisterous **Carnevale** (in February); for four consecutive Sundays there's an amazing parade of floats, or *carri* – colossal, lavishly designed papier-mâché models of politicians and celebrities.

The **train station** is 600m back from the seafront. **Buses** (Lazzi, CAT and CLAP) stop nearer the centre; turn right along the seafront, past Piazza Mazzini, to find the **tourist office**, at Viale Carducci 10 (June–Sept daily 9am–1pm & 4–7pm; Oct–May Mon–Fri 9am–1pm & 4–7pm, Sat 9am–1pm; ☎0584.962.233, *www.versilia.turismo.toscana.it*). The town has literally hundreds of **hotels** in all price brackets; one inexpensive option is *Villa Amadei*, just west of the tourist office at Via F. Gioia 23 (☎0584.45.517; ②). Of the dozens of **restaurants**, the long-established Liberty-style seafront villa *Montecatini*, Viale Manin 8 (☎0584.962.129; closed Mon) is a sound mid-priced choice. Summer sees Viareggio's **dance clubs** fill with holidaying Florentines:

WALKS IN THE ALPI APUANE

There are **walks** throughout the **Alpi Apuane**, which loom behind the Riviera della Versilia and are now protected as a Parco Naturale. Altitudes are relatively low (the summits crest 1900m), conditions are easy and distances are short – you're never very far from civilization. Tourist offices in Marina di Massa and Lucca have leaflets, maps and guidance for walkers, as do the **Ufficio Promozione del Parco delle Apuane**, Via Corrado del Greco 11 in Seravezza, partway between Viareggio and Massa (☎0584.756.144, *www.parcapuane.toscana.it*), and the Club Alpino Italiano in the Palazzo Ducale in Lucca (Mon–Fri 7–8pm; ☎0583.582.669).

One access point is the lovely village of **STAZZEMA**, served by bus from Pietrasanta and with the simple **hotel** *Procinto*, Via IV Novembre 21 (☎0584.777.004; ②). Trail #5 is a gentle climb from Stazzema through chestnut woods to the Procinto, a huge table-top crag, below which is the **Rifugio Forte dei Marmi** (open daily June–Aug; rest of year weekends only; dorm-bed L20,000/€10.33; ☎0584.777.051). This is an easy day-trip, with time to explore above the *rifugio* and drop in for a snack on the way back down to Stazzema on trails #121 or #126.

---

the most famous joint is *La Capannina* on the Viale Franceschi seafront (summer daily 9am–6am), despite its exorbitant entrance fee of up to L50,000/€25.82.

Carrara

The capital of Massa-Carrara, Tuscany's northernmost province, is **Massa**, a modern, unappealing town that is more or less merged with its adjacent beach resort of **Marina di Massa** in a sprawl of undistinguished holiday development. Nearby **CARRARA** sits just inside the Ligurian border, 28km north of Viareggio, and enjoys a fame that far outstrips its modest size. For the mountains here have been a principal source of **marble** since the ancient Romans; everyone from Michelangelo to Henry Moore has tramped up here in search of the perfect block. Carrara is still the world's largest producer and exporter of marble, shipping out 1.5 million tonnes a year from the container port plumb in the middle of **Marina di Carrara**. But quiet Carrara itself has a pleasant, rural feel and comes as a relief after the holiday coast.

From the central **Piazza Matteotti**, the pedestrianized Via Roma heads north to the pleasant Piazza Accademia, with steps down (west) to the old town and Carrara's Romanesque-Gothic **Duomo**, graced with a lovely Pisan-style marble facade. Heart of the old town is gracious **Piazza Alberica**. This is the focus for the town's display of contemporary marble sculpture, the biennial **Scolpire all'Aperto** (late July to early Oct), when the town invites internationally renowned artists to create new works in public. For the low-down on marble, there's an impressive **Museo Civico di Marmo** on Viale XX Settembre, 2km south of town (Mon–Sat: June–Sept 10am–8pm, May & Oct 10am–5pm, Nov–April 8.30am–1.30pm; L6000/€3.10), served by CAT buses from Piazza Matteotti. Any short trip into the interior brings you to the startling sight of the marble **quarries**. To get a closer view, take a bus (hourly from Via Minzoni) towards **Colonnata**, 8km northeast of Carrara, and get off before the village at the "*Visita Cave*" signs by the mine – if you're driving, follow the "*Cava di Marmo*" signs from the village. You'll see a huge, blindingly white marble basin, its floor and sides perfectly squared by the enormous wire saws used to cut the blocks that litter the surroundings.

Carrara-Avenza **train station** is close to the Marina di Carrara seafront, and is served by regular **buses** which run 4km inland to drop off at Carrara's central Piazza Matteotti. Carrara town has no **tourist office**; the nearest one is at Piazza Menconi 6 on the Marina di Carrara seafront (Mon–Sat 8.30am–12.30pm & 4–8pm; ☎0585.632.519, *www.bicnet.it/aptms*), from where Navigazione Golfo dei Poeti (see p.151) runs **boats** to Portovenere and the Cinque Terre (June–Sept daily; around L35,000/€18.08). Carrara's two **hotels** are the spartan *Da Roberto* on Via Apuana (☎0585.70.634; ②), and the more salubrious *Michelangelo*, Corso Fratelli Rosselli 3 (☎0585.777.161, fax 0585.74.545; ④), with parking and a jolly manager. The HI **hostel** *Apuano* is at Via delle Pinete 237 in Marina di Massa (☎0585.780.034, fax 0585.774.266; L18,000/€9.30; mid-March to Sept), alongside plenty of **campsites**. The excellent *Il Via* **restaurant**, Via Roma 17 (☎0585.779.423; July & Aug closed Mon, rest of year closed Sun) has a quality mid-priced **vegetarian** *menu fisso*. Elsewhere are *Roma di Prioreschi*, Piazza Cesare Battisti 1 (closed Sat), and *La Tavernetta*, Via Ghibellina 1 (closed Mon). A choice spot for wine and snacks is the *Enoteca* at Viale Verrazzano 11e (closed Sun).

Livorno

LIVORNO, 18km southwest of Pisa, is Tuscany's third largest city and one of Italy's largest ports – a status which invited blanket bombing during World War II. Its rebuilt commercial centre is not pretty, but a poke around the back streets will reveal a network of picturesque canals and hump-backed bridges, a lively streetlife that benefits from a very un-Tuscan ethnic diversity, and plenty of places to sample top-quality **seafood**. What you won't find are the very things Tuscany is famous for: art, architecture and tourists.

Livorno's port was developed under the **Medici**. In 1618, they declared it a **free port** and instituted a liberal constitution which prompted an influx of Jews, Greeks, Spanish Muslims, English Catholics and a cosmopolitan throng of other refugees. Livorno flourished, and attracted a community of English expatriates (including Shelley) whose cack-handed anglicization of the city's name into **Leghorn** is still in use.

The old **Porto Mediceo**, has fishing boats spilling back into the canal quarter and unfortunately under a cruise liner blocking the view out to sea. Sangallo's **Fortezza Vecchia** flanks the harbour, about 100m north of Livorno's sole surviving nod to Renaissance art – the statue of the **Quattro Mori**, overlooking the busy waterfront road at Piazza Micheli. This bizarre work decorates an inept 1595 statue of Ferdinando I with the addition of four chained Moors by Pietro Tacca (1623), tacked on either as a celebration of the success of Tuscan raids against North African shipping, or merely as slaves cowering beneath Medici glory. Either way they stand as a poignant and shocking harbourside symbol for this multiracial city. The **Museo Civico Giovanni Fattori**, devoted to Fattori and the late-nineteenth-century Macchiaioli movement, Italy's milk-and-water version of Impressionism, is housed in the extravagant Villa Mimbelli, 1km south at Via San Jacopo in Acquaviva 65 (Tues–Sun 10am–1pm & 4–7pm; L8000/€4.13; bus #1).

The broad Via Grande heads inland to **Piazza Grande**, which features the **Duomo**, a postwar reconstruction. Via Cairoli curls around the duomo and partway along, Via Buontalenti leads off to the ochre **Mercato Centrale** that stands at the heart of a boisterous street-market. The canal near here was the limit of the Medici port city; follow it northeast to the ugly treeless expanse of Piazza della Repubblica on one side, and Piazza XX Settembre on the other. The latter is the home of the **Mercatino Americano** – a cultural endowment of stationed American troops – that sells army surplus clothing, fishing and camping gear and flick-knives. From the Mercato Centrale, Via della Madonna strikes north into the **Venezia** district, Livorno's most attractive quarter, with crumbling old tenement buildings and the Fortezza Nuova ringed around by a network of quiet canals. August sees the area come alive for the *Effetto Venezia*, a free **street carnival** of jazz and world music.

Bus #2 from the station and Piazza Grande curls up to the hilltop **Santuario di Montenero**, 6km south, which was a pilgrimage site long before the marshes below

FERRIES FROM LIVORNO

There are dozens of **ferry** sailings from Livorno, to **Corsica** (Bastia or Porto Vecchio), **Sardinia** (Olbia, Golfo Aranci or Cagliari), **Sicily** (Palermo) and the Tuscan islands. Nearly all ferries to Corsica and Sardinia leave from alongside the **Stazione Marittima**, west of the centre behind the Fortezza Vecchia, although some (and boats to Sicily) depart from **Varco Galvani**, a long way west of town. Ferries to Capraia and Elba leave from the central **Porto Mediceo**. Check with the tourist office and the companies themselves for times and prices, and **reserve** well ahead in summer. If you're taking a car to Sardinia, most companies offer discount deals if you cross to Corsica and drive the 180km to the southern tip of the island – often this means the subsequent ferry to Sardinia is free. For a full list of ferries to Sardinia, see p.1025; and to Elba, see opposite.

FERRY COMPANIES

Corsica Ferries, Stazione Marittima, Calata Carrara (☎019.215.511, *www.corsicaferries.com*). To Bastia (Corsica).

Corsica Marittima, Stazione Marittima, Calata Carrara (☎0586.210.507, *www.corsicamarittima.com*). To Bastia and Porto Vecchio (Corsica).

Etruria Shipping, Porto Mediceo (☎0586.263.319). To Portoferraio (Elba).

Grandi Navi Veloci (Grimaldi), Varco Galvani, Calata Tripoli, Porto Nuovo (☎010.589.331, *www.grimaldi.it*). To Palermo (Sicily).

Lloyd Sardegna/Linea dei Golfi, Varco Galvani, Calata Assab, Porto Industriale (☎0565.222.300, *www.lloydsardegna.it*). To Olbia and Cagliari (Sardinia).

Moby Lines, Stazione Marittima, Calata Carrara (☎0586.826.823, *www.mobylines.it*). To Bastia (Corsica) and Olbia (Sardinia).

Sardinia Ferries, Stazione Marittima, Calata Carrara (☎019.215.511, *www.sardiniaferries.com*). To Golfo Aranci (Sardinia).

Toremar, Porto Mediceo (☎0586.896.113, *www.toremar.it*). To Capraia.

were populated. A clutch of stalls and cafés surrounds the eighteenth-century **church**, and you'll find quiet footpaths and plenty of vantage points. Last bus down is at 8.45pm daily.

Practicalities

The **train station** is 2km east of the centre; take city bus #1 or #2 to Piazza Grande. ATL **buses** from Piombino drop off on Piazza Grande; Lazzi buses from Florence, Pisa and Lucca arrive on Piazza Manin. The **tourist office** is just off Via Cairoli at Piazza Cavour 6 (Mon–Fri 9am–1pm, Tues & Thurs also 3–5pm; ☎0586.898.111, *www.livorno.turismo.toscana.it*).

The best **hotel** is the eighteenth-century villa *La Vedetta*, on the Montenero hill at Via della Lecceta 20 (☎& fax 0586.579957, *www.tuscany.net/vedetta*; ⑤), with modern decor, parking, and spectacular panoramic views. Livorno has a rash of cheap hotels, some of which – around the harbour and station – are grim dives. *Milano*, Via degli Asili 48 (☎0586.219.155, fax 0586.219.129; ②) is a pleasant exception. *Villa Morazzana* is a **hostel** in the hills, Via di Collinet 86 (☎0586.500.076, fax 0586.502.426; L25,000/€12.91). The **campsite** *Miramare*, Via del Littorale 220 (☎0586.580.402, fax 0586.883.338, *gallirisaliti@liternet.it*; May–Sept), is a short way south of town.

Italians travel to Livorno just to eat seafood and, specifically, to feast on the local dish *cacciucco*, a spicy seafood stew served with garlic toast. A choice **restaurant** if you can spare L70,000/€36.15 per head is *Le Chiave*, Scali delle Cantine (☎0586.888.609; closed Wed). There are dozens of more affordable options: *Antico Moro*, Via Bertelloni 59

(☎0586.884.659; closed Mon–Sat lunch and all day Wed) is a pleasant locals' haunt with excellent *cacciucco*. *Café d'Etoile*, Via Indipendenza 13 (closed Sun), is a breezy café off Piazza Cavour serving fresh salads and snacks. On Venezia's canalsides you'll find the attractive couscous-house *Mediterraneo*, Scali Ponte di Marmo 14 (closed Tues), and *The Barge*, a waterside pub with English beers and food, Scali Ancore 6 (closed Sun).

Elba

Mountainous **ELBA** is the third-largest Italian island after Sicily and Sardinia – 29km long by some 19km wide. It has exceptionally clear water, fine white-sand beaches, and a lush, wooded interior, superb for walking. It's now well and truly embracing package tourism – planes bring in a million tourists during August alone – and yet almost everyone comes for the beach resorts: even in the height of summer, inland villages remain mostly quiet. **Portoferraio** is very much the capital, a characterful port town overlooked by a warren of old alleys. Elsewhere, the most attractive towns are **Capoliveri** and **Porto Azzurro** in the southeast and little **Marciana** in the west, the last of these providing access to woodland hikes and the impressive chair lift up to **Monte Capanne** (1018m). **Biodola** occupies an idyllic sweeping bay near Portoferraio that is largely free from the island's otherwise remorseless beach culture.

FERRIES TO ELBA

The main port of departure to Elba is **PIOMBINO**, 75km south of Livorno – not a great place to stay, since it was flattened in World War II and these days makes its living from a giant steelworks. If you're arriving by train, you'll probably have to change at **Campiglia Maríttima** station, from where connecting trains run through the town to Piombino Maríttima. At the port, you'll find plenty of ticket outlets for all ferry companies. Most people head for Portoferraio, to where ferries run every day of the year, the first around 6am and the last around 9pm (earlier and later in high summer; L10,000/€5.16, plus about L60,000/€30.99 for a car). If you're looking to cut costs, get the bargain-priced ferry to Rio Marina (L6000/€3.10). Port taxes add a few thousand lire.

From Piombino, Toremar, Moby and Etruria Shipping **ferries** shuttle regularly to Portoferraio (summer every 30min; winter every 2hr; takes 1hr); Toremar also serve Rio Marina (2–3 daily) and Porto Azzurro (summer 1 daily). Toremar's **rapid ferry**, or *linea veloce*, serves Portoferraio (summer 2 daily; takes 40min) and Rio Marina (summer 3 daily; takes 30min). Toremar's **hydrofoil**, or *aliscafo*, glides to Cavo (summer 5 daily; winter 3 daily; takes 20min) and Portoferraio (summer 4 daily; takes 30min). Etruria Shipping ferries run **from Livorno** to Portoferraio (1 daily; 3hr).

FERRY COMPANY OFFICES

To book a place on any ferry, phone or visit the office at your port of departure.

Etruria Shipping Porto Mediceo, Livorno (☎0586.263.319); Calata Italia 20, Portoferraio (☎0565.915.555).

Moby Nuova Stazione Marittima, Piombino (☎0565.225.211, *www.mobylines.it*); Via Ninci 1, Portoferraio (☎0565.9361) or Viale Elba 4, Portoferraio (☎0565.914.133).

Toremar Nuova Stazione Marittima, Piombino (☎0565.31.100, *www.toremar.it* and *www.etruscan.li.it/torepi*); Calata Italia 23, Portoferraio (☎0565.918.080, *www.toremar-elba.it*); Calata Voltoni 20, Rio Marina (☎0565.962.073); Banchina IV Novembre 26, Porto Azzurro (☎0565.95.004); Via Michelangelo 54, Cavo (☎0565.949.871).

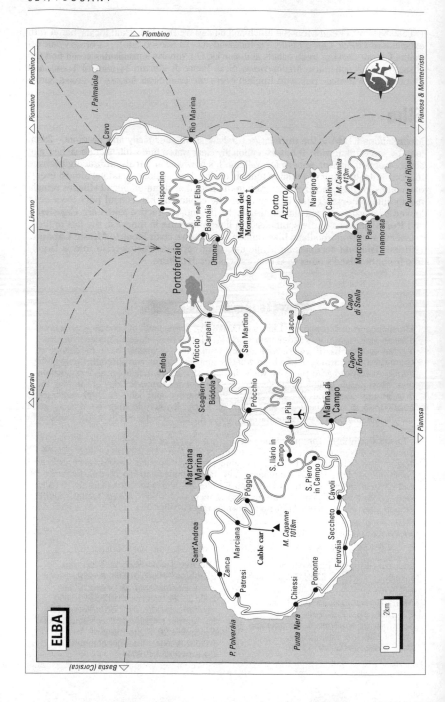

ELBA

Historically, Elba has been well out of the mainstream. The principal industry from ancient times until World War II was **mining**, both of iron ore and of the extensive mineral deposits. The **Romans** wrote of "the island of good wines" (Elban wines are still among Tuscany's finest). In later centuries control passed from Pisa to Genoa and on to the Medici, Spain, Turkey and finally France – a cosmopolitan mix that has left its legacy on both architecture and cultivation. Most people know the island as the place of exile for **Napoleon**, who, after he was banished here in May 1814, revamped education and the legal system, built roads and modernized the economy before escaping back to France in February 1815. The epic "Hundred Days" that followed culminated in his final defeat at Waterloo.

All seven Tuscan islands, and the seas around them, form the **Parco Nazionale Arcipelago Toscano**, the largest protected marine park in Europe, administered from Via Guerrazzi 1 in Portoferraio (☎0565.919.411, *www.islepark.it*).

Getting around the island

ATL **buses** serve just about every settlement on the island (no service after 8pm). One-way **fares** for all but the longest trips are L3500/€1.81, or you could get a **pass** for L11,000/€5.68 (one day) or L30,000/€15.49 (six days). In addition, council minibuses run several times a day between town centres and their outlying beaches in the summer season. **Boats** are also much used to reach out-of-the-way beaches, and are well advertised at all ports. Renting a **bike** or a **scooter** is a good way of exploring the island, see p.527, but **car rental** is less advisable: roads to the beaches and around the major resorts can get nastily congested in high season, and winter bookings can be hard to come by, since companies don't pay insurance off-season.

Portoferraio and around

PORTOFERRAIO is the hub of the island's transport system, has an atmospheric old quarter of stepped alleys and old churches, and lives a life quite separate from the hectic comings-and-goings of the huge ferries which dock nearby. All **boats** slide past the old quarter with its Medici-built harbour to dock at the main Calata Italia. The tallest building in town – an unmissable Fifties-style eyesore known as the *Grattacielo* (skyscraper) – rises ten storeys above the quay, and houses the island's main **tourist office** (☎0565.914.671, *www.arcipelago.turismo.toscana.it*): in summer, there's a desk up the first set of stairs (Mon–Sat 8am–8pm, Sun 8am–2pm), but in winter you must go up another flight (Mon–Sat 8am–1.30pm & 3.30–6pm). The Web sites *www.elbalink.it* and *www.elbatuttanatura.com* have a great deal of information. The Comunità Montana, Viale Manzoni 4 (☎0565.938.111), can provide a contour **hiking** map.

From the quayside, head up a short flight of steps to the old quarter's "back entrance", the **Porta a Terra**. From here, steep alleys fan out on different levels; follow Via del Carmine up to the picturesque little tree-shaded **Piazza Gramsci**, perched above the old port with a café and romantic views. Via Victor Hugo (the novelist spent his boyhood in Portoferraio) continues through another tunnelled gateway up to the highest point of the old quarter and Napoleon's residence-in-exile, the **Villa dei Mulini** (Mon & Wed–Sat 9am–7.30pm, Sun 9am–1pm; L9000/€4.65; joint 3-day ticket with Villa di San Martino L15,000/€7.75). The villa was purpose-built on a well-chosen site with grand views of the bay, and is a fair-sized old building – though undoubtedly not what the emperor was used to. Inside you'll find a gallery with Empire-style furniture, a Baroque bedroom with an absurdly over-gilded bed, a library of two thousand books sent over from Fontainebleau, and various items of memorabilia. The peaceful back garden looks down over the rocky headland.

Stepped alleys head down from the villa through the old quarter, passing the arts centre **Pinacoteca Foresiana** (Mon–Sat 9.30am–12.30pm; July & Aug also

6pm–midnight; L4000/€2.06), with a small collection of paintings and Napoleonic ephemera. The heart of the old town is **Piazza della Repubblica**, lined with cafés. Adjacent is the rather drab Piazza Cavour, from where the old Medici gate, the **Porta a Mare**, heads through to the U-shaped port. In the shadow of the Martello tower on the farthest point of the U is the fascinating **Museo Archeologico** (Mon–Sat: July–Aug 9.30am–12.30pm & 6pm–midnight; rest of year 9.30am–12.30pm & 4–7pm; L4000/€2.06), whose best displays are the various jars and amphorae salvaged from Roman shipwrecks, still full of preserved olives and fish.

From the bus station – round the side of the *Grattacielo* on Viale Elba – take bus #1 southwest into the hills for 5km to the **Villa di San Martino** (Tues–Sat 9am–7.30pm, Sun 9am–1pm; L9000/€4.65; joint three-day ticket with Villa dei Mulini L15,000/€7.75). The arrow-straight avenue leading up to the house is designed to impress, even if the villa itself – bought by Napoleon's sister Elise just before the emperor left the island for good – is a rather chilly affair, with a drab Neoclassical facade enlivened with "N" motifs. The monograms were the idea of Prince Demidoff, husband of Napoleon's niece, and it was he who created the Napoleonic museum. The interior halls of the Neoclassical palazzo are devoted to temporary art exhibitions. Instead, head left of the facade to the ticket office, and then up flights of stairs to the back of the site; here you'll find Napoleon's modest summer retreat. Of the handful of Empire-style rooms, the best is the **Sala Egizio**, decorated with Nilotic scenes to commemorate the Egyptian campaign.

West of Portoferraio, buses head 7km to **ÉNFOLA**, a headland flanked by sandy beaches, and then wind above the coast to the village at the end of the road, **VITICCIO**. From here a footpath covers ground inaccessible to vehicles for 2km south across a prominent headland to picturesque **SCAGLIERI**, fronted by a shop, a bar (which rents bikes and mopeds) and a pizzeria-restaurant. The beaches here are some of the best on the island. Just round the bay sits **BIODOLA** – little more than a road, a couple of hotels and a superb stretch of white sand. The main town of the area, **PROCCHIO**, lies around the next headland to the south: with its traffic, buzzing bars and shops, it's not a place to get away from it all, but the sea is good and the white sand similarly excellent.

Practicalities

You should book a **ferry ticket** for your return journey well in advance in summer, (see opposite). Tourist office staff will often phone around to try and find **accommodation**, as will the Associazione Albergatori, Calata Italia 20 (summer daily 8.30am–12.30pm & 3–7pm; ☎0565.914.754, toll-free ☎800.903.532, *www.albergatori.isoladelba.it*). Otherwise, you could ask in bars about **private rooms** or book a self-catering **apartment** through the tourist office. The best **hotel** in terms of its sense of exclusive isolation and impeccable service is the *Park-Hotel Napoleone*, a nineteenth-century mansion beside the emperor's villa at San Martino (☎0565.918.502, fax 0565.917.836, *www.elbalink.it*; ⑧; mid-April to mid-Oct). The white sand beach at Biodola is overlooked by the luxury *Hermitage* (☎0565.936.911, fax 0565.969.984, *www.elba4star.it*; ⑨; April–Oct); north along this coast is the decent *Danila* in Scaglieri (☎0565.969.915, fax 0565.969.865; ④). Portoferraio's best choices are the comfortably done-up old *Ape Elbana*, Salita Cosimo dei Medici 2 (☎ & fax 0565.914.245, *apelbana@elba2000.it*; ④), pleasant *Villa Ombrosa*, Viale De Gasperi 3 (☎0565.914.363, fax 0565.915.672; ⑤) and clean but spartan *Nobel*, Via Manganaro 72 (☎0565.915.217, fax 0565.915.415; ③).

The Associazione Campeggi (FAITA), Viale Elba 7 (☎ & fax 0565.930.208, *campeggie@ouverture.it*) can help out with bookings for the island's **campsites**. The shaded *Enfola* (☎0565.939.001, fax 0565.918.613; April to mid-Oct) is west from Portoferraio on the scenic coast road. On the hillside above Biodola beach is *Scaglieri* (☎0565.969.940, fax 0565.969.834, *www.campingscaglieri.it*; April to mid-Oct). Lacona,

Elba's camping hotspot on the coast 7km south of Portoferraio, has a flat foreshore crowded with bars and discos and nearby *Lacona* (☎0565.964.161, fax 0565.964.330, *www.camping-lacona.it*) set in pine woods.

Portoferraio's **restaurants** can be poor value. Notable exceptions include the characterful, mid-priced *Osteria Libertaria*, on the Medici harbourfront at Calata Matteotti 12 (closed Mon); and *Trattoria La Barca*, one street back at Via Guerrazzi 60 (☎0565.918.036; closed Wed), considered the best restaurant in town. For a real treat, book well ahead at the expensive terrace restaurant of the *Park-Hotel Napoleone* at San Martino (☎0565.918.502; closed in winter); the classic Tuscan cuisine is exquisite, but the multilingual maitre d's service really stands out as something special. Back in town, upmarket *Caffè Roma* fronts the harbour, a bright, lively place open all day for coffee and snacks, and then during the evening as a **bar**. *Enoteca Torchio*, close by in Via dell'Amore, has a bit more elbow room.

Listings

Bike, scooter, car and boat rental Main agencies are all near the quay: TWN, Viale Elba 32 (☎0565.914.666); BW's, Via Manganaro 15 (☎0565.930.491, fax 0565.930.492, *www.bwsplanet.com*); Rent Chiappi, Piazza Citi 5 (☎0565.914.366, fax 0565.916.779, *www.rentchiappi.it*); and Tesi (Maggiore/Budget), Calata Italia 8 (☎0565.930.212, fax 0565.915.368, *tesi@elbalink.it*). Cicli Brandi, Via Carducci 33 (☎0565.914.128) are mountain-bike specialists. From any of these outlets, the per-day rate for a small car is around L90,000/€46.48; a 50cc scooter L50,000/€25.82; a mountain-bike slightly less than that, and an ordinary bike L25,000/€12.91. A 5m boat (35–40hp) costs around L250,000/€129.11 a day (no licence needed).

Ferry information Return ferries to Piombino are often packed, and you should book your return as far in advance as possible; shop around between the three operators on both price and convenience (make sure to add in port taxes). Toremar are on the portside road at Calata Italia 23 (☎0565.918.080), and also let you book train tickets; Moby are just round the corner at Viale Elba 4 (☎0565.914.133) and also by the port at Via Ninci 1 (☎0565.9361); and Etruria Shipping are at the Ilva travel agency at Calata Italia 20 (☎0565.915.555). To Bastia, fast Corsica Marittima boats cost around L36,000/€18.60 (Calata Italia 22; ☎0565.914.648, *www.corsicamarittima.com*; April–Sept 2 weekly; 90min).

Internet access Joinelba, Via Concia di Terra 40 (☎0565.919.178, *www.joinelba.com*).

Left luggage In the bus station (daily 8am–8pm; L2500/€1.29 per piece per day).

Markets Behind Piazza Cavour is the covered food market (Mon–Sat 7am–1pm & 4–8pm, Sun 7am–1pm) which, aside from fruit and veg, has bottles of Elba's acclaimed DOC wines, *rosso* and *bianco*. The weekly Friday market in Piazza della Repubblica focuses on clothes and bric-à-brac.

Parking The car park opposite the bus station on Viale Elba is free. Cars are banned from the old quarter during the summer.

Pharmacy Centrale, Via Cavour 20 (☎0565.914.026).

Post office Piazza della Repubblica in the old town (Mon–Fri 8.15am–7pm, Sat 8.15am–12.30pm).

Eastern Elba

Eastern Elba comprises two tongues of land, each of them dominated by mountain ridges. The northeast corner was formerly mining country, as the reddish rocks bear testament, but is these days given over entirely to beach tourism. The main road east from Portoferraio heads through **Rio nell'Elba**, once the major mining town of the east, to **RIO MARINA**. Tourism and ferry links have replaced iron ore as the town's principal source of revenue; if you're stuck here, the one **hotel** is the *Rio*, Via Palestro 31 (☎0565.924.225, fax 0565.924.162; ④), next to the scrubby public gardens overlooking the port. Some boats stop at picturesque **CAVO**, 9km north of Rio Marina; its clutch of **hotels** includes the bargain three-star *Maristella* on the water (☎ & fax 0565.949.859; ③; April–Sept), and one of its most pleasant **restaurants** is mid-priced *La Scogliera*, with tables overlooking the beach.

Porto Azzurro and Capoliveri

The resort of **PORTO AZZURRO** was heavily fortified by Philip III of Spain in 1603. Today his fortress is the island's prison; a walk round the outer ramparts brings you to a shop selling crafts made by the inmates. The town's small, pretty old quarter, closed to traffic, centres on bustling **Via d'Alarcon**. Choice of the lacklustre **hotels** is *Belmare*, Banchina IV Novembre 21 (☎0564.95.012, fax 0565.958.245, *belmare@ elbalink.it*, ③). The *Arrighi* **campsite** north of town at Barbarossa (☎0565.95.568, fax 0565.957.822; April–Nov) gives straight onto the beach. Busy town **restaurants** serve identikit pasta-based nosh, including the friendly *Lo Scoglio*, Via Cavour 15 (closed Wed in winter). *All'Arco Antico* on Via d'Alarcon has snacks and pizzas from L7000/€3.61. Plenty of places rent **bikes**, boats and scooters, including BW's, Via Provinciale 10 (☎0565.920.196, *www.bwsracing.it*). Motorboats shuttle across the bay to the sandy beach at **Naregno**.

CAPOLIVERI, 3.5km southwest of Porto Azzurro and overlooked by Monte Calamita, is the best of the towns on Elba's eastern fringe, a prosperous inland centre whose close-knit lanes have made few concessions to tourism. Capoliveri makes an ideal base for visits south to the fine **beaches** at Morcone, Pareti and Innamorata, but **accommodation** is limited: try at the comfortable two-star *Villa Miramare* in Pareti (☎ & fax 0565.968.673; ③). The *Sugar Reef* **bar** and music venue 1km south of Capoliveri at La Trappola (☎0336.381.035, *www.sugar-reef.com*) feeds the town's nightlife image, with dance parties all summer long (daily 11pm–5am). In summer, municipal minibuses run hourly between Capoliveri and nearby beach towns until 1am.

Western Elba

The main road west from Portoferraio heads to prim **MARCIANA MARINA**, whose traffic-filled promenade of bars, restaurants and trinket shops does nothing to lure you into staying. You can **rent a bike** or scooter for a trip inland from TWN, Via Dussol 45 (☎0565.997.027) and access the **Internet** at Foto Berti, Via Cavour 5 (daily 9am–1pm, 5–8pm & 9–11.30pm). Aquavision (☎0328.709.5470) operates trips on the **M/N Nautilus**, which has glass panels below the waterline (daily: April–Oct 3.30pm; also July to mid-Sept 10am; L30,000/€15.49; takes 2hr).

A winding road heads south for 5km into the hills to **POGGIO**, a village renowned for its mineral water and its tight medieval centre, with decorated doorways and a patchwork of cheerful gardens. One of Elba's leading **restaurants**, *Da Publius*, Piazza XX Settembre 13 (☎0565.99.208; closed Mon) has great views and steep prices for its classic Elban cooking (including *cacciucco* and wild boar with mushrooms). The near- by *Monte Capanne*, Via Pini 1 (☎ & fax 0565.99.083) serves more affordable food in a lovely, peaceful setting and doubles up as Poggio's **hotel** (②).

Marciana and Monte Capanne

The high, isolated village of **MARCIANA**, up 4km of switchbacks from Poggio, is the oldest settlement on Elba. It's the most alluring place on the island, perfectly located between great beaches and the mountainous interior. Its steep **old quarter** is a delight, narrow alleys, arches, belvederes and stone stairs festooned with flowers and climbing plants that culminate at the twelfth-century **Fortezza Pisano** (closed to the public, but with great views). The only **accommodation** options are a handful of rooms and apart- ments available at *Bar La Porta* (☎0565.901.275; ③), located in Piazza Umberto at the gateway to the village. The best **restaurant** is the award-winning *Osteria del Noce*, high up at Via Della Madonna 19 (☎0565.901.284; closed Tues except in summer), with excellent mid-priced food and a terrace with spectacular views. Way up beside the Fortezza at Via del Pretorio 64 is little *Monilli*, a bar and paninoteca open daily until 2am perched over a wooded hillside.

WALKS AROUND MARCIANA

Various **walking** trails head out from Marciana, both up to Monte Capanne and on scenic, quiet routes down to the coast. Before setting off, you should pick up the local *Comunità Montana* **map** or consult the Portoferraio tourist office, and make sure you have water and a sunhat.

Trail #1 is a circular route starting from the southern end of the village, which passes the fifteenth-century **Oratorio di San Cerbone** (1hr) and continues beyond the junction with trail #6 and up to the summit of the mountain (where you could take the *cabinovia* down again); you then retrace your steps and take trail #6 west across open country to La Stretta, then skirt Monte Giove back to Marciana (total 8.5km; 4hr 30min).

A different route heads uphill west of Marciana – the path begins at the *Osteria del Noce* – for about 30min to the **Santuario della Madonna del Monte**, the island's most celebrated shrine, a Renaissance church built to house a stone mysteriously painted with an image of the Virgin. From the church, trail #3 again skirts round Monte Giove to La Stretta, then continues jigging on switchbacks west and down through fragrant woodland and scrub to hit the coast at **Chiessi** (total 12km; 6hr).

The main draw of Marciana is half-a-kilometre south of the village – the base-station of a **cabinovia** (cable car) that climbs 650m to the summit of **Monte Capanne** (1018m), Elba's highest point. "Cable car" is a misnomer: it's a series of small exposed cages, each of which is big enough for two people to stand up in, that are hooked onto a continually running cable: the open-air ride might give you the flutters. It runs in summer only (April–Oct daily 10am–12.15pm & 2.45–6pm; L13,000/€6.71 one way or L21,000/€10.84 return; takes 20min), lifting you slowly above the wooded hills and eventually above the tree-line to a levelled platform with a café. From here, it's a short scramble to the summit, from where the views are suitably stupendous. Another local attraction is one of Tuscany's very few **vegetarian restaurants**, *Vegetariano alla Cabinovia* (☎0565.901.029; closed in winter), by a brook in the woods alongside the *cabinovia* base-station, which boasts an affordable menu of falafel and tabbouleh, lentils, seitan and tofu, wholewheat pasta and organic wine.

The western coast and Marina di Campo

The spread-out village of **SANT'ANDREA**, 6km west of Marciana, just off the coast road, is one of Elba's trendiest retreats; divers are drawn here by the crystal-clear seas. **Hotels** are not expensive, most of them discreetly set amid near-tropical vegetation; just above the beach is the eco-friendly *Ilio* (☎0565.908.018, fax 0565.908.087, *www.ilio.it*; ③), which uses all biodegradable materials and has a pleasant, helpful manager. A little west, the road hugs the coast for a lonely, scenic drive round to **CHIESSI** and **POMONTE**, each of them with a small stony beach, beautifully clear water and little commercialism. By **FETOVAIA** on the southwestern tip of the island you're back to beach development, but the sandy beach is superb – and a big car park prevents some of the chaos of other Elban resorts. About 2km east of Fetovaia is a stretch of **nudist** beach.

MARINA DI CAMPO was the first resort on Elba and is now the largest. The huge white **beach** and clean water are what make the place suffocatingly popular. There's also all the tourist frippery and nightlife you'd expect in any major seaside centre, as well as a **tourist office**, Piazza dei Granatieri (Mon–Wed, Fri & Sat 8am–8pm; ☎0565.977.969). Internet Planet on Via Carducci has **Internet** access (daily 10am–midnight; L4000/€2.06 for 15min). The affordable **restaurant** *L'Aragosta*, Via Bologna 3 (closed winter), has fresh fish served daily, while *Il Gazebo*, Piazzetta Torino, is a **bar** specializing in wholewheat *panini*, pizzas, *calzoni* and hot-dogs.

The islands around Elba

None of the small islands dotted around Elba is easy to reach. **Gorgona**, near Livorno, and **Pianosa** (*www.pianosa.is.it*), 14km southwest of Elba, both house maximum-security prisons, but the latter permits day-trippers. Granite **Montecristo** pokes an impressive 645m above the waves 45km south of Elba, and also receives a few day-trippers. Various companies run full-day excursions **from Elba**: Linee di Navigazione Arcipelago Toscano go to Capraia, Montecristo and Giglio from Porto Azzurro (☎0565.921.009, *www.elbacrociere.com*), and to Capraia from Portoferraio (☎0565.914.797); and NapoleonElba, based in Portoferraio (☎0565.915.899, *www.napoleonelba.it*), go to Pianosa from Marina di Campo. Prices are upwards of L50,000/€25.82, and often include a guide and a meal. Toremar ferries also serve Pianosa from Porto Azzurro (1 weekly).

CAPRAIA, 30km northwest of Elba, is lovely and largely unspoilt. Its former use as a penal colony (up until 1996) ensured that the terrain remained largely untouched, and the local council has since backed environmental protection. The scrubby, almost tree-less island has a knobbly spine of 400m hills, with the eastern slope shallow and riven with valleys, and the western coast featuring cliffs rising almost sheer from the sea. Most people come for the excellent deep-sea **diving**. Toremar **ferries** run from Livorno (at least 1 daily; takes 2hr 30min; L20,000/€10.33) – their pre-sunrise service (Thurs 4.50am) is a memorable way to make the crossing.

From the harbour to the village of **CAPRAIA ISOLA**, overlooked by the **Fortezza di San Giorgio**, is a gentle walk. The Pro Loco **tourist office** is at Via Roma 2 (☎0586.905.138). The Cooperativa Parco Naturale, Via Assunzione 42 (☎0586.905.071, *agparco@tin.it*) **rents boats** – motorized dinghies (L140,000/€72.30 per day) and kayaks (L15,000/€7.75 per hour). The Capraia Diving Service (☎0586.905.137, *cds@omnimedia.it*), at Via Assunzione 72 have equipment for rent. The main **hotel** is the comfortable four-star *Il Saracino*, Via L. Cibo 40 (☎0586.905.018, fax 0586.905.062; ⑥), although there's also the small, attractive *Pensione Da Beppone* near the water (☎ & fax 0586.905.001; ③), numerous private rooms, and the **campsite** *Le Sughere* (☎ & fax 0586.905.066; May–Sept) behind the church. The best **restaurant** is *Vecchio Scorfano*, Via Assunzione 44 (closed winter). A good well-signposted **walk** leads up from the village into the uninhabited interior, passing springs and – on a branch trail – an isolated tarn known as **Lo Stagnone**. The path leads up to **Il Semaforo**, just below the summit of Monte Arpagna (410m), where a ravine between peaks gives a stunning view westwards across open water to Corsica. The rough trail heads steeply down to a lighthouse on the rugged western coast. Alongside a watchtower on the southernmost tip of land is the narrow inlet of **Cala Rossa** – a spectacular place to swim, in sparkling clear water beneath cliffs of fiery red.

The Maremma coast

The **Maremma** is a loose term derived from *maríttima* that refers to the coastal strip and inland hills of the Provincia di Grosseto, Tuscany's southernmost province. This was the northern heartland of the Etruscans but was depopulated in the Middle Ages as wars disrupted the drainage schemes and allowed malarial swamps to build up behind the dunes. The area became almost synonymous with disease, and nineteenth-century guides advised strongly against a visit – even though *butteri* cowboys roamed freely then, as now, taking care of the region's half-feral horses and its celebrated white cattle. Today, the provincial capital of **Grosseto** remains pretty uninspiring, though there are some patches of scenery – notably the **Monti dell'Uccellina**, protected in the **Parco Naturale della Maremma**, and the wooded peninsula of **Monte Argentario**, main departure point to the island of **Giglio**.

Grosseto and around

Until the mid-nineteenth century, **GROSSETO** was a malaria-ridden backwater. The draining of the marshes, however, which was finally effected under Mussolini, has transformed it into a provincial capital for the Maremma. Grosseto was rebuilt after the war with a rash of dreary condominiums and is deservedly undervisited, though you may well find yourself passing through.

Piazza Dante, at the heart of the old town, has a quirky statue showing Leopoldo II protecting Mother Maremma and crushing the serpent malaria under his foot. The adjacent **Duomo** was started in 1294 but virtually nothing is left to suggest antiquity: the white-and-pink marble facade is a product of the nineteenth century, while the interior has suffered repeated modifications. Its finest artworks are on display in the **Museo Archeologico**, Piazza Baccarini 3 (Tues–Sun: May–Oct 10am–1pm & 5–8pm; Nov–April 9am–1pm & 4–6pm; Nov–Feb closed Tues–Fri afternoons; L10,000/€5.16; *www.gol.grosseto.it/maam*); most interest is in rooms 24–34, the **Museo d'Arte Sacra**, with a handful of good Sienese paintings, notably Sassetta's *Madonna of the Cherries* and a Byzantine *Last Judgement* by Guido da Siena. **San Francesco**, just north of the museum, has a few patches of fresco and an early crucifix by Duccio; from here you can walk round the **walls**, a trip of about forty minutes and one of the more rewarding things Grosseto has to offer.

Most mainline **trains** on the Pisa–Rome coastal line stop in Grosseto, where you can change for Siena or Orbetello. Head from the station 100m ahead on Via Trieste to the **tourist office** on the second corner, Via Fucini 43c (Mon–Fri 9am–1pm & 4.30–6.30pm, Sat 9am–noon; ☎0564.414.303, *www.grosseto.turismo.toscana.it*); they have information on the whole province, which includes Massa Maríttima (see p.558), Pitigliano (see p.568) and Giglio (see p.533). At the next corner, head right on Via Roma for 700m past a Fascist-era post office and piazza into the old town. Central **hotels** include *Appennino*, Viale Mameli 1 (☎0564.23.009, fax 0564.416.134; ②).

The Monti dell'Uccellina

The hills and coastline of the Monti dell'Uccellina are protected as the **Parco Naturale Regionale della Maremma**, set to be upgraded to a Parco Nazionale – recognition for an area that, it is claimed, is the last virgin coastal landscape on the Italian peninsula, 12km south of Grosseto. This breathtaking piece of countryside combines cliffs, coastal marsh, *macchia*, forest-covered hills, pristine beaches and some of the most beautiful stands of umbrella pines in the country. It is a microcosm of all that's best in the Maremma, devoid of the bars, marinas, hotels, roads and half-finished houses that have destroyed much of the Italian littoral. There is no public road access – all drivers should park in **ALBERESE** (scene, in August, of a *butteri* rodeo), near the Visitors' Centre on Via del Fante (☎0564.407.098, fax 0564.427.278). RAMA city **buses** #15 and #16 run irregularly from Grosseto station to Alberese (Mon–Sat); otherwise, take a taxi (L30,000/€15.49).

Admission to the park (daily: mid-June to Sept 7am–dusk, rest of year 9am–dusk; L7000/€3.61) secures a basic **map** and a place on an hourly bus that runs 10km into the hills, dropping you at the trailhead **Pratini**. From Pratini, you're left to your own devices, or you can book ahead for a place on a 3hr or 5hr **guided walk** (summer Wed, Thurs, Sat & Sun; L5000/€2.58 extra). Most people head straight onto the *Strada degli Olivi*, which leads to the superb **beach**, an idyllic curving bay backed by cliffs and wooded hills. The circular **Trail 1** (*San Rabano*; 6km; 5hr) climbs a ridge and passes the ivy-covered eleventh-century ruined abbey of San Rabano. The last return buses from Pratini or Alberese are around 5.30pm in summer, earlier in winter.

Monte Argentario

The high, rocky terrain of **Monte Argentario** (*www.monteargentario.it*), 37km south of Grosseto, is as close to wilderness as southern Tuscany comes. The interior is mountainous, reaching 635m at its highest point, and the coast is sectioned dramatically into headlands, bays and shingle beaches. Much of the area is still uninhabited scrub and woodland, badly prone to forest fires but still excellent walking country.

Long ago, Monte Argentario was an island. Over several thousand years, inshore currents built up two narrow sand spits (*tomboli*) between the mountain and the mainland, creating a lagoon between them. The ancient town of **Orbetello** occupied a peninsula sticking out into the lagoon; then the Romans built a causeway to link Orbetello to the Argentario, forming a third spit of land and dividing the lagoon in two. Orbetello's strange location is about the most exciting thing about it, and on summer weekends the roads over the northern Tombolo della Giannella sandbar and through Orbetello become bottlenecks as tourists pile in to the resorts of **Porto Ercole** and **Porto Santo Stefano**.

Orbetello and around

ORBETELLO is an unassuming place, graced with palm trees, the pastel-coloured remnants of its Spanish walls, and a lively passeggiata each evening along its main street, Corso Italia. It was probably Etruria's leading port, though little evidence of an ancient past remains: the sixteenth-century Spanish fortifications are the town's conspicuous feature. The **train station** is 4km east at Orbetello Scalo. **Buses** originating in Rome or Grosseto run from Orbetello station to the bus stops near the **tourist office** at Piazza della Repubblica 1 (daily: July & Aug 10am–12.30pm & 5–9pm; April–June, Sept & Oct 10am–12.30pm & 4–8pm; ☎0564.861.226). Choice **hotel** is the simple, friendly and very central *Piccolo Parigi*, Corso Italia 169 (☎0564.867.233, fax 0564.867.211; ③). Most of the area's thirteen **campsites** are on and around the lagoon; plump for the *Feniglia* (☎0564.831.090, fax 0564.867.175; April to mid-Oct), the only site on the southern Tombolo di Feniglia. Orbetello's best **restaurant** for a treat is the *Osteria del Lupacante*, Corso Italia 103 (closed Tues), but less pricey options include the *Cantuccio*, Via Mentana 7 (closed Mon), which has a small garden in summer.

Roads from Orbetello head north and south around the base of Monte Argentario. On the south side is intimate **PORTO ERCOLE**, with an attractive old quarter and a fishing-village atmosphere. Though founded by the Romans, its chief historical monuments are two **Spanish fortresses**, facing each other across the harbour. At the entrance to the old town, a plaque on the stone gate commemorates the painter **Caravaggio**, who in 1610 keeled over with sunstroke on a beach nearby and died of a fever; he was buried in the parish church of Sant'Erasmo. From the village, you can easily **walk** across the Tombolo di Feniglia, which is barred to traffic and is a prime spot for birdwatching over the lagoon. Finest **restaurant** for fish and seafood is the classy *Gambero Rosso*, Lungomare Andrea Doria (☎0564.832.650; closed Wed). On the north side of the Argentario is **PORTO SANTO STEFANO**, more popular and developed than its twin. You'll probably stay only as long as it takes to get a **ferry** to the island of Giglio (see opposite).

The Tarot Garden

Unbroken sand stretches down the coast east of Orbetello, with a lagoon and nature reserve at **Lago di Burano** and plenty of opportunities for camping in the dunes. The gently shelving seabed makes for good swimming.

Bang on the Lazio border 20km east of Orbetello, in a landscape of dust, scrub and clammy heat, is one of the oddest and most engaging works of modern art in the region. The **Giardino dei Tarocchi**, or Tarot Garden, is the life-long dream of Niki de St-Phalle, wife of the late Swiss artist Jean Tinguely. Since 1978, St-Phalle has been devoting herself to constructing this physical interpretation of the tarot deck – chunky, brightly coloured cartoon figures of the **Devil**, the **Guardian Angel**, the **Hanged Man** and others loom well above the treetops, arranged around a curvaceous, arcaded **courtyard** tiled in shards of mirror and shimmering, multi-coloured plastic. The symbolism of the garden may be obscure, but kids of all ages will love it. Don't let its isolation or its priciness put you off: you might well find this fiery-loined Devil speaking to you more clearly from his remote hillside than Michelangelo's "must-see" *David* in the heart of Florence ever could. The garden has limited **opening hours** (mid-May to mid-Oct Mon–Sat 2.30–7.30pm; L20,000/€10.33; Nov–May first Sat of month 9am–1pm; free *www.nikidesaintphalle.com*). There's no public **transport**, but the sculptures are visible about 1km north of the main Livorno–Rome "Via Aurelia" highway, near the village of Pescia Fiorentina. The nearest **train station** is Chiarone, 4km south – a **taxi** from here will save on the L50,000/€25.82 fare you're likely to run up from Orbetello.

The island of Giglio

In winter, just 1300 people live on pint-sized **GIGLIO**, 15km west of Monte Argentario, but the island has become so popular with holidaying Romans that in July and August you may find that there's standing room only on the ferries. Yet it's well worth staying: most visitors are day-trippers, and few of them explore the unspoilt interior, a mix of barren granite outcrops and reforested upland. The island is rich in mouflon, peregrine falcons, kestrels and buzzards, and is the only place outside North Africa to shelter wild mustard.

Small, rock-girdled **GIGLIO PORTO** hosts eight of the island's thirteen hotels. The view from the ferry is wonderful as the town draws closer, its pale-coloured houses offset by a backdrop of terraced vineyards and framed between two lighthouses – one red, one green. The narrow harbourfront drag is crammed with a mix of touristy restaurants and boat mechanics, but behind the **Torre del Saraceno**, built by Ferdinand I in 1596, you'll find a tranquil, barely visited little inlet, with the wall of a Roman eel farm below the waterline.

There's a **tourist office** hut on the waterfront (April–Oct daily 9am–1pm & 4.30–7pm; ☎0564.809.400, *www.isoladelgiglio.it*). Most **hotels** open only in summer, such as the modest *La Pergola*, on the waterfront Via Thaon de Revel, at no. 30 (☎0564.809.051; ④; April–Oct). *Demo's*, at the end of the harbour, no. 31 (☎0564.809.235, fax 0564.809.319, *www.hoteldemos.com*; ⑤; April–Oct) has lovely top-floor rooms that offer a seaview flooded with morning sunshine; they also have a discount deal with Monaci Parking in Porto Santo Stefano (see box). The most visited quayside **restaurants** are *Doria* and *Margherita*, both offering standard fishy specials;

FERRIES TO GIGLIO

The embarkation point for Giglio is **PORTO SANTO STEFANO**, served by regular **buses** from Orbetello train station and town. Both Toremar (☎0564.810.803, *www.toremar.it*) and Maregiglio (☎0564.812.920, *www.maregiglio.com*) operate **ferries** to Giglio Porto (summer hourly; winter 4–5 daily; takes 1hr; L10,000/€5.16). Toremar also has slightly pricier **hydrofoils**, which cross in half the time. It's usually no problem to buy your ticket at the port and board immediately. You should leave your **car** at Porto Santo Stefano; Monaci is the most trustworthy parking company, run from the "Recapito Garage" hut on the waterfront (L12,000/€6.20 per day; ☎0564.810.438).

the food at *Demo's Hotel* is better, and comes with beach views. **Buses** depart every thirty minutes (7.30am–8.30pm) from behind the harbourfront for the island's other villages. You can rent transport from the little office beside *Pergola* restaurant (☎0338.432.0011): a **moped** is L10,000/€5.16 per hour, a **mountain-bike** half as much.

GIGLIO CASTELLO, perched on the highest point of the island, was for a long time the only settlement and the sole spot safe from pirate attack. Buses stop near a vine-covered patio **bar** in the large Piazza Gloriosa, also the entrance to the granite **fortress** and maze-like medieval quarter. *Santi* at Via Marconi 20 (closed Mon in winter) is among the the island's best, and priciest, **restaurants**. A minor road winds from Castello 9km south all along the spine of the ridge to **Punta del Capel Rosso**, the southernmost tip of the island – a wild, lonely bike-ride or 3hr hike. Walking from Castello across country down to either Campese or Porto takes less than an hour. At the western end of the island road, **GIGLIO CAMPESE** is a tiresomely overgrown resort. Its selling-point is Giglio's best **beach**, a fine stretch of sand curving for 2km from a huge phallic rock which the tourist brochures are too modest to photograph. There's a handful of unappealing hotels and, 500m north, the *Baia del Sole* **campsite** (☎0564.804.036, fax 0564.804.101, *baia.delsole@flashnet.it*; May–Sept).

GIANNUTRI is a rocky and deserted half-moon islet 15km southeast of Giglio. The resident Roman Enobardi family left behind ruins of their marble-clad villa, which you can explore, but the island's remoteness and lush flora are much more appealing. **Day-trips** are run by Mareglio (☎0564.812.920) from Giglio Porto (Tues–Fri 10am) and from Porto Santo Stefano (summer daily 10am).

SIENA AND AROUND

SIENA is the perfect antidote to Florence, a unified, modern city at ease with its medieval aspect, ambience and traditions – indeed, exultant about them. It's a place not easily read by outsiders, and to get anything meaningful from a visit you'll need to stay at least one night; too many visitors breeze through on a day-trip.

Self-contained and still part-rural behind its medieval walls, Siena's great attraction is its cityscape, a majestic Gothic ensemble that could be enjoyed without venturing into a single museum. The physical and spiritual heart of the city is the great scallop-shaped piazza **il Campo**, loveliest of all Italian squares and scene of the thrilling **Palio** bareback horse-race. Siena's **Duomo** and **Palazzo Pubblico** are two of the purest examples of Italian Gothic architecture, and the best of the city's paintings – collected in the **Museo Civico** and **Pinacoteca Nazionale** – are in the same tradition; the finest example of Sienese Gothic is Duccio's *Maestà*, on show in the outstanding **Museo dell'Opera del Duomo**. More frescoes fill the halls of **Santa Maria della Scala**, the city's hospital for over 900 years and now its premier exhibition space.

For a hundred years or so, in the twelfth and thirteenth centuries, Siena was one of the major cities of Europe. Virtually the size of Paris, it controlled most of southern Tuscany and its wool industry, dominated the trade routes between France and Rome, and maintained Italy's richest pre-Medici banks. This era reached an apotheosis with the defeat of a much superior Florentine army at the battle of **Montaperti** in 1260. Although the result was reversed permanently nine years later, Siena embarked on an unrivalled urban development under the guidance of its mercantile governors, the **Council of Nine**. From 1287 to 1355 the city underwrote the completion of its cathedral and then the **Campo** and its exuberant **Palazzo Pubblico**. The prosperity came to an abrupt halt with the **Black Death**, which reached Siena in May 1348; by October, two-thirds of the 100,000 population had died. The city never fully recovered (the population today is 60,000) and its politics, always factional, descended into chaos. In 1557 Philip II gave up Siena to **Cosimo de' Medici** in lieu of war services, and the city subsequently became part of Cosimo's Grand Duchy of Tuscany, and fell into decline. The lack of subsequent development explains Siena's astonishing state of preservation: little was built and still less demolished. Since World War II, Siena has again become prosperous, due partly to **tourism** and partly to the resurgence of the **Monte dei Paschi di Siena**. This bank, founded in Siena in 1472 and currently the city's largest employer, is one of the major players in Italian finance. It today sponsors much of Siena's cultural life, co-existing, apparently easily, with one of Italy's strongest left-wing councils.

The most popular trip from Siena is northwest to the picturesque multi-towered village of **San Gimignano**. Far fewer people take the trouble to sample the ancient Etruscan town of **Volterra**, a highly rewarding stop en route west from Siena to Pisa.

Arrival and information

Siena's **train station** is 2km northeast of town, down in the valley. It has a counter selling city bus tickets (Mon–Sat 5.50am–7.30pm; L1400/€0.72). To get into town, cross the road and take just about any city **bus** heading left (#3, #9 to Tozzi; #4, #7, #8, #14, #17, #77 to Garibaldi/Sale; #10 to Gramsci) all of which drop off about 100m north of Piazza Matteotti on the northern edge of the centre. Most **intercity buses** arrive on Viale Tozzi, the road running alongside Piazza Gramsci, or at La Lizza nearby, but note that many now avoid the centre and terminate at the train station instead. Coming from Florence **by train**, you may need to change at Empoli (takes 1hr 45min); **by bus**, there are hourly SITA expresses (takes 1hr 15min).

The **tourist office** is at no. 56 on the Campo (April–Oct Mon–Sat 8.30am–7.30pm; Nov–March Mon–Fri 8.30am–1pm & 3–7pm, Sat 8.30am–1pm; ☎0577.280.551, *www.siena.turismo.toscana.it*). "Ecco Siena" **guided walks** (in English) start from outside the office (April–Oct Mon–Sat 4.30pm; L35,000/€18.08; last 2hr 30min).

Accommodation

Finding **accommodation** is barely less of a struggle than in Florence. An alternative to contacting hotels directly is to let **Siena Hotels Promotion** do the work for you – phone, fax or email bookings through them for any of the city's thirty-odd hotels are free (☎0577.288.084, fax 0577.280.290, *info@hotelsiena.com*, *www.hotelsiena.com*). If you arrive without a reservation, go to their booth on Piazza San Domenico (Mon–Sat 9am–8pm; winter closes 7pm), where over-the-counter bookings for the same night cost L3000/€1.55. **Pro Tur** offers a similar service, based within the Parcheggio Il Campo parking garage at Via Mattioli 9c (Mon–Fri 9am–1pm & 3–7pm, Sat 9am–1pm; ☎0577.45.900, fax 0577.283.145, *info@protur.it*, *www.protur.it*). Note that hotels are booked solid at **Palio** time (early July and mid-Aug).

Hotels

Bernini, Via della Sapienza 15 (☎ & fax 0577.289.047, *www.albergobernini.com*). Friendly, well-situated one-star hotel near San Domenico, with good-value shared-bath rooms. Midnight curfew. ③.

Cannon d'Oro, Via Montanini 28 (☎0577.44.321, fax 0577.280.868). A stylish, friendly and well-maintained thirty-room two-star hotel tucked down an alleyway east of Piazza Matteotti. ④.

Centrale, Via Cecco Angioleri 26 (☎0577.280.379, fax 0577.42.152). A block north of the Campo, up on the third floor. Friendly staff, good location, but no lift. ③.

Certosa di Maggiano, Via Certosa 82 (☎0577.288.180, fax 0577.288.189, *www.relaischateaux.fr/certosa*). A former monastery in the countryside 1km southeast of Siena that offers luxurious comfort in its few, tasteful rooms and an alluring retreat from worldly affairs in its library, cloister and tranquil terrace. ⑨.

Chiusarelli, Viale Curtatone 15 (☎0577.280.562, fax 0577.271.177, *web.tin.it/chiusarelli*). Pleasant old three-star hotel with fifty airy rooms, a garden and private parking steps from Piazza Matteotti. ⑤.

Duomo, Via Stalloreggi 38 (☎0577.289.088, fax 0577.43.043, *www.hotelduomo.it*). Pleasant three-star, located in a residential area. Rooms are unremarkable, other than those with rooftop views of the duomo. Free parking at Parcheggio Il Campo. ⑤.

Garibaldi, Via Duprè 18 (☎0577.284.204). Seven no-nonsense rooms above a quality low-price trattoria just south of the Campo. Midnight curfew. ②.

Palazzo Ravizza, Pian dei Mantellini 34 (☎0577.280.462, fax 0577.221.597, *www.palazzoravizza.it*). Genteel old-style hotel in a pleasant backwater of town, also with a quality restaurant and charming little garden for afternoon tea. Free parking. ⑦.

La Perla, Via delle Terme 25 (☎0577.47.144). Regular one-star pensione with all-en suite rooms, in a very central location overlooking Piazza Indipendenza, just north of the Campo. Curfew 1am. ③.

Piccolo Hotel Etruria, Via delle Donzelle 3 (☎0577.288.088, fax 0577.288.461, *hetruria@tin.it*). Small, central two-star, with some pokey rooms and a 12.30am curfew, but with parking nearby. Beats the *Tre Donzelle* next door. ③.

Piccolo Hotel Il Palio, Piazza del Sale 19 (☎0577.281.131, fax 0577.281.142, *web.tin.it/pichotpal*). Perfectly located for bus arrivals (right near all the bus stops), but 200m north of the centre, with clean, good-sized rooms and extremely friendly, helpful staff. ④.

Santa Caterina, Via E.S. Piccolomini 7 (☎0577.221.105, fax 0577.271.087, *www.sienanet.it/hsc*). A three-star hotel ten minutes' walk southeast of the Campo, with the benefit of air-conditioning and private parking. ⑥.

Villa Scacciapensieri, Via di Scacciapensieri 10 (☎0577.41.441, fax 0577.270.854, *web.tin.it/villascacciapensieri*). Glorious country villa 3km north of Siena, with every luxury including a pool. ⑧.

Hostel and campsite

Campeggio Siena Colleverde, Strada di Scacciapensieri 47 (☎0577.280.044, fax 0577.333.298, *campingsiena@siena.turismo.toscana.it*). Secure, well-maintained campsite 2km north of town (bus #3 or #8), with a pool. April–Oct.

SIENA'S MUSEUMS

In the last couple of years, Siena's museum directors have grasped the nettle of customer service and, unlike Florence's disorganized shower, have come up with a full deck of excellent-value discounted **museum passes**. They're buyable at any of the participating museums, but all permit only a single entry to each place.

The cathedral authorities (*www.operaduomo.it*) have two passes. One is valid for three days, giving entry to the **Museo dell'Opera**, the **Baptistry** and the **Libreria Piccolomini** for just L4500/€2.32. The other is a five-day pass for L13,000/€6.71, which covers these three plus the **Oratorio San Bernadino**, the **Museo Diocesiana** and the church of **Sant'Agostino**. The Civic Museum Authorities have their own two-day pass for L17,000/€8.78, which gives entry to the **Museo Civico** (but *not* the Torre del Mangia), **Santa Maria della Scala** and the **Palazzo delle Papesse**. Finally, there's the combined **Siena Art Itinerary** ticket, which is valid for seven days and gives entry to all nine places mentioned so far (minus the Torre del Mangia) for a bargain L29,000/€14.98.

The **Pinacoteca Nazionale** is run by a separate body from all the above, and is not included on any of the passes.

It's now possible to **book ahead** for admission to any of the city's museums, by phone, fax or online through the Centro Servizi of the city council (☎0577.226.238 or 0577.41.169, fax 0577.226.265, *www.comune.siena.it*). Queues are not as excessive as in Florence, so booking is not vital, but there is one perk – it knocks L1000/€0.52 off admission to Santa Maria della Scala.

Ostello Guidoriccio, Via Fiorentina 89, Stellino (☎0577.52.212, fax 0577.56.172). Non-HI 111-bed hostel 2km northwest of the centre; take bus #3, #10 or #15 from Piazza Matteotti or, if you're coming from Florence, ask the bus driver to let you off at "Lo Stellino" (just after the Siena city sign). Curfew 11pm. L29,000/€14.98.

The City

Everything is easily walkable from the great central square of the **Campo**, which is built at the intersection of a configuration of hills that looks, on the map, like an upside-down Y. Each arm of the Y counts as one of the city's *terzi*, or thirds, and each has its principal thoroughfare, leading out from the Campo on elevated ridges: humdrum **Banchi di Sotto** in the Terzo di San Martino on the southeast; bustling, shop-lined **Via di Città** in the Terzo di Città on the southwest; and elegant **Banchi di Sopra** in the Terzo di Camollia on the north. The central core of alleys – almost entirely medieval in plan and appearance, and closed to traffic – can get a little disorientating, and it's surprisingly easy to lose your fix on the Campo, masked as it is by high buildings. The huge **Duomo** (and attendant museums, including the unmissable **Museo dell'Opera del Duomo** and **Santa Maria della Scala**) sits on a hill above Via di Città, looking across the deep Fontebranda valley north to the equally huge church of **San Domenico** occupying its own hill; getting from one to the other involves a lot of stairs, or a big semi-circular detour in order to stay on a level.

The Campo

The Campo is the centre of Siena in every sense: the main streets lead into it, the Palio is held around its perimeter, and in the evenings it is the natural place to gravitate towards, for visitors and residents alike. Don't spurn the chance to soak up the atmosphere last thing at night, when the amphitheatre curve of the piazza throws the low hum of café conversation around in an invisible spiral of sound, drowned out in the daytime. Four hundred years ago, Montaigne described it as the most beautiful square in the world; you'd find it hard to dispute his words.

When the Council of Nine were planning the piazza in 1293, this old marketplace, which lay at the convergence of the city quarters but was a part of none, was the only possible site. The piazza, completed in 1349, was created in nine segments in honour of the council. It was, from the start, a focus of city life, the scene of executions, bullfights, communal boxing matches, and, of course, the Palio. St Bernardino preached here, holding before him the monogram of Christ's name in Greek ("IHS"), which the council placed on the facade of the Palazzo Pubblico, alongside the city's she-wolf symbol – a reference to Siena's legendary foundation by Senius, son of Remus.

At the highest point of the Campo the Renaissance makes a fleeting appearance with the **Fonte Gaia** (Gay Fountain), designed and carved by Jacopo della Quercia in the early fifteenth century but now replaced by a poor nineteenth-century reproduction. The badly eroded original has been newly restored for display in Santa Maria della Scala.

The Museo Civico

The Palazzo Pubblico (also known as Palazzo Comunale), with its 97m belltower, the Torre del Mangia, is the focus of the Campo, occupying virtually its entire south side. Its three-part windows pleased the council so much that they ordered their emulation on all other buildings on the square. The palazzo is still in use as Siena's town hall, but its principal rooms have been converted into the **Museo Civico** (daily: July & Aug 10am–11pm; March–Oct 10am–7pm; Nov–Feb 10am–6.30pm; *www.comune.siena.it/museocivico*) – a

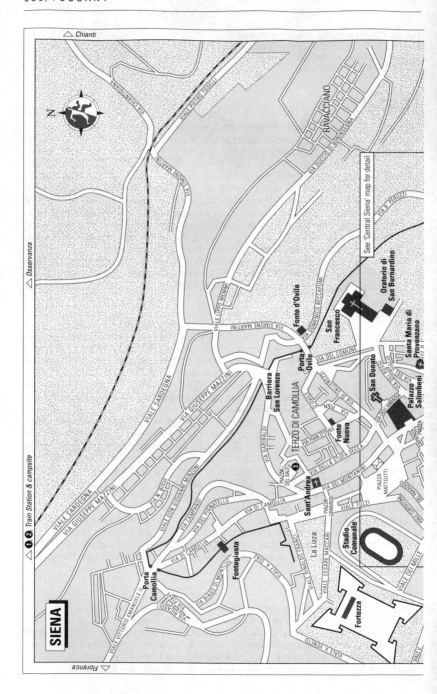

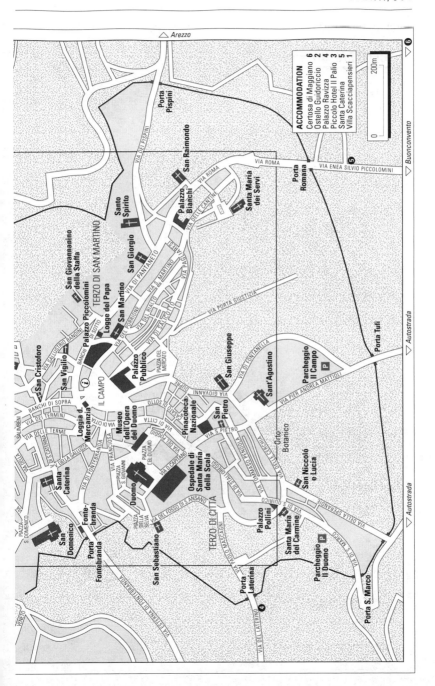

△ Arezzo

Porta
Pispini

VIA DEI PISPINI

San Raimondo

VIA ROMA

Santo
Spirito

Palazzo
Bianchi

Santa Maria
del Servi

VIA ENEA SILVIO PICCOLOMINI

Porta
Romana

San Giovannanino
della Staffa

TERZO DI SAN MARTINO

San Giorgio

VIA DI PANTANETO

VIA DEL CANTINE

Palazzo Piccolomini

San Martino

Logge del Papa

VIA DEL PORRIONE

VIA DEL MARTINO

VIA PAG

VIA PORTA GIUSTIZIA

San Cristoforo

San Vigilio

BANCHI BANDINI

VIA DI CITTA

PIAZZA DEL MERCATO

Palazzo
Pubblico

San Giuseppe

VIA DI FONTANELLA

Porta Tufi

IL CAMPO

BANCHI DI SOPRA

VIA DELLE TERME

Loggia d.
Mercanzia

Museo
dell'Opera
del Duomo

Pinacoteca
Nazionale

San
Pietro

Sant'Agostino

Parcheggio
Il Campo

VIA PIER ANDREA MATTIOLI

△ Autostrada

△ Buonconvento

VIA SALIMBENI

Santa
Caterina

VIA DELLA GALLUZZA

VIA DI FONTEBRANDA

VIA DI STALLOREGGI

PIAZZA DEL DUOMO

Ospedale di
Santa Maria
della Scala

Orto
Botanico

San Niccoló
e Lucia

VIA DI CITTA

PIAZZA
S. GIOVANNI

Duomo

VIA DEL CAPITANO

VIA DEL FOSSO DI S ANSANO

San
Domenico

Fonte-
branda

Porta
Fontebranda

PIAZZA
DELLA
SELVA

San Sebastiano

VIA DI STALLOREGGI

Palazzo
Pollini

Santa Maria
del Carmine

Parcheggio
Il Duomo

VIA DELLA SPERANDIE

Porta
Laterina

VIA DEL LATERINO

VIA DI S MARCO

Porta S. Marco

△ Autostrada

ACCOMMODATION
Certosa di Maggiano   6
Ostello Guidoriccio   2
Palazzo Ravizza   4
Piccolo Hotel Il Palio   3
Santa Caterina   5
Villa Scacciapensieri   1

0   200m

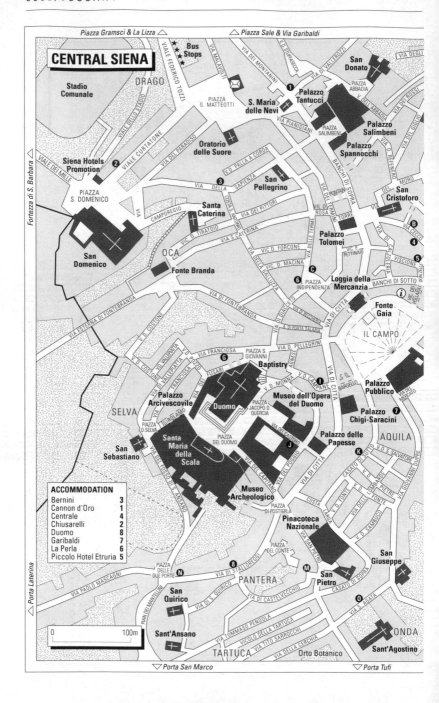

CENTRAL SIENA

Piazza Gramsci & La Lizza △ △ Piazza Sale & Via Garibaldi

★★★ Bus Stops

DRAGO

Stadio Comunale

PIAZZA G. MATTEOTTI

S. Maria delle Nevi

San Donato

PIAZZA ABBADIA

1 Palazzo Tantucci

PIAZZA SALIMBENI

Palazzo Salimbeni

Palazzo Spannocchi

Oratorio delle Suore

2 Siena Hotels Promotion

PIAZZA S. DOMENICO

3 San Pellegrino

Santa Caterina

San Cristoforo

San Domenico

OCA

Fonte Branda

Palazzo Tolomei

B

4

5 VISCIONE

C

6 PIAZZA INDIPENDENZA

Loggia della Mercanzia

BANCHI DI SOTTO

i

Fonte Gaia

IL CAMPO

PIAZZA S. GIOVANNI

G Baptistry

Palazzo Arcivescovile

SELVA

Duomo

PIAZZA JACOPO D. QUERCIA

Museo dell'Opera del Duomo

I

Palazzo Pubblico

Palazzo Chigi-Saracini 7

San Sebastiano

Santa Maria della Scala

PIAZZA DEL DUOMO

J

Palazzo delle Papesse

K

AQUILA

Museo Archeologico

PIAZZA DI POSTIERLA

Pinacoteca Nazionale

San Giuseppe

ACCOMMODATION

Bernini	3
Cannon d'Oro	1
Centrale	4
Chiusarelli	2
Duomo	8
Garibaldi	7
La Perla	6
Piccolo Hotel Etruria	5

PIAZZA DELLE DUE PORTE

N

8

PANTERA

M

San Pietro

San Quirico

O

Sant'Ansano

TARTUCA

Orto Botanico

ONDA

Sant'Agostino

0   100m

Porta Laterina △

Fortezza di S. Barbara △

△ Porta San Marco ▽ Porta Tufi

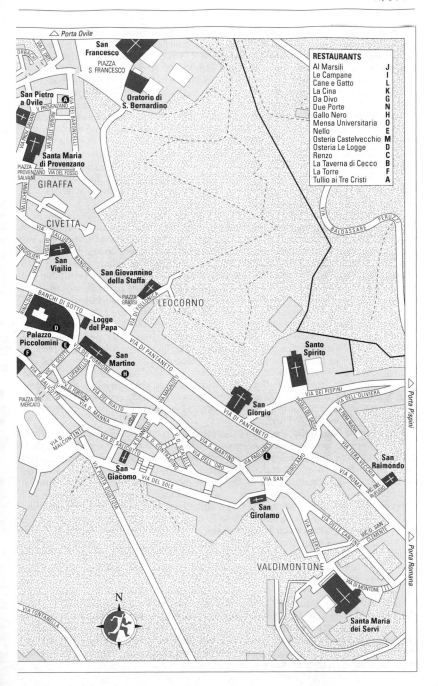

RESTAURANTS

Al Marsili	**J**
Le Campane	**I**
Cane e Gatto	**L**
La Cina	**K**
Da Divo	**G**
Due Porte	**N**
Gallo Nero	**H**
Mensa Universitaria	**O**
Nello	**E**
Osteria Castelvecchio	**M**
Osteria Le Logge	**D**
Renzo	**C**
La Taverna di Cecco	**B**
La Torre	**F**
Tullio ai Tre Cristi	**A**

series of grand halls frescoed with themes integral to the secular life of the medieval city. If you have time or inclination for only one of Siena's museums, make it this one. **Admission** to the Museo Civico is L12,000/€6.20, to the Torre del Mangia L10,000/€5.16. A joint ticket for them both is L18,000/€9.30 or for multi-entry tickets see box on p.536. An audioguide for the museum, available in English, costs L7000/€3.61.

At the top of the stairs, you're directed through a disappointing five-room picture gallery to the **Sala del Risorgimento**, painted with nineteenth-century scenes of Vittorio Emanuele, first king of Italy. Across the corridor is a series of frescoed rooms, the **Sala di Balìa** (or dei Priori; room 10), the **Anticamera del Concistoro**, and the grand **Sala del Concistoro**. Room 13, the **Vestibolo**, holds a gilded bronze of the *She-Wolf suckling Romulus and Remus* (1429), an allusion to Siena's mythical founding. Alongside is the **Anticappella**, decorated between 1407 and 1414 by Taddeo di Bartolo. Behind a majestic wrought-iron screen by Jacopo della Quercia is the **Cappella del Consiglio**, also frescoed by di Bartolo and holding an exceptional altarpiece by Sodoma and exquisite inlaid choir-stalls.

All these are little more than a warm-up for room 16, the great **Sala del Mappamondo**. Taking its name from the now scarcely visible frescoed cosmology – a circular map by Lorenzetti – the room was used for several centuries as the city's law court, and contains one of the greatest of all Italian frescoes. Simone Martini's fabulous *Maestà* (Virgin in Majesty) is a painting of almost translucent colour, painted in 1315 when Martini was thirty. The richly decorative style is archetypal Sienese Gothic and Martini's great innovation was the use of a canopy and a frieze of medallions to frame and organize the figures – lending a sense of space and hint of perspective that suggest a knowledge of Giotto's work. The fresco on the opposite wall, the *Equestrian Portrait of Guidoriccio da Fogliano*, is a motif for medieval chivalric Siena and was, until recently, also credited to Martini. Art historians, however, have long puzzled over the anachronistic castles, which are of a much later style than the painting's signed date of 1328. A number of historians – led by the American Gordon Moran (whom the city council accused of being a CIA agent and for a while banned from the building) – interpret the *Guidoriccio* as a sixteenth-century fake, while others maintain that it is a genuine Martini overpainted by subsequent restorers. The newly revealed fresco below the portrait, of two figures in front of a castle, is meanwhile variously attributed to Martini, Duccio and Pietro Lorenzetti.

The adjacent **Sala della Pace** holds Ambrogio Lorenzetti's *Allegories of Good and Bad Government*, frescoes commissioned in 1338 to remind the councillors of their duties. This is one of Europe's most important cycles of medieval secular painting, and includes the first-known panorama in Western art. The walled city shown is clearly Siena, and the paintings are full of details of medieval life; their moral theme is expressed in a complex iconography of allegorical virtues and figures. *Good Government* (the better-preserved half) is dominated by a throned figure representing the *comune*, flanked by the Virtues and with Faith, Hope and Charity buzzing about his head. To the left, Justice (with Wisdom in the air above) dispenses rewards and punishments, while below her throne Concordia advises the Republic's councillors on their duties. *Bad Government* is ruled by a horned demon, while over the city flies the figure of Fear, whose scroll reads: "Because he looks for his own good in the world, he places justice beneath tyranny. So nobody walks this road without Fear: robbery thrives inside and outside the city gates."

Some fine panel paintings by Lorenzetti's contemporaries are displayed in the **Sala dei Pilastri** to one side. Take time to climb the stairs up to the rear **loggia**, where you can crane your neck to see the current council chambers, also frescoed. From the loggia you can see how abruptly the town ends: buildings rise to the right and left for a few hundred metres along the ridges of the Terzo di San Martino and Terzo di Città, holding a rural valley in their embrace.

THE SIENA PALIO

The **Siena Palio** (*www.comune.siena.it/palioprova*) is the most spectacular festival event in Italy: a twice-yearly bareback horse race around the Campo, preceded by days of preparation, medieval pageantry and chicanery. Only ten of the *contrade* can take part in any one race; these are chosen by lot, and their horses and jockeys are also assigned at random. The only rule is that riders cannot interfere with each others' reins. Otherwise, anything goes: each *contrada* has a traditional rival, and ensuring that it loses is as important as winning oneself. Jockeys may be bribed to throw the race or whip a rival or a rival's horse; *contrade* have been known to drug horses and even to ambush a jockey on his way to the race. This is primarily a show for the Sienese; for visitors, in fact, the undercurrent of brutality and the bragging, days-long celebration of victory can be quite a shock.

The race has been held since at least the thirteenth century. Originally it followed a circuit through the town, but since the sixteenth century it has consisted of three laps of the **Campo**, around a track covered with sand and padded with mattresses to minimize injury to riders and horses (though this does occur, and the Palio is a passionate subject for animal-rights supporters). There are normally two Palios a year, with the following build-up:

June 29/August 13: The year's horses are presented in the morning at the town hall and drawn by lot. At 7.15pm the first trial race is held in the Campo.

June 30/August 14: Further trial races at 9am and 7.45pm.

July 1/August 15: Two more trial races at 9am and 7.45pm, followed by a street banquet in each of the *contrade*.

July 2/August 16: The day of the Palio opens with a final trial at 9am. In the early afternoon each *contrada* takes its horse to be blessed in its church (it's a good omen if the horse shits). At around 5pm the town hall bell begins to ring and riders and *comparse* – equerries, ensigns, pages and drummers in medieval costume – proceed to the Campo for a display of flag-twirling and other pageantry. The **race** itself begins at 7.45pm on July 2, or 7pm on August 16, and lasts little more than ninety seconds. There's no PA system to tell you what's going on. At the start (in the northwest corner of the Campo) all the horses except one are penned between two ropes; the free one charges the group from behind, when its rivals least expect it, and the race is on. It's a hectic and violent spectacle; a horse that throws its rider is still eligible to win. The jockeys don't stop at the finishing line but keep going at top speed out of the Campo, pursued by a frenzied mass of supporters. The **palio** – a silk banner – is subsequently presented to the winner.

There are viciously expensive stands for dignitaries and the rich (booked months ahead), but most spectators crowd for free into the centre of the Campo. For the **best view**, you need to have found a position on the inner rail by 2pm (ideally at the start/finish line), but be prepared to stand your ground; people keep pouring in right up until a few minutes before the race, and the swell of the crowd can be quite overwhelming. Toilets, shade and refreshments are minimal, and you won't be able to leave the Campo until at least 8.30pm. **Hotel rooms** are extremely difficult to find, and if you haven't booked, reckon on either staying up all night or travelling in from a neighbouring town. The races are shown live on national TV and repeated endlessly all evening.

All year round, Cinema Moderno on Piazza Tolomei screens a twenty-minute **film** explaining the history and drama of the race, dubbed into various languages (Mon–Sat, in English on the half-hour 9.30am–5.30pm; L10,000/€5.16).

Off to the left of the Palazzo Pubblico's internal courtyard, opposite the entrance to the Museo Civico, a door gives access to the 503 steps of the **Torre del Mangia** (daily: July–Sept 10am–11pm; March–June & Oct 10am–7pm; Nov–Jan 10am–4pm; see opposite for admission), which gives fabulous views across town and countryside. The tower takes its name from its first watchman – a slothful glutton (*mangiaguadagni*) who is commemorated by a statue in the courtyard.

The Loggia della Mercanzia and around

Gaps between buildings behind the Fonte Gaia lead up to the junction-point of the three main streets of Siena, marked by the fifteenth-century **Loggia della Mercanzia** – reluctantly Renaissance, with its Gothic niches for the saints – that was designed as a tribune house for merchants to do their deals. From here, Banchi di Sopra heads north (see p.545), and Via di Città curves west (see p.544). If you follow **Banchi di Sotto** east, you soon reach the **Logge di Papa** with, alongside it, the **Palazzo Piccolomini**, a committed Renaissance building by Bernardo Rossellino, the architect employed at Pienza by the Sienese Pope Pius II (Aeneas Sylvius Piccolomini).

The Duomo and around

Few buildings reveal so much of a city's history and aspirations as Siena's **Duomo**. Complete to virtually its present size around 1215, it was subjected to constant plans for expansion. An initial project, early in the fourteenth century, attempted to double its extent by building a baptistry on the slope below and using this as a foundation for a rebuilt nave, but the work ground to a halt as walls and joints gaped under the pressure. Eventually the chapter hit on a new scheme to reorient the cathedral, using the existing nave as a transept and building a **new nave** out towards the Campo. Again cracks appeared, and then, in 1348, came the Black Death. With the population halved and funds suddenly cut off, the plan was abandoned once and for all. The part-extension still stands at the north end of the square – a vast structure that would have created the largest church in Italy outside Rome. Despite all the abandoned plans, the duomo is a delight. Its style is an amazing conglomeration of Romanesque and Gothic, delineated by bands of black and white marble. The **facade** was designed in 1284 by Giovanni Pisano, who with his workshop created much of the statuary – philosophers, patriarchs and prophets, now replaced by copies. In the next century the **Campanile** and a Gothic **rose window** were added. The mosaics in the gables, however, had to wait until the nineteenth century, when money was found to employ Venetian artists.

The use of black and white decoration is continued in the *sgraffito* marble **pavement**, which begins outside the church and takes off into a startling sequence of 56 panels adorning the **interior** (daily: mid-March to Oct 9am–7.30pm; rest of year 7.30am–1pm & 2.30–7pm; free). They were completed between 1349 and 1547, with virtually every artist who worked in the city trying his hand on a design. The finest are reckoned to be Beccafumi's *Moses Striking Water from a Rock* and *Sacrifice of Isaac*, just beyond the dome area. However, you're unlikely to see much of the pavement, which is now protected by underfoot boarding for all but a few weeks a year in August, when the full effect is on show (exact dates vary). The zebra-striped interior is equally arresting above floor level, with its line of popes' heads set above the pillars, the same hollow-cheeked scowls cropping up repeatedly. The greatest individual artistic treasure is Nicola Pisano's **pulpit**, with its elaborate high-relief detail of the *Life of Jesus* and *Last Judgement*. In the north transept is a bronze statue by **Donatello** of an emaciated *St John the Baptist*, companion piece to his equally ragged *Mary Magdalene* in Florence, and the Renaissance High Altar is flanked by superb candelabra-carrying angels by Beccafumi.

Midway along the nave, on the left, is the entrance to the stunning **Libreria Piccolomini** (same hours; L2000/€1.03, for multi-entry tickets see box on p.536; *www.operaduomo.it*). The library was commissioned by Francesco Piccolomini (who for ten days was Pius III) to house the books of his uncle Aeneas (Pius II), and to celebrate Aeneas's life in a series of crystal-sharp, brilliantly colourful frescoes by Pinturicchio. The cycle begins to the right of the window, with Aeneas attending the Council of Basel as a secretary, then, in subsequent panels around the walls, presenting himself as envoy to James II of Scotland; being crowned poet laureate by Holy

Roman Emperor, Frederick II; representing Frederick on a visit to Pope Eugenius IV; and then – as Bishop of Siena – presiding over the meeting of Frederick III and his bride-to-be Eleanora outside Siena's Porta Camollia. The next panels show Aeneas' being made a cardinal in 1456; being elected pope two years later; and then launching a call for a crusade against the Turks, who had just seized Constantinople. His best-remembered action was the canonization of St Catherine, shown in the penultimate panel. The last fresco shows his death at Ancona.

Santa Maria della Scala

Opposite the duomo is the **Ospedale di Santa Maria della Scala** (daily: April–Oct 10am–6pm; Nov–March 10.30am–4.30pm; L10,000/€5.16; for multi-entry tickets see box on p.536; *www.santamaria.comune.siena.it*). For nine hundred years up until the 1980s, this vast complex served as the city's main hospital. Today its wonderful interiors are being gradually converted into a major centre for art and culture, revealing works that have been inaccessible to all but the most determined of visitors for centuries.

To the left of the ticket desk is the church of **Santissima Annunziata** (also with its own door onto the piazza), blandly remodelled in the fifteenth century but with a bronze statue on the high altar of the *Risen Christ* by Vecchietta, with features so gaunt the veins show through the skin. The other way from the ticket desk leads into a vestibule, the **Cappella del Manto**, with a strikingly beautiful fresco of *St Anne and St Joachim* (1512) – parents of the Virgin – by Beccafumi. Having failed to conceive during twenty years of marriage, the pair are each told by an angel to meet at Jerusalem's Golden Gate and kiss (the scene depicted in the fresco), a moment which symbolizes the Immaculate Conception of their daughter. Adjacent is a long hall, partly used as a bookshop; left off this hall is the vast **Sala del Pellegrinaio**, formerly used as the main hospital ward and entirely frescoed with scenes intended to record the hospital's history and promote the notion of charity toward the sick and orphaned. Their almost entirely secular content was extraordinary at the time they were painted (after 1440 and well before Renaissance ideas took hold). Off to the left, in room 12, is the frescoed **Cappella del Sacro Chiodo** (also known as the Sagrestia Vecchia), which once housed a nail (*chiodo*) from the Passion.

Stairs lead down to the **Oratorio di Santa Caterina della Notte**, an oratory that belonged to one of a number of medieval confraternities that maintained places of worship in the basement vaults of the hospital. It's a dark and strangely spooky place, despite the plethora of decoration – you can easily imagine St Catherine passing nocturnal vigils down here. Also on this level is a series of rooms devoted to documenting the continuing restoration of the original **Fonte Gaia** from the Campo. Stairs lead down again to the oratory and meeting-room of the **Società di Esecutori di Pie Disposizioni** (Executors of Benevolent Legacies), oldest of the lay confraternities, which house a wooden crucifix said to be the one which inspired St Bernadino to become a monk.

In the south wing of the hospital, with its own entrance from the piazza, is the small **Museo Archeologico** (Mon–Sat 9am–2pm; also second & fourth Sun of month 9am–1pm; free), displaying mostly Etruscan artefacts.

The Museo dell'Opera del Duomo

Tucked into a corner of the proposed new nave of the duomo is the impressive **Museo dell'Opera del Duomo** (daily: mid-March to Sept 9am–7.30pm; Oct 9am–6pm; Nov to mid-March 9am–1.30pm; L6000/€3.10; for multi-entry tickets see box on p.536; audio-guide L5000/€2.58 extra; *www.operaduomo.it*). A tour starts on the top floor: room 1 houses the stark, haunting Byzantine icon known as the **Madonna dagli Occhi Grossi** (of the Big Eyes), the duomo's original altarpiece, as well as panels depicting St

---

SIENA'S CONTRADE

Siena takes great pride in its division into neighbourhoods, or **contrade**, ancient self-governing wards that formed a patchwork of tribal identity within the fabric of the city and that still flourish today, helping to foster tight bonds of community and contributing to Siena's surprisingly low crime rate. Each of the seventeen *contrade* has its own church, social club and museum. Each, too, has a heraldic animal motif, displayed in a fountain-sculpture in its neighbourhood piazza. Allegiance to one's *contrada* – conferred by birth – remains a strong element of civic life, and identification with the *contrade* is integral to the competition of the Palio. You'll often see groups of *comparse* practising flag-waving and drum-rolling around town.

The *contrade* **museums**, with their displays of Palio trophies, are open to visitors during the build-up to the Palio and at other times by appointment (ask the tourist office to book for you at least a week in advance).

Bernardino preaching in the Campo and Piazza San Francesco. Pass through to the tiny entrance to the **Panorama dal Facciatone** – this leads to steep spiral stairs climbing the walls of the abandoned nave. The sensational view is definitely worth the two-stage climb, but beware that the topmost walkway is narrow and scarily exposed.

Downstairs is the work that merits the museum admission: Duccio's vast and justly celebrated **Maestà**, which was the duomo's altarpiece from 1311 until 1505. This is one of the superlative works of Sienese art, its iconic, Byzantine spirituality accentuated by Duccio's flowing composition, his realization of the space in which action takes place, and a new attention to narrative detail in the panels of the predella and the reverse of the altarpiece which are now displayed to its side. Downstairs again, back on ground-floor level, is the **Galleria delle Statue**, with Donatello's delicate ochre *Madonna and Child* flanked by huge, elongated, twisting figures by Giovanni Pisano. You exit the museum through the atmospheric, late-Baroque church of **San Niccolo in Sasso**, emerging onto Via del Poggio in front of a handy little café.

The Baptistry

The **Baptistry** (daily: mid-March to Sept 9am–7.30pm; Oct 9am–6pm; Nov to mid-March 10am–1pm & 2.30–5pm; L3000/€1.55; for multi-entry tickets see box on p.536; *www.operaduomo.it*) is unusual in being placed beneath the main body of the duomo; it is on Piazza San Giovanni, reached by steps which curl around the back of the duomo. The chapter responsible for the font (1417–30) must have had a good sense of what was happening in Florence at the time, for they commissioned panels by **Ghiberti** (*Baptism of Christ* and *John in Prison*), local sculptor **Jacopo della Quercia** (*The Angel Announcing the Baptist's Birth*), and a superbly dramatic *Herod's Feast* by **Donatello**. The lavishly frescoed walls, largely by Vecchietta, almost overshadow the font.

Along Via di Città

Via di Città is the main thoroughfare linking the duomo with the Campo, and is lined with shops and plenty of explorable side-alleys, as well as being fronted by some of Siena's finest private palazzi. The **Palazzo Chigi-Saracini** at no. 82 is a Gothic beauty, with its curved facade and rear courtyard. Almost opposite, at Via di Città 126, is the fifteenth-century **Palazzo delle Papesse**, Siena's museum of contemporary art (daily noon–7pm; L9000/€4.65; *www.comune.siena.it/papesse*). Its four airy floors house excellent temporary exhibits covering anything from architecture to video art, displayed in rooms, some with nineteenth-century frescoes, that still conserve many of their original Renaissance structural and decorative features.

Via di Città continues to a small piazza from where Via San Pietro leads left (south) to the fourteenth-century Palazzo Buonsignori, now the home of the **Pinacoteca Nazionale** (Mon 8.30am–1.30pm, Tues–Sat 9am–7pm, Sun 8am–1pm; L8000/€4.13). The collection is a roll of honour of Sienese Gothic painting. The first rooms – two storeys up – hold a host of gilded, thirteenth-century Madonnas; in room 7–8, two tiny panels recently attributed to Sassetta – *City by the Sea* and *Castle by a Lake* – are described as the first-ever landscape paintings entirely devoid of religious purpose. Down one flight are Renaissance works by such as Sodoma, whose panel of the *Deposition* (room 32) and frescoes from Sant'Agostino (room 37) show his characteristic drama and delight in costume and landscape. The gallery's topmost storey is devoted to the **Collezione Spannocchi**, a miscellany of Italian, German and Flemish works, including the only painting in the museum by a female artist – *Bernardo Campi Painting Sofonisba's Portrait* by Sofonisba Anguissola, a neat little joke in which the artist excels in her portrait of Campi, but depicts his portrait of her as a flat stereotype.

South of the Pinacoteca Nazionale is the church of **Sant'Agostino** (mid-March to Oct daily 10.30am–1.30pm & 3–5.30pm; L3000/€1.55 or for multi-entry tickets see box on p.536; *www.operaduomo.it*), with outstanding paintings by Perugino (a *Crucifixion* in the second altar of the south aisle) and Sodoma (*Adoration of the Magi* in the Cappella Piccolomini). A nice walk loops southwest along Via della Cerchia into a studentish area around the church of **Santa Maria del Carmine** (which contains a hermaphrodite *St Michael and the Devil* by Beccafumi). Via del Fosso di San Ansano, north of the Carmine square, is a country lane above terraced vineyards which leads to the Selva (Rhinoceros) *contrada*'s square, from where the stepped Vicolo di San Girolamo leads up to the duomo.

North of the Campo

Exploring only slightly beyond the touristed central alleys between the Campo and the duomo reveals much more of the bustling everyday life of the city. North of the Campo, the main street **Banchi di Sopra** leads through the commercial heart of town to **Piazza Matteotti**, home of the main post office, north of which lies the workaday neighbourhood of the Terzi di Camollia. The church of **Santo Stefano** fronts one of the nicest *contrada* squares in the city, home of the Istrici (Porcupine), while the road emerges from the walls at the northern Porta Camollia, inscribed "Siena opens her heart to you wider than this gate." The northwest corner of the city is occupied by a stadium and the gardens of **La Lizza**, which lead up to the bastions of the **Fortezza di Santa Barbara**, rebuilt by the Medici and now housing the comprehensive wine collection of the *Enoteca Italiana* (see p.548*)*.

San Domenico

Monasteries were essentially rural until the beginning of the thirteenth century, when the idea of an exclusively meditative retreat was displaced by the preaching orders of friars. Suddenly, in the space of a few decades, orders began to found monasteries on the periphery of the major Italian cities. In Siena the two greatest orders, the Dominicans and Franciscans, located themselves respectively to the west and east. **San Domenico**, a vast brick church west of Piazza Matteotti (daily: April–Oct 7am–1pm & 3–6.30pm; Nov–March 9am–1pm & 3–6pm; *www.essentia.org/basilicacateriniana*), was founded in 1125 and is closely identified with St Catherine of Siena (see box overleaf). Inside on the right is a raised chapel with a contemporary portrait of the saint by her friend Andrea Vanni. Her own chapel, on the south side of the enormous, airy nave has frescoes by Sodoma of her swooning (to the left of the altar) and in ecstasy (to the right), as well as a reliquary containing her head.

ST CATHERINE OF SIENA

St Catherine of Siena was born on March 25, 1347, the 24th child of Jacopo Benincasa, a dyer, and Lapa of Duccio de' Piacenti. Her path to beatification began early, with a vision aged six of Christ as pope, followed a year later by a vow of perpetual virginity. Her family tried to drill some sense into her by forcing her to work at household chores, but when her father discovered her at prayer one day with a dove fluttering above her head, he realized her holy destiny. Catherine took the Dominican habit aged sixteen, experienced a mystical "Night Obscure", and then began charitable works in post-plague Siena before turning her hand to politics. She prevented Siena and Pisa from joining Florence in rising against Pope Urban V (then absent in Avignon), and then, in 1376, travelled herself to Avignon to persuade Pope Gregory XI to return to Rome. It was a fulfilment of the ultimate Dominican ideal – a union of the practical and mystical life. Catherine returned to Siena to a life of contemplation, retaining a political role in her attempts to reconcile the 1378 schism between the Popes and Anti-Popes. She died in Rome in 1380, and was the first woman ever to be **canonized** – by Pius II in 1461. Pius IX made her **co-patron of Rome** in 1866; Pius XII raised her to be **co-patron of Italy** (alongside St Francis) in 1939; and then John Paul II declared her **co-patron of Europe** in 1999.

The **Casa Santuario di Santa Caterina** – St Catherine's family house, where she lived as a Dominican nun – is just south of the church, down the hill on Via Santa Caterina (daily: summer 9am–12.30pm & 2.30–6pm; winter 9am–12.30pm & 3.30–6pm; free). The building has been much adapted, with a Renaissance loggia and a series of oratories – one on the site of her cell. At the bottom of the hill, through the Oca (Goose) *contrada*, is the **Fonte Branda**, the best-preserved of Siena's medieval fountains and, according to Sienese folklore, the haunt of werewolves, who would throw themselves into the water at dawn to return in human form.

The Oratorio di San Bernardino

St Bernardino, born in the year of St Catherine's death, began his preaching life at the chill monastic church of **San Francesco**, across the city to the east. Alongside the church is the **Oratorio di San Bernardino** (mid-March to Oct daily 10.30am–1.30pm & 3–5.30pm; L4000/€2.06; for multi-entry tickets see box on p.536; *www.operaduomo.it*), with a beautifully wood-panelled upper chapel frescoed by Sodoma and Beccafumi. In the lower chapel are seventeenth-century scenes from the saint's life, which was taken up by incessant travel throughout Italy, preaching against usury and denouncing political strife; his sermons in the Campo, it is said, frequently went on for the best part of a day. He was canonized in 1444, and – because of his dictum on rhetoric, "make it clear, short and to the point" – was made patron saint of advertising in the 1980s. The attached **Museo Diocesano di Arte Sacra** (same hours and ticket) contains an array of devotional art from the thirteenth to the seventeenth centuries.

Eating, drinking and nightlife

Although Siena has a swathe of places at which to **eat** well, the city feels distinctly provincial after Florence. The main action of an evening is the passeggiata from Piazza Matteotti along Banchi di Sopra to the Campo – and there's not much in the way of **nightlife** to follow. For most visitors, though, the Campo, the city's universal gathering place, provides diversion enough, while the presence of the university ensures a bit of life in the **bars**.

Restaurants

Siena used to have a poor reputation for **restaurants** but over the last few years a range of new, imaginative *osterie* has signalled a general rise in standards. Local **specialities** include *pici* (thick, hand-rolled spaghetti with toasted breadcrumbs), *finocchiona* (minced pork flavoured with fennel), *pappa col pomodoro* (bread and tomato soup), and *fagioli all'uccelletto* (white bean and sausage stew).

Putting together a **picnic** in the Campo or elsewhere is easy: you can buy pizza by weight from many central hole-in-the-wall places, or phone an order ahead for quality, fresh-baked pizza (whole or by the slice) from *Mister Pizza*, Via delle Terme 94 (☎0577.221.746; closed Sun). Gourmet supplies are at the extravagantly stocked food store Manganelli, Via di Città 71. *Natural Planet*, Via delle Terme 70, has organic foods. The **covered market** south of the Campo in Piazza del Mercato is also good for picnic provisions, and every quarter has its bakery.

We've divided the listings below by price: **expensive** means an average full meal (excluding wine) costs above L60,000/€30.99 per person; **inexpensive** means you can eat for L25,000/€12.91 or less; **mid-priced** is between the two.

Inexpensive and mid-priced

La Cina, Casato di Sotto 56. Quiet, affordable Chinese restaurant 150m from the Campo. The food is adequate, and makes a change from pizza and spaghetti. No closing day.

Da Divo, Via Franciosa 29 (☎0577.286.054). Book a table in the atmospheric subterranean vaulted dining-room to savour hearty mid-priced Tuscan food that, on its day, is well above average. Closed Sun in winter.

Due Porte, Via di Stalloreggi 62. One place to head for in the quiet southwestern districts, with a large Tuscan menu, lower prices than you'd expect and an open terrace at the back. Closed Mon.

Gallo Nero, Via del Porrione 65 (☎0577.284.356, *www.gallonero.it*). Quirky, vaulted place, offering a Tuscan menu for around L30,000/€15.49, or a six-course medieval menu for half as much again, boasting dishes such as bittersweet duck with cheese ravioli and chicken in sweet wine with fruit. Closed Mon lunch.

Mensa Universitaria, Via Sant'Agata 1. The university canteen has full meals for around L15,000/€7.75, pasta dishes for less. Closed Aug.

Osteria Castelvecchio, Via di Castelvecchio 65 (☎0577.49.586). Adventurous, first-rate and nicely informal mid-priced osteria, the best bet for vegetarians (plus plenty of meat too). Menus change daily. Closed Tues & July.

Renzo, Piazza Indipendenza. Light, uncomplicated meals at terrace tables on a quiet enclosed piazza off Via di Città. Closed Thurs.

La Taverna di Cecco, Via Cecco Angiolieri 19 (☎0577.288.518). Attentive service, moderate prices and heavenly rabbit and rocket salad. Closed Wed.

La Torre, Via Salicotto 7. Friendly, studentish place off the Campo with a local ambience serving home-made pasta and excellent grills. No menu, so follow the advice of the waiters. Closed Thurs.

Tullio ai Tre Cristi, Vicolo Provenzano 1 (☎0577.280.608). A Sienese institution since 1830, this is the neighbourhood restaurant of the Giraffa contrada and is draped with heraldic banners to accompany its traditional fare – roast boar, steaks, tripe and some pastas. Terrace tables in summer. Closed Tues.

Expensive

Le Campane, Via delle Campane 6 (☎0577.284.035). High-quality Sienese cuisine at a small, formal restaurant just below the duomo. Set menus – *di terra* or *di mare* – cost around L60,000/€30.99. Closed Mon.

Cane e Gatto, Via Pagliaresi 6 (☎0577.287.545). Don't be put off by the lack of any menu: this restaurant serves superb Tuscan *cucina nuova* on its seven-course *menu degustazione* for L80,000/€42.32 without wine. Closed Thurs.

Al Marsili, Via del Castoro 3 (☎0577.47.154). Elegant and upmarket large restaurant with good local dishes (including some choice for vegetarians) and attentive service. The *risotto al limone* is

SWEET TREATS

Most Sienese buy **ice cream** at one or the other end of the passeggiata – either at the *Nannini Gelateria* at the northern end of Banchi di Sopra, or *La Costarella*, where Via di Città meets Via dei Pellegrini. Siena is also famous for a whole range of **cakes**, including the trademark **panforte** – a dense and delicious wedge of nuts, fruit and honey – and biscuits like *cavallucci* (aniseed, nut and spice) and *ricciarelli* (almond). All are best brought fresh by the *etto* (hectogram – 100g) in any of the bakeries or *pasticcerie* along Banchi di Sopra; the gift-packaged boxes aren't as good.

worth dallying over, plus they have more exotic dishes such as guineafowl with prunes, pine-nuts and almonds. L50,000/€25.82 buys a memorable meal. Closed Mon.

Nello, Via del Porrione 28 (☎0577.289.043). Sienese specialities at their best: try pumpkin-flower ravioli, roast rabbit, or beef fillet with rocket and *pecorino*, all bolstered by pasta freshly made daily. Around L50,000/€25.82 per head. Closed Mon.

Osteria Le Logge, Via del Porrione 33 (☎0577.48.013). The best-looking restaurant in Siena, in an old bookcase- and cabinet-lined pharmacy off the Campo. Good pasta and some unusual *secondi*, but the quality of the food – once exceptional – is these days merely above average; L75,000/€38.73 for a full meal. Closed Sun.

Bars and cafés

There are pleasant **bars** all over town. *L'Officina*, Piazza del Sale 3a, has around a hundred bottled beers and others on tap. Of the terrace **cafés** ringing the Campo, *Bar Fonte Gaia* stays open later than most, but otherwise they're much of a muchness. The garden of the *Palazzo Ravizza* hotel, Pian dei Mantellini 34, is a lovely tranquil spot for a cup of tea on a hot afternoon. The *Enoteca Italiana* inside the Fortezza (Mon noon–8pm, Tues–Sat noon–1am) is the country's only national **wine** collection. Its cellar stocks and exhibits every single Italian wine (almost a thousand of them) and there's a **bar** – at its best in the early evening – where you can order by the glass or bottle. At various times of year it stages promotions highlighting particular wine regions, and even hosts the odd concert.

Nightlife and entertainment

You'll spot posters for city **events** at Piazza Matteotti, and the Siena supplement of *La Nazione* newspaper has details of the day's concerts and films. You can catch **live bands** at *L'Officina* bar, Piazza del Sale 3a, and at the disco-bar *Al Cambio*, Via di Pantaneto 48, but otherwise your only chances are at the low-key **Siena Jazz** in the last week of July and the gigs organized for the PDS-Communist Party **Festa dell'Unità** throughout the summer.

Siena has prestigious **classical** concerts throughout the year. The Accademia Chigiana is the driving force, staging the *Estate Musicale Chigiana* cycle all summer, and the *Settimana Musicale Senese* in late July, often featuring a major opera production. Venues vary from the duomo and Sant'Agostino to out-of-town locations such as the atmospheric ruined abbey of San Galgano. Tickets start at L15,000/€7.75, bookable through the tourist office or from mid-July onwards in person at the Accademia Chigiana, Via di Città 89 (daily 3–7pm; ☎0577.46.152, *www.chigiana.it*).

Listings

Books Tempo Libero, Casato di Sotto 20 (closed Mon) is a smaller, friendlier place than the big bookstores such as Libreria Senese, Via di Città 64.

Bike rental DF Bike, Via Massetana Romana 54 (☎0577.271.905); Automotocicli Perozzi, Via del Romitorio 5 (☎0577.223.157).

Bus information Ticket offices beneath Piazza Gramsci have information on all routes. The Sienese bus company is called TRA-IN – don't confuse its name or logo for anything to do with trains! Lazzi or TRA-IN run roughly half-hourly to Poggibonsi, where you must change for San Gimignano (buy a through ticket), and half-a-dozen times daily to Montalcino and Montepulciano. Note that some buses to the hill-towns south of Siena now depart from the train station, not from Piazza Gramsci. Lazzi and SITA also run regularly to Florence (take an express), and to Massa Marittima, Volterra and Rome.

Car rental Avis, Via Simone Martini 36 (☎0577.270.305); Hertz, Viale Sardegna 37 (☎0577.45.085).

Hospital Santa Chiara, Via Roma 67 (☎050.992.111).

Internet access Internet Train, Via di Città 121 and Via Pantaneto 54; MegaWeb, Via Pantaneto 132; MediaNet, Via Paradiso 10 (closed Sun). All have long daily opening hours and charge L3000/€1.55 for 15min (less for students).

Laundry Wash & Dry, Via Pantaneto 38 (daily 8am–9pm); OndaBlu, Casato di Sotto 17 (daily 8am–10pm).

Left luggage At the TRA-IN bus information centre below Piazza Gramsci (daily 7am–7.45pm; L5000/€2.58 per piece for one day only). At the train station, there are self-service lockers on platform 1 (L3000/€1.55 per 6hr).

Lost property Comune di Siena, Casato di Sotto 23 (Mon–Fri 9am–12.30pm, Tues & Thurs also 3–5pm).

Market A huge weekly market sprawls over La Lizza (Wed 8am–1pm).

Parking The two biggest parking garages – run by the same company and clearly signposted – charge around L2500/€1.29 per hour (daily 7am–11pm) but are misleadingly named: "Parcheggio Il Campo" and "Parcheggio Il Duomo" are a long way south of either the Campo or the duomo, just inside the Porta Tufi and Porta San Marco respectively. Parking outside the city gates is free. Tourists are permitted to drive through the old town alleys only in order to check in at their hotel.

Police The *Questura* is on Via del Castoro (☎0577.201.111).

Post office Piazza Matteotti (Mon–Sat 8.15am–7pm).

Taxi Radio Taxi ☎0577.49.222; taxis wait on Piazza Matteotti.

Train information ☎1478.88.088. To save you the journey out to the station ticket office (daily 5.50am–8.25pm), you can buy train tickets at the tourist office on the Campo (closed Sun), the main post office on Piazza Matteotti (closed Sun), Bar Bottega del Caffè, Banchi di Sotto 39 (closed Sun) and the Tabaccheria, Via Cavour 85 (no closing day).

San Gimignano

SAN GIMIGNANO, 27km northwest of Siena, is perhaps the most-visited small village in Italy. Its stunning hilltop skyline of towers, built in aristocratic rivalry by the feuding nobles of the twelfth and thirteenth centuries, evokes the appearance of medieval Tuscany more than any other sight. And the town is all that it's cracked up to be: quietly monumental, very well preserved, enticingly rural, and with a fine array of religious and secular frescoes. However, from Easter until October, San Gimignano has very little life of its own, and a lot of day-trippers. If you want to reach beyond its facade of quaintness, you should come well out of season; if you can't, then aim to spend the night here – the town takes on a very different pace and atmosphere in the evenings.

San Gimignano was quite a force to be reckoned with in the early Middle Ages. It was controlled by two great families – the Ardinghelli and the Salvucci – and its 15,000 population (twice the present number) prospered on agricultural holdings and its position on the Lombardy-to-Rome pilgrim route. At its heyday, the town's walls enclosed five monasteries, four hospitals, public baths and a brothel. **Feuds**, however, had long wreaked havoc: the first Ardinghelli–Salvucci conflict erupted in 1246. Whenever the town itself was united, it picked fights with Volterra, Poggibonsi and other neighbours. These were

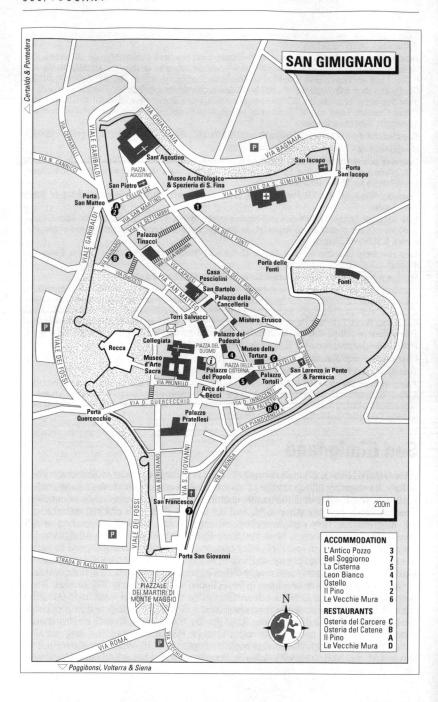

halted only by the **Black Death**, which devastated the population and – as the pilgrim trade collapsed – the economy. Subjection to Florence broke the power of the nobles and so their tower-houses, symbolic in other towns of real control, were not torn down; today, 15 of an original 72 survive. At the beginning of the last century, travellers spoke of San Gimignano as "miserably poor"; its postwar history has been one of ever-increasing affluence, through **tourism** and the production of an old-established but recently rejuvenated white **wine**, Vernaccia. The famous *Festival Internazionale* (*www.fts.toscana.it*) fills a couple of weeks in late July with **opera**, **ballet** and concerts of symphonic and chamber **music** on an open-air stage in Piazza Duomo; consult the tourist office for full details.

Arrival, information and accommodation

San Gimignano has very few direct buses from anywhere other than the ugly industrial town of **Poggibonsi**, 8km east: you're likely to have to call in here to transfer. From Poggibonsi train station (on the Florence–Empoli–Siena line), walk the length of platform 1, exit the gates and cross the road to reach the bus bays. TRA-IN buses drop off at both San Gimignano's main gates, **Porta San Giovanni** in the south and **Porta San Matteo** in the north. From each, the main streets Via San Giovanni and Via San Matteo climb to meet in the middle of town at the interlocking squares of **Piazza Duomo** and **Piazza della Cisterna**, where you'll find the Pro Loco **tourist office**, Piazza Duomo 1 (daily: March–Oct 9am–1pm & 3–7pm; Nov–Feb 9am–1pm & 2–6pm; ☎0577.940.008, *www.sangimignano.com*).

Accommodation is bookable for free through a branch of Siena Hotels Promotion, located just inside the southern gate at Via San Giovanni 125 (summer Mon–Sat 9am–7pm; winter Mon–Sat 9.30am–12.30pm & 3–6pm; ☎0577.940.809, fax 0577.940.113, *hotsangi@tin.it*). They can also give details of **private rooms**, which charge ③ prices.

Hotels

L'Antico Pozzo, Via San Matteo 87 (☎0577.942.014, fax 0577.942.117, *www.anticopozzo.com*). An upmarket eighteen-room three-star, occupying a fifteenth-century town house. ⑥.

Bel Soggiorno, Via San Giovanni 91 (☎0577.940.375, fax 0577.907.521, *hbelsog@libero.it*). Similar quality, price and facilities to the *Leon Bianco*. The 22 rooms are smallish but beautifully appointed. ⑥

La Cisterna, Piazza Cisterna 24 (☎0577.940.328, fax 0577.942.080). Elegant town hotel (established 1919), built into a medieval ensemble; some rooms have views onto the piazza or over the valley. ⑤.

Il Pino, Via Cellolese 4 (☎0577.942.225, fax 0577.940.415). A lovely five-room guesthouse above a trattoria just inside the Porta San Matteo. ②.

Leon Bianco, Piazza Cisterna 13 (☎0577.941.294, fax 0577.942.123, *www.see.it/sangimignano*). Tasteful three-star hotel with air-con, in a fourteenth-century town mansion alongside the *Cisterna*. Also with a roof terrace for breakfast, drinks and lounging. ⑥.

Le Vecchie Mura, Via Piandornella 15 (☎ & fax 0577.940.270, *vecchiemura@iol.it*). A couple of doubles above a restaurant, with welcoming owners and superb views. ②.

Hostel and campsite

Campeggio Il Boschetto (☎0577.940.352, fax 0577.941.982; April–Oct). The nearest campsite (with bar and shop), 3km downhill from Porta San Giovanni at Santa Lucia, off the Volterra road.

Ostello, Via delle Fonti 1 (☎0577.941.991). A 75-bed HI hostel, well positioned just north of the central piazzas. Reports suggest it could be better-run, and the breakfast is thin. L26,000/€13.42.

The Town

You could walk from one end of San Gimignano to the other in about fifteen minutes. It deserves at least a day, however, both for its frescoes and its lovely surrounding

A single *biglietto cumulativo*, overpriced at L20,000/€10.33, covers admission to most of the town's orthodox **museums** – the Collegiata/Duomo, Museo d'Arte Sacra, Museo Civico, Torre Grossa and Museo Archeologico/Spezieria. You can buy it from any of the participating places, but it's only worthwhile if you're visiting most of them. Not included are the wackier private concerns such as the Museo della Tortura.

countryside. From the southern gate, **Porta San Giovanni**, the palazzo-lined **Via San Giovanni** leads to the interlocking main squares, the Piazza della Cisterna and Piazza del Duomo. On the right of the street, about 100m up, is the former church of San Francesco – a Romanesque building converted, like many of the *palazzi*, to a wine shop. You enter the **Piazza della Cisterna** through another gateway, the **Arco dei Becci**, part of the original fortifications built before the town expanded in the twelfth century. The square itself is flanked by an anarchic cluster of towers and *palazzi*, and is named after the thirteenth-century public cistern, still functioning in the centre. To the left (northwest) of the square is one of the old Ardinghelli towers; a Salvucci rival rears up behind. An arch leads through to the more austere **Piazza Duomo**, with further towers and civic *palazzi*.

The Collegiata

The plain facade of the Duomo, or more properly the **Collegiata**, since San Gimignano no longer has a bishop, could hardly provide a greater contrast with its interior (Mon–Fri 9.30am–7.30pm, Sat 9.30am–5pm, Sun 1–5pm; Nov–March closes 5pm daily; closed Jan & Feb; L6000/€3.10; for details of combined entry ticket see box above). This is one of the most comprehensively frescoed churches in Tuscany, with cycles of paintings filling every available space, their brilliant colours set off by Pisan-Romanesque arcades of black and white striped marble. Entrance is from the side courtyard, where you'll also find the small **Museo d'Arte Sacra** (April–Oct daily 9.30am–7.30pm; Nov–March 9.30am–5pm; L5000/€2.58; joint ticket with Collegiata L10,000/€5.16; for details of combined entry ticket see box above).

The Collegiata's three principal **fresco cycles** fill the north and south walls, plus two short side walls which protrude from the east (exit) wall of the facade. The **Old Testament** scenes on the north wall, completed by Bartolo di Fredi around 1367, are full of medieval detail in the costumes, activities and interiors. They are also quirkily naturalistic: there are few odder frescoes than the depiction of Noah exposing himself in a drunken stupor. The cycle (which reads from left to right, top to bottom) follows the story of the **Flood** with those of **Abraham and Lot** (their trip to Canaan), **Joseph** (his dream; being let down the well; having his brothers arrested, and being recognized by them), **Moses** (changing a stick into a serpent before the Pharaoh; the Red Sea; Mount Sinai) and **Job** (temptation; the devil killing his herds; thanking God; being consoled). Above, note the beautiful fresco depicting the *Creation of Eve*, in which Eve emerges from the rib of the sleeping Adam. The **New Testament** scenes opposite (begun 1333) have a disputed attribution – either Barna da Siena or Lippo Memmi. They impress most by the intensity of their emotional expression: in *The Kiss of Judas*, the focus of eyes is startlingly immediate. One of the most dramatic scenes is the *Resurrection of Lazarus*, in which a dumbstruck crowd witnesses the removal of a door to reveal the living Lazarus in the winding bandages of burial. An altogether different vision pervades Taddeo di Bartolo's **Last Judgement** (1410), with paradise to the left and hell to the right. This is one of the most gruesome depictions of a customarily lurid subject, with no-holds-barred illustrations of the Seven Deadly Sins.

San Gimignano's most important Renaissance artwork is the superb fresco cycle made by Domenico Ghirlandaio for the small **Cappella di Santa Fina**. The subject is a local saint, born in 1238, who was struck by a dreadful and incurable disease at the age of ten. She gave herself immediately to God, repented her sins (the worst seems to have been accepting an orange from a boy), and insisted on spending the five agonizing years until her death lying on a plank on the floor. The fresco of the right-hand lunette shows Fina experiencing a vision of St Gregory. Opposite it is a much more accomplished work, the *Funeral of St Fina* – Raphael is said to have been especially impressed with it – showing the saint on her deathbed with the towers of San Gimignano in the background. Ghirlandaio left a self-portrait: he's the figure behind the bishop who is saying Mass.

The Museo Civico

The Palazzo Popolo, the other key component of Piazza Duomo, is partly given over to council offices, but most of the building is devoted to the **Museo Civico** and the **Torre Grossa**, the only one of San Gimignano's towers which you can climb (both March–Oct daily 9.30am–7.20pm; Nov–Feb Mon–Thurs, Sat & Sun 10.30am–4.20pm; museum L7000/€3.61, tower L8000/€4.13, joint ticket L12,000/€6.20; for details of combined entry ticket see box opposite).

The lovely courtyard was built in 1323. A loggia opens on the right, from which justice and public decrees were occasionally proclaimed (hence the subject matter of its frescoes). Stairs lead up to a picturesque little balcony and the ticket office. The first room, frescoed with hunting scenes, is the **Sala di Dante** – the poet visited as Florence's ambassador to the town in 1299, making a plea here for Guelph unity. Most of the paintings are Sienese in origin or inspiration, and the highlight is Lippo Memmi's *Maestà* (1317). Off the Sala di Dante are busts of a winsome *Santa Fina* (1496) and *San Gregorio* by Pietro Torrigiano. Highlights upstairs include two outstanding tondi by **Filippino Lippi**. Rooms off to the right hold a triptych by **Taddeo di Bartolo** depicting *Scenes from the Life of St Gimignano* (1393) – with the saint holding the eponymous town on his lap – and **Lorenzo di Niccolò's** *Scenes from the Life of St Bartholomew* (1401), which includes a graphic depiction of the saint being flayed alive. The most enjoyable paintings are hidden away in a small room off the stairs, frescoes of wedding scenes completed in the 1320s by the Sienese painter Memmo di Filipuccio that are unique in their subject matter: they show a tournament where the wife rides on her husband's back, followed by the lovers taking a shared bath and then climbing into bed – the man managing to keep on the same red hat throughout.

The rest of the town

A few steps east of Piazza della Cisterna at Via del Castello 1 is the new Museo Criminale Medioevale, or **Museo della Tortura** (daily: mid-July to mid-Sept 9am–midnight; rest of year 10am–7pm; L15,000/€7.75). This offers an array of instruments (most, chillingly enough, sourced from private collections) designed to inflict pain or death – everything from thumbscrews and chastity belts to an electric chair. The historical notes are scholarly but the place reeks of a distasteful, seedy prurience. Via di Castello continues east past the Romanesque **San Lorenzo in Ponte** (with fragments of a dramatic *Last Judgement* fresco) to a rural lane which winds down between vineyards to the city walls; just beyond the public wellhouse or **Fonti** stretches open countryside.

A backstreet off Piazza Duomo shelters the **Mistero Etrusco**, Vicolo dell'Oro 1 (daily 10am–1pm & 1.30–6pm; L10,000/€5.16, *www.etruscanmysterymuseum.it*), which uses imagined backdrops, dynamic lighting and sound to spice up what is essentially a static display of Etruscan artefacts. The place is just too small to be worth the admission fee. On the opposite side of the square, a signposted lane leads up to the **Rocca**, the old fortress, with its one surviving tower and superb views. It was built, at local expense, by the Florentines "in order to remove every cause of evil thinking from the inhabitants" after their union with the *comune*. Later, its purpose presumably fulfilled, it was dismantled by Cosimo de' Medici. Nowadays it encloses an orchard-like public garden, with figs, olives and a central well.

Via San Matteo is one of the grandest and best preserved of the city streets, running north from Piazza Duomo to the main **Porta San Matteo** gate. Before the gate, Via XX Settembre heads east to the former convent of Santa Chiara, which now houses the interesting **Museo Archeologico** (daily 11am–6pm; L8000/€4.13 or see box on p.552 for details of combined entry ticket). In the same complex is the **Spezieria di Santa Fina**, fragrant halls filled with exhibits from the sixteenth-century spice and herb pharmacy of the town's Santa Fina hospital – ceramic jars full of strange potions and hanging bunches of dried herbs. From 2001, the building will also house a **Galleria d'Arte Contemporaneo**. The northernmost corner of town is occupied by the large church of **Sant'Agostino** (daily 7am–noon & 3–7pm; winter closes 6pm), with an outstanding fresco cycle behind the high altar by Benozzo Gozzoli on the *Life of St Augustine* (1465), which provide a superb record of life in Renaissance Florence. Read from low down on the left, the panels depict the saint – who was born in what is now Tunisia in 354 – being taken to school and being flogged by his teacher, studying grammar at Carthage university, crossing the sea to Italy, his teaching in Rome and Milan and being received by Emperor Theodosius. Then comes the turning-point, when he hears St Ambrose preach and, while reading St Paul, hears a child's voice extolling him *"Tolle, lege"* (take and read). After this, he was baptized and returned to Africa to found a monastic community. The depiction of his death almost exactly prefigures Ghirlandaio's Collegiata fresco of the death of St Fina.

Eating and drinking

San Gimignano isn't famous for its **food** – there are too many tourists and too few locals to ensure high standards. However, the tables set out on the car-free squares and lanes, and the good local wines, make for pleasant dining.

Little *Gelateria di Piazza*, Piazza della Cisterna 4, has unquestionably the best **ice cream** in Tuscany. Owner Sergio stopped entering competitions after he retained the *Gelatissimo d'Italia* in 1998 – because he kept winning. Framed plaudits cover the walls. His incomparable pistachio flavour is made from finest-quality Sicilian nuts, and his trademark *crema di Santa Fina* is perfumed with saffron, but you'd be hard-pushed on a hot afternoon to beat the trio of peach, champagne with grapefruit, and *vernaccia*, the last fragrant sorbet made from the crisp local white wine. Avoid poor-quality imitators on the same piazza.

Il Pino, Via San Matteo 102 (☎0577.942.225). First choice: a lovely interior, with a specialist focus on *antipasti* and dishes sprinkled with truffle. No need to pay more than L30,000/€15.49. Closed Thurs.

Osteria del Carcere, Via del Castello 13 (☎0577.941.905). A relatively new and informal place with young owners, serving Tuscan cuisine with an innovative edge. Closed Wed.

Osteria del Catene, Via Mainardi 18 (☎0577.941.966). Thoroughly reliable spot for straightforward Tuscan cooking, plus an extensive wine list. Closed Wed.

Le Vecchie Mura, Via Piandornella 15 (☎0577.940.270). Housed in an old vaulted stable off Via San Giovanni, with a good atmosphere, fair-value pizzas and quality set meals. Closed Tues & lunch.

Listings

Bike and scooter rental Bruno Bellini, Via Roma 41 (☎0577.940.201).

Bus information You can buy tickets and get timetables from the tourist office in Piazza Duomo. Last buses to Siena and Florence leave from Porta San Giovanni about 8.30pm.

Internet access Cartoleria La Tuscio, just outside Porta San Matteo, or the craft shop at Via XX Settembre 24b; both charge L3000/€1.55 for 15min.

Market Piazza Duomo and Piazza Cisterna (Thurs morning).

Parking There are five pay car-parks dotted around the walls which work out about the same as the town-centre hotels' parking rates. Driving within the walls is forbidden unless you have a chit from your hotel, and the police will ticket you if you try (or if you park outside the Porta San Giovanni).

Taxis ☎0577.940.499 and ☎0577.940.049.

Volterra

The dramatic location of **VOLTERRA** – built on a high plateau enclosed by volcanic hills midway between Siena and the sea – prompted D.H. Lawrence to write that "it gets all the wind and sees all the world... a sort of inland island." Its walled medieval core is atmospheric and not excessively touristed. Everything is made from the yellow-grey stone *panchino*, and you can often find seashells embedded in the paving of streets and squares. **Etruscan** Volterra (Velathri) flourished through a combination of its alabaster mines and an impregnable position, attributes that ensured its survival through the Roman era and beyond. Its isolation was, however, its downfall. Under **Florentine** control from 1360, it proved unable to keep pace with changing and expanding patterns of trade, and the town itself began to subside, its walls and houses slipping away to the west over the **Balze** cliffs, which form a dramatic prospect from the Pisa road. Today, Volterra – part of the Provincia di Pisa – occupies less than a third of its ancient extent.

The Town

Dominating the almost totally medieval square of **Piazza dei Priori**, the **Palazzo dei Priori** is the oldest town hall in Tuscany, begun in 1208, which may have served as the model for Florence's Palazzo Vecchio. If you find the tower open, pay for the spectacular views from the top (which reputedly stretch to Corsica). Upstairs inside the palazzo (Mon–Fri 10am–1pm, Tues & Thurs also 3–6pm, Sat & Sun 10am–1pm & 2–6pm; L2000/€1.03) is the **Sala del Consiglio**, used as the town's council chamber without interruption since 1257. Its end wall is frescoed with a huge *Annunciation* by Orcagna; just outside, workers are currently restoring Francesco Fiorentino's fresco of the *Crucifixion*.

Leaving the square west past the tourist office, you come to a crossroads overlooked by the **Torre Buomparenti**. South (left) on Via Roma is the **Museo d'Arte Sacra**, a rich four-room collection (daily: March–Oct 9am–1pm & 3–6pm; Nov–Feb 9am–1pm; joint ticket with Museo Guarnacci and Pinacoteca L13,000/€6.71), which includes a silver reliquary bust of *St Ottaviano* by Antonio del Pollaiuolo and a beautiful sixteenth-century alabaster ciborium. Via Roma continues into the slightly down-at-heel cathedral square, with the Pisan-Romanesque **Duomo** (consecrated in 1120) and **Baptistry** (late-thirteenth century). The best of the duomo's works is a sculpture of the *Deposition* (1228) in the south transept, disarmingly repainted in its original bright colours. Behind the baptistry is an old foundling's hospital decorated by della Robbia. Via Marchesi heads south to a lush area of grass, trees and shade known as the **Parco Archeologico** (daily 10am–noon & 4–7pm; free). There's not much archeology about the place – a few odd lumps of rock, said to be part of a Roman bathhouse – but it's a beautiful part of the town to lie around for a few hours, and there is a good-value café in one corner. Overlooking the park to the east is the Medicean **Rocca**, with rounded bastions and a central tower; it's one of the great examples of Italian military architecture and for the last 150 years has been a prison for lifers and hard cases. The first turning off Via Marchesi is Via Porta dell'Arco, which runs downhill to the **Arco Etrusco**, an Etruscan gateway, third-century BC in origin, built in cyclopean blocks of stone. The gate was narrowly saved from destruction in the last war during a ten-day battle between the partisans and Nazis.

VOLTERRA'S ALABASTER

Alabaster is a form of crystallized chalk that has a delicate, milky texture and lends itself to the sculpture of fine, flowing lines and close ornamental detail. In even quite large blocks, it is translucent. The Etruscans and Romans extensively mined Volterra's alabaster for sculpting. Up until the 1960s, there were large alabaster factories throughout the town centre, but – not least because of the quantity of dust they threw up – large-scale production was moved to outlying areas. These days, only about a dozen artisans are permitted to maintain workshops in the centre of town, and Volterra's famous art school is the only one in Europe to train students to work alabaster.

You'll spot plenty of alabaster shops dotted around the centre – most are outlets for factories that produce machined pieces from the tasteful to the tacky. *Alab'Arte*, down the alley alongside the Museo Guarnacci at Via Orti S. Agostino 28 (☎0588.87.968), is one of the few to stick to hand-production, turning out sculpted pieces for as little as a few thousand lire.

North (right) from the Torre Buomparenti is the beautiful Renaissance Palazzo Minucci-Solaini, now housing the **Pinacoteca Comunale** (daily: March–Oct 9am–7pm; Nov–Feb 9am–2pm; joint ticket with Museo Guarnacci and Museo d'Arte Sacra L13,000/€6.71). The key works are Florentine: Ghirlandaio's marvellous *Christ in Glory*, Luca Signorelli's *Annunciation* and, best of all, Rosso Fiorentino's extraordinary *Deposition*. This is one of the masterpieces of Mannerism, its figures, without any central focus, creating an agitated tension from sharp lines and blocks of discordant colour. It's been described as symbolizing the dilemma of a lost generation (it was painted in the decade which culminated in the sack of Rome) and has also been dubbed blasphemous for its vision of a smiling Christ. On the same street as the Pinacoteca is the newly opened **Palazzo Viti**, Via dei Sarti 41 (daily 9am–1pm & 2.30–6pm; closed Tues morning; L7000/€3.61), an extensively frescoed Renaissance mansion filled with alabaster, everything from 2m-high alabaster candelabra to alabaster tiles laid in the floor of the ballroom.

The Museo Guarnacci

The **Museo Guarnacci**, 500m east of Piazza dei Priori at Via Don Minzoni 15 (same hours and ticket as Pinacoteca, see above) is one of Italy's major archeological museums. On display are entirely local finds, including some 600 Etruscan **funerary urns**. Carved in alabaster, terracotta or local sandstone or limestone, they date from the fourth to first centuries BC, and follow a standard pattern: below a reclining figure of the subject (always leaning on their left side), bas reliefs depict domestic events, Greek myths or simply a symbolic flower – one for a young person, two for middle-aged, three for elderly. The vast collection is organized by theme, with informative notes in each room. Key highlights are **upstairs**: past a large Roman mosaic transferred here from Volterra's baths is the **Urna degli Sposi**, a rare and artistically unique clay urn lid which features a disturbing double portrait of a husband and wife, all piercing eyes and dreadful looks. The star piece is the exceptional **Ombra della Sera** ("Evening Shadow"), an elongated nude that is unique in that it has been personalized and individualized – most of the figurines in nearby cases are generic. This piece was much admired by the twentieth-century Swiss sculptor Alberto Giacometti, who drew inspiration for his famous elongated figures from this Etruscan artist's visualization of the long evening shadows cast in hilltop Volterra.

The Balze cliffs

To reach the much-photographed eroded **Balze** cliffs, follow the Via Ricciarelli northwest from the Piazza dei Priori. As Via San Lino, this passes the church of **San**

Francesco, with fifteenth-century frescoes of the *Legend of the True Cross* by Cenni di Cenni, before leaving town through the Porta San Francesco. From here, follow Borgo Santo Stefano and its continuation, Borgo San Giusto, past the Baroque church and former abbey of **San Giusto**, its dilapidated but striking facade framed by an avenue of cypress trees. At the *Balze* (almost 2km west of Piazza dei Priori) you gain a real sense of the extent of Etruscan Volterra, whose old walls drop away into the chasms. Gashes in the slopes and the natural erosion of sand and clay are made more dramatic by alabaster mines, ancient and modern. Below are buried great tracts of the Etruscan and Roman city, and landslips continue – as evidenced by the ruined eleventh-century **Badia** monastery ebbing away over the precipice.

Practicalities

Regular **buses** run to Volterra from Siena, Florence and Livorno, with a couple a day from Poggibonsi; all arrive on the south side of the walls at Piazza Martiri, from where it's a two-minute walk to the central Piazza dei Priori. The helpful **tourist office** is at no. 20 (daily: April–Oct 9am–8pm; Nov–March 10am–1pm & 2–6pm; ☎0588.87.257, *www.volterratur.it*). They can book accommodation for free and rent you an **audioguide** (L15,000/€7.75), available in English, for a self-guided town tour. Avoid the Pro Volterra information office round the corner at Via Turazza 2 – they're not half as helpful or clued-in. There are free **car parks** on the northern side of the walls. Walking tours are run by Viaggi ATUV just off Piazza Martiri (☎0588.86.333, *volterraviaggi@biemmepro.it*) – one hour (L12,000/€6.20) or four hours including a drive to an agriturismo farm for a light lunch (L40,000/€20.66).

Volterra's most attractive **hotel** is the sixteenth-century *Villa Nencini*, in a peaceful, panoramic setting west of the centre at Borgo Santo Stefano 55 (☎0588.86.386, fax 0588.80.601, *villanencini@sirt.pisa.it*; ④). At the eastern end of town is the *San Pietro* independent **hostel**, Via del Poggetto 2 (☎ & fax 0588.85.577; L24,000/€12.39), and anyone can stay in a cell-with-a-view at the *Sant'Andrea* **convent** in the northeast outskirts (☎0588.86.028; L27,000/€13.94, or slightly more for en suite). The **campsite** *Le Balze* is 1km west of town, Via di Mandringa 115 (☎& fax 0588.87.880; April–Sept).

As a renowned centre for hunting, Volterra's **restaurant** menus are dominated by wild boar (*cinghiale*), hare (*lepre*) and rabbit (*coniglio*). Most places are moderately priced. *Ombra della Sera*, Via Gramsci 68 (closed Mon), is a pleasant local haunt, while the vaulted gloom of *Vecchia Osteria dei Poeti*, Via Matteotti 55 (closed Thurs) is the most characterful spot for Volterra's gamey cuisine. *Don Beta*, Via Matteotti 39 (closed Mon) offer relief in the form of inexpensive pizzas and light meals. *Il Toscano*, on Vicolo delle Prigioni, has **Internet** access.

SOUTHERN TUSCANY

The inland hills of **southern Tuscany** are the region at its best, an infinite gradation of trees and vineyards that encompasses the *crete* – a sparsely populated region of pale clay hillsides – before climbing into the hills around Monte Amiata. Southwest of Siena towards the sea is gentle **Massa Maríttima**, a memorable but little-visited hill-town that presides over a marshy coastal plain. Magnificent monastic architecture survives in the tranquil settings of **San Galgano** and, a short distance east, **Monte Oliveto Maggiore**, which boasts the additional attraction of some marvellous frescoes. The finest of the hill-towns to the south of Siena is **Montepulciano**, with its superb wines and an ensemble of Renaissance architecture that rivals neighbouring **Pienza**.

Further south, the tourist crush is noticeably eased in smaller towns and villages that are often overlooked by visitors gorged on Florentine art and Sienese countryside.

Wild **Monte Amiata** offers scenic mountain walks, **Saturnia** has some remarkable sulphur springs, and isolated **Pitigliano** is one of the most dramatically sited medieval
towns in the region, nurturing the amazing story – and scant remains – of what was
once Tuscany's strongest Jewish community.

Massa Maríttima

The road south from Volterra over the mountains to **MASSA MARÍTTIMA** is little
explored and scenically magnificent: classic Tuscan countryside which is given an
added surreal quality around **Larderello** by the presence of *soffioni* (hot steam gey-
sers), huge silver pipes snaking across the fields, and sulphurous smoke rising from
chimneys amid the foliage. There are three or four **buses** daily to Massa from Volterra
(change at Monterotondo), one from Grosseto and two from Florence and Siena. It
sees none of the crowds of San Gimignano, and even Volterra looks crowded in comparison.

Massa, like Volterra, has been a wealthy **mining** town since Etruscan times. In 1225,
on the heels of a declaration of independence, it passed Europe's first-ever charter for
the protection of miners; in the century afterwards, before Siena took over in 1335, its
exquisite **Duomo** went up and the population doubled. The trend was reversed in the
sixteenth century, and by 1737, after bouts of plague and malaria, it was a virtual ghost
town. Massa gained its "Maríttima" suffix in the Middle Ages when it became the leading hill-town of this coastal region, even though the sea is 20km distant across a silty
plain. Its recovery began with the draining of coastal marshes in the 1830s.

Blocks of new buildings mar an approach, but the medieval splendour of **Piazza
Garibaldi**, just up from the bus stops, overshadows all that. This exquisite example of
Tuscan town planning showcases the thirteenth-century **Duomo**, set on broad steps at
a dramatically oblique angle to the square. The cathedral is dedicated to the sixth-
century St Cerbone, whose claim to fame was to persuade a flock of geese to follow him
when summoned to Rome on heresy charges. Its airy **interior** (daily: 8am–noon &
3–6pm) features eleventh-century carvings of grinning, cross-eyed faces – powerful
and primitive, in dramatic contrast to the severe, polished Roman sarcophagus nearby.
A modest **Museo Archeologico** occupies the Palazzo del Podestà opposite (April–June
Tues–Sun 10am–12.30pm & 3.30–7pm; July & Aug daily 10am–12.30pm & 3.30–7pm;
Nov–March closes 5pm; L5000/€2.58) – worth visiting for the town's undisputed masterpiece, a superb *Maestà* altarpiece by Ambrogio Lorenzetti, coloured in vivid pink,
green and tangerine, with Cerbone and his geese lurking in the corner. Off the other
side of the piazza is the **Centro Espositivo di Arte Contemporanea**, Via Goldoni 5
(Tues–Fri 5–7pm, Sat & Sun 11am–1pm & 4–7pm; L3000/€1.55), which includes an
engaging collection of late-nineteenth-century painting.

Otherwise, barring a couple of limited-interest museums devoted to mining, aim for
the picturesque lane Via Moncini, which climbs steeply to the quiet Gothic **upper
town**: as you emerge beneath an impressive but militarily useless arch onto **Piazza
Matteotti**, facing you is the **Torre del Candeliere**, part of the thirteenth-century
Fortilizio Senese. The tower is climbable for a stupendous panorama (summer daily
11am–1pm & 3.30–7.30pm; L3000/€1.55).

Practicalities

The **tourist office** is just below Piazza Garibaldi at Via Norma Parenti 22 (summer
Mon–Sat 9am–12.30pm & 4–7.30pm, Sun 10am–1pm; winter Tues–Sat 10am–1pm;
☎0566.902.756, *www.amatur.it*). Massa's only central **hotel** is *Il Sole*, Via Libertà 43
(☎0566.901.971, fax 0566.901.959; ③); otherwise go for the pleasant, refurbished *Duca*

Statue in Padua's Prato della Valle

Neptune fountain, Bologna

Looking down the Arno to the Ponte Vecchio, Florence

GREG EVANS

"The Gates of Paradise", Florence

LEE KAREN STOW

Farmhouse shrine to the Madonna

CHRIS COE, AXIOM

Abbazia di Sant'Antimo, Tuscany

LUKE WHITE, AXIOM

Villa Adriana

W. MATTHEW, TRIP

Spoleto, Umbria

GREG EVANS

Contrada members, the Palio, Siena

PETER WILSON

The baldacchino, Saint Peter's, Rome

PETER WILSON

Coliseum, Rome

MATTHEW HANCOCK

Piazza Navona, Rome

JIM HOLMES, AXIOM

Campo de'Fiori, Rome

del Mare, just below town at Via Dante Alighieri 1 (☎0566.902.284, fax 0566.901.905, www.cometanet.it/ducadelmare; ③). Better **restaurants** than those lining Piazza Garibaldi include the characterful *Osteria del Viaggiatore*, Via Norma Parenti 35 (☎0566.902.093; closed Mon), with innovative, pricey takes on Tuscan staples, and *Il Gatto e La Volpe*, down the alley Vicolo Ciambellano (☎0566.903.575; closed Mon), offering jugged hare, stuffed rabbit and wild boar. *Pizzeria Barbablu*, up at Piazza Matteotti 5, has excellent *pizza gialla* (a pizza base sprinkled with saffron, scamorza and parmesan cheeses, and rocket) and outside tables where you can watch your afternoon vanish as the hands on the Torre del Candeliere's eccentric clock scoot round twelve hours in a single hour. The **pub** *Del Priore*, Via Libertà 34, has good beer and a blues jukebox.

Make time in summer for the **Toscana Foto Festival** (*web.tiscalinet.it/ toscanafotofestival*), with photo exhibits and workshops at venues around town in late July, and a prestigious show of the cream of the crop running until late August.

The crete

South of Siena stretches classic Tuscan countryside known as the *crete* – a sparsely populated region of pale clay hillsides dotted with sheep, cypresses and the odd monumental-looking farmhouse. These tranquil lands were one of the heartlands of medieval monasticism in Tuscany. The Vallombrosan order maintained their main house at Torri just south of Siena, the Benedictine order had theirs at Sant'Antimo near Montalcino (see p.567), while the Cistercians founded the convent and abbey of **San Galgano**; now ruined, this is one of the most alluring sights in Tuscany, complete with its hilltop chapel housing the **sword-in-the-stone**. The region's grandest monastery is southeast of Siena at **Monte Oliveto Maggiore**.

San Galgano

The **Abbazia di San Galgano**, 26km northeast of Massa Maríttima, midway on the road to Siena, is perhaps the most evocative Gothic building in all Italy – roofless, with a grass field for a nave, nebulous patches of fresco amidst the vegetation, and panoramas of the sky, clouds and hills through a rose window. In the twelfth and thirteenth centuries, local **Cistercian** monks were the leading power in Tuscany. The abbots exercised powers of arbitration in city disputes, and at Siena the monks were the city's accountants. Through them, the ideas of Gothic building were imported to Italy. The order began a hilltop **church** and monastical buildings here in 1218, but their project to build a grand abbey on the fertile land below was doomed to failure. Building work took seventy years up to 1288, but then famine struck in 1329, the Black Death in 1348, and mercenaries ran amok in subsequent decades. By 1500, all the monks had moved to the security of Siena. The buildings mouldered until 1786, when the belltower was struck by lightning and collapsed. Three years later, the church was deconsecrated, and the complex was abandoned for good.

These days, the main appeal of the **abbey** (daily: May–Sept 8am–8pm; Oct–April 8am–6pm) is its state of ruin, although work to halt the advance of Mother Nature is under way and there are concerts of classical music held during the summer (see p.548 for more). Andrei Tarkovsky filmed the finale of *Nostalgia* here.

On the hill above, the unusual round Romanesque church of **Monte Siepi** commemorates the spot where Galgano – a local twelfth-century knight – renounced his violent past by thrusting his sword into a stone. Amazingly enough, Galgano's **sword in the stone** has survived, protected under glass as an object of veneration. A sidechapel preserves the decaying remains of a man's hands: local legend has it that two wolves companions of Galgano – tore them from a robber who had broken into the saint's tomb.

There are two or three **buses** daily between Massa Maríttima and Siena which pass within sight of the abbey. To one side of the abbey building, in the old vaulted scriptorium, is a small **tourist office** (daily: March & April 10.30am–4pm; May–Sept 10am–6.30pm; Oct 10.30am–5pm; Nov–Feb 11am–3pm; ☎0577.756.738). The small café opposite, run by the *Cooperativa Agricola San Galgano*, has **rooms** (☎0577.756.292; ③), and can stump up sandwiches and simple meals. In its grounds is the **Centro Italiano Rapaci**, or Raptor Centre; it's open all summer (Mon, Tues & Thurs–Sun 10.30am–1pm & 2.30pm–dusk; L6000/€3.10; ☎0330.932.671), but restricts displays of falconry to August only.

Monte Oliveto Maggiore

It takes some effort to visit the **Abbazia di Monte Oliveto Maggiore**, but the rewards are clear: Tuscany's grandest monastery is sited twenty six kilometres southeast of Siena in one of the most beautiful tracts of Sienese countryside, and houses one of the most absorbing Renaissance **frescoes** you'll find anywhere. By car, you can approach from the crossroads town of Buonconvento, climbing quickly into forests of pine, oak and cypress, and then into the olive groves that enclose the monastery. One afternoon bus daily from Siena's train station goes to the village of Chiusure, 2km east of the abbey.

When Pius II visited in 1463, it was the overall scene that impressed him: the architecture, in honey-coloured Sienese brick, merging into the woods and gardens that the monks had created from the eroded hills of the *crete*. A wealthy Sienese noble, who had been struck blind and had experienced visions of the Virgin, came to this remote wilderness in 1313 and lived the life of a hermit, soon drawing a following. Within six years, the pope recognized his order – the **Olivetans**, or White Benedictines – and over the following two centuries this, their principal house, was transformed into one of the most powerful monasteries in the land. It was only in 1810, when the monastery was suppressed by Napoleon, that it fell from influence. It is today maintained by a small group of Olivetan monks, who supplement their state income with a hi-tech centre for the restoration of ancient books. At the **gatehouse**, there's a good café-restaurant, *La Torre* (☎0577.707.022, closed Tues), from where an avenue of cypresses leads down the hill to the abbey. Signs at the bottom of the slope direct you along a walk to **Blessed Bernardo's grotto** – a chapel built on the site where the founder lived as a hermit – and there's also a **shop**, selling herbal cures and liquors (Mon–Sat 10am–noon & 3.45–6pm, Sun 9.30–10.45am & 3.45–6pm).

The **abbey** (daily 9.15am–noon & 3.15–6pm; winter closes 5pm) is a huge complex, though much of it remains off-limits to visitors. The entrance leads to the **Chiostro Grande**, covered by a series of frescoes depicting the *Life of St Benedict*, the man traditionally regarded as the founder of Christian monasticism. The cycle begins on the east wall, just on the right of the door into the church, and was begun in 1497 by Luca Signorelli who painted nine panels in the middle of the series that start with the depiction of a collapsing house. The colourful Antonio Bazzi, known as Il Sodoma, painted the remaining 27 scenes between 1505 and 1508; he was by all accounts a lively presence, bringing with him part of his menagerie of pets, which included badgers, depicted at his feet in a self-portrait in the third panel. There's a sensuality in many of the secular figures – the young men especially, as befits his nickname, and also the "evil women" (originally nudes, until protests from the abbot). The **church** (entered off the Chiostro Grande) was given a Baroque remodelling in the eighteenth century and some superb stained glass in the twentieth. Its main treasure is the choir stalls, inlaid by Giovanni di Verona and others with architectural, landscape and domestic scenes (including a nod to Sodoma's pets with a cat in a window). Stairs lead from the cloister up to the **library**, again with carving by Giovanni; sadly, it has had to be viewed from the door since the theft of sixteen of its twenty codices in 1975.

. **BUONCONVENTO**, 9km southwest, has unappealing outskirts but a perfectly preserved medieval village at its heart, sheltering the **hotel-restaurant** *Roma* (☎0577.806.021, fax 0577.807.284; ③; restaurant closed Mon). Regular **buses** from Siena's train station to Buonconvento head on to Montalcino, or to Pienza and Montepulciano.

Montepulciano and around

The highest of the Tuscan hill-towns, at more than 600m, **MONTEPULCIANO** is built on a long, narrow ridge 65km southeast of Siena, along which coils the main street, the **Corso**, flanked by a series of dark alleys which drop away to the walls, providing slivers of views between Renaissance *palazzi* out over the rolling countryside. Henry James, who compared the town to a ship, spent most of his time here drinking – a sound policy, in view of the excellent local table wine and the more refined and much-celebrated **Vino Nobile**. The town is set in superb walking country and is not yet overrun by day-trippers. A short distance east is the little Etruscan town of **Chiusi**.

Arrival, information and accommodation

TRA-IN **buses** run roughly every hour between Buonconvento, Torrenieri (change for Montalcino), San Quírico d'Órcia, Pienza and Montepulciano – some of them begin from Siena – while LFI buses run regularly between Montepulciano, Chiusi, and its **train** station.

Montepulciano's spiralling, tortuous streets are incredibly steep, and **orientation** can get confusing. The main entrance to the town – at the lowest point – is the northern gate, the **Porta al Prato**, terminus of all buses; from here, the Corso climbs south through the town (changing its name from Via di Gracciano to Via di Voltaia, then to Via dell'Opio) until it reaches the southern gate, the **Porta delle Farine**, where inter city buses also drop off. From here, the main street (Via del Poliziano, then Via di San Donato) continues its coiling path up and around to enter the main **Piazza Grande** from the south. The stiff climb on foot takes an unrelenting quarter-hour; or you could resort to the LFI town minibuses which run on a loop every 20min, starting and ending at the Porta al Prato (L1400/€0.72). The official **tourist office** is at the very top of town, Piazza Grande 7 (April–Sept Mon–Sat 10am–1pm & 3–7pm, Sun 9.30am–1pm; Oct–March Mon–Sat 9am–4pm; ☎0578.717.484, *www.vinonobiledimontepulciano.it*). Don't be taken in by substandard imitators on lower streets. You can rent **mountain bikes** for L30,000/€15.49 per day from Cicloposse, Via Matteotti 45 (☎ & fax 0578.716.392, *biketuscany@bccmp.com*). **Parking** is free below the eastern walls.

Cheapest **accommodation** is the three rooms above *Ristorante Il Cittino*, Vicolo della Via Nuova 2 (☎0578.757.335; ①); another low-end option is *La Terrazza*, a pleasant two-star **hotel** at Via Piè al Sasso 16 (☎ & fax 0578.757.440; ②). The elegant *Marzocco* is at Piazza Savonarola 18 (☎0578.757.262, fax 0578.757.530; ④), but it's beaten for location and facilities by *Albergo Duomo*, Via San Donato 14 (☎ & fax 0578.757.473; ⑤). You might also consult the tourist office about **private rooms** – most notably those at *Il Riccio*, Via Talosa 21 (☎0578.757.713; ③). As a last resort, you could get the bus 8km east to **Chianciano Terme**, a huge, characterless spa resort with over 200 hotels.

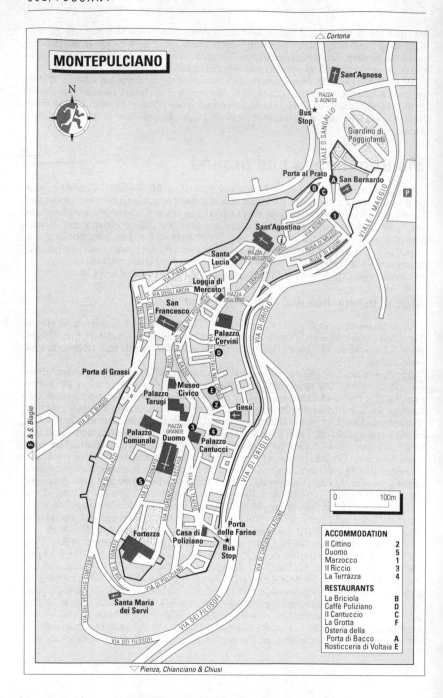

MONTEPULCIANO

N

△ *Cortona*

✝ Sant'Agnese

PIAZZA S.AGNESE

Bus
Stop ★

VIALE D. SANGALLO

Giardino di
Poggiofanti

P

Porta al Prato

Ⓐ San Bernardo

Ⓑ
Ⓒ

VIALE I MAGGIO

Ⓘ

Sant'Agostino ✝ Ⓘ

VIA ROMA

RUGA DI MEZZO

RUGA DI FIORI

Santa
Lucia ✝

PIAZZA / MICHELOZZO

VIA DEL CORSO

VIA GRACCIANO DEL CORSO

Loggia di
Mercato

PIAZZA
DELL'ERBE

VIA DI ORIOLO

VIA PIANA

VIA DEGLI ARCHI

VIA DEL PAOLINO

VIA DEL GIARDINO

San
Francesco ✝

VIA DEL POGGIOLO

Palazzo
Cervini

VIA PIE AL CORSO

VIA DI VOLTAIA NEL CORSO

Ⓓ

Porta di Grassi

VIA RICCI

VIA PIE AL SASSO

Museo
Civico

Ⓔ

Palazzo
Tarugi

Ⓖesù

Ⓔ

VIA DI ORIOLO

VIA DI S.BIAGIO

Palazzo
Comunale

PIAZZA
GRANDE
Duomo ✝

Ⓑ

Ⓒ

Palazzo
Cantucci

Ⓔ

VIA DI COLLAZZI

Ⓔ

VIA DI S.DONATO

VIA FIORENZUOLA VECCHIA

VIA DEL TEATRO

VIA DI CIRCONVALLAZIONE

△ & S. Biagio

Fortezza

Casa di
Poliziano

Porta
delle Farine ★

Bus
Stop

VIA DEL VECCHIO CIMITERO

VIA DI S.DONATO

Santa Maria
dei Servi ✝

VIA DI POLIZIANO

VIA DEI FILOSOFI

VIA DEI FILOSOFI

0   100m

▽ *Pienza, Chianciano & Chiusi*

ACCOMMODATION

Il Cittino	2
Duomo	5
Marzocco	1
Il Riccio	3
La Terrazza	4

RESTAURANTS

La Briciola	B
Caffè Poliziano	D
Il Cantuccio	C
La Grotta	F
Osteria della Porta di Bacco	A
Rosticceria di Voltaia	E

The Town

Montepulciano's unusually consistent array of Renaissance *palazzi* and churches is a reflection of its remarkable development after 1511, when, following intermittent alliance with Siena, the town finally threw in its lot with Florence. In that year the Florentines sent **Antonio Sangallo the Elder** to rebuild the town's gates and walls, which he did so impressively that the council took him on to work on the town hall and a series of churches. The local nobles meanwhile hired him, his nephew, Antonio Sangallo the Younger, and later the Modena-born **Vignola** – a founding figure of Baroque – to work on their own *palazzi*. The work of this trio is totally assured in conception and execution, and makes a fascinating comparison with Rossellino's Pienza.

Sangallo's first commission was Montepulciano's main gate, the **Porta al Prato**, at the north end of town. Inside the gate the **Corso** begins. In the first square, beside the *Albergo Marzocco*, is a stone column bearing the heraldic lion (*marzocco*) of Florence. Just beyond is the church of **Sant'Agostino**, designed by the earlier Medici protégé, Michelozzo, who also carved the relief above the door. Within are good Sienese paintings by Lorenzo di Credi and Giovanni di Paolo. Across the street a medieval **tower house**, a rare survival in Montepulciano, is surmounted by the commedia dell'arte figure of Pulcinella, who strikes out the hours on the town clock; most un-Tuscan, it is said to have been put up by an exiled bishop from Naples.

About 100m further along is **Piazza dell'Erbe** overlooked by the Renaissance **Loggia di Mercato**, which marks a fork in the street. A right turn off the Corso brings you up steeply to a beautiful little piazza fronting the church of **Santa Lucia**, which has a fabulous *Madonna* by Signorelli in a chapel on the right. Just below Santa Lucia, Via del Poggiolo runs down to the church of San Francesco and continues – as the imposing Via Ricci – up to the Piazza Grande past the Sienese-Gothic Palazzo Neri-Orselli, home to the **Museo Civico** (closed for renovation at the time of writing), an extensive collection of small-town Gothic and Renaissance works.

From Piazza dell'Erbe, the Corso continues to the left past further *palazzi*. A long, pleasant stroll through an untouristed part of town brings you onto the quiet, countryfied lane of Via di Poliziano, which loops briefly outside the walls and alongside south-facing vistas up to the Baroque **Santa Maria dei Servi**, before climbing steeply back into town alongside the old **Fortezza**, now part-occupied by houses.

Piazza Grande, Montepulciano's theatrical flourish of a main square, is built on the highest point of the ridge, and is worth the climb. Its most distinctive building is the **Palazzo Comunale**, a thirteenth-century Gothic mansion to which Michelozzo added a tower and rustication in imitation of the Palazzo Vecchio in Florence. You can climb the **tower** for free (daily 9.30am–12.30pm), and on fabled clear days the view supposedly stretches to Siena. Two of the *palazzi* on the square were designed by Sangallo. The **Palazzo Tarugi**, by the lion and griffin fountain, is a highly innovative building, with a public loggia cut through one corner; it originally had an extension on the top floor, though this has been bricked in. Headier pleasures await at the **Palazzo Cantucci**, one of many buildings scattered about the town that serve as *cantine* for the wine trade, offering free *degustazione* (tastings) and sale of the Vino Nobile. Sangallo and his contemporaries never got around to building a facade for the plain brick **Duomo** across the square (daily 9am–1pm & 3.30–7pm). Its interior is an elegant Renaissance design, and it's scattered with superb sculptures by Michelozzo. The finest of the church's paintings is the Sienese **Taddeo di Bartolo**'s iridescent altarpiece of the *Assumption*, a favourite subject among Sienese artists. The piece was commissioned in 1401 at a time when Montepulciano was briefly under Siena's sway; the choice of an artist and a subject with resonance for Florence's old enemy must have been as much political as aesthetic.

Sangallo's greatest commission came in 1518, when he was invited to design the pilgrimage church of **San Biagio** on the hillside below the town. It's a fifteen-minute walk from the centre: aim for the Porta di Grassi, a couple of levels below the north side of Piazza Grande, from where Via San Biagio slopes down to the church. This was the second-largest church project of its time after St Peter's in Rome, and exercised Antonio until his death in 1534. The result is one of the most serene Renaissance creations in Italy, constructed from a porous travertine whose soft honey-coloured stone blends perfectly into its niche in the landscape. A deeply intellectualized building, its major architectural novelty was the use of freestanding towers to flank the facade (only one was completed). Within, it is spoilt a little by Baroque trompe l'oeil decoration, but remains supremely harmonious. Scarcely less perfect is the nearby **Canonica** (rectory), endowed by Sangallo with a graceful portico and double-tiered loggia.

Eating, drinking and entertainment

One **café** is worth a special mention. *Caffè Poliziano*, at Via di Voltaia nel Corso 27 (daily 7am–midnight), is a tearoom from 1868 restored to a classic Art Nouveau design; it serves pastries and pots of tea as well as moderately priced full meals. *Rosticceria di Voltaia*, Via di Voltaia nel Corso 86 (no closing day), is a plain, sociable little **restaurant**; cosy *La Briciola* on Via delle Cantine (closed Wed) serves quality wood-fired pizza. Just inside the Porta al Prato are a clutch of good options. *Osteria della Porta di Bacco* (aka *Fattoria Pulcino*), Via di Gracciano nel Corso 106 (☎0578.757.948), is a quiet, characterful old stone-arched place; nearby is *Il Cantuccio*, Via delle Cantine 1 (☎0578.757.870; closed Mon), with a standard Tuscan menu enlived by items such as *coniglio alla medievale* (roast rabbit). Opposite San Biagio church is the very pleasant *La Grotta* (☎0578.757.479; closed Wed), serving mid-priced classic Tuscan cuisine in a sixteenth-century building with its own garden.

Vino Nobile di Montepulciano has been acclaimed since medieval times and today boasts a top-rated DOCG mark. Local vineyards offer tastings in the town (generally free, but often requiring advance notice) – the tourist office has a complete list, and can organize a **wine-tasting** ramble for you. Some of the many places to check out include the venerable *Contucci*, Via San Donato 15 (☎0578.757.006), which can trace the family line in Montepulciano back a thousand years; *Cantina Del Redi*, Via di Collazi 5 (☎0578.716.092, *info@cantinadelredi.com*); and *Borgo Buio*, Via Borgo Buio 10 (☎0578.717.497, *www.borgobuio.it*; closed Thurs). Even if you can't afford Vino Nobile, ordering a cheap carafe of house *rosso* anywhere in Montepulciano will turn up a fragrant, silky smooth and highly memorable wine.

Every July, the three-week **Cantiere Internazionale d'Arte** (*www.cantiere.toscana.nu*) presents exhibitions and concerts around town, and the last Sunday in August sees the **Bravìo delle Botti**, a barrel-race in medieval costume.

Chiusi

CHIUSI, 14km east of Montepulciano, is a useful transport hub, but this sleepy place is worth more than an hour or two's stopover – its quietly extraordinary cathedral, Christian catacombs and an Etruscan labyrinth could well entice you into delaying an onward journey. **Chiusi Scalo**, an unattractive suburb, is the default stop for all intercity buses, and is where the train station is located. The town centre, **Chiusi Città**, is 2km west; it's a short walk from the bus stop up Via Marconi to the main street, **Via Porsenna**, named after a semi-mythical Etruscan king of the sixth century BC. Here you'll find the modest **Museo Etrusco** (Mon–Sat 9am–8pm; Sun 9am–1pm; L8000/€4.13), with numerous sarcophagi, a few terracottas with traces of ancient paint, and the odd treasure – notably the enigmatic Gualandi Urn. If you're interested in seeing some of the Etruscan **tombs** outside town, ask one of the museum guards to take you (they hold the keys); the famous frescoed Tomba della Scimmia (of the Monkey), off-limits for many years, was opened to the public with much fanfare in May 2000 and is now visitable on pre-booked guided tours (Tues, Fri & Sat 4pm; ☎0578.20.177).

Outside the museum is Piazza Duomo, an elegant little square paved in glittering marble with the Romanesque **Duomo**, one of Tuscany's oldest, which was built in the sixth century almost entirely from Etruscan and Roman blocks. Inside is a wealth of decoration; although much of the mosaic work on the walls is nineteenth-century, the marble columns – each with a different capital – the mosaic floor and the alabaster font are all Roman. The **Museo della Cattedrale** alongside (daily: June to mid-Oct 9.45am–12.45pm & 4–7.30pm; mid-Oct to May 9.30am–12.45pm & 3–6pm; L3000/€1.55) has a small collection of silverware and codices, and gives access to the **Labyrinth of Porsenna** (L5000/€2.58 extra), which leads you through the atmospheric tunnels of the Etruscan water-catchment system below the piazza to a huge Roman cistern and then up inside the twelfth-century campanile. You can also arrange here to meet a guide at the entrance to the **Catacombs of Santa Mustiola**, 2km east of town, which were used by early Christians in the fourth and fifth centuries (tours daily 5pm; April–Sept also 11am; L6000/€3.10).

The helpful **tourist office** (April–Sept Mon–Sat 9am–1pm & 3.30–7.30pm, Sun 9am–1pm; Oct–March daily 9am–1pm; ☎0578.227.667) is opposite the duomo. There's one central **hotel**, the basic *La Sfinge*, Via Marconi 2 (☎0578.20.157, fax 0578.222.153; ②), with more options at Chiusi Scalo. The best **restaurant** is friendly *La Solita Zuppa*, Via Porsenna 21 (☎0578.21.006; closed Tues), with an inventive menu offering lots of soups and items such as *tagliolini al ginger*. The gourmet-oriented *Zaira*, nearby at Via Arunte 12 (☎0578.20.260; closed Mon in winter), is listed in various gastronomic guides for its pricey "Etruscan" fare – boar, pigeon and the like.

Pienza and around

PIENZA, 11km west of Montepulciano, is as complete a Renaissance creation as any in Italy, established in an act of considerable vanity by **Pope Pius II** as a Utopian "New Town". The transformation of the village of Cortignano, where Pius was born, began in 1459 under the architect **Bernardo Rossellino**. The cost was astronomical, but the cathedral, papal and bishop's palaces, and the core of a town (renamed in Pius's honour) were completed in just three years. Pius lived just two more years, and of his successors only his nephew paid Pienza any regard: the city, intended to spread across the hill, stayed village-sized. Today, with a population of 2500, it still has an air of emptiness and folly – a natural stage set, where Zeffirelli filmed *Romeo and Juliet*.

Traffic converges on **Piazza Dante**, just outside the main gate, Porta al Murello, and from here the **Corso** leads straight to Rossellino's centrepiece, **Piazza Pio II**, which deliberately juxtaposes civic and religious buildings – the Duomo, Palazzo Piccolomini (papal palace), Bishop's Palace and Palazzo Pubblico – to underline the balance between Church and Town. The square makes the usual medieval nod to Florence in its town hall, but it is otherwise entirely Renaissance in conception.

The **Duomo** (daily 8am–1pm & 2.30–7.30pm) has one of the earliest Renaissance facades in Tuscany; the interior, on Pius's orders, took inspiration from the German hall-churches he had seen on his travels, and remains essentially Gothic. The chapels house an outstanding series of Sienese altarpieces, commissioned from the major painters of the age – Giovanni di Paolo, Matteo di Giovanni, Vecchietta and Sano di Pietro. How long the building itself will remain standing is uncertain. Even before completion a crack appeared, and after an earthquake last century it has required much buttressing – the nave currently dips crazily towards the back of the church. The airy crypt, with a separate entrance (Mon, Tues & Thurs–Sat 10am–noon & 3.30–5.30pm; L1500/€0.77), displays some sixteenth-century tapestries. Pius's residence, the **Palazzo Piccolomini**, is alongside the duomo. You're free to walk into the courtyard

---

HIKES IN THE PARCO DELLA VAL D'ORCIA

There are plenty of interesting **hikes** in the area around San Quírico and Montalcino comprising the **Parco della Val d'Órcia**, full details of which are in *Walking the Val d'Orcia*, an English pamphlet by the Touring Club Italiano, available at the park office, Via Dante Alighieri 33 in San Quírico (☎0577.898.303, *www.parcodellavaldorcia.it*).

A moderately challenging trail runs from **Bagno Vignoni** out to the castle restaurant at Ripa d'Orcia and back (12km; 4hr). From 100m before the car-park, a cart-track rises through vineyards and olive groves to Rocca di Vignoni, the hamlet of Vignoni and on to Podere Bellaria, after which is a junction. One route heads right (north) to San Quírico, the other left (south) through a scenic landscape up to the castle. Backtracking 500m down the castle hill you'll find a signposted path leading right, down through foliage to a broken bridge over the Orcia river; don't cross, but follow the left-hand riverbank back to Bagno Vignoni.

There's an easy trail from **Montalcino** to San Quírico, crossing shadeless clay hills and dipping through vineyards (13km; 4hr), or you could cycle it, with rental bikes from *Lorenzo Minocci*, Viale Strozzi in Montalcino (☎0577.848.282). From the northern Porta Burelli, a track drops down to Gli Angeli and crosses the paved road in front of Podere La Casaccia, heading into an area of hummocks until you reach the provincial highway. Follow the road right for a few hundred metres, coming off at Podere Fiesole and heading east across clay ground to Podere Casello and Poderi Pian dell'Asso. Cross the train track and a couple of streams before climbing to Podere Belladonna and the chapel of Madonna di Riguardo. A rising and falling path covers the last 1.5km into San Quírico.

---

and through to the original "hanging garden" behind to the left, with a triple-tiered loggia offering a superb view over the valley. The **apartments** above (Tues–Sun: summer 10am–12.30pm & 4–7pm; winter 10am–12.30pm & 3–6pm; L5000/€2.58) include Pius II's bedroom, library and other rooms filled with collections of weapons and medals. Further mementos of the pope – notably his English-made embroidered cope – are across the piazza in the excellent **Museo Diocesano** (summer Mon & Wed–Sun 10am–1pm & 2–6.30pm; winter Sat & Sun 10am–1pm & 3–6pm; L8000/€4.13).

Practicalities

Regular **buses** between Montepulciano and Buonconvento pass through Pienza and San Quírico d'Órcia. Pienza is also a gentle day's **walk** from Montepulciano on an old cross-country route through the walled village of Monticchiello. The **tourist office** (daily 9am–1.30pm & 3–7.30pm; ☎0578.749.071, *www.chianciano.turismo.toscana.it*) is in Piazza Pio II opposite the duomo and offers a self-guided 50min Walkman tour of the town (L10,000/€5.16). Pienza has pleasant self-catering **apartments** at *Giardino Segreto*, Via Condotti 13 (☎0578.60.452, *mucci@ftbcc.it*; ③), and the fabulously romantic **hotel** *Chiostro di Pienza*, a converted Franciscan monastery at Corso Rossellino 26 (☎0578.748.400, fax 0578.748.440; ⑦). Its **restaurant** (closed Mon), with expansive terrace views, is the best in Pienza, but pricier than most. The *Falco*, a simple trattoria in Piazza Dante (closed Fri), and friendly *Latte di Luna*, just inside the walls at Via San Carlo 2 (closed Tues) are more affordable. You can get beers and *crostini* at *Sperone Nudo*, Via Marconi 5 (closed Mon), and there's plenty of **picnic food**: Pienza is centre of a region producing *pecorino* sheep's cheese, and has gone overboard on natural food shops.

San Quírico d'Orcia and Bagno Vignoni

SAN QUÍRICO D'ORCIA, a rambling old village, stands at a crossroads 8km west of Pienza. Despite being a major stop for TRA-IN (Siena–Montepulciano), RAMA

(Siena–Arcidosso) and SIRA (Montalcino–Rome) buses, its old town is quiet and rather decayed, with an exceptionally pretty Romanesque **Collegiata** church. With your own transport, head for the stunning *Castello Ripa d'Órcia*, an isolated castle **hotel-restaurant** 5km southwest of town down a gravel road (☎0577.897.376, fax 0577.898.038, *info@castelloripadorcia.com*; ⑨).

You can **rent bikes** from Valenti Alfiero, Via delle Madonnina 28 in Pienza (☎0578.748.465) to follow a country track south to the medieval baths at **BAGNO VIGNONI**, 6km southeast of San Quírico (also served by bus). Its central square is occupied by an arcaded Roman *piscina*, or open pool; the springs still bubble up at a steamy 51°C, and the old, flooded piazza with its backdrop of the Tuscan hills and Renaissance **loggia** – built by the Medici, who, like St Catherine of Siena, took the sulphur cure here – made a memorable scene in Tarkovsky's film *Nostalgia*. The *piscina* has been out of bounds for bathing for some years, but you can bathe in the sulphur springs at the characterful *Posta Marcucci* **hotel** just below the village (☎0577.887.112, fax 0577.887.119, *www.hotelpostamarcucci.it*; ⑥; pool free to guests, L12,000/€6.20 to others). Pius II's fifteenth-century summer retreat overlooking the *piscina* is now the romantic *Albergo Le Terme* (☎0577.887.150, fax 0577.877.497, *albergoleterme@tin.it*; ④). Best **restaurant** is the excellent *Antica Osteria del Leone*, Via dei Mulini 3 (☎0577.877.300; closed Mon).

Montalcino

MONTALCINO is another classic Tuscan hill-town, 20km west of Pienza. Set within a full circuit of walls and watched over by a *rocca*, it looks tremendous from below – and from above, the surrounding countryside strewn with vineyards, orchards and olive groves is equally impressive. Montalcino produces a top-notch DOCG **wine**, Brunello di Montalcino, reckoned by many to be the finest in Italy, and is a quiet place, affluent in an unshowy way from its tourist trade. For a time in the fifteenth century, though, the town was of great symbolic importance: it was the last of the Sienese *comune* to hold out against the Medici, the French and the Spanish after Siena itself had capitulated. This role is acknowledged at the Siena Palio, where the Montalcino contingent – under its medieval banner proclaiming "The Republic of Siena in Montalcino" – takes pride of place.

The main street, Via Mazzini, leads from **Piazza Cavour** at the north end of town to the **Piazza del Popolo**, an odd little square set beneath the elongated tower of the town hall, based in all but its dimensions on that of Siena. An elegant double loggia occupies another side with, opposite, a wonderful and rather Germanic nineteenth-century café, the *Fiaschetteria Italiana*, that is very much the heart of town life. Steps beside the café lead up to the excellent **Museo Civico e Diocesano** (Tues–Sun: April–Oct 10am–6pm; Nov–March 10am–1pm & 2–6pm; Jan–March closes 5pm; L8000/€4.13; joint ticket including Rocca ramparts L10,000/€5.16). The quality of the art on show is out of all proportion to the size of the town, and takes in a wealth of Sienese painting and early sculpture. Following Via Ricasoli south brings you to the **Rocca** fortress (daily 9am–7.30pm; winter closes 6pm). Impressively complete, this encloses a public park and plush *enoteca*. You can also get access to the ramparts from here (L4000/€2.06, or joint ticket from Museo Civico L10,000/€5.16).

Regular buses arrive from Buonconvento and Siena, most of which pass first through **Torrenieri**, from where connections head to Pienza and Montepulciano, and to Arcidosso and Abbadia San Salvatore. Montalcino's bus stop is at the north end of town in Piazza Cavour. The tiny Pro Loco **tourist office** is near the Piazza del Popolo at Costa del Municipio 8 (Tues–Sun: May–Sept 10am–1pm & 2–5.45pm; Oct–April 10am–1pm & 3–5pm; ☎0577.849.331, *www.digitamiata.com/promontalcino*). **Hotels** are uninspiring, with the *Giardino*, Via Cavour 2 (☎ & fax 0577.848.257; ③) prone to street noise; and the *Giglio*, Via Saloni 49 (☎ & fax 0577.848.167; ③), generically renovated. **Private rooms** are a better bet: try *Locatelli Maria Pia*, Via Spagni 3 (☎0577.847.150; ②). The best **restaurant** is *Cucina di Edgardo*, Via Saloni 21 (☎0577.848.232; closed Wed), swanky and a tad pretentious; *Grappolo Blu*, on Via Scale di Moglio off Via Mazzini (☎0577.847.150; closed Fri), is more down-to-earth. Best pizza in town is at *San Giorgio* on Via Saloni (closed Mon), while *La Griglieria del Corso*, Via Matteotti 19 (closed Mon) has a chill cabinet full of salads and meats to eat in or take out, plus wood-fired pizzas and fresh pasta. *Circolo Arci* is a pleasant **bar-café** in an arcaded courtyard opposite the Museo Civico.

Monte Amiata

At 1738m, the extinct volcano of **Monte Amiata** is the highest point in southern Tuscany. Rising from the comparative desolation of the *crete* in a succession of hills forested in chestnut and fir, it is visible for miles around. A circle of towns rings its lower slopes, but the only one worth visiting for its own sake is **Abbadia San Salvatore**; nonetheless, old castles and bucolic countryside makes the area a good detour. Towns such as Abbadia and, on the western slope, **Arcidosso**, are refreshingly cool for summer walking, and in winter are the nearest ski resorts to Rome. **Buses** serve Abbadia San Salvatore from Siena, Buonconvento, Chiusi and Montepulciano; those from Rome and Grosseto to Abbadia pass first through Arcidosso. Avoid the Monte Amiata **train** station – it's 45km away.

The centre of activity is **ABBADIA SAN SALVATORE**, which shelters at its heart a perfect, self-contained medieval quarter. The Benedictine **abbey**, around which the village developed, was founded under the Lombards and rebuilt in 1036. Today a mere fraction remains of the original, and most remnants date from the Middle Ages; the highlight is a large and beautiful eighth-century **crypt**, its 35 columns decorated with Lombard motifs. The town sees plenty of summer visitors, up here for the landscape, cool breezes and some good easy walks: best is the **Anello della Montagna**, a 29km path which circles the mountain between 900m and 1300m – a long day's walk, or easily manageable in sections round to Arcidosso. In July and August, buses shuttle up to the **summit**, offering a panorama that stretches to the sea. The **tourist office**, Via Adua 25 (Mon–Sat 9am–1pm & 4–6pm; ☎0577.775.811, *info@amiata.turismo.toscana.it*) is headquarters for the Amiata region. Best of the numerous **hotels** are the *Cesaretti*, Via Trento 37 (☎0577.778.198; ①), and the central *San Marco*, Via Matteotti 13 (☎ & fax 0577.778.089; ③).

ARCIDOSSO is another summer walking centre, with prosperous new development surrounding a well-preserved medieval quarter. Six buses daily connect to Abbadia. The *Gatto d'Oro* is a modern **hotel** on Via dei Venti (☎ & fax 0564.967.074; ③), and there's a small **tourist office** at Via Ricasoli 1 (☎ & fax 0564.966.083). Good **walks** include a ramble to to the village of Montelaterone, 3km northwest, passing the Romanesque **Abbadia Santa Maria ad Lamulas**. More demanding is the hike up **Monte Labbro** (1193m) 10km south (also accessible by dirt road), which has, on its summit, the ruins of a church established by Davide Lazzaretti, founder of the Jurisdavidical Church, a Christian movement which campaigned for social reform in the turbulent 1870s. Lazzaretti was murdered by the Carabinieri in 1878, and is still remembered by locals.

Pitigliano and around

Tuscany's deep south, on the Lazio border, is its least-touristed corner. **PITIGLIANO**, the largest town of the area, is best approached along the road from Manciano, 15km west. As you draw close, the town soars above you on a spectacular outcrop of tufa, its quarters linked by the arches of an immense aqueduct. **Etruscan** tombs honeycomb the cliffs, but the town was known for centuries for its flourishing **Jewish** community (see box below). It has today a slightly grim grandeur, due to its mighty **fortress** and the tall and largely unaltered alleys of the old Jewish ghetto.

Immediately through the main city gate is **Piazza Garibaldi**, flanked by the fortress and aqueduct (1543) and with views across of houses wedged against the cliffside. Within the fortress is the Renaissance **Palazzo Orsini** (Tues–Sun 10am–1pm & 3–7pm; winter closes 5pm; L5000/€2.58), its lovely interiors filled with jewellery and ecclesiastical ephemera; also in the fortress is the **Museo Civico** (same hours; L5000/€2.58), with an interesting collection of Etruscan vases and trinkets. The fortress backs onto **Piazza della Repubblica**, Pitigliano's elongated main square. Beyond lies the old town proper, a tight huddle of arches and medieval alleys. The left fork, Via Zuccarelli, brings you to Vicolo Manin and the **synagogue** and attached **Mostra Ebraico** (Jewish Exhibition; Mon–Thurs, Fri 10am–noon, Sun 10am–noon & 3–5pm; donations). Pitigliano's eighteenth-century synagogue part-collapsed in the 1960s, and lay derelict until renovation in 1995. The grand stone arch, and the stairs leading up to the women's gallery are the only survivors of the old building, along with plaques commemorating visits made by grand dukes Ferdinand III in 1823 and Leopold II in 1829. Although the Jewish community is virtually gone (see box below), Florentine, Livornese and even American couples still choose to tie the knot here. Staff are happy to show you around the old ghetto, which includes a **bakery** on Via Marghera with a Star of David in its barred window. A few minutes' walk beyond, at the western end of town, you can see traces of the **Etruscan wall** below the Porta Capisotto.

Three RAMA **buses** daily from Manciano and Grosseto, three from Orbetello and one from Siena drop off on **Piazza Pettruccioli** just outside the city gate. The tiny **tourist office** at Via Roma 11 (June–Oct Tues–Sun 10am–1pm & 3–6pm) has maps of the *Vie Cave*, ancient Etruscan paths that weave between tombs and cliffside caves all around the town. With its untouristed lanes and the drama of its cliff-edge site, Pitigliano makes a memorable overnight stop. The only **hotel** is *Guastini*, Piazza Petruccioli 4 (☎0564.616.065, fax 0564.616.652, *www.laltramaremma.it*; ②), with a good

---

THE JEWS OF PITIGLIANO

Jews began moving to Pitigliano from Rome in the thirteenth century. The community flourished until the annexation of the area by the Medici in 1608, when new laws forced the Jews to live in a **ghetto** and wear red clothing as a mark of identification. The granting of **religious freedom** throughout Tuscany by the last Medici ruler, Gian Gastone, in 1735, gave the town a new lease of life. Over the next 125 years, Jewish workshops and artisans on present-day **Via Zuccarelli** thrived, and there was even a Jewish university that attracted students from around Europe. By 1860, a third of the town, or some 2200 people, were Jewish.

It was Italian **Unification**, not the Holocaust, which brought about the end. In the new Italy, individuals felt freer than before to marry across religious lines, and the removal of a Catholic Papal State in central Italy gave Jews a new freedom to travel; many headed to the southern ports to take ship for Palestine. By 1900, there were barely a hundred Jews left in Pitigliano. With the surrender of Italian forces in 1943, the town's Jews were forced into **hiding**, and virtually all were protected from the Nazis by local Christian families. But by 1945 most felt unable to stay on, and departed for Rome, Livorno and Florence (all of which have large Jewish communities). Pitigliano's **synagogue** closed in the late 1950s, and today, in what was formerly one of the centres of Jewish learning in southern Europe, there are just three Jewish residents left.

restaurant; also check out the award-winning mid-priced *Osteria Il Tufo Allegro*, Vicolo della Costituzione 1 (closed Tues).

Terme di Saturnia

SATURNIA, 23km northwest of Pitigliano, is renowned for its sulphurous **hot springs**. Plenty of buses run from Pitigliano west through Manciano to Orbetello on the coast (see p.532), and there are three daily **buses** north along the minor road from Manciano to Saturnia (8am, 2pm & 6pm). Be sure to get off at the springs (*Le Terme*) and not at Saturnia village. The last return bus is at 1pm, but it shouldn't be too hard to hitch back. The large **spa complex**, with fierce admission charges, a vast pool and a five-star hotel (*www.termedisaturnia.it*) is 6km north of the village of Montemerano; some 200m before it (as the road takes a sharp curve) follow a dirt track off to the right, unsignposted but usually signalled by a cluster of cars and vans. Two minutes' walk from here brings you to the **cascatelle**, sulphur springs that burst from the ground, forming natural rock-pool jacuzzis of warm, turquoise water, in which you can lie around for hours submerged up to your neck. Entrance is unrestricted and free, but you'll need a shower to wash off the sulphur smell, which can linger for days. The nearest **hotel** is the excellent *Albergo-Ristorante Stellata* (☎0564.602.978; ⑤), in an isolated spot 1km down from the falls on the road to Manciano, while the **campsite** *Poggio alle Querce* (☎0564.602.568) is at Montemerano.

EASTERN TUSCANY

The Valdarno, or Arno Valley, upstream from Florence is a solidly industrialized district; there's no compelling stop before you reach the provincial capital, **Arezzo**, visited by foreigners in their thousands for its Piero della Francesca frescoes, and by Italians in even greater numbers for its antique trade. South of Arezzo is the ancient hill-town of **Cortona**, whose picturesquely steep streets and sense of hilltop isolation make it an irresistible place to stopover.

Arezzo

AREZZO, 65km southeast of Florence, has a charming old quarter, unspoilt enough to catch the eye a few years back of local folk-hero and deliberate clown of Italian cinema **Roberto Benigni**. Many key scenes in his Oscar-winning *La Vita è Bella* (Life Is Beautiful) were filmed in Arezzo, and strolling on its quiet streets is like a breath of fresh air after days spent doing battle with Florence's big-city grind.

Arezzo was a major Etruscan and Roman city, and was a prosperous independent republic in the Middle Ages, until, in 1289, its Ghibelline loyalties precipitated military defeat at the hands of Guelph Florentines. In the arts, Petrarch, Pietro Aretino and Vasari, all native Aretines, brought lasting prestige to the city, yet it was an outsider who gave Arezzo its permanent Renaissance monument – **Piero della Francesca**, whose extraordinary **frescoes** belong in the same company with Masaccio's in Florence and Michelangelo's in Rome. Today, the local economy relies on innumerable jewellers and goldsmiths (the city has the world's largest gold manufacturing plant) and on the **antiques** trade: Piazza Grande has showrooms filled with the sort of furniture you put in a bank vault rather than in your living room and once a month – on the first Sunday and the Saturday preceding it – a vast **Fiera Antiquaria** (see *www.comune.arezzo.it*) occupies the square. The array of some 600 stalls is fun to browse though, but don't expect any bargains, even among the more junk-laden stalls on the fringes.

Arrival, information and accommodation

Arezzo is a major stop for **trains** between Florence and Rome, and is also served by a branch line from Perugia. **Buses** from Siena and elsewhere arrive diagonally opposite the train station. There are two distinct parts to Arezzo: the **old town**, on the higher parts of the hill, and the newer quarters which occupy the gentler slopes directly in front of the train station.

The **tourist office** is beside the train station, at Piazza della Repubblica 28 (April–Sept Mon–Sat 9am–1pm & 3–7pm, Sun 9am–1pm; Oct–March Mon–Sat 9am–1pm & 3–6.30pm; on Fiera weekends year-round Sat 9am–6pm & Sun 9am–1pm; ☎0575.377.678, *www.arezzo.turismo.toscana.it*). Informative **walking tours** are run by AAAGIT (Arezzo Associazione Accompagnatori Guide e Interpreti Turistici), daily in summer at 10am (L15,000/€7.75) and 9pm (L20,000/€10.33; min 4 people) starting from their office at Via Vasari 13 just off Piazza Grande (office open Mon–Sat 9.30am–12.30pm; on Fiera weekends Sat & Sun 9.30am–6pm; ☎0575.356.859).

Accommodation is hard to come by – doubly so when the Fiera is on. The best **hotel** is the *Cavaliere Palace*, Via Madonna del Prato 83 (☎0575.26.836, fax 0575.21.925, *www.cavalierehotels.com*; ⑤), centrally situated but rather run-of-the-mill. *La Toscana*,

Via Marco Perennio 56 (☎0575.21.692; ②), is a quality one-star with and without en suite rooms; failing that, plump for good-value *Astoria*, Via Guido Monaco 54 (☎0575.24.361, fax 0575.24.362; ②). The non-HI **hostel** *Villa Severi* is 1km east of the old town at Via Francesco Redi 13 (☎0575.299.047; L28,000/€14.46; meals L17,000/€8.78).

The Basilica di San Francesco

In the heart of the old town, off to the left of the main Corso Italia and not far from its summit, stands the church of **San Francesco**, home to Piero della Francesca's celebrated **fresco** cycle in the choir (which has now been walled off and renamed the Cappella Bacci; see below). After centuries of damp and neglect, and some poor restoration early in the twentieth century that did more harm than good, work began in 1985 to consolidate and restore the badly damaged frescoes. On April 7, 2000 – fifteen years and ten billion lire later – the brilliantly coloured frescoes were revealed in full, with details visible that had been obscured by dust and grime for centuries. They are worth as much time as you can give them.

You can visit the church during normal hours (Mon–Fri 9am–noon & 2–7pm, Sat 9am–6.15pm, Sun 1–6.15pm; Nov–March Sat & Sun closes 5.45pm), but to get access to the chapel holding the frescoes, and to see them close-up, you have to **book in advance** on ☎0575.900.404, since only 25 people are allowed in at any one time – on slow weekday mornings you might walk straight in, but during Arezzo's hectic monthly Fiera you're likely to find the chapel booked solid. The **ticket office** is in the bookshop a few doors to the right of the church (daily 8.30am–7.30pm; *www. pierodellafrancesca.it*); **admission** to the church is free, but to the frescoed chapel is L10,000/€5.16, which includes an excellent audio-guide.

Built after 1322, the plain basilica earned its renown in the early 1450s, when the local Bacci family commissioned **Piero della Francesca** to continue the decoration of the choir. The theme chosen was **The Legend of the True Cross**, a story in which the wood of the Cross forms the link in the cycle of redemption that begins with humanity's original sin. Piero painted the series in narrative sequence, working continuously until about 1457. However, he preferred to arrange them according to the precepts of symmetry: the two battle scenes, for example, face each other across the chapel, rather than coming where the story dictates. As is always the case with this mystical painter, smaller-scale symmetries are present in every part of the work: the retinue of the Queen of Sheba (middle right wall) appears twice, in mirror-image arrangement, and the face of the queen is the same as that of the Empress Helena (middle left wall). This orderliness, combined with the pale light and the statuesque quality of the figures, create an atmosphere of spirituality that is unique to Piero, a sense of each incident as a part of a greater plan.

The fresco cycle

The complex story begins with the **Death of Adam** (top right wall), when a sprig from the Tree of Knowledge is planted in Adam's mouth. Below (to the left), **Solomon** orders a bridge to be built from wood taken from the tree that grew from Adam's grave. The visiting **Queen of Sheba** kneels, sensing the holiness of the wood, and then later (to the right) tells Solomon of her prophecy that the same wood will be used to crucify a man. Solomon then orders the beam to be buried (back wall, middle right).

The two most striking scenes have benefited hugely from cleaning. With the encrustation of dirt over the centuries, the **Dream of Constantine** (back wall, lower right) was always thought to be a night scene, but restoration has shown it in fact to depict early morning. As the angel descends to the tent of the sleeping emperor, bringing a vision of victory under the sign of the Cross, dawn is breaking behind the mountains to banish the constellation of Ursa Minor. Constantine's stolid guards keep watch, waiting, stiff with cold, for sunrise. Alongside, the **Victory of Constantine** (lower right wall), shows the emperor's defeat of his rival Maxentius, and his later baptism; part of the wall is damaged, but the sky is suffused with what the critic Sir Kenneth Clark has called "the most perfect morning light in all Renaissance painting".

Under torture, **Judas the Levite** (back wall, middle left) reveals to St Helena, mother of Constantine, the burial places of the three crosses from Golgotha, and then the three are excavated (middle left wall); the **True Cross** is recognized when it brings about a man's resurrection. Arezzo appears as Jerusalem in the top left. Then the Persian king Chosroes, who had stolen the Cross, is defeated by Emperor **Heraclius** (lower left wall); on the right he kneels awaiting execution. Heraclius returns the Cross to Jerusalem (upper left wall).

The rest of the town

Piero della Francesca's frescoes are the main reason to visit Arezzo, but the town's other highlights fit nicely into a pleasant afternoon stroll through the hilly lanes. Further up the Corso northeast of San Francesco you'll come to the steeply sloping **Piazza Grande**, which may look familiar from the film *La Vita è Bella*. The grand, imposing piazza is bordered on the east side by wooden balconied apartments and on the west by the apse of Santa Maria (see below) and the tiered facade of the **Palazzetto della Fraternità dei Laici**, with a Gothic ground floor and fifteenth-century upper storeys. The northern side is formed by the beautiful **Loggia di Vasari**, designed by Giorgio Vasari, court architect to the Medici, in the sixteenth century. Backing onto the square is the twelfth-century **Pieve di Santa Maria** (daily 8am–6pm) with its unmistakeable fourteenth-century campanile, known locally as "the tower of the hundred holes" for its many double-arched windows. The arcaded facade, elaborate yet severe, belongs to a Romanesque type associated more with Pisa and western Tuscany, and the church is doubly unusual in presenting its front to a narrow street rather than to the town's main square. The carvings of the months over the portal are a perfect Romanesque group, dating from the 1210s; in the tranquil interior, the raised sanctuary – the oldest section of the church – supports Pietro Lorenzetti's *Madonna and Saints* polyptych, painted in 1320 and restored rather nastily.

At the highest point of town looms the large and unfussy **Duomo** (daily 7am–12.30pm & 3–7pm), its harmonious appearance belying its history. Begun in the late thirteenth century, it was virtually finished by the sixteenth, but the campanile comes from the nineteenth and the facade from the twentieth. The stained-glass windows, made by Guillaume de Marcillat around 1520, let in so little light that his other contributions to the interior – the paintings on the first three bays of the nave – are virtually invisible. The tiny fresco nestled against the right side of the tomb is **Piero della Francesca**'s *Maddalena*, his only work in the town outside San Francesco.

A short distance west of the duomo is the thirteenth-century church of **San Domenico** (daily 8am–1pm & 3.30–7pm). The high altar has a *Crucifix* painted by a twenty-year-old **Cimabue** in 1260, and there are tatters of frescoes all round the walls. Signs point the way to the nearby **Casa Vasari**, Via XX Settembre 55 (Mon & Wed–Sat 8.30am–7.30pm, Sun 8.30am–12.30pm; free), designed in lurid style by the celebrated biographer-architect-painter for himself. Down the slope, at Via San Lorentino 8, the fifteenth-century Palazzo Bruni-Ciocchi houses the **Museo Statale d'Arte Medievale e Moderna** (Tues–Sun 8.30am–7.30pm; July–Sept Sat until 11pm; L8000/€4.13), with a collection of paintings by local artists and majolica work dating from the thirteenth to the eighteenth centuries.

All the principal sights are in the upper part of town, with the exception of the **Museo Archeologico** (daily 8.30am–7.30pm; L8000/€4.13), which occupies part of a monastery built into the wall of the town's Roman amphitheatre, to the right of the station at Via Margaritone 10. Most impressive are the marvellously coloured coralline vases produced here in the first century BC – their skill and artistry demonstrate how the Aretines achieved a reputation throughout the Roman world as consummate craftspeople.

Eating and drinking

An unmissable stop-off is the town's oldest **café** – *Caffè dei Costanti* on Piazza San Francesco (closed Mon). The high interior of the place drips character, from its long stone counter to its genteel *Sala de Tè* at the back. *Il Gelato* is another fine gelateria at Via dei Cenci 24, and *Pasticceria Carraturo*, Corso Italia 61 (closed Tues), is a nineteenth-century tearoom with a diner-style restaurant upstairs.

Arezzo's **restaurants** more than atone for its dull hotels. *Fiaschetteria de' Redi*, Via de' Redi 10 (☎0575.355.012; closed Mon) is a gloomy old stone-floored wine-bar-cum-osteria. Cosy *Antica Osteria L'Agania*, Via Mazzini 10 (☎0575.295.381; closed Mon) has rustic-style food, as does *Il Saraceno*, Via Mazzini 6a (☎0575.27.644, *www.ilsaraceno.com*; closed Wed). *La Buca di San Francesco*, alongside San Francesco church (☎0575.23.271, *space.tin.it/cucina/fmdef*, closed Mon eve & Tues), is a pricier spot for Tuscan cooking. *Ristorante Logge Vasari* is under the arches overlooking Piazza Grande (☎0575.25.894; closed Wed), the best place in town for a memorable meal-with-a-view.

Listings

Bus information Atam runs city buses, and some out-of-town routes. Its office "Atam Point", the building with the curving roof in the station forecourt (Mon–Sat 6.45am–7.40pm; ☎0575.382.651), sells tickets and has timetables for all bus companies.

Hospital Ospedale San Donato, Via De Gasperi (☎0575.3051).

Internet access Global Service Phone Center, Piazza Guido Monaco 8 (daily 9am–1pm & 3–8.30pm).

Parking There's free parking in the new town on Via Mecenate and Via XX Aprile, and at the top of the old town on Via Pietri, outside the northern walls.

Police Carabinieri ☎112; Polizia ☎113; local police ☎0575.906.667.

Post office Via Guido Monaco 34.

Taxis Radio-Taxi ☎0575.382.626.

Train information ☎1478.88.088.

Cortona

Travelling south from Arezzo you enter the **Valdichiana**, reclaimed swampland that is now prosperous cattle country, producing the much-prized Florentine *bistecca*. From the valley floor a long road winds up through terraces of vines and olives to the hill-town of **CORTONA**, 20km south of Arezzo, from whose heights you can see Lago Trasimeno. A scattering of Etruscan tombs aside, the steep streets are dominated by medieval architecture that claws its way around a knife-edge ridge, with barely a patch of level ground anywhere. Traffic is restricted, which accentuates the sense of hilltop isolation – although the quantity of summer visitors can diminish the atmosphere. Even without its art treasures, Cortona would be a good place to rest up, with pleasant hotels, excellent restaurants, and an amazing view at night of the villages of southern Tuscany glittering in the distance.

The main arrival point for buses and cars is **Piazza Garibaldi**, from where the only level street in town, Via Nazionale, connects to **Piazza della Repubblica**, which is overlooked by the grandstand staircase of the squat Palazzo del Comune. Just behind is **Piazza Signorelli**, named after Luca Signorelli (1441–1523), Cortona's most famous son, and site of the **Museo dell'Accademia Etrusca** (Tues–Sun: April–Sept 10am–7pm; Oct–March 10am–5pm; L8000/€4.13; *www.accademia-etrusca.net*), where an enormous hall contains cabinets of prized Etruscan stuff, surrounded by second-rate paintings. The major exhibit – honoured with its own bijou temple – is an Etruscan bronze lamp from the fifth century BC, its circumference decorated with alternating male and female squatting figures. Elsewhere there are ranks of Etruscan figurines, jewellery and masses of unlabelled domestic odds and ends. The painter Gino Severini (1883–1966), another native of Cortona and an acolyte of the Futurist firebrand Filippo Marinetti, gets a room to himself. With pre-booking (☎0575.630.415), museum experts can guide you around a handful of Etruscan tombs outside town.

Piazza Signorelli links with Piazza Duomo, where the **Duomo** (daily 8am–noon & 3–6.30pm) sits hard up against the city walls, overlooking the precipice. It was raised on the ruins of a pagan temple, but progressive rebuilding work has muffled the original Renaissance construction. It remains a cool and tranquil refuge from the sometimes wearing commercialism of the town centre. To the right of the altar is an illuminated vitrine holding a reliquary said to contain a fragment of the True Cross. Across the little piazza, a couple of churches have been knocked together to form the **Museo Diocesano** (Tues–Sun: April–Sept 9.30am–1pm & 3.30–7pm; Oct–March 10am–1pm & 3–5pm; L8000/€4.13), with a small collection of Renaissance art plus a fine Roman sarcophagus, carved with fighting centaurs.

Climbing from Piazza della Repubblica on Via Santucci and then Via Berrettini brings you into the upper town. A further work by Signorelli can be found in the unassuming church of **San Nicolò**, reached by veering right across Piazza della Pescaia at the far end of Via Berettini, then heading up the stepped Via San Nicolò. Ring the bell on the left-hand side wall, and the caretaker will take you to Signorelli's double-sided altarpiece, revealed by a neat hydraulic system that swivels the picture away from the wall. Signorelli's fresco of the *Madonna, Child and Saints* on the left is reminiscent of his more famous work in Orvieto.

From Piazza della Pescaia, a steep path leads up to **Santa Margherita** (daily 7.30am–noon & 3–7pm), resting place of St Margaret of Cortona, the town's patron saint. The daughter of a local farmer, she spent her long years of widowhood helping the poor and sick of Cortona, founding a hospital that stood close to the site of this church. Her tomb, with marble angels lifting the lid of her sarcophagus, was created in the mid-fourteenth century, and is now mounted on the wall to the left of the chancel, while her remains are on display in a glass coffin directly behind the chancel.

Practicalities

Trains from Arezzo, Florence, Rome and Perugia stop either at Camucia-Cortona station, or at Teróntola; both have buses shuttling into Cortona. Regular LFI **buses** arrive from Arezzo and Chianciano, the latter a transfer point from Montepulciano. All of them stop on **Piazza Garibaldi**, close to the **tourist office** at Via Nazionale 42 (April–Sept Mon–Sat 8am–1pm & 3–7pm, Sun 9am–1pm; Oct–March Mon–Fri 8am–1pm & 3–6pm, Sat 8am–1pm; ☎0575.630.352).

Best **hotel** is the four-star *San Michele*, Via Guelfa 15 (☎0575.604.348, fax 0575.630.147, *www.cortona.net/sanmichele*; ⑥), closely followed by the friendly three-star *Italia*, a restored seventeenth-century mansion with a stunning fifth-floor panoramic terrace, at Via Ghibellina 7 (☎0575.630.254, fax 0575.605.763, *www.emmeti.it*; ④). Downmarket choice is the *Athens*, Via S. Antonio 12 (☎0575.630.508, fax 0575.604.457; ③; June–Sept), often filled by students from the University of Athens, Georgia. Otherwise, there's an excellent, central HI **hostel** *Ostello San Marco*, Via Maffei 57

(☎0575.601.392; mid-March to mid-Oct; L19,000/€9.82); and *Istituto Santa Margherita*, Via Battisti 15 (☎0575.630.336, fax 0575.630.549) with meal-less dorms (L23,000/€11.87) and en suite rooms (②).

Choice of the **restaurants** is *La Loggetta*, overlooking Piazza della Repubblica (☎0575.630.575; closed Mon), where a memorable meal will cost around L50,000/€25.82; check out too the characterful and sometimes boisterous *Tonino* in Piazza Garibaldi (☎0575.630.500; closed Tues). *Grotta di San Francesco*, Piazzetta Baldelli 3 (☎0575.630.271; closed Tues), is less self-conscious than either, almost as good, and less expensive. *Fufluns*, Via Ghibellina 3, prides itself on a long list of pizzas, *focaccia* and cheeseburgers. *Caffè La Saletta*, Via Nazionale 28, has good local wines and inexpensive crepes. US-style *Route 66*, Via Nazionale 78 (closed Mon), churns out food and beers until 3am.

If you're around in late July, check out posters advertising **Umbria Jazz**, which seeps over into Cortona for a concert or two of top-line names. The main annual party is the gutbusting **Sagra della Bistecca** in mid-August, devoted to lauding – and barbecuing – the succulent flesh of the Valdichiana's beef herds.

East of Arezzo

Arezzo is the springboard for the Piero della Francesca art itinerary. Once you've taken in della Francesca's paired portraits of the Duke and Duchess of Urbino in the Uffizi in Florence, and the *Legend of the True Cross* and *Maddalena* in Arezzo, head east into the attractive Valtiberina (Tiber Valley) for more.

MONTERCHI is famous as the home of the *Madonna del Parto*, the only representation of the pregnant Madonna in Renaissance art. The village is off the main SS73 road to Sansepolcro, and is served by four buses daily from Arezzo. Signposts direct you to an ex-primary school on Via della Reglia, the painting's new home (Tues–Sun 9am–1pm & 2–7pm; Oct–March closes 6pm; July & Aug also 9pm–midnight; L5000/€2.58). Della Francesca shows two attendant angels drawing back the flap of a small pavilion to reveal the pregnant Virgin, who places her hand on the upper curve of her belly, her eyes downcast. No other Renaissance artist produced anything comparable to its poise and gravity. Note that the picture is an object of pilgrimage: attendants clear the museum of visitors when local pregnant women come to pray to the Madonna.

SANSEPOLCRO, 25km northeast of Arezzo by regular SITA **buses** (also served by **trains** from Perugia and Città di Castello), makes its living as a manufacturer of lace and Buitoni pasta. Piero della Francesca was born here in the 1410s, and, despite short periods away, he spent much of his life in the town. Sansepolcro's modest, wheelchair-friendly **Museo Civico**, in the centre at Via Aggiunti 65 (daily: June–Sept 9am–1.30pm & 2.30–7.30pm; Oct–May 9.30am–1pm & 2.30–6pm; L10,000/€5.16) houses perhaps della Francesca's greatest painting. The spectral *Resurrection* – originally painted for the adjoining town hall in the 1450s and moved here in the sixteenth century – is an image that has occasioned plenty of exotic prose. Kenneth Clark's description at least has the virtue of being provocative: "This country god, who rises in the grey light while humanity is asleep, has been worshipped ever since man first knew that the seed is not dead in the winter earth, but will force its way upwards through an iron crust." In a more prosaic vein, Aldous Huxley's pronouncement that this is the greatest painting in the world may have saved Sansepolcro from bombing in 1944: before the attack, a British officer recalled Huxley's description and delayed the air-raid. Occupying German forces peacefully withdrew from the town shortly afterwards. Elsewhere in the museum, an earlier della Francesca masterpiece, the *Madonna della Misericordia* polyptych, epitomizes the graceful solemnity of his work. Other pieces that attract attention are a sadistic *Martyrdom of St Quentin* by Pontormo and a painted standard by Luca Signorelli, a student of della Francesca.

Around the town, lesser art treasures are to be found in the **Duomo**, with its tenth-century carved image of the crucified Christ, and in the church of **San Lorenzo**, which has a *Deposition* by Rosso Fiorentino, painted within half-a-century of della Francesca's last works but seeming to belong to another world.

Sansepolcro's little **tourist office** is on Piazza Garibaldi behind the museum (daily: June–Sept 9.30am–1pm & 3.30–6.30pm; Oct–May 10am–noon & 3.30–5.30pm; ☎0575.740.536, *www.sansepolcro.net*). Best **hotel** is the welcoming *Fiorentino*, Via Pacioli 60 (☎0575.740.350, fax 0575.740.370; ③), in business since 1807 and with rooms both en suite and not. It also has a characterful **restaurant** (closed Fri), while *Tirar Tardi*, Via San Antonio 5 (closed Mon), is a convivial *enoteca* which also serves up hearty local cuisine.

North of Arezzo

Once you pull clear of the textile factories on Arezzo's northern fringes, you enter the **Casentino**, a lush agricultural area with high, often walled towns that see few tourists. Thick woodland of oak, beech and pine covers much of the upper slopes, remnants of the forests that used to supply timber to the shipyards of Pisa, Livorno and Genoa. The principal attractions are two tranquil monasteries located way up in the hills, Franciscan **La Verna** and Benedictine **Camáldoli** – though neither is easy to reach without a car, and both require booking for an overnight stay.

Buses from Arezzo are shadowed by the private LFI **train** line, which runs more or less hourly from Arezzo to **BIBBIENA**, the chief town of the Casentino.

St Francis of Assisi established a retreat in 1213 at the mountaintop site of **LA VERNA**, 23km east of Bibbiena on a ridge between the Arno and the Tiber, and it was here eleven years later that he received the stigmata, a badge of sanctity bestowed on nobody before. Now a site of pilgrimage, the rustic monastic village still has the atmosphere of a retreat, and its various churches and chapels hold some of the greatest of **Andrea della Robbia**'s glazed terracotta artworks: a stunning *Annunciation* in the nave of the main church as well as a giant *Crucifixion* in the smaller Cappella delle Stimmate and an altarpiece of the *Assumption* in the Cappella di Santa Maria degli Angeli. A chapel within the basilica holds various relics of St Francis (the habit that Francis was wearing when he received the stigmata is an object of much veneration in Florence's Ognissanti church), and you can also visit various cliffside sites where the saint prayed and meditated. The sanctuary is open to visitors daily from 6am to 8.30pm, though no public transport runs even close, and in midwinter the winding access road is often impassable. Book well in advance to **stay** at the monastery (☎0575.5341, fax 0575.599.320; ①; meals L26,000/€13.42). The minimum stay is generally three days, but one or two days are possible at a relative premium (full board L78,000/€40.28).

CAMÁLDOLI, 18km north of Bibbiena, was where, at the start of the eleventh century, St Romualdo founded a particularly ascetic order of the Benedictines amidst dense woodland. The monks soon attracted pesky pilgrims, and so, to preserve the community's integrity, Romualdo built a second monastery partway down the hillside specifically in order to welcome visitors and to work on maintaining the natural environment – and also to let the monks on the hilltop concentrate on their prayers. The much-rebuilt lower complex has a lovely little church and a sixteenth-century **pharmacy**, which now sells herbal products (closed Wed in winter; *www.camaldoli.com*), and still offers the chance to **stay**: the one-star *La Foresta* (☎ & fax 0575.556.015; ②) has rooms with and without private bathroom, near the more comfortable three-star *Il Rustichello* (☎0575.556.020, fax 0575.556.046; ④). The surrounding forests of pine and fir remain pristine and beautiful, thanks largely to the monks' efforts – they plant around 5000 saplings every year – and an hour's walk up the hill brings you to the original monastic residential quarters, the **Eremo** (Hermitage), with twenty little cottages set in the woods, and an incongruously lavish Baroque church (Mon–Sat 8–11.30am & 3–6pm, Sun 8–10.45am, noon–12.30pm & 3–6pm). The monks live here in complete silence and isolation from each other. Six **buses** a day run to Camáldoli from Bibbiena train station.

travel details

TRAINS

Arezzo to: Assisi (12 daily; 1hr 35min); Bibbiena (every 30min; 50min); Bolzano (5 daily; 7hr 30min); Chiusi (hourly; 1hr); Florence (hourly; 1hr); Foligno (11 daily; 1hr 50min); Orvieto (14 daily; 1hr 20min); Perugia (11 daily; 1hr 15min); Poppi (15 daily; 57min); Rome (hourly; 1hr 40min); Teróntola-Cortona (12 daily; 30min); Trento (5 daily; 7hr 30min); Udine (5 daily; 7hr); Venice (5 daily; 5hr 10min); Verona (5 daily; 7hr).

Empoli to: Florence (every 30min; 25min); Pisa (every 30min; 25min); Siena (every 30min; 50min–1hr 20min).

Florence to: Ancona (hourly; 3hr 30min–6hr); Arezzo (hourly; 1hr); Assisi (11 daily; 2hr 35min); Bari (12 daily; 8hr 15min–9hr); Bologna (every 30min; 1hr–1hr 30min); Bolzano (14 daily; 4hr 10min–5hr 50min); Empoli (every 20min; 25min); Foligno (11 daily; 2hr 55min); Genoa (hourly; 3hr 10min–4hr 30min); Lecce (7 daily; 10hr 25min–12hr); Livorno (12 daily; 1hr 30min); Lucca (hourly; 1hr 5min–1hr 50min); Milan (18 daily; 2hr 50min–4hr 50min); Naples (2 daily; 4hr); Perugia (11 daily; 2hr 10min); Pisa central (every 30min; 55min); Pisa airport (hourly; 1hr); Pistoia (hourly; 30–45min); Prato (every 30min; 20min); Rimini (hourly; 2hr 30min–4hr); Rome (hourly; 2hr 15min–3hr 30min); Rome Fiumicino airport (1 daily; 3hr); Trieste (9 daily; 5hr–6hr 15min); Udine (10 daily; 5hr 20min–6hr); Venice central (hourly; 3hr 25min–4hr 10min); Venice-Mestre (10 daily; 2hr 45min–3hr 20min); Verona (14 daily; 2hr 40min–3hr 40min); Viareggio (hourly; 1hr 30min–2hr 25min).

Grosseto to: Cécina (10 daily; 1hr); Florence (1 daily; 2hr 20min); Livorno (15 daily; 1hr 15min); Orbetello (10 daily; 30min); Pisa (15 daily; 1hr 30min); Rome (10 daily; 1hr 30min); Siena (6 daily; 1hr 20min).

Livorno to: Florence (12 daily; 1hr 30min); La Spezia (5 daily; 1hr 20min); Pisa (every 20min; 15–30min); Rome (every 30min; 3–4hr).

Lucca to: Florence (every 30min; 1hr 5min–1hr 50min); Pisa (every 30min; 30min); Pistoia (every 30min; 45min); Prato (every 30min; 1hr); Viareggio (every 30min; 30min).

Pisa to: Empoli (every 30min; 35min); Florence (hourly; 1hr); Livorno (every 20min; 15min); Lucca (every 30min; 30min); Viareggio (every 30min; 20min).

Pistoia to: Bologna (hourly; 1hr); Florence (every 30min; 30–45min); Lucca (every 30min; 45min); Viareggio (every 30min; 1hr 15min).

Prato to: Bologna (10 daily; 1hr); Florence (every 30min; 20min); Lucca (every 30min; 1hr); Pistoia (every 30min; 15min); Viareggio (every 30min; 1hr 30min).

Siena to: Asciano (12 daily; 35min); Buonconvento (11 daily; 25min); Chiusi (12 daily; 1hr 35min); Empoli (hourly; 50min–1hr 20min); Grosseto (8 daily; 1hr 20min).

BUSES

Arezzo to: Città di Castello (15 daily; 1hr 30min); Cortona (hourly; 1hr); Sansepolcro (17 daily; 1hr).

Chiusi to: Montepulciano (14 daily; 45min).

Cortona to: Arezzo (hourly; 50min); Chianciano (4 daily; 1hr).

Florence to: Castellina in Chianti (3 daily; 1hr 35min); Greve in Chianti (3 daily; 1hr 5min); Poggibonsi (10 daily; 1hr 20min); Poppi (9 daily; 2hr 5min); Radda in Chianti (3 daily; 1hr 40min); Siena (21 daily; 1hr–2hr 30min); Volterra (6 daily; 2hr 25min). In addition to these state-owned SITA services, numerous independent bus companies operate from Florence to most Tuscan towns, including Arezzo, Grosseto, Lucca, Pisa, Pistoia, Prato, Sansepolcro and Viareggio.

Livorno to: Piombino (8 daily; 2hr); Pisa (every 30min; 20min).

Lucca to: Florence (30 daily; 1hr 15min); La Spezia (7 daily; 2hr 20min); Livorno (3 daily; 1hr 20min); Pisa (35 daily; 40min); Pisa airport (3 daily; 1hr 30min); Prato (9 daily; 2hr 15min); Viareggio (30 daily; 40min).

Massa Maríttima to: Piombino (2 daily; 25min); San Galgano (2 daily; 1hr); Siena (2 daily; 1hr 40min).

Montalcino to: Buonconvento (hourly; 35min); Monte Amiata (2 daily; 1hr); Siena (6 daily; 1hr).

Montepulciano to: Buonconvento (7 daily; 1hr); Chianciano (every 30min; 25min); Chiusi (every 30min; 50min); Pienza (7 daily; 20min); San Quirico (7 daily; 40min); Torrenieri (7 daily; 50min).

Pisa to: Florence (hourly; 1hr 10min); La Spezia (7 daily; 1hr 20min); Livorno (every 30min; 20min); Viareggio (hourly; 20min).

San Gimignano to: Poggibonsi (17 daily; 35min).

Siena to: Abbadia San Salvatore (3 daily; 1hr 20min); Arezzo (4 daily; 2hr); Buonconvento (10 daily; 35min); Florence (30 daily; 1hr 30min–3hr); Grosseto (4 daily; 2hr); Massa Maríttima (4 daily; 1hr 40min); Montalcino (6 daily; 1hr); Montepulciano (4 daily; 1hr 20min); San Galgano (3 daily; 40min); San Gimignano (16 daily; 1hr–1hr 30min); Volterra (6 daily; 2hr).

Viareggio to: Pisa (every 30min; 35min).

Volterra to: Florence (4 daily; 2hr); Siena (5 daily; 1hr).

FERRIES

Livorno to: Capraia (1–2 daily; 3hr); Portoferraio (1 daily; 4hr).

Piombino to: Portoferraio (10–18 daily; 1hr).

Porto Santo Stefano to: Giglio Porto (2–8 daily; 1hr).

CHAPTER NINE

UMBRIA

O ften referred to as "the green heart of Italy", **Umbria** is a predominantly beautiful region of rolling hills, woods, streams and valleys, and despite the growing number of visitors has largely retained an unspoilt air. Within its borders it also contains a dozen or so classic hill-towns, each resolutely individual and crammed with artistic and architectural treasures to rival bigger and more famous cities. To the east, pastoral countryside gives way to more rugged scenery, none better than the dramatic twists and turns of the Valnerina and the high mountain scenery of the Parco Nazionale dei Sibellini.

Umbria was named by the Romans after the mysterious **Umbrii**, a tribe cited by Pliny as the oldest in Italy, and one that controlled territory reaching into present-day Tuscany and the Marche. Although there is scant archeological evidence pertaining to them, it is known that their influence was mainly confined to the east of the Tiber; the darker and bleaker towns to the west – such as Perugia and Orvieto – were founded by the **Etruscans**, whose rise forced the Umbrii to retreat into the eastern hills. Roman domination was eventually undermined by the barbarian invasions, in the face of which the Umbrians withdrew into fortified hill-towns, paving the way for a pattern of bloody rivalry between independent city-states that continued through the Middle Ages. Weakened by constant warfare, most towns eventually fell to the papacy, entering a period of economic and cultural stagnation that has continued almost to the present day.

Historically, however, Umbria is best known as the birthplace of several saints, **St Benedict** and **St Francis of Assisi** being the most famous, and for a religious tradition that earned the region such names as *Umbra santa*, *Umbra mistica* and *la terra dei santi* ("land of saints"). The landscape itself has contributed much to this mystical reputation, and even on a fleeting trip it's impossible to miss the strange quality of the Umbrian light, an oddly luminous silver haze that hangs over the gentle curves of the land.

After years as an impoverished backwater, Umbria has begun to capitalize on its charms. Foreign acquisition of rural property is now as rapid as it was in Tuscany twenty years ago, though outsiders have done nothing to curb the region's renewed sense of identity and youthful enthusiasm, nor to blunt the artistic initiatives that have turned

---

ACCOMMODATION PRICE CODES

Throughout this guide, prices per person are given for **youth hostels** and assume Hostelling International (HI) membership. **Hotel** accommodation is coded on a scale from ① to ⑨, reflecting the cost of the cheapest double room in each establishment in high season. The price bands to which these codes refer are as follows:

① Up to L60,000/€30.99
② L60,000–90,000/€30.99–46.48
③ L90,000–120,000/€46.48–61.98
④ L120,000–150,000/€61.98–77.47
⑤ L150,000–200,000/€77.47–103.29

⑥ L200,000–250,000/€103.29–129.11
⑦ L250,000–300,000/€129.11–154.94
⑧ L300,000–400,000/€154.94–206.58
⑨ over L400,000/€206.58

(See p.32 for a full explanation.)

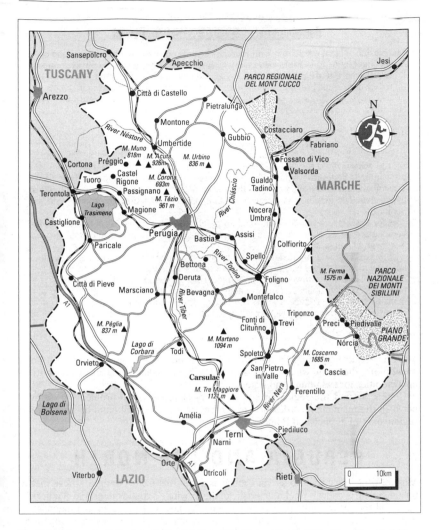

Umbria into one of the most flourishing cultural centres in Italy. Headline-grabbing earthquakes in 1997 briefly dented tourist numbers, but they have had a negligible long-term effect – at least as far as visitors are concerned – as the majority of sights suffered little damage.

Most visitors head for **Perugia, Assisi** – with its extraordinary frescoes by Giotto in the Basilica di San Francesco – or **Orvieto**, where the duomo is one of the greatest Gothic buildings in the country. For a taste of the region's more understated qualities, it's best to concentrate on lesser-known places such as **Todi, Gubbio**, ranked as the most perfect medieval centre in Italy, and **Spoleto**, for many people the outstanding Umbrian town. Although there are few unattractive parts of the Umbrian landscape (the factories of Terni and the Tiber Valley being the largest blots), some districts are

---

REGIONAL FOOD AND WINE

The cuisine of landlocked, hilly Umbria relies heavily on rustic staples – pastas and roast meats – and tends to be simple and homely. But the region is also the only area outside Piemonte where **truffles** are found in any abundance, and their flavourful shavings find their way onto eggs, pasta, fish and meat – at a price that prohibits overindulgence.

Meat plays a leading role – especially **pork**, which is made into hams, sausage, salami and, most famously, into *la porchetta*, whole suckling pig stuffed with rosemary or sage, roasted on a spit and any vegetarian's nightmare. **Game** may also crop up on some menus, most often as pigeon, pheasant or guinea fowl, though it's not unknown to be offered songbirds such as thrush (*tordo*), usually as a paté. The range of **fish** is restricted by the lack of a coast, but trout and crayfish are pulled out of the Nera, Clitunno and Scordo rivers, while the lakes of Piediluco and Trasimeno yield eels, pike, tench and grey mullet. **Vegetable** delicacies include tiny lentils from Castelluccio, beans from Trasimeno, and celery and cardoons from around Trevi. Umbrian **olive oil**, though less hyped than Tuscan oils, has a high reputation, particularly that from around Trevi and Spoleto.

As for desserts, Perugia is renowned for its **chocolate** and pastries. **Cheeses** tend to be standard issue, although some smaller producers survive in the mountains around Norcia and Gubbio.

Umbria is best known outside Italy for fresh, dry white **wines**. Orvieto, once predominantly a medium-sweet wine, has been revived in a dry style, though the original *abboccato* is still available. However, the pre-eminence of Orvieto in the domestic market has been successfully challenged by Grechetto, a cheap and almost unfailingly reliable wine made by countless producers across the region. Umbria's quest for quality is also reflected in the tiny Montefalco DOC region, which produces excellent reds, and around Perugia and Assisi.

---

especially enticing: principally the mountainous **Valnerina**, **Piano Grande** and **Lago Trasimeno**, the last of which is the largest lake in the Italian peninsula, with plenty of opportunities for swimming and watersports.

Getting around the region by public transport presents no problems. Distances between the main sights are short, and there are excellent rail links both within the region and to Florence and Rome.

PERUGIA AND THE NORTH

Most of what you'll want to see in Umbria is accessible from **Perugia**, whose metropolitan bustle is entirely uncharacteristic of the province's rustic hinterland. Trains run out to all the major highlights, complemented by fast new roads and an extensive if complicated bus network. The north is bleaker than much of the region, short on towns and communications but home to **Gubbio**, one of Italy's medieval gems, and **Città di Castello**, less obviously pretty but with a quiet charm and a couple of worthwhile sights, not least a good little picture gallery, as well as tracts of high, wooded countryside. Out to the west is the placid and low-hilled **Lago Trasimeno**, scenically less spectacular but preferable to the dreary Tiber Valley northwards.

Perugia

The provincial capital, **PERUGIA** is the most obvious, if not the most picturesque, base to kick off a tour of Umbria. As usual the centre of town is still medieval, but it's

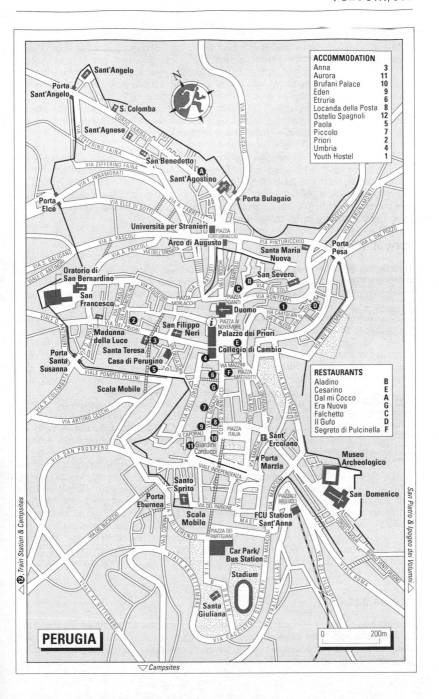

ACCOMMODATION

Anna	3
Aurora	11
Brufani Palace	10
Eden	9
Etruria	6
Locanda della Posta	8
Ostello Spagnoli	12
Paola	5
Piccolo	7
Priori	2
Umbria	4
Youth Hostel	1

RESTAURANTS

Aladino	B
Cesarino	E
Dal mi Cocco	A
Era Nuova	G
Falchetto	C
Il Gufo	D
Segreto di Pulcinella	F

Sant'Angelo
Porta Sant'Angelo
S. Colomba
VIA DEL BULAGAIO
CORSO GARIBALDI
Sant'Agnese
VIA ZEFFERINO FAINA
VIA ZEFFERINO FAINA
San Benedetto
VIA F. INNAMORATI
Sant'Agostino
Porta Elce
VIA ELCE DI SOTTO
VIA A. FABRETTI
Porta Bulagaio
Università per Stranieri
PIAZZA FORTEBRACCIO
VIA A. PASCOLI
Arco di Augusto
VIA PINTURICCHIO
Porta Pesa
VIA A. PASCOLI
VIA DELL'EREMITA
Santa Maria Nuova
VIA E. DAL POZZO
VIA S. GALIGANO
Oratorio di San Bernardino
San Severo
VIA DEL SOLE
San Francesco
PIAZZA MORLACCHI
VIA BONTEMPI
Duomo
PIAZZA DANTI
VIA CARTOLARI
PIAZZA IV NOVEMBRE
San Filippo Neri
Palazzo dei Priori
Madonna della Luce
Santa Teresa
Collegio di Cambio
Casa di Perugino
VIA MAZZINI
Porta Santa Susanna
VIALE POMPEO PELLINI
PIAZZA MATTEOTTI
Scala Mobile
VIA P. COLOMBATA
VIA ARTURO CECCHI
CORSO VANNUCCI
V. CAPORALI
PIAZZA ITALIA
Sant' Ercolano
Giardini Carducci
VIALE INDEPENDENZA
Porta Marzia
Museo Archeologico
Santo Sprito
Porta Eburnea
VIA DEL PARIONE
PIAZZALE BELLUCCI
San Domenico
Scala Mobile
VIA D. LORENZO
FCU Station
Sant'Anna
PIAZZA DEI PARTIGIANI
Car Park/ Bus Station
BORGO VENTIGGIANO
Stadium
VIA DEL FILOSOFI
VIA XX SETTEMBRE
Santa Giuliana
VIA CACCIATORI DELLE ALPI

◁ ⑫ Train Station & Campsites

San Pietro & Ipogeo dei Volumni ▷

▽ Campsites

0   200m

PERUGIA

surrounded by miles of fairly ugly suburbs and not a little industry. Buitoni, the pasta people, have a big works, and Italy's best chocolate, Perugino, is made here. Come summer the streets become claustrophobic and exhausting, so if your idea of Umbria is rural peace and quiet and lolling around old hill-towns – and really that's what the region is about – you probably won't want to spend a lot of time here. On the other hand, there's a day's worth of good sightseeing plus some big-city attractions.

The main draw in the summer is **Umbria Jazz**, Italy's foremost jazz event, whose line-ups may well tempt you into staying – past stars have included Sting, Stan Getz, Gil Evans and Wynton Marsalis. Information and tickets are best sussed out well in advance from the tourist office (see below).

The presence of the **Università Italiana per Stranieri** (the Italian University for Foreigners) is another plus. Set up by Mussolini to improve the image of Italy abroad, it's now run as a private concern and gives the town a welcome dash of style and an unexpectedly cosmopolitan flavour. The big state university also means there's an above-average number of films, concerts and miscellaneous cultural events, which can be somewhat lacking in the rest of the region.

Arrival and information

Arriving on the state train network you'll find yourself to the south-west of the centre at **Piazza Vittorio Veneto**: from here it's a fifteen-minute ride on just about any of the buses that pull up outside the station (bus #6, #7, #9, #11 or #15 – anything to Piazza Italia or Piazza Matteotti will do). City bus tickets (valid for 20, 40 or 70min; L1200/€0.60, L1400/€0.72 and L1700/€0.88 respectively) are available from a small booth over to the left as you exit the station. Don't walk – it's a steep haul on busy roads. If you're coming on the private FCU (Ferrovie Centrale Umbra) lines from Todi or Terni to the south, or from Città di Castello or Sansepolcro to the north, you'll arrive at the much more central **Stazione Sant'Anna**, near the bus terminal at **Piazza dei Partigiani**. From this large square you can jump on a *scala mobile* (escalator) as it wends its way through weird subterranean streets to **Piazza Italia**.

If you're arriving by **car** be prepared for hassle: all the town's approaches are up steep hills and the signposting leaves plenty to be desired. The centre is closed to traffic at peak times, and you'll do best to leave your car at the main train station and take a bus. Alternatively you could head towards one of the big peripheral car parks – Piazza dei Partigiani is the largest and most convenient.

There's a **tourist office** just behind the Palazzo dei Priori in the Sala San Severo at Piazza IV Novembre 3 (Mon–Sat 8.30am–1.30pm & 3.30–6.30pm, Sun 9am–1pm; ☎075.573.6458, *info@iat.perugia.it*). There's also a small summer-only office at the train station (daily 8.30am–1.30pm). Both offices will provide advice on city events and help in finding accommodation. At the station and in Piazza Italia you'll see some Digiplan machines, which supply tourist information on computer print-out – great in theory but almost invariably broken. Check your **email** at *Internet Point*, Via Ulisse Rocchi 4 (Mon–Sat 10am–10pm, Sun 4–8pm; L7000/€3.62 per hr, Happy Hour Mon–Sat 10am–1pm & 8-10pm; L5000/€2.58 per hr; ☎0339.269.1728, *www.internetpointpg.it*) behind the duomo.

Accommodation

Perugia has plenty of **accommodation** in all price ranges, although during termtime long-stay students tend to monopolize the cheapest options. As in most of Umbria's main towns, it's a good idea to book in advance, especially during the Jazz festival in July, when room rates may well be raised.

Hotels

Anna, Via dei Priori 48 (☎ & fax 075.573.6304). Central one-star; rooms come with or without private bath. ②.

Aurora, Viale Indipendenza 21 (☎075.572.4819). Basic, clean and pleasant, though on a busy street. ③.

Brufani Palace, Piazza Italia 12 (☎075.573.2541, fax 075.572.0210, *www.sinahotels.com*). Perugia's smartest and most luxurious option. Very centrally located ⑧.

Eden, Via C. Caporali 9 (☎075.572.8102, fax 075.572.0342). A two-star just west of the Corso; all rooms are en suite. ③.

Etruria, Via della Luna 21 (☎075.572.3730). A one-star in a great position; some rooms have private baths. ②.

Locanda della Posta, Corso Vannucci 97 (☎075.572.8925, fax 075.573.2562). Perugia's first-choice if you want an upmarket treat, not as slick as the *Brufani* but a historic building where the likes of Goethe and Hans Christian Andersen stayed once upon a time. ⑦.

Paola, Via della Canapina 5 (☎075.572.3816). Popular place with nice rooms, all with shared bathrooms. Hard to find – follow signs for the *Umbria* (see below) off the Corso and then bear left. ②.

Piccolo, Via Bonazzi 25 (☎075.572.2987). As central as it gets, 10 rooms with a choice of private or shared bath. ②.

Priori, Via Vermiglioni 3 (☎075.572.3378, fax 075.572.3213). Perguga's first-choice mid-range hotel. Rooms are tastefully fitted out and there's a terrace overlooking the rooftops. The rooms vary greatly so ask to see a selection. ④.

Umbria, Via Boncambi 37 (☎075.572.1203, fax 075.573.7952). Basic, centrally located two-star, some rooms with private bathrooms. ③.

Hostels and camping

The town's original **youth hostel**, two minutes from the duomo, at Via Bontempi 13 (☎075.572.2880, *ostello.perugia.it*; closed 9.30am–4pm; dorm beds L18,000/€9.30), is perfectly situated though its midnight curfew may deter some. The brand-new **Ostello Internazionale per la Gioventù M. L. Spagnoli**, Località Pian di Massiano (☎075. 501/1366, fax 075.502.6805; L25,000/€12.91) is down near the main station and has its own restaurant.

The **campsites** *Il Rocolo*, Strada Fontana 1n (☎ & fax 075.517.8550; 15 June–15 Sept) and *Paradise d'Été*, Via del Mercato 29a, Strada Fontana (☎ & fax 075.517.3121) are 5km out of town at Località Colle della Trinità (Sulga bus marked "Colle della Trinità" from Piazza Italia or #9 bus from the station and a short uphill walk from the crossroads), but you're better off heading to the superior sites on Lago Trasimeno (see p.589).

The Town

Once you're safely in Piazza Italia **orientation** is straightforward. The town hinges around a single street, the Corso Vannucci, one of the country's greatest people-watching streets, packed from dawn through to the early hours with a parade of tourists and Umbria's trendsetters and wannabes. Named after the city's most celebrated artist, Pietro Vannucci, better known simply as Perugino, the Corso contains several of the key sights and a couple of Perugia's most atmospheric little cafés.

Piazza Quattro Novembre and the Palazzo dei Priori

At the far end of the Corso Vannucci is the big and austere **Piazza IV Novembre** (once a Roman reservoir), backed by the plain-faced **Duomo**, fully restored after damage caused by the 1983 earthquake. While the Baroque interior is big on size, it's pretty small on works of art and comes as a disappointment after the fifteenth-century facade. As a change from pieces of the True Cross, one of the chapels contains the Virgin's "wedding ring", an unwieldy 2cm-diameter piece of agate that changes colour according to the character of the person wearing it. The Perugians keep it locked up in fifteen boxes fitted into one another like Russian dolls, each opened with a key held by a different person. It's brought out for general public edification once a year on July 30. In one of the transepts there's an urn holding the ashes of Pope Martin IV, who died in the city after eating too many eels. Urban IV's remains are here too – he was reputedly poisoned with *aquetta*, an imaginative little brew made by rubbing white arsenic into pork fat and distilling the unpleasantness that oozes out.

Outside in the piazza (which is the town's main hangout), the centrepiece is the **Fontana Maggiore**, designed by Fra' Bevignate, the monk who had a hand in the shaping of Orvieto's cathedral, and sculpted by the father-and-son team, Nicola and Giovanni Pisano. Sculptures and bas-reliefs – depicting episodes from the Old Testament, classical myth, Aesop's fables and the twelve months of the year on the two polygonal basins were part of a carefully conceived decorative scheme designed to illustrate the city's glory and achievements.. By some canny design work they never line up directly, encouraging you to walk round the fountain chasing a point of repose that never comes.

Just opposite rises the gaunt mass of the **Palazzo dei Priori**, hyped as one of the greatest public palaces in Italy. Sheer bulk aside, it's certainly impressive – with rows of trefoil windows (from which convicted criminals were once thrown to their deaths), majestic Gothic doorway, and business-like Guelph crenellations – but the overall effect is rather grim; its real beauty derives from the overall harmony set up by the medieval buildings around it. The lawyers' meeting hall, the **Sala dei Notari** (daily 9am–1pm & 3–7pm; free), at the top of the fan-shaped steps, is noted for its frescoes: lots of colour, fancy flags, swirls and no substance – but worth a glance.

The small **Collegio della Mercanzia** (March–Oct Tues–Fri 9am–1pm & 2.30–5.30pm, Sat 9am–1pm & 2.30–6.30am, Sun 9am–1pm; Nov–Feb Tues & Thurs–Fri 8am–2pm, Wed & Sat 8am–5pm, Sun 9am–1pm; L2000/€1.03 or L6000/€3.10 with Collegio di Cambio) lies further down the Corso side of the palace at Corso Vannucci 15 hidden behind an innocuous door. The seat of the Merchants' Guild, it is covered entirely in intricate fifteenth-century panelling. A few doors down at Corso Vannucci 25, the impressive **Collegio di Cambio** (March–Oct Mon–Sat 9am–12.30pm & 2.30–5.30pm, Sun 9am–1pm; Nov–Feb Tues–Sat 8am–2pm, Sun 9am–12.30pm; L5000/€2.58 or L6000/€3.10 with the Collegio della Mercanzia) was the town's money exchange in medieval times. The superb frescoes on the walls were executed by Perugino at the height of his powers and are considered the artist's masterpiece; in true Renaissance fashion, they attempt to fuse ancient and Christian culture. Up on the door-side wall there's a famous but unremarkable self-portrait in which the artist looks like he had a bad lunch. The small chapel to the right of the Collegio is frescoed by Giannicola di Paolo (1519), the last important Umbrian painter influenced by Perugino.

The **Galleria Nazionale dell'Umbria** (Mon–Sat 9am–7pm, Sun 9am–1pm, closed first Mon of every month; L8000/€4.13) is on the upper floor of the palace complex, with the entrance through its opulently carved **doorway**. (You have to push past harassed-looking Perugians on their way to do battle with council bureaucracy on the other floors.) One of central Italy's best and most charming galleries, this takes you on a romp through the history of Umbrian painting, with one or two stunning Tuscan masterpieces (Duccio, Fra' Angelico, Piero della Francesca) thrown in for good measure. The entrance is worth every penny if you're the slightest bit interested in early and mid-Renaissance art, though a long-term restoration of the gallery was no sooner finished than the 1997 earthquake threw the new arrangements into jeopardy. Nonetheless, plans are in hand to extend the gallery across a large part of the palace's lower floors.

Just east of Piazza Danti along Via del Sole brings you to the church of **San Severo** (April–Sept daily 10am–1.30pm & 2.30–6.30pm; Oct–March Mon–Fri 10.30am–1pm &

2.30–4.30pm, Sat–Sun 10.30am–1.30pm & 2.30–5.30pm; L3500/€1.81) in Piazza Raffaello, known for its painting of *Holy Trinity and Saints* by Raphael, an artist who spent some five formative years in Umbria. Today it's the only **painting** by him still left in the region – Napoleon carted many of the artist's works off to France – except for a painted banner in the art gallery in Città di Castello (see p.592).

North and west of Corso Vannucci

The best streets to wander around for a feel of the old city are to the east and west of the duomo, **Via dei Priori** being the most characteristic. Just behind the Palazzo dei Priori in the Via della Gabbia there once hung a large iron cage used to imprison thieves and sometimes even clergy. In January 1442, according to a medieval chronicler, priest Angelo di Ferolo "was put back into the cage at midday, and it was very cold and there was much snow, and he remained there until the first day of February both night and day and that same day he was brought out dead". You can still make out long spikes on some of the lower walls, used as hooks for the heads of executed criminals. Medieval Perugia was evidently a hell of a place to be. "The most warlike of the people of Italy", wrote the historian Sismondi, "who always preferred Mars to the Muse". Male citizens played a game (and this was for pleasure) in which two teams, thickly padded in clothes stuffed with deer hair and wearing beaked helmets, stoned each other mercilessly until the majority of the other side were dead or wounded. Children were encouraged to join in for the first two hours to promote "application and aggression".

In 1265 Perugia was also the birthplace of the **Flagellants**, who had half of Europe whipping itself into a frenzy before the movement was declared heretical. In addition to some hearty scourging they took to the streets on moonlit nights, groaning and wailing, dancing in white sheets, singing dirges and clattering human bones together, all as expiation for sin and the wrongs of the world. Then there were the infamous **Baglioni**, the medieval family who misruled the city for several generations, their spell-binding history – full of vendetta, incest and mass-slaughter – the stuff of great medieval soap opera.

Via dei Priori passes **Madonna della Luce** (Madonna of the Light) on the north side after the medieval Torre degli Scirri, little more than a chapel dominated by an impressive altarpiece (by a follower of Perugino). The church takes its name from the story that in 1513 a young barber swore so profusely on losing at cards that a Madonna in a wayside shrine closed her eyes in horror and kept them closed for four days. The miracle prompted celebrations, processions and the building of a new church. Some way beyond is a nice patch of grass perfectly placed for relaxing with the crowd from the art school next door or for admiring Agostino di Duccio's colourful **Oratorio di San Bernardino**, whose richly embellished facade (1461) is far and away the best piece of sculpture in the city. Again to the north is what's left of San Francesco, once a colossal church, now ruined by centuries of earthquakes and neglect, but with a curiously jumbled and striking facade still just about standing.

From here you can wander along Via A. Pascoli, past the hideous university buildings, to the **Università Italiana per Stranieri** in Piazza Fortebraccio. The big patched-up gateway here is the **Arco di Augusto**, its lowest section one of the few remaining monuments of Etruscan Perugia. The upper remnant was added by the Romans when they captured the city in 40 BC. The university bar atmosphere is friendly and cosmopolitan, but don't expect much joy out of the Information Desk in the foyer. Terms run from April to December, and posters around the place give details of concerts and English films (especially in the summer).

About a minute's walk north on Corso Garibaldi is the sadly half-defunct **Sant'Agostino**, once Romanesque, now botched Baroque and filled with wistful signs explaining what paintings used to hang in the church before they were spirited to France by light-fingered Napoleonic troops. The church, however, is not entirely ruined: there's a beautiful choir (probably based on a drawing by Perugino) and a couple of patches of fresco on the left-hand wall, giving a tantalizing idea of what the place must once have been. Next door to the north side is the fifteenth-century **Oratorio di Sant'Agostino**, its ludicrously ornate ceiling looking as if it's about to erupt in an explosion of gilt, stucco and chubby plaster cherubs. Fifteen minutes' walk up the street is the fifth-century church of Sant'Angelo, situated in a tranquil spot and based on a circular pagan temple; the 24 columns, each made from a different stone, are from the earlier building.

Corso Cavour

The rest of Perugia's highlights are on the other side of town, grouped together on **Corso Cavour**, a busy and dustily unpleasant road in the summer, and just plain unpleasant the rest of the time. On the way over you could join the smooching couples in the small but well-kept **Giardini Carducci** (by Piazza Italia) to see why Henry James called Perugia the "little city of the infinite views". When the usual cloak of haze lifts on crisp winter mornings, half of Umbria is laid out before you, with the mountains of Tuscany in the distance.

Below the piazza you could take a short walk past the strange octagonal, but rarely open, church of **Sant'Ercolano** – built on the site where the head of Perugia's first bishop miraculously reattached itself to his body after the Goths chopped it off – and through the Porta Marzia, where a subterranean road of medieval houses (Via Baglioni Sotteranea) leads under the ruins of the Rocca Paolina (a once-enormous papal fortress destroyed by the Perugians at Unification). You come eventually to **San Domenico**.

The church, Umbria's biggest, has a desolate and unfinished air from the outside, with pigeons nesting where they shouldn't and grass growing from the pinky-orange marble, but it's also pretty in a big and sad sort of way. The original Romanesque interior, however, collapsed in the sixteenth century and the Baroque replacement is vast, cold and bare. Like Sant'Agostino, however, it's full of hints as to how beautiful it must have been – nowhere more so than in the fourth chapel on the right, where a superb **carved arch** by Agostino di Duccio is spoilt only by Victorian Christmas card-style decorations and a doll-like Madonna. In the east transept, to the right of the altar, is the **tomb of Benedict XI** (1324), another pope who died in Perugia, this time from eating poisoned figs. It's an elegant and well-preserved piece by one of the period's three leading sculptors: Pisano, Lorenzo Maitini or Arnolfo di Cambio, no one knows which. There's also another good choir, together with some impressive **stained-glass** windows – the second biggest in Italy after those in Milan Cathedral and a welcome splash of colour in the midst of all the mud-coloured paint.

Housed in the church's cloisters is the **Museo Archeologico Nazionale dell'Umbria**, at Piazza Giordano Bruno 10 (Mon–Sat 9am–1.30pm & 2.30–7pm, Sun 9am–1pm; L4000/€2.07). Before being hammered by Augustus, Perugia was a big shot in the twelve-strong Etruscan federation of cities, which is why this museum has one of the most extensive Etruscan collections around. There's also a sizeable section devoted to prehistory. If the Etruscans get you going you might try the outstanding local tombs, the **Ipogeo dei Volumni** (July & Aug Mon–Sat 9.30am–12.30pm & 4.30–6.30pm, Sun 9.30am–12.30pm; Sept–June Mon–Sat 9.30am–12.30pm & 3–5pm, Sun 9.30am–12.30pm; L4000/€2.07), seven kilometres east of the town at Via Assisana, Ponte San Giovanni (bus or train to Ponte San Giovanni and then a short walk). Though the best in Umbria, they're quite small and without any of the racy paintings found in some Tuscan tombs; and certainly not a patch on the graves at Tarquinia or Cerveteri (see p.754 and p.752). Visits are also restricted to a maximum of five people at a time and you're only officially allowed five minutes in the tombs themselves.

Further on down the Corso Cavour, advertised by a rocket-shaped belltower, is the tenth-century basilica of **San Pietro**, the most idiosyncratic of all the town's churches.

Tangled up in a group of buildings belonging to the university's agriculture department, the none too obvious entrance is through a frescoed doorway in the far left-hand corner of the first courtyard off the road. Few churches can be so sumptuously decorated: every inch of available space is covered in gilt, paint or marble, though a guiding sense of taste seems to have prevailed, and in the candle-lit gloom it actually feels like the sacred place it's meant to be. All the woodwork is extraordinary; the **choir** has been called the best in Italy, and there is a host of works by Perugino, Fiorenzo di Lorenzo and others.

Eating and drinking

Perugia's student population ensures that there is a plethora of reasonably priced places to eat out, from the many snack bars around the centre of town to simple *osterie* serving traditional Umbrian cuisine. Local dishes feature wild mushrooms, truffles and game often succulently combined with homemade egg pasta.

Pizzerias and restaurants

Aladino, Via della Prome 11 (☎075.572.0938). Just up Via del Sole from Piazza Danti and the cathedral, this well-regarded restaurant serves an inspired mixture of Umbrian and Sardinian cooking and has an interesting wine list. You'll need to book. Closed lunchtimes & all day Mon.

Cesarino, Piazza IV Novembre 45 (☎075.572.8974). A great central trattoria and a Perugia tradition. Booking advised. Closed Wed.

Dal mi Cocco, Corso Garibaldi 12. Good-value traditional dishes with a variety of set menus. Closed Mon.

Era Nuova, Via Baldo 6. One of the best pizzerias in town. Closed Fri.

Falchetto, Via Bartolo 20, just off Piazza Danti. A reliably good and easygoing place with a medieval interior. Closed Mon.

Il Gufo, Via della Viola 18. Excellent osteria with moderately priced regional cooking. Closed Sun & Mon.

Segreto di Pulcinella, Via Larga 8. A bustling pizzeria that's very popular with students. Closed Tues.

Cafés and nightlife

The city's liveliest **cafés** are clustered on Corso Vannucci, with the atmospheric old-world *Pasticceria Sandri* at no. 32 (closed Mon) a high spot for the sweet-toothed. The best place to indulge in local wines is at the *Enoteca Provinciale* at Via Ulisse Rocchi 16–18 (closed Sun), or for a selction of beers and whisky, there's the inevitable Irish **pub** – *Sullivan's* at Via del Bovaro 2 (closed Tues). The *Australian Pub*, Via del Verzaro 39 (closed Wed), is one of several places to lay on **live music**, with jazz available at the *Bar Morlacchi*, Piazza Morlacchi 6–8, and the *Contrappunto Jazz Club*, Via Scortici 4a (closed Mon). The majority of big **clubs** and discos are out of town; the most popular exception is the central *Sub Way*, Via delle Prome 22 (closed Thurs).

Lago Trasimeno

The most tempting option around Perugia – whose surroundings are generally pretty bleak – is **LAGO TRASIMENO**, an ideal spot to hole up for a few days, and particularly recommended if you want to get in some swimming, windsurfing or sailing. The lake is about 30km from Perugia and is well serviced by both train and bus. It's the biggest inland stretch of water on the Italian peninsula, the fourth largest in Italy overall, and, though you wouldn't think so to look at it, never deeper than seven metres – hence bath-like warm water in summer. And, because the tourist and fishing industries are the economic bread and butter of the surrounding towns, it's also clean. Large banks of weed drift in during the summer, but the council takes care of these, dumping them with little subtlety on the shore.

A winning combination of tree-covered hills to the north, Umbria's subtle light, and placid lapping water produces some magical moments, but on overcast and squally days the mood can turn melancholy. Not all the reed-lined shore is uniformly pretty either; steer clear of the northern coast and head for the stretches south of Magione and Castiglione if you're after relative peace and quiet. Be warned, too, that **unofficial camping** is not as easy as it looks, partly because a lot of the immediate shoreline is marshy, but mainly because most of the good spots have already been grabbed by locals.

There's some good **walking** in the vicinity, with treks possible up Monte Castiglione on the mule track from the Passo di Gosparani (7km north of Tuoro); up Monte Acuto from Montacuto (15km northeast on the Umbértide road); or up Monte Murlo from **Préggio**, a hill-village 7km north of Castel Rigone and worth a visit in its own right. If you feel less adventurous, there are twelve waymarked trails around the lake, starting from centres such as Panicale, Passignano and Castiglione del Lago; pick up the map-brochure *Itinerari Turistici del Trasimeno* from tourist offices.

If you have a car, this area is also a good point to cross the border into Tuscany to visit Cortona (see p.574).

Passignano

PASSIGNANO, a newish town with a medieval heart, strung out along the northern shore, is the lake's most accessible point, being served by seven daily buses and by hourly trains from Perugia and Terontola. Popular with those Italians whose idea of an outing is to spend the whole day in a car, the town in summer often resembles nothing so much as a big traffic jam. In the evenings, however, when people come flooding in from the surrounding campsites, the joint is jumping, with bars, discos and fish restaurants aplenty. There's a **tourist office** at Via Roma 38 (June–Sept daily 9am–noon plus Mon–Wed & Fri & Sat 4–7pm; Oct–May Mon–Fri 9am–noon & 3–6pm, Sat 9am–noon; ☎075.827.635), and about a dozen **hotels** – the best value of which are the *Florida*, Via II Giugno 2 (☎075.827.228; ③) and *Del Pescatore*, Via San Bernardino 5 (☎075.829.6063; ③), both comfortable places where all rooms are en suite, and the larger, smarter three-star *Trasimeno*, Via Roma 16a (☎075.829.355, fax 075.829.267; ③).

Somewhere along the lakeshore towards Tuoro, probably at Sanguineto ("the Place of Blood") or Ossaia ("the Place of Bones"), is the spot where the Romans suffered their famous clobbering at the hands of **Hannibal** in 217 BC. Hannibal was headed for Rome, having just crossed the Alps, when he was met by a Roman force under the Consul Flaminius. Things might have gone better for Flaminius if he'd heeded the omens that piled up on the morning of battle. First he fell off his horse, next the legionary standards had to be dug out of the mud, then – and this really should have raised suspicions – the sacred chickens refused their breakfast. Poultry accompanied all Roman armies and, by some means presumably known to the legionnaire in charge of chickens, communicated the will of the gods to waiting commanders in the field. With the chickens against him Flaminius didn't stand a chance. Hannibal lured him into a masterful ambush, with the only escape a muddy retreat into the lake. Sixteen thousand Romans, including the hapless commander, were killed.

Tuoro and Castel Rigone

The rambling village of **TUORO**, four kilometres west of Passignano and three kilometres' walk from the Trasimeno battlefield, is a quiet, dull little place giving road access into the desolate, beautiful mountains north of the lake – the best of the scenery within easy reach of Perugia. A hard-to-find drive and walkway have recently been laid out, starting and finishing just west of the village on the road to Cortona, that take in salient features of the old battlefield. Accommodation here is restricted to a single **hotel**, the eight-roomed *Volante*, at Via Sette Martiri 52 (☎075.826.107, fax 075.825.088; ②), plus a **campsite**, the *Punta Navaccia* at Via Navaccia 4 (☎075.826.357; April–Sept) in the nearby hamlet of **Punta Navaccia**.

The outstanding village of **CASTEL RIGONE**, 8km northeast of Passignano, sits in the mountains, with superb views and a small, geranium-strewn medieval centre. There are two smart, rather staid, hotels the better of which is the immediately obvious four-star *Fattoria*, Via Rigone 1 (☎075.845.322, fax 075.845.197; ⑤). Each of the hotels has a cavernous, unatmospheric restaurant, the only places for a bite to eat; neither is terribly good. A little outside the village is the Renaissance church **Madonna dei Miracoli**, somewhat out of place in the overall medieval context.

Castiglione del Lago

CASTIGLIONE DEL LAGO is the most appealing town on the lake and cuts a fine silhouette from other points around the shore, jutting out into the water on a fortified promontory. In the event it doesn't really live up to its distant promise, but is still a friendly, unpretentious place with enough charm and action to hold anyone's interest for a couple of days – longer if all you want to do is crash out on an (albeit modest) beach. It's easy to reach by slow train either from Chiusi (heading north) or Terontola if you're coming from Arezzo or Perugia. There are also nine buses daily from Perugia.

There's a good **tourist office** in the main Piazza Mazzini (Mon 8am–1.30pm, Tues–Sat 8am–1.30pm & 3–7.30pm, Sun 9am–1pm; ☎075.965.2484 or 075.965.2738, *info@iat.castiglione-del-lago.pg.it*) whose flashiness in such a small place gives a good idea of the town's considerable appeal to tourists. They have a lot of reasonable but characterless **rooms** on their books and apartments to rent on a weekly basis, usually a cheaper option if you can get a party together. Among the **hotels**, the top dog is the *Duca della Corgna*, Via B. Buozzi 143 (☎075.953.238, fax 075.962.2446; ④), with the *Trasimeno*, Via Roma 174 (☎075.965.2494, fax 075.952.5258; ③), hot on its heels; more atmospheric is the *Miralago*, Piazza Mazzini 6 (☎075.951.157 or 075.953.063, fax 075.951.924; ④), with views of the lake behind. Most of the **campsites** are off the main road some way south of the town. *Lido Trasimeno* (☎075.965.9350; April–Sept) on the shore north of the castle has good facilities (swimming, windsurfing school, sailing etc). Aside from the summer-only **restaurants** on the promenade, the place to eat game, fish fresh from the lake and other dishes is the *L'Acquario*, Via Vittorio Emanuele II 69 (☎075.965.2432; closed Fri, also Tues in winter) on the old town's single main street. The best **swimming** is at the public lido on the southern side of the promontory.

Regular boats make the trip out to the **Isola Maggiore**, one of the lake's three islands, a fun ride if you don't mind the summer crowds. There's a pretty walk round the edge of the island, and you should have no problem discreetly pitching a tent once everyone else has packed up and gone home. If not, there's one good, popular **hotel**, the three-star *Da Sauro*, Via Guglielmi 1 (☎075.826.168; ④), which also doubles as a fine restaurant that's especially known for its fish.

Panicale

The surrounding countryside is best appreciated from a reclining position on the beach. The low hills make a good scenic backdrop but they're not really worth exploring, though if you have a car you could pop into **PANICALE** to the south. It has some picture-postcard views of the lake, plus two easily missed Perugino paintings – the

Martyrdom of St Sebastian and a *Madonna and Child* – tucked away in the church of **San Sebastiano** (off Piazza Vittoria; custodian at Piazza del Mercato 13 holds key). During the town's April festa, thanks to some miraculous plumbing, the fountains run with wine; well worth investigating.

The Upper Tiber

Rome's great and famously polluted river, the Tiber, actually spends most of its short life in Umbria, rising in the Alpe della Luna (the mountains of the moon) above Sansepolcro. In its moderately pretty but rather unexciting upper reaches north of Perugia – largely given over to sheep and fields of tobacco – you're faced with the familiar problem that everything you don't want to see is easily accessible and everything you do is out of reach without your own transport. The **Ferrovia Centrale Umbra** and the fast N3 to Sansepolcro are perfect for **Città di Castello**, the area's only town of note, after which you'll probably want to strike east on the N257 across the mountains to Urbino (70km). The best reason to follow the Tiber is to stay on the trail of **Piero della Francesca's** mysterious and unsettling masterpieces at Sansepolcro, Arezzo and Monterchi.

The region's best aspect, in fact, is not the valley but the desolate countryside on either side, areas which, like the Valnerina in the east, give the lie to the notion of Umbria as some sort of pastoral idyll. With few roads and fewer villages, but thousands of hectares of natural woodland and abandoned pasture, it teems with wildlife, including many rare species of birds, deer, wild boar and even wolves, now apparently pushing further up the Italian peninsula every year. **Pietralunga** and **Apecchio** to the north are the best exploring bases, with a **campsite** at Candeleto close to the former (*La Pineta*, ☎075.946.0080, fax 075.946.0646; Jun–Sept), but there's obviously plenty of scope for freelance camping if you're geared up.

Umbertide and around

UMBERTIDE is largely modern and lightly industrial, having been bombed almost to oblivion in the last war, but – except in the tiny medieval centre – it doesn't come over as a place that had much going for it in the first place. It's useful for trips into the surrounding hills, but only if you have transport. The big castle, **Civitella Ranieri**, looms invitingly to the northeast, but it's privately owned, so don't be suckered into the steep climb for a closer look. **Monte Corona** (693m), 6km south, has some good views and the reasonably evocative remains of a fifteenth-century monastery. More worthwhile is the hill-village of **MONTONE** which harbours a surprisingly good collection of paintings and early medieval sculpture in the **Museo e Pinacoteca Comunale** (April–Sept Fri–Sun 10.30am–1pm & 3.30–6pm; Oct–March Sat & Sun 10am–1pm & 3–5.30pm; L6000/€3.10) in Via San Francesco, housed in the fifteenth-century Gothic former church of San Francesco; there's a small and intermittently open **tourist office** at Piazza Caduti del Lavoro (☎075.941.7099). Much further south – and with a car you could tackle this more easily as a day-trip from Perugia – is the **Abbazia di Montelabate**. While the immense adjoining church of Santa Maria is fairly ordinary, the eleventh-century crypt and fourteenth-century cloisters are medieval perfection.

Città di Castello and around

The Church's seventh-century nickname for **CITTÀ DI CASTELLO** was "castrum felicitas" (the castle of happiness), though why, when it had been all but obliterated by Totila, is hard to fathom. Today there's nothing terribly special about the place – unless you've drunk sufficient quantities of the local *Colli Altotiberini* wines or you happen to be in town during August for its renowned **Festival of Chamber Music**.

Once an important Roman centre – the grid-iron of streets is the only legacy – today the plain-bound site is drab and preserves only a handful of fairly mediocre medieval monuments. The town's only real merit, apart from some quiet, pleasant medieval streets and a bargain restaurant (see below), is its ten-roomed **Pinacoteca** at Via della Cannoniera 22 (Tues–Sat: late March to mid-July 9.30am–12.45pm & 3–6pm; mid-July to Sept 9.30am–12.45pm & 3–7.15pm; Oct to mid-March 10am–12.30pm & 3–5.30pm; L8000/€4.13), one of the region's best galleries after Perugia's. The collection makes up in quality what it lacks in quantity, taking in works by **Raphael**, **Signorelli**, **Ghirlandaio** and **Lorenzetti**, plus a wondrous *Maestà* by the anonymous fourteenth-century Maestro di Città di Castello. There are also several sculptures, the most notable by Ghiberti, and a glittering reliquary of Florentine origin, dating from 1420.

If you stop off, then the banal reworked **Duomo** in Piazza Gabriotti warrants a call for its museum (daily: April–Sept 10.30am–1pm & 3–6pm; Oct–March 10am–1pm & 3–5.30pm; L5000/€2.58), which contains the **treasure of Canoscio**, a precious hoard of sixth-century silver chalices dug up in 1932. The town's other more paltry offerings include a late-Renaissance **choir**, located in San Francesco's Cappella Vitelli, and the fourteenth-century **Palazzo Comunale**, an imposing but unfinished work by Angelo da Orvieto, who was responsible for the vastly more impressive palaces in Gubbio.

Città di Castello's **tourist office** in the Logge Bufalini in Piazza Matteotti (daily 9am–1pm & 4–7pm; ☎075.855.4922, *info@iat.citta-di-castello.pg.it*) deals with the whole Upper Tiber region and so is a useful stop if you're spending any time locally. The town's top-of-the-range **hotel** is the central *Tiferno*, Piazza R. Sanzio 13 (☎075.855.0331, fax 075.852.1196; ⑤). A cheaper, equally well-located alternative is the excellent modern one-star *Umbria*, Via dei Galanti 4, off Via Sant'Antonio (☎075.855.4925, fax 075.852.0911; ③), just inside the medieval walls, in the east of the old centre. There's also a pleasant, rural **campsite** at La Montesca, 1km west of town on the minor road to Monte San Marina – the *Montesca* (☎075.852.0808, fax 075.852.0786; May–Sept). Best of several good **restaurants** is *Amici Miei*, downstairs in a medieval cellar at Via del Monte 2 (closed Wed): there's no choice, but the menu changes daily and you get four wonderful courses including wine for a bargain L30,000/€15.50.

A couple of kilometres south of Città di Castello, in the hamlet of **GARAVELLE**, is one of Umbria's best **folk museums**, the Centro delle Tradizioni Popolari (Tues–Sun: summer 9am–12.30pm & 3–7pm; winter 9am–noon & 2–6pm; L5000/€2.58). Situated in the Villa Cappelletti, Via Marchese Cappelletti, this is basically an eighteenth-century farmhouse, preserved with all the accoutrements of daily life – pots, pans, furniture and so forth, plus a range of exhibits covering rural activities from wine making, weaving and carpentry through to the blacksmith's forge. Totally out of context, the museum also has a **model railway collection** (Mon–Fri 3–5pm).

Gubbio

GUBBIO is the most thoroughly medieval of the Umbrian towns, an immediately likable place that's hanging onto its charm despite an ever-increasing influx of tourists. The streets are picture-book pretty, with houses of rosy-pink stone and seas of orange-tiled roofs; the setting is equally gorgeous with the forest-clad mountains of the Apennines rearing up behind. A broad and largely unspoilt plain stretches out in front of the town, and the whole ensemble – especially on grey, windswept days – maintains Gubbio's tough, mountain outpost atmosphere.

A powerful medieval commune, and always important as the gateway to Ravenna and

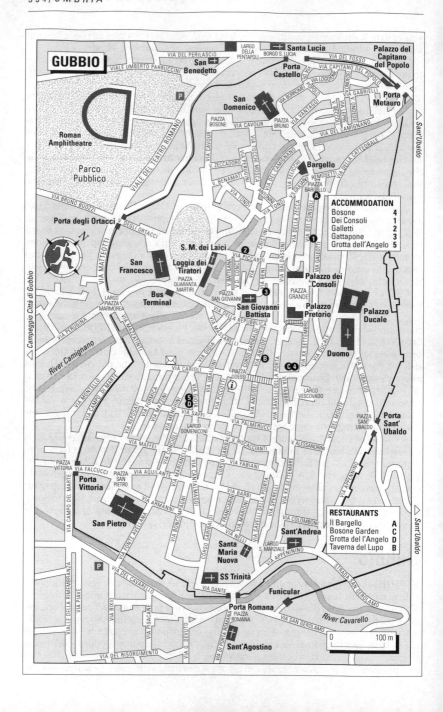

the Adriatic (it was a key point on the Roman Via Flaminia), these days it's a town apart, not really part of Umbria, Tuscany or Marche – the reason it's been spared the onslaught of the twentieth century and why getting here can be tricky.

Gubbio is easiest approached by **bus** from Città di Castello or Perugia on the lovely cross-country SS298 **road**. The nearest **train station** is at Fossato di Vico, 19km south on the Rome–Foligno–Ancona line; there are ten connecting shuttle buses to Gubbio from Monday to Saturday, six on Sundays.

The Town

Centre-stage is the immense and austere fourteenth-century **Palazzo dei Consoli**, whose crenellated outline and 98-metre campanile immediately grab your attention. Probably designed by Matteo Gattapone, who was also responsible for Spoleto's Ponte delle Torri, the palace took a couple of hundred years to build and required the levelling of vast tracts of the medieval town, mainly to accommodate the huge and windswept Piazza della Signoria. The lesser **Palazzo Pretorio** opposite was built to the same plan. Deliberately dominating and humbling, it was what medieval civic pride was all about, an attempt to express power and supremacy in bricks and mortar. Behind a plain square facade (there's a small hole top right where criminals were hung in a cage called *la gogna* – from *vergogna* or "shame") is a cavernous baronial hall, the Salone dell'Arengo, where council officials and leading citizens met to discuss business. The word "harangue" derives from *arengo*, suggesting proceedings frequently boiled over.

The **Museo Civico** (Tues–Sun: April–Sept 10am–1pm & 3–6pm; Oct–March 10am–1pm & 2–5pm; L7000/€3.62) is also based here, housing a typical miscellany, unremarkable except for the famous **Eugubine Tablets** (upstairs to the left), Umbria's most important archeological find. Discovered in 1444 by an illiterate shepherd, later conned into swapping his priceless treasure trove for a worthless piece of land, the seven bronze tablets are more or less the only extant record of the ancient Umbrian language, a vernacular tongue without written characters. The bastardized Etruscan and Latin of their religious texts was aimed at producing a phonetic translation of the dialect using the main languages of the day. Gubbio was close to the shrine of the so-called Apennine Jove, a major pagan deity visited by pilgrims from all over Italy, so the tablets were probably the work of Roman and Etruscan priests taking advantage of the established order to impose their religious cults in a region where their languages weren't understood. Most importantly, they suggest Romans, Etruscans and Umbrians achieved some sort of coexistence, refuting a long-held belief that succeeding civilizations wiped one another out.

Admission to the museum also gets you into the good five-roomed **Pinacoteca** upstairs, worth a look for works by the Gubbian School – one of central Italy's earliest, and a collection of ponderous fourteenth-century furniture. Try the door at the back for views from the palace's **loggia**. The palace also boasted 26 toilets; apparently it was the first in medieval Italy to have interior piped water.

To the north of the Piazza Grande lurks a not very inspiring thirteenth-century **Duomo**, partly redeemed by the odd fresco, twelfth-century stained glass, and some arches gracefully curved to emulate the meeting of hands in prayer. There are also a pair of carved **organ lofts** that for once don't look as if they'd be more at home in a fairground. The small adjoining cathedral **museum** is currently closed after a spate of thefts, but if you're lucky enough to find it open it's well worth five minutes, mainly for a florid Flemish cope, presented to the cathedral by Pope Marcellus II, who was born in Gubbio.

The plain-faced Gothic pile is overshadowed by the **Palazzo Ducale** in Via Federico da Montefeltro opposite (Mon–Sat 9am–7pm, Sun 9am–1.30pm; closed first Mon of the month; L4000/€2.07), built over an earlier Lombard palace by the Dukes of

Montefeltro as a scaled-down copy of their more famous palace in Urbino. The **courtyard** is particularly good, and the interior, though stripped of most of its original furniture and other trappings, is now open after years of restoration and well worth the admission.

On the hillside above the town stands the **Basilica of Sant'Ubaldo**, a place Gubbians drive to for their Sunday-morning walk, but pleasant enough for that. There's a very handy bar, plenty of shady spots to crash out, and some great views (even better ones if you can be bothered to climb up to the **Rocca**). There's not much to see in the basilica itself, except the body of the town's patron saint, St Ubaldo, whose missing three fingers were hacked off by his manservant as a religious keepsake. You can't miss the big wooden pillars (*ceri*) featured in Gubbio's annual **Corsa dei Ceri** (May 15), little known outside Italy but second only to Siena's Palio in terms of exuberance and bizarre pageantry. The rules and rigmarole of the 900-year-old ceremony are mind-boggling, but they boil down to three teams racing from Piazza della Signoria to the basilica, carrying the *ceri* (each representing a different saint) on wooden stretchers. By iron-clad tradition, the *cero* of St Ubaldo always wins, the other teams having to ensure they're in the basilica before the doors are shut by the leaders. There's hours of involved ritual at either end, vast crowds and plenty of drinking. A scholarly debate rages as to whether the whole thing's intrinsically religious (commemorating the day in 1155 Ubaldo talked Barbarossa out of flattening Gubbio), or a hangover from some pagan fertility rite. Nowadays the Church, not surprisingly, claims it as its own, but judging by the very phallic *ceri*, and the roar that goes up when they're raised to the vertical, there's something more than religion at play here.

There are several ways up to the basilica, one being via the steep track that strikes off from behind the duomo. However, it's quicker and far more fun – unless you have no head for heights – to take the **funicular** (summer 8.30am–7.30pm; winter reduced hours; return L9000/€4.65, one way L7000/€3.62) from Porta Romana, over on the eastern side of town; you jump on small two-person cradles, which then dangle precariously over the woods and crags below as you shudder slowly upwards. While you're waiting you could take in more of Ottaviano Nelli's paintings, tucked away in the thirteenth-century **Sant'Agostino** and **Santa Maria Nuova** nearby. The unusually lovely *Madonna del Belvedere* (1408) in the latter is a masterpiece of the detailed and highly decorative style for which he was famous. His most majestic efforts – seventeen frescoes on the life of the Virgin – are in **San Francesco**, the big church that dominates the Piazza dei Quaranta Martiri – the bus terminal – at the foot of the town. The piazza's named in memory of forty citizens shot by the Germans in 1944, a reprisal for partisan attacks in the surrounding hills.

Gubbio's **Porte della Morte**, the "doors of death", are as controversial as the phallic *ceri*. Almost unique to the town (there are a few others in Assisi and southern France), these are narrow, bricked-up doorways wedged into the facades of its medieval townhouses (with the best examples in Via dei Consoli). The party line is that they were used to carry a coffin out of a house, and then having been tainted with death, were sealed up out of superstitious fear. Nice theory, and very Italian, but judging by the constricted stairways behind the doors, their purpose was probably defensive – the main door could be barricaded, leaving the more easily defended passageway as the only entrance.

There are dozens of picturesque odds and ends around the streets, which are as wonderfully explorable as any in the region. The **Bargello** in Via dei Consoli, the medieval police station, is worth tracking down and gives you the chance to survey the adjacent **Fontana dei Matti** (the "fountain of the mad"), otherwise undistinguished but for the tradition that anyone walking round it three times will wind up mad. There's usually someone wondering whether to give it a go.

Practicalities

You shouldn't have any problem **staying** in Gubbio, though the place does get busy, and many of the hotels and restaurants are rather smart affairs aimed at well-heeled Italians. Check for cheap **rooms** in private houses with the **tourist office**, Piazza Odersi 6 (Mon–Sat 8.30am–1.30pm & 3–6pm, Sun 9.30am–12.30pm; ☎075.922.0790 or 075.922.0693, *info@iat.gubbio.pg.it*). You can check your **email**, at the *Caffè Centrale*, Piazza Oderisi 3 (7am–midnight; closed Mon; L10,000/€5.17 per hr; ☎075.922.2518, *www.seguceo.net*) near the bottom of Corso Garibaldi. For **hotel** accommodation, try the straightforward one-star *Galletti*, Via Piccardi 1 (☎075.927.7753; ②) with just seven rooms; the reliable two-star *Grotta dell'Angelo*, Via Gioia 47 (☎075.927.1747, fax 075.927.3438; ②); or the popular and perfectly placed *Albergo dei Consoli* at Via dei Consoli 59 (☎075.927.3335; ②) – though the nine rooms here are extremely plain. Moving up a notch, the spacious *Gattapone*, Via G. Ansidei 6 (☎075.927.2489, fax 075.927.2417; ④)with its peaceful garden is the best mid-range choice, while if you want a taste of a medieval palace with frescoed ceilings and lots of antiques, treat yourself to the three-star *Bosone*, Via XX Settembre 22 (☎075.922.0688, fax 075.922.0552; ④). For luxury, opt for the *Park Hotel ai Cappuccini*, Via Tifernate (☎075.92.34, fax 075.922.0323; ⑦) – an elegantly converted fourteenth-century monastery in parkland just outside of town, featuring a pool, gym, sauna and garden. Less than 2km south of town, the Città di Gubbio **campsite** (☎ & fax 075.927.2037; April–Sept) is in a pleasant setting and has a swimming pool.

Gubbio boasts a good selection of **restaurants**, including the smart *Taverna del Lupo* (closed Mon) at Via Ansidei 21, well worth a splurge for its classic Umbrian dishes and excellent truffle risotto; the much cheaper *Grotta dell'Angelo* (closed Tues), annexed to the *Grotta dell'Angelo* hotel, does very good basic meals in its wonderful dining room; and, if you want to dine outdoors, head for the *Bosone Garden* restaurant (closed Wed) on Via Mastro Giorgio, attached to the *Bosone* hotel. The best of the many cheap **pizzerias** is *Il Bargello* (closed Mon),Via dei Consoli 37.

Gualdo Tadino and around

GUALDO TADINO, like Gubbio, is distinct from the rest of Umbria and has a similarly rugged mountain-outpost character. Sprawling over the lower slopes of the Apennines, it is a bleakly medieval centre, hedged about with light industry and unplanned housing around the station and plain below. With Umbrian and Roman origins, its single historical claim to fame was as witness to the death of Totila the Hun, who was slain by the Romans under the town walls.

The only remarkable thing about the thirteenth-century Gothic **Duomo** is that the facade has two tiers instead of Umbria's usual three; the interior, done to death in the nineteenth century, has absolutely nothing to recommend it. The **Pinacoteca** housed in the angular San Francesco is more interesting, but is currently closed indefinitely (call the Vigili Urbani, ☎075.916.647 for latest details). Much space is given to local painters such as fifteenth-century Matteo da Gualdo, but the centrepiece is a polyptych by **Nicolò Alunno**, considered unsurpassed among the central Italian artists before Perugino came on the scene. Without the sugary quality of some Umbrian offerings – all soft-focus saints and dewy-eyed Madonnas – Alunno has a harder edge and a wider and more genuine range of emotion.

With little to detain you, you could easily soak up the atmosphere of the place between the frequent trains from Foligno and Fabriano. The cheapest **accommodation**, however, if you need it, is at the two-star *Centro Sociale Verde Soggiorno*, Via Bosco 50 (☎075.916.263, fax, 075.914.2951; ②), or the two-star *Dal Bottaio*, Via Casimiri 17

(☎075.913.230; ②). The best food is at *Gigiotto* (closed Wed & Nov), Via Morone 5, though service can be lacking. The **tourist office** *Pro Tadino* at Via Calai 39 (May–Sept Mon–Sat 9am–1pm & 3.30–7.30pm; ☎075.912.172) will fill in the gaps.

Nocera Umbra

Whether you make the fifteen-kilometre trip south to **NOCERA UMBRA** depends on whether you're sticking with Umbria or heading on to Urbino or Fabriano in Marche. This hapless little place was one of the worst affected by the 1997 earthquakes – the *centro storico* was almost completely levelled and will be under scaffolding for years to come. Nocera, or what's left of it, could just as easily be seen from Assisi, 20km away to the southwest and served by plenty of trains. Essentially a place for a flying visit – if that, at the time of writing – this is yet another hill-town, middling by Umbrian standards and with a sizeable new town on the valley floor to detract from its now battered medieval charms. It's most famous for its **mineral waters**, which you can sample at the public spa at **BAGNI DI NOCERA**, 4km southeast on the Colfiorito road. The waters are exported worldwide, and have been renowned since the sixteenth century, when people came from as far afield as Portugal and Turkey, lured by reputedly miraculous cures.

If you've got transport, the villages and hilly countryside to the east repay aimless exploration, and there's a scenic route over to Matelica (45km), midway between Fabriano and San Severino Marche, over in Marche (see p.655 and p.664 for more on these areas).

Parco Regionale del Monte Cucco

Some of Umbria's best upland scenery is to be found in the mountains east and north of Gualdo on the border with the Marche, much of it protected by the Parco **Regionale del Monte Cucco**. Where this area really scores is in its organized trails and backup for outdoor activities of every kind; if you want to don walking boots without too much fuss, this is one of the areas to do it – and **access** is easy, with buses from Gualdo to Valsorda and from Perugia, Gualdo, Gubbio and Assisi to Costacciaro.

The southernmost base for exploration of the park is the resort of **VALSORDA** (1000m), 8km northeast of Gualdo on the southern extremity of the park. You can tackle the straightforward trek (1 hr) up **Serra Santa** (1421m) on a track of motorway proportions carved out by pilgrims over the years. From the summit you could drop into the spectacular **Valle del Fonno** gorge and follow it down to Gualdo. Paths follow the main ridge from Valsorda north and south, and it's feasible to walk all the way to Nocera Umbra (6hr). Accommodation is thin on the ground, but there's a **campsite**, the *Valsorda* (☎075.913.261; June–Sept).

To get closer to the heart of the mountains head to the unpretentious and appealing **COSTACCIARO**, centre for all the park's outdoor pursuits and access point for the **Grotta di Monte Cucco**, at 922 metres the fifth-deepest cave system in the world. Above, the huge, bare-sloped Monte Cucco (1566m) is the main playground for **walkers**. The best place to go if you want to get seriously wet or muddy, or just tag along with a tour party, is the **Centro Nazionale di Speleologia,** Via Galeazzi 5 (down a side street off Corso Mazzini, ☎ & fax 075.917.0400 for details of tours, *www.cens.it*), one of the country's most energetic and organized outdoor centres; the *centro* also has hostel **accommodation** for L22,000/€11.36, but be sure to book ahead as the place is often full of school parties. For more comfort head for the country house hotel, *Villa Pascolo*, just outside of town, at Località Case Sparse di Villa (☎ & fax 075.917.0770; ②).

There are plenty of other places to stay in and around Costacciaro, the best of them being the *Monte Cucco da Tobia* in the Val di Ranco (☎075.917.7194; ②; Easter–Oct), a fabled mountaineers' and cavers' hangout. The tiny five-room, one-star *Il Torrione* in the village itself on Corso Mazzini (☎075.917.0740; ②) is convenient for walkers; as is the *Cappelloni*, Val di Ranco (☎075.917.7131; ②; May–Sept). The nearest **campsite** is the *Rio Verde* (☎075.917.0138; April–Sept) at **Fornace**, 3km north of Costacciaro. Freelance camping is prohibited within the *parco regionale*, but elsewhere you'll have few problems finding a discreet pitch for a tent.

ASSISI AND THE VALE OF SPOLETO

The broad southern sweep of the Vale of Spoleto constitutes Umbria's historic and spiritual heartland, boasting three or four of its most archetypal hill-towns – with **Assisi** and **Spoleto** the obvious highlights – plus great swaths of the sunny, pastoral countryside for which the region has traditionally been famous (though be prepared for the occasional blight of factories and unplanned housing). Everything is accessible from Perugia and within easy reach of the main routes, the railway to Terni and dual carriageway (N75) being particularly useful. Scenically inviting **Norcia** and the **Valnerina** are more tricky to reach but well worth the effort – the best approach if you don't have your own vehicle is by bus from Spoleto.

Assisi

ASSISI is already too well known, thanks to **St Francis**, Italy's premier saint and founder of the Franciscan order, which, with its various splinter groups, forms the world's biggest. Had the man not been born here in 1182 the town wouldn't be thronged with tourists and pilgrims for ten months of the year, but then neither would it have the **Basilica of St Francis**, one of the greatest monuments to thirteenth- and fourteenth-century Italian art. You'll probably feel it's worth putting up with the crowds and commercialism, but you may not want to hang around once you've seen all there is to see – something which can easily be done in a day. That said, Assisi quietens down in the evening, and it does retain some medieval hill-town charm. Ashtrays, key rings and other tacky paraphernalia are offset by geranium-filled window boxes, tranquil backstreets and some lovely buildings in the muted, pinkish stone that softens all towns in this area.

Arrival and information

Getting here is easy. **Buses** connect regularly with surrounding towns – especially Perugia – putting down and picking up in Piazza Matteotti, in the east of the town

---

ASSISI AND THE 1997 EARTHQUAKES

In the spring of 1997, earthquakes brought part of Assisi's famed **Basilica** crashing down, killing four people and destroying some of the building's less significant frescoes. But on no account be put off. While the event made world headlines, the damage to the rest of the town was overstated, the epicentre actually being near Colfiorito. Occasional precautionary scaffolding aside, there are very few tangible signs that anything ever happened and none of the famous frescoes were greatly affected. After several years of intense international support and dedicated, detailed work, both the Basilica's **Lower Church** and the spectacular **Upper Church** are now open, along with every other important monument in the town, with the exception of the church of San Pietro. In short, the disruption has, in fact, only prompted structural improvements and an overall refurbishment for Assisi's intrinsic and undiminished medieval appeal.

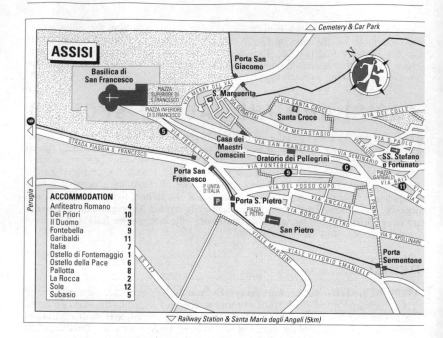

ASSISI

Porta San Giacomo

Basilica di San Francesco

△ Cemetery & Car Park

PIAZZA SUPERIORE DI S.FRANCESCO

PIAZZA INFERIORE DI S.FRANCESCO

S. Margherita

Santa Croce

Casa dei Maestri Comacini

Oratorio dei Pellegrini

SS. Stefano e Fortunato

Porta San Francesco

P UNITA D'ITALIA

Porta S. Pietro

PIAZZA S. PIETRO

San Pietro

Porta Sermentone

ACCOMMODATION

Anfiteatro Romano	4
Dei Priori	10
Il Duomo	3
Fontebella	9
Garibaldi	11
Italia	7
Ostello di Fontemaggio	1
Ostello della Pace	6
Pallotta	8
La Rocca	2
Sole	12
Subasio	5

▽ *Railway Station & Santa Maria degli Angeli (5km)*

above the duomo. In addition, one bus a day leaves for Rome and two for Florence, from Piazza Unità d'Italia. There are hourly **trains** to Foligno (via Spello) and Terontola (via Perugia), with connecting half-hourly bus services between the town and the station, which is 5km away to the south-west of the centre. The staff at the **tourist office**, currently housed in Piazza del Comune to the left of the Tempio di Minerva (Mon–Sat 8am–2pm & 3.30–6.30pm; Sun 9am–1pm; ☎075.812.534), do their best to help with accommodation and provide some useful maps and pamphlets. You can go **online** at *Bar del Corso*, Via Corso Mazzini, (☎075.812.989; daily 8am–10pm; L12,000/€9.30 per hr).

Accommodation

Assisi offers a wide range of **accommodation**, but the supply is often only just adequate for the number of visitors, so advance booking is highly advisable, and essential if you plan to visit over Easter or during the Festa di San Francesco (Oct 3–4) or Calendimaggio (May 21–22). The tourist office have a full list of lodgings, including over fifty **rooms** for rent, and will make reservations for you too. Spello is close enough to make seeing Assisi easy, and see below for options just outside town. Wherever you choose to stay, try to avoid the concentrations of rooms and hotels in Santa Maria degli Angeli or the grim village of Bastia, 4km out of Assisi.

Hotels

Anfiteatro Romano, Via Anfiteatro 4 (☎075.813.025). A good-value one-star in a very pleasant part of town. Choice of with or without bathrooms. ②.

Fontebella, Via Fontebella 25 (☎075.812.456, fax 075.812.941). The most elegant and intimate choice. Ask for a room on one of the top floors for great panoramas. ⑧.

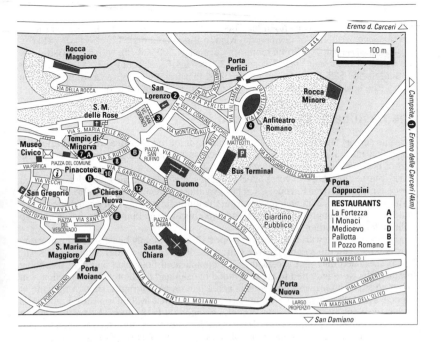

Garibaldi, Piazza Garibaldi 1 (☎075.812.624). An imposing restored palazzo in a quiet corner of town. ③.

Italia, Vicolo della Fortezza 2 (☎075.812.625, fax 075.804.3749; March–Oct). The most central one-star in an alley off the north side of Piazza del Comune. Basic but in an ideal location. ②.

Pallotta, Via San Rufino 6 (☎075.812.307). A two-star in a good location between the duomo and Piazza del Comune; also has a first-rate trattoria. ③.

Dei Priori, Corso Mazzini 15 (☎075.812.237, fax 075.816.804). A three-star slightly east of Piazza del Comune. Rooms vary greatly. ⑥.

La Rocca, Via di Porta Perlici 27 (☎075.812.284). Situated at the end of the street beyond the duomo. Quiet rooms, some with views, most have private bathrooms. ②.

Sole, Corso Mazzini 35 (☎075.812.373, fax 075.813.706). Functional two-star one minute's walk from the Basilica di Santa Chiara. Good option if everywhere else is full. ③.

Subasio, Via Frate Elia 2 (☎075.821.206, fax 075.816.691). Assisi's grande dame, old-world comfort with valley views and an enviable position – right next to the porticoes of the Basilica. ⑥.

OUTSIDE ASSISI

Hotel Sant'Andrea, Via Santa Caterina 2, Bettona (☎075.987.114, fax 075.986.9130, *www. hotelsantandrea.it*). Very comfortably converted medieval building, with an excellent restaurant, and a complimentary bus shuttle service to both Assisi and Perugia. ⑦.

Castello di Petrata, Pieve San Nicolò 22 (☎ & fax 075.815.451, *petrata@libero.it*). An elegantly converted fourteenth-century castle, 5km north of Assisi, with wonderful views over the valley and its own fine restaurant. ⑥.

Rooms, hostels and camping

The pick of the **private lodgings** is *Il Duomo*, Vicolo San Lorenzo 2 (☎075.812.742; ④), located in a tiny, flower-decked medieval alley (second left off Via di Porta Perlici, heading away from the duomo); full lists are available from the tourist office, which can also supply details of **pilgrim hostels**. There are two **regular hostels**: the *Ostello di Fontemaggio*, 3km east of town on the road to the Eremo delle Carceri (☎075.813.636 or 075.812.317, fax 075.813.749; rooms ②, dorms L17,000/€8.78), with a **campsite**; and the *Ostello della Pace* at Via di Valecchia 177 (☎075.816.767; rooms L27,000/€13.95 per person, dorms L22,000/€11.36), off the road that leads west of town from Porta San Pietro (the hostel is a 10min walk – signposted from Piazza Unita d'Italia).

The Basilica di San Francesco

Pilgrims and art lovers alike usually make straight for the **Basilica di San Francesco** (daily 6.30am–7.30pm; free), justifiably famed as Umbria's single greatest glory, and one of the most overwhelming collections of art outside a gallery anywhere in the world. Started in 1228, two years after the saint's death, and financed by donations that flooded in from all over Europe, it's not as grandiose as some religious shrines, though it still strikes you as being a long way from the embodiment of Franciscan principles. If you don't mind compromised ideals, the two churches making up the basilica – one built on top of the other – are a treat.

Most people start with Giotto in the **Upper Church**, mainly because it's the first one they come to, but the sombre **Lower Church** – down the steps to the left – comes earlier, both structurally and artistically. The complicated floor plan and claustrophobic low-lit vaults were intended to create a mood of calm and meditative introspection – an effect added to by brown-robed monks and a ban on photography, though the rule of silence is pretty much ignored by the scrums around the Cavallini frescoes. Francis lies under the floor in a **crypt** only brought to light in 1818 after 52 days of digging (entrance midway down the nave). He was hidden after his funeral for safekeeping, and nowadays endures almost continuous Masses in dozens of languages.

Frescoes cover almost every available space and span a century of continuous artistic development. Stilted early works by anonymous painters influenced by the Byzantines sit alongside Roman painters such as Cavellini, who with Cimabue pioneered the move from mosaic to naturalism and the "new" medium of fresco. They were followed by the best of the Sienese School, **Simone Martini** and **Pietro Lorenzetti**, whose paintings are the ones to make a real point of seeing.

Martini's frescoes are in the **Cappella di San Martino** (1322–26), the first chapel on the left as you enter the nave. He was given free rein in the chapel and every detail, right down to the floor and stained glass, follows his drawings, adding up to a unified scheme that's unique in Italy. Lorenzetti's works, dominated by a powerful *Crucifixion*, are in the transept to the left of the main altar. Vaults above the altar itself contain four magnificent frescoes, complicated but colourful allegories of the virtues on which Francis founded his order: Poverty, Chastity and Obedience. Once thought to have been the work of Giotto, they're now attributed to one of the church's army of unknown artists. The big feature in the right transept is Cimabue's over-restored *Madonna, Child and Angels with St Francis*, a painting Ruskin described as "the noblest depiction of the Virgin in Christendom." Look out for the famous portrait of Francis and for the much-reproduced fresco of St Clare on the wall to its left.

When open (see box opposite), the more straightforward **Upper Church**, built to a light and airy Gothic plan – that was to be followed for countless Franciscan churches – is a completely different experience. It's less a church than an excuse to show off **Giotto**'s dazzling frescoes on the life of St Francis. *Francis Preaching to the Birds* and *Driving the Devils from Arezzo* are just two of the famous scenes reproduced worldwide on cards and posters. The cycle starts on the right-hand wall up by the main altar and continues clockwise. Giotto was still in his twenties when he accepted the commission, having been recommended for the job by Cimabue, whose own frescoes – almost

ST FRANCIS

St Francis is the most extraordinary figure that the Italian church has produced, a revolutionary spirit who took Christianity back to basics. The impact that he had upon the evolution of the Catholic Church stands without parallel, and everything he accomplished in his short life was achieved by nothing more persuasive than the power of preaching and personal example. Dante placed him alongside another Messianic figure, John the Baptist, and his appeal has remained undiminished – Mussolini called him "il piu santo dei santi" (the most saintly of the saints).

The events of his life, though doubtless embellished by myth, are well chronicled. He was born in Assisi in 1182, the son of a wealthy merchant and a Provençal woman – which is why he replaced his baptismal name, Giovanni, with Francesco (Little Frenchman). The Occitan literature of Provence, with its troubadour songs and courtly love poems, was later to be the making of Francis as a poet and speaker. One of the earliest writers in the vernacular, Francis laid the foundation of a great Franciscan literary tradition – his *Fioretti* and famous *Canticle to the Sun* ("brother sun . . . sister moon") stand comparison with the best of medieval verse.

In line with the early life of most male saints, his formative years were full of drinking and womanizing; he was, says one chronicler, "the first instigator of evil, and behind none in foolishness". Illness and imprisonment in a Perugian jail incubated the first seeds of contemplation. Abstinence and solitary wanderings soon followed. The call from God, the culmination of several visions, came in Assisi in 1209, when the crucifix in San Damiano bowed to him and told him to repair God's Church. Francis took the injunction literally, sold his father's stock of cloth and gave the money to Damiano's priest, who refused it.

Francis subsequently renounced his inheritance in the Piazza del Comune: before a large crowd and his outraged father, he stripped naked in a symbolic rejection of wealth and worldly shackles. Adopting the peasant's grey sackcloth (the brown Franciscan habit came later), he began to beg, preach and mix with lepers, a deliberate embodiment of Christ's invocation to the Apostles "to heal the sick, and carry neither purse, nor scrip [money], nor shoes". His message was disarmingly simple: throw out the materialistic trappings of daily life and return to a love of God rooted in poverty, chastity and obedience. Furthermore, learn to see in the beauty and profusion of the natural world the all-pervasive hand of the Divine – a keystone of humanist thought and a departure from the doom-laden strictures of the Dark Ages.

In time he gathered his own twelve apostles and, after some difficulty, obtained permission from Pope Innocent III to found an order that espoused no dogma and maintained no rule. Francis himself never became a priest. In 1212 he was instrumental in the creation of a second order for women, the Poor Clares, and continued the vast peregrinations that took him as far as the Holy Land with the armies of the Crusades. In Egypt he confronted the sultan, Melek el-Kamel, offering to undergo a trial by fire to prove his faith. In 1224 Francis received the stigmata on the mountaintop at La Verna. Two years later, nursing his exhausted body, he died on the mud floor of his hovel in Assisi, having scorned the offer of grander accommodation at the bishop's palace. His canonization followed swiftly, in 1228, in a service conducted by Pope Gregory.

However, a split in the Franciscan order was inevitable. Francis's message and movement had few sympathizers in the wealthy and morally bankrupt papacy of the time, and while his popularity had obliged the Vatican to applaud while he was alive, the papacy quickly moved in to quash the purist elements and encourage more "moderate" tendencies. Gradually it shaped the movement to its own designs, institutionalizing Francis's message in the process.

Despite this, Francis's achievement as the first man to fracture the rigid orthodoxy of the hierarchical Church remains beyond question. Moreover, the Franciscans have not lost their ideological edge, and their views on the primacy of poverty are thought by many to be out of favour with the current pope.

ruined now by the oxidation of badly chosen pigments and further damaged in the 1997 'quake – fill large parts of the apse and transepts.

If time allows check out the **cloisters**, accessible from the rear right-hand side of the Lower Church, and the **Treasury** (April–Oct Mon–Sat 9.30am–noon & 2–6pm; L3000/€1.55), reached via the apse of the Lower Church. The latter, often passed by, contains a rich collection of paintings, reliquaries and general religious clutter given to the Franciscans over the centuries.

The rest of the town

Festooned with tourist trash, Via San Francesco leads back to the town centre. Halfway down on the right are the remains of the fifteenth-century **Oratorio dei Pellegrini** (daily 9am–noon & 3–8pm; free), the hospice for pilgrims, frescoed inside and out by local painters Mezzastris and Matteo da Gualdo – appealing but modest offerings after the basilica. The same goes for the **Museo Civico e Foro Romano** (daily: mid-March to mid-Oct 10am–1pm & 3–7pm; mid-Oct to mid-March 10am–1pm & 2–5pm; L5000/€2.07, or L10,000/€5.17 with Pinacoteca and Rocca Maggiore), housed in the crypt of the now defunct church of San Nicolo. For those with no interest in classical remains there's little here of more than curiosity value, but if ruins and ancient fragments appeal this is a treat, the more so as the museum includes an excavated street and other remains – probably part of the old Roman forum – buried under the tourist-thronged Piazza del Comune. The piazza is dominated by the so-called **Tempio di Minerva**, an enticing and perfectly preserved classical facade from the first century, concealing a dull, if beautifully restored, seventeenth-century Baroque conversion; it was the only thing Goethe was bothered about seeing when he came to Assisi – the basilica he avoided, calling it a "Babylonian pile".

On the other side of the piazza the much-restored Palazzo Comunale contains the town's **Pinacoteca** (Tues–Sun 10am–1pm & 3–7pm; shorter winter hours; L5000/€2.07, or L10,000/€5.17 with Rocca Maggiore and Museo Civico e Foro Romano), whose small but worthy Renaissance collection feels like a light snack after your previous artistic gorging. Francis's birthplace is next door, marked by a dreary new church.

A short hike up the steep Via di San Rufino brings you to the thirteenth-century **Duomo**, with a typical and very lovely three-tiered Umbrian facade and sumptuously carved central doorway. The only point of interest in a stultifyingly boring interior is the font used to baptize St Francis, St Clare and – by a historical freak – the future Emperor Frederick II, born prematurely in a field outside the town. Off the right nave, there's the small **Museo Capitolare** (Mon–Sat 10am–noon & 2–6pm; L2500/€1.29, or L4000/€2.07 with crypt), with a handful of good paintings and an atmospheric **crypt** (same hours; L2500/€1.29, or L4000/€2.07 with Museo Capitolare), entered down steps to the right of the facade. The cathedral makes a good point to strike off for the **Rocca Maggiore** (daily 10am–dusk; L5000/€2.07, or L10,000/€5.17 with Pinacoteca and Museo Civico e Foro Romano) one of the bigger and better preserved in the region, with some all-embracing views the reward after a stiff climb.

Below the duomo, on the pedestrianized Piazza Santa Chiara, stands the **Basilica di Santa Chiara** (daily 7am–noon & 2pm–dusk; free) burial place of St Francis's devoted early companion, who at the age of 17 founded the Order of the Poor Clares, the female wing of the Franciscans. By some peculiar and not terribly dignified quirk she's also the patron saint of television. The church was consecrated in 1265 and is a virtual facsimile of the basilica up the road, down to the simple facade and opulent rose window. Its engineering wasn't up to the same standards, however, and arches had to be added in 1351 to prevent the whole thing being undermined by crumbling foundations. Instead of art, the scantily decorated interior has the once-withered (it was restored by a specialist in Rome) and macabrely blackened body of St Clare herself and a Byzantine crucifix famous for having bowed to Francis and commanded him to embark on his sacred mission to repair God's Church.

You're not long off the Francis trail in Assisi. **San Damiano** (daily 10am–6pm; free), a peaceful spot of genuine monastic charm, is one of its highlights, and is easily reached by taking the Via Borgo Aretino beyond the basilica and following signs from the Porta Nuova, a steep downhill walk of about fifteen minutes. Original home to the Poor Clares, and one of St Francis's favourite spots (he is thought to have written his well-known *Canticle to the Sun* here), the church, cloisters and rustic setting preserve a sense of the original Franciscan ideals of humility and simplicity often absent in the rest of the town.

From the train station you can see the town's other major attraction, the vast and majestically uninspiring **Santa Maria degli Angeli**, built in the seventeenth century and rebuilt after an earthquake in 1832. Somewhere in its Baroque bowels are the remains of the **Porzuincola**, a tiny chapel that was effectively the first Franciscan monastery. Francis lived here after founding the order in 1208, attracted by its then remote and wooded surroundings, and in time was joined by other monks and hermits who built a series of cells and mud huts in the vicinity. Today the church is crammed full of largely fourth-rate works of art and bears no relation to the Franciscan ideal.

After you've exhausted the myriad Francis connections, Assisi has the usual churches, Roman remains and miscellaneous odds and ends that characterize most Italian towns of similar age. If you have time you could check out the **Roman amphitheatre** near Porta Perlici (east of the duomo) or the Romanesque church of **San Pietro**, brilliantly restored for once, in Piazza San Pietro.

Eating and drinking

Multilingual tourist menus proliferate in the town's **restaurants**, and prices can be steep. For straight pizzas there's *Il Pozzo Romano* in Via Sant'Agnese (closed Thurs), near Santa Chiara, and the superb *I Monaci*, Scaletti del Metastasio, whose entrance is in a stepped alley off the north side of Via Fontebella, a few steps down from Piazzetta Garibaldi (closed Wed). The excellent *Pallotta*, Via San Rufino 4 (closed Tues), is near some sticky tourist traps but is an unpretentious and welcoming trattoria – arrive early for a table at lunch. Moving upmarket, *La Fortezza*, Vicolo della Fortezza 2 (reservations essential in summer, ☎075.812.418; closed Thurs & Feb), has great food but slightly slow service. *Medioevo*, Via dell'Arco dei Priori 4b (booking advised, ☎075.813.068; closed Wed, Jan & July 1–21), just south off the Piazza del Comune, is highly recommended for a splurge on some eclectic cuisine that draws its inspiration from France, Germany and Austria as well as Italy.

Spello to Trevi

Ranged on broad terraces above the Vale of Spoleto, medieval and pink-stoned **SPELLO** is the best place for a taste of small-town Umbria if you haven't time or means to explore further, being easy to reach by road and rail (20min from Assisi or Spoleto). Emperor Augustus gave land in the adjacent valley to faithful legionaries who had reached the end of their careers, turning the town (Hispellum) into a sort of Roman retirement home in the process, an ambience it still rather retains.

The walls and three gateways are the most obvious Roman remnants. (Don't bother walking out to the paltry and overgrown remains of the old amphitheatre hidden away beyond the main highway to Assisi: you can see all you need to from the top of the town.) By far the most distinguished sight is **Pinturicchio's fresco cycle** in the thirteenth-century church of Santa Maria Maggiore, about a third of the way up the town's winding and steep main street on Piazza G. Matteotti. The number-two Umbrian painter after Perugino, he left other important works in Siena (the duomo), Rome (the Sistine Chapel, Borgia apartments) and a host of churches scattered over central Italy. The frescoes themselves are fresh and glowing from restoration, with Pinturicchio's famous details and colouring brought out to stunning effect. Unfortunately they're behind glass, which also means you can't get a closer look at the chapel's praised but faded fifteenth-century **ceramic pavement**. Almost immediately to the north of the church stands an excellent little art gallery, the **Pinacoteca Civica** (Tues–Sun: March–June & Oct 10am–1pm & 3.30–6.30pm; July–Sept 10am–1pm & 4–7pm; Nov–Feb 10am–1pm & 3–6pm; L5000/€2.58). It contains a handful of master-pieces by local Umbrian painters, notably Nicolò Alunno, as well as several rare pieces of sculpture. Look out in particular for the figure of Christ with moveable arms, once common, now extremely rare: during Holy Week the arms could be raised for cere-monies involving depictions of the Crucifixion and lowered for those depicting the Deposition and Resurrection. Further up the main street on the right stands **Sant'Andrea**, a striking Gothic church with another Pinturicchio painting in the right transept brightening up the gloomy interior. Also look out for the a looming crucifix attributed to the school of Giotto, and the mummified body of the beatific Andrea Caccioli, an early follower of St Francis, in the left transept.

Spello makes a reasonable base for visiting Assisi, with a good range of **accommo-dation** (albeit quite pricey), fair restaurants and a small summer-only **tourist office** at Piazza Matteotti 3 (daily 9.30am–12.30pm & 3.30–6.30pm; ☎0742.301.009 or 0742.651.408). *Il Cacciatore*, Via Giulia 42 (☎0742.651.141, fax 0742.301.603; ③), is an excellent-value two-star hotel, with fine views from some rooms and potentially noisier rooms looking out over the street. At the smarter *La Bastiglia*, Via dei Molini 17 (☎0742.651.277, fax 0742.301.159; ⑤), most of the rooms command a fine view. *Camping Umbria* (☎0742.651.772; April to early Oct) is the nearest **campsite**, 2km east of town at Chiona.

Spello's best **restaurant**, set in a vaulted medieval town house, is *La Cantina*, Via Cavour 2 (closed Wed), a friendly local place serving plenty of regional specialities – and wonderful fresh pasta. *Il Cacciatore* (closed Mon), attached to the hotel (see above), has middling food and service but a great terrace for al fresco dining. Towards the top of the main street, look out for *Bar Giardino* on the right, with a vast garden and panoramic terrace out back. A little further up, opposite the church of San Lorenzo, the *Pinturicchio* is a cheap and reliable trattoria; the *Bar Tullia*, to its left, is also good and has outside tables from which to take in the street life.

Foligno

To move on anywhere from Spello by public transport means a trip to **FOLIGNO** and a lull in proceedings, because it's a large modern town and flat in every sense of the word. Most of its star-turns were bombed out of existence in the war, and the place is now a mediocre provincial backwater sprawled over an unattractive plain. Its appear-ance wasn't helped by the 1997 earthquake, which hit the town relatively hard. However, much of what's left is conveniently grouped together in the central **Piazza della Repubblica**, and as you're likely to be passing through, a quick look isn't going to hurt. The town's also brimful of hotels and acts as a nodal point for trains and local village buses.

For the **tourist office** – at Corso Cavour 126 (☎0742.354.459 or 0742.354.165, *info@iat.foligno.pg.it*) – and bus station (Porta Romana), follow Viale Mezzetti west from the train station to Piazzale Alunno, and the office is on the southernmost corner. Continue up Corso Cavour and you hit the historic centre two minutes later. The grace-ful twelfth-century **Duomo** has two good Romanesque facades (there's an extra one, the better ones on the side) but the interior was finished off in the eighteenth century to predictable effect. The nearby **Palazzo Trinci** is the only thing worth making a real effort to see. The Trincis were Foligno's medieval big shots, with territory and influence extending over great swaths of Umbria, and their palace is an art-filled monument to wealth and power – all frescoed stairways, carved ceilings and general opulence, most of it restored in the 1990s. Inside are a small **archeological museum** and a **pinacoteca** (both currently closed for restoration), with good frescoes by the fifteenth-century Gubbian painter Ottaviano Nelli.

The only other monument that hints at Foligno's former glory is **Santa Maria Infraportas** (off Piazza San Domenico), a church of pagan origins in which St Peter himself is said to have conducted a Mass. The oldest bit of the current building (eighth century) is the Cappella dell'Assunta off the left nave, dominated by the town's most precious piece of art, a twelfth-century Byzantine mural.

If you need **to stay** in Foligno, the *Belvedere Hotel*, Via F Ottaviani 19 (☎0742.353.990, fax 0742.356.243; ③) just to the right of the station as you come out, on the same piazza but rather surprisingly pleasant. For snacks and full **meals**, right next to the side facade of the duomo, *La Bottega Barbanera*, Piazza della Repubblica 34, serves gourmet dishes in charming surroundings.

Bevagna

Connected to Foligno (8km) by a regular bus service, the serene attractive backwater of **BEVAGNA** is quieter and less visited than Spello, with a windswept **central square** of stark perfection. Flanked by two of Umbria's finest Romanesque churches (both untouched and creaking with age), the Piazza Silvestri dates from around the thirteenth century. The only exception is the fountain which, while blending perfectly, was installed in 1889. Look out particularly for the surreal and demented gargoyles over the doorway of the larger church, San Michele. And if it's open, check out the Palazzo Comunale, which was converted in the nineteenth century into one of Umbria's prettiest provincial theatres. Also worth seeking out is the impressive **Roman mosaic** (north side of Via Porta Guelfa; free) once part of a bath complex. This fine work shows octopus, lobsters, sea-centaurs and other creatures.

There's not a lot else to the town, other than the quaint attractiveness of the streets, but Bevagna does boast three charming **hotels**. The most central is *Il Chiostro di Bevagna*, Corso Matteotti (☎0742.361.987, fax 0742.369.231, *chiostro.bevagna @katamail.com;* ③) just off Piazza S. Silvestro, in an atmospheric renovated Dominican convent, with an original cloister. Down the same street, the *Palazzo Brunamonti*, Corso Matteotti 79 (☎0742.361.932, fax 0742.361.948, *www.brunamonti.com;* ④) is a sumptuous place with a period setting and trompe l'oeil decorations. *L'Orto degli Angeli* (☎0742.360.130, fax 0742.361.756, *www.ortoangeli.it;* ⑤) is the most luxurious and historic of them all; the mansion, with porticoes, gardens and a gourmet restaurant, has been in the same family since 1788. If you book in advance, it is possible to stay in the Santa Maria del Monte **convent** (☎0742.360.133; ②) courtesy of the Benedictine nuns at Corso Matteotti 15. There are also a couple of good **restaurants** in town: the *Ottavius*, Via del Gonfalone 4 (closed Mon), immediately south of Piazza Silvestri in the square in which the buses from Foligno and Montefalco stop; and the *Osteria del Podestà*, Corso Matteotti 67, which offers unusual regional specialities (closed Tues).

Montefalco

Bus is the only way to get from Foligno to **MONTEFALCO** by public transport, a pleasing and intimate medieval village that's home to a superb collection of paintings which definitely merit a morning. Its name, meaning Falcon's Mount, was glorified with the appendage *la ringhiera dell'Umbria* – "the balcony of Umbria" – a somewhat hyperbolic tribute to its, nevertheless wonderful, views. It was also the birthplace of eight saints, good going even by Italian standards. Nowadays the town's sleepy rather than holy, with only a stupendously ugly water tower and very slight urban sprawl to take the edge off its medieval appeal. The strong, blackberry-flavoured **local wine**, *Sagrantino Passito*, made from a grape variety found nowhere else in Europe, is well worth a try; there's a good little shop in the main square for this and other liquid purchases, the *Enoteca Benozzo Gozzoli*.

The lofty location was a godsend to Spoleto's papal governors, left high, dry and terrified by the fourteenth-century defection of the popes to Avignon. They took refuge here, and their cowering presence accounts for the rich decoration of the town churches, a richness out of all proportion to the town's size. The cavernous ex-church of **San Francesco**, off the central Piazza del Comune in Via Ringhiera Umbra (daily: 10.30am–1pm; also June–July 3–7pm; Aug 3–7.30pm; March–May & Sept–Oct 2–6pm; Nov–Feb 2.30–5pm; L7000/€3.62), houses the town's big feature, Benozzo Gozzoli's sumptuous **fresco cycle** on the life of St Francis. With Fra' Angelico, Gozzoli was one of the most prolific and influential Florentine painters to come south and show the backward Umbrians what the Renaissance was all about. Resplendent with colour and detail, the cycle copies many of the ideas and episodes from Giotto's Assisi cycle but, with 200 years of artistic know-how to draw on, is more sophisticated and more immediately appealing (if lacking Giotto's austere dignity). Among numerous other paintings in the church and excellent adjoining gallery are works by most of the leading Umbrians (Perugino, Nicolò Alunno, Tiberio d'Assisi) as well as a host of more minor efforts by local fifteenth-century artists. There are more early frescoes in **Sant'Agostino** across the main piazza in Via Umberto I, where you should also look out for some revered mummified bodies – one lot is halfway down the nave, and you can admire Beato Pellegrino, set out in a wardrobe at the top end of the left-hand nave.

The rest of the town is relatively low key but nice to wander and doesn't take long to see. Probably the most bizarre sight is the mummified body of St Clare (St Chiara), which languishes in the otherwise dismal church of the same name, five minutes' walk from San Francesco in Via Verdi (this is a second St Clare, not to be confused with the one in Assisi). Ring the bell and, if the nuns aren't deep in prayer, they may show you round the adjoining convent: in what turns out to be a fascinating behind-the-scenes look at monastic life, you're shown the remains of the saint's heart and the scissors used to hack it out. The story goes that Christ appeared to Clare, saying the burden of carrying the cross was becoming too heavy; Clare replied she would help by carrying it in her heart. When she was opened up after her death, a cross-shaped piece of tissue was duly found on her heart. Other strange exhibits include three of her kidney stones and a tree that miraculously grew from a staff planted in the garden here by Christ, during one of his appearances to Clare; the berries are used to make rosaries and are said to have powerful medicinal qualities.

Fifty metres beyond the church, preceded by a triple-arched Renaissance porch, is the chapel of **Sant'Illuminata**, strikingly if not terribly well frescoed by local painter Melanzio and others in 1510. Keep on heading out of town, turn left at the T-junction, and fifteen minutes of tedious walking brings you to **San Fortunato**, nicely situated amongst ilex woods and noted for the frescoes by Tiberio d'Assisi (1512), in the Cappella delle Rose (left of the main courtyard). Check out the macabre bundle of blackened bones under the altar of the main church, the remains of St Fortunato himself, martyred in 390.

Practicalities

There's no need to spend more than a morning in Montefalco, but if you do decide to stay – and it's a peaceful spot to rest up – there are two hotels in town. The tiny and quaintly old-fashioned *Ringhiera Umbra*, Via G. Mameli 20 1 (☎0742.379.166, fax 0742.379.166, *www.ringhieraumbra.com*; ③), or the fancier, *Hotel "Degli Affreschi"*, Via G. Mameli 45 (☎0742.379.243, fax 0742.379.643; ④) which is a bit closer to the main square. Residents have the use of the swimming pool at the modern sister hotel *Hotel Nuovo Mondo*, 2km outside of town on the main road. For grander dining than the *Ringhiera's* home-style **restaurant**, try the *Coccorone*, on the corner of Largo Tempestivi and Via Fabbri (closed Wed), where the chances are you'll have one of the best meals you're likely to have in Umbria – the *crespelle* (stuffed pancakes) and the *tiramisù* are especially good.

Should you want more **information** on the town, contact the tourist desk inside San Francesco (summer 10.30am–7.30pm, winter closes at 5pm; ☎0742.379.598).

Trevi

The best way to move southwards from Foligno is by train, which skirts the plain of Spoleto and whisks past the light industrial sites that blight the whole stretch of the valley to Terni and beyond. Not many people stop before Spoleto itself, giving **TREVI** and its towering position no more than an admiring glance. Its daunting inaccessibility is one of the reasons for its easy-going, old-fashioned charm; the feeling is of a pleasant, ordinary provincial town, unvisited and unspoilt. Beyond it lie vast expanses of olive groves, renowned for producing central Italy's finest oil. The town's also apparently famous for its celery.

The medieval centre, looming high on its hill, is 4km from the station, a dull and exhausting trek – take the connecting bus service instead. The **tourist office** at central Piazza Mazzini 6 (Mon–Sat 9.30am–1pm & 3.30–6pm; ☎0742.781.150) is invaluable for maps showing routes to the peripheral churches, which contain a sprinkling of Umbrian paintings. The most noteworthy are in **San Martino** and **Madonna delle Lacrime**, the latter containing excellent and well-restored works by Perugino and Lo Spagna. The twelfth-century **Duomo** of Sant'Emiliano at the town's highest point suffered more than usually violent nineteenth-century butchery of its innards, but is fine from the outside and conserves a series of sixteenth-century frescoes by Melanzio, a half-decent painter active in several villages locally.

The **Pinacoteca Comunale** (April–May & Sept Tues–Sun 10.30am–1pm & 2.30–6pm; June–July Tues–Sun 10.30am–1pm & 3.30–7pm; Aug daily 10.30am–1pm & 3–7:30pm; Oct–March Thurs–Sun 10.30am–1pm & 2.30–5pm; L5000/€2.58) in Largo Don Bosco, in the former Convento di San Francesco, houses a display of coins, ceramics and Roman trivia, several paintings by Umbrian masters and one outstanding work, a *Coronation of the Virgin* (1522) by Lo Spagna. Trevi's medieval governors commissioned this last painting as a copy of a more famous work by the Florentine Ghirlandaio, mainly because they couldn't afford the real thing.

Accommodation is limited to a single hotel, the rather bland but adequate three-star *Trevi*, at Via Fantosati 2 (☎0742.780.922, fax 0742.780.772; ⑤), though the tourist office (see above) may be able to come up with a few **private rooms** to rent. For food try the *Osteria La Vecchia Posta*, Piazza Mazzini 14 (closed Thurs except in July & Aug).

Fonti di Clitunno

A short hop from Trevi on the road south are the sacred **FONTI DI CLITUNNO** (daily: Nov–March 9am–1pm & 2–7pm; April to 15 Sept 9am–8pm; 16 Sept to end of Oct 9am–1pm & 2–6.30pm; ☎0743.521.141; L1500/€0.77), an unexpected beauty spot given the pockmarked surroundings. There's a certain amount of commercialized fuss and bother at the entrance, but the springs, streams and willow-shaded lake beyond – painted by Corot and an inspiration to poets from Virgil to Byron – are pure, languid romanticism. Unfortunately, the proximity of the noisy , with its roaring trucks and buses, comes very close to ruining the effect. The spa waters have attracted people since Roman times – the likes of Caligula and Claudius came here to party – but their major curative effect is allegedly the dubious one of completely extinguishing any appetite for alcohol. Earthquakes over the years have upset many of the underground springs, so the waters aren't as plentiful as they were, but they still flow as limpid as they did in Byron's day, the "sweetest wave of the most living crystal . . . the purest god of gentle waters . . . most serene of aspect and most clear . . . a mirror and a bath for Beauty's youngest daughters." A mini tourist office doles out background information in the summer.

A few hundred metres north is the so-called **Tempietto di Clitunno** (open 8am to sunset; free), looking for all the world like a miniature Greek temple but actually an eighth-century Christian church, cobbled together with a mixture of idiosyncrasy, wishful thinking and old Roman columns. It's only a small, one-off novelty, but still evocative, and with the bonus inside of some faded frescoes said to be the oldest in Umbria.

Spoleto

SPOLETO is perhaps Umbria's most compelling town and many people's central-Italian favourite. Known mainly for its big **summer festival** (see box on p.612), it's remarkable also for its thorough-going medievalism, an extremely scenic setting, and several of Italy's most ancient Romanesque **churches** (note that, excepting San Salvatore, Spoleto's churches close for the afternoon). Far more graceful and provincial a city than Perugia, nowadays it plays second fiddle politically to its long-time historical enemy, though for several centuries it was among the most influential of Italian towns. Two kilometres of well-preserved walls stand as testament to the one-time grandeur of its Roman colony, though its real importance dates from the sixth century when the Lombards made it the capital of one of their three Italian dukedoms. The autonomous **Duchy of Spoleto** eventually stretched to Rome, and by 890 its rulers had become powerful enough to lay claim to the imperial throne itself, making Spoleto, for a short time at least, the capital of the entire Holy Roman Empire. Barbarossa flattened the city in a fit of pique in 1155, and in 1499 the 19-year-old Lucrezia Borgia was appointed governer by her father, Pope Alexander VI. After that it was one long decline until about thirty years ago and the arrival of the festival.

Arrival, information and accommodation

Spoleto is easily reached by **train**, with regular services on the main Rome–Ancona line and local links with Foligno, Terni, Orte and elsewhere. The train station is just northwest of the lower town; shuttle buses to the centre depart from outside the station (get tickets from the station newspaper stand), as do services for Norcia (see p.617); other **buses** leave from Piazza Libertà and Piazza Garibaldi. The Spoleto **tourist office** is at Piazza Libertà 7 (daily 9am–1pm & 4–7.30pm; ☎0743.220.311, *info@iat.spoleto.pg.it*).

Inexpensive **rooms** are hard to come by when the festival's in full swing, but otherwise you shouldn't have too many problems. *Pensione dell'Angelo* is very central, above a busy trattoria at Via Arco del Druso 25 (☎0743.222.385; ③), but small and slightly dingy. Otherwise try the good, if slightly overpriced, *Aurora*, a perfectly situated *pensione* in an alley off Piazza Libertà at Via dell'Apollinare 3 (☎0743.220.315; ③), or the seven quiet and excellent rooms above *Il Panciolle* restaurant at Via del Duomo 4 (☎0743.45.677; ③). If you're prepared to spend more, the best of the central three-stars is the *Nuovo Clitunno*, Piazza Sordini 6 (☎0743.223.340, fax 0743.222.663; ④), or the *Charleston*, Piazza Collicola 10 (☎0743.220.052, fax 0743.221.244; ④) by the church of

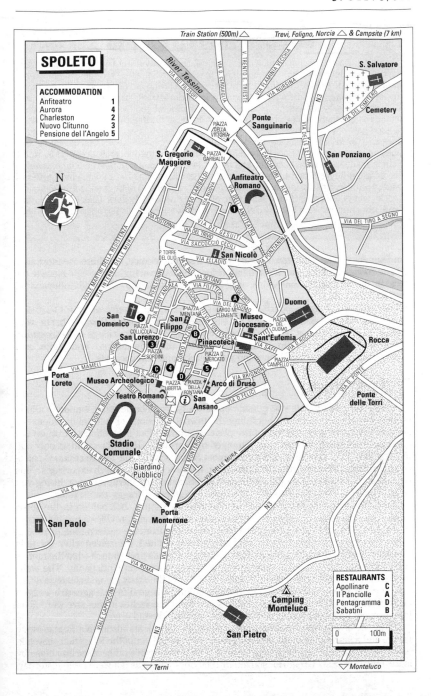

Train Station (500m) △   Trevi, Foligno, Norcia △ & Campsite (7 km)

SPOLETO

ACCOMMODATION
Anfiteatro	1
Aurora	4
Charleston	2
Nuovo Clitunno	3
Pensione del l'Angelo	5

S. Salvatore

Cemetery

Ponte
Sanguinario

San Ponziano

S. Gregorio
Maggiore

Anfiteatro
Romano

N

San Nicolò

Duomo

San
Domenico

San
Filippo

Museo
Diocesano

San Lorenzo

Pinacoteca

Sant'Eufemia

Rocca

Porta
Loreto

Museo Archeologico

Arco di Druso

Ponte
delle Torri

Teatro Romano

San
Ansano

Stadio
Comunale

Giardino
Pubblico

San Paolo

Porta
Monterone

Camping
Monteluco

San Pietro

RESTAURANTS
Apollinare	C
Il Panciolle	A
Pentagramma	D
Sabatini	B

0   100m

▽ Terni   ▽ Monteluco

THE FESTIVAL DEI DUE MONDI

Hosting Italy's leading international arts festival, the **Festival dei Due Mondi** (Festival of Two Worlds), has been a double-edged blessing for Spoleto – crowds and commercialism being the price it has had to pay for culture. Having already rejected thirty other Italian locations, the influential arts guru Giancarlo Menotti plumped for the town in 1958, attracted by its scenery, small venues and general good vibes. The ensuing jamboree is a great attraction if you're into music, dance or theatre, though the place forgoes a good part of its charm as a result. On top of the crowds, ticket prices for top companies and world-class performers can be off-putting, as can the jet-set, well-heeled cut of the audiences. Be warned too that while the festival's in progress you can expect packed hotels, madness in the restaurants and higher prices all round. At the same time there's an Edinburgh-type fringe and plenty of fellow travellers (plus lots of film, jazz, buskers and so on). Organizers, moreover, are increasingly looking to more avant-garde acts and wacky shows to recover the artistic edge of the festival's early days. Check out **tickets and information** from the **tourist office** on Piazza Libertà or the festival's own **box office** at Piazza del Duomo (☎0743.28.120).

San Domenico. The lower town is very much a second choice, but there are more likely to be rooms available, and it's still handy for the medieval highlights. The place to try here is the potentially noisy but well-renovated *Anfiteatro*, Via dell'Anfiteatro 14 (☎0743.49.853; ②).

Campsites are also a possibility. Closest is *Camping Monteluco* (☎0743.220.358; April–Sept), behind San Pietro and an easy downhill walk from Piazza Libertà, with (officially) only 35 places. The *Il Girasole* (☎0743.51.335) in the village of **Petrognano** (10km northwest of Spoleto; hourly buses from the train station) is a bigger and flashier affair, with a public swimming pool nearby and tennis courts.

The Lower Town

The first thing that greets you outside Spoleto's quaint Thirties-style station is a ludicrously out-of-place sculpture heralding the town's delusions of cultural grandeur – a shame, because the overall feel of the place is anything but pretentious. Through the gateway, the lower town was badly damaged by World War II bombing and its only real interest lies in a couple of churches, most impressively the fourth-century paleo-Christian **San Salvatore** (usually 7am–7pm). If you're not into church excursions a bus runs from the station up to Piazza Libertà, the heart of the medieval town, luring you with a superb skyline of spires, tiled roofs and splashes of craggy countryside.

San Salvatore is on the outskirts of the modern suburb, half-hidden in the **town cemetery**, whose spooky glimpse of the Italian way of death provides a morbid attraction in itself. The church was built by Christian monks from the eastern Mediterranean in the fourth century, since when it's hardly been touched. Conceived when the only models for religious buildings were Roman temples, that's pretty much what the monks came up with, the net result leaning more to paganism than Christianity. The walls inside are bare, the floors covered in fallen stone, and the dusty gloom is heavy with an almost eerie antiquity. Crumbling Corinthian columns from different ages are wedged awkwardly alongside one another, and at some point the arches in the nave were filled in to prevent total collapse. Try to visit at dusk to get the full effect.

In the vicinity is **San Ponziano**, unremarkable but for its distinctive Romanesque facade and a fascinating tenth-century **crypt** – if you can tempt the loquacious caretaker out of his cave-like house to show you it. The lower town's other attraction close by is the church of **San Gregorio**, started in 1069 but looking as if it were built yesterday, a result of recent cleaning and restoration. The tower and intriguing portico are made from a patchwork of fragments clearly pinched from earlier Roman remains, but it's the interior that commands most attention. Stripped back to their Romanesque state, the walls are dotted with substantial patches of fresco and interrupted by a series of unusual, rather intimidating stone confessionals. The presbytery is raised several metres above the level of the naves to allow for a masterful little **crypt**, supported by dozens of tiny pillars.

Tradition has it that somewhere under the church are the bones of ten thousand Christian martyrs killed by the Romans in the **amphitheatre** close by. There are still traces of the bloodbath visible in the military barracks up the road. No one seems to mind if you just walk straight in; bear right from the gateway for the best remains, none of which are terribly substantial. The ever-ingenious Romans apparently constructed special gutters to drain blood from the arena into the nearby Torrente Tessino, which ran crimson as a result. Now the river's full of rubbish and a long way from being a puddle, let alone a torrent.

The Upper Town

There's really no single central piazza in Spoleto, but the place to head for is **Piazza Libertà**. Here you are confronted by the much-restored first-century **Roman theatre** (Mon–Sat 9am–7pm, Sun 9am–1pm; L4000/€2.07), complete enough, if overshadowed by the gaudily painted buildings on all sides (it's entered from just down Via Sant'Agata, the street that drops west from the piazza). The worst of these offenders, the church and convent of **Sant'Agata**, absorbed much of the stage area in the Middle Ages and houses a small **archeological collection** of busts and stone fragments (same hours; entry with ticket for theatre). The theatre stage, such as it is, is used for festival and other performances throughout the summer. Its past includes a grisly episode in 1319 when four hundred Guelph supporters were rounded up by the Spoletans and dumped on the stage with their throats cut; the corpses were then pushed into a pile and burnt. The highlights of the museum are the *Lex Spoletina*, two Roman inscriptions that forbade the chopping down of trees in the sacred woods of **Monteluco**. The injunction must have worked because the forests, home to second-century hermits and later to St Francis, are still there, 8km east of the town. Take one of the hourly #9 buses from Piazza Libertà if you're not up to the very long and very stiff walk, and head away from the hotel-restaurant complex and accompanying crowds into the footpaths that cross the woods. You don't have to walk far before you're alone. The views are great on a good day, and it's a welcome relief from the summer maelstrom down in Spoleto itself.

Cutting into the adjoining **Piazza della Fontana** are more Roman remains, all far more humble than the vast wad of tourist blurb leads you to expect. Of the town's many arches from the period, the **Arco di Druso** (23 AD) straddling the entrance to the Piazza del Mercato is the only one not embedded in a wall. It was intended as a triumphal gateway to the old forum, and built to honour what must have been very minor campaign victories on the part of Drusus, son of Tiberius. The patched-up walls behind it are the city's oldest, built in the sixth century BC by the Umbrians, who otherwise are as mysterious and elusive as ever. To the right of the arch is what is described as a **Roman temple**, but unless you've a vivid imagination it's difficult to see it as anything other than a ditch. Pop into the adjacent church of **San Ansano** for a look at more of the temple and the wonderful fresco-covered crypt (down the stairs to the left of the high altar), originally the home of sixth-century monks.

Nowhere do you get a better sense of Spoleto's market-town roots than in the homely **Piazza del Mercato** beyond, whose main bar offers a fine opportunity to take in some colourful streetlife. Old women wash fruit and vegetables in a fountain, its crown embellished with an impressive clock, the men drink in the bars and swap unintelligible stall-holders' gossip, and tourists make barely a dent in the proceedings. The *alimentari* on all sides are a cornucopia of goodies, with a definite bias towards truffles and sticky liqueurs.

Turning the corners of the attractive streets hereabouts, it's a short walk to the **Duomo** (daily: March–Oct 8am–1pm & 3–6.30pm; Nov–Feb closes 5.30pm; free), whose facade of restrained elegance is one of the most memorable in the region. The careful balance of Romanesque and Renaissance elements is framed by a gently sloping piazza and lovely hanging gardens, but the broad background of sky and open countryside is what sets the seal on the whole thing. The church suffered like many in Italy from the desire of rich communities to make their wealth and power conspicuous, a desire usually realized by tearing the guts out of old churches and remodelling them in the latest style. This worked well on the thirteenth-century **facade**, which has an arched portico tacked on in 1491, but less well in the interior where Pope Urban VIII's architect, Luigi Arrigucci, applied great dollops of Baroque midway through the seventeenth century. His "improvements", luckily, are eclipsed by the apse's superlative **frescoes** by the great Florentine artist Fra' Filippo Lippi, dominated by his final masterpiece, a *Coronation of the Virgin* (1469).

He died shortly after their completion, the rumour being that he was poisoned for seducing the daughter of a local noble family, his position as a monk having had no bearing on his sexual appetite. The Spoletans, not too perturbed by moral laxity, were delighted at having someone famous to put in their cathedral, being, as Vasari put it, "poorly provided with ornaments, above all with distinguished men", and so refused to send the dead artist back to Lorenzo de' Medici, his Florentine patron. Interred in a **tomb** designed by his son, Filippino Lippi (now in the right transept), the corpse disappeared during restoration two centuries later, the popular theory being that it was spirited away by descendants of the compromised girl – a sort of vendetta beyond the grave.

You should also make a point of seeing the **Erioli Chapels** at the beginning of the right nave, primarily for a faded *Madonna and Child* (with Lago di Trasimeno in the background) by Pinturicchio (1497), and for the cruder frescoes in the adjoining chapel by the Sicilian artist Jacopo Santori. There's also a good **Cosmati marble floor**; Umbria's earliest documented painting (a *Crucifix* of 1187, by Alberto Sotio, behind glass at the beginning of the left nave); a colourful chapel further down the left nave containing a framed letter written by St Francis (one of only two to survive); and the inevitable **icon**, which Barbarossa gave to the town in 1185 to try to make amends for having flattened it thirty years earlier.

The **Pinacoteca** is stuck away in the farthest reaches of the Palazzo del Municipio, the town's council building (Tues–Sun 10am–1pm & 3–6pm; L5000/€2.58). You're sold a ticket at the entrance (which currently alternates between the front of the Palazzo del Municipio and a door to the rear almost opposite the entrance to Sant'Eufemia; see below), and then have to wait for someone to show you around the gallery on the upper floor. The handful of rooms are sumptuously decorated, and many of the paintings outstanding, though most are unlabelled. The best stuff is the early Umbrian work in the last of the rooms, particularly a couple of big canvases by a local follower of Perugino, **Lo Spagna**. Some of the more enthusiastic guides may also show you the remains of a Roman house nearby – admission is included with the pinacoteca ticket.

The medieval town's most celebrated **church** is the twelfth-century **Sant'Eufemia** (L3000/€1.55 or L5000/€2.58 with Museo Diocesano – see opposite), architecturally unique in Umbria for its *matronei*, high-arched galleries above the side-naves that served the purpose of segregating women from the men in the main body of the church. It was built over the site of the eighth-century Lombard ducal palace and appears to have been partly constructed from the remains of this and earlier Roman monuments; one or two of the completely mismatched columns are carved with distinctive Lombard motifs. The general dank solemnity of the place clearly points to an early foundation, and as one of the region's Romanesque highlights it warrants a few minutes of attention. Happily, the money from your admission fee does at least go towards the upkeep of the church – and, if you bought the combined-entry ticket, also lets you into the outstanding **Museo Diocesano** (daily: summer 10am–12.30pm & 3.30–7pm; winter 10am–12.30pm & 2.30–6pm; L4000/€2.07 or L5000/€2.58 with Sant'Eufemia), located up the stairs to the left of the church. The half-dozen rooms contain several surprisingly good paintings, including a *Madonna* by Fra' Filippo Lippi and an early Beccafumi, a room of old wooden statues and some wonderfully graphic votive panels offering thanks for salvation from a host of vividly illustrated mishaps.

The Rocca, Ponte delle Torri and San Pietro

If you do nothing else in Spoleto you should take the short walk out to the **Ponte delle Torri**, the town's picture-postcard favourite and an astonishing piece of medieval engineering. It's best taken in as part of a circular walk around the base of the Rocca or on the longer trek out to San Pietro (see below). Within a minute of leaving shady gardens in Piazza Campello you suddenly find yourself looking out over superb countryside (blighted only by the busy road way below, but this doesn't dominate), with a dramatic panorama across the Tessino gorge and south to the mountains of Castelmonte. There's an informal little bar, on the left before the bend, to help you enjoy the views.

The **Rocca**, everyone's idea of a cartoon castle, with towers, crenellations and sheer walls, was another in the chain of fortresses with which the tireless Cardinal Albornoz hoped to re-establish Church domination in central Italy, a primacy lost during the fourteenth-century papal exile to Avignon. It served until the early 1980s as a high-security prison – testimony to the skill of its medieval builders – and was home to, amongst others, Pope John Paul II's would-be assassin and leading members of the Red Brigade. It's approaching the end of some fifteen years of restoration, and will house, among other things, a museum devoted to the Duchy of Spoleto, but despite prodding from the EU – who put up much of the money for restoration – no date has been set for the grand opening.

The **bridge** is a genuinely impressive affair, with a 240-metre span supported by ten eighty-metre arches that have been used as a launching pad by jilted lovers for six centuries. Designed by the Gubbian architect Gattapone, who was also responsible for Gubbio's Palazzo dei Consoli, it was initially planned as an aqueduct to bring water from Meluco, replacing an earlier Roman causeway whose design Gattapone probably borrowed and enlarged upon. In time it also became used as an escape from the Rocca when Spoleto was under siege. The remains of what used to be a covered passageway connecting the two are still visible straggling down the hillside.

It's well worth crossing the bridge and picking up the **footpath**, which zigzags up from the left-hand side of the road and then contours left into peaceful countryside within a few hundred metres, giving great views back over the gorge. Alternatively, turn right on the road and make for the church of **San Pietro**, whose facade beckons from a not-too-distant hillside. If the idea of another church doesn't appeal you can easily double back to town on the circular Via della Rocca.

Though the walk to San Pietro is a longish one (2km), it's pleasantly shady with some good glimpses of Spoleto; the only thing to beware of on the country road (no pavements) are crazed Italians taking the bends too fast. The church would be undistinguished were it not for the splendid **sculptures** adorning its facade. Taken with Maitini's bas-reliefs in Orvieto, they are the best Romanesque carvings in Umbria, partly Lombard in their inspiration, and drawing variously on the Gospels and medieval legend for their complicated narrative and symbolic purpose. A particularly juicy scene to look out for includes the Death of a Sinner (left series, second from the top) where the

Archangel Michael abandons the sinner to a couple of demons who bind and torture him before bringing in the burning oil to finish the job. Fourth panel from the top (right series) shows a wolf disguised as a friar before a fleeing ram – a dig at dodgy monastic morals.

Eating and drinking

There are a couple of nameless bargain **restaurants** in Piazza del Mercato, at nos. 29 and 10, both catering mainly to Spoleto's labourers and market traders. The best basic trattoria is *Il Panciolle,* at Via del Duomo 3 (closed Wed), which has a wonderful terrace for al fresco meals: service can be slow, so settle in for a long lunch. For something more special, go to *Sabatini,* at Corso Mazzini 54 (closed Mon), the town's smartest spot (again with outside tables), or the nicely intimate *Apollinare*, Via Sant'Agata 14 (closed Tues): don't be put off by the blue and gold upholstery. More informal is the slightly cheaper and bistro-like *Pentagramma*, signposted off Piazza Libertà at Via T. Martani 4 (closed Mon). The place to drink in the evening is the main bar on the west side of Piazza del Mercato.

The Valnerina and Norcia

The **VALNERINA** is the most beautiful part of Umbria but is hard to get to without your own transport. Strictly translated as the "little valley of the Nera", it effectively refers to the whole eastern part of the region, a self-contained area of high mountains, poor communications, steep wooded valleys, upland villages and vast stretches of barren nothingness. Wolves still roam the summit ridges and are to be protected by a proposed (but long awaited) regional nature reserve. The area is a genuine "forgotten corner", deserted farms everywhere bearing witness to a century of emigration.

Six **buses** daily run from Spoleto station to Norcia (1hr 15min), calling at Piedipaterno (2 daily connections to Monteleone), Borgo Cerreto, Serravalle and villages in between (timetables from the tourist office in Spoleto, see p.610). The beautiful and tortuous N395 road from Spoleto is virtually the only access point until you hit the "main" SS209 and the more pastoral run up the Nera Valley towards Norcia. Mountains roundabout are around 1500m high, with excellent walking, creeping up as you move eastwards to about 2500m in the **Monti Sibillini**. It's difficult to explore with any sort of plan (unless you stick to the Nera), and the best approach is follow your nose, poking into small valleys, tracing high country lanes to remote hamlets.

More deliberately, you could make for **VALLO DI NERA**, most archetypal of the **fortified villages** that pop up along the Lower Nera. Medieval **TRIPONZO** is a natural focus of communications, little more than a quaint staging post and fortified tower (and a better target than modernish Cerreto nearby). **MONTELEONE** is the only place of any size for miles, with a fine church, and popular with trippers.

CASCIA figures large on the map, but is disappointing in actuality – largely modern, thanks to countless earthquakes over the years – and only recommendable to pilgrims in search of **St Rita**, whose presence, enshrined in the stupendously ugly twentieth-century **Basilica**, dominates both the new and earthquake-damaged hill-town. Rita's cult is enormous in Italy, particularly among women, who've virtually adopted her as their unofficial patron saint. There's not much a woman can suffer that Rita didn't suffer and then triumph over, which is the main reason for her universal appeal and why she's sometimes known as the "saint of the impossible". Apparently, the time to invoke St Rita is when an "ordinary" miracle isn't enough. A poor child of aged parents, she endured a forced marriage, followed by eighteen years of mistreatment from an alcoholic husband, who died in a brawl weeks after repenting his evil ways. Both sons died trying to avenge their father, leaving Rita alone in the world and, as a widow, unable to become a nun. A relaxation of convent rules did eventually allow her to take holy orders, a turnaround lauded as one of her "impossible" miracles.

Norcia

Small and stolid, the very pleasant mountain retreat of **NORCIA** is the only place of any size or substance in the Valnerina. Noted on the one hand as the birthplace of **St Benedict** – founder of Western monasticism – and on the other as the producer of Italy's top **salami**, it has an air of charming dereliction, and its low, sturdy houses (built to be earthquake-resistant) are a world away from the pastoral, fairy-tale cities to the west. It's friendly and appealing, though, and if transport allows, it can be the base for some good trips into neighbouring territory, particularly the famed Piano Grande (see overleaf). A big new road over the mountains into Marche looks set to open up the area – good news for local employment, which is scarce, but a possible challenge to the environment. Hang-gliders and winter sports enthusiasts are pouring in, another mixed blessing.

Taking in the town itself won't detain you long, but you may want to stay anyway, for the wonderful air and atmosphere. Most of the action is in the central **Piazza San Benedetto**, site of the Roman forum and presided over by a statue of Benedict. Apart from its facade, you can largely forget about the **Duomo** – destroyed by several earthquakes (the last big one was in 1979), and patched up to look like nothing on earth. The **Castellina** is more captivating: a papal fortress full of gaunt medieval echoes, it contains a fine little **museum** with fascinating old wooden sculptures and several surprisingly accomplished paintings. Unfortunately there doesn't seem to be enough money around to keep it open on a regular basis; if you're lucky enough to find it open, be sure to pop in. The fortress makes a strange bedfellow for the labyrinthine church of **San Benedetto**, which supposedly was built over the saint's birthplace but more likely was raised from the ruins of an earlier Roman temple. Inside there are a few paltry frescoes, nothing more, though the crypt contains the remains of a Roman-era house.

Meat-eaters would be daft not to try the deservedly famous **local pork products**. Anything that can be done to a pig, the Norcians apparently do – and supposedly better than anyone else. Even today, you still see butchers in other parts of Italy called *un nurcino*, after the town. If finances stretch, you could also indulge in the area's prized black **truffle**. The season runs from January to April (though you may come across the lesser prized summer truffles too), and several thousand lire will buy a light dusting over your tagliatelle. Plenty of shops, an attraction in themselves, are on hand to sell you all manner of local specialities, not just truffles, but also hams, the famed lentils of Castelluccio (see overleaf) and lots of rare mountain cheeses.

Moderate **hotels** are the central eight-roomed *Da Benito*, Via Marconi 4 (☎0743.816.670; ②), and the bigger *Monastero S. Antonio*, Via dei Vergini 13 (☎0743.828.208; ②), located at the far northwest corner of the upper town, open to all even though it's still a working convent. For a very comfortable modern option, try the *Salicone*, Via Montedoro (☎0743.828.076; ⑤) just outside the walls. Under the same management is the *Grotta Azzurra*, a comfortable three-star on Via Alfieri 12 (☎0743.816.513; ③) that is a fine and often lively hotel whose restaurant – *the Granaro del Monte* – is *the* best place to eat in Norcia, It's relatively inexpensive and set in huge medieval banqueting halls complete with suits of armour and huge, roaring fires. A more economical place to **eat**, but still central and excellent is the *Taverna de' Massari* (Via Roma 13; ☎0743.816.218; summer daily, winter closed Tues), located to the northeast of the central piazza, just behind the Basilica of San Benedetto.

Around Norcia – the Piano Grande and Preci

The eerie, expansive **Piano Grande**, 20km to the east of Norcia, is definitely one of Umbria's sights, an extraordinary prairie ringed by bare, whaleback mountains and stretching, uninterrupted by tree, hedge or habitation, for miles and miles. It's much photographed – especially in spring when it's ablaze with poppies – and was used by Zeffirelli as a setting in his Franciscan film *Brother Sun, Sister Moon*. The desperately isolated village of **CASTELLUCCIO** hangs above it at around 1400m; as the curious trickle in, it's no longer the sole reserve of shepherds, but remains an unspoilt base and the ideal starting point for any number of straightforward mountain walks. To plan routes, get hold of the 1:50,000 Kompass map no. 666 or the more detailed 1:25,000 CAI maps (the latter are often available in Norcia or Castelluccio's bars). There's no public transportation into the area, though you might try your luck at catching lifts in high season, when the skies are filled with hang-gliders. Once there rough **camping** is generally no problem, and there are a couple of two-star **hotel-restaurants** convenient for the plain and many walks: *La Sibilla*, in Castelluccio itself (booking advised, ☎0743.870.113; ③), which has an excellent restaurant, and the *Forca Canapine* (☎0743.823.007; ③), a big and comfortable ski-hotel on the Norcia-Arquata road, at the southern edge of the Piano Grande. You might also find rooms above the *Taverna di Castelluccio* bar (☎0743.870.158; ②), 100m from *La Sibilla*.

If you can't get out here the smaller **Piano di Santa Scolastica**, due south of Norcia, will give you a watered-down idea of what you're missing. Another worthwhile trip, if you're short of time to spend in aimless exploration, is the road north to **PRECI** and thus to Visso in Marche. Walled and castled Preci was known throughout Europe in the sixteenth century as a school for surgeons, their main trade being removal of kidney stones. However, they had a more notorious sideline – castrating young boys who were foolish enough to show operatic potential. A kilometre above nearby **PIEDIVALLE** is the beautifully sited Abbey of San Eutizio, one of the cradles of the Benedictine movement. Now only a pretty – if over-restored – twelfth-century Romanesque church stands on the site, but in its day the community of monks held sway over more than a hundred castles and local churches.

ORVIETO AND THE SOUTH

Towards its southern edge Umbria loses its pastoral mystical character and begins to feel like a flat foretaste of Rome and Lazio. **Terni**, its main focus, is a grim industrial city and little more than a watershed for regional transportation, though less than thirty minutes to the north are the classic hill-towns of **Orvieto** and **Todi**, too popular with tourists for their own good, perhaps, but still essential viewing. **Rail** is the key to getting about, with the single-track **FCU** branching off to Todi and thence to Perugia, complementing the **FS** line, which runs down from Spoleto to connect with the Rome–Florence route at Orte. Trains from Terni via Rieti are perfect if you intend to head south into Abruzzo: the branch-line ride to Sulmona is wonderful.

Terni and around

TERNI was the unlikely birthplace of one of the world's most famous saints, **St Valentine**, bishop of the town until his martyrdom in 273 and now entombed in his personal basilica at San Valentino, a village two kilometres to the southwest. A less romantic city however, would be hard to imagine. Terni's important arms and steel industries made it a natural target for Allied bombing in 1944, and eighty percent of the town was reduced to rubble, including, sadly, the best part of its Roman and medieval heritage. Rebuilding replaced what was lost with a grey grid-iron city straight out of postwar eastern Europe; it also put the arms industry back on its feet – the gun used to assassinate Kennedy was made here – and though the town no longer lives up to its nineteenth-century nickname of "the Manchester of Italy", hi-tech weaponry and the stench of chemicals aren't the most enticing of prospects. The **tourist office** (Mon–Sat 9am–1pm & 4–7pm; ☎0744.423.047, *info@iat.terni.it*), should you need it, is at Viale Battisti 7a – take Viale della Stazione from the station, and Viale Battisti is 300m up, on the right.

The Marmore waterfall

The best place to make for locally is the **Cascate delle Marmore** (train or bus from Terni), created by the Romans in 271 BC when they diverted the River Velino into the Nera during drainage of marshlands to the south. The highest waterfall in Europe (at 165m), it was boosted by the damming of Lago di Piediluco in the 1930s to satisfy the demands of industry for cheap hydroelectric power. Pictures of the falls in full spate adorn most Umbrian tourist offices, but what they neglect to tell you is that the water can be turned off at the flick of a switch (in favour of electric turbines), leaving a none-too-spectacular trickle. No two sources agree on when exactly the water is likely to be switched on, but the best chances of finding it running seem to be weekend lunchtimes and evenings when there's often a *son et lumière*. From July 15 to August 11 it also does the business on weekdays, between 5pm and 6.30pm. The observation platforms are below on the SS209 and above in the village of Marmore, with a steep path between the two. The green and luxuriant setting, tumbling water and expanses of gleaming polished marble add up to a spectacular show – shame about the factories round the corner, though.

Lago di Piediluco

If you want to carry on up the Velino Valley, **Lago di Piediluco** makes an attractive target. Surrounded by steep and thickly wooded hills, it's Umbria's prettiest lake, something like a miniature version of one of the northern Alpine lakes. Very dark and deep, the water's a bit on the cold side for swimming (and in places unsafe), though it's a big sailing and canoeing centre. The train station is at the western end, some distance from the town of **PIEDILUCO** itself, but perfect if you want to put up a tent on the southern, less-visited shore, or walk the scenic minor road on this shore to Monte Caperno. There's a quay here with boats to and from Piediluco, as well as a famous four-second **echo**, constantly and enthusiastically being tested. Piediluco is picturesque – with the lake on its doorstep it doesn't have to try too hard – but is filled by people escaping from Terni at the weekends. This said, if you're a fishing or watersports fan, or just need a quiet spot for your tent, you may want to go to ground for a couple of days. **Accommodation** can be tight: try the two-star *Lido* on the lake shore at Piazza Bonanni 2 (☎0744.368.354, fax 0744.368.292; ③), also a popular **restaurant** (no closing day). A top-notch place to eat is the *Tavoletta*, Via Forca 4 (closed Wed and parts of June and Oct). There's a big, and in high season usually packed, **campsite**, *Il Lago* (☎0744.369.199). If Piediluco seems too frenetic, you could always push on to neighbouring Cornello or Capolozza.

To the Abbazia di San Pietro in Valle

There are further worthwhile excursions from Terni, particularly if you're making for Norcia and the Valnerina from the south rather than Spoleto. The only route is the SS209, which follows the mountainous Nera Valley almost to its head. Buses make the run up to **Triponzo**, passing the valley's highlight en route – the Abbazia di San Pietro in Valle,

18km from Terni. You could, if tempted, stop off beforehand at **ARRONE** and **MONTE-FRANCO**, the first of several spectacularly sited **fortress villages** lining the valley. The Valnerina, now desolate and sparsely populated, was once the strategic and bustling hub of communications between the Kingdom of Naples and the Dukedom of Spoleto, and later a bone of contention between the Church and imperial armies – hence the castles.

FERENTILLO, the last village before the abbey, sprawls across two barren hillsides, guarded by twin fourteenth-century towers; it merits a brief stop only if the idea of **mummies** is appealing. Grotesquely propped up in the crypt of **San Stefano** (signposted off the main road; daily 10am–12.30pm & 2.30–5pm; reduced hours out of season; L4000/€2.07), these bizarre figures have been preserved by dry sandy soils and dessicating exposure to wind from south-facing windows. They include two French prisoners hung during the Napoleonic wars, a hapless Chinese couple from the last century who came to Italy for their honeymoon but died of cholera, and a pile of cheerfully leering skulls.

Much more enjoyable is to continue five kilometres up the valley to the **Abbazia di San Pietro in Valle** (daily: 10am–noon & 2–5pm; free), signposted from Colleponte, a kilometre away – and the real point of the exercise if you're not passing through simply for the scenery. Founded by the Lombard duke Faroaldo II, who retired to monastic life after being deposed by his son in 720, it was amongst the most powerful religious houses in Umbro-Romano, controlling vast tracts of land and dominating the lives of thousands of people. It's set high on the hillside near a thickly wooded cleft, the first impression being of a dull blockhouse affair, with nothing to hint at the splendour of the Lombard and Byzantine art inside. The faded frescoes (1190) that cover the body of the main church are the first tentative attempts to create a distinctively Italian art and move away from the stylized influence of Byzantine painting, an influence that nonetheless was to prevail until the advent of Pietro Cavallini, Cimabue and Giotto a century later. The **altar**, beautifully set off by the rose-coloured stone and rich Romanesque display all around, is a rare and important example of Lombard sculpture, carved with what look like pagan, almost Celtic figures and motifs. To each side are well-preserved Roman sarcophagi, backed by a profusion of gorgeously coloured frescoes. A doorway (not always open) leads to the twelfth-century campanile, a Lombard import of a type common in Rome and Lazio and distinguished by fragments and reliefs salvaged from the eighth-century church. There's also a faultless double-tiered cloister from the twelfth century, though access to this may be restricted as the complex's private owners – only the church belongs to the state – have opened an agriturismo (☎0744.780.316) in part of the abbey.

By following the SS209 past the walled, medieval village of **SCHEGGINO** you can pick up the Spoleto road into the Valnerina, a route covered on p.616. If you need to **stay** locally, Scheggino's *Albergo-Trattoria del Ponte*, Via del Borgo 17 (☎ & fax 075.61.131; ③), is the best bet. Even if you're just passing through, give their excellent **restaurant** (closed Mon & Sept 1–15) a try – the trout dishes with truffles are superb.

Carsulae

The building of the Via Flaminia in 220 BC between Rome and Ancona cemented Umbria's strategic importance as the crossroads of central Italy. Staging-posts and fully fledged colonies sprang up along its route, turning into modern-day Narni, Terni, Spoleto, and Spello. Some settlements, however, such as **CARSULAE**, 15km north of Terni, were subsequently abandoned in the wake of earthquakes and civil war. In its day this particular pile of stones was known as the Pompeii of central Italy, and both Tacitus and Pliny the Younger praised its beauty.

The surrounding plain, though rustic and peaceful, has little real interest, but the excavated remains are surprisingly impressive. The freely-accessible site – the largest Roman site in Umbria – is dominated by a church, **San Damiano**, made from materi-

als filched from the ruins (other stones and precious marbles went to build local houses), behind which runs a stretch of the original Via Flaminia, complete with grooves
made by carts and chariots, part of the arched northern gate, tombs, baths, wells, an
amphitheatre and all the other trappings of an ex-Roman town.

Narni and around

It's an easy thirty-minute hop on the train from Terni to **NARNI**, which claims to be the
geographical centre of Italy, with a hilltop site jutting into the Nera Valley on a majestic
spur and crowned by another of Albornoz's formidable papal fortresses. Commanding
one end of a steep gorge (about ten minutes of fairly spectacular train travel), it was
once the gateway into Umbria, the last post before the Tiber Valley and the undefend-
ed road to Rome. However, while the town retains a fine medieval character, the views
from its heights are marred by steel and chemical works around **Narni Scalo**, the new
town that's grown up in the valley below. The trick is to keep your gaze firmly fixed on
the gorge side of the walls and pretend the factories don't exist.

The heart of the **old town** (bus from the train station) has all the standard fittings:
the medieval piazzas, the warren of streets, a modest art gallery, the usual crop of
Romanesque churches, and a huge *rocca*, currently being restored. There's a **Roman
bridge** on the outskirts, the subject of considerable local hype. Goethe arrived in Narni
in the middle of the night and was peeved not to have seen it; he was only missing a
solitary arch in the middle of the river – just as easily viewed from the train.

In what's an appealing but relatively low-key centre, things revolve around the narrow **Piazza dei Priori**, where pride of place goes to the fourteenth-century **Palazza
dei Priori**, unremarkable except for a fountain and graceful **loggia** designed by the
Gubbian architect Gattapone. The gaunt and somewhat eccentric building opposite is
the Palazzo del Podestà, cobbled together by amalgamating three town houses and
adding some token decoration. The thirteenth-century Romanesque sculptures above
the main door are worth a glance, and there's a small **Pinacoteca** on the first floor
whose main feature is a superlative and much-copied canvas by Ghirlandaio. The bulk
of its paintings have been moved to a new gallery in the ex-church of San Domenico,
just a minute away in Via Mazzini, where there are key works by Benozzo Gozzoli and
Fiorenzo di Lorenzo, plus fourteenth- to sixteenth-century frescoes removed from
churches in surrounding villages. The walk down to the gallery offers a chance to look
at the tiny and easily overlooked church of Santa Maria in Pensole, unaltered since 1175
– you can still see the date above the door – and adorned across the width of its facade
with a marvellous carved frieze.

The twelfth-century **Duomo** merits a brief mention, chiefly because its front steps
are where the town hangs out. Inside, the Cosmati marble floor and a recently discovered ninth-century mosaic of Christ don't give much cause to linger.

There's no real reason for staying overnight in Narni, but should you want to there's
a collection of cheap but uninspiring **rooms** around the station, and a **campsite** out of
town at Monte del Sole (☎ & fax 0744.796.336; April–Sept). Otherwise, the best bet is
the cosy, central Piazza dei Priori, the *Dei Priori*, Vicolo del Comune 4 (☎0744.726.843,
www.loggiadeipriori.it; ③) which offers first-class meals at the lovely *La Loggia* restaurant (closed Mon & second half of July). The **tourist office** is at Piazza dei Priori 3
(☎0744.715.362; Mon–Sat 9am–1pm & 4–6pm, *info@iat.narni.tr.it*).

Amelia

AMELIA, 11km northwest of Narni and plonked on top of a sugar-loaf hilltop, is by
far the most tempting local excursion if the ruins don't appeal. Though not big on

monuments, it's fairly interesting and unvisited, noted mainly for its extraordinary cyclopean walls, claimed as some of the oldest and mightiest in Italy. Supported by their own weight and comprising vast polygonal blocks up to seven metres across, they reach a height of over twenty metres in places and date back, according to early Roman historians, to the Umbrian settlement of the eleventh century BC. Most of the town's churches were ruined in the nineteenth century, and art's thin on the ground – San Giacomo's **double cloister** and a **tomb** by **Agostino di Duccio** are the only highlights – but Amelia's charm is the typically Umbrian mixture of good views, medieval streets and lovely countryside close at hand.

The **tourist office** is at Via Orvieto 1 (☎0744.981.453, *info@iat.amelia.tr.it*). The local culinary speciality is a tooth-rotting combination of white figs, chocolate and crushed nuts (only available in winter), but for more substantial fare there are two good **restaurants**, both with rooms to rent: *Anita*, Via Roma 31 (☎0744.982.146, fax 0744.983.079; ③; restaurant closed Mon); and, just 1km north of town, *Le Colonne*, Via Roma 191 (☎0744.983.529; ②; restaurant closed Wed). For more elevated food, try the *Gabelletta*, Via Tuderete 20 (☎0744.982.159; closed Mon), housed in an elegant villa 3.5km northeast, on the road to Montecastrilli.

The drive on to Orvieto along the backroads is a treat: plenty of oak forests and fine walks, and the chance to catch one of Umbria's Romanesque highlights, the twelfth-century church of **Santa Maria Assunta** at Lugnano in Teverina.

Otrícoli

OTRÍCOLI, 15km south of Narni, is almost the last town in Umbria and a reasonable miniature of all the region's hill-towns. Its medieval delights, though, are eclipsed by the remains of Roman **Otriculum**, a ramshackle collection of ruins within easy walking distance of the village. To reach them get on the main road that bypasses the village, head downhill for 200m and take the signposted track that strikes off right towards the Tiber. So far no more than a trickle of tourists visits the colony – still largely unexcavated and evocatively draped in clinging undergrowth – but plans by the state to make them the centre of a vast archeological park mean they're headed for the big time.

Unusually, the settlement has no walls, mainly because it was more a pleasure garden than a defensive site, built as a sort of holiday village for Rome's hoi polloi, who travelled up from the capital by boat on the then still navigable Tiber. Turner stopped off to paint a picture (now in the Clore wing of the Tate Gallery in London), and in the sixteenth century Montaigne described the spot as "infinitely pleasant", though it probably won't stay that way for much longer. You can find **rooms** up in Otrícoli at the one-star, seven-room hotel *Umbria*, Via Roma 72 (☎0744.709.013; ②).

Todi

TODI is one of the best-established Umbrian hill-towns, at heart still a thriving and insular agricultural centre, but also a favoured trendy retreat for foreign ex-pats and Rome's arts and media types. In the way of these things the tourists haven't been far behind, particularly those from Britain, Germany and the US, but neither fact should deter you from making a day-trip: few places beat it for sheer location and fairy-tale medievalism. With a stunning and extremely daunting position, it makes a highly inviting prospect from below.

Getting there, and sussing out how to fit it into an itinerary, are likely to be your biggest problems. Basically you come either from Terni on the hourly FCU train or from Perugia, again by FCU or on one of the regular buses that stop below the town by the church of Santa Maria della Consolazione or higher up, just off the main square near San Fortunato. Moving on, in addition to the train, there's the option of a daily bus to Orvieto. Todi's **train stations** (there are two) are both in the middle of nowhere, and **buses** to the centre don't always connect with the trains. Ponte Rio is the one to go for: Ponte Naia, 5km distant, is marginally closer, but fewer trains stop there, bus shuttles are few and far between, and the uphill walk to town is one long slog.

The Town

The central **Piazza del Popolo** is why most people come here: just about every guide-book describes it as the most perfect medieval piazza in Italy, and although it lives up to this claim, the cars detract and the tone's a bit more gaunt and austere than you're led to expect. The **Duomo** at the far end, atop a broad flight of steps, is the main fea-ture – a meeting point of the last of the Romanesque and the first of the Gothic forms filtering up from France in the early fourteenth century. The square, three-tiered **facade** is inspired simplicity; just a sumptuous rose window (1520) and ornately carved doorway to embellish the pinky weathered marble – the classic example of a form found all over Umbria. Inevitably the interior is less impressive. There's some delicate nineteenth-century stained glass in the arched nave on the right, and a good altarpiece by Giannicolo di Paolo (a follower of Perugino), but an appalling sixteenth-century *Last Judgement*, loosely derived from Michelangelo's, defaces the back wall. The strikingly carved **choir** (1530) – of incredible delicacy and precision – is the region's best, with panels at floor level near the front depicting the tools used to carve the piece. The crypt contains a rambling collection of ancient Roman – and possibly Etruscan – fragments.

Back in the piazza, the other key buildings are the three **public palaces**, squared off near the duomo in deliberately provocative fashion as an expression of medieval civic pride – definitely trying to put one over on the Church. The adjoining Palazzo del Capitano (1290) and adjacent Palazzo del Popolo (begun 1213) are most prominent, thanks mainly to the stone staircase that looks like the setting for a thousand B-movie sword fights. Several films *have* actually been shot in Todi, lured by its relative prox-imity to Cinecittà and scenographic "authenticity". Most notable was the doomed *Cleopatra* – hence the yellowing photographs of a pouting Liz Taylor in some of the bars.

The Palazzo del Capitano houses the town's small **art gallery** and interesting little **Etrusco-Romano museum**, though don't be surprised to find that some minor "mishap" means the doors are closed on your arrival (both Tues–Sun: March & Sept 10.30am–1pm & 2–5pm; April–Aug closes 6pm; Oct–Feb closes 4.30pm; L6000/€3.10).

The **Palazzo dei Priori** (1293–1337) is the southernmost building in the square, with all the various crenellations, battlements and mullioned windows of the other palaces but with the difference that they've just been restored. It's been the seat of all the town's various rulers and today is still the town hall; if you can look like you're on council business you should be able to peep inside. Best place to enjoy the streetlife is from the **bar** down on its right-hand side, more of a locals' local than the flashy place halfway down the piazza (but which does do a good line in sandwiches).

Streets to the right of the duomo are quiet and dozy and worth a wander, though the single most celebrated sight in the town after the piazza is the church of **San Fortunato**. Set above some half-hearted gardens a very short stroll from the centre, it's an enormous thing given the size of the town – testimony to Todi's medieval wealth and importance. The squat, messy and clearly unfinished facade, an amalgam of Romanesque and Gothic styles, reflects the time it took to build (1292–1462) and at first glance doesn't exactly raise expectations. A florid **Gothic doorway** of arched swirls and carved craziness, however, is the first of several surprises, second of which is the enormous interior, recently highlighted by cleaning and several dazzling coats of whitewash. For once it's a light, airy and pleasing sort of size – a legacy of its Romanesque origins – rather than the aircraft-hangar dimensions that church builders seemed to indulge in for their own sake.

It marks the pinnacle of the Umbrian tradition for large vaulted churches, a style based on the smaller and basic "barn churches" common in Tuscany, which were distinguished by a single, low-pitched roof and naves and aisles of equal height. (San Domenico in Perugia, see p.588, is another example.) Also interesting is the increasing use of side-chapels, a habit picked up from Catalonia and southern France in the thirteenth century and made necessary by the rising demand for daily Masses as the Franciscans became a more ministering order.

There's another good **choir**, heavier and with more hints of the Baroque than the one in the duomo, as well as a few scant patches of Sienese fresco. The fresco by **Masolino di Panicale** in the fourth chapel on the right is a good example of this rare painter's work, though a bit battered. Some lovely **cloisters** to the rear (outside and to the right) round off a distinctive and worthwhile church.

Santa Maria della Consolazione (closed daily 1–3pm), completed in 1607, is thought to have been based on an earlier Bramante draft for St Peter's in Rome; the alternating window types in the cupola are a Bramante trademark. Victorian writers called it the best Renaissance church in Italy (pretty close to saying the best in the world). It's worth a look to judge for yourself, but doesn't merit a special journey.

Your time could be enjoyably spent taking a siesta in the rambling **Giardino Pubblico**, full of shady nooks and narrow pathways, and a cut above the normal town plot. There's also a kids' playground and a very small **Rocca**, both less noteworthy than the views, which are extensive though usually hazy. The gardens are best tackled via the stony track to the right of San Fortunato, less of a sweat than the path which comes up from Piazza Oberdan.

Todi's tourist offerings are soon exhausted, but if you want to go the whole hog, check the so-called **niches** in Piazza del Vecchio Mercato, all that's left of the Roman colony. The town's proud of them, but they don't amount to much: four big and slightly overgrown arches of completely unknown purpose. Two minutes' walk down the lane in the lowest corner of the piazza brings you to the tiny **San Carlo** or **Ilario** (1020), an ancient Lombard chapel well off the beaten track that's all too often locked to protect a set of frescoes by Lo Spagna. A few metres beyond the church, and next to a crumbling flower-strewn arbour, is the **Fonte Scarnabecco** (1241), an unusual arched fountain that's now all but redundant but as the town's lifeblood and social meeting place until the advent of piped water. During your wanderings look out for the **three sets of walls**, concentric rings that mark Todi's Umbrian, Roman and medieval limits; they're seen to best effect on Via Matteotti.

Practicalities

The **tourist office**, in the corner of the main square at Piazza Umberto I 6 (daily 9am–1pm & 4–7pm, closed Sun afternoon in winter; ☎075.894.3395, *info@iat.todi.pg.it*), also houses **telephone** booths and bus timetables. **Hotels** are in demand, especially during the increasingly popular Todi Festival (first ten days of Sept), and – except for one expensive four-star, the *Fonte Cesia*, Via Loernzo Leoni 3 (☎075.894.3737, fax 075.894.4677; ⑤) – are characterless modern affairs some way out of town. Ten minutes' walk straight down the main road from Porta Romana brings you to the *Tuder*, Via Maestà dei Lombardi 13 (☎075.894.2184, fax 075.894.3952; ③), an overpriced and functional place in an uninspiring spot. A short distance beyond it is the better located but rather fancy *Villa Luisa*, Via Angelo Cortesi 147 (☎075.894.8571, fax 075.894.8472; ④).

The town's best-known **restaurant** is the *Umbria* (☎075.882.390; closed Wed), behind the tourist office; prices are high and service can be slapdash, but the panorama from the terrace makes it all worthwhile; in season, book to be sure of an outside table. Cheaper alternatives include the excellent and unpretentious *Cavour* at Via Cavour 21 (closed Wed), and the basic *Pizzeria-Rosticceria* off Corso Cavour in Piazza B. d'Alviano (closed Mon after 8pm), a hundred metres from Piazza del Popolo.

Deruta and the Tiber Valley

North of Todi, the Tiber Valley broadens out into a flat plain edged with low hills and dotted with light industry. It's not somewhere you'll want to spend a lot of time, but there are one or two things worth catching if you're in no hurry to get to Perugia (though Marsciano, the area's main town, certainly isn't one of them).

Instead try to take in some of the **hill-villages** along the route – almost any you choose will boast a Romanesque church. Most are built over the graves of early monks and martyrs, the Tiber and Naia valleys having been amongst the earliest to be colonized by Christians fleeing Roman persecution, and thus the springboard of Umbria's powerful monastic tradition. The most rewarding churches are those you come upon by accident, in crumbling hamlets or in the midst of the ilex woods that blanket surrounding hills, but if you prefer to plan a visit the following are a cut above the rest: Viepri, Villa di San Faustino, Santa Maria in Partano, San Teranzano and the Abbazia di San Fidenzo.

If you don't get to the peripheral villages, **Madonna dei Bagni** is the one church on the main N3 that's definitely worth a look. Its walls are covered with hundreds of votive tiles left by pilgrims over 300 years, making a unique social document and occasionally wacky insight into the peculiarities of religious belief. Day-to-day life in the fields, the insides of houses, transport (from horse to carriage to car), clothes and so on are represented almost as cartoons, though the most entertaining tiles are those offered as thanks for "miraculous" escapes from dangerous and not so dangerous corners – a fall from a cow, a bite from a donkey, fire, flood and famine. A hundred tiles were stolen in 1980, and opening times have been curtailed to reduce the risk of a recurrence. The best time to try is Saturday morning, when it's not unknown for bus tours to show up; otherwise ask at the tourist office in Deruta, 2km up the road.

If you're travelling by car, one of the most charming options for **accommodation** in the area, handy for Todi, Perugia, Deruta and Assisi, is the bucolic *San Orsola* (☎0338.855.5361, *adimc@tiscalinet.it*; ③) a restored twelfth-century *casale*, just a few km off the main highway, near Schiavo di Marsciano. They offer spacious, comfortable rooms with a hearty buffet breakfast featuring their own fresh hens' eggs. An excellent **restaurant** 5km to the north is the *Piccolo Mondo*, at San Vito in Monte (☎075.870.8186; closed Mon), with an extensive menu of substantial regional dishes; phone for directions.

Deruta

The town of **DERUTA** is best known for its **ceramics** and seems to be devoted to nothing else. Some of the stuff is mass-produced trash, and some pieces so big you'd need a trailer to get them home, but most is beautiful – handmade, handpainted and, by general consent, Italy's best. The Romans worked local clay, but it was the discovery of distinctive blue and yellow glazes in the fifteenth century, allied with the Moorish-influenced designs of southern Spain, that put the town on the map. Some fifty workshops traded as far afield as Britain, and pieces from the period have found their way into most of the world's major museums. Designs these days are mainly copies, with little original work, though it's still very much the place for browsing and buying; avoid the roadside stalls and head for the workshops of the new town for the best choice and prices.

The **old town** on the hill isn't particularly compelling, but there's a mildly interesting **Museo-Pinacoteca** (April–June daily 10.30am–1pm & 3–6pm; July–Sept daily 10am–1pm & 3.30–7pm; Oct–March Mon & Wed–Sun 10am–1pm & 2.30–5pm; L5000/€2.58). Highlights of the three small rooms downstairs are paintings by Nicolò Alunno and Fiorenzo di Lorenzo, but most sections, not surprisingly, are given over to ceramics, largely unremarkable except for a **tiled floor** (1524) lifted wholesale from the town's parish church.

Torgiano

TORGIANO, 8km north, is the last worthwhile stop before Perugia. It's a fairly dull town but is home to a great little **museum** and Umbria's finest **wines**, the latter produced by Giorgio Lungarotti, one of the new breed of Italian producers and now something of a national celebrity. The unexpectedly interesting **wine museum** in Corso Vittorio Emanuele II in the Palazzo Graziani-Baglioni (daily: summer 9am–1pm & 3–7pm; winter closes 6pm; L5000/€2.58), offers a varied and comprehensive look at every aspect of viticulture and the best non-liquid reason for a visit. Any bottle with his name should be good, but particular wines to look out for include Lungarotti's Rubesco, Torre di Giano, Chardonnay and Castel Grifone; an excellent selection of wines are sold at good prices in the adjacent *enoteca*, and in shops and restaurants across Umbria and beyond.

Orvieto

ORVIETO, out on a limb from the rest of Umbria, is perfectly placed between Rome and Florence to serve as a historical picnic for tour operators. Tourists flood into the town in their millions, drawn by the **Duomo**, one of the greatest Gothic buildings in Italy. But once its facade and Signorelli's frescoes have been admired, the town's not quite as exciting as guides and word of mouth make out. This is partly to do with the gloominess of the dark volcanic rock (tufa) from which it's built, and, more poetically, because it harbours something of the characteristic brooding of Etruscan towns (it was one of the twelve-strong federation of Etruscan cities). Two thousand years on, it's not difficult to detect a more laid-back atmosphere in the cities east of the Tiber – sunnier and easier-going chiefly because they were founded by the Umbrians, a sunnier and easier-going people. All the same Orvieto is likeable, the setting superb, the duomo unmissable, and the rest of the town good for an enjoyable couple of hours. And there's always its renowned white **wine** if you're stuck with time on your hands.

Arrival, information and accommodation

First impressions of Orvieto from afar tend to be the ones that linger; its position is almost as remarkable and famous as its cathedral. The town, rising 300m sheer from the valley floor, sits on a tabletop plug of volcanic lava, one of four such remnants in the vicinity. Without a doubt, the best approach is by car through the hills to the southwest (from Bolsena, see p.764). It starts to look fairly average again from the dismal town around the train station, but hit the twisting three-kilometre road up to the old centre and you begin to get a sense of its drama and one-off weirdness. If you arrive by train the **#1 bus** makes the regular trip from the station to Piazza XXIX Marzo (buy two tickets at the platform bar – one for the return leg). Local bus tickets are also valid for the newly restored nineteenth-century **funicular** from the station forecourt to Piazza Cahen – a far nicer way of getting into the old town than the bus. Inter-town buses take you directly to

Piazza Cahen, Piazza XXIX Marzo, or Piazza della Repubblica, depending on the service. The **tourist office** is at Piazza del Duomo 24 (Mon–Fri 8am–2pm & 4–7pm, Sat & Sun 10am–1pm & 3.30–6.30pm; ☎0763.341.772, *info@iat.orvieto.tr.it*), with a room-finding service and plenty of maps and information. Check your **email** at *Caffè Montanucci*, Corso Cavour 23 (☎0763.341.261; L12,000/€6.20 per hr; 8am-midnight, closed Wed). Most of the town's nightlife and budget **rooms** are in Orvieto Scalo, the unlovely district around the station. The best low-cost central **hotels** are: the two-star *Duomo*, Via Vicolo di Maurizio 7 (☎0763.341.887; ③), in a comfortable restructured medieval building, round the corner from the cathedral; the pleasantly dated *Posta*, Via Signorelli 18 (☎0763.341.909; ③), two minutes from the duomo and offering a wide range of single and double rooms with and without private bathrooms; and the pleasant, three-star *Italia*, Piazza del Popolo 13 (☎0763.342.065; ④), the biggest central place (45 rooms) and thus likely to have space in an emergency. A little further from the centre, and therefore quieter, but still within easy walking distance of everything, are the good-value and well-appointed *Corso*, Corso Cavour 343 (☎0763.342.020; ④) and the slightly larger *Valentino*, Via Angelo da Orvieto 30–32 (☎0743.342.464; ④). The nearest **campsite**, the *Orvieto*, is 10km away on Lago di Corbora (bus to Baschi/Civitella); it's a three-star job with a swimming pool, and open all year, but rather out of the way (☎0744.950.240).

The Duomo

Burckhardt described Orvieto's duomo as "the greatest and richest polychrome monument in the world", while Pope Leo XIII called it "the Golden Lily of Italian cathedrals", adding that on the Day of Judgement it would float up to heaven carried by its own beauty. According to a tradition fostered by the Church, it was built to celebrate the so-called **Miracle of Bolsena** (1263), an event centred on a Bohemian priest travelling to Rome to shake off a heretical disbelief in transubstantiation – the idea that the body and blood of Christ are physically present in the Eucharist. While he celebrated Mass in a church near Lago di Bolsena, blood started to drip from the host onto the corporale, the cloth underneath the chalice on the altar. The stained linen was whisked off to Pope Urban IV, who like many a pope was in Orvieto to escape the heat and political hassle of Rome. He immediately proclaimed a miracle, and a year later Thomas Aquinas, no less, drew up a papal bull instigating the feast of **Corpus Domini**. The Church at the time, however, was in retreat, and the Umbrian towns were at the height of their civic expansion. It's likely that the building of an awe-inspiring cathedral in one of the region's most powerful *comuni* was less an act to commemorate a miracle than a shrewd piece of political opportunism designed to remind errant citizens of the papacy's power.

It was miraculous that the duomo was built at all. Medieval Orvieto was so violent that at times the population thought about giving up on it altogether. Dante wrote that its family feuds were worse than those between Verona's Montagues and Capulets – the original inspiration for *Romeo and Juliet*. The building was also dogged by a committee approach to design – even the plans took thirty years to draw up. Yet though construction dragged on for three centuries and exhausted 33 architects, 152 sculptors, 68 painters, and 90 mosaicists, the final product is a surprisingly unified example of the transitional Romanesque-Gothic style. Credit for guiding the work at its most important stage goes to the Sienese architect **Lorenzo Maitani** (c1270–1330), with the initial plans probably drawn up by Arnolfo di Cambio, architect of Florence's Palazzo Vecchio.

THE FACADE

The facade is the star-turn, owing its undeniable impact to a decorative richness just the right side of overkill. It's a riot of columns, spires, bas-reliefs, sculptures, dazzling and almost overpowering use of colour, colossally emphasized doorways and hundreds of capricious details just about held together by four enormous fluted columns. Stunning from the dwarfed piazza, particularly at sunset or under floodlights, it's not all superfi-

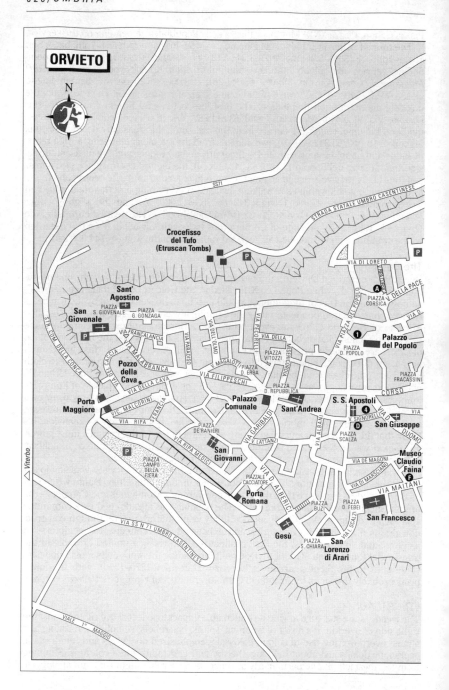

ORVIETO

N

Crocefisso
del Tufo
(Etruscan Tombs)

P

SS71

STRADA STATALE UMBRO CASENTINESE

VIA DI LORETO

P

Sant'
Agostino

PIAZZA
S. GIOVENALE — PIAZZA
G. GONZAGA

San
Giovenale

P

VIA FRANCALANCIA

VIA PARADISO

VIA DELL'OLMO

VIA PECORELLI

VIA DELLA

A

PIAZZA
CORSICA

VIA DELLA PACE

VIA PIAZZA DEL POPOLO

VIA D.

i

PIAZZA
D. POPOLO

Palazzo
del Popolo

STR. COM. DELLA CONCA

VIA D. CACCIA

VIA MALABRANCA

Pozzo
della
Cava

VIA DELLA CAVA

VIA MAGALOTTI

PIAZZA
VITOZZI

PIAZZA
D. ERBA

MISERICORDIA

VIA FILIPPESCHI

PIAZZA
D. REPUBBLICA

PIAZZA
FRACASSINI

CORSO

Palazzo
Comunale

Sant'Andrea

S. S. Apostoli

4

V. SIGNORELLI

VIA D.

VIA

Porta
Maggiore

VIC. MALCORINI

VIA RIPA

VIA SERANCIA

VIA GARIBALDI

V. LATTANZI

VIA ALBANI

PIAZZA
SCALZA

D

San Giuseppe

DUOMO

△ Viterbo

P

PIAZZA
CAMPO
DELLA
FIERA

PIAZZA
DE'RANIERI

VIA RIPA MEDICI

San
Giovanni

VIA DE' MAGONI

Museo
Claudio
Faina

F

VIA DI MARSCIANO

VIA D. ALBERICI

PIAZZALE
CACCIATORE

Porta
Romana

PIAZZA
BUZI

PIAZZA
D. FEBEI

VIA MAITANI

San Francesco

VIA SS N 71 UMBRO CASENTINESE

Gesù

PIAZZA
S. CHIARA

San
Lorenzo
di Arari

V. AT. SCALZA

VIALE 1° MAGGIO

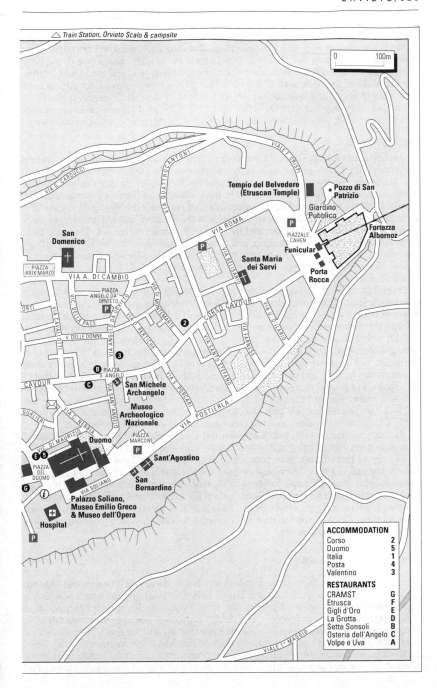

△ Train Station, Orvieto Scalo & campsite

0   100m

VIALE F. CRISPI

VIA QUATTROCANTONI

VIA G. CARDUCCI

Tempio del Belvedere
(Etruscan Temple)

Pozzo di San
Patrizio

Giardino
Pubblico

VIA ROMA

PIAZZALE
CAHEN

Fortezza
Albornoz

San
Domenico

VIA BELISARIO

Santa Maria
dei Servi

Funicular

PIAZZA
XXIX MARZO

VIA A. DI CAMBIO

VIA DI MONTEMARTE

Porta
Rocca

ORTI

PIAZZA
ANGELO DA
ORVIETO

VIA C. CAVOUR

CORSO CAVOUR

VIA DELLA PACE

VIA ANGELO DA ORVIETO

VIA DEL PERTICHE

❷

VIA DELLE DONNE

VIA CAVALOTTI

VIA FARNESE

VIA DEL LARIO

❸

CAVOUR

❸ PIAZZA
S. ANGELO

VIA SANTO STEFANO

❸

San Michele
Archangelo

VIA S. POPEARI

GUALTIERI

VIA C. NEBBIA

VIA SANT'ANGELO

Museo
Archeologico
Nazionale

VIA POSTIERLA

VIA DI MAURIZIO

PIAZZA
MARCONI

❺ Duomo

Sant'Agostino

PIAZZA
DEL
DUOMO

VIA SOLIANO

San
Bernardino

ⓖ

ⓘ

Palazzo Soliano,
Museo Emilio Greco
& Museo dell'Opera

☩ Hospital

P

ACCOMMODATION	
Corso	2
Duomo	5
Italia	1
Posta	4
Valentino	3

RESTAURANTS	
CRAMST	G
Etrusca	F
Gigli d'Oro	E
La Grotta	D
Sette Sonsoli	B
Osteria dell'Angelo	C
Volpe e Uva	A

VIALE 1° MAGGIO

cial gloss. The **four pillars** at the base, one of the highlights of fourteenth-century Italian sculpture, are well worth a close look. The work of Maitani and his pupils, they describe episodes from the Old and New Testaments in quite staggering detail: lashings of plague, famine, martyrdoms, grotesque mutilation, mad and emaciated figures, the Flagellation, the Massacre of the Innocents, strange visitations, Cain slaying Abel (particularly juicy), and only the occasional touch of light relief. In its day it was there to point an accusing finger at Orvieto's moral slackers, as the none-too-cheerful final panel makes clear, with the damned packed off to fire, brimstone and eternal misery.

THE INTERIOR

The inside (daily 7.30am–1pm & 2.30pm–dusk; free) is a disappointment, at least at first glance, as if the facade either took all the enthusiasm or all the money and the church was tacked on merely to prop everything else up. Adorned with alternating stripes of coloured marble similar to those found in the cathedrals of Siena, Florence and Pisa, it's mainly distinguished by **Luca Signorelli's** *Last Judgement* (1499–1504). Some claim it surpasses even Michelangelo's similar cycle in the Sistine Chapel, painted forty years later and obviously heavily influenced by Signorelli's earlier treatment. The cycle is on view again after years of restoration, and though you now have to pay for the privilege of seeing it, the admission's more than worth it (April–Oct Mon–Sat 10am–12.45pm & 2.30–7.15pm, Sun 2.30–6.45pm; Nov–March Mon–Sat 10am–12.45pm & 2.30–5.15pm, Sun 2.30–5.45pm; L3000/€1.55).

Several painters, including Perugino and Fra' Angelico (who completed two ceiling panels), tackled the chapel before Signorelli – a free-thinking and singular artist from nearby Cortona – was commissioned to finish it off. All but the lower walls are crowded with the movement of passionate and beautifully observed muscular figures, creating an effect that's realistic and almost grotesquely fantastic at the same time. Draughtsmanship and a delight in the human form are the frescoes' most obvious attributes, but there are plenty of bizarre details to hold the narrative interest. A mass of monstrous lechery and naked writhing flesh fills the *Inferno* panel, including that of the painter's unfaithful mistress, immortalized in hell for all to see. In another an unfortunate is having his ear bitten off by a green-buttocked demon. Signorelli, suitably clad in black, has painted himself with Fra' Angelico in the lower left corner of *The Sermon of the Antichrist*, both calmly looking on as someone is garrotted at their feet.

All this overshadows the twin **Cappella del Corporale**, which contains the sacred corporale itself, locked away in a massive, jewel-encrusted casket (designed as a deliberate copy of the facade), plus some appealing frescoes by local fourteenth-century painter Ugolino di Prete, describing events connected with the Miracle of Bolsena. The entire apse is covered in more frescoes by Ugolino, many of which were partly restored by Pinturicchio, who was eventually kicked off the job for "consuming too much gold, too much azure and too much wine". Also worth a mention are an easily missed *Madonna and Child* by Gentile da Fabriano and a beautifully delicate fifteenth-century font, both near the main doors.

The rest of the town

Next to the duomo on the right as you look at it is the **Museo dell'Opera del Duomo** (closed for restoration, excepting the Emilio Greco section), the main part of which is more charming for its atmosphere than for what it contains. There's probably no other Italian museum quite as chaotic and badly organized, though the restoration in progress may tidy things up a bit. Imagine opening up an attic that's been sealed for centuries, and you get the idea. Among the meaningless stone fragments, rusty keys, moth-eaten vestments, dusty pottery and woodwormy sculptures (all unlabelled), you'll unearth one or two gems, all the better for requiring a bit of rooting around to find them. There are paintings by Martini and Pastura (an artist from Viterbo influenced by Perugino), several important thirteenth-century sculptures by Arnolfo di Cambio and Andrea Pisano, and a lovely font filled with Escher-like carved fishes. The **Emilio Greco** section of the museum (Tues–Sun: April–Sept 10.30am–1pm & 3–7pm; Oct–March 10.30am–1pm & 2–6pm; L5000/€2.58, L8000/€4.13 for Biglietto Cumulativo, which includes Il Pozzo di San Patrizio – see below) comprises nearly a hundred works donated to the city by the artist who created the duomo's bronze doors in the 1960s, none of them profoundly interesting.

The wonderfully restored **Museo Civico** or Museo Faina, opposite the duomo (Tues–Sun: April–Sept 9am–1pm & 3–6pm; Oct–March 10am–1pm & 2.30–5pm; L8000/€4.13, or L5000/€2.58 if you hold a funicular or ATC bus ticket), has a predictable but superbly displayed collection of vases and fragments excavated from local tombs (it also offers some great **views** of the cathedral facade). These sixth-century-BC **tombs** (daily: summer 9am–7pm; winter closes 1hr before dusk; L4000/€2.07) are still visible just off the road which drops towards the station from Piazza Cahen and are worth tracking down for their rows of massive and sombre stone graves – though none have the grandeur or paintings of the more famous necropoli in Cerveteri and Tarquinia (see p.752 and p.754). Before leaving Piazza del Duomo enquire at the tourist office (see p.627) for details of a couple of companies who run fascinating tours into some of the vast labyrinth of **tunnels**, caves and store rooms that riddle the solf volcanic rock on which Orvieto is built: most date back to medieval times, and some to the Etruscan era.

As far as the town's **churches** go, they all pale beside the duomo, though they've a lot more going for them in terms of humility. The tiny Romanesque **San Lorenzo di Arari** is the perfect antidote, built in 1291 on the site of a church destroyed by monks from nearby San Francesco because the sound of its bells got on their nerves. Four recently restored **frescoes** on the left of the nave describe typically traumatic scenes from the life of St Lawrence. There's also an Etruscan sacrificial slab, which rather oddly serves as the Christian altar (*arari* meaning "altar").

From Piazzale Cacciatore there's a decent **walk** around the city's southern walls (Via Ripa Medici) with views over to a prominent outcrop of rock in the middle distance, part of the old volcanic crater. Ten minutes or so brings you to **San Giovenale**, whose rustic surroundings, on the very western tip of the *rupa*, Orvieto's volcanic plateau, are a far cry from the bustle of the duomo. It's not much to look at from the outside, but the musty **medieval interior** is the best (and oldest) in the town, though virtually no one makes the trek out to see it. The thirteenth-century Gothic transept, with its two pointed arches, rather oddly stands a metre above the rounded Romanesque nave, making for a hybrid and distinctive church, all of it exhaustively decorated with thirteenth- and fifteenth-century **frescoes**. Check out the *Tree of Life* fresco right of the main door and the macabre *Calendar of Funeral Anniversaries* partly covered by the side entrance.

From the church back to the centre of town Via Malabranca and Via Filippeschi are the best of the **medieval streets**, all tantalizing doorways and tiled roofs, but second-rate by the standards of neighbouring hill-towns. **San Andrea** is worth a mention, more for its strange twelve-sided **campanile** than the bits and pieces of the Roman and Etruscan city in the crypt. In the Piazza del Popolo, further up Corso Cavour (the town's pedestrianized main drag), there's a daily fruit and veg market plus the odd craft stall – in front of the recently restored **Palazzo del Popolo** (closed to the public).

Il Pozzo di San Patrizio (daily: April–Sept 10am–7pm; Oct–March closes 6pm; L6000/€3.10, or L8000/€4.13 with the Emilio Greco section of the duomo museum – see above), just off Piazzale Cahen, is the town's novelty act, a huge cylindrical well commissioned in 1527 by Pope Clement VII to guarantee the town's water supply during an expected siege by the Imperial Army (which never came). Water was brought to the surface by donkeys on two broad staircases, cannily designed never to intersect. It's a striking piece of engineering, 13m wide and 62m deep, named after its supposed similarity to the Irish cave where St Patrick died in 493, aged 133.

Eating and drinking

Cheap **restaurants** are grouped together at the bottom of Corso Cavour, though the best-value eating in the town is close to the duomo at the co-operatively run CRAMST, Via Maitani 15 (closed Sun). Deservedly popular with locals, it's a 450-seat canteen affair, offering a choice between restaurant and self-service pizzeria. Orvieto has recently spawned a whole crop of good little trattorias. *La Grotta*, Via Signorelli 5 (closed Mon), is good value, friendly and has been around longer than most. A touch cheaper and probably with better food to boot, is the *Volpe e Uva*, Via Ripa Corsica 1 (closed all day Mon & Tues lunch). Moving up a notch in price, both the *Sette Consoli*, Piazza Sant'Angelo 1a (closed Wed), and *Osteria dell'Angelo*, Corso Cavour 166 (closed Mon) are highly rated by Italian foodie guides, the *Osteria* being the better and slightly cheaper of the two. More traditional, and guaranteed to give you a reliable meal in old-world surroundings is the *Etrusca*, Via Maitani 10 (closed Mon). If it's romance you're after (and money's no object), the *Gigli d'Oro* in Piazza del Duomo (closed Wed) offers meals in the shadow of the cathedral facade.

The **wine bars** around the duomo are an expensive way of sampling the well-known Orvietan white, though the wine has inevitably suffered as a result of the mass-production methods employed to satisfy the demands of the international market. The most bizarre place to drink or buy the stuff is in *La Bottega del Buon Vino*, halfway down the steep Via della Cava at no. 26. It's located at the extreme east end of town, near Porta Maggiore. The *bottega* is partly in the cave from which the street gets its name and boasts an odd funnel-shaped well into the bargain; the tiny adjoining restaurant is also okay. Finally, there's great **ice cream** at *L'Archetto*, an ivy-covered gelateria right in the main piazza, to the north side of the duomo.

Around Orvieto

Moving on from Orvieto there are plenty of choices of destination. The obvious targets are Rome and Florence, both about ninety minutes away by train, but if you're in no hurry you might just as well head west. There are buses from Piazza Cahen to Viterbo (see p.704) and Bolsena (see p.764), both in Lazio. The road to Bolsena has some of the best views of Orvieto: it's where the postcard shots are taken from and was also where Turner set up his easel (the resulting picture's now in the Clore wing of London's Tate Gallery). The wooded pocket of countryside west of Orvieto around Castel Giorgio is pretty enough, but probably only worth bothering with if you're in a car. Depending on the route you've taken so far you could stay in Umbria and take a slow train north through Città della Pieve or follow one of two good routes east to Todi. The first of these runs through Monte Peglia, some of the region's classic hill country.

Monte Peglia

Monte Peglia is the generic name for the triangular expanse of land that rises between the Chiani Valley in the west and the Tevere in the east. It's wild, sparse and timeless countryside, with hilltop hamlets, olives, vines, herds of white oxen and miles of deserted roads and tracks – the archetype of the pastoral lowlands you find all over the region. Although the map marks several villages, most turn out to be no more than scattered farms, many of them abandoned. The only realistic way of tackling the remoteness is with your own transport.

You'll get the best quick taste of the area on the circuitous and beautifully deserted N79 from Orvieto Scalo to Todi; most of the traffic these days takes the newer and infinitely quicker route south of Lago di Corbara. Superb initial views of Orvieto peter out as the road climbs through many a hairpin into densely wooded hill country, with occasional glimpses (haze allowing) as far as Perugia.

The best of the scenery is north of the road, where the area's woods, rivers and fields are a haven for **wildlife**. It's about the only place in Umbria you'll see otters, for example, and is well known for the variety of its birds, who owe their immunity from the Sunday morning blast-anything-that-flies fraternity to an ancient tract of land – *una bandita demeniale di caccia* – where hunting has traditionally been forbidden.

It's quicker and almost equally scenic to take the N448 to Todi, which after meandering along the flattish southern shore of Lago di Corbara takes off into an unexpectedly dramatic **gorge** for the rest of the run onto Todi. Nobody seems keen to swim in the lake, and it's not used for any sort of watersports – and to be honest it doesn't actually look that inviting. Further on things get better, when the strange purple-red rocks of the gorge, along with sheer cliffs and forested slopes, add up to a more enticing package. The road's pretty quiet, with plenty of free-style **camping** and **picnic** opportunities as the valley flattens out towards Todi.

Città della Pieve

Città della Pieve is most famous as the birthplace of Perugino (1445–1523), but it has a modicum of charm that merits a short visit in its own right. Again, you're better off in a car, for the station is a long haul from the town and it's the sort of place that can easily be seen in an hour. From below, in the Tiber Valley, the town straggles along a distant ridge to the east, vaguely and mysteriously enticing, but once up in the streets it lacks the impact of other Umbrian towns, the chief appeal being the tiny red-bricked houses (there was no local building stone), old women knitting, and geraniums in profusion at every window. One of the streets, Via della Baciadonna, claims to be the narrowest in Italy, the width of a "woman's kiss", the translation suggests. If you prefer your poetry liquid, the town's fountains run with wine during its April *festa*.

Otherwise its only real interest lies in the handful of **Perugino's paintings**, which lie scattered around the town's fairly dismal churches, palaces and oratories, some of which – the **Palazzo della Corgna**, the church of **Sant'Agostino** and the **Oratorio di Santa Maria dei Bianchi** – have been united in a self-contained "circuit" known as the **Museo Aperto** with a single-ticket admission, available from any of the relevant attractions (summer, Easter & Christmas daily 10.30am–12.30pm & 4–7pm; Oct–April Fri–Sun 10.30am–12.30pm & 3.30–6.30pm; L3000/€1.55). If the small **tourist office** at Piazza Matteotti 4 (☎0578.299.375) is shut, there's a map of the town's few highlights outside the unremarkable duomo in Piazza Gramsci (or Piazza Plebiscito, depending on your politics).

The cathedral itself has a couple of late works that show **Perugino** in his worst light. The painter's reputation today, though still very high, is lower than it was in his own time, when contemporaries spoke of him in the same breath as Leonardo and Michelangelo. He trained with Leonardo da Vinci in Florence but largely remained faithful to the tenets of the Umbrian School – sublime misty landscapes behind ethereal religious subjects. His great facility enabled him to produce vast numbers of dewy-eyed saints and Madonnas, whose occasional absence of genuine religious sentiment horrified those who demanded sincerity above all else in devotional art. What in his youth had been profound and innovative gradually came to seem stilted and repetitive. Accused of merely replicating a successful formula, he also did nothing to discourage pupils finishing his works, adding his signature to some real shockers – especially in old age. He remains, however, one of the leading and most influential of the

Renaissance painters. The painting not to miss is *The Adoration of the Magi* in Santa Maria dei Bianchi, considered his greatest work still resident in Italy (Napoleon removed many to the Louvre in Paris), with lesser paintings in nearby **San Antonio Abate**, **San Pietro** and **Santa Maria dei Servi**.

travel details

TRAINS

Assisi to: Foligno (hourly; 15min); Perugia (hourly; 20min); Spello (hourly; 10min); Terontola (hourly; 1hr).

Città di Castello to: Perugia (hourly; 1hr); Sansepolcro (hourly; 15min).

Foligno to: Ancona (13 daily; 1hr 30min–2hr); Assisi (21 daily; 15min); Fabriano (14 daily; 40min–1hr); Fossato di Vico (14 daily; 40min); Gualdo Tadino (10 daily; 35min); Narni (18 daily; 1hr); Orte (hourly; 1hr–1hr 10 min); Perugia (hourly; 20–35 min); Rome (14 daily; 1hr 45min); Spello (hourly; 5min); Spoleto (hourly; 25min); Terni (hourly; 50min); Terontola (17 daily; 1hr 15min).

Orvieto to: Arezzo (12 daily; 1hr 20min); Chiusi (12 daily; 40min; connections to Siena, 1hr 30min); Florence (10 daily; 1hr 30min); Orte (17 daily; 30min); Rome (19 daily; 1hr 20min).

Perugia to: Assisi (hourly; 20min); Città di Castello (hourly; 1hr); Deruta (hourly; 20min); Foligno (hourly; 40min); Sansepolcro (hourly; 1hr 30min); Spello (hourly; 30min); Terni (hourly; 1hr 40min); Terontola (hourly; 35min); Todi (hourly; 50min).

Spoleto to: Foligno (hourly; 25min); Fossato di Vico (10 daily; 50 min); Narni (17 daily; 40min); Nocera Umbra (6 daily; 35min); Terni (hourly; 30min).

Terni to: Città di Castello (FCU line hourly; 2hr 30 min); Foligno (12 daily; 40min); Narni (17 daily; 15min); Orte (hourly; 25min); Perugia (FCU line; 4hourly; 1hr 20min); Sansepolcro (FCU line; hourly; 3hr); Spoleto (hourly; 20min); Todi (FCU line; hourly; 50min).

BUSES

Assisi to: Bettona (1 daily; 50 min); Foligno (10 daily; 50min); Gualdo Tadino (1 daily; 1hr 15min); Gubbio (2 weekly); Norcia and the Valnerina (1

daily; Mon–Sat from Santa Maria degli Angeli); Perugia (10 daily; 30min); Spello (10 daily; 40min).

Bevagna to Montefalco (3 daily; 20 min)

Foligno to Bevagna (3 daily Mon–Fri; 30 min); Montefalco (5 daily; 35min)

Gubbio to: Fossato di Vico (10 daily; 30min); Perugia (10 daily Mon–Sat, 4 daily Sun; 1hr 10min).

Montefalco to Bevagna (4 daily Mon–Sat; 20 min)

Narni to: Amelia (4–6 daily; 15min); Orvieto (6 daily; 1hr); Terni (4–6 daily; 30min).

Norcia to: Perugia (1 daily; 1hr 30min); Rome (1 daily; 3hr); Spoleto (5 daily Mon–Sat, 1 Sun; 1hr 10min); Terni (1 daily; 1hr).

Orvieto to: Amelia (6 daily; 1hr 15min); Narni (6 daily; 1hr 5min); Perugia (1 daily; 2hr 45min); Todi (1 daily; 50min); Terni (6 daily; 1hr 40min).

Perugia to: Ascoli Piceno (1–4 daily; 3hr); Assisi (3–12 daily; 30min); Bettona (2 daily; 40min); Castiglione del Lago (7–9 daily Mon–Sat; 1hr 15min); Florence (1 daily; 2hr); Gubbio (10 daily Mon–Sat, 4 daily Sun; 1hr 10min); Norcia (1 daily; 2hr 50min); Orvieto (1 daily; 2hr 25min); Passignano (7 daily Mon–Sat; 1hr 30min); Rome (2–6 daily; 2hr 30min); Rome Fiumicino airport (1–3 daily; 3hr); Siena (3–7 daily; 1hr 30min); Spello (4 daily Mon–Sat; 55min); Spoleto (1 direct daily Mon–Sat; 1hr 20min); Todi (5–7 daily; 1hr).

Spoleto to: Foligno (7 daily; 40min); Fonti di Clitunno (7 daily; 20min); Montefalco (2–3 daily Mon–Sat; 1hr); Norcia (5 daily Mon–Sat; 1 Sun; 1hr 10min); Perugia (5 daily; 1hr 20min); Rome (1 daily; 2hr 20min); Scheggino (5 daily; 1hr 10min); Terni (6 daily; 45min); Trevi (7 daily; 25min).

Todi to: Marsciano (2 daily; 1hr 30min); Orvieto (1 daily; 50min); Perugia (3 daily; 1hr); Terni (8 daily; 45min).

CHAPTER TEN

MARCHE

L ying between the Apennines and the Adriatic, **Marche** (sometimes anglicized as The Marches) is a varied region, and one you could spend weeks exploring. Large areas of it are unspoilt, particularly in the southwest between Macerata and the Sibillini mountains, where crumbling hill-villages make atmospheric bases for hikes into the stunning **Monti Sibillini** range. Not that all of Marche is free from tourism; much of its coastline is studded with modern grid-plan resorts, and ranks of sun-umbrellas fill many of its beaches. The area also has a fair amount of industry – in particular light engineering, shoe manufacturing and ceramics – heaviest around the port of **Ancona** and along the main road and rail route from Umbria.

Of Marche's old-fashioned and slightly forgotten seaside resorts, **Pésaro** is the largest with a Renaissance centre maintaining its dignity behind the package-tour seafront; for more interesting sunning and swimming it's a better idea to head to the south of Ancona to the **Cónero Riviera**, a spectacular stretch of coast, with small beaches nestling beneath the dramatic cliffs of Monte Cónero. **San Benedetto del Tronto** has six kilometres of beach, five thousand palm trees, and numerous discos, but is not exactly a happening place compared with say Rimini (see p.443). Really, though, the most appealing – and best known – of Marche's sights are the small hilltop town of **Urbino**, with its spectacular Renaissance palace, and the fortress of **San Leo**, just across the border from San Marino. Further south, **Macerata** is a sleepy university town surrounded by lovely countryside, and, right on the regional border, the fascinating city of **Áscoli Piceno** is a worthy stop-off on the way into Abruzzo (see p.781).

Getting around on public transport is not too much of a problem, though you'll obviously save time in the remotest parts of the region with your own vehicle. The provincial capitals – Urbino, Pésaro, Macerata, Ancona and Áscoli Piceno – are all well served by public transport; and Ancona is also a major port for ferries to Greece and Croatia. For hiking in the Sibillini, **Amandola** has the best bus service; if you don't mind relying on fewer buses, **Montefortino** is a prettier base.

ACCOMMODATION PRICE CODES

Throughout this guide, prices per person are given for **youth hostels** and assume Hostelling International (HI) membership. **Hotel** accommodation is coded on a scale from ① to ⑨, reflecting the cost of the cheapest double room in each establishment in high season. The price bands to which these codes refer are as follows:

① Up to L60,000/€30.99
② L60,000–90,000/€30.99–46.48
③ L90,000–120,000/€46.48–61.98
④ L120,000–150,000/€61.98–77.47
⑤ L150,000–200,000/€77.47–103.29

⑥ L200,000–250,000/€103.29–129.11
⑦ L250,000–300,000/€129.11–154.94
⑧ L300,000–400,000/€154.94–206.58
⑨ over L400,000/€206.58

(See p.32 for a full explanation.)

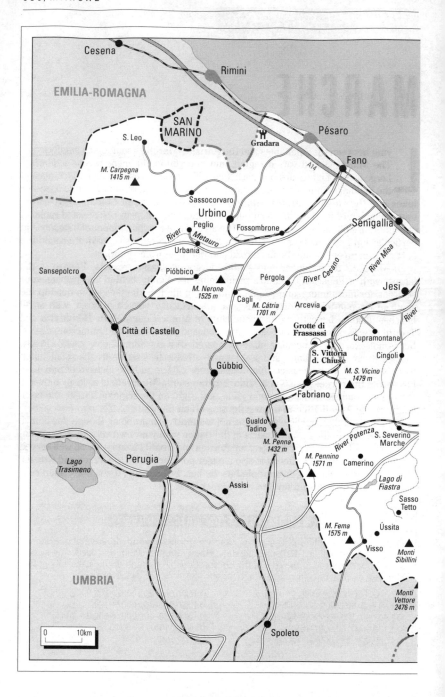

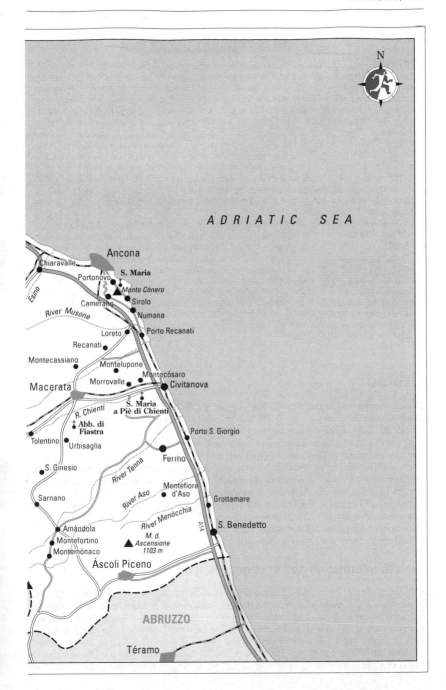

REGIONAL FOOD AND WINE

Marche is very much a rural region, its food a mixture of **seafood** from the long coastline and **country cooking** from the interior, based on locally grown produce – tomatoes, fennel and mushrooms. The most distinctive dish, often served at summer *festas*, is a sweet-and-sour mix of olives stuffed with meat and fried, then served with *crema fritta*, little squares of fried cream. Rabbit and lamb are popular, as is *papardelle alla papara*, wide, flat pasta with duck sauce, and, as in many other regions, truffles are considered a delicacy. The grand dish of **porchetta**, whole roast suckling pig, is ubiquitous in the Marche, both in its original large-scale form and in a fast-food version used to fill crisp bread rolls. Baked, stuffed dishes such as *vincisgrassi*, a rich layered dish of pasta, ham, bechamel and truffles, are found everywhere. A typical seafood dish from Ancona is *zuppa di pesce*, a fish soup flavoured with saffron, though you'll find excellent fish broths – known simply as *brodetto* – all along the coast. Puddings include *Cicerchiata*, balls of pasta fried and covered in honey, and *frappé*, fried leaves of filo-like pastry dusted with icing sugar.

Although it produces many very drinkable **wines**, the Marche region is best known for just one, **Verdicchio**, a greeny-gold white, excellent with fish, which is instantly recognizable due to its amphora-shaped bottle. This is in fact a hangover from a 1950s marketing ploy inspired by the ancient Greek custom of shipping wine from Ancona in clay amphorae, and, reputedly, by the shape of the actress Gina Lollobrigida. Today, however, many producers are selling their best Verdicchio in standard-shaped bottles – the one to look out for is Verdicchio dei Castelli di Jesi (see p.654 for more). The less well known local **reds** include one of Italy's finest, Rosso Conero, a light wine based on the Montepulciano grape and full of fruit; more common is Rosso Piceno, based on the Sangiovese grape. A Marche aperitif now back in fashion is **mistrà**, an aniseed liqueur generally drunk with coffee.

Urbino

During the second half of the fifteenth century, **URBINO** was one of the most prestigious courts in Europe, ruled by the remarkable Federico da Montefeltro, who employed some of the greatest artists and architects of the time to build and decorate his palace in the town. Baldassarre Castiglione, whose sixteenth-century handbook of courtly behaviour, *Il Cortegiane* (The Courtier), is set in the palace, reckoned it to be the most beautiful in all Italy, and it does seem from contemporary accounts that fifteenth-century Urbino was an extraordinarily civilized place, a measured and urbane society in which life was lived without indulgence.

Nowadays Urbino is Marche's most immediately likeable town, saved from an existence as a museum-piece by its lively university. There's a refreshing, energetic feel to the place, plenty of conducive places to eat and drink, and, although its nightlife is hardly wild, there are a few music bars hosting local bands and the like.

Arrival, information and accommodation

Urbino is served by regular **buses** from Pésaro, where they depart from Piazzale Matteotti and the **train station**, with the last one going at around 8pm. Buses also run regularly between Fano and Urbino. All buses stop in Borgo Mercatale, a terminus-cum-car park at the foot of the Palazzo Ducale which can be reached by spiral staircase, a lift or a series of steep narrow streets and flights of steps. Once up in the old centre, the **tourist office** is at Piazza Duca Federico 35, directly opposite the Palazzo Ducale (Mon–Sat: summer 9am–6pm; winter 9am–1pm & 3–6pm; ☎0722.2613 or 0722.2788).

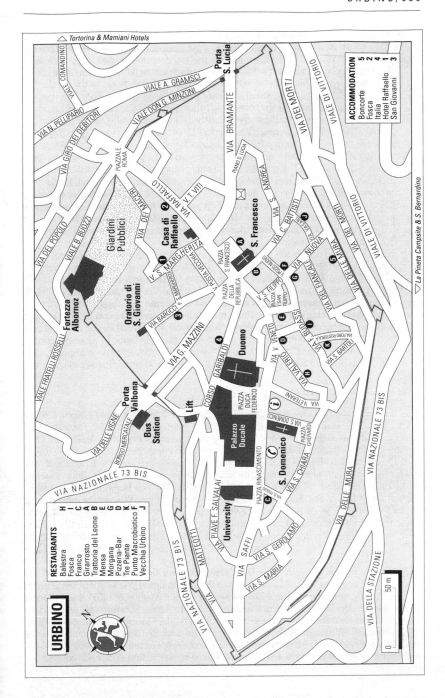

△ Tortorina & Mamiani Hotels

▽ La Pineta Campsite & S. Bernardino

ACCOMMODATION
Boncorte 5
Fosca 2
Italia 4
Hotel Raffaello 1
San Giovanni 3

URBINO

RESTAURANTS
Balestra H
Fosca I
Franco C
Girarrosto A
Trattoria del Leone B
Mensa E
Morgana G
Pizzeria-Bar D
Tre Piante K
Punto Macrobiotico F
Vecchia Urbino J

0   50 m

An economical **accommodation** option, although you need to stay more than 3 nights, is a **room in a private house**. You can get hold of a list at the tourist office but during term time you will be competing with the many students who lodge with families, so be sure to book in advance. Prices vary but expect to pay about the same as for a two-star **hotel** (price band ②–③). Otherwise, the cheapest hotel is the *Fosca*, Via Raffaello 67 (☎0722.2542; ①), a small studenty pensione on the top floor of a residential palazzo in the old town, (if the owner isn't there, call ☎0722.329.622 and someone will be along). Other good options are recently renovated *Italia*, Corso Garibaldi 32 (☎0722.2701; ②), and *San Giovanni*, Via Barocci 13 (☎0722.2827; closed July; ②), in the old town. This sixteenth-century Patrician house known as Palazzo della Spillara is a lovely old-style hotel with very courteous service and its own restaurant serving typical Marche dishes. *Hotel Raffaello*, Via Santa Margheria 38/40 (☎0722.4784 or 0722.4896, *www.poliedrosnc.com/hotelraffaellourbino*; ⑤) behind the Casa di Raffaello in the old town, has wide views over the pantiled roofs of Urbino. This former seminary provides 3-wheelers to pick up guests and luggage from the lower town. Alternatively try old-fashioned *Boncorte*, Via delle Mura 28 (☎0722.2463, *www.viphotels.it*; ⑦) just inside the city walls with views over the countryside. Breakfast is served in the tiny courtyard garden in summer.

If you have a car there are several hotel possiblities on the **outskirts** of town: *Tortorina*, Via Tortorina 4 (☎0722.308.100 or 0722.327.715; ⑤) is a tourist complex overlooking Urbino and the hills a ten-minute drive to the north of central Urbino with apartments, rooms, a gym and tennis courts. *Mamiani*, Via Bernini 6 (☎0722.322.309, *www.info-net.it/hotelmamiani*; ⑦) is chi-chi and corporate but might be good for a night's stay if everything else is full. For a much cheaper and more low-key option with great food and an open-air swimming pool, *Balcone sul Metauro* at Peglio near Urbania (☎0722.310.104; ②), a 30-minute drive south-west from Urbino, is a sound choice. There's a **campsite**, the *Pineta* (☎0722.4710, fax 0722.4738; April to mid-Sept), 2km south of Urbino beyond San Bernardino (see p.643); bus #4 or #7 drops you close by.

The Palazzo Ducale

The **Palazzo Ducale** (Mon 9am–2pm, Tues–Sat 9am–7pm, Sun 9am–7.30pm; L8000/ €4.13, including Galleria Nazionale – see below), whose *Facciata dei Torricini* overlooks the surrounding countryside, is a fitting monument to Federico. An elegant combination of the aesthetic and the practical, the facade comprises a triple-decked loggia in the form of a triumphal arch flanked by twin defensive towers. In contrast, the Palazzo's bare south side, forming one side of the long central Piazza Rinascimento, looks rather bleak, and it's only once you get inside that you begin to understand its reputation as one of the finest buildings of the Renaissance. Whereas a tour of most palaces of this size tends to reduce the visitor to a state of crabby exhaustion, the spacious rooms of the Palazzo Ducale instil a sense of calm. Indeed, although the palazzo now houses the **Galleria Nazionale delle Marche**, only the few remaining original Urbino works justify much attention, and until you hit these it's the building itself that makes the biggest impression.

Just inside the entrance, the **Cortile d'Onore** is your first real taste of what Urbino is about. The courtyard is not immediately striking – in fact if you've spent any amount of time in Italy, you'll have seen a host of similar ones already – but this is a prototype of the genre. Designed by Dalmatian-born Luciano Laurana, who was selected by Federico after he'd failed to find a suitably bold artist in Florence, it's at once elegant and restrained. Although each element, from the furling Corinthian capitals to the inscription proclaiming Federico's virtues, is exquisitely crafted, it's the way they work together that is Laurana's real achievement. Pilasters on the first floor echo columns on the ground floor, pale stone alternates with dark, and the whole is enhanced by the subtle interplay of light and shadow.

Off the cortile is the room that housed Federico's **library**, which in its day was more comprehensive than Oxford University's Bodleian Library. He spent fourteen years and over thirty thousand ducats gathering books from all over Europe, and employed forty scribes to make illuminated copies on kidskin, which were then covered in crimson and decorated with silver. They disappeared into the vaults of the Vatican after Urbino fell to the papacy in 1631, and all that's left of the room's former grandeur is one of the more outrageous representations of Federico's power – the Eagle of the Montefeltros surrounded by tongues of fire, symbolizing the artistic and spiritual gifts bestowed by Federico.

One of Italy's first monumental staircases takes you up to the first floor. Wandering through the white airy rooms, you'll see wooden doors inlaid with everything from gyroscopes and mandolins to armour, representing the various facets of Federico's personality. On carved marble fireplaces, sphinxes are juxtaposed with angels and palm trees with dolphins, while ceilings are stuccoed with such symbols of Montefeltro power as ermines, eagles and exploding grenades.

A famous portrait of Federico da Montefeltro by the Spanish artist **Pedro Berruguete** is worth seeking out (it's been moved about in recent years). Painted, as he always was, in profile (having lost his right eye in battle), Federico is shown as warrior, ruler, scholar and dynast; wearing an ermine-fringed gown over his armour, he sits reading a book, with his pale and delicate son, Guidobaldo, standing at his feet.

The most elaborately decorated part of the palazzo is the suite of rooms known as the **Appartamento del Duca**, behind the Facciata dei Torricini. Displayed here are **Piero della Francesca**'s two great works: the *Madonna of Senigallia*, a subtly coloured, haunting depiction of foreboding in which Mary flanked by two angels offers up her child; and the more perplexing *Flagellation*, where at the back of a cubic room Christ is being almost casually beaten, while in the foreground, in the courtyard, stand three figures: a beautiful youth and two older men. Perhaps the most persuasive intepretation of this much debated painting is that which holds that the foreground figure on the left is Ottaviano Ubaldini (Federico Montefeltro's senior counsellor), while the one on the right is Ludovico Gonzaga (grandfather of Federico's son-in-law), both of whom had been bereaved at the time the picture was commissioned; by this account the beautiful boy between them is the idealized projection of the boys they were mourning, and the picture as a whole is a meditation on the consolations of Christian faith. Also here is Raphael's compelling portrait of a gentlewoman, *La Muta*.

Still in the Appartamento del Duca, no painting better embodies the notion of perfection held by Urbino's elite than *The Ideal City*, long attributed to Piero but now thought to be by one of his followers. Probably intended as a design for a stage set, this famous display of perspective skill depicts a perfectly symmetrical and utterly deserted cityscape, expressing the desire for a civic order which mirrors that of the heavens.

Paolo Uccello's last work, the six-panelled *Profanation of the Host*, tells the story of a woman who sold a consecrated host to a Jewish merchant. She was hanged, and the merchant and his family were burned at the stake – the angels and devils are arguing over the custody of the woman's soul. The morbid theme and fairy-tale atmosphere that pervades the work may reflect the artist's depression at getting old: shortly after completing it, he filled in his tax return with the statement, "I am old, infirm and unemployed, and my wife is ill."

It's in the three most intimate rooms of the Duke's apartment you come to next that you get most insight into Federico's personality. A spiral staircase descends to two adjoining chapels, one dedicated to Apollo and the Muses, the other to the Christian God. This dualism typifies a strand of Renaissance thought in which mythology and

FEDERICO DA MONTEFELTRO

Federico was a formidable soldier, a shrewd and humane ruler, and a genuine intellectual, qualities which were due in part to his education at the Mantua school of the most prestigious Renaissance teacher, Vittorino da Feltre. Poor scholars and young nobles were educated together in Vittorino's classes and were taught self-discipline and frugal living as well as the more usual Latin, maths, literature and the courtly skills of riding, dancing and swordsmanship.

As the elder but illegitimate son of the Montefeltro family, Federico only became ruler of Urbino after his tyrannical half-brother Oddantonio fell victim to an assassin during a popular rebellion. Federico promptly arrived on the scene – fuelling rumours that he'd engineered the uprising himself – and was elected to office after promising not to punish those responsible for Oddantonio's death, to cut taxes, to provide an educational and medical service, and to allow the people some say in the election of magistrates.

Urbino was a small state with few natural resources and a long way from any major trading routes, so selling the military services of his army and himself was Federico's only way of keeping Urbino solvent. In high demand because of his exceptional loyalty to his employers, Federico's mercenary activities yielded an annual income equivalent to £7,000,000/US$11,200,000, a substantial portion of which was used to keep taxes low, thus reducing the likelihood of social discontent during his long absences. When he was at home, he seems to have been a remarkably accessible ruler: he would leave his door open at mealtimes so that any member of his 500-strong court might speak to him between courses, and used to move around his state unarmed (unusual in a time when assassination was common), checking up on the welfare of his people.

Between his military and political commitments, Federico found time to devote to the arts – he delighted in music, but his first love was architecture, which he considered to be the highest form of intellectual and aesthetic activity. He was a friend of the leading architectural theorist, Alberti, and according to his biographer, Vespasiano di Bisticci, Federico's knowledge of the art was unequalled: "Though he had his architects about him, he always first realized the design and then explained the proportions and all else; indeed, to hear him discourse . . . it would seem that his chief talent lay in this art, so well he knew how to expound and carry out its principles." The Dalmatian architect Luciano Laurana was scarcely known until taken up by Federico, while his later commissions included works from the more established Francesco di Giorgio Martini and one of the greatest of all painters and theorists of architecture, Piero della Francesca.

Christianity were reconciled by positing a universe in which pagan deities were seen as aspects of the omnipotent Christian deity.

Back on the main floor you come to the most interesting and best preserved of the palace's rooms, Federico's **Studiolo**, a triumph of illusory perspective created not with paint but with intarsia (inlaid wood). Shelves laden with geometrical instruments appear to protrude from the walls, cupboard doors seem to swing open to reveal lines of books, a letter lies in an apparently half-open drawer. Even more remarkable are the delicately-hued landscapes of Urbino as if viewed from one of the surrounding hills, and the lifelike squirrel perching next to an equally realistic bowl of fruit. The upper half of the room is covered with 28 portraits of great men ranging from Homer and Petrarch to Solomon and St Ambrose – another example of Federico's eclecticism.

The rest of the town – and San Bernardino

Urbino is a lively place, and its bustling streets – a pleasant jumble of Renaissance and medieval houses – can be a refreshing antidote to the rarefied atmosphere of the

Palazzo Ducale. Next door to the palace, the town's **Duomo** is a pompous Neoclassical replacement for Francesco di Giorgio Martini's Renaissance church, destroyed in an earthquake in 1789. There's a **museum** inside (daily 9am–noon & 2.30–6pm; L3000/€1.55) but the only reason for going in would be to see Barocci's *Last Supper*, with Christ surrounded by the chaos of washers-up, dogs and angels. Afterwards, trek up to the gardens within the **Fortezza Albornoz** (fortress daily 10am–4pm; gardens 10am–6pm; both free), from where you'll get great views of the town and the countryside. Close by is the **Oratorio di San Giovanni** (daily 10am–12.30pm & 3–5.30pm; L3000/€1.55), behind whose unfortunate modern facade is a stunning cycle of early fourteenth-century frescoes, depicting the life of St John the Baptist and the Crucifixion. Vividly coloured and full of expressive detail, so different from the cool economy of later Renaissance artists, the frescoes are at their liveliest in such incidental details as the boozy picnic in the background of the *Baptism of the Multitude*, or the child trying to escape from its mother in the *Crucifixion*. On Via Raffaello, the **Casa Natale di Raffaello**, birthplace (in 1483) of Urbino's most famous son, the painter Raphael (Mon–Sat 9am–1pm & 3–7pm, Sun 10am–1pm; L5000/€2.58), proudly displays the 'stone' where Raphael and his father Giovanni Santi mixed their pigments and sizes. There's one work by Raphael, an early *Madonna and Child*; the other walls are covered with reproductions and minor works by his contemporaries and Santi.

There's another fine Renaissance church just outside Urbino, that of **San Bernardino**, built atop a hill 2km south of town. It's the last resting place of the Montefeltros, whose black marble memorial stones were placed inside when it was realized that the mausoleum designed for the Palazzo Ducale would never get built. It was long thought to have been the work of Bramante, but is now attributed to Francesco di Giorgio Martini.

Eating, drinking and nightlife

There are plenty of reasonable places to **eat** in Urbino. The cheapest deal is the university *mensa* on Piazza San Filippo, which is open to student ID card-holders only. For those on a budget, there are any number of fast-food and self-service outlets: try the *Pizzeria-Bar* at Via V. Veneto 32 or *Franco* at Via del Poggio 1 (closed Sun), which is both a self-service place and a restaurant. The best of Urbino's sit-down pizzerias is the reasonably priced *Morgana*, Via Nuova 3 (closed Fri in winter), or you could try the slightly cheaper *Fosca*, Via Budassi 62 (closed Thurs). *Le Tre Piante,* Via Foro Posterula 1 (closed Mon), just off Via Budassi, has more interesting offerings, such as pasta dishes like *strozzapreti* – "strangled priests", with sausage, cream, mushrooms and peppers – or tagliatelle with lemon and prawns while *Trattoria del Leone*, on Via C. Battisti (closed Thurs), is an authentic sidestreet place serving good home-made pasta. *La Balestra*, Via Valerio 16, has tables inside and out and serves typical food from Montefeltro (as this part of the Marche is sometimes called) with a pizzeria that stays open until 3am, while *Vecchia Urbino*, Via Vasari 3/5 (closed Tues; booking advisable ☎0722.4447), is highly regarded for its truffles and specialities from Le Marche. For bargain **vegetarian** dishes you could do worse than to try *Un Punto Macrobiotico*, Via Nuova 6 (closed Sun) and for **ice cream**, go to *L'Orchidea* on Corso Garibaldi.

As for drinking and **nightlife**, the curiously named *Bosom Pub*, Via Budassi 24, has a good range of bottled beers, including Belgian classics, as well as decent sandwiches; there's also the *Cagliostro*, a kind of pub-restaurant at Via San Domenico 1, and *Gula* at Corso Garibaldi 23, where you can get cheap pizzas and good beer. If you're in search of live music, local bands tend to play at *Underground*, Via Barocci 16.

North of Urbino: Sassocorvaro and San Leo

The villages of northern Marche, though pleasant enough, cannot compete with the crumbling hill settlements further south, and the rarity of buses makes exploration by public transport something of an ordeal. There are a couple of places, however, that justify the effort.

Perched above a twee artificial lake some 30km northwest of Urbino by road, **SASSOCORVARO** is dominated by one of Francesco di Giorgio Martini's most ambitious fortresses (April–Sept daily 9.30am–12.30pm & 3–7pm; Oct–Mar Sat & Sun 9.30am–12.30pm & 2.30–6pm; L5000/€2.58 including folk musem). Like San Leo (see below) it was built to withstand the onslaught of the cannon, but as the site lacked San Leo's natural advantages, Francesco was forced to seek a strictly architectural solution. As far as possible, he did away with straight walls and built a grim and cunning fortress bulging with hourglass towers. Inside, it's something of a surprise to find an elegant Renaissance courtyard and an intimate and frescoed theatre – the fortress was built on the orders of Federico da Montefeltro for one of his condottieri, Ottaviano degli Ubaldini. It's a tribute to the strength of Francesco's architecture that the fortress was selected as a safe house for some of Italy's greatest works of art during World War II, including Piero della Francesca's *Flagellation* and Giorgione's *La Tempesta*, reproductions of which are on show.

There's also a museum of **folk life** (same hours and included in the castle admission ticket), with displays of traditional weaving, winemaking equipment and a mock-up of an old kitchen.

San Leo

The menacing fortress of **SAN LEO** (daily 9am–7pm; closes at least 1hr earlier in winter; L12,000/€6.19), clamped to the summit of a dizzying precipice in the northern tip of the Marche, has staggered generations of visitors with its intimidating beauty. Machiavelli praised it, Dante modelled the terrain of his Purgatory on it, and Pietro Bembo considered it Italy's "most beautiful implement of war". In fact it's not as impregnable as it seems: it fell to a succession of powers, most recently to the Fascists in World War II, who used it as an aircraft-sighting post. One of the few invaders to have been repelled was Cesare Borgia, despite his having first persuaded a weak-willed retainer to give him the key.

There's been a fortress at San Leo since the Romans founded a city on the rock. Later colonizers added to it as necessary until the fifteenth century, when Federico da Montefeltro realized that it was no match for the new gunpowder-charged weapons, and set his military architect, Francesco di Giorgio Martini, the task of creating a new one. The walls were built on a slight inward slope and backed with earth, thus reducing the impact of cannonballs and providing a rampart. Three large squares were incorporated for the manoeuvring of heavy cannons, and every point was defended with firing posts. San Leo's greatest advantage, however, remained its position, which allows unwelcome visitors to be spotted from a great distance.

From the eighteenth century San Leo was used as a prison for enemies of the Vatican, of whom the most notorious was the womanizing Count of Cagliostro, a self-proclaimed alchemist, miracle doctor and necromancer. At first the charismatic heretic was incarcerated in a regular prison, but on the insistence of his guards, who were terrified of his diabolic powers, he was moved to the so-called Pozzetto di Cagliostro (Cagliostro's Well), now the fortress's most memorable sight. The only entrance was through a trap door in the ceiling, so that food could be lowered to him without the warden running the risk of engaging Cagliostro's evil eye. There was one window, triple-barred and placed so that the prisoner couldn't avoid seeing San Leo's twin churches. Not that this had any effect – Cagliostro died of an apoplectic attack, unrepentant after four years of being virtually buried alive.

As well as the fortress, there's the pleasant old village to explore. Its two churches, though they failed to impress Cagliostro, are worth a visit. The **Pieve** was built in the ninth century, with material salvaged from a Roman temple to Jupiter, by Byzantine-influenced architects from Ravenna. The capitals, dimly lit by the tiny windows, are carved with stylized foliage; also notable is the raised sanctuary, designed to impress upon the common worshippers the elevated position of their social superiors. Sunk into the ground behind the church is a sixth-century chapel founded by and later dedicated to St Leo, whose body lay here until 1014 when Henry II, emperor of Germany, calling in at the town on his way home from defeating the Greeks and Saracens in Rome, decided to remove it to Germany. His plans were thwarted by the horses bearing the saint's body – after a short distance they refused to go any further, so St Leo's body was left in the small village of Voghenza near Ferrara.

The heavy lid of the sarcophagus remains in the twelfth-century **Duomo**, dedicated to the saint. Like the Pieve it's built of local sandstone and incorporates fragments from the Jupiter temple, on whose site it was raised. The best of these are the Corinthian capitals sitting on the stubby Roman columns in the raised sanctuary. Above them, vaults are supported on the heads of crouching caryatids – which are more aesthetically pleasing than structurally efficient, for the church walls and arches have been distorted by bearing the brunt of the weight. The lid of St Leo's sarcophagus is in the crypt, which is far older than the church and was perhaps once used for pagan worship, as evidenced by the primitive carvings on the wall behind the altar.

Getting to San Leo is a pain: you need to travel up the coast to Rimini (see p.443), then catch one of the three daily buses to the village from the train station. Once here, there's a **tourist office** at Piazza Dante 14 (daily: mid-July to 31 Aug 9am–11pm; autumn and winter 9am–6.30pm; rest of year 9am–7.30pm; ☎0541.916.306). There are only two **hotels** in San Leo: *La Rocca*, Via G. Leopardi 16 (☎0541.916.241; ③), which has a pleasant **restaurant** beneath its seven rooms; and *Castello*, Piazza Dante Alighieri 11/12 (☎0541.916.214; ③), a family-run hotel with stone colonnades on the main square.

Pésaro and around

Most of the tourists who come to **PÉSARO** visit for a beach holiday, attracted by the string of affordable three-star hotels and the easy, low-key family fun on offer. Germans and Brits are attracted by the cheap package holidays to Pésaro but it's a popular place among Italians too going through the daily ritual of beach, lunch, beach, passeggiata and ice-cream before dinner back at the hotel. The town is a bit of a backwater but pleasant enough nonetheless: with its long stretch of sandy beach, old centre with small craft and design shops to wander around. A lot of Pesaro dates from the 20s and 30s so it has rather has its day. Nevertheless, if you do find yourself strolling along the prom with an ice-cream in hand among all the grannies, you couldn't exactly call that unpleasant, and with regular transport connections to lesser-known towns like Gradara and Fano it makes a feasible base from which to explore the northern Marche.

The Town

The centre of town is the coolly dignified **Piazza del Popolo**, in which the rituals of the pavement café scene are played out against the sharp lines of sundry Fascist-period buildings and the Renaissance restraint of the **Palazzo Ducale**.

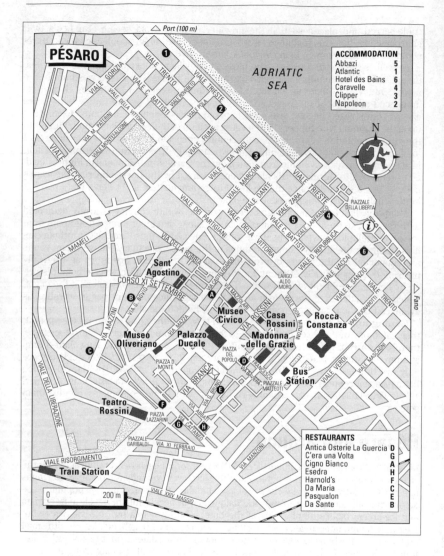

The most significant relic of Renaissance Pésaro, however, is Giovanni Bellini's magnificent *Coronation of the Virgin* polyptych, housed in the art gallery of the **Museo Civico** (July & Aug Tues–Sun 5–11pm; Sept–June Tues–Wed 9.30am–12.30pm, Thurs–Sun 9.30am–12.30pm & 4–7pm; L5000/€2.18, or L8000/€4.13 including Casa di Rossini). Painted in the 1470s for a church now known as Madonna delle Grazie (in Via San Francesco), the altarpiece situates the coronation not in some starry heaven but in the countryside around Pésaro, dominated by the castle of Gradara. Portraits of saints flank the central scene, ranging from the hesitant St Lawrence to the dreamy St Anthony, and below are a *Nativity* and scenes from the saints' lives. Although none of the gallery's other paintings can compare with the Bellini, don't miss Marco Zoppo's pietà, in which the dead Christ's muscled sensuousness prompts speculation on the artist's necrophiliac tendencies. Renaissance Pésaro was famous for its ceramics, and the museum houses a fine collection – ranging from a *Madonna and Child* surrounded by pine cones, lemons and bilberries from the workshop of Andrea della Robbia, to plates decorated with an Arabian bandit. The most striking piece, however, stands above the entrance to the museum – a ferocious snake-haired *Medusa* by the local artist Ferruccio Mengaroni.

A block beyond the museum, the old and narrow Via Castelfidardo leads down to Pésaro's most attractive street, the porticoed Corso XI Settembre. If you want to do more than just browse in its shops, take a look inside the church of **Sant'Agostino** – the choir stalls are inlaid with landscapes, Renaissance cityscapes, and, displaying a wit to rival the *studiolo* in the Palazzo Ducale in Urbino, half-open cupboards and protruding stacks of books.

On Via Mazza, the continuation of Via Castelfidardo, is Pésaro's archeological museum in the Palazzo Almerici, the **Museo Oliveriano** (July & Aug Mon–Sat 4–7pm; rest of year Mon–Sat 9am–noon; free; you may need to apply at the adjacent library, ☎0721.33.344), with a small but unusual collection of local finds. Among the relics from the Iron Age necropolis at nearby Novilara are a child's tomb filled with miniature domestic utensils and a tomb slab carved with pear-shaped figures rowing a square-sailed boat into battle. Even more intriguing is the collection of ex-votives – breasts, feet, heads and even a dog – collected not from an early Catholic church but from a Roman sacred grove at San Veneranda (3km from Pésaro), consecrated in the second century BC. Pride of place, however, goes to a bronze statue of a Grecian youth, exquisite even though it's a facsimile of a Roman copy of a fifth-century-BC Greek original.

In the other direction, the tree-lined grid of stucco hotels and gleaming apartments marks Pésaro's long sandy beachfront, punctuated by a handful of Art Deco villas, including one on Piazzale della Libertà whose eaves are supported by white plaster lobsters. On the way, at Via Rossini 34, the **Casa di Rossini** (July & Aug daily 5–11pm; Sept–June Tues–Sun 9.30am–12.30pm & 4–7pm; L5000/€2.58) houses a modest shrine of memorabilia to the composer, who was born here in 1792. The Teatro Rossini on Piazza Lazzarini hosts an opera festival in his honour every August.

Practicalities

Finding your way around Pésaro is no problem – Viale Risorgimento leads from the **train station** to the town's main axis, Via Branca–Via Rossini–Viale della Repubblica, which cuts straight through the historical town to the beach. Bisecting it at Piazza del Popolo are Corso XI Settembre, scene of the evening passeggiata, and Via San Francesco, which leads to the **bus station** on Piazza Matteotti. The main **tourist office** (daily: summer 8am–8pm; winter 9am–1pm & 4–7pm; ☎0721.69.341), is on the seafront on Piazzale della Libertà, at the end of Viale della Repubblica

Pick of the reasonably priced and convenient **hotels** along the seafront are *Caravelle*, Viale Trieste 269 (☎0721.370.450, *www.hotelcaravelle.net*; ③) a light, airy place with a swimming pool, bikes, a games room, and room prices that drop by almost a half in May and September; *Hotel des Bains*, Viale Trieste 221 (☎0721.34.957; ⑤), dating back to 1905 and though modernized many times since then, still with something of the 'belle epoque' about it; *Napoleon*, Viale Fiume 118 (☎0721.31.160; ④) geared up for families with its mini-suites, play room and water slides; and *Atlantic*, Viale Trieste 365 (☎0721.370.333, *www.hatlantic.com*; ⑤) with a retro feel in its Fifties-style lounge. Other hotels line the avenues which run parallel to the sea: *Abbazia*, Viale Trento 147 (☎0721.33.694; Apr–Sept; ②), is the budget choice though insists that you pay upfront; *Clipper*, Viale Marconi 53 (☎0721.30.915; ④) is relaxed and friendly despite the old-fashioned furniture and offers an alfresco buffet breakfast on the terrace. On the edge of town on the road south to Fano, *Villa Serena* Via S Nicola 6/3 (☎0721.55.211, *www.egm.it*; ⑦) is an atmospheric family-owned hotel stuffed with antiques and heirlooms, with a handful of guest rooms and a swimming pool in the rambling garden. Further afield, to rent a traditional stone **cottage** in the Pesarese Apennines contact the co-operative La Macina (☎0721.700.148, *cooplamacina@info-net.it*). The nearest **campsites** to Pésaro are at Fano and at Fiorenzuola (see opposite and below).

There's no shortage of affordable places to **eat**. For food on your feet, try *Harnold's* on Piazza Lazzarini; among pizzerias, *C'era una volta*, on Via Cattaneo (closed Mon), is good, cheap and popular – so long as you don't mind rustic decor and loud rock music. There's a fine ristorante/pizzeria called *Pasqualon* at Via G. Bruno 37 (closed Sun and first two weeks of June), or you could head instead to *Cigno Bianco*, Via Castelfiardo 6 (closed Wed), which bakes pizzas in a wood-fired oven and also serves full meals. Over to the east of town, *Da Maria*, at Via Mazzini 73 (closed Wed), is a chaotic, neighbourly trattoria specializing in fish, while *Trattoria Da Sante*, nearby on Via G. Bovio (closed Mon), also serves fish dishes at rock-bottom prices but has little atmosphere. The *Antica Osteria La Guercia* at Via Baviera 33, just off the Piazza del Popolo (closed Sun), does amazing pasta and fish dishes like *mal tagliati* and *cece e vongole* and is very reasonably priced; equally popular with locals is the fish restaurant *Esedra*, on the small piazza of the same name just off Via C Cattaneo (closed Mon), which serves wonderful ravioli with fresh sole and tomatoes, mixed fish kebabs and spaghetti with squid ink.

North of Pésaro

The most pleasant route north from Pésaro is the Strada Panoramica, a minor road winding through the coastal hills to **Gabicce Mare**, a large resort with a fine beach and an expensive clifftop disco.

If you want beaches without crowds, catch a bus to **FIORENZUOLA** and **CASTEL DI MEZZO**, just a few kilometres along the Strada Panoramica from Pésaro – tiny fishing villages, with minuscule beaches reached only by steep, narrow tracks. Most people visit them only to eat at the **fish restaurants**, so you should have the beaches to yourself. You can enjoy a fine *brodetto di pesce* at *Il Vento di Focara*, Via Fossa 1 (☎0721.208.522; closed Wed in winter), in Fiorenzuola – though it's wise to reserve in advance. En route, in a beautiful setting some 7km north of Pésaro, you'll also pass the *Panorama* **campsite** (☎0721.208.145; May–Sept).

Alternatively, you can escape beaches altogether by taking a trip to the sixteenth-century **Villa Imperiale** a sumptuous mansion in extensive grounds, with rooms decorated by Bronzino and Genga. Note that the villa is normally only open to the public on one day a week and that you have to visit by way of an organized tour; for details check with Pésaro's tourist office.

Gradara

Inland, to the north, is the castle of **GRADARA** (Mon 9am–2pm, Tues–Sat 9am–7pm, Sun 9am–8pm; L8000/€4.13) – not a place to go in season if you want to avoid crowds, as it's one of the main package-tour excursions. A fairy-tale confection of mellow red-brick and swallow-tail turrets, it's said to be the scene of a thirteenth-century scandal involving Francesca da Rimini, who committed adultery with Paolo da Malatesta, her husband's brother. The lovers were killed for their transgression and later consigned to hell by Dante – he meets their spirits in Canto V of the *Inferno*, where they are caught in a ceaseless whirlwind.

Inside the castle is a room decked out as the scene of the crime, with a sumptuously refurbished four-poster bed, fake wall hangings and an open book – Francesca tells Dante in hell that it was while reading the story of Lancelot and Guinevere that she and

Paolo first succumbed to their passion. Further reminders of the story are found in two nineteenth-century paintings: one showing the lovers (either dead or in a state of post-coital collapse) watched by the crippled husband; the other, less ambiguous, of the naked couple. Other rooms are furnished as a torture chamber, complete with spiked iron ball, handcuffs and lances, and as the guards' room, a strange mixture of tavern and armoury. After touring the castle, it's well worth taking a walk round the walls for the fine views over the surrounding hills. Incidentally, Francesca's unhappy spirit is said to wander the castle when the moon is full.

Fano

Fifteen minutes south of Pésaro by half-hourly bus, **FANO** has changed since Robert Browning came here in 1848, seeking relief from the heat and crowds of Florence: its beaches remain splendid but they now attract thousands of package tourists every year. As well as the sandy and sheltered Lido and the long, pebbly Sassonia there are further beaches at Torrette and Marotta to the south, both easily reached by bus. Fano is a pleasant enough place if a little humdrum, and comfortably combines its role as resort with that of small fishing port and minor historical town.

The Town

If you're coming to Fano by bus, you could ask to be dropped off at the crenellated **Porta Maggiore** and the remnants of the medieval defensive walls, on the southwestern side of the town centre. Behind them is a Roman gate, the **Arco di Augusto**, impressive despite having been truncated in the fifteenth century when Federico da Montefeltro blasted away its upper storey. You can see what it used to look like in a relief on the facade of the adjacent church of San Michele.

The Roman precursor of Fano, named Fanum Fortunae after its Temple of Fortune, stood at the eastern end of the Via Flaminia, which cut across the Apennines to Rome. The town is still built around a Roman crossroads plan: Via Arco di Augusto and Corso Matteotti follow the routes of the cardus and decumanus, and their junction is marked with a copy of a Roman milestone stating its distance from the capital (195.4 Roman miles). There are few other relics of Roman Fano, although the fifteenth-century **fountain** in the main square, along Via Mazzini, is dedicated to Fortune.

Overlooking the fountain are the reconstructed thirteenth-century Palazzo della Ragione and the fifteenth-century **Corte Malatestiana**, dating from the time Fano was ruled by the Malatesta family. Its most notorious member was Sigismondo, whose disagreements with the pope led to the siege of Fano (when the Arco di Augusto lost its top) and his excommunication. After the death of his first wife – whom he was suspected of having poisoned – Sigismondo remarried in Fano in 1449, holding a three-day banquet in the Corte Malatestiana. Rumours about Sigismondo's sinister interest in his wives' diet revived when, seven years later, his second wife also died unexpectedly, leaving him free to marry his long-time mistress, Isotta degli Atti (for more on the Malatestas, see opposite). The Corte is at its best nowadays on summer evenings, when its loggias, turrets and trefoil windows provide a backdrop for concerts. Inside there's a small **museum and art gallery** (summer Tues–Sat 8.30am–12.30pm & 5–7pm, Sun 8am–1pm; winter Tues–Sat 8.30am–12.30pm; L4000/€2.06) whose most striking exhibit is a mosaic of a winged figure riding a panther. Upstairs, the art gallery is worth visiting for an insight into the Victorian psyche, as it's here that you'll find Guercino's *The Guardian Angel*, a painting that entranced Browning during his stay here and inspired a poem of the same title. Expressing a wistful desire to take the place of the child depicted here learning how to pray, the gushingly sentimental poem became incredibly popular, and Italy was flooded with reproductions of the painting for holidaying Browning fans. The keenest disciples set up a club, membership of which was gained by travelling to Fano and sending the founder a postcard.

Less saccharine paintings are to be found in the Renaissance church of **Santa Maria Nuova** on Via de Pili, off the main square. The two works by Perugino, a **Madonna**, *Child and Saints* and an *Annunciation*, are both suffused with a calm luminosity, emanating as much from the figures as from the landscapes behind them.

A less demanding way of punctuating your sessions on the beach would be to browse through the classy shopping arcade tastefully laid out in the cloisters of the ex-convent of **San Domenico**.

Practicalities

The **train station**, where buses also stop, is ten minutes' walk from the seafront, at the end of Via Cavallotti. Fano's **tourist office**, at Via C. Battisti 10 (July & Aug Mon–Sat 8am–2pm & 4–7pm, Sun 9am–1pm; Sept–June Mon–Sat 9am–1pm & 4–7pm, Sun 9am–1pm; ☎0721.803.534), is well organized and has good maps of the town, hotel lists and the like. There are also seasonal offices at Torrette (Via Boscomarina 10) and Marotta (Via Viale C. Colombo 30), which open in July and August.

Two of the most reasonable **hotel** options are *Mare*, Viale Colombo 20 (☎0721.805.667; ②), an easy-going family-run pension with a shady garden and verandah a few blocks back from the sea, offering good home cooking and an excellent full board deal; and the more formal *Corallo*, at Via Leonardo da Vinci 3 (☎0721.804.200, *www.mobilia.it/corallo*; ③), on the seafront. There are plenty of **campsites** on the coast between Pésaro and Fano, such as *Norina* (☎0721.55.792) and *Marinella* (☎0721.55.795), both open from April to mid-October and easily reached by bus. South of Fano are the *Stella Maris* (☎0721.884.231) and *Torette* (☎0721.884.787) campsites, near the small resort of Torette, and many others are strung along the coast in between, all easily accessible by bus from Fano.

For **eating**, apart from numerous pizzerias and snack bars, there's *da Pep*, Via Garibaldi 19 (closed Mon), in the old town serving home-made pasta and fish dishes at reasonable prices, with tables outside in the shady cobbled street. Alternatively try the cheap and earthy fish taverna, *Quinta*, in the fishing harbour at Viale Adriatico (closed Sun), which caters mostly for fishermen, and the prices reflect this. Just around the corner from the port is a place with even lower prices: *Self Service "Al Pesce Azzurro"*, at Viale Adriatico 48 (June–Sept), specializes in cheaper fish like sardines, anchovies and mackerel.

Senigállia

Further down the coast, **SENIGÁLLIA** is an unprepossessing family resort with a good beach and with most of its tourist activity packed into a short season. Primarily a convenient place among locals for beach-lazing and swimming, though not special enough to travel any distance out of your way for, the lido part of town is cheerful enough in a low-key way in July and August though empty outside this period. The town centre focuses on the rickety **Foro Annonario**, a semicircular Neoclassical marketplace, behind which the imposing thirteenth-century **Rocca Roveresca** (May–Sept Tues–Sat 9am–1pm & 5–10pm, Sun 9am–1pm; L4000/€2.06), built for Federico da Montefeltro's son-in-law by Luciano Laurana, architect of the Palazzo Ducale in Urbino, is worth an hour of your time. A somewhat austere exterior is embellished by white stone brackets, while inside airily elegant Renaissance halls stand above an underground warren of vaulted storage rooms and dungeons. It seems that the Rocca was rarely used as a ducal residence – the fireplaces and beautiful spiral staircase show little sign of use. The cells, though, are a different matter: converted from cannon positions when the region fell to the pope, they have diminutive air-holes designed to inflict a slow and agonizing death on their occupants. Fine views are to be had from the towers, built in the fifteenth century when the Adriatic coast was plagued by Turkish bandits.

The Rocca overlooks Senigállia's scruffy and dilapidated sixteenth-century **Palazzo Ducale**, and the more interesting **Palazzo Baviera**. Now the seat of the *comune*, it still contains some original furniture and wall coverings, and its ceilings – stuccoed with sixteenth-century scenes from Greek mythology, Roman history and the Old Testament – are, to say the least, sumptuous.

Practicalities

The **tourist office** (July & Aug daily 8am–2pm & 4–7pm; Sept–June Mon–Sat 9am–1pm & 4–7pm; ☎071.792.2725), is behind the train station on Piazzale Morandi, a block from the beach. **Hotel** prices are on a par with the rest of Marche's resorts and rooms are predictably hard to come by in July and August. If you are set on staying, however, the seafront *Mareblù*, Lungomare Mameli 50 (☎071.792.0104; ③), with a swimming pool, is a good choice. With eighteen **campsites**, Senigállia is ideal if you've got a tent. Most of the hotels and all the campsites, including *Summerland* (☎071.792.6816; June–Sept), about 1.5km south of Senigállia at Via Podesti 236, which boasts a swimming pool and tennis courts, are along the coast; those to the south (Lungomare da Vinci) are reached by bus #2 and those to the north (Lungomare Mameli) by bus #1, both of which leave from the train station. If you want more independence, a number of places rent out bikes – ask at the tourist office for details.

Senigállia's liveliest street, Corso 2 Giugno (behind the Rocca), runs down to the Foro and the grim tunnel of arcades called the Portici Ercolani, which are the best hunting grounds for cheap **snacks**. For more substantial sit-down **meals**, *La Taverna*, at Via Fratelli Bandiera 55 (closed Sun), is a good deal, specializing in local dishes like *vincisgrassi*, a lasagne of ham, cream and truffles.

Ancona and around

Severely damaged by war and earthquakes, workaday **ANCONA** has a few historical monuments embedded in a tangle of commercial buildings. The modern centre is a bland grid of broad avenues and palm-shaded piazzas, while the station area, with its one-night cheap hotels, gaudy Chinese restaurants and heavy trucks travelling noisily to and from the port, will probably make you want to take the next train out. However, as the Adriatic's largest port it's a convenient departure point, and you may well pass through in order to catch one of the regular ferries to Greece and Croatia so for this reason you may find yourself making an overnight stop.

The Town

Regular buses run along the seafront from the train station to the port, passing the pentagonal **Lazzaretto**, built within the harbour in the eighteenth century as a quarantine station for immigrants. The port itself is headed by a well-preserved Roman arch, the **Arco di Traiano**, raised in honour of Emperor Trajan, under whose rule Ancona first became a major port. Behind it is the **Arco Clementino**, a piece of architectural self-congratulation by Pope Clement XII, who made Ancona a free port in the eighteenth century and thus considered himself Trajan's equal.

On a steep hill overlooking the port rises the town's Romanesque duomo. What survives of old Ancona is spread out below it, and a wander up the hill is the most pleasant way of filling in time before your ferry leaves. At the foot of the hill is Piazza della Repubblica, from which Via della Loggia leads past the **Loggia dei Mercanti**, whose Gothic splendours can be seen in all their glory now that the layers of grime have been cleaned off – you can make out the figures of medieval dignitaries and horsemen below its elaborately carved windows. Backtracking to Piazza della Repubblica, take a left into Corso Mazzini, where there's a long sixteenth-century **fountain** with 13 spouting heads, all with great expressions, attributed to Pellegrino Tibaldi

Equally appealing is the Romanesque church of **Santa Maria della Piazza**, its facade a fantasia of blind loggias and its portal carved with chunky figures and elegant birds. Behind the church, on Via Pizzecolli, is the town's **Pinacoteca Comunale** (Mon 9am–1pm, Tues–Sat 9am–7pm, Sun 3–7pm; L5000/€2.58). The highlight here is Titian's *Apparition of the Virgin*, a sombre yet impassioned work, with the Virgin appearing to a rotund and fluffy-bearded bishop in a stormy sunset sky. There's also a glorious *Sacra Conversazione* by Lotto, a view of sixteenth-century Ancona by Andrea Lilli, and an exquisite yet chilling *Madonna and Child* by Carlo Crivelli, with a mean-looking Mary pinching the toe of a rather pained Christ, incongruously flanked by bunches of apples and a marrow.

Beyond the gallery is the church of **San Francesco delle Scale**, named for the steps leading up to it. Titian's *Apparition* was painted for here, but today its most remarkable work is an almost orgasmic *Assumption* by Lotto. Further up the hill, the **Museo Archeologico** is not a bad place to spend an hour (June–Sept Mon–Fri & Sun 8.30am–7.30pm, Sat 9am–11pm; Oct–May Mon–Sat 8.30am–7.30pm, Sun 9am–8pm; L8000/€4.13), its wacky moulded ceilings vaulting over a collection of finds ranging from splendid Greek red- and black-figure craters to bright gold-leaf jewellery.

Passing the remains of the Roman amphitheatre, now capped with graffitied earthquake-shattered buildings, you climb up to the pink-and-white **Duomo** (or San Ciriaco). Though mostly built in a restrained Romanesque style, there's an outburst of Gothic exuberance in the doorway's cluster of slender columns, some plain, others twisted and carved. The simple and calm interior is built on a Greek-cross plan, enlivened by a cupola that from below resembles an elongated umbrella. The most memorable feature, however, is a screen along the edge of the raised right transept, one section of which is carved with eagles, fantastic birds and storks entwined in a tree, the other with saints.

Practicalities

Via Marconi and its continuation, Via XXIX Settembre, run straight along the coast up from the train station to the port and the centre of town. Via XXIX Settembre ends in the adjacent piazzas of Kennedy and Repubblica, from which the modern centre's three parallel avenues – Corso Stamira, Corso Garibaldi and Corso Mazzini – slice up to Piazza Cavour, while Via della Loggia runs up above the port to the alleyways of the old town. The main **tourist office** for Ancona and the Marche region is at Via Thaon de Revel 4 at the end of Viale della Vittoria (Mon–Fri 9am–2pm & 3–6pm, Sat 9am–1pm & 3–6pm, Sun 9am–1pm; July open til 7.30pm; ☎071.358.991, *www.le-marche.com*); there's also a seasonal office (June–Sept) at the Stazione Maríttima. The main **bus terminus** is Piazza Cavour, connected by regular bus with the **train station** on Piazza Rosselli. The **Stazione Maríttima**, where ferries dock, is connected with the train station by bus.

If you want to **stay** the night in Ancona there is no shortage of cheap and cheerful places: the *Dorico*, Via Flaminia 8 (☎071.42.761; ②), and *Gino*, Via Flaminia 4 (☎071.42.179; ③), are both fine, with the *Gino* serving good-value food. There are a cou-

---

ONWARDS TO GREECE AND CROATIA

Ferries leave from the Stazione Maríttima, a couple of kilometres (bus #1 or #1/4) north of the train station, close to the centre of town. The **tourist office** here (mid-June to mid-Sept daily 8am–8pm; ☎071.201.183) has timetables, and each of the main ferry lines has a ticket office (closed at lunchtime) – you can also buy tickets from the agencies all around the port. The main lines are Strintzis (☎071.207.3992 or 071.207.1068), who go to Corfu, Igoumenitsa and Patras in Greece and Minoan (☎071.201.708 and 071.56.789), and Superfast (☎071.207.0240, 071.207.0282 and 071.207.0283, *www.superfast.com*) who sail to Igoumenitsa and Patras. There's also Jadrolinija (☎071.204.305, *www.jadrolinkija.tel.hr/jadrolinija*) and Adriatica di Navigazione (☎071.204.915, *www.adriatica.it*) who sail to Croatia and the Dalmatian islands.

Charges on ferry lines depend on the speed of the crossing, with one-way fares starting at around L80,000/€41.32 per person to Croatia, if you are taking a car add another L80–90,000/€41,32–46,48. For the nineteen-hour journey to Patras in July and August, reckon on paying L167,000/€86.25 for an aircraft-style seat for the crossing (cabins are available) with Superfast; add L182,000/€93.99 for a car. There are no discounts for holders of InterRail and Eurail passes but outside high season prices drop by 25–30 percent, and there are 30 percent discounts on return journeys. You should book in advance, and you should always aim to arrive at the Stazione Maríttima a couple of hours before your ferry is due to depart.

---

ple more inexpensive hotels in the modern centre: the no-frills *Centrale*, Via Marsala 10, off Corso Garibaldi (☎071.54.388; ②), on the fourth floor (there's a lift) of a residential block and the centrally located *Milano*, Via Montebello 1 (☎071.201.147; ②). The most pleasant budget place to stay in Ancona is *Viale*, Viale della Vittoria 23 (☎071.201.861 or 204.053; ③), on the long avenue that leads to the blindingly white war memorial the Monumento ai Caduti (take buses #1, #1/3 or #1/4 from the train station), whose tiny courtyard garden is decked out with geraniums (breakfast is included in the price). Of the more upmarket options, the *Fortuna*, Piazza Rosselli 15 (☎071.42.633; ⑤), is new and slick, or if you can't get by without a pool, cocktail bar and health club aim for *Grand Hotel Passetto*, Via Thaon de Revel 1 (☎071.31.307, 071.31.308 or 071.31.309; ⑦), at the far end of Viale della Vittoria.

Piazza Roma is the place to hang out in Ancona – there are plenty of **cafés** with tables outside in the pedestrianized cobbled square, the busiest being *Caffè Lombardo* at the top of Corso Mazzini. If you're waiting for a bus on Piazza Cavour, *Caffè Cavour* is conveniently placed for good sandwiches and great pastries in its Sala de Thé. Of Ancona's **restaurants**, the first choice is *Clarice*, on Via del Traffico (closed Sun), off Corso Garibaldi (on the right as you walk up from the sea), an old-style, family restaurant in a cobbled side street with tables outside. It serves traditional, very reasonably priced food, with many local dishes on the menu. Second choice is *Osteria del Pozzo*, on Via Bonda (closed Sun), a narrow lane off Piazza del Plebiscito where diners tuck into seafood and pasta dishes, or *La Cantinetta* on Via Gramsci (closed Sun), just off Piazza del Plebiscito, a no-frills restaurant whose speciality is *Stoccafisso all'Anconetana* (a traditional recipe involving salt cod). For a good, inexpensive spread of roasted vegetables, pasta and seafood salads, cold meats and mozzarella head for the help-yourself lunchtime buffet at *Caffè Giuliani* on via Traffico with tables outside in a shady covered arcade (closed and Sun). For pizza, try *La Bussola* on Via Leopardi (closed Sun).

Inland: the Esino Valley and Fabriano

Cutting right across the Marche, the **Esino Valley** is broad and bland in the east, but narrows to a dramatic limestone gorge – the Gola di Rossa – just before the town of

Fabriano and the border with Umbria. Although Fabriano and Jesi are heavily industrialized, most of the valley is given over to agriculture and is best known for
Verdicchio, a dry white wine produced in the hilltop villages around Jesi. What most
visitors come for, however, are the vast Frasassi caves.

Jesi

Though its industrial development has led to **JESI** being known as "the little Milan of
the Marche", the historic centre of the town is well preserved. Clinging to a long ridge,
it's fringed by medieval walls and retains a scattering of Renaissance and Baroque
palaces. One of the most majestic of these, the Palazzo Pianetti, is home of the
Pinacoteca Civica (Tues–Sat 10am–1pm & 4–7pm, Sun 10am–1pm & 5–8pm;
L4000/€2.07). The highlight of its opulent interior is the magnificent 72-metre-long stuccoed, gilded and frescoed gallery – a Rococo fantasy of shells, flowers and festoons framing cloud-backed allegorical figures. The collection of paintings is best known for some
late works by **Lorenzo Lotto**, who unlike his contemporaries Titian and Giorgione,
chose to be an outsider from the Venetian artworld, opting instead for obscurity, working in such provincial Italian towns as Ancona and Recanati, Treviso and Bergamo. As a
result, until recently, he has been neglected though his use of colour and the expressive
intensity of his portraits is exceptional, and he was unique in combining this meticulous
realism with the southern European traditions of the High Renaissance.

In two graceful *Annunciation* panels (once part of a triptych), a hurried angel Gabriel
delivers the news to a more than slightly taken aback Virgin; and in the *Visitation*, the
setting is a simple domestic interior. Scenes from the refreshingly assertive life of St
Lucy (a polyptych) show Lotto's freshness of colour; the *Madonna delle Rose* is interesting for its naturalistic setting – with a baby Jesus trying to jump into the arms of a
grandfatherly St Joseph – as well as its allusions to Christian mysticism.

A stroll around town takes you past the Teatro Pergolesi, a vast eighteenth-century
opera house in Piazza della Repubblica, named after the composer Giovanni Battista
Pergolesi. Encircling the town are the massive ramparts, restructured in the fourteenth century and built on top of the foundations of Roman walls – an escalator takes
you through the ramparts, several metres thick, from the lower town to the upper town
(with steps back down again).

Verdicchio country

No wine is produced in Jesi itself – if you want to indulge in some wine sampling, head
for **CUPRAMONTANA**, accessible by bus from Ancona and Jesi, where one of the best
producers is Vallerosa Bonci, at Via Torre 17 (☎0731.789.129). Otherwise try
Colonarra, whose cellars, although disappointingly modern, have good wines, including a champagne-like sparkler called, naturally enough, Colonarra. The best time to
visit is on the first Sunday in October, when there's a parade and dancing, and the village streets are lined with stalls of wine and food for the **grape festival**. Theoretically,
this marks the eve of the harvest but, owing to hangovers, it's usually a couple of days
before anyone feels fit enough to start work.

The Frasassi caves and San Vittore Terme

Further up the Esino Valley, just after the Gola di Rossa, a road leads up from Genga
train station to the Frasassi gorge, carved by the River Sentino, which was also responsible for creating the eighteen kilometres of caves beneath it. The largest cave of the
Grotte di Frasassi (daily: 9am–12.30pm & 3–6pm, reduced hours on Sunday in low
season; 10 July–25 Aug open until 10.30pm; closed 10–30 Jan; tours every 30min;
L18,000/€9.30) was discovered only in 1971, and just over a kilometre of its caverns
and tunnels is now open to the public.

Inevitably, the most remarkable stalactite and stalagmite formations have been named: there's a petrified Niagara Falls, a giant's head with a wonderfully Roman profile, a cave whose floor is covered with candles, complete with holders, and a set of organ pipes. The vast Cave of the Great Wind, at 240m high, is one of the biggest in Europe – large enough to contain Milan Cathedral – and has been used for a series of experiments, ranging from sensory deprivation (as a possible treatment for drug addicts) to a sociological exploration of the dynamics that developed between a group of people sequestered there for a month.

Fabriano

Famous for two things – paper-making and Gentile da Fabriano, the best of the International Gothic artists – **FABRIANO** is now heavily industrialized and a dismal town at first sight. You're most likely to pass through on your way on to Umbria and Rome, and frankly there's little reason to stop off unless it's to visit the Museum of Paper and Watermarks (Tues–Sat 10am–6pm, Sun 10am–noon & 4–7pm; L6500/€3.36), housed in the ex-convent of San Domenico. The sort of place kids are dragged to on rainy days, it's owned by the biggest of Fabriano's paper mills, Miliani, which produces a staggering 900km of paper each day, including watermarked paper for banknotes of various currencies.

The Cónero Riviera

Just south of Ancona the white cliffs of **Monte Cónero** plunge straight into the sea, forming the northern Adriatic's most spectacular and enjoyable stretch of coastline. It's easily accessible, with the major resorts of **Portonovo**, Sirolo and Numana all linked by bus from Ancona, either from the train station or Piazza Cavour. **Sirolo and Numana** are now almost as crowded in July and August as the rest of the Adriatic resorts, the main difference being that their cliff-backed beaches are more picturesque. The most stunning stretch of coast, a series of tiny coves at the base of Monte Cònero between Portonovo and Sirolo, is best explored by boat – they leave from both bays. You can go just for the scenery or ask to be dropped off somewhere along the way for a few hours of swimming.

This stretch of coast is the home of Rosso Cónero wine, made from the same Montepulciano grape as Chianti, though less well-known than its Tuscan counterpart. Rarely found outside Italy, there's a chance to sample it at the Rosso Cónero **festival** at Camerano, 8km inland from Monte Cónero in the first week in September, with tastings, music and theatre.

Portonovo

Only 11km from Ancona **PORTONOVO** nestles beneath Monte Cónero, undeveloped save for two campsites and a few expensive hotels, one of which is sited in the Napoleonic fort that dominates the bay. Although its pebbly beach gets fairly busy in summer, the scenery is unbeatable, and the crowds are as nothing compared to those at Sirolo and Numana; even then, you can escape the crush if you're prepared to paddle and clamber to the few tiny beaches to the south. There's also a lovely Romanesque church, **Santa Maria**, perched above the beach at the end of an olean-der-lined path. At present you can see it only from the outside (ask at the nearby Hotel Fortino Napoleonico for details of how to get into the grounds), but this is enough – the clear light reflected from the sea bathes it in a golden glow, the shadows adding to the delicate interplay of arcades and wavily tiled roof. **The trail across Monte Cónero to Sirolo** begins in Portonovo, at a stairway to the right of the Hotel

Internazionale. Though rewarding, it's a steep and tricky hike, so don't attempt it without a map.

Portonovo is linked with Ancona by regular urban buses. Unfortunately all of the town's **hotels** are expensive – but at least there are some stylish choices. *Emilia*, Via Collina di Portonovo (☎071.801.117, *www.hotelemilia.com*; ⑦) is a five minute car journey inland – and uphill – from the beach. A light, modern hotel, the walls are covered with a huge contemporary art collection, a legacy of the Fifties and Sixties when artists were invited to pay for their stay with a piece of their work. The pool and many places to lounge tempt you to stay put but there are electric bikes on loan for short rides up into the Monte Cónero Park, and a shuttle service down to the beach. Down by the seashore in a converted fortress is *Fortino Napoleonico* (☎071.801.450, *www.fastnet.it/ market/fortino*; ⑦) built on the orders of Napoleon to stop the English landing to take on fresh water from Monte Cónero's springs, and now an upmarket hotel. There are some military touches in the suites but generally the hotel is chi-chi and grand. Otherwise there are two **campsites**, Camping Comunale La Torre (☎071.801.257; June to mid-Sept) is slightly cheaper; if it's full, try the Camping Club Adriatico (☎071.801.170; May to mid-Sept). For food, *Da Anna*, on the beach (closed Tues), is a great family-run fish **restaurant**.

Sirolo

Continuing south, **SIROLO** has an old centre of terraced cottages divided by neat cobbled streets. The main square, Piazza Veneto, is on the clifftop, with good views of the coast and Monte Cónero, and is home to a seasonal tourist office and a couple of bar-*gelaterie*. In season, buses run roughly every hour to the two beaches below, Sassi Neri and San Michele, of which San Michele, just to the north, is the better, with a section at the far end where nudism is tolerated. The town has won a blue flag for its clean waters for several years running, and in 2000 was one of only ten beaches in Italy to be awarded a "palma d'oro" for its unpolluted waters. Particularly inviting is the small beach close to the jagged mid-sea islets of the Due Sorelle, although you won't have it to yourself in peak season.

There is a good choice of **accommodation**: beach lovers should head for *Arturo*, Via Spiaggia 1 (☎071.933.0975; ②; June –Sept), right on the white shingle strand, a yellow house with green shutters and just seven rooms. It's a bus ride from Sirolo proper (or a long walk down and then back uphill) but it's the least expensive option in town. It has its own restaurant and there are other places to eat and drink in the evenings down at the beach. At the other end of the scale is *Rocco*, Via Torrioni 1 (☎071.933.0558; ⑥), built into the town gate and a short walk down the main street of Via Italia from the piazza. Once a thirteenth-century inn where St Francis is said to have slept, it's now a stylish seven-room hotel with an upmarket restaurant (closed Tues) serving refined, imaginative and very expensive food. Among more functional hotel alternatives, on Via Giulietti there are **rooms** at number 46 (☎071.736.0593; ③) with good triple and quadruple rooms as well as inexpensive doubles. Across the road *Stella*, Via Giulietti 9 (☎071.933.0704; ⑥) is a pleasant, modern hotel with large rooms. Other good choices are *Il Parco*, Via Giulietti 60 (☎071.933.0733; ③), with more dated decoration and a garden, and *Panoramic*, Via San Michele 8 (☎071.933.0659, *hotelpanoramic.sirolo @katamail.com*; ⑨) just off Via Giulietti, a friendly place with a sun terrace and a stunning view of the coastline. Sirolo's most attractive campsite is the *Internazionale* (☎071.933.0884; open May–Sept), set on tree-lined terraces at the bottom of the cliffs below Piazza Veneto, within sight and sound of the sea.

If you can afford to splurge in Sirolo, do it on a **meal** at the hotel *Rocco* (see above), or the equally expensive *Il Grottino* (closed Wed) on Via Ospedale, just off Via Italia, which serves Marche specialities in its stone-vaulted restaurant or outside on a terrace scented with jasmine plants. Otherwise you can eat more modestly at *La Taverna*, Via Italia 10, offering *enogastronomia*: local wine and salami, cheeses and bread, plus pizza by the slice. At *Hostaria Sara* next door at number 9 (closed Wed), diners can sample robust dishes in a no-nonsense atmosphere; the seafood antipasti, risotto and tagliatelle with fish sauce are especially recommended. Otherwise, during the day, the best eaterie by far is *Bar Pepi* down at the beach (daily May–Sept until 5pm), where workers from town go for lunch in summer. Back in town, for cocktails and **ice creams** with a sea view, head to *Il Grillo*, on Via Giulietti just below Piazza Veneto.

Numana

NUMANA, a small port with a large pebble beach, is more developed than Sirolo, and the main reason to go is to catch a boat to the offshore islets of Due Sorelle (June–Sept, roughly hourly 9am–3pm) for a spot of swimming and sunbathing. There is also the added attraction of a **museum** (Tues–Sun 8.30am–7.30pm; L4000/€2.06), filled mostly with relics of the Piceni tribe, who occupied the area between Senigállia and Pescara from the seventh century BC; the extent to which they were influenced by the Greeks, who set up a trading post nearby, is clearly visible in the red and black pots decorated with scenes from Greek mythology. If you want **to stay**, the *Scogliera*, Via del Golfo 21 (☎071.933.0622; ⑥), on a small headland at the northern edge of the bay is a modern and appealing place to stay, one of a score of three-star hotels, but otherwise you're better off staying in Sirolo, where there is also more choice of places to eat.

Loreto

One of Italy's most popular sites of pilgrimage, attracting four million visitors every year, **LORETO** owes its existence to one of the Catholic Church's more surreal legends. The story goes that in 1292, when the Muslims kicked the Crusaders out of Palestine, a band of angels flew the **house of Mary** from Nazareth to Dalmatia, and then, a few years later, whisked it across the Adriatic to Loreto. In the face of growing scepticism, the Vatican came up with the more plausible story that the Holy House was transported to Loreto on board a Crusader ship. Not surprisingly, though, this theory doesn't seem to have the same hold on the Catholic imagination, and the Madonna of Loreto continues to be viewed as the patron of aviators: Lindbergh took an image of the Madonna of Loreto on his landmark Atlantic flight in 1927, and a medallion inscribed with her image also accompanied the crew of Apollo 9. Among the Madonna of Loreto's more unlikely fans were Galileo, denounced and imprisoned as a heretic, and Descartes, who reckoned she'd helped him refine his philosophical method. For centuries she was also credited with military victories (presumably she was thought to have power over projectiles), though the builders of Loreto's basilica, aware that the site was vulnerable to Turkish pirates, decided not to rely on the Madonna's defensive capabilities, and accordingly constructed a formidable fortified church here.

Loreto's treasures were indeed covetable, the most costly and idiosyncratic being a golden baby donated by Louis XIII of France, weighing exactly the same as his long-awaited heir, the future Louis XIV. The basilica was ransacked in 1798 by Napoleonic troops, most of the plunder ending up on the shelves of the Louvre in Paris. Following Napoleon's demise, subsequent popes managed to retrieve many of the valuables, but the majority were stolen again in 1974, in what became known as the "holy theft of the century".

Numbering among its contributors such figures as Bramante, Antonio da Sangallo, Sansovino, Lotto and Luca Signorelli, the basilica is a must for anyone even mildly interested in the Renaissance. However, for the nonbeliever the atmosphere of devotional hard-sell can soon become stifling. Loreto can also be a distressing or a moving place, depending on your attitude to faith – between April and October so-called "white trains" bring the sick and terminally ill on three-day missions of hope, the main event being a Mass in Piazza della Madonna, outside the basilica.

The pilgrimage site

Had it been completed according to Bramante's design, the **Piazza della Madonna** would have been an ideal Renaissance square. It still looks pretty good, although Bramante's **Palazzo Apostolico** has only two of its projected three wings, and his low facade for the basilica, designed to make its elegant dome the piazza's focal point, was never built. Instead, the dome, masked by a fluid late-Renaissance facade, is best seen from the back. Here you can see how Baccio Pontelli, who had a hand in most of the Marche's fifteenth-century military architecture, fortified the church – the loggia that runs along the sides and around the nine apses has a dual role as a walkway for meditating monks and a battlement, looking down over the sturdy defensive walls.

Inside the basilica

The church's **interior** (daily: June–Sept 6am–7pm; Oct–May 6am–6pm) is the jumbled result of Bramante's, Sansovino's and Sangallo's attempts to graft Renaissance elements onto the late-Gothic structure. Clashing with the pointed arches of the nave, Loreto's raison d'être, the Santa Casa (Holy House), is encased in a marble cuboid designed by Bramante and encrusted with statues and reliefs. With typical Renaissance panache, pagan sibyls are juxtaposed with Old Testament prophets, all sharing in the honour of foreseeing Mary's life, scenes from which decorate the rest of the walls. The best are by Sansovino: a *Nativity* on the south side and an *Annunciation* on the front.

You may not be able to look around the Holy House itself as a service is usually being conducted for visiting pilgrims. A primitive stone building, it has no foundations and only three walls – cited by believers as proof of its authenticity (the basement and fourth wall were formed by a grotto which can still be seen in Nazareth) but seen by sceptics simply as evidence of the research undertaken by its fakers. Pride of place is given to a copy of the famous *Black Madonna of Loreto*; the medieval original, once crazily attributed to St Luke, was destroyed in a fire in 1921. Madonna and Child are usually to be seen swathed in an ornate but ill-fitting wrap known as a dalmatic, a practice started by Pope Pius VII in 1801 in celebration of the statue's return from the Louvre. Pope Julius II contributed the cannon shell hanging on the right-hand wall, attributing his miraculous escape from it to the Madonna of Loreto's missile-deflecting powers.

One of the most recent of the church's 25 chapels is the **Cappella Americana**, featuring a plane in recognition of the Madonna's role as patron of aviators. Of more artistic interest is the **Cappella del Crocifisso**, whose wooden *Crucifixion* is a triumph of Baroque ingenuity: viewed from the left, Christ appears to be still alive; from the centre, to be drawing his last agonized breath; and from the right, to be dead. Less theatrical is the **Sagrestia di San Giovanni**, frescoed by Luca Signorelli – most striking is the Conversion of St Paul, with its panic-stricken courtiers. The sacristy's inlaid cupboards, featuring a jumble of trompe l'oeil bric-a-brac, are influenced by those in the *studiolo* of Urbino's palace (see p.642).

Next door, in the **Cappella dei Duchi di Urbino**, commissioned by the last duke, Francesco Maria II della Rovere, is an *Annunciation* by Barocci, taking place before an open window through which the Palazzo Ducale can be seen. By far the most entertaining chapel, however, is the **Sagrestia di San Marco**, where vaulted frescoes feature prophets who seem to be resolving the knotty problem of the sex of angels by peering up their skirts. Ezekiel looks appalled, Zacharias flushed and embarrassed, Jeremiah delighted, and David utterly overwhelmed.

To the left of the Chapel of the Crucifix, a corridor leads to the sumptuously stuccoed atrium and the **Treasury**, its vault unremarkably frescoed by Pomerancio. The artist won the competition for the commission in 1604 thanks to Vatican manoeuvring, much to the chagrin of the loser, Caravaggio, who hired a cutthroat to slash Pomerancio's face.

The Museo-Pinacoteca
The items left behind in the treasury after the 1974 burglary are now kept in the Museo-Pinacoteca (Tues–Sun 9am–1pm & 4–7pm; donations requested) housed in the west wing of the Palazzo Apostolico. It shouldn't be missed, principally for the five paintings by Lorenzo Lotto that are held here, including his final work, *The Presentation in the Temple*. Plagued by neurosis and lack of money, Lotto finally joined the religious community at Loreto, and died here in 1556. Looking at *The Presentation*, with its rotund, crumbling priest and frail, almost skeletal nun, it would appear that he never found much inner peace. *Christ and the Adulteress* is an even more powerful work, with Christ surrounded by maniacally intense men and a swooning adulteress. For some light relief, take a look at the best of all the depictions of the Holy House's angel-powered flight – a copy of a fluffy-clouded fantasy by Giambattista Tiepolo.

Practicalities

Loreto is easily accessible by **train** from Ancona; the train station is some way out of town but connected with the centre by regular buses. The busiest periods are December 8–12 (the anniversary of the legendary flight), August 1–20, September 5–10, Easter, and from Christmas through to January 7; it's also pretty crowded throughout the summer, and finding accommodation can be difficult. All the cheap **hotels** are run by religious orders, the cheapest of which is that of the *Sorelle Francescane*, Via Marconi 26 (☎071.970.306; ①). If that's full, the **tourist office** at Via Solari 3 (Mon–Sat 9am–1pm & 4–7pm; Sun 9am–1pm ☎071.358.991) has a complete list. Otherwise, for something less spartan, try the central 1970s-style *Il Giardinetto*, just inside the Porta Romana on Corso Boccalini (☎071.977.135, *giardinetto@tin.it*; ③), or *San Gabriele*, Via Marconi 22 (☎071.970.160; ④), a 70-room hotel with terrazzo floors and eclectic furniture. *Centrale*, Via Solari 7 (☎071.970.173; ③), is a comfortable two-star with good reductions in low season and a vast and popular restaurant *Girarrosto* (see below). Within the city walls there are good deals in low-season at the *Pellegrino e Pace* on the edge of the main square at Piazza dell Madonna 5 (☎071.977.106; ④), especially if you are looking for a triple or quadruple room. Leading away from the piazza, at Corso Boccalini 69 is *Delfino Azzurro* (☎071.977.283; ③), a friendly two-star with a private garage. A couple of kilometres beyond the city walls, and connected by bus from the train station, is the **youth hostel** at Via Aldo Moro 46 (☎071.750.1026; L25–L35,000/€ 2.91–18.07).

Your best bet for places to **eat** is the *Ristorante Girarrosto* in Via Solari (closed Wed) for good, fresh pasta dishes, while the *Garibaldi*, further down the same street (closed Wed), serves great pizza as does the *Antica Pizzeria del Corso* at Corso Boccalini 74 (closed Mon).

Recanati and Porto Recanati

A few kilometres along the Macerata road from Loreto is **RECANATI**, a small town that makes a comfortable living from having been the birthplace of the opera singer Beniamino Gigli and the nineteenth-century poet Giacomo Leopardi. The visitor can wallow in Gigli memorabilia in the civic art gallery, or visit places that feature in

Leopardi's poems; if such acts of homage don't appeal, there's little point in coming to Recanati. It's attractive in a forgettable sort of way, but the provinciality soon becomes stultifying – Leopardi himself, though loving Recanati for its views of sea, hills and mountains, found most of its inhabitants stodgy and narrow-minded.

Recanati

On the central Piazza Leopardi, the town's **Pinacoteca Civica** (Tues–Sun 10am–1pm & 4–7pm; L6000/€3,09) is housed in the nineteenth-century **Palazzo Comunale**, a fussy mock-Renaissance symbol of Recanatese obtuseness – in order to build it they ripped down a fine medieval palace. All that remains of the original palace is the vast **Torre del Borgo**, glowering down on the municipal architecture that surrounds it. Once inside the gallery you can forget all this and lose yourself in Gigli's world, evoked by costumes worn by the great tenor, presents received by him (including a dagger from D'Annunzio), and, best of all, a replica of his dressing room. A crackly recording of his voice is often playing on a wind-up gramophone as a fitting accompaniment to the exhibits. The gallery itself has only two paintings worth spending time on, both by **Lotto**. There's a polyptych, complete save for its predella (which somehow ended up in Russia), and an *Annunciation*, better known as *The Madonna of the Cat* for the cat scuttling between the Madonna and angel – thought by some critics to represent the devil.

Turning left out of the piazza, the main street leads down to the **Palazzo Leopardi** (mid-June to mid-Sept daily 9am–8pm; mid-Sept to mid-June Mon–Fri 9am–6pm, Sat 9am–7pm; L7000/€3.61), where the poet was born in 1798 and which still contains his vast library of over 25,000 volumes. The odd name of the square in front of it, **Piazzuola Sabato del Villagio**, comes from one of Leopardi's poems, in which he observes a typical Recanati Saturday, with "a swarm of children shouting on the piazzuola". You're almost bound to meet crowds of schoolkids here, but their elation tends to come from relief at finishing the tedious tour of Leopardi's gloomy house. The best-known thing about the poet is his lack of success in love, which is typically blamed on his smothering mother, who still cut up his meat for him when he was 25. Leopardi sought solace in the view from the edge of town – on a good day it extends as far as the Apennines. The lower hills, which seem to roll endlessly towards the mountains, inspired his most famous poem, *Colle Infinito* ("Infinite Hills"), and a plaque with a line from it has been stuck on a wall, above a heap of rocks from Naples, where he died and is buried. Adding insult to injury, the place where he came to forget his failures with women has become a lovers' lane.

Porto Recanati

If you're not a fan of either Gigli or Leopardi, you may as well head straight to **PORTO RECANATI**, the nearest resort to Loreto. Its main street Corso Matteotti is headed by the turreted tower of a medieval castle; off it is a tiny old quarter of terraced cottages surrounded by hotels and apartment buildings. Apart from the beach, limited attractions include a **sailing and windsurfing school** (June–Aug) – details from the **tourist office** (summer Mon–Sat 9am–1pm & 4–7pm, Sun 9am–1pm; winter Mon–Sat 9am–1pm & 3–6pm; ☎071.979.9084) on the Corso – and four discos. When you tire of the beach you can visit an art gallery inside the **castle** (Mon–Fri 4–7pm; free), though sadly one of its two star attractions, a view of Venice attributed to Turner, was stolen in 1996; the other, a portrait of a peasant at work attributed to Miller, is still here however-er. Even better, the castle courtyard has an **arena** – a wonderfully atmospheric place to see films and theatre.

The cheapest **hotel** in town is the small, central one-star *Cacciatore*, at Corso Matteotti 11, (☎071.979.9234; ③). Slightly pricier, but much more comfortable is the

17-room *Bianchi Nicola* Via Rosselli 2 (☎071.979.9016; ④) or the *Bianchi Vincenzo* at Via Garibaldi 15 (☎071.979.9040; ④) whose rooms have balconies overlooking the sea. *Enzo* at Corso Matteotti 21/23 (☎071.759.0734; ⑤), is a glossy four-star. The *Pineta* **campsite**, to the south on Viale della Repubblica (☎071.979.9237), is reasonably convenient and has four-person bungalows as well.

Porto Recanati is best known for its *brodetto*, a classy fish soup cooked with nine varieties of fish, spiced with saffron and served with squares of toast. One of the best places to try it is the **restaurant** inside the *Bianchi Vincenzo* hotel (see above; closed to non-residents Mon) on the seafront – the chef is justifiably known as the *l'uomo del brodetto* (the "brodetto man") and conjures up other equally delicious dishes, including delicate seafood starters and a superb fish risotto. The *mago del brodetto* however (the "brodetto magician"), is the chef at the other Bianchi family hotel, *Bianchi Nicola* (also closed to non-residents Mon).

Macerata

A little-known provincial capital surrounded by Marche's loveliest countryside, **MACERATA** is one of the region's liveliest historical towns, thanks to its ancient university. Easy-paced and unpretentious, it's an ideal place to wind down in the evenings after exploring the province. For opera and ballet fans, its annual *Stagione Lirica*, held in Italy's best open-air venue outside Verona, is a must: in recent years it has drawn such heavyweights as Placido Domingo, Birgit Nilsson and José Carreras. And if you're the slightest bit interested in contemporary art, Macerata has a gallery that alone is reason enough for visiting the town.

The Town

Piazza della Libertà is the heart of the old town, an odd square in which the disparate buildings vie for supremacy. The Renaissance **Loggia dei Mercanti** was supplied by Alessandro Farnese, better known as Pope Paul III, the instigator of many architectural improvements to sixteenth-century Rome; sadly he did nothing else for the square, and the loggia is elbowed out by the bland **Palazzo del Comune** and overlooked by the dull **Torre del Comune**. The dreariest feature, however, is the mournful brick facade of **San Paolo**, a deconsecrated seventeenth-century church now used as an exhibition space.

Things buzz a bit more along the main passeggiata route, the boutique- and bar-lined **Corso della Repubblica**, which ends at **Piazza Vittorio Veneto** and the **Pinacoteca Civica** (Mon 4–7.30pm, Tues–Sat 9am–1pm & 4–7.30pm, Sun 9am–noon; free). The collection here, ranging from the Renaissance perfectionist Crivelli to Ancona-born futurist Cagli, isn't bad, but you might find the artworks on show in the **Palazzo Ricci** (Tues, Thurs & Sat 10am–noon & 4–6pm; free), off the square on Via Ricci, more challenging; they make up what is by any standards a fine collection of Italian contemporary art. There are two thrilling sculptures by Francesco Messina – a nerve-tingling nude of a dancer putting on her shoes, and a leaping horse. Enrico Baj's *Military Head* depicts a general decorated with assorted fabric on a background of upholstery material, and you might see a similarly satiric intent in Manzu's bronze bas-relief of a clutch of cardinals. There's also a good cross-section of work by the Italian futurists, followed by de Chirico's weird *Worried Muse*; de Chirico's brother, Alberto Savinio, provides the gallery's jokiest piece of social satire in the form of a painting of a richly dressed society woman whose long neck ends in a goose's head.

Seeing the rest of Macerata's sights doesn't take long. Via Ricci leads along towards the bleak **Piazza Mazzini**, below which is the Neoclassical **Sferisterio**, built in the early nineteenth century as an arena for *sphaera*, a traditional game that involved bashing a ball with a spiked iron glove. It was also used for bullfights, horse racing and mock jousts until, in 1921, the opera festival was inaugurated and the musicians took it over. It's rather dismal and not worth visiting, except for a performance.

Up Via Ciccarelli from Piazza Mazzini, the town's **Duomo** on Piazza Strambi is no architectural showpiece either – a workaday chunk of Baroque, which might have looked slightly more appetizing had its facade been finished. Inside there's a statue of Macerata's patron saint, Giuliano, whose path to sainthood sounds like something out of a Sunday tabloid. He arrived home to find two people in his bed and, thinking they were his wife and her lover, promptly killed them. Discovering he'd murdered his parents, he hacked one of his arms off in remorse – the severed limb is now kept in a church strongroom, encased in a sleeve of gold and silver. The relic is displayed on request, but a day's notice is required.

Practicalities

Old Macerata is wrapped around a hill, surrounded by modern suburbs that are home to the **train station**, a ten-minute walk south at the end of Viale Don Bosco. This is connected with Piazza della Libertà by frequent buses. **Buses** stop at the Giardini Diaz, directly below the old town on the western side, across Viale Puccinotti; some, however, do continue to a second, more convenient stop, from which it's a five-minute climb up stepped Piaggia delle Torre to Piazza della Libertà.

The **tourist office** is on Piazza della Libertà (Mon–Sat 9am–1pm & 4–7pm, Sun 9am–1pm; ☎0733.234.807). There are just a handful of **hotels** in Macerata, and if you're looking for somewhere fairly cheap you should try to book in advance; during the opera season (mid-July to mid-Aug), this is absolutely crucial. The top two choices are the *Arcadia* and the *Arena*; the *Arcadia*, Via P Matteo Ricci (☎0733.235.961; ④), in a quiet cobbled street in the historic centre between Piazza della Libertà and Piazza Mazzini has newly decorated bedrooms with huge beds and TVs; while the modern, friendly *Arena* at nearby Vicolo Sferisterio, off Piazza Mazzini (☎0733.230.931; ③), is tucked away in a small courtyard in a group of ancient stone buildings. Otherwise there's the *Residenza Lauri* at Via T. Lauri 6 (☎0733.232.376; ③), also central and reached via Corso Matteotti; its rooms are pleasant and there are triples and quadruples with kitchenettes also available. Macerata's four-star option is the medieval-style *Hotel Claudiani*, at Via Ulissi 8 (☎0733.261.400; ⑥), in an ancient, dark palazzo just off Corso Matteotti in the historic centre. If you have a car you may prefer to stay **out of town** at *Il Vecchio Granaio*, località Chiaravalle, Passo di Treia (☎0733.843.488, *turigest@tin.it*; ③) a former hunting lodge and now an agriturismo complex a twenty-minute drive from Macerata on the SS361 at the km 40,500 marker. The large guest rooms in the converted stable block are decorated with antiques and hunting prints, and superlative views of the hills are available from the communal sun terrace. There's a large swimming pool in the garden and the restaurant serves excellent food.

As for **food**, *Rusticanella Romana*, Corso della Repubblica 13, and *La Scaletta*, on the corner of Piaggia delle Torre and Via Rossi, both do decent takeaway pizza, while; *Narciso*, next to the Porta Montana (closed Tues), is a good place for breakfast. *Da Silvano* on Piaggia delle Torre, just off Piazza della Libertà (closed Mon and most of May) is an outstanding sit-down pizzeria. *Trattoria da Ezio*, Via Crescimbeni 65 (closed Sun), serves very reasonably priced food with fish specials on Wednesday and Friday, and "Thursday gnocchi". For a more indulgent meal, head for Macerata's most famous restaurant, *Da Secondo*, on Via Pescheria Vecchia (☎0733.260.912; closed Mon); they do a superlative *vincisgrassi*, a sinfully rich lasagne, along with excellent roast lamb and pigeon.

For more dedicated **drinking** (or indeed daytime sandwiches), there's the *Firenze* bar on Via Pescheria Vecchia, and the popular *Il Pozzo*, Via Costa 5, a student hangout that, sadly, closes at around 8pm. The kitschly tropical *Maracuia*, on Piazza V. Veneto, is a nice place to drink al fresco alongside Macerata's young and beautiful. Seats for the **opera** are bookable at the *Biglietteria dell'Arena Sferisterio*, Piazza Mazzini 10 (☎0733.230.735, fax 0733.261.570, *www.macerataopera.org*). Ticket prices range from L25,000/€12.91 to L170,000/€87.80.

East of Macerata

With its hills rising from the coast and rippling towards the Apennines, its medieval villages and scattering of Romanesque abbeys and churches, the area around Macerata is interesting to explore. You can get to most places by bus within a day, although if you're wanting to visit some of the more out-of-the-way hill-villages, you may find it more convenient to sleep over.

The Chienti Valley

From Macerata the road and rail line run east to the coast through the **Chienti Valley**, passing through some of the region's most characteristic hill-towns and two of its finest churches. About 10km from Macerata, close to the turn-off for Morrovalle, is the Romanesque church of **San Claudio al Chienti**, approached along a cypress-lined avenue. Carefully restored after years of use as a farm outbuilding, the church appears to be none the worse for its undignified past – you'd certainly never guess that the two cylindrical towers flanking its facade used to serve as grain silos. The upper storey, intended for church dignitaries, was entered through the elegant marble portal, while lesser mortals were directed to the tunnel-like door on the ground floor. The marble for the portal, like much of the church's fabric, was scavenged from a Roman village, Pausula, which once stood in the adjacent field. The interior is atmospheric enough, but needn't detain you for long.

Morrovalle

Above San Claudio, the hill-village of **MORROVALLE**, skirted by a stepped street which disappears through arched gates, is worth a visit only if you have your own transport.

The main piazza, tucked away at the top, is a tightly enclosed, even claustrophobic square, which for the past six centuries has been given over to municipal business. Flanked by the eighteenth-century Palazzo del Comune and squat Palazzo del Podestà (where Italy's first pawnshop was set up by St Bernard in 1428), is the Palazzo Lazzarini, built by those members of the Lazzarini family who survived their internecine battle for the privilege of ruling Morrovalle. The palazzo, though built in the fourteenth century, incorporates an earlier Romanesque-Gothic portal, possibly taken from a local church.

Montelupone

The even more remote **MONTELUPONE** is the most memorable of the district's walled hill-villages. Get there, if you can, in the early evening – the village is at its liveliest then, and looks particularly good glowing in the late sun. If it's clear, you can also catch a photographer's dream sunset from the belvedere: the view extends from Monte Cónero on the coast and across to the most beautiful of the Apennines, the Monti Sibillini.

You can get to Montelupone by (rare) bus from Macerata. Until the completion of a new **hotel** in Montelupone's historic centre, the nearest option is the *Moretti Dante*, on Via E. Fermi (☎0733.226.060; ②) a modern hotel a 10-minute drive away just off the SS571. It's casual and a bit chaotic at weekends when there are wedding and first communion parties but there are few other choices in the area. To get there from Montelupone take the road to Potenza, then turn left towards Recanati. The hotel is on the corner just before you reach the SS571.

Santa Maria a Piè di Chienti

Back in the valley, road and railway pass the ex-monastery of **Santa Maria a Piè di Chienti** (daily 8am–8pm) just after the fork for Montecósaro. It was built by Cluniac monks, who came to the area in the tenth century, draining the flood-prone river into channels and creating fertile land out of what had been a fever-ridden marsh. Situated close to the coast, the monastery was vulnerable to Saracen invasions, so the monks encircled it with ditches, which could be flooded in the event of a raid. The monastery survived until the early nineteenth century, when it was destroyed by Napoleonic troops, and now all that remains is the church itself. The facade was rebuilt in the eighteenth century, and the church's best external features are now its apses, decorated with fake pilasters and scalloped arcades. However, it's the interior (key from the adjacent bar) that's really special, its columns and arches bathed in the half-light that falls from the windowpanes of alabaster. After wandering around the vaulted chamber beneath the raised presbytery, and up the stairs to the galleries (narrow to ensure that they were climbed slowly, with a prayer on every step), you'll need to switch the lights on (by the right transept) to see the fifteenth-century frescoes properly. The best-preserved are in the apse, showing New Testament scenes in Renaissance settings, framed by fake mosaics and dominated by a stony-faced Christ.

Tolentino and around

Around 20km southwest of Macerata, **TOLENTINO** doesn't look much at first sight, girded as it is by ugly modern suburbs. But it improves markedly after you've crossed its turreted thirteenth-century bridge, a short way beyond which stands the **Basilica di San Nicola** (daily 7.30am–12.30pm & 3.30–7pm; free), the main reason for visiting the town. Its west front is a real feast for the eyes – a curly Baroque facade with a grinning sun instead of a rose window and a fancily twisting Gothic portal topped by an oriental-style arch enclosing a dragon-slaying saint. Inside, the most intriguing feature is the **Cappellone di San Nicola**, whose Gothic frescoes create a kaleidoscope of colourful scenes of medieval life. In fact, they are episodes from the life of Christ, painted in the fourteenth century by one of Giotto's followers, known only as the "Maestro di Tolentino". The most striking are *The Wedding at Cana*, with hefty servants carrying massive jugs of wine on their shoulders, *The Slaughter of the Innocents*, and *The Entry into Jerusalem*, in which an attempt at perspective is made by peopling the trees with miniature figures.

In the main piazza is the **Museo Internazionale della Caricatura** (Tues–Sun 10am–12.30pm & 3–6.30pm; winter closes 5.30pm; L5000/€2.58), which is filled with some of the world's best satirical cartoons. Just east of Tollentino is the imposing, fourteenth-century **Castello della Rancia**, which once harboured the notorious Renaissance mercenary Sir John Hawkwood.

San Severino Marche

Twelve kilometres north of Tolentino lies the old, silvery-grey town of **SAN SEVERINO MARCHE**, a pretty little place whose modern centre converges on an unusual elliptical square, **Piazza del Popolo**, surrounded by porticoes. Just above the piazza on Via Salimbeni the town's art gallery, known as the **Pinacoteca Tacchi-Venturi** after a local historian (July–Sept Tues–Sun 9am–1pm & 4.30–6.30pm; Oct–June Tues–Sat 9am–1pm plus alternate Sundays 9am–1pm; L4000/€2.06), is as good a reason as any for a visit, with a quite memorable assembly of pieces. A gilded polyptych of saints by Paolo Veneziano is followed by an even more sumptuous altarpiece by Vittore Crivelli, which centres on a china-doll Madonna weighed down in heavy gold embroidery. It's the frame that really catches your eye, though – an opulent confection of scalloped arches topped with urns from which spring gesticulating ecclesiastics. Other highlights are the works by the Salimbeni brothers, who were born and worked in San Severino in the fifteenth century; they are represented by delicate and expressive frescoes detached from local churches and a wooden polyptych of *The Marriage of St Catherine*. In the same building is the **Museo Archeologico**, (July–Sept Tues–Sun 9am–1pm & 4.30–6.30pm; Oct–June Tues–Sat 9am–1pm plus alternate Sundays 9am–1pm; L4000/€2.06), with relics from the Roman valley town of Septempeda, whose inhabitants, driven out by barbarian invasions in the sixth century, escaped up the nearest hill to found the forerunner of San Severino.

Other works by the Salimbeni brothers adorn two of San Severino's churches. One of these, the ancient **San Lorenzo in Doliolo**, at the top of Via Salimbeni, looks slightly odd thanks to a medieval brick tower standing on top of its stone portal. The Salimbeni frescoes, illustrating the story of St Andrew, are on the vault of the tenth-century crypt, looking far older and more primitive than they really are because of their antique surroundings; the back part of the crypt is thought to be a pagan temple dating back to the time of the refugees from Septempeda.

The other church – actually the old cathedral – is up in **CASTELLO**, the upper part of San Severino, a long and steep walk – although there are occasional buses from the main square. A lonely, evocative place, it was here that the Romans from Septempeda came, though as Castello continued to be the hub of religious and political life until the eighteenth century, any traces of them have long been covered over. Close to its thirteenth-century walls, sheltered by a Gothic portico, is the **Fontana dei Sette Canelle**, a seven-spouted fountain where you'll occasionally see women doing their washing. Right at the top, dwarfed by the medieval Torre del Comune, is the **Duomo Vecchio**, founded in the tenth century but with a Romanesque-Gothic facade, simple Gothic cloisters, and a much rebuilt interior. Not surprisingly, it's lost a bit of atmosphere with all these reconstructions, but the baptistry vault still has its Salimbeni frescoes. Also worth a look are the inlaid choir stalls and tomb of the town's patron, St Severinus.

For a congenial **place to stay** in San Severino, head for the *Due Torri*, Via San Francesco 21(☎0733.645.419, *duetorri@wnt.it*; ③), high above town in the Castello; spotless bedrooms in an old stone wing with green shutters, tiled floors and simple furnishings. There's a popular restaurant attached, which doubles as a shop, selling local delicacies, wines and spirits.

Ùssita and hiking territory

Some way south of San Severino, close to the border with Umbria and the Monti Sibillini, is **ÙSSITA**, a rather anonymous winter sports resort squeezed into a narrow valley at the foot of Monte Bove. Reachable by bus from Macerata, it's an accessible first base for **mountain hikes**, a seven- to eight-kilometre hike from the basic *Rifugio Forcella del Fargno* (June–Oct Sat & Sun; Aug daily; from within Italy ☎0330.280.690; from abroad phone the warden's private number ☎0733.230.812), from which there's a good choice of walks, including the ascent of the three-peaked mountain known as the **Pizzo Tre Vescovi** because it resembles three mitred bishops. The going can be tricky, as the upper peaks are covered in snow for most of the year, so you'll need a good map

(Kompass 666 is the best) and, if you can read Italian, the *CAI Guida dei Monti Sibillini* is helpful being packed with information on flora, fauna and local legends.

If you have your own transport or you don't mind road walking, you can also head up to the **Santuario di Macereto** (daily 7.30am–12.30pm & 3.30–7pm; free), set on a wild high plain above Ussita. It's no rustic chapel but a classy Bramantesque church built in the sixteenth century as a spiritual stopover for shepherds bringing their flocks up from their winter grazing grounds in the south, and it's surrounded by arcaded stalls for the animals.

South of Macerata: the road to Sarnano

With the Sibillini mountains on the horizon, snow-capped for most of the year, the route south from Macerata towards Sarnano ranks as one of the Marche's most beautiful. Ten kilometres along the road, on the edge of a dense wood, is the Romanesque-Gothic complex of the **Abbazia di Fiastra** (July to mid-Sept daily 10am–12.30pm & 3–6.30pm; Sun and rest of year closes one hour earlier; L5000/€2.58 for abbey and museum) a Cistercian abbey with a simple, pan-tiled brick cloister and monastic quarters adjoining a grandiose aisled church containing fifteenth-century frescoes of the Crucifixion with St Benedict and St Bernard. The abbey complex is a popular day out with locals and you'll see a steady stream of visitors looking round the abbey and its grounds, now a nature reserve. The abbey is still lived in and occasionally monks can be seen flitting across the cloister in their white hooded robes.

Other buildings in the complex include the eighteenth-century **Palazzo Giustiniani-Bandini**, where Wagner once stayed and whose wedding-cake facade was modelled on Buckingham Palace. The trails through the woods are a popular Sunday stroll, and you should take time to see the **Museo della Civiltà Contadina** (July 23 to August 27 daily 10.30am–12.30pm & 3.30–7pm; April to mid-October Sundays and national holidays 10.30am–12.30pm & 3.30–7pm; included in abbey ticket, see above), a folk museum laid out in the abbey's low-vaulted outhouses. Among the agricultural and weaving equipment is a decorated wagon such as most farming families would have owned right up until the middle of the twentieth century, using it as a manure cart, a wedding carriage, or whatever form of transport was needed. For some insight into the economics of marriage, take a look at the dowry lists, itemizing the value of household goods. There's also a small **archeological museum**, visitable on the same ticket, containing finds from the nearby Roman town of Urbisaglia.

A five-minute bus ride away, the site of **Urbisaglia** (April–Sept Mon–Wed & Sun 9.30am–1.30pm, Thurs–Sat 9.30am–1.30pm & 2.30–7.30pm; Oct–Mar Mon–Sat 9.30am–1.30pm; free; tour guides can be booked on ☎0733.506.566), or Urbs Salvia, was one of the Marche's most important Roman towns until it was sacked by Alaric in 409 AD. Its fame continued into the Middle Ages, when Dante invoked it as an example of a city fallen from glory in his *Paradiso*. So far an amphitheatre, theatre, baths and parts of the walls have been excavated, and frescoes of hunting scenes have been discovered in an underpassage.

South of Urbisaglia, the hill-town health resort of **SAN GINESIO** is justifiably known as the balcony of the Sibillini: the panoramic view from the gardens of the Colle Ascarano, just outside the town walls, stretches from the Adriatic and Monte Cónero to the Sibillini mountains and the highest of the Apennines, the Gran Sasso in Abruzzo. There's a fair amount to see in the town itself: its central piazza is dominated by one of the Marche's most unusual churches, the **Collegiata della Annunziata**, whose late-Gothic facade is decorated with filigree-like terracotta moulding. Rising above it are two campaniles, one capped by an onion dome and the other by what looks like a manicured cactus. Gothic frescoes adorn some of the chapels, and the crypt has frescoes by the

Salimbeni brothers – including a pietà in which Mary looks completely demented and Christ is so covered with nail-holes that he appears to have chicken pox.

Sarnano

Until a few years ago, **SARNANO**, south of San Ginesio, was a poor and virtually abandoned village. Recently, however, the town has woken up to the potential of its radioactive springs, known since Roman times to have wide-ranging curative properties, and has begun to develop itself into an exclusive spa resort. The medieval core, coiling in concentric circles around a gentle hill, has been subtly restored, and though it's now more of a showpiece than a living village, its narrow interconnecting cobbled streets and picturesque old houses make it an ideal place for an undemanding day's wandering. On the last weekend in May until mid-June every year, an arts and crafts fair draws in the crowds, with work by Italian craftsmen on sale at scores of temporary shop/exhibition spaces in and around the historic centre.

It's worth getting a map from the **tourist office**, Lago Enrico Ricciardi 1 just off Piazza della Libertà in the new town (Mon–Sat 9am–1pm & 3–6pm, Sun 9am–1pm; ☎0733.657.144), before heading up through **Porta Brunforte** into old Sarnano. Just inside is the fourteenth-century church of **San Francesco**, decorated with Palestinian plates, thought to have been brought to Sarnano by souvenir-collecting Crusaders. Its convent is now the seat of the *comune* and houses a fine **Pinacoteca** (Sat & Sun 10.30am–12.30pm & 4.30–7.30pm; L5000/€2.58. Open at other times by request ☎0733.659.923), the major item being a *Madonna and Child* by Vittore Crivelli.

Continue climbing to the summit of the town and you hit **Piazza Alta**, once the political and religious centre. When Sarnano fell under papal rule in the sixteenth century, the limitation of local power made participation in public life lose its allure; eventually, in the nineteenth century, the underused fourteenth-century **Palazzo del Popolo** was converted into a theatre. It also proved increasingly difficult to ordain priors, as Rome refused to accept those chosen by the people, and the **Palazzo dei Priori** became the prison. These and the square's other medieval buildings have all been restored in recent years and are worth a look; keys are held by the comune at Via Leopardi 1. At present the most interesting of the piazza's buildings is the thirteenth-century church of **Santa Maria di Piazza**, whose fifteenth-century frescoes include a figure known as the *Madonna with Angels*, for the host of celestial musicians and choristers surrounding her. The wooden statue of Christ on the altar has been saddled with one of popular tradition's looniest myths – if it's about to rain, his beard is supposed to grow. On the second Sunday in August, Santa Maria is the starting-point for Sarnano's annual medieval knees-up, or palio – though apart from the costumes and processions, it has more in common with a kids' sports day, featuring a tug-of-war, pole climbing, and a race in which the competitors have to balance jugs of water on their heads.

The two most affordable **hotels** in Sarnano are *Villa*, Via Rimembranza 46 (☎0733.657.218; ②), a shuttered villa in its own substantial garden 300m uphill from the tourist office and *Ai Pini*, Via F. Corridoni 101 (☎0733.657.183; ②), a similar hotel just past the sports ground. But for just a few lire more, you could stay at *Terme*, Piazza Libertà 82 (☎0733.657.166; ③), a substantial nineteenth-century brick palazzo with Art Nouveau flourishes and simple rooms with tiled floors. If you want to **ski** in winter, or to spend a few summer days in the mountains, there's a small resort, **Sasso Tetto**, 10km away – the cheapest hotel there is *La Sibilla* (June–mid-Sept & Dec–March; ☎0733.651.102; ①).

Southeast of Macerata: Fermo and Porto San Giorgio

Southeast of Macerata, a short distance from the coast, is the attractive old town of **FERMO**. Its web of streets is lined with medieval and Renaissance buildings, erupting out of which is a wooded peak crowned with a Romanesque-Gothic duomo. The town's most spectacular monument, however, is hidden from view – a first-century underground complex of thirty filter beds known as the **Piscina Epuratoria Romana**, originally designed to supply the Roman Imperial fleet with fresh water when it docked at the nearby port. Entered from Via Aceti, off the main Piazza del Popolo, it's something akin to a flooded cathedral, with its well-preserved vault and arches subtly lit and reflected in the dark, still water.

From Fermo a road descends to the resort of **PORTO SAN GIORGIO**, with a small fishing and sailing port and a long sandy beach. Its palms, pines and oleanders, and its sprinkling of Art Deco villas, make it a pleasant enough place, though the modern seafront is predictably bland. The best day to visit is on the second Sunday in July, for the *Festa del Mare*, when fish are fried in the open air in a giant frying pan – 5m across, it weighs 10,000 pounds and needs 3310 litres of oil to fill it.

The Monti Sibillini

With a mountain lake reddened by the blood of the devil, a narrow pass known as the gorge of hell and a cave reputed to have been the lair of an enchantress, the **Monti Sibillini** are not only the most beautiful of the Apennines, but they teem with ancient legends too.

The best way of exploring the Sibillini is on foot; even if you're not a seasoned hiker there are easy but stunning trails, while for diehard backpackers there are challenging long treks, too. The most agreeable bases are the medieval hill-villages that crown the Sibillini foothills, but there are also a number of *rifugi* if you want to be closer to the starting-points for walks. Most villages are served by buses, but they're few and far between and you'll do better with your own transport.

Amándola and around

Though perhaps not the prettiest of the Sibillini hill-villages **AMÁNDOLA** is easy to get to on public transport and makes one of the best bases for seeing the region. Its main sight is a **Museo della Civiltà Contadina** (daily 9am–noon & 3–6pm; free), housed in the ex-convent of the church of San Francesco. The collection is fascinating, ranging from wine-making and grappa-distilling apparatus to a hand-pulled ambulance and carts decorated with Fascist symbols. It's in the kitchen, though, that things really come alive – the clutter includes a jar of roasted barley (a coffee substitute), a sausage-making machine, mosquito spray, a primitive potty and a wooden baby-walker. Amándola is also a rather forward-looking place, holding an excellent week-long international **theatre festival** in the first week of September. Low on pretension and high on participation, the festival overcomes language barriers with mime and movement performances and workshops – the atmosphere is irresistible, and it's well worth sticking around for the whole week.

Otherwise, Amándola is a great place to unwind after a day's hiking. It has an excellent **hostel** in a converted eighteenth-century palazzo, the *Casa per Feria*, Via Indipendenza 73 (☎0736.848.598; L35,000/€18.08; in winter only open to groups of 15 or more) run by a co-operative and aimed particularly school parties – but open to individuals too. It has nine dorm-style rooms with en suite bathrooms each containing between four and seven beds. There's also a dining room in the basement. The only other hotel is the slightly run-down *Paradiso* at Via Umberto 1 (☎0736.847.468; ③), reached via steps leading from the steep narrow alleyway at the entrance to the main square: turn left at the top of the steps through the unmarked stone gateway. As an alternative, the restaurant *Savoy Valdaso* at Via C. Battisti 90 usually rents out **rooms** (☎0736.848.522; ③).

Around Amándola

One kilometre north of Amándola is the fifteenth-century church of **Santa Maria a Piè d'Agello** – no architectural masterpiece, but a fine country church, with slots in the window sills for offerings and a few simple frescoes, though many were destroyed by the lime with which they were covered in the seventeenth century. (It was thought, in plague-ridden times, that frescoes were unsanitary.)

Further along the Tenna Valley road you come to the abbey of **San Ruffino**, a thirteenth-century church built above catacombs. Their frescoes, dating back to the ninth and tenth centuries, indicate how long it was before Christianity was tolerated outside the main towns; in fact it wasn't until St Francis visited the area in the late eleventh century that Christianity took a hold and paganism finally began to decline.

Montefortino

A few kilometres south of Amándola, the hill-village of **MONTEFORTINO** is perhaps a prettier base than Amándola, touristy in season and dead quiet out, but less well served by buses. Primarily a place to wander and admire the Sibillini views, Montefortino also has a small **Pinacoteca** (daily 10am–1pm & 4–7pm), whose chief attractions are a polyptych by Alemanno – a follower of the Crivelli who took as much delight in painting embroidery as they did – and an arresting twelfth-century portrait of a man with a pipe and candle emerging from the darkness. Appropriately, given the necromantic traditions of the area, there's also an eighteenth-century painting of Circe with her occult apparatus. There's nowhere **to stay** actually in town, the nearest **rooms** are at the restaurant *Da Benito* (☎0736.859.515; ②) at the petrol station below town, just before the turn off to Ambro. If you have a car, however, you can take the road signposted Sanctuaria dell'Ambro, and head 5km west to Località Ambro, where you'll find a cluster of bars and market stalls at the weekend selling delicacies of the region and two places to stay. The friendly bar-restaurant with rooms *Peppiné* (☎0736.859.171; ②), offers simple accommodation and a menu including *tagliatelle casarecce* and lamb *cacciatore* (hunter style), while the *Ambro* (☎0736.859.170; ③), is a bigger slightly dour albergo also above a busy bar-restaurant, with a cheering menu which includes pasta with funghi porcini and *gorbani* (mountain greens), wild boar, kid and truffles.

Montemonaco and around

A short way south of Montefortino, **MONTEMONACO**, a walled medieval village of cobbled streets and yellow stone houses, is close to some of the Sibillini's most legendary sights. One, the **cave of the sibyl**, whose occupant gave her name to the mountain group (see p.839 for more on sibyls), is a two-hour walk west from the village, though periodic rockfalls can make this a less-than-rewarding excursion. The other, through the **Gola dell'Infernaccio** (Gorge of hell), southwest of the village, is a spectacular and fairly easy hike; buses run by the Infernaccio fork, from where it's a three-hour walk to the gorge. Even the approach to the gorge, down a narrow valley, is evocative: silent, except for the distant roar of the River Tenna seething through the Gola. Although a straightforward walk in summer, it can be hazardous in winter, as the memorial plaques on the cliffs at the entrance testify. Climbing up beyond the bridge, the path follows the river, squeezing its way under jagged overhanging rocks, accompanied by the deafening sound of raging water. After a second bridge the path forks, the lower leading to the tranquil source of the Tenna and the upper, more interestingly, in about half an hour, to the **Hermitage of San Leonardo**, occupied by a solitary monk.

The *Rifugio Monte Sibilla* (June–Sept Sat & Sun; mid-July to mid-Sept daily; ☎0736.856.422; for information from the *comune* at Montemonaco, call ☎0736.856.141), close to the cave, is the best base for climbing Monte Sibilla; without your own transport you'll have to walk. It lies about 6km east of Montemonaco along the path which eventually leads to the cave. As the path is only barely visible you'd be advised to take the Kompass *Monti Sibillini* map.

To do the best of the Sibillini treks, you need to travel 8km east from Montemonaco (though you'll either need to take a taxi or have your own transport) to **FOCE**, where you can stay in the *Taverna della Montagna* (☎0736.856.327; ②). The hike, through the **Valle del Lago di Pilato** and up to the **Lago di Pilato** and **Pizzo di Diavolo** (Devil's Peak), is fairly tough; you'll need the Kompass map, and you shouldn't attempt it at all outside the high summer months and only in good conditions, as the snows don't melt until June. Here, guarding the entrance to Umbria, stands **Monte Vettore** (2477m) the highest of the Sibillini peaks.

According to the legend of the lake, Pilate's body was dispatched from Rome on a cart pulled by two wild oxen, who climbed up into the Sibillini and ditched the corpse in the water here. In the Middle Ages it became a favourite haunt for necromancers seeking dialogues with the devil – stones inscribed with occult symbols have been found on its shores. Deciding they wanted to be rid of the magicians, the local lords one night put soldiers on guard around its shores. Nothing happened until the morning, when the soldiers discovered that the lake had turned red; assuming it was with the devil's blood, they fled. What in fact turned the water red was a mass of minuscule red *Chircephalus marchesonii*, a species of fish indigenous to Asia; a shoal was stranded here millions of years ago when the sea receded, and its descendants still thrive.

Áscoli Piceno and the coast

ÁSCOLI PICENO owes its existence to a woodpecker that led a band of nomadic shepherds to the wedge of land between two rivers on which the city now stands. At least, that's one of the many legends to have grown up around the origins of Áscoli and the Piceni tribe for whom it is named; other versions replace the woodpecker-guide with Diomedes or the son of Saturn, and the nomadic shepherds with veterans of the Trojan War or Greek traders. Whatever the truth, the Piceni were real enough, and the relics of their civilization suggest that they were a pretty emotional and impetuous lot: writing curses on missiles before firing them, gauging the intensity of grief by measuring the volume of tears, and losing a critical battle against the Romans when they interpreted an earthquake as a sign of divine wrath, and abandoned the fight.

Today the Ascolani seem initially to be reserved, as if in obedience to the aphorisms urging moderation, hard work and reticence that are inscribed on many of their houses. However, one taste of the exuberance that fills the central piazza of this good-looking medieval town in the early evening is enough to dispel such an impression. If you come for Mardi Gras, you'll be able to participate in the Marche's most flamboyant carnival, while on the first Sunday in August there's the Quintana, a medieval festival that incorporates a spectacular joust.

The Town

The central **Piazza del Popolo**, the stage for the evening passeggiata, is the place to get the feel of Áscoli. Paved with gleaming travertine and flanked by Renaissance porticoes, it's the setting for two of the city's finest buildings, the pleasantly jumbled **Palazzo dei Capitani del Popolo** and the refined Romano-Gothic San Francesco. The former dates from the late twelfth century, when the free commune of Áscoli was at its height. That anything of the building has survived is something of a miracle, for in 1535 a certain Giambattista Quieti set it on fire so as to incinerate a rebel barricaded inside.

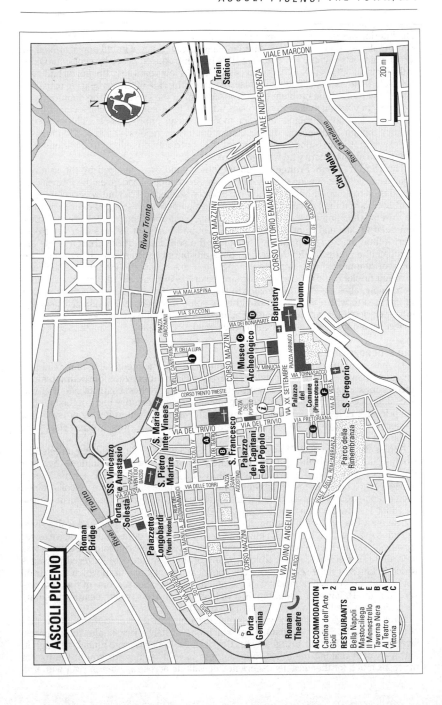

The interior was gutted but enough remained of the facade for a swift facelift to suffice. Rectangular windows were slotted into medieval arches, and a grand portal affixed, on top of which sits a statue to Pope Paul III, who reintroduced peace by replacing Quieti with a neutral outsider. Not that peace lasted long; a few years after the portal had been completed, the Ascolani, finding themselves under the rule of an overbearing papal representative, solved the problem by murdering him in the sacristy of the duomo.

When they weren't slaughtering each other, at least some of Áscoli's rulers found time to collect public money in order to finance city improvements. The sixteenth-century **loggias** that enclose the piazza are one of the results – each of a slightly different width, to correspond to the size of the contribution made by the various merchants and shopkeepers who worked there.

The church of **San Francesco**, on the other hand, was financed by the sale of a Franciscan convent outside the city, after Pope Alexander IV had given the Franciscans permission to move within its walls. Construction started in 1258 but wasn't completed until 1549, when the low cupola was added. It's a somewhat restrained church, with little to seize the attention except for the intricate west portal on Via del Trivio. Unless you need to cool and calm down after the heat and bustle of Áscoli's narrow streets, there's little point in going inside. Adjoining the south side of the church is the sixteenth-century **Loggia dei Mercanti**, once attributed to Bramante. It was once the scene of commercial wheeling and dealing; there are still niches cut into the back wall in which bricks could be checked for size before being purchased. Lower-scale commerce now takes place in the cloister to the north of the church, where market stalls fill the area to which the monks would have come to meditate. The church's smaller and older cloister is far prettier and remains tranquil, despite having been pressed into service as the garden of a Fascist-era office block.

San Vincenzo and around

Via Trivio continues up towards Piazza Ventidio Basso, the medieval commercial centre of town, now of interest for its two churches. **San Vincenzo e San Anastasio** is Áscoli's most distinctive church, with a fifteenth-century chessboard facade that was once filled out with frescoes. Beneath the mainly eleventh-century body of the building is a primitive crypt erected over a spring which was supposed to have leprosy-curing properties. Although the plunge bath is still there, the spring was diverted elsewhere in the last century.

Across the square, **San Pietro Martire** is a far less appealing building, erected by Dominican monks in the thirteenth century in order not to be outdone by their Franciscan rivals down the road. It's as austere and intimidating as St Peter the Martyr himself, who, between founding Dominican communities like that at Áscoli, gained such a reputation as a persecutor of religious sects that he became the patron of inquisitors after his murder by a couple of so-called heretics.

The dark **Via Soderini**, leading out of the square, forms the spine of Áscoli's riverside medieval quarter. Lined with buildings out of which the occasional defensive tower sprouts, it's an evocative street, giving you a clear idea of how rigorously the town was defended. Tiny streets fan out from it, many of them spanned by covered passages which in times of siege served as escape routes and as stations from which to pour oil down onto the heads of attackers. Of the defensive tower houses, one of the best preserved is the **Palazzetto Longobardi**, a virtually windowless twelfth-century building; it's been converted into a youth hostel (see p.674).

After exploring the quarter you can cut through to the river and the thirteenth-century gate, the **Porta Solestà**, from which one of Italy's largest and most impressively preserved **Roman bridges** spans the river. An underpassage tunnels through it, and it's worth making the effort to arrange to have it opened for you at the tourist office, as much for the uncanny experience of walking across an unseen river with traffic crossing just above your head as for the opportunity to examine colossal Roman masonry at close quarters.

To San Gregorio

There's little else of Roman Áscoli to see, except some sparse remains of a **Roman theatre**, on the southwest edge of town, close to the Roman **Porta Gemina**, or twin gate, at the beginning of the road to Rome. From the theatre a road leads up to the **Parco della Rimembranza**, for a great rooftop view of the town, and on to the steep and picturesque **Via Pretoriana**, whose small craft shops make it a good hunting ground for gifts. Close by, the fourteenth-century church of San Gregorio was ingeniously built around the remains of a Roman temple. Incorporated into the facade are two lofty Corinthian columns, originally imported by the Romans from Greece, and patches of *opus reticulatum* (diamond brickwork). In the adjoining convent is a tiny revolving door with the inscription *Qui si depositano gli innocenti* ("Here you deposit the innocent"), designed so that parents could remain anonymous when leaving unwanted children to the care of priests and nuns.

The duomo, pinacoteca and Museo Archeologico

With the pregnant caryatids on the facade of the **Palazzo del Comune** overlooked by the pompous **Duomo**, **Piazza Arringo** is a testimony to the flamboyance of Áscoli's Baroque architects. However, as the duomo shelters what is reckoned to be Carlo Crivelli's best work, and the Palazzo del Comune one of the Marche's best art galleries, the square's eccentric architecture does have its positive side.

In the duomo's flashy interior, chandeliers are suspended on strings of illuminated beads, the apse is painted with a fake Persian carpet, the pillar capitals and vault ribs are gaudily gilded, and the cupola is painted with late nineteenth-century frescoes of obscure Áscolani saints against a backdrop of impossibly blue skies and feather-mop palm trees. The **Crivelli polyptych**, in the Cappella del Sacramento, thus comes as a welcome relief. Even if Crivelli's penchant for rarefied opulence isn't to your taste, it has to be admitted that he did what he did with style and, in this work, with admirable psychological insight. The most arresting of the ten panels is the central pietà, in which the haggard expression of Mary, the bitter torment that distorts Christ's face, and Magdalene's frozen horror as she examines the wound in his hand are rendered all the more intense by the strict semicircular formation in which their heads are arranged.

The **Pinacoteca Civica** in the Palazzo Comunale (daily 9am–1pm & 3–7pm; L6000/€3.09) contains other pieces by Crivelli, and though they are in lousy condition and not as sophisticated as the duomo's polyptych they are engaging nonetheless. One shows the sprawling baby Christ, chin in hand, apparently mesmerized by an apple. Pietro Alemanno, Crivelli's follower, contributes an *Annunciation* featuring a view of medieval Áscoli bristling with towers, and there are also a few foreign works, most notably a *Portrait of a Woman* by Van Dyck.

If you want to know more about ancient Áscoli, you should also visit the **Museo Archeologico** (Mon–Sat 8.30am–1.30pm; L4000/€2.06), across the square. The collection includes Piceni projectiles inscribed with curses against their Roman enemies, jewellery, heavy bronze rings that were placed on the stomachs of dead women, and small test-tube-like containers used to assess the quality of grief by measuring the volume of tears.

Practicalities

Áscoli's train station is just east of the town centre, ten minutes' walk away, left off Viale Indipendenza. The **tourist office** is on the ground floor of the Palazzo dei Capitani del

Popolo on Piazza del Popolo (Mon–Fri 8am–1.30pm & 3–7pm, Sat 9am–1pm & 3–7pm, Sun 9am–1pm; ☎0736.253.045). You're likely to want to stay over, although there are only a couple of **hotels** in the centre and you will certainly need to book in advance. The most affordable option is a **youth hostel**, the *Ostello de' Longobardi*, open all year round and housed in a medieval tower bang in the historic centre at Via Soderini 16 (☎0736.259.007; L18,000/€9.30). The two central hotels are the small *Cantina dell'Arte*, Rua della Lupa 8 (☎0736.255.620; ②) a small place with 11 rooms and its own reasonably priced restaurant, and the smart *Gioli*, Viale de Gasperi 14 (☎0736.255.550; ⑤), which caters mostly for the business market

You can **eat** quite inexpensively, particularly at the lively *Bella Napoli*, Via Bonaparte 18–20 (closed Sun), off Piazza Arringo, Áscoli's best pizzeria. Alternatively try *Al Teatro*, Via del Teatro 3 (closed Mon), a small bar-restaurant with a garden and a long menu of classic dishes and pizza including alla *Tirolese*, or *Il Menestrello*, Via Pretoriana 32–34 (closed Tues) which serves moderately priced regular meals as well as pizzas. *Taverna Nera*, Rua Pietro Dini 13 (closed Mon) is a tiny neighbourhood place serving homemade pasta and other dishes. *Vittoria*, Via dei Bonnacorsi 7 (closed Sun) offers a good-value fixed-price menu at lunchtime and dishes like *fritto misto Ascolana* and fish kebabs. For more refined cuisine, try the *Mastrociliegia*, Via di Vesta 28 (booking advised, ☎0736.250.034; closed Sun), a convivial osteria-restaurant with a beamed ceiling and bare brick walls; the wine list is excellent and so is the food, in particular the polenta with boar or hare, gnocchi with butter and sage, tagliatelle with kid, and funghi porcini and truffles. For a **drink**, linger over a coffee or a cocktail at one of the tables outside *Bistro*, Via Vidacilio 12, or head for the famous Art Nouveau-style *Caffè Meletti* on Piazza del Popolo which makes its own superb amaro and anisette and is lined with mahogany cases filled with obscure bottles; the old men of Áscoli sit outside and converse on the topics of the day.

The Áscoli coast

Easily accessible by bus or train from Áscoli Piceno, **SAN BENEDETTO DEL TRONTO** is the most extravagant of the Marche's resorts. Known as the "Riviera delle Palme" for the five thousand palms that shade its promenade, and with six kilometres of sandy white beach, it'll give you a hedonistic buzz if you're in the mood for beaches, discos and passeggiata posing; if you're not, give it a miss. There are something like 120 **hotels**, details of which are available from the **tourist office** on Viale delle Tamerici (Mon–Sat 9am–1pm & 4–7pm, Sun 9am–1pm; ☎0735.592.237). Note that most places will insist on a full-pension arrangement in August. Of the central hotels just a few steps from the beach, *Sunrise*, Via San Giacomo 25 (☎0735.657.347; ⑤) is the top choice, with modern, airy rooms, pleasant management and plenty of sunloungers on a lush lawn. *Giacomino*, Via San Giacomo 20 (☎0735.753.631; ⑤), one road back from the beach is another cheerful place to stay with a large garden and rooms with balconies, many with a sea view, as well as its own private beach. Less central but near the seafront try *Girasole*, Lungomare Europa 126 (☎0735.821.62; ④), with a garden and balconies overflowing with flowers; *Taormina*, Via dei Mille 93 (☎0735.659.331; ④), a modern well-kept place and *Sayonara*, Viale Rinascimento 121 (☎0735.657.845; ④).

GROTTAMARE, a few minutes further up the coastal rail line, is a lower-key resort on the same model, but without San Benedetto's panache. If you want **to stay** try the *Villa Parco* hotel, at Lungomare della Repubblica 48 (☎0735.631.015; ④), a family house in a garden of roses and palm trees on the road running along the seafront. But if you have a car head the 8km inland to *La Campana*, at Contrada Menocchia 39, near the hill-town of Montefiore d'Aso (☎0734.939.012, *www.lacampana.it*; ⑤), an agriturismo complex of old stone with a great swimming pool on a terrace overlooking the Adriatic and the garden catches cooling breezes when the resorts are sweltering on the coast below. Bed and breakfast is available for most of the year except from July 22–August 25 when full board is obligatory; meals are made from vegetables from their organic garden and meat, cheese and buttermilk from their flock of sheep.

travel details

TRAINS

Ancona to: Bologna (33 daily; 2hr 5min–2hr 47min); Jesi (25 daily; 25min); Loreto (14 daily; 20min); Rome (10 daily; 3hr 45min); Porto S Giorgio and San Benedetto (25 daily; 42min & 1hr 8min respectively); Senigállia (27 daily; 25min).

Áscoli Piceno to: San Benedetto del Tronto (14 daily; 40min).

Macerata to: San Severino Marche (10 daily; 30min); Tolentino (10 daily; 20min).

Pésaro to: Ancona (36 daily; 45min); Fabriano (20 daily; 2hr 15min); Marotta (every 25 min; 20min); Torrette (every 25 min; 25min).

BUSES

Amándola to: Áscoli Piceno (3 daily; 1hr 15min); Fermo (4 daily; 1hr); Montefortino (5 daily; 25min); Montemonaco (5 daily; 25min); Porto San Giorgio (4 daily; 1hr 15min); Sarnano (7 daily; 30min).

Ancona to: Jesi (8 daily; 30min); Loreto (8 daily Mon–Sat; 1hr 5min); Macerata (6 daily; 1hr 30min); Numana (19 daily, 4 on Sun; 40min); Porto Recanati (5 daily Mon–Sat; 1hr); Senigállia (23 daily; 1hr); Sirolo (19 daily, 4 on Sun; 35min).

Áscoli Piceno to: Amándola (3 daily; 1hr 15min); Montefortino (3 daily Mon–Sat; 1hr 20min); Montemonaco (3 daily Mon–Sat; 1hr 30min); San Benedetto del Tronto (every 30min; hourly on Sun; 50min).

Macerata to: Amándola (5 daily; 1hr 30min); Fiastra (12 daily; 15min); Loreto (8 daily; 45min); Morrovalle Scalo (hourly; 15min); Porto Recanati (8 daily; 1hr); Recanati (8 daily; 30min); San Severino (4 daily; 50min); Sarnano (11 daily; 1hr); Tolentino (4 daily; 40min).

Pésaro to: Fabriano (6 daily; 2hr); Fano (every 30min; 15min); Gradara (hourly; 55min); Torrette (7 daily; 15min); Urbino (11 daily, 13 in term time; 50min).

Porto San Giorgio to: Fermo (every 30min; 15min).

Urbino to: Fano (10 daily; 1hr 15min).

INTERNATIONAL FERRIES

Ancona to: Corfu (summer at least 3 weekly; winter 3 weekly; 20–24hr); Croatia (summer 4 weekly; winter 3 weekly; 8hr); Igoumenitsa (summer at least 1 daily; winter 2–4 weekly; 24hr); Patras (at least 1 daily; 20–30hr).

CHAPTER ELEVEN

ROME AND LAZIO

O f all Italy's historic cities, it's perhaps **Rome** which exerts the most compelling fascination. There's more to see here than in any other city in the world, with the relics of over two thousand years of inhabitation packed into its sprawling urban area. You could spend a month here and still only scratch the surface. As a historic place, it is special enough; as a contemporary European capital, it is utterly unique.

Perfectly placed between Italy's North and South, and heartily despised by both, Rome is perhaps the perfect **capital** for a country like Italy. Once the seat of a great empire, and later the home of the papacy, which ruled its dominions from here with a distant and autocratic hand, it's still seen as a place somewhat apart from the rest of Italy, spending money made elsewhere on the corrupt and bloated government machine that runs the country. Romans, the thinking seems to go, are a lazy lot, not to be trusted and living very nicely off the fat of the rest of the land. Even Romans find it hard to disagree with this analysis: in a city of around four million, there are around 600,000 office-workers, compared to an industrial workforce of one sixth of that.

For the traveller, all of this is much less evident than the sheer weight of **history** that the city supports. There are of course the city's classical features, most visibly the Colosseum, and the Forum and Palatine Hill; but from here there's an almost uninterrupted sequence of monuments – from early Christian basilicas, Romanesque churches, Renaissance palaces, right up to the fountains and churches of the Baroque period, which perhaps more than any other era has determined the look of the city today. There is the modern epoch too, from the ponderous Neoclassical architecture of the post-Unification period to the self-publicizing edifices of the Mussolini years. All these various eras crowd in on one another to an almost overwhelming degree: there are medieval churches atop ancient basilicas above Roman palaces; houses and apartment blocks incorporate fragments of eroded Roman columns, carvings and inscriptions; roads and piazzas follow the lines of ancient amphitheatres and stadiums.

Inevitably, Rome is not an easy place to absorb on one visit, and you need to approach things slowly, even if you only have a few days here. You can't see everything on your first visit to Rome, and there's no point in even trying. Most of the city's sights can be

ACCOMMODATION PRICE CODES

Throughout this guide, prices per person are given for **youth hostels** and assume Hostelling International (HI) membership. **Hotel** accommodation is coded on a scale from ① to ⑨, reflecting the cost of the cheapest double room in each establishment in high season. The price bands to which these codes refer are as follows:

① Up to L60,000/€30.99
② L60,000–90,000/€30.99–46.48
③ L90,000–120,000/€46.48–61.98
④ L120,000–150,000/€61.98–77.47
⑤ L150,000–200,000/€77.47–103.29

⑥ L200,000–250,000/€103.29–129.11
⑦ L250,000–300,000/€129.11–154.94
⑧ L300,000–400,000/€154.94–206.58
⑨ over L400,000/€206.58

(See p.32 for a full explanation.)

approached from a variety of directions, and it's part of the city's allure to stumble across things by accident, gradually piecing together the whole, rather than marching around to a timetable on a predetermined route. In any case, it's hard to get anywhere very fast. Despite regular pledges to ban motor vehicles from the city centre, the congestion can be awful. On foot, it's easy to lose a sense of direction winding about in the twisting old streets. In any case, you're so likely to come upon something interesting it hardly makes any difference.

Beyond Rome, the region of **Lazio** inevitably pales in comparison, with relatively few centres of note and a landscape that varies from the gently undulating green hills of its northern sector to the more inhospitable mountains south and east of the capital. It's a fairly poor region, its lack of identity the butt of a number of Italian jokes, and it's the closest you'll get to the feel of the Italian south without catching the train to Naples. Much, however, can be easily seen on a day-trip from the capital, not least the ancient sites of **Ostia Antica** and the Roman Emperor Hadrian's villa at **Tivoli** – two of the area's most important ancient sites. Further afield, in the north of Lazio the Etruscan sites of **Tarquinia** and **Cerveteri** provide the main and most obvious tourist focus, the slightly gloomy town of **Viterbo** the best base; Romans, meanwhile, head out at weekends to soak up the gentle beauty of lakes **Bracciano**, **Vico** and **Bolsena**. The region east of Rome is sparsely populated and poor, though scenically appealing, its high hills unfolding beyond the main, rather dull, regional centre of **Rieti**. The south, on the other hand, is the one part of Lazio where you might want to spend a little longer, especially if you're beating a leisurely path to Naples. You can see coastal resorts like **Anzio** and **Nettuno** as a day-trip too, and they make the best places to swim while based in the capital. But the coast beyond demands more attention: resorts like **Terracina** and **Sperlonga** are relatively unknown outside Italy; and islands like **Ponza** one of the loveliest spots, out of season at least, on the entire west coast. Inland, much is mountainous and fairly inaccessible, but that's part of its appeal: the monasteries at **Subiaco** and **Montecassino** are just two worthwhile stops on what might be a rewarding and original route south.

ROME

Rome's early **history** is caked with legend. Rea Silvia, a vestal virgin and daughter of a local king, Numitor, had twin sons – the product, she alleged, of a rape by Mars. They were supposed to be sacrificed to the god but the ritual wasn't carried out, and the two boys were abandoned and found by a wolf, who nursed them until their adoption by a shepherd, who named them **Romulus and Remus**. As they grew into manhood, under the protection of the gods, they became leaders in the small community, and later laid out the boundaries of the city on the Palatine Hill. However, it soon became apparent that there was only room for one ruler, and, unable to agree on the signs given to them by the gods, they quarrelled, Romulus killing Remus and becoming in 753 BC the city's first **monarch**, to be followed by six further kings.

Whatever the truth of this story, there's no doubt that Rome was an obvious spot to build a city: the Palatine and Capitoline hills provided security, and there was, of course, the river Tiber, which could easily be crossed here by way of the Isola Tiberina, making this a key location on the trade routes between Etruria and Campania. Rome as a kingdom lasted until about 507 BC, when the people rose up against the tyrannical King Tarquinius and established a **Republic**, appointing the first two consuls and instituting a more democratic form of government. The city prospered under the Republic, growing greatly in size and subduing the various tribes of the surrounding areas – the **Etruscans** to the north, the **Sabines** to the east, the **Samnites** to the south. By the time it had fought and won the third Punic War against its principal rival, **Carthage**, in 146 BC, it had become the dominant power in the Mediterranean.

The history of the Republic was, however, also one of **internal strife**, marked by factional fighting among the patrician ruling classes, as everyone tried to grab a slice of the riches that were pouring into the city from its plundering expeditions abroad – and the ordinary people, or plebeians, enjoying little more justice than they had under the Roman monarchs. This all came to a head in 44 BC, when **Julius Caesar**, having proclaimed himself dictator, was murdered on 15 March, by conspirators concerned at the growing concentration of power into one man's hands. A brief period of turmoil ensued, giving way, in 27 BC, to the founding of the **Empire** under **Augustus** – a triumph for the new democrats over the old guard. Augustus heaved Rome into the Imperial era: he was determined to turn the city – as he claimed – from one of stone to one of marble, building arches, theatres and monuments of a magnificence suited to the capital of an expanding empire. Under Augustus, and his successors, the city swelled to a population of a million or more, its people housed in cramped apartment blocks or *insulae*;

crime in the city was rife, and the traffic problem apparently on a par with today's, leading one contemporary writer to complain that the din on the streets made it impossible to get a good night's sleep. But it was a time of peace and prosperity, the Roman upper classes living a life of indolent luxury, in sumptuous residences with proper plumbing and central heating, and the empire's borders being ever more extended, into other parts of Europe and the Middle East, reaching their maximum limits under the Emperor Trajan, who died in 117 AD. This period constitutes the heyday of the Roman Empire, a time which Gibbon called "the happiest times in the history of humanity."

The **decline of Rome** is hard to date precisely, but it could be said to have started with the Emperor **Diocletian**, who assumed power in 284 and divided the empire into two parts, east and west, while becoming known for his relentless persecution of Christians. The first Christian emperor, **Constantine**, shifted the seat of power to Byzantium in 330, and Rome's heady period as capital of the world was over, the wealthier members of the population moving east and a series of invasions by Goths in 410 and Vandals about forty years later only serving to quicken the city's ruin. By the sixth century the city was a devastated and infection-ridden shadow of its former self.

After the fall of the empire, the pope – who was based in Rome due to the fact that St Peter (the Apostle and first pope) was martyred here in 64 AD – became the temporal ruler over much of Italy, and it was the papacy, under Pope **Gregory I** ("the Great") in 590, that rescued Rome from its demise. In an eerie echo of the empire, Gregory sent missions all over Europe to spread the word of the Church and publicize its holy relics, so drawing pilgrims, and their money, back to the city, and in time making the papacy the natural authority in Rome. The pope took the name "Pontifex Maximus" after the title of the high priest of classical times (literally "the keeper of the bridges", which were vital to the city's well-being). The crowning a couple of centuries later of Charlemagne as Holy Roman Emperor, with dominions spread Europe-wide but answerable to the pope, intensified the city's revival, and the pope and city became recognized as head of the Christian world.

There were times over the next few hundred years when the power of Rome and the papacy was weakened: Robert Guiscard, the Norman king, sacked the city in 1084; a century later, a dispute between the city and the papacy led to a series of popes relocating in Viterbo; and in 1308 the French-born Pope **Clement V** transferred his court to Avignon. In the mid-fourteenth century, Cola di Rienzo seized power, setting himself up as the people's saviour from the decadent ways of the city's rulers and forming a new Roman republic. But the increasingly autocratic ways of the new ruler soon lost popularity; Cola di Rienzo was deposed, and in 1376 Pope **Gregory XI** returned to Rome. As time went on, power gradually became concentrated in a handful of **families**, who swapped the top jobs, including the papacy itself, between them. Under the burgeoning power of the pope, the city began to take on a new aspect: churches were built, the city's pagan monuments rediscovered and preserved, and artists began to arrive in Rome to work on commissions for the latest pope, who would invariably try to outdo his predecessor's efforts with ever more glorious self-aggrandizing buildings and works of art. This process reached a head during the **Renaissance**; Bramante, Raphael and Michelangelo all worked in the city, on and off, throughout their careers. The reigns of Pope **Julius II**, and his successor, **Leo X**, were something of a golden age: the city was once again the centre of cultural and artistic life, and site of the creation of great works of art like Michelangelo's frescoes in the Sistine Chapel, Raphael's *Stanze* in the Vatican Palace and fine buildings like the Villa Farnesina, Palazzo Farnese and Palazzo Spada, not to mention the commissioning of a new St Peter's as well as any number of other churches. However, in 1527 all this was brought abruptly to an end, when the armies of the Habsburg monarch, Charles V, swept into the city, occupying it – and wreaking havoc – for a year, while Pope **Clement VII** cowered in the Castel Sant'Angelo.

The ensuing years were ones of yet more restoration, and perhaps because of this it's the **seventeenth century** that has left the most tangible impression on Rome today, the vigour of the **Counter-Reformation** throwing up huge sensational monuments like the Gesù church that were designed to confound the scepticism of the new Protestant thinking. This period also saw the completion of St Peter's under **Paul V**, and the ascendancy of Gian Lorenzo Bernini as the city's principal architect and sculptor under the Barberini pope, **Urban VIII** – a patronage that was extended under the Pamphili pope, **Innocent X**.

The **eighteenth century** saw the decline of the papacy as a political force, a phenomenon marked by the occupation of the city in 1798 by Napoleon; **Pius VI** was unceremoniously sent off to France as a prisoner, and Napoleon declared another Roman republic, with himself at its head, which lasted until 1815, when papal rule was restored. Thirty-four years later a pro-Unification caucus under **Mazzini** declared the city a republic but was soon chased out, and Rome had to wait until **Garibaldi** stormed the walls in 1870 to join the unified country – symbolically the most important part of the Italian peninsula to do so. "Roma o morte", Garibaldi had cried, and he wasted no time in declaring the city the capital of the new kingdom – under **Vittorio Emanuele II** – and confining the by now quite powerless pontiff, **Pius IX**, to the Vatican until agreement was reached on a way to coexist.

The Piemontese rulers of the new kingdom set about building a city fit to govern from, cutting new streets through Rome's central core (Via Nazionale, Via del Tritone) and constructing grandiose buildings like the Altar of the Nation. **Mussolini** took over Rome in 1922, and in 1929 signed the **Lateran Pact** with Pope **Pius XI**, a compromise which forced the Vatican to accept the new Italian state and in return recognized the Vatican City as sovereign territory, independent of Italy, together with the key basilicas and papal palaces in Rome, which remain technically independent of Italy to this day. Mussolini's motivations weren't dissimilar to the popes, however, when he bulldozed his way through the Roman Forum and began work on the futuristic, self-publicizing planned extension to the city known as EUR.

Since **World War II**, Italy has become renowned as a country which changes its government, if not its politicians, every few months, and for the rest of Italy Rome has come to symbolize the inertia of their nation's government – at odds with both the wealthy north, and the poor south. Despite this, the city's growth has been phenomenal in the post-war years, its population soaring to close on four million and its centre becoming ever more choked by traffic. Though famous in the **Sixties** as the home of Fellini's *Dolce Vita* and Italy's bright young things, Rome is still, even by Italian standards, a relatively provincial place, and one which is in some ways still trying to lug itself into the twenty-first century. Great efforts were, however, made to prepare the city for the arrival of the **Millennium** and the millions of visitors who came to celebrate the Jubilee (Holy Year), and the city is looking better than ever. In many ways there has never been a better time to visit Rome.

Arrival, city transport and information

Rome has two **airports**: Leonardo da Vinci, better known simply as Fiumicino, which handles most scheduled flights, and Ciampino, where you'll arrive if you're travelling on a charter, or with one of the low-cost European airlines. **Taxis** in from either airport cost around L80,000/€41.32, more at night, and take 30–45 minutes; they're worth considering if you are in a group but otherwise the public transport connections are reasonable.

Fiumicino is connected to the centre of Rome by direct trains, which make the thirty-minute ride to Termini for L16,000/€8.26; services begin at 7.37am, and then leave hourly from 8.07am until 10.07pm. Alternatively, there are more frequent trains to Trastevere, Ostiense and Tiburtina stations, each on the edge of the city centre, roughly every twenty minutes from 6.27am to 11.27pm; tickets to these stations cost L8000/€4.13 and Tiburtina and Ostiense are just a short metro ride from Termini, making it a much cheaper (and not necessarily slower) journey; or you can catch city bus #175 from Ostiense, or city bus #492 or #649 from Tiburtina, to the centre of town. These cheaper alternatives do inevitably, however, involve a certain amount more bag-hauling.

There are no direct connections between the city centre and **Ciampino**. Hourly buses run from the airport to the Anagnina metro station, at the end of line A – a thirty-minute journey (L2000/€1.03), from where it's a twenty-minute ride into the centre. Failing that, you can take a bus from the airport to Ciampino overground train station, a ten-minute journey, and then take a train into Termini, which is a further twenty minutes (L4500/€2.32). The airline Go, incidentally, lay on their own bus to Piazza Santa Maria Maggiore, half an hour after the arrival of each of their flights, but it's no quicker and they charge L20,000/€10.33 one way.

Travelling by **train** from most places in Italy, or indeed Europe, you arrive at **Stazione Termini**, centrally placed for all parts of the city and meeting-point of the two metro lines and many city bus routes. There's a **left-luggage** facility here (daily 5.15am–midnight; L5000 per piece every 12hr); note that the Enjoy Rome office (see p.683) will also look after its customers' luggage. Among **other rail stations** in Rome, Tiburtina is a stop for some north–south intercity trains; selected routes around Lazio are handled by the Regionali platforms of Stazione Termini (a further five-minute walk beyond the end of the regular platforms); and there's also the COTRAL urban train station on Piazzale Flaminio, which runs to La Giustiniana – the so-called Roma-Nord line.

Arriving by **bus** can leave you in any one of a number of places around the city. The main stations include Ponte Mammolo (trains from Tivoli and Subiaco); Lepanto (Cerveteri, Civitavecchia, Bracciano area); EUR Fermi (Nettuno, Anzio, southern Lazio coast); Anagnina (Castelli Romani); Saxa Rubra (Viterbo and around). All of these stations are on a metro line, except Saxa Rubra, which is on the Roma-Nord line and connected by trains every fifteen minutes with the station at Piazzale Flaminio, on metro line A. Eurolines buses from outside Italy terminate on Piazza della Repubblica.

Coming into the city by **road** can be quite confusing. If you are on the A1 highway coming from the north take the exit "Roma Nord"; from the south, follow exit "Roma Est". Both lead you to the Grande Raccordo Anulare, which circles the city and is connected with all of the major arteries into the city centre – the Via Cassia from the north, Via Salaria from the northeast, Via Tiburtina or Via Nomentana from the east, Via Appia Nuova and the Pontina from the south, Via Prenestina and Via Casilina from the southeast, or Via Cristoforo Colombo from the southwest, and Via Aurelia from the northwest.

City transport

Like most Italian cities, even the larger ones, the best way to get around Rome is to **walk** – you'll see more and appreciate more. The city wasn't built for motor traffic, and it shows in the jams, the pollution, and the bad tempers of its drivers. That said, its **bus service**, run by ATAC, is, on the whole, a good one – cheap, reliable and as quick as the clogged streets allow. Rome also has a **metro**, which runs from 5.30am to 11.30pm, though it's not as useful as you might think, since its two lines are more directed at commuters from the suburbs than tourists in the city centre. Nonetheless, there are a few useful city-centre stations: Termini is the hub of both lines, and there are stations at the Colosseum, Piazza Barberini and the Spanish Steps.

When the buses and the metro stop, at around midnight, a network of **nightbuses** clicks into service, accessing most parts of the city through to about 5am; they normally

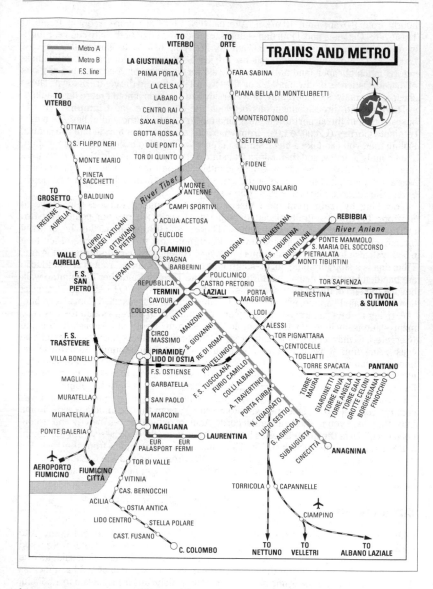

TRAINS AND METRO

- ▨ Metro A
- ▨ Metro B
- ▨ F.S. line

have conductors so you can buy a ticket on board (but keep spare tickets handy just in case); they are easily identified by the owl symbol above the "bus notturno" schedule. During the day there are also a few **tram** routes in operation, one of which – the #8, connecting Viale Trastevere with Largo Argentina – is brand new and very quick.

Flat-fare **tickets** on all forms of transport cost L1500/€0.78 each and are good for any number of bus rides and one metro ride within 75 minutes of validating them. Buy

USEFUL TRANSPORT ROUTES

BUSES

#23 Piazza Clodio–Piazza Risorgimento–Ponte Vittorio Emanuele II–Ponte Garibaldi–Via Marmorata–Piazzale Ostiense–Basilica di S. Paolo.

#64 Termini–Piazza della Repubblica–Via Nazionale–Piazza Venezia–Corso Vittorio Emanuele II–St Peter's.

#492 Stazione Tiburtina–Termini–Piazza Barberini–Via del Corso–Piazza Venezia–Largo Argentina–Corso del Rinascimento–Piazza Cavour–Piazza Risorgimento.

#660 Largo Colli Albani–Via Appia Nuova–Via Appia Antica.

#714 Termini–Santa Maria Maggiore–San Giovanni in Laterano–Baths of Caracalla–EUR.

#910 Termini–Piazza della Repubblica–Via Piedmonte–Via Pinciana (Villa Borghese)–Piazza Euclide–Palazetto dello Sport–Piazza Mancini.

TRAMS

#8 Viale Trastevere–Largo Argentina.

#19 Porto Maggiore–Viale Regina Margherita–Viale Belle Arti–Ottaviano–Piazza Risorgimento.

#30 Piramide–Viale Aventino–Colosseum–San Giovanni–Viale Regina Margherita–Villa Giulia.

them from *tabacchi*, newsstands and ticket machines located in all metro stations and at major bus stops. You can also get a **day pass**, valid on all city transport until midnight of the day purchased, for L6000/€3.10, or a **seven-day pass** for L24,000/€12.40.

The easiest way to get a **taxi** is to find the nearest taxi stand (*fermata dei taxi*) – central ones include Termini, Piazza Venezia, Piazza San Silvestro, Piazza di Spagna and Piazza Barberini. Alternatively, taxis can be radio paged (☎06.3570, 06.4994, 06.4157 or 06.5551). Only take licensed yellow or white cabs, and make sure the meter is switched on. To give you a rough idea of how much taxis cost, you can reckon that a journey from one side of the centre to the other will cost around L10,000/€5.17 – the supplement after 10pm is L5000/€2.58 and L2000/€1.03 more is added to every trip on a Sunday.

Information

There are **tourist information booths** at Fiumicino (daily 8.15am–7.15pm; ☎06.6595.6074), and at Termini (daily 8.15am–7.15pm; ☎06.487.1270 or 06.482.5078), although the long queues that often develop at both of these mean you're usually better off heading straight for the main **tourist office** at Via Parigi 5 (Mon–Fri 8.15am–7.15pm, Sat 8.15am–1.45pm; ☎06.4889.9253 or 06.4889.9255), five minutes' walk from Termini. They have free maps that should – together with our own – be ample for finding your way around. There are also **information kiosks** (see box overleaf) in key locations around the city centre (daily 9am–6pm) that are useful for free maps, directions (the staff usually speak English) and details about nearby sights. You might, however, be better off bypassing the official tourist offices altogether and going to **Enjoy Rome**, Via Varese 39 (Mon–Fri 8.30am–2pm & 3.30–6pm, Sat 8.30am–2pm; ☎06.445.1843), whose friendly, English-speaking staff run a free room-finding service; they also organize tours, and have a left-luggage service for customers. Their information is often more up to date and reliable than that handed out by the various tourist

INFORMATION KIOSKS

Spanish Steps, Largo Goldoni (☎06.6813.6061)
San Giovani, Piazza San Giovani in Laterno (☎06.7720.3535)
Via Nazionale, Palazzo delle Esposizioni (☎06.4782.4525)
Piazza Navona, Piazza delle Cinque Lune (☎06.6880.9240)
Castel Sant'Angelo, Piazza Pia (☎06.6880.9707)
Forum, Piazza del Tempio della Pace (☎06.6992.4307)
Trastevere, Piazza Sonnino (☎06.5833.3457)
Santa Maria Maggiore, Via del'Olmata (☎06.4788.0294)

offices, and they will also advise on where to eat, drink, and party, if you so wish.

For what's-on information, the city's best source of **listings** is perhaps *Romac'è* (L2000/€1.03, Thursdays), which has a helpful section in English giving information on tours, clubs, restaurants, services and weekly events. The English expat bi-weekly, *Wanted in Rome* (L1500/€0.78, every other Wednesday), is also a useful source of information, especially if you're looking for an apartment or work. If you understand a bit of Italian, there's *Time Out Roma* (L2000/€1.03; Thursdays), a weekly review full of listings as well as articles on the trendiest everything in Rome, and the daily arts pages of the Rome **newspaper**, *Il Messaggero*, which can be found in most bars for the customers to read, and lists movies, plays and major musical events. The newspaper *La Repubblica* also includes the "Trova Roma" section in its Thursday edition, another handy guide to current offerings. All of these publications are available from newsstands all over the city centre.

Accommodation

As you might expect, there is plenty of **accommodation** in Rome, and for much of the year you can usually expect to find something, although it's always worth booking in advance, especially when the city is at its busiest – from Easter to the end of October, and over the Christmas period. If you haven't booked, the Enjoy Rome office (see previous page) is your best bet; or try the Free Hotel Reservation Service (daily 7am–10pm; ☎06.699.1000), where multilingual staff will check out vacancies for you. The rooms offered by touts at Termini are rarely a good deal, and can often be rather dodgy; be sure you establish the (full) price beforehand, in writing if necessary, and only use them as a last resort.

Hotels and pensions

Many of the city's cheaper places are located conveniently close to **Termini**, and you could do worse than hole up in one of these, so long as you can tolerate the seediness of this district. The streets both sides of the station – Via Amendola, Via Principe Amedeo, Via Marghera, Via Magenta, Via Palestro – are stacked full of bargain hotels, and some buildings have several pensions to choose from, though you should be somewhat circumspect in the streets to the southwest of the station, parts of which can be a little *too* unsavoury, especially for women travelling alone. If you want to stay somewhere more central and picturesque, there are many hotels in the **centro storico**, some of them not that expensive, but they fill quickly – best phone in advance before heading down there. For more luxury surroundings, the area **east of Via del Corso**, towards Via Veneto and around the Spanish Steps, is the city's prime hunting ground for beautiful, upscale accommodation – although there are a few affordable options close by Piazza Spagna. Consider also staying across the river in **Prati**, a pleasant neighbourhood, nicely distanced from the hubbub of the city centre proper, and handy for the Vatican and St Peter's, or in the lively streets of **Trastevere**, again on the west side of the river but an easy walk into the centre of town.

Centro Storico and East of Via del Corso

Arenula, Via S. Maria de'Calderari 47 (☎06.687.9454, fax 06.689.6188, *www.hotel.arenula@flashnet.it*). Simple, clean rooms, each with their own bath, television and telephone. A great location, just a few minutes' walk from Trastevere, the Jewish Ghetto, and Campo de' Fiori. Bus #H or #63. ⑥.

Abruzzi, Piazza della Rotonda 69 (☎06.679.2021). Bang in front of the Pantheon, and as such you pay for the location. Rooms are clean but very simple, all with wash basins but none with private baths. No credit cards. Bus #64 or #492. ④.

Campo de' Fiori, Via del Biscione 6 (☎06.6880.6865, fax 06.687.6003). A friendly place in a great location close to Campo de' Fiori. Rooms come in all shapes and colours but are clean and pleasant. After six floors of stairs there are some great views to be had from their large roof terrace. Bus #64 or #492. ⑤.

Della Lunetta, Piazza del Paradiso 68 (☎06.686.1080, fax 06.689.2028). An unspectacular hotel, but in a nice location close to Campo de' Fiori. Simple, smallish rooms. No breakfast. Bus #64 or #492. ④.

Eradelli, Via due Macelli 28 (☎06.679.1265). A rather plain hotel with no-frills rooms, but well priced for its location just up the street from the Spanish Steps. Metro A Spagna. ⑥.

Firenze, Via due Macelli 106 (☎06.679.7240, fax 06.785.636). Just up the street from *Eradelli*, this recently renovated hotel is a bit more expensive but is worth it for its smart new rooms. Metro A Spagna. ⑥.

Grand Hotel Plaza, Via del Corso 126 (☎06.6992.1111, fax 06.6994.1575, *www.hotelplazarome.com*). There's a wonderful turn-of-the-century atmosphere to this hotel: its lobby and main bar are worth dropping into just to admire its glorious gilded and frescoed ceilings; the rooms are little more faded, but still very comfortable, and for the location the rates are about as low as you could reasonably expect. Metro A Spagna. ⑨.

Margutta, Via Laurina 34 (☎06.322.3674, fax 06.320.0395). Popular hotel handily located in the Corso/Piazza del Popolo shopping area. Three rooms have tiny private balconies. Reserve well ahead. Metro A Spagna. ⑤.

Navona, Via dei Sediari 8 (☎06.686.4203, fax 06.6880.3802). Completely renovated *pensione*-turned-hotel housed in a building that dates back to the first century AD. Very close to Piazza Navona and run by a friendly Italian-Australian couple. No credit cards; a/c available for L30,000/€15.49 extra a night. Bus #64 or #492. ⑤.

Primavera, Piazza San Pantaleo 3 (☎ & fax 06.6880.3109). Worth it for the location alone, in a grand building whose peaceful courtyard seems a world away from the noisy square outside. Its simple rooms overlook Corso Vittorio Emanuele, and are a couple of minutes' walk from both Piazza Navona and Campo de' Fiori. Bus #64. ⑤.

Santa Chiara, Via di Santa Chiara 21 (☎06.687.2979, fax 06.687.3144). A friendly, family-run hotel in a great location, on a quiet piazza behind the Pantheon. Nice rooms too, hard to beat for the price, which includes breakfast. Bus #64 or #492. ⑧.

Smeraldo, Via dei Chiodaroli 11 (☎06.687.5929, fax 06.6880.5495). Clean and comfortable hotel with a modern interior. All rooms have been recently renovated, with shiny new baths, televisions and a/c. Breakfast not included in the price. Bus #64. ⑤.

Sole, Via del Biscione 76 (☎06.687.9446, fax 06.689.3787). Almost overlooking Piazza del Campo de' Fiori, this place has pleasant rooms with televisions and phones, and a lovely, view-laden roof terrace. No breakfast, no credit cards. Bus #64. ⑥.

Zanardelli, Via G. Zanardelli 7 (☎06.6821.1392, fax 06.6880.3802). A new hotel run by the same family as the *Navona* – to which it is a more lavish alternative. Located just north of Piazza Navona, the building used to be a papal residence and has many original fixtures and furnishings. The rooms are elegant, with antique iron beds, silk-lined walls, and all modern amenities. Bus #70. ⑦.

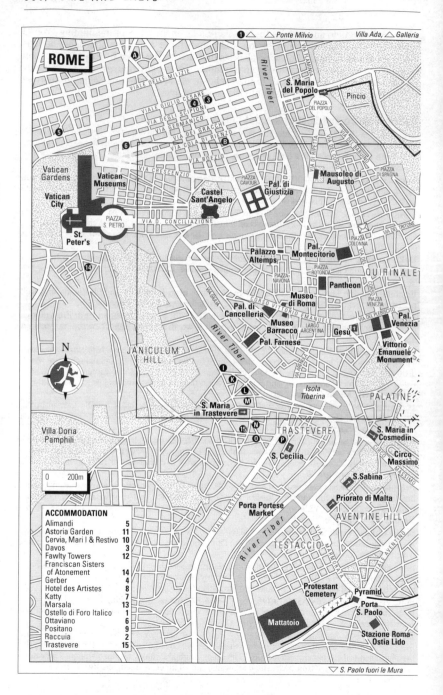

ROME

❶ △   △ *Ponte Milvio*   *Villa Ada,* △ *Galleria*

Ⓐ

River Tiber

VIALE DELLE MILIZIE

VIALE GIULIO CESARE

S. Maria
del Popolo

PIAZZA
DEL POPOLO

Pincio

VIA DEGLI SCIPIONI

Ⓓ Ⓒ

VIA GERMANICO

VIA DEI GRACCHI

Ⓔ

VIA COLA DI RIENZO

Ⓕ

VIA BOEZIO

Ⓖ

VIA CRESCENZIO

PIAZZA
CAVOUR

Pal. di
Giustizia

PIAZZA
DI SPAGNA

Mausoleo di
Augusto

Vatican
Gardens

Vatican
Museums

VIA COLA DI RIENZO

Castel
Sant'Angelo

VIA DELLA RIPETTA

VIA DEL CORSO

Vatican
City

VIA D. CONCILIAZIONE

PIAZZA
S. PIETRO

St.
Peter's

Palazzo
Altemps

PIAZZA
NAVONA

Pal.
Montecitorio

PIAZZA
COLONNA

VIA DEL TRITONE

PIAZZA
ROTONDA

Pantheon

QUIRINALE

PIAZZA
VENEZIA

VIA DEL PLEBISCITO

Pal.
Venezia

Ⓝ

River Tiber

Museo
di Roma

Pal. di
Cancelleria

CORSO VITTORIO EMANUELE

Museo
Barracco

LARGO
ARGENTINA

Gesù

JANICULUM
HILL

VIA ARENULA

Pal. Farnese

Vittorio
Emanuele
Monument

Isola
Tiberina

PALATINE

N

Ⓘ

Ⓚ

Ⓛ

Ⓜ

S. Maria
in Trastevere

S. Maria in
Cosmedin

Villa Doria
Pamphili

Ⓞ Ⓝ

TRASTEVERE

Circo
Massimo

Ⓟ

S. Cecilia

0   200m

S.Sabina

Priorato di Malta

VIA TRASTEVERE

Porta Portese
Market

AVENTINE HILL

River Tiber

TESTACCIO

Protestant
Cemetery

Pyramid

Porta
S. Paolo

Mattatoio

Stazione Roma-
Ostia Lido

▽ *S. Paolo fuori le Mura*

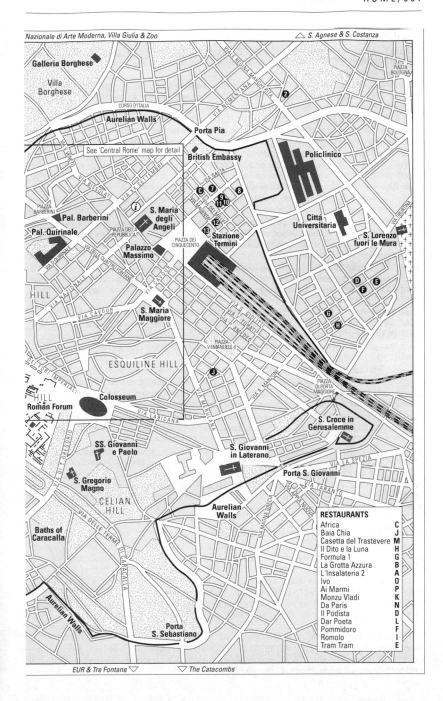

Nazionale di Arte Moderna, Villa Giulia & Zoo △ S. Agnese & S. Costanza

PIAZZA BOLOGNA

Galleria Borghese

Villa Borghese

VIA REGINA MARGHERITA

VIA NOMENTANA

CORSO D'ITALIA

Aurelian Walls

Porta Pia

❷

See 'Central Rome' map for detail

British Embassy

Policlinico

VIA BISSOLATI

VIA XX SETTEMBRE

VIA GAETA

PIAZZA BARBERINI

Pal. Barberini

ⓘ

S. Maria degli Angeli

PIAZZA DELLA REPUBBLICA

ⒸⒼ❼

❽

Città Universitaria

VIA TIBURTINA

Pal. Quirinale

VIA QUIRINALE

❾
❶❶❿

⓬

S. Lorenzo fuori le Mura

Palazzo Massimo

PIAZZA DEI CINQUECENTO

⓭

Stazione Termini

VIA DELLE QUATTRO FONTANE

VIA NAZIONALE

HILL

VIA CAVOUR

S. Maria Maggiore

ⒹⒻⒺ

VIA G. GIOLITTI

Ⓖ

Ⓗ

PIAZZA V. EMANUELE II

ESQUILINE HILL

Ⓙ

PIAZZA DI PORTA MAGGIORE

HILL
Roman Forum

Colosseum

VIA LABICANA

VIA MERULANA

VIA A. MANZONI

S. Croce in Gerusalemme

VIA DI S. GREGORIO

SS. Giovanni e Paolo

S. Giovanni in Laterano

VIA LA SPEZIA

S. Gregorio Magno

Porta S. Giovanni

CELIAN HILL

VIA LA TARANTO

VIA DELLE TERME

Aurelian Walls

VIA APPIA NUOVA

Baths of Caracalla

VIA MAGNA GRECIA

RESTAURANTS
Africa	C
Baia Chia	J
Casetta del Trastevere	M
Il Dito e la Luna	H
Formula 1	G
La Grotta Azzura	B
L'Insalateria 2	A
Ivo	O
Ai Marmi	P
Monzu Vladi	K
Da Paris	N
Il Podista	D
Dar Poeta	L
Pommidoro	F
Romolo	I
Tram Tram	E

Aurelian Walls

Porta S. Sebastiano

EUR & Tre Fontane ▽   ▽ The Catacombs

Termini and around

Astoria Garden, Via Bachelet 8 (☎06.446.9908, fax 06.445.3329). In a peaceful area east of Termini, a newly renovated hotel that was once the home of an Italian count. Rooms are pleasant, quiet and some have balconies. Metro Termini. ⑤.

Casa Kolbe, Via di San Teodoro 44 (☎06.679.4974, fax 06.6994.1550). In a quiet location not far from the Colosseum, this is a favourite with students and tour groups. Its rooms are simple, clean, and good value for the location. Metro B Colosseo. ④.

Cervia, Via Palestro 55 (☎06.491.057, fax 06.491.056, *hotelcervia@wnt.it*). Pleasant rooms in a lively *pensione* in the same building as the *Restivo* and *Mari* (see below). If you don't mind lugging your bags a few more steps, ask for the discounted rooms on the third floor. Metro B Castro Pretorio. ④.

Hotel des Artistes, Via Villafranca 20 (☎06.445.4365, fax 06.446.2368, *www.hoteldesartistes.com*). One of the better hotels in the Termini area. Exceptionally good value, spotlessly clean, and recently redecorated, with a breezy roof terrace, and email and Internet services for L10,000/€5.17 per hour. Also has dorm beds for L35,000/€18.08. Metro B Castro Pretorio. ⑤.

Elide, Via Firenze 50 (☎06.474.1367, fax 06.4890.4318). A *pensione* for the last fifty years, with clean, simple rooms and a friendly staff, a few minutes from Piazza della Repubblica. Metro A Repubblica. ③.

Fawlty Towers, Via Magenta 39 (☎06.445.4802). Playfully named accommodation, owned by the people who run Enjoy Rome, this place has both dorm beds (L35,000/€18.08) and clean and comfortable hotel rooms, some with private bath. There's a communal kitchen, Internet access, and a pleasant roof terrace. Metro Termini. ④.

Katty, Via Palestro 35 (☎06.490.079, fax 06.444.1216). A good-value *pensione* located in one of the nicer buildings on the east side of Termini. Rooms are quite pleasant and some have shiny new bathrooms. If you want to spend a bit extra, go up a floor to *Katty 2*, where all rooms have private baths, minibar, TV, phone, and a/c. Metro B Castro Pretorio. ③–④.

Mari, Via Palestro 55 (☎06.446.2137, fax 06.482.8313). Clean rooms in a friendly hotel run by three women, across the landing from the *Restivo*. No private bathrooms. Metro B Castro Pretorio. ③.

Mari II, Via Calatafimi 38 (☎06.474.0371, fax 06.4470.3311). Sister hotel to the Mari, and equally clean, though poorly situated east of Termini on a nasty little alley near a porno cinema. Metro Termini. ④.

Marsala, Via Marsala 36 (☎06.444.1262, fax 06.441.397). Handily situated two-star hotel 50m east of the station. Very clean, good-value rooms, and a friendly English-speaking staff. Metro Termini. ④.

Positano, Via Palestro 49 (☎ & fax 06.446.9101). Not glamorous, but certainly reasonably priced, with comfortable rooms two minutes' walk from Termini. Helpful management too. Metro Termini. ②.

Restivo, Via Palestro 55 (☎06.446.2172). Spotless rooms in a small *pensione* run by a sweet old lady. She stays up until all guests are safely back home, so it's best avoided if you're planning to party into the small hours. No private bathrooms. Metro B Castro Pretorio. ③.

Raccuia, Via Treviso 37 (☎06.4423.1406). A clean and family-run *pensione*, just a short walk from the Policlinico metro stop. A particularly good deal if there are three of you – L90,000/€46.48 for a triple room. Metro B Policlinico. ②.

Rosetta, Via Cavour 295 (☎ & fax 06.4782.3069). Family-run *pensione* in a nice location very close to the Colosseum. The small rooms are a bit shabby, but they're comfortable enough, and have private baths, TV, and telephone. No breakfast. Metro B Colosseo. ④.

Across the river: Trastevere and the Vatican

Alimandi, Via Tunisi 8 (☎06.3972.3948, fax 06.3972.3943). Close to the Vatican, this place boasts a friendly staff, a roof-top garden, and nicely furnished, good-value doubles, all with telephone and TV. Metro A Ottaviano. ⑥.

Arcangelo, Via Boezio 15 (☎06.687.4143, fax 06.689.3050). Clean, reliable hotel, with comfortable rooms in a quiet street not far from the Vatican. Metro A Ottaviano. ⑤.

Colors, Via Boezio 31 (☎ & fax 06.687.4030). Run by the people from Enjoy Rome, this is a smaller version of their popular *Fawlty Towers*, a hostel/hotel in a quiet neighbourhood near the Vatican. Dorm beds (L35,000/€18.08) and private rooms, are available. Everyone is very friendly, and there are kitchen facilities, a lounge with satellite TV, and a small terrace. Metro A Ottaviano. ④.

Davos, Via degli Scipioni 239 (☎06.321.7012, fax 06.323.0367). Simple, affordable *pensione* on a quiet street not far from the Vatican. Rooms are clean and quite basic, but all except one has a private bath. No credit cards. Metro A Lepanto. ④.

Gerber, Via degli Scipioni 241 (☎06.321.6485, fax 06.322.1001). A friendly staff and elegant comfortable rooms make this hotel great value for its convenient location on a quiet street not far from the Vatican. Even better, they give a 10 percent discount to *Rough Guide* readers. Metro A Lepanto. ⑤.

Ottaviano, Via Ottaviano 6 (☎06.3973.7253, *www.pensioneottaviano.com*). A simple *pensione*-cum-hostel near to the Vatican that is very popular with the backpacking crowd; book well in advance, fluent English spoken. No private bathrooms. Metro A Ottaviano. Dorm beds L35,000/€18.08; rooms ②.

Trastevere, Via Luciano Manara 24a/25 (☎06.581.4713, fax 06.588.1016). The place to come if you want to be in the heart of Trastevere, with all new furnishings, terracotta floors, and newly installed bathrooms in every room. They also have apartments with kitchens. Bus #H or #63. ④.

Hostels, convents, and student accommodation

Franciscan Sisters of Atonement, Via Monte del Gallo 105 (☎06.630.782, fax 06.638.6149). Pleasant rooms, all with private bath and close to the large peaceful garden, this place, near St Peter's, is popular with groups, and welcomes men and women, so it's best to book ahead; 11pm curfew; L55,000/€28.41 per person, with breakfast. Bus #64 to Piazza Cavour then bus #34.

Nostra Signora di Lourdes, Via Sistina 113 (☎06.474.5324). A swankily located convent – just a few minutes' walk from the Spanish Steps – with singles and doubles for women or married couples who can put up with a 10.30pm curfew. Bus #175. Reckon on paying around L50,000/€25.82 per person.

Ostello del Foro Italico, Viale delle Olimpiadi 61 (☎06.324.2571). Rome's official HI hostel, though not particularly central or easy to get to from Termini. You can call ahead to check out availability, but they won't take bookings – of any kind. L25,000/€12.91, including breakfast. Metro A to Ottaviano, then bus #32 to the hostel – ask the driver for the "ostello".

Sandy, Via Cavour 136 (☎06.488.4585). Run by the same folk as the *Ottaviano*, but with dormitories only. No breakfast; L37,000/€19.11. Metro B Cavour.

Suore Pie Operaie, Via di Torre Argentina 76 (☎06.686.1254). For women only, this place offers the cheapest beds in the city centre, although you need to book well in advance and there's a 10.30pm curfew. L25,000/€12.91 per person. Closed Aug. Bus #64.

YWCA, Via C. Balbo 4 (☎06.488.0460, fax 06.487.1028). Though only open to women and married couples, this is more conveniently situated than the HI hostel, just ten minutes' walk from Termini. Singles, doubles, and three-bedded rooms, for L80,000/€41.32 to L120,000/€61.98; all rooms include breakfast except Sun mornings and August. Midnight curfew. Metro Termini.

Camping

All Rome's **campsites** are some way out of the city, and, although easy enough to get to, they are not especially cheap. The closest site is *Camping Flaminio*, 8km north of the centre on Via Flaminia Nuova (L16,000/€8.26 plus L13,000/€6.71 per person; ☎06.333.2604); take bus #910 to Piazza Mancini, then transfer to Bus #200 (ask the driver to drop you at the "fermata più vicina al campeggio"; March–Oct). *Camping Tiber*, on Via Tiberina at Km1400 (L16,500/€8.52 plus 12,500/€64.56 per person; ☎06.3361.2314; March–Oct), is another good bet – spacious and friendly, with a bar/pizzeria, a swimming pool and really hot showers. It offers a free shuttle service (every 30min) to and from the nearby Prima Porta station, where you can catch the Roma-Nord service to Piazzale Flaminio (about 20min).

The City

Rome's **city centre** is divided neatly into distinct blocks. The warren of streets that makes up the **centro storico** occupies the hook of land on the left bank of the River Tiber, bordered to the east by Via del Corso and to the north and south by water. From here Rome's central core spreads east: across Via del Corso to the major shopping streets and alleys around the **Spanish Steps** down to the main artery of **Via Nazionale**; to the major sites of the **ancient city** to the south; and to the huge expanse

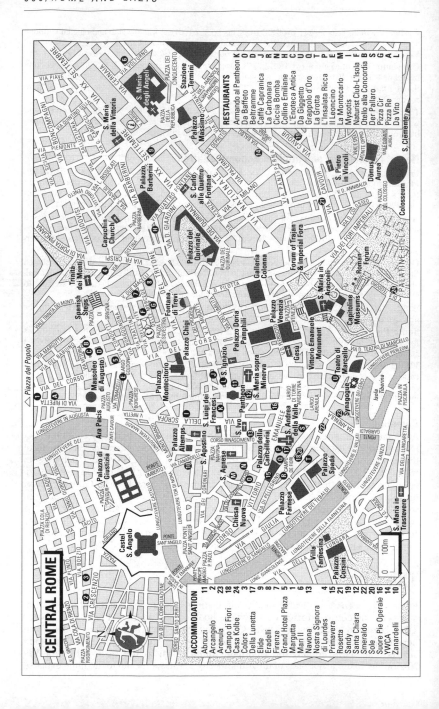

CENTRAL ROME

△ Piazza del Popolo

RESTAURANTS

Armando al Pantheon	K
Da Baffeto	O
Beltramme	J
Caffè Capranica	R
La Carbonara	C
Ciccia Bomba	N
Colline Emiliane	H
L'Enoteca Antica	Q
Da Giggetto	U
Grappolo d'Oro	D
La Grotta	T
L'Insalata Ricca	P
Il Leoncino	E
La Montecarlo	M
Mysotis	I
Naturist Club-L'Isola	F
Otello alla Concordia	B
Der Pallaro	S
Pizza Cir	G
Pizza Re	A
Da Vito	L

ACCOMMODATION

Abruzzi	11
Arcangelo	2
Arenula	23
Campo di Fiori	18
Casa Kolbe	24
Colors	3
Della Lunetta	17
Elide	9
Eradelli	8
Firenze	7
Grand Hotel Plaza	5
Margutta	5
Mari II	1
Navona	6
Nostra Signora	13
di Lourdes	4
Primavera	15
Rosetta	21
Sandy	19
Santa Chiara	12
Smeraldo	22
Sole	20
Suore Pie Operaie	16
YWCA	14
Zanardelli	10

VISITING ROME'S MUSEUMS AND ANCIENT SITES

There are a number of ways you can make visiting Rome's most important museums and ancient sites easier and cheaper. Museums and sites that are under the jurisdiction of the City of Rome – the Capitoline Museums, Palazzo Barberini, Palazzo Altemps and Palazzo Massimo, among others – can be visited on an all-in-one five-day ticket, which costs L30,000/€15.49 at any of those places it's valid. You can also visit the Plazzzo Altemps and Palazzo Massimo, together with the Palatine and Colosseum, on a L20,000/€10.33 **combined ticket** – again available at any of the places it's valid.

---

of the **Villa Borghese** park to the north. The left bank of the river is oddly distanced from the main hum of this part of the city, home to the **Vatican** and **Saint Peter's**, and, to the south of these, **Trastevere** – even in ancient times a distinct entity from the city proper, as well as the focus of much of the city's nightlife.

To see most of this, you'd be mad to risk your blood pressure in any kind of vehicle, and really the best way to **get around** the city centre and points east to Termini is to walk. The same goes for the ancient sites, and probably the Vatican and Trastevere too – although for these last two you might want to jump on a bus going across the river. Keep public transport for the longer hops, down to Testaccio, EUR, the catacombs, or other more scattered attractions.

Piazza Venezia and the Capitoline Hill

Piazza Venezia is not so much a square as a road junction, and a busy one at that. But it's a good central place to start your wanderings, close to both the medieval and Renaissance centre of Rome and the bulk of the ruins of the ancient city. Flanked on all sides by imposing buildings, it's a dignified focal point for the city in spite of the traffic, and a spot you'll find yourself returning to time and again.

Palazzo Venezia and the church of San Marco

Forming the western side of the piazza, the **Palazzo Venezia** (Tues–Sat 9am–1.30pm, Sun 9am–1pm; L8000/€4.65) was the first large Renaissance palace in the city, built for the Venetian Pope Paul II in the mid-fifteenth century and for a long time the embassy of the Venetian Republic. More famously, Mussolini moved in here while in power, occupying the vast *Sala del Mappamondo* and making his declamatory speeches to the huge crowds below from the small balcony facing onto the piazza proper. In those days the palace lights would be left on to give the impression of constant activity in what was the centre of the Fascist government and later the war effort; now it's a much more peripheral building, home to a museum of Renaissance arts and crafts made up of the magpie-ish collection of Paul II, and a venue for great temporary exhibitions (entrance price for temporary exhibitions varies). Adjacent to the palace on its southern side, the church of **San Marco**, accessible from Piazza San Marco (daily except Mon morning and Wed afternoon 8.30am–12.30pm & 4–7pm), is a tidy basilica rebuilt in 833 and added to by various Renaissance and eighteenth-century popes. Under restoration at the time of writing, it's a warm, cosy church, restored by Paul II – who added the graceful portico and gilded ceiling – with an apse mosaic dating from the ninth century showing Pope Gregory offering his church to Christ.

The Vittorio Emanuele Monument

Everything pales into insignificance beside the marble monstrosity rearing up across the street – the **Vittorio Emanuele Monument**, (Tues–Sun 9am–4.30pm; free) erected at the turn of the century as the "Altar of the Nation" to commemorate Italian Unification. Variously likened in the past to a typewriter (because of its shape), and, by American GIs, to a wedding cake (the marble used will never mellow with age), King Vittorio Emanuele II, who it's in part supposed to honour, probably wouldn't have thought much of it – he was by all accounts a modest man; indeed, the only person who seems to have benefited from the building is the prime minister at the time, who was (perhaps not entirely coincidentally) a deputy for Brescia, from where the marble was supplied. The monument has recently opened for the first time, and you can now climb to the immense semi-circular colonnade at the top, and the views are perhaps the best in Rome – not least because this is the one place you can't see the Vittorio Emanuele Monument. At the top of the stairs is the Tomb of the Unknown Soldier, flanked by eternal flames and a permanent guard of honour. Incidentally, the equestrian statue of the king is claimed to be the world's largest (its moustache is apparently 3m long) – though perhaps the greatest irony is that all this memorializes a royal dynasty that produced just four monarchs.

The Capitoline Hill

The real pity about the Vittorio Emanuele Monument is that it obscures views of the **Capitoline Hill** behind – once, in the days of imperial Rome, the spiritual and political centre of the Roman Empire. Apart from anything else, this hill has contributed key words to the English language, including, of course, "capitol", and "money", which comes from the temple to Juno Moneta that once stood up here and housed the Roman mint. The Capitoline also played a significant role in medieval and Renaissance times: the flamboyant fourteenth-century dictator Cola di Rienzo stood here in triumph in 1347, and was murdered here by an angry mob seven years later – a humble nineteenth-century statue marks the spot where he is said to have died. Michelangelo gave the piazza its present form, redesigning it as a symbol of Rome's regeneration after the city was sacked in 1527.

Santa Maria in Aracoeli

The church of **Santa Maria in Aracoeli** (daily: summer 7am–noon & 4–6.30pm; winter closes 5.30pm) crowns the highest point on the Capitoline Hill, built on the site of a temple to Jupiter where, according to legend, the Tiburtine Sybil foretold the birth of Christ. It's a steep climb to the top, reached by a flight of steps erected by Cola di Rienzo in 1348, but the church is worth it, one of Rome's most ancient basilicas. Inside, in the first chapel on the right, there are some fine frescoes by Pinturicchio recording the life of San Bernardino – realistic tableaux of landscapes and bustling town scenes. The church is also known for its role as keeper of the so-called "Bambino", a small statue of the child Christ, carved from the wood of a Gethsemane olive tree, that is said to have healing powers and was traditionally called out to the sickbeds of the ill and dying all over the city, its coach commanding instant right of way through the heavy Rome traffic. The Bambino was stolen in 1994, however, and a copy now stands in its place, in a small chapel to the left of the high altar.

The Campidoglio and Capitoline Museums

Next door to the steps up to Santa Maria, the **cordonata** is an elegant, gently rising ramp, topped with two Roman statues of Castor and Pollux, which leads to the **Campidoglio**, one of Rome's most elegant squares. Designed by Michelangelo in the last years of his life for Pope Paul III, who was determined to hammer Rome back into shape for a visit by Charles V, the square wasn't in fact completed until the late seventeenth century. Michelangelo balanced the piazza, redesigning the facade of what is now **Palazzo dei Conservatori** and projecting an identical building across the way, known as **Palazzo Nuovo**. Both are angled slightly to focus on **Palazzo Senatorio**, Rome's town hall. In the centre of the square Michelangelo placed an equestrian statue of Emperor Marcus Aurelius, which had previously stood for years outside San Giovanni in Laterano; early Christians had refrained from melting it down because they believed it to be of the Emperor Constantine. After careful restoration, the original is behind a glass wall in the Palazzo Nuovo, and a copy has taken its place at the centre of the piazza.

The Palazzo dei Conservatori and Palazzo Nuovo together make up the **Capitoline Museums** (Tues–Sun 9am–7pm; L12,000/€6.20 or for details of combined ticket, see box on p.691, free last Sun of month), now open again after a lengthy restoration, and featuring some of the city's most important ancient sculpture. Of the two museum buildings, it's the **Palazzo Nuovo** (on the left) that really steals the show. Just inside the entrance is the original Marcus Aurelius statue, and the first floor concentrates some of the best of the city's Roman copies of Greek sculpture into half a dozen or so rooms and a long gallery crammed with elegant statuary. There's a remarkable, controlled statue of the *Dying Gaul*, a Roman copy of a Hellenistic original; a naturalistic *Boy with Goose* – another copy; an original grappling depiction of *Eros and Psyche*; a *Satyr Resting*, after a piece by Praxiteles, which was the inspiration for Hawthorne's book the *Marble Faun*; and the red marble *Laughing Silenus*, another Roman copy of a Greek original. Walk through, too, to the so-called *Sala degli Imperatori*, with its busts of Roman emperors and other famous names, including a young Augustus, a cruel Caracalla, and a portrait of Helena, the mother of Constantine, reclining gracefully. And don't miss the *Capitoline Venus*, housed in a room on its own – a coy, delicate piece, again based on a work by Praxiteles.

The same ticket gets you into the **Palazzo dei Conservatori** across the square (though it must be on the same day) – a larger, more varied collection, with more ancient sculpture but also later pieces. You can either walk across the square itself, or follow a set of stairs down to the *Tabularium*, built in 78 BC as the state archives and recently converted into a gallery to connect the two museums. This way gives a marvellous view over the Forum and the chance to see the remains of the Temple of Vejovis, built here in 196 BC, directly under the Palazzo Senatorio, in the saddle between the two summits of the Capitoline Hill. Once on the other side, littered around the courtyard of the Palazzo dei Conservatori are the feet and other fragments of a gigantic statue of Constantine. Inside, in various **first-floor wings**, there are friezes and murals showing events from Roman history, a couple of enormous statues of popes Innocent X (by Algardi) and Urban VIII (by Bernini), the exquisite *Spinario* – a Hellenistic work from the first century BC showing a boy plucking a thorn from his foot – and the sacred symbol of Rome, the Etruscan bronze she-wolf nursing the mythic founders of the city; the twins themselves are not Etruscan but were added by Pollaiuolo in the late fifteenth century. Look, too, for the so-called *Esquiline Venus* and *Capitoline Tensa*, the latter a reconstructed chariot in bronze; and the soft *Muse Polymnia* and a gargantuan Roman copy of *Athena*. Upstairs, the **second floor pinacoteca** houses Renaissance painting from the fourteenth century to the late seventeenth century – well-labelled, with descriptions of each painting in Italian and English. The paintings fill half a dozen rooms or so, and highlights include a couple of portraits by Van Dyck and an intense *Portrait of a Crossbowman* by Lorenzo Lotto, a pair of paintings from 1590 by Tintoretto – a *Flagellation* and *Christ Crowned with Thorns* – and a very fine early work by Carracci, *Head of a Boy*. There are also several sugary works by Guido Reni, done at the end of his life. In one of two large main galleries, there's a vast picture by Guercino, depicting the *Burial of Santa Petronilla* (the legendary daughter of St Peter, who died young), which used to hang in St Peter's and arrived here via the Quirinale palace and the Louvre, to hang alongside several other works by the same artist, notably a lovely, contemplative Persian Sybil and a wonderful picture of Cleopatra cowed before a young and victorious Octavius. In the same room, there are also two paintings by Caravaggio, one a replica of the young *John the Baptist* which hangs in the Palazzo Doria-Pamphili, the other a famous canvas known as the *Fortune-Teller*. By this time you may be ready for a break, in which case you should go the building's new **bar and restaurant**, where a roof terrace gives unparalleled views over the city, as well as snacks, drinks and even lunch at fairly reasonable prices.

The Tarpeian Rock and San Pietro in Carcere

After seeing the museums, walk around behind the Palazzo Senatorio for a great view down onto the Forum, with the Colosseum in the background. On the right, Via del Monte Tarpeio follows, as its name suggests, the brink of the old **Tarpeian Rock**, from which traitors would be thrown in ancient times – so-called after Tarpeia, who betrayed the city to the Sabines. Steps lead down from here to the little church of **San Pietro in Carcere** (daily: summer 9am–noon & 2.30–6pm; winter 9am–noon & 2–5pm; donation expected), built above the ancient Mamertine Prison, where spies, vanquished soldiers and other enemies of the Roman state were incarcerated, and where St Peter himself was held. Steps lead down into the murky depths of the jail, where you can see the bars to which he was chained, along with the spring the saint is said to have created to baptize the other prisoners down here. At the top of the staircase, hollowed out of the honeycomb of stone, is an imprint claimed to be of St Peter's head as he tumbled down the stairs (though when the prison was in use, the only access was through a hole in the ceiling). It's an unappealing place even now, and you won't be sorry to leave – through an exit cunningly placed to lead you through the gift shop.

Immediately **north of Piazza Venezia** is the *centro storico* proper. It's here that most people find the Rome they have been looking for – the Rome of small crumbling piazzas, churches and fountains, blind alleys and streets humming with scooters and foot-traffic. This area was known in Roman times as the *Campus Martius*, a low-lying area outside the ancient city centre that was given over to barracks and sporting arenas, together with the odd temple. Later it became the heart of the Renaissance city, and nowadays it's the part of the town that is densest in interest, an unruly knot of narrow streets and alleys that holds some of the best of Rome's classical and Baroque heritage and its most vivacious street- and nightlife. Whichever direction you wander in there's something to see; indeed it's part of the appeal of Rome that even the most aimless ambling leads you past some breathlessly beautiful and historic spots.

Via del Corso

The boundary of the historic centre to the east, **Via del Corso** is Rome's main thoroughfare, leading all the way from Piazza Venezia at its southern end up to the Piazza del Popolo to the north. On its eastern side, it gives onto the swish shopping streets that lead up to Piazza di Spagna, on the western side the web of streets that tangles its way right down to the Tiber. Nowadays it is Rome's principal shopping street, home to a mixture of upmarket boutiques and chain stores that make it a busy stretch during the day, full of hurrying pedestrians and crammed buses, but a relatively dead one come the evening.

Galleria Doria Pamphili

Walking north from Piazza Venezia, the first building on the left of Via Del Corso, the Palazzo Doria Pamphili, is among the city's finest Rococo palaces. Inside, through an entrance on Piazza di Collegio Romano, the **Galleria Doria Pamphili**, Via del Collegio Romano 2 (Jan–Aug 15 & Sept–Dec Mon–Wed & Fri–Sun 10am–5pm;

L14,000/€7.23; private apartments tours every 30min 10.30am–12.30pm; L6000/€3.10) is one of Rome's best private late-Renaissance art collections. The Doria Pamphili family still lives in part of the building, and the first part of the gallery is made up of a series of **private apartments**, furnished in the style of the original palace, through which you're guided by way of a free audio-tour narrated by the urbane Jonathan Pamphili. Beyond here, the **picture gallery** extends around a courtyard, the paintings displayed in the style of the time, crammed in frame-to-frame, floor-to-ceiling. Just inside, at the corner of the courtyard, there's a badly cracked bust of Innocent X by Bernini, which the sculptor apparently replaced in a week with the more famous version down the hall, in a room off to the left, where Bernini appears to have captured the pope about to erupt into laughter. In the same room, Velazquez's famous painting of the same man is quite different, depicting a rather irritable character regarding the viewer with impatience. The rest of the collection is just as rich in interest. There is perhaps Rome's best concentration of Dutch and Flemish paintings, including a rare Italian work by Brueghel the Elder, showing a naval battle being fought outside Naples, a highly realistic portrait of two old men, by Quentin Metsys, and a Hans Memling *Deposition*, in the furthest rooms, as well as a further Metsys painting – the fabulously ugly *Moneylenders and their Clients* – in the main gallery. There is also Carracci's bucolic *Flight into Egypt*, painted shortly before the artist's death; two paintings by Caravaggio – *Mary Magdalene* and *John the Baptist*; and *Salome with the head of St John*, by Titian.

Sant'Ignazio
The next left off Via del Corso after the palace leads into **Piazza Sant'Ignazio**, a lovely little square, laid out like a theatre set and dominated by the facade of the Jesuit church of **Sant'Ignazio** (daily 7.30am–12.30pm & 4–7.15pm). The saint isn't actually buried here; appropriately, for the founder of the Jesuit order, he's in the Gesù church a little way south. But it's a spacious structure, worth visiting for its marvellous Baroque ceiling by Andrea del Pozzo showing the entry of St Ignatius into paradise, a spectacular work that employs sledgehammer trompe l'oeil effects, notably in the mock cupola painted into the dome of the crossing. Stand on the disc in the centre of the nave, the focal point for the ingenious rendering of perspective: figures in various states of action and repose, conversation and silence, fix you with stares from their classical pediment.

The Pantheon
Via del Seminario leads down to Piazza della Rotonda, where the main focus of interest is of course the **Pantheon** (Mon–Sat 9am–6.30pm, Sun 9am–1pm; free), which forms the square's southern edge, easily the most complete ancient Roman structure in the city and, along with the Colosseum, visually the most impressive. Though originally a temple that formed part of Marcus Agrippa's redesign of the Campus Martius in around 27 BC – hence the inscription – it's since been proved that the building was entirely rebuilt by the Emperor Hadrian and finished around the year 125 AD. It's a formidable architectural achievement even now, although like the city's other Roman monuments, it would have been much more sumptuous in its day. It was consecrated as a Christian site in 609 AD and dedicated to Santa Maria ai Martiri in allusion to the Christian bones that were found here; a thousand years later, the bronze roof was stripped from the ceiling of the portico by Pope Urban VIII, to be melted down for the baldachino in St Peter's and the cannons of the Castel Sant'Angelo. (Interestingly, some of the "stolen" bronze later found its way back here when, after Unification, the cannons were in turn melted down to provide materials for the tombs of two Italian kings, which are housed in the right and left chapels.) Inside, you get the best impression of the

engineering expertise of Hadrian: the diameter is precisely equal to its height (43m), the hole in the centre of the dome – from which shafts of sunlight descend to illuminate the musty interior – a full 9m across. Most impressively, there are no visible arches or vaults to hold the whole thing up; instead they're sunk into the concrete of the walls of the building. Again, it would have been richly decorated, the coffered ceiling heavily stuccoed and the niches filled with the statues of gods. Now, apart from the sheer size of the place, the main thing of interest is the tomb of Raphael, between the second and third chapel on the left, with an inscription by the humanist bishop Pietro Bembo: "Living, great Nature feared he might outvie Her works, and dying, fears herself may die."

Santa Maria sopra Minerva

There's more artistic splendour on view behind the Pantheon, though Bernini's **Elephant Statue** doesn't really prepare you for the church of Santa Maria sopra Minerva beyond. The statue is Bernini's most endearing piece of work, if not his most characteristic: a cheery elephant trumpeting under the weight of the obelisk he carries on his back – a reference to Pope Alexander VII's reign and supposed to illustrate the fact that strength should support wisdom. **Santa Maria sopra Minerva** (Mon–Sat 7am–7pm, Sun 8am–7pm) is Rome's only Gothic church, and worth a look just for that, though its soaring lines have since been overburdened by marble and frescoes. Built in the late thirteenth century on the ruins of a temple to Minerva, it is also one of Rome's art-treasure churches, crammed with the tombs and self-indulgences of wealthy Roman families. Of these, the Carafa chapel, in the south transept, is the best known, holding Filippino Lippi's fresco of *The Assumption*, a bright, effervescent piece of work, below which one painting shows a hopeful Carafa (the religious zealot, Pope Paul IV) being presented to the Virgin Mary by Thomas Aquinas; another depicts Aquinas confounding the heretics in the sight of two beautiful young boys – the future Medici popes Leo X and Clement VII (the equestrian statue of Marcus Aurelius, destined for the Capitoline Hill, is just visible in the background). You should look too at the figure of *Christ Bearing the Cross*, on the left-hand side of the main altar, a serene work that Michelangelo completed for the church in 1521.

Sant'Ivo

A few steps west of the Pantheon, on Corso del Rinascimento, the rather blank facade of the **Palazzo della Sapienza** cradles the church of **Sant'Ivo** (Sun 10am–1pm) – from the outside at least, one of Rome's most impressive churches, with a playful facade designed by Borromini. Though originally built for the most Barberini pope, Urban VIII, the building actually spans the reign of three pontiffs. Each of the two small towers is topped with the weird, blancmange-like groupings that are the symbol of the Chigi family (representing the hills of Monti Paschi), and the central cupola spirals helter-skelter-fashion to its zenith, crowned with flames that are supposed to represent the sting of the Barberini bee, their family symbol. Inside, too, is very cleverly designed, very light and spacious given the small space the church is squeezed into, rising to the tall parabolic cupola.

San Luigi dei Francesi

A short walk from here, at the bottom of Via della Scrofa, the French national church of **San Luigi dei Francesi** (daily except Thurs afternoon 7.30am–12.30pm & 3.30–7pm) is another church in the vicinity of the Pantheon that is worth a look, mainly for the works by Caravaggio. In the last chapel on the left are three paintings: the *Calling of St Matthew*, in which Christ points to Matthew, who is illuminated by a shaft of sunlight; Matthew visited by an angel as he writes the Gospel; and the saint's

martyrdom. Caravaggio's first public commission, these paintings were actually rejected at first, partly on grounds of indecorum, and it took considerable reworking by the
artist before they were finally accepted.

Piazza Navona and around

Just west of San Luigi dei Francesi, **Piazza Navona** is Rome's most famous square.
Lined with cafés and restaurants, pedestrianized and often thronged with tourists,
street artists and pigeons, it is as picturesque – and as vibrant, day and night – as any
piazza in Italy. It takes its shape from the first century AD Stadium of Domitian, the
principal venue of the athletic events and later chariot races that took place in the
Campus Martius. Until the mid-fifteenth century the ruins of the arena were still here,
overgrown and disused, but the square was given a facelift in the mid-seventeenth century by Pope Innocent X, who built most of the grandiose palaces that surround it and
commissioned Borromini to design the facade of the church of **Sant'Agnese in Agone**
on the piazza's western side. The story goes that the thirteen-year-old St Agnes was
stripped naked before the crowds in the stadium as punishment for refusing to marry,
whereupon she miraculously grew hair to cover herself. This church, typically
squeezed into the tightest of spaces by Borromini, is supposedly built on the spot
where it all happened.

Opposite, the **Fontana dei Quattro Fiumi**, one of three that punctuate the square,
is a masterpiece by Bernini, Borromini's arch-rival. Each figure represents one of the
four great rivers of the world – the Nile, Danube, Ganges and Plate – though only the
horse, symbolizing the Danube, was actually carved by Bernini himself. It's said that all
the figures are shielding their eyes in horror from Borromini's church facade (Bernini
was an arrogant man who never had time for the work of the less successful Borromini,
and their rivalry is well-documented) but the fountain had actually been completed
before the facade was begun. The grand complexity of rock is topped with an Egyptian
obelisk, brought here by Pope Innocent X from the Circus of Maxentius.

Bernini also had a hand in the fountain at the southern end of the square, the so-
called **Fontana del Moro**, designing the central figure of the Moor in what is another
fantastically playful piece of work, surrounded by toothsome dolphins and other marine
figures. In the opposite direction, just off the north side of Piazza Navona, there are
some visible remains of the **Stadium of Domitian** (Sat & Sun 10am–12.30pm;
L10,000/€5.17). You can visit these on one of the short, thirty-minute guided tours that
leave regularly at weekends, in English or Italian, and in doing so you can learn a little
more about the stadium and its relationship with present-day Piazza Navona. But to be
honest there's not a lot more to see than you can view from the street.

You might be better off spending any money you save on the Stadium in the antique
dealers of narrow **Via dei Coronari**, almost opposite. This street, and some of the
streets around, are the fulcrum of Rome's antiques trade, and, although the prices are
as high as you might expect in such a location, there is a huge number of shops (Via
dei Coronari consists of virtually nothing else), selling a tremendous variety of stuff,
and a browse along here makes for one of the city's absorbing bits of sightseeing.

Palazzo Altemps

Just across the street from the north end of Piazza Navona, Piazza Sant'Apollinare is
home of the beautifully restored **Palazzo Altemps** (Tues–Sat 9am–7pm, Sun
9am–6pm; L10,000/€5.17 or for details of combined ticket, see box on p.691; Sat & Sun
guided tours every hour, in English by request; L6,000/€3.10), nowadays home to part
of the Museo Nazionale Romano (the other half is in the Palazzo Massimo – see p.717),
and the cream of its collections of Roman statuary. On the ground floor, at the far end
of the courtyard's loggia, there's a statue of the Emperor Antoninus Pius, and, around

the corner, a couple of marvellous heads of Zeus and Pluto, a bust of Julia, the daughter of the Emperor Augustus, and a likeness of the philosopher Demosthenes, from the second century AD. There are two, almost identical statues of *Apollo the Lyrist*, a magnificent statue of Athena taming a serpent, pieced together from fragments found near the church of Santa Maria sopra Minerva, an *Aphrodite* from an original by Praxiteles, and, in the far corner of the courtyard, a shameless *Dionysus* with a satyr and panther, found on the Quirinal Hill. Upstairs you get a slightly better sense of the original sumptuousness of the building – some of the frescoes remain and the north loggia retains its original, late-sixteenth-century decoration, simulating a vine-laden pergola. Among the objects on display there is a fine statue of Hermes, a wonderful statue of a warrior at rest, and, most engagingly, a charmingly sensitive portrayal of *Orestes and Electra*, from the first century AD by a sculptor called Menelaus – his name is carved at the base of one of the figures. In a later room there is a colossal head of Hera, and – what some consider the highlight of the entire collection – the famous *Ludovisi throne*: an original fifth-century-BC Greek work embellished with a delicate relief portraying the birth of Aphrodite. Further on, the Fireplace Salon, whose huge fireplace is embellished with caryatids and lurking ibex – the symbol of the Altemps family – has the so-called *Suicide of Galatian*, apparently commissioned by Julius Caesar to adorn his Quirinal estate; at the other end if the room, an incredible sarcophagus depicts a battle between the Romans and barbarians in graphic, almost viscerally sculptural detail. All in all, an unmissable collection.

Sant'Agostino

Just east of Palazzo Altemps, through an arch, the Renaissance facade of the church of **Sant'Agostino** (daily 7.45am–noon & 4–7.30pm) takes up one side of a drab piazza of the same name. It's not much to look at from the outside, but a handful of art treasures might draw you in. Just inside the door, the serene statue of the *Madonna del Parto*, by Sansovino, is traditionally invoked during pregnancy, and is accordingly surrounded by photos of newborn babes and their blissful parents. But the biggest crowds gather around the first chapel on the left, where the *Madonna and Pilgrims* by Caravaggio (L500/€0.26 to switch on the lights) is a characteristic work of what was at the time almost revolutionary realism, showing two peasants with dirty limbs and clothes praying at the feet of a sensuous Mary and Child.

Piazza Montecitorio and around

Further on, **Piazza Montecitorio** takes its name from the bulky **Palazzo di Montecitorio** on its northern side, home since 1871 to the Italian parliament – though the building itself is a Bernini creation from 1650. The obelisk in the centre of the square was brought to Rome by Augustus and set up in the Campus Martius, where it formed the hand of a giant sundial. Just beyond, off Via del Corso, the **Palazzo Chigi** flanks the north side of **Piazza Colonna**, official residence of the prime minister. The **Column of Marcus Aurelius**, which gives the square its name, was erected between 180 and 190 AD to commemorate military victories in northern Europe, and, like the column of Trajan which inspired it, is decorated with reliefs depicting scenes from the campaigns.

The Mausoleum of Augustus and Aris Pacis Augustae

A little further up Via del Corso, off to the left, cut through to **Piazza del Augusta Imperatore**, an odd square of largely Mussolini-era buildings surrounding the massive **Mausoleum of Augustus** (guided tours Sat & Sun 11am; L10,000/€5.17), the burial place of the emperor and his family but these days not much more than a peaceful ring of cypresses, circled by paths, flowering shrubs and the debris of tramps. The mausoleum has been transformed into many buildings over the years, not least a fortress, like Hadrian's mausoleum across the river, but only recently has been opened to the public – although inside the passageways and central crypt, where the ashes of the members of the Augustan dynasty were kept, don't add much to the picture you get from the outside.

On the far side of the square, between the river and the mausoleum, the **Ara Pacis Augustae** or "Altar of Augustan Peace" (summer Tues–Sat 9am–7pm, Sun 9am–1pm; winter Tues–Sat 9am–4.30pm, Sun 9am–1pm; L4000/€2.07), is a more recognizable Roman remain, built in 13 BC to celebrate Augustus's victory over Spain and Gaul and the peace it heralded; although at time of writing closed to visitors until a new pavilion has been built to house it – expected in 2002. Much of the altar had been dug up piecemeal over the years, but the bulk of it was found during the middle half of the last century. It was no easy task to put it back together: excavation involved digging down to a depth of 10m and freezing the water table, after which many other parts had to be retrieved from museums the world over, or plaster copies made. But it's a superb example of imperial Roman sculpture and holds on its fragmented frieze the likenesses of many familiar names, most shown in the victory procession itself, which is best preserved on the eastern side. The first part is almost completely gone, but the shape of Augustus is a little more complete, as are the figures that follow – first Tiberius, then the priests with their skull-cap headgear, then Agrippa. The women are, respectively, Augustus's wife Livia, daughter Julia, and niece Antonia, the latter caught simply and realistically turning to her husband. Around their feet run various children clutching the togas of the elders, the last of whom is said to be the young Claudius.

Piazza del Popolo

The other side of Piazza del Augusto Imperatore, **Via di Ripetta** leads north to the oval-shaped expanse of **Piazza del Popolo** – a dignified meeting of roads laid out in 1538 by Pope Paul III (Alessandro Farnese) to make an impressive entrance to the city; it owes its present symmetry to Valadier, who added the central fountain in 1814. The monumental **Porta del Popolo** went up in 1655, the work of Bernini, whose patron Alexander VII's Chigi family symbol – the heap of hills surmounted by a star – can clearly be seen above the main gateway. During summer, the steps around the obelisk and fountain, and the cafés on either side of the square, are popular hangouts. But the square's real attraction is the unbroken view it gives all the way back down Via del Corso, to the central columns of the Vittorio Emanuele Monument. If you get to choose your first view of the centre of Rome, make it this one.

On the far side of the piazza, hard against the city walls, the church of **Santa Maria del Popolo** (Mon–Sat 7am–noon & 4–7pm, Sun 8am–1.30pm & 4.30–7.30pm) holds some of the best Renaissance art of any Roman church. It was originally erected here in 1099 over the burial place of Nero, in order to sanctify what was believed to be an evil place, but took its present form in the fifteenth century. Inside there are lovely frescoes by Pinturicchio in the first chapel of the south aisle, and the same artist also did some work in the Bramante-designed apse, which in turn boasts two fine tombs by Andrea Sansovino. The Chigi chapel, the second from the entrance in the northern aisle, was designed by Raphael for Agostino Chigi in 1516, though most of the work was actually undertaken by other artists and not finished until the seventeenth century. Michelangelo's protégé, Sebastiano del Piombo, was responsible for the altarpiece, and two of the sculptures in the corner niches, of Daniel and Habakkuk, are by Bernini. But it's two pictures by Caravaggio that attract the most attention, in the left-hand chapel of the north transept. These are typically dramatic works – one, the *Conversion of St Paul*, showing Paul and horse bathed in a beatific radiance, the other, the *Crucifixion of St Peter*, showing Peter as an aged but strong figure, dominated by the muscly figures hoisting him up. Like the same artist's paintings in the churches of San Luigi dei

Francesi and Sant'Agostino (see p.698), both works were considered extremely risqué in their time, their heavy chiaroscuro and deliberate realism too much for the church authorities; one contemporary critic referred to the *Conversion of St Paul*, a painting dominated by the exquisitely lit horse's hindquarters, as "an accident in a blacksmith's shop".

West of Piazza Venezia

Via del Plebiscito, a dark, rather gloomy thoroughfare, forges west from Piazza Venezia to the **Piazza del Gesù**, where the church of **Gesù**, a symbol of the Counter-Reformation and the Jesuit order (daily 6am–12.30pm & 4–7.15pm), was ideal for the large and fervent congregations the Jesuits wanted to draw – indeed, high and wide, with a single-aisled nave and short transepts edging out under a huge dome, it has since served as the model for Jesuit churches everywhere. The facade is by Giacomo della Porta, the interior the work of Vignola. Today it's still a well-patronized church, notable for its size (the glitzy tomb of the order's founder, St Ignatius, is topped by a huge globe of lapis lazuli – the largest piece in existence) and the staggering richness of its interior, especially the paintings of Baciccia in the dome and the ceiling's ingenious trompe l'oeil, which oozes out of its frame in a tangle of writhing bodies, flowing drapery and stucco angels.

Largo di Torre Argentina and around

Corso Vittorio Emanuele continues west from the Gesù, opening out eventually onto **Largo di Torre Argentina**, a good-sized square frantic with traffic circling around the ruins of four (Republican-era) temples and the channel of an ancient public lavatory, now home to a thriving colony of cats. This is not generally open to the public, but there's not a lot to see here – it's more a place to wait for a bus than to deliberately linger. On the far side of the square, the **Teatro Argentina** was in 1816 the venue for the first performance of Rossini's Barber of Seville, not a success at all on the night: Rossini was apparently booed into taking refuge in Bernasconi's pastry shop which used to be next door (now the Brek restaurant). Built in 1731, it is today one of the city's most important theatres, and has a small museum that can be visited by appointment. It is also thought, incidentally, that it was built over the spot where Caesar was assassinated. Nowadays, however, the **Crypta Balbi**, around the corner at Via delle Botteghe Oscure 31 (Tues–Sun 9am–7.30pm; L8,000/€4.13), is the area's principal point of interest, a new museum housed on the site of an old Roman imperial theatre and with displays covering the period from the fall of the Roman Empire to the late Middle Ages.

Sant'Andrea delle Valle

From Largo Argentina you can either push on down Corso Vittorio Emanuele or cut left towards the Tiber and right at Piazza Cairoli into the network of streets that centres on Campo de' Fiori. Taking the Corso route, you pass the church of **Sant'Andrea della Valle** (Mon–Sat 7.30am–noon & 4.30–7.30pm, Sun 7.30am–12.45pm & 4.30–7.45pm), which has the distinction of sporting the city's second-tallest dome (after St Peter's). Inside, it's one of the most Baroque of Rome's churches, a high, barnlike building, in which most of your attention is drawn not only to the dome, decorated with frescoes of the Glory of Paradise by Giovanni Lanfranco, but also to a marvellous set of frescoes in the apse by his contemporary Domenichino, illustrating the life of St Andrew, and centring on the monumental scene of his crucifixion on the characteristic transverse cross. In a side chapel on the right, you may recognize some good-looking copies of not only Michelangelo's pietà (the original is in St Peter's), but also of his figures of Leah and

Rachel, from the same artist's tomb of his patron, Julius II, in the church of San Pietro in Vincoli (see p.715).

Museo Barracco and Museo di Roma

A little further along, on the left at Piazza dei Baullari 1, is the so-called Piccola Farnesina palace, built by Antonio Sangallo the Younger, which now holds the **Museo Barracco**, a small but fine-quality collection of ancient sculpture that was donated to the city at the beginning of the twentieth century by one Baron Barracco (Tues–Sat 9am–7pm, Sun 9am–1pm; L10,000/€5.17). The first floor contains ancient Egyptian and Hellenistic pieces, while on the second floor are ceramics and statuary from the Greek classical period (essentially the fourth and fifth centuries BC). Across the street from the Museo Barracco, the eighteenth-century Palazzo Braschi is the home of the **Museo di Roma**, which hosts occasional exhibitions relating to the history of the city from the Middle Ages to the present day. The permanent collection is closed indefinitely, but contains paintings showing the city during different eras, frescoes from demolished palaces, and the open railway carriage that the nineteenth-century Pope Pius IX used for journeys out of the city.

Piazza Pasquino and around

Immediately behind the Palazzo Braschi, just south of Piazza Navona, the small space of **Piazza Pasquino** isn't quite what you'd expect from the scene of centuries of satire, but the battered torso of Pasquino itself, anonymous poker of fun at the rich and famous during the Middle Ages, still stands in the corner. It's most famous among a number of so-called "talking statues" in Rome, upon which anonymous comments on the affairs of the day would be attached – comments that had a serious as well as a humorous intent. Pasquino gave us our word "pasquinade", but nowadays the graffitied comments and photocopied poems that occasionally grace the statue are usually somewhat lacking in wit. **Via del Governo Vecchio** leads west from here into one of Rome's liveliest quarters, the narrow streets noisy at night, and holding some of the city's most vigorous restaurants and bars.

Chiesa Nuova

Just off Via del Governo Vecchio, back on Corso Vittorio Emanuele, the **Chiesa Nuova** is another highly ornate Baroque church, in contrast to its founder, St Philip Neri – an ascetic man who tended the poor and sick in the streets around here for most of his life. Neri died in 1595, after a relatively normal day of saintly tasks – his last words were "Last of all, we must die" – and was canonized in 1622, and this large church, as well as being his last resting-place (he lies in the chapel to the left of the apse), is his principal memorial. Inside, its main features include three paintings by Rubens hung at the high altar, centring on the *Virgin with Angels*, and, perhaps more obviously, Pietro da Cortona's ceiling paintings, showing the *Ascension of the Virgin* in the apse, and, above the nave, the construction of the church and Neri's famous "vision of fire", which he experienced in 1544.

Piazza Campo de' Fiori and around

At the southern end of Piazza della Cancelleria, in front of the palace, is one of several entrances to **Piazza Campo de' Fiori**, in many ways Rome's most appealing square, home to a lively **fruit and vegetable market** (Mon–Sat 8am–1pm), and flanked by restaurants and cafés. No one really knows how the square came by its name, which means "field of flowers", but one theory holds that it was derived from the Roman Campus Martius, which used to cover most of this part of town; another claims it is after Flora, the mistress of Pompey, whose theatre used to stand on what is now the northeast corner of the square

– a huge complex by all accounts, which stretched right over to Largo Argentina. You can still see the foundations in the basement of the *Da Pancrazio* restaurant, on the tiny Piazza del Biscione, and the semicircular Via di Grotta Pinta retains the rounded shape of the theatre. Later, Campo de' Fiori was an important point on papal processions between the Vatican and the major basilicas of Rome (notably San Giovanni in Laterano) and a site of public executions. The most notorious killing here is commemorated by the statue of **Giordano Bruno** in the middle of the square. Bruno was a late-sixteenth-century freethinker who followed the teachings of Copernicus and was denounced to the Inquisition; his trial lasted for years under a succession of different popes, and finally, when he refused to renounce his philosophical beliefs, he was burned at the stake.

Palazzo Farnese

Just south of Campo de' Fiori, **Piazza Farnese** is a quite different square, with great fountains spurting out of lilies – the Farnese emblem – into marble tubs brought from the Baths of Caracalla, and the sober bulk of the **Palazzo Farnese** itself, begun in 1514 by Antonio di Sangallo the Younger and finished off after the architect's death by Michelangelo, who added the top tier of windows and cornice. The building now houses the French Embassy and is closed to the public, which is a pity, since it holds what has been called the greatest of all Baroque ceiling paintings, Annibale Carracci's *Loves of the Gods*, finished in 1603. However, newly restored, even from the outside it's a tremendously elegant and powerful building; indeed, of all the fabulous locations that Rome's embassies enjoy, this has got to be the best.

Galleria Spada

Make do instead with the Palazzo Spada, back towards Via Arenula at Piazza Capo di Ferro 3, and the **Galleria Spada** inside (Tues–Sat 8.30am–7.30pm, Sun 8.30am–6.30pm; L10,000/€5.17) guided tours every hour, on the hour, included in the price); walk right through the courtyard to the back of the building. Its four rooms, decorated in the manner of a Roman noble family, aren't spectacularly interesting unless you're a connoisseur of seventeenth- and eighteenth-century Italian painting. But there are two portraits of the cardinal Bernadino Spada by Reni and Guercino, alongside works by the odd Italian-influenced Dutch artist (Van Scorel, Honthorst), and, among bits and pieces of Roman statuary, a seated philosopher, and the building itself is a treat: its facade is frilled with stucco adornments, and, left off the small courtyard, there's a crafty trompe l'oeil by Borromini – a tunnel whose actual length is multiplied about four times through the architect's tricks with perspective – though to see this you have to wait for one of the guided tours.

Via Giulia

Behind the Farnese and Spada palaces, **Via Giulia**, which runs parallel to the Tiber, was built by Julius II to connect Ponte Sisto with the Vatican. The street was conceived as the centre of papal Rome, and Julius commissioned Bramante to line it with imposing palaces. Bramante didn't get very far with the plan, as Julius was soon succeeded by Leo X, but the street became a popular residence for wealthier Roman families, and is still packed full with stylish *palazzi* and antique shops and as such makes for a nice wander, with features like the playful **Fontana del Mascherone** to tickle your interest along the way.

The Jewish Ghetto and around

By way of contrast, cross over to the far side of Via Arenula and you're in what was once the city's **Jewish Ghetto**, a crumbling area of narrow, switchback streets and alleys, easy to lose your way in, and with a lingering sense of age. There was a Jewish population in Rome as far back as the second century BC, and with the accruing of Middle Eastern colonies, their numbers eventually swelled to around 40,000. Revolts in the colonies led to a small tax on Jews and a special census and they were effectively ghettoized here in the mid-sixteenth century when Pope Paul IV issued a series of punitive laws that forced them into what was then one of Rome's most squalid districts: a wall was built around the area and all Jews, in a chilling omen of things to come, were made to wear yellow caps and shawls when they left the district. Later, after Unification, the ghetto was opened up, and although the Nazi occupation brought the inevitable deportations, the majority of Rome's Jewish population survived, and currently numbers 16,000 (around half Italy's total). This is nowadays, however, spread all over the city, and a couple of kosher restaurants and butchers are pretty much all that remains to mark this out from any other quarter of the city.

Via Portico d'Ottavia

The main artery of the Jewish area is **Via Portico d'Ottavia**, which leads down to the **Portico d'Ottavia**, a not terribly well-preserved second-century BC gate, rebuilt by Augustus and dedicated to his sister in 23 BC, that was the entranceway to the adjacent **Teatro di Marcello**. This has served many purposes over the years: begun by Julius Caesar, finished by Augustus, it was pillaged in the fourth century and not properly restored until the Middle Ages, after which it became a formidable fortified palace for a succession of different rulers, including the Orsini family. The theatre has been recently restored and provides a grand backdrop for classical concerts in the summer. Crossing to the other side of Via Portico d'Ottavia, follow your nose to **Piazza Mattei**, whose **Fontana delle Tartarughe**, or "turtle fountain", is a delightful late-sixteenth-century creation, perhaps restored by Bernini.

The Synagogue

The Ghetto's principal Jewish sight is the huge **Synagogue** by the river (Mon–Thurs 9am–4pm, Fri 9am–2pm, Sun 9am–noon; closed Sat & Jewish holidays; L10,000/€5.17), built in 1904 and very much dominating all around with its bulk – not to mention the carabinieri who stand guard 24 hours a day outside, ever since a PLO attack on the building in 1982. The only way to see the building is on one of the short guided tours it runs in English, afterwards taking in the small two-room museum. The interior of the building is impressive, rising to a high, rainbow-hued dome, and the tours, which are included in the price and leave very regularly, are excellent, giving good background on the building and Rome's Jewish community in general.

Piazza Bocca della Verità and around

Further along the river from the Synagogue lies **Piazza Bocca della Verità**, home to two of the city's better-preserved Roman temples – the **Temple of Portunus** and the **Temple of Hercules Victor**, long known as the temple of Vesta because, like all vestal temples, it is circular. Both date from the end of the second century BC, and although you can't get inside, they're actually fine examples of republican-era places of worship; and the Temple of Hercules Victor is, for what it's worth, the oldest surviving marble structure in Rome. More interesting is the church of **Santa Maria in Cosmedin** on the far side of the square (daily 9am–noon & 3–5pm), a typically Roman medieval basilica with a huge marble altar and a colourful and ingenious Cosmati-work marble mosaic floor – one of the city's finest. Outside in the portico, and giving the square its name, is the **Bocca della Verità** (Mouth of Truth), an ancient Roman drain cover in the shape of an enormous face that in medieval times would apparently swallow the hand of anyone who hadn't told the truth. It was particularly popular with husbands anxious to test the faithfulness of their wives; now it is one of the city's biggest tour-bus attractions. On the northern side, the square peters out peacefully at the stolid **Arch of Janus**, perhaps Rome's most weathered triumphal arch, beyond which the campanile of the church of **San Giorgio in Velabro** (daily 10am–12.30pm & 4–6.30pm) is a stunted echo of that of Santa Maria across the way. Inside, recently opened after a major restoration, this is one of the city's barest and most beautiful ancient basilicas, only the late-twelfth-century fresco in the apse, the work of Pietro Cavallini, lightens the melancholy mood. Cavallini's fresco shows Christ and His mother, and various saints, including St George on the left, to whom the church is dedicated – and whose cranial bones lie in the reliquary under the high altar canopy, placed here in 749 AD, shortly after the original basilica was built.

Isola Tiberina

Back by the river, you can see the remains of **Ponte Rotto** (Broken Bridge) – all that remains of the first stone bridge to span the river. Built between 179 and 142 BC, it collapsed at the end of the sixteenth century. Further upstream is **Ponte Fabricio**, which crosses to **Isola Tiberina**. Built in 62 BC, it's the only classical bridge to remain intact without help from the restorers (the Ponte Cestio, on the other side of the island, was partially rebuilt in the last century). As for the island, it's a calm respite from the city centre proper, its originally tenth-century church of **San Bartolomeo** worth a peep on the way across the river to Trastevere, especially if you're into modern sculpture – Padre Martini, a well-known local sculptor, used to live on the island, and the church holds some wonderful examples of his elegant, semi-abstract religious pieces.

East of Via del Corso

The triangular area on the **eastern side of Via del Corso**, bound by Piazza del Popolo, the Corso, the edge of the Villa Borghese and Piazza di Spagna, is travellers' Rome, historically the artistic quarter of the city, for which eighteenth- and nineteenth-century Grand Tourists would make in search of the colourful, exotic city. Keats and Giorgio de Chirico are just two of those who used to live on Piazza di Spagna; Goethe had lodgings along Via del Corso; and institutions like *Caffè Greco* and *Babington's Tea Rooms* were the meeting-places of a local artistic and expat community for close on a couple of centuries. Today these institutions have given ground to more latter-day traps for the tourist dollar: American Express and *McDonald's* have settled into the area, while Via dei Condotti and around is these days strictly international designer territory, with some of Rome's fanciest stores; the local residents are more likely to be investment bankers than artists or poets. But the air of a Rome being discovered, even colonized, by foreigners persists, even if most of them hanging out on the Spanish Steps are mostly flying-visit InterRailers.

Piazza di Spagna and the Keats-Shelley Memorial House

Via del Babuino leads down from Piazza del Popolo to **Piazza di Spagna**, a long straggle of a square almost entirely enclosed by buildings and centring on the distinctive boat-shaped **Barcaccia** fountain, the last work of Bernini's father. It apparently remembers the great flood of Christmas Day 1598, when a barge from the Tiber was washed up on the slopes of Pincio Hill here. At the southern end of the square, a **column** commemorates Pius IX's official announcement, in 1854, of the dogma of the Immaculate Conception.

Fronting the square, opposite the fountain, is the house where the poet John Keats died in 1821. It now serves as the **Keats-Shelley Memorial House** (Mon–Fri 9am–1pm & 3–6pm, Sat 11am–6pm; L5000/€2.58), an archive of English-language literary and historical works and a museum of manuscripts and literary mementos relating to the Keats circle of the early nineteenth century – namely the poet himself, Shelley and Mary Shelley, and Byron (who at one time lived across the square). Among many bits of manuscript, letters and the like, there's a silver scallop shell reliquary containing locks of Milton's and Elizabeth Barrett Browning's hair, while Keats's death mask, stored in the room where he died, captures a resigned grimace. Keats didn't really enjoy his time in Rome, referring to it as his "posthumous life": he was tormented by his love for Fanny Browne, and he spent months in pain before he finally died, confined to the rooming house with his artist friend Joseph Severn, to whom he remarked that he could already feel "the flowers growing over him".

The Spanish Steps
As for the **Spanish Steps**, which sweep down in a cascade of balustrades and balconies beside the house, the only Spanish thing about them is the fact that they lead down to the Spanish Embassy, which also gave the piazza its name. In the last century they were the hangout of young hopefuls waiting to be chosen as artists' models; nowadays the scene is not much changed, as the venue for international posing and fast pick-ups late into the summer nights. At the top is the **Trinità dei Monti**, a largely sixteenth-century church designed by Carlo Maderno and paid for by the French king. Its rose-coloured Baroque facade overlooks the rest of Rome from its hilltop site, and it's worth clambering up just for the views. But while here you may as well pop your head around the door for a couple of faded works by Daniele da Volterra, notably a soft flowing fresco of *The Assumption* in the third chapel on the right, which includes a portrait of his teacher Michelangelo, and a poorly lit *Deposition* across the nave. Poussin considered the latter, which was probably painted from a series of cartoons by Michelangelo, as the world's third greatest painting (Raphael's *Transfiguration* was, he thought, the best).

Piazza Barberini
From the church you can either continue left along past the Villa Medici, now housing the French Academy, to the Pincio terrace and the gardens of the Villa Borghese (see p.719), or head south down Via Sistina to **Piazza Barberini**, a frenetic traffic junction at the top end of the busy shopping street of Via del Tritone – named after Bernini's **Fontana del Tritone**, which gushes a high jet of water in the centre of the square. Traditionally, this was the Barberini quarter of the city, a family who were the greatest patrons of Gian Lorenzo Bernini, and the sculptor's works in their honour are thick on the ground around here. He finished the Tritone fountain in 1644, going on shortly after to design the **Fontana delle Api** ("Fountain of the Bees") at the bottom end of Via Veneto. Unlike the Tritone fountain you could walk right past this, a smaller, quirkier work, its broad scallop shell studded with the bees that were the symbol of the Barberinis.

Santa Maria della Concezione: the Capuchin Cemetery
A little way up Via Veneto, the Capuchin church of **Santa Maria della Concezione** was another sponsored creation of the Barberini, though it's not a particularly significant building in itself, only numbering Guido Reni's androgynous *St Michael Trampling on the Devil* among its treasures. The devil in the picture is said to be a portrait of Innocent X, whom the artist despised and who was apparently a sworn enemy of the Barberini family. But the **Capuchin cemetery** (Mon–Wed & Fri–Sun 9am–noon & 3–6pm; compulsory "donation"), on the right of the church, is one of the more macabre and bizarre sights of Rome. Here, the bones of 4000 monks are set into the walls of a series of chapels, a monument to "Our Sister of Bodily Death", in the words of St Francis, that was erected in 1793. The bones appear in abstract or Christian patterns or

as fully clothed skeletons, their faces peering out of their cowls in various twisted expressions of agony – somewhere between the chilling and the ludicrous.

Via Veneto
Via Veneto, which bends north from Piazza Barberini up to the southern edge of the Borghese gardens, is a cool, materialistic antidote to the murky atmosphere of the Capuchin grotto. The pricey bars and restaurants lining the street were once the haunt of Rome's Beautiful People, made famous by Fellini's *La Dolce Vita*, but they left a long time ago, and Via Veneto isn't really any different from other busy streets in central Rome – a pretty tree-lined road, but with a fair share of high-class tack trying to cash in on departed glory.

Via Rasella
Just off to the right of Via Veneto, **Via Rasella** was the scene of an ambush of a Nazi military patrol in 1944 that led to one of the worst Italian wartime atrocities – the reprisal massacre of 35 innocent Romans at the Ardeatine Caves outside the city walls. A memorial (see p.1104) now stands on the sight of the executions, and the event is commemorated every March 24.

Palazzo Barberini
On the other side of Piazza Barberini, the **Palazzo Barberini**, at Via Barberini 18, is home to the **Galleria di Arte Antica** (April–Oct Tues–Sat 9am–7pm, Sun 9am–8pm; Nov–March Tues–Fri 9am–5pm, Sat & Sun 9am–1pm; L12,000/€6.20 or for details of combined ticket, see box on p.691), consisting of a rich patchwork of mainly Italian art from the early Renaissance to late Baroque period. The building alone is worth the entrance fee, the epitome of Baroque grandeur, with a first-floor *salone* frescoed by Pietro da Cortona in one of the best examples of exuberant trompe l'oeil work there is – a manic rendering of *The Triumph of Divine Providence* that almost crawls down the walls to meet you. Broadly speaking, the collection proceeds chronologically across three floors of the building, starting with the first floor and ending on the third. Across the hall from the *salone*, the first floor displays early Renaissance works, notably Fra' Filippo Lippi's warmly maternal *Madonna and Child*, a richly coloured and beautifully composed *Annunciation* by the same artist, and Raphael's beguiling *Fornarina*, a painting of the daughter of a Travesteran baker thought to have been Raphael's mistress (Raphael's name appears clearly on the woman's bracelet) – although some experts claim the painting to be the work of a pupil. Look out also, in nearby rooms, for Bronzino's portrait of Stefano Colonna and an anguished *St Jerome* by Tintoretto – full of interesting detail, and clever use of light and shade. Among the upstairs works, there is a famous painting of *Beatrice Cenci*, fomerly attributed to Guide Reni, which moved Shelley to write a play about her tragedy, and a portrait of *Henry VIII* by Hans Holbein which feels almost as well-known – probably because the painter produced so many of the monarch. It's a stark contrast to the rather ascetic figure of *Erasmus of Rotterdam* by Quentin Matsys, which hangs next to it.

San Carlo alle Quattro Fontane and the Palazzo del Quirinale
Continue on up Via delle Quattro Fontane and you're at a seventeenth-century landmark, the church of **San Carlo alle Quattro Fontane** (Mon–Fri 9am–12.30pm & 4–6pm, Sat 9am–12.30pm). This was Borromini's first real design commission, and in it he displays all the ingenuity he later became famous for, cramming the church elegantly into a tiny and awkwardly shaped site that apparently covers roughly the same surface area as one of the dome-supporting piers inside St Peter's. Tucked in beside the church, the newly restored cloister is also squeezed into a tight but elegant oblong,

topped with a charming balustrade. Outside the church are the four **fountains** that give the street and church their name, each cut into a niche in a corner of the crossroads that marks this, the highest point on the Quirinal Hill, while to the left the featureless wall of the **Palazzo del Quirinale** (open second & fourth Sun morning each month 8am–1pm; L10,000/€5.17), a sixteenth-century structure that was the official summer residence of the popes until Unification, when it became the royal palace. It's now the home of Italy's president, but you can appreciate its exceptional siting from the **Piazza del Quirinale** at the far end on the right, from which views stretch right across the centre of Rome. The main feature of the piazza is the huge statue of the **Dioscuri**, or Castor and Pollux – massive five-metre-high Roman copies of classical Greek statues, showing the two godlike twins, the sons of Jupiter, who according to legend won victory for the Romans in an important battle.

Fontana di Trevi
Via della Dataria winds down from Piazza del Quirinale into the tight web of narrow, apparently aimless streets below, bringing you shortly to one of Rome's more surprising sights, easy to stumble upon by accident – the **Fontana di Trevi**, a huge, very Baroque gush of water over statues and rocks built onto the backside of a Renaissance palace; it's fed by the same source that surfaces at the Barcaccia fountain in Piazza di Spagna. There was a Trevi fountain, designed by Alberti, around the corner in Via dei Crociferi, a smaller, more modest affair by all accounts, but Urban VIII decided to upgrade it in line with his other grandiose schemes of the time and employed Bernini, among others, to design an alternative. Work didn't begin, however, until 1732, when Niccolò Salvi won a competition held by Clement XII to design the fountain, and even then it took thirty years to finish the project. Salvi died in the process, his lungs shot by the time spent in the dank waterworks of the fountain. The Trevi fountain is now, of course, the place you come to chuck in a coin if you want to guarantee your return to Rome, though you might remember Anita Ekberg throwing herself into it in *La Dolce Vita* (there are police here to discourage you from doing the same thing). Newly restored, it's one of the city's most vigorous outdoor spots to hang out.

Galleria Colonna
A short stroll south from the Fontana di Trevi brings you to the **Galleria Colonna**, at Via della Pilotta 17 (Jan–July & Sept–Dec Sat 9am–1pm; L10,000/€5.17; English guided tours at 11am, included in the price), part of the Palazzo Colonna complex and, although outranked by many of the other Roman palatial collections, worth forty minutes or so if you happen by when it's open, if only for the chandelier-decked Great Hall where most of the paintings are displayed. Best on the whole is the gallery's collection of landscapes by Dughet (Poussin's brother-in-law), but other works that stand out are Carracci's early – and unusually spontaneous – *Bean Eater* (though this attribution has been questioned), a *Narcissus* by Tintoretto and a *Portrait of a Venetian Gentleman* caught in supremely confident pose by Veronese.

The Roman Forums and the Palatine Hill

From Piazza Venezia **Via dei Fori Imperiali** cuts south through the heart of Rome's ancient sites, a soulless boulevard imposed on the area by Mussolini in 1932. Before then this was a warren of medieval streets that wound around the ruins of the ancient city centre, but as with the Via della Conciliazione up to St Peter's the Duce preferred to build something to his own glory rather than preserve that of another era. There is a long-standing plan to make this entire ancient part of the city into a huge archeological park which would stretch right down to the catacombs on the Via Appia Antica.

However, although excavations have been undertaken in recent years, they are continuing slowly. For the moment, if you want tranquil sightseeing you'll have to settle for coming on Sunday, when a long stretch from Piazza Venezia to Via Appia Antica is closed to traffic and pedestrians take to the streets to stroll past the ruins of the ancient city.

The Imperial Forums and around

One of the major victims of Mussolini's redesign was the **Forum of Trajan** on the north side of the road, a complex of basilicas, monuments, apartments and shops that was in its day the most sumptuous of the imperial forums, built here after the Forum proper had become too small at what was probably the very pinnacle of Roman power and prestige. It's currently fairly unrecognizable, the main section no more than a sunken area of scattered columns to the left of the road, fronting the semicircle of **Markets of Trajan** (summer Tues–Sat 9am–6pm, Sun 9am–1.30pm; winter Tues–Sat 9am–4pm, Sun 9am–1.30pm; L7000/€3.62), a tiered ancient Roman shopping centre that's also accessible from Via IV Novembre. Down below the markets, the Basilica Ulpia was a central part of the Forum of Trajan, an immense structure, now mostly hidden below ground level. It had five aisles and a huge apse at either end, and measured 176 metres long by 59 metres wide. At the head of the basilica, the enormous **Column of Trajan** was erected to celebrate the emperor's victories in Dacia (modern Romania) in 112 AD, and is covered top to bottom with reliefs commemorating the highlights of the campaign. The carving on the base shows the trophies brought back and there's an inscription saying that the column was dedicated by the Senate and People of Rome in 113 AD in honour of Trajan. Behind the Forum of Trajan, the **Torre delle Milizie** is fondly imagined to be the tower from which Nero watched Rome burning, although it's actually a twelfth-century fortification left over from days when Rome was divided into warring factions within the city walls.

The Roman Forum

The **Roman Forum** (summer Tues–Sat 9am–6pm, Sun 9am–1pm; winter Tues–Sat 9am–3pm, Sun 9am–1pm; free) is very near the top of most visitors' things to see in Rome. However, for many it's also one of the city's most disappointing sights, and you need an imagination and some small grasp of history to really appreciate the place at all. Certainly it holds some of the most ruined Roman ruins you'll see: the area was abandoned (and looted) for so long that very little is anything like intact. But these five or so acres were once the heart of the Mediterranean world, and are a very real and potent testament to a power that held a large chunk of the earth in its thrall for close on five centuries and whose influence reverberates right up to the present day – in language, in architecture, in political terms and systems, even in the romance that the last couple of hundred years have lent to its ruins.

Even in ancient times Rome was a very large city, stretching out as far as the Aurelian Wall in many places in a sprawl of apartment blocks or *insulae*. But the Forum was its centre, home to its political and religious institutions, its shops and market stalls, and a meeting-place for all and sundry – which it remained until the Imperial era, when Rome's increased importance as a world power led to the extensions nearby. The Forum never really recovered from this: neglect set in, a fire in the third century AD destroyed many of the buildings, and although the damage was repaired, Rome was by this time in a general state of decay, the coming of Christianity only serving to accelerate the process, particularly with regard to its pagan temples and institutions. After the later downfall of the city to various barbarian invaders, the area was left in ruin, its relics quarried for the construction in other parts of Rome during medieval and Renaissance times and the odd church or tower being constructed *in situ* out of the more viable piles. Excavation of the site didn't start until the beginning of the nineteenth century, since when it has continued pretty much without stopping: you'll notice a fair part of the site, especially up on the Palatine, closed off for further digs.

The **Via Sacra** runs directly through the core of the Forum, from below the Capitoline Hill in the west to the far eastern extent of the site and the Arch of Titus (where there's a handy exit for the Colosseum, see p.711). It was the best-known street of ancient Rome, along which victorious emperors and generals would ride in procession to give thanks at the Capitoline's Temple of Jupiter. The steps that line it just inside the main entrance are part of the **Regia**, or house of the kings, an extremely ancient group of foundations that date probably from the reign of the second King of Rome, Numa, who ruled from 715 to 673 BC. There was a shrine of Mars here, housing the shields and spears of Mars, which generals embarking on a war rattled before setting off. If the shields and spears rattled of their own accord it was a bad omen, requiring purification and repentance rites. The Regia later became the residence of Julius Caesar, who moved in here in 45 BC – an imperious act which at least in part led to his downfall. Opposite the Regia, the Temple of Antoninus and Faustina is the best-preserved temple in the forum, mainly because of its preservation since the seventh century as the church of **San Lorenzo in Miranda**. Next to the Regia, the pile of rubble with the little green roof is all that remains of the grandeur and magnificence that comprised the **temple to Julius Caesar** – the round brick stump under the roof marks the spot where Caesar was cremated, and around which the temple was built. The football pitch of broken columns to the right of the Via Sacra marks the site of the **Basilica Emilia**, built in the second century BC to house law courts, and, in the little booths and boutiques flanking it on the Via Sacra side, money-changers. Close by, a little marble plaque dedicated to **Venus Cloacina** marks the site of a small shrine dedicated to Venus where the Cloaca Maxima canal drained the Forum, which was originally marsh-land. The Cloaca Maxima reaches all the way to the Tiber from here, and still keeps the area drained.

A little way beyond, the large cube-shaped building is the **Curia**, built on the orders of Julius Caesar, although what you see now is a Diocletian reconstruction. One of the few whole structures left in the Forum, the Senate met here during the Republican period, and augurs would come to announce the wishes of the gods. Inside, three wide stairs rise left and right, on which about 300 senators could be accommodated with their folding chairs. In the centre is the speaker's platform, with a porphyry statue of a togaed figure. Otherwise, apart from the floor, elegantly patterned in red, yellow, green and white marble, there's not much left of its ancient decor, only the grey and white marble facing each side of the speaker's platform, which would once have covered the entire hall.

Immediately outside the Curia, the black, fenced-off paving of the **Lapis Niger** marks the traditional site of the tomb of Romulus, the steps beneath (usually closed) leading down to a monument that was considered sacred ground during classical times. To the right, the **Arch of Septimius Severus** was constructed in the early third century AD by his sons Caracalla and Galba to mark their father's victories in what is now Iran. The friezes on it recall Severus and his son Caracalla, who ruled Rome with a reign of undisciplined terror for seven years. There's a space where Galba was commemorated – Caracalla had him executed in 213AD, and his name expediently removed from the arch altogether.

To the left of the arch, the low brown wall is the **Rostra**, facing the wide-open scatter of paving, dumped stones and beached columns that makes up the central portion of the Forum, the place where most of the life of the city was carried on, and which, in ancient times, was usually crowded with politicians, tribunes and traders. Left of the Rostra, are the long stairs of the **Basilica Julia**, built by Julius Caesar in the 50s BC after he returned from the Gallic wars. A bit further along, on the right, the guard rails lead into a kind of alcove in the pavement, which marks the site of the **Lacus Curtius**

– the spot where, according to legend, a chasm opened during the earliest days and the soothsayers determined that it would only be closed once Rome had sacrificed its most valuable possession into it. Marcus Curtius, a Roman soldier who declared that Rome's most valuable possession was a loyal citizen, hurled himself and his horse into the void and it duly closed. Around the corner to the right, the enormous pile of rubble topped by three graceful Corinthinan columns is the **Temple of Castor and Pollux**, the Forum's oldest temple, dedicated in 484 BC to the divine twins or Dioscuri, the offspring of Jupiter by Leda, who appeared miraculously to ensure victory for the Romans in a key battle. The story goes that a group of Roman citizens were gathered around a water fountain on this spot fretting about the war, when Castor and Pollux appeared and reassured them that the battle was won – hence the temple, and their adoption as the protectors of Rome.

Beyond here, the **House of the Vestal Virgins** is a second-century AD reconstruction of a building originally built by Nero. Vesta was the Roman goddess of the hearth and home, and her cult was an important one in ancient Rome. Her temple was in the charge of the famed vestal virgins, who had the responsibility of keeping the sacred flame of Vesta alight, and were obliged to remain chaste for the thirty years that they served (they usually started at around age ten). If the flame should go out, the woman responsible was scourged; if she should lose her chastity, she was buried alive (her male partner-in-crime was flogged to death in front of the Curia). A vestal virgin could resign her post if she wished, and she had the benefit of residing in a very comfortable palace: four floors of rooms around a central courtyard, with the round **Temple of Vesta** at the near end. The rooms are mainly ruins now, though they're fairly recognizable on the Palatine side, and you can get a good sense of the shape of the place from the remains of the courtyard, still with its pool in the centre and fringed by the statues or inscribed pedestals of the women themselves.

Opposite the vestals' house, the curved facade of the **Temple of Romulus** (the son of the emperor Maxentius), dating from 309 AD, has been sanctified and serves as vestibule for the church of **Santi Cosma e Damiano** behind. Just past the temple, a shady walkway to the left leads up to the **Basilica of Maxentius**, which rises up towards the main road – in terms of size and ingenuity probably the Forum's most impressive remains. By the early fourth century, when this structure was built, Roman architects and engineers were expert at building with poured cement. Begun by Maxentius, it was continued by his co-emperor and rival, Constantine, after he had defeated him at the Battle of the Milvian Bridge in 312 AD. It's said that Michelangelo studied the hexagonal coffered arches here when grappling with the dome of St Peter's, and apparently Renaissance architects frequently used its apse and arches as a model.

Back on the Via Sacra, past the church of Santa Maria Nova, the **Antiquarium of the Forum** (daily except Mon 9am–5pm; free) houses a collection of statue fragments, capitals, tiles, mosaics and other bits and pieces. From the basilica the Via Sacra climbs more steeply to the **Arch of Titus**, which stands commandingly on a low arm of the Palatine Hill, looking one way down the remainder of the Via Sacra to the Colosseum, and back over the Forum proper. The arch was built by Titus's brother, Domitian, after the emperor's death in 81 AD, to commemorate his victories in Judea in 70 AD, and his triumphal return from that campaign. It's a much restored structure, and you can see, in reliefs on the inside, scenes of Titus riding in a chariot with Nike, goddess of Victory, being escorted by representatives of the Senate and Plebs, and, on the opposite side, spoils being removed from the Temple in Jerusalem. It's a long-standing tradition that Jews don't pass under this arch.

The Palatine Hill

Turning right at the Arch of Titus takes you up to the ticket booth and entrance to the **Palatine Hill** (summer Tues–Sat 9am–6pm, Sun 9am–1pm; winter Tues–Sat

9am–3pm, Sun 9am–1pm; L12,000/€6.20 or for details of combined ticket, see box on p.691, last tickets 1hr before closing), supposedly where the city of Rome was founded and holding some of its most ancient remnants. In a way it's a more pleasant site to tour than the Forum, larger, greener and more of a park – a good place to have a picnic and relax after the rigours of the ruins below. In the days of the Republic, the Palatine was the most desirable address in Rome (from it is derived our word "palace"), and the big names continued to colonize it during the imperial era, trying to outdo each other with ever larger and more magnificent dwellings.

Following the main path up from the Forum, the **Domus Flavia** was one of the most splendid residences, and, although it's now almost completely ruined, the peristyle is easy enough to identify, with its fountain and hexagonal brick arrangement in the centre. To the left, the top level of the gargantuan **Domus Augustana** spreads to the far brink of the hill – not the home of Augustus as its name suggests, but the private house of any emperor (or "Augustus"). You can look down from here on its vast central courtyard with maze-like fountain and wander to the brink of the deep trench of the **Stadium**. On the far side of the stadium, the ruins of the **Baths of Septimius Severus** cling to the side of the hill, the terrace giving good views over the Colosseum and the churches of the Celian Hill opposite.

Walking in the opposite direction from the Domus Flavia, steps lead down to the **Cryptoporticus** (closed for restoration), a long passage built by Nero to link the vestibule of his Domus Aurea with the Domus Augustana and other Palatine palaces, and decorated along part of its length with well-preserved Roman stucco-work. You can go either way along the passage: a left turn leads to the **House of Livia**, originally believed to have been the residence of Livia, the wife of Augustus, though now identified as simply part of Augustus's house (the set of ruins beyond). Its courtyard and some of the inner rooms are decorated with scanty frescoes.

Turn right down the passage and up some steps on the left and you're in the **Farnese Gardens**, among the first botanical gardens in Europe, laid out by Cardinal Alessandro Farnese in the mid-sixteenth century and now a tidily planted, shady retreat from the exposed heat of the ruins. The terrace here looks back over the Forum, while the terrace at the opposite end looks down on the church of San Teodoro, across to St Peter's, and down on the new excavations immediately below – the traces of an **Iron Age village** that perhaps marks the real centre of Rome's ancient beginnings. The large grey building here houses the Palatine **Antiquarium** (free), which contains a vast assortment of statuary, pottery, terracotta antefixes and architectural fragments that have been excavated on the Palatine during the last 150 years. Much like the Forum Antiquarium, its most interesting exhibits are the very oldest, including models of how the Palatine looked in the Iron Age.

The Colosseum, Celian Hill and beyond

Leaving the Forum by way of the Via Sacra, under the Arch of Titus, you see the huge **Arch of Constantine** to your right, placed here in the early decades of the fourth century AD after Constantine had consolidated his power as sole emperor. The arch demonstrates the deterioration of the arts during the late stages of the Roman Empire, in that there were hardly any sculptors around good enough to produce original work and most of the sculptural decoration here had to be removed from other monuments.

Across from here, the **Colosseum** (summer Tues–Sat 9am–6pm, Sun 9am–1pm; winter Tues–Sat 9am–3pm, Sun 9am–1pm; L10,000/€5.17 or for details of combined ticket, see box on p.691) is perhaps Rome's most awe-inspiring ancient monument, and one which – unlike the Forum – needs little historical knowledge or imagination to deduce its function. Originally known as the Flavian Amphitheatre (the name Colosseum is a much later invention), it was begun around 72 AD by the Emperor

Vespasian, who was anxious to extinguish the memory of Nero, and so chose the site of Nero's outrageous Domus Aurea (see p.714) for the stadium; the Colosseum is sited on a lake that lay in front of the vestibule of the palace, where Nero had erected a statue of himself as sun god. The lake was drained, and the Colosseum was – incredibly, given the size of the project – inaugurated by Vespasian's son Titus about eight years later, an event celebrated by 100 days of continuous games; it was finally completed by Domitian, Titus's brother, the third of the Flavian emperors. It is said that seventy thousand Hebrew slaves did the heavy work at the Colosseum. Fifty thousand cartloads of pre-cut travertine stone were hauled from the quarries at Tivoli, a distance of seventeen miles. In the depths of what must have been the muddy bottom of the lake, a labyrinth was laid out, walling in passages for the contestants and creating areas for assembling and storing scenery and other requirements for gladiatorial contests.

The overall structure was tastefully designed, with close attention paid to decoration. On the outside, the arena's three arcades rose in strict classical fashion – with Ionic, topped by Doric, topped by Corinthian, columns – to a flat surface at the top punctuated only by windows, where there was a series of supports for masts that protruded at the upper limit. These masts, 240 in total, were used to array a canvas awning over the spectators inside the arena. Inside, beyond the corridors that led up to the seats, lavishly decorated with painted stuccoes, there was room for a total of around 60,000 people seated and 10,000 or so standing; and the design is such that all 70,000 could enter and be seated in a matter of minutes – surely a lesson for designers of modern stadiums. The seating was allocated on a strict basis, with the emperor and his attendants naturally occupying the best seats in the house, and the social class of the spectators diminishing as you got nearer the top. There were no ticket sales as we conceive of them; rather, tickets were distributed through – and according to the social status of – Roman heads of households. These "tickets" were in fact wooden tags, with the entrance, row, aisle and seat number carved on them. Inside the amphitheatre, the labyrinth below was covered over with a wooden floor, punctuated at various places for trap doors which could be opened as required and lifts to raise and lower the animals that were to take part in the games. The floor was covered with canvas to make it waterproof and the canvas was covered with several centimetres of sand to absorb blood; in fact, our word "arena" is derived from the Latin word for sand.

The Celian Hill

Some of the animals that were to die in the Colosseum were kept in a zoo up on the **Celian Hill**, just behind the arena, the furthest south of Rome's seven hills and probably its most peaceful, still clothed almost entirely in woodland and with the park of **Villa Celimontana** at its heart. You can get in here by way of the entrance on **Piazza della Navicella**, a little way down Via Claudia, and you could do worse than take a stroll through, before moving on to a couple of worthwhile churches. Continuing up to the summit of the hill, you'll come to the church of **Santi Giovanni e Paolo** (daily 8.30am–noon & 3.30–6.30pm), marked by its colourful campanile and set in a once-peaceful square that's been invaded by adolescent autograph hunters since Silvio Berlusconi's TV studios moved in opposite. Originally founded by a Roman senator called Pammachius, the church is in a way a memorial to conscientious objection, dedicated to two dignitaries in the court of Constantine who were beheaded here in 361 AD after refusing military service. The relics of their house are downstairs, although this is currently closed for restoration – around twenty rooms in all, frescoed with pagan and Christian subjects. Inside the church, the railed-off square in mid-nave marks the shrine where the saints were martyred and buried.

From the church the road descends under a succession of brick arches to the church of **San Gregorio Magno** on the left (daily 9am–noon & 3–6.30pm), in a commanding position above the traffic drone of the road below, and looking over to the lollipop pines of the Palatine Hill opposite. Again, it's the story behind the church that's most interesting. It was from here that St Gregory dispatched St Augustine in the early seventh century to convert England to Christianity, and although the rather ordinary Baroque interior shows little evidence of it, the chapel of the saint does have a beautifully carved altar showing scenes from his life, and there's a room containing his marble throne. More impressive is the structure to the left of the church, made up of three chapels and surrounded by cypress trees. **Santa Silvia** and **Sant'Andrea** contain **frescoes** by Guido Reni, Domenichino and Pomarancio, while **Santa Barbara** treasures the table at which St Gregory fed twelve paupers daily with his own hands for years.

San Clemente

From the Colosseum, it's a short walk east down Via San Giovanni in Laterano to the church of **San Clemente** (Mon–Sat 9am–12.30pm & 3–6pm, Sun opens 10am), a cream-coloured twelfth-century basilica that encapsulates perhaps better than any other the continuity of history in the city – being in fact a conglomeration of three places of worship. The ground-floor church is a superb example of a medieval basilica: its facade and courtyard face east in the archaic fashion, and there are some fine, warm mosaics in the apse and a chapel with frescoes by Masolino. Downstairs (same hours as church; L4000/€2.07) there's the nave of an earlier church, dated back to 392 AD, with a frescoed narthex depicting, among other things, the *Miracle of San Clemente*. And at the eastern end of this church, steps lead down to a third level: a labyrinthine set of rooms including a dank Mithraic temple of the late second century, set among several rooms of a Roman house built after the fire of 64 AD. In the temple is preserved a statue of Mithras slaying the bull and the seats upon which the worshippers sat during their ceremonies. The underground river that formerly fed the lake in front of the Domus Aurea can be heard rushing to its destination in the Tiber, behind the Circo Massimo, a reminder that Rome is built on very shaky foundations indeed.

San Giovanni in Laterano

Continuing down the same street brings you out eventually at the basilica of **San Giovanni in Laterano** (daily: summer 7am–7pm; winter 7am–6pm). Officially Rome's cathedral and the seat of the pope as bishop of Rome, this was for centuries the main papal residence. However, when the papacy returned from Avignon at the end of the fourteenth century, the Lateran palaces were in ruin and uninhabitable, and the pope moved across town to the Vatican, where he has remained ever since. There has been a church on this site since the fourth century, the first established by Constantine, and the present building, reworked by Borromini in the mid-seventeenth century, evokes – like San Clemente or San Stefano – Rome's staggering wealth of history, with a host of features from different periods. The doors to the church, oddly enough, were taken from the Curia of the Roman Forum.

The **interior** has been extensively reworked over the centuries. Much of what you see today dates from 1600, when Clement VIII had the church remodelled for that Holy Year. The first pillar on the left of the right-hand aisle shows a fragment of Giotto's fresco of Boniface VIII, proclaiming the first Holy Year in 1300. Further on, a more recent monument commemorates Sylvester I – "the magician pope", Bishop of Rome during much of Constantine's reign – and incorporates part of his original tomb, said to sweat and rattle its bones when a pope is about to die. Kept secure behind the papal altar are the heads of St Peter and St Paul, the church's prize relics. Outside, the **cloisters** (daily 9am–5pm; L4000/€2.07) are one of the most pleasing parts of the complex, decorated with early thirteenth-century Cosmati work and with fragments of the original basilica arranged around in no particular order, including a remarkable papal throne assembly and various papal artefacts (not least the vestments of Boniface VIII) in a room off to the side.

Adjoining the basilica is the **Lateran Palace**, home of the popes in the Middle Ages and also formally part of Vatican territory. Next door, the **Baptistry** (daily: summer 9am–1pm & 5–7pm; winter 9am–1pm & 4–6pm; free) has been carefully restored, along with the side of the church itself, after a car bombing in 1993. It is the oldest surviving baptistry in the Christian world, a mosaic-lined, octagonal structure built during the fifth century that has been the model for many such buildings since. There are more ancient remains on the other side of the church, on Piazza di Porta San Giovanni, foremost of which is the **Scala Santa** (daily 6.15am–12.15pm & 3.30–6.30pm), claimed to be the staircase from Pontius Pilate's house down which Christ walked after his trial. The 28 steps are protected by boards, and the only way you're allowed to climb them is on your knees, which pilgrims do regularly – although there is also a staircase to the side for the less penitent. At the top, the chapel of **San Lorenzo** holds an ancient (sixth- or seventh-century) painting of Christ said to be the work of an angel, hence its name – *acheiropoeton*, or "not done by human hands".

Santa Croce in Gerusalemme

Across the far side of the square, the **Porta Asinaria**, one of the city's grander gateways, marks the Aurelian Wall, which leads around on its city side by way of Viale Carlo Felice to another key Roman church, **Santa Croce in Gerusalemme**, one of the seven pilgrimage churches of Rome (daily 6am–noon & 3.30–7pm). Built on the site of the palace of Constantine's mother St Helena, it houses the relics of the true cross she had brought back from Jerusalem. The building is mainly Baroque in style following an eighteenth-century renovation, but the relics of the cross are stored in a surreal Mussolini-era chapel at the end of the left aisle, and there are some very fine Renaissance apse frescoes, recording the discovery of the fragments. North of here, towards the rail tracks, the **Porta Maggiore** is probably the most impressive of all the city gates, built in the first century AD to carry water into Rome from the aqueducts outside.

The Esquiline Hill, Termini and beyond

On the far side of the main road, Via Labacana, from the Colosseum, the **Esquiline Hill** is the highest and largest of the city's seven hills. Nowadays it's a mixed area, but one which almost every traveller to Rome encounters at some point – not just because of key sights like Nero's Domus Aurea and the basilica of Santa Maria Maggiore, and the grand developments of post-Unification Rome around Via Nazionale and Via XX Settembre, but also because of Stazione Termini, whose tawdry environs are home to the lion's share of Rome's budget hotels.

The Domus Aurea

One of the Esquiline Hill's most intriguing sights is without doubt Nero's **Domus Aurea** or "Golden House" (daily 9am–8pm, guided tours obligatory; L10,000/€5.17, plus L6000/€3.10 for the obligatory tour, plus L2000/€1.03 reservation fee – L18,000/€9.30 in total; booking recommended, ☎06.3974.9907). The entrance is off Via Labacana, in the Parco Oppio, almost opposite the Colosseum. Built on the summit of the Oppian and into its sides after a fire of 64 AD devastated this part of Rome, the "house" was a vast undertaking, but it was not intended to be a residence at all; rather it was a series of banqueting rooms, nymphaeums, small baths, terraces and gardens, facing what at the time was a small lake fed by the underground springs that drained from the surrounding hills. Rome was used to Nero's excesses, but it had never seen anything like the Golden House before. The facade was supposed to have been coated in solid gold, there was hot and cold running water in the baths, one of the dining rooms was rigged up to shower flowers and natural scent on guests, and the grounds – which covered a full square mile – held vineyards and game. Nero didn't get to enjoy his palace for long – he died a couple of years after it was finished, and Vespasian tore a lot of the exposed facade down in disgust, draining its lake and building the Colosseum on top. Later Trajan built his baths on top of the rest of the complex, and it was pretty much forgotten until its wall paintings were discovered by Renaissance artists, including Raphael. When these artists first visited these rooms, they had to descend down ladders into what they believed at first was some kind of mystical cave, or grotto – giving us the word *grotesque*, which they used to describe their attempts to imitate this style of painting in their own work. The guided tours take in various covered fountains, service corridors, terraces and, most spectacularly, the Octagonal Room – domed, with a hole in the middle, which is supposed to have rotated as the day progressed to emulate the passage of the sun. Most of the rooms are decorated with fanciful depictions of people looking out of windows at you, garlands of flowers, fruit, vines and foliage, interspersed with mythical animals. Perhaps the best-preserved frescoes are in the room of Achilles at Skyros, illustrating Homer's story of Achilles being sent to the island of Skyros disguised as a woman to prevent him being drawn into the Trojan wars.

San Pietro in Vincoli

Steps lead up from Colosseum metro station to Via Terme di Tito and left into Via Eudossia, which leads to the tranquil piazza of the recently restored church of **San Pietro in Vincoli** (daily 8am–12.30pm & 3.30–6pm) – one of Rome's most delightfully plain churches, built to house an important relic, the chains that held St Peter when he was in Jerusalem and those that held him in Rome, which miraculously joined together. The chains can still be seen in the *confessio* beneath the high altar, in a beautiful gold and rock crystal reliquary, but most people come for the tomb of Pope Julius II at the far end of the southern aisle, which occupied Michelangelo on and off for much of his career and was the cause of many a dispute with Julius and his successors. Michelangelo reluctantly gave it up to paint the Sistine Chapel, and never again found the time to return to it for very long, being always at the beck and call of successive popes – who understandably had little interest in promoting the glory of one of their predecessors. No one knows how the tomb would have looked had it been finished, and the only statues that Michelangelo completed are the Moses, Leah and Rachel, which remain here in the church, and two Slaves which are now in the Louvre. The figure of Moses, however, pictured as descended from Sinai to find the Israelites worshipping the golden calf, and flanked by the gentle figures of Leah and Rachel, is one of the artist's most captivating works, the rest of the composition – completed by later artists – seeming dull and static by comparison.

Via Cavour and Santa Maria Maggiore

Steps lead down from San Pietro in Vincoli to **Via Cavour**, a busy central thoroughfare which carves a route between the Colosseum and Termini station. After about half a kilometre the street widens to reveal the basilica of **Santa Maria Maggiore** (daily: summer 7am–7pm; winter 7am–6pm), one of the city's five great basilicas, and with one of Rome's best-preserved Byzantine interiors – a fact belied by its dull eighteenth-century exterior. Unlike the other great places of pilgrimage in Rome, Santa Maria Maggiore was not built on any special Constantinian site, but instead went up during the fifth century after the Council of Ephesus recognized the cult of the Virgin and churches venerating Our Lady began to spring up all over the Christian world. According to legend, the Virgin Mary appeared to Pope Liberius in a dream on the night of August 4, 352 AD, telling him to build a church on the Esquiline hill, on a spot where he would find a patch of newly fallen snow the next morning. The snow would outline exactly the plan of the church that should be built there in her honour – which of course is exactly what happened, and the first church here was called Santa Maria della Neve ("of the snow"). The present structure dates from about 420 AD, and was completed under the reign of St Sixtus III, and survives remarkably intact, the broad nave fringed on both sides with strikingly well-kept mosaics, most of which date from the church's construction and recount incidents from the Old Testament. The chapel in the right transept holds the elaborate tomb of Sixtus V – another, less famous, Sistine Chapel, and is decorated with frescoes and stucco reliefs portraying events from his reign. It also contains the tomb of another zealous and reforming pope, St Pius V, whose statue faces that of Sixtus. Outside the Sistine Chapel is the tomb slab of the Bernini family, including Gian Lorenzo himself, while opposite, the Pauline Chapel is even more sumptuous, home to the tombs of the Borghese pope, Paul V, and his immediate predecessor Clement VIII. The altar, of lapis lazuli and agate, contains a Madonna and Child dating from the twelfth or thirteenth century. Between the two chapels, the *confessio* contains a kneeling statue of Pope Pius IX, and, beneath it, a reliquary that is said to contain fragments of the crib of Christ, in rock crystal and silver. Finally, the thirteenth-century mosaics of *Christ Pantocrator and the Legend of the Snow*, in the loggia above the main entrance, are definitely worth a look (daily 9.30am–6pm; L5000/€2.58), but for L5000/€2.58, they're hardly a bargain.

Santa Prassede and Santa Pudenziana
Behind Santa Maria Maggiore, off Via Merulana, the ninth-century church of **Santa Prassede** occupies an ancient site, where it's claimed St Prassede harboured Christians on the run from the Roman persecutions. She apparently collected the blood and remains of the martyrs and placed them in a well where she herself was later buried; a red marble disc in the floor of the nave marks the spot. In the southern aisle, the Chapel of Saint Zeno was built by Pope Paschal I as a mausoleum for his mother, Theodora, and is decorated with marvellous ninth-century mosaics that make it glitter like a jewel-encrusted bowl. The chapel also contains a fragment of a column supposed to be the one to which Christ was tied when he was scourged. On the other side of Via Cavour, the church of **Santa Pudenziana** on Via Urbana has equally ancient origins, dedicated to St Prassede's supposed sister and for many years believed to have been built on the site where St Peter lived and worshipped – though this has since been entirely discredited. There were for years two relics in the church, the chair that St Peter used as his throne and the table at which he said Mass, though both have long gone – to the Vatican and the Lateran, respectively. But the church still has one feature of ancient origin, the superb fifth-century apse mosaics – some of the oldest Christian figurative mosaics in Rome, though they've been tampered with and restored over the years.

Via Nazionale and Piazza della Repubblica
A couple of minutes' walk northwest from Santa Maria Maggiore, **Via Nazionale** connects Piazza Venezia and the centre of town with the area around Termini and the eastern districts beyond. A focus for much development after Unification, its heavy, overbearing buildings were constructed to give Rome some semblance of modern sophistication when it became capital of the new country, but most are now occupied by hotels and bland shops and boutiques. At the top of Via Nazionale, **Piazza della Repubblica** – formerly Piazza Esedra – is typical of Rome's nineteenth-century regeneration, a stern, once dignified but now rather shabby semicircle of buildings given over to cheap hotels, street vendors, travel agents and fast-food joints, and centring on a fountain surrounded by languishing nymphs and sea monsters.

The piazza actually follows the outlines of the exedra of the Baths of Diocletian, the remains of which lie across the piazza and are partially contained in the church of **Santa Maria degli Angeli** – not Rome's most welcoming church but giving the best impression of the size and grandeur of Diocletian's bath complex. It's a huge, open building, with an interior standardized by Vanvitelli into a rich eighteenth-century confection after a couple of centuries of piecemeal adaptation (started by an aged Michelangelo). The pink granite pillars, at nine feet in diameter the largest in Rome, are original, and the main transept formed the main hall of the baths; only the crescent shape of the facade remains from the original caldarium (it had previously been hidden by a newer facing), the vestibule (the tepidarium) and main transept. The meridian that strikes diagonally across the floor here was, until 1846, the regulator of time for Romans (now a cannon shot fired daily at noon from the Janiculum Hill).

Palazzo Massimo

Across from Santa Maria degli Angeli, through a seedy little park, the snazzily restored **Palazzo Massimo** at Largo di Villa Perretti is home, with the Palazzo Altemps (see p.697) to the Museo Nazionale Romano (Tues–Sat 9am–7pm, Sun 9am–2pm; L12,000/€6.20 or for details of combined ticket, see box on p.691), a superb collection of Greek and Roman antiquities, second only to the Vatican's, which has been entirely reorganized and features many pieces that have remained undisplayed for decades. The ground floor of the museum is devoted to statuary of the early Empire, including an unparalleled selection of busts of the emperors and their families. There are silver and gold coins from the seventh century BC to the first century AD, and, further on, a painted frieze from the first century BC showing scenes from the Trojan War and the legend of the founding of Rome. The top-floor gallery has a room devoted to the Flavian emperors – look out for the bust of Vespasian – and beyond there's more statuary from the imperial era, a room of bronze fittings from ships found at Lake Nemi, south of Rome, and some stunning frescoes from the country villa, north of Rome, of the emperor Augustus's wife Livia, depicting an orchard dense with fruit and flowers and patrolled by partridges, doves and other feathered friends. On the same floor, there are also some of the best mosaics ever found in Roman villas around the world – best of which are the floors from the Villa di Baccano on Via Cassia, including four mosaic panels taken from a bedroom, featuring four chariot drivers and their horses, so finely crafted that from a distance they look as if they've been painted.

Stazione Termini

Across the street is the low white facade of **Stazione Termini** (so named for its proximity to the Baths of Diocletian, nothing to do with being the termini of Rome's rail lines) and the vast, bus-crammed hubbub that is Piazza dei Cinquecento in front. The station is great, an ambitious piece of modern architectural design that was completed in 1950 and still entirely dominates the streets around with its low-slung, self-consciously futuristic lines. It has just received a huge and sleek renovation that has converted part of its cavernous ticket hall to retail and restaurant space and upgraded the building in general – making it a nice spot for a browse and a wander, and a marvellous place to catch a train. As for **Piazza dei Cinquecento**, it's a good place to find buses and taxis, but otherwise it and the areas around are pretty much low-life territory, and although not especially dangerous, not particularly a place to hang around for long either.

Via XX Settembre and Santa Maria della Vittoria

Just to the north of Termini, **Via XX Settembre** spears out towards the Aurelian Wall from Via del Quirinale – not Rome's most appealing thoroughfare by any means, flanked by the deliberately faceless bureaucracies of the national government, erected after Unification in anticipation of Rome's ascension as a new world capital. It was, however, the route by which Garibaldi's troops entered the city on September 20, 1870, and the place where they breached the wall is marked with a column. The church of **Santa Maria della Vittoria** here (Jan–July & Sept–Dec daily 6.30am–noon & 4.30–7.00pm) was built by Carlo Maderno and it has an interior that is one of the most elaborate examples of Baroque decoration in Rome: almost shockingly excessive to modern eyes, its ceiling and walls are pitted with carving, and statues are crammed into remote corners as in an over-stuffed attic. The church's best-known feature, Bernini's carving of the *Ecstasy of St Theresa*, the centrepiece of the sepulchral chapel of Cardinal Cornaro, continues the histrionics – a deliberately melodramatic work featuring a theatrically posed St Theresa against a backdrop of theatre-boxes on each side of the chapel.

Via Nomentana

At the north end of Via XX Settembre, the **Porta Pia** was one of the last works of Michelangelo, erected under Pope Pius IV in 1561, beyond which the wide boulevard of **Via Nomentana** leads up eventually to the church of **Sant'Agnese fuori le Mura** (Mon 9am–noon, Tues–Sat 9am–noon & 4–6pm, Sun 4–6pm), dedicated to the same saint who was martyred in Domitian's Stadium in 303 AD, and much as it was built by Honorius I in the seventh century, when he reworked Constantine's original structure. The apse mosaic is Byzantine in style and contemporary with Honorius's building, showing Agnes next to the pope, who holds a model of his church. Out of the narthex the custodian will lead you down into the **catacombs** (same hours as church; L8000/€4.13) that sprawl below the church, which are among the best-preserved and most crowd-free of all the city's catacombs. Indeed, if you only have time for one set of catacombs during your stay in Rome (and they really are all very much alike), these are among the best.

After the catacombs the guide will show you a further part of what is really a small complex of early Christian structures, the church of **Santa Constanza** (usually open the same hours as Sant'Agnese; free), which more than any other building in Rome, perhaps, illustrates the transition from the pagan to Christian city in its decorative and architectural features. Built in 350 AD as a mausoleum for Constantia and Helena, the daughters of the Emperor Constantine, it's a round structure which follows the traditional shape of the great pagan tombs (consider those of Hadrian and Augustus elsewhere in the city), and the mosaics on the vaulting of its circular ambulatory – fourth-century depictions of vines, leaves and birds – would have been as at home on the floor of a Roman *domus* as they were in a Christian church.

San Lorenzo

South and east of Via Nomentana, a short walk from Termini, the neighbourhood of **SAN LORENZO** spreads from the main campus of Rome's university, on the far side of Via Tiburtina, to the railway tracks – a solidly working-class district that retains something of its local air and is home to some good and often inexpensive local restaurants (see p.737). The area takes its name from the church of **San Lorenzo fuori le Mura** on Via Tiburtina, one of the seven great pilgrimage churches of Rome, and a typical Roman basilica, fronted by a columned portico and with a lovely twelfth-century cloister to its side (daily: summer 7am–noon & 4–7.30pm; winter closes 5.30pm). The original church here was built over the site of St Lawrence's martyrdom by Constantine – the saint was reputedly burned to death on a gridiron, halfway through his ordeal apparently uttering the immortal words, "Turn me, I am done on this side." Where the church of San Lorenzo differs is that it is actually a combination of three churches built at different periods – one a sixth-century reconstruction of Constantine's church by Pelagius II, which now forms the chancel, another a fifth-century church from the time of Sixtus III, both joined by a basilica from the thirteenth century by Honorius II. Because of its proximity to Rome's railyards, the church was bombed heavily during World War II, but it has been rebuilt with sensitivity, and remains much as it was originally. Inside there are features from all periods: a Cosmati floor, thirteenth-century pulpits and a Paschal candlestick. The mosaic on the inside of the triumphal arch is a sixth-century depiction of Pelagius offering his church to Christ; while below stairs, catacombs (presently closed for restoration) – where St Lawrence was apparently buried – lead a dank path from the pillars of Constantine's original structure. There's also a Romanesque cloister with well-tended garden that you can get into through the sacristy.

Villa Borghese and North Central Rome

Immediately above Piazza del Popolo, the hill known as the Pincio marks the edge of the city's core and the beginning of a collection of parks and gardens that forms Rome's largest central open space – the **Villa Borghese**, made up of the grounds of the seventeenth-century pleasure palace of Scipione Borghese, which were bought by the city at the turn of the century. It's a huge area, and its woods, lake and grass crisscrossed by roads are about as near as you can get to peace in the city centre without making too much effort. There are any number of attractions for those who want to do more than just stroll or sunbathe: a tiny boating lake, a zoo – a cruel affair well worth avoiding – and some of the city's finest museums.

The **Pincio Hill** isn't formally part of the Villa Borghese, but its terrace and gardens, laid out by Valadier in the early nineteenth century and fringed with dilapidated busts of classical and Italian heroes, give fine views over the roofs, domes and TV antennae of central Rome. Walking south from here, there are more gardens in the grounds of the **Villa Medici**, though as the villa is home to the French Academy, they can usually only be visited on selected days, when they host concerts and art shows.

Galleria Borghese

Situated on the far eastern edge of the Villa Borghese park, the **Galleria Borghese** (Tues–Sat 9am–7pm, Sun 9am–5pm; pre-booked visits only, every 2hr; reservations Mon–Fri 9am–7pm, Sat 9am–1pm call ☎06.32.810; L12,000/€6.20) is the best place to make for first, built in the early seventeenth century by Cardinal Scipione Borghese and turned over to the state when the gardens became city property in 1902. Recently reopened after a lengthy restoration, it has taken its place as one of Rome's great treasure houses and should not be missed.

The **ground floor** contains mainly sculpture: a mixture of ancient Roman items and seventeenth-century works, roughly linked together with late-eighteenth-century ceiling paintings showing scenes from the Trojan War. Highlights include, in the first room off the entrance hall, Canova's famously erotic statue of *Pauline Borghese* posed as Venus – Pauline Borghese, the sister of Napoleon and married (reluctantly) to the reigning Prince Borghese, was a shocking woman in her day, with grand habits. There are tales of her jewels and clothes, of the Negro who used to carry her from her bath, of the servants she used as footstools, and, of course, her long line of lovers. The statue was considered outrageous by everyone but herself: when asked how she could have posed almost naked, she simply replied, "Oh, there was a stove in the studio." Next door, there's a marvellous statue of David by Bernini – the face of which is a self-portrait of the sculptor – and, further on, a dramatic, poised statue of Apollo and Daphne that captures the split second when Daphne is transformed into a laurel tree, with her fingers becoming leaves and her legs tree trunks. Next door, the walls of the Room of the Emperors are walls flanked by seventeenth- and eighteenth-century busts of Roman emperors, facing another Bernini sculpture, *The Rape of Perseopine* dating from 1622, a coolly virtuosic work that shows in melodramatic form the story of the carrying off to the underworld of the beautiful nymph Perseopine. Finally, the so-called Room of Silenus contains a variety of paintings by Cardinal Scipione's faithful servant Caravaggio – notably the *Madonna of the Grooms* from 1605, a painting that at the time was considered to have depicted Christ far too realistically to hang in a central Rome church, so Cardinal Scipione happily bought it for his collection. Look also at *St Jerome*, captured writing at a table lit only by a source of light that streams in from the upper left of the picture, and his *David holding the Head of Goliath*, sent by Caravaggio to Cardinal Scipione from exile in Malta, where he had fled to escape capital punishment for various crimes, in the hope of winning a reprieve.

Upstairs houses the Galleria Borghese's **Pinacoteca**, literally one of the richest collections of paintings in the world, although unfortunately you're only allowed half an hour up here before having to leave. In the first room are several important paintings by Raphael, his teacher Perugino and other masters of the Umbrian school from the late fifteenth and early sixteenth centuries, not least Raphael's *Deposition*, done in 1507 for a noble of Perugia in memory of her son, and pillaged from Perugia cathedral by associates of Cardinal Scipione. Beyond, look also for the *Lady With a Unicorn*, and *Portrait of a Man*, both also by Raphael but misattributed earlier this century, and, over the door, a copy of the artist's portrait of a tired-out Julius II, painted in the last year of the pope's life, 1513. In further rooms there are more early-sixteenth-century paintings, prominent among which is Cranach's *Venus and Cupid with a Honeycomb*, of 1531, Lorenzo Lotto's touching *Portrait of a Man*, and, at the back of the building, a series of self-portraits done by Bernini at various stages of his long life. Next to these are a lifelike bust of Cardinal Scipione executed by Bernini in 1632, portraying him as the worldly connoisseur of fine art and fine living that he was, and a smaller bust of Pope Paul V, also by Bernini. Beyond here, in a further room, there is a painting of *Diana* by Domechino, showing the goddess and her attendants celebrating and doing a bit of target practice, and Titian's *Sacred and Profane Love*, painted in 1514 when he was about 25 years old, to celebrate the marriage of the Venetian noble Nicolo Aurelio (whose coat of arms is on the sarcophagus).

Galleria Nazionale d'Arte Moderna

The Villa Borghese's two other major museums are situated on the other side of the park, about a kilometre away along the Viale delle Belle Arti, and of these, the **Galleria Nazionale d'Arte Moderna**, Via delle Belle Arti 131 (Tues–Sat 9am–10pm, Sun 9am–8pm; shorter hours in winter; L8000/€4.13), is probably the least compulsory, a huge, lumbering, Neoclassical building housing a collection that isn't really as grand as you might expect, made up of a wide selection of nineteenth- and twentieth-century Italian (and a few foreign) names. The nineteenth-century collection, on the upper floor, contains a lot of marginal Italian masters (as well as a Van Gogh) but really isn't that compelling unless this is one of your areas of interest. The twentieth-century collection is more appealing, and includes work by Modigliani, De Chirico, Giacomo Balla, Boccione and other Futurists, along with the odd Cézanne, Mondrian and Klimt, and some post-war canvases by the likes of Mark Rothko and Jackson Pollock.

Museo Nazionale di Villa Giulia

The **Museo Nazionale di Villa Giulia** (Tues–Sat 9am–7pm, Sun 9am–1.30pm; L8000/€4.13), five minutes' walk away in the direction of Via Flaminia, is more of an essential stop, housing as it does the the world's primary collection of Etruscan treasures (along with the Etruscan collection in the Vatican), and a good introduction – or conclusion – to the Etruscan sites in Lazio, which between them contributed most of the artefacts on display here. It's not an especially large collection, but it's worth taking the trouble to see the whole, and it has recently been revamped so is looking very much at its best. The **east wing** houses bronze objects dating from the seventh and sixth centuries BC and a number of terracotta votive offerings of anatomical parts of the human body, their detail alluding to the Etruscans' accomplishments in medicine, although the most famous piece here is the remarkable Sarcophagus of the Married Couple from Cerveteri (see p.752), a touchingly lifelike portrayal of a husband and wife lying on a couch. Upstairs, in the rotonda overlooking the Married Couple, are bronzes, mirrors, candelabra, religious statues and tools. There is a model of a ploughman at work plodding along behind his oxen and a remarkably well-preserved two-wheeled funeral chariot. The **west wing** of the museum displays artefacts found outside Etruria proper but of obvious Etruscan provenance or heavily influenced by the Etruscans, most notably *Cistae* recovered from tombs around Praeneste (see p.769) – drum-like objects, engraved and adorned with figures, which were supposed to hold all the things needed for the care of the body after death. In the same room, look too at the marvellously intricate pieces of gold jewellery, delicately worked into tiny horses, birds, camels and other animals. There are also gold-washed silver dishes with Egyptian motifs – the Etruscans had close relations with North Africa; ostrich eggs, an Etruscan symbol of resurrection and rebirth, also imported from Africa; and mirrors, some of which have mythological events etched on their backs. Finally the museum's **atrium**, two storeys high, is devoted to the Faliscians, a people from northeast Lazio, who were closely affiliated with the Etruscans. There are gaudily coloured terracotta figures that leer, run, jump and climb, a drinking horn in the shape of a dog's head that is so lifelike you almost expect it to bark, and a bronze disc breastplate from the seventh century BC decorated with a weird, almost modern pattern of galloping creatures.

North Central Rome

The area north of Villa Borghese is the posh **PARIOLI** district – one of Rome's wealthier neighbourhoods, though of little interest to anyone who doesn't live there. Immediately east stretches the enormous public park of the **Villa Ada**, connected with Villa Borghese by Via Salaria – the old trading route between the Romans and Sabines, so called because the main product transported along here was salt. The Villa Ada was once the estate of King Vittorio Emanuele III and is a nice enough place in which to while away an afternoon, but otherwise not really worth the special journey from the centre of town. The **Catacombe di Priscilla** (Feb–Dec Tues–Sun 8.30am–noon & 2.30–5pm; L8000/€4.13 including tour), which you can reach from Via Salaria, are the only real thing to see – a frescoed labyrinth of tunnels that is visitable on regular (obligatory) guided tours and are home to a number of obviously Christian frescoes – Daniel in the lions' den, the resurrection of Lazarus, Noah, the sacrifice of Isaac – painted between the second and fourth centuries AD. However, other paintings, including something that is claimed as the earliest known depiction of the *Virgin and Child*, could in fact simply be a picture of a mother and child, both of whom were probably buried here.

On the far side of the Parioli district the Tiber sweeps around in a wide hook-shaped bend. These northern outskirts of Rome aren't particularly enticing, though the **Ponte Milvio**, the old, originally Roman, footbridge where the emperor Constantine defeated Maxentius in 312 AD, still stands and provides wonderful views of the meandering Tiber, with the city springing up green on the hills to both sides and the river running fast and silty below. On the northern side of the river, **Piazzale di Ponte Milvio** sports a cheap and cheerful market (Mon–Sat 8am–1.30pm) and a handful of bars and restaurants, and is ten minutes' walk southwest from the **Foro Italico** sports centre, one of the few parts of Rome to survive intact pretty much the way Mussolini planned it. Its centrepiece is perhaps the **Ponte Duca di Aosta**, which connects Foro Italico to the town side of the river, and is headed by a white marble obelisk capped with a gold pyramid that is engraved MUSSOLINI DUX in beautiful 1930s calligraphy. Beyond the bridge, an avenue patched with more mosaics revering the Duce leads up to a fountain surrounded by mosaics of muscle-bound figures revelling in healthful sporting activities. Either side of the fountain are the two main stadiums: the larger of the two, the **Stadio Olimpico** on the left, was used for the Olympic Games in 1960 and is still the venue for Rome's two soccer teams on alternate Sundays (see p.747). The smaller, the **Stadio dei Marmi** ("stadium of marbles"), is a typically Fascist monument, ringed by sixty great male statues, groins modestly hidden by fig leafs, in a variety of elegantly macho poses.

South Central Rome

On its southern side, the Palatine Hill drops down to the **Circo Massimo**, a long, thin, green expanse bordered by heavily trafficked roads that was the ancient city's main venue for chariot races. At one time this arena had a capacity of up to 400,000 spectators, and if it were still intact it would no doubt match the Colosseum for grandeur. As it is, a litter of stones at the Viale Aventino end is all that remains, together with – at the southern end – a little medieval tower built by the Frangipani family.

The Baths of Caracalla

Across the far side of Piazza di Porta Capena, the **Baths of Caracalla** Viale Terme di Caracalla 52 (summer Mon & Sun 9am–1pm, Tues–Sat 9am–6pm; winter Mon & Sun 9am–1pm, Tues–Sat 9am–3pm; L8000/€4.13), are much better preserved, and they give a far better sense of the scale and monumentality of Roman architecture than most of the extant ruins in the city – so much so that Shelley was moved to write *Prometheus Unbound* here in 1819. The baths are no more than a shell now, but the walls still rise to very nearly their original height. There are many fragments of mosaics – none spectacular, but quite a few bright and well preserved – and it's easy to discern a floor plan. As for Caracalla, he was one of Rome's worst and shortest-lived rulers, and it's no wonder there's nothing else in the city built by him. The baths have until recently been used for occasional opera performances during the summer (one of Mussolini's better ideas), but these have largely stopped due to damage to the site. Watch out for their re-emergence, though – it's a thrilling and inexpensive way to see the baths at their most atmospheric.

The Aventine Hill

Cross back over Viale Aventino after seeing the baths and scale the **Aventine Hill** – the southernmost of the city's seven hills and the heart of plebeian Rome in ancient times. These days the working-class quarters of the city are further south, and the Aventine is in fact one of the city's more upscale residential areas, covered with villas and gardens and one of the few places in the city where you can escape the traffic. A short way up Via Santa Sabina, the church of **Santa Sabina** (daily 7am–12.45pm & 3.30–6pm) is a strong contender for Rome's most beautiful basilica: high and wide, its nave and portico restored back to their fifth-century appearance in the 1930s. Look especially at the main doors, which are contemporary with the church and boast eighteen panels carved with Christian scenes, forming a complete illustrated Bible, which includes one of the oldest representations of the Crucifixion in existence. Santa Sabina is also the principal church of the Dominicans, and it's claimed that the orange trees in the garden outside, which you can glimpse on your way to the restrained cloister, are descendants of those planted by St Dominic himself. Whatever the truth of this, the views from the gardens are splendid – right across the Tiber to the centre of Rome and St Peter's.

There are other churches on the Aventine, and in any case it's a nice place to wander. Follow the road south past the **Priorato di Malta**, one of several buildings in the city belonging to the Knights of Malta, which has a celebrated view of the dome of St Peter's through the keyhole of its main gate. The little piazza in front of the main gate has marble triumphal insignia designed and placed here by Piranesi to celebrate the knights' dramatic history.

Testaccio

On the far side of Via Marmorata, below, the solid working-class neighbourhood of **TESTACCIO** groups around a couple of main squares, a tight-knit community with a market and a number of bars and small trattorias that was for many years synonymous with the slaughterhouse that sprawls down to the Tiber just beyond. In recent years the area has become a trendy place to live, property prices have soared, and some uneasy contradictions have emerged, with vegetarian restaurants opening their doors in an area still known for the offal dishes served in its traditional trattorias, and gay and alternative clubs standing cheek-by-jowl with the car-repair shops gouged into Monte Testaccio.

The slaughterhouse, or **Mattatoio**, once the area's main employer, is now home to the *centro sociale* "Villaggio Globale", a space used for concerts, raves and exhibitions, along with stabling for the city's horse-and-carriage drivers, a gymnasium, and a small gypsy camp. For years there has been talk of sprucing it up into a *chi-chi* affair of shops and restaurants, but so far nothing has happened, and it's likely to remain as it is for some time to come. Opposite the slaughterhouse, **Monte Testaccio**, which gives the area its name, is a 35-metre-high mound created out of the shards of Roman amphorae that were dumped here over some 600 years. The ancients were not aware of the fact that the terracotta amphorae could be recycled, and consequently broke them up into small shards and laid them down in an orderly manner, sprinkling quicklime on them to dissolve the residual wine or oil and so creating the mountain you see today. It's an odd sight, the ceramic curls visible through the tufts of grass that crown its higher reaches, the bottom layers hollowed out by the workshops of car and bike mechanics.

The Protestant Cemetery

On the opposite side of Via Zabaglia, Via Caio Cestio leads up to the entrance of the **Protestant Cemetery** (Tues–Sun 9am–5pm; donation expected), one of the shrines to the English in Rome and a fitting conclusion to a visit to the Keats-Shelley Memorial House (see p.704), since it is here that both poets are buried, along with a handful of other well-known names. In fact, the cemetery's title is a misnomer – the cemetery is reserved for non-Roman Catholics so you'll also find famous Italian atheists, Christians of the Orthodox persuasion, and the odd Jew or Muslim, buried here. It's a small and surprisingly tranquil enclave, crouched behind the mossy pyramidal **tomb** of one Caius Cestius, who died in 12 BC, and home to a friendly colony of well-fed cats. Part of Cestius's will decreed that all his slaves should be freed, and the white pyramid you see today was thrown up by them in only 330 days of what must have been joyful building.

Most visitors come here to see the grave of Keats, who lies next to his friend, the painter Joseph Severn, in a corner of the old part of the cemetery near the pyramid, his stone inscribed as he wished with the words "here lies one whose name was writ in water". Severn died much later than Keats but asked to be laid here nonetheless, together with his brushes and palette. Shelley's ashes were brought here at Mary Shelley's request and interred, after much obstruction by the papal authorities, in the newer part of the cemetery, at the opposite end. The Shelleys had visited several years earlier, the poet praising it as "the most beautiful and solemn cemetery I ever beheld". It had been intended that Shelley should rest with his young son, William, who was also buried here, but his remains couldn't be found (although his small grave lies nearby). Among other famous internees, Edward Trelawny lies next door, the political writer and activist, Gramsci, on the far right-hand side in the middle, to name just two – though if you're at all interested in star-spotting you should ask to have a look at the English booklet at the entrance.

From the Protestant Cemetery, you could make a long (hour or so) detour back into the city centre following the **Aurelian Wall**, built by the emperor Aurelian (and his successor Probus) in 275 AD to enclose Rome's seven hills, One of the best-preserved stretches runs between Porta San Paolo and Porta San Sebastiano: walk through Porta San Paolo and turn left, and follow the walls keeping them always on your left.

San Paolo fuori le Mura

Two kilometres or so south of the Porta San Paolo, the basilica of **San Paolo fuori le Mura** (daily 7.30am–6.30pm) is one of the five patriarchal basilicas of Rome, occupying the supposed site of St Paul's tomb, where he was laid to rest after being beheaded at Tre Fontane (see opposite). Of the five, this basilica has probably fared the least well over the years. It was apparently once the grandest of them all, connected to the Aurelian Wall by a mile-long colonnade of 800 marble columns, but a ninth-century sacking by the Saracens and a devastating fire in 1823 (a couple of cack-handed roofers spilt burning tar, almost entirely destroying the church) means that the church you see now is largely a nineteenth-century reconstruction, sited in what is these days a rather unenticing neighbourhood.

For all that, it's a very successful if somewhat clinical rehash of the former church, succeeding where St Peter's tries (but ultimately fails) by impressing with sheer size and grandeur: whether you enter by way of the cloisters or the west door, it's impossible not to be awed by the space of the building inside, its crowds of columns topped by round-arched arcading. Some parts of the building did survive the fire. In the south transept, the paschal candlestick is a remarkable piece of Romanesque carving, supported by half-human beasts and rising through entwined tendrils and strangely human limbs and bodies to scenes from Christ's life, the figures crowding in together as if for a photocall. The bronze aisle doors were also rescued from the old basilica and date from 1070, as was the thirteenth-century tabernacle by Arnolfo di Cambio. The arch across the apse is original too, embellished with mosaics donated by the Byzantine queen Galla Placidia in the sixth century that show Christ giving a blessing, angels, the symbols of the Gospels, and saints Peter and Paul. There's also the cloister, just behind here – probably Rome's finest piece of Cosmatesque work, its spiralling, mosaic-encrusted columns enclosing a peaceful rose garden.

EUR

From San Paolo, Via Ostiense leads south to join up with Via Cristoforo Colombo which in turn runs down to **EUR** (pronounced "eh-oor") – the acronym for the district built for the "Esposizione Universale Roma". It's quite a walk, so you'd be better off taking bus #714 from Termini or Metro line B. This is not so much a neighbourhood as a statement in stone: planned by Mussolini for the aborted 1942 World's Fair and not finished until well after the war, it's a cold, soulless grid of square buildings, long vistas and wide processional boulevards linked tenuously to the rest of Rome by metro but light years away from the city in feel. Come here for its numerous museums, some of which *are* worth the trip, or if you have a yen for modern architecture and urban planning; otherwise, stay well clear.

The great flaw in EUR is that it's not built for people: the streets are wide thoroughfares designed for easy traffic flow and fast driving, shops and cafés are easily outnumbered by offices. Of the buildings, the postwar development of the area threw up bland office blocks for the most part, and it's the prewar Fascist-style constructions that are of most interest. The **Palazzo della Civiltà del Lavoro** in the northwest corner stands out, Fascist-inspired architecture at its most assured – the "square Colosseum" some have called it, which sums up its mixing of modern and classical styles perfectly. To the south, **Piazza Marconi** is the nominal centre of EUR, where the wide, classically inspired boulevards intersect to swerve around an obelisk in the centre.

All the museums are within easy reach of here. On the square itself, the **Museo Nazionale delle Arti e delle Tradizioni Popolari** (Mon–Sat 9am–2pm, Sun 9am–1pm; L4000/€2.07) is a run-through of applied arts, costumes and religious artefacts from the Italian regions. Everything is labelled in Italian; bring a dictionary if you need it. The **Museo Nazionale Preistorico ed Etnografico Luigi Pigorini**, Viale Lincoln 1 (Tues–Sat 9am–2pm, Sun 9am–1pm; L8000/€4.13), is arranged in manageable and easily comprehensible order, but its prehistoric section is mind-numbingly exhaustive; the ethnographic collection does something to relieve things however, with artefacts from South America, the Pacific and Africa. In the same building, further down the colonnade, at Viale Lincoln 3, is the **Museo dell'Alto Medioevo** (Tues–Sat 9am–2pm, Sun 9am–1pm; L4000/€2.07), which concentrates on artefacts from the fifth century to the tenth century – local finds mainly, including some beautiful jewellery from the seventh century and a delicate fifth-century gold fibula found on the Palatine Hill. But of all the museums, the most interesting is the **Museo della Civiltà Romana**, Piazza Agnelli 10 (Tues–Sat 9am–7pm, Sun 9am–2pm; L5000/€2.58), which has, among numerous ancient Roman finds, a large-scale model of the fourth-century city – perfect for setting the rest of the city in context.

The Abbazia delle Tre Fontane

The antidote to EUR is just a short walk away, at the **Abbazia delle Tre Fontane**, a complex of churches founded on the spot where St Paul was martyred; it's said that when the saint was beheaded his head bounced and three springs erupted where his head touched the ground. In those days this was a malarial area, and it was all but abandoned during the Middle Ages, but in the second half of the nineteenth century Trappist monks drained the swamp and planted eucalyptus trees in the vicinity; they still distil a eucalyptus-based chest remedy here, as well as an exquisite liqueur, both sold – alongside wonderful chocolate bars – at the small shop by the entrance.

As for the churches, they were rebuilt in the sixteenth century and restored by the Trappists. They're not particularly outstanding buildings, appealing more for their peaceful location, which is relatively undisturbed by visitors, than any architectural distinction. The first church, originally built in 625, is the church of **SS Vincent and Anastasio**, which has a gloomy atmosphere made gloomier by the fact that most of the windows are of a thick marble that admits little light. The three fountains in the floor are supposedly the ones of the bouncing head of the saint but they have long since run dry. Further on, to the right, the church of **Santa Maria Scala Coeli** owes its name to a vision St Bernard had here: he saw the soul he was praying for ascend to heaven; the Cosmatesque altar where this is supposed to have happened is down the cramped stairs, in the crypt, where St Paul was allegedly kept prior to his beheading. Beyond, the largest of the churches, **San Paolo alle Tre Fontane** holds the pillar to which St Paul was tied and a couple of mosaic pavements from Ostia Antica.

Via Appia Antica: the Catacombs

During classical times the **Via Appia**, reachable by taking bus #218 from Piazza San Giovanni in Laterano, was the most important of all the Roman trade routes, the so-called "Queen of Roads", carrying supplies right down through Campania to the port of Bríndisi. It's no longer the main route south out of the city, but it remains an important part of early Christian Rome, its verges lined with the underground burial cemeteries or **catacombs** of the first Christians. Laws in ancient Rome forbade burial within the city walls – most Romans were cremated – and there are catacombs in other parts of the city. But this is by far the largest concentration, around five complexes in all, dating from the first century to the fourth century, almost entirely emptied of bodies now but still decorated with the primitive signs and frescoes that were the hallmark of the then-burgeoning Christian movement. Despite much speculation, no one really knows why the Christians decided to bury their dead in these tunnels: the rock here, tufa, is soft and easy to hollow out, but the digging involved must still have been phenomenal, and there is no real reason to suppose that the burial places had to be secret – they continued to bury their dead like this long after Christianity became the established religion. Whatever the reasons, they make intriguing viewing now. The three principal complexes are within walking distance of each other, though it's not really worth trying to see them all – the layers of shelves and drawers aren't particularly gripping after a while.

Via Appia Antica begins at the **Porta San Sebastiano**, built in the fifth century, a little way on from which the church of **Domine Quo Vadis** signals the start of the catacomb stretch of road. Legend has this as the place where St Peter saw Christ while fleeing from certain death in Rome and asked "Where goest thou, Lord?", to which Christ replied that he was going to be crucified once more, leading Peter to turn around and accept his fate. Continuing on for a kilometre or so you reach the catacombs of **San Callisto** (Jan–Oct & Dec Thurs–Tues 8.30am–noon & 2.30–5pm; L8000/€4.13). All third-century popes (of whom San Callisto was one) are buried here in the papal crypt, and the site features some well-preserved seventh- and eighth-century frescoes. A little way west from here, the catacombs of **San Domitilla** (Feb–Dec Mon & Wed–Sun 8.30am–noon & 2.30–5pm; L8000/€4.13) are quieter than those of San Callisto and adjoin the remains of a fourth-century basilica erected here to the martyrs Achilleus and Nereus. The labyrinth itself is Rome's largest, stretching for around 17km in all, and contains more frescoes and early wall etchings.

The catacombs of **San Sebastiano** (Jan–Oct & Dec Fri–Wed 9am–noon & 2.30–5pm; L8000/€4.13), 500m further on, are probably best for a visit, situated under a much renovated basilica that was originally built by Constantine on the spot where the bodies of the apostles Peter and Paul are said to have been laid for a time. Downstairs, half-hour tours wind around dark corridors showing signs of early Christian worship – paintings of doves and fish, a contemporary carved oil lamp and inscriptions dating the tombs themselves. The most striking features, however, are not Christian at all, but three pagan tombs (one painted, two stuccoed) discovered when archeologists were burrowing beneath the floor of the basilica upstairs. Just above here, Constantine is said to have raised his chapel to Peter and Paul, and although St Peter was later removed to the Vatican, and St Paul to San Paolo fuori le Mura, the graffiti above records the fact that this was indeed, albeit temporarily, where the two Apostles rested.

Trastevere

Across the river from the centre of town, on the right bank of the Tiber, the district of **TRASTEVERE** was the artisan area of the city in classical times, neatly placed for the trade that came upriver from Ostia and was unloaded nearby. Outside the city walls, Trastevere (the name means literally "across the Tiber") was for centuries heavily populated by immigrants, and this separation lent the neighbourhood a strong identity that lasted well into this century. Nowadays the area is a long way from the working-class quarter it used to be, and although you're still likely to hear Travestere's strong Roman dialect, you're also likely to bump into some of its many foreign residents, lured by the charm of its narrow streets and closeted squares. However, even if the local *Festa de' Noantri* ("celebration of we others"), held every July, seems to symbolize the slow decline of local spirit rather than celebrate its existence, there is good reason to come to Trastevere. It is among the more pleasant places to stroll in Rome, particularly peaceful in the morning, and lively come evening, as dozens of trattorias set tables out along the cobblestone streets – Trastevere has long been known for its restaurants (see p.741). The neighbourhood has also become the focus of the city's alternative scene and is home to much of its most vibrant and youthful nightlife (see p.743).

Porta Portese

The obvious way to approach Trastevere is to cross over from Isola Tiberina or from the pedestrian Ponte Sisto at the end of Via Giulia, both of which leave you five minutes from the heart of the neighbourhood. On a Sunday it's worth walking over the Ponte Sublicio to Porta Portese, from which the **Porta Portese** flea market stretches down Via Portuense to Trastevere train station in a congested medley of antiques, old motor spares, cheap clothing, trendy clothing and assorted junk – more touristy than it used to be, but still above all a Romans' market. Haggling is the rule, and keep a good hold of your wallet or purse. Come early if you want to buy, or even move – most of the bargains have gone by 10am, by which time the crush of people can be intense.

Santa Cecilia in Trastevere
Further north, on Via Anicia, is the church of **Santa Cecilia in Trastevere** (daily 10am–noon & 4–5.30pm), a cream, rather sterile church – apart from a pretty front courtyard – whose antiseptic eighteenth-century appearance belies its historical associations. A church was originally built here over the site of the second-century home of St Cecilia, whose husband Valerian was executed for refusing to worship Roman gods and who herself was subsequently persecuted for Christian beliefs. The story has it that Cecilia was locked in the caldarium of her own baths for several days but refused to die, singing her way through the ordeal (Cecilia is patron saint of music). Her head was finally half hacked off with an axe, though it took several blows before she finally succumbed. Below the high altar, Stefano Maderno's limp, almost modern statue of the saint shows her incorruptible body as it was found when exhumed in 1599, with three deep cuts in her neck – a fragile, intensely human piece of work that has helped make Cecilia one of the most revered Roman saints.

Santa Maria in Trastevere
There's more life on the far side of Viale Trastevere, the wide boulevard that cuts through the centre of the district, where **Piazza Santa Maria in Trastevere** constitutes the heart of old Trastevere. It was named after the church of **Santa Maria in Trastevere** in its northwest corner (daily 7.30am–12.40pm & 4–7pm), held to be the first Christian place of worship in Rome, built on a site where a fountain of oil is said to have sprung on the day of Christ's birth. These days people come here for two things. The church's mosaics are among the city's most impressive: those on the cornice by Cavallini were completed a century or so after the rebuilding and show the Madonna surrounded by ten female figures with lamps – once thought to represent the Wise and Foolish Virgins. Inside, there's a nineteenth-century copy of a Cosmatesque pavement of spirals and circles, and apse mosaics contemporary with the building of the church – Byzantine-inspired works depicting a solemn yet sensitive parade of saints thronged around Christ and Mary. Beneath the high altar on the right, an inscription – "FONS OLIO" – marks the spot where the oil is supposed to have sprung up.

Galleria Nazionale di Palazzo Corsini and the Orte Botanico
Cutting north through the backstreets towards the Tiber, the **Galleria Nazionale di Palazzo Corsini** at Via della Lungara 10 (Tues–Fri 9am–7pm, Sat 9am–2pm, Sun 9am–1pm; L8000/€4.13) is an unexpected cultural attraction on this side of the river, a rather highbrow collection, but with works by Rubens, Van Dyck, Guido Reni and

Caravaggio among its highlights, as well as a depiction of the Pantheon by Charles Clérisseau, when there was a market held in the piazza outside – though it's a rather fanciful interpretation, squeezing the Pyramid of Cestius and Arch of Janus into the background. You can also visit the chambers of Queen Christina, who renounced Protestantism, and, with it, the Swedish throne in 1655, and brought her library and fortune to Rome, to the delight of the Chigi pope, Alexander VII. She died here, in the palace, in 1689, and she is one of only four women to be buried in St Peter's.

The park of the Palazzo Corsini is now the site of the **Orto Botanico** (Mon–Sat 9.30am–5.30pm; L4000/€2.07), a good example of eighteenth-century garden design, with a wood of century-old oaks, cedars and conifers, a grove of acclimatized palm-trees, a herbal garden with medicinal plants, a collection of orchids that bloom in springtime and early summer – and, a nice touch, a garden of aromatic herbs put together for the blind; the plants can be identified by their smell or touch, and are accompanied by signs in Braille. The garden also has the distinction of being home to one of the oldest plane trees in Rome, between 350 and 400 years old.

Villa Farnesina

Much more interesting is the **Villa Farnesina** (Mon–Sat 9am–1pm; L6000/€3.10), across the road from the Palazzo Corsini, built during the early sixteenth century by Baldassare Peruzzi for the Renaissance banker Agostino Chigi and famous for its Renaissance frescoes. Inside you can view the Raphael-designed painting of *Cupid and Psyche* in the now glassed-in loggia, completed in 1517 by the artist's assistants, Giulio Romano, Francesco Penni and Giovanni da Udine. Vasari claims Raphael didn't complete the work because his infatuation with his mistress – "La Fornarina", whose father's bakery was situated nearby – was making it difficult to concentrate, and says that Chigi arranged for her to live with the painter in the palace while he worked on the loggia. More likely he was simply so overloaded with commissions that he couldn't possibly finish them all. He did, however, manage to finish the *Galatea* in the room next door, which he fitted in between his Vatican commissions for Julius II; "the greatest evocation of paganism of the Renaissance", Kenneth Clark called it, although Vasari claims that Michelangelo, passing by one day while Raphael was canoodling with La Fornarina, finished the painting for him.

The Janiculum Hill

From the Villa Farnesina, it's about a fifteen-minute walk up Via Garibaldi (bus #870 goes up from Piazza della Rovere) to the summit of the **Janiculum Hill** – not one of the original seven hills of Rome, but the one with the best and most accessible views of the centre. Via Garibaldi leads up past the church of **San Pietro in Montorio** (daily 7.30am–noon & 4–6pm), built on a site once – now, it's thought, wrongly – believed to have been the place of the saint's crucifixion. The compact interior is particularly intimate – it's a favourite for weddings – and features some first-rate paintings, among them Sebastiano del Piombo's graceful *Flagellation*. Don't miss Bramante's little **Tempietto** (daily 9am–noon & 4–6pm) in the courtyard on the right, one of the seminal works of the Renaissance, built on what was supposed to have been the precise spot of St Peter's martyrdom. The small circular building is like a classical temple in miniature, perfectly proportioned and neatly executed.

The Janiculum was the scene of a fierce 1849 set-to between Garibaldi's troops and the French, and the white marble **memorial** opposite the church is dedicated to all those who died in the battle. A little further up the hill, the **Acqua Paola** – constructed for Paul V with marble from the Roman Forum – gushes water at a bend in the road. At the top, the **Porta San Pancrazio** was built during the reign of Urban VIII, destroyed by the French in 1849, and rebuilt by Pope Pius IX five years later, and has recently been restored to house the new **Museum of the Roman Republic**

1848–49 – yet to open at the time of writing. Turn right to the crest of the hill, where, on Piazzale Garibaldi, there's an equestrian monument to Garibaldi – an ostentatious work from 1895. Just below is the spot from which a cannon is fired at noon each day for Romans to check their watches. Further on, the statue of Anita Garibaldi recalls the important part she played in the 1849 battle – a fiery, melodramatic work (she cradles a baby in one arm, brandishes a pistol with the other, and is galloping full speed on a horse) which also marks her grave. Spread out before her are some of the best views over the city.

The Vatican

On the west bank of the Tiber, directly across from Rome's historic centre, the **VATI-CAN CITY** was established as an independent sovereign state in 1929, a tiny territory surrounded by high walls on its far, western side and on the near side opening its doors to the rest of the city and its pilgrims in the form of St Peter's and its colonnaded piazza. It's believed that St Peter himself was buried in a pagan cemetery here, giving rise to the building of a basilica to venerate his name and the siting of the headquarters of the Catholic Church here. After reaching an uneasy agreement with Mussolini, the Vatican became a sovereign state, and nowadays has its own radio station, newspaper, currency and postal service, and indeed security service in the colourfully dressed Swiss Guards. Despite these trappings, you wouldn't know at any point that you had left Rome and entered the Vatican; indeed the area around the Vatican, known as the Borgo, is one of the most cosmopolitan districts of Rome, full of hotels and restaurants, and scurrying tourists and pilgrims. You may find yourself staying in one of many mid-range hotels located here, although unless you're a pilgrim it's a better idea to base yourself in the more atmospheric city centre and travel back and forth on the useful bus #64. However much you try, one visit is never anywhere near enough.

The Vatican Museums and St Peter's are open to visitors year-round – see individual accounts below for opening times. It's also possible to visit the **Vatican Gardens**, though only on one guided tour a day (Mon–Tues & Thurs–Sat except religious holidays 10am; L18,000/€9.30); visits last about two hours and tickets must be bought a few days ahead from the **Vatican Information Office** in Piazza San Pietro (Mon–Sat 8.30am–6pm; ☎06.6988.4466). You can also, if you wish, attend a **papal audience**: these happen once a week, usually on Wednesdays at 11am in the Audiences Room, and are by no means one-to-one affairs. It's often possible to get a place on one if you apply not more than a month and not less than two days in advance: send a fax with your name, your home address, your Rome address, and your preferred date of audience, to the Prefettura della Casa Pontificia (☎06.6988.3273, fax 06.6988.5863). If you want to send a postcard with a Vatican postmark, there are Vatican **post offices** on the north side of Piazza San Pietro and inside the Vatican Museums.

Castel Sant'Angelo

The best route to the Vatican and St Peter's is across **Ponte Sant'Angelo**, flanked by angels carved to designs by Bernini – his so-called "breezy maniacs". On the far side is the great circular hulk of the **Castel Sant'Angelo** (Tues–Sat 9am–10pm, Sun 9am–8pm; L12,000/€6.20), designed and built by the Emperor Hadrian as his own mausoleum (his ashes were interred here until a twelfth-century pope appropriated the sarcophagus, which was later destroyed in a fire). It was a grand monument, faced with white marble and surrounded with statues and topped with cypresses, similar in style to Augustus's mausoleum across the river. Renamed in the sixth century, when Pope Gregory the Great witnessed a vision of St Michael here that ended a terrible plague, the mausoleum's position near the Vatican was not lost on the papal authorities, who converted the building for use as a fortress and built a passageway to link it with the

Vatican as a refuge in times of siege or invasion – a route utilized on a number of occasions, most notably when the Medici pope, Clement VII, sheltered here for several months during the Sack of Rome in 1527.

Inside, from the monumental entrance hall a spiral ramp leads up into the centre of the mausoleum itself, passing through the chamber where the emperor was entombed, to the main level at the top, where a small palace was built to house the papal residents in appropriate splendour. After the Sack of Rome, Pope Paul III had some especially fine renovations made, including the beautiful frescoed *Sala Paolina* – you'll notice Paul III's personal motto, *Festina Lenta* ("make haste slowly"), scattered throughout the ceilings and in various corners of all his rooms. Elsewhere, rooms hold swords, armour, guns and the like, others are lavishly decorated with grotesques and paintings; don't miss the bathroom of Clement VII on the second floor, with its prototype hot and cold water taps and mildly erotic frescoes. Below are dungeons and storerooms (not visitable), testament to the castle's grisly past as the city's most notorious Renaissance prison – Benvenuto Cellini and Cesare Borgia are just two of its more famous detainees. From the quiet bar upstairs you'll also get one of the best views of Rome and excellent coffee.

Piazza San Pietro

The approach to St Peter's – **Via della Conciliazione** – is disappointing: typically, Mussolini swept away the houses of the previously narrow street and replaced them with this wide sweeping avenue, and nowadays St Peter's somehow looks too near, the vast space of Bernini's **Piazza San Pietro** not really becoming apparent until you're right on top of it. In fact, in tune with the spirit of the Baroque, the church was supposed to be even better hidden than it is now: Bernini planned to complete the colonnade with a triumphal arch linking the two arms, so obscuring the view until you were well inside the square, but this was never carried out and the arms of the piazza remain open, symbolically welcoming the world into the lap of the Catholic Church. The obelisk in the centre was brought to Rome by Caligula in 36 AD, and it stood for many years in the centre of Nero's Circus on the Vatican Hill (to the left of the church); according to legend, it marked the site of St Peter's martyrdom. It was moved here in 1586, when Sixtus V ordered that it be erected in front of the basilica, a task that took four months and was apparently done in silence, on pain of death.

Basilica di San Pietro

The piazza is so grand that you can't help but feel a little let down by the **Basilica di San Pietro** (daily: summer 7am–7pm; winter 7am–6pm), its facade – by no means the church's best feature – obscuring the dome that signals the building from just about everywhere else in the city. Built to a plan initially conceived at the turn of the fifteenth century by Bramante and finished off, heavily modified, over a century later by Carlo Maderno, St Peter's is a strange hotchpotch of styles, bridging the gap between the Renaissance and Baroque eras with varying levels of success. It is, however, the principal shrine of the Catholic Church, built as a replacement for the run-down structure erected here by Constantine in the early fourth century on the site of St Peter's tomb. As such, it can't help but impress, having been worked on by the greatest Italian architects of the sixteenth and seventeenth centuries, and occupying a site rich with historical significance.

In size, certainly, Saint Peter's beats most other churches hands down. Bramante had originally conceived a Greek cross plan rising to a high central dome, but this plan was altered after his death and only revived with the (by then) very elderly Michelangelo's accession as chief architect. Michelangelo was largely responsible for the dome, but he too died shortly afterwards, in 1564, before it was completed. He was succeeded by Vignola, and the dome was completed in 1590 by Giacomo della Porta. Carlo Maderno, under orders from Pope Paul V, took over in 1605, and stretched the church into a Latin cross plan, which had the practical advantage of accommodating more people and followed more directly the plan of Constantine's original basilica. But in so doing he completely unbalanced all the previous designs, not least by obscuring the dome (which he also modified) from view in the piazza. The inside, too, is very much of the Baroque era, largely the work of Bernini, who created many of the most important fixtures.

INSIDE ST PETER'S

You need to be properly dressed to enter St Peter's, which means no bare knees or shoulders – a rule that is very strictly enforced. Inside on the right is Michelangelo's other legacy to the church, his **pietà**, completed at the opposite end of his career when he was just 24. Following an attack by a vandal a few years back, it sits behind glass, strangely remote from the life of the rest of the building. Looking at the piece, its fame comes as no surprise: it's a sensitive and individual work, and an adept one too, draping the limp body of a grown man across the legs of a woman with grace and ease. As you walk down the **nave**, the size of the building becomes more apparent – and not just because of the bronze plaques set in the floor that make comparisons with the sizes of other churches. The **dome** is breathtakingly imposing, rising high above the supposed site of St Peter's tomb. With a diameter of 44 metres it is only 1.5 metres smaller than the Pantheon (the letters of the inscription inside its lower level are over six feet high); it is supported by four enormous piers, decorated with reliefs depicting the basilica's so-called **major relics**: St Veronica's handkerchief, which was used to wipe the face of Christ, and is adorned with His miraculous image; the lance of St Longinus, which pierced Christ's side; and a piece of the True Cross, in the pier of St Helen (the head of St Andrew, which was returned to the Eastern Church by Pope Paul VI in 1966, was also formerly kept here). On the right side of the nave, near the pier of St Longinus, the bronze statue of **St Peter** is another of the most venerated monuments in the basilica, carved in the thirteenth century by Arnolfo di Cambio and with its right foot polished smooth by the attentions of pilgrims. On holy days this statue is dressed in papal tiara and vestments. Bronze was also the material used in Bernini's **baldacchino**, the centrepiece of the sculptor's Baroque embellishment of the interior, a massive 26m high (the height, apparently, of Palazzo Farnese), cast out of 927 tonnes of metal removed from the Pantheon roof in 1633. To modern eyes, it's an almost grotesque piece of work, with its wild spiralling columns copied from columns in the Constantine basilica. But it has the odd personal touch, not least in the female faces expressing the agony of childbirth and a beaming baby carved on the plinths – said to be done for a niece of Bernini's patron (Urban VIII), who gave birth at the same time as the sculptor was finishing the piece.

Bernini's feverish sculpting decorates the apse too, his **cattedra** enclosing the supposed (though doubtful) chair of St Peter in a curvy marble and stucco throne. On the right, the **tomb of Urban VIII**, also by Bernini, is less grand but more dignified. On the left, the **tomb of Paul III**, by Giacomo della Porta, was moved up and down the nave of the church before it was finally placed here as a counter to that of Urban VIII. More interesting is Bernini's **monument to Alexander VII** in the south transept, with its winged skeleton struggling underneath the heavy marble drapes, upon which the Chigi pope is kneeling in prayer. The grim reaper significantly clutches an hourglass – the Baroque at its most melodramatic, and symbolic. On the left sits Charity, on the right, Truth Revealed in Time; to the rear are Hope and Faith.

An entrance off the aisle leads to the steeply priced **Treasury** (daily: summer 9am–6pm; winter 9am–5pm; L8000/€4.13). Along with some more recent additions, this holds artefacts from the earlier church: a spiral column (the other survivors form part of the colonnade around the interior of the dome); a wall-mounted tabernacle by Donatello; a rich blue-and-gold dalmatic that is said once to have belonged to

Charlemagne (though this has been called into question); the vestments and tiara for the bronze statue of St Peter in the nave of the basilica; and the massive, though fairly ghastly, late-fifteenth-century bronze tomb of Sixtus IV by Pollaiuolo – said to be a very accurate portrait. Back at the central crossing, steps lead down under Bernini's statue of St Longinus to the **Grottoes** (daily: summer 8am–6pm; winter 7am–5pm), where a good number of popes are buried, though to be honest none are particularly interesting. Far better is the ascent to the **roof and dome** (daily: May–Sept 8am–6pm; Oct–April 8am–5pm; L8000/€4.13 with elevator); the entrance is in the northern courtyard between the church and the Vatican Palace, on your way out as you exit through the crypt. You'll probably need to queue and, even with the lift, it's a long climb up a narrow stairway that spirals up the dome. The views from the gallery around the interior of the dome give you a sense of the enormity of the church. From there, the roof grants views from behind the huge statues onto the piazza below, before the ascent to the lantern at the top of the dome, from which the views over the city are as glorious as you'd expect.

The Vatican Museums

A fifteen minute walk from St Peter's (follow the signs out from the north side of the piazza), the only part of the Vatican Palace you can visit independently is the **VATICAN MUSEUMS** at Viale Vaticano 13 (Dec–March Mon–Sat 8.45am–12.45pm, last exit 1.45pm; rest of year Mon–Sat 8.45am–3.45pm, last exit 4.45pm; L18,000/€9.30; closed Sun, hols and religious holidays, except the last Sunday of each month when admission is free) – quite simply, the largest, richest, most compelling and perhaps most exhausting museum complex in the world; with a spanking new entrance that at least makes the queues at the height of the season much easier to bear. If you have found any of Rome's other museums disappointing, the Vatican is probably the reason why: so much booty from the city's history has ended up here, from both classical and later times, and so many of the Renaissance's finest artists were in the employ of the pope, that not surprisingly the result is a set of museums so stuffed with antiquities as to put most other European collections to shame.

As its name suggests, the Vatican Palace actually holds a collection of museums on very diverse subjects – displays of classical statuary, Renaissance painting, Etruscan relics, Egyptian artefacts, not to mention the furnishings and decoration of the palace itself. There's no point in trying to see everything, at least not on one visit. Once inside, you have a choice of **routes**, but the only features you really shouldn't miss are the Raphael Stanze and the Sistine Chapel. Above all, decide how long you want to spend here, and what you want to see, before you start; you could spend anything from 45 minutes to the better part of a day here, and it's easy to collapse from museum fatigue before you've even got to your most important target of interest. Be conservative – the distances between different sections alone can be vast and very tiring.

THE MUSEO PIO-CLEMENTINO, MUSEO EGIZIO AND MUSEO GREGORIANO ETRUSCO

To the left of the entrance, the small **Museo Pio-Clementino** and its octagonal courtyard is home to some of the best of the Vatican's classical statuary, including two statues that influenced Renaissance artists more than any others: the serene *Apollo Belvedere*, a Roman copy of a fourth-century BC original – and the first century BC *Laocoon*, discovered near Nero's Golden House in 1506 and depicting a Trojan priest being crushed with his sons by serpents sent to punish him for warning his fellow citizens of the danger of the Trojan horse. It is perhaps the most famous classical statue ever, referred to by Pliny who thought it carved from a single piece of marble, and written about by Byron – who described its contorted realism as "dignifying pain".

The nearby **Museo Egizio** isn't one of the Vatican's highlights. It has some vividly painted mummy cases (and two mummies), along with *canopi*, the alabaster vessels into which the entrails of the deceased were placed. There is also a partial reconstruction of the Temple of Serapis from Hadrian's Villa near Tivoli, along with a statue of his lover, Antinous, who drowned close to the original temple in Egypt and so inspired Hadrian to build his replica. Past the entrance to the Egyptian Museum a grand staircase leads up to the **Museo Gregoriano Etrusco**, which holds sculpture, funerary art and applied art from the sites of southern Etruria – a good complement to Rome's specialist Etruscan collection in the Villa Giulia. Especially worth seeing are the finds from a seventh-century BC tomb discovered near Cerveteri, which contained the remains of three Etruscan nobles, two men and a woman; the breastplate of the woman and her huge fibia (clasp) are of gold. Take a look at the small ducks and lions with which they are decorated, fashioned in the almost microscopic beadwork for which Etruscan goldsmiths were famous.

THE GALLERIES OF CANDELABRA, TAPESTRIES AND MAPS
Outside the Etruscan Museum, the large monumental staircase leads back down to the main route, taking you first through the **Gallery of Candelabra**, the niches of which are adorned with huge candelabra taken from imperial Roman villas. Beyond here the **Gallery of Tapestries** has on the left Belgian tapestries to designs by the school of Raphael which show scenes from the life of Christ, and on the right tapestries made in Rome at the Barberini workshops during the 1600s, showing scenes from the life of Maffeo Barberini, who became Pope Urban VIII. Next, the **Gallery of Maps**, which is as long (175m) as the previous two galleries put together, was decorated in the late sixtcenth century at the behest of Pope Gregory XIII, the reformer of the calendar, to show all of Italy, the major islands in the Mediterranean, the papal possessions in France, as well as the siege of Malta, the battle of Lepanto and large-scale maps of the maritime republics of Venice and Genoa.

THE RAPHAEL STANZE
Beyond the Gallery of the Maps, all visitors are directed to a covered walkway suspended over the palace courtyard of the Belvedere which leads through to the **Raphael Stanze**, the first of which, the **Stanza di Constantino**, was not in fact done by Raphael at all, but painted in part to his designs about five years after he died by his pupils, Giulio Romano, Francesco Penni and Raffello del Colle, between 1525 and 1531. It shows scenes from the life of the Emperor Constantine, who made Christianity the official religion of the Roman Empire. The enormous painting on the wall opposite the entrance is the *Battle of the Milvian Bridge* by Giulio Romano and Francesco Penni – a depiction of a decisive battle in 312 AD between the warring co-emperors of the West, Constantine and Maxentius. Further on, **Stanza di Eliodoro** is the first of the Raphael rooms proper, in which the fresco on the right of the entrance, *The Expulsion of Heliodorus from the Temple*, is an exciting piece of work, painted in 1512–1514 for Pope Julius II. The images of Heliodorus, the horseman and the flying men are adeptly done, the figures almost jumping out of the painting into the room, but the group of people on the left is more interesting – Pope Julius II, in his papal robes, Giulio Romano, the pupil of Raphael, and, to his left, Raphael himself in a rare self-portrait On the left wall as you enter, the *Mass of Bolsena* relates a miracle that occurred in the town in northern Lazio in the 1260s, when a German priest who doubted the transubstantiation of Christ found the wafer bleeding when he broke it during a service. The pope facing the priest is another portrait of Julius II. On the window wall opposite is the *Deliverance of St Peter*, showing the saint being assisted in a jail-break by the Angel of the Lord – a night scene, whose clever chiaroscuro predates Caravaggio by nearly one hundred years. It was painted by order of Pope Leo X, as an allegory of his imprisonment after a battle that took place in Ravenna a few years earlier. Finally, on the large wall opposite Heliodorus, *Leo I Repulsing Attila the Hun* is an an allegory of the difficulties that

the papacy was going through in the early 1500s, and shows the chubby cardinal, Giovanni dei Medici, who succeeded Julius II as Leo X in 1513.

The next room, the **Stanza della Segnatura** or pope's study, is probably the best known – and with good reason. Painted in the years 1508–11, when Raphael first came to Rome, the subjects were again the choice of Julius II, and, composed with careful balance and harmony, it comes close to the peak of the painter's art. The *School of Athens*, on the near wall as you come in, steals the show, a representation of the triumph of scientific truth, in which all the great minds from antiquity are represented. Plato and Aristotle discuss philosophy at the centre of the painting: Aristotle, the father of scientific method, motions downwards; Plato, pointing upward, indicating his philosophy of otherworldly spirituality, is believed to be a portrait of Leonardo da Vinci. Spread across the steps is Diogenes, lazily ignorant of all that is happening around him, while to the left Raphael added a solitary, sullen portrait of Michelangelo – a homage to the artist, apparently painted after Raphael saw the first stage of the Sistine Chapel almost next door.

The last room, the **Stanza Incendio**, was the last to be decorated, to the orders and general glorification of Pope Leo X, and in a sense it brings together three generations of work. The ceiling was painted by Perugino, Raphael's teacher, and the frescoes were completed to Raphael's designs by his pupils (notably Giulio Romano), most striking of which is the *Fire in the Borgo*, facing the main window – an oblique reference to Leo X restoring peace to Italy after Julius II's reign but in fact describing an event that took place during the reign of Leo IV, when the pope stood in the loggia of the old St Peter's and made the sign of the cross to extinguish a fire.

THE BORGIA APARTMENTS

Outside the Raphael Stanze, on the other side of the Sistine Chapel steps, the **Borgia Apartments** were inhabited by Julius II's hated predecessor, Alexander VI – a fact which persuaded Julius to move into the new set of rooms he called upon Raphael to decorate. Nowadays it's host to a largely missable collection of modern religious art, including liturgical vestments designed by Matisse, a *Landscape with Angels* by Salvador Dalí, and one of Francis Bacon's studies of Innocent X after Valazquez. But it's Pinturicchio's ceiling frescoes in the *Sala dei Santi* that are most worth seeing, typically rich in colour and detail, depicting the legend of Osiris and the Apis bull – a reference to the Borgia family symbol, a bull. Among other images is a scene showing St Catherine of Alexandria disputing with the Emperor Maximillian, in which Pinturicchio has placed his self-portrait behind the emperor – and also, clearly visible in the background, the Arch of Constantine. The figure of St Catherine is said to be a portrait of Lucrezia Borgia, and the room was reputedly the scene of a decidedly un-papal party to celebrate the first of Lucrezia's three marriages, which ended up with men tossing sweets down the fronts of the women's dresses.

THE SISTINE CHAPEL

Steps lead up from here to the **Sistine Chapel**, a huge barn-like structure built for Pope Sixtus IV between 1473 and 1481. It serves as the pope's official private chapel and the scene of the conclaves of cardinals for the election of each new pontiff. The ceiling paintings here, and the *Last Judgement* on the wall behind the altar, together make up arguably the greatest masterpiece in Western art, and the largest body of painting ever planned and executed by one man – Michelangelo. They are also probably the most viewed paintings in the world: it's estimated that on an average day about 15,000 people trudge through here to take a look; and during the summer and on special occasions the number of visitors can exceed 20,000. Bear in mind that the taking of pictures of any kind, including video, is prohibited in the chapel, and it is also officially forbidden to speak – although this is something that is rampantly ignored.

Upon completion of the structure, Sixtus brought in several prominent painters of the Renaissance to decorate the **walls**. The overall project was under the management of Pinturicchio and comprised a series of paintings showing (on the left as you face the altar) scenes from the life of Moses and, on the right, scenes from the life of Christ. Sixtus didn't have just anybody work on these: there are paintings by, among others, Perugino, who painted the marvellously composed cityscape of *Jesus giving St Peter the Keys to Heaven*, Botticelli – *The Trials of Moses* and *Cleansing of the Leper* – and Ghirlandaio, whose *Calling of St Peter and St Andrew* shows Christ calling the two saints to be disciples, surrounded by onlookers, against a fictitious medieval landscape of boats, birds, turrets and mountains. Some of the paintings were in fact collaborative efforts, and it's known that Ghirlandaio and Botticelli in particular contributed to each other's work. Recently restored, anywhere else they would be pored over very closely indeed. As it is, they are entirely overshadowed by Michelangelo's more famous work.

It was Pope Julius II who turned his attention to the **ceiling**; he was an avid collector and patron of the arts, and summoned to Rome the best artists and architects of the day, among them Michelangelo, who, through a series of political intrigues orchestrated by Bramante and Raphael, was assigned the task of decorating the Sistine Chapel. Oddly enough, Michelangelo hadn't wanted to do the work at all: he considered himself a sculptor, not a painter, and was more eager to get on with carving Julius II's tomb (now in San Pietro in Vincoli, see p.715) than the ceiling, which he regarded as a chore. Pope Julius II, however, had other plans, drawing up a design of the twelve Apostles for the vault and hiring Bramante to design a scaffold for the artist from which to work. Michelangelo was apparently an awkward, solitary character: he had barely begun painting when he rejected Bramante's scaffold as unusable, fired all his staff, and dumped the pope's scheme for the ceiling in favour of his own. But the pope was easily his match, and there are tales of the two men clashing while the work was going on – Michelangelo would lock the doors at crucial points, ignoring the pope's demands to see how it was progressing; and legend has the two men at loggerheads at the top of the scaffold one day, resulting in the pope striking the artist in frustration.

The **frescoes** depict scenes from the Old Testament, from the *Creation of Light* at the altar end to the *Drunkenness of Noah* over the door. The sides are decorated with prophets and sibyls and the ancestors of Jesus. Julius II lived only a few months after the Sistine Chapel ceiling was finished, but the fame of the work he had commissioned soon spread far and wide. Certainly, it's staggeringly impressive, all the more so for its recent restoration (financed by a Japanese TV company to the tune of $3 million in return for three years' world TV rights), which has lifted centuries of accumulated soot and candle grime off the paintings to reveal a much brighter, more vivid painting than anyone thought existed. The restorers have also been able to chart the progress of Michelangelo as he moved across the vault. Images on fresco must be completed before the plaster dries, and each day a fresh layer of plaster would have been laid, on which Michelangelo would have had around eight hours or so before having to finish for the day. Comparing the different areas of plaster, it seems the figure of Adam, in the key *Creation of Adam* scene, took just four days; God, in the same fresco, took three days. You can also see the development of Michelangelo as a painter when you look at the paintings in reverse order. The first painting, over the door, the *Drunkenness of Noah*, is done in a stiff and formal style, and is vastly different from the last painting he did, over the altar, which shows the artist at his best, the perfect master of the technique of fresco painting.

The **Last Judgement**, on the altar wall of the chapel, was painted by Michelangelo more than twenty years later (1535–41). Michelangelo wasn't especially keen to work on this either – he was still engaged on Julius II's tomb, under threat of legal action from the late pope's family – but Pope Paul III, an old acquaintance of the artist, was

keen to complete the decoration of the chapel. The painting took five years, again single-handed, but it is probably the most inspired and most homogeneous large-scale
painting you're ever likely to see, the technical virtuosity of Michelangelo taking a back
seat to the sheer exuberance of the work. The human body is fashioned into a finely
captured set of exquisite poses: even the damned can be seen as a celebration of the
human form. Perhaps unsurprisingly, the painting offended some, and even before it
was complete Rome was divided as to its merits, especially regarding the etiquette of
introducing such a display of nudity into the pope's private chapel. But Michelangelo's
response to this was unequivocal, lampooning one of his fiercer critics, the pope's master of ceremonies at the time, Biago di Cesena, as Minos, the doorkeeper of hell, with
ass's ears and an entwined serpent in the bottom right-hand corner of the picture. Later
the pope's zealous successor, Pius IV, objected to the painting and would have had it
removed entirely had not Michelangelo's pupil, Daniele da Volterra, appeased him by
carefully – and selectively – adding coverings to some of the more obviously naked figures, earning himself forever the nickname of the "breeches-maker". During the recent
work, most of the remaining breeches have been discreetly removed, restoring the
painting to its former glory.

THE BRACCIO NUOVO AND MUSEO CHIARAMONTI

Walking back from the Sistine Chapel takes you through the **Braccio Nuovo** and
Museo Chiaramonti, which both hold classical sculpture, although be warned that
they are the Vatican at its most overwhelming – close on a thousand statues crammed
into two long galleries – and you need a keen eye and much perseverance to make any
sense of it all. The **Braccio Nuovo** was built in the early 1800s to display classical statuary that was particularly prized, and it contains, among other things, probably the
most famous extant image of Augustus, and a bizarre-looking statue depicting the Nile,
whose yearly flooding was essential to the fertility of the Egyptian soil. The 300-metre-
long **Chiaramonti gallery** is especially unnerving, lined as it is with the chill marble
busts of hundreds of nameless, blank-eyed ancient Romans, along with the odd deity. It
pays to have a leisurely wander, for there are some real characters here: sour, thin-
lipped matrons with their hair tortured into pleats, curls and spirals; kids, caught in a
sulk or mid-chortle; and ancient old men with flesh sagging and wrinkling to reveal the
skull beneath.

THE PINACOTECA

The **Pinacoteca** is housed in a separate building on the far side of the Vatican's main
spine and ranks possibly as Rome's best picture gallery, with works from the early to
High Renaissance right up to the nineteenth century. Among early works, there are
pieces by Crivelli, Lippi and the stunning Simoneschi triptych by Giotto of the *Martyrdom
of SS Peter and Paul*, painted in the early 1300s for the old St Peter's. There are the rich
backdrops and elegantly clad figures of the Umbrian School painters, Perugino and
Pinturicchio, and Raphael has a room to himself, including, in climate-controlled glass
cases, the tapestries that were made to his designs to be hung in the Sistine Chapel during conclave, and three paintings including the *Transfiguration*, which he had nearly completed when he died in 1520, and which was finished by his pupils, the *Coronation of the
Virgin*, done when he was only 19 years old, and, on the left, the *Madonna of Foglino*,
showing saints John the Baptist, Francis of Assisi, and Jerome. Leonardo's *St Jerome*, in
the next room, is unfinished too, but it's a remarkable piece of work, with Jerome a rake-
like ascetic torn between suffering and a good meal. Caravaggio's *Descent from the Cross*
in the next room but one, however, gets more attention, a warts 'n' all canvas that unusually shows the Virgin Mary as a middle-aged mother grieving over her dead son, while
the men placing Christ's body on the bier are obviously models that the artist recruited
from the city streets – a realism that is imitated successfully by Reni's *Crucifixion of St*

Peter in the same room. Take a look also at the most gruesome painting in the collection, Poussin's *Martyrdom of St Erasmus*, which shows the saint stretched out on a table with his hands bound above his head in the process of having his small intestine wound onto a drum – basically being "drawn" prior to "quartering".

THE MUSEUMS GREGORIANO PROFANO, PIO CRISTIANO AND PIO CRISTIANO
Leaving the Pinacoteca, you're well placed for the further grouping of museums in the modern building next door. The **Museo Gregoriano Profano** holds more classical sculpture, mounted on scaffolds for all-round viewing, including mosaics of athletes from the Baths of Caracalla and Roman funerary work, notably the Haterii tomb friezes, which show backdrops of ancient Rome and realistic portrayals of contemporary life. The adjacent **Museo Pio Cristiano** has intricate early Christian sarcophagi and, most famously, an expressive third-century AD statue of the *Good Shepherd*. And the **Museo Pio Cristiano** displays art and artefacts from all over the world, collected by Catholic missionaries, and seems to be inspired by the Vatican's desire to poke fun at non-Christian cults as well as pat itself on the back for its own evangelical successes.

Eating

Rome is great place to **eat**: its denizens know a good deal about freshness and authenticity, and can be very demanding when it comes to the quality of the dishes they are served. Consequently, eating out is a major, often hours-long, activity in Rome, and the meals you'll enjoy generally range from good to truly remarkable. You'll find that most city-centre **restaurants** offer standard Italian dishes, although a few more adventurous restaurants have been popping up of late. At the geographical centre of the country, Italy's capital also has numerous establishments dedicated to a variety of regional cuisines, and a reasonable number of excellent ethnic restaurants. Rome is blessed with an abundance of good, honest **pizzerias** as well, churning out thin, crispy-baked pizza from wood-fired ovens. We've also listed a range of places serving **snacks** and, at the end of the section, the best of the city's **gelaterie** and **pasticcerie**. One final caveat: generally speaking it's hard to find truly bad food and rip-off prices in Rome. However, it may be wise to avoid places that are adjacent to some major monuments, such as the Pantheon, Piazza Navona, or the Vatican. The food in these places can be poor, and the prices truly outlandish, sometimes as much as three times the going rate. Near major sights, use the guide!

Lunch, snacks and self-service

Rome has plenty of places to refuel during a long day's sightseeing, and they don't all cater for tourists. Most bars sell *panini* and *tramezzini*, and there are plenty of stand-up rosticerrias, but the following are some of our favourite places for a good-quality, unpretentious **lunch or snack,** or just a sustaining cup of coffee.

Centro Storico and east of Via del Corso
Antico Forno, Via delle Muratte. The last thing you'd expect just by the Trevi Fountain: fresh pizza, a sandwich bar, a bakery and grocery store, all rolled into one – and open on Sundays.
Brek, Largo di Torre Argentina 1. A self-service restaurant, part of a chain, with a colourful cinema-theme décor. Everything is prepared fresh. Good for both a snack or a full meal.
Caffé Leonardo, Piazza Mignanelli 21a. Just around from the Spanish Steps, this bistro offers sandwiches and dozens of big, satisfying salads at amazing prices for the chic zone it's in.
Caffé Sant'Eustachio, Piazza Sant'Eustachio 82. Just behind the Pantheon you'll find what many feel is absolutely Rome's best coffee, usually served Neopolitan-style – that is, very, very sweet.

ROMAN FOOD AND WINE

Roman cooking is traditionally dominated by the offal-based earthy cuisine of the working classes, with a little influence from the city's centuries-old Jewish population thrown in. Although you'll find all sorts of pasta served in Roman restaurants, spaghetti is probably the most popular, as it stands up well to the coarse, gutsy sauces the Romans prefer: *aglio e olio* (oil and garlic), *cacio e pepe* (pecorino and ground black pepper), *alla carbonara* (with beaten eggs, cubes of pan-fried *guanciale* – cured pork jowl – or bacon, and pecorino or parmesan), and *alle vongole* (with baby clams). Fish is an integral, though usually pricey, part of Roman cuisine, and is most frequently eaten in Rome as salt cod – *baccalà*; best eaten Jewish-style, deep-fried. Offal is also important and although it has been ousted from many of the more refined city-centre restaurants, you'll still find it on the menus of more traditional places, especially those in Testaccio. Most favoured is *pajata*, the intestines of an unweaned calf, but you'll also find *lingua* (tongue), *rognone* (kidney), *milza* (spleen – delicious as a paté on toasted bread) and *trippa* (tripe). Look out too for *coda alla vaccinara*, oxtail stewed in a rich sauce of tomato and celery; *testerelle d'abbacchio*, lamb's head baked in the oven with herbs and oil; and *coratella*, lamb's heart, liver, lungs and spleen cooked in olive oil with lots of black pepper and onions. More conventional meat dishes include *abbacchio*, milk-fed lamb roasted to melting tenderness with rosemary, sage and garlic; *scottadito*, grilled lamb chops eaten with the fingers; and *saltimbocca alla romana*, thin slices of veal cooked with a slice of prosciutto and sage on top. Artichokes (*carciofi*) are the quintessential Roman vegetable, served "alla romana" (stuffed with garlic and roman mint and stewed) and in all their unadulterated glory as *alla giudea* – flattened and deep fried in olive oil. Another not-to-be-missed side dish is batter-fried squash or courgette blossom, stuffed with mozzarella and a sliver of marinated anchovy. Roman pizza has a thin crust and is best when baked in a wood-burning oven (*cotta a legna*), but you can also find pizza by the slice (*pizza al taglio*), always sold by weight.

Wine comes mainly from the Castelli Romani (most famously Frascati) to the south, and from around Montefiascone (Est! Est! Est!) in the north. Both are basic, straightforward whites, fine for sunny lunchtimes but otherwise not all that noteworthy. However, in most places you'll find a complete selection of Italy's best and most famous wines.

Filetti di Baccalà, Largo dei Librari 88. A fish-and-chip shop without the chips. Paper-covered Formica tables (outdoors in summer), cheap wine, beer and fried cod, a timeless Roman speciality. Located near Campo de' Fiori. Closed in August.

Il Forno di Campo de' Fiori, Campo de' Fiori 22. The *pizza bianca* here is a Roman legend, and their *pizza rossa* (with a smear of tomato sauce) follows close behind. Get it hot from the oven.

Herbier Natura, Via San Claudio 87. Just off Piazza San Silvestro, inside a lovely inner courtyard, this is a real oasis of calm away from the hectic and fumy traffic. Snacks or even a full lunch.

La Scaletta, Via della Maddalena 46–49. Very centrally placed *birreria* that's good for its great, reviving snacks, hot meals, or just a drink between sights.

Self-Service Luncheonette, Salita di San Nicola da Tolentino 19/21. Just up from Bernini's spouting Triton fountain at Piazza Barberini, this place has great food served cafeteria-style.

Zi Fenizia, Via Santa Maria del Pianto 64–65. Kosher pizza to go in the heart of the Jewish Ghetto, and also roasted chicken, *supplì*, burgers and *shawarma*.

Termini and around

Caffé Fantini, Via A. Depretis 77b. Cafeteria-style service, sandwiches, and a hot and cold buffet. A convenient place to break after seeing Santa Maria Maggiore.

Enoteca Cavour 313, Via Cavour 313. At the Forum end of Via Cavour, a lovely old wine bar that makes a handy retreat after seeing the ancient sites. Lots of wines and delicious (though not cheap) snacks and salads.

Trimani, Via Cernaia 37b. Classy wine bar (Rome's biggest selection of Italian regional vintages) good for a lunchtime tipple and gastronomic indulgence.

Across the river: Trastevere and the Vatican

Fidelio, Via degli Stefaneschi 3/7. Tucked away behind Piazza Sonino in Trastevere, a *vineria* with lunch and dinner possibilities, too.

Il Mondo in Tasca, Via della Lungaretta 169. This great little place, whose name translates as "The World in Your Pocket", offers *shawarma*, felafel, hummus, curry, pizza, chili con carne, couscous, salads, tandoori, moussaka, goulash, etc. Plus you can check your email and get a tarot reading.

Non Solo Pizza, Via degli Scipioni 95–97. Try a slice of pizza with sausage and broccoli or with courgette flowers. There's also the whole range of Roman fritters – *supplì, olive ascolane, fiori di zucca, crocchette*, etc. – and a complete selection of hot dishes.

Ombre Rosse, Piazza Sant'Egidio 12. People-watching spot that has become a Trastevere institution, especially for a morning cappuccino, but also for interesting light meals.

Da Venanzo, Via San Francesco a Ripa 137. Hole-in-the-wall pizzeria that does great slices, as well as roast chickens and potatoes, *supplì* and all the usual rosticceria fare.

Restaurants and pizzerias

There are lots of good places to eat in the **centro storico**, and it's still surprisingly easy to find places that are not tourist traps – prices in all but the really swanky places remain pretty uniform throughout the city. The area around **Via Cavour** and **Termini** is packed with cheap restaurants, although some of them are of dubious cleanliness; if you are not in a hurry, you might do better heading up to the nearby student area of **San Lorenzo**, where you can often eat far better for the same money. South of the centre, the **Testaccio** neighbourhood is also well endowed with good, inexpensive trattorias, and, across the river, **Trastevere** is Rome's traditional restaurant enclave. Even though the number of authentic "Trasté" trattorias has declined over recent years, you'll easily find good-to-great meals there, at all price levels.

Centro Storico and east of Via del Corso

Armando al Pantheon, Salita de' Crescenzi 30. (☎06.6880.3034) Surprisingly unpretentious surroundings and hearty food in a spot so close to the Pantheon. Good prices, too. Closed Sat pm and all day Sun.

Da Baffetto, Via del Governo Vecchio 114 (☎06.686.1617). A tiny, highly authentic pizzeria that has long been a Rome institution. Amazingly it's still good value, and has tables outside in summer, though you'll always have to queue.

Beltramme, Via della Croce 39. This very old-fashioned *fiaschetteria* (originally it sold only wine, by the *fiasco* or flask), two blocks from the Spanish Steps, is just about always packed and is fairly pricey, but if you want authentic Roman food, atmosphere and service the way it used to be, this is the place. No credit cards.

Caffé Capranica, Piazza Capranica 104 (☎06.679.0860). This restaurant, taverna and pizzeria all in one is admirably located on a quiet piazza near the Pantheon. Standard fare, well prepared, and average prices.

La Carbonara, Campo de' Fiori 23 (☎06.686.4783). The most expensive of the square's restaurants, but always busy, with plenty of outdoor seating and an excellent selection of antipasti. Try their homemade ravioli, *pappardelle* in wild boar sauce, or their namesake, *spaghetti alla carbonara*. Closed Tues.

Ciccia Bomba, Via del Governo Vecchio 76 (☎06.6880.2108). Very central, versatile pizzeria/trattoria that serves quality food for reasonable prices. Closed Wed.

L'Enoteca Antica, Via della Croce 76b (☎06.679.0896). An old Spanish Steps-area wine bar with a selection of hot and cold dishes, including soups and attractive desserts.

Colline Emiliane, Via degli Avignonesi 22 (☎06.481.7538). Many Italians consider the cuisine of the Emilia Romagna region to be the country's best. Try it for yourself, lovingly prepared by a family, oddly enough, from Le Marche. Closed Fri.

Da Giggetto, Via del Portico d'Ottavia 21–22 (☎06.686.1105). Roman-Jewish fare in the Jewish Ghetto, featuring deep-fried artichokes, *baccalà*, and *rigatoni con pajata*, along with good non-offal pasta dishes, eaten outside in summer by the ruins of the Portico d'Ottavia. Not cheap, but worth the splurge. Closed Mon.

Grappolo d'Oro, Piazza della Cancelleria 80 (☎06.686.4118). Curiously untouched by the hordes in nearby Campo de' Fiori. Genuine Roman cuisine in traditional trattoria atmosphere. Closed Sun.

La Grotta, Via delle Grotte 27 (☎06.686.4293). An out-of-the-way, cosy trattoria with a traditional, limited menu and the deeply authentic feel of old Rome. Outdoor seating in summer, towards the river from Campo de' Fiori. Closed Sun.

L'Insalata Ricca, Largo dei Chiavari 85/86 (☎06.6880.3656). An Anglo-American presence in a relaxed and slightly out-of-the-ordinary place, although it is just one of a Roman chain of six. Interesting, big salads, as the name suggests, wholefood options and reasonably priced Italian fare.

Il Leoncino, Via del Leoncino 28 (☎06.687.6306). Genuine, cheap and hectic pizzeria, just off Via del Corso – really one of the best for lovers of crispy Roman-style pizza, baked in wood ovens. No credit cards. Closed weekday lunchtimes.

La Montecarlo, Vicolo Savelli 12 (☎06.686.1877). Hectic pizzeria owned by the daughter of *Da Baffetto* (see previous page) and serving similar crisp, blistered pizza, along with good pasta dishes. Tables outside in summer, but be prepared to queue.

Myosotis, Via della Vaccarella 3–5 (☎06.686.5554). Excellent food, service and value at this slightly upscale restaurant a short walk from the Pantheon. Try the *maltagliati* or *stracci* if you like fresh pasta. Closed Sun.

Naturist Club – L'Isola, Via della Vite 14 (☎06.679.2509). A friendly vegetarian, semi-self-service restaurant at lunchtime, *Naturist Club* features wholegrain risottos, vegetable pies and fresh juices. In the evenings it becomes *L'Isola*, an affordable restaurant specializing in fish dishes. Closed Sun.

Otello alla Concordia, Via della Croce 81 (☎06.678.1454). This place used to be one of Fellini's favourites – he lived just a few blocks away on Via Margutta – and remains an elegant, yet affordable choice in the heart of Rome. Closed Sun.

Der Pallaro, Largo del Pallaro 15 (☎06.6880.1488). An old-fashioned trattoria serving a set daily menu for L32,000/€16.53, including wine. Located in a quiet piazza between Campo de' Fiori and Largo Argentina. No credit cards. Closed Mon.

Pizza Cir, Via della Mercede 43–45 (☎06.678.6015). A big, friendly pizza place that also has first courses, main courses, and desserts.

Pizza Re, Via di Ripetta 14 (☎06.321.1468). Authentic Neapolitan pizzeria made in a wood-stoked oven. Busy, so book. Closed Sun lunch.

Da Vito, Vdelle Colonnelle 5 (☎06.679.3842). Close by the Panetheon but hidden away, and very authentic, this trattoria has several set menus and an extensive à la carte selection. All the standards plus their own typically Roman specialities. Closed Wed.

Termini and around

Africa, Via Gaeta 26 (☎06.494.1077). Arguably the city's most interesting (Eritrean) food, and the first culinary sign of Rome's mostly recently arrived Ethiopian and Somalian population. Closed Sat.

Baia Chia, Via Machiavelli 5 (☎06.7045.3452). Near Santa Maria Maggiore, this Sardinian restaurant has lots of good fish starters and tasty first courses. Closed Sun.

Il Dito e la Luna, Via dei Sabelli 49/51 (☎06.494.0726). Creative Sicilian cuisine in a bistro-like San Lorenzo restaurant popular with thirty-something-ish Romans. Closed Sun.

Formula 1, Via degli Equi 13 (☎06.445.3866). Justifiably popular San Lorenzo pizzeria, with tables outside in summer. Closed Sun.

Il Podista, Via Tiburtina 224 (☎06.4470.0967). Owned and run by marathon-runners – hence, perhaps, the quickly served pizzas and fried food, along with typically Roman fare. Closed Sun.

Pommidoro, Piazza dei Sanniti 44 (☎06.445.2692). A typical, family-run Roman trattoria, with a breezy open veranda in summer and a fireplace in winter. Closed Sun.

Tram Tram, Via dei Reti 44–46 (☎06.490.416). Trendy, animated and smoky San Lorenzo restaurant, serving some fine Pugliese pasta dishes, notably seafood lasagne, and unusual salads. Reservations are recommended. Closed Mon.

Across the river: Trastevere and the Vatican

Ai Marmi, Viale Trastevere 53/59 (☎06.580.0919). Nicknamed "the mortuary" because of its stark interior and marble tables, this place serves unique "*supplì al telefono*" (deep-fried rice balls, so named because of the string of mozzarella it forms when you take a bite), fresh *baccalà* and the best pizza in Trastevere. A lively feel of the real Rome. Closed Wed.

Casetta de' Trastevere, Piazza de' Renzi 31–32 (☎06.580.0158). A traditional Trastevere eatery in every way. Beautiful setting, good food, low prices. Delicious *spaghetti alle vongole*. Closed Mon.

La Grotta Azzurra, Via Cicerone 62a (☎06.323.4490). Quiet, relaxing refuge after a day at the Vatican. Fish specialities and impeccable service at moderate prices. Closed Thurs.

L'Insalatiera 2, Via Trionfale 94 (☎06.3974.2975). A vegetarian restaurant specializing in regional Italian cuisine. Everything is home-made, including the wonderful desserts, such as chocolate and ricotta pie. No smoking. Closed Sun.

Ivo, Via di San Francesco a Ripa 158 (☎06.581.7082). *The* Trastevere pizzeria, almost in danger of becoming a caricature, but still good. Arrive early to avoid a chaotic queue. Closed Tues.

Monzù Vladi, Piazza San Giovanni della Malva 2 (☎06.589.5640). A welcome newcomer to Trastevere, this great restaurant specializes in fine Neapolitan cuisine. Go on Monday, Wednesday, or Friday, when the cheeses arrive fresh from Campania. Closed Sun.

Da Paris, Piazza San Callisto 7a (☎06.581.5378). Fine Roman Jewish cookery in one of Trastevere's most atmospheric piazzas. Also other traditional dishes. Closed Sun.

Dar Poeta, Vicolo del Bologna 45 (☎06.588.0516). Without any doubts, one of the top-ten pizzerias in Rome. Don't expect the typical crusty Roman pizza here; the margherita (ask for it *con basilico* – with basil) comes out of the oven soft and with plenty of good mozzarella on top. Closed Mon.

Romolo, Via Porta Settimiana 8 (☎06.581.3873). A Trastevere institution, apparently located in the very building where Raphael's lover, "La Fornarina", lived. Great garden setting in fine weather. Traditional Roman menu. Closed Mon.

Gelaterie and Pasticcerie

Dolci & Doni, Via delle Carrozze 85. A truly sumptuous array of pastries right in the heart of the city, just a few steps away from Piazza di Spagna. Tea and other snacks, too.

Doppia Coppia, Via della Scala 51. This Sicilian-owned Trastevere joint has some of the very best ice cream in town. Sublime consistency and unusual flavours.

Il Forno del Ghetto, Via del Portico d'Ottavia 1. Marvellous kosher Jewish bakery whose pies and pastries draw quite a crowd.

Il Gelato di San Crispino, Via della Panetteria 42. Considered by many to be the best ice cream in Rome. Wonderful flavours – all natural – will make the other *gelato* you've tasted pale by comparison.

Giolitti, Via Uffici del Vicario 40. An Italian institution that once had a reputation – now lost – for the country's top ice cream. Still pretty good, however, with a choice of seventy flavours.

Palazzo del Freddo di Giovanni Fassi, Via Principe Eugenio 65/7. A wonderful, airy 1920s ice cream parlour not far from Termini. Brilliant fruit ice creams and good milk shakes.

Pascucci, Via di Torre Argentina 20. *Frullati* central for the *centro storico*. Your choice of fresh fruit whipped up with ice and milk – the ultimate Roman refreshment on a hot day.

Tre Scalini, Piazza Navona 30. Bus #64 or #492. Open Thurs–Tues, 8am–1.30am. Piazza Navona institution that is renowned for its famous *tartufo* – death by dark chocolate.

Valzani, Via del Moro 37. One of the oldest of the city's pastry shops, still keeping up traditions. Closed June–15 Sept.

Drinking

There are plenty of **bars** in Rome, and although, as with the rest of Italy, most are functional daytime haunts and not at all the kinds of places you'd want to spend an evening, due in part to the considerable presence of Anglo-Americans, and the changing tastes of Italian youth, there are plenty of more conducive bars and pubs nowadays – and there's now an Irish pub practically on every corner in central Rome. There's also been a recent upsurge of interest in **wine bars** (*enoteche* or *vinerie*): the old ones have gained new cachet and newer ones, with wine lists the size of unabridged dictionaries, are weighing in too, often with gourmet menus to go with the wines they offer.

Bear in mind that there is sometimes considerable **crossover** between Rome's bars, restaurants and clubs: for the most part, the places listed below are drinking spots, but you can eat, sometimes quite substantially, at many of them, and several could be classed just as easily as nightclubs, with loud music and occasionally even an entrance charge. Although we've divided these listings into the usual **neighbourhoods**, the truth is the areas around Campo de' Fiori and the Pantheon, plus Trastevere and Testaccio, are the densest and most happening parts of town.

Centro Storico and east of Via del Corso

Bar del Fico, Piazza del Fico 26–28. Currently one of several hotspots in the area – just around the corner from *Bar della Pace*, and slightly cheaper. Outdoor heating in winter.

Bar della Pace, Via della Pace 5. Just off Piazza Navona, this is *the* summer bar, with outside tables full of Rome's self-consciously beautiful people.

Bevitoria Navona, Piazza Navona 72. Right by the Fountain of Neptune, a wine-tasters' tradition. Regulars swear it's the *only* place in Rome to drink Italian wine.

La Curia di Bacco, Via dei Biscione 79. This lively place looks like it was hollowed out of the ruins of the ancient Teatro di Pompeii, near Campo de' Fiori – and, in fact, it was. A young crowd, some good wines and interesting snacks.

The Drunken Ship, Campo de' Fiori 20–21. A lively meeting-point, with great music, tremendously popular with young Romans and foreign students. Happy hour 7–9pm.

Jonathan's Angels, Via della Fossa 18. This quirky bar, just behind Piazza Navona, certainly wins the "most decorated" award. Every inch (even the toilet, which is worth a visit on its own) is plastered, painted or tricked out in outlandish style by the artist-proprietor.

Lowenhaus, Via della Fontanella 16d. Just off Piazza del Popolo, a Bavarian-style drinking establishment with beer and snacks to match. Live jazz from 10pm onwards on Fridays.

Miscellanea, Via delle Paste 110a. Located halfway between Via del Corso and the Pantheon, this place was the first American-style bar in Rome, a boozy hangout of US students, and inevitably packed at night. Reasonable prices and the best-value sandwiches in town.

Rock Castle Café, Via B. Cenci 8. In the Jewish Ghetto, just across from Trastevere, a student hangout consisting of six medieval-style rooms, all for dancing and mingling.

Trinity College, Via del Collegio Romano 6. A warm and inviting establishment offering international beers and food. Food includes complete pub meals until 1am.

Victoria House, Via Gesù e Maria 18. Authentically dingy English-style pub, just a stone's throw from Piazza di Spagna. There's a non-smoking room, and a happy hour from 6pm to 9pm.

Vineria, Campo de' Fiori 15. Long-established bar/wine shop right on the Campo, patronized by devoted regulars, although it's recently been refurbished, and now also offers light meals. Closed Sun lunchtime.

Termini and around

Druid's Den, Via San Martino ai Monti 28. Appealing Irish pub near Santa Maria Maggiore with a genuine Celtic feel (and owners). It's not just for the homesick: it has a mixed expat/Italian clientele. Closed Mon.

Fiddler's Elbow, Via dell'Olmata 43. One of the two original Irish bars in Rome, one block closer to Santa Maria Maggiore than its rival the *Druid's*, and roomier, with a decidedly more Latin feel.

Monti D.O.C., Via G. Lanza 93. Comfortable Santa Maria Maggiore neighbourhood wine bar, with a good wine list and some nice food: quiches, salads and pastas. Closed Sun.

Rive Gauche 2, Via dei Sabelli 43. The San Lorenzo district's mythic dive, a smoky, noisy, cavernous evocation of intellectual Left Bank Paris – more or less. Happy hour till 9pm.

Across the river: Trastevere and the Vatican

Il Cantiniere di Santadorotea, Via di Santa Dorotea 9. In the heart of Trastevere, this place has some great wines and a range of delicious snacks. Closed Tues.

Clamur, Piazza del'Emporio 1. Large yet cosy Irish pub, on the trendy Testaccio side of the Porta Portese (Trastevere) bridge, offering the usual beers plus snacks.

Fiestaloca, Via degli Orti di Cesare 7. Mexico-by-the-Tiber-in-Trastevere with very mixed music and very Tex-Mex menu. You have to pay to get in at weekends – Friday L10,000/€5.17, drink included, Saturday L15,000/€7.75, drink included. Closed Mon.

Enoteca Malafemmina, Via San Crisogono 31. This Trastevere wine bar is one of the friendliest places in town. Some amazing wines and delicious light snacks ordered fresh from the first-class restaurant next door. Closed Wed.

Mr Brown, Vicolo del Cinque 29. This popular night-time hangout is on one of Trastevere's most charming detours. A young, fun-loving crowd, happy hour from 9pm to 10pm daily, cheap beers, and an assortment of salads, sandwiches and crepes. Closed Sun.

La Scala, Piazza della Scala 60. Perhaps the most popular Trastevere *birreria* – big, bustling and crowded, with a Texan-ranch-meets-McDonald's decor. Food too and occasional (dire) music.

Stardust, Vicolo de' Renzi 4. One of Trastevere's most authentic haunts, and just the place for all-night partying, with occasional live jazz.

Nightlife

Roman **nightlife** retains some of the smart ethos satirized in Fellini's film *La Dolce Vita*, and designer-dressing-up is still very much a part of the mainstream scene. Rome's **clubs** run the gamut. There are vast glitter palaces with stunning lights and sound systems, predictable dance music and an over-dressed, over-made-up clientele – good if you can afford it and just want to dance (and observe Romans in their natural Saturday-night element). But there are also places that are not much more than ritzy **bars** with music, and other, more down-to-earth places to dance, playing a more interesting selection of music to a younger, more cautious-spending crowd. Whichever you prefer, all tend to open and close late, and some charge a heavy entrance fee – as much as L25,000/€12.91, which usually includes a drink. During the hot summer months, many clubs close down or move to outdoor locations.

On the **live music scene**, there are plenty of small-scale summer offerings, but the chances of catching major rock and pop acts are virtually nonexistent, and getting worse. Big promoters book the cities up north, especially Milan and Bologna, and leave Rome entirely out of the loop. The city is also a bit of a backwater for the **performing arts**, and very few international performers of renown in any of the arts regularly put in an appearance here. Nevertheless, there is cultural entertainment available, and the quality is sometimes better than you might expect. In any case, what the arts here may lack in professionalism, they often make up for in the charm of the setting. Rome's **summer festival**, for example, organized by "Estate Romana", means that there's a good range of classical music, opera, theatre and cinema running throughout the warm months, often in picturesque locations. Other summer live-music offerings include **Testaccio Village**, and the **Festa dell'Unità**, both held in and around the old slaughterhouse in Testaccio. The Festa dell'Unità charges no admission and includes live music, dancing and an array of other entertainments, as well as ethnic eateries. **Testaccio Village** offers a different group every night during the warm months, followed by three outdoor **discos**, all for free on production of a very low-priced weekly pass – available at the ticket booth near the entrance.

Tickets and information

Rome has no comprehensive **ticket service**; you usually have to go to the venue in person some time before the event. However, you can first try Orbis, near Santa Maria Maggiore, at Piazza Esquilino 37 (Mon–Sat 9.30am–1pm & 4–7.30pm; ☎06.474.4776), or, not far from the Vatican, Box Office, Viale Giulio Cesare 88 (Mon 3.30–7pm, Tues–Sat 10am–1.30pm & 2.30–7pm; ☎06.372.0216), but these two provide only information by phone. If you have a credit card you may be able to save time by calling the Italian-language Prenoticket (Mon 3.30–5pm, Tues–Fri 10am–1pm & 2.30–5pm, Sat 10am–1pm; ☎06.520.721); let the recorded voice speak for about a minute, then dial 1 to select the reservation service. For **what's on information**, see p.684.

Clubs

Alien, Via Velletri 13/19 (☎06.841.2212). Currently one of the hippest clubs in Rome, with art and fashion shows, performance art and exhibitions as well as lots and lots of house music. Admission price L35,000/€18.08, though women are sometimes let in free. It also has a summer venue, *Alien 2 Mare*, in Fregene at Piazzale Fregene 5 (☎06.6656.4761).

Black Out, Via Saturnia 18 (☎06.7049.6791). Punk, trash and indie music, with occasional gigs by US and UK bands. Located out by San Giovanni in Laterano. Admission price L10,000–15,000/€5.17–7.75. Closed in summer.

Gilda, Via Mario de' Fiori 97 (☎06.678.4838). A few blocks from the Spanish Steps, this slick, stylish and expensive club is the focus for the city's minor (and would-be) celebs. Jacket required. Admission price L40,000/€20.66. Their summer venue, *Gilda-on-the-Beach*, is in Fregene, at Lungomare di Ponente 11 (☎06.6656.0649).

Goa, Via Libetta 13 (☎06.574.8277). Opened by famous local DJ Giancarlino and playing techno, house, and trance. There are sofas to help you recover after high-energy dancing; the decor changes every few weeks. Located near San Paolo. Admission price L15,000–30,000/€7.75–15.49.

Jam Session, Via del Cardello 13a (☎06.6994.2419). Just off Via Cavour, this place hosts a young crowd bopping to 1970s & 1980s disco tunes they couldn't possibly have heard first-time around. Wednesday is gay night. Admission price L10,000/€5.17 includes a drink.

Piper, Via Tagliamento 9 (☎06.855.5398). Established in the Seventies by singer Patty Pravo, this place has survived by undergoing a reincarnation every season. There are different nightly events (fashion shows, screenings, parties, gigs and the like), a smart-but-casual mixed-aged crowd, and a heavy pickup scene. Saturday nights are gay nights. Admission price is L15,000–35,000/€7.75–18.08 also depending on the night. Its summer venue, from the end of May to the beginning of September, is by the sea at the *AcquaPiper di Guidonia*, Via Maremmana, before the 23.9km marker (☎0774.326.538).

Gay bars, clubs and restaurants

L'Alibi, Via Monte Testaccio 44 (☎06.574.3448). Predominantly – but by no means exclusively – male venue that's one of Rome's oldest and best gay clubs. Downstairs there's a multi-room cellar disco and upstairs an open-air bar. There's a big terrace to enjoy in the warm months. Free admission Wed & Thurs; other nights L20,000/€10.33.

Baronato Quattro Bellezze, Via di Panico 23 (☎06.687.2865). Definitely one-of-a-kind, this place is owned and run by the inimitable Dominot, life-long drag chanteuse, who performs Piaf here on Thursday evenings. There's nothing else like it, at least not in Rome. Dominot is Tunisian by birth and the fare here is accordingly his home-made couscous. No admission charge.

Garbo, Vicolo di Santa Margherita 1A (☎06.5832.0782). A friendly Trastevere bar, with a relaxed atmosphere and a nice setting, just behind the main piazza. No admission charge.

L'Hangar, Via in Selci 29 (☎06.488.1397). One of Rome's oldest and least expensive gay spots, always crammed with young people. No charge to get in, you just take a ticket and pay when you leave for whatever you've had to drink.

Joli Coeur, Via Sirte 5 (☎06.8621.5827). Pretty far from the centre, in the Villa Ada area, but this club features Rome's only lesbian night every Saturday. Bus #310 or #63.

Le Sorellastre, Via San Francesco di Sales 1b (☎06.718.5288). This Trastevere bar and restaurant, serving Italian and international cuisine, is the only *exclusively* lesbian place in town. Closed Sun.

Rock and pop venues

Accademia, Vicolo della Renella 90 (☎06.589.6321). A popular Trastevere eatery and party spot for a youngish crowd, with live rock Mon & Wed evenings, otherwise a DJ.

Alpheus, Via del Commercio 36 (☎06.574.7826). Housed in an ex-factory off Via Ostiense, a little way beyond Testaccio, this has space for three simultaneous events – usually a disco, concert and exhibition or piece of theatre. Currently Fri night is gay night. Admission price L10,000–15,000/ €5.17–7.75, Wed free for students.

Blue Knight, Via delle Fornaci 8–10 (☎06.630.011). Right near St Peter's, the main floor here is a bar and gelateria, while downstairs there is almost always live acoustic music Thurs–Sat, usually starting at 10.30pm. No admission charge.

Caffè Latino, Via Monte Testaccio 96 (☎06.5728.8384). Multi-event Testaccio club with varied live music almost every night, as well as cartoons, films, and cabaret. There's also a disco playing a selection of funky, acid jazz and black music. Best at weekends when it gets more crowded. Admission price L15,000–20,000/€7.75–10.33.

Circolo degli Artisti, Via Casilina Vecchia 42 (☎06.7030.5684). A very large venue located beyond Porta Maggiore. A good range of bands, with frequent discos and theme nights, etc. Officially members only: L7000/€3.62 for a three-month membership.

Il Locale, Vicolo del Fico 3 (☎06.687.9075). Trendy joint that enjoys a lively, not to say chaotic, atmosphere, and some up-to-the-minute (mainly indie) music. Admission price L5000/€2.58.

Palacisalfa, Viale del Oceano Atlantico (no phone). A giant tent-like structure that is one of the city's two venues for major acts. It's inadequate, but Rome doesn't have much else. Metro B EUR Palasport.

Palaeur, Piazzale dello Sport (no phone). Immense sports arena out in EUR that's one of the two automatic choices for visiting megastars. Appalling acoustics and usually packed. Metro B EUR Palasport.

RipArte Café, Via Orti di Trastevere 7 (☎06.586.1852). Live music at 11pm every evening in an elegantly modern environment, where you can also eat – but best reserve ahead. Entrance L30,000/ €15.49.

Villaggio Globale, Lungotevere Testaccio (☎06.5730.0329). Situated in the old slaughterhouse along the river, this hosts concerts, club nights, performances and exhibitions almost every night. Winter months only. Opening hours depend on events. Admission price L5000/€2.58.

Jazz and Latin venues

Alexanderplatz, Via Ostia 9 (☎06.3974.2171). Rome's top live jazz club/restaurant with reasonable membership and free entry, except when there's star-billing. Reservations recommended.

Berimbau, Via dei Fienaroli 30b (☎06.581.3249). Plenty of live samba and strong Brazilian drinks and food in the heart of Trastevere. Admission price L15,000–20,000/€7.75–10.33, drink included.

Big Mama, Vicolo San Francesco a Ripa 18 (☎06.581.2551). Trastevere-based jazz/blues club of long standing. Closed July–Oct. Again, it's technically members only, but only costs L10,000/€5.17 a month, L20,000/€10.33 for a year.

Escopazzo, Via d'Aracoeli 41 (☎06.6920.0422). Friendly bar that attracts a thirty-something crowd and offers food and wine along with live concerts or jam sessions most nights. Free entrance.

Fonclea, Via Crescenzio 82a (☎06.689.6302). Located near the Vatican, this jazz/soul, funk and rock venue is fitted out like a British pub and has live music most nights. Happy hour 7–8pm. Free admission Mon–Fri and Sun, Sat L10,000/€5.17.

Gregory's, Via Gregoriana 54d (☎06.679.6386). Just up the Spanish Steps and to the right, an elegant nightspot featuring live jazz improvised by Roman and international musicians. Always crowded. Snacks on offer, too.

New Mississippi Jazz Club, Borgo Angelico 18a (☎06.6880.6348). Historical Vatican area jazz venue which also runs a music school. They serve cold buffet dinners, and concerts start at 10pm. Officially members only, but the annual fee is a mere L15,000/€7.75.

Classical music and opera

Rome's own **orchestras** are not of an international standard, and the city attracts far fewer prestigious orchestras and artists than you might expect of a capital. The city's main classical venue is the *Accademia Santa Cecilia* (see overleaf), and we've listed a number of other places where the city's other orchestras and musical associations perform. In the summer, concerts are staged in cloisters, in the Villa Giulia and Teatro di Marcello, just off Piazza Venezia, and in the ancient Roman theatre at Ostia Antica. In addition there are sponsored Sunday-morning concert cycles, such as the *Telecom Italia* one at the *Teatro Sistina*, Via Sistina 129 (☎06.482.6841), between November and April.

Rome's **opera** scene has long been overshadowed by that of Milan but is improving. The **Teatro dell'Opera** is located near Stazione Termini and Piazza della Repubblica, at Via Firenze 72 (box office daily 9am–4.30pm; English spoken; ☎06.4816.0255; metro A Repubblica). Rome's opera season runs from November to May. Nobody compares it to *La Scala*, but cheap tickets are a lot easier to come by, and important singers do sometimes perform here. Expect to pay at least L30,000/€15.49. In summer, the opera moves **outdoors** and ticket prices come down. Summer performances used to be held in a stunning setting at the ancient Baths of Caracalla, but that practice was terminated a few years ago due to excessive damage to the monument. The last few years the venue has been the Stadio Olimpico, but now the Teatro dell'Opera is air-conditioned that too may change.

Accademia Filarmonica Romana, Teatro Olimpico, Piazza Gentile da Fabriano 17 (☎06.326.5991). Classical standards and occasional contemporary works. Performances are on Thurs and run from October to early May. Tickets cost L30,000–60,000/€15.49–30.99.

Accademia di Santa Cecilia, Via della Conciliazione 4 (information ☎06.361.1064; box office ☎06.6880.1044). Year-round, the focus of the Rome classical music scene, with concerts by its own orchestra (Rome's best) and by visiting orchestras and artists. Most of the tickets are pre-sold by season pass, but for certain special events tickets can go for as little as L15,000/€7.75.

Gonfalone, Oratorio del Gonfalone, Via del Gonfalone 32a (☎06.687.5952). The season here runs from November to early June, offering performances of chamber music, with an emphasis on the Baroque, every Thursday at 9pm. Tickets cost L25,000/€12.91 and you can reserve by phone.

Istituzione Universitaria dei Concerti, Aula Magna of the Sapienza University, Piazzale Aldo Moro 5 (☎06.361.0051). Musical offerings ranging from Mozart to Miles Davis. Tickets cost L15,000–50,000/€7.75–25.82, and the season runs from October to April.

Film

There tends to be more and more **English-language cinema** on offer in Rome, partly due to foreign demand, but also because Italians are finally beginning to realize that they've been at a disadvantage culturally, linguistically and economically by being spoon-fed a steady diet of dubbed travesties. If you can understand Italian, you'll naturally also find current Italian productions available all over town.

Alcazar, Via Merry del Val 14 (☎06.588.0099). Trastevere cinema featuring mainstream American and English films.

Nuovo Olimpia, Via in Lucina 16 (☎06.686.1068). Very central, with two screens, and always featuring at least one foreign film in the original language.

Nuovo Sacher, Largo Ascianghi 1 (☎06.581.8116). Trastevere film theatre showing mainly foreign independent films in their original versions. L8000/€4.13, during the day, L10,000/€5.17 at night.

Pasquino, Piazza Sant'Egidio 10 (☎06.580.3622). Long-established in Trastevere as Rome's premier English-language cinema, with three screens showing recent general releases and the odd indie from Sundance, etc.

Quirinetta, Via. M. Minghetti 4 (☎06.679.0012). Centrally located, near the Trevi Fountain, and always showing films in the original language – most of them first-run mainstream American fare. A huge screen and great Dolby surround-sound.

Listings

Airlines Alitalia, Via Bissolati 11 (information ☎06.65.643; 24hr domestic flight information ☎06.65.641; international flights ☎06.65.642); British Airways, Via Bissolati 54 (☎06.485.480;

Fiumicino airport ☎06.6501.1513); TWA, Via Barberini 67 (☎06.47.211; Fiumicino airport ☎06.6595.4921). Note that most other airlines are either in or very close by Via Bissolati and Via Barberini.

Airport enquiries Fiumicino ☎06.6595.3640 or 06.6595.4455; Ciampino ☎06.794.941.

American Express Travel office and exchange facilities at Piazza di Spagna 38 (Mon–Fri 9am–5.30pm, Sat 9am–12.30; longer hours in the summer; ☎06.67.641).

Auto Club Italia (ACI) ☎06.49.981; 24hr recorded information ☎06.44.77. Italy's automobile club has an English-speaking staff that can help you with driving or repair information at little or no cost.

Bike and scooter rental Collalti, Via del Pellegrino 82 (☎06.6880.1084; closed Mon) does bike rental and repairs; Rent-a-Scooter Motoservices, Via F. Turati 50 (☎06.446.9222), is the best deal for scooters and offers a 10 percent discount to *Rough Guide* readers.

Books The Lion Bookshop, Via dei Greci 33 (☎06.3265.0437), is one of the city's biggest and best-stocked English-language bookshops, and has an English-speaking staff for enquiries. Try also the Anglo-American Book Co, Via della Vite 102 (☎06.679.5222); the Corner Bookshop, Via del Moro 48 (☎06.583.6942; no closing day), a tiny gem run by an English lady and her cat; the Economy Book Center, Via Torino 136 (☎06.474.6877); and Feltrinelli International, Via Orlando 84 (☎06.482.7878; no closing day), which has an excellent selection of English books and travel guides.

Car rental All the big names have desks at Fiumicino and Termini. In the city centre itself, there are, among others, Avis, Via Sardegna 38a (☎06.4282.4728), Hertz, Via Veneto 156 (☎06.321.6831), and Maggiore, Via Po 8 (☎06.854.8698).

Car repair Call ☎116 for emergency breakdown service. Otherwise, consult the ACI (see above) or the Yellow Pages under "Autoriparazioni" for repair shops.

Club Alpino Italiano Corso Vittorio Emanuele 305 (☎06.683.2684).

Dentist The Ospedale di Odontoiatria G. Eastman, Viale Regina Elena 287b (☎06.8448.3232), has a 24-hour emergency service.

Embassies Australia, Corso Trieste 25c (☎06.852.721, emergencies toll free at ☎800.877.790); Britain, Via XX Settembre 80a (☎06.482.5441); Canada, Via Zara 30 (☎06.445.981); Ireland, Piazza Campitelli 3 (☎06.697.9121); New Zealand, Via Zara 28 (☎06.441.7171); USA, Via Veneto 119 (☎06.46.741).

Emergencies Call ☎113. Both the Police and the Carabinieri have offices in Termini. Otherwise the most central police office is off Via del Corso in Piazza del Collegio Romano 3 (☎06.46.861), and there's a Carabinieri office in Piazza Venezia to the right of Via del Corso.

Exchange American Express (see above); Thomas Cook, Piazza Barberini 21a (Mon–Sat 9am–8pm, Sun 9.30am–5pm); Via della Conciliazione 23 (Mon–Sat 9am–8pm, Sun 9.30am–5pm).

Football Rome's two teams, Roma and Lazio, play at the Stadio Olimpico, on Via del Foro Italico, on alternate Sundays from September till May. The stadium is reachable by metro line A to Ottaviano, then bus #32, or by bus #910 from Termini. Lazio fans traditionally occupy the Curva Nord end of the ground, where a seat costs around L28,000; seats elsewhere, in the *distinti* (or corners) or the *tribuna* (or main stand) are quite a lot more expensive – reckon on paying around L100,00 for a decent *tribuna* ticket. Roma fans occupy the Curva Sud, and this is completely sold out to season ticket holders so you can expect to pay more to see Roma play. For information about ticket outlets and availability, try Lazio Point, Via Farini 34 (☎06.482.6688, Mon–Sat 9am–1pm & 2.30–5pm), the Lazio ticket office (☎06.323.7333), or the Roma team office (☎06.506.0200).

Gay contacts ARCI-Gay Caravaggio, Via Lariana 8 (☎06.855.5522), and ARCI-Lesbica Roma, Via dei Monti di Pietralata 16 (☎06.418.0369) are the Rome branches of the nationwide Italian gay organization. Otherwise there's gay information in English on ☎06.541.398, Mon evenings, 8.30am–10.30pm, or gay information in Italian on ☎167.162.966, Mon–Fri 2–4pm.

Hospital In case of emergency phone ☎113 or ☎118. Otherwise the most central hospitals with casuality departments are the Policlinico Umberto I, Viale del Policlinico 155 (☎06.49.971), and the Santo Spirito, Lungotevere in Sassia 1 (☎06.68.351), near the Vatican. The Rome American Hospital, Via E. Longoni 81 (☎06.22.551), is a private multi-speciality hospital with bilingual staff (☎06.678.6209).

Internet Bibli, Via dei Fienaroli 28 (☎06.588.4097), Internet access in a large, multipurpose bookstore in Trastevere, offering snacks, concerts, presentations and performances. Half an hour costs L8000/€4.13, an hour L12,000/€6.20. Try also Internet Café, Via Cavour 213 (☎06.4782.3051), an efficiently run, spacious, pleasant environment with Internet access, scanning and printing. Splashnet, Via Varese 33 (☎06.493.80450), also has laundry facilities so you can surf the Web while you get your washing done.

Laundry Onda Blu, at Via Principe Amedeo 70b and Via Lamarmora 12 (both daily 8am–10pm); Wash and Dry, Via Della Pelliccia 35 and Via Della Chiesa Nuova 15–16 (both daily 8am-10pm). All offer a wash including soap and tumble-drying for about L15,000/€7.75 for a 6kg (15lb) load. See also "Internet".

Libraries The British Council, Via delle Quattro Fontane 20 (Mon–Tues & Thu–Fri 10am–1pm, Wed 2–5pm; closed Aug & Christmas; ☎06.478.141), has a lending library, for which yearly membership costs L100,000/€51.65. Non-members are, however, allowed to use it for reference purposes for free. There's also a library at the American church of Santa Susanna, Via XX Settembre 14 (☎06.482.7510), which also has a good noticeboard for finding work, accommodation and so on.

Lost Property For property lost on a train call ☎06.4730.6682 (daily 7am–11pm); on a bus ☎06.581.6040 (Mon & Fri 8.30am-1pm, Tues–Thurs 2.30-6pm); on the metro ☎06.487.4309.

Pharmacies Piram, Via Nazionale 228 (☎06.488.0754), and Farmicia della Stazione, Piazza dei Cinquecento (☎06.488.0019), are both open 24hr, year-round.

Post Rome's main post office is at Piazza San Silvestro 18–20 (Mon–Fri 9am–6pm, Sat 9am–2pm; closes midday last Sat of each month). This is the place to pick up poste-restante mail.

Swimming pools There is an open-air public pool, Piscina delle Rose, Viale America 20 (June–Sept 15 daily 9am–7pm; L20,000/€10.33 a day, L14,000/€7.23 a half-day; ☎06.592.6717), in EUR (metro line B).

Train enquiries For general enquires about schedules and prices call ☎1478.88.088 (daily 7am–9pm).

Travel agents For discount tickets try CTS at Via Genova 16 (☎06.462.0431), and Corso Vittorio Emanuele II 297 (☎06.687.2672); both are open on Saturday mornings, when all the other travel agents are closed. Other good places to try are Viaggiare, Via San Nicola da Tolentino 15 (☎06.421.171), who have some English-speaking staff, and Elsy Viaggi, Via di Torre Argentina 80 (☎06.689.6460).

Tours The ATAC-run #110 bus tour is probably the best value for general orientation and a glance at the main sights. In summer it leaves Stazione Termini at 10.30am, 2pm, 3pm, 5pm, 6pm and costs L15,000/€7.75 for a three-hour jaunt, with twenty-minute stops at the Vatican, in Via dei Fori Imperiali and in Piazza Venezia. For the ultra-personal touch, Norman Roberson (☎06.5820.3105), one of the contributors to this guide, specializes in tours of the ancient sights and some of the larger galleries, as well as the Etruscan sites north of the city.

Out from the city: Tivoli and Ostia

You may find there's quite enough in Rome to keep you occupied during your stay. But Rome can be a hot, oppressive city, its surfeit of churches and museums intensely wearying, and if you're around long enough you really shouldn't feel any guilt about getting out to see something of the countryside around. Two of the main attractions visitable on a day-trip are, it's true, Roman sites, but just the process of getting to them can be energizing. **Tivoli**, about an hour by bus east of Rome, is a small town famous for the travertine quarries nearby, the landscaped gardens and parks of its Renaissance villas, and a fine ancient Roman villa just outside. **Ostia**, in the opposite direction from the city near the sea, and similarly easy to reach on public transport, is nowadays the city's main seaside resort (though one worth avoiding, see p.767 for more attractive options just a little further south), but it was home to the port of Rome in classical times, and the site is well preserved and worth seeing. Bear in mind, too, that a number of **other places in Lazio** – Lago di Bracciano (p.756) and the Etruscan sites north of Rome, the Castelli Romani (p.767), Palestrina and Subiaco (pp.769–70), and parts of the southern coast (p.772) – are close enough to the city to make a feasible day-trip, especially if you have access to a car.

Tivoli

Just 40km from Rome, perched high on a hill and looking back over the plain, **TIVOLI** has always been something of a retreat from the city. In classical days it was a retirement town for wealthy Romans; later, during Renaissance times, it again became the playground of the moneyed classes, attracting some of the city's most well-to-do families, who built their country villas out here. Nowadays the leisured classes have mostly gone, but Tivoli does very nicely on the fruits of its still-thriving travertine business, exporting the precious stone worldwide (the quarries line the main road into town from Rome), and supports a small airy centre that preserves a number of relics from its ritzier days. To do justice to the gardens and villas – especially if Villa Adriana is on your list, as indeed it should be – you'll need time; set out *early*.

The town

Most people head first for **Villa d'Este** (summer daily 9am–1hr before sunset; winter Tues–Sun 9am–1hr before sunset; L8000/€4.13 for house and grounds), across the main square of Largo Garibaldi – the country retreat of Cardinal Ippolito d'Este that was transformed from a convent by Pirro Ligorio in 1550, and now often thronged with visitors even outside peak season. They mainly come to see the fountains of the landscaped gardens, but the ground floor apartments have recently been restored and these ten rooms alone make the trip well worthwhile, frescoed with scenes of mythology and the history of Tivoli by Girolamo Muziano and Federico Zuccari in 1555–1560. Unfortunately, restoration is still going on in the gardens below, and you may find many of the famous fountains are temporarily closed. However, you can see the theatrical, magnificent Organ Fountain, which has been returned to its original glory and makes a most imposing sight as it dashes millions of gallons of water down the hillside. Among the other fountains you can see are the Fontana dell'Ovato, near the Organ Fountain, fringed with statues, behind which is a rather dank arcade, and the Rometta or "Little Rome", on the opposite side of the garden, which has reproductions of the city's major buildings and a boat holding an obelisk. Finally a word of warning: be sure to drink only from those fountains marked *acqua potabile*, and don't wade or splash in the other fountains – the water is basically sewage from the town above.

Tivoli's other main attraction is **Villa Gregoriana** (daily 10am–1hr before sunset; L3500/€3.81), a park with waterfalls created when Pope Gregory XVI diverted the flow of the river here to ease the periodic flooding of the town in 1831. Less well-known and less touristed than the d'Este estate, it has none of the latter's conceits – its vegetation is lush and overgrown, descending into a gashed-out gorge over 60m deep. There are two main waterfalls – the larger Grande Cascata on the far side, and a small Bernini-designed one at the neck of the gorge. The path winds down to the bottom of the canyon, scaling the drop on the other side past two grottoes, where you can get right up close to the pounding water, the dark, torn shapes of the rock glowering overhead. It's harder work than the Villa d'Este – if you blithely saunter down to the bottom of the gorge, you'll find that it's a long way back up the other side – but in many ways more rewarding; the path leads up on the far side to an exit and the substantial remains of a **Temple of Vesta**, which you'll have seen clinging to the side of the hill. This is now incorporated into the gardens of a restaurant, but it's all right to walk through and take a look, and the view is probably Tivoli's best – down into the chasm and across to the high green hills that ring the town.

Villa Adriana

Once you've seen these two sights you've really seen Tivoli – the rest of the town is nice enough but there's not that much to it. But just outside town, at the bottom of the hill, fifteen minutes' walk off the main Rome road (ask the Rome–Tivoli bus to drop you or take the local CAT #4 from Largo Garibaldi), **Villa Adriana** (daily 9am–1hr before sunset; L12,000/€6.20) casts the invention of the Tivoli popes and cardinals very much into the shade. This was probably the largest and most sumptuous villa in the Roman Empire, the retirement home of the Emperor Hadrian for a short while between 135 AD and his death three years later, and it occupies an enormous site. You need time to see it all; there's no point in doing it at a gallop and, taken with the rest of Tivoli, it makes for a long day's sightseeing. Spending L3500/€3.81 on the large-scale map they sell at the bookstore near the ticket booth helps make it all understandable.

The site is one of the most soothing spots around Rome, its stones almost the epitome of romantic, civilized ruins. The imperial palace buildings proper are in fact one of the least well-preserved parts of the complex, but much else is clearly recognizable. Hadrian was a great traveller and a keen architect, and parts of the villa were inspired by buildings he had seen around the world. The massive Pecile, for instance, through which you enter, is a reproduction of a building in Athens; and the Canopus, on the opposite side of the site, is a liberal copy of the sanctuary of Serapis near Alexandria, its long, elegant channel of water fringed by sporadic columns and statues leading up to a Temple of Serapis at the far end. Nearby, a museum displays the latest finds from the ongoing excavations, though most of the extensive original discoveries have found their way back to Rome. Walking back towards the entrance, make your way across the upper storey of the so-called Pretorio, a former warehouse, and down to the remains of two bath complexes. Beyond is a fishpond with a *cryptoporticus* (underground passageway) winding around underneath, and behind that the relics of the emperor's imperial apartments. The Teatro Maríttimo, adjacent, with its island in the middle of a circular pond, is the place to which it's believed Hadrian would retire at siesta time to be sure of being alone.

Practicalities

Buses leave Rome for Tivoli and Villa Adriana every twenty minutes from Ponte Mammolo metro station (line B) – journey time fifty minutes. Be sure to get on the buses that follow the Via Tiburtina route – much quicker. In Tivoli, the **bus station** is in Piazza Massimo near the Villa Gregoriana, though you can get off earlier, on the main square of Largo Garibaldi, where you'll find the **tourist office** (Mon 9am–2pm, Tues–Fri 9am–6.30pm, Sat 9am–3pm; ☎0774.334.522), which has free maps and information on **accommodation** if you're planning to stay over.

Ostia

There are two Ostias: one a rather over-visited seaside resort, **Lido di Ostia**, which is probably worth avoiding; the other, one of the finest ancient Roman sites – the excavations of the port of **Ostia Antica** – which are on a par with anything you'll see in Rome itself and easily merit a half-day journey out.

Lido di Ostia

The **LIDO DI OSTIA**, reachable by overground train from Magliana metro station on line B, has for many years been the number-one seaside resort for Romans and had suffered accordingly. However, the beaches here have recently been cleaned up, and the water's now more inviting: the best stretches are along the coastal road between Ostia and Torvaianica, and there are also nudist areas around the 8- or 9km marker. The town, though, is on the whole a poor outpost of the city, with little, if anything, to recommend it. Anzio or Nettuno, both of which are only an extra half an hour by train away from the city, and are also surrounded by beaches (the better ones being south of Nettuno), are a much better bet if you want to be beside the seaside.

Ostia Antica

The stop before Lido di Ostia on the train from Rome, the site of **OSTIA ANTICA** marked the coastline in classical times, and the town which grew up here was the port of ancient Rome, a thriving place whose commercial activities were vital to the city further upstream. The **excavations** (daily 9am–1hr before sunset; L8000/€4.13) remain relatively unvisited; indeed until the 1970s the site was only open one day a week and few people realized how well the port had been preserved by the Tiber's mud. Still relatively free of the bustle of tourists, it's an evocative site, and it's much easier to reconstruct a Roman town from this than from any amount of pottering around the Forum. It's also very spread out, so be prepared for a fair amount of walking.

Before visiting the excavations take a quick trip to the medieval **Borgo**, to the right as you come down off the pedestrian bridge – dominated by the Castello della Rovere (Tues–Sun 9.30am–2pm; free; obligatory guided tours every 20min). Built by Julius II when he was a cardinal, the castle was once a customs house collecting tolls from vessels sailing up to Rome. During the flood of 1587, the river changed course and left it in its present location – high and dry.

Backtracking from here to the site itself, the **Decumanus Maximus**, the main street of Ostia, leads west from the entrance, past the **Baths of Neptune** on the right (where there's an interesting mosaic) to the town's commercial centre, otherwise known as the **Piazzale delle Corporazioni** for the remains of shops and trading offices that still fringe the central square. These represented commercial enterprises from all over the ancient world, and the mosaics just in front denote their trade – grain merchants, ship-fitters, ropemakers and the like. Flanking one side of the square, the **theatre** has been much restored but is nonetheless impressive, enlarged by Septimius Severus in the second century AD to hold up to 4000 people. On the left of the square, the **House of Apulius** preserves mosaic floors and, beyond, a dark-aisled *mithraeum* with more mosaics illustrating the cult's practices. Behind here – past the substantial remains of the *horrea* or warehouses that once stood all over the city – the **Casa di Diana** is probably the best-preserved private house in Ostia, with a dark, mysterious set of rooms around a central courtyard, and again with a *mithraeum* at the back. You can climb up to its roof for a fine view of the rest of the site, afterwards crossing the road to the **Thermopolium** – an ancient Roman café, complete with seats outside, a high counter, display shelves and even wall paintings of parts of the menu.

North of the Casa di Diana, the **museum** (Tues–Sat 9am–4.30pm, Sun 9am–1pm) holds a variety of articles from the site, including a statue of Mithras killing a bull, wall paintings depicting domestic life in Ostia and some fine sarcophagi and statuary from the imperial period. Left from here, the **Forum** centres on the **Capitol** building, reached by a wide flight of steps, and is fringed by the remains of baths and a basilica. Continuing on down the main street, more **horrea** superbly preserved and complete with pediment and names inscribed on the marble merit a detour off to the right; although you can't enter, you can peer into the courtyard. Beyond, the **House of Cupid and Psyche** has a courtyard you can walk into, its rooms clearly discernible on one side, a colourful marbled floor on the other.

NORTHERN LAZIO

Northern Lazio is a quite different entity from the region south of the capital. Green and wooded in its central areas, its steadily more undulating hills hint at the landscapes of Tuscany and Umbria further north. There are few large centres, though, and interest is sparse: with determination (and, in some cases, a car), you can see much of it on day-trips from Rome. Foremost among the area's attractions is the legacy of the **Etruscans**, some of whose most important sites, scattered along the southern stretch of coast, are readily accessible by road or rail – necropoli mainly, but the only remains of a civilization that ruled the area for close on a thousand years. The **coast** itself is of very little appeal until you get close to the Tuscan border, and if you want to swim you'd be better off doing so inland, around lakes **Bracciano**, **Vico** or **Bolsena** – playgrounds for hot and bothered Romans on summer weekends. Between these, **Viterbo** is the main centre, a dour provincial town that can make a good base for visiting both the lakes and the region's **Mannerist villas and gardens**, though all over this central area bear in mind that touring without your own transport can be an uphill struggle. Over to the east, **Rieti** is the big centre, a rather bland and somewhat deservedly unvisited town on the way to Abruzzo. Beyond it lie the **lakes and mountains** of Terminillo and Amatrice, scenically spectacular, but again virtually out of reach without your own vehicle.

Etruria and the coast

D.H. Lawrence had pretty much the last word on the plain and low hills stretching north from Rome towards the Tuscan border: "A peculiarly forlorn coast," he lamented, "the sea peculiarly flat and sunken, lifeless looking, the land as if it had given up its last gasp and was now forever inert." His *Etruscan Places*, published in 1932, is one of the best introductions to both the Etruscans and their cities, which, one or two beaches excepted, are the main reasons for venturing out here.

Fregene and Ladispoli

For a so-called resort, **FREGENE** is one of the grimmest places imaginable. First main stop on the train out of Rome, its four kilometres of **beaches** – twenty years ago Lazio's trendiest – are blighted by the usual commercial tat and only slightly redeemed by huge stands of umbrella pines. Romans pile out here mainly for the fish restaurants and, in summer, to trawl the Roman clubs' seaside venues. The sand's marginally less crowded than at Ostia, but the gravy-coloured water fails every health and safety test going. Sunbathing slumbers are also disturbed by jets flying out of Fiumicino down the coast, and for decent, almost deserted beaches, you'd do better to stay on the train.

To Lawrence **LADISPOLI** was even worse, summed up in a thumbnail sketch: "Ladispoli is one of those ugly little places on the Roman coast," he wrote, "consisting of new concrete villas, new concrete hotels, kiosks and bathing establishments; bareness and non-existence for ten months in the year, seething solid with fleshy bathers in July and August . . . desecration put upon desolation." Nowadays, this is a little unfair: its apsect, to be sure, isn't the best; but its beaches are cleanest of those closest to Rome. There are plenty of places to swim about ten minutes' walk from the train station, although the best spot is further north, around half-an-hour away from the station at the **Torre Flavia** – a medieval construction restored in 1565 by an Orsini cardinal. The tower used to be about 200m from the shoreline; now it is 200m out to sea and collapsing elegantly into the water in four equal parts.

Cerveteri

The station at Ladispoli also serves **CERVETERI**, which provides the most accessible Etruscan taster if you're commuting from Rome – though be warned that the station is 7km away from the centre. Buses are more convenient, leaving from the Lepanto metro station (line A) in Rome every thirty minutes and dropping you at Piazza Aldo Moro in Cerveteri (a 1hr 20min journey). There's been a settlement here since the tenth century BC, when it was already known to the Greeks as an important trading centre. Cerveteri, the Roman *Caere*, was among the top three cities in the twelve-strong Etruscan federation, its wealth derived largely from the mineral riches of the **Tolfa hills** to the northeast – a gentle range which give the plain a much-needed touch of scenic colour. In its heyday the town spread over 8 km (something like thirty times its present size), controlling territory that stretched for 50km up the coast. The rot set in from 351 BC, when it became a dependency of Rome, having failed, like most of Etruria, to maintain a neutrality with the new power.

The present town is a thirteenth-century creation, dismissed by Lawrence – and you really can't blame him – as "forlorn beyond words". On arrival, make straight for the Etruscan **necropolis** (Tues–Sun: May–Sept 9am–7pm; Oct–April 9am–4pm; L8000/€4.13), just a kilometre away and signposted from the central piazza. The Etruscans constructed a literal **city of the dead** here, weird and fantastically well preserved, with complete streets and houses, some formed as strange round pillboxes carved from the living rock, others still covered in earth to create the tumuli effect that ripples over the surrounding plateau. The general span of the graves is seventh to first century BC: as far as anyone can make out, women were buried in separate small chambers within the "house" – easy to distinguish – while the men were laid on death beds (occasionally in sarcophagi) hewn directly from the stone. Slaves were cremated and their ashes placed in urns alongside their masters – civilized by comparison with the Romans, who simply threw their slaves into mass burial pits. The twelve or so showtombs, lying between the two roads that bisect the city, are grouped together beyond the entrance; they close in random rotation, so it's difficult to know in advance which ones are going to be open. If possible don't miss the **Tomba Bella** (Tomb of the Bas-Reliefs), **Tomba dei Letti Funebri** (Tomb of the Funeral Beds) and the **Tomba dei Capitelli**.

You could spend several hours wandering about here, but you might be better off heading back into town to the **Museo Nazionale di Cervéteri**, at the top of the old quarter in the sixteenth-century **Castello Ruspoli** (Tue–Sun 9am–7pm; free). This has two large rooms containing a fraction of the huge wealth that was buried with the Etruscan dead – vases, sarcophagi, terracottas and a run of miscellaneous day-to-day objects; most of the best stuff has been whisked away to Villa Giulia in Rome (see p.720). On the way to the museum, if the tombs have whetted your appetite you might want to make a stop at the little **trattoria**, *Tulchulcha*, on the necropolis road, where they serve a hearty country-style food backed up by crisp Cerveteri white wines: in summer you can eat on the terrace overlooking the town; in winter, there's a crackling fireplace to warm your chilled bones (no credit cards; closed Mon).

Civitavecchia

The only reasons to break a journey in **CIVITAVECCHIA**, 30km north, are to change trains or to pick up a **ferry to Sardinia** (see p.1025 for details of crossings); try to take a night crossing to save yourself the dubious pleasure of spending a night in town. The tourist office sells tickets, but you can book ahead (essential in the summer months) from many travel agents both in the town and in other parts of Italy. Otherwise, Civitavecchia is an ugly and forgettable port that's best avoided, with little to see beyond a small **Museo Archeologico** right in the centre of town on the corner of Largo Plebiscito, just off Viale Garibaldi (Tues–Sun 9am–7pm; free).

The **ferry docks** (closed Mon) are in the centre of the town at the end of Viale Garibaldi, ten minutes' walk from the train station. There's a **tourist office** between the two at Viale Garibaldi 40 (Mon–Fri 8am–1pm & 4.30–7pm; ☎0766.25.348). Should you get stuck, however, there are two functional **hotels**, the modern *Medusa* (☎0766.24.327; ③), near the 68,300km marker on Via Aurelia, which has nice, clean rooms, and the somewhat sleazy *Traghetto* (☎0766.25.920; ③), on Via Braccianese Claudia – passable if you're just overnighting on the way to Sardinia. As for **eating**, there are lots of cheap trattorias and pizzerias along the seafront Viale Garibaldi, and there's not much to choose between them – the *Santa Lucia*, Viale Garibaldi 38 (closed Wed in winter), close by the tourist office, does decent pizzas. *Trattoria Sora Maria*, just back from the water, off Largo Plebiscito on Via Zara (closed Fri in winter), is a nice place that's good for fish.

Tarquinia

TARQUINIA, about 15km further north, is the most touted of the Etruscan necropoli, and with good reason. As long as it is not overrun with fellow visitors, the site can be quite evocative and the actual town, partly walled and with a crop of medieval towers, is a pleasant place to pass an afternoon. The recently refurbished museum is the finest in the region outside of Rome and should not be missed.

The town

Apart from its old fortified district, which commanded the town approaches for several centuries and holds within its walls a twelfth-century Romanesque church, **Santa Maria di Castello** – notable for its rib vaulting, the first known example in Italy – it's the **Museo Nazionale Tarquiniense**, right on the main town square of Piazza Cavour (Tues–Sun 9am–7pm; L12,000/€6.20, including admission to the necropolis) that draws the crowds. It's not a large museum, and is all the better for that and for the fact that it is sensitively housed in an attractive Gothic-Renaissance palazzo. The ground-floor rooms contain some superb sculpted sarcophagi, many decorated with warm and human portraits of the deceased, while upstairs are displays of exquisite Etruscan gold jewellery, painted ceramics, bronzes, candlesticks, figures and heads, including the renowned winged terracotta horses (fourth century BC), probably from a temple frieze – a striking example of the Etruscans' skill in decorative terracotta. As well as having fine views over the surrounding countryside and down to the sea, the top floor is probably the most impressive part of the museum, with some of the best of the wall paintings from the nearby necropolis – relocated here due to their on-site deterioration, and displayed in re-creations of the tomb chambers. Several are particularly bright and realistic: one shows the lithe forms of dancers and musicians; another depicts athletes running and jumping, and a chariot race.

The site

It's the **necropolis** itself (Tues–Sun 9am–1hr before sunset; L12,000/€6.20 including admission to museum) though, which really makes the journey worthwhile, a warren of graves spread across a plateau on the southeast edge of the town that is all that's left of a city – the site of which is across the valley to the northeast of the necropolis – that was once the artistic, cultural and probably political capital of Etruria. Founded in the tenth century BC, its population is estimated to have been around 100,000, going into a gradual decline from the fourth century BC under the growing influence of Rome. Etruscan cities were built almost entirely of wood, so most vanished quickly – and those that didn't were redeveloped by the Romans, making this necropolis one of the few extant remnants of a culture that prevailed for something like 1000 years.

There are about four buses a day from Piazza Cavour to the necropolis, or it's a fifteen-minute walk: take Via Umberto I from Piazza Cavour, pass through the Porta Romana, skip the roundabout (Piazza Europa), follow Via IV Novembre/Via delle Croci up the hill, and the site is on the left. Excavations started in 1489, the first recorded in modern times, since when 6000 tombs have been uncovered (900 in 1958 alone), with many more apparently still to be unearthed. Grave-robbing is common (thieves are known as *i tombaroli*), and there are patrols; together with the growing influx of visitors, this means that only a limited number of tombs (usually about 12 each day) are open at any time. Etruscan burial places were often straight copies of houses (though less literally so here than at Cerveteri), filled with the clutter of daily life to provide the dead with all they might need in the afterlife. But the Tarquinia tombs have something else besides – **wall paintings**, the oldest of which date from about the seventh or eighth century BC. There's been much speculation about the purpose and style of these. The earliest paintings emphasize mythical and ritualistic scenes, but later works from the fourth century to the sixth century – in the Orco, Auguri, Della Caccia and Della Pescia tombs – show greater social realism, giving an insight into the habits, customs and scenes from the life of the deceased. The style of these later works is a mixture of Greek, indigenous Etruscan and even Eastern influences, their ease and fluidity pointing to a civilization that was at the pinnacle of its development. The Greek aspects are particularly important, representing the only allusions to Hellenistic monumental painting, a form that otherwise has largely vanished without trace. From the fourth century BC decadence sets in, with the appearance of increasingly morbid and purely necromantic drawings.

Practicalities
Tarquinia's **train station** is 2km below the town centre, connected with the central Barriera San Giusto, hard up against the city walls, by regular local bus; **buses** from Viterbo and Rome also drop you in Barriera San Giusto. The **tourist office** is just through the city gate at Piazza Cavour 1 (Mon–Sat 8am–2pm; ☎0766.856.38, *www.comune.tarquinia.vt.it*) and doles out maps of the town and other information. There are few places to **eat** and even fewer places to **stay** in town; indeed if you want to stay you're really better off on the coast at Tarquinia Lido (see below), where there's more choice. As for **eating**, there's a cosy trattoria-pizzeria, *Campanari*, at Piazza Cavour 11 (closed Mon), or the more upscale *San Marco* at Piazza Cavour 20 (closed Mon). Perhaps the most atmospheric place to drink is *Osterina il Grottino*, a rather dingy cave-like bar at Alberata Dante Aligheri 8 that serves wine siphoned out of barrels piled in the corner.

Tarquinia Lido
TARQUINIA LIDO, reachable by hourly bus from Barriera San Giusto via the FS station, is home to most of Tarquinia's real action. The *Albergo Miramare*, Viale dei Tirreni 36 (☎0766.864.020, no phone bookings accepted; ②), has reasonably priced double **rooms**, and there are three huge **campsites** here – and at Riva di Tarquinia to the north – hosting great herds of holiday-makers. The beaches are heavily developed, with restaurants, discos, sports facilities, "pubs", even cinemas, but might be just what you're looking for after dismal Tarquinia proper. The best bet, though, is to round off a day-trip with a quick dip and head back to the station.

North to the Tuscan border

Continuing north offers more peaceful opportunities for camping, though you'll probably want to skip **MONTALTO DI CASTRO**, a quiet but unexciting hilltop village famous throughout Italy for its huge, half-built nuclear power station. The plant became a *cause célèbre* for the country's emergent Green Party and was at the heart of the 1987 referendum voting against the country's nuclear power programme. After much government double-dealing, it's now going to be converted – at vast cost – to either oil or natural gas. If you can't resist sleeping in the eerie shadow of nuclear reactors, there are seafront **campsites** at Montalto Marina and Pescia Romana.

   VULCI, some 11km inland, is another **Etruscan site** (Tues–Sun 9am–1hr before sunset; L4000/€2.07) but, despite the presence of an estimated 15,000 tombs, has next to nothing much to see and is impossible to reach without your own vehicle; indeed it's really only worth bothering if you're particularly turned on by the Etruscans. Many of the tumuli have been ransacked and left to decay, though there's ample scope for scrambling around. There is a huge Etruscan temple platform made of tufa blocks that look as if they were quarried this year. Near that is a Roman villa and further on recent excavations have revealed Roman temples, walls and gate houses. More interestingly, north of these ruins, the **Ponte d'Abbadia** is a spectacular single-arched Etruscan-Roman bridge spanning a pretty ravine next to a ninth-century Templars' castle that houses a small **museum** of finds from the local necropoli (Tues–Sun 9am–7pm; L4000/€2.07).

The best and quietest of the **beaches** on this coast stretch north of Chiarone just over the border in Tuscany.

Lago di Bracciano and around

The closest of northern Lazio's lakes to Rome, **Lago di Bracciano** fills an enormous volcanic crater, a smooth, roughly circular expanse of water that's popular – but not too popular – with Romans keen to escape the summer heat of the city. It's nothing spectacular, with few real sights and a landscape of rather plain, rolling countryside, but its shores are fairly peaceful even on summer Sundays, and you can eat excellent lake fish in its restaurants.

The lake's main settlement is the town of **BRACCIANO** on the western shore, about half an hour by train from Rome San Pietro (direction Viterbo). It's a small town, dominated by the imposing **Castello Orsini-Odelscalchi** (April–Sept Tues–Fri 10am–7pm, Sat & Sun 9am–12.30pm & 3–7.30pm; Oct–March Tues–Fri 10am–5pm, Sat & Sun 10am–noon & 3–5pm; L11,000/€5.68), a late-fifteenth-century structure now privately owned by the Odelscalchi family, which was the last of the archery (as opposed to artillery) castles built in Europe and a handsome structure by any standards. The outer walls, now mostly disappeared, contained the rectangular piazza of the medieval town; nowadays it's unfortunately rather run-down, its interior home to rusting suits of armour and faded frescoes, but the view from the ramparts is worth the admission price alone. The best place to **swim** in the lake is from the beach at Via Argenti, below Bracciano town. You can rent a boat and picnic offshore; and the nearby trattorias are good and inexpensive. The shore between Trevignano and Anguillara also boasts fine swimming spots, as well as good **restaurants** in both of the towns. One of the best is the *Casina Bianca*, Via della Rena 100 (closed Mon), in Trevignano, which is inexpensive and serves fresh fish on a terrace overlooking the lake.

Lago di Vico and around

The smallest but most appealing of northern Lazio's lakes, and the only one deemed worthy of being declared a nature reserve, **Lago di Vico** is another former volcanic crater, ringed by appreciable mountains, the highest of which – Monte Fogliano – rises to 963m on the western shore. The **Via Cimina** traverses the summit ridges and is a popular scenic drive, dotted with restaurants, but there's a quieter road lower down (closed to cars) that skirts closer to the shoreline. The flatter northern edge, marshy in places, is the spot for discreet unofficial **camping**.

Getting around this part of Lazio is a sweat, and in an ideal world you'd have your own transport. Buses between Viterbo and Rome skirt the area, and two rickety branch rail lines spear around the lake from Orte. With careful scrutiny of the timetables both can just about be made to work for you. One of the rail lines ties in to the Rome–Viterbo line at Capranica, with halts at Ronciglione and Caprarola; the other winds up to Viterbo via Bomarzo.

Caprarola: the Palazzo Farnese

Over and above the lake's sheer prettiness, there's not much besides the odd attractive village and a scattering of Roman and Etruscan remains – none terribly interesting in their own right, but worthwhile if you can string several together. More properly deserving of individual attention is the **Palazzo Farnese** at **CAPRAROLA**, which, like the villas at Bagnaia and Bomarzo (see p.761–2), ranks among the high points of seventeenth-century Italian Mannerism.

The town is pleasant enough, owing its present prosperity to vast hazelnut groves that blanket the surrounding countryside, though you can't help feeling the place is simply an excuse for the **palace**, which stands huge and imposing at the top of the steep main street (Tues–Sun: March–Oct 9am–6.30pm; Nov–Feb 9am–4pm; L4000/€2.07, includes garden tour; *www.isa.it/tuscia/caprarola*). The building is clearly a masterpiece; Stendhal described it as a building where "architecture married Nature". Begun by Antonio di Sangallo the Younger for Pierluigi Farnese in the early 1520s, it was originally more a castle than a palace, situated at the centre of the lands belonging to the Farnese family. Later, Cardinal Alessandro Farnese took up residence here, in 1559 hiring Vignola to modify the building while retaining the peculiar pentagonal floor-plan. Vignola was an inspired choice. Apprenticed at Fontainebleau, he was among the most accomplished architects of the late Renaissance, and exemplifies the Mannerist style at its best in his creation at Caprarola, which celebrates the period's values of superiority of art over nature and style over substance, together with a self-satisfied, almost gloating eulogizing of the patron's virtues.

Of the palace's five floors only the *piano nobile* is open to the public, and there's no escaping a certain seediness that seems to have overtaken the place of late, both in the fag-ends and graffiti in the curving forecourt and in the state rooms themselves, which have lost all their furniture, suffering a cold, unlived-in feel as a result. There are frescoes from 1560, most of them by the brothers Zuccari chronicling the Farnese family's greatness, much lauded as the building's highlight (though some are embarrassingly crude and others terribly knocked about), and a monumental spiral staircase up to a circular courtyard.

The courtyard gives onto the main rooms of the *piano nobile*, huge and heavy with its thirty pairs of columns but considered to be one of Vignola's finest moments. The first and last rooms are perhaps the best, however, the first with a super-embellished grotto-like fireplace and pictures of local communities like Caprarola itself (the central scene is an imaginary one), the last, the *Sala del Mappomondo* – about the only place not given over to glorifying the Farnese clan – decorated with huge painted maps of the known world and a wonderful ceiling fresco of the constellations.

Outside there are twin **gardens** (guided tours Mon–Sat 10am, 1.30pm, 3pm & 5pm; same ticket as palace), divided into a south-facing summer terrace and an east-facing winter terrace, with plants and design appropriate to each. Look out for the artificial grotto and the stalactites, brought from a real cave and stuck on.

Practicalities

Without your own car, it's best to use Viterbo (see p.759) as a base and take one of the seven **buses** a day from there to Caprarola. This entails a very pleasant 45-minute ride through the wooded hills of the Monti Cimini that leaves you at the foot of the main street, from where it's a ten-minute walk to the palace at the top.

In any case Caprarola only has one **hotel**, the *Farnese* (☎0761.646.029; ②), a modern place way out on Via Circonvallazione on the Viterbo side of town (the Viterbo bus goes right past) that should be used in emergencies only.

For **food**, there's the *Trattoria del Cimino* midway down the main street at Via F. Nicolai 44 (closed Fri), and a pizzeria off to the left of Piazza Romei in front of the palace (closed Sun).

South of the lake

South of Caprarola lies a trio of towns, each good for about half an hour if you've got your own transport. **RONCIGLIONE** is closest, its old quarter nicely situated over one of the small east-running **ravines** that cut through the area. Turner thought it picturesque enough to paint, though Dickens later described it as "a little town like a large pig-sty". A couple of churches aside, there's little to see, but the **Pro Loco** at Corso Umberto I 22 (☎0761.625.460) can fill you in further.

SUTRI, 6km south, has more solid attractions, enclosed by part-medieval, part-Etruscan walls, with odd traces of cyclopean gateways. These days it's the self-styled "Gateway to Etruria" and claims to be the birthplace of Pontius Pilate. The site itself – on a rocky tufa outcrop between valleys – is the kind typically chosen by the Etruscans, and it has some Etruscan ruins that provide the town's one real draw: an **amphitheatre** south of the town off the main Via Cassia, carved completely from the solid rock (daily 9am–5pm; L10,000/€5.17). Later adapted by the Romans, it once had seating for 6000; on a smaller scale, classical concerts are still held here in the summer. Ask the custodian to show you the **Madonna del Parto**, a short walk away; an extremely ancient church, again carved from the rock, this was probably converted first from old Etruscan tombs and subsequently from a Mithraic temple.

NEPI is another charming little outcrop village, perched over three valleys surrounded by imposing tufa walls built by Alexander VI, Borgia, when he was a Cardinal. It has an interesting little **museum** (daily business hours; ask at the Town Hall), documenting the Roman Via Amerina, which starts here and continues on to Amelia in Umbria, but otherwise nothing tangible to see.

Leaving Nepi on the road to Civita Castellana about 2.5km brings you to **CASTEL SANT'ELIA**, a tiny village with an imposing gatehouse. Its principal attraction is the eleventh-century Romanesque **Basilica di Sant'Elia**, several hundred metres down in the valley to the southeast, a pleasant cypress-surrounded spot, with traces of an eighth-century church and twelfth-century frescoes in the apse. To gain entry you need to get the key from the local priest – easily found in such a small village; he'll give you the key in return for your passport and you give him a small tip when you return for your document.

Seven kilometres further on, the smart little town of **CÌVITA CASTELLANA,** situated on a peninsula of land over two ravines around 100m deep, was in ancient days known as Falerii, capital of an ethnic group known as the Faliscans, who spoke a Latin dialect but culturally were Etruscans. During the early Renaissance it became an important strong point in the northern defenses of Rome, and its **Rocca**, a huge fortress with an octagonal *Maschio*, or castle keep, now houses the museum of the Faliscans – a well laid-out and informative **museum** (Tues–Sun 9.30am–4.30 pm: free) that displays items relating to the Faliscans and their peculiar relationships with the Etruscans and the Romans. Also worth a visit is the Romanesque **duomo**, with splendid mosaics and a Cosmatesque floor.

VETRALLA, back up the Cassia, has been from the most ancient of days a strong defence between the Monte Cimini, Etruscan Tarquinia, and Viterbo and Rome. Nowadays there is not much to see here but it is a good jumping-off point for the Etruscan necropoli of **Grotta Porcina** and **Norcia**. Also, it has an excellent restaurant, *da Benedetta*, on Via della Pieta, a friendly place which has great homestyle cooking, home-made pasta, and their own wine and oil (closed Tues).

The medieval village of **BLERA,** a little way south of Vetralla, has a Fascist-era bridge spanning the valley of the Biedano river, soaring high over the stylish little Etrusco-Roman Ponte del Diavolo, and an even more ancient Etruscan bridge near the necropolis, on the north end of town. Blera's **necropolis** is one of the largest in the region, covering several kilometres of cliffs lining the valleys of both its little rivers.

From Blera you can follow the river on foot six kilometres **upstream** through the Parco Suburbano Marturanum, an archeology and wildlife preserve, to the charming little town of **BARBARANO ROMANO**, another Etruscan village built on a spur of land between two deep gorges. About 3km northeast, a paved road leads to the former Etruscan town of **SAN GIULIANO**, where there's yet another **necropolis** of cliff tombs up and down the river valleys that converge here. Of the more distinctive tombs, there is the imposing Tomba Cima, a large tumulus type with six chambers, numerous cliff tombs, and the Tomba Cervo, flanked by an ancient carved stair through the cliff to the plateau above. In the left wall of the stair is **an Etruscan** low-relief carving of a stag (*cervo*) being attacked by a wolf. On top of the central plateau, the little chapel of **San Giuliano** was built in the twelfth century, beyond which there are some so-called Roman **Baths** – in fact a grand hole in the ground reached by stairs leading to a large room and cistern of indeterminate age.

Finally, to the southwest of Blera, the tiny hamlet of **CIVITELLA CESI** is another Etruscan town where a local Etruscologist has reconstructed an **Etruscan village** that is authentic to the last detail. He casts bronze, throws pottery in the Etruscan style, even weaves cloth as the Etruscans would have done. Additionally he has a string of horses and can make the necessary arrangements for horseback camping trips of up to one-week duration throughout this part of Etruria at a cost of around L150,000/€77.47 per person per day (☎0761.415.031; fax 0761.415.096, *www.antiquitates.it*).

Viterbo and around

The capital of its province, and indeed of northern Lazio as a whole, **VITERBO** is easily the region's most historic centre, a medieval town that during the thirteenth century was once something of a rival to Rome. It was, for a time, the residence of popes, a succession of whom relocated here after friction in the capital. Today there are some vestiges of its vanquished prestige – a handful of grand palaces and numerous medieval churches, enclosed by an intact set of medieval walls. The town is a well-kept place and refreshingly untouched by much tourist traffic but only really worth staying in if you're keen to visit the surrounding area. If you aren't, it's worth knowing that buses and trains run frequently from Rome (buses are fastest) and you can comfortably see the town in a day.

The Town

If there is a centre to Viterbo it's **Piazza del Plebiscito**, an appropriately named square girdled almost entirely by the fifteenth- and sixteenth-century buildings that make up the town's council offices. The lions and palm trees that reflect each other across the square are Viterbo's symbol, and you'll see them repeated, in grandiose echoes of Venice, all over town. You can look in on the fine Renaissance courtyard of the main, arcaded building of the **Palazzo dei Priori** and also see the council chamber itself, decorated with a series of murals depicting Viterbo's history right back to Etruscan times in a weird mixture of pagan and Christian motifs – a mixture continued across the square in the church of **Sant'Angelo**.

There are a number of directions you can walk from the piazza. Most interesting is to take a right off the square down Via San Lorenzo, which leads past the pretty Piazza di Gesù to the macabrely named Piazza del Morte. Left from here takes you through Viterbo's oldest quarter, the **Quartiere San Pellegrino** – a tight mess of hilly streets hinged onto the arched axis of Via San Pellegrino. It's a nice neighbourhood, home to a number of art and antique shops, but half an hour should be more than enough time to see it all. In the opposite direction, Piazza San Lorenzo is flanked by the town's most historic group of buildings, notably the **Palazzo Papale** itself, a thirteenth-century structure whose impressive site, looking over the green gorge that cuts into central Viterbo, is best appreciated from its open Gothic loggia. You can peep into the Great Hall, venue of the election of half a dozen or so popes, but otherwise the palace is closed to the public, and you have to content yourself with a wander into the **Duomo** opposite, a plain Romanesque church that has an elegant striped floor and an understated beauty unusual among Italian churches.

Walking east from Piazza del Plebiscito, Via Roma soon becomes **Corso Italia**, Viterbo's main shopping street and the scene of a busy passeggiata of an evening. At its far end, steps lead up from Piazza Verdi to the nineteenth-century church of **Santa Rosa**, which holds the saint's corpse in a chapel in the south aisle – a faintly grotesque, doll-like figure with a forced grin, dressed up in a nun's habit; for a close-up view ring the bell on the right-hand side of the church entrance and someone will let you into the chapel. A good time to be in Viterbo is September 3 during the **festa**, when the *macchina* of Santa Rosa – the platform and altarpiece that hold the icon – is carried through the streets of the town to the accompaniment of much revelry and, later, fireworks.

After seeing Santa Rosa, the rest of Viterbo can't help but seem a bit sinister, and in any case you've seen it all except for one quarter, which is at the top of the hill above Piazza Verdi. Follow Via Matteotti up to **Piazza della Rocca**, a large square dominated by the fierce-looking **Rocca Albornoz**, home of the small **Museo Nazionale** (Tues–Sun 9am–7pm; L4000/€2.07), whose archeological collection includes displays of locally unearthed Roman and Etruscan artefacts. Just off the opposite side of the square, the church of **San Francesco** is also worth a quick look, a high and unusually plain Gothic church that is the burial place of two of Viterbo's popes – Clement IV and Adrian V – both laid in now heavily restored but impressive Cosmatesque tombs on either side of the main altar. The local open-air morning **market** (Mon–Sat) is nearby on Piazza San Faustino.

Outside the walls is the twelfth-century church of **Santa Maria della Verità**, whose fine early-Renaissance frescoes by little-known master Lorenzo da Viterbo in the Capella Mazzatosta were recently damaged by vandals and are under restoration. In the convent next door is the recently restored **Museo Civico** (Tues–Sun: summer 9am–7pm; winter 9am–6pm; L6000/€3.10), containing locally found antiquities from the Iron Age to the Roman imperial period, while the upper floors house an art gallery with paintings from the thirteenth to nineteenth centuries, including works by Sebastiano del Piombo.

Practicalities

Unusually for a small town, Viterbo has two **main train stations**: one, Porta Romana, is situated just outside the Porta Romana to the south of the town centre, around fifteen minutes' walk from Piazza del Plebiscito; and the other, Porta Fiorentina, is on Viale Trento just north of the city walls, close to Piazza della Rocca and handier for hotels and the centre of town. There's also a station serving the **COTRAL** Roma-Nord line in Località Riello, next door to Porta Fiorentina and about ten minutes' walk from Piazza del Plebiscito, where trains from Rome's Piazzale Flaminia station arrive. There's a **tourist office** on Piazza San Carluccio 5 (Mon–Sat 9am–1pm & 1.30–3.30pm; ☎0761.304.795) in the medieval part of town, which has free maps of Viterbo and the surrounding area and information on **accommodation**. Close by, Via della Cava, which winds up to Piazza della Rocca, has a couple of Viterbo's inexpensive hotels: the *Leon D'Oro*, Via della Cava 36 (☎0761.344.444; ④), is a decent three-star hotel – reasonably priced and friendly, with off-street parking; or you could try the cheaper, more basic *Roma*, down the street at Via della Cava 26 (☎0761.226.474; ③).

Finding **somewhere to eat** is no problem. *Schenardi*, Corso Italia 11 (closed Wed), is one of the nicest places for a lunchtime snack or a drink, and there are a number of cheap pizzerias on Via Matteotti and Via della Cava. The *Porta Romana*, in Via della Bonta, has excellent food, and is supremely friendly. Otherwise, try *La Scaletta*, Via Marconi 43 (closed Mon), for reasonably priced pizzas, or *Tre Re*, Via Marcel Gattesco 3 (closed Thurs), off Piazza dell'Erbe – a cosy place, popular with locals and a good venue for trying regional specialities. If you're feeling indulgent, the *Enoteca la Torre*, Via delle Torre 5 (☎0761.226.467) (evenings only; closed Sun), is Viterbo's culinary highlight: a slightly precious place, but serving wonderful food that is not overly costly if you select sparingly from the five or six courses on offer – and go easy on the huge and pricey wine list.

Around Viterbo: Bagnaia, Bomarzo and Tuscania

Viterbo makes by far the best base besides Rome for seeing much of northern Lazio, especially the places that aren't really feasible on a day-trip from the capital. The Mannerist villas of **Caprarola** (see p.756) and **Bagnaia** are a short distance away and easily reached on public transport, as are – from the same era – the bizarre gardens of **Bomarzo** and the shores of **Lago di Bolsena** (see p.763). Less excitingly, Viterbo is also connected by regular bus with **Tuscania**.

Bagnaia

BAGNAIA, about 5km east of Viterbo, isn't much of a town, but like Caprarola further south it's completely dominated by a sixteenth-century palace, the **Villa Lante**, whose small but superb **gardens** are considered Vignola's masterpiece and one of the supreme creations of Renaissance garden art – "the most lovely place of the physical beauty of nature in all Italy or in all the world", according to Sachaverell Sitwell. The villa is easily visited from Viterbo, using the hourly **bus** #6 from Piazza Martiri dei Ungheria or from the stop at the beginning of Viale Trento, or the less frequent trains of the Roma-Nord line.

A short walk up the hill from the main square, the **villa** is actually two villas, built twenty years apart for different cardinals but symmetrically aligned as part of the same architectural plan. They are closed to the public, but there's nothing much to write home about anyway; in contrast to Caprarola it's the **gardens** (Tues–Sun 9am–1hr before sunset; L4000/€2.07) that take pride of place – some of the best-preserved from the period and a summing up of Mannerist aspirations. The main group lie behind the villas, ranged over five gently sloping terraces, and are only visitable in the company of a guide. An attempt at a stylized interpretation of the natural world, they were an ambitious project, even by the standards of the time, depicting the progress of a river from its source in the hills to its outlet in the sea – represented here by a large parterre. The route takes in various watery adventures – waterfalls, lakes and the like – and among numerous fountains and low hedges there are plenty of humorous (or plain silly) touches, such as a maiden whose breasts spout water, a cascade designed as an elongated crayfish, and the so-called "wetting sports" – hidden sprays of water that drenched unsuspecting onlookers and were a big favourite of Mannerist funsters. Only the guide gets to play with these.

The adjoining **park** (Tues–Sun 9am–1hr before sunset; free), through which you can wander at will, has an even more ambitious narrative, attempting to describe through horticulture the progress of civilization from primitive times to the glories of the sixteenth century. In true Mannerist style almost as much weight is given to allegory as to architecture, both here and on the villas. The various square motifs that appear around the buildings, for example, were supposed to represent the perfection of heaven brought to earth.

Bomarzo

Twelve kilometres northeast of Bagnaia, the village of **BOMARZO** is home to another Mannerist creation, the **Parco dei Mostri** (daily dawn–dusk; L15,000/€7.75; *www. touring.it/bomarzo/index.html*) – and a greater contrast to the former's restrained elegance would be hard to find. It's still ostensibly a garden, but one look at the tangled wood and its huge, completely crazed sculptures is enough to see that this is Mannerism gone mad. Salvador Dali loved the surreal flavour of the place, even making a film here, and its strange otherworldly qualities – like a sixteenth-century theme park of fantasy and horror – have made it one of northern Lazio's primary tourist attractions.

Built in 1552 by the hunchbacked Duke of Orsini, the *Sacro Bosco* or "Sacred Wood", as he called it, set out to parody Mannerist self-glorification by deliberate vulgarity. Knocking the intellectual pretensions of the day through its mockery of idealized Arcadian retreats from society and Art's supposed "triumph" over Nature, it still retains the typically Mannerist calculated attempts at sensationalism. Apparently built by Turkish prisoners captured at the Battle of Lepanto (though this smacks of a Christian rationalization of the park's "heretical" features), the park has an Etruscan influence too, manifest in the plentiful urns and pine cones, and its madder moments are said to have been induced by a popular epic of the time, Ariosto's *Orlando Furioso*, a tale of lost sanity. The giant warrior at the entrance tearing apart a woodcutter comes from the story, a symbol of Orlando's madness, and deeper into the park an English prince pours Orlando's brains down an elephant's trunk – another symbol apparently, this time of the restoration of sanity. There are many other dank, mossy sculptures of tortoises, elephants, a whale, a mad laughing mask, dragons, nymphs, butterflies, and plenty of things you couldn't put a name to. There's a perfect octagonal temple, dedicated to Orsini's wife, and a crooked, slanting house that makes your head spin. Numerous cryptic inscriptions all over the park only add to the mystery.

Eight **buses** a day run from Viterbo to Bomarzo, from where the Parco dei Mostri is a signposted ten-minute walk. You can also get here by **train** – the nearest station is Attigliano-Bomarzo, on the Orte–Montefiascone–Viterbo link, but this is a five-kilometre walk from the park.

Tuscania

Sheep and then more sheep are the only thing that break the monotony of the wide, desolate country between Viterbo and Tarquinia until the towers of **TUSCANIA** come into view – all together an impressive sight, especially early in the morning when the sun is striking them full on. The town was used as the location of the Franco Zefferelli films *Romeo and Juliet* and *The Taming of the Shrew* but in 1971 it was flattened by an earthquake which killed several hundred people. A concentrated effort of civic planning and a healthy budget has restored it, and it's now a very tidy and clean reconstruction of what was once a run-down and seedy medieval town – well worth a wander.

The real point of a visit to Tuscania, however, lies in two justly celebrated **Romanesque churches** on the eastern edge of the town, close to the rocky outcrop of the old Etruscan settlement. From the central Piazza Basile take the Via Clodia until the unmistakable bulk of **San Pietro** (daily: summer 9am–1pm & 3–7pm; winter 9am–1pm & 2–5pm) looms into view. Considered one of the gems of the Italian Romanesque, it's an essentially thirteenth-century construction with eighth-century fragments of Lombard origin. Fronted by a threadbare grass piazza, which produces an odd courtyard effect, it's also flanked by the remains of a Bishop's Palace and two sturdy towers, the whole church having once been fortified as part of the town's defensive scheme. The intrinsic marble carving on the facade is a bizarre mix of mythological figures and Christian symbolism – look out for the dancer and a three-headed man spewing out a twisting vine – and may well come from an Etruscan temple. The interior is solemn and cavernous, with huge blunt pillars supporting curious notched arches, a feature known in Italian as *dentati* (literally "toothed"), a spiralling Cosmatesque pavement and some early twelfth-century frescoes in the transept, somewhat the worse for wear after the earthquake in 1971. Steps lead down underneath the chancel to a mosque-like crypt made up of 28 columns and ribbed vaulting.

The town's other focal point, **Santa Maria Maggiore** (same hours as San Pietro), is a stone's throw away down the hill, a less gracious affair than San Pietro, despite the fact that it was built slightly earlier in the same style. The arched marble doorway was probably added by Pisan sculptors in the twelfth century, and is surmounted by an almost naive white-marble Madonna and Child, and flanked by saints and biblical scenes. The rest of the ruddy stone facade is largely Gothic, only the left portal preserving the zigzags of Norman motif. Inside is the usual bare simplicity of the Romanesque – stone walls, the odd fresco (including entertaining scenes of the Last Judgment in the apse now, alas, fading fast) and, most remarkably, a font designed for total immersion.

The rest of the town is decidedly less impressive, boasting only a small **archeological museum** (Mon 3–7pm, Tues–Sun 9am–7pm; free), housed in the ex-convent of Santa Maria del Riposo on Via XX Settembre. In addition to the predictable Etruscan display, there's a collection of twelfth- to seventeenth-century ceramics, many taken from the walls of local houses.

Montefiascone, Lago di Bolsena and around

Heading north from Viterbo by road, there's little choice but to take the Via Cassia to **MONTEFIASCONE**, an unattractive journey, not improved by opting for the train, which runs alongside. Montefiascone rears up high, perched on the rim of an old volcanic crater, an Etruscan city and possibly the site of a huge temple to Voltumna – a sort of parliament for the heads of the twelve-city Etruscan Federation. The seventeenth-century **Duomo** is immediately striking, a huge octagonal pile that totally dominates the skyline, though it's less interesting than the twelfth-century church of **San Flaviano** a little way out of town on the road to Orvieto. An extraordinary Romanesque work, consisting of two interconnected but opposite-facing basilicas, the lower church contains several fourteenth- and fifteenth-century frescoes as well as the tomb of Bishop Giovanni Fugger, who reputedly died from knocking back too much of the local wine, *Est! Est! Est!*. Bumph from the **tourist office**, Via Cassia Vecchia (☎0761.83.201), regales you with other unlikely legends surrounding the brew and has details of **accommodation**, which includes the inexpensive hotel *Italia* at Piazzale Roma 9 (☎0761.826.058; ②) and a **campsite**, the *Amulasanta*, Via del Lago 77 (☎0761.85.294), out on the Marta road at Prato Roncone.

Buses run from Montefiascone to Orvieto (see p.626) and to most points on **Lago di Bolsena** – a popular destination, though rarely overcrowded. If you want to get away from it all and plan on spending some time here, head for the less-visited western shore, which is better for camping rough and more picturesque into the bargain. The lake, the largest crater lake in Europe, occupies the remains of a broad volcanic crater. The surrounding soil is immensely fertile, and there's a super-mild microclimate, with most of the shores intensely cultivated as a result. Dante praised the quality of its eels, though fishermen today are hampered by the so-called *sesse* – odd tide-like variations in the lake's level.

CAPODIMONTE, on the southern shore, is one of the more developed spots, an attractive town that pushes into the lake on a partly forested peninsula. The only sight worth a mention is the sixteenth-century **Castello Farnese** (closed to the public), an octagonal tower commanding the tip of the promontory, but there's good **swimming** from a tree-lined shore, and boat trips run out to the **Isola Bisentina**, which sports Etruscan tombs, five frescoed chapels, and another Farnese villa – the summer retreat of several popes. The nearest **campsite** is 1500m away at Località San Lorenzo, *Camping Bisenzio* (☎0761.871.202; May–Sept).

On the opposite shore, **BOLSENA** is the lake's main focus, a relaxed and likeable place that's worth a stop even if you don't intend to hang around. Medieval nooks and alleyways run off the single main drag, with a well-preserved fourteenth-century **castle** perched over the western end. Inside is the local **museum** (Tues–Sun: summer 9.30am–1.30pm & 4–8pm; winter 9.30am–1.30pm; free) with a modest collection of local Roman and Etruscan finds. The deconsecrated thirteenth-century church of **San Francesco** adds character to the town's main Piazza Matteotti and occasionally hosts concerts and small exhibitions, and the eleventh-century **Santa Cristina** conceals a good Romanesque interior behind a wide Renaissance facade added in 1494. St Cristina was the daughter of the town's third-century Roman prefect, who tortured her for her Christian beliefs, eventually throwing her into the lake with a stone round her ankles. Miraculously the stone floated and saved her life, becoming marked with the imprint of her feet – though she died at the tender age of 12 as a result of further mistreatment. The stone makes up the altar of the Cappella del Miracolo, off the left-hand aisle – an altar that also starred in the Mass of Bolsena (see p.733), when a sceptical priest was assured of the mystery of transubstantiation by real blood. Adjoining the chapel is the Grotta di Santa Cristina, once part of early Christian catacombs.

Set back a kilometre from the lake, the town itself tends to shut down come nightfall, when the **bars and restaurants** on the shore get into full swing. The closest of the **campsites**, most of which are a short walk out of town, is the *Campeggio Il Lago*, less than a kilometre away at Viale Cadorna 6 (☎0761.799.191; March–Sept); *La Pineta* is a similar distance from town at Viale Diaz 48 (☎0761.799.801; May–Sept). The cheapest **hotel** is the *Italia*, Corso Cavour 53 (☎0761.799.193; ②). For full details, call in at the **tourist office** at Piazza Matteotti 9 (summer Mon–Sat 9am–1pm & 4–8pm; winter Sat & Sun 9am–1pm & 4–8pm; ☎0761.799.923).

To the east of Bolsena stretches an extraordinary, almost lunar landscape, pitted with deeply eroded **canyons**, some wooded but most just bare, wasted slopes. At its heart lies the tiny village of **CIVITA DI BAGNOREGGIO**, known as "la città che muore" ("the city that is dying") due to the erosion of the rock beneath it. People have been emigrating from here since the sixteenth century, leaving behind a dwindling population in a strange, eerily deserted village that's also inhabited by a number of foreign artists. The village is slowly becoming a tourist attraction in its own right: there's a longstanding rumour that an Italian computer company has plans to buy up the place wholesale, but for the moment it's worth a visit just for its very weirdness. Stranded evocatively on an isolated rocky outcrop, the only access is on foot from the nearby village of **BAGNOREGGIO** (about 20min).

Due north of the lake, **SAN LORENZO NUOVO** is just one of many villages you'll pass through if you're continuing up by road to Siena. A planned settlement, centred on an octagonal piazza, it was constructed in 1774 to house the inhabitants of the village of San Lorenzo, who had been forced to move by the malaria that once ravaged the entire lake shore. By some architectural freak the design was copied from a suburb of Copenhagen. If you have time and transport, hilltop **GRADOLI**, a few kilometres west, is at the heart of a big wine area and has another palace built by the Farnese family. A rough road just beyond, from Latera, leads to the **Lago di Mezzano**, a beautiful and highly recommended spot if you're travelling with a tent.

Rieti and around

Pleasantly situated but rather dull, **RIETI** is capital of Lazio's largest province, occupying the plumb geographical centre of Italy – and with a plaque in Piazza di San Rufo to prove it. In the days of the Romans this was a key region, the so-called *Umbilicus Italiae*, and the Via Salaria or "Salt Road" traversing these parts formed an essential route for trading salt (extracted from the Tiber estuary) with the Sabines who lived up in these hills. But nowadays it's on its last legs, with the second lowest population density in the country (after Aosta) and a drift from the land that's more often associated with the south. Three-quarters of the rural population has moved from the countryside since 1950, most of them to Rome, and it doesn't look like changing: poor communications have deterred any sort of industrial initiative – something that is to the visitors' if not the locals' advantage, leaving Rieti's mountain-ringed plain almost entirely unscarred by factories or housing.

The Town

Rieti is really just somewhere to while away an hour waiting for a bus, unless you want to use it is a base for walks in the area (see below). Despite the tourist office's artful pictures of medieval walls and arches, the only traces of the medieval town you'll find are the **Duomo** and the **Palazzo Vescovile** off the main street and a short stretch of twelfth-century wall to the north of the centre. For those planning serious walking or camping trips, it's worth visiting the main **tourist office** at Piazza Vittorio Emanuele II (Mon–Sat 9.30am–1pm & 4–6pm; ☎0746.201.146, *www.apt.rieti.it*), who have maps of the town and, more importantly, detailed routes for **high-level walks** around Terminillo (see below). With their help you also shouldn't have problems planning a tour of the four **Franciscan monasteries** around Rieti, all connected one way or another with important episodes in the saint's life. They're all scenic enough, though without an abiding interest in St Francis you may not find them terribly exciting. The most famous is at **GRECCIO**, where Francis created the first ever Christmas crib, a real-life nativity scene complete with cows, for the benefit of locals; this is re-enacted every year on December 24, December 26 and at Epiphany on January 6.

Practicalities

Rieti's **train station** is just north of the town centre on the far side of Viale L. Morroni. By **train** from Rome it's around three hours to Rieti: there's no direct link and you have to change at Terni (and sometimes Orte) for a line that eventually continues to L'Aquila and Sulmona. The **bus station** is in Via Fratelli Sebastiani off Via Salaria, and several **buses** a day ply back and forth to Rome (a 2hr journey). If you need **to stay**, the *Serena*, Viale della Gioventù 17 (☎0746.270.930; ③), is probably the cheapest option close to the centre of town, and has a few cheaper rooms without baths. If you want to be in the centre itself, try the *Europa*, Via San Rufo 49 (☎0746.495.149; ③), which also has some cheaper rooms. You can **eat** inexpensively at *Pizzeria Il Pappamondo*, Piazza Cavour 63 (closed Tues), or, for a little more money, try *Bistrot*, on Piazza San Rufo 25 (closed Sun), a family-run place whose adventurous and varied menu changes daily.

Around Terminillo

Less than 20km from Rieti, reachable by way of a heart-stopping bus ride, **TERMINILLO** lies amidst 2000-metre-high mountains and scenery of almost Alpine splendour, a winter ski-resort that likes to think of itself as something of an elite tourist centre. As such it's dominated by clusters of big modern hotels, ski lifts and associated winter-sports paraphernalia. Terminillo is not an especially attractive place, more a string of ski-centres than a town, with facilities that seem rather out of place and redundant in summer, but there's plenty of off-season scope for walking and climbing in the hills around, including a series of refuges if you want to do more than stroll.

There's a **tourist office** at Via dei Villini 33 in Terminillo/Pian de Valli (daily: summer 9am–1pm & 4–8pm; winter 9am–1pm & 4–6pm; ☎0746.261.121), which can advise on ski conditions and **accommodation**. There's a **youth hostel**, the *Ostello della Neve*, at Terminillo/Campoforogna (☎0746.261.169; L18,000/€9.30). Contact the **Club Alpino Italiano**, Via Garibaldi 264b, in Rome (☎06.686.1011), for advance information on some of the most challenging hikes in the countryside around. One tremendous low-level hike is by way of **La Valle Scura**, 12km across country to Sigillo; ask at the tourist office for details. If you plan on trekking off into the wilderness, bear in mind that many slopes away from the ski-runs are thickly wooded, especially in the Vallonina towards Leonessa, and you often have to climb quite high before finding open country.

Another good base for hikes is **AMATRICE**, 65km northeast of Rieti, a rather drab grid-iron town laid out in 1529, famous only for having given birth to a pasta dish, *spaghetti all'Amatriciana*, with a spicy bacon and tomato sauce. Behind, the Monti della Laga rise to seriously high peaks – 2400m up – which continue on into Abruzzo's Gran Sasso (see p.786). The **tourist office** at Corso Umberto I 93 (☎0746.826.344) issue a detailed map with several marked paths, most of which start from rough roads above the hamlets of San Martino and Cappricchia. If you plan on staying, try the two-star hotel *La Conca* on Via della Madonnella 24 (☎0746.826.791; ②).

The Sabine Hills

The **Sabine Hills**, south of Rieti, are an altogether softer option than the mountains to the east. For an area so close to Rome this sees only a trickle of tourism – partly because there are no big sights and partly because it's difficult to get around in what is essentially a landscape of small villages and secondary roads. If you decide to bother with the region it'll be for the scenery, the best of which is east of the Via Salaria around **Lago del Turano** and **Lago del Salto**, where the village of **ROCCA SINIBALDA** provides a focus – though it's really no more than a fortified castle, surrounded by high wooded hills. Northeast of here, a great swath of desolate country centres around Monte Nuria (1888m) and Monte Moro (1524m) – walking and backpacking territory mostly, with the small **Lago Rascino** providing a wild and unspoilt destination, especially good for camping.

On the other side of the Via Salaria, many of the villages have been doubly destroyed, first in the Fifties by people emigrating to Rome, and then more recently – and ironically – by richer Romans returning to buy up holiday homes. The villages still look much as they always did – small self-contained nuclei on the tops of low hills – and varying degrees of medieval character are about all they've got going for them, though the rolling countryside between is moderately pretty. One undoubted highlight in a lacklustre area is the old Benedictine abbey at **FARFA**, situated in fine olive-covered countryside 6km from the village of Faro. Getting there by bus is difficult as connections are required, but the Rieti tourist office will be able to advise on the latest schedules. Founded in the fifth century and endowed by Charlemagne, it was one of the single most powerful abbeys in Europe for a while, with a huge economic base, a merchant fleet, even its own army, and rights to Aquila, Molise, Viterbo, Spoleto, Tarquinia and Civitavecchia – central Italy in effect. By the end of the Middle Ages, however, it was in decline, and most of its early medieval splendour has since been submerged under fifteenth- and sixteenth-century additions. The **Abbey Church** (summer Tues–Sat 9.30am–1pm & 4.30–7pm, Sun 10am–1pm & 4–7pm; winter daily 3.30–6pm; L5000/€2.58) is stacked with various treasures, including parts of the Carolingian pavement, the sculptural relief forming the pulpit base and a few eleventh-century frescoes in the belltower, but the **museum** (closed for restoration) is the main focus, collecting together parts of the abbey's heritage as well as local archeological fragments. Most fascinating is the **Cures Pillar**, a sixth-century BC Sabine inscription found in a local riverbed in 1982. It's the only example known, and, still undeciphered, it remains an emblem for studies of the previously ignored Sabine culture.

SOUTHERN LAZIO

The saying goes that the Italian South begins with the first petrol station south of Rome, and certainly there's a radically different feel to the **southern part of Lazio**, the green wooded hills north of the city having given way to a mix of flat marshy land and harsh unyielding mountains that has a poor, almost desperate look in places. Many skate straight through the area on their way south to Naples, and you may want to do the same. But if you've time, the **coast** is worth taking in on a more unhurried route south: its resorts, especially **Terracina** and **Sperlonga**, are fine places to take it easy after the rigours of the capital, and the **Pontine Islands**, a couple of hours offshore, are – out of high season at least – among Italy's undiscovered treasures. **Inland**, too, the landscape can be rewarding: the towns of the **Castelli Romani** are the most accessible taste of the region, easily assimilated on a day-trip from Rome; **Subiaco** to the east and the **Ciocaria** region to the south are more remote, but hold some of Lazio's most inspiring scenery – broad tree-clad hills and valleys sheltering small, unassuming towns.

The Castelli Romani and Alban Hills

Just free of the sprawling southern suburbs of Rome, the thirteen towns that make up the **Castelli Romani** date back to medieval times, since when these hills – the **Colli Albani** – have served as an escape for the rich and powerful from the summer heat of the city. It's a wine-growing area (the vines grow easily on the volcanic soil) and is now pretty heavily built-up, with most of the historic centres ringed by unprepossessing suburbs; and summer weekends can see Romans trooping out in huge numbers for lunch at local trattorias. But if you avoid the rush-hour times and peak-season holidays, the region is still worth the journey, either as a day-trip from Rome or on the way south through Lazio. By car, there are two obvious routes, both starting with Frascati and Grottaferrata and then spearing off at Marino along either the eastern or western side of Lago Albano. On public transport, COTRAL buses serve the area (every 30min; a 35min journey) from the terminus upstairs from the metro station Anagnina (line A).

Frascati and around

At just 20km from Rome, **FRASCATI** is the nearest of the Castelli towns and also the most striking, dominated by the majestic **Villa Aldobrandini**, built by Giacomo della Porta in 1598 for one Cardinal Aldobrandi. Since it still belongs to the family you can't actually get inside, but the **gardens** are open to the public (Mon–Fri: summer 9am–1pm & 3–6pm; winter 9am–1pm & 3–5pm; free). These are somewhat neglected these days, and sadly the potentially spectacular water garden at the rear of the villa is often switched off. But the view from the terrace in front of the house is superb, with Rome visible on a clear day. Frascati is also about the most famous of the Colli Albani wine towns: ask at the **tourist office** on Piazza Marconi 1 (Tue–Fri 8am–2pm & 4–7pm, Sat 8am–2pm; ☎06.942.0331) for details of local wine producers that run tours and tastings, or simply indulge in lunch at one of the many trattorias in town. Better yet, pick up a *porchetta* (whole roasted pork) sandwich from one of the stands on Piazza del

Mercato and head for one of the town's many *cantine* – you can take food in with you – where wine is sold by the litre from giant wooden barrels.

The tourist office can also give you more details of **Tusculum**, beautifully sited on a hilltop just outside Frascati. This was a favourite retreat of Roman patricians: Cicero had a villa here, but the resort was destroyed in 1191 by Pope Celestine III, the inhabitants moving down the hill to modern-day Frascati. Most of the Roman remains seem to have disappeared forever beneath the undergrowth; there's a small theatre, and the views, again, are fine.

Three kilometres or so down the road, **GROTTAFERRATA** is also known for its wine and its eleventh-century **Abbey** – a fortified Basilian (Greek Orthodox) monastery surrounded by high defensive walls and a now empty moat (daily: summer 6am–12.30pm & 3.30–7pm: winter 6am–12.30pm & 3.30–sunset; free). It's a timeless spot, the little church of Santa Maria inside with a Byzantine-style interior decorated with thirteenth-century mosaics and, in the chapel of St Nilo off the right aisle, frescoes by Domenichino. Through the inner courtyard there's a small museum (closed for restoration) displaying classical and medieval sculptures. **MARINO**, another 4km further on, isn't a particularly attractive place, though its wine is perhaps the region's best after Frascati and is distributed free on the first Sunday of October during its Sagra dell'Uva festival.

East of Lago Albano

The scenic Via dei Laghi skirts the eastern rim of **Lago Albano** until a winding road leads up to **Monte Cavo**, at 949m the second highest of the Colli Albani and topped with the masts and satellite dishes of the Italian military – who operate from nearby Ciampino airport. A temple to Jupiter once stood here, but now the only extant antiquity is the Via Sacra, which, about 1000m from the top, emerges from dense undergrowth, snaking down through the woods for a kilometre or so before disappearing again into thick bush.

On the far side of Monte Cavo, the road bears right for **ROCCA DI PAPA**, at 680m the highest of the Castelli Romani towns and one of its most picturesque, with a medieval quarter tumbling down the hill in haphazard terraces, and motor traffic kept to a strictly enforced minimum. The large main square, Piazza Repubblica, is modern and dull; instead, make for the small Piazza Garibaldi, a lively place in summer with a bar and restaurant, and soak up the views.

Castel Gandolfo and west of Lago Albano

Leaving Marino, the road joins up with the old Roman Via Appia, which travels straight as an arrow down the west side of Lago Albano. **CASTEL GANDOLFO** is the first significant stop, named after the castle owned by the powerful twelfth-century Genevose Gandolfi family and now best known as the summer retreat of the pope – though John Paul II is said to prefer visiting the mountains further north during the heat of the summer, much to the disgruntlement of the town. At over 400m above the rim of Lago Albano, it's a pleasantly airy place, but inevitably papal business predominates, especially on those Sundays between July and September when the pope traditionally gives a midday address from the courtyard of the Papal Palace. Unless you actually want to see the pope, it's best to avoid this. Better, if it's hot, to take advantage of the lake: there's a pleasant **Lido** just below the town, from where, if you've the energy, you can walk right around the lake in about two hours.

From Castel Gandolfo a panoramic road leads to **ALBANO LAZIALE**, probably the most appealing of the towns along the Via Appia, its large Piazza Mazzini looking south to the lovely Villa Comunale park, with sketchy remains of a villa that once belonged to

Pompey. The town also has other Roman remains. Along the high street, Corso Matteotti, the church of **San Pietro** was built over the foundations of the baths of a Roman garrison, which you can see built into the walls. Near the church of Santa Maria della Stella is the **museo civico** (Mon–Sat 9am–12.30pm, Sun 9am–noon, plus Wed & Thurs 4–7pm; L4000/€2.07), with a small but high-quality archeological collection, including Etruscan and Roman artefacts found locally. Walk along Via della Stella to the **Tomb of Horatii and the Curiatii**, just outside town on the Ariccia road, whose strange "chimneys" date from the Republican era. There's an **amphitheatre** too, on the hill above – in heavy ruin now, and currently closed, but once with room for 15,000 spectators.

The Via Appia continues on to **ARICCIA** across the nineteenth-century **Ponte di Ariccia** – from where you can see the arches of the old Roman viaduct just below – into the central piazza of the town, a well-proportioned square embellished with Bernini's round church of **Santa Maria dell'Assunzione**. Ariccia, incidentally, is famous for its *porchetta* – roast pork.

South of Lago Albano

GENZANO, two kilometres further on, also has a pleasant medieval centre, built around Piazza Frasconi, from where a road leads to the edge of Lago Albano's crater and sweeps down to the shore through dense woods. The town is the scene of the yearly Infiorata on Corpus Domini, usually in June, when Via Italo Belardi, which scales the hill from the piazza, is carpeted with flowers. A detour east will take you to **NEMI**, built high above the tiny crater **lake** of the same name. The village itself isn't much to write home about, but a cobbled road leads down to fields of strawberries that lie between the steep walls of the crater and the shores of the lake and make a good place to picnic. The town is known for its year-round strawberry harvest, in fact, and celebrates this on the first Sunday in June in the Sagra delle Fragole. On the northern shore of the lake you'll notice a large hangar-like building, which contains the scanty remains of two Roman pleasure boats said to have been built by Caligula.

Further southeast, **VELLETRI**, though larger, is scarcely more interesting, its largely modern centre rebuilt after extensive war damage and with a Baroque cathedral, the fourteenth-century Torre del Trivio and a small archeological museum among its scant sights.

Palestrina, Subiaco and the Ciociaria

Considering its proximity to the capital, it's a surprise that the **southeastern rim of Lazio** isn't more discovered; in fact it's one of the areas of Italy least known to tourists, for the most part a poor region of low hills edging into the mountains of Abruzzo that is bypassed by those heading south on the fast Autostrada del Sole.

Palestrina

PALESTRINA was built on the site of the ancient Praeneste, originally an Etruscan settlement and later a favoured resort for patrician Romans. "Cool Praeneste", as Horace called it, was the site of an enormous Roman Temple of Fortune, whose foundations more or less determine the extent of the modern town centre, which steps up the hillside in a series of terraces constructed on the different levels of the once vast edifice – the ruins of which you can see at every turn.

Buses run to Palestrina about every 45 minutes from Rome and take about 45 minutes, dropping you on Via degli Arcioni, from where you have to walk up the steep incline to the town centre. You can see this in no time. There's a much-changed **Duomo** with fragments of a Roman road at the top end of the right aisle and a copy of Michelangelo's *Pietà di Palestrina* – the original, is now in Florence. And the stepped streets of the place are appealing enough for some casual strolling. But you have to climb to the top of the town for the real attraction – the **Palazzo Colonna-Barberini**, which houses the **Museo Nazionale Archeologico Prenestino** (daily 9am–1hr before sunset; L4000/€2.07). Originally built in the eleventh century and greatly modified by Taddeo Barberini in 1640, this occupies the uppermost level of the Temple of Fortune, now largely modernized inside and containing a slightly faded display of artefacts. Among a number of Roman pieces, there's a torso of a statue of Fortune in slate-grey marble, a recently found sculpture, *Il Triade Capitolina*, other bits from the temple, and funerary cistae much like those displayed at the Villa Giulia in Rome.

At the top, the museum's prize exhibit is the marvellous first-century BC *Mosaic of the Nile*, which depicts the flooding of the river with a number of Egyptian scenes of life along the waterway from the source to the delta. Look closely and you'll notice a wealth of detail: there's a banquet going on under the vines on the left, soldiers and priests are grouped in front of the Serepaeum on the right, while the source of the river among the mountains is pictured at the top of the mosaic, where hunters and wild animals, labelled with Greek lettering, congregate. Outside the museum, your ticket admits you to the top **terrace** of the temple, the ruins of which command fine views over the surrounding countryside.

Subiaco

Around 15km northeast of Palestrina, **SUBIACO** (accessible by bus from Tivoli or direct from Rome), is beautifully set, pyramided around a hill topped by the Rocca Abbazia castle, close to Monte Liviato – one of Lazio's premier ski resorts. Founded as a purpose-built settlement to accommodate workmen building Nero's grand villa nearby (very meagre traces of which survive), during the fifth century Subiaco became the chosen contemplative base of St Benedict, who lived a life of seclusion and prayer in a cave on the slopes of a nearby mountain. St Benedict left after three years to found the monastery at Montecassino (see p.772), but his legacy lives on in the town, in the shape of two monastic complexes just outside.

The **Abbazia di Santa Scolastica** (daily 9am–12.30pm & 4–7pm; free) is the closer (and larger) of the two, a pleasant five-kilometre walk out of town along the Ienne road from the main bus stop and following the signs off to the left before the bridge. Dedicated to Benedict's sister, it's been heavily restored over the years: the facade, with the Benedictine motto *Ora et Labora* over the entrance, isn't original and the only features of any real age in the church inside are two cipolino marble pillars from Nero's villa. The three cloisters, though, are delightful: the first is from the Renaissance period; the second one of the oldest Gothic works in Italy, lushly planted and fragrant; and the third a Cosmati work with lovely arcades of pillars.

Continuing up the same road, the landscape grows more dramatic, after about fifteen minutes reaching the **Abbazia di San Benedetto** (daily 9am–12.30pm & 3–6pm; free) – a complex of two churches, chapels and other buildings clasping the rocky hillside on the precise site of St Benedict's cave. This is much the more interesting of the two monasteries: its church divides into several levels, the upper part decorated with frescoes of the fourteenth-century Sienese school and fifteenth-century Perugian school, the lower leading into the Sacro Speco – the actual cave where St Benedict lived, now left in its natural condition but for a serene statue by Raggi, a disciple of Bernini. From here a spiral staircase leads up to the chapel of San Gregorio, containing a thirteenth-century picture of St Francis that's reckoned to be the first ever portrait of the saint painted from life. In the other direction, stairs lead down to another chapel, from which Benedict would preach to shepherds, and a terrace which looks out onto the so-called "Holy Rose Tree" – in fact, a three-forked bush said to have been created by St Francis from a bramble.

Practicalities

You can comfortably see Subiaco and its monasteries on a **day-trip** from Rome, even using public transport: the bus journey takes around two-and-a-half hours and you can arrive in the town by lunchtime, eat, visit the monasteries in the afternoon and take an evening bus back to Rome (the last one leaves at 8.30pm).

The town's location may, however, make you want to linger: there's a reasonable **hotel** in the centre of town, the *Aniene*, at Via Cadorna 18 (☎0774.85.565; ②), which has an adequate **restaurant**, and the slightly more upmarket two-star *Miramonti*, Via Papa Giovanni XXIII, 4 (☎0774.83.243; ⑤), which has an excellent, if pricey (L80,000/€41.32 per person for dinner), restaurant. The **tourist office** at Via Cadorna 59 (Mon 8am–2pm, Tues–Sat 8am–2pm & 3.30–6.30pm; ☎0774.822.013) has full details of accommodation and transport links. If you're **heading south** there's an early bus out to Frosinone – from where you can get train or bus connections on to other points in Lazio and Campania.

The Ciociaria

From Subiaco the road heads south into a region known as the **Ciociaria**, a relatively remote corner of Lazio that takes its name from the bark sandals, or *ciocie*, worn here in days gone by. This hilly country was settled several centuries before the Romans by the Italic tribes – the Hernici, the Equii, the Volscians and the Sanniti – who built inaccessible and heavily fortified towns, the remains of which, due to their shrewd foreign policy of allying themselves with Rome, can still be seen today in the form of the extraordinary cyclopean walls of their citadels, quite unlike anything else in Italy.

The first town you come to, **FIUGGI**, is a spa resort whose bottled mineral water you will probably have already noticed in supermarkets, and which attracts health-conscious Italian tourists throughout the summer. It's not an especially appealing spot, its spa facilities, gardens and sports halls chic and pricey places that are either overflowing with crowds or (in winter) entirely dead.

From Fiuggi there's a choice of two routes, either west to Anagni or south to Alatri. **ANAGNI**, a former Hernici stronghold, is a well-preserved old place that produced a number of medieval popes from its powerful local Segni family, including Boniface VIII, whose **palace** (daily 9am–12.30pm & 3–6pm; L3000/€1.55) here was invaded in 1303 by representatives of Philip IV of France when he attempted to assert the absolute authority of the papacy. You can visit a few rooms in the palace, including the one where Colonna is said to have slapped Boniface – a statue of whom stands on the outside of Anagni's **Duomo**, an imposing Romanesque basilica dating from the eleventh century. Inside there's a fine Cosmatesque pavement, a thirteenth-century baldacchino, some important proto-Renaissance thirteenth-century frescoes in the crypt and a treasury containing some of the pontifical effects of Pope Boniface VIII.

In the opposite direction, **ALATRI** – the Hernici Aletrium – preserves its cyclopean walls from the sixth-century-BC acropolis. Built long before the more sophisticated stone-cutting techniques of the Romans, they are still very much intact – most impressively, perhaps, in the Porta di Falli, with its strident fertility symbols carved on the lintel. The town's streets wind around the citadel beneath the walls, cut by two square gateways (the arch hadn't yet been invented in Europe when this was built), inside of which the cathedral and Episcopal Palace stand on the site of the Hernici's ancient temples, since lost. The views, incidentally, are terrific.

FERENTINO, 10km west, also sports a good set of walls, though a hybrid one, modified by the Romans. You can get up to the old citadel here too, though it's 5km from the modern town's station (bus connection), and the cathedral there is regularly open. FROSINONE, 10km or so further south, is the main town of the Ciociaria but is of little interest, being a bland sprawling place with no obvious centre and barely any remains of the Hernici settlement. But it's a good place to pick up bus and train connections on to other points in Lazio and Campania: buses run west to Priverno from here, and from near there, you can pick up trains south or north and visit Fossanova abbey (see p.774). Trains also connect Frosinone's FS station (some way out of town but connected by bus) with Naples, Cassino and Caserta.

Further south: Cassino and the Abbey of Montecassino

The town of **CASSINO**, fifty minutes down the railway line from Frosinone, is the site of another important monastery, the **Abbey of Montecassino** (daily 9.30am–12.30pm & 3.30pm–6pm; free; *www.osb.org*), founded in 529 by St Benedict after he left Subiaco (see p.770), on a spot to which he was guided by three ravens. This was for many years one of the most important and influential monastic complexes in the Christian world, its monks spreading the word as far away as Britain and Scandinavia in between developing the tradition of culture and learning that was at the core of the Benedictine order. Ironically, its strategically vital position, perched high on a mountaintop between Rome and Naples, has been its downfall: this vantage point has been coveted and fought over by a succession of invaders, and over the years the abbey has been repeatedly destroyed. During World War II, the abbey came to be the lynchpin of the German presence in this part of Italy and, after a battle that lasted almost six months, the Allies – a mixture of Poles, New Zealanders and Indian troops – eventually bombed it to ruins in May 1944, sacrificing several thousand lives in the process. It was subsequently rebuilt, and the austere medieval style of its buildings has been faithfully re-created, but it's really more impressive for its position than for itself: much of the complex is not open to the public, and its sterile white central courtyard is engaging only for the views it gives over the surrounding hills and the Polish war cemetery below. The church, off here, in a hideously ornate Baroque style, has a small **museum** (same hours as abbey; L2000/€1.03) containing incunabula, old manuscripts and suchlike. But otherwise you can't help but feel that Montecassino's glory days ended firmly with the war.

The **town** below was fairly comprehensively destroyed, too, and has very little appeal. There's a **tourist office** at Piazza de Gasperi 10 (Mon–Sat 8.30am–1pm & 3.30–6.30pm, Sun 9am–noon; ☎0776.25.629, *www.apt.frosinone.it*), on the opposite side of the centre to the train and bus station, and another at Corso della Repubblica 23 (Mon–Sat 9am–noon & 4–7pm; ☎0776.26.842). Buses scale the mountain to the abbey from Piazza San Benedetto twice daily. If you need to stay, **hotels** are at least inexpensive – pick up a list from the tourist office.

The southern Lazio coast

The **Lazio coast to the south** of Rome is a much more attractive proposition than that to the north. Its towns have a bit more charm, the water is less polluted, and in the further reaches, beyond the dreary flats of the Pontine Marshes and Monte Circeo, the shoreline begins to pucker into cliffs and coves that hint gently at the glories that await in Campania further south – all good either for day-trips and overnight outings from the city, or for a pleasingly wayward route to Naples.

Anzio and Nettuno

About 40km south of Rome, and easily seen on a day-trip, **ANZIO** is the first town of any note, centre of a lengthy spread of settlement that focuses on a lively central square and a busy fishing industry. Much of the town was damaged during a difficult Allied landing here on January 22, 1944, to which two military cemeteries (one British, another, at nearby Nettuno, American) bear testimony. But despite a pretty thorough rebuilding it's a likeable resort, still depending as much on fish as tourists for its livelihood. The town's seafood **restaurants**, crowding together along the harbour and not unreasonably priced, are reason enough to come – try *Pierino* at Piazza C. Battisti 3 (closed Mon) – while the **beaches**, which edge the coast on either side, don't get unbearably thronged outside of August. Anzio is also a possible route on to the island of Ponza, for timings of **hydrofoils** (*www.vetor.it*) which leave daily in summer – ask at the **tourist office** on Piazza Pia 19 (daily 9am–1pm & 3.30–6pm; ☎06.984.5147).

NETTUNO, a couple of kilometres down the coast (and walkable by the coast road), is more of the same, but with slightly less beach space and water that's not quite so clear and calm. Again it's a mostly modern town, but there's a well-preserved old quarter, still walled, with a couple of decent trattorias on the main square – information from the **tourist office** at the port (daily: summer 9.30am–12.30pm & 5–7.30pm; winter 9.30am–12.30pm & 5–7.30pm but closed Sun afternoon; ☎06.980.3335, *www.eleweb.com/nettuno*).

The Pontine Marshes, Monte Circeo and San Felice Circeo

Beyond Anzio and Nettuno lie the **Pontine Marshes**, until seventy years ago a boggy plain prone to malaria that was populated by few except water buffalo. Julius Caesar had planned to drain the area but was assassinated before he could carry out his plan, and it was left to Mussolini to reclaim the region in 1928 – in a scheme that built a series of spanking new towns and provided an expanse of fertile, fresh farmland.

LATINA lies at the centre of the development, the provincial capital, founded in 1932, and centre of the thriving local agricultural economy, though of little interest now save for its transport connections. If you do end up here, it's instructive to at least have a brief walk around the town centre, which is something of a monument to Fascist architecture, with large open squares and sturdy-looking buildings interrupting broad avenues radiating out with classical uniformity from the central Piazza del Popolo.

Latina also makes an excellent base from which to visit the medieval town of **SERMONETA**, easily reachable by bus, and remarkable for its series of defensive walls erected over the centuries to protect it from the depredations of the Saracens and later from the wars between the papacy and Naples which raged throughout the Middle Ages. The outer walls have a massive gleaming white aspect that's reminiscent of Fascist architecture, but in fact they were put up by Cesare Borgia in the late 1400s when his father Alexander VI awarded this town to him. The earlier walls surround the historical centre and the defences around the castle, erected in the 1200s by the feudal Caetani family. This well-preserved castle is a near-perfect example of the medieval system of moats, porticuli, drawbridges and final defence tunnels designed to render the place practically inpregnable. As well as all the defence technology, there is a huge display of arms, armour, catapults and ancient cannon, and you can also see the vast cisterns and silos used to lay in supplies in times of conflict (Mon–Wed & Fri–Sun 9am–12.30pm & 2–5pm, closed Thurs; L5000/€2.58). To get a feel for Sermonetta, it's worth staying over, and the *Principe di Serrone* **hotel**, in the heart of the historic centre (☎0773.30.342; ④), is as good a place as any. There are also a number of good **restaurants and bars** nearby: *La Catena*, a moderately priced trattoria in the centre of town, serves decent local specialities (closed Mon; ☎0773.319.119), and on the way up the mountain there's *La Taparita*, a restaurant well favoured by the locals (also closed Mon; ☎0773.318.417)

Similarly easy to reach by bus from Latina (or by train and then taxi from Latina Scalo), **NINFA**, with its enchanting gardens, was another Cateani family stronghold. From the twelfth century, it was a thriving little fortified village with a castle keep in its centre, but it was abandoned during the Renaissance due to the spread of malaria. The inhabitants moved up the nearby mountain to Sermoneta, leaving a number of ruined medieval buildings, around which gardens here were created in the early twentieth century. There are all kinds of wild and domestic flowers, shrubs and trees, situated among little streams, waterfalls and ponds – very pretty, and worth the detour (April–Nov open first weekend of each month; guided tours only, last tour at 6pm; L12,000/€6.20).

Buses from Latina take about fifty minutes to reach **PRIVERNO**, another hilltop town, whose pretty main square is flanked by a Gothic town hall and a duomo from 1283 that apparently holds the relics of St Thomas Aquinas. About 5km south of the town, an hour or so walk or reachable by regular bus from Piazza XX Settembre, the **Abbey of Fossanova** (daily: summer 7am–noon & 4–7.30pm; winter 3–5.30pm; free) was where Aquinas died in 1274, en route between Naples and Lyon. This monastery of the Cistercian order may tempt you if you have time to spare before catching a train at the nearby Priverno-Fossanova train station, 2km beyond. Although it has been rather heavily restored, the simplicity of its thirteenth-century Burgundian Gothic church is refreshing after the gaudiness of Baroque churches. A door leads from here out to a plain Romanesque cloister, with a garden in the centre and a chapter house off to one side, with wide windows through which lay brothers could watch the services (the corridor on the far side of the cloisters was for their use). A door to the left leads through a small separate courtyard to the guest wing where, at the northern end, St Thomas is supposed to have breathed his last.

The area around **SABAUDIA**, another Mussolini-era new town, 20km from Latina on the coast, gives some impression of what the marshes were like before they were drained, poised between two lagoons that make up the coastal Lago di Sabaudia. A large area to the north of the town, the Selva del Circeo, four coastal lakes, the huge bulk of Monte Circeo to the south and the offshore island of Zannone together form the **Parco Nazionale del Circeo**, set up in 1934 to preserve something of the marshes' wildlife and almost sinister natural beauty. It's a fine spot for birds: all kinds of water species can be seen here – herons, buzzards, storks, fish hawks, and rare species like the peregrine falcon and Cavaliere d'Italia; and the flora includes eucalyptus groves, oaks, elms, ash and wild flowers in spring. **Monte Circeo** itself lies to the south of Sabaudia across several kilometres of gleaming water, the sandy beach coming to an end at the sixteenth-century **Torre Paola**, perched at the entrance of a canal linking Lago di Sabaudia to the sea. There's a little pier usually occupied by a group of fishermen, from where the road turns inland and skirts the northern slopes of the mountain, passing through splendid woods.

After about 4km a road branches off to the right and rounds the mountain to emerge at **SAN FELICE CIRCEO**, a picturesque village of pretty stone houses bleached yellow by the sun. In summer it becomes a fairly trendy spot, the marina chock-a-block with fancy motor launches and yachts, its sandy beaches crowded with glistening oiled bodies and its roads bumper to bumper with flashy cars. The small **Piazza Municipio** has a **tourist office** (summer daily 10am–noon & 5–8pm; winter Sat & Sun 10am–noon; ☎0773.547.77, *www.circeoprimo.it*) and an interesting local **museum** (July–Sept daily 6–10pm; free), from behind which a road winds its way up to the summit of the **mountain** and the site of an ancient **temple**. The views from here are marvellous: there's a large car park at the top, with a summer bar, near to which is the entrance to the sparse relics of a Roman town – *Circeii* – and its rather better preserved cyclopean walls, not unlike the constructions in the Ciociaria (see p.771).

Back in the village you can rest up on the beaches or, in season, rent a boat (☎0773.543.263) out to the famous **Grotta della Maga Circe**. For quieter swimming-spots, take the road towards the lighthouse, the "Faro di Torre Cervia", which after a couple of kilometres reaches a secluded rocky spot – great for snorkelling. The area is also well supplied with campsites and inexpensive hotels.

Terracina

A further 15km down the coast from San Felice (hourly buses), or, if you're coming from Rome, a short train ride on the local line to Monte San Biagio, **TERRACINA** is an immediately likeable little town, divided between a tumbledown old quarter high on the hill above and a lively newer area down by the sea. During classical times it was an important staging-post on the Appian Way, which reaches the sea here; nowadays it's primarily a seaside resort and one of the nicest along this stretch of coast, with good, ample beaches and frequent connections with the other points of interest around.

The town

The centre of the old quarter is **Piazza Municipio**, which occupies the site of the old Roman forum, complete with the original slabs, and now focuses on the colonnade of the town's **Duomo**, with its elegant mossy campanile. An endearing little church with a fine mosaic floor and a beautiful mosaic-studded pulpit, it was built within the shell of a Roman temple dedicated to Augustus.

Terracina's main attraction, and rightly so, is the **Temple of Jupiter Anxurus**, which crowns the hill above the town. Take the steps up from Piazza Municipio onto Via Anxur and follow this for 200m, from where you can either follow the winding road to the top (forty minutes) or, 100m after the sign to the temple, turn off right and climb up by way of a rocky path – which takes half as long. There's a convenient bar (closed lunchtimes) at the top to aid your recovery. The temple is believed to date back to the first century BC and was connected to Terracina by some lengthy walls, although all that's now visible is the base of the structure, in the form of an arched terrace from which the views are stupendous – Terracina boxed neatly below and the bay curving round on either side.

As for **beaches**, apart from a scrubby oval of sand fringing the town centre, they stretch north pretty much indefinitely from beyond the main town harbour and are large enough not to get overcrowded.

Practicalities

The **tourist office**, just off Via Leopardi (summer Mon–Sat 9am–1pm & 5–8pm, Sun 9am–1pm; winter shorter hours; ☎0773.727.759), has more information, hotel lists and a map of the town. **Bikes** are for rent at Caccia e Pesca, Via Roma 9, for around L8000/€4.13 a day.

There are a number of reasonably priced **hotels**, best of which is the very pleasant and friendly *Hegelberger*, up in the old town at Via San Domenico 2 (☎0773.701.697; ③); in the lower town there's the curiously named *For You*, right next to the beach on the Lungomare at Via Molise 2 (☎0773.731.501; ②), and the more basic *Vittoria*, Piazza Mazzini 1 (0773.727.603; ①).

The nearest **campsite** is the *Costazzurra* (☎0773.702.589), a fifteen-minute walk south along the coast road, and there are numerous other campsites outside town, especially on the stretch called Salto di Fondi.

When looking for a **place to eat**, you could do worse than stop in at *Pizzeria La Marina* on Piazza Repubblica (closed Mon), whose low-priced pizzas are very popular locally; if you want more choice of fare, the *Miramare*, Viale Circe 32 (closed Tues), at the end of Viale Vittoria, is also cheap and has a convivial terrace. Above the old town, seek out the excellent and lively *Vesuvio* on Via San Domenico (closed Wed), for seafood or pizzas cooked in a wood-fired oven.

Sperlonga

The coast south of Terracina is probably Lazio's prettiest stretch, the cliff punctured by tiny beaches signposted enticingly from the road. **SPERLONGA**, built high on a rocky promontory, is a fashionable spot locally, its whitewashed houses and narrow streets more Greek in feel than Italian, and sadly given over entirely to tourists during summer (though cars are not allowed into the centre). There are some excellent **restaurants** specializing in seafood along Via Cristoforo; a basic, modern **hotel**, the *Grazie* at Via M. A. Colonna 110 (☎0771.54.223; ③); and a few pricey *pensioni*, though these are often full and you might find it easier to hole up in Terracina and come to Sperlonga for the day, taking advantage of the half-hourly buses. Another possibility is the many **rooms** and apartments for rent at the height of the season; ask at the local **information office** (Thurs–Tues 9am–1pm; ☎0771.54.796). The **beach** is certainly worth stopping for: a lengthy strand to the south with the town as backdrop and abundant space.

Between Sperlonga and Gaeta the coast steepens markedly, with yet more appealing beaches and, if you're camping, any number of handy campsites. A couple of kilometres from Sperlonga, there's a small museum and the remains of the **Villa of Tiberius** (daily: summer 9am–9pm; winter 9am–4pm; L4000/€2.07) – worth a stop if you've got your own transport. The house was built around a large ornamental pool which extends into a large grotto in the cliff face. The **museum** (same hours and ticket as villa) holds finds from the villa, centrepiece of which is a large complex group of statues depicting scenes from Homer's *Odyssey* in the style of the Vatican's *Laocoon* (see p.732), possibly by the same sculptors.

Gaeta

Some 10km further on, **GAETA** lords it over the broad sweep of bay from its high, castle-topped headland, an appealing place at first sight (especially from the southern side), untidily piled up onto the pinnacle of its defensive rock. The fortress here was impregnable: it resisted Gothic and Saracen invaders and the town flourished under the Normans, some of its architecture dating back to that time – and earlier. The tiny church of **San Giovanni al Mare** (check with tourist office for opening times) by the water, hails from the tenth century; and on the summit of Monte Orlando, now a park, there's the classical tomb of one **Munatius Plancus**, the founder of Lyons, decorated with a frieze showing scenes of battle (daily: summer 9am–1pm & 4–8pm; winter shorter hours). Close by, a **terrace** gives fine views over the Serapo bay below, next to which the small church of **Santuario del Crocifisso** is built on a boulder breaching the chasm of Montagna Spaccata, literally suspended a few hundred metres above the sea.

But for all this, it's Gaeta's modern-day role as a naval port that is most apparent: much of the old town is closed off to the public (parts of the port and the castle itself) and the quayside bars advertise "burgers and chips" to entice visiting American servicemen off the warships that are often docked in the harbour. The main square, **Piazza del Municipio**, flanks the portside and is a lively enough spot, with a small Wednesday market; and there's a **tourist office** at Piazza XIX Maggio (June–Sept Mon–Fri 8am–2pm & 5–8pm, Sun 9am–1pm; ☎0771.461.165). But you'd do best to visit Gaeta for the **beaches** north of the headland – though be warned that these, especially the closest at Spiaggia di Serapo, can get quite packed and their frontages have been bought up almost exclusively by restaurants.

Formia

About five miles around the bay, hard under the glowering backdrop of the Monti Aurunci, **FORMIA** is not much more promising, a largely modern town but an important resort during Roman times. Cicero had a villa here, at which he was murdered by Mark Antony's soldiers in 44 AD for his opposition to the triumvirate that succeeded Caesar. There are good **beaches** to the north of the town centre and a **tourist office** at Viale Unita d'Italia 30–34 (summer Mon–Sat 8.30am–2pm & 5–8pm, Sun 9am–1pm; winter Mon, Wed, Fri–Sun 8.30am–2pm, Tues & Thurs 8.30am–2pm & 5–8pm; ☎0771.771.386). But otherwise Formia is more a stopover than a stop in its own right, with plentiful connections on to Naples, Rome and inland to Cassino, and regular ferries and hydrofoils to Ponza, one of the Pontine Islands (see below). If you're taking an early boat, the *Ariston* at Via Cristoforo Colombo 19 (☎0771.770.405; ③) is the most convenient **hotel** to the harbour but is expensive for what it is, and rather characterless; the *Del Golfo*, Piazzale Stazione Ferroviaria 1 (☎0771.790.037; ②), is much cheaper and not a great deal less convenient. For **food**, check out *Zi Anna Mare* on Largo Paone (closed Tues) for fresh fish and pizzas served on a terrace.

Minturno

A few kilometres south of Formia – and the next stop on the train – **MINTURNO** is the last town before the Campania border, a maze of tiny lanes and vaulted streets oddly reminiscent of an Arab *medina*. The main square is dominated by a massive crumbling **castle**, which was owned until the middle of this century by the Carraciolo-Carafa dynasty; a plaque on the west wall recalls a visit by St Thomas Aquinas in 1272. Behind, the town's **Duomo** is a Norman structure not unlike that of nearby Sessa Arunca or Ravello, with a similar colourfully mosaicked pulpit. About 4km south of town are the ruins of the ancient Roman port of **Minturnae** (daily 9am–7pm; L4000/€2.07), a once flourishing town afflicted by depopulation as this low-lying area became malarial. Most striking among the rubble are the remains of a restored amphitheatre (still used for concerts in summer), below which there's a small antiquarium containing finds from around the site and a broken-down aqueduct that runs for 2km southwest.

The Pontine Islands

Scattered across the sea between Rome and Naples, the **Pontine Islands** are one of Italy's least well-known island groupings, relatively unvisited by all except Italians. Volcanic in origin, only two of the islands are inhabited, **Ponza** and **Ventotene**, of which only Ponza supports any kind of tourist industry. Visit between mid-June and the end of August and you'll find this thriving, as people seek an alternative to crowded Cápri; at any other time the island is yours for the asking.

As for **getting to the islands**, you can reach **Ponza** from a number of points on the mainland during the summer. From **Formia**, there are year-round services every day except Wednesday, consisting of a twice-daily ferry and a twice-daily hydrofoil. There are also year-round ferries once daily from **Terracina** (twice daily in July and August), and at least twice-daily hydrofoils from **Anzio** (*www.vitor.it*) between June and September. Fares are similar from all ports, with ferries at around L19,000/€9.81 one-way and hydrofoils about double that – although they take less than half as long.

To reach **Ventotene** from the mainland you can go from **Formia** or **Anzio**: ferries run once daily; hydrofoils run twice daily except Tuesday. You can also travel **between the islands** of Ponza and Ventotene by hydrofoil twice daily.

Ponza

Even **PONZA**, the main island of the Pontine group, is manageably small, a sharp, rocky hunk of land only eight kilometres end to end and at its widest point just under two kilometres across. Ferries sail to **PONZA TOWN**, one of the most beautiful small towns in these parts: heaped around the bay in a series of neat pastel-coloured pyramids, its flat-roofed houses radiate out from the pink semicircle that curls around the fishing harbour. It makes a marvellous place to rest up for a while, having so far escaped the clutches of designer boutiques and souvenir shops; and, although there are not a lot of specific sights on the island, the town is a fun place for aimless wanderings, particularly at passeggiata time, when the crowds turn out to parade along the yellow-painted **Municipio** arcade of shops and cafés. For lazing and swimming, there's a small, clean **beach** in the town; and a ten-minute walk away, across the island, the **Chiaia di Luna** beach, a sheer sickle of cliff edged by a slender rim of sand – though be warned that the waves here are much choppier than those on the sheltered mainland-facing side of the island.

The only other real settlement on the island is **LA FORNA**, a wide green bay dotted with huddles of houses. There's a beach here, but a small grubby one, and you'd be better off following the path down from the road around the bay to the rocks and swimming from there: the water is lovely and clear, and, with the so-called **Piscina Naturale**, perfect for sheltered swimming when the fishing boats have finished for the day. For really secluded swimming, you can also take a boat from here (L7000/€3.62 per person return) around the headland to **Spiaggia Santa Lucia**, where you may well have the beach to yourself. Settlement straggles on from La Forna towards the sharp northern end of the island, where the road ends abruptly and a steep stony path (to the right) leads down to more rocks from which you can swim.

Practicalities
The **tourist office** in Ponza Town (Mon–Sat 9am–1pm & 4.30–7.30pm, Sun 9am–1pm; ☎0771.80.031) is on Via Molo Musco, up the hill from the Banca di Napoli on the right side of the harbour, and has maps and accommodation lists. You may well be accosted with offers of **rooms** as you get off the ferry: if so, a fair price is around the ③/② mark; otherwise, the woman at Via Chiaia di Luna 8 (☎0771.80.043) takes in visitors for a negotiable fee. **Hotels** are pricier; the cheapest in Ponza Town is the *Luisa*, on Via Chiaia di Luna (0771.80.128; ⑤); *Gennarino al Mare*, next to the town beach (0771.80.071; ⑥) is more expensive, but it's worth the splurge for its great seascape views, and boasts its own restaurant. You might also try the helpful people at *Immobiliare Turistica*, Via Roma 2 (☎0771.809.886), who rent out rooms and apartments year-round. In La Forna, the *Ortensia* (☎0771.808.922; ③) is the best and most convenient option location-wise. There's an island **bus service** connecting the port with other points on the island, including La Forna, roughly hourly. You can **rent scooters** from a place by the main harbour in Ponza Town, by the first tunnel, for L60,000/€30.99 a day. Motorboats, too, are a good (sometimes the only) way of seeing the most dramatic parts of the island, and will set you back around L70,000–80,000/€36.15–41.32 a day from a number of outlets around the harbour, or you could negotiate with Signora Lucia (☎0771.80.516).

For **food** you're spoilt for choice: there are plenty of restaurants in Ponza Town and most are good, albeit expensive. Try *Al Aragosta* in the harbour, which serves the local speciality of *zuppa di lenticchie* (lentil soup); the *Ippocampo*, in the Municipio above, does good pasta and fish; or check out the restaurant attached to the *Gennarino al Mare* hotel, (see above), or the restaurant called *Acqua Pazza* (☎771.80.643), which means "crazy water".

Ventotene

The only other inhabited Pontine island, **VENTOTENE** is quite distinct from Ponza, situated a fair way south, flatter and much less lush and green. It's also much smaller and, although it makes a nice stop on a leisurely route to Naples, it's unlikely to detain you for long. However, if you do decide to linger, there are a couple of places renting out rooms. The single town – village really – has a population of around 500, and its dusty piazza is home to a museum displaying finds from an imperial-era villa, remains of which you can see spread over the headland to the left of the village. On the other side, there's a small beach of grey volcanic sand.

travel details

TRAINS

Frosinone to: Caserta (8 daily; 1hr 10min); Cassino (12 daily; 1hr 10min); Naples (6 daily; 1hr 55min).

Priverno-Fossanova to: Terracina (10 daily; 40min).

Rome (Termini) to: Ancona (8 daily; 3hr 15min–6hr); Anzio/Nettuno (hourly; 1hr); L'Aquila (5 daily; 4hr 40min); Bologna (12 daily; 3hr 20min); Cerveteri* (11 daily; 45min); Civitavecchia* (8 daily; 45min); Florence (hourly; 2hr–3hr 30min); Formia (hourly; 1hr 25min); Latina (hourly; 35min); Milan (12 daily; 3hr–5hr 40min); Naples (hourly; 2hr 30min); Pescara (4 daily; 3hr 40min); Priverno-Fossanova (hourly; 1hr); Tarquinia* (5 daily; 3hr 30min).

* Trains also run from Rome Trastevere.

Rome (Laziale) to: Anagni (14 daily; 55min); Bracciano (8 daily; 40min); Palestrina (5 daily; 35min); Viterbo (6 daily; 2hr).

Rome (Magliania/metro B) to: Ostia Lido (every 20min; 30min).

Rome (Piazzale Flaminio/Roma-Nord line) to: Viterbo (5 daily; 2hr 45min).

Rome (San Pietro) to: Bracciano (8 daily; 40min); Viterbo (6 daily; 1hr 45min).

BUSES

Blera to: Civitella Cesi (Mon–Sat 4 daily, Sun 2 daily; 20min).

Frosinone to: Priverno (hourly; 50min).

Latina to: Sermoneta (Mon–Sat 12 daily, Sun 6 daily; 1hr).

Rome (Anagnina) to: Palestrina (16 daily; 45min).

Rome (EUR Fermi) to: Sabaudia (12 daily; 2hr 15min); San Felice (12 daily; 2hr 15min); Terracina (12 daily; 2hr 30min).

Rome (Ponte Mammolo) to: Subiaco (18 daily; 1hr 15min); Tivoli (every 20min; 1hr).

Rome (Via Lepanto) to: Cerveteri (every 30min; 1hr 20min); Civitavecchia (20 daily; 1hr 50min); Tarquinia (10 daily; 2hr 15min); Blera, via Bracciano and Barbarano Romano (Mon–Sat 6 daily, Sun 2 daily; 2hr).

Rome (Via Lepanto) to: Civita Castellana (via Nepi and Castel S. Elia) (12 daily; 1hr 30min).

Rome (Saxa Rubra) to: Viterbo, via Sutri and Vetralla (every 30min; 1hr 30min).

Rome (Tiburtina) to: Rieti (every 20min; 1hr 50min).

Subiaco to: Frosinone (3 daily; 2hr).

Terracina to: Cassino (3 daily; 2hr 30min); Formia (every 30min; 1hr 10min); Sabaudia (8 daily; 1hr 20min); San Felice Circeo (17 daily; 30min); Sperlonga (every 30min; 1hr).

Viterbo to: Bagnaia (11 daily; 20min); Bomarzo (6 daily; 30min); Caprarola (7 daily; 45min); Civitavecchia (8 daily; 1hr 30min); Tarquinia (11 daily; 1hr); Tuscania (14 daily; 30min).

FERRIES

Civitavecchia to: Cagliari (1 daily; 13hr); Golfo Aranci (2 daily; 9hr); Olbia (1 daily; 7hr).

Formia to: Ponza (2 daily; 2hr 30min); Ventotene (2 daily; 2hr 10min).

Terracina to: Ponza (2 daily; 1hr).

HYDROFOILS

Anzio to: Ponza (3 daily; 1hr 10min); Ventotene (2 daily; 1hr 10min).

Formia to: Ponza (2 daily; 1hr 15min); Ventotene (2 daily; 1hr 15min).

Ponza to: Ventotene (2 daily; 40min).

CHAPTER TWELVE

ABRUZZO AND MOLISE

One region until 1963, **Abruzzo** and **Molise** – previously just plain Abruzzi –
together make Italy's transition from north to south. Both are sparsely populated mountainous regions prone to earthquakes, and both have always been outside the mainstream of Italian affairs. You could spend a whole and very varied
holiday in **Abruzzo**. Bordered by the Apennines, it holds some of Italy's wildest terrain:
silent valleys, vast untamed mountain plains and abandoned hill-villages, as well as
some great historic towns, many of them rarely visited by outsiders. But this is only half
the story: the Abruzzesi have done much to pull their region out of the poverty trap,
developing resorts on the long, sandy Adriatic coastline and exploiting the tourist
potential of a large, mountainous national park.

   Molise is manifestly a part of the south, its countryside gentler than Abruzzo, its
mountains less forbidding, and its villages and towns usually modern and functional to

ACCOMMODATION PRICE CODES

Throughout this guide, prices per person are given for **youth hostels** and assume Hostelling International (HI) membership. **Hotel** accommodation is coded on a scale from ① to ⑨, reflecting the cost of the cheapest double room in each establishment in high season. The price bands to which these codes refer are as follows:

① Up to L60,000/€30.99
② L60,000–90,000/€30.99–46.48
③ L90,000–120,000/€46.48–61.98
④ L120,000–150,000/€61.98–77.47
⑤ L150,000–200,000/€77.47–103.29

⑥ L200,000–250,000/€103.29–129.11
⑦ L250,000–300,000/€129.11–154.94
⑧ L300,000–400,000/€154.94–206.58
⑨ over L400,000/€206.58

(See p.32 for a full explanation.)

withstand the shock of earthquakes. The lasting impression is of new, fast roads snaking across rolling countryside planted with grain, but although you can drive across Molise in less than an hour on the motorway it's not a region you can get the most out of by hurriedly passing through. This is a land which has long experienced peasant hardship; it still has a close affinity to traditional festivals and rituals, and demands time to be understood. Tourism is low-key: *tratturi* for example – ancient sheep-droving routes 111m wide – are gaining a new life as mountain-bike or horseback

REGIONAL FOOD AND WINE

Abruzzo is a mountainous region where agriculture is difficult and sheep-farming dominates. The diet of the area is consequently dominated by **lamb**: *abbacchio*, unweaned baby lamb that is usually cut into chunks and roasted; and *castrato*, castrated lamb, when the meat is often cooked as a casserole with tomatoes, wine, herbs, onion and celery (*intingolo di castrato*), while the innards are typically roasted in the oven (*alenoto di castrato*). Look out as well for *agnello a cutturo*, an aromatic herby casserole served with bread.

The other crucial ingredient in the region's cuisine is **chilli** (*peperoncino* in the rest of Italy, but known locally as *pepedinie*), used liberally in all kinds of dishes; in a region prone to magic and superstition, it is believed to be a cure for ailments ranging from neuralgia to arthritis.

Abruzzo is most famous for *maccheroni alla chitarra*, made by pressing a sheet of **pasta** over a wooden frame wired like a guitar; usually it is served with a tomato or lamb sauce. Other local pastas include the roughly cut *strengozze* and *maltagliati*, both inevitably served with a lamb sauce. Cheese tends to be *pecorino* – most often mature and grainy like parmesan, but you may come across young cheeses that are still mild, soft and milky.

The **wines** of Molise are rarely found outside the region. The most interesting vintages come from the Biferno Valley between Larino and Guglionesi, where a hearty Biferno red is made from a combination of the Montepulciano, Trebbiano Toscano and Aglianico grapes. The best-known wine of Abruzzo is Montepulciano d'Abruzzo, a heavy **red** made from the Montepulciano grape with up to 15 percent Sangiovese, commonly found as house red in the restaurants of Abruzzo, Molise and Rome. Montepulciano d'Abruzzo Cerasuola is a light **rosato** made from the same grapes; and Trebbiano d'Abruzzo is an often insipid dry **white** made from the Trebbiano d'Abruzzo and Trebbiano Toscano grapes. There are, however, a few quality producers: look out for wines from the Azienda Agricola Illuminati Dino and from the Azienda Agricola Pepe Emidio, both in the province of Téramo.

riding trails, served by occasional farmhouse guesthouses and riding stables along the way. Other focuses are the seaside town of Térmoli; one of Italy's least-visited Roman sites, Saepinum; and the hiking trails in the Matese mountains on the border with Campania. Don't expect to rush through, though; in both regions, getting around on public transport demands patience and the careful studying of bus and train timetables.

ABRUZZO

Over the last century or so, Abruzzo has become better known for its emigrants than for itself. These number Dante Gabriele Rossetti, film star Alan Ladd, and, most recently, Madonna, whose ancestors left Abruzzo to seek their fortunes in Britain and America. They left behind them hilltop villages and medieval towns overlooked by mountain ranges in which wolves, bears and chamois roamed and legends of witches and werewolves persisted.

Abruzzo has well and truly entered the twenty-first century; its coast is lined by a string of lucrative resorts, and its wolves, rounded up, enclosed and demystified, have become a major tourist attraction in its eponymous national park, the **Parco Nazionale d'Abruzzo** but there are still vast tracts of unspoilt countryside and villages where life is hard and strangers are a novelty. There's a strong, unshakeable sense of the provincial here, and although the region's costumes, crafts and festivals naturally appeal to tourists, there is little hype or sham.

L'Aquila, at the foot of Gran Sasso, and **Sulmona** just to its south, are the most visited of Abruzzo's historic towns. Both are good bases: Sulmona is more convenient if you're coming by train from Rome, L'Aquila if you're approaching from Umbria. The hill-villages around L'Aquila are worth visiting if you're based here for any length of time: those below the **Gran Sasso**, the Apennines' highest peak, are deeply rural places, where time can seem to have stopped in the fifteenth century; **Bominaco**, to the east, has two impressive churches, one a perfect and pristine example of the Romanesque, the other covered with Byzantine-style frescoes. The rail route from the Marche runs down the coast through Abruzzo's numerous grid-plan resorts – few of them anything special, but adequate sun-and-sand stopovers. The best of them is **Vasto**, with a gently shelving sandy beach and bus connections inland to the lively upper old town. Among other hill-towns worth visiting is **Atri**, whose cathedral protects a stunning cycle of frescoes.

South of Sulmona, Abruzzo feels more traditional. In **Scanno** the women wear costumes that – like the Scannese – originated in Asia Minor, and they make intricate lace on cylindrical cushions known as *tomboli*. Just down the road, **Cocullo** is a scruffy hill-village that on the first Thursday in May hosts one of Europe's most bizarre religious festivals, in which a statue of the local saint is draped with live snakes before being paraded through the streets.

L'Aquila

L'AQUILA is a pleasant mountain town overlooked by the bulk of the Gran Sasso mountain and is the main access point to the national park of the same name. The city was founded by a German emperor, and the story of its foundation is itself worthy of a Brothers Grimm fairy-tale: in 1242 Frederick II drew together the populations from 99 Abruzzesi villages to form a new city. Each village built its own church, piazza and quarter: there's a medieval fountain with 99 spouts, and the town-hall clock still chimes 99 times every night.

L'Aquila may no longer be the city of 99 churches, most of them having been destroyed in earthquakes, but two magnificent ones remain. And the city itself is a

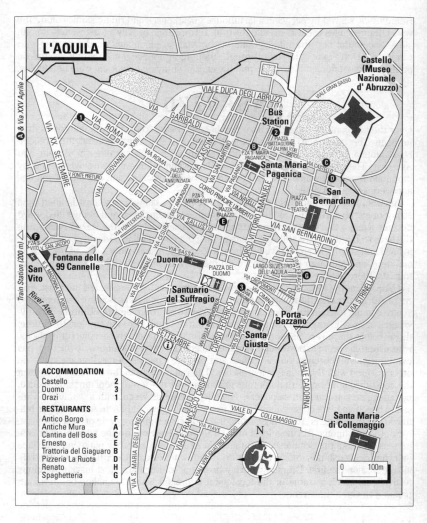

brighter place than you might expect – an appealing blend of ancient and modern, with a university, smart shops, bustling streets and a daily market where you can buy anything from black-market cassettes to traditional Abruzzese craftwork.

Arrival, information and accommodation

L'Aquila's **train station** is a good way downhill from the centre, connected with the main part of town by regular buses. Long-distance **buses** stop on Piazza Battaglione Alpini at the beginning of the old centre's main street, Corso Vittorio Emanuele. The **information booth** there has bus timetables covering L'Aquila province and connections to Rome. The **tourist office** is at the other end of the Corso, at Via XX Settembre

8 (March–Sept daily 9am–1pm & 4–7pm; Oct–April closed Sun; ☎0862.22.306). The **Club Alpino Italiano (CAI)** office is off Piazza del Duomo at Via Sassa 34 (Mon–Sat 7–8.15pm; ☎0862.313.304).

The main drawback of L'Aquila is its lack of cheap **hotels**, and you should definitely book in advance if you're planning to stay. The *Orazi*, at Via Roma 175 (☎0862.412.889; ①), a 10-minute walk from Piazza dell' Annunziata, is the cheapest option. Up from there is the modern, functional *Castello* on Piazza Battaglione Alpini (☎0862.419.147, fax 0862.419.140; ④) and the *Duomo* at Via Dragonetti 6 (☎0862.410.893, fax 0862.413.058; ④), housed in a quiet, eighteenth-century palace with views over Piazza del Duomo.

The City

L'Aquila's centre is relatively compact and easily seen on foot. Marking the northeastern entrance to the city centre is **Piazza Battaglione Alpini**, with the unusual Fontana Luminosa at its centre. Viale delle Medaglie d'Oro leads to the formidable **Castello**, built by the Spanish in the sixteenth century to keep the citizens of L'Aquila in order after an uprising. The Spanish forced the *Aquilani* to pay for the castle by imposing an annual tax and heavy fines. In the Fascist period the castle's surroundings were landscaped as a park, and, following the devastation wreaked by the Nazis in 1943, the building was renovated and the **Museo Nazionale d'Abruzzo** (Tues–Sun 9am–7pm; L8000/€4.13) established in the former barracks. The most popular exhibit here is the skeleton of a prehistoric mammoth found about 14km from L'Aquila in the 1950s, but the collection of works of art rescued from abandoned and earthquake-ravaged churches is also worth a brief visit. Among the clumsily painted wooden Madonnas, those by Silvestro d'Aquila stand out, spare, ascetic and nerved with inner strength, while the best of the paintings are the dreamy and mystical works attributed to Andrea Delitio, a fifteenth-century Abruzzese artist responsible for the region's best fresco cycle – in the cathedral at Atri (see p.799). The exhibit with the most sensational history is an elaborate silver crucifix by Nicola da Guardiagrele: after being stolen from L'Aquila's duomo and auctioned at Sotheby's, it's now kept for safety in the museum. The museum also hosts concerts throughout the year – check with the tourist office for details.

From Piazza Battaglione Alpini, arcaded **Corso Vittorio Emanuele** is L'Aquila's main street, lined with upmarket clothes shops, jewellers and cafés, and liveliest in the evenings when L'Aquila's youth turn out for the passeggiata. To the left down Via San Bernadino, the church of **San Bernardino** has a sumptuous, recently restored facade, with three magnificent white tiers bedecked with classical columns, pediments, friezes and inscriptions. Inside, the ceiling is luxuriously gilded and skilfully carved – in some places bold and chunky, in others as complex and sinuous as oriental embroidery. The glazed blue and white terracotta altarpiece by Andrea della Robbia is very fine, as is San Bernardino's mausoleum, sculpted by Silvestro d'Aquila, with their lively high-relief figures. As for San Bernardino, he was originally from Siena but died in L'Aquila, where his relics remain, ritually visited every year on his feast day by Sienese bearing gifts of Tuscan oil.

Corso Vittorio Emanuele leads on to the central **Piazza del Duomo**, more remarkable for its **market** (Mon–Sat 8am–2pm) than for its architecture. The duomo, having been destroyed on several occasions by earthquakes, now features a tedious Neoclassical front. More striking is the facade of the eighteenth-century **Santuario del Suffragio**, a voluptuous combination of curves, topped by a flamboyant honeycombed alcove. Tumbling down the hill below the piazza, steep stepped streets of ancient houses lead down to **Porta Bazzano**, one of the old city gates. Rather than heading straight there, take time to wander the abutting streets, lined with Renaissance and Baroque palaces. Some of these are still opulent, others decaying, providing an evocative backdrop for the church of **Santa Giusta**, whose rose window is decorated with twelve figures representing the various artisans who contributed to the building.

From Porta Bazzano, Via Porta Bazzano leads to the church of **Santa Maria di Collemaggio** (daily 9am–6.30pm). One of Abruzzo's most distinctive churches, its massive rectangular bulk is faced with a geometric jigsaw of pink and white stone, more redolent of a mosque than a church, pierced by delicate, lacy rose windows and entered through a fancy Romanesque arch. It was founded in the thirteenth century by Peter of Morrone, a hermit unwillingly dragged from his mountain retreat to be made pope by power-hungry cardinals who reckoned he would be easy to manipulate. When he turned out to be too naive even for the uses of the cardinals, he was forced to resign and was posthumously compensated for the ordeal by being canonized. Thieves stole his relics in April 1988, intending to hold them to ransom, but they were soon safely retrieved and returned to their grandiose Palladian-style sarcophagus. One of the few things Peter managed to do during his short reign was to install a Holy Door in the church – opened every year on August 28, when sinners pass through it to procure absolution.

Finally there's L'Aquila's best-known sight, the **Fontana delle 99 Cannelle**, outside the town centre close to the train station, tucked behind the medieval **Porta Riviera**. Set around three sides of a sunken piazza and overlooked by abandoned houses and the tiny church of **San Vito**, each water spout is a symbol for one of the villages that formed the city. This constant supply of fresh water sustained the *Aquilani* through the plagues, earthquakes and sieges to which the city was subjected, and was used for washing clothes until after the war.

Eating and drinking

L'Aquila has a decent selection of good, reasonably priced **places to eat**, ranging from places serving traditional Abruzzese fare to cheap and cheerful pizzerias catering for the town's student population. For a real treat head for *Ernesto*, in Piazza Palazzo (closed Mon & Sun), where you can indulge in *farfalline* with saffron and prawns, a soup of *farro* (emmer, a barley-like grain) with wild chicory, or lamb in a sauce of egg, local goat's cheese and artichoke hearts. *Antiche Mura*, at Via XXV Aprile 2 (closed Sun), is another good traditional restaurant, with a wide variety of local specialities – try *ceci e castagne* (chickpeas and chestnuts) or *coniglio allo zafferano* (rabbit scented with locally collected saffron) – as is *Trattoria del Giaguaro*, on Piazza Santa Maria Paganica (closed Mon evening & all day Tues); neither is especially expensive. *Renato* at Via della Indipendenza 9 (closed Sun) is a reliable choice close to Piazza del Duomo where the waiter will reel off the specials of the day based on produce from the market nearby. Away from the centre down the hill next to the 99 Cannelle is *L'Antico Borgo*, Piazza San Vito 1 (closed Tues) with excellent fish on Thursdays and Fridays; it makes a peaceful spot for lunch outside in summer. Seafood is a speciality too of *Pizzeria La Ruota* at Via Arco Terziarie 16, just off Via Castello (closed Tues). If you're on a really tight budget, there's the *Spaghetteria*, Via Fortebraccio 27 (closed Mon), for good-value pasta dishes. If all you want is a **snack** washed down with good wine, first choice is *La Cantina del Boss* (closed Sat evening & all Sun), Via Castello 3. Alternatively, several shops along Via Patini (between Piazza Palazzo and Piazza del Duomo) have all you need for a good picnic or lunch on the go.

The Gran Sasso and Campo Imperatore plain

Whether you approach Abruzzo from the Marche in the north or Rome in the west, your arrival will be signalled by the spectacular bulk of the **Gran Sasso** massif, containing by far the highest of the Apennine peaks. If you come by *autostrada* from the

Marche, you'll actually travel underneath, through a ten-kilometre tunnel, passing the entrance to a trailblazing particle-physics research laboratory bored into the very heart of the mountain range.

The massif itself consists of two parallel chains, flanking the vast **Campo Imperatore** plain which stretches for 27km at over 2000m above sea-level. This is a bleak but atmospheric place, overlooked by abandoned and semi-abandoned hill-villages, its rolling grasslands in places laid bare to reveal rocks, carved into moonscape ripples by the wind.

The itinerary below is an easy day's drive from L'Aquila. If you're dependent on public transport, it will take two days and you may have to content yourself with viewing the plain by cable car and taking buses up to the hill-villages from L'Aquila via the less interesting southern route.

Fonte Cerreto and the Corno Grande

The first leg, however, is easy. Bus #6 from L'Aquila's Corso Vittorio Emanuele runs regularly up to **FONTE CERRETO**, the gateway to Campo Imperatore – basically two hotels, a restaurant and a campsite clustered around a cable car station. Most of these were built in the Thirties as part of Mussolini's scheme to keep Italians fit by encouraging them to take exercise in the mountains. Ironically, he was imprisoned here in 1943, first at the *Villetta* inn in Fonte Cerreto, and then at the *Albergo-Rifugio Campo Imperatore*, a grim hotel at the top of the cable car route. Apparently it was with some trepidation that Mussolini stepped into the cable car, enquiring whether it was safe and then hastily covering his cowardice by adding, "Not for my sake, you understand, because my life is over. But for those who accompany me." *Il Duce* apparently spent his days at the hotel on a diet of eggs, rice, boiled onions and grapes, contemplating suicide. Hitler came to his rescue, dispatching an ace pilot to airlift him out in a tiny aeroplane, which is supposed to have terrified Mussolini almost as much as the cable car.

The **cable car** that so spooked Mussolini has been replaced by a new one which runs in winter for skiing and for the summer hiking season (1 July–15 November Mon–Sat 8.30am–6pm, Sun 7.30am–7pm; winter reduced service depending on snow fall; return journey L18,000/€9.30). A small **information office** (Fri–Mon 10am–12.30pm & 1.30–5.30pm) to the side of the *Villetta* hotel has details of walks and wildlife to be seen in the Gran Sasso park. You can still stay at the *Villetta* (☎0862.606.171; ④) though it's now a pleasant modernized hotel over a snack-bar; or *Villetta*'s larger sister hotel *Fiordigigli* (☎0862.606.172; ④) also at the base of the cable car. There's cheaper accommodation in two mountain refuges run by CAI: one of these is the *Ostello Campo Imperatore* (☎0862.400.011; L30,000/€15.50, or L55.000/€28.40 for dinner, bed and breakfast; 1 June to 15 Sept), which occupies the old cable car station; the other is the *Duca degli Abruzzi rifugio* (☎0347.623.2101; L50,000/€25.82 for dinner, bed and breakfast), several metres beyond. It's now the most popular starting-point for assaults on the Gran Sasso's highest peak, the **Corno Grande** (2912m).

Outside the summer months, the ascent of Corno Grande should only be attempted by experienced climbers, and at all times includes some fairly killing scree-climbing and alarming descents. Perhaps the most challenging route is the tough trek from the *Ostello Campo Imperatore* right across the mountain range, taking in the Corno Grande, sleeping over at the *Rifugio Franchetti* (☎0861.959.634; L30,000/€15.50, or L60,000/€30.98 for dinner, bed and breakfast; mid-June to mid-Sept), and then walking across to the Arapietra ridge. From here a ski lift will take you down to the ugly ski resort of Prati di Tivo – which nevertheless offers some of the best views of Gran Sasso – from where you can get a bus to the town of Téramo. If you're going to do any of the Gran Sasso trails, you'll need the CAI *Gran Sasso d'Italia* map, and should check out weather conditions from the CAI office in L'Aquila.

The Campo Imperatore plain

For non-hikers the road continues from Fonte Cerreto across **Campo Imperatore**, backed by awesome rocky massifs that have been prime fodder for film-makers over the years, masquerading as everything from the surface of Mars to a remote region of Tibet. Film crews and the occasional hiker apart, the only people you're likely to meet here are nomadic shepherds, who bring their flocks up to the plain for summer grazing after wintering in the south – a practice that has been going on since Roman times. Although the sheep are now transported by lorry rather than on foot, the shepherds' shacks sprinkled across the plain suggest that their living standards have changed very little.

The plain is fringed with hilltop villages, some with a few hotels and villas, others virtually abandoned. **CASTEL DEL MONTE** is a medieval village, heavily fortified and crowned with a ruined castle and church, that is now a minor tourist attraction. It was the scene of a chilling incident early this century when workmen discovered caves underneath them that were filled with clothed skeletons seated on cane chairs. This was the traditional way of burying the village's dead until 1860, when an outbreak of cholera alerted the inhabitants to the health hazard. All the skeletons that could be found were burned and those that weren't were lost forever when the cave was set alight and later filled in. As for the rest of the village, the steep streets and dark tunnels were designed to slow down invaders; windows, strategically placed high up, enabled the inhabitants to chuck hot oil down on the heads of unwelcome visitors. There are two **hotels**: the simple *Miramonti* with just ten rooms (with or without bathroom; ☎0862.938.142; ①) and the well-kept, chalet style *Parco Gran Sasso* (☎0862.938.484; ④) with wonderful, far reaching views; there's also a good little **osteria**, *La Pecora Nera*, on Via Sant'Angelo (closed Tues in winter).

Among the other hilltop villages which seem to have grown out of the yellow rock is **CALASCIO**, with castle and ruins of the old village crumbling above it. The bus from L'Aquila passes by, dropping you at the bottom of the hill, or stay on board until **SAN STEFANO DI SASSANIO** – a Medici stronghold in the fifteenth century, still with Tuscan-style loggias and Medici coats of arms stuck on the dilapidating and semi-abandoned houses. If you don't want to stay in the villages themselves and you have a car, one of the nicest bases for visiting the Campo Imperatore plain is in **Alanno** 8km north of the A25 motorway: there the seven-bedroomed hotel *Villa Alessandra*, Via Circonterranea 51 (☎085.857.3108; ④), more like a family home than a hotel, is furnished with an interesting collection of pictures and has an excellent restaurant; in summer, you can dine under a jasmine-scented pergola with the only sound the cicadas in the olive groves.

North of L'Aquila: Amiternum and San Vittorino

The countryside to the north of L'Aquila is undistinguished. **Lago di Campotosto**, encircled by bland hills and small tourist resorts, is one of the town's most popular nearby attractions, but is really just an artificial lake, regularly restocked with fish to keep the anglers happy. Closer to L'Aquila, and accessible by bus, are the theatre and amphitheatre surviving from the Sabine, and later Roman, city of **Amiternum** (daily 9am–1.30pm; free), now occasionally used for concerts and plays in the summer. Above Amiternum, **SAN VITTORINO** is hardly one of Abruzzo's more appealing villages, but it has a series of **catacombs** (currently closed for restoration) underneath its church that make for a dank and spooky way to pass an hour, with skulls and bones spilling out of coffin-shelves and the remains of St Vittorino stuffed underneath an altar. The local priest has the keys, and can be reached at ☎0862.461.695.

South to Sulmona: Bominaco

From L'Aquila, the SS17 follows the ancient route of the local shepherds across the saffron fields south to Sulmona. If you have your own transport, it's worth making a short detour on the way to see two of Abruzzo's most beautiful churches at **BOMINACO** (also accessible by bus from L'Aquila). The village itself is an inauspicious knot of grubby houses, but the endearingly askew and lichen-mottled facade of **San Pellegrino** conceals floor-to-ceiling frescoes in vivid hues reminiscent of a peacock's plume (if it's closed, contact Signor Cassiani, ☎0862.93.604, whose house is tucked behind a garage bearing the number two on the left of the main street; if he's out, try the village's bars). There's also an intriguing thirteenth-century calendar, with the signs of the zodiac looking down over lists of religious festivals and miniatures of men engaged in supposedly typical activities for the time of year – boozing in January, chopping wood in February, sleeping in March . . .

The church of **Santa Maria dell'Assunta**, just beyond, has a more coolly refined exterior, but its aloofness is tempered by monsters carved at the bases of the windows – notably a chimera with the face of a diabolic lion, flexing its talons and flicking its serpentine tail. Inside, the creamy-white carvings are so exquisitely precise that it seems the mason has only just put down his chisel. In fact they're 800 years old. There's been some restoration, but this is scarcely discernible, and the lack of the usual cracks and crumblings is uncanny. This is particularly striking in the extraordinary free-standing column, consisting of two entwined rolls of stone so supple and sensuous that you expect them to dimple to the touch. To get the keys, you'll need to search out Signor Cassiani (see above).

Sulmona and around

Flanked by bleak mountains and bristling with legends about its most famous son, Ovid, **SULMONA** is a rich and comfortable provincial town owing its wealth to gold jewellery and sugar almonds. An atmospheric little place, with a dark tangle of a historical centre lined with imposing palaces, its sights can be seen in a day, but the town makes a good base for exploring the surroundings, and you may want to stay longer.

Arrival, information and accommodation

Arrive in Sulmona **by bus** and you'll be dropped at the Parco Fluviale, just down the hill from the western end of the main street, Corso Ovidio. The **train station** is about 1km outside the centre of town; bus #A runs from the station along Corso Ovidio. The **tourist office** (daily 9am–1pm & 4–7pm; in winter closed Sat, Sun and some afternoons; ☎0864.53.276) is at Corso Ovidio 208. There's a second **information office** in the old pharmacy of the Palazzo SS Annunziata with maps and details of Sulmona's churches and palaces (daily: summer 9.30am–1pm & 4–8pm; winter 9.30am–1pm & 3.30–7.30pm; ☎0864.210.216).

The best of the cheaper options of **places to stay** is the *Centro Celestiniano*, a **hostel** in a former school between the bus station and the town centre at Via Matteotti 14 (☎0864.56.549; L35,000/€18.07 per person bed and breakfast); call them from the station and they will pick you up in their bus. Other cheap hotels are the *Stella*, at Via Mazzara 18, off Corso Ovidio (☎0864.52.653; ③), a relaxed, family-run establishment with much-needed renovations on the way, and the passable *Traffico*, Via degli Agghiacciati 17 (☎0864.54.080; ③). The most atmospheric of the town's affordable

hotels is the *Italia* (☎0864.52.308; ②) just behind Piazza XX Settembre – dusty and fusty though with plenty of personality and a nice owner (it's often fully booked by American students on summer courses). More upmarket is *Armando's*, on the edge of town at Via Montenero 15 (☎0864.210.783; ④).

The Town

Corso Ovidio, Sulmona's main street, cuts through the centre from the park-side bus terminus, leading up to **Piazza XX Settembre**, an intimate square that's home to the Art Nouveau **Gran Caffè** (closed Wed). Nowadays the elegant twists and curlicues of the wrought-iron lamps on its terrace have a soundtrack of blipping video games, but it makes a nice spot for sipping a drink. A couple of minutes back up Corso Ovidio, the **Annunziata** is Sulmona's architectural showpiece, a Gothic-Renaissance palazzo adjoining a flamboyant Baroque church. These days, its steps are a hangout for the town's lads during the evening passeggiata, but once they would have been crowded with Sulmona's ill and destitute: the Annunziata housed a hospital, a pharmacy and a store of grain, donated by the rich and shared out to the needy. It was established by a confraternity to take care of the citizens from birth until death, and most of the external decoration is designed to remind onlookers of the life process: around the first door is a tree of life; an allegorical frieze with scenes from the cultivation of the vine representing birth, marriage and death stretches right across the facade; a sunburst-style wheel of life stands above a window; and statues of saints gaze piously down from pedestals, firmly placing the symbolism in a Christian context. The most intriguing statue, however, is just inside the entrance: Ovid, metamorphosed from pagan poet of love into an ascetic friar. Inside the Annunziata are three **museums**: one (Tues–Thurs 9.30am–1pm & 4.30–7pm; Fri, Sat & Sun by request at tourist office; free) with exhibits on local costume and transhumance – the practice of moving sheep to summer pastures – and examples of work by Sulmona's Renaissance goldsmiths, a trade that continues here today, as evidenced by the number of jewellers' shops along the Corso. Another, the **Museo Civico** (Mon–Sat 9am–1pm, Sun 10am–1pm & 4–7pm; L1000/€0.52) has local sculpture and paintings from the sixteenth to seventeenth centuries; and a third the **Museo 'in situ'** (daily 9am–1pm & 3–8pm; free) shows the excavations of a Roman villa inhabited from the first century BC to the second century AD, abandoned suddenly along with many other houses in the valley when a landslide or an earthquake struck. Among the fragments of fabulously coloured wall painting are depictions of Pan, Eros, Dionysus and Ariadne, and there are several floor mosaics, all well-labelled. More monochromatic mosaics from a seventh century church and a Roman villa can be seen in excavations at the **church of Santo Gaetano** (open by appointment through the tourist office or contact Cooperativa Aprutium ☎0864.212.711, *aprutium@libero*.it).

The Corso's **shops** are also full of Sulmona's other great product – *confetti*, a confection of sugar almonds twisted with wire and ribbons into elaborate flowers. Through ingenious marketing the Sulmonese *confetti* barons have made gifts of their sugar almond sculpture *de rigueur* at christenings and confirmations throughout Catholic Europe. At Abruzzese weddings, bride and groom are painfully pelted with loose white *confetti*. Most apparent in the Corso's shops, however, are the brashly coloured giant daisies designed to tempt kids and tourists.

At Piazza XX Settembre, the weighty Romanesque portal of **San Francesco della Scarpa** was the only part of the church solid enough to withstand the 1703 earthquake. The church gets its name – delle Scarpe means "with the shoes" – from the fact that Franciscans wore shoes instead of the sandals worn by other monastic orders. Opposite, the impressive Gothic aqueduct, built to supply water to the town and power to its wool mills, ends at a fifteenth-century fountain, the **Fontana del Vecchio**, named for the chubby-cheeked old man on top. On the other side of the aqueduct is **Piazza**

Garibaldi, a vast square dominated by the austere slopes of Monte Morrone, on which the hermit Pietro Morrone lived until he was dragged away to be made pope (see p.786). There's a former nunnery in the corner – take a look at the courtyard, where there's a tiny door at which unmarried mothers were permitted to abandon their babies.

For centuries, women suffering from the opposite problem – infertility – would visit a Roman ruin outside the town once known as Ovid's Villa, where they would pray to the poet, who was seen as some kind of fertility god. A stone phallus then lay upon the steps although archeologists have now put paid to the myth by identifying the ruin as the **Sanctuary of Hercules Curinus**. The site is wonderfully evocative beneath a rocky crag topped by the hermitage of pope Celestino V, with fine views over the valley to the Maiella massif. To get there, take a bus to Bagnatura/Badia, get off after the prison and walk up the hill. On entering the site, (free access) remains of stairs, terrace and portico lie to the right; to the left is a small chamber dating back to the first century BC with substantial pieces of coloured plaster on the walls and with a well-preserved mosaic pavement decorated with leaping dolphins and a sheaf of thunderbolts, the symbol of Jupiter, Hercules's father. Devotees of Hercules would leave their offerings to the god on a stone block at the end of the wall backing this chamber and then continue up to the channelled spring, a sacred element for the cult. The Ovid connection continues at the spring where – so local legend has it – Ovid was caught making love to a fairy or (for sceptics) to the Emperor Augustus's granddaughter, Julia.

Eating and drinking

Sulmona has some excellent, reasonably priced **restaurants**. The chef at the *Italia* on Piazza XX Settembre (closed Mon), bases his dishes on traditional Abruzzese fare, but is ever inventing new variations – try his fresh cannelloni stuffed with ricotta and various secret ingredients. *Al Quadrivio*, Via Mazzara 38 (closed all Mon & Sun evening), also serves up some memorable food, like *carrati* – home-made *bucatini* with fresh tomato – while *Mafalda* at Via Solimo 20 (closed Sun in winter) is enjoyable in summer, when you can eat dishes like *maccheroni alla chitarra* in its walled garden. *Clemente*, Vico dell'Vecchio 11 (closed Thurs) serves home-produced salami and dishes such as *linguine d'Ovidio* (with pancetta and truffles), spicy *farfalle* with prosciutto and spinach, sausages, lamb roasted or grilled, and pastries made in-house. *Cesidio*, Via Solimo 25 (closed Mon), can be a bit hit-and-miss, but it too does some great pasta dishes, good crepes – even a truffle-based lasagne. The best **ice cream** is to be had at *Schiazza* and *di Marzio* both at the western end of Corso Ovidio, and for late-night boozing there are a couple of pseudo "pubs" – the *Basquiat* at Viale Stazione Introdacqua, though this is a bit of a walk from the centre, and the quintessentially Italian *Black Bull*, across the river by the Ponte Capograssi.

Around Sulmona: the western slopes of Maiella

The beautiful **Maiella** mountain range rises high above Sulmona, its steep wooded slopes and red and gold cliffs giving way to an upland plain as smooth as a cricket field. With your own transport you could explore it in a day; by bus, you either have to make a very early start or sleep over in one of the many villages with facilities for tourists.

One of the easiest places to reach is **PACENTRO**, a drab little village topped by a castle, most famous these days for the fact that the grandparents of Madonna emigrated from here. Back in the late 1980s, the mayor (who just happened to own the village's only pizzeria) decided to erect a statue to the pop star. The Church, feeling that Madonna was hardly an ideal role model for young girls, objected, and nothing ever came of the plan – though for a short while the village became accustomed to visits by armies of tabloid hacks. Pacentro is once again quiet, but it's worth stopping by for a memorable meal at the popular *Taverna di Caldora* on Piazza Umberto I (closed all day Tues & Sun evening).

The mountain-top forest of **Bosco Sant'Antonio**, on the bus route to Pescocostanzo, offers good hiking and picnicking. If you want to stay over, the *Hotel Sant'Antonio* (☎0864.67.101; ③) has reasonable doubles (near the cross country ski tracks in winter), as does the *Ristorante Faggetto* (☎0864.67.100; ④). Alternatively, after a morning in the woods you could move on to **PESCOCOSTANZO**, a well-preserved village with steep grey-and-white stone streets lined with craft workshops selling lace, gold filigree, wrought-iron work and woven rugs and bedspreads. As the sprawl of chalet-style apartments on the periphery suggest it's an extremely popular winter and summer resort. The best of the local crafts are to be found in the **Collegiata**, a fifteenth-century church at the head of the main street, with a magnificently carved and gilded Baroque ceiling and some superb wrought-iron work – lifelike putti and curling, delicate flowers incorporated into the iron chapel screen and the lampholders. The **tourist office** (daily 9am–1pm & 4–7pm; ☎0864.641.440) is on the main square. Among the **accommodation** in the village centre is *Valle Fura*, on Piazzale Seggovia (☎0864.642.229; ④) and some good B&B options: *Archi del Sole* comprises two houses in the historic centre on Via Porta Berardo (☎0864.640.007, *www.pescocostanzo.com/archidelsole*; ④); *Dell'Oca* is at Via Sant'Angelo in Piazza 16 (☎0864.640.007, *www.pescocostanzo.com/oca*; ④) and *Il Camoscio* on Via Maiella, just off the piazza where buses stop, offers doubles and cheaper quad deals (☎0864.641.436, *www.pescocostanzo.com/camoscio*; ④).

There's little reason for visiting the other village resorts unless you're going **skiing** or want somewhere cheaper to stay. The major centres for skiing are **ROCCARASO** and **RIVISONDOLI**. These are connected to Sulmona by a few trains as well as by bus, and accommodation prices are not high. Roccaraso has a modern centre because it was bombed flat in World War II. It is home to the **hotels** *Italia* Largo S Rocco 2 (☎0864.62.174; ③) and the *Locanda Duca Degli Abruzzi*, a simple place with shared bathrooms at Via Ovidio 19 (☎0864.62.176; ①), but both of these may insist that you take half-board. The resort of Rivisondoli has a bit more of the village left intact; for a **place to stay** there's the *Calypso* at Via G Marconi 93 (☎0864.641.910; ②). There are **tourist offices** at Roccaraso (daily 9am–1pm & 4–7pm; ☎0864.62.210) and Rivisondoli (daily 9am–1pm & 3–6pm; ☎0864.69.351).

South of Sulmona: Cocullo and Scanno

A tatty hill-village, connected by rare trains and even rarer buses with Sulmona, **COCULLO** is understandably neglected by outsiders for 364 days of the year. However, on the first Thursday in May it's invaded by TV crews, journalists, beggars, buskers, street-vendors and what seems like half the population of central Italy. Market stalls sell everything from digital watches to roast pork, and the roads – and on occasions even the nearby motorway – are crammed with parked cars and flustered traffic police. The reason for all this activity is Cocullo's weird **festival of snakes**, an annual event celebrated in memory of St Dominic, the patron saint of the village, who allegedly rid the area of venomous snakes back in the eleventh century.

It's an odd mixture of the modern and archaic. Everyone pours into the main square, while a wailing Mass is relayed from the church over aged speakers, competing with pulsing pop music and the cries of the beggars. After the service a number of snake-charmers in the crowd drape a wooden statue of St Dominic with a writhing mass of live but harmless snakes, which is then paraded through the streets in a bizarre celebration of the saint's unique powers (he was apparently good at curing snake-bites too). Actually, it is thought that Cocullo's preoccupation with snakes dates back to before the advent of the saint. In the pre-Christian era, local tribes worshipped their goddess Angitia with offerings of snakes, and it seems too much of a coincidence that Dominic's powers also related to the creatures. Scholars have attempted to rationalize the festival by drawing a parallel between snakes shedding their skins and the ancient Cocullans shedding their paganism for Christianity – but whatever the origins, Cocullo's festival is today more than anything a celebration of St. Dominic's power to attract enough tourist lucre in a day to keep the village going for a year. Incidentally, if you're suffering from toothache, he's also reckoned to have the power to cure it, the only snag being that you have to ring the church bell with the rope in your teeth.

Lago di Scanno ... and Scanno

Twenty kilometres down the road, but most easily accessible by bus from Sulmona, Scanno is another popular tourist destination, reached by passing through the narrow and rocky Saggitario Gorge, a spectacular drive along galleries of rock and around blind hairpin bends which widen out at the glassy green **Lago di Scanno**. Perched over the lake is a church, **Madonna del Lago**, encrusted with ex-votos and with the cliff as its back wall, and nearby there are boats and pedalos for rent, and a good restaurant, the *Trattoria sul Lago*. If you're planning on staying there's a **campsite** *I Lupi* (☎0864.740.100), 4km away at Villalago, but be warned that it is normally packed out in summer, especially during August.

A couple of kilometres beyond, **SCANNO** itself is a well-preserved medieval village encircled by mountains. Many of the women of the village still wear the traditional costume of long dark pleated skirts and bodices, with either a patterned apron for day-to-day wear or a brocade skirt and embroidered fez with coils of cord looped behind to conceal the hair on special occasions (with a white skirt for weddings). The skirts are made of wool – the village's staple industry in former times – and weigh around 12 kilos, but their heaviness doesn't prevent them from being worn for household tasks. As you wander round the village it soon becomes clear that far from being dismissed as an anachronism, older women dressed in this way are accorded great respect. The hat and the fact that at Scannese weddings the tradition was for women to squat on the floor of the church, has led scholars to believe that the Scannese originated in Asia Minor; Scannese jewellery also has something of the Orient about it – large, delicately filigreed earrings, and a star, known as a *presuntuosa*, given to fiancées to ward off other men. If you want to watch a goldsmith at work, go to the jewellers round the corner from the tourist office on the main square.

It's a pleasure strolling around the old town built into the steep hillside, the squares and alleyways lined with solid stone houses built by wool barons when business was good. However, Scanno is not some sort of museum piece. Though the population has dwindled it's a living village, with enough work available in Sulmona to keep people from moving away. Now that shepherding as a way of life is virtually finished, sheep have been replaced by tourists. A chair lift takes **skiers** up to a handful of runs on Monte Rotondo, operating also in the short summer season (July and August) when it's worth going up just for the view of lake and mountains, especially at sunset. In winter a skibus runs between Rome and Scanno once a day (journey time 1hr 50min; L60,000/€30.99 including ski-pass; ☎0864.747.774).

Scanno practicalities

The **tourist office** (summer daily 9am–1pm & 4–7pm; winter Tues–Sun 4–6pm; ☎0864.74.317) is at Piazza Santa Maria della Valle 12. Every August Scanno holds a **classical music festival**, and on January 17 a **lasagne festival** – more properly called the *Festa di San Antonio Abate*, involving the cooking of a great cauldron of lasagne and beans outside the door of the church, which is then blessed and doled out with a somewhat unholy amount of pushing and shoving. For the rest of the year sample traditional Abruzzese fare in the **restaurants**, best of which are the *Gli Archetti* (closed Tues) on Via Silla inside the Porta della Croce entrance to the old town; *La Volpe e l'Uva* a small, laid-back bar with music, a good wine list, and snacks in the form of crepes, cheese and salumi on Piazza San Rocco (closed Wed in winter); and *Birreria La Baita* above the village near the chair lift, serving excellent pasta dishes and snacks, with live music some Saturday nights. If you're **staying over**, the most atmospheric hotel is *Mille Pini* next to the chair lift at Via Pescara 2 (☎0864.74.387; ④), a large chalet with 22 rooms and several wood-floored lounges overlooking the village. There are also pine-clad mountain cabin rooms (with bath-tubs, a rarity in these parts, as well as showers) above *Birreria La Baita* – same price and phone number as *Mille Pini*. The cheapest options are the *Eden*, Viale della Pineta 10–12 (☎0864.74.328; ②) or *Pensione Nilde* between the lake and the village at Viale del Lago 101 (☎0864.74.359; ②); or for somewhere central and modern try *Seggiovia*, Via D. Tanturri 42 (☎0864.74.371; ③).

Southwest Abruzzo and the national park

Heading west towards Rome from Sulmona, road and railway skirt the **Fucino Plain**, an endless, unreal and utterly flat expanse of agricultural land whose only landmarks are the satellite dishes of Telespazio, Italy's biggest telecommunications complex. The Fucino was once Italy's third-largest lake, and is the largest lake in the world to have been artificially drained. Attempts to empty it began nearly two thousand years ago. The Marsi people who lived on its shores, fed up with the fact that it flooded every time the mountain snows melted, managed to persuade Emperor Claudius to build a six-kilometre-long outlet tunnel, designed to transfer the water from the lake into a nearby valley. On the day of the draining, the shores and surrounding mountains were packed with spectators: the proceedings were inaugurated by a mechanical Triton who rose up from the lake blowing a trumpet, whence a mock battle ensued, with warships manned by condemned criminals, after which Claudius gave the signal for the outlet gates to be opened. Unfortunately, the tunnel couldn't cope with the vast volume of water, and thousands of spectators, including members of the imperial party, only narrowly escaped being washed away. Frederick II attempted to open up the tunnel in 1240, but the lake was only finally drained in 1875, as much to gain agricultural land as to solve the flooding problem – though it has brought associated problems. The climate has grown humid, misty and mosquito-ridden, and it's clear that lakeside tourist developments would have been far more profitable than agriculture.

Celano, Avezzano and Alba Fucens

Fringing the plain is **CELANO**, a pretty village crowned by a turreted toytown castle and home to a new **Museo della Preistoria d'Abruzzo,** based on finds from a nearby lake village dating back to 3000 years BC (Mon–Sat 9am–7.30pm, Sun 2–7.30pm; free). *Hotel Le Gole* on Via Sardellino (☎0863.711.009, *www.hotellegole.it*; ⑤) makes an excellent base for the area, including Alba Fucens (see opposite). Built in 1998 in fauxFrancescan style around a central cloister it's a comfortable, professionally run, wellorganized place to stay, with great food at reasonable prices in its *Da Guerrinuccio* restaurant.

A little further west is **AVEZZANO**, an unfortunate city that was destroyed – along with 10,000 inhabitants – by an earthquake in 1915. It was rebuilt, but flattened again by World War II bombings. It's since been reconstructed, but the only reason for a visit is to get a bus out to the remains of a substantial **Roman colony** at Alba Fucens, or south to the Parco Nazionale d'Abruzzo (see below). **Buses** to Alba Fucens leave from outside the train station; there are around nine daily going there, about five coming back.

ALBA FUCENS was a garrison town of about 30,000 inhabitants, founded by the Romans in 304 BC to keep the surrounding tribes in check. Aerial photographs have identified remains spreading over three square kilometres, but only the area nearest to Albe has been excavated. The main street of the town, Via Valeria, originally ran to Rome, 68 Roman miles away, according to a milestone on the town's edge. Walking down the parallel street, you reach the marketplace, still with the walls and arches of the small shops that used to surround it. Beyond is a bar, consisting of a sink with pipes that once dispensed hot wine with honey and pine-resin; behind are the steam baths – you can see the holes in the raised pavement through which the steam rose. A good many statues, most notably a gargantuan marble Hercules, were also found, but these are now kept at Chieti's archeology museum (see p.802). Further on, above the amphitheatre, the beautiful Romanesque church of San Pietro has some excellent Cosmatesque inlaid and twisted marble decoration.

Tagliacozzo

Twenty minutes beyond Avezzano by train is **TAGLIACOZZO**, a picturesque town nestling beneath a pine-wooded cliff with an unspoilt Renaissance core that's well worth a wander. There are few focuses as such; the pleasure is more in discovering hidden corners, craft and gourmet food shops. The warren of small squares are enclosed by fourteenth- and fifteenth-century houses, a tangle of narrow streets and alleys, and the church of **San Francesco**, with its paper doily rose window and column capitals carved with twisting flowers and leaves. Above the church is the impenetrable **Palazzo Ducale** and the small **Teatro Thalia** – named, like Tagliacozzo itself, after the Greek muse of theatre. The story goes that the town was founded by Greeks from Mount Parnassus: next to San Francesco is a church dedicated to two Greek saints, Cosmo and Damiano, and there are supposedly still traces of Greek in Tagliacozzo's dialect.

There's a **tourist office** at Via Vittorio Veneto 6 that has leaflets and a map of the town (daily 9am–1pm & 4–7pm; ☎0863.610.318). Unfortunately many of Tagliacozzo's **hotels** have seen better days so it's not such a great stop-off; if you want to stay overnight, the cheapest hotels are *La Lucciola* on Via della Giorgina (☎0863.6501; ②) behind the station, and the rather run-down *Gatto d'Oro* on Viale Aldo Moro (☎0863.610.369; ②) with a restaurant with home cooking. For somewhere with marginally more facilities try the *Miramonti* also near the station on Via Vittorio Veneto (☎0863.6581; ④). You'll have no problem finding **somewhere to eat** as there are several scenic places around Piazza dell'Obelisco near the entrance to the old town. For home cooking in completely no-frills surroundings, *Petit Restaurant chez Nunzia*, Via XXIV Maggio 6 (closed Mon in summer and Mon & Sun evening in winter), parallel with Viale Aldo Moro, is friendly and family-run.

The Parco Nazionale d'Abruzzo

At four hundred square kilometres, the **Parco Nazionale d'Abruzzo** is Italy's third-largest national park and holds some of its wildest mountain land, providing a hunter-free haven for wolves, brown bears, chamois and a pair of royal eagles, along with some great walking. There are said to be around 70–100 bears in the park but sadly only 15–20 wolves, most of these lazing behind barbed wire at **CIVITELLA ALFEDENA**, impounded to prevent them mating with local dogs and stripped of the mystery that made stories of werewolves so prevalent around these parts. There are few big hotels in the park and development has largely been at agriturism level; the central village,

PESCASSÉROLI, is the most commercialized part of the park, liberally decorated with the park's cute logo – a brown bear looking as daft and cuddly as Winnie the Pooh – surrounded by campsites, holiday flats and hotels, and occasionally swamped by busloads of schoolkids and pensioners.

The best way to get away from the valley is to hike, and if you're not up for this there's not much point in coming here. There are several campsites with limited services (bathrooms, showers, grilling area, benches, and electricity), but at Easter and in July and August the numbers coming here can be immense and you'll have to put up with everything-but-the-kitchen-sink car campers, or with their heartier but less hardy compatriots in a hotel. The trick is to take advantage of the comprehensive information service, and get walking as quickly as possible: as soon as you get away from the vicinity of the tourist villages, the wild Apennine beauty really makes itself felt.

Information and walking routes

There is a **tourist office** at Via Piave (daily 9am–1pm & 4–7pm; ☎0863.910.097) in Pescasséroli, which also has a **museum** (daily 10am–1pm & 3–7pm; L10,000/€5.16) to fill you in on the park's flora and fauna. There's also an **Ufficio di Zona** behind the *municipio* (town hall) offering information on hiking in the park and with a map you can refer to (daily 9am–noon & 3–7pm; ☎0863.91.955). For organized trekking, mountain biking, horse riding and cross-country skiing, mountain-bike hire and CTS bus tickets, head for **Ecotur**, a co-operative at Piazza Vittorio Veneto 24 (daily 9am–1pm & 3.30pm–7pm; winter closed Sun; ☎0863.912.760, *www.pescasseroli.com*).

There are other offices in **Opi** (summer daily 9am–12.30pm & 4–7pm; winter closed Wed 9am–12.30pm & 3.30–6pm; ☎0863.910.622), where there's also a **chamois museum** (Easter & June–Sept daily 10am–1pm & 3–7pm; free); in **Villetta Barrea** (July 15 –Sept 15 daily 9.30am–1pm & 4–7pm; rest of year Sat & Sun 9.30am–1pm; ☎0864.89.333); and in **Barrea** (April–Oct daily 9am–12.30pm & 4–7pm). All have leaflets outlining specific walks that take less than an hour, and are gentle and very popular. They can also sell you a map (L10,000/€5.16) on which all **walking routes** are marked, along with an indication of the difficulty involved (F=easy, M=moderate, D=difficult), the time needed, and the flora and fauna you're likely to see on the way; there are nearly 150 different routes, starting from 25 letter-coded points, so making a choice can be difficult. The following are just suggestions, taking into account the ease of reaching the starting-point by bus.

From point #F2, 1km out of Opi on the SS83 (car park available) there's a two-and-a-half-hour walk through the **Valle Fondillo** – one of the loveliest parts of the park. This route is best followed very early in the morning, to avoid other hikers and have a small chance of seeing bears and chamois: if you do catch a glimpse of one, take care, keep quiet and don't panic – though they're extremely strong and will attack if under threat, it is almost unknown for them to harm walkers. Off this path runs #F1 via which you can climb **Mont'Amaro** (1862m) for great views over to Lake Barrea. Another good climb is up **Monte Tranquillo** (route #C3, about 2hr) about a kilometre out of Pescasséroli, taking the road to the left on entering the village, past the *Hotel Ivy*. The mountain (1841m) is crowned by a small sanctuary, dedicated to the black Madonna of Monte Tranquillo. From the summit you can either retrace your steps or take path #Q3 into the next valley, where you'll probably meet fewer fellow walkers. Your best chance of seeing some of the park's chamois is to take path #I1, turning left just before the youth hostel at Civitella Alfedena, and through the forested **Val di Rosa**, until the forest gives way to the grassy slopes where the chamois graze. A path zigzags from here up the slope to **Passo Cavuto**, and beyond to the *Rifugio Forca Resuni*. From here a path (#K6) descends into the **Valle Ianna'nghera** – where you may see bears – and back to Civitella Alfedena. This circuit should take six hours.

Note that from July to September, the two most popular routes – #F1 to Mont'Amaro and #I1 through Val di Rosa – are open by reservation **only**. For #F1, book onto a guided tour (in English by request, L15,000/€7.75) at the information point in Valle Fondillo. Access to #I1 is free in June but restricted from July 8 –Sept 10 to 50 walkers per day and 100 on Sundays and holidays. From Sept 16–Nov 5 it is free to walk #I1 during the week but access is restricted at weekends; book in person at the information point at Civitella Alfedena (L10,000/€5.16). During the rest of the year these two routes are open without restriction or fee, though guided tours can still be arranged.

Accommodation and restaurants

Pescassèroli is fairly well served by buses (from Avezzano, from Castel di Sangro on the border with Molise, and one bus daily to Rome in summer) so you may find it a convenient place to stay. In high season, there's little chance of finding a **room** on arrival; you need to book at least a month in advance. The cheaper places include *Al Castello*, a small, stone-built guesthouse with seven rooms decked with lace curtains and geraniums on Via Gabriele d'Annunzio off the main piazza (☎0863.910.757; ②), and *Peppe di Sora*, across the river on Viale B. Croce (☎0863.91.908; ③). Outside town *Paradiso*, Via Fronte Fracassi (☎0863.910.422, *a.paradiso@ermes.it*; ④) is an appealing place to stay. If you're coming here for a week or more B&B accommodation in a private house or an apartment rental are an option – the tourist office will supply you with a list though again, book a month in advance. Campers should manage to find space on one of the five **campsites**, of which the simplest three to reach are *dell'Orso* on the main approach road (SS83); and *Club Alto Sangro* (☎0863.912.264) and *Sant'Andrea* (☎0863.912.173) at Località Sant'Andrea off the SS83. *Dell'Orso* also has a **hostel**, open all year, but both site and hostel are currently closed for renovation (call ☎0863.91.955 for the latest information). *Panoramica* (☎0863.912.257) is out of the village at the foot of the *funivia* up to Monte Vitelle.

Among the other villages, Civitella Alfedena has a small **hotel**, *Antico Borgo* (☎0864.890.121; ②), and a **camping** area, *Wolf* next to the lake (☎0864.89.336). At Villetta Barrea, there's the reasonably priced *Degli Olmi* hotel, Via Fossata 8b (☎0864.89.159; ③); and two campsites – *Le Quite* (☎0864.89.141; summer) on the outskirts of the village and at Barrea *La Genziana* (☎0864.88.450), convenient for walkpoint #K up to the tiny mountain Lago Vivo or the larger Lago Montana Spaccata.

As for **eating out,** in most villages you'll find fairly cheap pizza and pasta, and general stores that will make up sandwiches for picnics. For local specialities it's worth heading for *La Baita*, on Piazzale Cabinovia (closed Tues in winter), in Pescassèroli; slightly more expensive is *Il Pescatore* in Villetta Barrea, where you can feast on superlative fish and pasta dishes.

Northeast Abruzzo: Téramo and around

Rising from the Adriatic and rolling towards the eastern slopes of the Gran Sasso, the landscape of northeast Abruzzo is gentle, and its inland towns are usually ignored in favour of its long, sandy and highly popular coastline. **TÉRAMO**, capital of the province of the same name, is a modern town with an elegant centre harbouring the remains of a Roman amphitheatre, theatre and baths and a treasure-filled cathedral. Maybe not much to draw you, but Téramo does have good bus and train connections with the northern Abruzzo coast, and if you're heading for the sea you may well pass through. **Buses** stop at **Piazza Garibaldi**, to which the **train station** is linked by regular city buses. Just off the piazza, down Corso S. Giorgio and then right onto Via Carducci brings you to the **tourist office** (May–Sept daily 9am–1pm & 4–7pm; winter closed Sun; ☎0861.244.222) at no. 17. In the other direction off Piazza Garibaldi is a reasonable **hotel**, the *Castello* (☎0861.247.582; ②), at Via del Castello 62. The **restaurant** in which to sample Abruzzese specialities is *Antico Cantinone*, at Via Ciotti 5 (closed Sun), and with the classic Teramano *virtù* on the menu: an elaborate version of minestrone. A newer place with an excellent wine list is *Sotto Le Stelle* at Via Nazario Sauro 50 (closed Sun); a good bet for local specialities including *chitarre*: pasta with meaty accompaniments. If you don't want to stay in Téramo itself, there's a good **hotel** between here and Ascoli Piceno in the Marche at the hill village of **Civitella del Tronto**: *Zunica*, at Piazza Filippi Pepe 14 (☎0861.91.319; ④) has small, modern rooms, excellent food in the restaurant, and a lively locals' bar on the ground floor.

Even if you're just passing through, look in on Téramo's main attraction, the **Duomo**, at the top of Corso San Giorgio, behind whose patchy facade lies a remarkable silver altarfront. It's worth squatting down for a good look at this (ask the sacristan to switch the lights on). Crafted by the fifteenth-century Abruzzese silversmith Nicola da Guardiagrele – also responsible for the statues of Mary and Gabriel that flank the church doorway – it has 35 panels with lively reliefs of religious scenes, starting with the Annunciation and moving through the New Testament, punctuating the narrative with portraits of various saints. Nicola was famous enough to feature in a sumptuous polyptych by a Venetian artist, Jacobello del Fiore, in a Baroque chapel to the left. Set into an ornate gilded frame are static portraits of saints, in rich blue, red and gold gowns, flanking the *Coronation of the Virgin*, and beneath it a model of Téramo, set against a gilded sky, with Nicola wearing a monk's habit on the left, Jacobello in the red gown on the right.

To the right of the duomo, Via Irelli leads to the heart of Roman Téramo, with fragments of the **amphitheatre**, and the more substantial walls of the **theatre**, where two of the original twenty entrance arches remain. Just behind Piazza Garibaldi at Viale Bovio 1 is the town's modest **museum** (Tues–Sun: summer 5–9pm; winter 10am–1pm; L10,000/€5.16) joint ticket with museo archeologico below), whose collection of local art over the centuries includes two appealing works – a lovely almond-eyed Madonna by a local fifteenth-century artist, Giacomo da Campli, and Campli's *Madonna Enthroned with Saints* – a polyptych in which the colours are lucid and the forms almost sculpted. The new **museo civico archeologico** off Via Carducci on Via Delfico (daily 9am–1pm & 4–7pm; mid-Jul–end Aug open until 11pm; L10,000/€5.16) is strong on Roman finds from excavations in Téramo and includes a first-century mosaic of an appealing lion among the forum columns and marble busts.

The northern Abruzzo coast

The **northern Abruzzo coastline** isn't at first sight the region's most appealing stretch, its ribbon of sand hugged for most of its considerable length by road and railway, studded with grids of beach umbrellas and flimsy cabins and lined with concrete-box apartment blocks and hotels. However, the beaches are good and frequently palm-fringed, there are plenty of campsites, and though the resorts may look bland they can be fun – especially if you're weary of travel or culture.

The coastal rail line ensures that access to the resorts couldn't be easier, though finding a hotel can be a problem, as the cheaper ones tend to be closed out of season and they get booked up in advance for most of the summer – your best bet at most of the coastal towns is to head straight for the tourist office on arrival.

The resorts

ALBA ADRIATICA is the most northerly of the Abruzzo resorts – a good place to stop off if you're heading on to Marche. **GIULIANOVA** has a rather forlorn old town perched above its resort quarter, although its five campsites (buses from opposite the train station) and connections with Téramo make it a useful stop off if you want a last swim before heading inland. Ten kilometres further south, **ROSETO DEGLI ABRUZZI** is modern and undistinguished but has views up the Vomano Valley towards the Gran Sasso. **PINETO**, a well-organized resort with a shady strip of pines and picnic tables between the beach and the town, is not bad for sunning and swimming if you are in the area. Every hotel is clearly signposted from the railway station and it's also a good base for visiting Atri (see below). There are lots of **campsites**, and twenty or so one- and two-star **hotels;** among them is *Jean-Pierre*, Via Michetti 70 (☎085.949.0587; ③) a friendly, family-run hotel slightly south of the centre. If everywhere is full, consult the **tourist office** in the Centro Polifunzionari on Via Mazzini (June–Sept daily 9am–noon & 4–7pm; Oct–May daily 9am–1pm and occasionally 3.30–6.30pm; ☎085.949.1745), who should be able to advise on where the vacancies are.

Atri

The approach to **ATRI**, about 10km inland from Pineto, is like travelling through the background of a Renaissance painting, with gently undulating hills planted with orderly olive groves giving way to a surrealist landscape of sleek clay gullies known as *calanchi*, water-eroded into smooth ripples, wrinkles and folds. Atri's duomo contains Abruzzo's greatest cycle of frescoes, and the town itself, with its narrow stepped and bridged streets, is one you're likely to be reluctant to leave.

Buses (see "Practicalities" overleaf) drop you near **Porta San Domenico**, the town's only surviving defensive gate. To get to the centre, walk through the gate and cut down one of the narrow sidestreets to the main street, which leads up to the central piazza, dominated by the thirteenth-century **Duomo**. Its facade is understated, pierced by a rose window and perforated by the holes in which scaffolding beams were slotted during construction. The inside is similarly simple, with patches of frescoes on the brick columns and – visible through glass set into the floor of the apse – an octagonal mosaic pavement decorated with sea horses, dolphins and fish, from the Roman baths over which the church was built. The duomo's highlight, however, is the cycle of **fifteenth-century frescoes** by Andrea Delitio on the apse walls. Delitio has been called the 'Piero della Francesca' of Abruzzo for his sophisticated use of architecture and landscape; but in contrast to Piero's cool intellectualism and obscure symbolism, Delitio places the religious scenes in realistic contexts. *The Birth of Mary*, for example, has servants giving the newly born baby a bath; in the vault the four Evangelists are placed in natural settings, the animals that are the emblems of the saints behaving as domestic pets; and back on the walls, the lives of the rich – especially in the *Wedding at Cana* and *Presentation in the Temple* – contrast with the lives of the poor, notably Mary, Joseph and the shepherds in the *Nativity*. The most emotionally charged scene is the *Slaughter of the Innocents*, in which the horror is intensified by the refined Renaissance architectural setting and the fact that the massacre is coolly observed from a balcony by Herod's party of civic bigwigs. One opulently dressed slaughterer slices a child with chill, technical accuracy as if it were a joint of meat; another holds a child upside down by the ankles, while the mothers weep wretchedly over the tiny corpses.

For a touch of light relief, head back up the right-hand aisle to see a piece of Renaissance kitsch – a font with four oversized frogs clinging to the basin. In the cloisters is the entrance to a cavernous Roman cistern, and there are more Roman relics outside the cathedral – the foundations of what was possibly a dye-works, complete with a vat. The town's two small **museums** (archeological and ethnographic) are both closed for restoration, but in any case the best thing to do in Atri is just wander around, strolling out to the belvedere for views, nosing into the many churches, or simply sitting in a café and watching the small-town life around you.

Practicalities

Regular **buses** make the trip from Pescara and Téramo as well as Pineto, and it's a journey that's undeniably worth making. You may well want to stay the night, and there's a great **hotel** – three-star quality at one-star prices – the *San Francesco* (☎085.87.287; ②), housed in an ex-convent next to the church of San Francesco on Corso Adriano. The best **restaurant** is *La Campana d'Oro* on Piazza del Duomo (closed Wed).

Loreto Apruntino

One of the most important market towns in the region is **LORETO APRUNTINO**, a quiet hilltop settlement with medieval origins 24km inland from Pescara. The labyrinthine old town is home to a score of **artisans' workshops** making knives, copper and iron pots and items in terracotta and decorated glass, which are open to the public (daily 4–7pm). Some tiny cantinas in the old town sell olive oil, for which the area has been awarded a DOP (*denominazione di origine protetta*) the equivalent of the DOC designation for wine. Loreto heaves with people on market day (Thursday) and in the evenings during the late-running passegiata, when it's a pleasure simply to do nothing much and for a moment be part of small town life. If you want a focus for your wanderings, just outside town is the fourteenth-century church of **Santa Maria in Piano** (daily 8am–noon & 3–7pm), with a series of frescoes in the right aisle in diverse styles dating from the fourteenth to sixteenth centuries, which celebrates the devotions of saints and apostles including St Thomas of Aquinas, protector of the city. At the top of the old town, on the end of a row of nineteenth-century palazzi, you'll find the church of **San Pietro Apostolo**. The church dates from the fifteenth and sixteenth centuries, with a Renaissance doorway decorated with the coat of arms of the Borboni, who chose this as their castle abbey.

Practicalities

Regular **buses** make the trip from Pescara (journey time 45mins). The **tourist office** is at Cia dei Normanni 8 (June–Sept Tues–Sun 9am–12.30pm & 4–7.30pm; Oct–May Tues–Sun 8.30am–1pm & 4–7.30pm; ☎ and fax 085.829.0484). There are some appealing **places to stay** in and around town: the castle dating back to 864 which tops the town has recently been turned into a grand hotel, the *Castello Chiola* (☎085.829.0690; ⑧). The huge, high-ceilinged rooms have been decorated in stately style and it has a glass-roofed, inner courtyard lounge, and a small swimming pool on a terrace overlooking the surrounding countryside. This is the only central hotel; outside town you can **eat** very well at hotel-restaurant *La Bilancia*, Contrada da Palazzo 11 (☎085.828.9321), or there's the welcoming agriturismo guest-house *Le Magnolie*, at Contrada da Fiorano 83 (☎085.828.9534; mobile 0335.384.180; ③) on a mixed farm cultivating olives, fruit trees, vegetables and cereal crops. The six bedrooms and three mini-apartments are furnished with flair; lunch and dinner are served on request. It's quite hard to find: the farm is on a minor road between the SS151 between Penne and Loreto Apruntino, and the SS81 between Penne and Pianella.

Pescara

The main town and resort of the Abruzzo coast is **PESCARA**, a bustling, modern place that's probably the region's most commercial and expensive city. If you're looking for somewhere to sunbathe there are much quieter places than Pescara's 16km beach; but now that ferries to Croatia and the islands of the Dalmatian coast have started running again you might find yourself using the city as a departure point, or there's a chance you might pass through for the train or bus connections.

Architecturally, Pescara isn't a distinguished town. In fact, its most striking sight is the central **train station**, strangely enough the most up-to-date in Italy, with a slick network of slinky escalators, smoked-glass screens and non-slip black rubber pavements. Opposite, the main street, **Corso Umberto**, is lined with designer boutiques and packed with the label-conscious Pescarese, who also hang out in the elegant cafés on **Piazza Rinascita**, known as Pescara's *salone*. If you've time to kill, you could visit the **Museo delle Genti d'Abruzzo** at Via delle Caserme 22 (Mon–Fri 9am–1pm & Mon, Wed, Fri 2.30–5pm; Sun 10am–1pm; L5000/€2.58), devoted to the life and popular traditions of the region; or visit the birthplace of the poet and mentor of Mussolini, **Gabriele d'Annunzio** (see p.225), at Corso Manthonè 101 (Tues–Sun 9am–1.30pm; L4000/€2.06). A third museum, the **Museo e Pinacoteca Cascella** at Viale G. Marconi 45 (Mon–Sat 9am–1pm, plus Thurs 4–7pm; L3000/€1.54) is for devotees of Art Nouveau and later twentieth-century art, with 500 lithographic prints, paintings, ceramics and sculptures including a stunning set of portraits (mounted on dinner plates) by the prolific Cascella family who lived and worked here.

Practicalities

Pescara has two **train stations**, though unless you're leaving the country you only need to use one, Stazione Centrale (the other, Porta Nuova, is only for ferry connections). Conveniently, **buses** to Rome (quicker than the train) and Naples leave from outside Stazione Centrale. The **tourist office** is at Via N Fabrizi 171 (daily 9am–1pm & 4–7pm; ☎085.4290.0212, *www.regione.abruzzo.it/turismo*) halfway up Corso Umberto between the train station and the seafront, on a turning to the right.

If you need to stay the nearest **campsites** are *Francavilla* (☎085.810.715) or *Paola* (☎085.817.525) at Francavalla al Mare – buses #1 and #2 stop outside. Most of the **hotels** are on the beach-front north of the river and the old town, although you can sleep more cheaply at somewhere like the *Corso* (☎085.422.4210; ③) to the right of the train station at Corso Vittorio Emanuele 292 or *Planet*, Via Piave 142 (☎085.421.1657; ②), up Corso Umberto from the train station, left onto Via M Forti and then right. A more upmarket choice (book a couple of weeks in advance) is the comfortable, shiny and businesslike *Alba*, Via M Forti 14 (☎085.389.145; ④). For **meals**, try the *Hosteria Roma*, Via Trento 86 (closed Sun), a small place off Corso Umberto with a short reliable menu, and low prices; or the *Cantina di Jozz* at Via delle Caserme 61 (closed all day Mon & Sun evening) – both do great Abruzzese food. Otherwise, try the gastronomically inclined *La Lumaca*, just down the road from the *Cantina* at no. 51 (closed Tues; booking advisable ☎085.451.0880). Corso Mathonè is the main street running through what remains of the old town of Pescara next to the river; here, among other good places to eat, you'll find *Locanda Manthonè*, recommended by the Pescarese for its good food at reasonable prices (no day of closure).

Chieti, Guardiagrele and Lanciano

Just twenty minutes by train from Pescara, **CHIETI** is a more pleasant place to stop over between trains. It holds Abruzzo's best museum by far, with an extensive collection of finds from the region, and the town itself has a relaxed and appealing provincial air.

Coming by train you arrive at Chieti Scalo, from where it's a short journey on bus #1 up the hill to Chieti proper, 5km away, which spreads over a curving ridge and has great views of the Maiella and Gran Sasso – and, when it's clear, out to sea. Buses arrive at **Piazza Vittorio Emanuele** alongside the chunky and much-reconstructed cathedral, from where the main **Corso Marrucini** cuts through the town centre to **Largo Trento e Trieste**. Behind the post office, off Via Spaventa, are the remains of three little

Roman temples. However, it's the **Museo Nazionale Archeologico di Antichitá** (June–Sept Mon–Fri & Sun 9am–8pm, Sat 9am–11pm; Oct–May daily 9am–7pm; L8000/€4.13) which is of most interest, laid out in a dignified villa encircled by a park beyond Piazza Trento e Trieste. It holds finds from Abruzzo's major sites: there's a Roman portrait-bust of an old man, in which the stone appears as soft, wrinkled and flaccid as real skin; a massive and muscly white-marble Hercules from the temple at Alba Fucens (see p.795); a bronze Hercules from the sanctuary outside Sulmona (see p.791), and an elegant, bone funeral bed from a tomb at Amiternum (see p.788). If you've seen Amiternum, look also at the frieze showing how its amphitheatre would have been in the first century, packed with bloodthirsty spectators at the gladiatorial games. Upstairs, don't miss the *Capestrano Warrior*, a statue of a Bronze Age warrior prince. It dates back to the time (sixth century BC) when a deified, hero-worshipped warrior leader was key to Bronze Age society. Statues like these in characteristic pose with the arms across the torso were set on the top of burial mounds to mark territory throughout the Adriatic and Central Europe and must have made an awesome feature of the landscape.

Remains of the occupants of Bronze Age tombs are laid out in the adjacent rooms – the men buried with armour and weapons, the women with jewellery, kitchen utensils, spindles, and in one case even a nail-brush. For more insight into prehistoric hygiene, head for the extraordinary exhibition about Paleolithic dental health, conclusions about diet being drawn from the state of the Paleolithic teeth.

Further digs in Chieti have uncovered the core of Teate, the main town of the Marrucini (an Italic tribe) which became a Roman colony in the first century BC. The site lies on the edge of central Chieti at the **Civitella archeological park** and includes the remains of temples, theatre, amphitheatre, thermal baths and a new museum. At the time of writing opening hours hadn't been set; for details call ☎0871.331.668.

Practicalities

The **tourist office** is on Via Spaventa, just off Corso Marrucino (daily 9am–1pm & 3–7pm; winter closed Sat & Sun afternoons; ☎0871.63.640). An affordable, central hotel is the *Garibaldi* at Piazza Garibaldi 25, which has **rooms** with and without bath (☎0871.345.318; ②). Around 3km away in the hills to the south-west of Chieti there's a place worth going out of your way to stay at: the welcoming, well-organized farmhouse guesthouse *Il Quadrifoglio* at Strada Licini 22, Colle Marconi (☎0871.63.400, *anndora @tin.it*; ③). There are six newly furnished bedrooms, an apartment with full kitchen and log-burning fire and a lounge, balcony and garden (with swing and climbing frame for children), with olive groves and oakwoods in one direction and far-reaching views in the other. Proprietor Anna Maria D'Orazio will cook an evening meal for guests if they want and also runs gourmet cooking courses (she speaks excellent English). Good-value **meals** can also be had in central Chieti at *Trattoria Nino*, Via Principessa di Piemonte 7 (closed Fri), near Piazza Trento e Trieste, and at *Primavera* on Viale B. Croce 69 in Chieti Scalo (closed Sun).

Near Chieti: Guardiagrele and Lanciano

From Chieti, most people head south to the lovely historical town of **LANCIANO**, taking in the smaller town of **GUARDIAGRELE** on the way if they have a car. The latter town enjoyed a literal golden age in the fifteenth century, when it was home to Nicola da Guardiagrele, a gold- and silversmith whose ornate crucifixes and altar-fronts can be seen in churches and museums throughout Abruzzo. Guardiagrele itself, however, has only one piece by Nicola – a silver processional crucifix in the church of **Santa Maria Maggiore**. The church's external fresco of St Christopher, by another great fifteenth-century Abruzzo artist, Andrea Delitio, was supposed to bring travellers good fortune.

It had its own share of luck in 1943 when it escaped being destroyed by the German soldiers who smashed the church's portico.

Lanciano, some 18km east of Guardiagrele, holds one of Abruzzo's most enticing and best-preserved historical quarters and is well worth the onward journey. As Italy's main producer of needles and host of an important wool and cloth fair, Lanciano was a major commercial centre during the Middle Ages, and the main **Piazza Plebiscito**, in the words of a contemporary, was invariably crowded with "peasants in red and blue jackets, Jews in yellow sashes, Albanians, Greeks, Dalmatians and Tuscans: there was an assortment of languages, it was a muddle, a nightmare. . ." The square is not much quieter now, a chaotic junction where the cathedral balances on a reconstructed **Roman bridge** – a testament of even earlier prosperity, built in the time of Emperor Vespasian to give easy access to the merchants of the Roman era.

Corso Roma leads out of the piazza and up to the church of **San Francesco**. Behind its austere rectangular facade are the relics of one of the more improbable miracles of the Catholic Church, the *Miracolo Eucaristico*. Contained in two reliquaries are five coagulated globules of blood and a fragment of muscular heart tissue, both 1200 years old. The story goes that during a communion service in the eighth century the bread became flesh and the wine blood in order to prove Christ's presence to a doubting monk. The relics have been forensically analysed by the Vatican's scientists, right down to their trace minerals, and the findings are presented in an exhibition, in which it is verified that the relics are indeed human blood and flesh, and that they both have the same blood group (AB) as that traced on the now discredited Turin shroud.

From the church, Via Fieramosca and Via Finamore climb up to the **Torri Montanare**, a bulwarked, multi-towered and crenellated stronghold as grim and impenetrable as when it was built in the eleventh century to protect the town's newly built residential quarters. You can walk along the walls, for great views of the Maiella mountain range, or descend to Via Santa Maria Maggiore to explore the appealingly crumbling houses of the medieval quarter, **Civitanova**, and Lanciano's most interesting church, **Santa Maria Maggiore**, which is open in the afternoon only. Built in the twelfth century, it's the best example of French Cistercian Gothic architecture in the region; the portal, surrounded by a series of columns carved into twists, zigzags and tiny leaves and flowers as elaborate as piped icing, is slightly crumbled, while inside there's a silver processional cross by Nicola da Guardiagrele, delicately decorated with biblical reliefs and hanging with silver incense baubles.

A few streets further on, a long flight of steps descends towards the centre. This marks the boundary of **Ripa Sacca**, the medieval Jewish ghetto – a series of the narrowest of stepped streets spanning out like ribs from a barely wider central spine. Here eighty Jewish families lived, obliged to observe a strict curfew, allowed to follow only certain professions, and forced to identify themselves by wearing a yellow sash at all times. A handful of the original houses remain on Via and Vico Santa Maria Maggiore, but even the later houses are in character. Below is the large and scruffy Piazza Garibaldi, and from there a flight of steps climbs up to Via degli Agorai, which was named after its fifteenth-century needlemakers. The same street skirts another wanderable quarter, **Lancianovecchia**, not as old as its name suggests but still something of a centre for the town's artisans.

Practicalities

Lanciano's **train station**, where **buses** also stop, is at the head of a broad avenue, off which Corso Trento e Trieste runs down to Piazza Plebiscito, where there's a **tourist office** (Mon–Sat 9am–12.30pm & 4–7pm; ☎0872.719.344). Lanciano's cheapest and most convenient **hotels** are the *Roma* just off Corso Trento e Trieste at Via Romagnoli 20 (☎0872.712.890; ②), the *Alba* on the edge of town on the road to the coast at Via Alba 1 (☎0872.714.640; ②), and the *De Paris* at Via Santa Giusta 113 (☎0872.711.170; ③).

The southern Abruzzo coast

The coast south of Pescara is less developed than the northern stretch; the long ribbon of sand continues, followed by the train line and punctuated with mostly small resorts. The largest, **FRANCAVILLA AL MARE**, is a characterless place, basically a continuation of Pescara. **ORTONA**, further along, is of most interest for its daily summer ferries to the Trémiti Islands (see p.888), its mainly reconstructed centre dominated by the shell of a castle and the massive dome of its cathedral. The town was at the centre of a six-week battle in 1943, fought over the territory between the Sangro and Moro rivers, which ended in the German occupation of Ortona and the deaths of thousands of Allied soldiers; there's a military cemetery 3km south of Ortona on the banks of the Moro.

On the other side of the river lies **SAN VITO**, a small resort and fishing centre with a pebbly beach and rocky coast. From here you can take a bus or – more fun – the gradient-scaling small-gauge railway inland to Lanciano (see p.802), or continue down the coast to the equally small resort of **FOSSACESIA**. The *Levante* hotel is right on the beach (☎0872.60.169; ③); 3km inland at Via S Giovanni in Venere 40 is *Golfo di Venere* (☎0872.60.541; ③) and a **campsite**, *Valle di Venere* (☎0872.608.282). Another campsite *La Foce* (☎0872.609.110) lies 4km up the coast next to the beach, just off the SS16 at the km 484,3 mark and is well equipped with shady pitches, bar, sailing and surfing facilities. On the way inland to Fossacesia itself is the creamy-gold Romanesque church of **San Giovanni in Venere**, which owes its name to the fact that it was built over a Roman temple dedicated to Venus the Conciliator and is visited by anyone seeking the return of peace within their family. The church, with its finely carved sandstone door and triple apse, is superbly sited among the undulating fields above the coast and is still a favourite outing for Abruzzese families – harmony now being sought by the treat of a hearty meal in the restaurant outside the church. If you're visiting at the weekend or during holidays and want the church to yourself, aim to get there at lunchtime, while everyone else is safely ensconced behind plates of pasta.

Vasto

VASTO, further south, close to the border with Molise, is a fine old city, overlooking the resort of **VASTO MARINA**. There are boats in the summer to the Trémiti Islands, plenty of campsites, and a handful of reasonable hotels along the broad sandy beach – palm-lined and beach-hutted in the centre, wilder and rockier to the north.

Vasto is all about beach, though if you're here for a day or so you should definitely get a bus from the new train station on the seafront to the upper town (they run roughly every 30min, a 10min journey), whose rooftops and campaniles rise above palms and olive groves. The centre of town is **Piazza Rossetti**, its gardens dominated by the chunky **Castello Calderesco**. The piazza is named after Gabriele Rossetti, a local eighteenth-century poet who is better known as the father of the Pre-Raphaelite poet Dante Gabriele Rossetti.

Just off the piazza, next to the small Duomo, stands the splendid Renaissance **Palazzo d'Avalos** (Oct–June Tues & Wed 4.30–8.30pm, Thurs–Sun 9.30am–12.30pm & 4.30–8.30pm; June–Sept Tues–Sun 8am–11pm), both of which have been restored. This was once the home of the poet and friend of Michelangelo, Vittoria Colonna, who was famous in her time for the bleak sonnets she wrote after her husband's death; nowadays it houses the town's **museum** (same hours as palazzo; L7000/€3.61 for the art gallery; L2000/€1.03 for the archeological museum; L2000/€1.03 for the costume museum; or L10,000/€5.16 for the whole lot). The best of its exhibits are some bellicose second-century bronzes, a third-century warrior with an arm missing, a collection of Greek coins – evidence of Vasto's early importance as an international trading city, and the beautiful clothes and battered old hobby-horse in the costume museum.

Alongside the palazzo, **Piazza del Popolo** is home to the **tourist office** (summer: Mon–Sat 9am–1pm & 4–7pm; winter open mornings only; ☎0873.367.312) and opens onto a panoramic promenade that takes you to Vasto's most memorable sight, the door of the church of **San Pietro**, surrounded by Romanesque twists and zigzags, standing isolated against a backdrop of sky, sea and trees, the rest of the church having been destroyed in a landslide in 1956.

Pleasant as the upper town is, most of the action is down by the beach in **Vasto Marina**, and you're more likely to want to stay in the numerous **campsites** along the coast. Most of them are off the SS16 towards Foggia; *Il Piopetto* is right on the beach and has pine-trees for shade (☎0873.801.466). The best of the cheaper **hotels** is *La Bitta* run by a lovely hospitable couple close to the free beach on Lungomare Cardella but open only in summer (☎0873.801.979; ②). It's a spacious airy hotel, with excellent food: fruit and veg come in fresh from the country every day. If you do want to stay in the upper town, try either *Dei Sette*, on Via San Michele, a ten-minute walk out of the centre past the stadium and the public gardens (☎0873.362.819; ③), or the *Palizzi*, a ten-minute walk in the opposite direction on the busy Corso Mazzini (☎0873.367.361; ②). The most peaceful bolthole has got to be *Villa Vignola* (☎0873.310.050; ⑥) a small white villa with 5 rooms, a tiny pebble beach, a garden for lounging in and a romantic terrace restaurant. serving such delicacies as marinaded prawns, stuffed baby squid, delectable home-made pasta and simple grilled fish. To find it, take the SS16 north out of Marina di Vasto, pass the turn-off for Vasto itself and keep going until you get to a sign pointing to the "Porto". Turn right here and then right again immediately after the railway line. As for **eating and drinking**, there are loads of pizzerias and "pubs" in Vasto Marina, although you might prefer to consider splashing out at *Villa Vignola* (no closing day) in Contrada Vignola (see above).

MOLISE

Gentler, less rugged and somewhat poorer than Abruzzo, **Molise** has more in common with southern than central Italy. Much of the region still seems to be struggling out of its past, its towns and villages victims of either economic neglect or hurried modern development. The cities, **Isernia** and **Campobasso**, are large and bland, rebuilt after earthquakes and fringed with factories erected by northern money that has been lured here by the low price of land and labour.

But Molise has its compensations. Just as the twentieth-century industrial tycoons have invaded Molise, scattering it with formula-built Anytowns, so, over 2000 years ago, the Romans charged into the region, forcing the native Italic Samnite tribes to leave their small villages and live in equally formula-built settlements. Molise still has a scattering of low-key Roman ruins – most interestingly at **Saepinum**, Italy's most complete example of a Roman provincial town and a site that's still well off the beaten tourist track. Wandering among the ruins, and looking out over the green fields to the mountains beyond, you get some inkling of what it must have been like for Italy's first Grand Tourists.

There are some interesting contradictions: traditions that would have been ancient two hundred years ago still persist. In many a new apartment block, Benetton-clad girls will be making lace alongside their grandmothers, and in the village of **Ururi**, settled by Albanian refugees in the fourteenth century, there's an annual chariot race, as barbaric as anything the Romans dreamed up.

Finally there's the sheer physical aspect of the place. Forty percent of Molise is covered by **mountains**, and although they are less dramatic than Abruzzo's there are masses of possibilities for hiking. A must is the trail up **Monte La Gallinola** in the **Matese** mountains, from where on a clear day the whole of the peninsula, from the Bay of Naples to the Adriatic, stretches out before you.

Isernia and around

ISERNIA was severely damaged for the eighth time by an earthquake in 1984, but after a slow recovery it has rebuilt its commercial centre so that it's now comparatively busy and bustling. Historically the city hasn't had much luck: much of the centre was destroyed in a bombing raid on September 10, 1943, and a monument to the 4000 who were killed – an anguished nude ankle-deep in fractured tiles, bricks and gutters – is the centrepiece of the square called, understandably, Piazza X Settembre.

Not surprisingly, not much of old Isernia survives. The city's main attraction is the **Museo Nazionale della Pentria e Isernia** (Tues–Sun 9am–1pm & 3–7pm; L4000/€2.06), in the heart of the old town at Piazza Santa Maria 8. In 1979 local road-builders unearthed traces of a million-year-old village here, the most ancient signs of human life yet found in Europe. The exhibits are backed up by computer demonstrations in four languages, including English, which reconstruct the village and put the ancient civilization in context. Contrary to the misleading publicity, there were no human remains found, just weapons, traps, traces of pigment thought to have been used as body paint, and animal bones, laid out to create a solid platform on the marshy land for the village.

Though unbeguiling in itself, Isernia can be a useful starting-point for exploring the rest of Molise: **buses** to local villages leave from Via XXIV Maggio, parallel with Corso Garibaldi, and longer-distance buses, including those to Rome and Naples, from outside the train station. The **tourist office** is at Via Farinacci 1 (Mon–Sat 8am–2pm; ☎0865.3992). You probably won't need to stay over, but if you do, *Sayonara* a three-star at Via G. Berti 131 (☎0865.50.992; ②) is the only central hotel. **Eating** prospects are better: there's a good traditional restaurant, *Taverna Maresca*, in the old town on Corso Marcelli (closed Sun). If you're on a budget, their pasta-, bean- or polenta-based first courses are filling and cheap; if you're not, you can gorge yourself on roast kid or lamb cooked in various mysterious but delicious ways.

Around Isernia

The countryside **around Isernia** is lush and gentle, at its best in spring, when the meadows are sprinkled with wild flowers. The valleys are headed by hill-villages, most of them run-down places ringed with new housing estates, and the rewards of exploring are principally those of being the first foreigner to have visited in ages. This is not always the most comfortable of experiences, and women can expect to be stared at, cat-called or even kerb-crawled – there's no chance of anonymity in a village where everyone knows everyone else. Getting around, too, isn't easy: buses are often organized around the school day, which means you'll have to leave either very early in the morning or at around 2pm – after that there may be no other bus until the next day.

Just outside **PIETRABBONDANTE**, northeast of Isernia, are the remains of a pre-Roman Samnite village, notably a well-preserved theatre (Tues–Sun 9am–dusk; free) set in a green field at the foot of Monte Caraceno. Further along the road, **AGNONE** is best known for having produced church bells for over a thousand years. The **Marinelli Pontifical Foundry** still makes bells in the traditional way, using a priest to bless the molten bronze as it's poured into the mould, which supposedly ensures that the bell's tones will be pure. A small **museum** can be visited (at noon for a guided half-hour tour; ☎0865.78.235). If you're into metalwork, Agnone is also famous for its coppersmiths, most of whom work on the main street.

To the west of Isernia, the bus calls at **Cerro al Volturno**, crowned by one of Molise's more spectacular castles, almost growing out of the grey rock on which it is perched. A few kilometres further on is **CASTEL SAN VINCENZO**, another pretty-from-a-distance hill-village: get off the bus below the village at the Cartiera (paper mill) and walk along the road to the left for about one kilometre, until you come to the abbey of **San Vincenzo al Volturno** (daily 10am–noon & 3.30–5.30pm; free, but offerings welcome) – a much-reconstructed complex now run by American nuns, with a crypt covered by a complete cycle of ninth-century frescoes in rich Byzantine colours, the only surviving example of ninth-century Benedictine art. Recently the remains of an earlier, eighth-century basilica of San Vincenzo Maggiore were discovered and these will eventually be open to the public too. At the **zona archeologico** nearby are the remains of a seventh-century monastery (in theory open daily 9am–noon & 3–6pm but call ☎0865.951.006 to book; guided tours L5000/€2.58).

About 20km to the south, but most easily accessible by train from Isernia, is the village of **VENAFRO**, topped by a derelict castle and with a Roman amphitheatre (just by the railway station) that was converted into an oval piazza in the Middle Ages. Most of the local finds are on display in the **Museo Archeologico Santa Chiara** (9am–1pm & 3–7.30pm; free) on Via Garibaldi.

Campobasso, Saepinum and the Matese

Home of a top-security prison and the National Carabinieri School, **CAMPOBASSO**, the regional capital, is about as appealing as you'd expect – a modern, rather faceless town that was once known for its cutlery industry. It's a good base, though, for the remarkable ruins at **Saepinum**, and if you're around in early June, its Corpus Christi *Sagra dei Misteri* procession is a spectacular event. Citizens are dressed as saints, angels and devils, inserted into fantastical contraptions and transported, seemingly suspended in midair, through the streets.

At any other time of the year the most notable attraction is the new **Samnite Museum** (summer daily 8.30am–7.30pm; winter Tues–Sun 9am–1pm & 3–7pm; free; ☎0874.412.265) at Via Chiarizia 12, with statues and archeological finds from the area. Steep alleys of the small, old upper town lead up to a couple of Romanesque churches – **San Bartolomeo**, which has eerily contorted figures carved around its main door, and **San Giorgio**, whose entrance displays a dragon surrounded by stylized flowers. The views at least are extensive, though they consist mostly of Campobasso's suburban sprawl. And there's little point carrying on up the hill to the monastery and sixteenth-century castle: the monastery is modern, and the castle now a weather station.

Should you need to sleep over, the nicest, most central **hotel** is the *Skandeberg*, near the station and museum at Via Novelli 31 (☎0874.413.341; ④), or there's the *Tricolore*, outside the centre on the road to Térmoli (☎0874.63.190; ②). The **tourist office** (Mon–Sat 8.30am–1.30pm; ☎0874.415.662) on Piazza Vittoria in the new town has details of local events and bus routes to elsewhere in the province.

Saepinum

It's **SAEPINUM**, a ruined Roman town to the south, close to the border with Puglia, that makes the stopover in Campobasso worthwhile. Three kilometres from the nearest village, surrounded by a lush plain fringed with the foothills of the Matese mountains, it's the best example in Italy of a provincial Roman town – and is tourist-free.

The main reason Saepinum is so intact is that it was never very important: nothing much ever happened here, and after the fall of the Roman Empire it carried on as the sleepy backwater it had always been – until the ninth century when it was sacked by

Saracens. Over the centuries its inhabitants added only a handful of farms and cottages, incorporating the odd Roman column or architrave, and eventually moved south to the more secure hilltop site of present-day Sepino. Some have now moved back and have rebuilt the farms and cottages on Saepinum's peripheries, contributing if anything to the site's appeal. Their sheep graze below an ancient mausoleum, chickens scratch around the walls, and the only sounds are from the geese and white peacocks.

There are a few more **buses** these days, so a visit to Saepinum no longer need take up most of the day, and there are now two **bar-restaurants** at the Porta Boiano and the Porta Tammaro so you don't need to take your own supplies. From Campobasso, either catch one of the two services that stop at Altilia (right outside the site) which leave the Campo Sportivo daily except Sunday at 7.50am and 1pm; or get a bus to **Sepino** (roughly every 2hr; to check schedules, call ☎0874.790.848) and walk the remaining 3km to Saepinum (you may be able to persuade the driver to detour to the "*zona monumentale*" – they sometimes will). Buses return to Campobasso from the archeological site at 8.15am and 1.35pm. Alternatively walk the 3km to the Sepino stop for more choices (no timetables are on display, but buses return daily except Sunday at 8.25am, 8.45am, 11.05am, 12.25pm, 1.35pm, 2.40pm, 6.05pm, 7.35pm; tickets on board).

The site

Depending on whether you arrive by bus or by car, entrance to Saepinum is through the **Porta Terravecchia** or the **Porta Tammaro**, two of the town's four gates. The site is bisected by the *cardus maximus*, still paved with the original stones, and crossed by the *decumanus maximus* – centre of town and home to the public buildings and trading quarters. On the left, grass spills through the cracks in the pavement of the **forum**, now used by the few local kids as a football pitch, bordered by the foundations of various municipal buildings: the comitium, the curia, a temple, baths, and in the centre a fountain with a relief of a griffin. Beyond the forum, on the left of the decumanus, the **Casa Impluvio Sannitico** contains a vat to collect rainwater, from the Samnite town that stood on the site before the Romans sacked it in 293 BC. Beyond lies the **Porta Benevento**, adjoining which is one of the two museums (both closed and neither due to reopen due to security problems) documenting the process of excavation, and with a section on more recent rural traditions. Until quite recently the village was passed through, as it had been for over 2000 years, by nomadic shepherds, moving their flocks between their winter grazing lands in the south and summer pastures in Abruzzo. The *trattura*, as it's called, still takes place, but in much reduced form by lorry and motorway. Further along the road is what must have been a welcome, if bizarre, landmark for generations of shepherds – an enormous stone cylinder resembling a modern water tower that is in fact the mausoleum of one of Saepinum's Roman citizens.

Back down the decumanus on the other side of the crossroads is the well-preserved **Basilica** that served as the main courthouse. Beyond is the most interesting part of the town – the octagonal macellum (marketplace), with its small stone stalls and central rain-collecting dish, and a series of houses fronted by workshops, with the small living quarters behind. This leads down to the best-preserved gate, the **Porta Boiano**, flanked by cylindrical towers and statues of prisoners celebrating some victory over barbarian invaders. Following the walls around, you reach the recently restored **theatre** and the second museum, which contains fragments of sculpture.

The Matese

One of Italy's least visited mountain ranges, scattered with high plains, forests and lakes, the **Matese** stretches between Molise and Campania. Wolves still wander its woods, and the peaks are home to eagles, falcons and hawks. The streams are well stocked with fish and the valleys full of the much-coveted *porcini* mushrooms.

Trains running between Isernia and Campobasso stop at **BOIANO**, a pleasant town overlooked by a densely wooded hill crowned with the remains of a castle. If you want to stay, the *Hotel Mary* at Via Barcellona 21 (☎0874.778.375; ②) is reasonably priced. There's also a good traditional **osteria**, the *Filomena* at Via Garibaldi 16 (closed Mon), featuring dishes such as *orrecchiette con broccoletti* and *spaghetti alla chitarra*. The town is a good starting-point for the hike (around 2hr) up **Monte Gallinola** – best done on a clear day when the views take in Italy's eastern and western coastlines. The road leads from beyond the central Piazza Pasquino up to a *rifugio*; from here a steep road, later a footpath, climbs through a forest to the Costa Alta, a mile-high pass whose views are good – though nothing compared to what you'll see when you get to the summit. The path then leads across ski-slopes to the base of Monte la Gallinola, where a track heads up to the top, from which you look down over the Lago del Matese, and, if weather permits, get the much-touted panoramic view.

You can, of course, see something of the Matese in more comfort, either taking a bus to the winter-sports centre of **CAMPITELLO MATESE** from either Boiano or Campobasso; or by staying over at the *Matese* (☎0874.780.378; ②) 9km from Campitello Matese at **SAN MASSIMO**, northwest of Boiano. From Boiano, take the road marked Castellone and San Massimo and, coming down from the mountains, take the left branch when the road forks.

Towards the coast: Larino and the Albanian villages

Halfway between Campobasso and Térmoli, **LARINO** is considerably more attractive than most Molise towns, its medieval centre clasped in the valley, relatively untouched by the concrete and pace of the modern industrial town that supports it. The highlight is its cathedral, but there are also some minor Roman relics in its small museum and a neglected amphitheatre in the modern town.

To the left of the **train station**, Via Gramsci leads down to old Larino. The main street widens out at Piazza Vittorio Emanuele, backing onto which is the **Palazzo Ducale**, whose **museum** (Mon–Fri 8am–2pm & 3.30pm –6.30pm; free) contains large Roman mosaics and a hoard of coins. On Via Gramsci, about halfway between the station and the *centro storico*, there's a garden that also has Roman ruins, including capitals and columns, and a sacrificial altar called the Ara Frentana. Close by is the **Duomo**, built in the early fourteenth century just after the town had been flattened by an earthquake and sacked by the Saracens, with an intricately carved Gothic portal.

The oldest part of the town starts beyond the duomo, but, appealing as the houses and steep alleys are, it is the glimpses of centuries-old streetlife that are more memorable – women making lace and preparing vegetables outside their houses, while the kids play at their feet and the men do absolutely nothing unless they're boozing in the bar.

If you take a bus from Piazza Vittorio Emanuele to the upper city, you'll jump a couple of centuries in five minutes. Modern Larino is a bustling place, built on the site of the original Samnite/Roman town. The large and overgrown **amphitheatre** off Via Viadotto Frentano, visible only from the street (Tues–Sat 9am–7pm, Sun 9am–1pm; free) gives some idea of the importance of early second-century BC Larinum, though apart from this the mosaic pavement off Viale Molise and a few fragments of walls, behind the Scuola Materna off Viale Giulio Cesare, are hardly sufficient clues to how Larino once looked. If you want to stay, the town's inexpensive **hotel** is in two parts: *Campitello* at Via Mazzini 9 and *Campitelli 2* (☎0874.822.666; ③) at Via Mazzini 16. Both are air-conditioned, are near the amphitheatre, and about a kilometre from the station.

The Albanian villages

URURI, 12km from Larino, and **PORTOCANNONE**, closer to the coast, are isolated villages, most easily reached by bus from Térmoli. Their isolation is such that 600 years after their ancestors emigrated from Albania, the locals still speak an Albanian-Italian dialect incomprehensible to outsiders. Portocannone's Romanesque church contains an icon of the Madonna of Constantinople, brought over by the original émigrés, and in Ururi, at the beginning of May, a **festival** is staged: a fierce and furious race through the village streets on gladiator-style carts, pulled by bulls and pushed by men on horseback with spiked poles. It's a ruthless business: the horses are fed beer before the race to excite them, and although the riders are supposed to push only the back of the carts, they are not averse to prodding the flanks of the bulls, who have already been given electric shocks to liven them up. The race itself is terrifying, but unforgettable, with bulls, carts and spikes hurtling past the frenzied crowds. There are almost inevitably injuries, and at least one person has been killed. If you want to go, the tourist offices at Campobasso and Térmoli will have the precise date.

The Molise coast

The brief stretch of the **Molise coast** is less developed than Abruzzo's. Its only real town, **TÉRMOLI**, a fishing port and quiet, undistinguished resort, makes for a relaxing place to spend a day. The beach is long and sandy and the old town, walled and guarded by a castle, has an interesting cathedral. It's also a departure point for ferries (June–Sept) to the Trémiti Islands (see p.888).

Térmoli is the place where Italian and Central European time is set – from the observatory inside the stark castle built above the beach in 1247 by Frederick II. Beyond the castle the road follows the old walls around the headland, holding what's left of the old town, focus of which is the **Duomo**. This is most notable for its Romanesque exterior, decorated all the way round with a series of blind arcades and windows – a feature introduced by Frederick II's Norman-influenced architects. Inside are the relics of St Timothy, best known for the letters he received from St Paul, who advised him on how to go about converting the Greeks. That he ended up in Térmoli is thanks to Térmolese Crusaders, who brought his bones back from Constantinople as a souvenir. The Térmolese hid them, fearing that if the Turks ever succeeded in penetrating the city they would seize and destroy them. In fact the relics were hidden so well they weren't discovered until 1945, during restoration work to repair bomb damage (the sacristan will show you them).

Térmoli's **tourist office** (Mon–Fri 8am–2pm & 5–6.30pm; Sat 8am–1pm; ☎0875.706.754) on Piazza M. Biga is difficult to find, tucked into a grotty car park beside the **bus station**. There's a second office open seasonally (daily 6pm–midnight) in Piazza Duomo in the old town, which promotes local crafts and Molise in general. The cheapest **hotel** is *Al Caminetto*, off the SS16 in Villaggio Airone, Via Europa 2 (☎0875.52.139; ②), served in high season by rare buses from Piazza Biga; on the same route are two **campsites**, *Cala Saracena* (☎0875.52.193; May–Sept) and *Azzurra* (☎0875.52.404). If you want to be closer to the train station, the *Corona*, opposite (☎0875.84.043; ⑤), is rather more expensive. A 200m walk from the station, *Rosary,* Lungomare Corso Colombo 24 (☎0875.84.944; ③) is smaller, old-fashioned, and handy for the old town and the beach. While here you should certainly have a meal in one of Térmoli's seafood **restaurants**. *Squalo Blu*, Via A. De Gasperi 49 (closed Mon), is worth a splurge – there's a splendid *menu degustazione* for L60,000/€30.99, though you can, of course, eat more modestly for less; and there are plenty of pizzerias and simple trattorias along Via Fratelli Brigada, the seafront and the parallel Via V. Emanuele III, if you want somewhere cheaper.

travel details

TRAINS

Avezzano to: Tagliacozzo (6 daily; 10min).

Campobasso to: Térmoli (14 daily; 1hr 45min).

L'Aquila to: Sulmona (13 daily; 1hr); Terni (9 daily; 2hr).

Isernia to: Campobasso (3–4 daily; 1hr).

Pescara to: Alanno (13 daily; 25min); Ancona (26 daily; 1hr 30min–2hr); Giulianova (40 daily; 20–30min); Pineto (22 daily; 15min); Rome (6 daily; 3hr 30min); Sulmona (21 daily; 1hr–1hr 30min); Térmoli (30 daily; 1hr); Vasto (21 daily; 55min).

Sulmona to: Alanno (13 daily; 45min); Avezzano (11 daily; 1hr 15min); Celano (9 daily; 1hr); Isernia (4 daily; 2hr 15min); Rivisondoli (6 daily; 45min); Roccaraso (6 daily; 50min).

Téramo to: Giulianova (12 daily; 25min).

Térmoli to: Foggia (30 daily; 1hr).

BUSES

Atri to: Pescara (12 daily; 1hr); Pineto (12 daily; 20min).

Avezzano to: Alba Fucens (10 daily; 20min); Pescasséroli (6 daily; 1hr 30min).

L'Aquila to: Bominaco (5 daily; 50min); Castel del Monte (5 daily; 1hr); Rome (16 daily; 1hr 40min); Sulmona (8 daily; 1hr 30min); Téramo (7 daily; 1hr 20min).

Chieti to: Rome (8 daily; 2hr 30min).

Isernia to Campobasso: (4–5 daily; 45min).

Pescara to: Áscoli Piceno (6 daily; 2hr 30min); Atri (12 daily; 1hr); Chieti (every 20min; 40min); L'Aquila (12 daily; 1hr 50min); Lanciano (8 daily; 1hr 45min); Loreto Apruntino (6 daily; 45min); Rome (8 daily; 3hr); Sulmona (2 daily; 1hr 30min).

San Vito to: Lanciano (9 daily; 10min).

Scanno to: Rome (skibus 1 daily; 1hr 50min; L60,000/€30.98 including ski-pass, call ☎0864. 747.774).

Sulmona to: Cocullo (1 daily; 45min); Pacentro (9 daily; 20min); Scanno (10 daily; 1hr).

Téramo to: Atri (3 daily; 1hr 40min).

FERRIES

Pescara to: Vis, Hvar, Brač and Spalato (1 weekly, Mon; 4hr, 5hr, 6hr 45min and 7hr 45min); Hvar, Korčula and Lastovo (1 weekly, Fri; 4hr 30min, 5hr 45min and 7hr).

Térmoli to: Trémiti islands (2 ferries and 3 hydrofoils daily; 45min –1hr 25min).

CHAPTER THIRTEEN

CAMPANIA

T
he region immediately south of Lazio, **Campania**, marks the real beginning of the Italian south or *mezzogiorno*. It's the part of the south too, perhaps inevitably, that most people see, as it's easily accessible from Rome and home to some of the area's (indeed Italy's) most notable features – Roman sites, spectacular stretches of coast, tiny islands. It's always been a sought-after region, first named by the Romans, who tagged it the *campania felix*, or "happy land" (to distinguish it from the rather dull *campagna* further north), and settled down here in villas and palatial estates that stretched right around the bay.

ACCOMMODATION PRICE CODES

Throughout this guide, prices per person are given for **youth hostels** and assume Hostelling International (HI) membership. **Hotel** accommodation is coded on a scale from ① to ⑨, reflecting the cost of the cheapest double room in each establishment in high season. The price bands to which these codes refer are as follows:

① Up to L60,000/€30.99
② L60,000–90,000/€30.99–46.48
③ L90,000–120,000/€46.48–61.98
④ L120,000–150,000/€61.98–77.47
⑤ L150,000–200,000/€77.47–103.29

⑥ L200,000–250,000/€103.29–129.11
⑦ L250,000–300,000/€129.11–154.94
⑧ L300,000–400,000/€154.94–206.58
⑨ over L400,000/€206.58

(See p.32 for a full explanation.)

You might, of course, find this hard to believe now, and anyone coming in search of the glories of the Bay of Naples is likely to be disappointed. Industry has eaten into the land around the city so as to render it almost unrecognizable, and even in the city the once-grand vistas are often cluttered by cranes and smoke-belching chimneys. Many people take one look and skate right out again, disappointed at such a grimy welcome.

But give the area time. **Naples** is the obvious focus, an utterly compelling city and one that dominates the region in every way. At just two-and-a-half hours by train from

REGIONAL FOOD AND WINE

The flavour of **Naples** dominates the whole of Campania. Nowhere else in Italy is street food so much part of the culture. Most importantly, perhaps, Naples is the true home of the **pizza**, rapidly baked in searingly hot wood-fired ovens and running with olive oil. There's no such thing as "Pizza Napoletana" here; in Naples, the crucial one is the *marinara* – not, as you might think, anything to do with seafood, but the basic Neapolitan pizza, topped with just tomato, garlic and a leaf or two of basil, *no* cheese. Street food also comprises fried pizzas topped with a smear of tomato and a square of mozzarella, and *calzone*, a stuffed fried pizza with ham and cheese or vegetables. *Friggiotore* sell other fried food: heavenly *krocche* (potato croquettes), *arancini* (rice balls) and *fiorilli* (courgette flowers in batter).

Naples is also the home of pasta and tomato sauce, made with fresh tomatoes and basil, and laced with garlic; it's a curious aspect of Neapolitan sauces that garlic, onion and parmesan are rarely combined. Aubergines and courgettes turn up endlessly in **pasta sauces**, as does the tomato-**mozzarella** pairing (the regions to the north and east of Naples are both big mozzarella-producing regions), the latter particularly good with *gnocchi*. **Seafood** is excellent all along the coast: clams combine with garlic and oil for superb *spaghetti alle vongole*; mussels are prepared as *zuppa di cozze* (with hot pepper sauce); fresh squid and octopus are ubiquitous. **Pastries** are good, too. Absolutely not to be missed is the *sfogliatella*, a flaky triangular pastry case stuffed with ricotta and candied peel, and the Easter cake, *pastiera*, made with ricotta and wheat berries. Further to the south, the marshy plains of the **Cilento** produce fabulous strawberries, artichokes and mozzarella cheese – much of the mozzarella that comes from here is made from pure buffalo milk, unmixed with cow's milk.

The volcanic slopes of Vesuvius are among the most ancient **wine-producing** areas in Italy: Ischia nowadays produces good **white** wine, notably Biancolella, while Cápri's is more everyday. Lacryma Christi, from the slopes of Mount Vesuvius and available in red and white varieties, can be reasonable. The best choices for a Campanian white, however, are Greco di Tufo and Fiano di Avellino; the **red** to go for is Taurasi, a rich wine made from the *aglianico* grape that can command high prices.

the capital, there's no excuse for not seeing at least this part of Campania, though of course you need three or four days to absorb the city properly, before embarking on the remarkable attractions surrounding it. The **Golfo di Napoli**, certainly, is dense enough in interest to occupy you for a good week: there are the ancient sites of **Pompeii** and **Herculaneum,** just half an hour away – Italy's best-preserved and most revealing Roman remains; there is the odd, volcanic **Campi Flegrei** area to the north of the city; and of course there are the islands, **Capri, Ischia** and **Prócida** – Capri swarms with visitors but is so beautiful that a day there is by no means time squandered, while Ischia, which is the largest island and absorbs tourists more readily, is a lively and attractive base from which you can explore the bay by ferry.

Inland Campania is, by contrast, a poor, unknown region for the most part, but the nearby towns of **Cápua** and **Caserta** repay visits and are easily seen on day-trips. Similarly **Benevento**, an old stop on the Roman route to Bríndisi, has its moments, though you might want to make this part of a wider trip through Campania's interior (or on to Puglia), bearing in mind that it's a difficult and not especially rewarding area to travel through. The area **south of Naples** has more immediate appeal – beach-bum territory on the whole, though certainly not to be avoided. **Sorrento**, at the far east end of the bay, is a major package-holiday destination but a cheery and likeable place for that; and the **Amalfi coast**, across the peninsula, is probably Europe's most dramatic stretch of coastline, harbouring some fantastically enticing – if crowded – beach resorts. Further south, the port of **Salerno** is an inviting place and gives access to the Hellenistic site of **Paestum** and the uncrowded coastline of the **Cilento** just beyond.

NAPLES

Whatever your real interest is in Campania, the chances are that you'll wind up in **NAPLES** – capital of the region and, indeed, of the whole Italian south. It's the kind of city laden with visitors' preconceptions, and it rarely disappoints: it is filthy, it is very large and overbearing, it is crime-infested, and it is most definitely like nowhere else in Italy – something the inhabitants will be keener than anyone to tell you. In all these things lies the city's charm. Perhaps the feeling that you're somewhere unique makes it possible to endure the noise and harassment, perhaps it's the feeling that in less than three hours you've travelled from an ordinary part of Europe to somewhere akin to an Arab bazaar. One thing, though, is certain: a couple of days here and you're likely to be as staunch a defender of the place as its most devoted inhabitants. Few cities on earth inspire such fierce loyalties.

In Naples, all the pride and resentment of the Italian south, all the historical differences between the two wildly disparate halves of Italy, are sharply brought into focus. This is the true heart of the *mezzogiorno*, a lawless, petulant city that has its own way of doing things. It's a city of extremes, fiercely Catholic, its streets punctuated by bright neon Madonnas cut into niches, its miraculous cults regulating the lives of the people much as they have always done. Football, too, is a religion here: frenzied celebrations went on for weeks after Napoli, with their hero Maradona to the fore, wrested the Italian championship from the despised north in 1987. Support is not as fanatical as it used to be, though the club is currently enjoying some success again in Italy's Serie A.

Music, also, has played a key part in the city's identity: there's long been a Naples style, bound up with the city's strange, harsh dialect – and, to some extent, the long-established presence of the US military: American jazz lent a flavour to Neapolitan traditional songs in the Fifties; and the Seventies saw one of Italy's most concentrated musical movements in the urban blues scene of Pino Daniele and the music around the radical Alfa Romeo factory out at Pomigliano. More recently, a distinctive style of

Neapolitan rap emerged from the *centri sociali* or "social centres" – groups of left-wing urban activists who challenge the establishment. The most famous exponents of this kind of rap are 99 Posse, who joined forces with Bisca to record *Guai a Chi ci Tocca* (*Trouble for Those who Touch Us*), which documented a brutal police attack on a peaceful student demonstration in Naples in 1994.

Some history

There was a settlement here, **Parthenope**, as early as the ninth century BC, but it was superseded by a colony formed by the Greek settlers at nearby Cumae, who established an outpost here in 750 BC, giving it the name Neapolis. It prospered during Greek and later Roman times, escaping the disasters that befell the cities around and eventually declaring itself independent in 763 – which it remained for close on 400 years, until the **Normans** took the city in 1139. The Normans weren't here for long: like the rest of this region, the city soon came under the rule of the Hohenstaufen dynasty, who stayed rather half-heartedly until 1269, when their last king, Conradin, was beheaded in what's now Piazza del Mercato, and the **Angevins** took over the city. With one exception – Robert the Wise, who was a gentle and enlightened ruler and made the city a great centre for the arts – the Angevin kings ruled badly, in the end losing Naples to Alfonso I of Aragon in 1422, thus establishing a **Spanish** connection for the city for the next 300 years. Following the War of the Spanish Succession, Naples was briefly ceded to the Austrians, before being taken, to general rejoicing, by **Charles of Bourbon** in 1734. Charles was a cultivated and judicious monarch, but his dissolute son Ferdinand presided over a shambolic period in the city's history, abandoning it to the republican French. Their "Parthenopean Republic" here was short-lived, and the British reinstalled the Bourbon monarch, carrying out vicious reprisals against the rebels. (The instigator of these reprisals was Admiral Nelson – fresh from his victory at the Battle of the Nile – who was famously having an affair with Lady Hamilton, the wife of the British ambassador to Naples. Under continuing Bourbon rule, or more accurately misrule, the city became one of the most populated in Europe, and one of the most iniquitous, setting a trend which still holds good today. For the rest of Europe, Naples was the requisite final stop on the **Grand Tour**, a position it enjoyed not so much for its proximity to the major classical sites as for the ready availability of sex. The city was for a long time the prostitution capital of the Continent, and its reputation drew people from far and wide, giving new meaning (in the days when syphilis was rife) to the phrase "see Naples and die".

More recently, Naples and its surrounding area have been the recipient of much of the money that has poured into the south under the **Cassa per il Mezzogiorno** scheme, and its industry is spreading, if not exactly booming. But the real power in the area is still in the hands of organized crime or the **Camorra**: much of the coastline west of the city – to Bagnoli – was built by Camorra money, and, although it's not at all publicized, little happens that matters here without the nod of the larger families. Not surprisingly, much government money has found its way into their hands too, with the result that there's been little real improvement in the living standards of the average Neapolitan: a very high percentage remain unemployed, and a disgraceful number still inhabit the typically Neapolitan one-room *bassi* – slums really, letting in no light and housing many in appallingly overcrowded conditions. In the late 1970s there was a cholera outbreak in part of the city, and until recently it was thought that the same thing could happen again. However, **Antonio Bassolino**, mayor of the city from 1993 until 2000, did much to promote Naples and its attractions, and the G7 summit, held here in June 1994, provided the impetus for a much-needed clean-up of the city centre. Bassolino was confident that supporting Naples' cultural strengths would boost local pride. Scores of neglected churches, museums and palaces were restored and now have extended opening times, particularly in the

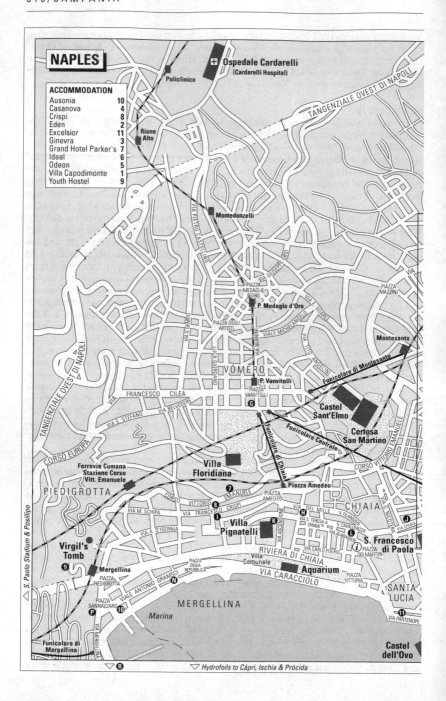

NAPLES

ACCOMMODATION

Ausonia	10
Casanova	4
Crispi	8
Eden	2
Excelsior	11
Ginevra	3
Grand Hotel Parker's	7
Ideal	6
Odeon	5
Villa Capodimonte	1
Youth Hostel	9

Ospedale Cardarelli
(Cardarelli Hospital)

Policlinico

TANGENZIALE OVEST DI NAPOLI

Rione Alto

Montedonzelli

VIA PIETRO CASTELLINO

VIA GIUSEPPE ORSI

PIAZZA MEDAGLIE D'ORO

P. Medaglie d'Oro

PIAZZA DEGLI ARTISTI

VIA SUAREZ

PIAZZA MAZZINI

VIA

VÓMERO

VIALE MICHELANGELO

VIA BERNINI

VIA TITO ANGELINI

Montesanto

Funicolare di Montesanto

VIA LUCA GIORDANO

P. Vanvitelli

PIAZZA VANVITELLI

G

Castel Sant'Elmo

VIA FRANCESCO CILEA

VIA BELVEDERE

VIA S. STEFANO

Certosa San Martino

Funicolare Centrale

CORSO EUROPA

Villa Floridiana

Funicolare di Chiaia

CORSO VITTORIO EMANUELE

PIEDIGROTTA

Ferrovia Cumana
Stazione Corso
Vitt. Emanuele

Piazza Amedeo

CORSO VITTORIO EMANUELE

7

PIAZZA AMEDEO

CHIAIA

VIA M. SCHIPA

8

VIA FRANCESCO CRISPI

I

DEL MILLE

V. FILANGIERI

H

VIA S. TERESA A CHIAIA

V. CAVALLERIZZA

J

VIA A. D'ISERNIA

Villa Pignatelli

K

VIA ASCENSIONE

V. ALABARDIERI

L

S. Francesco di Paola

i

PIAZZA DEI MARTIRI

Virgil's Tomb

9

VIA CARLO POERIO

RIVIERA DI CHIAIA

Mergellina

PIAZZA PIEDIGROTTA

Villa Comunale

Aquarium

PIAZZA VITTORIA

SANTA LUCIA

VIALE ANTONIO GRAMSCI

PIAZZA DELLA REPUBBLICA

N

VIA CARACCIOLO

PIAZZA SANNAZZARO

10

MERGELLINA

Marina

11

VIA PARTENOPE

Funicolare di Mergellina

P

VIA MERGELLINA

S. Paolo Stadium & Posillipo

R

Hydrofoils to Cápri, Ischia & Prócida

Castel dell'Ovo

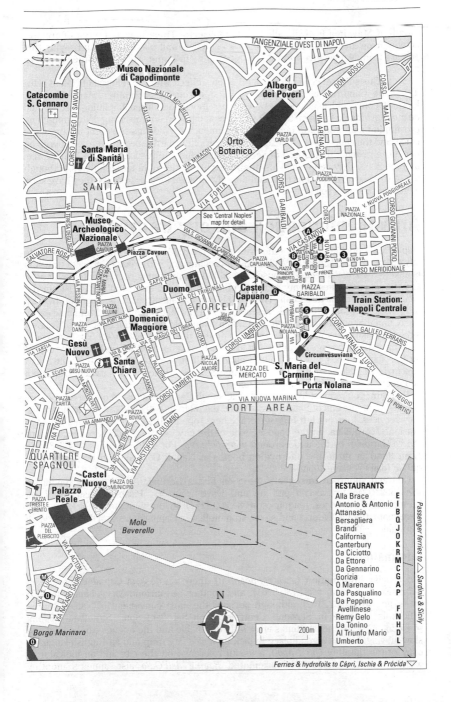

RESTAURANTS

Alla Brace	E
Antonio & Antonio	I
Attanasio	B
Bersagliera	Q
Brandi	J
California	O
Canterbury	K
Da Ciciotto	R
Da Ettore	M
Da Gennarino	C
Gorizia	G
O Marenaro	A
Da Pasqualino	P
Da Peppino	
Avellinese	F
Remy Gelo	N
Da Tonino	H
Al Triunfo Mario	D
Umberto	L

Passenger ferries to △ Sardinia & Sicily

Ferries & hydrofoils to Cápri, Ischia & Prócida ▽

month of May, in a festival called Maggio Aperto. There's been a burst of creative activity from local filmmakers, songwriters, artists and playwrights, and saying that you are from Naples gives you instant credibility in Rome, Milan and other northern cities.

Sadly, this surge of civic pride has received a check with the renewal of violent activity by the Camorra, in the person of "La Madrina" – godmother Maria Licciardi. Licciardi concocted an alliance between the Camorra families, maintaining that it would be more profitable for them to work together and pool resources from drug smuggling, prostitution and protection rackets. An argument over a drugs shipment fractured the truce, and the clans turned on each other. Four of Licciardi's people were murdered on her home ground, the suburb of Secondigliano, and she responded with brutal force: by June 2000, sixty people had lost their lives in a series of tit-for-tat killings. Although the "civilian" population has not been directly affected by these events, they have sorely dented the city's self-image.

Arrival, information and city transport

Naples' Capodochino **airport** (enquiries ☎081.789.6111) is a little way northwest of the city centre at Viale Umberto Maddalena. It is connected with Piazza Garibaldi (the stop is next to the *Hotel Cavour*) by buses #14 and #15 approximately every fifteen minutes, and the journey takes twenty to thirty minutes; buy tickets (L1500/€0.77) from the *tabacchi* in the departures hall. There is also an official airport bus, operated by CLP (enquiries ☎081.531.1706), which runs to Piazza Garibaldi and Piazza Municipio every thirty minutes between 6.30am and 11.30pm (6am–midnight in the opposite direction), although it isn't very much quicker and is double the price (L3000/€1.55); however, it does have the advantage of continuing to Molo Beverello, from where hydrofoils depart for the islands. Taxis, too, tend to take almost as long as buses to reach the centre, and cost up to L40,000/€20.66; if you do use one, make sure the meter is switched on when you get in (see opposite for more on taxis).

By train, you're most likely to arrive at Napoli Centrale, situated on the edge of the city centre at one end of Piazza Garibaldi, at the main hub of city (and suburban) transport services; there's a **left luggage** office here (open 24hr). Some trains also pull in to Stazione Mergellina, on the opposite side of the city centre, which is connected with Piazza Garibaldi by the underground *metropolitana*. For train enquiries ☎1478.88.088 (7am–9pm) or go to the information booths at Napoli Centrale and be prepared to queue (daily 7.30am–10pm).

City and suburban **buses** also stop on Piazza Garibaldi. SITA buses (enquiries ☎081.552.2176) to Salerno pull up and leave from Via Pisanelli, just off Piazza Municipio. CTP buses (enquiries ☎081.700.1111) to outlying towns like Avellino, Benevento, Cápua, Caserta and so on, stop on Piazza Capuana, just north of the Piazza Garibaldi.

Information

For **tourist information** (*www.ept.napoli.it*), there's a desk at Capodochino airport (Mon–Fri 9am–7pm; ☎081.780.5761), and another at Stazione Mergellina (Mon–Fri 9am–7pm; ☎081.761.2102), although perhaps the most convenient of Naples' tourist offices is the one in Stazione Centrale (Mon–Sat 9am–8pm, Sun 9am–1.30pm; ☎081.268.779), its opening times are a little unreliable and the queues can be long and slow-moving, but it's a good place to pick up a free city **map** and an English-language copy of the monthly *Qui Napoli*, a useful reference on the city and an indicator of **what's on**; the more youth-orientated *Pagine dell'Ozio* also appears monthly

(L2000/€1.03). In the centre, you'll find a tourist office on Piazza Gesù Nuovo (Mon–Sat 9am–8pm, Sun 9am–3pm; ☎081.551.2701), and another at Piazza dei Martiri 58 (Mon–Fri 8.30am–3.30pm; ☎081.405.311).

City transport

The only way to really **get around** Naples and stay sane is to **walk**. Driving can be a nightmare, and to negotiate the narrow streets, hectic squares and racetrack boulevards on a moped or scooter takes years of training. In any case, *not* to walk would mean you'd miss a lot – Naples is the kind of place best appreciated from street level.

For longer journeys – and Naples is a big, spread-out city – there are a number of alternatives, both for the city itself and the bay as a whole. **Public transport** comes under the care of Azienda Napoletana Mobilità (ANM). Its city **buses** are efficient, if crowded and slow, and are much the best way of making short hops across the city centre. The bus system is supplemented by the **metropolitana**, a small-scale underground network that crosses the city centre, stopping at about four stops between Piazza Garibaldi and Mergellina and runs eventually out to Pozzuoli and Solfatara in about half an hour; a new metro station at Piazza Dante will soon connect the city centre with Vómero and the hills. In addition, three **funiculars** scale the hill of the Vómero: one, the Funicolare di Chiaia, from Piazza Amedeo; another, the Funicolare Centrale, from the station at the bottom of Via Mattia, just off Via Toledo; and a third, the Funicolare di Montesanto, from the station on Piazza Montesanto. Another, the Funicolare di Mergellina, runs up the hill above Mergellina from Via Mergellina. **Tickets** for all ANM modes of transport cost a flat L1500/€0.77 and are available in advance from *tabacchi*, stations, or the transport booth on Piazza Garibaldi; an all-day ticket costs L4500/€2.32. Normal ANM tickets are valid for ninety minutes and allow any combination of bus or tram rides, plus unlimited trips within ninety minutes on an additional two means of transport – for example the metro, funicular (one trip only) or railway (one trip on the Ferrovia Cumana or the Circumflegrea lines – see overleaf).

If you need to take a **taxi** – and you should realize that they can be interminably slow – make sure the driver switches on the meter when you start (they often don't); fares start at L4000/€2.07 for the initial journey – minimum fare L6000/€3.10. Note that journeys to and from the airport incur an extra charge of L5000/€2.58; trips after 10pm or before 7am cost an extra L4000/€2.07; and those on public holidays an extra L3000/€1.55; all of which gives plenty of scope for confusion, and even resident Neapolitans are wary of the stunts taxi drivers pull to get a higher fare. There are taxi

---

USEFUL BUS ROUTES

#R2 Piazza Garibaldi–Corso Umberto–Piazza Bovio–Via de Pretis–Piazza Municipio–Corso Vittorio Emanuele–Via San Carlo–Piazza Trieste e Trento–Piazza Municipio–Via Medina–Via Sanfelice–Corso Umberto–Piazza Garibaldi

#R3 Piazza Trieste e Trento–Piazza Municipio–Riviera di Chiaia–Mergellina

#110 Piazza Garibaldi–Museo Archeologico–Museo di Capodimonte

#140 Via Santa Lucia–Mergellina–Posillipo Piazza Garibaldi–Pozzuoli

#152 Piazza Garibaldi–Piazza Municipio–Piazza Vittoria–Mergellina–Pozzuoli

#401 (night bus) Piazza Garibaldi–Riviera di Chiaia–Mergellina–Pozzuoli

#435 (night bus) Circular route from Stazione Centrale via Via Toledo and Piazza Trieste e Trento

For details on the frequency of the rail lines, see "Travel details", p.874.

ranks at the train station, on Piazza Dante and Piazza Trieste e Trento, or phone ☎081.556.4444 or 081.556.0202.

For solely **out-of-town trips** – around the bay in either direction – there are three more rail systems. The **Circumvesuviana** runs from its station on Corso Garibaldi right round the Bay of Naples about every thirty minutes, stopping everywhere, as far south as Sorrento, which it reaches in about an hour. The **Ferrovia Cumana** operates every ten minutes from its terminus station in Piazza Montesanto west to Pozzuoli and Báia. And the **Circumflegrea** line runs every twenty minutes, again from Piazza Montesanto, west to Cuma. Tickets are available at the stations, and are very reasonable.

Accommodation

Accommodation **prices** in Naples may come as a refreshing change after the north of Italy, but they're still not cheap, and the city being the kind of place it is you need to choose carefully from among the cheaper dives. A good many of these are conveniently situated around Piazza Garibaldi, spitting distance from the train station and not badly placed for the rest of town but rather insalubrious and noisy; others can be found in the lively and more atmospheric group on the far side of the *centro storico*, near the university. The station tourist office may point you somewhere good (it's certainly worth enquiring); if not, just follow the listings below – and don't, whatever you do, go with one of the touts outside the station. It's unlikely you'll be getting into anything dangerous but it *is* a possibility and in any case the room probably won't be up to much. Incidentally, if you can, try to **book in advance**, especially in high season, when the city does get crowded. Finally, it's worth knowing that the Naples youth hostel, and some of the hotels, offer cheap deals on ferry tickets to the islands, so ask around.

Hotels

Ausonia, Via Caracciolo 11 (☎ & fax 081.682.278). A two-star with a nautical theme, neatly placed in Mergellina, next to the stop for hydrofoils to the islands. Bus #R3 or #152. ⑤.

Bellini, Via San Paolo (☎ 081.456.996, fax 081.292.256, *hotelbellini@export.it*). This small, friendly hotel is a great budget option, ideally situated in the old town, just off Via dei Tribunali. ②.

Casanova, Via Venezia 2 (☎081.268.287, fax 081.269.792, *h.casanov@tin.it*). Station-area hotel run by an affable team. Pleasant, clean rooms, low prices, and a communal roof terrace. ③.

Crispi, Via Francesco Crispi 104 (☎ & fax 081.668.048, *lovenap@tin.it*). Well-established one-star hotel quite close to the Piazza Amedeo *metropolitana* stop. ⑤.

Eden, Corso Novara 9 (☎081.285.344, fax 081.285.690). One of the friendlier and more comfortable station-area choices, if rather noisy. Good rates for carriers of this book. ②.

Excelsior, Via Partenope 48 (☎081.764.0111, fax 081.764.9743, *www.excelsior.it*). An extremely plush upmarket hotel, wonderfully sited on the waterfront opposite the Castel dell'Ovo. ⑨.

Ginevra, Via Genova 116 (☎081.554.1757, fax 081.283.210, *hginevra@tin.it*). Welcoming place just to the right of the station that has fairly basic rooms looking onto a large plant-filled courtyard. Very handy if you're catching an early train. ②.

Grand Hotel Parker's, Corso Vittorio Emanuele (☎081.761.2474, fax 081.663.527, *www.thecharminghotels.com*). This upmarket and extremely comfortable hotel claims to be the oldest in Naples, and has hosted Oscar Wilde and Virgina Woolf, as well as King Vittorio Emanuale himself. With a high vantage-point over the city, the views from the dining room over the bay and east to Vesuvius are unparalleled. ⑧.

Ideal, Piazza Garibaldi 99 (☎081.269.237, fax 081.202.223, *www.export.it/ideal*). Large, newly renovated but basic hotel a few steps from the station. TV and phone in every room. Discounts for users of this book. ④.

Imperia, Piazza Luigi Miraglia 386 (☎ & fax 081.459.347). Friendly hotel with English-speaking management and a marvellous location in the heart of old Naples, a short walk from Piazza Dante.

Unspectacular but clean rooms, all with shared facilities; the only drawback is its location at the top of five arduous flights of stairs. ①.

Odeon, Via Silvio Spaventa (☎ & fax 081.285.656). Two-star hotel with decent doubles with TV, just two minutes from the station, off Piazza Garibaldi. ④.

Le Orchidee, Corso Umberto 7 (☎081.551.0721, fax 081.554.4390). A good central location, not far from the ferry port and just a short bus ride from Stazione Centrale. Large and elegantly furnished rooms, all with private bath. ④.

San Pietro, San Pietro ad Aram 18 (☎081.286.040, fax 081.553.5914). Friendly budget hotel off Corso Umberto on the right, just after you leave Piazza Garibaldi. A handy but slightly seedy location, and decent plain rooms. May have space when everything else is full. ③.

Villa Capodimonte, Via Moiariello 66 (☎081.459.000, fax 081.299.344). Ideally sited for seeing the Palazzo Reale di Capodimonte, this modern option is reasonably comfortable, and attractively located. It sits above the Sanità district (see p.830), which can be dangerous. ⑥.

Hostels and campsites

The cheapest place of all to stay in Naples is the official **youth hostel**, *Ostello Mergellina*, Salita della Grotta 23 (L29,000/€14.98, including breakfast; ☎081.761.2346, fax 081.761.2391). The hostel is in a nice location, if somewhat removed from the life of the city centre, and offers two-, four- and six-bedded rooms. The drawbacks are a midnight curfew and a three-day maximum stay during July and August. Take the *metropolitana* to Mergellina or the (slower) bus #R2 from Piazza Garibaldi to Piazza del Municipio; from here take the #R3 and get off at Piazza Sannazzaro from where the hostel is a five-minute walk to the north.

There are a number of **campsites** within a feasible distance of Naples. The closest is the *Vulcano Solfatara* site in Pozzuoli (see p.838) at Via Solfatara 161 (☎081.526.7413, fax 081.526.3482; April–Oct); take the *metropolitana* to Pozzuoli and walk ten minutes up the hill. When this is closed, you're probably best off going to one of the other sites around the bay – perhaps at Pompeii (see p.843), or, rather nicer, Sorrento (p.846), neither of which is more than an hour out from the city.

The City

Naples is a surprisingly large city, and a sprawling one, with a centre that has many different focuses. The area between Piazza Garibaldi and Via Toledo, roughly corresponding to the old Roman Neapolis (much of which is still unexcavated below the ground), makes up the old part of the city – the **centro storico** – the main streets still following the path of the old Roman roads. This is much the liveliest, most teeming part of town, an open-air kasbah of hawking, yelling humanity that makes up in energy what it lacks in grace. Buildings rise high on either side of the narrow, crowded streets, cobwebbed with washing; there's little light, not even much sense of the rest of the city outside – certainly not of the proximity of the sea.

But the insularity of the *centro storico* is deceptive, and in reality there's another, quite different side to Naples, one that's much more like the sunwashed Bay of Naples murals you've seen in cheap restaurants back home. **Via Toledo**, the main street of the city, edges the old centre from the **Palazzo Reale** up to the **Museo Nazionale Archeologico** and the heights of **Capodimonte**; to the left rises the **Vómero**, with its fancy housing and museums, and the smug neighbourhood of **Chiaia**, beyond which lies the long green boulevard of **Riviera de Chiaia**, stretching around to the districts of **Mergellina** and **Posillipo**: all neighbourhoods that exert quite a different kind of pull – that of an airy waterfront city, with views, seafood eaten *al fresco* and peace and quiet.

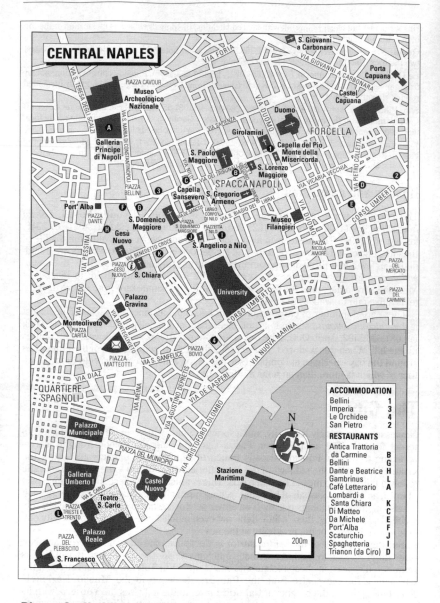

Piazza Garibaldi to Via Toledo: the centro storico

However you actually get to Naples, there's a good chance that the first place you'll see is **Piazza Garibaldi**, a long, wide square crisscrossed by traffic lanes that cuts into the city centre from the modern train station. It's the city's transport hub – most of the city buses leave from here, as do the *metropolitana* and Circumvesuviana lines – and one of its most hectic junctions; indeed it's Piazza Garibaldi, perhaps more so than any other part of the city, that puts people off Naples. The buildings aren't particularly distinguished, you're likely to be accosted on all sides by street hawkers selling a dubious array of pirate cassettes and cigarettes, underwear and sunglasses, and you need to have all your wits about you to successfully negotiate the traffic, which comes from all sides. Of late, the area around here has also become a centre for Naples' growing African community, with a number of African restaurants and Moroccan groceries.

Forcella and around

Piazza Garibaldi is good preparation for the noise, confusion, even menace that make up the rest of the city centre – especially in the streets around, which are sleazy and some of which are best avoided at night if you're alone. The other side of the square, the *centro storico* spreads west as far as Via Toledo – the tangled heart of Naples and its most characteristic quarter. Off the right corner of the square, the **Porta Capuana** is one of several relics from the Aragonese city walls, a sturdy defensive gate dating from 1490, delicately decorated on one side in Florentine Renaissance style. Across the road, the white and much renovated **Castel Capuano** was the residence of the Norman king William I, and later, under the Spanish, became a courthouse – which it still is.

Behind here, the **FORCELLA** quarter, which spreads down to Corso Umberto I, is the main city-centre stronghold of the Camorra and home to its most important families. It's also the city's open-air **market**, stamping-ground of yet more contraband tobacco dealers, cassette and sunglasses hawkers, and a quantity of food stalls – chickens sit in boxes waiting for the chop, after which they'll be plucked and cleaned up while you wait. As you might fast become aware, the trade in black-market ciggies is an old-established one and takes place throughout the city. It is, like just about every criminal activity in Naples, run by the Camorra, and it used to be a high earner for them. Nowadays, though, the big money is in drugs, and the people you'll see touting cigarettes are mainly little old ladies in need of some extra lira.

The two main streets of the *centro storico* are **Via dei Tribunali** and **Via San Biagio dei Librai** – two narrow streets, lined with old arcaded buildings, which lead due west on the path of the decumanus maximus and decumanus inferiore of Roman times, both charged with atmosphere throughout the day, a maelstrom of hurrying pedestrians, revving cars and buzzing, dodging scooters. Via dei Tribunali cuts up to **Via Duomo**, which ploughs straight through the old town to meet Corso Umberto I and Piazza Nicola Amore, laid out after a cholera epidemic in 1884 decimated this part of the city. On Via Tribunali, just before Via Duomo, you can't miss the **Capella del Pio Monte della Misericorda** (Mon–Sat 9am–2pm; free) – a beautiful octagonal chapel, with paintings by, among others, Caravaggio and Luca Giordano. The chapel was founded in the sixteenth century as a charity to raise money to ransom Christians held in the so-called Barbary States.

The Duomo

The **Duomo**, sharp on the right and tucked away unassumingly from the main street, is a Gothic building from the early thirteenth century (though with a late nineteenth-century neo-Gothic facade) dedicated to the patron saint of the city, San Gennaro. The church – and saint – are key reference points for Neapolitans: San Gennaro was martyred at Pozzuoli, just outside Naples, in 305 AD under the purges of Diocletian. Tradition has it that, when his body was transferred here, two phials of his blood liquefied in the bishop's hands, since which time the "miracle" has continued to repeat itself no less than three times a year – on the first Saturday in May (when a procession leads from the church of Santa Chiara to the cathedral) and on September 19 and

THE MIRACLE OF SAN GENNARO

If you're in Naples at the right time it's possible to attend the service to witness the **liquefaction of San Gennaro's blood**, but you must be sure to arrive at the cathedral early. The Mass starts at 9am, and queues begin to form two hours before that; arrive much after 7am and there's a chance you won't get in. Once the line of Carabinieri have opened up the church everyone will make a dash for the front; for a good view of the proceedings you'll have to join them – and pushing and shoving is, incidentally, very much part of the procedure. The atmosphere in the church throughout the service is a boisterous one. The preliminary Mass goes on for some time, the chancel of the church ringed by armed policemen and flanked by a determined press and photographic corps, until a procession leads out of the saint's chapel holding the (still solid) phial of the blood aloft, to much applause and neck-craning, and cries of "Viva San Gennaro". After ten minutes or so of emotional imprecations the reliquary is taken down from its holder and inspected – at which point, hopefully, it is declared to tumultuous applause and cheering that the saint's blood is indeed now liquid, and the phial is shaken to prove the point. Afterwards the atmosphere is a festive one, stallholders setting up outside the church and the devout queueing up to kiss the phial containing the liquefied blood – a process that goes on for a week.

December 16. There is still much superstition surrounding this event: San Gennaro is seen as the saviour and protector of Naples, and if the blood refuses to liquefy – which luckily is rare – disaster is supposed to befall the city, and many still wait with bated breath to see if the miracle has occurred. Interestingly, one of the few times this century Gennaro's blood hasn't turned was in 1944, an event followed by Vesuvius's last eruption. The last times were in 1980, the year of the earthquake, and in 1988, the day after which Naples lost an important football match to their rivals, Milan.

The miraculous liquefaction takes place during a special Mass in full view of the congregation – a service it's perfectly possible to attend (see box above), though the church authorities have yet to allow any close scientific examination of the blood or the "miraculous" process. Whatever the truth of the miracle, there's no question it's still a significant event in the Neapolitan calendar, and one of the more bizarre of the city's institutions.

The first chapel on the right as you walk into the cathedral is dedicated to San Gennaro and holds the precious phials of the saint's blood and his skull in a silver bust-reliquary from 1305. On the other side of the church, the basilica of **Santa Restituta** is almost a church in its own right, officially the oldest structure in Naples, erected by Constantine in 324 and supported by columns that were taken from a temple to Apollo on this site. The **Baptistry**, too (Mon–Fri 9am–noon & 4.30–7pm; L5000/€2.58) contains relics from very early Christian times, including a late fifth-century structure preserving fragments of contemporary mosaics and a font believed to have been taken from a temple to Dionysus. Downstairs, the **crypt** (same ticket as for the baptistry) of San Gennaro is one of the finest examples of Renaissance art in Naples, founded by Cardinal Carafa and holding the tombs of both San Gennaro and Pope Innocent IV.

Spaccanapoli

Across Via Duomo, Via Tribunali continues on past **Piazza Girolamini**, on which a plaque marks the house where, in 1668, Giambattista Vico was born – now the home of a well-known Camorra family. Vico was a late-Renaissance Neapolitan philosopher who advanced theories of cyclical history that were far ahead of their time and still echo through twentieth-century thinking: James Joyce's *Finnegans Wake* was based on his writings. Vico lived all his life in this district and was buried in the church of **Girolamini** (entrance on Via Duomo). Adjacent, you can look in on the recently

restored and impressive **Chiostro dei Girolamini**, built around a courtyard containing orange and medlar trees, and the **Quadreria dei Girolamini** (Mon–Sat
9.30am–1pm; free), a gallery containing paintings by Ribera, Solimena and Dürer,
among many others.

Further down Via Tribunali, on the left, the church of **San Lorenzo Maggiore** is a
light, spacious Gothic church, unspoiled by later additions and with a soaring Gothic
ambulatory at its apse – unusual in Italy, even more so in Naples, where garishly
embellished church interiors are the order of the day. It's a mainly thirteenth- and fourteenth-century building, though with a much later facade, built during the reign of the
Angevin king Robert the Wise on the site of a Roman basilica – remains of which are
in the cloisters. In a way it was at the centre of the golden age that Naples enjoyed
under Robert, the focus of its cultural activity. Petrarch stayed for a while in the adjacent convent, and Boccaccio is said to have met the model for his Fiammetta, believed
to be Robert's daughter, during Mass here in 1334.

Excavations beneath the church (April–Oct Mon–Sat 9am–1pm & 4–6pm, Sun
9am–1.30pm; Nov–March Mon–Sat 9am–1pm & 3.30–5.30pm, Sun 9am–1.30pm;
L5000/€2.58) have revealed what was once the Roman forum, and before that, the
Greek agora. You can walk along the old Roman pavement, passing a barrel-vaulted
bakery, a laundry and an area of sloping stone banquettes that were warmed underneath by a fire, where it is thought that people reclined and debated the great issues of
the day. What was likely to have been the town's treasury shows a remarkable resemblance to a contemporary bank, with visitors having to negotiate a security-conscious
double doorway before reaching the main area for business. The great tufa foundations
of the Roman forum were built over the earlier Greek agora; a scale model shows how
the latter was laid out, with the circular tholos, where some goods were sold, at its centre. It's a rare chance to see exactly how the layers of the city were built up over the
centuries, and to get some idea of how Naples must have looked back in the fifth
century BC.

You're now in the city's busiest and most architecturally rich quarter, the so-called
Spaccanapoli or "split-Naples" that's the real heart of the old city. Cut down to its other
main axis, **Via San Biagio dei Librai**, by way of **Via San Gregorio Armeno**, one of
the old city's most picturesque streets, lined with places specializing in the making of
presepi or Christmas cribs (see box below) – the last courtyard on the left is a good
place to see one of them in action if you're here at the right time of year.

Almost opposite is the arched portal of the church of **San Gregorio Armeno**, a sumptuous Baroque edifice with frescoes by the late seventeenth-century Neapolitan artist
Luca Giordano, not to mention two stupendously ornate gilded organs, one on each side
of the nave. Up above the south aisle, you'll notice a series of grilles through which the
Benedictine nuns of the **Chiostro di San Gregorio Armeno** next door would view the
services. You can visit the courtyard of the convent (entrance up the street and on the
left; daily 9.30–11.30am; free), which is a wonderfully peaceful haven from the noise outside, planted with limes and busy with nuns quietly going about their duties.

PRESEPI

Presepi (Christmas cribs) are a Neapolitan tradition kept up to this day, but the workshops along Via San Gregorio Armeno start turning them out well before Christmas.
The often-inventive creations now incorporate modern figures into the huge crib scenes,
which can contain moving water features, illuminated pizza ovens and tons of moss and
bark. "Goodies" such as Bassolino are distinguished from such "baddies" as Umberto
Bossi of the Lega Nord by their halos, while dear, departed saintly figures like Mother
Theresa, Princess Diana and Versace are also commemorated.

There's more work by Giordano back on Via Duomo, at no. 288 in the **Museo Filangieri**, which is currently closed indefinitely for restoration; contact the tourist office for updated information. Housed in the knobbly fifteenth-century Palazzo Cuomo and made up of the collection of Prince Gaetano Filangieri, it was reassembled after the original collection was burned by the Nazis in 1943. Giordano was easily the most prolific of all the Neapolitan painters, known as *Luca fa presto* or "Luca paint quickly", apparently from his father's habit of encouraging his astonishing output. He was the pupil of another well-known Neapolitan painter, Jose Ribera (otherwise known as "Il Spagnoletto"), whose work is also here, alongside the canvases of his contemporary and similar stylist Mattia Preti and an assortment of porcelain, old manuscripts and other bits and pieces.

More compellingly, west down Via San Biagio leads to the **Largo di Corpo di Nilo**, where a Roman statue of a reclining old man is a representation of the Nile, sculpted in Nero's time, and has a habit, it's claimed, of whispering to women as they walk by. The church nearby, **Sant'Angelo a Nilo**, has sculptures by Michelozzo and Donatello, the first Renaissance work to be seen in Naples. Further on, **Piazza San Domenico Maggiore** is marked by the **Guglia di San Domenico** – one of the whimsical Baroque obelisks that were originally put up after times of plague or disease, built in 1737. The **church** of the same name flanks the north side of the square, an originally – though much messed about – Gothic building from 1289, one of whose chapels holds a miraculous painting of the *Crucifixion* which is said to have spoken to St Thomas Aquinas during his time at the adjacent monastery.

North of here, Via de Sanctis leads off right to one of the city's odder monuments, the **Capella Sansevero** (Mon & Wed–Sat 10am–8pm, Sun 10am–1.30pm; L8000/€4.13), the tomb-chapel of the di Sangro family, decorated by the sculptor Guiseppe Sammartino in the mid-eighteenth century. The decoration, at least, is extraordinary, the centrepiece a carving of a dead Christ, laid out flat and covered with a veil of stark and remarkable realism, not least because it was carved out of a single piece of marble. Even more accomplished is the veiled figure of *Modesty* on the left, and, on the right, its twin *Disillusionment*, in the form of a woeful figure struggling with the marble netting of his own disenchantment. Look, too, at the effusive *Deposition* on the high altar and the memorial above the doorway, which shows one Cecco di Sangro climbing out of his tomb, sword in hand. You might also want to take a look downstairs. The man responsible for the chapel, Prince Raimondo, was a well-known eighteenth-century alchemist, and down here are the results of some of his experiments: two bodies under glass, their capillaries and most of their organs preserved by a mysterious liquid developed by the prince – who, incidentally, was excommunicated by the pope for such practices. Even now they make for gruesome sights – not for the queasy.

Continuing west, Via San Biagio becomes Via San Benedetto Croce, named after the twentieth-century philosopher who spent much of his life in this neighbourhood, living in the palace at no. 12. A little way down, the street broadens out at Piazza Gesù Nuovo, centring on another ornate **Guglia**, much larger than the San Domenico one and dating from 1750. On the right, the **Gesù Nuovo** church is most notable for its lava-stone facade, originally part of a fifteenth-century palace which stood here, prickled with pyramids that give it an impregnable, prison-like air. The inside is as gaudy as you might expect, in part decorated by the Neapolitan-Spanish painter Ribera.

Facing the Gesù church, the church of **Santa Chiara** is quite different, a Provençal-Gothic structure built in 1328 that was completely gutted during the last war and rebuilt with a bare Gothic austerity that's pleasing after the excesses opposite. There's not very much to see inside, only the tombs of the Angevin monarchs in the last chapel on the right, including Robert the Wise at the altar, showing the king in a monk's habit. But the attached convent, established by Robert's wife, Sancia, has a **cloister** (entrance to the left of the church: daily 8.30am–12.30pm & 4–6.30pm) that is truly one of the gems of the city, a shady haven lushly planted and furnished with benches and low walls covered with colourful majolica tiles depicting bucolic scenes of life outside.

Corso Umberto I, Piazza Municipio and the Palazzo Reale

Off the far left corner of Piazza Garibaldi, **Via Garibaldi** runs down to the sea, past the main Circumvesuviana terminal and, on the right, the **Porta Nolana**, a solid-looking Aragonese gateway that signals the entrance to Naples' main fish market – a grouping of streets lined with a wonderful array of stalls piled high with wriggling displays of fish and seafood. Behind, towards the water, the church of **Santa Maria del Carmine** dates back to the thirteenth century and is traditionally the church of the poor in Naples, particularly fishermen and mariners – the main port area is close by. Axel Munthe, the Swedish writer and resident of Cápri, used to sleep here after tending to victims of the 1884 cholera outbreak.

Just west, the still war-damaged **Piazza del Mercato** was for centuries home to the city's scaffold, and is a bleak, dusty square even now. There's little to detain you in this part of town, and you may as well cut back up to **Corso Umberto I**, which spears through the old part of the city, a long straight journey from the seedy gatherings of prostitutes and kerb-crawlers at its Piazza Garibaldi end, past many of the city's more mainstream shops, to the symmetrical **Piazza Bovio** and its elegant seventeenth-century Fontana del Nettuno.

From Piazza Bovio it's a short walk down to **Piazza del Municipio**, a busy traffic junction that stretches from the ferry terminal on the water up to the Palazzo Municipale at the top, dominated by the brooding hulk of the **Castel Nuovo** opposite – the "Maschio Angioino" – erected in 1282 by the Angevins and later converted as the royal residence of the Aragon monarchs. The entrance incorporates a triumphal arch from 1454 that commemorates the taking of the city by Alfonso I, the first Aragon ruler, and shows details of his triumph topped by a rousing statue of St Michael. These days the castle is mainly taken up by the offices of the Naples and Campania councils, but part is given over to the **Museo Civico** (Mon–Sat 9am–7pm; L10,000/€5.16), comprising a rather dull collection of fourteenth- and fifteenth-century frescoes and sculpture in the chapel and an array of silver and bronze objects.

Just beyond the castle, on the left, the **Teatro San Carlo** is an oddly unimpressive building from the outside; inside, however, you can see why this theatre was the envy of Europe when it opened in 1737 in time for Charles of Bourbon's birthday, for whom it was built. Destroyed by fire in 1816 and rebuilt, it's still the largest opera house in Italy and one of the most distinguished in the world (guided tours Sat & Sun 2–4pm; L5000/€2.58; tickets ☎081.797.2111). Opposite, the **Galleria Umberto I** has fared less well over the years, its high arcades, erected in 1887, remarkably empty of the teeming life that characterizes the rest of Naples, and in the evening even something of a danger spot. Its rather downbeat collection of shops can't compete with those of, say, Milan's Galleria, built ten years earlier – though you'll still pay way over the odds in its cafés.

Come out of the Galleria and you're on **Piazza Trieste e Trento**, more a round-about than a piazza, whose life you can watch while sipping a pricey drink on the terrace of the sleek **Caffè Gambrinus**. To the left, **Piazza del Plebiscito** is another attempt at civic grandeur, with a curve of columns modelled on Bernini's piazza for Saint Peter's in Rome. Until the early 1990s it was used as a car park and bus stop, but it has since been cleaned up and has become a favourite place to stroll of an evening; art features here have included a monumental pyramid of salt by Mimmo Paladino, a mountain of ancient furniture, armoires and kitchen tables by Jannis Kounellis and low-key *son et lumière* events. The church of **San Francesco di Paola** is floodlit at night, when it is at its most impressive. At other times its attempts at classical majesty (it's a copy of the Pantheon in Rome) only really work once you're standing under its enormous dome.

Opposite, the **Palazzo Reale** (Mon, Tues, Thurs, Fri & Sun 9am–8pm, Sat 9am–11pm; L8000/€4.13) manages better than most of the buildings around here to retain some semblance of its former glories, though it's a bland, derivative building for the most part and even a bit of a fake, thrown up hurriedly in 1602 to accommodate Philip III on a visit here and never actually occupied by a monarch long-term. Indeed it's more of a monument to monarchies than monarchs, with the various dynasties that ruled Naples by proxy for so long represented in the niches of the facade, from Roger the Norman to Vittorio Emanuele II, taking in among others Alfonso I and a slightly comic Murat on the way. Upstairs, the palace's first-floor rooms are decorated with fine Baroque excesses of gilded furniture, trompe l'oeil ceilings, great overbearing tapestries and lots and lots of undistinguished seventeenth- and eighteenth-century paintings. Best bits are the chapel, on the far side of the central square (you may have to ask someone to open this for you), with its finely worked altarpiece; the little theatre – the first room on the right – which is refreshingly restrained after the rest of the palace; and the terrace, which gives good views over the port and the forbidding Castel Nuovo. Look also at the original bronze doors of the palace at the bottom of the dwarfing main staircase, cast in 1468 and showing scenes from Ferdinand of Aragon's struggle against the local barons. The cannonball wedged in the bottom left-hand panel dates from a naval battle between the French and the Genoese that took place while the former were pillaging the doors from the palace.

Just south of Piazza del Plebiscito, Via Santa Lucia curves around towards the sea, the main artery of the **SANTA LUCIA** district – for years the city's most famed and characteristic neighbourhood, site of a lively fish market and source of most of the *O Sole Mio*-type clichés about Naples you've ever heard. It's a much less neighbourly place now, home to most of the city's poshest hotels on the streets around and along the seafront Via Partenope, though one or two decent restaurants make it a better-than-average place to come and eat. Down on the waterfront, seafood restaurants cluster around the grey mass of the **Castel dell'Ovo** or "egg-castle" – named for the whimsical legend that it was built over an egg placed here by Virgil in Roman times: it is believed that if the egg breaks, Naples will fall. Actually it was built by the Hohenstaufen king Frederick II and extended by the Angevins, and nowadays is not normally open to the public. But you can walk over the short causeway that connects its small island to the mainland and eat at one of the surrounding restaurants – which make an atmospheric if not always culinarily memorable place to spend the evening; *Bersagliera* on the landward side has great seafood and is the best option (see p.833).

From Piazza Trieste e Trento to Capodimonte

Piazza Trieste e Trento marks the beginning of the city's main shopping street, **Via Toledo** – or, to give it its official name, Via Roma – which leads north in a dead straight line, climbing the hill up to the national archeological museum and separating two very different parts of Naples. To its right, across as far as Piazza Gesù Nuovo, the streets and buildings are modern and spacious, centring on the unmistakeable mass of the Fascist-era central **Post Office**. The streets to the left, on the other hand, scaling the footslopes of the Vómero, are some of the city's most narrow and crowded, a grid of alleys that was laid out to house Spanish troops during the seventeenth century and is hence known now as the **Quartiere Spagnoli**. It's an enticing area, at least for visitors, in that it's what you expect to find when you come to Naples, with the buildings so close together as to barely admit any sunlight. But it's as poor a part of Italy as you'll find, home to the notorious Neapolitan *bassi* – one-room windowless dwellings that open directly onto the street – and as such a national disgrace.

Further up Via Toledo, just north of Piazza Carità on the edge of the old part of the city, the church of **Monteoliveto** was rebuilt after a sound wartime bombing, but it holds some of the city's finest Renaissance art, including a sacristy frescoed by Vasari, a rather startling almost life-size pietà of eight figures by Guido Mazzoni (the faces are said to be portraits) and two sculptural works by Antonio Rossellino – a nativity scene and the tomb of Mary of Aragon, daughter of Ferdinand I.

Continuing on up the hill, **Piazza Dante** is another Neapolitan square that looks as if it has seen better days, designed by Luigi Vanvitelli during the eighteenth century and cutting an elegant semicircle off to the right of the main road that focuses on a statue of the poet. There are a couple of restaurants here, and it's a turnaround point for buses, but otherwise – unless you want to take a right through the seventeenth-century **Port'Alba** into Piazza Bellini and the old part of the city – you may as well push on up the street to the archeological museum, housed in a grandiose, late-sixteenth-century army barracks on the corner of Piazza Cavour.

The Museo Archeologico Nazionale

Naples isn't really a city of museums – there's more on the streets that's worth observing on the whole, and most displays of interest are kept *in situ* in churches, palaces and the like. However, the **Museo Archeologico Nazionale** (Mon & Wed–Sun 9am–7.30pm; L12,000/€6.20; reachable direct by bus #110 from Piazza Garibaldi) is an exception, home to the Farnese collection of antiquities from Lazio and Campania and the best of the finds from the nearby Roman sites of Pompeii and Herculaneum. Currently the museum is undergoing a comprehensive restoration, and there's a good chance you won't be able to see it all. However, the most impressive sections are usually open, and you'd be mad to miss them, especially as they illuminate and enhance visits to Pompeii and Herculaneum.

The ground floor of the museum concentrates on sculpture from the **Farnese collection**, displayed at its best in the mighty Great Hall, which holds imperial-era figures like the *Farnese Bull* and *Farnese Hercules* from the Baths of Caracalla in Rome – the former the largest piece of classical sculpture ever found. The mezzanine floor holds the museum's collection of **mosaics** – remarkably preserved works all, giving a superb insight into ordinary Roman customs, beliefs and humour. All are worth looking at – images of fish, crustacea, wildlife on the banks of the Nile, a cheeky cat and quail with still-life beneath, masks and simple abstract decoration. But some highlights to look out for include a realistic *Battle Scene* (no. 10020), the *Three Musicians with Dwarf* (no. 9985), an urbane meeting of the *Platonic Academy* (no. 124545), and a marvellously captured scene from a comedy *The Consultation of the Fattucchiera* (no. 9987), with a soothsayer giving a dour and doomy prediction.

At the far end of the mezzanine is the fascinating **Gabinetto Segreto** (Secret Room), which reopened in 2000 after nearly thirty years. The room contains erotic material taken from the brothels, baths, houses and taverns of Pompeii and Herculaneum – to see the display, which lurks tantalizingly behind a partition, you need to obtain a timed ticket (no extra charge) from the entrance hall. The objects in the collection weren't always segregated in this way; it was the shocked Duke of Calabria who, having taken his wife and daughter to view the museum, decided that the offending objects should be removed from the gaze of ladies. From then until the time of Garibaldi they were kept under lock and key, disappearing again from public view in the twentieth century for long periods. The artefacts, from languidly sensual wall-paintings to preposterously phallic lamps, bear testimony to Roman licentiousness, although the phallus was often used as a kind of lucky charm rather than as a sexual symbol – cheerfully hung outside taverns and bakeries to ward off the evil eye. Free English-language tours of the Gabinetto are admirably serious and smut-free, though it is hard to repress a giggle at the sculpture of a man whose toga is failing to mask an erection, or at the graphic but elegantly executed marble of Pan "seducing" a goat.

Upstairs through the Salone della Meridiana, which holds a sparse but fine assortment of Roman figures (notably a wonderfully strained *Atlas* and some demure female figures – Roman replicas of Greek originals), a series of rooms holds the **Campanian wall paintings**, lifted from the villas of Pompeii and Herculaneum, and rich in colour and invention. There are plenty here, and it's worth devoting some time to this section, which includes works from the Sacrarium – part of Pompeii's Egyptian temple of Isis, the most celebrated mystery cult of antiquity – the discovery of which gave a major boost to Egyptomania at the end of the eighteenth century. In the next series of rooms, some of the smallest and most easily missed works are among the most exquisite. Among those to look out for are a paternal *Achilles and Chirone* (no. 9109); the *Sacrifice of Iphiginia* (no. 9112) in the next room, one of the best preserved of all the murals; the dignified *Dido abandoned by Aeneas and the Personification of Africa* (no. 8998); and the series of frescoes telling the story of the Trojan horse. Look out too for the group of four small pictures, the best of which is a depiction of a woman gathering flowers entitled *Allegoria della Primavera* – a fluid, impressionistic piece of work capturing both the gentleness of spring and the graceful beauty of the woman.

Beyond the murals are the actual **finds from the Campanian cities** – everyday items like glass, silver, ceramics, charred pieces of rope, even foodstuffs (petrified cakes, figs, fruit and nuts), together with a model layout of Pompeii in cork. On the other side of the first floor, there are finds from one particular house, the **Villa dei Papiri** in Herculaneum – sculptures in bronze mainly. The *Hermes at Rest* in the centre of the second room is perhaps the most arresting item, rapt with exhaustion, but around are other adept statues – of athletes, suffused with movement, a languid *Resting Satyr*, the convincingly woozy *Drunken Silenus*, and, in the final room, portrait busts of soldiers and various local big cheeses.

Piazza Cavour and Sanità

To the left of the archeological museum as you come out, **Piazza Cavour** is a busy traffic junction and bus stop. A short walk east, at 223 Via Foria, lies the **Orto Botanico** (Mon–Fri 9am–2pm, by appointment only; ☎081.449.759), founded in 1807 by Joseph Bonaparte and a detour worth making if you're interested in such things. Perhaps more intriguing is the enormously long facade, actually only one fifth of the originally conceived size, of the **Albergo dei Poveri** alongside, a workhouse built in 1751 that has been empty for years and forms a vast, oddly derelict landmark along the top side of **Piazza Carlo III**.

North of Piazza Cavour, you can stroll up through the old quarter of **SANITÀ**, following the tangle of streets for ten minutes or so up to the church of **Santa Maria della Sanità** on the piazza of the same name, a Dominican church from the early seventeenth century whose design was based loosely on Bramante's for Saint Peter's in Rome. There are paintings by Giordano and other Neapolitan artists inside, if you can get in, although perhaps of more interest are the **Catacombe di San Gaudioso** (guided tours in the mornings, afternoons by appointment only ☎081.544.1305; L5000/€2.58) underneath, an intriguing early-Christian burial ground full of skeletons and the fifth-century tomb of St Gaudioso, who was known, apparently, as the "African", due to the fact that he was a fifth-century bishop from North Africa.

Lifts link Sanità with Corso Amedeo up above, the main road up to Capodimonte. Walk under the bridge through to the rest of the teeming district, home to a couple of the city centre's larger hospitals and, close by one of them, another burial place, the **Catacombe di San Gennaro** (daily tours at 9.30am, 10.15am, 11am & 11.45am; L5000/€2.58), behind the huge Madre del Buon Consiglio church. These were discovered only recently, next to the originally eighth-century church of San Gennaro in

ASK IMAGES, TRIP

Posillipo, Naples, looking over Mergellina to Vesuvius

PETER WILSON

Porto di Levante, Vulcano

Convento dei Cappuccini, Palermo   Taormina

Temple of Neptune, Paestum

Tripe stall in Quartieri Spagnoli, Naples

Cloisters, church of Santa Chiara, Naples

NEIL SETCHFIELD

Palau, Sardinia

ROBERT HARDING

PETER WILSON

Festa di Sant'Efisio, Sardinia

Faraglioni, off Capri

Moenia, and hold early Christian frescoes and mosaics, newly restored and amazingly bright. Continuing the death theme is the **Cimitero della Fontanelle** (open last Sat of the month; free), made up of caverns containing the bones and skulls of – so it's said – plague victims, some of which have been "adopted" by visitors over the years in a weird kind of ex-voto cult. The cemetery is a good ten-minute walk from the bridge over Corso Amedeo, following Via della Sanità at first, then Via Fontanelle to its end; or bus #105 goes right there from Via Duomo.

The Palazzo Reale di Capodimonte

At the top of the hill, accessible by bus #110 from Piazza Garibaldi or #24 from Piazza Dante, the **Palazzo Reale di Capodimonte** – and its beautiful **park** (9am–1hr before dusk; free) – was the royal residence of the Bourbon King Charles III, built in 1738 and now housing the picture gallery of the Naples museum, the **Museo Nazionale di Capodimonte** (Tues–Sun 8.30am–7.30pm; L14,000/€7.23). The royal apartments, on the first floor, are smaller and more downbeat than those at Caserta (see p.859) but in many ways more enjoyable, not least because you can actually walk through the rooms freely. That said, you'll need a keen interest in the Bourbon dynasty to want to linger: high spots are the ballroom, lined with portraits of various Bourbon monarchs and other European despots, and a number of rooms of porcelain, some painted with local scenes and one in particular a sticky confection of Chinese scenes, monkeys and fruit and flowers from the Capodimonte factory here.

The museum is organized, not chronologically, but by collections: between them the Farnese and Bourbon rulers amassed a superb collection of Renaissance paintings and Flemish works, including a couple of Brueghels – *The Misanthrope* and *The Blind* – and two triptychs by Joos van Cleve. There are also canvases by Perugino and Pinturicchio, an elegant *Madonna and Child with Angels* by Botticelli and Lippi's soft, sensitive *Annunciation*. Later works include many Titians, with a number of paintings of the shrewd Farnese Pope Paul III in various states of ageing and the lascivious *Danae*; Raphael's austere portrait of *Leo X* and a worldly *Clement VII* by Sebastiano del Piombo; and Bellini's impressively coloured and composed *Transfiguration*.

Chiaia, Villa Communale, Mergellina and Posillipo

Via Chiaia leads west from Piazza Trieste e Trento into a quite different Naples from the congested *vicoli* of the *centro storico* or Quartiere Spagnoli, lined with the city's fanciest shops and bending down to the **Piazza dei Martiri** – named after the nineteenth-century revolutionary martyrs commemorated by the column in its centre. This part of town, the **Chiaia** neighbourhood, displays a sense of order and classical elegance that is quite absent from the rest of the city centre, its buildings well preserved, the people noticeably better heeled – although the upper part of the district, which spreads up the hill towards Vómero, is as maze-like and evocative as anywhere in the city.

From Piazza dei Martiri, you can stroll down to the waterfront and **Villa Communale**, Naples' most central city park and the place from where it's possible to appreciate the city best as a port and seafront city, the views stretching right around the bay from the long lizard of its northern side to the distinctive silhouette of Vesuvius in the east, behind the cranes and far-off apartment blocks of the sprawling industrial suburbs. The park itself sometimes hosts a large antiques and bric-a-brac market on Sunday mornings.

The road that skirts the park, **Via Caracciolo**, makes a nice way to walk around the bay to Mergellina, particularly in the early evening when the lights of the city enhance the views. On the way you might want to take in the century-old **Aquarium** (April–Oct Tues–Sat 9am–6pm, Sun 10am–6pm; Nov–March Tues–Sat 9am–5pm, Sun 10am–2pm; L3000/€1.55), though its rather glum collection of tanks containing fish, turtles, eels, octopuses and rays, together with a revolting array of pickled marine life, may put you off your dinner. Across from here, on the other side of Riviera di Chiaia, the gardens of the **Villa Pignatelli** (Tues–Sun 9am–2pm; L4000/€2.07) are a peaceful alternative to the Villa Communale, and the house itself, now a museum, is kept in much the same way as when it was the home of a prominent Naples family and a turn-of-the-century meeting place for the city's elite. It's tastefully furnished and by Naples standards low-key, its handful of rooms holding books, porcelain, the odd painting and a set of photos signed by various aristocrats and royal personages.

Villa Communale stretches around the bay for a good mile, at the far end of which lie the harbour and main square – Piazza Sannazzaro – of the **Mergellina** district, a good place to come and eat at night and a terminus for hydrofoils to the bay's islands. There's not a lot else here, only the dense and lovely **Parco Virgiliano** (Tues–Sun 9am–1pm), north of Piazza Sannazzaro, which holds the spot where the Roman poet Virgil is supposed to be buried, marked by a Roman monument. Nearby is an ancient tufa quarry and a disused tunnel, which once linked Naples to Pozzuoli. To get there, follow the Salita della Grotta from the other side of the tunnel off Piazza Piedigrotta. Of the other neighbourhoods nearby, the **Fuorigrotta** district, the other side of the Mergellina hill, is not of interest unless you're going to a football match, since it's home to Napoli's **San Paolo** stadium (see p.836 for details). Ditto **Posillipo**, further along the shore, which is an upmarket suburb of the city stacked with fat villas and pockets – though, again, people do come out here to eat.

Vómero

Like Chiaia below and Mergellina to the west, **VÓMERO** – the district topping the hill immediately above the old city – is one of Naples' relatively modern additions, a light, airy and relatively peaceful quarter connected most directly with the teeming morass below by funicular railway. It's a large area but mostly residential, and you're unlikely to want to stray beyond the streets that fan out from each of the three funicular stations, centring on the grand symmetry of **Piazza Vanvitelli**.

Come up on the Montesanto funicular (see map on pp.816–817) and you're well placed for a visit to two of the buildings that dominate Naples, way above the old city. Five minutes' walk away, the **Castel Sant'Elmo** (Tues–Sun 9am–7pm; L2500/€1.29) occupies Naples' highest point and is an impressive fortification, a fourteenth-century structure once used for incarcerating political prisoners and now lording it grandly over the streets below. Though still in use primarily as a military fortification, it nowadays hosts exhibitions, concerts and an annual antiques fair, as well as boasting the very best views of Naples.

Beyond the castle, the fourteenth-century **Certosa San Martino** has the next-best views over the bay and is also accessible, now being home to the **Museo Nazionale di San Martino** (Tues–Fri 8.30am–7.30pm, Sat & Sun 9am–11pm; L11,000/€5.68). Much of this, too, often appears to be under restoration, but the monastery itself, thoroughly Baroqued in the seventeenth century, and the views from its cunningly constructed terrace, are well worth the entrance fee – short of climbing Vesuvius as good a vista of the entire Bay of Naples as you'll get. The church, on the left of the entrance, is typically garish Baroque, with a colourful pavement and an *Adoration of the Shepherds* by Reni above the altar. In the museum proper, there are paintings by Neapolitan masters – Ribera, Stanzione, Vaccaro – and other rather dusty bits and pieces rescued from churches and the odd minor aristocrat, as well as historical and maritime sections displaying models of ships, and documents, coins and costumes recording the era of the Kingdom of Naples. The Baroque cloisters are lovely, though again rather gone to seed. The display of *presepi* or Christmas cribs (see box on p.825) is probably the most remarkable – and unique – aspect of the museum.

There's another museum up here, ten minutes' walk away in the Neoclassical **Villa Floridiana**, close to the Chiaia funicular, whose lush grounds (daily 9am–1hr before sunset) make a good place for a picnic. The **Museo Duca di Martina** (Tues–Sun 8.30am–7.30pm; L5000/€2.58) is, however, of fairly specialist interest, a porcelain collection such as you've never seen before, varying from the beautifully simple to the outrageously kitsch – hideous teapots, ceramic asparagus sticks and the like. There are examples (of course) of Capodimonte and Meissen, and eighteenth-century English, French, German and Viennese work – as well as a handful of pieces of Qing dynasty Chinese porcelain and Murano glass and exquisite non-ceramic items like inlaid ivory boxes and panels. On the whole, it's a small museum that's worth taking in before salivating over yet another view, this time from just below the villa.

Eating, drinking and nightlife

Neapolitan cuisine consists of simple dishes cooked with fresh, healthy ingredients (see box on p.813 for more on regional specialities). Also, as Naples is not primarily a tourist-geared city, most restaurants are family-run places used by locals and as such generally serve good food at very reasonable prices. There's no better place in Italy to eat pizza, at a solid core of almost obsessively unchanging places that still serve only the (very few) traditional varieties. You're never far from a food stall for delectable snacks on the move, or you can always pick something up from the city's street markets in La Forcella or the fish market at Porta Nolana.

Restaurants and pizzerias

Alla Brace, Via S. Spaventa 14–16. Good, cheap alternative just off Piazza Garibaldi that has well-priced pasta dishes and main courses. Closed Sun.

Antica Trattoria da Carmine, via Tribunali 330. An unobtrusive trattoria which boasts a great central location and serves up tasty standards – Don Carmine's seafood is particularly good. Closed Sun.

Antonio & Antonio, Via Francesco Crispi 89. A cheery no-nonsense place which dishes up enormous pizzas from L5000/€2.58. No closing day.

Bellini, Via Santa Maria di Constantinopoli 80. One of the city's most famous and longest established restaurants, though it's whispered that the place may be resting on its laurels. However, it still dishes up delicious pizzas and a very good selection of other, especially seafood, dishes. It also has a great convivial outside terrace on the street, screened by foliage. Closed Sun evenings.

Bersagliera, Borgo Marinaro. Fine food, especially seafood, though inevitably you pay for the location, slap next to the Castel dell'Ovo, and for the "*O Sole Mio*" minstrels who wander between the tables outside. Closed Tues.

Brandi, Salita Sant'Anna di Palazzo 1–2, off Via Chiaia. One of Naples' most famous pizzerias, said to be where they invented the *pizza margherita* in 1889 in honour of the visiting Queen Margherita of Savoy. Very friendly, serving pasta and (excellent) pizzas from L8000/€4.13. In the evening, the tables outside in the candlelit alley are a lovely place to sit. Closed Monday.

California, Via Santa Lucia 101. Another Naples institution, though a rather different one, serving a menu that's an odd hybrid of American and Italian specialities. Best for its full American breakfasts. Closed Sun.

Canterbury, Via Ascensione 6. Strangely named Chiaia restaurant near the Pignatelli museum that is one of the best-value places in the area. Pasta dishes are particularly good – try the *penne alla vodka*. Closed Sun.

Da Ciciotto, off Via Marechiaro, Posillipo. Hole-in-the-wall place where in fine weather you can sit outside and enjoy the bay. Good seafood and fish. To get there, follow Via Marechiaro to the end, where it opens out onto a small piazza. Take the steps off the far end that lead down to the sea. Turn sharp right at the bottom of the first flight. Closed Wed.

Dante e Beatrice, Piazza Dante 44. A long-established restaurant that trades slightly on its reputation, not least in its rather brusque service, although its menu of traditional Naples specialities is still not at all expensive – and you can eat outside. Closed Wed & late Aug to mid-Sept.

Da Ettore, Via Santa Lucia 56. An inexpensive, no frills, popular neighbourhood restaurant. Short, reliable menu includes pizza, with wines from Campania, Sicily and Tuscany. Closed Sun.

Da Gennarino, Via Capuana alla Maddelena 1–2. Again among the best pizzerias in the city, well situated (opposite the Porta Capuana) for hungry arrivals by train. Closed Mon.

Gorizia, Via Bernini 29. Unpretentious Vómero restaurant close to the Centrale and Chiaia funicular stops that does good antipasti, great mini-pizzas as well as a good selection of main courses. Try the speciality of the house – veal wrapped around prosciutto and mozzarella. Closed Wed.

Lombardi a Santa Chiara, Via B. Croce 59. Another well-known and well-respected pizza restaurant, and with a varied menu besides pizza. Closed Sun & most of Aug.

O Marenaro, Via Casanova. Around the corner from Piazza Garibaldi, opposite the CTP bus station, this is a great place to try *zuppa di cozze*, with a couple of tables outside. No closing day in summer; closed Wed in winter.

Di Matteo, via Tribunali 94. A terrific and well-located pizzeria – one of the best and most famous in the city; Bill Clinton popped in for a pizza during the 1994 G7 summit. Closed Sun.

Da Michele, Via Cesare Sersale 1–3. Tucked away off Corso Umberto I in the Forcella district, this is the most determinedly traditional of all the Naples pizzerias, offering just three varieties (allegedly the only three worth eating) – *marinara, margherita* and *ripieno*. Don't arrive late, as they sometimes run out of dough. Closed Sun.

Da Pasqualino, Piazza Sannazzaro 79. Inexpensive Mergellina restaurant with outdoor seating and great seafood and pizzas. A good bet also for takeaway pizzas if you're staying at the nearby youth hostel. Closed Tues.

Da Peppino Avellinese, Via S. Spaventa 31. The most welcoming and best value of the many options on and around Piazza Garibaldi, with terrific antipasti. Used by tourists and locals alike. Closed Sat in winter, otherwise open every day.

Port'Alba, Via Port'Alba 18. Old-established pizzeria just off Piazza Dante that has a wide-ranging menu including very good fish dishes, besides its excellent pizza. Said to be the oldest pizzeria in Italy. Closed Wed.

Spaghetteria, Via G. Paladino 7. Inexpensive plates of pasta in a youthful restaurant patronized by students from the nearby university. Also features a great-value *menu turistico* (L14,000/€7.23). Closed Sat lunchtime & Mon evening.

Da Tonino, Via Santa Teresa a Chiaia 47. Friendly and frenetic restaurant with large tables, around which everyone sits. Try their *pasta e fagioli* and *pasta e ceci* soups and, on Fridays especially, the *seppie in umido* – steamed cuttlefish. Closed Sun.

Trianon (da Ciro), Via P. Colletta 46. Lively Forcella pizzeria that is a nearby rival to *Da Michele* (above), but serving a wider range of pizzas. Open daily.

Al Triunfo Mario, Vico Il Duschesca 10. Great, cheap and popular eatery just off the Porta Capuana end of Piazza Garibaldi. Cheap pizza and pasta, and spit-roast chicken. Always full of locals and workers. Closed Mon.

Umberto, Via Alabardieri 30–31. A long-time popular choice among the professional classes of the Chiaia district, serving marvellous food in somewhat smooth and old-fashioned surroundings that belie the moderate prices. Closed Wed.

Cakes, snacks, ice cream

Attanasio, Vico Ferrovia, off Via Milano. Bakery that specializes in *sfogliatelle* (ricotta-stuffed pastries).

Gambrinus, Via Chiaia 1–2. The oldest and best-known of Neapolitan cafés, founded in 1861. Not cheap, but its aura of chandeliered gentility – and outside seating on Piazza Trieste e Trento – makes it worth at least one visit.

Café Letterario, Galleria Principe di Napoli 6–7. An elegant café inside the galleria, within striking distance of the Museo Nazionale. Also sells books and posters, and has Internet access (L5000/€2.58 for 30min; L10,000/€5.16 for 1hr).

Remy Gelo, Via F. Galiani 29a. Off Via Caracciolo, near the hydrofoil terminal, this place does superb ice creams and *granite*.

Scaturchio, Piazza San Domenico. Another elegant old Naples standard, it's been serving coffee and pastries in the heart of Spaccanapoli for decades. Has a small back room but is mainly a place to grab a quick coffee and pastry and move on.

Bars, clubs and theatres

The old part of the city is crammed with **bars**; the best thing to do is head for one of the lively and glamorous central squares where the local *ragazzi* hang out – try Piazza Bellini, a focal point for the gay community, or Piazza Gesù Nuovo. Bear in mind though, that things don't really get going till at least 9pm. For **nightclubs** you may – due to the licensing laws – have to obtain a *tesserino* or membership card to gain entry, which will cost upwards of L20,000/€10.33. For the best of the clubs head around the bay, ideally with your own transport, to the places situated in the beach areas north or south of the city; the *Qui Napoli* magazine has club listings.

For more highbrow **culture** there's the Teatro San Carlo, whose opera season runs from December to May, while the rest of the year is given over to classical concerts and ballet (box office Tues–Sun 10am–1pm & 4.30–6.30pm; ☎081.797.21.11). The Teatro Mercadante on Piazza Municipio (☎081.551.3396; tickets from L27,000/€13.94) is a stunning little eighteenth-century building, featuring the best of touring Italian theatre. Its long avant-garde tradition is upheld by Roberto de Simone, whose shows, such as the recent *La Gatta Cerontala*, are soaked in Neapolitan atmosphere.

Bars and Clubs

Chez Moi, Parco Margherita 12, near Piazza Amedeo. A great club which has been going strong since the Seventies, with a small dance floor and intimate lounges with waiter service. Frequented by an elegant crowd. Thurs–Sun 10pm–4am.

Internet Bar, Piazza Bellini 44, *www.internetbarnapoli.it*. A central and stylish little bar, where for L10,000/€5.16 an hour you can surf the Web. Mon–Sat 11am–2am.

Intra Moenia, Piazza Bellini 70. One of several trendy haunts on Piazza Bellini, where tables spread across the square. A lovely place to sit and read under the wisteria on a sunny day – it styles itself a "literary café". Substantial snacks and fancy ice creams are served, and there's a computer for Internet access (L5000/€2.58 for 30min). Daily 10am–2am.

Jasay Nightlife, Via Marina. This is a relatively new club located between the centre and the suburbs; it has an alternative focus and is part of a project to regenerate the port area. Oct–April Tues–Sun 9.30pm–4am.

La Mela, Via dei Mille 41. A legendary and long-established club with an exclusive clientele and a resident DJ. Dress up to get past the doorman. Thurs–Sun midnight–4am.

Madison Street, Via Sgambati 30c. A huge upmarket disco with themed events and a gay night on Saturdays. Open till late.

Michelemma Club, Via Campana 12, Pozzuoli (☎081.526.9743). An out-of-town option that's definitely worth the trip; centred round a lemon and orange plantation, it features a vibrant dancefloor and a concert hall, as well as a handy pizzeria.

My Way, Via Cappella Vecchia 30c, off Piazza dei Martiri. A funky nightclub with a cave-like dancefloor which plays a range of music, from salsa to house. Oct–April Thurs–Sat 10pm–4am.

Notting Hill Gallery, Piazza Dante 88a. A non-mainstream club geared to Brit pop plus garage and drum 'n' bass, with live music on Tuesday, Thursday and Saturday. Oct–May Tues–Sun 10.30pm–5am.

Otto Jazz Club, Piazzetta Cariati 23. A popular jazz club off Corso Vittorio Emanuele which also dips its toes into Neapolitan folk song. Has 200 cocktails on the menu. Daily 10pm–3am.

Velvet Underground, Via Cisterna dell'Olio 11. Plays an eclectic range of music including garage, and features live music by decent local bands. Oct–May 11pm–4am.

Virgilio Club, Via Lucrezio Caro 6, just below the Parco della Rimembranza, Posillipo. A fun and leafy outdoor disco that gets jam-packed on summer nights. June–Sept Sat 11pm–4am.

Listings

Airlines Alitalia, Via Medina 41–42 (☎081.542.5333); British Airways (☎147.812.266; Capodichino airport desk ☎081.780.3087); TWA, Via Cervantes 55 (☎081.551.3063).

Books English-language books from Universal, Rione Sirignano 1 (☎081.663.217).

British Council Library, via Morghen 31, Vomero (☎081.558.5817, *www.britishcouncil.it*). Features a limited range of literature, some reference books and a video library.

Car rental Avis, Via Piedigrotta 44 (☎081.761.1365); Europcar, Via Scarfoglio 10 (☎081.570.8426); Hertz, Via N. Sauro 21 (☎081.764.5323); Maggiore, Via Cervantes 92 (☎081.552.1900). These agents also have desks at Stazione Centrale and at the airport.

Consulates Canada, Via Carducci 29 (☎081.401.338); UK, Via Francesco Crispi 122 (☎081.663.511); USA, Piazza della Repubblica (☎081.583.8111).

Exchange Outside normal banking hours you can change money and travellers' cheques at the booth inside Stazione Centrale (daily 7am–9pm).

Football The Stadio di San Paolo in Fuorigrotta is the home of the Napoli side, who are currently in Serie A. To get to the ground, take the Ferrovia Cumana from Montesanto to Mostra and the stadium is right in front of you. Tickets, available from the offices facing you as you approach, or from the club's outlets in town, cost around L30,000/€15.49.

Funerals Death is big business in Naples, and you can still see the incredibly ornate traditional black hearses pulled by teams of horses on the streets of the city – the preferred way to go of Neapolitan fat cats and higher-ranking Camorra members. There are other, equally bizarre Neapolitan customs regarding death: a white hearse, for example, means a child or virgin has died; and despite official discouragement there are reports of some corpses being dug up by their families after burial, in a bizarre celebration centring on All Souls Day – November 2.

Hospital To call an ambulance, dial ☎081.752.8282, 081.752.0696 or 081.752.0850, or go to the Guardia Medica Permanente in the Palazzo Municipio, open 24hr.

Internet As well as the cafés and bars listed on p.834–5, try Internet Globe, on Via Carrozzieria (☎081.551.0306).

Language courses The Centro Italiano, Vico S. Maria dell'Aiuto 17 (☎081.552.4331, fax 081.552.3023), runs a selection of courses on Italian language and culture, ranging from an intensive two-week option (L420,000/€216.91) to a more relaxed three-month one (L780,000/€402.84), as well as specialist courses on cookery, the "Neapolitan crib", and archeology.

Lottery Along with San Gennaro, the lottery is a fanatically observed institution in Naples. Winning the lottery is seen, in a way, as the ultimate triumph over the system, and superstitions around it are rife – to the extent that there's even a book, *La Smorfia*, which interprets the meaning behind each lottery number. There are also people, called *assisti* (literally "guided ones"), who claim to have supernatural access to knowledge of what the winning numbers will be. If you're keen to see the lottery draw, it's made every Saturday noon at the Ufficio Lotto on Via San Biagio dei Librai, to the accompaniment of much hysteria.

Markets The Mercato dei Fiori (Flower Market) at Castel Nuovo kicks off every morning at sunrise, while Pignasecca on via Pignasecca is an atmospheric daily market, the stalls piled with fresh fruit, vegetables and seafood.

Pharmacies Late-night pharmacies work on a rotation system; ☎1100 for addresses of the three nearest open pharmacies from the point you are calling from, or look in *Il Mattino*. There's also a pharmacy at Napoli Centrale (Mon–Sat 8am–8pm).

Police ☎112; you can speak to an operator in English. The main police station is at Via Medina 75 (☎081.794.1111); you can also report crimes at the small police station in Stazione Centrale. To report theft of a car call ☎081.794.1436.

Post office The main post office is in the enormous building on Piazza Matteotti, just off Via Toledo (Mon–Sat 8.15am–7.20pm).

Telephones There is a Telecom Italia office at Napoli Centrale (open 24hr), though large queues form early evening. The office at Via Depretis 40 (also 24hr) is quieter.

Tours The Naples tourist office run guided bus tours of various parts of the city every Sunday morning beginning at 10.30am; details direct from one of their offices. Free guided excursions are organized by the Chamber of Commerce; ask at your hotel or at a travel agent (see opposite) for details and a voucher. You can also experience underground Naples on tours run by LAES (Sat & Sun 10am; ☎081.400.256), which leave from *Bar Gambrinus* on Piazza Trieste e Trento and take you through sewers and passageways that date back as far as 4000 years. Napoli Sotterranea run a similar tour (Sat & Sun; ☎081.296.944); the meeting point is Piazza San Gaetano. In summer you can also cruise Naples harbour by boat at night; departures are from Mergellina harbour twice each Saturday between mid-July and the end of August, three times on Sunday; in September just three times each Sunday evening. Tickets are available at the embarkation point or from the Piazza Gesù Nuovo tourist office.

Travel agents CTS, Via Mezzocannone 25 (☎081.552.7960), for discount tickets, budget flights and so on. You could also try Eurostudy, Via Mezzocannone 119 (☎081.552.0947).

THE BAY OF NAPLES

For the Romans, Campania and particularly the **Bay of Naples** was the land of plenty, a blessed region of mild climate, gorgeous scenery and an accessible location that made it a favourite vacation and retirement area for the city's nobility. Patrician Rome built villas here by the score – Hadrian had a house at Báia, for example – and towns like **Pompeii** and **Herculaneum** were among the richest in the imperial era: the "Bay of Luxury", Cicero called it. Later, when Naples became the final stop on northerners' Grand Tours, the bay became no less fabled, the relics of its heady Roman period only adding to the charm for most travellers.

It's a charm that is easy to detect – the landscape is still there and still as impressive, and the offshore islands of **Cápri**, **Ischia** and **Prócida** are no less enticing than they ever were, if immeasurably more crowded. But the fact is that these days it's hard to tell where Naples ends and the countryside begins. Northern money and Camorra speculation mean that the city now sprawls around the bay in an industrial and residential mess that is quite at odds with the region's popular image. The shoddily built *abusivi* – houses erected without planning permission – add an extra terror to living in a geologically unstable region; the Camorra and corrupt local officials were blamed for the tragedy at Sarno in 1998, when more than a hundred people were killed by a mudslide. You need to head some way out of the city before reaching anywhere you might want to stay for longer than an afternoon, especially if you want to swim. Even if the water is clean, the proximity of the bay's industry will make you think it isn't; and it's only when you reach lively **Sorrento** in the east, workaday **Pozzuoli** in the west, or any of the islands that you really feel free of it all. Luckily this is easy by way of the extraurban train services out of Naples (see p.820), or one of the bay's plentiful ferry connections: most of the places mentioned below are convenient for day-trips – though many obviously demand longer.

West from Naples: Pozzuoli and the Campi Flegrei

The area around Naples is one of the most unstable in the world. Vesuvius is only the best known of the many and varied examples of volcanic activity in the province, the most concentrated instances – volcanic craters, hot springs, *fumaroles* – being northwest of the city in the region known as the **Campi Flegrei** (Fiery Fields). This is the Phlegrean Fields of classical times, a mysterious place in turn mythologized by Homer and Virgil as the entrance to Hades and eulogized as the Elysian Fields for its beauty. These days most of the mystery is gone – like most of the bay, the presence of Naples dominates in the form of new building and suburbs – and much of the volcanic activity is extinct. But parts of the area still retain some of the doomy associations that first drew the ancients here, and there are some substantial remains of their presence – as well as some of the best and most accessible of Naples' nearby beaches.

Pozzuoli and the Solfatara

The first town that can really be considered free of Naples' sprawl is **POZZUOLI**, which sits on a stout promontory jutting out from the slender crescent of volcanic hills behind. Despite achieving some glamour as the hometown of Sophia Loren, it's an ordinary little place, nothing special but likeable enough, with ferry connections to the islands of Prócida and Ischia (see p.857 and p.853). And although you wouldn't want to stay here (unless you're a camper; see "Accommodation", p.821), it's a good first stop before travelling on to the rest of the Campi Flegrei. You can get there from Naples on the *metropolitana* from Piazza Garibaldi, or on the Ferrovia Cumanarail line from Montesanto station; both take about twenty minutes. Bus #152 also runs direct from Piazza Garibaldi.

Pozzuoli has suffered more than most of the towns around here from the area's volcanic activity. Twenty years ago a minor tremor caused a number of buildings to collapse, and subsidence is still a major – and carefully monitored – problem. The best time to come is on Sunday, when the whole town turns out for the morning fish market, afterwards eating lunch in one of several waterfront restaurants: *Il Capitano* (closed Tues) near the dock on Lungomare C. Colombo is decent; or there's *Don Antonio* (no closing day), up narrow Via Magazzini off the old port, which specializes in excellent fresh fish and seafood. In town there are a number of relics of the Romans' liking for the place. The rather overgrown **Anfiteatro Flavio** (daily 9am–1hr before sunset; L4000/€2.07), on Via Domiziana just north of the centre, was at one time the third largest in Italy and is still reasonably well preserved, although some parts are shut off to the public – a little illicit clambering over fences might enable you to get a better sense of the place. Not far from here, beyond the Cumana station between Via Roma and Via Sacchini, a **Temple of Serapide** sits enclosed within a small park, often flooded in winter, but, otherwise, accessible – and in fact since proved to be not a temple at all but a market hall from the first century AD. It's pretty ruined, but it is still possible to make out the shape of the building, its three freestanding marble columns eaten away halfway up by shellfish.

Just north of town, ten minutes' walk up the hill from the *metropolitana*/FS station (bus #152 from Piazza Garibaldi in Naples stops outside), the **Solfatara** (daily 9am–1hr before sunset; L8000/€4.13) is further, and tangible, evidence of the volcanic nature of the area, the exposed crater of a semi-extinct volcano – into which you can walk – that hasn't erupted for a couple of thousand years; in fact, it was a major tourist attraction in Roman times too. Not surprisingly, it's a weird place: steam rises from the rocks around and the grey-yellow ground is hot to the touch (and sounds hollow to the stamp), emitting eerily silent jets or *fumaroles* that leave the air pungent with sulphurous fumes. Some of the *fumaroles* have been covered artificially with brick, creating an almost unbearably warm, sauna-like environment into which you can bend if you can stand it, while others are just left open. You can hire a guide on site (from L25,000/€12.91) to steer you clear of the dangerous parts, but it's not really necessary – there's a clearly marked route and it's far more fun exploring the site on your own.

A short, three-minute walk further up the hill on the right, the sixteenth-century **Santuario di San Gennaro** (daily 9am–noon & 4.30–8pm) was built on the supposed site of the martyrdom of Naples' patron saint and holds a stone stained with splashes of his blood (he was beheaded) that apparently glows when his blood liquefies in Naples, which it does three times a year – see "The Miracle of San Gennaro" box on p.824.

Báia, Bácoli, Capo Miseno and Cumae

The next town along from Pozzuoli, reached in fifteen minutes by train from the Cumana station, by the Temple of Serapide, is **BÁIA**, a small port with a tiny, rather unattractive bit of beach and a set of imperial-era Roman ruins piling up on the hill above. This was one of the bay's most favoured spots in Roman times, a trendy resort at which all the most fashionable of the city's patricians had villas: the Emperor Hadrian died here in 138 AD and Nero was rumoured to have murdered his mother in Báia. Summer **tours** in a glass-bottomed boat explore the submerged villas along the coastline at Báia; contact the Associazione Aliseo (☎081.526.5780).

Immediately behind the station, remains of some enormous Roman baths leave you in no doubt of the town's function in ancient times. Steps lead up from the station square to the entrance to the **excavations** (daily 9am–1hr before sunset; L4000/€2.07) of a Roman palace of the first to the fourth century AD, structured across several levels. It's hard to tell what's what – the site is very ruined and there's little or no labelling – but it's an evocative location and can afford a happy hour of stumbling around among the stones and passages. Follow the steps down from the entrance level to the first terrace of the palace: the rooms on the right contain patches of Roman stucco-work depicting birds and mythical creatures and a statue of Mercury, beheaded by vandals in recent years. Below are the remains of a small theatre and an open space – a former *piscina* – bordered on one side by a pretty loggia now used for summer drama performances.

There are more ruins inland from Báia at **Lago d'Averno**, where Agrippa constructed a military harbour in 37 BC. The lake itself is the Lake Avernus of antiquity, a volcanic crater that the Greeks believed – and Virgil later wrote – was the entrance to Hades: birds flying over were said to suffocate with the toxic fumes that rose from the lake's murky waters, and sacrifices were regularly made here to the dark deities that lurked beneath the gloomy surface. Today it's more cheerful, no longer surrounded by thick forest (this was cut down by Agrippa), although there's not really any other reason to come – the water of the nearby sea is much more enticing for swimming.

A few kilometres down the coast from Báia, **BÁCOLI** has more Roman remains, an underground Roman reservoir, the **Piscina Mirabile**, and a small stretch of beach – more appealing than Báia's. However, if it's **beaches** you're after you'd be well advised to stay on the bus until **MISENO**, where, just beyond the lake of the same name, there's a very broad strand. You'll not find it empty by any means, but it's large enough to find yourself a space – and beach bars and restaurants abound.

If you've the energy, you can make the stiff climb to **Capo Miseno** from here, an almost level-topped hump at the furthest tip of the Campi Flegrei, though it's only really worth it if the weather's clear – the views back to Naples and up the coast to Gaeta are the main attraction. Otherwise push up to **CUMAE**, home to one of the most lauded of the ancient sites hereabouts.

The town of **Cumae** was the first Greek colony on the Italian mainland, a source of settlers for other colonies (Naples was originally settled by Greeks from Cumae) and a centre of Hellenistic civilization. Later it was home to the so-called Cumaean Sibyl, from whom Tarquinius purchased the Sibylline Books that laid down the laws for the Republic. The **site** (daily 9am–1hr before sunset; L4000/€2.07), a short walk from the bus stop, is spread over a large area and not at all comprehensively excavated. But the only part you're likely to want to see forms a tight nucleus close to the entrance. The best-known feature is the Cave of the Sibyl, a long dark corridor that was home to the most famous of the ancient oracles. The cave is rectangular in shape, with light admitted from a series of niches in the western wall; the Sibyl used to dispense her wisdom from the three large chambers at the far end of the forty-foot passageway, the most famous occasion being when Aeneas came here to consult her – an event recorded by the lines of Virgil posted up either side of the entrance.

But the best of Cumae is still to come. Climb up the steps to the right of the cave entrance and follow the winding Via Sacra past a constructed belvedere on the left and the fairly scanty remains of a temple on the right to the Acropolis. Here you'll find the remains of a temple to Jupiter, but it's the **views** that you really come for: from the far side of the temple way south across the shellfish-filled **Lago Fusaro** and the bottom corner of the coast; and, if you clamber down from the other side of the temple, north up the curving coast to the Gulf of Gaeta.

The coast north of Cumae

The coast north of Cumae up to the Lazio border is known as the **Costa Domiziana**, after the Roman road that leads north from here to join up with the Via Appia, and looks, at least from the heights of Cumae itself, enticingly empty – which it can be if you've a car to reach its more isolated spots. But most of the resorts along this stretch of coast are polluted and overdeveloped and hard to recommend for any kind of visit. **PINETA A MARE** is the closest resort to Cumae and fairly typical – tacky, rather dirty, and generally best avoided. **BÁIA DOMIZIA**, further north, close to the Lazio border, is much the same.

East from Naples: Ercolano to Sorrento

The coast **east from Naples** is no better, perhaps even a little worse than the coast west of the city – the Circumvesuviana train edging out through derelict industrial buildings and dense housing that squeezes ever closer to the track. Most people come here for the ancient sights of **Herculaneum** and **Pompeii**, or to scale **Vesuvius** – or they skip the lot for the resort town of **Sorrento**. All are easy day-trips, though Sorrento is easily worth a little more time and is a good base for seeing some of the Amalfi coast.

Ercolano: Vesuvius and the site of Herculaneum

The first real point of any interest is the town of **ERCOLANO**, the modern offshoot of the ancient site of Herculaneum, which was destroyed by the eruption of Vesuvius on August 2, 79 AD. It's worth stopping here for two reasons: to see the excavations of the site and to climb to the summit of Vesuvius – to which buses run from outside the railway station. A word of warning, though: if you're planning to both visit Herculaneum and scale Vesuvius in one day (and it is possible), be sure to see Vesuvius first, and set off reasonably early – buses stop running up the mountain at lunchtime, leaving you the afternoon free to wander around the site.

Herculaneum
Situated at the seaward end of Ercolano's main street, the site of **Herculaneum** (March–Sept 8.30am–7.30pm; Oct–Feb 8.30am–5pm; L16,000/€8.26) was discovered in 1709, when a well-digger accidentally struck the stage of the buried theatre. Excavations were undertaken throughout the eighteenth and nineteenth centuries, during which period much of the marble and bronze from the site was carted off to Naples to decorate the city's palaces, and it wasn't until 1927 that digging and preservation began in earnest. Herculaneum was a residential town, much smaller than Pompeii, and as such it makes a more manageable site, less architecturally impressive and less outside the modern mainstream (Ercolano virtually abuts the site), but better

preserved and more easily taken in on a single visit. Archeologists held for a long time that unlike in Pompeii, on the other side of the volcano, most of the inhabitants of Herculaneum managed to escape. However, recent discoveries of entangled skeletons found at what was the shoreline of the town suggest otherwise, and it's now believed that most of the population was buried by huge avalanches of volcanic mud, which later hardened into the tufa-type rock that preserved much of the town. In early 2000 the remains of another 48 people were found; they were carrying coins, which suggests they were attempting to flee the disaster.

Many of the houses on the site are kept locked, and you may have to ask one of the many attendants to open them up for you (in return for a tip). There are always plenty of guides hanging around, some English-speaking: if you can afford it, have one take you around the whole site; if you can't, tag along discreetly with an English-speaking group.

Because Herculaneum wasn't a commercial town, there was no central open space or forum, just streets of villas and shops, cut as usual by two very straight main streets that cross in the centre. Start your tour just inside the entrance at the bottom end of Cardo III, where you'll see the **House of the Argus** on the left, a very grand place judging by its once-impressive courtyard – although even this is upstaged by the size of the place across the street, the so-called **Hotel**, which covers a huge area, though you can only really get a true impression of its size from the rectangle of stumpy columns that made up its atrium. Further up, Cardo III joins the Decumanus Inferiore, just beyond which it's the large **Thermae** or bath complex which dominates – the domed frigidarium of its men's section decorated with frescoes of fish, its caldarium containing a plunge bath at one end and a scallop-shell apse complete with washbasin and water pipes. The women's section has a well-preserved mosaic of Neptune and glass shards in its window that are original. On the far side of the baths, across Cardo IV, the **Samnite House** and **House of the Wooden Partition** are both worth a peek inside, the Samnite House in particular, whose atrium is one of the most attractive in Herculaneum, with a graceful blind arcade all the way round and a hole in the roof still decorated with animal spouts. Next door but one, in the **House of the Carbonized Furniture**, there's a room with the marital bed still intact and portraits of the gent and lady of the house nearby – the former, in the room to the right, marked by a satyr, the latter voluptuously posed on the left-hand wall of an alcove. Close by, the dining room has pictures of Roman dishes – chicken, mushrooms and the like – while on the left as you enter there's a kitchen with an oven in the corner and a toilet on the other side. Beyond, the **House of the Neptune Mosaic** holds another sparklingly preserved mosaic floor, again including portraits of the owners of the household, and flower and vegetable frescoes which served in lieu of a garden; the concrete hatch to the right was a vomitarium, which allowed guests to relieve themselves of excess food before proceeding to the next course of their meal. Under the house is a **wine shop**, stocked with amphorae and with a coiled rope left as it stood when disaster struck.

Turning right at the top of Cardo IV takes you around to Cardo V and most of the rest of the town's **shops** – a variety of places including a baker's, complete with ovens and grinding mills, a weaver's, with loom and bones, and a dyer's, with a huge pot for dyes. Behind the ones on the left you can see the **Palestra**, where public games were held, although it's not actually possible to reach this. Further down on the right, the shop on the corner of Cardo V and Decumanus Inferiore has a well-preserved counter and urns for cereals or somesuch merchandise; another, further down Cardo V on the right, has a Priapic painting behind its counter. Cutting through to Cardo IV from here, the **House of the Wooden Partition** preserves its original partition doors under glass – evidence that it was the home of a poorer class of person than many of the buildings here. The next-door **House of Opus Craticium** is a very well-preserved example of a plebeian artisans' residence, and would have been divided into separate apartments; it gives a good impression of its original plaster and wood construction, complete with upper storey overhanging the streetfront. At the bottom end of Cardo IV, the **House of the Mosaic Atrium**, at the bottom, was a grand villa in its day and retains its mosaic-laid courtyard, corrugated by the force of the tufa. Behind here, the **House of the Deer** on Cardo V was another luxury villa, its two storeys built around a central courtyard and containing corridors decorated with richly coloured still-lifes and, as the centrepiece of one of its rooms, a bawdy statue of a drunken Hercules seemingly about to piss all over the visitors.

Close by, from the end of Cardo IV, a covered passageway leads down to another **baths** building on the left, which is in fact one of the most impressive – and intact – structures in Herculaneum, complete with extremely well-preserved stucco work and a pretty much intact set of baths; it also has a complete original Roman door, the only one in Herculaneum that wasn't charred by fire. Its damp mustiness makes it certainly the most evocative stop on a tour of the site, although it is prone to regular flooding and sadly often out of bounds altogether.

Mount Vesuvius

Since its first eruption in 79 AD, when it buried the towns and inhabitants of Pompeii and Herculaneum, **Mount Vesuvius** has dominated the lives of those who live on the Bay of Naples, its brooding bulk forming a stately backdrop to the ever-growing settlements that group around its lower slopes. It's still an active volcano, the only one on mainland Europe. There have been more than a hundred eruptions over the years, but only two others of real significance – one in December 1631 that engulfed many nearby towns and killed 3000 people; and the last, in March 1944, which caused widespread devastation in the towns around, though no one was actually killed. The people who live here still fear the reawakening of the volcano, and with good reason – scientists calculate it should erupt every thirty years or so, and it hasn't since 1944. It's carefully monitored, of course, and there is apparently no reason to expect any movement for some time. But the subsidence in towns like Ercolano below is a continuing reminder of the instability of the area, one of southern Italy's most densely populated: around half a million people would be immediately threatened by another eruption.

There are several ways of making the **ascent**. There are five buses a day from the Ercolano excavations (currently at 9am, 10am, 11.30am, 1.10pm & 2.10pm) to a car park and huddle of souvenir shops and cafés close to the crater; there is a **charge** of L9000/€4.65 to approach the crater, which includes a brief explanatory talk (in English). The bus costs L6000/€3.10 return and is much the cheapest way of doing things; the service is run by Trasporti Vesuviani (☎081.882.6787). Minibuses also run up to the crater from Ercolano, charging L10,000/€5.16 for a single or return ticket. There are plenty of taxis eager to take you up and wait while you see the crater for around L70,000/€36.15 all-in. If you have more energy, or have missed the bus and don't have that kind of money, you can also take the infrequent local bus (#5) from the roundabout near the train station to the end of the line and walk from there – a good couple of hours to the crater. One way of doing it might be to walk up and take the official bus back down (the last one descends at 5.30pm). The walk is certainly a pleasant one, winding through the fertile lower slopes of the volcano, covered with vines and olives, past the main lava flows of the 1944 eruption as far as the car park, which sits just above the greenery among the bare cinders of Vesuvius's main summit.

The walk up to the crater from the car park takes about half an hour, a stony stroll across reddened, barren gravel and rock on marked-out paths, though with nothing on your right to prevent you falling down the smooth side of the mountain – take care. At the top is a deep, wide, jagged ashtray of red rock swirled over by midges and emitting the odd plume of smoke, though since the last eruption effectively sealed up the main crevice this is much less evident than it once was.

The bay to Sorrento

Beyond Ercolano the bay doesn't really pick up: it's still hard to distinguish much countryside between the towns – most of which sadly seem more in tune with their proximity to the city than to the sea. TORRE DEL GRECO, the first place you reach, is famous for its coral industry, and you can still buy coral jewellery here, but the business is threatened by the polluted nature of the waters of the bay.

Further along, TORRE ANNUNZIATA is no more appealing at first sight, though about half a kilometre from the railway station there's a Roman villa, the **Scavi of Plantis** (March–Sept 8.30am–5.30pm; Oct–Feb 8.30am–4.30pm; L10,000/€5.16) that was covered, and preserved, by the 79 AD eruption. It was a sumptuous residence in its time, part of a suburb of Pompeii known as Oplontis, with elegant loggias, fine frescoes and graceful gardens, which have been sensitively reconstructed in the style of their day.

By the time you reach CASTELLAMMARE DI STABIA, a few kilometres further round the bay, the houses have begun to thin out a little. But the town isn't any more appetizing for all that, dominated by the ships and gantries of the Italian navy's military harbour here. Oddly enough, Castellammare is the kind of place people still come for a holiday, or at least for a cure: its **spas** are well known hereabouts and draw many for their healing properties. From the Circumvesuviana station you can take the funicular (daily every 30min: April–June 15 7.25am–5pm; June 16–Sept 15 8.25am–8.25pm; L8000/€4.13 return) up to the top of **Monte Faito** (1100m), a ten-minute journey that gives predictably dazzling views, although you need to walk for fifteen minutes or so at the top to get clear of the trees. However, on the whole you'd do better not to tarry here at all, instead hurrying on south to Salerno or west to Sorrento – both feasible jumping-off points for the Amalfi coast.

Pompeii

The other Roman town to be destroyed by Vesuvius – **Pompeii** – was a much larger affair than Herculaneum and one of Campania's most important commercial centres in its day. After a spell as a Greek colony, Pompeii came under the sway of the Romans in 200 BC, later functioning as both a moneyed resort for wealthy patricians and a trading town that exported wine and fish products, notably its own brand of fish sauce. A severe earthquake destroyed much of the city in 63 AD, and the eruption of Vesuvius sixteen years later only served to exacerbate what was already a desperate situation.

Vesuvius had been spouting smoke and ash for several days before the eruption and in fact most of the town had already been evacuated when disaster struck: out of a total population of 20,000 it's thought that only 2000 actually perished, asphyxiated by the toxic fumes of the volcanic debris, their homes buried in several metres of volcanic ash and pumice. **Pliny**, the Roman naturalist, was one of the casualties – he died at nearby Stabiae (now Castellammare) of a heart attack. But his nephew, Pliny the Younger, described the full horror of the scene in two vivid letters to the historian Tacitus, who was compiling a history of the disaster, writing that the sky turned dark like "a room when it is shut up, and the lamp put out".

In effect the eruption froze the way of life in Pompeii as it stood at the time – a way of life that subsequent excavations have revealed in precise and remarkable detail; indeed Pompeii has probably yielded more information about the ordinary life of Roman citizens during the imperial era than any other site: its social conventions, class structure, domestic arrangements and its (very high) standard of living. Some of the buildings are even covered with ancient graffiti, either referring to contemporary political events or simply to the romantic entanglements of the inhabitants; and the full horror of their way of **death** is apparent in plaster casts made from the shapes their bodies left in the volcanic ash – with faces tortured with agony, or shielding themselves from the dust and ashes.

The first parts of the town were discovered in 1600, but it wasn't until 1748 that **excavations** began, continuing more or less without interruption – after 1860 under the auspices of the Italian government – until the present day. Indeed, exciting discoveries are still being made, and a flood of new funds is being used to excavate a further twenty hectares of the site; it is hoped to resolve whether or not the survivors attempted, vainly, to resettle Pompeii after the eruption. A privately funded excavation has recently revealed a covered heated swimming pool, whose erotic wall-paintings have been deemed by the Vatican to be unsuitable for children. And, in a further development, a luxury "hotel" complex was uncovered in May 2000 during the widening of a motorway, slabs of stacked cut marble suggesting it was still under construction when Vesuvius erupted.

Bear in mind that most of the best mosaics and murals (from Herculaneum too) are in the archeological museum in Naples, and that as you can only see a small proportion of those found *in situ*, visits to both sites really need to be supplemented by an additional one to the museum (see p.829).

The site

The **site** of Pompeii (daily: March–Sept 8.30am–7.30pm; Oct–Feb 8.30am–5pm plus June–Sept evening *son et lumière* events; ☎081.854.5111, *www.pompeiisites.org*; L16,000/€8.26) covers a wide area, and seeing it properly takes half a day at the very least; really you should devote most of a day to it and take plenty of breaks – unlike Herculaneum there's little shade, and the distances involved are quite large: flat comfortable shoes are a must.

All of this makes Pompeii sound a bit of a chore – which it certainly isn't. But there is a lot to see, and you should be reasonably selective: many of the streets aren't lined by much more than foundations, and after a while one ruin begins to look much like another. Again, many of the most interesting structures are kept locked and only opened when a large group forms or a tip is handed over to one of the many custodians. It's worth studying the **site map**, which you'll find at every entrance – pins on the map indicate which areas are currently closed. To be sure of seeing as much as possible you could take a tour, although one of the pleasures of Pompeii is to escape the hordes and absorb the strangely still quality of the town, which, despite the large number of visitors, it is quite possible to do.

Entering the site from the Pompeii-Villa dei Misteri side, through the Porta Marina, the **Forum** is the first real feature of significance, a long, slim open space surrounded by the ruins of what would have been some of the town's most important official buildings – a basilica, temples to Apollo and Jupiter, and a market hall. Walking north from here, up the so-called Via di Mercurio, takes you towards some of the town's more luxurious houses. On the left, the **House of the Tragic Poet** is named for its mosaics of a theatrical production and a poet inside, though the "Cave Canem" (Beware of the Dog) mosaic by the main entrance is more eye-catching. Close by, the residents of the **House of the Faun** must have been a friendlier lot, its "Ave" (Welcome) mosaic outside beckoning you in to view the atrium and the copy of a tiny bronze dancing faun (the original is in Naples) that gives the villa its name.

On the street behind, the **House of the Vettii** is one of the most delightful houses in Pompeii and one of the best maintained, a merchant villa ranged around a lovely central peristyle that gives the best possible impression of the domestic environment of the city's upper middle classes. The first room on the right off the peristyle holds the best of Pompeii's murals actually viewable on site: the one on the left shows the young Hercules struggling with serpents; another, in the corner, depicts Ixion tied to a wheel after offending Zeus, while a third shows Dirce being dragged to her death by the bull set on her by the sons of Antiope. There are more paintings beyond here, through the villa's kitchen in a small room that's normally kept locked – erotic works showing various techniques of lovemaking (Greek-style, woman on top; Roman-style, man on top) together with an absurdly potent-looking statue of Priapus from which women were supposed to drink to be fertile; phallic symbols were also, it's reckoned, believed to ward off the evil eye.

Cross over to the other side of the site for the so-called **new excavations**, which began in 1911 and actually uncovered some of the town's most important quarters, stretching along the main Via dell'Abbondanza. The **Grand Theatre**, for one, is very well preserved and is still used for performances, overlooking the small, grassy, column-fringed square of the **Gladiators' Barracks** – not in fact a barracks at all but a refectory and meeting-place for spectators from the nearby amphitheatre. Walk around to the far left side of the Grand Theatre, down the steps and up again, and you're in front of the **Little Theatre** – a smaller, more intimate venue also still used for summer performances and with a better-kept corridor behind the stage space. As for the **Amphitheatre**, it's one of Italy's most intact and accessible, and also its oldest, dating from 80 BC; it once had room for a crowd of some 12,000 – well over half the town's population. Next door, the **Palestra** is a vast parade ground that was used by Pompeii's youth for sport and exercise – still with its square of swimming pool in the centre. It must have been in use when the eruption struck Pompeii, since its southeast corner was found littered with the skeletons of young men trying to flee the disaster. Just north of the Palestra, off Via Abbondanza, is the **House of Loreius Tiburtinus**, a gracious villa fronted by great bronze doors. Paintings of Narcissus gazing rapt at his reflection and Pyramus and Thisbe frame a water cascade; the water flowed down a channel and into the villa's lovely garden, which has been replanted with vines and shrubs.

One last place you shouldn't miss at Pompeii is the **Villa dei Misteri**, outside the main site, a short walk from the Porta Ercolano (same hours and ticket as main site). This is probably the best-preserved of all Pompeii's palatial houses, an originally third-century BC structure with a warren of rooms and courtyards that derives its name from a series of paintings in one of its larger chambers: depictions of the initiation rites of a young woman into the Dionysiac Mysteries, an outlawed cult of the early imperial era. Not much is known about the cult itself, but the paintings are marvellously clear, remarkable for the surety of their execution and the brightness of their tones and colours. They follow an obvious narrative, starting with the left-hand wall and continuing around the room with a series of freeze-frames showing sacrifice, flagellation, dancing and other rituals, all under the serene gaze of the mistress of the house.

Practicalities

To **reach Pompeii from Naples**, take the Circumvesuviana east from Torre Annuziata to Pompeii-Villa dei Misteri – about thirty minutes; this leaves you right outside the western entrance to the site. The Circumvesuviana also runs to Pompeii-Santuario, outside the site's eastern entrance, or you can take the roughly hourly mainline train (direction Salerno) to the main Pompeii FS station, on the south side of the fairly characterless modern town. From the main station ignore the taxi drivers offering to take you to the entrance for an extortionate fee – it only takes around ten minutes to walk. Head away from the station towards the tall belltower, turning left at the main square to follow the signs to "Pompeii Scavi". After around 200m you come to the eastern entrance, Porta di Nuceria on the right-hand side, the site itself screened by an avenue of trees.

It makes most sense to see Pompeii from Naples, and there's really no need to stay overnight, though if you get stuck or are planning to move on south after seeing Pompeii, there are plenty of **hotels** in the modern town and a large and well-equipped campsite – *Zeus* (☎081.861.5320), open all year, right outside the Pompeii-Villa dei Misteri station. Modern Pompeii's **tourist office** at Via Sacra 1 (Mon–Sat 9am–3pm; ☎081.850.7255), just off the main square, has plans of the site.

Sorrento

Topping the rocky cliffs close to the end of its peninsula, 25km south of Pompeii, the last town of significance on this side of the bay, **SORRENTO** is solely and unashamedly a resort, its inspired location and mild climate drawing foreigners from all over Europe for close on 200 years. Ibsen wrote part of *Peer Gynt* in Sorrento, Wagner and Nietzsche had a well-publicized row here, and Maxim Gorky lived for over a decade in the town. Nowadays it's strictly package-tour territory, but really none the worse for it, with little of the brashness of its Spanish and Greek equivalents but all of their vigour, a bright, lively place that retains its southern Italian roots. Cheap restaurants aren't hard to find; neither – if you know where to look – is reasonably priced accommodation; and there's really no better place outside Naples itself from which to explore the rugged peninsula (even parts of the Amalfi coast) and the islands of the bay.

Sorrento's centre is **Piazza Tasso**, built astride the gorge that runs through the centre of town; it was named after the wayward sixteenth-century Italian poet to whom the town was home and has a statue of him in the far corner. There's nothing much to see in Sorrento itself, but it's nice to wander through the streets that feed into the square, some of which are pedestrianized for the lively evening passeggiata. The local **Museo Correale di Terranova**, housed in the airy former palace of a family of local counts at the far end of Via Correale (Mon & Wed–Sat 9am–2pm, Sun 9am–12.30pm; L8000/€4.13), might kill an hour or so, with its examples of the local inlaid wood *intar-*

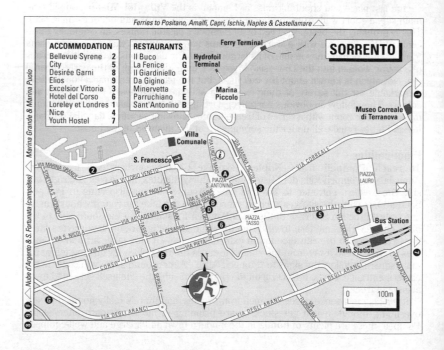

ACCOMMODATION
Bellevue Syrene	2
City	5
Desirée Garni	8
Elios	9
Excelsior Vittoria	3
Hotel del Corso	6
Loreley et Londres	1
Nice	4
Youth Hostel	7

RESTAURANTS
Il Buco	A
La Fenice	G
Il Giardiniello	C
Da Gigino	D
Minervetta	F
Parruchiano	E
Sant'Antonino	B

SORRENTO

Ferries to Positano, Amalfi, Capri, Ischia, Naples & Castellamare

sio work – most of it much nicer and more ingenious than the mass-produced stuff you see around town – along with various paintings of the Neapolitan school, the odd foreign canvas, including an obscure Rubens, lots of views of Sorrento and the Bay of Naples, and various locally unearthed archeological knick-knacks. Otherwise the town is entirely given over to pleasure and there's not much else to see, although it's nice to linger in the shady gardens of the **Villa Communale**, whose terrace has lovely views out to sea, and peek into the small thirteenth-century cloister of the church of **San Francesco** just outside, planted with vines and bright bougainvillea – a peaceful escape from the bustle of the rest of Sorrento.

Strange as it may seem, Sorrento isn't particularly well provided with **beaches**, and in the town itself you either have to make do with the small strips of sand of the **Marina Piccola** lido, right below the Villa Communale gardens and accessible by a lift or steps, or the rocks and tiny, crowded strip of sand at **Marina Grande** – fifteen minutes' walk or a short bus ride (roughly every 30min) west of Piazza Tasso. Both places cost around L5000/€2.58 a head for the day, plus charges for parasol and chair rental, although there is a small patch of sand, immediately right of the lift exit at Marina Piccola, that is free. If you do come down to either of these spots, it's a good idea to hire a pedal-boat (around L20,000/€10.33 an hour) and get free of the shore, since both beaches can get busy.

If you don't fancy the crowds in Sorrento, you can try the beaches further west. Twenty minutes' walk from the centre of Sorrento along Via del Capo (which is the continuation of Corso Italia), or a short bus ride from Piazza Tasso, there are a couple of options. You can either walk ten minutes or so from the bus stop down the Ruderi Villa Romana Pollio to some nice rocks, swathed with walkways, around the ruins of a Roman villa; or you could stroll 100m further west and take a path off to the right past the *Hotel Dania*, which shortcuts in ten minutes or so to **Marina Puolo** – a short stretch of beach lined by fishing boats and a handful of trattorias.

Practicalities

Sorrento's **train station** is located in the centre of town, five minutes from the main Piazza Tasso along busy Corso Italia. There's a **tourist office** in the large yellow Circolo dei Forestieri building at Via Luigi de Maio 35, just off Piazza San Antonino (Mon–Sat 8.45am–2.15pm & 3.45–6.15pm; ☎081.807.4033, *aastsorrento@libero.it*), which has maps, details on accommodation and information about excursions – including tours to the Venticano winery, where Greco di Tufo, Fiano di Avellino and Taurasi are produced. The travel offices on Piazza San Antonino can deal with bus and ferry enquiries and reserve tickets. Incidentally, if you don't want to rely on public transport, Sorrento, Corso Italia 210 (☎081.878.1386), close by the train station, rent cars and scooters, but check roadworthiness carefully before signing anything. Guarracino, Via Sant'Antonino 19 (☎081.878.1728), just off the piazza of the same name, rent bicycles.

As well as *Chaplin's* (see overleaf), there's a handy **Internet café** at Via Fuorimura 20 (*www.blublu.it*; Mon–Fri 10am–1pm, 4.30pm–midnight, Sat 10am–1pm, 5pm–1am; L3000/€1.55 for 15min, L5000/€2.58 for 30min, L10,000/€5.16 for 1hr).

ACCOMMODATION

Accommodation isn't really a problem, although during peak season you should definitely book in advance. There's a **youth hostel** at Via degli Aranci 160 (☎081.807.2925; L25,000/€12.91, including breakfast), five minutes' walk from the train station: to get there walk out of the station and turn left on the main road – Via degli Aranci is 200m down on the left. Among **campsites**, the closest choice is the *Nube d'Argento* site, close by the *Elios* at Via del Capo 12 (☎081.878.1344); if that's full, try the *Santa Fortunata*, about 1.5km from the centre at Via del Capo 39 (☎081.807.3579).

City, Corso Italia 221 (✆ & fax 081.877.2210). Fairly basic, but well placed for the action in town. ③.

Bellevue Syrene, Piazza della Vittoria 5 (✆ & fax 081.878.1024). A lovely nineteenth-century hotel, built on the remains of a Roman villa. Boasts glorious views and a private beach. ⑥.

Hotel del Corso, Corso Italia 134 (✆081.807.3157). Right by Piazza Tazzo, the del Corso is very pleasant, if a little rudimentary. ⑤.

Desiree Garnì (✆081.878.1563). Beautifully situated on top of the cliff to the west of town, and with stunning views. With its private beach (accessible by lift) and pleasant rooms it's a good option, and the owners go out of their way to be helpful. ③.

Elios, Via del Capo 33 (✆081.878.1812). Ten minutes' walk from the centre to the west of town, the Elios has terrific sea views and private parking. ③.

Excelsior Vittoria, Piazza Tasso 34 (✆081.807.1044, fax 081.877.1206, www.exvitt.it). This fabulously grand hotel has been owned by the same family since 1834; it sits right in the centre of town in a formal garden with a lemon and orange grove and a large pool; the lift from the swish terrace bar plunges straight down to the seafront. Immaculate but friendly service. ⑨.

Loreley et Londres, Via Califano 12 (✆ & fax 081.807.3187). Situated in a beautiful ancient building high on the cliffs on the eastern edge of the town centre, this is wonderful value. ⑤.

Nice, Corso Italia 257 (✆081.878.1650, fax 081.807.1154). A very convenient and centrally placed option; the en suite rooms are plain but clean. ④.

EATING

Sorrento has no shortage of **restaurants**, but in the more touristy places service can be slow and the food not up to scratch. If you just want a snack, *Bar Rita*, Corso Italia 219, can't be bettered, with a wide array of sandwiches, cakes and other delicious lunch items.

Il Buco, Rampe Marina Piccola 11, Piazza San Antonino. Just off the square down a cobbled alley, this is a fine option for lunch or dinner.

La Fenice, Via degli Aranci 11. A great place with a lively atmosphere. Closed Mon.

Giardiniello, Via Accademia 7. Just off Corso Italia, between Piazza Sant'Antonio and Via Tasso, this is a good, affordable pizzeria-ristorante with a small garden, specializing in fish, shellfish and barbecued meats. Closed Thurs.

Da Gigino, Via degli Archi 15. A great no-nonsense choice, with excellent pizzas and good pasta and main courses. Closed Tues except July & Sept.

Minervetta, Via del Capo 30. A great scenic option in a pension whose terrace restaurant perches a little way along Via del Capo on the right.

Parruchiano, Corso Italia 71. An enormous restaurant, very popular locally, with fine food and a wonderful enclosed garden setting. Closed Wed.

Sant'Antonino, Via Santa Maria delle Grazie, off Piazza Sant'Antonino. Terrific pizzas, and a garden as well. No closing day.

NIGHTLIFE

For **drinking**, stylish *Bar Ercolano*, right on Piazza Tasso, isn't as pricey as you'd think and is vibrantly sited. The terrace bar in the *Circolo dei Forestieri* is a genteel place to drink and has wonderfully romantic night-time views, as well as a dance floor, and for some vicarious glamour head for the beautiful outside bar at the *Grand Hotel Excelsior Vittoria* (see above), which looks across the bay to Vesuvius. *Bollicine*, a small wood-panelled wine bar on Via Accademia, is a smart place to sample a wide range of good Campanian wines. For late-night drinking, the pubs along Corso Italia are as good a place as any: try the capacious *English Inn*, Corso Italia 55, which has a free outside dance floor upstairs that gets packed in the summer; and *Chaplin's*, almost opposite, which provides Internet access, is open till late.

The islands

Guarding each prong of the Bay of Naples, the islands of Cápri, Ischia and Prócida between them make up the best-known group of Italian islands. Each is a very different

GETTING TO THE ISLANDS

Ferries and **hydrofoils** are run by three main companies: Caremar, Alilauro and SNAV, who operate from Naples' main harbour (the Molo Beverello) at the bottom of Piazza Municipio, and from the quayside at Mergellina. Between them, they depart for all of the islands from Naples, Pozzuoli and Sorrento, with some connections from Salerno, Amalfi and Positano. Whichever you take, day-trips are quite feasible; usually the last connection delivers you back on the mainland in time for dinner. On foot, you can simply buy tickets when you turn up at the offices at the port; in general it's better to buy a single rather than a return ticket since it doesn't work out more expensive and you retain more flexibility on the time you come back. Having said that, on summer Sundays (especially on Cápri, and especially by hydrofoil), it's a good idea to buy your return ticket as soon as you arrive, to avoid the risk of finding the last boat or hydrofoil fully booked.

The following is to give a rough idea of frequencies during the summer (they're greatly reduced off-season), and you should either look in *Qui Napoli*, check with the local tourist office or buy a copy of *Il Mattino* for specific timings. You can also phone the companies direct, if your Italian is up to it: Caremar (Molo Beverello ☎081.551.3882); Alilauro (☎081.761.1004, *www.lauro.it*); SNAV (☎081.896.9975); and Prócida Lines (☎081.896.0328).

HYDROFOILS

Naples (Molo Beverello)–Cápri (8 daily; 40min).
Naples (Molo Beverello)–Ischia (15 daily; 50min).
Naples (Molo Beverello)–Prócida (6 daily; 35min).
Naples (Mergellina)–Cápri (9 daily; 40min).
Naples (Mergellina)–Ischia (12 daily; 40min).
Naples (Mergellina)–Forio (Ischia) (6 daily; 50min).
Naples (Mergellina)–Casamicciola (Ischia) (6 daily; 50min).
Naples (Mergellina)–Prócida (7 daily; 30min).
Salerno–Cápri (2 daily; 1hr).
Sorrento–Ischia (via Naples) (4 daily; 1hr). Also 1 daily direct, and 1 daily via Cápri.
Sorrento–Cápri (12 daily; 20min).
Casamicciola (Ischia)–Prócida (7 daily; 30min).

FERRIES

Naples (Molo Beverello)–Cápri (6 daily; 1hr 15min).
Naples (Molo Beverello)–Ischia (8 daily; 1hr 20min).
Naples (Molo Beverello)–Prócida (7 daily; 1hr).
Pozzuoli–Ischia (14 daily; 1hr 40min).
Pozzuoli–Casamicciola (Ischia) (15 daily; 1hr 50min).
Pozzuoli–Prócida (14 daily; 1hr 10min).
Ischia–Prócida (6 daily; 40min).
Sorrento–Cápri (6 daily; 50min).
Salerno–Cápri (via Amalfi; 1 daily; 2hr).
Salerno–Ischia (via Amalfi and Positano; 1 daily; 2hr 30min).

creature, though. **Cápri** is a place of legend, home to the mythical Sirens and a much-eulogized playground of the super-rich in the years since – though now settled down to a lucrative existence as a target for day-trippers from the mainland. Visit by all means, but bear in mind that you have to hunt hard these days to detect the origins of much of the purple prose. **Ischia** is a target for package tours and weekenders from Naples, but its size means that it doesn't feel as crowded as Cápri, and plentiful hot springs, sandy beaches and a green volcanic interior make the island well worth a few days' visit, especially as you can easily visit other sites in the bay (including Pompeii and Herculaneum) by ferry from here. Pretty **Prócida**, the smallest of the islands and the least interesting – though the best venue for fairly peaceful lazing – remains reasonably untouched by the high season.

Cápri

Sheering out of the sea just off the far end of the Sorrentine peninsula, the island of **Cápri** has long been the most sought-after part of the Bay of Naples. During Roman times Augustus retreated to the island's gorgeous cliffbound scenery to escape the cares of office; later Tiberius moved the imperial capital here, indulging himself in legendarily debauched antics until his death in 37 AD. After the Romans left, Cápri was rather neglected until the early nineteenth century, when the discovery of the Blue Grotto and the island's remarkable natural landscape coincided nicely with the rise of tourism, and the island has never looked back, attracting a steady flow of artists and writers and, more recently, inquisitive tourists, ever since. The English especially have always flocked here: D.H. Lawrence and George Bernard Shaw were among more illustrious visitors, Graham Greene and Gracie Fields had houses here; and even Lenin visited for a time after the failure of the 1905 uprising.

Cápri tends to get a mixed press these days, the consensus being that while it might have been an attractive place once, it's been pretty much ruined by the crowds and the prices. And Cápri *is* crowded, to the degree that in July and August, and on *all* summer weekends, it would be sensible to give it a miss. But reports that the island has been irreparably spoilt are way overstated. Ischia is busy too, Prócida isn't nearly as interesting – or beautiful – and it would be hard to find a place with more inspiring views. It's expensive, though, especially if you sit and drink on its main squares. But prices aren't really any higher than at other major Italian resorts, and you can cut out the inflated expense of accommodation by visiting on a day-trip; indeed, in a couple of these you could see all of the island comfortably.

Marina Grande, Cápri town and around

Ferries and hydrofoils dock at **MARINA GRANDE**, the waterside extension of the island's main town, which perches on the hill above. You can take boats to the Blue Grotto (see opposite) from here, and there's a tourist office that doles out maps and other information, as well as any number of pricey waterside cafés and restaurants. It is, however, quickly exhausted, and you may as well take the **funicular** (daily: 6.30am–9pm; L1500/€0.77 one-way) up the steep hill to Cápri town itself; if the funicular is too crowded (as it surely will be in high season) you can also walk, which takes about twenty minutes; follow the road up from the far end of the harbour, from where steps lead all the way up across the crisscrossing road.

CÁPRI is the main town of the island, nestled between its two mountains, its houses connected by winding, hilly alleyways that give onto the dinky (almost toytown) main square of **Piazza Umberto**, crowded with café tables and, invariably, a lot of people. Sit on the steps and eat your lunch and watch the drinkers and diners digging deep for the (undeniable) ambience.

Of things to see in or near Cápri, the **Certosa San Giacomo** (Tues–Sat 9am–2pm, Sun 9am–1pm; free) on the far side of the town is a run-down old monastery with a handful of paintings, a couple of shapeless Roman statues dredged up from the deep and an odd, overgrown cloister given over in part to a music school. To the right of the monastery, the **Giardini Augustos** give tremendous views of the coast below and the towering jagged cliffs above, and from there you can wind down to either the beach below (rocks really), or, beyond, to **MARINA PICCOLA** – a small huddle of houses and restaurants around a few patches of pebble beach: reasonably uncrowded out of season, though in July or August you might as well forget it. Marina Piccola is also accessible by bus.

Up above the Certosa, and a further pleasant walk fifteen minutes through Cápri town, the **Belvedere del Cannone** has marvellous views, especially over the **Faraglioni** rocks to the left and Marina Piccola to the right. Further out of Cápri town, there are two walks worth doing out to the eastern edge of the island. One, up to the ruins of Tiberius's villa, the **Villa Jovis** (daily 9am–1hr before sunset; L4000/€2.07), is a steep thirty-minute hike from Piazza Umberto following Via Botteghe out of the square and Via Tiberio up the hill. It was here that Tiberius retired in 27 AD to lead a life of vice and debauchery and to take revenge on his enemies, many of whom he apparently had thrown off the cliff-face. You can see why he chose the site: it's among Cápri's most exhilarating, with incredible vistas of Ischia, Prócida and the bay; on a clear day you can even see Salerno and beyond. There's not much left of the villa, but you can get a good sense of the shape and design of its various parts from the arched halls and narrow passageways that remain. Below, there's another villa, the more recent **Villa Fersen** of one Count Fersen-Adelsward, a gay Swedish millionaire who built the house early this century apparently to entertain pick-ups from the town. Unfortunately its new owner has not seen fit to open it up to the public.

The other walk is to the **Arco Naturale**, an impressive natural rock formation at the end of a high, lush valley, a 25-minute hike from Cápri town, again following Via Botteghe out of the square but branching off up Via Matermania after ten minutes or so; you can get quite close to the arch due to the specially constructed viewing platforms. Just before the arch, steps lead down to the **Grotta di Matermania**, ten minutes away down quite a few steps – a dusty cutaway out of the rock that was converted to house a shrine to the Sybil by the Romans. Steps lead on down from the cave, sheer through the trees, before flattening into a path that you can follow back to the **Tragara Belvedere**, and, eventually, Cápri town – reachable in about an hour.

Anacápri and around

The island's other main settlement, **ANACÁPRI**, is more sprawling than Cápri itself and less obviously picturesque, its main square, **Piazza Vittoria**, flanked by souvenir shops, bland fashion boutiques and restaurants decked with tourist menus – Cápri without the chic. During the season, a chair lift operates from Piazza Vittoria up to **Monte Solaro** (March–Oct daily except Tues: 9.30am–5.30pm Nov–Feb 10.30pm–3pm; return L9500/€4.13, one way L7000/€3.62), shifting you up to the summit of the mountain at 596m high, the island's highest point, in about twelve minutes. At the top there's only a ruined castle and a café, but the location is very tranquil and the views are marvellous.

A short walk away from Piazza Vittoria down Via G. Orlandi, the church of **San Michele** is the village's principal sight, its tiled floor painted with an eighteenth-century depiction of the Fall that you view from an upstairs balcony – a lush work after a drawing by the Neapolitan painter **Solimena**, in rich blues and yellows, showing cats, unicorns and other creatures.

Continuing in the same direction, a good 45-minute hike away starting off down Via Lo Pozzo (or reachable by bus every twenty minutes from Piazza Vittoria), the **Blue Grotto** or Grotta Azzura is probably the island's best-known feature – though also its most exploitative, the boatmen here whisking visitors onto boats and in and out of the grotto in about five minutes flat (entrance L8000/€0.13, plus L7000/€3.62 for the rowing boat). The grotto is quietly impressive, the blue of its innards caused by the sun entering the cave through the water, but it's rather overrated, and the process is all over so quickly as to be barely worth the trip down here, let alone the extortionate fees. Technically, you can swim into the cave – it's not the exclusive preserve of the boatmen, though they'll try to persuade you otherwise – but the route through is so busy that unless you're a strong swimmer it's only advisable to try at the end of the day after the tours have finished. Incidentally, it's also possible to take a boat trip to the grotto direct from Marina Grande.

Time is much better spent walking in the opposite direction from Piazza Vittoria, past a long gauntlet of souvenir stalls to Axel Munthe's **Villa San Michele** (daily: March 9.30am–4.30pm; April 9.30am–5pm; May–Sept 9am–6pm; Nov–Jan 10.30am–3.30pm; L8000/€4.13), a light, airy house with lush and fragrant gardens that is one of the real highlights of the island. The Swedish writer and healer Munthe lived here for a number of years, and it's filled with his furniture and knick-knacks, as well as Roman artefacts ingeniously incorporated into the villa's rooms and gardens. Busts and bronzes abound: one statue of Hermes was given to Munthe by the city of Naples in thanks for his work in the city during the cholera epidemic of 1884 (see p.827); Corinthian capitals are converted as coffee tables, other surfaces topped with intricate Cosmati mosaic-work. His book *The Story of San Michele* – more the story of his life – is well worth a read.

Practicalities

There are **tourist offices** in Marina Grande (April, May & Oct Mon–Sat 8.30am–8.30pm, Sun 3.30–5pm; June–Sept Mon–Sat 8.30am–8.30pm, Sun 9am–1pm & 3.30–7pm; Nov–March Mon–Sat 9am–1pm & 3.30–6.45pm; ☎081.837.0634), and on Piazza Umberto in Cápri town (same hours; ☎081.837.0686). In Anacápri the tourist office is on Via G. Orlandi (Mon–Sat 9am–1pm & 3–6.30pm; ☎081.837.1524). **Getting around** the island, there is a decent bus service connecting all the main centres – Marina Grande, Cápri, Marina Piccola, Anacápri – every fifteen minutes; buses also run regularly down to the Blue Grotto from Anacápri; tickets cost L1500/€0.77 from *tabacchi*.

You'd be well advised not to **stay overnight** on Cápri: in peak season space is extremely limited, and the prices are through the roof; day-trips here from Naples or Sorrento are in any case easy. If you are keen to stay, however – and the island certainly is a lot quieter after the day-tripping crowds have gone home – you could try the *Quattro Stagioni*, Via Marina Piccola 1 (☎081.837.0041; ⑥), or the centrally placed *Stella Maris*, Via Roma 27 (☎081.837.0452; ④). If they are full, *La Prora*, very appealingly situated up above the *Stella Maris* on Via Castello (☎081.837.0281; ⑤), is an exceedingly pleasant place to stay, as is the excellent *Villa Esperia* on Via Sopramonte (☎081.837.0262; ⑤), a former Englishwoman's villa that has been recently renovated and has lovely views from its rooms, some of which have their own terrace. If you don't mind staying in Anacápri, the *Villa Eva*, Via La Fabbrica 8 (☎081.837.1365, *villa@capri.it*; ④), is perhaps the best-value place to stay on the island, a welcoming family-run hostel/hotel; phone from Piazza Vittoria and they'll pick you up. Otherwise go for the reasosnable and extremely friendly *Alla Bussola di Hermes* (☎081.837.1365, *hermes@libero.it*; ②), on Via Traversa La Vigna; it's basic but clean.

Even if you don't stay, **eating** can be an expense, and you might prefer to knock yourself up a picnic lunch: in Cápri town there are a supermarket and a bakery a little way down Via Botteghe off Piazza Umberto, and well-stocked *salumerie* at Via Roma 13 and 30. For sit-down food, one of the best places is *Da Gemma*, under the arches of old Cápri at Via Madre Serafina 6 (Oct–Feb closed Mon), a friendly, long-established place with a windowed main room overlooking the bay – good for seafood, and not that pricey. Down below, *Di Giorgio* is a surprisingly inexpensive restaurant in a good location (closed Tues), while on the other side of Piazza Umberto, *Pizzeria Aurora*, on Via

Fuorlovado (closed Tues) – the continuation of Via Botteghe – is pretty good value too. In Anacápri, *Materita* on Via G Orlandi, off Piazza Diaz (no closing day), is a fairly reasonable place to eat, and those staying at *Villa Eva* can get a bargain "tourist menu" at *Il Cucciolo* (no closing day), five minutes' away at Nuova Traversa Veterino 50. Somewhat nicer, though, *Da Giovanni*, near the Blue Grotto, is a great-value place to eat, especially by Cápri's standards. Take the cliffside path to the left of the Blue Grotto bus stop, away from the Grotto; ignore the pricey seafood places along the way, and follow the path right to the end. Giovanni is an artist who has set up a small restaurant under awnings on the cliff ledges here; his food and local wine are good and very reasonably priced and it's open daily in summer.

Ischia

Largest of the islands in the Bay of Naples, **Ischia** rises out of the sea in a series of pointy green hummocks, German, Scandinavian and British tourists flocking in large numbers during peak season to its charming beach resorts, thermal springs and therapeutic sands. Its reputation has always been poorer than Cápri's: it is perhaps not so dramatically beautiful, but you can at least be sure of being alone in exploring parts of the mountainous interior, and **La Mortella**, the exotic garden cultivated by the British composer William Walton and his widow Susana, is an unmissable attraction. Indeed, if you're after some beach lounging, good walking and lively nightlife within striking distance of Naples and the rest of the bay, it might be just the place.

Public transport is regular and easy to negotiate: buses go round the island from Ischia Porto every thirty minutes in both directions, stopping just about everywhere – they run on two circular routes, the CS and CD, basically one in each direction. Tickets cost L1800/€0.93 and are valid for an hour, although if you're going to be moving around a lot it's worth buying a day ticket for L5300/€2.74; a seven-day ticket is L23,000/€11.88.

Ischia Porto and Ischia Ponte

The main town of Ischia is **ISCHIA PORTO**, where most of the ferries dock, an appealing stretch of hotels, ritzy boutiques and beach shops planted with lemon trees and Indian figs fronted by golden sands: **Spiaggia San Pietro** is to the right of the port, accessible by following Via Buonocore off Via Roma; and the inexplicably named **Spiaggia degli Inglesi**, on the other side of the port, is reachable by way of the narrow path that leads over the headland from the end of Via Jasolino.

Otherwise the main thing to do is to window-shop and stroll along the main Corso Vittoria Colonna, either branching off to a further beach, the **Spiaggia dei Pescatori**, or following it all the way down to the other part of Ischia's main town, **ISCHIA PONTE**, a quieter and less commercialized centre. Here the focus is the **Castello Aragonese** (March to mid–Nov 9.30am till sunset; L12,000/€6.20, includes the lift to the top), which crowns an offshore rock but is accessible from a short causeway; its stunningly distinctive pyramid was one of the backdrops in the film *The Talented Mr Ripley*. Vittoria Colonna, the Renaissance poet and close friend of Michelangelo, spent much of her life here, following the seizure of her family's land by Alexander VI. The citadel itself where she lived is rather tumbledown now and closed to the public, but below is a complex of buildings, almost a separate village really, around which you can stroll. There's the weird open shell of a cathedral destroyed by the British in 1806, a prison that once held political prisoners during the upheavals of the Unification, and the macabre remnants of a convent, in which a couple of dark rooms ringed with a set of commode-like seats served as a cemetery for the dead sisters – placed here to putrefy in front of the living members of the community.

PRACTICALITIES

Ischia Porto's helpful **tourist office** is right by the quayside ferry ticket offices (Mon–Sat 9am–2pm & 3–8pm; ☎081.507.4211, *www.ischiaonline.it*); the **bus terminus**, with buses going to all other parts of the island, is just behind here.

There are plenty of **accommodation** options, though bear in mind that many close in low season. The *Monastero*, high in the *castello* in Ischia Ponte (☎081.992.435, *www.castelloaragonese.it*; ③), is perfect if you fancy a bit of seclusion and has tremendous views; it's due to be renovated in 2001, though the owner, an accomplished painter whose work adorns the walls, plans to maintain the simple austerity of the rooms, which once were the nuns' cells. Ischia Porto is better for access to the island's nightlife: the *Rosita*, Via Quercia 38 (☎081.993.875; ②), is a good-value choice a large place in a lush garden, two minutes from the bus terminus – as is the clean and appealing *Antonio Macri*, off the portside at Via Jasolino 96 (☎081.992.603; ③). Towards the pricier end of the scale is the *Hotel Continental Mare*, west of town at Via B. Cossa 25 (☎081.982.577, fax 081.992.505, *http://contimare.leohotels.it*; ⑤) which enjoys a splendid location above the sea and its own stretch of beach. Best of all though, is luxurious *Il Moresco* (☎081.981.355, fax 081.992.338, *www.ilmoresco.it*; ⑨), Via E. Gianturco 16, where Gwyneth, Jude et al stayed during the making of *The Talented Mr Ripley*. Housed in an elegant 1950s villa in the heart of Ischia Porto, but still managing to feel secluded, it boasts lovely swimming and thermal pools, comfortable rooms and friendly, attentive service.

For **eating**, *Mastù Peppe*, right by the tourist office and ferry quay (closed Mon), is cheap and quite good though the service can be slow; with a little more money, try *Gennaro*, across the harbour at Via Porto 64 (no closing day) where the food can be terrific but is rather hit or miss. For a real splash-out option, go for the superb *Alberto*, right on the seafront on Viale C. Colombo – the pretty restaurant, on stilts, over the sea, has immaculate service and beautifully presented seafood. In Ischia Ponte, *Cocogelo Alberto* (open daily), just to the right of the causeway which leads to the *castello*, has lovely sea views and dishes up great seafood.

As for **nightlife**, head for the lively run of late-night bars and cafés along Via Porto; best is the *Millennium Bar* which has a free dancefloor as well as serving during the day as a café with **Internet** access (2pm till late).

Casamicciola Terme and Lacco Ameno

The island is at its most developed along its northern and western shores – heading west from Ischia Porto. The first village you reach, **CASAMICCIOLA TERME**, is a spa centre with many hotels and a crowded central beach – though you can find a quieter one on the far side of the village. Ibsen spent a summer here, and the waters are said to be full of iodine (apparently beneficial for the skin and the nervous system), but otherwise you may as well push on to **LACCO AMENO**, a brighter little town, again with a beach and with spa waters that are said to be the most radioactive in Italy.

Lacco Ameno has two **museums** which are worth at least a peek. The first is accessed via the pink confection of the church of **Santa Restituta** on the main square (Mon–Sat 9.30am–12.30pm & 5–7pm, Sun 9.30am–12.30pm; L5000/€2.58). Persevere past a jumble of lamps and pots to the excavations below ground-level, where the graves of the island's inhabitants – "Proto Campanian", Hellenistic, Roman and Paleochristian – are piled on top of each other in bewildering but intriguing confusion. Amongst the displayed artefacts are Neolithic idols, Mycenean pottery, and a lovely fragment of Attic pottery, depicting a smiling reclining man.

Above the main square away from the sea in Villa Arbusto is the **Museo Archeologico di Pithecusa** (daily: April–Oct 9.30am–1pm & 5pm–7pm; Nov–March 9.30am–1pm & 3pm–9pm; L10,000/€5.16; *www.pithecusae.it*). This is an altogether more orderly affair with plenty of information in English, which displays finds from the acropolis of Monte di Vico, in continuous use from the eighth to the first centuries BC. Pithecusa (modern Ischia) was the first and most northerly Greek settlement in the West, a thriving and vital staging post at the western end of routes from the Aegean and the Levant – in addition to local artefacts, the museum displays grave goods imported from Syria, Egypt and Etruria. The epigram on the modest-looking Coppa di Nestore makes a light-hearted challenge to the cup mentioned in Homer's *Iliad*, while a ship-wreck scene on a locally made bowl is thought to be the oldest example of figurative painting in Italy.

La Mortella

Between Lacco Ameno and Forio is one of Ischia's highlights: the stunning garden of **La Mortella** (April–Nov Tues, Thurs, Sat & Sun 9am–7pm; L12,000/€6.20; ask the bus driver to drop you off), created by the English composer William Walton and his Argentinian widow Susana, who still lives here and, dressed in jewel-coloured Thai clothes, is a vibrant presence in the garden. The Waltons moved to Ischia, then sparsely populated and little-known to tourists, in 1949, forerunners of a coterie of writers and artists including Auden and Terence Rattigan. With the garden designer Russell Page they created La Mortella from an unpromising volcanic stone quarry, just the first phase of landscaping taking seven years to complete.

Paths wind up through the abundant site, which has some 300 rare and exotic plants. Near the entrance is a glasshouse sheltering the world's largest water-lily, **Victoria amazonica**, a gender-bending giant which flowers as a female with white petals, imprisons beetles for pollination purposes, and reopens later in the day with male organs developed and deep crimson petals. Above the glasshouse sits a charming terraced **tearoom/bar** where the lush strains of Walton's music can be heard, and an enclosure with bright hummingbirds flitting about. Paths loop through luxuriant foliage to the pyramid-shaped rock that holds Walton's ashes, a cascade guarded by a sculpted croc-odile and a pretty **Thai pavilion** surrounded by heavy-headed purple agapanthus. At the garden's summit, a belvedere provides superb views across the island.

Devotees of Walton's music shouldn't miss the prettily theatrical **museum** above the tearoom, which shows a video about the composer and features portraits by Cecil Beaton, a bust by Elizabeth Frink, and paintings and set-designs by John Piper. And it's well worth combing your visit to the garden with free **concerts** (April–July & Sept–Oct Sat & Sun 5pm), held in the adjoining recital hall, which provide a forum for students from Fiesole and Naples.

Forio

FORIO sprawls around its bay, another growing resort that is quite pretty behind its seafront of bars and pizzerias, focusing around the busy main street of Corso Umberto. Out on the point on the far side of the old centre (turn right at the far end of Corso Umberto), the **Chiesa Soccorso** is a bold, whitewashed landmark from which to sur-vey the town, a simple church, one of whose chapels preserves a wooden crucifix dis-covered among the rocks below after a storm in the early 1500s.

There are good **beaches** either side of Forio: the **Spiaggia di Chiaia**, a short walk to the north; to the south **Cava del Isola** which is popular with a young crowd; and the **Spiaggia di Citara**, a somewhat longer walk to the south along Via G. Mazzella. Here you'll find the **Giardini Poseidon** (April–Oct daily 8.30am–6.30pm; L45,000/€23.24 per day, L35,000/€18.08 for a half-day), an extensive complex of blissfully relaxing ther-mal baths on the seafront.

If you decide to **stay**, try the charming and central *Punta del Sole* on Piazza Maltese (☎081.989.156; ⑤), with balconied rooms set in a beautiful garden – or there's the more basic *Nettuno*, Via C. Piro 1 (☎081.997.140; ④). There are some good **eating** options here: head for the delightful *Umberto a Mare* (April–Oct) tucked under the Chiesa Soccorso, whose pretty whitewashed interior looks out onto the sea. If you have a car, take the road to Monte Epomeo and head for *Peppina di Renato* (closed Wed; April –June) where you sit on barrel seats to consume great pizzas; or just off the coast road heading south, is *Il Melograno* (April–Sept daily; Nov & Dec Wed–Sun), which does a modern take on traditional Ischia cuisine.

Sant'Angelo and around

Ischia is most pleasant on its southern side, the landscape steeper and greener, with fewer people to enjoy it. SANT'ANGELO is probably its loveliest spot, a tiny fishing village crowded around a narrow isthmus linking with a humpy islet that's out of bounds to buses, which drop you right outside. It's inevitably quite developed, centring on a square and harbour crowded with café tables and surrounded by pricey boutiques, but if all you want to do is laze in the sun it's perhaps the island's most appealing spot to do so. There's a reasonable **beach** lining one side of the isthmus that connects Sant'Angelo to its islet, as well as the nearby stretch of the **Spiaggia dei Maronti**, 1km east, which is accessible by plentiful taxi boats from Sant'Angelo's harbour (L4000/€2.07), or on foot in about 25 minutes – take the path from the top of the village.

Taxi boats will drop you at one of a number of specific features: one, the **Fumarole**, is where steam emerges from under the rocks in a kind of outdoor sauna; further along close by a couple of hotels is a path that cuts inland through a mini-gorge to the **Terme Cavascura**, where hot springs have been harnessed for you to pamper yourself thoroughly (daily 8.30am–1.30pm & 2.30–6pm; L16,000/€8.26 for swim & sauna; L35,000/€18.08 upwards for mud treatments).

Up above Sant'Angelo looms the craggy summit of Ischia's now dormant volcano, **Monte Epomeo**. Ischia Porto-bound buses make the twenty-minute trip up to **FONTANA**, a superb ride, with wonderful views back over the coast, from where you can climb up to the summit of the volcano. Follow the signposted road off to the left from the centre of Fontana: after about five minutes it joins a larger road; after another ten–fifteen minutes take the left fork, a stony track off the road, and follow this up to the summit – when in doubt, always fork left and you can't go wrong. About a fifty-minute climb in all, perhaps an hour, it's a steep haul and at times quite testing, especially at the end when the path becomes no more than a channel cut out of the soft rock. However, there are a couple of scenically placed cafés in which to gather your energies at the top, and the views from its craggy summit are stunning – right around the island and back across to the sprawl of Naples. Bear in mind, too, that you can drive to within about twenty minutes of the summit, leaving your vehicle by the signs for the military exclusion zone, if you don't think you can manage it there and back on foot; you can also rent a mule in Fontana; reckon on paying up to L35,000/€18.08 each way for this, though.

There are plenty of places to **stay** in and around Sant'Angelo; the cheaper places tend to be outside the village proper. Up in Succhivo, ten minutes' walk back in the direction of Forio (the bus passes right by), *Casa Guiseppina*, on the main road (☎081.907.771; half board obligatory, L60,000/€30.99), is excellent. On a rocky headland above Sant'Angelo itself, the *San Michele* (☎081.999.276; ⑤) is pricier but has a beautifully lush garden and terrace and a seawater pool. When it comes to **eating**, you might be wise to walk up to the next village along from Succhivo, Panza, where the *Da Leopoldo* restaurant (☎081.907.806; closed Mon–Sat lunchtimes; Nov–March call ahead to check opening times) is famous in these parts for its Ischian specialities (rabbit, great sausages and good antipasto table), cosy atmosphere and moderate prices. It is, however, a bit difficult to find: follow Via S. Gennaro from the main square of Panza for about ten minutes, and it's a little way past the *Hotel Al Bosco*. Alternatively, head north to the village of Serrara to *Il Bracconiere Alberto* (open daily), which also has a great local reputation for its Ischian cooking. In Sant'Angelo itself you could do worse than stoke up on the fine pizzas at the unpretentious *Da Pasquale* (no closing day), up in the old centre of the village; everywhere else is much of a muchness.

Prócida

A serrated hunk of volcanic rock that's the smallest and nearest island to Naples, **Prócida** has managed to fend off the kind of tourist numbers that have flooded into Cápri and Ischia. It lacks the spectacle, or variety, of both islands, though it compensates with extra room and extra peace. With a population of just 10,000, the island has few real population centres, its main town, **MARINA GRANDE** – where you arrive by ferry – a slightly run-down but picturesque conglomeration of tall pastel-painted houses rising from the waterfront to a network of steep streets winding up to the fortified tip of the island – the so-called **Terra Murata**. Part of this was once given over to a rather forbidding prison, now abandoned, but it's worth walking up anyway to see the abbey church of **San Michele** (Mon–Fri 9am–1pm & 2.30pm–sunset), whose domes are decorated with a stirring painting by Giordano of St Michael beating back the Turks from Prócida's shore. The views, too, from the nearby belvedere are among the region's best, taking in the whole of the Bay of Naples, from Capo Miseno bang in front of you right around to the end of the Sorrentine peninsula and Cápri on the far left.

For the rest, Prócida's appeal lies in its opportunities to swim and eat in relative peace. There are **beaches** in Marina Grande itself, on the far side of the jetty, and, in the opposite direction, beyond the fishing harbour, though both are fairly grubby. Similarly, **Spiaggia Chiaia**, just beyond the fishing harbour of nearby Coricella, is a reasonable bathing beach but isn't very large and can get crowded. You can walk there, or the Chiaioella bus stops nearby.

On the whole if you want to swim you're better off making the fifteen-minute bus journey from Marina Grande to **CHIAIOELLA**, where there's a handful of bars and **restaurants** around a pleasant, almost circular bay and a long stretch of sandy beach that is the island's best. By taking the road up from behind the beach you can cross the bridge onto the islet of **Vivara**, a nature reserve, very peaceful and overgrown. It's a refreshingly bucolic affair after the rest of the island, where the settlement is pretty much continuous.

Practicalities

The **tourist office** is by the water in the ferry terminal building (daily 9am–1pm & 3.30–6.30pm; ☎081.810.1968), close by where the buses stop; it has free maps and advice on accommodation. For **getting around**, a bus service connects Marina Grande with Chiaioella roughly every twenty minutes and coincides with all ferry and hydrofoil arrivals. There's not much choice if you want to **stay** on the island: there are only a handful of hotels, together with a couple of *pensioni*. Chiaioella is probably your best bet, where you can stay at the *Riviera* hotel, ten minutes' walk from the beach at Via G. de Procida 36 (☎081.896.7197, *riviera@poitel.it*; ③) – the bus goes right by – or *El Dorado*, Via V. Emanuele 236 (☎081.896.8005; ④), facing the sea on the eastern side of the island, an old mansion set in gardens and lemon groves. *Crescenzo*, at Via Marina Chiaiolella 33, is a three-star with a fine ristorante-pizzeria whose speciality is spaghetti with crab meat and courgette (☎081.896.7255, *hotel_crescenzo@iol.it*; ④). If these are full, there's the *Albergo Celeste*, between the *Riviera* and the harbour on the left, at Via Rivoli 6 (☎081.896.7488, *www.campnet.it/celeste*; ⑤). Be aware that at all of these places you *must* book in advance. For **camping**, there are five sites on the island, most within easy walking distance of the sea: try one of the two on Via IV Novembre: the *Caravella* (☎081.896.9230; May–Sept), and the *Vivara* (☎081.896.9242; June–Sept) –

both around 200m from the sea. To get to them, take the Chiaioella bus and get off at Piazza Olmo.

Eating is rather easier. In Marina Grande, restaurants line the waterfront Via Roma: *La Medusa*, opposite the ferry terminal (closed Tues), is not cheap but is very good; or economize at the friendly *Ristorante Il Cantinone*, Via Roma 55 (closed Mon), a popular locals' joint where wood-panelled walls add to the marine flavour and the antipasto is unmissable. In Chiaioella, you could try *Il Galeone*, right by the bus stop between the bay and the beach (no closing day). A number of **café-bars** in Marina Grande serve drinks and *gelati* – try *Capriccio* at Via Roma 99 or *Alexander* at no. 54 – while the *Number Two* on Via Libertà, which leads off Via Roma, is the main **nightclub**.

INLAND AND SOUTHERN CAMPANIA

Away from the coast Campania's appeal fades. The **interior** is a poor and remote region that few tourists visit – quite different from the populous and much-lauded coast. Large towns are few, travel can be slow and unless you're spending a long time in the area, or are an enthusiast for obscure ancient sites, there's not much of interest anyway. What places there are that might appeal – the royal palace at **Caserta**, the Roman amphitheatre at **Cápua**, the ancient town of **Benevento** – are best seen on a day-trip from Naples.

The **south** of the region, on the other hand, holds some of Campania's real gems. The glittering **Amalfi coast** is as spectacular a bit of shoreline as Italy has to offer, and worth a visit for just that, though you may find the tourist presence in high season a bit offputting. **Salerno**, at the far end of this stretch, is a genial working port and a jumping-off spot for the less-developed **Cilento** coast that stretches all the way to the border with Basilicata. Inland from here is also very undeveloped and difficult to reach without your own car. But it can be a rewarding area, its high hills and valleys sheltering some unspoilt routes and villages.

North of Naples: Caserta, Cápua and around

There's not much to draw you to the territory immediately north of Naples. The towns just outside the city – Casoria, Afragola, Acerra – are collectively known as the "**Triangle of Death**" for their Camorra connections and make up a bleak conurbation of poor housing and industrial messiness.

Caserta

Further inland, a short train or bus ride direct from Naples, **CASERTA**, incongruously surrounded by a sprawl of industrial complexes and warehouses that stretches all the way back to Naples, is known as the "Versailles of Naples" for its vast eighteenth-century royal palace, which utterly dominates the town. There's not much point in coming here if you don't want to see this; if you do, be sure to also see the old village of **Caserta Vecchia**, 10km north of the modern town, where the population lived before the building of the palace. To get there by car, more or less the only way, do a left onto Piazza Vanvitelli from the palace and carry straight on to the edge of town, following the road from there up into the hills. It's now almost entirely deserted but is a bucolic antidote to Caserta's soulless streets and has a nice main square and twelfth-century cathedral that is a fine example of southern Norman architecture. There are a couple of **restaurants** up here geared to wedding parties and Sunday excursionists from Naples and Caserta: try *A Marchesina* (no closing day), on the right of the street leading off the square from under the church tower; they do hearty sandwiches and strong local wine – which you can also buy in the adjacent shop. The local speciality, incidentally, is wild boar (and wild boar ham – *prosciutto di cinghiale*) – the animals are still plentiful in the surrounding hills.

The Palazzo Reale

The palace and its grounds are royal creations on the grandest of scales and made a fitting setting for the signing of the German–Italian armistice in 1945. Begun in 1752 for the Bourbon King Charles III to plans drawn up by Vanvitelli, and completed a little over twenty years later, it's an awesomely large complex, built around four courtyards, with a facade 245m long, nestling between two curving brick arms and overlooking a massive, classically ordered square. However, it's ultimately a dull structure that substitutes size for inspiration. Only the majestic central staircases up to the **royal apartments** (Tues–Sat 9am–2pm, Sun 9am–10pm; L8000/€4.13) hit the right note. And the apartments themselves are a grand parade of heavily painted and stuccoed rooms, sparsely furnished in empire style, some with great, overbearing classical statues and all, in their brazen, overstated display of wealth, pretty disgusting – not least in the smug portraits of the Bourbon dynasty, especially the one of the podgy Francis I with his brat-like children. There's little point in singling out anything of special significance: there isn't anything really, and it's the feel of the building and its pitiless overstatement that are the real attractions.

Behind the palace, the **gardens** too (Tues–Sun 9am–6pm; L4000/€2.07) are classically ordered and on no less huge a scale, stretching out behind along one central three-kilometre-long axis and punctured by myth-inspired fountains. The main promenade is longer than it looks from the palace (it's a good half an hour's walk or a short bicycle ride), and regular buses make the round trip, dropping you off at selected intervals along the way and turning round by the main cascade at the top, completed in 1779, which depicts Diana turning Actaeon into a stag. Walk to the top, look back at the palace, hop on a bus . . . and depart.

Santa Maria Cápua Vetere, Cápua and around

Regular buses run from Caserta, either from the bus/train station or the stop just to the left as you exit the palace, for the 6km to **SANTA MARIA CÁPUA VETERE** – a not especially pleasant journey past jutting signs, petrol stations and run-down housing. There's not a blade of grass in sight, and the feeling is one of grinding, hapless, urban poverty. There's not much to Santa Maria itself either, but in its day this originally Etruscan, later Samnite, city, then known as Cápua, was the second city of Italy, centre of the rich and important region of Campania and famous for its skill in working bronze. Its first-century-AD **amphitheatre** was once the largest in Italy after the Colosseum, and parts of it remain on the far side of town, a right turn shortly after Piazza San Francesco d'Assisi. In its day this held a reputed Roman gladiator school and barracks, and it was here that the gladiators' revolt, led by Spartacus, broke out in 73 BC – a revolt that was only put down after two years and four lost battles. The amphitheatre now is less well preserved than the Colosseum (though better than Pozzuoli's), having lost most of the surrounding tiers – and many of the remaining ones have been concreted over. But the network of tunnels underneath survives reasonably intact, and is accessible. You can also ask for the keys to a nearby **Mithraeum** across the road, down Via Antifeatro and then left down Via Morelli – one of the best preserved in the country and redolent with the bizarre, bloodletting rites that accompanied the cult of Mithraism.

There are heaps of rubble and a handful of artefacts dotted around the amphitheatre, not least a large piece of mosaic, but most of the finds have found their way to the

Museo Provinciale Campano in CÁPUA, 4km down the road (Tues–Sat 9am–1.30pm, Sun 9am–1pm; L8000/€4.13) – a smaller town than Santa Maria, settled by refugees when the original city was plundered in 856 by Saracens. Sited on the broad curve of the Volturno River, it's a marginally more attractive place than Santa Maria, but it's not really worth the trek (or even bus ride) if you're without a car.

If you do make it as far as Cápua, it may be worth pushing on to nearby SANT'AN-GELO IN FORMIS (there are regular buses from Cápua), where there's an ancient **church** built on the site of a temple to Diana that is now open again after years of restoration. Dating back to the tenth century, its most striking features are its entrance arches, whose pointed style suggests a strong Arab-Norman influence, and the vivid thirteenth-century frescoes inside, which depict various scenes in the life of St Paul. The church, reachable through a bombastic arch from 1860 that commemorates Garibaldi's victory over the Bourbons here, also has stirring views of the plain of Volturno, where he won his battle.

The area northwest of Cápua, the **Terra di Lavoro**, is a flat, fertile plain that's one of Campania's prime agricultural regions, yielding a healthy array of fruit and supporting plentiful herds of mozzarella-producing buffalo. The main town, SESSA AURUN-CA, has a pleasant centre of narrow arched streets and a Romanesque cathedral that has a pulpit similar to those at Salerno and Ravello. To the northeast of Campania is the peaceful **Parco Regionale del Matese**, good for quiet walks and cycle rides. The hospitable but rather pricey *Villa de Pertis* in the village of **Dragoni**, 5km outside the park boundary, offers **rooms** and a large self-catering apartment in an old country house (☎0823.866.619; ⑥). But otherwise there's not a lot to persuade travellers to stop, and most push straight on to Formia or Rome.

Benevento and around

BENEVENTO, further inland than Cápua or Caserta and reachable in about an hour and a half from Naples by bus, was another important Roman settlement, a key point on the Via Appia between Rome and Brindisi and as such a thriving trading town. Founded in 278 BC, it was at the time the farthest point from Rome to be colonized, and even now it has a remote air about it, circled by hills and with a centre that was (pointlessly) bombed to smithereens in the last war and even now seems only half rebuilt. Its climate also ranks among southern Italy's most extreme.

The Town

Buses from Naples drop you on the main square, where the **Duomo** is an almost total reconstruction of its thirteenth-century Romanesque original; what's left of its famous bronze doors, believed to be Byzantine, is now stashed inside. Left from here, the main street, **Corso Garibaldi**, leads up the hill, a once elegant thoroughfare lined with ancient palaces. Off to the left about halfway up, the **Arch of Trajan** is the major remnant of the Roman era, a marvellously preserved triumphal arch that is refreshing after the scaffolding and netting of Rome's arches, since you can get close enough to study its friezes. Built to guard the entrance to Benevento from the Appian Way, it's actually as heavy-handed a piece of self-acclaim as there ever was, showing the Emperor Trajan in various scenes of triumph, power and generosity. Further up Corso Garibaldi, the **Museo Sannio** (Tues–Sun 9am–1pm), in the cloister behind the eighth-century church of Santa Sofia, holds a selection of Roman finds from the local area, including a number of artefacts from a temple of Isis – various sphinxes, bulls and a headless statue of Isis herself. There are also terracotta votive figurines from the fifth century BC, and the cloister itself has capitals carved with energetic scenes of animals, humans and strange beasts – hunting, riding and attacking.

There are more bits and pieces from Roman times scattered around the rather battered old quarter of town, the **Triggio** – reached by following Via Carlo Torre off to the left of the main road beyond the cathedral. The **Bue Apis**, at the far end of Corso Dante, is another relic from the temple of Isis, a first-century BC sculpture of a bull. And in the heart of the old quarter there are the substantial remains of a **Teatro Romano** built during the reign of Hadrian – though it's been a little over-restored for modern use. In Hadrian's time it seated 20,000 people, rather less today as the upper level remains mossily decrepit, but it's still an atmospheric sight – looking out over the green rolling countryside of the province beyond and, like most of Benevento, relatively unvisited by tourists.

Practicalities

Benevento is roughly 60km from Naples, and **buses** run roughly every two hours from Piazza Garibaldi – an hour-and-a-half trip. **Trains** stop down the hill from the centre and are in any case slower and more infrequent. Benevento is easily seen on a day excursion and there's no need **to stay**, but if you're pushing on east to Fóggia and Puglia (to which there are regular train connections), or if you get stuck, the *Genova*, at Viale Principe di Napoli 130 (✆0824.42.926; ①), is an adequate hotel. For **food**, if you're just here for the day you're likely to be content with the snacks, pizza and *tavola calda*-style dishes at *Pizzeria Romana*, next door to the cathedral on the corner of Via Carlo Torre (no closing day). For evening eating there are adequate restaurants dotted on and around the main Corso Garibaldi.

Around Benevento

It's the countryside around Benevento that is of most appeal, and there are a handful of low-key attractions worth basing a tour around. Back towards Caserta from Benevento, just off the main road, **MONTESARCHIO** overlooks the Caudine Valley, a small town whose main claim to fame is its **Castle** – home to the powerful D'Avalos family in the sixteenth century and a stronghold for political prisoners in the nineteenth century. The poet Carlo Poerio was incarcerated here, a fact recorded by a plaque above the entrance. The town itself is worth a quick wander, no more, before moving on to **SANT'AGATA DEI GOTI**, way off the main road at the foot of the limestone massif of **Monte Taburno**. One of the best-preserved small towns of Campania, with hardly any disfigurement from building speculation (highly unusual in these parts), and an almost untouched, shuttered centre of small squares, old palaces and narrow vaulted streets that is host to a good Sunday-morning market, it's a nice place just to wander, especially if you can coincide with the market. Of a number of minor sights, there is a rather dank **Castle**, with some surprisingly well-preserved frescoes from the early eighteenth century, a slightly listing **Duomo**, with an elegantly carved thirteenth-century crypt, and any number of small churches and tiny courtyards. There's no real reason to stay, but if you do find yourself here in the evening, the castle's rather dimly lit **restaurant** makes for an atmospheric place to eat – not cheap, but serving imaginative food, washed down with good local red wine (no closing day).

The Amalfi coast

Occupying the southern side of Sorrento's peninsula, the **Costiera Amalfitana** lays claim to being Europe's most beautiful stretch of coast, its corniche road winding around the towering cliffs that slip almost sheer into the sea. By car or bus it's an incredible ride, with some of the most spectacular stretches between Salerno and Amalfi. If you're staying in Sorrento especially it shouldn't be missed on any account; in any case the towns along here hold the beaches that Sorrento lacks. The coast as a whole has become rather developed, and these days it's in fact one of Italy's ritzier bits of shoreline, villas atop its precarious slopes fetching a bomb in both cash and kudos. But the cliffs are so steep, and the towns' growth so inevitably constrained, that it seems unlikely that the Amalfi coast can ever become completely spoilt.

Coming **from Sorrento**, buses normally join the coast road a little way **west of Positano**. If the coast road is closed, however, which it is from time to time due to landslides and forest fires, the bus from Sorrento will take the alternative route, via Castellammare and Agerola, right over the backbone of the Sorrentine peninsula, which is itself a journey worth making – the bus zigzagging down the other side in a crazy helter-skelter of hairpin bends to join the road a few kilometres **west of Amalfi**.

Sant'Agata and Nocelle

If you've got your own transport, it's worth exploring the villages between Sorrento and Positano. **SANT'AGATA SUI DUE GOLFI**, as its name implies, gives great views of both the Golfo di Napoli and the Golfo di Salerno, and there is a great **restaurant** on the road between here and Positano, the *Stelluccia* (closed Wed). Try their specialities: mozzarella wrapped in ham slices, pasta with courgettes, and *agnello alla brace* – charcoal-grilled lamb. Just before you reach Positano, a road branches left up to the village of **NOCELLE**, where there's another **restaurant** – this time without a name – that has more unbeatable views over the coast (no closing day). The food is simple and well priced – reckon on L35,000/€18.08 for a full meal.

Positano, Praiano and the Grotta dello Smeraldo

There's not much to **POSITANO**, only a couple of decent beaches and a great many boutiques; the town has long specialized in simple beach clothes made from linen, georgette and cotton, as well as handmade shoes and sandals. But its location, heaped up in a pyramid high above the water, has inspired a thousand picture postcards and helped to make it a moneyed resort that runs a close second to Cápri in the celebrity stakes. Since John Steinbeck wrote up the place in glowing terms back in 1953, the village has enjoyed a fame quite out of proportion to its tiny size. Franco Zefferelli is just one of many famous names who have villas nearby, and the people who come here to lie on the beach consider themselves a cut above your average sun-worshipper.

Positano is, of course, expensive, and an overnight stay isn't recommended, although its beaches are nice enough and don't get too crowded. The main one, the Spiaggia Grande right in front of the village, is reasonable, although you'll be sunbathing among the fishing boats unless you want to pay over the odds for the pleasanter bit on the far left; there's also another, larger stretch of beach, Spiaggia del Fornillo, around the headland to the west, accessible in five minutes by a pretty path that winds around from above the hydrofoil jetty – although its central section is also a pay area. Nonetheless the bar-terrace of the *Puppetto* hotel (see opposite), which runs along much of its length, is a cheaper place to eat and drink than anywhere in Positano proper.

Buses to Positano drop off at the top of the village, from where it's a steep walk down or a short bus ride (every 30min) to the little square at the bottom end of Via Cristoforo Colombo, five minutes' walk from the seafront; **ferries** and **hydrofoils** from Cápri, Naples, Amalfi and Salerno pull in at the jetty just to the right of the main beach. There's a helpful **tourist office** just back from the beach by the church steps (daily 8am–2pm; ☎089.875.067). By far the cheapest **accommodation** in Positano is *Ostello Brikette* (☎089.875.857, *brikette@syrene.it*; ②; curfew Mon–Fri midnight, Sat & Sun 1am; lockout 10am–4pm), on Via G. Marconi 358, a100-metre walk uphill from the main bus-stop at Viale Pasitea along the coastal road from Sorrento to Amalfi. It's a clean and airy but somewhat spartan **hostel**; lower-floor male dorms are a little too close to the boisterously loud balcony area which does, however, offer stunning village and Mediterranean views. There's an Internet service (L10,000 per hr) and a bar. Alternatively, the *Bougainville*, right by the bus stop (☎089.875.047, fax 089.811.150; ③), is very pleasant and very central; less central, but handy for the Fornillo beach on Via Fornillo, are the *Maria Luisa* (☎089.875.023, fax 089.875.023; ③), the similarly priced but rather nicer *Casa Guadagno* (☎089.875.042, fax 089.811.407; ④), and the more expensive *Vittoria* (☎089.875.049, fax 089.811.037; ⑥). Consider also the *Puppetto* hotel (☎089.875.087, fax 089.811.517, *www.starnet.it/pupetto*; ⑤), which is very enticingly placed right by the beach.

For **food**, *Chez Black*, right behind Positano's beach (open daily), is a long-established seafood restaurant – their pizzas are the closest you'll get to a budget sit-down lunch in this location. *O Caporale*, just around the corner (closed Wed), is worth a try too and isn't too expensive whatever you have. If you're really strapped for cash, check out the *alimentari* by the tourist office at the foot of the church steps. At the other end of the price spectrum is *La Cambusa*, on the right as you approach the beach (closed Wed), where a full fish blowout will set you back L100,000/€51.65 a head.

PRAIANO is a little further along to the east, squeezed into a cleft in the rocks. It's smaller than Positano, but these days its two tiny centres – Véttica Maggiore on the Positano side, and Marina di Praiano on the Amalfi side – are often no less congested; indeed Praiano is becoming more so as its status as a fashionable resort increases. There is a small patch of beach, together with a couple of sandy coves close by, but food and **rooms** are again quite pricey. The *Casa Colomba pensione* (☎089.874.079, fax 089.874.392; ④), high above the main road just after the first tunnel, coming from Positano, has great views from its location at the top of 180 steps. *Onda Verde* (☎089.874.143, fax 089.813.1049, *www.starnet.it/onda_verde*; ⑤), perched on the cliff edge at Marina di Praiano, is a friendly place, or there are rooms to rent right on the harbour front – ask at *La Conchiglia* restaurant in Marina di Praiano (☎089.874.313; ②). In Véttica Maggiore there's also the *Tranquillità* **campsite** (☎089.874.084), on the seaward side of the main road, which also rents out bungalows, or the nearby *Continental* hotel (☎089.874.084, fax 089.874.779; ④), which also has a good **restaurant**. Otherwise the *Trattoria San Gennaro*, next to the church (closed Wed), with its good choice of local dishes, and *La Brace*, above the pharmacy (closed Oct–March), with its fresh fish and pizzas straight from the wood-fired oven, are especially popular at weekends.

Shortly after Praiano you pass the **Furore** gorge, which gashes into the mountainside just above the coast road, and a little further along, about 4km out of Praiano (reachable direct by taxi boat from either Praiano or Amalfi), the **Grotta dello Smeraldo** (daily: March–Oct 9am–5pm; Nov–Feb 10am–4pm; L5000/€2.58), one of the most highly touted local natural features. An elevator gets down to the level of the grotto, where you can tour the green-hued interior by boat – a mildly impressive but certainly not unmissable sight which includes a rather startling sub-aquatic nativity scene.

Amalfi

Set in a wide cleft in the cliffs, **AMALFI**, a mere 4km or so further east, is the largest town and perhaps the highlight of the coast, and much the best place to base yourself. It has been an established seaside resort since Edwardian times, when the British upper classes found the town a pleasant place to spend their winters. Actually Amalfi's credentials go back much further: it was an independent republic during Byzantine times and one of the great naval powers, with a population of some 70,000; Webster's *Duchess of Malfi* was set here, and the city's traders established outposts all over the Mediterranean, setting up the Order of the Knights of St John of Jerusalem. Amalfi was finally vanquished by the Normans in 1131, and the town was devastated by an earthquake in 1343, but there is still the odd remnant of Amalfi's past glories around today, and the town has a crumbly attractiveness to its whitewashed courtyards and alleys that makes it fun to wander through.

The town

The **Duomo**, at the top of a steep flight of steps, utterly dominates the town's main piazza, its decorated, almost gaudy facade topped by a glazed tiled cupola that's typical of the area. The bronze doors of the church came from Constantinople and date from 1066. Inside it's a mixture of Saracen and Romanesque styles, though now heavily restored, with a major relic in the body of St Andrew buried in its crypt, though the cloister – the so-called **Chiostro del Paradiso** (daily: April–Oct 9am–9pm; Nov–March 10am–5pm; L3000/€1.55) – is the most appealing part of the building, oddly Arabic in feel with its whitewashed arches and palms. There's an adjacent **museum** (same hours and ticket as the cloisters), with various medieval and episcopal treasures, most intriguingly an eighteenth-century sedan chair from Macau, which was used by the bishop of Amalfi; a thirteenth-century mitre sewn with myriad seed pearls, gold panels and gems; and three silver reliquary heads – two gravely bearded and medieval, the third an altogether more relaxed and chubby Renaissance character, with elaborately braided hair.

Almost next door to the duomo, in the **Municipio**, you can view the *Tavoliere Amalfitana*, the book of maritime laws that governed the republic, and the rest of the Mediterranean, until 1570. On the waterfront, the old **Arsenal** is a reminder of the military might of the Amalfi republic, and its ancient vaulted interior now hosts art exhibitions and suchlike. In the opposite direction you can follow the main street of **Via Genova** up through the heart of Amalfi and out the other side, to where the town peters out and the gorge narrows into the **Valle dei Mulini**, or "Valley of Mills", once the centre of Amalfi's high-quality paper industry. Apart from a rather desultory paper museum, there's not much to see here nowadays, despite the grandiose claims inferred by name, and it's hard to find a mill that is still functioning – although there is a shop on the left that makes and bottles its own *limoncello* (lemon liqueur), a speciality of the region.

Practicalities

Amalfi's most immediate focus is along the seafront, a humming, cheerfully vigorous strand given over to street stalls, a car park for the town's considerable tourist traffic, and an acceptably crowded **beach**, although once again the best bits are pay-areas only. There's a supremely unhelpful **tourist office** (Mon–Sat 8am–2pm & 4–7pm; ☎089.872.619), which may not even have so much as a map but it's worth a try; close by, at Corso delle Repubbliche 27, there's a **post office**. **Ferries** and **hydrofoils** to Salerno, Positano, Cápri and Ischia (see p.849) leave from the landing stage in the tiny harbour.

If you do want to stay – and Amalfi is the best place along this coast to find accommodation – there are a number of fair-priced **hotels**, among the cheapest of which are the centrally placed *Sant'Andrea* on the main square (☎089.871.145; ③) and the *Lidomare*, tucked away up to the left of the main square at Via Piccolomini 9 (☎089.871.332, fax 089.871.394; ③). On the western edge of the town is the swish *Hotel Santa Caterina* (☎089.871.012, fax 089.871.351, *www.hotelsantacaterina.it*; ⑧), an elegant villa with period furnishings; it has a great lift which plummets down from the bougainvillea-wreathed terrace to an arc of rocky beach. You might also consider staying in the adjacent village of Atrani (see opposite).

As for **eating**, *Trattoria da Gemma*, a short walk up Via Genova on the left (closed Wed), has a small, carefully considered menu, strong on fish and seafood, and a lovely terrace overlooking the street, although it's not one of the town's cheaper places. *Il Tari* (no closing day), a little further up on the left after Via Genova has become Via P. Capuano, *is* cheap and not at all bad; further up again, *Taverna del Duca* on Piazza Spirito Santo 26 (closed Thurs) has a cosy atmosphere, and their *fusilli del Duca* is well worth a try; while *Il Mulino* (no closing day), right at the top of the main street ten minutes' walk from the duomo, is a cheery and inexpensive family-run place used by locals that does good pizza and pasta dishes. If you fancy a bit of **nightlife**, carry on up the main street to the brand new *Roccoco Discopub* in the otherwise quiet Valle dei Mulini. Back in the centre of town, if all you want is a snack, the *Green Bar*, Via P. Capuano 46, has sandwiches, pizza slices, *calzone* and the like.

Atrani

A short walk around the headland (take the path off to the right just before the tunnel through the *Zaccaria* restaurant), **ATRANI** is an extension of Amalfi really, and was indeed another part of the maritime republic, with a similarly styled church sporting another set of bronze doors from Constantinople, manufactured in 1086. It's a quiet place, which benefits from all the attention bestowed upon its neighbour, with a pretty, almost entirely enclosed little square, Piazza Umberto, giving onto a usually gloriously peaceful (and free) patch of sandy **beach** – hard to believe the bustle of Amalfi is just around the corner. Another good reason for coming here is that it has a great **place to stay** in the *A Scalinatella*, Piazza Umberto 12 (☎089.871.492), hostel and hotel – a friendly, family-run establishment that offers excellent-value hostel beds (Easter–Sept L30,000/€15.49, including dinner; Oct–Easter L25,000/€12.91, including dinner) and regular private rooms (③) in various different buildings around town. Otherwise for **eating**, try *A'Paranza*, Traversa Dragone 2 (daily mid-June to mid-Sept; mid-Sept to mid-June closed Tues), a functional and friendly seafood trattoria with fabulous home-made pasta and a speciality of swordfish. You'll find the restaurant on the road that leads inland from the main square.

Ravello

The best views of the coast can be had inland from Amalfi in **RAVELLO**: another renowned spot, "closer to the sky than the seashore", wrote André Gide – with some justification. Ravello was also an independent republic for a while, and for a time an outpost of the Amalfi city-state; now it's not much more than a large village, but its unrivalled location, spread across the top of one of the coast's mountains, 335m up, makes it more than worth the thirty-minute bus ride up from Amalfi – although, like most of this coast, the charms of Ravello haven't been recently discovered. Wagner based part of *Parsifal*, one of his last operas, on the place; D.H. Lawrence wrote some of *Lady Chatterley's Lover* here; John Huston filmed his languid movie *Beat the Devil* in town (a film in which the locations easily outshine the plot); and Gore Vidal is just one of the best known of many celebrities who spend at least part of the year here.

The town

Buses drop off on the main **Piazza Vescovado**, outside the **Duomo**: a bright eleventh-century church, renovated in 1786, that's dedicated to St Pantaleone, a fourth-century saint whose blood – kept in a chapel on the left-hand side – is supposed to liquefy like Naples' San Gennaro once a year on July 27. It's a richly decorated church, with a pair of bronze doors, twelfth century, cast with 54 scenes of the Passion; inside, attention focuses on a monumental *ambo* of 1272, adorned with mosaics of dragons and birds on spiral columns supported by roaring lions, and with the coat of arms and the vivacious profiles of the Rufolo family, the donors, on each side. The superb bust, downstairs in the crypt, is also said to be a portrait of Signor Rufolo, alongside a collection of mosaics and reliquaries from the same era.

The Rufolos figure again on the other side of the square, where various leftovers of their **Villa Rufolo** (daily: June–Sept 9.30am–1pm & 3–7pm; Oct–May 9.30am–1pm & 3–5pm; L4000/€2.07) scatter among rich gardens overlooking the precipitous coastline; this is the spectacular main venue for concerts held during the prestigious Ravello music festival in July. If the crowds put you off – and you certainly won't be alone here – turn left by the entrance and walk up the steps over the tunnel for the best (free) view over the shore, from where it's a pleasant stroll through the back end of Ravello to the main square. Failing that, walk in the opposite direction to the **Villa Cimbrone** (daily 9am–sunset; L5000/€2.58), ten minutes away, whose formal gardens spread across the furthest tip of Ravello's ridge. Most of the villa itself, once frequented by the Bloomsbury Group, is not open to visitors, though it's worth peeking into the crumbly, flower-hung cloister as you go in and the open crypt down the steps from here – probably the only crypt with views over cliffs and open sea. But the gardens are entirely accessible, dotted with statues and leading down to what must be the most gorgeous spot in Ravello – a belvedere that looks down to Atrani below and the sea beyond.

Practicalities

Small orange Sita buses run up to Ravello from Amalfi roughly hourly from Piazza Flavio Gioià. It's not really worth staying – accommodation is much cheaper in Amalfi – but if you can't tear yourself away the **tourist office** on Piazza Vescovado (Mon–Sat: May–Sept 8am–8pm; Oct–April 8am–7pm; ☎089.857.096, *www.crmpa.it/EPT/ravello*) has information on **rooms**. If you have money to burn, the *Palumbo*, Via San Giovanni del Toro 16 (☎089.857.244, fax 089.818.133, *palumbo@amalfinet.it*; ⑨), is definitely the place to do it – one of Italy's best opportunities to experience real, old-world luxury in a magnificent location. If this seems too much, the *Parsifal*, back down the road, (☎089.857.144, fax 089.857.972; ⑤), easily competes on great views for quite a lot less.

Even if you don't stay, there are some marvellous places **to eat**, all doing their best to exploit the location, one of the best of which is the *Garden* through the tunnel off the main piazza on Via Chiunzi (no closing day), which has a wonderfully panoramic terrace. The *Cumpa Cosimo* restaurant at Via Roma 48 (no closing day) is good too, with decent local food and wine at moderate prices, while *La Colonna* at Via Roma 22 (no closing day) has an attractive courtyard and dishes up home-made pasta and fresh fish.

Amalfi to Salerno

The coast road maintains the attack on the senses beyond Amalfi, though the resorts grow less exclusive and for the most part less appealing. Around 4km beyond Atrani, **MINORI** is a pretty village with an appealing network of narrow streets behind its short tree-lined seafront and grey sandy **beach**. The remains of a Roman **villa** (daily 8am–8pm; free), dating from the first century AD, lie just off the main road into town from Amalfi, opposite the *Hotel Settebello*. They were discovered in 1932, and part of the site still lies unexcavated under the houses beyond, but you can visit the sunken peristyle, with its fish pond at one end, and the remains of a nymphaeum; and there are a couple of rooms housing an assortment of finds. If you want to **stay** in Minori, there are a few reasonable alternatives, the most affordable of which are the *Albergo Capri*, the large building on Via Dietro la Chiesa (☎089.877.417; ②), which starts from the arch supporting the church's belltower, just back from the far end of the seafront, and the nearby *Settebello* (☎089.877.619, fax 089.877.494; ③; half board obligatory in Aug). For **food**, try *La Botte*, around the corner from the Roman villa on Via Santa Maria Vetrano (closed Tues), where you can sit outside, or *Ristorante Giardinello* on Corso Vittorio

Emanuele (no closing day) with a lovely garden and fine seafood dishes. The **tourist office** (Mon–Sat 9am–noon & 4–7pm), on the main square of Piazza Umberto, has all the information you'll need.

MAIORI, 2km beyond Minori, is quite a different place altogether – a much louder, brasher place indeed than anywhere along the Amalfi coast, straggling along its huge stretch of beach for a kilometre or more in a long line of beach bars and restaurants. It's not especially enticing, particularly bearing in mind the rest of the coast, and you'd be well advised to move on, although it might be a place to base yourself if everywhere else is full. If you do stay, the *Pensione Rosa*, in a modern apartment building a block back from the seafront on Via degli Orti (☎089.877.031, fax 089.877.031; ②), and *Pensione Vittoria*, right by the sea on the corner of Corso Regina (☎089.877.652, fax 089.877.652; ②; full board obligatory in Aug), are both very convenient if you're here for the sea. When it comes to **food**, *Mammato*, right on the seafront (closed Tues), is a long-running favourite, with good fish and pizzas, while *Torre Normana* (no closing day) has a great setting by the sea and dishes up big pizzas.

After Maiori you may as well stay on the bus as far as **CETARA**, a tiny fishing village clasped tightly at the end of its narrow valley that has another very small beach, three restaurants and a hotel – the *Cetus* (☎089.261.388, fax 089.261.388; ④) – which has lovely rooms and a superb location perched on top of its own sandy cove, just past the village. A little further on, **VIETRI SUL MARE** is a larger and livelier town, split between its old centre heaped up towards the main road, the centre of a long-standing local ceramics industry, and a rather soulless waterfront area down below with numerous lidos lining its undeniably fine grey sand beach. It's not a place to linger – though the modern *Albergo Lloyd's Baia* (☎089.210.145, fax 089.210.186; ⑥) just east of town is a fairly decent if pricey accommodation alternative to Salerno – but if you have an hour or so to kill you should visit the **Solimene** factory (daily 9am–10pm). Housed in an amazing bulbous tiled building on the Salerno road – the bus goes right past – its shop is a treasure trove of brightly coloured mugs, jugs, pots and bowls. You can also wander into the workshop next door for a brief look at how it's done.

Salerno

Capital of Campania's southernmost province, **SALERNO** has much of the scruffy, disorganized charm of Naples: a busy, dirty port city that's well off most travellers' itineraries and so holds a good supply of cheap accommodation – making it a good base for both the Amalfi coast and the ancient site of Paestum further south. During medieval times the town's medical school was the most eminent in Europe. More recently, it was the site of the Allied landing of September 9, 1943 – a landing that reduced much of the centre to rubble. The subsequent rebuilding has restored neither charm nor efficiency to the town centre, which is an odd mixture of wide, rather characterless boulevards and a small medieval core full of intriguingly dark corners and alleys. But the town's siting, strung along the top of its gulf and looking across to the sheer wall of the Amalfi coast, is fine.

Arrival, information and accommodation

Salerno's **train station** lies at the southern end of the town centre on Piazza Vittorio Veneto. City and local **buses** pull up here; those from Paestum and further south arrive and leave from Piazza della Concordia, down by the waterside nearby; buses from Amalfi or Naples use the SITA bus station at Corso Garibaldi 119. **Ferries** and **hydrofoils** from Amalfi, Càpri and Positano (see p.849) arrive in the harbour.

For information, there's a **tourist office** on the corner outside the train station (Mon–Sat 9am–2pm & 3–8pm; ☎089.231.432, *eptinfo@xcom.it*), which has free maps, hotel lists and information on the Salerno area. If you're staying, there's a **youth hostel** about fifteen minutes' walk south from the station at Via Luigi Guercio 112 (☎089.790.251; dorms L12,000/€6.20, singles L20,000/€10.33, doubles L35,000/€18.08, triples L45,000/€23.24, quads L60,000/€30.99; closed 10.30am–5pm; curfew 1am); follow Via Torrione left out of the station and then do a left under the rail line up Via San Mobilio; it's the second street on the right. Alternatively, the town's cheaper **hotels** are handily placed along (or just off) Corso V. Emanuele, which leads north into the town centre from the station: try friendly *Santa Rosa*, at Corso V. Emanuele 16 (☎089.225.346; ②); you can use the **Internet** at the language school one floor down in the same building (Mon–Sat 9am–2pm & 3.30pm–8pm; L3000/€1.55 per hour). Right by the station is the more upmarket *Plaza*, Piazza Vittorio Veneto 42 (☎089.224.477, fax 089.237.311; ③).

The Town

There isn't a great deal to see in Salerno, but it's pleasant to wander through the vibrant streets of the centre, especially the ramshackle old medieval quarter, which starts at the far end of **Corso V. Emanuele**, lined with designer shops and heaving with people (especially on Saturdays), and has **Via dei Mercanti** as its main axis; the roads around, such as Via Giovanni di Procida, can sometimes feel like a social club rather than a commercial centre. To the right of Via dei Mercanti, up Via Duomo, the **Duomo** (daily 7am–noon & 4–8pm) squeezes into the congested streets, an enormous church built in 1076 by Robert Guiscard and dedicated to St Matthew. The main features are yet another set of bronze doors from Constantinople and, in the heavily restored interior, two elegant mosaic pulpits dating from 1173, as well as the quietly expressive fifteenth-century tomb of Margaret of Anjou, wife of Charles III of Durazzo. The crypt holds the body of St Matthew himself, brought here in the tenth century. Outside, the courtyard is cool and shady, its columns plundered from Paestum, centring on a gently gurgling fountain. Outside, turn right at the bottom of the steps for the **Museo Diocesano** (daily 9am–8.30pm; free), which, although its opening times are erratic, is worth a hammer on the door to see its large altar-front, embellished with ivory panels in the late eleventh century and the largest work of its kind in the world. Failing that, turn left out of the church, left at the bottom of the steps, left again and then first right, and 100m or so further on is the **Museo Provinciale** (Mon–Sat 9am–8pm, Sun 9am–1.30pm; free) – a largely dull museum that occupies two floors of an over-restored Romanesque palace. It's worth heading upstairs though, past the deadening array of fossils and fragments of ancient sculpture, to see the sensual *Head of Apollo*, a Roman bronze fished from the Gulf of Salerno in the 1930s.

Eating and drinking

Salerno isn't a tourist town, but it's a very sociable place with plenty of street life and an intriguing choice of **eating places**. If all you want is a bite at lunchtime, there is a good *tavola calda* at *Pranz Express*, Corso V. Emanuele 15 (closed Sun), and the fruit and vegetable market off to the left just before the end of Corso V. Emanuele is a good source for picnics, as are the *alimentari* and *panificio* outside the station by the *Plaza* hotel. Among sit-down options, the nearby *Trattoria da Rosalia*, tucked away at Via degli Orti 22 (closed Wed & Sun), a right turn off Corso V. Emanuele immediately after Via Diaz, is a reliable and inexpensive restaurant, used by locals, serving decent fish and seafood. Other than that, there are a number of places in and around the old town, and on the main roads – Via Roma and Lungomare Trieste – that sweep around by the sea. *Antica Pizzeria Vicolo delle Neve*, left off Via dei Mercanti about 50m past the duomo (closed Wed & lunchtimes) – one of the scruffiest streets in the old city – is a deliciously downbeat place with both pizzas and local specialities; *Il Caminetto*, five minutes' away at Via Roma 232 (closed Wed), is a little pricey but friendly; while *Ristorante Santa Lucia*, in between the two at Via Roma 182 (closed Mon), is the elegant haunt of Salerno's young and trendy. *Trianon*, Piazza F. Gioia (closed Sun lunchtime) sells many variations on the traditional, huge Neapolitan pizza – the best in the town.

As for **bars**, *Mennir* at Vicolo Giudaica 50 is a friendly, stylish place open in the evening for as long as its customers want to drink. A few doors away, *La Cantinella* offers a more traditional Italian atmosphere and cheap drinks, and is welcoming to foreigners. **Via Roma** is the place where things get really busy from around 9pm at night, with people crowding the street, talking and drinking. It's lined with good bars, from the unnamed, bustling place tucked into a corner at the northern end of the street, past *Easy Rider* which, despite the name, is an Irish pub, to the more ostentatiously trendy *Zen*.

Salerno hosts what claims to be the oldest **fair** in Europe – the Fieravecchia – on the first weekend in May, when townsfolk parade in medieval gear, food stalls are set up along the waterfront and a 2000-egg omelette is cooked down at the beach on a giant metal contraption. Incidentally, if you fancy a **swim** Salerno does have a scrappy bit of beach but swimming from there isn't recommended. Better to make the short bus journey to Vietri (see p.867) or even south to Paestum and make a day of it.

Paestum

About an hour's bus ride south of Salerno, the ancient site of **Paestum** (daily 9am–1hr before sunset; L8000/€4.13, L12,000/€6.20 for site plus museum) spreads across a large area at the bottom end of the **Piana del Sele** – a wide, flat plain grazed by buffalo that produce a good quantity of southern Italy's mozzarella cheese. Paestum, or Poseidonia as it was known, was founded by Greeks from Sybaris in the sixth century BC, and later, in 273 BC, colonized by the Romans, who Latinized the name. But by the ninth century a combination of malaria and Saracen raids had decimated the population and left the buildings deserted and gradually overtaken by thick forest, and the site wasn't rediscovered until the eighteenth century during the building of a road through here. It's a desolate, open place even now ("inexpressibly grand", Shelley called it), mostly unrecognizable ruin but with three golden-stoned **temples** that are among the best-preserved Doric temples in Europe. Of these, the Temple of Neptune, dating from about 450 BC, is the most complete, with only its roof and parts of the inner walls missing. The Basilica of Hera, built a century or so earlier, retains its double rows of columns, while the Temple of Ceres at the northern end of the site was used as a Christian church for a time. All are now sectioned off from the public and are undergoing various stages of restoration, though it's still possible to appreciate their scale and proportion. In between, the forum is little more than an open space, and the buildings around are mere foundations. But the **museum** (daily 9am–7pm; closed first and third Mon every month; L8000/€4.13, L12,000/€6.20 including site), across the road, holds finds from the site and around, including a set of archaic period Greek metopes from another temple at the mouth of the Sele River, a few miles north – brutish, rather crude scenes of fighting and hunting mainly. Much else is dull stuff, but you should see the fourth-century ceramics and the tomb paintings at the back of the building, one of which, from the so-called "Tomb of the Diver", a graceful and expressively naturalistic piece of work, is said to represent the passage from life to death.

Practicalities

It's perfectly feasible to see Paestum on a day-trip from either Salerno to the north or Agrópoli to the south (see p.870) – it's much nearer to the latter. However, you can also stay in one of the many **hotels** or **campsites** that are strewn along the sandy shore beyond the site. The **tourist office** on the main road close to the site entrance (Mon–Sat 9am–2pm & 3.30–7.30pm, Sun 9am–1pm; ☎0828.811.016) has details. Or just walk down to the beach (about fifteen minutes) and take your pick: the *Santa Lucia* (☎0828.811.133; ⑤) and *Poseidonia* (☎0828.811.101, fax 0828.722.123; ④, minimum half board obligatory in Aug) are among the cheaper **hotels**, close by the site to the left of where the main road hits the beach. For a relaxing one- or two-night stopover, try the *Tenuta Seliano* (☎0828.724.544; ④), a farm 1km outside Positano, which has a swimming pool and good food; the buffalo herd here produces milk for mozzarella. Most of the **campsites** are much of a muchness: the *Apollo* (☎0828.811.178) and *Mare Pineta* (☎0828.811.086) are two of the most central, to the right of the main beach road and well signposted. As for the **beach** itself, the development behind it is fairly tacky, and it's a bit grimy in places. But space, even in peak season, is rarely too much of a problem. For **food**, the *Apollo* restaurant, right by the temples, is not bad and is pleasantly located in an old building.

The Cilento

Immediately south of Paestum, the coastline bulges out into a broad mountainous hump of territory known as the **Cilento** – one of the remotest parts of Campania, thickly wooded with olives and chestnuts. The region divides into two distinct parts: inland, which is still wedded to a fairly traditional way of life, and the coast, which is where tourists go – although even in the main resorts you'll find far fewer people than further north.

The Cilento coast

After the sands of the Piana del Sele, the Cilento coast is fairly rocky territory, more suited to scuba-diving than sunbathing, though it does have sandy moments. **AGRÓPOLI**, the first town you reach, fifteen minutes out from Paestum, is a good base for the ruins (buses every hour), and its blend of the peaceful old quarter, heaped on a headland, and the new modern centre down below makes for a nice place to spend a few days, with a vivacious main-street passeggiata. The beaches aren't great – dirty on the north side of town, crowded to the south in the Lido di Trentova – but you can swim from the flat rocks in the harbour and the water's perfectly clean. For **accommodation**, the *Hotel Carola* in the harbour (☎0974.826.422, fax 0974.826.425; ③) is central and has attractive double rooms with balconies, or there's the *Serenella*, on Lungomare San Marco (☎0974.823.333, fax 0974.825.562; ③; full board obligatory in Aug), which has its own private beach. Agrópoli is also on the main Salerno–Reggio railway line and there's an excellent **youth hostel**, about one kilometre's walk from the station and conveniently close to the bus stop for Paestum, at Via Lanterna 8 (☎0974.838.364; March–Nov; L15,000/€7.75), which does full dinners for L14,000/€7.23, or half-meals for L7000/€3.62.

Santa Maria di Castellabate and around

Buses from Salerno run down the coast as far as the next town of **SANTA MARIA DI CASTELLABATE**, 8km south, but if you've time and energy it's preferable to walk from Agrópoli, taking the **dirt road** from behind the Lido di Trentova's tennis courts, which scenically skirts the hillsides past abandoned farmhouses, above rocky bays, eventually becoming a fairly good-quality track a little way before Santa Maria di Castellabate. This is another little resort, with a small harbour and bus connections south, along one of the most isolated stretches of the Cilento coast. There's a long **beach** of clean, golden sand just north of the town, the so-called "Zona Lago", close to where the path from Agrópoli comes out, with a number of **hotels** and **campsites**. *Hotel Tonino* (☎0974.965.082, fax

0974.965.082; ②) is the cheapest place to stay, while the pricier *Hotel Sonia* (☎0974.961.172, fax 0974.961.172; ④) enjoys a fantastic beach-front location. *La Duna* (☎0974.965.168) and *Trezene* (☎0974.965.027) are the best value of several campsites.

Above Santa Maria lies the ancient hill town of **CASTELLABATE**, surmounted by a castle that was begun in 1123, currently being restored. The twelfth-century basilica is worth a peek; the interior has been heavily made over in subsequent centuries, but there's a beautiful medieval triptych. You could round things off with a meal in *Il Calesse* by the castle (open daily), a terrific upmarket restaurant which also serves pizzas cooked in a wood-fired oven; its handsome terrace looks down to Santa Maria's beaches, with Cápri visible to the west on clear days.

SAN MARCO, three kilometres or so further along the coast from Santa Maria, is a picturesque, active fishing village which supplies fish to most of the villages along this part of the coast. Its tiny centre can get very crowded in summer. There are two hotels here, the *Antonietta* (☎0974.966.019, fax 0974.966.038; ②), ten minutes' walk from the harbour, and the grander *Hotel Hermitage* on Via Catarozza (☎0974.966.618, fax 0974.966.619, *www.hermitage.it*; ④), a family-orientated option with a pool and tennis courts. A narrow track leads from here down to **PUNTA LICOSA**, where there's a small harbour fringed by rocks from which you can swim. The offshore reef that's topped by a lighthouse is inhabited by lizards said to be of a unique species. To eat here, try the agreeable, if slightly expensive *Ristorante Leucosia*, just behind the dirt road five minutes' walk from the jetty (closed winter). From here you can either return to San Marco or follow the track around to **OGLIASTRO MARINA**, an attractive little village with a hotel and cheap *Pensione da Carmine* (☎0974.963.023; ①) – and some indifferent restaurants, and a long, rather grubby beach that in summer attracts a good number of holiday-makers.

Acciaroli, Marina d'Ascea and Velia

The facilities, and the beaches, improve the closer you get to **ACCIAROLI**, about 10km further south – one of the Cilento's larger resorts and a port for the hydrofoils plying the coast during summer. The railway joins the shoreline again at **MARINA D'ASCEA**, a fairly indifferent resort but surrounded by hotels and campsites, especially along the lengthy sand beach that stretches north to Marina del Casalvelino.

Close by, **MARINA DI VELIA** gives access to the site of **Velia** (daily 9am–1hr before sunset; L5000/€2.58) – comprising the ruins of the Hellenistic town of Elea, founded around 540 BC and an important port and cultural centre, home to its own school of philosophy. Later it became a favourite holiday resort for wealthy Romans, Horace just one of many who came here on the advice of his doctor. The decline of Velia parallels that of Paestum – malarial swamp rendering much of the area uninhabitable – though the upper reaches were lived in until the fifteenth century. There, however, the comparison ends: the remains of Velia are considerably more decimated than those of Paestum and the town was never as crucial a centre, with nothing like as many temples. At the centre of the ruins the **"Porta Rosa"**, named after the wife of the archeologist who conducted the first investigations, is one of the earliest arches ever found – and the first indication to experts that the Greeks knew how to construct such things. Up from here, the **Acropolis** has relics of an amphitheatre and a temple, together with a massive Norman tower – visible for some distance around.

Outside the site there's a restaurant, the *Amoroso* (no closing day) and beyond here a small beach – though this can get crowded in summer. There's another restaurant, too, *La Torre* (no closing day), 200m up the road going towards Agrópoli.

Palinuro

Cheerful **PALINURO**, too, further south, is worth a stop, named after the legendary pilot of the *Aeneid*, who is supposed to have drowned here. It's a much livelier place than anywhere else on the Cilento coast, and so can be packed out. But it's a good alternative to Agrópoli, both as a base for the site of Velia and a beach-bumming spot, and the harbour area to the east of town retains a certain fishing port authenticity. From the harbour, you can explore the stunning craggy coast of the Capo Palinuro, studded with a series of caves, either by taking a guided **boat tour** (L15,000/€7.75) or – more fun – by hiring a **motorboat** (L50,000/€25.82 for 2hr, plus around L20,000/€10.33 for petrol). For either of these options, ignore the touts and head for Alessandro's yellow gazebo on the beach, bearing in mind that the crucial instructions on how to use your motorboat will be given in Italian.

The best **hotel** option is *Hotel Residence La Torre* (☎0974.931.107, fax 0974.931.264, *latorre@xcom.it*; ④), just 10m from the glorious sandy beach by the harbour, where you'll find a sociable bar – a great place for a sundowner. In town, the attractive central **campsite** provides shade and has a rudimentary restaurant, with access to a sandy beach where steps from a series of rock pools take you straight into the sea. A number of good unpretentious **eating** options line Via Indipendenza, the best of which is friendly *L'Ancora* at no. 115; their speciality is *zuppa di pesce*, and the wood-fired oven turns out large and delicious pizzas. Alternatively, blow your last few lire at the *Da Carmelo* restaurant (sometimes closed Wed out of season), 2km south of town at Località Isca, whose fish and seafood is said to be the best for miles around.

East to Sapri

The last real resort, **MARINA DI CAMEROTA**, is less busy than Palinuro and has a shingly beach, three **campsites** and a couple of **hotels** – the *Brera* (☎0974.939.086; ②) is the more upmarket option, and only has seven rooms so it's essential to book ahead in season; or try *La Scogliera* (☎0974.932.019; half board obligatory, L50,000/€25.82) on the *lungomare*, near the beach. **POLICASTRO BUSSENTINO**, which lies 12km to the east, is a quiet resort too, with a crumbly *centro storico* and a shingle beach in a majestic setting, clasped by the high walls of the Golfo di Policastro. Or you can push straight on for another 10km to **SAPRI** – not much of a place in itself, but with an outstanding restaurant in *La Cantina I' Mustazzo* (and its next-door sister restaurant, *Cantina Ru Ranco*) on the main town square, Piazza Plebiscito, at which you can sample traditional Cilento cooking at its best and at very reasonable prices.

Inland Cilento

Inland the Cilento is lonely and often inaccessible, especially if you don't have your own transport. The train cuts through part of the region but doesn't stop, buses are few and far between, and in any case there are only a couple of proper roads winding across the rocky mountainsides. There are also few large settlements and little in the way of accommodation – although the countryside can be gorgeous, offering some splendidly panoramic routes, fine mountain walks and spectacular gorges and caves.

There are a number of villages you might structure a long day's car journey around. In the north, the caves of **CASTELCIVITA** (daily 10am–6.30pm; L8000/€4.14) form just one of several systems that riddle the Cilento, discovered by two brothers who got lost here in 1889 – one of whom died as a result, while the other was found to have gone totally insane. Guided tours every half-hour wind past intricate stalactites and under clusters of bats; whatever the weather outside, bring a sweater – it can get cold. If you enjoy these caves, you should also visit a similar system at **PERTOSA**, further inland, just off the main Salerno–Reggio *autostrada* (take the "Polla" exit). The caves here are in fact much larger than those at Castelcivita, and you tour them by boat, rowed along a subterranean river (summer daily 8am–7pm; short trip L10,000/€5.16, long trip L15,000/€7.75).

About 10km further south (though much longer by road), the village of **ROSCIG-NO VECCHIO** is an example of a typical Cilento village from the turn of the century, deserted now following a landslip but with a small museum of Cilento rural life in its old church (Sat & Sun 10am–noon & 4.30–6.30pm). Back towards the coast, **VALLO DELLA LUCANIA**, a little way inland from Velia, is an example of the more prosperous recent years here, the largest town inland and a lively place with a busy passeggiata of an evening. Three kilometres outside, the tiny village of **NOVI VELIA** is overshadowed by 1705-metre-high **Monte Sacro**, at the top of which is a **sanctuary** which has been a place of pilgrimage since 1323 – an odd, very remote complex of dormitories and churches and even a small post office that's open from the end of May until the beginning of October. With luck you should be able to stay the night.

Padula

Finally, there is one sight you should really try not to miss if you're touring this area by car: the vast **Certosa di San Lorenzo**, almost out of the Cilento off the Salerno–Reggio *autostrada* between Sala Consilina and Lagonegro, 1km or so below the town of **PADULA** ("Padula-Buonabitácolo" exit). The Carthusian monastery (daily 9am–7pm; L8000/€4.13) was begun in 1306 but is predominantly a Baroque building, its most impressive feature being an enormous central quadrangle. This would have been a hive of activity, with a foundry, stables, ovens and granaries, as well as the living quarters of the lay monks, who received postulants and pilgrims, but the whole complex fell into disuse following the supression of the monastery in 1816.

The playful sixteenth- to seventeenth-century facade of the monastery divided this lay activity from the seclusion of the "upper house", whose church, treasury and chapel are rich with intricate marquetry, swirling stucco, inset coloured marble and mother-of-pearl – it's hard to believe that in its heyday, the monastery's only 24 monks were housed amidst all this opulence. Despite the undeniable glories of the architecture – notably the grand staircase at the far end which swoops up to a gallery that is now closed to the public – the monastery has a rather desolate air. This might be due to the very excess of such a place in an area long blighted by poverty, or perhaps because it served as a prisoner of war camp for British soldiers during the Second World War, and subsequently fell into decay for many years before being opened to the public.

In the town of Padula itself, rather neglected but spectacularly sited, signs take you on an extremely circuitous route to the touching **Joe Petrosino museum** (daily 9.30am–1.30pm & 3.30–8pm; L3000/€1.55). Petrosino (see also p.1111) was born in Padula in 1860 and his family emigrated to the US when he was 14. The son of a tailor, he joined the New York Police Department, rising to the rank of Head of the Italian Squad. Returning to Italy in 1909 on an undercover mission to investigate links between the American "Black Hand" and Italian "Cosa Nostra", Petrosino was shot dead as he landed at Palermo. The museum, in the house where he was born, illustrates the humble conditions that spurred many people to emigrate to the US, as well as showing how the Petrosino legend entered popular culture both in the US and in Italy – a lurid cartoon strip, *Il Grande Poliziotto Italo-Americano*, immortalized the hero, who has a square and a school in New York dedicated to his memory.

Accommodation options are scarce, and you probably won't want to stick around for more than a night, but the obvious choice is the *Grand Hotel Certosa* (☎ & fax 0975.77046, *www.certosa.it*; ③), opposite the monastery on Viale Certosa – though it isn't quite as grand as the name suggests. A couple of minutes' walk from the hotel towards town you'll find a friendly and good-value **pizzeria/restaurant**, informally known as *Da Tonino*, with a few tables outside under a leafy canopy. Finally, the **Musica in Certosa** festival is a programme of chamber music featuring world-class musicians, usually held at the end of July (look out for posters around town) – concerts are free and held in a beautiful frescoed hall in the floodlit monastery.

travel details

METROPOLITANA/FS NAPLES

Gianturco–Piazza Garibaldi–Piazza Cavour–Montesanto–Piazza Amedeo–Mergellina–Piazza Leopardi (Fuorigrotta)–Campi Flegrei–Cavalleggeri d'Aosta–Bagnoli–Pozzuoli. Trains every 8min.

Circumflegrea (information ☎089.551.3328). Connects Naples Montesanto to Cuma, Lido Fusaro and Torregaveta with 6 departures daily. Departures every 20min for all stations to Licola.

Circumvesuviana (information ☎089.772.2444). This line runs between Naples and Sorrento, with many stops around the southern part of the bay, including Ercolano and Pompeii, every 20–30min.

Ferrovia Cumana (information ☎089.551.3328). Connects Naples Montesanto with Fuorigrotta, Agnano, Bagnoli, Pozzuoli, Báia, Fusaro and Torregaveta. Departures every 10min.

TRAINS

Benevento to: Fóggia (10 daily; 1hr 10min–1hr 40min); Naples (18 daily; 1hr 5min–1hr 55min).

Naples to: Agrópoli (15 daily; 1hr 40min); Benevento (18 daily; 1hr 5min–1hr 55min); Caserta (every 20min; 25–45min); Cassino (7 daily; 1hr 45min–2hr 5min); Fóggia (4 daily; 2hr 20min–3hr); Formia (hourly; 1hr); Paola (Calabria) (12 daily; 3hr–4hr); Rome (hourly; 2hr 40min); Salerno (hourly; 50min); Santa Maria Cápua Vetere (9 daily; 50min); Sapri (12 daily; 2hr).

Salerno to: Paestum/Agrópoli (9 daily; 35min); Sapri (hourly; 1hr 55min).

BUSES

Agrópoli to: Acciaroli (6 daily; 55min); Paestum (hourly; 15min); Salerno (hourly; 1hr 15min); Santa Maria di Castellabate (hourly; 30min); Sapri (1 daily; 3hr 30min).

Naples to: Amalfi (5 daily; 1hr 55min); Benevento (6 daily; 1hr 30min); Cápua (hourly; 1hr 15min); Caserta (every 20min; 1hr); Salerno (every 15–30min; 1hr 5min); Sant'Agata dei Goti (1 daily; 1hr 30min); Sorrento (1 daily at 8.45am; 1hr 20min); Pompeii Scavi (every 30min; 30min); Positano (1 daily at 8.45am; 1hr 55min).

Naples Capodochino airport to: Sorrento (2 daily; 1hr 15min).

Salerno to: Agrópoli (hourly; 1hr 15min); Amalfi (hourly; 1hr 10min); Naples (every 15–30min; 1hr 5min); Paestum (hourly; 1hr); Positano (every 1–2hr; 2hr); Sorrento (every 1–2hr; 2hr 45min); Vietri (every 20min; 20min).

Sorrento to: Amalfi (12 daily; 1hr 30min); Naples (1 daily at 6.35pm; 1hr 20min); Naples Capodochino Airport (2 daily; 1hr 15min); Positano (12 daily; 40min); Salerno (12 daily; 2hr 45min).

FERRIES AND HYDROFOILS

Naples to: Aeolian Islands/Milazzo (twice/thrice weekly in high season at 9pm; 12hr); Cagliari (weekly/twice weekly in high season; 15hr 30min); Palermo (daily at 5.30pm; 4hr); Sorrento (4 daily ferries/7 daily hydrofoils; 1hr 15min/40min).

Salerno to: Amalfi (12 daily hydrofoils; 40min); Positano (10 daily hydrofoils; 1hr 10min).

For details of ferry and hydrofoil connections between Naples, the Amalfi coast and Salerno and the islands, see p.849.

CHAPTER FOURTEEN

PUGLIA

Puglia is the long strip of land, 400km from north to south, that makes up the "heel" of Italy. It was for centuries a strategic province, colonized, invaded and conquered (like its neighbours, Calabria and Sicily) by just about every major power of the day, from the Greeks through to the Spanish. As elsewhere in the South, each ruling dynasty left its own distinctive mark on the landscape and architecture – as seen, for example, in the surviving traces of Roman agricultural schemes and the fortified medieval towns. There's no escaping some of the historical influences in Puglia. Perhaps most distinctive are the Saracenic kasbah-like quarters of many towns and cities, the one at **Bari** being the biggest and most atmospheric. The Normans endowed Puglia with splendidly ornate cathedrals; there's one at **Trani** which skilfully blends many strands of regional craft traditions from north and south. And the Baroque exuberance of towns like **Lecce** and **Martina Franca** are testament to the Spanish legacy. But if there's one symbol of Puglia that stands out, it's the imposing castles built by the Swabian Frederick II, all over the province – foremost of which are the **Castel del Monte** and the remnants of the palace at **Lucera**.

Clean seas and reliable sunshine have made Puglia a popular spot for holidays, with acres of campsite-and-bungalow type tourist villages – as well as a large number of flashy four-star hotels – principally serving tourists from Italy and Germany. The cities, however, including Bari, have little that's characteristic enough to warrant long stays: **Táranto** and its surroundings have fought a losing battle with the local steel industry, while **Bríndisi** is known and visited only for its ferry connections with Greece; even **Lecce** has little to hold you once you've trekked your way along modern boulevards to see the crazed confectionery of its Baroque churches. Nevertheless, there's a geographical diversity to Puglia that can be very attractive, though to get to the best of the province you either need your own transport or the patience to use the often erratic local buses. The very southern tip, the **Salentine peninsula**, is rocky and dry, more Greek than Italian, while there's plenty of barren mountain scenery in the undulating plateau of **Le Murge**, in the centre of the province. The best escape, though, is north to the mountains, forests and beaches of the **Gargano promontory** with some of the finest unpolluted sand and sea to be found anywhere on the Adriatic.

ACCOMMODATION PRICE CODES

Throughout this guide, prices per person are given for **youth hostels** and assume Hostelling International (HI) membership. **Hotel** accommodation is coded on a scale from ① to ⑨, reflecting the cost of the cheapest double room in each establishment in high season. The price bands to which these codes refer are as follows:

① Up to L60,000/€30.99
② L60,000–90,000/€30.99–46.48
③ L90,000–120,000/€46.48–61.98
④ L120,000–150,000/€61.98–77.47
⑤ L150,000–200,000/€77.47–103.29

⑥ L200,000–250,000/€103.29–129.11
⑦ L250,000–300,000/€129.11–154.94
⑧ L300,000–400,000/€154.94–206.58
⑨ over L400,000/€206.58

(See p.32 for a full explanation.)

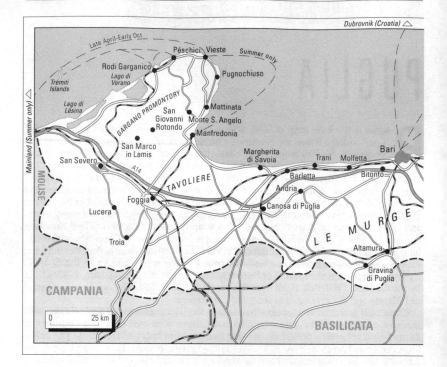

Getting around Puglia by public transport is fairly easy, at least as far as the main towns and cities go. FS **trains** connect nearly all the major places, while small, private lines head into previously remote areas – in the Gargano and on the edges of Le Murge. Most other places can be reached by **bus**, though as ever services are often infrequent or inconveniently early – a problem that can only really be solved by taking, or renting, your own **car**. Incidentally, if you're on your way **to Greece**, it's worth noting that you don't have to leave from Bríndisi: there are also departures from Bari and from **Otranto**, south of Lecce.

Fóggia and the Tavoliere

The broad sweep of the **Tavoliere plain** stretches from the Basilicata border to the edge of the Gargano massif – flat, fertile lands that are southern Italy's wheat bowl, and the source of the country's best pasta. It was the Romans who attempted the first intense cultivation of the area, parcelling the land up into neat squares for distribution to its pensionable centurions. This lent the land its chessboard appearance, from which the Tavoliere takes its name, but for the centurions the gift was a mixed blessing. **Fóggia** province proved to be an unhealthy place, an earthquake-prone swampland rife with malarial mosquitoes, and settlements here suffered from disease and disaster in fairly equal proportions. It wasn't until the advent of irrigation schemes in the 1920s that the mosquitoes lost their malarial bite and the area began to take on its present rich appearance. As the transport hub of the province, you will probably pass through Fóggia, though for more of an idea of what the Tavoliere is like, head for the walled town of **Lucera** or the little village of **Tróia**.

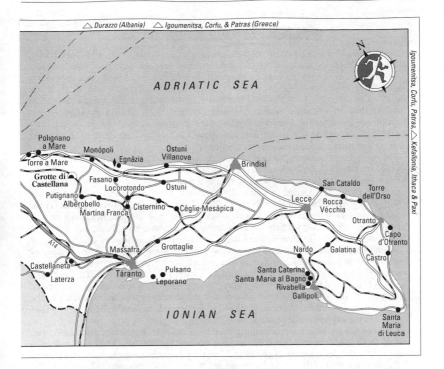

Fóggia

The Tavoliere's main town, **FÓGGIA**, looms out of the plain without warning, a fine starting-point for exploring northern Puglia and the Gargano promontory though in itself not that encouraging a stop. Although Fóggia flourished under Frederick II, who declared it an imperial residence and built a palace here, the town was devastated in turn by the French in 1528, an earthquake in 1731, and Allied bombs during World War II. Today the city's streets are all reassuringly earthquake-proof, wide and low-built, a modern layout that is handsome enough, but you're going to have to search hard in between the tree-lined boulevards for what is left of the old town.

What little there is lies scattered around the **Duomo**, which is to the left off Corso Vittorio Emanuele, the main drag that runs down from the central, fountained Piazza Cavour. The cathedral is an odd Romanesque–Baroque sandwich, the top part tacked on in the eighteenth century after the earthquake. Much of what was once notable about it was lost in the 'quake – particularly the tomb of Charles I of Anjou and a receptacle said to contain Frederick II's heart – but the crypt survived, and it features some finely decorated Romanesque capitals. A Byzantine icon, now housed in a chapel next to the presbytery, was reputedly discovered by eleventh-century shepherds in a pond upon which burned three flames; these flames became the symbol of the city.

While you're here, take a look at the nearby **Museo Cívico** on Piazza Nigri (daily 9am–1pm, weekdays except Wed also 5–7pm; free), reached by walking down the Corso to Via Arpi. Incorporated into the side of the building are three portals, one of which – the Porta Grande, with the thoughtful-looking eagles – is all that remains of Frederick II's imperial palace. Duck inside and there are the usual regional

REGIONAL FOOD AND WINE

The influence of Puglia's former rulers is evident in the region's food. Like the **Greeks**, Pugliesi eat lamb and kid spit-roast over herb-scented fires and deep-fried doughnut-like cakes steeped in honey; and like the **Spanish** they drink almond milk, *latte di mandorla*. Puglia is the source of eighty percent of Europe's pasta and most of Italy's fish; it produces more wine than Germany and more olive oil (even if it is not always of the finest quality) than all the other regions of Italy combined. It's famous for olives (from Cerignola), almonds (from Ruvo di Puglia), dark juicy tomatoes (often sun-dried), fava beans, voluptuous figs (fresh and dried), *cotognata* (a moulded jam made from quinces) and for its melons, grapes and green cauliflower.

The most distinctive local **pasta** is *orecchiette*, ear-shaped pasta which you will still see women making in their doorways in the old part of Bari. Look out too for *panzarotti alla barese*, pockets of pasta stuffed with *ragù* (meat sauce), egg and cheese or *ricotta* and *prosciutto* that are deep-fried in olive oil. Otherwise, there is a marked preference for short stubby varieties of pasta, which you'll find served with peppers, cauliflower, or even turnip tops (*cime di rapa*). Not surprisingly, fish and shellfish dominate many a menu. There are some good fish soups (*zuppe di pesce*) whose ingredients and style vary from place to place – the Brindisi version, for example, is dominated by eels.

As elsewhere in the south, lamb is the most common **meat**, often roast over rosemary and thyme branches, which impart a wonderful flavour. A local speciality is *gnummerieddi*, a haggis-like dish, made by stuffing a lamb gut with minced offal, herbs and garlic – best grilled over an open fire. There is little beef or pork, poultry is uncommon, and game is virtually nonexistent; as a result, horsemeat is popular, especially in the Salento area. To confound your prejudices, go for *braciole di cavallo*, horsemeat steaks cooked in a good rich tomato sauce.

Cheeses are a strong point, including *ricotta, cacioricotta, mozzarella, burrata, caprini* (small fresh goat's cheeses preserved in olive oil), and *fagottini* (small smoked cheeses, a speciality of the Fóggia area). If you're in Andria, try *burrata*, a creamy soft cow's cheese.

Puglia is the land of the grape. In recent years the region has exploited its hot, fertile plain to become one of the wealthiest parts of the south, and while much of its **wine** is pretty basic (the vast majority is used in Torinese vermouths) there have recently been immense improvements. Yields have been severely reduced, grapes have been picked at precisely the right moment, and modern technology has been introduced to great advantage. Wine-maker Kym Milne, for example, has created an excellent Chardonnay del Salento and a huge red Salice Salentino. Other wines to look out for include Primitivo di Manduria (another huge red) and Locorotondo, a straightforward, clean-tasting white, as well as dessert wines.

archeological finds; the more interesting section on local life and folklore was closed for restoration at the time of writing. If you're interested in such things, the modest **Museo di Storia Naturale** at Via Bellavia 5 (Tues–Sun: summer 9am–1pm & 5–9pm; winter 4–8pm; L3000/€1.55; take bus #8 or #12 from the train station) is dedicated to local flora and fauna, wth a small collection of Mediterranean shells.

That really is it, as far as Fóggia's sights go, though there are enough green spaces and shopping streets up in the new town to occupy any remaining time – something you might well have, as Fóggia is an important rail junction on the main Bologna–Lecce and Naples–Bari lines.

Practicalities

The **train station** is on Piazzale Vittorio Veneto, on the northern edge of town, a short walk from Piazza Cavour and the centre. FS services (information ☎1478.88.088) from here run to Manfredonia, while Ferrovie del Gargano (FG; toll-free information,

☎167.296.247; office to the left of the station entrance) trains go to Péschici Calenella. If you can stand getting to the station for 6am there's a combined train and ferry service (originating in Bari) that goes from Fóggia straight through to the Trémiti islands (see p.888).Tickets have to be bought from the station by 5pm the preceeding day. SITA **buses**, which serve the whole region, arrive at and depart from just outside the train station; their ticket office (☎0881.773.117 or 0881.773.425) is under the porticoes opposite the station; when this is closed, buy tickets at the *Kiwi Bar*, on the corner of Viale XXIV Maggio. There are also Ferrovie del Gargano buses to Manfredonia and Vieste. The **tourist office** (Mon–Fri 8.30am–1.30pm; ☎0881.723.650), a 15–20min walk into town, on the first floor at Via E. Perrone 17, off Piazzale Puglia, has a lot of good information on the province as a whole. If you are headed for the Gargano, *Tutto Gargano* (L5000/€2.58 from newsstands or free from the tourist office) is a great resource for accommodation and information on festivals and events; check out its site at *www.tuttogargano.com* too. For onward travel, there's a **CTS** office selling train, bus and air tickets with reductions for under-26s at Via Tugini 62 (Mon–Fri 9am–1pm & 5–8pm; ☎0881.708.269)

Staying in Fóggia is not a desperately attractive option; there are several rather rundown hotels near the station, but most are uninspiring and not particularly cheap; better bets are the recently renovated *Hotel Venezia*, Via Piave 40 (☎0881.770.903; ②), down Viale XXIV Maggio from the station, then third right. *Hotel Europa*, Via Monfalcone 52 (☎0881.721.057, *www.italiaabc.com*; ⑥), is more upmarket with smart rooms and helpful staff – again it's down Viale XXIV Maggio from the station, then second right. The grandest place in town is *Cicolella*, at Viale XXIV Maggio 60 (☎0881.688.890; ⑧), a businesslike hotel clad in black marble and cherry wood dating back to the early 1900s and offering attentive service. The only time that bed space will be short is at the beginning of May, during the **Fiera di Fóggia** – one of Italy's oldest fairs, although today simply a huge international agricultural affair held on the outskirts of the town.

There are several good **food** options: try *Il Rugantino*, Via Luigi Sturzo 23 (closed Mon), head down Corso Roma and turn left at the sanitorium – which offers great pizzas and other dishes; *Osteria Chacaito*, Via Arpi 62 (closed Sun), a typically Foggiese osteria with excellent wines near the Museo Civico; or spend a little more at *Da Pompeo*, Vico al Piano 14 (closed Sun), down Corso Vittorio Emanuele II and right at the Palazzo Vescovile – a good place to indulge in Pugliesi specialities. There is also a very good pizzeria a few steps from Piazza d'Italia and Corso Roma on Via Bari called *Le Arcate*, which doesn't look promising from the outside but which has a bright, modern interior and a fantastic inexpensive antipasti buffet as well as excellent cripsy pizzas.

Lucera

Just 18km west, within easy reach of Fóggia (hourly buses), **LUCERA** is a far better introduction to Puglia. A small town with a bright and bustling centre, it was once the capital of the Tavoliere, and it has a distinct charm, its vast castle dominating the landscape for miles around. It was once a thriving Saracen city: Frederick II, having forced the Arabs out of Sicily, resettled 20,000 of them here, on the site of an abandoned Roman town, allowing them complete freedom of religious worship – an almost unheard of act of liberalism for the early thirteenth century.

Buses arrive in Piazza del Popolo, from where it's only a short walk up Via Gramsci to the **Duomo**, which marks the centre of the medieval walled town. The cathedral – a dark, rather miserable building – was built in the early fourteenth century after Frederick II's death when the Angevins arrived and a conflict with the Saracens began. The Angevins won, and built the cathedral on the site of a mosque;

by the end of their rule, few of the town's original Arab-influenced buildings were left. However, the Arabic layout of Lucera survived and there's a powerful atmosphere here – best appreciated by wandering the narrow streets of the old town, peering into the courtyards and alleyways. Close to the cathedral, a little way down Via de' Nicastri, is the **Museo Cívico** (Tues–Sat 9am–1pm & 4–7pm, Sun 9am–1pm; L1500/€0.77), well stocked with Greek pottery and their Puglian copies. There are some fine mosaics and terracotta heads too, and the bust of a Greek youth said – rather optimistically – to be that of Alexander the Great. Also worth seeking out in town is the fourteenth-century **church of San Francesco** with a beautiful rose window and the moth-eaten clothes of 'Padre Maestro' or Francesco Antonio Pasani, a local saint-in-the-making, on display.

The other sights are all outside the old centre, most notably the **Castello** (Tues–Sun: summer 8am–8pm; winter 9am–1pm; free), built by Frederick and designed to house a lavish court which included an exotic collection of wild beasts. To get there from Piazza Duomo follow Via Bovio and Via Federico II to Piazza Matteotti and look for the signs. The largest in southern Italy after Lagopésole in Basilicata (see p.940), the castle commands spectacular views over the Tavoliere, stretching across to the foothills of the Apennines to the west and the mountains of Gargano to the east. Contained within the kilometre-long walls are the evocative remains of Frederick's great palace, fragments of mosaic work and fallen columns peering out of a dense undergrowth of wild flowers. The Roman **amphitheatre** is on the western edge of town and often holds concerts in summer.

Stopping over in Lucera wouldn't be a bad thing, although the functional *La Balconata* at Viale Ferrovia 15 (☎0881.546.725; ③) and *Al Passetto* at Piazza del Popolo 24 (☎0881.520.998; ③) are the only **hotels** in town (the latter has a fine restaurant closed Mon). There's a good farm B&B 5km outside Lucera, *Masseria Mezzana Grande* on the road to Bíccari (☎0881.529.915; ④), with large rooms, modern bathrooms and a private kitchen and sitting room for guests. Bear in mind that the B&B comes second to the farm's main business of growing grain, olives and almonds and book a couple of days ahead. As for **places to eat**: *La Tavernetta* Via Schiavone 7–9, behind the cathedral (closed Wed), is an excellent place for crispy pizzas cooked in a wood-fired oven, pasta dishes and local wine, while the new *Hostaria Lupus* Via Gramsci 10 (closed Tues in winter and July) in the old town offers a limited menu at moderate prices.

Tróia

Frequent buses also make the short ride (from either Lucera or Fóggia) to **TRÓIA**, 18km due south of Lucera. The locals seem curiously blasé as to the origin of their village's name; it means "slut" in Italian, which probably has its origins in Helen of Troy, but no-one is able to offer a logical connection with the village. Whatever the reason, the Tróiani atone for the name by having five patron saints, whose statues are paraded around town in a procession every July 9.

At all other times of the year the highlight in Tróia – an otherwise quiet, dusty village – is the fine **Duomo**, an intriguing eleventh-century blend of Byzantine and Apulian–Romanesque styles, with a generous hint of Saracen influence, too. The great bronze doors are covered with reliefs of animals and biblical figures, while above, surrounded by a frenzy of carved lions frozen in stone, is an extraordinary rose window. Distinctly Saracen in flavour, the window resembles a finely worked piece of oriental ivory, being composed of eleven stone panels, each one delicately carved. There's more exact detail inside too, including a curiously decorated pulpit and some ornate capitals.

West and south of Fóggia

Well off the beaten track in Fóggia province are some of the most handsome hilltop villages in this part of Italy. Most are little visited, and requests for information about them are likely to be met with a blank gaze at the tourist office. Indeed, although the area is slowly beginning to open up to visitors, it's still very much a quiet backwater of forests and hills.

Most remote is the scattering of settlements which lies to the **west of Lucera**, in the gentle **Monti di Daunia**. The inhabitants are Albanian in origin, first arriving in the fifteenth century to help fight the French and later as refugees fleeing from the Turks. It's hard to get here without your own transport, and there's not a lot here if you do.

South of Fóggia is more interesting. **BOVINO**, near the Campanian border, is a small and distinctly medieval village, with fragments of Roman fortifications and a thirteenth-century cathedral looking out over a fine landscape of undulating wooded slopes. The snag is that Bovino is an alarmingly steep seven-kilometre climb away from its train station, and if you're travelling by train **ORDONA**, over to the east, is probably an easier target. The ancient Daunic people of the Tavoliere once had a town here, sited on the banks of the River Carapelle, which was destroyed by Pyrrhus (using elephants) in the third century BC. Over what was left the Romans built Herdonia, large parts of which still survive. The **site** (free access) is a short walk south from the present village of Ordona, and there are the obvious remains of a forum and a small amphitheatre, as well as scantier pieces of a small basilica and two temples.

Manfredonia and Siponto

By Puglian standards, **MANFREDONIA** is a new town, a mere 600 years old, founded – as the name suggests – by Manfred, illegitimate son of Frederick II. The Austrians struck the first blow of World War I on Italian soil here by bombing the town's station in 1915, but this is really Manfredonia's only claim to fame. The town is seen more as the gateway to the Gargano promontory, and most people pass quickly through. Still, what the town lacks in historical sights is more than made up for by its sandy beaches, which stretch for miles down the coast.

The **Castello**, on Corso Manfredi, was started by Manfred and extended by the Angevins. Its huge bastions were added in 1607 by the Spanish to stave off a Turkish attack: they failed to do so, the Turks landing in 1620, ravaging the hapless inhabitants and destroying much of the town – though most of the protective walls still survive. The castle now houses the **Museo Nazionale** (daily except first and last Mon of the month: summer 8.30am–7.30pm & Sat 8–11pm; winter 8.30am–1.30pm & 3.30–7.30pm; L4000/€2.06), largely devoted to Daunic finds from the seventh and sixth centuries BC, particularly several stone stelae, thought to be tombstones, richly carved with images of armoured warriors, female figures and scenes from daily life.

SIPONTO, 3km south down the coast from Manfredonia, was once a thriving medieval port. But constant malarial attacks and damaging earthquakes have left it with little beyond its good sandy **beaches** to draw you – all no more than twenty minutes' walk or a short bus ride from Manfredonia's train station. They're signposted from town and in August you can expect them to be packed to the gills.

Practicalities

The easiest way to reach Manfredonia is by train from Fóggia: from the **station**, turn right and it's a short walk along Viale Aldo Moro to Piazza Marconi. Just across the square, Corso Manfredi leads up to the **tourist office** in the *comune* building in Piazza del Popolo (Mon–Fri 8.30am–1.30pm, plus Tues 3–6.30pm; ☎0884.581.998), which is a good source of maps and information on the Gargano area. If you're going to use Manfredonia as a base, there's no shortage of **accommodation**, but the better options are near the beach in Siponto – the *Sipontum*, Via G. di Vittorio 229 (☎0884.542.916; ②) is a good basic option. There are also **campsites** strung out south along the coast, the nearest 4km from town, although you'll probably have to walk there; check with the Manfredonia tourist office. The **hydrofoil** service to the Trémiti Islands, (June–Aug daily departs 8am; a 2hr journey; L34,000/€17.56 single), leaves from the harbour; **tickets** can be purchased in town from Agenzia Marittima Galli, Corso Manfredi 4 (Mon–Sat 8.30–12.30pm & 4.30–7pm; ☎0884.582.888), or from the Adriatica office in the harbour itself, one hour before departure.

There are plenty of **restaurants** in Manfredonia, one of the best of which is *Coppola Rossa*, Via dei Celestini 13 (☎0884.582.522; closed all day Mon & Sun evening), where you can feast on antipasti, *troccoli alla scoglio* (tiny pasta in a sauce of clams, eels, tomatoes and oil), *orecchiette* with scampi, or *ciambotta* (fish soup).

The Gargano promontory

The **Gargano promontory** rises like an island from the flat plains of the Tavoliere, geographically and culturally different from the rest of Puglia. Its landscape is remarkably diverse: beaches and lagoons to the north, a rocky, indented eastern coast and a mountainous, green heartland of oaks and beech trees – reminiscent of a Germanic forest rather than a corner of southern Italy. For centuries the promontory was extremely isolated, visited only by pilgrims making their way along the valley to Monte Sant'Angelo and its shrine. Nowadays tourism has taken off in a big way, especially on the coast around Vieste, but in 1991 the whole peninsula became a national park, helping to protect the Gargano from overbearing development and ensuring that much of the interior remains supremely unspoiled and quiet.

Approaches to the promontory are pretty straightforward. **FS trains** run from Fóggia to Manfredonia on the southeast side of Gargano, from where it's only 16km by **bus** to Monte Sant'Angelo, and there are buses straight up the coast as well. Alternatively, in the north of the region, **Ferrovie del Gargano** (FG toll-free information ☎167.296.247; ticket office in Fóggia) operates trains between Fóggia and Péschici-Calenella, from where a bus connects with Péschici. Note that most FG stations are quite a distance from the towns and villages they serve, so always go for the connecting bus if there is one.

Getting around in the interior can be a little more tortuous. **Buses** are run by two companies: SITA (☎0881.773.117 or 0881.773.425; ticket office in Fóggia) serves the inland towns and operates the inland route to Vieste; and FG, who run the trains and connecting buses in northern Gargano, roughly between San Severo and Péschici, and a coastal route to Vieste, via Manfredonia, Mattinata and Pugnochiuso. There is also a **ferry service** connecting Manfredonia, Vieste, Péschici, Rodi Garganico and most coastal towns, which goes on to the Trémiti Islands (p.888).

Monte Sant'Angelo and the pilgrim route

Just north of Manfredonia, perched almost 800m up in the hills, **MONTE SANT'AN-GELO** is the highest – and coldest – settlement in the Gargano. Pilgrims have trudged up the switchback paths and roads for centuries to visit the spot where the archangel Michael is said to have made four separate appearances, mostly at the end of the fifth century – making the sanctuary here one of the earliest Christian shrines in Europe

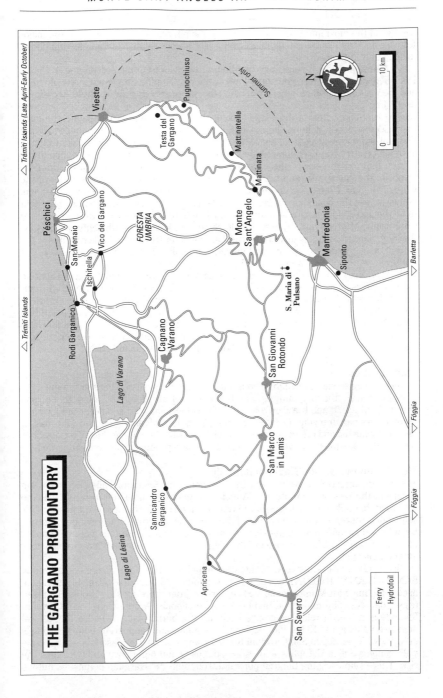

THE GARGANO PROMONTORY

Ferry — — —
Hydrofoil — · — · —

and one of the most important in Italy. Today, the pilgrims come by bus, and the major festivals on May 8 and September 29 every year attract locals from miles around who turn up in traditional dress.

SITA **buses** – which run every two hours from Manfredonia – drop you in Piazza Duca d'Aosta, from where you should follow the road uphill to the edge of the old town and the Via Reale Basilica, where you'll find the **Santuario di San Michele Arcangelo** itself (July–Sept daily 7.30am–7pm; Oct–June Mon–Sat 7.30am–12.30pm & 2.30–5pm, Sun 7.30am–7pm). Apart from a lean octagonal thirteenth-century campanile, the sanctuary seems rather plain on the outside, but from the small courtyard on the right a flight of stone steps leads down to the grotto – heralded by a magnificent pair of eleventh-century bronze doors, made in Constantinople, that form the entrance to the church built on the site of the cave in which the archangel first appeared (in 490). Opposite the campanile, another set of steps leads down to the nearby ruins of the **Chiesa di San Pietro**, behind which is the so-called **Tomba di Rotari** (9am–noon, otherwise see the custodian in San Michele) – an imposing domed tower once thought to be the tomb of Rothari, a seventh-century Lombard chieftain who was converted to Christianity. More prosaically, it's more likely to have been a twelfth-century baptistry; the large baptismal font is just on the right as you enter the tower. Little remains of the church itself, wrecked by an earthquake, but look out for the rose window – a Catherine wheel of entwined mermaids.

Back on Via Reale Basilica, it's an easy clamber up to the ruined Norman **Castello** for good views over the town and valley. From here, you can cut down through the narrow whitewashed streets of the old town to Piazza San Francesco d'Assisi and the **Museo Tancredi** (April–Sept Mon 8am–2pm, Tues–Sat 8am–2pm & 2.30–7pm, Sun 10am–12.30pm & 3.30–7pm; Oct–March Mon, Wed & Fri 8am–2pm, Tues & Thurs 8am–2pm & 4–7pm; L3000/€1.54), an arts and crafts museum with several interesting displays which explain the production of olive oil, wheat, wine and coal.

Practicalities

If you're going to stay overnight (though don't count on available beds at the main pilgrimage times), the only **hotels** are the *Rotary*, 1km along the road to Pulsano (☎0884.562.146; ③) and the *Sant'Angelo* nearby (☎0884.565.536; ④). There are a couple of **trattorias** worth trying: *Li Jalantuùmene*, Piazza de Galganis 5 (closed Jan), has an excellent wine list and offers good local specialities, while the *Medio Evo*, Via Castelli 21 (closed Mon in winter), serves home-made bread and produce from its own garden.

The pilgrim route: San Giovanni Rotondo

The ancient **pilgrim route** weaved its way along the Stignano Valley between San Severo in the west and Monte Sant'Angelo and until comparatively recently was the only road that linked the villages of the Gargano interior. With your own transport, it's still a good route to explore a couple of the region's most important religious centres. By public transport, though, the service and connections are sketchy but not impossible – if you want to follow any part of the pilgrim route by bus, you'll have to plan your itinerary carefully.

Direct bus services between Monte Sant'Angelo and the first village on the route, **SAN GIOVANNI ROTONDO**, run every two hours, although the village is better connected by bus with Manfredonia, a SITA service from there making around fourteen trips a day. Nestling under the highest peak hereabouts, Monte Calvo, San Giovanni Rotondo is no mean religious centre itself; it's the burial place of Padre Pio, a local priest who died in the 1960s. Pio received the stigmata and "appeared" before cardinals in Rome while asleep in San Giovanni Rotondo, and won an immense following – especially among Italian Catholics – for his model piety and legendary ability to heal the sick. There's no escaping his frail portrait throughout the Gargano peninsula, but it's especially prominent here; the **Santuario di Padre Pio** is extremely interesting as a celebration of this contemporary saint, beatified on 2 May 1998. The town takes its name from the **Rotonda di San Giovanni**, a building of indeterminate origin or purpose at the edge of the old town – like the Tomba di Rotari, it's thought to have been a baptistry, built on the site of an earlier pagan temple.

Nine kilometres further west, and looking splendidly out over the Tavoliere plain, **SAN MARCO IN LAMIS**, though considerably smaller than San Giovanni, is dominated by a huge sixteenth-century Convento di San Matteo, with a modern interior. Every Good Friday the town holds a noisy, lively – and originally pagan – affair called the **fracchie**, when huge bundles of burning wood are hauled through the streets to illuminate the town for the Madonna as she seeks Jesus.

Vieste and the Costa Garganica

About 15km north of Manfredonia, the road tunnels under a mountain to emerge in a softer, greener landscape. **MATTINATA**, a small but popular resort with good campsites, sits back from the coast, overlooking olive groves and pine trees that drop down gently to a magnificent stretch of beach. Beyond Mattinata the road splits: one branch (which the SITA bus takes) winds its way through the eastern part of the Foresta Umbra (see p.888), to Vieste; the coastal route (and the FG bus) runs up to **PUGNOCHIUSO**, a panoramic bay dominated by a vast Club Med holiday village. If you're interested, one of the easiest of the local **hiking trails** starts close by. The path is clearly marked off the Mattinata–Pugnochiuso road, about 3km north of Baia di Zagare, and the trail (around 3km each way) runs sharply down to a beach, the Spiaggia di Vignanótica. To reach the start of the trail, take the FG bus from Mattinata for Pugnochiuso/Vieste and ask to be let off at Località Mégoli.

Vieste
VIESTE juts out into the Adriatic on two promontories, the most easterly point of the Gargano peninsula. Fifty years ago there wasn't even a proper road here, but today Vieste, with its excellent beaches, is the holiday capital of Gargano (and Puglia), and the streets and sands are packed in August. Despite this it has managed to survive as a lively and inviting town, with an interesting historic core and active nightlife that warrant a stop of a day or two – certainly if you're planning to take the ferry from here to the Trémiti Islands.

The **old town** sits on the easternmost of the two promontories, at the tip of which stands the **Chiesa di San Francesco**, once a thriving monastery, and a **trabucco** – a cantilevered arrangement of beams, winches and ropes still used by fishermen to catch mullet. Made of wood, these structures are a feature peculiar to the rocky Gargano coast, probably Phoenician in origin, and the principle at least is straightforward. As mullet swim head to tail, a live mullet is attached to a line and used to entice others to swim over a net suspended below, which is then hoisted up to the platform. Visits can be arranged through the tourist office (see overleaf).

From the church, climb up Via Mafrolla, walking into the old town to Piazza Seggio. Straight ahead, Via Duomo is site of the so-called **Chianca Amara**, the "bitter stone", where as many as 5000 local people were beheaded when the Turks sacked the town in 1554. Further down, beyond the stone, the **Cattedrale**, eleventh century in origin but tampered with in the eighteenth century, is a cool retreat from the fierce glare of the sun in the whitewashed streets; and beyond here the **Castello** is another of Frederick II's installations – owned by the military now and not open to the public, but giving good views over the beaches and town.

You **arrive** by bus at Piazza Mazzini, to the west of the town centre; bear right from here along Viale XXIV Maggio, which becomes Corso Lorenzo Fazzini – the main street. At no. 8 is the main **tourist office** (Mon–Fri 8am–2pm, plus Tues & Thurs 4–7pm; ☎0884.707.495); there's another at Piazza Kennedy, in the centre of the old town (Mon–Fri 8am–2pm & 3–8pm; ☎0884.708.806). Though there's no shortage of **accommodation** in Vieste, you will need to book ahead in high season and budget options are hard to come by. First choice is the atmospheric, *Pensione al Centro Storico*, Via Mafrolla 32 (☎0884.707.030; ③), in the old town, with large, simple rooms, and a sun terrace overlooking the promontory where you can bring your own beer and take-out pizza and enjoy the sunset. With just thirteen rooms and many people coming back year after year you need to book well in advance (at Easter for August). Another option in the old town is the *Del Seggio*, Via Veste 7 (☎0884.708.123, *www.iqsnet.it/hotelseggio*; ④), with vertiginous views down to its swimming pool and private rocky beach, while around 500m north of the castle along the shore, the good-value *Albergo Vela Velo*, Lungomare Europa 19 (☎0884.706.303; ③), is a small, modern two-star. A little more upmarket is the *Hotel Punta San Francesco* at Via D Francesco 2 (☎0884.701.422; ⑤) with lovely views over the promontory and comfortable whitewashed rooms with terracotta tile floors. For **food**, the strangely named *Box 19*, Via Santa Maria di Merino 13 (closed Mon & Nov), serves excellent seafood such as *linguine all'astice* (lobster) and is fairly moderately priced.

From June to September there are ferry, catamaran and hydrofoil connections to the **Trémiti Islands** (see p.888) from Vieste; tickets are available from Gargáno Viaggi at Piazza Roma 7 (daily 9am–12.30pm & 5–9pm; ☎0884.708.501), from Vesta Travel, at Via Cavour 12 (June–Sept Mon–Sat 9am–1pm & 4–8pm; Oct–May Mon–Fri 9am–1pm & 4–8pm; ☎0884.701.522), or from the Adriatica office in the harbour. Otherwise, foot-passenger **ferries** (*motonave*) run between late April and early October; tickets from the agencies above or from the ticket office at the harbour (look for the "Vieste 1" sign).

Around Vieste

There are a number of day-trips worth making **around Vieste**. The most obvious move is to the **beaches**: there's a small one between the promontories, a second, San Lorenzo, to the north, and a third, Pizzomunno, just south of town; the last is much the nicest. Best of all, though, and certainly less crowded, is the marvellous Scialmarino beach, 4km up the coast towards Péschici – walkable if you don't have transport.

Otherwise, Vieste is an excellent base for seeing the grotto-ridden **coastline** around the Testa del Gargano, south of town, though the only way to do it properly is on an organized trip. Excursion boats for the grottoes leave from next to San Francesco church at 9am and 2.30pm, a three-hour trip; tickets, which cost around L20,000/€10.32 are again available from Gargáno Viaggi (see above) and SOL (daily Mar–Oct 9am–1.30pm & 2.30pm–7pm, July & Aug until midnight; ☎0884.701.558) at Via Tre Piccioni 5.

Péschici and northern Gargano

Atop its rocky vantage point overlooking a beautiful sandy bay, **PÉSCHICI** is a little smaller than Vieste and one of the most attractive village resorts in the Gargano. Though originally built in 970 as a buffer against Saracen incursions, its labyrinth of tiny streets and houses sporting domed roofs has a distinctly Arabic tinge. There's nothing to do beyond beach-lazing, although the town does make a good base for exploring parts of the coastline nearby, which is an interesting mixture of caves and defensive medieval towers. The easiest trips are to the grotto at **San Nicola**, 3km east of town (some buses), or 5km west to the **Torre di Monte Pucci** for some fine coastal views.

The FG **train** line ends at Calenella, a few kilometres west of Péschici but connected to the town by a bus. This, and other **buses**, drop you in the newer part of Péschici, from where it's a short walk down to the main street – Corso Garibaldi. For **accommodation**, the *Locanda Al Castello*, Via Castello 29 (☎0884.964.038; ③), down a narrow lane of whitewashed houses in the old town, has rooms over an excellent restaurant/pizzeria, while *Hotel d'Amato* off the SS89 next to the beach (☎0884.963.415, *www.hoteldamato.it*; ⑤), the sister hotel of *Sole* in San Menaio (see below), offers modern rooms, a restaurant, bar and two swimming pools. The *Elisa*, right next to the beach at Via Marina 20 (☎0884.964.012; ⑤), is a simple place with a good-value restaurant downstairs (try their fish soup). *Solemar*, a couple of kilometres west of the resort at Località Valle Scinni (☎0884.964.186; ③), is a large modern hotel with its own garden leading down to a sandy beach. There's also a **campsite**, the *Baia San Nicola* (☎0884.964.231), 2km east along the coast at Punta San Nicola. For **eating**, there are scores of resturants, pizzerias, gelaterias and bars in the old town, scene of a lively passeggiata that goes on all evening. As well as the *Locanda Al Castello* (see above), there is a less expensive option in the *Fra Stefano* at Via Forno 8 (closed mid-Sept to May). Outside the old town the *Grotta delle Rondini* (closed Nov–March), is situated in a natural cave near the port, while *La Collinetta* on the coast road to Vieste (closed Nov to mid-March) serves interesting seafood at resonable prices.

Ferries to the Trémiti islands from Péschici (calling at Rodi Garganico on the way) leave at around 9am from the port, taking 1hr 15min and costing L45,000/€23.24 for the return trip (the ferry brings everyone back at around 5pm). You can buy tickets onshore next to the boat right up until departure.

West along the coast and onwards

Sticking with the coast, there's a string of white sandy beaches stretching from San Menaio to **RODI GARGANICO** – originally a Greek settlement ("Rodi" is derived from Rhodes) and nowadays, with its beaches and fast hydrofoil links with the Trémiti Islands, a highly popular resort in summer. Again, it's full and expensive in August, but come a couple of months either side and it can be delightful. **SAN MENAIO** is much quieter than Rodi – more compact and with fewer villas – and even in high season it's easy to get away from it all by walking a few hundred yards south along the strand. *Sole, Lungomare 2* (☎0884.968.621, *www.hoteldamato.it*; ④), is an attractive 1920s **hotel** built right next to the sea, and room prices include sunlounger and umbrella on their private sandy beach. There's also a pleasant, shaded **campsite** called *Internazionale* (☎0884.968.528; May–Sept), just off the SS89 a few minutes' walk from the beach. From Rodi Garganico, both road and rail skirt the large **Lago di Varano**, a once-malarial swamp which swallowed the ancient Athenian town of Uria in the fourth century BC. The region around the lake, its villages traditionally poor and backward, is probably the least-visited part of the Gargano promontory – though the lake itself is full of eels and attracts a great variety of birdlife, particularly curlews and warblers. Further west, the thin **Lago di Lésina** is a highly saline shallow lagoon, cut off from the sea by a twenty-seven-kilometre stretch of sand dunes. It's still mercifully free from development – unlike the northern spit of Varano, which is slowly beginning to fill with campsites.

Alternatively, from Cagnano Varano the FG train line cuts southwest, skirting the promontory, inland to **SAN SEVERO**, a small market town known for its wines but otherwise not a place where you'll want to do much more than change transport. The FG line from here terminates at Fóggia, but the FS trains that stop here continue on down the coast to Bari.

Inland Gargano: Vico del Gargano and the Foresta Umbra

The **interior** of the Gargano promontory can make a cool break from its busy coast, though it's not possible to see much of it without your own transport. **VICO DEL GARGANO** is the nicest of the villages and firmly off the beaten track, sited on a hill surrounded by citrus groves and with a creakingly ancient centre full of steep, tangled streets. It's also right on the edge of the **Foresta Umbra** (or "Forest of Shadows") which stretches right across the centre of the Gargano massif – 11,000 hectares of pines, oaks and beeches, hiding a rich variety of wildlife, roe deer especially – and is the last remnant of an ancient forest which once covered most of Puglia. The area was designated a national park in 1991 and there are numerous marked **walks** through the forest and a **Centro di Vísita** (☎0884.565.579, *www.parcogargano.it*) in the middle which doles out advice and information.

Public transport is distinctly thin on the ground, but you're most likely to find a bus from Vieste – check with the tourist office there (see p.886).

The Trémiti Islands

A small group of islands 40km off the Gargano coast, the **Trémiti Islands** – Isole Trémiti – are almost entirely given over to tourism in the summer, when the tiny population is swamped by visitors. Despite this, the islands remain relatively unspoilt and the sea crystal clear.

The islands were traditionally a place of exile and punishment in the past. Augustus banished his granddaughter Julia to the islands, while Charlemagne packed his father-in-law off here (minus eyes and limbs) in the eighth century. Monks from Montecassino, on the mainland, first set about building a formidable fortress-abbey on one of the islands in the eleventh century, which managed to withstand frequent assault by the Turks. Later, during the eighteenth century, the islands returned to their old role as a place of confinement for political prisoners, though the Bourbons, concerned at the decline in the local population, shipped in 200 women from the Neapolitan taverns to encourage a recovery.

There's either a **hydrofoil or catamaran** service to San Nicola from Manfredonia (June–Sept 1 daily; a 2hr journey; L34,000/€17.56 single) and a service from Vieste (June, July & Sept 1 daily, Aug 3 daily; a 1hr journey; L24,000/€12.39 single) runs during the summer. **Ferries**, or *motonave* (foot passengers only), from Vieste, Péschici and Rodi Gargánico operate between late April and early October (1 daily; a 1hr 40min journey; L45,000/€23.24 return).

The islands

The main Trémiti group consists of three islands: San Nicola, San Domino – the biggest – and Capraia, of which only the first two are inhabited. Most **ferries** arrive at **SAN NICOLA**, where you can wander around the monastic fortress and the tiny church of **Santa Maria a Mare**, built by the monks in the eleventh century on the site of an earlier ninth-century hermitage. San Nicola is rugged and rocky with no beaches, although there is nude bathing on its east side and good swimming to be had off the whole island.

Ignore the offers of pricey boat trips to the other islands and instead jump on the regular ferry which takes about a minute to cross to **SAN DOMINO**. It's a greener island than its neighbour, its pines offering a welcome shade from the heat. Although there is a sandy **beach** – Cala delle Arene – right where the ferry lands on the northeast side of the island, it gets packed in the summer. Your best bet is to follow the signs for the *Villaggio TCI* (see opposite) and make for the west of the island and its quieter coves such as Cala dello Spido or the Punta di Diamante for walking; **maps** are pinned up in some of the bars or can be bought from souvenir shops. **Accommodation** on the islands is limited to San Domino and is largely full-board only in high season: count on paying about L30,000/€15.49 a night per person. The *municipio* on San Domino holds a list of **private rooms**, or you could try the most appealing of the small hotels,

Pensione Pineta (☎0882.463.202; ②), a whitewashed villa in pine trees near some quiet rocky coves just outside the tiny village centre. Alternatively there's the *Albergo La Nassa* (☎0882.463.345; ③), on the footpath into the village, or *Albergo Gabbiano* (☎0882.463.410; ⑥) in the village itself at Piazza Belvedere; it's essential to book ahead for all three. A cheaper alternative is to **camp** at the *Villaggio TCI* (☎0882.463.402); you can rent tents for around L31,000/€16.01 a night if you haven't brought your own. Bear in mind, too, that provisions have to be ferried across from the mainland, so **eating out** can be a costly exercise – buy some picnic food before you get on the boat. Mosquitoes tend to be a serious problem in the summer months, so be prepared.

Along the coast to Bari

The first part of the coastal route south from Manfredonia is unremarkable, flat lands given up to saline extraction. You won't, anyway, be able to come this way by train or bus – though there is a direct coastal road. First stop, by rail at least, isn't until **MARGHERITA DI SAVOIA**, at the edge of the Tavoliere, a small town that boasts the country's oldest working salt pans, dating to the third century BC. Beyond here, though, the rest of the coastline is easily accessible by public transport; most places have stations on the main Bologna–Lecce rail line. It's a varied stretch and there are two enjoyable stops, at Trani and Molfetta.

Barletta

The first place that's really worth a stop is **BARLETTA**, nearly 60km round the coast from Manfredonia – an indifferent and rather shabby town really, but meriting some attention if you happen to be passing on the second weekend in September, when it's the venue of one of Puglia's largest pageants, the **Disfida** ("the Challenge"). The event re-enacts an occasion in 1503 when thirteen Italian knights challenged thirteen French knights to a duel for control of the besieged town. They had been drinking together and, following a brawl, the Italians won and the siege was lifted.

For the rest, Barletta's dowdy atmosphere says little about its former importance as a medieval Crusader port, the only relic of its earlier days a five-metre-high statue in the town centre known as the **Colosso** – said to be the largest Roman bronze in existence, and a relic from the Venetian sacking of Constantinople in 1204. Towering dourly over pedestrians on Corso Vittorio Emanuele, its identity is a mystery, although most money is on Valentinian I, one of the last Eastern Roman emperors. Over the way from here, the thirteenth-century **Basilica del Santo Sepolcro** has been restored to its original thirteenth-century simplicity. The only other place of any interest, is the **Castello** (Tues–Sun 8am–2pm & 4–7pm; L5000/€2.58), which has a collection of antiques, coins and armour and is home to the **Galleria de Nittis** (same hours and ticket), with paintings by the nineteenth-century artist Giuseppe de Nittis, a local lad who spent most of his short but prolific life in Paris, painting under the influence of the Impressionists. You can also visit the reconstructed **Cantina della Disfida**, where the original Challenge occurred, on Via Cialdini (same hours and ticket).

Practicalities

The **tourist office** at Piazza Ferdinando d'Aragona 95 has information on the town (Mon–Fri 8am–2pm, plus Tues & Thurs 4–7pm; ☎0883.531.555). **Accommodation** options are limited here, but try the simple *Pensione Prezioso*, Via Teatini 11 (☎0883.520.046; ②). The **restaurant** situation is more promising: try the reasonable *Antico Forno* on Via Milazzo 29 (closed Mon), or the popular and appealing *Buca dei 13* on Via Municipio 61 (closed Sun).

Trani

Thirteen kilometres down the coast from Barletta, **TRANI** is a very different kind of place, with a cosmopolitan air not found in any of the other towns nearby. One of the most important medieval Italian ports, it was a prosperous trading centre with a large mercantile and Jewish community, during the Middle Ages rivalling Bari as a commercial port and in the fourteenth century powerful enough to take on the domineering Venetians.

Twentieth-century Trani is still a prosperous place, its elegant buildings spruce and smart. Centrepiece of the town is the cream-coloured eleventh-century **Duomo** (daily 8.30am–noon & 3–6pm), overlooking the sea on a large open piazza at the edge of the old town. Dedicated to San Nicola Pellegrino, it consists of no fewer than three churches, stacked on top of each other like an inverted wedding cake – the facade austere but lightened by a pretty rose window. The interior is slowly being restored to its original Norman state, the stark nave displaying a timbered ceiling, while near the presbytery fragments of a twelfth-century mosaic have been uncovered. Below the vaulted crypt is the earlier church of Santa Maria della Scala, whose marble columns are Roman, while further down the Ipogeo di San Leucio is an early Christian underground chamber dating from the sixth century. Back outside, the **Castello** (Mon–Sat 9.30am–12.30pm, Sun 9am–7.30pm; L4000/€2.06) is visible from Piazza Duomo, recently restored and reopened to the public after years of service as a prison. A wander through the adjacent streets gives an impression of the medieval city, not least in the names that echo the town's mercantile and Jewish origins – Via Sinagoga, Via Doge Vecchia and Via Cambio ("Street of the Moneychangers"). The **Palazzo Caccetta** on Via Ognissanti is a rare example of fifteenth-century Gothic architecture; the **Chiesa di Ognissanti**, close by, was a twelfth-century chapel of the Knights Templar, once part of a hospital for injured Crusaders. Sadly, it's unlikely to be open, but if you hang around someone may appear with a key.

Practicalities

If you're going to stick around in Trani, you can get information at the **tourist office** at Via Cavour 140 (Mon–Fri 9am–1.30pm plus Tues & Thurs 3–7pm in high summer; ☎0883.588.830), just down the road from the **train station**, which is at the far end of Via Cavour; there's also a seasonal tourist information kiosk (☎0883.43.295) on the central Piazza della Repubblica. Further along towards the sea, near the public gardens, the *Padri Barnabiti* on Piazza Tiepolo is a *foresteria* with cheap single and double **rooms** and great views of the harbour and piazza below (☎0883.481.180; ②; reception closed 1–5pm, curfew 1am). For **eating**, try the meaty sandwiches of *Premiata Norcineria Umbra* at Via Ognissanti 120 – the good-value *panzerotti* at the *Pizzeria Lopetuso* at Via Aldo Moro 73; or there's excellent fish (at very reasonable prices) at *La Nicchia*, Corso Inbriani 22 (closed Thurs).

Molfetta

The last stop worth making on this stretch of coast is at **MOLFETTA**, a working port, unashamedly non-touristy and all the better for it, with a twelfth-century **Duomo** that's a mishmash of styles from the Romanesque and Byzantine eras and a tiny alleywayed old centre – once an island – that's home to one of the biggest fishing fleets on the southern Adriatic. There are no beaches as such, but it's a busy, evocative place, its waterfront active with visiting ships and thronged by an evening passeggiata that sweeps down to the docks to watch the gorgeous sunsets over the Adriatic. You probably won't want to stay, but if you do there's one central **hotel**, the *Tritone* on Via Piave 11 (☎080.397.1069; ③). If you feel like something to **eat** try the *Bistrot*, at Corso Dante

33 (closed Wed) or for **snacks** the *Al Duomo*, next to the duomo, has outdoor tables, ideal for watching Molfetta amble by.

Bari

Commercial and administrative capital of Puglia, a university town and the *mezzogiorno's* second city, **BARI** has its fair share of interest. But although an economically vibrant place, it harbours no pretensions about being a major tourist attraction. Primarily people come here for work or to leave for Greece on its many ferries.

Bari was already a thriving centre when the Romans arrived. Later the city was the seat of the Byzantine governor of southern Italy, while under the Normans Bari rivalled Venice, both as a maritime centre and, following the seizure of the remains of St Nicholas, as a place of pilgrimage. Since those heady days Bari has declined considerably. Its fortunes revived briefly in 1813 when the king of Naples foisted a planned expansion upon the city – giving the centre its contemporary gridded street pattern, wide avenues and piazzas. And Mussolini instituted a university and left a legacy of strident Fascist architecture. But the city was heavily bombed during the last war, and today its vigorous centre is a symbol of the south's zeal for commercial growth at the expense of local identity and character.

Arrival and information

Bari is a fairly compact city, running from the train station in the gridded new city down to the bulging old centre, the *cittàvecchia*, in just ten blocks. There are three train stations in Bari. The **Stazione Centrale** is in Piazza Aldo Moro, on the southern edge of the modern centre; it serves regular FS trains and those of the private Ferrovia del Sud-Est line (FSE information ☎080.546.2111), which run down to Gagliano del Capo (see p.899 for more on this route). Nearby, at Piazza Aldo Moro, the separate **Stazione Bari-Nord** is for trains run by the private FerroTramViaria company (FTV information ☎080.523.2202), connecting Bari with Andria, Barletta, Bitonto and Ruvo di Puglia. Adjacent to this, on Corso Italia, is the **Stazione FAL Apulo-Lucane**; trains and buses from here are run by Ferrovia Apulo-Lucane (FAL train information ☎080.572.5227; bus information ☎080.572.5215) and go to Altamura, Gravina, and Matera and Potenza in Basilicata.

Buses complicate the issue even further: from the coastal towns north of Bari you'll arrive at Piazza Eroi del Mare; SITA buses from inland and southern towns pull up in Largo Sorrentino (behind the train station); Marozzi buses from Rome arrive either here or on Piazza Aldo Moro. Buses of the private rail line FAL, from Basilicata, arrive at their station on Corso Italia, while FSE buses from Brindisi pull in at their station on Largo Ciaia. **Ferries** from Albania, Croatia, Turkey, Israel, Montenegro and Greece (Igoumenitsa, Corfu and Patras) all use the Stazione Marittima, next to the old city, connected with the main FS train station by bus #20. The **airport** is about 9km northwest up the coast, there is an Alitalia bus that connects with arrivals and drops at the central train station.

THE BARESI BAG SNATCHERS

A **word of warning**: the Baresi take a positive delight in portraying the old city as a den of thieves, and certainly strolling through the narrow alleys with your camera in full view isn't particularly wise. Bag snatching by young kids on mopeds (the *topini*, or "little mice") isn't as rife as it once was, but neither is it extinct. Keep your wits about you.

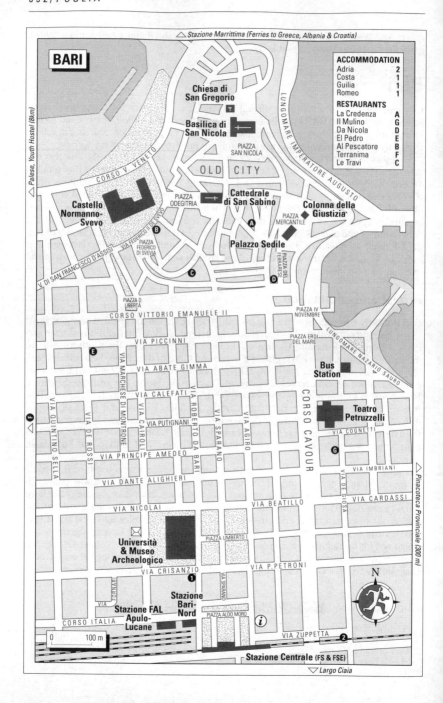

BARI

Stazione Marrittima (Ferries to Greece, Albania & Croatia)

Chiesa di San Gregorio

Basilica di San Nicola

PIAZZA SAN NICOLA

OLD CITY

LUNGOMARE IMPERATORE AUGUSTO

CORSO V. VENETO

Castello Normanno-Svevo

PIAZZA ODEGITRIA

Cattedrale di San Sabino

Colonna della Giustizia

PIAZZA MERCANTILE

Palazzo Sedile

VIA FEDERICO DI SVEVIA

PIAZZA FEDERICO DI SVEVIA

V. DI SAN FRANCESCO D'ASSISI

PIAZZA DEL FERRARESE

PIAZZA D. LIBERTÀ

CORSO VITTORIO EMANUELE II

PIAZZA IV NOVEMBRE

VIA PICCINNI

PIAZZA EROI DEL MARE

LUNGOMARE NAZARIO SAURO

VIA ABATE GIMMA

VIA MARCHESE DI MONTRONE

VIA CALEFATI

VIA CAIROLI

VIA ROBERTO DA BARI

VIA SPARANO

VIA AGIRO

Bus Station

VIA PUTIGNANI

Teatro Petruzzelli

VIA QUINTINO SELLA

VIA DE ROSSI

VIA PRINCIPE AMEDEO

CORSO CAVOUR

VIA COGNETTI

VIA IMBRIANI

VIA DANTE ALIGHIERI

VIA DE GIOSA

VIA CARDASSI

VIA NICOLAI

VIA BEATILLO

Università & Museo Archeologico

PIAZZA UMBERTO I

VIA P. PETRONI

VIA FORNARI

VIA CRISANZIO

VIA SPARANO

N

VIA

Stazione FAL Apulo-Lucane

Stazione Bari-Nord

PIAZZA ALDO MORO

CORSO ITALIA

0   100 m

VIA ZUPPETTA

Stazione Centrale (FS & FSE)

Largo Ciaia

Palese, Youth Hostel (8km)

Pinacoteca Provinciale (300m)

ACCOMMODATION	
Adria	2
Costa	1
Guilia	1
Romeo	1
RESTAURANTS	
La Credenza	A
Il Mulino	G
Da Nicola	D
El Pedro	E
Al Pescatore	B
Terranima	F
Le Travi	C

Getting around, your best bet is to walk – not a bad option in such a small city. **Buses** are bright orange and run from 5.30am until around 11pm, mostly focusing on Piazza Aldo Moro.

The **tourist office** is at Piazza Aldo Moro 33a, in a small cul de sac to the right as you come out of the main train station (Mon–Sat 8.30am–1pm; ☎080.524.2244), and has maps and information on the city.

Accommodation

There are several handy and affordable **hotels** one block from the station in the apartment building at Via Crisanzio 12: *Costa* (☎080.521.9015; ⑤), is the nicest, with simple but attractive rooms and air conditioning on the way. Next door, on the ground floor, the rooms at the *Romeo* (☎080.523.7253; ③), are all doubles with TVs and bathrooms, while upstairs is *Pensione Giulia* (☎080.521.6630; ②), run by a pleasant couple, with some rooms en suite. A more upscale choice in the same area is the *Adria*, right out of the station on Via Zuppetta (☎080.524.6699; ④); prices are cheaper if you opt for an inward-facing room without private bathroom or TV. Although it's a bit of a trek out of town, there's a decent **youth hostel** near the beach at Palese, 8km up the coast (currently closed for renovation; check with the tourist office for the latest details); it can be reached on bus #1 from Piazza Aldo Moro; get off at the Villaggio dell'Aeronautica and walk 300m. If you're under 30, you can **camp** for free between June and September at *Pineta San Francesco* (currently closed; phone ☎080.523.2716 for the latest details) on the outskirts of the city – reachable on bus #5 from the main train station or bus #1 from Corso Cavour. Otherwise, the nearest campsite is *Camping Sea World*, 6km south of the city at SS Adriatica 78 (☎080.549.1175); take bus #12 from Teatro Petruzzelli.

The City

There's not a lot to the **new city** of Bari, bar a good museum or two. Its straight streets are lined with shops and offices, relieved occasionally by the odd piazza and bit of greenery, best of which is the starting-point of the evening passeggiata, **Piazza Umberto I** – usually full of stalls selling jewellery, books and prints. Off the piazza, the university building houses an excellent **Museo Archeologico**, which is unfortunately closed for restoration at present. If it's re-opened by the time of your visit, it's well worth a look for anyone interested in the region's history: it holds a good selection of Greek and Puglian ceramics and a solid collection of artefacts from the Daunic, Messapian and Peucetic peoples – Puglia's earliest inhabitants. Afterwards, cut to the right for tree-lined **Corso Cavour**, Bari's main commercial street, which leads down to the waterfront. Right along here, in the Palazzo della Provincia, the **Pinacoteca Provinciale** (Tues–Sat 9am–1pm & 4–7pm, Sun 9am–1pm; L5000/€2.58) is a local art collection of mainly southern Italian stuff, twelfth- to nineteenth-century, with strong work by the fifteenth-century Vivarini family.

The old city

Even if you're only in Bari to catch a ferry, try to make time for a wander around the **old city**, an entrancing jumble of streets at the far end of Corso Cavour that's possibly the most confusing place to walk around in southern Italy. Its labyrinth of seemingly endless passages weaving through courtyards and under arches was originally designed to spare the inhabitants from the wind and throw invaders into a state of confusion. This it still does admirably, and even with the best of maps you're going to get lost. Life is lived very much outdoors, and on summer evenings, it's full of people sitting outside their kitchen doors.

FERRIES FROM BARI

International ferry services run from Bari to Greece, Albania and Croatia. Travel agents around town often have a wide variety of offers on **tickets**, one such place is CTS at Via Fornari 7 (☎080.523.6671), who give a discount on student/youth fares. Once you've got your ticket, you must report to the relevant desk at the Stazione Maríttima at least two hours before departure. As a general rule, you will save twelve to twenty percent if you buy a return ticket. Embarkation tax is L6,000/€3.09 per vehicle plus L6,000/€3.09 for each passenger. Prices given below are for travel in high season.

ALBANIA

Hydrofoil services to **Albania** are operated by La Vikinga Lines, bookable through Portrans at the Stazione Maríttima (☎080.523.2429) or at Corso A. de Tullio 6 (☎080.521.1416), departing Bari daily at 9.30am and 4.30pm and returning from Durazzo at 9.30am and 3.30pm; the journey takes three-and-a-half hours and costs L210,000/€108.45 one way.

Adriatica runs a car ferry to Durazzo four times a week in July and August (currently Mon, Wed, Fri & Sat); the journey takes eight hours (from L110,000/€56.81 per person, L180,000/€92.96 per car). Adriatica has offices at Via Liside 4 (☎080.553.1555) and Stazione Maríttima (☎080.523.5825, *www.adriatica.it*).

CROATIA

Jadrolinija operates three catamaran services a week to Dubrovnik in **Croatia**: mid-June to mid-Sept (currently Thur, Fri & Sat) with four during Aug (Thur–Sun); tickets cost from L78,000/€40.28 per person, from L63,000/€32.53 per cabin. Journey time is 7–8 hours. Contact Jadrolinija through P. Lorusso & Co, Via Piccinni 133 (☎080.521.2840) and at the Stazione Maríttima (☎080.521.7118 or 080.527.5439) or book online at *www.jadrolinija.tel.hr/jadrolinija*.

GREECE

Ferry services to **Greece** are operated by Ventouris – bookable through P. Lorusso & Co, Via Piccinni 133 (☎080.521.2840) and at the Stazione Maríttima (☎080.521.7118 or 080.527.5439) – and Superfast ferries (*www.superfast.com*), through Portrans at Corso A. de Tullio 6 (☎080.521.1416) and at the Stazione Maríttima (☎080.523.2429). Ventouris runs services to Corfu and Igoumenitsa; one-way prices are L79,000/€40.80 per person plus L176,000/€90.90 extra for a cabin (both with reductions for students), and a max of L100,000/€51.64 extra for a car. The service to Igoumenitsa takes 11hr 30min and runs from March to September (March 4 weekly: Apr–Sept daily). The service to Corfu takes 10 hours and runs from the end of June to late August (high season daily; beginning and end of the season twice weekly). Superfast runs to both Igoumenitsa and Patras from mid-Feb to end of December and the seats cost L89,000/€46.00; the journeys take nine and fifteen hours respectively.

Specific sights are few. The **Basilica di San Nicola** (daily 9am–1pm & 4–7pm; museum Tues–Fri 10am–noon), in the heart of the old city, was consecrated in 1197, as an inscription at the side of the main door testifies, to house the relics of the saint plundered a century earlier from southern Turkey. From the outside it all looks thoroughly Norman, especially the twin fortress-like towers, but it's a misleading impression: the right-hand tower predates the church, the other was added later for balance, and even the simple nave is shattered by three great arches and an ornate seventeenth-century ceiling. The real beauty of the church lies in its stonework: the twelfth-century altar canopy is one of the finest in Italy, the motifs around the capitals the work of stonemasons from Como; and the twelfth-century carved doorway and the simple, striking mosaic floor behind the altar are lovely, prey to a very heavy Saracen influence. Best of all is the twelfth-century episcopal throne behind the altar, a superb piece of work supported by small figures wheezing beneath its weight. Down in the crypt are the remains of the saint, patron of pawnbrokers and sailors (and of Russians, who made the pilgrimage here until 1917). Behind the tomb-altar, the richly decorated fourteenth-century icon of the saint was a present from the King of Serbia.

It's not far from the basilica to Bari's other important church, the **Cattedrale di San Sabino** (daily 8.30am–1pm & 4–7pm), off Piazza Odegitria, dedicated to the original patron saint of Bari, before he was usurped by Nicholas, and built at the end of the twelfth century. It's well worth coming just for the contrast: uncluttered by arches, it retains its original medieval atmosphere, and – unlike the basilica – a timbered roof. The cathedral houses an icon, too, an eighth-century work known as the *Madonna Odegitria*, brought here for safety from Constantinople by Byzantine monks. It's said to be the most authentic likeness of the Madonna in existence, having been taken from an original sketch by Luke the Apostle, and it's paraded around the city at religious festivals.

Across the piazza the **Castello Normanno-Svevo** (Tues–Sat 9am–1pm & 3.30–7pm, Sun 9am–1pm; L4000/€2.06) sits on the site of an earlier Roman fort. Built by Frederick II, much of it is closed to the public, but it has a vaulted hall that provides a cool escape from the afternoon sun. You can also see a gathering of some of the best of past Puglian artistry in a display of plaster-cast reproductions from churches and buildings throughout the region – specifically from the Castel del Monte, the cathedral at Altamura, and an animated frieze of griffons devouring serpents from the church of San Leonardo at Siponto.

Eating and drinking

For **snacks** and sandwiches, try the *Piazza Roma,* a restaurant/coffee bar at the corner of Via Sparano across from the Stazione Centrale or the *Bar Oceano*, Corso Cavour 49. Two budget **restaurants** in the old city are *Le Travi* on Largo Chiurlia (closed Mon), where you can have a complete meal for L20,000/€10.32, and *Da Nicola*, off Piazza del Ferrarese (closed Sun), where meals can be had for a remarkable L15,000/€7.74. Also worth trying is the good self-service *El Pedro*, at Via Piccinni 152 (closed Sun), which specializes in traditional Italian cuisine. Rather more interesting and not much more expensive is the *Cafe Batafobrele/Restaurant Terranima*, at Via Putignani 213–215 (closed Sun), with a daily menu of regional specialities, and a relaxed atmosphere. The pricey no-nonsense *Ristorante al Pescatore*, Via Federico II di Svevia 8 (closed Sun), just east of the castle, does fine fish, though it can cost anything up to L50,000/€25.82 a head. For a lively atmosphere, head for *Ristorante Pizzeria Il Mulino*, Via de Giosa 7 (closed Wed), alongside the Teatro Petruzzelli, off Corso Cavour, or *La Credenze*, Via Verrone 15/Arco Sant'Onofrio (closed Wed), in the old city where you can eat such typically Barese dishes as *orecchiette* with cauliflower.

Listings

Beach The nearest beach is north of the city; take bus #1 from Teatro Petruzzelli to Palese/Santo Spirito. To the south, there are beaches at Torre a Mare and San Giorgio – both reached on bus #12 from Stazione Centrale or #12/ from Teatro Petruzzelli.

Exchange Outside banking hours in Piazza Aldo Moro, inside Stazione Centrale.

Hospital Ospedale Consorziale Policlinico, Piazza Giulio Cesare (☎080.547.3111).

Police Via G Murat (☎080.529.1111).

Post office The main office is behind the university in Piazza Battisti (Mon–Fri 8am–7.30pm, Sat 8.30am–noon).

Travel agents CTS, Via Fornari 7 (☎080.523.6671).

Le Murge

Rising gently from the Adriatic coast, **Le Murge** – a low limestone plateau – dominates the landscape to the south and west of Bari. Around 50km wide and 150km long, it's generally divided into "Low" and "High" Murge: the further away from the coast you are, the higher and more barren it gets. The towns in the region are not natural holiday destinations: the area is sparsely populated, especially further inland, and the small settlements that exist are rural backwaters with a slow pace of life. But they do make an interesting day out from the more popular coastal towns, or a good stopover if you're heading for the region of Basilicata. There are some buses and trains from Bari, but, as always, without your own car travelling very extensively can be difficult.

The Low Murge

The main town of the Low Murge is **ANDRIA**, a large agricultural centre easily reached from Barletta or Bari that's at its best during its Monday-morning market – otherwise it has little to hold you. It was, though, a favourite haunt of Frederick II, who was responsible for the main local attraction these days, the **Castel del Monte**, 17km south – the most extraordinary of all Puglia's castles and one of the finest surviving examples of Swabian architecture (daily: April–Sept 10am–1.30pm & 2.30–7pm; Oct–March 10am–1.30pm; L4000/€2.06; ☎0883.569.848). Official guides here offer free tours in English, although donations are appreciated; from April to September they are based at the castle's Pro Loco cabin, but from October to March you need to contact the Pro Loco office in Andria (☎0883.592.283, *www.proloco.andria.ba.it*). Sadly, there is only an infrequent bus service from Andria – contact the Pro Loco office there or the castle itself for timetables.

Begun by Frederick in the 1240s, the Castel is a high, isolated fortress precisely built around an octagonal courtyard in two storeys of eight rooms. A mystery surrounds its intended purpose. Although there was once an iron gate which could be lowered over the main entrance (as tell-tale grooves in the portal show), there are no other visible signs of fortification, and the castle may have served as a mere hunting lodge. Nonetheless the mathematical precision involved in its construction, and the preoccupation with the number eight, have excited writers for centuries. It's argued the castle is in fact an enormous astrological calendar, also that Frederick may have had the octagonal Omar mosque in Jerusalem in mind when he designed it; but despite his recorded fascination with the sciences, no one really knows. There is only one record of its use. The defeat of Manfred, Frederick's illegitimate son, at the battle of Benevento in 1266 signalled the end of Swabian power in Puglia; and Manfred's sons and heirs were imprisoned in the castle for over thirty years – a lonely place to be incarcerated.

West of Andria, on the edge of the Low Murge, **CANOSA DI PUGLIA** used to be a thriving commercial centre but has never really recovered from its destruction by the Saracens. Today it's worth a stop perhaps for its **Duomo** – uninteresting from the outside but with a wealth of treasures in its beautiful eleventh-century interior. The bishop's throne behind the altar, carved with plants and animals and supported by a couple of rather fed-up looking elephants, dates from 1079. Adjacent is a tomb with a solid bronze door, richly engraved in an Arab fashion, its occupant Bohemond – the son of the Norman Robert Guiscard.

About the same distance east of Andria (but best reached by hourly bus from Molfetta), the old centre of **RUVO DI PUGLIA** is a more attractive stop, with a quiet, timeless atmosphere. In the autumn, the pavements of the old town are strewn with almonds, spread out to dry in the sun as they have been for centuries. The town was also once famous for its pottery, the locals strong on copying Greek designs to great effect. Just across from the **tourist office** on Via Vittorio Veneto 48 (Mon–Fri 10am–noon & 7.30–9pm, Sat & Sun 10am–noon; ☎080.361.5419), the **Museo Jatta** in Piazza Bovio (daily 8.30am–1.30pm, plus Sat 2.30–7.30pm; free) houses a dusty collection of the home-made stuff as well as some beautiful Greek originals, including a fifth-century BC crater depicting the death of Talos. Ruvo's thirteenth-century **Duomo**, tucked into the tightly packed streets of the town's old quarter, is also well worth some of your time. Its beautiful portal is guarded by animated griffins balancing on fragile columns, while recent work has restored the interior to its original state – exposing some of the sixteenth-century frescoes that used to cover the walls. What distinguishes Ruvo's cathedral, though, is the sheer amount of decoration that survives on the outer walls, like the rose window and the arches tapering off into human and animal heads.

There's a similar cathedral in **BITONTO**, just a few kilometres south-east out of Bari (20min by train), again with fiercely animated portals and a thirteenth-century pulpit with a bas-relief depicting Frederick and his family. Bitonto is also the centre of olive oil production in Puglia and is a fairly attractive place to visit anyway; pottering around the maze-like medieval centre makes for a pleasant afternoon's escape from the city noise of Bari.

The High Murge

Around 45km south of Bari (and reachable by train), **ALTAMURA** is the largest town in the High Murge, an originally fifth-century-BC settlement fortified by the Peucetians – parts of whose town still remain. You'll see bits of the walls as you come in from the station, over 4m thick in places. Destroyed by the Saracens, the ancient town lay abandoned until the thirteenth century, when Frederick restocked a new settlement with Greeks and built the high walls from which the town derives its name. Given its many historical layers, it's perhaps appropriate that Altamura is home to one of southern Italy's best **archeological museums** (July–Aug daily 8.30am–7.30pm; Sept–June Tues–Sat 8.30am–1.30pm & 2.30–7.30pm, Sun 8.30am–1.30pm; free) on Via Santeramo 88. The collection here traces the history of the people of the Murge from prehistory to late medieval times, with plenty of first-rate finds from all over the peninsula.

Altamura's most striking feature, however, is its **Duomo**, a mixture of styles varying from Apulian-Romanesque to Gothic and Baroque. The original thirteenth-century structure was badly damaged by an earthquake and suffered further in the sixteenth century when it was restyled: the portal and rose window were moved round to what had been the apse, and a couple of campaniles were tacked on – the pinnacles added later when Baroque was all the rage. Thankfully, the intricately carved medieval portal survived the switch, while the interior is still suitably austere. Take a look, too, at the tiny church of **San Niccolò dei Greci** on Corso Federico di Svevia; built by the Greek colonists in the thirteenth century and in which they celebrated their Orthodox religion for over 400 years.

Twelve kilometres west, not far from the border with Basilicata, lies **GRAVINA DI PUGLIA** – a castle-protected town clinging to the edge of a deep ravine. During the early barbarian invasions the locals took refuge in the caves along the sides of the ravine, a move that seems to have paid off until the arrival of the Saracens, who promptly massacred every cave-dwelling inhabitant. Under the Normans, though, the shattered town settled down to a quieter life as a fiefdom of the wealthy pope-producing Orsini family, whose mark – an enormous spread eagle – is all over town. In the dilapidated old quarter, the cave-church of **San Michele delle Grotte**, a dark, dank affair hewn out of the rock, holds bones that are said to be the remains of victims of the last Saracen attack, almost a thousand years old; guided **tours** in English of this and other cave churches are arranged by Leone Pino on ☎0339.208.3028. The **museum**

(Tues–Sat 9am–noon & 4–6pm, Sun 9am–1pm; L5000/€2.58) in Piazza Santomasi contains archeological finds, Bourbon arms and uniforms as well as sixteenth and seventeenth-century paintings, but more engaging, certainly if you couldn't get into San Michele, is the reconstruction of San Vito Vecchio, another cave-church, set up on the ground floor with some remarkable tenth-century Byzantine frescoes. There's also a new **archeological museum** on Piazza Benedetto Tredicésimo (Tues–Sat 9am–1pm & 4–7pm; free) with artefacts found around the ancient town.

Down the coast from Bari: to Monópoli and Egnázia

The coast south of Bari is a craggy stretch, with rock-hewn villages towering above tiny sandy coves. Just ten minutes by FS train from Bari (or bus #12 from Piazza Aldo Moro), **TORRE A MARE** provides one of the easiest escapes from the city, situated on a rocky ledge high above two large caves, though its ease of access from Bari means it can get quite crowded. There'll be fewer people around another twenty minutes on, at **POLIGNANO A MARE**, which, despite a newfound popularity remains fairly low-key. It's a small port, with a scuffed, whitewashed medieval centre, perching on the edge of the limestone cliffs, and the kind of place people head for on a Sunday to watch the waves crashing against the rocks or to sunbathe on the clifftops. If you don't have a car it is best reached by train, although there is a bus service, run by FSE, from Largo Ciaia in Bari. If you'd like to **stay**, the appealing *Covo dei Saraceni*, Via Conversano 1A (☎080.424.1177; ④) sits right on the rocks with modern rooms – some with large balconies and private terraces – a restaurant with panoramic views, and a laid-back atmosphere. For some fine fish, make your way to the **restaurant** attached to the hotel *Castellinaria*, Contrada S. Giovanni, where a full meal will set you back around L65,000/€33.57.

    MONÓPOLI, 8km further down the coast, was, like Polignano, once controlled by the Venetians and was a trading centre originally populated by the ancient Egnazians, whose maritime know-how lives on in what is still a large commercial port. Other than the goings-on at the dockside, there's not a lot to see, though the old town is worth wandering through, its steep narrow streets revealing fragments of its Venetian past. A brief scout around might take in the **Museo della Cattedrale** on Largo Cattedrale (closed at the time of writing, but phone to check ☎080.742.253), which contains some beautiful examples of religious art, including a tenth-century Byzantine reliquary, and the tiny chapel of **Santa Maria Amalfitana** (if closed, see custodian at the church of San Francesco d'Assisi, near the *municipio*) tucked away on Largo Plebiscito – built in the twelfth century by wealthy merchants from Amalfi on the site of an earlier cave-church, which is now the crypt. *Camping Santo Stefano* lies to the south of town next to the beach, an abandoned abbey and a restaurant (bus 3/S goes there from Monópoli). The **Pro Loco** is contactable on ☎080.808.533.

Egnázia and Fasano

There's more of interest south of the town, at the site of the ancient city of **Egnázia** (daily 8.30am–1.30pm & 2.30pm–dusk; L4000/€2.07; ☎080.482.9056), or Gnathia; if you don't have your own transport, it's best reached from **Fasano** (call Fasano's tourist office for timetable; ☎080.441.3086). Egnázia was an important Messapian centre during the fifth century BC, fortified with over two kilometres of walls, large parts of which still stand in the northern corner of the ruined town – up to 7m high. It was later colonized by the Greeks and then the Romans (in 244 BC), who built a forum, amphitheatre, a colonnaded public hall and temples: one was dedicated to Syria, a goddess popular with the early Romans who – according to Lucian – was worshipped by men dressed as women. Horace is known to have dropped by here to see the city's famous altar, which ignited wood without a flame.

At the turn of the first century AD, the Emperor Trajan constructed the **Via Egnázia**, a road that ran down to Bríndisi and continued from what is now Durres in Albania, via Thessaloniki, right the way to Constantinople, marking Egnázia's importance as a military and commercial centre. Parts of the road survive, running alongside the Roman public buildings. With the collapse of the Roman Empire, however, the city fell to subsequent barbarian invasions, and was almost completely destroyed by the Gothic king Totila in 545 AD. A community struggled on here, seeking refuge in the Messapian tombs, until the tenth century when the settlement was finally abandoned. There's a new on-site **museum** (same hours and ticket) housing a fascinating array of artefacts, including examples of the distinctive earthenware for which the ancient town was prized.

There are some excellent **places to stay** in the area around Egnázia. *Masseria Marzalossa* (☎080.441.3024, *www.marzalossa.puglianet.it*; ④) is a beautiful seventeenth-century house with swimming pool and large walled garden. The house has been in the owner's family for several generations and is packed with pictures and mementoes. To find it, follow the signposts on the tiny country road leading from Fasano to Cisternino. In **Selva di Fasano** – a hill station of villas in lush gardens above the town of Fasano – are *La Silvana*, Viale dei Pini 87 (☎080.433.1161; ③) an unpretentious hotel with large, simply decorated rooms, Moorish arches over balconies and plenty of terrace space. Alternatively, there's the modern, glitzy *Sierra Silvana*, Via Don Bartolo Boggia (☎080.433.1322, *htlsierra@mail.media.it*; ④) with regular rooms and *trulli* in the grounds that you can stay in; it's the perfect place to lounge by the pool for the day or take their free shuttle bus to the beach 15km away.

The FSE line:
Castellana Grotte to Martina Franca

Meandering lazily down towards the **Valle d'Itria**, the Ferrovia Sud-Est passes through some of the prettiest of Puglia's landscapes. The olive gradually loses ground to vineyards and cherry and peach orchards, neatly partitioned off by dry-stone walls. About 40km out of Bari are the **Grotte di Castellana** (guided tours every thirty minutes daily: April–Sept 8.30am–1pm & 2.30–7pm; Oct–March 9am–noon & 2–5pm; L25.000/€12.91 for 3hr tour, L15.00/€7.75 for 1hr tour excluding Grotta Bianca; ☎080.499.8211), a spectacular set of underground caves. The barren limestone terrain of Le Murge, which touches the region, swallows rivers whole (south of the Ofanto, near Barletta, few rivers make it to the sea), producing a landscape cut by deep ravines and pitted with caverns and grottoes. At Castellana, a lift takes you down to the largest of the caverns, La Grave, 60m below ground, which was used as the local rubbish dump until its accidental discovery in 1938. From here, there's over a kilometre of strangely formed caves to explore, ending in the most impressive of them all, the Grotta Bianca – a shimmering sea of white stalagmites and stalactites.

To **get to the caves**, simply follow the signs from the station, from where it's about 500m to the grotto. Tours leave roughly every hour and take around an hour and three quarters.

PUTIGNANO, next stop down the line, marks the beginning of the Valle d'Itria. It's really only worth a call if you happen to be in the area when its riotous carnival explodes at the beginning of February. But there is a grotto here, too, if you haven't already had your fill – this one of glistening pink alabaster, about 1km north of town, signposted Grotta di Putignano.

After Putignano the natural gives way to the constructed, and **trulli** come to dominate the landscape: cylindrical, whitewashed buildings with grey conical roofs tapering out to a point or sphere, often adorned with painted symbols. Confined to this part of Puglia, their ancient origins are obscure, though few today date back more than a couple of hundred years. Apart from their intrinsic beauty, there seems no special reason for building houses like this, and certainly no reason for them popping up here – though many theories abound, one claiming that the dome-shaped houses are much cooler in the baking Puglian summers. Certainly they make full use of local building materials and are remarkably easy to adapt: when you need more room, you simply knock a hole in the wall and build another next door (see p.1108 for more on *trulli*).

If you want to take a closer look, **ALBEROBELLO** is the best place, where there's a large local concentration of *trulli* – around 1500 packing Alberobello's narrow streets; most are south of the town centre, on and around Largo Martellotta, past the **tourist office** at Piazza Ferdinando IV (☎080.432.5171) from the station. Inevitably, there is a certain amount of tourist tat to go with all this, and proprietors of *trulli* given over to displays of woolly shawls, liqueurs and other souvenirs practically drag in passers-by. If you want to complete the *trulli* experience by **staying** in one, *Hotel Dei Trulli*, Via Cadore 31 (☎080.432.3555, *www.inmedia.it/hoteldeitrulli*; ⑦) comprises a dozen or so of the conical cottages, shaded by pine trees and with a pool next door. To admire the distinctive architecture from a safe distance, settle in at the shady terrace of the *Il Guercio di Puglia* **restaurant**, on Largo Martellotta itself (closed Wed), which serves a vast (and rather variable) array of antipasti. A more upmarket alternative is *Il Poeta Contadino*, at Via Indipendenza 21 (Sept–June; closed Mon lunchtime & Sun evening), whose specialities include *puré di fave con cicoria* (broad beans with wild chicory) and *cavatelli con cime di rapa* (pasta with turnip tops). Wine buffs shouldn't pass up a browse around the *Enoteca Anima del Vino*, on Largo Martellota 93, with its good assortment of local **wines** and excellent *cotognata* from Maglie; *Bar Ailanto* (across the way) serves an excellent **coffee** *granita*.

Just a few kilometres south, **LOCOROTONDO**, which owes its name to its circular layout, gives good views over the whole area, speckled with red- and grey-roofed *trulli* in a sea of olives, vines and almond trees. Distractions here include more wine – phone to make an appointment for a tour (in Italian) of the ultra-modern winery at the Cantina Sociale Co-operativa di Locorotondo, Via Madonna della Catena 99 (☎080.431.1644; tours must be booked a couple of days in advance by fax 080.431.1213). For edible **local specialities**, check out *Centro Storico* at Via Eroi di Dogali 6 (closed Wed in winter), an excellent trattoria where you can savour hearty *orecchiette,* served with meat sauce and creamy white cheese (*ragù e caciotta*) or with turnip tops (*cime di rapa*).

Martina Franca

The *trulli* are still plentiful by the time you reach **MARTINA FRANCA**, a surprising town with a tangible Moorish flavour and a lively passeggiata at weekends. It is reputed to have been founded by Tarentine settlers fed up with constant Saracen attacks during the tenth century, but it was the Angevin prince of Táranto who bolstered the community in the early fourteenth century by granting it certain tax privileges. The town derives its name from this – *franca* meaning duty or stamp. Today its centre shelters within an unprepossessing approach of tower blocks, a medieval core adorned with some of the most subtle and least overbearing examples of architecture from the Baroque period you'll find.

Through the **Porta di Santo Stefano**, which marks the entrance to the old town, Piazza Roma is dominated by the vast **Palazzo Ducale**, dating from 1688 and now housing the town hall, but with a handful of rooms open to the public most mornings – most of them smothered in classically eighteenth-century Arcadian murals by a local artist. Just across the square, narrow Via Vittorio Emanuele leads right into the old town and Piazza Plebiscito, fronted by the vast Baroque facade of the **Chiesa di San Martino**, an eighteenth-century church built on the site of an earlier Romanesque structure, of which only the campanile survives. From adjacent Piazza Immacolata you can either bear left down Via Cavour, with its Baroque palazzi and balconied streets, or wander further into the old town, the roads running around the edge of the surviving fourteenth-century town walls offering an excellent panorama of the Valle d'Itria, with its neatly ordered fields dotted with *trulli*. Indeed, if you're further interested in finding out about life in the *trulli*, there's a **Museo della Civiltà dei Trulli** (closed for restoration; ☎0831.381.409), 7km from Martina Franca on the road to Ceglie Messápico.

The best time to visit Martina Franca (so long as you secure your accommodation well in advance) is during the **Festival della Valle d'Itria** (☎080.480.5100) held from the end of July until the first week in August, one of the most important events on the Italian musical calendar, with opera, classical, jazz music and the like. Although tickets aren't cheap, it's a congenial and unpretentious event; information is available from the festival office in the Palazzo Ducale.

Practicalities

There's a spasmodic bus service from the **FSE train station** up to the centre of town; otherwise you'll have to walk for 15 minutes – left out of the station and up Viale della Libertà to Corso Italia, which leads to the old town centre. The **tourist office** on Piazza Roma 35 (June–Sept Mon–Fri 8.30am–1pm & 5–7pm; Sat 9am–12.30pm; Oct–May Mon–Sat 8.30am–1pm plus Tues & Thurs 5–8pm; ☎080.480.5702) has good maps of the town. The cheapest **hotel** is the *Hotel da Luigi* on Via Táranto, Zona G (☎080.430.1324; ②), though this is 2km out of town and at festival time you won't get a room here. One of the best of the pricier options in town is the comfortable *Dell'Erba*, Via dei Cedri 1 (☎080.430.1055, *hoteldellerba@italiainrete.net*; ⑤), with a swimming pool, restaurant and plenty of sun terraces. If you base yourself in Martina Franca for three days or more, there's the opportunity to stay in a traditional apartment in the old town – an atmospheric choice. Studio apartments for two work out at L130,000/€67.14 per night, plus linen charge; contact *Villaggio In* (☎080.480.5911).

As for **eating** in Martina Franca, you'll get an excellent meal at *La Cantina*, Vico 1 Lanucara 12 (closed Mon) – try the pasta with beans (*bucatini con fagioli*) or lamb (*orecchiette con sugo di castrato*) and broad beans with wild chicory, though the food is cheaper down Corso dei Mille (off Corso Italia); or head straight for the town's best pizzas at *La Panca*, Via Spirito Santo 14, off Via Bellini. If you're after **snacks** or picnic food, *Fratelli Ricci*, the butcher at Via Cavour 19 (closed Mon), sells roast meats in the evenings and stocks a wonderful example of *capocollo*, a local cured pork salami. There are good *piadine*, dotted with cheese, rocket and tomatoes (among other combos), to be had from *Smile*, on the corner of Piazza Umberto near the entrance to the old town – to find it, look for the queue.

Táranto

There are numerous legends connected with the origins of **TÁRANTO**. It was variously founded by the Spartan deity Phalanthus; Taras, the son of Neptune; or – perhaps more likely – illegitimate Spartans born while their fathers were away fighting. Whatever the truth is, Taras, as it was known to the Greeks, was a well-chosen site and soon became the first city of Magna Graecia, renowned for its wool, its oysters and mussels, and its dyes – the imperial purple was the product of decayed Tarentine molluscs. Resplendent with temples, its acropolis harboured a vast bronze of Poseidon that was one of the wonders of the ancient world. Sadly, little remains of ancient Taras or even

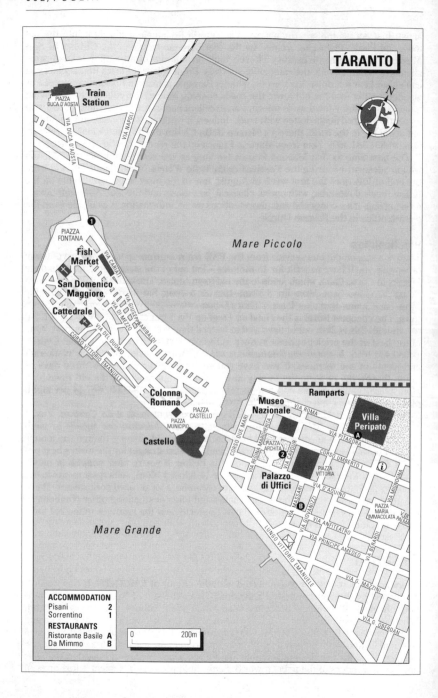

of later Roman Tarentum, their monuments and relics confined to the great museum in the modern city. After being destroyed by the Romans, Táranto was for years little more than a small fishing port, its strategic position on the sea only being recognized in Napoleonic times. It was home to the Italian fleet after Unification, and consequently heavily bombed during the last war, since when attempts to rejuvenate the town have left its medieval heart girdled by heavy industry, including the vast Italsider steel plant that throws its flames and lights into the skies above.

Finding your way around is easy. The city divides neatly into three distinct parts: the northern spur is the industrial part of town, home of the steel works and train station. Cross the Ponte di Porta Napoli and you're on the central island containing the old town. And the southern spur holds the modern city centre (the Borgo Nuovo), the administrative and commercial hub of Táranto, linked to the old town by a swing-bridge.

The City

In Greek times the island holding the **old town** wasn't an island at all but part of the southern peninsula, connected by an isthmus to the southern spur. Here the Greeks raised temples and the acropolis, while further south lay the residential districts. There's one extant fragment of ancient Táranto – the Doric **columns**, re-erected in a corner of **Piazza Castello**, which once adorned a temple of Poseidon. The rest of the tiny island is a mass of poky streets and alleyways, buttressed by scaffolding seemingly to prevent the whole place from falling down. The Aragonese **Castello** (now owned by the navy) at the southern end surveys the comings and goings of warships and fishing boats. The narrow canal they slide through, between the city's two inland "seas", was built in the late nineteenth century, on the site of the castle's old moat. "Seas" is a bit of a misnomer: the Mare Piccolo is really a large lagoon, home to Táranto's famous oysters and the Italian navy; and the Mare Grande is really a vast bay, protected by sea walls and the offshore fortified island of San Pietro.

At the heart of the old town lies the eleventh-century **Cattedrale**, which once did duty as a mosque – dedicated to Táranto's patron saint, Cataldo (Cathal), a seventh-century Irish monk who on returning from a pilgrimage to the Holy Land was so shocked by the licentiousness of the town's inhabitants that he decided to stay and clean the place up. His remains lie under the altar of a small chapel that bears his name – "a jovial nightmare in stone", Norman Douglas thought. As for the rest of the church, recent restoration has stripped away most of the Baroque alterations, and fragments of a Byzantine mosaic floor have been revealed. The columns of the nave, too, are ancient, pillaged from the temples that once stood on the island, their delicately carved capitals depicting tiny birds nestling among the stone foliage. A few blocks away, check out the city's **fish market**, on Via Cariati, a lively affair where the best of the local catch is displayed at the crack of dawn: octopi lie dazed, clams spit defiantly at you, while other less definable creatures seem preoccupied with making a last dash for freedom before the restaurateurs arrive – some of the city's finest restaurants are just across the road.

It's a short walk across the swing-bridge to Táranto's **modern centre** – though this, like Bari's, has limited charms, its wide streets laid out on a grid pattern that forms the centre of the city's passeggiata, around piazzas Vittoria and Archita. Nearby, the **Villa Peripato** was *the* place for the Tarentini to take their early-evening stroll at the turn of the century, but today's gardeners seem to be fighting a losing battle with the undergrowth.

The only real attraction in this part of town – and it's a gem when it's fully functioning – is the **Museo Nazionale** on Corso Umberto I at no. 41, which offers a fascinating insight into the ancient splendour of Taras. With something in excess of 50,000 pieces of Greek terracotta alone, it's one of the largest collections in the world. The museum has been undergoing a lengthy restoration and expansion; in the meantime the most important part of the collection is on show in twenty rooms in the **Palazzo Pantaleo**, Via Pantaleo (daily 8.30am–7.30pm; free; ☎099.471.3511) next to the sea and 200m from the cathedral in the old town. The **Tarentine Collection** is the main part of the museum. Most prominent in the collection is the Greek sculpture – including two beautiful busts of Apollo and Aphrodite dating from the fifth century BC – but there's Roman scuplture, too. Finds from the city's necropolis include the *Sarcophagus of the Athlete*, from 500 BC, its original painted decorations still intact, complete with the remains of the young athlete within. Mosaics (second to fifth century AD) depicting wild animals and hunting scenes found at Egnázia (see p.898), are due to be shown at the museum on Corso Umberto when it reopens. Highlight, however, will be the Sala degli Ori (Room of Gold). Magna Graecia's wealth was well catered for by the goldsmiths of Taras, who created earrings, necklaces, tiaras and bracelets with minute precision, all delicately patterned and finely worked in gold filigree. Some of the best examples of their work will be on display.

Practicalities

All **buses** arrive and depart from Piazza Castello, except FS connections with Metaponto and Potenza, which arrive at Piazza Duca d'Aosta, just outside the **train station**. To save you the 25-minute walk from the station, buses #1, #3 and #8 run to Corso Umberto in the modern city. Get off just after the huge Palazzo di Uffici and you're close to the **tourist office** on Corso Umberto I at no. 113 (Mon–Fri 9am–1pm & 2.30–6.30pm, Sat 9am–noon; ☎099.453.2392). Timetables for **city buses** are posted in the AMAT office just around the corner on Via Margherita 34.

Accommodation can be a real headache. There are cheap hotels in the old town, around Piazza Fontana, but most are grotty and some may be unsafe for lone women; the best choice is the *Sorrentino*, on Piazza Fontana 7 (☎099.470.7456; ②), run by a woman, her daughter and two cats. There are more pleasant but characterless options in the modern city: cheapest of these is the basic *Pisani* at Via Cavour 43 (☎099.453. 4087; ②).

For **meals**, check out the tourist menu at the *Ristorante Basile*, Via Pitagora 76 (closed Sat), and the good – and very fairly priced – local specialities at *Da Mimmo*, one block up at Via Giovinazzi 18 (closed Wed).

Around Táranto

With transport – public or private – it's fairly easy to get away quickly from the city. One of the best targets, and only 13km to the southeast, is the attractive coast beyond the adjacent small towns of **LEPORANO** and **PULSANO** – white sandy beaches flanked by pine woods. CTP, Circolare Rossa and Circolare Nera buses come out this way (check with the tourist office for timetables), and there are **campsites** nearby – *Santomay* at Viale delle Margherite, Località Gandoli (☎099.533.2275), and *Porto Pirrone* on the coast at Località Marina di Leporano (☎099.533.4844; May–Sept). If you want to swim, consider the other direction too, 15km west of the city, where a series of empty beaches stretches right along the **Golfo di Táranto** into Basilicata, pine woods again providing a cool escape from the August sun. The train stops at several small stations along this coast if you want to explore it further.

Inland from Táranto, due east of the city, the mildly undulating lands were once known as as "Albania Salentina" after the large numbers of Albanian refugees who settled here during the late fifteenth century, following the forced conversion of the Albanian population to Islam by the Turks. One of these Albanian settlements is **GROTTAGLIE**, only fifteen minutes by CTP bus from Via di Palma, honeycombed with caves, the *grotte* from which the town takes its name. It's been a centre of earthenware production since the tenth century and, tucked away in the potters' quarter, under the shadow of Grottaglie's massive fourteenth-century castle, they're still making convincing replicas of ancient Greek ceramics. The town's roofs, walls and pavements – in fact any part of the town with a flat surface – are covered with stacks of earthenware pots, plates and amphorae.

Northwest of Táranto

Inland and **northwest** of the city, the scenery changes dramatically, gorges and ravines marking a landscape that's closer to that of Basilicata than Puglia. **MASSAFRA**, about 15km from Táranto (regular trains and FSE buses from Piazza Castello), is split in two by a ravine, the Gravina di San Marco, lined with grottoes dating mainly from the ninth to the fourteenth centuries. Many contain cave-churches, hewn out of the rock by Greek monks and decorated with lavish frescoes. All such sites in Massafra are visitable only by guided tours (at 10am and 6pm; L7000/€3.62) arranged by the **tourist office** at Via Vittorio Veneto 15 (Mon–Fri 9am–noon & 4–7pm; ☎099.880.4695). A Baroque staircase runs down to the eighteenth-century **Santuario della Madonna della Scala**, built onto an earlier cave-church, which features a beautiful fresco of a *Madonna and Child*, dating from the twelfth to the thirteenth centuries – beyond which more steps lead down to an eighth-century crypt. The nearby **Cripta della Buona Nuova** houses a thirteenth-century fresco of the Madonna and a striking painting of Christ Pantocrator. About 200m away, at the bottom of the ravine, is a mass of interconnected caves known as the **Farmacia del Mago Greguro**, now in a pretty pitiful state but once used by the medieval monks as a herbalist's workshop.

Fifteen minutes further west by SITA bus (from Piazza Castello), **CASTELLANETA** clings to the edge of another ravine, 145m deep and 350m wide, commanding some spectacular views over the Golfo di Táranto and the mountains of Basilicata. It, too, has a sprinkling of cave-churches, though it's better known as the birthplace of Rudolph Valentino – to whom the locals have erected a statue on the windy town square.

Easily the most spectacular of the ravine towns is **LATERZA**, close to the border of Basilicata, also reachable by SITA bus from Piazza Castello. It's situated on the edge of one of the largest gorges in Puglia, 10km long, 200m deep and 500m wide in places – a Puglian "Grand Canyon", complete with buzzards and kites. As in the other ravine towns, the walls are scoured with cave-churches, over 180 of them dating from the eleventh century, of which about thirty can be visited. Contact the **Pro Loco** office on Via Galilei 3 for information.

Bríndisi

Hopping across the peninsula from the Ionian Sea to the Adriatic Sea, **BRÍNDISI** lies 60km east of Táranto, once a bridging point for Crusading knights and still strictly a place for passing through. The natural harbour here, the safest on the Adriatic coast, made Bríndisi an ideal choice for early settlers. In Roman times, the port became the main crossing point between eastern and western empires, and later, under the Normans, there came a steady stream of pilgrims heading east towards the Holy Land. The route is still open, and now Bríndisi – primarily – is where you come if you're **heading for Greece** from Italy. First impression on arriving is that the entire town is full of shipping agents; and this, when all is said and done, is the town's main business. But even if you're leaving the same night you'll almost certainly end up with time on your hands. You could just while away time in a bar or restaurant down the main Corso Garibaldi, but the old town is pretty compact and, although it isn't brimming with ancient monuments, has a pleasant, almost oriental, flavour about it – and a few hidden

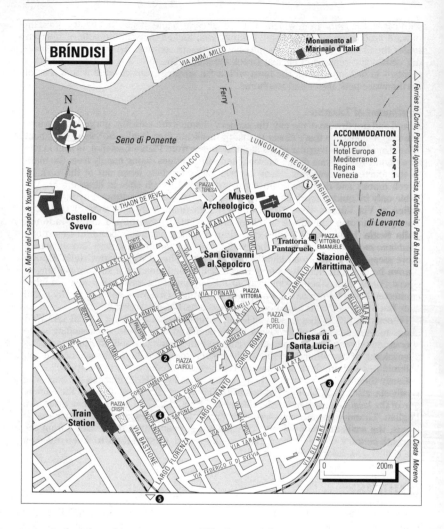

gems tucked down its narrow streets. What's more, the town's evening passeggiata is one of the south's most boisterous.

The town and around

The top of a broad flight of steps known as the **Scalinata Virgiliana** (Virgil's Steps) marks the end of the ancient Via Appia, which ran all the way from the Porta Capena in Rome. A marble tablet in the corner of the piazza marks the supposed site of the house in which Virgil died, in 19 BC. Via Colonne, with its seventeenth- and eighteenth-century palazzi, runs up to the **Duomo** – a remarkable building, if only for the fact that it's survived seven earthquakes since its construction in the eleventh century. Just outside is

ONWARDS TO GREECE: FERRIES, TICKETS AND SOME TIPS

AGENTS

There is a staggering array of **agents** selling ferry tickets to Greece, and you must take care to avoid getting ripped off. Ignore the touts clustered around the train station in high season, who specialize in selling imaginary places on non-existent boats, and *always* buy your ticket direct from the company's office or an approved agent. Among the **reliable agencies** are UTAC Viaggi, near the Standa at Via Santa Lucia 11 (☎0831.524.921); Grecian Travel, near the harbour at Corso Garibaldi 79 (☎0831.568.333), who can also handle bookings to Turkey and give advice on the more seaworthy seasonal offers which crop up; Discovery, Corso Garibaldi 102/104 (☎0831.525.400, *discovery@tin.it*) who also sell onward ferry tickets to the Cyclades and Crete; and Appia Travel, Via Regina Margherita 8/9 (☎0831.521.684) who sell Transalpino tickets and bus tickets to Rome and other destinations as well as ferry tickets. **Peak period** (roughly mid-July to mid-August) is calamitous, and less reputable agents make crass overbookings: book well in advance or travel a month either side of these dates.

FERRY COMPANIES

Ferry companies can't always be trusted either. Many appear overnight in July and August operating craft of questionable seaworthiness. As a rule (though there are honourable exceptions), nearly all the reliable companies' ferries sail at night (between 9pm and 10.30pm); only the pirates depart during the day. The companies listed below are long-established and their ferries will at least get you there: Adriatica (*www.adriatica.it*), c/o Adria (☎0831.523.825) on the first floor of the Stazione Marittima; to Corfu, Igoumenitsa and Patras; Hellenic Mediterranean Lines, Corso Garibaldi 8 (☎0831.528.531), to the same destinations, and also to Kefallonia, Paxos and Ithaca with connections for Lefkadha and Zakinthos included in the price; Fragline, Corso Garibaldi 88 (☎0831.590.310), to Corfu and Igoumenitsa.

Adriatica run three times a week throughout the year and daily late June to mid-Sept; the others operate frequent services between April and October. For full **schedules**, get a timetable from the agencies or the companies concerned.

PRICES AND BOARDING

Prices vary considerably according to season. On the whole, Adriatica are the most expensive, Fragline the cheapest: you'll be looking at a one-way, low/mid-season fare to Corfu/Igoumenitsa or Patras of L65,000–130,000/€33.57–67.14 per person, depending on whether you want a cabin or not; L70,000/€36.15 extra for a car. There are reductions of around 20–50 percent on the return fare if you book with the same company you are travelling out with. InterRail and Eurail **passes** are valid, while holders of Italian rail passes get discounts on some services. Everyone pays an **embarkation tax** – currently L12,000/€6.20 per person or per car, L30,000/€15.49 per camper van.

Leaving Italy, you must present your boarding card to the authorities at the Stazione Marittima (first floor); do it as soon as you have your ticket to avoid the crowds. Then, you should go to the terminal **at least two hours** before the ship's departure, and make sure that any stopover you are making on the way to Patras is clearly marked on your ticket. Don't forget to **stock up on food and drink** in Bríndisi's supermarkets, as there are some serious mark-ups once on board.

---

the **Museo Archeologico Provinciale** (daily 8.30am–1.30pm plus Tues 3.30–7pm; free). In addition to ornaments and statues from the necropoli that lined the Via Appia in Roman times, several rooms accommodate bronzes recovered in underwater exploration nearby, as well as finds from the excavations at Egnázia (see p.898). Follow Via Tarentini from here and bear left for the tiny round church of **San Giovanni al Sepolcro**, an eleventh-century baptistry. It's a little dark and decrepit inside, but you can just make out some of the original thirteenth-century frescoes. And there are more frescoes, this time a century older, in the **Chiesa di Santa Lucia**, just off Piazza del Popolo.

Bríndisi's most important medieval monument is further afield: the **Chiesa di Santa Maria del Casale** (check with the tourist office for hours and ring for entrance at the gate) – a three-kilometre bus ride from town; take bus #4 (from the train station) and ask the driver when to get off. Built by Philip of Anjou at the end of the thirteenth century, it's an odd mixture of styles, the facade an Arabic mass of geometric patterns, worked in two shades of sandstone, and the portal with an almost Art Deco touch to it. The stark interior is rescued from gloom by some fourteenth-century frescoes depicting allegorical scenes relating to the Day of Judgement, a vision of hell designed to scare the living daylights out of the less devout.

Practicalities

Arriving by **ferry** from Greece leaves you at one of three landing stages: two of these are on Via del Mare, at the **Stazione Marittima** from where it's a few minutes' walk to Piazza Vittorio Emanuele and the bottom of Corso Garibaldi, and another twenty minutes up to the central **train station** the other side of the town centre in Piazza Crispi. The other disembarkation point is at **Costa Moreno**, a couple of kilometres south-east of town, there's no bus to the centre, so take the ferry (7am–midnight; L800/€0.41) to the Stazione Marittima, or a taxi. Marozzi **coaches** linking the town with Rome (3 daily; ☎0831.597.884) and Miccolis coaches connecting it with Naples (3 daily; ☎0831.560.678) arrive at and depart from near the tourist office on Viale Regina Margherita. For **transport around town**, lots of buses run down Corso Umberto and Corso Garibaldi; taxis sit in ranks outside the train station. The **tourist office** is at Piazza Dionisio off Lungomare Regina Margherita (Mon–Fri 8.30am–2.00pm & 3–7pm Sat 8.30am–1pm; ☎0831.523.072).

Nearly all the ferries leave in the evening so **accommodation** isn't usually a problem. If you do need to stay, there's the no-frills *Venezia*, Via Pisanelli 6 (☎0831.527.511; ①), or fairly cheap rooms at the *Hotel Europa*, Piazza Cairoli 5 (☎0831.528.546; ②). More upscale choices are the clean but rather dated *Regina*, Via Cavour 5 (☎0831.562.001; ⑤), *L'Approdo*, Via del Mare 50 (☎0831.529.667; ④), with small, restful air-conditioned rooms, or the slick *Mediterraneo*, Via Aldo Moro 70 (☎0831.582.811; ⑥), a Best Western hotel. There's also a **youth hostel**, 2km out of town in Casale at Via Brandi 2 (☎0831.413.123, hostelbrindisi@hotmail.com; L18,000/€9.29),where you can rent a bed for the day (L9,000/€4.64) if you've got a night departure, with full use of their facilities including hot showers and email. The hostel is reachable on bus #3 or #4 from the train station, walkable in fifteen minutes by following the strategically placed yellow signs through town, or you can call them for a free pick-up service from town (they'll drive you back to the port or to the beach later too if you ask nicely).

It's not difficult to **eat** cheaply in Bríndisi; the whole of Corso Umberto and Corso Garibaldi (particularly the port end) is smothered in bars and restaurants staffed by waiters who will chase you down the street with copies of the menu. You should be able to grab a complete meal for under L20,000/€10.33. For twice as much you can have a memorable meal at the acclaimed *Trattoria Pantagruele*, Via Salita di Ripalta 13 (closed all day Mon & Sun evening, plus weekends in July & Aug), which serves very good local dishes, especially seafood.

Listings

Car rental Europcar at the airport (☎0831.413.817).

Exchange To buy/sell Greek drachmas, avoid the numerous exchange offices in town and stick to the banks, who shouldn't clobber you with exorbitant charges – though they might need persuading to deal with you. Banco di Napoli and Credito Italiano are both on Corso Garibaldi. The exchange office at the Stazione Marittima is open on Saturdays until 9pm, and the one at the main train station on Sundays, too.

Police station (☎0831.543.111).

Post office Main office on Piazza Vittoria (Mon–Fri 8.30am–1pm & 3–6pm, Sat 8.30am–noon).

Taxis (☎0831.597.901).

Train information (☎0832.668.233).

West of Bríndisi: Ostuni

OSTUNI, 40km northwest of the town and just 35 minutes away by train, is one of the most stunning small towns of southern Italy. Situated on three hills at the southernmost edge of Le Murge, and an important Greco-Roman city in the first century AD, its old centre spreads across the highest of the hills, a gleaming white splash of sun-bleached streets and cobbled alleyways, dominating the plains below. The maze of well-preserved, winding streets makes for a fascinating amble (the evening passeggiata is also well worth sticking around for, especially at the weekend), and there are some exceptional views – particularly from Largo Castello over the woods to the north. Bits of cavorting Baroque twist out of unexpected places, including an ornamented eighteenth-century obelisk, 21m high, dedicated to St Oronzo, which stands in Piazza della Libertà (aka Piazza St Oronzo) on the southern edge of the old town. The **Chiesa delle Monacelle**, on the main drag from the upper town to the main piazza, has displays on prehistory (daily 9am–1pm & 4.30–10.30pm; winter closes 7.30pm; L3000/€1.55), the highlight of which is "Delia", the skeleton of a pregnant young woman found in a crouched position, her bones decorated before burial. You'll find the **tourist office** on Corso Mazzini in the old town during the summer (Mon–Fri 9am–12.30pm & 6–9pm, Sat & Sun 6–9pm; ☎0831.301.268), and at Via Dottor V. Continelli 47 in the new town during the rest of the year (Mon–Fri 8am–2pm & 5–7pm; ☎0831.303.775).

Ostuni's proximity to a popular sandy coastline, 7km away, makes budget **accommodation** tricky to find. The tourist office can help with private **rooms** in town, or you can go for one of two unremarkable but cheap, central hotels: the *Hotel Orchidea Nera* on Via Mazzini 118 (☎0831.301.366; ②), or the *Tre Torri*, at Via Vittorio Emanuele 298 (☎0831.331.114; ③). If the budget can stand it, you could always opt for the beautiful, antique-filled four-star hotel *Al Castello Marchesale*, Via Scipione Petrarolo 7 (☎0831.305.925; ⑥). An alternative is to stay out of town in a farmhouse B&B: *Masseria La Salìnola* (☎0831.330.683, *www.agriturism.com/Salinola*; ③) has doubles and small apartments on a traditional estate surrounded by olive groves, with a swimming pool (in high season) and bikes. It's quite tricky to find: in town, look out for the neon sign of Bar Manhattan on the ring road, turn right at the roundabout, then head for San Michele; after 1.7km you'll see the *Masseria* on your left. Other agriturismo places are *Masseria Asciano* (☎0831.330.712, *www.italiainrete.net/asciano*; ②) a traditional white house with guest rooms on an olive-oil producing estate, 3km out of Ostuni on the Torre Pozzella road; and *Masseria Lamacavallo* (☎0831.330.703, *www.stelfair.com/ostuni/lamacavallo*; ⑤) on the same road to Torre Pozzella, 4km from Ostuni at Contrada Lamacavallo with apartments with kitchenettes in the farmhouse.

There are a number of excellent **restaurants** in Ostuni: try *Osteria del Tempo Perso*, at Via Tanzarella 47 (closed all day Mon & lunchtimes except Sun; reservations advised, ☎0831.303.320), for good-value *fave e cicoria* (broad beans with chicory), *orecchiette con cime di rapa* (pasta with turnip tops) and grilled meat. *Vecchia Ostuni*, Largo Lanza 9, just off Piazza della Libertà, is another good choice with a vast array of antipasti including deep-fried courgette flowers, snails in a piquant tomato sauce, twists of mozzarella, and pickled peppers. At the top of the town, *Antiche Pietanze*, on Via P Vincenti is a small place up a set of narrow whitewashed steps offering regional food at moderate prices (the set menu is good value). On summer Saturdays Ostuni buzzes when hordes of people (mostly young) drive in from the countryside around, meet up with their friends, pack out the **bars and cafés** and listen to the music coming from the sound system on Piazza della Libertà; *Hampton's Pub* facing this main square is the most glamorous of the chill-out zones. For **snacks**, try the particularly good cookies, bread, and *focacce* with onion that come out of *Lu Furne* at Via Petrarolo 28, at Porta Nova.

Of the **coastal resorts** accessible from Ostuni, there's more happening at **Ostuni Villanova** than Ostuni Marina: if you want to stay here, go for the modern *Baia del Re* at Villanova (☎0831.970.144; ⑤).

Lecce and the Salentine peninsula

A fast 40km south from Bríndisi, Baroque **Lecce** is a place to linger, with some diverting Roman remains and a wealth of fine architecture scattered about an appealing old town area. It's also a good starting-point for excursions further into the **Salentine peninsula**, which begins south of the city. In keeping with the city's long association with traders and settlers, the landscape here begins to take on a distinctive Greek flavour, a mildly undulating region planted with carob, prickly pear and tobacco. The Adriatic coast is pitted with cliffs, topped with ruined watchtowers, with rugged coves and caves right the way down to the **southern cape**. The hinterland, by comparison, is more barren, although there's again a Greek element to it, with its tiny, sun-blasted villages growing out of the dry, stony, red earth and the flat-roofed houses painted in bright pastel colours.

Lecce

Whether or not you like the Baroque style, you can't fail to be impressed by the exuberant building styles on display in **LECCE**, though the fact that they are firmly in the grip of a largely unremarkable modern city does detract from the enjoyment. Previously prey to opportunist attack, the city began a settled era signalled by the defeat of the Turkish fleet at Lepanto in 1571. The subsequent arrival of religious orders (Jesuits, the Teatini and Franciscans) brought an influx of wealth which was reflected in the building of opulent churches and *palazzi*, and it's this architectural extravagance that still pervades today's city. The flowery style of "Leccese Baroque" owed as much to the materials to hand as to the skills of the architects: the soft local sandstone could be intricately carved and then hardened with age. Unfortunately, modern pollution is in danger of ruining many of the buildings, keeping the mass of stonemasons and carpenters who still work in Lecce well occupied.

The city

Start in **Piazza Sant'Oronzo**, the hub of the old town, named after the first-century bishop of Lecce who went to the lions under Nero. His bronze statue lurches unsteadily from the top of the **Colonna di Sant'Oronzo** that once stood at the end of the Via Appia in Bríndisi. It resurfaced here in 1666 to honour Oronzo, who was credited with having spared the town from plague ten years earlier. The south side of the piazza is taken up by the weighty remains of the **Anfiteatro Romano**, which probably dates from the time of Hadrian. In its heyday it seated 20,000 spectators, and it's still used in summer for concerts and plays. Sadly, though, most of its decorative bas-reliefs, of fighting gladiators and wild beasts, have been removed to the town's museum for safekeeping, and nowadays it looks rather depleted.

The best of Lecce's Baroque churches are all a short distance from Piazza Sant'Oronzo. The finest, certainly the most ornate, is the **Basilica di Santa Croce**, just

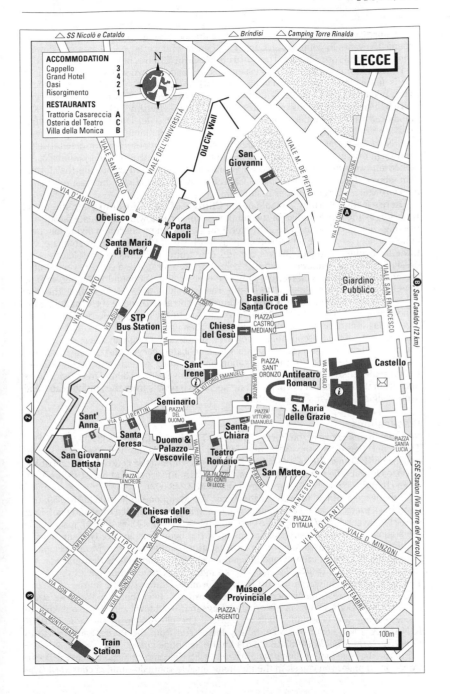

△ SS Nicolò e Cataldo   △ Brindisi   △ Camping Torre Rinalda

LECCE

N

ACCOMMODATION
Cappello   3
Grand Hotel   4
Oasi   2
Risorgimento   1

RESTAURANTS
Trattoria Casareccia   A
Osteria del Teatro   C
Villa della Monica   B

Old City Wall

VIALE DELL'UNIVERSITA

VIALE SAN NICOLO

VIA D'AURIO

San Giovanni

VIALE M. DE PIETRO

VIA DI PRIULI

VIA COLONNELLO A. COSTADURA

Obelisco

Porta Napoli

Santa Maria di Porta

VIA TRENTA PRATO

VIALE TARANTO

VIA ADUA

VIA PALMIERI

STP Bus Station

Basilica di Santa Croce

PIAZZA CASTRO MEDIANO

Chiesa del Gesù

Giardino Pubblico

VIALE SAN FRANCESCO

△ B — San Cataldo (12 km)

Sant' Irene ⓘ

VIA AUG. IMPERATORE

PIAZZA SANT' ORONZO

Antiteatro Romano

VIA 25 LUGLIO

Castello

VIA VITTORIO EMANUELE

Seminario

Sant' Anna

VIA G. LIBERTINI

PIAZZA DEL DUOMO

Santa Teresa

Duomo & Palazzo Vescovile

VIA PALAINI

Santa Chiara

PIAZZA VITTORIO EMANUELE

S. Maria delle Grazie

PIAZZA SANTA LUCIA

San Giovanni Battista

PIAZZA TANCREDE

Teatro Romano

VIA PERRONI

San Matteo

VIA FRANCESCO RUBICHI

FSE Station (Via Torre del Parco)

Chiesa delle Carmine

VIALE GALLIPOLI

VIA LOMBARDIA

VIA CAIROLI

PIAZZA D'ITALIA

VIALE OTRANTO

VIALE D. MINZONI

VIA DON BOSCO

VIA MONTEGRAPPA

VIALE ORONZO QUARTA

Museo Provinciale

PIAZZA ARGENTO

VIALE XX SETTEMBRE

Train Station

0   100m

to the north, whose florid facade, the work of the local architect Antonio Zimbalo, took around 150 years to complete, its upper half a riot of decorative garlands and flowers around a central rose window. The **Church of Santa Chiara**, in the opposite direction on Piazza Vittorio Emanuele, is an essential stop; loaded down with ornament, its interior is full of little chapels groaning with garlands and gilt. There's more Baroque extravagance on offer on Via Vittorio Emanuele, where the **Church of Sant'Irene** houses the most sumptuous of Lecce's Baroque altars – lavishly frosted and gilded, and smothered with decoration. Nearby, facing onto Piazza del Duomo, the **Seminario** holds an impressively ornate well, carved stone masquerading as delicately wrought iron. Next door, the balconied **Palazzo Vescovile** adjoins the **Duomo** itself, twelfth century in origin but rebuilt entirely in the mid-seventeenth century by Zimbalo. He tacked on two ornate facades and an enormous five-storeyed campanile that towers 70m above the square. The plain **Castello di Carlo V**, to the east of Piazza Sant'Oronzo, is currently under restoration.

There's further work by Zimbalo in the **Church of San Giovanni Battista** (or del Rosario), by the Porta Rudiae in the southwest corner of town – the ornate facade and twisting columns fronting some extremely odd altars, dumpy cherubim diving for cover amid scenes resembling an exploding fruit bowl. But if the Baroque trappings of the town are beginning to pall, there's the odd relic from other eras too, not least a well-preserved **Teatro Romano** (currently being restored for use as a concert venue) near the **church of Santa Chiara**, the only one of its kind to be found in Puglia, with its rows of seats and orchestra floor still remarkably intact. There's also the fine Romanesque church of **Santi Nicolò e Cataldo** (entrance through the cemetery gate; generally open mornings) built by the Normans in 1190, with a cool interior that reveals a generous hint of Saracen influence in the arches and the octagonal rounded dome. Little remains of the frescoes that once covered its walls, though an image of St Nicolò can be found on the south side, together with a delicately carved portal. One more stop you should make, near the railway station on the other side of town, is the **Museo Provinciale Castromediano** (Mon–Fri 9am–1.30pm & 2.30–7.30pm; free), which has finds from the old Roman town, including decorative panels from the amphitheatre and some religious gold- and silverwork.

Practicalities

Regional **buses** arrive at the Porta Napoli, the FSE bus station (☎0832.347.634) on Via Torre del Parco, or the STP bus station on Via Adua. FSE and FS **trains** (☎0832.668.233) use the same station, a kilometre south of the centre at the end of Via Oronzo Quarta. The **tourist office** is on Via Vittorio Emanuele II at no. 24 (Mon–Tues 10am–1pm & 5–7pm, Weds–Sat 10am–1pm; ☎0832.248.092).

The cheapest **place to stay** is the *Oasi*, Via Mangionello 3 (☎0832.351.359; ②), though it's pretty basic. If your budget will run to it, give yourself a treat and book in at the Art Nouveau *Grand Hotel*, Viale Oronzo Quarta 28 (☎0832.309.405; ④), just outside the station – for once, a fairly salubrious area; the bedrooms are pretty plain, but the building is gorgeous. Also near the station *Cappello*, Via Montegrappa 4 (☎0832.308.881; ②), is friendly and efficiently run. More imposing is *Risorgimento*, Via Augusto Imperatore (☎0832.242.125; ⑤), a sandstone palazzo dating back to the early 1900s with elegant interiors, just off Piazza S Oronzo. Otherwise, the tourist office can help you find a reasonably priced private **room** or check out the Web site *www.caffeletto.it* for B&B options in historic buildings in the old town and on the outskirts of Lecce – many are beautiful, albeit at a price. The closest **campsite** is at **TORRE RINALDA**, 10km north of Lecce; hourly buses run from the Piazza Sant'Oronzo to *Camping Torre Rinalda* (☎0832.382.161) on the Salentine coast.

For **meals**, head for the *Villa della Monica*, Via SS Giacomo e Filippo 40 (closed Tues), where, in summer, you can sit in the gleaming marble, fountain-studded courtyard. The best choice in town for homely cuisine is *Trattoria Casareccia* on Via Colonnello A. Costadura 19 (closed all day Mon & Sun evening), although the *Osteria del Teatro* on Via Palmieri 26 (closed Sun) serves up a good *purè di fave e cicoria*.

The eastern peninsula: Otranto and the southern cape

The quickest escape from Lecce to the coast is to **SAN CATALDO**, popular with the locals, and with sandy beaches served by buses from Lecce's Villa Comunale. Without your own transport, though, you won't be able to see anything else of the coast south of San Cataldo until Otranto. With a car it's a pleasant route south along a rocky shoreline littered with ruined towers, a legacy of the defences erected against Turkish incursions. You'll pass several low-key resorts. Just south of **SAN FOCA** there's a spectacular rockpool, the Grotta della Poesia, big enough to swim in; while **ROCCA VECCHIA** still displays traces of its ancient Messapian walls. **TORRE DELL'ORSO**, a couple of kilometres beyond, takes its name from the tower which stands on a stony promontory, the surrounding coves pockmarked by the remains of houses and tombs cut out of the rock. If you're looking to **stay**, the *Casa del Turista* at San Foca (☎0832.841.006; ②) is right on the coastal road. Between Torre dell'Orso and Otranto lie the **Laghi di Alimini**, two lakes surrounded by extensive pine woods, another popular green stop on this otherwise barren coast; there's **camping** here at *Camping Frassanito* (☎0836.803.005; May–Sept).

Otranto

OTRANTO, a minuscule town nestling around its harbour, makes an ideal base for exploring this part of the Adriatic. It's only an hour by train from Lecce (change at Maglie) and still very much a quiet Puglian backwater with a beach that was one of the ten cleanest in Italy in 2000 – though summer ferry services to Albania and a Club Med affair nearby attract visitors in the height of summer. Its history, however, is decidedly grim. One of the last Byzantine towns to fall to the Normans, in 1070, Otranto remained a thriving port for Crusaders, pilgrims and traders. But in 1480 a Turkish fleet laid siege to the town, which held out for fifteen days before capitulating. It's said that as a punishment the archbishop, upon capture, suffered the indignity of being sawn in half, a popular Turkish spectacle. Nearly 12,000 people lost their lives and the 800 survivors, refusing to convert, were taken up a nearby hill and beheaded. Otranto never really recovered, though the town does feature one glorious survivor of the Turkish attack inside its cathedral.

This, the **Cattedrale di Santa Maria Annunziata** (daily 8.30am–noon & 4–7pm), down a small alleyway just to the left of the castle, is a Romanesque structure with a rose window added in the fifteenth century and a marble-columned nave adorned by an extraordinary **mosaic floor**, a multicoloured tapestry in stone. Composed in three distinct but interconnecting parts, the mosaic stretches the length of the nave, centring on its main theme of the "Tree of Life", adorned with zodiacal signs and scenes from the medieval calendar and flanked by two smaller trees in the aisles depicting biblical scenes. Historical and animal figures are shown as a mix of myth and reality – Alexander the Great, King Arthur, the Queen of Sheba, crabs, fish, serpents and mermaids. The work of a twelfth-century monk, for all its rough simplicity the mosaic provides a captivating picture, empowered by a delightful child-like innocence.

Not far from the cathedral, the town's Aragonese **Castello** (daily 10am–noon & 6–10pm; free) juts out into the bay, defending the harbour. Recently restored, its walls incorporate fragments of Roman and medieval inscriptions, while Charles V's coat-of-arms looms from its portal. Outside on a dusty square, old men still play a highly animated form of *boules*, impervious to passers-by. Out on the southern edge of town is the hill, covered with cypress trees, where the survivors of the Turkish siege were beheaded. At the top of the hill, the sixteenth-century **Chiesa di San Francesco di Paola** holds inscriptions of the names of the victims, together with a vivid description of the terrible events of July 1480.

There's also a variety of musical and theatrical events in Otranto throughout summer, usually centred around the castle, and an annual **festival** commemorating the "800 Martyrs" on August 13–15. Details and other information are available from the **tourist office**, Via Pantaleone 12 in the new town (daily: July & Aug 8.30am–1pm & 3.30–9.30pm; Sept–June 8am–2pm; ☎0836.801.436). If you want **to stay** in Otranto, your best bet is the light, modern *Bellavista*, Via Vittorio Emanuele 4 (☎0836.801.435; ④), right in the centre of things near the beach, just outside the old town; the nearest **campsite**, *Camping Hydrusa*, is on Via del Porto (☎0836.801.255; May–Sept), signposted from the port. There are some excellent **restaurants** in town, such as *Da Sergio* on Corso Garibaldi (closed Sun in winter), and *La Duchesca* at Piazza Castello 17 (closed Mon in winter), while the air-conditioned self-service restaurant *Boomerang*, at 13/14 Via Vittorio Emanuele II, by the park next to the beach, services delicious well-priced fresh antipasti, pasta and simple meals. Alternatively, in nearby Frassanito, *Da Umberto*, along the road to San Cataldo (closed Sun in winter), does great fish dishes.

If you're heading to **Albania**, Icaria Line (☎0836.801.005) operates a ferry service there. One-way, low-season tickets cost L40,000/€20.66 per person, plus L5000/€2.58 embarkation tax; L45,000/€23.24 per car.

To the southern cape

From Otranto, all the way down to the cape at Santa Maria di Leuca, the coastline is steep and rugged. **CAPO D'OTRANTO**, 5km south of Otranto, is the most easterly point on the Italian peninsula, topped by a lighthouse and the rather desolate ruins of a seventh-century abbey. On clear mornings there's a commanding view across the straits, the mountains of Albania visible about 80km away. (On seriously clear days they say you can even see Corfu, 100km away.) **CASTRO**, about 30km down the coast, is the nicest of the towns around here. Fortified by the Aragonese in the twelfth century, it lies slightly inland, 100m above the small fishing hamlet of Castro Marina, the rocky creek serving as a harbour – and reputedly the landing place of the Trojan hero Aeneas. The area hereabouts is full of grottoes; the most spectacular and easiest to reach is the **Grotta Zinzulusa**, a little way north of Castro Marina. An iridescent mass of stalactites and stalagmites, its dark waters are home to a rather odd species of blind fish. If you feel confident enough to explore a grotto by swimming, ask around in **Marina d'Andrano** (about 6km down the coast from Castro Marina) for the un-signposted **Grotta Verde**, which is splendidly phosphorescent.

There isn't really much to draw you down as far as **SANTA MARIA DI LEUCA**, a somewhat barren spot that's a fitting "land's end", with a scattering of Neolithic remains and an uninspiring marina. The once-supposed "end of the world" is marked by the tiny church of **Santa Maria Finibus Terrae**, built on the site of an ancient temple dedicated to Minerva, which stands perched on the white limestone cliffs. But it's all a bit of an anticlimax: even the cape isn't really the southernmost point, that distinction going to the Punta Ristola, a little to the west. You can get down this far, or at least as far as **Gagliano del Capo**, by train: it's at the end of the FSE rail line, just 5km from the cape.

The western peninsula: Galatina, Nardo and Gallipoli

About half an hour down the rail line from Lecce, **GALATINA** is one of the most intriguing of the Salentine towns. It remained a key Greek colony well into medieval times, while retaining Greek customs and language up until the present century.

Today, it's an important centre of the Italian tobacco industry, with much of the weed grown in the fields around, as well as being famed for its excellent local **wine**; stop by at *Bellone* on Via Soleto 2 (closed Thurs afternoon & all day Sun) for good pasta and wine, including hard-to-find local pasta shapes that are produced in-house. In the old part of town, the church of **Santa Caterina in Galatina** (daily 9am–noon & 5–7pm) is also well worth a look for the stunning fourteenth-century frescoes that cover its interior.

Most interestingly, Galatina is the only place in the Salentine where the phenomenon of **tarantulism** still survives. Once a year, on the feast day of Saints Peter and Paul (June 28/29), the devout gather at the church dedicated to the saints to perform a ritual – the origins of which go back to the outbursts of mass hysteria that swept Europe in the wake of frequent plagues from the fourteenth century onwards. Victims of the dreaded tarantula bite would come here to give thanks for their survival from the spider's venom. Actually, the tarantula itself wasn't the culprit, but another smaller spider. In any case, the bite induced hallucinogenic symptoms, vomiting and paranoia, and those bitten believed that the only way to survive was to sweat the poison out of the system. This gave rise to a frenzied dance, which could last for days. During the nineteenth century the tarantella, as it was known, was modified into the colourful, popular dance that is still performed here today.

Fifteen kilometres west of Galatina, reachable by train, **NARDO** is a busy little town with a long and turbulent history of sackings, rebellions and occupations. Despite that, the centre of town, based around Piazza Antonio Salandra and Piazza San Domenico, retains some fine buildings in a more or less preserved state: there's an odd amalgam of ornately sculpted palazzi and bold facades, a fortified town hall and an eighteenth-century *guglia*, or obelisk, similar to the one in Ostuni.

By way of contrast, first impressions of **GALLIPOLI** (not the World War I battlefield in Turkey) are fairly uninspiring. The new town sprouted on the mainland once the population outgrew its original island site in the eighteenth century, and all that remains of the once-beautiful city (the Kalli-pollis) of the Greeks is a rather weather-beaten fountain, which sits in the new town near the bridge. Over the bridge things get more interesting: the old town itself is a maze of meandering and twisting whitewashed streets, with tiny tomatoes, hanging on the walls to dry, providing a sudden blaze of colour alongside the fishing nets. Only the familiar Aragonese castle, which squats in one corner of the island, serves as a reminder that this is still Italy.

For **accommodation**, try the *Pensione Pescatore* on Riviera C. Colombo 39 (☎0833.263.656; ④), an attractive hotel in the old quarter with some rooms which overlook the sea and a good restaurant (closed Mon) serving seafood-orientated home cooking. Alternatively, there's the simpler hotel, *Le Conchiglie*, Via delle Perle 12 (☎0833.209.039; ②), outside the centre at Località Conchiglie. There is also a good **campsite**, 5km to the north: *La Vecchia Torre* (☎0833.209.083; May–Sept) at Rivabella on the coast road to Santa Maria al Bagno. If you want to eat in Gallipoli, head for the **trattoria** *Da Sarino*, at Via de' Cordova 8 (closed Fri), and gorge yourself on *zuppa di pesce* or *spaghetti ai frutti di mare*.

Beaches

There are some excellent **beaches** along this part of the coast, all fairly accessible by bus from Gallipoli. The Baia Verde, just to the south of the town, is highly popular in summer, though the coves and small sandy beaches to the north, near the tiny villages of **Santa Caterina** and **Santa Maria al Bagno**, are better. Although there's been a spate of hotel building in recent years, the stretch of coast between here and Nardo is lined with villas in lush gardens, still it's a good place to rest up for a while and see the coast.

travel details

TRAINS

Altamura to: Gravina in Puglia (7 daily; 20min).

Bari to: Alberobello (FSE, 17 daily; 1hr 30min); Altamura (13 daily; 1hr 10min); Andria (hourly; 1hr); Barletta (hourly; 50min); Bitonto (hourly; 20min); Bríndisi (hourly; 1hr–1hr 30min); Fasano (20 daily; 30min); Gravina in Puglia (3 daily; 1hr 15min); Grotte di Castellana (FSE, hourly; 50min); Lecce (hourly; 1hr 30min–2hr); Locorotondo (FSE, hourly; 1hr 40min); Martina Franca (FSE, hourly; 1hr 50min); Molfetta (14 daily; 25min); Monópoli (20 daily; 25min); Naples (2 daily; 3hr 45min); Ostuni (hourly; 1hr); Polignano a Mare (22 daily; 30min); Putignano (FSE, hourly; 1hr); Rome (6 daily; 4hr 30min–5hr 15min); Ruvo di Puglia (hourly; 40min); Spinazzola (3 daily; 1hr 15min–1hr 45min); Táranto (7 daily; 2hr 30min); Torre a Mare (hourly; 10min); Trani (hourly; 40min).

Barletta to: Canosa di Puglia (13 daily; 20min).

Bríndisi to: Lecce (hourly; 20–50min); Ostuni (hourly; 20–40min).

Fóggia to: Bari (hourly; 1hr 30min); Barletta (17 daily; 20min); Brindisi (17 daily; 2hr 50min); Fasano (17 daily; 2hr 15min); Lecce (17 daily; 3hr 15min); Manfredonia (9 daily; 30min); Molfetta (hourly; 1hr 5min); Monópoli (17 daily; 2hr); Ostuni (17 daily; 2hr 30min); Péschici (5 daily; 2hr 15min); San Severo (5 daily; 40min); Trani (hourly; 50min).

Lecce to: Bari (hourly; 2hr); Otranto (7 daily; 1hr); Gallipoli (9 daily; 1hr); Gagliano del Capo (10 daily; 1hr 30min); Naples; (5 daily; 5hr 30min) Rome (4 daily; 6hr 20min).

Martina Franca to: Táranto (8 daily; 40min).

San Severo to: Péschici (7 daily; 1hr 40min).

Táranto to: Bari (15 daily; 1hr 15min); Bríndisi (10 daily; 1hr); Castellaneta (10 daily; 25min); Grottaglie (11 daily; 15min); Massafra (12 daily; 15min); Metaponto (3 daily; 50min); Reggio di Calabria (3 daily; 6hr 10min).

BUSES

NB: the bus service on Sundays is drastically reduced.

Bari to: Andria (6–7 daily; 1hr 30min); Barletta (3–4 hourly; 1hr 25min); Canosa di Puglia (10 daily; 2hr 10min); Margherita di Savoia (8 daily; 1hr 45min); Molfetta (3–4 hourly; 40min); Trani (3–4 hourly; 1hr 5min).

Fasano to: Savelletri and Egnazia (6 daily; 20 min); Selva Fasano (4 daily; 10min).

Fóggia to: Manfredonia (18 daily; 50min); Vieste (1 daily; 2hr 45min); Troia (24 daily; 40min).

Manfredonia to: Bari (1 daily; 2hr 20min); San Giovanni Rotondo (14 daily; 40min); San Marco in Lamis (10 daily; 1hr); Monte Sant'Angelo (every 2hr; 55min); Vico del Gargano (2 daily; 2hr 15min); Vieste (2 daily; 1hr 40min).

Molfetta to: Ruvo di Puglia (hourly; 30min).

Péschici to: Rodi Gargánico (3 daily; 35min); San Severo (1 daily; 3hr); Vico del Gârgano (1 daily; 45min).

Rodi Gargánico to: Foresta Umbra (2 daily; 1hr 5min); Vico del Gârgano (2 daily; 40min).

Vico del Gargano to: Ischitella (9 daily; 15min).

Vieste to: Fóggia (1 daily; 2hr 45min); Manfredonia (3 daily; 1hr 40min); Péschici (9 daily; 45min).

FERRIES

Manfredonia to: Vieste/Péschici/Rodi Gargánico (mid-June to mid-Sept 1 daily; early June & late Sept 4 weekly; April–May 2 weekly; 2hr 40min–5hr 20min).

HYDROFOILS

Trémiti Islands to: Manfredonia (1 daily June–Sept; 2hr); Vieste (June, July & Sept 1 daily; Aug 3 daily; 1hr).

INTERNATIONAL FERRIES

Bari to: Corfu (daily; 9hr); Dubrovnik, Croatia (5 weekly; 7–8hr); Durazzo, Albania (2–3 daily; 3hr 30min–8hr); Igoumenitsa (daily; from 9hr); Patras (daily; from 15hr).

Bríndisi to: Corfu (at least 1 daily; 9hr 30min); Igoumenitsa (at least 1 daily; 10hr 30min); Kefallonia (daily; 15hr); Patras (daily; 14hr); Paxi (2 weekly July & Aug; 12hr 15min); Zante (2 weekly July & Aug; 19hr).

CHAPTER FIFTEEN

CALABRIA AND BASILICATA

More than any other of the regions of the Italian South, **Calabria** and **Basilicata** represent the quintessence of the *mezzogiorno*. Culturally impoverished, underdeveloped and – owing to emigration – sparsely populated, these rural regions were long considered only good for taxation, and even then they were mismanaged. Although agriculture was systematized to an extent when these lands formed a part of Magna Graecia, by the time the Normans arrived there was little infrastructure or defence against the depredations of maritime raiders. Moreover, the feudal era didn't really die here until the Bourbons were ejected at Unification, and remnants of the older society persist in the widespread system of patronage and an exaggerated use of titles. Respect for authority co-exists with a deep scepticism and an apathy and inertia vividly described by Carlo Levi in his *Christ Stopped at Eboli* – a book that for many Italians was the introduction to the very deep problems besetting the *mezzogiorno*.

Indeed, this area is if anything even more marginalized than it was before Unification, when it was at least the geographical centre of the Bourbon state, and today talk of the Two Nations of Italy is most strikingly manifest in what can seem a very distant region from the emphatically European north – to which its people provide a reluctant supply of cheap labour. But despite lingering attitudes on both sides that perpetuate this gulf, much has changed in the south, to the extent that the picture drawn in Levi's book would hardly be recognized today, thanks largely to a massive channelling of funds since the war to finance huge irrigation and land-reclamation schemes, industrial development and a modern system of communications, all helping to set the southern economy on its feet. Unemployment remains the highest in the country, and emigration is still very much a reality, but malaria has been eradicated, previously unproductive land made fertile, and construction is under way everywhere – though

---

ACCOMMODATION PRICE CODES

Throughout this guide, prices per person are given for **youth hostels** and assume Hostelling International (HI) membership. **Hotel** accommodation is coded on a scale from ① to ⑨, reflecting the cost of the cheapest double room in each establishment in high season. The price bands to which these codes refer are as follows:

① Up to L60,000/€30.99

② L60,000–90,000/€30.99–46.48

③ L90,000–120,000/€46.48–61.98

④ L120,000–150,000/€61.98–77.47

⑤ L150,000–200,000/€77.47–103.29

⑥ L200,000–250,000/€103.29–129.11

⑦ L250,000–300,000/€129.11–154.94

⑧ L300,000–400,000/€154.94–206.58

⑨ over L400,000/€206.58

(See p.32 for a full explanation.)

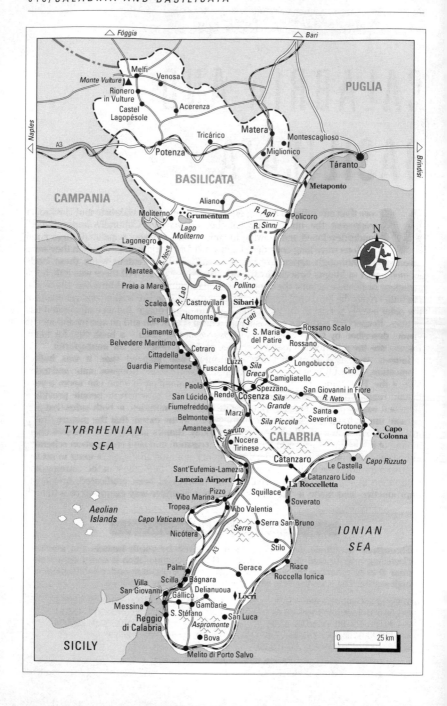

REGIONAL FOOD AND WINE

The food of Calabria is similar to that of Campania, but tends to have a rougher approach. **Greek influence** still pervades in the form of aubergines (eggplant), sword-fish and sweets incorporating figs, almonds and honey; otherwise it has the common trademarks of the south – plenty of pasta, pork and cheeses such as mozzarella, *cacio-cavallo*, mature provolone and pecorino. Basilicata is another poor region, mountainous and sparsely populated, relying on pasta, tomatoes, bread, olives and pork. A fondness for **spicy food** shows in the popularity of all types of peppers and, unusually in Italy, ginger (*zenzero*), which is thrown into many dishes. **Strong cheeses**, like matured ricotta – to match the strength of other ingredients – are favoured.

Cirò is the success story of Calabrian wine making, an old **wine** that has been given some modern touches and now shifts bottles outside its home territory. Not surprisingly, given its far-south position, Calabria also turns out sweet whites such as Greco di Bianco. The **aglianico** grape makes a star appearance in Basilicata: Aglianico del Vulture is the region's only DOC, but other wines worth trying are the sweet, sparkling Malvasia and Moscato.

---

often hand-in-hand with the forces of organized crime and with frequently dire consequences for the physical aspect of the land.

The **landscape** provides the main reason to come to Basilicata and Calabria: artistically they are the most barren regions in Italy, but the combination of mountain grandeur and a relatively unspoilt coastline, often in close proximity, give them a powerful appeal, and one only beginning to be exploited by the tourist industry. Two of the main cities, **Cosenza**, lying just inland of the Tyrrhenian coast, and **Reggio**, at its southern tip, lie within the shadow of the forested slopes of the **Sila massif** and the craggy wilderness of **Aspromonte**, respectively, and Cosenza also holds Calabria's most compelling old centre, in striking contrast to the progressive and prosperous sheen of its modern counterpart. In Basilicata, **Potenza** is useful as a transport hub for the string of medieval towns lying to the north, although the town holds none of the fascination of the region's second city, **Matera**, whose distinctive *sassi* – cavelike dwellings in the heart of the town – give it a uniquely dramatic setting. Of the coasts, it's the **Tyrrhenian** that is most engaging, with spots like **Maratea**, **Tropea** and **Scilla** favourite hideaway resorts for discerning Italian and foreign visitors. The **Ionian** coast, on the other hand, can be bleak and is visited mainly for its **ancient sites** – relics of the once mighty states that comprised the Greek colonies known as Magna Graecia.

Good **transport** services exist, but in hilly and coastal areas a car is useful, especially to penetrate some of the more far-flung inland areas. Once arrived somewhere, park up as soon as you can as a vehicle can only be an encumbrance in the smaller places. Walking around, you'll notice a general suspicion of strangers, especially in rural areas, though it's reassuring to remember that violence against strangers is very uncommon, even in Calabria, where the crime rate is notoriously high. As for sexual harassment, this is still a reality in some parts of the south – macho values prevail and women travelling alone will often be stared at (see p.57 for some hints on dealing with the more persistent specimens of southern manhood).

The northern Tyrrhenian coast

The northern stretch of the Tyrrhenian coast takes in both Calabria and Basilicata, of which the latter – a brief mountainous slice – is the most inspiring stretch and probably the most visited part of the entire region, its sheer cliffs and rocky coves refreshingly unspoilt by the holiday industry.

The obvious stop here is **Maratea**, hemmed in by the mountains and offering some first-rate beaches, which get overcrowded in summer. Once in Calabria, the holiday complexes intrude on the mainly mountainous littoral, though there are some absorbing places to break the journey, notably the towns of **Diamante**, **Belvedere** and **Amantea**, and plenty of good swim-stops in between. Following the coast down, the main SS18 runs alongside the railway line, though the frequent trains don't always stop at smaller places.

Maratea

The main – indeed the only – town on Basilicata's Tyrrhenian seaboard, **MARATEA** is a picturesque cluster of localities scattered along the cliffy coastline, mostly dedicated to the holiday industry during summer but perfectly peaceful outside the peak period. The old inland centre, known simply as **Maratea Paese**, is a knot of steep, narrow alleys and squares worth nosing around, though lacking any vital attractions. More compelling are the straggling, long-abandoned ruins of **Maratea Antica** behind and above town up the five-kilometre road to **Monte San Biagio** (624m), from which memorable views extend over the Golfo di Policastro. The peak is dominated by the **Redentore**, an enormous marble Christ, arms akimbo, symbolically positioned with its back to the sea, looking towards the mountains of the interior. Opposite the statue, and looking as if it were about to be crushed under the giant's feet, is the **Santuario di San Biagio**, built on the site of a pagan temple dedicated to Minerva and now the destination of a procession during the town's main festivities on the second Sunday of May, when a statue of the patron saint is carried up the hill.

Maratea's chief allure, however, is the beautiful rocky coastline hereabouts and the string of coastal offshoots where the hotels and restaurants are located. Most of the action – and accommodation – is in or around the *frazione* of **Fiumicello**, 5km north of Maratea Paese, though the chic elite who have colonized much of the area prefer to be seen in the snazzier bars and restaurants of **Maratea Porto**, directly below Maratea Paese – if nothing else, a pleasant place to stroll around and gawp at the yachts. The whole area is well endowed with sandy **beaches**, including a good one below Fiumicello; most are well signposted, but don't hesitate to explore the less obvious ones.

Practicalities

Most **trains** stop at the main Maratea station, at the bottom of Maratea Paese, from where it's a five-minute minibus or taxi ride (or a fifteen-minute walk) to Fiumicello. There is a second, less-used station, Maratea Scalo (at Marina di Maratea), 5km south of the main station. For **getting around**, a summer-only minibus service (every 1hr–1hr 30min; L1000/€0.52, tickets bought on board) connects Maratea Porto, Fiumicello, Marina di Maratea, and Maratea Paese in that order. The **tourist office** is on Fiumicello's main street (Mon–Sat: May–Sept 8am–2pm & 3–8pm; Oct–April 8am–2pm, also Tues & Thurs 3–6pm; ☎0973.876.908).

Accommodation can be hard to come by at any time, and in high season is often expensive, with many hotels obliging half-board during the peak period. Many close outside the summer months, though one good choice that's open all year, and has plenty of space, is the *Fiorella* (☎0973.876.921; ③), just outside Fiumicello at Via Santa Vénere 21 (near the petrol station). If you want to stay by the sea, there are a couple of options: the *Settebello* (☎0973.876.277; ⑤; May–Oct) overlooks the beach at Fiumicello; or move down to the remoter Marina di Maratea where the *Calaficarra* (☎0973.879.016; ③; end June to Sept) sits only a couple of minutes from Maratea Scalo station, and consequently is rather subject to overnight train rumble. A cheaper alternative to hotels around Maratea, and one that avoids the half-board requirement, is to rent **rooms** (lists available from the tourist offices); in central Fiumicello, for example, Giovanni Talarico offers spotless accommodation with sparkling views across to the mountains at Via Santa Vénere 29 (☎0973.877.040; ②; July–Aug). The nearest **campsite** is *Camping Maratea* at Castrocucco (☎0973.877.580; mid-June to mid-Sept), 5km south of Maratea Scalo station and 10km south of Maratea Paese; it's reachable on infrequent minibuses in July and August only, or by taxi.

There are dozens of **restaurants** in the area. Some of the best are in Fiumicello, where, on the main Via Santa Vénere, *La Bússola* is a plain pizza-and-beer joint, whose good and cheap pizzas generally pull in a strong local crowd (no closing day). Further down the main road towards the beach, at no. 97, *Da Felicia* has outdoor seating and serves fresh fish at reasonable prices (closed Sun in winter).

Into Calabria

South of Maratea, the road soon drops to reveal the flat coast of Calabria, on the other side of the River Noce. The first town you reach, **PRAIA A MARE**, is typical of the resorts along this coast – lively in the summer, deserted the rest of the time, and with a handful of **campsites**, **hotels** and **pizzerias** to choose from. On the beach, a six-teenth-century bastion faces the rocky **Isola di Dino** a little way out, where there are caves and grottoes visitable by renting a boat from the pebbly beach. Behind the town another **grotto** is the home of a widely venerated Madonna. The story goes that the people of nearby Aieta attempted repeatedly to remove this image to their own church, but each time it disappeared and was found back here, where they were eventually forced to let it be. More recently, however, the image disappeared for good, though a replacement was quickly and pragmatically installed.

Beyond Praia, **SAN NICOLA ARCELLA** has a lovely wide **beach**, from which – through a series of passages and a tunnel – you can get to other, emptier beaches. There is a good **pizzeria** here – *L'Incontro*, in Via Aldo Moro (closed Sun) – and a couple of **hotels**, the *Brillantino*, in the old centre (☎0985.3419; ②), and the pricier *Villa Príncipe* (☎0985.3125; ③), with fine views, near the south entrance to the village at Corso Umberto 8. The next town south, **SCALEA**, is quite different – Calabria at its worst, with the natural beauty of the location overwhelmed by an avalanche of unchecked development encircling a largely abandoned nucleus. Yet the old quarter still manifests a certain resilient vitality and there are even a couple of good **places to eat** here – for example the pizzeria *Il Borgo Antico* (signposted near Largo Nazionale; daytime only, closed Mon–Fri autumn & winter) – but the main reason to stop is to view the ruins of the Norman/Aragonese **castle** and a frescoed eleventh-century Byzantine **chapel**, bombed by both sides during World War II: it's signposted from Largo Nazionale, up Via Santa Maria. Pick up the key from the famiglia Grisolia nearby at no. 18.

South of Scalea, the banks of the River Lao hold the sparse remains of ancient **Laos**, colonized by the Sybarites following the destruction of their city (see "Sibari", p.947). The seaside town of **CIRELLA** was also a Sybarite colony, devastated by Hannibal, then Romanized; the theatrical ruins of **Cirella Vecchia**, overlooking the SS18, are of a later date, the result of a French bombardment in 1806 (though local lore attributes other, more sinister explanations, most notably a plague of ants). From behind the ruins a road forks inland to the hilltop villages of **Grisolia** and **Maiera**, close together on the map but actually divided by a gully, across which villagers conduct conversations with each other.

Five kilometres down the coast, the chic seaside town of **DIAMANTE** glistens on its small promontory. The walls of the narrow whitewashed lanes have been adorned with striking modern murals, making for an intriguing wander around, and there are a couple of good, moderately priced fish **restaurants** with outside seating down by the seafront at Spiaggia Piccola (beyond the *mole*): most relaxed is the *Taverna del Pescatore* (Oct–May closed Tues), with views over the small port.

BELVEDERE MARITTIMO, some 10km down the coast, overlooks its unexceptional marina from a spur a little way inland; it's an imposing and elegant town, full of greenery and having little of the air of neglect typical of Calabria's older centres. At the top, an impressive **castle** stands guard; originally a Norman construction but rebuilt under the Aragonese, whose coat-of-arms can be seen above the main gate. The inside has been gutted, however, and it's closed to the public. Down in **Belvedere Marina**, the best place to eat is the *Milleluci* on Via Grossi (mid-Sept to mid-May closed Tues), which serves pizzas baked in a wood-fired oven alongside such specialities as *gnocchi di patata alla pescatora*.

There are good **beaches** around **CITTADELLA**, 6km further south, while the next village down, **CETRARO**, has a good **bar** with delicious snacks and ices – the *Caffé Mulini* on Via Macchia di Mare – a useful place to cool off from the beach. If you wanted to stay around here, Cetraro has a choice of **hotels**, including the good-value *Piazza*, on Via Lungo Aron (☎0982.92.026; ②), and the more basic *Meridionale*, on Via De Seta (☎0982.91.262; ①). **GUARDIA PIEMONTESE** was once the home of a community of Walser refugees, Swiss Protestants who settled in the north of Italy in the thirteenth century but were brutally suppressed by the Inquisition in 1560, as the name of one of the gates round the still partly intact city walls recalls: Porta del Sangue ("Gate of Blood) on Piazza della Strage ("Slaughter Square"). From here, with the wind blowing in the right direction, you can't fail to notice the musty odours emitted from **Terme Luigiane**, a popular hot springs lower down the hill.

Paola and south to Amantea

Fourteen kilometres down the coast, **PAOLA's** size and importance are partly due to its function as the main rail and road junction for Cosenza, and partly to its **Santuario di San Francesco di Paola**, in a ravine above the town. Not to be confused with Francis of Assisi, this St Francis spent most of his life in the town and, as Calabria's principal saint, is venerated throughout the south. People visit the shrine at all times of year, but particularly during the week leading up to the May 4 **festa** – when a fair occupies the town, with daily festivities culminating in the carrying of his statue into the sea and a grand display of fireworks on the beach at midnight. There are several **hotels** and **trattorias** around the station by the sea and, a stiff ten-minute climb up, a couple of good **pizzerias** near the central piazza above – the *Eureka*, in Via del Cannone (closed Tues), with outdoor eating in summer, and *Le Arcate*, through the arch at Via Valitutti 5 (mid-Sept to June closed Mon). If you're looking for a place to **stay** however, **SAN LÚCIDO**, 6km south, is a more attractive town with a satisfying warren of alleys and squares in its clifftop old quarter; the spruce *Hotel Irma* (☎0982.81.330; ③) is a handy *pensione* near the station and the seafront, and there are **trattorias** nearby.

The series of small towns and villages that follow on further down the coast are all split between the original centres located higher up from the shore, perched on the edge of the Catena Costiera coastal range, and more modern marinas – good for the beach life but visually uninteresting. The older villages are difficult to get to but, if you can manage it, are worth the hike or twisty drive. **FIUMEFREDDO** has cobbled streets leading to a lovely piazza perched above a sheer drop (great for sunsets), though a hilariously incongruous modern statue in the square detracts somewhat from the scenic splendour. To one side of the village stands a quirky, dilapidated **castle** – a good picnic spot – with semipornographic murals inside by Salvatore Fiume, also responsible for the statue in the main piazza. **BELMONTE**, just beyond, has a mausoleum – easily visible as you pass below – dedicated to its most famous son, **Michele Bianchi**, one of the *quadrumvirate* of Fascists who marched on Rome in 1922, and for a while Mussolini's deputy. **AMANTEA** is the largest and liveliest of the chain, with beaches – either in the town itself, or better ones 3km south at **Córica** – and a handful of **fish restaurants**, best of which is *Locanda di Mare*, at the junction of the SS18 coastal road with the town's main shopping street, Via Margherita (Oct–May closed Mon) Round the corner from the restaurant, on the same street, is the small, tidy **pensione** *Margherita* (☎0982.41.337; ②), while 300m north along the SS18, the *Mediterraneo* at Via Dogana 64 (☎0982.426.364; ③) which has more comfort at higher prices. For local information ask at the **tourist office** at the top of Via Margherita (summer Mon–Sat 9am–noon & 5–8pm; winter Mon–Fri 7.30am–1.30pm, plus Mon & Wed 2.30–5.30pm; ☎0982.41.785). As for things to see, walk a few metres beyond the tourist office to see the fifteenth-century church and convent of **San Bernardino di Siena**, with majolica decoration and a *Madonna* by Antonello Gagini. Further up, at the top of the old town, a crumbling **castle** (always open; free) affords grand views over Amantea and the surrounding coast; those in the mood for castle ruins might like to visit another example crowning the nearby inland village of **Aiello**.

Cosenza and around

COSENZA, Calabria's first town of any size if you're travelling from the north, is also the region's most interesting, and makes a useful base to explore the surrounding area, particularly the **Sila** mountains. Historically it has always played an important role in the commercial and intellectual life of Calabria (Norman Douglas wrote, with characteristic hyperbole, "for acute and original thought this town can hardly be surpassed by any other of its size on earth"), and recently the town has generated a degree of wealth which – while still some way below most of Italy – has in the last twenty years or so literally transformed the landscape. New construction, much of it featureless and ugly, has sprouted everywhere, while its boldly designed university is expanding fast, helping to create a strong regional awareness and self-confidence.

Completely enclosed by mountains – the Sila on the east, the Catena Costiera separating it from the sea to the west – Cosenza is the meeting point of two rivers, the Crati and the Busento. Somewhere beneath the latter, tradition has the burial place of **Alaric the Goth**, the barbarian who gave the western world a jolt when he prised open the gates of Rome in 410 AD. Struck down for his sins by malaria while journeying south, he was interred here along with his booty, and the course of the river deviated to cover the traces, lending Cosenza a place in history and giving rise to countless, fruitless projects to discover the tomb's whereabouts.

The Town

The two rivers form a neat division between old and new Cosenza, with the main artery of the newer town, **Corso Mazzini**, running off north from near their junction. This is where most of the shops and banks are, and – by day – it's the liveliest place to be. Most of the things worth seeing, however, are located in the old part, the **centro storico**, a compact knot of steps and alleys rising up to a sturdy Swabian castle in the southern part of town. Much of the old town has been abandoned in favour of the newer suburbs to the north, but the area has recently pulled itself out of a long period as the haunt of *mafiosi*, delinquents and prostitutes, and attracted many small businesses in the form of boutiques and bars, making it a pleasant focus for walking and drinking until late. By day there's a tranquillity here that the rest of the town lacks, while by night the main street, **Corso Telesio**, is the place to be, especially in summer when it is closed to traffic.

From Piazza Valdesi on the far side of the bridge, Corso Telesio curves up into the old quarter's confusion of narrow streets. The road is named after Cosenza's most

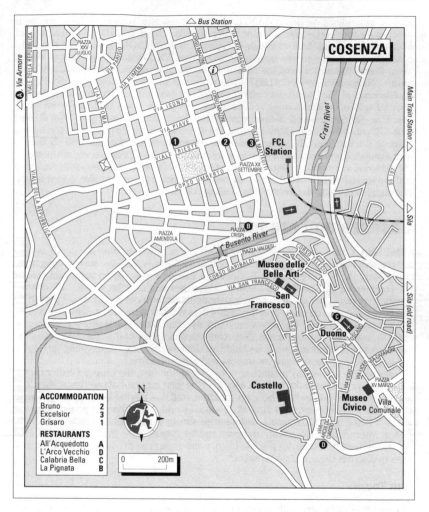

famous son, **Bernardino Telesio**, the sixteenth-century humanist philosopher and major influence on the other great Calabrian philosopher, Tommaso Campanella. Halfway up, Cosenza's stately **Duomo** stands in a square of tall *palazzi*. Consecrated on the occasion of Frederick II's visit to the city in 1222, its Provençal Gothic style was later modified by Baroque accretions – though sporadic restorations have undone much of the damage to the facade. The interior – a mixture of Romanesque, Gothic and Baroque styles – has a Roman sarcophagus carved with a hunting scene, in a good state of preservation, and, in the north transept, the lovely tomb of Isabella of Aragon, who died in Cosenza in 1271 while returning with her husband Philip III – seen kneeling beside her – from an abortive Crusade in Tunisia. But the duomo's most venerated item lies in the first chapel on the left: a copy of a thirteenth-century Byzantine icon, the *Madonna del Pilerio*, which was once carried around the country during times of plague. The original is in the **Museo delle Belle Arti** (Tues–Sun 9am–1pm & 3–7pm; free), housed for the forseeable future in a restoration workshop behind the cloisters of the church and convent of **San Francesco d'Assisi** on the street of the same name, reached from Via del Seggio, an alley leading up from Corso Telesio. The unsigned **Laboratorio di Restauro**, which also displays a Byzantine reliquary crucifix made by Greek craftsmen in Palermo and presented by Frederick II at the consecration of the cathedral, is located at the third door to the left behind the church (Mon–Fri 9.30am–1pm & 3.30–6pm; free). The church itself, a much-restored thirteenth-century complex badly damaged in World War II, has paintings by Wilhelm Borremans in the sumptuous St Catherine chapel on the right of the nave.

From St Francis, climb up to Corso Vittorio Emanuele, following it until you reach the little track on the right leading to the formidable **Castello** (summer Mon–Fri 9am–12.30pm & 4–6pm; winter closed; free), another Frederick II construction reduced to its present condition by a series of earthquakes. The inside is bare but sensitively restored, and hosts occasional exhibitions and concerts in summer, but it makes a good spot at any time for a breath of clean air and to enjoy the superb view over Cosenza and the surrounding mountains. You can also reach the castle from Cosenza's most elegant square, **Piazza XV Marzo**, at the top of Corso Telesio, where there is a shady public garden, and the **Accademia Cosentina** houses the **Museo Civico** (Mon & Thurs 9am–1pm & 3.30–6pm, Tues, Wed & Fri 9am–1pm; free), which sports a rather scanty collection of prehistoric and classical bric-a-brac from the surrounding area and a few paintings.

Practicalities

Arriving by bus you will be deposited at the **bus station** below Piazza Fera, from which it's a twenty-minute walk down the length of Corso Mazzini to the hotels and the *centro storico*. Arriving by train, you will have to take a bus (every 20min) from the **train station** a little way outside town – tickets from inside the station at the bar. There's a **left-luggage** office here (7am–8pm) and two **car rental** agencies charge identical prices – useful for excursions into the Sila – Hertz (☎0984.31.081) and Maggiore (☎0984.482.144); note, however, that parking spaces in Cosenza itself are a valuable commodity.

The main **tourist office** is at Corso Mazzini 92 (Mon & Wed 7.30am–1.30pm & 2–5pm, Tues, Thurs & Fri 7.30am–1.30pm; ☎0984.27.271), and there is an office specifically for the *centro storico* behind the duomo in Via Toscano (Mon–Thurs 9am–1pm & 4–6pm, Fri 9am–1pm; ☎0984.813.336). Primarily used by business travellers, Cosenza's **hotels** are mainly brash and expensive, but there are some more modest choices close to each other in the centre, namely the spacious and comfortable *Excelsior* in Piazza Matteotti (☎0984.74.383; ③); the modest, rather gloomy pension *Bruno* at Corso Mazzini 27 (☎0984.73.889; ①), and the more business-like *Grísaro*, around the corner on Viale Trieste, (☎0984.27.952; ③), which has parking for guests.

There is more choice when it comes to **eating** places: the best deal in town is at the small (but unmarked) *La Pignata* on Piazza Crispi (closed Sun), where you can have a complete meal for L20,000/€10.33. In summer the most congenial place to be is *All'Acquedotto*, a pizzeria/*birreria* below the old aqueduct, at the end of the winding Via Arnone and Viale della Repubblica, with great views over the valley (no closing day). In the old town, *L'Arco Vecchio*, above Piazza XV Marzo on Via Archi di Ciaccio, and *Calabria Bella* (closed Tues), in Piazza Duomo, which has outside seating in summer, are more formal choices, both serving traditional local dishes. But it's the **cafés** and **bars** of Cosenza's old quarter that are most fun, including a couple of very lively *birrerias* that stay open late: *The Beat*, serving beers and snacks opposite the duomo; and one of the town's two local Irish pubs, the *James Joyce*, on Via Cafarone (closed Mon), which charges up to L10,000/€5.17 for entry when there's live music in the basement (usually at weekends, when it's heaving). Just up from here, at Via Liceo 9, the *Caffè Telesio* is another congenial – and quieter – place for a late-night drink or meal, serving a range of cocktails, beers, and *frullati* inside, where the decor suggests an outdoor café in Rome's Trastevere. For coffees and *cornetti* during your daytime strolling, stop off at the old-fashioned *Caffè Renzelli*, up past the duomo. The best **ice creams** in town are from *Zorro*, at the bottom of Corso Telesio.

Around Cosenza

People spending any time in Cosenza will be mostly interested in excursions into the **Sila** (see below), but some of the villages dotted around the surrounding hills should-n't be ignored – especially in summer, when the heat and humidity settle on the town and the focus tends to move out of the city and into the hills, where most of the Cosentine population have their roots and family homes. With the village population swollen too by emigrants back for the summer, the streets are thronged until late, and at night the view over the bowl of the valley is magnificent, with glittering threads and clusters of light. It is also in the summer that the village **festas** normally take place, with each *comune*, or municipal administration, vying to outdo the others in terms of spectacle and expense.

The villages of the **Presila**, on the eastern slope of the valley, have a reputation for late-night revelry and some good **trattorias** – try *U'Fuccularu*, in **Pedace** (closed Mon), or *Dal Barone* in **Pianette di Rovito** (closed Wed) – and **birrerias** (such as *La Grotta* in **Spezzano della Sila**, which also serves snacks). On the other side of the valley the hilltop village of **RENDE** holds the prize for the tidiest village in the region: it has good views and an absorbing little **museum** (daily 9am–6pm; free) in the Palazzo Zagarese, on Via de Bártolo, devoted to local folk art, costumes, cuisine, music, the Albanian community and emigration. Rende also boasts a good choice of places to eat and drink, including the good-value **pizzeria** *L'Arco*, at Via Costa 4 (closed lunchtime & Tues), with a panoramic terrace. South of Cosenza, **MARZI** has *La Cisterna*, an agri-turismo where you can eat local dishes and also **stay** (☎0984.961.277; ②), making a good base for excursions into Sila; the attached stables provide opportunities for **rid-ing**. The village is best reached by bus or from the *autostrada*, just south of Rogliano; from Marzi, follow signs for Contrada Pezzapane.

Northeast of Cosenza, above the village of **LUZZI**, stands the **Abbazia di Sambucina**. A Cistercian abbey founded in the twelfth century and long the centre of this order of monks throughout the south, it has a beautiful, lightly pointed portal (rebuilt in the fifteenth century) and the original presbytery.

Buses for the villages depart from the **bus station** in Cosenza, below Piazza Fera, but to get the most out of these places you should ideally have your own transport, as sevices normally stop at nightfall. An interesting (but slow) way to get to the Presila during the day (and beyond, into the Sila) is by **train**, on the Cálabro-Lucane (FCL) line: this leaves twice a day from the small station east of Piazza Matteotti for Camigliatello (see opposite), offering marvellous glimpses over the Cosenza valley as it twists and grinds up the mountain through woods and over rivers.

The Sila

Covering the widest part of the Calabrian peninsula, the **Sila** massif is more of an exten-sive plateau than a mountain range, though the peaks on its western flank reach heights of nearly 2000m. It's divided into three main groups, the Sila Greca, Sila Grande and Sila Piccola, the last two of which are little more than an administrative division, while the former – although the least entrancing scenically – is distinguished by the Albanian villages from which it takes its name.

At one time the Sila was one huge forest and was exploited from earliest times to provide fuel and material for the construction of fleets, fortresses and even for church-building in Rome, resulting in a deforestation that helped bring about the malarial conditions that for centuries laid much of Calabria low. The cutting of trees is now strictly controlled, and since the regional government recognized the potential of the area and imposed restrictions on building and hunting, there is plenty here for the outdoors enthusiast, in summer as a relief from the heat of the towns or coasts and in winter for downhill or cross-country skiing. The other seasons have their own charms: spring, when the woods are a riot of wild flowers, and autumn, for the full gamut of decaying colour and – a local speciality – wild mushrooms.

The Sila Greca

Deforestation has had the most devastating effect on the **Sila Greca**, the most norther-ly part of the massif, leaving mainly cultivated rolling highlands in place of the dense woods. But the area is easily accessible from the Ionian coast or the *autostrada* inland, and if you have a car it's worth the detour to investigate some of the **Albanian villages** scattered around these hills. These mountain communities have their origin in the fif-teenth century, when colonies of Albanians in flight from Muslim invasions were allowed to settle in some of the poorest areas of the peninsula by Irene, princess of Bisignano and daughter of **Skanderbeg** – the Albanian warrior-king, whose fiery image adorns many a main square in these parts. The villages retain to this day the shabby, untended look of straitened circumstances, visually unexciting and with few buildings or treasures of great artistic merit. **SAN DEMETRIO CORONE** is the most interesting, containing an Italo-Albanian *Collegio* charged with the task of guarding what remains of the Albanian heritage. Annexed to this is the church of **Sant'Adriano**, a structure that still shows elements of its Byzantine and Norman origins, including some Norman paving depicting the various animals which roamed the woods that once covered these hills – lions, serpents and panthers. Really, though, it's the annual festi-vals that show these villages at their best, and you should try to make your visit coin-cide with one if you can. Along with the opportunity to see their elaborate costumes and hear some gutsy singing, it may be the only chance of hearing the authentic language – a fifteenth-century version of modern Albanian – which has only recently been replaced by *calabrese* dialect as the everyday language in these parts. Festivals take place in the villages of **Santa Sofia** (July 15 & 16), **San Cosmo** (September 26 & 27), **Vaccarizzo** (March 31–April 2), and **San Giorgio** (April 2).

The Sila Grande

Densely forested, and the highest, most extensive part of the Sila range, the **Sila Grande** has Calabria's main **ski slopes** as well as the region's three principal **lakes** – all artificial (for hydroelectric purposes) and much loved by fishing enthusiasts, who come out in force at weekends. The best base for day-trips is Cosenza, but if you want to spend any time up here it would be much better either to camp or lodge in a hotel; campsites enjoy good lakeside locations, but the hotels are mainly in the towns and vil-lages, and many close out of season (March–July, Oct & Nov).

The towns vary greatly. **SAN GIOVANNI IN FIORE**, in the heart of the Sila, is the area's biggest, but also the dreariest. For winter-sports enthusiasts and summer trekkers alike, **CAMIGLIATELLO** is the best-known of the resorts, a functional place that's well connected by bus with Cosenza, though it lacks any intrinsic charm. Centred on Via Roma, the town has three ski slopes of its own and another at Moccone (3km to the west) and a confusion of hotels, restaurants and souvenir shops; if you fancy **skiing**, the slopes have facilities for renting equipment (about L30,000/€15.50 per day) and offer tuition (group lessons are about L15,000/€7.75 per person per hour). The Sila terrain also makes ideal **riding** country, though most stables are open in summer only; one exception that's open all year is Maneggio Sila (☎0360.283.252), 3km from Camigliatello on the Cecita road. The numerous **hotels** in town can be expensive; for moderate rates in plain rooms try the *Miramonti* in Via Forgitelle (☎0984.579.067; ②) or the *Leonetti* at Via Roma 42 (☎0984.578.075; ②), or opt for more comfort at only slightly higher prices at the *Meranda* (☎0984.578.022; ③) just off Via Roma. For a **snack** in Camigliatello, *Lo Spuntino* on Via Repaci, off the other side of Via Roma, has excellent *panini* and other fast food, while Moccone has a good-value **trattoria**, the aptly named *Si Mangia Bene e Si Spende Poco* (closed Mon) which has a well-deserved reputation. Contact the **tourist office** at the top of Via Roma (erratic hours, officially Mon–Fri: summer 8.30am–1pm & 3.30–7pm; winter 9.30am–12.30pm & 4–6pm; ☎0984.578.243) for the latest information on accommodation, hiking and the state of the slopes: they can supply brochures and maps on **walking routes** in the area, though you can also pick up these from some of the bars scattered around the Sila. You need to understand Italian to read the route descriptions, and the map is not perfect, but it can be helpful as a broad guide to the relative lengths of the paths, and for switching from one to another.

From Camigliatello, you could hike for 15km – or take the bus – to **Lago Cecita**, the best starting-place for expeditions to **La Fossiata**, a conservation area that resembles a national park on the American model, with tidy wooden fences along the roads and numerous picnic spots. It is always possible to find your own space, but it's a good idea, too, to follow the planned routes set out by the *Corpo Forestale* – paths can run out on you when you least expect it. There's a **hotel** here, the *Cecita* (☎0983.579.074; ③), on the lakeside at Località San Giovanni Paliático. Owing to concerns about littering and the risk of fires, camping in the area is forbidden except in the **campsite** near the hotel – also called *Cecita* (☎0983.24.039). Elsewhere, there are a couple of sites 15km south on the banks of Lago Arvo (see below). If you choose to descend the steep slopes from La Fossiata to remote **LONGOBUCCO**, atmospherically enclosed at the bottom of a narrow valley, there's the useful *Hotel Stella* (☎0983.72.082; ②), offering simple accommodation and a restaurant – phone ahead.

Camigliatello is also a useful starting-point for a ramble that takes in the area's highest peaks, following the *strada delle vette* ("road of the peaks") for 13km through pine and beech woods before forking off and up to the three **peaks** of Monte Scuro, Monte Curcio and, highest of all, Monte Botte Donato (1928m). The trail, which is often snowbound between December and May, continues on down to **Lago Arvo** and the resort of Lorica, from which it is a shorter distance than following the *strada delle vette* to reach Botte Donato. Or you can save the sweat and take the chair lift from the località Cavaliere, just outside town. **LORICA**, like Camigliatello, is dedicated to tourism in the height of the winter and summer seasons, but its lakeside location makes it a more relaxed spot, with lots of places for picnicking under the pines and observing the antics of the black squirrels that inhabit them. The town is connected with Cosenza by **bus**, arriving in the morning and returning in the afternoon, and there is a **campsite** which also rents out bungalows, *Lago Arvo*, occupying a picturesque lakeside location just outside the town (☎0984.537.060). The only hotel currently functioning is the *Ruscello*, near the ski slope in località Cavaliere. Rates are low for most of the year, but half- or full-board is required in peak seasons (☎0984.537.274; ③).

The Sila Piccola

Bounded by Lago Ampollino in the north, Catanzaro and the Ionian coast in the south, the **Sila Piccola** is the region's most densely forested section, centring on the **Foresta** di **Gariglione** – much reduced from its extent a century ago but still impressively thick, with fir, beech and the gigantic turkey oak from which it derives its name. Its designation as national park protects it from further plundering, though it is not so well adapted for walking as La Fossiata. Apart from the odd resort, it's a sparsely populated area, and most of its villages are in any case unattractive.

More interesting than most is **BELCASTRO**, on the southern fringes of the range. Watched over by a Norman castle, it is claimed to be the birthplace of St Thomas Aquinas, whose family once held the town in fief. Further west, on the SS109, the mountain village of **TAVERNA** has long historical associations but is best-known today as the home of Calabria's foremost seventeenth-century painter, **Mattia Preti**, whose Spanish-looking works can be seen in four of the local churches, notably **San Domenico** – in which, in a corner of his portrait of St John the Baptist, is a self-portrait with the artist dressed as a Knight of Malta holding a paintbrush. Leaving the village it's 25km down a winding road to the regional capital of Catanzaro.

The southern Tyrrhenian coast

The province of Catanzaro begins at the Savuto River, and from here down to Reggio the SS18, *autostrada* and main rail line all run parallel along the coast, apart from the stretch of the Tropea promontory. Immediately after the river, a few kilometres inland from the resort of Lido di Falerna, the hill-village of **NOCERA TIRINESE** (buses run from the station on the coast) is famed for the flagellants who – literally – paint the streets red every Easter during a religious festival that grips the whole village with fervour. Wailing processions sway through the streets, and teams of two sprint between churches, one holding a cross, the other beating himself with a spiked brush; his freely flowing blood is then splashed over the doors of the houses to protect those within – not to be washed off until it happens naturally with the rain. One of the few examples of this kind of ritual bloodletting still to be found in the south, and not at all a mere tourist event, it's worth catching if you're around here at the right time.

Thirteen kilometres further down the coast, between Capo Súvero (marked by its lighthouse) and Lido di Gizzeria, is a fine **swimming spot**, a sandy spit with a freshwater lake close by, surrounded by palms and bamboo. The plain that stretches east from here, the **Piana di Sant'Eufemia**, is the narrowest part of the Calabrian peninsula, much of it reclaimed only in the last hundred years from malarial swamp: the mosquitoes remain but they no longer carry the disease. **LAMEZIA** has Calabria's main **airport** (most international flights are summer only), while **SANT'EUFEMIA-LAMEZIA** is the **rail and road junction** for Catanzaro and the Ionian coast. Heading south on the highway you begin a slow ascent on the long viaduct that is one of the engineering feats of the Autostrada del Sole, the views growing more inspiring as it rises above the coast to the high tableland of the Tropea promontory.

Pizzo

Following the railway or the SS18, you might want to spend some time in the picturesque little town of **PIZZO**, neatly placed for the **beaches** around Tropea and site of a small **castle** (daily: summer 9am–1pm & 5–10pm, winter 9am–1pm & 3–7pm; free) overlooking the sea just off the main Piazza della Repubblica. Built in 1486 by Ferdinand I of Aragon, it holds the room in which the French general **Murat** was imprisoned, with some of his personal effects and copies of the last letters he wrote, and the terrace where he was shot in October 1815. Murat, Napoleon's brother-in-law and one of his ablest generals, met his ignominious end here after attempting to rouse the people against the Bourbons to reclaim the throne of Naples given to him by

Napoleon; the people of Pizzo ignored his haughty entreaties, and he was arrested and court-martialled.

A couple of kilometres north of the centre, you might drop in on the **Chiesetta di Piedigrotta** (daily 9am–1pm & 3–7.30pm), a curious rock-hewn church by a sandy beach, signposted off the coastal SS22. Created in the seventeenth century by Neapolitan sailors rescued from a shipwreck, the church was later enlarged and its interior festooned with eccentric statuary depicting episodes from the Bible. Most of this was the work of a local father-and-son team, and it was augmented by another scion of the family in 1969, who restored the works and contributed some of his own, including a quirky scene showing Fidel Castro kneeling before Pope John XXIII and President Kennedy. You can see some of the inside through the windows if the church is closed.

Pizzo has a Pro Loco **tourist information** office which doubles as an insurance agency (or visa versa), located under the arches at the bottom of Piazza della Repubblica (Mon–Sat: summer 9am–1pm & 5–9pm; winter 9am–1pm; ☎0963.531.310). There's a comfortable **place to stay** in Pizzo, right on the main square, the *Hotel Murat*, with good views over the coast from some rooms (☎0963.534.201; ⑤); alternatively, there's the rather characterless *Sonia*, right by the Chiesetta di Piedigrotta on Via Prangi (☎0963.531.315; ②), which requires at least half-board in August. If you have transport, you might consider a first-rate agriturismo further north on the main road out of town (200m before the Agip station), *A Casa Janca* (☎0963.264364; ⑥), where full-board weighs in at an extra L150,000/€77.50 per person per night. Furnished in traditional rustic style, the place is locally renowned for its **restaurant**, where non-guests can also dine. Other places to eat in the centre of town include a good trattoria under the arcade in Piazza della Repubblica, *Il Porticato* (closed Wed), or walk down to the port area for a range of seafood restaurants, one of them, *La Nave* (closed Wed), in the form of a ship. Between April and July sample the **tuna** or **swordfish**, for which Pizzo is a fishing centre. Make sure you also sample the famous local **ice cream**, though you can also find *gelato di Pizzo* in bars and restaurants up and down the coast.

Vibo and the Tropea promontory

Pizzo is a starting-point for the coastal rail line that rings the **Tropea promontory**; trains run from a separate **station**, Pizzo Calabro, near the port (if you're coming from the north, you need to change at Lamezia). The first stop, **VIBO MARINA**, is the major port and industrial centre of this stretch of coast, with regular departures to the Aeolian Islands (see p.976) between June and September. Some 10km above the port and served by the mainline station of Pizzo-Vibo Valentia, the larger town of **VIBO VALENTIA** has a history that goes back to Greek times, when it was known as **Hipponion** (fragments of whose walls are still standing 2km north of town). Because of its strategic importance, Vibo has always held a prominent position in Calabria's history: under Murat it was a provincial capital with a flourishing cultural life, inhabited by grandees whose memory survives in the street names and in the many surviving palaces – mostly now in a state of decay. Vibo's restoration as a provincial capital may change the town's backwater feel, but in the meantime it's a place to stop at chiefly to view the impressive **Museo Archeologico**, housed in the Norman castle superbly sited at the top of the town (daily 9am–7pm; L4000/€2.07). The display, with labelling and explanations in Italian (but still comprehensible), includes Greek and Roman vases, figurines, *pinakes* (terracotta plaques) and military hardware from the sixth century BC on. The museum is brilliantly designed, incorporating the towers and stairs from the Norman construction, and you should leave time after seeing the interior for a walk round the lofty walls for the distant views out to sea and inland over the rolling countryside. Back in the town centre, there's an **information office** (Mon–Fri 7.30am–1.30pm, plus Mon & Wed 2–5pm; ☎0963.42.008) on Via Forgiari, off the main

Corso Vittorio Emanuele. Central **hotels** in town include the *Risorgimento* on Via Collelle (☎0963.41.125; ③) and the plainer *Miramonti* on Via Protetti (☎0963.41.053; ②), and there's a good **trattoria** round the corner from the *Risorgimento* at Via Francica 2, *Le Arcate* (closed Sun lunch).

West of Vibo the golden sands of the Tropea promontory stretch invitingly into the Tyrrhenian Sea – one of the least spoilt and most scenic parts of Calabria. Take your choice among the numerous **beaches** – mostly clean and sandy, though relatively crowded at the height of the season – and **campsites**, for example *Squalo 33* (☎0963.391.945) at picturesque **BRIÁTICO**; all sites around here are open summer only.

Twelve kilometres southwest along the coast from Briático, **TROPEA** can claim to be the prettiest town on the whole of the southern Tyrrhenian coast, and (after Maratea) the most fashionable, with a seaside charm missing from many of the other Calabrian resorts, and not yet entirely eroded by the annual influx of tourists. The buildings have character without being twee – see particularly the lovely Norman **Cathedral** at the bottom of Via Roma, whose interior harbours a couple of unexploded American bombs from the last war (one accompanied by a grateful prayer to the Madonna), a Renaissance ciborium and a statue of the Madonna and Child from the same period. The central apse also has a much-venerated fourteenth-century icon of the Virgin Maria of Romania. The views from the upper town over the sea and the church of **Santa Maria dell'Isola** on its rock are superb, and on a clear day you will see the cone of Strómboli and sometimes other Aeolian Islands looming out of the horizon. There are good beaches all around and, in season at least, plenty of **accommodation** – though it's wise to book all the same. Cheapest are the hotels *Vulcano* on Via Campo Sopra (☎0963.61.674; ②) and *Virgilio* in Viale Tondo (☎0963.61.978; ③), both of which oblige half- or full-board in high season. One that doesn't is the *Miramare* (☎0963.61.570; ④) on Via Libertà, the road heading south out of town, a fairly standard hotel with small rooms. As for **eating**, Tropea has more trattorias per square metre than any other town in Calabria, often with budget-priced tourist menus, though of varying standards. With outdoor seating in Largo Mercato, behind the central Piazza Ércole, *Tre Fontane* offers a good selection of dishes, while fish fans will appreciate the *Osteria del Pescatore*, a vaulted cellar around the corner from the cathedral in Via del Monte (closed in winter). For other evening entertainment, *Donegan*, the **pub** attached to the *Miramare* hotel, serves Guinness on tap as well as *panini* and other snacks, and hosts occasional live music. The Pro Loco **tourist office** is in Piazza Ércole (summer daily 9am–1pm & 4.30–9pm, July and Aug open till 10pm; winter Mon–Sat 9am–1pm & 4–8pm; ☎0963.61.475).

Further around the promontory, **CAPO VATICANO** holds some of the area's most popular beaches, including **Grotticelle**, which is spacious enough to get away from the bustle and has a **campsite** immediately above it, *Quattro Scogli*, where you can rent self-contained **apartments** for about L40,000/€20.67 a head in low season, rising to L60,000/€30.99 (☎0963.663.126; May–Oct). The nearest **hotel** to this beach, the *Grotticelle* (☎0963.663.157; ③), lies a few minutes' walk further up the road. The next beach up, a couple of kilometres further, **Tonicello**, also has a campsite, *Costa Verde*, with mini-apartments for rent, rising from L400,000/€206.70 weekly for two, to L1,150,000/€598.00 in high season (☎0963.663.090; May–Sept). **Information** can be had from a summer-only office in San Nicolo di Ricadi, three kilometres inland, at Via Vaisette 17, near the *Bar Shaker* (daily 9am–12.30pm & 5–8pm; ☎0963.663.119). To the south of Capo Vaticano, the road teeters high above the sea before reaching **NICÓTERA**, eleven kilometres down, built in its present position by Robert Guiscard. The Castello Ruffo here contains a small **archeological museum** of finds from the area and a collection of folkloric items (both free), but keeps very irregular hours: you're most likely to find someone to let you in during the mornings. There's also a

Cathedral, with work by Antonello Gagini, and far-reaching views south over the **Piana**, Calabria's second plain of any size, mostly dedicated to olive cultivation. Directly below the town, Nicótera's marina has wide beaches with a couple of summer-only **campsites** at their southern end.

Inland to the Serre

Inland of Vibo, 8km beyond the *autostrada* (and connected by frequent local buses), the village of **SORIANO** is dominated by the remains of the church and monastery of **San Domenico** – one of the largest and richest houses of the Dominican Order in Europe until it was wrecked by earthquakes in 1659 and 1783. The monastery produced four popes, two of whom can be seen on canvas in the modern adjoining church, along with a miraculous portrait of St Dominic said to be painted by no human hand. The majestic ruins still manage to render an idea of the size and wealth of the complex, which must have once striven to out-dazzle the nearby Carthusian monastery at Serra San Bruno (see below).

From Soriano, buses leave for the leafy uplands of the **Serre**, a little-known area that's well worth a visit for its lush green slopes and shady glens. In its thick beech and oak forest it's still possible to see black-faced *carbonari* making charcoal in the traditional way, cooking the wood in conical ovens resembling miniature smoking volcanoes. **SERRA SAN BRUNO**, a secluded village in the heart of the Serre, holds the area's only **hotel**, the *Certosa* (☎0963.715.538; ②), on Via Vittorio Emanuele. Most visitors come for the famous Carthusian abbey twenty minutes' walk south of town, the **Certosa di Santo Stefano del Bosco**. Built on land granted by the Norman Count Roger in 1090 to St Bruno, the founder of the strict Carthusian order who lent his name to the village, the abbey grew in wealth and influence, accumulating vast portions of land in Calabria and Sicily before being almost completely destroyed by a series of earthquakes in 1783. Rebuilt, it is still going strong, although much reduced from its former glory; one of the monks (now dead) was rumoured to have been one of the American airmen who flew on the atomic-bomb missions to Japan. Only men are allowed to visit the ruins of the old monastery inside (Mon–Sat 11am–noon & 4–5pm; ring the bell for entrance). There is also a small **museum** here that's open to everyone and holds relics of the abbey's illustrious past (April–Sept daily 9am–1pm & 3–8pm; Oct–March Tues–Sun 9.30am–1pm & 3–6pm; L3500/€1.81).

A couple of kilometres further down the road, the little basilica of **Santa Maria del Bosco** stands on the site of the first church founded here by St Bruno. You can see the cave where the saint is said to have prayed, and a pond with his statue kneeling in the middle. Legend has it that when the saint died in 1101 he was buried on this spot, the spring gushing forth when his bones were later dug up to be transferred to the abbey. The water is prized by devotees, who gather to bathe here on Whit Monday, when a statue of St Bruno is brought from the abbey. Beyond the church, 5km south, a left turn onto the SP110 brings you to a stunningly beautiful but very twisty road that climbs and dives on its way to the Ionian coast, taking in the village of Stilo (see p.953).

South to Reggio

Back on the Tyrrhenian coast, the Mesima river marks the border of the province of Reggio di Calabria. The towns around here are mostly new and unattractive, partly due to the fact that the area is one of the most seismically active in Italy – the epicentre of the notorious 1783 earthquake was at nearby Oppido. The small Tropea rail line connects with the main line at Rosarno, eighteen kilometres beyond which is **PALMI**. Situated a little way above the town (take Via San Giorgio, close to the exit onto the SS18), is the excellent **museum complex** in **La Casa della Cultura Leonida Repaci**

(Mon & Thurs 8am–2pm & 3–6pm, Tues, Wed & Fri 8am–2pm; L3000/€1.55), named after a local writer and artist. It incorporates an archeological section, holding pieces of pottery and various excavations from the sea bed; paintings including work by Tintoretto and Guercino; a gallery of modern art and sculpture, mainly by southern Italian artists such as Guttuso but also including works by Modigliani, De Chirico and Carlo Levi; a section devoted to local composer Francesco Cilea; and Calabria's best collection of folklore items.

From Palmi the tall TV mast on Sicily's northern tip is already visible, but the best view of Sicily and the Calabrian coast is some 5km down the road, at **Monte Sant'Elia**, the first elevation of the Aspromonte massif (see p.936). From this balcony, perched on cliffs that plunge vertically down to the sea, you can see the two volcanoes of Etna and Strómboli on a clear day; there is a **campsite** behind and a tourist village. The spot is believed to have been named after St Elia Speleotes, who lived in these parts (in a cave, which can be visited on the road leading into Aspromonte from Melicucca) and whose body, when he died aged 94, proved unburnable by the Saracens. Earlier, when his body was washed, the water was used for curing another holy man's toothache.

From here south, the proximity of Sicily becomes the dominant feature looking out to sea, and the stretch of the *autostrada* that dives down to Villa San Giovanni can claim to be one of the most panoramic in Italy, burrowing high up through mountains with the Straits of Messina glittering below. Travelling by train or following the old coastal road, you skirt the so-called Costa Viola, passing through **Bagnara**, famous for its swordfish, and **SCILLA**, ancient Scylla, with a fine sandy **beach** and lots of action in the summer. This was the location of a six-headed cave monster, one of two hazards to mariners mentioned in the **Odyssey**, the other being the whirlpool Charybdis, corresponding to the modern Cariddi located 6km away on the other side of the Strait. Crowning a hefty rock, a **castle** separates the fun and frolics on the main beach from the fishing village to the north. The only **place to stay** in town is the *Pensione Le Sirene* (booking advisable in summer, ☎0965.754.121; ②): try to get one of the four front rooms facing the sea – the others are just mediocre. There are several good fish **restaurants** along the seafront, including *U Bais* (closed Mon); on the piazza in the upper town, *Vertigine* has a terrace with tables for snacks or full meals overlooking the sea (Sept–June closed Mon).

From Scilla it's just 9km to **VILLA SAN GIOVANNI** (hourly buses), worth stopping at only as a point of embarkation for Sicily. The state-run FS **ferries** leave from directly behind the station about every thirty minutes and arrive at the train station in Messina (see p.982) in about forty minutes; if you're travelling by **car** it's more convenient to catch one of the private Caronte ferries (under the train tracks to the right of the station), which leave approximately every fifteen minutes and pull in closer to the entrance to the *autostrada*. Both companies charge around L2000/€1.03 for foot passengers and L33,000/€17.16 for cars. If you're heading for Reggio, take a train or one of the hourly Salzone **buses** from outside the station.

Reggio province

The southernmost province of Calabria – **Reggio** – is, in some ways, the apotheosis of all that makes the Italian south so distinctive. Encapsulating many of the problems to be found throughout the region, it is a place where hope has run out, stymied by the obstacles that stifle every initiative. Significantly, emigration from this part of Italy has long been the highest, and continues to be high, though with the narrowing of the international job market the number of escape routes is constantly diminishing. At the same time the land itself, once the heart and soul of the southern peasant culture and economy, is increasingly being abandoned in the face of low returns and high expectations

△ The Port   △ Autostrada

REGGIO DI CALABRIA

Museo Nazionale

VIALE AMENDOLA

PIAZZA NAVA

PIAZZA INDIPENDENZA

Train Station (Reggio Lido)

VIA TORRIONE

VIA D'ANNUNZIO

CORSO VITTORIO EMANUELE

CORSO GARIBALDI

VIA II SETTEMBRE

LUNGAMARE MATTEOTTI

VIA TRIPEPI

VIA TORRIONE

VIA POSSIDONEA

VIA GIULIA

VIA GIUDECCA

Straits

of

Messina

VIA OSANNA

VIA ASCHENEZ

VIA CATTÓLICA DEL GRECI

PIAZZA ITALIA

VIA FOTI

VIA FURNARI

CORSO VITTORIO EMANUELE

VIA CAMPANELLA

VIA VITRIOLI

CORSO GARIBALDI

Castello

VIA POSSIDONEA

Duomo

VIA CROCEFISSO

PIAZZA DUOMO

VIA XXI AGOSTO

VIA SAN FRANCESCO DI PAOLA

VIA SPANO

VILLA COMUNALE

Airport & SS 106 △

VIA BIXIO

VIA BATTISTI

ACCOMMODATION
Hotel Diana   1
Hotel Mundial   2

RESTAURANTS
Bonaccorso   B
Gnam Gnam   A

Train Station (Reggio Centrale)

PIAZZA GARIBALDI

0   100m

▽ 2

– no one expects to share in the get-rich-quick society by tilling fields. Misery and delinquency are more evident here than in other parts of the south, earthquakes more frequent, the landscape more extreme in all ways, with dilapidated villages lying stranded among mountains, which are themselves torn apart by wide *fiumare*, or riverbeds – empty or reduced to a trickle for nine-tenths of the year, but swelling with the melting of the winter snows to destructive torrents.

Reggio di Calabria

REGGIO DI CALABRIA, the provincial capital, was one of the first ancient Greek settlements on the Italian mainland, and today, with a population of over 180,000, is the town in the region that shows most evidence of urban decline – an untidy mix of heavy industry, slum housing, and pot-holed streets. Traces of elegance survive, not least in the superb seafront that faces Messina across the Straits, while its main street, Corso Garibaldi, stretching for two kilometres across the centre of town, has one of the most animated passeggiatas in Calabria. But the absence of any buildings of historical note testifies to the violence of the earthquakes that have repeatedly devastated the area, the most recent – and most destructive – of which flattened the city in 1908.

Much of Reggio's air of shabby neglect has its roots in deep-seated social problems, specifically the stranglehold that the Calabrian Mafia, or **'ndrangheta**, continues to have on the town. Locally this phenomenon is referred to as the *piovra*, or octopus, whose tentacles penetrate all aspects of the city's life (*tangente*, or protection money, is tacitly understood to be paid by all shopkeepers and business people in most parts of Reggio), while the town is periodically convulsed by bloody *faide* (feuds) between rival families over control of the drugs trade.

Closely linked to the *'ndrangheta*'s hold on the city is the high rate of unemployment in the province (20–30 percent), which has provoked a general attitude of scepticism and indifference towards any attempt to improve the situation. Occasional outbursts of media interest, or the election of reforming councils, rarely make a lot of difference: politicians of all persuasions are held to be intrinsically corrupt, and *clientelismo*, the complicated network of political favours and obligations, is – like the *'ndrangheta* itself – too entrenched.

Most visitors to Reggio, however, will see little of the seamier side of the political scene here, let alone Mafia violence. There are few, in any case, who choose to spend much time in the city, which is not exactly bulging with unmissable attractions. It does possess, however, the **Museo Nazionale** at the Lido end of Corso Garibaldi (daily except first and third Mon of the month 9am–7pm, May–Sept also open until 11pm on Sat; L8000/€4.13), which holds the most important collection of archeological finds in Calabria. Most of the items inside date from the Hellenic period, with examples from all the major Greek sites in Calabria, including the famous *pinakes* or carved tablets from the sanctuary of Persephone at Locri. The most renowned exhibits in the museum are the **Bronzi di Riace**: two bronze statues dragged out of the Ionian Sea in 1972 near the village of Riace. They are shapely examples of the highest period of Greek art (fifth century BC), attributed to Phidias or followers of his school, and especially prized because there are so few finds from this period in such a good state of repair. Around them are detailed explanations of the recovery and cleaning-up of the statues that preceded their tour around the country, when they caused a minor sensation. Now they seem almost forgotten in the well-lit basement they share with another prize exhibit – a philosopher's head from the fourth century BC. Upstairs, in contrast, you can see examples of Byzantine and Renaissance art, including work by Antonello da Messina.

Other sights in the city can be quickly encompassed. Off Corso Garibaldi, the **duomo**, rebuilt after the earthquake of 1908, resembles an ice cream confection and contains little of interest. The remains of the **castello aragonese** on Piazza Castello, make a pleasant backdrop for summer festivities. The **lungomare** seaside esplanade is mostly ruined by road and rail, but has some sections where there's more space and a view. As you gaze over the Straits of Messina, you probably won't catch sight of the semi-mythical phenomenon known as the **Fata Morgana**, which appears as a shimmering, magical city of turrets and towers – quite unlike the city of Messina. The legend is said to be connected with Arthurian myths brought south by the Normans, but some locals swear they have witnessed it, suggesting it may be a meteorological pheonomenon – best conditions are apparently an absolute stillness of the air and water.

Practicalities

If you're **arriving** by train, get off at **Reggio Lido** for the port or museum. Buses end up at the **Reggio Centrale** station, a kilometre or so down the long Corso Garibaldi. For getting around, make use of **city buses** for saving legwork from one end of town to the other; tickets cost L1000/€0.52 from kiosks and *tabacchi*. For information, there's a small **tourist office** inside the Centrale station (Mon–Sat 8am–8pm; ☎0965.27.120), and a larger one at Corso Garibaldi 329 (Mon–Sat 7.45am–1.45pm & 2–8pm; ☎0965.892.012).

The Centrale station area is also where you'll find Reggio's best-value **hotel**, the basic, but clean and modern, *Mundial* at Via Gaeta 9 (☎0965.332.255; ③). At the other end of the Corso, near the Lido station, the *Lido* at Via Tre Settembre has cheerful rooms (☎0965.25.001; ④), while the large and shabby *Diana* (☎0965.891.522; ③) at Via Vitrioli 12, mid-way along the Corso, should be a last resort. There are plenty of **eating** places around Corso Garibaldi, ranging from the pricey but rated *Bonaccorso* near the main train station at Via Bixio 5 (closed Fri), which offers a L35,000/€18.20 set-price menu, to the *paninoteca* and *spaghetteria Gnam Gnam* at Via Furnari 22 (closed Sun), a popular place with students and workers at lunchtime. There's a **pub** near the museum on the corner of Via d'Annunzio and Corso Vittorio Emanuele serving crepes, *panini* and other snacks, or you could venture out to the far more fashionable *Ritrovo Morabito*, a bar with tables selling ice cream and pastry on Via Vallone Petrara (from Piazza Nava, follow Viale Améndola for nine blocks, turning right onto Via Cardinale Portanova and right again onto Via Vallone Petrara). More centrally, the **bars** around Piazza Duomo have good – though pricey – snacks, while the best **gelateria** in town is *Césare*, a kiosk on Piazza Indipendenza. Off Via Améndola, Piazza del Pópolo has a daily morning fruit and veg **market** and occasional evening concerts in summer; other summer entertainments take place on Reggio's seafront, which is partly closed to traffic in August.

From Reggio's port you can reach Messina in fifteen minutes by *nave veloce*, or **fast ferry** (Mon–Sat 12 daily, Sun 6 daily; L5000/€2.58); by car you have to go from Villa San Giovanni (see p.933). There's also a regular **hydrofoil** service (summer 5 daily; winter 1 daily; L34,000/€17.68) to the Aeolian Islands (see p.976).

Aspromonte

Most visitors to Reggio province leave without having ventured into the great massif of **Aspromonte**, the last spur of the Apennines on the tip of Italy's boot, and displaying an even more pronounced dialogue between mountain scenery and seascape than elsewhere in Calabria. You can be on a beach and a ski slope within the same hour, passing from the brilliant, almost tropical vegetation of the coast to dense forests of beech and pine that rise to nearly 2000m. The physical aspect of the range varies enormously, depending on which side you enter from: coming up from the Tyrrhenian coast you pass through endless olive groves that are the thickest and tallest in the region, whereas on the Ionian side the mountains have the empty, arid look of desert peaks.

Santo Stefano

Access is easiest from the Tyrrhenian side, from Bagnara or Gállico, from which frequent buses leave for Delianuova or Gambarie. The most scenic route is the SS184 from Gállico, which winds through profusely terraced groves of vine and citrus to the village of **SANTO STEFANO**, famous as the birthplace and final resting-place of the last of the great brigands who roamed these parts, **Giuseppe Musolino** (1875–1956). Occupying a sort of Robin Hood role in the popular imagination, Musolino was a legend in his own lifetime, the last thirty years of which he spent in jail and, finally, a lunatic asylum – the penalty for having led the *Carabinieri* on a long and humiliating dance up and down the slopes of Aspromonte during his profitable career.

While he was alive, he was warmly regarded by all who might otherwise have paled at the mention of brigandage, and even now he is seen as a local hero – described even by a village policeman as *"una persona onestissima"*, the most honest of people. Musolino's victims were rich, or corrupt, or informers, and he was never known to refuse a plea for help from those in need. It is hard to know how much is myth, but the romantic aura that surrounds him is partly due to the fact that brigandage, with which the region was rife during the Bourbon period and for which the tormented mountainscape of Aspromonte provided a natural refuge, was also a political gesture of rebellion and little to do with the organized crime that has succeeded it. Just above the village, in the cemetery, you can see Musolino's grave, now renovated but until recently daubed with the signatures of people come to pay their respects.

Gambarie

GAMBARIE, a little further up amid thick woods, is a fully fledged holiday town, used as a skiing resort in the winter and a cooling-off place for overheated *reggini* (from Reggio) in the summer. There is a **ski slope** from the top of **Monte Scirocco** (1660m), connected by a sporadically working chair lift, and a small choice of **hotels**, including the surprisingly good-value *Grande Albergo Gambarie* in Piazzale Miramare (☎0965.743.012; ③). Ask here or at any of Gambarie's larger hotels about rental facilities for skiing equipment. When the mountain is not snowbound, Gambarie is also a good base for walks in the area: for Aspromonte's highest peak, **Montalto** (1955m), start down along the SS183 towards Melito, turning off left after three or four kilometres onto a broken road, after which it's another 16km to the top, marked by a bronze statue of Christ gazing steadily out over the Straits of Messina – a memorable view. If you still have any energy there is another track that descends steeply for another 10km to the *santuario* of **Madonna di Polsi**, inhabited only by the monks of the monastery there. A large **fair** takes place here every year on the first two days of September – an unashamedly pagan event that involves the slaughter and sale of large numbers of goats. The monastery can put you up, or else camp in the area.

Delianuova and the coastal route

Continuing on down along the SS183 will bring you eventually to the Ionian coast at Melito di Porto Salvo, a tortuous but highly scenic route with views over towards Sicily. Going up the same road from Gambarie (in the opposite direction) leads twenty-six kilometres along a plain and through more forest to **DELIANUOVA**, another resort, though not as busy as Gambarie, with a trattoria, a *birreria* and one **hotel**, the *Aspromonte 2001* (☎0966.963.012; ②). Another path from here leads up to Montalto (about a five-hour hike). Halfway between Gambarie and Delianuova, a turn-off on the right will take you to the **Cippo Garibaldi**, a modern monument in the woods commemorating the spot where the hero, having emerged from his retirement in the summer of 1862 with the intention of marching on Rome, was ignominiously captured by the troops of King Vittorio Emanuele II, in whose name he had raised the banner.

The **coastal route** along Italy's toe-tip also offers some interesting excursions into the mountainous inland Aspromonte, road and rail line running south out of Reggio through the series of small nondescript towns adorned by a profusion of cactus, agave, banana trees and date palms, and surrounded by the extensive plantations of citrus that are a feature of the Reggio area. Look out in particular for the bergamot, a fruit resembling a yellow orange whose essence is used as a base for expensive perfumes – one of the principal exports of this area and until recently, because of the precise conditions required for its cultivation, not found anywhere else in the world.

Campsites abound along this coast, attached to sandy beaches in varying states of cleanliness, and mostly open only in summer. Visible to the right, as you travel eastwards, is the inland village of **PENTEDÁTTILO**, which owes its name to the Greek word for "five-fingered", on account of the curiously shaped rock on which it stands. Norman Douglas likened it more to an upturned molar, and Edward Lear, travelling through the area in 1848, thought it "perfectly magical" – though its old Byzantine centre has largely been abandoned in favour of a new and ugly town just below.

You are now in the **Zona Grecánica**, named after the villages on these southern slopes of Aspromonte that were settled by Greeks some two thousand years ago and that still retain some traces of the Greek language in the local dialect. One such village is **BOVA**, perched on a crag 15km inland from its seaside satellite, Bova Marina. Bova is a remote place, with a view justifiably described by Lear as "truly magnificent", although the thick oak forests he saw then no longer exist. From the remains of the **castello** at the top, you can map out some alluring excursions into the wild country around: there are no hotels here but the countryside is one of the loveliest and most isolated parts of Aspromonte. Around the corner of the coast, another route into Aspromonte takes you by way of the village of **SAN LUCA**, known to *Calabresi* as the home of the writer **Corrado Alvaro**, whose novels (*Gente di Aspromonte* is one) describe the lives of the people living in these mountains. The region is also known for its reputation as a *'ndrangheta* stronghold: the triangle of land between the villages of San Luca, Plati and Cimina is a favourite area for holding kidnap victims, often for months at a time, and is periodically – usually following accusations of apathy on the part of the government – a target for army operations to root out the hiding places. From San Luca a road continues up, leading after 20km to the Santuario della Madonna di Polsi (see p.937) and from there to the peak of Montalto. The road is asphalted for only half the way and careers up some pretty hairy mountainsides, but is worth the sweat for the near-Himalayan landscape and the numerous possibilities for picnicking and walking. Local people will warn you against travelling alone in these parts, to which you should pay heed without necessarily following their advice.

Potenza and around

Basilicata's regional capital, **POTENZA**, has suffered more than most southern towns from the effects of earthquake and war, which have robbed it of much of its historical heritage. There is still considerable restoration work in progress, and despite the dust in summer continuing improvements have helped to make Potenza a lively, go-ahead place and an excellent base for visiting some of the smaller towns and villages of inland Basilicata, most of which are conveniently situated on the main routes to – or from – the outside world.

The Italian mainland's highest provincial capital, Potenza is built on a spur between two valleys, and presents an unpromising vista from afar, seemingly consisting of nothing but characterless modern blocks surrounded by unsightly and polluting industrial works. The town is also a trial for drivers, its confusing one-way streets clogged with traffic and almost devoid of parking spaces (make sure you're not parked illegally – tickets and fines are freely distributed). But perseverance pays off, for the animated centre, focused on the narrow, partly pedestrianized **Via Pretoria**, is a maze of alleys and small, sequestered squares, well stocked with bars and restaurants and at its best during the nightly passeggiata. The most important sight here, off the main **Piazza Prefettura** (also known as Piazza Pagano), is the church of **San Francesco,** which contains a Byzantine-style icon of the Madonna del Terremoto and an elaborate sixteenth-century tomb. In the modern districts spread out below, the only compelling attraction is the **Museo Archeologico Provinciale** (Mon, Wed & Sun 9am–1pm, Tues, Thurs & Sat 9am–1pm & 4–7pm; free) in Rione Santa Maria (north of the centre), home to the region's most important collection of finds from the prehistory of Lucania, and some good ceramics, terracottas and statuettes from Greek Metapontum.

Potenza has three **train stations**, all connected but not all serving the same routes. The central Potenza Città station has a line to Acerenza and Gravina in Puglia, and links with Potenza Inferiore, on the other side of town, which in turn has trains to Rionero, Melfi, Ferrandina (for Matera), Metaponto, Taranto, Fóggia and Salerno; Stazione Superiore in Rione Santa Maria is a stop on the line to Rionero, Melfi and Fóggia. The independent Ferrovie Appulo-Lucane (FAL) line links all three and also serves Bari and the Potenza area. **Drivers** would be well advised to park below the centre around Viale Marconi, from where escalators and lifts connect with Via del Pópolo, a few steps away from Piazza Prefettura. Most **buses** leaving for destinations within Basilicata leave from Piazza Crispi; buses for Salerno, Naples and Rome leave from Piazza Bologna. Frequent **city buses** connect the modern districts with Via Vaccaro and Corso Umberto in the city centre (tickets from *tabacchi* and bars; L1000/€0.52), as do several lifts (free) and rickety stairways. There is a **tourist office** at Via Alianelli 4, off Piazza Prefettura (Mon–Fri 9am–1pm & 4.30–7pm, Sat 9am–12.30pm; ☎0971.21.812).

Central **accommodation** includes the small and basic *Europa*, at the bottom of Via Pretoria (☎0971.34.014; ③), and the rather gloomy *Miramonti* at Via Caserma Lucania 30 (☎0971.22.987; ②), whose rooms are adequate though charmless. For a little more comfort, pay extra at the *Tourist*, Via Vescovado 4 (☎0971.25.955; ④), a big place with good facilities at the eastern end of Via Pretoria, below Piazza Bonaventura. If these are full, there's the very ordinary *Galgano* at Via Vaccaro 428 (☎0971.52.125; ②), a brief bus ride or a thirty-minute walk from the centre and difficult to find: it's signposted from a roundabout at the bottom of Via Vaccaro (from Potenza Inferiore station, turn left and keep walking for twenty minutes). When you want **to eat** you can do so well and cheaply in the brick-vaulted *Trattoria al Duomo* in Via Serrao (closed Sun), just around the corner from Potenza's cathedral (to the right of it), which serves excellent pasta dishes, including a delicious *orecchiette alla boscaiola* (pasta with a rich sauce of mushrooms and ham). Alternatively, the *Taverna Oraziana* on Via Flacco is a pleasant, casual place, occupying yet another cellar at the bottom of steps at the western end of Via Pretoria (closed Wed, and Sun evening). On the northern edge of the old town, the *Due Torri*, on the street of the same name, is a more upmarket place, though the prices are certainly reasonable (closed Sun). Potenza has a few good **pubs**: the *Barracuda*, in Via Caserma Lucania (closed daytime and Mon), near Piazza Matteotti, serving *panini* and other **snacks**, and *Goblin's*, right on the central Piazza Prefettura, which serves Irish draught beer and also makes a good breakfast stop for its *cornetti* and chocolate *faggotti*. Another good drinking-spot, popular with a younger crowd, is *Carpe Diem*, round the corner from the *Barracuda* at Via XX Settembre 27, enjoying a view over the valley. The management here also operates Potenza's main venue for **live music**, located in the suburbs; just check the posters or ask for details of what's on.

South of Potenza: Grumentum and Moliterno

To the south, just inside the border with Campania and close to a lake formed by the damming of the River Agri, lies ancient **GRUMENTUM**, one of the principal cities of Roman Lucania and the site of two victories over the Carthaginians, most memorably that of 207 BC when Hannibal lost 8000 of his men and four elephants. At two spots along a narrow country lane (well signposted) are the remains of a theatre, a basilica, baths and an amphitheatre, with fragmentary mosaics among the ruins of the houses, and there is a modern **museum** (daily 9am–7pm; free) showing finds over two floors, most notably a bust of Livia, wife of Emperor Augustus.

Following the destruction of the town by the Saracens between 872 and 975, many of Grumentum's inhabitants fled to the nearby town of **MOLITERNO**, a few kilometres up the road, later a Norman stronghold that guarded the western approaches into Basilicata. The birthplace of a clutch of local literati, it possesses the remains of the **Castle** and several mediocre churches.

North of Potenza

It's the region to the north of Potenza that is the most interesting historically, with several towns from the Norman era and some good examples of their brand of hybrid architecture. All are connected by bus with Potenza, and most are on the main Potenza–Fóggia rail line.

Acerenza

The venerable stronghold of **ACERENZA**, northeast of Potenza, is not so easy to reach by public transport, although it does have a station on the FAL line to Gravina, in Puglia, a few kilometres below the town itself, connected by a regular bus service to the top. It's worth the effort for the grand panorama and its famous **Cattedrale** (daily 9.30am–12.30pm & 4–7pm), from which it is thought the name of Basilicata derives (it was the bishop of this basilica who exercised jurisdiction over the territory around). Constructed in the eleventh century but rebuilt in its present Romanesque form in 1281, probably by French Angevin architects, the cathedral has a time-worn exterior, though the cupola at the top is a recent addition, following the earthquake of 1930. Inside, its crypt is a rare example of the impact of the Renaissance in Basilicata.

Castel Lagopésole and Monte Vulture

West of here, following the main road north out of Potenza towards Fóggia, the massive castle of **Castel Lagopésole** (daily: summer 9.30am–1pm & 4–7pm, winter 9.30am–1pm & 3–5pm; free) is visible long before you reach it, dominating the surrounding country and dwarfing the village at its base. This was the last and greatest of Frederick II's castles, and was said to be his favourite for the rich hunting grounds in the woods around (now farmland), though the building itself was still unfinished by the time of the emperor's death in 1250. You can visit the chapel and some of the royal apartments. Note the two sculpted heads on the outside of the keep, one representing Beatrice, Frederick Barbarossa's second wife, the other Barbarossa himself (Frederick II's grandfather), on whom you may just distinguish the ass's ears for which he was famous. If you need a **meal** around here, *Falcon's Castle* at the bottom of the hill should fit the bill.

North of the village, the truncated cone of **Monte Vulture** becomes increasingly evident – Italy's only volcano east of the Apennines and now a national park with a large range of fauna and flora. A road leads up through thick woodland to two lakes that occupy the former crater – **Lago Grande** and **Lago Piccolo** – separated by a thin strip of land entirely given over to bars, pizzerias and souvenir shops, the area being a favourite for weekend trippers from Naples and Fóggia. Though signs exhort visitors to be tidy, the litter and clutter conspire to ruin what is a genuine beauty spot. If you want to stay over, you can choose from several **hotels** and two **campsites**, one right on the shore of the Lago Piccolo.

Melfi

From the lakes a road runs down to the historic town of **MELFI**, long a centre of strategic importance, taken by the Normans in 1041 and their first capital in the south of Italy. It was in the formidable **Castle** at the top of the town that Pope Nicholas II formally recognized the conquests of Robert Guiscard over the Byzantines and Saracens, thereby legitimizing the piratical Normans and confirming their place in the embattled history of the south. It was here also that Guiscard imprisoned his first wife Alberada, and from where, in 1231, Frederick II issued his *Constitutiones Augustales*, reckoned to be the most comprehensive body of legislation promulgated since the time of Charlemagne. Repeatedly damaged by earthquakes, the castle now contains a **museum** (Mon 2–8pm, Tues–Sun 9am–8pm, L5000/€2.58) housing prehistoric finds and objects from the Greek, Roman and Byzantine eras, including ceramics, jewellery and a candelabra carved with the goddess Ea abducting the manly looking infant Kephalos. A separate door from the courtyard gives access to the museum's most celebrated item, an exquisitely carved Roman sarcophagus from the second century, the so-called *sarcofago di Rapolla*, showing the image of the dead girl for whom it was made, reclining on cushions, with five statuettes of gods and heroes on the sides.

In the centre of town off Via Vittorio Emanuele, is the **Duomo**, originally twelfth-century but rebuilt following earthquakes. After the 1930 quake, a Byzantine-style Madonna and Child fresco was brought to light, which you can see to the left of the altar; a chapel on the right also has a Madonna, in her role as protectress of the city – a copy of the original statue stolen from here in 1982. The cathedral's campanile has miraculously survived the various cataclysms: the two black stone griffins symbolized the Norman hegemony in the South and are visible everywhere in Melfi, having been adopted as the town's emblem.

Melfi has a decent, very cheap **hotel**, the *Savoia* at Viale Savoia 21 (☎0972.23.710; ①), though it's rather difficult to find: behind the cathedral turn right at Piazza IV Novembre, then left at Via Camassa, then left again onto Viale Savoia. You'll find a pleasant **restaurant/pizzeria** a little way down from the cathedral at Via Vittorio Emanuele 29, the *Delle Rose* (closed Mon), with outdoor seating in summer.

Venosa

If Melfi preserves the appearance of a dark medieval town, **VENOSA** has an attractive airiness, a harmonious place, rich with historical associations. Known in antiquity as Venusia, it was in its time the largest colony in the Roman world, and much is made of the fact that it was the birthplace of Quintus Horatius Flaccus, known to Italians as Orazio and to the English as **Horace** (65–68 BC); his supposed house lies past the cathedral on the right. Venosa's web of narrow streets is full of reminders of the town's long past. The tomb of the Roman general Marcellus, ambushed and killed by Hannibal here in 208 BC, is off Via Melfi, while a medieval washing-place lies near the duomo on the old town's long main street, Corso Vittorio Emanuele. At the top of this street, a formidable Aragonese **Castello** dominates the spacious and arcaded Piazza Umberto, and houses a well-presented **archeological museum** (daily 9am–8pm, sometimes open until 11pm on Sat; L5000/€2.58), displaying finds from local excavations, mainly coins, frescoes, fragments of mosaics and older prehistoric remains from the Vulture area. Many of the Roman exhibits here were unearthed in Venosa's **archeological park**, a twenty-minute walk away at the far end of the *corso* (daily: March 9am–6pm; April–Sept 9am–7pm; Oct & Feb 9am–5.30pm; Nov & Jan 9am–5pm; Dec 9am–4.30pm; free). Here you can see the sketchy remains of Roman baths and houses as well as a paleo-Christian baptistry, while across the road lies an amphitheatre (for which you must ask at the ticket-office for entry), and there are Jewish catacombs further along the road.

The excavations are overlooked by Venosa's most striking attraction, the **Abbazia della Trinità** (daily 8am–1pm & 3–5.30pm), a complex of churches begun in the mid-eleventh century that was the resting place of a number of Norman bigwigs, including Robert Guiscard. The first and greatest of the Norman adventurers in southern Italy, he's thought to be buried along with three of his brothers in a single uninscribed tomb on the right of the nave, while his divorced first wife Alberada occupies a slightly nobler tomb on the opposite side. The church also displays murals and mosaics, including a good fresco of the Byzantine St Apollonia hidden in the recess of an arch in front of Guiscard's supposed tomb; more frescoes showing Christian imagery can be seen in the crypt. Backing on to the older church, the Chiesa Nuova was begun in around 1100, a gigantic construction that was too ambitious to be properly finished – only the lower part of the walls and the apse were completed, incorporating fragments from the Roman ruins.

Venosa has an excellent **place to stay**, the *Orazio*, a beautifully restored old house at Corso Vittorio Emanuele 142 (☎0972.31.135; ③); it's well worth telephoning ahead to guarantee a room. If it's full, you'll have to make do with the *Villa del Sorriso*, a modern place a couple of kilometres west of the centre at Via Appia 135 (☎0972.35.975; ②). As for **restaurants**, your best bet is *Il Grifo*, behind the church of San Filippo Neri across from the castle, where you can enjoy such dishes as *pastoni all' erbe* – ravioli with spinach and ricotta smothered in fresh herbs (closed Tues).

Matera and around

The interior of the **province of Matera** has a great deal in common with Potenza province – a wide, empty terrain, much of it given over to agriculture and pasture, much of it good for nothing in particular. Run-down, depopulated, its bare clay hills appear, in Carlo Levi's words, "a sea of white, monotonous and treeless", dotted with solitary villages that are cut off from each other and the rest of the world. Little to recommend for an action-packed tour, then, but plenty of the timeless atmosphere portrayed by filmmakers like Rosi and Bertolucci.

Matera

The town of **MATERA** itself is unique, with a degree of culture and elegance unusual by southern standards and, in its **sassi** – dwellings dug out of the ravine in tiers – one of the country's oddest urban features. The *sassi* are mainly abandoned now, an eerie troglodyte enclave occupying the lower regions of the city. But until thirty years ago this part of the city was still populated by the poorest of the *materani*.

During the 1950s and 1960s, fifteen thousand people were forcibly removed from the *sassi* and rehoused in modern districts on the outskirts of town. Since then the area has been officially cleaned up and is being gradually repopulated, and in 1993 was made a World Heritage Site. Nowadays it's hard to picture the squalor that previously existed here, as described by Levi's sister, in *Christ Stopped at Eboli*, who compared the *sassi* to Dante's *Inferno*, so horrified was she by their disease-ridden inhabitants. "Never before have I seen such a spectacle of misery," she said. The children had "the wrinkled faces of old men, emaciated by hunger, with hair crawling with lice and encrusted with scabs. Most of them had swollen bellies and faces yellowed and stricken with malaria." Pursuing her, they begged not for coins but for quinine.

The Town

Divided into two sections – the Sasso Caveoso and Sasso Barisano – the *sassi* district can be entered from a number of different points around the centre of town, some signposted, some not. The **Strada Panoramica dei Sassi**, newly built with an eye to tourism, weaves through both zones and is a useful reference point, but you need to leave this to penetrate the warren and its *chiese rupestri* or **rock-hewn churches**. One, **Santa Maria de Idris**, perched on the conical Monte Errone that rises in the midst of the *sassi*, has frescoes dating from the fourteenth century. Another, the tenth-century **Santa Lucia alle Malve** in the so-called Albanian quarter (settled by refugees in the fifteenth century), has Byzantine-style frescoes dating from 1250. Other churches have a more orthodox appearance but are worth a visit; **San Pietro Caveoso**, for example, at the centre of the Caveoso district (Santa Lucia alle Malve lies behind it), is rather over-zealously restored and has a wooden ceiling and frescoes. If you want to explore the **caves** and more *chiese rupestri* on the far side of the ravine, you can cross the river further up towards the Sasso Barisano, though you'd do well to take a supply of drinking water – the excursion is further than it looks – up to an hour if you don't stray off the track. To get the most out of the whole area equip yourself with an *itinerario turistico* and a map, both available from the tourist office (see overleaf). Better still, for a commentary and access to parts of the *sassi* you might otherwise miss on your own, you can join a guided **tour**; the Nuovi Amici dei Sassi, at Piazza Sedile 20 (☎0835.331.011), or Tour Service Matera, at Piazza Vittorio Veneto 42 (☎0835.334.633), charge around L15,000/€7.80 per person for groups of four or more; or negotiate with one of the freelancers on the spot, who ask around L15,000–30,000/€7.80–15.60 according to the length of the tour and the size of your party.

The more animated face of the old town has its centre at **Piazza Vittorio Veneto**, a large and stately square which in the evening is cleared of traffic and given over to a long procession of shuffling promenaders. The *materani* take their evening passeggiata seriously, and the din of the crowds rising up out of this square can be like the noise from a stadium. Matera's modern quarters stretch out to the north and west of here, but most of the things worth seeing are along the Via San Biagio and Via del Corso.

Winding off from the bottom end of the piazza, the narrow Via del Corso leads down to the seventeenth-century church of **San Francesco d'Assisi**, whose ornate Baroque style was superimposed on two older churches, traces of which, including some eleventh-century frescoes, can be visited through a passage in the third chapel on the left. In the main church are eight panels of a polyptych by Bartolomeo Vivarini, set above the altar. Behind San Francesco, on Piazza Sedile, the imposing structure on the right was formerly a convent, then the town hall, and is now a conservatory dedicated to the eighteenth-century composer Egidio Duni, a native of Matera who settled in Paris, where he was largely responsible for popularizing Neapolitan comic opera among the pre-revolutionary aristocracy. Via Duomo leads off to the right, a good place to view the sprawling *sassi* below. The **Duomo**, which effectively divides this area into two, was built in the late thirteenth century and retains a strong Apulian-Romanesque flavour. Between the figures of Peter and Paul on the facade is a sculpture of the patron of Matera, Madonna della Bruna. Her feast day, the Sagra di Santa Bruna, is celebrated on July 2, when her statue is carried in procession three times round the piazza before being stormed by the onlookers, who are allowed to break up the papier-mâché float and carry off bits as mementos. At the back of the building you can see a recently recovered fresco from about 1270 showing scenes from the Last Judgement.

From Piazza San Francesco, continue down into Via Rídola to admire the elliptical facade of the **Chiesa del Purgatorio**, gruesomely decorated with skulls. A little further on is the essential **Museo Rídola** (Mon 2–8pm, Tues–Sun 9am–8pm, also summer Wed & Sat until 11pm; L5000/€2.58), housed in the ex-monastery of Santa Chiara and containing an extensive selection of prehistoric and classical finds from the Matera area, including Bronze Age weaponry and beautifully decorated Greek plates and amphorae. A few metres on, at the end of Piazzetta Pascoli, the Palazzo Lanfranchi holds a **Pinacoteca** with an assortment of seventeenth- and eighteenth-century paintings, but the real draw here is the **Centro Carlo Levi** (free), containing a good cross-section of Levi's vivid canvases, as well as the long mural, *Lucania* 1961; annoyingly, the palazzo is currently only sporadically visitable, though this should change once restoration work is complete. – check first at the tourist office (see below)

Practicalities

Matera's **train station** is on Piazza Matteotti and is served by the FAL line, linked to Altamura (in Puglia, for connections to Bari and Gravina) and to Ferrandina (for connections to Metaponto or Potenza); **buses** also stop here. Trailing down from Piazza Matteotti, Via Roma has the town's **tourist office** – actually just off it at Via de Viti de Marco 9 (Mon & Thurs 9am–1.30pm & 4–6.30pm, Tues, Wed, Fri & Sat 9am–1.30pm; ☎0835.331.983). Via del Corso, leading off the main Piazza Veneto (at the bottom of Via Roma), has the **telephone** office and the **main post office**.

If you're flush, Matera's best **hotel** is the *Sassi*, right in the heart of the Sasso Barisano district and not far from the duomo at Via San Giovanni Vecchio 89 (☎0835.331.009; ④), its rooms gouged out of the tufa and affording marvellous views. Other choices in town include the *Píccolo*, a smart, modern place at Via de Sariis 11 (☎0835.330.201; ④) and the elegant but pricey *Albergo Italia,* in Via Rídola (☎0835.333.561; ⑤), while the only budget hotel is the very plain *Albergo Roma*, at Via Roma 62 (☎0835.333.912; ②). There is, however, an unofficial **youth hostel** in two converted guest rooms in the *Sassi Hotel* (see above), well-sited and with dormitory beds going for L30,000/€15.60 per night: apply at the hotel.

There is more choice and better value among Matera's **restaurants**. The *Trattoria Lucana* is a good family-run place at Via Lucana 48 (closed Sun & 2 weeks in Sept), or enjoy the view over the *sassi* at the atmospheric *Il Terrazzino*, Via San Giuseppe 7 (closed Tues evening). There is a pizzeria in Piazza Sedile, and a much rowdier affair, *La Panca*, a bit further out from the centre in Via Giolitti (closed Mon), ten minutes' walk from Piazza Vittorio Veneto up Via XX Settembre and Via Annunziatella. There's also a pizzeria, *Il Castello*, at the Angevin castle above Via Lucana, with outdoor seating in summer (Oct–May closed Wed). *Hemingway*, in Via Rídola (closed Mon in winter) is an elegant bar/pasticceria with tables in the square, while in Sasso Barisiano, the *Caffè del Cavaliere* in Piazza San Pietro Barisano (closed Mon) – the more populous end of the ravine dwellings – is an evocative place for a coffee or late-night drink.

Around Matera

Twenty kilometres south of Matera and connected by rail, the hilltop town of **MONTESCAGLIOSO** was once a Greek settlement and is now the site of a magnificent ruined eleventh-century Benedictine abbey, the **Abbazia di Sant'Angelo**. There are good views from here over the Bradano Valley. On the same line, but more conveniently reached by bus (the train station is 10km below the town), is the lively medieval town of **MIGLIÓNICO**, with a finely preserved fifteenth-century bastion at one end, with views all around. It was here in 1481 that the *congiura dei baroni* was held, a meeting of rebellious barons who formed a league in opposition to Ferdinand II of Aragon, from which the castle assumed the name *Castello del Malconsiglio*.

The SS7, which heads west from here, is the Roman Via Appia, and is a far preferable route to the SS407 (Basentana) that runs parallel. Buses only touch on it intermittently, so it's best covered with your own transport. Tracing the ridge between the Bradano and Basento valleys, it takes in some magnificent country and a number of good stopoffs. **TRICÁRICO** is another old hilltop village, quite important in its time, with a **Duomo** originally constructed by Robert Guiscard. Further south, **ALIANO** is the village in which Carlo Levi set *Christ Stopped at Eboli*. Called Gagliano by Levi, it's reachable by bus from **Pisticci**, on the Matera train line. Apart from the yellow "welcome" sign on the outskirts of the village and a general air of well-being, the place has not significantly changed since he was there. Nothing is missing: the church, the piazza where the Fascist mayor gave his regular addresses to the impassive peasants and which gives onto the steep drop of the *fossa del bersagliere* and a striking view over the Agri and the "endless sweep of clay, with the white dots of villages, stretching out as far as the invisible sea" that Levi knew so well. You can see the rather grand house where he stayed at the bottom of the village ("away from the gaze of the mayor and his acolytes"), near which is a **museum** (free) housing some personal items of Levi's and articles of folkloric interest; to visit, telephone ☎0835.568.074 or 0360.506548, or call at the *Bar Centrale* on the main street – where, incidentally, there is also a basic **restaurant.**

The northern Ionian coast

From Táranto, in Puglia (see p.901) to Reggio, at Italy's toe-tip (see p.933), the **Ionian coast** is a mainly flat sandy strip, sometimes monotonous but less developed than the Tyrrhenian side of the peninsula, and with cleaner water. The **northern** section, from **Metaponto** to **Capo Colonna**, consists of a mountainous interior backing onto an empty seaboard, punctuated only by holiday resorts, a plethora of campsites – overflowing, in the summer months, with legions of Italians – and some notable historical sites. Of these, the most significant are connected with the periods of Greek occupation, the most recent of which was that of the Byzantines, who administered the area on and off for 500 years, leaving their traces most strikingly in the hilltop town of **Rossano**. A thousand years earlier, the clutch of Greek colonies collectively known as Magna Graecia rose and fell, of which Metapontion, Sybaris and Kroton, all on this stretch of the Ionian coast, were some of the greatest. Although only the first of these has been properly excavated, there are museums in all, describing an era that was – culturally and intellectually – the brightest moment in the history of Basilicata and Calabria. All the coastal towns are well connected by rail and bus, while places inland are linked by local buses from the coast. The SS106 road, which skirts this coastline, is mostly straight and fast.

The Basilicata coast

The most extensively excavated of the Greek sites, and the only place of any real significance on the Ionian coast of Basilicata, is at **METAPONTO**, an important road and rail junction connecting the coastal routes between Táranto and Reggio with the interior of Basilicata – to Potenza by train and Matera by bus. Metapontion was settled in the eighth century BC and owed its subsequent prosperity to the fertility of the surrounding land – perfect for cereal production (symbolized by the ear of corn stamped on its coinage) and its position as a commercial centre. Pythagoras, banished from Kroton, established a school here in about 510 BC that contributed to an enduring philosophical tradition. The city's downfall came as a result of a series of catastrophes: absorbed by Rome, embroiled in the Punic Wars, sacked by the slave-rebel Spartacus, and later desolated by a combination of malaria and Saracen raids.

Lido di Metaponto and the Zona Archeologica

Metaponto today is a straggling, amorphous place, comprising train station, museum and ruins. Arriving at the station, you're 3km from the **LIDO DI METAPONTO**, where there are sandy, well-equipped **beaches**, numerous **campsites** and a handful of hotels. Two of the campsites – the *Lido* (☎0835.741.884) and *Magna Grecia* (☎0835.741.855) – also have bungalows available (both ③); all have their own beaches and the bigger ones have tennis, discos and other facilities. For moderately priced **hotels**, try the well-equipped *Kennedy*, at Via Jonio 1 (☎0835.741.960; ②), or the drably old-fashioned *Sacco Dipendenza*, in Via Olimpia (☎0835.741.930; ③; June–Sept); both are about 1km from the station, off the Lido road.

For the first batch of ruins, take the next turning on the right after the Lido junction (coming from the station) and follow the narrow lane down to the wide site – signposted **Zona Archeologica** – which has the remains of a theatre and a Temple of Apollo Licius. The latter is a sixth-century BC construction that once possessed 32 columns, but you need some imagination to picture its original appearance. In a better state of preservation is the **Temple of Hera**, or Tavole Palatine, 2–3km north, where the main SS106 crosses the Bradano (take one of the buses to Táranto from Metaponto station). With fifteen of its columns remaining, it is the most suggestive remnant of this once mighty state. A selection of other survivals can be seen at the **Museo Archeologico Nazionale** (Mon 2–8pm, Tues–Sun 9am–8pm; L5000/€2.58), opposite the sanctuary of Apollo Licio, about a kilometre outside Metaponto town (and well signposted). The exhibits are mainly fourth- and fifth-century statuary, ceramics and jewellery, though administrative and financial problems have meant that only a small fraction of the finds are displayed, and work on a new wing has stopped indefinitely. Nonetheless, there is a fascinating section on the new insights revealed by the study of fingerprints on shards found in the artisans' quarter, and look out too for examples of the famous coins.

Policoro

There's a similar collection of antiquities at the **Museo Nazionale della Siritide**, 25km down the coast, just behind the village of **POLICORO**. The museum (daily 9am–6pm; L5000/€2.58) contains clay figurines and jewel-bedecked skeletons among other material taken from the zone between the Sinni and Agri rivers, in its time one of the richest areas on this coast and site of the two Greek colonies of **Siris** and **Heraclea**. The first of these, after which the museum is named, reached such a position of wealth and eminence that the other colonies were persuaded to gang together in the middle of the sixth century BC to put an end to Sirian ambitions. Heraclea was founded on the same spot by Tarentines in 432 BC with the aim of driving a wedge between the Achaean cities of Metapontion and Sybaris to the north and south. It was here that Pyrrhus, king of Epirus, first introduced elephants to the Romans, and although winning the first of two battles in 280 BC, suffered such high losses that he declared another such victory would cost him the war – so bequeathing to posterity the term "Pyrrhic victory".

Into Calabria: Síbari and Rossano

Shortly after crossing the Sinni River you enter Calabria, skirting the base of the lofty Monte Pollino. Inland, look out for the **Castle** at **ROCCA IMPERIALE**, built by Frederick II in the style of Lagopésole and Lucera. Imposing from a distance, its state of abandon becomes more obvious as you approach, but the views from its crumbling walls are impressive. Further inland, at the medieval village of **ORIOLO**, there's another **Castle**, this one from the fifteenth century and in a better state of preservation, from which you can continue inland into Basilicata and the woods around **Senise**, or loop back to the coast at **ROSETO**, the site of another of Frederick II's castles, prominent at the side of the road. In Norman times this spot marked the boundary between the territories controlled by Robert Guiscard and his brother Roger.

Síbari

The mountainous slopes soon give way to the wide **Piana di Síbari**, the most extensive of the Calabrian coastal plains, bounded by Pollino to the north, the Sila Greca to the west and the Sila Grande in the south. The rivers flowing off these mountains, which for centuries kept the land well watered and rich, also helped to transform it into a stagnant and malarial mire, and although land reclamation has restored the area's fertility, without visiting the museum and excavations at **Síbari** you could pass through the area with no inkling of the civilization that once flourished on these shores.

Long one of the great archeological mysteries tantalizing generations of scholars, the site of ancient Sybaris was only definitely identified in the late 1960s, when aerial and X-ray photography confirmed that the site previously known to be that of Roman Thurium was also that of Sybaris. There are in fact three separate levels of construction that have been unearthed here, one Greek and two Roman, one on top of the other. Together these make up one of the world's largest archeological sites, covering 1000 hectares (compared to Pompeii's 50), though only 10 hectares have so far been dug up, and the great riches that the excavations were expected to yield have not yet come to light; there have been too many other settlements on this same spot, not to mention the marauders who regularly passed through the area.

The wealth of the city – said to number 100,000 in population and have dominion over half a million – was only one factor in its fame, around which myth and documentary evidence have combined to produce a colourful muddle of anecdotes. The city's laws and institutions were apparently made to ensure the greatest comfort and well-being of its citizens, including the banning from the city of all noisy traders, such as metalworkers, and the planting of trees along every street for shade. Cooks were so highly prized that they were apparently bought and sold in the marketplace for great sums and were allowed to patent their recipes, while inventions ascribed to the Sybarites include pasta and the chamberpot. This was all too much for the Crotonians, who, under their general Milo (more famous as a much-garlanded Olympic athlete) sacked and destroyed the city in 510 BC, diverting the waters of the river over the site to complete the job.

The **excavations** lie across the rail lines some 4km south down the SS106, on the right-hand side (daily 9am–1hr before sunset; free). Most of the excavations belong to the Roman period, but something of the earlier site might still be turned up – the silt and sand of the river bed has yet to be explored properly, work having been effectively halted for much of the last twenty years due to shortage of funds. Of the Roman city, the remains are at least impressively displayed and maintained, including baths, a patrician's house with mosaics, and a decumanus (claimed to be the widest in existence). Just off the site, a small room contains individual finds including some Greek exhibits, mainly ceramic shards, though nothing that would have raised much excitement in the numerous enthusiasts who long sought this spot. There's more to be seen, from here and other local sites, at the **Museo della Sibarite** (daily 9am–7.30pm; L4000/€2.07), located down a left-turn about a kilometre before the excavations, on the banks of the River Crati.

Monastery of Pathirion and Rossano

There are remnants from more recent times further south, near the village of **SANTA MARIA DEL PATIRE**, where the **Monastery of Pathirion** sits among groves of olive and holm-oak at the end of a road built by Austrian prisoners during World War I. Its well-preserved church – a simple basilica – has sweeping views over the Sibari plain and the mountains around, but is the only intact relic of the monastery, which lies in ruins below – an extensive complex that had its centre at nearby Rossano and rivalled the holy mountain of Athos in Greece as a centre of monastic learning.

Twelve kilometres away, the resort of **ROSSANO SCALO** has far outstripped its parent-town of **ROSSANO** in terms of size and bustle, and most of the holiday-makers who frequent its beaches never even get round to visiting the hilltop town, 7km up an awkward winding road – something that has helped to preserve the old centre from excessive development. The foremost Byzantine centre in the south, Rossano was the focus of a veritable renaissance of literature, theology and art between the eighth and eleventh centuries, a period to which the town's greatest treasures belong. Its majolica-tiled **Cattedrale** is an Angevin construction largely rebuilt after the 1836 earthquake but has a much-venerated ninth-century Byzantine fresco, *Madonna Achiropita*, whose Greek epithet, meaning "not painted by hand", refers to its divine authorship. The over-decorated interior boasts a wooden ceiling and a mosaic floor near the altar, though most of the artworks here suffer from neglect. Next to the cathedral, the **Museo Diocesano** (July to mid-Sept daily 9am–1pm & 4.30–8.30pm; mid-Sept to June Tues–Sat 9.30am–12.30pm & 4–7pm, Sun 10am–noon & 4.30–6.30pm; L4000/€2.07) contains the famed *codex purpureus Rossanensis*, or Purple Codex, a unique sixth-century manuscript on reddish-purple parchment illustrating the life of Christ. The book, which was brought from Palestine by monks fleeing the Muslim invasions, is open at one page, but you can leaf through a good copy and see, among other things, how the Last Supper was originally depicted, with Christ and his disciples not seated but reclining on cushions round the table, and all eating from the same plate. Other items in this tiny museum include a fifteenth-century icon painted on both sides and formerly at Pathirion, and several pieces of silverware of superb artistry. In contrast to the duomo's grandiosity, the diminutive church of **San Marco**, at the end of Corso Garibaldi on the edge of town, retains a primitive spirituality. The five cupolas of the tenth- or eleventh-century construction, surrounded by palms on a terrace that looks out over the gorge below, impart an almost Middle Eastern flavour; to see the stark white interior, enlivened only by six frail columns and a poorly maintained fresco, ask at the Cooperativa Neilos at their office at Piazza Duomo 25 (☎0983.525.263). They are also equipped to supply **information** on the area.

Hotels are few and far between, all in the lower town, and they aren't cheap. Try the *Murano*, right by the sea on Lido Sant'Angelo (☎0983.511.788; ③), or, 50m up from the level crossing, the *Scigliano* (☎0983.511.846; ⑤), though if you have transport you'll find a better deal at the *President* (☎0983.511.375; ④), a couple of kilometres north up the SS106. All are rather characterless modern places but prices should include breakfast. Alternatively, a kilometre north from Rossano Scalo on the seafront road, you'll find chalets for rent at the local **campsite**, *Torino* (☎0983.512.394). Back in the old town, the best **trattoria** lies just off Piazza Anargiri, *La Villa*, in Via San Bartolomeo, with alfresco eating in summer (closed lunchtimes & Tues); there's another, more casual evenings-only place, *La Bizantina*, right outside San Marco, or try *Le Arcate* near the cathedral. All of these places also serve pizzas.

Crotone and around

South of Rossano there is an empty stretch of beaches; inland are the vineyards of Cirò, the source of Calabria's best-known **wine**. Crossing the River Neto into the fertile **Marchesato** region, the approach to **Crotone** (the ancient Greek city of Kroton) is blighted by a smoky industrial zone – not the most alluring entry into a city but a rare thing in Calabria, and a reminder of the false hopes once vested in the industrialization of the region.

Crotone

The site of ancient Kroton has been entirely lost, but in its day this was among the most important colonial settlements of Magna Graecia, overshadowed by its more powerful neighbour Sybaris but with a school of medicine that was famous throughout the classical world and closely linked with the prowess of the city's athletes, who regularly scooped all the honours at the Olympic Games back in Greece. In 530 BC the mathematician and metaphysician Pythagoras took up residence in Kroton and established an aristocratic party based on his ideas which eventually gained control, though the political turmoil that resulted from the sack of Sybaris led to their banishment from the city. Kroton went on to be the first of the Greek cities in Calabria but was increasingly destabilized by internal conflicts and the external threat of the encroaching barbarians, eventually being destroyed by the Romans. A resurgence of sorts occurred in the thirteenth century when it was made the main town of the Marchesato region, a vast feudal domain extending from the Neto to the Simeri rivers, held by the powerful Ruffo family of Catanzaro. But its prosperity was always hindered by the scourge of malaria, which poisoned every initiative and debilitated its people, provoking the author George Gissing – himself a victim of malaria during his visit in 1897 – to condemn Crotone as "a squalid little town".

In recent times Crotone has been mired in drugs and crime, though the city's elevation in 1995 as one of Calabria's new provincial capitals may finally revitalize the area. In fact, past the ugly industry defacing the northern approaches, the old centre retains an agreeable, unspoiled character, and the town makes a good base for the **beaches** that spread to the south and for the Greek ruins at Capo Colonna (see overleaf). On the old town's main Corso Vittorio Emanuele, the **Duomo**'s chief draw is an icon of the Black Madonna, usually locked away, but displayed during May when, at midnight on the third Saturday, it is paraded through the town en route to Capo Colonna; the following evening it's transported back to the duomo by sea – the highlight of a week of festivities during which the seafront is jammed with stalls. At the end of the Corso, the church of the **Immacolata** has an ossuary in its crypt, containing hundreds of neatly piled skulls grinning under electric candle-light. Further up Via Risorgimento, the brand new **Museo Archeologico Nazionale** (daily except first and third Mon of month 9am–8pm; L5000/€2.58) holds the best collection of finds from Magna Graecia on the Ionian coast. Alongside good examples of Greek and Roman coins, information about and fragments from the excavations at Crotone and its various colonies, lists of the Olympic winners who hailed from the city and maps of the digs (the main one right next to the main industrial complex), the cool and airy rooms display an array of items from Capo Colonna. Most noteworthy of these is the so-called **Treasure of Hera**, a beautifully restored group of bronze statuettes – including a sphinx, a gorgon, a horse, a winged siren and a very rare nuraghic boat from Sardinia – found in a tomb at Capo Colonna in 1987, and dating from the seventh to the fifth centuries BC. The most dazzling item is a gold diadem, expertly worked with garlands of leaves and sprigs of myrtle.

At the top of the road, the eighteenth-century **Palazzo Morelli**, which stands on the corner of Piazza Castello is one of several palaces built by Spanish nobility that surround the **Castello**, itself locally referred to as Charles V's but actually constructed by the Spanish viceroy Don Pedro di Toledo in 1541. Within, you can gaze over the sturdy ramparts to the town and sea below, and visit the **Museo Cívico** (Tues–Sat 9am–1pm & 3–8pm, Sun 9.30am–12.30pm; L3000/€1.55), a diverting exhibition of old maps and photos of Crotone and around, plus coins and sundry heraldic devices. The ticket also allows you into the **Torre Comandante**, one of the sentinel towers (same hours).

Arriving by **train** you will need to take either a taxi or bus to cover the 1.5km to the centre of town, Piazza Pitagora, and most of the hotels. There's a **tourist office** at Via

Torino 148, obscurely sited halfway between the station and the old town (Mon & Wed 7.30am–1pm & 2.30–5.30pm, Tues, Thurs & Fri 7.30am–1pm; ☎0962.23.185). The **bus** office is on Via Ruffo, a couple of streets east of Piazza Pitagora, where most provincial and regional buses arrive. Nearby, the small and clean *Pace* at Via Cutro 56 (☎0962.22.584; ③) is central Crotone's cheapest **accommodation** choice, after which comes the rather dingy *Italia*, over the arcades of Piazza Vittoria, just off Corso Vittorio Emanuele (☎0962.23.910; ②), and the much fancier *Capitol* (☎0962.24.996; ④), at the bottom of the Corso at Piazza Umberto 61.

Below the *Italia*, the *Caffè Italia* is good for snacks, *cornetti* and refreshing *latte di mándorla* (almond milk). For something more substantial, there is no shortage of **restaurants** in this part of town, ranging from the basic *Mary* pizzeria with its wood-fired oven, opposite the *Pace* hotel (closed Sun), to *Al Mio Ristorante* at Via Nicoletta 8 (closed Sun), which has good-value set-price meals. For seafood, try the *Ristorante Da Peppino* in Piazza Umberto (closed Mon).

Inland to Santa Severina

From Crotone's bus office on Via Ruffo there are a couple of departures daily to **SANTA SEVERINA**, on the eastern fringes of the Sila Piccola (see p.928). A Byzantine fortified town built on a hilltop, it's well worth a detour, principally for the Norman castle that dominates it. Rebuilt by Robert Guiscard on the ruins of a Byzantine stronghold and remodelled by the Swabians and Angevins, the newly renovated castle holds a first-rate **museum** (Aug daily 9am–1pm & 3–10pm; Sept–July Tues–Sun 9am–1pm & 3–7pm; L6000/€3.10), ranging through all parts of the construction from the foundations to the first-floor rooms. Exhibits include Byzantine artefacts, sundry arms and artillery and a scale model of the castle, as well as an informative overview of military architecture in Calabria and temporary exhibitions upstairs. From the stout battlemented walls long views extend over the hilly surroundings towards the mountains of Sila, and nearer at hand over the elongated square of the old town. On the other side of the piazza, whose flagstones are studded with symbols of the zodiac, the **duomo** lies adjacent to an eighth-century Byzantine **baptistry** (9am–noon & 3–7pm) which preserves traces of frescoes of the saints, Greek inscriptions on the capitals and its original font. On the other side of the duomo, the **Museo Diocesano** also repays the visit (Mon–Sat 9am–1pm & 3–8pm, Sun 3–10pm; L4000/€2.07), containing a painfully graphic fifteenth-century Christ on the cross, an early printed edition of the Bible, and – its greatest treasure – the *Spilla Angioina*, a broach from about 1300, studded with gold, pearls and rubies. The bars in the square serve snacks, and if you're looking for a full **meal** in Santa Severina, try the *Locanda del Re* on the steps below the castle (closed Mon & 2 weeks in Sept), but there's nowhere to stay in town.

Capo Colonna to Le Castella

Another worthwhile excursion from Crotone is to the famed column at **Capo Colonna** on Calabria's extreme eastern point, for which you have to drive or walk 11km along the coast. The column is a solitary remnant of a vast structure which served as the temple for all the Greeks in Calabria. Dedicated to Hera Lacinia, the temple originally possessed 48 of these Doric columns and was the repository of immense wealth before being repeatedly sacked as Magna Graecia and Hellenism itself declined. The object of Gissing's pilgrimage to Crotone, and a feature of his fevered visions as he lay on his sick bed (he eventually left without seeing it), it remained forever a mirage for him as he strained his eyes on the Crotone seafront, as unattainable as his attempts to recapture the glories of ancient Greece.

There are some excellent **bathing spots** not far south of here. **CAPO RIZZUTO** is a spit of land with a choice of sandy or rocky inlets to swim from. In winter the resort is dead, but it can get quite congested in the height of summer and difficult to find a place to stay. Nearby **LACASTELLA** is another busy holiday spot, but not yet strangled by tourism. It would be hard to spoil the beautifully sited Aragonese **castle** on an islet just off the main town (always open; free). As the Golfo di Squillace's only anchorage for large ships, the site was fortified from the fourth century BC and was later held by the Aragonese and Angevins, sold in perpetuum to the Duke of Carafa for 9000 ducats in 1496, and, the target of repeated Turkish raids, was finally abandoned at the end of the eighteenth century. Entering from the seaward side, you can climb up its restored tower (a torch will help) and examine an extent of wall built using the ancient method of alternating regular slabs with rectangles of loose stones and mud. You could swim off the rocks here, though you'll probably be more tempted by the arc of beach to the south. If you're seduced into **staying**, you can't do better than *L'Aragonese* (☎0962.795.013; ② full-board obligatory in Aug), right opposite the castle, with a **restaurant** below – ask for a sea-facing room. There are a couple of other hotel options in town if this is full, alternatively look for houses advertising *camere*. The nearest **campsites** are the *Costa Splendente* (☎0962.795.131) and *Marinella* (☎0962.799.810), both a couple of kilometres to the west and open June to September.

The southern Ionian coast

The southern part of Calabria's Ionian seaboard is less developed than the rest of the region, perhaps because it's less interesting scenically and most of the seaside towns and villages strung along it are unappealing. If you like sandy **beaches**, though, this is where to find them – either wild and unpopulated or, if you prefer, glitzy and brochure-style, as at **Soverato**. At **Locri** there is the region's best collection of Greek ruins and, overlooking the coast a short way inland, the craggy medieval strongholds of **Squillace** and **Gerace**, and **Stilo**, with its jewel of Byzantine church-building, the **Cattólica**.

Catanzaro

There's plenty of bustle at **CATANZARO LIDO**, a rather overworked resort with a handful of swish hotels and eating-places, the first beach stop for the people of Calabria's regional capital, **CATANZARO**. If you're aiming to visit this hilltop city just out of sight of the coast, regular buses leave from outside the Lido's main train station every twenty minutes or so (tickets from *tabacchi* or the ticket office in the station), and trains on the Cálabro-Lucane line operate hourly from an anonymous white building up the road. Best of all is the funicular which climbs to the bottom of the main drag, Corso Mazzini, every thirty minutes (L2000/€1.03). Drivers unwilling to cope with the traffic, lack of signs and one-way systems would do well to park their vehicles at the Lido.

Despite its fine position, Catanzaro has little innate charm: a crowded, overdeveloped, traffic-ridden city, it's a useful base for the Sila Piccola (see p.928) and is within a short ride of some five-star beaches, but is otherwise best avoided. It has much in common with its northern neighbour, Cosenza (see p.923), and perhaps for this reason they share an implacable rivalry. Both are inland mountain towns within sight of the Sila range, although Catanzaro also has a view over the sea, from which frequent strong winds keep the town relatively free of the sticky heat that can clog Cosenza during the summer months. Both towns have also been subject to repeated devastations of human and natural causes, though Catanzaro has suffered the most, being almost entirely demolished by a 1783 earthquake and robbed of any residual character by postwar property speculation.

An animated stream of cars and people, **Corso Mazzini** is the axis around which lies almost everything that is worth seeing in Catanzaro – though, to be frank, it doesn't amount to much. Step into the huge eighteenth-century Baroque church of the **Immacolata** to see four of the few remaining examples of the work of the Neapolitan Caterina de Iuliani: biblical scenes modelled in wax, rather difficult to make out clearly because they need to be kept away from excessive heat and light. Behind the town hall on the left of the Corso (heading down), Villa Trieste holds the **Museo Provinciale**, most notable for its Greek, Roman and Byzantine coin collection, though there is also a motley assortment of local and other southern Italian art (including a canvas signed by Antonello da Messina). At present, however, the museum is almost permanently closed for lack of funding, but check it out anyway: if you can't get in, the tranquil **public garden** on the ravine's edge makes a good spot for a breather, the haunt of card-players and couples in clinches, and with views over one of the two viaducts that tether Catanzaro to the surrounding hills – much used for suicides, they say, before the higher *viadotto* was built on the other side.

Practicalities

Most local and long-distance **buses** stop at the top of Via Milano (off Via Indipendenza, a northern extension of Corso Mazzini), which is also where the FCL **train station** is. The **tourist office** is off Corso Mazzini at Via Mancuso 11 (Mon & Wed 7.30am–1.30pm & 2–5pm, Tues, Thurs & Fri 7.30am–1.30pm,; ☎0961.741.764). An overnight **stay** in Catanzaro isn't recommended, but if you get stuck the cheapest and most central choice is the *Belvedere* in Via Italia (☎0961.720.591; ②), with rooms with or without bath. The town isn't much better off for **places to eat**, though you'll find most trattorias and snack bars along or just off Corso Mazzini. Halfway along, on the narrow Via Salita Rosario, is *Da Salvatore* (closed Mon), a favourite lunchtime haunt of locals, while further down, opposite the funicular station in Piazza Roma, *La Funicolare* is a good fast-food joint serving pizzas, *panini* and beers.

La Roccelletta and Squillace

Continuing on down the Ionian coast, a side-road signposted to San Floro and Borgia leads off right for the entrance, about a hundred metres up, to the ruined basilica of Santa Maria della Roccella, or **La Roccelletta**. Half-hidden in an olive grove, this partly restored red brick shell is all that remains of what was once the second-largest church in Calabria (after Gerace). Of uncertain date, though probably Norman in origin and founded by Basilian monks, its sheer size still has a mighty impact on the unsuspecting viewer. Much of the building material used in its construction came from the remains of the Roman town of Scolacium, the excavations of which can be seen in the **zona archeologica** (daily 9am–1hr before sunset; free) nestled among the olives behind the church. The best-preserved item here is a **theatre**, once able to hold some 3500 spectators, and thought to have been abandoned following a fire some time after 350 AD. Elsewhere on the site are the scanty remains of baths, and an **antiquarium** displaying finds from the site – mainly statuary, pottery and coins.

Five kilometres further south along the coast, at Lido di Squillace, is the turn-off for the old town of **SQUILLACE**, 8km up in the hills, once an important centre but now just a mountain village, isolated on its high crag. There are lofty views to be enjoyed over the Gulf and beyond Catanzaro as far as the Sila Piccola, and the **Castle** (currently under restoration) is one of the most romantic collections of ruins in Calabria. But the place is probably most renowned for its associations with **Cassiodorus**, whose monastery was located in the vicinity – though all trace of it has long since disappeared. Cassiodorus (480–570), scholar and secretary to the Ostrogoth, Theodoric, used his position to preserve much of Italy's classical heritage against the onset of the Dark Ages and the book-burning propensities of the Christians. Retiring to spend the last thirty years of his life in seclusion here,

Cassiodorus composed histories and collections of documents which have been of invaluable use to historians. There's a **restaurant** below the castle, La Cripta, which also serves pizzas (closed Mon).

The coast to Locri

South of Squillace, the golden sands of **COPANELLO** and **SOVERATO** beckon, two resorts that are increasingly attracting the international market. The private lidos hold sway here, charging L5000–10,000/€2.58–5.17 for a day under a parasol on a clean **beach** with access to a bar, but it's easy to find free beaches if you fancy more seclusion. Soverato has a handful of two-star **hotels** among the grander establishments, for example the *San Vincenzo* (☎0967.21.106; ②), at Corso Umberto 296, and the *Riviera*, on Via Regina Elena (☎0967.25.738; ②), both of which have **restaurants**. If you want to go up a peg or two, opt instead for the well-equipped *Gli Ulivi*, Via Moro 1 (☎0967.21.487; ⑤), which has its own strip of beach, or the more modest *Del Golfo* on Via Marina (☎0967.21.307; ④), well-sited by the sea but without a restaurant. The local **campsite**, *Glauco,* lies in Località San Nicola, a kilometre north (☎0967.25.533; closed winter).

The coast south assumes a bare, empty look that it keeps until the outskirts of Reggio, though with views of the distant mountains of the Serre and Aspromonte to stave off monotony. Regular **buses and trains** connect the towns along the coast and buses link inland villages. On the far side of Monasterace a turn-off where the bus stops leads to **STILO**, 11km up the side of the rugged Monte Consolino. An influential centre at different periods, Stilo is best known for the tiny tenth-century Byzantine temple, the **Cattólica** (daily: summer 8am–8pm; winter 7am–7pm; donations requested), which can be reached by car by taking the first hairpin on the right at the end of the village, or on foot by climbing a series of alleys from the village's main street, Via Tommaso Campanella. Once a base for hermits and Basilian monks in the south of Calabria, this perfectly proportioned temple is reckoned to be the best-preserved monument of its kind, though it has little remaining inside of its former glory, apart from some damaged frescoes and four slim, upturned columns taken from an older temple.

The name of **Tommaso Campanella** occurs everywhere in Stilo, a reminder of the village's links with this Dominican friar and utopian philosopher (1568–1639). Campanella was hounded by the Inquisition principally for his support of the Copernican model of the solar system, and spent some thirty years in prison for the heretical theories expounded in his book, *City of the Sun*. Eventually fleeing to Paris, he became the protégé of Cardinal Richelieu. The shell of **San Domenico** church, part of the convent where he lived, can be seen by following Via Campanella to the Porta Stefanina at the end of the village. Halfway along the road, look into the thirteenth-century **Duomo**, its ogival Gothic portal the only part remaining from the original construction. Note, too, along with other Byzantine and Norman reliefs, the surreal pair of feet stuck onto the wall on the left of the door, taken from a pagan temple and symbolizing the triumph of the Church.

Stilo has a pair of **hotels**, both open in summer only. The more appealing of the two is the *San Giorgio* at Via Citarelli 8 (☎0964.775.047; ③; May–Sept), just off the main Via Campanella, housed in the seventeenth-century palace of the Lamberti counts and furnished in nineteenth-century style, with a garden and pool. The *Città del Sole*, on Viale Roma heading towards the Cattólica (☎0964.775.588; May–Sept; ④), has a contrastingly impersonal, corporate atmosphere, with modern rooms and facilities. In both, make sure you get a room enjoying the wide views over the Ionian. Both have **restaurants** (open to non-guests), though the *San Giorgio*'s is only open June to September. The only other place in town to eat is a basic pizzeria, *Oenotria*, on Viale Roma (closed Sun).

The resort of **RIACE**, where the Bronzi di Riace were found (see p.935), lies 7km south of Monasterace, though it has little to stop for beyond its sandy beaches – a far better place to pause would be **ROCCELLA IÓNICA**, another resort 13km down the coast, surmounted by the remains of a medieval castle. Once the stronghold of local feudal overlords, the princes of Caraffa, the ruins are now too precarious to allow entry, but they make a striking backdrop for a **jazz festival** at the end of August which takes place in an amphitheatre below, attracting international names: contact the tourist office at Reggio for details (p.936). At sea-level, the town is lively enough to make a decent overnight stop, with one **hotel**, the functional and reasonably priced *Mediterraneo* in the central Piazza XXV Aprile (☎0964.863.388; ②), near the train station. There's a fish **restaurant** and pizzeria, *Il Veliero* (closed Wed), just beyond the level-crossing at the bottom of the square, though if you have transport it's well worth heading 3km south out of town on the SS106, where *La Cascina*, a well-restored farmhouse from 1899, serves up excellent meals at very moderate prices (closed Tues).

Locri and Gerace

Continuing south, you soon come to the most famous classical site on this coast, **Locri Epizefiri** (daily 9am–1hr before sunset; free), some 3km beyond the resort town of **LOCRI**. Founded at some time in the seventh century BC, the city of Locris was responsible for the first written code of law throughout the Hellenic world. Its moment of glory came in the second half of the sixth century when, supposedly assisted by Castor and Pollux, 10,000 Locrians defeated 130,000 Crotonians on the banks of the River Sagra, 25km north. Founding colonies and gathering fame in the spheres of horse rearing and music, the city was an ally of Syracuse but eventually declined during Roman times. The walls of the city, traces of which can still be seen, measured some five miles in circumference, and the excavations within are now interspersed over a wide area among farms and orchards. Your own transport would be useful for some of the more far-flung features, though the most interesting can be visited on foot without too much effort, including a fifth-century-BC Ionic temple, a Roman necropolis and a well-preserved Graeco-Roman theatre. In any case make a stop at the **museum** (daily except first & third Mon of month; 9am–8pm; L4000/€2.07) to consult the plan of the site, and examine the most recent finds, including a good collection of **pinakes**, or votive ceramics – though some of the best items have been appropriated by the Museo Nazionale at Reggio.

After the Saracens devastated Locris in the seventh century AD, the survivors fled inland to found **GERACE**, on an impregnable site that was later occupied and strengthened by the Normans. At the end of a steep and tortuous road 10km up from modern Locri, its ruined **castle** stands at one end of the town on a sheer cliff; it's usually accessible, though officially the site is out of bounds due to the very precarious state of the paths and walls. Easier to visit is the **Duomo** (daily: April–July 9.30am–1pm & 8pm; Aug 9.30am–1pm & 3–9pm; Sept & Oct 9.30am–1pm & 3–7pm; Nov–March 9.30am–1pm & 3–6pm;), founded in 1045 by Robert Guiscard, enlarged by Frederick II in 1222 and today still the biggest church in Calabria. Its simple and well-preserved interior has twenty columns of granite and marble, each different and with various capitals; the one on the right nearest the altar in *verde antico* changes tone according to the weather. The Treasury below (L2000/€1.03), which you pass on the way up to the nave, contains religious knick-knacks. Two other churches from the same period that are worth a look are **San Francesco** and **San Giovanello**, at the end of Via Caduti sul Lavoro (to the left of the duomo's main entrance), both showing a nice mix of Norman, Byzantine and Saracenic influences. They are usually closed: ask at the nearby *tabacchi* about access.

travel details

TRAINS

Cosenza to: Camigliatello (Ferrovia Cálabro-Lucane; 2 daily; 1hr 20min); Naples (every 2hr; 3hr 40min–4hr 15min); Paola (hourly; 20min); Rome (2 daily; 5hr 30min–6hr 15min).

Matera to: Bari (Ferrovia Appulo-Lucane; 8 daily; 1hr 30min).

Metaponto to: Bari (6 daily; 2hr); Cosenza (2 daily; 2–3hr); Ferrandina (for Matera) (10 daily; 35min); Reggio (4 daily; 4hr 40min–6hr 45min); Síbari (hourly; 1hr–1hr 35min); Táranto (hourly; 45min).

Paola to: Cosenza (hourly; 30min); Naples (hourly; 3–5hr); Reggio (hourly; 2hr); Rome (every 1–2hr; 5hr).

Potenza (Inferiore) to: Fóggia (every 2hr; 2hr); Metaponto (9 daily; 1hr 30min); Salerno (hourly; 2hr); Táranto (6 daily; 2hr 15min).

Reggio to: Catanzaro (6 daily; 2hr 25min–4hr 15min); Naples (every 1–2hr; 4hr 35min–9hr 10 min); Paola (hourly; 1hr 45min–6hr); Rome (hourly; 6hr 15min–11hr); Táranto (4 daily; 5–8hr).

BUSES

Cosenza to: Camigliatello (hourly; 1hr); Catanzaro (Mon–Sat 8 daily; 1hr 45min); Naples (1 daily; 5hr); Rome (3 daily; 6hr).

Matera to: Metaponto (Mon–Sat 4 daily; 50min); Potenza (Mon–Sat 2 daily; 1hr 30min).

Potenza to: Matera (Mon–Sat 2 daily; 1hr 30min); Naples (4 daily; 2hr); Rome (2 daily; 3hr 30min).

Tropea to: Capo Vaticano (June–Sept 4 daily; 20min).

FERRIES AND HYDROFOILS

Reggio to: Messina (12 daily; 20min).

Villa San Giovanni to: Messina (every 15min; 45min).

CHAPTER SIXTEEN

SICILY

I like Sicily extremely – a good on-the-brink feeling – one hop and you're out of Europe . . .

D. H. Lawrence in a letter to Lady Cynthia Asquith, 1920

The Sicilians aren't the only people to consider themselves, and their island, a separate entity. Coming from the Italian mainland, it's easy to spot that **Sicily** (Sicilia) has a different feel, that socially and culturally you *are* all but out of Europe. Occupying a strategically vital position, and as the largest island in the Mediterranean, Sicily's history and outlook are not those of its modern parent but of its erstwhile foreign rulers – from the Greeks who first settled the east coast in the eighth century BC, through a dazzling array of Romans, Arabs, Normans, French and Spanish, to the Bourbons seen off by Garibaldi in 1860. Substantial relics of these ages remain: temples, theatres and churches are scattered about the whole island. But there are other, more immediate hints of Sicily's unique past. A hybrid Sicilian language, for a start, is still widely spoken in the countryside; the food is noticeably different, spicier and with more emphasis on fish and vegetables; even the flora echoes the change of temperament – oranges, lemons, olives and palms are ubiquitous.

Sicily also still promotes a real sense of **arrival**. The standard approach for those heading south from the mainland is to cross the Straits of Messina, from Villa San Giovanni or Reggio di Calabria: this way, the train-ferry pilots a course between *Scylla* and *Charybdis*, the twin hazards of rock and whirlpool that were a legendary threat to sailors. Coming in by plane, too, there are spectacular approaches to either of the coastal airports at Palermo and Catania.

Once on land, deciding **where to go** is largely a matter of time. Inevitably, most points of interest are on the coast: the interior of the island is often mountainous, always sparsely populated and relatively inaccessible. The capital **Palermo** is a memorable first stop, a bustling, noisy city with an unrivalled display of Norman art and architecture and Baroque churches, combined with a warren of medieval streets and markets. From modern and earthquake-ravaged **Messina**, the most obvious trips are to the chic resort of **Taormina** and the lava-built second city of **Catania**. A skirt around the foothills, and even up to the craters of **Mount Etna**, shouldn't be missed on any visit to

---

ACCOMMODATION PRICE CODES

Throughout this guide, prices per person are given for **youth hostels** and assume Hostelling International (HI) membership. **Hotel** accommodation is coded on a scale from ① to ⑨, reflecting the cost of the cheapest double room in each establishment in high season. The price bands to which these codes refer are as follows:

① Up to L60,000/€30.99
② L60,000–90,000/€30.99–46.48
③ L90,000–120,000/€46.48–61.98
④ L120,000–150,000/€61.98–77.47
⑤ L150,000–200,000/€77.47–103.29

⑥ L200,000–250,000/€103.29–129.11
⑦ L250,000–300,000/€129.11–154.94
⑧ L300,000–400,000/€154.94–206.58
⑨ over L400,000/€206.58

(See p.32 for a full explanation.)

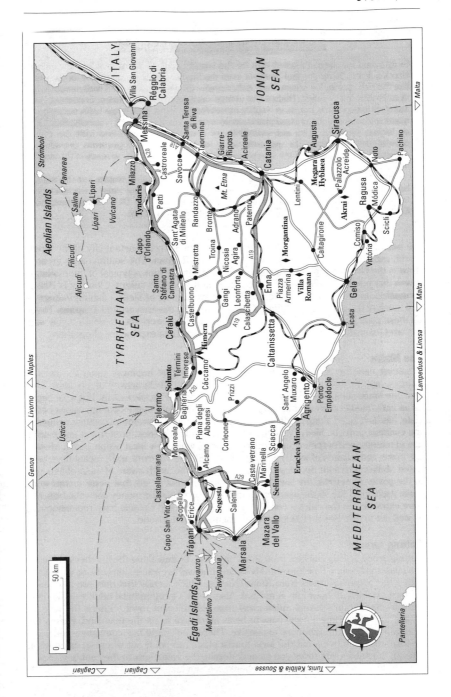

ITALY

Villa San Giovanni
Réggio di Calabria

IONIAN SEA

Messina

Santa Teresa di Riva
Taormina
Giarre-Riposto
Acireale

Catania

Augusta
Siracusa

Megara Hyblaea

Palazzolo Acreide

Akrai

Noto

Pachino

Ragusa
Módica
Scicli

Comiso
Vittória

Gela

Lentini

Caltagirone

Villa Romana

Morgantina

Piazza Armerina

Enna

Calascibetta
Leonforte
Agira
Nicosia

Licata

Porto Empédocle
Agrigento

Sant'Angelo Muxaro

Caltanissetta

Gangi

Castelbuono

Troina

Mistretta

Randazzo

Bronte

Adranò
Paternò

Mt. Etna

Savoca
Castroreale

A20

Milazzo
Tyndaris
Patti

Capo d'Orlando

Sant'Agata di Militello

Santo Stéfano di Camastra

Cefalù

Himera

Términi Imerese

Soluntо

Cáccamo
Bagheria
A20

Palermo

Monreale

Piana degli Albanesi

Prizzi

Corleone

Alcamo

Castellammare

Scopello
Capo San Vito
Érice
Trápani

Segesta
Salemi

Marsala

Mazara del Vallo

A29

Castel vetrano
Marinella
Selinunte

Sciacca

Eraclea Minoa

MEDITERRANEAN SEA

TYRRHENIAN SEA

Aeolian Islands
Strómboli
Panarea
Salina
Lipari
Lipari
Vulcano

Alicudi
Filicudi

Ústica

Égadi Islands
Lévanzo
Favignana
Maréttimo

Pantelleria

0   50 km

N

△ Genoa   △ Livorno   △ Naples

△ Cagliari   △ Cagliari

△ Tunis, Kelibia & Sousse

▷ Lampedusa & Linosa   ▷ Malta

▷ Malta

Piazza Armerina

REGIONAL FOOD AND WINE

Sicily's food has been tinkered with by the island's endless list of invaders, including Greeks, Arabs, Normans and Spanish, even the English. Sicily is famous for its **sweets**, like the rich *cassata* ice cream dish, and *cannoli* – fried pastries stuffed with sweet ricotta and rolled in chocolate. Dishes like orange salads evoke North Africa; **couscous** is a more obvious pointer. Just as in Naples, **street food** is all over, with rice balls, potato croquettes, fritters and dinky-sized pizzas made to be clutched in a hand. Naturally, **fish** like anchovies, sardines, tuna and swordfish are abundant, teamed often with the ever-popular pasta in dishes like *spaghetti con le sarde*. **Cheeses** are pecorino, provolone, *caciocavallo* and, of course, the sheep's-milk ricotta which goes into so many of the sweet dishes.

Wine making in Sicily is associated mainly with the fortified **Marsala**, but the island has also made a name for itself as a producer of quality everyday wines such as Corvo (red and white) and Regaleali (white). These names have no DOC designation, but **Corvo** in particular is found all over Italy – a tribute to its quality.

---

the island; while to the south sit **Siracusa**, once the most important city of the Greek world, and a Baroque group of towns centring on **Ragusa**. The south coast's greatest draw is the Greek temples at **Agrigento**, while inland, **Enna** is typical of the mountain towns that provided defence for a succession of the island's rulers. Close by is **Piazza Armerina** and its Roman mosaics, and to the west, most of Sicily's fishing industry – and much of the continuing Mafia activity – focuses on the area around **Trápani**. To see all these places, you'll need at least a couple of weeks – more like a month if you want to travel extensively inland, a slower and more traditional experience altogether.

The Mafia

Whatever else the **Mafia** is, it isn't an organization that impinges upon the lives of tourists, and it's unlikely you'll come into contact with Mafia activity of any kind. That said, the Mafia does exist – and for very real historical and social reasons. But what began as an early medieval conspiracy, to protect the family from oppressive intrusions of the state, has developed along predictable lines. Throughout the twentieth century, alongside the endemic poverty, Sicily has endured a system of allegiance, preferment and patronage of massive self-perpetuating proportions, from which few local people profit. Most of the towns and villages of western Sicily are tainted, and Palermo and Trápani have been noted Mafia centres for decades. But travellers won't be much aware of the problem, due to the power of *omertà*, the law of silence. All this is not to say that **petty crime** won't make itself felt. Take all the usual precautions concerning your money and valuables, and have extra care in the cities – certain parts of Palermo and Catania have reputations it's as well not to test. See p.1109 for a fuller discussion of the issue.

Getting around

Getting around Sicily can be a protracted business. **Trains** along the northern and eastern coasts (Messina–Palermo and Messina–Siracusa) are extensions of – or connected with – the "express" trains from Rome/Naples, which means that they are frequently delayed. At least an hour late is normal. Also, Sicily's geographical oddities often conspire to place train stations miles away from the relevant town – check the text for details, and don't expect a rail pass to be as much use as on the mainland. **Buses** are generally quicker though more expensive. There's no single bus company – SAIS and AST are the main two – but the local tourist office can point out where to catch what. Pick up timetables wherever you go and, despite the assertions to the contrary, expect there to be little (if any) service anywhere on a Sunday.

PALERMO AND AROUND

Unmistakeably the capital of Sicily, **Palermo** is fast, brash, loud and exciting. Here the Sicilian fusion of all things foreign – art, architecture, culture and lifestyle – exists at its most extreme: elegant Baroque cheek by jowl with Arabic cupolas, Byzantine street markets swamping medieval warrens, Vespas parked against Spanish *palazzi*. It's a fascinating place to be, as much for just strolling and consuming as for its specific attractions. But Palermo's monuments, when you can get to them through the tight streets and swirling traffic, are the equal of anything on the mainland: the city's unique series of Baroque and Arabic-Norman churches, the unparalleled mosaic work and excellent museums all stand much wider comparison.

You could easily spend a week in Palermo without ever leaving the city's limits. But make time for at least one day-trip: the capital has several traditional bolt-holes if you want a break from the bustle, most obviously the heights of **Monte Pellegrino** and the fine beach at **Mondello**. If your interest has been fired by the city's great Norman heritage, you won't want to miss the famous medieval cathedral of **Monreale**, just a few kilometres west; or you might like to take one of the year-round ferries or hydrofoils to **Ústica**, 60km northwest of Palermo – a tiny volcanic island with enough impressive grottoes and coastal walks to occupy any remaining time.

Palermo

In its own wide bay underneath the limestone bulk of Monte Pellegrino, and fronting the broad, fertile Conca d'Oro (Golden Shell) Valley, **PALERMO** is stupendously sited. Originally a Phoenician, then a Carthaginian colony, this remarkable city was long considered a prize worth capturing. Named Panormus (All Harbour), its mercantile attractions were obvious, and under Saracen and Norman rule in the ninth to twelfth centuries Palermo became the greatest city in Europe – famed for the wealth of its court, and peerless as a centre of learning. There are plenty of relics from this era, but it's the rebuilding of the sixteenth and seventeenth centuries that shaped the city as you see it today.

It's worth making Palermo your first stop in Sicily. It's the island's main transport centre, and it boasts Sicily's greatest concentration of sights. Quite apart from the Arab influence in its finest churches, there's more than a hint of the city's eastern past in its undisciplined centre, a sprawling, almost anarchic mass with no real focus: great pockets of medieval alleys, nineteenth-century piazzas, twentieth-century bombsites and contemporary office blocks all conspire to confuse what is essentially a straightforward street grid. Money from Rome and from the European Union has been earmarked for a redevelopment of the city centre, and, despite signs of improvement, the obstacles remain huge: this is partly due to the age-old system of kickbacks for contracts and tenders to bent politicians and the Mafia, which have creamed off much of the money. One of the few to stand up against this state of affairs has been **Leoluca Orlando**, who, following his deposition by his own Christian Democrat party in 1990, went on to found and lead the anti-Mafia and anti-Masonic party, **La Rete**, and he continues to make progress against the forces of graft and corruption as Palermo's mayor. While doubtless retaining his place on the Mafia's hit list, Orlando's prominence on the national stage has helped to focus attention on reform of the city's institutions and reverse the tendency of neglect and decay that has characterized the city for centuries.

The essential sights are all pretty central, and if you are disciplined enough you could get around them in a couple of days. Paramount are the hybrid **Cattedrale** and nearby **Palazzo dei Normanni** (Royal Palace), with its superb, mosaic-decorated chapel, the

Cappella Palatina; the glorious Norman churches of **La Martorana** and **San Giovanni degli Eremeti**; the Baroque opulence of **San Giuseppe dei Teatini** and **Santa Caterina**; and three magnificent **museums** – inspiring collections of art, archeology and ethnography.

This historical jumble of treasures has its downside. Many people have continued to live in their medieval ghettos, unemployment is endemic, the old port largely idle and petty crime commonplace. Some areas – La Kalsa and area around La Cala in particular – can be positively dangerous if you're not careful, and every *pensione* owner will warn you to watch your money and camera. Don't be paranoid, though: things are not significantly worse than any other European city, and the only rule is to avoid any quiet neighbourhood, especially at night.

Arrival, information and transport

Palermo's **airport** is at Punta Raisi, 31km west of the city, from where fairly regular buses run into the centre, stopping outside the Politeama Garibaldi theatre on Piazza Ruggero Séttimo, and finally outside the *Hotel Elena*, at the Stazione Centrale; the first bus is at 5am, the last departure timed for the last flight arrival (17 daily, a 45min journey; L7500/€3.90; enquiries ☎091.580.457). Note that for the return journey, departures leave every thirty minutes from 5am to about 10.30pm from outside the *Hotel Elena*, and follow the same route. Taxi fares for the same trip run to around L65,000/€33.80 per car, though you might be able to negotiate a lower price, see opposite.

Trains all pull in at the Stazione Centrale (24hr train enquiries ☎147.888.088), at the southern end of Via Roma, close to the cheap accommodation; buses #101 and #102, and two circular minibus services – *linea gialla* and *linea rossa* – connect with the modern city from outside the station.

Country- and island-wide **buses** serve terminals all over Palermo: AST operate out of Piazza Lolli and Via Balsamo for Bagheria, Corleone, Módica and Ragusa; Cuffaro services depart from Via P. Balsamo 13 for Agrigento; SAIS leave from Via P. Balsamo 16 for Rome, Caltanissetta, Catania, Enna, Piazza Armerina, Messina, Siracusa, Noto, Cefalù and Términi Imerese; and Segesta go from Via P. Balsamo 26 (for Rome and Trápani).

All **ferry** and **hydrofoil** services dock at the Stazione Maríttima, just off Via Francesco Crispi, from where it's a ten-minute walk up Via E. Amari to Piazza Castelnuovo; see p.971 for details of ferry companies and destinations.

Information
Palermo's main **tourist office** is at Piazza Castelnuovo 34 (Mon–Fri 8.30am–2pm & 2.30–6pm, Sat 8.30am–2pm; ☎091.605.8351 or 091.583.847); it has free maps of the city and province, a booklet published every two months (*Agenda*) containing reams of tourist information, including current events and transport information, and also provides a list of accommodation in and around the city. There are two smaller offices, which can at least provide maps: at the airport (open for incoming flights), and at Stazione Centrale (Mon–Fri 8.30am–2pm & 2.30–6pm, Sat 8.30am–2pm). There's also a kiosk on Piazza Bellini (Mon–Thurs 9am–7pm, Fri & Sat 8.30am–8.30pm; Sun 9am–1pm & 3–7pm). For more complete **city listings** and a rundown of what's on, pick up a copy of the local paper, *Il Giornale della Sicilia*, available from any newsstand.

City transport
Palermo is very much a city in which to **walk**, but you'll find getting around exclusively on foot exhausting and impractical. The **city buses** (run by AMAT) are easy to use, covering every corner of Palermo and stretching out to Monreale and Mondello. There's a flat fare of L1500/€0.78 for any number of journeys made within the same

hour, or you can buy an all-day ticket for L5000/€2.58, while tickets for the *linea gialla* and *rossa* minibus services cost just L1000/€0.52 for a day's use – all are available from the glass booths outside Stazione Centrale, or at the southern end of Viale della Libertà, in some *tabacchi*, and wherever else you see the AMAT sign; validate tickets in the machine at the back of the bus the first time you use them. Buses run until around 11pm, when night-services (generally one an hour) take over on all the major routes. The main city **bus rank** is outside Stazione Centrale. Otherwise, don't be afraid of jumping into a **taxi** (ranks outside the train station and in other main piazzas, or call ☎091.513.311), a cheap and safe way to get around at night – just make sure the meter is switched on, or you have checked the price beforehand.

Accommodation

Most of Palermo's budget **hotel accommodation** choices lie on and around the southern ends of Via Maqueda and Via Roma, roughly in the area between Stazione Centrale and Corso Vittorio Emanuele. Beyond the Corso the streets begin to widen out and the hotels get more expensive, though there are a few exceptions. If you're **camping**, take bus #616 from Piazza Vittorio Veneto (itself reached by #101 or #106 along Viale della Libertà from Piazza Castelnuovo) out to **Sferracavallo**, 13km northwest, where there are two all-year sites: the *Trinacria* on the seafront on Via Barcarello (☎091.530.590) and the cheaper *Ulivi* on Via Pégaso (☎091.533.021).

Alessandra, Via Divisi 99 (☎091.616.7009, fax 091.616.5180). Small, modern rooms with TV and telephone in a well-maintained building. It's at the corner with Via Maqueda, which means the rooms are overlooking that noisy street. ②.

Cortese, Via Scarparelli 16 (☎091.331.722). Buried in back streets just a step away from the Ballarò market, it's a ten-minute walk from Via Maqueda and Piazza Pretoria, but it's comfortable, clean and safe. Follow the signpost down Via dell'Università. ②.

Grande Albergo Sole, Corso Vittorio Emanuele 291 (☎091.581.811, fax 091.611.0182). Old-fashioned but relatively luxurious, with a roof terrace. Rooms without a bath are considerably cheaper and rates drop by 50 percent in low season. Prices include breakfast. ④.

Orientale, Via Maqueda 26 (☎091.616.5727). This marble-studded palazzo near the station has plenty of atmosphere, but rooms are mostly pokey. ②.

Petit, Via Principe di Belmonte (☎091.323.616). Tidy choice in this traffic-free part of the road, near the port and Piazza Castelnuovo, though with only six rooms, it's often full. ②.

Posta, Via Gagini 77 (☎091.587.338). On a street parallel to Via Roma, the hotel is central but quiet. Most rooms are en suite (⑤), all are modern and clean, and the service is polite. Garage parking available at L15,000/€7.80 per day. ④.

Principe di Belmonte, Via Principe di Belmonte 25 (☎091.331.065). With clean rooms and good facilities, this is a sound choice close to the port ③.

Santa Lucia, Via Francesco Crispi 258 (☎091.589.902). A useful budget stop for anyone using the port, clean but basic. ①.

Sausele, Via V. Errante 12 (☎091.616.1308, fax 091.616.7525). Clean and secure, this Swiss-managed hotel represents good value though can be noisy at night. Take the first right off Via Oreto, behind the station. ③.

Tonic, Via Mariano Stábile (☎ & fax 091.581.754). Smart, spacious hotel in the modern town, with plenty of rooms, all with private facilities. Friendly, English-speaking staff, longer-stay discounts, and parking and bike storage on request. ④.

The City

Historical Palermo sits compactly around one central crossroads, the **Quattro Canti**, which is at the core of four distinct quarters. The **Albergheria** and the **Capo** quarter, the latter beyond the cathedral, lie roughly west of Via Maqueda; the **Vucciria** and old harbour of La Cala and the **La Kalsa**, lie to the east, closest to the water. In these areas

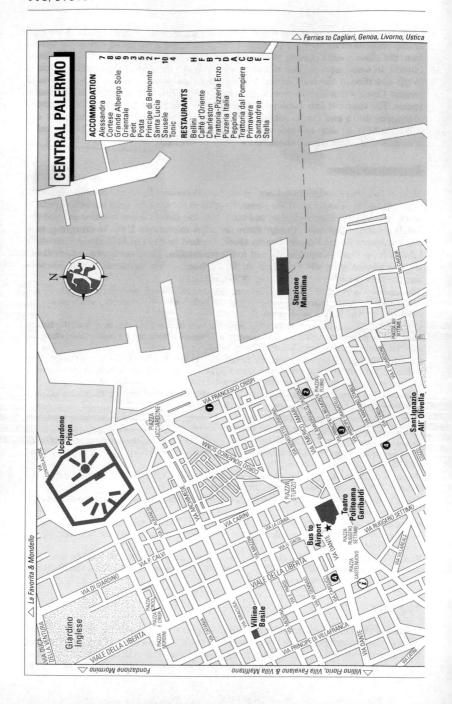

△ Ferries to Cagliari, Genoa, Livorno, Ustica

CENTRAL PALERMO

ACCOMMODATION

Alessandra	7
Cortese	8
Grande Albergo Sole	6
Orientale	9
Petit	3
Posta	5
Principe di Belmonte	2
Santa Lucia	1
Sausele	10
Tonic	4

RESTAURANTS

Bellini	H
Caffé d'Oriente	F
Charleston	B
Trattoria-Pizzeria Enzo	J
Pizzeria Italia	D
Peppino	A
Trattoria dal Pompiere	C
Primavera	G
Santandrea	E
Stella	I

Stazione Marittima

N

Ucciardone Prison

△ La Favorita & Mondello

Giardino Inglese

VIA DUCA DELLA VERDURA

VIALE DELLA LIBERTA

PIAZZA UCCIARDONE

VIA CONSOLARE

VIA FRANCESCO CRISPI

CORSO DOMENICO SCIMA

VIA BENEDETTO GRAVINA

VIA EMERICO AMARI

VIA PRINCIPE DI BELMONTE PIAZZA FLORIO

VIA AMMIRAGLIO GRAVINA

VIA MARIANO STABILE

VIA M. GIARDINONE

VIA CAVOUR

PIAZZA XIII VITTIME

Sant'Ignazio All' Olivella

VIA SPINUZZA

VIA ZERBA

VIA ARCHIMEDE

VIA A. ALBANESI

VIA CARINI

VIA P. CALVI

VIA DI GIARDINO

VIA LA LUMIA

VIA N. TURRISI

VIA M. AMARI

Bus to Airport ★

VIA DANTE

Teatro Politeama Garibaldi

PIAZZA RUGGERO SETTIMO

VIA RUGGERO SETTIMO

VIA VILLAFRANCA

PIAZZA STURZO

VIA DAITA

VIA V. GERMANO

VIA PARISI

Villino Basile

VIA SIRACUSA

VIA CATANIA

VIA MESSINA

PIAZZA MORDINI

PIAZZA P. CRISPI

PIAZZA G. CESARE

VIA DANTE

PIAZZA CASTELNUOVO

VIA PRINCIPE DI VILLAFRANCA

VIALE DELLA LIBERTA

△ Villino Florio, Villa Favaloro & Villa Malfitano

△ Fondazione Mormino

△ Villino Florio, Villa Favaloro & Villa Malfitano

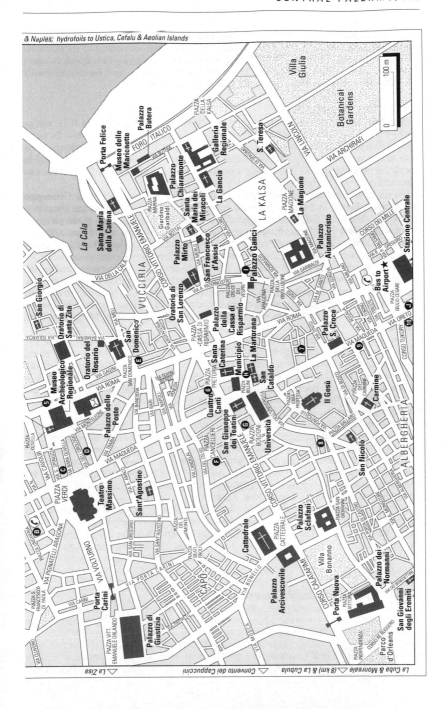

& Naples; hydrofoils to Ustica, Cefalu & Aeolian Islands

you'll find virtually all the surviving ancient monuments and buildings of the city, in a confusing chronological jumble. Each quarter, too, retains something of its medieval character in a system of run-down labyrinthine streets and alleys which speak volumes about the quality of life behind the rich churches and sights. Don't be unnecessarily wary though – most areas are perfectly safe in the daytime.

Around the Quattro Canti

Heart of the old city is the **Quattro Canti**, or "Four Corners", erected in 1611: not so much a piazza as a dingy Baroque crossroads that divides old Palermo into its quadrants. You'll pass this junction many times, awash with traffic and with newspaper vendors sitting under the ugly fountain water spouts, and it's worth one turn around to check the tiered statues – respectively a season, a king of Sicily and a patron of the city – in each concave "corner".

On the southwest corner (entrance on Corso Vittorio Emanuele), **San Giuseppe dei Teatini**, begun in 1612, is the most harmonious of the city's Baroque churches. Inside there's a wealth of detail – especially in the lavish side chapels – given plenty of contrasting space by 22 enormous supporting columns in nave and dome. Outside, across Via Maqueda, is **Piazza Pretoria**, floodlit at night to highlight the nude figures of its great central fountain, a racy sixteenth-century Florentine design since protected by railings to ward off excitable vandals. The piazza also holds the restored *municipio*, plaque-studded and pristine, while towering above both square and fountain is the massive flank of **Santa Caterina** (closed, except at Easter), Sicilian Baroque at its most exuberant, every inch of the enormous interior covered in a wildly decorative, pustular relief-work, deep reds and yellows filling in between sculpted cherubs, Madonnas, lions and eagles.

The entrance to Santa Caterina is on **Piazza Bellini**, just around the corner, the site of two more wildly contrasting churches. The little Saracenic red golfball domes belong to **San Cataldo**, a squat twelfth-century chapel on a palm-planted bank above the piazza (Mon–Fri 9am–3.30pm, Sat 9am–12.30pm, Sun 9am–1pm). Never decorated, it retains a good mosaic floor in an otherwise bare and peaceful interior. The understatement of this little chapel is more than offset by the splendid intricacy of the adjacent **La Martorana** (Mon–Sat 9.30am–1pm & 3.30–7pm, Sun 8.30am–1pm; closes 5.30pm in winter) – one of the finest survivors of the medieval city. With a Norman foundation, the church received a Baroque going-over – and its curving northern facade – in 1588. Happily, the alterations don't detract from the power of the interior, entered through the slim twelfth-century campanile, which retains its ribbed arches and slender columns. A series of spectacular **mosaics**, animated twelfth-century Greek works, are laid on and around the columns supporting the main cupola. A gentle Christ dominates the dome, surrounded by angels, the Apostles and the Madonna to the sides. The colours are still strong, the admirable craft work picked out by the sun streaming in through the high windows. Two more original mosaic panels have been set in frames on the walls just inside the entrance to the church: a kneeling George of Antioch (the church's founder) dedicating La Martorana to the Virgin and King Roger being crowned by Christ – the diamond-studded monarch contrasting with a larger, more dignified Christ.

The Albergheria and the Palazzo dei Normanni

The district just to the northwest of the train station – the **Albergheria** – hasn't changed substantially for several hundred years. A warren of tiny streets and tall leaning buildings, it's an engaging place to wander, much of the central area taken up by a street market that all but conceals several fine churches. Via Ponticello leads down past the Baroque church of **Il Gesù** (daily 7.30–11.30am), the first Jesuit foundation in Sicily and gloriously decorated inside, to **Piazza Ballarò** – along with adjacent **Piazza del**

Carmine the focus of a raucous daily market, with bulging vegetable stalls, unmarked drinking dens and some good snack stalls.

At the westernmost edge of the quarter, over Via Benedettini, is the Albergheria's quietest haven, the deconsecrated church of **San Giovanni degli Eremiti** (Mon–Sat 9am–7pm, Sun 9am–1pm; L8000/€4.13) – St John of the Hermits. Built in 1132, it's the most obviously Arabic of the city's Norman relics, with five ochre domes topping a small church that was built upon the remains of a mosque. A path leads up through citrus trees to the church, behind which lie its celebrated late-thirteenth-century cloisters – perfect twin columns enclosing a wild garden.

From San Giovanni it's a few paces to the main road, where, if you turn right and then veer left up the steps, you'll climb out of the fast traffic to gaze on the vast length of the **Palazzo dei Normanni** or Palazzo Reale (entrance on Piazza Indipendenza). A royal palace has always occupied the high ground here, above medieval Palermo. Originally built by the Saracens, the palace was enlarged considerably by the Normans, under whom it housed the most magnificent of medieval European courts – a noted centre of poetic and artistic achievement. Sadly, there's little left from those times in the current structure. The long front was added by the Spanish in the seventeenth century and most of the interior is now taken up by the Sicilian regional Parliament (which explains the security guards and the limited opening hours).

Of the **Royal Apartments**, the only part now open to the public is happily the most sumptuous, the so-called **Sala di Ruggero** (Mon, Fri & Sat 9am–noon; free), decorated with lively twelfth-century mosaics of hunting scenes. Descend a floor to the beautiful **Cappella Palatina** (Mon–Sat 9am–noon & 3–5pm, Sat 9am–noon, Sun 9–10am & noon–1pm), central Palermo's undisputed artistic gem. The private royal chapel of Roger II, built between 1132 and 1143, its interior is immediately overwhelming – cupola, three apses and nave entirely covered in twelfth-century **mosaics** of outstanding quality. As usual, it's the powerful representation of Christ as Pantocrator which dominates the senses, bolstered here by other secondary images – Christ blessing, open book in hand, and Christ enthroned, between Peter (to whom the chapel is dedicated) and Paul. Unlike the bright pictures of La Martorana the mosaics here give a single, effective impression, fully expressing the faith that inspired their creation.

The Cattedrale, the Capo and the modern city

Spanning Corso Vittorio Emanuele, on the far side of the Palazzo dei Normanni, the early sixteenth-century **Porta Nuova** commemorates Charles V's Tunisian exploits, with suitably grim, turbaned figures adorning the western entrance. This gate marked the extent of the late medieval city, and the long road beyond heads to Monreale.

The Corso runs back towards the centre, past the huge bulk of the **Cattedrale** (Mon–Sat 7am–7pm, Sun 8am–1.30pm & 4–7pm; free) – a more substantial Norman relic than the palace. It's an odd building, with the fine lines of the tawny stone spoilt by the late eighteenth century addition of a completely out-of-character dome. Still, the triple-apsed eastern end and the lovely matching towers are all original, dating from 1185. And despite the Catalan-Gothic facade and arches, there's enough Norman carving and detail to rescue the exterior from mere curiosity value. The same is not true, however, of the inside: it is grand enough but cold and Neoclassical, the only items of interest are the fine portal and wooden doors (both fifteenth century) and the royal **tombs**, containing the mortal remains of some of Sicily's most famous monarchs – including Frederick II and his wife Constance. There's also a **treasury** (daily 9.30am–5.30pm; L1000/€0.52) to the right of the choir: a sumptuous collection which includes a jewel- and pearl-encrusted skull cap and three simple, precious rings, all enterprisingly removed from the tomb of Constance of Aragon in the eighteenth century.

From the cathedral you can bear left, around the apses, and up into the **CAPO** quarter, one of the oldest areas of Palermo and another tight web of impoverished streets, unrelieved by space or greenery. Just around the corner from Piazza del Monte is the fine church of **Sant'Agostino** (Mon–Sat 7am–noon & 4–5.30pm, Sun 7am–noon), built in the thirteenth century. Above the main door (on Via Raimondo) there's a gorgeous latticework rose window; inside, some calm sixteenth-century cloisters; and – along Via Sant'Agostino, behind the market stalls – a sculpted fifteenth-century doorway attributed to Domenico Gagini.

The stalls of the clothes **market** (daily 8am to around 8pm) along **Via Sant'Agostino** run all the way down to Via Maqueda and beyond, the streets off to the left gradually becoming wider and more nondescript as they broach the area around the late-nineteenth-century **Teatro Mássimo**. Strictly Neoclassical in style, this is a monumental structure, supposedly the largest theatre in Italy, and beautifully cleaned up after years of closure; unless you book an appointment to visit (☎091.589.575), the interior is best appreciated during one of the classical concerts held here November and May).

The theatre marks the dividing line between old and new Palermo and beyond here there's little that's vital, though plenty that is grand and modern. Via Maqueda becomes **Via Ruggero Séttimo**, which cuts up through the gridded shopping streets to the huge double square made up of **Piazza Castelnuovo** and **Piazza Ruggero Séttimo**. Dominating the whole lot is Palermo's other massive theatre, the **Politeama Garibaldi**, which also houses the city's **Galleria d'Arte Moderna** (Tues–Sat 9am–8pm, Sun 9am–1pm; L6000/€3.10) – a vibrant collection of twentieth-century Sicilian art and sculpture.

The Vucciria, archeological museum and old harbour

Via Roma, running from Stazione Centrale, is a fairly modern addition to the city, all clothes and shoe shops. It's nothing like as interesting as the parallel Via Maqueda, consisting mostly of tall apartment blocks that conceal hotels, but stick with it as far as the church of Sant'Antonio. Behind here – down the steps – is the sprawling **Vucciria market** (daily 8am to around 8pm): winding streets radiating out from a small enclosed piazza, wet from the ice and waste of the groaning fish stalls. There are a couple of restaurants, some very basic bars and all manner of food and junk on sale. Other than early morning when the action is at its most frenzied, lunchtime is a good time to stroll around here – the stallholders take a break at card schools set up around packing cases and trestle tables, or simply slumber among their produce.

The northern limit of the market is marked by the distinctive church of **San Domenico** (Tues–Fri 9am–11.30pm, Sat & Sun 9am–11.30pm & 5–7pm), with a fine eighteenth-century facade that's attractively lit up, and an interior of tombs containing a horde of famous Sicilians. Parliamentarians, poets and painters, they're of little interest to foreigners except to explain the finer points behind Palermitan street naming. The **oratory** behind the church (Oratorio del Rosario; Mon–Fri 9am–1pm & 3–6.30pm, Sat 9am–1pm; free but tipping is usual) contains stucco work by Serpotta and a masterful Van Dyck altarpiece, painted in 1628 before the artist fled Palermo for Genoa to escape the plague.

From Piazza San Domenico, Via Roma continues north, passing (on the left) Palermo's main post office, the gargantuan **Palazzo delle Poste**. Built by the Fascists in 1933, it's a severe concrete block, with a wide swathe of steps running up to ten unfluted columns that run the length and height of the building itself. The grandiosity of the post office is brought down to size by the sixteenth-century convent behind, which now houses the **Museo Archeologico Regionale** (daily 9am–1.15pm, also Tues, Wed & Fri 3–6.15pm; L8000/€4.13), a magnificent collection of artefacts, mainly from the western half of the island, displayed on three floors. Two cloisters hold anchors and other retrieved hardware from the sea off the Sicilian coast, Egyptian and Punic remains in rooms to either side, and Roman sculpture – notably a giant enthroned Zeus. In rooms at the far end of the cloisters are numerous stelae and other inscribed tablets, and reconstructions of the assembled stone **lion's head water spouts** from the so-called "Victory Temple" at Himera (fifth century BC), the fierce animal faces tempered by braided fur and a grooved tongue which channelled the water. There are also finds from the temple site of Selinunte, on the southwest coast of the island, highpoint of which – indeed of the museum – is the **Salone di Selinunte**, a room that gathers together the richly carved metopes from the various temples. Sculpted panels from the friezes which once adorned the temples, the metopes are appealing works of art depicting lively mythological scenes: the earliest, dating from the sixth century BC, are those representing the gods of Delphi, the Sphynx, the rape of Europa, and Hercules and the Bull. But it's the friezes from Temples C and F that really catch the eye, vivid fifth-century-BC works – such as Perseus beheading the Medusa with a short sword. Upstairs has also plenty to reward a lengthy dawdle: lead water pipes with stopcock excavated from a site at Términi Imerese, some 12,000 votive terracotta figures, and two bronze sculptures – the life-like figure of an alert ram (third century BC), originally one of a pair, and the glistening, muscular study of Hercules subduing a stag, found at Pompeii.

The juxtaposition of different styles begins again in earnest if you cross back over Via Roma and head towards the water. The church of **Santa Zita** (also called Santa Cita, or San Mamiliano), on quiet Via Squarcialupo, suffered grave damage during the war, though it has since been restored, and is justly known for its marvellous **oratory** (Mon–Fri 9am–1pm & 3–6pm, Sat 9am–1pm; ring the bell if closed, or ask in the church in front): repository of one of Serpotta's finest works – the *Battle of Lépanto* – and some rich mother-of-pearl benches. Striking wealth indeed when you step back outside and consider the neighbourhood, the depressed inertia of whose streets spreads to the thumb-shaped inlet of the old harbour, **La Cala**. This was once the main port of Palermo, stretching as far inland as Via Roma, but the rot set in during the sixteenth century when silting caused the water to recede to its current position. All the heavy work eventually moved northwards to docks off the remodelled postwar streets, and La Cala has been left to the few fishing boats that still work out of Palermo.

La Kalsa and the Galleria Regionale

The air of abandon if anything intensifies in the southeastern quarter of old Palermo. Worst hit by the war and allowed to decay since, these are some of the poorest streets in the city, within some of the most desolate urban landscapes imaginable. But, alongside the bombsites, you'll find a number of Palermo's most remarkable buildings and churches – and a surprising amount of greenery.

Indeed, Palermo's only central park, **Villa Giulia**, is just a few minutes' walk along Via Lincoln from the train station: an eighteenth-century garden that provides a welcome escape from the traffic. Attractions include aromatic gardens, a kiddies' train, bandstand, deer and ducks and a botanical garden (Mon–Fri 9am–6pm, Sat & Sun 9am–1pm; L6000/€3.10).

Cut back to Piazza Garibaldi and walk north, turning off down Via Magione for the church of **La Magione** (Mon–Sat except for services 8–11.30am & 3–6.30pm, Sun 8am–1pm), one of the city's more graceful spots, approached through a palm-lined drive. Built in 1151, the simple Norman church was subsequently given to the Teutonic knights as their headquarters by Henry VI. Today, it's strikingly sparse, inside and out, the reason becoming clear as you step around the back to look at the finely worked apse: you're standing on the very edge of **La Kalsa**, an area subjected to saturation bombing during World War II, because of its proximity to the port. Planned by the Saracens, the quarter (its name is from the Arabic *khalisa*, meaning "pure") looks old, shattered and – even in daylight – vaguely threatening. In parts it is no more than a huge bombsite, with scarred and gutted buildings on all sides, and on maps it just appears as a blank space. It goes without saying that this is one of Palermo's more notorious areas for street crime, with young pickpockets and racing Vespas adding to the thrills.

Beyond Piazza della Kalsa is Via Alloro with, at its seaward end, the **Palazzo Abatellis**, a fifteenth-century palace revamped since the war to house Sicily's **Galleria Regionale** (Mon, Wed, Fri & Sat 9am–1.30pm, Tues & Thurs 9am–1.30pm & 3–7.30pm, Sun 9am–12.30pm; L8000/€4.13), a stunning medieval art collection. Inside, there's a simple split: sculpture downstairs, paintings upstairs, the one exception to which, a magnificent fifteenth-century fresco of the *Triumph of Death*, is displayed in the former chapel, coating an entire wall. It's a chilling study by an unknown (possibly Flemish) painter in which Death is cast as a skeletal archer astride a galloping, spindly horse, trampling bodies planted by his arrows. The other masterpiece on the ground floor is among the works of fifteenth-century sculptor Francesco Laurana (room 4), whose white marble bust of Eleonora of Aragon is a calm, perfectly studied portrait.

Upstairs there's no shortage of excellent Sicilian work, including a fourteenth-century Byzantine mosaic of the Madonna and Child, and paintings and frescoes from the fifteenth century vivid in their portrayal of the coronation of the Virgin, a favourite theme. This floor, too, contains a collection of works by Antonello da Messina (1430–79), including three small portraits of Saints Gregory, Jerome and Augustine and the celebrated *Annunciation*, a placid depiction of Mary, head and shoulders covered, right hand slightly raised.

Via Paternostro, which runs west off Via Alloro, curves north passing the striking thirteenth-century church of **San Francesco d'Assisi** (daily 7am–12.30pm & 4.30–6pm), whose portal, picked out with a zigzagged decoration, is topped by a wonderful rose window. The harmonious design is, for once, continued inside: all the Baroque trappings have been stripped away to reveal a pleasing stone interior, some of the chapels displaying excellently worked arches. To the side of the church, at Via Immacolatella 5, is the renowned **Oratorio di San Lorenzo** (Mon–Sat 9am–noon), harbouring stucco scenes from the lives of St Lawrence and St Francis by Serpotta.

Nearby, Corso Vittorio Emanuele runs straight down to the water, ending in the Baroque gate, **Porta Felice**, begun in 1582 as a balance to the Porta Nuova to the west. The whole area beyond the gate was flattened in 1943, and has since been rebuilt as the ugly **Foro Italico** promenade, from where you can look back over the harbour to Monte Pellegrino. Back beyond the Porta Felice, around the corner from the **Palazzo Chiaramonte**, second largest of Palermo's palaces and ex-headquarters of the Inquisition, is the engaging **Museo delle Marionette** at Via Butera 1 (Mon–Fri 9am–1pm & 4–7pm, Sat 9am–1pm; L5000/€2.58), the definitive collection of puppets, screens and painted scenery in Palermo. A traditional Sicilian entertainment, puppet theatres are now mainly staged for the benefit of tourists. The stories are usually based on the exploits of the hero Roland (Orlando), a dashing knight in combat against Saracen invaders, usually culminating in a great battle. It's all great fun, and in summer the museum puts on free shows (the *Spettácolo dei pupi*): check at the tourist office or museum for days and times.

The outskirts

Even if you don't have the time to see everything in the old centre there are several places beyond – on the outskirts of the modern city – that warrant investigation. Some, in fact, shouldn't be missed on any visit to Palermo; others are strictly for fans of the Norman period; and one is decidedly ghoulish, for the strong of stomach only.

The third of Palermo's showpiece museums lies on the edge of **La Favorita**, a large park around 3km north of Piazza Castelnuovo (bus #106 or #806 from Politeama or Via della Libertà). The **Museo Etnografico Pitrè** (daily except Fri 9am–8pm; L6000/€3.10) is *the* seminal exhibition of Sicilian folklore and culture on the island.

There's all the work traditionally associated with Sicily – a wealth of carts painted with bright scenes from the story of the Paladins, a reconstructed puppet theatre (with performances in the summer; ask at the tourist office), and dozens of the expressive puppets, scenery backdrops and handbills lining the walls. Fascinating, too, are the other Sicilian artefacts, including a whole series of intricately worked terracotta figures, dolls and games, bicycles, painted masks, even a great, flowery iron bedstead.

To track down the rest of central Palermo's **Norman relics** entails a lot of fairly fruitless scurrying around the southern and western parts of the city; in any case, much of what survives is often locked up or under restoration. Bus #124 runs west from the Politeama to **La Zisa** (from the Arabic, *el aziz*, "magnificent"), a huge palace begun by William I in 1160, with a fine exterior and a rich, well-crafted Islamic interior (Mon–Sat 9am–7pm, Sun 9am–1pm; L5000/€2.58). Closer to the centre, about 1km beyond Porta Nuova at Corso Calatafimi 100, is **La Cuba**, the remains of a slightly later Norman pavilion that formed part of the same royal park as La Zisa, now tucked inside an army barracks, but well-restored and open to the public (Mon–Sat 9am–7pm, Sun 9am–1pm; L4000/€2.07). The best excursion, however, is south to the eleventh-century church of **San Giovanni dei Lebbrosi** (Mon–Sat 9.30–11am & 4–5pm), reachable on bus #211, #226 or #231 from the Stazione Centrale. Just off Corso dei Mille, at Via Cappello 38, this is one of the oldest Norman churches in Sicily, reputedly founded in 1070 by Roger I; its squat tower is topped by a red dome, with a second dome over the apse, while its windows are just narrow slits.

For real attention-grabbing stuff, take bus #327 from Piazza Indipendenza southwest along Via dei Cappuccini as far as Via Pindemonte. Close by, in Piazza Cappuccini, the **Convento dei Cappuccini** (daily 9am–noon & 3–5pm; L2500/€1.29) retained its own burial ground for several hundred years, placing its dead in catacombs under the church. Later right up until 1881, others were also interred here. The bodies (some 8000 of them) were preserved by various chemical and drying processes – including the use of vinegar and arsenic baths – and then placed in niches along corridors, dressed in suits of clothes provided for the purpose. Descending into the catacombs is like having a walk-on part in your own horror film. The rough-cut stone corridors are divided according to sex and status, different caverns reserved for men, women, the clergy, doctors, lawyers and surgeons. Suspended in individual niches, the bodies have become vile, contorted, grinning figures – some decomposed beyond recognition, others complete with skin, hair and eyes fixing you with a steely stare. Those not lining the walls lie in stacked glass coffins, and it's a distinctly unnerving experience to walk among them. Follow the signs for the sealed-off cave containing the coffin of two-year-old Rosalia Lombardo, who died in 1920 but looks like she's simply asleep, thanks to a series of embalming injections.

Eating and drinking

For **snacks**, the *Ferrara*, just to the left of the train station in Piazza Giulio Cesare, and the *Mágico*, Corso Vittorio Emanuele 244, are reliable options and both also offer bargain lunches, while you can eat good **ice cream** and snack lunches including *arancini* at *Mazzara*, a bar-pasticceria at Via Magliocco 15 (on the corner of Piazza Ungheria). For authentic Sicilian fast food, *Antica Focacceria San Francesco*, off Corso Vittorio Emanuele at Via A. Paternostro 58, is an old-time place with marble-topped tables. **Markets** all offer a variety of typically Sicilian takeaway food – boiled octopus, liver-filled bread rolls and cooked artichokes – as well as fruit and vegetables. Best are the Ballarò, in the Albergheria (see p.964), and the Vucciria, off Via Roma (p.966). And there's an Upim **supermarket** at the corner of Piazza San Domenico and Via Roma. The most popular restaurants get packed at weekends, full of people intent upon a night out rather than just a meal. Recommended restaurant options range from "Inexpensive"

(L25,000) to "Moderate" (L25,000–40,000), "Expensive" (L40,000–70,000) and "Very Expensive" (over L70,000) according to the amount one person might expect to pay for a full meal including wine and cover charge.

Bellini, Piazza Bellini. The best bet for alfresco pizzas; outdoor tables are in the shadow of La Martorana church. Service is, however, somewhat slapdash. Closed Tues. Moderate.

Caffé d'Oriente, Piazza Cancellieri. Hidden away at the top of Via Celso (an alley off Via Maqueda near Corso Vittorio Emanuele), this place swims with North African atmosphere. Couscous and other specialities are served in the square. Closed Mon. Moderate.

Charleston, Piazza Ungheria 30 (☎091.321.366). For a special treat try Palermo's most celebrated high-class restaurant. Formal and stylish, it serves exquisite cuisine, with regular forays into other Italian regions to supplement its Sicilian specialities. Between mid-June and late September, the restaurant shifts to the beach at Mondello (see opposite). Reservations advised. Closed Sun. Very Expensive.

Trattoria-Pizzeria Enzo, Via Maurolico 17/19. The city's best bargain for three-course meals – hefty portions and daft prices. Closed Fri. Inexpensive.

Pizzeria Italia, Via Orologio 54 (opposite Teatro Mássimo). The best place in town for pizzas, attracting large queues. Closed lunchtime except Sun & also all day Mon from Oct to May. Inexpensive.

Peppino, Piazza Castelnuovo 49. A full restaurant menu is offered alongside some good pizzas. It's touristy, but in a good location. Closed Wed & Aug Moderate.

Trattoria dal Pompiere, Via Bara Olivella 107 (opposite Teatro Mássimo). It's a bit seedy, but the pizzas are spot on. Inexpensive.

Primavera, Piazza Bologni 4. Close to the cathedral with outdoor seating, this is a popular trattoria with home-style cooking. Closed Mon. Moderate.

Santandrea, Piazza Sant'Andrea (☎091.334.999). Chic and popular restaurant a stone's throw from Piazza San Domenico and the Vucciria market. There are no menus, dishes are seasonal and generally delicious. Book early to eat alfresco. Closed Tues & Jan. Expensive.

Stella, Via Alloro 104. Seafood pasta and grilled fish served in the lovely courtyard of this little restaurant in La Kalsa. Closed Sun & Mon lunch in summer, Sun lunch & Mon in winter. Moderate.

Bars and nightlife

The strangest thing about Palermo's fast lifestyle is that it virtually stops at around 8pm. Apart from a perfunctory passeggiata between the Teatro Massimo and Piazza Castelnuovo, in most areas everything is quiet outside after dark. In summer, most young people head for Mondello (see opposite), and buses run there and back all night. Still, for an outdoor, early-evening **drink**, Via Principe di Belmonte is a good spot – closed to traffic, and with several popular places – for coffees and beers. Evening crowds also congregate at the nearby *Bottiglieria del Mássimo*, a wine bar with pavement seating at Via Spinuzza 59, and, at the bottom of this street, in the bars on Piazza Olivella, opposite the archeological museum; all of these remain open until late. For a refreshing non-alcoholic drink on the hoof, the stand-up *Pinguino* at Via Ruggero Séttimo 86 serves famous milkshakes and a range of non-alcoholic cocktails, and also has excellent ice cream (closed Mon).

If it's **discos** and **video bars** you're after, what exists is all in the new, northern section of the city, along Viale Strasburgo, or along Via Generale Arimondi (beyond the Giardino Inglese). Otherwise, there are **cinemas** on Via Cavour and Via E. Amari, and, on Mondays (winter only), English-language films at the Fiamma Cinema, Largo Abeti 3, on the corner of Via Libertà and Via Notarbártolo (☎091.625.1868).

Listings

American Express Via E. Amari 40 (Mon–Fri 9am–1pm & 4–7pm, Sat 9am–1pm; ☎091.587.144).

Bookshops Large selection of English books from Feltrinelli, Via Maqueda 395, opposite Teatro Mássimo.

Car rental Avis, Via Enrico Amari 91 (☎091.586.940); Hertz, Via Messina 7e (☎091.331.668); Maggiore, Viale Alcide de Gásperi 79 (☎091.517.305); Sicily By Car, Via M. Stábile 6 (☎091.581.045). All of these also have desks at Punta Raisi airport.

Consulates Netherlands, Via Roma 489 (☎091.581.521); UK, Via Cavour 117 (☎091.326.412); US, Via Vaccarini 1 (☎091.305.857). For nationals of most other countries, the nearest consulates are in Naples or Rome.

Exchange There are exchange offices open outside normal banking hours at Punta Raisi airport (daily 7.50am–1.20pm & 2.35–8pm) and Stazione Centrale (daily 8am–12.30pm & 3–7pm).

Ferry and hydrofoil companies Grandi Navi Veloci, services to Genova and Livorno (at the port at Calata Marinai d'Italia; ☎091.587.404); Siremar, to Ústica (Via Crispi 120; ☎091.582.403); SNAV, to Naples and the Aeolian Islands (Via Principe di Belmonte 55; ☎091.333.333); Tirrenia, to Naples, Genoa and Cágliari (at the port on Via Molo; ☎091.602.1111).

Gay information ARCI Gay, Via Genova 7 (☎091.335.688).

Hospital Civico Regionale Generale, Via Carmelo Lazzaro (☎091.666.1111). For emergency first aid ☎091.288.141.

Internet Access Accademia Internet, Via Cala 64 (☎091.611.8483); Internet Café, Via Candelai (Tues–Sun from 7pm; ☎091.327.151).

Left luggage Stazione Centrale (daily 6am–10pm; L5000/€2.58 per 12hr); Stazione Maríttima (daily 7am–7pm; L2000/€1.03 per 24hr).

Newspapers English newspapers and magazines from the newsagents at the southern corner of Via Ruggero Séttimo and Piazza Castelnuovo.

Pharmacist All-night service at Via Roma 1, Via Roma 207 and Via Mariano Stábile 177.

Police Central city station at Piazza Vittoria (☎091.210.111).

Post office Main post office is the Palazzo delle Poste on Via Roma (Mon–Fri 8.10am–7.30pm, Sat 8.10am–1.30pm). Poste Restante closes at 1.15pm daily.

Telephones Offices on Piazza Giulio Césare, opposite the train station (daily 9am–10pm); and Via Príncipe di Belmonte 92 (Mon 4–7.30pm, Tues–Sat 9am–1pm & 4–7.30pm).

Travel agents CTS, Via Garzilli 28 (Mon–Fri 9am–1pm & 4–7.30pm; ☎091.611.0713).

Women's movement ARCI Donna, Via di Giovanni 14 (☎091.345.799).

Around Palermo

Palermo is a busy city with few quiet spaces and fewer parks, so any respite is welcome. Even on just a short visit to the city, try to include some of the trips below – all easy day (or half-day) excursions.

Monte Pellegrino and Mondello

Splitting the city from the bay at Mondello (see below) is **Monte Pellegrino**, to which the ride itself is as good a reason as any to go (bus #812 from the Politeama theatre) – an impressive route through a green belt of trees, cacti and scrub, and with views over Palermo and its plain. The bus drops you at the **Santuario di Santa Rosalia** (daily 7am–8pm), a cave in the hillside where the bones of the city's patron were discovered. A chapel was promptly built over the entrance in 1625: supposedly miraculous water trickles down the walls, channelled and collected by steel plates, and fancy lighting illuminates a bier containing a statue of the saint, around which there's invariably a scrum. A small road to the right of the chapel leads to the summit, a half-hour's walk, affording more splendid views, while paths and trails cover the rest of the mountain top.

If this isn't your bag, the other obvious trip from central Palermo is the short (11km) run to **MONDELLO**, a small seaside resort tucked under the northern bluff of Monte Pellegrino. It features one of Sicily's best stretches of sand (rather than the more usual stones), the two-kilometre beach curving round to a tiny working harbour and the remnants of a medieval tower. There's a line of restaurants overlooking the water and the fish, naturally, is temptingly fresh. Alternatively, you could grab some of the excellent snack food from the waterfront stalls and hit the beach. Although often crowded, summer nights at Mondello are fun – the scene of Palermo's real passeggiata. In winter it's more laid-back, and rarely very busy, but the restaurants and snack stalls are still open and it's usually warm enough to swim. To get to Mondello, take bus #806, or #833 in summer, from the Politeama theatre or Viale della Libertà – a half-hour ride.

Monreale

Whether or not you get to mountain or beach, you really shouldn't miss Sicily's most extraordinary medieval mosaics in the cathedral at **MONREALE** (Royal Mountain). This small hill-town, 8km southwest of Palermo, commands unsurpassed views down the Conca d'Oro Valley, with the capital shimmering in the distant bay. Bus #309 or #389 runs frequently from Piazza dell'Indipendenza, and the journey up the valley takes twenty minutes. Monreale's Norman **Duomo** (daily 8am–6pm) flanks one side of Piazza Vittorio Emanuele. The rather severe, square-towered exterior – though handsome enough – is no preparation for what's inside: the most impressive and extensive area of Christian medieval mosaic work in the world, the apex of Sicilian-Norman art.

The cathedral, and the town that grew up around it in the twelfth century, both owe their existence to young King William II's rivalry with his powerful Palermitan archbishop, the Englishman Walter of the Mill. William endowed a new monastery in his royal grounds in 1174; the abbey church – this cathedral – was thrown up in a matter of years. This haste accounts for the splendid uniformity of the cathedral's galaxy of coloured mosaics, all bathed in a golden background.

The **mosaics** were almost certainly executed by Greek and Byzantine craftsmen, and they reveal a unitary plan and inspiration. Once inside, your eyes are immediately drawn across the wooden ceiling to the all-embracing half-figure of Christ in benediction in the central apse: an awesome and pivotal mosaic, the head and shoulders alone almost twenty metres high. Underneath sit an enthroned Madonna and Child, attendant angels and, below, ranks of saints, each individually and subtly coloured and identified by name. Worth singling out here is the figure of Thomas à Becket (marked *SCS Thomas Cantb*), canonized in 1173, just before the mosaics were begun, and presumably included as a show of support by William for the papacy. The nave mosaics are no less remarkable, an animated series that starts with the Creation (to the right of the altar) and runs around the whole church. Most scenes are instantly recognizable: Adam and Eve, Abraham on the point of sacrificing his son, a positively jaunty Noah's Ark; even the Creation, shown in a set of glorious, simplistic panels portraying God filling his world with animals, water, light . . . and people.

Ask at the desk by the entrance to climb the **tower** (L2000/€1.03) in the southwest corner of the cathedral. The steps give access to the roof and leave you standing right above the central apse – an unusual and precarious vantage point. It's also worth visiting the **cloisters** (Mon–Sat 9am–7pm, Sun 9am–1pm; L8000/€4.13), part of William's original Benedictine monastery. The formal garden is surrounded by an elegant arcaded quadrangle, 216 twin columns supporting slightly pointed arches – a legacy of the Arab influence. No two capitals are the same, each a riot of detail and imagination: armed hunters doing battle with winged beasts; flowers, birds, snakes and foliage. Entrance to the cloisters is from Piazza Guglielmo, in the corner by the right-hand tower of the cathedral.

Ústica

A volcanic, turtle-shaped island 60km northwest of Palermo, **ÚSTICA** is one of the more appealing destinations for a quick jaunt away from the city. Colonized originally by the Phoenicians, the island took its name from the Latin *ustum*, or "burnt", a reference to its blackened, lava-strewn appearance. Exposed and isolated, it had a rough time throughout the Middle Ages, its scant population repeatedly harried by pirates who used the island as a base. Even as late as the 1890s the few inhabitants were nearly all exiled prisoners. Today, Ústica's fertile uplands are just right for a day's ambling, while the rough coastline is touted as a skin-diver's paradise, the clear water bursting with fish, sponges, weed and coral. Less adventurous types can easily take a boat trip through Ústica's rugged grottoes and lava outcrops.

The little port of **ÚSTICA TOWN**, where the boats dock, features a museum devoted to underwater finds from the area, a bank, a dozen restaurants and a handful of places to stay. All these facilities sit around a sloping double piazza, just five minutes' walk uphill from the harbour. **Ferries** and **hydrofoils** operate roughly once or twice daily from Palermo (from the Stazione Maríttima): the cheapest summer passage is around L19,000/€9.88 one way by ferry, rising to L31,000/€16.12 on the hydrofoils, but they complete the journey in less than half the time. (Tickets from Siremar – see "Listings" for Palermo, p.971.) Ústica town has a couple of good **hotel** choices: the attractive *Clelia*, at Via Magazzino 7 (☎091.844.9039; ④), with a roof terrace overlooking the sea, and the very basic but friendly *Locanda Castelli*, Via San Francesco 16 (☎091.844.9007; ①). Alternatively, ask about **private rooms** at the *Bar Centrale* on the piazza, or look for *camere* signs. A good central place to **eat** is *Da Mario*, opposite the *Bar Centrale*, a small, simple trattoria where superb fish dinners with wine cost around L35,000/€18.20 (no closing day), or if you want a view, dine at *La Luna sul Porto* below the piazza and above the port on Via Vittorio Emanuele (closed Tues).

THE TYRRHENIAN COAST

From Palermo, the whole of the rugged **Tyrrhenian coast** is accessible by rail and road, offering at times a spectacular ride past deserted coves and rocky beaches. Aside from spots of interest at and around **Bagheria** and **Términi Imerese**, the first real attraction is **Cefalù**, a beach resort and cathedral town. There are few essentaial stops beyond, though the quiet seaside towns further east are all nice enough for a short break. Also, buses run inland from the larger resorts, providing access to the northern **mountain chains**, the Madonie and the Nebrodi. Many of the hill-towns here are worth a visit – especially **Cáccamo** and **Castroreale**, quiet airy places with castles and good hiking at hand. Unfortunately, the easternmost part of the coast, around **Milazzo** – Sicily's second largest port – is fairly grim and industrial. However, there's an easy escape route to the desolate **Aeolian Islands**, visible from much of the Tyrrhenian coast and reached by ferries and hydrofoils from Milazzo, hydrofoils from Messina, and, during the summer, hydrofoils from Palermo and Cefalù.

Bagheria, Solunto, Términi Imerese and Cáccamo

Although it's tempting to head straight for Cefalù, there are some enticing diversions before that – and they can also be seen on day-trips from Palermo. Road and railway cut eastwards, across Capo Zafferano, to reach the rural town of **BAGHERIA**, a ten-minute ride by train. Scattered across the town, a seventeenth- and eighteenth-century summer retreat, is a series of (largely neglected) Baroque country villas, on which the city's nobility stamped their mark. Most are privately owned, and closed to the public, but there is access to the **Villa Palagonia** (daily 9am–12.30pm & 4–6.30pm;

L5000/€2.58) on Piazza Garibaldi. Noted for its menagerie of eccentric gargoyles, the villa is only ten minutes' walk from the train station (left out of the station onto Corso Butera, then left).

You might combine a trip to Bagheria with a tour around the Graeco-Roman town at **SOLUNTO** (the ancient Solus), one stop further on the train (the station is called Santa Flavia-Solunto-Porticello). The **site** (Mon–Sat 9am–1hr before sunset, Sun 9am–12.30pm; L6000/€3.10) is about a half-hour walk north from the station, beautifully stranded on top of Monte Catalfano. There's a **museum** at the entrance, as well as the impressive remains of Roman houses (some with mosaics) and shops, a well-preserved agora and a fragmentary theatre – all looking down on the small bay below, guarded by the medieval **Castello di Solanto**.

Another twenty minutes on, **TÉRMINI IMERESE** has an upper town whose cliff-edge belvedere is another excellent vantage-point for views of the curving shore. The grand piazza holds a seventeenth-century cathedral studded with four sixteenth-century statues, and the **Museo Civico** (Tues–Sat 9am–1.30pm & 4–7pm, 3–6pm in winter, Sun 9am–1.30pm; free), over the other side of the piazza, is worth a peek for the remains from the ancient Greek site of Himera, 20km to the east. Términi, after a prosperous Greek and Carthaginian period, was also a Roman spa, and in the shaded, congested lower town are the remains of the former baths, covered now by a hotel in Piazza delle Terme, the stylishly old-fashioned *Grand Hotel delle Terme* (☎091.811.3557; ⑥), close to the little port. Términi would be a fair place to spend the night, though there's only one other **hotel**, *Il Gabbiano*, at Via Libertà 221 (left out of the station, a 20min walk; ☎091.811.3262, *www.ilgabbianohotel.neomedia.it*; ④), which in August, also has a basic annex with shared bathrooms (②). The nearest **campsite**, *Himera* (☎091.814.0175), is at Buonfornello, 15km east of town; take the bus from outside the train station.

Buses from Términi's train station also run regularly to **CÁCCAMO**, 10km south. The small town, a jumble of little houses astride a craggy hill, is dominated by a sturdy, battlemented twelfth-century **Fortezza**, its sheer walls built on a crag that falls away down into the valley below. Though it's propped up by scaffolding, you should at least be able to climb up to the gates of the castle for views over the steeply stepped streets; for entrance, try ringing at the door of the custodian at Corso Umberto 6.

Cefalù

Despite the recent attentions of Club Med and a barrage of modern building outside town, **CEFALÙ** remains a fairly small-scale fishing port, partly by virtue of its geographical position – tucked onto every available inch of a shelf of land beneath a fearsome crag, La Rocca. Roger II founded a mighty cathedral here in 1131 and, as befitting one of the most influential early European rulers, his church dominates the skyline, the great twin towers of the facade rearing up above the flat roofs of the medieval quarter. Naturally, it's the major attraction in town, but most visitors are equally tempted by Cefalù's fine curving sands – the main reason why the holiday companies have moved in in such great numbers in recent years. Still, it's a pleasant town, and nothing like as developed as Sicily's other package resort of Taormina.

Halfway along Corso Ruggero, the main pedestrianized road through the old town, the **Duomo** (daily: summer 8am–noon & 3.30–9pm; winter closes 6.30pm) was built – partly at least – as Roger's thanks for fetching up at Cefalù's safe beach in a violent storm. Inside, covering the apse and presbytery, are the earliest and best-preserved of the Sicilian church mosaics, dating from 1148. The **mosaics** follow a familiar pattern. Christ Pantocrator dominates the central apse, underneath is the Madonna flanked by archangels, and then the Apostles. Although minuscule in comparison with those at Monreale (see p.972), these mosaics are just as appealing and, most interestingly, display a quite marked artistic tradition. Forty years earlier than those in William's cathedral, they are thoroughly Byzantine in concept: Christ's face is elongated, the powerful eyes set close together, the outstretched hand flexed and calming.

In high season, when Cefalù's tangibly Arabic, central grid of streets is crowded with tourists, you'd do best to visit the cathedral early in the morning, before succumbing to the lure of the long sandy **beach** beyond the harbour. There are a couple of other places that are also worth venturing to: the **Museo Mandralisca** (daily: 9am–7pm; Aug 9am–midnight; L8000/€4.13), at Via Mandralisca 13 (across from Piazza Duomo), has a wry *Portrait of an Unknown Man* by the fifteenth-century Sicilian Master Antonello da Messina; and **La Rocca**, the mountain above the town, holds the megalithic so-called Tempio di Diana, from where paths continue right around the crag, inside medieval walls, to the sketchy fortifications at the very top. If you want to stay over, choose between the very pleasant *Pensione delle Rose* (☎ & fax 0921.421.885; ③), at Via Gibilmanna, twenty minutes out of town along Umberto I, where some of the rooms have private terraces, or the pricier *La Giara*, in the heart of the old town at Via Veterani 40 (☎0921.421.562, fax 0921.422.518; ⑤), well-equipped, with an affable management and a big terrace. The best place to **eat** on a budget is the *Arkade Grill*, off Corso Ruggero at Via Vanni 9 (closed Thurs in winter), which offers a good-value tourist menu in summer. For more elegant dining, the friendly *La Brace*, Via XXV Novembre (closed Mon & mid-Dec to mid-Jan), serves a wonderful two-course meal for around L28,000/€14.56 (three courses for L48,000/€24.96). The **tourist office** is on the main street at Corso Ruggero 77 (June–Sept Mon–Sat 8am–8.30pm; Oct–May Mon–Fri 8am–2.30pm & 3.30–7pm, Sat 9am–1pm; ☎0921.421.050) and has free maps and accommodation lists. There are three **hydrofoils** a week to the Aeolian Islands from mid-June to mid-September.

The coast to Milazzo, and inland routes

The best stretches of the Tyrrhenian coast all lie east of Cefalù: clean stony beaches backed for the most part by extensive orange and lemon groves. The train stops at several small, attractive seaside resorts, where there's often cheap accommodation, and there are buses south, into the hills, from various points on the coast.

Frequent trains stop at **SANTO STEFANO DI CAMASTRA**, a ceramics town and small-time resort, where there's a cheap *locanda*, the *U Cucinu*, at Via Nuova 75 (☎0921.331.106; ①). Another 30km east, **SANT'AGATA DI MILITELLO** has a small working fishing fleet, which means excellent fish in the local restaurants. The busy summer resort has a long pebbly beach, and you can stay here at the *Locanda Miramare*, Via Cosenz 3, next to the train station (☎0941.701.773; ②).

Further down the coast, rounding the cape, there are good **beaches** at Capo d'Orlando itself, and from **Patti**'s main square you can catch a bus (3 daily) to Tìndari and the ruins of ancient **Tyndaris** (daily 9am–2hr before sunset; L4000/€2.07, includes museum). Founded in 396 BC, it was one of the last Greek settlements in Sicily and retains its Greek walls. Most of the remains, though, are Roman, including some house ruins and a theatre with splendid views over the sea, together with finds collected in a **museum** (same hours as site; included in site ticket).

There's not much else to stop for before Milazzo; indeed the better destinations are all south and inland, away from the increasingly built-up coast. The SS185 cuts one of the grandest routes on the island, climbing gently into the hills to **Novara Di Sicilia**. Creakingly medieval, the decrepit streets and alleys are pleasant to wander around and the small town offers terrific views over the mountains and sea. A closer target is the hill-town of **CASTROREALE**, to the northeast, just 8km south of Barcellona train station on the coast – to which it's connected by local buses (up to 7 daily). This is another extraordinarily sited town, defended in past days by the fourteenth-century

---

GETTING TO THE AEOLIAN ISLANDS

Sailings **from Milazzo** operate daily and are frequent enough to make it unnecessary to book (unless you're taking a car), although bear in mind that there is a reduced service between October and May – and that even moderately rough weather can disrupt the schedules. The **shipping agencies** are down by the harbour and open usual working hours as well as just before all departures – Siremar (Via dei Mille 19; ☎090.928.3242) for ferries and hydrofoils, SNAV (Via dei Mille 33; ☎090.928.7821) for hydrofoils only, and NGI (Via dei Mille 26; ☎090.928.3415) for ferries only. Hydrofoils are more frequent and twice as quick, but almost twice as expensive as the ferries: Milazzo to Lipari costs around L13,000/€6.76 one way on the ferry, L22,000/€11.44 on the hydrofoil.

There are summer services, too, from **Naples** and **Reggio di Calabria** on the Italian mainland; elswhere in Sicily, services run from **Messina** and, in summer, **Palermo** and **Cefalù** (see "Travel details", p.1018, for an outline of schedules and crossing times).

---

castle of Frederick of Aragon, the tower of which survives on top of the pile: it does duty these days as a **youth hostel** (☎090.974.6398; L18,000/€9.36; April–Oct). Even if you can't stay the night, Castroreale is well worth seeing and provides ample opportunity for aimless wandering through the stepped streets, past badly restored sixteenth-century churches and fine nobles' houses.

Milazzo

At the base of a thin spit of land poking into the Tyrrhenian Sea, **MILAZZO** is not the sort of place you're likely to make a beeline for. Disfigured by a giant oil refinery, the coast around is noisy and smelly. However, it's the main port of departure for the **Aeolian Islands** (see box above for details of sailings), which means, at best, a couple of hours in town awaiting the ferry/hydrofoil – at worst a night in one of the **hotels**. Near the dock, try the *Central*, Via del Sole 8 (☎090.928.1043; ②), a cheery little place with clean, shared bathrooms, or the *California*, opposite, at Via del Sole 9 (☎090.922.1389; ②), family-run and friendly, offering rooms with private facilities. With a car, you could spend a bit more to stay by the beach on the promontory north, at the *Riviera Lido* (☎090.928.7834; ⑤), in Località Corrie on the Strada Panoramica. The local favourite for fish **meals** is *Il Covo del Pirata*, Lungomare Garibaldi 47–48 (closed Wed except Aug), while the best place for pizza is the economic *Pizzeria Tonino*, at Via Manzoni 4 (closed Thurs in winter), right in the centre. **Buses** (including the Giuntabus service from Messina) stop on the quayside. The **train station** is 3km south of the centre, but local buses run into town every thirty minutes during the day, dropping you on the quayside or further up in Piazza della Repubblica. Milazzo's **tourist office** is at Piazza Duilio 20 (Mon–Fri 8am–2pm & 3–6.30pm, Sat 8am–2pm; ☎090.922.2865), just back from the harbour.

If there's time to kill, you might like to poke around the restored **Castle** (guided tours hourly Tues–Sun: March–May 10am–noon & 3–5pm; June–Aug 10am–noon & 5–7pm; Sept 10am–noon & 3–6.30pm; Oct–Feb 9am–noon & 2.30–3.30pm; L6000/€3.10) which sits inside a much larger and older walled city, complete with its own cathedral.

The Aeolian Islands

Volcanic in origin, the **Aeolian Islands** lead a precarious existence in the buffeted waters off the northern Sicilian coast. They are named after Aeolus, the Greek god who kept the winds he controlled shut tight in one of the islands' many caves. According to

Homer, Odysseus put into the Aeolians and was given a bag of wind to help him home, but his sailors opened it too soon and the ship was blown straight back to port. More verifiably, the islands were coveted for their mineral wealth, the mining of obsidian (hard, glass-like lava) providing the basis for early prosperity. Later their strategic importance attracted the Greeks, who settled on Lípari in 580 BC. The Greeks' powerful fleet kept rivals at bay until the islands fell to the Carthaginians, who in turn were pushed out by the Romans in 252 BC. Thereafter began a period of decline: the islands became a haven for pirates and a place of exile, a state of affairs that continued right into the twentieth century with the Fascists exiling their political opponents to Lípari.

It's only comparatively recently that the islanders stopped scratching a subsistence living and started welcoming tourists. Emigration had virtually depopulated some of the islands, and even now the more remote ones are sorely stretched to maintain a decent living. That said, you won't be alone if you come to the islands during the summer months: the central group of Vulcano, Lípari, Panarea and Salina are pretty well known to a gradually increasing crowd of devotees. Lípari, particularly, is expensive in high season and is rapidly becoming rather a hip resort. But get out to the minor isles or come in blustery winter for a taste of what it was like twenty – or a hundred – years ago: unsophisticated, rough and beautiful.

Getting there is easiest from Milazzo (see box opposite), with year-round ferries and hydrofoils connecting the port with all the islands. **Getting around** in summer is easy as ferries (*traghetti*) and hydrofoils (*aliscafi*) link all the islands. In winter, services are reduced and in rough weather cancelled altogether, particularly on the routes out to Alicudi and Filicudi. You can take cars to Lípari and Salina but bikes are better and you can rent them on the spot.

In high season (Easter and July/August), **accommodation** is scarce and you'd be wise to phone in advance, especially if you want to visit Strómboli. You may also find that many places insist that you pay for **half-board**). Many hotels and *pensioni* drop their prices by up to fifty percent from October to March, while **renting apartments** or **private rooms** is an economical option too. There are **campsites** on Vulcano, Lípari and Salina – but note that camping rough is illegal. **Restaurants** can be expensive, since much of the food (as well as much of the water on some islands) has to be imported. In many places there's not always the option of a cheap pizzeria, so if money is tight, expect to do some self-catering.

There are **banks** on Lípari, Salina and Vulcano (summer only), and you can change money in post offices, travel agencies and major hotels throughout the islands, but the rates aren't good. **Electricity** has only slowly come to some islands, and if you're spending any time on Alicudi, Filicudi or Strómboli, a torch isn't a bad investment.

Vulcano

Closest to the Sicilian mainland, **VULCANO** is the first port of call for ferries and hydrofoils – around an hour and a half on the slowest crossing. From the harbour of **PORTO DI LEVANTE**, you can walk up to the main crater of the volcano in around an hour; the last volcanic explosion here was in 1890. A second hike is to **Vulcanello**, the volcanic pimple just to the north of the port, spewed out of the sea in 183 BC, and there's good walking to be had around the rest of the island, too. Less energetically, just fifteen minutes' walk from Porto di Levante, across the neck of land separating it from Porto di Ponente, there's an excellent black-sand **beach**. On the way you'll pass Vulcano's sulphurous mud baths and hot springs bubbling into (and warming) the sea. If you opt for a wallow in the mud, be warned you'll reek of it for days afterwards, and don't wear any jewellery, because it will be stained and corroded.

A summer-only **tourist office** operates at Porto di Levante (June–Sept daily 7.30am–1.30pm; ☎090.985.2028) which has information on **rooms**. There isn't a huge choice, but try the amenable *Casa Sipione*, at the end of a path beside the church (☎090.985.2034; ②; June–Sept); otherwise try the *La Giara*, welcoming and quiet at Via Provinciale 18 (☎090.985.2229; ⑤; April to mid-Oct), or the functional *Agostino*, in the piazzetta near the mud baths (☎090.985.2342; ④). On the Porto Ponente side, *Residence Lanterna Bleu* (☎090.985.2178; ④; closed mid-Dec to mid-Jan) is a series of two- and three-bed apartments with kitchen. The cost of **food** is exorbitant here, and you have to choose carefully from the battery of restaurants along the road that bends around from the port. *Da Maurizio* (closed Nov–Easter), just beyond the Siremar agency, has a nice shady garden and good food, and there's a fairly reasonable tourist menu on offer. Overlooking the sea at Porto di Ponente, *Baia di Ponente* is worth the splurge for a delicious meal on the attractive candlelit terrace (☎090.9850; closed Oct–May). For cheaper **pizzas**, *Il Palmento* (closed Nov–Easter), just up from the mud baths, is not bad.

Lípari

There are regular daily hydrofoil services from Vulcano on to **Lípari**, by far the most popular of the islands – and the most diverse. The group's main port and capital, **LÍPARI TOWN** is a thriving little place prettily bunched between two harbours, **arrival** at which is one of *the* island experiences: hydrofoils dock at the Marina Corta, a tiny harbour formed by a church-topped mole and dwarfed by the castle that crowns the hill above; ferries steam straight past, around the mighty sixteenth-century walls of the fort, to dock at the Marina Lunga, a deep-water harbour curving around to the north as a long beach.

The upper town within the fortress walls, the **Castello**, forms the main focus of interest. Finds from the site, which has been continuously occupied since Neolithic times, have enabled archeologists to date other Mediterranean cultures. Alongside the well-marked **excavations**, there's a tangle of dilapidated churches flanking the main cobbled street, and several buildings (including the seventeenth-century bishop's palace) that make up the separate arms of the **Museo Eoliano** (daily: summer 9am–1.30pm, classical section also 3–7pm; winter 9am–1.30pm, classical section also 3–6pm; last entries 1hr before closing; L8000/€4.13) – a lavish collection of Neolithic pottery, late Bronze Age artefacts, and Greek and Roman vases and statues, most of it dug up outside. Down below, the streets wind around the base of the fortified hill and down to the harbours. The town is reliant upon tourism these days – as the restaurants and craft shops testify – but it's all fairly small-scale.

The **tourist office** at Corso Vittorio Emanuele 202 (Sept–June Mon–Fri 8am–2pm & 4.30–7.30pm, Sat 8am–2pm; July & Aug Mon–Sat 8am–2pm & 4–10pm; ☎090.988.0095) can provide a useful hotel list, good for all the Aeolian Islands, but in July and August especially, it makes sense to listen to the offers of **rooms** as you step off the boat. Expect to pay around L50,000–70,000/€26–36.40 per person in August, L35,000/€18.20 at other times of the year, for something with a shower, kitchen and balcony or terrace. Otherwise, good places to try include *Enza Marturano*, Via Maurolico 35 (☎0368.322.4997 or 090.981.2544; ④), whose four bright rooms are ranged around a communal lounge/kitchen; *Enzo Il Negro*, Via Garibaldi 29 (☎090.981.3163; ③; closed Dec), a roomy place with a roof terrace near the hydrofoil port; *Europeo*, Corso Vittorio Emanuele 98 (☎090.981.1589; ④; April–Sept), on the main drag and consequently often full; and the *Neri*, Via G. Marconi 43 (☎090.981.1413; ⑥), a fine old mansion that serves breakfast on a lovely terrace, and which halves its rates in low season. The nearest **campsite** is 3km away at the southern end of the fishing village of Canneto (see opposite) and is called the *Baia Unci* (☎090.981.1909; Easter to Sept); the bus from Lípari stops outside. There's an UPIM **supermarket** and various *alimentari* and bakeries on the main Corso.

The town's numerous **restaurants and pizzerias** have (often poor) tourist menus at around L25,000/€12.91; even the cheaper places impose exorbitant 15 or 20 percent service charges that'll boost your bill. *Bartolo*, Via Garibaldi 53 (closed Fri Oct–June), has great wood-fired pizzas, while *Trattoria d'Oro*, Via Umberto I 32 (closed Oct–Dec), and *A Sfiziusa*, Via Roma 29 (closed Fri Oct–April), are both decent backstreet trattorias. For a gastronomic treat, the expensive *E'Pulera*, Via Diana (☎090.981.1158; mid-May to mid-Sept), specializes in traditional Aeolian food and is set in a romantic courtyard-garden.

The **rest of the island** is easy to reach on a network of regular **buses**, which leave from a stop by the Marina Lunga, opposite the service station. Around here too are a couple of **scooter and bike rental** outfits, such as Da Marcello, Via Sottomonastero (L70,000–120,000/€36.40–62.40 a day for scooters, L10,000–20,000/€5.17–10.34 a day for bikes; ☎090.981.1234). Lípari is a good place to book a **boat excursion**: the main agencies are Viking, Vico Himera 3 (☎090.981.2584), also with a kiosk at the Marina Corta; and La Cava, Corso Vittorio Emanuele 124 (☎090.981.1242). Typically, you'll pay around L60,000/€31.20 for an all-day trip which lets you visit and swim off Panarea and then see the evening explosions off Strómboli; day-trips to Panarea or Vulcano, allowing plenty of swimming, are around half that price.

CANNETO, a fishing village with a pebbled beach and a couple of hotels, also makes an pleasant excursion. From here the road climbs north, passing an excellent sandy beach (the Spiaggia Bianca) a couple of kilometres out of Canneto, before reaching the stony beach at **Porticello**. West of Lípari, the road clambers up the hill to **Quattrocchi** ("Four Eyes"), a three-kilometre hike that ends in glorious and much-photographed views over Vulcano and the spikey *faraglioni* rocks that puncture the sea between the two islands. Keep on the road to **Pianoconte**, which has a couple of pizza restaurants that are popular in the evenings, and just after the village, a side road slinks off down to the old Roman thermal baths at **San Calógero**. This is a particularly fine walk, across a valley and skirting some impressive cliffs. It takes about half-an-hour from Pianoconte.

Salina

North of Lípari, **Salina**'s two extinct volcanic cones rise out of a fertile land which produces capers and white *malvasia* wine by the bucketload. Again, it's excellent walking country (though there are bus services between the main villages) and you get some marvellous vantage points over the other islands.

The main island port is **SANTA MARINA DI SALINA**, on the east coast, visually unexciting but a relaxed enough spot to linger awhile. You can find **private rooms** here if you ask around, or try *Catena de Pasquale* at Via Francesco Crispi 17 (☎090.984.3094; ②). Of the **hotels** and *pensioni*, you're most likely to find room at *Mamma Santina*, Via Sanità 40 (☎090.984.3054; ③), signposted to the left off the main street of Via Risorgimento. This also serves **meals**, or you can indulge in the excellent local antipasto, slabs of swordfish and wine by the carafe at the *Portobello* above the port (closed Nov). **LINGUA**, 3km south, makes a pleasant alternative base, with accommodation at *'A Cannata* (☎090.984.3161; ④), near the church, where some of the rooms come with a terrace and wonderful views of Lípari, or *Il Delfino*, right on the *lungomare*, with attractive rooms attached to its locally renowned restaurant (☎090.984.3024; ③). In both places, half- or full-board is compulsory in peak season.

Trails cut right across Salina, in particular linking Santa Marina with the peak of **Monte Fossa delle Felci** (962m), the sanctuary of Madonna del Terzito and the south coast at Rinella. Take the bus to the sanctuary – any between Santa Marina/Malfa and Leni/Rinella pass right by it – and start there, saving yourself the first three hundred metres of climbing. Don't go overloaded, wear strong shoes, and take plenty of water.

Most ferries and hydrofoils also call at the little port of **RINELLA**, on the island's south coast; if you want to move straight on, **buses** meet the boat arrivals on the quayside (and call here several times a day in addition). Notices at the port advertise **rooms** for rent and there's a nice little **hotel**, too, *L'Ariana* (☎090.980.9075; ⑤), above the port to the left, which requires half- or full-board mid-June to mid-Sept. The village is also the site of the island's one **campsite**, *Tre Pini* (☎090.980.9155; May–Sept), with a bar-restaurant.

Panarea

Panarea, to the east, is the smallest of the Aeolians but easily the most scenic. Only 3km by 1.5km, no cars can squeeze onto the island's narrow lanes to disturb the tranquillity, though heavily laden three-wheelers are common. Indeed, Panarea's cosy intimacy has made it into something of a ghetto for the idle rich. Nevertheless, either side of high season you can find reasonably priced accommodation if you persevere. Panarea's population divides itself among three hamlets on the eastern side of the island, Ditella, San Pietro and Drauto, with the boats docking at **SAN PIETRO**. It's always worth asking around for **rented rooms** – *Trattoria da Francesco* on the harbourside and several houses on Via San Pietro, up from the port, oblige – but bear in mind that the supply of accommodation on the island simply can't meet the demand in July and August. The two cheapest **hotels** are the *Casa Rodà* (☎090.983.006; ④) and the *Bottari* (☎090.983.268; ⑤), both on Via San Pietro and both open summer only. For a splurge, you could try one of the two more luxurious hotels at San Pietro, the *Raya* (☎090.983.101; ⑧; mid-April to mid-Oct), on a hill to the left, or the nearby *Cincotta* (☎090.983.014; ⑧; April–Sept): both have wonderful terraces and facilities, and rates plummet outside high season. The hotels also house Panarea's best **restaurants**, though you can eat more modestly by the harbour at *Trattoria da Francesco*, while *Casa Rodà* has a garden-restaurant serving pizzas in the evenings (both closed in winter).

Half an hour's walk south of San Pietro is the island's one sandy **beach** and, high above here on the other side, **Punta Milazzese**, where a Bronze Age village of 23 huts was discovered in 1948. The site is thought to have been inhabited since the fourteenth century BC, and pottery found here (displayed in Lípari's museum) shows a distinct Minoan influence. Elsewhere, there are hot springs at San Pietro and, at **CALCARA** to the north, a beach and sea that sometimes steam – one effect of the island's *fumarole*.

Strómboli

Despite the regularity of the volcanic explosions, which throw up noise and flashes – and occasionally chunks of rock – throughout the day, people have always lived on **Strómboli**. All the action is limited to one volcanic trail (the Sciara del Fuoco), on the northwest side of the volcano, and the eastern villages, with their white houses standing out against the green slopes, are safely settled. Most of the many hotels and rooms to let on Strómboli are here, in the adjacent parishes of San Vincenzo, San Bartolo and Piscità, often grouped together as **STRÓMBOLI** town and something of a chic resort since Rossellini and Ingrid Bergman immortalized the place in the 1949 film *Strómboli*. From the quayside, the lower coastal road runs around to the main beaches of **Ficogrande** and, further on, **Piscità**, the island's best ashy beach. It's around 25 minutes on foot from the port to here. The other road from the dock cuts up into the "village", where as Via Roma it runs to the church of **San Vincenzo**, whose square offers glorious views of the offshore islet of **Strombolicchio**. Beyond the square, along Via Vittorio Emanuele III, it's another fifteen minutes' walk to the second church of **San Bártolo**, above Piscità.

In summer, the quayside is thick with three-wheelers and touts from the various rooms places waving cards; prices start at around L45,000/€23.40 per person. If you want to try and book a **room** in advance, the following places are all worth contacting: the *Pensione Stella*, at Via Filzi 14 (☎090.986.722; ④), which has attractive, raftered rooms; the remoter *Villa Petrusa* (☎090.986.045; ⑤; April–Oct), where there's an attractive garden, or still further out, the friendly *Pensione Brasile*, Via Soldato Cincotta, in the Piscità district (☎090.986.008; ③). The best **restaurant** in the village is *Il Canneto* (closed Oct–Easter), up from the port, though you'll find cheaper fare and good **pizzas** further up the road at *La Trottola*, a popular place where you can eat for well under L40,000/€20.66 (Easter–Sept, though pizzas available in winter at weekends). At night, there's no better spot for lingering than *Bar Ingrid*, in the square by San Vincenzo church, open until late.

On the other side of the island, the hamlet of **GINOSTRA** is a peaceful place of typical white Aeolian houses on terraces. There's excellent accommodation here, too, at the *Locanda Petrusa* (☎090.981.2305; ③; Easter–Oct), which has three spacious rooms with terraces and a shared bathroom, and also serves meals.. **Hydrofoils** run back to Strómboli three times a day in summer (three a week in winter), but these are susceptible to cancellation because of rough waters.

Guides for the **ascent of the volcano** are readily available in Strómboli village and cost around L35,000/€18.20 per person. The climb up takes three hours; you get an hour or so at the top watching the pyrotechnics, and it then takes another two hours to descend. Although there are signs suggesting otherwise, many people make the hike alone: it's not dangerous provided you stick to the marked paths. The **route** starts a few minutes' walk beyond San Bartolo church (see opposite), where a fork bears left and then climbs upwards for an easy forty minutes to *L'Osservatorio*, a bar-pizzeria (closed in winter) with a wide terrace and a view of the volcano. Beyond this point, you'll need to be properly equipped: good shoes, a sunhat and plenty of water (a minimum of two litres per person) are essential. If you intend to spend the night at the top take a sweater, waterproofs, groundsheet, sleeping bag, torch and food, and bed down in one of the lava shelters until dawn. Do not, under any circumstances, come down in the dark without a guide, and if it clouds over or starts to rain heavily, stay put until it clears.

The main **boat trips** offered are tours around the island, calling at Ginostra and Strombolicchio (3hr; L25,000/€13); and trips out at night to see the Sciara del Fuoco by boat (1hr; L25,000/€13). A friendly outfit is run by Pippo – of Società Navigazione Pippo (☎090.986.135 or 0338.985.7883) – who has a stand in front of the *Beach Bar*.

THE IONIAN COAST: MESSINA TO SIRACUSA

It's Sicily's eastern **Ionian coast** which draws most visitors, attracted by some of the island's most exciting sights – natural and constructed. The most likely arrival point is **Messina**, which receives a constant stream of ferries bearing trains across the Straits from Calabria. **Taormina**, most chic of the island's resorts and famed for its remarkable Graeco-Roman theatre, is an hour's train ride south, and lava-built **Catania**, Sicily's second city, is another hour beyond: both places (indeed the whole of this part of the coast) are dominated by the massive presence of **Mount Etna**, Europe's highest volcano. A road and a narrow-gauge, single-track railway circumnavigate the lower slopes of Etna, passing through a series of hardy towns surrounded by swirls of black rock spat from the volcano. Further south, out of the lee of Etna, lie traces of the ancient Greek cities that once lined the southeastern coast. **Megara Hyblaea** has the most extensive remains, and the route concludes in **Siracusa** – formerly the most important and beautiful city in the Hellenistic world.

Messina and south

MESSINA may well be your first sight of Sicily; and – from the ferry – it's a fine one, the glittering town spread up the hillside beyond the sickle-shaped harbour. Sadly, the image is shattered almost as soon as you step into the city, bombed and shaken to a shadow of its former self by a record number of disasters. Plague, cholera and earthquakes all struck throughout the eighteenth and nineteenth centuries, culminating in the great earthquake of 1908 that killed 84,000 people, levelled the city and made the shore sink by half a metre overnight. Allied bombing raids in 1943 didn't help, undoing much of the post-earthquake restoration.

Today, the remodelled city guards against future natural disasters, with wide streets and low, reinforced concrete buildings marching off in all directions. Not surprisingly, it is a pretty dull spectacle, and most of what interest there is resides in Messina's active port area. Take time at least to walk up Via I Settembre from the train station to Piazza del Duomo. The traffic-cluttered paved square was laid out in the eighteenth century, while the **Duomo** itself (daily 7.30am–11.45pm & 4.30–7pm, 3.30–6pm in winter) is a faithful reconstruction of the medieval cathedral built by Roger II. The facade retains its grand doorways and some original sculpture: inside, most of what you see – from the marble floor to the painted wooden ceiling – has been retouched and rebuilt. The detached **campanile** reputedly contains the largest astronomical clock in the world. Be there at noon and you get the full show, a visually impressive panoply of moving gilt figures including a crowing cock, roaring lion and a succession of doves and angels accompanying the Madonna.

Much of what was salvaged from the various disasters now resides in the **Museo Regionale** (summer Mon, Wed & Fri 9am–1.30pm, Tues, Thurs & Sat 9am–1.30pm & 4–6.30pm, Sun 9am–12.30pm; winter Mon, Wed & Fri 9am–1.30pm, Tues, Thurs & Sat 9am–1.30pm & 3–5.30pm; L8000/€4.13), 3km north of the centre – a 45-minute walk along Via della Libertà, or bus #28 from Piazza Cairoli or Via Garibaldi, or buses #76, #77, #78 and #79 from Via Garibaldi or the train station. A great deal has been painstakingly stuck and plastered back together in this beautifully laid-out museum, including a couple of Caravaggios, commissioned by the city in 1604. There are also damaged works by Antonello da Messina, a few good Flemish pieces and the city's rescued archeological remains as well.

If you're in Messina in mid-summer, you may coincide with the feast of the Assumption, or **ferragosto**, August 15, when a towering carriage, the *Vara* – an elaborate column supporting dozens of papier-mâché putti and angels, topped by the figure of Christ stretching out his right arm to launch Mary heavenwards – is hauled through the city centre. Late at night, one of Sicily's best **firework displays** is held on the seafront near Via della Libertà.

Practicalities

Trains all use the **Stazione Centrale** by the harbour, adjacent to the **Stazione Maríttima** – where the train-ferries from Calabria dock. Other **ferries** and **hydrofoils** (to and from Villa San Giovanni, Reggio di Calabria and the Aeolian Islands) dock at quays further to the north, on Via Vittorio Emanuele and Via della Libertà. SAIS **buses** for Taormina and Catania leave to the right of the train station, while those for Milazzo (for onward connections to the Aeolian Islands) depart from the Giuntabus office at Via Terranova 8 (at the corner of Viale San Martino). There are two **tourist offices** just outside the train station: one on Piazza della Repubblica (Mon–Thurs 8.30am–1.30pm & 3–6pm, Fri–Sat 8am–1pm; ☎090.672.944); the other behind the station on Via Calabria (Mon–Sat 8am–6.30pm; ☎090.674.236); both can supply you with free maps, Aeolian Island ferry timetables and accommodation lists.

Unless you arrive late in the day, it's hardly necessary to **stay over** in Messina. Still, there are a couple of basic options on Via N. Scotto, an alley on the south side of Piazza della Repubblica, beyond the SAIS office: the *Mirage*, at no. 3, with all rooms en suite (☎090.293.8844; ②); and the sprucer *Touring*, at no. 17 (☎090.293.8851; ②). If you would prefer something a little slicker, more business-orientated, try the modern *Excelsior* (☎090.293.1431; ④), near Piazza Cairoli at Via Maddalena 32. There's a **campsite**, *Il Peloritano* (☎090.348.496), out beyond Punta del Faro on the northern coast; take bus #81 to Rodia from the train station. Messina has a good choice of **restaurants**, in which you should try the swordfish, freshly caught and a local speciality; May and June are the best months for this, before the water gets too warm. *Lungomare da Mario* is a good choice, opposite the hydrofoil dock at Via Vittorio Emanuele (closed Wed except Aug); otherwise try *Osteria del Campanile*, Via Loggia dei Mercanti 9, off Piazza del Duomo (closed Sun), for surprisingly good pasta, or the basic but good *Pizzeria del Capitano* at Via dei Mille 88, close to Piazza Cairoli (closed Mon). For good *panini* and other cold **snacks**, head for *Salumeria Nucita*, an *alimentari* at Via Garibaldi 125 (closed Wed evening & Sun). There's an **internet point** at Via Garibaldi 225 (Mon–Sat 8am–2pm & 4.30–8.30pm).

The coastal route south

Try to take the train, rather than the slower bus or road option, **south from Messina**, since the line follows the rough, stony shore pretty much all the way: on a clear day there are spanking views over to Calabria.

Santa Teresa Di Riva is the first recognizable resort, with an oversized beach, though it's nothing to shout about. The straggling village is more attractive as a jumping-off point for the foothills of the **Monti Peloritani**, the long mountain range that cuts south from Messina. Buses from Santa Teresa twist the 4km up to **SAVOCA**, a peaceful hill-village, evocatively sited up in the clouds. Houses and three churches perch precariously on the cliff sides in clumps, a tattered castle topping the pile. Signs in the village point you to the **Cappuccini monastery** whose catacombs (Tues–Sun: summer 9am–1pm & 4–7pm; winter 9am–1pm & 3–5pm; donation requested) maintain a selection of mummified bodies, two to three hundred years old, in niches, dressed in their eighteenth-century finery, the skulls of less complete compatriots lining the walls above. More offbeat delight is at hand in the village's *Bar Vitelli*, used as the scene of Michael Corleone's betrothal in Coppola's film *The Godfather*; there are old curios inside, and terrace tables outside. Two kilometres on, **Casalvecchio Siculo** has even better valley views from its terraces and is the nearest village to the Norman monastery of **San Pietro e Paolo**, a twenty-minute hike away. Built in the twelfth century, its battlemented facade and double domes are visible from quite a distance, and the church betrays a strong Arabic influence.

Taormina

TAORMINA, high on Monte Tauro and dominating two grand sweeping bays below, is Sicily's best-known resort. The outstanding remains of its classical theatre, with Mount Etna as an unparalleled backdrop, arrested passing travellers when Taormina was no more than a medieval hill-village. Goethe and D.H. Lawrence are the two big names touted by the tourist office; Lawrence was so enraptured that he lived here (1920–23) in a house at the top of the valley cleft behind the theatre. Although international tourism has taken its toll over recent years, Taormina still retains much of its small-town charm. The one main traffic-free street is an unbroken line of fifteenth- to nineteenth-century palazzi and small, intimate piazzas, and there is an agreeably crumbly castle and rows of flower-filled balconies. The downside is that between June and

August it's virtually impossible to find anywhere to stay, and the narrow alleys are shoulder-to-shoulder with tourists. April, May or September are slightly better, but to avoid the crowds completely come between October and March, when it's often still warm enough to swim.

Arrival, information and accommodation

Trains pull up at Taormina-Giardini station (left-luggage office 6am–10pm) on the water's edge, way below town. It's a very steep thirty-minute walk up to Taormina (turn right out of the station and then, after 200m, left through a gap in the buildings, marked "Centro"). Much better (certainly if you have luggage) is to arrive by bus or take one of the fairly frequent local buses that pick up outside the train station. The **bus terminal** is on Via Pirandello in Taormina itself: bear left up the road from the terminal, turn through the Porta Messina, and the main street, **Corso Umberto I**, lies before you. The **tourist office** (Mon–Sat 8.30am–2pm & 4–7pm; ☎0942.23.243) is in the fourteenth-century Palazzo Corvaja, off Piazza Vittorio Emanuele, the first square you come to; pick up a free map, accommodation listings and bus timetables, and programmes for summer events in the theatre.

Finding a bed in summer is a time-consuming business; only a handful will be both available and affordable, so start looking early. The best prices are for **rented rooms**, for example close to the public gardens at the *Leone*, Via Bagnoli Croce 126 (☎0942.23.878; ②); nearer the Greek theatre at Via Iallia Bassa 20 (☎0942.24.776; ②), with incredible roof-terrace views, or else the tiny but cheap and central *Diana* at Via di Giovanni 6 (☎0942.23.898; ②). A big step up in price gets you a **hotel** room at the pleasant *Pensione Elios* at Via Bagnoli Croce 98 (☎0942.23.431; ⑤) or the *Pensione Svizzera*, at Via Pirandello 26 (☎0942.23.790; ⑤), just up from the bus terminal and enjoying excellent views from its spacious rooms. A family-run place, the *Pensione Villa Greta* (☎0942.28.286; ⑤) is warmly recommended: ten minutes' walk out of town on the road up to Castelmola, it has superb balcony views as well as a dining room with good home cooking.

The nearest **campsite**, *San Leo* (☎0942.24.658), is on the cape below town (next to the *Grande Albergo Capo Taormina*): take any bus running between Taormina and the train station. Better sites are further afield, at Letojanni and Giardini-Naxos (see opposite) – the latter where you might also continue your search for a room if you've had no luck in Taormina.

The Town

The **Teatro Greco** (daily 9am–1hr before sunset; L8000/€4.13) – signposted from just about everywhere – is where you should make for first, if only to acquaint yourself with Taormina's remarkable siting, with panoramic views encompassing southern Calabria, the Sicilian coastline and snow-capped Etna. That it was founded by Greeks in the third century BC is the extent of the theatre's Hellenistic connections, for the visible remains are almost entirely Roman. It was rebuilt at the end of the first century AD, when Taormina thrived under imperial Roman rule, and the reconstruction changed the theatre's character entirely. The impressive Roman scene building, for example, is Sicily's only surviving example but can only have obscured the views of Etna – presumably a major reason for the theatre's original siting. Likewise, the stage and lower seats were cut back to provide more room and a deep trench dug in the orchestra to accommodate the animals and fighters used in Roman gladiatorial contests. Between July and August the theatre hosts an international **arts festival** including film, theatre and music (tickets and information from the tourist office).

There are a few other Roman vestiges around town, including a much smaller **Odeon** (originally used for musical recitations) next to the tourist office. Really, though, Taormina's attractions are all to do with strolling the flower-decked streets and alleys, and window shopping in the converted ground floors of the mansions along the Corso. Centre of town is Piazza IX Aprile, with its restored twelfth-century **Torre dell'Orologio** and terrace overlooking Etna and the bay – though don't sit down at the inviting outdoor cafés unless you have a substantial bankroll. Give yourself time to hike up to the **Castello** by way of a stepped path leading up from the main road behind the tourist office, from where you can continue on to **Castelmola**, 5km above and seemingly growing out of its severe crag. It's about an hour's climb to the village (though there are buses), while another couple of hours beyond are the heights of **Monte Venere** (885m) – take the path behind Castelmola's cemetery – for the last word in local vistas.

Eating

Eating in Taormina can be an expensive business, though most places have tourist menus of varying standards and prices. Among the **trattorias**, *Il Baccanale* in Piazza Filea, off Via Bagnoli Croce (closed Thurs in winter), serves good grilled sardines at outdoor tables, while below Porta Messina the *Trattoria da Nino* cooks up basic but good pasta and seafood dishes at Via Pirandello 37 (closed Fri in Nov–Feb), and *Terrazza Angelo*, Corso Umberto 38 (closed Thurs in Nov–Easter), does good seafood and pizzas, and has a panoramic terrace. For **pizzas** and pasta in lively surroundings, there's *Mamma Rosa*, Via Naumachia 10 (closed Nov), and the more secluded *La Botte*, Piazza Santa Domenica 4 (closed Mon in winter), both touristy but serving good hearty meals at their outdoor tables. For snacks, there's an indoor **market** off Via Cappuccini (mornings only, Mon–Sat) and a good **rosticceria** just up from Porta Messina, on the corner of Via Timeo and Via Patricio.

Taormina's beaches – and Naxos

The **coastline** below town is unquestionably appealing – a mixture of grottoes and rocky coves – but too many of its beaches are either private lidos (which you have to pay to use) or simply too packed in summer to be much fun.

Closest beach to town is at **Mazzarò** with its much-photographed islet. There's a **cable car** service (L3000/€1.55) that runs every fifteen minutes from Via Pirandello and a steep path that starts just below the cable car station. If you're still searching for a bed there are a dozen small **hotels** here, though get the tourist office to phone first. The beach-bars and restaurants at **Spisone**, north again, are also reachable by path from Taormina, this time from below the cemetery in town. From Spisone, the coast opens out and the beach gets wider. With more time you might explore **Letojanni**, a little resort in its own right with rather more ordinary bars and shops, a few fishing boats on a sand beach, two campsites and regular buses and trains back to Taormina.

Roomier and better for swimming are the sands south of Taormina at **GIARDINI-NAXOS**, and to a lesser extent at the holiday village of Recanati, beyond. Be prepared to pay to use the beach, a few hundred lire for access, a couple of thousand for a sunbed. The wide curving bay of Giardini – easily seen from Taormina's terraces – was the launching-point of Garibaldi's attack on the Bourbon troops in Calabria (1860) and, as significantly, the site of the first Greek colony in Sicily. An obvious stop for ships running between Greece and southern Italy, it was the site of a settlement in 734 BC, named Naxos after the Naxian colonists. It was never very important, and the extensive **excavations** (daily: Easter–Sept 9am–7pm; Oct–Easter 9am–4.30pm; L4000/€2.07) are very low-key – a long section of ancient, lava-built city wall, two covered kilns and a sketchy temple. But it's a pleasant walk there through the lemon groves (bus from Taormina to Naxos/Recanati and follow the "Scavi" signs), and you can see some of the finds in a **Museo Archeologico** by the entrance to the site (same ticket).

Giardini itself, the long town backing the good beach, is an excellent alternative source of accommodation and food. Prices tend to be a good bit cheaper than in Taormina and in high season, if you arrive by train, it's probably worth trying here first. Recommended **places to stay** are *La Sirena*, Via Schisò 36 (☎0942.51.853; ②), by the pier with views over the bay, and the central *Villa Pamar*, Via Naxos 23 (☎0942.52.448; ③), behind the tourist office, both offering good value for their central locations. For **eating**, the best and the cheapest is the restaurant-pizzeria attached to the seafront *Lido Europa* (opposite the Chiesa Immacolata); good pizzas and fresh pasta are also to be had at *Fratelli Marano*, Via Naxos 181. For terrace seating and views of the bay, visit *Da Angelina* beyond the port on Via C. Eubea (Nov–Feb closed Wed) – it does fine fish soup. **Buses** run half-hourly to Giardini from Taormina, the last one at midnight in summer and 10.30pm at other times; the last one back is at 11.40pm in summer, otherwise 7.35pm, from the stop on the seafront opposite the Chiesa Immacolata.

Around Mount Etna

Mount Etna's massive bulk looms over much of the coastal route south from Taormina. One of the world's largest volcanoes, it really demands a separate visit, but if you're pushed for time you'll have to content yourself with the ever more imminent views of its eastern flank as you head along the coast to Catania. With time, you can make the circular route to Catania on the slow train around the volcano, the **Circumetnea** – one of Sicily's most interesting rides – and stop off on the **volcano** itself. Reaching the lower craters below the summit is eminently possible, on foot or by mountain-bus – either way a thrilling experience.

South down the coast: Acireale, Aci Trezza and Aci Castello

The train is best if you're travelling directly to Catania, a fast route which hugs the coast. The only major town on the way is **ACIREALE**, 35km south of Taormina. Well sited a couple of kilometres above the rocky shore, and a noted spa centre, Acireale was rebuilt directly over the old lava streams after the 1693 earthquake. Aside from the views along the coast from its pretty public garden, the town's worth a stop for its several striking examples of Sicilian Baroque in the crowded central streets. A good time to come is at *Carnevale* (February/March), when Acireale hosts one of Sicily's best festivals, with flower-decked floats and fancy dress parades clogging the streets for five noisy days.

Acireale takes its name from the local river Aci, in Homeric myth said to have appeared following the death of the shepherd Acis at the hands of the giant, one-eyed cyclops Polyphemus. Other nearby villages take the name too, like **Aci Trezza** and **Aci Castello**, a few kilometres south (both reachable on the Messina–Catania bus route). Between the two, just offshore, the jagged points of the **Scogli dei Cicopli** stand: Homer wrote that the now blinded Polyphemus slung these rocks, broken from Etna, at Ulysses as he and his men escaped from the Cyclops in their ships. The three main sharp-edged islets present an odd sight, and it's a good half day's entertainment to get off the bus at Aci Trezza and walk the couple of kilometres south along the rough coast to Aci Castello. The **Castello** itself (Tues–Sun: summer 9am–1pm & 4.30–7.30pm; winter 9am–1pm & 3–5pm; free) is a terrific thirteenth-century building that rises above the sea in splinters from a volcanic rock crag. In summer the rough, lava-spattered coastline around town is popular for sunbathing and swimming, while Aci Castello has a couple of small restaurants, handy for lunch. Very frequent buses connect the two villages with Catania.

The Circumetnea railway: Giarre-Riposto to Catania

If you don't have the time to reach the summit of Etna, then the **Circumetnea** railway provides alternative volcanic thrills. A private line, 114km long, it runs around the base of the volcano through fertile vegetation and the strewn lava from more recent eruptions – a marvellous ride. The line begins in the twin town of **Giarre-Riposto**, thirty minutes by train or bus from Taormina; mainline FS trains will drop you at Giarre, the second stop of the Circumetnea line. Rail passes are not valid on this route, and if you make the entire trip to Catania, allow five hours; tickets cost L10,000/€5.17 one way, L20,000/€10.33 return.

The closest town to the summit is **RANDAZZO**, a dark medieval town built entirely of lava. Although dangerously near Etna, Randazzo has never been engulfed; when the 1981 eruption took it to the point of evacuation, the lava-flow finally stopped just outside town. Poke around the gloomy streets – dingily authentic despite the fact that much of the town has been heavily restored after being bombed to bits in 1943, when it figured as the last Sicilian stronghold of the Axis forces.

If you want to break the journey around Etna then Randazzo is probably the place to stay, despite the fact that the only **accommodation** is the uninspiring *Scrivano* (☎095.921.126; ④), behind the Agip petrol station on Via Regina Margherita. You could, anyway, give Randazzo a couple of hours and pick up the next Circumetnea train for Catania – or the regular branch line (rail passes valid) to Taormina-Giardini.

Mount Etna: the ascent

The bleak lava wilderness around the summit of **Etna** is one of the most memorable landscapes Italy has to offer. While circling its lower slopes by road or rail is fine for the views, it can only be second best to the spectacular ascent – an expedition which should not be undertaken lightly. At 3323m, Etna is a fairly substantial mountain, and one of the world's biggest active volcanoes. Some of its eruptions have been disastrous: in 1169, 1329 and 1381 the lava reached the sea; in 1669 Catania was wrecked and its castle surrounded by molten rock; while this century the Circumetnea railway line has been repeatedly ruptured by lava flows and, in 1979, nine people were killed on the edge of the main crater.

This unpredictability means that it's no longer possible to get close to the main crater. An **eruption** in 1971 destroyed the observatory supposed to give warning of just such an event; another in 1983 brought down the cable car that provided access to the crater, and the volcano has been in an almost continual state of eruption since 1998. All this is not to say you'll be in any danger, provided you heed the warnings as you get closer to the top.

There are several **approaches** to the volcano. If you have a car you can enjoy some of the best scenery, on the north side of the volcano, by taking the road that leads up from Linguaglossa. On **public transport**, though, you'll need to come via **Nicolosi**, on the southern side of Etna and an hour from Catania by bus. A winter ski resort and last main stop before the steeper slopes begin, it's a good place to pick up information – from the small **tourist office** at Via Garibaldi 63 (daily 8.30am–1pm, summer also 4–7.30pm), the main road that runs through Nicolosi. There are several **hotels** too, a couple in town, the rest on the road out, as well as a **campsite** – all signposted and detailed on full lists available from the information office.

Although there are frequent buses to Nicolosi from Catania, only one (around 8am from outside Catania train station) continues to **Rifugio Sapienza**, the mountain refuge-cum-hotel that marks the end of the negotiable road up the south side of Etna. Everywhere here the slopes are dotted with earlier, spent craters, grass-covered on the lower reaches, like black pimples further up. At the car park beyond the road there's a line of souvenir shops, a couple of restaurants and the *Rifugio Sapienza* (☎095.911.062; ②)) itself. Arriving on the early-morning bus, you should have enough time to make the top and get back for the return bus to Catania – it leaves around 4.45pm from the refuge.

There are two ways **up the volcano** from the refuge. You can either take the **cable car** (L35,000/€18.20 return) to the *Rifugio Montagnola*, from where jeeps will drop you just below the main crater (L68,000/€35.36 ticket includes cable car, jeep and the guide both ways; April–Oct/Nov); or you can **walk**, following the rough minibus track. Really it all depends on finances and time: walking up will take between three and four hours, the return obviously a little less. However you go, at whatever time of year, take warm clothes, good shoes or boots and glasses to keep the flying grit out of your eyes.

As you climb, the ground under your feet is alternately black, grey or red depending on the age of the lava. The more recent stuff lies in great folds, and earlier minor craters are signposted. The highest you're allowed to get (on foot or in the bus) is 2900m, and though there's only a rope across the ground to prevent you from climbing further, this would be a foolish act – gaseous explosions and molten rock are common this far up. From the turn-around point for the jeeps you can look up to the summit, with smoke puffing from the southeast crater immediately above. Higher still is the main crater: depending on the weather conditions you may see smoke from here too and, if you're lucky, spitting explosions. If you've walked, you'll be glad of the **bar** set up in a wooden hut here, one of the odder places in the world to sip a cappuccino.

Catania

First impressions don't do much at all for **CATANIA**, on an initial encounter possibly the island's gloomiest spot. Built from black-grey volcanic stone, its central streets can feel suffocating, dark with the shadows of grimy, high Baroque churches and *palazzi*; and the presence of Etna dominates everywhere, in the buildings, in the brooding vistas you get of the mountain at the end of Catania's streets – even the city's main street is named after the volcano.

Yet fight the urge to change buses and run: Catania is one of the most intriguing, and historic, of Sicily's cities. Some of the island's first Greek colonists settled the site as early as 729 BC, becoming so influential that their laws were eventually adopted by all the Ionian colonies of Magna Graecia. Later, a series of natural disasters helped shape the city as it appears today: Etna erupted in 1669, engulfing the city, the lava swamping the harbour, which was then topped by an earthquake in 1693 that devastated the whole of southeastern Sicily. The swift rebuilding was on a grand scale, and making full use of the local building material, Giovanni Vaccarini, the eighteenth-century architect, gave the city a lofty, noble air. Despite the neglect of many of the churches and the disintegrating, grey mansions, there's still interest in what, at first, might seem intimidating. Delving about throws up lava-encrusted Roman relics, surviving alongside some of the finest Baroque work on the island.

Arrival, information and accommodation

The **Stazione Centrale**, for all mainline trains, is in Piazza Giovanni XXIII, northeast of the centre (train information ☎147.888.088). If you're changing on to the round-Etna train, the **Stazione Circumetnea** is at Corso delle Province 13, just off Corso Italia (information ☎095.531.402 or 095.374.842). The **airport**, Fontanarossa (☎095.730.6266 or 095.730.6277), is 5km south and is the entry point of most charter flights to Sicily. To get into the city, take the Alibus (every 15min, 5am–midnight; L1300/€0.68) from right outside, which runs to the central Piazza Stesicoro (on Via Etnea) and to Stazione

Centrale in around 20 minutes. A taxi from the rank outside the airport will cost around L35,000/€18.20 for the same journey.

All **buses**, both regional from Catania province and island-wide, stop at various points in Piazza Giovanni XXIII, across from the train station. Of the bus companies, AST (☎095.746.1096; timetables are pinned to posts and there's a ticket office at Via L. Sturzo 230, on the east side of the square) stop opposite the station and serve Acireale, Carlentini, Etna (*Rifugio Sapienza*), Lentini and Nicolosi; Etna Trasporti (☎095.530.396) leave from Via d'Amico 181, at the back of the piazza, for Caltagirone, Piazza Armerina, Gela, Giardini-Naxos and Taormina; Interbus (☎095.532.716), going to Acireale, Giardini-Naxos, Taormina, Siracusa and Ragusa, also depart from Via d'Amico 181, as do SAIS (☎095.536.168) to Agrigento, Enna, Caltanissetta, Messina/Taormina, Nicosia, Noto, Pachino, Palermo and Siracusa.

Immediately outside the Stazione Centrale you'll find ranks of AMT **city buses**: #1/4, #4/7, #4/27, #4/39 and #431 run into the centre, along Via VI Aprile and Via Vittorio Emanuele to Piazza del Duomo; the #4/8 also takes you to Via Etnea. Other central pick-up points are Piazza del Duomo itself, Piazza Stesicoro, and Piazza Borsellino (below Piazza del Duomo), where there's a stop for the airport Alibus and for buses #4/27 and #5/38, which serve the campsites. **Tickets** (L1300/€0.68) are valid for any number of journeys within ninety minutes and are available from *tabacchi*, the newsagents inside Stazione Centrale or the booth outside the station. The same outlets also sell a Biglietto Giornaliero (L3500/€1.82), valid for one-day's unlimited travel on all local AMT bus routes.

There's a **tourist office** (daily 9am–7pm; ☎095.730.6255) inside Stazione Centrale, with English-speaking staff. The main office (daily 9am–7pm; ☎095.730.6233 or 095.730.6222, fax 095.316.407) is signposted off Via Etnea, at Via Cimarosa 10. There's also an **information office** at the airport (daily 8am–9pm; ☎095.730.6266 or 095.730.6277).

Accommodation

There are lots of **places to stay** in Catania, and some real bargains if you hunt around. Around Via Etnea, *Pensione Gresi*, Via Pacini 28 (☎ & fax 095.322.709; ②) and the *Rubens*, Via Etnea 196 (☎095.317.073, fax 095.321.1277; ②) are among the best budget choices, clean and simple, though they fill quickly. Further down at Via Vasta 10, on the corner with Via Etnea, *La Collegiata* (☎095.315.256; ③) has a little more character, occupying a restored Baroque palazzo. If you want to stay nearer the station, the *Holland* is a good choice at Via Vittorio Emanuele 8 (☎095.533.605; ②), with a multi-lingual Dutch owner and vaulted frescoed ceilings. Around Piazza del Duomo, the *Savona* at Via Vittorio Emanuele 210 (☎095.326.982, fax 095.715.8169; ②) is a solid choice, or try the pleasant new **youth hostel** near the fish market in Piazza Currò (☎095.533.605; L26,000/€13.52), where breakfast is included in the price. There are three **campsites** (with lidos and cabins available) a short way south of the city on Lungomare Kennedy; take bus #4/27 or #5/38 (the latter service operates in summer only) from the train station or Via Etnea.

The City

Catania's main square, **Piazza del Duomo**, is a handy orientation point and a stop for most city buses: Via Etnea steams off north, lined with the city's most fashionable shops and cafés; fish market and port lie behind to the south; train station to the east; the best of the Baroque quarter to the west.

It's also one of Sicily's most attractive city squares, rebuilt completely in the first half of the eighteenth century by Vaccarini and surrounded with fine Baroque structures. Most striking of these is the **Municipio** on the northern side of the piazza, finished in

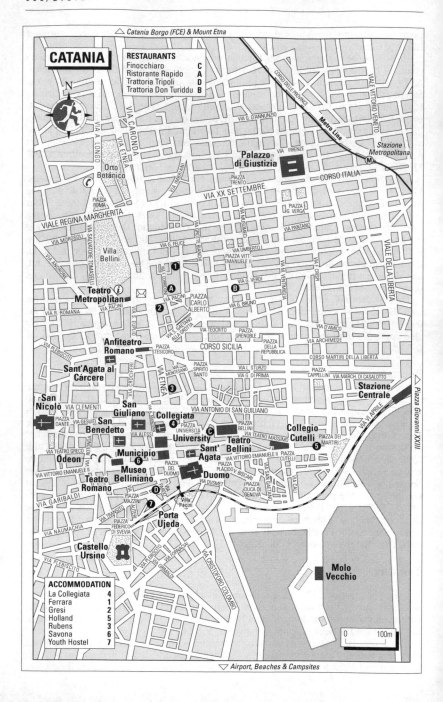

△ *Catania Borgo (FCE) & Mount Etna*

CATANIA

RESTAURANTS
Finocchiaro   **C**
Ristorante Rapido   **A**
Trattoria Tripoli   **D**
Trattoria Don Turiddu   **B**

ACCOMMODATION
La Collegiata   **4**
Ferrara   **1**
Gresi   **2**
Holland   **5**
Rubens   **3**
Savona   **6**
Youth Hostel   **7**

▽ *Airport, Beaches & Campsites*

1741, though to admire it properly you'll have to gain the central reserve of the piazza. Here, the **elephant fountain** is the city's symbol, the eighteenth-century lava elephant supporting an Egyptian obelisk on its back.

Cross back for the **Duomo** (daily 8am–noon & 5–8pm) on the piazza's eastern flank. Apart from the marvellous volcanic-rock medieval apses (seen through the gate at Via Vittorio Emanuele 159), this was pretty much entirely remodelled by Vaccarini, whose heavy Baroque touch is readily apparent from the imposing facade on which he tagged granite columns from Catania's Roman amphitheatre (see below). The interior is no less grand: adorned by a rich series of chapels, notably the Cappella di Sant'Agata to the right of the choir, which conceals the relics paraded through the city on the saint's festival days.

Nearby is Catania's open-air **market**, a noisome affair with slabs and buckets full of twitching fish, eels and shellfish and endless lanes full of vegetable and fruit stalls, as well as one or two excellent lunchtime trattorias. The roads wind through a pretty dilapidated neighbourhood to an open space punctured by the **Castello Ursino**, once the proud fortress of Frederick II. Originally the castle stood on a rocky cliff, over the beach, but following the 1669 eruption, which reclaimed this entire area from the sea, all that remains is the blackened keep. The **Museo Cívico** (Tues–Sat 9am–1pm & 3–6pm, Sun 9am–1pm; free) is housed inside, its central chambers hung with retrieved mosaic fragments, stone inscriptions and tombstones, while other rooms hold an extraordinarily delightful range of items, including a Greek terracotta statuette of two goddesses being pulled in a sea carriage by mythical beasts and a seventeenth-century French pistol, inlaid in silver and depicting rabbits, fish and cherubs.

Back towards the centre, dingy **Piazza Mazzini** heralds perhaps the most interesting section of the city. Everything close by is big and Baroque, and **Via Crocíferi** – which strikes north from the main road, under an arch – is lined with some of the most arresting religious and secular examples, best seen on a slow amble, peering in the eighteenth-century courtyards and churches. At the bottom of the narrow street, the house where the composer Vincenzo Bellini was born in 1801 now houses the **Museo Belliniano** (Mon–Fri 9am–1.30pm, Sun 9am–12.30pm; free), an agreeable collection of photographs, original scores and other memorabilia. A local boy, Bellini notches up several tributes around the city, including a piazza, theatre and park named after him, a berth in the duomo and the ultimate accolade, *spaghetti Norma*. Cooked with tomato, ricotta and aubergine sauce, and named after one of Bellini's operas, it's a Catanian speciality.

West from here, the **Teatro Romano** (Mon–Sat 9am–1pm & 3–7pm, Sun 9am–2pm; L4000/€2.07) was built of lava in the second century AD on the site of an earlier Greek theatre, and much of the seating and the underground passageways are preserved, though all the marble which originally covered it has disappeared. Further west, down Via Teatro Greco, the pretty crescent of Piazza Dante stares out over the unfinished facade of **San Nicolò**, the biggest church in Sicily, stark and empty of detail both outside and in following its partial eighteenth-century restoration. The builders are in again now, but there's usually someone around in the early morning to show you the echoing interior – virtually undecorated save for a meridian line drawn across the floor of the transept. The church is part of the adjoining **convent**, also under restoration and, in terms of size at least, equally impressive.

Nearby, a few minutes' walk north, the little twelfth-century church of **Sant'Agata al Cárcere** (Tues–Sat 4–7pm, Sun 9.30am–noon), with its strong defensive walls, couldn't be less roomy. It was built on the site of the prison where St Agatha was confined before her martyrdom, and a custodian lets you into the third-century crypt – now bright with electric candles. From here, you drop down into **Piazza Stesicoro**, the enormous square that marks the modern centre of Catania, one half of which is almost entirely occupied by the closed-off, sunken, black remains of Catania's **Anfiteatro Romano**, dating back to the second or third century AD. In its heyday, the amphitheatre could hold around 16,000 spectators, and from the church steps above you can see the seating quite clearly, supported by long vaults.

Eating and drinking

You'll rarely do better for eating than in Catania, where fresh **fish** is a speciality. The *Ristorante Rapido*, Via Corridoni 17 (closed Sun), off Via Pacini, is probably Catania's best-value restaurant – great at lunch, with a bargain *pranzo completo*. Worth trying too is the *Trattoria Tripoli*, Via Pardo 30 (closed Sun), close by the fish market, where you can try the fried fish and *spaghetti alla Norma* specialities. For a more expensive meal, *Ristorante Finocchiaro*, off Piazza dell'Università at Via E. Reina 13, has excellent antipasti and unusual local dishes, and at *Don Turiddu*, Via Musumeci 50, there's no menu, just a splendid parade of antipasti and fish at the entrance for you to take your pick (closed Sun & Aug). For **snacks**, *Savia*, Via Etnea 302, opposite the main entrance to the Villa Bellini, is one of the town's finest stand-up café-bars, open since 1899.

Catania's student population ensures a fair choice of youthful **bars and pubs** – some with live music – which stay open late. In addition, the *comune* operates *café concerto* periods during the summer, when the streets and squares of the old town, between Piazza Università and Piazza Bellini, are closed to traffic between 9pm and 2am. The bars here all spill tables out onto the squares and alleys, and live bands keep things swinging until the small hours.

Listings

American Express c/o La Duca Viaggi, Via Etnea 63 (☎095.316.155); Mon–Fri 9am–1pm & 4–7.30pm, Sat 9am–noon (but not for cashing cheques).

Car rental Avis, at airport (☎095.340.500) and Via V. Giuffrida 19 (☎095.445.536); Maggiore/Budget, at airport (☎095.340.594); National Car Rental, at airport (☎095.340.252); Hertz, at airport (☎095.341.595) and Via P. Toselli 16 (☎095.322.560); Holiday Car Rental, at airport (☎095.346.769).

Emergencies ☎113 for all emergency services.

Hospital Ospedale Vittorio Emanuele, Via Plebiscito; Ospedale Generale Garibaldi, Piazza S. Maria di Gesù 7; S. Tomaselli, Via Passo Gravina 185; for any of these, call ☎095.759.1111.

Pharmacies Caltabiano, Piazza Stesicoro 34 (☎095.327.647); Croce Rossa, Via Etnea 274 (☎095.317.053); Europa, Corso Italia 105 (☎095.383.536).

Police Emergencies ☎112; Carabinieri, Piazza Giovanni Verga 8 (☎095.537.822).

Post office Main post office and poste restante at Via Etnea 215, close to the Villa Bellini (Mon–Sat 8.30am–7.30pm).

Telephones Offices at Corso Sicilia 67, at the airport (both daily 9am–8pm), and at Via A. Longo 54 (daily 8am–9.45pm), next to the botanical gardens.

Travel agents La Duca Viaggi, Via Etnea 63–65 (☎095.316.155); Elisea, Corso Sicilia 31 (☎095.312.321); Etnea Viaggi, Corso Sicilia 109 (☎095.327.080); Viaggi Wasteel, Piazza Giovanni XXIII (☎095.531.511).

The plain of Catania

Compared to the interest further north, there's a real paucity of places if you're looking for another halt before Siracusa. Trains and buses cut right across the **Piana di Catania**, known to the Greeks as the Laestrygonian Fields after the cannibalistic Laestrygones who were reputed to live there: it's a pretty ride but with absolutely no reason to get off until **LENTINI**, half an hour or so out of Catania. Lentini was founded in 728 BC, probably to restrict any further northward expansion by the Corinthians in Siracusa. Built far inland, unusual for a Greek colony, it prospered before succumbing to the Romans under Marcellus, who slaughtered some 2000 of the inhabitants in 214 BC. The ancient city – some defences, a necropolis and part of a main gate – lies a twenty-minute walk south of the nearby upper town of **CARLENTINI**, which you can also reach directly by bus from Catania. There's no real point in getting out at Carlentini itself, though it has a fairly pleasant central square with bars: most buses also stop in Piazza San Francesco on the outskirts of Carlentini, closer to the zone, as do buses #1 or #2 from Lentini's train station. The **Zona Archeológica** (daily 8am–2pm; free) is then five minutes' signposted walk away, spread over the two hills of San Mauro and Metapíccola. There isn't a huge amount to see here, but it's a nice site, with good views over the valley. Most of the interesting bits are on display in the local **Museo Archeologico** in Lentini's Piazza del Liceo (Mon–Sat 9am–5pm, Sun 9am–noon; free), where finds include a reconstruction of the gate.

If this doesn't grab you then trains and direct buses from Catania run around the southern spur of the Golfo di Catania to **AUGUSTA**, oil port and naval base. It's more pleasant than it sounds, built (like Siracusa) on a small islet connected to the mainland, and there are beach resorts to the north, one at **BRUCOLI** together with a fifteenth-century castle. But the real reason to stay would be as a base for visiting the nearby site of **Megara Hyblaea**, around 10km south, across the bay. Founded by Greeks a few years before Siracusa, the city enjoyed a fair living from sea-trade and pottery until destroyed by first Gelon in 483 BC and later the Romans. The large **site** shows a Doric temple, some tombs and houses, an eighth-century BC agora, as well as a small **museum** (Mon–Sat 9am–7pm; free) with plans, photos and some finds. Unfortunately, it's not easy to get to without your own transport: the only possibility is to take a local train from Augusta to Megara-Giannalena, from where it's still a fair hike, though you could reduce it to a kilometre by walking along the rails and climbing up at the road bridge.

The last stretch of the journey to Siracusa, by train especially, is a nightmare of **rampant industrialization**. As far as Priolo, the track skirts the largest concentration of chemical plants in Europe, a stinking, Meccano-built mesh of pipes and tanks that has irreversibly polluted the local sea and air. People living in the coastal villages have had to be evacuated and their houses destroyed, the environment deemed unfit for human habitation.

Siracusa

It's hardly surprising that **SIRACUSA** (ancient Syracuse) – an easily defendable off-shore island with fertile plains across on the mainland and two natural harbours – should attract the early Greek colonists, in this case Corinthians who settled the site in 733 BC. Within a hundred years, the city was so powerful that it was sending out its own colonists to the south and west; and later Siracusa was the island's main power base – indeed, the city's history reads as a list of Sicily's most famous and effective rulers.

Some history

Syracuse first assumed its almost mythic eminence under **Gelon**, the tyrant of Gela, who moved his rule to the city in 485 BC to increase his power: it was he who began work on the city's Temple of Athena, later to become the Christian cathedral of Syracuse. It was an unparalleled period of Greek prosperity in Sicily, while the extent of a wider Siracusean influence was indicated by the defeat of the Etruscans (474 BC), who had been causing trouble for Greek towns on mainland Italy. It was a growing influence which troubled Athens, and in 415 BC a fleet of 134 triremes was dispatched to take Syracuse – only to be blockaded and the fleet destroyed. Those who weren't slaughtered as they ran were imprisoned in the city's stone quarries.

Under **Dionysius the Elder**, the city became a great military base, the tyrant building the first of the Euryalus forts and erecting strong city walls. As the leading European power, Syracuse more or less retained its prime position for two hundred years until it was attacked by the Romans in 215 BC. The subsequent two-year siege was made long and hazardous for the attackers by the mechanical devices contrived by **Archimedes** – who, as the Romans finally forced victory, was killed by a foot soldier.

From this time, Syracuse withered in importance. It became, briefly, a major religious centre in the early Christian period, but for the most part its days as a power were done: it was sacked by the Saracens and most of its later Norman buildings fell in the 1693 earthquake. Passed by until this century, the city suffered a double blow in World War II when it was bombed by the Allies and then, after its capture, by the Luftwaffe in 1943. Luckily, the extensive ancient remains were little damaged, although decay and new development have reduced the attractions of the modern city. It's an essential stop on any tour of the island, but it's getting daily more difficult to picture the beautiful city which Plutarch wept over when he heard of its fall to the Romans.

Some **orientation** pointers are useful. The original Greek settlement was on the fortified island of **Ortygia**, compact enough to see in a good half-day's stroll and almost completely late medieval in character. The Greek city spread onto the mainland in four distinct areas: **Achradina**, over the water from Ortygia, was the city's commercial and administrative centre and today encompasses the new streets that radiate out from the train station; **Tyche**, to the northeast, was residential and now holds the archeological museum and the city's extensive catacombs; **Neapolis**, to the west, is the site of the fascinating archeological park based on ancient Syracuse's public and social amenities; while **Epipolae** stretches way to the northwest, to the city's outer defensive walls and the Euryalus fort.

Arrival, information and accommodation

The **train station** is on the mainland, about a twenty-minute walk from either Ortygia or Neapolis. If you're not staying, dump your bags in the **left luggage office** in the station (6am–9.30pm; L5000/€2.58 for 12hr) and strike off for one or the other. AST **buses** arrive either in Piazza della Poste, just over the bridge on Ortygia (where there's also an office doling out timetables for regional and city bus services), or else in Piazzale Marconi, in the modern town; SAIS buses stop in Via Trieste, close by Piazza della Poste.

The main **city bus** stops are in Piazza Archimede and Largo XXV Luglio on Ortygia, and along Corso Umberto on the mainland; tickets cost L1500/€0.78, valid for 90 minutes. For maps, accommodation listings, details of performances in the Greek theatre, and other **information**, visit the **tourist office** at Via Maestranza 33 (Mon–Fri 8.30am–2pm & 2.30–5.30pm, Sat 8.30am–2pm; ☎0931.464.255, fax 0931.60.204), or at Via San Sebastiano 43 (daily 8.30am–1.30pm & 3.30–6.30pm, closed Sun in winter; ☎0931.481.200, fax 0931.67.803). The main **post office** is in Piazza della Poste; **telephones** (8am–10pm) are at Via Teracati 46 close to the Parco Archeologico.

Accommodation choices aren't spectacular and in high season you must make an advance reservation. For staying on Ortygia the *Gran Bretagna* is a popular lodging at Via Savoia 21 (☎0931.68.765; ②), or you could try the elegant *Domus Mariae*, Via Vittorio Veneto 76 (☎0931.24.858; ⑤), which has luxury facilities and views to the sea. Most stylish of all is the *Grand Hotel* (☎0931.464.600; ⑧), a veteran haunt of the rich and famous in a prime position overlooking the Porto Grande, at Viale Mazzini 12. The cheaper hotels are all on the mainland, for example the *Milano*, Corso Umberto 10 (☎0931.66.981; ③), a rather cramped choice, and around the train station you'll find the *Aretusa*, at Via Francesco Crispi 75 (☎ & fax 0931.24.211; ②), and the *Centrale*, at Corso Umberto 141 (☎0931.60.528; ①), both plain and functional. The private **youth hostel**

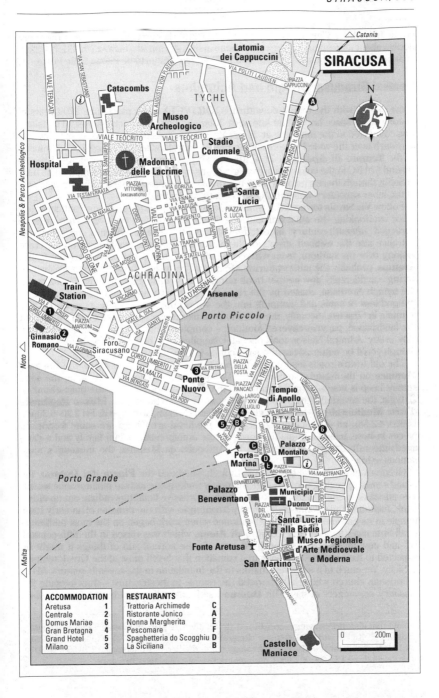

△ Catania

SIRACUSA

N

Latomia
dei Cappuccini

VIA POLITI LAUDIEN

PIAZZA
CAPPUCCINI

VIALE TERACATI

VIA SAN SEBASTIANO

VIA AUGUSTO VON PLATEN

(i)

Catacombs

TYCHE

Ⓐ

**Museo
Archeologico**

VIALE TEOCRITO

VIALE TEOCRITO

**Stadio
Comunale**

VIA LORINO

RIVIERA DIONISIO IL GRANDE

Neapolis & Parco Archeologico △

Hospital

VIA DEL SANTUARIO

**Madonna
delle Lacrime**

PIAZZA
VITTORIA
(excavations)

VIA TESTAFERRATA

VIA DI NATALE

VIA GORIZIA

VIA ENNA

VIA RAGUSA

VIA AGRIGENTO

VIA BIGNAMI

**Santa
Lucia**

PIAZZA
S. LUCIA

VIA MONTE GRAPPA

VIA FILISTO

CORSO GELONE

VIA M. CARABELLI

VIALE LUIGI CADORNA

VIA TRAPANI

VIA STATELLO

VIA MOSCO

A C H R A D I N A

VIA D'ARSENALE

**Train
Station**

VIA EPICARMO

Arsenale

VIA F. CRISPI

CORSO UMBERTO I

⓵

PIAZZA
MARCONI

VIALE A. DIAZ

VIA DANTE

VIA R. MARGHERITA

Porto Piccolo

**Ginnasio
Romano**

⓶

VIA ELORINA

**Foro
Siracusano**

CORSO UMBERTO I

VIA PALERMO

Noto △

VIA MALTA

VIA BENGASI

VIA RODI

⓷

**Ponte
Nuovo**

VIA ERITREA

PIAZZA
DELLA
POSTA

PIAZZA
PANCALI

VIA TRIESTE

VIA TRENTO

LARGO
XXV
LUGLIO

**Tempio
di Apollo**

VIA RESALIBERA

RIVA GARIBALDI

VIA XX SETTEMBRE

VIA SAVOIA

⓸

Ⓑ

O R T Y G I A

VIA MIRABELLA

LUNGOMARE DI LEVANTE

⓹

RIVA NAZARIO SAURO

VITTORIO VENETO

Ⓒ

**Porta
Marina**

Ⓓ

Ⓔ

PIAZZA
ARCHIMEDE

**Palazzo
Montalto**

VIA DA ROMA

(i)

Ⓖ

VIA MAESTRANZA

Porto Grande

VIA GEMMELLARO

Ⓕ

**Palazzo
Beneventano**

FORO ITALICO

Municipio

PIAZZA
DEL
DUOMO

Duomo

VIA PICHERALE

VIA LARGA

VIA ROMA

VIA CAPODIECI

**Santa Lucia
alla Badia**

Fonte Aretusa ⊺

**Museo Regionale
d'Arte Medioevale
e Moderna**

San Martino

LUNGOMARE ORTIGIA

△ Malta

VIA CASTELLO MANIACE

0   200m

**Castello
Maniace**

ACCOMMODATION	
Aretusa	1
Centrale	2
Domus Mariae	6
Gran Bretagna	4
Grand Hotel	5
Milano	3

RESTAURANTS	
Trattoria Archimede	C
Ristorante Jonico	A
Nonna Margherita	E
Pescomare	F
Spaghetteria do Scogghiu	D
La Siciliana	B

out at Belvedere, Viale Epipoli 45 (☎0931.711.118), is currently closed and there are doubts about its reopening. The nearest **campsite**, *Agriturist Rinaura* (☎0931.721.224), is 5km away – take bus #21, #22 or #23 from Corso Umberto or Piazza delle Poste.

Central Siracusa: Ortygia and Achradina

A fist of land with the thumb downturned, **ORTYGIA** stuffs more than 2700 years of history into a space barely one kilometre long and half a kilometre across. The island was connected to the mainland at different times by causeway or by bridge: today you approach over the wide Ponte Nuovo to Piazza Pancali, where the sandstone remnants of the **Tempio di Apollo** sit in a little green park surrounded by railings. Erected around 570 BC in the colony's early years, it was the first grand Doric temple to be built in Sicily, though there's not much left to provoke the senses: a few column stumps, part of the inner sanctuary wall and the stereobate can be made out.

Follow Via Savoia towards the water and you fetch up on the harbour front, an active place overlooking the main harbour, the Porto Grande. Set back from the water, a curlicued fifteenth-century limestone gateway, the **Porta Marina**, provides one entrance into the webbed streets of the old town. The walk uphill ends on a terrace looking over the harbour, from where you slip down to a piazza encircling the **Fonte Aretusa**, probably the most enduring of Siracusa's romantic locations. The freshwater spring – incidentally now neither fresh nor a spring – fuelled an attractive Greek myth: the nymph Arethusa, chased by the river god Alpheus, was changed into a spring by the goddess Artemis and, jumping into the sea off the Peloponnese, reappeared as a fountain in Siracusa. Actually, there are natural freshwater springs all over Ortygia, but the landscaped, papyrus-covered fountain – complete with fish and ducks – is undeniably pretty. Admiral Nelson took on water supplies here before the Battle of the Nile, though you'd be better advised to sip a coffee in one of the cafés nearby.

The old town's roads lead on, down the "thumb" of Ortygia, as far as the **Castello Maniace** on the island's southern tip. Thrown up by Frederick II in 1239, the solid square keep is now a barracks and is off-limits to visitors. Back on the main chunk of Ortygia, the severe thirteenth-century Palazzo Bellomo houses the **Museo Regionale d'Arte Medioevale e Moderna** (Tues–Sat 9am–1.30pm, also Wed & Fri 2.30–6.30pm; L5000/€2.58), an outstanding collection of medieval art. There are some wonderful pieces in here, including notable works by the omnipresent Gagini family and a damaged fifteenth-century *Annunciation* by Antonello da Messina, the museum's most famous exhibit.

Ortygia's most obvious attractions, though, surround the **Piazza del Duomo**, the island's most appealing spot (though currently undergoing radical maintenance work). The piazza is an elongated space from which impressive buildings radiate out up either flank, including the seventeenth-century **Municipio** with the remains of an early Ionic temple in its basement. This was abandoned when work began on the most ambitious of all Siracusa's temples, the **Tempio di Atena**, which was raised in the fifth century BC and now forms the basis of the duomo. In the normal run of things it might be expected to have suffered the eventual ruination that befell most of the Greek temples in Sicily. Yet much of it survives, thanks to the foundation in the seventh century AD of a Christian church which incorporated the temple in its structure – thus keeping the masonry scavengers at bay. The **Duomo** itself makes the grandest statement about

---

Note that it's worth buying a **combined ticket** if you're planning to see Siracusa's major sights: a ticket for the Museo Regionale and the Museo Archeologico costs L10,000/€5.17; for the Museo Archeologico and the Parco Archeologico L12,000/€6.20; or for all three L15,000/€7.80. Combined tickets are valid over two days.

Ortygia's continuous settlement, with twelve of the temple's fluted columns, and their architrave, embedded in its battlemented Norman wall. Inside, the nave of the Christian church was formed by hacking eight arches in the cella walls.

Buses run from Largo XXV Luglio over Ponte Nuovo and into **ACHRADINA**, the important commercial centre of ancient Syracuse. Although nowadays there's little of interest here, you may find yourself staying in one of the hotels scattered around its modern streets. The **Foro Siracusano** was the site of the agora, the marketplace and public square, and there are a few remains still to be seen – though the dominant feature is the war memorial in its garden, a Fascist monument of 1936. The only other ancient attraction left in the area is the **Ginnasio Romano**, off Via Elorina behind the train station: not a gymnasium at all, but a small first-century AD Roman theatre – partly sunken under moss-covered water – and a few pieces of a temple and altar.

Tyche and Neapolis: the archeological museum and park

TYCHE, north of the train station, is mainly new and commercial, and if you want to see the best of Siracusa's archeological delights you might as well take the bus straight from Ortygia and save your legs. Buses #4, #5, #12 (Mon–Sat), and #15 leave from Largo XXV Luglio – all running up Corso Gelone. Get off at Viale Teocrito and signposts point you east for the archeological museum and west for Neapolis. It's best to take the museum first: it's good for putting the site into perspective and is unlikely to be packed first thing in the morning.

The **Museo Archeologico** (Tues–Sat 9am–2pm, also Mon, Wed & Sat 3.30–6.30pm; may open Sun morning; last entry 1hr before closing; L8000/€4.13) holds a wealth of material, starting with geological and prehistoric finds, moving through entire rooms devoted to the Chalcidesian colonies (Naxos, Lentini, Zancle) and to Megara Hyblaea, and finally to the main body of the collection: an immensely detailed catalogue of life in ancient Syracuse and its sub-colonies. Most famous exhibit is the *Venus*, at the entrance to the Syracuse section: a headless figure arising from the sea, the clear white marble almost palpably dripping. Attempt also to track down the section dealing with the temples of Syracuse; fragments from each (like the seven lion-gargoyles from the Tempio di Atena) are displayed alongside model and video reconstructions. There's an explanatory diagram at the entrance to the circular building and everything is colour coded: pick the sector you're interested in and follow the arrows, prehistory starting just to the left of the entrance.

NEAPOLIS, to the west, is now contained within a large **Parco Archeologico** (daily 9am–2hr before sunset), reachable on bus #4, #5 or #6 from Largo XXV Luglio. Although you don't pay for the initial excavations, seeing the Greek theatre and quarries – easily the most interesting parts – costs L8000/€4.13, paid at a separate entrance. The **Ara di Ierone II**, an enormous altar of the third century BC on a solid white plinth, is the first thing you see, across the way from which is the entrance to the theatre and quarries. The **Teatro Greco** is very prettily sited, cut out of the rock and looking down into trees below. It's much bigger than the one at Taormina, capable of holding around 15,000 people, though less impressive scenically. But the theatre's pedigree is impeccable: Aeschylus put on works here, and around the top of the middle gangway are a set of carved names which marked the various seat blocks occupied by the royal family. Greek dramas are still played here in even-numbered years, as wooden planking over the surviving seats testifies.

Walk back through the theatre and another path leads down into a leafy quarry, the **Latomia del Paradiso**, best known for its unusually shaped cavern that Dionysius is supposed to have used as a prison. This, the **Orecchio di Dionigi** (or "Ear of Dionysius") is a high, S-shaped cave 65m long: Caravaggio, a visitor in 1586, coined the name after the shape of the entrance, but the acoustic properties are such that it's not impossible to imagine Dionysius eavesdropping on his prisoners from a vantage point above. A second cave, the **Grotta dei Cordari**, used by the ancient city's ropemakers, is shored up at present.

Keep your ticket from the theatre and Latomia del Paradiso, as it will also get you into the elliptical **Anfiteatro Romano**, back up the main path past the altar and through a gate on your right; you have to see this last. A late building, dating from the third century AD, it's a substantial relic with the tunnels for animals and gladiators clearly visible. Again, some of the seats are inscribed with the owners' names.

Castello Eurialo

For terrific views over the city and relief on hot and crowded days, it's worth the brief excursion a few kilometres west of Siracusa to the military and defensive works begun under Dionysius the Elder to defend the port from land attack. Added to and adapted over a couple of centuries, they basically consisted of a great wall which defended the ridge of **Epipolae** (the city's western limit), and the massive **Castello Eurialo** (daily until 1hr before sunset; free) – *the* major extant Greek fortification in the Mediterranean. There are three defensive trenches, the innermost leading off into a system of tunnels and passages. Climb up to the castle proper, its long keep and the lower walls and towers providing hearty views over the oil refineries and tankers of the coast north of the city, and over Siracusa itself.

Bars and pizzerias share the view, and make this a viable place for an evening out. **Buses** #9, #11 and #12 run from the Corso Gelone, outside the archeological park, to the village of Belvedere; the site is just before the village, on the right, a fifteen-minute ride.

Eating and drinking

Many of Siracusa's **restaurants** are overpriced, but there are some good-value places. *Spaghetteria do Scogghiu*, Via Scina 11, has a huge selection of cheap pasta and is popular at night. *La Siciliana*, Via Savoia 17 and *Nonna Margherita* at Via Cavour 12 on Ortygia, have a wide range of good pizzas which often draw queues. For fish, the *Trattoria Archimede*, Via Gemmellaro 8, is frequented by locals, while *Pescomare*, just off Piazza del Duomo at Via Landolina 6, serves pizzas too, in an atmospheric, plant-filled old courtyard. For top-quality nosh, take a taxi or hike out to the rustic *Ristorante Jonico*, Riviera Dionisio il Grande 194 (☎0931.655.40; closed Tues), where a meal of superb antipasti and staggeringly delicious fresh fish will cost around L60,000/€31.20. Good **bars** and cafés are easy to come by, two of the best being the outdoor *Bar Ortygia*, at the Fonte Aretusa, and the *Bar Del Ponte*, at the end of the Ponte Nuovo on Ortygia – a good breakfast place, this one.

THE SOUTHERN COAST
AND THE INTERIOR

It's tempting to give Sicily's long **southern coast** a miss, especially if you're short on time as there are few major sites. But to do so would be to ignore some of the most appealing places on the island. The whole region, coast and hinterland, marks a welcome break from the volcanic fixation of the blacker lands to the north: here the towns are largely spacious and bright, strung across a gentler, unscarred landscape that rolls and pitches down to the sea.

Sicily's southeastern bulge was devastated by a calamitous seventeenth-century earthquake and the inland rebuilding, over the next century, was almost entirely

Baroque in concept and execution. **Ragusa** dominates, a splendid town on two levels, the older lower town much abandoned but still with its share of grandiose buildings. Elsewhere, similar vigorous Baroque towns mushroomed, like little **Módica** to the south and – the undisputed gem – **Noto** to the east.

Down on the **coast** itself there's a line of small-town resorts which stretches from the southeastern cape, **Capo Passero**. There are decent beaches but often the coastline is marred by industrial development and pollution, as at **Gela**, although its extensive Greek fortifications are worth a look. More vital, further west, is **Agrigento**, sitting on a rise overlooking the sea above its famed series of Greek temples.

Slow cross-country trains and limited exit motorways do little to encourage stopping in the island's **interior**, but it's only here that you really begin to get off the tourist trail. Much of the land is burned dry during the long summer months, sometimes a dreary picture, but in compensation the region boasts some of Sicily's most curious towns. **Enna** is the obvious target, as central as you can get, the blustery mountain town a pace apart from the dry hills below. There are easy trips to be made from here, north into the hills and south to **Piazza Armerina** and the fabulous Roman mosaics and to airy, ceramic-studded **Caltagirone**.

Ragusa and the southeast

The **earthquake of 1693**, which destroyed utterly the towns and villages of south-eastern Sicily, had one positive and lasting effect. Where there were ruins, a new generation of confident architects raised new planned towns in an opulent Baroque style. All were harmonious creations, Catania the grandest, Noto the most eagerly promoted by the tourist board. But there is a bagful of other towns too, less visited but all providing surprising pockets of grandeur amid the bare hills and deep valleys of the region.

Ragusa

Best base for any exploration of the area is **RAGUSA**, a busy and likeable provincial capital with an encouraging, friendly atmosphere. The destructive earthquake split the city in two: the old town of Ragusa Ibla, on a jut of land above its valley, was comprehensively flattened, and within a few years a new town emerged, on the higher ridge to the west. Ibla was stubbornly rebuilt around its medicval ruins, while its new rival developed along grander, planned lines. All the business and industry relocated in the prosperous upper town, where oil is the latest venture – derricks scattered around modern Ragusa's higher reaches.

You'll arrive here, in the **upper town**: all **buses** stop outside the **train station**, and a left turn takes you along the main road and over the exposed Ponte Nuovo, spanning a huge cleft in the ridge. All the interest in modern Ragusa is on the other side, the gridded Baroque town slipping off to right and left on either side of the steeply sloping Corso Italia. To the right, down the Corso on a wide terrace above Piazza San Giovanni, stands the **Duomo**, conceived on a grand, symmetrical scale. Finished in 1774, its tapered columns and fine doorways are a fairly sombre background to the vigorous small-town atmosphere around. Back towards the train station, underneath the Ponte Nuovo, there's an important **Museo Archeologico** (daily 9am–1.30pm & 4–7.30pm; L4000/€2.07) dealing mainly with finds from the archeological site of Kamarina (sixth century BC) on the coast to the southwest.

But it's **RAGUSA IBLA**, the original **lower town**, where you'll probably while away much of the day, its weather-beaten roofs straddling the outcrop of rock about twenty minutes' walk away. The main attraction, the church of **San Giorgio** – stridently placed at the top of Piazza Duomo – is one of the masterpieces of Sicilian Baroque, built by Rosario Gagliardi and finished in 1784. The glorious three-tiered facade, sets of triple columns climbing up the wedding cake exterior to a balconied belfry, is an imaginative work, though typically not much enhanced by venturing inside. As with Gagliardi's other important church in Módica (see below), all the beauty is in the immediacy of the powerful exterior.

The whole town – deathly quiet at lunchtime – is ripe for aimless wandering. Gagliardi gets another credit for the elegant rounded facade of **San Giuseppe** in Piazza Pola, a few steps below the duomo, while Corso XXV Aprile continues down past abandoned *palazzi* to the **Giardino Ibleo** (daily 8am–8pm) – gardens that mark the very edge of the spur on which the town is built. If you can't face the walk back to the upper town, bus #1 or #3 makes the trip, hourly, from Piazza Pola.

Sadly, there's nowhere to stay in Ragusa Ibla, and even up in the main part of town **accommodation** is limited to a very few fairly expensive hotels. The cheapest, *San Giovanni*, Via Traspontino 3 (☎0932.621.013; ②), is at the train station end of the lower Ponte dei Cappuccini, while the *Montreal* on Via San Giuseppe is far better equipped but considerably more expensive (☎ & fax 0932.621.133; ④). There's a good, basic **restaurant** in Via S. Anna 117 the *Ristorante Orfeo*, with large, full meals for around L30,000/€15.60 (closed Sun), while *La Grotta* is good for pizzas at Via Cartia, off Via Roma (closed Wed). The best deal in Ibla is to be had at *U Saracinu*, on Via del Convento (closed Wed), near the duomo, good Sicilian cooking with North African touches. Also in Ragusa Ibla, you can sit outside for nourishing meals at *La Béttola* in Largo Camarina (closed lunchtime & Mon). The *Caffè Trieste*, Corso Italia 76–78, is a decent **café-bar** with an enticing savoury snack and pastry selection.

Comiso and Módica

The best of the rest of the Baroque southeast can be seen in easy trips from Ragusa. If you came from the west you might already have passed through **Comiso**, its green centre dominated by the twin domes of two impressive churches. If you didn't, the journey in itself is worth making, up over a barren 600-metre-high plateau looking away to the distant sea. The wild countryside hereabouts continues to impress as you head beyond Ragusa, the route to **Módica**, half an hour to the south, a case in point. As the bus swirls down past Ragusa Ibla and climbs through some rugged hills, all the vegetation seems to have been pulled into the valleys below, the tiered slopes bare and rocky. Módica itself is an enjoyable place to spend half a day. A powerful medieval base of the Chiaramonte, the upper town is watched over by the magnificent eighteenth-century facade of **San Giorgio**, a worthy rival to the church of the same name in Ragusa Ibla. It's thought that Gagliardi was responsible for this too: the elliptical facade is topped by a belfry, the church approached by a symmetrical double staircase which switchbacks up across the upper roads of the town.

Noto

The real highlight of any tour of the Baroque southeast, despite the collapse of its duomo, is further afield at **NOTO**. Easily the most harmonious post-earthquake creation, for a time, in the mid-nineteenth century, it replaced Siracusa as that region's provincial capital. Indeed, despite its architectural identification with the Baroque towns around Ragusa, Noto is best reached from Siracusa – around half an hour's journey by bus or train. Planned and laid out by Giovanni Battista Landolina, adorned by Gagliardi, there's not a town to touch Noto for uniform excellence in design and execution. Sadly it has long been afflicted by pollution and heavy traffic. Much of the traffic has now been diverted, and most of the central monuments have recently emerged from years of restoration work, but parts of the centre are still obscured, reducing Noto's visual impact.

Now pedestrianized, the main Corso is lined with some of Sicily's most captivating buildings, all a rich honey colour – from the flat-fronted church of **San Francesco**, on the right, along as far as Piazza XVI Maggio and the graceful, curving church of **San Domenico**. And Piazza Municipio is arguably Sicily's finest piazza with its perfectly proportioned, tree-planted expanses. The **Duomo,** finished in 1770, but now closed due to the unfortunate collapse of the dome in 1996, is hemmed in by two palaces of remarkable decorative quality. Opposite, the **Municipio** (or Palazzo Ducezio) is flanked by its own green spaces, the arcaded building presenting a lovely, simple facade of columns and long stone balconies. Head up the steep **Via Corrado Nicolaci**, an eighteenth-century street that contains the extraordinary **Palazzo Villadorata** (no. 18), its six balconies supported by a panoply of griffins, galloping horses and fat-cheeked cherubs, but at present in the hands of the restorers.

Staying in Noto wouldn't be a bad alternative to Siracusa, though you'll have to move sharp to get a room at the only pensione in town, *Albergo Stella*, Via F. Maiore 44 (☎0931.835.695; ②; closed Nov), on the corner of Via Napoli. Find out about **rented rooms** from the **tourist office** in Piazza XVI Maggio (April–Sept Mon–Sat 8am–2pm & 3.30–6.30pm, also Sun in summer 9am–1pm; ☎ & fax 0931.836.744), or else stay at Noto Marina, 8km southeast, where the cluster of holiday hotels includes the *Meeting* on Viale Lido 0931/812.344; ④), impeccably clean with all mod cons and views to the sea. There's a good **restaurant** here too. In Noto, you can eat at the straightforward *Trattoria Giglio*, just to the side of the town hall at Piazza Municipio 8–10 (closed Sat), where the cooking has a Spanish flavour, or try the small *Trattoria del Carmine*, Via Ducezio 9, which serves popular *cucina casalinga* at low prices.

West to Gela

Most of the coastal section west of Capo Passero is pretty inaccessible without your own transport. Even then, to be frank, there's not a lot worth stopping for, the odd sea-side town awash with new holiday apartments but little individual character; camping offers the best opportunity to enjoy the sandy beaches around here. The railway line touches down at Pozzallo and trains then loop north, through Módica, Ragusa and Comiso before cutting back down to the coast at Gela.

GELA couldn't present a worse aspect as the train edges into town, through a petro-chemical mess of futuristic steel bubbles and pipes. There are fine dune-backed beaches in the vicinity but there must be serious doubts about the cleanliness of the water. Once, though, Gela was one of the most important of the island's Hellenic cities, founded in 688 BC, and under Hippocrates and Gelon rivalled even Syracuse as the island's political hub. But, smashed by the Carthaginians, ancient Gela was abandoned to the encroaching sands. Modern Gela was the first Sicilian town to be liberated in 1943, but otherwise – beyond an excellent archeological museum and a fine set of defensive walls – is almost entirely without interest.

If you want to see these, best leave your bags at the train station **left-luggage office** – there's really no need to stay longer than half a day. Outside the station (also where buses pull up) turn right down the main road and, at the junction, bear right for the town centre and the main Corso Vittorio Emanuele, at either end of which are Gela's two sights. To the left, a twenty-minute walk, Gela's **Museo Archeologico** (daily 9am–1.30pm & 3–7pm; L4000/€2.07) is notable largely for its excellent collection of painted vases: mainly seventh- to fifth-century BC, the black-and-red jugs and beakers were Greek Gela's speciality. Outside the museum a small acropolis has been uncovered, a few walls and a single temple column from the fifth century BC. There are more archeological remains at the other end of town – along the Corso and then a left fork into Via Manzoni, which runs parallel to the sea as far as the red gates of the site, a hefty three- to four-kilometre walk. Here, at **Capo Soprano**, is a remarkable series of **Greek fortifications** (daily 9am–1hr before sunset; free) dating from the fourth century BC. Preserved by the sand, the walls stand nearly eight metres high in parts, made up of perfectly fitted stone blocks topped by a storey of brick – now covered in protective glass panels. It's a beautiful site, with waves crashing onto a particularly fine, duned stretch below.

Agrigento

Though handsome, well sited and awash with medieval atmosphere, **AGRIGENTO** is not visited for the town itself. The interest instead focuses on the substantial remains of Pindar's "most beautiful city of mortals", a couple of kilometres below. Here, strung out along a ridge facing the sea, is a series of Doric temples – the most captivating of Sicilian Greek remains and a grouping unique outside Greece.

The site

In 581 BC colonists from nearby Gela and from Rhodes founded the city of Akragas between the rivers of Hypsas and Akragas. They surrounded it with a mighty wall, formed in part by a higher ridge on which stood the acropolis (and, today, the modern town). The southern limit of the ancient city was a second, lower ridge and it was here, in the so-called "Valley of the Temples", that the city architects erected their sacred buildings during the fifth century BC.

A road winds down from the modern city to the **VALLE DEI TEMPLI**, buses dropping you at a car park between the two separate sections of archeological remains (the eastern and western zones), and then the museum (see opposite). The **eastern zone** is unenclosed and is at its crowd-free best in early morning or late evening. A path climbs up to the oldest of Akragas's temples, the **Tempio di Ercole** (Hercules). Probably begun in the last decades of the sixth century BC, nine of the original 38 columns have been re-erected, everything else scattered around like a waiting jigsaw puzzle. Retrace your steps back to the path which leads to the glorious **Tempio della Concordia**, dated to around 430 BC: perfectly preserved and beautifully sited, with fine views to the city and the sea, the tawny stone lending the structure warmth and strength. That it's still so complete is explained by its conversion (in the sixth century AD) to a Christian church. Restored to its (more or less) original layout in the eighteenth century, it's kept its lines and slightly tapering columns, although it's fenced off to keep the crowds at bay. The path continues, following the line of the ancient city walls, to the **Tempio di Giunone** (or Hera), an engaging half-ruin standing at the very edge of the ridge. The patches of red visible here and there on the masonry denote fire damage, probably from the sack of Akragas by the Carthaginians in 406 BC.

The **western zone** (daily 8.30am–1hr before sunset; L4000/€2.07), back along the path and beyond the car park, is less impressive, a vast tangle of stone and fallen masonry from a variety of temples. Most notable is the mammoth construction that was the **Tempio di Giove**, or Temple of Olympian Zeus. The largest Doric temple ever known, it was never completed, left in ruins by the Carthaginians and further damaged by earthquakes. Still, the stereobate remains, while on the ground, face to the sky, lies an eight-metre-high *telamone*: a supporting column sculpted as a male figure, arms raised and bent to bear the temple's weight. Other scattered remains litter the area, including the so-called **Tempio dei Dioscuri** (Castor and Pollux), rebuilt in 1832 and actually made up of unrelated pieces from the confused rubble on the ground.

Via dei Templi leads back to the town from the car park via the excellent **Museo Nazionale Archeologico** (daily 9am–1pm, plus Wed–Sat 3.30–5.30pm; L8000/€4.13) – the bus passes by outside. The extraordinarily rich collection is devoted to finds from the city and the surrounding area; best displays are the cases of vases (sixth to third century BC) and a reassembled *telamone* stacked against one wall. Nip over the road on the way out for the **Hellenistic-Roman quarter** (daily 9am–1hr before sunset; free), which contains lines of houses, inhabited intermittently until the fifth century AD, many with mosaic designs still discernible.

The modern city
It would be a mistake not to scout round modern Agrigento, modern only in comparison with the temples. Thoroughly medieval at its heart, its tiny stepped streets and fine churches look down over the Valle dei Templi and beyond to the sea. The main street, **Via Atenea**, starts at the eastern edge of the old town, above the train station, the streets off to the right harbouring ramshackle *palazzi* and the church of **Santa Maria dei Greci**. Built over a Greek temple of the fifth century BC, the flattened columns are visible in the nave, while an underground tunnel reveals the stylobate and column stumps, all part of the church's foundations.

Practicalities
Trains arrive at Agrigento Centrale station at the edge of the old town; don't get out at Agrigento Bassa, as it's 3km north of town. **Buses** use the terminal in Piazza Roselli, near the post office, while **city buses** to the temples and the beach at San Leone leave from Piazza Marconi, outside the train station, as does the bus to Porto Empédocle for ferries to the Pelágie Islands (see overleaf). Buy city bus **tickets** (L1500/€0.78) from kiosks or *tabacchi*, not on the bus. The old town stetches west of the three main interlocking squares, piazzas Marconi, Aldo Moro and Vittorio Emanuele. Via Atenea is Agrigento's principal artery, running west from Piazza Aldo Moro, with the **tourist office** at its eastern end, at via Cesare Battisti 15 (Mon–Fri 8.30am–1.45pm, also Wed 4–7pm; ☎0922.20.454).

Finding **somewhere to stay** in Agrigento shouldn't be a problem, except perhaps in peak season. The *Bella Napoli*, Piazza Lena 6 (☎ & fax 0922.20.435; ②), at the western end of the old town, is one of the better budget choices, but can be a little noisy. Otherwise try the smartish *Belvedere*, Via San Vito 20 (☎ & fax 0922.20.051; ③), or the friendly *Concordia*, Piazza San Francesco 11 (☎0922.596.266; ③), both clean and pleasant choices. If you want to spend a little more, you can stay right in the archeological zone at the *Villa Athena*, Via dei Templi (☎0922.596.288; ⑦), with a pool and big windows soaking up the views. You can **camp** 6km away at the coastal resort of **SAN LEONE**, at *Internazionale San Leone* (☎0922.416.121); bus #2 or #2/ from outside the train station (every 30min until 9pm).

You can try the **food** and local wine at *La Forchetta*, next door to the *Concordia* hotel, with outdoor seating but nothing fancy; an unadvertised *menu turistico* keeps the bill down. If you're budgeting, make your way to the *Atenea*, a friendly family-run trattoria in Via Ficari, a quiet courtyard just off the Via Atenea (closed Sun except July–Aug). In the same neighbourhood, at Via Giambertoni 2, the *Ambasciata di Sicilia* (☎0922.20.526; closed Mon) is small but has a view-laden terrace and serves a mean *antipasto rustico* and delectable fresh fish. Right overlooking the temples below the centre, *Le Caprice* at Via Panoramica dei Templi 51 is professionally brisk but maintains high gastronomic standards in its classic Italian cooking – a good spot for lunch or dinner. With a car, you could head out to the moderate-to-expensive *Del Vigneto* at Via Cavaleri Magazzeni 11, south of the temples off the SS115 (☎0922.414.319; July & August closed Mon; Sept–June closed Tues & Nov); the regional dishes served here are superb.

Eraclea Minoa

From Agrigento you're well poised for moving on into western Sicily, and frequent buses get you to Sciacca in around two and a half hours. If you can, though, first drop in on the other important local Greek site, **ERACLEA MINOA** – originally named Minoa after the Cretan king Minos, who chased Daedalus from Crete to Sicily and founded a city where he landed. The Greeks settled here in the sixth century, later adding the tag Heraklea. A buffer between the two great cities at Akragas, 40km to the east, and Selinus, 60km west, Eraclea Minoa was dragged into endless border disputes, but in spite of this it flourished. Most of the remains date from the fourth century BC, Eraclea Minoa's most important period, three hundred years or so before the town declined.

The **site** (daily 9am–1hr before sunset; L4000/€2.07) is finely situated right on the coast, at the mouth of the River Platani. Apart from the good **walls**, once 6km long, which survive in interrupted sections, the main attraction is the sandstone **theatre**; some of the finds are held in a small on-site **museum**. While you're here, you'll be hard put to resist a trip down to the **beach**, one of the best on Sicily's southern coast, backed by pine trees and chalky cliffs. At the foot of the road from the site, a couple of bar-restaurants sit right on the beach; at one, *Lido Gabbiano*, you can rent **rooms** (☎0339.813.7907; ②); or there's a **campsite** nearby with cabins, *Camping Eraclea* (☎0922.847.310; May–Sept). Without your own transport, you can get here between June and September by buses from Cattolica Eraclea or from the SS115, both accessible from Agrigento, but outside the summer months you're going to have to do some tough walking: take any bus running between Agrigento and Sciacca and ask the driver to let you off at the turning; it's 5km west of Montallegro, on the SS115, and the site is another 4km from there. Heading on, walk west from the site turning and you should be able to flag down a bus going to Sciacca.

The Pelagie Islands

The remote and barren **Pelagie Islands** (Isole Pelagie) are simply dry rocks, south even of Malta and bang in the middle of the Mediterranean. Throughout history they've been neglected, often abandoned, their only days of importance destructive ones: in 1943 the Allies bombed the main island, Lampedusa, prior to springing into Sicily; and Colonel Gaddafi of Libya provided a repeat performance in 1987 when he retaliated against the American bombing of Tripoli by despatching missiles (off-target, it turned out) at Lampedusa's US base. That said, the only danger you're likely to face now is a rough sea crossing from Porto Empedocle. Don't come expecting an action-packed time – things move slowly here, though that shouldn't deter you from the range of water activities which the islands have to offer. The sun and sea are the main events, and the overriding sensation is one of remoteness.

Most travellers will get to the islands by **ferry** from **PORTO EMPÉDOCLE**, the ugly port town 6km south of Agrigento: buses run there hourly (#8, #9 or #10 from outside Agrigento's train station). It costs around L50,000/€26 one way to Linosa (a 6hr journey), L65,000/€33.80 to Lampedusa (an 8hr journey); tickets can be bought from the harbour-side Siremar office and travel agents in Agrigento. The only way to cut this time would be to **fly** from Palermo to Lampedusa, which will cost you around L150,000/€78 one way, L190,000/€98.80 for a weekend return.

Ferries call first at **LINOSA**, a volcanic islet, a pretty-quiet place with four extinct craters, some lavial beaches and not much else in the way of sights. The only village has a few hundred inhabitants, rather fewer cars and a minimal road system. The

Algusa (☎0922.972.052; ⑤), is the only **hotel** and you need to make a reservation in advance if you want to stay; there's also an unofficial **campsite**. The other ferry stop is at **LAMPEDUSA**, 50km south and much bigger. Around 4000 people live here, mostly in the town of the same name, the majority making their living from fishing or the tourist industry. It's a flat, dry island with more in common with Africa than Europe, the main attraction the beaches and the sea – bitingly clean and offering some of the best swimming and skin-diving in the Mediterranean. You should have no trouble finding somewhere to stay on Lampedusa except during July and August, when it's vital to book: most of the many **hotels** are a few minutes' walk from the beach, and most have double rooms in the ③ category and above. During the high season you will be expected to take full or half board; at the cheaper end of the scale there's the basic *Mir Mar* (☎0922.970.093; ③), very close to the beach, or the comfortable *Belvedere* (☎0922.970.188; ④), situated in the town. There are a couple of official **campsites**, too, including *La Roccia* (☎0922.970.055) at Cala Greca. If you arrive by boat out of season, it's more than likely that you'll be touted accommodation.

Inland to Enna

The most scenically rewarding parts of Sicily's **interior** are in the east, primarily the hill-towns and villages that lie in a wide half-circle to the north of Enna – which is where you should head if you want to see the region by public transport.

    Coming from Agrigento, however, there are several worthwhile routes – most only practicable for travellers with transport. One route goes by way of **Sant'Angelo Muxaro** (daily buses from Agrigento), beyond which begins the most convoluted **approach to Palermo**, the twisting road climbing up to 1000m at Prizzi, from where there are occasional bus services down to **Corleone**. A fairly large town for these parts, it lent Mario Puzo's fictional Godfather, Don Corleone, his adopted family name – and it's the name of one of Sicily's most notorious real-life Mafia clans. There is a bus from Corleone to Palermo, another 60km, though drivers won't want to miss the diversion into the higher hills around **PIANA DEGLI ALBANESI**: one of the most interesting of Sicilian towns, a fifteenth-century Albanian colony whose Greek Orthodox inhabitants still wear the costume and speak the tongue of their ancestors. Any celebration brings out the festive garb, but the best time to visit is at Easter when the local ceremonies form a marked contrast to the island's Catholic rites. At other times of the year entertainment is limited, though a stroll down the steep main street – Via Giorgio Kastriota – reveals street signs in Albanian and gives a glimpse of the town's three churches. Only 25km from Palermo, Piana degli Albanesi could also be seen on a daytrip from the capital; regular buses leave from outside the train station; the last one back to Palermo leaves at 7.45pm.

    The other option from Agrigento, better if you want to head on to the most appealing parts of the interior, is the **route to Enna**. There's a local bus service that connects up the nearer places, while trains make the journey too, up through gentle, tree-planted slopes and then across the hilltops. At Canicatti the line splits, trains running south to Licata, on the coast. Better to keep on to **CALTANISSETTA**, capital of its province and a brisk modern town, which (with its couple of hotels) is a possibility for day-tripping to Enna and Piazza Armerina (see p.1007); the bus timetables, for once, are kindly disposed. Caltanissetta's only tangible attraction is the worthy **Museo Civico** (daily except for last Mon of month 9am–1pm & 3.30–7pm; L4000/€2.07) on Via Napoleone Colajanni, close to the train station, which contains some of the earliest of Sicilian finds, including vases and Bronze Age sculpted figures. From Caltanissetta it's a short bus ride to Enna – don't take the train as Enna's train station is way outside town.

Enna

From a bulging V-shaped ridge almost 1000m up, **ENNA** lords it over the surrounding hills of central Sicily. The approach to this doughty mountain stronghold is still as formidable as ever, the bus climbing slowly out of the valley and looping across the solid crag to the summit and the town. For obvious strategic reasons, Enna was a magnet for successive hostile armies, who in turn besieged and fortified the town, each doing their damnedest to disprove Livy's description of Enna as *inexpugnabilis*.

Despite the destructive attention, most of Enna's remains are medieval and in good shape, with the prize exhibit the thirteenth-century **Castello di Lombardia** (daily: Easter–Oct 8am–8pm; Nov–Easter 9am–1pm & 3–5pm; free), dominating the easternmost spur of town. A mighty construction with its strong walls complete, it guards the steep slopes on either side of Enna, its six surviving towers (out of an original twenty) providing lookouts. From the tallest, the Torre Pisana, the magnificent views take in Enna itself, some rugged countryside in all directions and, if you're lucky, Mount Etna.

In the centre of town virtually all the accredited sights lie stretched out along and around **Via Roma**, which descends from the castle. It's a narrow street, broken by small piazzas – one of which fronts the hemmed-in **Duomo**, dating in part from 1307. The spacious sixteenth-century interior (usually open afternoons) features huge supporting alabaster columns, the bases of which are covered with an amorphous, writhing mass of carved figures. Outside, behind the apses, the **Museo Alessi** (daily 8am–8pm, closes 10pm in July–Sept; L5000/€2.58) fields a rich collection of local church art, old coins and the impressive contents of the cathedral's own treasury. There's a second museum too, equally good: the **Museo Archeologico** (daily 8am–7.30pm, last entry at 6.30pm; L4000/€2.07), just over the way in Piazza Mazzini, covering Neolithic to Roman times and including a fine series of painted Greek vases.

Via Roma slopes down to the rectangular **Piazza Vittorio Emanuele**, focal point of the evening passeggiata. Off here, there's a long cliff-edge belvedere, while the bottom of the piazza is marked by the plain, high wall of the **Chiesa di San Francesco**, whose massive sixteenth-century tower previously formed part of the town's system of watchtowers. This linked the castle with the **Torre di Frederico**, which stands in isolation in its little park in the largely modern south of the town. An octagonal tower, 24m high, it's a survivor of the alterations to the city made by Frederick of Aragon who added a (now hidden) underground passage linking it to the *castello*.

Practicalities

All long-distance and most local buses use the **bus terminal** on Viale Diaz in the new town – turn right out of the terminal, right again down Corso Sicilia and it's around a ten-minute walk to Piazza Vittorio Emanuele. Enna's **train station** is five kilometres below town, though a local bus runs roughly hourly to the town centre (but only at selected times on Sunday, when you may have to take a taxi). You can reach everywhere in Enna itself very easily on foot, though buses for Pergusa (#5; roughly every 30min, 7am–9.30pm) leave from outside San Francesco church; tickets (L1500/€0.78) are bought from *tabacchi* and valid for one hour. Information, as well as a good, free **map** of Enna, is available from the **tourist office** at Via Roma 413 (Mon–Sat 9am–1pm & 3.30–6.30pm; ☎0935.528.228, fax 0935.528.229).

There's only one **hotel** in Enna, the dead-central *Grande Albergo Sicilia* in Piazza Colaianni (☎0935.500.850, fax 0935.500.488; ⑤), which has bright, clean rooms, some with views. If it's full (or too expensive) you'll have to take a bus to nearby **PERGUSA** instead, supposedly the site of Hades' abduction of Persephone to the underworld. These days the famed Lago di Pergusa is encircled by a motor-racing track, alongside which are several hotels, including the clean and functional *Miralago* (☎0935.541.272;

②) and the much pleasanter and better-equipped *Garden* (☎0935.541.694; ④), both with their own restaurants.

For **meals** in Enna, the *Marino*, near the castle at Via C. Savoca 62 (closed Wed), provides pizzas, pastas and local specialities in a simple environment. *La Fontana*, Via Vulturo 6 (no closing day) has good home-cooking and friendly service, while considerably more costly, but worth every lira, is the *Ristorante Ariston*, Via Roma 353 (closed Sun); expect to pay around L50,000–60,000/€26–31.20 for a full meal with wine. The **market** in Enna is held on Tuesdays (8am–2pm) in Piazza Europa, below the Torre di Federico II.

North of Enna

Some of the most fascinating, unsung towns of the Sicilian interior are within easy reach of Enna: to the north, along roads which wind either over mountain ranges to the Tyrrhenian coast or en route to the foothills of Mount Etna. Both directions provide spectacular rides and, unlike destinations further west, are feasible by bus.

Closest to Enna, across the valley and accessible by regular buses from Enna's bus and train stations, is medieval **Calascibetta**, its tightly packed buildings perched above a sheer drop on the eastern side. Beyond Calascibetta, it's around forty minutes by bus to **Leonforte**, with its roots firmly in the seventeenth century. The most notable sight here is **La Gran Fonte**, less a fountain than a range of 24 water spouts set in a sculpted facade of embossed roses and figures, built in 1651. It's about 300m on foot down from the Chiesa Matrice (or follow the signs at the western end of the village if you're driving), overlooking the hills on the edge of town. Buses run further east to **Agira**, again well sited with sparkling views down over the surrounding hills. The bus route continues through Regalbuto and, eventually, to Catania, a journey that strikes through land that was fiercely contested during the short Sicilian campaign of World War II.

If you time it right, you can catch one of the three Interbus buses a day linking Agira with **Troina**, a tortuous thirty-kilometre ride to Sicily's highest town (1120m). Hardly surprisingly, the journey there is the real event. Without a car you'll probably have to retrace your steps as the two onward routes – east to Cesarò and west to **NICOSIA** – are long, mountainous hauls, not to be hitched lightly. Nicosia, though, can be reached by bus from Enna, changing at Leonforte (as well as directly from Palermo), another momentous ride rewarded by an ancient medieval town of cracked palazzi and the remains of a Norman castle. It's an evocative little place, worth an **overnight stop** if you can: there's a comfortable, modern hotel a 15-minute walk from the centre, *La Pineta*, in Località San Paolo (☎0935.647.002; ③), with its own restaurant.

Piazza Armerina and around

To the **south of Enna**, less than an hour away by bus, **PIAZZA ARMERINA** lies amid thick tree-planted hills, a quiet, unassuming place mainly seventeenth and eighteenth century in appearance, its skyline pierced by towers, the houses huddled together under the joint protection of castle and cathedral. All in all, it is a thoroughly pleasant place to idle around, though the real local draw is an imperial Roman **villa** that stands in rugged countryside at Casale, 5km southwest of Piazza Armerina. Hidden under mud for 700 years, the excavated remains reveal a rich villa, probably a hunting lodge and summer home, decorated with polychromatic mosaic floors that are unique in the Roman world for their unrivalled quality and extent.

Buses drop you in Piazza Sen. Marescalchi, in the lower town. The old town is up the hill, centred around Piazza Garibaldi, off which is the **tourist office**, at Via Cavour

15 (Mon–Fri 9am–2pm, also Wed 3.30–6.30pm; ☎0935.680.201). The only central **hotel** choice is the rather noisily sited *Villa Romana*, Via A. de Gasperi 18 (☎ & fax 0935.682.911; ④), which only has a few rooms without bath at a lower price. You'd do much better to secure a room at the *Mosaici da Battiato*, in Contrada Paratore (☎ & fax 0935.685.453; ②; closed late Nov to late Dec), 4km out of town at the turn-off to the villa, which is just a kilometre from the hotel. A friendly place, it has twenty-three rooms with bath and a grill-restaurant where you can eat very well for under L30,000/€15.60. Taxis here won't be prohibitively expensive, while the bus to the mosaics passes right by. Immediately across from here, *La Ruota* (☎0935.680.542) has space for **camping**. For **eating**, *La Tavernetta*, in town at Via Cavour 14 (closed Sun), isn't bad value for money, or alternatively try *Da Pepito*, Via Roma 140 (closed Tues evening in winter), opposite the park, which serves tasty Sicilian dishes.

The Villa Romana

There is a **bus service** between May and September to **get to the villa** from Piazza Armerina, leaving Piazza Sen. Marescalchi at 9am, 10am, 11am and 4pm, 5pm and 6pm; the return service is on the half-hour, starting at 9.30am. Otherwise you'll have to take a taxi or **walk** the six kilometres: head down Via Matteotti or Via Principato and follow the signs; it takes around an hour on foot and is an attractive walk. It's also feasible to visit on a day-trip **from Caltanissetta** or **Enna** (see p.1006), but check the bus schedules before setting out.

The **Villa Romana** (daily 9am–6.30pm; L8000/€4.13) dates from the early fourth century BC and was used right up until the twelfth century when a mudslide kept it largely covered until comprehensive excavations in the 1950s. It's been covered again since to protect the mosaics, with a hard plastic and metal roof and walls designed to indicate the original size and shape, while walkways lead visitors through the rooms in as logical an order as possible. The mosaics themselves are identifiable as fourth-century Roman-African school, which explains many of the more exotic scenes and animals portrayed; they also point to the villa having had an important owner, possibly Maximianus Herculeus, co-emperor with Diocletian.

The **main entrance** leads into a wide courtyard with fountains, where the **thermae** (baths) group around an octagonal *frigidarium* and a central mosaic showing a lively marine scene. A walkway leads out of the baths and into the villa proper, to the massive central court or **peristyle**, whose surrounding corridors are decorated with animal head mosaics. From here, a balcony looks down upon one of the villa's most interesting pictures, a boisterous **circus scene** showing a chariot race. Small rooms beyond, on either side of the peristyle, reveal only fragmentary geometric patterns, although one contains probably the villa's most famous image, a two-tiered scene of ten girls, realistically muscular **figures** in Roman "bikinis", taking part in various gymnastic and athletic activities.

Beyond the peristyle, a long, covered corridor contains the most extraordinary of the mosaics: the **great hunting scene**, which sets armed and shield-bearing hunters against a panoply of wild animals. Along the entire sixty-metre length of the mosaic are tigers, ostriches, elephants, even a rhino, being trapped, bundled up and down gangplanks and into cages, destined for the Games back in Rome. The square-hatted figure overseeing the operation is probably Maximianus himself: his personal area of responsibility in the imperial Tetrarchy was North Africa, where much of the scene is set.

Other rooms beyond are nearly all on a grand scale. The **triclinium**, a dining room with three apses, features the labours of Hercules, and a path leads around the back to the **private apartments**, based around a large basilica. Best mosaics here are a **children's circus**, where tiny chariots are drawn by colourful birds, and a **children's hunt**, the kids chased and pecked by the hares and peacocks they're supposed to snare.

Caltagirone

CALTAGIRONE, an hour's ride southeast from Piazza Armerina, is one of the least known of Sicily's inland towns, with a fine central body of monumental buildings that dates from the rebuilding after the 1693 earthquake. As the town is a noted centre of ceramics, the effect is lightened by tiled decoration found all over Caltagirone, most effectively as flowers and emblems flanking both sides of a bridge (the Ponte San Francesco) on the way into the centre. The grandest statement, though, is made by the 142 steps of **La Scala**, which cut right up one of Caltagirone's hills to a church at the top, the risers in between each step covered with a ceramic pattern, no two the same. **Accommodation** in the centre is rather limited, but *La Scala 2* (☎0933.51.552, fax 0933.57.781; ②) has rooms to rent right in the main square at Piazza Umberto I, no. 1, and the comfortable hotel *Monteverde* (☎0933.53.682, fax 0933.53.533; ③), just south of the town at Via Industrie 11, also has a good **restaurant**. In town, the *Scala*, right by the bottom of the eponymous steps, is not cheap but it does some good dishes and the location is unbeatable, with a mountain stream splashing through (closed Wed).

TRÁPANI AND THE WEST

The **west** of Sicily is a land apart. Skirting around the coast from **Trápani** – easily the largest town in the region – it looks immediately different: the cubic whitewashed houses, palm trees, active fishing harbours and sunburned lowlands seem more akin to Africa than Europe; and historically, the west of the island has always looked south. The earliest of all Sicilian sites, the mountain haunt of **Érice**, was dominated by Punic influence, the Carthaginians themselves entrenched in **Marsala**, at Sicily's westernmost point, for several hundred years; while the Saracen invaders took their first steps on the island at **Mazara del Vallo**, a town still strongly Arabic at heart. The Greeks never secured the same foothold in Sicily's west as elsewhere, although the remains at **Segesta** and **Selinunte** count among the island's best.

Trápani

Out on something of a limb, **TRÁPANI** is an attractive enough town, though with little to keep you more than a day or two – more a stopover, perhaps, en route to the offshore Égadi Islands (see p.1012) or inland to Érice (see p.1011). A rich trading centre throughout the early Middle Ages, halfway point for Tunis and Africa, Trápani has suffered years of decline since then, and today suffers from its remote position on Sicily's western tip, despite the revitalization of the huge salt pans to the south of town. Beyond the gridded streets of modern Trápani, however, its old centre still retains a busy feel, and there are a couple of museums worth checking out.

The Town

Trápani's **old town**, broadly speaking the area west of the train station, sports a mix of often incongruous architectural styles, something that harks back to Trápani's past as a complex medieval Mediterranean trading centre. It's particularly true of the medieval Jewish quarter, a wedge of hairline streets and alleys that holds one of the city's most characteristic buildings, the **Palazzo della Giudecca** on Via Giudecca – sixteenth-century, with a stone-studded tower and finely wrought Spanish-style Plateresque windows. Just up from here, Trápani is at its most engaging, Corso Italia preceding a confused set of three piazzas, enlivened by their surrounding churches: one doorway of the sixteenth-century **Chiesa di Santa Maria di Gesù** (Via San Pietro) is defiantly Renaissance in execution, and further up, on Piazzetta Saturno, the church of **Sant'Agostino** is even earlier, fourteenth-century and retaining a Gothic portal and delicate rose window.

Off the Piazzetta, Via Torrearsa neatly splits the old town. West of here Trápani's layout becomes more regularly planned, while the main drag and shopping street, the elegant **Corso Vittorio Emanuele**, changes name to Via Carolina and then Via Torre di Ligny as it runs towards the **Torre di Ligny** – utmost point of the scimitar of land that holds the old town. The squat tower hides Trápani's **Museo Civico di Preistoria** (Mon–Sat 9am–12.30pm & 4–7.30pm; reduced hours in winter; L3000/€1.55), an archeological collection of local finds, worth an hour or so, and the water here is clean enough should you want to swim off the rocks. Finish off your circuit at the daily **market**, at the northern end of Via Torrearsa – fish, fruit and veg sold from the arcaded Piazza Mercato di Pesce, and with several lively bars in the area.

Celebrations and processions at Easter in Trápani are given added piquancy by the carriage around town on Good Friday of the **Misteri**, a group of life-sized eighteenth-century wooden figures representing scenes from the Passion. At other times they are on display in the exuberantly sculpted **Chiesa del Purgatorio** (daily 4–6.30pm, plus Lent daily 10am–noon & 4–7pm; free), on Via Domenico Giglio, near the junction with Via Francesco d'Assisi.

Except on arrival, you hardly need to set foot in the newer parts of the city. The only incentive is the interesting **Museo Nazionale Pepoli** (Mon–Sat 9am–1.30pm, Sun 9am–12.30pm; L5000/€2.58), a good three-kilometre bus ride away in the drab heart of modern Trápani: take bus #24, #25 or #30 from Corso Vittorio Emanuele, Via Libertà or Via Garibaldi, and get off at the garden outside the Santuario Santissima Annunziata, the fourteenth-century convent which houses the museum. Approached through bird-filled cloisters, the collection includes a bit of everything, from Gagini statuary and local archeological finds to delicate seventeenth-century coral craftwork, some nice prints and drawings, and a grim wooden guillotine of 1789.

Practicalities

Come to Trápani by land from the east of the island and you'll arrive in the modern part of town: most **buses** (including those to and from Érice) pull up at the terminal in Piazza Malta; **trains** stop just around the corner in Piazza Umberto I. Exceptions to the rule are the fast **buses** for Palermo and Agrigento, which leave from the Egatour office, Via Ammiraglio Staiti 13. **Ferries** and **hydrofoils** for the Égadi Islands, Pantelleria, Cagliari and Tunis dock at the adjacent Molo di Sanita. For information, accommodation listings and free maps, visit the **tourist office** in Piazzetta Saturno (Mon–Sat 8am–8pm, Sun 9am–noon; ☎0923.29.000, fax 0923.24.004).

Finding somewhere to stay at Easter will be tricky, unless you book well in advance, but at other times rooms are easy to come by. Cheapest of the **hotels** is the *Messina*, Corso Vittorio Emanuele 71 (☎0923.21.198; ①), a bit dingy and often booked out; alternatively, try the smarter and more professional *Maccotta* on Via degli Argentieri (☎0923.28.418; ③), or the comfortably modernized *Nuovo Russo* at 4 Tintori 4 (☎0923.22.166; ③). The nearest **campsite** is a twenty-minute bus ride away at Lido Valdérice (☎0923.573.086; April–Sept) – there are seven buses daily (not Sun in winter) to the turn-off, from which it's a 15-minute walk.

Eating is particularly enjoyable in Trápani. The *Trattoria Safina*, opposite the train station at Piazza Umberto I (closed Fri except July & Aug), is a real bargain; for fine pizzas seek out *Pizzeria Mediterranea*, Corso Vittorio Emanuele 195 (closed Thurs), opposite Piazza Jolanda – a takeaway joint with a couple of rooms at the back. Better-class meals are on offer at *P&G*, Via Spalti 1, near the station (☎0923.547.701; closed Sun & Aug), a semi-formal place with local *busiate* pasta.

Érice and Segesta

The nearest and most exhilarating ride from Trápani is to ÉRICE, forty minutes away by bus. It's a mountain town with powerful associations: creeping hillside alleys, stone buildings and silent charm. Founded by Elymnians, who claimed descent from the Trojans, the original city was known to the ancient world as Eryx, and a magnificent temple, dedicated to Venus Erycina, Mediterranean goddess of fertility, once topped the mountain. Though the city was considered impregnable, Carthaginian, Roman, Arab and Norman forces all forced entry over the centuries. But all respected the sanctity of Érice: the Romans rebuilt the temple and set 200 soldiers to serve as guardians of the shrine; while the Arabs renamed the town Gebel-Hamed, or Mohammed's mountain.

If it's fine, the views from the terraces of Érice are stupendous – over Trápani, the slumbering whales of the Égadi Islands and on very clear days as far as Cape Bon in Tunisia. Scout around the town at random: the most convoluted of routes is only going to take you a couple of hours and every street and piazza is a delight. You enter through the Norman **Porta Trápani**, just inside which the battlemented fourteenth-century campanile of the **Duomo** did service as a lookout tower for Frederick III of Aragon. From here there's no set route, though passing through pretty **Piazza Umberto** with its couple of outdoor bars is a good idea; and a natural start or finish could be made at the ivy-clad Norman **Castello** at the far end of town. This was built on the site of the famed ancient temple, chunks of which are incorporated in the walls.

Hardly surprisingly, **staying** in Érice means paying through the nose and booking in advance. The only relatively cheap choices are the smart *Edelweiss*, in Cortile Padre Vincenzo, a cobbled alley off Piazzetta San Domenico (☎0923.869.420; ④), and, just outside town, the *Ermione*, Via Pineta Comunale 43 (☎0923.869.138, fax 0923.869.587; ⑤), 1950s-style and with seaward views. More economical is the **youth hostel** (☎0923.869.144; L30,000/€15.60), outside the town walls on Viale delle Pinete, but it's usually open June–September only, and even then is often fully booked – check with the helpful **tourist office** (Mon–Sat: 8am–2pm; ☎0923.869.388) on Viale Conte Pepoli, which also dishes out maps. If you're coming for the day you may want to bring a picnic since **restaurant** prices in Érice are vastly inflated. However, many places offer a tourist menu, such as the *Re Aceste*, Viale Conte Pepoli 45 (closed Wed & Nov), whose terrace overlooks the plain below town. There's higher-quality fare at *La Pentolaccia*, Via Guarnotti 17, housed in an old monastery and moderately priced (closed Fri), and at the more formal and correspondingly pricier *Monte San Giuliano*, entered through a medieval gateway at Vicolo San Rocco 7 (☎0923.869.595; closed Mon and 2 weeks in Nov & Jan).

The Temple of Segesta

If time is limited, it's hard to know which to recommend most: the heights of Érice or Trápani's other local attraction, the temple at **Segesta** (daily 9am–2hr before sunset; L8000/€4.13). Although unfinished, this Greek construction of 424 BC is one of the most inspiring of Doric temples anywhere and, along with the theatre, virtually the only relic of an ancient city whose roots – like those of Érice – go back to the twelfth century BC. Unlike Érice, though, ancient Segesta was eventually Hellenized and spent most of the later period disputing its borders with Selinus to the south. The temple dates from a time of prosperous alliance with Athens, the building abandoned when a new dispute broke out with Selinus in 416 BC.

The **temple** itself crowns a low hill, beyond a café and car park. From a distance you could be forgiven for thinking that it's complete: the 36 regular white stone columns, entablature and pediment are all intact, and all it lacks is a roof. However, get closer and you see just how unfinished the building is: stone studs, always removed on completion, still line the stylobate, the tall columns are unfluted and the cella walls are missing. Below the car park, a road winds up through slopes of wild fennel to the small **theatre** on a higher hill beyond; there's a half-hourly minibus service if you don't fancy the climb. The view from the top is justly lauded, across green slopes and the plain to the sea, the deep blue of the bay a lovely contrast to the theatre's white stone – not much damaged by the stilted motorway snaking away below.

Without your own transport, **getting to Segesta** involves a twenty-minute uphill walk from Segesta-Tempio, to which there are four buses a day from Piazza Malta in Trápani, the last one returning at around 6pm, and three daily trains from Trápani stopping here on their way to Palermo. There are more frequent trains connecting Trápani and Palermo with the station of **CALATAFIMI**, signposted 4km away (the town itself is a further 4km away). There's also a cheap and modern **hotel** in Calatafimi, the *Mille Pini*, Piazza F. Vivona 4 (☎0924.951.260; ②), if you want to stay the night in the quiet surroundings: there are good views from some windows.

The Égadi Islands

Of the various islands, islets and rock stacks that fan out from the west coast of Sicily, the three **Égadi Islands** (Isole Égadi) are best for a quick jaunt – connected by ferry and hydrofoil with Trápani. Saved from depopulation by tourism, in season at least you're not going to be alone, certainly on the main island, Favignana. But a tour of the islands is worthwhile, not least for the caves that perforate the splintered coastlines. Out of season things are noticeably quieter: come between April and July and you may witness the bloody Mattanza, an age-old slaughter in this noted centre of tuna fishing.

All **transport** (ferries and hydrofoils several times daily in summer) to the islands departs from Trápani's Molo di Sanità; tickets are available from the booth on the dockside on Via Ammiraglio Staiti. Though less frequent, ferries are, as always, much cheaper.

FAVIGNANA, island and port town, is first stop for the boats from Trápani, a good base since it has virtually all the accommodation and the Égadi's only campsites. Only 25 minutes by hydrofoil from the mainland, the island attracts a lot of day-trippers, keen to get onto its few rocky beaches. But get out of the main port and it's easy enough to escape the crowds, even easier with a bike. (There's a bike rental shop, Isidoro, at Via Mazzini 40; around L10,000/€5.17 a day.) Caves all over the island bear prehistoric traces and many are accessible if you're determined enough. Otherwise, the two wings of the island invite separate walks; best is the stroll around the eastern part, past the bizarre ancient quarries at Cala Rossa and taking in Lido Burrone, the island's best beach, only 3km from the port. Best **hotel** choice for value and comfort is the modern *Egadi*, Via C. Colombo 17 (☎ & fax 0923.921.232; ③), right in the centre of Favignana town, and there are two **campsites** outside town – an easy walk and both well signposted.

LÉVANZO, to the north, looks immediately inviting, its white houses against the turquoise sea reminiscent of the Greek islands. The steep coast is full of inlets and, again, is riddled with caves. One, the **Grotta del Genovese**, was discovered in 1949 and contains some remarkable Paleolithic incised drawings, 6000 years old, as well as later Neolithic pictures. To arrange to see the cave you'll have to contact the guardian, Natale Castiglione, who lives at Via Calvario 11 (call ☎0923.924.032 during summer; weekends only in winter), near the hydrofoil quay. There are two **hotels** on Lévanzo, both just above the only road and with good views over the sea; the cheaper one is the *Paradiso* (☎0923.924.080; ②), and a little further up the side road, the *Pensione Dei*

Fenici (☎0923.924.083; ③), is much fancier. In summer, both places demand half- or full board. However, you should be able to get **rooms** in private houses if you ask around the port.

MARÉTTIMO, furthest out of the Égadi Islands, is the place to come for solitude. Very much off the beaten track, it's reached by only a few tourists. More white houses are scattered across the rocky island, while there's a bar in the main piazza and two restaurants. The spectacular fragmented coastline is pitted with rocky coves sheltering hideaway **beaches**, and there are numerous gentle **walks** which will take you all over the island. Again, although there are no hotels on Maréttimo you should be able to rent a room by asking at the café in the main square.

Trápani to Palermo: the coastal route

Frequent buses run north from Trápani, cutting away from the coast until reaching **SAN VITO LO CAPO** at the very nib of the northwestern headland. There are some good sands nearby, while the cape itself is only a stride away; and there are several **campsites** too – best value are *La Fata* (☎0923.972.133) and *La Pineta* (☎0923.972.818), both open all year. San Vito is a popular local holiday spot and you don't have to camp – there are several fairly good **pensioni** in the village, as well as trattorias and bars catering to the summer crowds. The *Sabbia d'Oro*, behind the church at Via Santuario 49 (☎0923.972.508, fax 0923.621.163; ③), has decent rooms with spacious separate bathrooms, while the main Via Savoia has at least three places offering rooms up to ④; cheapest is the *Costa Gaia* (☎0923.972.268; ②), which is basic but clean. You'll get plenty more comfort at the *Hotel Capo San Vito*, right on the beach at Via San Vito 3 (☎0923.972.284, fax 0923.972.559; ⑤; April–Oct), with a good terrace restaurant. There's no shortage of places to **eat**; for dishes with a Tunisian influence try *Tha'am* at Via Duca degli Abruzzi 32 (closed Wed in winter), off Via Savoia.

You'll have to return to Trápani for onward transport. Buses or, more frequently, **trains** cut across the headland to **CASTELLAMMARE DEL GOLFO**, another popular resort built on and around a hefty rocky promontory which is guarded by the squat remains of an Aragonese castle. The local **train station** is 4km east of town; a bus meets arrivals and shuttles you into Castellammare, passing the **campsite** *Nausica* (☎0924.33.030; May–Sept) and the beach on the way. However, if you're looking for a place to stay you could do much better by moving the ten kilometres west up the coast to Scopello; there are four buses a day (Mon–Sat) from the **bus station** on Via della Repubblica off the main Via Segesta.

The road to **SCOPELLO** from Castellammare forks just before the village, with one strand running the few hundred metres down to the **Tonnara do Scopello**, set in its own tiny cove. This old tuna fishery is where the writer Gavin Maxwell lived and worked in the 1950s, basing his *Ten Pains of Death* on his experiences there. It's almost too picturesque to be true – not least the row of abandoned buildings on the quayside and the ruined old watchtowers tottering on jagged pinnacles of rock above the sea. The actual village of Scopello perches on a ridge a couple of hundred metres above the coastline, comprising little more than a paved square and a fountain, off which run a couple of alleys. In summer, particularly, you'd do well to book in advance if you want **to stay** here, and be prepared to accept half-board terms in the pensions. *La Tranchina* at Via A. Diaz 7 (☎0924.541.099; ④, including breakfast) has comfortable rooms with decent plumbing and an English-speaking owner. *La Tavernetta*, next door at no. 3 (☎0924.541.129; ③), has similarly pleasant rooms, some with distant sea views. At the *Torre Benistra*, just around the corner at Via Natale di Roma 19 (☎0924.541.128; ②), the price includes half-board, and the **food** here is probably the best in the village. The nearest **campsite** is *Baia di Guidaloca* (☎0924.541.262; April–Sept), 3km south of

Scopello and a stone's throw from the lovely bay of **Cala Bianca**, where there's good swimming; the bus from Castellammare passes right by.

The southern entrance to the **Riserva Naturale dello Zíngaro** is just 2km from Scopello, the first nature reserve to have been established in Sicily, comprising a completely unspoiled seven-kilometre stretch of coastline backed by steep mountains. At the entrance, there's an **information hut**, where you can pick up a plan showing the trails through the reserve. It's less than twenty minutes to the first beach, **Punta della Capreria**, and 3km to the successive coves of **Disa**, **Berretta** and **Marinella**, which should be a little more secluded.

East of here (and the train from Trápani stops at every town before Palermo) it's a strange – often unpleasant – coastal mixture of industrialization and tourist development. The wide and fertile gulf provides some good views though, and there's the occasional beach that beckons. The last few towns that line the gulf, **Balestrate**, **Trappeto** and, inland, **Partinico** are more interesting for what they were, and to some extent still are – infamous centres of Mafia influence and social and political neglect. **Daniel Dolci**, a social reformer of remarkable persistence, first came to Trappeto in 1952 from wealthy northern Italy. He was appalled. "Looking all around me, I saw no streets, just mud and dust. Not a single drugstore – or sewer. The dialect didn't even have a word for sewer." Dolci inaugurated a programme of self-help among the local people, building community and cultural centres, promoting local education – things that cut right across the traditional areas of influence in the Mafia-ridden west of Sicily. It's a story told in the words of the local people in Dolci's extraordinary book *Sicilian Lives*: vital reading if you intend to pass this way.

Marsala and Mazara del Vallo

Another section of the western rail loop runs **south from Trápani** down the coast, pretty much within sight of the sea all the way, trains ploughing across the cultivated plain, past white, squat houses and distant burned hills. The region flaunts its tangible non-Greek heritage even more in **MARSALA**, 10km on, which takes its name from the Arabic Marsah-el-Allah, the port of Allah. Once the main Saracenic base in Sicily, since the late eighteenth century Marsala has been better known for the dessert wine that carries its name, something every bar and restaurant will sell you.

The centre of Marsala is extremely attractive, a clean sixteenth-century layout that's free of traffic and littered with high, ageing buildings and arcaded courtyards. But – pleasant as the town is – save your energy for two excellent museums. The most central, behind the cathedral at Via Garraffa 57, is the **Museo degli Arazzi** (Tues–Sun 9am–1pm & 4–6pm; L2000/€1.03), whose sole display is a series of eight enormous hand-stitched wool and silk tapestries depicting the capture of Jerusalem – sixteenth century and beautifully rich, in burnished red, gold and green. Afterwards, walk out to the cape (follow the main Via XI Maggio to Piazza della Vittoria and bear left towards the water); one of the stone-vaulted warehouses that line the promenade holds the equally impressive **Museo Marsala** (daily 9am–1.30pm, plus Thurs–Sat and alternate Sun 4–7.30pm; L4000/€2.07). An archeological museum of quality, its major exhibit is a reconstructed Punic warship once rowed by 68 oarsmen, probably sunk during the First Punic War, and rediscovered in 1971. Other bits and pieces on display are from the excavated site (mostly Roman) of Lilybaeum. If you want a **meal** in Marsala, head for the wood-panelled *Trattoria Garibaldi* at Piazza Addolorata 5 (closed Mon) for good local dishes.

Half an hour further on, **MAZARA DEL VALLO** is Sicily's most important fishing port and a place of equal distinction for the Arabs and Normans who dominated the island a thousand years ago. The first Saracen gain in Sicily, Mazara was Arabic for 250 years until captured by Count Roger in 1075: the island's first Norman parliament met in the town 22 years later, and a relic of that period is the tiny pink-domed Norman chapel of **San Nicolò**, on the edge of the harbour. North Africans crew the colourful fishing boats that block the harbour and river, the old city kasbah once more houses a Tunisian community. Wandering around the harbour area is the most rewarding thing to do in Mazara, although you can spend an enjoyable hour or so as well in the remodelled Norman **Duomo**, which shelters some Roman and Byzantine remains, and poking around the **Museo Civico** (Mon–Fri 9am–1.30pm, plus Tues & Thurs 4–6pm; free) in Piazza del Plebiscito, just off Mazara's main square. Hotel **accommodation** includes the dauntingly large but very comfortable *Hopps Hotel*, at Via G. Hopps 29 (☎0923.946.133; ⑤), at the eastern end of the Lungomare Mazzini. If you're budgeting, choose the *Kristallo* (☎0923.932.688; ③), at Via Valeria 36, not far from the station off Corso Armando Diaz. A good **restaurant** for regional dishes in the town is *La Béttola* at Corso Diaz 20, opposite the train station (closed Sun).

Castelvetrano to Sciacca

There's very little else to stop for around the western coast; even less inland, which is crossed by one major road, the SS188 which runs from Marsala to Salemi, centre of a prosperous wine-making region. But the southernmost chunk of Sicily's western bulge is easily reached by train and has several places worth more than a cursory glance if you have the time.

CASTELVETRANO isn't necessarily one of them. If anyone stops at all, it's to take in the nearby Greek ruins at Selinunte, though this can be much better done from the adjacent fishing village of Marinella (see below). But the centre of Castelvetrano is handsome and you may be intrigued enough by the story of Sicily's most famous bandit, **Salvatore Giuliano**, to want to stop. Less a Robin Hood figure than a political pawn caught between the regrouping Mafia and the Sicilian separatists after World War II, Giuliano got a sympathetic press – and much covert support – from the local people hereabouts. But like all true folk heroes he was eventually betrayed, his bullet-riddled body found in one of Castelvetrano's courtyards in 1950.

To **get to Selinunte**, take the bus for **MARINELLA** from Piazza Reina Margherita (5 daily; 25min). The village, right next to the site, is no longer the isolated place it once was, with new buildings going up in the centre and the seafront slightly top-heavy with trattorias and *pensioni* these days. But it remains an attractive place, certainly if you're planning to make use of the fine sand **beach** that stretches west from the village to the ruins. **Buses** pull up on the road that leads down to the seafront, where the main **hotels** and restaurants are situated. First choice here is the *Lido Azzurro*, Via Marco Polo 98 (☎ & fax 0924.46.256; ③), a charming villa with sea-facing balconies. Opposite the temple car park, the sign pointing to "Chiesa" leads to the old abandoned train station, just before which you'll find the cheaper *Pensione Costa D'Avorio*, at Via Argonauti 10 (☎0924.46.207; ③), a secluded and clean *pensione*. There are also two **campsites** virtually next to each other on the main road, though they are 1500m north of the village: the *Athena* (☎0924.46.132) and *Il Maggiolino* (☎0924.46.044), both open all year; the bus from Castelvetrano passes right by them. Of the many **restaurants**, *Baffo's*, at Via Marco Polo 51, is good value, with a wide selection of fish dishes. In the residential district, the ristorante-pizzeria *Africa*, in Via Alceste, serves crispy pizzas from a wood-burning stove, good antipasti and a reasonable tourist menu.

Selinunte: the site

The most westerly of the Hellenic colonies, the Greek city of Selinus – **Selinunte** in modern Italian – reached its peak in the fifth century BC when a series of mighty temples was erected. A bitter rival of Segesta (see p.1011), whose lands lay adjacent to the north, the powerful city and its fertile plain attracted enemies hand over fist, and it was only a matter of time before Selinus caught the eye of Segesta's ally, Carthage. Geographically vulnerable, the city was sacked by Carthaginians, any recovery forestalled by earthquakes that later razed the city. Despite the destruction, which left the site completely abandoned until it was rediscovered in the sixteenth century, the ruins of Selinus have exerted a romantic hold ever since.

The **site** of Selinus is set back behind the main part of Marinella village, split into two parts with temples in each, known only as Temples A–G. The two parts are enclosed within the same site, with the car park and **entrance** (daily 9am–1hr before sunset; L8000/€4.13, tickets sold until 2hr before sunset) lying through the landscaped earthbanks that preclude views of the east group of temples from the road. The first stop is at the **East Group**. Shrouded in the wild celery which gave the ancient city its name, the temples are in various stages of reconstructed ruin: the most complete the one nearest the sea (Temple E), the northernmost (Temple G) a tangle of columned wreckage six metres high in places. The road leads down from here, across the (now buried) site of the old harbour to the second part of excavated Selinus, the **acropolis**, a site containing what remains of the other temples (five in all), as well as the well-preserved city streets and massive, stepped walls which rise above the duned beach below. Temple C stands on the highest point of the acropolis, and there are glorious views from its stones out over the sparkling sea: from this temple were removed some of the best metopes, now on show in Palermo's archeological museum (see p.967).

Sciacca

FS **buses** leave from outside Castelvetrano train station three times daily (1 on Sun) for Sciacca, picking up at the abandoned Selinunte station in Marinella village. **SCIACCA**'s upper town is skirted by good medieval walls which form high sides to the steep streets, rising to a ruined Spanish castle. Below, the lower town sits on a clifftop terrace overlooking the harbour, a place where it's easy to while away time drinking in the coastal views. Hot springs at **Monte San Calogero**, 8km from town, kept the Romans healthy and are still in use. Get there on bus #4 every hour from Sciacca; ask for details at the **tourist office**, Corso Vittorio Emanuele 84 (Mon–Sat 9am–2pm; ☎0925.86.247, fax 0925.84.121).

With an active harbour here and some good beaches close by, Sciacca makes a nice place to **stay** over, though there's precious little choice – the only central option being the *Paloma Bianca* at Via Figuli 5 (☎0925.25.667, fax 0925.25.130; ③), a rather uninspiring business-travellers' hotel, but comfortable enough. You could spend a little more money on the plusher *Grand Hotel delle Terme*, Viale Nuove Terme 1 (☎0925.23.133; ③), on the cliffs to the east of town, set in its own park with outstanding views out to sea. The nearest **campsite**, *Baia Makauda* (☎0925.997.001; June–Sept), lies 9km east of town at Località San Giorgio Tranchina, most conveniently reached by taxi if you don't have your own transport.

Pantelleria

Forty kilometres nearer to Tunisia than to Sicily, **PANTELLERIA** is the most singular of Sicily's outlying islands. Volcanic, it has been settled since Neolithic times and later supported a Phoenician colony in the seventh century BC. Its strategic position kept it in the mainstream of Sicilian history for years: developed as one of the main Mediterranean bases by the Fascists during World War II, Pantelleria was bombed without mercy by the Allies in May 1943 as they advanced from North Africa. In part,

GETTING TO PANTELLERIA

Siremar **ferries** from Trápani (June–Sept 1 daily; Oct–May 1 daily Mon–Sat) take just under six hours to reach Pantelleria, for a deck-class fare of around L43,000/€22.36 one way, less outside the high season. The **hydrofoil service**, also from Trápani, is twice as fast and twice the price; it currently operates from mid-June to mid-September, on Wednesday, Friday and Sunday.

Pantelleria is 45 minutes' **flight** from Trápani (1 daily), or 50 minutes from Palermo (at least 2 daily): the normal one-way fare from either is around L140,000/€72.80, but there are special offers at weekends, and discounts are available from mainland travel agencies and the Cossira office on the island.

this explains the morose appearance of the island's main town (also called Pantelleria) – thrown up in unedifying concrete.

There are no beaches of any kind in Pantelleria, its rough black coastline mainly jagged rocks, but the **swimming** is still pretty good in some exceptionally scenic spots. Inland, the largely mountainous country offers plenty of **rambling** opportunities, all an easy moped- or bus-ride from the port. If you're spending any length of time on Pantelleria, a novel accommodation option is to stay in one of the local **dammuso** houses: a throwback to the buildings of Neolithic times, their strong walls and domed roofs keep the temperature down indoors; many are available for rent (through Call Tour, Via Cágliari 52 ☎0923.911.065). The main drawback is the **cost of living**: there are only a few hotels, where the cheapest rooms start at L80,000–100,000/€41.60–52 a double, while food (and water) is mostly imported and therefore relatively expensive. The best times to visit are May/June or September/October, to avoid the summer's ferocious heat.

Practicalities

PANTELLERIA TOWN is the site of most of the island's accommodation and facilities. The **airport** is 5km southeast of town; a bus connects with flight arrivals and drops you in the central Piazza Cavour. **Arriving by sea**, you'll disembark right in the centre of town. The local **buses** leave from Piazza Cavour, with regular departures to all the main villages on the island – there are no services on Sundays. The few **hotels** in town include the *Miryam*, Corso Umberto I (☎0923.911.374; ④), bright and pleasant inside despite rather glum external appearances, which is at the far end of the port, near the castle; and the *Port Hotel* (☎0923.912.680; ⑤), nearer the dock at Via Borgo Italia 6, with harbour-facing but fairly functional rooms; half- or full-board is required in August. The nearby *Khamma*, at Via Borgo Italia 24 (☎0923.912.680; ⑤), also on the harbourfront, offers three-star comforts at relatively bargain rates. There's no **campsite** on the island. Probably the best place to **eat** in town is *Il Cappero*, Via Roma 31, just off the main piazza (closed Mon in winter), which serves the local ravioli stuffed with *tumma*, fresh fish (including large tuna steaks) and popular pizzas. There's a good *antipasto* table too. The best-placed trattoria in town is *Il Dammuso*, Via Borgo Italia (near the *Miryam*), a trendy place with large windows opening right onto the harbour; the long menu includes great fish and pizzas.

Around the island

There are seven daily **buses** along the southwest coast to Scauri, passing on the way the first of the island's strange **sesi**, massive black Neolithic funeral mounds of piled rock, with low passages leading inside. On foot, it's just over an hour from the *sesi* to **Sataria**, where concrete steps lead down to a tiny square-cut sea pool. In the cave behind are more pools where warm water bubbles through, reputed to be good for curing rheumatism and skin diseases.

Along the northeast coast to Kamma and Tracino (6 daily buses), get the bus to drop you at the top of the route down into **Gadir**, a small anchorage with just a few houses hemmed in by volcanic pricks of rock. From here it's an easy, fairly flat hour's stroll to the charming **Cala Levante**, a huddle of houses around another tiny fishing harbour. Where the road peters out, bear right along the path at the second anchorage and keep along the coast for another five minutes until the **Arco dell'Elefante**, or "Elephant Arch", hoves into view, named after the hooped formation of rock that resembles an elephant stooping to drink.

The main inland destination is Pantelleria's main volcano, the Montagna Grande, whose summit is the island's most distinctive feature seen from out at sea. Buses (4 daily) run from the port for the crumbly old village of **Siba**, perched on a ridge below the volcano. To climb the peak of **Montagna Grande** (836m), keep left at the telephone sign by the *tabacchi* here, and strike off the main road. From Siba, another (signposted) path – on the left as you follow the road through the village – brings you in around twenty minutes to the **Sauna Naturale** (or Bagno Asciutto). It's little more than a slit in the rock-face, where you can crouch in absolute darkness, breaking out into a heavy sweat as soon as you enter.

travel details

TRAINS

Agrigento to: Palermo (5–10 daily; 2hr); Términi Imerese (5–10 daily; 1hr 40min).

Catania to: Caltagirone (7–9 daily; 2hr); Enna (3–6 daily; 1hr 30min); Gela (5–8 daily; 2hr 40min); Messina (1–2 hourly; 1hr 30min); Palermo (1–4 daily; 3hr 30min); Randazzo (11 daily; 3hr); Siracusa (1–2 hourly; 1hr 30min); Taormina (1–2 hourly; 1hr).

Enna to: Caltanissetta (4–7 daily; 25min); Catania (6–8 daily; 1hr 30min); Palermo (1–4 daily; 2hr 10min–5hr 30min).

Messina to: Catania (1–2 hourly; 1hr 30min); Cefalù (10–16 daily; 2hr 45min); Palermo (9–15 daily; 3hr 30min–6hr); Taormina (1–2 hourly; 35min–1hr).

Palermo to: Agrigento (5–10 daily; 2hr); Castelvetrano (1–6 daily; 2hr); Catania (4–5 daily; 3–4hr); Cefalù (1–2 hourly; 1hr); Enna (4–5 daily; 2hr); Marsala (1–5 daily; 3hr); Mazara del Vallo (1–5 daily; 2hr 30min); Messina (11–18 daily; 3hr–4hr 30min); Milazzo (12–18 daily; 2hr 30min–3hr 40min); Términi Imerese (1–2 hourly; 30min); Trápani (6–8 daily; 2hr 15min–3hr 30min).

Ragusa to: Gela (5–10 daily; 1hr 20min); Módica (7–12 daily; 20min); Noto (9 daily; 1hr 30min).

Randazzo to: Riposto (6 daily; 45min).

Siracusa to: Catania (9–17 daily; 1hr 20min); Gela (4 daily; 3hr 40min); Messina (10–17 daily; 3hr 15min); Noto (4–11 daily; 30min); Ragusa (3–5 daily; 2hr 20min).

Taormina to: Catania (1–2 hourly; 50min); Messina (1–2 hourly; 45min–1hr 15min); Randazzo (2 daily during school terms; 1hr 30min); Siracusa (10–14 daily; 2hr 15min).

Trápani to: Castelvetrano (4–9 daily; 1hr 10min); Marsala (4–11 daily; 30min); Mazara del Vallo (4–10 daily; 50min); Palermo (5–11 daily; 2–3hr); Segesta-Tempio (3 daily; 25min).

BUSES

Schedules below are for Monday–Saturday services; on Sundays, services are either drastically reduced or non-existent.

Agrigento to: Catania (11 daily; 2hr 50min); Gela (3 daily; 1hr 30min); Palermo (4 daily; 2hr); Porto Empédocle (every 30min; 20min); Trápani (3 daily; 3hr 40min–4hr 20min).

Castelvetrano to: Agrigento (9 daily; 2hr); Marinella (4 daily; 20min); Marsala (7 daily; 40min); Mazara del Vallo (7 daily; 20min); Trápani (7 daily; 1hr 30min).

Catania to: Acireale (1–2 hourly; 50min); Agrigento (11 daily; 2hr 50min); Caltagirone (11 daily; 1hr 30min); Enna (6 daily; 1hr 20min); Gela

(7 daily; 2hr); Lentini (hourly; 1hr); Messina (1–2 hourly; 1hr 35min); Nicolosi (hourly; 40min); Noto (5 daily; 1hr 40min); Palermo (hourly; 2hr 40min); Piazza Armerina (4 daily; 2hr 50min); Ragusa (8 daily; 3hr); Siracusa (hourly; 1hr 20min); Taormina (hourly; 1hr).

Enna to: Caltanissetta (4 daily; 50min); Catania (6 daily; 1hr 20min); Gela (4–5 daily; 1hr 20min); Piazza Armerina (7 daily; 40min).

Messina to: Catania (1–2 hourly; 1hr 35min); Giardini-Naxos (7 daily; 50min–2hr); Milazzo (hourly; 45min); Palermo (4 daily; 3hr 15min); Randazzo (4 daily; 2hr 15min); Taormina (hourly; 1hr–1hr 40min).

Milazzo to: Messina (hourly; 45min).

Palermo to: Agrigento (4 daily; 2hr); Bagheria (hourly; 20min); Catania (hourly; 2hr 40min); Cefalù (3 daily; 1hr); Enna (4 daily; 1hr 45min); Messina (5 daily; 3hr 15min); Piana degli Albanesi (10 daily; 30min); Siracusa (3 daily; 3hr 15min); Términi Imerese (6 daily; 40min); Trápani (hourly; 2hr).

Piazza Armerina to: Caltagirone (6 daily; 1hr); Enna (7 daily; 30min); Palermo (6 daily; 2hr–2hr 30min).

Ragusa to: Módica (every 30min; 20min).

Siracusa to: Caltagirone (1 daily; 2hr); Catania (hourly; 1hr 20min); Noto (every 30min; 40min); Piazza Armerina (1 daily; 2hr 30min); Ragusa (6 daily; 1hr 30min).

Taormina to: Castelmola (5–6 daily; 20min); Catania (hourly; 1hr).

Trápani to: Agrigento (3 daily; 3hr 5min–4hr 5min); Érice (9 daily; 40min); San Vito Lo Capo (7 daily; 1hr 15min).

FERRIES

The services detailed here refer to the period from June to September; you should expect frequencies to be greatly reduced or suspended outside these months, especially to the Aeolian Islands.

Lípari to: Alicudi (5 weekly; 4hr); Filicudi (6 weekly; 2hr–2hr 25min); Milazzo (4–6 daily; 2hr); Naples (3–6 weekly; 13hr 45min); Panarea (1–2 daily; 2hr); Salina (1–2 daily; 50min); Strómboli (5–8 weekly; 4hr 15min); Vulcano (3–5 daily; 25min).

Messina to: Villa San Giovanni (every 20min; 40min).

Milazzo to: Alicudi (5 weekly; 6hr); Filicudi (5–6 weekly, 5hr); Ginostra (3–6 weekly; 6hr); Lípari (5–6 daily; 2hr); Naples (3–6 weekly; 17hr); Panarea (3–8 weekly; 5hr–8hr 30min); Salina (3–4 daily; 3hr–3hr 40min); Strómboli (5–8 weekly; 7hr); Vulcano (3–4 daily; 1hr 30min).

Palermo to: Cágliari (1 weekly; 14hr 30min); Genoa (1 daily; 20hr); Livorno (3 weekly; 17hr); Naples (1 daily; 11hr); Ústica (1 daily; 2hr 20min).

Porto Empédocle to: Lampedusa (1 daily; 8hr 15min); Linosa (1 daily; 5hr 45min).

Trápani to: Cágliari (1 weekly; 11hr); Favignana (1 daily; 1hr); Lévanzo (3 daily; 55min–1hr 40min); Maréttimo (1 daily; 3hr); Pantelleria (1 daily; 5hr 45min).

HYDROFOILS

Again, most of the services listed are greatly reduced or suspended outside the summer season.

Cefalù to: Lípari (3 weekly; 2hr 45min); Palermo (3 weekly; 1hr); Vulcano (3 weekly; 3hr).

Lípari to: Alicudi (3–4 daily; 1–2hr); Capo d'Orlando (1–2 daily; 1hr); Cefalù (3 weekly; 3hr); Filicudi (4 daily; 1hr–1hr 35min); Ginostra (2 daily; 1hr–1hr 25min); Messina (3–6 daily; 1hr 20min–3hr); Milazzo (hourly; 55min); Naples (1–2 daily; 5hr 30min); Palermo (2 daily; 4hr); Panarea (8–10 daily; 25–55min); Salina (hourly; 25–50min); Strómboli (7–9 daily; 1hr 15min–1hr 45min); Vulcano (hourly; 10min).

Messina to: Lípari (5–6 daily; 1hr 20min–2hr 35min); Reggio di Calabria (hourly; 25min); Vulcano (5–6 daily; 1hr 20min–3hr 25min).

Milazzo to: Alicudi (2 daily; 2hr 45min–3hr); Filicudi (2 daily; 2hr 20min); Ginostra (3 daily; 1hr 45min–2hr 30min); Lípari (hourly; 45min–1hr); Panarea (4–6 daily; 1hr 15min–2hr 20min); Salina (6–15 daily; 1hr 30min); Strómboli (4 daily; 1–3hr); Vulcano (hourly; 40min–1hr).

Palermo to: Cefalù (3 weekly; 1hr); Lípari (2 daily; 3hr 30min–4hr); Naples (1 daily; 4hr); Ústica (2–3 daily; 1hr 15min).

Pantelleria to: Trápani (3 weekly; 2hr 15min).

Trápani to: Favignana (10 daily; 20min); Lévanzo (10 daily; 15–35min); Maréttimo (3 daily; 1hr 5min); Naples (3 weekly; 6hr 45min); Pantelleria (3 weekly; 2hr 30min); Ústica (3 weekly; 4hr).

Ústica to: Favignana (3 weekly; 2hr); Naples (3 weekly; 4hr); Trápani (3 weekly; 2hr 30min).

FLIGHTS

Palermo to: Lampedusa (2 daily; 45min); Pantelleria (2–4 daily; 50min).

Trápani to: Pantelleria (1 daily; 45min).

INTERNATIONAL FERRIES AND CATAMARANS

Catania to: Malta (2–5 weekly; 3–11hr).

Trápani to: Tunis (1 weekly; 8hr 15min).

CHAPTER SEVENTEEN

SARDINIA

A little under 200km from the Italian mainland, slightly more than that from the North African coast at Tunisia, **Sardinia** is way off most tourist itineraries of Italy: D.H. Lawrence found it exotically different when he passed through here in 1921 – "lost", as he put it, "between Europe and Africa and belonging to nowhere." Your reasons for coming will probably be a combination of plain curiosity and a yearning for clean beaches. The island is relatively free of large cities or heavy industry, and its beaches are indeed some of the cleanest in Italy and are on the whole uncrowded, except perhaps for peak season, when ferries bring in a steady stream of sun-worshippers from what the islanders call *il continente*, or mainland Italy. But Sardinia offers plenty besides sun and sea – the more so if you are prepared to penetrate into its lesser-known interior.

Although not known for its cultural riches, the island does hold some surprises, not least the remains of the various civilizations that passed through here. Its central Mediterranean position ensured that it was never left alone for long, and from the Carthaginians onwards the island was ravaged by a succession of invaders, each of them leaving some imprint behind: Roman and Carthaginian ruins, Genoan fortresses, a string of elegant Pisan churches, not to mention some impressive Gothic and Spanish Baroque architecture. Perhaps most striking of all, however, are the remnants of Sardinia's only significant native culture, known as the **nuraghic** civilization after the 7000-odd *nuraghi* that litter the landscape. These mysterious, stone-built constructions, unique to Sardinia, are often in splendid isolation, which means they're fairly difficult to get to without your own transport, but make the effort to see at least one during your stay – or failing that, drop in on the museums of Cágliari or Sássari to view the lovely statuettes and domestic objects left by this culture.

On the whole, Sardinia's smaller centres are the most attractive, but the capital, **Cágliari** – for many the arrival point – shouldn't be written off. With good accommodation and restaurants, it makes a useful base for exploring the southern third of the island. The other main ferry port is **Olbia** in the north, little more than a transit town but well geared for accommodation and conveniently close to the jagged northern coast. The **Costa Smeralda**, a few kilometres distant, is Sardinia's best-known resort

---

ACCOMMODATION PRICE CODES

Throughout this guide, prices per person are given for **youth hostels** and assume Hostelling International (HI) membership. **Hotel** accommodation is coded on a scale from ① to ⑨, reflecting the cost of the cheapest double room in each establishment in high season. The price bands to which these codes refer are as follows:

① Up to L60,000/€30.99
② L60,000–90,000/€30.99–46.48
③ L90,000–120,000/€46.48–61.98
④ L120,000–150,000/€61.98–77.47
⑤ L150,000–200,000/€77.47–103.29

⑥ L200,000–250,000/€103.29–129.11
⑦ L250,000–300,000/€129.11–154.94
⑧ L300,000–400,000/€154.94–206.58
⑨ over L400,000/€206.58

(See p.32 for a full explanation.)

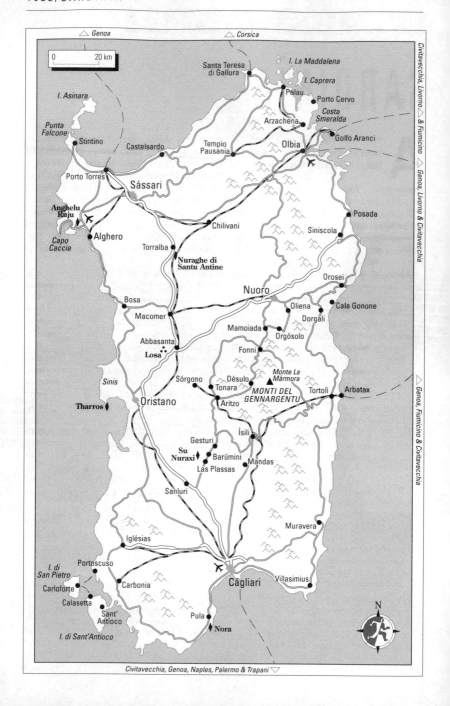

REGIONAL FOOD AND WINE

Sardinian cooking revolves around scintillatingly fresh ingredients simply prepared: seafood – especially **lobster** – is grilled over open fires scented with myrtle and juniper, as is meltingly tender **suckling pig**. This means that there is little pork left to be made into salami and other cured meats, although a few wild boar escape the fire long enough to be made into *prosciutto di cinghiale*, a ham with a strong flavour of game. Being surrounded by sparkling seas, Sardinians also make rich, Spanish-inspired **fish stews** and produce **bottarga**, a version of caviar made with mullet eggs. **Pasta** is substantial here, taking the form of *culigiones* (massive ravioli filled with cheese and egg) or *maloreddus* (saffron-flavoured, *gnocchi*-like shapes), while cheeses tend to be made from ewe's milk and are either fresh and herby or pungent and salty – like the famous **pecorino Sardo**. The island is also famous for the quality and variety of its bread, ranging from parchment-like *carta da musica* wafers to chunky rustic loaves intended to sustain shepherds on the hills. As in Sicily, there is an abundance of light and airy **pastries**, frequently flavoured with lemon, almonds or orange flower water.

Vernaccia is the most famous Sardinian wine: a hefty drink reminiscent of sherry and treated in a similar way – the bone-dry version as an **aperitif** and the sweet variant as a **dessert wine**. Other wines worth seeking out are Mandrolasi, an easy-drinking **red**, and Cannonau di Sardegna, a heady number much favoured by locals. Among the **whites**, look out for dry Torbato or the full-flavoured Trebbiano Sardo, both perfect accompaniments to local fish and seafood.

area and lives up to its reputation for opulence. The prices may preclude anything more than a brief visit, although there are campsites for those outside the ranks of the super-rich.

Both Olbia and Cágliari have airports, as does Sardinia's main package destination of **Alghero** – a fishing port in the northwest of the island that has been known to British holiday-makers for years, yet retains a friendly, unspoiled air. But Alghero's main attraction is its Spanish ambience, a legacy of long years in which the town was a Catalan colony, giving it a wholly different feel from the rest of the island. Inland, **Nuoro** has impressive literary credentials and a good ethnographical museum. As the biggest town in Sardinia's interior, it also makes a useful stopover for visiting some of the remoter mountain areas, in particular the **Gennargentu** range, covering the heart of the island. This is where you can find what remains of the island's traditional culture, best embodied in the numerous village **festivals**.

Some history

Anyone seeking the true Sard identity must refer all the way back to the island's prehistory, the one period when it enjoyed an undisturbed prosperity. Although little is known about the society, plenty of traces of this era survive, most conspicuous of which are the rough constructions known as *nuraghi*, mainly built between 1500 and 500 BC both for defensive purposes and as habitations. They can be seen everywhere in Sardinia, the biggest ones all in the heart of the island: at **Su Nuraxi**, north of Cágliari, and, between Oristano and Sássari, at **Losa** and **Sant'Antine**.

This nuraghic culture peaked between the tenth and eighth centuries BC, trading with the **Phoenicians**, amongst others, from the eastern Mediterranean. But from the sixth century the more warlike **Carthaginians** entered the scene, with their capital less than 200km away near present-day Tunis. Their campaign to control the island was halted only by their need to concentrate on the new military threat to their power, the Romans. Caught in the middle, the Sards fought on both sides until their decisive defeat in a campaign in 177 and 176 BC, during which some 27,000 islanders were slaughtered. A core of survivors fled into the impenetrable central and eastern mountains, where they retained their independence in an area called Barbaria by the Romans, known today as the **Barbágia**.

The Romans left little behind apart from some impressive remains at **Nora**, near **Cágliari**, and **Tharros**, west of Oristano – two Carthaginian sites later enlarged by Roman settlers – and a strong Latin element which survives in the Sardinian dialect today. The fall of Rome was followed by barbarian raids, then, briefly, in the sixth century AD, by the **Byzantines**, whose only significant monument is **Cágliari**'s church of **San Saturno**.

The relative emptiness of Sardinia's coasts today is largely due to the twin effects of malaria and the Muslim raids which continued sporadically for over 500 years, prompting the construction of the numerous watchtowers which can still be seen. In the eleventh century ecclesiastical rights over Sardinia were granted to the rising city-state of Pisa. **Pisan** influence was mainly concentrated in the south, based in **Cágliari**, where the defences they built still stand, and Pisan churches can be found throughout Sardinia, often marooned in the middle of the Sardinian countryside – like Santa Trinità di Saccárgia and San Pietro di Sorres (see p.1053).

By the end of the thirteenth century, Pisa found itself out-manoeuvred by its rival **Genoa**, which established power-bases in Sássari and the north. But when, in 1297, Pope Boniface VIII gave James II of Aragon exclusive rights over both Sardinia and Corsica in exchange for surrendering his claims to Sicily, **Spain** entered the scene. The islanders' cause was led by **Arborea**, the area around present-day Oristano, and championed in particular by **Eleanor of Arborea**, a warrior along the lines of Boadicea and Jeanne d'Arc. Eleanor succeeded in stemming the Spanish advance, but after her death in 1404 Sardinian resistance crumbled and the Aragonese triumphed.

Traces of Spain's long dominion survive in the island's dialects and in the sprinkling of Gothic and Baroque architecture in churches and palaces. The best example of both is at **Alghero**, where the people still speak a strong Catalan dialect and the whole town has the air of a Spanish enclave. Nearby **Sássari** also shows strong Spanish influence, as do the festivities in the town of **Iglésias**, west of **Cágliari**.

During the War of the Spanish Succession (1701–20), **Cágliari** was bombarded by an English fleet and briefly occupied. Treaties followed, ceding the island first to Austria, then to Victor Amadeus, Duke of Savoy. His united possessions became the new **Kingdom of Sardinia**.

The years that followed saw a new emphasis on reconstruction, with the opening of schools, investment in industry and agriculture, and the building of roads, most famously the **Carlo Felice highway** which runs the length of the island – today the SS131. But Savoy's quarrels became Sardinia's, and in 1793 the island found itself threatened by **Napoleon**, who led an unsuccessful attempt at invasion in 1793. Later, **Nelson** spent fifteen months hovering around the island's coasts in the hunt for the French fleet that led up to the rout at Trafalgar in 1805. Throughout this long wait, during which Nelson never once set foot on shore, he sent a stream of letters to London urging that steps be taken to secure Sardinia – at the time the only neutral shore in this part of the Mediterranean: "God knows", he wrote, "if we could possess one island, Sardinia, we should want neither Malta, nor any other."

Garibaldi embarked on both his major expeditions from his farm on one of Sardinia's outlying islands, **Caprera**, and the Kingdom of Sardinia ended with the **Unification of Italy** in 1861. Since then, Sardinia's role as part of a modern nation-state has not always been easy. The phenomenon of **banditry**, for example, associated with the hinterland and the Gennargentu mountains in particular, was largely the continuation of old habits into the new age. Outbreaks of lawlessness were ruthlessly suppressed, but there was little money available to improve the root causes of the problem, nor much interest in doing so.

Ironically, it was Mussolini who initiated some of the most far-reaching land reforms, including the harnessing and damming of rivers, the draining of land, the introduction of agricultural colonies from the mainland, and the founding of the new towns of **Carbónia** and **Fertília**.

After World War II, Sardinia was granted the same autonomous status as Sicily, Valle d'Aosta and Alto-Adige, giving the island control over such areas as transport, tourism, police, industry and agriculture. The *Cassa per il Mezzogiorno* fund was extended to Sardinia, and the island was saturated with enough DDT to rid it of malaria forever. But despite the improvements, much rancour is still felt towards a central government that has imposed on the island, among other things, one of the largest concentrations of NATO forces in the Mediterranean. Campaigning against this presence, and ultimately for complete independence from Rome, albeit with limited popular support, is the **Partito Sardo d'Azione**, or Sardinian Action Party.

Getting to Sardinia

There are frequent daily **flights** from the Italian mainland to the island's three main airports, at **Cágliari**, Olbia and Fertília (for Alghero and Sássari), and there is a limited service to the small airport outside Arbatax in summer. The flights, which take about an hour, are mainly operated by Alitalia and Sardinia's own Meridiana, and cost L150,000–250,000/€77.47–129.11 for a one-way ticket from Rome or Milan to **Cágliari**, Alghero or Olbia, with a myriad of special deals and weekend discounts worth asking about. Direct flights from UK and other European cities are mainly confined to the summer months, when you might expect to pay, for example from the UK, about £250 return.

Considerably cheaper than flying are the **ferries** from mainland Italy, as well as from Sicily, Tunis, Corsica and France (see box below). You should make bookings several

From	To	Line	No. per week	Duration
FERRIES TO SARDINIA				
Civitavécchia	Arbatax	Tirrenia	2	11hr
Civitavécchia	Cágliari	Tirrenia	7	15–17hr
Civitavécchia	Golfo Aranci	FS & Sardinia	7–14	7–9hr
Civitavécchia	Olbia	Tirrenia & Moby Lines	7–14	8hr
Genoa	Arbatax	Tirrenia	1–2	17–20hr
Genoa	Cágliari	Tirrenia	2 (July–Sept only)	21hr
Genoa	Olbia	Tirrenia	3–7	14hr
Genoa	Porto Torres	Tirrenia	5–7	13hr
Livorno	Golfo Aranci	Sardinia	1–7 (not Jan)	10hr
Livorno	Olbia	Moby Lines	3–14	10hr
Naples	Cágliari	Tirrenia	1–2	17hr
Palermo	Cágliari	Tirrenia	1	14hr
Trápani	Cágliari	Tirrenia	1	11hr
Tunis	Cágliari	Tirrenia	1	36hr
HIGH-SPEED FERRIES				
Civitavécchia	Golfo Aranci	Tirrenia	5–10 (April–Oct only)	3hr 30min
Civitavécchia	Olbia	Tirrenia	7–28 (June–Sept only)	4–6hr
Fiumicino	Arbatax	Tirrenia	2 (July–Sept only)	5hr
Fiumicino	Golfo Aranci	Tirrenia	14–28 (June–Sept only)	4hr
Genoa	Olbia	Tirrenia	3–7 (June–Sept only)	6hr
Genoa	Porto Torres	Tirrenia	7–14 (June–Sept only)	6hr
La Spezia	Golfo Aranci	Tirrenia	7 (June–Sept only)	6hr

months in advance for summer crossings, even if you're on foot; sailings in July and August can be fully booked up by May. Basic **prices** range from about L35,000/€18.20 to about L95,000/€49.40 per person, depending on the season and the route taken: a reclining armchair costs about L15,000/€7.80 on top of this, a **berth** L30–40,000/€15.60–20.66 on top, while the charge for a vehicle starts at L105,000/€54.60 for a small **car** in low season. Look out for discounts applying to return tickets bought in advance within certain periods, and for special deals for car plus two or three passengers. Fares on the **high-speed ferries** (*mezzi veloci*) are L140,000–155,000/€72.80–80.60 on the Civitavécchia–Olbia route, L130,000–180,000 /€67.60–93.60 from Genova.

Getting around the island

Once on the island, you can rely on a good network of public transport covering all but the remoter areas. There is the island-wide bus service run by ARST and the private PANI for longer hauls between towns, while trains connect the major towns of **Cágliari**, **Sássari** and **Olbia**, with smaller narrow-gauge lines linking with Nuoro and Alghero.

If you're planning to use the buses a lot between June and September, consider investing in a *biglietto turístico*: available during this period from main ARST offices, they're valid on all ARST buses. The 7-day version costs L61,500/€31.98; 14 days cost L105,000/€54.60, and they are also available for 21 or 28 days.

CÁGLIARI AND THE SOUTH

Cágliari has been Sardinia's capital at least since Roman times and is still its biggest town, with the busiest port and the greatest concentration of industry. Intimidating as this may sound, Cágliari is no urban sprawl: its centre is small and compact enough to be easily manageable on foot, offering both sophistication and charm in the ragge-taggle of narrow lanes crammed into its high citadel.

The main attractions here are the **archeological museum** with its unique collection of nuraghic statuettes, the city walls with their two **Pisan towers** looking down over the port, and the **cathedral** – all within easy distance of each other in the old centre. There is also a sprinkling of Roman remains, including an impressive **amphitheatre**. More evocative ruins from this period can be seen 40km out of town at **Nora**, the most complete ancient site on the island. Other places worth visiting from Cágliari include the famous *nuraghe* of **Su Nuraxi**, a compelling sight surrounded by the brown hills of the interior. Off the coast west of Cágliari are moored the islands of **Sant'Antíoco** and **San Pietro**, while the Spanish-tinged town of **Iglésias** makes an appealing inland destination during its flamboyant Easter festivities.

Cágliari

Viewing Cágliari from the sea at the start of his Sardinian sojourn in 1921, D.H. Lawrence compared it to Jerusalem: ". . . strange and rather wonderful, not a bit like Italy". Today, still crowned by an old centre squeezed within a protective ring of Pisan fortifications, **CÁGLIARI** is less frenetic than any town of equivalent size on the mainland, with a population of nearly a quarter of a million spread around its modern outskirts in mushrooming apartment blocks. Its setting is enhanced by the calm lagoons (*stagni*) behind the city and along the airport road, the habitat for cranes, cormorants and flamingos. In the centre, the evening promenades along Via Manno are the smartest you'll see in Sardinia, dropping down to the noisier Piazza Yenne and Largo Carlo Felice, around which most of the shops, restaurants, banks

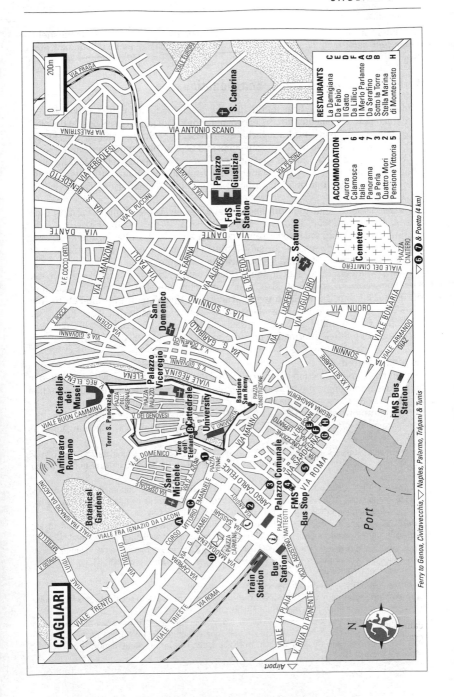

CAGLIARI

RESTAURANTS

La Damigiana	C
Da Fabio	E
Il Gatto	D
Da Lillicu	F
Il Merlo Parlante	A
Da Serafino	G
Sotto la Torre	B
Stella Marina	
di Montecristo	H

ACCOMMODATION

Aurora	1
Calamosca	6
Italia	4
Panorama	7
La Perla	3
Quattro Mori	2
Pensione Vittoria	5

Ferry to Genoa, Civitavecchia, ▷ Naples, Palermo, Trapani & Tunis

and hotels are located. At the bottom of the town, the arcades of Via Roma shelter shops and bars, in between which African and Asian traders jostle for pavement space.

Arrival, information and accommodation

Cágliari's **port** lies in the heart of the town, opposite Via Roma; there's a tourist office here that opens to coincide with the arrival of **ferries**. The **airport** sits beside the city's largest *stagno* (lagoon): facilities include a **bureau de change** and an information office (daily: mid-June to mid-Sept 8am–8pm; mid-Sept to mid-June 9am–1pm & 4–6pm; ☎070.240.200). An ARST bus service into town runs at least every ninety minutes from 6.15am until midnight to Piazza Matteotti and takes fifteen minutes (tickets from the shop behind the information office); otherwise a taxi ride costs around L25,000/€12.91.

Piazza Matteotti holds the **train** and **bus stations** and is the terminus for most **local buses**, tickets (L1300/€0.68) for which are sold at the booth; FMS buses for Sant'Antonio and Carbonia leave from Via Roma and Via C. Colombo (behind Piazza Deffenu); and the FdS station, for slow trains to Arbatax, is a twenty-five minute walk from Piazza Matteotti, at Piazza Repubblica (on Via Dante).

Piazza Matteotti also has a tourist information kiosk (March–Oct Mon–Sat 8am–8pm, July to mid-Sept also Sun 9am–7pm; Nov–Feb Mon–Sat 8am–2pm; ☎070.669.255), but the **main tourist office** is at Via Mameli 97 (mid-Feb to May Mon–Sat 9am–7pm; June–Aug daily 8am–8pm; Sept Mon–Sat 8am–8pm, Sun 9am–2pm; Oct to mid–Feb Mon–Fri 9am–5.30pm, Sat 8am–1.30pm; ☎070.664.195). There's also a toll-free information line for the whole island (☎800.013.153).

Accommodation

Cágliari has a good selection of budget **hotels**, though availability may be restricted in high season, and single rooms are at a premium at all times. The biggest concentration of places is on or around the narrow Via Sardegna, running parallel to Via Roma. The nearest **campsite** is beyond **Quartu Sant'Elena**, a 45-minute bus ride east along the coast, where the *Pini e Mare* (☎070.803.103; mid-June to mid-Sept) has bungalows as well.

Aurora, Salita Santa Chiara (☎070.658.625). A modest pensione in a delapidated palazzo behind Piazza Yenne. The plain and reasonably clean rooms are always popular so it's best to book ahead. ①.

Calamosca, Viale Calamosca (☎070.371.628). Comfortable upmarket option; this is the nearest hotel to Poetto (see p.1030), Cágliari's summer suburb, and also has its own beach, but space is limited in peak season and there's no direct bus link to the centre of Cágliari. ④.

Italia, Via Sardegna 31 (☎070.660.410). Smart but rather characterless choice on this road, mainly used by business travellers and groups. All rooms are modern and well-equipped, without views. ④.

Panorama, Viale Armando Diaz 231 (☎070.307.691). Big and expensive and a twenty-minute walk from the centre, but you enjoy the best views over Cágliari from this top-class hotel, not to mention the pool and other facilities. ⑥.

La Perla, Via Sardegna 18 (☎070.669.446). Very basic rooms, some en suite. ②.

Quattro Mori, Via Angioy (☎070.668.535). Well-placed but erratic: ask to see the rooms first – some are bright and cheerful, others downright shabby. ③.

Pensione Vittoria, Via Roma (☎070.657.970). Located in the heart of town but undisturbed by street-noise, this good place has clean and sizeable rooms, though you may prefer the slightly pleasanter and pricier ones in the *AeR Bundes Jack*. The latter, run by the same family, is on the floor below the *Vittoria*. ③.

The City

Almost all the wandering you will want to do in Cágliari is encompassed within the old quarter, known as Castello. The most evocative entry to this is from the monumental **Bastione San Remy** on Piazza Costituzione, whose nineteenth-century imperialist tone is watered down by the graffiti and weeds sprouting out of its walls. It's worth the haul up the grandiose flight of steps inside for Cágliari's best views over the port and the lagoons beyond. Sunset is a good time to be here, or whenever you feel like a pause from sightseeing-fatigue, its shady benches conducive to a twenty-minute siesta.

From the bastion, you can wander off in any direction to enter the intricate maze of Cágliari's citadel, traditionally the seat of the administration, aristocracy and highest ecclesiastical offices. It has been little altered since the Middle Ages, though the tidy Romanesque facade on the **Cattedrale** (daily 8am–12.30pm & 4–8pm) in Piazza Palazzo is in fact a fake, added in this century in the old Pisan style. The structure dates originally from the thirteenth century but has gone through what Lawrence called "the mincing machine of the ages, and oozed out Baroque and sausagey".

Inside, a couple of massive stone **pulpits** flank the main doors: they were crafted as a single piece around 1160 to grace Pisa's cathedral, but were later presented to Cágliari along with the same sculptor's set of lions, which now adorn the outside of the building. Other features of the cathedral that are worth a glance include the ornate seventeenth-century **tomb** of Martin II of Aragon (in the left transept), the **aula capitolare** (off the right transept), containing some good religious art, and, under the altar, a densely adorned **crypt**. Hewn out of the rock, little of this subterranean chamber has been left undecorated, and there are carvings by Sicilian artists of the Sardinian saints whose ashes were said to have been found under the church of San Saturno (see overleaf) in 1617. Also here are the tombs of the wife of Louis XVIII of France, Marie-Josephine of Savoy, and the infant son of Vittorio Emanuele I of Savoy and Maria-Teresa of Austria, Carlo Emanuele, who died in 1799.

The cathedral stands in one corner of the square, flanked by the eighteenth-century **Palazzo Viceregio** (Tues–Sun: May–Sept 9.30am–1.30pm & 4–8pm; Oct–April 9am–1pm & 3–7pm; L4000/€2.07), or Governor's Palace – formerly the palace of the Piemontese kings of Sardinia, though rarely inhabited by them, its stately rooms today holding regular exhibitions – and by the graceful archbishop's palace, both the work of the same architect, Davisto, in 1769.

At the opposite end of Piazza Palazzo a road leads into the smaller Piazza Indipendenza, location of the **Torre San Pancrazio**, one of the main bulwarks of the city's defences erected by Pisa after it had wrested the city from the Genoans in 1305 (though these did not prevent the Aragonese from walking in just fifteen years later). It's worth ascending the tower (Tues–Sun: May–Sept 9.30am–1.30pm & 4–8pm; Oct–April 9am–1pm & 3–7pm, last admissions 15min before closing; free) for the magnificent views seawards over the old town and port. From here it's only a short walk to Via dell'Università and the city's second major bulwark, the **Torre dell'Elefante** (same hours as above), named after a small carving of an elephant on one side. Like the other tower, it has a half-finished look, with the side facing the old town completely open.

Through the arch at the top of Piazza Indipendenza, Piazza dell'Arsenale holds a plaque recording the visit made by Cervantes to Cágliari in 1573, shortly before his capture and imprisonment by Moorish pirates. Across the square, the **Cittadella dei Musei** stands on the site of the former royal arsenal, housing the city's principal museums. The main attraction is the **Museo Archeologico** (Tues–Sun: April–Sept 9am–2pm & 3–8pm; Oct–March 9am–7pm; L5000/€2.58), a must for anyone interested in Sardinia's past. The island's most important Phoenician, Carthaginian and Roman finds are gathered here, including busts and statues of muses and gods, jewellery and coins, and funerary items from the sites of Nora and Tharros. But everything pales beside the museum's greatest pieces, from Sardinia's **nuraghic** culture. Of these, the most eye-catching is a series of bronze statuettes, ranging from about thirty to ninety centimetres in height, spindly and highly stylized but packed with invention and quirky humour. The main source of information about this phase of the island's history, these figures represent warriors and hunters, athletes, shepherds, nursing mothers, bulls, horses and wild animals. Most were votive offerings, made to decorate the inside of temples, later buried to protect them from the hands of foreign predators.

The other museums contrast wildly with each other, but each is worth exploring. The smallest and most surprising is the **Mostra di Cere Anatomiche** (daily 9am–1pm & 4–7pm; free), which displays 23 wax models of anatomical sections, gruesome reproductions of works made by the Florentine Clemente Susini at the start of the nineteenth century. Further up, the **Museo d'Arte Siamese** (Tues–Sun 9am–1pm & 4–8pm; L4000/€2.07) holds a fascinating assemblage of items from Southeast Asia – the collection of a local engineer who spent twenty years in the region – including Siamese paintings of Hindu and Buddhist legends, Chinese bowls and boxes, Japanese statuettes and a fearsome array of weaponry. Lastly, the excellent **Pinacoteca** (daily 8.30am–7pm; L4000/€2.07) contains mostly Catalan and Italian religious art from the fifteenth and sixteenth centuries. Look out in particular for the trio of panel paintings next to each other on the top level: the panel frame of *San Bernardino* by Joan Figuera and Rafael Thomas, *Annunciation* by Joan Mates, and *Visitation* by Joan Barcelo.

Turning right out of Piazza dell'Arsenale, Viale Buon Cammino leads to Viale Fra Ignazio and the entrance to the **Anfiteatro Romano** (Tues–Sun: April–Oct 9am–1pm & 3.30–7.30pm; Nov–March 9am–5pm; free). Cut out of solid rock in the second century AD, the amphitheatre could hold the entire city's population of about 20,000. Despite the decay, with much of the site cannibalized to build churches in the Middle Ages, you can still see the trenches for the animals, the underground passages and several rows of seats. Turning left out of the amphitheatre, walk a few minutes down Viale Fra Ignazio da Laconi to the **Botanical Gardens** (daily: April and mid-Sept to Oct 8am–1.30pm & 3–6.30pm; May to mid-Sept 8am–1.30pm & 3–8pm; Nov–March 8am–1.30pm; L1000/€0.52), one of Italy's most famous, with over 500 species of Mediterranean and tropical plants – a shady spot on a sizzling afternoon.

Heading east from the centre, there is little to see in Cágliari's traffic-thronged modern quarters beyond the banks and businesses, the one exception being the fifth-century church of **San Saturno** (Mon–Sat 9am–1pm), Sardinia's oldest and one of the most important surviving examples of early Christian architecture in the Mediterranean. Stranded on the busy Via Dante close to the FdS station on Piazza Repubblica, looking Middle Eastern with its palm trees and cupola, the basilica was erected on the spot where the Christian martyr Saturninus met his fate during the reign of Diocletian. Around the sturdy walls, which withstood severe bombardment during World War II, lie various pieces of flotsam from the past: four cannonballs, fragments of Roman sarcophagi and slabs of stone carved with Latin inscriptions. The interior is bare of decoration, though it's nonetheless impressive, with tall glass walls added to the sides, through which you can see an excavated necropolis.

Poetto

When you need a break and a bathe, head for the suburb of **Poetto**, a fifteen-minute bus ride from Piazza Matteotti past Cágliari's Sant'Elia football stadium. Poetto has six kilometres of fine sandy **beach**, with small bars and showers conveniently nearby; some stretches are lidos where you pay a standard daily rate for entry (about L5000/€2.58), and deckchairs and parasols are available for rent (L5000–10,000 /€2.58–5.17), along with pedalos and wind-surfing equipment.

One end of the strip, rearing above a small marina, is the **Sella del Diávolo** ("Devil's

Saddle"), aptly describing the shape of the rock that juts into the sea; most of it is now a military zone and therefore off limits. The name is connected with a legend relating how the Archangel Gabriel won a battle here against the devil himself. The name of Cágliari's gulf, Golfo degli Angeli, is also a reference to this celestial tussle.

Eating, drinking and nightlife

Cágliari has a great range of **restaurants**, many clustered around Via Sardegna. Almost all have competitively-priced tourist menus, which aren't at all bad though they don't offer very much choice. Recommended restaurant options range from "Inexpensive" (L25,000) to "Moderate" (L25,000–40,000), or "Expensive" (L40,000–70,000) according to the amount one person might expect to pay for a full meal including wine and cover charge. For a morning **coffee** or afternoon tea, Piazza Yenne makes a pleasant, relatively traffic-free alternative to the bustling cafés on Via Roma, while, outside the centre, Poetto is a blitz of bars, fairgrounds and ice-cream kiosks – a good place to while away a summer evening. Cágliari also has a couple of lively places for late-night **drinking**, listed below.

La Damigiana, Corso Vittorio Emanuele 115. Good fixed-price meals popular with locals are served in this basic place. Closed Mon evening, and Tues evening from Oct–Easter. Inexpensive.

Da Fabio, Via Sardegna 90, on the corner with Via Concezione. Easy-going trattoria which offers tourist menus and pizzas and has an English-speaking boss. Closed Mon & two weeks in Sept. Moderate.

Il Gatto, Viale Trieste 15, just off Piazza del Cármine. Away from the port, and with a smarter feel than the places there, this little restaurant offers immaculately prepared seafood and meat dishes. Closed Sat lunch & all day Sun. Moderate.

Da Lillicu, Via Sardegna 78 (☎070.652.970). Serves a small but reliable range of authentic Sard specialities on marble tables. It's very popular with locals, so you'll need to book ahead. Closed Sun. Moderate.

Il Merlo Parlante, Via Portascalas. Hidden down an alley off the middle of Corso Vittorio Emanuele, this small but popular students' hangout offers beer, *panini* and music until late. Closed daytime. Inexpensive.

Da Serafino, at Via Sardegna 109 and Via Lepanto 6. Popular place offering honest, local dishes served without formality, extremely good value. Closed Thurs & Aug. Inexpensive.

Sotto La Torre, Piazza San Giuseppe. Located opposite the Torre dell'Elefante, a great place for a snack and a drink from early morning to late at night. Tables in small, stylish rooms help create a relaxed atmosphere. Inexpensive.

Stella Marina di Montecristo, Via Sardegna 142 (☎070.666.692). Tucked away at the end of the strip, where Via Sardegna meets Via Regina Margherita, this is a great choice for seafood-lovers, worth booking at weekends. Closed Mon. Moderate–Expensive.

Listings

Airlines Alitalia, Via Caprera 12 (☎070.60.101); Meridiana, Via Rossi 27 (☎070.669.161).

Airport Flight information for Alitalia ☎070.240.079; Meridiana ☎070.240.169; Volare ☎070.212.8263.

Automobile Club d'Italia Via San Simone 60 (☎070.283.000).

Car rental Pinna, airport (☎070.241.125); Ruvioli, Via Mille 11 (☎070.657.969) and airport (☎070.240.323); Hertz, Piazza Matteotti 8 (☎070.651.078) and airport (☎070.240.037).

Ferries Tirrenia, Via Campidano 1 (☎070.666.065); ticket office also at Stazione Maríttima.

Festivals Sant'Efisio: May 1–4, including a procession to the saint's church at Nora.

Hospital Via Peretti 21 (☎070.543.266).

Laundry Coin-operated laundry at Via Ospedale 109 (daily until 10pm; last wash at 9pm).

Post office Piazza del Cármine (Mon–Fri 8am–6.40pm, Sat 8.10am–1.20pm). Closes at 4pm on last day of month (or noon, if this falls on a Sat).

Telephones Via Angioy (daily 8am–10pm).
Travel agents CTS, Via Balbo 4 (☎070.488.260); Sardamondial, Via Roma 9 (☎070.668.094); Viaggi Orrù, Via Roma 95 (☎070.659.858).

Nora

The easiest excursion you can make from Cágliari is to the waterside archeological site at **NORA**, 40km south of the city. In July and August two daily ARST buses follow the coast past Sardinia's biggest industrial complex at Sarroch, where the huge refinery imports eighteen million tonnes of oil annually, mainly from Libya. At other times of the year you'll have to get off at **PULA** (10 buses daily), and then walk the 3km to the sea. It's worth going to Pula anyway, as the village **museum** (daily: April–Oct 9am–8pm; Nov–March 9am–6pm; L5000/€2.58, or L8000/€4.13 including site at Nora) gives a good explanation of the Nora finds.

Founded by the Phoenicians and settled later by Carthaginians and Romans, **Nora** (daily: April–Oct 9am–8pm; Nov–March 9am–6pm; L5000/€2.58, or L8000/€4.13 including museum) was abandoned around the third century AD, possibly as a result of a natural disaster. Now partly submerged under the sea, the remains on land include houses, Carthaginian warehouses, a temple, baths with some well-preserved mosaics, and a theatre in an equally good state of repair. The rest is rubble, though its position on the tip of a peninsula gives it plenty of atmosphere.

Outside the site stands the rather ordinary-looking eleventh-century church of Sant'Efísio, site of the saint's martyrdom and the ultimate destination of Cágliari's three-day May Day procession. Behind the church is an exquisite sandy bay, lapped by crystal-clear water, but rapidly transformed into day-tripper hell in season. The nearest **hotel** lies a kilometre away on the road back to Pula, *Su Guventeddu* (☎070.920.9092; ③), offering bright, quiet rooms, with a recommended restaurant downstairs; in the village itself there's the basic *Quattro Mori* at Via Cágliari 10 (☎070.920.9124; ①), and, further along the same road at no. 30, the better-equipped *Sandalyon* (☎070.920.9151; ③).

The coast south has a few of Sardinia's most exclusive hotels, biggest and flashiest of which is the *Forte Village*, spread over a huge area, and catering largely to package groups (mid-April to mid-Nov; ☎070.92.171, fax 070.921.246; ⑧), though luxury-lovers might prefer the more select *Flamingo* (late April to mid-Oct; ☎070.920.8361, fax 070.920.8359; ⑦), where you can stay in hotel rooms or in detached villas; the half-board requirement bumps up the price. There are fine beaches all down this coast, especially around **Chia**, while beyond **Capo Spartivento**, the coastal road offers terrific views over a deserted cliff-hung coastline, sheltering a few small sand beaches which are accessible on an infrequent bus service in summer.

Su Nuraxi and around

Even if you only get to see one of Sardinia's *nuraghi*, make a point of visiting **SU NURAXI** (daily 9am–1hr before sunset; L8000/€4.13), the biggest and most famous of them, and a good taste of the primitive grandeur of the island's only indigenous civilization. The snag is access: the site lies a kilometre outside the village of **BARÚMINI**, 50km north of Cágliari, to which there are only two daily ARST buses, calling here en route to Désulo and Samugheo. The site lies fifteen minutes' walk west of the main crossroads at Barúmini's centre.

Su Nuraxi's dialect name means simply "the *nuragh*", and not only is it the largest nuraghic complex on the island, but it's also thought to be the oldest, dating probably from around 1500 BC. Comprising a bulky fortress surrounded by the remains of a village, Su Nuraxi was a palace complex at the very least – possibly even a capital city. The central tower once reached 21m (now shrunk to less than 15m), and its outer defences and inner chambers are connected by passageways and stairs. The whole complex is thought to have been covered with earth by Sards and Carthaginians at the time of the Roman conquest, which may account for its excellent state of preservation: if it weren't for a torrential rainstorm that washed away the slopes in 1949, the site may never have been revealed at all. There's a **restaurant** and bar nearby, and a handy **hotel** choice on Barúmini's Via Cavour, *Sa Lolla* (☎070.936.8419; ③). If this is full, the nearest alternatives are either 20km south off the SS131 at **SANLURI**: the modern *Mirage* (☎070.930.7100; ②), on Via Carlo Felice, or about the same distance northeast at **ÍSILI**, a stop on the FdS line, where the clean and friendly *Cardellino*, on Via Dante (☎0782.802.004; ①), is the cheapest of the four choices in town.

The skyline south of Barúmini is punctuated by the extraordinary conical hill of **Las Plassas**, its round peak strewn with the fragments of a twelfth-century **castle** sticking up like broken teeth – a landmark for miles around. North and west of the town extends the high plain of **Giara di Gésturi**, the last refuge of Sardinia's wild ponies. You'll need a little luck and a lot of cunning to spot these small, shy creatures, but in any case it's excellent high ground for walking, at an altitude of around 600m. Spring is the best season to visit, when the area is a stopover for migrating birds. Again, though, the problem is access. Dedicated hikers can explore a good part of the plain on foot from the village of Gésturi, a stop on the Cágliari–Désulo and Cágliari–Samugheo bus routes.

West of Cágliari: Sant'Antíoco and San Pietro

On the main island, only two places west of Cágliari warrant a brief stop-off: **Iglesias**, surrounded by abandoned mine-shafts but best known for its numerous churches and Spanish-flavoured Holy Week celebrations; and nearby **Carbonia**, a coal-mining centre founded by Mussolini in 1936 – its regimented streets and planned workers' houses still imbued with the Duce's presence. Both are connected to Cágliari by the FMS line, and from Iglesias there are bus connections to **Portoscuso**, the port for ferries to **San Pietro**. This island, and neighbouring **Sant'Antíoco**, can just about be visited from Cágliari in a day, but you'd do better staying over. Although well-frequented holiday destinations in summer, the islands have not yet become too developed; in fact accommodation is on the scarce side, and if you're thinking of staying, be sure to book ahead.

Sant'Antíoco

SANT'ANTÍOCO, the larger of the southwest islands, is linked by causeway to Sardinia's coast and served by six daily FMS buses from Cágliari, about a two-hour ride. The port area of the island's town (also called Sant'Antíoco) is just on the other side of the causeway. Nelson's flagship, the *Vanguard*, having suffered severe damage in a storm, put in here shortly before the Battle of the Nile in 1798. The vessel was rerigged in four days, though Nelson deplored the fact that, on account of Sardinia's recently declared neutrality in the French Revolutionary War, the ship's company was not allowed ashore. "We are refused the rights of humanity," he wrote to Lady Nelson.

The core of the upper part of Sant'Antíoco has been continuously inhabited since Phoenician times and was an important base both for the Carthaginians and the Romans, commanding the whole of Sardinia's southwest coast. Here, on Piazza Parrochia, at the top of Via Regina Margherita, the twelfth-century church of **Sant'Antíoco** was built over Christian **catacombs**, which were in turn enlarged from an existing Carthaginian burial place; you can visit these dingy corridors, with authentic skeletons and reproductions of ceramic objects unearthed during excavation, on a guided tour (summer Mon–Sat 9am–noon, 3–6pm & 7–8pm, Sun 10–11am & 4–8pm; winter Mon–Sat 9am–noon & 3–6pm, Sun 10–11am & 4–8pm; L4000/€2.07). Near the entrance to the catacombs stands a statue of St Antiochus, plainly showing his Mauretanian origins; his feast day, on the second Sunday after Easter, is a four-day affair with traditional songs, poetry recitations, dancing, fireworks and a procession to the sea.

Further down Via Regina Margherita, a small **museum** (site and museum daily: summer 9am–1pm & 3.30–7pm, closes one hour earlier in winter; L8000/€4.13) displays finds from the excavations of the Phoenician, Carthaginian and Roman cities that once occupied the surrounding territories. The exhibits represent a tiny fraction of the second-largest collection of Carthaginian discoveries after Carthage itself; the bulk of which is presently stored away until a new on-site museum has been completed. Nonetheless, this small collection is worth a cursory glance for its few ceramic objects and items of jewellery, and for the maps and diagrams of the site.

The same ticket allows you into Sant'Antíoco's archeological zone, signposted up a side-road outside the church, about a kilometre's walk away towards the sea. The most impressive remains are of an extensive **Punic tophet**, or burial site, dedicated to the Carthaginian goddess Tanit, this burial site once covered the entire hill where the old city now stands. The numerous urns scattered about here (interspersed with modern reproductions) were long believed to contain the ashes of sacrificed first-born children, but this is now thought to have been Roman propaganda: the urns, it seems, contained the cremated remains of children still-born or dead from natural causes. Apart from the *tophet*, the archeological zone also contains the well-preserved ruins of a temple and an exhibition of more bits and pieces dug up from the area.

Returning into the town on Via Necrópoli, you can use your ticket for the museum and archeological zone for a small but engrossing **Museo Etnográfico** (daily: summer 9am–1pm & 3.30–7pm; winter 9am–1pm & 3.30–6pm): one capacious room crammed to the rafters with examples of rural culture – tools, agricultural implements, craftwork, bread- and pasta-making equipment, most of them only recently superseded by modern machinery – all enthusiastically explained (in Italian) by a guide.

There are three **hotels** in town: the somewhat dowdy *Eden* (☎0781.840.768; ④), right next to the church of Sant Antíoco, where half- or full-board is required in August, and two smaller places on the main road between the port and the church: the *Hotel del Corso*, at Corso Vittorio Emanuele 32 (☎0781.800.265, *www.hoteldelcorso.it*; ⑤), which has a panoramic roof-terrace, and the more modest *Moderno* at Via Nazionale 82 (☎0781.83.105; ③). Other, more inspiring places lie in or around the small resort of **Calasetta**, ten kilometres north along the coast and the end-of-the-line for the FMS bus from Cágliari: try for example *Cala di Seta*, at Via Regina Margherita 61 (☎0781.88.304, fax 0781.31.538; ④), or the *Bellavista*, standing above a lovely arc of beach a short walk north of town (☎ & fax 0781.88.211; ③). There's also a **campsite** nearby, *Le Saline* (☎0781.88.615), just southwest of Calasetta.

San Pietro

Every day nine to thirteen **ferries from Calasetta** do the five-kilometre hop to **SAN PIETRO** (40min; L4000/€2.07): if you're in a car, you'll need to join the queue in good time, as summer sees a lot of congestion – and make sure you get a return ticket.

San Pietro's dialect is pure Piemontese, two and a half centuries after the Savoyan king Carlo Emanuele III invited a colony of Ligurians to settle here after their eviction from the island of Tabarca, near Tunisia. The settlers were later abducted and taken back to Tunisia in one of the last great pirate raids, but were returned once the pirates' ransom demands had been met. The island's only town, **CARLOFORTE** (named after the king), is attractive and lively in summer, and is close to various panoramic beauty spots and mainly rocky beaches.

The few **hotels** are concentrated in Carloforte, where the most stylish choice is undoubtedly the *Hieracon* at Corso Cavour 63 (☎0781.854.028; ④) – right from the port, as you leave the ferry – though you might try the plainer *California*, Via Cavallera 15 (☎0781.854.470; ③), a ten-minute walk left along the port. Availability is extremely limited in summer, but if you are stuck without a booking, ask around for **rooms for rent**, or contact the **tourist office** opposite the port at Piazza Carlo Alberto III (Mon–Fri 9am–noon; ☎0781.854.009). There is a **campsite** at LA CALETTA (☎0781.852.112; June–Sept), 8km from Carloforte and accessible by bus from Piazza Carlo Emanuele, marked "La Caletta".

ORISTANO AND NUORO

Sardinia's smallest province, Oristano, was created as recently as 1975 out of bits hacked off the provinces of Cágliari and Nuoro, but it roughly corresponds with the much older entity of Arborea, the medieval *giudicato* which championed the Sardinian cause in the struggle against the Spaniards. Then as now, **Oristano** was the region's main town, and today it retains more than a hint of medieval atmosphere.

The Punic-Roman town of **Tharros** is similar to Nora in appearance and worth a visit if you gave Nora a miss. Even older traces are to be seen at **Abbasanta**, where the nuraghic remains of **Losa** give an insight into Sardinia's prehistory. North up the coast, the predominant flavour at the riverside town of **Bosa** is also medieval, with its sturdy fort, and is within striking distance of a lovely unspoilt stretch of coastline.

Bosa is the only west-coast point of the province of Nuoro, which covers most of Sardinia's interior and its barren eastern coast. This area is little travelled by tourists, which no doubt has helped to preserve the last remnants of Sardinia's traditional culture as well as a largely unspoiled natural environment. Scattered over the woodland and pasturage are isolated villages, of which the provincial capital, **Nuoro**, is only a larger, drabber version, though it is a useful transport junction and base for excursions.

Oristano

ORISTANO is a flat, unprepossessing place, whose old walls have been mostly replaced by busy boulevards. However, the centre has a relaxed and sophisticated ambience, and although it is four kilometres from the sea, the town is attractively surrounded by water, its lagoons and irrigation canals helping to make this a richly productive agricultural zone. The southern lagoon, the **Stagno di Santa Giusta**, is one of the two homes of Sardinia's flamingo population: if they're not at Cágliari they're bound to be here, sharing the water with the coracle-like flat-bottomed boats still used by the lagoon's fishermen.

The Town

In the heart of the town is Oristano's central symbol, the marble statue of **Eleonora d'Arborea**, presiding over the piazza named after her. Eleanor was the *giudice* of the Arborea region from 1384 to 1404 and is the best known and best loved of Sardinia's medieval rulers, having been the only one who enjoyed any success against the island's aggressors. Ensconced in the last of Sardinia's *giudicati* to remain independent of the Aragonese, Eleanor united local resistance and, despite the desertion of her husband, Brancaleone Doria, to the enemy, succeeded in negotiating a treaty in 1388 that guaranteed her a measure of independence. She later backed this up by a tactical alliance

SA SARTIGLIA

The rituals of Oristano's flamboyant **Sa Sartiglia** festival perhaps originated with knights on the Second Crusade, who in the eleventh century may well have imported the trappings of Saracen tournaments to Sardinia. In the period of the Spanish domination, similarly lavish feasts were held for the ruling knights at regular intervals throughout the year. In time, these celebrations took on a more theatrical aspect and became merged with the annual Carnival – the Sa Sartiglia is now a three-day festival that closes the Carnival period, ending on Shrove Tuesday. Highlights of this costumed pageant include horseback parades and trials of equestrian prowess, all judged by a white-masked arbiter known as **Su Componidori**. Selected from among the "knight" contestants, the *Componidori* represents the continuation of the *giudice*'s role and is decked out in a bizarre pastiche of medieval garb – the process of dressing him is itself a highly formal ceremony, conducted in public at the beginning of each day.

In fact all the participants are masked and costumed, and the whole affair exudes a theatrical spirit unrivalled by Sardinia's other festivals. The climax of the proceedings is the joust after which the festival is named, when the mounted contestants attempt to lance a ring, or *sartiglia*, suspended in the air, charging towards it at full gallop.

with the Genoans, and it was with Genoan help that Brancaleone, returned to the fold, managed to occupy Sássari on her behalf.

Eleanor's military achievements collapsed soon after her death from plague in 1404, though the most enduring benefit of her reign survived her by several centuries: the formulation of a **Code of Laws** (*Carta di Logu*), first mooted by her father Mariano IV but embodied by Eleanor in a legal document in 1395. Covering every aspect of civil legislation, this document was adopted in 1421 by the Aragonese and extended throughout the island. As the eighteenth-century English lawyer and traveller John Tyndale put it: "The framing of a body of laws so far in advance of those of other countries, where greater civilizations existed, must ever be the brightest ornament in the diadem of the Giudicessa." Eleanor's statue, carved in 1881, shows her bearing the scroll on which the laws were written, while inset panels depict her various victories.

Although it's called the **Casa di Eleonora**, the fine house – now derelict – at Via Parpaglia 6–12 (left off Via La Marmora, which leads off the piazza) could not in fact have been her home, as it was built over a century after her death. She is unequivocally buried in the fourteenth-century church of **Santa Chiara**, in the parallel Via Garibaldi.

Off Via Parpaglia, Piazzetta Corrias holds Oristano's **Antiquarium Arborense** (July–Sept Tues–Sun 9.30am–1pm & 5–7.30pm; Oct–June daily 9am–8pm; L4000/€2.07), one of Sardinia's most absorbing museums, housed in a sixteenth-century merchant's house. As well as rotating exhibitions of its extensive collection of nuraghic, Phoenician, Roman and Greek artefacts, there's a gallery of medieval and Renaissance art and an imaginative scaled-down reconstruction of Roman Tharros.

At one end of Via Parpaglia, linked to Piazza Eleonora d'Arborea by the narrow pedestrianized Corso Umberto, is Piazza Roma, where pavement bars are clustered around the base of the **San Cristóforo** bastion, erected by the *giudice* Mariano II in 1291. This was the fulcrum of Oristano's fortifications, the only other survivor of which is the smaller **Portixedda** ("little gate") tower, at the bottom of Via Mazzini (off Via Roma). Both are open for visits during the summer, each holding a small display of odds and ends relating to local history.

Oristano's **Duomo** stands in a spacious square up Via Duomo, which is behind Piazza Eleonora. Though started in the thirteenth century, most of the present duomo is a Baroque renovation, retaining only parts of the apses from its original construction.

With the fourteenth-century onion-roofed belltower and the next-door seminary, it forms an atmospheric ensemble.

At the other end of Via Duomo stands the nineteenth-century church of **San Francesco**, incorporating the remains of a much older Gothic building. The space in front, merging with Piazza Eleonora d'Arborea, forms the main arena for Oristano's annual **Sa Sartiglia** (see box opposite).

Practicalities

Oristano's **train station** is at the eastern end of town, a half-hour walk from the centre, or linked by a local bus every forty minutes or so. The ARST **bus** station is on Via Cágliari, while PANI buses pull in at Via Lombardia, ten minutes from Piazza Roma down Via Tirso. The **Pro Loco** tourist office is off Via Duomo at Via Vittorio Emanuele 8 (Mon–Fri 9am–12.30pm & 4–7.30pm, mid-July to mid-Sept also Sat 9am–noon; ☎0783.70.621); the **main tourist office** is currently opposite the bus station at Via Cágliari 278 (July–Sept Mon–Fri 8am–2pm & 4–7pm, Sat & Sun 9am–1pm; Oct–June Mon–Fri 8am–2pm, also Tues & Wed 4–7pm; ☎0783.74.191), though is due to move to a more central location in Piazza Eleanora; in summer there is also a handy kiosk on Piazza Roma (daily 9am–1pm & 4.30–8.30pm).

Accommodation

Oristano is badly off for accommodation, with just six **hotels** listed, and these often full. You'll need to book way ahead if you want to stay during the Sa Sartiglia festivities in particular. The cheapest and friendliest is also the most difficult to find – the *Píccolo Hotel*, at Via Martignano 19 (☎0783.71.500; ③), in an area of unmarked streets behind Piazza Martini, near Via del Cármine. Also centrally located, the *Isa* in Piazza Mariano (☎0783.360.101; ④) is comfortable though rather bland, while the run-down *Cama*, in Via Vittorio Véneto, is a convenient choice near the train station (☎0783.74.374; ④). North of the centre on Piazza Italia, *Villa delle Rose* (☎0783.310.101, fax 0783.310.117; ③) is a good choice on a quiet piazza, with solidly furnished rooms, each with a spacious bathroom, or you can go more upmarket and stay at the central, business-traveller's *Mistral*, at Via Mártiri di Belfiore (☎0783.212.505, fax 0783.210.058; ④), with an unprepossessing appearance but bright rooms.

The nearest **campsite** is 6km away at **MARINA DI TORRE GRANDE**, Oristano's lido. The *Torre Grande* (☎0783.22.228; May–Sept), 150m from the sea, is reachable on frequent buses from the ARST bus station.

Eating and drinking

Oristano is better off for **restaurants**, including the central and reliable *Trattoria Gino*, off Piazza Roma at Via Tirso 13 (closed Sun), which has a good-value menu with traditional Sardinian items like *ravioli sardi* (made with butter and sage) and *sebadas* (cheese-filled pastry-cases topped with honey). A few doors along, the modishly modern *Ciccio & Dessi* offers a complete contrast, serving snacks and full, moderately priced meals; some tables are in the garden (closed Sun evening & Mon). Via Parpaglia's *Trattoria del Teatro* is touristy but handy, also cooking up novelty pizzas lunchtimes and evenings (closed Sun). For a cheap and basic pizza, head for *La Torre* on Piazza Roma (closed Mon), where the speciality is *pizza ai funghi porcini*. You might like to finish your meal with a glass of Oristano's celebrated *Vernaccia* dessert wine. For late-night drinking or daytime snacks, the hip and cool *Lolamundo Café* in Piazzetta Corrias has tables in the piazza and DJs in the evenings on Fridays and Saturdays (closed Sun).

Around Oristano: Tharros

Many people come to Oristano just to visit the Punic and Roman ruins at **Tharros**, twenty-odd kilometres from Oristano and served by two ARST buses daily. Like Nora, Tharros is pitched on a limb of land surrounded by water, though in this case it's a clenched fist, dominated by a sturdy Spanish watchtower. The peninsula forms part of the mouth of the Golfo di Oristano and was settled by Phoenicians as early as 800 BC. Tharros grew under Carthaginian occupation and then, after 238 BC, was revitalized by the Romans, who furnished it with the baths and streets that you see today. The town was finally abandoned in 1070 in favour of the more secure Oristano, then a small village.

The **site** (daily: 9am–1hr beofre sunset; L8000/€4.13) consists mostly of Punic and Roman houses arranged on a grid of streets, of which the broad-slabbed Decumanus Maximus is the most impressive. Another, the Cardo Maximus, has a deep open sewer visible alongside it. But the things you'll notice immediately on entering the site are the solitary remnants of a first-century BC Roman temple, with only two of its four Corinthian columns still upright. There are also baths and fragments of mosaics from the Roman city, and a wall and remains of a tophet from the earlier Punic settlement. Like Nora, there is much more submerged underwater, as a result of subsidence.

Near the site stands the fifth-century church of **San Giovanni di Sinis**, which vies with Cágliari's San Saturno for the title of oldest Christian church in Sardinia. Further back up the road towards Oristano (signposted off the Tharros road) is the sanctuary of **San Salvatore**, whose main interest is in a subterranean fourth-century chamber dedicated to Mars and Venus, complete with faded frescoes of Venus, Cupid and Hercules – ask the custodian to let you see it. The sanctuary forms the focus of a wild **festival** on the first weekend of September, the main feature of which is a race run at dawn to the village of **Cabras**, 8km away, by the town's boys. Barefoot and clad in white shirts and shorts, they bear aloft the statue of San Salvatore in a re-enactment of a frantic rescue mission undertaken four centuries ago to save the saint from Moorish attackers.

Bosa

North of Oristano, a brief bus ride from the rail and road junction of **Macomer** takes you to **BOSA** and the coast. Stranded in the middle of one of Sardinia's last remaining stretches of deserted coastline, and so far overlooked by the tourist industry, the town huddles on the banks of the Temo river around a hilltop castle. From the riverside the corridor-like streets of the old district, **Sa Costa**, ascend the contours of the hillside, full of medieval gloom. To explore these backstreets, take any road leading up from the **Cathedral**, on the northern side of Bosa's main bridge. Keep climbing for about twenty minutes to reach Bosa's **Castle** (summer daily 10am–noon & 4–7pm; erratic hours in winter; free), erected by the Malaspina family in 1122 – there's also a road that skirts the back of town, leading round to the castle gate. From the castle ramparts you can pick out the ex-cathedral of **San Pietro**, an eleventh-century construction with a lovely Gothic facade added by Cistercian monks a couple of hundred years later. From the bridge, it's a two-kilometre walk along the river to the church.

In the other direction, **BOSA MARINA** lies 5km downstream on what was the town's original site before its inhabitants shifted to a more defensible position. Today it is a conventional minor resort with a small choice of hotels and trattorias, its tiny port and beach in the lee of the islet of Isola Rossa, now linked to the mainland and guarded by an old Spanish watchtower.

Practicalities

Bosa's **tourist office** is at Via Azuni 5 (summer daily 10am–1pm & 6–9pm; erratic hours in winter; ☎0785.376.107). Most of the **hotels** are in Bosa Marina, though Bosa does have one fine old palazzo just across the river, *Sa Pischedda* (☎0785.373.065; ③). Though convenient for the beach, Bosa Marina has a fairly uninspiring bunch of hotels, though these include the friendly *Costa Corallo* on Via C. Colombo (☎0784.375.162; ④), and you will also find here one of Sardinia's very rare **youth hostels**, close to the beach on Via Sardegna (☎0785.375.009; L20,000/€10.33; April–Sept) The nearest **campsite**, *Turas* (☎0785.359.270; June–Sept), is a couple of kilometres south down the coast from Bosa Marina (connected by bus in summer).

There are surprisingly few **restaurants** in the area, though there's a good choice in the centre of town. One of the best is the semi-formal *Borgo Sant'Ignazio* (☎0785.374.662; closed Oct–April Tues), in an alley above the Corso, Via Sant'Ignazio 33, which cooks up delicious local specialities; the hotel above is a comfortable accommodation option. The restaurant attached to the *Sa Pischedda* (no closing day) is handy but the food is rather indifferent. If you have your own transport or don't mind the lengthy walk on the north bank of the river, you can eat sumptuously at the highly rated *Mannu* (☎0785.375.306), which serves superlative Italian and Sard dishes at rather steep prices. It's attached to the hotel of the same name on Viale Alghero, equidistant from Bosa and Bosa Marina, which would make a further accommodation option, though the rooms (④), while comfortable enough, don't really compensate for the poor location.

For **snacks** and refreshments, you can sit under the palms at *Bar-Café Taverna*, on Piazza Cármine (closed Tues in winter).

Nuoro and the interior

Heading east from Macomer on the private FCS line, you can reach **Nuoro** in around two hours; the alternative is to take a PANI bus all the way from Oristano (4 daily; 2hr). The huge central province of Nuoro has little in common with Sardinia's modern sun-and-sand image. For many, though, it's the most interesting part of the island, dotted with small and isolated villages which have never known the heel of foreign conquerors. Their inhabitants have retained a fierce sense of independence and loyalty to their traditions, and this is especially true in the ring of the once almost impenetrable **Gennargentu mountains**, centred on the island's highest peak, **La Mármora** (1834m). These mountains form the core of the **Barbágia** region, called Barbaria by the Romans who, like their successors, were never able to subdue it, foiled by the guerrilla warfare for which these hidden recesses proved ideal.

Nuoro

"There is nothing to see in Nuoro: which to tell the truth, is always a relief. Sights are an irritating bore," wrote D.H. Lawrence, though he omitted to mention the town's superb position beneath the soaring peak of Monte Ortobene and opposite the sheer and stark heights of Sopramonte. In many respects **NUORO** is little different from the other villages of the region, but no place on the island can match its extraordinary literary fame. This was the town Lawrence made for in his Sardinian excursion of 1921, when it appeared to him "as if at the end of the world, mountains rising sombre behind". The best-known Sard poet, **Sebastiano Satta** (1867–1914) was Nuorese, as was the author **Grazia Deledda** (1871–1936), who won the Nobel Prize for Literature in 1927 in recognition of a writing career devoted to recounting the day-to-day trials and passions of local villagers. For **Salvatore Satta** (1902–75) – no relation to Sebastiano – "Nuoro was nothing but a perch for the crows", as he wrote in his semi-autobiographical masterpiece, *The Day of Judgment*; his only work, it was published posthumously to great acclaim. The last century has witnessed few changes in this insular town despite the unsightly apartment blocks, administrative buildings and banks superimposed upon it.

Nuoro's **old quarter** is the most compelling part of town, spread around the pedestrianized hub of **Corso Garibaldi**, along which a buzzing passeggiata injects a bit of life into the place. After poking around this area, head up past the duomo to see the town's impressive **Museo Etnografico** (daily: mid-June to Sept 9am–8pm; Oct to mid-June 9am–1pm & 3–7pm; L5000/€2.58) on Via Antonio Mereu, a ten-minute walk from the Corso. The museum has Sardinia's most comprehensive range of local costumes, jewellery, masks, carpets and other handicrafts, arranged in a modern purpose-built complex. Examples and explanations of traditional musical instruments from around the island are also displayed, together with a fascinating array of old photographs. On Via Deledda, off Piazza San Giovanni, is the **Casa di Grazia Deledda** (same hours as Museo Etnografico; free), the well-to-do home of Nuoro's literary star, restored and furnished and displaying various photos and mementos. A more contemporary note is sounded in Nuoro's new **Museo d'Arte Nuorese**, just off the Corso on Via Satta (Tues–Sun: June–Sept 10am–1pm & 4–8pm; Oct–May 10am–1pm & 4.30–8.30pm; L5000/€2.58), a collection of twentieth-century and contemporary art from the whole island, with a preponderance of local artists. Displayed on three floors, the works are refreshingly diverse, and there are also temporary exhibitions of modern Italian art.

Nuoro's traditional face is again to the fore at the town's biggest annual **festival**, one of the most vibrant events on the island's calendar. Taking place over the penultimate Sunday of August, when dancing and dialect singing are enthusiastically performed, and August 29, the day of a long procession to Mount Ortobene (see opposite), the **Festa del Redentore** is the opportunity to see as many as 3000 of Sardinia's local costumes, worn by participants from all over the island, in particular the villages of Barbágia (see p.1042).

Practicalities

Nuoro's **train station** is a half-hour walk from the centre of town along Via La Mármara, along which stop frequent **city buses** (tickets from the shop inside the station). ARST **buses** stop outside the station, while PANI buses stop at Via Brigata Sássari (parallel to Via La Mármara). There's a **tourist office** on Piazza Italia (March–Sept daily 9am–1pm & 3.30–7pm; ☎0784.30.083); in winter go directly to the administration office on the third floor (Mon, Thur & Fri 9am–1pm, Tues & Wed 9am–1pm & 3.30–6.30pm; ☎0784.30.083). There's another private information office at Corso Garibaldi 155, which has material on excursions beyond Nuoro (Easter–Sept Mon–Sat 10am–1pm & 4–7pm, also Sun in Aug; Oct–Easter Mon–Sat 10am–1pm; ☎0784.38.777).

Nuoro is hopelessly ill-equipped for the few tourists who pass through, but you can usually find a place to **stay** at the *Mini Hotel*, neat, friendly and centrally located at Via Brofferio 31 (☎0784.33.159; ②); alternatively try Signora Jacobini's unofficial hotel at Via Cedrino 31, off Piazza Italia (☎0784.30.675; ②), or the business-class *Grillo*, near the ethnographic museum at Via Monsignor Melas 14 (☎0784.38.678; ③). The town is better off for **restaurants**, for example the excellent *Tascusi* at Via Aspromnte 13, off the top end of the the Corso, where local dishes are served in simple white rooms decorated with Sard art (closed Sun). Alternatively, round the corner at Via Monsignor Bua 13, try *Il Portico*, a slightly more formal place also serving delicious local food (closed Sun). You'll find a more boisterous atmosphere at *Ciusa*, a pizzeria-restaurant popular with the Nuorese at Viale Ciusa 53, on the western end of town (closed Mon

Oct–May). For a lunchtime **snack**, there's *Il Mio Bar*, a handy sit-down **bar** on Via Mereu, between the museum and the duomo (closed Sun), while *Bar Nuovo* at the top of Corso Garibaldi (closed Wed) and *Bar Cambosu* round the corner on Piazza Vittorio Emanuele (closed Mon) are amenable places for breakfasts and evening drinks.

Monte Ortobene

From Nuoro's Piazza Vittorio Emanuele you can take a local bus (3–10 daily) up to the summit of **Monte Ortobene**, 8km away, from where there are striking views over the gorge separating Nuoro from the Sopramonte massif. This is the venue for Nuoro's **Festa del Redentore** on August 29, when a procession from town weaves up the mountain to the bronze **statue** of the Redeemer at the top (955m). Poised in an attitude of swirling motion, the statue is probably the best vantage point, with dizzying views down to the valley floor. The woods round about are perfect for walks and picnics, and there are possibilities for horse riding at the signposted *Locanda Sedda Ortai*. Delicious – but pricey – local **dishes** can be had at *Fratelli Sacchi* on Monte Ortobene (closed Mon), also signposted off the only road up the mountain. There are also **rooms** available here between April and October (☎0784.31.200; ③).

Oliena

The nearest village to Nuoro is **OLIENA** (4–11 buses daily from Nuoro), 12km distant on **Monte Corrasi** and visible across the deep valley south of the provincial capital. Rising to 1349m, this dramatically rugged limestone elevation forms part of the Sopramonte massif, famed as the haunt of bandits until relatively recent times. Oliena itself prefers its reputation as the producer of one of the island's best wines, a dry, almost black concoction that turns lighter and stronger over the years.

Organized **trips** around Sopramonte's caves and crags leave from Oliena. Contact one of the operators in the village, for example Levamus at Via Vittorio Emanuele 27 (☎0784.285.190) or the Cooperativa Turística Enis, 3km outside town in Localitá Maccione (☎0784.288.363), which also has **rooms** (②) and pitches for camping.

Orgósolo

Deeper into the mountains, at the end of a straggly eighteen-kilometre road running south from Oliena, **ORGÓSOLO** is stuck with its label of bandit capital of the island. The clans of Orgósolo, whose menfolk used to spend the greater part of the year away from home with their flocks, have always nursed an animosity towards the settled crop-farmers on the Barbágia's fringes, a tension that occasionally broke out into open warfare. On top of this there was the tension between rival clans, which found expression in large-scale sheep-rustling and bloody vendettas, such as the *disamistade* (enmity) that engulfed Orgósolo at the beginning of this century. The feud arose from a dispute over the inheritance of the village's richest chieftain, Diego Moro, who died in 1903, and lasted for fourteen years, virtually exterminating the two families involved. Between 1901 and 1954, Orgósolo – population 4000 – clocked up an average of one murder every two months.

Perhaps the village's most infamous son is **Graziano Mesina**, the so-called "Scarlet Rose", who won local hearts in the 1960s by robbing only from the rich to give to the poor and only killing for revenge against those who had betrayed him. Roaming at will through the mountains, even granting interviews to reporters and television journalists, he was eventually captured and incarcerated in Sássari prison. Escaping in 1968, he was recaptured near Nuoro and flown by helicopter the same day to appear on television in Cágliari. Mesina last surfaced in July 1992, when he was dispatched to

Sardinia from a mainland prison to help negotiate the release of Farouk Kassam, an eight-year-old boy held hostage for seven months in the Barbágia (see below).

Saddled with this semi-legendary background, it is inevitable that Orgsóolo should play host to a constant dribble of visitors hoping to find some traces of its violent past amid the shabby collection of breeze-blocked grey houses. But the villagers have obliged the tourists by providing a vivid collection of **murals**, some of them covering whole houses and shops, portraying village culture, most illustrating the oppression of the landless by the landowners, or demanding Sardinian independence. One of them seems intended to shock unsuspecting newcomers: a scarlet face painted onto a rock below the entrance to the village, as if lying in wait.

Nine to eleven **buses** daily ply the route to Orgósolo from Nuoro (4 on Sun), so it's not necessary to stay over. Should you want to, however, there are a couple of **hotels**: the basic *Petit* on Via Mannu (☎0784.402.009; ②) and the panoramic and slightly smarter *Sa e Jana*, on Via Lussu, at the southern edge of the village (☎0784.402.437; ②), with stupendous views and a good **restaurant**.

The Barbágia

There are dozens of small villages like Orgósolo in the **BARBÁGIA**, interconnected by twisting mountain roads and still, as Salvatore Satta described them at the start of the twentieth century, "minuscule settlements as remote from one another as are the stars". The elderly folk in these tight communities are just about the only people on the island who still routinely wear the traditional local costumes, which otherwise are likely to be seen only during one of the numerous small festivals that punctuate the year. Each village has at least one, for which preparations are made months in advance.

Mamoiada, 11km west of Orgósolo, is the scene of a highly pagan carnival romp, when masked *mammuthones* representing hunted animals march through the streets, decked in sheepskin with their backs arrayed with rows of jangling goat-bells. **Ottana**, on the northern fringes of the area – and reckoned to be the dead centre of Sardinia – vies with Mamoiada for its masked and horned carnival horrors, but is otherwise unremarkable. **Fonni**, 13km due south of Mamoiada and at 1000m the island's highest village, has less gruesome costumed processions in its festivals of the Madonna dei Mártiri, held on the Monday following the first Sunday in June, and on San Giovanni's day on June 24. Close to the island's highest peaks, the village has become one of the main centres of the Barbágia region, and holds a couple of comfortable hotels (see opposite).

Each of these villages was until recently primarily a community of shepherds, whose isolated circumstances and economic difficulties in the postwar years led to widescale emigration and, among those who stayed behind, a crime wave. Sheep-rustling and internecine feuding came to be replaced by the infinitely more lucrative practice of the **kidnapping** and ransoming of wealthy industrialists or their families. This phenomenon reached epidemic proportions during 1966–68 when scores of Carabinieri were drafted into the area to comb the mountains for the hide-outs, rarely with any success. Recent years, however, have seen a lull in the kidnaps, apart from occasional high-profile cases such as that of Farouk Kassam, an eight-year-old who was abducted on the Costa Smeralda and held for seven months in 1992, having part of his ear cut off by his kidnappers to accelerate the ransom payment.

Nowadays, shepherds send their children to university, or they go to seek work in mainland Italy and don't come back. They leave behind slowly atrophying village communities whose salvation is deemed to lie in a greater awareness of their tourism potential as centres for outdoor activities. The **Gennargentu** chain of mountains – the name means "silver gate", referring to the snow that covers them every winter – have the island's only **skiing** facilities on Sardinia's second-highest peak of **Monte Bruncu Spina** (1829m).

Practicalities

Various Barbágia villages offer **accommodation** from which to explore the region, all of them connected by bus with Nuoro and with each other. Nearest to Nuoro is **Fonni**, 33km south (13–14 buses daily, 6 on Sun), where there is the flashy modern *Cualbu* (☎0784.57.054; ③) on Viale del Lavoro and the much more personal, *Cinghialetto* on Via Grazia Deledda (☎0784.57.660; ③), both with their own restaurants. **Désulo**, a further 26km south (1 bus daily, not Sun), has a wider choice, including the good-value *Maria Carolina*, on Via Cágliari (☎0784.619.310; ②), and the basic *La Nuova* on Via Lamármora (☎0784.619.251; ①). At **Tonara**, 14km to the west of Désulo (1 bus daily), you'll find a couple of small hotels: the *Belvedere* (☎0784.63.756; ②) and *Su Toni* (☎0784.63.420; ①), very similar places with adequate en suite accommodation and restaurants. Finally, **Aritzo**, 15km south of both Désulo and Tonara (1 bus daily), has a choice of five hotels: try the old-fashioned but comfortable *Moderno*, at the top of the village on Via Kennedy (☎0784.629.229; ③), with a small garden and restaurant, or the modern and slightly bland *Castello*, on the main Corso Umberto (☎0784.629.266; ②).

These villages all make good bases for **mountain treks**, best undertaken in spring and summer. From Désulo, for example, it is possible to reach the area's highest peak, La Mármora, by a twelve-kilometre path. Along the way you may see wild pigs, vultures and deer, though you would be lucky to spot one of the rare mouflon, an elegant wild goat with long curved horns – its numbers have been decimated by hunting. For fuller details on walks, you can obtain a booklet from Nuoro's tourist office (see p.1040).

The eastern coast

Nuoro province's long **eastern seaboard** is highly developed around the resorts of Siniscola and Posada, but further south it preserves its desolate beauty, virtually untouched apart from a couple of isolated spots around **Orosei** and **Cala Golone**, and, further down, the small port of **Arbatax**. Frequent daily buses connect Cágliari and Nuoro with Tortolí, which is close to Arbatax. Tortolí, and Arbatax are also on the narrow-gauge railway which follows an inland route to Cágliari, with a change at Mandas; the full journey from the coast to Cágliari takes seven dawdling hours.

Dorgali and Cala Gonone

Centre of the renowned **Cannonau** wine-growing region, **DORGALI** attracts a lot of tourists in summer, both for its craftwork and on account of the recent growth of Cala Gonone, a small port 10km away. Dorgali's **restaurants** and **hotels** are generally cheaper than its neighbour's: try the *San Pietro* (☎0784.96.142; ②) for bargain lodgings.

CALA GONONE is reached by going south out of town and turning left into the tunnel that brings you through the rock wall, from which the road plunges down to the bay. Beautifully sited at the base of the 900-metre-high mountains, this once tiny settlement was until recently accessible only by boat. Now hotels and villas dominate the scene, though these have not entirely spoilt the sense of isolation, and it is worth a visit if only to take advantage of the numerous boat tours to the secluded coves up and down the coast. Among the best are **Cala Luna** and **Cala Sisine**, though if you are here for a short time you would do well to choose a tour that combines pauses at these swimming stops with exploration of the deep grottoes that pit the shore.

Most famous of these is the **Grotta del Bue Marino** – one of the last refuges of the Mediterranean monk seal, or "sea ox", in Italian waters, before the last colony moved on, probably at about the same time that the tourists moved in. It's a good expedition, anyway, since this is among Sardinia's most spectacular caves, a luminescent gallery filled with remarkable natural sculptures, resembling organ pipes, wedding cakes and even human heads – one of them is known as *Dante*, after a fondly imagined resemblance to the poet. Boat trips from Cala Gonone cost around L10,000/€5.17, and entry to the cave is about the same.

There's no lack of **hotels** in Cala Gonone. Near the port and beaches are the lively, bougainvillea-covered *Cala Luna* (April–Oct; ☎0784.93.133; ③), with direct access to the beach; the *Píccolo* (☎0784.93.232; ③), a fairly plain place that's open year-round, just up the hill from the harbour, and *La Conchiglia* (☎0784.93.448; ④; March to mid-Oct), smaller and smarter, and also with seafront views. There's a wide choice of **places to eat**, ranging from fast food to gourmet parlours (though mostly closed in winter). In the latter category, the restaurant attached to the *Miramare* hotel, on Piazza Giardini, is rated highly for its fish dishes (closed Oct–April), while *Il Faro*, just beyond on Via Dándolo, is a more relaxed place for pizzas and seafood. The restaurant at the *Pop* hotel on Via Marco Polo is cheap and boisterous.

Hikes from Cala Gonone and Dorgali

South of Cala Gonone lies one of Sardinia's last truly untouched tracts: swerving inland along the ridge of the Flumineddu River, walled on the other side by the Sopramonte massif, the new road brings you into a majestic mountain landscape, largely devoid of human life. There are several long-distance hikes which can be made in these wild parts, one of which – a two- to three-day hike – follows the coast **from Cala Gonone** to Cala Sisine, at which point the route wanders inland, up the Sisine canyon, as far as the solitary church of San Pietro, from which a track leads down to Baunei. A second, shorter hike follows the course of the Flumineddu River **from Dorgali** and takes you after a couple of hours into the **Gorropu gorge**, though further exploration requires mountaineering skills and even dinghies to negotiate the small lakes in the heart of the gorge, which also terminates at Baunei.

A good first port of call for those interested in **walks** and excursions is Sa Domu De S'Orku, a bunker-like building near the turn-off for Urzulei. It houses a bar, a shop, and the Società Gorropu (☎0782.649.282), an informal hiking centre where you can look at routes and maps and talk to the staff about destinations, such as the Supramonte massif. Guided walks are also on offer, costing L20,000–100,000/€10.33–51.70 per person according to the size of your party and the route you choose.

Tortolí and Arbatax

From Baunei the road descends steeply to **TORTOLÍ**, 5km inland from the port of **ARBATAX**, itself little more than a paper factory, a few bars and restaurants, and a port from which ferries ply to Genoa, Fiumicino and Civitavécchia three or four times weekly (daily in summer). The small beach here is famous for its red rocks, but there are better bathing spots outside town – especially to the south, where there is a series of sand and rock beaches at **Lido Orri**. There's a **tourist office** at Arbatax station (daily: June–Sept 7.30am–1.30pm & 5–8pm, July & Aug closes 10.30pm; Oct–May closed; ☎0782.667.690) that has information on sea **excursions**, including to the Grotta del Bue Marino for L35,000–45,000/€18.20–23.40 (see p.1043); in winter Tortolí's Pro Loco on Via Mazzini is open 9am–noon (☎0782.622.824). For **ferry tickets**, the Tirrenia office is near the port, on your right as you walk towards the station (Mon–Fri 8.30am–1pm & 4–8pm or 3.30–7.30pm in winter, Sat 8.30am–1pm, plus Wed & Sun 10pm–midnight).

There are several small **hotels** in the Arbatax area, most of them difficult to reach on foot. The only reasonably priced one lies a couple of kilometres south of the port in the Porto Frailis district, near a good beach, the *Gabbiano* (☎0782.623.512; ③). Otherwise, head towards Tortolí, where there is a small selection, including the pleasant *Splendor* on Viale Arbatax (☎0782.623.037; ③) – opposite the Esso station on the other side of the rail tracks – and, further up on the left (on the corner with Via Sarcidano), *Dolce Casa* (☎0782.623.484; ③; June–Sept), a clean and comfortable place run by an expatriate Englishwoman and her husband. There's a **campsite** in Porto Frailis, *Telis* (☎0782.667.323; May–Sept), which also has bungalows to rent. Frequent buses connect Tortolí, Arbatax and Porto Frailis.

As for **restaurants**, there are a few seafront places in Arbatax itself; in the Porto Frailis district, one of the best is *Il Faro*, overlooking the beach, and with a good choice of fish.

OLBIA, GALLURA AND THE COSTA SMERALDA

The largest town in Sardinia's northeastern wedge, **Olbia** owes its recent phenomenal growth to the huge influx of tourists bound for one of the Mediterranean's loveliest stretches of coast, the **Costa Smeralda**, whose five-star development has transformed the economy of the entire island. Elsewhere on the coast it's still possible to have fun without stacks of money: there are miles of shoreline still undeveloped and a profusion of minor islands, over sixty in all, which you can explore on various boat tours. A daily ferry service from **Palau** links the biggest islands of **Maddalena** and **Caprera**, while further west **Santa Teresa di Gallura** boasts some superb coves and beaches.

This indented northern shore fringes the region of **Gallura**, whose raw red and wind-sculpted granite mountains imbue the area with its unique edge-of-the-wilderness appeal. There is a hidden world within here that most tourists never discover, thickly forested with the cork-oaks which, after tourism, provide most of Gallura's revenue.

Olbia

When the English barrister John Tyndale visited **OLBIA** in the 1840s, he compared its Greek name, meaning "happy", with the state he found it in: "A more perfect misnomer, in the present condition of the town, could not be found. . . The whole district suffers severely from *intemperie*. The wretched approach across these marshes is worthy of the town itself. The houses, none of which have an elegant or neat appearance, are built mostly of granite, and are whitewashed, as if to give a greater contrast to the filth and dirt within and around them."

The "*intemperie*" of which Tyndale complained was malaria, which, together with the marshes and the filth, has long vanished as a result of the land-drainage schemes and DDT-saturation of the 1950s. Olbia today is once more a happy place, enjoying its new-found income from the tourists pouring through the docks and airport. Few of these tourists stay, however, for Olbia – the least Sardinian of all the island's towns – is awash with traffic and ugly apartment blocks which spoil what might once have been an attractive seafront. All the same its numerous bars and restaurants are generally crowded with tourists, sailors from the port and US service personnel from the NATO base on Palau and the Maddalena archipelago, who venture into town to spend their dollars and stalk the main Corso Umberto.

If you're stuck for an afternoon here, you might as well visit Olbia's only item of historical interest, the little basilica of **San Símplicio**, on the street of the same name. The simple granite structure is set in a piazza apart from Olbia's bustle, making it a good

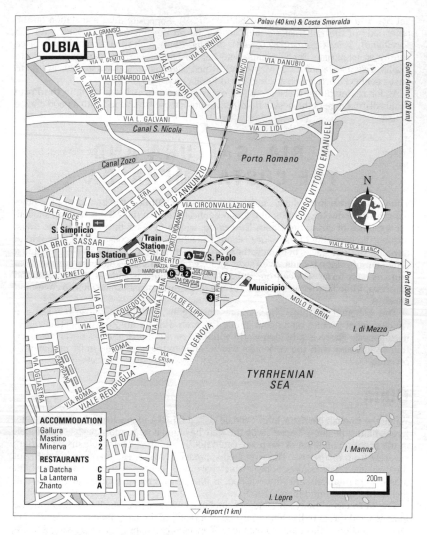

spot for a sit down. Claimed to be the most important medieval monument in the whole of Gallura – a region hardly famed for its artistic heritage – the church formed part of the great Pisan reconstruction programme of the eleventh and twelfth centuries. Its murky interior has three aisles separated by pillars and columns recycled from Roman constructions, and even the stoup for the holy water was formerly an urn that held cremated ashes. Along the walls is an array of Roman funerary slabs, with fragments of inscription still visible on some.

The church is the venue for Olbia's biggest **festa**, six days of processions, costumed dancing, poetry recitations, traditional games and fireworks around May 15, commemorating San Símplicio's martyrdom in the fourth century.

Arrival, transport and information

Ferries from Civitavécchia, Genova and Livorno (see box on p.1025) dock at the island of Isola Bianca, connected to the mainland by a two-kilometre causeway along which you can walk or take an hourly #3 bus; alternatively take a train from Olbia's main station. There are Tirrenia offices at the port (daily 8.30am–1pm & 5–11pm; ☎0789.24.691), and agencies at the bottom of Corso Umberto, where you can pick up tickets for Tirrenia, Moby Lines and Sardinia Ferries services (all agencies Mon–Sat 8.30am–1pm & 4.30–7.30pm). Sardinia Ferries for Livorno leave from Golfo Aranci, 15km up the coast (9 buses daily); their office in Olbia is at Corso Umberto 4 (☎0789.25.200). Book early for all departures.

Olbia's **airport** is connected by half-hourly buses (#2) to the central Piazza Regina Margherita; tickets cost L1300/€0.68 and can be bought from the airport bar. Taxis cost about L25,000/€12.91. Note that there is a summer-only bus service (5 daily) that departs from the airport for the **resorts** of Arzachena, Palau and Santa Teresa di Gallura (see p.1050), obviating the need to go to Olbia at all if you're bound for the beach-chequered coast or for Corsica.

Trains for Sássari and Cágliari run several times daily from the station just off Corso Umberto, which has a **left-luggage office** (daily 7.30am–8.30pm). There is also a station at the ferry quay, though not all trains stop here. The ARST **bus station** is round the corner on the Corso (also reachable by walking along the train station platform).

The **tourist office** is on Via Piro, a sidestreet running off the Corso (mid-June to mid-Sept Mon–Sat 8.30am–1pm & 4–7pm, Sun 8.30am–1pm; mid-Sept to mid-June Mon–Sat 8.30am–1pm; ☎0789.21.453). There are further offices at the port and airport, but these are open in summer only, and then only for arrivals and departures.

Accommodation and eating

Olbia has several good, central **hotels**, though most are on the expensive side. Cheapest choice lies just along from the tourist office on Via Vespucci, the *Mastino* (☎0789.21.130; ②), with somewhat shabby rooms, though these may improve as at the time of writing it was in the process of changing hands. Round the corner on Via Garibaldi, the *Minerva* (☎0789.21.190; ③) offers more comforts, while at the *Gallura* at Corso Umberto 145: (☎0789.24.648; closed Dec; ⑤), you get TVs, minibars, air-conditioning and breakfast thrown in, and there's a first-class restaurant on the ground floor. The nearest **campsite** is at Località Cugnana (☎0789.33.184; mid-May to Sept), 10km north of town; it's also the closest to the Costa Smeralda, and consequently can get crowded. There's a pool and bungalows are also available (④); from Olbia, 4–5 buses daily stop right outside.

As for **eating**, the small and elegant *Zhanto*, just off the Corso on Via delle Terme (closed Sun), offers good value and is always busy with locals; it serves pizzas at lunchtime. Also good for pizza is the subterranean *La Lanterna*, off the other side of the Corso on Via Olbia (closed Wed), which offers a **vegetarian** choice too. *La Datcha*, near the central Piazza Margherita at Via Cavour 3 (no closing day), is an *osteria* with good-value dishes-of-the-day and some benches outside. *Caffè Cosimino*, on Piazza Margherita (closed Sun), is a good place for coffees and fresh *cornetti*; with seating both inside – where the walls have faded photos of old Olbia – and outside.

The Costa Smeralda

The **Costa Smeralda** is a strictly defined ten-kilometre strip between the gulfs of Cugnana and Arzachena, beginning about 12km north of Olbia. Legend has it that the Aga Khan stumbled upon the charms of this jagged coast when his yacht took shelter from a storm in one of the narrow creeks here in 1958. Four years later the fabulously wealthy tycoon headed a consortium of businessmen with the aim of exploiting this wild coastal strip, and was easily able to persuade the local farmers to part with their largely uncultivable land – though stories have circulated ever since of the stratagems used to dupe the locals into selling their property for a fraction of its value.

The consortium's plans were on a massive scale, limited only by the conditions imposed by the regional government. These included proper sewage treatment and disposal, restrictions on building, and the insistence that the appearance of the landscape should not be unduly changed. On this last point the developers were only partly successful. Although you won't see any multi-storey hotels, advertising hoardings, fast-food restaurants or garish filling stations, neither will you find a genuine fishing village surviving in these parts, nor anything like the kind of raucous local markets you'll see in other parts of the island, and the luxurious holiday villages have a bland, almost suburban feel about them.

You can make your own mind up by taking a look at the "capital" of Costa Smeralda, **PORTO CERVO**, connected to Olbia by ARST buses (4–6 daily Mon–Sat). The "local"-style rustic-red architecture here is overwhelming in its artifice, embodying the dream of an idyllic Mediterranean village without any of the irritations of real life. Fascinating to wander round, crime- and litter-free, Porto Cervo is a child's playground on a massive scale. The huge yachting marina is a curiosity in itself, awash with the baubles of the ultra-rich, its gleaming ranks overlooked by the **Stella Maris** church. A modern whitewashed design by the Roman architect Michel Busiri Vici, who was also responsible for the grotto-like shopping arcade in Porto Cervo's centre, it houses a good *Mater Dolorosa* by El Greco.

You'll need your own transport to get to the sequestered **beaches**, none of them clearly marked; just follow any dirt track down to the sea – the rougher it is, the more promising. Try ones at **Cappriccioli**, **Rena Bianca** and **Liscia Ruia**, all dotted down the coast south of Porto Cervo.

The Golfo di Arzachena

At least seven buses daily leave Olbia on the coast road north that takes in Arzachena, Palau and Santa Teresa di Gallura. **ARZACHENA** is a not particularly inspiring inland town, though it has a useful **tourist office** in its central Piazza Risorgimento (Mon–Fri 8am–1.30pm & 3–7pm, Sat 8am–1.30pm; ☎0789.82.624) and a handful of mostly expensive **hotels**. Most economical of these, the *Citti*, lies just outside town on the main road to Palau at Viale Costa Smeralda 197 (☎0789.82.662; ④), and boasts a small pool, while *Casa Mia*, on the other side of Arzachena off the Olbia road at Via Torricelli 3 (☎0789.82.790; ⑤) has a garden and restaurant; both have significantly lower rates outside the peak season.

Outside the luxury zone but sharing many of the Costa Smeralda's natural advantages, the **Golfo di Arzachena** is a deep narrow bay with facilities concentrated around the resort village of **CANNIGIONE** – a small fishing port and yachting resort linked by buses (4–5 daily) with Arzachena. Virtually all Cannigione's hotels are over the ⑤ mark, and most are open only from Easter to October: one of the few remaining open all year, and also one of the cheapest, is the *Hotel del Porto*, right in front of the port on Lungomare Andrea Doria (☎0789.88.011; ⑤), offering fairly standard holiday accommodation with good views. There's a **campsite** a kilometre or two inland and south of Cannigione, the *Golfo di Arzachena* (☎0789.88.583), which also has bungalows and a large pool, but the more attractive site lies a couple of kilometres beyond Cannigione round the bay in the **LACONIA** district, the *Villaggio Isuledda* (☎0789.86.003; April to mid-Oct), right on the shore, with excellent bathing spots. Two **buses** a day link the area to Cannigione and Arzachena.

The Maddalena Islands

From **PALAU**, 10km up the coast from Cannigione, ferries leave once or twice an hour (L4000/€2.07 per person, L10,000/€5.17 for a medium-sized car) for the main island of the Maddalena archipelago, **La Maddalena**, from which you can reach **Caprera**, the island on which Garibaldi spent the last third of his life. Drivers should be warned that, in high season, it's a hectic bustle for tickets, and long queues are common.

La Maddalena

It takes twenty minutes to cross what Nelson called "Agincourt Sound" from Palau to the port and sole town on **LA MADDALENA**. The town, bearing the same name as the island, is a cheerful place with a population of about 15,000, swollen by a large number of Italian and US sailors who lend the town a garrison feel. Their headquarters are on the eastern side of town, a drab area of barracks and sentries, though the main military installations and submarine base are situated on the neighbouring island of Santo Stéfano – briefly captured by Napoleon in 1793 in an abortive attempt to take Sardinia.

Most of the action takes place in the narrow lanes between Piazza Umberto I and Cala Gavetta (the marina for small boats), a five-minute walk from the ferry port (heading left) and site of the **tourist office** (summer Mon–Fri 8am–2pm & 4–7pm, Sat 8am–7pm; winter closes 2pm Sat; ☎0789.736.321). The town is not particularly well off for **hotels**. Cheapest are the *Arcipélago* at Via Indipendenza Traversa 2 (☎0789.727.328; ④), which is hard to find (but signposted), offering modern, quiet and comfortable rooms a fifteen-minute walk east from the ferry port, and the state-run *Gabbiano*, at Via Giúlio Césare 20 (☎0789.722.507; ④), panoramically sited on the shore beyond Cala Gavetta but rather old-fashioned. Addresses of **rooms** to rent are available from the tourist office, or you could ask around in bars. There are also three **campsites**, all outside town: *Il Sole*, on Via Indipendenza (☎0789.727.727; mid-June to mid-Oct), and *Maddalena*, in the Moneta district (☎0789.728.051; June to mid-Oct) are both on the way to Caprera; or there's *Abbatoggia* (☎0789.739.173; June–Sept), close by some good beaches in the north of the island; the last two also have bungalows available (②).

Buses run to various parts of the island from near the Banco di Sardinia at the end of Via XX Settembre (every 30min in summer; every 2hr in winter). A good way of getting round the island is on a **bike or moped**, which can be rented from any of the outlets on the seafront walking towards Cala Gavetta for about L10,000/€5.17 a day for a bike, or L50,000/€25.82 a day for a *motorino*. The island invites aimless wandering and offers a variety of sandy and rocky beaches in mostly undeveloped coves. The **beaches** on the northern and western coasts are most attractive, particularly those around the tiny port of Madonetta, 5km west of La Maddalena, and at Cala Lunga, 5km north of town.

Caprera

Between October and May half of **CAPRERA** is closed off for military purposes, but there is always plenty of space left to roam this protected woody parkland, which is undeveloped apart from Garibaldi's house in the centre and a Club Med complex that offers the island's only tourist facilities.

Giuseppe Garibaldi (1807–82) came to live in Caprera in 1855, after a twenty-year exile from Italy. It was from here that he embarked on his spectacular conquest of Sicily and Naples in 1861, accompanied by his thousand Red-Shirts, and it was here that he

returned after his campaigns to resume a simple farming life. Having bought the northern part of the island for £360, he spent much of his time writing his memoirs and some
bad novels. His neighbour was an Englishman named Collins, with whom he had some
celebrated disagreements concerning their wandering goat-herds, as a result of which
Garibaldi built a wall dividing their properties, which can still be seen. After Collins's
death in 1864 a group of English admirers provided the money for Garibaldi to buy the
rest of Caprera from his ex-neighbour's family.

The **museum** (daily: June–Sept 9am–6.30pm; Oct–May 9am–2pm; L4000/€2.07) is
in Garibaldi's old house, the elegant South American-style **Casa Bianca**, which has
been preserved pretty much as he left it. Visitors are escorted past the bed where he
slept, a smaller one where he died, various scrolls, manifestos and pronouncements, a
pair of ivory-and-gold binoculars given to him by Edward VII and a letter from London,
dated 1867, conferring on him honorary presidency of the National Reform League. A
stopped clock and a wall-calendar indicate the precise time and date of his death.

The tour ends with Garibaldi's tomb in the garden, its rough granite contrasting with
the more pompous tombs of his last wife and five of his children. Garibaldi had requested to be cremated, but following the wishes of his son Menotti his corpse was stuffed.
In 1932, fifty years after his death, his tomb was opened to reveal the body perfectly
intact.

Santa Teresa di Gallura

The bus from Olbia and Palau to **SANTA TERESA DI GALLURA**, Sardinia's most
northerly port, passes a succession of lovely bays, some dramatic rocky coastline, and
a handful of campsites. Santa Teresa's **tourist office** is on the main Piazza Vittorio
Emanuele (June–Sept daily 8.30am–1pm & 3.30–8pm; Oct–May Mon–Fri 9am–1pm &
3.30–6.30pm, Sat 9am–1pm; ☎0789.754.185); there is also a summer-only booth down
by the port. Moby Lines, Saremar and Sardinia Ferries operate sailings from here to
Bonifacio in Corsica (4–18 daily; 1hr; L13,000–18,000/€6.76–9.36).

Among Santa Teresa's plentiful central **hotels**, good, relatively cheap choices include
the plain and secluded *Scano* on Via Lázio (☎0789.754.447; ③) and the more elegant *Da
Cecco*, at Via Po 3 (☎0789.754.220; Easter–Oct; ③), both of which, like most other hotels
here, demand at least half-board in July and August. There are several more hotels outside town, where they are best placed to take advantage of some of Sardinia's most
alluring **beaches**, all with superb views over to Corsica, just 11km away. To the east,
Punta Falcone and **La Marmorata** are popular spots, while 3km west of Santa Teresa,
Capo Testa is one of Sardinia's finest bathing localities, a rocky promontory surrounded by turquoise sea. In the latter area, you can stay comfortably and cheaply at
Bocche di Bonifacio (☎0789.754.202; April to mid-Oct; ③), which also has good-value
apartments to let, though these are usually booked up in peak period.

SÁSSARI, ALGHERO
AND LOGUDORO

The western half of the province is a green, fertile region, hilly but not so craggily
scenic as Gallura. The provincial capital, **Sássari**, is for many the island's most interesting town, with its crowded medieval centre and teeming squares. As a holiday destination, however, it has limited appeal, being inland and lacking enough entertainment
to fill more than a couple of afternoons or evenings here. More popular is **Alghero**, the
island's oldest resort as well as its major fishing port. Further inland, the heartlands of

the old *giudicato* of **Logudoro**, the "Land of Gold", offer some striking examples of Pisan architecture, their refinement in sharp contrast to the ramshackle but equally grand *nuraghi*, of which the area has a rich selection.

Sássari

Sardinia's second city, **SÁSSARI**, combines an insular, traditional feel, as embodied in its well-preserved tangle of lanes in the old quarter, with a forward-looking, confident air that is most evident in its modern centre. Historically, while Cágliari was Pisa's base of operations during the Middle Ages, Sássari was the Genoan capital, ruled by the Doria family, whose power reached throughout the Mediterranean. Under the Aragonese it became an important centre of Spanish hegemony, and the Spanish stamp is still strong, not least in its churches. In the sixteenth century the Jesuits founded Sardinia's first **university** here, and the intellectual tradition has survived, particularly in the political sphere. In recent years, Sássari has produced two national presidents – Antonio Segni and Francesco Cossiga – as well as the long-time head of the Italian Communist Party, Enrico Berlinguer (1922–84) – a cousin, incidentally, of the Christian

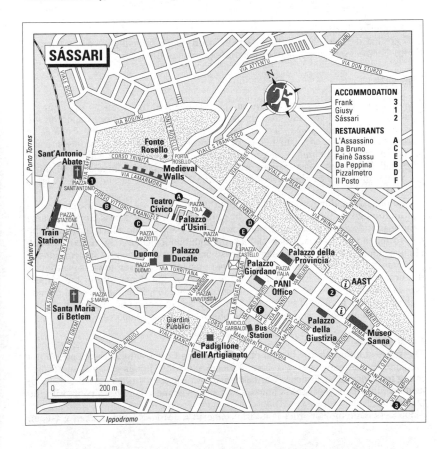

SASSÁRI'S FESTIVALS

One of Sardinia's showiest festivals – the **Cavalcata** – takes place in Sássari on **Ascension Day** (the fortieth day after Easter, usually the penultimate Sunday of May), the highlight of a month of cultural activities. Northern Sardinia's equivalent to Cágliari's Sant'Efisio festival, it attracts hundreds of richly costumed participants from villages throughout the province and beyond. Originally staged for the benefit of visiting Spanish kings or other dignitaries, it lapsed until its revival forty years ago by the local branch of the Rotary Club. The festival is divided into three stages, the morning featuring a horse-back parade and a display of the embroidered and decorated costumes unique to each village, after which there is a show of stirring feats of horsemanship at the local race course, ending with traditional songs and dances back in Piazza Italia.

On the afternoon of **August 14** there is a much more local affair – **I Candelieri**, linked to the Pisan devotion to the Madonna of the Assumption. It became a regular event when an outbreak of plague in Sássari in 1652 mysteriously abated on the eve of the feast of the Assumption, since when the ritual has been repeated annually as a token of thanks. The rumbustious event involves bands of *gremi*, or medieval guilds of merchants, artisans and labourers, decked out in Spanish-style costumes and bearing gigantic wooden "candlesticks", 8m tall, through the old town.

Democrat Cossiga.

Note that if you're coming to Sássari by **train**, you'll probably have to change at Ozieri-Chilivani station, outside the nondescript town of Chilivani.

The City

The **old quarter**, a network of alleys and piazzas bisected by the main Corso Vittorio Emanuele, is a good area for strolling around. Take a break from your wanderings to look at the **Duomo**, whose florid facade is Sardinia's most imposing example of Baroque architecture, added to a simpler Aragonese-Gothic base from the fifteenth and sixteenth centuries. Behind it, the eighteenth-century **Palazzo Ducale** now houses the town hall. On the other side of the Corso, **Piazza Tola** retains its medieval feel and is the venue of a daily market, overlooked by the Renaissance facade of the **Palazzo d'Usini**.

The only other thing worth searching out in the old town is the late-Renaissance **Fonte Rosello**, at the bottom of a flight of dilapidated steps accessible from Corso Trinità, in the northern part of the old town. Fed by a spring in which throngs of the city's women used to scrub their clothes, the fountain is elaborately carved with dolphins and four statues representing the seasons, the work of Genoese stonemasons.

Connected by a series of squares to the old quarter, the **newer town** is centred on the grandiose Piazza Italia. Leading off the piazza is Via Roma, site of the **Museo Sanna** (Tues–Sat 9am–7pm, Sun 9am–1pm; L4000/€2.07), Sardinia's second archeological museum. It's a good substitute if you've missed the main one at Cágliari; like the Cágliari museum, its most interesting exhibits are nuraghic sculptures.

Practicalities

The **train station** is at the bottom of the old town's Corso Vittorio Emanuele, with a luggage deposit that closes at 8.45pm. All local and ARST **buses** arrive at and depart from the semicircular Emiciclo Garibaldi, south of the tourist office. PANI buses run from Via Bellieni 5, just off Via Roma. ARST buses connect **Fert'lia airport** with the bus station.

Sássari's **main tourist office** is at Viale Umberto 72 (Mon–Fri 9am–1.30pm & 4–6pm;

☎079.231.331), but there is a handier one next to the museum at Via Roma 62 (same hours except closed Fri afternoon; ☎079.231.777). **Staying** in Sássari can be a real problem, and you'd do well to phone ahead to ensure availability. If you don't mind the somewhat primitive, bathless rooms, the most characterful of Sássari's two central budget options is the tumbledown *Sassari* Hotel, at Viale Umberto 65 (☎079.239.543; ①), but the lacklustre *Giusy* (☎079.233.327; ②), conveniently near the station on Piazza Sant'Antonio, has more comfort. The next step up is quite a leap, the relatively luxurious *Frank*, Via Armando Diaz 20 (☎079.233.327; ④), in the modern town. On the other hand, you'll find a good range of **restaurants** in town, such as *Il Posto*, a friendly trattoria in the new town at Via Enrico Costa 16 (closed Sun), where you can eat moderately priced pastas and pizzas. In the old town, the basic *Da Peppina*, in Vicolo Pigozzi (closed Sun), an alley off Corso Vittorio Emanuele, is a good place to sample the local speciality of horsemeat, or try the cosier but pricier *L'Assassino* on Vicolo Ospizio Cappuccini, a lane on the other side of the Corso (closed Sun). At *Fainè Sassu*, off Piazza Castello at Via Usai 17 (closed Sun & June–Sept), the menu is confined to another *sassarese* speciality: *fainè*, a sort of pancake made of chickpea flour, either plain or cooked with onions, sausage or anchovies. Further along this street, *Pizzalmetro* serves **pizzas** to eat in or take away (closed Sun), or sit outside *Da Bruno*, a cheap pizzeria on Piazza Matteotti (closed Wed).

Around Sássari: inland Logudoro

Inland from Sássari there are few places you would consider staying at, but there are a couple that are well worth a stop en route to somewhere else – though a car is generally necessary. In the middle of the **Logudoro** countryside, right on the main Sássari–Olbia SS 597 some 15km from Sássari (and also glimpsed from the Sássari–Chilivani train), rises the tall belltower of **Santa Trinità di Saccárgia**, its conspicuous zebra-striped facade marking its Pisan origins. Built in 1116, the church owes its remote location to a divine visitation, informing the wife of the *giudice* of Logudoro that she was pregnant. It has survived remarkably well, with lovely Gothic capitals at the top of the porch as you enter the rather gloomy interior, where there is little to distract attention from the stark walls apart from some crude thirteenth-century frescoes.

There is another Pisan relic 30km south of Sássari – the twelfth-century church of **San Pietro di Sorres**, perched on a bluff with sweeping views, near the villages of Bonnanaro and Borutta. Formerly a cathedral, the church shows more French influence in its ornate style than Sardinia's other Pisan churches, being grander and tidier, though the interior is disappointing.

A couple of kilometres further on, the road leads straight past one of the island's greatest prehistoric monuments, the **Nuraghe Sant'Antine** (daily 9am–1hr before sunset; L4000/€2.07 or L5000/€2.58 including Museo di Torralba – see below). Located in the heart of the so-called Valle dei Nuraghi, an area liberally dotted with the ancient structures, this one stands only a few hundred metres from **TORRALBA** train station, making the site easily visitable. Of the dozens here, this nuraghic palace is the biggest and most impressive – hence its common name **Nuraghe Majore** – and is thought to date back to the fourteenth century BC. Overlooking the scattered ruins of a village as well as later Carthaginian and Roman additions, the central complex consists of three external bastions connected by a defensive wall, grouped around the original massive three-storey tower, with walls up to five metres thick and sixteen high. You can find out more by employing the services of an English-speaking guide for L3000/€1.55.

The **Museo di Torralba** (daily: May–Sept 9am–8pm; Oct–April 9am–5pm; L4000 /€2.07, or L5000/€2.58 including Nuraghe Sant'Antine), two and a half kilometres north in the village of Torralba, features a small collection of finds from the site as well as a model of the *nuraghe*'s original appearance and details of its excavation. There are also rooms devoted to local costumes, with fascinating old photos, and a garden of mainly Roman bits and pieces.

Alghero

ALGHERO is a very rare Italian phenomenon: a tourist town that is also a flourishing fishing port, giving it an economic base entirely independent of the summer masses. The predominant flavour here is Catalan, owing to a wholesale Hispanicization that followed the overthrow of the Doria family by Pedro IV of Aragon in 1354, a process so thorough that it became known as "Barcelonetta". The traces are still strong in the old town today, with its flamboyant churches, wrought-iron balconies and narrow cobbled streets named in both Italian and Catalan. Beyond the stout girdle of walls enclosing this historic core, the new town's grid of parallel streets has little of interest beyond its restaurants and hotels.

Arrival and accommodation

Trains arrive some way out of the centre, but regular buses connect the station to the port. **Buses** arrive in Via Catalogna, on the Giardino Púbblico. Alghero's efficient **tourist office** (May–Sept Mon–Sat 8am–8pm, Sun 9am–1pm; Oct–April Mon–Sat 8am–2pm; ☎079.979.054) is at the top end of the Giardino Púbblico, its multilingual staff equipped with reams of maps, accommodation lists and tour details.

Alghero's best-value **hotel**, and the only one located in the old town, is the *San Francesco*, at Via Machin 2 (☎079.980.330; ④), just behind San Francesco church, with all of its clean and quiet rooms en suite. If it's full, try the very basic but clean *Normandie*, an apartment on Via Enrico Mattei, south of the old town, between Via Kennedy and Via Giovanni XXIII (☎079.975.302; ②), or the *San Giuan*, a modern holiday villa with bland, airy rooms, located north of the centre and near the beaches at Via Angioy 2 (☎079.951.222; ④). Two kilometres out of town, *La Mariposa* **campsite** (☎079.950.360; April to mid-Oct) has direct access to the beach. Alghero's *Giuliani* **youth hostel** (☎079.930.353; L14,000/€7.28) is actually 6km along the coast at FERTILIA, reachable by local bus, but call first to check availability.

A good way to get around the town and its environs is by **bike**: Cicloexpress, off Via Garibaldi at the port, charge L50,000/€25.82 per day for a scooter, L20,000/€10.33 for a mountain bike, and L15,000/€7.80 for a regular bicycle.

The Town

A walk around the old town should take in the series of seven defensive **towers** which dominate Alghero's centre and its surrounding walls. From the **Giardino Púbblico**, the **Porta Terra** is the first of these massive bulwarks – known as the Jewish Tower, it was erected at the expense of the prosperous Jewish community before their expulsion in 1492. Beyond is a puzzle of lanes, at the heart of which the pedestrianized Via Carlo Alberto, Via Principe Umberto and Via Roma have most of the bars and shops. At the bottom of Via Umberto stands Alghero's sixteenth-century **Cattedrale**, where Spanish viceroys stopped to take a preliminary oath before taking office in Cágliari. Its incongruously Neoclassical entrance is round the other side on Via Manno; inside, the lofty nave's alternating pillars and columns rise to an impressive octagonal dome.

Most of Alghero's finest architecture dates from the same period and is built in a similar Catalan-Gothic style. Two of the best examples are a short walk away: the **Palazzo d'Albis** on Piazza Cívica and the elegantly austere Jewish palace **Palau Reial** in Via Sant'Erasmo.

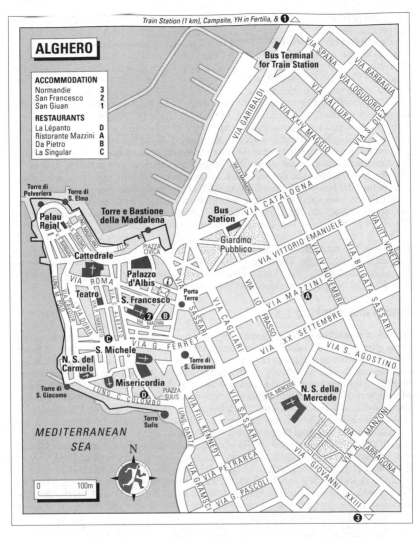

Outside the old quarter, most of the tourist activity revolves around the **port**, its wide quay nudged by rows of colourful fishing boats and bordered by bars. The town's beaches begin further north, backed by hotels, many of the older ones converted from villas formerly owned by the expatriate community of central Europeans who fled here after World War I.

Neptune's Grotto and ancient sites
The best of the excursions you can take from the port is to **Neptune's Grotto**, with boats departing several times daily in summer: tickets cost L17,000/€8.84, not counting the entry charge to the grotto. The forty-five-minute boat ride west along the coast

takes you past the long bay of Porto Conte as far as the point of **Capo Caccia**, where the spectacular sheer cliffs are riddled by deep marine caves. They include the **Grotta Verde** and **Grotta dei Ricami** – visited on some tours – but the most impressive is the **Grotta di Nettuno** itself (daily: April–Sept 9am–7pm; Oct 10am–5pm; Nov–March 9am–2pm; L15,000/€7.80), a long snaking passage delving far into the rock, into which 45-minute tours are led, single-file, on the hour every hour, past dramatically lit and fantastical stalagmites and stalactites.

A cheaper alternative to the boat is to drive to Capo Caccia or take a **bus** from the main bus terminal (3 daily in summer; 1 in winter; L3400/€1.77 one way, L6300/€3.28 return). Once you are deposited at the end of the line, there's a 654-step descent down the Escala del Cabirol, a highly scenic route whose Catalan name means "goat's steps", presumably a reference to the only animal that could negotiate the perilous path before the construction of the stairway in 1954. Make sure you time your arrival at the cave in time for the next tour: the descent takes 10–15 minutes. On the way back, leave some time before the bus goes for a well-earned ice cream at the bar opposite the steps.

With your own vehicle, you can also visit two sites 10km outside Alghero. The necropolis of **Anghelu Ruju**, a pre-nuraghic cave complex of thirty-six hypogea (daily: March–Sept 9am–7pm; Oct–Feb 9.30am–4pm; L4000/€2.07, or L7000/€3.62 with guide), is on the road to Porto Torres, near the airport. On the road to Porto Conte, you'll pass the **nuraghe di Palmavera** (same hours and price as Anghelu Ruju) on your right, comprising a ruined palace dating from around 1100 BC and surrounded by fifty or so circular huts, one of which, with a central stool surrounded by a stone bench, is believed to have been used for meetings and religious gatherings.

Eating and drinking

Alghero's **restaurants** are renowned for their fish and seafood, always fresh, inventively prepared and tastefully presented; spring and winter are the best seasons. Remember when ordering that most places price fish by weight – two–three *etti* (an *etto* is 100g) usually gets you a healthy portion. For a first-rate – and fairly pricey fishy feast, head for *La Lépanto*, off Piazza Sulis at Via Carlo Alberto 135 (☎079.979.116; closed Mon in winter), also offering delicious meat dishes. Slightly less expensive, but less atmospheric, *Da Pietro* deals out straightforward seafood dishes at Via Machin 20 (closed Wed in winter). If you hanker for something meatier, *La Singular* on Via Arduino uses mostly land-based recipes (closed Mon except Aug), while in the right-angled streets of the new town, at Via Mazzini 59, the no-nonsense *Ristorante Mazzini* (no closing day) serves standard Italian dishes at reasonable prices and has a wood-fired oven for pizzas. For snacks, the fast-food joints by the port aren't bad.

There is an abundant supply of decent **bars** to repair to when required. The *Café Latino*, with an entrance in Via Manno, has parasols on the city wall overlooking the port, and serves ices and snacks as well as drinks, while the *Mill Inn* in Via Maiorca has beers and occasional live music.

Stintino and Pelosa

The tiny village of **STINTINO**, on Sardinia's northwestern tip, was until recently nothing more than a remote jumble of fishermen's cottages jammed between two narrow harbours. Fortunately its discovery by the tourist industry has not drastically altered it, and it remains a small, laid-back village and the only centre in the tongue of land forming the western arm of the **Golfo di Asinara**. Most of the sunning and swimming takes place further up the coast at La Pelosa, but the only cheapish **accommodation** in the area is in Stintino itself: the simple *Lina* at Via Lepanto 38 (☎079.523.071; ③), overlooking the Porto Vecchio; the smarter and more central *Silvestrino* at Via Sássari 12 (☎079.523.007; ⑤), which has an excellent trattoria that specializes in lobster soup; and the small and neat *Geranio Rosso*, Via XXI Aprile (☎079.523.292; ⑤), which has a pizzeria on site – the last two require at least half-board in summer. It's worth finding out about renting **apartments** in and around Stintino, available for as little as two or three days and costing about L40,000–75,000/€20.80–39 per person, depending on the season: contact Stintours (☎079.523.160) on Lungomare C. Colombo for information and bookings, where you can also rent **cars, mopeds** and **bikes**. Between two and six **buses** a day go to Stintino from Sássari, and there are organized bus trips from Alghero in the summer months.

Four kilometres up the road from Stintino a collection of tourist villages clutter up the otherwise idyllic promontory of **La Pelosa** – reached by taxi or rented transport from Stintino. Hotels and self-catering apartments back some of Sardinia's most deluxe **beaches**, with views out to the isles of Piana and the larger, elongated **Asinara**, the only known habitat of a miniature white ass from which the island takes its name, and previously a prison-island. In summer, you can explore it on daily boat excursions from Stintino, leaving at about 9.30am, returning at 5.30pm; the full visit including swimming-stops and guide costs around L55,000/€28.60.

travel details

TRAINS

Alghero to: Sássari (7–11 daily; 35min).

Arbatax to: Cágliari (May–Sept 1–2 daily via Mandas; 7hr).

Cágliari to: Arbatax (May–Sept 1–2 daily via Mandas; 7hr); Macomer (6–7 daily; 1hr 45min–3hr); Olbia (4–5 daily via Oristano and/or Ozieri-Chilivani; 4hr 30min); Oristano (hourly; 1hr–1hr 30 min); Sássari (3–4 daily direct or via Oristano and/or Ozieri-Chilivani; 3hr 20min–4hr 30min).

Macomer to: Nuoro (2–4 daily; 1hr 30min).

Nuoro to: Macomer (2–4 daily; 1hr 25min).

Olbia to: Cágliari (3 daily direct or via Ozieri-Chilivani; 3hr 40min–4hr); Golfo Aranci (4–6 daily; 20min); Macomer (3–4 daily direct or via Ozieri-Chilivani; 2hr 15min); Oristano (3–4 daily direct or via Ozieri-Chilivani; 2hr 40min–3hr 30min); Sássari (5–6 daily direct or via Ozieri-Chilivani; 2hr).

Oristano to: Cágliari (hourly; 1hr–1hr 30 min); Macomer (8–11 daily; 1hr); Olbia (5–6 daily direct or via Ozieri-Chilivani; 3hr); Sássari (4–5 daily direct or via Ozieri-Chilivani; 2hr 20min–3hr).

Sássari to: Alghero (8–11 daily; 35min); Cágliari (4 daily; 3hr 20min–4hr); Macomer (4 daily; 1hr 45min); Olbia (4 daily; 2hr); Oristano (4 daily; 2hr 40min).

BUSES

Alghero to: Bosa (4 daily; 1hr 10min–1hr 45min); Olbia (1 daily; 2hr); Sássari (hourly; 1hr).

Cágliari to: Macomer (5 daily; 2hr 30min); Nuoro (4 daily; 3hr 30min); Oristano (5 daily; 1hr 35min); Sássari (7 daily; 3hr 15min–3hr 50min).

Macomer to: Bosa (3 daily; 30min); Cágliari (5 daily; 2hr 15min); Nuoro (4 daily; 1hr); Oristano (5 daily; 50min); Sássari (4 daily; 1hr 15min).

Nuoro to: Cágliari (4–6 daily; 3hr 30min–5hr); Olbia (3–7 daily; 1hr 45min); Sássari (2–5 daily; 1hr 45min–2hr 30min).

Olbia to: Alghero (1 daily; 2hr); Arzachena (8–13 daily; 1hr 40min); Nuoro (6–7 daily; 1hr 45min); Palau (9–14 daily; 1hr); Porto Cervo (4–6 daily, not Sun in winter; 45min); Santa Teresa di Gallura (5–7 daily; 2hr); Sássari (Mon–Sat 2 daily; 1hr 40min).

Oristano to: Cágliari (5 daily; 1hr 25min); Macomer (5 daily; 1hr); Nuoro (4 daily; 2hr); Sássari (4 daily; 2hr 15min).

Sássari to: Alghero (hourly; 1hr); Bosa (1–5 daily; 2hr 10min); Cágliari (7 daily; 3hr 15min–3hr 45min); Olbia (Mon–Sat 1 daily; 1hr 45min); Stintino (3–8 daily; 1hr 15min).

FERRIES

Arbatax to: Civitavécchia (1–2 weekly; 10hr 30min); Fiumicino (mid-July to early Sept 2 weekly; 5hr 30min); Genoa (1–2 weekly; 16–20hr).

Cágliari to: Civitavécchia (1 daily; 14–17hr); Genoa (mid-July to early Sept 2 weekly; 20hr); Naples (1–2 weekly; 16hr 15min); Palermo (1 weekly; 13hr 30min); Trápani (1 weekly; 11hr).

Golfo Aranci to: Civitavécchia (1–21 weekly; 3hr 30min–8hr); Fiumicino (late June to early Sept 2–3 daily; 4hr); La Spezia (late June to early Sept 1 daily; 5hr 30min); Livorno (1–14 weekly; 9–10hr).

Olbia to: Civitavécchia (1–6 daily; 4hr–8hr); Genoa (3–14 weekly; 6–13hr); Livorno (June–Sept 4–7 weekly; 9hr).

Palau to: Genoa (April–Sept 1–4 weekly; 12hr); La Maddalena (2–4 hourly; 20min); Naples (April–Sept 1–2 weekly; 14hr).

Porto Torres to: Genoa (5–21 weekly; 6–13hr).

INTERNATIONAL FERRIES

Cágliari to: Tunis (1 weekly; 23hr 15min).

Palau to: Porto Vecchio, Corsica (April–Sept 1–2 weekly; 2hr 30min).

Porto Torres to: Toulon, France (April–Sept 1 weekly; 16hr).

Santa Teresa di Gallura to: Bonifacio, Corsica (4–18 daily; 1hr).

THE HISTORICAL FRAMEWORK

A specific Italian history is hard to identify. Italy wasn't formally a united country until 1861, and the history of the peninsula after the Romans is more one of warring city states and colonization and annexation by foreign powers. It's almost inconceivable now that Italy should fragment once again, but the regional differences remain strong and have even, in recent years, become a major factor in Italian politics.

EARLY TIMES

A smattering of remains exist from the Neanderthals who occupied the Italian peninsula half a million years ago, but the main period of colonization began after the last Ice Age. Evidence of **Paleolithic** settlements dates from this time, around 20,000 BC, the next development being the spread of **Neolithic** tribes across the peninsula, between 5000 and 6000 years ago. More sophisticated tribes developed towards the end of the prehistoric period, between 2400 and 1800 BC; those who left the most visible traces were the **Ligurians** (who inhabited a much greater area than modern Liguria), the **Siculi** of southern Italy and Latium, and the **Sards**, who farmed and raised livestock on Sardinia. More advanced still were

migrant groups from the eastern Mediterranean, who introduced the techniques of working copper. Later, various **Bronze Age** societies (1600–1000 BC) built a network of farms and villages in the Apennines, and on the Sicilian and southern coasts, the latter population trading with Mycenaeans in Greece.

Other tribes brought Indo-European languages into Italy. The Veneti, Latins and Umbrii moved down the peninsula from the north, whilst the Piceni and the Messapians in Puglia crossed the Adriatic from what is now Croatia. The artificial line between prehistory and history is drawn around the eighth century BC, with the arrival of the **Phoenician** alphabet and writing system. Sailing west along the African coast, the Phoenicians established colonies in Sicily and Sardinia, going on to build trade links between Carthage and southern Italy. These soon encouraged the arrival of the **Carthaginians**, who set themselves up on Sicily, Sardinia and the Latium coast, at the same time as both **Greeks** and **Etruscans** were gaining influence.

ETRUSCANS AND GREEKS

Greek settlers colonized parts of the Tuscan coast and the Bay of Naples in the eighth century BC, moving on to **Naxos** on Sicily's Ionian coast, and founding the city of Syracuse in the year 736 BC. The colonies they established in Sicily and southern Italy came to be known as **Magna Graecia**. Along with Etruscan cities to the north they were the earliest Italian civilizations to leave substantial buildings and written records.

The Greek settlements were hugely successful, introducing the vine and the olive to Italy, and establishing a high-yielding agricultural system. Cities like **Syracuse** and **Tarentum** were wealthier and more sophisticated than those on mainland Greece, dominating trade in the central Mediterranean, despite competition from Carthage. Ruins such as the temples of **Agrigento** and **Selinunte**, the fortified walls around Gela, and the theatres at Syracuse and Taormina on Sicily attest to a great prosperity, and Magna Graecia became an enriching influence on the culture of the Greek homeland – Archimedes, Aeschylus and Empedocles were all from Sicily. Yet these colonies suffered from the same factionalism as the Greek states, and the cities of Tarentum, Metapontum, Sybaris and Croton were united only when faced with the threat of outside invasion. From 400 BC, after Sybaris was razed to the ground, the other colonies went into irreversible economic decline, to become satellite states of Rome.

The **Etruscans** were the other major civilization of the period, mostly living in the area between the **Tiber** and **Arno** rivers. Their language, known mostly from funerary texts, is one of the last relics of an ancient language common to the Mediterranean. Some say they arrived in Italy around the ninth century BC from western Anatolia, others that they came from the north, and a third hypothesis places their origins in Etruria. Whatever the case, they set up a cluster of **twelve city states** in northern Italy, traded with Greek colonies to the south and were the most powerful people in northern Italy by the sixth century BC, edging out the indigenous population of Ligurians, Latins and Sabines. Tomb frescoes in Umbria and Lazio depict a refined and luxurious culture with highly developed systems of divination, based on the reading of animal entrails and the flight of birds. Herodotus wrote that the Etruscans recorded their ancestry along the female line, and tomb excavations last century revealed that women were buried in special sarcophagi carved with their names. Well-preserved chamber tombs with wall paintings exist at **Cerveteri** and **Tarquinia**, the two major sites in Italy. The Etruscans were technically advanced, creating new agricultural land through irrigation and building their cities on ramparted hilltops – a pattern of settlement that has left a permanent mark on central Italy. Their kingdom contracted, however, after invasions by the **Cumans**, **Syracusans** and **Gauls**, and was eventually forced into alliance with the embryonic Roman state.

ROMAN ITALY

The growth of **Rome**, a border town between the Etruscans and the Latins, gained impetus around 600 BC from a coalition of Latin and Sabine communities. The **Tarquins**, an Etruscan dynasty, oversaw the early expansion, but in 509 BC the Romans ejected the Etruscan royal family and became a **republic**, with power shared jointly between two consuls, both elected for one year. Further changes came half a century later, after a protracted class struggle that resulted in the **Law of the Twelve Tables**, which made patricians and plebeians equal. Thus stabilized, the Romans set out to systematically conquer the northern peninsula, and after the fall of Veii in 396 BC, succeeded in capturing **Sutri** and **Nepi**, towns which Livy considered the "barriers and gateways of Etruria". Various wars and truces with other cities brought about agreements to pay harsh tributes.

The **Gauls** captured Rome in 390, refusing to leave until they had received a vast payment, but this proved a temporary reversal. The Romans took **Campania** and the fertile land of Puglia after defeating the **Samnites** in battles over a period of 35 years. They then set their sights on the wealthy Greek colonies to the south, including Tarentum, whose inhabitants turned to the Greek king, **Pyrrhus of Epirus** for military support. He initially repelled the Roman invaders, but lost his advantage and was defeated at **Beneventum** in 275 BC. The Romans had by then established their rule in most of southern Italy, and now became a threat to Carthage. In 264 they had the chance of obtaining **Sicily**, when the Mamertines, a mercenary army in control of Messina, appealed to them for help against the Carthaginians. The Romans obliged – sparking off the **First Punic War** – and took most of the island, together with Sardinia and Corsica. With their victory in 222 BC over the Gauls in the Po Valley, all Italy was now under Roman control.

They also turned a subsequent military threat to their advantage, in what came to be known as the **Second Punic War**. The Carthaginians had watched the spread of Roman power across the Mediterranean with some alarm, and at the end of the third century BC they allowed **Hannibal** to make an Alpine crossing into Italy with his army of infantry, horsemen and elephants. Hannibal crushed the Roman legions at Lago Trasimeno and Cannae (216 BC), and then halted at Capua. With remarkable cool, considering Hannibal's proximity, **Scipio** set sail on a retaliatory mission to the Carthaginian territory of **Spain**, taking Cartagena, and continuing his journey into **Africa**. The Carthaginians recalled Hannibal, who was finally defeated by Roman troops at **Zama** in 202 BC. It was another fifty years before Carthage was taken, closely followed by all of Spain, but the Romans were busy in the meantime adding **Macedonian Greece** to their territory.

These conquests gave Roman citizens a tax-free existence subsidized by captured treasure, but society was sharply divided into those enjoying the benefits, and those who were not. The former belonged mostly to the **senatorial party**, who ignored demands for reform by their opposition, the popular party. The radical reforms sponsored by the tribune **Gaius Gracchus** came too close to democracy for the senatorial party, whose declaration of martial law was followed by the assassination of Gracchus. The majority of people realized that the only hope of gaining influence was through the army, but **General Gaius Marius**, when put into power, was ineffective against the senatorial clique, who systematically picked off the new regime.

The first century BC saw civil strife on an unprecedented scale. Although Marius was still in power, another general, Sulla, was in the ascendancy, leading military campaigns against northern invaders and rebellious subjects in the south. Sulla subsequently took power and established his dictatorship in Rome, throwing out a populist government which had formed while he was away on a campaign in the east. Murder and exile were common, and cities which had sided with Marius during their struggle for power were punished with massacres and destruction. Thousands of Sulla's war veterans were given confiscated land, but much of it was laid to waste. In 73 BC a gladiator named **Spartacus** led 70,000 dispossessed farmers and escaped slaves in a revolt, which lasted for two years before they were defeated by the legions.

JULIUS CAESAR AND AUGUSTUS

Rome became calmer only after Sulla's death, when **Pompey**, another general, and **Licinus Crassus**, a rich builder, became masters of Rome. Pompey's interest lay in lucrative wars elsewhere, so his absence from the capital gave Julius Caesar the chance to make a name for himself as an orator and raiser of finance. When Pompey returned in 60 BC, he made himself, Crassus and Caesar rulers of the **first Triumvirate**.

Caesar bought himself the post of consul in 59 BC, then spent the next eight years on campaigns againt the **Gauls**. His military success needled Pompey, and trouble began. Pompey eventually turned against his colleague, giving Caesar the chance to hit back. In 49 BC he crossed the river **Rubicon**, committing the offence of entering Roman territory with an army without first informing the Senate, but when he reached the city there was no resistance – everyone had fled, and Caesar became absolute ruler of Rome. He spent the next four years on civil reforms, writing his history of the Gallic wars, and chasing Pompey and his followers through Spain, Greece and Egypt. A group of enemies within the Senate, including his adopted son **Brutus**, conspired to murder him in 44 BC, a few months after he had been appointed ruler for life. **Octavian**, Caesar's nephew and heir, Lepidus, and Marcus Antonius **(Mark Anthony)** formed the **second Triumvirate** the following year. Again, the arrangement was fraught with tensions, the battle for power this time being between Anthony and Octavian. While Anthony was with **Cleopatra**, Octavian spent his time developing his military strength and the final, decisive battle took place at **Actium** in 31 BC, where Anthony committed suicide.

As sole ruler of the new regime, Octavian, renaming himself **Augustus Caesar**, embarked on a series of reforms and public works, giving himself complete powers despite his unassuming official title of "First Citizen".

THE EMPERORS

Tiberius (AD 14–37), the successor to Augustus, ruled wisely, but thereafter began a period of decadence. During the psychopathic reign of **Caligula** (37–41) the civil service kept the empire running; **Claudius** (41–54) conquered southern Britain, and was succeeded by his stepson **Nero** (54–68), who murdered his mother Agrippina and his wife Octavia, moving on to violent persecution of the **Christians**. Nero committed suicide when threatened by a coup, leading to a rapid succession of four emperors in the year 68. The period of prosperity during the rule of the **Flavian** emperors (Vespasian and his sons Titus and Domitian) was a forerunner for the **Century of the Antonines**, a period named after the successful reigns of Nerva, Trajan, Hadrian, Antonius and **Marcus Aurelius**. These generals consolidated the empire's infrastructure, and created an encouraging environment for artistic achievement. A prime example is the formidable bronze equestrian statue of Marcus Aurelius in Rome – a work not equalled in sophistication until the Renaissance.

A troubled period followed under the rule of Marcus Aurelius' son **Commodus** (180–93) and his successors, none of whom were wholly in control of the legions. Artistic, intellectual and religious life stagnated, and the balance of economic development tilted in favour of the north, while the agricultural south grew ever more impoverished.

BARBARIANS AND BYZANTINES

In the middle of the third century, incursions by **Goths** in Greece, the Balkans and Asia, and the **Franks** and **Alamanni** in Gaul foreshadowed the collapse of the empire. **Aurelian** (270–75) re-established some order after terrible civil wars, to be followed by **Diocletian** (284–305), whose persecution of Christians produced many of the Church's present-day saints. **Plagues** had decimated the population, but problems of a huge but static economy were compounded by the doubling in size of the army at this time to about half a million men. To ease administration, Diocletian **divided the empire** into two halves, east and west, basing himself as ruler of the western empire in Mediolanum (Milan). This measure brought about a relative recovery, coinciding with the rise of **Christianity**, which was declared the state religion during the reign of **Constantine** (306–337). **Constantinople**, capital of the eastern empire, became a thriving trading and manufacturing city, while Rome itself went into decline, as the enlargement of the senatorial estates and the impoverishment of the lower classes gave rise to something comparable to a primitive feudal system.

Barbarians (meaning outsiders, or foreigners) had been crossing the border into the empire since 376 AD, when the **Ostrogoths** were driven from their kingdom in southern Russia by the **Huns**, a tribe of ferocious horsemen. The Huns went on to attack the **Visigoths**, 70,000 of whom crossed the border and settled inside the empire. When the Roman aristocracy saw that the empire was no longer a shield against barbarian raids, they were less inclined to pay for its support, seeing that a more comfortable future lay in being on good terms with the barbarian successor states.

By the fifth century, many legions were made up of troops from conquered territories, and several posts of high command were held by outsiders. With little will or loyalty behind it, the **empire floundered**, and on New Year's Eve of 406, Vandals, Alans and Sueves crossed the frozen Rhine into Gaul, chased by the Huns from their kingdoms in what are now Hungary and Austria. Once this had happened, there was no effective frontier. A contemporary writer lamented that "the whole of Gaul is smoking like an enormous funeral pyre". Despite this shock, worse was to come. By 408, the imperial government in Ravenna could no longer hold off **Alaric** (commander of Illyricum – now Croatia), and he went on to **sack** Rome in 410, causing a crisis of morale in the west. "When the whole world perished in one city," wrote Saint Jerome, "then I was dumb with silence."

The bitter **end of the Roman Empire** in the west came after **Valentinian III**'s assassination in 455. His eight successors over the next twenty years were finally ignored by the Germanic troops in the army, who elected their general **Odoacer** as king. The remaining Roman aristocracy hated him, and the eastern emperor, **Zeno**, who in theory now ruled the whole empire, refused to recognize him. In 488, Zeno rid himself of the Ostrogoth leader **Theodoric** by persuading him to march on Odoacer in Italy. By 493, Theodoric had succeeded, becoming ruler of the western territories.

A lull followed. The Senate in Rome and the civil service continued to function, and the remains of the empire were still administered under Roman law. Ostrogothic rule of the west continued after Theodoric's death, but in the 530s the eastern emperor, **Justinian**, began to plan the reunification of the Roman Empire "up to the two oceans". In 536 his general **Belisarius** landed in Sicily and moved north through Rome to Ravenna; complete reconquest of the Italian peninsula was achieved in 552, after which the Byzantines retained a presence in the south and in Sardinia for 500 years.

During this time the **Christian Church** developed as a more or less independent authority, since the emperor was at a safe distance in Constantinople. Continual invasions had led to an uncertain political scene in which the **bishops of Rome** emerged with the strongest voice – justification of their primacy having already been given by Pope Leo I (440–461), who spoke of his right to "rule all who are ruled in the first instance by Christ". A confused period of rule followed, as armies from northern Europe tried to take more territory from the old empire.

LOMBARDS AND FRANKS

During the chaotic sixth century, the **Lombards**, a Germanic tribe, were driven southwest into Italy. Rome was successfully defended against them, but by the eighth century the Lombards were extending their power throughout the peninsula. In the middle of that century the **Franks** arrived from Gaul. They were orthodox Christians, and therefore acceptable to Gallo-Roman nobility, integrating quickly and taking over much of the provincial administration. The Franks were ruled by the Merovingian royal family, but the mayors of the palace – the Carolingians – began to take power in real terms. Led by **Pepin the Short**, they saw an advantage in supporting the papacy, giving Rome large endowments and forcibly converting pagans in areas they conquered. When Pepin wanted to oust the Merovingians, and become King of the Franks, he appealed to the pope in Rome for his blessing, who was happy to agree, anointing the new Frankish king with holy oil.

This alliance was useful to both parties. In 755 the pope called on the Frankish army to confront the Lombards. The Franks forced them to hand over treasure and 22 cities and castles, which then became the northern part of the **Papal States**. Pepin died in 768, with the Church indebted to him. According to custom, he divided the kingdom between his two sons, one of whom died within three years. The other was Charles the Great, or **Charlemagne**.

An intelligent and innovative leader, Charlemagne was proclaimed King of the Franks and of the Lombards, and patrician of the Romans, after a decisive war against the Lombards in 774. On Christmas Day of the year 800, Pope Leo III expressed his gratitude for Charlemagne's political support by crowning him **Emperor of the Holy Roman Empire**, an investiture that forged an enduring link between the fortunes of Italy and those of northern Europe. By the time Charlemagne died, all of Italy from south of Rome to Lombardy, including Sardinia, was part of the huge **Carolingian Empire**. The parts which didn't come under his domain were Sicily and the southern coast, which were gradually being reconquered by Arabs from Tunisia; and Puglia and Calabria, colonized by Byzantines and Greeks.

The task of holding these gains was beyond Charlemagne's successors, and by the beginning of the tenth century the family was extinct and the rival Italian states had become prizes for which the western (French) and eastern (German) Frankish kingdoms competed. Power switched in 936 to **Otto**, king of the eastern Franks. Political disunity in Italy invited him to intervene, and in 962 he was crowned emperor; Otto's son and grandson (Ottos II and III) set the seal on the renewal of the Holy Roman Empire.

POPES AND EMPERORS

On the death of **Otto III** in 1002, Italy was again without a recognized ruler. In the north, noblemen jockeyed for power, and the papacy was manipulated by rival Roman families. The most decisive events were in the south, where Sicily, Calabria and Puglia were captured by the **Normans**, who proved effective administrators and synthesized their own culture with the existing half-Arabic, half-Italian south. In **Palermo** in the eleventh century they created the most dynamic culture of the Mediterranean world.

Meanwhile in Rome, a series of reforming popes began to strengthen the church. **Gregory VII**, elected in 1073, was the most radical, demanding the right to depose emperors if he so wished. **Emperor Henry IV** was equally determined for this not to happen. The inevitable quarrel broke out, over a key appointment to the archbishopric of Milan. Henry denounced Gregory as "now not pope, but false monk"; the pope responded by excommunicating him, thereby freeing his subjects from their allegiance. By 1077 Henry was aware of his tactical error and tried to make amends by visiting the pope at **Canossa**, where the emperor, barefoot and penitent, was kept waiting outside for three days. The formal reconciliation thus did nothing to heal the rift, and Henry's son, **Henry V**, continued the feud, eventually coming to a compromise in which the emperor kept control of bishops' land ownership, while giving up rights over their investiture.

After this symbolic victory, the papacy developed into the most comprehensive and advanced centralized government in Europe in the realms of law and finance, but it wasn't long before unity again came under attack. This time, the threat came from **Emperor Frederick I** (Barbarossa), who besieged many northern Italian cities from his base in Germany from 1154. **Pope Alexander III** responded with ambiguous pronouncements about the imperial crown being a "benefice" which the pope conferred, implying that the emperor was the pope's vassal. The issue of papal or imperial supremacy was to polarize the country for the next two hundred years, almost every part of Italy being torn by struggles between **Guelphs** (supporting the pope) and **Ghibellines** (supporting the emperor).

Henry's son, **Frederick II**, assumed the imperial throne at the age of three and a half, inheriting the Norman **Kingdom of Sicily**. Later linked by marriage to the great **Hohenstaufen** dynasty in Germany, he inevitably turned his attentions to northern Italy. However, his power base was small, and opposition from Italian comune and the papacy snowballed into civil war. His sudden death in 1250 marked a major downturn in imperial fortunes.

THE EMERGENCE OF CITY STATES

Charles of Anjou, brother of King Louis IX of France, defeated Frederick II's heirs in southern Italy, and received **Naples** and **Sicily** as a reward from the pope. His oppressive government finally provoked an uprising on Easter Monday 1282, a revolt that came to be known as the **Sicilian Vespers**, as some two thousand occupying soldiers were murdered in Palermo at the sound of the bell for vespers. For the next twenty years the French were at war with **Peter of Aragon**, who took Sicily and then tried for the southern mainland.

If imperial power was on the defensive, the papacy was in even worse shape. Knowing that the pontiff had little military backing or financial strength left, **Philip of France** sent his men to the pope's summer residence in 1303, subjecting the old man to a degrading attack. Boniface died within a few weeks; his French successor, Clement V, promptly moved the papacy to **Avignon**.

The declining political power of the major rulers was countered by the growing autonomy of the cities. By 1300, a broad belt of some three hundred virtually **independent city states** stretched from central Italy to the northernmost edge of the peninsula. In the middle of the century the population of Europe was

savagely depleted by the **Black Death** – brought into Europe by a Genoese ship returning from the Black Sea – but the city states survived, developing a concept of citizenship quite different from the feudal lord-and-vassal relationship. By the end of the fourteenth century the richer and more influential states had swallowed up the smaller **comune**, leaving four as clear political front runners. These were **Genoa** (controlling the Ligurian coast), **Florence** (ruling Tuscany), **Milan**, whose sphere of influence included Lombardy and much of central Italy, and **Venice**. Smaller principalities, such as Mantua and Ferrara, supported armies of mercenaries, ensuring their security by building impregnable fortress-palaces.

Perpetual vendettas between the propertied classes often induced the citizens to accept the overall rule of one **signore** in preference to the bloodshed of warring clans. A despotic form of government evolved, sanctioned by official titles from the emperor or pope, and by the fifteenth century most city states were under princely rather than republican rule. In the south of the fragmented peninsula was the **Kingdom of Naples**; the **States of the Church** stretched up from Rome through modern-day Marche, Umbria and the Romagna; **Siena, Florence, Modena, Mantua** and **Ferrara** were independent states, as were the **Duchy of Milan**, and the maritime republics of **Venice** and **Genoa**, with a few odd pockets of independence like Lucca, for example, and Rimini.

The commercial and secular city states of late medieval times were the seed bed for the **Renaissance**, when urban entrepreneurs (such as the Medici) and autocratic rulers (such as Federico da Montefeltro) enhanced their status through the financing of architectural projects, paintings and sculpture. It was also at this time that the Tuscan dialect – the language of Dante, Petrarch and Boccaccio – became established as Italy's literary language; it later became the nation's official spoken language.

By the mid-fifteenth century the five most powerful states – Naples, the papacy, Milan, and the republics of Venice and Florence – reached a tacit agreement to maintain the new balance of power. Yet though there was a balance of power at home, the history of each of the independent Italian states became inextricably bound up with the power politics of other European countries.

FRENCH AND SPANISH INTERVENTION

The inevitable finally happened when an Italian state invited a larger power in to defeat one of its rivals. In 1494, at the request of the Duke of Milan, **Charles** VIII of France marched south to renew the Angevin claim to the Kingdom of Naples. After the accomplishment of his mission, Charles stayed for three months in Naples, before heading back to France; the kingdom was then acquired by **Ferdinand II of Aragon**, subsequently ruler of all Spain.

The person who really established the Spanish in Italy was the Habsburg Charles V (1500–1558), who within three years of inheriting both the Austrian and Spanish thrones bribed his way to being elected Holy Roman Emperor. In 1527 the imperial troops sacked **Rome**, a calamity widely interpreted at the time as God's punishment to the disorganized and dissolute Italians. The French remained troublesome opposition, but they were defeated at Pavia in 1526 and Naples in 1529. With the treaty of Cateau-Cambresis in 1559, Spain held Sicily, Naples, Sardinia, the Duchy of Milan and some Tuscan fortresses, and they were to exert a stranglehold on Italian political life for the next 150 years. The remaining smaller states became satellites of either Spanish or French rule; only the papacy and Venice remained independent.

Social and economic troubles were as severe as the political upheavals. While the papacy combatted the spread of the **Reformation** in northern Europe, the major manufacturing and trading centres were coming to terms with the opening up of the Atlantic and Indian Ocean trade routes – discoveries which meant that northern Italy would increasingly be bypassed. Mid-sixteenth-century **economic recession** prompted wealthy Venetian and Florentine merchants to invest in land rather than business, while in the south high taxes and repressive feudal regimes produced an upsurge of banditry and even the raising of peasant militias – resistance that was ultimately suppressed brutally by the Spanish.

The seventeenth century was a low point in Italian political life, with little room for manoeuvre between the papacy and colonial powers. The Spanish eventually lost control of Italy at the start of the eighteenth century when, as a result of the War of the Spanish Succession, Lombardy, Mantua, Naples and Sardinia all came under Austrian control. The machinations of the major powers led to **frequent realignments** in the first half of the century. Piemonte, ruled by the Duke of Savoy, Victor Amadeus II, was forced in 1720 to surrender Sicily to the Austrians in return for Sardinia. In 1734 Naples and Sicily passed to the Spanish Bourbons, and three years later the House of Lorraine acquired Tuscany on the extinction of the Medici.

Relatively enlightened Bourbon rule in the south did little to arrest the economic polarization of society, but the northern states advanced under the intelligent if autocratic rule of Austria's **Maria Theresa** (1740–80) and her son **Joseph II** (1780–92) who prepared the way for early industrialization. Lightning changes came in April 1796, when the French armies of Napoleon invaded northern Italy. Within a few years the French had been driven out again, but by 1810 Napoleon was in command of the whole peninsula, and his puppet regimes remained in charge until Waterloo. Napoleonic rule had profound effects, reducing the power of the papacy, reforming feudal land rights and introducing representative government to Italy. Elected assemblies were provided on the French model, giving the emerging middle class a chance for political discussion and action.

UNIFICATION

The fall of Napoleon led to the Vienna Settlement of 1815, by which the Austrians effectively restored the old ruling class. **Metternich**, the Austrian Chancellor, did all he could to foster any local loyalties that might weaken the appeal of unity, yet the years between 1820 and 1849 became years of revolution. Uprisings began in Sicily, Naples and Piemonte, when **King Ferdinand** introduced measures that restricted personal freedom and destroyed many farmers' livelihoods. A makeshift army quickly gained popular support in Sicily, and forced some concessions, before Ferdinand invited the Austrians in to help him crush the revolution. In the north, the oppressive laws enacted by **Vittorio Emanuele I** in the Kingdom of Piemont sparked off student protests and army mutinies in Turin. Vittorio Emanuele abdicated in favour of his brother, Carlo Felice, and his son, **Carlo Alberto**; the latter initially gave some support to the radicals, but Carlo Felice then called in the Austrians, and thousands of revolutionaries were forced into exile. Carlo Alberto became King of Piemont in 1831. A secretive, excessively devout and devious character, he did a major volte-face when he assumed the throne by forming an alliance with the Austrians.

In 1831 further uprisings occurred in Parma, Modena, the Papal States, Sicily and Naples. Their lack of co-ordination, and the readiness with which Austrian and papal troops intervened, ensured that revolution was short-lived. But even if these actions were unsustained, their influence grew.

One person profoundly influenced by these insurgencies was **Giuseppe Mazzini.** Arrested as Secretary of the Genoese branch of the Carbonari (a secret radical society) in 1827 and jailed for three months in 1830, he formulated his political ideology and set up **"Young Italy"** on his release. Among the many to whom the ideals of "Young Italy" appealed was **Giuseppe Garibaldi**, soon to play a central role in the **Risorgimento**, as the movement to reform and unite the country was known.

Crop failures in 1846 and 1847 produced widespread **famine** and **cholera outbreaks**. In Sicily an army of peasants marched on the capital, burning debt collection records, destroying property and freeing prisoners. Middle- and upper-class moderates were worried, and formed a government to control the uprising, but Sicilian **separatist** aims were realized in 1848. Fighting spread to Naples, where **Ferdinand II** made some temporary concessions, but nonetheless he retook Sicily the following year. At the same time as the southern revolution, serious disturbances took place in Tuscany, Piemonte and the Papal States. Rulers fled their duchies, and Carlo Alberto altered course again, prompted by Metternich's fall from power in Vienna; he granted his subjects a constitution and declared war on Austria. In Rome, the pope fled from rioting and Mazzini became a member of the city's republican triumvirate in 1849, with Garibaldi organizing the defences.

None of the uprisings lasted long. Twenty thousand revolutionaries were expelled from Rome, Carlo Alberto abdicated in favour of his son Vittorio Emanuele II after military defeats at the hands of the Austrians, and the dukes returned to Tuscany, Modena and Parma. One thing which did survive was Piemonte's constitution, which throughout the 1850s attracted political refugees to this cosmopolitan state.

CAVOUR AND GARIBALDI

Nine years of radical change began when **Count Camillo Cavour** became Prime Minister of Piemonte in 1852. The involvement of Piemontese troops in the Crimean War brought Cavour into contact with Napoleon III at the Congress of Paris, at which the hostilities were ended, and in July 1858 the two men had secret talks on the "Italian question". Napoleon III had decided to support Italy in its fight against the Austrians – the only realistic way of achieving unification – as long as resistance was non-revolutionary. Having bargained over the division of territory, they waited for a chance to provoke Austria into war. This came in 1859, when Cavour wrote an emotive anti-Austrian speech for Vittorio Emanuele at the opening of parliament. His battle cry for an end to the **grido di dolore** (cry of pain) was taken up over Italy. The Austrians ordered demobilization by the Piemontese, who did the reverse.

The war was disastrous from the start, and thousands died at Magenta and Solferino. In July 1859, Napoleon III made a truce with the Austrians without consulting Cavour, who resigned in fury. Provisional governments remained in power in Tuscany, Modena and the Romagna. Cavour returned to government in 1860, and soon France, Piemonte and the papacy agreed to a series of plebiscites, a move which ensured that by mid-March of 1860, **Tuscany** and the new state of **Emilia** (duchies of Modena and Parma plus the Romagna) had voted for **union with Piemonte**. A secret treaty between Vittorio Emanuele and Napoleon III ceded Savoy and Nice to France, subject to plebiscites. The result was as planned, no doubt due in part to the presence of the French Army during voting.

Garibaldi promptly set off for Nice with the aim of blowing up the ballot boxes, only to be diverted when he reached Genoa, where he heard of an **uprising in Sicily**. Commandeering two old paddle steamers and obtaining just enough rifles for his thousand Red Shirts, he headed south. More support came when they landed in Sicily, and Garibaldi's army outflanked the 12,000 Neapolitan troops to take the island. After that, they crossed to the mainland, easily occupied Naples, then struck out for Rome. Cavour, anxious that he might lose the initiative, hastily dispatched a Piemontese army to **annex the Papal States**, except for the Patrimony around Rome. Worried by the possibility that the anti-Church revolutionaries who made up the Red Shirt army might stir up trouble, Cavour and Vittorio Emanuele travelled south to Rome, accompanied by their army, and arranged plebiscites in Sicily, Naples, Umbria and the Papal Marches that offered little alternative but to vote for annexation by Piemonte. After their triumphal parade through Naples, they thanked Garibaldi for his trouble, took command of all territories and held elections to a new parliament. In February 1861, the members formally announced the **Kingdom of Italy.**

Cavour died the same year, before the country was completely unified, since Rome and Venice were still outside the kingdom. Garibaldi marched unsuccessfully on Rome in 1862, and again five years later, by which time Venice had been subsumed. It wasn't until Napoleon III was defeated by Prussia in 1870 that the French troops were ousted from Rome. Thus by 1871 **Unification** was complete.

THE WORLD WARS

After the Risorgimento, some things still hadn't changed. The ruling class were slow to move towards a broader based political system, while living standards actually worsened in some areas, particularly in Sicily. When Sicilian peasant farmers organized into **fasci** – forerunners of trade unions – the prime minister sent in 30,000 soldiers, closed down newspapers and interned suspected troublemakers without trial. In the 1890s capitalist methods and modern machinery in the Po Valley created a new social structure, with rich **agrari** at the top of the pile, a mass of farm labourers at the bottom, and an intervening layer of estate managers.

In the 1880s Italy's **colonial expansion** began, initially concentrated in bloody – and ultimately disastrous – campaigns in Abyssinia and Eritrea in 1886. In 1912 Italy wrested the Dodecanese islands and Libya from Turkey, a development deplored by many, including **Benito Mussolini**, who during this war was the radical secretary of the PSI (Partito Socialista Italiano) in Forlì.

WORLD WAR I AND THE RISE OF MUSSOLINI

Italy entered **World War I** in 1915 with the chief aims of settling old scores with Austria and furthering its colonial ambitions through French and British support. A badly equipped, poorly commanded army took three years to force Austria into defeat, finally achieved in the last month of the war at Vittorio Veneto. Some territory was gained – Trieste, Gorizia, and what became Trentino-Alto Adige – but at the cost of over half a million dead, many more wounded, and a mountainous war debt.

The middle classes, disillusioned with the war's outcome and alarmed by inflation and social unrest, turned to Mussolini, now a figurehead of the Right. In 1921, recently elected to parliament, Mussolini formed the Partito Nazionale Fascista, whose **squadre** terrorized their opponents by direct personal attacks and the destruction of newspaper offices, printing shops, and socialist and trade union premises. By 1922 the party was in a position to carry out an insurrectionary **"March on Rome"**. Plans for the march were leaked to Prime Minister Facta, who needed the king's signature on a martial law decree if the army were to meet the march. Fears of civil war led to the king's refusal. Facta resigned, Mussolini made it clear that he would not join any government he did not lead, and on October 29 **was awarded the premiership**. Only then did the march take place.

Zealous **squadristi** now urged Mussolini towards **dictatorship**, which he announced early in 1925. Political opposition and trade unions were outlawed, the free press disintegrated under censorship and Fascist takeovers, elected local governments were replaced by appointed officials, powers of arrest and detention were increased, and special courts were established for political crimes. In 1929, Mussolini ended a sixty-year feud between Church and State by reorganizing the **Vatican** as an autonomous Church state within the Kingdom of Italy. (As late as 1904, anyone involved in the new regime, even as a voter, had been automatically excommunicated.) By 1939, the motto "Everything within the State; nothing outside the State; nothing against the State" had become fact, with the government controlling the larger part of Italy's steel, iron and ship-building industries, as well as every aspect of political life.

WORLD WAR II

Mussolini's involvement in the **Spanish Civil War** in 1936 brought about the formation of the "**Axis**" with Nazi Germany. Italy entered **World War II** totally unprepared and with outdated equipment, but in 1941 invaded Yugoslavia to gain control of the Adriatic coast. Before long, though, Mussolini was on the defensive. Tens of thousands of Italian troops were killed on the Russian front in the winter of 1942, and in July 1943 the Allied forces gained a first foothold in Europe, when Patton's American Seventh Army and the British Eighth Army under Montgomery landed in Sicily. A month later they controlled the island.

In the face of these and other reversals Mussolini was overthrown by his own Grand Council, who bundled him away to the isolated mountain resort of Gran Sasso, and replaced him with the perplexed **Marshal Badoglio**. The Allies wanted Italy's surrender, for which they secretly offered amnesty to the king, Vittorio Emanuele III, who had coexisted with the Fascist regime for 21 years. On September 8 a radio broadcast announced that an **armistice** had been signed, and on the following day the Allies crossed onto the mainland. As the Anglo-American army moved up through the peninsula, German divisions moved south to meet them, springing Mussolini from jail to set up the **republic of Salò** on Lago di Garda. It was a total failure, and increasing numbers of men and women from Communist, Socialist or Catholic parties swelled the opposing partisan forces to 450,000. In April 1945 Mussolini fled for his life, but was caught by partisans before reaching Switzerland. He and his lover, Claretta Petacci, were shot and strung upside down from a filling station roof in Milan's Piazzale Loreto.

THE POSTWAR YEARS

A popular mandate declared Italy a republic in 1946, and Alcide de Gasperi's **Democrazia Cristiana** (DC) party formed a government. He remained in power until 1953, sustained by a succession of coalitions. Ever since then, the regular formation and disintegration of governments has been the norm, a political volatility that reflects the sharp divisions between rural and urban Italy, and between the north and the south of the country. A strong manufacturing base and large-scale agriculture have given most people in the north a better material standard of living than previous generations, but the south still lags far behind, despite such measures as the establishment in 1950 of the Cassa del Mezzogiorno development agency, which has pumped much-needed funds into the region.

During the 1950s Italy became a front-rank industrial nation, massive firms such as Fiat and Olivetti helping to double the Gross Domestic Product and triple industrial production. American financial aid – the Marshall Plan – was an important factor in this expansion, as was the availability of a large and compliant workforce, a substantial proportion of which was drawn from the villages of the south.

The DC at first operated in alliance with other right-wing parties, but in 1963, in a move precipitated by the increased politicization of the blue-collar workers, they were obliged to share power for the first time with the **Partito Socialista Italiano** (PSI). The DC politician who was largely responsible for sounding out the socialists was **Aldo Moro**, the dominant figure of Italian politics in the 1960s. Moro was prime minister from 1963 to 1968, a period in which the economy was disturbed by inflation and the removal of vast sums of money by wealthy citizens alarmed by the arrival in power of the PSI. The decade ended with the "**autunno caldo**" ("hot autumn") of 1969, when strikes, occupations and demonstrations paralysed the country.

THE 1970S AND 1980S

In the 1970s the situation worsened: bankruptcies increased, inflation hit twenty percent, and unemployment rocketed. More extreme forms of unrest broke out, instigated in the first instance by the far right, who were almost certainly behind a bomb which killed sixteen people in Piazza Fontana, Milan in 1969, and the Piazza della Loggia bombing in Brescia five years later. **Neo-fascist terrorism** continued throughout the next decade, reaching its hideous climax in 1980, when 84 people were killed and 200 wounded in a bomb blast at Bologna train station. At the same time, a plethora of left-wing terrorist groups sprang up, many of them led by disaffected intellectuals at the northern universities. The most active of these were the **Brigate Rosse** (Red Brigades). Founded in Milan in 1970, they reached the peak of their notoriety eight years later, when a

Red Brigade group kidnapped and killed Aldo Moro himself. A major police offensive in the early 1980s nullified most of the Brigate Rosse, but a number of hardline splinter groups from the various terrorist organizations – especially right-wing ones – are still in existence, as was proved in 1988 by the murder of an aide of the prime minister.

Inconsistencies and secrecy beset those trying to discover who was really responsible for the terrorist activity of the Seventies. One Red Brigade member who served 18 years in jail for his part in the assassination of Aldo Moro recently asserted that it was spies working for the **Italian secret services** and not bona fide members of the group who masterminded the operation. Alberto Franceschini told a parliamentary commission on terrorism in March 1999 that he believed that Brigade members Mario Moretti and Giovanni Senzani were both secret service plants who had infiltrated the group. Their involvement coincided with a particularly bloody phase of activity at a time when **Renato Curcio**, the orginal leader of the Red Brigades was betrayed to the authorities; the details of the kidnapping implied that certain privileged information was available; and both Moretti and Senzani were exceptional in being allowed to travel to the US when it was the usual US policy to refuse Italian Communists visas.

A recent report prepared by the PDS (Italy's party of the democratic left) for the same parliamentary commission stirred up controversy again in summer 2000. The report referred to the Establishment's **"strategy of tension"** in the 1970s and early 1980s in which it was said that indiscriminate bombing of the public and the threat of a right-wing coup were devices to stabilize centre-right political control of the country. The perpetrators of bombing campaigns were rarely caught, said the report, because "those massacres, those bombs, those military actions had been organized or promoted or supported by men inside Italian state institutions and, as has been discovered more recently, by men linked to the structures of United States intelligence". "Other bombing campaigns were attributed to the left to prevent the Communist Party from achieving power by democratic means" said Valter Bielli, PDS MP, and one of the report's authors. The report drew furious rebuttals from centre-right groups and the US embassy in Rome.

Yet the DC government survived, sustained by the so-called "historic compromise" negotiated in 1976 with **Enrico Berlinguer**, leader of the **Partito Comunista Italiano** (PCI). By this arrangement the PCI – polling 34 percent of the national vote, just three points less than the DC – agreed to abstain from voting in parliament in order to maintain a government of national unity. The pact was rescinded in 1979, and after Berlinguer's death in 1984 the PCI's share of the vote dropped to around 27 percent. The combination of this withdrawal of popular support and the collapse of the Communist bloc led to a realignment of the PCI under the leadership of **Achille Occhetto**, who turned the party into a democratic socialist grouping along the lines of left-leaning parties in Germany or Sweden – a transformation encapsulated by the party's new name – the **Partito Democratico della Sinistra** ("Democratic Party of the Left").

In its efforts to exclude the left wing from power, the DC had been obliged to accede to demands from minor parties such as the **Radical Party**, which gained eighteen seats in the 1987 election, one of them going to the porn star Ilona Staller, better known as **La Cicciolina**. Furthermore, the DC's reputation was severely damaged in the early 1980s by a series of scandals, notably the furore surrounding the activities of the P2 Masonic lodge, when links were discovered between corrupt bankers, senior DC members, and fanatical right-wing groups. As its popularity fell, the DC was forced to offer the premiership to politicians from other parties. In 1981 Giovanni Spadolini of the Republicans became the first non-DC prime minister since the war, and in 1983 **Bettino Craxi** was installed as the first premier from the PSI, a position he held for four years.

Even through the upheavals of the 1970s the national income of Italy continued to grow, and there developed a national obsession with **Il Sorpasso**, a term signifying the country's overtaking of France and Britain in the economic league table. Experts disagreed as to whether Il Sorpasso actually happened (most thought it hadn't), and calculations were complicated by the huge scale of tax evasion and other illicit financial dealings in Italy. All strata of society were involved in the withholding of money from central government, but the ruling power in this **economia sommersa** (submerged economy) was, and to a certain extent still is, the **Mafia**, whose contacts penetrate to the highest levels in Rome. The most traumatic proof of the Mafia's infiltration of the political hierarchy came in May 1992, with the murders of anti-Mafia judges **Giovanni Falcone** and **Paolo Borsellino**, whose killers could only have penetrated the judges' security with the help of inside information.

TO THE PRESENT DAY

The murders of the immensely respected Falcone and Borsellino might well come to be seen as marking a fault-line in the political history of modern Italy, and the late 1980s and early 1990s saw the rise of a number of new political parties, as people become disillusioned with the old DC-led consensus. One, Leoluca Orlando's La Rete ("Network"), was founded specifically to counter the Mafia in Sicily, but rapidly evolved into a coalition of groups opposed to the vested interests in the country's town halls and businesses. More successful has been the right-wing **Lega Nord** (Northern League), whose autocratic leader, **Umberto Bossi**, capitalized on northern frustration with the state, which they see as supporting a corrupt south on the back of the hard-working, law-abiding north. The Northern League's official aim is now a federation, with Italy divided into two or three parts; they have already dubbed the north "Padania" and minted a separate, unofficial currency (worthless in reality, but a powerful symbol of intent). Formerly a marginalized firebrand, Bossi is now one of the most feared men in Italian politics. The newer **Alleanza Democratica**, or Democratic Alliance, led by the more circumspect **Mario Segni**, offers a less divisive alternative to middle-of-the road voters, while the fascist MSI, renamed the **Alleanza Nazionale** (AN), or National Alliance and now a wide coalition of right-wingers led by the persuasive Gianfranco Tini (who calls himself a post-fascist), has gained ground in recent years.

In 1992 the new government of **Giuliano Amato** – a politician untainted by any hint of corruption – instigated the biggest round-up of Mafia members in nearly a decade, issuing 241 arrest warrants in Operation Leopard. However, this was nothing compared to the arrest in Palermo, at the beginning of 1993, of Salvatore "Toto" Riina, the Mafia **capo di tutti capi** (boss of bosses) and the man widely believed to

have been behind the Falcone and Borsellino killings. The arrest of Riina followed the testimony of numerous supergrasses; the result of the trials was that key members of the establishment began to be openly implicated in Mafia activities. For example, it was exposed that a murdered associate of the former prime minister **Giulio Andreotti** was the Mafia's man in Rome, a top-level fixer who would arrange acquittals from the Supreme Court in exchange for support. (Bettino Craxi once called Andreotti a fox, adding "sooner or later all foxes end up as fur coats.")

However, it was Craxi himself who was one of the first to fall from grace, at the beginning of the postwar Italian state's most turbulent period – **1992–96**. Craxi was at the centre of the powerful Socialist establishment that ran the key city of Milan, when in February 1992, a minor party official, Mario Chiesa, head of a Milan old people's home, was arrested on corruption charges. It was realized before very long that Chiesa represented just the tip of a long-established culture of kickbacks and bribes that went right to the top of the Italian political establishment, not just in Milan, nicknamed **tangentopoli** ("bribesville"), but across the entire country. By the end of that year thousands in the city were under arrest and the net was spreading. What came to be known as the **Mani Pulite** or Clean Hands investigation, led by the crusading Milan judge, Antonio di Pietro, was under way.

The mood of the country changed almost overnight. Suddenly people wanted the politicians, the party officials, all those who had been taking their slice of **tangentopoli**, out of office. The established Italian parties, most notably the Christian Democrats and the Socialists, were almost entirely wiped out in the municipal elections of 1993. Di Pietro's zeal in tracking down the villains, and in asserting the power of the judiciary over the political establishment, captured the imaginations of the nation in a series of televised trials, and it seemed that no one who had been part of the old order was safe.

The establishment wasn't finished yet, however, and the national **elections of 1994** saw yet another political force emerge to fill the power vacuum: the centre-right **Forza Italia** or "Come On Italy", led by the media mogul **Silvio Berlusconi**, who used the power of his TV stations to build support, and swept to power as prime minister in a populist alliance – his "Freedom Pole" coalition – with Bossi's Lega Nord and the fascist National Alliance. The fact that Berlusconi was not a politician was perhaps his greatest asset, and most Italians, albeit briefly, saw this as a new beginning – the end of the old, corrupt regime, and the birth of a truly modern Italian state. However, as one of the country's top northern industrialists, and a former crony of Craxi, Berlusconi was as bound up with the old ways as anyone. Not only did he resist all attempts to reduce the scope of his media business, with which, as prime minister, there was a clear conflict of interest, but in time it also emerged that he himself was to be investigated, in a series of inquiries into the tax dealings of his Fininvest group.

Despite the resignation of di Pietro at the end of 1994, Berlusconi was himself forced to resign after the withdrawal of Bossi's Lega Nord from the coalition, and the government collapsed. For once elections were not seen as a solution; instead President Scalfaro leaned on some of the less political, and therefore less corruptible, members of the leadership to form a new, relatively non-partisan government that would institute the necessary economic and political reforms. Led by the relatively colourless finance man **Lamberto Dini**, this administration managed to stagger on into 1995, if only because of the ongoing political crisis, but by the time 1996 arrived things had once again descended into chaos, with none of a number of compromise candidates able to put together a government. In an attempt to break the deadlock, Scalfaro called elections for April 1996.

Meanwhile, the trial of Giulio Andreotti, perhaps the most potent symbol of the sleazy postwar years, at last went ahead in Palermo and he had to answer charges of a long-term conspiracy with the Mafia. Andreotti, seven times Prime Minister of Italy and a senator for life, denied any association, and was acquitted in October 1999 aged 80 after a trial that lasted 5 years, with prosecution evidence depending on the testimony of Mafia informants. In January 1999, Craxi was convicted with twenty others of corruption in connection with kickbacks involving ENEL, the state electrical company. He was sentenced to five years in prison, but died a year later in exile in Tunisia.

Antonio Maccanico succeded Dini but was unable to form a convincing government. For the first time in Italy's history a broad centre-left alliance was formed; known as the **ulivo** (the "olive tree"), and led by **Romano Prodi**, head of the small **Partito Popolare Italiano** (the PPI, or Italian Peoples' Party), it succeeded Maccanico's government. In terms of numbers, ulivo was made up mostly of the PDS (the Democratic Party of the Left), though in order to gain a majority in the Chamber of Deputies the government formed alliances with most of the other parties, including the Lega Nord and the newly created Italian Communist Party, split from the Rifondazione Communista (the Marxist residue of the former PCI) in October 1998.

Compared with the turmoil of the early 1990s, the political situation had reached a fairly even plateau. The Christian Democratic party had dissolved; the shift from proportional representation to a first-past-the-post system had begun; and a trend towards two large coalitions – one to the centre-left and the other to the centre-right – indicated a major break from the fragmented, multiparty political landscape of the postwar era. In the mid- to late-1990s attention shifted to the economy. A series of austerity measures to bring down inflation and reduce public spending began as a prelude to the entry of the lira into the **ERM** (Exchange Rate Mechanism of the European Union). Italians were keen to join, in preparation for the single currency, the **euro**, and full economic and monetary union (EMU). They perceived huge benefits; if the euro was strong then interest rates would be low and they would be able to pay off their vast national debt. In addition, the federalism that other Europeans often fear is seen as a positive advantage in Italy – in 1998, **La Repubblica** noted how dissatisfied Italians were with rule by their own politicians, and how they would be much happier if decisions were made in Brussels. Austerity measures, including cuts in pensions and healthcare benefits (to facilitate Italy's qualification to join EMU in January 1999) provoked demonstrations in Rome and elsewhere.

In October 1998, the relatively prolonged period of stability ended when the Prodi government was defeated in a parliamentary vote of no confidence, carried by a majority of one. The implications of another round of political upheaval were too serious to ignore: with less than three months to the launch of a common European currency, the threat of global recession, and imminent NATO strikes against Serbia, Italy needed a credible government. President Scalfaro acted quickly and appointed the former leader of the Communist PDS, **Massimo D'Alema**, as Prime Minister designate. The government lasted for eighteen months before he quit after overwhelming defeat in regional elections in April 2000. President Carlo Azeglio Ciampi appointed Italy's finance minister and former PM, **Giuliano Amato**, to head up a weak centre-left coalition dominated by the Democratic Party of the Left (PDS).

Meanwhile, the popularity of the Alleanza Nazionale, with its anti-immigration policies, reflects a residual **racism** in present-day Italy. When a black woman was chosen as Miss Italy in 1996, she was criticized for being "unrepresentative of Italian beauty". And a clampdown on prostitution in 1998, which caused passionate national debate, was as much about disapproval of the thousands of immigrant African women making a living this way as it was about "cleaning up the streets".

The untangling of the corrupt systems of party favours and organized crime continues apace. Even di Pietro, the architect of Operation Clean Hands, came under investigation in 1997, though many regarded this as a political move to discredit him. The most influential public figure to have been tried in the late nineties, however, was **Berlusconi**, who was **convicted** and sentenced in August 1998 to two years and nine months in jail; Perhaps not surprisingly, Berlusconi has since been acquitted of a number of the charges against him, and, although further offences have come to light (bribing the judiciary among them), the ongoing proceedings have served more as a background to his resurgent politial career than anything else, with Forza Italia triumphing in the European elections of 1999, and doing well, too, in Italy's regional elections of April 2000.

These polls were a disaster for the ruling left coalition, and the prime minister Massimo d'Alema decided to call it a day immediately afterwards, bringing back Giuliano Amato, a long-established political fixer of the left, as the country's 58th prime minister since World War II. At the time of writing Amato was going to stagger through to the next general election in April 2001, but the left coaltion clearly doesn't pin too many hopes on him beating the more-popular-than-ever Berlusconi, and have looked to the slick and successful mayor of Rome, **Francesco Rutelli** to lead them.

In this way, Italian politics are perhaps much the same as they ever were, with one coalition quickly succeeding another. However, there is a feeling that the investigations of the early 1990s lanced a boil and that the country is moving on. The public sector now appears to operate slightly more for the benefit of its users than for state employees and cultural and artistic institutions have been renovated and injected with new funds.

In the Church's **Holy Year**, damaging evidence emerged of the extent to which the Catholic Church, motivated by anti-Communist ideology, helped the Nazis during World War II by laundering money and supplying intelligence about allied invasion plans. It seems that the **Vatican** may soon face the same scrutiny that the political system has undergone during the last decade.

On an everyday level Italians are concerned to improve their quality of life and are ready to try out new measures, among them **car-free** days in Rome, Florence, Milan and 143 other towns and cities, where for several consecutive Sundays at the beginning of 2000, cars and lorries were banned between the hours of 10am to 6pm (a central government fund of £300m paid for improved, subsidised transport on these days and free entry to museums and galleries). A **Slow Cities** movement is carrying the idea of a more tranquil, less stressed urban way of life forward, campaigning on a variety of issues including better food (less fast food) and a healthier environment.

PAINTING AND SCULPTURE

Italy's contribution to European painting and sculpture far surpasses that of any other nation. This is in part due to the triumph of the Renaissance period, but Italy can also boast many other remarkable artistic achievements, from the seventh century BC to modern times. The country's fragmented political history has led to strong regional characteristics in Italian art: Rome, Pisa, Siena, Florence, Milan, Venice, Bologna and Naples all have distinctive and recognizable traditions.

THE ETRUSCANS

Italian artistic history begins with the **Etruscans**, whose culture spanned the seventh to the first centuries BC. Etruscan art was distinct from that of Greece, then the dominant nation both politically and artistically, though in many other respects it consistently shows the impact of contemporary trends in Greece. Many of the finest Etruscan **sculptures** date from the sixth century BC. Among the best examples, both now in the Villa Giulia in Rome, are the *Apollo and Herakles* from Veio, and the *Sarcophagus of a Married Couple* from Cerveteri, the reclining figures of the latter a typical motif of Etruscan art – the faces realistic and expressive, with prominent eyes and enigmatic smiles, but otherwise scant attention paid to human anatomy. Depictions of animals, both real and imaginary, were also common,

most famous among which are the *Chimera* from Arezzo, now in the Museo Archeologico in Florence, and Rome's own emblem, the *She-Wolf*, in the Palazzo dei Conservatori – both from the fifth century BC.

Surviving Etruscan **wall paintings** are surprisingly numerous, especially considering that (apart from a few at Paestum) all of their Greek counterparts in Italy have vanished. The most outstanding array is in Tarquinia, which preserves examples ranging from the sixth to the first century BC; another fine group is at Chiusi. These paintings were at first of a religious or magic nature, initially intending to provide an amenable environment for the dead. Later, visionary views of the afterlife were attempted. With their bold drawing, bright colours and lively details, they have an immediate visual appeal.

THE ROMANS

Like the Etruscans, the **Romans** were heavily indebted to the Greeks for their art forms, happily adapting Greek models to suit their own purpose, though they had little taste for the aesthetic values that had played such a key role in Greek art. Admittedly, the great heroic statues of the Greeks were highly prized. Many were brought to Rome, while others were extensively imitated and copied, and some of the most famous pieces of Roman **sculpture** – the *Apollo Belvedere* and the *Venus of Cnidos* in the Vatican, the *Medici Venus* in the Uffizi – are actually Roman copies of lost Greek originals, though they are successful pieces of work in their own right.

The Empire's own contribution to artistic development is exemplified by Roman **portraiture**, which usually eschewed idealization in favour of an objective representation of the physical features, typically showing a bony facial structure, bare forehead, pursed lips and large eyes. Only occasionally, as in the reigns of Augustus and Hadrian, was this image softened. Marble portrait busts have survived in vast quantities, but the bronze equestrian statues – a particularly effective means of stressing the power and charisma of the emperor – were later melted down. Only that of Marcus Aurelius in Rome survives.

The Romans also made full and varied use of relief sculpture, not least in the carvings which adorned the front of **sarcophagi**, their main form of funerary art, and on the **triumphal arches** and **columns** erected to celebrate military victories. Some of these, like Trajan's Column in Rome, which dates from the second century AD, display a virtuoso skill and attention to detail in their depiction of great deeds and battles.

In the domestic environment, **wall paintings** were an essential feature, though relatively few survive. In Rome itself, there are the *Esquiline Landscapes* and *Aldobrandini Wedding*, and the frescoes from the Villa Livia, while the best examples are those preserved in the towns of Pompeii and Herculaneum after their submersion by the eruption of Mount Vesuvius in 79 AD. Some of these remain in situ, notably the spectacular paintings in the Villa dei Misteri; others have been moved to the Museo Nazionale in Naples. In general, a huge range of subject matter was tackled – landscapes, portraits, still lifes, mythologies and genre scenes – while both realistic and stylized approaches to the depiction of nature were attempted.

EARLY CHRISTIAN ART

The **early Christian** period saw an almost total rejection of sculpture, other than for sarcophagi, though the remarkable wooden doors of Santa Sabina in Rome – featuring the earliest known representation of the Crucifixion – are a notable exception. The earliest murals were created in the Roman catacombs, and show no great stylistic innovation, but increasingly Christian painters began to render a sense of expression to the facial features, in order that the emotions of pain, sorrow and ecstasy could be depicted, along with a richly symbolic pictorial vocabulary. But the early Christians favoured **mosaics** rather than painting as a medium. This painstaking art form had hitherto been associated with floor decoration, but it proved ideal for the decoration of the early churches, its inappropriateness for the depiction of movement in many ways responsible for the rigid artistic forms which took an increasing grip. The earliest surviving cycle, in Santa Maria Maggiore in **Rome**, dates from the second quarter of the fifth century, and is fairly small-scale. The slightly later group in the Mausoleo di Galla Placidia in **Ravenna**, the city which had by then assumed the status of capital of the western empire, are more monumental, their

daring geometric patterns, elaborate imagery and sublime colouring representing perhaps the first great milestone of Christian art.

Ravenna continued as a centre of artistic innovation when a century later it became in effect the Italian capital of **Byzantine** culture and politics. Many magnificent mosaic series were created, and three sets in particular far surpass in quality anything produced in Constantinople itself, or indeed anywhere else in its empire: at the church of San Vitale, where the mosaics are the central focus of the architecture itself; Sant'Apollinare Nuovo, whose two frieze processions were quite unlike anything previously seen in Italian art; and the church of Sant'Apollinare in Classe, whose apse mosaics exude a unique sense of peace and mystery.

THE MIDDLE AGES

Italy at first played a rather subsidiary role in the Europe-wide re-emergence from the Dark Ages. The **Byzantine tradition** proved surprisingly durable, particularly in Venice and Sicily, which both retained strong trading links with Constantinople. Throughout the twelfth century, Byzantine craftsmen proved that the art of mosaic was far from exhausted, providing works that are worthy successors to those at Ravenna in the Cappella Palatina of Palermo and the duomos of Cefalù and Monreale, and of course the Basilica of San Marco in Venice.

Many Italian **fresco cycles** of the period still show traces of Byzantine influence, and the style was also a feature of the great eleventh-century Benedictine art movement fostered by the abbey of Montecassino. Sadly, nearly all the products of this school have vanished, though the murals in Sant'Angelo in Formis near Capua give an approximate idea of what they must have looked like.

Because of the cost of frescoes, from the second quarter of the twelfth century **panel paintings** became increasingly important, particularly in Tuscany. Subjects fell into three main categories: the Madonna and Child with saints; the portrait of a saint surrounded by scenes from his life; or the *Christus Triumphans*, a large painted crucifix showing an open-eyed Christ with outstretched hands.

The art of **sculpture** was initially slow to revive after its long period in the doldrums, but it came to occupy a crucial role throughout

Europe during the Romanesque period, with Lombard and Emilian masons playing a key role in its dissemination. Just after the turn of the twelfth century, a master by the name of **Wiligelmo** carved at Modena what may well be the earliest of the great cathedral porches – a form that was to become one of the outstanding features of European medieval art. His bas-reliefs feature expressive figures grouped with considerable narrative skill, and they suggest at least some familiarity with classical works. The same sculptor may also have carved the magnificent episcopal throne in San Nicolò in Bari. **Nicolò**, a pupil of Wiligelmo, seems to have been responsible for most of the other great portals of northern Italy – those of the Sacra di San Michele, San Zeno in Verona, and of the cathedrals of Verona, Ferrara, Piacenza and Cremona. Towards the end of the century, this style was developed in and around Parma by **Benedetto Antelami**, who created the graceful *Deposition* relief in the cathedral, the profuse and lively decoration of the baptistery.

THE PRECURSORS OF RENAISSANCE

The distinction between **Gothic** and **Renaissance**, so marked in the painting and sculpture of other countries, is very blurred in Italy. In the mid-thirteenth century, what is normally considered one of the key planks of the Renaissance – the rediscovery of the full sense of form, beauty and modelling characteristic of classical art – had already occurred with the statues of the Porta Romana in **Capua**, fragments of which are preserved in the town's museum. These were commissioned by Emperor Frederick II, who wished to revive memories of the grandeur that was Rome. Increasingly, Italians came to believe that it was northern barbarians who had destroyed the arts, which it was now their own duty to revive.

A sculptor of south Italian origin who was doubtless familiar with the work at Capua, **Nicola Pisano** (c1220–84), developed this style, in four major surviving works – the pulpits of the Pisa Baptistery and the duomo in Siena, the Arca San Domenico in Bologna and the Fonte Gaia in Perugia. His figures have a sure sense of volume, with varying levels of relief used to create an illusion of space. **Arnolfo di Cambio** (c1245–1310), his assistant on some of these projects, developed the mix of classical

and Gothic features in his own works, which include the famous bronze *St Peter* in Rome, and the *Tomb of Cardinal de Braye* in San Domenico in Orvieto. The latter defined the format of wall tombs for the next century, showing the deceased lying on a coffin below the Madonna and Child, all set within an elaborate architectural framework.

Of even greater long-term significance was the achievement of **Giovanni Pisano** (c1248–1314), who abandoned his father's penchant for paganism, adopting instead new and dramatic postures for his figures which were quite unlike anything in the previous history of sculpture. This is nowhere more evident than in the statues he created for the facade of the duomo in Siena, which are placed high up rather than round the portals, and are a world away from their static counterparts on French cathedrals.

It was only in the last three decades of the thirteenth century that Italian painters finally began to break away from the time-honoured Byzantine formulas, a new sense of freedom initiated by **Pietro Cavallini** (active 1273–1308) in Rome and developed by the Florentine **Cimabue** (c1240–1302), who introduced rounded forms to his fresco of *The Madonna of St Francis* in the lower church at Assisi. His masterpiece, the Passion cycle in the upper church, is sadly ruined, but enough remains to give evidence of the overwhelming tragic grandeur it must once have possessed.

Whereas Cimabue's works were still rooted in the Byzantine tradition, and made no attempt to break away from a flat surface effect, a huge leap was made by his pupil and fellow Florentine, **Giotto di Bondone** (1266–1337), whose innovations were to define the entire subsequent course of Western art. Giotto decisively threw off the two-dimensional restrictions of painting, managing to give his pictures an illusion of depth. Thanks to having better materials at his disposal than Cimabue, his *Life of St Francis* in the upper church at Assisi survived remarkably well until the 1997 earthquake; his decoration of the Scrovegni Chapel in Padua, however, is still in good condition. These two great cycles are the best examples of Giotto's genius in all its many facets. Among these are such basic principles as a sense for the significant, unencumbered by surplus detail; the convincing treatment of action, movement, gesture and emotion; and total command over technical matters like figure modelling, foreshortening, and effects of light and shade.

THE FOURTEENTH AND EARLY FIFTEENTH CENTURIES

In spite of these momentous developments, the path towards the Renaissance was not to follow a continuous or consistent course. Indeed, the leading local school of painters in the fourteenth century was not that of Florence, but of neighbouring **Siena**, which had very different preoccupations. This had a great deal to do with the father figure, **Duccio di Buoninsegna** (c1255–1318), who did not go along the revolutionary path of Giotto, but instead breathed a whole new life into the Byzantine tradition. Duccio's sense of grandeur is well conveyed by the central panel of his masterpiece, the *Maestà*, in the Museo dell'Opera del Duomo of his native city. However, it is the small scenes of this vast altarpiece which bring out his best quality: that of a masterful storyteller, adept at arrangement, grouping and the depiction of expression, feeling and movement. Colour, which in Giotto is merely used to bring out the forms, becomes a leading component in its own right.

In spite of the presence in the city of the vibrant statues of Giovanni Pisano, subsequent Sienese painters found Duccio's narrative art the more potent model. **Simone Martini** (c1284–1344) began his career by painting a fresco counterpart of Duccio's *Maestà* in the Palazzo Pubblico, though his most celebrated work in this building, the commemorative *Equestrian Portrait of Guidoriccio da Fogliano*, is now widely regarded as a fake. His refined, graceful style depended above all on line, colour and decorative effects – seen to best effect in the cycle of *The Life of St Martin* in the lower church in Assisi and in the sumptuous, cunningly designed *Annunciation* in the Uffizi. The latter was painted in collaboration with his brother-in-law **Lippo Memmi** (d1357), who independently painted the *Maestà* in the Palazzo Pubblico in San Gimignano, and may also have been responsible for the dramatic New Testament frescoes in the Collegiata of the same town, traditionally ascribed to the otherwise unknown **Barna**.

Another Sienese painter who worked at Assisi was **Pietro Lorenzetti** (active 1306–45); his frescoes there show the impact of Giotto, and have a sense of pathos which is uncharacteristic of Sienese painting. His brother **Ambrogio Lorenzetti** (active 1319–47) was a more original artist, whose main achievement was the idiosyncratic *Allegory of Good and Bad Government* in the Palazzo Pubblico, which shows painting being used for a secular, didactic purpose for the first time and raises the landscape background to a new, higher status, with an awareness of perspective uncommon for this date. The other notable Sienese sculptor of the period was the mysterious **Lorenzo Maitani** (c1270–1330), who is associated with one work only – the wonderfully lyrical reliefs on the most sumptuous facade in Italy, that of the duomo in Orvieto.

In **Florence**, meanwhile, a whole group of painters consciously followed Giotto's style, without materially adding to it. The most talented was **Maso di Banco** (active 1320–1350), who was particularly skilled at conveying the master's sense of plastic form, while the most faithful was **Taddeo Gaddi** (d1366), whose son **Agnolo Gaddi** (d1396) carried the Giottesque tradition on to nearly the end of the century. **Bernardo Daddi** (c1290–1349), on the other hand, combined this tradition with aspects of the Sienese style. The sculptor **Andrea Pisano** (c1290–1348) succeeded Giotto as master mason of the campanile. The reliefs he executed for it, plus the bronze door he made for the baptistry, translate Giotto's pictorial language back into a three-dimensional format.

A reaction against the hegemony of the Giottesque style came with **Andrea Orcagna** (c1308–68) who was equally prominent as a painter and sculptor, developing a flowery, decorative idiom seen to best effect in the tabernacle in Orsanmichele. The paintings of Orcagna and his school re-established the hierarchical tradition of the Byzantines, and rejected the importance of spatial depth.

At the very end of the fourteenth century, the **International Gothic** style, originating in the Burgundian courts, swept across Europe. This introduced a new richness to the depiction of landscape, animals and costume, though it was unconcerned with intellectual matters. Its dissemination in Italy was largely due to **Gentile da Fabriano** (c1370–1427), whose *Adoration of the Magi* in the Uffizi (one of his relatively few surviving compositions) shows the gorgeously opulent surface effects of this style at its best. Another leading practitioner was

Masolino da Panicale (c1383–1447), who is best known for having begun the famous fresco cycle in Santa Maria del Carmine in Florence. In the same city, the new movement influenced Lorenzo Monaco (c1372–1425), whose work bridges the Florentine and Sienese traditions.

International Gothic took a particularly firm grip in Verona, chiefly through Antonio Pisanello (1395–1455). The latter's fame rests partly on his prowess as a medallist, and only a tantalizing handful of his paintings remain, notably the frescoes in the Veronese churches of Sant'Anastasia and San Fermo, and the Palazzo Ducale in Mantua, which magically evoke the idealized courtly world of fairy tales. Numerous drawings prove these were based on patient observations of nature – something that was to be a key element in the unfolding of the Renaissance.

THE FLORENTINE RENAISSANCE

A date often given for the start of the Renaissance is 1401, when the Florentine authorities announced a public competition for the right to make a second door for the baptistry. Candidates had to submit a trial piece of The Sacrifice of Isaac, a stiff test presenting problems of narrative, expression, movement and spatial arrangement, in which scenery, animals and both nude and draped figures had to be adequately depicted. The most audacious solution, which can be seen in the Bargello, was provided by Filippo Brunelleschi (1377–1446), who in the process fully mastered the science of perspective. He failed to win, and in disgust gave up sculpture in favour of architecture, but the new possibilities opened up by his command over visuals, and the impetus they provided for other artists to experiment and discover, mark the transition from medieval art to modern.

Brunelleschi's mantle was taken over by Donatello (c1386–1466), who began his long career by creating a new kind of freestanding statue to adorn Florence's churches, which became the artistic symbol of the city. These heroic, larger-than-life figures are shown with their feet planted firmly on the ground, displaying facial expressions of great energy and concentration. A typical example is the St George made for Orsanmichele, below which was placed an extraordinary carving of the saint slaying the dragon which uses the art of per-

spective for the first time in stone sculpture, as well as pioneering the technique of very low relief. With the bronze David, now in the Bargello, Donatello helped bring the nude – the ultimate figurative challenge – back into the mainstream of art; and he also revived another lost art, the bronze equestrian statue, with the Monument to Gattamelata in Padua.

The victor of the baptistry door competition was Lorenzo Ghiberti (1378–1455), who thereafter devoted almost the rest of his life to the project. Ghiberti initially showed no interest in perspective, and remained loyal to most of the old Gothic formulas, his first set of doors merely refining Andrea Pisano's techniques. However, his second set of doors, known as the Gates of Paradise, show how his style evolved under the influence of classical antecedents, creating a sense of space and illusion, and imbuing the grouping and characterization of the figures with a gently lyrical touch.

Donatello's collaborator Nanni di Banco (c1384–1421) was another to achieve an individual mix of the Gothic and Renaissance idioms, notably in The Four Saints on Orsanmichele. Another architect-sculptor, Bernardo Rossellino (1409–64), created in the Monument to Leonardo Bruni in Santa Croce the prototype of the sort of niche tomb that was to prevail for the rest of the century.

Luca della Robbia (1400–82) began his career as a sculptor of marble and bronze, working in a classically derived style, but a very different one from the essentially serious approach of his contemporaries. However, after Luca invented the art of glazed terracotta, he abandoned other forms of sculpture, laying the foundation for a highly lucrative family business which was continued by his nephew Andrea della Robbia (1435–1525).

The painter Masaccio (1401–28) belongs with Brunelleschi and Donatello as a key figure of the early Renaissance. His Trinity fresco in Santa Maria Novella must have startled his contemporaries, its perfect sense of depth and perspective giving the illusion of peering into the solid wall on which it was painted. Masaccio collaborated with Masolino, most notably in the fresco cycle in Santa Maria del Carmine. In this, the scenes are pared down to the essentials; the figures have a heroic quality and dignity, with their gestures depicted at the moment of maximum intensity. A single source of light is used, with shadows cast accurately.

Fra' Angelico (1387/1400–55), like Ghiberti in sculpture, combined new techniques with the Gothic tradition. A devout Dominican monk, his pictures show a rapt, heavenly vision. Colour is a telling ingredient: Angelico's ethereal blue was inimitable, the rest of his palette hardly less fetching. Frescoes in the cells of his own monastery of San Marco, intended as aids to contemplation, rank as his most important body of work. Late in his career, Angelico was called to the Vatican, where he frescoed the Cappella Niccolina, employing a style which had by then lost all Gothic traces.

Fra' Filippo Lippi (c1406–69) gradually moved away from the style of his master Masaccio to develop a greater sense of drama, seen to best effect in the frescoes in the cathedral at Prato. His later panels show a highly personal, mystical vision, characterized by wistful Madonnas, playful children and poetic landscapes. Fra' Angelico's only follower of note was **Benozzo Gozzoli** (c1421–97), whose work lacks any sense of profundity, but possesses undeniable decorative charm, best seen in the frescoes in the Palazzo Medici-Ricardi in Florence.

The city's most eccentric painter was **Paolo Uccello** (1396–1475), who was obsessed by the problems of perspective and foreshortening. His *Sir John Hawkwood* in the duomo was a deliberate piece of trompe l'oeil, though its effect is marred by the use of different vantage points, a characteristic common to his paintings, in which he tried to find as many lines as possible to lead the eye inwards. **Domenico Veneziano** (1406–61) was one of the most admired artists of the day, but only a few works by him survive, notably the *serene **St Lucy Altar*** in the Uffizi, which shows his talent for spatial arrangement and gentle, pastel-like colouring. **Andrea del Castagno** (c1421–57), in contrast, favoured harsh, strong colours, and an exaggerated dramatic pose for his figures, as can be seen in *The Last Supper* in Sant'Apollonia. In the series of *Famous Men* in the Uffizi he initiated a Florentine trend by vividly translating onto canvas the late sculptural types of Donatello.

Halfway through the century, a new versatility was brought to Florentine art by **Antonio Pollaiuolo** (c1432–98), who was active as a painter, sculptor, engraver, goldsmith and embroidery designer. Pollaiuolo was renowned for the advances he made in the depiction of anatomy and movement; he was also one of the first to grapple with the next great challenge facing Renaissance painters, namely how to move beyond making all parts of a picture accurate and realistic, while at the same time creating a satisfying compositional whole. Another painter-sculptor was **Andrea del Verrocchio** (c1435–88), whose fame as a teacher has unfairly drawn attention away from his own wide-ranging achievements. His *Christ and St Thomas* on Orsanmichele shows crafty compositional skills in fitting two statues into a space intended for one, and marks a move away from classicism, as does his equestrian *Monument to Bartolommeo Colleoni* outside San Zanipolo in Venice. Other Florentine sculptors of this period preferred a much softer approach. **Desiderio da Settignano** (1428–64) made sensitive busts of women and children, and used Donatello's technique of low relief to create scenes of the utmost delicacy. **Mino da Fiesole** (1429–84), **Antonio Rossellino** (1427–79) and **Benedetto da Maiano** (1442–97) showed broadly similar preoccupations, all concentrating on grace and beauty of line.

Subjects drawn from classical mythology became an increasingly important part of the repertoire of Florentine painters in the second half of the fifteenth century, in large part owing to the humanist culture fostered at the court. One of Italy's most distinctive artists, **Sandro Botticelli** (c1445–1510), created the most famous and haunting images in this field, notably *The Birth of Venus* and *Primavera*, both now in the Uffizi. His late work shows a deliberate archaism, perhaps as a result of the religious fanaticism of the time.

Filippino Lippi (1457/8–1504), the result of Fra' Filippo's affair with a nun, came to fame with his completion of Masaccio's frescoes in Santa Maria del Carmine. He developed a style based on that of Botticelli, though with a more consciously antique feeling. Another painter with pagan tastes was the reclusive **Piero di Cosimo** (c1462–1521), who was at his best in enigmatic mythological scenes. Meanwhile, vivid new frescoes were created for Florence's churches by **Domenico Ghirlandaio** (1449–94), whose works are now chiefly remembered for their documentary interest, being tilled with portraits of contemporary notables and vivid anecdotal details.

THE FIFTEENTH CENTURY ELSEWHERE IN ITALY

Although the fifteenth century brought a rich crop of artists working throughout Italy, including many places which previously had little tradition of their own to draw on, no other city came near to matching the depth and consistency of the fifteenth-century Florentine School.

However, although the technical innovations pioneered in Florence were to have an enormous influence, they were by no means slavishly followed. Sienese painters proved the continuing vitality of the colourful narrative approach of the previous century, modified by the impact of International Gothic. The works of **Sassetta** (c1392–1450), which are often impregnated by a sense of mysticism, do make some concessions to the new theories of spatial composition, but this is an essentially subordinate feature. The finest Sienese artist of the century was the sculptor **Jacopo della Quercia** (1374–1438), whose style is essentially linear, though with classical tendencies modified by knowledge of the most advanced northern European art of the day. He was given important public commissions in his native city, such as the overall supervision of the baptistry font and the Fonte Gaia. However, his masterpiece is his last work, the reliefs on the facade of San Petronio in Bologna, which show a vigorous approach fully comparable with those of the great Florentines. His main follower was the Florentine-born **Agostino di Duccio** (1418–81), another sculptor heavily dependent on line, whose work abounds with nervous energy. His masterpiece, executed in collaboration with **Matteo de' Pasti** (c1420–67), is the joyous series of low reliefs in the Tempio Malatestiano in Rimini.

Another artist associated with the Rimini project was the Tuscan **Piero della Francesca** (1410/20–92), who cast an overwhelming influence over the development of painting in central Italy. A painstaking worker, Piero was also active as a mathematician, hence the importance of perspective and symmetry in his compositions. His figures are painted with a cool sense of detachment yet have a grave, monumental beauty. Piero was also one of the great painters of light, in the blue skies which illuminate his gentle landscapes, and in more dramatic effects, such as in *The Dream of Constantine*, part of his most substantial commission – the fresco cycle in San Francesco, Arezzo.

Melozzo da Forlí (1438–94) was the closest follower of Piero della Francesca, showing a similar interest in perspective, and apparently inventing a favourite Renaissance trick device called *sotto in su*, an extreme form of illusion in which figures painted on a ceiling appear to float in space. Another inventive pupil of the same master was **Luca Signorelli** (1450–1523), who developed the ideas of dramatic movement pioneered by Pollaiuolo. In spite of obvious defects, such as harsh colours, stiff drawing and a tendency to overcrowd his compositions, Signorelli was responsible for some of the most heroic paintings of the day. His profound knowledge of anatomy was to be an enormous influence on the succeeding generation, and he used the nude to achieve the most spectacular effects, notably in the frescoes in Orvieto's duomo.

Pietro Perugino (1445–1523), probably yet another pupil of Piero, developed in a quite different way from Signorelli, producing calm altarpieces featuring soft and beautifully rounded figures set against serene Umbrian landscapes. His collaborator **Bernardino Pinturicchio** (c1454–1513) was a purely decorative artist whose work has no pretensions to depth, but is nearly always fresh and pleasing, particularly in his larger schemes such as the Libreria Piccolomini in the duomo in Siena.

The first important Renaissance painter in northern Italy was **Andrea Mantegna** (c1431–1506), who represents the apogee of classical influence. Steeped from an early age in the art of the Romans, Mantegna's ideal vision of the antique world permeates nearly all his work, even becoming the predominant element in many of his sacred compositions, together with a phenomenal technical skill, and daring use of unorthodox vantage points – best seen in the grief-laden *Dead Christ* in the Brera, Milan. In total contrast is the exuberant decoration for the Camera degli Sposi in Mantua, one of the artist's few works based on direct observation rather than classical inspiration.

Padua in the mid-fifteenth century became an important training ground for artists, thanks to the early successes of Mantegna, and the ten-year stay of Donatello. One of its offshoots was the group of painters active in Ferrara: **Cosmè Tura** (c1431–95), **Francesco del Cossa** (1435/6–77) and **Ercole de' Roberti** (1448/55–96). Tura's figures are highly charged, with mannered poses and claw-like hands, typically set against fanciful architecture very different from the idealized townscapes painted by other Renaissance artists. Cossa's outline is sharper, his figures energetic rather than theatrical, his colours more resplendent; he too favoured architectural backgrounds, particularly of ruins. Roberti's essentially small-scale style combines something of the pathos of Tura with Cossa's emphasis on colour and line.

Also trained in Padua was the Brescian **Vincenzo Foppa** (1427/30–1515/6), who subsequently became the leader of the Milanese school. His best works have a certain grandeur of conception, and a subdued sense of colouring. His main follower was **Ambrogio Bergognone** (1450/60–1523), who is particularly associated with the Certosa di Pavia. This great building project was also the main outlet for the talents of the leading Lombard sculptors of the day, notably **Giovanni Antonio Amadeo** (1447–1522), whose other main work is the decoration of the Cappella Colleoni in Bergamo.

Venice, as always, remained something of a law unto itself. Even in mid-century, the sculptures of **Bartolomeo Bon** (c1374–1464/7) and the crowded panels of **Michele Giambono** (active 1420–62) showed the city's continuing preference for late-Gothic forms. Something of a transition can be seen with the **Vivarini** family – **Antonio** (c1419–80), his brother **Bartolomeo** (c1430–91) and his son **Alvise** (c1445–1505) – who gradually introduced a sense of spatial perspective and an increased attempt at characterization. **Carlo Crivelli** (c1430–95) was also associated with them. One of the most inventive and idiosyncratic artists of the day, Crivelli abandoned Venice, preferring commissions from churches in small towns in Marche, which he executed in a deliberately archaic style. His altarpieces are claustrophobically opulent, characterized by strong drawing, rich colours, elaborate detail and a superfluity of decoration, with incidental still lifes a common ingredient.

Another, and far more influential, artistic dynasty was that of the **Bellini** family – **Jacopo** (c1400–70) and his sons **Gentile** (c1429–1507) and **Giovanni** (c1430–1516). The latter was the most significant, standing as a major influence on Venetian painters to come. Though influenced by his brother-in-law Mantegna, Bellini's overall effect is very different, with a soft beauty of both colour and outline. He painted a seemingly endless series of variations on subjects such as *the Madonna and Child* and pietà, yet always managed to make each very different. His larger altarpieces concentrate attention on the foreground, and arrange the figures in such a way that there is a parallel plane behind, rather than the more usual receding landscape. Gentile Bellini was essentially a history painter who epitomized the penchant for highly detailed depictions of Venetian life.

Vittore Carpaccio (c1460–1523) continued this narrative tradition, and two complete cycles by him can still be seen in Venice: that of *St Ursula* in the Accademia, and of *St George and St Jerome* in the Scuola di San Giorgio degli Schiavoni. A love of the picturesque also pervades his altarpieces, which generally give due prominence to fantastic landscapes and resplendent Renaissance buildings.

Venetian Renaissance sculpture was dominated by yet another dynasty, the **Lombardo** family: **Pietro** (c1438–1515) and his sons **Antonio** (c1458–1516) and **Tullio** (c1460–1532). Their strongly classical style was particularly suited to funerary monuments, the best of which are in San Zanipolo. They were also talented decorative carvers, as can be seen in the interior scheme for their own church of Santa Maria dei Miracoli.

Closely associated with the Venetian school was the only important southern Italian painter of the Renaissance, **Antonello da Messina** (c1430–79), who spent the last years of his life in the city. Antonello combined Italian painters' achievements in perspective and foreshortening with the ability to reproduce a variety of textures (skin, velvet, hair, wood) in the naturalistic way that was typical of contemporary Flemish artists; and it was through contact with their work that he introduced oil painting to Italy. His pictures have a strong sense of pathos, and some of his most arresting images are simple devotional pictures, which follow the same format he favoured for his secular portraits.

THE HIGH RENAISSANCE

Just as the beginning of the Renaissance is linked to the specific circumstances of the competition for the Florence Baptistry doors, so the climactic part of the era, known as the High Renaissance, is sometimes considered to have started with the mural of *The Last Supper* in Santa Maria delle Grazie in Milan, painted in the last years of the fifteenth century by **Leonardo da Vinci** (1452–1519). Apart from its magnificent spatial and illusory qualities, this painting endowed each of the characters with identifiable psychological traits, and successfully froze the action to capture the mood of a precise moment. His use of *sfumato*, a blurred outline whereby tones gradually but imperceptibly changed from light to dark, was of crucial importance to his ability to make his figures appear as living beings with a soul – a technique best seen in his portraits.

In Florence, the most original painter of the generation after Leonardo was **Fra' Bartolommeo della Porta** (c1474–1517), who was caught up in the religious fanaticism that also influenced Botticelli. As a device to stress the otherness of the divine, he clad the figures in his religious compositions in plain drapery, rather than the colourful contemporary costumes which had hitherto been fashionable. He also did away with elaborate backgrounds and anecdotal detail, concentrating instead on expression and gesture. **Mariotto Albertinelli** (1474–1515), who worked with him in the same workshop in San Marco that had once been run by Fra' Angelico, painted in a broadly similar but less austere manner. **Andrea del Sarto** (1486–1530), on the other hand, was the one Florentine artist who shared the Venetian precept of colour and shade as being the most important ingredients of a picture. His figures are classical in outline, aiming at a balance of nuance, proportion and monumentality.

These Florentines, however, stood very much in the shadow of **Michelangelo Buonarroti** (1475–1564), with whom the Renaissance period reaches its climax. Michelangelo's first love was the creation of marble statues. He had little interest in relief, and none at all in bronze or clay, believing that the slow building up of forms was too simple a task for a great artist. His technique is illustrated most graphically in the unfinished *Slaves* in Florence's Accademia, who seem to be pushing their way out of the stone. The colossal early *David*, also in the Accademia, shows his mastery of the nude, which thereafter became the key focus of his art. In spite of claiming to be a reluctant painter,

Michelangelo's single greatest accomplishment was the ceiling fresco of the Sistine Chapel, one of the world's most awe-inspiring acts of individual human achievement. Its confident and elated mood is offset by the overpowering despondency of *The Last Judgement* on the end wall, painted three decades later. His later works are more abstract, as seen in the pietàs in the Museo dell'Opera in Florence and the Milan Castello, which contrast sharply with the formal beauty of his youthful interpretation of the scene in St Peter's.

Raphael (1483–1520) stands in almost complete antithesis to his rival Michelangelo, though the personal friendships he forged with his powerful patrons were as significant in raising the status of the artist as was the latter's less compromising approach. A pupil of Perugino, he quickly surpassed his teacher's style, going to Florence where he became chiefly renowned for numerous variants of the *Madonna and Child* and *Holy Family*. Raphael also developed into a supreme portraitist, skilled at both the psychological and physical attributes of his sitters. His greatest works, however, are the frescoes of his Roman period, notably those in the Stanze della Segnatura in the Vatican and the Villa Farnesina. Influenced by Michelangelo's achievement in the Sistine Chapel, Raphael's late works show him moving towards a large-scale, more dramatic and mannered style, but his early death meant that the continuation of this trend was left to his pupils.

Closely related to the classicizing tendency of Raphael is that of the Florentine-born sculptor **Andrea Sansovino** (c1467–1529), whose grandiose tombs in Santa Maria del Popolo in Rome, with standing effigies of the *Virtues*, set the tone for sixteenth-century funerary monuments. His pupil **Jacopo Sansovino** (1486–1570) took his name and carried on his tradition, spending the latter part of his career in Venice, where although principally active as an architect, he also made monumental sculptures which are inseparable from the buildings they adorn. **Sebastiano del Piombo** (c1485–1547), on the other hand, stood as a direct rival to Raphael in Rome, striving to transfer Michelangelo's heroic manner to panel painting. In this, he was only variably successful, though he was a highly sensitive portraitist.

Meanwhile **Antonio Correggio** (1489/94–1534) managed to carve out a brilliant career for himself in Parma. His three ceiling frescoes there develop the illusionistic devices of Mantegna, marking Correggio out as a precursor of the Baroque. One of the great painters of mythological scenes, he was also a relentless explorer of the dramatic possibilities of light and shade. Another fine exponent of the contrasts of light was the Ferrarese **Dosso Dossi** (1479/90–1542), a romantic spirit who created fantastic landscapes peopled with sumptuously dressed figures.

The golden period of Venetian painting, ushered in by Bellini, continued with his elusive pupil, **Giorgione** (1475–1510), whose short life is shrouded in mystery. One of the few paintings certainly by him is *The Tempest* in the Venice Accademia, whose true subject matter baffled even his contemporaries. In it, the figures are, for the first time in Italian art, completely subsidiary to the lush landscape illuminated by menacing shafts of light. The haunting altarpiece in the duomo of his native town of Castelfranco Veneto is also almost certainly his, but many other paintings attributed to him may actually be by one of many painters who maintained something of his poetic, colourful style. Some of these, notably **Vincenzo Catena** (c1480–1531) and **Palma il Vecchio** (c1480–1528), developed recognizable artistic personalities of their own. **Lorenzo Lotto** (c1480–1556) was the most distinctive of this circle, travelling widely throughout his career, assimilating an astonishing variety of influences.

Giorgione's influence is also marked in the early works of **Titian** (c1485–1576), the dominant personality of the Venetian school and one of the most versatile painters of all time. His art embraced with equal skill all the subjects that were required by the Renaissance – altarpieces, mythologies, allegories and portraits. Even more than Michelangelo, he was able to pick and choose his patrons, and was the first artist to build up a truly international clientele. As a portraitist of men of power, Titian was unrivalled, setting the vocabulary for official images which was to prevail until well into the seventeenth century. His complete technical and compositional mastery was already apparent in relatively early works such as the *Assumption* in I Frari, the first example of what was to become a Venetian speciality: a panel painting specially designed to fit an architectural space. Towards the end of his life, Titian abandoned his bravura and brilliant palette in favour of a very free style, stretching the possibilities of oil paint to their very limits.

Giovanni Antonio Pordenone (1483/4–1539) was a provincial north Italian painter strongly influenced by Giorgione and Titian. More obviously in direct descent from the Venetian masters was the school of Brescia. **Giovanni Girolamo Savoldo** (active 1508–48) showed particular adeptness at light effects, and was a pioneer of night scenes, while **Alessandro Moretto** (c1498–1554) was one of the most incisive portraitists of the Renaissance, and seems to have been responsible for introducing the full-length form to Italy. His altarpieces are more variable, but often have a suitably grand manner.

THE LATE RENAISSANCE

The perfection of form achieved in the late Renaissance was the culmination of centuries of striving. As artists could not hope to improve on the achievements of Michelangelo and Raphael at their peak, they had to find new approaches. As a result, **Mannerism** was born. This was a deliberately intellectual approach, aimed at flouting the accepted rules, notably by distorting the senses of scale and perspective, exaggerating anatomical details, adopting unlikely poses for the figures, and using unnaturally harsh colours.

One artist commonly labelled a Mannerist is **Giulio Romano** (c1499–1546), one of the most gifted of Raphael's assistants, whose frescoes in the Palazzo Te in Mantua, which he himself built, show the style at its most grandiose, notably in *The Fall of the Giants*, occupying a room to itself. A leading light in the adoption of Mannerism in Florence was **Rosso Fiorentino** (1494–1540), together with **Jacopo Pontormo** (1494–1556) and **Agnolo Bronzino** (1503–72). Pontormo, a brilliant draughtsman, was the most talented of this group, an able decorator and an inquiring if understated portraitist. Bronzino was highly prolific, but only his portraits of royal and noble personages have much appeal today, their detachment, concentrating more on the beauty of their clothing, casting an enormous influence on official portraitists down the centuries. **Giorgio Vasari** (1511–74), originally from Arezzo, was responsible for many of the frescoes in the Palazzo Vecchio, although he is now chiefly famous for his series of biographies of artists, which marked the birth of art history as a discipline.

Another Florentine Mannerist whose writings have helped secure his fame is the sculptor **Benvenuto Cellini** (1500–71), the author of a racy *Autobiography* which offers a fascinating insight into the artistic world of the time. Though he was successful in finding favour at courts all over Europe, only a few of his sculptures, all of a very high quality, survive. The *Bust of Cosimo I*, in the Bargello, marks the departure of the portrait from realism, creating instead a new heroic image. His *Perseus*, in the Loggia dei Lanzi, forms a fitting counterpart to Donatello's late *Judith*, and completely outclasses the *Hercules and Cacus* in the square outside by his rival **Baccio Bandinelli** (1493–1560).

By far the most influential Florentine Mannerist, however, was **Giambologna** (1529–1608), a sculptor of French origin. His favourite medium was bronze, and he established a large workshop which churned out miniature replicas of his most important compositions. These typically show figures in combat, and are designed for the spectator to walk around, rather than examine from only one viewpoint. His most famous image is the typically androgynous *Mercury*, in a conscious rebuttal of the approaches of both Donatello and Michelangelo, this figure appears to float in the air, in the boldest attempt ever made by a sculptor to defy the laws of gravity.

One of the most individualistic Mannerists was **Domenico Beccafumi** (1486–1551), who provided a somewhat unusual end to the long line of Sienese painters, though his emphasis on colour was utterly typical of that city. He was a master of decorative effect, as witnessed by his illusionist frescoes in the Palazzo Pubblico, and his large altarpieces for Sienese churches, which show a particular concern for light and shade, perspective effects, and deep emotions. In Parma, the paintings of Francesco Mazzola, known simply as **Parmigianino** (1503–40), retained something of the consciously refined approach of Correggio, with their exaggeratedly sinuous figures, though his portraits reveal considerable spiritual insight. His decorative scheme for Santa Maria della Steccata typifies the Mannerist penchant for surplus ornament and demonstrates the fertility of his imagination.

Venice, as ever, followed its own distinctive late-Renaissance path, having no taste for the sort of Mannerism practised elsewhere in Italy. **Jacopo Tintoretto** (1518–94) aimed at an ideal based on the drawing of Michelangelo and the colour of Titian, though in fact the heroic style he forged had only superficial resemblances to his mentors. To heighten the sense of drama, he used a battery of other methods: unorthodox vantage points, elongated figures, and unexpected positioning of the main subject on the canvas.

In strong contrast to Tintoretto, the other leading Venetian painter of the day, **Paolo Veronese** (1528–88), was a supreme decorator on a grand scale. Indeed, some of his best work was conceived for architectural settings, such as San Sebastiano in Venice and the Villa Barbara in Masèr. Veronese's love of pomp and splendour, however, is carried over into his easel paintings, which revel in warm, glowing colours and monumental figures, with little sense of gravitas. He fell foul of the Inquisition as a result of the inclusion of German soldiers (which put him under suspicion of Protestant sympathies) and other anachronistic and surplus detail in a huge banquet scene (now in the Venice Accademia) purporting to represent *The Last Supper*. He responded by changing the title to *A Feast in the House of Levi*.

Alessandro Vittoria (1525–1608), a pupil of Jacopo Sansovino, embellished Venice's churches with sculptures that have much in common with Mannerist productions elsewhere in Italy, but are more classically modelled. **Jacopo Bassano** (1510–92) was trained in the city, but preferred to work in the provincial town after which he takes his name, where he was by far the most remarkable of a dynasty of painters. As a setting for his religious panels, he painted the small town and country life of his day as it really was. He also popularized the inclusion of animals and heaped piles of fruit and vegetables – features eagerly taken up by later northern European artists – and was a superb painter of light and shade, using heavy daubs of colour and strong chiaroscuro.

Another remarkable artist working well away from the main centres was **Federico Barocci** (1535–1612) of Urbino. His paintings were painstakingly executed, their soft rounded forms mirroring the comforting religious image propagated by the Counter-Reformation, and with an emphasis on light and movement that was to some extent anticipatory of the Baroque to come.

THE BAROQUE AGE

The leadership of Italian art away from the sterility of late Mannerism came initially from cities that had hitherto played a minor role in its development. Bologna was the first to come to prominence, through the academy founded there in 1585 by members of the **Carracci** family – **Lodovico** (1555–1619), **Agostino** (1557–1602) and **Annibale** (1560–1609). This was by no means the first attempt to set up a training school for artists, a concept rendered necessary by the blow the Renaissance had dealt to the old workshop tradition, but it was far more successful than any previous venture. Annibale was easily the greatest and most versatile artist of the three, breathing a whole new life into the classical tradition. His frescoes in the Palazzo Farnese in Rome offer a fresh and highly imaginative approach to mythological scenes, as well as being brilliant examples of illusionism. A more serious intent is noticeable in the artist's canvases, which introduce an emotional yet untheatrical content to well-ordered religious subjects. He was also a major landscape painter, pioneering the sort of luscious scene with a subsidiary subject from the Bible or classical literature which was later to be developed in Rome by the great French painters, Claude and Poussin.

An entirely different but equally novel approach was taken by **Michelangelo da Caravaggio** (1573–1610), whose violent and wayward life led him from Milan to Rome, Naples, Malta, Sicily and most of the way back again. Caravaggio was the great master of chiaroscuro, which he used to even more dramatic effect than Tintoretto. He also used what seemed like shock tactics to his patrons in the Church, stripping away centuries of idealized tradition to present biblical stories as they might have seemed at the time. Real-life peasants, beggars, ruffians and prostitutes were all used as models for the figures, to enhance the realistic impact. His original canvases for commissions such as those for the Roman churches of San Luigi dei Francesi and Santa Maria del Popolo were sometimes rejected, though he always managed to find a private buyer. His impact on the great European Golden Age of

seventeenth-century painting was immense, spawning whole schools of Dutch and French derivatives, along with Rembrandt, Rubens, and most of the great Spanish masters.

In Italy, Caravaggio's art had an immediate impact on the older **Orazio Gentileschi** (1563–1639), who was particularly keen on its tenebrist effects. The Mantuan **Bartolomeo Manfredi** (c1580–1620) extended the master's style to such genre subjects as card games and soldiers in guardrooms. And Caravaggio's style was brought to Naples by **Giovanni Battista Caracciolo** (c1578–1635), inspiring the city's painters to raise Naples from its traditionally marginal position in Italian art to a place, throughout the seventeenth century, at the very forefront.

The first important follower of the Carracci in Bologna was **Guido Reni** (1575–1642). In the nineteenth century, Reni was ranked as one of the supreme artists of all time, but suffered a slump in reputation when a reaction against artistic sentimentality set in; it is only very recently that his genuine gifts for the expression of feeling have been given their proper due. Among other Carracci pupils, **Domenichino** (1581–1641) was a faithful follower of the style, extending its hold on Rome, though he was better at its more decorative and idealized aspects. **Guercino** (1591–1666) merged the classical and realistic styles, imbuing chiaroscuro effects with a subtlety very different to that favoured by Caravaggio and his followers.

Giovanni Lanfranco (1582–1647), originally from Parma, combined the Carracci style with elements borrowed from Correggio. His frescoes in Rome and Naples have a greater sense of movement and technical trickery than those Domenichino was painting at the same time, and mark the beginnings of High Baroque painting. In turn, his own work was made to seem out-of-date by **Pietro da Cortona** (1596–1669), who introduced a sense of fantasy and freedom that was far more ambitious than anything previously attempted. His ceiling in the Palazzo Barberini presented the illusion of opening on to the heavily populated heavens above, with figures seen *di sotto in su* – apparently teeming down into the hall below. For a century, this was to be the sort of monumental painting favoured in Rome; it was also spread to Florence by Cortona himself, by means of a series of frescoes in the Palazzo Pitti.

The High Baroque style was essentially a Roman phenomenon, born out of the super-confident mood in the world capital of Catholicism as a result of the success of the Counter Reformation. Its overwhelmingly dominant personality was **Gianlorenzo Bernini** (1598–1680), a youthful prodigy who had created an entirely new sculptural language while still in his early twenties. Such works as *David* and *Apollo and Daphne*, both in the Villa Borghese, were the first great marble statues since Michelangelo, yet in their independence of form showed a decisive rejection of the concept of belonging to the block from which they were carved, drawing the spectator into the scene and asserting the primacy of the emotions – a key concept of the Baroque. Though only an occasional painter (he in fact spent more time as an architect), Bernini adopted painterly techniques for his work, using different materials for contrast, exploiting sources of light, and using illusionist techniques, producing a drama best seen in *The Ecstasy of St Theresa* in Rome's Santa Maria della Victoria, which goes so far as to re-create the atmosphere of a theatre by the inclusion of a gallery of onlookers.

So overwhelming was the impact of Bernini's art that most other sculpture of the period is but a pale imitation of it. One of the few sculptors not to be overawed was the Tuscan **Francesco Mochi** (1580–1654), who made two magnificent equestrian monuments in Piacenza. **Alessandro Algardi** (1598–1654) of Bologna managed a brilliant career in Rome as a bitter rival of Bernini, promoting a sculptural version of the Carracci style.

In Venice, the versatile Genoese **Bernardo Strozzi** (1581–1644) tried to revive memories of the great sixteenth-century masters. His exuberant early works are generally more successful, showing the influence of Rubens: they typically have very free brushwork, luminous colours and pronounced modelling. In Naples, **Massimo Stanzione** (1585–1656) combined something of the approaches of Carracci and Caravaggio, though his most original works are his detailed, colourful portraits. A much more aggressively Caravaggesque idiom is apparent in the work of **Artemisia Gentileschi** (c1597–1651), daughter of Orazio, who was particularly adept at lurid subjects. She enjoyed a remarkable degree of independence and status for a woman of her day, and has attracted a great deal of attention from modern feminists, having a fair claim to the title of "the greatest ever female painter". **Salvator Rosa** (1615–73) painted landscapes that have a wild, mystical quality very different from those of the classical painters of Bologna and Rome. Characteristically, they are populated by bandits or witches, or have an allegorical theme. **Mattia Preti** (1613–99), who originally hailed from the artistic backwater of Calabria, painted some of the most effective canvases in Caravaggio's idiom, excelling at its tenebrist aspects. His later work is more influenced by Roman Baroque, using brighter colours and pronounced spatial effects. In these, he resembles **Luca Giordano** (1632–1705), the main Neapolitan painter of the second half of the century. Giordano was renowned for his ability to paint quickly, and he ranks among the most prolific artists of all time. His output employs a whole variety of styles and is uneven in quality, but shows remarkable technical facility. The last major Baroque painter active in Naples was **Francesco Solimena** (1657–1747), whose large crowded compositions show the full theatricality of the style.

Meanwhile, the Roman vogue for spectacular illusionistic ceilings was continued by **Giovanni Battista Baciccia** (1639–1709), who was warmer in colour and even more audacious in approach than Pietro da Cortona. His most famous decoration is that in the Gesù, which boldly mixes painted and stucco figures. An even greater command of pyrotechnics, however, was displayed by the Jesuit **Andrea Pozzo** (1642–1709) on the ceiling of Sant'Ignazio, whose illusion is designed to be seen from only one specific point.

THE EIGHTEENTH CENTURY

The decline of Italian art in many of its most celebrated strongholds gathered pace in the eighteenth century, a slump from which only Venice and Rome stood apart. In the case of the former, its pre-eminence was due to a revival of its grand decorative tradition after a century's gap. This gave it a leading position in European **Rococo**, the ornate derivative of late Baroque.

An updated version of the style of Veronese was first fostered by **Sebastiano Ricci** (1659–1734), whose work is superficially similar to Veronese's, but has an airier, lighter feel.

A more individual approach is apparent in the work of **Giovanni Battista Piazzetta** (1683–1754), an outstanding draughtsman whose joyful and harmonious paintings give the impression of a free and easy approach, yet which were actually the result of meticulous planning. Venice also boasted a notable female portraitist in **Rosalba Carriera** (1675–1757), who was the first artist to use pastel as an independent medium.

By far the most accomplished exponent of Venetian Rococo, and one of the greatest decorative artists of all time, was **Giovanni Battista Tiepolo** (1696–1770). His work is best seen in an architectural setting, where his illusionistic approach compares favourably with those of the earlier Roman artists in its colour, handling, spatial awareness, sense of fantasy and depth of feeling. The finest schemes were made for foreign patrons (in Würzburg and Madrid), but there are some excellent examples in Udine, Vicenza and Stra, and several in Venice itself, notably the Palazzo Labia and Ca'Rezzonico.

His son, **Giovanni Domenico Tiepolo** (1727–1804), aided him on many projects and painted in a broadly similar style, though he had a more obvious eye for satire. Also active in Venice were a number of painters who specialized in painting views of the city as mementos for its aristocratic visitors. The best known of these was **Antonio Canaletto** (1697–1768), whose images, often painted on the spot and with the use of a camera obscura, have defined the popular conception of the buildings and lifestyle of Venice ever since. However, they are an idealized representation, with spatial arrangements and even individual buildings altered. Canaletto's nephew, **Bernardo Bellotto** (1721–80), closely followed his style and applied it to cities all over Europe, but took a more literal approach, stressing topographical exactness. A more sombre, musing mood is present in the Venetian views of **Francesco Guardi** (1712–93), who used a darker palette. His emphasis on transitory light effects foreshadowed the French Impressionists, while his figures have a greater vivacity than those of Canaletto. Genre scenes were also much in demand with visiting tourists, and **Pietro Longhi** (1702–85), who had a limited technique but ready sense of humour, vividly characterized the Venetian life of his day for the benefit of this market.

Among non-Venetian painters, the Genoese **Alessandro Magnasco** (1667–1749) is particularly distinctive, often combining into one picture his two favourite themes of mannered landscapes ravaged by the elements and ecstatic monks at prayer. In Rome, the tourist demand for views was met by **Giovanni Paolo Panini** (c1692–1765), who painted both the ruins of the classical period and the modern buildings of the day. These are surpassed, however, by the grandiose large-scale etchings of **Giovanni Battista Piranesi** (1720–78), which fully exploit the dramatic contrasts of light and shade possible in the black-and-white medium.

The latter can be seen as an early manifestation of **Neoclassicism**, a movement which began in the middle of the century, inspired partly by a reaction against Baroque excesses, and partly by the excitement caused by the discovery of Pompeii and Herculaneum, though many of its leading exponents were foreigners resident in Rome. Neoclassicism aimed at the complete revival of the arts of the ancients, a trend that was particularly marked in sculpture, which had a far larger legacy to borrow on than painting. It is best seen in the works of **Antonio Canova** (1757–1822), which show great beauty in modelling, though a certain frigidity in the depiction of emotions. His statues are often highly erotic in effect: the several monuments he made in honour of Napoleon include life-sized nude depictions, one of which is now in the Brera, Milan.

THE NINETEENTH CENTURY

If the eighteenth century was a lean time for Italian art, the nineteenth century was even worse, Paris becoming the overwhelmingly dominant European trendsetter. **Francesco Hayez** (1791–1882) was perhaps the most successful painter at work in the first half of the century, continuing the Neoclassical manner in his history scenes and highly finished portraits.

Towards the 1850s the Romantic taste for realism was reflected in an interest in the country's scenery, immortalized by various local schools: the **Scuola di Posillipo** and the Palizzi brothers (Giuseppe, 1812–88, and Filippo, 1818–99) in Naples; the **Scuola di Rivara** in Piedmont; **il Piccio** (1804–73) in Lombardy; and the **Macchiaioli** in Tuscany. The Macchiaioli were a group of painters based in Florence, who held comparatively modern and definable aims. Their name derives from the Italian word for a blot, as they made extensive use of individual patches of light and dark colour, which was used to define form, in opposition to the super-smooth Neoclassical approach then in vogue. The guiding spirit of the movement was **Giovanni Fattori** (1825–1905), who painted scenes of military life (based on his experiences fighting in the Wars of Independence of 1848–9) and broad landscapes using very free brushwork and compositional techniques. The group's chief theorist, **Telemaco Signorini** (1835–1901), came to be influenced by the painting of Corot and the Barbizon School, and later followers moved to Paris, to become accepted as peripheral members of the Impressionist circle.

The turn of the century drew, once again, on international trends. Symbolism was chiefly represented by the haunting *femmes fatales* of **Gaetano Previati** (1852–1920) and the subtler compositions of **Giovanni Segantini** (1858–99), who coupled naturalism with imagination. **Giuseppe Pellizza da Volpedo** (1868–1907) experimented with **Divisionismo**, the Italian version of Seurat's Pointillisme. His most famous work, *The Fourth State*, is a striking depiction of the inevitable progress of the working class as outlined by Marx.

Compared with painting, the development of nineteenth-century **sculpture** was somehow delayed. The Canova influence seems to have been hard to escape, and works from this period often demonstrate great skill but little originality. Favourite subjects were portraits and, in typically Romantic fashion, historical characters with heavy revolutionary overtones, such as *Spartacus* by **Vincenzo Vela** (1820–91). Vela's work, together with the later efforts of **Lorenzo Bartolini** (1777–1850), introduced a more naturalistic touch while still retaining a high degree of finish. A more dramatic change of direction occurred through the Neapolitan **Vincenzo Gemito** (1852–1929), who dared to leave smoothness aside and concentrated on movement. **Mario Rutelli** (1859–1941) developed a naturalistic and lively style, taking inspiration from Hellenistic sculpture and specializing in bronze figures for fountains and equestrian monuments, which have since become famous Roman landmarks (the Fontana delle Naiadi in Piazza della Repubblica and **Anita Garibaldi**, on the Janiculum Hill, for example).

Yet the most innovative experiments would only be made by **Medardo Rosso** (1858–1928), who managed to capture the fluidity and elusiveness of the fleeting moment in the third dimension, influencing, among others, Rodin. After the latter's death in 1917, Guillaume Apollinaire acclaimed Rosso as "the greatest living sculptor"; his wax and bronze sculptures, when properly lit, seem to emerge softly from the shadows. Rosso, however, lived and worked in Paris for most of his life.

THE TWENTIETH CENTURY

The only Italian artist born within the last two hundred years to have gained truly universal recognition is **Amedeo Modigliani** (1884–1920). Although most of his adult life was spent in Paris, Modigliani's work is recognizably Italian, being rooted in the tradition of the Renaissance and Mannerist masters. Primitive African art, then being appreciated in Europe for the first time, was the other main influence on his highly distinctive and essentially linear style. His output consists almost entirely of sensuous reclining female nudes, and strongly drawn, psychologically penetrating portraits.

In 1909 an attempt to break France's artistic monopoly was launched – ironically enough, in Paris – by the **Futurists**, who aimed to glorify the dynamism of the modern world, including the key role of warfare. Their approach was similar to the recently founded Cubist movement in aiming to reproduce several sides of an object at the same time, but differed in striving to convey movement as well. **Umberto Boccioni** (1882–1916) was the most resourceful member of the group, which never recovered from his death in World War I – for which, true to his principles, he had volunteered. His erstwhile colleagues later developed in different directions. **Giacomo Balla** (1871–1958) painted in a variety of styles, ranging from the academic to the abstract. **Gino Severini** (1883–1966) joined the Cubists after the latter had become more interested in colour, then turned to mural and mosaic decorations, before reverting, towards the end of his life, to a sense of fantasy that was characteristic of his Futurist phase. **Carlo Carrà** (1881–1966) did a complete about-face from his Futurist origins, aiming to revive the representationalism of the old Italian masters.

Carrà teamed up in 1917 with **Giorgio de Chirico** (1888–1978) to form **Pittura Metafisica**, which reacted against both the mechanical approach of Cubism and Futurism's infatuation with the modern world, cultivating instead a nostalgia for antiquity. The movement, which established a school in Ferrara, was influenced by Surrealism, and had in particular a penchant for the presence of unexpected, out-of-place objects; de Chirico's **Metaphysical Interiors** show rooms littered with all the fetishes of modern civilization. Architectural forms of a strange and rigid nature are another recurring theme in his work of this period, though like Carrà he later abandoned this in favour of a consciously archaic approach.

Other Italian painters of the twentieth century to have gained an international reputation include **Giorgio Morandi** (1890–1964), who was strongly influenced by de Chirico and specialized in haunting still lifes – very precisely drawn and often in monochrome. Also touched by the Metaphysical tradition was **Filippo de Pisis** (1896–1956), whose huge output is experimental in nature, often exploring sensation and the unexpected; consequently, it is highly uneven in quality.

If Futurism had been the official art of the Fascist regime, after World War II any self-respecting artist had to be a Communist, or at least display left-wing sympathies. However, unanimity in political ideas didn't generate agreement on how these ideas should be expressed. Realists such as **Renato Guttuso** (1912–1987), who believed in figurative painting and focused on dramatic subjects, were opposed by Formalists like Renato Birolli (1905–1959), who were moving towards experimental, non-figurative art. Italy's leading practitioner of abstraction was **Alberto Burri** (1915–95), best known for his collages of waste materials with a thick blob of red or black paint. One of the most successful experiments in Formalism was **Spazialismo**, a group founded by **Lucio Fontana** (1899–1968) with the aim of integrating the third dimension with the two-dimensional format of traditional painting.

Between 1960 and 1970 the antithesis between Realism and Formalism was resolved with the so-called **Informal Art** that originated from a rejection of the establishment, an attitude shared by both European and American artists (New York having by now become the modern alternative to Paris). Since contemporary society was viewed as hostile, the artist wanted to affirm his or her own individuality without even attempting to communicate or to represent reality in any immediately recognizable way. The work of art became equated with the artist's individual gestures, such as Lucio Fontana's sharp cuts in the canvas. Particular importance was attached to the materials on which the informal artist impressed his mark: wood, cloth, metal scraps, plastic were cut, torn, and burned to emphasize the purely "gestural" value of the work.

However, not all artists took themselves that seriously. **Piero Manzoni** (1933–1963) parodied both "the artist's gesture" and the deliberate lack of any communicative content by a series of provocative experiments à la Warhol, from *Consecration of the Art of the Hard-boiled Egg*, where cooked eggs available for public consumption were given added value by the artist's thumb print, to *Lines*, traced on a piece of paper rolled up and sealed into a container. But the most sensational of these statements was perhaps his *Merda d'Artista* (literally, "Artist's Shit"), mercifully tinned and sealed but outrageously sold by weight at the current price of gold.

After this eloquent comment on art as self-expression, the focus shifted once more to materials and techniques, particularly as a response to an exhibition of American pop art at the prestigious Venice Biennale in 1964. Italian artists such as **Michelangelo Pistoletto** (b1933) rediscovered the creative possibilities of the mixed media collage (pioneered by Burri), with cheap materials still enjoying popularity and sometimes even attaining subject-matter status. Meanwhile, politics made a quiet exit from the art scene.

A parallel development in terms of a "return to reality" was Minimalism (yet another US creature), which concentrated on the mechanical process of constructing the artwork, again using unsophisticated materials (steel, iron, concrete) and elementary geometrical shapes. The traditional divide between painting and sculpture, already blurred by Fontana, seemed to be gone for good, as Minimalist artists such as **Rodolfo Aricò** (b1930) and **Mario Surbone** (b1932) played ambiguous games with depth and surface.

Along these lines came the so-called **Arte Povera** ("Poor Art"), a post-Minimalist movement whose leading figure was **Jannis Kounellis** (b1936), an artist of Greek origin who produced 3D installations and performances using odd media mixes (such as cotton and steel). Another representative of this "school", which flourished mainly between the late Sixties and the mid-Seventies, is **Mario Merz** (b1925), who uses found objects and materials (glass sheets, twigs, metal scraps) to create installations that convey a sense of fragility and danger.

Figurative art made a comeback at the end of the Seventies with the work of **Francesco Clemente** (b1952), **Enzo Cucchi** (b1949), **Sandro Chia** (b1946) and **Mimmo Paladino** (b1948), usually referred to, in the veritable jungle of twentieth-century art movements as **Transavantguardia** or **Neo-Expressionist** painters. Not only was the human figure rehabilitated but so too were the traditional media, from oil on canvas, to watercolour, pastel, and even fresco. After a long spell of sulky anti-commercialism, Italian painting seemed to have finally made up with the public.

Generally speaking, modern Italian sculptors have been more successful than painters in reinterpreting Italy's heritage in a novel way.

Giacomo Manzù (1908–91) aimed to revive the Italian religious tradition, in a highly personal manner reminiscent of Donatello, whose technique of very low relief he used extensively. His best-known work is the bronze door of St Peter's on the theme of death, a commission awarded following a highly contentious competition in 1949. **Marino Marini** (1901–80) specialized in another great theme of Italian art, that of the equestrian monument – examples of his work are now displayed in a museum specially devoted to Marini in Florence – while the elegant portraits and female nudes of **Emilio Greco** (1913–95) stand as an updated form of Mannerism.

Although there is nothing truly ground-breaking about the Italian sculpture or painting of the last few years, there are a couple of interesting artists who have been well-received in the international forum. Video-artist **Grazia Toderi** (b1963) uses images of water to discuss transformation and existence, while Padua-born **Maurizio Cattelan** (b1960) creates witty, thought-provoking installations that explore themes of Italian popular culture. Unnerving work like *bidibidobidiboo* (1996) and *La Nona Ora* (1998) hide a lonely despondency behind their laconic humour.

Gordon McLachlan,
with contributions by **Catherine McBeth**

ARCHITECTURE

Even if Italy's architecture has not been so consistently influential as its painting and sculpture, the country still boasts a remarkable legacy of historic buildings, an almost unbroken tradition stretching back over more than 2500 years. As in the other arts, strong regional distinctions are evident in most of the main architectural periods.

THE GREEKS AND ETRUSCANS

The earliest important structures still standing in Italy were built by the peninsula's **Greek** colonizers of the sixth century BC. These exhibit the same qualities characteristic of the classical architecture of Greece itself: a strong but simple outline, a rigorous adherence to balanced proportions, a total unity of design featuring a logical system of horizontals and verticals, and extensive use of decoration to emphasize the structure. This architecture, which principally made use of marble, was based on three great **classical orders**, each of which consisted of an upright column, sometimes resting on a base, topped by a capital and an entablature of architrave, cornice and frieze.

Doric, the grandest and plainest of these orders, was used for the **temples** which are the chief glory of the Greek style, dedicated to gods yet always human in scale, never rising very high, nor appearing in any way overblown. A fine group can be seen on the Italian mainland at **Paestum**; the others – at Agrigento,

Selinunte, Segesta and Siracusa – are in **Sicily**. They are older and less refined than the Parthenon in Athens, but their state of preservation compares favourably with any of their counterparts in Greece. Significantly, the Temple of Concord in Agrigento, the most complete of all, was saved by being transformed into a Christian church, while the Temple of Athena in Syracuse was incorporated into the duomo, where it still remains.

The Greeks were also inveterate builders of open-air **theatres** – generally set against hillsides, with seats for the spectators hollowed out of the rock. Siracusa's Greek theatre is one of the best preserved of its period; that of Taormina, with the peerless backdrop of Mount Etna, also dates back to the Greeks, but was extensively remodelled by the Romans.

A very different form of architecture was practised during the same period in central Italy by the **Etruscans**, but unfortunately little Etruscan architecture remains above ground, as their Roman conquerors engaged in a deliberate programme of obliteration. The few surviving examples include the city walls of Volterra and Cortona, from the sixth century BC, and the gateways at Volterra and Perugia, from about three centuries later. However, Etruscan tombs survive in abundance, mainly at Cerveteri and Tarquinia in northern Lazio.

THE ROMAN PERIOD

In architecture, as in many other fields, the **Romans** borrowed from and adapted Greek models. Just as was the case with other art forms, however, their approach to building shows marked differences, particularly in their preference for order and usefulness above beauty. Functional building materials were favoured, and only from the time of Augustus, which marked the softening of the Roman image, are marble and stucco much in evidence, and then usually for facing purposes only. Furthermore, towns were laid out wherever possible in a regular planned grid format, to the model of a military camp.

Although they used the three Greek orders (preferring the Corinthian, with its elaborate acanthus leaf capital), and invented two more of their own, the Romans relegated the column from the essential structural role it had performed under the Greeks to one that was merely decorative. Instead, they concentrated on solid constructions, employing the rounded forms of the arch and dome, and focusing attention on the end walls. **Vaulting** was the Romans' major contribution to architectural development. Their use of an early type of concrete rather than timber frames enabled them to span much larger spaces and build much higher than the Greeks had ever done; indeed, their achievements were unequalled until the nineteenth century. Accordingly, they were able to create an architecture which perfectly expressed their own preoccupations of power and glory.

Roman architecture once dominated Europe, showing no appreciable regional variations, and many of the most impressive individual monuments still standing lie outside Italy. However, the most important ensembles are to be found in **Rome** itself, its original seaport of **Ostia**, and the residential towns of **Pompeii** and **Herculaneum** (which were both submerged by the massive eruption of Mount Vesuvius). The heart of a Roman city was its **forum**, a square usually set at the intersection of the two main streets. Its buildings were the focus of all the main aspects of public life: worship, politics, law, finance, trading, shopping and meeting. In time, it often became too small for all these functions: the Roman Forum itself, which largely dates from the days of the Republic, is an extreme case in point, and successive emperors found it necessary to lay out separate new forums in the city.

Each forum usually contained several **temples**, of which notable examples survive in Palestrina, Tivoli, Assisi and Brescia. At first, these tended to follow the Greek model, with the front entrance given due prominence, and often preceded by a flight of steps. Later, circular designs were increasingly favoured, as with the Temples of Vesta in Rome. A circular design was also chosen for the **Pantheon** in Rome, which is not only the greatest temple of all, and the only complete building to have survived from the days of imperial Rome, but is also one of the all-time masterpieces of both engineering and architecture, its dome still one of the largest in the world.

The main public building in Roman towns was the **basilica**, which was used for meetings and administration. In many respects, it was rather like a Greek temple turned inside out, consisting of a large hall terminating in an apse, with aisles to the side, often bearing galleries and with a sloping vault which was lower than that of the main section. No complete examples survive in Italy, but some idea of the development of this type of building can be had by comparing the fragments of the basilicas of Trajan and Maxentius in Rome, which are nearly two centuries apart in date. The former was colonnaded, and had a flat wooden roof, while the latter (as can clearly be seen in the surviving aisle) had a sturdy concrete vault borne by five massive piers.

In the field of leisure, the **thermae** played a key role. These vast edifices had hot, warm and cold baths, as well as halls for all kinds of other activities – those of the Emperors Caracalla and Diocletian, both in Rome, from the third and fourth centuries AD, provide the most potent reminder of their splendour. Roman **theatres** differed from those of the Greeks in being constructed above ground, and in having a semicircular *orchestra*. The Teatro di Marcello, completed under Augustus, is the only survivor in Rome itself; it is also notable for marking the use of superimposed orders in architecture for the first time. However, the Romans as a rule much preferred the atmosphere of their **amphitheatres**, which were used to stage gladiatorial contests and other public spectaculars. These were elliptical in shape, and of very solid construction, using a variety of materials. The outer wall, pierced by rows of arches, had a massive effect; inside, the seats were grouped in tiers. Rome's so-called Colosseum is the best preserved; others are to be found in Verona, Cápua, Pozzuoli and Pompeii.

Roman **houses** fall into three main categories. The *domus* or town dwelling was grouped symmetrically around an atrium and one or more peristyle courts. A more rambling plan characterizes the *villa*, a patrician country residence which tended to be decorated with porticoes and colonnades, and have rooms specially aligned to catch both the sun and the shade. Poorer Romans lived in *insulae*, tenement-type constructions with several floors, which were often vaulted throughout and grouped symmetrically in streets and squares. Few Roman **palaces** remain. The most important is the misleadingly named Villa Adriana in Tivoli, replete with fantastical re-creations of buildings the Emperor Hadrian had seen on his travels, along with grottoes, terraces and fountains. From a century earlier, Nero's fabled Domus Aurea in Rome survives only in part.

Roman law forbade burial inside the city walls, and the Via Appia became the favoured site, lined by cylindrical, tower-like **mausoleums**, the finest being that of Cecilia Metella. A similar but larger structure, of the Emperor Augustus, was the first to be built in the city centre. Another in honour of Hadrian was by far the most spectacular funerary monument built by the Romans, but was later converted into the Castel Sant'Angelo.

The **triumphal arch** was a specifically Roman creation, usually erected to celebrate military victories and richly adorned with bas-reliefs, the whole surmounted by a large sculptural group, usually of a horse-drawn triumphal chariot. Several of these arches can be seen in Rome; others are in Ancona, Aosta, Benevento, Rimini and Susa.

Another Roman invention was the **aqueduct**, which was built to transport water to the towns. These were undecorated and purely functional, with the water running down a very gentle gradient along a channel at the top. Nonetheless, they often have a majestic sweep, particularly when the lie of the land dictated the building of several tiers. Traces of aqueducts can be seen south of Rome, though the most impressive surviving examples are in other countries. The Romans also excelled at building **bridges**. There were eleven spanning the Tiber in the capital in imperial times; these have mostly been replaced or altered, but the Pons Fabricius remains substantially intact. Other bridges which have changed little are the graceful Ponte di Solesta in Ascoli Piceno, which is of a single arch only, and the five-arched Ponte di Tiberio in Rimini.

EARLY CHRISTIAN AND BYZANTHINE

The **early Christians** in Italy initially had to practise their religion in private houses and underground in **catacombs** hollowed out of the rock. Those in Rome are the most famous, but other impressive groups can be seen in Naples and Siracusa. When Christianity was legalized and officially adopted by the Roman Empire, it was hardly surprising that its architecture should base itself very directly on secular imperial models. In particular, **churches** adopted a basilican format. They were generally raised over the graves of martyrs, whose tombs were kept in the crypt, directly below the high altar. In

time, they would invariably be orientated towards the east, though in the early churches it was quite normal to face exactly the opposite way. For the interior, columns were often taken from demolished secular buildings.

In **Rome** itself, much the best-preserved church of this time is Santa Sabina, which dates from the fifth century. Its exterior is of a stark simplicity, the plain brick walls pierced only by large windows; the interior shows the move towards regular columns. The larger contemporary basilicas of Santa Maria Maggiore and San Paolo fuori le Mura, though both much altered down the centuries, still clearly show the variations in the basilican plan. **Transepts** were introduced, as a result of a conscious desire to simulate the shape of the Cross; double aisles were also employed, except at Santa Maria Maggiore. Also of this period is San Giovanni in Laterano, which pioneers the Italian preference for a separate, octagonal **baptistry**.

The basic basilican style flourished in the city for centuries, and little in the way of development is discernible between the seventh-century Sant'Agnese and the ninth-century Santa Maria in Cosmedin, or even the twelfth-century San Clemente, though the last is unusually archaic.

The next significant buildings are those of the subsequent imperial capital, **Ravenna**. These are understandably more famous for the resplendent mosaics which adorn their interiors, but they are also of major architectural significance, marking the appearance in Italy of the **Byzantine** style, whose most distinctive characteristic was the development of the dome. Under the Romans, this by necessity had to rest on a circular base; by the use of pendentives, the Byzantines were able to erect a dome on square foundations. The earliest of the surviving Ravenna monuments, the Mausoleum of Galla Placida, dating from about 430, provides a good illustration of this. The church of San Vitale, an ingenious design of an octagon within an octagon, is also remarkable. The other churches here are basilican in form; a curiosity is that the apse is semicircular inside, but has a polygonal exterior. Their cylindrical **campaniles** were added later, probably in the ninth century. These are the earliest freestanding belltowers – from then on, a popular characteristic of Italian churches – to have survived, though the form was actually pioneered in Rome.

Italy's most purely Byzantine buildings are to be found in the Venetian lagoon, whose prosperity was dependent on its eastern trade. The duomo of **Torcello**, originally seventh-century but extensively remodelled in the early eleventh century, is the oldest of these; Santa Fosca on the same island is in the same style. However, the Byzantine heritage is seen to best effect in the basilica of San Marco in **Venice** itself. This was also much altered in the eleventh century, but the basic layout of the original ninth-century building, modelled on the Church of the Holy Apostles in Constantinople, was preserved. With its five bulbous domes, its Greek-cross plan and sumptuous mosaic decoration, it stands as the supreme Byzantine monument of its time.

ROMANESQUE

The European emergence from the Dark Ages in the tenth and eleventh centuries is associated in architecture with the **Romanesque** style, which in Italy draws heavily on the country's own heritage. Features not commonly found in other countries include a continued attachment to the basilical plan, and to cupolas raised on domes, the use of marble for facing, the presence of separate baptistries and campaniles, and the employment of the arch for decorative rather than purely structural reasons.

Strong regional variations are apparent. The churches of the **Lombard plain** most resemble those of northern Europe, and were among the most internationally influential. Their most dominant features are their tall, stately towers, which are unbuttressed and adorned with pilaster strips. They usually have a projecting vaulted porch on the facade, resting on a base of lions, above which a wheel window serves as the principal source of light for the nave. Decoration is otherwise concentrated in the apse, which often has an open dwarf gallery and corbels delicately carved with grotesque heads. Rib vaulting – revolutionary in its day – was sometimes used inside. The duomo in **Modena** is particularly outstanding, as are the characteristic trios of duomo, campanile and baptistry at **Parma** and **Cremona**.

All these are surpassed by the highly distinctive style of **Pisa**, which can be seen all over the city but is particularly associated with the Piazza del Duomo, which adds a burial ground (the Camposanto) to the normal group of three,

and has the rare advantage of a spacious verdant setting away from the commercial centre. Although the ensemble was begun in the mid-eleventh century and only finished three hundred years later, it shows a remarkable sense of unity. The buildings all have marble facing, and their exteriors, in a design conducive to catching wonderful light effects, have open arcaded galleries, which rise all the way to the facade gable – and all the way round the building. A broadly similar approach was adopted in the neighbouring cities of **Lucca** and **Pistoia**.

An even more idiosyncratic Romanesque style was fostered in the earliest surviving buildings of **Florence** – the baptistry, San Miniato and Santi Apostoli, plus the Badia in Fiesole. The overall layout of these buildings is typical enough of the time, but the continued use of mosaics and marble panelling in the interiors is suggestive of the Byzantine era, while the overall elegance of form shows a debt to Roman models.

In **southern Italy** there was a marriage of Byzantine and Romanesque styles, as can be seen at San Nicola in Bari and the duomos of Salerno, Amalfi, Troia, Trani, Molfetta and Bitonto. An even more intoxicating mix is found in **Sicily**, where the island's traditions were freely welded into an exotic confection which is wholly unique. Sturdy Norman towers are often found in concert with Byzantine domes and mosaics and Saracenic horseshoe arches and stalactite vaulting. The duomo of **Monreale** – and in particular its fabulous cloister with dazzling mosaics and richly carved capitals – is particularly outstanding. Those of **Cefalù** and **Palermo** are also notable, as are three surprising parish churches, all in the capital – La Martorana, San Cataldo and San Giovanni degli Eremiti. Palermo also has two outstanding palaces which show the same mix of styles: the Palazzo dei Normanni and La Zisa.

THE GOTHIC PERIOD

The **Gothic** style, which placed great emphasis on light and verticality, and was associated with the pointed arch, rib vault, flying buttress and large traceried windows, progressed from its mid-twelfth-century French origins to become the dominant architectural force of medieval Europe. But although it was used in Italy from the early thirteenth century to the early fifteenth century, its lifespan here was far shorter than elsewhere, and the forms it took quite different from those of other countries. In many ways, Italy was wholly unsuited to the Gothic, which remained essentially a northern European creation. The pointed arch was foreign to a country steeped in classicism, while the hot climate meant that only small windows were required, or interiors would become stifling. For the same reason, the giant portals of northern Gothic were unwanted; moreover, the large numbers of statues in the round they required were anathema to a nation reared on relief carvings.

In Italian Gothic architecture the emphasis is still on the **horizontal**: buildings seldom rise very high, and often have wooden roofs rather than stone vaults. **Colour** plays a far more important role than in any other country, as do walls covered with marble facing, mosaics and frescoes. A great deal of attention was lavished on **facades**, but these were again often purely decorative, with no architectural relationship to the structure behind. Many of the most characteristic features of Gothic, such as soaring steeples and graceful pinnacles, flying buttresses and elaborate vaults, are hardly to be found in Italy at all.

As elsewhere in Europe, the spread of the plain early-Gothic style in Italy is associated with the reforming Cistercian order of monks. The abbey of **Fossanova**, which was complete by the first decade of the thirteenth century, is an outstanding example of their architecture, as well as an unusually complete example of a medieval monastic complex. In a similar manner are the monasteries of San Galgano near Siena (now in ruins) and the collegiate church of Sant'Andrea in Vercelli. However, the most outstanding early-Gothic church in Italy is the basilica of San Francesco in **Assisi**, which was built in the wake of the saint's death in 1226. It is a wholly original, symbolical design, with the lower church dark and mysterious, the upper light and airy, each provided with ample wall space which in time was duly filled with appropriate fresco cycles.

Nothing quite like San Francesco was ever built again, but the churches of the Franciscan and Dominican orders became a dominant feature of many cities. In accordance with the emphasis placed on preaching, these were typically barn-like structures, intended to hold a large congregation. They were invariably of brick, but differed considerably in plan. The most imposing are the late-thirteenth-century Santa Croce and Santa Maria Novella in **Florence**, and their fourteenth-century counterparts in **Venice** – I Frari and San Zanipolo.

Though there were relatively few important building projects of the Gothic period, they generally took on a spectacular nature. The duomo in **Siena** is arguably the most sumptuous Gothic cathedral ever built, and boasts a resplendent facade in which sculptures were used in a wholly unorthodox and challenging way. **Florence**'s duomo has gained world fame through its Renaissance dome, but in essentials it is a highly inventive Gothic design, whose final shape had already been determined by the mid-fourteenth century. Its detached campanile, unbuttressed and faced with coloured marbles and reliefs, illustrates the continuing Italian preference for this form. **Orvieto** shows the tendencies of Italian Gothic at its most extreme: the interior architecture is plain, and remarkably close in spirit to an early Christian basilica, whereas the facade surpasses even Siena's for ornateness, with its narrative bas-reliefs, brightly coloured marbles and mosaics. Only the duomo of **Milan**, begun in the late fourteenth century but not finally completed until the nineteenth century, uses much of the stock vocabulary of northern European cathedral architecture, no doubt owing to the fact that German masons were partly responsible for its construction. Yet even here the gleaming white marble and pronounced geometric nature of the design are wholly Italianate.

The scale of this project seems to have inspired that of the nearby Certosa di Pavia, near **Pavia**, the most extensive monastic complex in the country. Here, however, notice was paid to changing artistic tastes, with the result that it progressively moved away from its Gothic origins. San Petronio in **Bologna**, which was started around the same time, was a parish church intended to rival any cathedral, and to surpass them all in length. Work, however, was abandoned on the belated completion of the nave. From a century earlier, another idiosyncratic design worthy of mention is the pilgrimage church of il Santo in **Padua**. This has an essentially Gothic plan, even including a French-style chevet with radiating chapels. However, the facade is derived from the Lombard Romanesque, while the seven large domes are evidence of the continued attraction of Byzantinism.

In the field of military architecture, the most imposing thirteenth-century **castles** were built in southern Italy by Emperor Frederick II, most impressive of which is the celebrated **Castel del Monte**, which combined classical and Gothic elements in a plan of monotonous regularity, with an octagonal shape used for towers, perimeter walls and courtyard. Frederick's castle at **Lucera** was transformed later in the century by the Angevins, who also built the Castel Nuovo in **Naples** – later altered to serve as a palace in succeeding centuries.

Among fourteenth-century constructions, the Fortezza at **Volterra** is an archetypal medieval castle set high on a hill, with cylindrical keep, round towers, massive outer walls and machicolations. Of the palatial fortresses begun around this time, those of **Mantua, Ferrara** and **Verona** are particularly outstanding, the last guarded by a strongly fortified **bridge** over the Adige. Italy's other famous Gothic bridge, the Ponte Vecchio in Florence, presents a total contrast, with jewellers' shops along its length.

In the late thirteenth century, the rise of civic pride led to a passion for building majestic **town halls**, often crowned by a slender tower. The most imposing are the Palazzo Pubblico in Siena and the Palazzo Vecchio in Florence. These same cities, along with many more in central Italy, are rich in Gothic **mansions** of the patrician class. However, the most distinctive residences in the country were built in **Venice**. The Ca' d'Oro is the most refined, whereas the Ca' Fóscari and Palazzo Giustinian have a compensating monumental grandeur. All were modelled on the **Palazzo Ducale** in Mantua, arguably the greatest secular European building of its time, which ingeniously combines Gothic and Islamic styles on its exterior walls, with evidence of the classical influence in its courtyards and interiors.

THE EARLY RENAISSANCE

The Gothic style maintained a firm hold over northern European architecture until well into the sixteenth century. In **Florence**, however, it had been supplanted by the second decade of the fifteenth century by the new, classically derived **Renaissance** style, which soon spread throughout Italy. Its conquest of the rest of Europe, if belated, was absolute, establishing an architectural vocabulary which remained unchallenged until the nineteenth century, and still maintains a footing even today. From here on, the history of architecture becomes a history of architects. Previously, major buildings had been designed and built by lodges under masons whose fame was seldom wide or long lasting. To some extent this had been modified in Italy by the appointment of famous painters and sculptors for the most prestigious commissions. This trend continued in the Renaissance period and was undoubtedly a factor in ensuring that all major buildings were aesthetically pleasing – a casual relationship which was lost in later centuries as architecture shed its dilettante connotations and became professional in outlook, with full-time practitioners emerging for the first time.

Both the format of modern architecture and the profession of architect were in many respects the single-handed creation of **Filippo Brunelleschi** (1377–1446). Having been unsuccessful in the competition for the Florence Baptistry doors, he turned away from his original training as a sculptor, devoting himself to a careful study of the building practices and techniques of the ancients. He subsequently won another major local competition, that for the duomo's dome. It was only by reviving Roman methods of herringbone brickwork, and by inventing suitable hoisting machinery, that Brunelleschi was able to give the final shape to this otherwise Gothic construction, which ever since has served as the focal point of the city, and provided a model for all subsequent domes. In his key original buildings – the Ospedale degli Innocenti, the churches of San Lorenzo and Santo Spirito and the Cappella Pazzi – Brunelleschi seems to have been inspired as much by the distinctive Romanesque legacy of his native city as by ancient Rome. His designs are majestic but uncomplicated; they are entirely original, and in no sense an archeological revival of any previous style.

Two more Brunelleschi innovations – a new type of urban palace, and a central plan for church design – are best illustrated in buildings by **Michelozzo di Bartolommeo** (1396–1472). The Palazzo Medici-Riccardi established the form of Florentine mansions for the rest of the century – a severe facade of three bands: rusticated stonework in the basement, smoother stones in the middle and smooth ashlar upstairs, an overhanging cornice, and a compensatingly light inner courtyard. In the church of Santa Annunziata, Michelozzo modelled the tribune on a circular Roman temple in the first centrally planned church design to be built in the Renaissance period; with Santa Maria delle Grazie in **Pistoia** he extended this concept to the entire building. His light and airy library in San Marco is a mould-breaker in its own right; its format of a central nave flanked by aisles was used throughout the Renaissance.

Even more influential was **Leon Battista Alberti** (1404–72). One of the most complete personifications of Renaissance Man, Alberti was above all a writer and theorist, the author of the first architectural treatise since Roman times; he designed buildings, but always relied on other architects to build them. Far more archeological in taste than Brunelleschi, he set out to give new life to such Roman forms as triumphal arches and pedimented temple fronts. He also articulated the theory of harmonic proportions, which, in emulation of musical intervals, adopted certain ratios of measurement – first put into practice in the facade of Santa Maria Novella. With the Palazzo Rucellai, he solved the problem of how to make the facades of Florentine palaces seem less austere and Gothic in feel by the simple expedient of introducing thin pilaster strips. Alberti's most original creations, however, are outside Florence. Although unfinished, his design for the Tempio Malatestiano in **Rimini** is a magnificent fragment, cloaking the old Franciscan church with a covering inspired by the same town's great Roman monuments. An even more resplendent facade was designed for Sant'Andrea in **Mantua**. Its elements are carefully repeated in the interior, a vast space which daringly omits aisles in favour of a single nave with side chapels.

Bernardo Rossellino (1409–64), who was the builder of the Palazzo Rucellai, used its basic form again in the Palazzo Piccolomini in **Pienza**, where he was also responsible for the duomo and the surrounding buildings. This was part of the most ambitious planning scheme of the day, the laying out of a complete new papal town. Like many subsequent Renaissance projects, it remains incomplete, available funds failing to match the grandeur of inspiration. The creation of ideal towns was the main preoccupation of Antonio Averlino known as **Filarete**

(c1400–69), the second main architectural theorist of the day. He himself built very little, other than part of the Castello Sforzesco and the huge, symmetrical Ospedale Maggiore, both in **Milan**.

Of the next generation of Florentine architects, **Giuliano da Maiano** (1432–90) introduced the Renaissance style to **Siena** with the Palazzo Spannochi, and also built the duomo in **Faenza**. The last phase of his career was spent in **Naples**, where he was responsible for the Porta Capuana and chapels in the church of Monteoliveto. **Giuliano da Sangallo** (1445–1516) was the first to apply Renaissance principles to the layout of villas, and his work in **Florence** includes the Palazzo Strozzi, the most ambitious palace of the century, and the heavily antique cloister of Santa Maria Maddalena dei Pazzi, in which Ionic columns boldly take the place of arches.

The most complete and refined early-Renaissance palace was built in the comparative obscurity of **Urbino**, where a cultivated humanist court flourished. **Luciano Laurana** (c1420–79), an obscure architect of Dalmatian origin, is credited with the overall plan, as well as the building of the elegant courtyard, and the ornate chimneypieces and doorways which are key features of the interior. Also attached to Urbino was the Sienese **Francesco di Giorgio Martini** (1439–1501/2), who is thought to have built the exquisite loggia overlooking the hills, as well as two domed churches: San Bernardino in Urbino itself and Santa Maria del Calcinaio in Cortona. Like many other Renaissance architects, he worked extensively on military projects, specializing in hilltop castles with pioneering defences against artillery. **Ferrara** was another small court where the Renaissance prospered, thanks in large part to an ambitious extension to the town designed by **Biagio Rossetti** (1447–1516), which included numerous churches and palaces, the most original of which is the Palazzo dei Diamanti, named after the diamond shapes used on its facade. **Venice** remained attached to the Gothic style until the 1460s. When the Renaissance finally took root, it was given a pronounced local accent, with hangovers from Byzantinism in the preference for rich surfaces and mystical spatial effects. Architects still enjoyed nothing like the prestige they had gained in Florence, and it was only as a result of nineteenth-century research that

Mauro Coducci (c1440–1504) emerged from obscurity to be identified as the builder of many of the city's best buildings of this time – the churches of San Michele in Isola, San Giovanni Crisostomo and Santa Maria Formosa. His rival **Pietro Lombardo** (c1435–1515) was less concerned with the central tenets of the Florentine Renaissance than with using them to update the Venetian-Byzantine tradition. The tiny church of Santa Maria dei Miracoli, for which he and his sons also made the decoration, shows his highly ornate style at its best.

THE HIGH RENAISSANCE AND MANNERISM

The ornate facades characteristic of the Venetian Renaissance were to some extent repeated all across northern Italy, notably in the early buildings of **Donato Bramante** (1444–1514) in **Milan**. These include the church of San Satiro, which ingeniously incorporates a ninth-century chapel and makes up for the lack of space to build an apse by including a convincing trompe l'oeil of one; the centrally planned east end of Santa Maria delle Grazie, which completely outclasses the Gothic nave; and a series of cloisters for Sant'Ambrogio.

With the French invasion of the city in 1499, Bramante fled to **Rome**, where his enthusiasm coincided nicely with the papal authorities' desire to rebuild the city in a manner worthy of its imperial heyday, and the **High Renaissance** in architecture was born. This centred on the demolition of the fourth-century basilica of **St Peter's**, and its replacement by a vast new church. Bramante provided a design that was the ultimate in central planning, a Greek cross with four smaller Greek crosses in its arms. This project took well over a century to complete, by which time Bramante's plan had been altered out of all recognition, with only the piers of the dome surviving. Bramante's surviving masterpiece in Rome is the tiny Tempietto of San Pietro in Montorio, whose grandeur is out of all proportion to its size.

Bramante's position as leading architect in Rome was taken over by **Raphael** (1483–1520). His painting activities left him little time for this, but his few buildings were enormously influential. The Chigi chapel in the church of Santa Maria del Popolo brought to fruition the interest in centralized temples first evident in his early panel of *The Marriage of the Virgin*

(now in the Brera, Milan). It is deliberately set apart from the rest of the church, and opulently adorned with statues, bronze reliefs, paintings, marbles and mosaics, its richness reflecting that of the patron, the papal banker. His pupil **Giulio Romano** (c1492–1546) was active mainly in **Mantua**, where he consciously distorted the elements of classical architecture, thus beginning the Mannerist style. The Palazzo Te establishes an organic unity between house and garden, as well as between architecture and interior decoration. The artist's own house in the same city is very different but equally inventive, while his design for the duomo is an early example of a building concerned above all with effect, the intention being to "suck" the viewer towards the high altar.

Baldassarre Peruzzi (1481–1536), originally from Siena, built the most graceful of **Rome**'s High Renaissance palaces, the Villa Farnesina, which is arguably the outstanding secular monument of the time, featuring an unusual U-shaped plan with two superbly frescoed ground floor loggias and an upstairs hall with illusionistic architectural perspectives. The Palazzo Massimo alle Colonne from late in his career successfully overcomes the difficulties of its sloping site by means of a highly original convex facade. Peruzzi also built the pentagonal Villa Farnese in Caprarola in collaboration with **Antonio da Sangallo the Younger** (1485–1546), with whom he also worked on St Peter's. Sangallo's most important independent work, however, is the strongly classical Palazzo Farnese, the most spectacular Roman palace of its time.

Michelangelo Buonarroti (1475–1564) only took up architecture in middle age. His approach was in direct contrast to Alberti's, using plans only as a rough guide, and making constant changes throughout the period of execution. None of his major buildings were finished in his lifetime: his earliest commissions in **Florence** – San Lorenzo's Sagrestia Nuova (which forms a piece with his own sculptures) and the Biblioteca Laurenziana (where every element of the decoration is closely tied to the architecture) – already show an original approach to building. Like Giulio Romano, he adopted an entirely new attitude to space, and turned the vocabulary of classicism to suit his own ends. In **Rome**, he invented the giant order – columns and pilasters rising through two or more storeys – for his palaces on the Piazza del Campidoglio. Other major projects were the conversion of the central hall of the Baths of Diocleti, into the church of Santa Maria degli Angeli, and the work on St Peter's.

The High Renaissance was introduced to **Venice** by **Jacopo Sansovino** (1486–1570), who fled from Rome after its sacking by French troops in 1527. Sansovino quickly became the leading architect in the city, and erected a series of public edifices – the Zecca, the Loggetta and the Libreria Sansoviniana – which transformed the area around San Marco. The last-named is one of the most joyous, festive designs of the Renaissance, a highly successful compromise between classical precision and Venetian love of surface ornament.

Michele Sanmicheli (c1484–1559) spent much of his career on military projects, building the fortifications of his native **Verona**, including three dignified gateways, and the Fortezza at the entrance to Venice's Lido. He also built very grandiose palaces in both cities, which are especially notable for their facades of richly detailed stonework: the Palazzo Grimani on the Canal Grande and the Palazzo Bevilacqua in Verona are among the finest. The Cappella Pellegrini in San Bernardino, Verona, develops the idea of Raphael's Chigi chapel, while the later pilgrimage church of Madonna di Campagna in the same city is one of the most ambitious centrally planned churches of the sixteenth century.

Italy's most erudite and internationally influential architect was the Paduan **Andrea Palladio** (1508–80), who distilled features from all his great predecessors, welding them into a distinctive personal style. Palladio is associated above all with the city of **Vicenza**, which he adorned with a magnificent series of palaces, beginning with the so-called Basilica. In a spectacular piece of conjectural archeology in the same city, he built the Teatro Olimpico, the first permanent theatre since the days of antiquity. The villas he created for aristocratic clients in the surrounding countryside were much imitated elsewhere; indeed, they served as the model for British country houses until well into the nineteenth century. In the most famous, La Rotonda, Palladio put the architect's ideal of a central plan to secular use for the first time, and introduced identical temple-like fronts on all four sides of the building.

Genoa developed a distinctive architectural character of its own during the High Renaissance thanks to **Galeazzo Alessi** (1512–72), who made the most of the sloping sites common to this hilly city. His huge palaces typically feature monumental staircases and courtyards set on different levels. He also designed the commanding hilltop church of Santa Maria in Carignano, which borrows Bramante's plan for St Peter's.

In **Florence**, the Mannerist style took firm root in the wake of Michelangelo. **Bartolomeo Ammannati** (1511–92) is best known for his additions and amendments to the Palazzo Pitti, which more or less determined its final form, and for the graceful Ponte San Trinità. **Bernardo Buontalenti** (c1536–1608) was the city's quirkiest architect, celebrated mainly for the grottoes in the Bóboli Gardens and his designs for court spectaculars. Yet he also worked in a conventional idiom, as witnessed by the Fortezza Belvedere, the Tribuna of the Uffizi and the facade of Santa Trinita.

Both Ammannati and Vasari worked in Rome in collaboration with Jacopo Barozzi, known as **il Vignola** (1507–73), on the Villa Giulia, the city's finest expression of the Mannerist delight in architecture mingled with landscape gardening. Vignola also succeeded Michelangelo as architect of St Peter's, but his chief importance lies in the way he prepared the ground for the new Baroque style. The Gesù, mother church of the Jesuits, the order on which the Counter-Reformation was to depend so much, was Vignola's most important commission, and one which was imitated all round the world. His design was based on Alberti's Sant'Andrea in Mantua, eliminating the aisles and using the nave pilasters and lighting effects to draw the eye towards the high altar.

Vignola died before the Gesù was complete, leaving the facade to be built by **Giacomo della Porta** (c1537–1602). This imperious front places emphasis on the portal, and presents a highly unified design in which every component plays an essential role. Della Porta was also responsible for the construction and final shape of the dome of St Peter's, making it more ornate than Michelangelo had intended.

While Rome moved confidently into a new era, the High Renaissance was kept alive in northern Italy by Palladio's most faithful follower, **Vincenzo Scamozzi** (1552–1616). He completed many of Palladio's unfinished designs, and added the brilliant perspective stage set to the Teatro Olympico. Many of his original works imitate Palladio's most famous buildings: he built a broadly similar theatre at Sabbioneta, and modelled San Nicola da Tolentino in Venice on Il Redentore.

THE BAROQUE

Although it may be difficult to pinpoint the exact period when **Baroque** began, it is recognizably a distinctive style in its own right. Politically, its birth is inexorably linked to **Rome**, a city which needed to reflect in a wealth of new buildings the brash, self-confident mood it had acquired as a result of the Counter Reformation, its architecture expressing both the pomp and mystery of the religious approach then being propagated. Architects became concerned with daring spatial effects, with rendering movement by the use of curvaceous lines and dazzling tricks of light, and with rich decoration of which painting and sculpture were integral components.

The first architect to build wholly within the new idiom was **Carlo Maderno** (1556–1629). Maderno's reputation has been sullied by his association with a major architectural failure, the completion of St Peter's by the addition of a nave and facade, which destroyed the balance of the Greek-cross plan and masked the view of the dome. Yet Maderno was really only marginally at fault: the clergy had always disliked the democratic nature of centrally planned churches, and it was the new hieratic spirit of the age which prompted the need for the extensions. The highly original facade of Santa Susanna and the dome of Sant'Andrea della Valle prove that Maderno was actually a highly capable designer. He also started Rome's most important seventeenth-century palace, the Palazzo Barberini, though this was much altered by later hands.

The overall appearance of Baroque Rome is owed above all to **Gianlorenzo Bernini** (1598–1680). Like Michelangelo, Bernini only took up architecture in mid-career, by which time he had established his reputation as the leading sculptor of the day. His fusion of the arts was to be one of the keynotes of the Baroque. His principal architectural achievements were in the field of town planning: he revamped the Piazza Navona, in the centre of which he placed a monumental fountain to his own design. Most brilliant of all was his

surprisingly simple rearrangement of the square in front of St Peter's into an oval shape, with two sets of colonnades grouped to symbolize the embracing arms of the Church. The nearby Scala Regia is an equally clever design, with the steps, columns and vault all diminishing in size towards the summit to give a far greater feeling of grandeur than the restricted space would seem to allow.

Francesco Borromini (1599–1667), at first Bernini's assistant, but later his bitter rival, was the most daring and inventive Baroque architect. His attitude to decoration was very different to Bernini's, whose sculptural training he did not share. To him, architecture was sculpture in its own right, and he treated the entire wall surface plastically, favouring monochromal effects instead of colours. Even in his first commission, San Carlo alle Quattro Fontane, Borromini showed his total disregard for convention, creating a stunning spatial design based on a complex series of shapes, with two equilateral triangles resolved into an oval at the level of the dome, and a circle in the lantern above. The facade, added later, was highly influential in its mixed use of concave and convex effects. Most of Borromini's subsequent buildings suffered from the handicap of having been begun by other architects. Nevertheless, he achieved many highly unusual effects, notably in Sant'Ivo alla Sapienza, and in the seemingly independent towers flanking the dome of Sant'Agnese, a motif that was subsequently much imitated. Borromini's most prestigious commission was the internal remodelling of San Giovanni in Laterano, which transformed the early Christian basilica into a vast Baroque temple.

The third main architect of Baroque Rome was **Pietro da Cortona** (1596–1669). Surprisingly, Cortona desisted from the union of the arts beloved of Bernini, preferring instead whitewashed interior walls. Nonetheless, his mature work combines elements from both Borromini and Bernini: the facade of Santa Maria della Pace, for example, makes considerable play with concave and convex shapes, yet takes this further by rearranging the square in which it is set to form a kind of foyer.

Elsewhere in Italy, only a handful of seventeenth-century architects stand comparison with their Roman contemporaries. One of these was **Francesco Maria Ricchino** (1583–1658), whose buildings in **Milan** bear direct comparison with the most progressive designs in Rome. **Bartolomeo Bianco** (c1590–1657) adorned **Genoa** with some of the century's finest palaces, proving a worthy successor to Alessi in the way he turned the sloping ground to his advantage.

The leading Baroque architect in **Naples** was the Lombard **Cosimo Fanzago** (1591–1678), whose early buildings, notably the cloisters of the Certosa di San Martino, are restrained and classically inspired. Another south Italian centre for a distinctively exuberant, wilful form of Baroque was the little town of **Lecce**, which was adorned with a series of churches and public buildings by a group of architects whose leading light was **Giuseppe Zimbalo** (active 1659–86).

The only major Baroque architect in **Venice** was **Baldassarre Longhena** (1598–1682). His fame rests chiefly on the votive church of Santa Maria della Salute, whose distinctive domed silhouette makes the most of its prominent site. Longhena also built two of the Canal Grande's finest palaces, the Ca' Pésaro and the Ca' Rezzonico, though here he did little more than update Sansovino's forms.

Turin, which had previously played no significant part in Italian art and architecture, progressively took over from Rome as the leading centre of the Baroque. **Carlo di Castellamonte** (1560–1641) drew up an ambitious plan of the city, and built the Piazza San Carlo as its centrepiece. Even more significant was the arrival of the monk **Guarino Guarini** (1624–83), who was a brilliant mathematician as well as architect. Guarini was unusual among Italians in his interest in both Gothic and Islamic styles of building, but the prime influence on his development was Borromini. He used his mathematical skills to inflate the Roman architect's essentially small-scale approach into the grand manner in such commissions as the Collegio dei Nobili and the Palazzo Carignano. Both the Cappella della Santa Sidone, built at the east end of the duomo to house the Turin Shroud, and San Lorenzo feature fantastic conical domes and pyrotechnic spatial effects using a wide variety of shapes.

After a gap of a generation, Turin attracted another remarkable architect, the Roman-trained Sicilian **Filippo Juvarra** (1678–1736). In a twenty-year sojourn in the city, he was responsible for a wealth of buildings, including the planning of new districts, churches, palaces and countryside villas. His imposingly sited Superga basilica combines the pilgrimage church and monastery in a single unit, and is by far the finest of its type in Italy, fully worthy of comparison with its central European counterparts. However, Juvarra's masterpiece is the Palazzina di Stupinigi, an extravagantly decorous villa which uses a triaxial hexagonal design instead of the conventional rectangle.

In **Sicily**, the disastrous earthquake of 1693 led to a wholesale demand for new buildings. Accordingly, the island is richly endowed with flowery late-Baroque creations which are the nearest Italian equivalents to French and German Rococo. Essentially, they are derivative in nature, paying a heavy debt to Borromini as well as to the Churrigueresque style of Spain. The most individualistic architect was **Giovan Battista Vaccarini** (1702–68), who was particularly associated with the laying out of **Catania**. However, the much smaller planned town of **Noto** provides an even more visually satisfying ensemble.

NEOCLASSICISM

The **Neoclassical** style, which reacted against the sumptuousness of late Baroque by returning to the most basic principles of classicism, is generally considered to have begun in **Rome** in the mid-eighteenth century. Yet long before that, while the century was still young, a number of architects in **Venice** had decisively moved against Baroque excesses, notably **Giovanni Scalfarotto** (1690–1764), whose San Simone Piccolo is demonstrably derived from the Pantheon.

Giovanni Battista Piranesi (1720–78) did more than anyone to popularize the Neoclassical approach in Rome. His inspired large-scale engravings of the city's ruins rank among the all-time masterpieces of graphic art, and were to have a wide circulation. His theoretical writings asserted the superiority of the architecture of classical Rome over Greece, and advocated a reinterpretation of its forms as the basis for a new style. As a practising architect, Piranesi is known only for Santa Maria del Priorato, a heavily symbolical church for the Knights of Malta, set in a pentagonal square.

A remarkable synthesis of late Baroque and Neoclassicism was achieved by **Luigi Vanvitelli** (1700–73) in the colossal royal palace of **Caserta**, whose ornate apartments with their long vistas show all the swagger of the old style, whereas the exterior has all the calm restraint of the new. His pupil **Giuseppe Piermarini** (1734–1808) became the leading Neoclassical architect in Milan, where he designed several severe palaces with long, unadorned facades, along with what became Italy's most prestigious opera house, La Scala.

Another celebrated theatre, La Fenice in **Venice**, is the best-known building by the city's most committed exponent of Neoclassicism, **Giannantonio Selva** (1751–1819). Although gutted by fire early in 1996, the opera house will almost certainly be rebuilt, as it was after an earlier fire in 1836. A certain French influence pervades the work of **Giuseppe Valadier** (1762–1839), who was given responsibility for remodelling the interiors of the cathedrals of Spoleto and Urbino while still in his twenties. Later he was based in Rome, where his commissions included the triumphal arch on the Ponte Milvio and the laying out of the Piazza del Popolo.

As with the other visual arts, architecture in Italy was in the doldrums for most of the nineteenth century. Because of the all-pervasiveness of the classical tradition, there was little of the confident modern reinterpretation of other styles which characterizes northern European building of this period. Only **Giuseppe Japelli** (1783–1852) stands as an exception to this. His masterpiece, the Caffè Pedrocchi in **Padua**, is firmly Neoclassical, but its extension is neo-Gothic, while his Teatro Verdi in the same city is based on Rococo, and his villas are modelled on Palladio.

The nineteenth century also saw some impressive examples of town planning. One of these was in **Trieste**, where the waterfront area was redesigned. In **Turin**, the work of the previous century was continued by the laying out of the Piazza Vittorio Veneto and Piazza Carlo Felice at opposite ends of the city. Later, **Alessandro Antonelli** (1798–1888) adorned the city with a huge iron supported tower, the Mole Antonelliana, originally intended as a synagogue, but converted into a museum.

The most original piece of planning was in **Milan**, whose status as the commercial hub of the emergent nation-state is symbolized by the construction of the Galleria Vittorio Emanuele II by **Giuseppe Mengoni** (1829–77) – Italy's first important example of design in iron and glass,

and the initiator of a trend for covered shopping areas throughout Europe.

With the accomplishment of complete Italian Unification in 1870, **Rome** had to be supplied with new streets and buildings worthy of a great modern capital; inevitably, the most monumental classical style possible was chosen, and it was only a partial success. The most strikingly visible – if not the most aesthetically pleasing – late-Neoclassical addition to the city's patrimony is the huge white marble Monument to Vittorio Emanuele II by **Giuseppe Sacconi** (1853–1905).

THE TWENTIETH CENTURY

A reaction against the nineteenth-century infatuation with the imitation of historical styles came with the **Art Nouveau** movement, whose sinewy forms dominated European architecture and design in the early years of the new century. In Italy, where it was known as **Liberty**, its impact was less extensive than in most other countries and also more restrained. **Giuseppe Sommaruga** (1867–1917) was the most talented exponent; the most important of his buildings is the Palazzo Castiglioni in Milan.

Of far more long-lasting significance to the overall direction of Italian architecture was the **Futurist** movement, manifested in the visionary drawings of **Antonio Sant'Elia** (1888–1916), who envisaged a vibrant high-rise metropolis of the future dominated by frenetic activity and rapid transport systems operating on several levels. Sant'Elia's death in World War I meant that none of these visionary projects was ever realized. The only construction that gives a vague idea of what Futurist architecture might have been is the Monument to the Fallen in **Como**, which is based on a design by Sant'Elia for a lighthouse. The executant architect was **Giuseppe Terragni** (1904–43), the major exponent of **Rationalism** in Italy. This movement was strongly influenced by the ideas of the Bauhaus movement in Germany, and sought to use new materials in a modern way, to capitalize on space and light for a modern revolution where rational lines were cleared of the decorations and elaborations of past styles. Terragni founded the Gruppo 7, composed of Italy's seven most progressive inter-war architects, who fought to have Rationalism accepted above classicist architecture as the official architecture of Fascism. Terragni built several other works in Como, the most accomplished of which is the Casa del Fascio, originally the local Fascist Party headquarters.

During the twenty years of **Fascism**, Mussolini directed a massive building programme which left cities, towns and villages across the country shadowed by institutional buildings built in a monumental style reminiscent of those of ancient Rome. The colossal dimensions and imperial paraphernalia adopted by architects like **Marcello Piacentini** (1880–1960), Mussolini's favourite architect, who was responsible for the Piazza della Vittoria in **Brescia**, tended to be favoured over Rationalism. New towns like Sabaudia and Littoria near Rome were designed as prototype communities for the new "empire". But World War II put a stop to the building programmes and later caused the destruction of much of the built fabric of Italy's urban centres.

After the war the themes of memory, relationship with history and the search for a new identity became the central concerns of Italian architecture. The story of postwar architecture begins with two **memorials**: the monument to the 35 civilians killed in the massacre of the Ardeatine Caves in Rome and the monument to the victims of the German concentration camps in Milan's Cimitero Monumentale. The latter was designed by the studio BPR, a successful practice before the war called BBPR: the first "B", Gian Luigi Banfi, was killed in Mauthausen concentration camp towards the end of the war. The postwar years were also the years when **New Realism** dominated Italian culture from cinema to literature. It was a new language, free from the ties of the recent Fascist past. The critic **Bruno Zevi** (1918–1999) wrote about organic architecture as the architecture of democracy, where forms were freed from the strictures of straight lines in favour of curves.

Huge rebuilding programmes were undertaken as much to provide employment as to repair the devastation suffered during the war. Endless motorways were laid across the country and working class neighbourhoods were built on the outskirts of cities, public money often being used to subsidize private financial and speculative interests. The architecture was often subordinate to the political interests involved, and in the worst cases New Realism became synonymous with nostalgia and populism. However, as this approach flourished in Rome, there was a different atmosphere in Milan. **Ernesto Nathan Rogers** (1909–1969) of BPR (a close relative of the British architect Richard Rogers) was the personality behind the theory of continuity, the necessity for continuity with the ideals of prewar Rationalism without negating its critical revision. The most significant example of this architecture is the Torre Velasca by BPR in Milan. The giant *torre civica* is an intellectual interpretation of the disappearing medieval city.

During the Fifties and Sixties architectural tendencies or movements were overshadowed by the work done by several individual characters who defy categorization, the most important being Ignazio Gardella, Carlo Scarpa, and Pier Luigi Nervi. **Ignazio Gardella** (1905–1999) rejected exhibitionism in favour of the value of materials and forms. His most representative works are the Casa Borsalino in **Alessandria** and the Padiglione d'Arte Contemporanea (PAC) in the Villa Reale in **Milan**, recently reconstructed after being destroyed by a Mafia bomb in 1993. The work of **Carlo Scarpa** (1906–1978) on the other hand, was infused with a very personal poeticism, always on the verge of refined excess. His exquisite detailing is superbly exemplified in the restoration of the Castelvecchio in **Verona** as a museum, and the reorganization of the Fondazione Querini Stampalia in Venice. **Pier Luigi Nervi** (1891–1979), an engineer, practised throughout the political turmoil of the twentieth century, unaffected by fashions or prevailing styles, and popularized the use of reinforced concrete. Among his prestigious postwar commissions are exhibition halls in **Turin**, whose amazing wide-span vaults recall his aircraft hangars destroyed during the war; the buildings for the 1960 Olympic Games in **Rome** and the Papal audience chamber in the Vatican. Nervi also provided the engineering core of Italy's most famous skyscraper, the Grattacielo Pirelli in Milan by **Gio Ponti** (1891–1979).

In the mid-Sixties the myths of New Realism were substituted by technological myths and egalitarian utopias. But the projects remained on the drawing board and paradoxically the radical social architects, like Andrea Branzi and Ettore Sottsass, found their only creative outlet was through **industrial design**, in particular, pieces commissioned by a wealthy, cultured elite. From this moment on, Italian architecture has been essentially architecture on the page – written or drawn – characterized by a lack of common thinking. The most important contributions have been **theoretical** (Giorgio Grassi and Aldo Rossi), and other architects have even become painters or writers (Massimo Scolari and Arduino Cantafora).

The few Italians who do construct are only able to build their best works abroad: for example **Giorgio Grassi** (b.1935), with his restoration of the Roman theatre in Sagunto in Spain, and **Renzo Piano** (b.1937), with the Pompidou Centre in Paris, in collaboration with Richard Rogers, and the Contemporary Art Museum for the Menil Collection in Houston, USA. It is perhaps significant that the two most important works of Italian architecture in the last twenty years have been a temporary installation, the Teatro del Mondo, built for the Biennale di Venezia in 1979, and a cemetery, that of San Cataldo, Modena, both by **Aldo Rossi** (1931–1997).

In the last few years, however, there have been signs of a reviving interest in architecture, and international competitions have multiplied. Renowned architects from abroad have been called in to work on historically and culturally important projects: **Zaha Hadid** (b.1950) for the contemporary arts centre in Rome; **David Chipperfield** (b.1953) for the extension to the cemetery of San Michele in Venice; and **Enric Miralles** (1955–2000) and **Benedetta Tagliabue** (b.1963) for the new school of architecture in Venice. It remains to be seen whether this will bring with it more work for home-grown talent.

Gordon McLachlan
with contributions by **Lucy Ratcliffe**

VERNACULAR ARCHITECTURE

Architecture isn't just about palaces and churches, and it's interesting to see how domestic architecture has developed, especially with regard to the siting and layout of small towns and farming settlements, both of which have had at least as much impact on the landscape of Italy as the country's better-known monumental architecture.

THE HILL-TOWNS

Throughout the Middle Ages in Italy, the countryside was unsafe and unhealthy and the land in many places remained uncultivated, either swamp or barren. As late as the fifteenth century, wolves still prowled within a few miles of Florence, in a landscape populated largely by brigands and deer. The topography of the countryside, with its abundance of hills and mountains rising steeply from fertile plains, provided natural sites for fortified settlements which could both remove the population from the malarial swamps and bandits and preserve the limited fertile land for cultivation.

In the period of their greatest expansion – between the twelfth and fourteenth centuries – **hill-towns** sprang up all over. Many were superimposed on early Etruscan cities – **Chiusi** and **Cortona** – or cave dwellings, as in **Sorano**. **Matera,** in Basilicata, grew from a very early settlement of grottoes formed by the natural erosion of volcanic rock (tufa) along the side of a high ravine. The houses that evolved from these caves (called sassi – literally "rocks") remained in use until 1952 when they were condemned. Though most hill-towns were built within high and sometimes battlemented perimeter walls, the fortress aspects of many sites obviated the need for additional protection. Houses in **Pitigliano** (in Tuscany), for example, rise like a natural extension of the rock outcropping on which they sit. The sheer drop afforded by these sites (often extended by the use of towers) enabled inhabitants to make good use of gravity by dropping a crushing blow onto the heads of enemies attempting to scale the walls. It was also a good way of dispatching the dead as well as a simple form of rubbish

disposal. After the revolution in fortifications between the thirteenth and fifteenth centuries, and the introduction of gunpowder and cannon reduced the need for enormous vertical drops, towers grew shorter and were adapted to newer methods of warfare.

Although many hill-towns were genuinely self-contained communities, the countryside remained under the political and economic control of the cities and of the communes, and the Grand Dukes and Church officials who ran them, particularly in north and central Italy. Each city-state set up satellite towns of its own, to protect trade routes (whether at sea or on land), or to operate as garrisons for soldiers, weaponry and food in case of war (or civil insurrection). Siena established the fortified hill-town of **Monteriggioni** in the early thirteenth century along an important route from Rome into France which also passed through **San Gimignano**. **San Miniato** was also set up as a fortified town by Emperor Frederick II (still quarrelling with the papacy) to take advantage of and protect this same route. At roughly the same time, Florence founded similar frontier outposts, setting up **San Giovanni Valdarno**, **Scarperia** and **Firenzuola**, all within ten years. Fewer towns emerged in the south during this period, partly because there were fewer cities: of the 26 Italian towns with populations of more than 20,000 in the thirteenth century, only three were in the south.

Hill-towns share many features, whatever the impetus for their original development. They are almost always densely built settlements, constructed with materials found on or near their site, which adds to the impression that they arise naturally from their geological foundations. They usually rely on just one or two simple dwelling types endlessly repeated. **Strómboli**, one of the Aeolian islands off the north coast of Sicily, is an example of the rich effects created by repetition of a single, very basic dwelling type, in this case a simple cube. In most hill-towns, houses are built right up to the edge of – and often open out directly onto – the narrow passageways and streets. This reflects the more integral links between the productive activities of the medieval household (carried out on the ground floor) and the street immediately outside which not only became an extension of the works inside but also served as a kind of shop, linked to a wider network of merchants, traders and exchange. Altogether, many more functions were carried out publicly in the streets, traces of which are still visible in the surviving evidence of public fountains and wash-houses, wells, and communal ovens. Streets in medieval hill-towns were even more crowded than they are today; houses had overhanging wooden balconies, used to dry and store a variety of foods. Supports for these balconies (or the holes which held them) can still be seen on the fronts of many houses.

Hill-towns still preserve a great deal of their medieval character. The very characteristics which made them useful for purposes of defence and isolation made them unsuitable for later growth and redevelopment in response to changing circumstances. There are exceptions – in the late-fifteenth century the village of Corsignano near Montepulciano was transformed into the little Renaissance town of **Pienza** to commemorate the birthplace of Pope Pius II. But in general, there is little evidence of urban planning, or the country's more recent economic history, in hill-towns.

SETTLEMENTS OF THE PLAIN

Though variations abound, the basic types of settlements on the plains and in coastal areas reveal a great deal about the impact of urban political and economic activity on the development of the countryside. Distinct waves of development correspond to changes in the fortunes of city merchants and in the accumulation of capital required for agricultural investment. Accumulation, in turn, depended on economic prosperity and on relatively long and uninterrupted periods of peace.

Just as the economic incentive for rural development derived from the towns, so did the building style. The **house-tower** (*la casa-torre*), which spread first through the Mugello, Chianti and Casentino districts between the thirteenth and fifteenth centuries, was really a transplanted version of the tall, square, fortified city house, using construction techniques borrowed from urban models, particularly from the fortified towns of Bologna, Perugia, and Siena. The defensive character of the house-tower can be read from the thickness of its walls, from its restricted openings high off the ground and from its height.

Over successive centuries, the house-tower gradually lost its defensive character, re-emerging as a **dove tower** (*la torre columbaia*),

protruding from the centre of a new form of extended dwelling which had been wrapped around it. Doves and pigeons were not only adept at killing snakes and consuming weeds but also provided valuable meat for the table and manure for agricultural use. Though this functional role gradually fell away, the dove tower became a ubiquitous feature of domestic architecture across almost all of central and southern Italy, and still remains an important decorative element in contemporary villas.

The house to which the dove tower belongs is the **casa della mezzadria**, the classic Renaissance country villa, widespread across Tuscany, Umbria and Marche as well as other areas in central and northern Italy. Usually square in plan, it was built using a combination of brick, stone and terracotta under a tent-like roof with the dove tower at its apex. Depending on its location and the urban models to which it harks back, it might boast a portico at ground level (typically Florentine), and a loggia at first-floor level (typically Arentine), or neither a portico nor loggia but a flat wall on the front facade (more common in the area around Siena).

The house derives its name from the system of sharecropping by which most of the land was farmed. Under this system, *la mezzadria* (based on the word *mezza* – "half"), the peasant farmer, in exchange for half the seed, yielded up half the annual produce to his landowner. This gave the landlord no incentive either to invest in stock or to introduce new agricultural methods. At the same time, it impoverished the labour force, compelled by increasing debt to supply free labour – which was used, among other things, to build the main house. Used only occasionally by the landlord, the house was the primary residence of the estate manager *(il fattore)*, who was the agent and overseer of urban capital invested in the countryside. Because this system paid workers in kind rather than in cash, it inevitably tied agriculture to the limited production of subsistence goods and so failed to encourage specialization (based on natural advantages) and the commercial innovations that modern agriculture required.

By contrast, the alluvial plain across north and central Italy encouraged specialization very early on. Large-scale investment in reclamation and irrigation is necessary to create and sustain arable land, something that was first undertaken by the Benedictines and Cistercians in the eleventh to thirteenth centuries. The enormous commercial enterprises that resulted from this catered for commercial markets in rice, silk and dairy products, and bore some resemblance to the monasteries whose functions they replaced and extended. Square in plan and built around a massive enclosed courtyard which could extend for 150 metres or more, the architecture of the farming complex (*la casa della Pianura Padana*) was often stark with high rectangular porticoes supported by square columns sometimes running along three sides of the enclosed interior space.

Normally, the estate accommodated four basic elements which were architecturally distinct: the owner-manager's house which was more elaborate in design and often taller than the other buildings; housing for workers, tenement-like in character, with external balconies running along the upper floors used to dry and store crops like rice; stables for cows and other animals; and stables for horses with hay lofts above. This last feature is easily recognizable from a distance by virtue of the striking patterns of brickwork used to create large grates for the ventilation of hay. An overall operation of this kind of enterprise was convincingly portrayed in Olmi's *film The Tree of Wooden Clogs* (see p.1121), set in nineteenth-century Lombardy. Today many of these courtyards are inhabited by independent small farmers, each cultivating their own smallholding; others are abandoned. On the eastern side of the plain, around the Ferrara district, where agriculture has become most mechanized, the stables and storage areas of enclosed-court complexes have become truly vast.

At the more modest end of the spectrum, the house of the **independent farmer** (*la casa colonica)* is to be found all over Italy, adapted to local materials and customs. Of simpler construction, it often consists of a kitchen and bedrooms sitting on top of animal sheds and agricultural stores (common in central and north Italy), but equally, the barn and house might form separate wings or entirely separate buildings, as is typically found along the slopes of the Apennines running the entire length of the country.

SOUTHERN ITALY

In southern Italy (particularly Campania and Puglia), the **masseria** is a more common type of farming settlement. Dominating vast tracts of land which were derived from feudal estates and ultimately from the landed properties of the Roman emperors (*latifondia*), these complex structures are massive and set in isolated countryside where they are entirely closed to the outside world. Consisting of a dense cluster of separate buildings, *masserie* were sometimes enclosed by a high perimeter stone wall into which round defence towers were built. They could, however, also consist of a lower grouping of buildings more loosely bound within a larger area. At its largest a *masseria* virtually operated as a self-contained village incorporating church, school, medical clinic and shop within its precinct, in addition to accommodating the full range of agricultural requirements for stabling, housing (of day labourers called *braccianti*) and a wide variety of storage. In their purest, least-altered form, village *masserie* are still visible in parts of Sicily.

Trulli, found along the coast of Puglia and inland, form one of the most remote, curious and ancient types of farm settlement in Italy. Of uncertain origin (possibly Cretan or North African), and appearing in Italy some time between 2000 and 1000 BC, *trulli* consist of clusters of single circular rooms, each covered by a conical roof made of overlapping rough stone tiles and topped by decorative symbolic pinnacles. Built as primitive agricultural communities, the profusion of conical roofs (each dwelling contributing two or three) produces a startling effect on the landscape.

Ellen Leopold

MAFIA, 'NDRANGHETA, CAMORRA: SOCIALIZED CRIME IN SOUTHERN ITALY

"And the Mafia – what's this Mafia that the newspapers are always talking about?" "Yeah, what is the Mafia, after all?" Brescianelli chimed in. "It's a very complicated thing to explain", Bellodi said. "It's . . . incredible, that's what it is."
Leonardo Sciascia, *The Day of the Owl*

Few modern social phenomena have been more misinterpreted and misunderstood than the Mafia, 'ndrangheta and Camorra, the three names designating organized criminal activity in Sicily, Calabria and Naples respectively. In some sense it is no surprise that there should be misunderstandings. Numerous hindrances lie in wait for the would-be Mafia observer. Most important of these may be the secrecy in which the Mafia shrouds itself, a secrecy assured by the vow of silence known as omertà, which surrounds all those who, however unwillingly, come into contact with it.

An example: at 2am, July 10, 1988, three associates of the Camorra boss Antonio Bardellino were gunned down on the streets of his hometown of Aversa, just outside Naples, by members of a rival clan. The gunfight lasted thirty minutes. A few minutes after the last shots were fired, the police arrived. While they removed one of the corpses from the street, a man in a nearby apartment opened his window to ask in a derisory tone – "Anything happen down there?" As Leonardo Sciascia shows in his penetrating portrait of the Mafia world cited above, one knows better than to witness a Mafia crime.

Another, less dramatic, hindrance to making sense of the **Mafia, 'ndrangheta** and

Camorra is the complexity of these phenomena. They are distinct organizations, based in particular territories, but they also have numerous common characteristics, not to mention continuous dealings with one another. The Mafia and *'ndrangheta* especially have similar, interwoven, histories – unless otherwise specified, in this article the term Mafia will be used to indicate them both. The Neapolitan Camorra, for all its similarities, is something of a case unto itself, and will be considered separately.

Until recently organized crime was generally viewed as a southern problem, an issue of "special" interest to those with a criminal curiosity. But with the *Mani Pulite* investigations in the 1990s it became clear that these organizations are thoroughly enmeshed in the fabric of Italian society as a whole, and that understanding Italy is hardly possible without reference to them. Certainly they are not something that can be eradicated with one trial, defeated in one year or even in ten; indeed to move beyond the Mafia would require the total transformation of Italian society, politics and economic life. Those that ask what shape Italy will have in the 21st century therefore also need to ask what role the Mafia, *'ndrangheta* and Camorra will play in it.

MAFIA AND 'NDRANGHETA

The one thing most mafiologues agree on is that the Mafia as a thing *does not exist*. When a defendant in a 1960s Mafia trial was asked if he belonged to the Mafia he responded, "I don't know what the word means". This criminal was not so much evading the question as confessing a real perplexity. Mafiusi never call themselves, or one another, mafiosi, but rather *amici* (friends) or *uomini d'onore* (men of honour). In the words of one noted mafiologue, the defendant above "knew individuals who are called mafiosi, not because they belong to a secret sect but rather because they behave in a particular fashion, that is in a Mafia-like fashion".

What does it mean to behave in a Mafia-like fashion? "It means *to make oneself respected, to be a man of honour*, capable of vindicating by force any offence against his enemy," writes another Mafia expert, Pino Arlacchi. Honour and respect clearly have rather different meanings here than those that most people attach to them. A man is an *uomo d'onore* when he acts according to the prevailing codes of courage, cleverness and ferocity, never hesitating to resort to violence and trickery to gain the upper hand.

What gradually emerges from this portrait, however, is a sort of confusion between the Mafia as a "state of mind, a philosophy of life, a moral code, prevailing among all Sicilians" (Luigi Barzini), and organized criminal activity, delinquency and social deviance. In southern Italy, the border between the two is often unclear.

Two aspects of **southern Italian culture** in particular seem to have contributed to the birth and development of the Mafia as a criminal organization. The first is the generally positive value this culture has given to assertiveness, aggression and the ability to impose one's will on others. The meek, mild and naive may be saints in their afterlives, but in this life they are, quite simply, fools. The fundamental Neapolitan phrase, *ca'nisciun e'fesso* ("I'm no fool") – with its implication "you won't get the best of me" – sums up the milieu of dominance and submission in which the southern Italian lives.

A second, related aspect is the southern Italian attitude towards the state. Even today, the relationship of the southern Italian (and of many northern Italians as well) to the state is one of profound distrust. The state, its institution and laws, are not something in which one participates as a citizen but are rather things which challenge the citizen's independence, interfering with his family's sacred autonomy. This attitude towards the state may have its origins in the long succession of invading powers that ruled southern Italy over the centuries (Norman, French, Catalan, and so on). And also in the distance that separated the mass of peasant-farmers (*contadini*) working on huge estates (*latifondi*) from their absentee landlords residing in Naples or Palermo. Certainly Unification did little to help matters in the south, transferring as it did the capital from Naples to Rome and replacing the Bourbon monarchy with the Turin-based House of Savoy. Whatever the case, the space of distrust between citizen and state is the space in which the Mafia has prospered.

ORIGINS AND DEVELOPMENT

However, there is much more to the Mafia than this, and a look at more recent history shows that Mafia criminality is no longer what it used to be. The Mafia has come a long way from the traditional, feudal ways of the nineteenth century to become an entrepreneurial Mafia moving in the circles of international finance, and of drugs and arms dealing. With this transformation has come a change in the Mafia's relationship to society at large, from one of widespread sympathy and support to that of dismay and alienation.

The word "Mafia" first appears in written documents around the time of Italian Unification, and, although its etymological origins are debatable, many speculate that it derives from the Arabic word *mu'afah* meaning "protection". In 1863 a play entitled *I Mafiusi della Vicaria*, based on the life of a Palermo prison, was a roaring success among the high society of Sicily's capital, giving the word its first extensive usage. When the city rose against its new Italian rulers three years later, the British consul described a situation where secret societies were all-powerful: "*Camorre* and *maffie*-elected juntas share the earnings of the workmen, keep up intercourse with outcasts, and take malefactors under their wing and protection."

The Mafia's appearance at this time is historically significant, its rise paralleling that of the young Italian state. Indeed, in the words of Leonardo Sciascia: "a history of the Mafia would be none other than the history of the State's complicity – from the Bourbons to the Savoys to the Republic – in forming and encouraging this unproductive and parasitic class of power."

Which isn't to say it hadn't existed before in a different form. Early versions of the Mafia were to be found in the Sicilian countryside during the long centuries of foreign rule. This vast, mountainous island was virtually impenetrable to the distant authorities in Naples, Madrid or wherever, and "law and order" had to be maintained by local, semi-official authorities. The Bourbons, for example, in the early nineteenth century entrusted their campaign against brigands and bandits to "companions at arms", which consisted of ex-brigands who would be pardoned in return for assistance in helping to catch and prosecute their old friends, the brigands at large. Usually, however, these "companions", instead of catching the brigands would negotiate a kind of peaceful settlement between the bandit who had committed some theft and the offended party. In this way local social harmony was maintained without the direct intervention of central government.

Another early Mafia activity was that of a certain type of rural "**middleman**" who handled negotiations between property owners, landlords, sharecroppers and dayworkers. During the first half of the nineteenth century, the great estates were divided up numerous times in the crown's attempt to challenge the power of local barons and proprietors. The early mafiosi grew fat off the tensions that these social changes generated, intimidating sharecroppers into accepting unfavourable contracts and dayworkers into accepting low wages, while persuading proprietors and landlords to cede control over their land to them, so fulfilling the important social function of mediation. As E.J. Hobsbawm noted: "we can't say that the Mafia was imposed upon the Sicilians by someone. In a certain sense it expressed the needs of all the rural classes and served their interests in varying ways."

The main characteristic of the traditional, rural Mafia, then, is that of the **mediation of social conflict**. And by the late nineteenth century these mediators had turned into true mafiosi with well-established codes of honour and a semi-formal, though unwritten, form of organization. Though much has changed in the Mafia world, its organization, based on the family, is much the same today as it was a hundred years ago.

The Mafia **family**, however, is not really a domestic unit at all, but a conglomeration of people, some blood-relations and others not, who gather together in the pursuit of illicit aims. Each family takes on the name of the village it comes from (Corleone, for example) or the quarter of a city which it controls (in Palermo – Ciaculli, Santa Maria di Gesù, Porta Nova, etc). Above the families is something called the **commission**, a kind of governing body made up of representatives from all the major groupings. In each family there is a body of "soldiers", presided over by lieutenants, who are in turn presided over by the *capo* or *padrino* ("godfather") and his assistants. Families, in turn, ally themselves in **cosche**, meaning the crown of the artichoke (symbolizing the solidarity of many), which act in coordination with other *cosche*, all of which together form the *onorata società*, the totality of organized crime in Sicily.

All of this sounds much neater than in fact it is. Periods of peace, when everyone feels comfortable in their place, when territories are respected and pacts observed, are relatively rare. More often there are wars between and within families, and between and within *cosche*.

There is little or no documentary proof of the rise to power of the "Honoured Society", but most writers agree that between the 1890s and 1920s its undisputed boss was **Don Vito Cascio Ferro**, who presided over a period of unprecedented Mafia peace. Don Vito generated such fear and respect (virtual synonyms in the world of the Mafia) that no theft occurred in Palermo of which he did not receive a substantial cut. Already at this time the Sicilian underworld and its younger cousin in America, the "Black Hand", or **Cosa Nostra** (meaning literally "our thing"), were well co-ordinated. When Joe Petrosino, head of the Italian squad of the New York Police Department, secretly arrived in Palermo to study the relations between the *onorata società* and the Cosa Nostra, Don Vito was there at the waterfront to shoot him down. Don Vito later declared, "in all my life I've only killed one person, and I did it selflessly . . . Petrosino was a courageous adversary – he deserved to die in dignity, not by the hand of just any old assassin". The rise to power of the American Mafia at this time was no accident. Mafia-style groupings and loyalties flourished among the hundreds of thousands of Sicilians who emigrated to America in the early decades of the twentieth century, emigrants who had need of their own forms of social and economic security in a country where they lacked the full franchise. In addition to this the Sicilian Mafia suffered considerable setbacks at the hands of the Fascist authorities and many mafiosi fled to the US for safer operations.

Ferro's career ended with Mussolini's anti-Mafia purges, instigated to clear the ground for the establishment of a vigorous Fascist structure in Sicily. Il Duce sent the legendary prefect, **Cesare Mori**, to Sicily, granting him almost limitless powers to suppress the Mafia. Most importantly, Mori understood that the only way to beat the Mafia was on its own terms: "if the Sicilians are afraid of the mafiosi, I'll show them that I'm the meanest mafiosi of them all." He had understood that in the Sicily of the time it was indeed necessary to fight fear with fear.

This brief, Fascist chapter in the campaign against the Mafia foreshadows certain aspects of the debate over what legal and governmental forms the fight against the Mafia should take today. In particular it raises the question of how much the law should be circumvented by authorities in the attempt to wage an effective fight against the Mafia, and to what extent "extraordinary powers" should be granted to combat this "extraordinary" form of criminality. While opponents of the more "repressive" approach exemplified by Mori agree that the Mafia can be more effectively fought with the tools of repression, they ask what the cost of this might be to society as a whole. A dark example of such a battle won at the cost of civil liberties is the fight against terrorism in the late 1970s and early 1980s, when hundreds of innocent men and women were imprisoned.

If Mori, the Fascist, on the one hand, did much to reduce the powers of the Mafia, the Americans, on the other, did a good deal to restore them. When the Allies prepared for their landing in Sicily in 1943, they relied on the Mafia for crucial intelligence information and logistical support for the execution of Operation Husky. One of these informers was **Lucky Luciano**, with whom the US Navy consulted frequently while he was serving his thirty- to fifty-year prison sentence. Luciano not only provided them with important information and connections for the American landing in southwest Sicily but helped them to catch a group of Nazi saboteurs who were operating in New York. After the war the US expressed their gratitude by letting him go free, sending him to his home country where, in Naples, he would play a key role in developing links between the Sicilian, Neapolitan and American underworld.

The most important introduction with which Luciano provided the Allies was that of **Don Calógero Vizzini**, head of the Mafia of all Sicily during and immediately after the war. Don Caló was instrumental in clearing the way for the American landing and, afterwards, in helping the Allied Military Government establish itself in Sicily. In order to maintain political control of the island the Allies relied heavily on the Mafia: of the 66 cities on the island, 62 were entrusted either to mafiosi or men connected with the Mafia. **Don Vito Genovese**, the figure on which Mario Puzo modelled Don Corleone in *The Godfather*, was one of these men. After

helping the Americans, and the Mafia, to consolidate their power in Sicily, Genovese returned to the US to become head of the Cosa Nostra.

The Mafia was left in a good position to take advantage of the extraordinary economic growth which Italy underwent in the first two postwar decades. Moreover, in the south there was a key novelty which helped the Mafia secure its economic and political base: billions of dollars of government funding were sent here for an "extraordinary intervention" designed to modernize the region and bring it up to par with the wealthy north. The Mafia exploited the situation with ruthless efficiency, landing crucial and lucrative government contracts by intimidating all competitors into not even tendering bids. Needless to say, the Mafia-firm bid would be two to three times the appropriate amount necessary to complete the job.

THE NEW MAFIA

It was during the post-war years that the Mafia underwent a fundamental transformation, from a predominantly rural organization with a role of mediation, to an active criminal society, with its power base in the cities, and interests in construction, real estate and drugs smuggling. The modern Mafia may keep up a "clean and legal" front, but the economic basis for their civilized decorum is predominantly drugs and, to a lesser extent, the arms trade, kidnapping and extortion. In the 1950s the Mafia helped to found and develop an international drug market that extended its influence to all four corners of the globe. Experts estimate that more than half of the world's heroin trade is controlled in Palermo. The dizzying profits are "laundered" – invested in legal activities, all traces of their illicit origin having vanished.

Part of the Mafia's postwar success, then, can be traced to the ability to become "entrepreneurs" in high-risk, high-profit international trade while maintaining a respectable social front as businessmen in both the local and national economy. The strength of the Mafia organization would not make sense, however, without the presence of another factor which explains its ability to continue to recruit. The chronic unemployment that plagues southern Italy ensures that there will always be a reserve army of idle, able-bodied men who have been denied access to legal employment. And to these unemployed men, an invitation to work for the Mafia is often an offer they simply cannot refuse.

In almost complete symbiosis with the culture and economy of southern Italy, the Mafia has thus established itself in every area of politics and society, obtaining a more modern form of bourgeois respect, based not on fear but economic power. It is a form of economic power, however, whose costs to society are high, one which diverts human energy, initiatives and funds from the public sphere where they can be more democratically managed and accounted for. Also, the plague of drug addiction on which the Mafia grows fat, and its perennial family wars, have thoroughly traumatized both Sicilian and Italian society. The death count has grown too high for the people to remain sympathetic with these mafiosi who, stripped of all folklore and Hollywood hype, reveal themselves for what they are: rapacious criminals bent on personal accumulation at all costs.

The state responded to the growing power of the Mafia with a **Parliamentary Commission** that sat between 1963 and 1976, posing enough of a threat to the underworld to provoke a change of tactics by the Mafia, who began to target state officials in a sustained campaign of terror which continues to this day. In 1971 Palermo's chief public prosecutor, Pietro Scaglione, became the first in a long line of **cadaveri eccellenti** – illustrious corpses – that has included journalists, judges, lawyers, left-wing politicians and police chiefs. A new peak of violence was reached in 1982 with the ambush and murder in Palermo's city centre of **Pio La Torre**, regional secretary of the Communist Party in Sicily, who had proposed a special government dispensation to allow lawyers access to private bank accounts.

One of the people attending La Torre's funeral was the new Sicilian prefect of police, **General dalla Chiesa**, a veteran in the state's fight against the Red Brigade, and whose dispatch promised renewed action against the Mafia. He began investigating Sicily's lucrative construction industry, which proved an effective means of investing drug profits. His scrutiny of public records and business dealings threatened to expose one of the most enigmatic issues in the Mafia's organization: the extent of corruption and protection in high-ranking political circles, the so-called **Third Level**. But

exactly one hundred days after La Torre's death, dalla Chiesa was gunned down, together with his wife, in Palermo. The whole country was shocked, and the murder revived questions about the depth of government commitment to the fight. In his engagement with the Mafia, dalla Chiesa had met with little local co-operation, and had received next to no support from Rome, to the extent that his son had accused the politicians of isolating his father. The Italian president and senior cabinet ministers were present at the prefect's funeral, and were pelted with coins by an angry Sicilian crowd – an expression of disgust which has since been repeated at the funerals of other prominent anti-Mafia fighters.

THE MAXI-TRIALS AND THE OUTLOOK

This more critical attitude to the Mafia permeated throughout Italian society. A scandal in 1981, surrounding the so-called **"Propaganda Due"** (P2) masonic lodge, also helped to mobilize public opinion against the Mafia when it was discovered that numerous high-ranking politicians, bankers, military men and even members of the Vatican were involved in a secret masonic organization with Mafia connections. A year later, the first anti-Mafia law in history was passed by the Italian parliament.

Of equal import has been a wave of *pentitismo* (repentance or confession) in which, for the first time, mafiosi are revealing the secrets of their organization, thereby breaking the promise they make during their initiation when they declare, "may my flesh burn if I do not maintain this promise", becoming one of the *pentiti*. **Tommaso Buscetta**, a high-ranking Mafia member, was one of the first to break with *omertà*, setting in motion the Palermo **"maxi-trials"** or *maxiprocessi* in 1986, the largest ever held against the Mafia. Never before had so high-ranking a member of the commission turned on his "friends". His revelations about the most intimate high-level dealings of the *onorata società* were a breakthrough for the campaign against the Mafia both in Italy and in the US, and led to important prosecutions against members of the massive heroin and cocaine network between Palermo and New York known as the "pizza connection".

The decisions taken by the "maxi-trial" court in Palermo in December of 1987 were hailed as a substantial, if partial, victory of the forces of law and order in Italy. The fears of most seasoned Mafia fighters, however, were soon confirmed: as soon as the media-hype surrounding the "maxi-trial" ended, and the public – and government – turned its attention to other matters, the Mafia went back to business as usual. The Mafia fighters (judges, special investigators, police, parliamentary commissions), deprived of all-important media attention and government support, once again were engaged in a losing battle.

In the late Eighties the battle intensified. In 1988, Parliament granted vast, unprecedented powers to the High Commissioner for the Fight Against the Mafia, making him the most powerful anti-Mafia commissioner in postwar history. The Mafia responded, with typically brutal efficiency, by instigating a new series of **murders** of prominent officials. The first of these was that of **Salvatore Lima**, a former mayor of Palermo turned Euro-MP who was in the Mafia's thrall; he was killed perhaps as a warning to any other establishment figures who were seen not to be adequately "protecting" their Cosa Nostra paymasters. Shortly after, the Mafia turned its attention to two of its most prominent opponents, the **judges Giovanni Falcone** and **Paolo Borsellino**. The nation was appalled that two such well-known anti-Mafia figures could be disposed of so easily, and the anti-Mafia feeling intensified in direct proportion to the growing anti-Establishment mood in the country: it was only the politicians that allowed the Mafia to continue to exist and prosper, the thinking went, so why not get rid of them, and the rest, surely, would follow?

The murders led to a special Carabinieri unit being sent to Sicily in a calculated show of force by the state – something that might have seemed a somewhat empty gesture but for the arrest, in January 1993, of **Salvatore Riina**, or "Don Toto", after 24 years on the run. Riina sat at the head of the Cosa Nostra, the **capo di tutti capi** ("boss of all bosses"); it was he who was largely responsible for turning it into the sophisticated multinational corporation it is today, expanding into the lucrative global drugs trade and laundering the profits worldwide; he too who probably ordered the murders of La Torre, dalla Chiesa, Falcone and Borsellino. While it is true that Riina's conviction the following year did not significantly abate the level of Mafia violence in Sicily, there is a belief that his arrest marked a turning point in the fight against the Mafia, a sign that the political establishment had finally lost patience with the Cosa Nostra and its murderous deeds – it is said, after all, that until his arrest Riina walked around the streets of Corleone quite openly, and could have been picked up at any time.

There were accusations, too, that Riina had links with politicians at the highest level in Rome, a suggestion apparently supported by the infamous *bacio*, a kiss he was supposed to have exchanged with the seven-times prime minister, **Giulio Andreotti**, according to *pentiti* revelations in 1994. In April that year, the anti-Mafia commission implied that Andreotti was the Mafia's man in Rome, when it found that Salvatore Lima (see above) had had Mafia connections and that Andreotti had been protecting him. Along with stories emerging about Andreotti's possible involvement in the murder in Rome of the journalist **Carmine Pecorelli** in March 1979, the political stalwart – notorious for his cunning and survival skills – went on trial on charges of Mafia association, which ended four years later with his complete acquittal, largely on account of the dubious nature of the testimony offered against him by the *pentiti* "supergrasses". The only lasting effect of this *cause célèbre* has been to throw into question the state's reliance on Mafia informers, who are often themselves mass-murderers and keen to grasp any opportunity for escaping heavy sentences, and for wreaking personal revenge.

Statements by *pentiti* and others accused of Mafia associations were also at the bottom of investigations into former prime minister **Silvio Berlusconi** and his Fininvest consortium, and were considered serious enough to warrant a raid on Berlusconi's Milan headquarters by an elite anti-Mafia unit in July 1998. Despite these whiffs of scandal, the interminable delays and legal niceties of the trials have caused many Italians to lose much interest in their outcomes. The very concept of Mafia involvement has become increasingly irrelevant with each new report of political and business corruption that emerged during the 1990s. As the mayor of Venice remarked, in response to whispers of Mafia involvement in the fire that destroyed La Fenice opera house in 1996, "Claiming it was burnt by the Mafia is about as useful as saying it was attacked by alien spacecraft."

Meanwhile, new blows against leading Mafia figures were being scored with the capture in 1995 of **Leoluca Bagarella**, Riina's successor and brother-in-law, and **Natale D'Emanuele**, alleged to be the financial wizard behind the Mafia in Catania. Bagarella (whose hideout turned out to be a luxury apartment overlooking the heavily guarded home of two of the anti-Mafia judges who had helped catch him) was the convicted killer of the chief of the Palermo Flying Squad in 1979, while D'Emanuele was said to traffic in arms throughout Italy, the hearses and coffins he used in his nefarious operations comically reminiscent of 1930s Chicago. The following year another of Riina's heirs, **Giovanni Brusca**, was captured – like Bagarella, he was thought to have been involved in Falcone's assassination – and two other bosses, **Vito Vitale** and **Mariano Troia**, were netted in 1998. Brusca was believed to have been responsible for the strangling of the eleven-year-old son of a Mafia informer, whose body was then disposed of in a vat of acid – an act that provoked general outrage in 1996. Popular anger resurfaced when it emerged that Brusca was being given special treatment and a monthly income as a *pentito*.

Such revelations only increase the general feeling in the south that evil can go unpunished and that the Mafia will always survive. One of the worst massacres in recent years took place in the Sicilian town of Vittoria in 1999, showing that the gunmen had never simply disappeared, while, with the Mafia in Sicily on the defensive, many believe that the less organized and more reckless Calabrian *'ndrangheta* has expanded to fill the vacuum, forging links with arms and drugs traffickers based in the Balkans. Other experts maintain that the Mafia dons have indeed retired from direct involvement in crime and instead are acting as "consultants" for other criminal gangs, reaping a share of the profits in return for their connections and expertise.

At the same time, extortion remains widespread: directors such as Salvatore Tornatore (of *Cinema Paradiso* fame) are thought to have paid out large sums for their Sicilian films, while recent figures have suggested that more than 90 percent of companies in Campania, Calabria and Sicily pay **tangente** (protection money) to do business. With this in mind, legislation was introduced in March 1999 entitling businesses which have been bombed or burned down for not paying *tangente* to compensation and relocation grants. In the long run, it is probably at this ground level that there is any hope of extirpating the Mafia from Italian society. However many businessmen and politicians are uncovered for their Mafia associations – and Andreotti's defenders have pointed out that it is impossible for anybody in Italian political life *not* to have had contacts with the forces of organized crime – it is the culture of denial and *omertà* among ordinary people which is the greatest block to ending the Mafia's grip on southern Italian life.

THE CAMORRA

Though in recent years the Neapolitan **Camorra** has in many ways become indistinguishable from the Mafia and *'ndrangheta*, conducting similar illicit activities in the drug trade, extortion, building speculation and suchlike, and often working in collaboration with them, its origins are quite distinct from its southern cousins. While the Mafia and *'ndrangheta* were predominantly rural phenomena until World War II, the Camorra has always been an urban animal, a secret underworld organization of gambling and gaming. Today, a main Camorra activity is that of the clandestine lottery, which shadows the official one run by the state. Instead of buying an official ticket you buy one printed by the Camorra. The winning numbers are those drawn by the official lottery, but the Camorra version has significant advantages: if you win you're paid immediately (instead of waiting a year or two); and, clearly, you pay no taxes.

Though the Mafia has outshone, or outshot, the Camorra over the past century, the Camorra is much older and was already a well-established and ill-reputed criminal society at the beginning of the nineteenth century. In the bustling Bourbon capital there were huge sums of wealth to be controlled by aspiring men of the underworld, and there were few commercial transactions in the city of which the *camorristi* did not get a substantial cut, known as the *taglio* or *tangente*. Even today, a great number of Neapolitan businesses pay a monthly sum to the Camorra for "protection" – which of course means protection from the Camorra itself.

Until World War II the Camorra was a relatively traditional organization, performing the familiar social functions of mediation and the maintenance of a kind of harmony, by whatever violent and parasitic means. Against a background of profound transformations in postwar Naples, and the arrival of the American-trained gangster **Lucky Luciano**, the Camorra turned to the traffic in contraband cigarettes and drugs. Like the Mafia, the Camorra has become entrepreneurial, and the name of the clan which commanded Naples until recently, the New Organized Camorra, suggests that the new Neapolitan underworld is structured more like a commercial firm than a family.

Although Camorra practice is to retain its business in all corners of the globe, its cardinal rule is to maintain its connection to the culture of the region, to the popular quarters of Naples. Such is the case of the **Giuliano** family, the clan based in Forcella, the district near the train station, which controls the centre of Naples. Though members of the family have become millionaires many times over, moving comfortably in the international circles of high society, the family still lives in the centre of one of Naples' most run-down quarters, in a *basso*, or one-room, ground-floor apartment. A friend from Forcella once explained this apparent contradiction: "These *camorristi*, for however powerful they become, realize that outside their quarter, their territory, they're nobodies, provincial hoods. They stay here because this is where they count, this is where their respect and control is beyond dispute."

Ironically, the "traditional", neighbourhood character of such a Camorra clan as the Giuliano family creates a clash between good neighbourliness and delinquency. By producing and dealing heroin, the Camorra, Giulianos included, have inflicted upon Naples one of the great social tragedies in contemporary Italy, as evidenced by the used needles that litter the streets of the city. This paradox was brought home to the Giuliano family in the autumn of 1987 when one of their own, seventeen-year-old Ciro, died of a heroin overdose. What followed was unprecedented: the grandfather/godfather of the family forbade the funeral to take place in his native quarter, making it pass through a street behind Forcella. He wanted to signal to his "people" that something was wrong, that something had to change. This strange admonition, however, did not deter the thousands of mourners from following the funeral cortege, and the 25 limousines bearing flowers from "friends" made clear that it wasn't just any seventeen-year-old who had died.

The other ground-breaking aspect of this incident was the reaction of **Nunzio Giuliano**, the boy's father. Soon after his son's death, Nunzio began a campaign (in the papers, and at public gatherings) against the heroin trade and the Camorra's perpetration of it – in general terms, taking care not to incriminate any kin. Many saw this as a potential turning point in the Camorra's operations in Naples, while others, less optimistic, viewed it as little more than an act of showmanship, a piece of theatre, to divert attention from the real workings of the Camorra and an embarrassing family tragedy.

The late 1990s saw the body-count in Naples overtaking that of the Mafia and '*ndrangheta*, with the high tally of innocent victims caught in the crossfire making the headlines. As Camorra **women** get in on the act for the first time (see p.1048), often taking over the roles of their dead or incarcerated husbands and brothers, the situation is as chaotic and desperate as ever, and there is no sign yet of the same kind of intensive investigations that the anti-Mafia commission has set in motion in Palermo.

Recent years have seen alliances forged with criminal organizations in Russia and the Balkans, creating a greatly expanded scope for dealing in illegal immigration, prostitution and arms trafficking. Evidence has surfaced of Camorra involvement in musical piracy – illegal recordings in Italy account for some twenty percent of the total music retail market – leading to the arrest in 1999 of 14 members of a Neapolitan organization calling itself "Quadrifoglio", also involved in counterfeiting and money-laundering and thought to be close to the Contini clan. The creation of the single market in the EU has further extended the Camorra's arm, as seen by the exposure in 2000 of a scandal in Brussels where it was found to be bribing officials to subsidize and market "butter" which contained beef tallow, cosmetics oils and chemicals – but no milk products.

Nelson Moe,
with contributions by **Rob Andrews**

CINEMA

From the earliest days of the cinema, the Italians have always been passionate movie-lovers and movie-makers. But it was with their films of the postwar period, and the shift from studio-based films to the use of the country's actual town and landscapes, that Italy came to the forefront of world cinema. Their style and technique were ground-breaking, and the use of real locations added a dimension, a mood, which made Italian cinema linger longer in the memory. The endless expanse of the Po Valley plain in Obsession, the steaming sulphur springs outside Naples in Voyage to Italy, the deserted, off-season seaside resort of Rimini in I Vitelloni, created an atmosphere that could never have been achieved in a studio.

THE BACKGROUND

The Italians were once famous for their silent costume epics, pre-World War I dramas that had monumental backdrops and crowd scenes – a leftover from the Italian grand opera tradition. They were often set in the period of the Roman Empire, anticipating the Fascist nostalgia for ancient Rome by at least a decade. **Giovani Pastrone**'s **Cabiria** (1913), set in Babylon, was the most sophisticated and innovative of these, with spectacular sets and lighting effects that the American director D. W. Griffiths imitated in his masterpiece **Intolerance** (1916). This borrowing of Italian expertise by Hollywood gave

the Taviani brothers the story for their **Good Morning Babylon** (1986).

Even in its early stages the Italian cinema was handicapped by the economic problems that were destined to keep it lagging behind the American industry. The reason for this was not simply lack of funds, but also an inability on the part of the government to realize what a moneyspinner the indigenous film-making talent could be, and what the unregulated influx of foreign films into Italy would mean for the home market. In addition to this, the Americans themselves began making films in Italy, attracted by the cheap labour, the locations, and the quality of the light, thereby devastating the already fragile indigenous industry. An American film crew arrived in 1923 to make an epic version of **Ben Hur**. Three years prior to this, 220 films were made in Italy; by 1927 the number had dropped to around a dozen a year.

The Fascist regime (1922–43) was surprisingly slow to recognize the potential, in both economic and propaganda terms, of the cinema. But in 1934 Mussolini did begin to mete out financial support. He also limited the number of foreign imports, had film added to the arts festival in Venice, and in 1937 inaugurated "Cinecittà", the film studio complex just outside Rome. From 1938 to 1944 the proportion of Italian productions to imports rose rapidly, though home-produced films would never account for more than a third of the total number of films distributed in the country.

Films made during the Fascist period featured glorious victories from the past (the Romans again), and from the present – the war in Ethiopia, for example. During this time, although not all movies were vehicles for propaganda, no films could be made that were overtly critical of the regime. Most popular at the time were the escapist, sentimental, "white telephone" films, so-called because the heroine would have a gleaming white telephone in her boudoir, Hollywood-style – a touch of the exotic for the average Italian at the time, who rarely even saw such a thing, let alone owned one.

Italians were not, however, cut off from what was going on in world cinema between the wars, and the ideas and techniques of Eisenstein and, even more so, of French directors, particularly Renoir, Pagnol and Carne, began to filter through. Likewise with literature: probably the biggest single influence on the emerging generation of Italian film-makers was the American novel. Hemingway, Faulkner and Steinbeck spoke directly to the young generation: their subjects were realistic, their stylistic approach was fresh, even raw, and the emotion seemed genuine.

It was not surprising, then, that the late 1930s and early 1940s should see an element of documentary-style realism creep into film-making. Contemporary social themes were addressed; non-professional actors were sometimes used. Directors – even those with the official stamp of approval – made the occasional realistic documentary, with none of the bombast or gloss of the typical Fascist film. It was on films such as these that future neo-realist directors such as Visconti, Rossellini and De Sica, and the writer Zavattini, worked their apprenticeships, learning techniques that they would draw on a few years later when they were allowed to unleash their creative imaginations.

A film made in 1943 caused a considerable stir. When it was first shown, Mussolini's son, Vittorio, walked out, exclaiming "This is not Italy!" But Mussolini allowed it to be distributed anyway, probably because there was nothing politically controversial in it. The film was **Luchino Visconti**'s **Obsession**, an unauthorized adaptation of the American novel **The Postman Always Rings Twice** by James M. Cain. Visconti transposed this low-life story of adultery and murder to northern Italy, the characters playing out their seedy tragedy in the relentlessly flat landscape of the Po Valley and among the surreal carnival floats in Ferrara. It showed two ordinary people in the grip of a violent passion, so obsessed with each other that they bring about their own destruction. The original negative was deliberately destroyed when the official film industry was moved north to Mussolini's Saló Republic on Lago di Garda. **Obsession** was something new in the Italian cinema: it had an honesty and intensity, a lack of glamour, that pointed the way to the "neo-realist" films of the immediate postwar period.

THE NEO-REALISTS

The end of the war meant the end of Fascist domination of everything, including the film industry; but Italy was left emotionally as well as physically shattered. It now seemed important to film-makers to make sense of the intense experience the Italian people had undergone, to rebuild in some way what had been destroyed.

As the tanks were rolling out of Rome in 1945, **Roberto Rossellini** cobbled together the bare minimum of finances, crew and equipment and started shooting **Rome, Open City**. He used real locations, documentary footage, and low-grade film, and came up with a grainy, idiosyncratic style that influenced not only his Italian contemporaries, but also the American film noirs of the late 1940s, and the grittily realistic films of the early 1950s – as well as the French New Wave of the 1960s.

Neo-realism had no manifesto, but its main exponents – Rossellini, De Sica and Visconti – expounded the following aims, even if they didn't always stick to them: to show real people rather than conventional heroes (using non-actors), real time, real light, real places (shooting on location, not in studios). Their intention was to present the everyday stuff of life and not romantic dreams.

Unusually for an "art" film, **Rome, Open City** was a box office hit. It had a good emotional, even melodramatic, story, with touches of humour, and packed a terrific moral punch. Set in a downbeat quarter of occupied Rome, it is about a partisan priest and a communist who join forces to help the resistance. The Nazis are depicted as effeminate and depraved, while the partisans – including a band of children – are the true heroes, though Rossellini seems to pursue immediacy at the expense of making political statements.

This was the first in Rossellini's so-called "war trilogy". It was followed by **Paisà** (1946), which traced the Allied occupation north from Sicily to the Po Valley, in six self-contained episodes; and the desolate **Germany, Year Zero** (1947), set in the ruins of postwar Berlin, about a child whom circumstances push to suicide.

In these, as in other neo-realist films, children are seen as the innocent victims of adult corruption. **Vittorio De Sica**'s **Shoeshine** (1946) is an anatomy of a friendship between two Roman boys, destroyed first by black-marketeers, then by the police. A young boy is the witness to his father's humiliation in De Sica's **Bicycle Thieves** (1948) – also set in the poorer quarters of Rome – when he sees him steal a bicycle out of desperation (a bicycle means getting his job back) and immediately get caught. The child's illusions are dashed, and the blame is laid on society for not providing the basic human requirements. At the time *Bicycle Thieves* was called the only truly communist film of the postwar decade, but in retrospect the message, as in *Rome, Open City*, seems politically ambiguous. Crowds are seen as hostile and claustrophobic, and the only hope seems to lie in the family unit, which the hero falls thankfully back on at the end.

This conflict between Catholic and Marxist ideology is a recurrent theme in Italian cinema, from Rossellini through to Pasolini, and the Taviani brothers in the 1980s, and it's often this that gives their films the necessary tension. More than anyone, Visconti exemplifies this dichotomy. Born an aristocrat in the famous Milanese family, and sentenced to death (though not executed) for being anti-Fascist in 1944, he was influenced by the writings of Antonio Gramsci, and right up until his death in 1976 veered between two milieux for his films – the honest, suffering sub-proletariat, and the decadent, suffering upper classes.

In 1948 Visconti made a version of the nineteenth-century Sicilian author Giovanni Verga's novel **The House by the Medlar Tree**, about a family of fishermen destroyed by circumstance, which he filmed as **The Earth Trembles**. It was shot on location on the stark Sicilian coast, using an entire village as cast, speaking in their native Sicilian (with an Italian voice-over and subtitles). He adapted the story to incorporate a Marxist perspective, but this fades from view in the pervading atmosphere of stoic fatalism, closer to Greek tragedy than to the party line. Something else that detracted from the intended message was the sophisticated visual style: stunning tableaux such as the one where the wives, dressed in black, stand waiting for their husbands on the skyline, looking out to sea, prompted Orson Welles to remark that Visconti shot fishermen as if they were Vogue models. Indeed, style constantly threatened to overtake content in Visconti's work, culminating in the emotionally slick **Death In Venice** (1971).

THE END OF NEO-REALISM

By the early 1950s, neo-realism was on the way out. Social problems no longer occupied centre stage, and film-makers now concentrated on the psychological, the historical, even the mag-

ical side of life. There were several reasons for this, not least that the trauma of World War II had receded, and cities (and lives) were being rebuilt. As Rossellini said in 1954, "you can't go on making films about heroism among the rubble for ever". Directors wanted to move on to new themes. Another reason for the break was government intervention. The cinema industry was in the doldrums, and the Christian Democrat minister Giulio Andreotti had banned any more neo-realist films from being made on the grounds that social criticism equalled communism. The Cold War was just beginning.

Neo-realist films had in any case, with one or two exceptions, rarely been good box office. Of Italian-made films, the general public tended to prefer farces, historical dramas, or comedies. The Neapolitan comic actor Totò – who had a colossal career spanning scores of films and several decades – was a particular favourite. In **Toto looks for a Home** (1949), he and his family search for somewhere to live in the postwar ruins of Rome, in a comic variation on a neo-realist theme. It was a sign of the times that people preferred to laugh at their problems rather than confront them.

De Sica meanwhile had moved on from the unremitting pessimism of *Bicycle Thieves* to a fantastic fable set in Milan, **Miracle in Milan** (1950), about a young man who is given a white dove which possesses the power to grant the wishes of everyone living in his slummy suburb. Surreal special effects are used to create a startling impact, for example in a shot of the hero and heroine flying high above the pinnacles of Milan cathedral on a broomstick. The moral is still a neo-realist one, but with a change of emphasis: art and imagination can help your problems disappear for a while, but won't solve them.

In 1954 **Visconti** made **Senso**, another adaptation of a nineteenth-century novel but worlds away from **The Earth Trembles**. It opens to the strains of Verdi in the Venice opera house, La Fenice, one night in 1866, and is Visconti's view of the politically controversial Unification, portrayed through the lives of a few aristocratic individuals. It was a theme he would return to in **The Leopard** (1963). **Senso** was the first of Visconti's historical spectaculars, and the first major Italian film to be made in colour.

THE FIFTIES AND THE NEXT GENERATION OF DIRECTORS

Neo-realism was dead, but the next generation of film-makers – Fellini, Pasolini, Bertolucci, Antonioni, Rosi – could not help but be influenced at first by its ideals and techniques, though the style each of them went on to evolve was highly personal.

Federico Fellini, for one, saw neo-realism as more a world-view than a "school". His early films, such as **La Strada** (1954), follow a recognizably realistic storyline (unlike his later movies), but the whole feeling is different to the films of the 1940s. His characters are motivated by human values rather than social ones – searching for love rather than solidarity. All through his long career Fellini used films as a kind of personal notebook in which to hark back to his youth. **I Vitelloni** (1953) is set in an unrecognizable Rimini, his birthplace, before the days of mass tourism; **Amarcord** (1974) is again set in Rimini, this time under Fascism. He also explores his own personal sexual fantasies and insecurities, as in **Casanova** (1976), and **The City of Women** (1980).

But Fellini isn't all nostalgia and sex. There are philosophical themes that run through his work, not least the gap between reality and illusion. The heroine of **The White Sheikh** (1952) falls in love with the Valentino-type actor playing the romantic lead for "photo romance" comics (being shot on the coast outside Rome), and has her illusions dashed when reality intervenes and he makes a bungling attempt to seduce her. **Casanova** too is an oddly (and deliberately) artificial-looking film. It wasn't actually shot in Venice, and the water in the lagoon is in fact a shaken plastic sheet – an odd backlash against the real landscapes of the neo-realists.

Religion is also a theme in Fellini's work, and he's at his best when satirizing the Roman Catholic Church, as in the grotesque clerical fashion parade in **Roma** (1971), or the malicious episode in **La Dolce Vita** (1960) where a couple of children claim to have had a vision of the Virgin Mary, and create the press event of the month.

Pier Paolo Pasolini, murdered in mysterious circumstances in 1975, was a practising Catholic, a homosexual and a Marxist, as well poet and novelist. His films reflected this

cocktail of ideological and sexual tendencies, though in a less autobiographical way than Fellini's. They're also far more disturbing and challenging: **Theorem** (1968) intercuts shots of a spiritually empty middle-class Milanese family, which a mysterious young stranger insinuates himself into, with desolate scenes of a volcanic wasteland. **The Gospel According to Matthew** (1963) is a radical interpretation of a familiar story (and an excellent antidote to Zeffirelli's syrupy late-Seventies **Jesus of Nazareth**) in which Jesus is not a man of peace but the champion of the sub-proletariat and the enemy of hypocrisy. It was filmed in the surprisingly biblical-looking landscape of the poorer regions of southern Italy – Puglia and Calabria – and used the peasants of the area in the cast. Pasolini's **Decameron** (1971) was a record hit at the box office because of its explicit sex scenes, though the director's intention had been political rather than salacious, with Boccaccio's fourteenth-century tales transposed from their original middle-class Florentine setting to the dispossessed of Naples.

Otherwise, the real box-office earners in the 1960s and 1970s were the so-called "spaghetti westerns", shot in the Arizona-look-alike interior of Sardinia, the best of which were directed by **Sergio Leone**.

Bernardo Bertolucci started out as Pasolini's assistant, and shared his politics, though his own films are more straightforward and accessible. **The Spider's Strategem** (1969), filmed in the strange, star-shaped Renaissance town of Sabbioneta near Mantua, was the first of many feature films sponsored by RAI, the Italian state TV network, and is about the anatomy of a destructive father-son relationship with constant flashbacks to the Fascist era. Another early film, **The Conformist** (1970), adapted from the novel by Alberto Moravia, had the spiritually empty hero (or rather, anti-hero) search for father-substitutes in Fascist Rome – again a dream-like jumble of flashbacks. **The Conformist** was Bertolucci's first step on the path to world recognition; subsequent projects, from **Last Tango in Paris** (1971), through **1900** (1976), **La Luna** (1979), the Oscar-winning **The Last Emperor** (1988) and the ill-judged **The Sheltering Sky** (1990), have made him one of the country's most commercially successful directors.

Michelangelo Antonioni again had a neorealist background, but in the films he made in the 1960s and 1970s he shifted the emphasis from outward action and social realism to internal and psychological anguish. The locations he chose – the volcanic landscape of Sicily for **L'Avventura** (1964), the bleak townscape of industrial Milan in **La Notta** (1961), the impersonal Stock Exchange building in Rome for **The Eclipse** (1962), the alienating oil refineries and power plants at Ravenna for **The Red Desert** (1964) – made perfect settings for what were almost cinematic equivalents of existential novels.

The Neapolitan director **Francesco Rosi** made a series of semi-documentary "inquiry" films attacking various aspects of the Italian establishment: the Sicilian mafia in **Salvatore Giuliano** (1962), the construction industry mafia in Naples in **Hands Over the City** (1963), the army in **Just Another War** (1970), and vested interests of all kinds in **The Mattei Affair** (1972). Not that these are dry analyses of Italian society: the viewer has to sort through the pieces of evidence – the newsreel footage, the half-heard comments, the absence of comment – to come to his or her own conclusions about the truth, in kind of do-it-yourself mystery stories.

Later on, in the late 1970s and 1980s, Rosi went in a more personal direction. **Christ Stopped at Eboli** (1979) is a surprisingly unincisive critique of "the problem of the south", set in a poverty-stricken mountain village in Basilicata. **Three Brothers** (1980) looks at three different political attitudes, as the brothers of the title, reunited for their mother's funeral back home in Puglia, argue, reminisce and dream. Oddly enough, in 1983 Rosi made a completely apolitical film of the opera **Carmen**.

NOSTALGIA... TO THE PRESENT

Italian cinema of the Seventies and Eighties was dominated by foreign co-productions and TV-sponsored films, which, like elsewhere, led to a loss of national identity and audiences were eroded by the successive onslaughts of television, video and TV deregulation. Some directors tried to address this problem by focusing on purely Italian themes, others by looking to the past.

Ermanno Olmi's The Tree of Wooden Clogs (1978) has a Bergamasque cast speaking dialect with Italian subtitles, and did well at the box office worldwide. **Bernabo of the Mountains** (Mario Brenta, 1994) is a similarly eloquent portrayal of the people and landscape of the Cadore and the Po Valley. Also prominent among current Italian directors are the **Taviani brothers**, whose **Padre Padrone** (1977), a mini-epic set in Sardinia that details the showdown between an overbearing father and his rebellious son, and **Kaos** (1984), an adapation of Pirandello stories shot in scenic Sicily, are both loving of the Italian landscape and redolent of a time past. Together with **Good Morning Babylon** (1986), these films have put the brothers' work centre-stage internationally.

Among the themes of this period, nostalgia was a keynote, typified by **Giuseppe Tornatore's** Oscar-winning **Cinema Paradiso** (1988), shot in the director's native village near Palermo. Much of the film comprises flashbacks to the boyhood years of the central figure, Salvatore, who goes on to become a successful film director; he returns to the village for a funeral, only to find that the magical Cinema Paradiso of his childhood is about to be razed to make way for a car park. Similarly, in **Ettore Scola's Splendor** (1989), the owner of the cinema in a small provincial town is forced to sell up to a property developer because of declining audiences and debt. This is, however, a far less saccharine film than *Cinema Paradiso*, and is less a lament for a lost past than a tirade against the impoverishing aspects of TV culture. In a similar vein, **Michael Radford's Il Postino** (1994) is a poignant and gently humorous tale, set in 1930s Italy, which follows the artistic and political awakening of the central character, played by Italian comic Massimo Troisi (who sadly died soon after the film's completion).

In the Nineties films emerged that were re-evaluating and questioning with their subject matter, which often led to a hard-hitting, realistic edge to their presentation. **Mario Martone's** atmospheric films **Death of a Neapolitan Mathemetician** (1991) and **L'Amore Molesto** (1995) deal with the subject of mortality, the latter telling the story of a young woman who goes back to Naples to live with her dying mother, and in the process, examines some key themes in her own life. His **Rehearsal for War (Teatro di Guerra**, 1998) examines the war in the former republic of

Yugoslavia and the power of the imagination in our perception of evil. Meanwhile, directors such as **Marco Risi** specifically deal with social problems – his **Ragazzi Fuori** follows the lives of half a dozen youngsters fresh out of prison, and the sequel, **Mery per Sempre** (1988), shows them back inside.

Other directors, like **Nanni Moretti**, are idiosyncratic, funny and equally penetrating in their exploration of contemporary life. Moretti's **Dear Diary** (Caro Diario; 1994) is in three parts, covering such diverse subjects as twentieth-century architecture, children and telephones, Pasolini's unsolved murder, the myth of rural idyll, and Moretti's own fight against cancer. Much of the film is spent following Moretti on his scooter through Rome, or travelling by ferry from one island to another. Moretti's earlier films are equally restless. The **Red Lob** (**Palombella Rossa**; 1989), whose title refers to a technique in water polo – the film takes place over the course of a match – is a political reflection on the Italian Communist Party, as it was then known. **The Mass is Over** (**La Messa è Finita**; 1985) tells the story of a priest who, called back to Rome after serving a remote community for ten years, is confronted by the city's overwhelming problems, forcing him to question the value of his vocation. Moretti himself appears to be continually questioning the worth of everything, including his own work; indeed, he went too far for some critics in **Aprile** (1998), which focuses on his inability to decide how to finish his films – or even whether to finish them. Although it wasn't as well received as his earlier works, it's still a very funny film; in it, Moretti feels an obligation to make a film about Italian politics in the 1990s, but is continually sidetracked by his real passions, including the birth of his first child.

Like Moretti, other directors have used metaphor to comment on present-day politics. **Gianni Amelio**'s political drama **Open Doors** (**Porte Aperte**, 1989), from Leonardo Sciacia's novel of the same name, is set in Fascist Palermo just before World War II, but its subject matter – a liberal judge being obstructed in his investigations of all-pervasive corruption – is particularly apposite today. From the same director, **Stolen Children** (**Il Ladro di Bambini**; 1992) is better known outside Italy, dealing with corrupt society as seen through the ～ of a child. Amelio made no new work for

five years until **The Way We Laughed** (**Così Ridevamo**; 1998), the story of two brothers leaving rural Sicily for Turin in the late 1950s. The film is divided into six chapters, each telling the story of one day in their lives between 1958 and 1964. Amelio himself says that the film is about an Italy that doesn't exist any more. Its relevance to today is in its depiction of the brothers' quest for money and a better life, and how the present-day malaises that Italy is experiencing have their roots in the betrayals and violence in the late Fifties and early Sixties.

Returning to the corruption theme, the nicely titled **The Brownnose** (**Il Portaborse**; 1991) by **Daniele Luchetti**, satirizes the favoured Italian way of outwitting the system and getting things done – the oiling of the wheels of bureaucracy by means of gifts and bribery involves the anti-hero in all manner of scrapes. In a case of life imitating art, the film's release just predated the cataclysmic "Operation Clean Hands" (see p.1072).

In this rather soul-searching period of Italian film-making, the films of **Gabriele Salvatores** have dealt with groups of Italians abroad, often cut adrift, or seeking escape. His **Mediterraneo** (1991) shows eight reluctant Italian sailors stranded on a Greek island in 1941, and recounts their gradual integration into local life, while **Marrakech Express** (1989) has a group of seven setting off for Morocco in search of their friend, and **Puerto Escondido** (1992) explores life for an Italian in a commune in Mexico.

An Oscar-winning work by **Roberto Benigni**, known for such slapstick-style movies as **Johnny Stecchino** (1992) and **The Monster** (1996), suggests that Italian film-makers may be again willing to tackle subjects unconnected with the country's political tribulations. Benigni's **La Vita è Bella** (**Life is Beautiful**; 1997) bravely addresses the Holocaust and dares to combine comedy with genocide. A parent's desire to protect the innocence of their child, rather than the Holocaust itself, is the theme of the film and Benigni (who also plays the lead role with his wife, Nicoletta Braschi, as his co-star) distinguishes between laughing *at* the Holocaust and laughing *in* the Holocaust; visual gags, dramatic tension and a poignancy that's almost unbearable at times permeate the film. In answer to critics who accuse them of treating a painful subject with too much levity, Benigni claims that Italian Holocaust surviviors are only just beginning to talk about the events of more than fifty years ago and that a film like *La Vita è Bella* is justified if it opens up debate.

Certainly other films seem to be finding the money for production now that the subject is being aired. A new film by **Andrea and Antonio Frazzi, Il Cielo Cade (The Sky will Fall**; 2000) deals with the loss of innocence through the violence and betrayals of war. Set in a Tuscan villa in the final year of World War II, it's a moving, at times funny and tragic account of events seen through the eyes of two children billetted with their aunt and uncle, both German Jews. Based on a real-life story by Lorenza Mazzetti, in the film, Isabella Rossellini turns in a strong performance as the mother.

More provocative still, **Daniele Cipri** and **Franco Maresco**'s **Toto Che Visse Due Volte (Toto And His Two Lives**; 1998), set in Sicily, ruffled a few feathers with its religious and sexual themes (including a depiction of a statue of the Virgin Mary being assaulted). Critics disliked the film's clumsiness, but this iconoclastic work didn't trouble the establishment. When it was banned by the film censors, the deputy prime minister – a film buff – responded by disbanding their board.

With a final backward look, **Sicilia! (Sicily!**; 1999), is a beautifully judged adaptation of Elio Vittorio's classic anti-fascist novel, *Conversation in Sicily*. A Franco-Italian collaboration directed by **Danièle Huillet** and **Jean-Marie Straub**, the film tells the story of the main character Silvestro's return to his home in Sicily in the 1930s after an absence of fifteen years, and includes some gentle comedy as the protagonist discovers among other things both his father's and his mother's infidelities.

On a different note, **Lucky and Zorba** (1999) is an Italian animation directed by **Enzo D'Aló** and shot using English voices. It is loosely based on a novel by the Chilean novellist Luis Selpulveda, about an orphaned seagull (Lucky) taught to fly by his friend Zorba, a cat. Fastmoving and action packed, it's a noteworthy example of a European animated film that can rival Hollywood offerings. Continuing the fantasy theme, the sexually explicit costume drama

Amor nello specchio (Love in the Mirror; 1999), is an interesting twist on Commedia dell'Arte directed by **Salvatore Maira**. Set in the seventeeenth century and shot on location in Italian theatres from the period, a troupe of actors (with Anna Galiena, Peter Stormare and Simona Cavallari) are riven by jealousies and romantic conflict as they plan their performance for the King of France – a kind of risqué version of *Shakespeare in Love*. Though made for very different age-groups and audiences both films illustrate the huge variety of subject matter in current Italian cinema, where familiar themes are given a recognizably Italian treament.

Director **Gabriele Muccino**'s coming of age story **Come te nessuno mai (But Forever in the Mind**; 1999) is an interesting take on the US high-school comedy genre: his very Italian students are highly politicized, planning strikes and taking part in a 24-hour sit-in, both of which provide a backdrop for the inevitable angsting and first love.

FRONT OF HOUSE

Those bored by the endless nostalgia of the last decades of the twentieth century welcome the embracing of previously taboo subjects by filmmakers, with many looking to Naples and Sicily as the most vibrant sector of the film industry. Revitalization has been taking place not just behind the camera, but also in front of the screen, with Rome foremost among Italian cities in wooing the public away from its TV and back into the **cinemas**. The old cinema halls of the 1930s so deeply mourned in films like *Cinema Paradiso* and *Splendor* are being brought back to life in Rome (if they haven't already been pulled down), financed by the film industry itself at the "encouragement" of the city council. New multiscreen complexes have supplemented the historic Pasquino and Nanni Moretti's Nuovo Sacher, and the red-tape restricting filming on location in the city has been much reduced. By all accounts this has been a success: in the *Dolce Vita*-era there were three hundred cinema halls in the city – in 2000, this figure was about to be exceeded and other Italian cities are reported to be set to follow the Roman example.

Sheila Brownlee and **Celia Woolfrey**

BOOKS

A comprehensive background reading list for Italy would run on for dozens of pages, and would include a vast number of out-of-print (OP) titles. Most of our recommendations are in print, but those that aren't shouldn't be too difficult to track down. Where titles are published by different companies in the UK and US, the UK publisher is given first in each listing, followed by the publisher in the US; if a title is available in one country only, we have specified which. University Press is abbreviated as UP.

TRAVEL AND GENERAL

Anne Calcagno (ed), *Travelers' Tales: Italy* (OP in UK; Travelers' Tales). One of the latest offerings in this excellent series of travel anthologies – not just full of evocative period detail by the likes of H.V. Morton, but with good contemporary writing too, by Tim Parks, Lisa St Aubin de Teran and others, specifically commissioned for this volume. Along with this guide, a perfect introduction to the richness and variety of the country.

Vincent Cronin, *The Golden Honeycomb* (Harvill Press; OP in US). Disguised as a quest for the mythical golden honeycomb of Daedalus, this is a searching account of a sojourn in Sicily in the 1950s. Although overwritten in parts, it has colourful descriptions of Sicily's art, architecture and folklore.

Charles Dickens, *Pictures from Italy* (Penguin). The classic mid-nineteenth-century Grand Tour, taking in the sights of Emilia, Tuscany and Rome, and Naples, in elegant, measured and incisive prose.

Norman Douglas, *Old Calabria* (Northwestern UP; Marlboro Press). The chronicle of Douglas's travels around the south in the early part of this century. Evocative and descriptive, though riven with digressions. See also the slightly earlier *Siren Land* (OP), which focuses on Cápri and Sorrento.

Johann Wolfgang Von Goethe, *Italian Journey* (Penguin). Surprisingly readable account of a journey all through the peninsula at the end of the eighteenth century, a classic of travel writing and a decisive point in Goethe's own transition from Sturm und Drang to classicism.

Henry James, *Italian Hours* (Penguin). Urbane travel pieces from the young James; perceptive about particular monuments and works of art, superb on the different atmospheres of Italy.

D.H. Lawrence, *D.H. Lawrence and Italy* (Penguin). Lawrence's three Italian travelogues collected into one volume. *Sea and Sardinia* and *Twilight in Italy* combine the author's seemingly natural ill-temper when travelling with a genuine sense of regret for a way of life almost visibly passing away – classic travel writing, supremely evocative of the spirit of place. *Etruscan Places*, published posthumously, consists of his more philosophical musings on Etruscan art and civilization, and remains much the most illuminating book to read on the period.

Norman Lewis, *Naples '44* (Eland; OP in US). Lewis was among the first Allied troops to move into Naples following the Italian surrender in World War II, and this is his diary of his experiences there. Part travelogue, part journalism, this is without question the finest thing you can read on World War II in Italy – and, despite its often bleak subject matter, among the most entertaining. Lewis' more recent *In Sicily* (Cape in UK), is a broad contemporary portrait of the island he has married into and returns to frequently. Subjects range from reflections on Palermo's ruined *palazzi* to the impact of immigration, and there's plenty on the Mafia.

Mary McCarthy, *The Stones of Florence/Venice Observed* (Penguin; Harcourt Brace). A mixture of high-class reporting on the contemporary cities and anecdotal detail on their histories; one of the few accounts of these two cities that doesn't read as if it's been written in a library.

James Morris, *Venice* (Faber; Harcourt Brace, titled *The World of Venice*). Some people think this is the most acute modern book written about any Italian city, while others find it unbearably fey. At least give it a look.

H.V. Morton, *A Traveller in Italy* (Methuen; OP in US); *A Traveller in Rome* (Methuen; PMA Communications, both OP) and *A Traveller in Southern Italy* (Methuen; PMA Communications, both OP). Morton's leisurely and amiable books were written in the 1930s, long before modern tourism got into its stride, and their nostalgic charm has a lot to do with their enduring popularity. But they are also packed with learned details and marvellously evocative descriptions.

William Murray, *Italy: the Fatal Gift* (OP). Murray spent several years in Italy shortly after the last war, and this is a collection of essays inspired by his time there, and many return visits since. Skilfully combining personal anecdote and contemporary Italian history and politics, it's one of the most insightful introductions to the country and its people you can buy. Hopefully someone will see fit to reprint it.

Eric Newby, *Love and War in the Apennines* (Picador; Lonely Planet). Anecdotal, oddly nostalgic account of the sheltering of the author by local people in the mountains of Emilia-Romagna in the closing months of World War II. Newby's *A Small Place in Italy* (Picador; Lonely Planet), recounting his life in a small farmhouse at the foot of the Alps, is equally evocative, and reads much more "authentically" than other expatriates-in-Italy tales.

HISTORY, POLITICS AND SOCIETY

The Longman History of Italy (OP in UK, Addison-Wesley). This eight-volume series covers the history of Italy from the end of the Roman Empire to the present, each instalment comprising a range of essays on all aspects of political, social, economic and cultural history. Invaluable if you've developed a special interest in a particular period.

Pino Arlacchi, *Mafia Business* (OP). Rather academic account of how the Mafia moved into big business, legal and illegal, its argument contained in the book's subtitle *The Mafia Ethic and the Spirit of Capitalism*. The author has served on the Italian government's Anti-Mafia Commission, which makes him supremely qualified to judge accurately the Mafia's cutting edge.

Luigi Barzini, *The Italians* (Penguin; Atheneum). Long the most respected work on the Italian nation, and rightly so. Barzini leaves no stone unturned in his quest to pinpoint the real Italy.

Jerome Carcopino, *Daily Life in Ancient Rome* (Penguin; Yale UP). Detailed but never dull, this is a seminal work of Roman social history.

John Cornwell, *A Thief in the Night* (OP). An investigation into the death of the "three-day pope", John Paul I, told as a fast-paced detective story. A good read for devotees of conspiracy theory, although more cynical types will probably wonder whether it isn't all a lot of fuss about nothing.

Christopher Duggan, *Fascism and the Mafia* (Yale UP). Well-researched study of how Mussolini put the Mafia in their place. Duggan uses this account for his thesis that there's no such thing as the Mafia, that it was dreamed up by Italians seeking a scapegoat for their inability to control the delinquent society.

Giovanni Falcone, *Men of Honour: The Truth about the Mafia* (OP). The most incisive analysis of the mafioso mentality, by the investigating magistrate assassinated by the mob in May 1992.

Alan Friedman, *Agnelli and the Network of Italian Power* (OP). Agnelli publicly didn't like this when it came out, and no wonder. Friedman's book was among the first pieces of journalism to properly pull no punches on the dynastic and anti-democratic power network that is at the heart of Italian society. If you're intrigued by the inertia of Italian postwar politics, it's a must.

Edward Gibbon, *The Decline and Fall of the Roman Empire* (Penguin; Wordsworth). Awe-inspiring in its erudition, Gibbon's masterpiece is one of the greatest histories ever written, and one of the finest compositions of English prose. Penguin also publish an abridged version for those without the time to tackle the entire work.

Paul Ginsborg, *A History of Contemporary Italy* (Penguin). A very readable account of postwar Italian history. Economic, social and political influences are bound together in a fascinating account of contemporary events.

Michael Grant, *A History of Rome* (Faber; Prentice Hall). Straightforward and reliable summary of an impossibly complicated story.

Christopher Hibbert, *Rome: The Biography of a City* (Penguin). The history of Italy's capital made easy. As ever, Hibbert is readable and entertaining, but never superficial, providing by far the most comprehensive brief account of the city through the ages yet published. The companion volumes, *Venice: The Biography of a City* (OP) and *Florence: The Biography of a City* (Penguin; OP in US), are particularly good on the changing social fabric in those cities, and have more coverage of the twentieth-century than most; excellent illustrations too. Another foray into an episode of Italian history, Hibbert's *Garibaldi and his Enemies* (Penguin; OP in US), is a popular treatment of the life and revolutionary works of Giuseppe Garibaldi, thrillingly detailing the exploits of "The Thousand" in their lightning campaign from Marsala to Milazzo.

Norman Lewis, *The Honoured Society* (Eland; OP in US). Famous account of the Mafia, its origins, personalities and customs. Certainly the most enjoyable introduction to the subject available, though much of it is taken up with the story of banditry – really a separate issue – and his lack of accredited sources leaves you wondering how much is conjecture.

Valerio Lintner, *A Traveller's History of Italy* (Windrush Press; Interlink). Brief history of the country, from the Etruscans right up to the present day. Well written and sensibly concise, it could be just the thing for the dilettante historian of the country. Lots of tables and chronologies for easy reference.

Clare Longrigg, *Mafia Women* (Vintage in UK). Fascinating look at the new, active role of women within organized crime in the 1990s, mainly in Naples and Sicily. Intimidation and fear are shown to be the oil that turns the Mafia wheels, the supreme place of the family appearing to justify almost any outrage or amount of complicity.

Patrick McCarthy, *The Crisis of the Italian State* (Palgrave; St Martin's Press). Subtitled *From the Origins of the Cold War to the Fall of Berlusconi and Beyond*, this is a detailed but quite readable analysis of the root causes and major events of the "Clean Hands" political crisis of the Nineties.

John Julius Norwich, *The Normans in Sicily* (Penguin). Accessible, well-researched story of the Normans' explosive entry into the south of Italy and their creation in Sicily of one of the most brilliant medieval European civilizations. Just as stimulating is his *A History of Venice* (Penguin; Vintage), the most engrossing treatment of the subject that's available.

Giuliano Procacci, *History of the Italian People* (Penguin; OP in US). A comprehensive history of the peninsula, charting the development of Italy as a nation-state.

Ute Ranke-Heinemann, *Eunuchs for the Kingdom of Heaven* (OP). Entertaining, erudite and witty critique of the Catholic Church's attitude to sex.

Charles Richards, *The New Italians* (Penguin in UK). Vivid snapshot of Italy in the early 1990s, replete with entertaining pen-portraits of the major players. Richards has a good eye for a telling anecdote, though the social analysis is occasionally a bit too slick.

Donald Sassoon, *Contemporary Italy* (Longman; Addison-Wesley). Slightly academic background on the country and its institutions.

Renate Siebert, *Secrets of Life and Death: Women and the Mafia*, translated by Liz Heron (Verso). History and analysis of the patriarchal nature of Mafia organizations, which are held to be the apotheosis of the masculine society of Italy's south. Poignant first-person narratives give background to the account, exploding the myth of the Mafia as protecting the weak and defending women, who continue to be used as drug mules and decoys. The author is a German-born professor of sociology at the University of Calabria.

Denis Mack Smith, *The Making of Italy 1796–1866* (OP in UK; Holmes & Meier). Admirably lucid explanation of the various forces at work in the Unification of Italy.

Denis Mack Smith, *Italy and its Monarchy* (Yale UP). Learned and entertaining account of Italy's short-lived monarchy, whose kings ruled the country for less than a century. Reveals Vittorio Emanuele II and co. as a bunch of irresponsible and rather dim buffoons that the country was glad to be rid of. The same author has also written a couple of excellent biographies, *Mazzini* (Yale UP) and *Mussolini* (Phoenix Press; OP in US).

Claire Sterling, *The Mafia* (HarperCollins, OP in US). Thorough piece of Mafia scholarship, showing to a disturbing degree just how little Mafia power has been eroded by the state's onslaught of recent years. Followed up by *Crime Without Frontiers* (Warner; OP in US), which looks at the worldwide expansion of organized crime.

Alexander Stille, *Excellent Cadavers* (Vintage). Important new book that traces the rise, successes, failures and eventual assassinations of anti-Mafia magistrates Giovanni Falcone and Paolo Borsellino, as well as dishing the dirt on Andreotti and Craxi.

ART, ARCHITECTURE AND ARCHEOLOGY

Michael Baxandall, *Painting and Experience in Fifteenth-Century Italy* (Oxford UP). Invaluable analysis, concentrating on the way in which the art of the period would have been perceived at the time.

Anthony Blunt, *Artistic Theory in Italy 1450–1600* (OP in UK; Oxford UP). Cogent summary of the aesthetic ground rules of Renaissance art, but – contrary to the impression given by the writer's patrician tone – far from the last word. The author's *Baroque Rome* (Oxford UP) is a broad examination of Rome's Baroque architecture in two volumes.

Jacob Burckhardt, *The Civilization of the Renaissance in Italy* (Penguin). Nineteenth-century classic of Renaissance scholarship.

Robert Etienne, *Pompeii, The Day a City Died* (Thames and Hudson/Harry N. Abrams). Archeologically and historically rigorous, yet highly accessible, account of the life and death of Pompeii.

J.R. Hale (ed), *Encyclopaedia of the Italian Renaissance* (Thames & Hudson). Exemplary reference book, many of whose summaries are as informative as essays twice their length; covers individual artists, movements, cities, philosophical concepts, the lot.

Frederick Hartt, *History of Italian Renaissance Art* (Thames & Hudson; Harry N Abrams). If one book on this vast subject can be said to be indispensable, this is it. In view of its comprehensiveness and acuity, and the range of its illustrations, it's something of a bargain.

Howard Hibberd, *Bernini* (Penguin; Viking). Standard overview of the life and work of the central figure of Roman Baroque.

Peter Humfrey, *Lorenzo Lotto* (Yale UP). A lavishly illustrated, scholarly reappraisal of the Renaissance painter who was a contemporary of Titian and Giorgione, and whose finest achievements were his portraits.

Michael Levey, *Early Renaissance* (OP). Precise and fluently written, and well illustrated; probably the best introduction to the subject. Levey's *High Renaissance* (OP) continues the story in the same style.

Peter Murray, *The Architecture of the Italian Renaissance* (Thames & Hudson; Schocken). Begins with Romanesque buildings and finishes with Palladio – valuable both as a gazetteer of the main monuments and as a synopsis of the underlying concepts.

Peter and Linda Murray, *Art of the Renaissance* (Thames & Hudson). Serviceable thumbnail sketch, useful for preparing the ground before a trip to Italy.

T.W. Potter, *Roman Italy* (British Museum Press; University of California Press). Learned illustrated survey of Roman society based on archeological sources. Essential reading if you're interested in the period.

John Shearman, *Mannerism* (Penguin; Viking). The self-conscious art of sixteenth-century Mannerism is one of the most complex topics of Renaissance studies; Shearman's brief discussion analyzes the main currents, yet never oversimplifies nor becomes pedantic.

Giorgio Vasari, *Lives of the Artists* (Oxford Paperbacks; Oxford UP). New abridgement of the sixteenth-century artist's classic work on his predecessors and contemporaries. Includes essays on Giotto, Brunelleschi, Mantegna, Leonardo, Michelangelo, Raphael, and more. The first real work of art history and still among the most penetrating books you can read on Italian Renaissance art. The unabridged version was published in 1996 by Everyman's Library.

SPECIFIC GUIDES

Helena Attlee and Alex Ramsay, *Italian Gardens* (Ellipsis). Evocatively photographed (by Alex Ramsay), this is a guide to more than sixty of the peninsula's most beautiful gardens. Both practical and up to date, the guide provides histories and descriptions, as well as detailed information on locations, facilities, opening times, and accessibility.

Amanda Claridge *Oxford Archeological Guides: Rome* (Oxford UP). A well-written and excellently conceived concise guide to the ancient city, a good investment if that is your particular area of interest.

Tim Jepson, *Wild Italy* (Aurum Press; OP in US). Guide to the flora and fauna of the Italian peninsula by a *Rough Guide* contributor.

Gillian Price, *Walking in the Dolomites* (Cicerone in UK). Lively and informative specialized guide to the best walks in the Dolomites. Cicerone also publish guides to Alta Via 1 & 2 and to various Vie Ferrate (see p.238 for more on these peculiarly Italian phenomena).

Victoria Pybus, *Live and Work in Italy* (Vacation Work Publications). Accessible and informative handbook on all aspects of living and working in Italy, including regional differences.

ANCIENT LITERATURE

Catullus, *The Poems of Catullus* (Penguin; Oxford UP). Although his name is associated primarily with the tortured love poems addressed to Lesbia, Catullus also produced some acerbic satirical verse; this collection does full justice to his range.

Cicero, *Selected Works* (Penguin; Viking). The rhetorical prose of Cicero was for many Renaissance scholars the paragon of literary style, and his political ideas provided similarly fertile material for discussion. Penguin publish half a dozen volumes of his work.

Juvenal, *The Sixteen Satires* (Penguin). Savage attacks on the follies and excesses of Rome at the end of the first century and start of the second.

Livy, *The Early History of Rome* (Penguin). Lively chronicle of the city's evolution from the days of Romulus and Remus; Penguin also publish later instalments of those parts of Livy's history that have survived, including the gripping War with Hannibal.

Marcus Aurelius, *Meditations* (Penguin; Viking). The classic text of Stoic thought, written by one of the few Roman emperors it's easy to admire.

Ovid, *Metamorphoses* and *Erotic Poems* (both Penguin). The mythical tales of the Metamorphoses have been so frequently quarried by artists that they can be enjoyed both as literature and as a key to some of the masterworks of Renaissance and later art. His elegiac love poems have a sexual candour that makes them seem almost modern.

Petronius, *Satyricon* (Penguin). Fragmentary, spicy narrative written by one of Nero's inner circle; Fellini's film of the same name gives a pretty accurate idea of the tone.

Plautus, *Pot of Gold, and other plays* (Penguin; Oxford UP). The most popular playwright of his time, whose complicated plots provided a model for Renaissance comedies such as The Comedy of Errors.

Seneca, *Four Tragedies and Octavia* (Penguin; Viking). Violent, fast-paced drama from Nero's one-time tutor; the only plays to have survived from the Roman Empire.

Suetonius, *The Twelve Caesars* (Penguin; Viking). The inside story on such vile specimens as Caligula, Nero and Domitian; elegantly written and appalling.

Tacitus, *Annals of Imperial Rome* (Penguin; Viking). Covers much of the terrain dealt with by Suetonius, but from the stance of the diligent historian and serious moralist.

Virgil, *The Aeneid* (Penguin). The central work of Latin literature, depicting the adventures of Aeneas after the fall of Troy, and thus celebrating Rome's heroic lineage.

ITALIAN CLASSICS

Dante Alighieri, *The Divine Comedy* (Penguin). No work in any other language bears comparison with Dante's poetic exegesis of the moral scheme of God's creation; in late medieval Italy it was venerated both as a book of almost scriptural authority and as the ultimate refinement of the vernacular Tuscan language. A new translation, by Mark Musa, is printed in full in *The Portable Dante* (Penguin).

Ludovico Ariosto, *Orlando Furioso* (Penguin; Oxford UP). Italy's chivalrous epic, set in Charlemagne's Europe; has its exciting moments, but most readers would be grateful for an abridged version.

Giovanni Boccaccio, *The Decameron* (Penguin). Set in the plague-racked Florence of 1348, this assembly of one hundred short stories is a fascinating social record as well as a constantly diverting comic sequence.

Baldassare Castiglione, *The Book of the Courtier* (Penguin). Written in the form of a series of dialogues held in the court of Urbino, this subtle, entertaining book defines all the qualities essential in the perfect gentleman; the idealistic converse of Machiavelli.

Benvenuto Cellini, *Autobiography* (Penguin). Shamelessly egocentric record of the travails and triumphs of the sculptor and goldsmith's career; one of the freshest literary productions of its time.

Giacomo Leopardi, *Leopardi*, tr. Eamon Grennan (Princeton UP). Generally considered the greatest Italian poet since Dante, and a formative influence on the poets who followed, Leopardi has never had a big following in the English-speaking world, a situation that may change with this new, gutsy translation by Grennan, an Irish poet.

Niccolo Machiavelli, *The Prince* (Penguin). A treatise on statecraft which actually did less to form the political thought of Italy than it did to form foreigners' perceptions of the country; there was far more to Machiavelli than the realpolitik of *The Prince*, as is shown by the selection of writings included in Penguin's anthology *The Portable Machiavelli* (Viking in US).

Alessandro Manzoni, *The Betrothed* (Penguin). No pool-side thriller, but a skilful melding of the romance of two young lovers and a sweeping historical drama, all suffused with an almost religious sense of human destiny. First published in 1823, but reissued in 1840 after Manzoni had improved the novel's diction through study of the Tuscan dialect – a landmark in the transition towards linguistic nationalism.

Petrarch, (Francesco Petrarca) *Selections from the Canzoniere* (Oxford Paperbacks; Oxford UP). Often described as the first modern poet, by virtue of his preoccupation with worldly fame and secular love, Petrarch wrote some of the Italian language's greatest lyrics. This slim selection at least hints at what is lost in translation.

Marco Polo, *Travels* (Penguin; Viking). Buttonholing account of Polo's journey to the court of Kublai Khan, and his seventeen-year stay there; engaging even when the stories are clearly fanciful.

Leonardo da Vinci, *Notebooks* (Oxford Paperbacks; Oxford UP). Miscellany of speculation and observation from the universal genius of Renaissance Italy; essential to any understanding of the man.

MODERN ITALIAN LITERATURE

Giorgio Bassani, *The Garden of the Finzi Continis* (Quartet; Harcourt Brace). Gentle, elegiac novel, set in the Jewish community of Ferrara during the Fascist period, on the eve of the mass deportations to Germany. Infused with a sense of regret for a Europe that died with the war.

Enrico Brizzi, *Jack Frusciante has Left the Band* (Grove Press). Pacy, unrequited-love story set in Bologna. Rebellious Alex D endures life with his parents (whom he calls Matron and The Chancellor) while not getting anywhere with his girlfriend, the enigmatic but totally insecure Aidi. Some great descriptions of the overpowering pressure to conform in an Italian provincial town, the book is also memorably poignant at times.

Gesualdo Bufalino, *The Keeper of Ruins* (Harvill; OP); *The Plague Sower* (Eridanos); *Blind Argus* (OP) and *Night's Lies* (Harvill). One of Sicily's most esteemed twentieth-century writers, Bufalino arrived late on the literary scene, publishing his first novel, *The Plague Sower*, when he was into his sixties. Most of his output has now been translated.

Aldo Busi, *Seminar on Youth* (Carcanet; OP in US); *Confessions of a Panty-Hose Salesman* (Faber; OP in US) and *Sodomies in Eleven Point* (Faber; OP in US). Busi is something of an *enfant terrible* in the Italian literary world, but his tales of gay escapades around northern Italy go beyond the mere showy; indeed his somewhat impenetrable style masks a humanity and wit that is rare in much recent Italian fiction.

Ann and Michael Caesar (eds), *The Quality of Light* (Serpent's Tail). Anthology of contemporary Italian writers, including work by Primo Levi and Gianni Celati, as well as many other less well-known writers like the starkly realistic Pier Vittorio Tondelli.

Italo Calvino, *If on a Winter's Night a Traveller* (Minerva; Harcourt Brace). Calvino's fiction became increasingly concerned with the nature of fiction itself, and this involuted, witty novel marks the culmination of the process. Other titles include *The Castle of Crossed Destinies* (Vintage; Harcourt Brace) and *Invisible Cities* (Minerva; Harcourt Brace); *Difficult Loves* and *Mr Palomar* (both Minerva; Harcourt Brace).

Gianni Celati, *Voices from the Plains* (Serpent's Tail). Chance encounters on a walk down the Po provide the focus for these atmospheric tales. The four understated novellas in *Appearances* (Serpent's Tail) pay similarly close attention to the specific locales of Emilia-Romagna.

Gabriele D'Annunzio, *Halcyon* (OP). Self-regarding dandy, war hero and worshipper of Mussolini, D'Annunzio was perhaps the most complex figure of twentieth-century Italian literature; this extended lyric sequence – a troubled idyll set on the Tuscan coast – contains much of his finest poetry.

Umberto Eco, *The Name of the Rose* (Minerva; Harvest). Allusive, tightly plotted monastic detective story. Check out also his equally hyped, though rather more impenetrable, *Foucault's Pendulum* (Vintage; Ballantine), and the allegorical *Island of the Day Before* (Minerva; Penguin).

Dario Fo *Plays I* (Methuen; Books Britain). This collection includes a trio of Fo's most famous plays – *Mistero Buffo*, *Accidental Death of an Anarchist* and *Trumpets and Raspberries* – along with two previously unpublished short works. The Nobel Prize-winner fabulously weaves together contemporary politics, surreal farce and the traditions of *commedia dell'arte*.

Carlo Emilio Gadda, *That Awful Mess on Via Merulana* (Quartet; OP in US). Superficially a detective story, this celebrated modernist novel is so dense a weave of physical reality and literary diversions that the reader is led away from a solution rather than towards it; it enjoys the sort of status in Italian fiction that *Ulysses* has in English.

Natalia Ginzburg, *Family Sayings* (OP). The constraints of family life are a dominant theme in Ginzburg's writing, and her own upbringing is the source material for this characteristically rigorous yet lyrical work.

Giuseppe di Lampedusa, *The Leopard* (Harvill; Pantheon). The most famous Sicilian novel, written after the war but recounting the dramatic nineteenth-century transition from Bourbon to Piemontese rule from an aristocrat's point of view. A good character-study and rich with incidental detail, including some nice description of the Sicilian landscape.

Carlo Levi, *Christ Stopped at Eboli* (Penguin; Noonday). First published in 1945, this novel, set in a remote region of Basilicata, to which Levi was exiled under the Fascists, was the first to awaken modern Italy to the plight of its southern regions.

Primo Levi, *If This is a Man/The Truce* (Abacus; Collier, published as *Survival in Auschwitz*); *The Periodic Table* (Penguin; Schocken). Levi's experiences in Auschwitz are the main subject of *If This is a Man*, while *The Truce* records his eight-month journey back to Turin after his liberation. Levi's training as a chemist forms the background of *Periodic Table*, a mixture of autobiographical reflections and practical observations. The amorality of the Third Reich and its repercussions are the recurrent subjects of Levi's later works, all of which show an unwavering exactitude of recollection and judgement.

Elsa Morante, *History* (Steerforth Press). Capturing daily Roman life during the last war, this is probably the most vivid fictional picture of the conflict as seen from the city.

Alberto Moravia, *Roman Tales* (OP). Collection of stories, first published in the Fifties, which show the underbelly of a rapidly changing city; it is evocative both of the city and its people. *The Conformist* (Prion; Steerforth Press) is a psychological novel about a man sucked into the abyss of Fascism by his desperation to conform; *The Woman of Rome* (Steerforth Press) is an earlier work, a teeming and sensual novel, centred on the activities of a Roman prostitute.

Pier Paolo Pasolini, *A Violent Life* (Carcanet; OP in US). Pasolini's writing is preoccupied with the demise of local, dialect-based cultures of agrarian Italy in the face of modernization. His super-naturalistic evocation of life in the slum areas of Rome caused a scandal when it was published in 1959, but is now considered one of the classics of Italian postwar fiction. See also the collection of short stories, *Roman Nights and Other Stories* (Quartet; OP in US), and *A*

Dream of Something (OP) – Pasolini's pastoral tale of growing up in Friuli in the late Forties.

Cesare Pavese, *Moon and the Bonfire* (Peter Owen; OP in US); *Devil in the Hills* (Peter Owen; OP in US). Exploring the difficulties of achieving an acceptance of one's past, *Moon and the Bonfire* was written shortly before Pavese's suicide at the age of 42; *Devil in the Hills* is an early collection of tales of adolescence in and around Turin.

Luigi Pirandello, *Six Characters in Search of an Author* (Penguin; Dover); *The Late Mattia Pascal* (Andre Deutsch; Marsilio) and *Eleven Short Stories* (Dover). His most famous and accomplished work, *Six Characters...*, written in 1921, contains many of the themes that dogged Pirandello throughout his writing career – the idea of a multiple personality and the quality of reality. *The Late Mattia Pascal* is an early novel (1904), entertainingly written despite its stylistic shortcomings; while the collection of short stories is perhaps the best introduction to Pirandello's work.

Umberto Saba, *Ernesto* (OP). Lyrical autobiographical novel by the Triestine poet, recollecting youth and homosexuality. Marvellous translation.

Leonardo Sciascia, *Sicilian Uncles* (OP); *The Wine Dark Sea* (Granta; New York Review of Books); *Candido* (Adelphi; OP in US) and *The Day of the Owl* (Granta; OP in US). Writing again and again about his native Sicily, Sciascia has made of that island "a metaphor of the modern world". Economically written, Sciascia's short stories are packed with incisive insights, and infused with the author's humane and sympathetic views of its people.

Ignazio Silone, *Fontamara* (Redwords; New American Library); *Bread and Wine* (OP in UK; New American Library). From his exile in Switzerland, Silone wrote about his native Abruzzo, and about the struggle for social justice. *Fontamara* tells the tale of a small village driven to revolt against its landlords and the Fascist thugs sent to enforce their rule; *Bread and Wine*, a more introspective work, examines the parallels between Silone's political commitment and religious belief. The two works, together with *The Seed Beneath the Snow*, are published in one volume by Steerforth Press, titled *The Abruzzo Trilogy*.

Italo Svevo, *Confessions of Zeno* (Everyman's; Vintage). Complete critical indifference to his early efforts so discouraged Svevo that he gave up writing altogether, until encouraged by James Joyce, who taught him English in Trieste. The resultant novel is a unique creation, a comic portrait of a character at once wistful, helpless and irrepressible.

Giovanni Verga, *Short Sicilian Novels* (Dedalus); *Cavalleria Rusticana* (Penguin) and *I Malavoglia, or The House by the Medlar Tree* (Dedalus). Verga, born in the nineteenth century in Catania, spent several years in various European salons before coming home to write his best work. Much of it is a reaction against the pseudo-sophistication of society circles, stressing the simple lives of ordinary people, though sometimes accompanied by a heavy smattering of "peasant passion", with much emotion, wounded honour and feuds to the death.

Elio Vittorini, *Conversations in Sicily* (OP in UK; New Directions). A Sicilian emigrant returns from the north of Italy after fifteen years to see his mother on her birthday. The conversations of the title are with the people he meets on the way, local villagers and his mother, and reveal a poverty- and disease-ridden Sicily, though the scenes are affectionately drawn. In the US, New Directions publish an excellent anthology of his writings, *A Vittorini Omnibus* (OP in UK).

William Weaver (ed.), *Open City: Seven Writers in Postwar Rome* (Steerforth Press). A nicely produced anthology of pieces by the cream of Italy's twentieth century novelists – Bassani, Silone, Ginzburg, Moravia, among others – selected and with an introduction by one of the most eminent Italian translators of recent years.

AN ITALIAN MISCELLANY

Lindsey Davis, *Venus in Copper; Shadows in Bronze* (Arrow; Ballantine). These crime novels set in the age of the Emperor Vespasian are shot through with sparkling comedy, and follow super-sleuth Marcus Didius Falco as he unpicks mysteries and dastardly doings.

Michael Dibdin, *Ratking, Vendetta, Cabal* (all Faber; Vintage); *Dead Lagoon* (Faber; Vintage). Dibdin's Aurelio Zen is a classically eccentric, loner detective, and this is a classic series of well-plotted detective yarns. However, Dibdin is as interested in the country as he is in his characters, and these novels tell us plenty about the way Italian society operates. Most recent in the series are *Cosi Fan Tutti* (Faber; Vintage) set in Naples, *A Long Finish* (Faber; Vintage) in which Zen is sent to Piemonte on the trail of the murderer of a noted wine maker, and *Blood Rain* (Faber), set in Catania, with more of his own personal life revealed along the way. A supremely palatable way to read about Italy and Italians.

E.M. Forster, *A Room with a View* (Penguin). Set in and around Florence, this is the ultimate novel about how the nature of the Italian light, temperament and soul can make the English upper classes lose their heads.

Marius Gabriel, *House of Many Rooms* (Bantam). Psychological thriller and study of human relationships set in San Francisco and Italy.

Nathaniel Hawthorne, *The Marble Faun* (Penguin). A nineteenth-century take on the lives of Anglo-American expats in the Eternal City – sculptors, passionate lovers, devotees of Classical Purity – the usual mad mix and excessive goings-on that you'll still find today.

Ernest Hemingway, *Across the River and Into the Trees* (Arrow; Scribner). Not at all Hemingway's best work, and full of the self-loathing of the writer's final years, but the odd flash of fine prose paints Venice as a vivid foil to this quiet tale of a military man at the end of his life and tether.

Patricia Highsmith, *The Talented Mr Ripley* (Vintage). The novel follows the fortunes of the eponymous hero through Italy as he exchanges his own identity for that of the man he has murdered. Recently released as a movie, starring Gwyneth Paltrow and directed by Anthony Minghella.

Thomas Mann, *Death in Venice* (Minerva; Dover). Irascible and ultra-traditional old novelist visits Venice to recover after a breakdown and becomes obsessed with a beautiful young boy, awakening an internal debate about the nature of beauty and art to which the city is a fitting and resonant backdrop.

Allan Massie, *Augustus* (Sceptre; Carroll & Graf); *Tiberius* (Sceptre; OP in US); *Caesar* (Sceptre; OP in US). A trilogy of novels that tells the stories of the three emperors as if they were recently discovered autobiographies. Massie's historical precision and careful dramatization hold up well.

Frances Mayes, *Under the Tuscan Sun* (Bantam; Broadway Books). Follow the trials and triumphs of American author and boyfriend as they renovate a farmhouse near Cortona, interspersed with recipes. The echoes of Peter Mayle in Provence will put many off.

Ian McEwan, *The Comfort of Strangers* (Vintage). An ordinary young English couple fall foul of a sexually ambiguous predator in a Venice who is never named, but evoked by means of arch little devices such as quotes from Ruskin.

John Mortimer, *Summer's Lease* (Penguin). The chattering classes revel in Chiantishire. Not exactly profound, but hugely entertaining.

Magdalen Nabb, *Death in Springtime*, *Death in Autumn* and many other titles (OP). Thrillers that make the most of their settings in low-life Florence and the wild Sardinian hills where shepherds dabble in a spot of kidnapping.

Michael Ondaatje, *The English Patient* (Picador; Vintage) The novel that inspired the Anthony Minghella film starring Juliette Binoche and Ralph Fiennes. A nurse cares for her patient, burnt beyond recognition, in an abandoned Italian monastery during World War II as his true identity, and the story of the passionate but doomed affair he has survived, are uncovered.

Tim Parks, *Italian Neighbours* (Vintage; Fawcett) *An Italian Education* (Minerva; Avon), and *Europa* (Vintage; Arcade). Novelist Tim Parks married an Italian woman and has lived in Italy since 1981. Through deftly told tales of family life, his first two books examine what it means to be Italian, and how national identity is absorbed. His later novel, *Europa*, was shortlisted for the Booker prize in 1997; a bawdy, savage tale of love gone wrong, it's set among a group of academics travelling to lobby the European Parliament in Strasbourg. Tragic but very funny.

Daphne Phelps, *A House in Sicily* (Virago; Carroll & Graf). An Englishwoman inherits a grand house in Taormina and turns it into a guest house to make ends meet. This allows vignettes of eminent guests – Bertrand Russell, Tennessee Williams, Roald Dahl – as well as of the locals, though her patronizing take on some of these, including the local Mafia don, grates, and her anglocentric, provincial style are off-putting.

Susan Sontag, *The Volcano Lover*, (Vintage/Anchor). A profound and surprising novel, based on the notorious affair between Nelson and Lady Hamilton, wife of the volcano-fixated English ambassador to Naples. The self-absorbed protagonists indulge their various obsessions – romantic and geological – as Vesuvius smoulders in the background and the Bourbon court wallows in dissolution and incompetence. An absolute must-read for visitors to Naples.

Stendhal, *The Charterhouse of Parma* (Oxford Paperbacks; Modern Library). Panoramic nineteenth-century French novel that dramatizes the struggles and intrigues of the Italian papal states before Unification. A wonderful read, and a good insight into the era to boot.

Irving Stone, *The Agony and the Ecstasy* (Mandarin; New American Library). Stone's dramatized life of Van Gogh is well-known, filmed with a memorably angst-ridden Kirk Douglas in the title role. Here Stone gives the same treatment to Michelangelo, popular "faction" that is entertaining even if it doesn't exactly get to the root of the artist's work and times. Great fun, though.

Lowri Turner, *Gianni Versace: Fashion's Last Emperor* (OP in UK; Trans-Atlantic). Fashion editor Turner's 'photo-biography' of the late designer suggests that Versace and the man who allegedly gunned him down were murdered by the Mafia. A strange mix of reportage, interspersed with 90 colour photographs of supermodels and Versace's own glamorous homes.

Barry Unsworth, *After Hannibal* (Penguin; W.W. Norton) and *Stone Virgin* (Penguin; W.W. Norton). The author lives in Umbria, where the former novel is set. *After Hannibal* is a black comedy of expat life, where a diverse cast of characters in the process of being betrayed each confide in the same local lawyer. The earlier *Stone Virgin*, set in Venice, is based around a conservation expert who falls under the spell of a statue of the Madonna he is working on – and of a member of the family who owns it.

Roger Vailland, *The Law* (OP in UK; Hippocrene). This evocation of life in a small Pugliese town, of its people, etiquette, and harsh tradition, is tight, considered and utterly convincing.

Edith Wharton, *Roman Fever & Other Stories* (Prentice Hall; Collier). The title story of this collection recounts two old women's stingingly bitchy reminiscences about their adolescence in Rome.

Jeanette Winterson, *The Passion* (Vintage; Grove Press). Whimsical tale of the intertwined lives of a member of Napoleon's catering corps and a female gondolier.

FOOD AND DRINK

Burton Anderson, *Wines of Italy* (Mitchell Beazley; Millers). Comprehensive pocket guide to the regional wines and winemaking techniques of Italy.

Antonio Carluccio, *Carluccio's Complete Italian Food* (Quadrille; Rizzoli). Based on the BBC TV series. Carluccio's passion for food goes right back to basics; his message is that a meal – however humble or grand – is only as good as the land or sea from which its ingredients come.

Elizabeth David, *Italian Food* (Penguin). The writer who introduced Italian cuisine – and ingredients – to Britain. Ahead of its time when it was published in the Fifties, and imbued with all the enthusiasm and diversity of Italian cookery. An inspirational book.

Keith Floyd, *Floyd on Italy* (Michael Joseph in UK). Glossy pictures and fairly straightforward recipes – strong on game and fish – all delivered in Floyd's rumbustious style.

Patience Gray, *Honey from a Weed* (Prospect; The Lyons Press). The author lived and worked in basic conditions in various Mediterranean countries, and in this intriguing blend of cookbook and autobiography, she describes roughing it and cooking it.

Valentina Harris, *Italia! Italia!* (Seven Dials in UK); *Recipes from an Italian Farmhouse* (Conran Octopus). All the classics, pizzas and pastas, with regional recipes and anecdotes from local and regional tradiitions.

Marcella Hazan, *The Classic Italian Cookbook* (Macmillan; OP in US) and *Marcella Cucina* (Macmillan; HarperCollins). The best Italian cookbook for the novice in the kitchen, *The Classic Italian Cookbook* is a step-by-step guide that never compromises the spirit or authenticity of Hazan's subject. She draws her recipes from all over the peninsula, emphasizing the intrinsically regional nature of Italian food. Her latest, the fully illustrated *Marcella Cucina*, combines regional dishes and anecdotes.

Fred Plotkin, *Italy for the Gourmet Traveller* (Kyle Cathie; Little Brown). Comprehensive, region-by-region guide to the best of Italian cuisine, with a foodie's guide to major towns and cities, a gazetteer of restaurants and specialist food and wine shops, and descriptions of local dishes, with recipes.

Mary Taylor Simeti, *Sicilian Food* (Grub Street; OP in US). Starting with the oldest and most elemental components of the Sicilian diet, this book offers a collection of recipes and evocations of the dishes' origins: from the culinary innovations of Arab and Norman invaders to the ritual luxuries of Sicily's aristocracy.

LANGUAGE

The ability to speak English confers prestige in Italy, and there's often no shortage of people willing to show off their knowledge, particularly returned emigrati. However, even in the main cities and resorts you'll need to use at least some Italian, and in more remote areas you may well find no one speaks English at all.

PRONUNCIATION

Wherever you are, it's a good idea to master at least a little **Italian**, a task made easier by the fact that your halting efforts will often be rewarded by smiles and genuine surprise. In any case, it's one of the easiest European languages to learn, especially if you already have a smattering of French or Spanish, both of which are extremely similar grammatically.

Easiest of all is the **pronunciation**, since every word is spoken exactly as it's written, and usually enunciated with exaggerated, open-mouthed clarity. The only difficulties you're likely to encounter are the few **consonants** that are different from English:

c before e or i is pronounced as in **ch**urch, while ch before the same vowels is hard, as in **c**at.

sci or **sce** are pronouced as in **she**et and **she**lter respectively.

The same goes with **g** – soft before e or i, as in geranium; hard before h, as in **g**arlic.

gn has the ni sound of our on**i**on.

gl in Italian is softened to something like li in English, as in stal**li**on.

h is not aspirated, as in **h**onour.

When speaking to strangers, the third person is the polite form (ie lei instead of tu for "you"); using the second person is a mark of familiarity or disrespect. Italians don't use "please" and "thank you" as much as we do: it's all implied in the tone. If in doubt, err on the polite side.

Most Italian words are **stressed** on the penultimate syllable. In written Italian, **accents** (either ´ or `) have traditionally been used to denote stress on other syllables, but the acute (') accent is more rarely used these days. In the text we've used acute accents only when we feel it's necessary to help you get the pronunciation right – eg Pésaro where the accent indicates that the stress should be on the **e**, not the a. Note that the endings -**ia** or -**ie** count as two syllables, hence trattoria is stressed on the **i**.

You'll find variations in **dialect** all over the country. Neapolitan especially can be difficult to understand, and the Sicilian dialect is different enough from conventional Italian as to be almost a separate language. But everywhere people will slip into more orthodox Italian if they see you're a foreigner.

ITALIAN WORDS AND PHRASES

BASICS

Good morning	*Buon giorno*	Today	*Oggi*
Good afternoon/		Tomorrow	*Domani*
evening	*Buona sera*	Day after	*Dopodomani*
Good night	*Buona notte*	tomorrow	
Hello/goodbye	*Ciao* (informal; to strangers	Yesterday	*Ieri*
	use phrases above)	Now	*Adesso*
Goodbye	*Arrivederci*	Later	*Più tardi*
Yes	*Si*	Wait a minute!	*Aspetta!*
No	*No*	Let's go!	*Andiamo!*
Please	*Per favore*	In the morning	*Di mattina*
Thank you	*Grázie*	In the afternoon	*Nel pomeriggio*
(very much)	(*molte/mille grazie*)	In the evening	*Di sera*
You're welcome	*Prego*	Here/There	*Qui/Là*
All right/that's OK	*Va bene*	Good/Bad	*Buono/Cattivo*
How are you?	*Come stai/sta?*	Big/Small	*Grande/Piccolo*
(informal/formal)		Cheap/Expensive	*Económico/Caro*
I'm fine	*Bene*	Early/Late	*Presto/Tardi*
Do you speak	*Parla inglese?*	Hot/Cold	*Caldo/Freddo*
English?		Near/Far	*Vicino/Lontano*
I don't understand	*Non ho capito*	Vacant/Occupied	*Libero/Occupato*
I don't know	*Non lo so*	Quickly/Slowly	*Velocemente/Lentamente*
Excuse me	*Mi scusi/Prego*	Slowly/Quietly	*Piano*
Excuse me	*Permesso*	With/Without	*Con/Senza*
(in a crowd)		More/Less	*Più/Meno*
I'm sorry	*Mi dispiace*	Enough, no more	*Basta*
I'm here on holiday	*Sono qui in vacanza*	Mr . . .	*Signor . . .*
I'm British/Irish/	*Sono britannico/a irlan-*	Mrs . . .	*Signora . . .*
dese/a		Miss . . .	*Signorina . . .*
American/	*americano/a*		
Australian/	*australiano/a/*		(*il Signor, la Signora, la Signorina*
New Zealander	*neozelandese/a*		when speaking about someone else)
I live in . . .	*Abito a . . .*		

DRIVING

Left/right	*A sinistra/A destra*	No entry	*Senso vietato*
Go straight ahead	*Sempre diritto*	Slow down	*Rallentare*
Turn to the right/	*Gira a destra/*	Road closed/	*Strada chiusa/*
left	*sinistra*	under repair	*lavoro in corso*
Parking	*Parcheggio*	No through road	*Vietato il transito*
No parking	*Divieto di sosta/*	No overtaking	*Vietato il sorpasso*
	Sosta vietata	Crossroads	*Incrocio*
One way street	*Senso único*	Speed limit	*Limite di velocità*

SOME SIGNS

Entrance/Exit	*Entrata/Uscita*	Closed for restoration	*Chiuso per restauro*
Free entrance	*Ingresso líbero*	Closed for holidays	*Chiuso per ferie*
Gentlemen/Ladies	*Signori/Signore*	Pull/Push	*Tirare/Spingere*
WC/Bathroom	*Gabinetto/bagno*	Out of order	*Guasto*
Vacant/Engaged	*Libero/Occupato*	Drinking water	*Acqua potabile*
Open/Closed	*Aperto/Chiuso*	To let	*Affitasi*
Arrivals/Departures	*Arrivi/Partenze*	Platform	*Binario*

SOME SIGNS (Cont')

Cash desk	Cassa	Danger	Perícolo
Go/walk	Avanti	Beware	Attenzione
Stop/halt	Alt	First aid	Pronto soccorso
Customs	Dogana	Ring the bell	Suonare il campanello
Do not touch	Non toccare	No smoking	Vietato fumare

ITALIAN NUMBERS

1	uno	14	quattordici	70	settanta
2	due	15	quindici	80	ottanta
3	tre	16	sedici	90	novanta
4	quattro	17	diciassette	100	cento
5	cinque	18	diciotto	101	centuno
6	sei	19	diciannove	110	centodieci
7	sette	20	venti	200	duecento
8	otto	21	ventuno	500	cinquecento
9	nove	22	ventidue	1000	mille
10	dieci	30	trenta	5000	cinquemila
11	undici	40	quaranta	10,000	diecimila
12	dodici	50	cinquanta	50,000	cinquantamila
13	tredici	60	sessanta		

ACCOMMODATION

Hotel	Albergo/hotel	Is breakfast included?	È compresa la prima colazione?
Is there a hotel nearby?	C'è un albergo qui vicino?	Do you have anything cheaper?	Ha niente che costa di meno?
Do you have a room . . .	Ha una cámera . . .	Full/half board	Pensione completa/ mezza pensione
for one/two/three person/people	per una/due/tre persona/e	Can I see the room?	Posso vedere la cámera?
for one/two/ three night/s	per una/due/ tre notte/i	I'll take it	La prendo
for one/two week/s	per una/due settimana/e	I'd like to book a room	Vorrei prenotare una cámera
with a double bed	con un letto matrimoniale	I have a booking	Ho una prenotazione
with a shower/bath	con una doccia/un bagno	Can we camp here?	Possiamo campeggiare qui?
with a balcony	con una terrazza	Is there a campsite nearby?	C'è un camping qui vicino?
hot/cold water	acqua calda/freddo	Tent	Tenda
How much is it?	Quanto costa?	Cabin	Cabina
It's expensive	È caro	Youth hostel	Ostello per la gioventù

QUESTIONS AND DIRECTIONS

Where? (where is/ where are . . . ?)	Dove? (Dov'è/ Dove sono . . . ?)	Can you tell me when to get off?	Mi può dire di scendere alla fermata giusta?
When?	Quando?	What time does it open?	A che ora apre?
What? (what is it?)	Cosa? (Cos'è?)	What time does it close?	A che ora chiude?
How much/many?	Quanto/Quanti?		
Why?	Perché?	How much does it cost (. . . do they cost?)	Quanto costa? (. . . Quanto cóstano?)
It is/there is (is it/ is there . . . ?)	C'e . . . ?		
What time is it?	Che ora è/Che ore sono?	What's it called in Italian?	Come si chiama in italiano?
How do I get to . . . ?	Come arrivo a . . . ?		
How far is it to . . . ?	Cuant'è lontano a . . . ?		
Can you give me a lift to . . . ?	Mi può dare un passaggio a . . . ?		

TRAVELLING

Aeroplane	Aeroplano	What time does it leave?	A che ora parte?
Bus	Autobus/pullman		
Train	Treno	When is the next bus/train/ferry to . . . ?	Quando parte il prossimo pullman/treno/traghetto per . . . ?
Car	Macchina		
Taxi	Taxi		
Bicycle	Bicicletta	Do I have to change?	Devo cambiare?
Ferry	Traghetto	Where does it leave from?	Da dove parte?
Ship	Nave		
Hydrofoil	Aliscafo	What platform does it leave from?	Da quale binario parte?
Hitch-hiking	Autostop		
On foot	A piedi	How many kilometres is it?	Quanti chilómetri sono?
Bus station	Autostazione		
Railway station	Stazione ferroviaria	How long does it take?	Quanto ci vuole?
Ferry terminal	Stazione maríttima		
Port	Porto	What number bus is it to . . . ?	Che número di autobus per . . . ?
A ticket to . . .	Un biglietto per . . .		
One-way/return	Solo andata/andata e ritorno	Where's the road to . . . ?	Dové la strada per . . .
Can I book a seat?	Posso prenotare un posto?	Next stop please	La prósima fermata, per favore

PHRASEBOOKS AND DICTIONARIES

The most user-friendly phrasebook is the Rough Guides' own Italian, arranged dictionary-style for ease of access and with a host of cultural tips and slang expressions. Among dictionaries, Collins publish a comprehensive series: their Gem or Pocket dictionaries are fine for travelling purposes, while their Concise is adequate for most language needs.

GLOSSARY OF ARTISTIC AND ARCHITECTURAL TERMS

AGORA Square or market place in an ancient Greek city.

AMBO A kind of simple pulpit, popular in Italian medieval churches.

APSE Semicircular recess at the altar (usually eastern) end of a church.

ARCHITRAVE The lowest part of the entablature.

ATRIUM Inner courtyard.

BALDACHINO A canopy on columns, usually placed over the altar in a church.

BASILICA Originally a Roman administrative building, adapted for early churches; distinguished by lack of transepts.

BELVEDERE A terrace or lookout point.

CALDARIUM The steam room of a Roman bath.

CAMPANILE Belltower, sometimes detached, usually of a church.

CAPITAL Top of a column.

CATALAN-GOTHIC Hybrid form of architecture, mixing elements of fifteenth-century Spanish and northern European styles.

CELLA Sanctuary of a temple.

CHIAROSCURO The balance of light and shade in a painting, and the skill of the artist in depicting the contrast between the two.

CHANCEL Part of a church containing the altar.

CIBORIUM Another word for Baldachino, see above.

CORNICE The top section of a classical facade.

CORTILE Galleried courtyard or cloisters.

COSMATI WORK Decorative mosaic work on marble, usually highly coloured, found in early Christian Italian churches, especially in Rome. Derives from the name Cosma, a common name among families of marble workers at the time.

CRYPT Burial place in a church, usually under the choir.

CRYPTOPORTICUS Underground passageway.

CYCLOPEAN WALLS Fortifications built of huge, rough stone blocks, common in the pre-Roman settlements of Lazio.

DECUMANUS MAXIMUS The main street of a Roman town. The second cross-street was known as the Decumanus Inferiore.

ENTABLATURE The section above the capital on a classical building, below the cornice.

EX-VOTO Artefact designed in thanksgiving to a saint. The adjective is ex-votive.

FRESCO Wall-painting technique in which the artist applies paint to wet plaster for a more permanent finish.

LOGGIA Roofed gallery or balcony.

METOPE A panel on the frieze of a Greek temple.

MITHRAISM Pre-Christian cult associated with the Persian god of Light, who slew a bull and fertilized the world with its blood.

NAVE Central space in a church, usually flanked by aisles.

PANTOCRATOR Usually refers to an image of Christ, portrayed with outstretched arms.

PIANO NOBILE Main floor of a palace, usually the first.

POLYPTYCH Painting on several joined wooden panels.

PORTICO Covered entrance to a building, or porch.

PRESEPIO A Christmas crib.

PUTTI Cherubs.

RELIQUARY Receptacle for a saint's relics, usually bones. Often highly decorated.

SGRAFFITO Decorative technique whereby one layer of plaster is scratched to form a pattern. Popular in sixteenth-century Italy.

STEREOBATE Visible base of any building, usually a Greek temple.

STUCCO Plaster made from water, lime, sand and powdered marble, used for decorative work.

THERMAE Baths, usually elaborate buildings in Roman villas.

TRIPTYCH Painting on three joined wooden panels.

TROMPE L'OEIL Work of art that deceives the viewer by means of tricks with perspective.

GLOSSARY OF WORDS AND ACRONYMS

ALISCAFO Hydrofoil.

ANFITEATRO Amphitheatre.

AUTOSTAZIONE Bus station.

AUTOSTRADA Motorway.

BIBLIOTECA Library

CAPPELLA Chapel.

CASTELLO Castle.

CENTRO Centre.

CHIESA Church.

COMUNE An administrative area; also the local council or town hall.

CORSO Avenue or boulevard.

DUOMO/CATTEDRALE Cathedral.

ENTRATA Entrance.

FESTA Festival, holiday.

FIUME River.

FUMAROLA Volcanic vapour emission from the ground.

GOLFO Gulf.

LAGO Lake.

LARGO Square.

LUNGOMARE Seafront road or promenade.

MARE Sea.

MERCATO Market.

MUNICIPIO Town hall.

PAESE Place, area, country village.

PALAZZO Palace, mansion, or block of flats.

PARCO Park.

PASSEGGIATA The customary early evening walk.

PIANO Plain.

PIAZZA Square.

PINACOTECA Picture Gallery

PONTE Bridge.

SANTUARIO Sanctuary.

SENSO UNICO One-way street.

SOTTOPASSAGGIO Subway.

SPIAGGIA Beach.

STAZIONE Station.

STRADA Road.

TEATRO Theatre.

TEMPIO Temple.

TORRE Tower.

TRAGHETTO Ferry.

USCITA Exit.

VIA Road (always used with name, eg Via Roma).

ACRONYMS

AAST Azienda Autonoma di Soggiorno e Turismo.

APT Azienda Promozione Turistica.

ACI Automobile Club d'Italia.

CAI Club Alpino Italiano.

DC Democrazia Cristiana (the Christian Democrat party).

EPT Ente Provinciale per il Turismo (provincial tourist office); see also APT .

FS Ferrovie dello Stato (Italian State Railways).

IVA Imposta Valore Aggiunto (VAT).

MSI Movimento Sociale Italiano (the Italian Fascist party).

PDI Partito Democratica della Sinestra; new name for the Italian communist party.

PDS Partito Democratico della Sinistra (the former Italian Communist party).

PSI Partito Socialista Italiano (the Italian Socialist party).

RAI The Italian state TV and radio network.

SIP Italian state telephone company.

SS Strada Statale; a major road, eg SS18.

GLOSSARY OF STREET NAMES

Italian streets form a kind of outdoor pantheon of historical figures. A jumble of artists, thinkers, politicians, generals and saints, in roughly equal proportions, intersect with each other in blind disregard for sense or chronology. The mad mix of heroes (and a very few heroines) constantly reminds the visitor of just how much Italians relish their past. Almost all of the following appear in every major Italian city.

Bassi, Ugo (1801–1849). A priest from Bologna who, as a fervent and eloquent supporter of Garibaldi and his cause, became one of its most important martyrs when he was condemned to death and shot by the Austrians.

Bellini. The name of both a Venetian family of fifteenth-century painters (Jacopo and sons Gentile and Giovanni), and a nineteenth-century Sicilian composer of operas (Vicenzo), best known for *Norma* and *La Sonnambula*.

Bertani, Agostino (1812–1886). A Milanese doctor, who organized the medical and ambulance services for Garibaldi's campaigns and became one of his closest associates and shrewdest strategists.

Bixio, Nino (1821–1873). Loyal companion-at-arms to Garibaldi, who enlisted and disciplined civilian volunteers to fight some of the critical battles of the Unification era.

Buonarroti, Filippo (1761–1837). Tuscan revolutionary and friend of Robespierre, who was involved with Gracchus Babeuf in the short-lived Conspiracy of Equals in Paris, May 1796.

Calatafimi. First decisive battle in Garibaldi's Sicilian campaign, May 1860.

Cappuccini. Monks whose characteristic brown robes and peaked white hoods have lent their names to the Italian coffee drink with hot milk.

Carducci, Giosue (1835–1907). Patriotic poet of the Risorgimento who won the Nobel Prize for literature in 1907.

Cavour, Camillo di (1810–1861). Prime Minister of Piemonte who relied on diplomatic cunning to promote the interests of his northern kingdom in the Unification of Italy.

Crispi, Francesco (1819–1901). Reforming prime minister of the late nineteenth century.

D'Annunzio, Gabriele (1863–1938). Nationalist writer who refurbished Italy's past with sex and violence and who lived out some of his fantasies as a Fascist military adventurer.

Dante Alighieri (1265–1321). Medieval Italian poet known for his three-part poem, *The Divine Comedy*.

De Gasperi, Alcide (1881–1954). A prominent anti-Fascist imprisoned by Mussolini, and the first Catholic Prime Minister of modern Italy in 1945, aligning his country with the West by joining NATO.

Depretis, Agostino (1813–87). Italian prime minister on three occasions during the late nineteenth century. His administrations are remembered for the stagnation and corruption they engendered.

Foscolo, Ugo (1778–1827). Nineteenth-century poet, dramatist and critic who left Venice under Austrian rule to settle in England where he became a commentator on Petrarch, Dante and Boccaccio.

Garibaldi, Giuseppe (1807–1882). Italy's unquestioned nationalist hero, and the tag on most Italian towns' most prominent boulevards or squares. Streets are full of his exploits and the supporting cast of comrades (see Bassi, Bertani, Bixio, Calatafimi, I Mille, Turr).

Giolitti, Giovanni (1842–1928). Prime minister five times between 1892 and 1921. He sponsored an electoral reform bill which extended male suffrage and won workers the right to organize and strike.

Goldoni, Carlo (1707–1793). Venetian dramatist much influenced by Moliere, who wrote more than 250 comedies.

Gramsci, Antonio (1881–1937). One of the founders of the Italian Communist Party. Arrested by Mussolini in 1928 and held until just before his death, his influential writings from prison on the political role of culture and intellectuals remain controversial fifty years on.

Leopardi, Giacomo (1798–1837). A lyric poet plagued by ill-health and melancholy whose patriotic verses were taken up by the Unification.

Machiavelli, Nicolo (1469–1527). Political scientist and author of *The Prince* whose name outside Italy has become synonymous with unprincipled political opportunism.

Manin, Daniele (1804–1857). Leader of a revolution in Venice which proclaimed a republic in March 1948 and was overrun by the Austrians shortly thereafter.

Manzoni, Alessandro (1785–1873). Liberal Catholic writer and playwright whose historical novel *I promesi sposi* (*The Betrothed*), set in seventeenth-century Milan, is still required reading in Italian schools.

Marconi, Guglielmo (1874–1937). Developer of the wireless system, sending messages across the Straits of Dover in 1899 and across the Atlantic in 1901.

Matteotti, Giacomo. A Socialist in the Italian Parliament who was murdered by Fascist thugs for his public denunciation of the 1924 elections which gave Mussolini majority control. In what has become known as Mussolini's Watergate, the incident had a brief chance of stopping Il Duce in his tracks – but didn't.

Mazzini, Giuseppe (1805–1872). Propagandist of Italian Unification whose influence was spread through the organization (Giovine Italia) Young Italy which he founded to promote the national cause.

I Mille (The Thousand). The name given to the largely untrained band of civilian volunteers (made up of students, workers, artists, journalists and every kind of adventurer) who were mobilized in 1860 for Garibaldi's successful Sicilian campaign.

Moro, Aldo. Post-war prime minister who was kidnapped and murdered by the Brigate Rosse in May 1978.

Puccini, Giacomo (1858–1924). A member of the fifth generation of a family of professional musicians, and composer of many popular operas, including *Madame Butterfly*, *La Bohème* and *Tosca*.

Quattro Novembre (November 4). Anniversary of the 1918 victory in the war.

Ricasoli. An ancient and distinguished Tuscan family name. The nineteenth-century Baron Ricasoli (an ally of Cavour and very briefly prime minister) has been eclipsed by the relatively greater prominence of his family's vineyards, known particularly for their Chianti.

Ricci, Matteo (1552–1610). Early Italian missionary to China.

Risorgimento. The nineteenth-century movement to unify Italy and liberate the country from foreign domination.

Savonarola. A fifteenth-century Dominican friar and prophet of doom, who inspired a famous book-burning (which included Boccaccio's *Decameron* among the forbidden texts), and was himself burned in 1498.

Togliatti (1893–1964). Co-founder (with Gramsci and others) of the Italian Communist Party, which, in 1956, adopted his programme for an "Italian Road to Socialism".

Turr, Stefan. A Hungarian colonel in Garibaldi's army and close associate who helped acquire arms for the volunteer army (The Thousand) to mount the campaign in Sicily.

Umberto I and II. Kings of Italy, respectively, between 1878 and 1900 and for a brief period in 1946.

Vasari, Giorgio (1511–1574). The father of modern art history, whose *Lives of the Artists* traced the story of art from ancient Rome through to his own contemporary – and fellow Tuscan – Michelangelo.

Venti Settembre (September 20). The day Italian troops stormed into Rome in 1870, marking the final stage of Unification.

Venticinque Aprile (April 25). Anniversary of the 1945 liberation.

Ventiquattro Maggio (May 24). Date in 1915 when Italy declared war on Austria-Hungary.

Verdi, Giuseppe (1813–1901). Hugely popular and prolific composer of operas who became a national hero.

Vespri Siciliani. Massacre of the Angevin French in Sicily in 1282, carried out (according to legend) while vesper bells were ringing, in retaliation for the savage colonization of the island by the Angevin. Verdi used the story for an opera in 1855.

Vittorio Emanuele II and III. Respectively, the first king of unified Italy, from 1861 to 1878, and from 1900 until 1946. Very often the main street of towns are named after Vittorio Emanuele II – an overly grand accolade for a dull and unenlightened ruler.

Volturno. A river near Capua, and the name given to an important battle led by Garibaldi against the Bourbons in October 1860.

INDEX

Don't bury your head in the sand!

Take cover!

with Rough Guide Travel Insurance

UK Freefone 0800 015 09 06
Worldwide (+44) 1243 621 046
Check the web at
www.roughguides.com/insurance

ROUGH GUIDES

Worldwide cover, for Rough Guide readers worldwide

Insurance organized by Torribles Insurance Brokers Ltd, 21 Prince Street, Bristol, BS1 4PH, England

Stay in touch with us!

**ROUGHNEWS is Rough Guides' free newsletter.
In three issues a year we give you news, travel
issues, music reviews, readers' letters and the
latest dispatches from authors on the road.**

I would like to receive ROUGHNEWS: please put me on your free mailing list.

NAME . . . .

ADDRESS . . . .

Please clip or photocopy and send to: Rough Guides, 62–70 Shorts Gardens, London WC2H 9AH,
England or Rough Guides, 375 Hudson Street, New York, NY 10014, USA.

IF KNOWLEDGE IS POWER,
THIS ROUGH GUIDE IS A POCKET-SIZED BATTERING RAM

THE MILLION-COPY BESTSELLER

THE ROUGH GUIDE TO
The
Internet
Angus J. Kennedy

2001 EDITION • FOR PCs AND MACS

£6.00
US$9.95

Written in plain English, with no hint of jargon, the Rough Guide to the Internet will make you an Internet guru in the shortest possible time. It cuts through the hype and makes all others look like nerdy textbooks

AT ALL BOOKSTORES • DISTRIBUTED BY PENGUIN

www.roughguides.com

Check out our Web site for unrivalled travel information on the Internet.
Plan ahead by accessing the full text of our major titles, make travel reservations and keep up to date with the latest news in the Traveller's Journal or by subscribing to our free newsletter ROUGHNEWS - packed with stories from Rough Guide writers.

ROUGH GUIDES: Travel

Alaska
Amsterdam
Andalucia
Argentina
Australia
Austria

Bali & Lombok
Barcelona
Belgium &
  Luxembourg
Belize
Berlin
Brazil
Britain
Brittany &
  Normandy
Bulgaria
California
Canada
Central America
Chile
China
Corsica
Costa Rica
Crete
Croatia
Cuba
Cyprus
Czech & Slovak
  Republics

Dodecanese &
  the East Aegean
Devon &
  Cornwall
Dominican
  Republic
Dordogne & the
  Lot
Ecuador
Egypt
England
Europe
Florida
France
French Hotels &
  Restaurants
  1999
Germany
Goa
Greece
Greek Islands
Guatemala
Hawaii
Holland
Hong Kong &
  Macau
Hungary

Iceland
India
Indonesia
Ionian Islands
Ireland

Israel & the
  Palestinian
  Territories
Italy
Jamaica
Japan
Jordan
Kenya
Lake District
Languedoc &
  Roussillon
Laos
London
Los Angeles
Malaysia,
  Singapore &
  Brunei
Mallorca &
  Menorca
Maya World
Mexico
Morocco
Moscow
Nepal
New England
New York
New Zealand
Norway
Pacific
  Northwest
Paris
Peru
Poland
Portugal
Prague
Provence & the
  Côte d'Azur
The Pyrenees
Romania
St Petersburg
San Francisco

Sardinia
Scandinavia
Scotland
Scottish
  highlands and
  Islands
Sicily
Singapore
South Africa
South India
Southeast Asia
Southwest USA
Spain
Sweden
Switzerland
Syria

Thailand
Trinidad &
  Tobago
Tunisia
Turkey
Tuscany &
  Umbria
USA
Venice
Vienna
Vietnam
Wales
Washington DC
West Africa
Zimbabwe &
  Botswana

AVAILABLE AT ALL GOOD BOOKSHOPS

ROUGH GUIDES: Mini Guides, Travel Specials and Phrasebooks

MINI GUIDES

Antigua
Bangkok
Barbados
Beijing
Big Island of Hawaii
Boston
Brussels
Budapest
Cape Town
Copenhagen
Dublin
Edinburgh

Florence
Honolulu
Ibiza & Formentera
Jerusalem
Las Vegas
Lisbon
London Restaurants
Madeira
Madrid
Malta & Gozo
Maui
Melbourne
Menorca

Montreal
New Orleans

Paris
Rome
Seattle
St Lucia
Sydney
Tenerife
Tokyo
Toronto
Vancouver

TRAVEL SPECIALS

First-Time Asia
First-Time Europe
Women Travel

PHRASEBOOKS

Czech
Dutch
Egyptian Arabic
European
French
German
Greek

Hindi & Urdu
Hungarian
Indonesian
Italian
Japanese
Mandarin
  Chinese
Mexican
  Spanish
Polish
Portuguese
Russian
Spanish
Swahili
Thai
Turkish
Vietnamese

AVAILABLE AT ALL GOOD BOOKSHOPS

ROUGH GUIDES:
Reference and Music CDs

REFERENCE

Blues:
  100 Essential CDs
Classical Music
Classical:
  100 Essential CDs
Country Music
Country:
  100 Essential CDs
Drum'n'bass
House Music
Hip Hop
Irish Music
Jazz

Music USA
Opera
Opera:
  100 Essential CDs
Reggae
Reggae:
  100 Essential CDs
Rock
Rock:
  100 Essential CDs

Soul:
  100 Essential CDs
Techno
World Music

World Music:
  100 Essential CDs
English Football
European Football
Internet
Money Online
Shopping Online
Travel Health

ROUGH GUIDE MUSIC CDs

Music of the Andes
Australian Aboriginal
Bluegrass
Brazilian Music
Cajun & Zydeco
Music of Cape Verde
Classic Jazz
Music of
  Colombia
Cuban Music
Eastern Europe

Music of Egypt
English Roots Music
Flamenco
Music of Greece
Hip Hop
India & Pakistan
Irish Music
Music of Jamaica
Music of Japan
Kenya & Tanzania
Marrabenta
  Mozambique
Native American
North African
Music of Portugal
Reggae
Salsa
Samba
Scottish Music
South African Music
Music of Spain
Sufi Music
Tango

Tex-Mex
West African Music
World Music
World Music Vol 2
Music of Zimbabwe

AVAILABLE AT ALL GOOD BOOKSHOPS

MUSIC ROUGH GUIDES ON CD

The Rough Guide To The Music Of Italy

'There isn't a single track that doesn't leap out
and command your attention. This is exactly what
Rough Guides are all about – and it's just great' –*Taplas*

Artists include: **Daniel Sepe, Tenores Di Bitti,
Riccardo Tesi, La Macina, Banda Ionica,
Barabàn, Re Niliu and Totore Chessa**

Available from book and record shops worldwide or order direct from
World Music Network, Unit 6, 88 Clapham Park Road, London SW4 7BX
tel: 020 7498 5252 • fax: 020 7498 5353 • email: post@worldmusic.net

Hear samples from over 50 Rough Guide CDs at
WWW.WORLDMUSIC.NET

NORTH SOUTH TRAVEL
Great discounts

North South Travel is a small travel agent offering excellent personal service. Like other air ticket retailers, we offer discount fares worldwide. But unlike others, all available profits contribute to grassroots projects in the South through the NST Development Trust Registered Charity No. 1040656.

For **quotes** or queries, contact Brenda Skinner or Bridget Christopher, Tel/Fax 01245 608 291. Recent **donations** made from the NST Development Trust include support to Djoliba Trust, providing micro-credit to onion growers in the Dogon country in Mali; assistance to displaced people and rural communities in eastern Congo; a grant to Wells For India, which works for clean water in Rajasthan; support to the charity Children of the Andes, working for poverty relief in Colombia; and a grant to the Omari Project which works with drug-dependent young people in Watamu, Kenya.

Great difference

Email brenda@nstravel.demon.co.uk
Website www.nstravel.demon.co.uk

ATOL
75401

rth South Travel, Moulsham Mill, Parkway, Chelmsford, Essex, CM2 7PX, UK

Will you have enough stories to tell your grandchildren?

©2000 Yahoo! Inc.

Yahoo! Travel

DO YOU YAHOO!?

Lost cash.

One travel adventure you can live without.

Travel smart.
Carry American Express® Travelers Cheques.
They're safer than cash.

Whether you're surfing Baja, backpacking Europe, or just getting away for the weekend, American Express Travelers Cheques are the way to go. They're accepted virtually everywhere around the world — at hotels, stores, and restaurants. Simply sign the Cheques and use them as you would cash.

American Express Travelers Cheques never expire. And if they're lost or stolen, they can be replaced quickly — usually within 24 hours. Pick them up at any participating American Express Travel Service location, bank, credit union, or AAA office.

American Express Travelers Cheques.
Don't leave home without them.®

© 2000 American Express   TCST-00

Travelers
Cheques